The Trial

The DOJ's Suit to Block Penguin Random House's Acquisition of Simon & Schuster

Nearly Complete Transcripts and Comprehensive Coverage

By Publishers Lunch

Publishers Lunch has been the "daily essential read" for the book publishing business for twenty years and is the largest-circulation news communication in the world for publishing professionals. Publishers Marketplace is the website associated with Publishers Lunch—providing round-the-clock news and analysis, deal reports, job listings, and many unique databases and tools that help publishing professionals find critical information, connect with each other, and do business better electronically.

Publishers Lunch
2 Park Place, #4 Bronxville, NY 10708
Info@publishersmarketplace.com
www.publishersmarketplace.com

Michael Cader, Founder and Principal Reporter
Robin Dellabough, Projects Director
Katy Hershberger, Principal Reporter
Kathy Smith, Editor
Erin Somers, Reporter
Cover design by Wendy Palitz
Layout by Julie Ink

print ISBN: 9781948586559

PART ONE: THE BEGINNING

PROLOGUE

For three short but endless weeks in August 2022 in the E. Barrett Prettyman Federal Courthouse in Washington, DC, something extraordinary occurred in Courtroom 12. Eight publishing CEOs; four publishers; six literary agents; other executives; and two economics experts took the stand to answer questions about how publishing works. The focus was the market for high-advance "anticipated best selling books" [ATSB, in the accepted terminology]. But the testimony broadly covered how publishing works and sometimes doesn't work; the competitive landscape among publishers large and small; and the process through which literary agents sell books to publishers, along with some insights into corporate publishing plans for the future.

The point of the proceedings was to determine whether Judge Florence Y. Pan would block Penguin Random House from acquiring Simon & Schuster as a violation of the Clayton Antitrust Act. On Halloween eve she did just that, finding, "The government has presented a compelling case that predicts substantial harm to competition as a result of the proposed merger of PRH and S&S."

The Trial was the biggest industry event in a decade, and the effect of both the testimony and the ruling – the first time a major merger of book publishers has been blocked by the court – will be felt for years to come. For those of us following along, it was exciting and tense and boring and illuminating and hilarious and infuriating and ridiculous. We laughed, we cried, it was much better than Cats. For many it has been the summer obsession, mostly riveting, if occasionally unsettling. Ironically it was "Must See TV" that no one outside of a few dozen court-going stalwarts actually saw.

At Publishers Lunch, we covered the day-to-day developments fairly exhaustively, writing about 35,000 words over three weeks, and we shared some relevant trial transcript excerpts as well. But the full record of the proceedings was not publicly available and has likely been read in full by a similarly small audience. Everyone followed the trial, but almost no one knows everything that happened.

So in the great book publishing tradition of preserving and sharing landmark papers and reports, the staff of Publishers Lunch presents this massive compilation of The Trial, supplemented by a revised version of our own daily coverage, along with other key pre- and post-trial documents, and the judge's final opinion.

We believe it is important to preserve and share the complete account of What Happened In August, and how the judge came so easily to this significant decision. (Or, in this case, nearly complete: Portions of the trial were closed to the public, and some testimony came from taped depositions, which were transcribed ahead of time for the court and not included in the daily, live transcripts. Also, some material, including key bits of data, was either redacted entirely, or shown quickly on hard-to-view slides. It is possible that the "exhibits" officially admitted into evidence will be made public at a later date, so far they have not been.) As book people, we all value the significance of the full, narrative record. Plus, the collected testimony and supplementary coverage presented here stands as one of the best books on publishing we have ever read — and, as you will see, one of the longest.

For the sake of readability, we have edited out daily "court business" and smoothed out or even corrected some of the speech informalities. (Some of our favorite changes included substituting "backlist" for "backless"; BookTok for "Book Talk"; and GUPPIs for "guppies".) While the testimony is presented in chronological order, we have organized each person's testimony into individual chapters, regardless of whether they appeared on one or more days.

The testimony and all of the related exhibits and documents was riveting — and revealing — to anyone interested in the business of book publishing. The answers were constrained by the questions being asked and the very nature of an antitrust case, but along the way plenty was revealed.

For all the bluster and amusing quotes, real jobs and real advances and careers are potentially at stake whatever the outcome. (As we learned, there is perhaps 2000 hours of work involved from both the author and the publishers on each and every book, whether anticipated sales are large or modest.)

The verdict is in, but everyone in publishing will continue to wrestle with what happened those three weeks in Washington. It's important to understand that this was not "publishing on trial" or a "publishing trial" of any kind: This was an antitrust trial. (The DOJ's John Read actually addressed some of this in the beginning of his closing argument.) It sounded like us in publishing, but it wasn't really about us.

Antitrust trials are technical and complicated and have little to do with the nuances of the businesses involved. They are about market definition, market concentration and market constraints, and about pricing power and econometric models. Most of the witnesses work in publishing, but all of the testimony was defined and constrained by the questions asked. The witnesses were all prepped with key case points in mind, and it's the rare person who can speak naturally when sitting in a courtroom on the witness stand. The government's case relied on reasserting a small number of key points and trying to put words in people's mouths — or take words from the occasional discovery document and give them great import; just as the defense's case was focused on poking holes in those DOJ points and reinforcing a few simple contrary points.

The government brought a very focused case about the small set of authors and deals that win contracts of $250,000 or more every year (or about 1200 projects a year, as we learned). It was the DOJ, not anyone in publishing, that had no regard — in an antitrust case — for the other tens of thousands of authors and books brought to market every year.

Trial by tweet is an incomplete way for the broader community to experience and assess what happened these past three weeks, and publishing will be reckoning with some of the soundbites for some time to come. (A simple example is the reference to non-big-five publishers as "farm teams." The line comes from a long memo the late Carolyn Reidy wrote to her boss at CBS as the company was preparing to merge back with Viacom, in a document designed to make her business sound as a good as possible. It was introduced before the trial — in fact, it was quoted in the DOJ's original complaint. The publishing executives asked about that remark at trial rejected both the term and the idea it represented, as did Viacom's attorney Stephen Fishbein in his closing on Friday. And yet the phrase landed in the judge's final opinion as well.) But we were left with a fulsome supply of pull-quotes and slights without context — and authors, and agents, and staff and trading partners will all need context and care in the days to come. This book is intended to help provide that context.

SETTING THE SCENE

Before the trial began on August 1, we compared the must-follow proceedings to the closely-watched January 6 hearings that had recently wound down for recess just four-tenths of a mile away. In our day-to-day coverage, we dubbed the trial A3 for brevity (August/Antitrust; three weeks of trial)—and suggested it could be viewed by many in publishing in a similar vein as J6: A laborious investigation culminates with a public airing of findings that few expect to alter the course of the events, no matter what they might hope for or believe is just. Just like J6, however, we predicted, the case made at A3 will matter for putting things on the record, and it just may surprise us all. Indeed, by the third week of the trial, within the courtroom Judge Florence Pan appeared to be aligning herself with many of the prosecution's key arguments.

Also like J6, as we predicted, A3 did indeed include a few surprise witnesses, some redacted material, taped depositions played in court, and some odd or embarrassing stories and quotes that will not bear on the actual outcome but will still be hard to forget.

Monopsowhat?

Back in those innocent days of July, 2022, most people in publishing (and the world at large) were pretty unfamiliar with monopsony, which is the formal basis of the Department of Justice's case.

In their original complaint, the DOJ alleged that allowing PRH to acquire S&S "would likely result in substantial harm to authors" by "leaving hundreds of authors with fewer alternatives and less leverage." They suggested that the combined company would be a monopsonist: "A hypothetical monopsonist of anticipated top-selling books would profitably reduce advances paid to authors of anticipated top-selling books by a small but significant, non-transitory amount."

So what is monopsony? Simply put, monopsony is a market dominated by a single buyer—whereas monopoly is a market dominated by a single seller. As this document from the FTC puts it, "A 'monopsony' is a single (or dominant) buyer dealing with multiple sellers. In important respects, monopsony is the mirror image of monopoly." A monopolist "forces up the market price for what it sells by restricting the amount it produces" while a monopsonist "forces down the market price for what it buys by restricting the amount it buys."

There are very few controlling monopsony cases or precedents that would guide the court in a case like this. But the case against PRH is more than just a standard merger challenge, as evidenced by Attorney General Merrick Garland making the announcement of the action last November. The Biden Administration has proclaimed a more aggressive position that concentration in general is hurting the American economy and installed more pro-active regulators with both Lina Khan as chair of the FTC and Jonathan Kanter as leader of the DOJ's Antitrust Division.

And in the White House's 2022 economic report, a full chapter (No. 5) focuses on the lack of competition in labor markets in particular as a key focus for remedy: "Increased enforcement of antitrust laws would also alleviate labor market monopsony and therefore its negative effects on wages, equality, and race- and gender-based pay gaps. . . . It can also be used to block mergers that would concentrate labor markets excessively and to penalize large employers that use illegal methods to obtain or maintain labor monopsonies. Though some of these uses of antitrust law have been rare until recently, the Executive Order on Promoting Competition calls for agencies to make greater use of antitrust law to promote competition in labor markets. For example, the DOJ and the FTC have begun the process for revising the merger guidelines, and have called for public comment on labor market implications. . . . These and other polices can begin relieving the historical burdens on disadvantaged groups of workers, helping to reduce inequality and bolster economic output and growth."

So this is no ordinary case for the DOJ, but rather what they hope will be a signature case in paving the way for more monopsony-based actions that look to preserve competition for workers (rather than the previous focus on worrying solely about prices to consumers).

For some more background on monopsony and the judicial standards to be applied, a friend pointed us to this journal article by University of Tennessee College of Law distinguished professor Maurice E. Stucke, "Looking at the Monopsony in the Mirror." As he notes in the introduction, "Despite the increasing interest in monopsony and buyer power, relatively few cases have actually been brought. Given the relatively few antitrust cases, the legal standards for monopsony claims are less developed than for monopoly claims."

As Prof. Stucke explains, while a monopolist needs a very high market share, a monopsonist can exert a dominating influence with a relatively modest market share: "Since firms can enjoy monopsony power with market share below 50 percent, agencies and courts cannot reflexively import the market share thresholds from monopolization cases to monopsonization cases."

He notes that, "The U.S. competition authorities recognize the difficulty, 'in the abstract, to state market share thresholds for such monopsony concerns.' Rather than rely on market share thresholds alone to find monopsony power, they encourage the courts to consider several interrelated factors:

(1) a large market share on the part of the purchaser;

(2) an upward sloping or somewhat inelastic supply curve in the input market; and

(3) an inability or unwillingness for new purchasers to enter the market or current purchasers to expand the amount of their purchases in the market.

This is the correct approach."

The Pre-Trial Briefs: DOJ and PRH State Their Cases

The trial really began on July 25, when the Department of Justice and Penguin Random House both filed their formal pre-trial briefs, framing in advance the core arguments and counterpoints they both intended to make at trial.

As in their original complaint, the DOJ focused on their core argument that the acquisition of Simon & Schuster "would further entrench the largest publishing giant in the United States (and the world) and give the merged company control of nearly half of the market to acquire anticipated top-selling books [ATSB] from authors." They alleged that the "merger would likely result in authors of anticipated top-selling books receiving smaller advances, meaning authors who labor for years over their manuscripts will be paid less for their efforts and fewer authors will be able to earn a living from writing."

Below we try to line up points of interest from the two separate briefs on a sequence of topics of interest, while calling out some key bits on statistics cited and evidence from industry figures the parties expect to present. We focus on the publishing business issues, and leave aside for now details on some of the more legalistic arguments (most importantly a dispute on whether or not the government meets the bar of showing that the merger is presumptively illegal and that the market shares they assert "adequately capture the market's competitive conditions").

1. Is the Relevant Market . . . Relevant?

Given the government's primary allegation as cited above, one initial and primary hurdle for the Court is whether ATSB are an identifiable, relevant market at all.

DOJ: This Is A $1 Billion Annual Market

As the DOJ defines it, "Anticipated top-selling books can be identified by the advances publishers pay to authors because those advances are based on the publishers' assessment of the volume of future book sales."

That market, the government argues, is highly-concentrated already and very sizable, with the five largest trade publishers controlling 90 percent or more such titles in 2020, when deals within the ATSB parameters comprised $1 billion in advances. Elsewhere in the brief, DOJ cites similar but slightly different statistics, saying that publishers outside of the Big 5 "collectively account for only about 9% of anticipated top-seller acquisitions, with no single small publisher having more than 2% market share." In yet another slightly different measure, they add, "Defendants' expert's own agency data reveal that the Big 5 dominate the market for anticipated top-sellers with a collective 94% market share." (As it turned out, the "agency data" was a smaller set of information from 18 literary agencies collected by the defense's economics expert Dr. Edward Snyder. The government's broader set was said to come from over 60 publishers, and represent the market at large.)

Within that ATSB market, the DOJ tabulates, "the combined firm would be a giant in the market for the acquisition of publishing rights to anticipated top-selling books, with a market share of 49%." As detailed at trial, that's a combination of PRH's 37% share, and S&S's 12% share. (The DOJ's assertions roughly align with the smaller pool of data at PublishersMarketplace.com, where a combined PRH and S&S comprised 45.5 percent of ATSB in 2020 and 2021.)

PRH: This Is A Subset of 2% of All Books Published

Without looking at the $1 billion annual dollar value of ATSB, the publisher argues DOJ is looking at "one very small segment of the market to acquire U.S. book rights: the set of about 1200 books . . . or about 2% of all books published by commercial publishers. The government treats this tiny price segment as a 'sub-market' and gives it a label—the market for the rights to 'anticipated top-selling books'—that is entirely unknown to industry participants." In their view, "the government tries to erase 98% of the market" in a quest for where concentration might be felt.

Smaller still, though, they say the DOJ only alleges an effect on the 7 percent—or roughly 85 books—for which PRH and S&S were the two top bidders. "Alleged harm to 85 books does not constitute a substantial lessening of competition by any definition." As, "Anecdotes about some of those acquisitions out of thousands of books published each year cannot establish substantial harm to competition."

Elsewhere, they itemize in a different way, based on that smaller set of "agency data" derived in discovery: "Actual data from agents show that from 2018 to 2021, PRH and S&S were the top two bidders in only 21 acquisitions out of 299 in this price segment, or just 7%."

2. What About That $250,000 Price Level?

DOJ: There Are Multiple Reasons to Look At Significant Deals and Higher

The government notes: "As the Court will hear at trial, both PRH and S&S recognize $250,000 as a significant threshold in their ordinary business operations: they require higher-level approvals and additional documentation to make an offer of $250,000 or more for a book. This type of internal business practice is recognized in the caselaw as a basis for defining a market."

Then they make a glaring error: "For example, industry journal Publisher's Weekly uses thresholds to categorize book deals, and uses $250,000 to define a 'significant deal' when agents and publishers submit announcements of their deals." (If they don't understand the difference between *Publisher's Weekly* [sic] and Publishers Marketplace, the defendants might ask, how well does the government understand publishing at all . . . ?)

For good measure, though, The DOJ says their expert witness Dr. Nicholas Hill looked at different monetary levels—cutoffs of $150,000, $350,000, $500,000 and $1 million"—and found "market shares do not change meaningfully" as those lines are drawn differently.

PRH: This Isn't A Thing

As far as the publisher is concerned: "Industry participants do not apply common objective criteria to identify which authors to target as likely to receive advances of $250,000 or more. There are no separate publishers who target such authors, and no separate imprints or departments within publishers that cater separately to such authors."

Rather, "The most one can say about this price segment is that larger publishers more often acquire books than do smaller publishers. But that fact—which is true at all price levels—does not demonstrate either that the largest publishers distinctly target books in this segment, or that authors treat such publishers as a distinct market."

As for us, the publisher gets the source right, though they declare us "cute." A footnote indicates: "The government relies heavily on Publishers Marketplace reports of book deals, which use cute designations to describe different deal-size thresholds, i.e. deals up to $50,000 are 'nice'; those up to $100,00 are 'very nice'; those up to $250,000 are 'good'; those up to $500,000 are 'significant'; and larger deals are 'major.' Those designations do not purport to identify different markets or bargaining conditions. On the government's contrary view, the designations would implausibly define five distinct book-acquisition 'markets.'"

In a revised unredacted filing, PRH revealed this rebuttal as well: "The government will also cite some publishers' internal requirements for additional approval of advances exceeding certain amounts (sometimes $250,000), the evidence will show that these approval thresholds are also arbitrary—i.e., they have never been fixed to collect a set of books with unique shared characteristics—and have varied over time."

3. Are Publishers Outside of The Big 5 Viable Competitors For the Biggest Books?

PRH: We Can Lose Auctions to 20 Publishers Or More, and This Will Be Just One Fewer

Flipping the lens here to start with the defendant, PRH argued that a large number of publishers can compete and win the auction for any given big books, representing a broadly competitive marketplace: "Collectively, in fact, smaller publishers—which include elite publishers like Norton and Scholastic, and global giants like Amazon and Disney—outpace one or more of the largest publishers in acquisitions every year. Slice and dice the market any way you want, and you will find vigorous competition to acquire books, especially books that one or more publishers believe are most likely to succeed with consumers."

The said, "The evidence will show that existing Big 5 rivals can easily expand and actively plan to do so. Other rivals among the top twenty also can easily increase their acquisitions—they already possess the needed talent, experience, and reputation. Numerous top twenty rivals plan to meaningfully expand, including Disney, Chronicle, Candlewick, and others. And entirely new publishers started by well-known editors have recently gained share and become increasingly effective competitors. Given this ease of expansion and entry, market shares are a highly unreliable predictor of post-merger competitive conditions."

By their math, "The merger at most reduces the number of publishers that pose a meaningful competitive threat in any given acquisition from 'very many' to 'still very many, but one fewer.'" Even if market shares and participants were an issue, "viewed strictly through the government's structural lens, the merger changes the effective number of potential acquirors for any given book from six (the five largest plus all others in aggregate) to five. And the government has not cited any case rejecting a merger on the basis of market concentration alone, where five market participants remained in active competition."

DOJ: The Big 5 Are Unto Themselves In Most Cases, And Everyone Knows It

The government cited a Bertelsmann board document that characterized the US publishing market as an "oligopoly" of the Big 5 and quoted an email from former S&S CEO Carolyn Reidy to her boss at ViacomCBS noting that the non-Big 5 publishers "rarely compete with us in auctions for new properties" and often serve as "farm teams" as evidence that in most cases, the market for the biggest books is focused on the largest publishers.

"While Defendants may try to confuse the record by pointing to isolated instances of a non-Big 5 publisher winning a particular book, the market share data tell the story: smaller publishers are not sufficient competitive constraints on the Big 5, and they cannot replace the competition that would be lost by allowing the Defendants to merge to a 50% share of the market."

As an example, they indicate that Abrams CEO Michael Jacobs "will testify that Abrams gets 'outbid all the time by publishers who are willing to pay . . . more for books than we are' because Abrams has limited resources and there is a 'limited number' of things Abrams can 'really lean into' and 'make investments that make sense for us.'"

More broadly, "The evidence demonstrating that the Big 5 are close competitors who leave small publishers far behind in competing for anticipated top-selling books matters because it illustrates that those smaller publishers will not be a meaningful competitive constraint on the combined firm such that they could overcome the presumption of illegality."

The government also asserted that the Big 5 are advantaged in making big books work in the marketplace, and PRH claims it is the best of all: "The Big 5 are best able to offer authors the extensive and sophisticated infrastructure of editorial, production, marketing, and publicity support needed to produce a topselling book, and the sales and distribution networks necessary to place a book into the hands of readers. For example, a marketing presentation titled 'The Penguin Random House Advantage' touts the company's 'industry-leading supply chain and specialized sales team for every kind of retail channel' as a competitive advantage and proclaims, 'we get our books into consumers' hands faster and more reliably than our competition.'"

4. Do Agents Control the Market For Big Books, or Publishers?

Here we get into deep chicken-and-egg territory in a dispute that will long outlive this three-week trial.

PRH: Agents Run the Sale, Starting with Who Gets to Bid

The publisher argues that agents are really in control of who gets to bid on, and ultimately acquire, ATSB, and the power and leverage of agents in where they submit and whom they advise selecting (since the highest bid does not always win the rights to the title) trumps the publishers' power of the purse. "Market concentration also ignores the competitive effect of agents' control over the acquisition process.

Publishers do not participate in acquisitions proportionally to their market shares—the agent decides which publishers to invite, and how many. Those invitations are not based on market shares, which are not even known to the agent.

". . . Among other competitive factors that market shares cannot account for, acquisitions in this industry are controlled by agents, who use their skill and experience to decide which publisher(s) to invite to consider a given book and which acquisition format will best serve their clients' interests.

As they put it elsewhere, "acquisitions are controlled by literary agents acting on authors' behalf. The agent determines the 'rules; for each acquisition, decides which publishers may compete for each acquisition, and controls what information about bidding to share. When an author brings her agent a book, the agent uses her skill and experience to determine how and to whom to pitch the book."

DOJ: Agents Can't Create Competition In A Lopsided Market, and Publishers Have Certain Uncrossable Lines

The government claims "testimony at trial will show that Defendants' argument is not grounded in reality. Agents are not powerful sellers that can counteract the anticompetitive harms from the merger. As Defendants' purported expert Jennifer Walsh admitted at deposition, literary agents are part of a fragmented industry. They are numerous and diffuse, with agents belonging to many different agencies, including many small or even solo agencies. Most literary agents have more limited resources compared to PRH and S&S, which are part of multibillion-dollar companies that have access to business development and strategy teams and vast amounts of data.

Beyond that, "Agents are not omnipotent. Agents cannot control whether publishers are interested in a book. Agents cannot control a publishing house's internal bidding rules, including whether it prohibits its imprints from bidding against each other for a book. Nor can an agent control how a publisher values a book. Agents cannot control how much a publisher bids for a book. Agents cannot even always control the scope of rights that they can sell; a recent example is that the Big 5 publishers have all but refused to acquire books unless audio rights are included."

More broadly, "Agents cannot manufacture competition. In addition, an agent cannot conduct an auction if the only imprints that are interested in a book are all in the same publishing house."

The government also reminds us of the importance of advances, and how few of those ATSB actually earn out: "An author of an anticipated top- selling book typically receives a generous advance. More than 85% of author contracts for anticipated top-selling books never earn out their advance, even several years after publication. Thus, the amount of the advance is all the more important because the vast majority of authors never receive royalties beyond the amount of the initial advance. Indeed, because authors of anticipated top-selling books seldom earn out their advance, literary agents and authors focus on the amount of the advance in negotiations with publishers and rarely negotiate royalties beyond the advance."

5. After the Merger, Will Advances Go Up or Down or Neither?

Even if there is an identifiable market for ATSB (as many would concede); and even if the merger produces a high-level of concentration in that market (as many would say seems self-evident); that still begs what may be one of the payoff questions: Does that mean that advances for big books will go down from the diminished number of big houses—and can the government prove that expectation—or that they will go up because of intensified competition from everyone else for the projects they want?

DOJ: Competitors, And Our Expert, Expect Big Advances to Moderate

Among the evidence the government said it would present at trial, "Industry participants anticipate that the merger is likely to lead to lower advances for authors. For example, Hachette CEO Michael Pietsch is expected to testify that [redacted] and Kensington CEO Steven Zacharius has testified that he 'would expect that [advances] go down since there will be less competition for those authors.'

"The Court will hear testimony from several literary agents that they expect the merger will lead to lower advances for authors. . . . Executives from the remaining Big 5 publishers will testify that the combined firm will be so dominant that it will be able to employ exclusionary tactics such as restricting printing capacity or access to distribution networks to make it more difficult for the remaining Big 5 publishers to compete against the combined firm."

Beyond that, the DOJ planned to rely on highly technical models from their expert Dr. Hill that they said "demonstrates that a hypothetical monopsonist publisher would likely reduce advances to authors of anticipated top-sellers because an insufficient number of those authors would switch to self-publishing in response to such a reduction" and other measures.

The government also alleged there is "some evidence" that Random House's acquisition of Penguin in 2013 "harmed authors of top-selling books by reducing advances and the overall output of books published." They cited redacted testimony from literary agents, and claim "internal PRH documents confirm the anticompetitive harm from the 2013 merger."

PRH: We Will Make More Money, and Authors Will Make More Money

You will not be surprised to hear that the publisher took the opposite approach. Not only will the merger not reduce advances for big books, it will actually increase that pool of money. PRHSS will make more money and have more to bid, the reasoning goes, and their competitors will step up their allocation of big advances in order to compete: "The merger instead will enhance competition by creating efficiencies that will enable the combined entity to make better offers to more authors, especially for those books most likely to succeed with consumers. And by making the combined entity a stronger competitor downstream, it will incentivize other publishers to compete harder to acquire the books they, too, need to win sales among consumers." Also, they say, "With greater net income, the combined company will not only offer higher advances, it will also bid on more books from more authors—an author benefit the government ignores entirely."

They claimed the government's own expert posits only a low level of harm and "would reduce advances by about 6% on average" ($29.3 million per year). Whereas PRH's expert Professor Edward Snyder "will opine that the merger will produce gains for the merged entity that will translate to an increase in total annual author compensation for all U.S. book rights of $75 million to $107 million in 2025."

That larger argument—which said that a combined PRH and S&S would be so powerful and so profitable that it will spend vastly more on advances (and royalties) than the companies spend now separately—was breathtaking in its own way if you reflect on it (in part because it seems to demonstrate the government's argument, that the combined company would be remarkably, unbeatably profitable). And it also showed us for the first time how Bertelsmann and PRH came to the unprecedented multiple in agreeing to pay $2.175 billion for S&S.

The publisher cites its own pre-merger analysis, expressed in the "PRH Efficiencies Model," to demonstrate "four distinct ways in which the merger will improve the combined entity's net income over what each entity could achieve separately."

First was their belief that "PRH's premier supply chain" will increase the sales at retail for S&S authors and distribution clients, estimated at an increase of between $26 million to $46 million a year by 2025 (the target date for all of the projections).

Second is an expectation of lower variable costs—from reduced returns and lower PPB, freight and marketing—since "PRH has consistently reduced the 'return rates' of previously acquired companies by incorporating their books into PRH's distribution system, and it expects to do the same for S&S's return rate." That was projected to save $21 million to $24 million a year.

Third—and most telling or controversial—was a reduction in operating costs of between $81 million and $95 million annually. That appears to primarily target job cuts everywhere except editorial, along with unspecified systems integration and other operating efficiencies, e.g. "reducing duplicative sales, marketing, and administrative positions. PRH does not eliminate editorial roles after acquisitions—it considers editorial expertise additive, not redundant—but 'de-duplicating' other positions will reduce costs significantly."

During the trial, the community took greater note of the portentous $81 million target seemingly based on extensive job cuts, which became a minor sensation, even though we had already sleuthed it out earlier for Publishers Lunch readers. A PRH spokesperson then clarified that from that figure, $31 million related to the elimination of third-party contracts; $25 million was from warehouse consolidation and space and storage savings; and $25 million was said to be from processing and IT/ systems and back-office projects.

Fourth was savings of $10 million on "real estate costs by reducing redundant properties and consolidating employees into existing PRH offices."

PRH declared with confidence: "They are not speculative, but instead are verified by past experience: in prior mergers, PRH achieved efficiency benefits even greater than expected, creating access to more money it has deployed to win the most attractive books and thereby better compete downstream." Also, by their account, "the 2013 merger had no negative effect on author advances. In fact, advances trended upwards in subsequent years."

Verified the PRH's experiences but—tellingly during trial—not verified by any independent third party, which led Judge Pan to declare all of the testimony about those planned efficiencies and projected additional author revenues as inadmissible.

6. Further Learnings

Revised, unredacted versions of the pre-trial briefs then revealed some additional details of interest, among them: When bidding for Simon & Schuster, Bertelsmann CEO Thomas Rabe expressed that the company faced "a disadvantage in the auction due to antitrust risks, which are likely to be greater in our case than with all other bidders." To overcome the "antitrust risks," the government said, "Bertelsmann paid hundreds of millions of dollars over the next-highest bidder."

We also learned that:

- PRH earned 58% of its revenue from backlist books in 2020. (S&S's backlist earnings are still blacked out.)
- Literary agent Ayesha Pande, on the government's witness list, "will testify that the proposed merger likely will make it more difficult to get sizeable advances for authors from diverse backgrounds because there will be fewer editors to whom she can submit diverse stories."
- Pande and another agent (at trial, Christy Fletcher) "testified that the 2013 [Penguin and Random House] merger reduced competition for authors' works and resulted in lower author advances; they expressed concern that the proposed acquisition of S&S could lead to similar "downward pressure" on advances.
- On that point, Dr. Hill will testify that the 2013 merger "led to lower compensation for authors of anticipated top-selling books. The relevant data shows that authors of anticipated top-selling books earned on average just under $100,000 less per advance in the two years following the 2013 merger than they did in the two years leading up to the merger. Furthermore, average advances for authors of anticipated top-selling books decreased by about 15% compared to advances for authors of all books."

More Pre-Trial Skirmishes

A week before the actual trial began, Judge Pan ruled on various pre-trial motions. Among them:

Bidding Policy

The government moved to exclude any mention of PRH CEO Markus Dohle's pledge that PRH and S&S imprints would continue to bid against each other after the merger, arguing the policy is unenforceable and irrelevant to whether the merger should be approved. Judge Pan concluded "that the unenforceability of the bidding policy goes to weight and not admissibility. It, potentially, has some relevance."

Printing

PRH had moved to exclude evidence about Bertelsmann's significant US book printing capabilities was denied, on technical grounds. The printing-related evidence was admissible.

The DOJ had argued, with success, that the company's printing ability had bearing on "multiple issues in this case." Those include:

"(1) the extent to which printing availability affects choices authors have when selling a book to publishers, (2) Defendants' claim that new entrants could quickly and easily enter the market, and (3) the extent to which existing competitors could readily expand their output."

The DOJ said they were advancing a concern expressed by multiple publishers: "The heads of several Big 5 publishers and smaller publishers testified about their concerns about the impact of the merger on an essential part of book publishing: the printing of books. If there were a change in the supply chain as a result of the transfer of books from S&S to Bertelsmann's Printing Group, already stretched capacity would be further limited, and PRH could favor the printing of its own books, to the potential disadvantage of external printing clients of the Bertelsmann Printing Group."

They alleged those concerns are fueled by Bertelsmann and PRH's own documents, which would later be presented at trial: "Bertelsmann and PRH recognize the significance of their control of printing resources: their own documents tout that it is a huge competitive advantage in attracting authors to be the sole publisher has a printing asset in its family."

Also, "During depositions of third-party publishers, a number of witnesses testified that they were concerned about the impact of the merger on PRH's future provision of printing and distribution services to other publishers."

The government said the issue was also important because "it is relevant to the choices authors have when selling a book to publishers."

Jennifer Rudolph Walsh's Testimony

There was another dispute over whether former literary agency Jennifer Rudolph Walsh, hired to testify on behalf of PRH, would be deemed an "expert" and allowed to opine about whether the merger would affect the market for top authors' properties. Here Judge Pan initially ruled in favor of the government, but then changed her position during trial as she began to hear from other publishing veterans.

Notable from Walsh's pre-trial declaration was her disclosure of the compensation for her testimony, "I am being compensated with a guaranteed minimum fee of $250,000 against a rate of $2,000 per hour and an additional $10,000 per day spent at trial."

PRH's "Efficiencies Model"

There were oral arguments over the admissibility of PRH's internal calculations of all the money they will save after the merger—and thus, as they have argued, all of the extra money that will flow through in part to authors. Judge Pan clearly took a dubious initial view of PRH's position, and we saw that view sustained during the trial: "I will say that my review of the expert reports and the evidence on this leaves me a little skeptical about what you're telling me."

She did agree to hear preliminary testimony from Snyder and PRH executive Sansigre "to figure out if this is verifiable." "I'm still interested in, like, who's supposed to do the verifying. I'm not convinced that it should be me, but I'm willing to hear more on that." But that's done "with the understanding if I find it's not [verified or verifiable], we don't need to get into all the rest of the testimony on this issue because that will save us some time."

PREAMBLE TO THE TRIAL

UNITED STATES DISTRICT COURT FOR THE DISTRICT OF COLUMBIA
United States of America,
Plaintiff,
vs.
Bertelsmann SE & Co. KGaA, et al.
Defendants.
Civil Action No. 1:21-cv-02886-FYP
Bench Trial—a.m. session
Washington, D.C.
August 1, 2022
Time: 9:30 a.m.

THE COURT: Good morning. All right. So this case is here for trial, and I think there's some preliminary matters that we should address.

I did receive a proposed order regarding the handling of confidential information, which I'm prepared to sign today. I just wanted to confirm that the proposed order was circulated among the third parties, and I just want to understand the procedure you followed to make sure that we've done what we can to make sure there are no objections from the third parties.

MS. STRICK: Good morning, Your Honor.

I don't think we have circulated that to the third parties, but we can do that this morning. And we spoke to them individually to discuss what was going to be stipulated.

THE COURT: Okay. That's fine. Then I will hold off on signing it until you've circulated it to them, and if you want to make any amendments to it, that's fine.

Okay. And I do appreciate the parties working together on that. I think it's a good procedure that you've proposed.

All right. I think there's also another preliminary matter regarding the presentation of evidence of efficiencies from the merger that the defendants had planned to introduce. I'll note I received an email from the parties saying that they had not been able to reach an agreement on this, and I wanted to check in with the parties to see if you've made any progress on that before we address it.

MR. SCHWARZ: Good morning, Your Honor. Mel Schwarz for the United States.

Unfortunately, no. I don't think we're that far apart with respect to one of our two options. We're trying to get, following Your Honor's suggestion, to get the verification issue—if I can call it that—neutral word—resolved before we have other evidence, a lot of other evidence. And we proposed either that Mr. Sansigre—and perhaps, I think, they also want to call Malaviya on that issue. We were prepared to do it out of order later this week; Wednesday afternoon, Thursday would be convenient for us.

Then if they didn't want to do that, which they definitely did not, apparently, we suggested that we hold off witnesses that we might otherwise examine on efficiencies issues and move that to their case. And if they agreed to call Sansigre and Malaviya before so we could resolve that issue and before Dr. Snyder testified.

THE COURT: No, I understand.

MR. SCHWARZ: Okay. And I think part of our problem is that they don't want to contemplate cutting anything off at the verification level.

THE COURT: No, I understand. So let me just say a few words on the record before we get into the details of this discussion.

You can have a seat, Mr. Schwarz. Thank you.

MR. SCHWARZ: You said I can sit? I didn't hear you.

THE COURT: Yes. Yes, please.

The background on this is the government filed a motion *in limine* to preclude certain expert testimony of Dr. Snyder related to efficiencies that the defendants believe that this merger will create, and there was a motion *in limine* to preclude that evidence under Rule 702 because the expert testimony was not reliable, not based on sufficient facts and data.

I'll note that I considered this a very standard motion *in limine*, a motion to preclude evidence, not a dispositive motion, as the defendants have stated. I think of a dispositive motion as a motion to dismiss or a motion for summary judgment that disposes of the case or a cause of action in the case. This is a Rule 702 motion. I've seen many of these in many cases. I've never considered them dispositive motions, and I've never heard of any other party characterize them as such.

In any event, one argument made by the government was that this evidence about efficiencies that was used in Dr. Snyder's analysis was not verified and not verifiable. The parties dispute whether the efficiencies evidence must be verified in order to be admissible or whether such evidence just must be verifiable. And they also dispute whether the evidence is, in fact, verifiable.

I heard oral argument on this issue at our last hearing because I thought that the government's argument on this point was potentially meritorious. I determined that I should hear evidence about the verifiability of the efficiencies before ruling. And if this were a jury trial, I would have heard the evidence before trial, made a ruling on the motion before the trial. But because this is a bench trial, I thought that we had leeway to hear this evidence during the trial.

But I asked the parties to please meet and confer about how this evidence could be presented so that I could address the issue of verifiability first, and if I determined to grant the government's motion, then we would not have to hear the other evidence about efficiencies that is part of Dr. Snyder's analysis, and there's plenty more evidence, and I thought it would be more efficient to proceed this way.

And so I was very surprised when I received a bench memo from the defendants that appeared to forget or overlook that we had had this conversation in court. I thought perhaps I had not been clear, but I went back to the transcript, pages 58 and 59. I said, "Is there a way to efficiently present this so that we don't have to hear evidence if I don't need to get there, because we can't even get past verifiable?"

And I also said, "Let's make sure that we present the evidence in a way that I can address this issue first without having to get into other things we might not need to get into if this is dispositive of this particular analysis."

So I guess my first question is, Mr. Petrocelli or Mr. Frackman, whoever is speaking for the defendants on this, why have you filed a bench memo that disregards what I said in my first hearing?

MR. PETROCELLI: Your Honor, we thought that we had not done a good job of explaining our position the first time, and so that's the reason we filed the bench memo.

Your Honor, I don't really think there's much of a difference between where the parties stand right now. We had agreed to let them recall our witnesses after Mr. Sansigre testified. They could call any one of them back. They don't have to ask any questions about efficiencies. If they're calling our witnesses in their case in chief, in our case, we would present Mr. Sansigre and some others, and then if they wanted to examine our witnesses, they could do so.

The only issue, which I tried to explain in the email, was that there are a couple of third-party witnesses in the plaintiff's case, including the first witness, that we have questions about, and a couple of others, regarding things that relate to efficiencies. Probably we're talking about no more than about—with cross and direct for these witnesses, probably a half an hour at most.

I understood the government's position to be that we couldn't ask any witnesses any questions, including third-party witnesses, about anything related to efficiencies, and we, obviously, can't call those witnesses back in our case in chief to ask them five minutes of questions. That was the only area where we differed.

THE COURT: All right. Well, to be clear, this discussion that we had at our prior hearing was about Dr. Snyder's expert testimony about efficiencies, and that doesn't mean that you can't mention efficiencies in other parts of the trial.

MR. PETROCELLI: Okay.

THE COURT: So with that understanding, are we straight?

MR. PETROCELLI: I think we're good, Your Honor. Yes, we've agreed that we'll call Sansigre and Malaviya before Dr. Snyder. We've also agreed that they can recall any of our witnesses if they want to ask them about efficiency questions after the testimony of Dr. Sansigre; so they don't have to be concerned about that now. And we just have a handful of efficiency-related questions that you'll see today even; and you'll see that they're really of no consequence and no burden on the government.

THE COURT: So I would even consider—and I want to let the parties have some leeway to decide how they want to do this—hearing just the evidence about verifiability from Sansigre or whoever else you want to call on that and then hearing Dr. Snyder just about verifiability, but I don't know if that disrupts your presentation too much.

MR. PETROCELLI: No. No. And to be clear, that's the way it's been set up, Your Honor; that Sansigre and Malaviya, who has a little piece that leads into Sansigre, will lay out the evidence regarding the verifiability of the efficiencies.

If you want to have argument at that point, whether we go forward on efficiencies, we will do so. And then after that, Your Honor, we're prepared to call Professor Snyder who touches upon the verification issue, but actually he's there for two other issues: pass-through and merger specificity. He's not really the verifying person; that's Sansigre.

THE COURT: I understand, but I think it would be appropriate to ask him why he didn't verify.

MR. PETROCELLI: I'm sure they can ask him those questions, and Your Honor can as well.

THE COURT: All right. Thank you.

MR. PETROCELLI: Okay.

THE COURT: All right. Thank you. Anything else from the government on this point, or are we resolved?

MR. SCHWARZ: Following Your Honor's suggestions—and I think, hopefully, we can get this resolved at least before we have to have a lot of our own rebuttal evidence. That will at least save that much time and perhaps others.

THE COURT: Thank you.

MR. SCHWARZ: One other scheduling issue, which the defendants have asked that a gentleman named John Glusman who cannot testify, I believe, until any time after August 8th, be able to be called in our case. Reluctantly, because although they waited for a month to figure this out, we'll agree to do that, Your Honor, just so you understand it's not our witness; it's theirs.

THE COURT: I understand. Thank you for accommodating them. Are there any preliminary matters before we go to opening statements?

MR. CANTOR: Good morning, Your Honor. Daniel Cantor from O'Melveny & Myers.

On Saturday evening at around 6 o'clock, we were notified by the government that during their opening statement they're going to be playing about a 5-minute video clip from the deposition of Mr. Sansigre. We were informed this morning that there would also be deposition clips from Mr. Dohle played during opening.

Your Honor, we believe that this is improper and that the government should be precluded from including those video clips in their opening statement. As Your Honor well knows, an opening is supposed to be the outline of the case and not the evidence in the case. And while the rules have changed over time and different courts have different approaches in terms of how much evidence they will allow someone to mention during openings, the guiding point has always been that it has to be evidence.

And in this case, what they're proposing to play is not, in fact, evidence. Mr. Sansigre and Mr. Dohle will both be testifying live in this trial. The government did not designate either Mr. Sansigre or Mr. Dohle's deposition testimony as something that they would or even might play during the trial.

So the video of the depositions was never going to be an exhibit at trial. And it's totally improper, therefore, Your Honor, for them to be displaying a piece of nonevidence during their opening statements.

THE COURT: Can I ask you a question?

MR. CANTOR: Sure.

THE COURT: Is it your position that the substance of what will be said in those video clips is not admissible evidence?

MR. CANTOR: No, Your Honor. We're not taking the position that they couldn't ask questions of the live witness along those lines, but it is inappropriate to put the video testimony in. It would be inappropriate for them to quote from the deposition transcript, the written deposition transcripts themselves. What they're free to do is ask questions. And if they get an answer that they think gives rise to impeachment, then they can use the written transcript in that way, but this is totally—

THE COURT: Okay.

MR. CANTOR:—aside from that, Your Honor.

THE COURT: Okay. So is the difference between what you're objecting to and what you think is permissible, them saying the evidence will show that and then stating those things versus showing a video of what they think the evidence will show?

MR. CANTOR: That is exactly it, Your Honor.

I mean, the traditional way one does an opening is to say we believe the evidence will show X, Y, and

Z. We will talk to Mr. Sansigre in this case. We believe he will say this, that, or the other thing. It's not permissible, especially when it cannot ever be evidence in the case, for them to say, here's what Mr. Sansigre had to say during his deposition.

THE COURT: Okay. Thank you. Does the government want to respond to that?

MR. CANTOR: Thank you.

MS. STRICK: Your Honor, first, under Rule 32(a)(3), deposition testimony of officers can be used for any purpose. Deposition video clips have played in openings since 2002. I can list some cases, Northfield Insurance Company v. Royal Surplus Lines Insurance, from 2003, WL 25948971, in which a court's Rule 32(a)(2) saying party depositions are permitted and allowing video clips to be played.

Other cases that allowed video clips to be played, MDI Partners, L.P. v. Chronicle Publishing Company, from 2002, WL 32349903. And there are others.

This is a bench trial. We're putting this in to say this is not an exhibit. We're putting this in to show the evidence will show. To the extent that defendants are worried about how this is characterized, both witnesses for the defendants are going to be in the court later and they can question them about this.

So we think that this is just permitted, both under Rule 32(a)(3) and just plain common sense.

THE COURT: Okay. Thank you.

MR. CANTOR: Your Honor, may I respond to that?

THE COURT: I don't think that's necessary. I'm just going to overrule your objection at this time. I think that the government's raised a good point. This is a bench trial, and so to the extent it might be more prudent to be cautious if a jury were involved; this is just going to be before me, and I think this objection is pretty narrow. Because while the government can say the evidence will show that and state what the witnesses will say consistent with what was in their deposition, I don't think there's much difference between them saying that and just playing the deposition tape itself.

And the defense has said that they don't object to the substance of what is in those videotapes. That's not inadmissible evidence, and so this really is a presentation issue. And given that it's a bench trial, I'm going to overrule your objection.

MR. CANTOR: Thank you.

THE COURT: All right. Are there any other preliminary matters before we begin?

MS. STRICK: Your Honor, just one more.

Later today if there's time, we plan on playing a deposition video of the witness for Kensington. Right now we have two versions available. Because there's confidential information, one of that is entirely to be played in closed court. The other one the confidential clips are interspersed. So we have attempted to have one section which is confidential information with enough context and the other one which can be played—that would be played in closed court. The other one, nothing is confidential; could be played in open court.

We have sent that to defendants, who I believe are looking and confirming that they're fine with this, but we wanted to know if you had a preference as to which would be played, if we play the Kensington deposition.

THE COURT: Are you contemplating that we would have an open-court session where you would play part of the video and then go to closed court and play the confidential part?

MS. STRICK: Correct. Or because it's interspersed, we wanted to give you the option as well to play it all in closed court.

THE COURT: You mean the whole thing in closed court?

MS. STRICK: Yes. We can give the court reporter, then, the transcript which will show which portions are actually confidential, which aren't for the record, but just for your—so you can—so—because things are interspersed, we just wanted to make sure that if you wanted something that would be a little chopped up, but that could be played in video now versus giving you a—

THE COURT: I see. Thank you.

I would err on the side of openness, if possible. So I would like to play what we can play in open court in open court before going to a closed session.

MS. STRICK: Okay.

THE COURT: I think that's an important part of this trial, to be as transparent as possible and let the public see as much as they can.

MS. STRICK: Thank you very much.

THE COURT: All right. And if there are no further preliminary matters, I'll hear the government's opening.

OPENING ARGUMENTS

We covered the trial's opening arguments lightly in Publishers Lunch, since all of the presentations built only slightly on the extensive pre-trial briefs, with a few facts and rhetorical flourishes added in.

The DOJ made clear to equate authors with workers or laborers in general—an advance is "compensation for a job"—and to parry PRH's argument that only a "tiny sliver" of authors might suffer harm by saying "it's real money to real people. . . . Most authors of anticipated top sellers never earn a penny beyond their advance. [85% of authors for high advance books do not earn out, the DOJ says.] The thousands of authors whose income is at stake need, deserve and are entitled to protection."

The $1 billion in advances of $250,000 or more that the government is focused on is said to comprise "roughly 70 percent" of advances overall. (There is a little confusion on this point; Read actually said "More significantly, that 1 billion accounts for roughly 70 percent of what defendants spend on advances every year." But the judge and others in further questioning took that to mean not just defendants but either the Big 5 together or the industry as a whole.)

Judge Pan asked later on if that equated to consumer sales as well—e.g. do big advance books comprise 70 percent of sales?, which they clearly do not—as well as confirmation that two percent of the books sold to publishers every year account for some much of the advances paid.

On the evidence regarding Bertelsmann's big role in the US printing industry that the parties skirmished over pre-trial, the government showed they will use that to argue about how hard it might be for smaller publishers to rise up and fill the void after the merger. Smaller companies "are actually beholden" to Bertelsmann for scarce printing resources, and can't become meaningful competitors.

The DOJ played a few bits of testimony from PRH CEO Markus Dohle and executive Manuel Sansigre, the cheap point of which was not to highlight their answers so much as to dwell on their very lengthy pauses before even answering the questions.

In an amusing slip, at one point the DOJ's lead attorney John Read accidentally said "murder" instead of merger, and at the end of his opening he appeared to become very emotional when mentioning the team that supported him in the case.

PRH's attorney Petrocelli directly attacked the DOJ for trying to "think this is kind of a test case" for "using antitrust laws to prevent harm to labor markets." While "some mergers do pose real monopsony risks . . . the situation here is quite different." Speaking to the power of agents in a folksy way, as part of the argument that authors and "agents will continue to have many competitive options," he cited the saying, "The way you know the agents have all the power is that the publishers always pay for lunch."

He also claimed, as part of their challenge to the idea of a distinct market for books that draw higher prices at auction, that, "If you think about it, your honor, every book starts out as an anticipated top seller in the gleam of the author's eye, right?"

Petrocelli worked hard, per their brief, to establish that there is vigorous competition in auctions, from the other Big 5 publishers—"they compete; they win; they're not going anywhere"—as well as "more than 30 smaller publishers" who "compete for and win books for $250,000 or more." In a new factoid, he said non-Big 5 publishers win or come in second in 23 percent of the auctions.

S&S's lead attorney Stephen Fishbein followed with a few well-chosen points, underscoring that "Simon & Schuster will be sold to somebody" and it is "the other book publishers that can attain the highest efficiencies" in buying the house. He noted that HarperCollins and HBG "had no problem with the elimination of an independent S&S if they were the buyer."

OPENING STATEMENT FROM DEPARTMENT OF JUSTICE

MR. READ: May it please the Court.

This proposed merger must be stopped. It would, in defendants' own words, cement Penguin Random House's dominance in the American publishing market. Penguin Random House is already the largest book publisher in the United States. If it acquires Simon & Schuster, it will get even bigger; more than twice the size of its next largest competitor.

Your Honor, there will be significant evidence during this trial about advances paid in the publishing industry. Those advances are the main way that publishers pay authors for their books. The vast majority of advances that publishers pay go to authors of anticipated top sellers. After firms combine, they will own nearly half of that market. The new super-sized Penguin Random House will exercise outside influence over what books get published in this country and how authors are compensated.

This is an industry that's already concentrated. In fact, no publishers have cracked the inside circle of that Big 5 in almost three decades. This merger would make that concentration worse. Indeed, the merger is so problematic, it is presumptively illegal. The merger will reduce compensation, harming authors who are the creative lifeblood of this industry.

As the evidence will show, the industry trades in ideas and creativity in work that's deeply meaningful to the people who author it. Those books, both nonfiction and fiction, have shaped modern political discourse, and social and economic discourse. This lawsuit is designed to protect those authors of those books.

This current competition between Penguin Random House and Simon & Schuster benefits those authors. You will hear Dr. Nicholas Hill—he's the United States economic expert—testify using assumptions in defendants' favor; that if this merger goes through, he predicts Penguin Random

House authors will receive $40,000 less per anticipated top seller, and Simon & Schuster authors will receive $100,000 less per anticipated top seller.

The authors of those anticipated top sellers aren't just the elite or those already making a lot of money. In that group are journalists who need the advances to take a sabbatical from her job, to finance a socially beneficial investment in a project. It includes public figures who are ready to share their memoirs and the fiction author who's already toiled uncompensated for years to write their dream novel before finally selling it to a publisher.

The author's advance is compensation for their work, for a job. To put simply, these funds are essential to an author's livelihood, just like a salary. It's essential to an employee of a company. That's what it's like. And in most circumstances, these advances are paid out in installments over years. So to think an author who receives a $250,000 advance may only be paid $60,000 a year, that's real money to real people.

Some authors have anticipated top sellers sell so well that they earn additional royalties later. But as I'll explain shortly, most authors of anticipated top sellers never earn a penny beyond their initial advance. The evidence will show that the advance is, essentially, the whole ball game for those authors. The thousands of authors whose income is at stake need, deserve, and are entitled to the protection of the Clayton Act.

Finally, competition for anticipated top selling books matters. Defendants suggest that competition in this marketplace can be sacrificed to the corporate bottom-line because it only includes 2 percent of the books. Let's unpack that. The evidence will show that those 2 percent of books account for more than $1 billion in annual spending by the publishing industry. More significantly, that $1 billion accounts for roughly 70 percent of what defendants spend on advances every year.

These are the books that sell, that consumers demand, and that most influence our public discourse. Anticipated top selling books are not some little corner of the book market.

This market is the bread-and-butter business for publishers like Penguin Random House and Simon & Schuster. That's why they compete so fiercely for these authors. They compete by offering bigger advances, better editorial services, better art design, superior promotion, marketing support, and the other services that authors need to have their book be a success.

The competition matters. I'm going to talk later about what the data shows and how close they compete because of that data. But let me share with you one example of how beneficial the competition is between Penguin Random House and Simon & Schuster to an individual author. Your Honor will hear during the trial about an author who wanted to write a compelling memoir of her life. We'll not refer to that author by name or her title right now so we don't invade her privacy, because we want to talk more compellingly about the competition for her work and what it means.

Both Penguin Random House and Simon & Schuster highly valued this book internally and anticipated it would be very successful. The author's memoir generated a lot of interest initially in the industry. And so we begin, on the slide, the morning of February 24th. There are initially seven bidders. Penguin Random House is top at $550,000. Simon & Schuster next at 510; Hachette at 300. And they're followed by Macmillan, HarperCollins, Norton, and Bloomsbury. Those two smaller publishers each bid at $100,000 or less.

The next day there's additional bidding, and at midday—and then there's bidding until 6:00 p.m. Penguin Random House has raised its bid to $645,000 and leads. Simon & Schuster is a close second at 625. Hachette is still in the game at $605,000. All the other participants did not raise their bid, and they drop out at levels below $300—250,000.

The next day bids were submitted around 10:30 in the morning, and you see a three-bidder horse race. Penguin Random House, as you see, comes out at top at 685. Simon & Schuster at 665. And Hachette's right there in third place at 650. But that's Hachette's last bid.

The next day, from 10:30 a.m. to 6:00 p.m., Penguin Random House bid back and forth, back and forth, alternating in rounds raising at $20,000 increments. The highest bid goes to 705. Then it goes to 725. Simon & Schuster's last bid comes in at 745, end of the day, and then Penguin Random House tops at 765. Hachette long ago dropped out.

The next day at 10:40 in the morning, Simon & Schuster raises its bid to 765, passing—or 785, passing Penguin Random House. A few minutes later, Penguin Random House takes the lead again with a bid of $805,000.

Then before 3:40, Simon & Schuster matches Penguin Random House at 805. But Penguin Random House comes in a few minutes later with another $20,000; wins the bidding with the high of 825. Penguin Random House's high bid of 825 comes well after Hachette drops out. Remember when it was at 650? The only two remaining bidders were the defendants.

It was only Simon & Schuster's aggressive independent bidding that forces Penguin Random House to more fully pay what it believes the author's book is worth. This author's labor benefits by close to $200,000 because Simon & Schuster alone continues to compete against Penguin Random House. That competition is worth protecting. And there are many other examples you're going to hear of during this trial; examples that would be lost if this merger proceeds.

One note, this auction is a little unique in that all the Big 5 originally participated. Often only some of the Big 5 participate. And then the loss of Simon & Schuster matters even more.

Now defendants' attempt to disparage the facts of this loss and others by suggesting that in a conservative estimate of harm by our economist, over tens of millions of dollars are at stake each year. I think they called that minuscule in one of the writings before this Court.

In all the numbers and evidence the Court will hear, let's not lose this: Whether it's $200,000 for one author or tens of millions for many authors for many books, competition results in authors being paid more fully for their hard labor. There's no good reason to lessen that competition so those minuscule amounts of money can flow to Bertelsmann. Frankly, tens of millions of dollars year in, year out are not minuscule for most of us, and they're certainly not trivial for the authors who often work hard to write these books.

During trial, economist Nick Hill will walk more fully through the effects of the merger. Yet certain parts of his analysis don't need very much explanation, like how important the Big 5 are to the authors of the anticipated top sellers. This bar chart shows how many of the books with advances greater than $250,000 each publisher has acquired. You see on the left, Penguin Random House in dark blue, and Simon & Schuster in green; towering over every other publisher in the industry, even other members of the Big 5 after the merger.

Dr. Hill listed first in order of share of acquisitions, the publishers, the combined share of Penguin Random House and Simon & Schuster's almost half the market. And the share of all the Big 5 is 90 percent of the market.

Then you see five small publishers, each with about 1 percent share each. And then just for convenience, we've aggregated all the other small publishers. They all have a fraction of a percent—and there's scores of them—and they total about 5 percent each.

Now, we expect, Your Honor, defendants will elicit testimony of a publisher winning one prominent author here—one of these small ones—winning one publisher here and another one winning another publisher there. And, of course, that's why they have some share, but their wins are relatively rare as evidenced by their low share.

In contrast, Penguin Random House, Simon & Schuster, HarperCollins, Hachette, and Macmillan—all the bars to the left—they're called the Big 5 because they've long dominated the industry. They've got the capital, they've got editorial capacity, marketing, sales force; most importantly, reputation. Reputation to successfully churn out best sellers time after time and convince authors that they're the ones to do it. They have the ability to take on the risk of an inexpensive book that may not sell well.

The internal documents of Penguin Random House acknowledge how dominant it is. They indicate the merger was designed to, quote, cement Penguin Random House as the largest dominant publisher in the United States, and it does.

Here's one of the clips we talked about earlier. It's the CEO of Penguin Random House. He's here today, and you'll hear how he reluctantly had to agree that this merger cements Penguin Random House as number one in the industry.

(An audio-video recording was played.)

MR. READ: If Penguin Random House cements its dominance in the United States market, hardens it so it does not need to worry about rivals overtaking it, that benefits one and only group, its shareholder, its owner, Bertelsmann.

Now, during this opening I'd like to cover some industry background, the legal standard for the merger, the product market, competition in the marketplace and harm, and, finally, some of the mitigating factors that defendants argue.

But before we cover those topics, I just want to give you a brief overview of the types of witnesses you'll hear from and the kinds of evidence you'll hear.

First, you'll hear from literary agents, such as Ayesha Pande, and famed author Stephen King. Based on their years of experience, they'll explain how the publishers acquire the rights to books, the importance of competition in obtaining a fair price for an author's labor. They'll help you see through an author's eyes what your options are if you craft an important book and need a publisher who can make that book a success.

In addition to agents and authors, Your Honor will hear from editors at defendants and other companies. They'll explain the internal process for valuing a book, for using comparables to determine the likely success of a book, and how they compete to win books for competitors.

Your Honor will also hear from the CEOs of each one of the Big 5 publishers in person, including today the CEO of Hachette. You'll also hear from the CEOs of several smaller publishers by deposition. These CEOs will provide you with a rich record for your decision. The big—the Big 5 CEOs will describe how they compete with other Big 5 publishers, and the CEOs of the smaller publishers will tell you about how uneven the playing field is for them, which will make it clear that these small publishers cannot suddenly grow and expand to replace the force of Simon & Schuster.

You'll then hear late in the government's case, the expert Dr. Hill. He's an economist. He's been recognized in several courts as an expert. He's testified both in support of and against the Department of Justice and Federal Trade Commission. He will explain as a matter of economics how the acquisition of anticipated top selling books are a market and the shares of that market. He'll discuss the degree of competition from smaller publishers, barriers to expansion that small publishers face. He'll estimate for you, even though he doesn't have to, the harm authors will face based on well-accepted economic models.

If defendants present a viable efficiencies defense, you'll hear in rebuttal the testimony of Dr. Hammer, an accountant, to talk about the viability of their claim. You'll also hear Dr. Hill probably in rebuttal to respond to any claims by defendants' expert.

Finally, you'll see contemporaneous documents of the merging parties and other industry players that corroborate the key points of the testimony and all the elements necessary for the defendants—for the United States to prove its case.

So let's begin with the background. And we're mindful Your Honor has read lengthy pretrial briefs; so I'll be brief here. I just want to highlight a few things that the witnesses will speak to. Authors typically work with a literary agent to sell the publishing rights to a book, and that's either in direct negotiations or in an auction. And the key term is the advance because that's guaranteed compensation to the authors. There are—there are prepayment of royalties, and the reality is that 85 percent of the time, an author of anticipated top selling books, that's all they get is the advance, is the whole payment. These advance payments are not lump-sum windfalls.

While we think about books like fiction books you curl up with, there's also included in this a lot of nonfiction books. And for a nonfiction writer, like a professor who's writing about a moment in history or a journalist who's doing investigative reporting, that advance goes to traveling for interviews. It goes to original research. It goes to hiring a photographer or an illustrator for the materials in the book.

That advance is paid out over time; so it's not one lump-sum payment for an author. And Your Honor will hear that even if the advance does not earn out, if the author does not get royalties later, the publisher can still make money on the book. Often does.

As we get to this final bullet about imprints, I wanted to note that Penguin Random House is the result of years of consolidation. Its name tells that story. Penguin and Random House. Those were two separate large publishers, part of the Big 6 of American publishing, that merged to bring it down to a Big 5. As a result, you're about to see, Penguin Random House owns 90 U.S. publishing imprints, most of which it has acquired over this time.

This slide gives a sense of the breadth and scope of Penguin Random House and Simon & Schuster's imprints. By the way, imprints are brand names of different publishing groups, which I think Your Honor knows, with different editorial focus. Now, it can be a challenge to keep track of which publishing house controls which imprints. Included in this list, the Penguin Random House imprints are such well-known publishers as Crown, Ballantine, Bantam, Del Rey, Delacorte Press, Clarkson Potter, Viking. And I could go on, but I don't want to go too fast for the court reporter.

And Simon & Schuster has imprints that are well known, such as Atria, Scribner, and Gallery. And each of these imprints—this is what shouldn't be lost—is under the control of senior management. Your Honor will hear evidence advancing that senior management has and undoubtedly will continue to change and consolidate these imprints. They ensure these imprints row in the same direction, and particularly the level of advance—of advances at issue; senior management ensures that different imprints don't competitively undercut each other.

Let's spend a moment on the market. You may have wondered which authors are most likely harmed by this merger. So we've defined a market around that with that question in mind. And, therefore, our proof at trial will focus on authors of anticipated top selling books. These books are, by definition, expected to sell well. And authors of these books usually, therefore, receive a generous advance.

We'll use $250,000 and greater as a threshold for anticipated top selling books. But that doesn't mean there isn't harm on the other side of that $250,000.

In fact, the Court will see that choosing a significantly higher or lower threshold does not materially affect the analysis. This marketplace is so concentrated, it's presumptively illegal whether the threshold is $100,000 or $1 million.

As we turn to the legal standard, I want to clarify something defendants put in their pretrial brief. The standard here is what may occur, not what is likely to happen. Congress made this clear in the plain text of Section 7 of the Clayton Act. That prohibits mergers whose effect, quote, may substantially lessen competition. Congress intended courts to stop industry trends toward consolidation in their incipiency before they, quote, tend to create a monopoly.

This statute, the Clayton Act, Your Honor is about to deal with, is different than most; right? It makes you anticipate the future rather than determine past events.

Recognizing the difficulties of projecting the future, Section 7 of the Clayton Act only requires the Court to determine whether a lessening competition may occur.

Let's read how Judge Posner expanded on this point, which has been adopted by the D.C. Circuit in Heinz. Judge Posner noted that Section 7 does not require proof that a merger or other acquisition has caused higher prices. All that's necessary is that the merger create an appreciable danger of such consequences in the future. A predictive judgment, necessarily probabilistic and judgmental rather than demonstrable is called for. We're likely to come back to this point again, Your Honor, because we respectfully request that the Court reject defendants' invitation to raise the bar on the burden. It's no higher than the plain text of the Clayton Act. The merger should be enjoined if this—if this consolidation may lessen competition. Recognizing the difficulty improving what the future may hold and to fulfill

Congress's intent, the Supreme Court also created a presumption that a merger is illegal if the merger significantly concentrates a market. That presumption began in the Philadelphia National Bank case before the Supreme Court, and the Supreme Court presumed harm to competition when the merged firm significantly concentrated that market by merging to 30 percent. Your Honor will see that this merger well surpasses that 30 percent threshold, as we're looking close to half the market.

Now, today courts and enforcement agencies have adopted a more sophisticated mathematical analysis of the market concentration. We call it the Herfindahl-Hirschman Index, or HHI. The D.C. Circuit and other appellate courts have adopted that HHI analysis and test to determine whether a presumption applies. And as you can see, that—thresholds are 2,500; that the post-merger concentration is. And the merger needs to increase concentration by 200.

Dr. Hill will explain how the merger easily surpasses those standards that the D.C. Circuit has recognized, and you will learn that the presumption applies even if the threshold from our definition is lowered, as I spoke before, even to a hundred thousand.

Here the presumption is strong. Dr. Hill will testify the HHI numbers will exceed 3,100 and well exceed 800 because of the merger. What that means is that if defendants cannot rebut the presumption that applies, this merger cannot proceed. When, as here, the presumption of illegality is triggered, courts shift the burden to defendants to show that the benefits of the merger are so compelling that they overwhelm this presumption of illegality.

As the D.C. Circuit stated, the defendants need to produce evidence showing that the market share statistics give an inaccurate account of the merger's probable effect on competition. That comes from Heinz. Your Honor will see defendants cannot meet that burden, which is not surprising.

And case after case in this Court's circuit, courts have found defendant's attempts to rebut the presumption insufficient and enjoined the challenged merger. Those cases include cases by your colleagues from H&R Block, Sysco, Staples, Aetna, Anthem, Wilhelmsen, the D.C. Circuit in Heinz Beech-Nut, CCC Holdings, and Tronox.

Your Honor, this gives me the opportunity to respond to two unusual arguments defendants raised in their pretrial brief. First, defendants claim that the HHIs and the presumption of illegality from concentrating a market don't apply to what antitrust lawyers call a unilateral case.

Defendants' claim is just wrong. Unilateral effects cases are those where the merger gives the merging party the power to profitably worsen prices on its own.

Defendants' characterization of the case law and academic literature in the pretrial brief is, frankly, misleading. We will have more to say about that in our post-trial briefing but wanted to put you on notice of that. Suffice it to say that courts, such as Anthem, Aetna, Sysco, and others, routinely apply the presumption to unilateral effects cases. It's not controversial.

Second, defendants spend some time in their pretrial brief asserting this merger should proceed because any anticompetitive harm suffered by authors is insufficient on its own to establish a violation of law. They, essentially, say that even if Your Honor finds that authors will be harmed, you should reject the government's case because we haven't shown that that will lead to fewer books.

Economists call this an output effect. First, defendants cite no case law for this novel attempt to increase the government's burden, and we discussed relevant cases in our opening—in our pretrial brief on that as well. For example, a court that blocked the purchase of Penn Grade crude oil without requiring any proof of a reduction in output. We'll have more to say about that in our post-trial briefing as well. But, frankly, it should be a nonissue.

While it's not the government's burden to show that the supply of books will go down, let's take a moment to listen to the Penguin Random House's CEO, Markus Dohle, explain in different context what happens when you lower advances to authors. This takes a moment as Mr. Dohle gives thought to the response.

(An audio-video recording was played.)

MR. READ: The government could but won't simply rely on the presumption of illegality. Your Honor will hear testimony and receive documentary evidence from market participants that validates what the shares show; that Penguin Random House will dominate the market if the merger proceeds, and that the Big 5 stand apart from the other publishers.

The merging parties understand this. You will see their internal documents corroborate the implication of the high market shares. This document was drafted by the former CEO of Simon & Schuster Carolyn

Reidy. She, sadly, passed away in May 2020. She created this document in 2019 in response to questions asked during due diligence from the merger of Viacom and CBS; and CBS had owned Simon & Schuster.

Viacom executives wanted Ms. Reidy's input to better understand and analyze her business. She describes for them the threat level of large and of small publishers. With regard to large publishers she writes, "The U.S. publishing market is made of what is known as the 'Big 5.'"—[Penguin Random House] dominates with the largest market share, followed by Harper Collins and then [Simon & Schuster]. Hachette is a close fourth, followed by Macmillan. These companies are our biggest competitors, especially for books by already bestselling authors and celebrities, since they are the most likely to come up with high advance payments required and are known for their strong editorial and publishing skills."

Note that Ms. Reidy understood even before this proposed merger that Penguin Random House dominates, and she understood that competition is especially fierce between Penguin Random House and Simon & Schuster and the other Big 5 for bestselling authors. And the reason is because those publishers can come up with the high advance payments required, and have the strong editorial and publishing skills.

Next Ms. Reidy addresses competition from the small publishers. She writes, "There are myriad smaller publishers . . . they too can compete with us for the bestseller list at any one time . . . but they rarely compete with us in auctions for new properties. Often these publishers become farm teams for authors who then want to move to a larger, more financially stable major publisher."

Ms. Reidy's turn of phrase about farm teams—minor league baseball teams that nurture raw talent and then lose them to the big league teams once the talent is ready to succeed—is especially apt. Her message that all those smaller publishers rarely compete in auctions for big sellers, that they act as farm teams developing talent for the Big 5 publishers that later acquire them is consistent with the implication of the market share data you will see.

Turning to product market. The defendants spent a lot of time in their pretrial brief attacking the product market in this case. They say it's not recognized by the industry, it's not supported by economics, but those arguments won't square with the evidence. The product market we focused on here draws from Ms. Reidy's recognition that the Big 5, especially, compete for bestselling authors and celebrities. The product market is based on how the industry actually operates. It's confirmed by economic analysis. In fact, the $250,000 line means something in defendants' own business. Per its own policies, defendants require higher approval levels and documentation before offering $250,000 or higher advances.

Let's talk about why we define a relative market in the first place. Courts define a relevant market to focus their inquiry where the Supreme Court says, in fact, competition exists. As an initial matter, we note that the defendants don't seriously dispute that the hypothetical monopolist's test is satisfied here. What's that mean?

Economic experts in courts look to that test to answer that question of whether there is a relevant product market. In other words, whether there are insufficient alternatives to protect authors if the market goes to a monopoly. Here there's little disagreement that a monopoly publisher or, more technically, a monopolist publisher could harm authors of anticipated top sellers by lowering advances because those authors don't have a good alternative. Self-publishing is an unappealing option for most authors of anticipated top selling books.

Now, defendants quibble—unlike most cases—is that authors can protect themselves. It's not that authors cannot protect themselves by choosing self-publishing; rather, they argue there's no proper line or boundary that can be drawn.

But that misses the point. Line drawing exists to help the Court evaluate the potential anticompetitive effects of the merger.

The drawing of the line and the specific line that is drawn isn't an end to itself. The reality is an industry rarely presents a court with a perfectly drawn bright line that can be used to separate where there's harm and where there's not. That's why courts say that the boundary line for a market does not need to be defined by perfect, quote, metes and bounds. Any reasonable boundary line here will show the importance of the Big 5 and Penguin Random House's dominance after the merger.

Broad markets, like the essentially unchallenged market for all books acquired, can include submarkets, which the Supreme Court has said made themselves, quote, constitute product markets for antitrust purposes. This anticipated top seller market is such a submarket. Defining a market around those authors who will most likely be harmed follows the law in this and other circuits.

Listed on this slide are three cases from this district that define the market around the set of customers most likely to be targeted or harmed by the merger. These cases all illustrate that line drawing for market definition purposes need not be surgically precise but, rather, is done to provide the courts with a useful framework for analyzing the likely effects of the proposed merger.

In Anthem, the court recognized a market bounded around national customers of health insurance; meaning in that case, those that had 5,000 or more employees. Customers with 4,900 employees were excluded from the market, even though that didn't mean they weren't harmed.

In Staples, the court analyzed the market around large customers, which were defined as those customers who spent over 500,000 or more on office supplies. Those customers who spent a little less were out of the market.

In Wilhelmsen, the Court approved a market of global fleets consisting of companies of ten or more vessels. It excluded those fleets of nine or fewer ships. Emphasizing the point that the boundary line does not have to be—have perfect precision around where the competition of—competitive harm would end, the Court approved the cutoff of ten vessels because of, quote, its roundness and simplicity. Roundness and simplicity are far from the hypertechnical precision defendants insist are required.

The Wilhelmsen court noted that the parties had high market shares both above and below the round number. The court indicated it was sufficient. There was enough competitive harm among those customers with ten vessels or more to enjoin the merger, and that's all true here.

Focusing on anticipated top sellers is consistent with Ms. Reidy's statement about where the Big 5 especially compete. It's also consistent with the Ninth Circuit decision in an antitrust case in another creative industry, movies. When looking at how movies would be affected by the alleged anticompetitive conduct, the Ninth Circuit upheld a product market of industry-anticipated top grossing films. That proper product market distinguished those movies that were anticipated to be successful and forged the anticompetitive conduct would cause the most harm from those not so anticipated. We do the same here.

Our common sense tells us that the competition looks different for anticipated top selling books and other books. And the economics supports that. These columns, which Your Honor will see evidence of later in trial, show that the competitive environment for books looks very different where advances are high and where they are low. This will come from Dr. Hill.

To show the change in the competitive success of the small publishers, the columns are reoriented. So at the bottom in dark purple are the small publishers all grouped together. And then above them are the Big 5 in descending order, with Penguin Random House in dark blue, and Simon & Schuster in green, and the other Big 5.

On the left, the small publishers—this is for the advance of $250,000 or above—the small publishers account for a 9 percent share. By comparison on the right, looking at acquisitions below $250,000 that are much smaller, you see there the small publishers have a much larger share of 45 percent.

The contrast with the columns on the right and the left is stark. On the right, the small publishers are sizable, but they've clearly lost their competitive punch at the higher advanced levels, where they're no longer selling books to small niche audiences or books that have limited sales potential.

You will hear testimony—and this information comes from the data of that defendants' expert. You will hear testimony from large and small publishers that confirm this data; that the small publishers find less success and compete less aggressively for advances above $250,000.

We wanted to play one clip. You will hear this deposition clip during trial. It's from Liate Stehlik. She's a senior publishing executive at HarperCollins, and she testifies the smaller publishers are not in the very expensive auctions because they can't absorb the losses.

(An audio-video recording was played.)

MR. READ: There will be more to that testimony that Your Honor will hear. As you previewed—where you draw the line here is not particularly sensitive. The shares show that Penguin Random House will dominate no matter how—the metric used as a threshold for anticipated top selling books.

We're going to put on the screen one more slide from Dr. Hill to make this point. This slide shows different columns for different thresholds of advances. On the far left is if you used a threshold of $150,000 for an anticipated top seller. Next column is $250,000 in yellow because that's what we're using. And then you can see 350, 500, 1 million. What is important is that the blue and the green, the Penguin Random House and the Simon & Schuster at the bottom, you see that they're approximately 50 percent regardless of the threshold.

You see that the blue, green, red, lighter blue, and orange—the Big 5—are about 90 percent regardless of the threshold. The key is that regardless of the threshold, this merger is anticompetitive, presumptively illegal, and we could draw the line at 150 or a hundred thousand. We could have captured more volume of commerce and, theoretically, more harm, but we wanted to be conservative, and we chose $250,000.

But either way, it's a huge market with huge concentration. Let's turn to the marketplace competition and harm.

Penguin Random House's and Simon & Schuster's vigorous, head-to-head competition for anticipated top sellers has resulted in higher advances, better service, more favorable contract terms, which has real-world consequences for authors.

When I began, Your Honor, I talked about that author who benefited by $200,000. That's far from an isolated incident.

You're going to hear other evidences of head-to-head competition that will be lost by this merger. I won't go through those now, but I will tell you that Simon & Schuster and Penguin Random House know that they compete frequently against each other, and they don't like losing to each other. You're going to see four examples just from their documents that are illustrative. The first one, "We also lost the homeless auction to Crown"—which is a Penguin Random House imprint. "This was the third beauty contest we lost this week to PRH." These are all Simon & Schuster documents.

The next. "I did everything I could and we lost to Random House . . . Frustrating."

Third, another auction. "I'm concerned that if we offer less than $8 million, [the agency] will go back to PRH. [The agent] said they were willing to offer more."

Another. "Portfolio"—another Penguin Random House imprint—"offered $1 million for World." That means world rights. "To win the book, we'll have to offer $1.1 million . . . I think we should top Portfolio . . . for the following reasons . . . I don't want to let [Penguin Random House] steal an author we've invested in and developed."

This harm is not limited to auctions alone. If Simon & Schuster is negotiating with an author, both sides know that if Simon & Schuster does not offer enough, the author can turn to Penguin Random House, Simon & Schuster's biggest competitor, to get another quote.

Now, these former competitors seek to be partners.

Your Honor will see not only individual examples of competition, but data, specifically diversion-ratio data, which quantifies the extent of the competition. The data on diversion will indicate that the market shares accurately portray the degree of competition. Simon & Schuster loses more book contracts to Penguin Random House than anyone else, and Penguin Random House loses a significant amount to Simon & Schuster as represented by a significant share.

The data will show there's little diversion to the small publishers reflecting their small shares accurately reflect their limited competitive strength.

We expect, Your Honor, defendants will spend a lot of time at trial pointing to dozens of small publishers, many so small they have a fraction of a percent, and claim that just the existence of all of them means the merger cannot substantially harm competition. You'll see examples of a small publisher nurturing a top selling author and that author staying loyal to the small publisher. But you'll also hear why these small publishers remain small publishers and that none of them have been able to grow to become one of the Big 5 in over 30 years.

If we think about all that's happened in business and commerce in the last 30 years—the rise of the internet, how books are sold, how other commodities are sold—and it's remarkable to think that the Big 5 remained unchanged with the exception of what used to be the Big 6—these small publishers have never established a reputation for churning out best seller after best seller like the Big 5 have. They do not possess the same assets.

Please listen to the testimony of Michael Jacobs. He's going to testify by video. He's the CEO of Abrams. It's one of the small publishers, although it's one of the bigger ones. And he testifies to the reality of things that Abrams as a small publisher is constantly outbid.

(An audio-video recording was played.)

MR. READ: Your Honor, a small publisher has to really, really believe in a particular book and be willing to stretch for it because it cannot as routinely and as cost-effectively turn that book into lots of sales. And after the merger, these small publishers are not to magically start stretching further to win more anticipated top selling books as they do today.

We spend a moment on harm. Because of the presumption of illegality and its application, we could end the analysis here. But while the government doesn't have to show evidence of harm, you'll see some at trial. For example, consider Christy Fletcher. Ms. Fletcher is a successful literary agent. She was on defendants' initial witness list, and she lived through the prior merger of Penguin with Random House. Based on her experience, she testifies of her concern that authors would potentially receive less for their labor if this merger is handled in the same way as the last one. Please listen.

(An audio-video recording was played.)

MR. READ: Dr. Hill will provide for you a quantification of a potential harm to authors, and as I said earlier, he predicts using a standard economic model and conservative assumptions that it will harm Penguin Random House anticipated top selling authors by $40,000, and Simon & Schuster top selling authors by a hundred thousand. Losing a hundred thousand in advances can't help but affect the quality and number of books those authors write. Imagine any other industry where the losses were a hundred thousand for the laborers.

The prediction in—the model makes about the impact is consistent with the other evidence the Court will see about the importance of head-to-head competition and the expectation by industry participants that the merger will pay for lower advances—will lead to lower advances for authors. In addition to head-to-head competition, Your Honor will also hear evidence that the merger leads to an increased risk of what we call tacit or explicit coordination among the remaining major competitors.

As stated by the trial court in this district in CCC Holdings, merger law rests upon the theory that where rivals are few, firms will be able to coordinate their behavior, either by overt collusion or implicit understanding, in order to restrict output and achieve profits above competitive levels. The theory follows that absent extraordinary circumstances, a merger that results in an increase in competition—concentration above certain levels raises the likelihood of interdependent anticompetitive conduct.

That implicit understanding referred to can simply be that once one firm becomes dominant in the market, the other firms decide to play follow the leader in their choices about how to compensate authors or the terms in which they set for authors. But this implicit or expected understanding is generally—one thing to note is this implicit understanding is not actionable generally under the antitrust laws once the merger is approved. It's too late. There's no legal action an author or the government can take after the merger to prevent publishers from interdependently choosing to just follow the lead of Penguin Random House. As a result, the same presumption of illegality I discussed earlier attaches to coordinated effects cases.

And the court puts the burden, quote—it's from the same court—on the defendants to demonstrate structural barriers unique to the industry that are sufficient to defeat the ordinary presumption of collusion that attaches to a merger.

Defendants will not be able to make that showing. We already know that in this industry a court found coordination—specific, that Simon & Schuster and Penguin—before the merger with Random House—were both found by the Second Circuit to have colluded to raise ebook prices. After this merger, the market will be even more ripe for coordination, even simple legal coordination of a follow-the-leader variety.

Penguin Random House's unsurpassed position as the dominant publisher will give it greater ability and incentive to punish any other publisher it believes is acting as a maverick and not following the industry lead.

Let's turn to the last part of the presentation.

Defendants have raised one purported defense, efficiencies, and identified three other mitigating factors: expansion, agent power, and the promise of internal bidding.

Efficiencies are a common defense theme, but they're easy for optimistic business executives to puff up, and for that reason—and it's hard for courts to get underneath them and test them. For that reason, the Supreme Court long ago rejected efficiencies as a defense. The Court of Appeals expressed skepticism of them. And in this circuit, efficiencies have never justified an otherwise anticompetitive merger.

As this Court is well aware, to even begin to consider efficiencies, they have to be verified. There are other important requirements, but if the claimed efficiencies can't be verified by someone independent of the parties, the inquiry ends. Your Honor will see that defendants' rosy efficiency claims have not been verified by any independent actor.

In a deposition where he spoke as a corporate representative on efficiencies, a 30(b)(6) deposition,

Manuel Sansigre, who we're about to introduce to you, explained his investment spreadsheet; how it's a top-down model, and how he could not know if Penguin Random House could achieve these efficiencies until he had more confidential data and discussions with Simon & Schuster, which they had not done while the deal was pending. Let's meet Mr. Sansigre.

(An audio-video recording was played.)

MR. READ: Based on testimony like that, there will be no evidence of verifiable efficiencies and nothing to weigh against the harm of the merger.

Turning to the last three mitigating factors. With regard to the claim of injury, the idea behind that claim is that the small publishers will suddenly grow so they can replace the competitive pressure that comes from Simon & Schuster. Defendants won't make such a showing. There are, and Your Honor will see, high barriers to expanding and becoming a major publisher that can meaningfully compete to routinely acquire anticipated top selling books.

There have been no changes among the Big 5 publishers for decades, with the exception of some being bought out.

That's hardly a story of powerful entry. Your Honor will hear testimony from the CEO of one small publisher explaining that it is, quote, very difficult, end quote, to compete against the Big 5 for books with an advance of $250,000 or higher.

To combat the fact that existing small publishers have been unable to grow in the anticipated top-selling market over time, defendants' expert identified four brand-new companies that entered, and these are his poster examples of new entry. But the entry defendants' expert will point to has been minuscule, as Your Honor will see.

These are charts from Dr. Hill's report. They're based on data from defendants' expert, and they show how small that new entry is. Each column represents a different year. For simplicity, the shares of the Big 5 are all combined at the bottom and have a steady 90 percent. The smaller publishers are combined and have the rest of the share, which has been steady, except the big four poster examples have had their actual share combined. And in bright red, there are small slivers, as you see, in the very last year. That's the extent of new entry that defendants' expert points to.

Your Honor will also hear—and let it not be lost—that Amazon entered the publishing industry with a splash about a decade ago. Even with all its scales and resources, Amazon has had to retrench, and now it's just one of the many small competitors with a 1 percent share or less.

And then Your Honor will hear testimony that there's a shortage of book printing capacity in this country. One of the printing providers is a Bertelsmann subsidiary, a sister company to Penguin Random House. Many publishers that defendants claim will expand to compete against Penguin Random House post-merger are actually beholden to the Bertelsmann printing company and its capacity.

The CEOs of HarperCollins and Macmillan will come before you. They're expected to testify that even they—with their large share and size—will find it harder to compete afterwards against Penguin Random House because of the printing and the retailing muscle that Penguin Random House will have.

What they face, as big publishers install their expansion, exists in spades for the smaller publishers.

The next mitigating factor, agent power. Your Honor will hear from defendants that the agents control the auctions, just like your real estate agent does when selling your home; but the evidence will show that just because agents have alternative ways to ask for bids, it doesn't prevent the harm from the loss of competition from losing an aggressive bidder.

The real estate agent can't manufacture competition and desires an enthusiastic bidder. A different auction approach can't substitute for that.

Ms. Fletcher, a long-time agent, who we showed the clip of before, succinctly and, obviously, testified—and you will hear it—quote, with fewer bidders, it's harder to drive the advances up.

Let's turn to the last mitigating factor, the promise to have Simon & Schuster continue to compete. No court has ever approved a merger based on a promise quite like this. In fact, it's hard to find another case where defendants have made such a flimsy promise to justify the merger. The fact that Penguin Random House is making it implies that this merger is a bad deal for authors. Here's a slide showing when the deal was announced. A lot of authors and agents were on Twitter expressing their concern about the harmful effects, and here are some of those tweets.

The result is Penguin Random House has been working to assuage those concerns, and as part of that effort, it's promised what it has not done before in—contrary to its current policy; that even though there are no other bidders for a book, it's going to let Simon & Schuster and Penguin Random House imprints go after head to head, driving up prices and increasing Penguin Random House's own costs.

Beyond that public relations promise, the public—who this promise is supposed to protect—can't enforce it.

Penguin Random House will still control those imprints. It will still be able to combine them together, focus them on different genres so they aren't competing for the same books; and nobody outside of Penguin Random House is going to be able to verify or monitor the promise.

Let's hear the last video clip. This is from the CEO of Kensington, Steve Zacharius. He's another small publisher, although one of the largest, and he testifies to the economic irrationality of the promise. Let's hear a fellow CEO explain it.

(An audio-video recording was played.)

MR. READ: Given the Supreme Court's Copperweld decision, which allows 100 percent-owned subsidiaries to legally collude, Penguin Random House at any time can stop Simon & Schuster from competing legally. Defendants are asking you to bet on their goodwill; that they'll continue their promise in perpetuity. But goodwill bends often to exigencies of time, earning statements, market demands. And authors shouldn't bear that risk.

I'd like to conclude. Over the next few weeks, Your Honor will have the opportunity to hear several DOJ attorneys conduct examination given their knowledge of the case and hard work in gathering the evidence. We're a team. And what will be clear that comes from that team is that if this merger is allowed to proceed, Penguin Random House will achieve its stated goal of cementing itself as number one in the United States. That will be good for Penguin Random House's business but bad for the marketplace of ideas, for the authors who contribute to that, and its sacrifices paid to the authors for market consolidation, which is bad.

At the conclusion of all this evidence, Your Honor, it won't surprise you that we will ask the Court to use the Clayton Act to protect authors and the publishers [sic] who read the book of authors and to enjoin this merger.

Thank you.

THE COURT: Thank you, Mr. Read. Can I ask you two questions? First, what was the Second Circuit case that found coordination in the industry?

MR. READ: I'm sorry?

THE COURT: What was the Second Circuit case that found coordination in the industry?

MR. READ: United States v. Apple, Your Honor.

THE COURT: Okay. And another question. I haven't seen this in everything I read, but do the sales and the downstream market for books correlate strongly to the level of advances paid?

MR. READ: Yes.

THE COURT: So if anticipated top selling books account for 70 percent of advances, do 70 percent of books sold have advances paid of more than $250,000?

MR. READ: If I understand the question right, yes. Your Honor will see that there's a correlation between the size of the advance and the success of the book in retail sales, yes.

THE COURT: Okay. All right. Thank you.

OPENING STATEMENTS FROM BERTELSMANN/PRH AND VIACOMCBS/S&S

MR. PETROCELLI: Thank you. For the record, Daniel Petrocelli for defendants Bertelsmann and Penguin Random House.

And I speak more slowly than Mr. Read. I may go a little bit over an hour, but I'll try to keep it within that time.

THE COURT: All right.

MR. PETROCELLI: So, Your Honor, as you know, Section 7 of the Clayton Act requires the government to prove that the likely effect of the merger is to substantially lessen competition. We submit the trial evidence will show the government cannot meet that burden. And although it's not our burden, we also suggest, Your Honor, the evidence is going to show just the opposite; that the combination of these two firms, Penguin Random House and Simon & Schuster, will only enhance the fierce competition that exists both downstream and upstream in the publishing business. Author advances are not going to go down. They will continue to go up.

Now, when we look at how we got here, Your Honor, what we see is what I call an incredible shrinking of the government's case. And I say that—the reason that—the first question the government would have examined as it does in all mergers is whether this merger would harm consumers. The answer was a resounding no. There's no harm to competition in the sale of books. There's no higher prices to booksellers, no higher prices to book readers, no fewer books, no reduction in quality, no harm at all to consumers or booksellers as a result of this merger.

And the reason for that, Your Honor, is that the downstream market is not concentrated. Publishers of all types and sizes compete aggressively to sell the books that readers want to read; and the government will concede that after this merger, there will continue to be robust competition downstream.

If you could just look at these shares. This is the public version; so I've kept some numbers off of here, Your Honor. And also I will tell you that this is based on Dr. Hill's data. And as I will show you in a minute, the actual shares for Penguin Random House and Simon & Schuster are significantly less.

But this is what the downstream market looks like, and you're also going to hear that Penguin Random House has been losing share downstream for years to non-Big 5 publishers, as well as self-publishing.

Now, why am I showing this to you, Your Honor? Why are we talking about the downstream case when this is a monopsony case? Because it means that every one of those publishers downstream has a strong incentive to compete and sell books, which, in turn, means that they must compete vigorously upstream to get the books the readers want.

Remember, Your Honor, this is not a case where we're dealing with a product component, like brakes on a car. The product that's being acquired upstream is the product the publishers are competing to sell downstream, and every book is unique. We're not dealing with bushels of wheat. Every book is a new product that has never existed before, and the competition to win that book is zealous, because if you don't win that book, you have nothing to sell.

When the government concluded there was no harm downstream, they went looking upstream into the market for the acquisition of all books. And when it filed this case last year, if you go back to the complaint, you'll see that the government alleged that the merger would substantially lessen competition in this overall book market; but as events have unfolded, as events—as the evidence has come out, including their own expert, they cannot make that claim. They cannot support that claim.

And here—here's a graph or a chart of the upstream acquisition market. This is an unconcentrated market. It will remain unconcentrated after the merger, and importantly—although the government, I'm sure, ran it—there is no presumption, no HHI that is triggered in this market for all trade books.

And now I would ask that the public-facing monitor be turned off. I'll—and if you look at these pie charts, here's the downstream. And this is what I want to point out to—to Your Honor. With better data—this was prepared by Dr. Hill using data reported by booksellers. When you look at all of the book sales, not just to retailers, but also to institutions, al places, like—and libraries—Penguin Random House's share, Your Honor, is—is just a little bit of half that number that you see. And the same is true of Simon & Schuster. Because this chart prepared by Dr. Hill doesn't take into account the sale of all books.

So not able to show any harm to the overall trade book acquisition market, what did the government do next, Your Honor? And that whole market, Your Honor, is about 55,000 to 65,000 books a year that are published. So the government went looking for harm, and what they did is they shrunk their case down to a tiny corner of this market, focusing only on those acquisitions where an advance of $250,000 or more per book is paid.

And I heard Mr. Read talk about how it doesn't matter if it's 300 or 100. In a sense he's right, Your Honor, because those—if it's 100, that 2 percent is probably 1 percent.

And if it's a 300—or $350,000 threshold, it's probably no more than about 3 or 3 and a half percent. So we're talking no matter how much they want to slide the $250,000 number, we're talking about a tiny increment of the overall market.

So what the government is telling us in this trial is we know the overall market is competitive. We know there is no harm to 98 percent of all acquisitions. But if you look way down there in that tiny corner, we may have some harm. And so what did they do? They hired the expert to conduct a mathematical analysis of transactions in that little corner.

And as you will hear, he applied a counterfactual model; one that always finds harm from any horizontal merger. And there are a number of problems with that. I won't detail them now.

But I'll just say this: The way those models work, Your Honor, is they focus solely on transactions where the models assume the merging parties were the final two bidders with the two highest bids. And so the models assume one lost out to the other, and they ask what would happen if you removed one of those two top bidders from those transactions. How much would eliminating that runner-up affect the advances paid in those transactions?

And I'd like to make this point, because it took me a while to really understand it, but the model is predicting harm only when post-merger a book is acquired by the combined firm, and only when it can be assumed that pre-merger Penguin Random House and Simon & Schuster would have been the final two bidders.

Now, putting aside the dubiousness of that proposition, I'm sure the government expected that PRH and S&S would frequently be the top two bidders given their focus on just this tiny 2 percent market.

But, again, look what happened when Dr. Hill ran his model, his second score auction model in this 2 percent of the market, it projected that PRH and S&S would be the two top bidders in only 12 percent of some 1200 acquisitions in that market. Twelve percent. So, Your Honor, that's 145 books a year. And when you use more accurate real-world data, the 12 percent figure is actually 7 percent, a grand total of 85 books a year.

So that's why we're here. They're asking the Court to block this important merger for under a hundred books a year. And although Dr. Hill didn't run his dollar-harm value, we did. And it projected a reduction in total author advances of $29 million annually out of advances paid annually in this 2 percent segment of the market of more than 1 billion, not to mention, several billions across the entire actual market. And, Your Honor, that 29 million is without correcting for a single error or omission, which reduces the harm to zero.

So even if you accept the 29 million—and before correcting for the flaws, there are at least two immediate problems. One, of course, is the harm is not substantial. But, more importantly, Your Honor, the prediction isn't reliable. Nobody demands perfection in modeling. But the figures here are so low that they leave no margin of error and no confidence that, in fact, there is any harm. If you tweak any of the dials on the model, even just a little, or you include any of the projected efficiencies that go to the benefit of the authors, the projected harm rapidly diminishes to zero.

So that's how we got here, an incredibly shrinking case shriveled down all the way to statistical insignificance. In simple terms, the government has created an artificial market to create artificial concentration to create artificial harm.

So mindful that you've read everything—we've learned that by now, Your Honor—we're going to be—I'm going to be careful not to try to repeat, you know, the dense briefing.

But I do want to highlight some of the insurmountable problems in the government's case that the evidence will expose, but I want—what I want to start with, though, is at least an implicit underlying theme of the government's case—which was alluded to by Mr. Read.

There's been a lot of attention recently in antitrust circles about using antitrust laws to prevent harm to labor markets. And the government may think this is kind of a test case for this mission, and, if so, I submit they picked the wrong case. We take no issue with the idea that mergers can harm labor markets. Some mergers do pose real monopsony risks.

You can imagine when three hospitals in a town merge or the only two local lumber mills merge, it's easy to see how wages might be depressed. A nurse or a mill worker can't drive a couple of hundred miles to find a better-paying job, or they don't want to substitute their job for some local fast-food or other job. In other words, they can be stranded.

The situation here is quite different, Your Honor.

Agents have and will continue to have many competitive options to get their works published. They have agents who, as you will hear, will control and do control the bargaining process with publishers. The agents have a number of tools in their toolbox to get the best possible deals for their authors in their negotiations with publishers. And, you know, there's a saying in the publishing industry that the way you know the agents have all the power is that the publishers always pay for lunch.

And that is particularly true, Your Honor, when we're talking about agents' leverage in negotiating the top 2 percent of all acquisitions with six-, seven-, and eight-figure author advances. You can be sure that agents will be able to resist and counter any attempt if a publisher or the merged firm were silly enough to try to lower an advance. It would take an agent no less than five minutes to knock on another publisher's door who would like nothing more than to win a book, especially one the government would say is anticipated to be a top seller.

Let me start with the market definition, which, of course, the government has the burden to prove. It has to be a distinct cognizable market, but why is this important? The reason it's so important, particularly in this case, is because the wrong market definition can lead to serious mistakes.

Antitrust law operates on the core assumption that competition promotes greater market output, meaning lower prices and more goods for consumers. But if you just focus on the 2 percent or the one part of a market and ignore the rest, you could end up blocking a merger, Your Honor, that will expand overall output and enhance consumer welfare. So to avoid that outcome, courts have always insisted that right up-front, the government must identify a market that includes all products that actually compete with one another. And the evidence is going to be overwhelming that the government's proposed product market is fundamentally wrong.

As you heard, the government bases this merger challenge on a so-called market for anticipated top selling books, which it further defines to mean books with advances of at least $250,000. Now, what you're going to hear is that no one in the publishing business has ever heard of this before. It does not exist. The critical point is that the only defining characteristic of a book in the government's alleged market, the only way to know whether it's in or out of the market, is that it was ultimately acquired for an advance of at least $250,000. And we submit the government's case fails right there. The price segment of books that after bargaining were acquired for advances of $250,000 or more is just that. It's a price segment in an overall market. It is not a distinct market of its own.

The courts do not recognize markets based solely on price, where the price is just a continuum of the same product sold for different values. What the courts do recognize,

Your Honor, are markets based on price where the products themselves have distinctive characteristics other than just the amount paid for them.

Now, I won't go through all of the practical indicia factors from the Supreme Court's Brown Shoe case, but the key takeaway is this: The evidence will be—will be irrefutable that nobody in the industry treats books that yield advances of $250,000 or more as if they exist in their own category of competition separate from other books.

You will hear from agents and editors that nobody uses the term "anticipated top selling books." Publishers do not have editors or imprints or divisions dedicated to books where they plan to offer more than $250,000. Publishers have no special marketing services, no special distribution channels, no special printing facilities used for books $250,000 or over. And that's what distinguishes this case from the ones Mr. Read mentioned; cases like Syufy, Staples, and Whole Foods.

Now, let me mention a few words about Syufy because it has a superficially appealing similar product definition for the exhibition of, quote, industry anticipated top-grossing films. Unlike this case, that market definition made sense. We were dealing with films that are already completed, and they had all characteristics that enabled industry participants, in the words of the court in that case, to identify, quote, from an ex-anti perspective, this particular subset of films as different, meaningfully and categorically from other films, including facts such as they were filmed by major directors. They had big stars. They involved larger budgets. They had distinctive exhibition bookings in first-class theaters.

But interestingly, Your Honor, one factor the court did not identify as a basis for defining the market there was the prices that were paid to the script authors for rights to develop and distribute the film prior to production, which would be parallel to what the government is saying here.

There are no agreed-upon objective criteria that this industry applies in advance to determine which books will yield advances for $250,000 and which will not. When you get right down to it, Your Honor, what the government is sort of imagining is that you could take the approximately 55,000 books that are published every year, you could give them to a panel of participants, and you could ask them and they should be able to identify the books where the advances were $250,000 or more, and that's completely implausible.

Now, when—there are authors, Your Honor, whose books everyone knows in advance will command large advances. John Grisham. We're going to see Stephen King tomorrow. Celebrities like Dolly Parton, public figures like President Obama and Michelle Obama. But I think, as Mr. King himself will acknowledge, these authors and their books are not what this alleged market is about. They're going to be the first to admit, they will not be harmed by this merger.

And this is an important point in this case because when you hear vague terms like "high advances" or "significant deals" and you're thinking about obvious hit books, that's not what the government means by $250,000 or more. These big-ticket authors command advances vastly more—often in the millions, tens of millions—than $250,000.

And the government has not purported to draw a price boundary that is so small as to capture only those transactions. So what they're focusing on in their price segment are authors who are debut authors, unknown authors, lesser-known authors. These are the authors to obtain advances of $250,000 or more, but not because they fall into some category recognized by the industry, but because it happens to be that somebody decided as a result of an auction or negotiation to pay that author $250,000 or more.

And, yes, that editor who bought that book may have hoped and even anticipated that the title would be a top seller. But, Your Honor, when you think about it, every book starts out as an anticipated top seller in the gleam of an author's or editor's eye; right? Every book is a dream.

Where—where—this is a business of out—outcoming, not algorithms. And sometimes dreams come true. And sometimes they don't. And the history of publishing is littered with very, very high advance books that flop and very, very low advance books that soar.

And, you know, it's interesting, but you asked that question at the end about whether there was a correlation between advance—books that have high advances and—and whether—I think you said 70 percent of the market using Mr. Read's figure—whether those books constitute 70 percent of sales. And, you know, to my knowledge, nobody on either side of—of this aisle here has done that calculation.

I think it might be difficult to do, but it may be doable. I would—I would think, Your Honor—and I hazard a guess here—that there may be just a rough correlation, but I think what you would see is that 70 percent of sales are not high-advance books. I think you would see a number lower than that. For one reason, half the sales in the downstream market are backlist sales, and you would have to—

THE COURT: I'm sorry. What sales?

MR. PETROCELLI: Backlist sales. They're—they're books that were published a long time ago or more than a year ago. But we're going to take—we're going to take a look at that.

But my point here is that you cannot define an antitrust market on the idea that you think a book is going to be a top seller.

We heard Mr. Read mention, in order to try to support this market definition, that, for example, publishers have internal approval levels and some—and PRH might have one such level at $250,000; that has nothing to do with—with the market definition. These publishers have all kinds of different internal approval levels depending on who the—who the executives and who the editors are, and they change all the time, Your Honor, and there's no categorical difference between the books themselves. That's the key. It's just based on somebody needs someone's approval if you go above a certain level.

Now, the last market definition point I want to mention is the government's focus on the Big 5. Again, on this market definition point, the government is suggesting that only five publishers can provide services for authors with $250,000 advances or more. And they're just completely wrong about that, Your Honor.

There are many publishers who provide those same services. I mean, because the Big 5 are bigger, they provide more of them, but they're the same services that are being provided by everybody, including elite publishing houses like Norton, and Scholastic, Abrams, Hay House, not to mention some of the largest companies in the world like Amazon and Disney.

More than 30 publishers compete for and win books with advances of $250,000 or more. And there is no strict market-defining division between the Big 5 and these other major publishers. They all provide first-class services to authors at all price levels.

At the end of the day, the government is just putting out a price level, and that's the only differentiating factor in their market; and by their own logic, that line could be drawn anywhere. It could be a hundred thousand, could be $500,000, could be $5 million.

So, again, Your Honor, treating an arbitrary 2 percent of the overall market as its own antitrust market would be putting the Court in the position of disregarding the continuing and enhanced competition throughout the other 98 percent of the real market. That's where the government couldn't find harm. That's where they should have stopped. And the only reason I suggest they came up with this tiny 2 percent market is to create high concentration in order to trigger a presumption of harm that we say has no place in this case.

So let me talk about the presumption. Obviously, the—the HHA [sic] was calculated and the presumption is triggered according to the numbers. But to be clear, it was based on this 2 percent of the market, and if you ran the HHI for the entire market, no presumption would be triggered. Okay? And although a lot of weight is being put on this presumption by the government, as you saw from Mr. Read's opening statement, the government cannot prevail on a presumption alone.

The D.C. Court made that clear in Baker Hughes that the HHI presumptions cannot guarantee litigation victories. Because to allow the government, quote, virtually to rest its case at that point, leaving the defendant to prove the core of the dispute would grossly inflate the role of statistics in actions brought under Section 7.

Now, to rebut the presumption, just to give an overview of the legal framework, our burden is a burden of production, Your Honor, not of persuasion. We have to produce evidence showing that the market shares alone do not accurately capture effects on competitive conditions.

And once we rebut that presumption, the presumption vanishes and the government has to prove their case without the benefit of a legal presumption, which, after all, is a substitute for evidence. Now they have to actually produce the evidence to show—to show harm.

And the evidence that you'll see in the trial, Your Honor, readily and easily rebuts the presumption and demonstrates that market shares do not actually capture real-world competitive effects. And here are just some of the key reasons that I'll run through.

First, strong competitive rivals. Judge Mehta put the point well in the Sysco case. "[E]ven if the merging parties had large market shares, if they were not particularly close competitors, then the market shares might overstate the extent to which the merger would harm competition."

Now, that was not a problem in Sysco where you had these two giant companies who were neck and neck merging and other competitors were a far, far, far distant third. And so as a result, if you go into that case, Your Honor, those two companies lost to each other, more than they lost to all the other competitors combined. So it was very easy to see how eliminating the biggest sellers' only serious competitor would cause a material increase in prices. That was a sale—that was a monopoly—monopoly case, not a monopsony case.

This case is completely different, and it's exactly what Judge Mehta was referring to. Despite significant combined market shares, the merging parties—S&S and PRH—they are not particularly close competitors, and that's because you, obviously, have three other major publishing houses, the three other members of the Big 5: HarperCollins, Macmillan, and Hachette. They compete, they win, and they're not going anywhere.

But you have the other publishers in the top 30, the names I mentioned before, like Norton, Scholastic, Abrams, Disney, Amazon, and the government showed you Figure 8 from Dr. Hill's report to suggest that the non-Big 5 publishers acquire only an insignificant number of books for advances of $250,000 or more, and that's just contrary to the facts.

When you add up all those Big 5 publishers' market shares—excuse me. When you add up all those non-Big 5 publishers' market shares collectively, they win about as many books in the government's 2 percent price segment as do individual members of the Big 5.

And this is a confidential chart. If I could have it displayed for the benefit of the Court, Pam.

What you're also going to hear, Your Honor, is that the non-Big 5 publishers collectively win or come in second in about 23 percent of auctions. So in a real sense, this is not a five-to-four merger but a six-to-five merger. And as I said earlier, Your Honor, PRH and S&S are rarely the top two bidders in acquisitions; 12 percent according to the government; 7 percent according to more accurate bidding data. Either way, whether it's 12 percent or 70 [sic] percent, that means that Penguin Random House and Simon & Schuster are not close competitors with each other in about almost 90 percent of acquisitions in the government's market.

The next—the next factor I want to point out is about the agents and their acquisition formats, and Mr. Read alluded to that. I believe he anticipated some of the points I was going to make. But the evidence will be undisputed that agents have complete control over how acquisitions are structured, and, more importantly, that market shares play no role whatsoever in that process.

Most acquisitions, Your Honor, are one-on-one negotiations where you don't have a runner-up. The agent negotiates a deal with the author's existing publisher, or she may decide to negotiate with a single editor she thinks is the right match. There's a lot of matchmaking that goes on in this business between editor and author. Or the editor might submit a work to a number of editors, but then preempt—pre-empt the work from the market to take it off the market. And sometimes the editors will—or the agent will put the book through an auction.

However she decides to proceed, the one thing they do not do is choose a process based on a publisher's upstream market shares. So before this case and the government's pursuit of this theory, I believe it's fair to say that no one in publishing, Your Honor, has ever even calculated upstream shares. It's not a relevant factor in the way the business is conducted.

The next point I'll make on the last one on here is about the ease of expansion, and we heard a little bit about that as well. Now, this is actually important, Your Honor, because the HHI presumption relies entirely on static backward-looking shares. It just assumes that after the merger the market will be exactly the same, except that you're combining two of the entities. But what happens if, as the government claims, the post-merged entities start driving prices down to below-market levels?

In that situation, the guidelines in case law tell us that if other rivals, other publishers here, would have the ability and the incentive to step in and pick up that slack, then it is not appropriate to rely on existing market shares alone to project reduced competition. And that's what the evidence will show here.

If the—if Penguin Random House after this merger were foolish enough to begin unilaterally pushing down prices, you can be sure that other publishers would jump in at the opportunity to grab valuable books. And I'm not talking just about new entrants, although there are several that have emerged recently, as you'll hear.

But this applies with more force to expansion by existing publishers; those who are already active in the $250,000 market and perhaps those who are less active. These existing publishers already have skilled and experienced editors. They already have the knowledge and the infrastructure required to successfully acquire books at any advance level, and some already have plans to expand by increasing their book acquisitions.

Mr. Read mentioned the printing issue as a potential obstacle to expansion. That's not a credible argument, Your Honor. It is true that Bertelsmann owns printing facilities, but there will be no evidence that it favors Penguin Random House and no basis for assuming it would do so after the merger. It's just pure speculation. The deals between PRH and Bertelsmann for printing are at arm's length; and Bertelsmann serves many different publishers in the industry. So we believe all of that, and more that you'll hear, readily rebuts the presumption.

So now where does that take us? What is the additional evidence absent the assumption the government has to prove harm?

Well, you're going to hear, Your Honor, about several sources of evidence. One of them will be other publishers, starting with Mr. Pietsch this afternoon, who's the CEO of Hachette.

Now, let's be—let's be fair about this. The other publishers, the big publishers, in particular, they don't want this merger to go through; right? They think Penguin Random House will be able to compete more aggressively, buy more books, drive up the price, and they're going to have to pay more. When you think about it, under the government's theory where advances are going to go down, these publishers should be happy about this merger. They should be supporting it because there would be lower prices for advances, but that's not what's happening here.

We're also—we're also going to see a number of—hear about a number of anecdotal accounts, as Mr. Read mentioned, where Penguin Random House and Simon & Schuster were the final two bidders. And we are not going to dispute,

Your Honor, that there are instances when both of those companies are the final two bidders. Of course, that happens.

But to the 50 or so examples that the government may show the Court, there's a remaining 1,150 examples that they're not going to show the Court where Penguin Random House and Simon & Schuster were not—were not one and two, were not the final two bidders.

The government will rely heavily on emails, like the one the late Ms. Reidy wrote, and my colleague Mr. Fishbein will address that. But I'll just say one thing about the kind—those kinds of documents you'll see. Those documents, by and large, all say the same thing; that the five big publishers all compete against each other, and they do. That's what it means to be the five biggest. But they're not saying that competition is weak or that competition is soft. You're not going to see anything like that, and they're not saying that there are no other 5, 10, or 20 largest publishers who never compete, because the data shows they do.

But, Your Honor, what you won't see are the kind of internal documents, for example, that we saw in Sysco where the merging parties each referred to each other as the primary competitor, the main rival, the only rival, because nobody in this business thinks Penguin Random House and Simon & Schuster are each other's only or main rivals.

You will see documents to the contrary, like this one published by a News Corp on behalf of its company HarperCollins, discussing how highly competitive the market is, how there's competition with all publishers. And, importantly, competition could also come from new entrance as barriers to entry in book publishing are low. And that was the point that I was making to you before. You don't have to go out and—and get a couple of billion dollars of capital to build a facility, a manufacturing plant or a fabrication plant.

And here's another one by HarperCollins, which has to be displayed confidentially. This one was just a few months ago, Your Honor, back in January after the merger was announced.

And what you will see—and I won't say it out loud, Your Honor, but the—the statement that's in yellow and underlined about authors' spending—and this is after this merger was announced—is completely contrary to the government's suggestion that advances are going to go down. The last piece of evidence—and we did not hear too much about it in the—

THE COURT: I'm sorry. Can you put that up again.

MR. PETROCELLI: Should I proceed?

THE COURT: I'm sorry. That increase reflects an increased number of books, not advances per book?

MR. PETROCELLI: That's how I would read it, Your Honor, or it could be both.

THE COURT: Thank you. Go ahead. Thank you.

MR. PETROCELLI: Yes. I want to say a few words about the government's modeling by Dr. Hill. And as Your Honor knows, the model is only good if it fits, and fits the real world meaningfully enough to give you meaningful results, and our position is his models do not fit because he's modeling an outcome of an auction that's not representative of how books are usually acquired. Think—think, as you've read, the second-score model assumes an auction where the highest bidder is the winner, but that winner pays the runner-up price. Doesn't pay the winning price, pays the runner-up price.

The theory is the runner-up constrains the amount of the winning bid. The model then tries to determine what would happen to the price in those auctions if the merger removed that runner-up. That inquiry makes sense, if at all, if there's a runner-up bid.

And here's the problem: Most acquisitions do not have a runner-up bid that constrains the amount of the winning bid at all. I think, as I indicated, half of the acquisitions occur without multiple bidders. And where there are multiple bidders, agents often use a best-bid auction where the publishers are invited to submit a blind bid.

And that's not the only fit problem. Dr. Hill's model assumes every publisher participates in every acquisition in that post-merger. Because of the combination of the two firms, there will be one fewer bidder. That's one of the reasons the model always predicts harm, but that's not how it works. Not all publishers are invited to bid on a book. And even when they are, they don't always participate. So agents can readily find other editors—other editors and publishers to pitch a book to or submit a book to. It's not a closed universe.

And there are also other problems, such as inflated profit margins and other inaccurate inputs that Professor Snyder will go over in detail.

On efficiencies, Dr. Hill's models also do not take into account any efficiencies. And efficiencies are important, Your Honor, in assessing the incentive effects of the merger. Because here the government is looking at the dynamics that potentially create downward pressure on advances, we also need to evaluate the dynamics that create upward pressure on advances. And that's the only way to understand and project what effects a merger will have.

And here there is uniform agreement that merging Simon & Schuster will create efficiencies. You're going to hear it from Mr. Pietsch of Hachette, Mr. Murray of HarperCollins, Mr. Berkett of Simon & Schuster; and the government's own expert, Ms. Hammer, acknowledges there would be efficiencies from a transaction like this. And this is another confidential exhibit with—with more specific information about that.

And we've had a lot of discussion about verify. I think when Your Honor finally gets to hear the extensive work that went into the efficiencies model prepared by the company that included not just Mr. Sansigre, but also vetted by financial groups at Bertelsmann, I think Your Honor will see that they're not hardcore numbers taken, you know, off the top of his head, but was a result of a couple of hundred hours of hard work to develop these synergies. And the Court will hear that evidence. And the Court raised questions about what its role is.

Your role, Your Honor, is not to be the verifier. Your role is to evaluate the verification evidence that you receive, just like any other evidence, and determine whether it's credible, whether it's reasonable, whether it's persuasive. And the witness will go through each—each of the items, and you'll—you'll make the judgment yourself whether—whether that process produced estimates. Remember, we're not talking about hardcore numbers. We're talking about future estimates that are reliable.

Now, we don't need to prove any efficiencies at all in this case because we don't believe there can be any demonstration of harm, but—but even a portion of the efficiencies here would be sufficient to counteract the government's claimed harm because it is so small.

I will—I want to mention one thing about this independent bidding, which Mr. Read mentioned. For decades, Your Honor, Penguin Random House has had internal competition among its imprints. This is not something new that it just came up with, and it's in the DNA of the company. And why do they do it? We heard that clip from one of the editors questioning—you know, you're just negotiating against yourself. Maybe so, Your Honor.

But that is the best way the company believes that it can win the book. Because what they're trying to do is match the most passionate editor with the author and the agent for that particular book. And one editor may say it's worth a hundred thousand dollars in the same company, and the other editor may say it's worth a million dollars. And so there is vibrant internal competition that has gone on, and it's the belief of the company that this is the best way to achieve success in winning the book and fostering a partnership, a long-standing partnership, not just the one-off transaction between the author and the publisher. And the—the author community recognizes it. The agent community recognizes this, and—and they exploit this. They often submit proposals to multiple imprints.

So what—the statement Mr. Dohle had made was to try to calm anxiety, that somehow that was going to be disrupted. No, the answer was it was not. But he went beyond that, and he said that post-merger, he'll allow S&S not only to internally compete against each other, just like the Penguin Random House editors do, but he'll even let competition go on even when S&S and PRH are the only bidders remaining in an auction, let's say, or in some kind of negotiation.

And we're not resting our case on that. Okay? And we don't need that to win this case at all, but the idea is also wrong, Your Honor, that the day after the merger or year after, he can just pull the plug on that, he can just renege on it, which is sort of the suggestion being made, because that would destroy all trust and credibility that the company has nourished over generations.

On coordinated effects, I think it's sufficient to say there's no evidence at all to support that theory. Dr. Hill barely mentioned it in his report, and we don't believe he will testify that the merger is more likely to increase coordination among publishers. For obvious reasons, Your Honor, because there isn't any price transparency in this business, there's no way for publishers to coordinate or follow prices of other deal terms. They're not public, and they're not visible. And you will hear that the agents control and keep that information tightly to themselves.

There was a reference about the old ebooks case, the Second Circuit case, and to be clear, Bertelsmann and Random House were not parties to that case, Your Honor.

So in closing, let me say this: Bertelsmann has been in the publishing business for almost 200 years. Its mission is to serve readers around the world for generations to come.

There is universal agreement, even among those who oppose this merger, Your Honor, that Bertelsmann and Penguin Random House are the best stewards and home for these important and iconic Simon & Schuster imprints. That is where they can continue to flourish. That is where they can continue to spur competition for the benefit of authors, booksellers, and readers. And we submit the evidence you will hear will leave no doubt about that. Thank you for your patience.

THE COURT: Okay. Thank you, Mr. Petrocelli.

So just a follow-up on the question I asked Mr. Read. Is it correct, then, that 2 percent of the books account for 70 percent of the advances? Because he uses the 70 percent number, and you're saying it's only 2 percent—

MR. PETROCELLI: I believe—I believe—on the acquisition side, yeah, I believe that's correct, but I'll double-check if I'm—and let you know if I'm mistaken.

THE COURT: Okay. Thank you.

MR. FISHBEIN: Thank you, Your Honor.

Stephen Fishbein for ViacomCBS and Simon & Schuster. And, Your Honor, I'm not going to repeat what Mr. Petrocelli said, but I would like to take just a few minutes to address briefly what the evidence will show from the perspective of ViacomCBS and Simon & Schuster. And let me start with why ViacomCBS is selling Simon & Schuster and why they chose to sell it to Penguin Random House.

ViacomCBS, which changed its name this year to Paramount Global, is a global media company. They own television networks, the Paramount Pictures film studio, and the Paramount Plus streaming service.

In recent years, ViacomCBS has chosen to focus on those core business activities of television, film, and streaming. To align with that strategic focus, ViacomCBS's CEO in March of 2020 announced publicly that Simon & Schuster would be sold.

And he explained book publishing is a great business, but it's not television, it's not film, it's not streaming. So we're going to sell it.

Your Honor, the evidence will show that that decision to sell Simon & Schuster is a firm one. Simon & Schuster will be sold to somebody, and that somebody, if it's not Penguin Random House, is very, very likely to be another book publisher because it's the other book publishers who can obtain the highest efficiencies that we've been talking about by combining their operations with Simon & Schuster.

Now, the Court—the government, Mr. Read, said that he's going to call as witnesses some of the other publishers who are going to complain that this transaction is anticompetitive. Two of those major publishers, Harper and Hachette, made their own efforts to acquire Simon & Schuster. And the CEOs of those publishers are going to say eliminating an independent Simon & Schuster is going to be bad for competition. But the Court, of course, should be aware that they had no problem with the elimination of an independent Simon & Schuster if they were the ones acquiring it.

And, of course, they stand to benefit if the Court blocks the transaction because that gives them another chance to accomplish what they failed to do the first time.

Now, Your Honor, you'll hear from our witnesses why they chose Penguin Random House over these other bidders.

Obviously, Bertelsmann has offered to pay over $2 billion, was an important consideration, but as everybody agrees and Mr. Read said, the book publishing business, you know, it's as much an art as an industry. And I think the people in this business, they recognize that in important ways they're stewards of an important part of our culture.

And you're going to hear from the Simon & Schuster CEO, from others, that with those considerations in mind, they do believe that Penguin Random House is an excellent home for Simon & Schuster and for the legacy they've built; for the reasons that Mr. Petrocelli said, deep respect for publishing. They've been in the business since the 19th century; author-friendly, and a commitment to the independence of Simon & Schuster on the creative side, creative and editorial independence.

Now, the government in their opening gave a lot of attention, a lot of emphasis, to the words of a Simon & Schuster employee who you're not going to hear from as a witness, which is Carolyn Reidy, the former and, unfortunately, deceased CEO. And the government has touted that that document that they put up on the screen—let me give you some context for that.

Ms. Reidy wrote those notes over three years ago. The circumstances were that she was presenting her business during due diligence to Viacom and the lead-up to the merger between Viacom and CBS back in 2019. And as is common in due diligence exercises, she wanted to present Simon & Schuster in the best possible light that she could, and that's not just an inference from the circumstances.

The email chain on top of that document said—that Ms. Reidy says to her colleague: Am I presenting this positive enough? Am I making it look positive enough? So what did she say when she was trying to make Simon & Schuster look good?

One thing she said was that the four other major publishers are significant competitors—I think she said the biggest competitors—of Simon & Schuster.

And we don't dispute that. We don't dispute that there's competition, significant competition, with the Big 5. What we do dispute is treating the Big 5 as a unit. And Mr. Read continuously—and the government, you'll hear—they're always saying Big 5 instead of HarperCollins, Hachette, and Macmillan, as if this Big 5 is a monolith and it's, you know, one monopolistic entity.

What the evidence will show is that HarperCollins—a strong second—ferociously, continuously, unrelentingly competes with Simon & Schuster, as does Hachette and Macmillan. And we can't lose sight of the fact that in addition to all the other competitors beyond the Big 5—the Big 5 itself, there's tremendous competition.

Now, Ms. Reidy also in those comments that—that they put up, she described the publishers outside the Big 5 as—I forget—minor league or farm teams. And if I may, Your Honor, I think the government is swinging for the fences with that analogy, and I look forward to what the evidence is going to show in this case as to whether that analogy holds up; whether the smaller publishers are really like farm teams, where their purpose is to groom people for the majors. Let's see whether they compete with each other and what the story is in terms of movement from big publishers to small, et cetera, and we'll come back to that in due course.

In any event, those are Ms. Reidy's words, but we can't really know what she meant by that because she's not here to—to explain it. And she certainly didn't address the central issue here; is whether advances would go down if there were a merger between Simon & Schuster and Penguin Random House.

And, Your Honor, with—I respectfully submit that the Court will find much more persuasive than these three-year-old comments that were done about a different merger from somebody who can't explain them—you will find much more persuasive the testimony of the current CEO of Simon & Schuster, Jon Karp, who took the helm when Ms. Reidy passed away several years ago. He's a witness. He's going to testify.

And he and his colleagues are going to explain to you, they work with editors—excuse me—with authors and with agents every day, and they will explain and give you specific examples that there are many, many, many options for authors, including the other Big 5, small and medium publishers, recent upstarts, Amazon, and self-publishing.

And just on the recent upstarts, you know, Mr. Read put up that slide. He said, well, today the recent upstarts don't have much of a share. You know, by definition, the recent entrants are recent, and we don't have to show that they already have a significant share. The analysis is prospective, what will happen in the future. And the very fact that small publishers are motivated, people are motivated to create small publishing companies, even today, and that they have a hope of success in the future shows that, you know, they have a reputation, they have—anticipate success. And you're going to hear plenty of evidence about that, about new entrance into the market.

The ultimate issue, Your Honor, and what the government has to prove is that a combined Penguin Random House/Simon & Schuster would dare to lower advances to their highest paid authors and that they would get away with it. Not only would losing those authors—the government—I think Mr. Read said that Simon & Schuster is going to lower advances by a hundred thousand dollars—I assume he meant per book—which is a significant amount. Not only would that deprive Simon & Schuster of the books that it needs to capture the attention of readers, but the evidence will show that HarperCollins, Macmillan, Hachette, Norton, Scholastic, Amazon, many other competitors would happily step in if Simon & Schuster underpays authors or mistreats them in some way.

Your Honor, lowering author compensation for Simon & Schuster would be biting the proverbial hand that feeds them. The government will not be able to show that such reductions are likely, much less that they're substantial, and we respectfully submit that the government will not be able to prove its case.

Thank you.

PART TWO: TESTIMONY OF GOVERNMENT WITNESSES

MICHAEL PIETSCH, CEO, HACHETTE BOOK GROUP

On its opening day, the A3 antitrust trial went quickly from the excitement of the long-anticipated event—with cameras set up outside awaiting the non-arrival of Stephen King, due Tuesday, and long security lines for the many visitors—to the slow tedium of an actual trial, establishing a foundation with witnesses and trying to provide a crash course in the basics of book publishing.

The good news for both sides—and all sides—is that Judge Florence Pan clearly lived up to her reputation as a rising star heading for the Court of Appeals. Throughout the day, she showed clear command of her court—irritated at PRH's attorneys appearing not to comply with her orders on the evaluation of the verifiability of the publisher's "efficiencies model," and ready to grant the government leeway in showing some brief witness videos in their opening argument. And clear command of the material, even as it got into the weeds of auction procedures, regularly interjecting with her own questions, which demonstrated the close attention she was already paying to the details. (She asked HBG CEO Michael Pietsch, on hearing that most big advances don't earn out, "Does your business rely on some of your books wildly overperforming?") Judge Pan was also flexible and ready to reconsider her own rulings as she learns more about publishing. After listening to Pietsch testify, she decided to "allow the opinion testimony of the industry participants who have substantial experience"—including Jennifer Rudolph Walsh testifying for the defense, after initially thinking "it didn't seem she had the expertise to opine about predicting what would happen in the market."

The DOJ began their case with Pietsch as their first witness. Pietsch said it was his "expectation that having these two extremely large companies" merge "will limit the high advances in many cases."

He saw that coming from the obvious situations, in which S&S and PRH would have been bidding against each other, but also observed that "the more bidders . . . the more the upward pressure on bidding," since "publishers often revise their estimates of what they are willing to bid on a book upward—the kind of auction fever, that anyone who's been in an auction understands." That all "leads me to believe that successful winning bids at auction will be lower" if S&S and PRH merge.

Pietsch said he was advocating for authors getting the most the market will bear because, "I think the book is the greatest creation of humankind and people who write books are incredibly admirable, often heroic . . . I still think authors will do better in a world that has more competition among major publishers than it would have if this merger is approved."

Pietsch also expressed concern that with a merged PRHSS there is "likely to be a reduction in title count," since he observed a big decline in Penguin's title count following their acquisition by Random House.

He noted that PRH already "often has much better terms than us" with big retailers and is concerned that "one company as gigantically dominant as Penguin Random Simon would give them such financial advantages" over everyone else. As for effects on bidding and auction processes, Pietsch noted that it was after Random House acquired Penguin "when agents began using best bids" auctions with some frequency "instead of a round robin" with fewer available bidders, since they were essentially pitting PRH against everyone else.

In Cross-Examination, PRH attorney Daniel Petrocelli tried to establish that Pietsch was primarily suggesting the effected titles would only be ones where S&S and PRH previously had bid against each other—which the defense is arguing is a very small pool of about 85 deals a year—though Pietsch continued to point to larger effects. And he had Pietsch confirm that HBG's own bidding would not change as a result of the merger.

Among the industry details illuminated is that HBG compiles a list, informally called The Ones That Got Away, monitoring books they lost at auction for $500,000 or more, to see how those books ultimately performed in the marketplace and help refine their own assumptions during big auctions. They recorded 302 "losses" over a recent four-year period, losing 124 books to PRH. Approximately 15 auctions were lost to companies outside of the Big 5 (once you eliminate HMH, now that it is part of HarperCollins).

Asked what the analysis showed by Judge Pan, Pietsch said, "It stands as a kind of caution against big advances. . . . The lesson that's taken away again and again is, thank goodness we stopped bidding when we did, because, even at the advance we offered, we would have lost money." While noting that some books they have lost "went on to be gigantically successful," still, "we usually come away saying, it's a good thing we didn't succeed in acquiring that book."

Pietsch confirmed the company currently has annual sales of about $800 million, and said about $300 million of that annually comes from backlist (which is low for the Big 5, since historically HBG has had a smaller backlist and their biggest imprints have been more frontlist focused. PRH, on the other hand, got 58 percent of sales from backlist in 2020.) He told the court, "around half the books we publish make a profit of some kind." And he confirmed that HBG does have executive approvals of advances above different levels for the company's different publishing groups, ranging from $100,000 to "just above" $250,000 depending on the group.

Pietsch noted that he wanted Lagardere to bid to acquire Simon & Schuster but the parent company "did not submit a bid." And he confirmed that, if the merger is blocked and S&S were to come back on the market, "it is my hope they would bid" to buy the company. He told Petrocelli when challenged on that ambition, "My concern is not about a 5-to-4 merger. It is about the creation of one super-dominant publisher that is so far out of scale with all other publishers."

TESTIMONY OF MICHAEL PIETSCH, CEO, HACHETTE BOOK GROUP

DIRECT EXAMINATION

BY MR. VERNON:

Q. Good afternoon, Mr. Pietsch.

A. Good afternoon.

Q. Can you state your name for the record.

A. Michael Pietsch.

Q. What is your title?

A. Chief executive officer.

Q. And when did you become CEO?

A. '13—2013, January.

Q. And just for the record, you're CEO of which company?

A. Of Hachette Book Group.

Q. Can you briefly describe the publishing jobs that you held prior to joining Hachette?

A. Very briefly, my first publishing job was an intern at a small publisher in Boston in 1977; then an assistant and then editor at Charles Scribner's Sons, from 1979 to 1985. From 1985 to '91, I was editor, senior editor at Harmony Books, a division of Crown; and from 1991 I came to Little, Brown as executive editor; and was after that Editor in Chief, and publisher at Little, Brown for about a dozen years before becoming CEO.

Q. Let me ask you to take one step back. For the jobs that you held prior to working at Hachette, what was your involvement in acquiring books, if any?

A. In all of my jobs before becoming CEO of Hachette, before joining Hachette, except as an intern, my job was to acquire books.

Q. And I think you said when you came to Hachette, you worked for Little, Brown. Did I get that right?

A. Yes. Little, Brown is one of the imprints of Hachette Book Group at this time.

Q. Can you describe the jobs that you held at Little, Brown.

A. At Little, Brown, first I was an executive editor, which has been an honorific. I was an editor. My job was to find books for publication, persuade the company to invest in them, and then to oversee working with the author on the book, editing it, and then working with the publishing company to bring the book into the world.

After being executive editor, I was Editor in Chief. As Editor in Chief, my job was to continue acquiring books for publication and to oversee the staff of editors who worked at Little, Brown, for probably about a dozen editors who have the same job or the same basic role. My job was to manage them and to work with them on their—on their solicitation of books and the way they—they brought them forward and brought them into the world. And then, after, I became publisher. Do you want me to describe that job?

Q. Yeah. If you can please describe what the publisher job entails.

A. Yes. Of course. The publisher job is the person who—for that imprint or division, in this case it was an imprint—is responsible for the totality of the publishing that that imprint does; for acquiring books, for overseeing the staff of editors, staff of publicists, the staff of marketers and designers; who all work together to bring in books and bring them into the world.

The publisher's responsibility is the P&L for that group; to invest wisely and effectively in attracting books, paying advances against royalties, getting good rights, grants, and then publishing the books with force, fervor, effectiveness, getting them. . . . The publisher's job is the profitability of the imprint they oversee. They're responsible for hiring, managing, developing the people in all these areas who work with books, and doing so in a way that is profitable for the—the publishing company that oversees and employs them.

Q. And can you briefly describe your responsibilities as CEO.

A. As CEO I'm responsible for the profitability and strategy and direction and personnel of the Hachette Book Group, which is the U.S. division of Hachette Livre, a French—a global publishing company based in France.

And the CEO's job is to oversee all of the publishing divisions and all the other parts of the company that work with the publishing divisions. And those are the groups like the sales force, the central marketing group, the central communications group, legal, contracts, the warehouse and operations of the fulfillment of orders, the sales force that solicits orders from retailers and work with those retailers to bring books out. Managing an editorial group that works with the publishing teams on the copyright team; the production group that—that works with manufacturers to obtain paper, get the books manufactured, get them delivered.

Basically, the totality of the publishing company in the United States is my responsibility. I'm responsible for delivering a profit to our shareholder; I'm responsible for making sure that we're well staffed with creative and talented, hard-working individuals in all roles; and for looking into the future and imagining what the business might be in the future and preparing our company to meet the demands we see coming soon on—and to be competitive.

Q. As CEO of Hachette, what involvement, if anything, do you have in acquiring books?

A. As CEO I oversee all of the publishing divisions. All the publishers of our publishing groups report to me. And I work with them on the books—the kind of books they decide to go after, what their strategy is, how they stand out in the marketplace; and make sure they work with them to make sure they have strong teams of editors and marketers and publicists, and work with them to attract and acquire books.

I'm specifically responsible for overseeing the advances they pay to authors above a certain level. All the publishers have a certain authorization level they can authorize in advance, up to a certain amount, above which they need to come to me for approval on those higher-advance books. I am more involved in looking at the projects with them and discussing them with them the—their assumptions in signing the book up and—and how it will stand out in the market.

I also acquire books myself. I continue to edit a few books a year as CEO. And so I'm directly involved in acquiring books in that role.

Q. Why do you still as CEO continue to edit books personally?

A. Having been an editor for most of my career, I've found in working with writers directly, extraordinarily gratifying, challenging. It enlarges me. And it's the central—it's the core work of our company; working with authors on the books that they're creating and how they complete them in making the book they want it to be. And then working with them to bring the book into the world effectively.

I've always found that book—that work just kind of soul filling, gratifying, important. And because it's the core work of our company, I find doing that as CEO keeps me in touch with the work that all the publishing teams are doing; and it's also a good representation to the world of authors and agents that this company is led by someone who works directly with authors and knows what their experience is like and what they're looking for in publication.

Q. Can you briefly list a few of the noteworthy books that you've edited personally over the course of your career?

A. I—one of the first was I had the pleasure of editing a posthumous Ernest Hemingway memoir called *The Dangerous Summer* when I was an editor at Scribner.

In fiction, I've worked with a broad range of writers. I've worked with James Patterson on dozens and dozens of his thrillers. I worked with the thriller writer Michael Conway on many of his books as editor. The great George Pelecanos, the great D.C. crime writer, I've worked with as editor on many of his books. Walter Mosley. So I've worked a lot in suspense fiction and thrillers.

In literary fiction, I've worked with Donna Tartt on her novel *The Goldfinch*; with J. K. Rowling on her first novel for adults, *The Casual Vacancy*. Worked with David Foster Wallace on *Infinite Jest* and his posthumous book, *The Pale King*.

In nonfiction I've worked with Stacy Schiff on her book *Cleopatra*, and her forthcoming book about Samuel Adams called *The Revolutionary*, a book called *The Witches*. I worked with John Feinstein, a D.C. sports writer, on *A Good Walk Spoiled*, on many of his books.

And I love music, and I've worked with a bunch of musicians. I've worked with Keith Richards of the Rolling Stones on his memoir called *Life*; and with Chuck Berry on his book which was called *The Autobiography*. Those are a few.

Q. How many years of experience do you have in the book publishing business?

A. Right on 45 years.

Q. How many years of experience do you have acquiring books?

A. At least 40.

Q. And I won't hold you to a specific number, but approximately how many books have you acquired over the course of your career?

A. I'm guessing the range of three to four hundred.

Q. What is Workman Publishing?

A. Workman Publishing is a publishing company that was founded by Peter Workman around 50 years ago that specialized in—specializes in creative nonfiction, practical nonfiction, books for—books for children. Many kinds of books of—descriptive books with very creative formats: books with wheels on them, books with magnifying glasses inside them, books with beads. Very creative nonfiction publishing group that Hachette Book Group acquired last September.

Q. I'm sorry. Can you say it again. When did Hachette acquire Workman?

A. September of 2021.

Q. What is Black Dog & Leventhal?

A. Black Dog & Leventhal is a publisher of illustrated and art books that was distributed—a distribution client of Workman for many years and that Hachette Book Group acquired, I think, around seven years ago.

Q. Let me ask you, first, to explain a few things and a few concepts in the publishing industry. I'm going to start by asking you just to describe some of the work that publishers do. Can you explain what work do publishers do with respect to the design and editing of books?

A. Publishers sign a contract with an author to publish their work and as part of that contract, first on the editing side, the editor—the publishers employ editors whose job it is to work with the author, to read the manuscript, to read the outline—to work with them to make the book everything that the author wants it to be, and that the publisher at the same time believes they can sell effectively and market effectively.

That's work that can happen all in one-fell swoop or it can happen over many, many years, depending on the pace of the writing and the way the author wants to work with the publisher. Publishers employ designers who create the jacket art that is the face of the book that's brought into the world; is intended to make it visible, exciting, pair with what's inside the book and attract the purchases. They also design the interior—the interior, the text, the type, the headlines; and, in the case of illustrated books, very, very complicated interplay of images and texts.

Q. What work, just at a high level, do publishers do to help publicize books?

A. I would say that it's an extremely important part of the publisher's function. There are tens of thousands of books that are published every year; and every one of them is competing not just with all the other books published, but all the other available entertainments and the activities that people could be doing at any time. So getting attention for any one book at any one moment is a gigantic, gigantic challenge that publishers fight hard to accomplish. So publicity, getting publicity for the book is hugely, hugely important when you bring your book into the world.

People don't know that any one book exists unless they hear about it in various ways, or unless they come upon it in the bookstore and happen to pick it up and find it interesting.

Q. What work do publishers do to help that—to help ensure that books get sold and promoted at retailers?

A. Most publishers have a very large sales force. It's a team of executives and employees who interact with all of the retailers who sell books, which covers the range from independent bookstores, with bookstores who do nothing but sell books; chain bookstores, like Barnes & Noble or Books-A-Million, that do nothing but sell books and some games and sidelines. And then all the other kind of retailers who carry books as part of their mix of products that they make available for their customers, like Walmart, and Sam's Clubs and Targets and . . . I'm drawing a blank for a minute on the whole range. But you think of all the places you find books. Costco is another major retailer. And there are places like—there's clothing stores that sell books. So our sales force is working with the companies that—that sell books, the retailers that sell books, as well as companies that don't sell books yet, and we want to persuade them to carry books as part of their mix. Through Workman, we work with a place called Tractor Supply, which is a farm and tractor supply store that carries books.

And, of course, there's the whole range of digital retailers—Amazon and Apple and Google—who sell books as part of their product mix. And we have executives working constantly with them. And our goal is to make them aware of the books that we publish, to bring them the ones that are best suited for their customers, persuade them that they should stock these books if they're a physical retailer. And then work with them on how to make the book stand out within their store; how it's displayed, how it's discounted, what assortment it might be included in. So our job is to work with these retailers to help them sell books in a way that's profitable for them and, of course, profitable for us.

Q. Who are the Big 5 publishers?

A. The Big 5 is a common term for the five largest publishers of general interest books for adults and children. They are—Penguin Random House, by far the largest; HarperCollins; Simon & Schuster; Hachette Book Group; and Macmillan are the five in order of size.

Q. Can you explain how an advance works, focusing on trade book publishing?

A. Yes. In signing a contract with an author to publish their book, our contract includes a grant of rights of the ability to sell it in a particular territory, often North America, sometimes around the world, including translation rights. And it includes a guarantee of a royalty that they will pay the author for each copy that's sold. And the royalty's different depending upon the format of the book, whether it's a hardcover, a trade paperback, mass-market paperback, ebook, downloadable audio. Each of them has a different royalty rate that we pay on each copy sold. And then there are royalties we pay on books that are licensed for translation or, for instance, for serialization in a magazine. Each of those rights that we can exploit has a royalty rate.

In competition—in signing books up, authors usually would like to be paid in advance for their work before it's published. So what's called an advance is an advance against future royalty earnings that we agree to pay to the author as part of the contract, and the advance is recouped from each sale in each of those formats until the royalty is earned equal the advance paid, after which we pay the author for the royalties on future earnings.

And the advance is not recoupable by the author if the sales do not rise to the level of the advance. I'm sorry. It's not recouped by the publisher. I misspoke.

Q. Can you explain what the term "earning out" means?

A. Earning out. I'm sorry. I was getting ahead. Earning out is what I was just describing. Earning out is if we pay an author in advance of a hundred thousand dollars for the rights to publish the book, once the total royalty or earnings from all formats rise to a hundred thousand dollars, the book has earned out.

Q. For Hachette, how often do Hachette's books earn out the advance?

A. Roughly half the time. About half the books we publish earn out their advances.

Q. At the higher-advance levels, meaning above $200,000 for Hachette, how often does Hachette's books earn out the advance?

A. I don't have a specific statistic for that, but—a large proportion of the books we pay high advances for do not recover their advances.

Q. And I think you may have described this briefly, but if a book does not earn out, does the author need to pay the advance back?

A. It does not. And I just want to say, I believe I misspoke when I said half of our books do not earn out. I don't have that number clear in my head. It's probably a little more than half that don't earn out their advance. I don't have a specific statistic about that in my head.

Q. So let me see if I can just clarify. For books where the advance is above $200,000 for Hachette, roughly how often do books earn out the advance?

A. At the higher-advance levels, $200,000 and above—this is an educated guess, I've not done an analysis of this—I would say at that level, around half of the books we publish earn back their advance.

Q. In your experience, what financial term is the most important when Hachette is negotiating with agents and authors?

A. The advance against royalties is the term upon which the negotiations and auctions are based. It's almost entirely always on the advance against royalties.

Q. Why is that? Why is the most important term for negotiations the advance?

A. Well, authors are devoting a great deal of work and long, long stretches of time to creating the book, and they want to be paid for their work. And the way that they often decide who they're going to be published by is in a competitive situation where the highest advance for the book is what gets the publisher the right to publish the book. Authors are looking to maximize their earnings. Almost all the authors we work with are represented by literary agents who, likewise, are looking to maximize their own earnings.

Q. In your experience, how often do authors turn down an offer with a higher advance to accept an offer with a lower advance but a higher royalty rate?

A. That is extraordinarily rare, that the royalty rate is the foundation for a decision like that. The deciding factor is almost always the size of the advance.

Q. Can you explain what a work-for-hire deal is?

A. A work-for-hire deal is a deal in which the author does not receive royalties. They simply are paid a flat fee for the work on their book, and that's the amount that they earn regardless of how many copies the book sells.

Q. In your experience, how often do authors turn down an offer with a higher advance to accept a work-for-hire offer?

A. I can't think of a single occasion that's been the case.

Q. What relationship, if any, is there between the sales that Hachette expects for a particular book and the advance?

A. The advance we pay is based on our projection—the advance that we're willing to pay is based on our projection of how many copies we think we can sell of a particular book. So the relationship is an extremely close one. We're willing to pay a higher advance when we think we can sell more copies.

Q. And let me come back to the 50 percent figure for earning out really quickly. I think you said at one point, 50 percent of advances earn out. Was that for books above $200,000 or books at all advance levels, or what was it for?

A. That was for the higher-advance books. It's not a figure I have in my head for all the books we publish.

Q. Okay. What is an auction?

A. In the context of book publishing, an auction is a situation in which a literary agent or the representative of an author approaches multiple publishers to solicit their interest in publishing a particular book. And if they find themselves in a situation where there's multiple publishers who've indicated an interest in making an offer to publish the book, they decide how they want to sell the book, how to choose among those publishers, and they often set it up in the form of an auction.

And it's an auction, like in many other kinds of businesses, where they ask each of the bidders to make an opening bid. And then a common approach after that is called a round-robin auction in which the person with the lowest opening bid is approached and told what the highest bid at that point is and told that in order to stay in the auction, they have to offer above the highest bid. And if they don't, they're dropped out. If they do, then that's the bid that's brought to the next highest bidder. And it keeps going around like that until there's one publisher left who wins the rights to the book.

Q. Let me ask you to list briefly the most common auction formats that you see, other than the round-robin, which you described. And then after you list them, I'll ask you to describe them.

A. The round-robin auction is the most common form of auction.

There's what is called a best-bids auction in which the agent will tell interested publishers that they just get one shot, and they say what they think they want to bid, and that's it. They don't get a chance to improve it after that.

And then there are many variations of that; where an agent will say, I will accept opening best bids and then the three first best bids will get to proceed into subsequent rounds as a way of extracting the highest possible advance.

And then there are others that are much looser. Some agents offer a book to a lot of publishers and just keep talking to them about what they're offering without really telling anyone else what's going on until they found what's the best bid that way.

The industry doesn't have rules defining how books can be sold. Agents are all independent operators who set up the sale of the books they represent and the way that they think is going to be most effective for them and their client.

Q. Can you explain what acquiring books through an option means?

A. In our contract with an author, we have what is called an option clause. And I believe most publishers have this. And it is an option to consider first, before it's submitted elsewhere, the author's next book, usually in the form of an outline or proposal. It usually has a term on it—a time term. Usually it's a period of 30 or 60 days that the publisher who published the previous book may consider and discuss with the author what their offer will be for the next book. From my experience, there aren't any that are really binding in terms of setting a price in advance. It's simply an option to consider before it goes elsewhere.

Q. When Hachette acquires a book in a situation in which no other publishers have bid, what factors affect the advance that Hachette offers?

A. We can find ourselves in a situation in which no other publisher has bid in quite a few ways. Sometimes an agent submits a book to many publishers and only one publisher is interested in making an offer. In which case, we make an offer that we think is an amount that we feel that we can have a profitable publication with. It's an advance that will allow the author to write the book. In that negotiation, you're negotiating only against the author's willingness to write the book. They can say, well, no, for that amount of money I would just rather not, or I would rather go try a different one.

Other situations in which we're not bidding against another publisher can be in a situation of an option publication, such as you just mentioned, where the author comes back to us and wants to publish their next book. And, usually, the agent will say what kind of advance they are looking for based on their experience of the book's previous sales and their hopes for the next book. Sometimes we'll say first what we would like to offer. So that's a negotiation without another party.

There's a negotiation in which it is implicit or explicit that the agent is able to—if we do not reach agreement—to take the book on the market and bring in bids from other parties.

Q. So I think you said in those negotiations, the agent could implicitly or explicitly take the book to other parties. What effect, if any, does that have on the advance that Hachette offers in that situation?

A. We end up bidding against what we imagine the market would be if the book were taken out. So it can lead to us increasing our offers quite significantly.

Q. Can you explain what a pre-empt is?

A. A pre-empt is the term for a pre-emptive offer on which a publisher attempts to acquire a book without going through a competitive process. So a publisher will, in that situation, say to the agent: We love this book so extraordinarily much and we feel we're the perfect publisher for it. We have a great plan for it. And to make this really easy for you, we're going to bring you an advance. And name an advance that is appropriate that—that they think is high enough that it will be worth the agent's and author's while to say we won't go through the competitive process and perhaps not end up with this publisher.

So it's an attempt to take on a book without going through the competitive process.

Q. When Hachette acquires a book through a pre-empt, what factors affect the advance that Hachette offers?

A. When we're calculating a pre-empt, we want to bring an advance that we believe the agent will consider a good advance; that they will think, yes, there's a chance that if I take this to auction, I might not get this much or this is the range that it might end up at. And so we try to offer a high advance that we think will be compelling to the agent; in addition, along with our enthusiasm and the marketing proposals we're bringing.

Q. What effect, if any, does the advance that the agent could get in an auction affect the advance that Hachette offers in a pre-empt?

A. In a pre-empt conversation with the agent, the agent can say, I know I could get a million dollars for this book at auction. I'm just not going to consider that if you're not at a level. So there could be kind of a—the publisher who's made the pre-empt is bidding against what they think the market will be, and with the agent's help and guidance often.

Q. Let me ask you one question about contracts, author contracts. When Hachette signs a contract to pay an advance to an author, how many books does that contract typically cover?

A. Each contract is different. Most of our book contracts are for one book at a time. We have contracts for two books, three books. Usually when there's a series; when the books connect to each other, that's quite common. It's quite common in children's book publishing, and we have authors we sign contracts for 30 books at a time. I wouldn't say authors. We have one author we have signed a contract for 30 books at a time.

THE COURT: Can I ask a question.

THE WITNESS: Yes.

THE COURT: If you're in a pre-empt situation and the agent doesn't accept your pre-empt, do you then bid in the auction or are you not allowed?

THE WITNESS: The leverage in making a pre-emptive offer is that if the agent does not accept our offer, then we usually say, well, then we're taking the offer off the table. When you put the book out for auction, we'll come back in and we'll bid in whatever format you set up the auction in. And the leverage is that the agent is risking that in that situation; the high bid might be less than what we tried at a pre-empt. But, yes, we will almost always say, yes, we're still interested in publishing this book, even if we can't win it by a pre-empt.

THE COURT: Okay. Thank you.

Q. Briefly, can you explain what backlist means with respect to trade book publishing?

A. Backlist is a term for all the books that a publishing company has in its back catalog. It's the books that it has published in the past, acquired in the past, published in the past, and has the rights to continue publishing in all formats.

So it's in opposition to frontlist. Frontlist is what we call the books we're bringing out at this time, the books that are new that we're trying to get a lot of excitement around as they're coming into the world.

Backlist is the body of books that we continue to sell year after year after year. And the backlist is the financial foundation of a publishing company, certainly the Big 5 publishing companies, because backlist is all the books that continue selling because retailers know they have customers for them. They continue to reorder them, to stock them, and they require much less work and much less investment for the publisher to sell. So they're much more profitable. The backlist is the most profitable part of a publisher's portfolio of publications.

Q. I think you said backlist is the financial foundation for a publisher like Hachette.

A. Yes.

Q. If I got that right, can you explain what you meant by that?

A. What I mean is that Hachette and the other major publishers, the Big 5—and Scholastic, kind of the biggest children's book publisher—all have these books that we keep in stock, we make available electronically and through physical bookstores and that are reordered routinely. And they're very, very profitable.

They take less work than new books. They require much less marketing work. And in almost all those cases, the advance for the book is long since earned back. So they're extremely, extremely profitable, and they're the foundation because that's revenue and profit that the publisher keeps achieving year after year after year; so it's very reliable.

As opposed to the frontlist, which is extremely high risk, and a lot of the frontlist books lose money and deliver a very, very poor margin to publishers.

Q. Let me switch gears slightly and ask you briefly about Hachette's publisher services business. And I think my first question is: Can you explain what that business is?

A. Our publisher services business is a business where we take on distribution and order fulfillment and sometimes sales solicitation for smaller publishers who choose not to take on the expense of building their own warehouse and doing all that operations work. So it's the way we leverage our systems. Our fulfillment systems are order-to-cash systems, but by providing the service at a markup for a fee to smaller publishers.

Q. Is the publisher services business sometimes referred to as distribution?

A. Distribution is usually what it's referred to as, yes.

Q. When Hachette provides distribution services to another publisher, who does the publicity on behalf of that other publisher's book? Is it Hachette or the other publisher?

A. It's the other publisher. We provide distribution fulfillment and, occasionally, sometimes sales services. The originating publisher does their own marketing and publicity.

Q. You may have anticipated my next question. When Hachette provides distribution services to another publisher, who does the marketing on behalf of the books of that other publisher? Is it Hachette or the other publisher?

A. It's the other publisher; the originating publisher.

Q. When Hachette provides distribution services to another—to another publisher, does Hachette share a portion of its backlist revenue with that publisher?

A. No.

Q. Briefly, can you just explain what book printing is.

A. The books we publish have a physical form. And book printing is a service we obtain from companies that specialize in printing; usually many kinds of printed products, but including books. Printing is setting ink on the pages, binding the pages up, printing the covers, printing the jackets—manufacturing the covers, printing the jacket that's wrapped around the covers, the hard covers of a hardcover book, and bringing it all together into a book.

Q. And just at a very high level, can you explain some of the issues that Hachette has seen with printing capacity in recent years?

A. In recent years, a number of the largest print printers in the U.S. have gone out of business. Where there was reliable capacity for most of my career and several printers against who we could negotiate with to get good terms, there are now far fewer printers. And their capacity to print all the books that are offered to them to print is very strained. So printings have been delayed; hard to get; and much, much more expensive in recent years, in ways I have never seen before.

Q. Does Hachette own any book printing companies?

A. It does not.

Q. Mr. Pietsch, let me ask you now about competition to acquire books. Let me first ask you, do you have an understanding of which publishers Hachette loses to most frequently when it's competing to acquire books?

A. Yes. When competing to acquire books, Hachette loses most frequently to the other Big 5 publishers.

Q. Let me ask you to step back and just explain, what's the basis for your understanding of which publishers Hachette loses to most frequently?

A. The basis of that is hearing from the publishers the outcomes of the books that they have bid for with my approval and from analyses we do.

Q. And what analyses are those?

A. We do keep track of the books that we bid on that we do not acquire when the advance is above a certain level. We have a report that we colloquially call "The Ones That Got Away." And it's a report on the books where we bid $500,000 or more as an advance and did not succeed in acquiring the book. And in the course of business, the business managers of all the publishers, when an offer like that is made and we don't succeed in acquiring it, they keep track of it. They keep track of what we know of the bid that won the auction.

And we look back on that once a year to see what books from the past that we're tracking have been published and we look at the sales that are recorded publicly to try to get a sense of whether we made the right decision when we decided to stop bidding, wherever we stopped bidding, just as a learning tool. And part of that report is a tracking of the publishers who won the bids.

Q. And do you have an understanding of which publishers Hachette competes with most frequently when Hachette is competing to acquire books?

A. The publishers we're competing with most frequently align with market share. We compete most frequently with Penguin Random House, then Harper Collins, Simon & Schuster, Macmillan in that order. And we lose to them kind of in that frequency, in that order.

Q. And let me ask you, what's the basis for your understanding when you talk about which publishers Hachette competes with the most?

A. The basis of my understanding is experience of years and years and years of auctions and hearing who we lost to. And it's almost always one of the other Big 5. There are occasions when it's someone outside that group, but they're few.

Q. Okay.

THE COURT: Can I ask a question? So you said you had "The Ones That Got Away"—

THE WITNESS: Yeah.

THE COURT:—list, and you track to see how the sales went compared to the bids you gave.

THE WITNESS: Exactly.

THE COURT: Do you have, I guess, a general sense of how you've been doing in terms of your bidding?

THE WITNESS: We track, obviously, the ones that we acquire of a certain level. And there's a way of tracking the ones we don't succeed in acquiring. And this report stands as a kind of caution against the high risk of big advances because—the lesson that's taken away again and again is: Thank goodness we stopped bidding when we did because, even at the advance we offered, we would have lost money.

But very, very frequently, the winning bid in our calculation is a money loser. There are exceptions to that. There are books that we've lost that went on to be gigantically successful. But across the broad run of business, we usually come away saying: Oh, that's a good thing we didn't succeed in acquiring that book.

THE COURT: Thank you.

Q. Let me ask you about some different advance levels. When Hachette is competing to acquire books with an advance of $100,000 or higher, which publishers does it lose to most frequently?

A. Most frequently, it loses to the imprints of the other Big 5 publishers.

Q. When Hachette is competing to acquire books with an advance of $250,000 or higher, which publishers does it lose to most frequently?

A. Definitely the other Big 5 publishers.

Q. When Hachette is competing to acquire books with an advance of $100,000 or higher, which publishers does it compete against most frequently?

A. It is most frequently competing with the imprint of the other Big 5 publishers.

Q. When Hachette is competing to acquire a book with an advance of $250,000 or higher, which publishers does Hachette compete with most frequently?

A. Most frequently the same: the other Big 5.

Q. In your mind, in your view, which publishers do you view as Hachette's main competitors with respect to the acquisition of books with an advance of $100,000 or higher?

A. We consider the other Big 5 publishers our main competitors in those situations.

Q. And in your mind, which publishers are Hachette's main competitors with respect to the acquisition of books where the advance is $250,000 or higher?

A. The Big 5.

Q. For books with an advance of $100,000 or higher, how frequently does Hachette lose to a non-Big 5 publisher?

A. Quite seldom.

THE COURT: I'm sorry?

THE WITNESS: Quite seldom.

Q. For books with an advance of $250,000 or higher, how frequently does Hachette lose to a non-Big 5 publisher?

A. Quite rarely.

Q. Do you have an understanding of the competitive advantages Hachette has when it's competing against non-Big 5 publishers to acquire books?

A. When competing with non-Big 5 publishers, our biggest advantage is a willingness to take on risk in the form of high advances. We simply have seen over time that we have much greater capacity for that than smaller publishers do.

Because of the size of our list and the prominence of the authors we publish, we have stronger relationships with media. We have strong relationships with retailers. We have programs in place with major retailers to promote certain of our books that I believe are stronger than those that smaller publishers who don't have big successes as often.

Q. Before we get into these advantages, let me just ask you, what's the basis for your understanding of the competitive advantages Hachette has when it competes with non-Big 5 publishers to acquire books?

A. It's both an observation over the years in the industry and seeing how often we are in those competitive situations and how often we win auctions and from our experience in acquiring smaller publishing companies and seeing what their business terms are, what their advance risk tolerance is, what their ability to get major media for their books is.

Q. And which smaller publishers are you referring to?

A. I'm thinking in particular of our having acquired companies like Perseus Books and Workman Publishing.

Q. Let me ask you about Workman for a minute. What advance levels did Workman focus on before Hachette acquired it when Workman was trying to acquire books?

A. Workman sought to acquire books with very, very, very low advances or no advances. Their approach to the market was to not take on unearned advance risk but to invest instead in books that they thought had a very strong chance to backlist, to sell over time, and to invest in the quality of the product to make it distinctive rather than paying high advances in the high-risk marketplace where you are trying to get a great amount of media attention or review attention for a book. So they would offer an advance of $200,000 or more extremely, extremely rarely.

Q. You mentioned some competitive advantages that Hachette has when it's competing with non-Big 5 publishers to acquire books. I'm going to try to go through all of them. I think the first one you mentioned was willingness to take on the risk of higher advances. Can you explain what you meant by that?

A. What I meant is simply—we bid more. We are willing to go to advances in the six figures and even higher six figures more often than smaller publishers are.

I'm not sure I answered your question. Can you repeat it, please?

Q. Let me back up a little bit. If a book with a significant advance doesn't sell well, talking about a Hachette book for the moment, how does that affect Hachette financially?

A. Well, anytime a book with a high advance does not sell well, we have a loss on that title. And those losses are part of our overall P&L. We have a tolerance for a fairly high level of unearned advance for books that have a loss because we are massive—not massive; compared to other publishers, we're not massive—but we have an $800 million company in revenues and we can afford to take the risk because we have a fairly large foundation of backlist books that are reliably profitable. So that gives us more range for taking these risks on books that could become significant bestsellers, could become very profitable, could become backlist books for the future.

Q. In your experience, how does Hachette's ability to absorb the losses that could come from a high-advance book that doesn't sell well compare to the ability of a non-Big 5 publisher to absorb those losses?

A. My understanding from the companies we've acquired and from observation of the industry, our ability to absorb those losses is much, much greater because on a much smaller financial basis if you're a $50 million company or a $25 million company; advance losses of several million dollars in a year can have a really big detrimental effect on your profitability and on your margin. And your investors may just say: Why are you doing this? This doesn't make sense. You're losing money or you're not making the kind of profit that I expect you should be making. So the high risk on the frontlist is much less tolerable when you have a small financial basis and can't absorb it because you have much bigger revenues and much bigger backlist revenues.

Q. So you just mentioned backlist. And let me ask you, how does Hachette's backlist affect its ability to compete to acquire books with non-Big 5 publishers?

A. The fact that Hachette's backlist sales, which as I said before are sales that are highly profitable because the advances are usually earned out or long ago written off and the marketing cost is quite low and the sales cost is quite low—I just lost track of your question in the middle of that answer. I apologize.

Q. That's fine. I'll repeat it. I think it was: How does Hachette's backlist affect its ability to compete with non-Big 5 publishers to acquire books?

A. Our backlist brings in about a third of our annual revenues, so $300 million a year roughly, a little less. And it's very profitable revenue. So we have a big financial foundation that allows us to take on risk. A smaller company without a big backlist does not have that big a cushion and their frontlist risks can affect their annual financial performance in a much, much more significant way.

Q. Now, earlier, when you listed the competitive advantages that Hachette has when competing with non-Big 5 publishers to acquire books, I think you mentioned stronger relationships with media. Can you explain what you meant by that?

A. Sure. Each of our publishing imprints has a portfolio of authors that they publish, many of them quite, quite prominent and with long-established relationships with different media outlets who, you know, use their works for their own content, for their magazines, newspapers, TV shows, radio programs.

So the publicists for our publishing imprints get noticed. Their calls get returned. Their emails get answered because the producers and bookers for these programs and media outlets know that this is a person who brings them good stuff at different times. So they have a presence; they have reputation; they have valuable connections. The smaller publishers simply don't have the same scale. They can't count on getting the attention of these influencers in the same way.

Q. And I think one of the things you mentioned was strong relationships with retailers when you were talking about the competitive advantages that Hachette has when it's competing with non-Big 5 publishers. Can you explain what you meant by that?

A. Yes. The major publishers, again, do so much business with these major retailers that we developed programs with them to promote our books in certain ways; we're able to do this because of our size. Because we bring them a lot of bestsellers, they're willing to take a risk with us to put a particular book on an end cap or a visible display. And sometimes those displays are written into our contract with them. We can arrange to have a certain amount of display space over the course of the year for our books.

And smaller publishers without that volume of successful publishing simply don't have that leverage, don't have that kind of relationship with retailers and don't have those kind of commitments.

Q. Let me switch topics a little bit and ask you about entry.

THE COURT: Before you do that, let me ask a question here.

I'm just trying to understand your business. And it seems that if you are making bids and giving advances and 50 percent of them are not earning out. Does that mean that the ones that do earn out have to overperform from what you expected and those are the ones who become your backlist? Is that right? Some of them have to overperform to make up for the ones that don't. Am I right?

THE WITNESS: A book can be profitable without earning back its advance. The advance is one of the costs along with manufacturing costs and shipping costs and warehousing costs and fulfillment costs, marketing costs. You can have a book that you paid $100,000 for and it only earns $80,000 in royalties, but it has sold enough with those other costs that you have a profit. It's not as profitable as it would have been if the book were fully earned out.

I think that's part of the answer to your question, but I don't think it was the whole thing.

THE COURT: Does your backlist consist of some books that didn't earn out but they're still profitable?

THE WITNESS: There are some in the backlist that have not yet earned out that are—but by and large, it's made up of books that are earned out.

THE COURT: I see.

So my original question was: Does your business model rely upon some portion of your books wildly overperforming to make up for the losses of the ones that don't perform, don't earn out?

THE WITNESS: Yes. You have identified a feature of our business, which is that on the frontlist portion, we're very hit-driven. When a book is successful, it can be wildly successful. There are books that sell millions and millions of copies, and those are financial gushers for the publishers of that book, sometimes for years to come.

And so that's one of the reasons that publishers are willing to take on risk after risk after risk, out of the optimism that they're going to be able to get the world's attention and make something sell in numbers far beyond what they envisioned when they paid the advance that they paid.

THE COURT: How often do you get one of those gushers?

THE WITNESS: The thing I'm describing now, a gusher, is once a decade or something. . . . For instance, I don't know if you know the *Twilight* series of books. Hachette published the *Twilight* series of books, and those made hundreds of millions of dollars over the course of time.

Right now, the novels of Colleen Hoover are topping the bestseller lists in really, really huge numbers and the publishers of those books are making a lot of money. You probably remember *The Girl With the Dragon Tattoo.*

THE COURT: Sure.

THE WITNESS: You know, that series. So something like that. It really becomes the absolute industry leader. Or the *Fifty Shades of Grey* series. So once every five years, ten years, those come along for the whole industry and become the industry driver that's drawing people into bookstores because there's such a commotion about them. So those can be a huge part of the business when they occur.

THE COURT: Thank you. Go ahead. Sorry.

Q. Focusing on industry for a moment, in the past 30 years, have you seen any new publishers enter the market and become strong competitors for Hachette with respect to acquiring books with an advance of $250,000 or higher?

A. I have not. No.

Q. What advantages does Hachette have when competing with new publishers, publishers that have just entered the market, for books with an advance of $250,000 or higher?

A. Our advantages over new entrants are really substantial, which are the relationships with retail herbs that I talked about earlier, business terms with retailers. We negotiate the financial terms with each of the retailers and wholesalers that we work with. And, given our scale, we have terms of a certain favorableness. When we acquire smaller companies, we see that their terms are not nearly as favorable. They have to pay a lot more to get the book into a store than we do.

Please repeat the question.

Q. Sure. When Hachette is competing with new publishers, meaning a publisher that's just entered the market, for a book with an advance of $250,000 or higher, what advantages does Hachette have over those new publishers?

A. We have the advantage of the backlists and size that allows us to take a lot of risks. I mean, we bid advances in the $100,000, $250,000 and up. We make offers of that size routinely, quite frequently, thousands of times, you know. Let me restate that: I wouldn't say thousands of times, but certainly hundreds of times each year.

And I think new entrants—maybe they have infinite funding, but most new entrants have backers that are looking for a return. And return on these new books, new publications, as I said, is quite unreliable. A lot of the books that we bid significant sums for do not meet their expectations and lose money. Also, the new entrants won't have the access to the media and marketing outlets that we have through long relationships. And we've published many successful books over time, so we have a kind of credibility that new entrants don't have.

Q. How does Hachette's track record with publishing companies in the past affect its ability to compete with new publishers, if at all?

A. I think I just said when talking about relationships with the media, our track record of having success means that media interlocutors of various kinds are willing to talk to us and hear our pitch and consider our books for them.

And on the retail front, I think retailers because of our broad list and repeated successes are more likely to consider our books because we've shown we can market them effectively and make bestsellers, so they are willing to join us in making a book prominent in their stores.

Q. How long does it take to build a large backlist?

A. Building a backlist is something that these big publishers are doing constantly. All these big publishers are built up through acquisition, through conglomeration over many years of a lot of smaller companies, adding their backlist, adding their backlist, adding their backlist. So the Big 5 all have these backlists through conglomeration. That's a big part of what publishers are buying when they buy another publishing company, is this backlist that's a reliable contributor going forward.

And once again, I need you to repeat the question.

Q. Let me ask you a slightly different question. How long would it take a publisher to build a backlist organically, meaning in a way that is not through acquisition?

A. Building a backlist organically takes a really long time. I mean, it's a question kind of what you're considering appropriate scale here. To build a backlist the size of any of the Big 5, I don't think it's possible or conceivable that any publisher starting now could do it in 100 years. It just takes these massive publishing entities, or these agglomerations of backlists.

So I have the example of Workman. That's been in existence for little over 50 years and really focused from the start on publishing for the backlist and acquiring books specifically to obviate the risk of unearned advances publishing fiction. They just focus on nonfiction, aiming for the backlist.

And over 50 years, they grew to a company of around $100 million to $110 million in revenue, with a significant part of their sales, $70 million say, coming from backlist titles. So that's one example of a publisher that set out to do that and it took 50 years to get to that. And they still put themselves up for sale.

Q. Why does it take a long time to build a backlist comparable to Hachette's organically?

A. It takes a long time to build a backlist of the scale of Hachette's or any of the other larger Big 5 because only a certain number of books make it through and continue to be books that sell on and on and on. Most of the frontlist books, the new books that we publish each year, don't go on and have a significant life for years and years afterwards. I would say the majority of the books we publish, after a relatively small number of years, are not selling in very significant numbers.

Q. How long does it take to build the relationships that Hachette has with media executives and the other people that Hachette works with to publicize books?

A. The relationships we build up with media and other influencers, again, it's something that a publisher works on constantly over long, long stretches of time of success of building relationships, of returning to the same people, bringing new people in. Each publisher has a big team of marketing publicity specialists who are working constantly on developing these relationships. And it takes a long time.

Q. Why does it take a long time to build the relationships that Hachette has with the people that help Hachette publicize a book?

A. The people that help us publish the book, all these media entities who we go to to bring our books to the attention of the world, they're all being pitched by every other publisher and movie company. And many of them are covering all kinds of entertainment media. And just to get their attention is hard. They're pitched everything that exists anywhere.

And so to get them to pay attention to your emails or return your phone calls or come out to lunch or come to your pitch event, it takes a long time in developing a lot of credibility. They just don't have that much time. And they have to divide up their time where they think it's going to be most reliably rewarded, and so they come to the Big 5.

Q. Would you say that it is easy or difficult for a publisher to enter the part of the trade book business that focuses on books with an advance of $250,000 or higher?

A. I think it's very difficult to enter a business at that level. As I've looked back over my years in publishing, I have not seen a publisher enter and achieve a scale anything close to what the Big 5 publishers have.

Q. Why do you think it's very difficult for a publisher to enter the part of the trade book publishing market that focuses on books with an advance of $250,000 or higher?

A. I think it's hard because the rate of success is so low. . . . Just because the publisher pays $250,000 or $500,000 or a million dollars for a book does not guarantee that a single person is going to buy it. A lot of what we do is unknowable and based on inspiration and optimism. So that's one of the reasons it's hard.

Q. How difficult or easy would it be for a non-Big 5 publisher to grow, to get to the point where it could compete on an even playing field with Hachette for books with an advance of $250,000 or higher?

A. Is it hard or easy, did you say?

Q. Right.

A. Again, I think it's demonstrably very, very hard because I haven't seen it happen in 45 years. And in fact, I've seen the contrary happen. Each time the smaller publishers of scale, in recent years, are continually being acquired by other Big 5 publishers, because their owners and investors do not want to continue to support them and think they're going to maximize their investment not by continuing to grow independently, but by selling off to the other Big 5. That's what's happened to Houghton Mifflin Harcourt. It was just recently acquired by HarperCollins. That's the largest of the non-Big 5 publishers before that. And Workman was, I think, the next largest. Perseus we acquired five or six years ago. It was around $80 million in revenue at the time.

So the significant independent publishers find it a challenging environment such that instead of growing and trying to compete in this high-risk area, they've almost all shaped their list to avoid the highest-risk areas. They almost all do not publish fiction; they almost all are careful about advance levels; they tend to specialize in particular areas of nonfiction where they can develop an expertise and find a way to reach a core audience, because they're really good in a particular area.

So when I look at the companies we've acquired, Perseus and Workman, and I look around the industry, what I see is the significant independent publishers tend to be focused on nonfiction in a particular area of expertise, health and well-being, illustrated books, rather than competing in the kind of books that go for the whole market, which is what the Big 5 are doing constantly. We are publishing books that we think we can sell to any general-interest reader. The smaller independent publishers tend to focus in a particular area. And as I said, none of them in my career in the industry has grown to be a significant competitor.

Q. Let me ask you about Amazon.

A. Sure.

Q. How frequently does Hachette compete with Amazon to acquire books with an advance of $100,000 or higher?

A. Extremely rarely.

Q. How frequently does Hachette compete with Amazon to acquire books with an advance of $250,000 or higher?

A. Extremely rarely.

Q. What advantages does Hachette have when Hachette is competing with Amazon to acquire books?

A. Excuse me. Well, Hachette has the advantages we've talked about before, which is a broad list of successful publications for general-interest readers over many decades. That gives us the advantage of credibility with media and influencers in getting our books noticed.

We also have the advantage of being able to sell our books in all the retail outlets that carry books, which includes, chain stores, independent bookstores, all the Targets and Walmarts and all those stores that carry books.

Amazon, to my understanding, has a very, very limited range of offering outside their own platform. They can obviously sell books on the Amazon digital and physical platforms, and do so and promote them heavily. But their ability to get their books into other outlets is extremely limited by the behaviors of those other retailers.

Q. Do you view Amazon as a significant competitor for Hachette with respect to acquiring books?

A. Not at all.

Q. Why do you say that?

A. Because we almost never encounter them in auctions. When we do, it's a very particular case. It's a case where there's someone who was once a bestselling author and whose sales are declining but whose name is so big that it is still something that attracts readers' attention. And they will occasionally bid a significant amount.

And that's the rare occasions when we encounter them in an auction, for someone who was once a bestselling author, because they find value, I believe, in having a name author in their general offering. But that is really the only time we encounter them with levels of a significant advance. My understanding is that they do not want to take on significant advances.

And I know from reporting and conversation that they did consider entering mainstream publishing over a decade ago. They started an Amazon publishing program that was intended to be competitive and in which they bid in auctions, paid a lot of money for a bunch of books and tried to develop a team to bring them into the world. And they closed it down very, very suddenly. They closed it down very quickly after some very visible failures.

And from conversations with senior executives there who left the company, I'm told that they just found them business-nonsensical, that it didn't fit their idea of what they should be doing with their business, taking these very, very high risks on books whose salability and profitability was entirely unpredictable.

Q. Let me ask you now about self-publishing. Do you view self-publishing as a significant competitor for Hachette when Hachette is trying to acquire books with an advance of $100,000 or higher?

A. I do not consider that a threat in that situation at all because . . . self-published authors can't pay themselves an advance against royalties and they don't have the ability to attract the attention of media. We're talking about how hard it is for small publishers. Imagine how hard it is for for one person who has a book they published entirely on their own to say: Give me your attention. Review my book. Promote my book. And so they simply don't have access to the general-interest market that we and the other Big 5 publishers address routinely. That's our business.

Self-publishing is almost entirely digital. And it's wonderful to buy—the volume of self-published titles is enormous. Anyone can publish a book, and it's a wonderful thing. But it is not competitive with what we do.

Q. How often does Hachette make an offer with an advance of $100,000 or higher and then learn that the author decided to self-publish instead?

A. I truly can't think of a time that that's happened.

Q. How does the availability of books in retail stores compare for a Hachette book as compared to a self-published book?

A. Self-published books are almost not seen at all in retail stores.

Q. What benefits does Hachette provide to an author that in your view the author would not get from self-publishing?

A. Benefits that Hachette provides or the Big 5 publishers provide include the ability to get the book reviewed, to get it noticed, to get it distributed in physical bookstores, to have it professionally edited and designed.

We provide a broad, broad range of services in addition to the advance that we pay. So we provide financial benefits, marketing benefits, publicity benefits, professionalism, the ability to license the book in foreign countries that an individual author who self-published usually has no ability to do.

Q. Now, let me change topics slightly and turn back to auctions.

How does the number of bidders change over the course of an auction to acquire a book?

A. How does the number of bidders change—

Q. Right.

A.—over the course of a single auction? As I stated earlier, when an auction is in a round-robin format, it starts off with as many interested parties as the agent has been able to solicit at the start of it. And then it gets smaller and smaller until there's one publisher left bidding.

Q. When an auction narrows to just having two bidders, what causes the advance to go up after the auction is narrowed to two bidders?

A. The same thing that causes it to go up before that point. The agent will constantly communicate to the bidder with the lower bid what the high bid is that they have to top to stay in. And it's limited only by the appetite for risk that the two publishers have for that particular project.

Q. Can you explain some of the reasons why Hachette might drop out of an auction?

A. Yes. At the start of bidding for every book we bid on, we do an estimate of the sales level that we anticipate for the book and the costs that will be associated with the book—whether it's the manufacturing costs, the marketing costs—and look at the amount of royalties that will be earned by the book based on the sales at the level we anticipate. And we do our best to limit the auction for a level where we will still have a good profit at that level of sale.

Q. Is it fair to say that Hachette sometimes drops out of an auction because the advance gets higher than the advance that Hachette is willing to pay?

A. Yes. That is exactly the reason we would drop out.

Q. Will the merger of Penguin Random House and Simon & Schuster change the level at which Hachette drops out of an auction?

A. When we are dropping out, it's because there are bids that are higher than ours going on after us. The identity of the other publishers is not relevant. We'll drop out because we have reached the point at which we think it no longer makes sense to continue bidding more.

Q. Let me try to walk you through an example. Let's say there's an auction where, before the merger, Hachette drops out of the auction at $500,000. And then after that, Penguin Random House and Simon & Schuster stay in the auction and the book ultimately gets sold for $700,000. Are you with me so far?

A. Yeah.

Q. If that same auction were to happen after the merger, at what level would Hachette drop out?

A. We would still drop out at the $500,000 that we had decided was our limit at the start of the auction.

Q. So will the merger of Penguin Random House and Simon & Schuster change the level at which Hachette drops out of an auction?

A. No, it won't.

Q. Let me step back one minute. Remind me: How many years of experience do you have acquiring books?

A. Around 40.

Q. And how many books have you acquired over the course of your career?

A. As an editor, acquiring around—I assume it's 300 to 400. But as a publisher and CEO, there are many, many more beyond that that I've overseen the acquisition of, the setting of an advance limit.

Q. Based on your experience, do you have an expectation as to how the merger of Penguin Random House and Simon & Schuster will affect advances, if at all?

A. Yes. I have—it's my expectation that—

MR. PETROCELLI: Your Honor, may I approach on this one?

THE COURT: Yes.

MR. PETROCELLI: You know, this is a question that I think we're going to be hearing from a lot of witnesses. At least it'll be asked of a lot of witnesses. I'm just looking for, I guess, a little clarity. With respect to the motion that we had regarding Jennifer Rudolph Walsh, this is one of the questions the Court indicated she could not be asked or she could not testify about. And she has, you know, years and years and years of experience.

And it's really sort of the identical question that's being asked here. And so I would object on that basis based on your prior ruling.

But if your Honor's going to allow this question, I'm just giving you a heads-up that probably you're going to have a lot of witnesses being asked the same question.

THE COURT: I think you're right with respect to the motion that we had about Ms. Walsh. The issue was, she had industry expertise about how it works. Based on what I reviewed, it didn't seem she had the expertise to opine about predicting what would happen in the market.

But as I hear this witness's testimony, I am feeling more willing to reconsider that and allow her to testify about that and allow other witnesses in the industry, because as I listened to Mr. Pietsch's testimony, it seems that 30, 45 years in the industry, an industry where there's been significant consolidation in the past, I think that perhaps it does provide a basis to talk about what is expected to happen.

It's not an opinion that's going to be undergirded by data and analysis like the experts.' But I think I'm going to reconsider that and I'm going to allow the opinion testimony—

MR. PETROCELLI: Thank you, your Honor.

THE COURT:—of the industry participants who have substantial experience. So you may answer.

THE WITNESS: Could you repeat the question,

Q. Sure. Based on your experience, what effect, if any, do you think the merger of Penguin Random House and Simon & Schuster will have on advances?

A. It's my expectation that having these two extremely, extremely large publishers combined into one entity will limit the high advances paid in many cases for two reasons. One is in those cases where the last two remaining publishers in an auction are from those two houses right now. They bid against each other freely, Penguin Random House and Simon & Schuster.

It is my experience both with myself and from observation around the industry and in conversations with agents that all the major publishers allow to some degree their separate imprints to bid against each other as long as there is still a bidder from a different house.

And the combination of Penguin Random House and Simon & Schuster will eliminate one of the major houses from that and decrease the number of rounds an auction goes to.

There is another way, which is during the course of the auction, publishers often revise their estimate of what they are willing to bid on a book upward. It's the kind of auction fever that anyone who's been in an auction understands, that the interest of other parties validates their own sense of what a book is worth.

And they will come back to their publisher or the publisher to meet with a new P&L saying: We've been thinking about this. There's a lot of excitement. We actually think that rather than selling 100,000 copies, this book is—we have a good chance of selling 150,000 copies, and we would like to bid more.

And the more bidders there are in rounds, the more excitement of that kind, the more upward pressure there is in auctions. So I believe that in general, auctions—the price paid at auction can increase because of the number of participants.

I saw when Random House acquired Penguin that that's when agents began using the best-bids approach instead of a round robin because, as some of them told me, they felt that there were fewer participants in a round robin because the publishers did not allow their imprints to be the last two remaining.

And the Penguin imprint of Random House to my knowledge does not even allow its internal imprints to bid against each other. They pool their bids into one house bid in order to not have multiple bids coming from within the same part of Random House.

So I think all those factors will lead me to believe that the successful—the winning bids at auction will be lower with Penguin Random House owning Simon & Schuster.

Q. What does the phrase "title count" mean?

A. Title count is a term which means just the number of—it can mean the number of new books published in a year. That's one thing we measure. Then title count is the total number of books a publisher has to offer for sale.

Q. What effect, if any, do you think the merger of Penguin Random House and Simon & Schuster will have on title count?

A. My experience of acquisitions and my observations lead me to believe that it will decline. I have observed that in the four or five years after Random House acquired Penguin—at the time of the acquisition Penguin and Random House were publishing around 2500 titles a year each year.

In the years after the acquisition, the number of titles published from the Penguin imprints declined from 2500 to 1500 a year, where the Random House side's published imprints continued to publish around 2500 titles a year.

Q. Let me switch topics briefly. I think you and I shook hands as we saw each other walking in the line for the courtroom this morning. Do you remember that?

A. I do. Yeah.

Q. Other than that, have we met since your deposition?

A. No.

Q. Let me switch topics again. In your experience, do agents frequently lie to you or to Hachette about the offers that they have received from other publishers?

A. I do not have experience of literary agents lying. That's what you asked, right?

Q. Right.

A. And they vary a great deal in what they communicate about an auction, about its participants, about the financial outcomes. But I've never experienced an agent lying to me. No.

Q. Why is that?

A. I think they find it in their self-interest to tell the truth because—I guess it is quite likely that a lie will out and they will not be trusted anymore if publishers feel they can't trust their statements about where an auction is, what the bid is or anything like that. Publishers would be loath to do business with them.

Q. Who selects the format of an auction?

A. The agent controls that.

Q. Who decides—can an agent change the format of an auction in the middle?

A. As I said earlier, there really are no fixed rules. Agents do sometimes change the format midway through. They might have started it in rounds and feel like: This is taking too long; it's been through six rounds now; we're going to best bids. So everybody give us best bids.

Or they might start as saying it's best bids and then come back and say: Well, we're actually going in rounds now because we had three best bids that were quite close to each other, so I'm going to change it and go in rounds now.

So they really decide how they want to sell their books. And publishers work with them.

Q. Earlier, I think you said you think the merger of Penguin Random House and Simon & Schuster will lead to lower advances for some books. Is that right?

A. Yes.

Q. Why do you think the merger will lead to lower advances for some books even though agents control the format of an auction?

A. I believe that lower advances will be the outcome of having fewer parties bidding against each other during the course of the auction. And when it's down to just two because—or however many, you know, 85, however many imprints Penguin Random House has, I don't know the number, but many, many imprints. And Simon & Schuster has another 40 or 50.

So instead of all these different imprints that might bid against each other, there will be less chances for the Penguin Random House and Simon & Schuster imprints to be the last two bidding and there will be fewer. If they go to the house bid system that Penguin uses, that would mean fewer participants in the auction overall to kind of drive up the rate, the rate of bidding.

Q. Let's switch topics slightly again. Before the merger of Penguin Random House and Simon & Schuster was announced, was Hachette interested in acquiring Simon & Schuster?

A. Hachette Book Group's parent company, Hachette Livre, was interested in acquiring Simon &

Schuster.

Q. Did Hachette or Hachette Livre submit a bid for Simon & Schuster?

A. Hachette Livre did not submit a bid for Simon & Schuster.

Q. And what about the part of Hachette that is not Hachette Livre? Does that part—

A. No. Hachette Livre was our parent company. They're the party that would have been bidding, not the Hachette Book Group.

Q. If Simon & Schuster were to come on the market again, would Hachette submit a bid for Simon & Schuster?

A. It is my hope that they would. It is my belief that they would intend to try again, even though they did not succeed in making a bid last time.

Q. If advances were to go down after a merger, wouldn't that be good for Hachette in some sense?

A. If advances were to go down? I suppose it is possible that we would buy some books at a lower advance than we might have, so on the advance front it would be good. But I think there are many, many other ways in which Penguin Random House acquiring Simon & Schuster would not be good for us.

Q. So you anticipated my next question. Why are you concerned about the merger even though advances going down would in some sense be good for Hachette or could be good for Hachette?

A. Having as much of the trade publishing business controlled by one entity, as Penguin Random Simon would control, I believe it would have several negative effects: One, as I said, I think there's likely to be a reduction in title count because when publishers conglomerate they tend to look at imprints that are very similar and say: We don't need these two competing against each other; we don't need two business imprints; we don't need two—whatever that they tend to say. Let's choose the one that's doing better and not keep the other one. And we saw after Random House acquired Penguin, quite a few of Penguin's imprints were closed. So I think there's a potential loss of offering.

I think there's a loss in sort of variety and originality. I think Penguin Random House has a very strong dominant central culture, which in my view is somewhat conservative. And Simon & Schuster has its own strong separate culture. And I feel that there's a danger of some kind of homogenization and lack of originality in publishing that might originate.

I also think that having one company as gigantically dominant as Penguin Random Simon would be would give them such financial advantages. I know from negotiations with retailers that Penguin Random House often has much better terms with them than we do. They don't tell us the terms; but we are able to ask, Are our terms on a par with our peers?

And we are often told: You're on par with all your peers except one. And it's very clear that they're talking about Penguin Random House having better terms. So I think that they already have financial advantages against us. So that's selfish.

I think it would be harmful to us in terms of our ability to compete with them because of the profitability that that gives them.

So title count, competition, loss of culture.

And then lower advances to authors. I think those are the major concerns I have about one company controlling so much of the market.

Q. And why are you concerned about lower advances to authors?

A. Why I'm concerned about that? I mean, I'm in this business because I think the book is the greatest creation of humankind and people who write books are incredibly admirable, often heroic. I'm here because I love authors. I'm in this business because I love authors and books. And I think it's good, though, for each book we compete for—to try to have an advance that is as high as it needs to be but no higher, I still think authors will do better in a world that has more competition among major publishers than it would have if this merger is approved.

Q. Let me turn to one document. There's a binder in front of you. It's got a white cover on it.

A. Uh-huh.

Q. I'm going to ask you to turn to PX 790.

Your Honor, Hachette has designated this document as confidential, so we would ask that we not show it on the public screen. But we think we can talk around the issues and talk through it in open court, if that makes sense.

Ms. Hare, can you show PX 790 on the judge's screen?

Q. And, Mr. Pietsch, let me know when you're at the right page.

A. I'm on that page.

Q. You are?

A. Yes.

Q. So the title of this—I'll just read it. The Bates number ends in 1061. And the title is: Titles Not Acquired Over $500,000 By Division. Is that right?

A. Yes.

Q. What information does this document contain?

A. This is a document that I mentioned earlier. This is what we call the Titles Not Acquired. We call it "The Ones That Got Away" report. This tracks books for which we offered $500,000 or more in advance and did not succeed in acquiring. I've said, we do our best to learn what the winning bid was, who the winning publisher was, and then over time look back at how many copies that book has sold as a way of educating ourselves about the outcome of the risks we attempted to take but did not succeed in taking.

Q. Who originally had the idea for tracking this information in this way?

A. This is something that I started doing when I was the publisher of Little, Brown; and then we expanded it to all Hachette divisions more recently.

Q. How does Hachette use this document?

A. As I've said, Hachette uses this document to learn, to look at the assumptions that we made when we were bidding for a book and then consider those assumptions against the outcome and try to learn if we were making faulty assumptions. Did we overestimate or underestimate the publicity platform of the book? Did we not understand how well this particular story might connect with the market? So we look at each one and try to see if there's something that can guide our future investments, acquisitions.

Q. Let me ask you to turn to the next page. It has the title "Titles Not Acquired, Hachette Book Group, Titles through June 2021." Then there's a thing labeled "Scorecard" in the upper left. Let me know when you're there.

A. Yes.

Q. Focusing on the scorecard, this states—this lists a total of 302 losses over a four-year time period. Is that right?

A. That's right.

Q. The time period is 2017 to 2021. Is that right?

A. That's right.

Q. And the first row, the PRH row, there were 124 losses to Penguin Random House. Is that right?

A. That's right.

Q. There's a row at the bottom labeled "Other." Do you see that?

A. I do.

Q. And it shows 50 losses labeled Other over a four-year time period. Is that right?

A. That's right.

Q. Does that mean that 50 of the 302 losses were to non-Big 5 publishers?

A.It does not.

Q. What books are included in this row labeled as "Other"?

A. "Other" captures a lot of circumstances. One is situations in which we know what we bid, but we did not learn who the winning bidder was. And that's the largest part. Almost half of those 50 is titles where we don't know the outcome.

The second-largest group is titles acquired by Houghton Mifflin Harcourt, which is now part of HarperCollins. I think out of this 50, 15—or 15 out of the total of 302 were titles acquired by non-Big 5 publishers.

Q. So you mentioned Houghton Mifflin Harcourt. Is that right?

A. That's right.

Q. They're often known as HMM?

A. That's correct.
Q. Who acquired them?
A. HarperCollins.
Q. I think you said 15 out of the 302 losses, approximately, were to non-Big 5 publishers. Is that if you count HMH as a Big 5?
A. No. That's not ounting HMH.
Q. I'm sorry. If you were to count HMH as not part of the Big 5, approximately how many losses out of that 302 are to non-Big 5?
A. Say that one more time, please.
Q. I've confused myself. If you were to count HMH as not being a Big 5 publisher, even though it was later acquired by Harper, how many approximately of the 302 losses would be to a non-Big 5 publisher?
A. I think that would bring it up to a little under 30.
Q. So I don't want to ask you for specific percentages. But in general, for the books listed in this chart, which publishers did Hachette lose to most frequently?
A. For the publishers were not the Big 5, who did we lose to most frequently?
Q. Oh, no. I'm sorry. Overall.
A. Overall, we lost most frequently to Penguin Random House, followed by HarperCollins, followed by Simon & Schuster, followed by Macmillan.
Q. Is it possible—
A. So there's some cases listed in here where we had one imprint that dropped out at 500 and another one did not and they acquired the book.
Q. Is it possible that this chart misidentifies the winning publisher for a small number of books?
A. It does. This graph is not the purpose of this. It's a scorecard that I think our finance team created because they thought it was interesting. The original impetus of the report was the title-by-title analysis that we could learn from.
So I can't speak—I can't say this is all the time that it captures everything. I can't say it captures everything accurately. It's not something I ever see in this scorecard. I don't oversee it in that way.
Q. Do you think any errors, meaning any misidentifications of winning publishers, would change the bottom-line conclusion that for most of the books listed in this chart Hachette lost to the Big 5?
A. No. It definitely would not.
Q. And when did you create the original titles on the document?
A. I don't remember when it began. It was something I started tracking when I was at Little, Brown, which I have left almost ten years ago.
Q. And what years does this version of the document cover?
A. This document covers 2017 to '21.
MR. VERNON: Your Honor, at this time we would pass the witness.
THE COURT: Thank you. Let me ask you one more question. Would you say that some bidders in the market are more conservative than others and are known for being so? Because it seems to me you said that you have sort of a 50 percent earn-out rate on books that get advances of $250,000 or more. And I've seen a number in things I've read in this case that some people have 85 percent of books that don't earn out.
So would you say that you're more conservative than other players in this market generally speaking or can that not be generalized?
THE WITNESS: I'm not sure that we're more conservative. Our business does have quite a few very large parts that are conservative. We have two imprints, Little, Brown and Grand Central, which are kind of big, mainstream going-out-to-the-heart-of-the-market imprints. And then we have a children's book division called Little, Brown Books for Young Readers that goes very aggressively and is competitive with all these other imprints.
I think of our competitors as having a lot more imprints that are making big bids like this than we do, because we just have those two or maybe three.
Then we have our imprints that are very cautious. The Perseus Book Group has five imprints that tend

to go above $250,000 much more rarely. So they have a much, much better rate of earn-out.

And Workman, newly acquired, has the same approach. So we have big parts of our business that earn out more often than the two kind of heart-of-the-market imprints do.

THE COURT: Thank you.

MR. VERNON: Can I follow up on that quickly, your Honor?

THE COURT: Yes.

Q. Mr. Pietsch, do you have a specific recollection of how frequently Hachette's books earn out at specific advance levels?

A. I don't have a specific recollection. No.

Q. Would looking at your deposition testimony possibly help you remember?

A. Okay. Sure.

Q. Let me ask you to turn in your binder to your litigation deposition. It's the last tab. It says Deposition 4/5/2022. Please turn to Page 263, Lines 5 through 18. And please read that to yourself and let me know when you're ready.

A. Yes.

Q. How often do Hachette's books earn out the advance at the higher advance levels?

A. The great majority of the books that we pay high advances for do not earn out their advances.

MR. VERNON: Thank you.

Now I pass the witness.

CROSS-EXAMINATION

BY MR. PETROCELLI:

Q. Mr. Pietsch, hi. I'm Dan Petrocelli. I represent Bertelsmann and Penguin Random House. How are you today?

A. I'm very well. Thank you.

Q. We've not met before, have we?

A. No, we have not.

Q. So before I jump into some of the questions I had planned to ask you, I thought I might follow up on some of your last answers and some of the questions the judge asked you.

A. Uh-huh.

Q. When you were talking about how many times you earn out and don't earn out, when you don't earn out, when the publisher doesn't earn out, you can still earn a profit. Right?

A. In a few cases. Mostly, you lose money. But in some cases you can not earn out and make a profit.

Q. Well, when you say in most cases you would lose money, you bake into your projections, right, about how much a book is going to sell? You do, like, a P&L pro forma when you're bidding for a book. Right?

A. Yes.

Q. Okay. And you project the sales. Right?

A. Yes.

Q. And then you have certain cost categories that you subtract. Right?

A. Yes.

Q. What are those? What are those categories?

A. Advances, unearned advances, manufacturing costs, planned costs, marketing costs, distribution costs.

Q. And what was the second one? Did you say unearned advances?

A. Yes. I said first royalties and then—perhaps I misspoke. What I meant to say was royalties followed by unearned advances.

Q. Now, if a book doesn't sell as projected, but it covers your costs that you just identified, you can still make money on the book. Right?

A. We can. Yeah.

Q. Okay. Do you keep track of how many times you actually make money on a book as opposed to lose

money on a book?
A. We look back over our performance on our high-earning titles quite rigorously over each year. I'm not sure what you mean by "keep track."
Q. You know, for every book that you publish, do you at some point go back and calculate whether you made any profit at all or you lost money?
A. We do a P&L for every title we publish—that's correct—after publication.
Q. And you have to wait a long time, though, to see—for the sales to go through. Right?
A. Yes. We do one after one year, after two years and after three years.
Q. And then there could even be sales beyond that as well. Right?
A. There are sometimes. Yes.
Q. But typically, if there are sales beyond three years, then you're doing pretty well on that book and the authors likely earned out. Right?
A. Not at all. No. Not remotely true.
Q. What's your batting average, then? How often do you make money, even if it's a small amount, on a book?
A. I don't have that figure clear in my head. I think it's around half the books we publish make a profit of some kind.
Q. Okay. Thank you for that. Now, you spoke recently. You gave a YouTube presentation for an organization a couple of weeks after your deposition was taken in this case. Right? For the Book Industry Study Group?
A. I spoke to the BISG. That's correct.
Q. You also wrote an article for *Publishers Weekly* at the end of last year. Right?
A. That's right.
Q. And in both of those, the article and your speech, you indicated that the publishing industry has not just survived the COVID crisis, but has actually thrived. Right?
A. Yes. I did say that.
Q. Okay. And you also said that—let me make sure I get the right quote here. You also said that most publishers, most publishers, are reporting record revenues and profits for the past two years. Right?
A. Those publishers that publicly report their results have all said that the unique combination of factors that COVID brought were extremely positive for the book industry. Yeah.
Q. Okay. And you didn't indicate that the only publishers who were reporting record revenues were the Big 5. Correct?
A. To my knowledge, the only publishers that report their revenues and profits publicly are the Big 5, plus perhaps Bloomsbury, which is English, an English company with U.S. imprints.
Q. But to be clear, when you gave the speech, you didn't make that clarification. You just said: Most publishers are reporting record revenues. True?
A. Those who report. Yes. You said "are reporting." So that—
Q. And you didn't even say "those who report."
A. No. I did.
Q. You said "most publishers." Correct?
A. That's correct.
Q. And you also indicated that even beyond the pandemic years, we're living in a great age for publishers, authors and readers. Right?
A. I did say that. Yeah.
Q. And you said: Industry revenues have grown year after year for decades, excluding a recession and a disruption or two, but we are in an industry that's just kept growing. You said that, too. Correct?
A. I was speaking very positively. Yes. I did say that.
Q. Now, you indicated in your speech that there were a number of immediate crises and long-term crises. Do you recall that?
A. I do. Yes.
Q. And none of the immediate or long-term crises included consolidation. Correct?

A. I chose not to speak about consolidation in that public address because of this ongoing matter of PRH acquiring Simon & Schuster.
Q. And your company's been pretty active in acquiring other companies. Right?
A. Yeah. It has.
Q. Just so we have a complete record on that, you acquired Workman just last year. Right?
A. Excuse me.
Q. Do you need a break?
A. No. I just needed to clear my throat.
Q. You acquired Workman just last year. Right?
A. That's right.
Q. A couple of years before that, you acquired a publisher called Worthy?
A. Yes.
Q. And before that, Perseus?
A. That's correct.
Q. And before that, Black Dog & Leventhal?
A. Yes.
Q. And as CEO of Hachette Book Group, you oversaw each of those acquisitions?
A. Yes; and more.
Q. Okay. And you also acknowledged in your direct exam that your parent company tried to acquire Simon & Schuster. Right?
A. My parent company considered the offering and did not make an offer.
Q. You personally were involved in the analysis of the Simon & Schuster opportunity for Hachette. Correct?
A. Yes.
Q. And you recommended that Hachette make an offer to acquire Simon & Schuster. Correct?
A. That's true.
Q. And you are aware that your parent company has expressed an interest in acquiring Simon & Schuster if this merger were not to proceed. Correct?
A. Yes. That's true.
Q. And you will continue to support the acquisition of Simon & Schuster were this merger not to proceed. Correct?
A. Simon & Schuster is a great publishing company. I would be very happy for my parent company to acquire it. Yes.
Q. So given that you would be very happy to acquire Simon & Schuster, I assume, then, that you would not be concerned in that circumstance about a 5-to-4 merger. Correct?
A. My concern is not about a 5-to-4 merger. It is about the creation of one super-dominant publisher that is so far out of scale with all other publishers.
Q. I would appreciate it if you just answered my questions little more directly.
You're not—you were not concerned about a 5-to-4 merger per se. Correct?
A. That's correct.
Q. And if you were to succeed in acquiring Simon & Schuster, you don't have any intention of lowering author advances, do you?
A. First, I would not be the one acquiring it; my parent company would be the one acquiring it. And it is not at all known who would be leading that entity. So would I be in a position to do that? I can't say. I do not expect the—repeat the question.
Q. Okay. If this merger were not to proceed and your parent company were to acquire Simon & Schuster, would it be your intention to lower author advances?
A. You're speaking of this as though it's something I would be doing. My parent company would be acquiring Simon & Schuster.
Q. Sir, I'm asking whether you would support a decision, if you would make a recommendation as the CEO of Hachette: We succeeded in acquiring Simon & Schuster; we should now lower advances?

A. No. I would not make that recommendation.

Q. Okay. And am I correct that you also would not make a recommendation to start reducing titles?

A. I cannot say that that is true.

Q. You might want to recommend to reduce titles?

A. If Hachette Livre owned Simon & Schuster, we would look at the publishing program of all the imprints. And it is possible we could expand. It's possible we could reduce. I really don't have an opinion on that in the absence of the information that would come with acquisition, which we never got to see because we did not make an offer.

Q. But it wouldn't be your purpose in closing imprints down in order to take advantage of the concentration to reduce author advances. That wouldn't be your purpose, right, in reducing title count and closing imprints down?

A. I'm sorry. Say that again, please.

Q. Yeah. If the merger went through, you indicated you might want to close some imprints down. Is that what you said?

A. No. That's not what I said.

Q. Then I didn't hear you.

A. I said I don't have enough information about Simon & Schuster to have any judgment about whether expanding imprints or reducing them might be an appropriate next step.

Q. Okay. Well, let me ask you this: As the person who made a recommendation to your parent company to bid for Simon & Schuster just a year ago, did you do an analysis whereby you informed your company that you could reduce title count as a result of the merger?

A. We did not do such an analysis. That's true.

Q. As part of your analysis, did you indicate to your parent company that you could reduce author advances?

A. No.

Q. Did you project in any financial estimates or analysis a reduction in author advances?

A. We did not.

Q. You did project efficiencies, though. Right?

A. We did.

Q. Okay.

MR. PETROCELLI: And I'd like to show the witness Defendants' Exhibit 288. This may be a confidential exhibit.

Q. So you have in front of you Defendants' Exhibit 288. And you understand this to be a March 2020 presentation concerning the potential acquisition of Simon & Schuster. Correct?

A. That's right.

Q. Okay. And if you could turn to page—and to be clear, you believed that the combined company of Hachette and Simon & Schuster would experience certain synergies and cost savings. Correct?

A. That's true.

Q. Okay. And if you look at Slide 17 in Exhibit 288, you will see a description of the types of costs and other synergies that are discussed there. Correct?

A. Yes.

Q. And if you look at the next page—and I won't say the number out loud—that's Slide 18. You will see on the right-hand side in euro an estimate for the full synergies. Correct?

A. That's right.

Q. And in U.S. dollars, that number would be roughly the same. Correct?

A. It would now.Yeah.

Q. Excuse me?

A. It would now.Yes.

Q. And it was around the same number back in 2020. Right?

A. It was a little higher, the conversion rate. Yeah.

Q. Now, I'd like to go back to your testimony about the lowering of advances—all right?—if this merger were to go through. If the merged company were to lower advances, you would have an opportunity to win more books. Right?

A. If the merged company—

Q. Yeah.

A.—were to—

Q. Were to lower author advances and proposals being made to authors, you know, through the agents, if they said, you know, Now we're merged and now we can lower advances, like the Government was saying, if they actually tried to do that, you could win more books.

A. I don't see that logic.

Q. You're saying you could not win more books?

A. I don't believe that that is the case. I think that we make each acquisition decision title by title based on what we believe we can sell it at; and that would continue to be the case. In certain situations, if we were the last two bidders left at the top, we might acquire the book for less than it might have gone for without another publisher bidding. I do not see how that would lead us to buy more books.

Q. To be clear, what you're saying is that, merger or not, your bidding would be the same as before. Right? You're going to bid as much as you think it's worth and not more. Right?

A. That is correct.

Q. Okay.

A. Yes.

Q. But if they lowered the bid—

A. If you lowered the bid—

Q. Excuse me. If the merged company were to lower its bid below the level—your highest level, you would win the book in that circumstance?

A. I'm sorry. I need you to repeat the question. I didn't understand it.

Q. Yes. If the merged firm were to lower its bid below your highest valuation that you were willing to bid, that would be a circumstance in which you would win a bid that previously you might not have?

A. I'm not following your logic that we would offer less as a merged company than we would offer as just Hachette. The merged company would still come up with what it thinks the book is worth and bid up to that amount. We wouldn't lower it.

Q. I'll give you an example. If pre-merger your top number was $500,000, okay, and Simon & Schuster or Penguin Random House bid $600,000 and won the book, but after the merger they bid $400,000, and your number is still $500,000, in that circumstance, you would have a higher bid and you might be selected. Correct?

A. I think you don't understand the logic of offering at an auction. I don't understand how a combined Simon & Schuster and Random House would offer $400,000 where separately they might have offered 600. If they had one of their publishers that wanted to offer $600,000, that would be the bid that carried the day.

Q. Well, can you just accept my hypo?

A. No. I don't accept it, is what I'm saying.

Q. And it's because you don't believe that the merged company would actually lower its bid?

A. No. What I was saying was that in situations where they were the last two publishers bidding, they would stop bidding each other up at a certain level when they were the last two, but not that they would agree to offer less than either one of the entities thought it was worth.

Q. And you're talking about an auction situation. Right?

A. I am. Yeah.

Q. But what if it were not an auction?

A. Okay.

Q. What if it were just an agent playing—getting a number from the merged firm and getting a higher number from you? In that circumstance, you would win?

A. If we have the higher bid, yes. We would win, most likely.

Q. Now, your view that the merged firm could lower advances is in a situation where the final two bidders pre-merger would have been Simon & Schuster and Penguin Random House, and let's say Hachette might have been third. But post-merger, now we don't have Simon & Schuster and Penguin Random House one and two, because now they're merged. And in that situation, you think that they could lower an advance. Correct?

A. In that situation, they could be the highest bidder for the book, win the book and not pay as much as they might have been willing to had they been competing with each other.

Q. Okay. Because the constraint that one imposed on the other pre-merger is now gone in that situation?

A. If they are, yes, in their own financial self-interest not bidding against each other when they're the only remaining publishers.

Q. But if you're bidding against anybody other than Penguin Random House and Simon & Schuster, you don't see a reduction in advance in that scenario. Correct?

A. No. Outside of the merged company, I think everything continues as it was.

Q. My question was: If you were bidding against another firm, let's call it HarperCollins, and not Simon & Schuster/Penguin Random House, you would not see that circumstance leading to a lower bid, to a lower advance. Correct?

A. To a lower advance for the author ultimately? Is that what you're saying?

Q. Correct.

A. That is correct.

Q. And in the situation where you do think there's a potential—I think you testified in your deposition that it was conceivable. Do you recall using that word?

A. I don't have the context you're talking about.

Q. The context in which you're bidding against Simon & Schuster and Penguin Random House post-merger.

A. I do not understand the question. What is conceivable?

Q. What you said in your deposition, am I correct, that the lowering of an advance was not likely or probable, but conceivable?

A. Forgive me for not understanding your question. Please repeat it.

Q. I'll take you to your deposition. Could you turn to Page 59, Line 11 through Line 19. Do you have your deposition in front of you?

A. I am opening it now.

Q. Okay.

A. What lines?

Q. Line 11.

A. Okay.

Q. Question: Does it follow that if advances go down that Hachette would pay less in advances?

In those situations where the last two bidders were Hachette and the combined Penguin Random House/Simon & Schuster, it is conceivable that the lack of a third party, if that third party were either PRH or Simon & Schuster, would—it would to [sic] lead lower ultimately winning advances.

And you gave that testimony. Correct?

A. I did. I'm trying to understand it.

Q. And could you look at Lines 21, Page 59? 21 to 60.

A. Yes.

Q. Other than in the case where the final two bidders were Hachette and Penguin Random House/Simon & Schuster, are there other instances where you believe that advances will go down?

Answer: No.

That was an accurate answer you gave. Right?

A. As I said this morning, I believe there are also situations where the smaller number of bidders in an auction will also in many cases lead to ultimately higher bids.

Q. We'll get to that. But that's the answer you gave in your deposition?

A. That is correct.

Q. Now, one question I have about that is, when you are bidding post-merger, you're not going to know whether you're bidding against Simon & Schuster/Penguin Random House. Correct?

A. In most cases, we do not know who we are bidding against. That's correct.

Q. And if you don't know who you're bidding against, you're not going to be able to make an assumption that you're bidding against Simon & Schuster/Penguin Random House, that therefore in that situation there might be a lower advance offered. You're just not going to know. Right?

A. It sounds like—I will say it sounds to me like you're saying that a lower advance offered means we're offering less. Is that what you're saying?

Q. No; that—well, I want to get to that. But Penguin Random House and Simon & Schuster are lowering. That's what the Government is claiming.

A. We will not know if we don't know who the other bidder is that it is a Penguin Random House/Simon & Schuster bid. That's correct.

Q. I think, as you testified earlier, your strategy post-merger in bidding is not going to change at all, correct, no matter who you're up against? Right?

A. Our strategy will still be to—yeah. I don't see our strategy changing. No.

Q. It's also the case when you are bidding for books against other publishers, it's quite common that with respect to the same book, different publishers and different editors could value it very differently. True?

A. Absolutely. Absolutely.

Q. And that happens often. Right?

A. That is—that is—

Q. And that's because every book is unique. Correct?

A. Absolutely correct.

Q. And I believe you confirmed in your direct, but just to make sure, Hachette would not drop out of an auction at any different rate post-merger versus pre-merger. Right?

A. That's correct.

Q. When Penguin—you gave some testimony about the merger in 2013 between Penguin and Random House. Do you recall that?

A. When Random House acquired Penguin?

Q. Yes.

A. Okay.

Q. Yes. First of all, you didn't see any kind of decrease in author advances as a result of that merger. Right?

A. I did not observe any.

Q. And you've never done any analysis to determine if there was any reduction in author advances as a result of that merger. Correct?

A. That is true.

Q. Now, with respect to the reduction in title count, did I understand you to say that as a result of the 2013 merger, there was a reduction in Penguin Group's title count by some 1,000 titles?

A. That is what I observed. Yes.

Q. Now, are you saying that that was as a result of the merger or that would have occurred independent of the merger?

A. I cannot speak to causality. I observed—I just keep track of the title count of our competitors each year and observed that over time at the same time that I observed several Penguin imprints being closed down.

Q. With respect to the reduction in title count, you understood that there was an industry trend going on around that time regarding a reduction in mass-market paperback books. Correct?

A. In that time, there were, yes. Some publishers were cutting back on their mass-market publishing. Yes.

Q. It's fair to say that the demand for mass-market paperbacks had decreased significantly. Correct?

A. That has been a steady trend. Yes.

Q. And did you understand that the Penguin Group was overindexed in mass-market books at or around the time of the merger?

A. I did not understand that. No.

Q. That was a phenomenon that affected all publishers?

A. Many publishers cut back their mass-market paperback title count in that period. Random House also has mass-market publishing, and their title count stayed the same.

Q. Now, did I also understand you to say that as a result of that 2013 merger that there was closure of imprints?

A. Yes.

Q. And did you—you attribute that to the merger?

A. I noticed that it happened after the merger.

Q. Well, do you know how many imprints the merged firm Penguin Random House closed following 2013?

A. I do not have a count. No.

Q. If I told you it was 32 imprints that were closed, would that be consistent with your knowledge?

A. As I said, I observed imprints I knew of closing. I didn't have any sense of a count.

Q. And do you know how many they opened during that same period of time?

A. No, I don't.

Q. And if I told you that Penguin Random House opened 32 imprints during that same period of time, is that consistent with your knowledge?

A. I was not aware of that. No.

Q. And your company also closed imprints. Right?

A. Yes. Our company has closed some.

THE COURT: I'm sorry. Could I ask a clarifying question?

What's the relationship between the imprints and the title counts?

THE WITNESS: Imprints are a unit of a publishing group or a larger company that publishes books. So an imprint is responsible for bringing out a certain number of titles a year. An imprint employs editors, publicists, marketing teams, designers. And so an imprint is a sub-unit of a publishing company.

THE COURT: So if you close an imprint, you necessarily reduce your title count because that imprint's not producing titles?

THE WITNESS: When an imprint is closed, that usually means that the people that are employed at that imprint for acquiring books and publishing them are let go and that they stop acquiring books.

THE COURT: And that's why the title count goes down?

THE WITNESS: That is an outcome of that—that imprint's title count would disappear. It would not be acquiring new titles.

BY MR. PETROCELLI:

Q. Well, the total title count would be reduced unless you opened up new imprints. Right?

A. I'm sorry?

Q. Total title counts might go down unless you opened up new imprints that created new titles. Right?

A. A publisher can do that as well. Yes.

Q. And in—

THE COURT: I'm sorry, Mr. Petrocelli. Does the title count include backlist or only—

THE WITNESS: No. When we're talking about title count here, we're talking about the new titles issued each year under the aegis of a particular imprint.

THE COURT: I'm sorry, Mr. Petrocelli. Go ahead.

Q. You closed Weinstein Books in 2017. Right?

A. That's correct.

Q. And you closed Da Capo Lifelong/Da Capo Press in 2018–2019?

A. We merged that into a—we created a new imprint called Hachette Books that took on that publishing and those editors.

Q. And you also closed Grand Central's Life & Style imprint?

A. Yes.

Q. And FaithWords and Worthy. Right?
A. That's incorrect. Those are both ongoing imprints, FaithWords and Worthy. Very much alive.
Q. Now, you gave a lot of testimony about the Big 5. So let me just follow up a bit on that. You have in front of you a spreadsheet which is a document identical to the one that you were shown on your direct examination, except this is marked as Defense Exhibit 220 rather than the Plaintiff's exhibit because I had put some tabs on there to make it easier for you to turn to certain pages.
A. Thank you.
Q. Do you have that in front of you?
A. I do.
Q. At the beginning, let me just direct you to the front page that you testified about, the scorecard up in the top corner.
A. Yes.
Q. Okay. And again, you're keeping track of the offers that your company makes $500,000 and above that you're unsuccessful. Right?
A. That's correct.
Q. Okay. And you indicated that the "Other" category includes the non-Big 5 publishers. Right?
A. It does. Yes.
Q. And at the time that that scorecard was prepared, HMH was a non-Big 5 publisher. Right?
A. That's correct.
Q. So the number you have there is about 30, then, for the non-Big 5 publishers. Right?
A. That's my rough estimate from memory. Yes.
Q. Now, have you actually gone through that document to confirm that the other 20 are not—are not non-Big 5 publishers?
A. I have not gone through it myself. No.
Q. Were you just guesstimating?
A. No. I was given an analysis after our deposition when this was the subject of a lot of questioning and I kept saying I do not know what these other 50 are.
Q. Who gave you that analysis?
A. Counsel.
Q. Your counsel?
A. Yeah.
Q. That was after the deposition?
A. That's right.
Q. But at the deposition, you indicated that it was essentially for non-Big 5 publishers. Right?
A. What I indicated at the deposition was that I did not know what made up those 50 other titles.
Q. Let me take you through a couple of those non-Big 5 titles, if you wouldn't mind, where you were unsuccessful.
A. Sure.
Q. By the way, just to clarify something, one of the items on—or the names on the scorecard is HBG. The judge asked you about that. That stands for Hachette Book Group.
Right?
A. Right.
Q. Now, your company allows your imprints to bid against each other. Correct?
A. As long as there is another party outside Hachette bidding. Yes.
Q. Okay. So do you know any other company that allows imprints to bid against one another within the same corporation?
A. As I testified earlier, I believe all the other Big 5 publishers allow the imprints within the company to bid against each other as long as there are outside bidders. So yes, I do.
Q. Now, you indicated that you thought the Penguin Group may have a different policy?
A. That is my understanding.
Q. Well, if I told you that the Penguin division within Penguin Random House is free to bid against any

other imprint in any other division, you wouldn't quarrel with that. Right?

A. No. I was speaking about imprints within the publishing—the Penguin Group of Random House, not bidding against each other, but rather putting in a house bid. The Penguin Group house bid can be against other Random House side imprints, to my knowledge.

Q. So just to explain that a little more—

A. Sure.

Q.—Penguin Random House has several divisions. Right?

A. Right.

Q. And in each division are a number of imprints. One is the Penguin division; one is the Random division; one is the Knopf Doubleday division.

A. Right.

Q. And then there's two children's divisions. Right?

A. Right.

Q. And each of those divisions has a number of imprints. Right?

A. Yes.

Q. Within—and across those divisions, imprints are permitted to bid against one another. Right?

A. Except the imprints on the Penguin Group are put in a house bid even—but it can be against an imprint or multiple imprints from the other parts of Random House. Yes.

Q. The Penguin house bid can—they can bid against any—

A. Yes.

Q.—of the other imprints?

A. Yes. Absolutely.

Q. And your company has that same practice of allowing internal bidding, provided there's an external bidder. Right?

A. That's right. Yeah.

Q. The reason you have that practice is because you think it's good for your business. Right?

A. That's right.

Q. And you think it helps you to match up the author and the work with the right editor and give you a greater opportunity to win a book. Right?

A. We want our publishers to be competitive, and in some cases that includes being competitive with each other. That causes them to move faster and work harder and have better chances of winning the book.

Q. Okay. So let me just walk through a few instances where your company lost to a non-Big 5 company. Okay?

A. Uh-huh.

Q. And just one final thing before I do that. If you go back to that scorecard under HBG—

. . . Under HBG, you have a total of nine. Those are nine times when one of your imprints won a bid against another or more of your imprints. Right?

A. That's right.

Q. Now we go to the page on the Bates numbers on that document you have in front of you, Exhibit—

If you could go to Bates No. 1065. And what I have attempted to do—and I apologize for not doing it first for your Honor—I tabbed those in the order in which I'm going to walk you through them, 1, 2, 3, 4, 5. Do you see

the numbers on the yellow tabs?

A. Bates No. 1065?

Q. Yeah. But if you go look at yellow Tab No. 1, you'll be there.

A. Got it.

Q. And that's at page Bates No. 1065.

A. Uh-huh.

Q. So it's row 61. And it's the situation where—again, all of these are cases where Hachette lost to a non-Big 5 for an amount over $500,000. Right?

A. Yes.
Q. Okay. I'm not going to identify the amount that you folks bid. Okay?
A. Okay.
Q. The first one was a loss to Chronicle. Correct?
A. I'm sorry. I'm on the page. I'm just seeing when—it doesn't point me to a particular one.
Q. Row 61.
A. I'll look at the screen instead of the document. Thank you.
Q. Do you see that?
A. I do.
Q. And you lost Chronicle, and I won't tell you the amount of the winning bid, for a book called *Elements of Flavor* in 2020. Right?
A. Right.
Q. You lost to Chronicle also two other books, one called *Songteller*, Dolly Parton's book. Correct?
A. That's correct.
Q. And also Snoop Dogg's book, *From Crook to Cook*. Right?
A. Yeah.
Q. So that's three losses to Chronicle there. Scholastic—you lost to Scholastic for Brittney Cooper's *Stand Up!* right?
A. (Nods in the affirmative.)
Q. You have to answer audibly.
A. Yeah.
Q. You lost to Abrams on a book called *The Book of Zeewee*. Is that right?
A. I can't read it on the screen, but I'll take your word for it.
Q. And *Super Attractive.* Right?
A. Sounds right.
Q. Grove Atlantic, Ruth Coker Burks' *All the Young Men*?
A. I'm taking your word for it. I cannot see that on my screen or on my page.
Q. Tyndale, Beth Moore's *Making It Matter*. Correct?
A. I think that might be a misunderstanding—misidentification. I believe Tyndale is owned by HarperCollins.
Q. That would be Row 94.
A. It says Tyndale House. Yes.
Q. And Disney: *Ellie Engel Saves Herself*. Right?
A. Yeah.
Q. And one more. Spiegel & Grau: *Echoes Within*. Correct?
A. What is the date of that?
Q. Page—excuse me?
A. What date is that?
Q. I don't have the date in front of me. But it would be in the last couple of years.
A. Let me find it.
Q. Page 1079, Row 265. Do you see that, Alison Smith's *Echoes Within*?
A. Yes.
Q. Now, Spiegel & Grau, by the way, is a relatively new publisher. Right?
A. That's correct.
Q. Okay. And they obviously—well, they would have bid more than $500,000 to win that book. Right?
A. Absolutely. I'm not saying that that never happens. I say it happens very, very rarely and is hard to sustain over time for companies without backlists.
Q. Your company is not set up such that it has a special division for books that go for advances of $250,000 or above. Right?
A. No. That happens across many of our imprints.
Q. Excuse me?

A. No. That happens across many of our imprints.

Q. What happens?

A. Offering advances among—of $250,000 or more. I'm saying it happens across the company.

Q. So my question is: You don't have, like, a special division, a special group, that handles acquisitions of 250 and above. That could happen in any of your imprints. Right?

A. Several of our imprints choose not to bid at that level. But any one of the imprints that makes a case to offer that much is supported in that bid because we have the wherewithal across our whole company to support that level of risk.

Q. You don't have any separate marketing channels or distribution—marketing services or distribution channels for just books that happen to have an advance of 250 or above. Correct?

A. No. We do not divide our company that way.

Q. And you don't have approval levels within your company based on $250,000, do you?

A. We have advance approvals right around that. All our publishers have advance approval levels and they are all clustered right around that number. Almost everyone in the company has to come to me for approval at that level or higher.

Q. But there are various numbers, right, ranging from $100,000 and above? Right?

A. From $100,000 to just above $250,000. Yeah.

REDIRECT EXAMINATION

BY MR. VERNON:

Q. Mr. Pietsch, Mr. Petrocelli asked you about some testimony you gave in your deposition. Do you remember that?

A. I do.

Q. He asked you about some testimony that you gave on Page 59 where you discussed a situation in which the merger might lead to lower advances. Do you remember that?

A. Yes.

Q. Did you describe in your deposition any other situations in which the merger might lead to lower advances?

A. Not to my recollection.

Q. Let me ask you to turn to Page 58, again going back to your litigation deposition. Let me ask you to read Lines 10 through 20 on Page 58 to yourself and then let me know when you're done.

A. Yes.

Q. Setting that aside, do you recall which circumstances you explained in your deposition when you thought the merger would cause advances to go down?

A. When Simon & Schuster and Penguin Random House were the last two bidders in an auction, in those situations it is likely that the bidding would stop when they were the last two bidders. And the advance would be lower than if they continued competing against each other.

Q. I think counsel also asked you if you had observed an effect on advances from the merger of Penguin and Random House.

Do you remember that?

A. Yes.

Q. Do you recall in your deposition testifying about whether you had an expectation as to whether the merger of Penguin and Random House would have affected advances?

A. Yes. I said that I thought it would.

Q. And what effect did you expect it to have had?

A. I think the acquisition of Simon & Schuster by Penguin Random House would lead to lower advances.

Q. I'm sorry. I intended to ask you about the merger of Penguin and Random House.

A. Oh, I'm sorry. Forgive me.

Q. That's okay.

A. Please ask it again.

Q. Do you recall testifying in your deposition about whether you had an expectation about whether the merger of Penguin and Random House would have led to lower advances?

A. Yes. I expected that Random House's acquisition of Penguin would have led to lower advances for the same reason that their acquiring Simon & Schuster would.

Q. Let me ask you to turn back to PX 790, which is the—again the win/loss document we've been discussing. Let me know when you're ready.

A. Yes.

Q. First of all, did Hachette create this document for purposes of this litigation?

A. No.

Q. Did Hachette create this document for purposes of the DOJ's regulatory review?

A. No.

Q. I tried to count during counsel's examination—I think he asked you about ten losses to non-Big 5 publishers that are recorded in this document. Does that sound right?

A. Sounds right. Yeah.

Q. How many losses in total are recorded in this document?

A. We lost 302 auctions in this document.

Q. And I believe counsel only showed you one loss to Scholastic. Is that right?

A. That sounds right.

Q. Did counsel show you any losses to self-publishing?

A. No.

THE COURT: I just had a final question. I thought you said if there's a smaller number of bidders there could be a downward pressure on advances, including fewer round robins. Did I write—

THE WITNESS: I said that in answer to a question at trial, but not in the deposition.

THE COURT: I see. Thank you.

MR. PETROCELLI: May I ask a couple follow-up questions?

THE COURT: You may.

BY MR. PETROCELLI:

Q. On the 2013 merger, Hachette didn't pay any lower author advances as a result of that merger. Right?

A. Not to our knowledge.

Q. And you never reported to anybody in the company or to your superiors that there had been a reduction in author advances as a result of the 2013 merger. Correct?

A. That's true.

Q. And one other question that I neglected to ask you the first time around: Does Hachette coordinate with other publishers on advance amounts to be offered to authors?

A. There's only one circumstance that we've ever done that, and that's a collaborative publication of books by President Clinton and James Patterson with Knopf and Little, Brown.

We don't collaborate, but we agree to offer an advance to publish books jointly. Other than that, there's never been any—never any collaboration or coordination with other publishers.

Q. And is it fair to say that Hachette does not intend to start coordinating with other publishers on advance amounts if this merger were to go through? Right?

A. That's correct.

Q. If the merger is approved, will that make it more likely for Hachette to coordinate with other publishers on author advance amounts?

A. No, it will not.

THE COURT: I had one more question, actually. I had forgotten to ask this. You had said that you tend to lose to other bidders in proportion to their market shares?

THE WITNESS: That's correct.

THE COURT: Does that mean that if the combined entity has almost 50 percent of the market share you would expect them to bid in about 50 percent of the auctions? I know it's not precise.

THE WITNESS: Yeah. I would expect that the combined entity would be bidding in more auctions because bids come from individual editor's, publisher's enthusiasm and there would be more imprints—

THE COURT: Oh, imprints within the combined entity?

THE WITNESS: Yeah; than, from Simon & Schuster Group added to all the imprints of Penguin Random House. They would be bidding in total in more auctions.

THE COURT: Thank you. Any questions based on my questioning?

MR. VERNON: I actually do have one question. I apologize.

Q. I think you testified Hachette does not allow its imprints to compete against each other unless there is an outside bidder. Did I hear that correctly?

A. That's correct.

Q. Why do you do that?

A. Once we have only Hachette imprints bidding, then the bidding—continuing to bid each other up would hurt the company's collective P&L. At that point, we ask the author and agent to make a choice between the two. We allow the two imprints who are left to match at the higher bid of the two if they were at different levels at the end and ask the author and agent. And that's just financial self-interest.

MR. VERNON: Thank you, your Honor. We have no further questions.

THE COURT: Thank you. Thank you very much, Mr. Pietsch. You can step down.

AYESHA PANDE, AYESHA PANDE LITERARY

Ayesha Pande at Ayesha Pande Literary was one of just a couple of literary agents that DOJ called to testify directly at length in the A3 trial, but when her appearance concluded on Tuesday morning, it left some people wondering how her evidence supported the case against the merger.

She did ratify the government's argument that the Big 5 are unto themselves in terms of their ability to consistently pay big advances and bring to bear best-in-breed marketing, publicity and sales clout. Pande noted that even for her authors who have published successfully with a smaller, independent house, "it often has been the preference of the author to publish their next book with a larger publisher, ideally one of the Big 5." Both because "it would have a better chance at success with more substantial resources being brought . . . as well as higher advances."

Given that she represents a number of authors from under-represented communities, she said: "Because of being under-represented, it already makes it slightly more challenging to find homes [for their books]." The merger "would limit that choice even more. And I believe overall advances for my clients would be suppressed."

On cross-examination, however, PRH lead attorney Daniel Petrocelli successfully demonstrated that very few of Pande's clients have been in bidding situations for anticipated bestselling books in which S&S and PRH were the final two bidders.

In fact, among the eight significant deals or better she provided information on during deposition, six were bought by PRH and none were bought by S&S. Five of the eight were exclusive submissions, option books or pre-empts. They also elicited that almost all of Pande's auctions for 33 books sold in very nice deals or better have been at full round robin auctions. Her auctions have been best bids—albeit, at least in some cases, best bids with two or three rounds.

Of that bigger pool of 33 books, only one was bought by S&S. In another case, S&S was the high bidder, but the author selected a lower bid—"by tens of thousands of dollars" according to Petrocelli—from a PRH imprint.

At the end of her testimony Judge Pan followed the evidence and asked, "Is it correct that if Simon & Schuster and PRH were merged, it wouldn't have affected any of the deals on this list?" The answer was yes. Judge Pan also asked Pande, regarding her anticipated big books, if "you treat such books differently" (as the DOJ has posited), which she also affirmed.

TESTIMONY OF AYESHA PANDE, AYESHA PANDE LITERARY

DIRECT EXAMINATION

BY MS. LICHT:

Q. Good afternoon, Ms. Pande.

A. Good afternoon.

Q. I'm going to get started by asking you some questions about your professional background. How long—

THE COURT: Can you have her state her name and spell her name for the record.

BY MS. LICHT:

Q. Ms. Pande, could you state your name and spell it for the record, please.

A. My name is Ayesha Pande, A-Y-E-S-H-A P-A-N-D-E.

Q. How long have you been in the publishing industry?

A. 32 years.

Q. What was your first position in publishing?

A. I worked as an editorial assistant for a small independent publisher.

Q. Have you held any other positions in publishing since that time?

A. Yes, I have.

Q. Can you tell me about some of those positions?

A. I worked at Readers' Digest as a research editor and then as an editor for Readers' Digest Condensed

Books. And then I held editorial positions at Crown Publishers, which was a division of Random House; HarperCollins; and Farrar, Straus and Giroux, which is an imprint at Macmillan.

Q. How long did you work as an editor in total?

A. 15 years.

Q. Approximately how many book acquisition negotiations did you participate in as an editor?

A. I don't remember an exact number, but I would say several dozens.

Q. Are you currently employed?

A. Yes, I am.

Q. What is your current position?

A. I am the founder and president of my agency, Ayesha Pande Literary.

Q. When did you found Ayesha Pande Literary?

A. In 2007.

Q. Why did you decide to become a literary agent?

A. I felt that my particular set of experiences, my passions, my interests were better suited to advocating on behalf of authors.

Q. How would you describe the mission of your literary agency?

A. The mission of my agency arose out of my realization as a biracial woman and an immigrant that there weren't a lot of narratives that represented my particular experience of being an outsider, being other, that those stories that I was looking for that reflected that experience I couldn't really find in the publishing industry.

And so I thought that it would benefit me to look for those stories and to represent clients who wrote those kinds of stories.

And over the years, that has become somewhat of a mission, a mandate for my agency, where we deliberately look for those kinds of narratives and voices and we seek to support and amplify those voices.

Q. Where is your business located?

A. It is located in Harlem, New York City.

Q. How many people does Ayesha Pande Literary employ?

A. There's ten of us all together.

Q. How many authors does Ayesha Pande Literary represent?

A. Approximately 300.

Q. And does that include both fiction and nonfiction authors?

A. Yes.

Q. What about you personally? How many authors do you represent?

A. Approximately 50.

Q. Is that also fiction and nonfiction authors?

A. Yes.

Q. How has your agency grown over the years?

A. When I first started, I was solo and I had a very small handful of clients. And I remained independent and on my own for several years and then I started adding other agents to my company. So there's eight agents all together now.

And we also recently launched a speakers bureau.

Q. Can you tell me about some of the authors you represent and their notable achievements?

A. Yes. We—I specifically represent both novelists, prizewinning, award-winning novelists, scholars, journalists, activists. That's both in fiction and nonfiction.

Q. Have the books written by your authors been nominated or won any awards in recent years?

A. Yes. They've won numerous awards in recent years, including the PEN/Bingham Prize, the National Book Award, the PEN/Bellwether Prize and many others.

Q. Are you a member of any professional organizations?

A. Yes. I am a member and also a board member of the AALA, which is the Association of American Literary Agents.

Q. What are your responsibilities as a board member of the AALA?

A. Aside from attending meetings and voting on various initiatives, I'm also a founding member of our DEI committee, where we're also supporting a mentorship and a fellowship program that's designed to bring more people of color into the industry.

Q. What does DEI stand for in that context?

A. Diversity, equity and inclusion.

Q. How many members does the AALA have?

A. Approximately 500.

Q. I'm going to turn to some questions about what it is that you do as a literary agent and how you sell the rights to publish your authors' books. So at a high level, what do you do as a literary agent?

A. As an agent, the first job that I do is to find promising, aspiring authors. And once we decide to work together, once I decide to represent them, I work with them to develop their projects. That can be editing manuscripts; it can be helping them to refine their nonfiction ideas for a book proposal. It can take anywhere from six months to two years to really hone and refine a project and get it ready for submission.

Q. How are you compensated as a literary agent?

A. We are compensated via commissions that we receive after we have sold a project to a publisher.

Q. What is the commission that you typically receive?

A. For domestic rights, it's typically 15 percent.

Q. Do you have an understanding of whether that is typical for literary agents?

A. Yes. That's pretty standard.

Q. When an author's book is ready to be sent out to prospective publishers, what do you do?

A. I work together with my clients to put together a submission. That means writing a submission letter, putting together a submission list, thinking about which might be the most qualified editors and publishing houses to submit to; and then once all of that is in place, I actually send it out to editors.

Q. How do you decide which editors may be especially interested in a particular book?

A. I weigh a number of different factors, including the kinds of books that they have acquired in the past, how effectively the publishing house for which they work has published those kinds of books. And also, I weigh the ability of a publishing company to pay an appropriate compensation for the work.

Q. Do you prioritize editors at certain publishers when making your submissions?

A. I would say that in the first round of submissions, I prioritize mostly editors from what we call the Big 5 publishers, because I find that they are most likely to pay an appropriate advance for my clients.

Q. Why is it important that your authors are compensated appropriately?

A. Well, by the time we send out the project, very frequently they have already spent many hours over many years working on the project. By the time I even start representing the book, it's usually already a finished manuscript that they've spent years writing. So it makes sense that all of those many hours of labor should be reasonably compensated.

Q. Looking beyond the financial compensation to authors, in your experience, what types of services do publishers provide to authors?

A. Well, of course editorial services and then everything that goes into producing a book, including designing a cover, typesetting the book, marketing and publicizing the book, distributing the book. Yeah. I think those are the most important things.

Q. Does the quality of those services matter to you?

A. Yes. Very much.

Q. Why?

A. The way that a publisher positions a book in the marketplace and then the ways in which they promote the book to potential audiences is crucial in ensuring the success and longevity of that book.

Q. Are there any other publishers to whom you typically submit books in a first wave of submissions?

A. I frequently include what I would refer to as some of the mid-sized publishers, such as Bloomsbury and Grove and Norton.

Q. Why do you submit to mid-sized publishers like Bloomsbury, Grove and Norton in addition to the Big 5 publishers?

A. Submitting to a broad range of publishers is more likely to lead to competition and therefore a more reasonable advance.

Q. How would you characterize the competition in terms of advance level offered by a mid-sized publisher such as one of the ones you mentioned compared to an imprint of the Big 5?

A. If I anticipate that the advance is going to be below six figures, there's a reasonable expectation that they can compete with the Big 5 publishers. So yes.

Q. When would you move to a second round of submissions?

A. There's a point when enough of the publishers in the first round of submission have passed on a book that in order for me to achieve success in publishing the book or in selling the book to a publisher I have to include other publishers as well.

Q. Who are some of the other publishers to whom you submit books in a second wave of submissions?

A. I would say they fall into two categories: the smaller independent publishers, like Graywolf, Pegasus, Melville House, Tin House; and then the ones that I would refer to as the relative newcomers, the ones that have cropped up in the last year or two.

Q. Taking those separately, thinking about the smaller independent publishers that you mentioned, why do you typically not include those smaller publishers in a first wave of submissions?

A. In my experience, they don't have the resources to pay adequate advances, as much as I love working with them. The advances that I've received from them in the past have been very modest.

Q. Can you give me an example of or compare an advance given by a smaller, independent publisher compared to an advance that one of your clients has received from a Big 5 publisher?

A. The advances that I've received from the small publishers have tended to be somewhere below 10,000. And the advances from the Big 5, of course, have a broad range, but I would say a modest advance from a Big 5 would be somewhere around 25,000 to 30,000.

Q. You also mentioned some newcomers. Who are you referring to there?

A. There's a house that was recently launched by two industry veterans called Spiegel & Grau. There's another one called Zando Projects. There's Astra House. There's Zibby Owens' new publishing company called, I believe, Zibby Books. Those are the ones.

Q. And why do you not include some of those new publishers in a first wave of submissions?

A. Because I think it takes a long time for a publisher to establish itself in the industry. A publisher's lasting success, its longevity, depends on them having a substantial list of books that they've published and that continue to receive or generate revenues. And all of these publishers are still too new to have really proven themselves.

Q. How often do you submit a book to more than one editor at Penguin Random House?

A. Always.

Q. Why always?

A. Well, first of all, there's many, many imprints at Penguin Random House and therefore many potential homes for my clients' books. But also, in order for me to ensure the greatest chance of success, I simply cannot not submit to those imprints at Penguin Random House.

Q. With respect to Penguin Random House, could you decide to not submit to any of their imprints at all?

A. I would say no.

Q. Why not?

A. I don't believe I would be doing my clients any favors by not submitting to Penguin Random House when on average they make up approximately 30 or so percent of my submissions. So leaving them out would really shrink the possibilities.

Q. I'm going to focus my next few questions on what happens after you've submitted a book to editors. What are the next steps you take after making those submissions?

A. I follow up with editors to determine the level of interest. And depending on whether there's interest from more than one publisher, I determine how I will go about soliciting offers by setting what's called a closing.

Q. Is there anything you can do to control the number of editors who express interest in a book?

A. No.

Q. Is there anything you can do to control the number of editors who make an offer to publish a book?

A. No.

Q. Is there anything you can do to control how much an editor offers to acquire a book?

A. No.

Q. What are some of the different methodologies you use to sell an author's book to a publisher?

A. It depends on whether the book is a debut or a first novel or a nonfiction project by an author, in which case I would hopefully set a closing and request something like best bids from multiple publishers, "best bids" just meaning asking them at a particular time and at a particular date to send in what their best offer is for a particular project.

If it is a repeat book for an author who's already under contract, which we call an option, then I would first submit it to that publisher exclusively and, if they make an offer, negotiate with them.

Q. What can you do if you don't think that the option offer made by a publisher is sufficient for your author?

A. At that point, I can decide to decline that offer and then send the book out widely to other publishers.

Q. How many interested bidders do you need to hold a best-bids auction?

A. Anywhere above two.

Q. Do you ever sell books in a preempt?

A. Yes.

Q. Under what circumstances would you sell an author's book in a preempt?

A. When I have sent the book out to multiple publishers and there's a lot of interest, one of those publishers or one of those editors at those publishing houses may decide to try and take that book off the table by making what we call a preemptive offer. So they would approach me and say: Would you consider accepting this offer rather than going to a best-bids kind of situation?

Q. And if you don't think that the preempt offer is sufficient in terms of the compensation offered, can you then seek additional offers from other publishers?

A. Yes. I can decide not to accept that preempt offer and then move on to the closing.

Q. In your experience, how does the number of interested editors impact which of these methodologies are available to you to sell the book?

A. I'm sorry. Could you repeat that question?

Q. Yes. Let me ask a slightly different question. How do you choose which kind of methodology to use to sell a book?

A. It really depends on how many editors at different publishing houses have expressed interest. The preferred scenario is if there are several interested publishers so that I can move toward a competitive closing. If there's just interest from one publisher, then I have to try and negotiate in good faith with that publisher.

Q. In your experience, does having multiple editors interested in a book impact the likely advance that is offered?

A. Yes. In my experience, having a competitive situation tends to lead to a higher advance.

Q. In your experience, when multiple editors are interested in a book, how often is a publisher outside the Big 5 involved?

A. Very rarely.

Q. In your experience, how often has a publisher outside the Big 5 won a competitive situation for a book?

A. Frankly, I don't remember a time when a publisher outside of the Big 5 has won any kind of competitive situation for a book.

Q. I'm going to turn now to some questions about the contract terms that you negotiate on behalf of your authors. What are some of the most important contract terms that you negotiate?

A. I would say the single most important contract term is the advance. And after that, it would be the rights, including translation rights and the other rights included in the package that the publisher is seeking to acquire, and the royalty rates.

Q. Why is the advance the most important term that you negotiate on behalf of your authors?

A. Because in a large number of cases, it may be the only compensation that the author will receive for their work.

Q. Approximately what percentage of the authors represented by your agency have earned out their advance?

A. On the more generous side, I would say 20 percent.

Q. From your experience, how are advances usually paid out?

A. This has been something that's shifted in the time that I have been in publishing. And now the standard payout tends to be in quarters.

Q. What have you observed to be the typical schedule for a payout in quarters?

A. The first payment is on the signing of the contract. After the next payment comes on what we call delivery and acceptance, which is when the editor officially accepts the manuscript and declares it ready to be sent off to the copy editor.

And then the third payment is upon publication of the book. And the final payment is usually 12 months later or for the paperback publication.

Q. So how long does it take on average for an author to earn their entire advance in your experience?

A. It can take between three or four years for the entire advance to be paid out.

Q. What have some of your clients done to support themselves in the time between beginning work on their book and receiving their full advance?

A. They teach; they work in coffee shops; they work in nonprofit organizations; they're journalists.

Q. You mentioned royalties. Do you typically negotiate royalties with publishers?

A. No. There's a standard set of royalties, and it's very hard to negotiate or to have any kind of movement.

Q. When you say that royalties are standard in the industry, what is your basis for that statement?

A. In all the publishing contracts that I have with many different publishers across the industry, the royalties tend to be the same except for maybe academic presses, where they're significantly lower.

Q. Can you walk me through what those standard royalties are by format?

A. I will try. The hard-cover royalties are 10 percent of the retail price for the first 5,000 copies sold. The second 5,000 copies, so from 5,000 to 10,000 copies, receive 12 and a half percent. And then it's 15 percent of the retail price thereafter.

The paperback is a straight 7 and a half percent. And then ebooks are 25 percent net. And audio, digital downloads are also 25 percent of net.

Q. Thank you. You mentioned that the payout structure had shifted over time and is now typical in quarters. What was the payout structure typically before that?

A. The standard payout used to be in thirds.

Q. In your experience, who determines what territorial format or other rights are available to be sold with a book?

A. When I send out what I call a closing notice, I also include the rights that I am offering on behalf of my client. But usually, those are whether we're offering world rights or North American only. So they refer to territories and several other rights; for example, first serial. The right to publish an excerpt prior to publication may or may not be offered. And then there's certain sets of reserve rights like film and television rights, dramatic rights, things like that.

But there are quite a number of rights that are really not negotiable in my experience.

Q. What are some of the rights that are nonnegotiable in your experience?

A. E-book is one of those rights and audio is one of those rights. Now the new territory that seems to be sort of a little bit in contention is NFTs.

Q. Are there circumstances in which you would prefer to reserve the audio rights for your author?

A. I would always prefer to reserve the audio rights for my author.

Q. Why is that?

A. If I sell those rights to the publisher, the publisher then controls those rights, and any revenues from those rights will only come to my client after the entire advance has been earned out.

If on the other hand I control those rights on behalf of my client, I can offer those rights to audio publishers and provide another income stream directly to my client.

Q. In the past several years, have you been successful reserving audio rights on behalf of any of your authors?

A. Only for—with the smaller publishers that don't have their own audio division.

Q. I want to talk now about the marketing and publicity efforts that a publisher puts into a book after it is acquired.

In your experience, have you seen any connection between the level of an advance that a publisher offers and the marketing and publicity effort that the publisher puts into selling the book?

A. Yes. I would say that there's a pretty clear relationship between the level of the advance and the amount of resources that the publisher invests in the marketing and publicity of the book.

Q. Is there an especially critical time for marketing a new book?

A. Yes. In the month immediately leading up to publication, when the publisher starts pitching the book to news outlets and other media, and then in the six to eight weeks right after publication.

Q. Why is that an especially critical time?

A. It's when you have the best possibility of gathering attention for the book. And then when it's out in stores is when you want to make sure to maximize sales, because bookstores don't actually hold onto those books for very long, you know. So if the books don't sell after the first eight or so weeks, they tend to disappear from the shelves. So while the book is visible and out there is when we want to have the most attention for the book.

Q. In your experience, how do Big 5 publishers support books in terms of marketing and publicity compared to publishers outside the Big 5?

A. In my experience, they tend to have greater resources. I'm just reminded of a time when I sold a book to one of the smaller publishers and the editor was also the subsidiary rights manager and also the publicist and would stay in her office late in the evening stuffing envelopes to send to media outlets. And the head of the publishing house was also the marketing manager and the sales manager because the totality of the employees was maybe three or four. And now I currently have a book under contract with one of the Big 5 and we are meeting weekly with my client's marketing and publicity teams, which consist of six to eight members of just her team devoted to the marketing and publicity of her book.

THE COURT: Before we stop, I just had a couple questions, which I'll forget if I wait until tomorrow. How many publishers do you typically submit to when you do your first wave of submissions?

THE WITNESS: I think it depends a little bit on how much attention or interest I think I can get in the book. But anywhere between 15 and 25.

THE COURT: And you said that you pretty much always submit to Penguin Random House. How often do you submit to Simon & Schuster?

THE WITNESS: Always.

THE COURT: So you always submit to both of those?

THE WITNESS: Yes.

THE COURT: Thank you so much.

BY MS. LICHT:

Q. Ms. Pande, when you say you submit to 15 to 25 different publishers, are you referring to separate publishing houses or editors?

A. Editors.

Q. I am going to turn to a few questions about some offers for authors after they have published their first book. In your career as an agent, when one of your authors has published a successful book with a small publisher, have they gone on to publish their next book with that same publisher?

A. In my experience, that has often been the preference of the author.

Q. To publish their—

A. To publish their next book with a larger publisher, ideally with one of the Big 5.

Q. And what is your understanding of why your authors' preference is to publish their next book with a larger publisher?

A. Because the next book would have a better chance of success with more substantial resources being brought to promoting and publishing the book from one of the Big 5 as well as, of course, higher advances.

Q. Can you give me any examples of authors that you would represent that have moved from a smaller publisher to a larger publisher for their subsequent book?

A. Yes. Should I mention the authors by name?

Q. That's up to you.

A. I have had several authors who have moved from small publishers to larger publishers. One of the authors is Lady Hubbard. Her first book was published by Melville House. And for her second book, she moved to Harper Collins.

My author Lisa Ko moved from Algonquin to Penguin Random House. Those are just a couple of examples.

Q. In your career, have you observed situations when it is difficult for an author to move publishers after publishing their first book?

A. It's definitely more difficult if the sales for the first book have been modest.

Q. And why is that?

A. The sales of books are generally easily accessible via various databases to prospective publishers, and it's one of the elements that they weigh when they are considering acquisition of another book. If the sales of the first book have been modest, then frequently it's more challenging for the publisher to distribute larger numbers of books into those bookstores.

Q. I would like to ask a few questions about your experiences with mergers in the publishing industry. In your career, have you experienced any mergers between publishers?

A. Yes, I have.

Q. Which ones?

A. When I was an editor at Crown, the Random House, the group of which Crown was a part, was acquired by Bertelsmann, and later as an agent, I witnessed the merger of Penguin and Random House, I believe in 2013.

Q. Did you see any changes in the publishing industry as a result of any of those mergers?

A. In each case, I saw layoffs. They usually happened in waves. The first round of layoffs usually tended to be in the administrative or back office part of the publishing house distribution sales, the warehouses, and then eventually we also saw imprints that maybe overlapped in terms of their mandates or goals being merged and also editors being laid off as a result.

Q. And in your time as a literary agent, how did changes like that impact the number of editors to whom you could submit bids on behalf of your authors?

A. In my experience, with the merging of imprints and the reduction overall of editors, I found that there were fewer editors to whom to submit my projects.

Q. And what did you experience from having fewer editors to whom to submit your projects?

A. It made it more challenging to sell my clients' books because there was less choice.

Q. Based on your experience with previous mergers in the publishing industry, have you thought about whether you would have to change your approach to making submissions if Penguin Random House acquires Simon & Schuster?

A. Yes, I have thought about it. And, of course, I would always still have to include editors at Penguin Random House in my first round of submission, but I would probably also include some of the newcomers and maybe some of the smaller independent publishers in the first round.

Q. And why would you include some of those newcomers and smaller publishers in the first round?

A. To guarantee the best possible chance of finding a home for my clients' projects.

Q. How do you think that changing your approach in this way would compare to the current way that you submit including an independent Simon & Schuster?

A. Sorry. Could you repeat that question?

Q. Sure. How would changing your approach to submissions in that way impact the compensation that you think you can receive for your authors?

A. Well, if I am submitting largely to editors in the Big 5 in my first round of submission, I can anticipate a certain level of advance which I think would be reduced if I have independent publishers in the mix.

Q. Given the mission of your agency, do you think that the authors you represent may be affected by the proposed transaction?

A. I do believe that overall they will be impacted by the proposed merger. I think overall it will limit the choice, the number of editors and imprints and publishing houses that would be a good home for my clients.

And I just want to state that my clients, because of being underrepresented, already makes it slightly more challenging to find homes, editors, and publishing houses that have the appropriate experience to publish those books with the kind of expertise that is required. So it would limit that choice even more. And I believe overall advances for my clients would be suppressed.

Q. In your experience as a literary agent, have you seen authors decide not to publish a book at all if they did not receive a sufficiently high advance?

A. I have experienced once or twice during my career when a client has chosen not to go forward with publishing a book because the advance was too modest.

Q. Do you think that the proposed acquisition of Simon & Schuster by Penguin Random House may make it more difficult for certain authors to publish their books going forward?

A. It's already always a conversation that I have with my clients. And I believe that after the merger, it would have to be something that we would have to seriously anticipate, that we may get advances that will not allow them to move forward with the publication of their book.

THE COURT: I'm sorry, can you go back to your testimony about how you would change your approach to sending out submissions because it wasn't clear to me why with this merger you would include the independent and smaller publishers because, I guess, there's the practice in the industry of having imprints within the same publishing house compete against each other. So can you say more about that?

THE WITNESS: The imprints within the larger houses can only compete against each other, at least that's the rule for Penguin Random House, when there are other houses also in the mix. So recently a colleague of mine received an offer from a Penguin Random House imprint, and another Penguin Random House imprint was also interested but was not allowed to bid higher because they were not allowed to top each other or compete against each other.

So it's always important to have houses outside of the Big 5 in the mix, and also the more houses you have or publishers you have competing against each other makes it more likely to get offers. And the more offers you have, it's more likely to get competition going amongst the different houses.

THE COURT: Thank you. You may proceed, Ms. Licht.

MS. LICHT: Thank you, Ms. Pande. I will pass the witness.

CROSS-EXAMINATION

BY MR. PETROCELLI:

Q. Good morning, Ms. Pande. I'm Dan Petrocelli.

A. Good morning.

Q. I represent Penguin Random House and Bertelsmann.

I wanted to follow up, and I think where I will begin is the question the judge asked you or at least that general subject matter.

You are aware that Penguin Random House for many, many years has allowed its imprints to internally bid against one another provided there's an external bidder in the mix, right?

A. Yes.

Q. And what I mean by that is, within each division of Penguin Random House, there are a number of imprints, right?

A. Yes.

Q. And those imprints across divisions can compete and bid against each other, correct?

A. Correct.

Q. And the agent doesn't typically tell the publishers the identity of all of the bidders, correct?

A. In my experience, almost the minute that I submit a project to one of the Penguin Random House imprints, one of the first things that the editor asks me is what other imprints also have a submission in.

Q. Is it your practice to always identify who all the participants are by name?

A. Yes.

Q. Okay. And you understand that other agents may not do that?

A. I can't speak for other agents.

Q. Okay. Fair enough. Fair enough. And in order to keep the internal bidding going within the imprints at Penguin Random House, do you make an effort to always try to have an external bidder in the process?

A. In order for me to have the best possible chance of getting the highest possible offer, I send it out widely to all the five. So usually there is another publishing house in the mix for an initial submission. Of course, I have no control over which editors end up being interested.

Q. And to the extent that other publishers, other imprints outside of Penguin Random House, are interested and continue in the process with you, then Penguin Random House imprints can continue to bid each other up, correct?

A. Yes, correct.

Q. Okay. And when you say you always disclose the names of the other bidders, do you mean you always disclose the name of the other Penguin Random House bidders, or do you also always disclose the outside bidders?

A. Only the Penguin Random House bidders.

Q. Ah, okay. Well, thank you for that clarification. So to be clear, when you are involved in selling one of your books and you have external bidders and you have a number of internal Penguin Random House bidders, you don't tell the Penguin Random House imprints who the outside imprints or bidders are, correct?

A. Correct.

Q. Okay. Thank you.

And I hear your concern about the merger. And to be clear, though, you are not aware of any plans by Penguin Random House post merger to lay off editors, are you?

A. I am not aware of any plans.

Q. Okay. Or to close down imprints, right?

A. No.

Q. Okay. And you have heard that they will continue to allow the Simon & Schuster imprints to bid against one another and against the Penguin Random House imprints just as the company has been doing for many years, correct?

A. I have seen Mr. Dohle's announcement to that effect, yes.

Q. Okay. So in order to try to get through this a little bit more efficiently, I would like to show you the list of book titles and other information that you provided the parties. It's confidential, so I am going to give you the exhibit.

There's no objection to it. And what I have done is I have had a copy of this highlighted with different colors to make it easy to find things. And that will be displayed on the screen for the judge and yourself, and it will be a lot faster to follow some of my questions.

But you do recall providing the parties with a list of books that you have sold in the last few years for $50,000 or greater, correct?

A. Yes, I do.

Q. And there were 33 such books, correct?

A. I believe so.

MR. PETROCELLI: Okay. So with that, I would like to hand the witness Exhibit 263.

May I approach, Your Honor?

THE COURT: Yes.

MR. PETROCELLI: Thank you. Here's the color coded one. Your Honor, may I move Exhibit 236 into

evidence?
THE COURT: Any objection?
MS. LICHT: No objection.
THE COURT: That will be admitted. (Defendant's 236 received in evidence.)
BY MR. PETROCELLI:
Q. Ms. Pande, am I pronouncing your name correctly, Pande?
A. Yes.
Q. And feel free to use the exhibit that I have given you because this is not a memory contest. Okay? So among the 33 books, over $50,000 that you sold, 8 were sold at an amount for $250,000 or more, correct?
A. Correct.
Q. And I've highlighted those 8 in yellow.
A. In yellow.
Q. Okay. And I would like to first ask you some questions about the 8, and then I am going to follow up about the 33.
And the 8, for the record, are books 16—and I am going to refer to these as much as possible by number on your exhibit. Okay?
So they are books 16, 21, 23, 24, 25, 28, 32, and 35, is that correct?
A. Yes.
Q. Thank you. With respect to those eight books then, it is correct that none of them involved a situation where Penguin Random House and Simon & Schuster were the final two bidders, correct?
A. Correct.
Q. Of the eight books that you sold for more than $250,000, none of them were sold to Simon & Schuster, correct?
A. Correct.
Q. On the other hand, six of the eight were sold to Penguin Random House, correct?
A. Correct.
Q. And those would be books No. 16, 21, 23, 24, 25, and 35, is that correct?
A. That is correct.
Q. Okay. And of those six books, two were sold to Penguin Random House without your offering them to Simon & Schuster, correct?
A. Correct.
Q. Okay. And it's also true that of the eight books you sold for more than $250,000, none was sold in a round robin auction, correct?
A. Correct.
Q. And for the record, five of the eight were sold by way of exclusive submissions pursuant to an option or otherwise or a preempt, and those would be books 16, 21, 24, 28, and 32, correct?
A. Did you include a preempt as one of the–
Q. I did.
A. Because book 16 was offered to a broad range of publishers, but it was preempted by the imprint.
Q. Right, I did include preempts. So, again, five of the eight, the numbers I just gave you, were exclusives, options,
or preempts, correct?
A. Correct.
THE COURT: May I ask a question? I'm sorry, Mr. Petrocelli. If there are multiple submissions and then a preempt, did the multiple submissions drive up the price of the preempt?
THE WITNESS: I would imagine that the editor understands that it was submitted widely and the editor anticipates that there may very well be other interest. And so in order for them to secure the book, they would offer a more aggressive price, a more aggressive advance.
THE COURT: Thank you.
THE WITNESS: So preemptive offers tend to be quite high because it has to incentivize us to be willing

to take the book off the table and not offer it in a competitive situation.

THE COURT: Okay. Thank you. I'm sorry to interrupt, Mr. Petrocelli. Go ahead.

BY MR. PETROCELLI:

Q. We are focused on the eight books for $250,000 or more. We went through five. The other three were sold by best bid, correct, and those would be books 23, 25, and 35?

A. Yes.

Q. Okay. I now want to ask you some questions about all 33, not just confined to the 8 that were 250 and above. Okay? Of the 33 books, Simon & Schuster won the book only once; that would be book 11, correct?

A. Correct.

Q. And that was an occasion when PRH did not bid, correct?

A. Correct.

Q. You had submitted the proposal to four different PRH imprints, Penguin Press, Riverhead, Viking, Knopf, and Random House—That's actually five.

A. Yes.

Q. And none of them bid, right?

A. Yes.

Q. It's also true that with respect to the 33 deals, the 33 book deals, there was not a single instance when Penguin Random House was the winning bidder and Simon & Schuster was the second highest bidder, correct?

A. I believe that's correct.

Q. There was one occasion where Simon & Schuster was the highest bidder, but Penguin Random House won as an underbidder, correct?

A. Correct.

Q. And that would be book 7, correct?

A. Correct.

Q. And Penguin Random House underbid that by tens of thousands of dollars. I don't want to say the number, right?

A. Correct.

Q. Okay. We were talking about book 7. That was a best bid auction, right?

A. Yes.

Q. And only the two publishers submitted bids; no one else, correct?

A. Correct.

Q. And it's also true that typically Simon & Schuster is not the runner up in the auctions that you do from time to time, correct?

A. In my recent experience, no. In those last few years, no, that has not been the case where Simon & Schuster have been the runner up.

Q. With respect to all 33 books, Ms. Pande, 21 of the 33 were sold by exclusive submissions or preempts. For the record, those would be, and you can follow along if you would like, books 8, 9, 10, 12, 15, 16, 17, 19, 20, 21, 22, 24, 27, 28, 29, 30, 31, 32, 33, 34, and 37, correct?

A. I do think that we need to differentiate between an exclusive submission for a book where I am submitting to an editor or a publishing house because I believe it is the best fit for that particular book and an exclusive submission which I am contractually required to do because of the option clause in the contract.

So a lot of the ones that you have just pointed out are ones where it is the second or third book with the same publisher, and so the option clause required me to send it to that publisher exclusively.

Q. And with that clarification, those were all instances then where there was, for the reasons you have articulated, an exclusive submission or preempt, correct?

A. Correct.

Q. And following up on your clarification with respect to the submissions because of the contract option—

A. Yes.
Q.—now, that contract option provides for a period of time, generally 30 days or so, when you have to give the existing publisher an opportunity to negotiate for the book?
A. Yes, exclusively.
Q. Correct. But you understand that if you can't make a deal in that period of time, you can take the book to market, right?
A. I can take the book to market.
Q. Okay. Now, I just identified the 21 out of the 33 that were sold by way of exclusives or preempts, so let me turn to the other 12. Okay? 4 of those 12, books 7, 23, 25, and 35, were best bids. Those are the ones I previously went over with you.
A. Yes.
Q. And there were two other best bids, book 14 and book 36, correct?
A. Yes.
Q. So out of the 12 that we are referring to now, 6 of the 12 were best bids, correct?
A. I believe so.
Q. Now, with respect to the remaining 6 out of the total of 33, do you know how those were sold?
A. Not off the top of my head.
Q. I will give you the numbers. Book 11, starting there, and if you don't remember, that's fine.
A. For book 11, it was multiple submissions, but we received only one expression of interest, and so I negotiated with that editor.
Q. The next book would be—forgive me, and you closed the deal with that?
A. We closed the deal with that Simon & Schuster editor, yes.
Q. No. 13?
A. That was a multiple submission, and I asked for best bids and we received two offers.
Q. And your author picked the best one, highest one of the two?
A. I believe it was the highest one, yes.
Q. Okay. Book No. 18?
A. Again, multiple submissions and we received—I can't exactly remember, but multiple offers, four or five offers.
Q. And how did it end, in a best bid?
A. It was a best bid, yes.
Q. Okay. That was No. 18, is that right?
A. Correct.
Q. No. 26?
A. The same thing, multiple submissions that resulted—it was a best bids that resulted in multiple offers.
Q. No. 38?
A. The same.
Q. And No. 39?
A. The same.
Q. Okay. Thank you.
THE COURT: Ms. Pande, is it correct that if Simon & Schuster and PRH were merged, it wouldn't have affected any of the deals on this list?
THE WITNESS: Correct.
THE COURT: Thank you.
MR. PETROCELLI: Your Honor, I don't have anything more. Thank you. Thank you, Ms. Pande.
THE COURT: Any redirect?
MS. LICHT: Yes, Your Honor.

REDIRECT EXAMINATION

BY MS. LICHT:

Q. Ms. Pande, while we are looking at Defendant's Exhibit 263 here, I believe you testified that there are eight deals here for $250,000 or more?

A. Correct.

Q. And of those eight, how many deals were made with an imprint of Penguin Random House?

A. I believe it's six.

Q. And with respect to the two of eight that were not made with an imprint of Penguin Random House, to whom did you sell those books?

A. One of the Big 5. I can't remember which one though.

Q. Let me use this handy highlighting.

A. Harper Collins and the former Houghton Mifflin, which is also Harper Collins.

Q. And those are books?

A. Those are books that I sold for above $250,000 that did not go to Penguin Random House.

Q. So of all the deals that you made for an advanced level of $250,000 or more, how many of those went to an imprint of what is now a Big 5 publisher?

A. All of them.

Q. Do you have a sense of why that is?

A. My sense, based on my experience as an agent, is that the Big 5 are the only publishers that can, with any consistency, pay advances at that level.

Q. Counsel for Penguin Random House asked you about the internal bidding rules at Penguin Random House. Is there anything you can do as a literary agent to determine whether those imprints are adhering to the internal bidding rules at Penguin Random House?

A. No. It's a matter of trust.

Q. Thank you very much, Ms. Pande.

MS. LICHT: Your Honor, I have no further questions.

THE COURT: Thank you. I have one more question which might spark more questions from the parties.

If you think that a book that you are working on, a project that you are submitting, is going to be a best seller or is going to generate a lot of sales, do you treat that differently from other books? Is that different to you, the different category of books to you?

THE WITNESS: Ideally, I hope that every single book that I send out is going to be a best seller. That said, there are some which for various reasons I think I might get a lot more interest in, and so I try to create as much interest as possible by sending it out as widely as I possibly can.

THE COURT: And so you do treat such books differently?

THE WITNESS: Yes.

THE COURT: Any questions based on my questioning?

MS. LICHT: No, Your Honor.

RECROSS-EXAMINATION

BY MR. PETROCELLI:

Q. Following up on Your Honor's question, if you think this is going to be a book that will sell more, as the judge was asking you, I understood you to say that you will send it out more widely to try and generate more buzz, right?

A. Yes.

Q. So by more widely, is there sort of a number you have in mind? Is there a general practice of how many imprints you would send it out to?

A. I don't have a particular number in mind, but for a book that I am maybe not so certain of the interest, I may be more selective in sending it out to a small group of editors basically just to test the waters. And for a book that I anticipate would be big, I send it out to every single imprint that I think could be a possible good fit for that book.

Q. Okay.

A. And that may be anywhere between 25 and 35 imprints.
Q. What do you then do after that, if you could kind of walk us through it?
A. I follow up with editors, either via email or phone call, to assess their reaction.
Q. And what happens if you get a good reaction?
A. If I get a good reaction from a substantial number of editors, then I think about what my, quote/unquote, closing strategy would be, in other words, what strategy I will use to solicit offers.
Q. And in those situations, is that where you might have a preempt opportunity?
A. Well, I have no control over that. That is a strategy that the editor would employ.
Q. But in circumstances where you are getting a lot of positive feedback, is that when you might get a preempt?
A. In some instances, an editor might try to preempt the book, yes.
Q. And then, let's say, if you do get a preempt, you might close it on the preempt, right?
A. I may.
Q. And if you don't get a preempt, what would be your next step?
A. If I choose not to accept a preempt because I believe that there is a higher advance to be gained by offering it to a broader range of publishers and soliciting bids from a broader range of publishers, then I would decide on the date and the time and methodology of how to solicit the offers either via some sort of best bid or hybrid thereof.
Q. And of the 33 books on the exhibit that you have, would any of those books, and you can identify it by number if you would like, fall into the category that you are now describing going back to the judge's question where you thought this could be a big seller?
A. Yes. No. 25 was one where I was pretty certain that I was going to get significant interest.
Q. And forgive me, I don't have the exhibit in front of me, but how did 25 end up?
A. It ended up with multiple offers and went to a division of Penguin Random House.
Q. On a best bid?
A. It was, I think, a two- or three-round best bids.
Q. Okay.
A. So best meaning the publishers or the highest offering publishers get a chance to improve their offer after they have made their initial offer.
Q. That's No. 25, you said? A. Correct.
Q. Okay. Thank you.
MR. PETROCELLI: No further questions, Your Honor.
THE COURT: Thank you.
So the authors of these books that people have a sense are going to do well, do you think that they are looking for different things in the contracts and different services than other authors?
THE WITNESS: Taking this particular book as an example, this author's first book was published by a small independent publisher which in the meanwhile has been acquired by Hachette, and it did extremely well and it also won a couple of awards. And so, yes, my conversation with my client at that point was that here was an opportunity to select the publisher that could, not only publish the book in the best way possible, but also pay the best possible advance. So the timing really suited itself to that. When we are offering debut works, we don't always have that same opportunity because the author has not necessarily proven themselves to be a sure seller.
THE COURT: So that goes with a different approach that you take with a book that you anticipate is going to be a good seller, that you advise your client of the different options that they might have that they otherwise would not?
THE WITNESS: Yes, correct.
THE COURT: I understand. Any further questions?
BY MR. PETROCELLI:
Q. What was the book number you were referring to in response to the judge's question?
A. Book No. 25.

MR. PETROCELLI: Thank you, Your Honor.
THE COURT: Any follow-up, Ms. Licht, based on my question?
MS. LICHT: No, Your Honor. Thank you.
THE COURT: You may step down, Ms. Pande. Thank you very much.
THE WITNESS: Thank you, Your Honor.

STEPHEN KING, AUTHOR

"My name is Stephen King; I'm a freelance writer." So began what proved to be the most entertaining testimony of the trial, even if may not have had great bearing on the case. (Though Judge Pan was clearly as charmed as everyone else to have the renowned author on the stand. When he was dismissed, smiling, broadly, she said, "It was a real pleasure to hear your testimony.")

King noted he was testifying voluntarily, because, "I think that consolidation is bad for competition; that's my understanding of the book business." As he recalled, "When I started there were hundreds of imprints, started by people with idiosyncratic interests." Now, "it becomes tougher and tougher for writers to find enough money to live on," citing a recent Authors Guild survey on how little money most authors make. As he put it, "The more companies there are, the better it is." He concurred with the prosecution's position that houses outside of the Big 5, "That's like the minor leagues for writers."

Extending the baseball metaphors—which were abundant since the trial began—"there are only so many shops" left to negotiate with in publishing, whereas a baseball player has 32 teams to choose among. "You can't hit 'em if you can't see 'em," he said.

Challenged on a couple of the defense's mitigating factors, such as new entrants playing a meaningful role, he replied: "Could a new publisher suddenly show up? They show up all the time, but they don't have the traction. . . . The Big 5 are pretty entrenched."

Asked about PRH's announced policy to let S&S continue to bid independently, King retorted, "You might as well say you're going to have a husband and wife bidding against each other for the same house. The idea is a little bit ridiculous when you think about it." He suggested the internal bidding "would not reach the wild sort of enthusiasm that I remember from the 70s and the 80s." Rather, "It's going to be very gentlemanly, and it will sort of be like, after you, no, after you."

At the same time, he underscored the positive effect of recent competition among streaming networks, citing a "huge hunger for content, content, content. . . . The streaming networks have been a gold rush for writers."

While King provided a delightful and humble recounting of his career and his path to enormous success—"As far as I was concerned, I was living the dream. I was writing full-time and the bills were paid"—it was also clear that he has not needed or tried to shop his books for many years after settling into his happy profit-sharing deal with Scribner long ago. PRH's attorney did not perform any Cross-Examination.

TESTIMONY OF STEPHEN KING, AUTHOR

DIRECT EXAMINATION

BY MR. SCHWARZ:

Q. Good morning, Mr. King. Mel Schwarz.

A. Good morning.

Q. Would you mind stating for the record your occupation, please?

THE COURT: I'm sorry, could you have him state his name for the record. We all know who he is, but I think we need to get that the for the record.

BY MR. SCHWARZ:

Q. Would you please state your name.

A. My name is Stephen King. I'm a freelance writer.

Q. Thank you. When, sir, did you publish your first book?

A. 1974.

Q. And that book was?

A. *Carrie.*

Q. And with whom did you publish that book?

A. I'm sorry?

Q. With whom, who was the publisher?

A. That was Doubleday.
Q. Did you have an agent to negotiate that book?
A. No, I did not.
Q. And was that deal with Doubleday, was that a one-book deal or a two-book deal?
A. That was a one-book deal. And they had an option for the second book. They had the first look on the second book.
Q. And what, if you don't mind saying, was the advance that you received on that book?
A. It was $2,500.
Q. And I take it ultimately that book became a movie?
A. Yes, it did.
Q. And did you receive some royalties for the movie as well?
A. No. I've never seen a single dollar from the movie. But Signet published a movie tie-in edition and that did very well.
Q. And was there a second book, I take it, with Doubleday?
A. Yes. The second book was *Salem's Lot.*
Q. And did you receive an advance for that book?
A. $7,500.
Q. And I take it you did not have an agent for that book either?
A. No, sir.
Q. Did there come a time when you did decide to hire an agent?
A. Yes.
Q. Who was that?
A. That was Kirby McCauley.
Q. And did you hire Mr. McCauley after book two with Doubleday or sometime later?
A. No. It was later than that. I did a two-book contract with Doubleday for two novels that were—well, actually it was a novel and a book of short stories. *The Shining* was the novel. And the book of short stories was called Night Shift. And at that time I was having trouble selling some short stories. A lot of the markets had dried up. And I talked to my editor at Doubleday, Bill Thompson and said, gee, I just can't seem to sell these stories; maybe I need an agent. And Bill said on behalf of the company, oh, no, you don't need an agent. We will sell your stories for you. And they did not. They sold one story called "I Know What You Need," but the other ones just languished, and if I am going on, tell me I am going on too far.
Q. No.
A. It was a literary party for a romance writer named Helen Van Slyke and Kirby McCauley was at this party. And I knew him as somebody who had agented a lot of old-time horror and fantasy writers. And I complained to him about not being able to sell any of my short stories. And he said, I will sell them for you. And he did.
Q. Okay. Thank you. And these initial books that you published with Doubleday without an agent, did any of them become best sellers?
A. Yes.
Q. Which ones?
A. *Carrie* was a best seller in paperback. *The Shining* was the first hardcover best seller. And Night Shift was also a best seller.
Q. And I take it you earned out your advance on those books?
A. Yes.
Q. And received royalties hopefully?
A. Yes.
Q. Okay. Good. Are any of those books still in backlist with Doubleday?
A. Yes, they are still in the backlist.
Q. And they continue to earn money for Doubleday and for you, I hope?
A. Yes.

Q. Okay. And Doubleday is now part of PRH, Penguin Random House?
A. Yes.
Q. So at what stage did Mr. McCauley then negotiate the contract for you? Was this after book five or—
A. Well, I did *Carrie*, *Salem's Lot*, *The Shining*, *Night Shift*, and a book called *The Stand* with Doubleday. And they were still paying very, very small advances. And I talked to Kirby about it. And Kirby said, we can do better than that. And I said, well, I would like to stay with Doubleday. I feel a lot of loyalty to the company that picked me out of the slush pile and I like my editor very much and I would like to stay with Doubleday. And Kirby said, well, we will go to Doubleday first if you want, but really, they will probably try to lowball you.
So we went to Doubleday and offered them three books for $2 million. And the man who's negotiating on Doubleday's behalf, a man named Robert Banker, laughed and walked out of the restaurant where we were meeting.
Q. And did you ultimately come to an agreement with Doubleday or with another publisher?
A. No, we did not.
Q. By the way, do you have a recollection of what year this was?
A. I think it must have been 1979 or 1980.
Q. And do you have a recollection of whether Mr. McCauley then negotiated with other publishers, if so, who they were?
A. Well, yes. Doubleday had sold the paperback rights to all of my books to New American Library. And the editor there, the Editor in Chief, Elaine Koster, was a fan of mine. She thought that I had great potential that I hadn't reached. And so the first person that he went to was Elaine Koster who agreed to pay $2 million for three books.
Q. And you signed that deal? That was the deal that you made at that point?
A. Yes, sir, I did.
Q. And that was with which publisher?
A. That was with New American Library which was a subsidiary of Times Mirror at that time. And New American Library was a paperback publisher, strictly paperback, so they sold the hardcover rights to Viking Press.
Q. And Viking is now part of Penguin Random House?
A. Yes. Viking is now a part of the Bertelsmann business. They were not at that time. They were an independent publisher.
Q. And do you recall how many books you published with those two publishers?
A. No, not offhand. I think probably in the neighborhood of ten.
Q. Okay. And you recall whether those ten were best sellers?
A. They were all best sellers, yes.
Q. And did all of them earn out, that is, you received royalties beyond the advance in those cases?
A. Yes, sir.
THE COURT: I'm curious, Mr. King, if you ever went back to Robert Banker. Did you ever go back to Robert Banker who laughed at your $2 million offer and talk to him about this?
THE WITNESS: Robert Banker retired shortly after that.
THE COURT: Thank you.
BY MR. SCHWARZ:
Q. So did there come a point in time then—was Mr. McCauley still your agent, by the way, through these ten books?
A. Yes, he was the agent through those ten books.
Q. Did he negotiate with other publishers with respect to publishing any of those ten books as you went down the road through the years?
A. No. I had loyalty to Viking Press.
Q. And I take it you were also satisfied with the compensation you were receiving at that point?
A. Yes.
Q. Did you make any efforts during that period to try to see whether you were receiving, shall we say,

the market rate for what you were doing?

A. Well, it never really crossed my mind, sir. The major thing was I was able to pay the mortgage and I was able to put money away for the kids' education. I didn't have to finance the car. As far as I was concerned, I was living the dream. I was writing full-time. I enjoyed what I was doing. And the bills were paid. That was the big deal, right there.

Q. But I take it there did come a point in time when you considered changing publishers?

A. Yes.

Q. Do you recall about what time frame that was?

A. I think probably around 1993 or 1994, toward the end of
the '90s I became a little bit–

Q. End of the '80s or '90s?

A. Around the end of the '80s, excuse me, I became a little bit downhearted, a little bit down on Viking Press, and I felt they weren't trying as hard as they used to.

Q. At that point was Mr. McCauley still your agent or was he gone?

A. Yes. And then at some point around 1987 or 1988, Kirby and I parted ways, and he stopped being an agent.

Q. And so—

A. He retired, if you will.

Q. And who became your agent at that point?

A. Well, my business manager at that time, Arthur Greene, became my interim agent. He didn't really know the business, but he did the best he could.

Q. And did he negotiate a deal at that point with another publisher?

A. Well, first he tried to negotiate a deal with Viking. And at that point I think that the mergers had begun and he wanted an equal amount of money to what Tom Clancy was making in advance. In other words, I think what Arthur wanted was something like $64 million for three books. And it was way above what the projected royalties would have been, but he wanted to keep up with Clancy. It was not a good business decision because he wasn't a real agent.

But in any case, I took it as a sign that I was supposed to leave Viking. The parting was amicable enough, but I was glad to go.

Q. And did your agent then talk to other publishers as far as you know?

A. Well, the man who became my agent, Chuck Verrill, spoke to Arthur and said that Simon & Schuster or the subsidiary Scribner would be a good fit and that there were editors there that were anxious to work with me and they had a creative plan for growing the books. And eventually that's where we went.

Q. Did you speak with any other publishers that you can recall besides Scribner?

A. No. There was a list of publishers we had sort of planned on going to. I think that we had planned at some point that there would be an auction, but it never happened because Scribner came forward with this offer and people who were obviously enthusiastic about the books. And I was delighted to go there.

Q. And I take it you felt the money being offered was appropriate or adequate?

A. Well, what they offered at that time was almost like a copublishing deal where I would share in a lot more than 10 percent or 15 percent of the royalties, that I would get 40 to 50 percent, but I would have to share in the expenses, the publicity, and I would have to do a certain amount of promotion of the books and that sort of thing, which I was happy to do because I loved the people that I was working with.

Q. And you had a pretty good track record of best sellers at that point, I take it?

A. I did.

Q. Is it your understanding that that kind of a deal is somewhat unusual or special?

A. My understanding was that it was very unusual.

Q. Limited to very successful authors, is that right?

A. Say it again.

Q. Limited to very successful authors?

A. I can only speak for myself. I'm the only one I know of that had that deal.

Q. That makes it unusual, yes. And did you talk to the potential agent during those negotiations with

Scribner?

A. Well—

Q. Excuse me. I may have misspoken. Did you talk to the editor at Scribner that you might be working with?

A. Yes. I talked to Susan Moldow and Nan Graham both, and we connected on a level that was—they cared about the books and they thought that the books were serious entertainment, and I loved that.

Q. And has Ms. Graham been your editor at Scribner since that time?

A. Yes. Nan has edited the books since then. Chuck Verrill edited the first two or three books with Scribner, and then he moved on to an agency, Darhansoff & Verrill, and became my agent. And I think that Arthur Greene was glad to give that position up to somebody who knew the book business. Chuck became my agent and Nan Graham became my editor, and she's still my editor.

Q. So during this consideration of shifting from Viking to Scribner, do you recall you or your agent talking to any other publishers?

A. No.

Q. Do you know what I mean when I say the Big 5?

A. Yes.

Q. Okay. Did you talk to any non-Big 5 publishers then?

A. Well, I published books with small presses. Is that what you mean?

Q. No. I meant during this particular–

A. No.

Q. Was there any particular reason why you focused then on the Big 5 in your considering switching from Viking?

A. Well, I wanted to stay with Scribner because they had a long and honorable record of people who had published with them like F. Scott Fitzgerald and Hemingway and just, you know, a lot of Thomas Wolfe and people that I idolized, but also

because they were able to reach into the chain bookstores. They had salespeople everywhere. They had a wonderful distribution network, and I realized that I was going to reach bookstores from coast to coast and that was great. That was great. They are a muscular firm. They were not going to just be in specialty bookstores. They were going to be everywhere.

Q. I think you were mentioning that—let me withdraw that. Have you published then continuously since that time at least some of your books with Scribner?

A. Have I published with Scribner?

Q. With Scribner since that time, at least most before your books?

A. Yes, most of the books.

Q. And have all the ones with Scribner been best sellers as far as you can recall?

A. Yes.

Q. Now, did there come a time when you published one or more books with other publishers?

A. Yes.

Q. Can you recall the first such occasion?

A. I think the first book that I published with another press was maybe just near the end of the Doubleday period. It was a book called *The Gun Slinger*. And it was published with—help me here.

Q. I don't recall either. I'm sorry. It's okay. It was—

A. Grant, Donald Grant, publisher.

Q. I assume that's not a Big 5 publisher?

A. No.

Q. And why did you go with them?

A. Because it wasn't the sort of book that Doubleday wanted or that Viking wanted. It wasn't a crafted best seller. There was a series of five connected stories set in a kind of western world that was also fantastical. It just seemed wrong for the sort of reputation that I had as the, quote/unquote, scary guy. It was different so . . .

Q. Okay. So after *The Gun Slinger*, what was the next occasion you could recall—

THE COURT: I'm sorry, I have to ask. How did *The Gun Slinger* do?

THE WITNESS: In hard cover, it sold probably 1,500 copies because there were illustrations by Michael Whelan and the fan community liked that. And Donald Grant at that time sold those books. He would go around in his station wagon to conventions and put them in what they called the huckster room, which was rooms, sales rooms, and they would sell there. They were not in bookstores or anything.

And what happened to me was, when I did publish *Pet Cemetery*, which was later to fulfill a contractual obligation with Doubleday, without even thinking about it on what they call the ad card where you print the other books previously written by this author, I put on *The Gun Slinger*, *The Dark Tower*, and the outcry from all these people was, what is this book. I've never heard of this book. Where is it. I must read it. And my reaction to a lot of that was, don't be so grabby. You don't necessarily get everything. Yes, it's America, you can get all the toothpaste and toilet paper you want, but that doesn't mean you can necessarily get this book.

But eventually it was done in paperback, and then anyone who wanted it could read it. But that was not a best seller.

THE COURT: Did it sell well in paperback?

THE WITNESS: In paperback it became a best seller. But in hard cover, with only 1,500 copies, it could not become a best seller.

THE COURT: Thank you.

BY MR. SCHWARZ:

Q. And so let's move on to your next non-Big 5 publication that you can recall.

A. Well, I published a book called *The Colorado Kid* with a paperback publisher called Hard Case Crime.

Q. And why did you go with them?

A. Because I admired that line of paperbacks. They were kind of retro detective stories, hard boiled, you know. They were the kind of stories about heroic men and women in distress and that sort of thing. They were like from the '50s, you know. And every cover had a picture of a semi-dressed woman and a guy with a gun or something. And they were detective stories.

And this was really different from the sort of things that I was doing with Viking at that time, and so I went to Hard Case Crime and the editor, the only employee of the company, Charles Ardai, said we would be delighted to do it, and they did it.

Q. Is there any particular reason or reasons why are you didn't publish that book with Viking?

A. It didn't fit the mold.

Q. And did that book make money for Hard Case Crime?

A. Oh, yes.

Q. Was that something you wanted to happen

A. Yes. I was delighted for it to happen because Hard Case Crime was sort of on the bubble. There was no—we weren't sure—I didn't think that it would survive. I mean, there are paperback publishers that go in there all the time, from Monarch Books to Berkley Books, to—I don't know. Some of the big boys are still around because they are part of other publishing groups, but a lot of the indies are gone, and I thought that Hard Case Crime might go that way.

And they were doing a service to people who love that kind of fiction. So I was delighted to be able to pitch in. And it didn't hurt me. I got a royalty on the books. I didn't get much of an advance, but that was okay.

Q. And did there come a point then after Hard Case Crime when you published the book or books with another publisher?

A. I published two small novellas with a company called Cemetery Dance. There was one called *Blockade Billy*, which was a baseball story, and there was one called *A Face in the Crowd*, which I cowrote with Stewart O'Nan, an acclaimed literary writer, and that was another baseball story. So we did those.

Q. And why did you go with Cemetery Dance as opposed to Viking or Scribner or whoever you were with at the time?

A. Well, they didn't fit. They didn't fit the mold. And also they were too long to be short and too short to be long. They were novellas, which is kind of an awkward literary form, and Rich Chizmar, who was the editor and publisher of Cemetery Dance, was happy to do it.
Q. Did your financial success play any part in your willingness to go with the smaller publisher?
A. Absolutely.
Q. Perhaps we ought to clarify for the record, in what way?
A. Well, the rent was paid. The kids were doing fine in college. Their college educations were paid. And I could afford to do it. There comes a point where, if you are very, very fortunate, you are able to stop following your bank account and start following your heart. And that's what I did. It was wonderful. It was great. It was great to be able to do that.
Q. Okay. I think that's enough of that history, but do you belong to any writers associations, sir?
A. I am a member of The Authors Guild of America. I am a member of PEN America.
Q. Are you a member of something to do with mysteries?
A. Yes, I am a member of the Mystery Writers of America, too, the MWA.
Q. And do they publish newspapers or periodicals?
A. Yes, they do.
Q. Do you read them at all?
A. I read the MWA one, which is more interesting. I have a tendency to kind of skim through the others, I guess you would say.
Q. As far as you can recall, those periodicals tend to report the developments in publications in the industry or at least with respect to those genres?
A. Yeah. The Mystery Writers of America will usually talk about writers who have made book deals and they are very bullish, if you will, on new writers who publish mystery novels. And sometimes they will talk about writers who have gotten a three-book contract with this publisher or that publisher. They rarely talk about money. That's considered a bit vulgar.
Q. Has your son, by the way, become an author?
A. Both of my sons write books, yes.
Q. At least one of them writes under a pen name?
A. Yes, my older son. It wasn't exactly a pen name. His name is Joseph Hillstrom King, and he published under the name of Joe Hill. And he sold a number of stories, if you want to call them a selling, sometimes he would get $25, sometimes contributors' copies, to little magazines like *Sewanee Review* or—I can't remember the other ones. But eventually there were enough short stories for a collection which he called *20th Century Ghosts*. And he shopped that around to the major publishers, the Big 5. I can't remember if Joe had an agent at that point or not. I don't think that he did.

But eventually the book reached a small press in England, PS Publishing, and they agreed to publish it. And Joe was very pleased. And I was very pleased that that happened without any recourse to my name, to his famous father.

And one of the stories in that book, "The Black Phone," has become an extremely popular movie just this year. So hooray for Joe. I'm glad.
Q. Did he also recently have a number one *New York Times* best seller?
A. I don't think that—I don't know. Not to my knowledge, but he's had several best sellers.
Q. So let's switch gears a bit. Are you here voluntarily, sir?
A. Yes, sir.
Q. So why did you come?
A. Well, I came because I think that consolidation is bad for competition. That's my understanding of the book business.

And I have been around it for 50 years. When I started in this business, there were literally hundreds of imprints, and some of them were run by people who had extremely idiosyncratic tastes, let's say. And those businesses one by one were either subsumed by other publishers or they went out of business.

But, you know, I think that it becomes tougher and tougher for writers to find enough money to live on. The Authors Guild of America did a survey in 2018. It stuck in my mind that writers who were writing full-time, as an average, they make like $20,300, which is below the poverty line.

And so, the more companies there are, the better it is. You have to think of writers as just another artisan and the publishers as a shop where they take items on consignment. And if they are able to sell them, they are able to buy more from that particular artisan.

But the shops have closed one by one. There are fewer and fewer. There are a number of independent publishers, and those publishers, the indies who look at works like my son's work who are new writers who don't have a reputation, those writers go to the independent book dealers, and there are fewer and fewer of them because they are being squeezed. And the reason they are being squeezed is because they don't get the shelf space that they used to in the bookstores because the majors take a lot of that shelf space up.

And that's like the minor leagues for writers. That's where writers learn their chops. And sometimes they step up to the Big 5 which would become, I think, the big four if this deal goes through. And that's just the way it goes.

And then a lot of times when writers like Raymond Carver, who published in small magazines, become something that's considered special, one of the big publishers will poach them. So, it's a tough world out there now. That's why I came.

Q. Thank you. I think you may have already identified some of this, but let me just ask you, what attributes of the Big 5 publishers make them appealing to authors?

A. The distribution for one. The fact that they have very deep pockets for another thing. They can pay, if they choose, huge advances. They have a publicity network. They have publicity departments. And they are able to tap into the social media now. They are able to get advanced copies out to reviewers and they are able to put up a platform.

Not every book is successful because of that, but when a publisher really gets behind a book, particularly a big publisher, the chances are that that book is going to probably succeed on some level.

Now, maybe lightning won't strike the way it does with a writer like Colleen Hoover, who is suddenly, you know, the biggest thing in the world or the *Fifty Shades of Grey* woman. Sometimes lightning strikes out of nowhere, but mostly the big publishers have a distribution network, an advertising network, publicity. They are able to have access to film producers and get copies out to them. They are able to generate buzz.

Q. Are there developments in other media that you consider relevant to your views on the limitations on competition that might develop if this merger went through?

A. Well, it's interesting to me, maybe not to anybody else, but it's interesting to me that as the book world has contracted over my time in this business, this is a strange business because it mingles with art. It's a strange place to be.

But at the same time, the publishing world has contracted little by little. There's been this explosion of content, of fictional content, on the streaming networks, on the networks, and all at once, there is a huge demand. Shops have opened.

If you think about the book row of artisans and shops closing, all at once there's this other market where you have Netflix to start with and, boom, Hulu comes along, I don't know HBO Max, Showtime, Stars, Bravo, and the list goes on and on. And what this means is that there's this huge hunger for content, content, content. It's gotten to the point where it's been years since I have had a property that hasn't sold or been optioned to somebody because they are so hungry for anything.

Q. And has that increase in the number of other media, streaming media and whatnot, affected the price of manuscripts for those media?

A. Say again. I don't understand.

Q. Has the increase in the number of streaming services and other services caused the price paid by them for that content to go up?

A. Yes. The streaming networks have been a gold rush for writers, for screen writers primarily and television writers, but also they have picked up a number of books. We talk about so-called minimalist writers, writers who might make anywhere from $22,000 on upward to, say, maybe a hundred thousand dollars or maybe a little bit more, and one of those writers is a man named Thomas Perry who's written some fantastic suspense novels. And FX just paid him a certain amount of money. I don't know how much. But I envy him anyway. They did a show with Jeff Bridges and John Lithgow called *The Old Man*, and it's based on a Thomas Perry book.

Good for him. It's delightful. When that happens, I'm always happy. I am happiest when it happens to me, but I am happy when it happens to others.

THE COURT: Well, it seems like it's happened to you many times.

BY MR. SCHWARZ:

Q. I was about to clarify that. How many best sellers have you had, sir?

A. I don't know, probably 60, 62, 65.

Q. So a lot of lightning. That's great.

A. A lot, yes.

Q. Do you have a view on whether or not the agents could take actions sufficient to deal with or keep competition at the same level after this merger happens?

A. I don't think that's a very—I don't think that starts really as a viable position because there are only so many shops. Right now there are five shops, five big publishers. It's a different thing. Let's say if you are an agent and your specialty is baseball teams, you have something like 32 different teams that you could negotiate with. But when it comes to big publishers, there are five.

You know, the baseball players have a saying, you can't hit them if you can't see them. And you can't sell books competitively if there are only so many people in competition.

Q. Do you have a view about whether or not any new publishers could fill the gap if the merger were to take place here from five to four in the Big 5?

A. It's impossible to say.

Q. Meaning that it's too speculative?

A. Well, it's speculative. If you are saying could a new publisher suddenly show up in the marketplace, they show up all the time and they don't have a great deal of success because they don't have the traction that the Big 5 do. The Big 5 are pretty entrenched.

Q. And are you familiar with the promise that Penguin Random House has made to keep Simon & Schuster imprints bidding after this merger were permitted?

A. Yes, I am familiar with that.

Q. And do you think that that would salvage the competitive levels in the industry as they are now?

A. Well, you might as well say you're going to have a husband and wife bidding against each other for the same house. The idea is a little bit ridiculous when you think about it. So I really think that there might be a certain amount of bidding, but it would not reach the wild sort of enthusiasm that I remember from the '70s and '80s where they talked about auctions in *Publishers Weekly* and phones ringing off the hook and bids coming in and at 5:00 the auction is going to close and oh, my God. That's not going to happen. It's going to be very gentlemanly, and it will be sort of like, after you, no, after you.

Q. On that note, I will pass the witness.

THE COURT: All right. Thank you. Mr. Petrocelli is going to have some questions for you.

MR. PETROCELLI: Good morning. Mr. King. I am Dan Petrocelli. I represent Penguin Random House and Bertelsmann. I want to, first of all, congratulate you on your extraordinary success over such a glorious career. I would love one day to sit down over a cup coffee and chat more with you, but as far as today is concerned, I don't have any questions for you.

Thank you for your testimony.

THE COURT: Thank you.

MR. SCHWARZ: I guess I have no redirect.

THE WITNESS: Am I done?

THE COURT: You're done. Thank you very much for coming in. It was a real pleasure to hear your testimony.

THE WITNESS: Thank you very much.

THE COURT: You may step down.

DENNIS EULAU, COO, SIMON & SCHUSTER

Much of the questioning of S&S CFO and COO Dennis Eulau occurred in closed court, and during the public testimony he was a reluctant witness.

We did report a few interesting details gleaned from his appearance, however. We learned that ViacomCBS's bankers LionTree gave the sale of S&S the code name, Project Typeface.

We also were presented with an email Carolyn Reidy had written to her boss Bob Bakish and others in 2020, as S&S looked to move their printing contract from Quad to LSC (now Lakeside). Reidy wrote: "Strong indications are that Quad will be selling its book trade business to Bertelsmann who owns Penguin Random House. We would not want to be 100 percent beholden to a competitor for printing."

Part of the government's point in calling Eulau was read into the record—and have him concur with—a memo former S&S CEO, the late Carolyn Reidy, wrote in 2019, characterizing the publisher to her boss as part of the diligence done in connection with the merger of Viacom and CBS in 2019. Reidy's writings were offered to support some of the government's basic contentions. She wrote:

"The U.S. publishing market is made up of what is known as the Big 5. PRH dominates with the largest market share followed by Harper Collins and then S&S. Hachette is a close fourth followed by Macmillan. These companies are our biggest competitors especially for books by already best-selling authors and celebrities since they are the most likely to come up with the high advance payments required and are known for their strong editorial and publishing skills."

She also wrote, "Publishing houses and imprints gain reputations based on the successes they have published."

Regarding smaller publishers, Reidy noted, "they rarely compete with us in auctions for new properties." And she wrote, "Often these publishers become farm teams for authors who then want to move to a larger, more financially stable major publisher."

TESTIMONY OF DENNIS EULAU, COO, SIMON & SCHUSTER

DIRECT EXAMINATION

BY MR. MATELSON:

Q. Good morning. Would you state and spell your name for the record, please, sir.

A. Sure. Dennis Eulau, D-E-N-N-I-S E-U-L-A-U.

Q. And where are you employed?

A. Simon & Schuster.

Q. What is your job title?

A. Chief financial officer and chief operating officer.

Q. And you have held that job title since about 2012, is that right?

A. 2010.

Q. To whom do you report?

A. Jonathan Karp, chief executive officer.

Q. And your current responsibilities include overseeing all the financials for Simon & Schuster, correct?

A. That's correct.

Q. And you also have responsibilities for the sales department, book manufacturing, and the warehousing and distribution functions of Simon & Schuster, is that right?

A. That's correct.

Q. You also advise the CEO on high-level strategy issues, right?

A. We discuss them, yes.

Q. And you are sometimes asked to weigh in on bids that Simon & Schuster is making for authors, right?

A. Weigh in? You would have to clarify that.

Q. Sometimes you are asked for your input or advice on bids, correct?

A. Not often.

Q. Okay. But from time to time, you do?
A. From time to time.
Q. And you have worked at Simon & Schuster continuously since 1995, is that right?
A. That's correct.
Q. I want to go back through a little bit of your job history. You were named senior vice president and general manager of adult publishing in 2001, is that right?
A. I believe that's correct.
Q. And in 2007 you were promoted to executive vice president of operations for all of Simon & Schuster?
A. That sounds correct also.
Q. And then you added the title of chief financial officer for all of Simon & Schuster in 2009, is that right?
A. Again, that sounds close to accurate, yes.
Q. And you started your career in the trade book business?
THE COURT: Could you stop leading the witness.
MR. MATELSON: I'm sorry, Your Honor. This is an adverse witness, adverse party witness. He's called under Rule 611.
THE COURT: All right. Go ahead.
MR. MATELSON: Thank you.
BY MR. MATELSON:
Q. Sorry to repeat my question. Is it correct that you have been in the trade book publishing business since 1990?
A. That's correct.
Q. And before Mr. Karp became CEO, you reported to his predecessor Carolyn Reidy for over 20 years?
A. Yes, I did.
Q. Now, you are familiar with the term Big 5? We have heard that in the trial. But you are familiar with the term Big 5 in the publishing industry?
A. Yes, I am.
Q. And, again, that refers to Penguin Random House, Simon & Schuster, Hachette, Harper Collins, and Macmillan, right?
A. Yes.
Q. And you consider those Big 5 publishers to be Simon & Schuster's peers, right?
A. Yes, I do.
Q. And they are the five biggest publishers in the trade book publishing world, right?
A. I agree with that also.
Q. And when we are talking about trade book publishing, that's something that's different from other types of books such as educational publishing and professional book publishing, right?
A. I agree with that also, yes.
MR. MATELSON: We have some exhibit binders. May we distribute those, Your Honor?
THE COURT: Yes.
BY MR. MATELSON:
Q. Mr. Eulau, from time to time you track how the financial performance at Simon & Schuster compares to the other Big 5 trade publishers, correct?
A. From time to time we report on that, yes.
Q. All right. I want to look at an example. This is going to be in your binder in front of you. If you could turn to the first tab. It's marked PX529.
A. Yes, I have that.
Q. All right. Now, the first page of this exhibit is a series of emails about an upcoming meeting that you are having with the CFO of ViacomCBS in August 2020, is that right?
A. That's correct.
Q. All right. And in the top email in this chain, you say you are attaching a work chart and a 2020

budget package for the CFO?
A. Yes.
Q. If you could flip ahead to just past the org charts, there's a presentation called Simon & Schuster, a global leader in publishing, do you have that?
A. Yes.
Q. This presentation was created by Simon & Schuster?
A. It was.
Q. And it's the 2020 budget presentation to ViacomCBS, right?
A. Yes.
Q. And as part of your job, you are responsible for determining the budget that is presented to ViacomCBS corporate managers, correct?
A. At that time, that's correct.
Q. All right. And you reviewed and provided input into the slides in this presentation?
A. I did.
MR. MATELSON: Your Honor, we move PX529 into evidence.
THE COURT: Any objection?
MR. FISHBEIN: No objection.
THE COURT: That will be admitted. (Plaintiff's 529 received in evidence.)
BY MR. MATELSON:
Q. Let me ask you to turn the page one more time. This is internal slide two of the deck. And the title of this slide is S&S OI profit margin exceeds competitors. Do you see that?
A. I do.
Q. OI refers to, just so we know our terms, operating income?
A. Yes.
Q. And the word competitors here is referring to Penguin Random House, Harper Collins, and Hachette, right?
A. Yes.
Q. What you are showing on this page is how your margins compare to those of your competitors?
A. How we estimated them, yes.
Q. And generally speaking, you compare your performance of Simon & Schuster to Penguin Random House, Harper Collins, and Hachette because those are the largest publishers in trade publishing, is that right?
A. That was why we would have done it, yes.
Q. Okay. We can now set that down to the side. You mentioned earlier that you worked closely with the former CEO Carolyn Reidy, before her passing. Now, she viewed the Big 5 publishers as Simon & Schuster's main competitors for authors, isn't that right?
A. Yes. She would view it as that, yes.
Q. I want to show you next in your binder, the next tab, which is what we have marked as PX530, please.
A. Okay.
Q. All right. Now, again, there's a cover email with an attachment, is that right?
A. Yes.
Q. And the cover email is an exchange that you had with Ms. Reidy in May of 2019?
A. Yes.
Q. All right. And she sent you the email at the bottom of the page, the first page.
A. Yes.
Q. And in that email, she's sending you an attachment and she wrote, can you read this and see if you think I have any errors, slash, things I shouldn't say or suggestions of what I should say, right?
A. I see that.
Q. And then you reviewed the draft and you responded in the top email on this page with a suggestion?
A. Yes.

Q. All right. And if we could turn to the attachment, which is called publishing call. In the upper left, you will see it says project constellation, diligence discussion agenda. Are you with me?
A. Yes.
Q. And do you recall that the diligence referred to here was the diligence done in connection with the merger of Viacom and CBS Corporation in 2019?
A. I believe that's what this was about, yes.
Q. So you were aware that Viacom and CBS were—had a common parent company but were separate entities until they joined in 2019?
A. Yes.
Q. Now, the attachment has a series of topics and then responses below them in all capital letters and bold font. Do you see that?
A. I do.
Q. And you know from working with Ms. Reidy that when she was preparing material for presentation, she would write out in all capital letters and bold font, correct?
A. She would normally do it that way, yes.
Q. So based on that experience, you think it's fair to say that Ms. Reidy was the author of the text in this document that's in capital letters and bold font?
A. Yes.
MR. MATELSON: Your Honor, we offer PX530 into evidence.
THE COURT: Any objection?
MR. FISHBEIN: No objection.
THE COURT: It will be admitted. (Plaintiff's 530 received in evidence.)
BY MR. MATELSON:
Q. When Carolyn Reidy was the chief executive officer, you often spoke to her multiple times a day, is that fair?
A. That's correct.
Q. And did you talk to her about things like sales?
A. Yes.
Q. And high-level strategy issues?
A. Yes.
Q. And sometimes you discussed with her efforts to acquire author content?
A. Again, not very often.
Q. Okay. But from time to time?
A. It was my main job responsibility.
Q. You did?
A. From time to time we would speak, yes.
Q. And your view was that Ms. Reidy was very capable as the chief executive officer of Simon & Schuster, right?
A. Yes, that's my view.
Q. And you saw her as an expert in the publishing industry?
A. I did.
Q. And she had a combination of editorial knowledge and business acumen in your mind, right?
A. Yes.
Q. And she ran a great organization at Simon & Schuster, fair?
A. I believe she did.
Q. And her reputation in the publishing industry that you observed was that she was smart and tough, right?
A. I agree with that.
Q. Now, turning back to the document in front of you, I want to start at the top where it says publishing. And in the first subject that's listed under there reads, business overview and differentiation. (a) competition. Describe the competitive landscape and the threat from other large publishers Penguin

Random House, Hachette, Harper Collins, Macmillan versus smaller independent publishers versus self-publish alternatives. Do you see where I am reading?

A. I do.

Q. So I want to now go through some of the comments below that. First look at the first three sentences of the document. And those read, as you note, the U.S. publishing market is made up of what is known as the Big 5. PRH dominates with the largest market share followed by Harper Collins and then S&S. Hachette is a close fourth followed by Macmillan. These companies are our biggest competitors especially for books by already best-selling authors and celebrities since they are the most likely to come up with the high advance payments required and are known for their strong editorial and publishing skills. Do you see that?

A. I do.

Q. Your experience with Ms. Reidy, she regarded the Big 5 publishers as Simon & Schuster's biggest competitors for authors, right?

A. Yes.

Q. And you agree with that as well, right?

A. I do agree with that.

Q. And that's based on what you have been able to observe in your time at Simon & Schuster, right?

A. In just my observations, yes.

Q. And what you have observed during your tenure is that in instances where Simon & Schuster does not acquire an author, typically that author will go to another Big 5 publisher, correct?

A. In my experience, that would be my observation, yes.

Q. And looking back again at the third sentence that I read to you, it's accurate that, generally speaking, the Big 5 are the most likely to come up with the high advance payments required, as she wrote here?

A. Yes.

Q. And one reason, in your view, that the Big 5 are the most likely to come up with the high advance payments is because they are the most able to afford to, right?

A. I agree with that.

Q. And another reason that you think they are the most likely to come up with high advance payments is they have a history of success doing so, right?

A. Yes.

Q. And in that same sentence, at the very end, it refers to their strong editorial and publishing skills. Do you see that?

A. I do.

Q. And you understand the phrase publishing skills refers to everything you do to publish a book and get it out there such as marketing and sales?

A. I do.

Q. And having a good sales and marketing team helps maximize the sales of your titles, correct?

A. It does.

Q. If I could ask you to move down now a little lower on this page, it's the third paragraph in capital letters. And I will direct you to the first sentence. It reads, publishing houses and imprints gain reputations based on the successes they have published. Do you see that?

A. I do.

Q. And you agree that publishing houses and imprints gain reputations based on the successes they have published, right?

A. I do.

Q. Having a successful reputation is important to being a successful publishing house going forward, right?

A. Can you repeat that? I'm not sure what you mean by that.

Q. So the question was, having a successful reputation is important to being a successful publishing house, fair?

A. I believe it is.

Q. Okay. You believe that having a reputation for success is important for attracting authors to Simon & Schuster, right?

A. I believe reputation is important, yes.

Q. And the basis for your view is that if a publisher proves its success in a particular category, then other authors in that same category want to be published by you to have similar success, right?

A. I believe so. There's other sides to that also where sometimes they don't want to be together with everyone else that was in the genre, but I mostly agree.

Q. So in general, that's a fair statement?

A. Yes.

Q. Let's look at another paragraph in the same document. It's the last paragraph on that page. Do you see that there's some statements there about smaller publishers?

A. Yes.

Q. And one thing Ms. Reidy says is, they rarely compete with us in auctions for new properties. Do you see that part of it?

A. I do.

Q. Okay. And you don't disagree with Ms. Reidy on that, do you?

A. I do not. I did not disagree with her and I do not.

Q. Going to the next sentence, it says, often these publishers become farm teams for authors who then want to move to a larger, more financially stable major publisher. And again, you don't have a basis to disagree with Ms. Reidy about that, right?

A. I do not.

Q. We can take that exhibit down. You can set that aside. Now, you are familiar with the book pricing process at Simon & Schuster as part of your job?

A. I review pricing.

Q. Simon & Schuster does not consider the size of the advance payment to the author when it's determining the list price of the title, does it?

A. It does not.

Q. Different topic. Self-publishing, you are aware that some authors choose to self-publish their books?

A. Yes.

Q. You agree that self-publishing is not a threat to the core business of Simon & Schuster, correct?

A. My view is it's not a threat to our core business, no.

Q. At one time you thought self-publishing might be a threat in the romance category back when the book *Fifty Shades of Grey* first came out, right?

A. Back at that time, self-publishing definitely seemed to be more of a threat.

Q. So that was about 10, 12 years ago?

A. You said threat to core business. Of course, it's always a threat to a certain category or subject matter.

Q. Okay. But that book came out, *Fifty Shades of Grey*, we are talking about 10 or 12 years ago?

A. Yes.

Q. But then what you saw after that was that the potential threat from self-publishing never really materialized, correct?

A. It definitely changed, it seems, over time. It was definitely talked about more during that time frame as being a major threat.

Q. Okay. But the threat, from what you have seen, the threat never really materialized, right?

A. In my opinion, it did not.

Q. Also I wanted to ask you about Amazon Publishing. You are aware that Amazon opened a publishing business called Amazon Publishing a number of years ago?

A. Yes.

Q. And what you have observed since then is that Amazon Publishing has tried but did not end up being successful in acquiring major authors, right?

A. In my opinion, they didn't seem to be successful in major author acquisitions, correct.

Q. I would like to get back to your binder and take a look at another document. If you could open it up to PX663, third tab.
A. I have it.
Q. You have it? Okay. Now, the first page of this exhibit is a cover email from someone at a firm called LionTree and it's going to you and others. And the subject is, materials provided to buyers in phase one, right?
A. Yes.
Q. And LionTree is an advisory firm that ViacomCBS worked with to help find a buyer for Simon & Schuster?
A. That's correct.
Q. It's a lengthy exhibit, but I want to look at one of the attachments called Project Typeface MP. And there is a Bates number at the bottom that ends in 225. The title should be Simon & Schuster Management Presentation. So let me know when you have found it.
A. I have that.
Q. All right. So Project Typeface refers to the sale of Simon & Schuster in 2020?
A. That's correct.
Q. And this document is the management presentation that Simon & Schuster gave to potential buyers in September 2020, right?
A. I believe this would be the one, yes.
Q. And you and Mr. Karp met with each of the potential buyers and walked them through this presentation?
A. We did.
Q. And if you go to actually the third page of the document, it's numbered slide 2, there's your picture along with Mr. Karp as the presenters, right?
A. That's me.
Q. All right. And the purpose of this presentation was to provide information to potential buyers before they submitted their initial offers to Simon & Schuster, right?
A. That's correct.
Q. Bertelsmann, for example, was one of the bidders that you presented to?
A. Yes.
Q. And LionTree asked Simon & Schuster to help assemble the information to present to the buyers, right?
A. They asked for information.
Q. And you and your team helped get them the information they asked for?
A. We got them any information they wanted, yes.
Q. And you helped answer any questions that LionTree had?
A. I did.
Q. And you had a chance to review and discuss the contents of this management presentation with LionTree before it was provided to the buyers, right?
A. Yes, and answered questions that they had.
Q. In your dealings with LionTree, you were truthful and accurate, correct?
A. Yes.
MR. MATELSON: Your Honor, we move PX663 into evidence.
THE COURT: Any objection?
MR. FISHBEIN: No objection, Your Honor.
THE COURT: That's admitted. (Plaintiff's 663 received in evidence.)
MR. MATELSON: Thank you.
BY MR. MATELSON:
Q. I want to talk about the topic of backlist books first. If I could ask you to go to what's numbered—it's the internal slide 44 in this presentation. The Bates number ends in 269, if that's helpful.
A. Okay. I have it.

Q. And the title of this slide is Sales Breakdown?
A. Yes.
Q. Okay. And there's a chart in the upper right titled Frontlist and Backlist Percentage of Total U.S. Gross Sales. Do you see that?
A. I see that.
Q. I don't want to mention any numbers due to confidentiality, but does this accurately show the percentage of backlist sales versus frontlist sales that Simon & Schuster had for these years?
A. It does.
Q. And the upper part of the bar chart is the backlist percentage?
A. Yes.
Q. If I could ask you then to turn back a few pages to—it's internal slide 41 in the deck titled Financial Highlights?
A. Okay. I got it.
Q. This lists some of the financial highlights you wanted to show the buyers?
A. LionTree did, yes.
Q. One of the things that's mentioned here is, continually refreshed backlist continues to be a source of stability. Do you see that?
A. Yes.
Q. Now, you agree that Simon & Schuster's backlist is a source of stable revenue for the company?
A. I agree with that, yes.
Q. Another highlight that's mentioned here is that Simon & Schuster has industry-leading margins. Is that right?
A. I agree with that.
Q. Okay. Now, moving ahead one page to slide 42. Again, I think we will avoid mentioning any numbers, but this shows the sales projections that were provided to the bidders, right?
A. Yes.
Q. And if I could ask you to just look at the commentary section on the right, the second bullet from the top reads, backlist projected to continue strong performance seen in recent years. Do you see that?
A. I do.
Q. And the chart on the lower left of this page shows the projected growth in gross backlist revenues through 2024?
A. Yes.
Q. Also in the commentary section on the lower left side, there's a bullet that reads, given Simon & Schuster's recent run of commercially successful frontlist titles and investment in future author advances, management expects the backlist to be consistently replenished by strong sellers. Do you see where I was reading?
A. Yes.
Q. And what this is saying is that the frontlist feeds the backlist, right?
A. Yes.
Q. Another fact about backlist books is that they have lower return rates than frontlist books, correct?
A. On average, yes.
Q. And by return rates, we are talking about the proportion of books returned unsold by retailers?
A. That's correct.
Q. High return rates can be costly for publishers, is that fair?
A. That's fair.
Q. And backlist books tend to have lower return rates because there's established demand for them, right?
A. That's also fair.
Q. We can set that document aside. Thanks. Let me switch gears again. You mentioned before that one of your job responsibilities is book production which would include contracts with printing companies, right?

A. That's correct.
Q. Printing books in a timely way is important to Simon & Schuster, isn't it?
A. Yes, it's important.
Q. And one reason it's important is that if you miss a planned publication date for a new book, your marketing and publicity efforts for the book can be wasted, right?
A. That could be one reason, yes, that's important.
Q. And another situation where it's important to have timely printing is when you are doing a reprint of a book that's already out in the market, right?
A. Yes. You are about to go out of stock, yes, you need a reprint.
Q. Right. And that's because there's a demand from readers, and if a printer is late, you can lose sales, right?
A. That's correct.
Q. Simon & Schuster needs the ability to print one-color trade books on short notice, right?
A. Yes, we do.
Q. Like if a book is selling well, you want to replenish the stock so you don't run out, right?
A. That's correct.
Q. And having printing capacity is also important for Simon & Schuster when you are competing for authors, correct?
A. I'm not sure what you mean by that.
Q. Well, it's important when you are competing for authors that you have printing capacity to print their books, right?
A. Yes. I'm assuming if authors hear that you can't print books, they wouldn't want to be published by you. I agree with that.
Q. In fact, the first phone call you get when a book goes out of stock is from the author's literary agent asking why the book isn't available?
A. That could be. That's often, yes.
Q. And you get those kind of calls continuously?
A. Yes.
Q. If Simon & Schuster lost access to adequate printing capacity, that would adversely impact your ability to convince authors to publish with Simon & Schuster, correct?
A. That would be an issue.
Q. And if you couldn't get enough printing capacity, your sales would fall, correct?
A. Yes. You need books to sell them, yes.
Q. And you are aware that there's limited book printing capacity in the United States today?
A. There seems to be a finite amount of capacity.
Q. You agree that it's limited, right?
A. I guess, I'm not sure—I mean, limited, there's a finite capacity. There has been very much in the last two years been issues with getting enough capacity. It ebbs and flows.
Q. In fact, it's already been affecting Simon & Schuster's business because you have to spread out larger titles at the printers, right?
A. When you say effective business, we have been dealing with the capacity limitations. We have been printing our books.
Q. Right. So I am asking, sometimes you have to spread out large print jobs at the printer because there's not enough capacity to do them at the same time, right?
A. Right, that's what we would do and will do.
Q. The two printers that Simon & Schuster relies on the most are Bertelsmann and LSC?
A. We have a major amount of work that goes through those two printers, yes.
Q. And you believe that Bertelsmann and LSC are the best equipped printers to handle the volumes that Simon & Schuster needs, right?
A. Yes.
Q. You don't know of anyone else in the United States that has the same capacity as Bertelsmann and

LSC, correct?
A. At the volumes we place with them, I think those are the ones we rely on, yes.
Q. And Simon & Schuster can't put large quantity jobs at small printers, right?
A. If you have time to print, you can. Again, I'm not sure what the range you are talking about, but you can get a fairly large volume out of printers even if they keep your book on press.
Q. But for most of your large quantity jobs, you are not going to small printers, correct?
A. That's right, we would rather not, yes.
Q. Now, you have done some print jobs overseas due to the lack of capacity in the United States, right?
A. That's correct.
Q. One disadvantage of printing overseas is that it takes more time than printing in the United States, right?
A. Yes.
Q. And there can be unforeseen shipping delays, for example, at ports?
A. Yes.
Q. Now, Simon & Schuster entered into a new printing contract with LSC back in 2020, is that right?
A. Yes, we did.
Q. And Simon & Schuster committed a certain amount of its print work to LSC?
A. Yes, we did.
Q. Now, before this LSC agreement, Simon & Schuster was primarily using a printer called Quad, is that right?
A. Yes, for our contracted work, yes, we use Quad.
Q. And in early 2020, you learned that Quad was about to be sold to Bertelsmann, correct?
A. Yeah. I don't know exact timing, but yes, at some point we had that thought, yes.
Q. All right. So to help with our discussion on this, let me ask you to turn to your next tab in your binder, which is PX682.
A. Okay. I have it.
Q. All right. And what we have marked as PX682 is an email string between Carolyn Reidy, Bob Bakish, and others concerning a printing contract for approval, right?
A. That's correct.
Q. Mr. Bakish was the CEO of ViacomCBS?
A. Yes.
Q. And in the first email on the string, which the text is on the second page, Ms. Reidy is writing to Mr. Bakish seeking approval for the LSC printing contract, right?
A. That's correct.
Q. And you reviewed this email with Ms. Reidy before she sent it off?
A. Yes.
Q. And you are also copied on this email string?
A. Yes, I am.
Q. And Simon & Schuster did enter into the printing contract with LSC that's discussed here?
A. Yes, we did.
MR. MATELSON: Your Honor, we offer PX682 into evidence.
THE COURT: Any objection?
MR. FISHBEIN: No objection.
THE COURT: That will be admitted. (Plaintiff's 682 received in evidence.)
BY MR. MATELSON:
Q. In the body of the email on page 2, Ms. Reidy wrote to Mr. Bakish, and this is in sort of the middle of the paragraph, strong indications are that Quad will be selling its book trade business to Bertelsmann who owns Penguin Random House. We would not want to be 100 percent beholden to a competitor for printing.
Do you see where I was reading?
A. I do.

Q. And you agreed with Ms. Reidy that Simon & Schuster would not want to be beholden to a competitor for printing capacity, correct?
A. At a hundred percent, correct.
Q. And that's because you never want a competitor to be in control of your business?
A. That's correct.
Q. And one reason you didn't want Bertelsmann to have control of your printing is they might allocate a larger part of their business to Penguin Random House versus other publishers, right?
A. It could be a concern, yes.
Q. And a printing company usually prints from many publishers at once, right?
A. Yes, they do.
Q. And a printer has the ability to prioritize among those jobs, right?
A. They do.
Q. So if you are printing at a competitor of yours, the competitor could potentially prioritize its own titles over Simon & Schuster's titles, right?
A. Potentially.
Q. And if a competitor did that, it could adversely affect Simon & Schuster's business, right?
A. It could.
Q. If Simon & Schuster doesn't get the books it needs from the printer, then you can't sell them and your sales would decrease, right?
A. That's correct.
Q. A competitor could also raise your printing costs if you don't have an alternative, correct?
A. If you don't have an alternative, correct.
Q. And the desire not to be beholden to a competitor was an important reason that Simon & Schuster moved volume to LSC, correct?
A. Yes. It was one of the reasons, yes.
Q. And you saw it as an important reason, right?
A. We did, yes.
MR. MATELSON: Your Honor, I am going to pause my questioning here. I have a number of other questions of Mr. Eulau that really relate primarily to the efficiencies issues in the case. And as I understand the agreement we have with defendants, Mr. Eulau can be recalled at a future time to answer those questions. So with that understanding, I would pass the witness.
THE COURT: All right. Thank you.

CROSS-EXAMINATION

BY MR. FISHBEIN:

Q. Good morning, Mr. Eulau.
A. Hello.
Q. Mr. Eulau, I just want to get a couple of aspects of your job responsibilities clear. In your career at Simon & Schuster, have you held any positions outside of sales, finance, or operations?
A. No.
Q. In your career at Simon & Schuster, have you ever been a publisher or an editor? Have you ever had those positions?
A. No.
Q. And have you ever had a position supervising publishers or editors?
A. I have not.
Q. And I thought I saw on the transcript what may have been an error so I want to clarify. You said something about your main job. What is your main job at Simon & Schuster?
A. I would say my main job is financial oversight.
Q. And is your main job content acquisition or creative editing or publishing?
A. It is not.
Q. So, for example, let's just say during the last five years, have you spoken to any agents about

acquiring books, book rights from authors, in the last five years?
A. I have not.
Q. Have you submitted bids to agents in connection with auctions for books?
A. I have not.
Q. Have you ever participated in a book auction?
A. I have not.
Q. How many books in your career have you personally acquired?
A. I have not acquired books.
Q. As part of your finance function, do you track or compile lists of who Simon & Schuster competes with or loses to in competitions for books?
A. I do not.
Q. Let me ask you some questions about—if you have it in front of you, I think it's Plaintiff's Exhibit 530, the memo that Ms. Reidy sent to you, the email. Do you have that in front of you?
A. I do.
Q. And we will turn, not to the cover page, but to the actual memo. And my first question is do you recall receiving these notes back in May of 2019?
A. I see them here, and I have reviewed them many times, but no, I don't recall specifically receiving them at any particular time, no.
Q. Yeah, that's what I'm asking you. Do you have a memory of receiving these back in May of 2019?
A. I do not.
Q. Do you have a memory of reading them back in May of 2019?
A. May of 2019, I do not.
Q. Do you recall discussing this email with Ms. Reidy when she sent it to you back in May of 2019?
A. I do not recall discussions.
Q. Now, the government asked you—I think it's in the bottom paragraph. There's a comment about smaller publishers. Mr. Eulau, do you know which publishers compete in auctions with Simon & Schuster?
A. Which compete, I do not.
Q. Because you don't follow auctions or who's bidding and that sort of thing, correct?
A. I do not.
Q. And you don't know how often various publishers compete in auctions with Simon & Schuster?
A. Or in the mix, I do not. I do not know.
Q. You know, the government showed you, I think it was, a management presentation, and there was a photo of you and Mr. Karp, right? And from what you are saying, I take it that you are sort of responsible for the financial side?
A. Operations.
Q. Okay. And is there some other executive at the company other than you that would be more familiar with the day-to-day of who's competing against Simon & Schuster in auctions for books?
A. Yes. It would be the publishers and Jonathan Karp.
Q. Okay. And I think you said, you had no reason to disagree that authors sometimes move from small publishers to larger ones. Are you aware, though, that sometimes authors have success and stay with smaller publishers? Are you aware of that?
A. I am not aware specifically, but I'm sure it happens.
Q. Have you heard of Michael Lewis, for example, the author?
A. I have.
Q. I mean, just based on what you know about the publishing industry, is he someone you know is successful?
A. I believe he's successful, yes.
Q. Do you know if he moved to a Big 5 publisher?
A. I do not know. I do not think so.
Q. Do you know who publishes him?

A. I believe Norton.
Q. Okay. And then are you familiar with a book series called *Diary of a Wimpy Kid* by Jeff Kinney?
A. Yes, I am familiar.
Q. Is that a successful series?
A. I think it's very successful, yes.
Q. And do you know where he's published?
A. I think it's Abrams, but I'm not sure.
Q. Do you know, for example, if he, after having success, moved to a Big 5 publishing company?
A. I don't believe he has.
Q. Fair to say you don't track this, right? You don't have knowledge of who stays and who goes, is that fair?
A. I do not track it.
Q. Okay. And by the way, do you know whether there are any authors who have published with a Big 5 and then subsequently choose to publish with non-Big 5 publishers?
A. I do not.
Q. Do you track that?
A. I do not track that.
Q. Let me show you what I am going to mark—what's already marked for identification as Defendant's Exhibit 405. Your Honor, can I hand this up? It's the only exhibit I am going to add here.
THE COURT: Yes.
MR. FISHBEIN: May I approach?
THE COURT: Yes.
THE WITNESS: Thank you.
BY MR. FISHBEIN:
Q. Mr. Eulau, I am showing you what's been marked as Defendant's Exhibit 405, which is an email chain between you and Ms. Reidy, May 6, 2019. Do you see that?
A. I do.
Q. And do you see about halfway down, there's the email where Ms. Reidy sent to you the presentation that the government asked you about?
A. Yes.
Q. And then do you see the conversation continues above that?
A. Yes.
MR. FISHBEIN: Your Honor, I will offer Defendant's Exhibit 405, I believe without objection.
MR. MATELSON: Right, no objection.
THE COURT: That will be admitted. (Defendant's 405 received in evidence.)
BY MR. FISHBEIN:
Q. Mr. Eulau, is this a continuation of the email chain that the government showed you?
A. Yes, it is.
Q. It is the same email chain, is that right?
A. It looks—yes, it is.
Q. Just with an additional conversation, is that correct?
A. That's correct.
Q. So if I could direct your attention, Ms. Reidy writes to you after you made a proposed edit to her. She says, only correction, positive enough, question mark. Do you see that?
A. Yes.
Q. What did you understand her to mean by positive enough?
A. It was a management presentation and we wanted to make sure we were looked at in a positive light, just looked at as positive as an organization, as a publishing house.
Q. So in a positive light to management, is that fair?
A. Yes, that's correct.
Q. Thank you. Now, the government attorney asked you about Amazon as a competitor. And I think in

your answer you said something like, based on my view. Did I hear that right?
A. You did.
Q. And what did you mean by that, based on your view?
A. Just what I see and the dialogues that I would have with publishers, editors.
Q. Okay. Now, do you, yourself, follow sort of what Amazon Publishing has done in recent years or how successful they are?
A. I do not.
Q. Do you know, for example, whether Amazon has recently been in auctions against Simon & Schuster?
A. I do not.
Q. Do you know whether recently Amazon has been able to get independent bookstores to carry books published by Amazon?
A. I do not know.
Q. Do you know whether Simon & Schuster has pursued authors who have chosen Amazon instead?
A. I do not.
Q. And then similar to self-publishing, is it fair to say that that's also based on sort of what comes to your attention?
A. Yes.
Q. And I think you said that there was a time when self-publishing was a threat to romance. Is that right?
A. It was a threat in general at one point. It was more in the dialogue, day-to-day dialogue, about self-publishing.
Q. And I think you mentioned that from time to time, there are genres that are affected by self-publishing. Did I hear that right?
A. I said something to that effect.
Q. So the romance genre, just what's your understanding of what happened with the romance genre in self-publishing?
A. That seemed to stay more in the self-publishing area, and it seemed to expand.
Q. I'm sorry, what expanded?
A. Romance authors self-publishing.
Q. Okay. Now, do you follow self-publishing in the sense of looking to see who the self-publishers are and to what extent there's crossover with major publishers?
A. Crossover, I do not look at that in that way.
Q. Have you ever discussed self-publishing with an author or an agent?
A. No.
Q. Do you know if there are Simon & Schuster authors who have threatened to self-publish?
A. I do not.
Q. Let me ask you about printing. And the government showed you an exhibit. I don't think we are going to need to look at that exhibit. As I understand what you said, there was a time when a significant portion of your printing was with a company called Quad. Is that right?
A. That's correct.
Q. And by the way, what type of books was that for?
A. Mostly black and white, hard cover, and trade paper, but it was predominantly black and white hard cover.
Q. Do Simon & Schuster have other types of books that are printed?
A. Yes.
Q. This is just one segment of Simon & Schuster printing?
A. That's correct.
Q. And you said most of it was with Quad, is that right?
A. Yes.
Q. And when you were printing with Quad, were they owned by Bertelsmann?

A. They were not.
Q. I understood at some point they became owned by Bertelsmann, and you switched some of the quantity, is that right?
A. Correct.
Q. To a company called LSC?
A. Yes, now called Lakeside.
Q. Is Lakeside owned by Bertelsmann?
A. It is not.
Q. And how has that worked out for Simon & Schuster in terms of the things the government asked you about, namely having capacity and being able to fulfill your needs?
A. It just worked out.
Q. So LSC has worked out for you?
A. Yes.
Q. And they are a non-Bertelsmann printer?
A. Yes.
Q. You said that printing capacity, I think you used the term ebbs and flow. Is that right?
A. Yes.
Q. What did you mean by that?
A. Sometimes in a given month, there might be some large quantities printed by any number of printers, and you find capacity issues at that point. So it ebbs and flows, and sometimes you will find a certain month during the year when there's capacity.
Q. When there are periods where there are limitations of capacity, what have you done to try to address that to make sure that Simon & Schuster's books get printed?
A. Spread it out, get a limited capacity over the last few years. We've done a lot internationally, and we have used a lot before smaller printer.
Q. When you say internationally, what you are referring to?
A. Asia, Italy, Germany.
Q. When you say smaller printers, what are you referring to?
A. Just the smaller printer are spread out in the country, some in Canada, many in the U.S.
Q. On the smaller printers, some of those are also in the U.S—
A. Yes.
Q.—or Canada? And has Simon & Schuster been able to find enough printing capacity between LSC and international and small—the sources that you are mentioning?
A. Yes, we have.
Q. Has Simon & Schuster been able to avoid being beholden to any one printing company including Bertelsmann?
A. Yes.
Q. And is that by spreading it around, as you described?
A. Yes. We didn't spread it around for that reason. There was capacity issues throughout the industry.
Q. Now, you were asked about whether a printer could prioritize their own titles over Simon & Schuster. Have you had that problem with Bertelsmann?
A. I have not.
Q. And you were asked whether a printer could raise its prices to somehow disadvantage you? Have you had that problem with Bertelsmann as a printer?
A. No.
Q. You were shown a slide about margins, and I think there was a phrase industry-leading margins—
A. Yes.
Q. How do you compare your margins to other players in the industry?
A. It's mostly by piecing together public information. It's not—there is a chance it's not a hundred percent accurate. We just do the best we can.
Q. So Bertelsmann is not a public company, right?

A. Exactly.
Q. So do you have access to the actual cost structure of Bertelsmann?
A. Do not.
Q. So is it fair to say that's kind of an estimate based on what you can find?
A. It's an estimate based on what's reported in the industry trades, trade publications.
Q. When we are talking about margins, are we talking about just your book-selling operations or are we talking about all of Simon & Schuster's operations?
A. When we are talking about margins, it's the complete operation.
Q. Does that include, for example, your third party distribution business?
A. It does.
Q. And how do the margins of your third party distribution business compare to your book publishing business?
A. The question depends on how you allocate costs, but we do see it as a higher margin.
Q. I'm sorry, a higher margin?
A. Higher margin.
Q. Where, in which part?
A. I'm sorry, can you repeat that.
Q. Yes. The higher margin is in the third party distribution or the book publishing?
A. Third party distribution.
Q. Have you attempted to compare Simon & Schuster to other publishers by accounting for the different ratios of third party distribution to direct publishing?
A. We have not.
MR. FISHBEIN: That's all I have, Your Honor.
THE COURT: Thank you.

REDIRECT EXAMINATION

BY MR. MATELSON:

Q. Mr. Eulau, you mentioned that it's not your main job to work on the editorial side of the business, right?
A. To work on the editorial side, it's not my job at all. It wouldn't just be not my main job.
Q. What you said, I believe, earlier was that you are consulted from time to time about author acquisitions, right?
A. Sometimes when there's large acquisitions, they will show me the sales histories and what they are comparing against, yes.
Q. And in your time at Simon & Schuster, 25 or more years, you have been able to observe all aspects of the business, right?
A. That's correct.
Q. And you mentioned having dialogues with other executives and being able to observe things that are happening at the company. I think when Mr. Fishbein was asking, you said you do have those conversations, right?
A. I do.
Q. And so you know enough about some aspects of the business to give testimony today. For example, Mr. Fishbein asked you about self-publishing, and you offered some opinions there. You have enough knowledge to do that, right?
A. I have enough knowledge to give my opinion, yes.
Q. That's based on your experience in the industry, that opinion?
A. Yes.
Q. And the printing topic, there are certain times of the year when there are more capacity constraints than others at printing facilities, is that right?
A. There are certain times of the year that the larger books usually are printed, yes.
Q. For example, leading up to the Christmas holiday season to get books into the stores in time, there's

often a capacity crunch at that time of the year, right?
A. There is often. We call it the fall season, yes.
Q. Are there other times in the year when you see capacity crunches?
A. It could happen at any time.
Q. You talked about one-color printing. That's the vast majority of the printing that Simon & Schuster does for adult books, correct?
A. It is the majority, yes.
Q. And you also talked a little bit about the margin analysis that we looked at in one of the documents where you compared Simon & Schuster's margins to your competitors, right?
A. Yes.
Q. Now, you mentioned that is an estimate, right?
A. Yes.
Q. But you believe it's a reliable estimate, right?
A. I believe the estimate.
Q. Okay. And it was reliable enough to report to ViacomCBS management, right?
A. Yes.
Q. And you also said the same thing to potential buyers at Simon & Schuster, that Simon & Schuster had the highest margins in the industry, right?
A. We had a schedule showing that, yes.
MR. MATELSON: I have nothing further. Thank you.
THE COURT: Thank you. You can step down, sir.

JONATHAN KARP, CEO, SIMON & SCHUSTER

A good portion of initial questioning of S&S CEO Jonathan Karp seemed like the pilot for a "Deals Court" reality show, as the DOJ's Jeffrey Vernon walked through a number of competitive situations in which S&S and PRH were the final two bidders for projects of scale.

But before we get to the deals, there were other pertinent details raised during Karp's testimony, which was a mix of cheerful, well-prepared answers along with some equivocations that were impeached—five times—by things he had said differently in the past, mostly during a deposition when the merger was first being investigated.

Throughout the trial (and afterwards) there was unfounded speculation, in a series of hypotheticals, that if the merger is quashed by the court S&S might get sold to a private equity company, and that company might want to cut staff and expenses, rather than invest and grow. (This despite the testimony that PRH—and other bidders—is counting on capturing "efficiencies" that would also reduce some staff and resources.)

But in September 2020, as the auction for the publisher was nearing the end, Karp clearly took the opposite position, and advocated for selling the publisher to a financial buyer because he thought it would be better for the staff.

Karp had written to Alex Berkett—the ViacomCBS executive overseeing the sale: "Although I really do understand why strategics [other publishers] are the most likely option, if there is a financial buyer who is willing to match the top bid, that outcome would be better for the employees of S&S, and arguably the larger book publishing ecosystem." (As we reported previously, PRH's internal assessment of post-merger "efficiencies" projects a reduction in operating costs of between $81 million and $95 million annually, from unspecified systems integration and other operating efficiencies, e.g. "reducing duplicative sales, marketing, and administrative positions," as "'de-duplicating' other positions will reduce costs significantly.")

During his testimony, Karp confirmed that—like at HBG, and as the government asserted in their opening—all acquisitions for $250,000 or more require his approval. But he insisted it had nothing to do with significant deals standing out from all others and said, "It's an arbitrary number, for corporate governance." S&S also has editors write a "justification memo," instituted by the late Carolyn Reidy, written after the deal is secured. "She felt that if editors were spending more than $200,000, they should be able to articulate their reasons why."

Karp indicated that S&S gets about 75 percent of its sales from the US (though earlier, DOJ documents indicated the publisher's US sales were $760 million in 2020, when their total reported sales were $901 million, or 84 percent).

In the Deals Court portion of Karp's testimony, the DOJ walked through—with redactions—a set of eight deals in which advances were increased when S&S and PRH were the only remaining bidders, demonstrating how competition between the two has yielded higher payments in some instances. Those deals included:

- An author Karp had been pursuing for 12 years, to whom he offered $5 million when he worked at Twelve/HBG—unsolicited—and then $6 million a number of months later, for world English. After Crown bid $7.5 million plus $2.5 million in bonuses, S&S won the book for $8 million.
- A book for which bidding stood at $645,000 when others dropped out. Allison Callahan and Eamon Dolan lost the book to Dial Press for $825,000.
- A book which got to $1.1 million, and then Atria and Libby McGuire won for $1.5 million in a final two-way round of best bids.
- A deal in which Aimee Bell won a book by going from $525,000 to $535,000 plus two bonuses totaling $100,000.
- A book in which S&S was tied with Penguin Press at $750,000 and lost.
- A Dawn Davis deal that stood at $575,000 when just two bidders remained. S&S's "top number was $750,000" and Viking won the book in final best bids.

- A book for which Portfolio had bid $1 million, and S&S, which had a $700,000 floor, topped for $1.1 million

Later in the session, Karp offered another deal "as recently as three weeks ago" as a counter-balance in which he said they were "in a seven-figure auction with Amazon." even though he had previously said—in deposition—that they do not frequently compete with Amazon to acquire books.

The most amusing moment came after the DOJ displayed an email in which Karp had bemoaned, "This was the third beauty contest we lost to PRH this week." As the DOJ's attorney was explaining a beauty contest to the court, and asked Karp for confirmation of the explanation, he replied instead: "Pulchritude!"

Mr. Vernon said, "Pulchritude?" Karp answered, "Yes, it's beauty." And Vernon returned, "Beauty. Okay. I should have guessed that you would have a big vocabulary as the head of a publishing house."

In cross-examination, S&S attorney Stephen Fishbein led Karp through a separate list of books they lost to HarperCollins, not PRH, all for seven figures, highlighting deals for Dave Grohl, Ben Shapiro, longtime Atria novelist Kate Morton, who "recently left us," and Brad Meltzer.

Karp also explained that "more than 50 percent" of their acquisitions are not at auction—comprising option books, exclusive submissions, and books they commission or elicit. He underscored that they "approach authors ourselves directly. We are going out and trying to find our own books."

That review of big books lost to other houses, from the Big 5 and beyond, continued in testimony on Wednesday morning. Also notable Wednesday was Karp's explanation of why he "thinks Amazon as a publisher is underestimated" by people. "It seems like they are getting more aggressive" in their acquisitions again. He also said the retailer's "bestseller list is, in my view, more important than *The New York Times* bestseller list" and they base many of their acquisitions on Amazon sales data.

When one of Colleen Hoover's books that is published by Amazon rather than Simon & Schuster made the ABA's bestseller list recently—showing that independent bookstores were carrying and selling an Amazon-published title, "What that says to me is, the Rubicon has been crossed."

Also notable was Karp explaining that his emailed remark to author John Irving—"I'm pretty sure that the Department of Justice wouldn't allow Penguin Random House to buy us, but that's assuming we still have a Department of Justice"—was made the day after ViacomCBS was putting the publisher up for sale. And the remark was a response to an email from Irving, speculating on the irony of his work going back to Random House in the end, since they were his first publisher. "I was responding humorously to his ironic remark," Karp said. As to his knowledge at the time about "the Department of Justice regulatory process on antitrust issues, Karp allowed, "I think you could say quite accurately that I was almost entirely ignorant. My parents wanted me to go to law school and I didn't listen!"

Fishbein's Deals Court tour also walked Karp through a number of significant deals or better that the house had to FSG, Flatiron, Norton, and Scholastic, as well as—at least in the occasional instance—Hay House, Princeton University Press and Harvard Business Review Press. (In redirect, however, the prosecution showed internal emails on the Hay House and PUP titles where Libby McGuire expressed surprise—"Wow, I didn't know they pay big advances"—and Julia Cheiffetz opined that, "They do that, the university presses, buy one big book a year. . . ."

Unstated in the defense's presentation of bids in which S&S was the animating underbidder is that, should the merger go through, there would be even more transactions in which final bids could pit PRH against everyone else.

Karp's amended view that Amazon Publishing and self-publishing are both viewed as a "threat" to his business appeared to be based on a single example: The recent auction in which Amazon bid, but still lost, a seven-figure project, cited Tuesday; and a "very highly regarded neuroscientist" who "asked to be released from his contract so he could self-publish . . . only a few months ago" because "he just thought he could make more money that way."

The prosecution countered with a few more deals of their own—including one in which S&S beat out Dutton with a two-book bid of $1.1 million, and "didn't have to go to $1.5 million," which was their planned high bid. The DOJ's Jeffery Vernon used it to suggest, "for those books, the agent doesn't have enough power to force Simon & Schuster to pay the maximum that it was willing to pay."

Similarly, the DOJ demonstrated that the big publishers have all independently come to have "a no audio, no deal rule," as Scribner publisher Nan Graham put it, again suggesting, "the agent did not have enough power to convince S&S to acquire the book without acquiring the audio rights."

Marketing and midlist were topics that Judge Pan and Karp engaged in lively exchanges over. At one point, Karp claimed, asked when marketing budgets are set, that: "We often decide late in the process after we have heard the reactions from readers. In fact, literary agents frequently ask us to guarantee marketing dollars. And we don't do it because we don't want to be locked into a plan when we acquire the book."

Judge Pan wanted to know, "Putting aside the advance, books that [authors/agents] expect to sell well, they can ask you for things, like, can you commit certain marketing dollars? And do they ask you, for example, can you get this book reviewed in *The New York Times*, can you get my author on the Today Show, things like that?"

Karp said, "You would be a fool to make that kind of promise because we can't control that." But the judge was "trying to figure out if the negotiating process with these anticipated top selling books is different from everybody else's negotiation. I saw in one of the defense exhibits, there was a budget for 'glam' and 'wardrobe.'"

They both agreed glam budgets were "hilarious," though the judge asked seriously, "But you can't demand that unless you are an anticipated top selling books author, right? That's not a term that everybody gets, am I right?"

Karp said it was a more common ask from talent agencies. "It doesn't come up that often. You have to be pretty glamorous to ask for that." He noted, "John Irving isn't asking for a glam budget." The court was also shown a bid that had an "as is" clause on the manuscript. "That's something you would only offer to an anticipated top selling books, not just to anybody, right?" asked the Judge. Karp acknowledged, "I think that's a fair assumption to make."

The judge also noticed, "There was also something in one of the exhibits about a compelling marketing plan. [Which is how Karp said Norton had won a book away from them.] And that was a factor in which publisher and author chose. So if you know it's going to be a hot auction, a lot of interest, do you spend more time developing a compelling marketing plan?"

Answer: "Yes. . . When you really want the author, you jump through hoops." He then said marketing plans aren't dependent on the expected advance at all. "A lot of the times when you do these marketing plans, you don't know what the book will wind up selling for. So, you know, you could do it for any reason. sometimes editors just do them because they really want the book and they are just showing that they are going the extra mile."

In a different exchange, Karp told the court, "The idea that any publisher can make a book a best seller is false."

But Judge Pan asked: "But you are telling them that you can better their chances so that's why they should come with you; because you have a broad distribution network, you have relationships with sellers, you can raise the profile of their book, you can create buzz, you are saying all those things, right?"

To which Karp responded, "The problem is, after you have had two meetings, if you are an author, after you have had two meetings and everyone says the same thing in the meeting, you don't believe it. And a lot of the time . . . your success is like taking credit for the weather. And you can't really make those assurances to authors." He added later in the exchange, "I have much more humility about my role in the publishing process now than I did ten years ago, I think that so much depends on luck, so much depends upon factors that are out of your control."

Later, Judge Pan and Karp seemed equally baffled on trying to define midlist, and engaged in a who's-on-first exchange. "Midlist is anything," Karp said. "It's funny. When I got into the book business, midlist was anything that you paid, you know, 50 or 75 thousand dollars for or even 25 thousand dollars for."

"So would a midlist book now be $150,000 or . . ." the Judge reasonably asked. "No," Karp said. "It could be $25,000. It could be anything."

With all the sensible confusion of someone trying to apply logic to the terminology of publishing,

"Midlist implies there's a low list," the Judge wisely inferred. "I'm just trying to figure . . ." Karp explained, "Midlist is a word that publishers use that doesn't mean anything unfortunately. . . . No author would want to be on low list." [That's why it's called a nice deal, friends.] "I think maybe the best way of saying it is you are hoping," Karp suggested.

A few side notes as well:

–Agents and authors will want to file away that Karp told the judge about marketing to independent booksellers: "We create advance readers editions. It doesn't cost a lot of money to do."

–The DOJ indicated, "If consummated, [Karp] would receive a significant bonus"—"a standard provision of the contract that I was offered when I was CEO."

–In an unexpectedly fraught question, they asked who Karp would report to if the merger does through: "[Markus Dohle] has not actually discussed anything other than to say that we would remain independent and that we would have the same kind of creative and entrepreneurial freedom that we have today."

–At one point, Karp noted: "I don't think it's a particularly generous thing to refer to these really great [non-Big 5] publishing companies as farm teams. They publish a lot of authors we would love to publish and a lot of authors who actually have come to us and then gone back to them. So I just don't think it's an apt analogy."

–One of the more newsworthy revelations that has little bearing on the case is that one of the deals in which S&S was outbid by HBG (rather than PRH) was a forthcoming book by Dr. Ben Carson, who Karp said will write about "his experiences in the Trump Administration and his thoughts on race." S&S lost the book despite a "mid-six-figure offer."

Judge Pan Rules

During Karp's testimony, we made the point that among the most important takeaways was the extent to which it was already clear that Judge Pan was clearly very smart, learning quickly about publishing, and not allowing herself to be distracted by posturing from either side of the dispute.

In the opening session on Tuesday morning, at the end of testimony and cross-examination from literary agent Ayesha Pande, Judge Pan had inferred, "Is it correct that if Simon & Schuster and Penguin Random House were merged, it wouldn't have affected any of the deals?" (The answer was, yes.)

Then towards the end of the Karp first day of testimony, she challenged him directly with some questions. Her reasoning suggested she had registered a strong impression that more competition—and competitors—leads to bigger advances for some authors.

Judge Pan's questions came as Karp was being cross-examined by S&S's attorney, Stephen Fishbein. As Karp was suggesting that sales, publicity and marketing efforts do not vary by advance level and "sometimes . . . don't even know how much we've spent on the books," Judge Pan interjected with some incredulity, saying, "This is quite interesting to me."

Pan asked, "If you pay a lot for a book, like one of these million dollars books that you've been chasing for ten years, you're not going to market that harder than another book? You're not going to get it reviewed, you're not going to create a buzz about that book?"

Karp did a turnabout, and acknowledged, "We have to market those books quite arduously, definitely."

The Judge pressed, "And more than your run of the mill book because you're not getting a reviewer for every one of your books."

Karp replied, "You have to pick your shots, that's definitely true. . . . the big obvious books that we spent a lot of money for, they definitely have to be marketed and publicized aggressively, although sometimes we're paying that kind of money because the author takes care of a lot of that."

The Judge continued her skepticism: "I'm sure they're expecting from you a high level of attention."

Karp noted, "They definitely are." But again, he tried to qualify his answer, explaining that sometimes "it's in the read" as publishing people say. "And when it's in the read and when people have that kind of a euphoric reaction, as they did to a book like *Sea Biscuit*, for example, it doesn't matter what we paid, people just get behind it."

And again on Wednesday morning, he said underscored, "We fall in love with books that we pay five-figure advances for. Love is supposed to be blind."

Judge Pan brought him back to the matter at hand, though: "You're saying there's no correlation between the books and the read that you've paid more for the book and the read that you're going to promote?"

Karp conceded, "I certainly think that when we've paid a lot for a book, everybody knows that there's extra pressure on us to earn it back."

Mr. Fishbein tried to extricate them, asking about the advance level for what was being called "big books" and Karp said, "I'm thinking in the hundreds of thousands of dollars"—after denying there was anything different about books acquired for six figures or more. (That is in the range of the DOJ's posited anticipated best sellers).

He added, "A lot of those books are called make books and the idea is that it's up to the publisher to make them." Fishbein was trying to establish that there is no "separate marketing program for books at 300 (thousand) versus 250 (thousand)" but that parsing may have missed the mark.

Shortly thereafter, Judge Pan interjected again, after Karp said books they compete with PRH for are "a small fraction of the books we compete for." She asked, in "A pre-empt or a best bids auction, isn't your bid going to be higher if you perceive that there are more bidders or more competition out there?" Shortly thereafter she said, "In any kind of competitive situation you're going to bid higher if you think there's more competition, more people in the pool?"

Here Karp suggested, "I think that does color our thinking to some extent. But I also think that when you want it, it doesn't matter how many people are competing against you."

But she opined back, "It does seem that throughout this trial, there's this sort of sense—competition raises advance levels, less competition lowers them, and that's consistent with the idea that anytime there's a competitive situation, whether it's a round robin or any other type, you're going to try harder because you might have to bid more in order to win, because more people are in it, the bids are probably going to be higher."

On Wednesday morning, Judge Pan revisited some of her key questions with Karp. She wanted to know the percentage of anticipated top-selling books that are acquired in competitive situations, and Karp said, "I never counted." With more questions, she elicited from him, "I do think a lot of the higher-priced books we acquire are acquired" that way, conceding it's "more likely that they would be sold in a competitive situation." At the same time, at least a few highly-sought after books are acquired outright: "When we acquired Bruce Springsteen, he never talked to anyone else."

As she had asked previously, once again Judge Pan probed a number of times to try to determine the "correlation between the books that are paid the highest advances and how they sell." She noted, "It seems that there must be some correlation; I'm trying to figure out how strong it is."

Karp noted, "We have not actually authoritatively studied that, and that may be a weakness on our part." But generally he agreed with her impression from testimony so far that, "About half the books we publish make money and a much lower percentage of them earn back the advance."

On the correlation, the judge said, "There must be some correlation, or else you wouldn't be in business," to which Karp replied, "Well, it's a precarious business."

He also allowed that, "There's a fairly common truth—you make the most money on the midlist books" on authors like Laura Dave or Colleen Hoover, who are not acquired for a lot of money but go on to sell in huge quantities. He also opined, "I believe that the authors you build over time turn out to be the most profitable." Not made explicit yet in any of these exchanges is that the most successful authors get a higher effective royalty rate through high advances which may not be expected to "earn out," while still yielding a healthy profit for both the publisher and the author. In higher-advance situations, the publisher has to earn their advanced money back, whereas in low-advance situations, the author is hoping that the publisher's efforts will earn them more money. "Midlist" books that become bestsellers are so profitable because they earn regular royalties (often with follow-on bonuses or adjustments to the next contract), rather than a higher effective royalty.

It was also evidenced through Karp's testimony about a number of deals that the publisher sets a number it is willing to pay—as Michael Pietsch said HBG does—but it will bid less and generally only go up to their maximum amount if forced to by another bidder.

During the same conversation, in which Fishbein was trying to demonstrate that agents are in control and the publishers "entertain" them, Karp echoed PRH lawyer Daniel Petrocelli's opening remark: "I take them to lunch regularly. . . . The publisher always pays. And I mean that literally and metaphorically." Asked to explain, he added, "We pay for lunch and we pay the advances!" (On Twitter, after the opening arguments, agents have been suggesting they would gladly pay for lunch if they get more power and better deals.)

Karp also told Fishbein he is "not a big fan" of the term Big 5: "I think that it's parochial and ethnocentric. There are a lot of really good publishers all over the country. I don't think it's all about us."

TESTIMONY OF JONATHAN KARP, CEO, SIMON & SCHUSTER

DIRECT EXAMINATION

BY MR. VERNON:

Q. Good afternoon, Mr. Karp.
A. Good afternoon. How are you doing?
A. I'm fine. Thank you.
Q. Good. Can you state your name for the record.
A. Jonathan Karp.
Q. And what is your title?
A. I'm the President and chief executive officer of Simon & Schuster.
Q. I think this is right. You have 32 years of experience in the book publishing business; is that correct?
A. Thirty-three.
Q. Thirty-three. And before working at Simon & Schuster, you worked at Random House and Hachette; is that right?
A. Yes.
Q. And you started working at Simon & Schuster in 2010; is that right?
A. Yes.
Q. You became the President of Simon & Schuster's adult group in 2018; is that right?
A. Yes.
Q. As president of Simon & Schuster's Adult Publishing Group, you oversaw all of the Simon & Schuster divisions that publish adult books; is that fair?
A. Yes.
Q. You became the CEO of Simon & Schuster in May of 2020?
A. Yes.
Q. Except for the first two years, you have been involved in negotiations with authors and agents for all of your publishing career; is that fair?
A. Yes.
Q. So you have approximately 31 years of experience in negotiating with authors and agents; is that right?
A. Yes.
Q. Let me ask you about competition. Authors benefit from competition between Penguin Random House and Simon & Schuster, fair?
A. They benefit from competition among all publishers.
Q. Including Simon & Schuster and Penguin?
A. Yes.
Q. For example, competition between Penguin Random House and Simon & Schuster has led to higher advances for authors, hasn't it?
A. That's happened, and, again, the competition throughout the publishing industry has led to higher advances.
Q. Head-to-head competition between Simon & Schuster and Penguin Random House is quite common, correct?
A. Well, head-to-head competition is relatively rare in the full picture of the total number of deals that

we do.

Q. Let's walk through some examples. For these questions, I'm going to refer to a book and author confidentiality document that's in the front of every binder in the front fold.

So if you open it up, it's a list of books and titles. Don't show this to the public. It lists the title of a book and the name of an author, and then a number?

A. Yes.

Q. So let me just explain this because we're trying to be sensitive to confidential information. We are going to talk about the advance dollars and the offer dollars so you can say the dollar of the advance. Does that make sense?

But we're trying not to say the name of a book, the name of an author, the name of an agent, or information that could identify the book or the author like their profession. Does that make sense?

A. Yes.

Q. Okay. If you have any questions about which portions of a document have been marked as confidential, you can look at your screen. Right there.

A. Oh, yeah. Got it.

Q. Your screen will have redactions; the binder in front of you does not. If you have any questions, please stop me, because we are trying to be sensitive.

A. Got it.

Q. Let me start you with book 58, it's the last one on your list. Simon & Schuster and Penguin Random House competed to acquire this book; is that correct?

A. We were negotiating and I found out near the end that Penguin Random House had made an offer.

Q. You personally handled much of the negotiations over this book; is that correct?

A. Yes.

Q. You offered $6 million for book 58; is that correct?

A. That's part of it. We started lower.

Q. Let me see if I remember correctly. You first offered $5 million for book 58; is that right?

A. Right.

Q. And then a few days after you offered $5 million, you increased the offer to $6 million; is that right?

A. Right.

Q. After that, you learned that Penguin Random House had offered $7.5 million for the book; is that correct?

A. Are there documents?

Q. Sure, we can go to a document: Let me ask you to turn in your binder to PX643, so that the PXs are in the front, and let me know when you're ready.

A. Okay. So the reason I wanted to check was because the $6 million offer was about eight or nine months earlier. So we did increase the offer, as you said, but there was about a nine-month—eight- or nine-month gap between that.

Q. Let me just walk you through the document quickly. First, PX643 is an email chain with the top email from you to Ms. Reidy dated November 6th, 2019; is that correct?

A. Correct.

MR. VERNON: Your Honor, we have prepared a redacted version. May we show it to the public?

THE COURT: You may.

MR. VERNON: Thank you.

BY MR. VERNON:

Q. There is an email from you, starting at the bottom of the first page, and the substance of the email starts at the top of the second page. Do you see that?

A. Yes.

Q. In the first sentence at the top of page 2, you write: As you will recall, we made a confidential $6 million world English offer for the author in January. Do you see that?

A. Yes.

Q. Halfway through the second line, you write: Unfortunately, a person whose name we are redacting, urged him to consider an offer from Crown, which has put $7.5 million on the table, with $2,500,000 in bonuses.

Did I read that correctly?

A. Yes.

Q. And Crown is an imprint of Penguin Random House; is that correct?

A. That's correct.

Q. In the second-to-last line of this paragraph, you write: They will not go back to Crown if we offer $8 million for world English rights.

Did I read that correctly?

A. You did.

MR. VERNON: The United States, Your Honor, moves to admit PX643.

THE COURT: Any objection?

MR. FISHBEIN: No objection.

THE COURT: That will be admitted. Thank you. (Plaintiff's Exhibit PX643 received into evidence.)

BY MR. VERNON:

Q. You were concerned that the agent would go back to Crown if Simon & Schuster did not offer $8 million for this book; is that correct?

A. Yes. I also think that the reason it wasn't exactly between us and Crown is because anybody could have offered for an artist of this magnitude. And so when we were making our offer, it was a nine-month lag. I had a feeling that there was a possibility that we were going to have to increase our offer. In this case, it was Crown, but it really could have been anybody.

Q. Let me ask you to turn to PX613. And before we do that, can I just say, let's not show this document on the public screen, if we can turn it off, because there's one thing that we just don't want to show, but I think we can talk about it in open court. So can you turn it to PX613 in your binder. And let me know when you're there.

A. 613?

Q. Right, 613.

A. Okay.

Q. PX613 is an email with the top email from you to Ms. Reidy dated November 7th, 2019. Do you see that?

A. Yes.

Q. And this is about the same book, book 58?

A. Yes.

Q. In your email at the top, the only paragraph, the second line down, you write: I'm concerned that if we offer less than $8 million, the agency will go back to PRH. She said they were willing to offer more. Did I read that correctly?

A. You did.

MR. VERNON: The United States moves to admit PX613.

THE COURT: Any objection?

MR. FISHBEIN: No objection.

THE COURT: That will be admitted. (Plaintiff's Exhibit PX613 received into evidence.)

BY MR. VERNON:

Q. Competition from Penguin Random House was directly relevant to your reasoning when you decided to increase the offer from $6 million to $8 million, correct?

A. Well, it's more complex than that. I've been after this author for almost 12 years. I actually made an offer for this author when I was working for Hachette. I'd offered $5 million then.

People have been after pursuing this author for decades. And I believe that the literary agent in this deal was going to negotiate hard regardless of who the competitor was. As I said, in this instance, it happened to be Penguin Random House, but it could have just as easily been someone else.

Q. Let me ask you to turn to your day 2 of your CID deposition transcript. So there's three deposition transcripts in the back; it's the second one. Before I point you to a specific page, can I ask you, fair to say

I did take your deposition in this case?
A. Oh, it was—yes, that's very fair, it was about 14 hours.
Q. That's okay. Touché.
A. Day 2?
Q. It's day 2.
A. Okay. I see it. I'm there.
Q. It's the one that starts August 13th. And you were under oath for that deposition?
A. Yes.
Q. Let me ask you to turn to page 368, line 17 through 24. Let me know when you're there; I'll turn to them.
A. 353?
Q. 368.
A. 368. Okay. I'm there.
Q. Lines 17 through 24: Question: Was competition from Penguin Random House irrelevant to Simon & Schuster's reasoning when it increased its offer for the author from $6 million to $8 million?
Answer: The competitive offer was directly relevant.
Did I read that correctly?
A. You did.
MR. VERNON: The United States moves to admit this both for impeachment and for the substance of the testimony.
MR. FISHBEIN: Your Honor, I would object because the answer continues on 369 in a way that I believe is not inconsistent with his testimony. So he should be able to at least—
THE COURT: Just a moment. Can I read that?
The objection is overruled. I'm going to admit it for the purposes stated by the government. I don't see that as being consistent with what he said here, okay?
BY MR. VERNON:
Q. In your mind, Penguin Random House was the stalking horse that the agent used to increase Simon & Schuster's offer from $6 million to $8 million, correct?
A. Well, I do say in this deposition that I think it is consistent. I knew when I started that we probably weren't going to get it for $5 million. It was just a matter of time. It was a matter of how far we got pulled up. It happened to be in this case Penguin Random House was the manipulative stalking horse to pull us up. It could have been anybody. That's what I said.
Q. But for this book, in your mind, Penguin Random House was the stalking horse that the agent used to increase the offer from 6 to 8; is that correct?
A. Yes.
Q. And author 58, this author did agree to publish this book with Simon & Schuster; is that right?
A. Yes.
Q. Let me ask you about book 41.
THE COURT: And I just want to note for the record that in the first testimony for Mr. Karp, he denied that the Penguin Random House offer was directly relevant and that's why I think that that was properly admitted because you admit it in your deposition—
THE WITNESS: All right.
THE COURT:—that it was directly relevant.
THE WITNESS: I apologize.
THE COURT: I just want to note for the record my ruling. All right. Go ahead.
BY MR. VERNON:
Q. Let me ask you about book 41, Mr. Karp. And let me ask you to turn to, in your binder, to PX557. Let me know when you're ready and I'll take a second to get there too.
A. PX41?
Q. 557, I think it's the second one from the front.
A. It says PX43. And I see PX34.

THE COURT: The second tab.
MR. VERNON: 557.
THE COURT: 557.
THE WITNESS: Oh, 557. I'm sorry.
MR. VERNON: No. That's okay. It's a big binder. It's true.
THE WITNESS: I'm there.
MR. VERNON: Your Honor, we have prepared a redacted version of this document. May we show it to the public?
THE COURT: You may.
BY MR. VERNON:
Q. Mr. Karp, this is an email chain with the top email from Mr. Dohle to you, dated February 26th, 2020; is that right?
A. Yes.
Q. And this email chain relates to the bidding for book 41; is that correct?
A. Yes.
Q. Let me ask you to turn to page 6, which ends in the Bates number at the bottom of 500.
A. Okay.
Q. About halfway or a little more than halfway down, there is an email from the agent for this book; is that right?
A. Yes.
Q. And the agent writes that the auction is down—and I'm paraphrasing here—that the auction is down to two bidders; is that correct?
A. Yes.
Q. And you later learned that the other bidder was Penguin Random House; is that right?
A. I'd just like to take a moment to read this if that's okay.
Q. That's fine.
A. Can you please repeat your question.
Q. Sure. You later learned, after the email on page 6, that the other bidder for this book was Penguin Random House; is that fair?
A. I believe I learned it after the auction was over.
Q. Okay.
A. I'm not 100 percent sure, but I believe that I learned it after the auction was over.
Q. Going back to this email, the agent writes—and, again, I'm paraphrasing—that the high bid was currently 645, so Simon & Schuster would need to bid $665,000 to stay in the auction. Is that correct?
A. Yes.
Q. And in the next email up, there's an email from Ms. Callahan, who's an editor, I think, at Simon & Schuster; is that right?
A. Yes.
Q. She bids $665,000; is that right?
A. Right.
Q. Let me ask you to turn to the next page, 499.
At the bottom of page 499, there's another email from the agent who says, the auction is back to you—again, I'm paraphrasing—at $685,000. Simon & Schuster needs to bid 705 to stay in. Is that right?
A. Right.
Q. And then at the very top of this page, Ms. Callahan bids $705,000; is that right?
A. Right.
Q. And after that, Simon & Schuster and the other bidder go back and forth a couple more times; is that fair?
A. Yes.
MR. VERNON: The United States moves to admit PX557.
THE COURT: Any objection?

MR. FISHBEIN: No objection.
THE COURT: That's admitted. (Plaintiff's Exhibit PX557 received into evidence.)
BY MR. VERNON:
Q. Let me ask you to turn to PX588. And let me know when you're there.
A. Okay.
Q. This is an email chain with the top email from Ms. Reidy to you, dated February 26th, 2020; is that right?
A. Right.
MR. VERNON: Your Honor, we have prepared a redacted version. May we show it to the public?
THE COURT: You may.
BY MR. VERNON:
Q. And this email also relates to the bidding for the same book, book 41; is that correct?
A. Right.
Q. Let me ask you to focus on the email from you that is second from the top, do you see that, to Ms. Reidy?
A. Yes.
Q. You write in this email: We were bidding only against Dial/Random for three rounds from $650,000 onward. We asked the agent to go to best bids and he refused. We matched at $805,000 and Random added $20,000 dollars and won. Did I read that correctly?
A. You did.
Q. And you referred to Dial and Random. Those are imprints of Penguin Random House; is that correct?
A. Yes.
Q. So what you know now is the only bidders for the last several rounds of the auction for this book were Simon & Schuster and Penguin Random House; is that fair?
A. Fair.
Q. And your email states that near the end of the auction, Random House offered $805,000; is that correct?
A. Yes.
Q. And then Simon & Schuster matched the $805,000 offer; is that correct?
A. We did.
Q. And after that Random House, increased its offer to 825 and won; is that correct?
A. That's correct. It's worth noting there were several other bidders in this auction, though, before it reached that final level between the two of us.
Q. Let me ask you this. You think that during the last several rounds of this auction, competition between Penguin Random House and Simon & Schuster pushed up the advance from $650,000 to $825,000, correct?
A. That's what happened.
Q. Okay.
MR. VERNON: The United States moves to admit PX588.
THE COURT: Any objection?
MR. FISHBEIN: No objection, Your Honor.
THE COURT: That's admitted. Thank you. (Plaintiff's Exhibit PX588 received into evidence.)
BY MR. VERNON:
Q. Let me try to ask you about the next book which is going to be book 39. And I'll do this. Let's turn to PX700 in your binder. And let me know when you're there.
A. All right. I'm there.
MR. VERNON: Your Honor, we have prepared a redacted version. May we show it to the public?
THE COURT: You may.
BY MR. VERNON:
Q. Mr. Karp, this is an email chain with the top email from Ms. Reidy to you, dated February 22nd,

2019; is that correct?
A. Yes.
Q. Let me ask you to focus on the second email, which is from you, towards the top. You write: The auction for book 39 went on all week. There were initially seven bidders from 11 imprints, including Gallery and Atria. Do you see that?
A. Yes.
Q. And Gallery and Atria, those are two imprints of Simon & Schuster; is that right?
A. Yes.
Q. You then write: "Gallery dropped out at $750,000. It was down to PRH and Atria in the final best bid part of the auction, with the high bid at the time being $1.1 million." Did I read that correctly?
A. You did.
Q. Then you write: Libby—and Libby refers to Libby McGuire; is that correct?
A. Correct.
Q. She is the publisher of Atria; is that right?
A. Yes.
Q. "Libby and I decided to go all the way to the approved $1.5 million level because that was always our number. We didn't want to risk losing it, and Libby remained confident throughout the process. We won." Did I read that correctly?
A. You did.
Q. So this—the auction for this book initially included several publishers; is that correct?
A. Eleven imprints, seven bidders.
Q. The only two bidders in the final round were Penguin Random House and Simon & Schuster, is that right?
A. This is written after the fact. I didn't know that the other bidder was Penguin Random House, but, yes, we were the only two bidders at the very end.
Q. The high bid prior to the final round was $1.1 million; is that right?
A. Yes. And the agent went to the best bids.
Q. During the final round, Simon & Schuster increased its bid from $1.1 million, or possibly less, to $1.5 million; is that correct?
A. It's correct because that was the number we had in our heads all along. And we were looking straight ahead, we weren't looking at the competition. We just wanted to publish this book.
Q. And Simon & Schuster won this book; is that correct?
A. We did.
MR. VERNON: The United States moves to admit PX700.
THE COURT: Any objection?
MR. FISHBEIN: No objection.
THE COURT: That's admitted. (Plaintiff's Exhibit PX700 received into evidence.)
BY MR. VERNON:
Q. Let me ask you now about book 48. And I think the easiest way to do this is to ask you to turn to PX632 in your binder. And let me know when you're ready.
A. Okay.
MR. VERNON: Your Honor, we have prepared a redacted version. May we show it to the public?
THE COURT: Yes, you may.
BY MR. VERNON:
Q. This is an email chain where the top email is from Amy Bell to you, dated June 8th, 2020; is that right?
A. Yes.
Q. About halfway down this first page, there is an email from Ms. Bell; is that correct?
A. Yes.
Q. And she is an editor at Simon & Schuster; is that fair?
A. Yes.

Q. She writes, and I'm paraphrasing, that the auction is down to two bidders; is that correct?
A. Correct.
Q. And at this time, you didn't know who the other bidder was; is that fair?
A. Yes.
Q. But after this, you did go back and forth against that other publisher; is that correct?
A. Correct.
Q. So here, Ms. Bell states that after Simon & Schuster bid $525,000, the other bidder matched Simon & Schuster's $525,000 offer; is that correct?
A. Correct.
Q. And then after the other bidder matched Simon & Schuster's $525,000 offer, Simon & Schuster increased its bid to $535,000 and added two bonuses totaling $100,000; is that correct?
A. Correct.
Q. And then Simon & Schuster won the book; is that right?
A. We did.
MR. VERNON: United States moves to admit PX32.
THE COURT: Any objection?
MR. FISHBEIN: No objection.
THE COURT: That will be admitted. (Plaintiff's Exhibit PX32 received into evidence.)
BY MR. VERNON:
Q. Next book I want to ask you about is book 38. Simon & Schuster bid on book 38; is that correct?
A. Correct.
Q. Let me ask you to turn to PX716. Let me know when you're there.
A. I'm here.
MR. VERNON: Your Honor, we have prepared a redacted version. May we publish to the public?
THE COURT: You may.
BY MR. VERNON:
Q. This an email chain with the top email from you dated November 3rd, 2018, to Ms. Reidy; is that right?
A. Yes.
Q. In your email at the top, you write, we were even with Penguin Press on a book at $750,000 and lost. Do you see that?
A. Yes.
Q. And you also forwarded an auction chart that the agent emailed you; is that correct?
A. Yes.
Q. Can you turn to the next page. And the next page, there is—what appears to be a chart; is that fair?
A. Yes.
Q. The chart shows seven publishers on the left; is that right?
A. I see eight.
Q. Eight. I'm sorry. And at the bottom, it says Houghton Mifflin. Do you see that?
A. Yes.
Q. Is that HMH?
A. Yes.
Q. The other seven publishers are all imprints of the Big 5; is that fair?
A. That's correct.
Q. And this chart shows that for the last two rounds of this auction, meaning rounds four and five, the only bidders were Penguin Random House and Simon & Schuster; is that correct?
A. That is correct.
Q. May I ask you another question. Penguin Random—
MR. VERNON: I'm sorry, Your Honor, the United States moves to admit PX716.
THE COURT: Any objection?
MR. FISHBEIN: No objection, Your Honor.

THE COURT: That will be admitted. (Plaintiff's Exhibit PX716 received into evidence.)

BY MR. VERNON:

Q. Simon & Schuster lost three books to Penguin Random House in one week; is that correct?

A. Is there a document?

Q. We can go to a document. And you can set that one aside. Let me ask you to turn to PX559. Let me know when you're there.

A. I'm there.

MR. VERNON: Your Honor, we have prepared a redacted version. May we publish?

THE COURT: You may.

BY MR. VERNON:

Q. This an email chain, with the top email from you to Ms. Reidy, dated September 27th, 2019; is that fair?

A. Yes.

Q. In this email, you write in the second paragraph: This was the third beauty contest we lost this week to PRH.

Do you see that?

A. I do.

Q. And a beauty contest is a situation where two publishers' offers for the same book are similar financially and the publishers then compete on non-financial terms or factors to win the book; is that correct?

A. Pulchritude.

Q. Pulchritude?

A. Yes, it's beauty.

Q. Beauty. Okay. I should have guessed that you would have a big vocabulary as the head of a publishing house. As an example, in a beauty contest, Simon & Schuster and Penguin Random House might try to compete to convince the author that they will do the best job marketing a book; is that fair?

A. That they have the best vision for publishing the book overall. It could be many things. Sometimes it's the editorial connection. Sometimes it is the marketing or the publicity. Sometimes it's just the sum of the enthusiasm that the house has.

Q. And in this email, you state that Simon & Schuster lost three beauty contests in one week to Penguin Random House; is that fair?

A. It was an ugly week. But you'll also find emails bemoaning losses to HarperCollins and Macmillan and our other competitors.

Q. I understand. Just since we have limited time, let me ask you to try to focus on my question, and then I'm sure your counsel will be able to ask you about that?

A. You got it.

Q. Let me ask you to turn to PX624.

MR. VERNON: Your Honor, I'm sorry, the United States moves to admit PX559. I think there are no objections.

THE COURT: Any objection?

MR. FISHBEIN: No objection.

THE COURT: That will be admitted. (Plaintiff's Exhibit PX559 received into evidence.)

BY MR. VERNON:

Q. Back on PX624, this is an email chain with the top email from you, dated June 16th, 2019; is that right?

A. Yes.

MR. VERNON: Your Honor, we have prepared a redacted version. May we show it to the public?

THE COURT: You may.

BY MR. VERNON:

Q. This email relates to book 55; is that correct?

A. It does.

Q. And for this book, you did everything that you could and you lost to Random House; is that correct?
A. That is correct.
Q. And Random House is a part of Penguin Random House; is that correct?
A. Yes.
Q. And you found that frustrating; is that right?
A. I found it frustrating until the book came out, and then I was relieved because it lost a lot of money and it sort of proves how you never really know anything.
MR. VERNON: The United States moves to admit PX624. I believe there are no objections.
THE COURT: Any objection?
MR. FISHBEIN: No objection.
THE COURT: Okay. That will be admitted. (Plaintiff's Exhibit PX624 received into evidence.)
BY MR. VERNON:
Q. Let me ask you about book 44. Oh, I'm sorry, I'm referring to the confidentiality.
A. Right.
Q. Do you see that book 44?
A. Oh, yes.
Q. Do you remember that one?
A. I remember that one, too.
Q. Penguin Random House and Simon & Schuster competed for this book; is that fair?
A. There were other bidders, too.
Q. But you did compete with Penguin Random House; is that correct?
A. We found out after the fact that we were competing with them, yes.
Q. Okay. Let me ask you to turn to PX569. And let me know when you're ready.
MR. VERNON: Your Honor, we have prepared a redacted version. May we show it to the public?
THE COURT: Yes, you may.
THE WITNESS: Okay. I'm there.
BY MR. VERNON:
Q. This is an email chain with the top email from you, dated June 30, 2020; is that right?
A. Right.
Q. Let me ask you to turn to the second page. The bottom of this page, there's an email from Dawn Davis. Do you see that?
A. Yes.
Q. At this time, Ms. Davis was an editor at Simon & Schuster; is that fair?
A. Yes
Q. She writes: Just spoke to the agent and went to 600 as the other player was at 575. The one other offer is on behalf of one bidder.
Did I read that correctly?
A. That's right.
Q. So by the time that Simon & Schuster offered $600,000 for this book, the only bidders were Simon & Schuster and one other publisher; is that right?
A. That is fair. It's also fair that our top number in this auction was 750.
Q. And you later learned that the other publisher that you were bidding against at this point was Penguin Random House; is that fair?
A. We learned after the auction was over that they went higher than we did.
Q. Let me ask you—
A. Our top number, we stayed actually at our top number. I don't think we got pulled up by them.
Q. Let me ask you to turn to page 1.
A. Page 1? I'm sorry, the document.
Q. The first page.
A. Yes.
Q. At the bottom, there's another email from Ms. Davis. Do you see that?

A. Yes.
Q. She writes that the other publisher has advanced to 625. Is that fair?
A. Yes.
Q. And she writes that Simon & Schuster is advancing to 650. Is that right?
A. That's right.
Q. And then after that, the agent called for best bids; is that right?
A. Right.
Q. And as you alluded to earlier, after the agent called for best bids, Simon & Schuster increased its offer to $750,000; is that correct?
A. Yes. I wrote: We all thought it was worth 750, so I'm okay with going there if that's what you want to do.
Q. And then Simon & Schuster lost this book to Penguin Random House; is that correct?
A. That's correct.
Q. It was Viking, I think, was the imprint?
A. Yes.
MR. VERNON: United States moves to admit PX569, and I believe there are no objections.
MR. FISHBEIN: No objection.
THE COURT: All right. That will be admitted. (Plaintiff's Exhibit PX569 received into evidence.)
BY MR. VERNON:
Q. Let me walk you through one more book. I'm going to ask you about book 30, and I think I'll do that by referring you to PX729.
A. PX729.
Q. It's maybe about two-thirds of the way back.
A. I see it.
MR. VERNON: Your Honor, we have prepared a redacted version. May we show it to the public?
THE COURT: You may.
BY MR. VERNON:
Q. This is an email chain where the top email is from you to Ms. Reidy dated March 7th, 2018; is that correct?
A. Yes.
Q. This relates to the bidding for book 30; is that correct?
A. Yes.
Q. At the top of your email the very first paragraph, you write: Carolyn, we're finally at the end of the author 30 auction. We took a $750,000 floor with 10 percent topping. The author met with other publishers and Portfolio offered $1 million for world. To win the book, we'll have to offer $1.1 million. Did I read that correctly?
A. Yes.
Q. Let me see if I can break this down. Simon & Schuster initially offered $750,000 for the book; is that correct?
A. I think we might have even started lower than that before there was a book proposal. But in this iteration of the memo you're reading, yes, it's at that level.
Q. And just try to simplify it. At some point, Simon & Schuster bid 750 for this book; is that fair?
A. Yes.
Q. After Simon & Schuster offered—
THE COURT: Sorry, can I just ask: What does 10 percent topping mean?
THE WITNESS: 10 percent topping means that wherever the auction ended, no matter who else was bidding, we would have the right to own the book if we agreed to pay 10 percent more.
THE COURT: Thank you.
BY MR. VERNON:
Q. Portfolio made the highest bid in the auction; is that right?
A. They did.

Q. And Portfolio is an imprint of Penguin Random House; is that right?
A. Yes.
Q. Portfolio bid $1 million for the book; is that correct?
A. Yes.
Q. And after that Simon & Schuster exercised the topping privileges; is that fair?
A. Yes.
Q. So Simon & Schuster offered $1.1 million; is that correct?
A. We did.
Q. And then Simon & Schuster won; is that fair?
A. Yes.
Q. And just to simplify it a little more, initially, or at least at some point, Simon & Schuster offered 750, then Penguin Random House offered a million, then Simon & Schuster offered $1.1 million; is that correct?
A. Right. We thought we were going to get pulled up, but the author had been with us his whole career and so he tested the market with our blessing, which ended—it was an amicable understanding that we had.
Q. One of the reasons that you offered $1.1 million for the book was that you did not want to let Penguin Random House steal an author that you had invested in and developed; is that fair?
A. Well, I list three points in this memo. That was the least important point. In this case, it happened to be PRH, but I wouldn't have wanted to lose this author to anybody, he's a young, promising author. So you're right on the facts, but I don't agree on the context.
Q. Let me just read the document. In the second paragraph, you say: I think we should top Portfolio for the following reasons. Do you see that?
A. Yes.
Q. And then the third reason says: Three, I don't want to let PRH steal an author we've invested in and developed. Did I read that correctly?
A. Absolutely right. We also believed the book was a stronger book, and that he was going to have a long career. Those are the two more important reasons.
MR. VERNON: The United States moves to admit PX729.
THE COURT: Any objection?
MR. FISHBEIN: No objection.
THE COURT: That will be admitted. (Plaintiff's Exhibit PX729 received into evidence.)
BY MR. VERNON:
Q. Let me step back and ask you about competition overall.
When Simon & Schuster is competing to acquire books, the publishers that it bids against most frequently are Penguin Random House, HarperCollins, Hachette and Macmillan; is that correct?
A. Well, we compete against a broad range of publishers. At the higher end, those are the ones who are most often there, but we compete against a much broader range than the ones you mentioned; and any one of them is capable of winning the book in the end.
Q. Let me try to ask again. When Simon & Schuster is competing to acquire books, the publishers that it competes against most frequently are Penguin Random House, HarperCollins, Hachette, and Macmillan; is that correct?
A. It seems to be that way at the higher end.
Q. Let me ask you to look back at your CID deposition, day two, page 459. I'm going to point you to line 6 through 11 and let me know when you're there.
A. 459?
Q. Right.
A. Okay.
Q. Mr. Read's question: I'll try to be more precise. Are the other Big 5 publishers in your experience the competitors against which Simon & Schuster bids most frequently for author acquisitions? Answer: Yes. Did I read that correctly?

A. You did.

MR. VERNON: United States moves to admit this testimony for impeachment and as a party admission.

THE COURT: Any objection?

MR. FISHBEIN: Your Honor, I do have an objection to the party admission. I believe this is the CID deposition at which the adverse party is not allowed to cross-examine and essentially not allowed to object. This is during the investigation. It's not like a deposition where the represented party can object and ask questions. So I'm not sure that—

THE COURT: What would have been the basis of an objection to this?

MR. FISHBEIN: I'm sorry?

THE COURT: What would have been a basis of an objection to this?

MR. FISHBEIN: No, only that it's coming in as the truth. In other words, a prior consistent statement—a prior inconsistent statement is for impeachment unless it's under oath, subject to cross-examination.

THE COURT: Was this under oath?

MR. FISHBEIN: It was under oath, but it was not subject to cross-examination. I think it's not like a regular litigation.

THE COURT: I don't think it has to be a subject of cross-examination, because grand jury is admissible.

MR. FISHBEIN: I'm sorry?

THE COURT: I don't think it needs to be subject to cross-examine because grand jury testimony is admissible.

MR. FISHBEIN: Well, Your Honor—

THE COURT: So your objection is overruled.

MR. FISHBEIN: Okay.

BY MR. VERNON:

Q. Penguin Random House, HarperCollins, Hachette, and Macmillan and Simon & Schuster are sometimes referred to as the Big 5; is that fair?

A. Yes.

Q. In your experience, the other Big 5 publishers are the publishers that Simon & Schuster loses to most frequently; is that correct?

A. That seems to be the case, yes.

Q. Let me ask you about why that seems to be the case. It's fair to say that the Big 5 publishers have certain advantages over smaller publishers; is that correct?

A. What do you mean by advantages?

Q. I'll be a little more specific. Big 5 publishers have an advantage in publishing new print bestselling books because of their marketing and publicity assets; is that correct?

A. I think that that is a prevailing piece of conventional wisdom. And I'm not going to disagree. I do think that a lot of us believe that a good editor, a good publicist, and a sales rep is enough. So there are some people who believe you need a lot of people to publish a lot of books, but I also think that a smaller publisher can be just as effective for any given book.

Q. Setting aside the editorial issue that you mentioned, it's fair to say that one advantage that Big 5 publishers have over other publishers in publishing new print bestselling books, they have an advantage because of their marketing and publicity assets; is that correct?

A. I think some people think that, yes.

Q. Let me ask you what you think. Is it fair to say you think that Big 5 publishers have an advantage in publishing new print bestselling books because of their marketing and publicity assets; is that correct?

A. I think that now, but if I were working for a small publisher, I might think that I'd be just as good.

Q. Okay. But you do agree, you think Big 5 publishers have an advantage in publishing new print bestselling books because of their marketing and publicity assets, fair?

A. It's not the way I put it, but I can't disagree with you.

Q. I just want to see if I can understand. You do agree Big 5 publishers have an advantage in publishing new print bestselling books because of their marketing and publicity assets; is that correct?

A. I'm not trying to be difficult. I think that anybody can publish a book well. So I don't know what you mean by having an advantage. An advantage over who, the smaller publishers?

Q. Let me ask you to turn to day one of your CID deposition, page 250, lines 2 through 8.

A. Which page?

Q. 250. Let me know when you're there. This reads: It sounds like you're—it is your testimony that at least for print books that are new books, the Big 5 publishers do have an advantage in making those books into bestsellers because of their publicity and marketing assets; is that correct? Answer: That's correct. Did I read that correctly?

A. Yes.

MR. VERNON: The United States moves to admit this for impeachment and as a party admission.

THE COURT: Any objection?

MR. FISHBEIN: Your Honor, when he asked the question, he did not include the part about making it a bestseller. I'm not trying to quibble, but I think there could be a difference. I mean, the witness said, as a general matter. The question in the deposition is making it to bestsellers. So maybe he could ask witness that way, and then if it's inconsistent, he can use it.

THE COURT: Your objection is overruled. Based on the context of the testimony, this is inconsistent.

BY MR. VERNON:

Q. Focusing for a moment on Simon & Schuster, Simon & Schuster's track record of success can also give it a competitive advantage in acquiring books; is that correct?

A. Yes.

Q. You have described Simon & Schuster as having decades of credibility and success for nonfiction books; is that correct?

A. Yes.

Q. And having decades of credibility and success can be a helpful selling point with authors at times; is that correct?

A. Correct.

Q. And Simon & Schuster is particularly strong as a publisher for certain categories of books; is that fair?

A. Yes.

Q. For example, Simon & Schuster is particularly strong for biographies and memoirs; is that correct?

A. Yes, and we're getting stronger in a lot of other categories.

Q. Well, like what?

A. Well, we just started a practical nonfiction lifestyle imprint.

Q. Simon & Schuster is also particularly strong for nonfiction books on current events, politics and history; is that right?

A. Yes.

Q. Now, let me ask you to turn back to the advantages that Simon & Schuster has. You have described the publishing business as having a portfolio business model; is that right?

A. Right.

Q. And the portfolio model refers to publishers publishing a broad range of books by a variety of different imprints; is that correct?

A. Correct.

Q. Fair to say there is a risk inherent in every book that Simon & Schuster publishes?

A. Well, I think that you never know how many copies you're going to sell, and so I do think that there are risks, some are bigger than others.

Q. It's fair to say there's a risk that when Simon & Schuster pays a significant advance and the book does not sell well, Simon & Schuster could lose money; is that correct?

A. That's correct.

Q. And having a broad range of books and imprints helps Simon & Schuster manage that risk; is that correct?

A. Yes.

Q. Okay. I've asked you a series of questions about publishers. Let me ask you a question about self-publishing. Self-publishing is definitely not a big threat to Simon & Schuster, correct?
A. Well, my view has changed on that since our deposition.
Q. Well, let me ask you first. You did testify at your deposition, I asked you if you would say that self-publishing was a big threat to Simon & Schuster and you testified that you would not say that at all; is that correct?
A. I said that then, and some things have happened since then that have made me change my thinking.
Q. And at the time of your deposition, you've been in the business for approximately 30 years; is that correct?
A. That's right.
Q. Let me ask you now about Amazon. Simon & Schuster does not frequently compete with Amazon to acquire books; is that correct?
A. Well, that's one of the things that's changed actually. And as recently as three weeks ago, we were in a seven-figure auction with Amazon. So I know that I have some prior statements about that, but I don't feel that way anymore.
Q. You did testify in your deposition that Simon & Schuster does not frequently compete with Amazon to acquire books; is that correct?
A. I said that and we were in a seven-figure auction with them just three weeks ago.
Q. Let me ask you a few more questions about how competition works. In your experience when Simon & Schuster is competing with other publishers to win a book, the term that is most important is the advance; is that correct?
A. I think you'd have to say that's correct.
Q. Authors do not frequently turn down offers with a higher advance because they want to accept offers with better royalty rate terms; is that correct?
A. Well, there are some authors who would rather have higher royalty rates. So I would say they're in the minority, but there are some.
Q. So it's fair to say then that authors do not frequently turn down offers with a higher advance because they want to accept offers with better royalty rate terms; is that correct?
A. Correct.
Q. Focusing again on advances, fair to say the advances that Simon & Schuster offers are based on how many books it predicts it will sell; is that correct?
A. That's the main factor. But we also have estimates for subsidiary rights, which can add to the value of the offer.
Q. Is it fair to say that if everything else is equal, when Simon & Schuster anticipates that a book will sell better, Simon & Schuster will be more willing to pay a higher advance; is that correct?
A. If everything—if what else is equal? You said if everything else is equal?
Q. I'm sorry, go ahead.
A. You said if everything else is equal. What do you mean?
Q. Everything else about the book that you mentioned subsidiary rights. If you hold subsidiary rights constant, it's fair to say that if Simon & Schuster anticipates that a book will sell better, it will be more willing to offer a higher advance; is that correct?
A. Yes.
Q. Your approval is required for any offer to acquire a book that includes an advance of $250,000 or higher; is that correct?
A. That's right.
Q. And Simon & Schuster editors have to write what's known as a justification memo for all books they acquire when the advance is $250,000 or higher; is that correct?
A. I believe that they have to write it if it's $200,000. I'm not 100 percent sure, but I think that if it's over 200, they have to write it.
Q. Let me ask you to refer to your litigation depo, which is the third depo in your binder, the last one, page 59. Let me know when you're there.

A. Okay.

Q. Lines 13 through 17, Question: And Simon & Schuster editors also have to write a memo when the advance is $250,000 or higher; is that correct? Answer: That is a justification memo, yes, that is correct.

Did I read that right?

A. Right. And since this, I think I was just misinformed when I said that to you. I think it actually is 200. But I'm not 100 percent sure. It's either 200 or 250, I can tell you that.

Q. Okay. Let me change topics and ask you about the relationship between advances and output. You have seen authors decide not to write a book because the advance they have been offered is not high enough; is that fair?

A. That's happened.

Q. Fair to say that happens every year; is that correct?

A. It happens every year? Well, I can think of one example, but I don't know if it happens every year.

Q. Let me ask you to turn to day one of your CID deposition, page 306. It's the first deposition tab.

A. Okay. Well, I said that. I didn't remember saying it.

Q. That's okay. Let me just read this for the record. Page 306, lines 7 through 17, this reads: Question: Have you seen instances in which an author, a person who was considering writing a book, doesn't obtain any type of advance they thought they would, and so they just don't write the book? Answer: Yes. Question: How common is that? Answer: Well, it happens. I don't know how many times a year it happens, but it certainly happens every year, something like that happens.

Do you see that?

A. Yes.

MR. VERNON: United States moves to admit this testimony for impeachment and as a party admission.

THE COURT: Any objection? All right. That will be admitted. (Plaintiff's Exhibit CID deposition, page 306, 7–17 received into evidence.)

BY MR. VERNON:

Q. This is an email chain where the top email is from you, dated January 26th, 2020; is that correct?

A. Yes.

Q. And we won't say the name, but in this email, you're discussing Simon & Schuster's efforts to acquire a specific book; is that fair?

A. That's fair.

Q. In the first paragraph starting at the top, halfway through the first line, you write: I believe the agent is telling you the truth when she says they can't do it for less than $350,000. Assume they're each making $150,000 a year and they want to take a full year off. They're just trying to break even after paying the commission. Did I read that correctly?

A. You did.

Q. So in this email what you are saying is that if the advance wasn't above $350,000, it wouldn't make financial sense for the people who are writing the book to take the year off and write the book; is that correct?

A. That's what I was thinking, yes.

MR. VERNON: The United States moves to admit PX656.

THE COURT: Any objection?

MR. FISHBEIN: No, no objection.

THE COURT: That will be admitted. (Plaintiff's Exhibit PX656 received into evidence.)

BY MR. VERNON:

Q. Let me change topics and ask you about bidding via imprints. First question: Simon & Schuster has many different imprints; is that fair?

A. It has many different imprints? Yes.

Q. And Simon & Schuster does not allow its imprints to bid separately for the same book; is that correct?

A. That's right, they all bid together.

Q. And you previously worked at Random House; is that correct?

A. Yes.

Q. When you worked at Random House, imprints within Random House were allowed to bid independently as long as there was an outside competitor bidding against them; is that correct?

A. That's correct.

Q. And you believe that having multiple imprints from the same publisher bidding on the same book rarely drives up the advance for that book; is that correct?

A. Having multiple imprints—can you just repeat the question, I'm sorry.

Q. Sure. You believe that having multiple imprints from the same publisher bidding on the same book rarely drives up the advance for that book, correct?

A. I've written that, yes.

MR. VERNON: Your Honor, let me pause for a second. I have a very small number of questions on efficiency that I think will take possibly a minute but less than five minutes. I spoke with Mr. Fishbein and asked him if it was okay if we do that now just so we don't have to bring Mr. Karp back for a short amount of time.

THE COURT: That's fine.

MR. VERNON: Okay.

BY MR. VERNON:

Q. Is it fair to say you were not closely involved in the work that Viacom did to analyze efficiencies; is that right?

A. That's correct.

Q. But you know that it's possible that a new owner of Simon & Schuster might lay off some Simon & Schuster employees; is that correct?

A. It's possible.

Q. And you think it would be very hard to prove that those layoffs would lead to higher advances for authors; is that correct?

A. I don't recall saying that, but if you have—you seem to have a lot of things of me saying things that I don't remember, so I'm hesitant to answer your question without knowing the context.

Q. Let me just ask you for your opinion. I mean, you think it would be very hard to prove that those layoffs, meaning layoffs after a merger, would lead to higher advances for authors, correct?

A. I don't think I know enough to answer that question.

Q. Okay. Well, let me ask you to turn to page 40 of your day one CID deposition and line 24. Let me know when you're there.

A. Okay.

Q. I'll start on line 23, actually. Question: Let me give you an example. So if after a merger, the new owner of Simon & Schuster lays off some of Simon & Schuster's employees, would that automatically mean that Simon & Schuster's authors or new authors would get higher advances, or is there no relationship? Answer: I think it would be very hard to prove any correlation. Did I read that correctly?

A. That's what I said.

MR. VERNON: The United States moves to admit this testimony for impeachment and as a party admission.

THE COURT: Any objection?

MR. FISHBEIN: Same objection as before, Your Honor.

THE COURT: All right. That's overruled. This will be admitted. (Plaintiff's Exhibit CID deposition and line 23 received into evidence.)

MR. VERNON: That'll be the end of my efficiencies section.

THE COURT: Thank you.

BY MR. VERNON:

Q. Simon & Schuster has had several very strong years recently; is that correct?

A. That's correct.

Q. For example, Simon & Schuster's sales in 2020 were its highest ever up until that year; is that right?

A. That's right.

Q. And in 2021, Simon & Schuster beat its sales record from 2020; is that correct?
A. Yes.
Q. And at your deposition earlier this year, you said that you thought Simon & Schuster was off to a strong start in 2022; is that correct?
A. Correct.
Q. And I think you gave an interview to the press where you said Simon & Schuster was defying gravity so far in 2022. Did I get that right?
A. Right.
Q. Fair to say Simon & Schuster has been a successful publisher for many years; is that correct?
A. Yes. 100 years. Well, actually, 98.
Q. Simon & Schuster is not struggling to compete, correct?
A. We are not.
Q. Simon & Schuster has not merged with Penguin Random House yet; is that fair?
A. Yes, that's fair.
Q. So Simon & Schuster has been successful for many years even though it has not yet merged with Penguin Random House; is that correct?
A. That's correct.
Q. And you think Simon & Schuster will be successful in the future even if it does not merge with Penguin Random House; is that correct?
A. Yes, I believe that Simon & Schuster is a strong company.
Q. And you believe Simon & Schuster will be successful in the future even if it does not merge with Penguin Random House; is that correct?
A. I believe that.
Q. Let me look at a few documents you wrote discussing the merger. Let me ask you to turn to PX655. Let me know when you're ready.
A. PX655, okay.
Q. It's about halfway through.
A. PX655. That's weird, I'm just having trouble finding it. Oh, I see what it is. Okay. Go ahead.
MR. VERNON: Your Honor, we've prepared a redacted version. May we show it to the public?
THE COURT: You may.
BY MR. VERNON:
Q. This is an email chain dated March 5th, 2020, where the top email from you to John Irving; is that correct?
A. That's right.
Q. Mr. Irving is your favorite author; is that correct?
A. Yes.
Q. You've had a working relationship with Mr. Irving for eight or nine years; is that fair?
A. Something like that. It might be a little longer. I've known him longer.
Q. In your email at the top, you write: Thanks, John, I'm pretty sure that the Department of Justice wouldn't allow Penguin Random House to buy us, but that's assuming we still have a Department of Justice. Did I read that correctly?
A. You read it exactly right, yes.
Q. And you wrote that because Penguin Random House was the largest trade book publisher, correct?
A. That's what I said, yes.
MR. VERNON: The United States moves to admit PX655.
THE COURT: Any objection?
MR. FISHBEIN: No objection.
THE COURT: That'll be admitted. (Plaintiff's Exhibit PX655 received into evidence.)
BY MR. VERNON:
Q. That wasn't the only time you questioned the idea of merging with a competitor, right?
A. I'm sorry?

Q. This PX655 was not the only time you questioned the idea of merging with a competitor; is that correct?
A. It was not the only time. I don't remember the other times.
Q. Let me ask you to turn to PX634.
A. Oh, okay. Okay.
MR. VERNON: Your Honor, the United States has prepared a redacted version. May we publish?
THE COURT: You may.
MR. VERNON: Let me just say a word about the redactions so I know we're not messing anything up. In the number two paragraph, there are some words that have been redacted here that I think I've cleared with Simon & Schuster's counsel that we say out loud but we couldn't change the redactions at the last minute.
THE COURT: Okay.
BY MR. VERNON:
Q. This is an email chain where the top email is from you dated, September 11, 2020; is that correct?
A. Correct.
Q. And you're emailing Alex Berkett; is that right?
A. Yes.
Q. He was the Viacom executive managing the sale process for Simon & Schuster; is that fair?
A. Yes.
Q. Halfway down the page, there's an email from you with two numbered paragraphs. Do you see that?
A. Yes.
Q. In the second paragraph, you refer to financial buyers. Do you see that?
A. Yes.
Q. Financial buyers are companies that do not already own a business that competes with Simon & Schuster, correct?
A. That's right.
Q. Strategic buyers are buyers that do own companies that compete with Simon & Schuster; is that fair?
A. Yes.
Q. You write here in this number two paragraph: "Although I really do understand why strategics are the most likely option, if there is a financial buyer who is willing to match the top bid, that outcome would be better for the employees of S&S, and arguably the larger book publishing ecosystem." Did I read that correctly?
A. Yes.
Q. And despite your concern about harm to the book publishing ecosystem, Viacom agreed to sell Simon & Schuster to your largest competitor, correct?
A. I'm not so sure that my concerns were a key factor in their decision.
Q. Fair to say Viacom did agree to sell Simon & Schuster to Simon & Schuster's largest competitor?
A. Yes.
MR. VERNON: The United States moves to admit PX634.
THE COURT: Any objection?
MR. FISHBEIN: No objection, Your Honor.
THE COURT: That will be admitted. (Plaintiff's Exhibit PX634 received into evidence.)
MR. VERNON: I apologize, I just don't remember. If I did not move to admit PX655, I would also move to admit that one.
THE COURT: I think you did move to admit. That will be admitted. (Plaintiff's Exhibit PX655 received into evidence.)
MR. VERNON: The United States passes the witness.
THE COURT: All right. Thank you.
MR. VERNON: Thank you, Mr. Karp.
MR. FISHBEIN: Your Honor, we have some binders as well.
THE COURT: All right. I'm glad we got rid of the plastic water bottles since we can't get rid of the

binders.

MR. FISHBEIN: Our binders are smaller.

THE COURT: Thank you.

CROSS-EXAMINATION
BY MR. FISHBEIN:

Q. Mr. Karp, let me ask you just, you addressed it a little bit, but a little background on Simon & Schuster. When was the company founded, how long has it been in business?

A. It was founded in 1924, by Richard Simon and Max Schuster.

Q. And just generally, briefly, can you explain to the Judge how it's organized, do you have divisions? What do you do?

A. Well, we have obviously adult publishing, children's publishing, audio books. We have international divisions in Canada, Australia, India, and the United Kingdom. And we also have a distribution business.

Q. There's been some discussion about imprints. Approximately how many imprints are there at Simon & Schuster?

A. About 50.

Q. And about how many new books do you publish each year?

A. About a thousand.

Q. Now, you mentioned that you had some operations outside the United States. What percentage roughly of your business is within the United States?

A. It's somewhere around 75 percent. Quite a lot of it.

Q. You know, since you became CEO, have you continued to be involved in the book acquisition process?

A. Yes.

Q. What are some of the significant books that you've published over your career, yourself, that you've been involved in?

A. Well, I've either edited or published books by Bob Woodward, John Irving, Walter Isaacson, Doris Goodwin, Susan Orlean, Hillary Clinton, John McCain, Ted Kennedy, Bruce Springsteen, Brian Grazer, and, since we're here, Ruth Bader Ginsburg. But she only did one book with us and she didn't like our cover and she overruled us.

Q. Mr. Karp, I'm going to ask you to just slow down a little bit.

A. Sorry.

Q. Especially when you're doing lists like that. The court reporter will appreciate it. How many books have you personally been involved in the acquisition of over your career?

A. More than a thousand.

Q. And now, did you personally acquire those or those include ones where you participated as a supervisor?

A. Oh, I'm sorry. I personally acquired hundreds. And I've supervised the acquisition of more than a thousand.

Q. The government showed you some emails where there were bidding between various publishers. Do you remember that?

A. Yes.

Q. And is it fair to call some of those are what we would call auctions; is that right?

A. That's right.

Q. Now, are there other ways that Simon & Schuster acquires books other than auctions?

A. Yes, there are at least three that I can think of. And there are more than 50 percent of the deals that we do. So one way is we're negotiating exclusively with an author who we've already published, so that's an option author. And a lot of our authors repeat, we place a real value on those relationships, we want them to continue book after book after book. So that's a big, big part of it.

The second way is we approach authors ourselves directly, sometimes before an agent is involved, but certainly before another publisher is involved. Simon & Schuster actually had its origins in going out and getting the books. There was a profile written of the founders in 1939 in *The New Yorker*, and 80 percent of the books that they acquired back then were their own ideas. So we still very much try to keep that spirit alive and we are going out and trying to find our own books, and those are also exclusive opportunities.

And then there are the books where the agents come to us exclusively because they think we're the right publisher or because the editor expressed interest in somebody.

Q. So I think you've mentioned three types of what you call exclusives, which I believe are options or where you approached the author exclusively or where the agent approaches you exclusively; is that right?

A. Right.

Q. And in an exclusive situation like that, are you responding when you're negotiating the advance to a bid from another publisher?

A. No.

Q. In that context, the exclusive, is there a runner-up bidder?

A. No.

Q. How do you set the advance level in an exclusive situation of the type that you just described?

A. It's a conversation with the author's representative, and we want to be fair so what we try to do is we try to give them a context for the offer that we're making, and that context is usually the sales of books that are either similar in subject matter or books that, I guess, that the author has published, maybe that would be another way. So if the author has a track record, we would look at the author's previous sales.

Sometimes also just sort of the tenor of the moment you're in can make a book seem more relevant or bigger.

Q. Now, we've also heard testimony in this case about a type of acquisition called a pre-empt. Are you familiar with that?

A. Yes.

Q. And I'm not going to ask you to describe it, we've heard about it. But in a pre-empt situation, are you responding to a bid from another publisher?

A. No, you're initiating a bid.

Q. And in a pre-empt situation, is there a runner-up bidder?

A. No.

Q. Now, with auctions, are they all the same type or are there different types?

A. They're different.

Q. What are the principal type of auctions?

A. Well, there are round robin auctions where you're finding out what the previous bid is and you're topping it. That's a common kind of auction.

There's also different kinds of best bids auctions. So there are gradations of bids where they'll do best bids once, twice, three times.

And then there's a one-time best bid where you don't know who you're competing against, how many people there are, you're just flying blind.

Q. And why is it that you're saying that you're flying blind in a best bid?

A. Because you have absolutely no idea what anybody else is doing.

Q. Now, I think you said less than half are auctions, but can you just explain a little bit on what basis are you saying that less than half of your acquisitions are auctions?

A. Well, the reason why I can say that with some confidence, is because we have so many repeat authors. And so a lot of the people who we publish year after year constitute a good part of our list. So those are continuing business relationships, where they're happy with us, we're happy with them, and we try to find a fair accommodation on the terms.

Q. Of the auctions, do you have any idea of sort of what portion are the best bid type where you said you were flying blind, as opposed to round robin, where you are informed about the level of other bidding?

A. I can't quantify it, but it does seem to me that more and more, we are in some version of a best bids auction.

Q. In your experience, Mr. Karp, in multi-bidder situations where you do get some insight into the levels of the other publishers, what level of variation, if any, is there between different offers that different publishers make for any given book?

A. There's a broad range of different offers.

Q. And to what do you attribute that? We're talking about the same book but you're saying there's a range of offers. Why is that?

A. Well, in a word, subjectivity. I think that people read differently, and they have different enthusiasms, they have different interests and they have different metabolic reactions to the book.

But I also think that certain editors and publishers have a kind of inner confidence about certain kinds of books. And so sometimes they'll bid more because they've had success with a certain kind of book. Conversely, they may bid more because they really want to carve a niche that they haven't yet succeeded at. So sometimes people pay more because they have a lot of books like that, and other times they pay more because they don't have any books like that.

Q. Mr. Karp, does the advance level that an author receives predict whether the book will be successful?

A. I wish it did but it doesn't.

Q. And I'm going to ask you to give an example and you can name a book and an author, but I don't want you to give specific advance amounts. We're going to talk about general ranges of advance amounts, okay?

A. Sure. Early in my career, I acquired a book about horse racing by a writer named Laura Hillenbrand, called *Sea Biscuit*, and it was actually sold for well under the number that this.

Q. $250,000?

A. Yes, well under that. And a lot of the conventional wisdom in the publishing world was that books on horse racing don't sell. But I was too young to know that. And it was actually a phenomenal best seller. It was an instant number one best seller, it sold millions of copies. So that was an example.

Q. And what about the other way. I think when the government was asking you questions, there was one where you said the bids were high and it ended up not being successful. Are there any that you've been involved in? And, again, don't say anything specific about the advance amount.

A. Well, actually, there was more than one that the government mentioned but I didn't want to interrupt him.

Q. Okay. Anyway, can you just give an example of a type of book?

A. Sure. There was a book by a spiritual leader who had an Internet following in the millions, and our offer was over seven figures as well, and unfortunately his following did not follow him to the bookstores.

Q. Now, Mr. Karp, you've been talking with the government also about sort of your method, your approach to acquiring books. Is that something that you've discussed with the editors and publishers at Simon & Schuster, giving them guidance about book acquisition?

A. Yes.

Q. Let me show you what is marked as Defense Exhibit 71, it's tab 1 in the binders, and just let me know when you have that. Do you have that, Mr. Karp?

A. Yes.

Q. This is an email from you to a group of people, it's dated November 17th, 2019. Did you recognize the email?

A. I do.

Q. The subject is Guideline for Editors on Acquisitions. Do you see that?

A. Yes.

MR. FISHBEIN: Your Honor, I offer Defense Exhibit 71.

THE COURT: Any objection? 71 is admitted. (Defendants Exhibit 71 received into evidence.)

BY MR. FISHBEIN:

Q. Mr. Karp, in the "to" line, there's a list of people, Jennifer Bergstrom, Jofie Ferrari-Adler, Nan Graham, Libby McGuire, et cetera. Who are they?

A. These are the publishers of our various imprints.

Q. And what does that mean, to be—I think we've heard about editors. Can you explain to the Judge what a publisher of an imprint is?

A. The publishers are the deciders. They're the people who the editors come to when they want to sign up a book.

Q. And in the first line of this email here, it says: "Thanks for the good conversation on Friday." Do you know what that refers to?

A. Yes, we have a monthly meeting of our publishers.

Q. And the subject matter of this email, Guidelines for Editors on Acquisitions, has that been the subject of discussion at your publisher meetings?

A. Yes.

Q. Directing your attention to the number list. Do you see the No. 1 on the first page there?

A. Uh-huh.

Q. And if you could just read the first two sentences there out loud.

A. "You will be rewarded for enterprise and imagination and for creating your own opportunities. The highest praise will go to those who make things happen and acquire projects before they are submitted widely."

Q. Is that something you've discussed with the publishers at Simon & Schuster?

A. Yes.

Q. And what do you mean by that?

A. Well, I mean I want them to show initiative, think for themselves, have their own ideas, go out and find writers who excite them.

Q. And then if you look at the second paragraph, you write: "Whether or not there is wisdom in crowds, being part of a pack is not the best way to distinguish yourself." Do you see that?

A. Yes.

Q. And has that been the subject of conversations that you've had with publishers at Simon & Schuster?

A. It is.

Q. And what did you mean by that?

A. Well, I meant that when you're just reacting to the crowd, when you're falling under the spell of social influence, I don't think that you're publishing a book for the right reasons. I think you have to have it in your core why you believe that a book is worth publishing.

Q. If you can turn the page, Mr. Karp, and I'm just going to ask you maybe to slow down just a little.

A. I'm sorry.

Q. Give the court reporter a little bit of a break. On number 4, if you could read the first sentence there out loud?

A. "Simon & Schuster will be a better publishing company if we're driven by editors who think for themselves and acquire the books they want to buy, without focusing on the competition or needing to have their judgment validated by other bidders."

Q. And is that something that you've discussed with the publishers at Simon & Schuster?

A. Yes.

Q. And what did you mean by that?

A. Well, I meant that, again, that they should think for themselves, and that they should want the book for the right reasons, because if they have the right reasons for wanting the book, I believe we'll publish it better and the book will ultimately be more successful.

Q. And what did you mean specifically by without focusing on the competition or needing to have their judgment validated by other bidders?

A. Well, I think sometimes people get into these auctions and they think that because everybody else likes it, it must be good. It's kind of like the Pied Piper. And so I am trying to encourage independence of imagination here.

Q. Mr. Karp, does this mean that you discourage auctions at Simon & Schuster?

A. Not at all. As you can see, we compete in auctions all the time.

Q. Now, the Department of Justice in their complaint refers to a category of books that they refer to as anticipated top selling books. Is that a category that you have referred to in your professional career?
A. No.
Q. And have you heard anybody else in the publishing industry refer to a category of anticipated top selling books?
A. I have not heard that phrase.
Q. Does that category make sense to you based on your experience as an identifiable category of books?
A. I don't think so, because I don't think that people can agree on what an anticipated top selling book is.
Q. And why is that? What is your view as to why there is not agreement on that?
A. Well, again, it's about the subjectivity of reading and about the—and the alchemy of publishing. The thing that's so interesting about working in the publishing business is that a certain group of people can come together and they can have a vision of what a book can be and they might be exactly the right people and they might have the right vision; however, just as often, they could be wrong.
Q. Mr. Karp, you explained to the government when they were asking you that you approve offers for advances above $250,000; is that right?
A. Yes.
Q. And you mentioned there was a memo, and I think you said you weren't certain whether it was 200 or 250 that the memo gets written. Can you first tell us, what is this memo that's done?
A. The memo is for corporate governance. It's called a justification memo. And my predecessor instituted it because she felt that if editors were spending more than $200,000, they should be able to articulate their reasons why.
Q. Is that done during the acquisition process or afterwards?
A. It's done afterwards.
Q. Now, with respect to the approval level, and just so we're clear, that means you personally as CEO have to approve above 250; is that correct?
A. Correct.
Q. Has always been the cut-off for your approval?
A. No, that number has moved around. It's an arbitrary number that I set for corporate governance.
Q. When did you set that?
A. I set it when I became CEO in May of 2020.
Q. And why did you pick $250,000?
A. Because it was in the middle area of where some other people were.
Q. Meaning what? What do you mean other people were?
A. Some people were above 250 and some people were below 250.
Q. But when you say, some people, can you—
A. Some publishers. Some of the people acquiring the books. Some of the people who had the authority to approve acquisitions.
Q. And, again, just so we're clear, when you say publisher, you're talking about within Simon & Schuster internally?
A. Within Simon & Schuster internally and internationally, yes.
Q. But still at Simon & Schuster?
A. Yes.
Q. You're not talking about other publishing companies?
A. Only Simon & Schuster.
Q. Okay. So there were different levels within Simon & Schuster and you harmonized it at 250; is that fair?
A. I harmonized it at 250.
Q. How does that 250 threshold apply to an offer for multiple books and let me just give you an illustration. If you do a two-book deal and each book is $150,000 for a total of $300,000, does that require your approval?

A. I'd still have to approve that because it's over the $250,000 level.
Q. Okay. But each book in that scenario is only 150, right?
A. But the total offer is over, yes.
Q. Okay. But if each book is only—is under 250, why do you have to approve it?
A. Because for corporate governance, I want to know about any time we're spending over $250,000 on an author.
Q. Is there any difference in the process of editing, meaning like revising, giving comments, or marketing or selling a book based on the advance level?
A. No. You have to work just as hard on every book because you never know which one is going to break out.
Q. So, if I gave you 100 books before they were put on the market, so you had the book, you had the proposal, but you don't know what anybody offered and you don't know how much it sold, could you identify in advance which ones would garner advances of $250,000 and above?
A. I could pick them, but I would probably be wrong.
Q. And why do you say that?
A. Because, first of all, my own judgment might be off. I could just guess wrong, as I've done many times. But the other thing is I wouldn't be able to assess what the other people thought the books were worth, because they'd have the same subjective frame.
Q. Now, with respect to books that you publish, is the editorial staff, the people that actually edit the books, is that any different based on whether it's above $250,000 or below 250 in advance?
A. No.
Q. And what about the editorial process, the process of going back and forth with an author, does that vary by advance level?
A. No, it doesn't.
Q. And then what about the marketing and production and sale, does that vary by advance level?
A. It doesn't. And sometimes those people don't even know how much we've spent on the books.
Q. So—
THE COURT: Can I ask about this, because this is quite interesting to me. If you pay a lot for a book, like one of these million dollars books that you've been chasing for ten years, you're not going to market that book harder than another book?
THE WITNESS: Oh.
THE COURT: You're not going to get it reviewed, you're not going to create a buzz about that book?
THE WITNESS: We have to market those books quite arduously, definitely.
THE COURT: And more than your run of the mill book because you're not getting a reviewer for every one of your books.
THE WITNESS: You have to pick your shots, that's definitely true.
I think, thought, that what happens, I mean, yes, the big obvious books that we spent a lot of money for, they definitely have to be marketed and publicized aggressively, although sometimes we're paying that kind of money because the author takes care of a lot of that because they have enough of their own reach so that they can actually do a lot of that work themselves.
THE COURT: But I'm sure they're expecting from you a certain level of attention.
THE WITNESS: They definitely are. But it's also true that there's some books, and this really does happen just as often, that the publishing houses fall in love with and they champion them regardless of what's been paid, and that's because of—the phrase that people use in publishing houses is, it's in the read. And when it's in the read and when people have that kind of a euphoric reaction, as they did to a book like *Sea Biscuit*, for example, it doesn't matter what we paid, people just get behind it.
THE COURT: You're saying there's no correlation between the books and the read that you've paid more for the book and the read that you're going to promote.
THE WITNESS: I certainly think that when we've paid a lot for a book, everybody knows that there's extra pressure on us to earn it back. I certainly agree with that.
THE COURT: Okay. Thank you.

BY MR. FISHBEIN:

Q. When you're talking about big books where you're saying there's an expectation that you're going to ping hard—push hard—what kind of advance level are you talking about there?

A. Big books?

Q. Yeah.

A. Well, it could be any level really. I mean I'm thinking in the hundreds of thousands of dollars.

Q. So we've heard some testimony about, for example, books by presidents and that sort of thing for many millions of dollars. You know, for that kind of book, is there some pressure to make sure that you're doing a good effort on marketing?

A. Sure, yeah, that's all hands on deck.

Q. Okay. And between books at $100,000 or $200,000, $300,000, $400,000, $500,000, in that range, does the marketing vary correlated to how much of an advance you're paying?

A. The marketing varies. And a lot of those books are called make books and the idea is that it's up to the publisher to make them.

Q. But what I'm saying is, do you have a separate marketing program for books at 300 versus 250?

A. No. No.

Q. Or 200 versus 300?

A. No.

Q. So in those hundreds of thousands of dollars ranges, do you have separate marketing, publicity programs based on the advance amount?

A. Not at all.

Q. And I think you mentioned the people who were involved, what people are you referring to?

A. The people in marketing and publicity mostly.

Q. Do they know on a given book how much you paid for it?

A. They often don't know. And our sales force rarely knows.

Q. What about the customers? Are the customers any different based on the advance level?

A. No.

Q. And the pricing, is the pricing any different based on the advance level?

A. No.

Q. And in your questioning by the government, you referred to, or there was some discussion about, literary agents. What percentage of your authors that you deal with have agents?

A. The majority of them. I would even say probably the vast majority of them.

Q. And what is the role of a literary agent?

A. Well, the first role is obviously fiduciary. Their job is to get the best terms that they can get that would be most favorable to the author.

But they do a lot more than that. They are partners in the endeavor. They're frequently involved in the editing. They're involved in the marketing. They're a sounding board. And most important of all, they are a moderating and mediating voice when the publisher wants the author to do something and the author doesn't quite see it that way.

Q. How would you describe the relative roles of the publisher and the agent in structuring the acquisition process?

A. The agent is in control.

Q. So like who decides which publishers are going to receive a submission?

A. The agent.

Q. And who decides what kind of process it's going to be, like you mentioned the different types of auctions or an exclusive?

A. The agent.

Q. And you mentioned that sometimes you know certain information about other bidders and sometimes you don't. Who decides that?

A. The agent discloses whatever information the agent wants to disclose.

Q. Do you entertain agents as part of your job?

A. I do.
Q. Like in under what circumstances?
A. I take them to lunch regularly.
Q. And who pays?
A. The publisher always pays. And I mean that both literally and metaphorically.
Q. How do you mean it metaphorically?
A. We pay for lunch and we pay the advances.
Q. Now, let me turn to auctions. While a book auction is in progress and before it's concluded, what kind of information do you typically have about who the competitors are?
A. We rarely know anything. Sometimes we know the number of people we're bidding against, but sometimes the agents don't even disclose that.
Q. And what about after the auction is concluded, then do you have any different information?
A. After the auction is concluded, the agents usually tell us who we were competing against. They very rarely don't.
Q. Now, in response to one of the government's questions, you made a comment, and it was in your deposition transcript as well, that in a given auction, it could be anybody that you were competing with. Do you remember that?
A. Yes.
Q. And what are you referring to when you say it could be anybody that you're competing with?
A. It could be one of the major publishers who are the focus of this trial or it could be any number of other publishers.
Q. Have you heard the term Big 5?
A. I have. I'm not a big fan of it.
Q. Do you use that term yourself?
A. I don't.
Q. And why is that?
A. I think that it's parochial and ethnocentric. There are a lot of really good publishers all over the country. I don't think it's all about us.
Q. So let me ask you about some of the competition. Let's start with Penguin Random House. I take it from the documents that you were shown on your direct examination, that Simon & Schuster does compete with Penguin Random House for the acquisition of books, correct?
A. Correct.
Q. And are there situations in which Simon & Schuster pursues a book and when Penguin Random House does not compete?
A. Yes.
Q. What would those situations be?
A. Well, first of all, if it was a recurring author or an author who has already got a relationship with us, they would never hear about the project and that's a lot of our books.
Q. Are there situations in which Simon & Schuster competes with Penguin Random House and there's also other publishers that are competing for the same book?
A. Yes.
Q. And what kind of situation would that arise in?
A. Well, that could be any number of the kinds of auctions that there are.
Q. How often does it happen in a book acquisition that it comes down to Simon & Schuster competing only with Penguin Random House and nobody else?
A. I think that's a small fraction of the books that we compete for, a small fraction.
Q. And you mentioned that in any given year, I think you said you publish more than a thousand books. How many do you compete for, just roughly, if you have any idea?
A. Where it's head to head with Penguin Random House?
Q. No, just in total, what's the universe that you're competing for?
A. I—

Q. If you don't have an exact number, that's fine. I'm just asking for the general if you know it.
A. I don't know it. You know, I don't think it's a lot.
Q. No, let me—I'm sorry, let me be clear. You said you publish a thousand books a year, correct?
A. Yes.
Q. But do you compete for more books than you publish?
A. Oh, yes, we do, yes.
Q. And do you have any idea for how many?
A. Oh, it's probably twice as many. We probably wind up offering on twice as many books as we actually get to publish.
Q. So thousands of books a year?
A. Yes.
Q. And, I'm sorry, you said the situation out of those thousands where you're head to head with Penguin Random House and nobody else is what?
A. It's not a lot. It's a small fraction.
THE COURT: Can I ask you a question?
THE WITNESS: Yes.
THE COURT: In the situations where it's a pre-empt or a best bids auction, isn't your bid going to be higher or do you perceive that there are more bidders or more competition out there?
THE WITNESS: Yes.
THE COURT: So 50 percent of your books, there's no competition at all because you're just negotiating with the agent, and then 50 percent, there's some kind of competition, sometimes it's a round robin, sometimes it's a best bid, sometimes it's a pre-empt. There are other people interested. In any kind of competitive situation you're going to bid higher if you think there's more competition, more people in the pool?
THE WITNESS: I think that we frequently do ask how many people are involved and I think that does color our thinking to some extent. But I also think that when you want it, it doesn't matter how many people are competing against you. You've heard the counts already where there was one other bidder and I was going to pay any price and bear any burden.
THE COURT: Yes. I think that there are human emotions involved in some of these bidding situations.
THE WITNESS: Yes.
THE COURT: But it does seem that throughout this trial, there's this sort of sense, competition raises advance levels, less competition lowers them, and that's consistent with the idea that anytime there's a competitive situation, whether it's a round robin or any other type, you're going to try harder because you might have to bid more in order to win, because more people are in it, the bids are probably going to be higher.
THE WITNESS: Right.
THE COURT: Okay. Thank you.
BY MR. FISHBEIN:
Q. Yeah, I mean, do you always know how many other bidders there are?
A. No.
Q. And so even in the competitive situations, there are some where you don't know how many bidders; is that fair?
A. There are some where we don't know.
Q. And I take it from what you said before, that even where you do know, you typically don't know who they are; is that right?
A. That's—we rarely know who they are.
Q. The Department of Justice showed you some emails where you noted some losses to Penguin Random House. Do you remember that?
A. Yes.
Q. And you said that you also had emails that noted losses to others; is that right?
A. Right.

Q. What were you referring to there?
A. Well, I guess there was HarperCollins.
Q. Let me stop you there. So HarperCollins. Who are they?
A. HarperCollins is a publishing company that's owned by the Murdoch family, and they are part of News Corp. They are the second largest publisher after Penguin Random House in terms of their sales revenue.
Q. And do you compete with them?
A. We do.
Q. And what's your assessment of them as a competitor?
A. They are a strong formidable competitor with us in many categories.
Q. I'd like to show you Defense Exhibit 188, it's tab 3. And do you see this, Mr. Karp, it's an email chain between you and Libby McGuire. It's called pre-empt offer, dated June 16th, 2021.
MR. FISHBEIN: And I believe this is confidential, Your Honor, and so I would ask that either a redacted copy be shown or that it not be shown in the gallery.
THE COURT: Okay. I see a redacted copy on the screen.
BY MR. FISHBEIN:
Q. Do you recognize the email, Mr. Karp?
A. Yes.
MR. FISHBEIN: Your Honor, I offer Exhibit 188.
THE COURT: Any objection?
MR. VERNON: No objection.
THE COURT: 188 is admitted. And I think the redacted version can be shown. (Defendants' Exhibit 188 received into evidence.)
BY MR. FISHBEIN:
Q. And if we go about two-thirds of the way down the page, Mr. Karp, this involved a pre-empt offer on a particular book, correct?
A. Correct.
Q. And in the context of that, if you look about two-thirds down the page, do you see the sentence that starts, I'm sober?
A. Yes.
Q. And it says, "I'm sobered by Brian Murray's comments in yesterday's Publishers Marketplace about how HarperCollins was going to be more aggressive in its offers because the market is growing." Do you see that?
A. Yes.
Q. Who is Brian Murray?
A. He's the CEO of HarperCollins.
Q. And what is it that you were referring to there?
A. He made public comments that his company was going to be bidding more aggressively in auctions—or, actually, bidding more aggressively for authors period.
Q. And why were you sobered by that?
A. Because it meant that we were going to have to bid more if we wanted to win those authors.
Q. And then you also say, "He made similar comments about eight years ago to his editors and it set off a frenzy." Do you see that?
A. I do.
Q. And then at the top, you see, you wrote, "Yes, the HarperCollins strategy from eight years ago worked." Do you see that?
A. I did.
Q. What does that refer to?
A. HarperCollins made a strategic decision to increase their market share by bidding aggressively in auctions and it was something that our editors knew at the time. It was something that we knew.
Q. And that was eight years ago from about, from 2021, so around 2013?

A. Yes.
Q. And do you know, was there consolidation in the publishing business around that time, around 2013?
A. Yes, that was the year that Penguin and Random House combined.
Q. And is it your testimony that that HarperCollins aggressiveness contributed to upward pressure on advances notwithstanding any consolidation?
MR. VERNON: Objection; leading.
THE COURT: Sustained. Can you rephrase?
MR. FISHBEIN: Sure.
BY MR. FISHBEIN:
Q. So 2013, there was some consolidation; is that correct?
A. Correct.
Q. And your reference here to, in 2013, HarperCollins' strategy from eight years ago working as what?
A. I'm sorry, can you repeat the question.
Q. What is that a reference to?
A. Uh-huh.
Q. The statement that HarperCollins strategy from eight years ago.
A. It was a strategy of acquiring books more aggressively.
Q. Was that in the 2013 time frame as far as you recall?
A. Yes.
Q. Now, to the extent that you were sobered by Mr. Murray's comments about being aggressive, is your concern about HarperCollins dependent in any way on whether Simon & Schuster goes forward with its merger with Penguin Random House?
A. No.
Q. In other words, if the merger goes forward, will you continue to be sobered or concerned about HarperCollins' competitiveness?
A. We will continue to be concerned about HarperCollins.
Q. Has HarperCollins successfully competed against Simon & Schuster for books with advances over $250,000?
MR. VERNON: Objection; leading.
THE COURT: Overruled.
THE WITNESS: Yes, HarperCollins has competed with us on numerous books, and we've lost plenty of book to see HarperCollins.
BY MR. FISHBEIN:
Q. I'm going to go through some examples with you and you can name the authors and the books, but we're going to talk about advance levels in ranges, broad ranges, and not give specific amounts, is that okay?
A. Sure.
Q. Okay. So can you tell me, give me an example of a book that you lost to HarperCollins for above $250,000?
A. Dave Grohl, the musician, rock star, that was over seven figures. We really want—
Q. Let me just stop you there. Who is Dave Grohl?
A. Dave Grohl is a musician and rock star.
Q. And did Simon & Schuster bid for the book by Mr. Grohl?
A. Yes, we did.
Q. And why was it that you were interested in that?
A. Well, we've had a lot of success publishing musicians, I mentioned Bruce Springsteen. We've also published Bob Dylan and Linda Ronstadt, a lot of entertainers through the years, and we thought that Dave Grohl would be a very exciting addition to that list and we pursued it quite aggressively and we lost.
Q. And again, the range, just generally, very broad range that you offered for that was what?
A. It was over—it was a seven figure offer.
Q. Okay. And it ended up going to HarperCollins?

A. Yes.
Q. Anybody else that you lost to HarperCollins?
A. There was a political writer, Ben Shapiro, who has a very popular podcast and a large following. We also competed with HarperCollins for that. They have a very strong list of conservative authors. And we also lost that for an offer in the seven-figure range.
Q. When you say offer, meaning your offer was in the seven-figure range?
A. Our offer was in the seven-figure range and so was theirs.
Q. Do you have any authors who published with Simon & Schuster who then left Simon & Schuster for HarperCollins?
A. Kate Morton, the novelist, who we published for many years, recently left us for HarperCollins. It was also a seven-figure deal.
Q. Any others in particular that you happen to recall?
A. We competed for Brad Meltzer, the novelist. We also lost that.
Q. Again, just very generally, what was the range?
A. That was also a seven-figure deal.
Q. Now, the government showed you some emails where you expressed disappointment and frustration about losing to Harper—excuse me, Penguin Random House. How did you feel about losing these books that you just listed to HarperCollins?
A. I was equally frustrated.

CROSS-EXAMINATION (Resumed)

BY MR. FISHBEIN:

Q. We are going to start where we left off. You were telling us about competition with some of the other publishers. I would like to turn to Hachette. Is Hachette a company that Simon & Schuster competes with for books?
A. Yes.
Q. And can you give us a description of Hachette as a competitor in your view.
A. Another strong competitor. They have a lot of fiction and nonfiction. Malcolm Gladwell, David Baldacci, a lot of blockbuster fiction. Nicholas Sparks works with high quality, broad range of books, practical books, literary books.
Q. Mr. Karp, again, I am going to ask you, try to slow down a little bit.
A. Sorry.
Q. You do tend to speak quickly and we want to go easy on the court reporter. Does Hachette compete with Simon & Schuster to acquire books at advance levels above $250,000?
A. Yes.
Q. Can you think of any illustrative examples of that?
A. There was a popular movie star, singer, and we were competing to publish his book. And it was sold for over—for seven figures plus, and we lost that book to Hachette.
Q. Again, Mr. Karp, unless I tell you otherwise, you can name the author or the book—
A. Oh, it was—
Q. Hold on.—but we are not going to name specific advances. We are just going to use the general ranges. If I want to do it a different way, I will tell you. Who was the author of that book?
A. Jamie Foxx.
Q. And why were you interested in that book?
A. Well, he had a very funny idea for it. And he was—he's obviously a tremendously talented performer. And he was also a comedian, so we thought it would be funny.
Q. And on direct the government showed you some emails in which you were disappointed and frustrated in losing books to Penguin Random House. Do you remember that?
A. Yes.
Q. And what was your reaction to losing this Jamie Foxx book to Hachette?
A. I was disappointed. I was very frustrated.

Q. Any others with Hachette as examples?
A. Well, we competed to publish Dr. Ben Carson, and we did not prevail in that auction.
Q. Who is he?
A. He was a best selling author, number one best selling author actually. One of his books sold north of 500,000 copies. He had quite an inspirational story about his time as a surgeon. This was a book about his experience in the Trump administration and his thoughts on race.
Q. Who did you lose that to?
A. We lost that to Hachette.
Q. Again, just generally the range of offer you made for that?
A. It was a mid-six figure offer.
Q. Let me turn to Macmillan. Do you know them?
A. Yes.
Q. And what is your assessment of Macmillan as a competitor of Simon & Schuster?
A. Another strong competitor. They have—Macmillan is the home of FSG, Farrar, Straus & Giroux, one of the great publishers of award-winning fiction and nonfiction. Holt. They have many, many other imprints as well.
Q. You mentioned FSG, Farrar, Straus & Giroux, what is their specialty?
A. Works of high literary quality.
Q. If you are competing against them for literary fiction, do they have any particular advantages in your mind?
A. Well, they have a long reputation, so they can claim that when they publish a writer, that writer will be following in the tradition of other great award-winning Nobel laureates.
Q. When you say award-winning, how are their awards associated with an imprint?
A. How are awards—
Q. In other words, when you say that there's awards associated with FSG, what are you referring to?
A. Nobel Prizes, national book awards, Pulitzer prizes.
Q. Are you aware of another imprint Flatiron at Macmillan?
A. Yes.
Q. Are there any celebrities in particular associated with that?
A. Oprah Winfrey has an imprint with Flatiron.
Q. Does that affect the attractiveness of their marketing pitch when you are competing against them, in your opinion?
A. It does.
Q. How so?
A. Oprah Winfrey obviously has such a huge following both on TV and online that when she endorses a book, it becomes an instant best seller.
Q. Has Simon & Schuster competed with Macmillan for books with advances over $250,000?
A. Many times.
Q. And are there any authors that were Simon & Schuster authors who then moved to Macmillan?
A. Yes.
Q. And who are some of those?
A. Two that come to mind are Alec McGillis, former *Washington Post* reporter who wrote a book about Amazon for FSG; and Noam Scheiber, a *New York Times* labor reporter who was recently—who recently—who's book was recently acquired by FSG.
Q. And both of them have previously published with Simon & Schuster?
A. Yes.
Q. And did you make offers to keep those authors?
A. Yes, we did.
Q. And, again, just by general range, were those offers above or below $250,000?
A. They were above $250,000.
Q. How about auctions, can you think of any auctions recently where you competed against Macmillan?

A. Yes. There was one by a New York writer Jiayang Fan, and it was a memoir about her relationship with her mother. It was a really powerful piece of writing. We very much wanted to publish it.

Q. And who did that go to?

A. That went to FSG as well.

Q. And, again, just generally by a range, what was the level of the offer for advance that you made for that book?

A. It was high. It was over seven figures.

Q. Let me show you an exhibit. If we could—if you could look in your book at tab 21, it's Defendants' Exhibit 21.

MR. FISHBEIN: This is a confidential document, so, Your Honor, I think we are showing a redacted version.

THE COURT: Okay.

BY MR. FISHBEIN:

Q. Mr. Karp, this is an email chain between you and Carolyn Reidy from November 2018. Do you see that?

A. Yes.

Q. And there's a title that I am not going to read out, but that's the title of the book that was being discussed, is that correct?

A. Correct.

MR. FISHBEIN: Your Honor, I would offer Defendants' Exhibit 21.

THE COURT: Any objection?

MR. VERNON: No objection.

THE COURT: That will be admitted. (Defendant's 21 received in evidence.)

BY MR. FISHBEIN:

Q. If you can turn to the second page, the first thing I want to ask you about is, can you tell from there what advance level Simon & Schuster bid for this book?

A. $875,000.

Q. And that's on the second page?

A. Yes.

Q. Okay. And did you approve that?

A. I did.

Q. And then if you go up, the top email on that same second page, it's blacked out, but there's a person there. It's from a person who's name I won't mention to Dawn Davis. Who is Dawn Davis?

A. Dawn Davis at the time was the publisher of 37 Ink, which is an imprint within Simon & Schuster.

Q. And without naming who the email is from, what type of person is that?

A. Literary agent.

Q. Okay. And so what did Simon & Schuster learn from the literary agent as to what happened for this book where you bid $875,000?

A. Well, she writes that this was such a tough decision given our two amazing options, the final publishers were home to the author's most important supporters and mentors, and Oprah was one of the mentors.

Q. Okay. And does it say in here, if you look to the second paragraph, what the level was that Macmillan won this book at?

A. Oh, a million.

Q. So you bid 875, and they won it for a million?

A. Yes.

Q. And if you go to the next page, the first page.

A. Yes.

Q. Okay. Towards the bottom, do you see there's a sentence, and this is coming from Dawn Davis, your editor, correct?

A. Yes.

Q. And it says, I knew it was Oprah as she's working on the television show. This is the fourth book I have lost to her. Do you see that?
A. Yes.
Q. And who is the her in that sentence as far as you understand?
A. The her was definitely Oprah.
Q. So, again, the government showed you, I think, an email on direct where you commented that you had lost several books to Penguin Random House. Do you remember that?
A. I do.
Q. Is Penguin Random House the only other publisher to whom you lose multiple books?
A. Not—no. We lose them—we lose them to all of our major competitors.
Q. Let me turn now to—we have talked about HarperCollins. We have talked about Hachette. We talked about Macmillan. Right? So let me turn to some other publishers. Does Simon & Schuster compete for the acquisition of books from publishers other than Penguin Random House, HarperCollins, Hachette, and Macmillan?
A. Yes.
Q. And I am going to—I know you have had some testimony about Big 5. I am going to refer to them as non-Big 5. Okay?
A. Okay.
Q. Is there any particular genre that the non-Big 5 focus on? In other words, what genres do they cover of books?
A. They cover many of the same categories that we cover.
Q. There was testimony in this case to the effect that the non-Big 5 focus more on nonfiction. Is that correct in your experience?
A. No.
Q. Let me turn first to Norton. Do you know anything about them?
A. Yes.
Q. Who are they and what is your assessment of them as a competitor?
A. Norton is a superb publishing company. They publish a—they publish fiction including an award-winning novelist Richard Powers. And they have a broad range of books in all categories.
Q. Does Simon & Schuster compete with Norton for books with advances of $250,000 or more?
A. Yes.
Q. And can you give us an example of a book in that category?
A. Well, Neil deGrasse Tyson.
Q. Who is he?
A. The astrophysicist.
Q. And what kind of book was it?
A. It was a book about—it was his writing on science and faith and trying to square the two.
Q. And was Simon & Schuster interested in that book?
A. Very interested.
Q. And general range, don't give any specific numbers, what was the range of advance offer that you made?
A. It was a seven-figure advance.
Q. And where did Mr. deGrasse Tyson end up going?
A. He decided to stay with Norton for that book.
Q. There was some discussion yesterday about marketing. Do the non-Big 5, to your understanding, have marketing programs for their authors?
A. Yes.
Q. And have you ever had situations where authors chose a non-Big 5 over you because of marketing?
A. Yes.
Q. Let me show you another exhibit. It's Defendants'
Exhibit 54. On this one, Mr. Karp, this is tab 12, we are not going to mention the name of the author or

the book title. Okay?
A. Right.
MR. FISHBEIN: Your Honor, I am going to show a redacted version to the public.
THE COURT: Thank you.
BY MR. FISHBEIN:
Q. Exhibit 54, do you recognize that as an email chain between you and Stephanie Frerich?
A. Yes.
Q. Who is she?
A. She's executive editor at Simon & Schuster.
Q. And don't say the name, but do you see in the subject line is the name of an author and then it says auction?
A. Yes.
MR. FISHBEIN: Your Honor, I offer Defendants' Exhibit 54.
THE COURT: Any objection?
MR. VERNON: No objection.
THE COURT: That will be admitted. (Defendants' 54 received in evidence.)
BY MR. FISHBEIN:
Q. Mr. Karp, if you can look at the bottom of the first page, can you tell us what the deal was that was being considered here?
A. It was a two-book deal for two books. And she's kind of a humorous writer.
Q. Okay. And the amount, if you just look at the bottom paragraph, on this one, we can say what the amounts are, what was the proposal from Simon & Schuster in terms of how much to pay in advance?
A. A total advance of $400,000, and it would be divided among the two books, $150,000 for a novel and $250,000 for a nonfiction book.
Q. There's an email from you to Ms. Frerich, and you say, okay with me. What does that represent?
A. I approved the offer.
Q. And if you look above that, you sent an email back to
Ms. Frerich—I'm sorry, Ms. Frerich sent an email to you that starts, just heard from, and then there's a name.
A. Right.
Q. The name, don't say what the name is, but do you understand who that person is?
A. It was the agent.
Q. Could you just read what you heard from the agent.
A. They went with Norton mostly because of their marketing team who was at the meeting and conveyed a compelling plan.
Q. Did it surprise you, Mr. Karp, that this author chose Norton over you because of marketing?
A. It didn't because, as I have said, you can have a really good marketing plan or team with just a few people. It doesn't take a lot.
Your Honor, I was thinking about the question you asked me—
Q. Mr. Karp, we will get back to that.
A. Okay.
Q. I had intended to ask clarifications about that.
A. Okay.
Q. While we are still on Norton, you mentioned Richard Powers was a Norton author. Are there any other authors with Norton that are authors that Simon & Schuster would be interested in?
A. There certainly are.
Q. Who is that?
A. Well, I'll start with Michael Lewis who I think is one of the best nonfiction writers at work today. We would love to publish Michael Lewis. He's been with Norton virtually his entire career.
Q. Anybody else?
A. I think Mary Roach, who is a very, very entertaining science writer. She would also be somebody we

would love to publish. I have asked her agent many times through the years whether we could publish Mary Roach and I have been unsuccessful.

THE COURT: Who is her publisher?

THE WITNESS: Norton.

BY MR. FISHBEIN:

Q. We have been talking about Norton. Let me turn to another one. Do you know a publisher name Scholastic?

A. Yes.

Q. Who are they? What do they do?

A. Scholastic is a publisher of children's books. They are a giant. I think their revenue is over $1.6 billion a year.

Q. And when you say children's, one question I have is, we have sometimes heard in the case and in the briefing and whatnot a category called young adult.

A. Yes.

Q. Is that different or the same than children's?

A. Young adult is one of the major categories of children's books. There are picture books, then there are middle-grade books, and then there are young adult books. And so you follow the trajectory of a child's growth.

Q. When you say that Scholastic does children's, does that include young adult?

A. Very much so. They are very strong in that category.

Q. Does Simon & Schuster compete with Scholastic for books where the advance is $250,000 or more?

A. Regularly.

Q. Are there any examples of Simon & Schuster authors who have moved to Scholastic for books that you wanted?

A. Yes. Two of our best selling authors in the young adult category have written books for us and also written books for Scholastic when we were not able to pay them enough. So one of them is Cassandra Clare who is one of the very best selling young adult authors at work. And the other is Scott Westerfeld.

Q. I just want to understand, there was a time when these two authors published books with Simon & Schuster, is that right?

A. Yes. They still do, but they also publish books with Scholastic.

Q. And for the new books that went to—or for the books that went to Scholastic, did Simon & Schuster express an interest in those?

A. We offered for them.

Q. And those authors did what after you offered?

A. The agent took the offer that came from Scholastic instead.

Q. Okay. And, again, just generally, no specific numbers, were the offers you made above or below $250,000?

A. They were above 250.

Q. Have you heard of a publisher called Hay House?

A. I have.

Q. What do you know about them?

A. They are a mind, body, spirit publisher. They specialize in those categories. They are based in California. They have a very strong online teaching business where their authors conduct courses online, and they also are very strong at promoting their authors' books.

Q. Does Simon & Schuster compete against Hay House for books with advances above $250,000?

A. Yes, we have.

Q. And can you give us any examples of that?

A. There was a book on—it was a diet book.

Q. And, again, if you don't—

A. It was High Fiber Keto.

Q. Okay. So did Simon & Schuster bid for this High Fiber Keto book?

A. We did.
Q. And, again, general range, what was the range of advance that you were bidding?
A. It was in the mid six—it was north of—it was a mid six figure or higher. I can't remember exactly.
Q. Was it above $250,000?
A. Well above that.
Q. Who won that auction?
A. Hay House.
Q. Are you familiar, Mr. Karp, with what are known as academic book publishers?
A. Yes.
Q. What are those?
A. They are publishers affiliated with universities in some way and, you know, oftentimes the presses are a little bit independent, but they are—they are basically university presses.
Q. Does Simon & Schuster compete with university presses for books with advances of $250,000 or more?
A. We do.
Q. And are you familiar with Princeton University Press?
A. Yes.
Q. Is that one of the university presses that you mention?
A. Yes.
Q. And can you give us any examples of books where you competed with Princeton University Press?
A. There was a book by a writer named Ruha Benjamin on race and health care. And we very much wanted to publish that book, and she chose Princeton University Press instead of us.
Q. And did you bid for it?
A. Yes.
Q. And was the bid above or below $250,000?
A. It was above $250,000.
Q. How about Harvard Business Review, is that another academic press?
A. Yes—well, actually, yes, they—again, they are—they are spun off from Harvard Business School. I don't know exactly the nature of their financial attachment to Harvard Business School, but they are connected to it in some way. They are a very successful publisher of business books.
Q. Do you recall any examples where Simon & Schuster competed with them for books with advances over 250?
A. Yes. The author of a book called Blue Ocean Strategy had a new book, and we wanted to publish their book.
Q. Did you bid for that?
A. Yes.
Q. Generally, what was the level of the advance that you offered?
A. Around a million dollars.
Q. And they chose to go to Harvard Business Review, correct?
A. Correct.
Q. Now, you have listed a bunch of non-Big 5 publishers. Have you ever heard the non-Big 5 publishers referred to as farm teams?
A. I have in the—in recent moments.
Q. Where did you hear that?
A. I guess it was in either one of the pretrial briefs or around that time.
Q. Okay. And I want to make sure I establish the right foundation here. Do you know anything about baseball?
A. Yes.
Q. Based on your 33 years in publishing and your knowledge of baseball, do you agree with that analogy, that the non-Big 5 publishers are like farm teams?
A. I don't.

Q. And why not?
A. Well, because usually when you are on a farm team, you want to get off the farm team and you want to get to the majors. And I don't think it's a particularly generous thing to refer to these really great publishing companies as farm teams. I mean, they publish a lot of authors we would love to publish and a lot of authors who actually have come to us and then gone back to them. So I just don't think it's an apt analogy.
Q. You mentioned that there are authors that stay with the smaller publishers. And I think you mentioned some of them, Michael Lewis, Richard Powers, Mary Roach. Are those examples?
A. Right. Michael Lewis actually had a book with Knopf. He had been published very successfully. Norton broke him out. They published his first book, Liar's Poker. It was a foundational book. It's still in print. He heard the siren song of Knopf and he went and published a book with them. It was a political book. It didn't do particularly well, and he went back to Norton and stayed there forever. I'm sorry. I was talking fast on that.
Q. You mentioned, I think, Richard Powers and Mary Roach as other authors, for example, that have stayed with Norton?
A. Yes.
Q. And in your view, are those authors staying with Norton because they have no other choice among the Big 5?
A. They are staying with Norton because they are loyal to Norton in the same way that Simon & Schuster authors like David McCullough have been loyal to us. He's been with us for over 50 years.
Q. You mentioned there are some authors that go the other way, that they will publish with a Big 5 and subsequently publish with a non-Big 5. Does that happen?
A. That does happen.
Q. Any examples of those?
A. Martha Nussbaum, the philosopher and legal theorist, published a book with us, then she published a book with a smaller publisher. I believe it was Norton. She's also published with many university presses. We are going to be publishing her book this fall on animal rights.
Q. You had mentioned Scholastic. They are not in the Big 5,
correct?
A. They are not in the Big 5.
Q. Those authors there, they had published with you first, is that correct?
A. The Scholastic authors?
Q. Yes, Mr. Westerfeld and Clare.
A. Yes.
Q. And after publishing with you, is that when they went to Scholastic?
A. Yes.
Q. Okay. Has the landscape of publishing— excuse me. Has the landscape of publishers who compete for books changed in recent years?
A. It has.
Q. How so?
A. Well, it's a dynamic landscape. And there are new publishing companies.
Q. Who are some of the new publishing companies that have come into the business in the last few years, last two or three years?
A. One of them is Spiegel & Grau.
Q. Who is Spiegel & Grau?
A. Spiegel & Grau is an upstart company. Julie Grau and Cindy Spiegel are two very highly regarded former Penguin Random House publishers.
Q. Let me just ask you a question. On your direct examination, Mr. Vernon asked you some questions about the importance of track record. Do you remember that?
A. Yes.
Q. So are you saying that the founders of Spiegel & Grau, they previously were with Penguin Random

House?

A. Yes.

Q. And so what kind of track record do Ms. Spiegel and Ms. Grau have in the publishing industry?

A. They are among the best publishers of their generation. I have known them for a long time.

Q. Do they have a track record, though, of prior successes?

MR. VERNON: Objection.

THE COURT: Overruled.

THE WITNESS: They have had a lot of success. *Orange is the New Black*; Bryan Stevenson's book *Just Mercy*; Ta-Nehisi Coates, *Between the World and Me*; those books were all published by Spiegel & Grau.

BY MR. FISHBEIN:

Q. When they were at Penguin Random House, is that right?

A. When they were at Penguin Random House.

Q. By the way, do you know how they do their distribution of books to retail stores?

A. Yes. They are affiliated with Ingram. I spoke to them about distributing their books, and they chose Ingram.

Q. And does Simon & Schuster have a third party distribution business?

A. Yes.

Q. Can you just very, very briefly explain to the judge what that is.

A. We distribute the books of smaller publishers and take a commission on it.

Q. And so do I understand from your testimony that you asked Spiegel & Grau if you could distribute for them?

A. Yes.

Q. And who did they choose?

A. Ingram.

Q. Who is Ingram? Tell us a little bit about what Ingram is.

A. Ingram is a wholesale distributor. They distribute books from many, many publishers throughout the country. They get them into bookstores.

Q. And is Ingram associated with any of the Big 5 publishers?

A. Well, they—I believe that they service many of them.

Q. Are they owned by any –

A. Oh, no.

Q. So you mentioned Spiegel & Grau. Any other new entrants—

THE COURT: Can I ask, have Spiegel & Grau published any blockbusters like the ones you mentioned since they have been independent?

THE WITNESS: They had—they just launched a year or two ago, and their first book was a *New York Times* best seller. It was called *Fox and I*.

THE COURT: So one?

THE WITNESS: That's the one I am aware of.

THE COURT: Okay.

BY MR. FISHBEIN:

Q. Any other new entrants?

A. Zando, which is, I think, X-A-N-D-O. No, Z-A-N-D-O.

Q. Who started Zando?

A. That was started by Molly Stern. Molly Stern is another former publisher from Penguin Random House. She was the publisher of Crown where she published Michelle Obama's book. She's best known in my mind for having published *Gone Girl* by Gillian Flynn, which was one of the best selling suspense novels of the decade.

Q. And has Zando done anything different from other publishers in terms of how it markets itself or publicizes its offering to authors?

A. Molly Stern is an innovative publisher. And she has affiliated with public figures who have broad followings, large followings. And by affiliating with those figures, she's creating imprints with them so that they can choose books and help her make those books better known to the public. It's a smart idea.

Q. And do you view Zando as a potential competitor of Simon & Schuster?

A. They are a potential competitor, yes.

Q. Anybody else that you would name as new—

THE COURT: I'm sorry. And has Zando published any blockbusters?

THE WITNESS: I don't know whether they have published many books yet. They are just getting started.

BY MR. FISHBEIN:

Q. Have you seen Zando in any auctions?

A. We have competed with them in an auction recently, and it was above the 250 level. And I also know that there's a book that they have signed up that has a lot of online preorders that suggest to me that it's about to become a best seller. It hasn't come out yet.

Q. Any other new entrants in the last couple of years?

A. Yes. Astra or Astra House, which is a new company that is backed, financially backed, by Thinkingdom, which is one of the largest Chinese book companies. And they have actually started an adult imprint, a children's imprint, and they recently bought a science fiction and fantasy publisher.

Q. Mr. Karp—

MR. FISHBEIN: And I don't know if Your Honor had a question about that.

THE COURT: Just wondering about their track record.

THE WITNESS: I don't know anything about—again, they are relatively new, but I don't know about their track record.

THE COURT: Okay.

BY MR. FISHBEIN:

Q. Mr. Karp, do existing publishers that have been in the publishing industry already ever expand their title counts or offerings?

A. Yes.

Q. And can you give us some examples of existing publishers who for whatever reason expanded?

A. Well, Bloomsbury, which is the publisher of Harry Potter in the UK, they set up a New York—or an American office in New York, and they have expanded here into fiction and nonfiction. They have a number one best selling author Sarah Maas, M-A-A-S-S, I think.

And then there's also—well, I mean, Hachette has obviously expanded. They created a science fiction imprint called Orbit. Flatiron, which is part of Macmillan, has very intelligently gone into a category that's called new adult which is between YA, young adult, and older fiction. So it's sort of trying to hit the, you know, people in their late teens and early 20s.

Q. What about Simon & Schuster, under your watch—

A. Well, I mentioned yesterday that we started a practical nonfiction lifestyle imprint called Simon Element.

Q. And what's involved? Like if you want to go into a new area and increase your title count and expand, what do you need to do?

A. It doesn't take much. All it takes is, you know, a publisher with a vision or a couple of really good editors. It's basically an investment in talent.

Q. Where do you find that talent? Where do you find editors and publishers with the experience you want?

A. Well, you can find them—you know, I look everywhere. You can find them in other parts of the media. We have hired people from magazines, online. We find them sometimes from other publishing companies.

Q. Is there a movement between the publishing companies in terms of people hiring each other?

A. Yes.

Q. Let me switch topics. You mentioned Amazon on your direct testimony. Does Amazon compete with Simon & Schuster for the acquisition of books from authors?

A. They do.

Q. And just what is your understanding of Amazon as a publisher, not a distributor, as a publisher of books?

A. I think Amazon as a publisher of books is underestimated. They have over—they have about 50 editors. They have a lot of imprints. They have imprints in the general categories, fiction and nonfiction. They have a romance imprint. They have a science fiction and fantasy imprint. They have something that even we don't have, literature in translation, award-winning international fiction and nonfiction. I think it's mostly fiction. And I have read—I think they have published possibly more than we have published in terms of international fiction translated.

Q. Mr. Karp, is there anything about Amazon, when you are competing with various publishers and you are talking to authors, is there anything about Amazon's offering that makes it different than other publishers?

A. Yes. Obviously, given the number of people searching on Amazon for products, that gives them a huge advantage because when people go onto Amazon, they—if the book isn't there for what they are searching for, they could create that book. That's one theory I have.

But even if that doesn't happen, they know what people are buying and they have access to that data. Their best seller list in my view is more important than *The New York Times* best seller list because it's in realtime. It's hourly. And I look at that Amazon best seller list regularly, every day.

Q. Mr. Karp, has Amazon's status as a publisher for acquiring books from authors, has that changed over time?

A. Yes.

Q. In what way?

A. Well, they have been—they were very aggressive, and then they weren't so aggressive. And now they are—it seems like they are getting more aggressive.

Q. Are there any recent developments in terms of distribution of Amazon-published books that affects your view?

A. Yes. We are currently publishing the hottest author in the country. Her name is Colleen Hoover. Colleen Hoover is a cultural phenomenon. And she may even turn out to be on the same scale as something like *Fifty Shades of Grey* or *Twilight*. Her books are selling at a tremendous rate, unlike anything we have seen in a long time.

To put this in some perspective, her novel *It Ends With Us* is the first book to sell a million copies this year in trade paperback. And the most amazing thing about that is that it's an old book. It came out in 2017.

Q. If we could—I think I was asking about Amazon and recent developments with Amazon.

A. Yes. Oh, I'm sorry. I got distracted. So Colleen Hoover is hot. She's so hot that she made the independent best seller list, the independent bookstores' best sellers list. This is a list that is from only independent book sellers.

And the reason why this is so significant is that independent book sellers up to this point had refused to carry books from Amazon. And Colleen Hoover has published with both Amazon and Simon & Schuster. And her Amazon book was on the independent book sellers' best seller list.

So what that says to me is that a Rubicon has been crossed. One of the competitive advantages that the traditional publishers have had over Amazon through the years is that independent book sellers wouldn't take books from Amazon because independent book sellers felt threatened by Amazon.

So when I saw Colleen Hoover's Amazon book on the independent best seller list, that was a Rubicon, that was different, and that said to me that they are more of a threat than I thought.

Q. Are there any other authors other than Colleen Hoover who you have pursued who chose Amazon?

A. Yes. Dean Koontz is a best selling novelist of suspense and horror. And we made a significant offer for his books and we lost that to Amazon.

Q. And again, just general range –

A. It was a seven-figure offer.

Q. All right. And then what about auctions, do you ever see Amazon in auctions?

A. Yes.
Q. When was the last time that happened?
A. Well, last time was a few weeks ago.
Q. And what was the, again just general, what was the range of offer that Amazon made?
A. Seven figures.
Q. Who won that?
A. We won it.
Q. There was some discussion yesterday about self-publishing. And I think you said—or you were confronted with and you acknowledged that in an earlier deposition in this case, you had said that self-publishing was not a major threat. Is that fair?
A. I had said that in the context of a series of questions that spun me in that direction.
Q. And do you remember whether you addressed self-publishing again in a subsequent deposition as part of the same case?
A. I did.
Q. And so if you look at your—I think it's—does he have the document?
A. It's right up here, I think, if it didn't move.
Q. If you look at the February 17, 2022 transcript—do you have that?
A. Yeah, I have it.
Q. Page 128, line 17 to 22. I'm sorry.
A. Page 128.
Q. Hold on. Hold on. Hold on. My mistake. It's—yes, it's page 180, lines 17 to 22. Just tell me when you have it.
A. Okay. I'm there.
Q. Do you see you were asked the question, now I want to go back to my question from before—
A. Yes.
Q.—which is, self-publishing is not a big threat to Simon & Schuster, correct?
A. Right.
Q. And you said, I actually have changed my opinion about that. I am seeing more of a threat now. Do you see that?
A. Yes.
Q. Okay. So your change of opinion, is it fair to say, goes back to the depositions in this case?
A. Correct.
Q. And is the market static, by the way? Does the market change generally in terms of competition?
A. The market is dynamic.
Q. And do your opinions evolve about competition as the market changes?
A. Yes.
Q. So I want to ask you, based on your experience—you can put that to the side. Based on your experience until today, so currently, you know, what is your view of self-publishing as competition in the publishing industry?
A. I think it's more—I think it's more of a threat than I thought.
Q. Why is that?
A. Well, actually, recently, we had an author, a very highly regarded neuroscientist affiliated with a major university, and he was under contract to us for a significant advance. And he asked to be released from his contract so that he could self-publish because he felt he could make more money that way. It had nothing to do with us. He just thought he could make more money that way. And he had heard that from—
Q. I don't want to ask you about what you heard from other people who heard from other people. Okay. And when did that occur? When did that occur that this author threatened to go self-publishing?
A. This was only a couple—a few months ago. It was recent.
Q. You mentioned Colleen Hoover, and I think you said she's published with Atria and she's published with Amazon. Is that correct?

A. Yes.
Q. Does she publish anywhere else?
A. She publishes with Hachette, and she also self-publishes.
Q. Currently?
A. Currently. She's a free agent. She can do what she wants.
Q. Are there any recent developments relating to internet promotion relating to self-publishing that affect your view?
A. Yes.
Q. And what is that?
A. Kickstarter, which is a site where anyone can go and raise money for anything. There is a best selling—*New York Times* best selling author in the science fiction and fantasy category. His name is Brandon Sanderson. I believe he's published by both Macmillan and Penguin Random House.
He went onto Kickstarter and announced that he would be offering four of his novels to anybody who wanted them if they wanted to donate to Kickstarter. And he raised over $42 million.
Q. Do you remember when that was, Mr. Karp?
A. That was this year, I think.
Q. Any other examples of Kickstarter or Kickstarter-like publishing that you are aware of?
A. I have subsequently become aware of *Good Night Stories for Rebel Girls*, which is a series of books. It's now actually become a whole company. And these are stories to give young girls confidence. And it's been very successful, and it's actually resulted in an entire company.
Q. Okay.
A. And it started on Kickstarter.
Q. So taking what you just said about Kickstarter and then you mentioned Ms. Hoover who self-publishes and you mentioned the incident with the scientist, what is your assessment going forward prospectively of self-publishing in terms of competition with major publishers?
A. I think really from the advent of online—really, once the internet became popular, you know, we heard the phrase disintermediation. And I don't understand why that wouldn't be a possible prospect for any best selling author, to just disintermediate, to go straight to the internet and sell directly if you have a following.
Q. Mr. Karp, I am going to switch gears. Based on your experience making and approving advances to authors, do you have a view or sense of whether advance levels have changed since 2010?
A. Have they changed? Well, yes.
Q. And in your view, how have they changed?
A. I think they have gone up.
Q. Do you recall in 2013 Random House acquired Penguin?
A. Yes.
Q. In your view, did that have any effect on advance levels when those two companies combined?
A. I couldn't say that that combination had any effect one way or the other.
Q. Mr. Karp, do you coordinate with employees of other publishers about the terms on which you acquire books from authors?
A. No.
Q. Have you agreed with other publishers what terms you will offer authors like royalty rates, audio rights, and that sort of—
A. No.
Q. Are you more likely to coordinate with other publishers and book acquisition terms if Penguin Random House merges with Simon & Schuster?
A. No.
Q. On the audio, do you get audio rights when you get print rights from authors?
A. Yes, we do.
Q. Do you buy print rights without the audio rights?
A. We don't. We don't do that.

Q. Why is that?
A. Because we believe that the audiobook is the product of our work. We work with the writers to develop the book. We help make the book better. We design it. We produce it. And we believe that the audiobook is an extension of our work in the same way that the ebook is or the paperback is.
Q. Is the fact that you pursue the audio as well as the print, is that something that you have ever discussed with other publishers?
A. No.
Q. Let me show you another exhibit. It's going to be Plaintiff's Exhibit 577, which is tab 18 in your binder. Do you recognize this?
A. This is *The Storm in the Spring*?
Q. Yeah.
A. Yeah.
Q. And actually, let's not –
A. I'm sorry.
Q. I am not going to mention any figures, actually, on this, so that's okay.
A. Okay.
Q. So am I right that this is a package of information about a book that you published?
A. Yes.
MR. FISHBEIN: I am going to offer Plaintiff's Exhibit 577.
THE COURT: Any objection?
MR. VERNON: No, Your Honor.
THE COURT: It will be admitted. (Plaintiff's 577 received in evidence.)
BY MR. FISHBEIN:
Q. I want to flip to the spreadsheet, I think it is. It starts with 1 of 4. It's about three pages in, Mr. Karp.
A. Yes.
Q. Do you know what that document is?
A. Yes. That's a P&L.
Q. What is a P&L?
A. A profit and loss statement. It's the projections we make, our estimations for how the book will perform in the marketplace.
Q. Do you do—when in the process do you do these in terms of when you actually bid at an auction and make an advance offer?
A. We do them before we decide to acquire the book.
Q. Do you use this in any way in trying to figure out what advance you want to pay?
A. Yes.
Q. If you look with me, and I don't know what page you have, it says 2 of 4 on the bottom?
A. Okay.
Q. Do you have it?
A. I am looking at yours. Yeah, I think I've got where you are.
Q. I just want to make sure. There's a Bates No. VCBS and it ends in 9708.
(There was an interruption by the court reporter.)
MR. FISHBEIN: VCBS and it ends in 9708
THE WITNESS: That's what I am looking at.
BY MR. FISHBEIN:
Q. Do you see on that page there's a line that says gross margin?
A. Yes.
Q. Don't give me the numbers, but what does that represent?
A. The gross margin is the amount of money contributed to the company after it's been produced but before certain fixed costs.
Q. How does the advance factor into the calculation of the gross margin?
A. Well, we obviously want to have a positive number there.

Q. And then there's another line that says operating income. Do you see that?
A. Yes.
Q. There's a percentage all the way to the right. Do you see that?
A. Yes.
Q. What does that reflect?
A. That reflects the profit that we have after our fixed expenses, our salaries, the cost of distributing the book, warehousing.
Q. Now, internally at Simon & Schuster, do you have any goals or targets for either of those figures, gross margin or operating income margin?
A. We do.
Q. For—don't tell me what the targets are, but for which ones?
A. For both.
Q. Just so I understand, there's—in setting the advance, you have a target for gross margin and operating income margin?
A. Yes.
Q. And the operating income margin is after fixed expenses?
A. That's right.
Q. Okay. And again without giving a specific number, can you give us just a range or an idea—first of all, the operating income margin, is the goal for it to be positive or negative?
A. We always want it to be positive.
Q. And in what general area, without giving a specific –
A. Double digits.
Q. Okay. Mr. Karp, I think you might have wanted to say something about this, but I did want to come back and ask for some—ask you to elaborate a little bit on some terms you used yesterday when the judge was asking you about marketing. Okay?
A. Yes.
Q. And the judge asked you about marketing for—I think she referred to million-dollar books. And you said, sometimes we are paying that kind of money because the author takes care of a lot of that. Do you remember that?
A. That's exactly what I wanted to elaborate on.
Q. Please explain.
A. So a lot of the time, not all the time, but a lot of the time when we are paying these big advances, the authors have quite a bit of their own infrastructure with them. They have their own publicists. They have their own social media people. They have their own newsletters.
So they actually are able—we are able to offload a good amount of the work, not all the time, but that is actually a factor in why we sometimes pay these big advances, because the authors are actually capable of helping us a lot.
Q. So let me ask you, Mr. Karp, you said, for example, that Ms. Hoover is—who is the best selling Simon & Schuster author currently?
A. Right now it's Colleen Hoover.
Q. Does she have the highest marketing budget that Simon & Schuster pays?
A. No.
Q. Why is that?
A. She's the queen of TikTok, and so she has a huge following on TikTok.
Q. Now, you also said yesterday, and I think this was also in answer to the judge's questions, you said, this really does happen just as often that publishing houses fall in love with and they champion them regardless of what's being paid. Do you remember that?
A. Yes, it's true.
Q. And so what did you mean by that, and can you give some examples?
A. Sure. We really do fall in love with—we fall in love with books that we pay five figure advances for. You know, it doesn't—love is supposed to be blind. It really is. And so—and we are often wrong, you

know, by the time we—by the time we get to publish a book. I mean, there are famous stories about books that the publishers pay a lot of money for and then the sales force fell in love with a completely different book.

The *Lovely Bones*, actually, I heard that story when I was at Hachette. That was a book that they never pushed, but the sales force embraced it.

Recently, we had two novels, Simon & Schuster did. One of them was acquired for twice as much as the other one. The other one was a book that was—it was actually a book called *The Last Thing He Told Me* by Laura Dave. And it was not the most expensive book we had acquired.

She had never been a best selling author before, but she wrote the book of her life. It was her sixth book, and it exploded when she was published. We just announced that we have sold over 2 million copies of *The Last Thing He Told Me*. It's been on *The New York Times* best seller list for a full year. It wasn't about what we paid for Laura Dave. It was the way we reacted to it. And you often don't know that when you sign the book up.

Q. Mr. Karp, when in the process are estimations made about how much marketing dollars you are going to use for a particular book?

A. We actually—this is interesting. We often decide late in the process after we have heard the reactions from readers. And, in fact, literary agents frequently ask us to guarantee marketing dollars. And we don't do it because we don't want to be locked into a plan when we acquire the book.

Q. So when you—

THE COURT: So can I ask, when they ask you to commit marketing dollars, that's for the books that they expect to sell well or else they couldn't make that demand on you, correct?

THE WITNESS: It tends to—you know, it doesn't—yes, they expect it to sell well, but sometimes they ask for it—it could just be an author who has a lot of cachet. It doesn't always correspond to the advance but—

THE COURT: Putting aside the advance, books that they expect to sell well, they can ask you for things like can you commit certain marketing dollars?

THE WITNESS: Yes, they can. We rarely—

THE COURT: And do they ask you, for example, can you get this book reviewed in *The New York Times*, can you get my author on the Today Show, things like that?

THE WITNESS: You would be a fool to make that kind of promise because we can't control that. *The New York Times Book Review* is completely independent. The TV producers decide what they put on the air.

THE COURT: I understand. I am just trying to figure out if the negotiating process with these anticipated top selling books is different from everybody else's negotiation. I saw in one of the defense exhibits, there was a budget for glam and wardrobe.

THE WITNESS: That's hilarious.

THE COURT: Yes, hilarious, but you can't demand that unless you are an anticipated top selling books author, right? That's not a term that everybody gets, am I right?

THE WITNESS: You are right. Although, I would say—the people who ask for these glam budgets, they tend to be represented by talent agencies. And so they are used to asking for that for their movies, and it's kind of a—

THE COURT: It's not a standard term in a book contract?

THE WITNESS: Thankfully, no. John Irving isn't asking for a glam budget.

THE COURT: No. And then there was an as-is term I saw in one of the emails. Like one of the factors in the auction was the publishing house that won, so they will take the book as is. That's something you would only offer to an anticipated top selling books, not just to anybody, right?

THE WITNESS: I think that's a fair assumption to make.

THE COURT: Okay. Thank you.

BY MR. FISHBEIN:

Q. How often do you—like the glam budget, is that a common thing that you agree to?

A. It's not. It doesn't come up that often. You have to be pretty glamorous to ask for that.

Q. Now, you did tell the judge that, in general, the more you pay in an advance, the more expectation there is that you are going to try to earn back the advance? That sounds reasonable. Is that fair?

A. Yes.

Q. Is there any specific advance level, like particular advance level, that demarcates, you know, when you are going to be more intensive about marketing a book?

A. No. And, in fact, a good editor worries about every book that he or she acquires, making every book profitable. I certainly know from my own experiences that you feel personally responsible when you ask the company to spend money on a book, so you work just as hard on every book because you never know.

Q. And then—

THE COURT: Can I follow up on that? I'm sorry, Mr. Fishbein. There was also something in one of the exhibits about a compelling marketing plan. I saw that in one of exhibits. And that was a factor in which publisher and author chose. So if you know it's going to be a hot auction, a lot of interest, do you spend more time developing a compelling marketing plan?

THE WITNESS: Yes.

THE COURT: Thank you.

BY MR. FISHBEIN:

Q. Do you ever do marketing plans for books with advances below $250,000?

A. Yes.

Q. Under what circumstances?

A. When you really want the author, you jump through hoops.

Q. But did you hear me, that for books with advances below $250,000, do you ever do marketing plans?

A. Sure.

Q. Is there any advance level or even range of advance level where you have internal guidance where you say, okay, above this, we are going to do marketing plans, and below this, we won't?

A. No. And also, a lot of the times when you do these marketing plans, you don't know what the book will wind up selling for. So, you know, you could do it for any reason. Sometimes editors just do them because they really want the book and they are just showing that they are going the extra mile.

Q. So what are the factors, what are the factors that go into your decision as to whether to put together a marketing plan, whether to offer glam or whether to offer an as-is clause? What are the factors?

A. It really does come down to the personal passion that the company is radiating for the project. There is no hard and fast rule for any of this. Each book is different.

Q. And is there any hard and fast or even soft advance level that dictates either the intensity or the quality of what you are going to do on marketing?

A. No.

Q. You were shown an exhibit—I think you just mentioned Mr. Irving, who, I guess, is not getting a glam budget, as I understand it. You were shown an email exchange with him. It's Plaintiff's Exhibit 655. If you could take a look at that.

A. Is it one of your—it's not in mine. It's in the—the government showed it to you.

A. Okay. 655.

Q. Yeah. And this is the one where you corresponded with John Irving. It's already in evidence, March 5, 2020. Do you remember it?

A. Oh, I remember vividly.

Q. Okay. And you said on direct that you wrote this to him and that Penguin Random House was the largest trade book publisher. Do you remember that testimony?

A. Yes.

Q. First of all, what position at Simon & Schuster did you hold in March—on March 5, 2020?

A. I was the publisher of Simon & Schuster, and I was more—and head of the adult trade group, but more significantly, I was John Irving's editor.

Q. Were you CEO—

THE COURT: (Inaudible.)

THE WITNESS: I wish I had. No. I edited *In One Person* and *Avenue of Mysteries* and his forthcoming book, which was called *The Last Chairlift*. And I am willing to say under oath that it is one of his very best. And it's coming out in October. And he's been working on it for six years.

THE COURT: Excellent. Thank you.

BY MR. FISHBEIN:

Q. Mr. Karp, March 5, 2020, when in the sale process was that? When in the process of selling Simon & Schuster was that?

A. It was around the day after it was announced, we were put up for sale.

Q. Did you know at that time who the bidders were or who would acquire Simon & Schuster?

A. I had given no thought to any process at all. We had just found out that we were being put up for sale. I wasn't the CEO. I was acting as his editor when I wrote that.

Q. How was it that you focused on Penguin Random House?

A. I focused on Penguin Random House because he sent me an email which is on the same page where he writes, naturally, I am inclined to imagine an ironic sale. Generally irony is more satisfying in fiction than in real life such as S&S is bought by Penguin Random House and I find myself back in the hands of publishers I thought I left. I mean, in the U.S. and the UK, because he's still published by Penguin Random House in Canada, but that's how I imagine things in fiction, ironically.

And I was responding humorously to his ironic remark. And Mr. Vernon asked me a lot about this in the deposition and—

Q. We don't have to get into the deposition.

A. Okay.

Q. Let's stick with what happens in the courtroom. Let me ask you this though. At that time, March 5, 2020, what was your level of knowledge, if any, about the Department of Justice regulatory process on antitrust issues?

A. I think you could say quite accurately that I was almost entirely ignorant. My parents wanted me to go to law school and I didn't listen.

Q. Did you subsequently communicate again with Mr. Irving on the subject of the transaction?

A. I did.

Q. And if you could look at tab 20, it's Defendants' Exhibit 154. Do you recognize this, Mr. Karp, as an email chain between you and John Irving on November 25, 2020?

A. Yes.

MR. FISHBEIN: Your Honor, I offer Defendants' Exhibit 154.

THE COURT: Any objection?

MR. VERNON: No objection.

THE COURT: That will be admitted. (Defendants' 154 received in evidence.)

THE COURT: I'm sorry, which tab is this?

MR. FISHBEIN: Tab 20, Your Honor.

THE COURT: Thank you.

MR. FISHBEIN: I will give you a second to get to that.

BY MR. FISHBEIN:

Q. While you are doing that, the date, Mr. Karp, November 5, 2020, when was that in the chronology of the sale process of Simon & Schuster?

A. That was the same day that our sale was announced to Penguin Random House.

Q. Okay. So now it's known that you are selling to Penguin Random House?

A. Now I know.

Q. Okay. And if you turn to the second page, there's a letter that starts, Dear colleague, what is that? You don't have to describe it in detail, but what is it?

A. It's a letter that I sent to all Simon & Schuster employees expressing my elation that we have been sold to Penguin Random House.

Q. And do you see that Mr. Irving or somebody, and I think we have blacked out the email addresses, wrote—who did you send that to here?

A. I sent it to John Irving and his wife, who's also his—who also acts as his literary agent, Janet.

Q. And then you got something back. And do you see at the top of the second page, it says, my second thought was to check in with you and make sure you are feeling good about this. Do you see that?

A. Yes.

Q. And then you responded. And what did you say?

A. I said, yes, I am delighted by the outcome.

Q. Did you mean that at the time?

A. I still mean it.

Q. At the time when you said to John Irving who—were you still involved with him as an author at that point?

A. Yes. As an editor, you mean. Yes, I am still involved with him, yes.

Q. And when you told John Irving that you were delighted with the Penguin Random House transaction, did you believe at that time that the transaction would harm authors in any way?

A. Definitely not.

Q. Mr. Karp, do you have any plans to decrease advances to authors if this merger goes through?

A. No.

Q. Do you have any plans to decrease title count if this merger goes through?

A. No.

Q. Have you made any projections to decrease advances or title counts post merger?

A. No.

Q. And why is that? Why haven't you made a plan that you are going to be able to decrease advances in light of the merger?

A. Well, because we have a growth mind-set and we believe that the way to continue to grow is to publish more books.

Q. Do you have any views on what the results would be if you did try to lower advances?

A. Yes. I think that we would face something of a rebellion from our staff because editors want to have the latitude to sign up the books they want to sign. And I think that the literary agent community would react quite badly to it.

Q. And is that view informed by any experiences that you actually have had in your career?

A. Yes. I immediately thought of what happened around 2008 or 2009 when Houghton Mifflin announced that they were going to freeze acquisitions of new books. And there was an outcry, and it hurt them badly.

Q. For what period of time, you know, based on your experience in the market, during what period of time did that hurt them?

A. Certainly in the subsequent years. I mean, I recall at least one significant editor left. I think more than one left. And I think it was something that literary agents remembered. I heard agents tell me at the time, well, I am not submitting to them.

Q. Mr. Karp, do you have a view on how the proposed Simon & Schuster Penguin Random House merger will affect Simon & Schuster authors?

A. I think it would be good for Simon & Schuster authors.

Q. Why?

A. Well, first of all, the culture of the company is quite analogous to what Simon & Schuster is about. This is a company that is wholeheartedly committed to nurturing its authors. Penguin Random House is known for treating its authors well. They are a good corporate citizen. And I think that they are part of a larger company, Bertelsmann, that has a long commitment to books going back to 1835, nearly 200 years. And it's a pure play book publishing company.

Having worked now at a media company that has sold us or is trying to sell us, I think that being part of a company that is wholeheartedly committed to books will really matter to our authors.

It's a good culture. It's also a privately owned company which I think gives them the opportunity to invest for the long term.

Q. Thank you, Mr. Karp.

MR. KIM: I will pass the witness.

THE COURT: Let me just ask a couple questions before you begin, Mr. Vernon.

Mr. Karp, when you said 50 percent of the books that are acquired by Simon & Schuster are acquired through noncompetitive means, like through options or because of a prior relationship—

THE WITNESS: At least 50 percent.

THE COURT:—did you mean all the books or just the anticipated top selling books?

THE WITNESS: All the books we publish.

THE COURT: Is there a different number for anticipated top selling books?

THE WITNESS: I have never counted.

THE COURT: Do you think it's more or less?

THE WITNESS: So you are asking me what percentage of the so-called anticipated best selling books do we acquire competitively in auctions?

THE COURT: Not just—well, whatever is competitive. I think of competitive not just as sort of round robin auctions but best bids things and preemptive, anything that's not just a one-on-one negotiation.

THE WITNESS: I have never counted. I am trepidatious about saying anything more than that. I do think that a lot of the high-priced books we acquire are acquired in those manners that you've outlined.

THE COURT: Okay. So you think about the same as other books, same proportion as other books, 50 percent?

THE WITNESS: I don't know.

THE COURT: Do you think anticipated top selling books are more likely to be sold in a competitive situation than—

THE WITNESS: I think it's possible. I think that that's more likely than the other way. I think it's more likely that they would be sold in a competitive situation.

But the only reason I am hesitating is because sometimes, I mean, you really are negotiating—you know, with some of these major talents, you go to them and you put a big enough number out there so that they never talk to anybody
else.

THE COURT: Right. But the reason it's big is because you think other people are interested?

THE WITNESS: Right. So when we acquired Bruce Springsteen, he never talked to anyone else.

THE COURT: Interesting. So I just have a couple of questions for you. You have been in the business a long time so you have worked with a lot of authors. When you are working with an author who thinks their book is going to do well, someone with a track record or someone who is famous, do they approach the process very differently from somebody who is just trying to get their foot in the door, they are just trying to get their big break, trying to publish their first book? Can you talk about those differences?

THE WITNESS: You know, that's funny because I've wondered about that myself. Sometimes, you know, the most famous best selling authors are actually the calmest because they have been to the top of the mountain and they are relaxed and they are just hands off. Whatever do you is fine. And they are actually—some of them are a total joyride.

THE COURT: Stephen King didn't seem to care too much about the terms—

THE WITNESS: He's a pleasure and such a generous writer too, so generous to his colleagues, to other writers. The ones who were trying to make it are sometimes the—because they have all that energy and because they have that drive, they can push harder, but they sometimes get better results because of it.

THE COURT: So it seems that the well-established authors probably have the leverage to ask for more, but they don't really use the leverage because they have made it?

THE WITNESS: There's that. There's also kind of an equanimity that comes with experience. And you realize that a lot of the success depends upon events that are out of your control.

The idea that any publisher can make a book a best seller is false. We don't make that promise because anybody making that promise would be, you know, putting themselves in a very dangerous credibility place.

THE COURT: But you are telling them that you can better their chances so that's why they should come with you, because you have a broad distribution network, you have relationships with sellers, you can raise the profile of their book, you can create buzz, you are saying all those things, right?

THE WITNESS: The problem is, after you have had two meetings, if you are an author, after you have had two meetings and everyone says the same thing in the meeting, you don't believe it. And, you know, a lot of the time it's like taking success for the weather, taking—I'm sorry, it's like taking credit for the weather. Your success is like taking credit for the weather. And you can't really make those assurances to authors.

I think that—I'm sure you have heard this before, and maybe—I really do believe that it does usually come down to the editor and the publisher. It usually does come down to a personal connection or a spark or a shared sensibility.

I was talking to an editor just last night. He's got a novel exclusively. He spent two hours on the phone with the author. He thinks he has a chance of getting that book, not because of what we are going to pay, but because he understood what the author cared about and the author had read a couple of the books that he had worked on and they talked about it. And, you know, one of the books he had edited was one of the three seminal books for this author.

That's why she wants to go with him. It doesn't have to do with his marketing plan or the promises he's making because it's very hard to deliver on those promises. We can't control how people read a book.

I mean, the thing that has confounded me, I have much more humility about my role in the publishing process now than I did ten years ago, I think that so much depends on luck, so much depends upon factors that are out of your control.

THE COURT: I see. So here's another question for you. How strong is the correlation between the advances paid and the books that are ultimately sold?

I know that the level of advance reflects the P&L which reflects your expectation of the amount sold, but I'm interested in—and the advance reflects the judgment of professional people with a lot of experience in the industry, yet it seems that 85 percent of the books don't pay out, but it looks like 50 percent of them are profitable.

I'm just trying to get a sense of that correlation between—like, for example, if anticipated top selling books account for 70 percent of the advances, are 70 percent of the books being sold in the downstream market books that had advances of—high advances over 250? Like what's the correlation? How strong is it?

THE WITNESS: All right. That's a great question. I will tell you that we have not actually authoritatively studied that. That may be a weakness on our part. We haven't actually looked at it that way.

The statistics you cited do seem basically right to me, that about half of the books we publish make money, and a much lower percentage of them earn back the advance we pay. I think that's basically right.

Whether the books we have paid the most money for actually provide the greatest source of our profit or our sales revenue is a question I that don't know the answer to. I have an opinion, and there is evidence to this in my email.

I believe that the authors you build over time ultimately turn out to be the most profitable for the company because you publish them over time, and there is—I think there's a fairly common truth that publishers hold which is that you make money on the midlist books. You make money on the books that come out of nowhere and of become phenomenons. Like *The Last Thing He Told Me* or Colleen Hoover, these were not books that we paid stratospheric advances for at first but—

THE COURT: How often does that happen?

THE WITNESS: Well, it happens. It happens every year. And maybe the reason why we remember those cases more is because they validate our role as publishers. We saw the talent early, and our dreams were realized. So you are more likely to remember that.

THE COURT: Are the midlist books likely to be ones that you anticipated some sale, but they just over performed—

THE WITNESS: That's what happens.

THE COURT: So they are anticipated top selling books, but they were really—the sales were beyond what you anticipated?

THE WITNESS: There are a lot of books that are acquired for anywhere from $50,000, $75,000, upwards into the hundreds of thousands. It's a broad band of books. And, look, I really do believe—there were many books that I acquired for five figures when I was an editor. And I had hopes that they would be best sellers. And some of them became best sellers. So it didn't—you know, it's not where you start. It's where you finish.

THE COURT: Like Carrie?

THE WITNESS: Yeah.

THE COURT: Yeah, I'm just trying to get a sense of how the market we are talking about now plays into the downstream market. And it seems like there must be some correlation. I'm just trying to figure out how strong it is because the advances reflect your expectations of sales, and there must be some correlation or else you wouldn't be in business.

THE WITNESS: Well, it's a precarious business. But, you know, there are a lot of things we do that don't cost a lot of money that actually really do seed word of mouth.

I don't know whether you have heard anyone else talk about the role that independent book sellers play, but we spend a lot of time—we create advance readers editions. It doesn't cost a lot of money to do. And a year, nine months in advance, we mail out these readers' editions or we email them digitally to book sellers, and that's where a lot of word of mouth begins. And you really—that part of the business—I mean, I don't want you to come away from this testimony thinking that midlist books are just a once-in-a—you know, once-in-a-while thing. They are the core of our business.

THE COURT: So how do you define midlist?

THE WITNESS: Midlist is anything—it's funny. When I got into the book business, midlist was anything that you paid, you know, 50 or 75 thousand dollars for or even 25 thousand dollars for. The numbers have gone up, as I have indicated. Advances have been rising throughout my 30-year career. They have only gone in one direction. I remember when—

THE COURT: So now midlist would be higher?

THE WITNESS: Yeah. I mean, I remember—when I got into the business, I remember that spending a hundred thousand dollars on a book was considered a lot of money. And now that's, I guess, a relatively low advance to the people who are looking at this.

THE COURT: So would a midlist book now be 150 or —

THE WITNESS: No. It could be $25,000. It could be anything. I mean, there was a book we published for under a hundred—

THE COURT: Midlist implies there's a low list. I'm just trying to figure—

THE WITNESS: Midlist is a word that publishers use that doesn't mean anything unfortunately. It just means—I mean, nobody—I don't think any publisher would ever have much of a career if they started using the words low list. No author would want to be on low list.

THE COURT: It's something just below what would be an anticipated top selling, it's a midlist. Like, you think it's going to be okay, but you are not anticipating it's going to be a big one?

THE WITNESS: I think maybe the best way of saying it is you are hoping.

THE COURT: Last question. What about the backlist, has the backlist consisted disproportionately of books that had high advances because you are anticipating that they would do well and end up on the backlist?

THE WITNESS: Completely unpredictable. A lot of books catch on over time and they just sell and sell and sell, and they never started out that way. They just—you know, either because the author is a force of nature and keeps talking about it or people that—word of mouth.

I mean, word of mouth is the most electric galvanizing aspect of why people read and buy books. So we put it out there, and then whatever happens happens.

THE COURT: And finally, do you expect to see publishers bidding at auctions at least roughly in proportion to their market share? Like, say, you know, Penguin Random House has 30 percent now. Do you expect them—I have heard that they are in all the auctions, but maybe they are winning 30 percent of them. A publisher's presence in an auction is correlated to their market share on some level. Is that—

THE WITNESS: Well, look, I will defer to the economists on that, but I think that it would—you are asking me to guess. And it would seem to me that if you are publishing more books, you are more likely to be present in these multiple submissions just because you are publishing more books. I guess it's a tautology.

THE COURT: Okay. Thank you.

MR. VERNON: Good morning. May I proceed?

THE COURT: Yes.

REDIRECT EXAMINATION

BY MR. VERNON:

Q. Let me follow up on the last point. I think the judge asked you if other publishers' performance at auction—or participation in auctions would be correlated to market shares. And I think you said, if you publish more books, you are more likely to participate. Did I get that roughly right?

A. That's—I think that's what I just said, yes.

Q. Penguin Random House is the largest trade book publisher, correct?

A. They are.

Q. So you would expect Penguin Random House to be the publisher that you bid against the most, correct?

A. I think so, yes.

Q. Let me ask you about the question of books that are acquired in different scenarios meaning competitive, noncompetitive, auction, non-auction. Can we talk about that for a minute?

Let's start with preempts. When you are making an offer that's a preempt, one of the things that affects the advance you offer is that you are trying to make an advance offer that is high enough to preempt further bidding, is that correct?

A. Correct.

Q. Now, let me ask you about books that are acquired in situations where no one has bid yet, no other publishers have bid yet like an exclusive negotiation or an option. Is that okay?

A. Yes.

Q. For those books, one of the factors that affects the advance that you offer is that you know that if you don't make a high enough offer, the agent can take the book and shop it to other publishers, is that correct?

A. Yes.

Q. So in that situation, you are not bidding against other publishers, is that correct?

A. That's right.

Q. But the threat that the book could go to auction does affect the advance that you offer for those books, is that correct?

A. Absolutely. That threat is there with every relationship, Mr. Vernon. Any author we currently publish, there's always the risk that if you don't treat them well, they are going to go somewhere else.

Q. Let me switch topics slightly.

You would receive—I am not going to ask you about the specific number, but it's fair to say you would receive a significant bonus if the merger of Penguin Random House and Simon & Schuster goes through, is that correct?

A. It's a standard provision of the contract that I was offered when I was CEO. It wasn't something I asked for. And it certainly isn't affecting my testimony.

Q. Let me just make sure I understand. If the merger is consummated, you would receive a significant bonus, is that correct?

A. Yes.

Q. And if the merger does through, who would your boss be?

A. I haven't actually talked about anything beyond this regulatory review with Markus Dohle. He has not actually discussed anything other than to say that we would remain independent and that we would have the same kind of creative and entrepreneurial freedom that we have today.

Q. It's fair to say that, if the merger goes through, you would expect to have a role at the combined company, is that correct?

A. I haven't really thought much about it, but yes. Yes, I would like to. I would rather not do my job interview right now with you, if that's okay.
Q. If the merger goes through, you would report to Mr. Dohle directly or indirectly. Is that fair?
A. We haven't discussed it.
THE COURT: Do you have a lot, Mr. Vernon, because we should take a break at some point?
MR. VERNON: I am happy to take a break now, Your Honor.
THE COURT: Let's take a break for 15 minutes. Please don't talk to anyone about your testimony during the break.
THE WITNESS: You got it.
(A recess was taken at 11:01 a.m.)
THE COURT: Good morning again.
THE COURTROOM DEPUTY: Court in back in session. Please be seated and come to order.
THE COURT: All right. Ready when you are, Mr. Vernon.
MR. VERNON: Thank you, Your Honor.
BY MR. VERNON:
Q. Mr. Karp, can I ask you to turn to defendants' binder, which is the smaller one, tab 1. Let me know when you are there.
A. Yes.
Q. Just for the record, it's DX71. I believe's already been admitted. The top email is from you, Mr. Karp, dated November 17, 2019, is that correct?
A. Yes.
Q. I think your counsel asked you some documents (sic) about this question (sic) yesterday, is that right?
A. Yes.
Q. Let me ask you to turn to the second page. If you look at the paragraph number 3 at the top, do you see that?
A. Yes.
Q. You were—in this page, you are describing some limits on the extent to which Simon & Schuster imprints should be competing with each other. Is that fair?
A. I would phrase it that I was asking them—I was asking them not to duplicate work.
Q. Let's just read this point three. At the top it says, collegiality matters more than internal competition.
A. Yes.
Q. Do you see that?
A. Yes.
Q. Then you say, we will thank and honor editors who defer to more enthusiastic colleagues or to those who have established a prior relationship with the author on submission. Did I read that correctly?
A. Yes. That parenthetical remark was very important. I was trying to—part of what I was trying to do was create a clear path for people who had shown initiative and enterprise and forged a relationship with a new writer.
So as I testified previously, I don't believe that internal competition has any effect on what we ultimately offer. So I am fine with internal competition, and we often have editors bidding together. But if there are too many of them, I just think that some of them are wasting their time. That's all.
Q. So it's fair to say that in this paragraph, you are saying that there are some situations in which Simon & Schuster editors should not be bidding for the same book, is that fair, or at least you would discourage it?
A. I would discourage it in some cases.
Q. Let me ask you to look at No. 7 –
A. Yes.
Q.—at the very bottom.
It says, try to bail out on submissions in which there are more than two imprints in the building pursuing the project especially if you think your chances aren't as good as the other two imprints in the building.

Did I read that correctly?

A. Yes, you did.

Q. Again, in this paragraph you are saying that there should be some circumstances in which editors from different Simon & Schuster imprints should not be bidding on the same book, is that fair?

A. Yeah. I think that there's too much of a pack mentality sometimes and it's just not a good use—it's more about efficiency than anything else.

Q. Let me ask you to change topics a little bit, and you can set that document aside. Yesterday, in response to questions by Mr. Fishbein, you said that the bids that Simon & Schuster offers are subjective. Is that fair?

A. Yes.

Q. As an example, there are some situations in which an editor can value a book higher or even significantly higher than other editors. Is that fair?

A. Yes.

Q. And we also talked yesterday about how a larger number of bidders can lead to higher advances. Do you remember that?

A. Yes.

Q. And one reason that's the case is that with more bidders, there's a greater chance that there will be a bidder who values the book higher or even significantly higher than the other bidders. Is that fair?

A. I'm not a game theorist, but I think that that—that seems like a reasonable expectation to me.

Q. Okay. Let me ask you a different question. There are more publishers who can compete for books with a $10,000 advance than there are who can compete with a $1 million advance. Is that correct?

A. That seems to be correct.

Q. So I take it you disagree with the $250,000 cutoff, but you don't disagree with the general idea that there are fewer competitors at the higher advance levels. Is that correct?

MR. FISHBEIN: Can I object to higher advance levels.

THE COURT: Overruled.

THE WITNESS: Well, the thing is, there are—you know, I am sure that, you know, Norton or Scholastic or Abrams or Bloomsbury, they are all paying massive advances, you know, well into the seven figures for certain authors. It's just about picking your shots more than anything else. So I—that's my answer to your question.

BY MR. VERNON:

Q. Let me go back to my question. You do not disagree with the general idea that there are fewer competitors at the higher advance levels, is that correct?

A. In those—in the auctions, I agree with you, yes, in the auctions. In the exclusive negotiations, I have no way of knowing.

Q. Okay. If the government's expert in this case were to do calculations that showed that the market shares of non-Big 5 publishers are very different, below $250,000 in terms of advances than they are above $250,000, you wouldn't be in a position to dispute that, is that correct?

A. I am not in a position to dispute that.

Q. In response to questions by Mr. Fishbein, you talked about competition with non-Big 5 publishers, is that fair?

A. Yes.

Q. Mr. Fishbein asked you, and I tried to count, about two losses to Norton, two losses to Scholastic, one to Hay House and one to, I think, Harvard. Do you remember that?

And those losses were over a period of several years, is that fair?

A. Those were the ones—those losses were some of the ones over a period, I think, of the three years that we looked at for this case.

Q. Mr. Fishbein did not show you a document where Simon & Schuster lost three books in one week to Norton, is that fair?

A. That's fair.

Q. In my examination before, I asked you about instances—some instances in which Penguin Random

House and Simon & Schuster were the last two bidders in an auction, is that fair?
A. Yes.
Q. And there are many other instances in which Simon & Schuster and Penguin Random House were the last two bidders, is that fair?
A. There are other examples in your binder.
Q. Let's go through some of them.
A. Oh, really?
Q. Let me ask you to turn to PX697. Let me know when you are ready, and also give me a minute to get there.
A. PX697. All right. I'm there.
Q. This is an email chain with the top email from you dated July 29, 2021, is that correct?
A. Yes.
Q. And just as a precaution, let me remind you, we can talk about the advance levels, but let's try not to name the author, the agent, or the book title.
A. Got it.
Q. Just to be safe.
A. Okay.
Q. But this email relates to the bidding for a book where the author's name is in the subject of the email at the top, is that fair?
A. Yes.
Q. Let me ask you to focus on the fourth email down from Leah, I might mispronounce her last name, Trouwborst
A. Yes.
Q. She writes, I just got the call that the author went with Talia Krohn at Crown for an offer that was, quote, virtually identical to ours. PPG was the third bidder and was at the same level. Did I read that correctly?
A. Yes.
Q. And PPG is the Penguin Publishing Group, which is part of Random House, is that fair?
A. Yes.
Q. And Crown is also part of Penguin Random House, is that fair?
A. Yes.
Q. This email states, the top three bidders for this book were Simon & Schuster and two imprints from Penguin Random House, is that fair?
A. Yes.
MR. VERNON: The United States moves to admit PX697.
THE COURT: Any objection?
MR. FISHBEIN: No objection.
THE COURT: That will be admitted. (Plaintiff's 697 received in evidence.)
BY MR. VERNON:
Q. Please turn to PX574, and let me know when you are ready.
A. Okay.
Q. This is an email chain from Ms. Kennedy—the top email is from Ms. Kennedy, dated August 5, 2020, is that fair?
A. Yes.
MR. VERNON: Your Honor, we had prepared a redacted version. May we show that to the public?
THE COURT: You may.
BY MR. VERNON:
Q. Let me ask you to focus on the email from Ms. Painton at the bottom.
A. Yes.
Q. Ms. Painton is another editor at Simon & Schuster, is that fair?
A. She's the editor in chief.

Q. Her email, the subject line says, it's a tie, is that right? It's a tie. A phone call could help. Do you see that?
A. I should be able to. Hold on a second.
Q. I think we might have highlighted it on your monitor.
A. Oh, I'm sorry.
Q. That's okay.
A. Yeah.
Q. And then she writes, and I will just paraphrase, in the first email that Simon & Schuster was up against Crown and Portfolio for a specific book that we won't name out loud, is that correct?
A. That's correct.
Q. And, again, Crown and Portfolio are Penguin Random House imprints, is that correct?
A. That's correct.
Q. This email states that there was a three-way tie between Simon & Schuster and two Penguin Random House imprints, is that correct?
A. Correct.
MR. VERNON: The United States moves to admit PX574.
THE COURT: Any objection?
MR. FISHBEIN: No, Your Honor.
THE COURT: That will be admitted. (Plaintiff's 574 received in evidence.)
BY MR. VERNON:
Q. I will just do one more. Please turn to PX530. This is an email chain with the top email from Ms. Reidy dated June 18, 2019, is that fair?
A. Yes.
MR. VERNON: Your Honor, we have prepared a redacted version. May we show it to the public?
THE COURT: You may.
BY MR. VERNON:
Q. The email chain relates to a bidding for a book that is listed in the subject like of this email, is that correct?
A. Correct.
Q. Focusing on the email at the top from you—sorry, the second email from the top. You write, the author is deciding between Hilary Redmond at Random House and Karyn Marcus at Gallery. Did I read that correctly?
A. Yes.
MR. VERNON: The United States moves to admit PX590.
THE COURT: Any objection?
MR. FISHBEIN: No, Your Honor.
THE COURT: That will be admitted. (Plaintiff's 590 received in evidence.)
BY MR. VERNON:
Q. Counsel asked you—and I am going to have to turn back to the smaller binder. Counsel asked you about a situation in which you bid against Hay House. Do you remember that?
A. Yes.
Q. I think it was the High—A *High Fiber Keto.*
Q. Right.
A. Not a book I have read, by the way.
Q. Let me ask you to turn to defendants' binder, the smaller binder, DX38, which I believe is tab 13 if I wrote that correctly.
This is an email chain with the top email from Ms. Maguire dated March 13, 2019, is that right?
A. Yes.
Q. The subject of her email at the very top says, we lost *High Fiber Keto* to, dot, dot, dot, is that right?
A. Yes.
Q. And then at some point, she identifies Hay House as the winner, is that correct?

A. Correct.
Q. And in the email at the very top, there's an email from Ms. Maguire, is that right?
A. Yes.
Q. I think we mentioned this yesterday, but she is the publisher of—
(There was an interruption by the court reporter.)
MR. VERNON: I'm sorry. I'll try to slow down.
BY MR. VERNON:
Q. She is the publisher at Atria and she reports to you, Mr. Karp, is that fair?
A. Yes.
Q. She writes, wow, I didn't know they pay big advances. Do you see that?
A. Yes.
Q. Fair to say she's referring to Hay House?
A. Yes.
Q. So she's not saying in this email that Simon & Schuster frequently competes with Hay House for big advances, is that fair?
A. Yes.
Q. Let me ask you to turn to tab 15 in defendants' binder. Let me know when you are there.
A. I'm there.
MR. VERNON: The United States moves to admit DX38.
THE COURT: Any objection?
MR. FISHBEIN: No objection.
THE COURT: That will be admitted. (Defendants' 38 received in evidence.)
BY MR. VERNON:
Q. Now let me ask you to turn to tab 15, which is DX131.
A. Tab 13?
Q. 15.
A. I'm there.
Q. This is an email where the top email is from Ms. Maguire, is that right?
A. Yes.
Q. Dated October 5, 2020, is that right?
A. Right.
Q. And this email relates to the book by—and I forget the first name, but the last name is Ruha.
A. Ruha Benjamin.
Q. And that was one of the bidding episodes that you discussed with Mr. Fishbein, is that right?
A. Right.
Q. And you lost this book to Princeton, is that right?
A. Princeton University Press.
Q. There's an email—the second email from the top is from Julia Cheiffetz. Do you see that?
A. Yes.
Q. She's another editor at Simon & Schuster, is that right?
A. Yes. She's the publisher of this imprint, One Signal Press.
Q. She writes, I found out it was Princeton University Press. They do that, the university presses, buy one big book a year, dot, dot, dot. Did I read that correctly?
A. That's — yes.
Q. And then in the email at the top, Ms. Maguire writes, wow, I had no idea they pay that much. Did I read that correctly?
A. Yes.
Q. So both Ms. Cheiffetz and Ms. Maguire in this email are not saying that they complete frequently at the higher advance levels with Princeton. Is that fair?
A. Yes.
Q. Let me switch subjects a little bit.

THE COURT: Is that admitted?
MR. VERNON: I'm sorry, Your Honor. United States moves to admit DX131.
THE COURT: Any objection?
MR. FISHBEIN: No objection.
THE COURT: That would be admitted. (Defendants' 131 received in evidence.)
BY MR. VERNON:
Q. You have not done a quantitative study analyzing how frequently non-Big 5 publishers are the runner up when Simon & Schuster wins a book. Is that fair?
A. Correct.
Q. If the defendants' expert in this case did a study and concluded that Big 5 publishers are the runners up—I'm sorry. Can I restart my question?
If the defendants' expert did a study and concluded that the Big 5 publishers are the runner up for most of the books that Simon & Schuster wins, you would not be in a position to dispute that, is that correct?
A. Correct.
Q. And, in fact, that would be consistent with your testimony that Simon & Schuster competes with the Big 5 the most, is that correct?
A. That's—yes, that's what I have said. Although, I have also said that we compete with everybody, but the most often in auctions at a high level with the other major four publishers.
Q. Let me ask you, I think you mentioned three recent imprints when you were answering questions for Mr. Fishbein. I think they were S&G, Zando, and Astra. Is that right?
A. Right.
Q. You haven't calculated the market shares for those firms, is that correct?
A. That's correct.
Q. If the government's expert calculated their shares, you wouldn't be in a position to dispute his calculations, is that fair?
A. That's fair.
Q. You also discussed Amazon with Mr. Fishbein, is that fair?
A. Yes.
Q. You haven't calculated Amazon's market share, is that correct?
A. I haven't. I wish somebody would.
Q. If the government's expert in this case calculated Amazon's market share, you wouldn't be in a position to dispute that, is that correct?
A. Correct.
Q. In response to questions from Mr. Fishbein, I think you said that you do see Amazon in auctions. Did I get that correct?
A. Yes.
Q. Let me ask you to turn to the litigation deposition in the government's binder. I think it's page 207. Let me know when you are there, and give me a second to get there too.
THE COURT: What's the date on that?
MR. VERNON: It's the very last one. I think it was February 15 or roughly that. February 17.
THE WITNESS: What page?

BY MR. VERNON:
Q. Page 207, lines 5 through 14. Are you there?
A. Yes.
Q. Mr. Read's question, it's fair to say—I mean, you would agree with me that Amazon rarely competes with Simon & Schuster to acquire a book, is that correct?
There's an objection.
Answer, yeah, right now their—right now we do not find ourselves in auctions with Amazon, but they are—and they are omnipresent in many other aspects of our publishing.
Did I read that correctly?

A. Yes.
MR. VERNON: United States moves to admit page 207, lines 5 through 14 for impeachment and as a party admission for substance.
MR. FISHBEIN: (Inaudible.)
(There was an interruption by the court reporter.)
THE COURT: Would you come up to the microphone, please.
MR. FISHBEIN: Yes. On this one I do have an objection because he testified that the auction was two weeks ago. So it doesn't seem inconsistent to have said in a deposition in February of '22 that right now we do not find ourselves in auctions with Amazon, and to say on the stand that I was in an auction with Amazon two weeks ago, that doesn't seem consistent to me.
THE COURT: I do think the record reflects that this witness's view on this matter has changed over time. But I think that this is still admissible.
MR. FISHBEIN: If I may, Your Honor, he's saying—in February of '22, he's saying as of right now.
THE COURT: Yes. He says presently we do not find ourselves in auctions with Amazon.
MR. FISHBEIN: Right. And now he's saying—
THE COURT: And now he's saying he just had one two weeks ago.
MR. FISHBEIN: Right.
THE COURT: I think that is not inconsistent, Mr. Vernon.
MR. VERNON: May I address that briefly, Your Honor?
THE COURT: Yes.
MR. VERNON: The testimony I wrote down from the direct that I remember, and I might be remembering it wrong, was he said, we do find ourselves in auctions with Amazon. This, I think that first three lines, is inconsistent with that. And there's also a question of why something would have changed after the deposition.
THE COURT: This deposition was February of 2022. We are now in July of 2022. Back then he said, we do not find ourselves in auctions with Amazon. Now he says I had an auction two weeks ago. I mean, it's not a strong difference or point.
MR. VERNON: I will move on, Your Honor.
THE COURT: Yes. I am going to sustain the objection.
BY MR. VERNON:
Q. You also referred to two books that had Kickstarter campaigns, is that correct?
A. Correct.
Q. One of them was—or at least two authors, and one of the authors was Brandon Sanderson, is that right?
A. Yes.
Q. And the other book was, I think, *Good Night Girls*. Did I get that correct?
A. I think it's called *Good Night Stories for Rebel Girls*.
Q. Was the author for *Good Night Stories* a Simon & Schuster author before he or she did the Kickstarter campaign?
A. To the best of my knowledge, I believe this was a self-published book. I don't think we have any connection with that author.
Q. Was Mr. Sanderson a Simon & Schuster author before he did the Kickstarter campaign?
A. No.
Q. Your knowledge about these two Kickstarter authors comes from where?
A. I read about the *Good Night Stories for Rebel Girls* in a trade publication.
Q. So you haven't seen any Simon & Schuster authors leave Simon & Schuster to start a Kickstarter campaign, is that fair?
A. That's right.
Q. Let me ask you about the merger emails quickly.
You will remember there was the first email in March of 2020 with Mr. Irving, is that correct?
A. Could we look at those?

Q. Yes, we can. I believe the first one was PX655.
A. PX655. Okay. Here it is. Okay. You've got it up it on the screen. Okay.
Q. This was the email where you said you thought the Department of Justice—
(There was an interruption by the court reporter.)
BY MR. VERNON:
Q.—would not allow Penguin Random House to buy Simon & Schuster. That's what this email says, is that fair?
A. That's what my joke says, yes.
Q. And I think you said in response to questions from Mr. Fishbein that this was right after the sale was announced and so you hadn't thought about it very much. Is that right?
A. I certainly hadn't thought very much about antitrust at that point.
Q. Now let me ask you to turn to PX634.
A. 634.
Q. Let me know when you are there.
A. Yes.
Q. And this is the email with the number two paragraph where you discuss—you mention harm—arguable harm to the larger book publishing ecosystem from a merger with a strategic buyer, is that right?
A. Yes.
Q. And this email is six months later, is that correct?
A. And in those six months, I had become CEO and really educated myself. I was in a completely different place then. So actually there's a big difference about those six months.
Q. Let me ask you another question. I think in response to questions from counsel yesterday, you talked about agents. Is that right?
A. Yes.
Q. Now, let me ask you, you sometimes give editors approval to offer up to a certain dollar amount for a book, is that fair?
A. Publishers, yes, I give them approval, yes.
Q. And Simon & Schuster sometimes acquires books for less than the maximum amount that you approved, is that correct?
A. Yes.
Q. So for those books, the agent doesn't have enough power to force Simon & Schuster to pay the maximum that it was willing to pay, is that correct?
A. Well, the only thing is, a lot of those offers that I clear people to, I do it—and there's a lot of email to this effect. I ask them to go with their worst case scenario, you know, what's the most you would absolutely have to pay if you had to. That's different than what we want to pay.
MR. VERNON: Your Honor, may I approach with two documents?
THE COURT: Yes.
BY MR. VERNON:
Q. Let me mark for identification purposes the first document as PX984. Just for the record, it's an email chain where the top email is from Mr. Karp dated November 18, 2019, and the Bates number at the end ends in 356.
This is an email relating to the bidding for a book by the author who is listed in the subject of the email at the top, is that fair?
A. Yes.
Q. In your email at the very top, you say Libby and Lindsey have a good feel for this kind of fiction. I think this is the kind of author they can build, so we will start low and go to $750,000 per book if necessary. Do you see that?
A. Yes.
Q. We may not have to. Let me ask you to turn to the second document that I identified.
MR. FISHBEIN: (Inaudible.)
(There was an interruption by the court reporter.)

THE COURT: I'm sorry, Mr. Fishbein. Before you speak, come to the microphone just to do the court reporter a favor.

MR. FISHBEIN: These two documents, as far as I know, are not on the exhibit list. I am wondering, before Mr. Vernon goes forward in reading them, whether he's offering them.

MR. VERNON: It's partly for impeachment, Your Honor, but after I go through the questions, I will move to admit them also.

THE COURT: I think that's permissible. It's for impeachment purposes. Go ahead.

BY MR. VERNON:

Q. Let me ask you to look at the second document. We will mark this as PX985. Just for the record, this is an email where the top email chain is from Ms. Reidy dated November 20, 2019, is that correct?

A. Yes.

Q. And this is about the same author and the same book in the previous email, is that correct?

A. Yes.

Q. In your email, second from the top, you write, we beat Dutton with the same bid they had, $1.1 million for two books, so we didn't have to go all the way to $750,000 per book. Did I read that correctly?

A. Yes.

Q. And Dutton is an imprint of Penguin Random House, is that correct?

A. Yes.

THE COURT: I am so sorry, Mr. Vernon. I just went back and looked at the transcript, and I don't know that this is impeaching what Mr. Karp said. And reading back, before you started introducing these documents, he said, I asked them to go with their worst case scenario. You know, that's the most you would absolutely have to paid if you had to. That's different from what we want to pay. I don't see these documents as impeaching this testimony.

MR. VERNON: Let me address that briefly, Your Honor. This is meant to impeach something he said yesterday. My vague memory of it was a discussion of how the agents have power.

And so the idea with these documents is that whatever power the agents have doesn't do enough to force them to bid the maximum they are willing to pay. That's what I was trying to impeach.

THE COURT: I see. Mr. Fishbein, do you want to address that?

MR. FISHBEIN: I think that's very attenuated impeachment, Your Honor. These are not on the exhibit list. It would be one thing if they directly contradicted something, but I don't think it's even disputed that they don't always pay the top amount. He could just ask him, and I think his answer would be that's correct.

THE COURT: I think I agree with Mr. Fishbein on this one, Mr. Vernon. I don't think Mr. Karp has said that they always pay the most that they have authorized. I think he said that's different from what they want to pay. And I think these documents merely reinforce that same point. So I am going to sustain the objection on these documents.

MR. VERNON: I will move on.

THE COURT: Okay.

BY MR. VERNON:

Q. Simon & Schuster almost never acquires books without acquiring audio rights, is that fair?

A. Yes.

Q. Agents sometimes ask Simon & Schuster to buy books without also buying audio rights, is that correct?

A. That has happened, yes.

Q. But Simon & Schuster generally does not acquire books without also acquiring audio rights, is that right?

A. Correct.

Q. Let me ask you to turn to PX652 in your binder.

A. Okay.

Q. This is an email relating to the bidding for book 44, is that correct?

A. Correct.
MR. VERNON: We have prepared a redacted version. May I show it to the public, Your Honor?
THE COURT: Yes, you may.
BY MR. VERNON:
Q. Let me ask you to turn to the bottom of page 3. There's an email from Dawn Davis. Do you see that?
A. Yes.
Q. She writes, and I'm paraphrasing, that the agent is not including audio rights for this book. Is that correct?
A. Correct.
Q. At the bottom of page 2, there's an email from Chris Lynch. Do you see that?
A. Yes.
Q. He writes, I know this is a book we would all love to publish, but I hope that we would walk away if audio rights are not part of the deal. Did I read that correctly?
A. Correct.
Q. And then there's an email from Ms. Graham. Do you see that?
A. Yes.
Q. At the very bottom of her email, she says, I hate to give this book up, but I'm afraid I have to agree with Chris. Do you see that?
A. Yes.
Q. And then please turn to the bottom of the first page.
A. Yes.
Q. There's an email from you where you write, I agree with all of you. Did I read that correctly?
A. Yes. Chris Lynch is the publisher of our audio division, so I was supporting him because obviously his division depends upon us having the audio rights.
Q. And then at the top, there's an email from Ms. Graham. Do you see that?
A. Yes.
Q. She writes, thanks, Jon. Let me know if you would like me to draft it. You have a lot to do. It would be very interesting to see whether PRH, Hachette, Harper, or Macmillan participate. My understanding is that they have the no audio, no deal rule—they too have the no audio, no deal rule. Did I read that correctly?
A. Yes.
MR. VERNON: United States moves to admit PX652.
THE COURT: Any objection?
MR. FISHBEIN: No objection.
THE COURT: That's admitted. (Plaintiff's 652 received in evidence.)
BY MR. VERNON:
Q. Let me ask you to turn to PX568.
A. Okay. I'm here.
Q. This is another email relating to the bidding for this same book, is that correct?
A. Correct.
MR. VERNON: Your Honor, we have prepared a redacted version. May we publish?
THE COURT: You may.
BY MR. VERNON:
Q. The top email is from you dated June 25, 2020, is that correct?
A. Correct.
Q. Let me ask you to turn to the bottom of the second page.
A. Yes.
Q. There's an email from the agent for this book, is that right?
A. Yes.
Q. And I'm paraphrasing, but he writes that he's going to restart the auction but include audio rights, is that right?

A. Right.
Q. So for this auction, the agent did not have enough power to convince Simon & Schuster to bid to acquire the book without acquiring audio rights, is that correct?
A. All I know is that we pushed back and he dropped them. I don't know what his thinking was or why he did.
Q. But the agent did restart the auction and include audio rights according to this email, is that correct?
A. That's absolutely right.
MR. VERNON: The United States moves to admit PX568.
THE COURT: Any objection?
MR. FISHBEIN: No objection.
THE COURT: That will be admitted. (Plaintiff's 568 received in evidence.)
MR. VERNON: Your Honor, the United States has no further questions, but we would like to thank Mr. Karp.
THE WITNESS: Thank you, Mr. Vernon.
THE COURT: Thank you very much.
MR. FISHBEIN: (Inaudible.)
(There was an interruption by the court reporter.)
THE COURT: Mr. Fishbein, you must talk into the microphone.
MR. FISHBEIN: I have two questions about one document that he referred to when you were speaking to him, Your Honor, if I may.
THE COURT: You may.
MR. FISHBEIN: Okay.

RECROSS-EXAMINATION

BY MR. FISHBEIN:

Q. Mr. Karp, when the judge was asking you about any relationship between advances and how books sell, do you remember you said, it's in my email? If you could turn to tab 1, Defendants' Exhibit 71 that's already in evidence.
A. Yes.
Q. And this was the email where you were giving guidelines on acquisitions, is that right?
A. Yes.
Q. And if you would look at paragraph 1, can you read paragraph 1 starting with most of our biggest.
A. Most of our biggest titles are not acquired in fevered auctions. Our most successful authors tend to be writers we build over time or acquire in routine ways, outreach, options, limited submissions. I'm speaking of people like Brad Thor or David McCullough or Walter Isaacson or Doris Kearns Goodwin.
Q. Is this what you were referring to when you made a comment in your email about which of your books is successful?
A. Yes.
Q. In the parenthetical when it says outreach, what does that refer to?
A. Outreach is encouraging editors to go out and find writers who they want to work with.
Q. Is that one of the categories of exclusives?
A. Yes.
Q. And then options, I think we know, but can you say quickly what that is.
A. Options are repeat authors whose next work we want to acquire.
Q. Is that also an exclusive situation?
A. It is.
MR. FISHBEIN: Thank you, Your Honor.
COURT: Thank you. You may step down, Mr. Karp. Thank you very much for your testimony.

ADRIANA PORRO, RESEARCH ANALYST, DEPARTMENT OF JUSTICE

DIRECT EXAMINATION

BY MS. RIKER:

Q. Would you please state and spell your name for the record.
A. Of course. My name is Adriana Porro; spelled A-d-r-i-a-n-a P-o-r-r-o.
Q. I'd like to talk a little bit about your background. Where do you work?
A. I work at the antitrust division of the Department of Justice.
Q. And what is your title?
A. My formal title is statistician, but, internally, I'm referred to as an RA, a research analyst.
Q. And what is an RA?
A. An RA is somebody who works predominantly with economists, and that's kind of the lingo that they normally use. But I work with data, most predominantly, and coding. Those are my—
Q. How long have you worked at the antitrust division?
A. As of September, it will be three years.
THE COURT REPORTER: Can you pull the microphone just a little bit closer to you.
THE WITNESS: Yes.
THE COURT REPORTER: Thank you.
THE WITNESS: Absolutely.

BY MS. RIKER:

Q. Have you had the same title the whole time?
A. Yes, I have.
Q. What did you do before working at the antitrust division?
A. This is my first job after I graduated from college.
Q. What degree did you get?
A. I have B.A.s in economics and art history.
Q. Ms. Porro—
THE COURT: You're not using your art history background, are you?
THE WITNESS: No. No, I'm not.

BY MS. RIKER:

Q. Ms. Porro, what was your assignment on the Penguin Random House/Simon & Schuster team?
A. My assignment was to oversee an accurate summarization of the documents that I was presented with.
Q. What do you mean by that?
A. More specifically, I mean a summarization of the bidding details that were in the documents that I reviewed.
Q. What did you create for your assignment?
A. For my assignment, I created 27 summaries.
Q. And what do you mean by "bidding details"?
A. Yeah. By bidding details, I mean information about the different bidding events that were captured within the documents, such as—would it help for an example? Such as the participants within a bidding event, the amount of money or bid—for a particular bid, things like that.
Q. When did you start working on the 27 summaries?
A. I started working on the summaries in May.
Q. May of this year?
A. Yes. Sorry.
Q. And did you have any role in the department's investigation of the Penguin Random House/Simon & Schuster merger?
A. So in July of the last year—2021—I was asked to help out with doing a quick data check on a data production that was received for this matter.

Q. What do you mean by "data check"?
A. Yes. So it's very normal course, preliminary, at a high level, just identifying if there are any issues with the data, any breaks or if the data is corrupted, and just flagging that for an economist.
Q. Did you have any role in analyzing the data once the data check was complete?
A. I did not.
Q. And how long did you work on that data-check project?
A. I'd say it was about two weeks.
Q. And when was the data-check project?
A. July of 2021.
Q. Other than the data-check project, did you have any role in the department's investigation of Penguin Random House and Simon & Schuster's merger?
A. I did not.
Q. And did you have any involvement in the recommendation to sue?
A. I did not.
Q. Did you attend team meetings?
A. I believe I may have attended one team meeting when I was doing the data check, but nothing beyond that.
Q. Did you work on any data analysis for the government's expert?
A. I did not.
Q. Ms. Porro, I'd like to turn to your binders. Let me grab them.
MS. RIKER: May I approach?
THE COURT: Yes, you may.
THE WITNESS: Thank you.
THE COURT: Thank you.

BY MS. RIKER:

Q. Okay. Ms. Porro, I'd like you to open the binder in front of you that contains exhibits that have been marked for identification purposes as PX 932-B through PX 958-B. And are you familiar with PX 932-B through PX 958-B?
A. Yes, these are the summaries that I created.
MS. RIKER: Two housekeeping items about the binders. They include two copies of each summary. The top copy has a red box around confidential material, and there is a clean copy behind each of those. And second, in the front of the binders there should be a key that ties the author names with the master key.
So the key uses the last two digits of the PX number. So for the purposes of this exam, the PX number and the last two digits of the PX number can be used interchangeably to refer to the confidential author names and book titles.
THE COURT: Thank you.

BY MS. RIKER:

Q. Ms. Porro, are these the summaries you created?
A. Yes, they are.
Q. Starting with the big picture, what types of information are summarized in PX 932-B through PX 958-B?
A. At a high level, details about the bidding event from the documents I reviewed are captured in my summary. So information about participants, bid values, a bit about the structure of the bidding event, and the winner, things like that.
Q. How did you decide what to include in the summaries?
A. Yes. So I wanted my summaries to be direct and succinctly summarize the information that I found—that I read in my documents. And since the documents revolved around the particular bidding event, I wanted to highlight and call out those details. So identifying the participants, the bids that they made, and more about the structure.
Q. What types of documents did you summarize in PX 932-B through PX 958-B?

A. I looked at a variety of documents. Some were email chains. Others were meeting minutes, information about potential acquisitions, and spreadsheets; maybe like an agent spreadsheet, for example.

Q. And at a high level, what types of entities produce these documents?

A. Yes. So I looked at documents from Simon & Schuster, Penguin Random House, other third-party publishers, and agents.

Q. And how many documents did you review to prepare the summaries?

A. I believe I reviewed around 250 documents.

Q. And earlier you mentioned spreadsheets. Does the number of documents that you reviewed include spreadsheets?

A. Yes, it does.

Q. And how would you describe the volume of information contained in spreadsheets that you reviewed?

A. Yeah. The vast majority of the workbooks that I reviewed had tens of thousands of observations and multiple tabs of information.

Q. Did you review the same type of information to prepare each of the summaries, PX 932-B through PX 958-B?

A. Yes, I did.

Q. And is the same types of information summarized in each of PX 932-B through 958-B?

A. Yes, it is.

Q. Let's walk through how you prepared the summaries. How much time did you spend preparing them?

A. I believe I spent over 200 hours on the summaries.

Q. What did you spend those 200 hours doing?

A. Yes. That's a long amount of time. So I'd say that the biggest category of time—I'll break them down into—that time into just sections, if that's helpful. So the largest section of time that I spent was on reading the documents. I had no prior information about the industry or things like that, and so I was reading the documents for comprehension of understanding, what information is present, what is information that's being discussed, or what are meeting minutes.

And then—so I'd say the longest time was spent reading for comprehension.

And then the second bucket of time, I'd say, was making sure that the tables that were in the summary, like validating the values and tables in the summary and making sure that the information in the documents was accurate and supported those values. So verification was also there and also involved looking at the documents again.

And then I'd say the third bucket—that's kind of associated with the second—was while I was reviewing the documents to make sure that the values in the table were correct and consistent, I also made sure to cite the documents and cite them accurately. So that was another component of incorporating the citations and making sure that the citations were correct.

And then I'd say the last chunk of time was on just making sure that my summaries were standardized; and if a change was made to one of the 27 summaries, it would need to be carried over and consistent for all of them. So I did that.

And the last, last thing I did—sorry—was I made a few edits to the summaries after my deposition.

Q. What's involved in reviewing all the documents for comprehension?

A. Yes. Lots of reading. And not in the sense of skimming, because I know that's some type of reading, but as I did not know what was going on, I wanted to—sorry. Before I started, I wanted to spend the time with the documents to make sure that I understood what was happening and picking up nuances or things like that. So lots of intensive reading.

Q. And how did you validate the information in the tables in the summaries?

A. Yes. I cross-referenced the values that were in the tables to the documents that I reviewed.

Q. And where did the templates come from for the summaries?

A. Yes. So as I had never made a summary before for a legal audience, I wasn't sure exactly where to start. So I asked for help from my team to give me examples of what a summary could look like. And so I worked on—and evolved—my summaries based on those initial templates.

Q. And what did you do so you could feel comfortable that you were viewing the complete set of documents for each bidding event?

A. Yes. So if I was reviewing a particular bidding event and I had some questions about—maybe a little bit of ambiguity, I'm not quite sure I'm understanding what's happening here, I asked if there were any other documents that could speak to this particular event or this particular point in time. And I asked the team about that.

Q. And you mentioned that you revised the summaries after your deposition. Why did you do that?

A. So I made my edit specifically to clarify ambiguities that were brought to my attention during my deposition.

Q. And did you follow the same process for all of the summaries?

A. Yes, I did.

MS. RIKER: Your Honor, I move to admit Ms. Porro's summaries of the bidding events, PX 932-B through PX 958-B into evidence.

THE COURT: Any objection?

MR. SHORES: No objection, Your Honor.

THE COURT: All right. Those would be admitted. (PX 932-B through PX 958-B admitted into evidence.)

MS. RIKER: At this point I'd like to walk through a few of the summaries. Your Honor, may we publish the redacted summaries to the public monitors?

THE COURT: Yes.

BY MS. RIKER:

Q. Ms. Porro, would you please turn in your binder to PX 937-B.

A. Yes. Thank you. I have it up.

Q. And without referring to the name of the author or the title of the book, what is PX 937-B?

A. This is one of the summaries of a bidding event that I looked at.

Q. Now, I'll ask about the table in a minute, but first I want to talk about the information above the table. What information is above the table?

A. Above the table I'm highlighting the winning publisher and imprint of this particular bidding event or auction, the winning advance value, and the date in which the auction or bidding event took place.

Q. Who was the winning publisher for PX 937-B?

A. For this particular example, Penguin Random House was the winner.

Q. And how did you confirm that Penguin Random House won PX 937-B?

A. So referring to my footnotes, I cite two separate documents supporting this conclusion.

Q. What was the winning advance for PX 937-B?

A. The winning advance was $550,000.

Q. How did you confirm the winning advance for PX 937-B?

A. So looking specifically at my footnotes, I cite to an advance spreadsheet that's kept by, in this case, Penguin Random House that details all of their acquired titles for a certain period of time and the advance that corresponds to that.

Q. Did you follow the same process for confirming the winning publisher and advance for each of the other summaries, PX 937—or 932-B through PX 958-B?

A. Yes, I did. And I would like to clarify that Simon & Schuster also has a similar advance spreadsheet that I looked at.

Q. Above the table there's also a date. What does the date represent?

A. Yes. The date captures the time range—or a general month, time frame of when the bidding event or auction took place.

Q. And there's not a footnote next to the date. How did you confirm the date?

A. So I pieced together the date or identified the general time frame by looking at the dates within the emails that I looked at pertaining to a particular bidding event.

Q. And, Ms. Porro, please turn your attention to the table in PX 937-B. At a high level, what information is captured in the table?

A. Yes. So in the table, I wanted to highlight and clearly communicate what happened within the bidding event; so information on the participants, the general structure of the bidding event, and information about the bids.

Q. And let's look at the first column in the table labeled publisher and then with imprint in parenthesis. What's this column showing?

A. This column captures the different identities of the bidders in this particular auction. So the first name, Penguin Random House, is the publisher, and then the imprint is in parentheses. So Viking, the imprint of Penguin Random House, and the division, PPG, Penguin Publishing Group.

Q. How did you decide which publishers and imprints to list in the table for PX 937-B?

A. I identified the publishers for which I had the information that they bidded—oops. Excuse me—that they bid, and I confirmed that these were the only two bidders in this auction by ref-—by being able to see the number of bids that were placed in that particular round. And that's the final row of the table.

Q. Did you use the same process for listing publishers and imprints in each of PX 932-B through 958-B?

A. Yes, I did.

Q. And the row for PRH has PPG before Viking. What does PPG refer to?

A. PPG refers to Penguin Publishing Group.

Q. And why do you include the information—why did you list Penguin Publishing Group next to the PRH bid?

A. Absolutely. So to my understanding, Penguin Random House has multiple divisions of—in their publishing group, and individual imprints from those divisions bid. So I specifically wanted to call out the division in my table because in other bidding events, there can be multiple divisions within Penguin Random House that are bidding. So I wanted to make sure that it was clear in a distinction of—these are the imprint or imprints that bid and if they're from this division.

Q. And what abbreviations did you use for the other Penguin Random House divisions?

A. Yes. I believe I used KDD for Knopf Doubleday, and then PPG—I'm sorry. RH for Random House, and I think that captures—I think that covers it.

Q. Did you use the same naming convention for the PRH divisions for all of the PRH bids in each of the other summaries?

A. Yes, I did.

Q. Looking at the other headers in the table, one is initial offer and the other is best bids with final offer in parentheses. Why did you organize the bids for PX 937-B into these two columns?

A. Yes. So specifically for the column titles in my table, I pulled directly from language that was used in the documents that I reviewed. So if the first round were called initial offers and the second round was called best bids, I pulled that language directly from the documents.

Q. And did you use the same naming convention for the column headers in each of the other summaries, PX 932-B through PX 958-B?

A. Yes. I sourced the titles based on information that I saw in the documents pertaining to a particular bidding event.

Q. And the last header, best bids final offer, seems to cover two columns. What information is captured in those two columns?

A. Yes. So the final offer column includes not only the final advance that was made as the bid but also differentiating bidding details for the final bids.

Q. Why did you include differentiating—or what do you mean by "differentiating bidding details"?

A. Yes. So as this was the final round bid, I know that terms generally are significant, and so I called out information that had—that gave insight and was included in the final offer.

And, specifically, I made sure to highlight in this column information that differentiated bids. So, for example, if—in this case, both PPG and Viking and S&S decided to propose something of—like the same—the same feature of their bid, I would not call that out. I just wanted to highlight the differences, as it was important that my summary be readable and concise, and highlighting the differences is an

important part of that.
Q. And do all the summaries include those differentiating bid details?
A. Not all of them, no.
Q. Why not?
A. If there was a situation in which the final offers had all of the same bidding characteristics, I didn't call those out.
Q. And how did you indicate the source for the information that you cite in your summaries?
A. Yes. All of the citations and sources for the numbers and information cited are in the footnotes.
Q. And I want to raise one minor issue in PX 937-B. There is no Footnote 3. Why not?
A. Yes. Unfortunately, that is a formatting issue. It—as I was implementing my edits after my deposition, deleting certain fields that previously had a footnote caused a little bit of a formatting mix-up. But I want to stress that all of the information is still fully present and correctly accounted for in the footnotes, and the footnotes themselves still correspond to the correct number in the table.
Q. And in the other summaries that do not have a Footnote 3, is it for the same reason?
A. Yes, it is.
Q. Okay. You can put aside PX 937-B.
THE COURT: I'm sorry. Can you explain how the bonus would be paid in this deal? Do you remember?
THE WITNESS: Why I mentioned a bonus?
THE COURT: No. I'm wondering how the bonus works. Maybe you're not the right witness for this, but I'm just wondering if it—when does that bonus get paid in this deal?
THE WITNESS: To my understanding—so I highlighted—if it was one bonus, I used the word bonus and then put the value. And if there were a series of multiple bonuses, I used the word bonuses and summarized those. I did not call out the terms in which the bonus would be received, if that makes sense—
THE COURT: Okay.
THE WITNESS:—in my summaries.
THE COURT: Okay. I'll ask another witness. Thank you.
THE WITNESS: Sorry.
BY MS. RIKER:
Q. I don't want to go through each summary in detail, but I would like to ask some questions about how you handled certain situations in your summaries.
A. Uh-huh.
Q. So if—do any of your summaries, Ms. Porro, indicate that some information was unknown?
A. Yes, they do.
Q. I'd like to look at an example with some unknown information. If you would please turn to PX 935-B, and let me know when you're there.
A. Great. I have the document open.
Q. Looking at the table in PX 935-B, would you explain your use of the abbreviation UNK?
A. Yes. So specifically in this example, I use the abbreviation UNK to represent that's an unknown value for that particular cell in my table. So in this case, for example, for Macmillan, I had information from my documents that Macmillan bid. I just didn't know what the monetary value of their bid was. So they bid, but I don't know the value. So unknown represents that. And then the total number of bids collected is unknown. So I'm not sure the information was not present in the documents to indicate the total number of bids collected in the first round. So I represent that by UNK.
Q. And for the total number of bidders, did you leave out any bidders that you knew about in the table?
A. No, I did not.
Q. And did you use unknown where it appears the same way in each of the summaries, PX 932-B through 958-B?
A. Yes, I did.
Q. Would you look at the row for Penguin Random House. And it lists the imprint as house bid. What

does that mean?

A. I used the terminology house bid to indicate when multiple imprints submitted bids together from a particular publisher. Or in this case, for Penguin Random House, a particular division.

Q. How did you indicate which imprints participated in the house bid?

A. I called out the—and identified—all of the imprints who participated in each round in the footnotes for the bid corresponding to every round.

Q. And it appears that Crown and Random House participated in the Random House division bid through all four rounds of the auction. But how would you have indicated if one of them had dropped out in the bidding?

A. Yes. So if one of them had dropped out, I would have noted in the footnote, in this round this imprint dropped out. The bidder—the imprint who bid in this round is X.

Q. Did you use the same method for indicating the imprints that participated in a house bid where it appears the same way in each of the other summaries, PX 932-B through PX 958-B?

A. Yes, I did.

Q. Ms. Porro, there's a see, s-e-e, signal at the beginning of—in Footnote 15 through 18 and PX 935-B. Why did you use a see signal there?

A. Yes. So I used a see signal to indicate that I had information in the documents to identify that whatever particular value I put there was the number of bids for that particular round. So using Round 2 as an example in the documents, I was able to identify that there were two bids collected in Round 2. However, the documents did not explicitly say the words two bidders or two bids.

Q. And have you been made aware of any information that suggests that any other publisher bid in Rounds 2 through 4 of PX 935-B?

A. I have not.

Q. And did you use the see signal where it appears the same way in each of the other summaries, PX 932-B through 958-B?

A. Yes, I did.

Q. Okay. You can put aside PX 935-B. Ms. Porro, in any of the summaries, did you ever have documents indicating differing amounts for the same bid?

A. Yes, I did.

Q. Let's look at an example. Please turn in your binder to PX 932-B.

A. Thank you. I have that open.

Q. Does PX 932-B contain an example of a bid that has a different—example of bids that have different amounts in the documents you reviewed?

A. Yes, it does.

Q. And where is that?

A. That would be for Simon & Schuster's Round 1 bid.

Q. And how did you indicate that there were different values for that bid in the documents you reviewed?

A. Yes. So when—I indicated that there were two different—that there were differing values by noting in the footnote, specifically, using a but-see to identify the document that had differing information. And I used—I called out the quote from the document to identify what the language was. But, more specifically, I determined the value to put in the table by relying on if I was faced with two different documents that had differing information, if one of them had information from a source.

So that being the editor or publisher submitting their bid or an agent receiving the bid. So a source on either end of the bid, I used that information and put that in the table and used the but-see signal to call out any other information that was there.

Q. And did you use the but-see signal where it appears the same way in the endnotes for each of the other summaries PX 932-B through 958-B?

A. Yes, I did.

Q. And PX 932-B lists the third and fourth bidders as Publisher A and B. Would you explain what that means?

A. Yes. So in this particular situation, from the documents, I knew that four bids were collected in Round 1. And also from the documents, I was able to determine that—the identity of two of the bidders, Penguin Random House and Simon & Schuster. I was not able to identify the identities of the third and fourth publisher. So I used Publisher A and Publisher B as placeholders to say this is a publish—like this is an unknown publisher and this is another unknown publisher.

Q. And did you use the same naming convention for unknown publishers where they appear in each of the summaries, PX 932-B through 958-B?

A. Yes, I did, but I would like to say as well, if there's a Publisher A in one summary and a Publisher A in another summary, those—I'm not trying to draw equivalencies. They're not supposed to represent the same person. It's just based on the number of publishers that I did not know the identity of.

Q. Thank you.You can put aside PX 932-B.

A. Okay.

Q. And, Ms. Porro, in any of the summaries, do you ever know a range for a bid but not an exact value?

A. Yes.

Q. Okay. Let's look at an example. Would you turn in your binder to PX 950-B, and let me know when you're there.

A. Okay. I have the summary open. Thank you.

Q. Looking at the Round 2 bid for Hachette, why'd you put the bid value as greater than 270 and less than $290,000?

A. Yes. So, specifically, for this example, I had information that Hachette bid in Round 2, and I didn't know their exact bid. However, for this particular auction, the agent used specific auction rules that were the order of bids collected in rounds after Round 1 are set by the value of bids in the first round.

So, specifically, the first bidder in Round 2 was the lowest bidder in Round 1, and they have to improve upon the highest bid in Round 1.

So because of the order of bids in Round 1—and I knew all of the values there—I could place the order in which bids were received. So I know that Hachette bid after Penguin Random House—Random House division, imprint Crown. So the first cell in Round 2. And I knew that they bid before Simon & Schuster, who bid $290,000. So because of the order, I could place that their bid was somewhere between $270,000 and $290,000 dollars.

Q. And how did you know the auction rules for PX 950-B?

A. Yes. The auction rules were explicitly stated in the documents that I looked at.

Q. And looking at the initial best-bid round, why did you list HarperCollins and Hachette's bids as less than $510,000?

A. So the agent set terms, again, for this particular round and said the top two bidders from this round will proceed to the final best-bids round, which is the next column. And I knew the values of the bids for Simon & Schuster and Penguin Random House, and I know that they both proceeded to the final best-bids round.

So I know that the four active bidders in Round 3 were given the opportunity to bid, but I wasn't sure of the value of their bids; but knowing that they didn't progress, I knew they had to be lower than the lowest of the highest bids in the initial best-bids round.

Q. And did you use the greater-than and less-than symbols where they appear the same way in each of PX 932-B through 958-B?

A. Yes, I did.

Q. And in the initial best-bids round in 950-B, the table says two to four bids were received. Why did you use a range there?

A. Yes. So I used a range here because I knew from the documents with certainty that Simon & Schuster and Penguin Random House bid in the initial best-bids round, but I wasn't sure—I didn't have the evidence in the documents to indicate whether or not HarperCollins and Hachette actually made a bid. So to account for that ambiguity, I used the range of two to four bids.

THE COURT: I just want to take a pause while my law clerk gets my laptop. I keep forgetting to bring it back and forth with me, because I'm doing these motions, as the motions judge, through the breaks.

Let me ask. I think these exhibits are very clear. I think that you did a really good job and the notes are very self-explanatory. And so I'm wondering: Is it necessary to go into the detail that we're going into about how these exhibits were put together?

And it could be that I need to ask Mr. Shores: Are you planning to challenge the way these were put together?

MR. SHORES: Your Honor, we just have a very brief set of questions that won't go into the details of how they were put together.

THE COURT: Okay. So with that in mind, do you think you could maybe shorten and summarize what you've been doing?

MS. RIKER: Sure. You know, I was going to go through a couple of examples of other places where it may be actually clear on the face of the summary what was intended, but let me look. I think there are one or two examples that would be helpful to go through, and then we can pass Ms. Porro.

THE COURT: That's fine.

BY MS. RIKER:

Q. And, Ms. Porro, I'd like to look at the number of bids row in PX 950-B. And in Round 2, the number of bids is four advancing, five bids total. What does that mean? And we're on PX 950-B.

A. Thank you so much. I closed my binder. 950. Okey dokey. I'm sorry. Would you mind repeating that.

Q. No problem. In Round 2 the number of bids is listed as four advancing, five bids total.

A. Yes.

Q. What does that mean?

A. Yes. So in this particular case, five bids were received in this round. However, one of them was a terminal bid—whoops. Sorry. One of them was a terminal bid or a last bid by one of the publisher participants. So it didn't contribute towards advancing the auction. It just counted as their last bid. It didn't follow the auction rules. So they were considered out and not progressing the auction further. So I wanted to make sure that their final bid was captured in my summary, and that is in the five bids total in parentheses, but noting that only four of the other bidders were continually advancing and were considered as active participants.

Q. Thank you. I'd like to look at—you can put aside PX 950. I'd like to look at PX 954. And how many—in the number of bids row for Round 3, the table says one bid, partial round. Would you explain what you meant by that.

A. Yes. So in this particular auction, the first bid was collected in Round 3, and then the agent moved the auction to best bids. So a bid was still received, but the auction changed and it was immediately put into the best-bids round. So I noted the number of bids collected in that official Round 3 round, which is one bid, and then indicated that it's a partial round. So there wasn't—everyone didn't just decide to drop out and not bid in that round. It was just expedited.

Q. Thank you.

MS. RIKER: Those are all the questions I have for now, Your Honor. I pass the witness.

THE COURT: Okay. Thank you.

CROSS-EXAMINATION

BY MR. SHORES:

Q. Good afternoon, Ms. Porro.

A. Good afternoon.

Q. My name is Ryan Shores, and I'm counsel for Paramount and Simon & Schuster. I'm just going to ask you a few questions about your summaries.

A. Okay.

Q. So there are 27 summaries in total; is that correct?

A. That's correct.

Q. And my understanding is that each of these summaries represents an instance in which Penguin Random House and Simon & Schuster were among the last two bidders; is that correct?

A. Yes, that's correct.

Q. And so there's no instances, for example, on which Penguin Random House only competed against HarperCollins? No instances like that?

A. No. These summaries capture head to heads; so instances where both Penguin Random House and Simon & Schuster are present.

Q. Right. And not just present, but they're both among the last two bidders; isn't that correct?

A. I believe the focus was more that they were both in the auction, less that—I'm sorry. I don't know.

Q. Okay. Well, I'll represent to you that I reviewed them—

A. Okay.

Q.—and Penguin Random House and Simon & Schuster are among the last two bidders in each of the final stages.

A. Okay.

Q. None of the summaries show any instance in which an agent negotiated exclusively with just one publisher; is that correct?

A. No. These bidding events include multiple bidders.

Q. Okay. Now, these summaries span, as I understand it, about three and a half years; is that right? Let's take a look. I don't want you to have to guess. If we could look quickly at PX 957-B.

A. Uh-huh.

Q. And you see at the top there where it says January 2018?

A. Yes, I do.

Q. And then let's take that down and look at PX 933-B. And the date on this acquisition is August of 2021. Do you see that?

A. Uh-huh.

Q. So January 2018 to August 2021, about a three-and-a-half-year period; is that fair?

A. Yes, between these two examples.

Q. Okay. And in the summaries, you've included titles where the ultimate winning advance was above $250,000; is that correct?

A. I'm not sure off the top of my head.

Q. Okay. Well, again, I'll represent to you that it includes titles where the advance—winning advance was above $250,000, and I think we saw some examples of those, didn't we?

A. Yes, sir. Apologies. I didn't hear your question.

Q. Oh, that's okay. That's okay. And then some of the summaries reflect titles where the winning advance was below $250,000; is that right?

A. I believe so, but I would need to look at all of them too.

Q. Okay. Well, let's take a look quickly at an example. How about 934-B. Do you want to take a look at that one?

A. Great. Yes. I have that open, and I see the $160,000 advance.

Q. Right. Okay. And that's below $250,000; right?

A. Yes, it is.

Q. Now, Ms. Porro, you didn't have any role in deciding which titles for which summaries would be created; is that correct?

A. That's correct. I did not choose the documents that I reviewed.

Q. And do you have an understanding of why these particular 27 titles were selected from all of the books published over a three-and-a-half-year period?

A. I do not.

Q. And do you know how many trade books are published each year in the United States?

A. I do not.

Q. Well, I'll represent to you that there's more than 55,000 trade books published in the United States each year, which over a three-year period would be roughly 165,000 books.

A. Okay.

Q. And my question, Ms. Porro, is: Did you do any type of statistical analysis to determine whether 27

is statistically significant relative to the tens of thousands of books published each year?
A. I did not perform any statistical analyses for my assignment. That was not my assignment.
Q. Okay. Thank you, Ms. Porro.
A. Thank you.
MS. RIKER: No further questions, Your Honor.
THE COURT: All right. Thank you. You can step down. Thank you very much for your testimony.
THE WITNESS: Thank you so much, Your Honor.

MARKUS DOHLE, CEO, PENGUIN RANDOM HOUSE

Penguin Random House CEO Markus Dohle took the stand as the DOJ's lead attorney John Read took over the questioning for the first time in the trial. Much of his questioning of Dohle was based on, and bounded by, a number of key documents—which meant Dohle's answers were more direct than many of his predecessors in the trial.

The point of the exercise, from the government's perspective, was to introduce documents that reinforce some of the main arguments they have been trying to establish, for Dohle to confirm and offer context on.

They were intended to link up to points in DOJ's pre-trial brief, opening arguments, and subsequent repeated lines of questioning at trial, so we'll try to highlight those attempts in sub-headers below.

Does Bertelsmann Think US Trade Publishing Is An "Oligopoly"?

That's what it said on a slide prepared for a Bertelsmann board discussion, considering what at the time was a hypothetical purchase of a competitor like Simon & Schuster. The "structure" of the US trade publishing business was described as: "Oligopoly, in addition to PRH, only four other major trade publishers." Dohle said, "I remember that being on a slide. I disagreed with it."

Does the Reputation and Legacy of the Big 5 (As Well As Their Backlist) Give Them Structural Advantages Over Everyone Else That Are Hard to Equal?

Another item in the same document described "Barriers to entry" as, "High (especially reputation, sales)." While conceding that "reputation certainly helps" in attracting the best authors, Dohle noted, "The reputation of the editor and publisher is more important than the reputation of the publishing house; that's my view."

"Most of the money is in just a few books"; Top Sellers, Often Books with High Advances

Another document was a presentation from PRH US CEO Madeline McIntosh to some "famous public figures" considering starting a publishing company or imprint—held up to illustrate how PRH pitches its strengths when it is trying to win business rather than a legal case.

At one point it says, "Agent landscape fragmented, with a few big agencies, but large number of smaller players along with non-agent representatives" (which is quoted in DOJ documents regarding the power balance of publishers and agents).

It also says, "In most cases, publishers acquire rights in fast-moving auctions." A large item notes that, "Out of every 100 books published, 35 are profitable" (and 50 on a contribution basis). Here Dohle said, "I call it the Silicon Valley of media. We are angel investors in our authors and their dreams, their stories. That's how I call my editors and publishers: angels." More specifically, the presentation indicates, the "top 4% of profitable titles drive 60% of profitability."

The same document says, "In general, higher advances books are correlated with more book sales—however, there are always exceptions."

New Entrants Are Not Much of A Competitive Threat Because of the Long Path to Profits

In a follow-up document advising the public figures against starting a publishing company—even backed by PRH—they noted a "company will always have a higher cost structure than an imprint" and stated, "No history of companies starting from scratch achieving profitability within a 3–5 year period." The DOJ is using this to rebut the idea that new entrants pose a credible challenge to the market power of PRHSS in ATSB.

Bertelsmann's Ownership of Book Printers Gives PRH A Strategic Advantage

Read's questioning and documents about PRH's relationship with Bertelsmann's printing assets brought about an interesting set of answers. In an internal PRH document with meeting notes from April 2019 about the company's relationship with Bertelsmann's Berryville Graphics, Sue Malone Barber wrote: "Markus reiterated the importance of, and strategic advantage of, acting like a vertically integrated company." The notes also indicate, "We are the only publisher with a printer in the family and that is a huge competitive advantage in attracting authors (our ability to get books and supply the market better than anyone else)."

Here Dohle replied, "I've never seen an author pitch that includes printing as an argument to come to us." He added, "But what I'm doing here, I'm addressing to the executives of the printing group . . . that they should do their job as contractually committed." He also said on the stand, a few times, that Berryville "has been a competitive disadvantage for some time." He said in the April meeting he was, "hugely frustrated with them" and he wanted them "to fulfill their contractual obligations with us. . . . They should do their job." The notes said it was "critically important for BVG + PRH to focus on improvement now." For more context, Dohle said Bertelsmann does about 30 percent of their one-color printing in the US, and LSC (now Lakeside) is their largest printer.

Amazon Is Not Considered A Publishing Threat, Nor Is Self-Publishing

Another document was a draft of an email to his boss Thomas Rabe in early 2019 on his future with the company that Dohle sent to himself and family for review. He wrote about early "rejection of the Apple-introduced Agency Model for eBooks, making us a witness instead of a defendant," to which Read—who led that prosecution as well—proclaimed, "Well done!"

Also "key to this phase was the way we chose to work with Amazon, which ultimately led to windfall profits and the merger with Penguin."

A different document from April 2020 encouraged PRH executives—right at the height of the early pandemic, when physical retail was closed—to provide Amazon with the highest level of service. "Large publishers are our (main) competitors—Amazon is (mainly) our customer, in all book formats."

On the subject of Amazon, Bertelsmann board meeting minutes from right before the final deal to acquire S&S was approved in September 2019 report Dohle, "saw little danger in Amazon's self-publishing activities since PRH operated on a different quality level. Nor was he expecting Amazon to launch a book streaming service."

Information On Market Share and Profits

While we're less clear on where the DOJ was going with this, back to the draft mail to Rabe, Dohle also wrote: "In these years, 2012–2016, we have chosen to run our business in order to optimize shareholder profit and cash flow (versus market share and sales)." On multiple occasions during the testimony, Dohle expressed clear frustration with PRH's steady decline in market share—though here, Read was trying to imply that was a choice, and had a specific remedy. . . .

PRH Wanted to Grow Share, Which Meant Buying More ATSB, E.g. Books for $250k And Up

Another fraught document from August 2020 on the PRH US agenda 2020 acknowledged, to PRH USA CEO Madeline McIntosh, "I know that not achieving our key success factor [of "profitable market share growth"] is frustrating for both of us." Dohle said the document was an encouragement to "stop the market share decline, and buy more of the books in demand." There was a "hypothesis" in the document that "U.S. market share loss comes from publishing."

Dohle said he was, "Telling her to get more involved!" Another item said, "Involve/use me in negotiations as much as you can." In the document he called for McIntosh to have, "More deep involvement with content acquisitions: team meetings for acquisitions greater than 250/500K to get more content (increase appetite for more risk)." In questioning Dohle said, "I randomly used those numbers. I would love her to get involved in every book acquisition over $100,000."

To which Read replied dryly, "My observation, Mr. Dohle, is that you do very little randomly." Shortly thereafter, PRH attorney Daniel Petrocelli got Dohle to add, "Everything is random in publishing; that's why we have that name. So the founder thought. . . . Success is random. Bestsellers are random. So that's why we are the Random House."

Later it was elicited in redirect that—yes, the government invented the awkward phrase "anticipated top selling books" to stand for hotly sought or big books, but Dohle acknowledged the house uses the term "key authors." "I hope we have a lot of key authors." And they are interested in getting "attractive authors" to publish with them.

And After the Merger, They Will No Longer Have to Bid As Aggressively

Much was made of PRH's decline in market share since the Penguin merger—at least by their measures—and Dohle positions the S&S acquisition as an expensive necessity to get them back to where they were: "We are paying $2.2 billion to refill our market share for the most part—that shouldn't have happened. In the future, we want to grow with the market and that's sufficient." (By PRH's analysis of Bookscan data, they lost four points of market share from 2013 to 2019, down to 21 percent. The government didn't challenge any of this data—probably because their case is all about the share of big/expensive books, not all books.)

What Read was trying to demonstrate at the end of his questioning was that when PRH lost market share, they bid more aggressively on higher-priced books. "One way to grow market share is to be more aggressive in bidding for content from authors. Correct?" A. Correct.

In looking to buy S&S, PRH is trying to buy back market share in one big chunk: "Another way to grow share is to acquire a company with a lot of market share. Correct?" A. Correct.

After which they will not need to spend as heavily to buy share—implying, but not saying out loud, that they will be less aggressive in paying authors. Read will likely quote this in his closing argument, so let's put it here:

Read: "After this merger, Penguin Random House U.S. will not have as strong a need to grow share? Yes or no."

Dohle: "Yes. Growing with the market is enough."

Read: "Let me make sure I got that. After this merger, Penguin Random House will not have as strong a need to grow its share?"

Dohle: "Yes."

But later Dohle refuted that idea—in a redirect from Read himself about bringing "key authors" to the PRH. Dohle underscored, "If we want to grow, we have to invest more into books in a very competitive marketplace so our author commitments costs are going up."

One other exchange towards the end elicited more internal disagreement over some of the consolidation and reorganization of the company, reading partial texts from February 2021 to Divya Sawhney and Nihar Malaviya.

"TR [Bertelsman chief executive Thomas Rabe] has heard the Penguin story many times" Dohle texts to his colleagues. "It's really poor what happened," since, "It's simple, we lost [redacted] million contribution and then got them back through efficiencies." A follow up text says, "We really screwed it on the product side post-merger."

Here Dohle explained in court, "Given the fact that we have this market leading sales and distribution services, control group, our third-party distribution clients went up, my conclusion is that we haven't been able to acquire and publish enough of the books that readers want to buy. So the problem with our market share development has to be on the content side." He also noted, "I take full responsibility for everything that happens in the company because I'm the global CEO."

There is also reference to having "only discussed the risk that MMC and G created for us," He wrote, "We consolidated, and I couldn't stop it and didn't do enough downtown."

A contrite Dohle in court said, "For a long time, I've had a different vision for our organization, and I acknowledge that this is strong language . . . so I apologize for the passionate language." He explained, "These are private text messages to my closest collaborators in the company, and I display some passion and frustration here about our development, about the development of Penguin Random House and the fact that I could not prevail with my opinion for many years how to organize our company, so I couldn't convince my boss and I couldn't convince Ms. McIntosh."

The judge wanted to know, "When you say consolidated, do you mean consolidated imprints?" Dohle said, "It is more about how we are above the imprints."

Afterwards, a company spokesperson noted that the comment was presented out of context. She added that Dohle also said on the stand he takes full responsibility for all aspects of the business, and that more fully, this particular exchange was to evaluate a number of ongoing ways to improve processes in the increasingly competitive landscape and take greater risks in response.

Dohle on Bidding

During his testimony, Dohle made news twice with revisions of his bidding pledge, and a musing on a change in PRH's own house bidding policy.

First Dohle made what community members may see as an extension of his previous commitment to treat Simon & Schuster as an external bidder after the merger.

Asked by Read how the policy would apply to *one-on-one negotiations*—such as situations in which an author wants to move houses from one group to the other—Dohle said, "We're going to keep that external, too; that's my understanding." Pressed on the point by Read regarding direct negotiations and not just competitive bidding situations, such as if an author believes an option clause offer is too low, Dohle offered, "Our publishers and editors see their colleagues as some of their fiercest competitors. And he reiterated in answer to the question, "We want to keep those external and independent."

Dohle also said of the bidding policy, when asked if it could be reversed in the future by another CEO, "Unfortunately we couldn't find a legally binding way of doing it," suggesting that would have been his preference if possible. (You could infer that the legally binding reference might have had something to do with negotiations with the DOJ before the suit was filed.)

Later, Dohle said he and Madeline McIntosh are considering an even bigger change for PRH US.

Dohle said "We are considering—no decision yet—to even broaden the opportunity" that their S&S bidding pledge provides, to apply to PRH US imprints as well. He added, "I think it's a good decision for us without any material financial impact."

Judge Pan did push back on Dohle's suggestion that if he were ever to renege on his bidding pledges it would have serious repercussions among agents and author. "Correct me if I am wrong, agents are not going to not take your money because you're doing this if you're the high bidders; they're still going to choose you."

Here he evaded the question and replied that, "The fact of the matter is that the agents told me that their concern is perception rather than based on data." And he does not expect "a material financial impact because of the rareness of, in round robin auctions, Penguin Random House and Simon & Schuster being the last bidders."

Other Learnings

Some other elements of publishing rather the legal interest came up during the course of Dohle's testimony. Here are a few:

- The defense has been pointing to Spiegel & Grau as a well-financed upstart that could pose a competitive threat to them in the future—even though, as DOJ attorney John Read asked this morning, Julie Grau and Cindy Spiegel left PRH after their imprint was discontinued in early 2019.

  Dohle interjected, "I disagreed with that decision and tried to move that imprint and Cindy and Julie into another publishing division, but I didn't succeed." Asked if the line was discontinued because it wasn't profitable enough, Dohle said, "That is my understanding that that was the rationale," though he added later, "I disagree with the assessment that they didn't have a profitable business." In their new venture, "I'm sure they are going to succeed."
- At one point, Dohle revealed that PRH was an underbidder in the recent auction for Britney Spears' memoir—though the book is coming from Simon & Schuster, which the government did not point out.
- On Bertelsmann's acquisition of two former Quad printing facilities, Dohle confirmed our earlier

report that they only paid about $15 million, and he said Bertelsmann is executing a five-year plan to invest $75 million in those facilities at his urging. Dohle says PRH US prints only about 30 percent of their books with Bertelsmann plants, down from 40 percent five years ago, in part because, "They were just not able to fulfill their contractual commitments."

- A historical document indicated that there "were discussions about our children's imprints and how they are going to be organized in the future"—and "about how we might bring [them] together into one community of imprints." A company spokesperson indicated to PL that this was one of a variety of past scenarios considered and no such plans are in the works.
- On a point the prosecution has raised repeatedly, with less direct success when questioning Simon & Schuster CEO Jonathan Karp, Dohle conceded regarding self-publishing that, "Most traditional authors continue to be published traditionally. . . . Today, it doesn't keep me up at night anymore. Today, the biggest threat is all-access models for books" [e.g. unlimited subscription offerings].

He said later, as he has said in the past, that such models "will have a tectonic influence on the revenue pool of the industry," particularly since "20 to 25 percent of the heavy readers account for 80 percent of the revenue." If the industry moves to all-access subscriptions, "physical retail will be gone in two to three years" and "we'll be dependent on a few Silicon Valley or Swedish companies." Later in the day, he said of such models, "We think it's going to destroy the publishing industry." The DOJ tried to suggest PRH uses its market power to prevent or slow the growth of such competitors. "At least with us, they would have no growth, correct."

But Dohle said he has not decided yet what to do about Simon & Schuster's existing participation in such platforms: "I haven't made a decision and I'm going to think about it post-closing. I don't know to what extent they participate. So I'm going to look at it in detail once I'm able to look at it and allowed and then I will make a decision."

A different internal document, Bertelsmann board minutes from September 2020, indicated that Dohle was not "expecting Amazon to launch a book streaming service."

- PRH US CEO Madeline McIntosh can approve any offers up to $2 million (raised from a previous $1 million), at which point they need his approval—though he has never withheld that approval. And Dohle has a $75 million governance threshold before he needs approval from Bertelsmann, which he has never reached.
- More figures. PRH paid out "a little more than $1 billion globally" in advances and royalties in 2021. By our calculations, that would account for about 21 percent of total company sales for the year ($4.76 billion based on the average exchange rate). Dohle said that roughly two-thirds of that was paid by PRH US. (About 29 percent of last year's $2.691 billion in US revenue.) Dohle added that advances are higher in the US and that in 2021, PRH US committed an "all-time high" of around $650 million in author advances alone.
- A graph calculating changes in market shares from 2013 through 2019 showed that sales of PRH Publisher Services distribution clients in that period went from $385 million to $602 million. (If you extrapolate that PRH distribution clients grew at market rates or better the following two years, though would put their gross sales volume at over $725 million by the end of 2021.)

Amazon "is a supply chain machine. Very efficient. Very low return rates. Roughly 5 percent when the industry collectively 15 years ago was perhaps at 30 percent. The growth of Amazon has actually reduced the return rates."

TESTIMONY OF MARKUS DOHLE, CEO, PENGUIN RANDOM HOUSE

DIRECT EXAMINATION

BY MR. READ:

Q. Welcome, Mr. Dohle.

MR. READ: Your Honor, I think we have preplaced the binders for Mr. Dohle's examination.

THE COURT: Yes. Thank you.

BY MR. READ:

Q. Mr. Dohle, you have in front of you two binders, One contains your depositions and the other are some of the exhibits we'll go through today.

THE COURT REPORTER: I'm sorry. Could I have the witness state and spell his name for the record, please?

BY MR. READ:

Q. Please state your full name for the record.

A. Markus Dohle.

Q. Mr. Dohle, I'd like to cover a few basic background facts with you first. Okay?

A. Sure.

Q. Would you tell us your current title?

A. Yes. I'm the chief executive officer of Penguin Random House globally and I'm also a member of the executive board of Bertelsmann.

Q. Thank you. I'm going to go just briefly through some of your background. Mr. Petrocelli may go through more of your success and your career. But I just wanted to ask you, were you made the CEO of Random House in 2008?

A. That's correct.

Q. And then in 2013, with the merger of Penguin, you became CEO of the Penguin Random House combined entity?

A. Correct.

Q. And you mentioned you're a member of the Bertelsmann board. Is that it?

A. That's right.

Q. And the board you're a member of is the executive board?

A. The executive board of Bertelsmann. Correct.

Q. Yes.

A. That's correct.

Q. That's an operating board that sets strategy?

A. Yes. It's an operating board. It sets the strategy and it's also responsible for the implementation of the strategy.

Q. And you serve on that board with Mr. Thomas Rabe, the CEO of Bertelsmann?

A. Yes. He's the chairman and CEO of Bertelsmann.

Q. Maybe just a few more questions on your background. You have worked with Bertelsmann your whole adult life. Correct?

A. That's correct. Almost 30 years. I'm a lifer in the company.

Q. Good for you. And Bertelsmann—let's just spend a moment describing it. It's a diversified media company with companies it owns in television and magazines and publishing and music and other things?

A. We call it an international diversified media services and education company. It operates in eight divisions.

And Penguin Random House is a very special one because the whole company was built on books and started to publish books almost 200 years ago and grew after the Second World War with book clubs in particular around the world.

Q. And the relationship between Penguin Random House and Bertelsmann is that Bertelsmann owns 100 percent of Penguin Random House?

A. That's correct.

Q. We have placed in that first notebook—the first tab is an organization chart—it's actually a demonstrative. We prepared it hopefully to help the Court as we talk about some of the names and some of the entities. So I want to go through it and see if it's accurate. Okay?

A. Sure.

THE COURT: Is that Binder 1?

MR. READ: It's on Binder 1. The tab is "org chart."

BY MR. READ:

Q. Mr. Dohle, this org chart was given to your attorneys on Tuesday. Have you had a chance to look at it?

A. No, not in detail.

Q. Well, we've simplified the org chart, given the complexity. I just want to go through a few items of people we may talk about with you or with others and make sure we have it accurate. Okay?

A. Sure.

MR. READ: Well, first, your Honor, I would like to mark for identification this as PX—I don't know your naming designation—Demonstrative 1. Would that be sufficient?

THE COURT: That's fine. Well, you have it marked as PX 79.

MR. READ: Oh, we did? No. That's the next one.

THE COURT: Oh, that's the next one.

MR. READ: Yes.

THE COURT: Thank you. Demonstrative 1 is fine.

BY MR. READ:

Q. So, Mr. Dohle, you're listed at the top of this demonstrative as the CEO of Penguin Random House. And that's accurate?

THE COURT: Can you show that to the public?

MR. READ: Yes.

BY MR. READ:

Q. That's correct. Right?

A. Yeah. That's right.

Q. And then it lists several direct reports to you. I just want to focus on a couple of them here that might appear later.

A. Sure.

Q. Divya Sawhney is—

THE COURT REPORTER: I'm sorry, counsel. For the record, can I please see what you're reading from? The ELMO or a paper copy is fine.

MR. READ: Oh, sure. Is that all right?

MR. PETROCELLI: It takes three people to use an ELMO, your Honor.

THE COURT: How many lawyers does it take? (Laughter.)

MR. READ: I remember when this was high-tech. I never learned it.

THE COURT: Please proceed.

MR. READ: Yes.

BY MR. READ:

Q. Mr. Dohle, underneath you in the center a little to the left is Divya Sawhney. Do you see her name?

A. (Nods head in the affirmative.)

Q. She's the global strategy and corporate development officer for PRH?

A. That's correct.

Q. She reports directly to you. We got that right. And Manuel Sansigre is to the right. And he's the senior vice president of global mergers and acquisitions?

A. Correct. Yes.

Q. And he reports directly to you?

A. Correct.

Q. And then I think just one other we'll address with you, perhaps today, is on the left second row is Esther Guerra. Do you see her name?

A. Yes.

Q. She's an executive assistant. Correct?

A. Yes. She works for several executives, but also for me. She reports directly to me.

Q. And sometimes she forwards emails for you. Right?

A. She works for several executives, but also for me. And she reports directly to me.

Q. That's a yes?
A. Yes.
Q. And then we listed Madeline McIntosh as reporting to you. She's the CEO of Penguin Random House U.S. Correct?
A. Correct.
Q. And you have a number of other reports from other CEOs of other countries that report to you as well?
A. Ten more CEOs reporting to me around the world. Correct.
Q. And then reporting to Madeline McIntosh are in the next row six presidents and publishers of different groups within Penguin Random House. Correct? Do you see that?
A. Correct.
Q. And the first of those is Allison Dobson. She's the president of the publishing group at Penguin Random House?
A. That's right.
Q. What are some of the most well-known imprints in the Penguin Publishing Group that Allison Dobson oversees?
A. There is Penguin Press; there is Viking; there is Riverhead; there is Putnam; and Dutton. So these are some of the imprints within the Penguin Publishing Group, adult publishing group.
Q. And Bertelsmann acquired those imprints when it combined Penguin and Random House in 2013?
A. That's right.
Q. And then next to her is Maya Mavjee. She's the president and publisher of the Knopf Doubleday Group?
A. That's right.
Q. What are some of the most significant imprints in that group?
A. It's of course Alfred A. Knopf, the very Alfred A. Knopf imprint. It's Vintage; it's Doubleday; it's Pantheon as part of that group. It's Nan Talese books, many other imprints.
Q. And those imprints were acquired by Bertelsmann in previous acquisitions?
A. When Bertelsmann acquired Random House in 1998, Knopf and some of those imprints were part of that. And Doubleday Bertelsmann acquired in 1985, so it became part of the community family of imprints back then in the mid-'80s.
Q. Thank you. And then to the right of Maya Mavjee is Gina Centrello. She's the president and publisher of the Random House Group. Correct?
A. That's right.
Q. And what are some of the most significant imprints there?
A. Of course the Random House imprint, the founding imprint of Random House, 1923, Bennett Cerf. There is Bantam Books; there is Ballantine; One World. Many, many others.
Q. And you already—I think you testified that Bertelsmann acquired Random House earlier. Right?
A. That's correct. In 1998.
Q. And then Barbara Marcus to the right is the president and publisher of Random House Children's Books?
A. That's correct.
Q. What are a couple of well-known imprints there?
A. Well, there are Schwartz Books; there is the Random House's children's imprint; there is Dial Press; there are many smaller imprints part of the Random House Children's Books Group.
Q. And then to just wrap this up, Jennifer Loja is the president of the Penguin Young Readers Group and then Amanda D'Acierno is the president and publisher of the Penguin Random House Audio Publishing Group. Correct?
A. That's correct.
Q. And for Jennifer Loja, just a couple of the imprints in her group?
A. There is a Penguin Young Readers imprint; there is Dutton Books For Young Readers; there is Putnam; sort of a lot of brand names that also have smaller imprints.

Q. Okay. Now that we have a little better understanding of Penguin Random House, let's go to the final line. On the final line, we see Nihar Malaviya, third to the right. Right? Correct?
A. Correct.
Q. He's here in the court today as a corporate representative for Bertelsmann?
A. For Penguin Random House?
Q. For Penguin Random House. Correct. You're the corporate representative for Bertelsmann. Right?
A. That's correct.
Q. And Mr. Malaviya is the chief operating officer for Penguin Random House U.S.?
A. Yes. And he has a dotted line to me and he's also a member of the global executive committee. So we work very closely together. He reports directly to Madeline, but he also does a lot globally for Penguin Random House on the operations side, the back-end side of the business.
Q. We're going to move on, but is there anything inaccurate in this chart other than it doesn't include the whole universe of Penguin Random House and Bertelsmann relations?
A. No. It's correct.
Q. I'd like to get one preliminary out of the way, Mr. Dohle. And that is, this is a merger about the planned purchase of Simon & Schuster. So I just want to make sure we have in the record an agreement to buy Simon & Schuster. So if we could do that.
A. That's right.
Q. Would you turn in your binder, the big one, to one of the latter tabs, No. 885.
A. The same binder, right?
Q. Right. They should be in numerical order, so it's at the end.
A. 0080. And then?
Q. It's near the end of your binder. They're all in numerical order. 885.
THE COURT: It's the second-to-the-last tab.
THE WITNESS: I'm on 885.
BY MR. READ:
Q. We're just going to make sure we have this in the record. This is a copy, Mr. Dohle, of the purchase agreement between ViacomCBS and Bertelsmann signed November 24, 2020. Correct?
A. That's right.
Q. And your signature is on the next-to-the-last page of this whole document? Take your time.
A. Yes. That's my signature.
Q. And Penguin Random House is a party to this agreement to buy Simon & Schuster?
A. Correct.
MR. READ: Your Honor, I move to admit PX 885, the purchase agreement.
THE COURT: Any objection?
MR. PETROCELLI: None, your Honor.
THE COURT: That will be admitted. (Whereupon, Plaintiff's Exhibit No. 885 was entered into evidence.)
BY MR. READ:
Q. Let's put this aside. Again, I just wanted that for the record.
Let me ask you a couple questions. Before Viacom bought [sic] Simon & Schuster for sale, Bertelsmann discussed internally at the board level the idea of acquiring Simon & Schuster. Right?
A. Can you ask that question?
Q. Yeah. Let me ask it again. Before Viacom put Simon & Schuster up for sale, did Bertelsmann have at its board level some meetings where it discussed the idea of buying Simon & Schuster?
A. Yes. There were rumors about the sale of Simon & Schuster for many years, more than a decade. Yes.
Q. And in those board meetings, as Bertelsmann considered the idea of buying Simon & Schuster, did it consider whether in the marketplace of publishing there were barriers to entry?
A. I remember documents that include that.
Q. And did Bertelsmann consider whether the market was structured as an oligopoly?

A. I remember that being on a slide. I disagree with it.

Q. Well, let's turn to that slide, This is going to be in that same notebook, PX 80, 0080. It should be about the third tab.

A. Yeah. I'm on it.

Q. Mr. Dohle, this document may be a little more unwieldy than the others, Here's why: It's got parts that are in German. Right? So what we have done is the parts that are in German—let me just tell you, this is a document that's a cover and some attachments. And so the parts that are in German, we have tabs behind that for English translation and then certifications of those translations. So, for example, the cover is partly in German. So Tab 80-A. is the English translation and 80-B is the translation certificate.

A. I'm familiar with that from our depositions.

Q. In the second, there's another attachment; and so that's—80-C is the English version and 80-D is the certificate. And then the one we're going to spend time on is the attachment in German that's 80-E, with 80-F being the translation certificate. Okay? So as we work through this kind of unwieldy document.

A. Sure.

Q. Let's turn first to Tab 80-A, the cover email as translated, and see if we can identify the document.

A. Yes.

Q. And this document was sent from Esther Guerra. Correct?

A. Correct.

Q. And we established she's your executive assistant?

A. Yes.

Q. And it was sent on October 22nd, 2019?

A. There was a typo in my name. But that's fine.

Q. We'll forgive her. It was sent on October 22nd, 2019?

A. Correct.

Q. And it was sent to Divya Sawhney, among others, was copied on it as the strategy officer?

A. Correct.

Q. It lists some attachments in this cover. Do you see the list of attachments?

A. I do.

Q. One of the attachments, the last one, is called in German Kapitalallokation?

A. Yeah.

Q. I assume that's the English translation? It looks pretty close.

A. Yeah. It was not even translated here. Yeah. Kapitalallokation.

Q. That's right. It's not translated here. You received these materials on or around October 22nd, 2019?

A. That's correct.

Q. And this was all done for a board meeting in Germany in later October?

A. All the documents that we discussed basically at the board meeting.

MR. READ: Your Honor, we'd move to admit PX 80 and then PX 80-A. through 80-E.

THE COURT: Any objection?

MR. PETROCELLI: No.

THE COURT: Those will be admitted. (Whereupon, Plaintiff's Exhibit Nos. 80 and 80-A. through 80-E were entered into evidence.)

BY MR. READ:

Q. You were present at the board meeting for which these documents were created?

A. That's right.

Q. Let's turn to 80-E, Tab 80-E, the capital allocation presentation.

Are you there, Mr. Dohle?

A. D?

Q. 80-E, as in elephant.

A. Thank you. Yeah.

Q. The purpose of this capital allocation attachment to this board meeting in preparation for the board meeting was to envision potential investment opportunities that Bertelsmann might make. Correct?

A. Correct.
Q. And let's turn—so basically it was to cover the ideas of: How could Bertelsmann invest its money? And there are four ideas that are discussed in this presentation. Correct?
A. It's a high-level blue sky exercise to think about future investments and capital allocation for those. Correct.
Q. Correct. And one of the ideas was to discuss buying Simon & Schuster?
A. Correct.
MR. READ: Your Honor, there have been some redactions in this document. If we may publish the next slide, which is Slide 13.
THE COURT: Yes.
BY MR. READ:
Q. Would you turn to Slide 13, Mr. Dohle?
A. Sure.
Q. That's where we're going to spend our time.
A. I'm on 13 now.
Q. The title of this slide is PRH B1/B2. What does the B1 and B2 stand for?
A. Can you ask that question again, Mr. Read?
Q. Are those Bertelsmann options, PRH B1/B2 at the top title?
A. Yeah. It shows on the right-hand side a complete acquisition and a partial acquisition. So yeah. That resonates.
Q. And the rest of the title is "Purchase of competitor (here: Simon & Schuster)" and then it goes on. Do you see that?
A. Yes.
Q. And on the left hand—
THE COURT: I'm sorry. Mr. Read, there's a discrepancy in my exhibits. It just looks different in the binder than on the screen, It's a different document, though it has the same Bates—
MR. READ: Let's make sure. Is the Bates stamp you're looking at 216, your Honor?
THE COURT: It is. But it looks like a different document.
MR. READ: At least on the public screen is a redacted version. I don't know if your Honor has seen that, too.
THE COURT: It just looks like a completely different document. Let me just pass this to you, Mr. Read. Maybe I'm missing something. I want to make sure.
MR. READ: We had late-night binder issues.
THE COURT: This is what I have in my binder with the Bates stamp 216, which looks different.
MR. READ: There's a very different document. Maybe it's on Slide 13.
THE COURT: Thank you.
MR. READ: It could be. It's a PowerPoint, your Honor. So every page has the same Bates stamp on it.
THE COURT: Oh, I see.
MR. READ: So we may have been on the wrong page.
BY MR. READ:
Q. So the title—this is Slide 13 of the presentation, a PowerPoint. Correct?
A. Correct.
Q. And the title is "Purchase of competitor (here: Simon & Schuster)"?
A. Yes.
Q. And on the left of this slide is the—underneath Classification of Projects, it says "Strategic thrust." Do you see that?
A. I do.
Q. And to the right of that it says "Boosting core business consolidation." Do you see that?
A. Correct.
Q. And then below that, let's go to the market characteristics. Do you see market characteristics below Classification of Projects?

A. Yes.
Q. And then to the right of that, there is—let's go straight to it. There's a third one down that says "structure." Do you see that?
A. Yes.
Q. And then after that it's "Oligopoly in addition to Penguin Random House only for our major trade publishers." Do you see that line in this board document?
A. Yes.
Q. And then there's a footnote there, Footnote 2. Do you see that?
A. I do.
Q. And if you look at the bottom of this slide, Footnote 2, do you see it identifies four large U.S. publishers: Hachette, HarperCollins, Macmillan and Simon & Schuster?
A. Yes.
Q. And those four with Penguin Random House would be the Big 5 in the United States?
A. That's what they are called.
Q. Let me just ask you a couple questions related to this. Would you agree that there's not many mid-sized publishers left?
A. Not really. To give you some context, take Scholastic. That company is as large as Macmillan and Hachette or larger than some of the Big 5. So I don't like that expression. They are pretty large companies in the United States. Globally, Scholastic's revenue is about $1.4 billion.
Q. If a mid-sized publisher were to have testified that "There are not many of us left," would he be wrong?
A. How do you—I don't know how to define a mid-sized publisher.
Q. Over $100 million in revenues.
A. On top of my head, there is Disney, Amazon, Callisto, Sourcebooks, ReaderLink, just to mention a few.
Q. And they all have over $100 million in book revenues?
A. At least that's my understanding. That's my understanding.
Q. These board materials were sent a week in advance of the board meeting, were they not?
A. Can you ask that question again?
Q. Were these board materials sent about a week in advance of the board meeting that you attended?
A. That's correct.
Q. And at this board meeting, your testimony is no one discussed this oligopoly statement contained in the materials?
A. I don't remember it. It was a very short board meeting. The agenda shows that we had for this topic, for this whole deck, 45 minutes. I don't know how many slides; perhaps 40, 45. I'm not even sure whether we discussed this slide back then. And certainly I disagree with the oligopoly definition.
Q. At the board meeting at this time, no one disputed in the board materials this oligopoly statement?
A. Not in advance of the meeting. That's correct.
Q. And not at the meeting?
A. No.
Q. And then below this statement, two lines down, it says "barriers to entry."
Do you see that?
A. Yes.
Q. And the line continues: "High (especially reputation, sales)." Do you see that?
A. I do.
Q. And the word "reputation" here is referring to the reputation a publishing house has to have. Right? That a publishing house has to earn?
A. That's my understanding, that the author of the document meant that.
Q. And you would agree that a publishing house needs a good reputation so that authors will want to sell the rights of their books to the publishing house?
A. The reputation of the editors and publishers is more important than the reputation of the publishing

house.
Q. Right.
A. That's my view.
Q. A. publisher without a good reputation for success will find it challenging to attract the best authors?
A. Authors select their editors and publishers more than they select their publishing house because that's the reason why they often move with their editors when they switch houses, if that makes sense.
Q. You would agree that a publisher without a good reputation for success will find it challenging to attract the best authors?
A. Reputation certainly helps.
Q. It's an important aspect to the success of a publishing house?
A. It resonates with me.
Q. I'm sorry?
A. That resonates with me.
Q. So we have the timing right, this board meeting where Bertelsmann discussed buying Simon & Schuster occurred about six months before Viacom publicly announced the sale of Simon & Schuster. Correct?
A. Correct.
Q. Let's put this exhibit aside for a second. I just have a couple of questions on this point.
In trying—later, after the announcement by Viacom of the sale, in trying to acquire Simon & Schuster, you advocated that Bertelsmann be willing to pay a substantial premium over the next largest bidder. Correct?
A. I wanted Bertelsmann to go to the highest level possible in order to get the asset. Correct.
Q. And you thought it should be willing to pay a premium over the next highest bidder?
A. I didn't know where they were, the other bidders. But I certainly only looked at us and advocated for the highest possible bid that we could actually—call it "afford."
Q. And you thought paying a premium for Simon & Schuster would be worth it?
A. I don't remember that. But I might have said it.
Q. Penguin Random House is the largest book publisher in the United States?
A. That's correct.
Q. And if Penguin Random House combines with Simon & Schuster, it will cement Penguin Random House as number one in the United States?
A. It will increase our market share and bring it back, by and large. In 2013, we lost a lot of market share. So it will refill the market share that we've lost in the market.
Q. Will it cement Penguin Random House as the number one in the United States?
A. It increases our market share. Yes.
Q. So yes, it does cement Penguin Random House as number one in the United States?
A. Correct.
Q. Let's turn to another topic. It relates to the reputation and barriers to entry, Okay? Would you agree that starting a new publishing business is very hard?
A. We are establishing new imprints, small imprints from scratch, every year. So we do it regularly. But I would agree it's not easy.
Q. Okay. Let's talk about an independent publishing company, not an imprint. You would agree that a new startup, independent publishing company, can face years of losses before turning a profit?
A. If they get lucky and their first publications are successful, I wouldn't say that they necessarily make losses. But it could certainly be the case in the ramp-up phase of a publishing house.
Q. Well, let's follow up on that. Would you turn to PX 151.
MR. READ: There have been some redactions in this document for confidentiality reasons. Your Honor, may we, when we get there, publish the redacted version?
THE COURT: Yes.
THE WITNESS: I'm on 151, Mr. Read.

BY MR. READ:

Q. Sure. The cover email is from Madeline—from you to Madeline McIntosh. Correct?

A. Correct.

Q. And this cover email is dated August 8, 2019?

A. Yes.

Q. And given the redactions, the document is entitled—it's the proposed name of a new imprint books update. Do you see that?

A. I do.

Q. And it attaches a document that—called Penguin Random House offer imprint presentation both in a PowerPoint and a .pdf. format. Do you see that?

A. I do.

Q. And you write to Ms. McIntosh: Attached, please find the presentation for the redacted imprint. I guess these are very famous public figures, right, that this imprint is going to?

A. That's correct.

Q. And it says: David has reviewed with Gina and we will send to—it's an individual who's associated with those very famous public figures, correct—later today?

A. That's correct.

Q. And Gina is Gina Centrello, who we talked about in the org chart. Right?

A. Correct.

Q. She's the president and publisher of Random House?

A. Correct.

MR. READ: Your Honor, I'd move to admit PX 151.

THE COURT: Any objection?

MR. PETROCELLI: The unredacted version will remain under seal?

THE COURT: Yes. That will be admitted. (Whereupon, Plaintiff's Exhibit No. 151 was entered into evidence.)

BY MR. READ:

Q. We're going to talk about the attachment, Mr. Dohle. This attachment and document relates to an imprint you're considering creating with a very famous public figure. Correct?

A. That's right.

Q. More specifically, you wanted to help this famous public figure to get started as a publisher?

A. Correct.

Q. Would you turn to the attached presentation? And specifically, Slide 4. Are you there, Mr. Dohle?

A. Yes, I am.

Q. And the title of this slide is "Content rights landscape"?

A. Correct.

Q. On the left-hand side, it has a little icon for author and agent. Do you see that?

A. Yes.

Q. And underneath that, let's look at the second bullet, where it's written: Agents typically submit manuscripts to multiple publishers, but sometimes make exclusive submissions. Do you see that?

A. Yes.

Q. And then the last bullet. Let's make sure we've got that. It says: Agent landscape fragmented, with a few big agencies, but large number of smaller players along with non-agent representatives?

A. Yes.

Q. On the right-hand side, do you see the publisher—so those were descriptions of authors and agents, were they not?

A. Correct.

Q. On the right-hand side, do you see the publisher icon?

A. Yes.

Q. And the second bullet under that says: In most cases, publishers acquire rights in fast-moving competitive auctions. Do you see that?

A. Yes.
Q. Those acquisitions—those acquisitions are fast-moving in that they can take place over just a few days or weeks. Right?
A. Correct.
Q. And in most cases, the publishers acquire those rights in competitive auctions, is what it says. Right?
A. That's on the page.
Q. The next bullet reads: Publishers pay an advance to agents in exchange for a bundle of rights.
Do you see that?
A. I do.
Q. And here on this slide, you're providing basic industry facts to the executives working with this famous public figure about the industry?
A. Yes. We try to educate them.
Q. Would you turn to Slide 9 of this presentation.
A. I am on Slide 9, Mr. Read.
Q. The title of this is "Publishing is a portfolio business with profitability driven by a small percentage of books." Do you see that?
A. I do.
Q. Sometimes you call the publishing business a portfolio business, don't you?
A. Yes. We invest every year in thousands of ideas and dreams, and only a few make it to the top. So I call it the Silicon Valley of media. We are angel investors of our authors and their dreams, their stories. That's how I call my editors and publishers: angels.
Q. And the idea is that by publishing a lot of titles, you can manage risk better?
A. Can you ask that question again, Mr. Read? I didn't get it.
Q. The idea is that by publishing a lot of titles, you can spread out and manage risk better?
A. It's rather this idea of Silicon Valley, you see 35 percent are profitable; 50 on a contribution basis. So every book has that same likelihood of succeeding.
Q. Part of the idea of having a portfolio business is being able to spread the risk among a lot of bets?
A. Yes. That's statistically and mathematically not true, but that's the idea.
Q. And then the first row to the right on the right column, it says: Book profitability is primarily driven by revenues generated and advance paid. Do you see that?
A. Yes, I do.
Q. And advance is a cost that affects the profitability of a book?
A. It does.
Q. And then below that, on the right-hand side, it says top 4 percent—one more down: Top 4 percent of profitability titles drive 60 percent of profitability. Do you see that?
A. Yes. That's how risky our business is.
Q. Most of the money is in just a few books. Correct?
A. That's what it says, it means.
Q. And that's the reality. Right?
A. Yeah. It's the books that you don't pay a lot for and become runaway bestsellers.
Q. Well, let's unpack that a little bit. The top 4 percent of profitability titles drive 60 percent of the profitability.
A. Correct.
Q. Those are the ones that sell the most?
A. And cost the least.
Q. They're the ones with the highest revenue?
A. Correct.
Q. And then in the last item on this page in that column, it says: In general, higher advance levels are correlated with more book sales; however, there are always exceptions. Do you see that?
A. I do.
Q. You would agree that books that sell well are more likely to have received higher advances?

A. Books that sell—can you ask that again?

Q. Would you agree—maybe we'll see which way it goes—would you agree that books that sell well are more likely to have received higher advances?

A. There is a correlation, but that does not flow through to profitability necessarily.

Q. Okay. Well, let's just stop at the correlation. Let's make sure we get that.

A. Correct.

Q. So it is correct that books that sell well are more likely to have received higher advances?

A. There is a correlation.

Q. Is it also true that those books that have received higher advances are more likely to sell well?

A. There is a wide range; and some big advances flop completely and don't sell anything. But there should be a correlation. I agree with that.

Q. Yeah. And there's risk in this, isn't there? That's why you need a portfolio?

A. There is a lot of risk with each book. Each book is unique and has a lot of risk.

Q. Let's turn to Slide 10, if we may. The title of this slide is Overall New Imprint Profitability.

Do you see that?

A. I do.

Q. And the illustrative graph here divides time into three segments: an investment phase, a build phase and a steadier-state phase. Do you see that?

A. I do.

Q. And the idea here is you're teaching this famous public figure and his staff the different phases a new imprint would face if they were to choose to start one?

A. It's illustrative. But yes.

Q. Yes. And you chose illustratively to have the investment phase be zero to three years?

A. Yes.

Q. And the idea there in the initial first three years is that there can be initial losses because the books are not yet published?

A. Yes.

Q. So the idea is, there's a time period where an imprint or a new publishing house is acquiring books, waiting for those books to be written, waiting for those books to be printed, before it can ever start to recoup its investment and make sales?

A. Correct.

Q. You would agree that when an existing publisher changes their acquisition strategy, it can take two to three years to see the results of that strategy?

A. I can. That's right. Let's put this exhibit aside and turn to PX 79. It's a little earlier in your tab.

Q. And the reason is again there's a lag time in changing strategy and acquiring books and then seeing the results because the books have to later be actually written and printed and marketed and sold?

MR. READ: Let's put up a confidential version. Do we have one? Thank you.

BY MR. READ:

Q. Do you have PX 79 in front of you, Mr. Dohle?

A. I do.

MR. READ: Again, there's some confidentiality with this, so we've made some redactions, your Honor. May we publish the redacted version?

THE COURT: Yes.

MR. READ: Did I move to admit the prior exhibit, PX—no. I did. Yes.

BY MR. READ:

Q. This exhibit was—the cover email was sent on Saturday, September 14, 2019. Correct?

A. Correct.

Q. And that's a little less than a month after the prior presentation that we just discussed?

A. Yes.

Q. And this email was sent from Divya Sawhney, your chief strategy operator, to several people. Correct?

A. Yes.
Q. One of those is you?
A. Yes.
Q. And also included is Nihar Malaviya and Manuel Sansigre, who we have discussed in the org chart. Correct?
A. Correct.
Q. The title of this slide is Regroup Meeting. Do you see that it's a regroup meeting?
A. Yes.
Q. And so the idea is that there's going to be an additional presentation to these famous individuals?
A. Correct.
MR. READ: Your Honor, I move to admit PX 79.
THE COURT: Any objection?
MR. PETROCELLI: No, your Honor.
THE COURT: It'll be admitted. (Whereupon, Plaintiff's Exhibit No. 79 was entered into evidence.)
BY MR. READ:
Q. And again, you were looking to help these public figures get started in publishing? That's the purpose for these presentations in this slide—in these presentations?
A. To be involved with the imprint [indiscernible] that would be run by us in the day-to-day business.
THE COURT REPORTER: Could you repeat your answer, sir?
THE WITNESS: We wanted them to involved in the imprints, but we would run it for them, basically.
BY MR. READ:
Q. Would you turn to Slide 7, please, of this presentation.
A. I'm on 7.
Q. The slide is entitled "Considerations on key takeaways, potential routes to build enterprise value." Do you see that?
A. I do.
Q. And on the left-hand side, you see just below that "potential routes." Right?
A. Yes.
Q. And a little below that you see something that looks like a decision tree. For A, you can create; and it says "Create an imprint" or "Create a company." Do you see that?
A. I do.
Q. Let's look at that second row about creating a company. Okay?
A. Yes.
Q. The line under it reads: Company will always have a higher cost structure than an imprint and will take a longer time to achieve profitability. Do you see that?
A. I do.
Q. And company there is a publishing company? That's what we're talking about?
A. Yes.
Q. And below that, it reads: No history of companies starting from scratch achieving profitability in a three- to five-year time period. Do you see that?
A. That's on the page.
Q. And that was the information conveyed, the background information about the industry conveyed to these famous public figures?
A. We did.
Q. To the right of what we've been reading, it says under Assessment For This Area: Not a viable option. Correct?
A. For those figures we mean, because they thought they come to an enterprise value headline much faster. So they were overestimating it, I guess.
Q. Let's make sure we understand. You recommended to these public figures against starting a publishing company even with Penguin Random House's help?
A. Because of their goals. Yes.

Q. And part of the information you conveyed was that there was three to five years of—that no publishing company had achieved—had a history of profitability even in a three- to five-year time period?
A. It needs some incubation, some financing to build a publishing company. I think that goes across all industries.
Q. Correct. There's been some mention in this trial about the new publishing company Spiegel & Grau. You've heard of them. Right?
A. Yes.
Q. And you know Ms. Spiegel and Ms. Grau?
A. Very well. Indeed.
Q. They used to work at Penguin Random House?
A. For a very long time. For decades.
Q. And they had an imprint at Penguin Random House?
A. They did.
Q. What was the name of that imprint?
A. Spiegel & Grau.
Q. And that imprint was shuttered?
A. Before that they ran Riverhead for a long time, just for context.
Q. The Spiegel & Grau imprint was shuttered by Penguin Random House?
A. That's correct.
Q. The rationale was it wasn't profitable enough even with Penguin Random House's resources and muscle behind it?
A. Correct. I disagreed with the decision and tried to move that imprint and Cindy and Julie into another publishing group at Penguin Random House, but I did not succeed.
Q. Cindy is Cindy Spiegel?
A. And Julie Grau.
Q. Julie Grau. So you disagreed with it, but the decision was made to shutter their imprint because it wasn't profitable enough?
A. That is my understanding, that that was the rationale.
Q. And now they've started their own business?
A. That's correct.
Q. And they have no backlist?
A. Correct.
Q. They do have a successful book. One. Right?
A. Yeah. They are buying—they started very competitively buying bigger books and smaller ones, and I'm sure they're going to succeed.
Q. You don't know if they're turning a profit yet, do you?
A. No. Of course not.
Q. And there's no guarantee of their success?
A. No.
Q. And you can't testify that these two editors that were let go for running an imprint that wasn't profitable enough are a significant competitive threat to Penguin Random House?
A. First of all, part of their business was also One World. They actually started it, which was successful. So I disagree even with the assessment that they didn't have a profitable business.
But putting that aside, I very much believe in them given their reputation as editors and publishers in the industry. I'm sure they are going to succeed. And they have good financing, I guess, because they are buying big books.
Q. Let's turn to another topic, Mr. Dohle. Let's talk about printing for a second.
A. Sure.
Q. Okay?
A. Sure.
Q. It's been difficult for publishers to print their books in a timely fashion over the last couple of years.

Correct?

A. Oh, yeah. The book market has been growing 20 percent.

Q. And on several occasions over the last couple of years, even Penguin Random House has encountered printing capacity issues for its one-color books?

A. That is correct. We had to move publishing dates and we had out-of-stocks. Correct.

Q. I think the record's clear from before, but just so we've got it, one-color books are black-and-white books?

A. Correct, Mr. Read.

Q. And even Penguin Random House has not been able to avoid some books going out of stock because of these printing capacity issues?

A. That's right.

Q. And the publication of several titles in the fall of 2020 were moved later in time because of the unavailability of printing capacity?

A. That's right.

Q. And the fall of 2020 is an important release time generally because you can make sales for the Christmas holiday season?

A. Very important.

Q. Would you agree that a significant portion of sales that are lost due to a book being out of stock are lost forever?

A. Whether it's significant or not depends on whether it's a long seller or a short seller, But some of that sales is lost forever.

Q. So let's just make sure we're clear. When a book's out of stock, there are sales that are lost forever for that book?

A. That's right.

Q. Please turn to PX 983 in your tab. It's the last one in the notebook. Are you there, Mr. Dohle?

A. Yes, I am.

Q. And again, there have been some redactions of this for confidentiality. But—

MR. READ: May we publish this to the courtroom, your Honor?

THE COURT: You may.

BY MR. READ:

Q. PX 983 is an email sent by Sue Malone Barber to you and others. Is that correct?

A. Correct.

Q. The subject line is: Meeting recap, 4–25 BVG PRH fall planning update. Do you see that?

A. Yes.

Q. What does BVG stand for?

A. It stands for Berryville Graphics, which is part of the Bertelsmann Printing Group.

THE COURT REPORTER: Could you repeat the name of the company, please?

THE WITNESS: Berryville Graphics. Berryville. It's an hour from here. And it's the old Doubleday printing company that we acquired with Doubleday in the 1980s. Berryville Graphics, part of the Bertelsmann Printing Group.

MR. READ: Your Honor, I move to admit PX 983.

THE COURT: Any objection?

MR. PETROCELLI: No.

THE COURT: That will be admitted. (Whereupon, Plaintiff's Exhibit No. 983 was entered into evidence.)

BY MR. READ:

Q. Mr. Dohle, you don't know of any other publisher besides Penguin Random House who has a printing group in its corporate family?

A. In the U.S., that's correct.

Q. And Penguin Random House has a huge—has a significant competitive advantage in attracting authors by having a printer in the corporate family, doesn't it?

A. Well, the printing group has been a competitive disadvantage for Penguin Random House in recent years. But I see that line here in the minutes, and printing is part of supply chain. And it could be an advantage.

Q. Well, let's spend a moment and back that up and make sure we've got it. Looking at the document—and I think you're looking at the third bolded area down the page that starts with: Markus reiterated the importance of, and strategic advantage of, acting like a vertically integrated company.

Right? Is that part of what you're looking at?

A. Yes.

Q. And what do you mean in the publishing industry—how does a vertically integrated company work when you're talking about a printer and a publisher?

A. Sure. We have dozens of printers for black-and-white, one-color, in North America and even beyond. But most of our volume is being printed in North America.

Our four-color work, so illustrated books and children's books, picture books, are mainly printed in China, but also in Europe. And we have dozens of suppliers. We call it a multivendor strategy. And printing companies have multi-publishing house, multi-client strategies.

Q. In a vertically integrated company with a printer and a publisher, the printer can work with the publisher to help supply their needs and make sure that they have the capabilities—the books they need to keep in stock. Right? That's the advantage?

A. It's an arm's-length relationship with them. We have a contract like other publishers, too. But what I'm addressing here is they have become a disadvantage because they have not for years fulfilled their contractual obligation with us, and I'm obviously frustrated. If you read the whole thing, the whole minutes, I'm very frustrated with them. And—period.

Q. Let's make sure we're level-set. Bertelsmann owns both this Berryville Graphics enterprise and the printing?

A. And more printers.

Q. And more printers. 100 percent owner?

A. Correct.

Q. It's 100 percent owner of Penguin Random House?

A. Correct.

Q. And you would like the printing to support the publishing?

A. I would like them to fulfill their contractual obligations, to not run out of stock. That's correct.

Q. In the second bullet, under what we just read in bold, it says: "We are the only publisher with a printer in the family, and that is a huge competitive advantage in attracting authors (our ability to get books and supply the market better than anyone else)." Do you see that?

A. I do.

Q. And that's accurate?

A. I've never seen an author pitch that includes printing as an argument to come to us. But what I'm doing here, I'm addressing to the executives of the printing group, which I ran once myself before Penguin Random House and Random House, that they should do their job as contractually committed.

Q. And do you believe if Penguin Random House can get the printing group to work closely with the publishing group, that can help Penguin Random House attract authors by persuading them that Penguin Random House will be able to get the books into stock?

A. That was what is on the page.

Q. Right. And you would not be surprised if there are other publishers in this country who are concerned that they may be at a competitive disadvantage in acquiring authors because they cannot get the necessary printing at a fair price or at all?

A. If I may, two things: Around 30 percent of our one-color hard-cover entry paperback volume is being printed with Bertelsmann in the United States.

LSC is the largest supplier for us. And every printer can work very closely with publishing houses. And printing books is part of the supply chain. So having that system part of the supply chain distribution system is important. And I have that history in printing, So it's an arm's-length relationship that we have.

The only advantage, Mr. Read, that we have is we have the same shareholder. And what I did is I lobbied and pitched to Bertelsmann to invest into Berryville and the other printing companies of Bertelsmann. I also pitched to Bertelsmann to reopen the then shut-down capacity of Quad/Graphics because I wanted to keep that capacity in the market even though we didn't have a contract with Quad. So we have the same shareholder.

And Bertelsmann agreed to acquire Quad and to invest over the next five years some $75 million into more capacity for one-color in the United States.

Q. And you're a corporate representative of that common shareholder. Right? You're on the board of that common shareholder, Bertelsmann?

A. That is correct.

Q. Let me ask you this. Let me go back. You would agree it's a genuine concern that other publishers have that they may be at a disadvantage in acquiring authors because they're not as able to acquire the printing they need at a fair price or at all?

A. I can see that. And they certainly would have been able to acquire Quad. I think we acquired it for $15 million or whatnot. But actually, I lobbied to reopen the shut-down capacity for everyone in the market without having even a contract with Quad/Graphics.

Q. Mr. Dohle, let's turn to a different topic. I want to talk about the commitment you've made to treat the bids from Simon & Schuster imprints and auctions and how you're going to treat them after the merger. Okay?

A. Sure. Sure.

Q. You would agree that you can reorganize Penguin Random House and Simon & Schuster soon after the merger closes?

A. I made a commitment to the agent community in my letter that I would keep the ecosystem of Simon & Schuster imprints together, So I have made a commitment on that topic that we keep that ecosystem and history of imprints together.

Q. You can combine imprints after you close? You have that ability?

A. On the Simon & Schuster side?

Q. On either side.

A. Well, that would violate my commitment that I made to the agent and author community.

Q. And you've committed not to close any imprints?

A. No.

Q. You have not made that commitment?

A. Correct.

THE COURT: So how would that violate your commitment?

THE WITNESS: You mean the closing of imprints?

THE COURT: I'm sorry. I thought he asked you: You can combine imprints? You said that would violate your commitment. And then he said: Did you make that commitment? And you said no.

THE WITNESS: I think what Mr. Read then asked was: Can you close imprints?

And I said yes. The commitment that I made to the agent community was that I would keep Simon & Schuster—the ecosystem of imprints together and would not move imprints around to Random House and combine imprints with Penguin Random House. That's part of my letter, if I recall correctly, from February 2022.

BY MR. READ:

Q. It's a normal course of business to combine imprints?

A. When imprints cannot—if we think they cannot become profitable—and that happens—what happens then is in most cases that we bring the backlist and the to-be-published frontlist, and hopefully the editors, under the roof of another imprint. I'll give you an example. When we said that Gotham shouldn't be an imprint anymore, we brought the backlist and the frontlist and some of the editors to—I think it was Viking at the time. So the books continued to live, but the imprint name is gone.

Q. In the past, Penguin Random House has consolidated different imprints and publishing groups. Right?

A. That's correct.

Q. For example, the Crown Group was combined with . . . ?

A. Random House.

Q. And Penguin Putnam was combined with—was it Berkley?

A. Berkley NAL. Correct.

Q. And sometimes—well, you've had discussions about combining the children's imprints at Penguin Random House and Simon & Schuster?

A. We are talking about divisions with a community of imprints that we might bring together into one community of imprints. But the imprints is, of course—the imprints are the driving factor of our business.

But yes. There were discussions about how we organize our children's imprints—I think we have some 35 children's imprints—and how they are going to be organized in the future. Yes.

Q. I want to go back to the Crown consolidation with Random House and just make sure I understand it there. Crown was reorganized at one point in time, so it was less focused on fiction and more focused on nonfiction. Do you recall that?

A. That's right.

Q. So it's—the genre and focus of that imprint were changed?

A. Correct.

Q. And editors were moved from Crown that had previously done fiction into another imprint that—

A. The fiction editors moved to Random House, Ballantine, Bantam and other imprints. Correct.

Q. So imprints can be specialized, and that specialty can change. Right?

A. Yes.

Q. And your commitment to the agent community doesn't prevent you from changing the focus of imprints so that they are more complementary and less overlapping each other.

Correct?

A. Correct.

Q. Let's talk a little more directly about acquisitions in the commitment.

A. Sure.

Q. Is your promise—yes or no—essentially to have Penguin Random House continue what it is already doing with regard to acquisitions?

A. It goes beyond.

Q. It goes beyond. Right. Because today, you stop internal bidding when there's no outside bidder?

A. At Penguin Random House today. And with Simon & Schuster, we will be going beyond that. We will treat them as an external bidder.

Q. Let's talk about the logic of your policy today. Okay?

A. Sure.

Q. The reason that you stop the bidding today when there's no outside bidder is because Penguin Random House has already won the auction?

A. Correct.

Q. So if there's two Penguin Random House imprints, as long as there's a third one, you keep bidding. The outside one drops out. And then you stop the bidding because the two Penguin Random House imprints have already won the auction?

A. We count on the agent to notify us that we are the last ones. Correct.

Q. And that's logical and makes business sense today?

A. I don't know how often it happens. But yes.

Q. So this will be new to have Penguin Random House and a company it owns, Simon & Schuster, continue to bid against itself even when there's no other bidder and it's already won the auction?

A. That's correct.

Q. The reason you made this commitment was you had heard that agents still had concern about—concerns about Penguin Random House and Simon & Schuster coming together?

A. Correct.

Q. You would agree that Bertelsmann has no legal obligation to continue this commitment after the merger closes?

A. Unfortunately, we couldn't find a legally binding way of doing it.

Q. If Bertelsmann were to ever sell Penguin Random House and Simon & Schuster, the new owner would have no legal commitment?

A. That's my understanding.

Q. And you have an employment contract with Bertelsmann, don't you?

A. I do.

Q. And it lasts—it expires in a few years? We can just do it rough.

A. It does.

Q. And there's no legal constraint on the future CEO to continue this commitment you've made?

A. Correct.

Q. Today—let's talk about a slightly different way to acquire books. Today, if an agent is negotiating with Simon & Schuster and Simon & Schuster offers that agent and that author too little, that agent can threaten to go to Penguin Random House for a better offer. Right?

A. Correct.

Q. After the merger, if the agent is negotiating with Simon & Schuster and Simon & Schuster offers too little, is it your testimony that it will be just as effective that that agent can threaten to go to a Penguin Random House imprint to get a better offer?

A. Yes, it is. At Penguin Random House, our publishers and editors see their colleagues as some of their fiercest competitors today.

Q. Your commitment to the public was related to auctions. Correct?

A. Yes, which is a small, small sliver of the overall deals we do, especially the expensive deals we do.

Q. It did not cover negotiations one on one with authors, did it?

A. We are going to keep that external, too. So if an author wants to move an existing author [sic] from Penguin Random House to Simon & Schuster or the other way around, they can certainly do that in the future. That's my understanding.

Q. So before this commitment applied to auctions, and now it applies to negotiations as well?

A. We want to keep them as external and independent as possible.

Q. Let's go to a slightly different topic. If author advances are significantly reduced by this merger or any other reason, that would have a negative impact on the diversity of stories that will be published?

A. I've said that many, many times publicly in the context of the industry moving to an all-access business model, and I've given speeches and interviews about it. Correct.

Q. Correct. So regardless of the reason, if author advances are significantly reduced, that will have a negative impact on the diversity of stories that will be published?

A. Correct. And tectonic shifts in business model would certainly allow for that.

Q. And there is a correlation between author income and the diversity of stories being published?

A. If you add the word "significant," I support that.

Q. And you would agree that reduced author income means fewer authors will be able to make a living from writing?

A. I didn't get that, Mr. Read.

Q. You would agree that reduced author income means fewer authors will be able to make a living from writing stories?

A. Adding the word "significant," I support that.

Q. And you would agree that reduced author income will have an impact on the output of books?

A. Correct. If it's significantly reduced, yes.

Q. Let's turn to another slightly different topic. I want to—let's just turn to tab—PX 412.

A. The same binder, Mr. Read?

Q. Same binder. 412.

A. Sure. I found it.

Q. And PX 412 is an email that you composed and initially sent to yourself and some family members?

A. That's right.

Q. And it's dated January 14, 2019?
A. That's right.
Q. And it's an email you are composing and considering sending to Mr. Rabe. Right?
A. Who is my boss. Correct.
Q. In it, you are expressing your thoughts about your future with Bertelsmann and Penguin Random House?
A. That's right.
Q. And you are writing up some of your successes for Mr. Rabe. Correct?
A. I gave him a little bit of the history. Correct.
MR. READ: PX 412, your Honor, has some redactions. May I publish the document to the public with those redactions?
THE COURT: You may.
MR. READ: And I move to admit PX 412.
THE COURT: Any objection?
MR. PETROCELLI: No, your Honor.
THE COURT: It'll be admitted. (Whereupon, Plaintiff's Exhibit No. 412 was entered into evidence.)
BY MR. READ:
Q. Let's start with—since it's a draft, it's a little hard to see the paragraph breaks. There is in the third paragraph kind of what should be the start of a fourth paragraph.
Do you see it says: The first phase, 2008–2012, was marked by a cultural, commercial and financial transformation of Random House? Do you see that?
A. I do.
Q. And then below that, the last two lines of that paragraph, let's just read the first of those last sentences. It says: "A. series of decisions followed, from halving digital royalty rates from 50 percent to 25 percent to the (initial) rejection of the Apple-introduced agency model for ebooks, making us a witness instead of a defendant in the U.S. Department of Justice (DOJ) lawsuits against the five other major publishers and Apple." Do you see that?
A. Yes.
Q. And so one of the things is, you were taking credit for not getting sued in that Apple ebooks case. Correct?
A. I do.
Q. Well done.
A. Thank you.
Q. Well done. I give you credit for that. Well done. And then before that, in that same sentence, you talk about ebook royalty rates were halved, they used to be 50 percent and are now 25 percent. Do you see that?
A. Yes.
Q. And there exists today a few authors who were grandfathered in and who still get 50 percent royalty on ebooks. Correct?
A. Correct.
Q. But now the rate is generally 25 percent?
A. That's right.
Q. And you were taking some credit here for lowering that royalty rate on ebooks?
A. Random House was basically a pioneer in trying to entice authors and agents to give them ebook rights. It goes back to 1998, when Bertelsmann and Random House and Barnes & Noble started together the Rocket e-Book. So there was no device, really, for ebooks. You had to download them on your computer. So we basically experimented with different business models and tried to entice authors and agents to give us ebooks rights. It was 50 percent for some. Then we went to a royalty rate on wholesale prices after that, 50 percent.
And then I think the entire media industry basically went to—for other media categories, too, to a 75/25, 25 of net receipt. And so the book industry also did in a way.

And, yes, those 50 percent were grandfathered.

There was a lot of testing and experimenting going on, especially at Random House ventures, as we call it.

Q. Let's make sure we got some of—at least the basic facts. So initially, in ebooks, there were some authors who were getting 50 percent royalty for their ebooks?

A. Correct. And they still get it, as you mentioned.

Q. Under the grandfather provisions. But now, authors are not getting that. They're getting 25 percent as ebook royalties. Correct?

A. That is correct. But the question is: What is the denominator of the 25 and 50 percent? Those are different denominators.

Q. And you are taking some credit, at least in this email to your family as you form your thoughts, of having that ebook royalty rate being reduced?

A. If you interpret that that way, I can agree with that.

Q. Now, I want to talk about a related—or another change in authors. Today, Penguin Random House most commonly pays authors the advance in four installments. Correct?

A. Correct.

Q. And those are paid out over time?

A. Correct.

Q. About 25 percent at each time period?

A. Yes.

Q. And it waits from the initial signing to the acceptance of the—

A. Delivery and acceptance, publication.

Q.—to publication?

A. Subsequent formats.

Q. And subsequent formats. So that can be a period of years over which the advance is paid. Right?

A. In some cases, it is. Danielle Steel publishes eight books a year with us, so it goes faster for some, but it can take years. Correct.

Q. Right. For a nonfiction writer who has to do some research, it can take years to go and get all those payouts?

A. Correct.

Q. And isn't it true that there was a period of time where authors got their advances in three installments instead of four?

A. I don't recall whether that was our rule. What I do know is that some of our big authors get it even in two installments. And I'm—and I don't know, Mr. Read, whether it changed from thirds to quarters as a rule.

Q. Let's go to the next full paragraph of this document. It says: "The second phase (2012–2016) was about becoming Penguin Random House." Do you see that?

A. I do.

Q. And then below that, there is a sentence that reads: "The value creation of Penguin Random House merger is between"—and we're going to make confidential the exact amounts of the value creation—"including world market leader premium." Do you see that?

A. I do.

Q. And so you were again thinking of some credit in the value creation of Penguin Random House, which you should. Right?

A. Yes.

Q. I wanted to focus on this idea of world market leader premium that you wrote. Do you see that?

A. Yes.

Q. Is there a premium for being a market leader?

A. I would agree with that in enterprise value. I give you an example. We did ten years ago, or 11, when we were still Random House and already the market leader, we did an external valuation of Random House. And we did the same exercise again last year. And the valuation, external valuation, of Penguin

Random House, Bertelsmann's book business globally, went significantly up, also because Penguin Random House, yeah, is present on all continents and publishes great books. So that's what it means. It has a premium in valuation.

Q. And that enterprise value premium is because the market leader can be perceived as having the ability to generate greater profits?

A. That's not what I mean with the premium. It is that the brand Penguin Random House is so strong. Random House was strong already. With Penguin, it became even stronger.

People pay a premium independent from the underlying KPIs. That's what it really means.

Q. So the enterprise value if somebody were to purchase Penguin Random House would be greater, right, because it's a market leader?

A. Yes.

Q. And that—

THE COURT: Sorry. What is a KPI?

THE WITNESS: Key performance indicators, meaning revenue and profit.

BY MR. READ:

Q. And the enterprise value being larger can come because there's a potential for more profits by being market leader?

A. That's a matter of size globally in the end of the day. Yes.

Q. And that can come from two ways, either better at pricing or better at lower costs?

A. A market leader should have some economies of scale if they do a good job.

Q. And that economies of scale is a lowering of costs?

A. Yes.

Q. And another way to lower costs is to not have to pay authors as much? Yes or no.

A. Theoretically, yes.

Q. In the next sentence, it says: "In these years, 2012–2016," we're referring to, "we have chosen to run our business in order to optimize shareholder profit and cash flow (versus market share and sales)."

Do you see that?

A. I do.

Q. And in optimizing profit and cash flow, you were not prioritizing market share growth. Correct?

A. Yeah. I've been frustrated with our market share development. And at least, despite the fact that we've lost market share, we could achieve our goals in terms of cash flow and profitability.

Q. So you've been very successful on profitability. Correct?

A. Correct.

Q. And on market share, you'd like to do better?

A. Much better.

Q. And the priority at this time, 2012 to 2016, had been to focus on cash flow for dividends to your shareholders and profits?

A. I would have loved to gain market share, but we lost market share almost of the size of Simon & Schuster since the merger.

Q. And the focus, the priority, was to get cash flow for dividends to your shareholders then, Pearson and Bertelsmann, and profitability?

A. What I mean here is that we did not achieve our sales revenue and market share goals, but at least we delivered what our shareholders expected from us.

Q. So the output was a little less, but the profits were good?

A. The whole industry got more profitable during that time because of the shift to online and e-commerce. Correct.

Q. And you ran the business in a way to prioritize profits over share growth?

A. I'm looking back here. I ran the business in order to actually increase my market share, which hopefully would have resulted in more cash flow. But we could not achieve that goal.

Q. Well, why do you have in this sentence "in order to optimize shareholders' profit and cash flow versus market share and sales"? Why did you put the word "versus" there?

A. I don't know.
Q. Did you make a choice to prioritize profits and cash flow over market share growth?
A. I didn't, Mr. Read. I always want to grow at least with the market. But we lost significant market share.
Q. So why did you write this when you're talking about your successes?
A. What I'm saying is that we delivered on profit and cash flow. And I'm honestly unhappy with our revenue and market share development. Why I used "versus," this letter was never sent. It was only sent to me. I don't recall.
Q. Let's go to a different topic, Mr. Dohle. Let's talk about Amazon.
Q. This combination of Penguin Random House and Simon & Schuster does not serve as a countermeasure to Amazon. Correct?
A. Correct.
Q. And acquiring Simon & Schuster will not give Penguin Random House any ability to negotiate better terms against Amazon?
A. No. Not at all.
Q. Would you turn to PX 157.
MR. READ: Your Honor, there have been some redactions for confidentiality, I think, on this one—or maybe not. No redactions.
THE COURT: Okay.
MR. READ: So if we may put it up on the screen.
BY MR. READ:
Q. Are you there at 157, Mr. Dohle?
A. I am.
Q. This is an email you wrote and sent on April 1st, 2020?
A. Yes.
Q. Not on April Fool's, though?
A. My April Fool's blog. Yeah.
Q. It's entitled Markus's GEC blog?
A. Yes.
Q. And you sent it to your global executive committee?
A. That is correct.
Q. Would you tell the Court what constitutes the global executive committee at Penguin Random House?
A. It is a body, a governance body, of my direct reports, the 11 CEOs globally that report to me and the group service functions, like CFO and strategy and communications and legal. We saw them before on the slide. It's some 17 people on that board. And with me, we are 18, I think.
Q. These are your leaders at Penguin Random House?
A. Yes. And my direct reports. Correct.
MR. READ: Your Honor, I move to admit PX 157.
THE COURT: Any objection?
MR. PETROCELLI: No, your Honor.
THE COURT: It will be admitted. (Whereupon, Plaintiff's Exhibit No. 157 was entered into evidence.)
BY MR. READ:
Q. You begin this email or blog stating: Uber-resource your most important priorities. Do you see that?
A. I do.
Q. And you end that with an exclamation point?
A. Correct.
Q. And I think later in this document, you say this is a mantra you learned early in your career?
A. Yes. I'm an engineer by education. So yes.
Q. Let's talk about what your most important priorities are and uber-resourcing them, then.

The last sentence of the second paragraph, if we can find that, says Amazon was becoming—

MR. READ: Jordan, actually, maybe it's the paragraph—the last sentence above that. You've got it exactly right, Jordan. It's actually—let's go one paragraph up. It's—I count the uber-resource as a paragraph. I apologize. It's my fault.

BY MR. READ:

Q. So it's the paragraph that starts: This is a mindset and mantra. There's where we're going to go.

And we're going to go to the last sentence of that paragraph, where it reads: Thus, Amazon was becoming the most important priority in terms of our book sales besides preserving the diversity of booksellers and ensuring a competitive marketplace for books in the future. Do you see that?

A. Yes.

Q. And what you're doing here is you're starting to encourage your executives to provide Amazon with the highest service levels. Right?

A. Correct. First of all, I encourage them to read the book, and I recommend it highly to everyone here: *The Theory of Constraints*.

Q. Thank you. And in the next paragraph, the second-to-the-last sentence, you write to your team, your executives: "Large publishers are our (main) competitors and Amazon is (mainly) our customer in all book formats." Do you see that?

A. Yes, I do. And I like two times putting "main" into parentheses.

MR. READ: Your Honor, may we publish it to the gallery?

THE COURT: You may.

BY MR. READ:

Q. The main competitor of Penguin Random House is not Amazon. That's what you're telling your executives?

A. Well, I'm saying large publishers are our competitors, and in parentheses "main."

Q. So the main competitors for Penguin Random House are the large publishers?

A. If I wanted to say that, I—why would I actually add the parentheses? What I'm saying is, large publishers are all competitors. And in parentheses, yes, a main. And Amazon is our customer. Our largest, you know. It was mainly our customer, So that's what I am saying.

Q. Right, you wanted your executives to know that Amazon is more of a customer than a competitor?

A. They are a lot of things. But the most important role is to be a customer.

Q. And the large publishers are the competitors they should focus on?

A. If you want to interpret it that way, that's fine. The whole industry is our competitor and Amazon is our advertiser, is our competitor in self-publishing, in traditional publishing, but it's mainly our customer. That's correct. That's the biggest part.

Q. And the main publishers—the large publishers I can interpret you telling your executives are the competitors that they should mainly be focused on?

A. I hope they focus on the entire competition for books. But large publishers we encounter very often, given their size. Correct.

Q. In the end, this document—the point is, you do not want to fight Amazon in any way, shape or form?

A. Where do I say that?

Q. I'm just asking you the question. You do not want to fight Amazon in any way, shape or form?

A. Amazon as a customer, I always wanted to have a very good relationship and very good interfaces with. They are by far globally our largest customer and also in the United States. I never fight my customers. On the publishing side, we compete with them. And yeah. They get a lot of advertising dollars from us, too.

Q. Let's turn to self-publishing. I'd like to ask a few questions there. You would agree that self-published books have very limited sales?

A. Self-publishing is a hundreds and hundreds of millions of dollars business in the United States. Given the number of books that are self-published, on average, it's pretty low.

Q. So for most authors, self-published books have very limited sales? For most authors?

A. For most authors?

Q. Yeah.

A. For most authors, sales are low.

Q. And self-published books tend to provide authors with very limited income?

A. If you are not Brandon Sanderson, Colleen Hoover and many, many others who make a lot of money in self-publishing, given the millions of books that are being self-published, most of them don't sell. Correct.

Q. Well, you would agree the best authors don't choose self-publishing because they like the advances that publishers like Penguin Random House provide?

A. I just mentioned a few big, big authors, including the largest author in 2022, Colleen Hoover, who actually self-publishes books. But she also publishes books in the traditional way with publishers.

Q. Let me try that question again. The best authors don't choose self-publishing because they like the advance that publishers like Penguin Random House provide?

A. If you think they are not the best authors, that's correct.

Q. The best authors also choose to sell their books to Penguin Random House instead of self-publishing because they enjoy the services that Penguin Random House brings on the creative side, such as editing and cover design. Correct?

A. That is correct.

Q. And the best authors enjoy Penguin Random House's ability to reach members and Penguin Random House's marketing and other services?

A. Most traditional authors continue to be published traditionally. And that is correct.

Q. Your experience is that self-published books tend to be lower quality with a lower price point?

A. Yes. Most of them are. Correct.

Q. And you would agree that self-publishing presents only a limited competitive threat to publishers like Penguin Random House?

A. Today, it doesn't bring me up at night anymore. There was a time ten years ago when it was considered a big threat. Today, the biggest threat is all-access models for books. Correct.

Q. Let me make sure I've got that. So earlier in time, self-publishing was a greater threat than it is today. That threat from self-publishing has receded?

A. Their growth has slowed down a little bit the self-publishing growth as far as I understand it. There was a time when a lot of traditionally published authors, especially in the genre fiction, romance category, chose to pursue the self-publishing route. And that was some ten years ago. And that has not continued at the same pace. Correct.

Q. So ten years ago, self-publishing was more likely to keep you up at night than it is today?

A. That's right.

Q. Let's take one document on this, PX 445. Would you turn there, please?

A. The number again, Mr. Read?

Q. 445.

A. Same binder? Yes. I have it. I'm on it, Mr. Read.

Q. These are the minutes of a Bertelsmann's supervisory board meeting?

A. Correct.

Q. This is the board meeting that was convened on November 5th, 2020?

A. Correct.

Q. Just a few weeks before the final offer was made to secure Simon & Schuster. Right?

A. That's right.

Q. These are the minutes that were drafted later on December 17th, 2020?

A. After we signed the contract. Correct.

MR. READ: Your Honor, I'd move to admit PX 445.

THE COURT: Any objection?

MR. PETROCELLI: No, your Honor.

THE COURT: That will be admitted. (Whereupon, Plaintiff's Exhibit No. 445 was entered into evidence.)

MR. READ: And this is a significantly redacted document, but if we could put it on the public screen for the portion that's not?

THE COURT: Yes.

BY MR. READ:

Q. Would you turn to Page 3 of these minutes. By the way, this is a board meeting you were present at. Right?

A. I think it was all virtual because of COVID. But I attended it virtually from New York.

Q. Okay. You attended from New York virtually. And then so we're going to focus on the unredacted portion on Page 3, where you're asked some questions. Okay?

A. Okay.

Q. The paragraph begins, "With respect to the planned acquisition." It's the third paragraph. Are you there, Mr. Dohle, together?

A. Yes. I see it.

Q. "Mr. Levy asked whether the acquisition would not cause an increase in the existing cluster risk relating to Amazon." Do you see that?

A. Yes.

Q. And what does the word "cluster risk" refer to there? Is that a German expression?

A. It means that, given the size of Amazon as a customer globally, whether it would increase—call it our dependency on Amazon, given the fact that Simon & Schuster also, I assume Amazon is the largest customer of them as well, so we would increase our volume with Amazon globally significantly, and whether that dependency would result in additional risks.

Q. And you told them it would not?

A. Correct.

Q. And then a little deeper into this paragraph—it may be a little hard to find—it says: "He saw little danger in Amazon's self-publishing activities since Penguin Random House operated on a different quality level." Do you see that?

A. I do.

Q. And so you were telling the board that you didn't fear Amazon's self-publishing activities because it operated on a different quality level?

A. "And limited risk" is absolutely fair.

Q. And you agree today that self-published books operate on a different quality level?

A. And that it's a limited risk. Correct.

Q. Let's talk about some competitors to Penguin Random House.

A. Sure.

Q. And maybe let's ground you in your observations. You have authority to approve—well, if an advance exceeds $2 million, it needs your permission before the offer can be made. Right?

A. For the U.S., that is the threshold when I sign off. Correct. $2 million.

Q. And so your role, given that threshold, is more limited in acquiring books than some of the editors that are more day-to-day involved?

A. Correct. I love to be involved, but it's limited, given the threshold.

Q. So let's ask when you're involved. When you're involved, most of Penguin Random House's losses in acquiring books are to the other Big 5 publishers?

A. Given their size—I don't track it; but given their size, I would say—I would say that's correct.

Q. And because of their size, that gives you a sense of how often you think you're running up against them in acquiring books?

A. I mean, their collective size in the marketplace, I think we encounter them more often than the rest of the market.

Q. Right. Given their collective size and share, that gives you a sense of how often you think you're running up against them?

A. And the sense is that it's more often at that level than the rest of the market. Correct.

Q. Right. At a lower level, you might see more of the rest of the market. Correct?

A. That's correct.
Q. You cannot name any instance in which you were involved where Penguin Random House lost a book to Disney?
A. To . . . ?
Q. To Disney.
A. No, I don't.
Q. And you cannot name any instance in which you were involved where Penguin Random House lost a book to Abrams?
A. That is correct. At that level, I don't recall any.
Q. And you cannot name any instance in which you were involved where Penguin Random House lost a book to Scholastic?
A. At that level, that's correct.
Q. You cannot recall any instance where you were involved where Penguin Random House—well, you cannot recall any instance where Penguin Random House lost an author to a non-Big 5 with an advance over $2 million?
A. We just recently lost after my deposition on that topic, for example. It was not really an auction, but we lost a book of a celebrity, Britney Spears in that case, to another big house. And if I may, very often—
Q. Can I just make sure? So you're talking about a loss to a Big 5 publisher?
A. That is correct.
Q. I just wanted to focus on smaller publishers. But I've got your testimony. That's fine.
A. I'm sorry.
Q. Let me turn to a different topic, if I may. And I don't know if—how much longer we're going to need to go. Let's turn to PX 87.
MR. READ: This document has some redactions, your Honor, but may we publish the redacted version to the public?
THE COURT: You may.
THE WITNESS: I see it, Mr. Read.
BY MR. READ:
Q. Thank you. This is an email you sent on Saturday, August 16, 2020?
A. I did.
Q. And you sent it to Madeline McIntosh?
A. Correct.
Q. And it attaches a document called PRH U.S. agenda for 2020?
A. Yes.
Q. And on this—
MR. READ: Your Honor, I'd move to admit PX 87.
THE COURT: Any objection?
MR. PETROCELLI: No.
THE COURT: That will be admitted. (Whereupon, Plaintiff's Exhibit No. 87 was entered into evidence.)
BY MR. READ:
Q. So Item 1 on the cover says, "As we have discussed, profitable market share growth continues to be the—capitalize "the"—"key metric for our owners and for us." Do you see that?
A. Yes.
Q. And you talked earlier about KPIs, key performance indicators?
A. Yeah. You have to stop the loss of market share. Most important.
Q. And so that market share growth is extremely important to you and Bertelsmann?
A. Organic market share growth. Yes.
Q. And you've been discussing this with Ms. McIntosh multiple times?
A. Many times.
Q. So you're now focused more on growth and less on cash flow?

A. No. I say profitable market share growth. So of course we want to make contribution with that growth; and with that, add to our cash flows.

Q. So let's turn to the attachment entitled "PRH (U.S.) priorities for the next two to three years." Do you have that?

A. I do, Mr. Read.

Q. The first item at the top says "1," in bold: "Increase our market share, outperform the market, profitable market share growth." That's the goal, right?

A. Absolutely.

Q. And then the second—I want to talk about the second bullet in bold: "Content, acquisition, focus and involvement." Do you see that?

A. Yes.

Q. And then under that, there's an underlined word "hypothesis." Do you see that? "U.S. market share loss comes from publishing"?

A. Yes.

Q. And then—so you're working on a remedy to—where the market share loss is coming from. Right?

A. Correct.

Q. And the next line, the dash has—and this is—you're sending this to Madeline McIntosh. Right?

A. Yes.

Q. It says, "More deep involvement with content acquisitions: Team meetings for acquisitions greater than 250/500 K dollars to get more content (increase appetite for risk a notch)." Do you see that?

A. I do.

Q. And what you're doing is you're asking or directing Madeline McIntosh to personally get more involved in content acquisitions?

A. Correct. The level before was like $1 million, I think, her official signoff. And I encouraged her, given the importance of getting the books that are in demand with end consumers, to top the market share loss, to get more involved.

Q. And you're telling her to get—and your hope is that her involvement would increase the appetite for risk in acquiring books. Right?

A. We want to encourage our editors to buy the books that they are passionate about.

Q. And not be so risk averse?

A. To increase their risk appetite.

Q. And be a little more aggressive?

A. Sure.

Q. And you wanted Ms. McIntosh more personally involved at advance levels of $250,000 and advance levels of $500,000?

A. Yes. That clearly sends a signal into the organization.

Q. And you wanted Penguin Random House to acquire more books in the $250,000 and $500,000 advance range?

A. I randomly used those numbers. I would love for her to get involved in every book acquisition over $100,000.

Q. My observation, Mr. Dohle, is you do very little randomly. Let me ask this question: Ms. McIntosh's involvement at $250,000 in acquiring more books with more appetite for risk would help Penguin Random House grow its share?

A. Yes. We want to pay more for acquisitions in order to get the books and stop the market share drain and publish more books that are in demand and that readers like.

Q. And you wanted her to focus on—this is an area for her to focus—$250,000, $500,000, get personally involved with teams and be more aggressive?

A. Go for it. Pay more.

Q. Because it would make a difference in the market share for Penguin Random House if she were to do that?

A. If we buy more books, I would hope so, that they sell.

Q. And there's enough books in that segment that it can make a difference for the market share of Penguin Random House?

A. Sure.

Q. We've been talking about Penguin Random House wanting to grow share and as a result increasing its appetite for risk a bit. That means that you want Penguin Random House to be paying a little more in advances to win books?

A. Or even much more. And it also says: Involve me. Use me. I love that stuff. I love to negotiate and to win books and negotiate with agents and support our editors in the negotiation strategies to get the books to Penguin Random House. I love that.

Q. One way to grow market share is to be more aggressive in bidding for content from authors. Correct?

A. Correct.

Q. Another way to grow share is to acquire a company with a lot of market share. Correct?

A. That is correct.

Q. Early in this testimony, we discussed Penguin Random House cementing its position as the number one publisher in the U.S. with this merger. Do you remember that testimony?

A. I do.

Q. After this merger, Penguin Random House U.S. will not have as strong a need to grow share. Correct?

A. I think it doesn't speak to our performance that we are paying almost $2.2 billion to refill our lost market share for the most part. That shouldn't have happened. And in the future, we want to grow at least with the market. And that's sufficient.

Q. Let me try that question again. After this merger, Penguin Random House U.S. will not have as strong a need to grow share? Yes or no.

A. Yes. Growing with the market is enough.

Q. Let me make sure I got that. After this merger, Penguin Random House will not have as strong a need to grow its share?

A. Yes.

MR. READ: No further questions, your Honor. I pass the witness, your Honor.

THE COURT: Thank you. Mr. Petrocelli?

CROSS-EXAMINATION

BY MR. PETROCELLI:

Q. Mr. Dohle, did you—I'm going to take you back to that comment Mr. Read made that you do nothing randomly, no pun intended.

A. Everything is random in publishing. That's why we have that name. So the founder thought: Everything is random. Success is random, Bestsellers are random, So that's why we are the Random House.

Q. And that is the real origin of the name Random. Correct?

A. Correct.

Q. Okay.

A. It's a creative business.

Q. Well, did you pick $250/500,000 because it represented something associated with the anticipated top selling books?

A. At that point and until this lawsuit, I hadn't ever heard about that term.

Q. Okay. So I want to start from the beginning. But something caught my attention when you were answering questions and you were talking about what you perceived to be the biggest threat to publishing today. And you referenced "all access." Can you explain what that is and why that is a threat in your view?

A. Sure. I'm happy to. And I try to be concise.

There are a lot of all-access models in media. We all know about NetFlix; we all know about Spotify and other media categories. And we also know what it has done to some industries. The music industry has lost in the digital transformation approximately 50 percent of its overall revenue pool. And with all-access now, it's growing a little bit.

Q. Well, what is all-access?

A. All-access is basically a subscription model. You pay a monthly subscription fee, call it $9.99, and then you have access to the entire catalog, the entire content, all music, frontlist and backlist music.

Q. I'm talking about in the book industry.

A. In the book industry, we had two sort of attempts in the last ten years to establish all-access models in the industry. One was with ebooks ten years ago, around ten years ago, which resulted in a few startups like Oyster and Scribd and others. Scribd still exists.

And it resulted in Amazon for competitive reasons starting Kindle Unlimited, which is their subscription model. They are an all-access model. And it has thrived in the industry.

Then in the last years, basically, we had another all-access model development for digital downloads, for digital audio books. And around the world, many companies established the all-access models, subscription models, for digital audio books.

I think it's the biggest threat to the industry and especially to author income and author royalties and also author advances, because if this industry goes all-access, in this industry if we can get access to all books in digital formats by paying $9.99 a month, and in the family accounts all family members get it for free, it will have a tectonic influence on the revenue pool of the industry, on author advances ultimately and on author royalties and author income.

And I think that will have an impact on the diversity of stories that will be published.

Q. Does—

A. There is no need to do it. We provide as publishers between 10 and 30 hours of entertainment for a very reasonable price in Á La Carte, and all-access would have a huge impact.

One of the most important reasons, if I can add that, your Honor, 20 percent, around 20 to 25 percent of the readers, the heavy readers, account for 80 percent of the revenue pool of the industry of what consumers spend on books. It's the really dedicated readers.

If they got all-access, the revenue pool of the industry is going to be very small. Physical retail will be gone—see music—within two to three years. And we will be dependent on a few Silicon Valley or Swedish internet companies that will actually provide all-access, and authors are going to lose.

Q. Does Penguin Random House participate in any such all-access programs?

A. Not at all. And we go even further when we sell rights internationally. Even like in international markets, we don't let those rights become part of all-access. We think it's the biggest threat for author income.

Q. Okay. So let me go back to the beginning. What is the mission of Penguin Random House?

A. Well, we have a clear larger purpose, a clear "why." And that is that we want to create the future of books and reading, reading in long form, for generations to come.

And that generations to come is really important for us. So the children's books segment is really, really important for us. We know that reading in long form and immersing yourself into complex stories and characters creates empathy and human values in young people.

And we take our societal assignment as publishers really, really seriously. We think that books matter. And reading matters in our society. And we call our business culture and commerce, in that order.

Q. You indicated you've been with Bertelsmann your entire career and with Penguin Random House or its predecessors going back to 2008. Is that right?

A. That's right.

Q. Before we get into your work, what do you do outside of work? Do you have any interests?

A. Yes. I have a family and I love sport. But that's outside.

But I also am very engaged as an active citizen. Active citizenship is important for me in how I grew up and was raised in the '70s and '80s. And it's also important for Bertelsmann. So I serve on a lot of nonprofit boards and I'm very engaged in our community, small and large.

Q. What are some of the boards you serve on or associations with which you're affiliated?

A. Very quickly, I'm a board member of Pan America, the organization that fights for freedom of expression and protects authors and journalists, which becomes not only international, but also domestically more and more important and also celebrates literature. I'm the executive vice president of Pan America.

I am a board member of the National Book Foundation that also gives the National Book Awards and promotes reading and literature across the country, across the United States, with all their programs that they provide.

I've been a board member of the Association of American Publishers for many, many years and served as the chairman. They are for some years—they of course fight for copyright and, here on the Hill, lobbying to protect authors and copyright and the creators of intellectual properties—property.

I am a board member of the Atlantic Council here in D.C, a think tank that becomes more and more important. Again, the Transatlantic community, of course, given the war in Europe, is becoming more important. I'm on the international advisory board there.

I'm a member of the Council on Foreign Relations and I'm also serving on the Bertelsmann Foundation here in North America, which is based here in D.C.

THE COURT REPORTER: Excuse me. Did you say "wall" in Europe?

THE WITNESS: "War." Well, hopefully, we don't get a wall again. I grew up on the one side of it, on the better side.

BY MR. PETROCELLI:

Q. Mr. Dohle, who owns Bertelsmann?

A. 81 percent of Bertelsmann is being owned by the nonprofit Bertelsmann Foundation and 19 percent by the founding family in their sixth generation.

Q. What is the Bertelsmann Foundation?

A. The Bertelsmann Foundation is the largest nonprofit operating foundation in Europe. That's what it is.

Q. What does it do?

A. It was founded 45 years ago. The founders always thought an active citizenship and giving back to society, which they did with their publishing, of course, but in 1977 they decided to donate their wealth, 81 percent of it, back to society. And they call Bertelsmann an institution for society, which it actually is.

They wanted to tackle the mega challenges back then already. And they created the foundation that tackles from the get-go demographic change, healthcare for all, education, immigration, labor markets and inequality. More recently, they also get very engaged in environmental issues, climate change. So they are still on the mega challenges that we face today.

Q. And you say they had an office here in Washington?

A. They have an office here in Washington. And they don't give money, your Honor. They are an operating foundation. They are a think tank. And what they do is they try to help public institutions and governments to make better decisions based on data to tackle those mega challenges of our time and generation.

Q. With the profits that Bertelsmann earns, what is its policy regarding investments in its flagship book business?

A. We are a diversified company. The profits are reinvested in their eight divisions. And I always say we have unlimited access to cash flow to invest into our business. I've never seen them limit us in any way, shape or form in terms of investments.

Q. What kind of significant investments has Bertelsmann made in its U.S. publishing business, let's say, over the last 10 or 15 years?

A. Sure. So first of all, they encourage us—it's a content company—they encourage us to invest into content in order to at least grow with our—the markets grow with the markets that we operate in.

So content, most important. It drives everything. It's the only revenue- and profit-generating object of this business. So they encourage us to invest into it, number one.

Number two—

Q. Before you go to number two, on the subject of content, can you estimate, let's say, in 2021 how much in author advances and royalties you paid out by Penguin Random House worldwide and in the

U.S.?

A. Yeah. I track those numbers, Mr. Petrocelli. It was around—a little bit more than a billion dollars globally, two-thirds roughly in the U.S. And that reflects also the size of our U.S. market.

It's a little bit more in terms of author costs that we have here. Advances are really high in the U.S. market. And with that [indiscernible]—

THE COURT REPORTER: Sorry. I missed that.

THE WITNESS: I said ballpark, two-thirds of that in the U.S. in terms of author costs. And that reflects the market size. It's a little bit more than that, given the market we operate in here in the U.S.

BY MR. PETROCELLI:

Q. Okay.

A. So—and 2021, we also in the U.S. had an all-time high in terms of new author commitments, meaning acquisitions of books, and the advance commitments that we go into by signing those contracts. Actually it was for Penguin Random House an all-time high around $650 million last year.

Q. Okay. I got you. I cut off. You were going to go to number two. First was content.

A. Number two, very quickly, they encourage us also to invest heavily into reaching readers around the world. So publishing is about supporting creators, supporting authors and to perfect the story and the product, meaning the book, before we launch it into the world. And it's about reaching the largest audience for the author with sales and distribution and all the back office that is involved in it.

So it's creativity and reach. That's what publishing in essence is about. So they encourage us to invest heavily into reaching the largest readership globally for our books, number two.

Number three, if the opportunity comes along, they also encourage us to increase the community of imprints, the community of small- and medium-sized publishing houses that we operate around the world. In the U.S., almost 100; globally, more than 300. So if a merger and acquisitions opportunity come along, they also support us to look into it and perhaps acquire that.

Q. I want to go back to the supply chain. How much has been invested in the supply chain for Penguin Random House in the last 10 or 15 years?

A. Let me focus on the U.S. We have a lot of supply chain—

Q. Just the U.S.

A. Sure. We've invested more than $250 million into upgrading and into getting books to readers in the United States and more than $150 million since the merger with Penguin.

Q. And can you just briefly explain what improvements have been made and how it's enhanced the delivery of books?

A. Sure. So I try to be concise.

I had a life—a long life, eight years—in distribution. So actually it goes to the core of where I started my career in books. And I'm very excited about it. But let me be very short here.

So what we've done in essence is we've invested into speed, the speed of distribution and replenishment of our books. And you do that by establishing more warehouses in the country. That helps. Right?

Because it reduces the distance. We have a West Coast facility now, distribution center, and ten years ago we only had an East Coast and Midwest facility. You invest in warehouse technology to have a faster turnaround time of your authors. You invest into seven-days-a-week delivery for your customers to actually increase the speed.

So several investments. You invest into freight, because you deliver in smaller chunks. And what it does, it makes the whole chain more efficient for retailers and for us.

And the best news is, it always makes sure that the books are on the shelves. And readers can only buy books if they are on the shelves, of course. So it's good for readers; it's good for retailers; it's good for revenues; it's good for authors; and ultimately for us.

Q. What is a return rate and how has your enhanced supply chain affected return rates?

A. Yeah. That was one of the ideas back then, to reduce return rates.

So if you speed up your supply chain and your replenishment time, you can actually deliver books in 48 hours, countrywide. What it does is it takes out inventory out of the whole chain. So booksellers don't have that much cash in inventory because they can order more quickly and they get it so quickly back on the shelves. That makes retailers much stronger financially and more sustainable.

And that was the idea back then. We wanted to support physical retail and keep those stores open and strengthen them financially.

It also reduces the return rate because there's less inventory in the chain. Right? And if books don't sell, you get fewer books back. And that is good for retailers; that's good for publishers. It makes everything more efficient and profitable.

Q. You know, I did—my apologies—skip a brief description of your career. So if you could just briefly describe it. You mentioned you were in printing. Maybe you could just tell the judge what areas of the publishing business you've worked in.

A. So in five sentences, I've basically worked in the entire value chain of books in the almost 30 years at Bertelsmann. And I did it in reverse. So I started with sales and distribution for eight years, I ran distribution centers, even, and the interface to retailers which I—yeah—which I had a long life in. That was eight years, the first eight years.

Then I moved a step back in the value chain of books. So before you distribute books and sell books, you have to produce them and to print and bind them. So I ran printing companies for Bertelsmann around the world, including the United States, for six years.

And then I went another step back in the value chain of books and Bertelsmann decided to send me to New York to become part of the content acquisition, the book-making, the publishing of the books. Before you print them, you have to acquire them.

So—and that's what I've done for 14 years-plus, Random House and Penguin Random House.

Q. Does Bertelsmann impose a budget on what Penguin Random House can spend on acquiring books in a year?

A. As much as we want. I've never—we have unlimited access to cash.

Q. Does Bertelsmann have to sign off on any book deals?

A. There is a governance threshold. Mine is $2 million. We talked about that. Bertelsmann's is $75 million, I've never had to ask them to sign off.

Q. Do you impose a budget on the U.S. operating company run by Madeline McIntosh?

A. No. I want her to invest more.

Q. And you were asked questions about your approval level, which is $2 million and above. Have you ever turned down a request to approve a book at your level?

A. It's not the CEO's job to value a book. The answer is no. The editors do.

Q. You were asked questions about printing. I'd like to go back to that. There was a back-and-forth you had about whether printing gives Penguin Random House a competitive advantage, and Mr. Read showed you that document. Do you recall that?

A. I do.

Q. I think that was Exhibit 983. I just wanted the record to be clear. Do you think there's any advantage that Penguin Random House has because its parent company owns a printing company?

A. The only advantage that I see is that I can convince Bertelsmann, given their important publishing business in the United States, to invest more into printing to help us keep our books in stock. I was quite successful in convincing Bertelsmann to almost green-light $100 million into printing capacity equipment and acquiring Quad.

Q. And have you—have those investments in printing been made by the Bertelsmann Printing Group?

A. There is an investment plan for the existing companies of about 75 million and we are—it's a five-year plan. And then there is the acquisition of Quad. That was also part of it.

And as I said, we print 30 percent of our hard covers and trade paperbacks with Bertelsmann. So the entire industry benefits from them. And because of us, the Quad plants were reopened again.

Q. In your—

THE COURT: May I ask, why don't you publish more of your books within Bertelsmann?

THE WITNESS: You mean print, right?

THE COURT: Print. Yes. Print.

THE WITNESS: So actually, five years ago, it was 40 percent. We're just not able to fulfill the commitments. And so the volume has been declining over many, many years with them. And we've always said it's very important to have a multivendor strategy for us and it's very important for them to print for a lot of publishing houses in order to flatten out the capacity load of their machines throughout the year.

BY MR. PETROCELLI:

Q. In your experience, has the Bertelsmann Printing Group given Penguin Random House a priority or preference when it comes to printing?

A. No. I've been frustrated with them because of their underperformance.

Q. Okay. I wanted to talk a little bit about the 2013 merger.

A. Sure.

Q. But I thought it might be helpful first if you could just kind of go back in time and tell us sort of the key milestones in Penguin Random House's growth in the U.S. starting with Bertelsmann's first appearance in the U.S. publishing business.

A. As I said this morning, 1977, Bantam. 1985, '86, Doubleday Dell—it became Bantam Doubleday Dell. 1998, Random House. The groups became Random House together. 2013, Penguin Random House.

Q. And you became the U.S. CEO in 2008. Correct?

A. Of Random House in 2008. The global CEO of Random House. Correct.

Q. And you then were instrumental in recommending and supporting the merger with Penguin?

A. I was responsible for it. I ran the project.

Q. And what was your rationale for that merger?

A. The same as it is here with Simon & Schuster: We were convinced that, given our investments in supply chain, back then already into speed, into in-stock rates, into faster replenishment, we were convinced—and it's widely acknowledged in the retail community—that we could sell more of the Penguin books by giving their imprints access to the, by far, best sales and supply chain network in the country.

On the creative side, if I may add that, I always said: This is the most boring merger of all time, quote.

The only thing we are doing is we are bringing two communities of imprints, Random House and Penguin, communities of imprints, into one. And they continue to act editorially, creatively and entrepreneurially independent.

We are just a larger community of imprints. We keep the creative side always untouched. It's business as usual.

Q. Now, with respect to the structure of that deal, the owner of Penguin was Pearson Company. Right?

A. Correct.

Q. And so the two of you, Bertelsmann and Pearson, co-owned Penguin Random House for a number of years. Right?

A. Yeah. This is not the place to explain why it was a noncash deal. So there were reasons for that, for another time. But it was a noncash deal.

So they valued their respective businesses globally and then they settled actually in that case without me. I had to recuse myself because I became the CEO. They settled on a split of shares. And Bertelsmann owned 53 percent of the company, Penguin Random House, the newly founded company, and Pearson 47. So Bertelsmann would be the majority and fully consolidate the business and Pearson became a quasi-financial investor.

Q. Ultimately, was Pearson bought out?

A. Yeah. Very happy with that. Bertelsmann bought out Pearson. It makes the governance easier for me as CEO.

And in two steps: In 2018, Bertelsmann brought 22 percent. So it became 75 versus 25 percent Pearson.

And just after the COVID pandemic hit, in April 2020, Bertelsmann acquired the remaining 25 percent of Penguin Random House. And now we are 100 percent Bertelsmann again.

Q. Based on your experience with that merger and running the company thereafter, did the 2013 merger between Penguin and Random House result in a reduction in titles published by the company?

A. No. Not at all.

Q. Was there a reduction in titles that occurred at some point after that merger?

A. Yes, there was.

Q. What was the source of it?

A. The source were market forces. I think that we've heard about during this week already.

And very quickly, it was a time when genre fiction, especially romance and science fiction to a certain extent, mystery, suspense novels, but romance is a very good example, many of those heavy readers of romance novels at that time switched to self-published stories. A very different price point. 99 cents, $1.99, away from what we call mass-market trade paperbacks.

Q. Now, what is a mass-market trade paperback?

A. The mass-market trade paperback is the sort of small-format mass-market book, as we call it, like it is a trade paperback, but a smaller format. It has been declining for the last 25 years, forever.

But we had a step change around '14, '15, with this trend that so many consumers went away from mass-market books into electronic ebooks in particular and self-published books.

And that movement of consumers who moved on from mass-market books, that resulted in retailers dedicating less and less shelf space. Some of them would list out, would not really carry anymore, like Walmart at the time, mass-market books, especially big-box retailers. So less and less shelf space. No distribution for those books anymore because of shrinking shelf space. And again, it was a step change.

So we had—we had to adjust that. Penguin, especially Berkley NAL, was traditionally, overindexed in that business, and we had to adjust that.

Q. And was that a trend that affected the industry in general?

A. Very much so. All publishers. I think we've even heard about this week already. And it was happening years after the merger, sort of '15, '16, '17, for the most part.

Q. Did you close any imprints as a result of the merger?

A. No. We never touch creative because of an acquisition or increasing the number of imprints in our community. The answer is no.

Q. Is it not correct that some 32 imprints were closed after 2013?

A. I've heard that number, around 30. It's interesting what happens in ten years. I explained this morning what happens. Normally, backlist, frontlist, and editors move on.

We also opened, started, almost the same number of imprints exactly in the last ten-ish years or nine-ish years since the merger. So we were more than 90 imprints on July 1st, 2013. And today, we are also more than 90 imprints in the United States. So that also shows that we invest into startups, into new imprints, every year.

Q. And—

A. More than 30 imprints were opened.

Q. In connection with the 2013 merger, did you make any plans in advances of the merger to reduce author compensation?

A. No. Not at all.

Q. And did you direct the company in any way, shape or form to reduce author compensation after the merger?

A. No.

Q. Talking about now competition, you were asked a number of questions about that by Mr. Read. First of all, is it part of your responsibilities to track competition with other publishers?

A. Very much so. Yes.

Q. Do you track it downstream?

A. Only market shares, consumer market shares and retail market shares. And I'm quite competitive about that. Yes. Yes, I do.

Q. Do you track upstream? By "upstream," I mean with respect to the acquisition of books.

A. No.

Q. Are you aware of any industry publications that provide market share information regarding the acquisition of books?

A. No. A. few deals are being publicized in *Publishers Weekly* and then there is this Publishers

Marketplace anecdotal reporting of some deals. But we don't track that.

Q. You don't—

A. No one really tracks analytically sort of upstream shares or whatnot. We all look into: What are the books that are in demand?

Q. So let's focus, then, on downstream. What are the main sources of information that you track and rely on for assessing downstream competition in market shares?

A. There are two main sources. Both have their advantages and their flaws. One is being done by the Association of American Publishers. I'm a board member, as I said. It's called AAP StatShot. And how it works is it—let me go directly to annual data. More than 2,000 publishers report their billing, their revenue, the books they sell into retail for that given year across all formats and across all channels.

Q. By "all channels," does that mean—what does that mean, beyond booksellers?

A. Educational channels, special markets like gas stations, Williams-Sonoma, whatnot.

Q. Libraries?

A. Of course libraries which is of course an important societal assignment for publishers and especially for us at Penguin Random House. We take that very seriously for the reading culture.

Now—but they just report their revenues. And that's the most holistic. If 2,000 publishers, more than 2,000 publishers in the United States, report their revenues, then it is actually the most holistic database that you can have. And then AAP makes some adjustments and so on for self-publishing, So it is accepted as—there are flaws, but it is accepted as the most holistic database to measure market share.

Q. And it includes physical ebooks and audio?

A. Sure. Yes.

Q. And all formats of physical?

A. (No audible response.)

Q. What's the other source?

THE COURT REPORTER: Sorry. I didn't hear an answer.

THE WITNESS: Yes, it does.

MR. PETROCELLI: Thank you.

BY MR. PETROCELLI:

Q. What is the other source of market share data for the downstream market?

A. The other source is BookScan. And BookScan reports weekly and consumer sales across many channels. So it basically reports books that are being sold through the register to end consumers. And it only tracks print, physical books. And it tracks around 70 to 75 percent of the physical sales.

Amazon actually reports to BookScan as the largest bookseller in America and also the chains, of course, Barnes & Noble, Books-A-Million and also the independent bookstores.

Q. You need to slow down. You need to slow down, because I'm having trouble hearing what—

A. So since it's 70 percent, your Honor, of 70 to 75 percent of print, if you multiply those two numbers, it reflects 50 percent of the book market. Right? 75 percent of our books are print books that we sell in America, around 75. And it tracks 70 percent of those print sales. So it's around 50 percent of the overall market, but a very relevant one.

Q. What is your market share under the AAP StatShot information?

A. Ballpark, 15 percent.

Q. And what is it under BookScan?

A. A little bit more than 20, 21.

Q. You indicated in answering some of Mr. Read's questions that you were losing market share and have been losing market share. Is that true?

A. Correct.

Q. Okay. So I want to talk about that.

MR. PETROCELLI: Let me actually do this by showing a document that's in the binder, your Honor. And it is exhibit—Defendants' Exhibit 76. And this is a confidential document. Is that right? That particular slide is not, I'm told. Okay.

BY MR. PETROCELLI:

Q. Do you have that in front of you? You have the slide in front of you, right, from that exhibit? Okay. And so you'll see that this is from a presentation dated December 2019.

A. Correct.

Q. And what was the purpose of this presentation?

A. To look at our market share development since the merger between Penguin and Random House in the retail consumer marketplace.

Q. Okay.

MR. PETROCELLI: Your Honor, I would ask that Defendants' Exhibit 76 be admitted into evidence.

THE COURT: Any objection?

MR. READ: No objection, your Honor.

THE COURT: It will be admitted. (Whereupon, Defendants' Exhibit No. 76 was entered into evidence.)

BY MR. PETROCELLI:

Q. Can you turn to Slide 1, I believe it is? Do you have that in front of you?

MR. PETROCELLI: Can we put it on the monitor? Next page, please.

THE WITNESS: Next.

MR. PETROCELLI: Keep going. There you go.

BY MR. PETROCELLI:

Q. Okay. So let's go over this slide. This has to do with your lost market share?

A. Yeah. It unfortunately has.

Q. And the timeframe here is 2013 through 2019. Is that right?

A. Correct.

Q. And you'll see a number of lines. And starting with the bottom line, it has "clients" next to it. What is that?

A. Okay. Very quickly, the client development is our—those are our third-party distribution clients. The clients are publishers that we distribute and sell in the marketplace. So they use the same wonderful distribution and sales network that we've established over the years.

Q. So to be sure, these clients are using Penguin Random House's supply chain. Right?

A. Our wonderful supply chain. They've grown significantly, you know. You see the 200 million here. Above is the Penguin Random House development in the dotted—

Q. I'm not there. Yes. I'm going to do this. So the clients—

A. Excuse me.

Q.—the clients show growth from 2013 to 2019. Right?

A. Correct.

Q. Okay. Now, the next line up, the solid line, says PRH U.S. What is that?

A. That is our PRH U.S. core business of our company, a little bit more than $2 billion here. We can see in 2013 we were $2.3 billion and in 2019 also $2.3 billion. $2.290 it starts, actually, in 2013. So we could unfortunately not increase our revenues.

Q. What is the dotted line?

A. The dotted line is a simulation. And it basically indicates if we had grown with the market.

And then on the right-hand side is another dotted line bucket. We would have grown around $400 million during that timeframe to $2.7 billion. If we had been able to grow with the market, the company would be $400 million roughly larger than it actually was.

Q. Okay. Let's go up to the next line, so the one that says the Big 5. Do you see that?

A. Yeah.

Q. Now, first of all, what is included in the line for the Big 5?

A. Yeah. We are not in that bucket. What we did here, because of their size, we included Hachette, Macmillan, HarperCollins, Simon & Schuster and we added Scholastic into that line. I remember it back then. We discussed I think market share numbers of course on a weekly and monthly basis. But this was a longer period of time, and we are not in that.

So they had grown their revenues from $3 billion, I guess, to $3.7 billion. Those five companies.

Q. And what's the next line up under All Others?

A. All Others are—is the rest of the market outside of the Big 6, if I may, excluding Scholastic, which is again a $1.4 billion company, larger than some of the Big 5.

THE COURT: I'm sorry. I thought you said Scholastic for this was included with the Big 5.

THE WITNESS: It is Big 5, but not—we are out. We are separate. And the Big 5 means the Big 4, if you will, plus Scholastic.

BY MR. PETROCELLI:

Q. I was asking you about All Others. Is that everybody other than the five in the Big 5 and Penguin Random House?

A. That is correct. It's the rest of the market—

Q. Okay.

A.—which basically grew their revenues and end consumer sales by $1 billion. This is BookScan, so it's really end consumer sales.

MR. PETROCELLI: Pam, can I just now focus on the market share box on the right?

THE WITNESS: You also see at the top, if I may, Mr. Petrocelli, the overall market, your Honor, grew from $9 billion to more than $11 billion. What a great market the book market is. It's always growing. So $9 billion to $11 billion. That's $2 billion. And, of course, more than 20 percent.

And in the last two years, 2020 and 2021, the book market in the U.S. grew again by 20 percent. So it was like a hockey stick during COVID. The industry is thriving.

BY MR. PETROCELLI:

Q. And did you—

A. That's also the reason for some supply chain issues globally and locally and for some printing issues. That business is growing so quick.

Q. In the last two years, did Penguin Random House keep up with the market?

A. Unfortunately, not. So we lost a little bit more. It slowed down, our losses, And we are heavily investing. 2021: Record commitments, new advance commitments for the future.

But yeah. You know, we are still in turnaround phase.

Q. And can we just take a look at the summary box, the market share?

A. Yeah.

Q. That recaps the different growth levels. Right?

A. It does.

Q. So Penguin Random House went from a 25 percent market share down to a 21 percent market share. Is that right?

A. Ballpark, yes.

Q. Now, what does this tell you who you lost that market share to?

A. Well, since the other big companies here, Big 5, including Scholastic, they were 33, then went down. So it's sort of up and down, which is creative volatility. They're still at 33 percent.

But that includes many acquisitions that these companies have done. For example, HarperCollins bought Harlequin, a big global publisher, $400 million in revenue at the time. That's what I recall, $400 million. So their acquisitions.

We have not really acquired. In the U.S., two very small companies.

But the 33 percent includes their nonorganic acquisitions. But they could keep their market share all in all. The market share that we lost went to clients and "all others." Clients are also "all others," smaller publishers. So that's some 43 percent in 2019, if I see that correctly.

And in the last two years, that fragmentation of the market towards "all others," away from the big publishing houses in consumer demand and sales, have actually accelerated again last year. 50 percent of the revenue. And books basically that were being sold in America were sold by smaller publishers.

Q. What in your estimation based on your analysis and your experience—

THE COURT: I'm sorry. I didn't catch that. 50 percent of the revenue last year was from smaller publishers?

THE WITNESS: Yeah. This is 2019. So it's actually 38 percent plus 5 percent plus Scholastic. I have put now Scholastic into that bucket, away from the Big 5.

By let's say it's 43 percent here outside of the Big 6, including Scholastic. That was 2019.

During COVID, your Honor—I was just giving you the 2021 numbers—the trend has continued. Smaller publishers have outperformed the large houses. And in 2021, around 50 percent of the books sold in America were sold by publishers outside of the Big 5.

BY MR. PETROCELLI:

Q. And what's the reason for that, based on your analysis of the market over the last ten or so years?

A. This trend has been going on for a long time. And it started even before 2013. And the main reason for the industry fragmenting is the shift to online and e-commerce. Every second book in America, ballpark, is being sold via e-commerce.

Q. You mean 50 percent?

A. 50, five zero. It has leveled the playing field in the marketplace between larger houses and smaller houses.

Q. How so?

A. First of all, Amazon today—amazon.com has 50 million books available. Five zero million books available.

A bookstore, a good independent bookstore, has around 50,000 different books available, SKUs as we call it, 60,000 titles available. Amazon has 50 million.

The second point is that—

THE COURT: For our transcript, when you said SKUs, you meant S-C-U, not S-K-E-W?

BY MR. PETROCELLI:

Q. What does SKU stand for?

A. Like—

Q. Stock keeping units? Is that what you meant when you said SKUs?

A. It's not units; it's titles.

Q. I think her Honor asked what the SKU stands for.

A. That's how we sort of just call it sometimes, sort of a—

THE COURT: Is it S-K-U?

THE WITNESS: Can someone help me?

THE COURT: How do you—

THE WITNESS: I don't even know how we spell it.

MR. PETROCELLI: Your Honor, I think it's S-K-U.

THE COURT: That's fine. I just wanted to know for our transcript.

THE WITNESS: It's—we can settle on "titles." I shouldn't have used that word.

BY MR. PETROCELLI:

Q. So let's get back on track, okay?

A. The second point is that it is not a human being involved, a bookseller. An algorithm decides what is being presented and made visible and discoverable for an end consumer online. It makes a huge difference.

THE COURT: You mean at Amazon?

THE WITNESS: At Amazon and other outlets for e-commerce like Apple and Google and barnesandnoble.com. And so it's not only Amazon. Amazon is of course by far the largest e-commerce player in books, and it started as a bookstore almost 30 years ago. But there are still a few others, even though it's perhaps 20 percent of the e-commerce.

So it's an algorithm that decides. So in the past, with our great sales force, we basically had a lot of influence on which books are being presented, frontlist and backlist in bookstores. And smaller publishers might have been here and there underrepresented. But today, in this market, where e-commerce dominates, the algorithm dominates, it has completely leveled the playing field. That is number two.

So especially from a backlist perspective, the large publishers, if you follow BookScan, large publishers have lost backlist market share. Why? Because all the backlists of the world that has ever existed is now being made available on Amazon when in the past we had perhaps a good share of a bookstore in terms of our backlist and smaller publishers had a smaller share.

So they have gained frontlist market share, but they've also gained backlist market share. And that has made them much stronger financially. Return rates is another thing in e-commerce. You can—

BY MR. PETROCELLI:

Q. Can I stop you right there? How has online delivery of books assisted smaller publishers efficiency-wise?

A. Sure. So we know that in the end of the day, Amazon is a supply chain machine. Right? So they are super efficient. And since we also are interested in efficiencies and efficient delivery, we work very well with them on that interface.

As we can see, our distribution clients, they greatly benefit from that, gaining their share by 25 percent from 4 to 5 percent in the marketplace in these eight years or six years or—six years, seven years.

So Amazon is a supply chain machine. Very efficient. Very low return rates. Roughly 5 percent when the industry collectively 15 years ago was perhaps at 30 percent.

The growth of Amazon has actually reduced the return rates. And it's not only the freight and the handling of the product that costs money; unfortunately, many of the books that are being sent back can't be sold anymore and are going to be destroyed. We actually donate millions of books every year, but that has limits.

So the print paper, binding, everything is actually involved in that. So it's a very, very important level for profitability.

And the shift to online has made publishers more profitable and leveled the playing field. So the risk assessment for smaller publishers has become much more favorable over the last decade. And we can see that, and them being very competitive and gaining retail and end consumer market share as we speak.

Q. Does that have any impact on smaller publishers' ability to pay author advances?

A. I'm sure it has.

Q. In what way?

A. If you know that 50 percent of your business is at a maximum return rate of 5 percent and it's a very important factor of your risk assessment, and if you know that your books are being featured side by side, frontlist and backlist, with all publishers, and an algorithm decides which book is being made visible for an end consumer, presented to an end consumer, it makes you financially stronger. And I'm sure you are more willing to invest into content and to take your risk a notch up.

Q. Your what?

A. Your advance a notch up.

Q. Let me turn to another subject that Mr. Read asked you about, and that is the internal competition that goes on in the company.

A. Okay.

Q. So just to clarify, the practice has been for some time that the imprints can compete against one another across divisions. True?

A. Signature service to the industry at Penguin Random House for decades.

Q. Okay. And the limitation on that is when there is an auction and an agent discloses that there's no other external bidder, then the internal bidding at Penguin Random House stops. Right?

A. Correct.

Q. Okay. Why do you allow these imprints to compete against one another?

A. The essence of publishing, the foundation of this business, is that every book idea finds the most passionate editor with the largest vision for the book. And the largest vision for the book, the biggest passion for the book, has a high correlation to the advance the editor wants to pay for the book. And with that, hopefully, also in more sales.

The essence of publishing is that every author finds the most comfortable home publishing imprint, the team, the editor of course, but then also the publishing team, the publisher, the imprints, marketing and publicity staff. So we want to make sure to provide the perfect match. I call it the perfect match in publishing.

Everything is bottom up. It's one book at a time. So the perfect match is between book idea and editor and author and imprint. And internal bidding makes that possible and supports that idea.

Q. And within each imprint, can you give the Court a description of the types of positions that each imprint has besides the editor?

A. Sure. There is the publisher; there is—

Q. What's the difference between the publisher and an editor?

A. The acquiring editor is the acquiring editor who edits the books.

The publisher in many cases still edits books but also runs sort of a group of and supervises a group of editors and helps with everything and is also responsible for the entire process, which includes then copy-editing, of course, art and design, the interior design of the book, the jacket design of the book, setting the pub date and then together with production setting the first print run of the book.

So publisher: Responsible for the whole thing.

Editor: Underneath responsible for of course perfecting the product in collaboration with the author.

You have—in imprints, normally you have some publicity staff. You have dedicated publicity and marketing people. And yeah. They need to be very close to the books and the authors, too. That's it.

Q. So just a brief detour here, but sort of the timeline of a book, right? You win the bid, hopefully. The book is being written with the editor and publisher involvement. Right? And then once that manuscript is done, what then happens?

A. Yeah. When you win a book, very often the book is not through being written, as we know. The book idea, there might be an outline, a chapter or a manuscript. So it depends on—you know, every book is unique, like its own startup. It never existed.

And then comes of course first of all acceptance and delivery. So you finalize the manuscript and it goes into copy-editing. Then the interior design starts of the book. We want to make it beautiful inside. We try to create the most compelling jacket for it. You develop a marketing and publicity plan.

Q. Let me stop you there. You develop a marketing and publicity plan before the book is sold?

A. Yes.

Q. And let's go back a step. When the book is being negotiated and you're trying to win the book, we've heard that companies, including Penguin Random House, have a profit-and-loss projection that they make. Right?

A. Yeah.

Q. Where—

A. We call it the book P&L, the acquisition P&L. Correct.

Q. On that acquisition P&L, there's a projection of the number of units sold. Right?

A. And the corresponding revenues.

MR. READ: I was going to object to leading, but it went by fast.

MR. PETROCELLI: I don't think this is controversial, but I'm trying to speed it up. But I'll try not to lead.

BY MR. PETROCELLI:

Q. Does the P&L contain any kind of provision for marketing and publicity?

A. At Penguin Random House we put for every book a 2 percent cost of marketing into our book P&L, which means 2 percent of the revenue, the anticipated revenue, the projected revenue. So it's basically 2 percent of that projected revenue is the so-called acquisition P&L—call it "budget"—in terms of marketing.

Q. Is 2 percent used for all books regardless of advance level?

A. That's correct.

Q. Okay.

THE COURT: But that changes, then, depending on how much you pay for the book. It's more marketing for books with higher advance?

THE WITNESS: It's more for books with higher projected revenues. It is not 2 percent of the advance; it's 2 percent of the projected revenues of that book.

THE COURT: I see. But the advances are correlated with the projected revenues?

THE WITNESS: Correct.

THE COURT: Okay. Thank you.

BY MR. PETROCELLI:

Q. And after the book goes through the process of being edited and the design and all of that, when does—you were saying the marketing plan was being prepared. When does the company start to try to sell the book? And in particular, do they try to sell it before it's actually available?

A. Sure. We sell it in months before it's available. We sell it into bookstores, to booksellers, months before it's available.

Q. Months?

A. Months before the publication date.

Q. And during—and then it has to be printed and bound and delivered. Right?

A. Correct.

Q. When during that process does a company find out if the book is going to be well received?

A. Yeah. Only after a publication date, when end consumers either decide to buy it or not. And as we know, there is the return right. We are not really selling books; we are providing booksellers with books, and they can send it back and get full credit for it.

So we only know once the book is on sale whether end consumers decide to choose it.

Q. Are there any other ways in which you find out if in advance of the book being made, for example, it's going to be popular?

A. You know, we try to sort of think about certain, is there buzz? Is there word of mouth? Are people excited about the story internally? And have we heard externally? We have advance reading copies for booksellers. Is there buzz around it?

Q. Slow down a little bit. What are advance reading copies?

A. So we—for some books, we actually produce the so-called ARCs, advance reading copies, and we send them to booksellers, to bloggers, to journalists. And so the editor would write a letter, an accompanying letter, and present that book.

And we hope that booksellers love it and create buzz with their customers and also that media and bloggers and—you know, would discuss it and like it, too.

THE COURT: Is now a good time for a break, Mr. Petrocelli?

MR. PETROCELLI: Yes.

THE COURT: Let's take our lunch break at this time. And we'll resume again at 2:00.

Please don't talk about your testimony, Mr. Dohle.

THE WITNESS: Sure. Sure. I won't.

THE COURT: Thank you.

(Thereupon, a luncheon recess was taken, after which the following proceedings were had:)

CROSS-EXAMINATION (Continued)

BY MR. PETROCELLI:

Q. So I got a little off on a detour at the end of the morning session. I want to go back to the internal bidding issue, okay?

A. Okay.

Q. So are you oriented there now?

A. Sure.

Q. Okay. So Mr. Read asked you about your commitment to the agent and author community and I'd like to follow up on that. And there was some back and forth also about what would violate your commitment. So just so we can be very clear on the record, your commitment to the agent and author community was exactly what?

A. It is that if, in a competitive bidding situation in an auction, there are only Penguin Random House and Simon & Schuster imprints left in that auction, the auction would not stop but continue so Simon & Schuster imprints would be treated like an external bidder.

Q. And what would violate that commitment?

A. Taking that commitment away and treating Simon & Schuster like an internal bidder would undo it and violate it.

Q. And you indicated that it's not a legally binding commitment, right?

A. Unfortunately not.

Q. Okay. So is there any reason why you couldn't just renege on it the day after this merger was cleared?

A. Oh, yes.

Q. What's the reason?

A. Well, my experience in almost 30 years in business and in the publishing industry is if you grant your trusted business partners, in this case, agents and authors, an additional service, an additional, call it advantage, you are unable—practically unable to take it away. It would undermine that trustful relationship. I think it would damage our business in that agents and authors would not appreciate it and would feel betrayed.

So if you grant a service, it is practically not possible to take it away.

Q. Okay.

THE COURT: Can I follow up on that? What do you think agents and authors would do if you reneged?

THE WITNESS: The agent community would, of course, argue against it because it is something that we granted them, we gave it to them, like we gave them video rights 50 years ago and we never got them back, like we granted book sellers in the Depression to be able to send books back 90 years ago and we could never take it back and returns still exist in the industry, we talked about that, it's one of the few industries on the planet that has such a right.

There are so many examples for it. So if you give terms, whether it's to customers, better terms of business or whether it's authors and agents, from my perspective, you better continue with that business practice.

THE COURT: Are there other examples you give are industry-wide practices, things like video rights and return rights, you would be the only publisher in the industry to do this. And I don't think, correct me if I am wrong, agents are not going to take your money because you're doing this if you're the high bidders, they're still going to choose you.

THE WITNESS: If I undid it?

THE COURT: Yes.

THE WITNESS: The fact of the matter is that the agents told me that their concern is rather perception than based on data, number one. Number two, I don't think that for us, that external bidding rule has a material financial impact because of the rareness of, in round robin auctions, Penguin Random House and Simon & Schuster being the last bidders.

I'm also considering it to broaden it for Penguin Random House. I think the notification happens very, very rarely, the notification of agents on the Penguin Random House side. So what Ms. McIntosh and I are considering, no decision yet, is to even broaden the opportunity, but no decision yet.

I think it's a good decision for us without any material financial impact.

But I agree with you that it's—the comparisons are like we do something or industry-wide, I don't know who started the returns and perhaps others had to also agree to it, but it's an industry-wide practice, you're absolutely right.

THE COURT: Go ahead, Mr. Petrocelli.

MR. PETROCELLI: Thank you, Your Honor.

BY MR. PETROCELLI:

Q. So let's talk a little bit about your pursuit of the Simon & Schuster transaction.

A. Mr. Petrocelli, also, we have in our plan for the new company going forward for the next years, we would have never thought about there is room for reducing author commitments or whatnot.

Part of our business plan is to increase our author investments. So we would have never thought of any impact here in a way that would reduce.

Q. So in connection with the pursuit of the Simon & Schuster transaction, just following up on what you just said, was there ever any internal planning, calculations or even discussions about reducing author compensation?

A. And even this external bidding or whatnot so rarely, it didn't come to our minds so basically, our projections are to grow the newly combined company and not lose market share again. We are basically paying $2.2 billion to actually replace our lost market share in this case. And that includes, of course, if we want to grow, we have to invest more into books in a very competitive marketplace so our author commitments and author costs are going up.

Q. So post-merger your plan is to continue to grow?

A. That is part of our official business plan and investment proposal.

Q. Is that organic growth?

A. That's correct.

Q. Now, just briefly on the S&S, Simon & Schuster transaction, how did you come about and how did you get interested in recommending this to Bertelsmann?

A. There had been rumors for more than a decade that one day CBS Viacom today, Paramount Global, would—might sell Simon & Schuster. I remember 10, 15 years ago everyone thought Amazon would actually buy them.

So when we heard that there is an opportunity, I immediately informed Bertelsmann and recommended to be in the process and try to acquire Simon & Schuster.

Q. Now, I'd like to have you just briefly describe to the Court your rationale for the transaction, but I want to be careful here, because we have an agreement that we're not going to get into the subject of efficiencies.

A. Okay.

Q. So that'll be for another day. So you can save that. But just generally, what was your thinking behind pursuing the transaction and recommending it to the company?

A. Sure. I told Bertelsmann that I'm convinced that we are the best home for the community of imprints of Simon & Schuster, for the following reasons.

I was convinced, like I was convinced in the Penguin Random House case, which is widely seen as a big success also at Bertelsmann, that if we allow the Simon & Schuster books, frontlist books and the catalog, their rich catalog, to be call it plugged into our market leading supply chain that we've invested more than $250 million into, it would make the books more available on the shelfs in more sales outlets, domestically and internationally, and it would result in higher sales, which retailers, authors, via royalties, and readers would benefit from and ultimately also Penguin Random House would benefit from that.

And then on top of that come economies of scale that give us the opportunity to bid more for a book.

I'm not talking about efficiencies, only economies of scale and still make a sufficient profit.

Q. Okay. Thank you. I think I just have one final topic I'd like to ask you about. You understand the government is asserting that there's a market that consists of anticipated top selling books which had further defines to mean books sold for $250,000 advances or more. You understand that?

A. I understand that.

Q. Okay. Does Penguin Random House have any setup in its company designed specifically to deal with that segment of the advances?

A. No.

Q. Does it have any special editorial group or designated editors to negotiate and acquire books at 250 and above?

A. No.

Q. Does it have any specific editorial services for that group?

A. No.

Q. Does it have any special marketing or public relations group designed just to deal with larger advance books?

A. No.

Q. Does it have any special sales processes or procedures to deal with large advance books?

A. No.

Q. And by that I meant books 250 and above.

A. No, we don't.

Q. Okay. And is their sales force, do they always know the advances associated with a book?
A. No, not at all, we don't share advances with our sales force.
Q. And is there any specific method of distribution associated with books with advances of $250,000 or more?
A. No.
Q. And same would be true with printing, right?
A. Correct.
Q. Does the company have any kind of customer—excuse me, not customer, but author reports or break-ups dividing authors into categories that their advances are $250,000 or above?
A. Not that I'm aware of.
Q. Are you aware of any $250,000 thresholds discussed at trade shows or industry conventions?
A. No.
Q. When you look at market share data, have you ever looked at shares for books acquired for more than $250,000 as opposed to those under $250,000?
A. No.
Q. Have you ever asked your team to prepare any reporting that separates books acquired for $250,000 or more from books acquired for less?
A. No, I haven't.
Q. Have you ever provided reporting to your superiors at Bertelsmann, separating books acquired for $250,000 or more from books acquired for less?
A. No.
MR. PETROCELLI: Thank you, Your Honor.
THE COURT: Thank you, Mr. Petrocelli.
MR. PETROCELLI: I pass the witness.
MR. READ: May I proceed, Your Honor?
THE COURT: Yes, you may.

REDIRECT EXAMINATION

BY MR. READ:

Q. Good afternoon, Mr. Dohle.
A. Hello, Mr. Read.
Q. I want to follow up on a couple of the printing questions that Mr. Petrocelli asked you.
A. Sure.
Q. And let's go back to PX983 if we could. It's the last one.
A. Thank you.
Q. Yeah, let me ask some preliminary questions before we get into the document.
A. I have the document in front of me.
Q. Yeah. At Bertelsmann, you were an advocate for the investment by Bertelsmann into the printing assets, right?
A. That's correct.
Q. And one of the reasons is you want something to show for that asset with regard to Penguin Random House publishing? You want there to be some benefit to Penguin Random House publishing, that's why you advocated investing into the printing assets?
A. I hope we would.
Q. Yeah. And if you could look at the final bullet below where we talked before, so it's above the next steps. Do you see that?
A. I see that.
Q. And that bullet reads, "Penguin Random House is willing to help with financial incentives to increase our capacity and make it financially attractive to print Penguin Random House's allocated units even if overall capacity goes down." Do you see that?
A. I do.

Q. So Penguin Random House was willing to work with, invest with Berryville Graphics to work together like a vertically integrated company?

A. No.

Q. Well, you were hoping to invest in Berryville Graphics to help them?

A. I'm happy to give context. This is now '19, this is before COVID. So our contractual commitments were not fulfilled. They said they have labor issues, no one comes in at the weekend and stuff.

And we were willing to give them, to help them financially even and, say, hey, we know it's a tough business, printing is a tough business, I was in it for many years so I know it very well firsthand, and I also ran the U.S. publishing printing companies. We are willing to help. We have done the same with LSC and supported them with financial support and bonuses if they get the job done.

Q. Let me re-ask the question and highlight what I should have. The effort to invest and help Berryville even with all these labor shortages and other issues illustrates how important having the printing capacity is for a publisher like Penguin Random House?

A. That's correct, Mr. Read.

Q. In response to some of Mr. Petrocelli's final questions about, are there tracking $250,000 and above authors, you recall those questions, isn't it true that Penguin Random House sometimes tracks key authors?

A. In which way?

Q. It sometimes discusses and categorizes authors as key authors?

A. Might be, yes.

Q. Yeah. And these are the kinds of authors Penguin Random House wants to recruit?

A. I hope we have a lot of key authors, but we also have dreams of authors that we would love to publish.

Q. So there is a concept of some authors being important and wanting to recruit and cultivate?

A. If we have an opening and a chance to get attractive authors on board, we immediately go in and try to get them to Penguin Random House, sure.

Q. Yeah. Attractive authors is a good word, right? It signifies those authors that are particularly important to Penguin Random House?

A. Authors that our editors would love to publish.

Q. Okay. And so categorizing that idea of authors that editors love to publish, that's something that Penguin Random House tries to do, tries to figure out that group?

A. No.

Q. No?

A. On a Penguin Random House level? That happens on an editorial level.

Q. But it happens within the company?

A. Editors have, I'm sure, dream authors that they would love to publish.

Q. Let's go to one of the discussions you had with Mr. Petrocelli. He presented you a chart about sales over time. We don't need to look at the chart, but you walked through it carefully of Penguin Random House's sales being down a bit on share and others.

A. I don't like that chart, yeah.

Q. Okay, we won't show it to you. No bad dreams. That was a chart about retail sales. Let's just make sure we've got it, right?

A. Yeah.

Q. So it's about sales to Barnes & Noble and all sorts, it's not about author acquisitions?

A. And consumer spending.

Q. Yeah. It's not about top seller author acquisitions and that kind of share?

A. Overall.

Q. I want to understand a little bit the kinds of books that are included in that data, okay? You said the data came from BookScan?

A. Correct.

Q. And let's talk a little bit about the kinds of books that are included in that BookScan data.

A. Sure.
Q. You're aware that that includes the sale of Bibles? It includes the sale of Bibles, King James version, some of the other versions of Bibles. That's included in that data?
A. Correct.
Q. I mean, it includes coloring books?
A. Yes.
Q. Dictionaries?
A. If they have an ISBN, sure.
Q. Encyclopedias?
A. That's my assumption.
Q. Magic trick books?
A. Can you repeat that.
Q. Magic books, magic trick books?
A. Yes.
Q. Calendars?
A. Yes.
Q. Puzzles?
A. Correct.
Q. Sudoku and crossword puzzle books?
A. Correct.
Q. Diaries, journals?
A. Do they have ISBNs? Do they have like BookScan? I don't know the answer to that question.
Q. Math workbooks?
A. Educational books? I don't know the answer to that question, Mr. Read.
Q. SAT or study aids?
A. Yes, we publish many.
Q. It includes back list books?
A. Correct.
Q. So books like Stephen King's *Carrie*, right?
A. Correct.
Q. It includes books that are out of copyright like *Don Quixote*?
A. Yes.
Q. And so this is a measurement that's of something different than what we're talking about at this trial, right?
A. Yes, it's the books that are in demand and the development of our share of those books in the marketplace.
Q. And does Penguin Random House ever measure its share of *New York Times* bestsellers?
A. I think someone counts them in the industry, but all bestsellers lists are so different from each other. We are looking at *The New York Times* bestseller list, correct, we are looking at that.
Q. That's something you look at?
A. Oh, yeah.
Q. And Penguin Random House's share in that looks very different, doesn't it?
A. I don't measure it. I don't know.
Q. So as you observed Penguin Random House's share in this big book market, that includes puzzles and coloring books, work-for-hire books, right?
A. Yes.
Q. As you've considered that and measured that, has Penguin Random House ever thought about lowering its retail prices in order to stem those share losses?
A. Not to my knowledge. I think we are very competitive in our pricing.
Q. Right. And so you've never pulled the lever of retail price in order to solve the share issue?
A. I don't even think it would have resolved the demand issue for our books. We also do coloring

activity and we have a publishing house. Dorling Kindersley, they very rarely buy a book with an advance. They actually create their own intellectual property. We also own the Eric Carle, *Very Hungry Caterpillar* intellectual property. So we are in many of those businesses that you just mentioned like coloring activity. We've done that for many years for Disney, and we are also in the college work for hire, we are in our own development of the intellectual property. We are not only in the advance business.

Q. Right. From your perspective, it's a big business and you have aspects working on color books, you'd like to make more sales there, more sales of Eric Carle's book?

A. Sure.

Q. And what's going on in those areas can be different than what's going on in the areas where you're acquiring titles of books that hope to sell well?

A. *Ceteris paribus* from 2013 to 2019, there weren't tectonic shifts. So at least from a development perspective, it shows that we have not been able to publish enough books with enough demand.

Q. So we talked a little bit about the share falling and not looking at price to solve it.

A. Correct.

Q. I want to follow up on some questions Mr. Petrocelli asked you about subscription models, okay, right. And to level set, these are the Netflixes of books, right, you pay $9.99 a month and you read all you can, right?

A. Correct.

Q. And these are models that Penguin Random House refuses to participate in?

A. That is correct.

Q. No books are found on Kindle Unlimited?

A. That is correct.

Q. But the small publishers choose to provide books to Kindle Unlimited?

A. My understanding is that some publishers give them some sort of very deep backlist books, very deep and slow moving backlist books. Others give them more. We give them nothing.

Q. And one of the reasons Penguin Random House is withholding content from these subscription models is it hopes to not have them grow and have the success of a Netflix because you think that'll be bad for the industry?

A. We think it's going to destroy the publishing industry, And it will have a huge effect on author income and, with that, on the diversity of stories that will be published, and we have had multiple discussions with the agent community and by and large they support that view.

Q. I just want to make sure. I know there's a lot of things going on. Penguin Random House withholds its contents from these subscription models to help prevent their growth?

A. "To help prevent their growth." They are growing and if the end consumer goes there, we might participate, but we don't think it's good for writing and for writers.

Q. What if I asked the question, does Penguin Random House not participate in those subscription models to slow their growth?

A. At least with us, they would have no growth, correct.

Q. And some consumers like these models?

A. They exist, so—yes.

Q. And Simon & Schuster participates in these models to some degree?

A. Correct.

Q. And after the merger, you plan to pull Simon & Schuster's books from those models?

A. I haven't made a decision and I'm going to think about it post closing. I don't know to what extent they participate. So I'm going to look at it in detail once I'm able to look at it and allowed and then I will make a decision.

Q. Maybe one final question in this area. Participating in those subscription models would allow Penguin Random House to sell more copies of its books?

A. Correct, they are not reflected in BookScan or in AAP, but it would allow us to sell more books if those people who would use them actually in the subscription model are those who wouldn't buy them anyway in retail.

Q. Let me turn to another set of questions Mr. Petrocelli asked you. I think the discussion was around how Amazon has leveled the playing field for all the publishers. Is your contention that the small publishers can sell through Amazon just as well as Penguin Random House?

A. Yes.

Q. And you're not telling authors that, correct?

A. If an author asks me, I would tell the truth.

Q. The Penguin Random House pitch to the agent community is that it's better able to sell their books than the small publishers, even through an enterprise like Amazon?

A. We are working on instruments and tools like metadata, like search engine optimization, to sell more books through Amazon. It's not measurable yet, especially not in our market share, perhaps one day it will be. It's early days.

Q. Let's just spend a moment on that. Penguin Random House has hired a number of data scientists to help in the sale—with sales from Amazon, right?

A. To help with how to manage the fact that an algorithm sells our books or presents our books going forward, It is one of the many things they do.

Q. Right. So Penguin Random House has hired data scientists to try and figure out these algorithms so that its books get better presented on Amazon than its competitors' books?

A. One of the many efforts that we pursue, correct.

Q. And Amazon—I'm sorry, Penguin Random House pays Amazon to improve its search results?

A. There is something that is available to our publishers, it's called Amazon Marketing Services, AMS, and all publishers can spend money and give it to Amazon to have hopefully better search results.

Q. Sure. And you're looking to uber-resource Amazon to be successful with them because they're a major partner and they sell a lot of books and you're channel agnostic and just want to sell the books?

A. Mr. Read, April 1st, 2020, was the time when all physical retail was shutting down and Amazon was the only shop in town, and I said, hey, now it's 100 percent of our market, there is no other outlet, we have to focus and uber-resource.

Q. Let me phrase that differently then. You're still working closely with Amazon as a major partner to sell as many books through them as you can?

A. Yes, it's one of the areas where we did zigzagging. We were always a good retail partner with Amazon, and not like other publishers.

Q. And you would agree these small publishers haven't hired the data scientists that Penguin Random House has to work with the algorithms at Amazon to try to make those algorithms work for their books?

A. I think the entire industry understands that they have to complement their creativity with a little bit more of a data-driven approach because of the fact that this business shifts online, not digital, it shifts—the physical format, thank God, has prevailed, but ecommerce is a very different way of selling books. And I think the entire industry acknowledges that.

Q. Did you testify with Mr. Petrocelli that Penguin Random House, one of the rationales for the deals, it's going to improve the discoverability of Simon & Schuster books?

A. Yes, we think invisibility, discoverability and availability of our books. And we work on all these three areas, correct.

Q. And so one of the rationales for the deal is your belief that Penguin Random House can help the Simon & Schuster books be more discoverable and sell better than Penguin Random House is currently able to do?

A. Ultimately, yes. I don't have evidence for that yet. It's too early. I can't prove it.

Q. And so there is, in your mind, some differentiating ability between Penguin Random House's ability to sell books and other publishers' ability to sell books.

A. It would be good to have a competitive advantage one day. So we are striving for it. We built one in supply chain.

Q. Let's dig in a little more to why the share of Penguin Random House has been falling or not been growing.

Now, Hachette, Macmillan, HarperCollins and Simon & Schuster's share has been growing according to the charts you showed?

A. On the slide, it was actually 33 percent, 2013 and the same number in 2019 on the slide. So it was not growing. And granted, Scholastic was part of that control group.

And what I said is that they haven't been growing even though they had much more M&A activity during those six years than we had.

Q. Let me rephrase that. So the control group, HarperCollins, Hachette, Macmillan, Simon & Schuster—

A. And Scholastic.

Q.—and Scholastic, they were doing better over time than Penguin Random House. That was the point of that slide, right?

A. One of the many points. Not the most important one.

Q. And I'm going to save some of this for an efficiencies discussion if we have that. But I want to dig in a little bit to why that share is falling.

Your belief is that after the merger of Penguin Random House, the organization screwed up the product side?

THE COURT: I'm sorry, I don't understand that question.

BY MR. READ:

Q. Your belief is that the reason Penguin Random House's share didn't grow is that the book business was mismanaged?

A. Given the fact that we have this market leading sales and distribution services, control group, our third-party distribution clients went up, my conclusion is that we haven't been able to acquire and publish enough of the books that readers want to buy.

So the problem with our market share development has to be on the content side.

Q. And one of your conclusions is on the contents side, it has been mismanaged?

A. Number one, for the most part of the last ten years, I was the U.S. CEO of that business, so I take full responsibility for everything that happens in the company because I'm the global CEO, but I also take responsibility for the first years between '13 and '18 before Madam McIntosh took over.

I think we could become more aggressive, nimble, agile, faster on the contents side in order to make sure we acquire enough books that have enough demand to grow with the market, correct.

Q. You think some of the consolidations that were done by current management led to a loss of title count and revenues?

A. I don't want to go back to the mass market phenomenon. I think we had that. And what happened years after the merger to resolve the overindexed genre fiction footprint of Penguin, I think that everything that is important in publishing happens on an editorial and imprint level, and everything above that is not that important.

Q. Let's present to you PX136. Can we get that circulated?

A. Is it the same?

Q. It's not in your binder.

MR. READ: We will not put these on the screen, Your Honor, because we have not resolved whether there are confidentiality issues.

BY MR. READ:

Q. Let me know when you've had a chance to look through these, please.

MR. PETROCELLI: Your Honor, since this document is not included with the exhibits—

THE COURT: You have to come to the microphone.

MR. PETROCELLI: Apologies. Since this document was not included in the exhibits to be shared for today's examination, we haven't had a chance to review it for confidentiality, so I would ask that it be not publicized at this moment until we can discuss it, okay?

THE COURT: That's fine, Mr. Petrocelli. This will remain under seal for the time being.

MR. PETROCELLI: Thank you.

THE COURT: But we can remain in open session?

MR. READ: I think we can do this in open session.

BY MR. READ:

Q. Mr. Dohle, these are five tweets from you around the time period of February 4th, 2021?

A. I don't tweet but they are text messages.

Q. I'm sorry, they are text messages, yes.

THE COURT: Okay.

THE WITNESS: I'm not a tweet.

Q. No. Thank you. And these are texts to Divya Sawhney and Nihar Malaviya, two people who report to you either by dotted line or by direct reports?

A. That is correct.

Q. And the first text said, "TR has heard the Penguin story many times." Do you see that?

A. I do.

Q. And TR stands for Thomas Rabe?

A. Correct.

Q. And then you go on, "It's simple, we lost," and then you have a number contribution—first of all, after the number, you have the word "Mio." Do you see that? M-I-O?

A. M-I-O?

Q. We lost?

A. We lost million.

Q. That's your word for million?

A. That stands for million.

Q. So "We lost X million contribution and then got them back through efficiencies." That's what you texted, right? And then you continue, "It's really poor what happened, He still portrays it as a success," right?

A. Correct.

THE COURT: By contribution, does that mean sales or revenues?

THE WITNESS: No, contribution means—it's sort of a definition for a certain profit and it means contribution is after you—it's the profit after you pay for your variable cost and it means you make contribution to your fixed cost.

If you cover your variable and fixed cost, we call it profit after full cost. Contribution is profit after variable cost. So it's a definition of profit, not revenues.

BY MR. READ:

Q. I'm going to skip the next couple sentences.

A. Thank you.

Q. Just out of respect. Although, could you help the Court and tell Judge Pan who the "her" is in that sentence. It's Madeline McIntosh, isn't it?

A. That's correct.

Q. And then the next text you send, a little over an hour later, you write, "We really screwed it on the product side post-merger." Do you see that?

A. Correct.

Q. And you're talking about the Penguin Random House merger?

A. I do, I think I explained it sufficiently before what I mean.

Q. Yeah. And on the products side, you're talking about acquiring the books and publishing the books and getting the books?

A. Correct, the creative side of the business.

Q. Then if you turn forward to the texts at 1:01 p.m., the Bates number is 600 if you prefer that way. Do you have this?

A. I have it.

Q. And this is, again, a text to you to the same two individuals, Ms. Sawhney and Mr. Nihar Malaviya. Are you there?

A. Correct.

Q. And then you say, "We only discussed the risk that MMC and Gina created for us," right?

A. Correct.
Q. And MMC is Madeline McIntosh?
A. Yes.
Q. And Gina is Gina Centrello?
A. Correct.
Q. And you write, "We consolidated, and I couldn't stop it and didn't do enough downtown. Back then, I still thought," and then you have a call about one of these individuals. Do you see that?
A. Yes, I do, Mr. Read.
Q. And your point of your text there is that the consolidations that had occurred had harmed Penguin Random House's growth?
A. For a long time, I've had a different vision for our organization, and I acknowledge that this is strong language. These are private text messages to my closest collaborators in the company, and I display some passion and frustration here about our development, about the development of Penguin Random House and the fact that I could not prevail with my opinion for many years how to organize our company, so I couldn't convince my boss and I couldn't convince Ms. McIntosh.
And I had a clear opinion on it, so I apologize for the passionate language.
Q. I just want to spend maybe one more document a little more time on this reason why Penguin Random House's share hasn't been growing.
THE COURT: Can I ask, when you say consolidated, do you mean consolidated imprints?
THE WITNESS: No. That's the point of what we might discuss later in the trial.
THE COURT: Okay.
THE WITNESS: It is more about how we are organized above the imprints. Everything that happens in publishing is about one book at a time and one imprint at a time. The rest is overhead, and that includes me. That is not so important, and for a long time, I had a very clear opinion of what to do, but it seems like I could not prevail.
BY MR. READ:
Q. Your point, Mr. Dohle, or your observation, is that Penguin Random House has too many layers of management in acquiring books?
A. Yes.
Q. And that has stunted its growth?
A. It certainly hasn't helped. But I want to go further. We have also some functions in publishing divisions has nothing to do with imprints, like production and other areas, finance departments that could be a little bit more centralized. But that goes into other areas.
So it's not just sort of publishing layers, it's more than that, when I address my vision for the companies' organization above the imprints.
Q. I'm going to do this lightly because if we have to, we'll spend more time after the efficiencies.
Your observation is that, in contrast, Simon & Schuster is super lean in how it acquires books?
A.They have done certainly better in the marketplace than Penguin Random House has, so I think that it's good to at least compare and benchmark how they do things and potentially learn from them and adopt that.
MR. READ: No further questions, Your Honor.
THE COURT: Thank you.

RECROSS-EXAMINATION

BY MR. PETROCELLI:
Q. Just briefly and because the Judge asked about consolidation, I wasn't sure if the answer was clear and I know you don't want to get into efficiencies. But did this consolidation debate that you had have anything to do with eliminating editors on reducing acquisitions of books?
A. No.
Q. Okay. Thank you.
THE COURT: Thank you.

THE WITNESS: It's just an internal reorganization.
THE COURT: I understand. Thank you. Anything else, Mr. Read?
MR. READ: No.
THE COURT: Thank you, Mr. Dohle. Thank you for your testimony.
THE WITNESS: Do I leave everything here or do I take it?
THE COURT: It's up to your counsel. Do you want that back?
THE WITNESS: Thank you, Mr. Read. I will put my mask on and leave.
THE COURT: Did you want to admit 136?
MR. READ: Yes, Your Honor. Thank you.
THE COURT: It would be under seal. Any objection, Mr. Petrocelli?
MR. PETROCELLI: I'm sorry?
THE COURT: I'm asking if you object to the admission of Exhibit 136 under seal?
MR. PETROCELLI: That last document. No, Your Honor.
THE COURT: That will be admitted. Thank you, Ms. Calloway. (Plaintiff's Exhibit 136 received into evidence.)
THE COURT: You can step down Mr. Dohle.

BRIAN TART, PUBLISHER, VIKING

Viking president and publisher Brian Tart gave a good account of how his acquisition process works, spread out over two days—with the second day of testimony presented by video since he became ill over the weekend.

We reported two notable moments from his appearance. The first was among the more widely-quoted exchanges of the entire trial. Towards the end of Tart's first appearance on the stand, Judge Pan offered this apt inference: "You're saying that's fake, it's not real, the marketing budget isn't really what's in the P&L. . . . The P&L is really fake. Am I wrong?"

The answer? "No . . . I mean, it's what we do. And I can't dismiss it but in the art and science of publishing, it's—. . . We get a lot wrong with the P&L."

Another bit of amusement came when after Tart discussed having passed on bidding for both *Where the Crawdads Sing* and *The Life-Changing Magic of Tidying Up*. "Were those books anticipated top sellers?" he was asked.

"Not to me," he replied.

In Cross-Examination, however, the government's Meagan Bellshaw noted, "While those books may have gotten away from you, they didn't get away from Penguin Random House, right?" (Indeed, they were published by Putnam and Ten Speed Press.)

More broadly as to books that sell for less than the $250,000 floor for ATSB, Tart testified that "less than a quarter" of Viking's list—approximately 20 books per season or 60 per year—is acquired at that level. He noted, "You can take some chances with those, you can get really creative in terms of how you publish them, I think, and so that's kind of why we do it." Tart told the judge that those are "authors we're growing" who "have aspirations and expectations just like others on the list" and that "we have the same conversations with those authors as we do with authors with big advances."

Tart discussed anticipated sales numbers in P&Ls, and when pushed by Bellshaw, conceded that they are an educated guess. The sales data from comp titles reflect the market they were published into, or the current market, Tart said, but those numbers may not reflect the market in two to three years when the book they are acquiring may be published. "That is very difficult, nearly impossible to predict," he said.

Tart explained the difference between publicity and marketing to the Judge, and–surprising anyone who has ever sent or received a galley–said that publicity and marketing plans are generally made six weeks before the publication of a book. But Bellshaw brought up emails in which Viking discussed publicity potential before acquiring a title. "Is it fair to say that you started thinking about the level of publicity before you even bid on the book?" she asked. "Yes."

TESTIMONY OF BRIAN TART, PUBLISHER, VIKING

DIRECT EXAMINATION

BY MS. BELLSHAW:

Q. Good afternoon, Mr. Tart.

A. Good afternoon.

Q. Can you please state your name for the record?

A. Brian Tart.

Q. Mr. Tart, you're the president and publisher of Viking Penguin; is that correct?

A. Yes.

Q. And Viking Penguin is a group at Penguin Random House that consists of several different imprints?

A. Yes.

Q. Viking Penguin is comprised of Viking Books, Penguin Books, Penguin Classics, Pamela Dorman Books, Penguin Life, and The Open Field?

A. Yes.

Q. And Viking Penguin is part of the Penguin Publishing Group; is that right?

A. Yes.

Q. And Penguin Publishing Group is a division within Penguin Random House?
A. Yes.
Q. And you report to Allison Dobson, the President of Penguin Publishing Group?
A. Yes.
Q. And you have been president and publisher of Viking Penguin since 2020?
A. I was the publisher of Viking in 2015 and then made the publisher of Penguin Books in 2020. So Viking and Penguin in 2022—I mean, in 2020.
Q. So starting in—just to make sure I have this clear. Starting in 2015, you were the president and publisher of Viking Books which is an imprint at Penguin Random House?
A. Yes.
Q. And then in 2020, you also became president and publisher of Penguin Books?
A. Yes.
Q. And so together that's Viking Penguin?
A. Yes.
Q. And then you started as an editor at Dutton in 1998?
A. At Penguin at the time, yes.
Q. And did Penguin become Dutton?
A. I had started my career in publishing in 1992 at Bantam Books but I moved to Dutton in 1998, which was part of Penguin.
Q. Is it right that you've been a member of different publishing entities within the Penguin group for about 24 years?
A. Yes. I was with Penguin from 1998 until the merger, 2013, I think that was. And then I was still at Dutton until 2015 and then I moved to Viking.
Q. As president and publisher of Viking Penguin, you were responsible for overseeing editorial, marketing, and publicity for all of the books published by Viking Penguin; is that right?
A. Yes.
Q. The Viking Penguin website, which I assume you're familiar with, describes Viking Penguin as a legendary imprint that was founded in 1925 with a distinguished list of extraordinary writers. Do you agree with that description of Viking?
A. Yes.
Q. At Viking, you publish around 70 new hard cover books a year?
A. It's more like 60. I aspire to 70, but I don't often get there, or I haven't published that number in the last couple of years. It's more like 60.
Q. Is it right that about half of those books are fiction books?
A. Again, that's my aspiration. That's kind of how I like to balance the list, but it doesn't always end up that way.
Q. Can you tell me some of the fiction authors and books that Viking has worked with recently?
A. Sure. We publish Amor Towles, author of *The Lincoln Highway* and *The Gentleman in Moscow* and his first book, *The Rule of Civility*. We've published this year NoViolet Bulawayo's book *Glory*, which just got long listed for the Booker Prize, which is great.
We're the publisher of Matt Haig, *The Midnight Library*, Jojo Moyes, her books, *Giver of Stars* was the last one. I can happily go on.
Q. Thank you. If you aspire to publish about half of your books as fiction books, is that correct, that the other half you aspire to publish is nonfiction books?
A. Yes.
Q. And can you tell me some of the nonfiction authors and books that Viking has worked with recently?
A. Sure. Adam Grant, we just published his book, *Think Again*. Vaclav Smil, we just published his book, he's an academic, about *How the World Really Works*, which has done really well for us. We've published some history, *Blood and Ruins* by Richard Overy. Generally publish history, biography and kind of wide range of narrative nonfiction.
Q. Now, turning to Penguin Books, Penguin Books is a paperback book publisher?

A. Not exclusively. Sometimes we'll do hard covers in Penguin Books. Sometimes paper-over-boards, which is kind of a hybrid paperback but it's mostly a paperback publisher.

Q. Penguin Book publishes some paperback originals—or some originals every year; is that right?

A. Yes.

Q. But Penguin Books is primarily a backlist publisher?

A. We have a robust, big backlist, but we do keep the frontlist active and we put a lot of time into those—the new books that we publish as paperback originals.

Q. Backlists are books that are at least a year past their publication or initial sales date; is that right?

A. That's the way that I think of it at Viking Penguin. It can change from, I think, house to house, but that's the way that we—that I view it, at Penguin Viking.

Q. And once books move from Viking's frontlist; am I correct that they go to the Penguin Books' backlist?

A. Yes.

Q. And so books actually—strike that. And I think you described the Penguin Books backlist as robust. Is it correct that the Penguin Books backlist has approximately 2,500 active titles currently in print being sold?

A. Yes, that's number that I think about with the backlist. I think that's right.

Q. And having a large backlist is an important way to make money in publishing, right?

A. I spend a lot of time as a frontlist publisher without a backlist. When I was at Dutton, it was just the frontlist without a backlist. And then those first couple years at Viking, I didn't have a backlist either.

So I place great importance on it because it provides a certain stability. You can count on, or you think you can count on certain sales coming out of the backlist that you can't always count on from a frontlist. So I really myself appreciate having a backlist. Not a lot of people focus on the backlist. Everyone's really interested in the new book, the thing that's being talked about in the media and things like that.

But I think a backlist is important.

Q. And I think you may have mentioned this in your answer, but that's because having a large backlist helps provide a stable source of revenue?

A. If you have a backlist that people want to read, that you can refresh, that is valuable, that you can keep those books selling, yes, I look at it as a good way of gaining revenue and having some stability to your imprint.

Q. And would you agree that the backlist revenues make up more than half of Viking Penguin's combined annual revenues?

A. I think if you're including all of the Penguin backlist in that, yes, it's likely that it's more than half.

Q. And you consider Penguin's backlist when thinking about acquiring new books for Viking, correct?

A. I'm very proud of the Penguin backlist. I think it's a real selling point. I think authors want to be published there. And so, yes, I like to talk about it a lot, I like to invite writers to join us and be published by Penguin one day. So I think of it as a prestige imprint that authors hopefully will want to be a part of.

Q. And part of your strategy in acquiring books for Viking is to look for books that will continue to sell well on the Penguin Books backlist, right?

A. Yes, I'm looking to build a future backlist through my Viking hard covers that eventually will go into Penguin paperbacks.

Q. I'd like to ask you a few questions about how Viking buys the books that it publishes. One method that Viking uses is to bid on the rights to a particular book in an auction process, right?

A. Yes.

Q. And when Viking is bidding on a book at auction, part of your role is to work with the editor to shape Viking's approach to acquiring a book; is that fair?

A. Yes, we work with the editor, also with other people in my group, the associate publisher, talking to marketing and publicity, certainly the editors in chief, so it's kind of a wide group of people that talk about these acquisitions. But I'm part of it, yes.

Q. And you're responsible for approving the level of advance that Viking will bid for a particular book?

A. Yes.

Q. And you're personally authorized to approve advances up to $250,000?
A. Yes.
Q. And then above $250,000, you need approval from a higher level Penguin Random House executive?
A. I get approval from Allison Dobson.
Q. And she's your boss?
A. Yes.
Q. When deciding what advance to offer an author for a particular book, Viking will put together a profit and loss statement or P&L; is that correct?
A. Yes.
Q. And the P&Ls include an estimate of anticipated future sales for the book?
A. They include—we put in numbers that are based on a comparative title that we feel is close to the book that we're trying to buy, that we think is—either has an editorial affinity or the author has a similar kind of author platform or it's a category that is similar to the one we're trying to publish. So once we find that, then we take those sales figures, or the approximation of those, and put them into the P&L, right.
Q. So you take the sales figure from the comparative title and put them into the P&L?
A. Yeah, it's kind of like a guidepost. It's kind of directional. We're guessing in X amount of years that we're going to be publishing this book, what the numbers are going to be. So the way we look at is trying to find a comparative title that's close to it that we think is going to justify that.
Q. And then the anticipated sales in the P&L are used to help determine the appropriate level of advance to offer the author, right?
A. The sales, the comparative sales that we put in are then calculated and we get out of that a suggested advance.
Q. The higher the projected sales in the P&L, the higher the advance Penguin Random House is willing to offer to an author, correct?
A. The P&L also has a number of other imports, like the cost of publishing and stuff like that. It calculates shipping and printing and marketing and other costs that are involved.
And so what we get out of that is a suggested advance, taking in those costs, based on the sales and then we get a suggested advance.
Q. And generally speaking, higher the projected sales correspond to higher advances, correct?
A. That does affect the advance, yes.
Q. And you would agree with me that the higher the advance that Penguin Random House pays an author, the more risk there is to Penguin Random House in buying the book, right?
A. Certainly, when you pay a higher advance, you have to sell more books to justify that. But, I don't know how much I think of that in terms of risk because we're really just trying to buy the book and if we really believe in the book, we'll take an acceptable amount of risk to do that. So I think I understand the question correctly, so in that, there is risk involved as the advance goes up, but for me, I don't really think of it as that being riskier than pretty much most of the deals that I do.
Q. So the higher advance levels require a book to achieve bigger sales levels, right?
A. Yes, the higher the sales equate to a higher advance in the P&L.
Q. And the bigger the sales number, the harder it is to meet, right?
A. You know, the more sales that you're trying to get, yes, I guess it could make it more difficult.
Q. And so you would agree that because the numbers are bigger, there is more risk involved in offering an author a larger advance, right?
A. Yes, I can see that.
THE COURT: I'm sorry, doesn't it depend on how well you estimate? Because if you're very spot on, then the risk is not greater at any price level if your estimates of how much you're going to sell are accurate.
THE WITNESS: Honestly, we're very rarely spot on with those estimations.
THE COURT: Okay. Do you tend to skew too high or too low or is it just random?
THE WITNESS: It is a really wide range.

THE COURT: Okay.

THE WITNESS: So we use the acquisition P&L for all the acquisitions. But down the road, we don't refer to it again because of that.

BY MS. BELLSHAW:

Q. It's fair to say that if the P&Ls were not at least somewhat reliable, you wouldn't continue to use them for all of your acquisitions, right?

A. We continue to use it for acquisitions, but in terms of when we're actually publishing the book and so forth, we're not referring back to the acquisition P&L often, if at all.

Q. Turning to negotiations with authors and their agents, you have a standard set of royalty rates that you offer, correct?

A. We do—

Q. I don't mean to interrupt you, but I'm going to ask you not to say any of the specific numbers out loud just for confidentiality reasons.

A. Right. Thank you for that. We offer royalty rates. Sometimes they're negotiable, not all of them, for me, at Viking Penguin. I don't think all of them are negotiable. But, yes, we offer a kind of set rate.

Q. You have a standard set of royalty rates, correct?

A. I guess I'm thinking of the hard cover royalty rate as not necessarily standard because that can be negotiable.

Q. Even if it can be negotiated in some cases, you have a standard starting point for your royalty rates, correct?

A. We often start at the same place, yes.

Q. And so you very occasionally offer an increased royalty rate for your hard cover books correct?

A. Yes.

Q. But you don't offer variations on royalty rates for other forms of books, correct?

A. Correct.

Q. And agents don't often ask you to deviate from the standard royalty terms during book negotiations?

A. I think that the hard cover rate is in play. I think that does get negotiated. But the others, no.

Q. But you would agree with me that even if the hard cover rate is sometimes in play, it is not often the subject of negotiation with agents?

A. Often? It comes up, and when it comes up, I'm not surprised. But it doesn't come up every time.

Q. You would agree that agents and authors want to work with publishers that have a track record of successfully publishing books, right?

A. Yes, I think agents and authors want to be part of a list that they admire.

Q. And Viking has a track record of successfully publishing books?

A. Yes.

Q. And Viking it also known for publishing award-winning books; is that right?

A. Yes.

Q. Viking's reputation for publishing award-winning books helps it to acquire new books and new authors, right?

A. I like to think so. Certainly I'm not alone in that, but I do think it helps.

Q. And you would agree that literary agents want to sell to publishers like Viking who can win awards and be nominated for awards?

A. I think certain agents it matters, certain authors it matters. Certainly it doesn't matter to everybody, but for some it does.

Q. And awards can help generate the sales of books, right?

A. I've seen that happen, yes.

Q. In addition to auctions, Viking also acquires some of its books through preempts, right?

A. Yes.

Q. And you would consider a preempt to be a competitive situation?

A. Yes.

Q. When you make a preempt offer, you don't know if other publishers are also submitting bids, right?

A. No, we don't know.
Q. Viking also acquires rights to books through exclusive submissions?
A. Yes.
Q. Viking acquires less than 10 percent of its books via exclusive offers, right?
A. Yes, for new authors, authors that we haven't worked with before, and authors who haven't been sent out widely. I think for that 10 percent, I mean, those are authors that agents come to us and say, I think you'd be the right publisher for this. So why don't we try and do a one-on-one negotiation and see if we can come to a deal because to me you're the right person. So that happens roughly around 10 percent of the time or less.
Q. And setting aside contract options, would you agree that exclusive offers account for less than 10 percent of the time in terms of overall acquisitions at Viking?
A. You know, sometimes books are sent out widely and it ends up that we're the ones who are interested or most interested and that turns into a one-on-one negotiation. So that certainly happens, which would raise that percentage up. But that would be the other one-on-one kind of negotiation that we would do.
Q. And thinking about exclusive offers is when the agent comes to you, rather than sending out books more widely, that is less common, right, for overall acquisitions?
A. For when an agent decides we're the publisher they want to work with so here's an exclusive look, yes. That's what I think is under 10 percent, around 10 percent.
Q. And if an agent brings an exclusive opportunity to you but Viking and agent can't negotiate an agreement as part of those discussions, the agent can always take the book to other publishers, right?
A. Yes.
Q. Mr. Tart, during the next part of this exam, I'm going to ask you a question about some specific books and auctions that Viking has bid on. To protect confidentiality, I'm going to ask that you not say the names of any authors or book titles out loud, and we're also going to avoid other identifying information and agent's names, okay?
A. Okay.
Q. In the front pocket of your binder, you should find a list of authors and book titles next to a number. I'm going to refer to the books and authors in my questions by the number that is listed there on the chart. So if you're ever confused about what book I'm talking about or what author I'm talking about, you can let me go and take a look at your chart.
A. Okay.
Q. So let's start with book 44.
A. Okay.
Q. If you could take a look at your binder, tab marked PX320. Just let me know when you have it.
A. Okay. I have it.
Q. PX320 is an email chain with a top email dated June 23rd, 2020, from Wendy Wolf to you and others at Penguin Random House about an auction for book 44. Is that right?
A. Yes.
Q. And Ms. Wolf is an executive editor at Viking?
A. Yes.
MS. BELLSHAW: Your Honor, I move to admit PX320.
THE COURT: Any objection?
MS. RUDZIN: No objection, Your Honor.
THE COURT: That will be admitted.
MS. BELLSHAW: Permission to publish a redacted version to the public.
THE COURT: Yes. (Plaintiff's Exhibit PX320 received into evidence.)
BY MS. BELLSHAW:
Q. Mr. Tart, you were involved in Viking's bid for book 44, right?
A. Yes.
Q. The auction for book 44 began as a rounds auction; is that right?

A. Yes.
Q. And a rounds auction contains multiple rounds of bidding, correct?
A. Correct.
Q. In each round publishers take turns submitting bids?
A. Yes.
Q. And then the rounds continue as long as the participants are still bidding?
A. Yes.
Q. Looking at the last page of PX320, Viking submitted its first bid for book 44 for $250,000, right?
A. Yes.
Q. If you could please turn to PX324. PX324 is an email chain with a top email dated June 29th, 2020, from Ms. Wolf to you and others at Penguin Random House discussing the auction for book 44; is that right?
A. Yes.
MS. BELLSHAW: Your Honor, I move to admit PX324.
THE COURT: Any objection?
MS. RUDZIN: No objection.
THE COURT: That will be admitted.
MS. BELLSHAW: Permission to publish the redacted version?
THE COURT: Yes. (Plaintiff's Exhibit PX324 received into evidence.)
BY MS. BELLSHAW:
Q. Looking at the first email in the chain, Ms. Wolf wrote, "It's down to us versus one house, from two imprints, which I'm assuming is some S&S configuration, probably including Atria." You understand S&S here to refer to Simon & Schuster, correct?
A. Yes.
Q. And Atria is a Simon & Schuster imprint?
A. Yes.
Q. Do you recall this auction began with several bidders?
A. I can't remember from this where it started or how many bidders was in at that point.
Q. According to Ms. Wolf's email, at this point, only Viking and one other bidder are still in the running for book 44, right?
A. Yes, that would indicate that there were other bidders at the beginning of the auction.
Q. And Ms. Wolf believes that the other bidders still in the running for book 44 is Simon & Schuster?
A. She believes that, yes.
Q. And in response to Ms. Wolf's email, you write back, "I say, $500,000." Viking increased its bid to $500,000 at this point; is that correct?
A. Yes, we made a $500,000 offer.
Q. Mr. Tart, if you would please—I'm sorry? Oh, I thought I interrupted you.
A. Oh. No.
Q. If you would please turn to PX326. PX326 is an email chain with a top email dated June 30th, 2020, from Ms. Wolf to you regarding the auction for book 44 again; is that right?
A. Yes.
MS. BELLSHAW: Your Honor, I move to admit PX326 into evidence.
THE COURT: Any objection?
MS. RUDZIN: No objection.
THE COURT: It will be admitted. (Plaintiff's Exhibit 326 received into evidence.)
MS. BELLSHAW: Permission to publish a redacted version?
THE COURT: Yes.
BY MS. BELLSHAW:
Q. In the email exchanges between you and Ms. Wolf in PX326, Ms. Wolf is keeping you updated on several additional rounds of bidding for book 44; is that right? And you should feel free to take a look at the email if you need to.

A. Yes, she's telling me what's going on in the auction.
Q. And part of what she's telling you about the auction for book 44 is that there have been several rounds of bidding, correct?
A. Yes.
Q. And in each round, Viking raised its bid for book 44?
A. Yes.
Q. If you turn to the third page of PX326, and the top email is from you and you write, "We should really push him to go to best bids now if they come back at $650,000." The "him" there is referring to the agent running the auction?
A. Yes.
Q. And prior to this email, at this point, Viking has bid $625,000 for book 44, right?
A. Yes.
Q. And at this point, you're suggesting that Ms. Wolf push the agent to end the round bidding and go to best bids instead, right?
A. Yes, I'm saying she should suggest that to the agent.
Q. And if you look at the email on the top of the second page of PX326 from Ms. Wolf to you at 11:08 a.m., Ms. Wolf writes, "Best bids by 5:00 p.m." So the agent has agreed to go to best bids?
A. The agent decided it was time for best bids, yes.
Q. Later down—a few sentences later, Ms. Wolf writes, "Since the other house is, or at least was, a house bid of two, I'm presuming it's S&S/Atria and S&S has political best seller chops like no other right now." Ms. Wolf is telling you again that she thinks your competition for book 44 is Simon & Schuster?
A. She thinks that, yes.
Q. Turning to the first page. You respond to Ms. Wolf's email and write, "Maybe $775,000 gives us a shot." Do you see that?
A. I do.
Q. And Viking did submit its best and final offer for book 44 for $775,000?
A. Yes, we did.
Q. If you would please turn to tab 39 in your binder. sPX39 is an email dated July 6th, 2020, from Allison Dobson to others at Penguin Random House, copying you, regarding book 44; is that right?
A. Yes.
MS. BELLSHAW: Your Honor, I move to admit PX39.
THE COURT: Any objection?
MS. RUDZIN: No objection.
THE COURT: That'll be admitted. (Plaintiff's Exhibit 39 received into evidence.)
MS. BELLSHAW: Permission to publish a redacted version, Your Honor?
THE COURT: Yes.
BY MS. BELLSHAW:
Q. In the bottom email of PX39, Ms. Wolf writes that "In the auction for book 44, PRH prevailed over a house bid from Nan Graham and Dawn Davis at S&S." Nan Graham and Dawn Davis at the time were editors at Simon & Schuster, right?
A. I think they were publishers and editors but, yes.
Q. At Simon & Schuster?
A. At, yes, Simon & Schuster.
Q. You write in response, "We got this one and over stiff competition." Viking ultimately had to increase its bid for book 44 from an initial offer of $250,000 to $775,000, right?
A. That was our final bid, yes. Our first bid and our final bid.
Q. Mr. Tart, Viking sometimes offers bonuses to authors when trying to acquire a book; is that right?
A. Yes.
Q. And a bonus is an additional payment on top of an advance?
A. Yes, I think of it as an additional advance.
Q. Bonuses are different from advances, though, because they're not guaranteed payments, right?

A. Correct.
Q. When negotiating for a book, there are certain rights that Viking must acquire before it will agree to buy the book, right?
A. At Viking Penguin, I try and buy print rights, book rights and audio rights. I think that's very important to what we do. So I always try and buy all those rights.
Q. And you would not buy a book that does not include audio rights, correct?
A. For me, no, I think it's very important to have those rights.
Q. And you've turned down multiple large projects since at least 2015 because the agent wouldn't include audio rights, correct?
A. I don't know about the time of that, honestly, but I don't think I would have bid on a book without audio rights.
Q. I'll ask you to look at tab PX328 in your binder. And please let me know when you're there.
A. Yes.
Q. PX328 is an email chain with a top email dated August 14th, 2020, from Patrick Nolan to you; is that right?
A. Yes.
MS. BELLSHAW: Your Honor, I move to admit PX328.
THE COURT: Any objection?
MS. RUDZIN: No objection.
THE COURT: That will be admitted. (Plaintiff's Exhibit 328 received into evidence.)
MS. BELLSHAW: Your Honor, may we publish a redacted version?
THE COURT: Yes.
BY MS. BELLSHAW:
Q. Mr. Nolan is a publisher with Penguin Books; is that right?
A. He is the publisher of Penguin Books, yes.
Q. Now, on the bottom of the first page of PX328 and going on to the second page, there's an email from you to Mr. Nolan dated August 14th, 2020, where you're discussing audio rights as part of your book negotiations. Do you see that?
A. Yes.
Q. I'd like to direct your attention to the second paragraph of that email, starting with "For at least the last five years." In that paragraph, you write, "For at least the last five years, but more likely the last ten years, we have bought everything with audio." And you're referring to audio rights there?
A. Yes, audio rights.
Q. Further down in the paragraph, you wrote, "We have to get those rights." Again, referring to audio rights, correct?
A. Yes.
Q. A sentence later you write, "We have walked away from much bigger deals because of it. Remember when Amazon was offering seven figures on audio before books were sold to publishers, we turned down big book after big book until agents realized we would not play in an auction without audio." Did I read that correctly?
A. Yes.
Q. "And now they always sell us audio." You're referring to agents there, correct?
A. Yes.
Q. And now agents always sell you audio?
A. Or if they don't want to sell us audio, then I wouldn't bid on it.
Q. You can set that aside. Thank you. Would you please turn to tab 197 in your binder. I'd like to ask you a few questions about book 29. And if you need a remainder of which book that is, please refer to your chart.
A. Can you remind me what tab?
Q. 197.
A. Thank you.

Q. PX197 is an email chain with the top email dated October 6th 2020, from you to Casey Blue James and others at Penguin Random House, is that right?
A. Yes.
MS. BELLSHAW: Your Honor, I move admit PX197.
THE COURT: Any objection?
MS. RUDZIN: No objection.
THE COURT: That will be admitted.
MS. BELLSHAW: Permission to publish a redacted version?
THE COURT: You may. (Plaintiff's Exhibit 197 received into evidence.)
BY MS. BELLSHAW:
Q. Mr. Tart, Ms. James works in the office of the president of Penguin Publishing Group; is that right?
A. Yes.
Q. When more than one imprint in Penguin Publishing Group is interested in bidding on a particular book, your understanding is that Ms. James' job is to coordinate with those imprints; is that right?
A. Yes, she takes care of the house bid for us.
Q. A. house bid is when multiple imprints from the same division bid on a book together at the same price?
A. It is for the Penguin Publishing Group. When it's more than one imprint within that group, we assemble a house bid, and so it's one bid coming from that group which the number of imprints can vary as to who's in that auction or not, but that's how we handle it.
Q. And then if the house bid is the winning bid, the author will decide which imprint he or she wants to work with?
A. Yes.
Q. Looking at PX—
THE COURT: I'm sorry, how often does it happen that you have a house bid?
THE WITNESS: Pretty regularly, yeah. It's not uncommon.
THE COURT: Okay.
BY MS. BELLSHAW:
Q. Looking at PX197, Ms. James' email in the middle of the page, she writes, "PP had been thinking of offering $300,000 to get the meeting." Do you see that?
A. Yes.
Q. You understand that PP here refers to Penguin Press?
A. Yes.
Q. And Penguin Press is another Penguin Publishing Group imprint?
A. Yes.
Q. In the auction for book 29, Penguin Press and Viking submitted an initial house bid together, correct?
A. Correct.
Q. And the initial house bid for book 29 was $300,000?
A. Yes.
Q. Would you please turn to tab 161.
A. Got it.
Q. PX161 is an email chain with a top email dated October 13th, 2020, from you to Casey Blue James and Allison Dobson at Penguin Random House regarding book 29; is that right?
A. Yes.
MS. BELLSHAW: Your Honor, I move to admit PX161.
THE COURT: Any objection?
MS. RUDZIN: No objection.
THE COURT: 161 will be admitted. (Plaintiff's Exhibit 161 received into evidence.)
MS. BELLSHAW: Permission to publish a redacted version, Your Honor.
THE COURT: You may.

BY MS. BELLSHAW:

Q. Looking at the email from Andrea Schulz to you in the middle of the page, Ms. Schulz is the Editor in Chief at Viking?

A. Correct.

Q. Ms. Schulz wrote, "We made a bid to get the meeting of $300,000. We discovered that the high bid of that round was $450,000 from Scribner." Scribner is a Simon & Schuster imprint, correct?

A. Yes.

Q. Aside from Simon & Schuster, the only other bidders for book 29 that are identified in this email are Penguin Random House imprints; is that correct?

A. Yes, those are the only imprints discussed in the email.

Q. And Ms. Schulz is informing you that Simon & Schuster has the highest bid at $450,000 for book 29?

A. Yes.

Q. If you would please turn to the tab marked PX41. PX41 is an email chain with a top email dated October 14, 2020, from Casey Blue James to you and others at Penguin Random House regarding the auction for book 29, right?

A. Yes.

MS. BELLSHAW: Your Honor, I move to admit PX41.

THE COURT: Any objection?

MS. RUDZIN: No objection.

THE COURT: That will be admitted. (Plaintiff's Exhibit 41 received into evidence.)

MS. BELLSHAW: Permission to publish a redacted version, Your Honor?

THE COURT: Yes.

BY MS. BELLSHAW:

Q. Viking submitted a best bid for book 29 for $550,000, correct?

A. Yes.

Q. And Penguin Press submitted its own best bid for $700,000, according to the email?

A. Yes.

Q. So Viking's bid for $550,000 was $250,000 higher than its initial bid; is that correct?

A. Yes. Yes.

Q. And Penguin Press went up $400,000, right?

A. Yes.

Q. Thank you. You can set that aside.

THE COURT: I'm sorry, I thought that you would submit one number for both groups, but this looks like two numbers.

THE WITNESS: It is. It is. This happens also where even though we're not competitive on the advance, we still want the agent to know that we were thinking of the book higher than we initially offered. So sometimes publishers will put in a bid knowing that it might not be competitive on the advance level but because they want the agent to know, I wasn't thinking of this at $300,000, I was actually thinking of it at 550.

THE COURT: I see. Okay.

BY MS. BELLSHAW:

Q. When two imprints at the Penguin Publishing Group are submitting a bid for the same book, there's no requirement that they bid the same amount; is that right?

A. I'm sorry, can you say that again.

Q. When two separate imprints at the Penguin Publishing Group are bidding for the same book like we saw with book 29, there's no requirement that they both submit the same amount for the advance, correct?

A. Correct.

Q. But you can choose to submit a house bid for the same amount together, correct?

A. Yes. And sometimes you'll defer to the other—to the higher bid and not place your bid. And sometimes you'll stretch to match that bid which will make it a house bid, or sometimes you'll do what we did here which was bring in your lower bid just so they know.

THE COURT: Does each imprint have its own budget or what's the limit on what they can bid?

THE WITNESS: Overall budget for advances or—

THE COURT: Yeah, for each imprint, because given that they have the same parent company, it seems that Viking could have gotten approval for 700 if Penguin rested.

THE WITNESS: Yes. I could have but I didn't see it, I felt the book was valued at this level and I didn't want to push farther. Possible the editor wanted to. That happens often. But as much as we want books, we have to be able to walk away at a certain level. So we do it sometimes. Just because another imprint wants to pay more doesn't mean that I'm convinced that we should.

THE COURT: But you don't have a set budget, like you can't go above this amount for the year or anything like that?

THE WITNESS: No, I don't have a budget like that.

THE COURT: Okay. Thank you.

BY MS. BELLSHAW:

Q. Mr. Tart, I'd like to ask you a few more questions about options where multiple Penguin Random House imprints are participating in the auction. As we've seen and as you told Your Honor, it's not unusual for more than one Penguin Random House imprint to participate in a single auction, right?

A. Right.

Q. And Penguin Random House has rules governing when imprints can compete against one another?

A. Yes.

Q. If you would please turn to tab 332, PX332. PX332 is an email chain with a top email dated October 26th, 2020, from Allison Lorentzen to you and Andrea Schulz; is that right?

A. Yes.

Q. And Ms. Lorentzen is an executive editor at Viking?

A. Yes.

MS. BELLSHAW: Your Honor, I move to admit PX332.

THE COURT: Any objection?

MS. RUDZIN: No objection.

THE COURT: 332 will be admitted. (Plaintiff's Exhibit 332 received into evidence.)

MS. BELLSHAW: Permission to publish a redacted version?

THE COURT: Yes.

BY MS. BELLSHAW:

Q. Mr. Tart, I'd like to direct your attention to the bottom email in PX332 from Ms. James. Ms. James is sending an email to an agent whose name I'm not going to say for confidentiality reasons. And it appears she is submitting bids to an agent on behalf of Viking and another Penguin Publishing Group imprint; is that right?

A. Yes.

Q. Ms. James explains to the agents in her email, "You are likely already quite familiar with the Penguin Random House bidding rule, but I always like to reiterate it in advance just in case. As long as there's a third non-PRH party still in the auction, Penguin and the other PRH U.S. divisions can bid against each other. "When it gets down to just PRH bids, though, we can only match each other. We can't further bid each other up." You understand PRH in Ms. James' email to refer to Penguin Random House?

A. Yes.

Q. And Ms. James' explanation to this agent of the Penguin Random House bidding rule is consistent with your understanding of that rule?

A. It is.

Q. When Viking bids on a book at auction, you have your editors ask whether there are any other Penguin Random House imprints bidding as well, correct?

A. We usually ask if there's any other Penguin imprints. So, because we have to do a house bid, if it's the other Penguin Publishing Group imprints.

Q. In your experience when agents provide information about whether there are Penguin Publishing

Group imprints bidding, they tell you the truth?
A. Yes.
Q. In your experience, agents are generally trustworthy in communicating about their auctions or other competitive processes?
A. Yes.
Q. I'd like to turn now from competition among the imprints to competition among the divisions at Penguin Random House. Multiple divisions within Penguin Random House can also choose to bid against one another for the same book, correct?
A. Yes.
Q. And just so that we're talking about the same thing, the adult divisions at Penguin Random House are Penguin Publishing Group, which is your division; Random House, and Knopf Doubleday; is that correct?
A. Yes. I'm in the Penguin Publishing Group. I don't run the Penguin Publishing Group.
Q. Yes. Thank you. Viking Books is part of the Penguin Publishing Group?
A. Yes.
Q. Penguin Random House has rules limiting how and when those divisions can compete against one another for the same book, right?
A. In that there needs to be an external bidder for us to bid against each other.
Q. If you would please turn to PX54. PX54 is an email with a top email from Ms. Dobson to you and others at Penguin Random House dated April 14th, 2020, correct?
A. Yes.
MS. BELLSHAW: Your Honor, I move to admit PX54 into evidence.
THE COURT: Any objection?
MS. RUDZIN: No objection.
THE COURT: 54 will be admitted. (Plaintiff's Exhibit 54 received into evidence.)
MS. BELLSHAW: Permission to publish a redacted version?
THE COURT: You may.
BY MS. BELLSHAW:
Q. Now, if you could refer to your chart briefly, I know there are multiple books referenced in this email. I'm going to be asking you questions about book 76. In the second paragraph of your email to Ms. Dobson at the bottom, you're describing Viking's discussions with the author of book 76; is that right?
A. Yes.
Q. And Viking had a contract option to buy the author's next novel, right?
A. Yes.
Q. Meaning that Viking had a contractual right to make the first offer for book 76?
A. We have in our contracts usually an option clause, which means if we publish the book, we get a right to offer on the next book exclusively.
Q. And the author for book 76 had previously published books with Viking?
A. Yes.
Q. And so the option at issue in this email is from that contract on the author's previous novels?
A. Yes.
Q. If Viking couldn't reach a deal for book 76 within some window of time, the author had the right to offer the books to other publishers, right?
A. Yes.
Q. You write in your email to Ms. Dobson, "We offered $150,000 for the new novel and they turned us down and are going out widely with it." So Viking offered $150,000 for book 76, correct?
A. Yes, it's untitled, but I'm assuming that, yes, that's what we did.
Q. Viking offered $150,000 for the new novel by the author referenced on the chart for book 76?
A. Yes.
Q. But the author rejected Viking's offer for the new novel in favor of shopping it around to other buyers, correct?

A. Yes.
Q. You write to Ms. Dobson in the next sentence, "We would like to invoke the PRH policy/rule/process where other imprints can bid on this but not more than our $150,000." Do you see that?
A. Yes.
Q. Looking at the email that Ms. Dobson writes to you in response in the second paragraph, she writes, "The PRH rule is that if an agent next goes exclusively to a PRH division, they would have to live within our bid," meaning that if the agent for book 76 next brought it to a Penguin Random House division, that division could not bid more than $150,000 for the book?
A. Yes.
Q. Ms. Dobson goes on to write, "However, if he takes it to an action:—I think he means auction?
A. I think so, too.
Q. "If he takes it to an auction, within the auction situation with competitive bidders, by the rule, Knopf or Random House could bid to the level of the market." And I think that RH is for Random House. Would you agree?
A. Would I agree that RH is for Random House?
Q. Yes.
A. Yes.
Q. Both Knopf and Random House, as we just discussed, are divisions of Penguin Random House?
A. Yes.
Q. So under the rule as Ms. Dobson describes it, if an imprint's bid on an option is rejected, no other imprint may bid more for that book unless the agent also submits the book to at least one non-Penguin Random House bidder, correct?
A. Yes. I think of it as an extension of our overall bidding policy that there has to be another external bidder in order to go up.
Q. Ms. Dobson continues a few sentences later, "That said, there are some books where there are bad feelings and we just ask the other divisions to back off." Did I read that correctly?
A. Yes.
Q. So if there are hard feelings, one imprint can ask the rest of Penguin Random House not to bid on the author's work?
A. I don't know. That's not a situation that really has ever come up with me. So I don't really have a specific example of it.
MS. BELLSHAW: Thank you, Mr. Tart. The United States passes the witness.
THE COURT: Thank you. Can I just ask, in this particular situation, would you enter the auction and bid 150?
THE WITNESS: We did bid 150.
THE COURT: Okay.
THE WITNESS: We did bid 150 and they turned us down.
THE COURT: But then can you enter the auction in case someone else enters the bid at 150 or would you not do that?
THE WITNESS: I wanted the book at 150 so if I thought that could get me the book at 150, I would do that.
THE COURT: Okay.
THE WITNESS: It didn't seem to be an opportunity for me to do that, but, yeah.
THE COURT: You mean they didn't invite you to the auction.
THE WITNESS: Yeah.
THE COURT: I see. Thank you.
MS. RUDZIN: Good afternoon, Your Honor. Abby Rudzin from O'Melveny & Myers.
THE COURT: Good afternoon.
MS. RUDZIN: Hello, Mr. Tart. Actually, we also have a Captain Crunch decoder ring, if I could hand that up, please. Okay.

THE COURT: Is there a binder that goes with this?
MS. RUDZIN: No.
THE COURT: Okay. Just—
MS. RUDZIN: It just allows him to talk about it first.

CROSS-EXAMINATION

BY MS. RUDZIN:

Q. I'd like to start with just a few follow-ups to what Ms. Bellshaw was talking to you about. She asked you about if the advance is higher, the risk is higher?
A. Uh-huh.
Q. That isn't always true, correct?
A. You know, I think I was just thinking about, as the advance is higher, it could be—you have to sell more copies to justify that advance and that may be more difficult, but it's entirely dependent on the book.
Q. Well, let me put it this way. A $2 million advance from Ms. Obama's next book is presumably less risky than a $2 million advance for a no-name's first collection of short stories, correct?
A. Correct.
Q. And Ms. Bellshaw also asked you some questions about book 44, the auction for book 44. Just so the record is clear, did you at any time during the auction know that Simon & Schuster was in the auction?
A. No.
Q. Would it have made a difference to how you bid?
A. No.
Q. Ms. Bellshaw asked you whether you consider the backlist when thinking about your advance, and you explained that it's prestige that maybe you could pitch to the author, right?
A. Uh-huh.
Q. Does the revenue you get on the backlist help you decide what advance to offer?
A. No. I'm thinking about the book. The value that I would need to be able to acquire the book. I'm not thinking about where that money would come from.
Q. Is backlist the only way to have revenue to be able to offer advances?
A. No, certainly—no, there are plenty of other ways.
Q. If you could turn to PX328, please. This is the email about your explanation on insisting on audio rights; correct?
A. Yes.
Q. If you could please look at the first paragraph of the email that Ms. Bellshaw read and read from "the audio book benefits" through the end of the paragraph.
A. Yes. "The audio book benefits entirely from the book's publicity, marketing, packaging, positioning, editing, et cetera. All things I know you know. But maybe you haven't thought that through.
"We can't give up 40 percent of the market for this book. The outside audio players do almost zero marketing, certainly nothing approaching our marketing and publicity, they get a free ride."
Q. And is this still consistent with your view today about why you insist on audio rights?
A. Yes.
Q. You told the Judge that Penguin pretty regularly does house bids. Why is that?
A. I think agents send their submissions out to a number of publishers and we act independently on what we're interested to buy. Sometimes we'll come up on the same proposals or manuscripts that we want to buy.
Q. In other words, it's routine for imprints within the Penguin Group to compete against each other, correct?
A. Yes.
Q. And that obviously is true of imprints in the Random House division and Knopf Doubleday division as well, correct?
A. Yes.
Q. The difference is, though, there's—

THE COURT: Should you be leading this witness?
MS. RUDZIN: I didn't mean to be. I'm sorry. I'll rephrase.
BY MS. RUDZIN:
Q. If we could just go back to the beginning a little bit and if you just tell us how long you've been in publishing.
A. I've been in publishing, it will be 30 years next month.
Q. So you've been acquiring and editing books for almost 30 years now?
A. The first two years mostly copying and filing, but after that, yes, acquiring and editing.
Q. Acquiring and editing books for 28 years. Can you tell us maybe over that long career, what your favorite book is that you've personally acquired and edited?
A. It's a very tricky question, but I'm very proud of a book, *A New Earth* by Eckhart Tolle that I edited and published back in 2005, found it to be foundational text, a book that matters to a lot of people and will continue. I think it's a book that's changed lives and will continue. I think it's something that people will be reading for a long time, so I'm very proud of that one.
Q. And you mentioned Viking acquires about 60 books a year. How many books—strike that. You mentioned that Viking publishes about 60 books a year. How many books does Viking acquire each year?
A. Well, since we have to acquire books in order to publish them and since sometimes the books we acquire do not deliver on time, sometimes they don't deliver at all, I usually want to acquire more books in a year than I publish. So around 70 or more. In fact, the first book I bought when I was at Viking in 2015, I'm still waiting to be delivered.
Q. And I'd like to turn to the acquisition process itself since you're the first actual acquiring editor we've heard from. From your perspective, can you just tell us generally what are the different ways Viking acquires books?
A. For the most part, it's one-on-one negotiations. That can happen through an option that we have or agent who comes to us exclusively because they want us to be the publisher or a book that's been sent out widely that we end up in a one-on-one negotiation.
And then the other—and then we can acquire book through an auction or through a preempt, by preempting the auction.
Q. Backing up for a minute, who decides whether Viking even has the opportunity to bid on a book?
A. The agent.
Q. Does Viking end up offering on every book that is submitted to it?
A. No.
Q. Do you like acquiring books through one-on-one negotiations?
A. I find it very difficult. I think you are basically bidding against the author's expectations and the agent's expectations. I find it hard to convince them otherwise. There's no other bidder, there's no other market inputs, you know there's competition out there, and so I think those are some of the hardest deals to put together.
Q. What about when negotiating to keep a repeat author, how do those usually go?
A. Those can be very tricky. And the trickiest ones are when an author has had great success with a book or success with a book because oftentimes the agent is looking to have a deal that is based on or close to those numbers for that book, but a previous success does not always mean future success, and so those become—some of my costliest mistakes have happened in that.
Q. I hate to do this to you but if you can give us an example of one of your big mistakes, and I'd caution you to not name the book or the author if you're going to give the advance amount?
A. Yes. Author B and title B was a great success for Viking. We sold more than 3 million copies of the book. We loved working with the author, felt it was very identifiable with our imprint. Looking forward to the next book idea. The author sent in the next book idea, which we all really liked, thought it was really strong really looking forward to continuing the relationship.
But the agent had expectations that were much higher than our expectations for it. I was thinking about trying to do a deal around $2 million and the agent really wasn't budging from $5 million, so I thought it was important to do the deal. I thought if it went out widely, we could lose it. I didn't want to do that. So I

agreed to the $5 million deal. We published the book and it didn't perform all that well. We sold about 100,000 copies or so, which is pretty good, but it doesn't justify a million dollars advance.

Q. And how was the agent able to get you to pay $5 million if you were thinking of paying $2 million?

A. I didn't want to lose the author. I felt it would look bad for Viking if we had such a great success with the book and we didn't even try to continue to work with the author. I thought I think it's—the imprint can take a hit if a big author leaves. People wonder why they couldn't keep the author, why they couldn't make these things work.

Q. Do you ever go ahead and say, okay, the author can walk away?

A. You know, sometimes I just can't reach the expectations. And when that happens, the author can take it out widely and often will leave.

Q. Can you give us an example, again, without naming the author and the advance?

A. Yes, this would be author G and this author was a house author. We published a number of books with this author. We had great success with title G. And because of that great success, we went into a new contract. We spent $2 million on that. It underperformed. We sold around 50,000 copies. But we still wanted to continue with the author because we really liked working with him. You know, some books work, some books don't. And so we bid but closer to the book that sold around 50,000 copies. The author and the agent wanted more, thought they could get more, so in this case, I didn't think I could move up so they went out widely with it and they ended up selling the book to another publisher for 50 percent more than I was looking to pay, so I lost—the author did leave.

Q. And in a situation like that, has it ever been the reverse where Viking takes an author from another house?

A. Yes, I brought Elizabeth George, she's a crime writer, over from HarperCollins, she writes the Inspector Lynley series. It was a PBS television series. I followed her career for a long time, I really wanted to work with her. The agent knew that and came to me when he didn't think HarperCollins thought they could grow her audience anymore. So asked me if I thought I could, I thought I could, I gave an offer that was more than what he had been offered. So she came to me and I've worked with her ever since, five books in, very successfully.

Q. When you're in that one-on-one negotiation, are you thinking about competition?

A. Absolutely. I'm thinking the competition is there it's—I think it's been a pretty robust market for—in terms of advances, so I always think about the competition.

Q. Are you thinking about Simon & Schuster?

A. No, I'm not thinking specifically about any publisher. I'm just thinking about the competitive market for books.

Q. You explained you could take a book by preempt which we've heard a lot about. If Viking attempts to preempt a book and the preempt offer is rejected, does Viking go to the auction to try to get the book anyway?

A. You could. You can go into the auction, but I wouldn't bid more than I offered as a preempt.

Q. And that's just a policy you have?

A. That's just the way I feel about it. I don't think—you know, if I give a preempt, I'm asking the author and agent to take it at that amount, and if they think that's not my highest amount, why would they ever take it. So I have to be consistent when I make a preempt offer.

Q. And in that case, does Viking ever win the auction for less than it offered as a preempt?

A. If I go—if I were to go into an auction? That can happen, yes.

Q. You also participate in auctions, correct?

A. Yes.

Q. What kind of auctions does Viking buy books in?

A. Pretty much every auction that agents set up. It could be a rounds auction, it could be also a round robin auction, it could be a best bid auction, it can be a better best auction, it can be a combination of all three all at the same time. It happens.

Q. What type of auction do you see more frequently?

A. I don't track it, so I don't really know. But I would assume it's better, best, best bid auctions.

Q. Let's take those one at a time. What's a best bids option?

A. So that's a one-time only bid. You have one chance to buy the book. Then the agent is not going to come back to you to refine the offer. That's your opportunity to buy it. So it's just a one round bid.

Q. And do you like those because they get over faster?

A. No, I don't like those. I think they're very difficult. It's very difficult to value that.

You know, you're kind of valuing it in the dark. You don't know about any other bids. You don't know all that much information. So it's hard.

Q. Can you give us an example where you think you missed the mark in a best bids auction and maybe lost a book to a non-peer agent imprint, let's say, and again, please don't say the author out loud.

A. Yes, author E and title E was a manuscript that I read that I loved. It was kind of speculative fantasy fiction. I thought it was brilliant, start of a great career. It was going to be a trilogy and so I put together a bid of $825,000 for three books to buy it. I thought that was a great bid considering only one of the books was written and there was some work to be done. But it showed a lot of promise.

And I went to the auction and I lost the auction to a bid that was over $2 million.

Q. Do you know who made that bid over $2 million?

A. It was Flatiron from Macmillan.

Q. Macmillan, you said?

A. Macmillan, yes.

Q. What's a better best auction?

A. So it starts off as a best bid auction but then there's another round. So oftentimes that second round is a round you have to compete to get into, meaning not everybody goes through to the second round, but it's a two-round auction.

Q. Do you have an understanding of why the agent wouldn't let everyone into the second round? Isn't more bidders better?

A. I think what they're doing is trying to make the first bid as aggressive as possible so that there's as high of an initial bid as possible and the way to do that is to say, if you're not high enough, you won't be invited to make a second bid.

Q. Did the agents always enforce that kind of narrowing of the field in the second round?

A. No, there's some leeway there for sure. They'll say, I'm only allowing three bidders in, but if the bid come in and they want to include another bid, they'll just say, I'm allowing four bids in.

Q. Talking about the difference between a single round best bid auction and a two round better best bid auction, do you always know in advance which kind you're in?

A. No, I think the rules change pretty regularly. And so sometimes you think you're in a best bid option and then it's going to turn into a better best auction, or sometimes you think you're in a rounds auction and then there's a call for best bids, one final bid out of a rounds auction. So things do change.

Q. In those best bid auctions or better best bid auctions, does the PRH rule about requiring an external bidder have any application?

A. Not in a best bid auction.

Q. And that's because even if the agent expects only PRH imprints to bid, every imprint is still allowed to go ahead and put its best bid in?

A. Yes.

Q. Does Viking ever do round robin auctions?

A. Yes, we do.

Q. And how do those work?

A. They're usually set up in two ways. One is a round will start and then you'll find out what the highest bidder was of that round and then you'll have to beat that in the following round. Or it goes publisher by publisher, and someone bids X and then the next publisher bids Y, so on and so on until everyone has bid and then it goes to the next round and starts at that high bid.

Q. When you say publisher by publisher, do you mean publishing house or publisher persons such as yourself?

A. It would be on the imprint level.

Q. So it goes imprint by imprint?

A. Yes.

Q. In all of these different auction formats, does Viking win only if it ultimately offers the highest advance?

A. No, sometimes you can win as an underbidder.

Q. Why would the author choose an imprint that's offering a lower advance?

A. Sometimes they want to work with a certain editor, sometimes they want to be on a certain list, sometimes it can be about other things that the publisher might be bringing, but it's not always about the advance.

Q. If the agent tells you that there are a lot of bidders in the auction, does that affect how you value the book?

A. I try not to let it affect how I value the overall book, but it could affect how I bid in the auction. And it is a factor, something that we take into account. But I try not to be too reactive to that just because you can't verify it, you don't know how many people are actually going to show up, you don't know if they are as passionate about it as you are. There's lots of things you have to assume in that and it's—so it makes it hard.

Q. What happens if you learn that there aren't that many bidders?

A. Well, I can't get complacent then either because we always say it only just takes one bidder, one committed bidder to outbid you. So if you think there aren't going to be a lot of bidders and you try and lower your offer, you really could set yourself up for being outbid by somebody for a book that you really want. It's also unlikely we know that there's going to be few bidders, agents don't often tell us that.

Q. Ms. Bellshaw asked you earlier if you thought agents were trustworthy. Do you recall that?

A. Yes.

Q. And—but if there are only a few bidders, you think the agent is trustworthy, wouldn't she tell you that?

A. You know, I think we all accept that the agents are trying to get the best deal for their authors and that they're going to make decisions, changing auction rules, giving us information, withholding some information, that they feel is in the best interest of their author. So we are—or I accept that. I don't think that's being dishonest.

Q. Do you know who you are bidding against during an auction?

A. Very rarely. You know, do we know the other—what imprints are bidding against us in an auction, almost never.

Q. How would you learn?

A. The agent would tell us.

Q. How are communications with the agent about negotiating and bidding usually handled?

A. We encourage editors to do it by phone because it's a relationship business between the editor and the agent and you can learn things over the phone much better than you can over email. And it's also an opportunity for the editor to pitch themselves to find out maybe there's one special thing we need to do in order to win the auction. So we always encourage a call.

Q. Does Viking hold meetings to discuss the book proposals that you're considering?

A. Yes, we have weekly editorial meetings.

Q. What happens at those meetings?

A. We discuss acquisitions, passes books we're going to pass on, things like that.

Q. Do you keep minutes from the meetings?

A. We do.

Q. Do those minutes list all the books that Viking has won and lost since the last meeting?

A. They would include a number of the books that we talked about at the meeting but not all of them. We wouldn't include books that we've signed a non-disclosure agreements about. Sometimes agents don't make you sign a non-disclosure agreement, but they ask you to keep a project confidential, so that wouldn't appear on the minutes as well.

Some repeat authors, that's kind of like house business, doesn't make it to the editorial meetings, so those might not be on that list either.

Q. So a submission that isn't discussed at a meeting isn't going to be in the meeting minutes, right?

A. Right.

Q. Stepping back, how do you value a book you're considering acquiring?

A. It is as much an art as a science. It always starts with the editors' enthusiasm. It comes from the editor. They read a book, they get excited by it, they bring it—ask other people to read it, that excitement kind of grows. That's really where it starts. And from there, we will run a P&L.

Q. And you discussed with Ms.—(Cellular telephone interruption)

THE COURT: We have a rule of no electronics in the gallery.

GALLERY VOICE: I'm sorry.

THE COURT: Okay. Thank you.

BY MS. RUDZIN:

Q. You discussed with Ms. Bellshaw that the first thing you put in the P&L is an estimate of how many copies you can sell, right?

A. Yes.

Q. And as you discussed with the Judge, you don't usually get it right, right?

A. Correct, it's really a guess.

Q. I assume you often overestimate how well you sell a book?

A. We can, yes.

Q. So this time I'll ask you for a more positive example. Can you give us an example where you understated how well you would sell a book?

A. Yes, this is a happier example. When we were acquiring the next book from Matt Haig, we were basing it on the success of his previous book, *How to Stop Time*. And at that point, it had sold around 20 or 25,000 copies. So we put that into the P&L, we thought that would be what we could do. We made an offer for the book based on those numbers. And the book went on—it is just about to sell its 3 millionth copy in a couple months. So we wildly underestimated that one.

Q. You also mentioned that another input in the P&L is the cost of selling the books, right?

A. Yes.

Q. How do costs, if at all, how do they impact the advance range suggested by the P&L?

A. Generally, the higher the cost would mean the lower the profit.

Q. If the costs included in the P&L were lower, would that have any impact on the advance amount suggested by the P&L?

A. Yes, it would give us a higher advance where we could still make a profit.

Q. Are you limited in offering an advance that's suggested by the P&L?

A. So after we run the P&L and we look at the suggested advance that is on the P&L, we always talk about it, is this the right number, do we think this is going to take it, is this just wishful thinking that we want to buy the book at this level and are we going to be able to do it. So we do look at it and then we start to talk about, is this going to be enough to buy the book.

Q. And are there any factors you would consider in trying to go beyond the P&L?

A. Yes. You know, is this a start of a writing career I want to be a part of, is there a long-term relationship that we can build here that I want to stretch for, is it a category that's growing? Is it like a book that we just had great success with? Is it a book that can win awards? Is there a prestige to publishing this? There's a lot of factors that can go into that.

Q. How do you weigh all those different factors and decide how much to stretch beyond the P&L?

A. It comes back down to kind of a gut feeling that you have when you put it all together. Can we stretch for this? Do we really want this book? I think what we really figure out is this a book that we have to publish, and if it is, then we'll find a way to stretch.

Q. In your experience, is it common for different imprints to value the same book differently?

A. Yes.

Q. And why is that?

A. Again, editor enthusiasm, imprint profile. We are distinct. I think we offer different things, and so certain books can do really well at one imprint but maybe not do as well in another. So that's kind of how I feel about publishing.

Q. Can you give us an example of a book that you didn't think would necessarily do well at Viking but maybe did better somewhere else?

A. This is a particularly painful example, yes. But we read a manuscript called *Where the Crawdads Sing*. We talked about it, we didn't think it was going to be a big book, we didn't even make a bid on it. My colleagues at Putnam published it and they've made a success out of it.

Q. We know what happened. I know it's painful but you can give us one other example of a book you let get away?

A. This is my personal example. I had in *The Life-Changing Magic of Tidying Up* by Marie Kondo. I didn't know what to make of it. And I didn't even make a bid on that book. And ultimately that's kind of changed the world in some way and sold millions of copies in the process.

Q. Were those books anticipated top sellers?

A. Not to me.

Q. How did it make you feel when those books turned out to be huge after you had thought they weren't worth anything?

A. I felt terrible. I felt like I wasn't doing my job. But there's a kind of gallows humor around editors about this. We do talk about the books that got away. Not really the books that got away, the books we didn't even try for that were big successes. So it's kind of a club you get initiated into over time, and every editor has a story like it.

Q. Switching gears, whom do you consider to be Viking's competitors?

A. Because we're a broad based imprint and general interest, I think most publishers are competitors of mine. I think that within Penguin Random House and I think of that outside of Penguin Random House.

Q. Does Viking compete with imprints from Macmillan, for example?

A. Yes. We'll complete with Houghton, Farrar, Straus and Giroux.

Q. Are there any particular imprints at HarperCollins that Viking competes with?

A. We compete with William Morrow and Ecco.

Q. And what about at Hachette?

A. Little, Brown.

Q. Does Viking compete with imprints from Simon & Schuster?

A. Yes, Scribner.

Q. While we're on this topic, do you see Scribner or Simon & Schuster more generally as a more important competitor?

A. No, I don't single them out. I think of the broad group of publishers as all being competitive with me.

Q. Does Viking compete with any smaller publishers?

A. Yes, they would be different for fiction and nonfiction, but I believe we do.

Q. So let's start with fiction. What are some small publishers you see as competitors for fiction?

A. I think Grove is a really interesting publisher. I admire their list a lot. What they do specifically with literally fiction is great. And so I consider them competitors, as well as Graywolf, an award winning publisher, also really strong literary fiction.

Q. What about in nonfiction?

A. I compete with Norton. I think they have a similar profile to Viking Penguin in that they're very academic focus. So I do think of them as competition. And then on the wellness self-help side, I compete with Hay House.

Q. Can you give us an example of a book you lost to Norton?

A. We were interested—just checking here—we were interested in a book by Elizabeth Hinton, a Yale University professor. She was writing a book on race in America, history of race in America, it was brilliant, we were very excited about it. We were not the only ones. There was a lot of excitement around that book. And Norton ended up pre-empting it for $2-.

Q. And do you think that was more than 250 per book?

A. Yes.

Q. Do you have any losses of examples to Hay House?
A. Yes. Author H, and who was the author of H1, which was a big success for us. We did really well with this book, we were looking to continue with her. She delivered a proposal for a new book ten years after the success of this book, maybe more. But we were excited by it. We made an offer of 750 for it. The agent turned it down and went out widely with it and Hay House bought it for a million dollars, plus a profit-sharing deal.
Q. Any other books you think you've recently lost to Hay House?
A. There was a recent wellness title, author I, title I. We bid 175 in the auction and they won it at 250.
Q. Hay House paid?
A. Yes.
Q. Thank you. You mentioned that Viking competes with other Random House imprints. Can you explain how that works if the imprints are in a different division?
A. Yes. From the other divisions, we would treat them as any other bidder. You know, we still would need an outside bidder to be part of an auction, but we would treat them as an outside bidder unlike the Penguin Publishing Group where we would put together a house bid.
Q. Can you give us an example of a book Viking recently lost to a Penguin Random House imprint outside Penguin?
A. Yes, this would be author D and title D. This was one of those best bid auctions, meaning like there was only one bid, they weren't coming back to us. We were really excited about this. Loved the book. We made an offer of 1.250. I thought for sure that was a winning bid, but we lost it to Knopf at 1.5.
Q. And because that was a single round best bids, the external bidding rule you mentioned wouldn't apply, correct?
A. Correct.
Q. You told Ms. Bellshaw that in a rounds auction if it gets down to just PRH imprints, then you can't bid each other up, right?
A. Correct.
Q. How often does that happen in your experience?
A. Not often because what happens is agents just call for best bids, and then they get an extra round out of it.
Q. And when they're calling for best bids at the end of a rounds auction, it doesn't matter about whether they think only PRH imprints are going to show up in that last best bids round?
A. Right, we're allowed to bid.
Q. When acquiring books does the advance level of $250,000 for a book have any significance to you?
A. No.
Q. Does the advance level for a book indicate how well it will sell?
A. No, it doesn't. For example, in 2021, my best—my most profitable book in 2021 was *The Lincoln Highway*. The advance for that was more than $2 million.
Q. Who's the author on that one?
A. Amor Towles.
Q. Okay.
A. And in 2020, my most profitable book was *The Midnight Library*, Matt Haig, and the advance for that was under $200,000.
Q. Is that an anomaly?
A. No, it happens. If you were to look at my 2020 list, of the top most profitable books on my 2020 list, three of them would have advances in the seven figures, two of them would have advances of 150 or below.
Q. How does Viking decide the level of marketing support a book will receive?
A. We decide on the basis of how the book is setting up, is it looking to be successful, is there potential that we're going to be able to turn this into a successful publication.
Q. When does Viking make that decision?
A. So I try and make it as late as possible, often six weeks before we're about to publish a book.

Q. And why is that?

A. There are three reasons. One is because I want to know if we're publishing into a moment. Is there something happening in the culture that's going to help me lift this book up.

The other is, are there new marking tools and new ways to reach audiences. The pace of change in marketing so extreme right now it's overwhelming. And what I think is going to help me sell a book or reach an audience today is not the same from three months ago or certainly six months ago. There's new things that we're learning, new tools that we're trying. So I want to use the ones that are most relevant at that point.

And then the other part I have a lot of feedback that I get through the process of setting up a book. I hear from my salespeople, I hear from the media, I hear from foreign publishers, I know if a book is sold to TV, movies, things like that. All of that informs the way I'm going to publish the book and how I'm going to position it. So the closer I make the marketing decisions to publication, the better.

Q. Does the level of advance determine the amount of marketing support a book gets?

A. No, not for me, because normally we've contracted for these books years before, or at least a year before but mostly years before, and so these other things that—it's not on my mind.

I do know the advances, and so it's not completely separate by any stretch, but I keep advances confidential, and so my marketing staff and my publicity staff, they don't know what we pay for books.

Q. Can you give us an example of a book that you didn't pay a high advance for but you ended up putting a lot of marking support behind it?

A. Yes, we had a book called *Fiona and Jane* by Jean Chen Ho. This was a collection of stories. We bought a collection of stories and we bought a novel, but we were publishing the collection of stories first, mid-five-figure advance for that.

And honestly, we all thought it's very hard to make a success out of short stories. It's not an easy thing to do. Our expectations were pretty modest for it.

I brought the book to our sales conference, our sales team went absolutely nuts over the book. They read it, they were like, we can do a lot with this, this is a big book; and we listened to them and we changed how we were positioning it, we put her on a pre pub tour, virtual tour. We used the galley at trade shows. We spent a lot of time being creative about what we could do marketing-wise and so forth. We thought of it as a bigger book because of these inputs we were getting from the sales group and because people were really responding to it.

So we published the book. Seven, eight months later now, we've sold around 17,000 copies, which for a collection of short stories, I think is really great, definitely double what I thought we would do. And I think when we publish it in paperback at the end of the year, it's going to be a real success. We turned it into a great story for her career.

Q. Even though it started out as a five-figure advance?

A. Correct.

THE COURT: Can I go back to something you said before? You said in your 2020 list of the most profitable, three had advances in the seven figures and two were below 150?

THE WITNESS: Yes.

THE COURT: How big was the list, what was in between?

THE WITNESS: I think the first two books were seven-figure deals, and then the third most profitable, I think, was 150. And then another seven-figure deal and then the fifth most profitable was 100.

THE COURT: So how big is this list?

THE WITNESS: Oh, I'm sorry, we published 60 books—59 or 60 books that year.

THE COURT: Oh, okay. So when you say of your 2020 list, the most profitable, three had advances in the seven figures, two below 150, then 55 had advances between 150 and seven figures?

THE WITNESS: No. I meant the very top. I meant the top five most profitable books on that list, of which there are probably 60 books on that list.

THE COURT: Okay, so of the top five—

THE WITNESS: Correct.

THE COURT:—three had advances of seven figures and two were below 150?

THE WITNESS: Yes.
THE COURT: Okay. Thank you.
BY MS. RUDZIN:
Q. Unfortunately I'm going to ask you to give an example of the other way, where you had a high advance book and you didn't put marketing support behind it very much.
A. This is author C, title C. This is a book I loved, it's a thriller, I fell for it completely, has a great twist at the ending, really excited about publishing it. We spent $900,000 to acquire it. Again, brought it to my salespeople. And I didn't get the reaction I was expecting, nobody was talking to me about the twist at the end and it was because they couldn't get there because it wasn't page turning which is the worst thing you can hear about a thriller.
And so we tried all sort of things. We thought well, maybe it's not a thriller, maybe it's domestic suspense. Maybe it's not domestic suspense. Maybe it's a book about female friendship. We just tried different ways to get people to just keep reading the book.
But it didn't happen. And by the time I published it, I didn't have a lot of partnerships with boo stores, I didn't get a lot of media, all those imprints that I was getting books like *Fiona and Jane* and other successes, I wasn't getting on this. So while I thought—I was hoping I could sell around 200,000 copies of this book, I ended up selling about 20,000.
Q. But you paid a $900,000 advance so why didn't you just put more money into marketing to try to recoup that advance?
A. Because it wouldn't have made a difference. I couldn't—it would have been throwing good money after bad, to be honest. I don't find that marketing money can create a success. I think it can amplify it. I think you can find new audiences with it.
I think you can make a book much, much bigger with marketing for sure, but it's—I find it very difficult to create success out of whole cloth just through marketing. And I would have done it if I could have paid for it, if I could have turned this into a success, I would have done it, but I couldn't.
Q. Is it fair to say by the time you're making the decision about marketing of the book, the advance is a sunk cost?
A. I think that's fair to say.
THE COURT: So when you do your P&L to decide what advance to offer, I've heard other evidence in this case, that that includes—the costs include like a variable cost for marketing.
THE WITNESS: Yeah, that's in the P&L.
THE COURT: Yeah. Which means that the marketing budget in the P&L is going up and down depending on what you think the sales are going to be. But you're saying that's fake, it's not real, the marketing budget isn't really what's in the P&L.
THE WITNESS: I don't go back to that original P&L to decide my marketing budget.
THE COURT: Interesting.
THE WITNESS: Mainly because—
THE COURT: The P&L is really fake. Am I wrong?
THE WITNESS: No.
THE COURT: Okay.
THE WITNESS: No. I mean, it's what we do. And I can't dismiss it entirely, but in the art and science of publishing, it's—you know.
THE COURT: Okay.
THE WITNESS: We get a lot wrong with the P&L.
MS. RUDZIN: May I proceed, Your Honor?
THE COURT: You may proceed.
MS. RUDZIN: Thank you.
BY MS. RUDZIN:
Q. Just quickly when you talk about marketing, is that corporate marketing or is there a Viking specific marketing department?
A. Penguin Random House has a big, great corporate marketing department but Viking Penguin has its

own marketing department, most imprints have their own marketing department. And in our marketing department, we are title specific. So while we get market research, audience affinities, data analytics from the corporate marketing group, which is incredibly helpful, they don't really touch the titles like we do so we come up with the creative, we come up with the marketing all around the titles within our own imprint.

Q. And to the Court's question about the marketing spend in the P&L, we've also heard that sometimes imprints give a marketing plan to the agent as part of the bid for the book, right?

A. Yes.

Q. What does that have to do with how you actually end up marketing the book?

A. Very little. It's really an expression of how much we love the book and how creative we can be. But usually we're sending those out years in advance of actually publishing the book. So they're pretty obsolete by the time we publish.

Q. Quickly, this case is about books that go for $250,000 advance or more. Is that a high level advance to you?

A. No. I don't consider 250 a high level advance. You know, I consider seven figures mid—multiple seven figures being a high level advance.

Q. So a book that you think is really going to sell well is getting seven figures, right?

A. I mean, not always, but more so than I would think $250,000.

Q. Are the negotiations over a book that will cost more than $250,000 different than a book that ends up costing less than $250,000?

A. No.

Q. What about a book that you're paying an advance of $8 million for?

A. Yes, that is a different level of what you're negotiating. That is a very—it's very rare to be up around that level, but when you are, you're negotiating a different kind of beast.

Q. And is there a threshold or a line where it tips from being just a nice, ordinary, we think it might do well book and we really think this is going to fly book?

A. In terms of the advance?

Q. Yes.

A. No.

Q. Does Viking give the same editorial support to a book if it goes for less than $250,000 than a book that goes for more than $250,000?

A. No.

Q. Is the sales support the same or dependent on the advance level in any way?

A. Yes, the sales support is the same.

Q. Does Viking have different printing and distribution services for books that go for more than $250,000?

A. No.

Q. Would your answer to any of those questions change if the figure was $100,000?

A. No.

Q. What about $350,000?

A. No.

Q. Is there any advance threshold at which Viking treats books differently?

A. No.

Q. Just to be clear—

THE COURT: I thought you just said $8 million.

THE WITNESS: Oh—there is—yes, there is a several million advance level would make me think.

BY MS. RUDZIN:

Q. Well, just to be clear, the printing, distribution, editorial services, those aren't different based on the advance even for an $8 million book, right?

A. Right.

Q. They're printed on the same paper and same printer?

A. Yes.

THE COURT: Can I just ask about this, because I've seen other evidence in this case, other email chains with other deals where things did make a difference, like a budget for glam, like makeup, wardrobe, negotiating about royalty rates, taking a book as is. I mean, that must kick in at some level—and I just think of the advance as some way of identifying the books that are the most desirable. It's like sort of a rough way of calculating that. Don't those things come in at some level when they wouldn't for a book that's less desirable?

THE WITNESS: My experience is they come in for certain kinds of books, like celebrity books you talk about glam, you don't ever talk about glam with fiction really or certain other kinds of books that you're doing, it's really a specific kind of book that you would be negotiating that. So I don't really consider it so much advance based as I do kind of type of book.

THE COURT: What about the royalty rates and the as is, like something that everybody wants, don't you throw in things like this?

THE WITNESS: Yeah, I don't—I'm not sure what "as is" means.

THE COURT: It was another email chain I saw where they said one editor would just take it as is, like they're not going to change it, they're going to give the author—

THE WITNESS: The manuscript.

THE COURT:—make the author have their way with it.

THE WITNESS: That's pretty rare.

THE COURT: Yeah.

THE WITNESS: It hasn't really come up with me.

THE COURT: And what about negotiating royalty rates?

THE WITNESS: Yes, that will happen. You know, as I said, it's usually hard cover, which we'll negotiate. Very rarely, if ever, will I negotiate the other royalty rates, but if it were to happen, it would be at that very, very top tier advance level.

THE COURT: Okay. So when you're negotiating royalty rates, around what advance level are you doing that?

THE WITNESS: For the hard cover royalty rates, pretty much any level.

THE COURT: Any level?

THE WITNESS: I might not give it or I might give it—usually agents use some leverage when they're asking for that. They haven't yet accepted your offer and they'll say, I'd love to accept this but if you give me to a 15 percent hard cover rate then I might do it.

THE COURT: And so when would you give it and when would you not? How would you decide?

THE WITNESS: If I think it's going to determine if I get the book or not, like if I think, oh, if I give this, they're going to agree to the book, then I would give them.

THE COURT: So the more desirable books.

THE WITNESS: More desirable? Well, the books that I—yeah, I guess.

THE COURT: The more important books.

THE WITNESS: The books that I want to buy that I think are really important for us to buy in our list. And if I think the agent would give it to me if I give them that term.

THE COURT: Right. But is that ultimately driven by competition for the book?

THE WITNESS: Yeah. Yes, it is.

THE COURT: Okay.

THE WITNESS: Yes.

THE COURT: Thank you. Go ahead.

BY MS. RUDZIN:

Q. I just want to clean one thing up, Mr. Tart, because we might have been talking past each other. Does Viking give the same editorial support to books without regard to the advance level?

A. Yes.

Q. Okay. So it does not have different editorial support for a book that goes for more than $250,000, right?

A. No.
Q. Thank you. So back to where we were just ending, are you saying a book that gets only $100,000 advance is going to be or can be treated the same way and perform the same way as a book that gets a million-dollar advance?
A. Yes. You know, I published a book, book A. in title A, which had a million-dollar advance. We set this up really well. We had a book club for it, it was a debut, but we put a lot behind it. And we turned it into a *New York Times* best seller. And really were selling the book week in and week out. It became, I think, just a great success. Four weeks after that book, we had a similar book, same kind of book that we were publishing, this time by author F and title F. We paid $100,000 for this book. We also had a book club picked for this book. It also hit *The New York Times* best seller list in its first week out. Both of those were debuts. It also had almost eerily similar week to week sales as the other book that I'm talking about. And over a year later, if you look at the sales, they're almost exactly the same, hundreds of thousands of copies sold of these two books. And if you look at the marketing, we did the exact same thing. We spent the same marketing on it because we were reaching the same audience, too. The only difference really was one book we spent a million dollars to acquire and the other book we spent $100,000 to acquire.
Q. Just a few quick last questions on the advance. Based on your experience, what's been happening to advances over the course of your career?
A. My experience is that they've only gone up.
Q. And is that true after the merger between Penguin Random House?
A. Yes.
Q. And based on that experience, do you think Penguin Random House acquiring Simon & Schuster will impact the advances that authors receive?
A. I think advances are just going to continue to go up.
Q. Does Viking plan to offer lower advances if Penguin Random House acquires Simon & Schuster?
A. No.
Q. Why not?
A. Because I don't think I'd be able to buy the books if I did.
Q. Well, what happens if Viking doesn't offer a high enough advance for a book?
A. Most likely we would lose the book, and that won't change when Penguin Random House buys Simon & Schuster.
MS. RUDZIN: Thank you very much, Mr. Tart.
THE COURT: Thank you. Ms. Bellshaw.
MS. BELLSHAW: Thank you, Your Honor.

REDIRECT EXAMINATION

BY MS. BELLSHAW:

Q. Good morning, Mr. Tart.
A. Good morning.
Q. Thank you for joining us by Zoom this morning. I'm going to do my best to get you out of here quickly. I have questions on just a few of the topics that Ms. Rudzin asked you about last week. I'm going to do my best to look at you sometimes but your screen is over here. Last week Ms. Rudzin asked you several questions about Viking's competitors. You would agree that you compete most frequently in auctions with other members of the Big 5; is that right?
A. You know, I often find out who wins the auctions but I don't always know who's in it. I would—I know that Simon & Schuster, Hachette, Macmillan, and HarperCollins are often in the auctions that I'm in, but I also think they aren't the only ones, but I don't always get that information.
Q. Fair to say that it would be unusual for Viking to compete in an auction without at least one member of the Big 5 present?
A. I think—I would expect one to be there, yes.
Q. You testified in response to Ms. Rudzin's questions about three instances where you lost books to non-Big 5 publishers. Do you recall that testimony?

A. I do.
Q. Including one book that you lost to Norton on a preempt, right?
A. Yes.
Q. And that you lost to Norton on a preempt means that Viking never submitted a bid for the Norton book; is that right?
A. I believe so, yes. I know we were talking about a bid but I don't think we had the opportunity to make the offer.
Q. You were deposed in this litigation in March of 2022, right?
A. Yes.
Q. And at that deposition, you recall that my colleague from the Department of Justice asked you questions about the publishers with whom Viking competes?
A. Yes.
Q. And do you recall that at that deposition, you could not identify a single instance where Viking bid on a book and lost the book to Norton?
A. Yes.
Q. Is it fair to say that at your deposition, you couldn't think of a single book that Viking bid on and lost to Norton because it doesn't happen very often?
A. I couldn't think of one at the time. And I had forgotten the instance where the book—that book was preempted.
Q. And fair that you couldn't think of any other instances where Viking lost a bid to Norton because it doesn't happen very often?
A. Yes.
Q. At your deposition, you also could not identify a single instance where Viking made an offer and lost to a non-Big 5 publisher; is that right?
A. Yes.
Q. And, again, you were able to identify some in response to your counsel's questions, but fair to say it's unusual for Viking to lose a book to a non-Big 5 publisher?
A For the ones that I find out—and we usually do find out who wins the auction, yes.
Q. You testified last week that the Penguin Random House bidding rule does not apply to best-bid auctions, right?
A. Correct, yes.
Q. That exception that imprints can bid against each other in a best-bid auction is not written down anywhere, right?
A. I don't know if it is.
Q. You also testified that sometimes an auction will start as a rounds auction and then the agent will decide to call for best bids, right?
A. Yes.
Q. And I just wanted to clarify, in that instance, Viking's best and final offer would be capped by whatever the existing highest Penguin Random House bid was, right?
A. Just so I'm clear, if we're in a rounds auction and they call for best bids, we can make a best bid based on our individual valuation, meaning the imprints valuation of the book. I don't really—I don't get what you mean by capped.
Q. So if you're in a rounds auction where—and the agent calls for best bids and only Penguin Random House imprints remain to bid in the next round, which is a best-bids auction, you can match the other Penguin Random House imprints but you cannot exceed the Penguin Random House imprint bids; is that right?
A. That's not really my understanding of it. We often don't know what the other bids are from the other divisions at Penguin Random House. We would know what they are from the Penguin Publishing Group. And so you would have an opportunity possibly to join the highest bid from the Penguin Publishing Group. But we don't often know what the other divisions are doing, so it's—it doesn't really extend beyond our own division.

Q. Mr. Tart, you should have received a file of documents in your email. Did you receive that a few minutes ago?
A. I've been refreshing, but I haven't received it.
Q. So there were two emails that were sent. Have you received either of them?
A. I have not.
Q. We may need to come back to that because I think we're having technical difficulties and can't show the witness.
THE COURT: You can't share your screen and show from here?
MS. BELLSHAW: No, we've been unable to get on the WiFi this morning so we're not able to join the Zoom to share our screen.
THE COURT: Okay.
MS. BELLSHAW: So we may come back to that.
THE COURT: Can we see if we can get the WiFi up and running.
COURTROOM DEPUTY: I'm going to send an email.
MS. BELLSHAW: And we'll do our best to get back on in the meantime.
THE COURT: Okay.
BY MS. BELLSHAW:
Q. Mr. Tart, you mentioned two titles last week in your testimony that you consider to be books that got away, right?
A. I can't think exactly which ones you're speaking of.
Q. Marie Kondo's book, *The Life-Changing Magic of Tidying Up* and *Where the Crawdads Sing*?
A. Yes.
Q. Those books were both published by imprints of Penguin Random House, right?
A. Yes, they were.
Q. So while those books may have gotten away from you, they didn't get away from Penguin Random House, right?
A. Yes.
Q. I'd like to ask you a few questions about marketing. And actually, if I can pause just one moment, I think this may require a document.
THE COURT: Okay.
MS. BELLSHAW: I think we're going to ask defendant's counsel to please share their screen. They've graciously offered to do that.
THE COURT: Thank you very much.
BY MS. BELLSHAW:
So if we could, we'll step back and take a look at PX332, which was admitted into evidence last week. And so, Mr. Tart, this is going to be shared on your screen in just a moment.
A. Okay.
Q. Can you see the image?
A. I can.
Q. It may be a little bit small.
A. Just went away, the image.
MS. BELLSHAW: Could we not publish this to the gallery, the version they have may not be redacted. Thank you.
BY MS. BELLSHAW:
Q. So, Mr. Tart, looking back at this email, PX332, we looked at this last week. And the bottom email from Ms. James to an agent. The agent is laying out here the Penguin Random House bidding rule to the agent, correct?
A. Yes.
Q. Ms. Agent does—or Ms. James doesn't tell the agent in her email about the exception for best-bids auctions, right?
A. Yes.

Q. So Ms. James writes, "When it gets down to just PRH bids, though, we can only match each other, we can't further bid each other up." So she never lets the agent know that even though this auction is starting as a rounds auction, if the agent decides to go to best bids, the Penguin Random House imprints can bid against each other, correct?

A. She doesn't mention that, no.

Q. And if we could scroll up to the next email, please, the agent writes back to Ms. James—and in the middle of her email the agent writes, "And I can confirm there are non-PRH imprints in the mix. I'm asking that this next and final bid come in by 3:30 p.m. if that's possible." The agent here is moving to a best-bids round; is that correct?

A. Yes.

Q. And in doing so, she's confirming that there are non-Penguin Random House imprints in the mix?

A. Yes.

Q. And if Penguin Random House imprints are allowed to bid against each other in the best and final auction round, there will be no need for the agent to reassure Penguin that there are non-Penguin Random House imprints in the mix before moving to a best-bid format, correct?

A. In this scenario, I believe it's essentially a better best auction and she's confirming that there were non-Penguin Random House imprints who were in the—who made the last bid, meaning the first bid. And then, therefore, by going to best bids, it's understood that we can make a bid even if the bidders in the first round who are not PRH bidders end up not bidding.

Q. So if in the first round only Penguin Random House bidders had participated, you would not be able to participate in the next round?

A. That is my understanding, yes.

Q. Okay. Thank you, Mr. Tart. I wanted to ask you a few questions about marketing. You testified last week that Viking decides what level of marketing support to provide a book about six weeks before publication; is that right?

A. Yes.

Q. But is it correct that sometimes you do bring marketing and publicity in to help when you're thinking about how much to bid for a book?

A. Yes.

Q. If we could look at PX327, please?

THE COURT: Can this be shown to the gallery?

MS. BELLSHAW: Do you have redactions on your version? No. My apologies, Your Honor.

THE COURT: Okay. Thank you.

BY MS. BELLSHAW:

Q. PX327 is an email chain with a top email dated June 30th, 2020, from Wendy Wolf to you; is that right?

A. Yes.

Q. And this is an email regarding the auction for book 44 that we discussed last week?

A. Yes.

MS. BELLSHAW: Your Honor, I move to admit PX327 into evidence.

THE COURT: Any objections?

MS. RUDZIN: No objection.

THE COURT: 327 will be admitted. (Plaintiff's Exhibit PX327 received into evidence.)

BY MS. BELLSHAW:

Q. Looking at the email from Ms. Schulz to you on June 15th, 2020, it is on the page with the Bates number ending in 1077 at the top. Thank you. Again, Ms. Schulz is the editor-in-chief at Viking books, right?

A. Yes.

Q. And this email from Ms. Schulz to you appears to be from early on in the auction process before Viking has submitted any bid for book 44; is that right?

A. I believe so, yes.

Q. Ms. Schulz is forwarding you the initial P&L and explaining why she thinks that Viking—that, I'm sorry, book 44 could be worth up to $700,000?

A. Yes.

Q. In explaining her valuation of book 44, Ms. Schulz identifies a comparative title and writes, "Lindsey is certain she could get that level of media attention and ongoing audience for the author of book 44." Lindsey refers to Lindsey Prevette, Viking Books' director of publicity, is that right?

A. Yes.

Q. Later, you forward the P&L for book 44 to your boss Allison Dobson. It's the email from Mr. Tart at—on June 16th at 10:17 a.m. And you say to him—you explain to Ms. Dobson in your email, "There is great publicity support for this." Do you see that?

A. Yes.

Q. So is it fair to say that for book 44, you started thinking about the level of publicity support to give book 44 early on before you even bid on the book?

A. Yes.

Q. Thank you. Mr. Tart, I just ask you to check and see if you have received the file that we sent this morning yet?

A. Yes, I did. I have it.

Q. Great. Thank you.

A. Thank you.

Q. You don't need to open anything right now but I may ask you to open a document in a moment.

A. Okay. Yep, it's here.

Q. Mr. Tart, you testified last week that a larger advance doesn't indicate how well that a book will sell. Do you recall that testimony?

A. Yes.

Q. And you gave some examples of a book that had received a high advance and sold really well and then also of a lower advance book that did well. Do you recall that?

A. Yes.

Q. Now, acknowledging that there will always be some outlier break-away hits or duds, you would agree that generally high advance books as a group sell more copies than lower advance books?

A. Looking at my list, I can see a wide range of books that succeed with high advances and books that succeed with low advances. It's possible, probable, that if you put them all together, you would sell more copies with the books that have higher advances, but I—at least for the Viking list, I do see a range at the top of the list for me in terms of which books are successful.

Q. And recognizing that, again, not every book will fall into these categories, you would agree that generally higher advance books correlate with higher sales than lower advance books, correct?

A. We certainly acquire them that way. And as you say, there are exceptions. It doesn't always go according to plan. I would think that, ultimately, that is the case, that the higher advance books would sell more, but I don't know I'd really spend time tracking them.

Q. Mr. Tart, you testified in response to Ms. Rudzin's questions that when estimating future book sales in the P&L, you don't usually get it right. Do you recall that testimony?

A. Yes.

Q. And you described the predicted sales and the P&Ls as a guess?

A. Yes.

Q. Is it fair to say it's an educated guess?

A. Yes, we do our best to get as close to it as we can in terms of the comp being realistic.

Q. And the P&Ls are based on sales data from comp titles whose success you believe you can emulate, right?

A. Yes.

Q. And you use your own experience and the experience of your editors to select the comp titles to include in the P&Ls?

A. Yes.

Q. And Viking uses comp titles to estimate future sales in the P&Ls because those give Viking a view of the market it is hoping to publish into, right?

A. I think the understanding is that it may be a view of the market at this moment or when those books were published, but it's not necessarily a view of the market in two, three, how many years we're actually going to publish the book. We do understand that that is very difficult, nearly impossible to predict.

Q. So when you prepare the P&Ls, they represent Viking's best estimate of how well a book will sell based on market conditions at the time the book is acquired, correct?

A. It takes in account a lot of factors. Best estimate or best guess is pretty close to me describing the process. But it is about the market that is existing or has existed more than trying to predict the market in how many years we're going to publish the book.

Q. And you submit these P&Ls to the finance department at Penguin, right?

A. Yes.

Q. And if the advance is above $250,000, you also submit them to your boss, the President of Penguin Publishing Group?

A. Yes.

Q. Thank you.

MS. BELLSHAW: No further questions. Thank you, Mr. Tart.

THE COURT: Thank you.

THE WITNESS: Thank you.

THE COURT: I have a question for Mr. Tart. Mr. Tart, I've heard, and it's my understanding, that the anticipated top selling books represent only 2 percent of the books that are actually published. And I was wondering if you could speak for a minute about the other 98 percent of the books and what the process is like to acquire the books with low advances, how low do those advances go, where there's no competition. I just want to get a general sense of the other books.

THE WITNESS: Okay. So by other books, is there a range, like an advance range you're look at?

THE COURT: Yeah, I guess maybe you can tell me below $100,000. Just books that there's—I guess there's not competition for those books; is that right? I'm just trying to understand what's going on with the other 98 percent.

THE WITNESS: Well, for us we do have a range of advance levels on our list every year. I do think a balance of that is really important, meaning a number of books that are in the seven-figure range, so forth, and then a number of books somewhere in the middle, and then some books in the five figures, low six figures, that you're acquiring for—oftentimes it's a number of reasons. One is it may not be that book that is going to be a breakout book but you feel the writer has a book in him or her that you want to invest in for the future. So the *Fiona and Jane* example is a pretty good one of that. I didn't really think that a collection of short stories would be as—we could do as much with it as we ended up doing. So we have, I'd say, less than a quarter of our list is in that range of low six figures to five-figure books. But we generally have a few on every list and we do three lists a year. So what is that? About 20 books a season. So of those, we have a handful that would be authors that were growing, books we're trying to set up in the best possible way that don't have big advances to it. And you can take some chances with those, you can get really creative in terms of how you publish them, I think, and so that's kind of why we do it.

THE COURT: I see. And so is it fair to say that there isn't really competition for books like that, that they're just authors that you're home growing?

THE WITNESS: There is often some competition but it's usually around that same level.

And then for the kind of mid-five-figure books—there may be just one other publisher or two who are interested, if that. But people generally see it at the same level so that's why the price doesn't go up.

THE COURT: And can you talk a little bit about those authors, like are they different to deal with? I just imagine you have a broad range of authors and author expectations.

THE WITNESS: I don't really get—no, I don't think they're different to deal with. I think they are excited to be published. I think they have ambitions and aspirations just like the others on the list. I think they're looking for opportunities in the same way. If opportunities come and people start to think those books could really do something, they are right there with us to help support it, promote it as much as possible. So we have the same conversations with those authors as we do with authors with bigger advances. We might not get as many opportunities, but we're trying to do the same thing.

THE COURT: And do you have more leverage over these authors? For example, you can offer them less money. Can you also not entertain things like bonuses and things like that? Front loaded royalties?

THE WITNESS: Yeah, sometimes that will come up even if it's one other bidder, you know. I think I tried to make the point that I usually have to decide about the other aspects, those other deal points when we still haven't yet bought the book. When there's leverage, the agent is saying, well, there's somebody else who's interested—who's close to you, but if you give me this or that, then it's yours, and that's usually when I'll negotiate to get the book. And so bonuses come up, even at the five-figure level. You know, mostly when you make an offer at the five-figure level and you're not going to get to six figures, the agents, a lot of agents try to get there with bonuses. So we do talk about bonuses at that level.

THE COURT: And how often in this kind of part of the market is there competition, or how often are you just picking your own people without competition?

THE WITNESS: It's unusual that we would be the only ones interested in a book. I think that happens certainly. We ultimately just don't often know how many people are interested in it. Just the agents kind of tell us what they want to tell us in order to get the best deal they can. So they'll say things like, well, I have interest but we'd like to go with you, or—So it kind of, sometimes it does end up being just a one-on-one negotiation with the agent at that level. We just don't really know. And I'm fine with that because if we want the book, we want the book, I want to get the deal. At that level, I still think there's opportunity for success so I'm happy to engage in those negotiations.

THE COURT: Thank you. Any questions based on my questioning?

MS. BELLSHAW: No, Your Honor. Thank you.

THE COURT: Thank you. Any questions from you, Ms. Rudzin?

MS. RUDZIN: Yes.

RECROSS-EXAMINATION

BY MS. RUDZIN:

Q. Mr. Tart, just so we're clear, you just told the Court that sometimes for lower advance books Viking might be the only one interested. Can that happen with higher advance books, books that go for more than 250 as well?

A. It can, yes.

Q. And just so we're clear, the *Fiona and Jane* example you gave where I think you testified last week that it was low or mid-five-figure advance, do you recall how you acquired that book?

A. It was, I believe, a two-book deal. We bought a collection of short stories and we bought a novel. I can't remember the circumstances of whether or not it was an auction, a best bid, but I know it was a two-book deal.

Q. Do you know whether it was a competitive bid situation?

A. I believe there was.

Q. So it's fair to say there is competition for books that sell below six figures, correct?

A. Yes.

Q. Ms. Bellshaw asked you about the publicity support for book 44. Can you explain the difference between publicity and marketing?

A. Yes, publicity is where we engage with the media to promote the book. The costs with publicity are often around book tours, or travel that might be—we might have to send an author to L.A. or Chicago or wherever for the publicity appointment, but they aren't marketing costs, we're not spending advertising costs on publicity.

Q. So in general, publicity is sort of free marketing versus marketing the company pays for, right?

A. That's the way we think of it.

THE COURT: I'm sorry, I didn't understand that. Can you explain that?

THE WITNESS: Yes.

THE COURT: Free marketing.

THE WITNESS: Yes, publicity is—I'm sorry.

THE COURT: I didn't understand the distinction between free marketing.

THE WITNESS: Okay. So publicity is where we're using the media, partnering with the media to spread the message of the book. We don't pay to get on television shows. We don't pay to get on NPR. We don't pay for review attention, things like that. So we will pay for advertising. We will pay for digital programs, things like that. But we consider those different than publicity. We make a distinction between publicity and marketing. We have a publicity department and we have a marketing department.

THE COURT: I see. Thank you.

MS. RUDZIN: If I could ask that Exhibit 332 be shown to Mr. Tart but not made public, please.

BY MS. RUDZIN:

Q. Mr. Tart, Ms. Bellshaw asked you about this auction and I think you said that you recalled it was a better best auction, correct?

A. Yes.

Q. Just to be clear, Ms. Bellshaw didn't quite understand that your bid was not capped in the second round because there were non-PRH bidders in the first round, right?

MS. BELLSHAW: Objection; leading, Your Honor.

THE COURT: Sustained. Also characterizing the other attorney, I don't think is appropriate.

MS. RUDZIN: Okay. So why don't you tell us about what you told Ms. Bellshaw about how the bidding rule worked in this auction, please?

THE COURT: I think that was clear ultimately. Let's move on.

BY MS. RUDZIN:

Q. Okay. So I'll ask a different question then. If the Random House division and Knopf division had been participating in this auction, what would you have known about their bids, if anything?

A. I most likely wouldn't have known about their bids. Just the Penguin bids.

Q. Would you have known if they were even in the auction?

A. Not necessarily, no.

Q. And finally, Ms. Bellshaw asked you about who you compete with in auctions and noted that Viking doesn't as often lose to non-Big 5 imprints. Who does Viking most often lose to?

A. It's a wide range of imprints around publishing. When I get that information, I really don't see a consistent imprint that I'm losing to.

Q. Do you have a sense of how many books you lose to other Penguin Random House imprints?

A. My feeling is we lose most often to other Penguin Random House imprints.

MS. RUDZIN: Thank you. Nothing further.

THE COURT: Thank you. Any questions, Ms. Bellshaw?

MS. BELLSHAW: Just a few, Your Honor.

THE COURT: All right.

FURTHER REDIRECT EXAMINATION

BY MS. BELLSHAW

Q. Mr. Tart, I think you just said a moment ago that if other Penguin Random House divisions were also bidding on a book, you wouldn't know what their bid was. Did I understand that correctly?

MS. RUDZIN: Objection.

THE WITNESS: Yes, in most circumstances–

THE COURT: I'm sorry. What's the objection?

MS. RUDZIN: He said, "You wouldn't know."

THE COURT: He can answer the question then. Overruled. You may answer the question.

THE WITNESS: In most circumstances, I don't know.

BY MS. BELLSHAW:

Q. But there are circumstances where you are competing in an auction and other Penguin Random House divisions are also competing in the auction where the divisions discuss their bids among one another, correct?

A. Yes, there are times when they're discussed at the division head level. I never have those discussions. I don't talk to the other publishers about it, neither do the editors, but it does happen on the division head level.
Q. And when it does happen at the division head level, you are sometimes made aware of those conversations, correct?
A. Yes.
Q. And sometimes the divisions at Penguin Random House will coordinate their bids when submitting them in an auction, correct?
A. We coordinate our bids on the Penguin Publishing side, but I don't know about that on the Penguin Random House.
Q. Mr. Tart, if you would look at the document that you received this morning marked PX336. Would you mind putting PX336 on the screen.
THE COURT: And that may not be shown to the gallery?
MS. BELLSHAW: If it's not redacted, it may not be shown. Apologies, Your Honor.
THE WITNESS: Is it possible to see it—there it is.
MS. BELLSHAW: Thank you. Mr. Tart, PX336 is an email chain with a top email dated June 14th, 2018, from Georgia Bodnar to you; is that right?
THE WITNESS: Yes.
MS. BELLSHAW: Your Honor, I move to admit PX336.
THE COURT: Any objections?
MS. RUDZIN: No objection, Your Honor.
THE COURT: That will be admitted. (Plaintiff's Exhibit PX336)
BY MS. BELLSHAW:
If you could look at the last email in the chain on PX336, it's an email from Casey Blue James to you and others at Penguin Random House. Do you see that?
A. Yes.
Q. And Ms. James is providing you an update on a bid that the Penguin Publishing Group had submitted for the book referenced here in the email, correct?
A. Yes.
Q. And then in Ms. James' email, she identifies several other bidders for the book referenced in PX336, including Penguin—offers to Penguin Publishing Group?
A. Yes.
Q. Knopf?
A. Yes.
Q. Knopf is a division of Penguin Random House, correct?
A. Yes.
Q. And then also RH. Is it your understanding that that refers to Random House?
A. Yes.
Q. And Ms. James is informing you that Random House has dropped out of the auction?
A. Yes.
Q. And then she writes, "Crown, currently their turn." Crown is also a division of Penguin Random House, correct?
A. Yes.
Q. Ms. James writes, "Basically the agent followed the rules, but PRH is now the main driver of value here. So we're agreeing to move up slowly." Do you see that?
A. I do.
Q. "Crown intends to bid $890,000, up only 5K. When it comes back to us, which should happen right after Crown, Allison suggests we also go up a mere 5K, to $895,000." Did I read that correctly?
A. Yes.
Q. Ms. James goes on, "Then we'll find out from Knopf at what level is comes to them and can continue to gauge." Do you see that?

A. Yes.

Q. So it's fair to say that there are auctions where the divisions of Penguin Random House coordinate the bids that they're submitting for a particular book, correct?

A. It does happen, it happened in this instance.

MS. BELLSHAW: Thank you. No further questions, Your Honor.

THE COURT: All right. Thank you. Thank you, Mr. Tart. I hope you feel better soon. And I appreciate you appearing by video despite being sick. Thank you very much for your testimony.

THE WITNESS: Thank you.

THE COURT: Thank you. So we're going to break for the day. All right. Thank you. So we're going to break for the day. Everybody have a good night. Thank you very much. Mr. Tart, you can step down.

DONALD WEISBERG, CEO, MACMILLAN PUBLISHERS

Macmillan CEO Don Weisberg continually described publishing as a "business of passion" during his testimony. He acknowledged that the sales department is often involved in acquisitions decisions, and that one reason to get approvals for high advances is to get more opinions on the project. "It's a business of gambling," he said. "The more people you have who feel great about a book . . . the better chance you have to succeed."

Like Michael Pietsch at HBG, the government's primary purpose in calling Weisberg was for when he opined on the merger: "I think less competition is going to change the dynamic. . . . The prices for the advances, the type of competition, new auction[s], I think it will have an impact across the board." That expected impact? "I think that the ultimate advances will change over time. My guess is less competition will long-term probably bring the advance levels down. [Based on . . .] Less competition. It's simple as that."

His reasoning, he said on being questioned further, is "just gut." Weisberg described PRH as already "so large at this point that it's intimidating. . . . It means that pretty much in almost every situation if they want to pay enough, they can get any book." Already, "we find them more often than not in pretty much every auction." At the same time, it was not spelled out how he would expect one gigantic, rich competitor that can bid for anything would actually lower advances.

When asked about how it would influence Macmillan's relationship with agents, he went on to speculate, "I think inherently when you have a company the magnitude of what's being proposed, it has to change. If I'm a smaller agent and I'm selling a book and they're one player that's incredibly bigger than everyone else, I think that will have an impact. They will have to change their behavior to deal with that."

While Macmillan does have various thresholds of advances that require executive approvals, those levels vary among divisions and were not declared in open court. Also, "We're not a terribly formal company." Weisberg said that Macmillan competes most often in auctions against PRH, and keeps an eye on Hachette's business, since they are the closest to Macmillan in size. An internal document showed that Macmillan celebrated growing its market share among the Big 5 in 2021 from about 10.4 percent to 12.2 percent. At one point in 2021, prior to HBG's acquisition, "There was a moment when we were fourth, I think" in size among the Big 5, and Weisberg agreed that Macmillan competes with the other major publishers. "And you're going to continue to try to claw every percentage of market share that you can at their expense, right?" S&S attorney Stephen Fishbein asked. "Yes."

Like most executives—with the exception of Jonathan Karp—Weisberg, too, does not consider self-publishing to be a threat. Fishbein brought up Brandon Sanderson's recent Kickstarter success—raising over $40 million to self-publish in print and ebook. Weisberg said it's "rare" and takes a "unique" person to want to coordinate production, distribution, and marketing in addition to writing. "He's an incredibly successful novelist and it's a feat," Weisberg said.

Also like other executives, Weisberg explained the balance in which sometimes books that get high advances work well and sometimes they don't. "When you fail, everybody feels it. When you fail large, everybody feels it a little more." But even if the company doesn't spend a lot on a book, he said, "if everyone in house reads a book and loves it, it becomes a big book." On marketing and promotion, he emphasized, "This is a business of one-to-one word of mouth. It's never been anything else."

Also learned along the way was that, as Fishbein noted in a question, "Macmillan committed to pay Nora Roberts for a multiple book deal over $30 million in that one year, 2020," and more than $10 million in 2021.

TESTIMONY OF DONALD WEISBERG, CEO, MACMILLAN PUBLISHERS

DIRECT EXAMINATION

BY MR. IHAN KIM:

Q. Good morning, Mr. Weisberg.

A. Good morning.

Q. If it helps, you can take off your mask, if that's all right with you.
A. Thank you.
Q. Thank you. Could you state your full name for the record, please?
A. My name is Donald Weisberg.
Q. And what's your current title right now?
A. Current title is chief executive officer of Macmillan Publishers.
Q. And how long have you had that position?
A. Soon to be two years.
Q. Okay. And at a high level, could you describe your responsibilities as CEO of Macmillan Publishers?
A. Yeah, I'm responsible for the Macmillan Publishers English-speaking worldwide. So it would be U.S., North America, England, U.K., South Africa, Australia, India.
Q. And when you say you're responsible for those areas, what do you mean by that responsibility?
A. All of the folks reporting to me, we're responsible for publishing the books in those areas.
Q. Could you describe your prior positions at Macmillan?
A. I was president of the Macmillan Publishing Group U.S., and I assume you're going to ask the responsibility, so I was primarily responsible for two areas, content and sales.
Q. And when you talk about content, what do you mean by that?
A. The books, buying and marketing and packaging the books.
Q. And who did you report to then when you were president of the U.S. part of Macmillan?
A. I reported to John Sargent, who's chief executive officer.
Q. You succeeded Mr. Sargent as chief executive officer?
A. I did.
Q. Could you give us a description of your work history in publishing prior to joining Macmillan, please?
A. Sure. I started in approximately 1974 working in a bookstore in Yonkers, New York. I did pretty much everything you can do in a bookstore. I ended up managing the bookstore.
I left, came to Bantam Books at that time as a telephone sales rep. Bantam became Bantam Doubleday Dell. Bantam Doubleday Dell became Random House. I worked numerous jobs, marketing, publishing, primarily sales. I left in around 2007, took a year off, and then came to Penguin and began working as the head of their children's division. Then Penguin was merged with Random House and I did the same thing for what was then Penguin Random House. I left approximately six, seven years ago, six years ago, to do what I previously described at Macmillan.
Q. Great. And just to back up about some of those roles, when you left Random House, what was your position then?
A. My title was Chief Operating Officer. I don't think I was actually—I had all of the responsibilities that a chief—typical chief officer—chief operating officer has, but that was my title.
Q. And could you give us just a short overview of what your responsibilities were then?
A. I'm sorry, which time? When I left Random House? Pick one.
Q. Yes, when you were Chief Operating Officer at Random House could you give us an overview of those responsibilities?
A. Yeah. When I left?
Q. Yes.
A. I left without a job.
Q. Just during the time you were COO, what were your responsibilities?
A. I had the sales department reporting to me. I had the warehouse reporting to me. I had production reporting to me, inventory, IT. I had most of the functions that a COO has without human resources and legal.
Q. And when you joined Penguin to work in their children's division, who owned Penguin at the time?
A. Who owned it.
Q. Yes?
A. Pearson.

Q. So that was prior to the merger between Penguin and Random House?
A. Correct.
Q. Going back to Macmillan, how would you describe Macmillan's business?
A. I'm sorry, I don't understand the question.
Q. Yeah, sure. So Macmillan Publishers publishes what kinds of books?
A. We publish commercial, nonfiction, fiction, bestsellers, across the spectrum, but primarily commercial.
Q. And does Macmillan have an owner?
A. We're owned by—yes, we're owned by the von Holtzbrinck Group out of Stuttgart.
Q. And who owns the von Holtzbrinck Group?
A. Combined with Stefan von Holtzbrinck and Christiane Schoeller are the two managing partners. They're the owners.
Q. Does Macmillan divide its U.S. publishing business into imprints?
A. Yes.
Q. And could you list those for us, please?
A. Yeah, St. Martin's, Tor, Celadon, Flatiron, Holt, Children's Group, the audio group, and I'm missing one. Farrar, Straus.
Q. About how many books, new books does Macmillan publish in any given year?
A. I use about a thousand as the number.
Q. And when—just to make sure people are clear as far as terms that we might be using, is there a difference between a work and a title when referring to books?
A. Yeah, a book can be published in a number of different formats so we count them both ways. So a typical book will also be a paperback, could be in two different versions of paperback, could be in audio. So a typical work would be four times versus a book once.
Q. So if a book is published in hard cover and paperback in the same year, would that count—are you referring to those as two separate titles but one work?
A. We refer to them both. I always get it mixed up, the actual semantics, but we refer to them both.
Q. Does Macmillan provide any services to other publishers?
A. Yeah, we distribute a number of smaller publishers, one larger one.
Q. And when distributing on behalf of other publishers, what sort of services are involved?
A. We offer them primarily sales—warehousing is the most important. Sales, for the most part, is the other.
Q. Any other services that you're providing in addition to those?
A. Not very much.
Q. I would just like to switch gears now and talk about acquiring books. First off, are you involved in Macmillan's process for acquiring books?
A. I am.
Q. And could you describe your involvement in the process?
A. Yeah, I ultimately approve books over a certain level from an advance perspective.
Q. Okay. And when you were president of Macmillan Trade U.S., your prior position, were you involved in acquiring books then?
A. Yes.
Q. And what was your involvement then?
A. My involvement was, I was involved in all the books but at different level, we give latitude to publishers to act on their own, either or I approve or I would go to John Sargent and John Sargent would go to Stefan von Holtzbrinck and he would approve, depending on the level of advance.
Q. And as far as the criteria you used to determine whether or not your approval was required in either of your positions at Macmillan, what were those criteria?
A. There would be certain levels of dollars.
Q. Okay. And when you talk about dollars, are you talking about the amount of the advance?
A. Yes. Understanding that, as an organization, we are not totally formal. So it changes sometimes

between imprints, it changes sometimes between days of the week. We are fairly loose about that.

Q. So without mentioning any specific numbers as far as those dollar thresholds, could you walk us through the different people involved in approving a potential acquisition for a book just in terms of the steps in the chain?

A. So assuming that a book comes in through an agent, it usually goes to an editor, the editor determines whether they're interested, what their level of passion and level of interest is. They usually take it to an editorial meeting. At that editorial meeting are, in some cases, 50 people. They talk about the book. They decide as a group. Now each imprint is different. So they may do it different ways. And each auction has a life of its own, each—so that also creates differences.

But assuming it's a traditional, it goes through the editorial meeting, then they get the salespeople involved and they give their opinions, and then depending on level of the auction, they go through a process of approvals through the person who reports to me, Jon Yaged, who's the President, and the publisher who reports to him and ultimately at a certain level it gets to me and at a certain level it gets to Stefan.

Q. Why are the salespeople involved in the process?

A. I would say that the salespeople are involved in most of the process. We'd like for the sales, because we'd like to get a sense of what expectations the sales department has in terms of advance—in terms of distribution levels.

Q. And when you're talking about distribution levels, what do you mean by that?

A. What they can get out in the marketplace. But just to back up for a second, when everything works perfectly and that's a portion of the time, when everything works perfectly, then the whole company is behind a book and the earlier you can get as many people involved and passionate about it, the more success you're more likely to have.

Q. Thinking about the rationale for these different levels of approvals you need, why do you have these different approval levels as the amount of the advance goes up?

A. I think some of it is history, some of it's tradition, and some—and a lot of it is—it's a business of gambling and so the more people you have that feel great about a book and feel passionate about where you are from the beginning of that book, the better chance you have to succeed.

Q. And what are the consequences of a book not succeeding at different advance levels?

A. Well, a lot of the books don't succeed. The consequences are all over the place in terms of the level of advance you pay, in terms of the write-off you have, in terms of the energy, as a company, you put behind something that doesn't work and the emotion that goes into that and the disappointment. I mean, every—it's a business of passion and everybody is really invested.

Q. As far as the books with larger advances that you have to approve compared to smaller advances that are approved at lower levels, is there a difference as far as consequences for Macmillan if a book is not successful as you described it?

A. Yes.

Q. And what would those consequences—those differences be?

A. It's—obviously has an impact on the bottom line if you're unearned advances are too large. It's a number of different factors. It's psyche, it's emotion, it's P&L, it's all of the things that go into what we are as a business. So when you fail, everybody feels it. When you fail large, everybody feels it a little more.

Q. So I'd like shift gears again and talk a little bit about the sales and marketing process for books. If I heard you correctly from a few minutes ago, you were part of selling books earlier in your career?

A. Yes.

Q. And you've been involved in marketing of books at different points in your career as well?

A. Yes.

Q. And is overseeing sales and marketing part of your current duties as CEO?

A. Yes.

Q. Can you describe the different ways that Macmillan publicizes and markets its books?

A. It's changing over time. Obviously, on social media and TikTok, all of the different ways you can market a book virally, that's changed a lot in the future. But essentially what we're trying to do is understand from a very early part who the market is, at the time we acquire a book, who the audience is, and then every device possible to find that audience. And as time has gone on, finding them earlier and earlier because presales and demand is a huge factor today, much more so than it is particularly with the ebooks and the marketplace changing. There's no one set of tools for a book. It's getting our customers excited about it. It's getting our consumers excited about it at the earliest possible stage. It's literally trying to move everybody in the direction of passion, of being passionate about a particular book, whether it's fiction or nonfiction, more so on fiction than nonfiction. So the beautiful part about our business is there's no one answer for any book. Every book is unique, every book is individual, and we do our best to treat them as such.

Q. When talking about the toolbox that you have, what are some of the different tools in your toolbox that you use to promote and sell these books?

A. I'm not the greatest person to ask that. I'm not in the day to day anymore. But I mentioned TikTok, which you can't control, because it's—what's the word I'm looking for. It needs to happen on its own naturally. We have all sort of online newsletters. We still do advertising. It's all across the board. Publicity for nonfiction is still the single most important tool you have. So getting an author on a talk show, getting an—we still do author tours. This is the business of one-to-one word of mouth. It's never been anything else and it's still not, just the devices have changed.

Q. Out of your roughly thousand books a year that you publish, how do you decide which books receive what attention from your sales and marketing efforts?

A. Again, it's varied. There's so many different ways. But the read is obviously critical, the author is always—I mean, at the end of the day, we're a company that is only as good as our authors are. And whether it's an author which we believe is somebody we can build over a long career or it's a one shot publicity, I mean, everyone is different. So it's really—it's one of the reasons why it's so difficult to explain.

Q. Do your sales expectations—let me start that question over again. Does your expectations of how well a book will sell determine when you're bidding on the book come into play at all when determining how to devote publicity and marketing efforts once the book is out?

A. Sure, yes.

Q. And how does that come into play?

A. Well, I think if you make a major—we're a certain-sized company and we have—you know, this is a business of risk, so if you make enough big bets and they fail, you're going to have a problem. So we want to make sure we make the right bets, and that's why we try to bring as many people as possible into the process. Sometimes you don't have that luxury, sometimes these things happen real quickly. So if you fail on your big bets that means others are going to have to work to offset that, and that's hard. So you want to make sure that certain some of your big bets, some of your big risks pay off.

Q. And when talking about big bets in the context of advances, how does that—how do those two terms interrelate with each other?

A. Well, since—I want to answer this correctly. I have eight divisions, seven acquiring divisions. So each one of them are making bets simultaneously, bets, taking risks, acquiring content. And so there's a number of them going on simultaneously. Sometimes it's determined by the advance you pay, sometimes it's determined by the passion you have for the books. So we may buy a book for less money but because everybody in house reads it and loves it, it becomes a big book. So it's not always defined by the same criteria.

Q. When trying to make these sort of priorities as far as your sales, marketing and publicity efforts, are there any particular terms you use to identify those titles?

A. I'm sorry, I don't understand the question.

Q. Are there any particular—is there sort of a term that you use to—as a shorthand for identifying the books that you really want to put a priority on?

A. I'm sorry, lead titles, there are lead titles versus—there's not really a term that comes to my mind because each one of the publishers are different. And so, believe it or not, the semantics change even within house. So nothing comes to mind.

Q. But lead titles is a term that's used by Macmillan every now and then?

A. Yeah, because you always have a hierarchy within your list. It happens naturally. It's the first title you present at sales conferences, it's the last title you present at sales conferences, it's the first title from an imprint. They take a life of their own on as they go through the process.

THE COURT: How do you define lead title?

THE WITNESS: I'm sorry.

THE COURT: How would you define lead title?

THE WITNESS: Top of the list. I mean, so if we spend a lot of money on a book and it's a book that everybody loves, it becomes a lead title. But that's not defined by the fact that we might spend a lot of money on it. It might be a title that we bought for not a lot of money but because person after person that has read it has raved about it and it becomes a lead title.

THE COURT: It's the ones that you're marketing–

THE WITNESS: More aggressively.

THE COURT: More aggressively. And how many are lead titles?

THE WITNESS: So I have seven divisions with books, they each have at least one every month that they're focused on. So, but it can change. It depends on the schedule.

BY MR. KIM:

Q. Changing gears a little bit, I'd like to talk about self-publishing. And when trying to acquire a book, does a prospect that an author could self-publish that book factor into your acquisition process at all?

A. Not terribly often. I mean, if at all, because if we're seeing it, then usually the author has decided they want to publish. So primarily not much.

Q. What's your basis for thinking that if an author has decided to not self-publish if you are seeing it at Macmillan?

A. I grew up in the publishing industry. I think most people want to be published. There are authors that have the ability and the capability but self-publishing takes an enormous amount of work. And I have to tell you, from somebody who's never written a book and never published the book, it feels to me like it's an enormous amount of work to write a book. So to want to write a book and do all of the other things that a company does is enormous amount of work. So it takes a unique kind of individual to do it on a grand—on a really great scale.

Q. And when talking about those other things that a publisher like Macmillan provides to an author what are some of those additional services?

A. We warehouse, we ship, we sell, we invoice, we bill, we credit, we do customer service, we manufacture. It's an enormous amount to take on yourself and write a book at the same time. There are certain people in the world who can do everything and they're incredible and more power to them.

Q. And just to be clear, when talking about books with larger advances, let's just say over 100 or $200,000, is self-publishing ever something that factors into how much Macmillan will offer for that book?

A. We offer based on what we think the value of the book is versus—or what we need to pay to have that author on our list. There are many different reasons that go into those decisions. I don't remember self-publishing being part of, personally, my decision, but I can't speak for all other people that are involved.

Q. So you mentioned just a few minutes ago that only a few people really have the ability to not just write the book but to handle all those other tasks. We heard the name Brandon Sanderson be mentioned a few times during the course of this trial. Are you familiar with Brandon Sanderson?

A. I am.

Q. And could you describe him for us?

A. He's an incredibly great selling, terrific science fiction and fantasy writer. He's prolific and he writes many books. We publish him and we publish him on the adult side. And he also has published his own books simultaneous—you know, at the same time. He's one of those people that can do everything.

Q. And does—do you know if Mr. Sanderson publishes with any other publishers other than

Macmillan?

A. He does, off the top of my head—I know he publishes with Penguin Random House in the young adult section.

Q. And the types of books he publishes with Macmillan versus the types of book he publishes with Penguin Random House—

A. He does adult books at Tor, and the young adult on the Random House side at the children's museum.

Q. And just to remind us, Tor is?

A. Tor is our science fiction and fantasy imprint that—at Macmillan. It's also known as Tom Doherty Associates, goes by both names.

Q. Are you familiar with Mr. Sanderson's Kickstarter campaign from earlier this year?

A. Somewhat, yeah.

Q. And as far as the ability of someone to mount a successful self-publishing Kickstarter, that appears to be—how would you describe the rarity of that compared to what other authors might be able to do?

MR. FISHBEIN: Objection; leading.

MR. KIM: I'm happy to rephrase.

THE COURT: Yeah, go ahead.

BY MR. KIM:

Q. Let me ask just first when you described Mr. Sanderson as one—as rare in terms of his ability to take on the tasks involved in self-publishing, why did you describe him that way?

A. It's just rare that somebody has the ability to do everything that he does and write these incredibly successful novels, and it's just—it's a feat.

Q. With those self-published books that Mr. Sanderson is putting into the marketplace, is Macmillan assisting at all with those? Is Macmillan assisting at all with the books that Mr. Sanderson is self-publishing?

A. Not that I'm aware of. I can't speak to the conversations that the author has with the agent, with the editor. But we're not financially involved.

Q. And as far as Mr. Sanderson's just history publishing with Macmillan, could you describe that briefly, please?

THE COURT: I'm sorry, can I just ask, if he's self-mixing are those ebooks or are they actually physical books?

THE WITNESS: No, he's doing it all. He's actually self-publishing ebooks and printing and warehousing and employing people. He's doing the soup to nuts.

THE COURT: But wouldn't he have to engage somebody like Macmillan to do the warehousing?

THE WITNESS: No, he's doing it all himself. That's what makes it so incredible.

THE COURT: Okay. Thank you.

MR. KIM: May I proceed, Your Honor?

THE COURT: Yes.

MR. KIM: Thank you.

BY MR. KIM:

Q. Could you describe briefly Mr. Sanderson's history of publishing with Macmillan?

A. To the best of my ability, he started off as working with Robert Jordan, who is this incredibly successful author of this series called *The Wheel of Time*, and he picked up writing with him mid-stream and then he wrote the books as they went on at the end, and they become enormously successful and then he became an enormously successful writer to himself, and I think he's one of two or three of the best-selling science fiction fantasy writers of today.

Q. Is Mr. Sanderson still publishing with Macmillan?

A. Yes.

Q. Has he published any books with Macmillan recently?

A. Yes.

Q. And is Macmillan planning on—does Macmillan currently have a schedule to publish any upcoming books by Mr. Sanderson?

A. Yes. Hopefully as many as he wants.

Q. Changing gears a little bit again, just like to talk about how Macmillan compares to other publishers. We've heard the term Big 5 used in this courtroom. Are you familiar with that term?

A. Yes.

Q. And do you consider Macmillan to be one of the Big 5 publishers?

A. Yes.

Q. Is there any one publisher Macmillan believes it competes against most often when it comes to acquiring books?

A. Yes.

Q. And who would that be?

A. Penguin Random House.

Q. And any reason why it would be Penguin Random House?

A. They're the largest and they publish across the board so we find them more often than not in pretty much every auction.

Q. Does Macmillan track any sort of measures of market share that it has compared to other publishers?

A. We look at BookScan, which provides data. But we look at it much more casually, I think, than most, it's not necessarily an arbiter of success for us.

Q. And when looking at BookScan information, first off, could you just give us an overview of the type of information that's captured in BookScan?

A. Yeah, it's primarily physical book sales, digital are harder to get. So it's primarily physical, and it measures the data from, I think, somewhere around 80 percent of the retail marketplace. So it's a good indicator of your books getting out there.

Q. When tracking Macmillan's performance, any particular competitors you focus on?

A. Probably the one that we focus most closely on from just a motivational perspective would be Hachette because they're the closest in size to us. So when we get closer, it gets more exciting, not that it, at the end of the day, makes that much of a difference, it's just fun.

Q. If we were to try and rank the Big 5 in terms of order of size, is there a place where you would put Macmillan that order rankling?

A. Today, we would be fifth. There was a moment when we were fourth, I think last year. Macmillan's philosophy for the most part is organic growth. Whereas most of our competition are making acquisitions so they—last year, two of them made acquisitions or at least two of them made acquisitions, so we—we're usually just a little bit below them.

Q. And when talking about being at fourth last year compared to being fifth now, who would have been—would you have traded places essentially between four and five last year to this year?

A. Yeah, that would be Hachette. We had an incredible year last year, not as good a year this year. That's what makes the difference.

Q. And was Hachette involved in any acquisitions last year that also changed its position?

A. Yes, they acquired Workman.

Q. Mr. Weisberg, if we could turn in your binder to a document that's marked PX829. And if we could keep this off the public screens due to the business information that's in here, please. We should have it on your monitor as well, sir. Do you see that? 829?

A. Yep.

Q. Mr. Weisberg, do you know what this document is?

A. I do.

Q. Could you describe it just generally for us.

A. It's a document that we created that tracks key performance indicators throughout our business. We primarily do this for our office in Stuttgart.

Q. And is this—and key performance indicators is sometimes abbreviated KPI?

A. Yeah. And green is good and red isn't.

Q. And this is for the end of the year 2021?

A. Yes.
MR. KIM: Your Honor, the United States moves PX829 into evidence.
THE COURT: Any objection?
MR. FISHBEIN: No objection, Your Honor.
THE COURT: That will be admitted. (Plaintiff's Exhibit PX829 received into evidence.)
BY MR. KIM:
Q. All right. Mr. Weisberg, I would just like to, for present purposes, look on the second page of this document, please, the second of two. Could you let me know when you're there?
A. Yep.
Q. And I don't want to focus on the specific numbers right now, but just the different indicators that are listed on the left-hand side of the page. About a third of the way down, there's a listed category, competitive metrics. Do you see that?
A. Yes.
Q. And then underneath that are different line items, BookScan share of Big 5 revenue for—with these five lines of different members of the Big 5. Do you see those?
A. Yes.
Q. And what are those percentages given trying to track?
A. A sense of where we are in terms of the Big 5. In terms of our major competitors, what market share we have.
Q. And so the percentages that are tracked over in the YTD actual December 2021 column, if we were to add those up, that should equal 100?
A. Yeah, pretty close.
Q. And so this—these metrics are only tracking competition against the Big 5 and not non-Big 5 publishers?
A. Yes.
Q. Then looking further down the page towards the bottom, there's a category for competitors' half-year financials. Do you see that?
A. Yes.
Q. And what are you trying to track there with that information?
A. It's an effort to look at them from a profit perspective, with the best of information we have available. We take it with a grain of salt.
Q. And when talking about them, it's only the Big 5 publisher—the other Big 5 publishers that you're tracking in that category?
A. Yeah, and primarily because they're public companies, we can see what we can see.
Q. Thank you. You can go ahead and put that document aside. All right. Mr. Weisberg, I'd like to turn to the proposed merger between Penguin Random House and Simon & Schuster. First off, when Viacom put Simon & Schuster up for sale, did Macmillan put in a bid to acquire Simon & Schuster?
A. No.
Q. Okay. Thank you. Now, just turning to the implications of the merger and how it might affect Macmillan—well, first I'd like to talk about author advances. Do you believe that competition for acquiring books will be affected by Penguin Random House acquiring Simon & Schuster?
A. I do.
Q. And in what way?
A. I think less competition is going to change the dynamic.
Q. And when you talk about less competition, what are you referring to?
A. Well, two of the major players becoming one.
Q. And when talking about the dynamic that's being changed, what are you referring to there?
A. The prices for the advances, the type of competition, new auction, I think it will have an impact across the board.
Q. And what sort of impacts are you thinking about when talking about those impacts on competition?
A. I think that the ultimate advances will change over time.

Q. And change in what way?
A. My guess is less competition will make the long-term probably bring the advance levels down.
Q. And what's your—what's the reasoning behind your thought that advances will go down?
A. Less competition. It's simple as that.
Q. Is that based on any of your experiences in the publishing industry?
A. No, it's just gut.
Q. Now, keeping in mind we're still in open court, as far as effects on Macmillan's relationships with agents, do you think those relationships might be affected if Penguin Random House combines with Simon & Schuster?
A. I don't know the answer to that regarding our relationships, but the fact that Penguin Random House, Simon & Schuster will be considerably larger as an entity, I imagine the relationships will change. I just don't know how.
Q. And in what other—are there any ways that those relationships could change that you're concerned about?
A. I think inherently when you have a company of the magnitude of what's being proposed, I think inevitably it has to change.
Q. And change in—
A. If I'm a smaller agent and I'm selling a book and there's one player that's incredibly bigger than everybody else, I think—I think that will have an impact. I think they'll have to change their behavior to deal with that.
Q. And how might that change in behavior affect Macmillan?
A. I think it will potentially make it harder for us to acquire books. I don't know this. We're dealing in a speculative world, but that would be my conjecture.
Q. When thinking about the Penguin Random House combination compared to earlier mergers you've been involved in, how do they—are there any ways to compare them in terms of the scale of the companies that are combining?
MR. FISHBEIN: Objection. I'm not sure. Maybe you misspoke. Are you talking about the two numbers or you wanted to compare the price?
MR. KIM: Oh, no. Sorry.
THE COURT: Just rephrase.
MR. KIM: Yes, more than happy to rephrase, Your Honor.
BY MR. KIM:
Q. When thinking about the Penguin Random House/Simon & Schuster combination, is there a way to think about the scale of that combination compared to earlier mergers that you've experienced in the publishing industry?
A. When Penguin Random House merged, they were one of two players in the business. Now, they're the one player in the business and they're merging with the third player in the business. It's so large at this point that it's intimidating.
Q. And as far as it being intimidating, what does that mean as far as how you have to think about prospects going forward?
A. It means that pretty much in almost every situation if they want to pay enough, they can get any book.
Q. Does Macmillan have plans to change how it bids for books if Penguin Random House acquires Simon & Schuster?
A. No, not today.
Q. If Penguin Random House acquires Simon & Schuster, does Macmillan plan on changing the number of books that it acquires?
A. There are no plans today.
MR. KIM: Your Honor, for the public session of Mr. Weisberg's testimony, those are all the questions I have for this time. I'll pass the witness for the public cross.
THE COURT: All right. Thank you.

MR. FISHBEIN: Thank you.

CROSS-EXAMINATION
BY MR. FISHBEIN:

Q. Mr. Weisberg, I'm Stephen Fishbein. I represent ViacomCBS and Simon & Schuster.
A. Nice to meet you.
Q. Nice to meet you. And we've never met before; is that correct?
A. That's correct.
Q. Mr. Weisberg, you mentioned that you were No. 5 within the Big 5, but you'd agree that Macmillan is a strong player in an overall competitive book market, correct?
A. Yes.
Q. And your publishing is very high quality, right?
A. I hope so, yes.
Q. And I'm going to give you a chance to brag a little bit. You mentioned some of your imprints. In fact, you have some of the finest imprints in the industry, isn't that fair?
A. I think so.
Q. So you mentioned Farrar, Straus and Giroux. Isn't that one of the very best literary fiction imprints?
A. Literary fiction and nonfiction.
Q. Okay. Just to give it some concrete indicia, how many Nobel prizes, do you know, have authors from FSG won?
A. I don't have that number off the top of my head.
Q. Would it surprise you if I said it was 25?
A. No.
Q. And you mentioned Flatiron, that's relatively new, right, last 8 years or so?
A. Yes.
Q. And would it surprise you if I said that your website indicates that it's had 72 *New York Times* bestsellers in the last eight years?
A. Yes, probably right.
Q. Probably right? Okay?
A. If it says so on the website, I buy it, yeah.
Q. The one you didn't mention is Oprah Winfrey. Don't you have an affiliation with her?
A. We do.
Q. What is that?
A. She has an imprint within Flatiron.
Q. An imprint within Flatiron. Oprah has a lot of influence in selling books, doesn't she?
A. Yes.
Q. So she has like a book club, right?
A. Yes.
Q. And if she puts the book on the book club, that's a big push for sales, right?
A. Yes.
Q. So having her have an imprint is an attraction to authors; isn't that true?
A. Yes.
Q. So Macmillan's high quality publishing, that's yielded strong financial results for you, fair?
A. Yes.
Q. Would it be fair to say that in the past two years for Macmillan were record breaking years of unprecedented growth and profit?
A. Yes.
Q. And would also be fair to characterize that during the past two years, Macmillan has achieved financial results that are nothing short of spectacular?
A. Yes. I really don't know how—they're pretty good.
Q. I'm not going to hide the ball. You issued a press release back in May, right?

A. Yes.
Q. Those are the terms you used to describe the business, right?
A. Yes.
Q. And you have a very positive outlook for sales and profits in 2022; isn't that fair?
A. Yes, though less so over the last few weeks and months.
Q. Okay. But—
A. But, yes.
Q. Okay. Now, your goal is to grow your market share among—well, let me—the government showed you some figures for your market share within the Big 5. Do you remember that?
A. Yes.
Q. And your goal is to grow that market share within the Big 5, correct?
A. Yes.
Q. And also overall in the market, right?
A. Yes.
Q. And let me show you, if we could, if you could turn back to that exhibit that the government showed you, it's Plaintiff's Exhibit A29. So I think it's in the binder that they showed you. And this is again non-public. And if you could go to the second page, I want to just ask you a couple questions, just make sure I understood it. So this is for the year 2021, your key performance indicators, correct?
A. Yes.
Q. And there's some comparisons to the prior year, right?
A. Yes.
Q. And so there's a column, for example, that says, YTD actual 2020?
A. Yes.
Q. And so is that the comparison between 2021 and 2020?
A. Yes.
Q. And so the government was asking you about the competitive metrics where it shows share of Big 5 revenue among the various Penguin Random House, HarperCollins, Simon & Schuster Hachette, and Macmillan; is that right?
A. Yes.
Q. And so if you look over to the right, there's a column that's called variance to last year. Do you see that?
A. Yes.
Q. And by the way, these figures, these are based on BookScan, right?
A. Correct.
MR. FISHBEIN: And, Your Honor, I've discussed this with Macmillan counsel. So certain things based on BookScan, we're going to go ahead and talk about the figures.
BY MR. FISHBEIN:
Q. So the variant shows what the difference was between 2020 and 2021, right?
A. Yes.
Q. And so there are two companies with negative numbers. Which companies lost market share within the Big 5 between 2020 and 2021?
A. PRH and S&S.
Q. And the others all gained, right?
A. Yes.
Q. If you look further down, it says, "Current EBIT and EBITDA." Do you see that?
A. Yes.
Q. These figures I'm not going to say out loud, Mr. Weisberg, but the year-to-date December 2021, that is your profit for 2021, correct?
A. Yes.
Q. And it's a six-digit number that ends up in a 2, right?
A. Yes.

Q. And then for 2020, it's a five-digit number that ends up in a 4, right? If I'm reading it right.
A. One of us isn't, but—
Q. I just want to make sure I'm looking at the right number. It's in the year-to-date actual 2020 column?
A. Oh, I see what you're saying.
Q. EBITDA is a five-digit number that ends up in a 4, right?
A. Yes.
Q. And then variance to last year, that's the percentage increase in your profits over the prior year, right?
A. Yes.
Q. And that's a number with a decimal that ends .7, correct?
A. Yes.
Q. So that's what you meant by the supremely positive profits, right?
A. Uh-huh, yes.
Q. Now, this issue about growing market share in the Big 5, that's something that was important to Macmillan and featured in various management presentations, right?
A. Yes.
Q. And if I could show you a defense exhibit—And, Your Honor, we have some binders which I will pass up to you and the witness. If you could look at Defense Exhibit 217, it's tab 2.
A. Yes.
Q. And this is a confidential document, although certain figures are not, and I will read those out loud, Your Honor. Do you recognize this, Mr. Weisberg?
A. I do.
Q. What is it?
A. It's a presentation, a monthly executive meeting we have where we present to our senior management.
Q. And when you present to senior management, you try to pick the information that's most relevant for the company, right?
A. Sometimes.
Q. I'm sorry?
A. Sometimes.
Q. Okay. Well, I'll ask you about some of them. Your Honor, the defense offers Defense Exhibit 217?
THE COURT: Any objection?
MR. KIM: No objection.
THE COURT: That will be admitted. (Defendant's Exhibit 217 received into evidence.)
BY MR. FISHBEIN:
Q. Mr. Weisberg, this was a presentation made in October of 2021, correct?
A. Yes.
Q. And if you turn to page 3, do you see the section on Macmillan Market Share?
A. Yes.
Q. And I am I right that you felt it was important that senior management understand that Macmillan in 2021 had grown its market share of the Big 5 from about 10.4 percent to 12.2 percent?
A. Yes.
Q. And that was something that you wanted to let—make sure everybody knew about, right?
A. Yes.
Q. And then if you turn to page 5, there's a summary of sales and market update. Do you see that?
A. Yes.
Q. And the only point under market is "year to date, we have taken approximately 2 percent of market share from the other Big 5 publishers." Do you see that?
A. Yes.
Q. And, again, that was important for your management to know, right?
A. Yes.

Q. And sometimes we use the term Big 5 and it makes it seem like that there's only one entity. But the fact is the Big 5 compete against each other, right?
A. Yes.
Q. And you compete strongly against the other Big 5; is that fair?
A. Yes.
Q. And you're going to continue to try to claw every percentage of market share that you can at their expense, right?
A. Yes.
Q. Now, in order to grow market share, you need to invest in book acquisitions, correct?
A. Yes.
Q. And is it true that you plan to spend more on author advances in the coming years than you do now?
A. I think from a budgeting process, yes. I don't know that's going to turn out to be accurate, but—
Q. Right, we can never know. But when I say plan–
A. Yes.
Q.—what you're projecting in planning your budgets?
A. Sure.
Q. Is that correct?
A. Yes.
Q. Now, one way to grow share is to compete for successful authors who are publishing at other houses, right?
A. Yes.
Q. In other words, hasn't it happened that Macmillan has gone after—
A. Sure.
Q.—or otherwise acquired an author who was with another publishing house?
A. Yes.
Q. And you've done that successfully, right?
A. Yes.
Q. Numerous times?
A. Okay, yes. Off the top of my head, I don't know what numerous times means, but, yes, we have.
Q. Okay. We'll go over one example. Who is Nora Roberts?
A. She's a bestselling commercial fiction writer.
Q. And do you know—
A.—and publisher.
Q. Do you know approximately how many of her books are in print?
A. Hundreds.
Q. I'm sorry?
A. Hundreds.
Q. Hundreds. No, no, I mean, how many units? What's the unit sales?
A. Millions and millions.
Q. Right. Would it surprise you if on your website you said that she has more than 500 million copies of her books in print?
A. Wouldn't surprise me.
Q. Now, she used to be at another publishing house, right?
A. Yes.
Q. Where was that?
A. Penguin Random House.
Q. And she came over while you were at Macmillan, right?
A. That is correct.
Q. And in 2020, as I understand it, Macmillan committed to pay Nora Roberts for a multiple book deal over $30 million in that one year, 2020, correct?
A. Yes, sounds correct.

Q. And then in 2021, you committed to pay her over $10 million?
A. Sounds correct.
Q. So a big author, right?
A. Big author.
Q. Now, I do want to ask you about those thresholds that you mentioned where you get—need approvals for various advance levels. And I understand we're not going to make that public, but in your binder in the front flap—
A. Which? This? I see–
Q. There's—
A. It says A, B, C.
Q. There's a defense exhibit—exactly—408.
MR. FISHBEIN: Your Honor, for identification, it's our Rosetta Stone decoder, which you should have as well, it's Defense Exhibit 408.
THE COURT: Yes.
BY MR. FISHBEIN:
Q. So, Mr. Weisberg, what I'll do is ask you to refer to that instead of saying the number out loud. So for the editors, to what level can they approve without the president or somebody else signing off?
A. Varying degrees less than letter A.
Q. Okay?
A. A or less.
Q. A or less. And does it—so what you're saying is there's no single number among the editors?
A. Different publishers have a little bit different criteria. As I mentioned before, we're not terribly a formal—
Q. Understand.
A.—company so some people have a little more latitude than others.
Q. Okay. But some of them can approve up to letter A?
A. Yes.
Q. Okay. And then what about you said, is it the president or the CEO that's at the next level?
A. President. I'm CEO and John Yaged is the president.
Q. And up to what level can—at what level does the president have to approve?
A. B and a little above.
Q. Okay. And then is there a level that you have to get approval from Germany?
A. C.
Q. That's C.
MR. FISHBEIN: Your Honor, I'd offer Defense Exhibit 408 just for the purpose of having those numbers in the record.
THE COURT: That's fine.
MR. KIM: No objection.
THE COURT: That will be admitted. (Defendant's Exhibit 408 received into evidence.)
BY MR. FISHBEIN:
Q. Why is it that you set that highest level for Germany? What's the point of that?
A. Number one, he would like approval on the money that's going out at that level and that's a negotiated level. Number two, it's prudent to get more people involved because you're making such critical decisions.
Q. Now, Mr. Weisberg, you've achieved the success that we've talked about. You've achieved that success in what you said was competitive market, correct?
A. Yes.
Q. And Macmillan competes, as you said, against the other Big 5, right?
A. Yes.
Q. But they also compete against many of the mid-sized and smaller publishers; isn't that true?
A. Yes.

Q. I'm sorry, I didn't hear that?
A. Yes.
Q. And so to take an example, are you familiar with Scholastic?
A. I am.
Q. Who are they?
A. Scholastic is the largest children's publisher, but also does book fairs, book clubs and educational publishing so they're in a lot of different areas of the children's marketplace.
Q. And are you especially familiar with them because I think you said you were in charge of Penguin's children's division, right?
A. Yes.
Q. And so I want to ask you about Macmillan and currently. Is it true that Macmillan competes with Scholastic regularly currently?
A. I would imagine, yes.
Q. I mean, they're a presence in the marketplace, right?
A. Sure.
Q. And they acquire books for advances above $250,000?
A. Yeah. I don't know that, but, yes, I assume so.
Q. Would you say that Scholastic is a very large player in children's and, in some cases, larger than the Big 5?
A. I don't understand the question.
Q. Let me direct you to your deposition. You have it in back of you, there's a tab.
A. Yep.
Q. And if you could just look at page 83, lines 8 to 11. Do you have it there? Just want to make sure you have your deposition.
A. Yes.
Q. Okay. And if you look on page 83, do you see there was a question, "When I'm referring to the Big 5, I'm referring to the Big 5 that we talked about earlier." And then you said, "Answer: But Scholastic is a very large player in children's, in some cases larger than the Big 5." Do you see that?
A. So when everybody talks about the Big 5—
Q. But let me just ask you, do you see that testimony there?
A. I do.
Q. Did you give that testimony?
A. Yes.
Q. And was that accurate?
A. Yes.
Q. What did you mean by that?
A. The Big 5 tends to talk about adult and children. When you're talking about just children, Scholastic is as big a player as some of the Big 5.
Q. So at least with children, you can arguably say it's the Big 6.
A. Yes.
Q. Now, Macmillan also views Amazon as a competitor, correct?
A. Yes.
Q. And would it be fair to say that Amazon's presence in the market has ebbed and flowed to some degree, it's changed over time?
A. Yes.
Q. So back in 2019, is it correct, a few years ago, that Macmillan viewed Amazon as a formidable competitor for the acquisition of high advance works; is that fair?
A. Define—I don't know that I would say the word "formidable." They were definitely a player, but formidable as in the other Big 5, Big 4, no.
Q. Okay. If you could again look at your deposition, and I'm going to direct you to page 96, and just tell me when you're there.

A. I'm there.

Q. Lines 18 to 23. And you were asked the following question and gave the following answer. "Question: In 2019, Macmillan viewed Amazon as a formidable competitor for the acquisition of high advance works, correct?"

A. I said yes.

Q. "Answer: Yes." You did say that?

A. Yes.

Q. And you thought that was true at the time?

A. Yeah, I think our definitions of the word formidable are probably different but, yes, I did say that.

Q. So in the last couple of years, like in the last year so, have you seen Amazon in high value auctions?

A. Not to my knowledge.

Q. I'm sorry?

A. Not to my knowledge.

Q. Okay. But you're aware that they do have the resources, if they want to, to acquire high level books, right?

A. Absolutely, yes.

Q. And, in fact, you fear that Amazon can again become a formidable competitor at any given moment; isn't that fair?

A. Yes.

Q. And that's because they could expand, right, they could change what they're doing now?

A. Right. Yes.

Q. We talked about self-publishing a little bit. And you mentioned it's challenging to self-publish certain books, right? I think that's what you said, right? You said it's a lot of work?

A. It's a lot of work, yeah.

Q. But let's distinguish between the Brandon Sanderson, which we'll come to a minute. Don't a lot of people self-publish through Amazon?

A. Yes.

Q. And Amazon has a platform where you basically load up what you wrote and then they distribute it for you electronically right?

A. Yes.

Q. As an ebook, right?

A. Yes.

Q. And you would agree with me that's not a lot of work, other than writing a book?

A. It's not a lot of work to do. It may not—to do it right, I think it's a lot of work.

Q. Okay. But the point is, you were talking about warehouses and things of that nature and physical distribution, that doesn't apply if—do you know the name of Amazon's self-publishing platform?

A. Yes. Just not at this time.

Q. Kindle Unlimited or something, or some Kindle?

A. They have a bunch of different imprints.

Q. I may have misspoke. But Amazon has a platform where you can load a book and then get it distributed electronically, right?

A. Yes.

Q. And that doesn't involve warehouses or anything else?

A. No.

Q. To your knowledge, aren't there thousands of people every year that self-publish books that way?

A. Yes.

Q. So now let's talk about—well, let me ask you this. Would you agree that self-publishing is especially attractive for authors who have a built-in following?

A. I think so. Yes.

Q. When I say a built-in following or built-in audience, you mentioned social media, right?

A. Yeah.

Q. And that's changed a lot in the industry recently, hasn't it?
A. Yeah.
Q. In other words, there are personalities who are Internet influencers or have a big TikTok following, right?
A. Sure.
Q. That can be very helpful in selling books?
A. Absolutely.
Q. That's one of the things you look at, right, when you're looking at acquiring an author, right?
A. Yes.
Q. Just wait for me to finish before you answer.
A. Sorry.
Q. And would you say that self-publishing is especially attractive to those people with the social media following?
A. Yes.
Q. And that's because they don't need the marketing publicity apparatus of a major publisher, they can do it themselves through social media?
A. Yes.
Q. And would you agree that those type of authors, meaning the ones with the built-in audience, are also authors who would command a high advance if they went to a traditional publisher like Macmillan or PRH?
A. That's a broad brush. I'm not sure that that's the—totally the answer. But a—yes.
Q. I guess I'd like to get a clean answer from you. Do you agree with that or not? In other words, do you agree that authors with a built-in audience for whom self-publishing is attractive, would you agree that those are the kind of authors that would command a high advance if they went to a traditional pleasure?
A. Define the size of built-in audience.
Q. I'm sorry?
A. Define the size of built-in audience.
Q. Okay. Well, I can—can you look at your deposition at page 202?
A. Yeah. 202.
Q. 202 at the top, lines 2 to 7. And you were asked the following question and gave the following answer. "Those type of authors, like Brendan Sanderson, who have a built-in audience, are also the type of authors that would command a high advance if they went to a traditional publisher like Macmillan or Penguin Random House, correct?" And you said, "Yes, yes."
A. Yes.
Q. Do you see that? And did you understand the question then when you answered it?
A. I think so but it was a very broad answer.
Q. Okay. So all I'm saying is that advances—in other words, one of the things you look at in figuring how much to pay is whether somebody has a social media following like that, right?
A. Yes.
Q. And you're willing to pay more if they have a significant following?
A. Yes.
Q. And those are the same people for whom self-publishing is attractive?
A. Yes.
Q. Now, Mr. Sanderson, I'm not going to go over the whole story again, but I take it that when—for the books he publishes at Macmillan, his advances are over $250,000, right?
A. I think so.
Q. Do you not know? You don't know what his advances are in particular?
A. We publish a lot of different books by Brandon, but I don't know that every one of his—
Q. Some of them are?
A. Some of them, yes.
Q. And I mean, you said that he was highly successful, right?

A. Yes.
Q. Now, do you know how much he raised on Kickstarter in his self-publishing campaign?
A. I know it's a lot. I don't know what the current number is.
Q. Right. Okay. Were you aware that it was in the vicinity of $40 million?
A. Yeah, yes.
Q. Now, let me ask you something. Like two years ago, would you have predicted that Brandon Sanderson could go to Kickstarter and raise $40 million to issue a series of hard copy and ebooks?
A. I don't mean to sound—but I tend not to predict those things, but, no.
Q. Okay. It was kind of surprising?
A. Yes.
Q. Okay. So would you agree that that's an example that the market changes?
A. Yes.
Q. You can't predict everything in book publishing, right?
A. No.
Q. You cannot predict what the next source of titles is going to be, right?
A. Correct.
Q. The government asked you a little bit about marketing and I just have a couple questions about that. You mentioned some methods, like TikTok, newsletters, advertising, and publicity tours, right. Now, do you do that for a range of books?
A. Yes.
Q. Of your books? Is there any like dollar cut-off of advance where you say we're only going to be that above this advance level, we won't do it below?
A. No, not that I'm aware of.
Q. I think you said the factors are the read, which I take it means the impression it makes on you when you read it; is that right?
A. Yes.
Q. And the author, your impression of the author?
A. Yep.
Q. And would another factor be kind of the cultural moment that you're releasing the book into?
A. Could be.
Q. So those are the factors that drive how you get behind a book for marketing?
A Plus more, yes, I'm sure.
Q. Those are among them?
A. But—yeah.
Q. And if there's a low advance book and those factors are there, you're going to get behind it, right?
A. Yes.
Q. And there's no cut-off of $100,000, 2-, 3-, 4-, where you say we're not doing it below that cut-off?
A. No.
THE COURT: Can I just ask you, do those books tend to have higher advances?
THE WITNESS: I'm sorry?
THE COURT: The books that you do get behind for marketing do they tend to have higher advances?
THE WITNESS: I think if you looked at them statistically, yes.
BY MR. FISHBEIN:
Q. Obviously there's plenty with lower advances that you get behind?
A. Yes.
Q. And they're probably also ones with high advances that you don't do as much marketing, for example, if the person has a big social media following. Let me ask this. I'll clarify.
A. Yeah, I'm not—
Q. For TikTok, I think you said you don't do that, right?
A. It's not that we don't do that. But TikTok is a—takes—usually takes a force of its own.
Q. Right.

A. It usually happens because people who are on TikTok love the book and talk to each other.
Q. Right.
A. So it's much more a natural—it's harder to try to create that.
Q. Yeah. In other words, Macmillan doesn't have to spend a lot of money to get notoriety on TikTok if the author already has a big TikTok following; is that fair?
A. That's fair.
Q. Now, you talked about some views on—you talked about some views on the merger. And isn't one of your concerns, Mr. Weisberg, that as a result of the merger, that you will have to compete with a larger, more formidable competitor?
A. Is that a concern? I'm sorry.
Q. Is that a concern of yours?
A. Yes.
Q. But you think you could do it, right?
A. I hope so, yeah.
Q. And specifically, I think—well, let me just ask you. Would you agree that the merged—in your view, the merged company could get better terms with respect to distribution?
A. I believe so, yes.
Q. And what does that mean, better distribution terms?
A. I think a company the size of what's being proposed will try to benefit from its scale with customers, with vendors, yeah.
Q. So let me break that up. By customers, you don't mean the people who read the books, you mean people like Amazon?
A. Correct.
Q. Independent bookstores that distribute them, right?
A. Correct.
Q. So we'll talk about Amazon first. How would scale, how would that advantage, the merged entity, in getting terms with Amazon?
A. I don't know how, I just know that it's possible—it's a conversation.
Q. Well, I think you said it was something you're concerned about, right?
A. Definitely.
Q. So are you concerned that Amazon will favor Penguin Random House Simon & Schuster in terms of promotion and distribution and discoverability?
A. Yes.
Q. And that would be obviously a benefit to the Simon & Schuster Penguin Random House authors who got the benefit of that, right?
A. I would imagine.
Q. And then what about at the independent book retailers. What does it mean that the combined entity scale would give them an advantage with the independent sellers?
A. I think there's inherent advantage if you walk in and you represent 60 percent or 50 percent of their bestselling titles, you can attempt to leverage benefits.
Q. And is some of that leverage, things like getting book placement on shelves—
A. Could be.
Q.—and advertising in a store?
A. Yeah.
Q. And again that would benefit the Simon & Schuster Penguin Random House authors?
A. Potentially, sure.
Q. I'm sorry, you've got to–
A. Yes.
Q. And you're also concerned, aren't you, Mr. Weisberg, that the combined entity would have resources such that they could outbid you in auctions?
A. Yes.

Q. Now, you said, and tell me if I'm misquoting you, I just wrote it down as you were writing, I think with respect to the advances, you said that it was your guess and just your gut that they might go down, right?
A. Yes.
Q. So you don't—you haven't performed any type of quantitative or qualitative analysis to support that, right?
A. No.
Q. And you haven't modeled the impact of the merger to author advances?
A. No.
Q. So really it's just—it's speculation; is that fair?
A. Yes.
Q. And then with respect to the agents, you mentioned that it could have an effect with agents, right, the merger?
A. Sure.
Q. But you don't know what that effect will be?
A. I don't.
Q. I guess if we wanted to get a better idea of that, we could ask the agents, right?
A. Yes.
Q. Now, to the extent that you're guessing or speculating about what might happen with advances, you understand that not all book acquisitions are auctions, right?
A. Correct.
Q. In other words, you can have an exclusive where it's a returning author and you're just negotiating with them, right?
A. Yes.
Q. You can go out and approach an author and just do a project you and them, correct?
A. Yes.
Q. So there can be a single submission where the author or agent just submits to you, right?
A. Could be, yes.
Q. And would you agree with me that to the extent that you're guessing or speculating that advances could go down, you will agree with me that that would not apply to situations like these exclusives where there's not direct head-to-head competition between publishers?
A. I don't know that.
Q. You don't know that?
A. I could agree with you but I don't know that.
Q. Right, because it's all kind of—
A. It's all speculative.
Q. It's all speculative. But to the extent you're speculating, wouldn't you agree that methods of acquisition like direct outreach and bilateral negotiations, you're not speculating that author advances will be impacted one way or the other for those?
A. When I said that I thought author advances would go down, I was talking across the board as a general. I wasn't talking specifically as an auction or as direct solicitation. I was just talking in general.
Q. Could you just, Mr. Weisberg, just take one more look at your deposition, it's page 48. And I'm going to read you the question and answer from line 18 on 48 to line 1 on 49.
A. Sorry, it's taking me a second.
Q. Just tell me when you're there.
A. 48 and 49?
Q. Yeah. So starting on 48, line 18, "Question: So in the methods of acquisition of direct outreach and bilateral negotiations, Macmillan does not speculate that the author advances will be impacted one way or another for those methods of acquisition as a result of the merger between Penguin Random House and Simon & Schuster, correct?" "Answer: Correct."
A. Correct.

Q. Did you give that testimony?
A. Yes.
Q. Was it true?
A. Both things that we just talked about can be true.
Q. Was your testimony–
A. Yes.
MR. FISHBEIN: Your Honor, I would offer that in evidence as well as a prior inconsistent statement under oath.
THE COURT: Any objection?
MR. KIM: No objection, Your Honor.
THE COURT: Okay. That will be admitted. (Plaintiff's Exhibit Deposition Line 18 on 48 to line 1 on 49 received into evidence.)
MR. FISHBEIN: That is all I have for the open section.
THE COURT: Okay. Thank you. Can I just follow up on that last line of questioning?
THE WITNESS: Yes, Your Honor.
THE COURT: If there's an exclusive negotiation, a bilateral negotiation, is the publisher's negotiating position influenced by its perception of whether there's demand for that book from other publishers, and therefore, would you have a higher—be willing to pay more in a bilateral negotiation if there's more competition generally?
THE WITNESS: Yes, I believe that to be the case. I believe that if you're bidding—if I'm bidding directly with somebody and I think is it is going to go on the open market, I might try to preempt getting there by offering more money.
THE COURT: Okay. And so if there's less competition, you would offer less, thereby potentially—
THE WITNESS: I'm not sure that we would think of it in that way. I think we think of it in terms of value of what we think we can sell and what the author is worth and all of the other things that go on with that. But if we're negotiating directly, the objective is to keep it off the marketplace.
THE COURT: I see.
THE WITNESS: Whatever that takes.
THE COURT: Whatever it takes to keep it off the marketplace.
THE WITNESS: Right.
THE COURT: I understand. Thank you.
MR. FISHBEIN: May I, Your Honor?
THE COURT: You may.

FURTHER RECROSS-EXAMINATION

BY MR. FISHBEIN:

Q. So you just referred to that in a direct negotiation. By the way, that's often with a returning author, right? In other words, somebody you've already published?
A. Yeah, that's a big part of it, yeah.
Q. A big part of it?
A. Yeah.
Q. So you're happy—in that scenario, you're generally happy with them, right?
A. Uh-huh.
Q. And they're generally happy with you?
A. Yes.
Q. And isn't what you're really trying to do is reach an agreement based on what the author thinks the value is and what you think the value is?
A. Yes.
Q. I think that's what you just referred to, right?
A. Yeah.
Q. You do things like compare, see what the last book was sold and see how that did and make an

estimate for the new one so you come up with your own value, right?
A. Yes.
Q. Wouldn't the primary driver of what you agree to in that situation be your view of the value of the book?
A. Our value of the book but also a value of the author. The author is an incredibly important part of this.
Q. Right.
A. And if we're negotiating with an author and we want the author long term, we may pay more because we want the author long term.
Q. Right.
A. So I don't think it's any one thing.
Q. Okay. But certainly two important factors are your own view of the value of the book and the author's view of the value of the book?
A. Yes.
MR. FISHBEIN: Thank you.
THE COURT: Thank you. Any redirect?
MR. KIM: Thank you, Your Honor. May I proceed, Your Honor?
THE COURT: You may.
MR. KIM: Thank you.

REDIRECT EXAMINATION

BY MR. KIM:

Q. Mr. Weisberg, when talking about self-publishing, you have authors currently published at Macmillan that have large social media followings?
A. Yes.
Q. Could you give examples of some of those, please?
A. Well, Brandon we talked about. There's a bunch of authors. Louise Penny on the St. Martin's side. A whole bunch of authors.
Q. And they are publishing with you instead of self-publishing, do I have that right?
A. Yes.
Q. When talking about Mr. Sanderson, are there any other authors that Macmillan works with that has similar sort of scale of a self-publishing effort?
A. Not that I'm aware of.
Q. And what makes Mr. Sanderson different in that way?
A. The willingness and the creativity and the brilliance to do it all himself. He's one of a kind.
Q. When talking about the willingness, what are you talking about there?
A. The willingness to actually start a distribution company. It's building an entire business while you're writing multiple books a year.
Q. Skip over and talk about Amazon. Mr. Fishbein had asked you several questions about your view of Amazon in 2019. How has your view changed since 2019 with respect to Amazon as a competitor when it comes to Amazon as a publisher that's acquiring books?
A. They've become much more low key as a publisher, but, keep in mind, Amazon is our biggest customer so for the most part we treat them as our biggest customer, one of our biggest customers.
Q. When you talk about Amazon being more low-key, what do you mean by that?
A. It means I haven't heard their name come up in auctions very often.
Q. And you said, I'm sorry, please?
A. Recently.
Q. Any particular reasons that you think—that you've been able to observe about Amazon's strategy when it comes to books and acquiring books?
A. I think they focused on the self-publishing. They focused on different areas of publishing, but they're not going after, from what I can see, the big authors.

Q. And when talking about big authors, how are you thinking about that sense of scale when we're talking about big?

A. I don't think about it in terms of numbers, but then—for a moment in time, 2019, they seemed like they were going to start to aggressively pursue competition with publishing. They backed off that, or seemingly backed off.

Q. And to go back to BookScan, just—and the relative shares of Macmillan versus other book publishers, first off, as far as BookScan goes, is it just the Big 5 that BookScan measures as far as retail sales?

A. No, I think they measure others. I think we broke it down to that.

Q. And why do you only break it out to the Big 5 as far as your tracking?

A. Because those are the people we tend to compete with on a regular basis, particularly in terms of author acquisition.

Q. But if you wanted to, to track it, those numbers would be available for going further down that list?

A. I think so.

Q. When it comes—jumping—apologies for jumping around a little bit here. When it comes to losing authors to Penguin Random House, have you lost significant authors to Penguin Random House?

A. Yes.

Q. And could you give examples of some of those. We don't need to go into numbers or any contractual deals?

A. The one that comes to mind is Lisa Scottoline.

Q. Do you remember about when that happened?

A. It's got to be about three years ago.

Q. And do you remember which imprint at Penguin Random House she went to?

A. I think it was Putnam.

Q. And do you remember which imprint at Macmillan that she left from?

A. St. Martin's.

MR. KIM: Your Honor, those conclude my questions for the open session. We're happy to start up—transition over to the closed session.

THE COURT: I have some questions.

MR. KIM: Yes.

THE COURT: Okay. So, Mr. Weisberg, there's been talk in this trial about how the anticipated top selling books are only 2 percent of the books that are published and they account for 70 percent of the advances. So I'm kind of interested in the other 98 percent of the books that account for 30 percent of the advances and if there are differences in the way those books are acquired. Can you talk a little bit about those books?

THE WITNESS: The difference is primarily in the financial level. But we're at auctions every day. And if you look at my particular imprints that I'm responsible for at Macmillan, you take Tor, which is the science fiction and fantasy, they're very rarely involved in large auctions. Their whole business is built on building and developing authors. We have an ebook division called Tor.com, which focuses on developing authors from novella to short story to novel to breakout work. So—and if you look at each of the different divisions, they all do it a little bit differently and they compete a little differently. So most of the books we buy are not the big mega-price books. They're most of the time—they're books that we pay a reasonable sum of money that we hope to—it's—specifically it's different on fiction and nonfiction, but using fiction as an example, we buy an author and hopefully we're looking for five books out so that the author grows with us and develops with us. So it's a different business. The fact that we're spending so much time on the 2 percent of the business, because we don't even talk—we have a—you know, backlist part of the business, romance, classics, all of the things that we do on an everyday basis represent a lot of our income.

THE COURT: I see. And so you're saying these are sort of a different set of authors, more ones that you're developing and investing in?

THE WITNESS: Well—or we can develop and invest in an author from a higher level too, but, yes.

THE COURT: But are you discovering them, is that the difference?

THE WITNESS: Discovering is a strong word. I mean, we're investing in them. At the end of the day, as a publisher, all we're about is about our authors. We're a mechanism for the authors to get their words out into the world. And there are lots of just different ways to do it. And fiction is very different than nonfiction. Children's is very different than adult.

THE COURT: And would you make any generalizations about the types of authors who are in the top 2 percent versus the other 98 percent?

THE WITNESS: They're mostly celebrities. As best a generalization as I can make. Going back to what we talked before, they're people with real high platforms, large platforms.

And it's different between, again, different between nonfiction and fiction, because in nonfiction, you're investing in somebody who is going to go out and do research for three years. So you're paying them to actually do the work in advance, whereas a novel, most of the time, you're receiving the novel fully—ready to be edited and ready to be worked with. So it's very different.

THE COURT: I see. And do you think it's less competitive for the other 98 percent of books versus the top 2?

THE WITNESS: No.

THE COURT: No.

THE WITNESS: No, I think in some cases, it's just as competitive. I don't think there's anybody, any editor that you'd meet that doesn't want to find that future story that they worked on. I used an example before, Louise Penny. We're working on Louise Penny's nineteenth book with us. When she started out, nobody necessarily knew who she was and the editor who bought her had that vision of breaking her out into the world and together they did something incredible with a lot of help from a lot of different people.

THE COURT: And when the editor identified her, were there other people competing for her?

THE WITNESS: Sometimes. And sometimes not. Sometimes they just—the other people reject authors. One of the old stories is that *The Hunt for Red October* was rejected by everybody before Naval Institute Press decided to buy it and then it became *The Hunt for Red October*. So there are always stories like that.

THE COURT: Okay. And then, sorry, last question. I've heard testimony in this trial about special terms that some people can negotiate, bonuses and front loading, and there was testimony about like a glam budget for one author. So are those things that you see more commonly in the anticipated top selling books or is that across the entire—

THE WITNESS: That's the top end.

THE COURT: That's top tier. Okay. Thank you. Any questions based on my questions?

MR. KIM: No, Your Honor.

MR. FISHBEIN: I do, Your Honor.

THE COURT: Okay.

FURTHER RECROSS-EXAMINATION

BY MR. FISHBEIN:

Q. Mr. Weisberg, the Judge was just asking some questions and she used the term anticipated top seller. Is that a category that you have in Macmillan?

A. No.

Q. And you were referring to certain, I think you said, mega sellers, did I get that right. Mega-sellers, celebrities?

A. Possibly. Celebrities, I know I said.

Q. Are there books in the 100 to $500,000 advance range that are not celebrities?

A. Sure.

Q. That's not a particularly high advance for Macmillan, is it?

A. No.

Q. So when you're talking to the Judge about–

A. Well, let me take that back. 100 to $500,000 is a large advance, I would take that back.

Q. But that includes books that are not by celebrities?

A. Correct.
Q. That are not the blockbusters that you referred to?
A. Yes.
Q. That could be a first-time author?
A. Could be.
MR. FISHBEIN: Thank you.
MR. KIM: May I follow up, Your Honor?
THE COURT: Yes.

FURTHER REDIRECT EXAMINATION

BY MR. KIM:

Q. Mr. Weisberg, when talking about those books with advances between $100 and $500,000, did those include books where Macmillan has expectations that they're going to sell particularly well?
A. Sure.
Q. And did those have—do those types of books include works that Macmillan thinks are going to be important for their literary or social value?
A. Absolutely. As I said to you before in the situation of Tor, that could be the top of their list.
Q. And are those books that Macmillan will—may identify as ones that it considers lead titles or otherwise put efforts behind them?
A. Could be.
MR. KIM: All right. Thank you. No more questions, Your Honor.
THE COURT: Okay. Thank you. And my last question is, the advances correlate to what you think the book is going to sell so—
THE WITNESS: Not always.
THE COURT: You're paying for—not always.
THE WITNESS: I mean, there are teams—I mean, if we're in a—if we're in an auction and the auction ends earlier, that's great, and sometimes the auction will end and we're paying more for a book that we might not think might benefit us at the time of publication but we think the author is somebody we want to publish forever and we think down the road will be special so we'll spend extra. I mean, it's hard for me to make statements about this that are accurate in every case because every auction is different.
THE COURT: Right, absolutely.
THE WITNESS: And every author is different.
THE COURT: But generally speaking, though, don't you use a P&L—
THE WITNESS: Yeah.
THE COURT:—to project the sales and decide what the advance is going to be?
THE WITNESS: Yeah.
THE COURT: That's what I've been hearing from everybody?
THE WITNESS: The whole concept of P&L is an interesting concept. But generally speaking, yes.
THE COURT: So there could be other factors but expected sales is generally a big part?
THE WITNESS: Yeah.
THE COURT: Okay. Thank you. Any questions based on my questioning?
MR. KIM: No, Your Honor.
MR. FISHBEIN: No, none at all.
THE COURT: Okay. Thank you.

NICHOLAS HILL, PARTNER, BATES WHITE ECONOMIC CONSULTING

The government's antitrust economics expert Dr. Nicholas Hill testified across multiple days, consolidated here into a single presentation (except for his rebuttal of the defense's expert at the very end of the trial). His initial presentation walked everyone through the typical if technical economic analyses of antitrust effects: Herfindahl-Hirschman index, the hypothetical monopsonist test, diversion ratios, second-score auction models, GUPPI analysis and more.

The "I am Spartacus moment" came towards the end his first day on the stand, when the ever-direct Judge Pan said: "So not being a Ph.D. in economics, I don't really understand the intricacies of these models. And I'm wondering if the dispute between the experts is more about the inputs as opposed to the methodology, because if the dispute's about the inputs, I think I understand that. But if the dispute is about the methodology, I feel like I have to understand this better."

The simple translation of the answer is that Hill believes he tested more options than the defense's expert Dr. Edward Snyder, and he maintains that all of his models roughly cohered, while Snyder favors the models that show the most favorable outcome for his clients. None of them are definitive alone, but Hill said that it's worth looking at the same information with many methodologies. "We're trying to get a holistic understanding of what diversion might look like. And we're looking at five different ways of looking at it." Hill also said he used multiple data sets on book deals and auctions—including a "comprehensive" data set of "advances paid for anticipated top sellers and other books from over 60 publishers"—while Snyder focused on a smaller sample of data from literary agents, only for transactions where there was "more or less" a complete account of the auction.

We cited the Judge's question with some levity, but it is telling—since there's good reason to believe that her decision on the case will rest squarely on the assessment of potential harm to authors. Will the two expert opinions cancel each other out, or give Judge Pan more reason to find one credible over the other? Absent firm economic hypotheses, will she be swayed by the historical evidence of events in which head-to-head competition clearly increased the advance? With anecdotal guesses that so far bid advances have tended to increase over time, will she be convinced by the defense's argument that PRHSS would make even more and pay more than ever to win the most attractive properties, or was she persuaded by the DOJ's leading of Markus Dohle to indicate that after the merger, the publisher will be less motivated to buy market share? (By the end of the trial, she did seem more persuaded by a number of Hill's arguments.) And if she finds harm or potential harm, does it potentially affect enough authors to move her to block the deal, or is it so limited as to not merit action?

One early question in the session was why Dr. Hill focused on books acquired for $250,000 or more. Hill argued that this is a market because publishers identify these books—ones with the broadest possible audience—and pay for them accordingly. The number of publishers competing for these Anticipated Top Selling Books is different from the number of publishers who compete for non-ATSB. Plus, ATSB authors almost always go with Big 5 publishers because the biggest publishers can deliver better marketing and distribution, and have a stronger reputation.

When Judge Pan asked, "Doesn't every author want that [better marketing, distribution, and reputation]?" Hill referenced Stephen King's testimony. According to Hill, King said that he'll publish his "bestsellers" with a Big 5 publisher, but when he "has a niche book that he thinks is targeting a hard-boiled crime demographic or a sci-fi or Western demographic, he seeks out a different type of publisher."

Hill said that he used the $250,000 threshold in part because we do at Publisher Marketplace—that's the level of significant and major deals—and because, as multiple publishers including PRH and S&S have testified, the Big 5 often "use $250,000 as an internal approval threshold." According to his research, the books and authors above that range are different, and are published differently, than those below that number. But also, he said, the results don't change much if the threshold is moved somewhat in either direction, either down to $150,000 or up to $350,000. As entered into evidence previously, another key point about ATSB is that "about 85 percent of them never earn out in my data. . . . So for a large swath of authors, the advance is the most significant part of their compensation. So it seemed a reasonable thing to study."

Hill explained his reasoning on how a merged PRHSS would cause advances to go down across the board, since with one fewer player the remaining Big 3 publishers could bid less aggressively and their probability of winning an auction would be higher.

Hill also used internal S&S and PRH emails to assert that the companies compete against each other, including someone at PRH remarking in an email, "Well, editor at S&S continues her role as imprint-wide nemesis."

Hill talked through a number of economics models that suggested PRH and S&S's market share and acquisitions outcomes. If you, like Judge Pan, want to spend some time contemplating some of the key figures and models ("Let me think about that for a second"), here's a bit of Hill's analysis by the numbers.

Lay people may have found it amusing—or ironic?—that publishers were laughed at during the trial for using "fake" acquisitions P&Ls that loosely posit assumptions that often have little correspondence with how things turn out, but they use the formula again and again.

Yet many of the standard economic models deployed in merger analysis are also predicting future outcomes based on elaborate hypotheticals and a modest set of historical inputs.

As indicated in opening arguments, from January 2019 to June 2020, Hill found PRH had 37% of the market share for ATSB. S&S had 12%.

According to defense economic expert Dr. Edward Snyder's model of agency data, there's an average 20% difference in the second and third bids for ATS and all contracts. So if what used to be the third bid becomes the runner up—which determines the advance by being the one to beat—advances could go down 20%.

The Diversion According to Share model, which Hill said is widely used in economics, states that "If an author leaves a publisher, the probability that it picked another publisher is proportional to that publisher's market share." The model showed that 20% of authors lost by PRH went to S&S and 40% of authors S&S lost went to PRH.

A study of competitive acquisitions showed that, when PRH lost a book, 19% of the time it went to S&S. When S&S lost, PRH won 60% of the time.

Looking at actual P&L results for titles, one model predicts between a $44,000 and $60,000, or 4–6% decrease, in advance per book for PRH authors. For S&S, Hill predicts a $105,000–140,000 or 11.5–15% decrease for S&S authors.

In subsequent testimony, Hill said he believes that the proposed mitigating factors—mainly the pledge to keep S&S as an independent bidding entity—are "unlikely to affect the anticompetitive effect of the transaction." Hill's reasons are built on qualitative evidence in the form of internal PRH and S&S emails. First, already "imprints can and do coordinate" before and during a bid. As an example, an email from the president of a PRH imprint said that bidding against another PRH imprint would drive up the price in an auction for themselves. Second, there would be less internal competition if imprints were reorganized to focus on different books—as evidenced by internal emails on the Random House and Crown integration. Also, imprints would be less likely to take an author from another imprint, with one email saying, "Of course we'd never poach another PRH author."

Much of Hill's early testimony centered on non-Big 5 publishers. According to his calculations, those publishers combined acquire 10 percent or less of ATSB. Even the expansion of some non-Big 5 publishers in market share in recent years is canceled out by the decline of others, so collectively their market share is flat. From 2019 to 2021 those publishers' collective market share didn't change, while PRH saw small growth.

When asked by DOJ counsel Ethan Stevenson if other Big 5 companies would expand to compete with PRHSS, Hill said it was "unlikely" that they'd have the "incentive" to expand. Judge Pan asked whether over time those companies would compete more aggressively. "When you realize you're less likely to lose a competition for your book on average . . . you bid a little bit less aggressively than you did prior to the merger," Hill said.

Hill also said that he disagrees with defense expert Snyder's assertion that agents will keep advances from going down. "Agents are a feature in many different markets and they don't have a magic wand,"

Hill said. (The "magic wand" was cited multiple times during the trial.) They "use the leverage created by competition to create better terms." If there's less competition, they can't fix it.

Hill couldn't give specific numbers, but, when analyzing whether Amazon competes for big books, said "I think you can see that Amazon's share in the market for ATSB is," he paused, "not high."

The lengthy Cross-Examination by defense attorney Randy Oppenheimer predominantly poked holes in Hill's models. Oppenheimer asked whether Hill's research found harm among all books, or just those acquired for $250,000 or more ("what you call anticipated top sellers" as he seemed loathe to give that term credence). Just ATSB.

Oppenheimer asked Hill a number of questions about auctions and small press acquisitions, prompting Judge Pan to remind him—three times—that Hill isn't a publishing expert or the best witness to speak to those issues.

Oppenheimer also asked why Big 5 companies acquire more ATSB. Hill said it was because of stronger reputations, that they are better able to bear risk, and they have distribution and marketing that helps appeal to authors. If these companies were simply bigger and buying more books overall, then the data on non-ATSB would look the same as ATSB, he said. Pan asked, "Isn't it possible that they just have the most money?" "Yes," Hill reiterated, "they're better able to bear risk."

Hill once again brought up a PRH editor "saying editor X at Simon & Schuster continues her role as imprint-wide nemesis." He suggested, "When that firm is no longer one of your competitors, I think it's reasonable that your behavior will change," he said.

The defense pointed again to the rough conclusion that Hill's Second Score Auction model predicts total harm of about $29 million. His reply: "Thinking about it in 'this is a very specific and exact prediction of harm' is less useful than thinking of it as 'consistent predictions from the models of harm are an indication that there's a substantial reduction in unilateral competition.'"

Judge Pan tried to get a handle on whether that model is actually predicting the future, or just reflecting the past: "So does your model just talk about the historical data and say, if these were merged, this would have been the harm, or is it predicting future harm?"

Hill said, "It's using the past data to predict the future. It essentially says, here are the market shares, here's how likely it is that one is number one and one is number two. And it makes predictions of harm based on that past data. And then I'm applying it to say, this is my prediction of what would happen in the future."

Based on his study of the data, Dr. Hill said about 50 to 60 percent of the transactions he studied were bilateral negotiations, and the rest—comprising auctions—were "roughly split between some form of best bids and some form of rounds."

Judge Pan asked, "If bilateral negotiations are more common than auctions, why didn't you build a bilateral negotiations model?" Hill explained he tried first price auction and negotiations models, but he didn't have sufficient data. "I tried to build a model that included all of the mechanisms in one grand model and—sadly, for my chances of winning the Nobel Prize, I failed in that endeavor," Hill said.

Defense counsel Oppenheimer again challenged Hill's models and the data input to them. Hill used the minutes of editorial meetings at 12 S&S imprints (out of 38) and 13 PRH imprints (out of about 100) to determine how often one party bids, and if they lost, how often the other was the winner. (Oppenheimer: "This was hard work for you right?" Hill: "It took a long time.") Oppenheimer referred to previous testimony that those minutes themselves are "haphazard" and "slapdash." He also repeatedly questioned, or misunderstood, the point of reading the minutes, asking whether the data tells us the runner-up for an auction, and Hill responding that that wasn't the goal of the analysis.

Oppenheimer also said that, assuming PRH participates in 37 percent of auctions and S&S in 12 percent, it's possible they'd never compete. Later, DOJ lawyer Ethan Stevenson asked Hill about the likelihood of that hypothetical. "I don't think it's likely that Simon & Schuster and Penguin Random would never compete with each other in an auction," Hill said.

Stevenson asked, "Did you reject any models because the harm predicted by the model is too low?" "I did not."

In his re-cross, Oppenheimer asked if it's possible that "the industry may be unmodel-able?" Hill said that there are challenges to modeling it, but the "second price [auction] and GUPPI models are reasonable."

TESTIMONY OF NICHOLAS HILL, PARTNER, BATES WHITE ECONOMIC CONSULTING

DIRECT EXAMINATION

BY MR. ETHAN STEVENSON:

Q. Dr. Hill, what is your academic training?

A. I have a Ph.D. in economics from the University of Warwick.

THE COURT REPORTER: Excuse me. What was the name of the university?

THE WITNESS: Sorry. Johns Hopkins University. Warwick is my undergraduate degree. Apologies.

BY MR. STEVENSON:

Q. What work have you done since obtaining your Ph.D. at Johns Hopkins?

A. After getting my Ph.D., I moved to the Department of Justice's antitrust division, where I worked as a staff economist for seven years. Then I moved to the Federal Trade Commission, to the bureau of economics, and I worked there for two years as a staff economist. Then I returned to the antitrust division for three years as a supervisory economist. And for the past five years, I've been a partner at Bates White Economic Consulting.

Q. At a high level, what were your responsibilities during your time at the antitrust distribution in the FTC?

A. When I was a staff economist, my responsibilities were to work directly on antitrust matters, primarily mergers, your Honor. And then when I returned as a supervisory economist, I supervised other economists who were working on such matters. And in that role, I also interacted frequently with the legal staff.

Q. Did you receive any awards while working for the government?

A. I did.

Q. Which ones?

A. For my work on and Aetna and Humana, I received the attorney general's award of distinguished service.

Q. What type of consulting work do you do with Bates White today?

A. So my practice largely focuses on mergers, but I work on other antitrust matters as well.

Q. Over the course of your time at the government and Bates White, how many mergers have you analyzed, roughly?

A. I don't have an exact number, but it's certainly more than 100.

Q. Have you analyzed mergers in different industries?

A. Yes. I've worked in a wide range of industries. I've worked on chemicals, airlines, healthcare, wireless telecom, wired telecom, defense. I've worked on—I'm not aware of a major industry I have not worked on.

Q. Have you ever published on the subject of merger analysis?

A. Yes, I have.

Q. Have you ever been recognized by a court as an economic expert in litigation?

A. Yes. I've been recognized four times.

Q. Which times?

A. Once in the Tronox matter, once in the Ivonik matter, once in Peabody/Arch and then once in the U.S. Sugar matter in Delaware.

MR. STEVENSON: Your Honor, at this point I would like to offer Dr. Hill as an expert in economics.

THE COURT: Any objection?

MR. OPPENHEIMER: No objection, your Honor.

THE COURT: He will be so qualified. One question: Have you ever testified on behalf of the defendants in an antitrust action?

THE WITNESS: Yes, your Honor. In Tronox and Arch/Peabody, I was on behalf of the FTC. In Ivonik, I was on behalf of the defendants against the FTC. Then in the recent sugar trial in Delaware, I was on behalf of the defendants against the Department of Justice.
THE COURT: Thank you. You may proceed.
MR. STEVENSON: Thank you. Dr. Hill, have you prepared a slide presentation to assist with your testimony today?
THE WITNESS: I have.
MR. STEVENSON: Your Honor, may we publish this slide presentation?
THE COURT: Any objection?
MR. OPPENHEIMER: Your Honor, we have no objection. We have an understanding with counsel that these are being used as part of 703 and 705 as his reliance materials. They're not coming in for the truth of the matter. And where there are exhibits that are to be introduced, they'll be done in the normal course.
THE COURT: All right. Do you agree with that?
MR. STEVENSON: Yes, your Honor. There are figures in the PowerPoint that we will—that I will likely move to admit. But—
THE COURT: But separately?
MR. STEVENSON:—those are separate. Those have exhibit numbers.
THE COURT: So anything that's not specifically moved for the truth will not be admitted for the truth.
MR. STEVENSON: Correct.
THE COURT: Got it.
MR. STEVENSON: We have a public version that we're going to display, but your Honor has a version that I think should be kept under seal in your binder. If you'd like, we can email a copy to chambers, too.
THE COURT: That's okay. Which binder should we be looking at?
MR. STEVENSON: The narrower one or the thinner one.
THE COURT: Okay.
MR. OPPENHEIMER: Sorry. I don't mean to interject, your Honor. Just by way of clarification, our understanding is that none of the demonstratives are coming in. They're just demonstratives. But those exhibits that are moved will be handled in due course.
MR. STEVENSON: Yes. That's correct.
THE COURT: Thank you.
BY MR. STEVENSON:
Q. Dr. Hill, does this slide give an overview of your testimony today?
A. It does, yes.
Q. Did the United States give you a particular assignment with regard to Penguin Random House's proposed acquisition of Simon & Schuster?
A. Yes.
Q. What was that assignment?
A. If we advance one more slide, please, you'll see a summary. My assignment was to evaluate the likely effect of the transaction on competition.
Q. How do you carry out that assignment?
A. So if you advance two more, please. I carried it out by using the merger analysis framework and the horizontal merger guidelines.
Q. At a high level, would you please describe the horizontal merger guidelines analysis—
A. Sure.
Q.—versus the framework?
A. Sure.
Q. Thank you.
A. Your Honor, typically one splits it up into sort of four buckets. One is market definition; one is market shares and concentration; one is competitive effects; and then one is looking at mitigating factors.
Q. Would you please summarize your high-level conclusions about this merger following the merger guidelines framework.

A. Sure. If we could advance one more slide, there's a summary. Your Honor, I think the relevant market here is the acquisition of U.S. rights to anticipated top sellers. I think the merger will substantially increase concentration in the market and result in a highly concentrated market.

I think that the qualitative and quantitative evidence show that the merger is likely to significantly reduce competition. And I think it's unlikely that the mitigating factors will fully mitigate the anticompetitive effects.

Q. Dr. Hill let's first focus on market definition, the first step in your analysis. Staying at a high level, what is the purpose of defining a market for antitrust analysis?

A. Sure. So if we could advance one more than slide, please. So I think, your Honor, the U.S. economy has many products and services. And considering all of those to analyze any particular merger is generally both unnecessary and very challenging. I think of market definition as accomplishing two things: Let's try to find an area where the parties compete with each other substantially and, two, identify all of the reasonable substitutes to the parties' products.

Q. Did you identify an area in which the parties compete significantly?

A. Yes, I did.

Q. What area was that?

A. The purchase of the U.S. rights for anticipated top sellers.

Q. What is an anticipated top seller?

A. So an anticipated top seller is a book that is expected to sell a significant number of copies.

Q. Who is the—who is selling the rights to anticipated top sellers?

A. Authors.

Q. Do you have an example of the type of book you're thinking about?

A. Yeah. I think you've heard testimony on this, your Honor. It's a book written by a celebrity or an important political figure, an established author. It may also be a first-time author who has a particularly strong book.

Q. Who primarily competes with the merging parties to purchase the rights to anticipated top sellers?

A. So the competition is from other publishers, particularly members of the so-called Big 5.

Q. Have you seen evidence that this is where the merging parties and other members of the Big 5 compete significantly?

A. Yes. If we could please advance one more slide. So this slide is a discussion of some of the evidence that's occurred in this trial. Without reading too much detail from the slides, I'll just direct your Honor to the last of the quotes here: For books with advances above a certain level, how frequently does Hachette lose to a non-Big 5 publisher? And the answer is: Quite rarely. And I think these other quotes are also consistent with the idea that there's a group of books for which publishers compete, particularly the Big 5.

Q. Other than publishers, what substitutes for the merging parties do you consider as part of your analysis?

A. I consider self-publishing.

Q. Is self-publishing a reasonable substitute to a publisher for authors of anticipated top sellers?

A. No. I don't believe.

Q. Have you seen any evidence that self-publishing is not a reasonable substitute?

A. Yeah. If we could please advance one more slide. So here again, your Honor, we'll see some testimony on this point. And I'll direct you to the bottom quote to begin with, your Honor: Self-publishing is a different market category, and we don't directly compete with it. And then in the top quote, you can also see an author talking about self-publishing compared to publishers. That doesn't mean there aren't authors who self-publish, but for the majority of authors who are publishing, other publishers are the best alternative to their current publisher.

Q. Collectively, what does the evidence on these two points tell you?

A. So the collective evidence shows, I think, that—your Honor, we talked about identifying an area where the parties meaningfully compete with one another. I think that's these anticipated top sellers. And then we talked about finding reasonable substitutes. I think that the other publishers are the most reasonable substitutes, such that one should include them when analyzing competition. And I think self-publishing is too distant to be included.

Q. To be clear, does the market for anticipated top sellers include all trade books or just anticipated top sellers?

A. It just includes anticipated top sellers.

Q. Is it common to define a market around only a subset of sellers?

A. Yeah. If we could please advance one more slide. This is some language, your Honor, from the hypothetical—from the horizontal merger guidelines. And it's talking about this idea of what are commonly called targeted customers, so the idea that some customers may be vulnerable, but other customers may not be. So in our context, we're thinking of sellers, your Honor. So some sellers could be harmed by a merger when others would not. And the merger guidelines have an example that they use of glass jar makers. If glass jar makers merged, some current customers could potentially switch to other substitutes. But it may be that, for example, baby food manufacturers really prefer having glass compared to some kind of metal and they would not be able to switch. And so this idea is that there may be some customers who are harmed when others are not.

Q. What needs to be true to define a market around only a subset of sellers?

A. So there's two conditions. And you can see them, your Honor, in the second of the two boxes here, the one at the bottom: differential pricing and limited arbitrage.

Q. What is differential pricing?

A. So if you're going to target particular sellers, your Honor, you have to be able to identify them and price to them differently.

Q. Can publishers price differently to authors of anticipated top sellers than other authors?

A. Yes.

Q. Why?

A. The negotiations between the publishers and the authors are an individual negotiation. So they are able to identify and they see either the book proposal or the close-to-finished manuscript. So they're able to identify, does it look like a book—and I believe the witness from Hachette described it as: Is this a book that is going to appeal to a broad audience—I apologize—potentially appeal to a broad audience?

Q. You mentioned arbitrage. What is that?

A. So arbitrage, if you're attempting to change—if you're attempting to target certain sellers, arbitrage would be the ability of the sellers to avoid that targeting by selling to a third party who would then sell to the publishers.

Q. Is arbitrage feasible in this market?

A. I don't believe so, your Honor.

Q. Why not?

A. So if an author were to sell the book to a third party, to then sell to a publisher, the publishers will still observe either the book proposal or the manuscript. I think the best case would be that—I mean, even in the best case, if they were successful, then it would be classified as not being an anticipated top seller and might earn a lower advance amount. So I don't think arbitrage is realistic here.

Q. Stepping back, does the market for anticipated top sellers meet the horizontal merger guidelines criteria for defining a market around a targeted seller group?

A. Yes. I think publishers can identify this group of authors, and authors can't easily avoid that targeting through arbitrage.

Q. Why did you define a market around only a subset of sellers to analyze this merger?

A. So authors of anticipated top sellers have different preferences for publishers and for self-publishing than other authors. And the competitive conditions that they face also are different.

Q. What is different about the preferences and competitive conditions for anticipated top sellers?

A. So authors of anticipated top sellers, these books that are aimed at a broad market, have more of a taste for strong distribution, strong marketing and a strong reputation. And similarly, on the supply side, there's only—the number of publishers that regularly compete to purchase these books is different for authors of anticipated top sellers than for other authors.

THE COURT: Don't all authors want all of those things, reputation, distribution, marketing?

THE WITNESS: Yes. So I think what I found helpful in this case was the testimony from Mr. King, who said when he's got one of his bestsellers, he is taking that to his Big 5 publisher who publishes it. And then when he has a niche book that he thinks is targeting a hard-boiled crime demographic or a sci-fi or Western demographic, he seeks out a different type of publisher. So I think there are—you know, these books by—if you're a major political figure and you're having your 15 minutes of fame, you want your book everywhere and get it sold. And you may have different preferences than authors who are doing different things. So I agree with you in general that they—everyone would like these things. But the intensity of the taste may vary.

BY MR. STEVENSON:

Q. How did you define an anticipated top seller?

A. So if we advance one more slide, I think we'll see something that's helpful here. So, your Honor, there's this idea of these types of books. And then the challenge for the antitrust analysis was: How are we going to find them in the data so we can perform analysis on them? And I defined them as books that receive an advance of $250,000 or more.

Q. Why did you use an advance threshold to—as the defining characteristic of an anticipated top seller?

A. So advances, as I believe you've heard, your Honor, are correlated with expected sales. And so this was a way of trying to get at what books are there that are expected to hit this broad market and sell a lot of books.

Q. How did you arrive at the $250,000 threshold in particular?

A. So there were a number of things that led me to $250,000, and they're displayed here on the slide. So one is Publishers Marketplace in their deal reports say if the deal has an advance of $250,000 or above, it's a significant or major deal. And then there are publishers, including the parties and some others, who use $250,000 as an internal approval threshold.

So, your Honor, for books above this level, an additional level of review is necessary.

Q. Are any of your opinions in this case sensitive to the exact threshold you used to define anticipated top seller?

A. No. So, your Honor, as we go through, you'll see that I've repeated many of my analyses for other thresholds to see if a small change away from $250,000 makes a significant difference. And the answer is no.

Q. Did you develop any quantitative evidence showing that authors of anticipated top sellers have different preferences than other authors?

A. Yes.

Q. What evidence did you develop?

A. So if we could advance one more slide, please.

Your Honor, here, these are some data looking at the share of books for authors of anticipated top sellers on the left and non-anticipated top sellers on the right. And one thing that immediately jumps out here is for the anticipated top sellers, the non-Big 5 are about 10—

MR. OPPENHEIMER: Your Honor, I believe this may be confidential.

THE COURT: Is that right?

MR. OPPENHEIMER: Can you take it down?

THE COURT: Let's turn it off while they discuss. I'll give you guys a moment to confer. Do you want to confer?

(Counsel confer privately.)

MR. OPPENHEIMER: May I make a suggestion, your Honor? May we keep this off the public slides and continue to display to the Court and we can resolve it? There may be a miscommunication involved. I'm not sure. Our records indicate it's confidential.

THE COURT: How long is it going to take you to resolve that?

MR. STEVENSON: I understood we met and conferred on this last night, and it was decided that the public versions of these slides were not confidential.

MR. OPPENHEIMER: May I ask for 30 seconds?

THE COURT: Yes.

MR. OPPENHEIMER: Thank you, your Honor.

(Counsel confer privately.)

MR. OPPENHEIMER: Your Honor, my apologies for the delay. It looks like that is the public version. My apologies.

THE COURT: Thank you. So we can display those.

THE WITNESS: Yes. So—and I will be careful about names, given the confidentiality.

So, your Honor, if we look on the left at anticipated top sellers, you can see the non-Big 5 are about 10 percent. On the right for non-anticipated top sellers, the non-Big 5 publishers are about 45 percent.

And you can also see significant differences for the parties, particularly for Penguin Random House. And in general, the Big 5 publishers are significantly larger for anticipated top sellers than for non-anticipated top sellers. So the authors of anticipated top sellers are making different choices than other authors.

MR. STEVENSON: Your Honor, the figure on this slide is a re-creation of PX 0963. And I move to admit PX 0963.

THE COURT: Any objection?

MR. OPPENHEIMER: No, your Honor.

THE COURT: That will be admitted. (Whereupon, Plaintiff's Exhibit No. 0963 was entered into evidence.)

BY MR. STEVENSON:

Q. Dr. Hill, why in your opinion do authors of anticipated top sellers select Big 5 publishers more frequently than other authors?

A. So I think it's for the advantages I listed earlier: for marketing, distribution and reputation.

Q. Did you prepare any evidence analyzing the importance of any of those factors?

A. I did.

Q. What evidence did you prepare?

A. We'll get to some of this in the course of the presentation. But there's one slide here that—if we could advance one more slide, please.

This, your Honor, is a look at marketing spend. This is from actual P&Ls, so actual spend on book titles. On the far left, we have zero to $250,000.

THE COURT: I'm sorry. When you say P&Ls, do you mean the P&Ls that they create before they bid or is this a different P&L?

THE WITNESS: These are actual results, not pre-bidding. And so this is what actually happened, your Honor.

THE COURT: Thank you.

THE WITNESS: On the left, we have the bucket for zero to $250,000. And then we have three other buckets, ranging up to $1 million, so three slices of anticipated top sellers. And you can see that the marketing spend for anticipated top sellers is higher than for non-anticipated top sellers.

MR. STEVENSON: Your Honor, this figure is a re-creation of PX 0972. I move to admit PX 0972.

THE COURT: Any objection?

MR. OPPENHEIMER: No objection.

THE COURT: That will be admitted. (Whereupon, Plaintiff's Exhibit No. 0972 was entered into evidence.)

BY MR. STEVENSON:

Q. Dr. Hill, have you had the opportunity to review the reports of Defendants' expert Dr. Edward Snyder in this case?

A. I have.

Q. What is your understanding of Dr. Snyder's view of your $250,000 threshold?

A. He believes it's arbitrary, is my understanding.

Q. Do you agree?

A. I don't.

Q. Why not?

A. So I think, your Honor, there's a reasonable basis for using this particular cutoff. If we look at the results, as we've just seen, the cutoff seems to identify a group of authors who have different preferences. So I think there's a reasonable basis for using it for those reasons.

But it's also true that if we change the threshold by a significant amount, so if we move it down or up a little bit, we get to substantively the same conclusions.

So I think the issue is perhaps not a particularly significant one. This particular cutoff is identifying a different group of authors, and the results don't materially change if you move a little bit up or down from this threshold.

THE COURT: So aren't you saying that the cutoff may be arbitrary, but it doesn't matter? At $250,000, that number could be arbitrary, but that doesn't matter.

THE WITNESS: I think "arbitrary" is too strong just in the sense, your Honor, that there were—in the industry, people do think of $250,000 as a cutoff. Different publishers have different cutoffs. So I'm not saying every publisher has it.

But Publishers Marketplace does use this particular cutoff. The parties use this cutoff.

So I think you could say: Is it absolutely 100 percent certain this is the threshold? The answer is no. Some anticipated top sellers are in our market, but they're not—or some books are in our market, but they're probably not anticipated top sellers, and vice versa. But the threshold is identifying a group of books and authors that are different than other authors. So I don't know if that helps.

THE COURT: I think so. Thank you.

BY MR. STEVENSON:

Q. Dr. Hill, now that we have identified your candidate market, I would like to take a step back and ask some basic questions about it. How big is the market for anticipated top sellers?

A. It's on the order of a billion dollars a year in commerce.

Q. Relative to your past experience analyzing mergers, how substantial a market is that?

A. It's a significantly sized market. I've worked on smaller cases and I've worked on larger ones.

Q. How much of publishers' advance spending goes towards anticipated top sellers?

A. So across all of the data that I have available, your Honor, it's about 70 percent of spending on anticipated—of advance spending is on anticipated top sellers.

Q. You've referenced advances a couple times. Why did you focus your analysis on advances?

A. Sure. So, your Honor, for anticipated top sellers, about 85 percent of them never earn out in my data. So that, as you know, means they didn't—royalties don't fully cover the advance.

So for a large swath of authors, the advance is the most significant part of their compensation. So it seemed a reasonable thing to study.

Q. How, if at all, does earning out an advance relate to the profitability of a particular title?

A. So a title can be profitable, your Honor, without the advance being earned out.

Q. Now I would like to ask a couple questions about the next step in your analysis. After identifying a candidate market—or after identifying the candidate market for this merger, did you do anything to determine that that market was properly defined for antitrust analysis?

A. Yes, I did.

Q. What did you do?

A. So I tested the market using the hypothetical Monopsonist test.

Q. At a high level, what is the hypothetical Monopsonist?

A. So, your Honor, the hypothetical Monopsonist test is a way of testing: Is the market too narrowly defined? Have we excluded from the market important substitutes from the perspective of authors?

Q. Again, what substitutes for the merging parties does your market for anticipated top sellers include?

A. So it includes all other publishers.

Q. Would you please remind us what substitutes it does not include?

A. It doesn't include self-publishing.

Q. Would you please explain to the Court how the hypothetical Monopsonist test works in this context?

A. Sure. So the idea, your Honor, is today we have competition among publishers for authors of anticipated top sellers. The test essentially asks: If I were to eliminate all of that competition, would advances increase by a significant amount? So we're in a sense testing: Is the competition today between publishers valuable? And we mean "valuable" in a very specific way. We mean: Would its elimination lead to worse outcomes for authors?

THE COURT: So "decrease." You said "increase."

THE WITNESS: I apologize, your Honor. Yes. Decrease.

BY MR. STEVENSON:

Q. Just to be clear, who is the hypothetical Monopsonist in in context?

A. So the hypothetical Monopsonist is the combination of all publishers. So everybody who's included in the market has now been Monopsonized, and they are the only publisher—the only owner of publishers.

Q. Why might the hypothetical Monopsonist not lower advances for one of the merging parties?

A. So one way that could happen, your Honor, is let's consider authors at Penguin Random House. So suppose that there's a Monopsonist of all publishers and it decides to lower advances at Penguin Random House. And if many authors—some authors at Penguin Random House will be unhappy. They're getting lower advances. Things are not as good as they were. Some of them will seek a new solution for their books.

If many of those authors would switch to self-publishing, which is outside the market, then the Monopsonist would lose those books. If many of those authors say: You know, I can't get a good deal with Penguin; I'm going to switch to Macmillan or Simon & Schuster, then most of them are switching inside the market and the Monopsonist is not really losing them; they're just switching to another publisher controlled by the Monopsonist.

So really the test is just asking: Are a lot of these authors going to leave and go to self-publishing? And if the answer is yes, then it's not a market. If the answer is no, then it is a market. So we're really trying to test how serious a constraint is self-publishing compared to other publishers.

THE COURT: Can I ask a question?

THE WITNESS: Sure.

THE COURT: Wouldn't this test hold true for all of the books? Like why does this test your market, which talks about books of $250,000 or more in terms of advance?

THE WITNESS: Yes, your Honor. You can also implement the test for all the books and ask the question for all authors: Is self-publishing not a sufficient substitute? So here, I've defined this group of anticipated top sellers because competitive conditions for them look different. So I want to analyze them separately. I'm going to test for them: Would those authors switch to self-publishing?

But I could equally—and in my reports, I do, your Honor—test: How about for all books? Would it also be the case that all authors don't have a strong taste for self-publishing and prefer publishers?

THE COURT: I see. So this tests whether the market you've chosen passes the Monopsonist test, but it doesn't necessarily validate your demarcation point at $250,000 or more?

THE WITNESS: That's fair, your Honor. What we're really testing here is, does this market—you know, remember, I said there are these two parts. Where do the parties compete significantly? And who should be in there competing with them when we analyze it?

The hypothetical Monopsonist test is addressing the second issue. It's saying: How many—should we include self-publishing in addition to all other publishers as significant competitors?

THE COURT: Thank you.

BY MR. STEVENSON:

Q. What type of evidence do you consider to assess whether self-publishing is a reasonable substitute for authors of anticipated top sellers?

A. So I looked at both quantitative and qualitative evidence about whether it's likely that authors would switch in large numbers to self-publishing.

Q. What quantitative analysis did you do?

A. I implemented the hypothetical Monopsonist test using what is known as the aggregate diversion ratio methodology.

Q. Excuse me. Before we move too far, you mentioned a term that I think we'll hear more about this afternoon or tomorrow, and that's diversion ratio. What is that?

A. So, your Honor, a diversion ratio essentially measures if one publisher, let's say Penguin Random House, were to lower advances and some authors were to leave, the diversion ratio from Penguin Random House to Simon & Schuster measures what proportion of those authors would switch to Simon & Schuster.

Similarly, you could do a diversion ratio if Penguin Random House lowers advances, what proportion of authors switch to publishers and what proportion switch to self-publishing.

Q. What is the aggregate diversion ratio methodology?

A. So if we could advance one more slide, please. So the aggregate diversion ratio methodology is a way of implementing the hypothetical Monopsonist test. It's part of an approach known as critical loss methods. And in these methods, your Honor, I think of there as being three steps.

So the first you can see in the red box here. We ask: How much switching to self-publishing would be necessary for the hypothetical Monopsonist to not decrease his advances—not decrease advances significantly? So that's Step 1, the critical diversion.

And then we're going to ask: What's the actual diversion? If this happened, if Penguin Random House lowered its advances, how much switching to self-publishing would there actually be?

And then the third step is we put them together. We say: If the actual diversion is less than the critical diversion, then the market is properly defined. So self-publishing is not a significant enough substitute to include in the market.

Q. How did you calculate the critical diversion?

A. So the critical diversion is collected using two inputs. One is the size of the decrease in advances. And here, I used 10 percent. And then the other input is a variable profit margin for the hypothetical Monopsonist.

Q. Why do you use the variable profit margin for the hypothetical Monopsonist?

A. That's a measure, your Honor, of how painful it is for the Monopsonist to lose a sale. So we're going to ask: How many sales would it lose and how profitable—how painful is that from a profit perspective?

Q. Let's go to the actual diversion. How did you calculate that?

A. So I did it two ways. Here, I did it, your Honor, using data on sales revenue for publishing and self-publishing. And then I also did it using win-loss data.

Q. How were you able to calculate a diversion ratio from sales data?

A. So here, your Honor, I was assuming that diversion would be proportional to sales. So I calculated all the sales for—all the revenue from publishing and all the revenue from self-publishing.

And I asked the question: If someone left Penguin Random House, they would switch in proportion to that. So if 90 percent of the revenue excluding Penguin Random House is from publishers and 10 percent is from self-publishing, then an author has a 90 percent chance of going to publishing rather than self-publishing.

Q. You mentioned win-loss data. And what are win-loss data?

A. So win-loss data—in the ordinary course of events, a firm may track when it loses an opportunity or wins one, your Honor. I think you heard Mr. Pietsch from Hachette talk about this, that Hachette tracks losses above a certain threshold.

So win-loss data here, you can use it to say: When Penguin Random House loses an author, how often does that author switch to publishers and how often does that author switch to self-publishing?

Q. How did your actual diversions compare to the critical diversion?

A. So if we could please advance one more slide. This table, your Honor, is summarizing our results. So we have one row from Penguin Random House and one row for Simon & Schuster. So in the Penguin Random House row, I'm asking: If Penguin Random House lowered advances by 10 percent, what is its critical diversion?

That's in the red column. And you can see, your Honor, it's about 75 percent.

So if 75 percent of the authors it lost went to self-publishing, that it wouldn't be profitable for it to decrease advances by that much. And when I say "it," I mean the hypothetical Monopsonist.

The first blue column is actual diversion using sales revenue. So you can see, your Honor, it's about 10 percent. And then in the second of the blue columns, we have the win-loss data. How often in Penguin Random House's win-loss data when it loses an author does that author switch to self-publishing? And the answer is about 1 percent of the time.

So in this case, both of the actual diversions are significantly below the critical diversion. And so the market is passing the hypothetical Monopsonist test.

And then the second row of the table is doing the same thing, except it's asking: If the hypothetical Monopsonist lowered advances for Simon & Schuster by 10 percent, would that increase the profits of the hypothetical Monopsonist? And you can see, your Honor, that there, too, the critical diversion is about 75 percent and the actual diversions are roughly 10 percent and 1 percent. So it again passes—comfortably passes the hypothetical Monopsonist test.

Q. What are the implications of passing the hypothetical Monopsonist test?

A. So the implications here are that the market is not too narrowly defined.

As you put it earlier, your Honor, we've tested whether we're including the right set of substitutes.

MR. STEVENSON: Your Honor, this figure with, I admit, a few cosmetic changes is a re-creation of PX 0969. I move to admit PX 0969.

THE COURT: Any objection?

MR. OPPENHEIMER: No objection, your Honor.

THE COURT: That will be admitted. (Whereupon, Plaintiff's Exhibit No. 0969 was entered into evidence.)

BY MR. STEVENSON:

Q. What is your understanding of Dr. Snyder's arguments regarding your hypothetical Monopsonist test?

A. Dr. Snyder argued, your Honor, that some publishers have never wanted an anticipated top seller, and they should be considered outside the market with the self-publishing. So when I'm testing the market, I should say: How much diversion would there be from publishers who ever won an anticipated top seller to publishers who have never published one and to self-publishing? So he wanted to expand the actual diversion by looking at diversion to publishers who have never presently won an anticipated top seller.

Q. Did you agree with that argument?

A. I don't.

Q. Why not?

A. So I think the market here includes all publishers. I'm thinking about all publishers competing with the parties.

But just to check, using Dr. Snyder's proposed approach, I reran the hypothetical Monopsonist test in my reply report. And when I include publishers who are not—who have never won an anticipated top seller, the results are the same. The market passes the hypothetical Monopsonist test.

Q. Before we move on, would you please summarize your conclusions regarding market definition in your analysis of this merger.

A. Sure. My conclusions are that there is a market for anticipated top sellers and that it is properly defined. It includes as alternatives all the publishers, including the parties.

Q. After concluding that the market for anticipated top sellers was properly defined, what was the next step in your analysis of this merger?

A. So, your Honor, having calculated—having identified a market and defined it, the next step is to calculate market shares and to calculate concentration in that market.

Q. Let's start by focusing on market shares. What is the purpose of calculating market shares?

A. So market shares, your Honor, can give an indication of the competitive significance of firms in the market.

Q. How did you calculate market shares in this case?

A. I used a data set of advances paid for anticipated top sellers and other books from over 60 publishers and I collected that all together and then I calculated market shares based on the number of titles won by each publisher for anticipated top sellers.

Q. How comprehensive are the data that you used?

A. I believe it to be comprehensive. I'm not aware of any missing anticipated top sellers.

Q. How does this data compare to—

THE COURT: I'm sorry. Over what period of time was that?

THE WITNESS: So, your Honor, it goes from January 2019 to June 2021. In the reply report, there's some extension of it to the end of 2021. But the data we're going to talk about today are focused on January 2019 to June 2021.

THE COURT: Thank you.

BY MR. STEVENSON:

Q. How does this data compare to data sets you've used to calculate market shares in other matters?

A. Favorably. It's a comprehensive data set. And it's what I would call contemporaneous, your Honor, so these are recently concluded situations in which a book was acquired. In some products or markets, you may have a firm that won a contract many, many years before; and so they still have significant shares, but they're not today actively competing. In some defense technology areas, that can be the case.

Q. Can you please share the results of your market share calculations with us?

A. Sure. If we could please advance one more slide. So again, your Honor, I'm trying to be careful here about not saying anything that'll get me into hot water in confidentiality.

If we look at the—this is a measure of the market shares and the market for anticipated top sellers. If we look on the far left, we can see the combined market share for Penguin Random House and Simon & Schuster. You can see Penguin Random House's share in blue and Simon & Schuster's share in green. And then you can see after that bars representing the other three Big 5 publishers. Then you can see five bars for some non-Big 5 publishers. And then the gray bar at the end, your Honor, represents all other publishers.

MR. STEVENSON: Your Honor, this figure is a re-creation of PX 0959. I move to admit PX 0959.

THE COURT: Any objection?

MR. OPPENHEIMER: No objection.

THE COURT: That will be admitted. (Whereupon, Plaintiff's Exhibit No. 0959 was entered into evidence.)

BY MR. STEVENSON:

Q. Dr. Hill, did you prepare a detailed table of your market share calculations?

A. I did.

Q. And—

A. If we—

Q. Go ahead.

A. I apologize.

Q. Please share that with us.

A. Yes. If we could please advance one more slide. Here is just a summary, your Honor, of the market shares on the previous slide, if you want to have exact numbers. But the—all the non-Big 5 publishers are being combined into one at the bottom.

Q. For the benefit of the record, what are the shares of Penguin Random House and Simon & Schuster?

A. So for Penguin Random House it's 37 percent. For Simon & Schuster, it's 12 percent.

Q. Did you perform any alternative market share calculations?

A. I did. If we advance one more slide. So, your Honor, here we're looking at market shares for different thresholds. So the market shares are displayed here as a vertical bar. You can see the color coding identifies each group of publishers, with purple again being all the non-Big 5 publishers.

The yellow is highlighting the cutoff of $250,000, your Honor. This is my definition of an anticipated top seller.

And then I also look at market shares with a threshold below that of $150,000, one above it of $350,000, then $500,000 and then $1 million.

What you can see, your Honor, is that by and large the market shares are fairly stable across these thresholds. The share of the non-Big 5 shrinks a little bit as the threshold increases. But by and large, I would say that the market shares look pretty similar across this.

MR. STEVENSON: Your Honor, this figure is a re-creation of PX 0960. I move to admit PX 0960.

THE COURT: Any objection?

MR. OPPENHEIMER: No objection.

THE COURT: That'll be admitted. (Whereupon, Plaintiff's Exhibit No. 0960 was entered into evidence.)

BY MR. STEVENSON:

Q. Let's switch our focus to market concentration. What is the purpose of market concentration—or measuring market concentration?

A. So market concentration can give an initial read on the likely competitive effects of a transaction. And here is some language from the merger guidelines talking about this in the first box, your Honor. And typically in looking at market concentration, one looks at two things: so the change in concentration that may result from a merger and then the level of concentration post-merger.

Q. How did you measure concentration in this case?

A. I used a standard antitrust measure known as the Herfindahl-Hirschman index. But it's very common to refer to this as the HHI for brevity.

Q. What is the HHI?

A. So to calculate the HHI, you square the share of each participant in the market and then you add up each of those squares. And that total number is the value of the HHI. So if there's a single firm in the industry, your Honor, it will have 100 percent market share. When I square that, I'll get 10,000. So that's the maximum value for the HHI. If there's so many firms in the market that they all have shares that are close to zero, and I square all those zeroes and add them up, I get zero. So the scale runs from zero to 10,000. The cutoff, according to the horizontal merger guidelines for highly concentrated, is 2500.

Q. So I'd like to follow up on that point. Are there certain HHI values that raise concern about harm to authors?

A. Yes. So more generally, a transaction—the language in the horizontal merger guidelines, your Honor, if you look at the second box here, says that a merger that causes—sorry—mergers that cause a significant increase in concentration and result in highly concentrated markets are presumed to be likely to enhance market power. So if the transaction increases the HHI by 200 points and results in an HHI above 2500, that merger is presumed to be likely to enhance market power.

Q. What were the results of your market concentration calculations?

A. Yeah. If we could please advance one more slide. This is a slide, your Honor, both summarizing my results and visualizing the thresholds that were described on the previous screen. So let me start by situating us a little bit in the graph.

If you look at the vertical axis, the one that's labeled "increase in HHI," this is the change in the HHI that will result from the merger.

And on the horizontal axis, the one that's labeled "post-merger HHI," this is the HHI in the market after the transaction, were the merger to be approved.

And then you can see, your Honor, there are two green dashed lines. The vertical dashed green line—to the right of this, these are values for which the post-merger HHI is greater than 2500. And the horizontal dashed line is labeled "increase in HHI greater than 200." So dots above this point increased HHI by more than 200 points. And then there's a pink region. Any dots in this area increase the HHI by more than 200 points and result in a highly concentrated market. And they're presumed to be likely to enhance market power. So that's sort of the visualization of what's called the structural presumption we saw in the previous slide. And then the dots here are representing the values I get if I use my data. So the blue dot is my data from January 2019 to June 2021. These are the data, your Honor, I used to calculate market shares. And you can see the post-merger HHI is about 3100, so above 2500. And the increase in the HHI is about 900, so above 200. And then the other dots, green, orange and red, these are looking at different years. So I calculated the concentration values not just for all of the data, but also for different years, to see if this result seemed to be robust.

Q. Did you examine market concentration using different advance thresholds to define an anticipated top seller?

A. I did. So if we could please advance one more slide. On this slide, your Honor, I'm looking both at different advance levels and different cuts of the data. So the shapes here are giving the advance level I'm using to define an anticipated top seller. So the triangles are $150,000. The circles are $250,000. The squares are $350,000. And diamonds are $500,000. And then I look at the data, both for the complete sample in blue and then also for 2019, 2020 and the first half of 2021. And you can see that for all of these different cuts of the data, these different thresholds, the transaction is presumed to be likely to enhance market power.

Q. Did you prepare a table that summarizes the detailed results of your concentration analysis?

A. Yes. If we could please advance one more slide. Here you see, your Honor, this is a table summarizing the precise numbers from the previous chart. The blue column here is my definition of an anticipated top seller. And then the other columns are looking at thresholds of $150,000, $350,000 and $500,000. And you can see for the definition of $250,000, the pre-merger HHI is 2,220. The increase in the HHI is 891. And the post-merger HHI is 3,111.

Q. After calculating market shares and market concentration, what is the next step in the economic analysis of a merger following the framework of the horizontal merger guidelines?

A. So the next step, your Honor, is to look at competitive effects.

Q. What are competitive effects?

A. So competitive effects are an attempt to estimate: What's the impact of losing competition in this market likely to be?

Q. What types of competitive effects are usually considered?

A. So if we advance one more slide, we have a summary of the two major types one looks at. Your Honor, they're unilateral effects and coordinated effects.

Q. What are unilateral effects?

A. So unilateral effects are when just the elimination of the head-to-head competition between the parties is by itself sufficient to reduce competition.

Q. What are coordinated effects?

A. Coordinated effects are when a transaction leads a group of firms in the industry to collectively pull their punches, to compete less aggressively in coordination with one another.

Q. Did you consider any general evidence regarding competitive effects?

A. I did.

Q. What evidence did you consider?

A. If we advance one more slide, please. Thank you.

So on this slide, your Honor, these are some testimony from literary agents and from an author talking about the transaction. And I'll just read the top one without identifying the speaker: I will be very disappointed if this merger is permitted. It's obviously anticompetitive in every direction.

So the other quotes here are variants of this, the idea that there are market participants who feel that the transaction is likely to be anticompetitive.

Q. Why did you consider this type of statement?

A. I think it's useful to look at the qualitative evidence and see what participants in the industry are saying about the transaction.

Q. Do all industry participants share the views that are displayed on the screen?

A. No.

Q. And are the views of industry participants who support the proposed merger consistent with your opinions in this case?

A. Yes. They can be. So, your Honor, some agents, for example, may have a clientele for which Penguin Random House and Simon & Schuster compete aggressively. So agents in that bucket may feel this transaction is likely to be harmful.

Some agents may not see a great deal of competition between Penguin Random House and Simon & Schuster for their authors. So people in the industry may have different views of whether the transaction's likely to significantly affect competition.

Q. Let's focus first on unilateral effects. We'll come back to coordinated effects. Why does head-to-head competition between the merging parties matter?

A. So if we advance one more slide, I believe.

Here we have some language just from the horizontal merger guidelines, thinking about unilateral effects. And I think, your Honor, here an example is probably the easiest to think about.

I believe you've seen some testimony about—I'll call them rounds options, where Simon & Schuster and Penguin Random House were the last two competitors and they competed with one another to push the advance up to a higher level than it otherwise would have been. Eliminating that competition between them would have resulted in a lower advance amount for that author. So that's an example of unilateral head-to-head competition whose elimination could have an adverse effect on authors.

Q. At a high level, what were your conclusions about the likely unilateral effects of this merger?

A. I think that the transaction is likely to substantially reduce unilateral competition, your Honor.

Q. What types of evidence did you consider to arrive at that opinion?

A. So I put it into four broad buckets. The first bucket we've already looked at, your Honor. It's evidence on concentration, so a presumption of an anticompetitive effect.

The second, there's evidence on—we'll look at some qualitative evidence that I've considered.

Third is diversion ratios, so an attempt to estimate directly how much head-to-head competition there is between the parties.

And then, fourth, economic models to try to simulate the effect of the merger.

Q. I know we already spoke about it, so I'll be brief. Why is market concentration relevant to unilateral effects analysis?

A. So a high level of concentration means that there's not a lot of competition in a market and a low level of concentration means there's a lot of competition. And the less competition there is, and if that competition is reduced by a merger, it can reduce head-to-head competition between parties.

Q. Let's now focus on the qualitative evidence that you referred to. What types of qualitative evidence did you consider regarding unilateral effects?

A. So I looked at two types, sort of general statements from the parties about competing head-to-head with one another and then more specific evidence about specific instances of that competition.

Q. Let's start with the general statements. Why did you consider those?

A. I think it's useful to look at the parties' documents and see: Are the parties perceiving themselves as competing with one another at a level?

Q. Did you see any evidence of that?

A. Yeah. If we could please advance one more slide, you'll see a summary of some of that evidence.

So if you look on the left-hand column, you have some evidence from Penguin Random House. And on the right-hand side, you have some evidence from Simon & Schuster.

On the upper left-hand corner, we have: "Well, editor at S&S continues her role as imprint-wide nemesis" from someone at Penguin Random House. So this is evidence of significant competition with Simon & Schuster.

And then if we look in the lower right-hand corner, we see a quote: "This was the third beauty contest we lost this week to PRH. There may have been a fourth we lost to PRH."

So again, this is evidence that the parties perceived themselves as competing with one another.

Q. Let's move on to the specific episodes that you referenced. Why did you consider that type of evidence?

A. So having looked at the high-level indications of competition between the parties, I think it's helpful to look at specific incidents to see how that loss in competition may manifest itself in the market.

Q. In what acquisition settings did the merging parties compete head-to-head?

A. So if we could advance one more slide, please. So here, your Honor, we have sort of five groups of potential competition or acquisition scenarios. So we have rounds auctions. This is auctions where publishers bid against one another in rounds. We have best bid auctions, where there may be a single round; hybrid auctions, which may be some combination of the two; negotiations, which may be a publisher negotiating with an author; and then finally what I've called poaching, so this would be one publisher trying to steal another publisher's established authors.

Q. We'll get to all these except actually the hybrid auctions. But let's focus first on rounds auctions. How do the merging parties compete in rounds auctions?

A. So, your Honor, here I think an example is pretty helpful. If we could please advance one more slide. So, your Honor, from looking at the transcripts, I believe you've seen several examples of this. I'll just walk through a few.

This is competition in 2020 for a memoir. We can see in the right-hand box at the lower left only Penguin Random House and Simon & Schuster left. Another publisher dropped out at $650,000. And then in the upper right of that box, Penguin Random House's offer of $825,000 is accepted after some back-and-forth between the parties.

So the author was driven up to 25 percent from the level of $650,000 to the advance that the author received of $825,000.

And then on the left, your Honor, we have some quotes just talking about the competition.

Q. In the rounds auctions, where the merging parties are the first and second bidders, can you determine what the extent of harm to an author might be?

A. Yeah. So here you can see, your Honor, the third-party publisher dropped out at $650,000. So if you imagine that Penguin Random House and Simon & Schuster were not competing against one another, after the $650,000 point, that's where the competition would stop. So you can compare the additional benefit of getting to $825,000 compared to $650,000.

Q. Have you observed other examples of similar auctions?

A. Yeah. If we can advance to one more slide, please. Your Honor, I'll do only this additional one. There are many more examples in my reports.

So here, again, we have an auction, this time for a biography as opposed to a memoir. And if I could focus you on the area where it says: Three publishers bid; highest third-party bid is $500,000. This is the last bid by a third party. And after that, Penguin Random House and Simon & Schuster bid against each other until the final advance amount of $750,000.

So here, the final advance went up about 50 percent from the level at which the third most interested publisher dropped out.

Q. Are examples of auctions like the ones you just discussed outliers?

A. No. As I said, there are many examples of this type in my expert reports. And it's also consistent with the quantitative evidence we'll see later.

Q. Let's move to best bid auctions. How do the merging parties compete in best bid auctions?

A. So again, I think here an example is helpful. If we could look at—move forward one more slide. So here, your Honor, we have two examples of best bid auctions. At the top we have a 2019 auction for a young adult novel. And the quote here says: "Sally's best bid for title is due tomorrow morning. As there are only three players, she says, 'I think we can be more guarded in our bidding.'"

And the second quote says, for a different auction: "Another editor and I discussed bringing our offer significantly down yesterday based on the sense I got from the agent that she doesn't have many interested bidders."

So this is a correlation between when you have a large number of bidders, you may need to be more aggressive in your bidding. And when you feel like there isn't as much competition, you can bid less aggressively. And if you have a lot of head-to-head competition with another firm, the elimination of that competition can lead you to bid less aggressively.

And sometimes it's helpful to think of that at extremes. If Penguin Random House never lost to Simon & Schuster, then in these best bid settings it may say post-merger: We never lost to these guys anyway, so we're not going to change our behavior.

If Penguin and Random House always lost to Simon & Schuster, they could say post-merger: This is great. The competition has softened significantly.

And then somewhere in between is the middle ground where they competed sometimes, but not always. And so you may soften—feel competition softened. How much it softened depends on how often you compete with the other party.

Q. Will the strategy of altering bids in reaction to softening competition only affect Penguin Random House and Simon & Schuster?

A. Not necessarily. So, your Honor, when you're thinking about a best bid auction, if you're putting in one bid on a house, you put—for example, or for a book, you're trading off two things: the probability that you win and the margin you can make if you win.

So if you bid a billion dollars, your probability of winning is very high, but your margin is probably going to be very low or negative. If you bid one dollar, your probability of winning is very low; but if you were to win, it could be an excellent deal for you.

And in between that, as a publisher you're playing off—if I bid higher, I win more often, but I get less margin. And when you've got those two things balanced, you say: This is the level I'm comfortable bidding, given the valuation I put on this book.

And so the parties, since they compete directly with one another, the transaction—if they compete significantly, then the transaction can increase the chance of winning for any given bid. And that gives you an incentive to bid slightly less aggressively.

Third parties may also have a second-order effect, where they observe that the merged firm is less aggressive and so they can also bid as they were before or even bid a little less aggressively because their probability of winning has also gone up.

Q. Is it necessary for publishers to know who they're bidding against for this merger to have the effect you're talking about?

A. No. And we already saw it in the case of rounds auctions. You don't necessarily need to know who you're bidding against. Here, for best bids, the really key thing is how you perceive the competitiveness of the field. If you think that there was a lot of competition between you and your merger partner and removing that competition will make the field less competitive, then you may bid less aggressively, even if you don't know who you're facing in a particular opportunity.

Q. Let's focus now on negotiations. How do the merging parties compete in negotiations?

A. Sure. So again, if we could advance one more slide, please. I think an example helps here. Here on the right-hand side, your Honor, we have little blue dots that are representing the stages in a negotiation. And the arrow is showing time moving from left to right and ending with the offer being accepted.

And for the moment, I'd like to focus on that graphic. So we can see if we look at the smallest of the blue dots, where Penguin Random House offers $1.5 million, and the agent counters $3 million for this book. The second round of negotiations: Penguin Random House increases its offer to $2.25 million; the agent counters with $3 million. And the Penguin Random House offer here is for two books. The agent then counters for $2.75 million. And then finally, Penguin Random House counters with $2.5 million for one book and a $500,000 bonus for a prior book. And that offer is accepted by the author. And then on the left, your Honor—so we have a negotiation here where the price went up from—or the advance went up from $1.5 million to $3 million. And on the left we have a quote from the president and publisher of the Penguin Random House imprint saying, "The agent says she is certain she can get over $3 million from someone at S&S." So this is an example of using the other party as leverage to get a better negotiated term. And a transaction that eliminates that leverage can reduce advances and harm authors.

Q. Have you observed any other examples of this negotiating dynamic?

A. Sure. I'll just do one more, if I may. If we could please advance one more slide. This is a similar dynamic, but it's for the Simon & Schuster side. Again, we can see the offers here start at—Simon & Schuster offers $1.5 million. The agent counters with $275,000. In the end, the accepted offer is $250,000. And we can see some quotes on the left. If we start with the top one: "I'm here to tell you that if this book made its way to 1745 Broadway," which is Penguin Random House's address, "we are talking 300 to 400 baseline. And if Knopf, not-so-little Random/Doubleday start all going after it, 500 to 750 easy." And so this is again one of the parties recognizing the competitive impact of the other. And in the middle, we see a similar quote just saying: "I'm certain the agent could get this and more on the open market."

Q. Finally, you mentioned instances where the merging parties poach each other's established authors. How, if at all, do those efforts affect authors?

A. So they can—they result in better terms for authors. It gives established authors a chance to realize the benefits of competition. And if we advance one more slide, we'll see an example of—two examples of this. So I'll just focus, your Honor, on the first one here. It's a quote from a senior vice president at Simon & Schuster talking about the fact that Simon & Schuster has successfully poached a pair of authors from Penguin Random House. And then the bottom quotes are: "Penguin Random House personnel discussing poaching a book from Simon & Schuster." So this existence of competition to take one's established authors is valuable.

Q. What conclusions, if any, did you draw from these episodes of head-to-head competition between the merging parties?

A. So I draw two conclusions. One, your Honor, I think they show that there's substantial head-to-head competition between the parties. And, two, I think they illustrate some of the mechanisms by which this head-to-head competition can be important for different acquisition formats.

Q. Did those episodes of head-to-head competition mean that the merging parties don't compete with other publishers?

A. No, they don't.

Q. Let's move on from the qualitative evidence you considered. And would you please remind us what other types of evidence you considered regarding unilateral effects?

A. So, your Honor, I also tried to directly identify how much or estimate how much head-to-head competition is there between the parties. And then I also looked at economic modeling to say: What would economic models predict about the likely effect of the merger?

Q. Let's start with your estimates of how much the merging parties compete head-to-head. How did you estimate that in this case?

A. So I used diversion ratios.

Q. Do the horizontal merger guidelines discuss the diversion ratios?

A. They do. So this slide here is talking about the fact that you can use diversion ratios to measure how much head-to-head competition between the parties there is. And the guidelines go on to say, your Honor, that when you're thinking about unilateral effects in a market for differentiated products, the really key point is the diversion between the parties. Is there significant division between the parties? And diversion to other parties is a second-order concern.

Q. I know you told us this earlier. But would you please briefly remind us what a diversion ratio is?

A. Sure. I think this time we can walk through an example, if we'd advance one more slide, please. So here, your Honor, we're trying to visually represent what diversion might look like. We start with Simon & Schuster and we're asking: What is a Simon & Schuster author's next best option? So if advances went down, where might that author go? And then on the right-hand side, we're representing diversion to Penguin Random House. What proportion of those lost authors would go to Penguin Random House? And then what proportion would go to other Big 5 publishers and then to the non-Big 5? And so this is—diversion here is measuring: How often is the next best alternative the other party? So how much head-to-head competition is there?

Q. How many sources of data did you use to estimate diversion in this case?

A. So in my initial report, I used four.

Q. And why did you use four data sources to estimate diversion?

A. So I think it's important to get as many estimates as you can on this diversion ratio, this head-to-head competition. No single one measure is perfect. But the more ways we can look at it, the more we can learn about it.

Q. Would you please list the four data sources you used to calculate diversion ratios.

A. Sure. So the first is I looked at diversion according to share. So I looked at data on market shares to try to estimate diversions. Second, I looked at win-loss data. Third, I tried, your Honor, to go through the documents and data and tried to identify when one party lost an auction, to whom did it lose? I call that the runner-up study. And then, fourth, I looked at editorial minutes.

Q. We'll break down all those results in a minute. But would you first tell us what the general results of your diversion ratio calculations were?

A. Sure. However I looked at it, your Honor, I found significant diversion from Simon & Schuster to Penguin Random House and from Penguin Random House to Simon & Schuster.

Q. Let's start with diversion according to share. What were the results of that diversion calculation?

A. So if we could advance one more slide, please. We'll see here for Penguin Random House to Simon & Schuster, so if Penguin Random House loses an author, what proportion of the lost authors go to Simon & Schuster? The answer is about 20 percent. And then on the right, for Simon & Schuster, if it loses a bunch of authors, we would expect about 40 percent to go to Penguin Random House.

Q. I know you explained this in the context of self-publishing earlier, but would you please remind us what diversion according to share means?

A. Sure. So, your Honor, diversion according to share means that market shares are reflective of how attractive a publisher is to authors. If an author leaves a publisher, the probability that it picked another publisher is proportional to that publisher's market share.

Q: Is that a common approach in antitrust economics?

A. Yes. It's widely used.

Q. What is your understanding as to why?

A. So as an—inside of a market is a default assumption. It's common to think that market shares are representing how attractive a firm is. If you have strong evidence that a particular pair of publishers are not close substitutes, or are closer-than-expected substitutes, then you may wish not to use diversion according to share. But in many settings, it's a reasonable approach to estimating diversion.

Q. Are there situations in which—and I think you just mentioned, but you might—when—excuse me. Let me try again. When might you not use market shares to calculate diversion ratios?

A. Sure. So, your Honor, I can give you two examples of one where you might not want to do it and one where you—well, two where you might not want to do it for different reasons. So if you imagine a market for passenger vehicles and you think, Well, minivans are in that market and sports cars are in that market. And if you have a merger between a sports carmaker and a minivan maker, you may think, most consumers aren't choosing between a sports car and a minivan. So even if I know their market shares, probably diversion is not going to be according to share there, because they're a little more distant. They're different groups of consumers. If you're thinking about a merger of brewers and you were thinking about Bud Light and Miller Lite, you might say: Wow, those are very close substitutes from the perspective of a lot of customers. Diversion's probably higher than according to share.

So when you have that kind of information, qualitative or quantitative, that makes you think: Diversion's probably not proportional to share. Then you may not want to assume that it is proportional to share, as I have here.

THE COURT: In your first example, with the minivans and the sports cars, how are you calculating market share? Market share of minivans and market share of the sports—

THE WITNESS: Yes. So if you did market shares of all passenger vehicles, your Honor, and let's say each was—

THE COURT: Oh, I see.

THE WITNESS: So then you would think, Oh, wait a minute. That's probably not a great assumption.

THE COURT: I see. So they're both in a broad general market, but they each specialize in different things?

THE WITNESS: That's correct. And in my beer example, it would be all beer. So you'd have high-end beers, imported beers. Two domestic light beers are probably really competing more closely with one another than you'd just guess from their share of all beer.

THE COURT: I see. Okay.

BY MR. STEVENSON:

Q. Have you seen any evidence in this case suggesting that publishers compete in ways that are not reflected in their market shares?

A. No. I would say on balance, the evidence suggests, if anything, there might be—yeah. I would say on evidence, on balance, the evidence is consistent with diversion according to share.

Q. Dr. Hill, I think you were at your second source of data to calculate diversion, which was the win-loss data. What was the result of your diversion calculation using the win-loss data?

A. Sure. If we could please advance one more slide. Here you see on the left, your Honor, for diversion from Penguin Random House to Simon & Schuster, the win-loss data is about 20 percent. And for Simon & Schuster to Penguin Random House, it's about 60 percent. So for Penguin Random House to Simon & Schuster, the two are very similar. For Simon & Schuster to Penguin Random House, the win-loss is giving a higher estimate than proportional to share.

THE COURT: So can you explain, like, the win-loss ratio? Like they won 19 percent?

THE WITNESS: Sure. So, your Honor, on the left here, I looked at: When Penguin Random House lost a competition, how often was Simon & Schuster the winner?

THE COURT: Oh, I see.

THE WITNESS: The answer was—

THE COURT: 19 percent of the time they lost to Simon & Schuster.

THE WITNESS: That's correct. On the other side, it's when Simon & Schuster lost. 60 percent of the time, Penguin Random House was the winner.

BY MR. STEVENSON:

Q. Are win-loss data commonly used by economists to estimate diversion ratios?

A. Yes. They're one of the most commonly used methodologies.

Q. So the merger guidelines discuss whether win-loss data are a useful source to estimate diversion?

A. Yes. The merger guidelines call them out as one source for estimating diversion.

Q. Do the merging parties contest whether their win-loss data are systematically maintained?

A. Yes. I think the parties would argue that their win-loss data is not systematically maintained. So it may include some competitions, your Honor, but not others.

Q. Given that, why did you nevertheless rely on it?

A. So in my experience, it's common for win-loss data to not be fully systematic. Salespeople will record some competitions and not others in other industries and in this industry. I nevertheless think it's useful to look at what records there are as part of a holistic look at the degree of head-to-head competition.

Q. Let's move to your third diversion calculation, which you referred to as the runner-up study. What were the results of that diversion calculation?

A. So if we advance one more slide, please. Yes. Thank you. So here, for Penguin Random House to Simon & Schuster, the runner-up study finds about 25 percent diversion. And for Simon & Schuster to Penguin Random House, it's about 60 percent.

Q. Will you please describe the methodology behind the runner-up study?

A. Sure. So this was an attempt, your Honor, to, as much as I could, look at when one party lost, did the other party win? And I did something similar to this on the Ivonik matter.

THE COURT: How is that different from the win-loss ratio?

THE WITNESS: It's really getting at a similar thing, your Honor, but I'd say there are two principal differences. My hope in the runner-up study was to look at as many of these competitions as I could. But the other difference—and the win-loss data, as you heard, is not necessarily systematically maintained. And then the other difference is in the runner-up study, your Honor, I was really looking for, I have concrete evidence that one party is first and the other party is second. In the win-loss data, we know that Penguin Random House records that it lost and Simon & Schuster won. But we don't necessarily know that Penguin Random House was the second closest bidder; we just know they competed.

BY MR. STEVENSON:

Q. Dr. Hill, I'd like to take a step back. I think you misspoke, which may have led to the confusion. Did you implement your runner-up study using books that you knew the merging parties won?

A. Yes. I started with books won by Penguin Random House and won by Simon & Schuster.

Q. And then from that, what were you trying to identify?

A. I was trying to identify the identity of the runner-up. Sorry if I was unclear.

Q. Is calculating diversion based on the identity of the runner-up when a party wins a common way to estimate diversion?

A. Yes.

Q. What were the criteria you used to select the books for which you attempted to find the runner-up?

A. So I used data from 2020 that had an advance amount of $500,000 or above.

Q. Why did you only examine books that received advances of $500,000 or more?

A. Two reasons: First, the study turned out to be a lot more time-consuming than I had expected. And it didn't seem fully feasible to do it for additional years or other advance amounts. And second, when I looked at $250,000 to $500,000, I was often finding there just wasn't an evidentiary record. I wasn't able to identify with much confidence who was the runner-up in the competition.

Q. Roughly how many books do you end up examining as part of this study?

A. Around about 285.

Q. You mentioned that you attempted to identify the runner-up for those books. What did that entail?

A. So, your Honor, I reviewed documents and data related to each of these wins by Penguin Random House and Simon & Schuster. In the end, I think I reviewed more than 1200 documents. And so I looked through and tried to see if I could determine from the emails, from any records, from agents, any data I had available, if one party won, who was the runner-up?

Q. Were there any books where you were unable to determine who the runner-up was?

A. Yeah. There were some books where I wasn't able to determine who the runner-up was. And I would split those into two categories. One was a category where I wasn't sure who the runner-up was, but I was sure it wasn't the other party. So I could keep those in the study and could classify them as "diversion to other," because I'm really looking at diversion from one party to another. And if I don't know exactly who it went to, but I know it didn't go to the other party, I can include it in the study. And then there was a second class of books, about 20 percent, where I just couldn't tell who the runner-up was. And those ones I excluded from the study.

Q. Now I'd like to ask a couple questions about your last source of data to calculate diversion, the editorial minutes. Will you please share the results of that calculation with us?

A. Sure. If we advance one more slide, please. So if we see for Penguin Random House to Simon & Schuster, the diversion is again about 20 percent, your Honor. And then for Simon & Schuster to Penguin Random House, the diversion's about 55 percent.

Q. What are editorial minutes?

A. So I think you heard the witness from Macmillan talking about editorial meetings, where the editorial staff at an imprint will gather weekly or with some other frequency and discuss books that are of interest to the imprint. These may be books that they have identified as of interest; they may be books they have won; it may be books they have lost. And I—your Honor, I looked for books that they had bid for, that either of the merging parties recorded in their editorial minutes that they had bid for.

Q. How were you able to use that information to estimate a diversion ratio?

A. So I was able to merge it with my advance data for anticipated top sellers and see how often, when one party bid for a book and lost that book, to whom did they lose? Did they lose to the other party? Did they lose to some other publisher?

THE COURT: So on this one, you wouldn't have to be number one and number two? It's just whoever ultimately won?

THE WITNESS: Yeah. It was—if you bid and you recorded it, then I was just asking: Did HarperCollins win? Did Simon & Schuster win? Correct, your Honor. And—yes. Sorry.

BY MR. STEVENSON:

Q. Go ahead.

A. I was just going to say, your Honor, these are all different ways of looking at it. I was trying to take a different approach each time.

Q. I would like to follow up on that. Given that a book appearing in a publisher's editorial minutes doesn't necessarily mean that the publisher was a runner-up, why did you use this methodology?

A. So I think it's—I still think it's a useful measure of how much competition there is. I don't know precisely who the runner-up is, but I know them. I know one publisher thought enough about it to record it in the editorial minutes. And then I'm going to ask: Who won? It could be HarperCollins; it could be

Macmillan; it could be Scholastic; it could be some other publisher. It could also be the party, the other party. And so that's what—I was just using a measure of how much competition there is.

Q. Stepping back, did you draw any conclusions from all four of your diversion ratio calculations?

A. Yeah. I mean, looking at them, I think that there is significant diversion both from Penguin Random House to Simon & Schuster and from Simon & Schuster to Penguin Random House.

MR. STEVENSON: Your Honor, this figure with a slight alteration is a version of PX 0970. I move to submit PX 0970.

THE COURT: Any objection?

MR. OPPENHEIMER: No.

THE COURT: That will be admitted. (Whereupon, Plaintiff's Exhibit No. 0970 was entered into evidence.)

BY MR. STEVENSON:

Q. Does Dr. Snyder propose an alternative way to measure diversion?

A. He does.

Q. Would you please briefly describe his approach?

A. Sure. So, your Honor, Dr. Snyder gathered bidding records from agencies and so he looked at: Can I gather information about competitions from the agency side? And in particular, he looked for instances in which there was a complete bidding record, so lists of who bid and how much. And then he asked: How often when one party was the winner was the other party the runner-up?

Q. Does Dr. Snyder have a view of your diversion calculations?

A. Yes. He feels that these estimates are not reliable and he prefers his estimate.

Q. And what is your opinion of Dr. Snyder's diversion estimate?

A. I think it's useful as part of the more holistic picture of "We now have five estimates of diversion, and I think it's useful to look at all five."

THE COURT: Were his results consistent with yours?

THE WITNESS: So I would say his results were consistent with mine. And we'll go through that in a minute, your Honor, in a little more detail.

BY MR. STEVENSON:

Q. Did you identify any flaws in Dr. Snyder's approach?

A. So, your Honor, Dr. Snyder did the best that he could. But his—he has a sample of the anticipated top sellers. And there are times when his sample does not appear to be representative of the population.

Q. What does it mean to not be representative?

A. So a sample is not representative of the population if the values that it has don't look like—are not likely to be drawn from a particular population. So if you were trying to estimate the average height of males in the United States and you sampled only professional basketball players, you might get a misleading view of the height of professional basketball players—or the men on average. Sorry.

THE COURT: So who did he sample?

THE WITNESS: So he sampled what he could—he can explain better than you his exact sample—I mean, better than me. I apologize. But he essentially looked for competitions in the agents' data where he had something close to a complete record, so some record recording who bid against whom and how much. And the challenge he had, as we'll see in a second—actually, if we can advance one more slide, we can probably talk about it a little bit. So, your Honor, this is sort of starting by looking at the problem. So here, the advance data are in blue. And the agency data, which is what Dr. Snyder calls his data set, are in red. And the variable we're summarizing here is the average contracted amount for an anticipated top seller. So you can see in the advance data, which contains all of the anticipated top sellers, the average for Penguin Random House—I don't know. Can I say these numbers or should I keep these off?

THE COURT: I can see the numbers. You don't need to—

THE WITNESS: Yes. You can see the numbers, your Honor.

THE COURT: They're higher.

THE WITNESS: So you can see they're significantly higher for the advance data than they are for the agency data. It's particularly true in the case of Simon & Schuster. And I think part of the issue here, your

Honor, is Dr. Snyder found more examples of Penguin Random House wins, because Penguin Random House has a larger market share, than he did Simon & Schuster. So for Simon & Schuster, he has about 22 competitions won by Simon & Schuster. And so the data look—they don't look representative of the average contract amount.

THE COURT: That's much fewer than Simon & Schuster would publish in a year.

THE WITNESS: Yes. If you look at the full advance data, the average contracted amount is much higher. For reasons that aren't clear to me, and I don't think they're clear to Dr. Snyder, his data has competitions that on average had much lower advance amounts. And he only has 22 events. So it's not a huge sample for Simon & Schuster. I mean, this Penguin Random House number, your Honor, if you do some statistical testing, it's within the 95 percent confidence interval. But the number on the right for Simon & Schuster is not. And it's not entirely clear why the sample of agency competitions is not representative for Simon & Schuster. But it's highly likely it's tied to the relatively small sample size.

THE COURT: And so it just depends on whether the agents were keeping complete records or not, basically?

THE WITNESS: Yeah. And Dr. Snyder's sample of agents wasn't random. We didn't go out and randomly sample agents. If you did that, you would—and some agents don't keep good data. So some, you just don't have a record for it. And it just turned out not to quite look like the population.

THE COURT: Okay.

BY MR. STEVENSON:

Q. Is there a worth—or is—or actually, I'll save that for a second. How did Dr. Snyder's diversion calculations compare to yours?

A. Sure. So if we could advance one more slide. This is what you were asking about earlier, your Honor. We'll start by looking at diversion from Penguin Random House to Simon & Schuster. You have my estimates in blue and then the agency data estimate is in red. So similar to the—I'd say his results here are broadly similar with my results.

Q. How did Dr. Snyder's diversion calculation of Simon & Schuster to Penguin Random House compare with yours?

A. So he found a lower estimate. If we advance one more—than some of my estimates. So here, your Honor, my estimates are in green and Dr. Snyder's estimate is in red. You can see that the three bars in the middle, the win-loss, runner-up and editorial minutes, are significantly higher. Proportional to share is higher; but statistically, the proportional to share and agency are statistically consistent with one another.

Q. Stepping back, what is your view of this group of diversion estimates?

A. So I think they all show significant diversion. Of this group, my preference is to take proportional to share. It's based on the largest sample.

Here we're seeing them all at once, your Honor, so let me be more systematic. If we look at Penguin Random House to Simon & Schuster, the numbers are broadly consistent with one another. The runner-up study is a little higher. But I think it's reasonable here to take proportional to share, about 20 percent. And then for Simon & Schuster to Penguin Random House, we see more variation. And in general, we have smaller sample sizes. But I think the 42 percent is a reasonable estimate for this group.

It's based on the largest sample. And if—and it's something of a midpoint in between the higher estimates and the lower estimate.

Q. You mentioned that Dr. Snyder's agency data sample was about 22. Don't you rely on some small samples to calculate diversion ratios?

A. Yes. The runner-up study, I think, is only slightly larger than the agency data for Simon & Schuster to Penguin Random House. The win-loss data and editorial minutes are a little bigger. And then proportional to share is using a much larger number of competitions, your Honor.

Q. Why did you nevertheless rely on those estimates despite their small sample sizes?

A. So I think here, your Honor, we're trying to get a holistic understanding of what diversion might look like. And we're looking at five different ways of looking at it. And I think each of them has their challenges. I think proportional to share is probably the most reliable here, especially given the largest sample size. But I think it's also helpful to look at all of the different estimates.

Q. Do you agree with Dr. Snyder that only his diversion estimates are reliable here?

A. No. I think it's more sensible to look at the set of five together.

Q. And we discussed the representativeness of a sample. Is a diversion estimate based on a representative sample worthless?

A. No. I think it's useful to look at all five of these estimates.

Q. Now that we've discussed diversion ratios, I would like to move on to the next step of your analysis, which was using an economic model to simulate the effect of the merger, I think you said. What is the point of using an economic model?

A. So economic models, your Honor, give us another perspective on the likely effect on unilateral competition.

Q. What kind of model did you use in this case?

A. I used what's known as the second score auction model.

Q. Why was this model developed?

A. It was developed by one of my former colleagues at the antitrust division to look at mergers in industries that use auctions or frequently use auctions to allocate goods and in which there's not—there's relatively low-quality information available, so you don't have a full history of all bids for most auctions.

Q. At a high level, what does the second score option model do?

A. So the second score auction model, your Honor, takes information at an aggregate level about the industry and uses that to simulate current competition. And then it says: Let's imagine that competition is changed by a merger. And it asks: What would the effect of that be on competition?

Q. To clarify, are the results of this model projected across all of the merging parties' anticipated top sellers or just ones that are sold by auction?

A. So the model itself is narrowly looking at the mechanism in the model as the second price auction, which is similar in some ways to a rounds auction. But I interpret this more broadly. I'm taking aggregate information about the industry and I'm using it to try to make a prediction about how competition may be affected.

Q. So would you tell us what a second score auction is?

A. Sure. So, your Honor, the way I think about it is there's an author who's trying to sell a book and publishers submit bids for that book. And the publisher with the most attractive bid wins and the publisher—but the price or—sorry—the advance depends upon the second most attractive bid.

Q. Why is the advance that the winner pays based on the attractiveness of the second best bid?

A. So in some sense, the advance ends up depending on the second-highest bidder. And so if you think about auctions, you often see in television or in movies an open outcry auction where there's an object and I say, I'll pay $10 and you say, I'll pay $15, and we keep bidding. And Mr. Stevenson says, I'll pay $25. And eventually, at some point, everybody drops out but the winner. And the point you stop at is the point that the second best bidder decides that they've had enough. They've hit their valuation. They're not going higher. That's where the price ends up. So that's the high-level intuition of what a second price auction looks like.

THE COURT: So does your model only look at a portion of the market, of the relevant market, because it only looks at the portion that uses auctions?

THE WITNESS: Yes. So technically, it's just looking at ones with auctions of a particular type. I again interpret it more broadly because what I'm going to give—the information I'm going to put into the model is the market shares and diversion, hence diversions between the parties, and then also an aggregate margin measuring their margin in all types of competitions. And it's going to try to translate those into a price effect. So whenever you're modeling, you have to make—to make progress, you have to make some assumptions and fix some things. And then in return, you get more precise predictions than just a measure of diversion. So we're getting a more precise prediction about whether harm is likely, but we have to make some modeling assumptions. And this model is often used in the context of mergers involving auctions.

THE COURT: I'm not sure I quite understand, because we're talking about a market where some of the acquisitions are done through auction, but a lot of them are not. But you're using the data for all of the transactions, including the ones that are not auctions, and plugging them into a model that talks about auctions.

THE WITNESS: That's correct.

THE COURT: Why does that work?

THE WITNESS: So I think the model is—at a high level, it's trying to ask a question of: What happens if competition is disturbed? And it is true it's using aggregate information on all types and using a specific mechanism to estimate it. But I think of it more holistically, as just we're using a particular mechanism of competition with our data to make a prediction. And we'll see that when I try other models to estimate the effect, we'll see that the second score auctions model is consistent with them even though they're using different models of competition.

BY MR. STEVENSON:

Q. Would you please explain to the Court how the second score model simulates the effect of the merger.

A. Sure. So again, it assumes—it takes aggregate information, makes a prediction about the outcome of current competition, and then it changes the competition so that the merged firm only submits one bid. So previously, it submitted two. Post-merger, it only submits the bid of—the higher bid of the two publishers.

Q. Does the model predict that some authors will be harmed by the merger?

A. It does.

Q. And when does the model predict that authors will be harmed?

A. So an author will be harmed if the parties are the first and second highest bidder for that author.

Q. Why is that?

A. So in those cases, your Honor, if you have a second score—a second price auction, the highest bidder wins and the second highest bidder sets the level of the advance. And what we're thinking about is, if you eliminate one of the parties, the second highest bid leaves the market, and now the advance is set by the third highest bidder. So when the parties are the first and second closest bidders, an author can be harmed.

THE COURT: I don't see why this wouldn't be true for any auction.

THE WITNESS: So I mean, I think at a high level, I think it's reasonable—I agree with you, your Honor. The specific mechanism here is saying auctions where the parties are first and second, and we're eliminating that competition and we're going to narrow in on that competition. But you could also interpret this as a broader statement about the average effect of the transaction. So what's the average effect of eliminating the head-to-head competition between the parties? I don't know if—

THE COURT: I guess what I'm confused about is, isn't it a truism that if you have an auction and you eliminate the top few, it's going to be a lower price?

THE WITNESS: Right. So, your Honor, the way—the example I might give is we talked about sort of an open outcry auction where we end up with the second highest bidder as setting the price. If you think about a best bids auction, where you, Mr. Stevenson and I all submit bids, then let's say I have the highest bid, your Honor. I will win; and the advance is the amount I bid.

So if I didn't know what you two bid, I could eliminate Mr. Stevenson. And if I bid the same, even though he's been eliminated, then the amount wouldn't change. But if I knew ahead of time that Mr. Stevenson—so to your point, if I knew that Mr. Stevenson was eliminated, I might say: Well, her Honor is bidding against me. Mr. Stevenson is not here. It's not going to be as aggressive. I'll bid less high. So your intuition is right that the general thing the model is testing is: How often are the parties first and second? And how often does that mean there's going to be some kind of reduction in competition? If they're rarely first and second, the model is going to predict no significant effect. If they're always first and second, there's going to be a big effect. And that is a general intuition, as you say, that I think applies across auctions.

THE COURT: You're saying it works for best bids auctions when you don't even know who is bidding?

THE WITNESS: In a different form. Right? Because in a best bids auction, the question is: Has the competition with the field decreased? Do I think there's less competition? And if I know that someone I compete with a lot has been eliminated, I may say: Okay. Now there's less competition. And I can bid less aggressively than I used to.

THE COURT: Okay.

THE WITNESS: So it varies depending on the specific format. But one way people sometimes think about it is, in an auction you're trying to beat the second best person and by as little as you have to. So you want to be highest, but by no more than is necessary. And that's kind of a common intuition. And in this particular model, it's using a second price setting. But again, I think that it's a more general idea of what's the effect of a merger in an industry with auctions.

BY MR. STEVENSON:

Q. To follow up on that, does this prediction of your model mean that the only authors who might be harmed by this merger are ones that would have had the merging parties as the top two bidders in an auction?

A. So again, narrowly in the model, in the second score auction model, those authors for whom the parties are number one and number two are the ones who are being affected. But the prediction of the model is going to be an average effect across all authors of the parties.

Q. That includes other acquisition types?

A. I'm using it for a much broader purpose. Yes.

Q. How does the second score model determine the extent of harm to authors?

A. So in this model, your Honor, the first—there's harm if the parties are number one and number two. And you remember I said, well, the effect of the merger is to eliminate the second highest bid. So now the advance is set by the third highest bid. If bids are very close together, everyone who bids has a very similar valuation for the book, then moving from the second best bidder to the third best bidder will have no big effect. If there's a big difference between the valuations of the second and third closest bidder, then the merger can have a more substantial effect. So the size of the effect depends upon the difference on average between the second best bidder and the third best bidder.

Q. Have you observed any evidence on the difference between the second best and third best bidders in book auctions?

A. Yes. If we could please turn the screens back on and advance one slide. Yes. Thank you. So, your Honor, this slide is looking for all contracts and for anticipated top seller contracts. Using Dr. Snyder's advance data, what's the average difference between the second and third highest publisher's bid? And you can see if we look at all contracts or anticipated top seller contracts, it's about 20 percent. Or for advance—anticipated top seller contracts, it's on the order of $100,000.

Q. You said that this was based on Dr. Snyder's advance data. I think you misspoke.

A. I apologize. It's his agency data.

Q. Have you observed any qualitative evidence regarding the distance between the second and third bidders?

A. Yeah. I think there's been a good deal of testimony. The testimony of Mr. Karp comes to mind of participants in the industry saying that there's often significantly different valuations of a book across publishers.

And this chart is essentially a qualitative—a quantitative version of that, finding that the second and third bidder are roughly 20 percent apart in their valuation and their bid.

THE COURT: This is an average. Did you find it was fairly consistent or is this—

THE WITNESS: No. It can vary significantly, your Honor. In some competitions, it may be high; and in others, the third bidder may be close.

BY MR. STEVENSON:

Q. Let's delve into the implementation of your model. What are the inputs to the second score auction model?

A. So if we could please advance one more slide. Thank you. Yes. So there are two key inputs here, your Honor. The first one is market shares. And the market shares are used to estimate how often the parties are the top two bidders. So using diversion according to share, how often is one party the winner and the other party the runner-up on average? And here, the higher the market shares for the party, the higher the diversion and the greater the predicted harm in the model. The second input is a variable profit margin. So this in the model is measuring how close together are publishers' bids to one another on average. If publisher bids are all very close together, then margins are going to be low. If there's significant variation, then margins will be higher. So a higher variable profit margin leads to greater variation in bids or is associated with greater variation in bids and leads to more harm. And smaller margins means more tightly clustered bids and it means less harm.

THE COURT: Why is there a correlation between variable profit margins and how close the bids are?

THE WITNESS: So if I—if we're all driving up to our valuation of the book, your Honor, and let's say you value the book at $500,000 and I value it at $250,000. I'll only drive you up to $250,000. So now you're getting a book you value for 500,000 for $250,000. So you can make a significant profit there. If I drive you up to 495, I've put you within $5,000 of your valuation. So you're going to expect to earn a lower margin because you have to pay a higher advance than you would if my valuation was lower.

THE COURT: Let me think about that for a second.

THE WITNESS: Sure.

THE COURT: How does that correlate with what I'm bidding compared with what other people are bidding?

THE WITNESS: So the closer all of our bids are, the—so you can think of your bid as being based on your valuation. You don't want to go above your valuation. And if the other bidders are very close to you, you get forced to bid up to your valuation and you're paying a significantly higher advance. So let's say the book is going to generate $500,000 in sales. You're right about that. That's going to be the value above the advance that you're going to get, but not counting the advance. If I force you to pay $495,000, you're only going to make a $5,000 profit on the book. If my valuation is very low, you're going to get the book for much lower than your valuation and your profit will be higher because you'll have to pay the author a lower advance.

THE COURT: I understand that. I'm just trying to understand the relationship between the bidders. Are you saying that if they're bidding around the same amount, they have the same variable profit margins?

THE WITNESS: Yes. Well, in general, I'm saying if there's less variation across them, we all sort of think the book is worth about the same, and we're all roughly correct, then there's not a lot of room for any of us to earn profit because we're all driving each other up. But if someone values it more highly and others value it more lowly—at a lower level, that dispersion creates the ability to get some additional profit that wouldn't be there otherwise.

THE COURT: But this is actual profit margin and not predicted profit margin.

THE WITNESS: Right. So in the model, the language here is a little bit loose, your Honor. In general, the idea is, in the actual profit margins, if there's—to earn a big profit margin, you have to be correct about it and it has to be the case that the other publishers don't value it as highly as you do. So on average, you're making more for a book because the competition for it is less intense.

THE COURT: I think I kind of understand that.

THE WITNESS: Yes. So maybe if we switch the context. If you imagine you were buying houses, fixing them up and then selling them, let's just say on average you have a pretty good sense of the valuations in the market, on average. And you're competing for a series of houses. If I'm in there and I have the same sense as you and I'm also pretty good at it, you and I are going to end up paying about what we think we can get for the house. So there's not a lot of room left over for us to make a profit margin. But if I don't value the houses, you look at a Victorian house and say, "Someone will really like this when it's fixed up," and a Victorian house is not to my taste, I won't push you up to bid the full value. So you can bid under what you think it's going to get. You get it for less than it's actually worth. And when you fix it up, you're able to sell it for more because I'm not right there pushing you to go up to the final value of the product.

THE COURT: So I understand what you're saying there. I'm just not sure how it plays into this analysis. I don't want to belabor this.

THE WITNESS: Sure. I think we'll see an actual example of this in a second. But the general point I was just trying to make here is just that when there's higher profit margins, there's generally going to be more harm. And the mechanism that's coming through is, when everybody is valuing things very closely together, there's just not a lot of room to make a profit. Everybody is really on it and they all know—they all value things very similarly.

THE COURT: Thank you.

BY MR. STEVENSON:

Q. Dr. Hill, do the horizontal merger guidelines discuss how profit margins are—may predict harm in auction settings?

A. Yes. I believe they do.

Q. What is your understanding of what the merger guidelines say?

A. I think they say that higher margins in the auctions are likely to be correlated with more harm.

Q. So we've been discussing margins for a couple minutes. How do you as an economist calculate a publisher's variable profit margin?

A. So a variable profit margin is sort of asking, your Honor, what's the incremental value of an additional book? If I add this additional book, how much additional revenue will it bring in? And how much additional will I have to pay to acquire it? And when you think about it in those terms, your Honor, let's say I'm already publishing 100 books and I'm thinking of adding one more book to get to 101. The new book will bring in some stream of revenue and it will lead to some incremental costs. So I'll have to pay for copies of the book, for example, to distribute it. But I won't have to pay myself the CEO's salary again. I won't have to pay rental on a warehouse where I store books. I can just use already-paid costs. So those are what we might call fixed costs. And then incremental costs are things like paying for the printing of the book, paying the advance to the author. And so in a variable profit margin, you're just asking: How much additional revenue do I get and how much additional cost do I have to bear?

Q. Can you describe in just a little more detail the intuition for why you don't consider fixed costs when calculating a variable margin? How did you calculate variable profit margins in this case?

A. So I used title-level P&L data. So, your Honor, to your earlier question, this is actual realized results. So what happened to each of these titles in terms of revenue and what happened to each of these titles in terms of costs?

Q. What did you do with the title-level P&L data?

A. So, your Honor, I calculated the revenue and then I split the costs into costs that were likely variable and costs that were likely fixed.

Q. And were there any costs that were difficult to categorize?

A. So for Simon & Schuster, it was relatively straightforward. For Penguin Random House, there was a category of costs called direct operating expenses, your Honor, that looked like some mix of both variable and fixed costs.

Q. What did you do with that category of costs?

A. I treated them—to be conservative, I treated them all as being variable.

Q. Why is that conservative?

A. It's conservative with respect to harm in the model because if I make Penguin Random House's margin lower, it reduces the predictions of harm in the model.

Q. Dr. Hill, would you please share the results of your model with us?

A. Sure. So if we could please advance one more slide. Your Honor, here on the left, we have the predicted average decrease in advances for Penguin Random House authors. It's about 4 percent. And on the right, we have the predicted decrease in advances for Simon & Schuster. And it's about 11.5 percent on average.

Q. How does that translate to dollar terms for the benefit of the record?

A. Sure. So for Penguin Random House, it's about $44,000 per book in advance reduction. For Simon & Schuster, it's about a $105,000 reduction per book.

THE COURT: That's all books, not just the ones at auction?

THE WITNESS: Right. This is—the prediction here is—I'm using it for all Penguin Random House authors and all Simon & Schuster authors, your Honor.

BY MR. STEVENSON:

Q. Just a minute ago we were discussing margins. Did Dr. Snyder calculate a different margin? I think that was redundant.

A. Yes. Dr. Snyder did calculate margins differently.

Q. Did he estimate the results of your model using his margins?

A. Yes, he did.

Q. Roughly, what were those results?

A. So at a high level, it reduced the harm by about 30 percent, your Honor.

THE COURT: For both?

THE WITNESS: Yeah. Your Honor, I can't quite remember the breakdown by firm. So that's an average breakdown across both.

BY MR. STEVENSON:

Q. Is a reduction in advances the only harm you expect to result from this merger?

A. Not necessarily. Your Honor, when we're creating these economic models, we often focus on something we can quantify; so prices in some mergers, in this case advances. So I focused on advances. But the—you know, the merger guidelines have language about these sorts of what are called merger simulations. It's more of a question about: How significant is the reduction in unilateral effects here? The specific numbers are not the thing to focus on. And the harm need not be restricted to advances. So it's more a question about: Is there a reduction in unilateral competition? And that could manifest itself in changes in advances; it could manifest itself in worse terms. But the model is actually measuring it in something that's quantifiable, which is the change in advances.

Q. We discussed the direct operating expenses of Penguin Random House. Did you investigate the results of your model treating those costs as fixed instead of variable?

A. Yes, I did. And if we could advance one more slide, please, we'll see those results. So here, your Honor, on the left, this is the Penguin Random House average effect per author. If we treat the direct operating expense as fixed, it's about a 6 percent reduction per book, or about $60,000 per book.

On the right, for Simon & Schuster, it's about a 15 percent reduction in advances, or about $140,000.

Q. Do you have a baseline version of your second score auction model?

A. Yeah. The one I presented in my initial report assumes that the direct operating expenses are variable. And I used that because it is conservative relative to assuming that they are all fixed. Somewhere in between, your Honor, I think is probably the correct number. There's some portion of the direct operating expenses that's variable and some portion that's fixed. So it's somewhere between the results on these two slides.

Q. Did you run your model for different advance thresholds that defined an anticipated top seller?

A. I did. I also ran the model, your Honor, using a threshold of $150,000 and I did it using a threshold of $350,000. And the results were, broadly speaking, similar. And then I also ran it for a special subset of authors, those who received an advance between $150,000 and $250,000. And the model also predicted that those authors would likely see a reduction in advances.

Q. Did Dr. Snyder criticize your modeling approach in this case?

A. Yes.

Q. Will you please briefly summarize his criticisms?

A. I think his top-level criticism is he disagrees with using the second score auction model to look at all competitive situations and all auctions.

Q. Do you agree with that criticism?

A. No. I think in modeling one always has to make some assumptions. And I think this is a reasonable model to look at the aggregate effect of the transaction.

Q. Do you conduct any analysis to assess Dr. Snyder's claims?

A. I did.

Q. What analysis did you do?

A. So I also tried to analyze the effect of the transaction using a series of models derived by the economists working on behalf of the parties that look at what are known as gross upward pricing pressure index. That's often shortened to an acronym of GUPPI.

Q. Could you please explain to the Court what GUPPI is?

A. So the GUPPI model was developed by two former head—chief economists at the Department of Justice and the FTC. It's an attempt to look at what is the change in incentives, the pricing incentives, of firms in the case—unilateral change in pricing incentives for the firms in a merger?

Q. And is GUPPI discussed in the horizontal merger guidelines?

A. Yes. If we advance one more slide, in the section of the guidelines, your Honor, that talks about unilateral competitive effects, there's language discussing the use of upward pricing pressure to estimate the effect of competitive—unilateral competitive effect.

Q. Why did you use these GUPPI models?

A. Dr. Snyder criticized the second score auction model for being focused on a particular second score auction. The GUPPI models developed by the parties' economists looked at three different types of auctions—sorry—of competitive situations. So it was a way of trying to answer Dr. Snyder's criticism.

Q. At a high level, would you please describe what the Defendants' economists developed with regard to the GUPPI models?

A. Sure. So they took the baseline GUPPI methodology and they looked at three mechanisms, your Honor. One was a best bids-type auction. One was a rounds auction. And then they looked at a hybrid approach, which is a rounds auction followed by negotiations.

Q. Did the Defendants' economists state which version is the most reliable?

A. Their preference, your Honor, is to take whichever of the three makes the lowest prediction about the aggregate price effect.

Q. Did you follow that approach?

A. I did not.

Q. Why not?

A. So that approach, as I understand it, is based on the idea that the agent will unerringly select the most advantageous of those mechanisms. I think it's probably more realistic to look at each of the different possibilities separately.

Q. What are the inputs to the GUPPI models?

A. If we could please advance—yes. Thank you. So here, your Honor, the GUPPI model takes similar inputs to the second score auction model. So first, it takes a measure of diversion and then it takes a variable profit margin.

Q. How do these inputs compare to the second score auction models?

A. So they're the same. In the second score auction model, we used market shares to estimate diversion. In GUPPI, we can—we also have a diversion estimate. And then both models take the variable profit margin.

Q. How does a diversion ratio affect the GUPPI model?

A. So the higher the diversion ratio, the higher the great predicted harm in the model.

Q. And how about the margin?

A. So as in the second score auction model, the higher variable profit margin leads to greater predicted harm.

Q. Which diversion ratio calculation did you use for the GUPPI models?

A. So, your Honor, here I used two. I used my estimate, which is diversion proportional to share, and then I used Dr. Snyder's estimate, which is based on his agency data.

Q. Which profit margin calculation did you use in the GUPPI models?

A. I used my calculation that treats the direct operating expenses as being variable.

THE COURT: That's the more conservative approach?

THE WITNESS: Correct, because it leads to a lower profit margin.

BY MR. STEVENSON:

Q. Would you please share the results of the GUPPI models with us?

A. Sure. If we could please advance one more slide. Thank you. So in this, your Honor, here we're looking at the multi-round bidding GUPPI model. So this is the equivalent to a rounds auction. On the left-hand side, we have Penguin Random House. So this is the average effect on Penguin Random House authors. The blue bars are the GUPPI estimate using diversion proportional to share. The green bars are the GUPPI results using the agency data to estimate diversion. And the orange bars are the second score auction models prediction. So under the multi-round bidding GUPPI model, the models predicting—using either my preferred diversions or Dr. Snyder's, it's showing significantly higher reductions in advances than the second score auction model. If we look on the right-hand side, we have the same information for Simon & Schuster. We can see that the GUPPI prediction using diversion proportional to share is about twice the size of the reduction for the second score auction model. And for the GUPPI using the agency data diversion, the value is about the same.

Q. The same as the second score auction model?

A. That's correct.

Q. What were the results of the GUPPI models for the best bid in hybrid scenarios?

A. If we could advance one more slide, please. Here you see—it turns out, your Honor, the single round in hybrid GUPPI models—so that was essentially a best bids-type model—and then a model where there's a rounds auction followed by negotiations, they ended up giving the same prediction.

So on the left, for Penguin Random House, the GUPPI model's predictions are similar to the second score auction model's prediction. On the right, for Simon & Schuster, using diversion proportional to share, the GUPPI model's effect is slightly smaller than for the second score auction model. And then for the GUPPI using Dr. Snyder's agency data, the prediction's about half the size but still significant.

Q. Stepping back, what conclusions, if any, did you reach from the results of the GUPPI models?

A. So I think the GUPPI models support the idea that the second score auction model is a reasonable approach to estimating harm here. It uses some different mechanisms for acquisitions of books and it reaches qualitatively similar results.

MR. STEVENSON: Your Honor, this figure and the one on the previous slide are collectively re-creations of PX 0964. I move to admit PX 964.

THE COURT: Any objection?

MR. OPPENHEIMER: No objection.

THE COURT: Thank you. It'll be admitted. (Whereupon, Plaintiff's Exhibit No. 1064 was entered into evidence.)

THE COURT: Can I ask a question?

THE WITNESS: Sure.

THE COURT: So not being a Ph.D. in economics, I don't really understand the intricacies of these models. And I'm wondering if the dispute between the experts is more about the inputs as opposed to the methodology, because if the dispute's about the inputs, I think I understand that. But if the dispute is about the methodology, I feel like I have to understand this better.

THE WITNESS: Sure. So let's take the second point first. I would say that Dr. Snyder and I disagree somewhat about the inputs. As you can see on these slides and the previous one, sometimes our diversions give different answers; and similarly, we saw if you give different margins, you get somewhat different results.

THE COURT: Yes. I understand that part.

THE WITNESS: Yes. And then similarly, which I won't go into in any detail here, because I understand it's going to be handled later, but if you include efficiencies, the way Dr. Snyder would like to, there are also different results. On the methodological differences, I think Dr. Snyder's concern is that he feels the second score auction model is not addressing all the different ways in which books are acquired. And I would say because it assumes the second score auction format.

THE COURT: But if I understood you correctly, you inputted data about all the different ways that books are acquired. But you made an assumption and put it into a second score auction framework. But the data is from all of the books. And so you are assuming, if we put that into this framework, we can get some idea of what the competitive effects would be. That's kind of what I understood you to be saying.

THE WITNESS: That's right. I think that's fair. And the second score auction model is often used in models with auctions in which the auctions may not be second score auctions. It's—but it's a way of—the thing about the second score auctions model, your Honor, without going into too many details, is it's very easy to solve, because in it, it turns out that everyone has an incentive to just—in certain circumstances, the competitors bid their true valuations. It works out that you just reveal your true valuation. And so it's very easy to solve. Under some circumstances, it gives the same predictions as best bid auctions or other formats. It's not guaranteed to do that, but it often does. So people often use it because economic models can be very hard to solve, especially best bid-type auctions. I tried to do a best bids auction here. And the data—you know, in a best bids auctions, if you're going to model it, you would really like to have data for every auction, who bid and how much they bid and when they bid. In some settings you have that information, your Honor, particularly ones involving public procurement. But here, you don't have that kind of information. So my attempts to do that—

THE COURT: Well, you have the agency data. But you think it's incomplete?

THE WITNESS: The agency data are incomplete. I tried to use something like the agency data to make a prediction, and I ended up with significantly higher price effects. And they were higher enough that I didn't think that they were credible based on what I knew about the market. And so I used the second score auction model. It's a widely used model. It's broadly reliable. So I thought it was a reasonable approach. And the—and then Dr. Snyder criticized it and I tried these GUPPI models, which look at a best bids setting; they look at a second price setting; and then they look at this hybrid setting, which is rounds followed by negotiations. So they're giving some flavor of a broader set of settings.

THE COURT: Is there a dispute about the methodology in the GUPPI analysis or just the inputs?

THE WITNESS: I don't believe so, your Honor, with the brief exception that the parties' economists said: You should look at the three GUPPI models and take the lowest. So they would say: Look at this slide. Don't think about the previous slide. My view is you should look at both of them when you're thinking about it. But I think—I don't believe that there's a dispute about that point.

THE COURT: Thank you.

THE WITNESS: And then if I may, your Honor, with respect to the second score auction model, there's also—one of the ways that the creator of the model talked about evaluating whether it's performing well is to compare the model takes—the model will take the inputs you give it, profit margins and market shares, and then it'll predict what margins should look like in the model. And you can compare those to actual margins and say: How well are these matching? My view is that the model—the match there is good. And Dr. Snyder, I believe, will testify that he doesn't think the match is good. So that's something that'll—you'll probably hear about that in addition.

THE COURT: Thank you.

BY MR. STEVENSON:

Q. Dr. Hill, before we move on from unilateral effects, will you please summarize your primary conclusions on the topic?

A. Yeah. So I looked at here four buckets of information about unilateral effects. So concentration, qualitative evidence, diversion ratios and economic models. And I think they're all consistent with the idea that the transaction will substantially reduce unilateral competition.

Q. Let's switch our focus to coordinated effects. Would you please remind us what coordinated effects are?

A. Sure. So if we advance one more slide, please. So this is language from the merger guidelines summarizing the idea of coordinated interaction. And essentially, the idea is a merger may reduce competition in a way that makes it easier for firms to pull their punches when competing with one another.

Q. What do you have in mind when you think of coordinated interaction?

A. So there's usually two types that one thinks about, your Honor. One is explicit coordination and the other is tacit coordination. Explicit, I think, is easier to think about. You could think of an example of this as being price-fixing or market allocation. So the firms in an industry get together and say: We're going to—today we're charging $5 when we're competing. Wouldn't it be better if we could charge $7? Let's all charge $7. So it's an explicit agreement. Or a market allocation: You take that half of the country; we'll take this half. And let's not compete because competition leads to lower margins. That's what explicit coordination might look like. Tacit coordination, your Honor, is through repeated interaction, firms learn that things go better when we don't compete aggressively for one another's business. And so they learn to be accommodating rather than to compete aggressively.

Q. And do explicit and tacit coordination share any features?

A. Yeah. I think at a high level for coordination, there are three things you think are necessary. One is you need some form of common understanding. You need an agreement that you're, be it tacit or explicit, that you're going to pull your punches. A second is the ability to monitor and detect. So you need to be able to see if other firms are adhering to the coordination. If you can't tell if anyone else is coordinating, it's very hard to coordinate. And then third is some form of punishment. So, your Honor, on this quote we see "Coordinated interaction involves conduct by multiple firms that is profitable for each of them only as a result of the accommodating reactions of the others." So when coordination is ongoing, it's often the case that the firms have a unilateral incentive to leave the coordination, to cheat. So we all agreed we'd fix prices at $7. I charge $6.95 and I steal the whole market. That's my incentive to cheat. So you need to be able to detect that. And then the third common element is you need some sort of punishment. If we—if someone leaves the coordination, how do we punish them for doing that and thereby incentivize them to stick with the coordination?

Q. Did you reach any opinions about the likelihood of coordinated effects arising from this merger?

A. I did.

Q. What were those opinions?

A. I think that the transaction is likely to increase the risk of coordination.

Q. How did you reach that opinion?

A. So if we can advance—oh, we're there. So this is some language, your Honor, from the horizontal merger guidelines. The guidelines sort of set three conditions for thinking about what it would look like for a merger to increase the risk of coordination. So number one is: The merger must significantly increase concentration and lead to a moderately or highly concentrated market. So we've seen that that's the case in this market.

Second, the market has to show some signs of vulnerability to coordinated conduct. And then, third, the agencies have a credible basis on which to conclude that the merger may enhance that vulnerability. So these three points are the framework I use to look at coordinated effects of this market.

Q. Let's start with this—the market's signs of vulnerability to coordinated conducted. Did you observe any of those?

A. I did. So if we could please advance one more slide. Your Honor, here I've listed some of the reasons why I think the market is susceptible to coordinated conduct. The first is there's some history here of coordination among publishers. Now, that coordination, which is—I'm thinking here of the ebooks price-fixing, which was in a different market. But in that coordination, the heads of five of the major six publishers were able to meet and come to an agreement. And that ability to reach an agreement, I think, raises the chance that there's a susceptibility to coordination. Second, coordination is more likely when you have a small number of significant firms. Your Honor, I think you've already seen evidence that here there's the Big 5. And so that makes it easier to monitor and detect. Your Honor, greater transparency typically makes coordinations easier because it aids in the monitoring and punishment. And I think here we see some hallmarks of that transparency. Fourth: frequency of purchase. Small, frequent purchases make coordination easier to sustain. Larger, regular purchases make coordination harder to sustain. And here, your Honor, we have a lot of frequent purchases. I think there's on the order of 1,000 anticipated top sellers a year. And then finally, there's some evidence that the reliance of other firms on the Big 5 publishers for printing and distribution may make it more challenging for them to disrupt any coordination should it appear.

Q. You mentioned that there's some hallmarks of transparency here. What are you referring to?

A. Sure. So I think, your Honor, you heard testimony today and also from some other publishers, including Mr. Pietsch and Mr. Karp, that information is available on who wins competitions. They may not know who they're competing with at the time, but they typically observe after the auction's over who was the winner. So there's an ability to know to whom you're losing. And if one of your established authors is poached, for example, you often know to whom they've switched.

Q. Why is the merger likely to increase the market's vulnerability to coordination?

A. So today, your Honor, we have the Big 5. And after the transaction, it'll be the Big 4. And reductions in the number of firms simplify monitoring detection. They can simplify punishment. And they can simplify reaching an agreement.

DIRECT EXAMINATION (Resumed)

BY MR. STEVENSON:

Q. Good afternoon, Dr. Hill.

A. Good afternoon.

Q. Do you recall yesterday the Court asked a couple questions about your $250,000 threshold?

A. I do.

Q. Could you please provide a little more insight into what role the $250,000 threshold plays in your analysis?

A. So, Your Honor, it's the cutoff I'm using to identify anticipated top sellers. I'm thinking of there's this group of these general interest books that have a potential for high sales, and $250,000 is how I am identifying them in the data. And then I also looked at other thresholds in the vicinity.

Q. Do you also recall yesterday the court asked a couple questions about how margins interact with your model?

A. I do.

Q. Does the profit margin of a publisher tell you on average the differences between the first and second bidders in an auction?

A. It's a measure of how competitive the competition is, Your Honor, so it can give you a sense of how much competition there was for books on average.

Q. How does the model take that information to determine the distance between the second and third bidders?

A. So the model is using that distance to make an estimate of the distance between the second and third bidder and, thus, the effect of the merger on competition.

Q. I would like to move on—

THE COURT: I'm sorry, can I just ask, so your variable margin numbers, are they an average of all the variable margins of all the books, or are they individual in each auction?

THE WITNESS: They are averaged across the title level P&Ls, Your Honor.

THE COURT: Okay. I'm sorry. Go ahead.

BY MR. STEVENSON:

Q. And by title level of the analysis, you mean all the anticipated top selling P&Ls?

A. Yes, sorry.

THE COURT: So for each publishing company of anticipated top sellers, you looked at their variable profit margin and you used the same one across all auctions?

THE WITNESS: So I calculated for Penguin Random House, Your Honor, and for Simon & Schuster because they are the ones for which I had the detailed P&L level data. And then in the case of the model, you use one margin to calibrate the model. So you can put in the Penguin Random House margin for Penguin Random House, and then the model would predict margins for other publishers, you can put in the Simon & Schuster margin, and then the model will predict margins for others, or you can use a blended average of two margins.

THE COURT: How does it predict the other bidders' margins?

THE WITNESS: So it uses the observed market shares, the margin for one publisher, and then the model of competition, which is a second score auction model, and then predicts margins for other publishers. And if you recall, Your Honor, I talked about you can use the predicted margins compared to the actual margins to see how well the model is fitting. And that's what you would do. If you calibrated the model using Penguin Random House's margin, then the model would predict Simon & Schuster's margin, and you can compare that margin to the observed margin for Simon & Schuster.

THE COURT: And the estimates are based on market share?

THE WITNESS: It's based on the market shares and also on the model of competition in the model.

THE COURT: Okay. I hope you don't mind my asking this. So when you did the market shares for HarperCollins, did you include Christian books and romance novels in their market share number?

THE WITNESS: So here I used all anticipated top sellers of general trade books. Things like an edition of the Bible that had $250,000 in sales, it would not have been included because it would be outside the general trade books. But otherwise, all of HarperCollins' books for which they paid more than—$250,000 or more would be included.

THE COURT: Okay. So anything over—but you said general trade books. Does that include any Christian books that are not the Bible?

THE WITNESS: Yes. There are—I was going to say general interest Christian books, but books that—I think the previous witness was—Mr. Murray was talking about some books, some Christian books, appeal to a broader audience, and then there are some that are sold exclusively through Christian bookstores.

THE COURT: But you included both the Christian bookstores and the general audience Christian books, just not Bibles?

THE WITNESS: I believe so. I believe if the advance was above $250,000. I would have to check the backup to be sure.

THE COURT: Okay. And then for the romance books, you included the Harlequin books if the advances were over 250?

THE WITNESS: That's my understanding, yes. I would have to check to be absolutely sure.

THE COURT: Okay. Thank you. Go ahead, Mr. Stevenson.

BY MR. STEVENSON:

Q. Dr. Hill, did you include Baker Publishing in your market share calculations?

A. Yes, I did.

Q. What is your understanding of the genres that Baker Publishing publishes?

A. Baker focuses on Christian books.

Q. I would like to focus now on mitigating factors which we previewed at tiny bit yesterday.

A. Sure.

Q. What are mitigating factors in the context of the—in the context of your economic analysis of a merger?

A. So, Your Honor, mitigating factors are things that could offset an otherwise anticompetitive effect from a merger.

Q. What mitigating factors did you consider in your analysis of this merger?

A. So there are four. If we could advance one more slide, please. So the first will be entry and expansion, Your Honor. Then I will talk a little bit about the role of literary agents. Then we will talk about the Penguin Random House bidding promise. And then efficiencies is the fourth.

Q. And I would ask you to save for today any efficiencies testimony. I think we will cover that in rebuttal if necessary.

A. Okay.

Q. What were your overall conclusions regarding mitigating factors in the context of this merger?

MR. FISHBEIN: Your Honor, can just I ask, I think the gallery is not seeing the public version.

THE COURT: Okay. Thank you, Mr. Fishbein.

THE COURTROOM DEPUTY: It's on.

THE COURT: Okay.

THE WITNESS: So my general conclusions were that the mitigating factors are unlikely to mitigate the anticompetitive effect of the transaction.

BY MR. STEVENSON:

Q. Let's start by discussing entry and expansion. What would entry and expansion look like in this context?

A. So expansion could be an existing publisher of anticipated top sellers competing more aggressively as a result of the merger, and entry could be the appearance of a new publisher who enters into publishing and competes for anticipated top sellers.

Q. At a high level, why are entry and expansion unlikely to offset the anticompetitive effects of the merger?

A. At high level, I think there are significant barriers to entry and expansion. And I think some of the existing competitors may not have an incentive to aggressively expand. And so yeah.

Q. Let's start with the barriers to entry and expansion. Did you observe any general evidence regarding barriers to entry and expansion in the market for anticipated top sellers?

A. Yes. If you could please advance one more slide. These are some quotes from the parties talking about the existence of entry barriers. I think the second of the three quotes here, Your Honor, high barriers to entry, no successful startups in the last decade, sort of summarizes the general tenor.

Q. Did you observe any other general evidence outside of the merging party statements?

A. Yeah. If we can advance one more slide, please. Here are some additional quotes, Your Honor. And the one that I would highlight is the one at the very top. The originator of the quote says, in 45 years in the business, I haven't seen a single company set out to compete in this general trade world and achieve it. No one has succeeded in creating a publisher—a publishing entity that is competitive with the Big 5.

Q. What are the barriers to entry and expansion in the market for anticipated top sellers?

A. If we can advance one more slide, you will see a list of them. One is the ability to manage risk. One is breadth of marketing. One is breadth of distribution. And one is reputation.

Q. We will get to the others in a couple minutes. Let's start with risk. Why is the ability to manage risk a barrier to entry and expansion in the market for anticipated top sellers?

A. Your Honor, I think you heard Mr. Murray testify about the riskiness of these larger books that are anticipated to have high sales and the challenges in financially bearing that risk.

Q. Have you seen any evidence that larger publishers are able to manage this risk?

A. Yes. If you could advance one more slide, please. This is some evidence from two larger publishers including Penguin Random House.

And the quotes here, Your Honor, are talking about the ability to manage that risk. And I would direct you in particular to the first quote on the left. By publishing a lot of tiles, you can manage your risk because you are not dependent on a few. When there's a very risky asset, the more of the risky asset you hold, the more you can mitigate the risk on average.

Q. Do large publishers do anything else to manage the riskiness of anticipated top sellers?

A. Yes. If you could please advance one more slide. I think there was some testimony about this earlier today as well. The Big 5 tend to have very large backlists that they can use to reduce their risk. And so here I would focus on the very bottom here. I mean, to build a backlist the size of any of the Big 5, I don't think it's possible or conceivable that any publisher starting now could do it in a hundred years. It just takes these massive publishing entities or these agglomerations of backlists. I think that's informative. And the second quote down as well, the fact that we have the largest and richest backlist in the industry is what gives us the latitude to take risks with new acquisitions every day. So these very large backlists form a basis for taking risks on the frontlist, Your Honor.

Q. In addition to the riskiness of anticipated top sellers, you mentioned the marketing demands. Why is that a barrier to entry?

A. The ability to effectively market a book to reach a broad audience of consumers and let the consumers know that this book is available for purchase is something that the Big 5 do better than other publishers.

Q. Have you seen any evidence of that?

A. Sure. If you advance one more slide, please. Thank you. So here you have again some evidence on this point, Your Honor. And I will direct you to the one at the top. So for print books that are new books, why is it the case that the Big 5 publishers have a leg up on some of the competition in making sure that those books become best sellers. And the answer is, because they can coordinate publicity and distribution and marketing at the time of release.

Q. You also mentioned distribution as another barrier to entry and expansion. Why is that?

A. So if the marketing of the book has created excitement about the book, it's important that the book be available in a wide variety of outlets for consumers to purchase it.

Q. Have you observed any evidence of distribution posing a barrier to entry and expansion?

A. Sure. If you advance one more slide here. I think here the second quote is perhaps the most revealing. We have strong relationships with retailers. We have programs in place with major retailers to promote certain of our books that I believe are more—are stronger than those that smaller publishers who are—who don't have their—have big successes as often. There's a good deal of qualitative evidence about the idea that distribution is stronger for the Big 5 than for others.

Q. Do all Big 5 publishers manage their own distribution?

A. Not fully, no.

Q. Which ones do not?

A. Four of the five, I believe, handle all their distribution functions. I think you heard testimony from Mr. Murray that HarperCollins does not do all of its own distribution. It does manage sales and some other parts, but it outsources part of that distribution.

Q. Why do you view distribution as a barrier to entry and expansion when HarperCollins, the second largest publisher in of your market, outsources some of its distribution function?

A. So I think the testimony from HarperCollins is that they view the sales function, which is part of distribution, as being crucial. This ability to reach all types of retailers, the independent bookstores that Mr. Murray spoke about to have your book in the airport bookstore, just to have a wide range of options for acquiring that book.

Q. Why can't smaller publishers just contract with a Big 5 publisher to get the benefits of a great distribution network?

A. Many smaller publishers do contract with a Big 5, Your Honor. I believe their view, if you look at the qualitative evidence, is that that puts a surcharge on top of their costs that the Big 5 don't typically bear.

Q. Finally, you mentioned reputation as a barrier to entry and expansion. Why is that?

A. So I think of reputation as having two parts. One is that authors would like to have a publisher who has a reputation for successfully publishing books that have a lot of sales to a general audience, and two, I think we have heard testimony from a number of entities saying that authors also are attracted by the prestige of some of the imprints of the Big 5.

Q. Have you seen any evidence on that point?

A. Sure. So this slide here is summarizing some evidence on those points, Your Honor. And I think the quote at the bottom here from a literary agent talking about the longevity and success is an important consideration for authors is a useful one.

Q. I would like to ask a few questions now about non-Big 5 publishers in particular. What did you conclude about these publishers—or excuse me, the likelihood that these publishers would expand to mitigate the anticompetitive effects of the merger?

A. I think it's low.

Q. Why is that?

A. We have talked, Your Honor, about some of the barriers expansion that the non-Big 5 face, and I also think that the quantitative evidence shows that they have had a small market share over time and that that share hasn't changed significantly.

Q. You mentioned quantitative evidence about their competitiveness today and over time. Could you share that with us, please.

A. Sure. If you could please advance one more slide. So this, Your Honor, is a chart looking at the market shares of the Big 5 publishers and the non-Big 5 publishers for various advance amounts. So we have the Big 5 publishers in blue and we have all of the non-Big 5 publishers in green.

And you can see that, Your Honor, if you cut the—however you cut the advance levels here, the share of the non-Big 5 publishers is 10 percent or less collectively.

Q. You mentioned that hasn't changed over time. What evidence have you seen of that?

A. If you could advance one more slide, please. Dr. Snyder identified in his report a group of non-Big 5 publishers that he argued had expanded from 2019 to 2021. So this chart here is looking at the left at the market share growth of those publishers, non-Big 5 publishers, and then on the right looking at the change in market share of other non-Big 5 publishers. And you can see that the expansions and the shrinkages essentially cancel one another out.

Q. What does that mean about the aggregate growth of the non-Big 5?

A. It's essentially flat.

MR. STEVENSON: Your Honor, this figure is a recreation of PX0977. I move to admit PX0977.

THE COURT: Any objection?

MR. OPPENHEIMER: No objection.

THE COURT: That will be admitted. (Plaintiff's 0977 received in evidence.)

BY MR. STEVENSON:

Q. How does the non-Big 5's share change over time compare to the merging parties'?

A. If we advance one more slide, there's a slide summarizing this. So on the left, we have the change over time in Penguin Random House's share, and it's somewhere between two and two and a half percent. Simon & Schuster is flat. And the non-Big 5 are essentially flat. Penguin Random House from 2019 to 2021 saw a small amount of growth. The non-Big 5's share, collective share, did not change materially.

MR. STEVENSON: Your Honor, this is a recreation of PX0967. I move to admit PX0967.

THE COURT: Any objection?

MR. OPPENHEIMER: No objection.

THE COURT: That will be admitted. (Plaintiff's 0967 received in evidence.)

BY MR. STEVENSON:

Q. In addition to this quantitative evidence, did you observe any qualitative evidence regarding the competitive significance of non-Big 5 publishers?

A. Sure. If you could advance one more slide, please. This is a slide summarizing some evidence on the question of how often the smaller publishers compete for anticipated top sellers. And I think it's consistent with what we see in the market shares, that the non-Big 5 publishers do compete but rarely.

Q. Did you consider any expansion plans of small publishers in your analysis or the lack thereof?

A. I did.

Q. What evidence did you observe on that?

A. So if we advance one more slide, please. Your Honor, on this slide and on the following slide, this is evidence from publishers. I am not sure which version you are seeing, Your Honor, but I think in your binder you have a version with the names of publishers included. This is a group of publishers discussing whether they are likely to expand. And so there's four publishers talking about it on this slide, and then—this is slide 78, Your Honor, if you are looking in the binder. And then slide 79 also summarizes four other publishers.

Q. We have been discussing entry and expansion at a relatively general level. Did you observe any recent examples of attempted entry?

A. Yes.

Q. What example?

A. Amazon's attempt to enter into publishing.

Q. Why is Amazon's attempt at entry relevant to your analysis of this merger?

A. I think Amazon's attempted entry is useful, Your Honor, to understand some of the barriers to entry given that Amazon is a large and successful organization.

Q. Have you observed any qualitative evidence regarding Amazon's attempted entry?

A. Sure. If you advance one more slide, please. You will see some quotes here from third parties, and you heard some testimony from Mr. Murray, Your Honor, about this earlier. So I direct you here in particular to the upper left. I don't know of any examples of Amazon competing with Penguin Random House in auctions to acquire books. It would be fair to say that I don't know any examples of auctions where Amazon has competed with us in the auction. I think these are indicative of how successful Amazon has been in competing for anticipated top sellers.

MR. STEVENSON: Could we please take down this slide for a moment just for a confidentiality issue. Thank you. What other evidence have you observed regarding Amazon's attempting entry?

I have also analyzed Amazon's market share in the market for anticipated top sellers. And if we could advance one more slide, we will see a summary of that evidence. And I won't speak to the specifics, but, Your Honor, I think you can see here that Amazon's share in the market for anticipated top sellers is not high.

MR. STEVENSON: Your Honor, this figure is a recreation of PX0968. I move to admit PX0968.

THE COURT: Any objection?

MR. OPPENHEIMER: No objection.

MR. STEVENSON: It's one of two figures in the exhibit, just to clarify. I would like to admit the entire exhibit. It's the full exhibit is in your binder.

MR. OPPENHEIMER: That's fine, Your Honor.

THE COURT: All right. That's admitted.

MR. STEVENSON: Apologies. It's just a stamping issue. (Plaintiff's 0968 received in evidence.)

BY MR. STEVENSON:

Q. I would like to ask a couple questions now about the remaining Big 5 expanding to mitigate the anticompetitive effect of the merger. Did you consider the possibility that that might happen?

A. I did.

Q. And what did you conclude?

A. I don't think it's likely that they will have the incentive to expand in response to an anticompetitive effect.

Q. Why not?

A. I think here it's helpful to think through the various acquisition mechanisms, Your Honor. If we start by thinking about a rounds auction, you heard testimony, for example, from Mr. Pietsch and also from Mr. Karp that at an auction, the publishers are bidding in a rounds auction up to their valuation. The transaction is not likely to change their valuations of the books they are competing for, so it's unlikely in a rounds setting that there is going to be a significant change in incentives for the other Big 5 publishers.

Q. How about other acquisition types?

A. So it varies again acquisition type by acquisition type. Your Honor, we discussed yesterday in a best bids type framework the effect is that a publisher is balancing the probability of winning against the margin if it wins. For the parties, by removing the head-to-head competition, they can significantly change the probability of winning and lead them to bid less aggressively. Other publishers won't have that, what we would call a first order effect. There may be an additional effect that they recognize over time that the parties are bidding less aggressive—or, sorry, the merged firm is bidding less aggressively, but they are unlikely to have an incentive to bid more aggressively.

THE COURT: I'm sorry. So over time, they are not going to bid more aggressively to compete with the combined entity?

THE WITNESS: Right. So there—this is a common feature in some economic models, Your Honor. If you recognize that competition has been softened but you are less likely to lose an auction for a particular book on average, then your incentive is to take some of that as a higher probability of winning and take some of it as a higher margin if you win. So you take a little bit of both, and that means you bid a little bit less aggressively than you did prior to the merger.

BY MR. STEVENSON:

Q. How might other Big 5 publishers' incentives be—excuse me. How might the incentives of other Big 5 publishers be affected in negotiations with authors?

A. The effect in negotiations will likely be similar to that in best bids. In a negotiation, the concern is that the book may go into the open market or go to another publisher. If there is a perception—for the parties, there is a recognition that a direct competitor has been removed and is not competing head-to-head with us. The non-Big 5—sorry, the other members of the Big 5 don't have that direct effect. But there can be a second order effect where they recognize that competition has softened because the merged firm bids less aggressively. So they may be unchanged or they may have a small diminution in their aggressiveness.

Q. At a high level, what is your understanding of Dr. Snyder's arguments regarding entry and expansion?

A. I believe that Dr. Snyder believes that there aren't—that entry is relatively easy into the market for anticipated top sellers and that there have been recent examples of entry that underline that.

Q. Let's break that down. Do you agree with Dr. Snyder's argument that entry and expansion are easy?

A. I don't believe so, Your Honor. I think there are significant barriers to entry and expansion.

Q. Do you agree with Dr. Snyder that examples of recent entry show that there are limited barriers to entry and expansion?

A. I think, Your Honor, there hasn't been evidence of significant entry and expansion by the non-Big 5 over the past three years. And I think there's qualitative evidence that the non-Big 5 face significant barriers to entry and expansion.

THE COURT: Did you consider whether other Big 5 publishers might merge themselves and consolidate?

THE WITNESS: I did not analyze that, Your Honor.

THE COURT: Is that a factor?

THE WITNESS: Typically what the—when looking at a particular merger, one thinks about what would happen if this merger occurred, because subsequent mergers may themselves be subject to evaluation or challenges and maybe—it's relatively speculative for me to guess there might be a merger between HarperCollins and Hachette, which that's complete speculation. I have no knowledge of such a merger, just to be clear.

BY MR. STEVENSON:

Q. Dr. Hill, I would like to focus on literary agents for a moment.

A. Sure.

Q. Did you consider the role that literary agents play in your analysis of this merger?

A. I did.

Q. What do you understand to be the role of literary agents?

A. I think Mr. King gave some very good testimony on the role of literary agents, the ways they can help an author to find a publisher for a manuscript or an idea.

Q. Did Dr. Snyder make any arguments regarding literary agents?

A. He did.

Q. What is your understanding of those arguments?

A. My understanding is his argument is that literary agents will make it unlikely that there will be harm from the transaction post-merger.

Q. Do you agree with that argument?

A. I don't.

Q. Why not?

A. I don't think that literary agents—their agents are a feature in many different markets, Your Honor, and—or, sorry, agents are a feature in many different markets, and they don't have a magic wand. They have experience in negotiations, and they use the leverage created by competition to get better terms. And if there's a significant reduction in competition, they can't fix that.

Q. Have you seen any evidence suggesting that this would be the case?

A When you say this would be the case.

Q. Oh, yeah, any evidence that literary agents would be unable to mitigate the anticompetitive effect of the merger.

A. Yeah. I think there's two broad buckets of evidence on that, Your Honor. One is that today publishers are earning a significant margin. If literary agents had a magic wand, then I would expect to see publishers not earning a margin. And then second, there are examples of competitions where the publishers were willing to pay more than they eventually did. And, again, if agents were so good at preventing any harm to authors, I wouldn't expect to see that.

Q. Would you please share an example with us of that happening?

A. Sure. If you can advance one more slide, please. So, Your Honor, this is an example from a Simon & Schuster acquisition. And you can see in the first—and the block of text here is going forward in time from top to bottom. So an editor writes, I think if we make a bold preempt offer, we can keep it out of a competitive environment. At auction I can see this going for well above a million. For our preempt, I would like to get approval up to $750,000, but try to get it for $500,000. But open to other strategies. And then the publisher writes, approved to offer up to $500,000, so I think start at $350,000 world. But happy to discuss the other strategies. And the author ended up accepting the offer for $350,000.

And the editor writes, thanks again for setting the right price and keeping me from overspending. So here's an example where the publisher was willing to spend more, but the agent wasn't able to extract all of that value.

Q. Dr. Hill, did you review Jennifer Rudolph Walsh's report in this case?

A. I did.

Q. What is your understanding of Ms. Walsh's arguments regarding literary agents?

A. There was some variation, but I believe Ms. Walsh's arguments are similar to Dr. Snyder's.

Q. Would you please tell us your opinions are of those arguments?

A. They are the same as my opinions with regard to Dr. Snyder, that I don't think literary agents are likely to significantly mitigate the anticompetitive harm.

Q. You mentioned that the Penguin Random House bidding promise was a mitigating factor you considered.

A. Correct.

Q. I would like to ask a couple questions about that. What is your understanding of the substance of Penguin Random House's promise with regard to Simon & Schuster?

A. So if we could advance one more slide, there's a slide summarizing some of what I understand to be the key terms. And I think at a high level, Your Honor, the second bullet here is sort of summarizing it. The idea that post-merger Simon & Schuster imprints will continue to bid as an external bidder with the caveat on the third bullet that there's some level at which competing bids from Simon & Schuster and Penguin Random House will be subject to review by the CEO.

Q. What did you conclude about the likelihood of this promise to mitigate the anticompetitive effects of the merger?

A. I think it's unlikely to mitigate the anticompetitive effects.

Q. Why do you think the promise is unlikely to mitigate the anticompetitive effects?

A. If we could advance one more slide, please, I think there's four reasons. One is that it's a unilateral promises, Your Honor, that can be revoked. Two is, even if the promise remains in effect, there are other methods that the merged firm could take to reduce competition. Three, today we observed that imprints can and do coordinate before and during acquisitions which could circumvent the bidding promise. And then fourth, there may not be an effect in some acquisition settings. My understanding—sorry, go ahead.

Q. Let's start with the first issue, that it's a unilateral promise. Have you seen evidence that the merged firm would have an incentive to limit bidding between Penguin Random House and Simon & Schuster imprints after the merger?

A. Sure. If you could advance one more slide, please. This is some testimony from a president of one of the Penguin Random House imprints talking about this question of, why today, if there's only two—of the only imprints left in a rounds auction are Penguin Random House imprints, why are they not allowed to compete against one another further? And I think the last answer here says, because ultimately we are the same company so, frankly, we would just be driving up the price of an auction amongst ourselves. So this is summarizing the incentive to try to limit competition when the competition is just down to Penguin Random House imprints.

Q. Have you seen any other evidence of this incentive?

A. Yeah. If you could please advance one more slide. This is a discussion or a quote from a non-Big 5 publisher saying, I have seen the press releases put out by Markus Dohle and how they are going to keep the imprints bidding against each other, but I know if I were leading that company, I would never allow that. I don't know why a CEO of a company would allow multiple imprints to bid against each other. I think this again speaks to the incentive of why a publisher can have an incentive to limit its competition between imprints.

Q. You mentioned that the merged firm would have other ways to reduce competition between its imprints. Could you give us an example of how that might happen?

A. Sure. There's this incentive, Your Honor, to limit the competition, and it could be realized in a number of ways. So if you advance one more slide here, this is a discussion of some reorganization of imprints particularly focused on Crown. And if we look at the top left bullet, the highlighted section says, of course, there will be less internal competition with the focused editorial profiles in our three divisions. So one thing that the merged firm could do, Your Honor, is reorganize imprints so that they don't overlap and compete with each other as closely, so particularly imprints of Penguin Random House and Simon & Schuster.

Q. And just to clarify, the example you just walked through is the Random House and Crown integration, is that right?

A. Correct.

Q. You also mentioned that there's evidence that imprints today coordinate during auctions and that they might do that in the future. What evidence have you seen of that?

A. So if we could please advance one more slide. Here we are just seeing some examples, Your Honor, of the way this typically works is in a bidding auction. So the second one here, for example, we are going to—we, Penguin Publishing, are going to coordinate with the Random House side. Everyone has agreed to $1.1 million. Okay. So these are settings where, either before or during an auction, imprints inside of PRH can completely legally coordinate with one another to agree not to compete fully. And so post-merger, the Penguin Random House imprints and the Simon & Schuster imprints as part of one corporate family could similarly coordinate. And then I would also direct Your Honor just to the last bullet here, or the last quote at the bottom, of course, we would never poach another PRH author. PRH editor is a really good colleague. She would never try and poach from you guys. So, again, even if there was a limit on the bidding promise, established authors who are up for renegotiation would lose the benefit of the head-to-head competition between Penguin Random House and Simon & Schuster.

Q. That leads to the next question I was going to ask. I think you mentioned that the promise may not affect certain acquisition types. What are you thinking about there?

A. So my understanding is the bidding promise applies to rounds auctions. The testimony on this wasn't entirely clear to me. But that's the format in which I think it applies. And in other formats like best bids or negotiations, the idea is not necessarily that you get to a situation where you know that there are just Penguin Random House imprints left, but rather, you recognize that a significant head-to-head competition—source of competition has left.

So, for example, in a negotiation, you recognize that the external threats if the author walks away from negotiation are lower, and so you have less incentive to price aggressively—or sorry, to offer an aggressive advance amount.

Q. We are almost finished, Dr. Hill, but before we wrap up, I would like to ask that, taking into account all the evidence we discussed yesterday and today and the analysis you have done, would you please summarize your overall conclusions of the likely effect on competition of the acquisition of Simon & Schuster by Penguin Random House?

A. Yes. My conclusion, Your Honor, is the transaction is likely to significantly reduce competition in the market for anticipated top sellers and that that reduction in competition is likely to harm authors.

MR. STEVENSON: Your Honor, I have no further questions, and I pass the witness.

CROSS-EXAMINATION

BY MR. OPPENHEIMER:

Q. Dr. Hill, in your earlier testimony, you spent some time explaining that you could set the advance level in your market that you're proposing at different levels without any real substantial effect on your analysis. Fair statement?

A. Yes, I don't think it has a qualitatively significant effect.

Q. Okay. What I want to do at the outset here is identify one area where I think you'll agree with me it does make a difference where we set that advance level. Would you agree with me that if we zoom out and look at the market for—acquisition market for all trade books, that we're looking at an unconcentrated market?

A. If you make the advance cut-off zero, so which I think is what you have in mind or you're saying all trade so all books, whether they got an advance or not, then I think it's unconcentrated, it's very close to—its either unconcentrated or very close to the line.

Q. You tested down to $100,000 when you did your market concentrations, right?

A. It was either 100 or 150.

Q. Okay. You didn't go below that, though, correct?

A. Correct.

Q. And when the government first filed its complaint in this case, it alleged—also alleged a market for all trade books, the acquisition of all trade books, correct?

A. Correct.

Q. And that would be equivalent to a market that did not have an advance level cut-off, correct?

A. Correct, that would be all trade books.

Q. Okay. And you've never done an HHI market concentration analysis on the market for the acquisition of all trade books, have you?

A. I don't believe so.

Q. Okay. But you know that Professor Snyder has, correct?

A. I did not recall that.

Q. Do you recall seeing in his work an analysis of the shares associated with the all trade book acquisition market?

A. There are shares in my report and I remember some from his, but I don't remember—sorry, they're all trade book shares in my report and in his report.

Q. Do you recall looking at Professor Snyder's rebuttal report in connection with your work?

A. Yes.

Q. Could I ask you to look at Professor Snyder's rebuttal report, and I'd like you to take a look at the plate VII .1, that's on page 84 of the professor's rebuttal report to your work.

A. I'm there, sir.

THE COURT: Where in the binders is that?

MR. OPPENHEIMER: Your Honor, that's the binder of expert reports, and it is tab No. 6 in your binder. And, Dr. Hill, it's tab No. 6 in yours as well.

THE WITNESS: Yes, I'm here.

BY MR. OPPENHEIMER:

Q. Okay. Does this refresh your recollection that Professor Snyder ran a concentration, an HHI analysis on the market for all trade book acquisitions?

A. Yes.

Q. And you would agree with me that he concluded that that market was not sufficiently concentrated to trigger the presumption of harm?

A. Correct.

Q. And you did not address this in your reply materials; is that correct?

A. That's correct.

Q. Do you have any reason to disagree with Professor Snyder's conclusions?

A. I think when I ran this, again, I got something close—we got slightly different results, but it's either unconcentrated or very close to it. It certainly doesn't trigger the presumption.

Q. Okay. Fair enough. We have no dispute, I take it, Dr. Hill, that when we look at the market for the acquisition of all trade books, we don't trigger the presumption of harm, there is insufficient concentration, correct?

A. Correct.

Q. Okay. Good. By the way, it's also your view, is it not, that the downstream market is not highly concentrated?

A. I believe that to be true, yes.

Q. And so just we're talking about the same things, I think we are, by downstream, I simply mean the retail sale books, right?
A. Correct.
Q. And you expressed that view in your report as well, right?
A. That is correct.
Q. And, again, just so we can table set here a little bit, you have not analyzed any potential harm or benefit to the downstream market from this merger, correct?
A. That is correct.
Q. And you have no opinion about that?
A. Correct.
Q. And also—
THE COURT: When you say harm, though, you mean concentration type harm or—what type of harm do you mean?
MR. OPPENHEIMER: Let me clarify. Thank you.
BY MR. OPPENHEIMER:
Q. By harm, I mean any type of harm or benefit to the downstream market from this merger?
A. Yes, Your Honor, I haven't looked at the downstream market in my analysis.
Q. And you're not offering an opinion about whether consumers in the downstream market will pay more or less for their books post-merger?
A. That is correct.
Q. Now, we've spent time talking about the advance level cut-off for the market that you're proposing and you've chosen 250 as your cut-off, correct?
A. That's correct, $250,000.
Q. Okay. But you're not proposing to define a market based solely on the amount of the advance, are you?
A. I use the amount of the advance to identify the group of anticipated top sellers.
Q. Understood. But if the only information you had was the amount of the advance, that would be inadequate for you to define a market, would you agree with me?
A. I don't know. It would depend on the circumstances. It would be fact-specific.
Q. But you're not testifying in this case, to be clear, that you have identified a market on the basis of price alone?
A. I would say that the definition of the market cut-off is based on a number of—is based on a range of evidence.
Q. And have you ever—ever in your work defined market on the basis of price alone?
A. I don't recall. I've worked on a lot of cases. I don't know.
Q. Are you familiar with any cases that have ever done that?
A. It would be a differentiated products case where you might define the high quality good market by picking a price cut-off, but I can't recall—yeah. I think typically one also looks at the qualitative photographs.
Q. And that's what you're trying to do in this case as well, correct?
A. I'm trying to consider all the evidence, yes.
Q. Okay. And what you're saying is that there's something qualitatively different, other than just the price, between the books that are in your price segment and those that are not; is that correct?
A. I would put it slightly differently. There's the set of books that are intended to sell—expected to sell a lot of copies and appeal to a broad audience. And I'm trying to identify them in a way so that I can analyze them. And I'm using this dollar cut-off to try to find that group. And the dollar cut-off may classify some as anticipated top sellers who are not and it may do the reverse.
Q. I'd like to get a little better handle on your understanding of a top seller. Is that literally any book for which a $250,000 advance was paid?
A. The way it's defined—I think it's—there's some intricacies around contracts with multiple books, but it is the—the way I'm defining it is general trade books above $250,000, with an advance above

$250,000 for the title.

Q. So any—just to be clear, any book that receives an advance—any trade book, that receives an advance over $250,000 is in your segmented market that you're proposing?

A. I believe so, yes.

Q. And we've had testimony about books that have been written by celebrities, you recall some of that?

A. Sure.

Q. And by repeat authors, the Clancys of the world. Do you recall that?

A. Yes.

Q. Okay.

A. Well, I don't recall Mr. Clancy specifically, but, yes.

Q. Your market segment, does it take into account that group as a special group or are they just lumped in with everybody else over $250,000?

A. The existing authors are included in the market.

Q. So you would put the authors who received advances of tens of millions of dollars in the same market as the author who receives $250,000?

A. Correct.

Q. Do you see any difference between those two groups of authors?

A. I mean, they receive a different advance amount.

Q. You see no other differences between them?

A. I mean, it can be the case that they have other differences and they still belong in the same market. So I've defined a market for all beer in the past and that may include lots of different brands of beer. And I've defined markets for premium beer, which is an industry term, you know. There may be products in a market that are different from one another but share some common characteristics.

Q. But you typically wouldn't put either of the two beers you mentioned in the same market as champagne?

A. Champagne—it depends. If you're defining an all alcohol market, I would put champagne in the market.

Q. Did you do anything to test whether authors who received advances of $250,000 and more should be segmented into different groups within your proposed market?

A. In some of my analyses, I looked at different advance buckets, but they tended to look fairly similar in those analyses.

Q. Did you give any consideration to the proposition that authors who receive tens of millions of dollars in advances might have more leverage in the negotiating situation or in the market generally over somebody earning $250,000?

A. I did not. I mean, from my perspective, the key question was how the competition that's eliminated by the merger might affect them.

Q. I'm hoping that we can be mercifully brief with the hypothetical monopolist test. Not because your description wasn't interesting but because it was a little complicated, and I think we can conclude that it really doesn't help us much. So tell me if I have this right, Dr. Hill. The hypothetical monopolist test—

A. My apologies, sir. You said monopolist twice rather than monopsonist.

Q. You're right, I reverse that all the time.

A. I do the same thing.

Q. Actually, the case we have is a bit unusual, isn't it, it's a buyer-seller case?

A. A merger of seller—or buyers, yes.

Q. Have you ever applied the hypothetical monopolist test to a buy side case?

A. Do you mean the hypothetical monopsonist or monopolist because you said monopolist.

Q. Fair enough. They're not literally the same formula but the hypothetical—have you ever previously applied a hypothetical monopsonist test?

A. I don't believe so.

Q. Do you know anyone who has?

A. I don't believe so.

Q. Now, correct me if I am wrong, but isn't it the case that the hypothetical monopsonist test that you conducted in this case doesn't tell us anything about whether we should be dividing the authors into different advance levels?

A. I think if—it does a little bit in the sense that arbitrage is part of the consideration. So the market is properly—the focus is largely on the group of competitive products. Who else is competing with the parties. But as part of the test, too, you're considering losses due to arbitrage as part of the test. So to the extent that the arbitrage is likely, which I think it's not, that would factor into your test.

Q. Well, an arbitrage here simply means an author would somehow circumvent the market by selling her work to somebody else or getting it to somebody else who would again sell it to the publisher, correct?

A. That's correct.

Q. And I think we all agree that—we're in agreement, are we not, that that's not happening and nobody's really arguing that it is, correct?

A. Right. So that's one of the two conditions for defining a market around a particular group of buyers—or sellers, I'm sorry.

Q. It may have been that my comment at the outset that this would be mercifully short was overly optimistic. But let me ask you this. Isn't it true that the only thing your hypothetical monopsonist test does is to rule out self-publishing as an alternative for any author who's being published if the publisher lowers the advance. That's all it does. It just rules out self-publishing?

A. No, it also does this other function which is to test whether arbitrage is likely here, which is one of the two conditions for defining a market around the targeted seller or targeted sellers, yes. So the major function here is identifying these publishers, but it's also part of the test to identify whether your targeting is feasible.

Q. Would you agree with me that you cannot use that test, because you ran it, to determine whether one group of publishers at a lower advance level could be distinguished from another group of publishers at a higher advance level?

A. I would say it tests whether the group of authors where you have to find it is an appropriate market. So it may be appropriate, you could define it lower at $150,000, it's not ruling out that there's another market or—and it's not ruling that there's not a market for $350,000.

But it is telling you that the $250,000 cut-off is appropriately defined.

Q. But also tells you that the $150,000 cut-off is appropriate, right?

A. I do you mean the test in general?

Q. I mean, it won't distinguish between 250 and 150, will it?

A. Right, but that's only because there isn't a risk of arbitrage. Had there been a risk of arbitrage, then you might reject the test at a lower or higher advance amount but not reject it at the 250 amount.

Q. But the way you've run the test, it won't tell us whether a cut-off should be at 250, 150, 100, it won't tell us any of that, will it?

A. It's not going to choose between them, but it tells you that at $250,000, there's not enough substitution to arbitrage to make it unprofitable for the hypothetical monopsonist to lower advances.

Q. All right. And my last question, I promise, is, you're not claiming that your hypothetical monopsonist test required you to choose 250 or any other specific advance level as a cut-off, correct; that we agree on?

A. Correct.

Q. Okay. Success. You also claim that authors, if I understand you correctly, but tell me if I've got it wrong, you claim that authors of books in your price segment have different publisher preferences; is that right?

A When you say my price segment, you mean $250,000 and above?

Q. Yes.

A. Yes.

Q. And they're more likely to select a Penguin Random House or Simon & Schuster, HarperCollins, Macmillan or Hachette than to select another publisher; is that right?

A. That's correct.
Q. And you say that's because there's something about the book that requires those publishers?
A. I think of it as the book has expectation of significant sales, and so the advantages the Big 5 can bring are more significant for those authors than some other authors.
Q. And you say the books in your price segment typically require strong editing, marketing, and distribution, fair?
A. Correct.
Q. And you claim that publishers like Penguin Random House, Simon & Schuster, HarperCollins, Macmillan and Hachette, they have these characteristics, right?
A. Correct.
Q. But you're saying that the other publishers out there in the world, they don't have these characteristics; is that what you're saying?
A. I would put it slightly differently. I would say that the—for this group of authors, we can see through their revealed choices that they have a stronger preference for the Big 5 vis-à-vis the non-Big 5 than do other—authors of other books.
Q. And just so we're clear, you're deriving that preference from the market shares?
A. In part, yes.
Q. Because you're saying that if those publishers have a larger market share, they're engaged in acquisitions with more authors, correct?
A. I'm sorry, could you say that last part.
Q. I'm sorry, yes. Because those authors have more market share, they're engaged with more acquisitions with authors?
A. You said because those authors, did you mean publishers?
Q. I probably misspoke. Let me try it again.
You infer from the fact that a publisher has a high market share, that they are preferred by the authors; is that correct?
A. That's part of the evidence, yes.
Q. Do you take into account that it may also reflect the preference that the publisher has?
A. Yes, there's—I apologize, go ahead.
Q. Okay.
A. No, sorry. My answer would be, yes, it may be a combination of push and pull. The preferences of the authors and the competitive set in terms of which publishers can effectively compete.
Q. Okay. So I want to go back now to the characteristics that you identified earlier that you say the publishers we identified had, the Penguin Random Houses and the HarperCollins and the Macmillans. Are you saying that people out of the—publishers out of the so-called Big 5 don't have the ability to edit, market, and distribute books that are expected to generate significant sales?
A. So, again, there's 10 percent of the market is accounted for for the non-Big 5. So I'm not saying they can never do it. I'm just saying there are barriers to them doing it as regularly and competing as effectively as the Big 5 do.
Q. So you don't dispute that authors—pardon me, I've done it again—that publishers outside of the so-called Big 5 are perfectly capable of rendering those services, they just don't do it as often?
A. Yeah, in some circumstances, they can do it, yes.
Q. All right. So let's take a look at an example. Would you turn to tab 10?
A. In the big one.
Q. Tab 10. And, Dr. Hill, and Your Honor, we're going to be talking about book A. Okay.
A. I think I'm there.
Q. Do you have that, Doctor?
A. I do.
Q. Thank you. All right. This identifies this as a transaction involving author A. Do you see that?
A. Which page are you on that has the author's name?
Q. Let me bypass one document. Let us go to tab 11.

A. Okay.
Q. And we can see from that quite quickly that we're dealing with author A. So if we go to tab 11. Let me know when you're there.
A. I'm there.
Q. Okay. Do you recognize this as one of the summary sheets provided during the course of discovery in this case?
A. I do.
Q. And you do recognize this as being part of your reliance list?
A. It looks like one of them. I don't recall this particular one, but, yes. This is a format I've seen before.
Q. Okay. Now, I can represent to you that this summary came as part of the agent investigation that you're familiar with?
A. Sure. That's fine.
Q. And it was anonymized by the agency when it was delivered to us.
And so what you're seeing on tab 11 was anonymized directly by the agency. I can represent it corresponds to book A in tab 10. That's our cheat sheet, okay?
A. Okay.
Q. It's that author and that title.
A. Got it.
Q. You can see from the summary page, if you go to 459, we should have that marked for you.
A. Yeah.
Q. Okay. You can see there that the form of this acquisition was a straight one-round best-bid auction. Do you see that in the notes there?
A. I do.
Q. Okay. And the—just so we're clear, the one-round best-bid auction, you understand to be everybody who's been invited to participate in the auction will submit their best bid?
A. Everyone who wishes to participate, yes.
Q. Well, let's back up one step even before that. Everyone whom the agent invited to participate and who elected to participate, correct?
A. Yes, everyone who is interested and is being contacted about participating will participate.
Q. These aren't public auctions, correct?
A. No.
Q. No. It is not common, based on your investigation, it is absolutely not common for agents to widely distribute sort of an open invitation to any form of auction, correct?
A When you say widely–
Q. Let me rephrase it. You would agree with me that agents, when they invite participants to any kind of auction in the publishing world, exercise thought and discretion about whom they invite?
A. Yes.
THE COURT: Is this the right witness to testify to the things that you're asking?
MR. OPPENHEIMER: Well, Your Honor, I think that, as we go forward, I think it will be a little bit clearer, because it has to do with the mechanism of harm in the case that is definitely part of his model.
THE COURT: Okay. I guess you should maybe phrase your questions in terms of what assumptions he made because he's not an expert on the publishing industry.
MR. OPPENHEIMER: I will, Your Honor.
THE COURT: Okay.
BY MR. OPPENHEIMER:
Q. So let's go to the summary page, 459.
A. I'm there.
Q. Okay. And now I want to take us to the summary bidding page, which is on 462.
A. I'm there.
Q. Okay. And do you see that the winner of the bid was Astra House?
A. I do.

Q. And that Astra House put in two bids, one for North America and one for global?
A. I do.
Q. And that the other two bidders on this book were Simon & Schuster and Penguin Random House. Do you see that?
A. Yes.
Q. And, by the way, their bids were under $250,000?
A. Correct.
Q. Does that mean that they did not think that this book was in your segmented market?
A. So using the—if one of them had won, this book would not be included in the market. If Aster House had not participated or if the author had selected them.
Q. Okay. Now, are you—Astra not one of the so-called Big 5 publishers, correct?
A. Correct.
Q. Are you saying that they cannot provide the editing, marketing, and distribution services needed for this book?
A. No.
Q. And would you agree with me that in this transaction, the agent must have thought that they had the capabilities to do all of those things for this book as well?
A. Well, I would say the key decision-maker would have been the author, but, yes, the author felt that Astra House was the best choice out of these bidders.
Q. Do you know who Astra Publishing is?
A. No.
Q. Do you know if they're a relatively recent entrant into the market?
A. I believe they may be one of Dr. Snyder's four examples of entrants.
Q. And do you have any familiarity with their recent bidding history?
A. I have familiarity with how often they've won, which is not a great deal.
Q. How often do you think they've won?
A Less than one percent of the time.
Q. I'm talking about Astra specifically, do you know how many—pardon me, how can acquisitions they've actually succeeded in securing?
A. Their total acquisitions?
Q. Yes.
A Of anticipated top sellers?
Q. Yes.
A. No.
Q. Okay. Do you have any idea within the last two years what their success rate has been?
A. Well, I have an idea of their market share. So if you count market share success rate, yes, it's been low.
Q. Market share is a picture of their wins at the time you take their market share, correct?
A. Correct.
Q. Right. It's not telling you what they're doing in terms of going-forward basis, right?
A. Right. But it goes—I believe it's from the reply report so it goes through the end of 2021.
Q. Can I have you take a look at tab 12?
MR. OPPENHEIMER: Your Honor, this is confidential.
THE COURT: All right.
BY MR. OPPENHEIMER:
Q. So I will be referring to some of this just by the placement on the page, and they should have been marked also for you, Dr. Hill. Do you see that?
A. I do.
Q. If you take a look at the first highlighted book, do you recognize it's the book we just talked about that was acquired by Astra, book A?
A. So I have a different title for—the book in the first row for me, the title ID begins with the word

"abolition." The second is the same title as the one I think you're referring to.

Q. I hate to do this, but I'll count down. If you go down to the ninth book on the list.

A Yep, that's it.

Q. I would say it and solve this easily for us, but if you see, it corresponds to A?

A. Correct.

Q. Okay. Do you see the next two acquisitions by Astra?

A. I do.

Q. And do you see that those were respectively in November of last year?

A. Correct.

Q. Do you see that each of those is in excess of $250,000?

A. I do.

THE COURT: Can you orient me about what this document is?

MR. OPPENHEIMER: Yes, Your Honor. This is a submission to us by the agent listing the acquisitions, the author, the date of the acquisition, and the amounts.

THE COURT: So this is a document from an agent?

MR. OPPENHEIMER: Correct.

THE COURT: Okay. Just one agent?

THE WITNESS: I don't think that's correct.

MR. OPPENHEIMER: Somehow, this is from the publisher.

THE COURT: Okay. From the publisher that's listed in the second column?

THE WITNESS: Yes.

MR. OPPENHEIMER: Yes, Your Honor.

THE COURT: Okay.

BY MR. OPPENHEIMER:

Q. And do you see the last acquisition in December also in your market?

A. I do.

Q. So you would agree with me that new entrants into the market, like Astra, are making acquisitions in your market segment?

A. Correct.

Q. And you realize this is a relatively new participant?

A. Correct.

Q. And would you dispute that Astra was established by well-known and well-respected publishing industry veterans?

A. I would not.

Q. Would you agree with me that Zando is another new entrant into the market?

A. I'm trying to remember if—

THE COURT: Again, Mr. Oppenheimer, he's not a publishing industry expert, so I don't understand why you keep asking him questions like this.

MR. OPPENHEIMER: Your Honor, I will move it forward.

BY MR. OPPENHEIMER:

Q. So I want to focus again on the characteristics of the books in your market. You say that they require the services that the Big 5 provide, correct?

A. I don't quite think I said they require that the Big 5 preside. We just saw an example of a non-Big 5 publisher winning. I would say that the Big 5 are better suited to compete for those books than the non-Big 5 are in general.

Q. Let's talk about another entity outside of the so-called Big 5, that's Norton Publishing?

A. Sure.

Q. Okay. Do you have any reason to believe that Norton Publishing can't provide the same services as the Big 5?

THE COURT: Again, Mr. Oppenheimer, he is not a publishing industry expert.

MR. OPPENHEIMER: Your Honor, I think one of the items that I'm trying to get into here a little bit is that part of the distinction of these books is that it's alleged that they need certain services, and so I'm exploring the degree to which those services are available by publishers throughout the publishing world. And the reason for that is that it is not limited to the Big 5 in any way.

THE COURT: Okay. I think—

MR. OPPENHEIMER: And these publishers have the ability to service those books?

THE COURT: I think he's agreed with you on that. Am I wrong?

THE WITNESS: No, I would say, I agree with you, Your Honor. They win about 10 percent of the time. They win more frequently for other types of books.

BY MR. OPPENHEIMER:

Q. Is the only distinction in your mind between the publishers who service your segment of $250,000 and higher the frequency with which those publishers service that segment?

A. No, I would say that it's more challenging for them to service—they being the non-Big 5, to service that segment than it is for the Big 5. And I think the qualitative and quantitative evidence supports that.

MR. OPPENHEIMER: Your Honor, could I beg the Court's indulgence for just a few more questions on that answer?

THE COURT: All right. Go ahead.

BY MR. OPPENHEIMER:

Q. Thank you. So if Norton bought a book at $500,000, is there something impeding it from rendering a full set of services to the author of that book?

A. When you say the full set of services, do you mean distribution and marketing?

Q. All the services that book needs to succeed in the marketplace?

A. I think it's more challenging for them than it is for the other members—or than for the members of the Big 5.

Q. With respect to the hypothetical one book bought at $500,000, what is the disadvantage that they set here?

A. The hypothetical book that you have in mind I can't tell you the exact disadvantage. It may be that that is a niche book that Norton acquired for a large advance amount and they are well-suited to publish. But in general, I think the evidence shows that the non-Big 5 are significantly less frequently acquiring these large books, and that people in the industry, including the Big 5 publishers, feel that there's a set of authors they are better set up to serve and publish.

Q. But you're not saying that the services that those publishers actually render are inferior to the services provided by the Big 5?

A. For a particular book that is acquired by the non-Big 5, the author has decided that—assuming that the Big 5 competed, that that—for that book, that non-Big 5 publisher is the best choice. And given the respective advance amounts offered.

MR. OPPENHEIMER: May we put up Plaintiff's Exhibit 963? Your Honor, this is previously admitted.

THE COURT: All right.

BY MR. OPPENHEIMER:

Q. This is confidential, sorry, only for our screens. You had made the point in prior testimony, Dr. Hill, that the participation by the publishing houses that are identified here, Penguin Random House, HarperCollins, Simon & Schuster, Macmillan, Hachette, are greater in the over $250,000 advance, correct?

A. They win more frequently in that.

Q. They win more frequently. And do you attribute that to their having special skills?

A. I think it's a mix of things. I think they have a stronger reputation. They're better able to bear risk, and they have the distribution and the marketing that helps them appeal to authors, which reputation, as well, helps appeal to authors.

Q. Is it possible that they also just are bigger and buy more books?

A. If they were just bigger and bought more books, the non-anticipated top seller numbers, I would expect to look more similar.

Q. That assumes that they would make their investments at all advance levels at the same rate?

A. I don't know if it assumes that or not. What I take away from this is we see authors of anticipated top sellers systematically choosing differently than authors of non-anticipated top sellers. To your point, it could be both a push and a pull thing. It could be author preference and it could be the—where each group of publishers feels most comfortable competing.

THE COURT: Or isn't it the case the biggest ones just have the most money?

THE WITNESS: They have the ability to bear risk that the others do not, yes, Your Honor, in general.

BY MR. OPPENHEIMER:

Q. When you say in general, you have not made a study of the capital constraints of the publishers in the industry, correct?

A. That's correct.

Q. All right. And you're aware that some of the new publishers are receiving funding?

A. I'm not aware of the funding of all of the non-Big 5 publishers.

Q. You haven't made a study of that, obviously?

A. Correct.

Q. And to the extent that we're talking about an entity such as Disney, you don't have any question about their ability to invest capital?

A. So I think there's a question of ability to invest capital and incentive to invest capital. A firm like Google may have lots of capital it could invest in this business but it's not focused on this business. So Disney may have—I think the testimony this morning from the gentleman—Mr. Murray was that he has a budget, but clearly News Corp. has more money than the size of his budget. There's a business rationale for the amount of money they commit to HarperCollins on a given year.

Q. Do you recall expressing a view at your deposition that you didn't think Disney had indicated a plan to expand its publishing?

A. I don't recall talking about its publishing generally. I recall we talked a little bit about if it said it was going to expand, where might it expand.

Q. And do you recall that you were asked if you were aware of any publisher that's non-Big 5 publisher who says they have an intent to expand and that you couldn't think of any?

A. I'll take your word for it. I don't recall but . . .

Q. Are you aware of Disney's plans one way or the other with respect to the expansion into publishing?

A. Into publishing or anticipated top sellers?

Q. Either.

A. No.

Q. Would you take a look at tab No. 28. This is an article from *Publishers Weekly* in April of 2021. I just want to ask you, it says, "Disney publishing is returning to that market with a launch of Hyperion Avenue."

A. I see that.

Q. And were you aware of Disney's stated intention to enter the publishing market with Hyperion?

A. I was not.

Q. And were you aware of any intention on the part of Disney to release 50 to 60 times a year through Hyperion?

A. No, I was not.

Q. Were you aware that the deposition in this case of Tonya Agurto was taken?

A. I believe I knew Disney was deposed, but I don't recall the details.

Q. Okay. Fair enough. I only ask because it's not in your reliance list. I'll represent to you that she was deposed in April of this year, 2022. I'll direct your attention to tab No. 28.

A. I'm there.

Q. This is in the exhibit binder still and it's tab No. 28.

A. I'm there.

Q. And this is Ms. Agurto's deposition?

A. Oh, I apologize.

Q. I'm sorry, it's in the deposition binder, pardon me.

A. I apologize. Which binder should I be looking for?
Q. Dr. Hill, it's the deposition binder.
A. So my deposition? Okay. I'm there.
Q. Would you take a look at the transcript at page 61, lines—starting at line 23?
THE COURT: I'm sorry, which transcript are we on?
MR. OPPENHEIMER: Yes, Your Honor. This is the deposition of Tonya Agurto.
THE WITNESS: I see it.
MR. OPPENHEIMER: That should be tab, for Your Honor, at page 61.
THE COURT: Okay.
BY MR. OPPENHEIMER:
Q. Do you see there that she says—she's asked whether the statement was accurate, that "within five years, Disney aims to release 50 to 60 titles through Hyperion Avenue"?
A. Yes.
Q. And she says "Yes," and that that plan still holds true as of April of this year?
A. Yes.
Q. And you were not aware of that?
A. Correct. Well, I knew that Disney had general plans to expand. I didn't know the specifics.
Q. Do you have any understanding of what price target, what segment Disney is targeting?
A. No.
Q. May I draw your attention to Ms. Agurto's testimony at page 120, line 20.
A. I'm there.
Q. Okay. Do you see she's asked, "Of the books that Hyperion Avenue has acquired to date, how many books received an advance of $250,000 or more?" And she answered, "The majority." Do you see that?
A. I do see that.
Q. That would put that squarely in the segmented market?
A. Some of them, yes, all those ones above 250.
Q. And then she's asked about "What about over 500;" and she'd say "Half, if not more than half"?
A. Correct.
Q. And then finally she's asked, "What about over a million dollars?" And she says, "Maybe a little less than a quarter."
A. Correct.
Q. So would it appear that Disney is aiming right into your market segment?
A. They appear to have plans to enter, yes.
Q. And just to be clear, if we go back—Pam, if we could put back up Plaintiff's Exhibit 963. Just to make the point, to the best of your knowledge, Disney is not in these data that are depicted in this bar graph, right?
A. Correct. These data are 2019 to 2021.
Q. Right.
A. Well, I don't know when—it doesn't give a date for these acquisitions so I don't know how many of them are or not included. If they were made in 2021, they'd be included.
Q. Okay. Right. So things keep changing?
A. Well—but the market share of the non-Big 5 stays pretty stable over this time period.
Q. Would you agree that the importance of the participation of the publishers in the competitive environment is how often they're bidding against each other?
A. No, I think that how often they win is probably a better reflection of their competitive significance.
Q. Well, let's take a look at a table from your report. Let's go to tab 1 of the exhibit book. This is also confidential.
A. Okay. I'm there.
Q. Okay. So this is your table of shares of purchases of more during the period January 2019 through June 2021; is that correct?
A. That's correct.

Q. And we can see here that you've created an entry for something called the non-Big 5?
A. Correct.
Q. Would you tell us who's in the non-Big 5?
A. Every other publisher with an anticipated top selling book that qualifies is here. Everything that's not the merged firm and then the other three members of the Big 5.
Q. And then as we read across, you're giving the market share for the acquisition of books in your book segment for the three years, plus an average for the total, correct?
A. Correct.
Q. And if we look over to 2021, the non-Big 5 collectively have a larger market share than Hachette and Macmillan; is that correct?
A. If you aggregate them into one firm, yes.
Q. And they have—collectively, they have the same market share as Simon & Schuster, correct?
A. Correct.
Q. And what that means is that as a group, they are bidding and winning titles above $250,000 at the same rate as individual Big 5 publishers?
A. Right, but they're not one firm. If you were to merge them into one firm and you were to calculate an HHI counting this as one firm instead of as diffuse firms, the concentration in the market would go up, because we—the concentration measure in the HHI gives more weight to large firms than to small firms.
Q. Well, I'm putting aside the HHI now and I'm just wanting us to take a snapshot of the market. And when you put together the non-Big 5 and their wins, they're operating as sort of a Big 6, would you say?
A. I would not. Again, if you wanted to call them the Big 6, then you would aggregate them into one firm and treat them as one firm. But they're diffuse firms. But I will agree that if you add up their market share, it's larger than Macmillan and Hachette's individual share.
Q. What is the significance in your mind of the fact that they're not a single firm?
A. Well, it means each one of them is winning a non-Big 5—or an anticipated top seller rarely.
Q. If you are a member of the Big 5 and you're contemplating competition, would you conclude that you're going to be competing with somebody in the non-Big 5 just about as often you're going to be competing with somebody who's in the Big 5?
A. Well, I mean, I think there's a couple of inferences. One is that the Hachettes and the Macmillans of the world, in this example, are regularly winning as often as all the members of the non-Big 5 combined. So it's telling something—telling us something about their ability to regularly compete at this level. These individual firms are not able to do that. They win collectively as often, but individually they win significantly less often. And so it's giving us some indication about how likely it is that they compete on a regular basis.
THE COURT: But can you answer Mr. Oppenheimer's question about from the perspective of a Big 5 publishing house in an auction, are they thinking, we're just as likely to have one non-Big 5 firm, whichever one it is, as likely as Hachette, which has, like, a similar share?
THE WITNESS: That's right. If you take them all collectively, that's roughly correct. Although the fact that they win so much more infrequently, raises the possibility that there are special cases, special cases are more likely for them than for the larger firms that win more regularly.
BY MR. OPPENHEIMER:
Q. Could I ask you a hypothetical, Dr. Hill. If you were an editor at Penguin Random House and you'd been invited to a best bid, didn't know who the other bidders were or how many there would be, wouldn't you think that your chances of having a bid from somebody outside the Big 5 was every bit as good as having a bid as somebody inside the Big 5?
A. Somebody outside compared to inside?
Q. Yes.
A. No. I mean, the rest of the Big 5 win on the order of—let me get this right—50 percent of the time and the non-Big 5 win about 10 percent of the time. If you remove Penguin Random House.
Q. If you were in that best-bid situation and you were trying to figure out how likely—let's say you were paying Penguin Random House.

A. Sure.

Q. And you were trying to figure out how likely it would be that Simon & Schuster would be bidding against you, what would you be thinking?

A. If I was Penguin Random House?

Q. Yes.

A. I would think about how often I've lost to Simon & Schuster in the past.

Q. So you'd look for competition where you were number one and number two in the bidding?

A. I might not know when I was number two because Penguin Random House, I think Mr. Karp testified, we don't often know—we don't necessarily know the ordering but we know who won. So I would probably look as Hachette does, for example, how often have I lost a book and the winner was one of the other firms.

Q. Do you have any understanding of what level of sales are associated with a $250,000 advance, retail book sales?

A. Yeah, as part of the runner-up study, I did briefly calculate this number. I tried to calculate for $100,000 in advance, what is the level of sales that typically is—justifies that in the P&L and I just don't recall the number.

Q. Did you determine whether it differed among publishers?

A. I was—for the runner-up study I was looking at—largely at books won by Penguin Random House and Simon & Schuster. I think I did it for the parties. I don't recall doing it for other publishers.

Q. Now, you're aware that more than 30 publishers have purchased titles with advances above $250,000 per title between 2019 and 2021?

A. I don't know the exact number but that sounds roughly correct.

Q. And would you agree that an increasing number of publishers have titles above $250,000 in the last three years?

A. I haven't studied that, whether the number of publishers has changed. It's probably in my report if you want me to look.

Q. If I could direct your attention to tab No. 46?

A. Of the Hill exhibits?

Q. Yes, please. This has been marked as Defendant's Exhibit 370.

A. I'm there.

Q. And it's from Professor Snyder's rebuttal report. It's his figure 9.3.

A. Yes, I see it.

Q. And do you see there it specifies the number of publishers who have made acquisitions in the minimum advance amounts from $100,000 to $500,000?

A. Correct.

Q. And do you see how those numbers have been climbing?

A. I do.

Q. Let's take a look at tab No. 2. This is Defendant's DX375. It's confidential.

A. I see it.

Q. Let's talk a little bit about some of the contracts that have been entered into by various publishers during this time period. You recognize this as Exhibit 9.8 from Professor Snyder's expert report?

A. I do.

Q. And the highest contract entered into during that time period was neither PRH nor S&S, correct?

A. That's correct.

Q. It was another publisher, publisher I, from that list?

A. I don't have your wheel but, yes, I think—yeah, I see that publisher.

Q. And the third largest contract entered into during this time wasn't even one of the Big 5, correct?

A. That's correct.

Q. It was a non-Big 5?

A. That is correct.

Q. And the largest per title—pardon me, the third largest per title acquisition was also by a non-Big 5, correct?

A. Oh, third largest. Yes—yes. Do you mean second largest or third largest?

Q. Third largest.

A. Per title, so the last column here?

Q. Yes.

A. I think.

Q. Do I have it wrong?

A. Am I wrong that the second largest is the sixth line and the third largest is the fifth line?

Q. You're correct. I stand corrected. Do you see that?

A. Yeah.

Q. Okay. Now, you'd mentioned earlier that it's important when publishers are making acquisitions to think about who may they be bidding against. Fair enough?

A. Correct.

Q. And do you recall from Professor Snyder's analysis of the agency data, that in the price segment that you proposed, 47 percent of the time that Penguin Random House or Simon & Schuster win in a multi bidder auction for books with advances over 250, the other party didn't even bid?

A. I don't recall that. I'm not disputing it. I don't recall that analysis.

Q. So that in the marketplace, according to the agency data, these parties are not bumping into each other half the time?

A. Yeah, I don't recall that calculation.

Q. If you accept my representation that that's Professor Snyder's conclusion in his report, would that indicate to you that Penguin Random House and Simon & Schuster are not always going after the same books even in the auction setting?

A. Yeah, if they don't bid it and run into each other, then they're not always going after the same book.

Q. Right. And the merging parties, you're not running into each other, and almost half the institutes are winning books?

A. According to your representation, correct. Is that for anticipated top sellers or all books?

Q. Correct. What you've called anticipated top sellers. And you would agree that based upon your own diversion calculations, HarperCollins is more likely to be the runner-up to Penguin Random House than Simon & Schuster for books in your price segment, correct?

A. Correct, although I'd also say with diversions, the guidelines are clear that when you're thinking about this competition, the key question is the diversion to the other party and second order of importance is diversion to third parties. But, yes, I would agree that HarperCollins is—for Harp—from diversion from Penguin Random House, HarperCollins would be second.

Q. And you would agree with me based on your research that HarperCollins, Macmillan, and Hachette are most likely to win or be runner-up—more likely to win or be runner-up to Simon & Schuster than Penguin Random House?

A. No, I wouldn't agree with that. What is your basis for that?

Q. Let's take a look at tab 49, which is figure 40 from your report. And it's confidential.

A. Okay. I'm there.

Q. So based on that, would you agree that HarperCollins, Macmillan, and Hachette are most likely to win or be the runner-up to Simon & Schuster more often than PRH?

A. This is from the agency data. Did you mean just restricted to the agency data? Or did you mean my general conclusions?

Q. No, based on the agency data.

A. I'm trying to remember the context here. Yeah, yeah.

Q. And this also reflects that HarperCollins is a more significant competitor to Penguin Random House than S&S, correct?

A. In this agency data, yes.

Q. Correct. And do you recall that in Professor Snyder's work, also based on the agency data, that in multi bidder acquisitions with an advance of at least $250,000, 54 percent of the time there was at least one bid from a non-Big 5 publisher?

A. I don't recall, but I don't have any reason to dispute that.

Q. And would you have any reason to dispute that 23 percent of the acquisitions for titles in ad-—with advances above $250,000 were either won by non-Big 5 publishers or a non-Big 5 publisher was the runner-up?

A. I don't know what to make of that statistic because you're—you've moved from 100 to 200 as the base. So I don't know how to interpret it, but I don't—I remember Dr. Snyder calculated that number.

Q. So you don't dispute the statistic, you question its relevance?

A. I just don't understand what point he's trying to make with that particular system. But if you think of 200 as the base, then it's close to the 10 percent I calculated for the Big 5 winning. So it seems directionally consistent with that.

Q. And if we go back to tab No. 1, which is your initial report, figure 25, by these calculations would you agree with me, based on this data, that the non-Big 5 collectively acquired as many titles for advances of $250,000 or more as Hachette during the time period?

A. Yes.

Q. And during that same time period, the non-Big 5 collectively acquired more titles in that price segment than Hachette or Macmillan?

A. I'm sorry, could you repeat that question. I apologize.

Q. Yeah, certainly. The non-Big 5 during this same time period collectively acquired more titles for advances of $250,000 than Hachette or Macmillan did?

A. Are you taking the full-time period?

Q. Yes.

A. Oh—

Q. Pardon me, just '21.

A Oh, '21, yes.

Q. And, in fact, the non-Big 5 collectively have acquired roughly as many titles as S&S did last year in the $250,000 and above price range?

A. And you're thinking 2021? Yes.

Q. Yes. So let's talk a little bit about direct competition between the parties, the merging parties. Your SSA model predicts harm in situations where Penguin Random House and Simon & Schuster are first and second, correct?

A. That's correct.

Q. And to be clear, your model only predicts harm when the two merging parties are first and second, correct?

A. Yeah, inside the mechanism of the model, that's correct.

Q. And the—I'm focusing on—we're now focusing on the second score auction model. We'll get to the GUPPIs in a minute.

And the second score auction model does not find harm if there's a reduction of one bidder—excuse me, does find harm if there's a reduction of one bidder, but that bidder was not—I apologize.

The second score auction model does not find harm if there's a reduction of a bidder but that bidder was not the winner or the runner-up, correct?

A. That's correct.

Q. And if a bidder who drops out isn't in first or second position, your model doesn't predict any harm?

A. That's correct.

Q. So the second score auction model is not showing, for example, that four bidders is necessarily worse than five?

A. It's not necessarily worse, correct.

Q. There's only a problem if the one who leaves the bidding is the runner-up, correct?

A. So narrowly inside the model, yes, that's correct.

Q. Well, let's—that's the only harm that the model is identifying, correct?

A. Yeah, using that second score auction format, the first and second bidders set the value. So if you remove others, it's not going to affect their valuation.

Q. And when you've expressed harm identified by the second score auction model, that is all we're talking about, correct?

A. The way I've expressed the harm is the average harm overall PR—Penguin Random House and Simon & Schuster authors.

Q. Model itself predicts that there will only be harm in those situations where Penguin Random House and Simon & Schuster are first and second, correct?

A. Right, but I'm spreading the harm out over all PRH and S&S authors.

Q. Well, we'll talk about that, but when you say that you're doing that—Well, we'll come back to that.

THE COURT: So does your model just talk about the historical data and say, if these were merged, this would have been the harm, or is it predicting future harm?

THE WITNESS: It's using the past data to predict the future. So it's saying—it essentially says, here are the market shares, here's how likely it is that one is number one and one is number two. And it makes predictions of harm based on that past data. And then I'm applying it to say, this is my prediction of what would happen in the future.

THE COURT: So does it analyze the past data?

THE WITNESS: Yes, Your Honor.

THE COURT: And say what would have happened if one of these guys dropped out?

THE WITNESS: That's correct. And then there's—and then I'm using it to make a prediction about the future.

THE COURT: And is your prediction different from what the past data said?

THE WITNESS: No, Your Honor, it's based on the past data.

THE COURT: So it's the same basically. You're saying—looking at the past data, if one of these two firms dropped out, this would have been the harm to the authors and we're going to predict that same harm would occur in the future?

THE WITNESS: That's correct. The one thing I would add is that, just to be clear, it's an aggregate prediction. I'm not feeding it information about every auction. Instead, I'm saying, on aggregate, the parties were winner—the parties have these market shares, and then the market is—the model says, if diversions according to share, that means they were runners-up this often.

THE COURT: I see.

THE WITNESS: But it doesn't—I haven't given it an auction by auction dataset, Your Honor.

THE COURT: I see. Thank you.

BY MR. OPPENHEIMER:

Q. And the based on the model, there is an implicit percentage of time when Penguin Random House and Simon & Schuster are first and second, correct?

A. Correct.

Q. That's 12 percent of the time?

A. Something like that, yeah.

Q. So they're only first and second, and the harm is only generated 12 percent of the time?

A. If you measure it against all auctions, including those won by others, yes.

Q. So 88 percent of the time they are not one and two?

A. That's correct, in the model, yes.

Q. Now, if we assume that, as I believe we have here, that there are about 1,200 books annually in your proposed market—by the way, are you comfortable with that number, about 1,200?

A. Yeah, I usually think of a thousand, but 1,200 is probably closer to the actual number.

Q. Okay. So if they are first and second, 12 percent of the time, then we're talking about harm computed on the basis of about 145 books?

A. Yeah. If it was a thousand, it would be 120 books.

Q. Fair enough.

A. Yeah, I can't do the–

Q. At 1,200—fair enough. Somewhere between 125 and 145 books?

A. Yeah.

Q. And you indicated in prior testimony that there was a price affect for each of the two companies that came out of your model, one for PRH and one for S&S, correct?

A. That's correct.

Q. And when you combine those in your analysis, you get an average advance reduction of about 6.1 percent for PRH and S&S authors; is that correct?

A. That's correct. But just to be clear, the individual firms have fairly different affects. It's more significant for Simon & Schuster because of their diversion to Penguin Random House is higher.

Q. Right. But on average, you're talking about roughly 6 percent?

A. Yeah, if you want to take an average, then 6 percent.

Q. And I don't believe that we have a disagreement on this, but if you apply that 6 percent to the advances on an annual basis, you're talking about a maximum amount of harm identified by the second score auction model of somewhere around 29- or $30 million a year?

A. So in the baseline run, that's right. If I use the version in which I treat all direct operating expenses as fixed, then the harm is higher.

But for the baseline, that number is, I believe, correct.

Q. Well, we'll talk about margins in a little bit. But so the basic harm identified by the model is somewhere in the neighborhood of 29 or 39—pardon me, 29- to $30 million year?

A. So that's what the baseline, which I think of as conservative, identified, yes.

Q. Does your analysis tell you at all how that harm will be arrayed over the authors in the price segment?

A. So I think of the model more as—the purpose of the modeling is to ask the question—so the answer to your question is, in the model itself, the harm is going to be to situations where Penguin Random House are number one and number two. But I think of the model more generally, consistent with the guidelines, as signif-—producing predictions of significant harm consistently and, hence, indicating that there's likely to be a unilateral effect.

Q. But in terms of actually measuring it, it's the numbers we're talking about?

A. You mean the $29 million?

Q. Correct.

A. Correct.

Q. I'm just asking, do you have any theory for how that is spread across the authors in the price segment?

A. So inside the model, it's going to be that harm is auctions where Penguin Random House is number one and Simon & Schuster is number two. But, in general, in the report, I treat it as average harm to Penguin Random House and Simon & Schuster authors.

THE COURT: Is it different if it's Simon & Schuster's number one and Penguin Random House is number two? Or does it not matter as long as they're both numbered?

THE WITNESS: The authors, Your Honor, for whom Simon & Schuster is number one, there's a larger effect for them because the—you can think of a merger that eliminates competition as internalizing that competition. From Simon & Schuster's perspective, it loses more often to Penguin Random House, and so removing that constraint has a bigger effect on it than it does on Penguin Random House.

BY MR. OPPENHEIMER:

Q. Would it be fair to say that the takeaway from the second score auction, if you're negotiating for the merged entity going forward, is that there's something like an overall 6 percent—should be an overall 6 percent reduction in advances?

A. I would tend to think a better prediction would be to say the relaxation of the competitive constraint's more significant than Simon & Schuster—for Simon & Schuster and less significant for Penguin Random House, and an aggregate, if you wanted to combine them, you could use the 6 percent.

Q. Is there any way for anyone at the merged entity post-merger to figure out which acquisitions to apply the price reduction on?

A. So if you think about a rounds type competition, so we've seen some examples of those, you don't need to think about reducing your behavior at all. The auctions in which you're competing head to head will simply have lower—a lower final advance.

For best bids or negotiations, it's just based on the idea of I think we saw some qualitative evidence of I'm negotiating with this author, I think there's a real chance they'll go to the other party, now that I know that threat is removed, I'll be less aggressive. But to your question, there's nothing in the model that says, if hypothetical book X appears, you should bid this much less on this book. I think—thinking about it in this is a very specific and exact prediction of harm is less useful than thinking of it as consistent predictions from the models of harm are an indication that there's a substantial reduction in unilateral competition.

Q. You would agree with me, as an economist, that there has to be a mechanism for harm to be effectuated?

A. I mean, could you say more about what you mean for—

Q. Sure. There could be a theoretical harm but no practical way it occurs, would you agree with me?

A. There may be cases where that's true, sure.

Q. So let's go back to a best-bids situation. And how would anybody who is invited from the merged entity to participate in that best-bids situation make use of the information from the second score auction?

A. So I wouldn't necessarily suggest they make use of the second score auction model. I didn't really develop it for their purposes. But I would think, if you think back to some of the qualitative evidence, there was a quote from Penguin Random House authors saying editor X at Simon & Schuster continues her role as imprint-wide nemesis. When you have that information that you're competing frequently with another firm and you know that firm is no longer one of your competitors, then I don't think it's unreasonable to think your behavior will change.

Q. Well, let's assume all we have is the second score auction model.

A. Okay.

Q. What would somebody representing the merged entity do when confronted with an invitation to a best bid? How would they use the results of the second score auction model to adjust their bidding behavior in that situation?

A. I mean, the model not designed for that purpose. I would not recommend to them, use this modeling to figure out your optimal bid in your next competition.

Q. Okay. Fair enough. So as a practical matter, the best-bid situation, we wouldn't use what I'll call the SSA, the second score auction?

A. I wouldn't recommend—I mean, the model is not designed to be—you could hire a management consultant to say, now we've—and you see these—and I'll just talk about other industries, management consultants can say, now that this competition is being removed, you can do these different things. This analysis was never intended to be something that could be given to people at either party and say, here's how you should change your bidding in the future in any auction format.

THE COURT: Can I ask you this? Is the upshot of your model, which applies to when the two merged parties are number one and number two, which is 12 percent of the time, so in 12 percent of the cases author advances will go down 6 percent?

THE WITNESS: Not quite, Your Honor. The 6 percent is spreading it out over all Penguin Random House and Simon & Schuster authors. So I take the prediction of harm in the model and then I say, if advances came down by that much, what would that look like if I spread it across all Penguin Random House authors.

THE COURT: But why would you spread it across to the people who weren't involved in the situation that the model addresses, which is when they're number one and number two?

THE WITNESS: Because I don't think of the model as just narrowly looking at that situation. Yes, that's the precise mechanism in the model, but I'm thinking of it more as just, can we use this specific model to make a more general evaluation of how likely harm is here.

THE COURT: So how do you make that leap between the specific model and general harm?

THE WITNESS: Yeah, if you wanted to, you could take it and go up to the more specific. Then that number would go up for those 12 percent. So you can look at it either as very high harm in 12 percent, or you can spread it out and say, 6 percent over about 50 percent of competitions. That doesn't really answer your question.

THE COURT: Yeah, I just don't understand how you're getting there.

THE WITNESS: So frequently, in economics, particularly in auctions, you may use a second score auction model or some other type of auction model to simulate what competition may look like. And here for the runner-up study, I looked through these bidding histories one after another, and there are many different formats. You can put them broadly into rounds or best bids or negotiations. But if you tried to build a model, you might end up with 150 different models because there are all these different types. So, you say, look, is my model capturing a key intuition here. And the key intuitions I was trying to capture is how often are the parties competing directly with one another and what do their margins look like. And broadly speaking, low margins mean there's lots of competition, very high margins mean little competition. So the model—that's how I think of the model generally at that level, and I'm trying to use it to use that general information to make a prediction. It predicts harm in that 12 percent, and then I'm spreading that over Simon & Schuster and Penguin Random House authors.

THE COURT: I still don't understand the spreading part, but never mind.

THE WITNESS: Yeah, I mean, so there's some language in the guidelines, Your Honor, in section 6.1, I think, talking about, in auctions, you can think about having the harm where I can't—or maybe it's 6.2—you can have a lot of harm in a few auctions or you can have a little harm or less harm in a lot of auctions. And it really depends on whether you're thinking the model is precisely right about how the world works. So I know it's not precisely right. Not every auction is a second score auction. And as I said, there are all these other mechanisms. But often in modeling, we take a step back from the very particulars and just say I can't make—you know, for example, it's using aggregate information about how often the parties compete. I don't have data for every auction who competed with whom and for how much.

THE COURT: But you're assuming that their second score auctions even when they're not in your model?

THE WITNESS: Correct, the model is using that mechanism and we're stepping back. And the alternative would be to try to build a separate model each of the mechanisms one observes, and there are many, many different mechanisms. And so then the question of the modeling is, by assuming the second score auction and using this aggregate information, are we grossly misrepresenting the way competition really works or do we think the model is a reasonable approximation. And so that's one of the reasons Dr. Snyder made this critique, and I compared the results to the GUPPI model to see, okay, let's try a model that's set up to look at rounds options, best bids, and hybrid and see if the results look similar.

THE COURT: Okay. Thank you.

MR. OPPENHEIMER: Let me go into the model just a little bit more.

THE COURT: Can I just ask a question before you begin? I've been thinking about your second score auction model, Dr. Hill. Tell me if this is correct. Does your model, it's assuming, given market shares and competitiveness of bids, that the two merging parties will be number one and number two in some number or percentage of competitions, not just in a round-robin type auction but all different types, best bids, any kind. But you're using an auction model because it's too complicated to model every different type of competitive situation, and so you're putting that data just into an auction model and then you're assuming that the results of the auction model can be extrapolated to apply to other types of bidding situations. Is that what it's doing?

THE WITNESS: That's fair, Your Honor, yes.

THE COURT: Okay. Thank you. You may proceed.

BY MR. OPPENHEIMER:

Q. Thank you, Your Honor. That was well put. I'd like to explore that just a little bit. Let's talk about what goes in the model, okay?

A. Sure.

Q. Am I right that there are two things, and only two things, that go in the model, margins and shares, correct?

A. Yes, and then there's the machinery of the model, but, yes, that's correct.

Q. Absolutely, the model version does all its things. But before we get there, and be patient here with me, but I want to, just at a high level, identify what margins we're talking about and what shares. So, first of all, the margins that go into the model are the margins of one of the two merging parties or some average of those two. Do I have that right?

A. That's correct.

Q. That's it. No margins from anybody else in the market?

A. That's correct.

Q. Okay. And the shares that go in are the shares of each of the merging firms. Is that also right?

A. Those are the ones that in end up mattering, yes, but you can—yes, that's fine.

Q. Let's go through some of the assumptions or protocols that drive this model at a high level, okay? And if I misstate something, so it's misleading about the model, you just tell me, okay.

A. Sure.

Q. So one assumption the model makes and, again, we're talking about the second score auction model, is that every acquisition is in the form of an auction, correct?

A. Correct.

Q. And not just any—I'm sorry.

A. Yeah, if you're applying it broadly as I am, that's correct.

Q. Well, we'll get to applying it broadly in a minute because I think that's important, but let me just, if I may, build up so we understand the modeling. So it makes the assumption that every acquisition is in the form of an auction.

A. The model is agnostic about that. I'm applying it to every auction.

The model is looking at second score—if you want to apply it to—broadly, yes, it's assuming all of these are second score auctions.

Q. And not just any kind of auction but a second score auction, correct?

A. That's correct.

Q. And candidly, I had not heard of a second score auction before this case. But in the second score auction, you do not pay your willingness to bid, do I have that right?

A. So in a second score auction model, the highest bidder wins and pays a price—or an advance that depends upon the second highest bid.

Q. Right. So the bidders in a second score auction never pay what they bid, they pay what the number two bidder bid; is that fair?

A. In a straight second price auction, that would be correct.

Q. Okay. And the second score auction does not assume that there are multiple rounds of bidding. Is that also true?

A. That's correct.

Q. And the second score auction assumes that everyone bids their maximum valuation in a single bid?

A. It doesn't assume that. That's a strategic implication of the format. If you have a format that's a second price auction, your incentive is to bid truthfully under some assumptions.

Q. So in the structure of the model, there is no learning, if you will, from an auction process, fair?

A. Could you say more about what you mean by learning?

Q. Sure. You don't have a situation where you begin to understand what other people are bidding. That's not a part of the model structure, correct?

A. The literal way it's structured is you all submit a bid and then the bids are revealed and the winner is determined.

Q. Right.

A. You can think of it as being an open outcry auction, where everybody bids until you run out of steam and the highest bidder is the only person left.

Q. Yeah, but it's not actually an outcry auction, right, because we're not—just to be clear, we're not literally watching people hold up a panel at Christie's with a bid, right? We—the model takes everybody's valuation and it does one run, so to speak, and picks the highest?

A. Yeah. You get to the same place, but the model itself is a structure as you submit one bid.
Q. Okay. And I think you believe that the most analogous, real-world auction to this would be what we've been calling round-robin auctions in the case?
A. Correct.
Q. And you say that's analogous because even it is not literal, correct?
A. Yeah, it's not a sealed bid, second price auction.
Q. And in your work, you never tried to calculate how many acquisitions in your data or in Professor Snyder's data were round-robin auctions?
A. Correct.
Q. And in the round-robin auction, the bidder knows what they have to pay to stay in the auction, correct?
A. They have a target they have to top, yes.
Q. Now, would it be fair to say that the most removed form of acquisition from the model used by the second score auction would be what we're calling a bilateral or one-on-one negotiation?
A. I don't have an easy basis for making that comparison. At any rate, it is not the same as—it is not the same mechanism as a negotiation.
Q. Okay. Let's talk just a little bit about best-bid auctions. Those are known as first price auctions, correct?
A. Typically, yes, you could call them that.
Q. And that means that the winner expects to pay the amount they bid if they win, correct?
A. Correct.
Q. What a lot of us think as an auction. So in a best bid, the runner-up bid does not set the price paid, correct?
A. That's correct.
Q. And obviously that's different than the second score structure where the winner is expecting to pay the price of the second highest bid or the runner-up?
A. Yes, though there are some situations in which first price auctions and second price auctions lead to equivalent outcomes. They're not necessarily the same outcome.
Q. And I believe you were clear, I just want to confirm from your deposition, that a single round best-bid auction is not a second score auction, correct?
A. Correct.
Q. And once again, you have not calculated how much—strike that, I'll come back to it. In a best-bid auction, is it fair to say that the competition is not affected by the amount of the second bid? Pardon me.
A. Yeah. It's—
Q. Yeah, that is actually my question. Let me say it again. In a best bid, the competition is not affected by the amount of the second bid?
A. The competition is not affected or—
Q. Correct, the outcome of a best bid is not affected by the amount of the second bid?
A. In a narrow sense, the winner pays their bid. If you knew you'd eliminated a competitor, then the best bid that—the bid that the winner would have submitted had that competitor not existed might have changed. But mechanically, when you open the sealed bids, you take the highest bid and that winner pays that amount.
Q. Right. I'm not sure, did I hear you say if you knew you had eliminated the second bidder, that would affect your bid?
A. Right. So what I'm—and just trying to distinguish between the mechanically, the winning bid is—sorry. The person with the highest bid pays that bid amount. It's not the case that the other competitors don't matter. It's just there, the price that's paid is not, when you open the bids, dependent on the second highest bid.
Q. Yeah, there's no pressure from the bid of the second place publisher in a blind bid?
A. I would disagree. So if you imagine, you and I are publishers and we are the only two publishers, if I eliminate your competition, then my bids might be different in a best-bid setting than when I know you're

there competing with me. But in a narrow sense, supposing you and I are competing and we open the envelopes and my bid is highest, I'm going to pay the amount I bid. It doesn't depend on the amount you bid.

Q. Correct. Because I think this is important, I want to make sure I understand.

THE COURT: I think I've got it.

MR. OPPENHEIMER: Okay, Your Honor.

BY MR. OPPENHEIMER:

Q. And best bids is a pretty common format of auctions in the publishing industry?

A. Yes, I would say so.

Q. And if you have no special information about the other bidders in a best bid and you're just participating and putting your bid in, you are not going to be affected by the amount of the second bid, correct?

A. Again, the way you're phrasing the question is on a borderline, because when you're thinking about a best-bid auction, you're thinking I—the higher I bid, the more likely I am to win. The higher I bid, the lower my expected margin given my valuation. And that first piece, how likely am I to win given a particular bid, so just take the value of $100,000, you're thinking about how often that will win based—is based on your perception of the competition. So that competition matters when you're forming your optimal bid. But mechanically once all the bids are in, everyone has figured out their optimal bid based on their beliefs about the competition and the envelopes are, let's just say it's sealed bids, you open the bids and the highest bid is the winner and that person pays their valuation. It is not determined by the second or third bid.

Q. At your deposition, you indicated that you thought about 30 percent of all acquisitions, including bilateral negotiations, were best bids. Is that still your view?

A. Yeah, I—so I looked back at my notes for the runner-up study. It's about 60 percent for bilateral negotiations, and then the remaining 40 percent are auctions. And then I will say the auctions are probably split about 50/50. So I would say 20—I don't know if—you said the number was 30. Look, the runner-up study is also a sample. I think your number is a reasonable estimate. It's somewhere—it's significant.

Q. Yeah, I think we're in agreement in essence, which is that the majority of the acquisitions are not auctions, they're bilateral negotiations?

THE COURT: The majority are. They're 60 percent.

THE WITNESS: Yeah, I would say somewhere around 50 to 60 percent will be negotiation. And then I would guess, and I haven't studied it systematically, that the auctions would be roughly split between some form of best bids and some form of rounds. But there are, you know—that's a very rough.

BY MR. OPPENHEIMER:

Q. Do you recall in your runner-up data that about 65 percent of the acquisitions were bilateral?

A. Yeah, something like that. I think it's 60, but maybe it's 65. I don't have the exact number.

Q. So a minority of the acquisition formats in the industry, as you understand it, correspond to round robins, which are the most closely analogous to the second score auction?

A. That's correct.

Q. And then the other forms of acquisition differ by varying degrees?

A. That's fair.

Q. Now, does the model take any historical inputs about any other publishers in the industry?

A. No, except to the extent that they affect the market shares or margins of the parties.

Q. There's no historical data?

A. As you enter the market shares and the margins, which are themselves affected by others, but the actual data you enter is determined—is based on the merging parties.

Q. And only the merging parties?

A. Correct.

Q. And the product of the calculation done by the second score auction pertains to harm only between the merging parties when they're first and second, correct?

A. Correct.

Q. Now, is it your testimony that the results of the second score auction are instructive with respect to the competitive constraints in a bilateral negotiation?

A. Yeah, I take them more broadly as being instructive about competition in general. Does it perfectly fit every mechanism? No, it doesn't.

Q. And if you only had bilateral negotiations to model, would you still use a second score auction model?

A. If everything in the industry was bilateral?

Q. Correct.

A. Yeah, I would probably try to build a negotiation model, and if it was unsuccessful, then I would consider either an auction model or a differentiated product model.

Q. But the SSA would not be your first choice for modeling bilateral negotiations?

A. If there were only bilateral negotiations, I would probably try to develop another kind as well.

Q. And is it fair to say that you have not undertaken an analysis—really, you have not undertaken an analysis to determine the percentage of time, other that than what you've testified to, beyond that you haven't examined a percentage of time that any particular acquisition format is used in the publishing industry, correct?

A. Correct.

THE COURT: If bilateral negotiations are more common than auctions, why didn't you build a bilateral negotiations model?

THE WITNESS: So, Your Honor, I tried to build an omnibus model that would start with a bilateral negotiation. If you were unable to reach an agreement, then you would move into a second score auction or a first—sorry, a rounds auction or a first price auction.

The model that ended up being the one I could effectively solve was the second price auction. And so as I told you, I experimented with the first price auction, I wasn't able to get results that I thought were credible, and I also didn't make a great deal of progress with the negotiations model. I also looked at just—there was a couple other model types I considered and didn't end up using.

THE COURT: So your choice of model depended in part on what the results were and if they just looked right to you?

THE WITNESS: It depended on whether I could get a model I could solve. So the challenge in a first price auction is that you're thinking about—and I'll give that just as an example. I as a bidder am thinking, what is the probability that I win if I bid $100,000. And to do that, the agents all have to form expectations about each other's bidding. And once you get into that, you get into a great deal of complications. What's nice about the second price setting is your strategic incentive is always to submit your true valuation and that turns out to be the optimal strategy. So it was the easiest one to solve. And the first price model can work, but you need a lot of data and I just didn't have the data to use any of the standard approaches.

BY MR. OPPENHEIMER:

Q. And, Dr. Hill, you would agree with me that agents play a very critical role in determining what type of acquisition process will be used for a book?

A. I would say agents and authors—I'm not an expert on that. Agents and authors come to an agreement about the format of the auction they're going to—or the acquisition format.

Q. Jointly, or however each author and her agent does it, they control the auction process or the acquisition process if it's a bilateral negotiation, right?

A. I wouldn't say control, because they may choose to—they may say, I'm having a best-bid auction and you invite ten people. That doesn't mean ten people are showing up for the auction.

Q. But it also means that if you're not invited as publisher, you don't get to participate at all, for example, right?

A. It may.

Q. And so the agents and the authors decide that, right?

A. The agent and the author can say, this is the format we're using, and then publishers can make a separate decision about whether to compete and how.

Q. So the agents can decide whether to do a round robin, correct?

A. The author can decide to do a round robin, yes.

Q. We can—we can stipulate, I'll use the author, you seem to prefer it, I think, the agent, we'll have more testimony later, but as we've said, let's focus on the economics. So agent-author. And they could decide what kind of round robin, how many rounds, for example?

A. The selling party can determine the number of rounds.

Q. They can decide what kind of information to distribute to the parties to the auction?

A. They can, but there are times when the participants buck the rules and do something they're not supposed to.

Q. Well, all right. And—

A. And I just say that because of having read all these documents, you'll see times where the rules are, you have to increase your bid by 10,000, and the publisher will say, I'm just going to bid my—I'm just going to match the existing bid or something like that.

Q. Okay. I mean, other than the good fortune of having some friends who are journalists and authors, everything I know about publishing I've only learned in this case. Perhaps we're similar in that regard.

But you would agree with me, though, that the acquisition process, whether it's an auction or some other form, can be changed mid-stream by the author and agent?

A. Yeah, I've seen settings where they'll say, we're doing a two rounds auction, and then they will call for best bids at the end, having not previously announced that.

Q. Right. And the ability of the author-agent to manipulate the process, and I don't mean that nefariously but just to control the process to their maximum benefit, that's not something that the second score auction model models, is it?

A. The second score auction model starts at the point at which second score auction has been selected. So, yes—so, no.

Q. So it doesn't take into account all the strategy behind maximizing value that can occur in choosing the type of acquisition process?

A. It is not thinking about choosing different acquisition processes.

Q. And it cannot—it does not take into account changes during the course of an acquisition that an author-agent may create to try to maximize value?

A. Right, although those changes may be maximized value or they may not be as valuable as something else.

Q. And in some cases, all the parties are somewhat constrained. In a case, for example, of a repeat author, where you have an option, where you have an obligation if you're doing a subsequent book with a publisher, to negotiate with them first, correct?

A. Correct.

Q. And there are different elements of those contracts, but basically that would require at least some period of bilateral negotiation before anybody could change the rules there, correct?

A. That's correct.

Q. And the second score auction doesn't model that, correct?

A. That's correct.

THE COURT: Except, tell me if I've got this right, doesn't your model assume, based on market shares—the market shares represent the deals that they've actually won, right?

THE WITNESS: Correct, Your Honor.

THE COURT: Historically. And they won them for whatever reason. It could be because of other factors like better distribution and sales or it could be—whatever it is, this is what they won so your model does take into account those other factors if the bottom line is these are the ones we won and the model is based on—because we're expecting, number one, to normally win this percentage, and, number two, to normally win that percentage, and we're going to use their margins to say how aggressively they're bidding, we would expect these results to happen in the market, because it's based on market share?

THE WITNESS: Yeah, exactly. I think at an aggregate level it is reflecting the level of competition, Your Honor.

THE COURT: But including everything that goes into that.

THE WITNESS: Correct. It's all of the different mechanisms.

And narrowly the model itself is not set up as a model where agents can change mechanisms, that would be very complex. But you're correct, I interpreted the way you are describing it, that I'm trying to use aggregate information to reflect broad competitive outcomes.

THE COURT: Right. I think I now understand what you did. Thank you.

THE WITNESS: Okay. Thank you.

BY MR. OPPENHEIMER:

Q. Do you think—further to Her Honor's question, do you believe that by taking the market share, which is the result of when it's done by a whole variety of different acquisition processes, that it makes the second score auction model suitable for just bilaterally—if it were just bilateral negotiations?

A. You mean if there were only bilateral negotiations?

Q. Yes.

A. As I said earlier, if it was only bilateral negotiations, if I could build a bilateral negotiation model, that would be my first choice.

Q. Because it would better depict the potential competitive harm from the merger, correct?

A. It could, if I could come to a—if I came to a bilateral model that I thought worked well, then, yes, that could—if then all negotiations were bilateral, then, yes.

Q. How does the model, Dr. Hill, determine the difference between the bid of the second bidder and the third bidder?

A. So that's determined using the margin.

Q. And what does the model do to make that assumption?

A. So the larger the margin, the—so at a high level, the larger the margin, the more the dispersion in the valuations of the bidders, and more the dispersion in the valuation of the bidders, the more significant the effect of eliminating one of those bidders. So if you recall, when I was talking about moving from number two to number three, the margin is giving us an insight into the distribution, essentially a way of estimating how far apart are number two and number three.

Q. Okay. And the model does not do anything to—let me put it this way—break down the information that goes in from shares. For example, the model is indifferent to—with respect to shares, what type of acquisition the shares reflect, correct?

A. Yes, you just give it to market share.

Q. Right. So if hypothetically the market one year was entirely bilateral negotiations for Penguin Random House and Simon & Schuster, the model wouldn't care in the sense that it would treat it as if we're still in auction?

A. The model, however—whatever the breakdown is the model is always treating them as auctions, yes.

Q. Would you refer to this as a stylized model, a model that stylizes the activity in publishing?

A. In publishing particularly?

Q. Sure.

A. I mean, I think of the model as more general. It's developed to use in situations where information is relatively scarce about auctions, but auctions are used to allocate goods.

Q. By the way, the second score auction model was developed primarily to deal with auction environments, correct, actual auction environments?

A. Correct.

Q. Yes.

A. But not necessarily second score auctions.

Q. Right. And when we talk about the origins of the model, do you have in mind the work by Miller in 2014?

A. Correct.

Q. So fair to say that his writings don't talk about the application of the model to bilateral negotiations?

A. Correct.
Q. He doesn't address it?
A. That is correct.
Q. Are you aware of anybody who has applied the second score auction model to bilateral negotiations?
A. No.
Q. You're the—this is the first time as far as you know that it's been done?
A. Correct.
Q. Okay. We're going to get into the GUPPI, which is a form calculation that you did not do in your first report, correct?
A. That's correct.
Q. But you did in your second. We'll talk about it. But on this point that we're talking about now about different forms of acquisition, would you agree with me that the GUPPI produces different harm results depending upon the different form of acquisition?
A. That's correct.
Q. And so it differs from the second score auction model in that critical respect?
A. So you can say that there are three different forms of the GUPPI model and two of those forms give the same result. That's the best bids and the hybrid, and then one, which is the rounds, gives a different result.
Q. And the one that would be the closer to, in your view, encompassing bilateral negotiations, would that be what you just called the hybrid model?
A. The hybrid model is rounds followed by negotiations. I don't know which of the three I would say is closest. I mean, that one has negotiations at the end so you could say that's closest in some ways.
But it is an auction followed by a negotiation.
Q. Okay. Well, and we'll get to it. But would it be fair to say at a general level that the GUPPI consistently produces lower harm results when it's looking at a bilateral negotiation versus an auction situation?
A. I don't believe I've analyzed the general results, but it's true that in the specifics here, the second—or the multi round GUPPI produces larger estimates of harm than the best bids and hybrid.
Q. So at least one of the calculations you're working, the GUPPI calculations, indicates that the difference in acquisition format can make a difference in the harm outcome?
A. Correct.
Q. Correct me if I am wrong, but in the second score auction that is not the case, correct?
A. The second score auction only has the second score mechanism so it just gives one prediction.
Q. It's just—it just does not distinguish between these different formats?
A. Correct. Well, again, narrowly, the model is a second score auction more generally, yeah.
THE COURT: In your second score auction model, how do you predict the third bidder? Is that a prediction? Because you're only putting in the margins for the top two.
THE WITNESS: Right. The margin is used inside the model to say, given these margins and these market shares, what is the likely dispersion of bidders. So how likely—you're—and large margins mean they're dispersed, which is more opportunity for harm.
THE COURT: Right.
THE WITNESS: And small margins mean all right on top of each other competing.
THE COURT: But those are the margins of Penguin Random House and Simon & Schuster, and it's just predicting, if you're going to win these percentages of at the time which the model predicts, then we would just expect the third through the fifth would be around here?
THE WITNESS: Right. So it takes one of those margins or a combination of the two, as Mr. Oppenheimer said, and then it predicts what margins look like for other participants.
THE COURT: But what's predicting, though, is given that you have to win this percentage of the time. Is that what's predicting it?
THE WITNESS: Yeah, and an assumption of what the distribution of bids looks like. And then it backs out, given this information, given these margins, these market shares, what does the distribution of

valuations look like.

THE COURT: So what's your assumption of what the distribution bid should look like, what's that look like?

THE WITNESS: It's a particular distribution. The name is currently escaping me, but there's a particular distribution the model uses as, this is what the distribution looks like. It's in the paperwork.

THE COURT: But typically in bids, in the analysis, is this what they look like?

THE WITNESS: It's called the Gumbel distribution, and it—you know, it's essentially—I don't believe I have any graphs of what it looks like. It will depend upon the information you enter. From the perspective of the model, the key thing is a big margin means lots of spread and a low margin means very little spread in the Gumbel distribution.

THE COURT: Okay.

THE WITNESS: So the—If I may, Your Honor, the way I think about it is, I've lost the second closest bidder, and I'm going to draw a third one. And if the distribution is very, very tightly packed, I'm just going to draw the same guy again.

THE COURT: Right.

THE WITNESS: If it's very dispersed–

THE COURT: They would be very close.

THE WITNESS:—I'll draw somebody who may be far away.

THE COURT: Okay.

BY MR. OPPENHEIMER:

Q. And when you take that first margin of one of the parties and you extrapolate as Her Honor described to the margin between the second and the third, it matters what distribution you choose, correct? In other words, you referred to the Gumbel method, right?

A. Right.

Q. And if you took a linear distribution, you get a different result?

A. If I haven't solved the model using a linear distribution, I could potentially change the results.

Q. So I'm just asking, the model is sensitive to the distribution assumptions you make when you're figuring out the difference, the space between the second bid and the third bid, right?

A. Correct, it may be. It will depend on the distribution—I haven't systematically studied that. But in general, Nate used—or Dr. Miller used the Gumbel distribution because he was able to get a solution using that distribution and it seemed reasonable.

I haven't gone through and tried, what would it look like if I used a different distribution for the bids.

Q. Okay. And just to be clear, the model is absolutely not looking at actual spreads between bidding parties in the publishing realm, correct? It's only taking the inputs of one or both of the merging parties and then extrapolating everything else?

A. That's correct.

Q. Would you say that the outcome of the second score auction model is sensitive to the inputs?

A. Yes.

Q. So if the shares aren't right or the margins aren't right, that is going to affect the outcome?

A. Different inputs—when you say sensitive, I would take it to mean different inputs can give different results. And so if you put in the wrong inputs, you could get the wrong results.

Q. Are you familiar with the revenue equivalency theorem?

A. Yes.

Q. Did you apply it here?

A Did I apply it here?

Q. Yes.

A. No.

Q. And is that because the conditions couldn't be met?

A. I don't recall evaluating that. The revenue equivalency theorem, Your Honor, at a high level, is just sometimes a second score auction and a—second price auction, that's the kind we've been talking about, and a first price auction, best bids, will give the same revenue to the seller of the goods, under certain conditions.

Q. But you didn't undertake that analysis here?

A. I did not. If that were to hold, then it would mean that you could apply the second score auction to best bid auctions.

Q. It would if it did?

A. Yeah.

Q. It hasn't been done in this case, correct?

A. That's correct.

Q. Okay. By the way, you're not aware of any actual second score auction being used in publishing, right?

A. Not of the form of one set of bids is submitted and the second highest is—sets the price.

Q. And presumably if agents thought that was a good way to sell books, they'd do it?

A. Well, remember, the round robin is very close and rounds in general share similarities with it.

Q. Let's go on to another assumption of the model. The model assumes in effect that every publisher bids in every auction, correct?

A. Correct.

Q. And obviously that's not true in reality either, right?

A. That's correct.

Q. And does that help explain why the second score auction will always show harm if you remove a competitor from the auction?

A. I don't think so. I think the model is—the model is capturing the fact that if you reduce unilateral competition, there will be some impact. And then the size of that competition depends on how important that competition is. If you have parties that are very small market shares, the model is going to predict a very, very small effect.

Q. But it will always predict some effect, correct?

A. It both parties have market share, they'll be some effect.

Q. By the way, this is true of both the models you use, both—but correct me if I am wrong, both the second score auction model and the GUPPI's, they will always show some harm, correct?

A. Correct, some.

Q. And that's why in the case of the GUPPI's, for example, when regulatory agencies use them, they typically think in terms of having some sort of safe harbor because the model will always show some harm?

A. So the creator of the GUPPI methodology, Dr. Shapiro, proposed a 5 percent GUPPI threshold, so, yes, his thinking was, look at a transaction, if you see a positive GUPPI, you need to think about whether it's likely that mitigating factors will offset that. So he proposed a 5 percent GUPPI, not price effect but a 5 percent GUPPI value.

Q. Right. And that simply speaks to the fact that there's always going to be a harm result so we have to put it in perspective when we look at it?

A. I think it's important to put in perspective the predictions of these models. And I was talking earlier about the guidelines language saying finding models that significantly—if you find the models significantly produce a prediction of harm, that's significant rather than focusing on the specifics of the prediction.

Q. So let's come back to our assumption that every publisher participates in every auction. You're aware that in multi bidder acquisitions, that it's almost invariably that there is a subset of the available publishers who are invited to bid, correct?

A. I mean, in general, I would say some auction—yeah, there's a variance in who decides to bid and in which auctions.

Q. And that's partly determined as we discussed earlier, by the author-agents' decision?

A. Yeah, the sellers can decide who they want to try to involve in the auction, yeah. Sure. Sure.

Q. And it's partly decided by the publishers' decisions, whether they like the book and want to participate?

A. That's fair.

Q. And the second score auction model doesn't model that at all, correct?

A. Correct.

Q. May I give you a hypothetical? If there are 20 publishers who are in a position to bid on a book in your proposed market and the agent elects to invite ten of those bidders—ten of those publishers to bid, would the model conclude that there was harm if one of the bidders in the group of ten that had been invited had to be replaced by a bidder from outside the ten?

A. Yeah, I mean, that hypothetical, I don't—I would have to—the model is set up the way it is as a modeling assumption. All the publishers are assumed to bid. I don't recall exactly where that—what that assumption is necessary for in the mechanics of the model. I don't recall it having a big effect, but I haven't systematically studied it.

Q. Fair enough.

THE COURT: Your model can't replace a bidder, that's what Mr. Oppenheimer is asking.

THE WITNESS: Right. I'm assuming in the market that the shares are represented.

THE COURT: Right.

THE WITNESS: So in that sense, it's because the shares are including all publishers.

THE COURT: They're all in, everybody's in.

THE WITNESS: Yeah.

BY MR. OPPENHEIMER:

Q. The other thing that the second score auction does is it assumes each bidder—I'm sorry, each publisher bids only once, correct?

A. That's correct.

Q. So it excludes the effect of imprint competition, for example, at Penguin Random House?

A. I mean, you could interpret it more broadly as it's looking at the outcome of how often Penguin Random House wins. It's not saying how often does a particular Penguin Random House imprint win. How often does Penguin Random House win and in what margin does it win.

THE COURT: Can we move on from the second score auction model now because I think I understand that now.

MR. OPPENHEIMER: Sure, Your Honor.

BY MR. OPPENHEIMER:

Q. So let's go to the GUPPIs. You did not include the GUPPIs in your first report?

A. That's correct.

Q. And I assumed you covered the field looking for what would work with the GUPPIs. I'm sorry, what would be the best modeling for purposes of this case?

A. I apologize, I didn't hear that question.

Q. It was not a particularly good question.

You did your best to find the best modeling for this case when you did your first report, correct?

A. Right.

Q. You did not include the GUPPI?

A. Correct.

Q. Did you consider using the GUPPI?

A. I did not.

Q. Any reason why you didn't consider them?

A. I mean, I think the first—the second price auction is a reasonable approach here, and that's the one I elected to use.

Q. You did look at the first score auction model and rejected it, correct?

A. I tried a number of first price auctions and rejected them.

Q. So were you just looking at auction models?

A. No, I also looked at negotiations. As I said, I tried to build a model that included all of the mechanisms in one grand model and it—sadly, for my chances of winning the Nobel prize, I failed in that endeavor.

Q. And you indicated before that, earlier, that—I think you referred to the GUPPI as a defendant's model or as a model the defendants would use used?

A. So for full context, I'd say the GUPPI was developed by two former heads of the chief economists, I apologize, at the Department of Justice and the FTC. But the defendants' economists in the advocacy phase took the GUPPI model and adapted it to three different settings that they then applied to the publishing industry.

Q. And you're aware that the GUPPI model that was used in the regulatory phase—did you modify it? Let me put that way. Did you modify the model that you used?

A. The only modification I'm aware of is the party's economists argued for taking the lowest of the three. So take all three models, see which prediction gives the lowest harm and use that as the estimate of harm.

Q. But you did not do that?

A. No, I presented the results of each of the three different models.

Q. When you say that, that's what you did here in this case, correct?

A. That's correct.

Q. And you haven't provided a mechanism by which we can combine those, correct?

A. No. I mean you could look at my results and pick the one that gives the lowest protection.

Q. We could. Should we do that?

A. The parties' economist would enthusiastically say yes.

Q. But is there a principled approach we should take to that?

A. I mean, sorry. I apologize.

Q. I interrupted you. I'm sorry. Is there are a principled approach we should be taking in that?

A. I mean, I think it's valuable to see all three of the results and if you wish to take the lowest you may. I think the idea they had behind motivating that was something you've been discussing, which is the idea that agents will choose the right mechanism to get their author the best deal. And so you should discard the high—the least—or the ones that result in the most harm because agents will adjust to that.

My view is it's probably in between those. There's some ability for agents and authors to adjust, but it may not be perfect, and so I think seeing the range of the predictions is probably more useful than just showing one set of them.

Q. And the harm outcomes or the difference in the harm outcomes between the three different GUPPIs are significant, yes?

A. The—yeah, they're multi round version predicts lot more harm than the second score auction model. And then the other model, depending on the inputs, is close or less than the predictions of the second score auction model.

Q. It's about—is it fair to say that that model you just mentioned is half of the other GUPPI model harm?

A. I haven't—I haven't done the comparison, actually. I've thought about the comparison of the GUPPI model to the second score auction model but not the internal comparison.

Q. Can we agree that it's not an inconsequential difference between the GUPPI results depending upon what type of acquisition they're modeling?

A. Yeah, the multi round GUPPI makes significantly larger harm predictions than the second score auction model. Depending on the inputs, I would say that the best bids and hybrid are either similar using my inputs or, for Dr. Snyder's inputs, it's about half the harm for Penguin—Simon & Schuster to Penguin Random House.

Q. And the GUPPI model is also sensitive to inputs, correct?

A. Correct, different inputs will result in a different prediction.

A. Your Honor, I'm good to my word, I will not go back into the SSA, but there's common thread between the two models. They basically use the same inputs, correct?

A. Very similar, yes.

Q. So I want to talk a little bit about the—

A. Let me, if I may, just the second score auction model is using the market shares to get diversions. So it's assuming according to share. In the GUPPI model, as I've done it here, you can input diversions without using market shares. So I used my estimates of diversion and I used some from Dr. Snyder as well.

Q. You know that—Your Honor pointed—just a point of privilege on one SSA matter. You make a good point, Dr. Hill, that I'd forgotten about, which is, you cannot literally put diversions into the second score auction model at all, can you?

A. You would have to re-work the baseline format of it.

Q. Right. And I understand you didn't do that, correct?

A. Correct.

Q. So you're putting shares into the SSA model, it's calculating the diversions?

A. Diversions are according to share. So, yes, you're essentially using diversion according to share in that model.

Q. And in the GUPPI model you can actually put in diversions?

A. You can put in different diversions, yes.

Q. Yeah.

THE COURT: But did you put in diversions according to share or a different diversion?

THE WITNESS: For the GUPPI, Your Honor, I did both, I did diversion according to share and then I did diversion according to Dr. Snyder's estimates.

THE COURT: Okay.

BY MR. OPPENHEIMER:

Both models—

THE COURT: I'm sorry. What were Dr. Snyder's inputs? Dr. Snyder had his own diversions?

THE WITNESS: Yeah, Dr. Snyder estimated diversion using his agency data. So he took his agency data and said, when one party was the winner, how often was the other party the second highest bidder and he took that as diversion. I used those diversion estimates in the model.

BY MR. OPPENHEIMER:

Q. Would it be fair to say that the second score auction model and the GUPPI are taking inputs and they're calculating how often the parties are number one and number two, versus actually looking at empirical data and seeing who's number one and number two?

A. I don't think I would go quite that far. I think the—in the second score auction model, you're using diversion according to share, so you're assuming that the market shares are informative about diversion. In the GUPPI framework, you have—you could push—I had those five estimates of diversion, Your Honor, you could put any five of those in you want or you could put in another five. So then question is—you know, those estimates, I think, are based on data from the marketplace.

THE COURT: But when you ran the GUPPI, you used diversion according to share, which is consistent with what the SSA model did, so then you can use the GUPPI to see if the SSA was in the right ballpark because you're using the same diversion data.

THE WITNESS: Correct.

THE COURT: Whereas Dr. Snyder used the agency data which is not complete.

THE WITNESS: Yeah. So I used—I put in both, so I did it using the—

THE COURT: Right.

THE WITNESS:—diversion according to share for the reason you said, it's my preferred estimate and it also allows us to say, what do things like look in the GUPPI compared to the second score auction model. And then I secondly said, Dr. Snyder has estimated diversion using the agency data. Let me see what results that gives in the GUPPI model.

THE COURT: I see. Okay. Thank you.

BY MR. OPPENHEIMER:

Q. So the—what were the—how did you compute the margins that you used for both the SSA model and the GUPPI model?

A. So I used title level P&Ls.

Q. Can you explain how did that work? How did you do that?

A. Sure. So for each title, you take the actual realized P&L and you look at the revenue that it earns and then you look at the costs, the incremental costs that were incurred in producing that.
Q. And now for that, did you look at actual data?
A. Yes.
Q. Did you look at the book level P&Ls?
A. Yes, it's at the title level.
Q. I'm going to try to simplify this for myself. In both cases you used two margins, correct, the SSA and the GUPPI, you used a weighted average?
A. Yes.
Q. Okay. And in the initial report that you did, I'm going to try to keep this—we can go into more detail, but in the initial report you did, you included operational expenses it in calculating PRH's margins, correct?
A. I used their direct operating expenses and treated them as all variable, correct.
Q. Would you explain for us what you mean by that?
A. So there's a category of costs, Your Honor, in the Penguin Random House cost data. That is called direct operating expenses. And in the calculating Penguin Random House's margin, I included those as all variable.
Q. Why is it important to determine whether they're variable?
A. So for the models you want to use a variable profit margin. And so I want to include variable costs and exclude fixed costs.
Q. And in the first report, you—can we call that Op Ex, is that what you called it?
A. I call it direct operating expenditure, but, sure, we can call it Op Ex.
Q. How did you treat the S&S Op Ex in calculating its margins in your first report?
A. So the Simon & Schuster P&Ls were arranged differently. It didn't have the—the title level P&Ls don't have the direct operating expenses. So they were excluded from the—they were treated as fixed costs.
Q. So in the first report, the PRH margins include Op Ex and the S&S margins exclude Op Ex, right?
A. That is correct.
Q. And when you exclude the Op Ex, I assume your margins go up?
A. Correct.
Q. Higher?
A Yep.
Q. Fewer costs?
A. Fewer variable costs.
Q. Fewer variable costs, thank you.
A But the margin goes down for Penguin Random House.
Q. Yes. Now, in the reply report, you changed that calculation in response to some criticisms that Professor Snyder had made, correct?
A. Yeah, Dr. Snyder criticized that, correct.
Q. And what you did the second time was that you took Op Ex out of Penguin Random House and you also kept it out of Simon & Schuster?
A. Correct.
THE COURT: I thought you did it both ways. Dr. Snyder's way and your way.
THE WITNESS: Yeah. So, Your Honor, I did. In the initial report, I treated them all as variable.
THE COURT: Right.
THE WITNESS: In my reply report, I treated them all as fixed. And then Dr. Snyder in his report did it where he went to the—so I used the title level P&Ls. As I said, the S&S title level P&Ls don't have direct operating expenses.
THE COURT: Right.
THE WITNESS: He went to aggregated cost P&Ls, which is where the costs were because, in my view, they're fixed costs so they're at this higher level P&L, and he made an estimate of what proportion of

those costs would be equivalent to the direct operating expenses and then he ran the second score auction model with a model using those margins. So we had sort of three different versions. In mine, I used direct operating expenses are variable for Penguin Random House, and they're fixed for Penguin Random House. And then—

THE COURT: You mean Simon & Schuster?

THE WITNESS: I'm sorry?

THE COURT: You mean Simon & Schuster? They were fixed for Simon & Schuster?

THE WITNESS: So for me, I treated them as variable and fixed within Penguin Random House, and then Dr. Snyder said, let's treat them as variable for Penguin Random House and for Simon & Schuster.

THE COURT: Okay.

THE WITNESS: And in mine, my two versions, those direct operating expenses are fixed for Simon & Schuster.

THE COURT: Why did you switch in your second report to fixed?

THE WITNESS: Yeah. So in my view, the direct operating expenses for Penguin Random House are some mix of variable and fixed.

THE COURT: Right.

THE WITNESS: And I wanted to see what were the two extremes like. I don't want to include fixed costs. I did originally to be conservative. So then I saw what it looked like if I treated them all as fixed. I didn't really have this problem on the Simon & Schuster front because the P&Ls aren't arranged in the same way.

THE COURT: Right.

THE WITNESS: Their direct operating expenses, in my view, Dr. Snyder will disagree, were somewhere else and were treated as fixed. So I felt comfortable excluding them, but I wasn't totally sure what to do with the Penguin Random House category.

THE COURT: Right. So you were being conservative the first time, but then the second time you did it the other way just to see what it would be like if you did it?

THE WITNESS: Yeah, the first time was conservative with respect to harm. So the model predicted less harm the way I did it. And when I ran it again in the reply report, it predicted more harm, Your Honor.

THE COURT: Which is predictable because you were not doing the conservative way.

THE WITNESS: Correct.

THE COURT: Okay. But the correct way analytically is to just include variable costs in the margin?

THE WITNESS: That's my view, yes. And that's commonly what one does. The truth here is somewhere in between—in my view, is somewhere in between the figure in my initial report, which is conservative, and the figure in my reply report is aggressive, because I think some of those costs really are variable, so somewhere in between there is what I think is the truth.

THE COURT: Okay. But you think Simon & Schuster—you think you're accurate on that because you think that their numbers are reflecting pure variable costs?

THE WITNESS: Yes, I think the costs—their P&Ls, I think I got the right set of variable costs.

THE COURT: Okay. I got it. Thank you.

BY MR. OPPENHEIMER:

Q. Okay. And there's a critical test that needs to be performed, is there not, on the second score auction to determine if it's going to produce reliable results?

A. Yes. So Dr. Miller's paper says, a first way to test the reliability of the model is to compare the actual margins to the predicted margins.

Q. Because if the predicted margins that result from the inputs don't accurately predict the actual margins, then there could be something wrong with the model, correct?

A. Yeah. If you see very big differences between predicted and actual margins, it's a warning sign that the model is not working well.

THE COURT: I'm not sure I understand that because you put in actual margins into the model.

THE WITNESS: Yeah, so, Your Honor, you put in one firm's margin or a blended margin. It's easiest to think about it in terms of the one firm. So suppose I put in Penguin Random House's margin, then the model is going to predict a margin for Simon & Schuster.

THE COURT: Oh, I see.

THE WITNESS: And I can say, does that look like the Simon & Schuster margin or does it not?

THE COURT: I see.

BY MR. OPPENHEIMER:

Q. And that test, that the accuracy of that prediction is a—pretty much a requirement to determine the reliability of the model, would you say?

A. I mean, I think Dr. Miller says it's a first check you can make. I think it's an important check to make.

Q. Now, in this case, the reply report margins that you used produced quite a difference, did it not, between the predicted margins and the actual margins?

A. So there's no hard-and-fast rule for how big a difference has to be. But I would say the reply report margins match less well than the initial report margins.

Q. You were recently involved in a case where this issue came up, this sugar case?

A. Correct.

Q. Could you just identify this for us, it's the sugar antitrust matter earlier this year?

A. Yes, it was Department of Justice versus, I think, U.S. Sugar and United Sugars, and there may be another—and Imperial Sugar.

Q. And you there were representing the defendants, correct?

A. Correct.

Q. And the—you argued there that the difference between the two firms predicted margins was just too great for that model to be relied upon?

A. Correct.

Q. And what was the—not talking about the absolute difference in the margins, but what was the percentage difference in the margins between the predicted margin and the actual margin?

A. So at a high level, and I may get the exact percentages wrong. There were two firms involved. If you calibrated the model using, I'll say, firm A, so you put in its margin, then firm B's margin increased by five or six times so its margin went from, let's say, ten to 50.

Conversely, if you used firm B's margin, then firm A's margin was cut by about 85 to 90 percent. So there was a pretty dramatic change in the margins.

Q. In terms of a percentage difference in the margins, do you have that in mind?

A. There was a figure in my report looking at—if you used both firms' margins, so you used a blended margin, the differences in the margins—I can't remember exactly what the figure was, honestly.

There's a very significant difference based on—Your Honor, in that case, there was a dispute about the geographic market and the parties had similar market shares, but I'll just represent radically different margins, and the model found that extremely confusing. In the model, similar market shares and very different margins just—it wasn't internally able to reconcile that, was my interpretation. Dr. Rothman, the expert on the other side, disagreed.

THE COURT: So in that case, the opposing expert used the SSA model under those market circumstances but similar market shares and wildly different margins, and you thought that the results were unreliable.

THE WITNESS: Correct.

THE COURT: Based on trying to compare the actual margins with the predicted margins?

THE WITNESS: That's a fair summary, Your Honor, yes.

THE COURT: Got it.

BY MR. OPPENHEIMER:

Q. And would the predicted margins in that case, would it be fair to say they were a couple of percent and the difference in the actual margin was about 16 percent?

A. With using—no, if you allocate—if you did it using firm A's margin to firm B's margin, the difference would have been on the order of about 21 percent. But it was about a 600 times increase. And if you did it the other way, the difference was about a 90, 85 to 90 percent decrease, but, again, about 25 points—or, sorry, 20 point decrease.

Q. Right. I know that the absolute margins were quite different in that case. But I'm simply asking if you turn the difference between the margins that were being predicted by the modeling in the sugar case and the percentages, do you recall what that would have been?

A. Do you want to know the margins of each firm?

Q. No, no, the difference.

A. Between the two firms? Without saying what the margins were, the difference between firm A and firm B was about 22 percent.

Q. 22 percent. And the second score auction in that case had predicted a difference of something like 2 percent, right?

A. It predicted the firms essentially had the same margin, correct.

Q. So very close. And but they were, in fact, off by some 20 or 21 percent, correct?

A. They were off by—but it's a little misleading to just think about that difference because one of them had a margin that was very small and so the difference was very dramatic in terms of percentages.

Q. Right. Now, have you done that analysis of the second score auction model here?

A. Yeah, I believe my initial report has the differences in the margins. If it's not, then it's in the reply report.

Q. If we take the margin analysis that was done in the reply report where we have Op Ex out of both margins, both PRH and Simon & Schuster, would you agree that the percentage difference in margins between the two companies is about 21 percent, 22 percent?

A. I don't recall, but there's a figure of it in either Dr. Snyder's report or mine.

Q. And would I be correct that if the model predicts that the difference should be about 3.7 percent?

A. I don't recall the exact numbers, but there's a demonstrative, I think, in my report that looks at this. I assume you're representing numbers you've taken from the report.

Q. Yeah. Well, I'm doing the best I can. I think so. And when Professor Snyder did his analysis, did you check on his analysis of how well the second score auction model predicted the difference in—the actual difference in margins?

A. Do you mean using his margins?

Q. That is correct.

A. There, I believe the difference was larger than in either of my two model runs.

Q. Do you recall that he said that model predicted that there should be a 2 percent difference, give or take, between the margins and it turned out to be almost 29 percent?

A. I don't recall the exact numbers. But his differences were certainly larger than mine.

Q. Okay. Fair enough. Would I be correct in saying that the only model that really satisfies the requirement that the SSA predicted margins be roughly—would be a good predictor of the actual margins is the margins you used in your first report?

A. I don't think you fairly characterized Dr. Miller's description. He says that it's an important test to look—of the validity of the model to look at how the actual and predicted margins line up. I think the model in the first report, using all direct operating expenses, is variable for Penguin Random House. The match is very close. It's less close when I treat them all as fixed. But I think it's still acceptable. For Dr. Snyder's version, I believe it's—I don't recall exactly. I think it's a larger difference than for either of mine.

Q. Would it be fair to say that if—of among all the options, that was the only one that comfortably fit from your point of view?

A. Again, there isn't a hard-and-fast rule. But I would say that one is certainly the closest match of any of the three models.

Q. And you've said a couple of times that there's no hard-and-fast rule. I just want to make sure we're clear, but there really is no standard for measuring this, is there?

A. That's fair. Often in economics, looking at margins is a way of evaluating a model and we don't have a yardstick you can use every time to say it's this much or that much. So it is a matter of judgment.

Q. And just to be clear, based on the analysis you did on this factor in the sugar case, you advocated that

that model—that SSA model was just not reliable?

A. I did not think it was reliable, that's correct.

Q. So let's talk about the outputs both models quickly in terms of the confidence you have in the outcomes of them.

A. Sure.

Q. So you've indicated that the second score auction model produced a downward pricing effect of about 6.1 percent, correct?

A. Yeah, about 4 percent for Penguin Random House, 11 and a half, say, for Simon & Schuster.

Q. And you're absolutely not saying that's the exact result, correct?

A. It's my best estimate; but, again, in modeling, I think, the—it is more directional than necessarily and entirely precise.

Q. And with respect to the SSA model, you don't have an estimate for the range of error in the model, do you?

A. That's correct.

Q. So the price effect could be 5 percent?

A. There isn't an estimate of the range of the effect.

Well, I would say to the extent that there's a range that—Dr. Snyder ran the model using different margins, I ran the model using different cutoffs, so it was run a number of different ways. But I can't give you a confidence interval around the 4 percent and the 11.5 percent. They could be larger, they could be smaller.

Q. At your deposition, you said it could be as low as 3 percent, correct?

A. Do you mean overall?

Q. Yes.

A. It could be as low as 3 or as big as 9, yeah. I don't have a confidence interval.

Q. So the outcomes—could it even be lower than 3 percent?

A. Yeah. I mean, there isn't—the model doesn't produce a confidence interval. I think that the model—the way I interpret the model is, there are these different buckets of evidence on unilateral effects and the model, both the SSA and the GUPPI models, predicting substantial harm is another form of inference about how likely all of the effects are. But I do not put too much weight on the specifics of the 4 percent and the 11 and a half percent.

Q. Could it go down to zero?

A. I don't think that would be consistent with the other evidence. So technically the model could have produced that but none of the runs I've seen of the model produce anything close to that.

Q. But I just want to be clear because you said not—something to the effect of not in consideration of the other evidence.

Just as a technical matter looking at the second score auction model, could the result go down to zero?

A. It doesn't have a confidence interval. It gives you a best estimate of the harm. If I put different inputs in, then you can get it down to zero if you give zero market share to the parties.

Q. But, Dr. Hill, I'm just talking about using the same inputs. But using the same inputs, it could go down to 3 percent?

A. There's no—we're trying to learn about the true unilateral effect of the merger, and this is one way of estimating it. It doesn't tell me what the true value it. Is gives me an estimate and I have other ways of estimating how likely the effect is. But I can't tell you what the true effect is based on this single model.

CROSS-EXAMINATION (Resumed)

BY MR. OPPENHEIMER:

Q. So I wanted to pick up where we left off and ask you some questions about market shares. Okay?

A. Okay.

Q. So market shares tell you who won; correct?

A. Correct.

Q. And market shares don't actually tell you how often two companies compete; correct?

A. You can use them to draw an inference, but in and of themselves, they are a record of who won.
Q. Exactly. And it's possible that you can have a situation where you have market shares that are quite different from the actual incidence of one-to-one competition in a market; correct?
A. That's correct.
Q. What I'd like to do—and Mr. Read and I may be the last champions of ELMO technology around here, but I'd like to use the ELMO for one illustration. Okay. Good. All right. So I'd like to just do a brief example and see if we're on the same page on this. I'd like you to assume, Dr. Hill, that you take the shares that you have used—So these are the two shares that you use in your report, respectively, for PRH and Simon & Schuster; correct?
A. That's correct.
Q. Okay. Now, I'd like to assume a world in which we're just in auctions. Okay? And I'd like you to further assume that each of these parties wins half the auctions they're in and loses half the auctions. Okay?
A. Okay.
Q. So what I'm going to do, I'm going to represent that—in this manner by saying that they're in auctions twice as often as they win. Okay?
A. Okay.
Q. Okay. So that would tell us the percentage of time that they are participants in an auction; correct?
A. Correct.
Q. So in that world, PRH—pardon me. This is all you need to know about my math. This is 74.
A. And my math.
Q. Okay. You get a pass then. All right. So in this world, PRH is in 74 percent of the auctions in the market, winning half the time; and Simon & Schuster is in 24 percent of the auctions in the market, winning half of the time. Agree?
A. Agreed.
Q. And they would never bump into each other?
A. They might or they might not.
Q. Fair enough. You—this could—absolutely knowing just this—be a situation—and this is only for illustrative purposes because we know they do bump into each, but this—in this scenario, they would never bump into each other?
A. By your assumption, yes, these are completely—they could never bump into each other if they—one competed in—if they competed in completely different auctions.
Q. Okay.
A. Yes.
Q. So we could have stipulated, you and I, that Penguin Random House has a 37 percent share of the book market and Simon & Schuster has a 12 percent share of the book market. And based on that alone, we would not know how often they encountered each other in the marketplace?
A. Yeah, as in my previous answer, we frequently draw the inference substitutions according to share, but it is not necessarily the case that they—substitution is according to share.
Q. And the notion that we can determine that people encounter each other in the market, actually compete head-to-head in the market, in proportion to their market shares is exactly what you said, an assumption; correct?
A. No. I mean, I think you also check the evidence. Do you see in other sources of information indication that they can compete more frequently or less frequently than according to share?
Q. Right. But if we're only looking at the market shares, it's just an assumption that it follows proportionately?
A. If we just had the market shares, then—and that was the only piece of information you would have; correct.
Q. Okay. And you saw—we talked about this yesterday in the agency data that Professor Snyder developed that PRH—that only about half the time that PRH and S&S wins, the others in that competition?

A. Could you refresh my memory on that, please.
Q. Sure. In about—in about half the contracts, the other party didn't even submit a bid; correct?
A. And you're talking just about auctions?
Q. Sure. We'll start there.
A. Well, is that—where is the number coming from? Is it for just auctions, or does it include renegotiations?
Q. Do—let's start with auctions. Do you know the answer to auctions?
A. I'm not familiar with that number. I'm familiar with the estimates of how often there are runners-up, but I don't know how often one participated when the other won.
Q. Okay. Let's just focus, then, on multi-bidder contracts and Professor Snyder's database.
A. Okay.
Q. Okay. And would you agree with me that in about half of the multi-bidder acquisitions, that when one party wins, the other party did not even submit a bid?
A. I believe we talked about that. I don't recall the number, but I have not analyzed it separately. So I don't need any reason to push back.
Q. Right. And just taking our—our market share example, if all you had was the market share, would you not be able to tell just from it how often Penguin Random House or Simon & Schuster were not the runner-up in any bidding from the market shares? Correct?
A. If you just know the market shares, then you would just know who won. You wouldn't have information, direct information, about who was the runner-up.
Q. Right. And you could say the same thing about who was number three for market shares—correct?—if you only had market shares?
A. If you only had market shares, you—I mean, you could draw an inference based on the shares, but they wouldn't be direct evidence on who was the third-place bidder.
Q. And the market shares don't tell you at all how often a publisher participates in a bid; correct?
A. That's correct.
Q. And they don't tell you at all how often—
A. Well, I apologize. They don't tell you exactly how often they participated, but, clearly, they'll tell you that PRH participated at least 37 percent of the time and S&S percent. So you couldn't narrow it down. But they would tell you they're participating at least as often as they want.
Q. Sure. That makes perfect sense. But you'd have no idea how often they bid in order to achieve those winnings?
A. Correct.
Q. Okay.
A. Except that it was more than their share, yes.
Q. Absolutely. And that's—that's what we showed on the ELMO.
THE COURT: So you have no sense of how often they win when they bid? That's not part of your analysis?
THE WITNESS: No, Your Honor. I didn't separately analyze that.
THE COURT: Okay.
BY MR. OPPENHEIMER:
Q. And a publisher's share could be smaller than their actual participation; correct?
A. So you mean they could win less than they bid?
Q. No. My question wasn't clear. A publisher's share, market share, could be less than the times they participate in a bid?
THE COURT: Should be, unless they're winning every time; right?
THE WITNESS: Yeah. So they bid more often than they win?
BY MR. OPPENHEIMER:
Q. Right. And it doesn't tell you—it doesn't tell you the ratio of their participation in bidding to their winning?
A. Correct.

Q. Okay.
A. Yeah, it—yeah.
Q. And it doesn't—it doesn't tell you how often they're a runner-up?
A. Correct.
Q. Okay. And, conversely, a publisher could be a runner-up more often than the share would predict?
A. Correct.
Q. So in addition to deriving your head-to-head competition percentage of 12 percent from a share analysis, you also looked at other sources, such as editorial minutes?
A. So I don't believe I derived the 12 percent. I think that was one of Dr. Snyder's calculations.
Q. It's implicit in your calculation, however; correct?
A. I don't know if I would—I mean, you could figure out something like that, but I never calculated it. But at any rate, to your question, yes, I also considered editorial minutes.
Q. Okay. And that was to get outside just looking at shares, to look at something else?
A. Yeah. As I said, I wanted to look at various different measures of diversion.
Q. Okay. So let's—let's start with the editorial minutes. You looked at editorial minutes from Penguin Random House and Simon & Schuster; correct?
A. Correct.
Q. No one else?
A. Correct.
Q. All right. And you—you understood when you were doing that that those minutes capture whatever books happened to be raised at a meeting that was of particular interest to that group?
A. The—the imprints are recording the books that they talk about in the editorial meeting, yes.
Q. But you know those editorial minutes aren't—they're not comprehensive?
A. They need not be; correct.
Q. And sometimes they're a little bit haphazard?
A. I mean, I've heard testimony. I haven't seen any quantitative evidence on that.
Q. And do you recall that one of the publishers at S&S referred to them as slapdash? Does that ring a bell?
A. I don't recall that, but I recall that there was some testimony that they may not be systematic.
Q. Okay. And you had to actually go through those minutes and try to decipher them and figure out as best you could who was first and who was second?
A. No. No, sir.
Q. So what were you actually looking for?
A. We were actually looking in the editorial minutes for opportunities that either Penguin Random House or Simon & Schuster submitted a bid for.
Q. And did you actually find throughout all of the editorial minutes evidence of who's number one and who's number two in the bidding?
A. No. I was looking for opportunities where Penguin Random House or Simon & Schuster bid, and then I identified who won the book using the anticipated top seller database.
Q. And did you on that basis assume that those two entities were winner and runner-up?
A. I used it as an estimate of that. So it's—the question was when one publisher bids, how often does the other publisher win. And if it was often HarperCollins, then that will be reflected. And if it's often one of the parties, that will be reflected.
Q. And could you actually tell from looking at the editorial minutes who was number one and number two?
A. No.
Q. Okay. And you didn't review all of the editorial minutes, correct?
A. I tried to review all—I think in the end I had data from PRH imprints and 12 Simon & Schuster imprints.
Q. Yes, I believe that's what your report says. Do you know how many—so 13 PRH imprints. Do you know how many imprints there are at PRH?

A. I believe they have about a hundred.
Q. Yeah. So 13 out of a hundred?
A. Right. But I took the data for all the ones I had.
Q. Sure. No. I—this was hard work for you; right?
A. It took a long time.
Q. Yeah. And it was basically having to review all these individually?
A. It turns out that you can do some of it by reading them in. Some of them are in a—sort of a standard format, Your Honor, so you can read it in and they'll have a standard language for identifying. But it turned out to be much more labor-intensive than I anticipated.
Q. Okay. And you got through 13 out of—out of a hundred-plus imprints?
A. I got through all the ones I had editorial minutes for.
Q. Okay.
A. But that was 13 out of roughly 100. I don't remember the exact number.
Q. And you reviewed 12 of the imprints at Simon & Schuster?
A. Correct.
Q. That—and they have—do you know how many imprints they have?
A. I don't.
Q. Does it refresh you if I say 38?
A. That sounds reasonable.
Q. Okay. So 12 out of 38 of Simon & Schuster. Now, you're aware from Professor Snyder's report that there are some inaccuracies in your editorial minutes data; correct?
A. When—I believe he identified cases where he said that the—they were not actually the runner-up, but that wasn't what I was trying to estimate.
Q. But you did—you did report winner and runner-up data from your review of the editorial minutes?
A. No. The goal in the editorial minutes was to say which books are important enough that one of the parties bid on and then how often was that book won by each of the other potential publishers. It was used as an estimate of how often they're first and second, but it was not actually an estimate of who was the winner and the runner-up.
Q. In what respect does it tell us who was first and second?
A. So it's useful to look at how often one party competes and the other party wins.
Q. But in each of these specific cases, you couldn't tell for the book that was the subject of the minutes you reviewed who was actually one and two?
A. That's correct.
Q. Now—
THE COURT: Can you give me a sense of how many auctions we're talking about in the editorial minutes?
THE WITNESS: Yes, Your Honor. It's—it's in my report. I believe it's on the order of about 75 or—75 for each publisher, and it—I was only able to do it for 2020, Your Honor.
MR. OPPENHEIMER: And—
THE WITNESS: I apologize, Mr. Oppenheimer. If you're interested, the number is in my report, and we could look it up, if you're—if you'd like to.
THE COURT: Okay.
MR. OPPENHEIMER: And your—
THE WITNESS: It's in the—should—
MR. OPPENHEIMER: If Your Honor is checking it, sure.
THE WITNESS: Sure. Let me just see.
THE COURT: Do you know where that would be?
THE WITNESS: Yeah. I believe it would be in the reply report, Your Honor.
THE COURT: The rebuttal?
THE WITNESS: My reply report.
THE COURT: Your reply report.

THE WITNESS: Oh actually, it's in the—so in the reply report on page 22, there's a figure summarizing it, Figure 13. So there's—in the reply report, Your Honor, that Figure 13 is summarizing. And then in the initial report on page 88, there's a table with the numbers. So it's 90 books for Penguin Random House, and it's 78 for Simon & Schuster. And that's page 88 of the initial report.

THE COURT: I see. Thank you.

THE WITNESS: Sorry about that.

BY MR. OPPENHEIMER:

Q. And do you have an understanding of the mechanism that Professor Snyder used to determine where the editorial minutes were actually not identifying the winner and the runner-up?

A. As I recall, he compared books that were in the editorial minutes to his agency data.

Q. And let's just pause on the agency data for a minute. You and Professor Snyder have collected information, would it be fair to say, that no one in the publishing industry has collected before?

A. I think that's fair to say, because we had access to data from multiple publishers.

Q. And the parties here, pursuant to confidentiality orders and whatnot, have been able to amass information about the activities of publishers that are not public?

A. Yeah. I mean, for example, the advance data has a complete record of all anticipated top sellers from 2019 to 2021.

Q. Your advance data is the—are you referring to your acquisition data?

A. I call it the advance data, but we could call it the acquisition data.

Q. Yeah. And so that—that data, just to be clear, that only tells you who won; correct?

A. It tells us the date, who won, and the amount.

Q. Yeah. Nothing about who was second or third or anything else?

A. That's correct, but I—to your point, I don't believe anyone has a data set of this type.

Q. Yeah. Understood. And you're aware that Professor Snyder collected bidding information with respect to almost a thousand acquisitions?

A. I don't remember the total number. There's—there's 22 Simon & Schuster wins and, I think, around 70 Penguin Random House wins.

Q. But you know there's well over 900 acquisitions in the agency database that was compiled by Professor Snyder and his team; correct?

A. Are you talking about anticipated top sellers or all books?

Q. Yes—no. Anticipated top sellers.

A. I don't recall the numbers, sir.

THE COURT: I'm sorry. What did you mean by 22 Simon & Schuster wins and 70 Penguin Random House wins?

THE WITNESS: So in the data, Dr. Snyder looks at competitions that were won by Simon & Schuster or Penguin Random House, and then he tries to estimate who was the runner-up, and then he calculates diversion using that methodology. So for Simon & Schuster, he has 22 auctions that were won by Simon & Schuster.

THE COURT: Out of 900? That doesn't seem right.

THE WITNESS: Yeah, that's why the 900 strikes me as being quite strange, and I calculated market shares using his data. And it also doesn't match that, but I—so I'm struggling to understand the 900.

BY MR. OPPENHEIMER:

Q. So of the 900, does it ring a bell that 360 are in the segment of $250,000-and-up advances?

A. Oh. So I just asked if you meant anticipated top sellers, and you said yes. But, in fact, the 900 includes non-anticipated top sellers?

Q. Correct. Did you understand that?

A. Oh, okay. No, no. That's why I asked you, and you said yes, but—

Q. I apologize. I probably misunderstood your question. So you understand there are 360 acquisitions in the agency database that involve the price segment that you're proposing?

A. That sounds correct, including both negotiations and auctions.

Q. Okay. And you understand that–

THE COURT: Wait. Can I just ask a second—I'm sorry. But if we're talking about 360 auctions and Penguin Random House, does that match up with their market share?

THE WITNESS: Yeah. Your Honor, if we look at the—my—if you would like to go—yes. So if you look in my reply report, I believe I have a table of market shares from Dr. Snyder's data.

THE COURT: Okay.

THE WITNESS: Let me find that quickly, if I can. It should be—I think it's Section 4.

THE COURT: Page 16?

THE WITNESS: Oh, rats. Ah. Oh. Let me see.

THE COURT: I think it's page 16.

THE WITNESS: Oh. Thank you, Your Honor. Oh, yeah. There we go. And the discrepancy for the 22 versus 360 is when Dr. Snyder is calculating his diversions, Your Honor, he uses auctions. Because in a—in a one-on-one negotiation, he may not have information about who's the runner-up. So when he's thinking about diversions, he says, let's look at ones where there was an auction and I can identify the runner-up. And then for the total share markets here, I believe we're using all the opportunities, and that would be the 360. And some of those, it's just not possible to say who the runner-up is.

THE COURT: Okay.

BY MR. OPPENHEIMER:

Q. Right. So you have to limit it to the ones where you can actually determine who was actually the runner-up; correct?

A. Dr. Snyder had a methodology for identifying it, which was to take the second-highest bidder and assume that was the runner-up. And I think he also only looked at auctions where he felt he had a complete record. So he didn't—if he felt like there might be missing bidders, he—I believe he excluded those opportunities.

Q. Right. Your understanding is that Professor Snyder's approach was to only rely on information where he could verify who was number one and number two; correct?

A. I don't believe he could verify number two. I think he assumed that the second-highest bidder would be the runner-up.

Q. All right. But if you couldn't determine the second-highest bidder, he would not base the calculation on it?

A. If he—I think he—I think he went further. He said if I don't have a complete record. I think this was his intention, and he—he'll be able to tell you that if he didn't feel he had the full record of the auction, then he didn't include that.

Q. Right.

A. Including knowing who the second-highest bidder was.

Q. Right. Those were part of his protocols for the agency study; correct?

A. I believe so.

Q. Okay.

THE COURT: When would the second-highest bidder not be the runner-up? You said he's assuming that. But if he has the complete data, isn't that the runner-up?

THE WITNESS: So, Your Honor, you may have heard about underbidders. There are cases where someone will bid a higher value but they will not be selected. So there's an example where a prominent political figure received a much higher bid but went with an underbidder who was about half the size of the—of the—the bid that didn't win.

BY MR. OPPENHEIMER:

Q. Right. Correct. A good example. And when that happened, Professor Snyder would control for that; correct?

A. I think he—I don't know how he—I don't recall how he—

Q. Okay. That's fine. He can go into more detail. But data all comes from agencies; correct?

A. The data comes from agencies, but not from all agencies.

Q. Correct.

A. He had some criteria for selecting which agencies were included.

Q. But all of the data that is in the agency data set comes from agencies?

A. I believe—yes.

Q. And all of the data sets that we're talking about in this case and that you're using, that's the only data set that comes exclusively from agencies; correct?

A. Exclusively from agencies would be correct, but the runner-up study uses agency data as well.

Q. Right. But would you agree with me that the agents are uniquely positioned to see the entirety of the competitive landscape of a bid or acquisition?

A. No. Because by looking in the runner-up study, for example, I know who is perceived as the second-best bidder rather than having to assume it was the second-highest bid.

Q. I just want to make sure I understand what you just said. You're saying that you have seen some anecdotal information that publishers are thinking about who they might be bidding against in certain circumstances?

A. I disagree with your characterization as anecdotal. And I think it goes back to your point, about being able to construct and Dr. Snyder have constructed data sets that no one else in the industry has the equal of.

Q. And would you agree with me that the parties who have a view—they can actually see who all the bidders were for a particular book—are the agents?

A. Yeah, I think that's fair.

Q. And that a vast amount of the information in that database is not now publicly known and has never been publicly known?

A. That's reasonable. Well, I would—yeah, the winner is always known, but there's parts of it that are unknown, certainly.

THE COURT: And can I just ask: If he's got 360 anticipated top seller auctions in his agency database, what percentage of all of the ATX auctions is that?

THE WITNESS: So in a given year, you can think that there's about a thousand to 1200. So over—I think his—I think his agency data covers four years. One way to think about it is Simon & Schuster would win about 100 anticipated top sellers in a year, give or take. So over four years it would win 400, and he has 22. I think those numbers are roughly correct. Others can check.

BY MR. OPPENHEIMER:

Q. And this was as a result of the quality-control protocol that you described earlier?

A. Well, and also I believe all of his agency data comes from subpoenas, and particularly from party subpoenas, but I'm not—I'm not a hundred percent sure which of the subpoenas were—

Q. All right. We'll have him explain in more detail. But a large—a large—and would you say unprecedented study?

A. I would—yeah, in the sense that it has never been done before.

Q. Okay. And let's go back now to the editorial minutes. And you're aware that Professor Snyder looked at the results of the editorial minutes examination and identified places where the winning publisher and runner-up publisher were not as identified in your conclusions about those minutes?

A. I—I disagree with the last part of your point there. I never intended in the editorial minutes to claim that these were necessarily the winner and the runner-up. It was, rather, to look at another source of information about how often the parties are losing to one another, but they can also be losing to others. So, similarly, in the editorial minutes, if the book is in, let's say, Simon & Schuster's editorial minutes and HarperCollins was the winner, then that would be counted as Simon & Schuster being the runner-up to HarperCollins.

Q. Let's take a look at Tab 2, which is—

A. Certainly, sir. Which—in the cross exhibits?

Q. In the thin book. The new thin book. This is Defendant's Exhibit 384. This is from Professor Snyder's rebuttal report. It's page 190 of his report, Exhibit X.9.

A. Sure.

Q. Do you recall seeing this—oh, I'm sorry. This is confidential. Do you recall seeing this report?

A. It is unprecedented.

Q. Did you recall seeing this report?

A. I do.

Q. Okay. And do you understand that when—that Professor Snyder had compared the results of your editorial analysis to the agency database? Do you understand that was his basic approach?

A. Correct.

Q. Okay. And what he did—there's a column that says Editorial Meeting Minutes Source. You understand that identifies whose editorial minutes these are; correct?

A. Correct.

Q. Okay. And then he identified the publisher who actually won based on the agency data in the next column?

A. Correct.

Q. And he identified the actual runner-up from the agency data in the last column; correct?

A. Correct.

Q. All right. And those conclusions about who was the winning publisher and who was the runner-up publisher differ from the conclusions you drew with respect to these titles in the editorial minute review; correct?

A. So, again, I disagree. The goal of the editorial meeting—minutes was never to say this is absolutely the winner and the runner-up. It was, rather, to ask a more general question: When one party is competing, how often is the other the winner? And I used it, to your point, to draw an inference about how often they were likely to be runner-up.

Q. So I understand, with respect to the titles that are identified in DX 384, were you suggesting that any inference whatsoever be drawn about whether Penguin Random House or Simon & Schuster were winner and runner-up with respect to these?

A. So here you've picked one side. If you look at other ones, you may have examples that go in the other direction. But at a high level, I looked at all of this information for the editorial minutes to get a sense of how often the parties compete. And I think it's a reasonable way to get us another look at how often are the parties winner and runner-up. That doesn't mean that if it's in one party's editorial minute as a bid, the other side was definitely the—and the other side was the winner, that they were definitely the runner-up.

Q. So can we agree, then, before we move on to win-loss data, that the editorial minutes don't tell us who's one and two?

A. I think they're informative about how often the parties are competing head to head. But the editorial minutes, if you look for who bid and who won, it does not tell you for sure that the bidder was the runner-up. Yes, we can agree on that.

Q. Okay. Let's turn to your win-loss data.

A. Sure.

Q. This was another source you looked at outside of shares. And this was a collection of materials you went through that the parties maintained that were records, as best they kept them, of literally who won and who lost in acquisitions?

A. Correct. It was if the—if the party maintaining the record lost, who was the winner. And then I believe I also looked at when one party won, who was the—the—the winner—or who was the—no, yeah. The loss side.

Q. Right. And—and I believe you've previously acknowledged that these only sporadically—the information of this type is only sporadically kept by the parties; correct?

A. My recollection of the letters about them said that they are not necessarily systematic.

Q. And that, in fact, they were sporadic; correct?

A. If you have that information, we can certainly review that. I don't recall that. It's—there's a footnote in my report about it. I don't recall the exact language.

Q. We can go to the footnote, if necessary. Let me just ask: Do you recall that the footnote indicated that Simon & Schuster said they had limited and unsystematic data on such bids?

A. Correct. That sounds right.

Q. Does that sound right? Okay. So can we agree that the win-loss data that was submitted to you by the parties was limited on systematic data?

A. On the side of Simon & Schuster, yes; and Penguin Random House had slightly different language, which—

Q. But, ultimately, to the same effect; correct?

A. I don't recall their exact language, but it was certainly to the effect that they were not systematic. They—they certainly represented that not every competition we're in is recorded in win-loss data; and that's certainly true given the number of observations.

Q. Okay. And the win-loss data produced by the parties doesn't tell you who the runner-up for any particular book is; right?

A. That's correct.

Q. Okay. And the—the data that was produced in this data set that you used doesn't tell you whether they were—whether the parties were second, third, fourth, fifth, or runner-up; correct?

A. Correct. All it tells you is one of them competed and—or it tells you that the party keeping the data competed, and then it tells you who the eventual winner was.

Q. Right. So in the win-loss database, the documents from PRH would perhaps let you know that it lost to Simon & Schuster or vice versa, but they don't in many cases even know who the runner-up is; correct?

A. That's correct.

Q. Okay. But in your calculation of diversion rates from these documents, you treated the win-loss data as if it established winner and runner-up; correct?

A. It's common in antitrust analysis, Your Honor, to look at win-loss data and use it to draw inference about head-to-head competition, and that's what I used it for. I took the estimates from the win-loss data, and I used them to estimate how much head-to-head competition there was.

Q. Even though they didn't actually tell you who was one and two?

A. They do not tell you if one party was the winner or the other was the runner-up. That is correct.

Q. When you—by the way, did you identify that qualification in your report?

A. That they don't actually tell you?

Q. Correct.

A. I don't recall my exact discussion of it.

Q. Okay.

A. But it's—to anyone who uses win-loss data regularly, it is not going to be a mystery.

Q. And you—you used the win-loss data to verify the diversion rates that you get for market share?

A. I used all my estimates of diversion. As I said, I think I considered the full range of them to get a picture of what diversion likely looks like.

Q. But just to be clear, you used the win-loss data to confirm the diversions that you got for market shares, even though they don't literally tell you who's one and two?

A. I think the way I would say it is the diversion, according to share, is based on the largest sample and is any preferred methodology. And I think the estimates from the other samples—the other methods are largely consistent with them, including the win-loss data and the editorial minutes.

Q. Neither of which actually tell you who's one and two; correct?

A. That's correct.

Q. Now, let's—and those were the—those were the three corroborations you made of the diversions proportional to shares—is that correct?—your win-loss database, which we've talked about, the runner-up database that we've talked about, and the editorial minutes; correct?

A. In my initial report, that's correct.

Q. Okay. Let's talk about imprint competition.

A. Okay.

Q. You agree that it's possible that Penguin Random House imprints finish first and second—can finish first and second in a given auction; correct?

A. It's possible, yes.

Q. And, in fact, that—that certainly can happen in a best-bid situation; correct?

A. In a best-bid situation, did you say?

Q. Yes.

A. Yes.

Q. And it even happens in other auctions that aren't best bids; correct?

A. It can, yes.

Q. Right. Now, if—if Simon & Schuster joins the Penguin Random House family of imprints, you understand that the intent is to treat them at least as another imprint? You understand that?

A. I don't understand that.

Q. Okay. You—

A. I understand the text of the bidding promise, but—I don't know exactly what you mean by treat them as at least another imprint.

Q. I want to divide this up so we separate questions about Mr. Dohle's letter. And just assuming for a moment that letter doesn't exist—you're familiar with the letter I'm talking about?

A. Correct, sir.

Q. Okay. Assume that doesn't exist. After the merger, as far as you know, all of the Simon & Schuster imprints will be moved over into the Penguin Random House company but they'll all still exist?

A. I believe there's been discussions of collapsing some of the children's imprints, but on the adult side, I'm not aware of any discussion of collapsing any of them.

Q. And you understand it is the long-standing practice of Penguin Random House to allow imprint competition in bidding; correct?

A. I would say limited imprint competition.

Q. What is the limitation you have in mind?

A. If the two Penguin Random House imprints are the last bidders, they are not allowed to—they can match—the lower of the two can match—or the lower imprints can match the higher, but they cannot go higher.

Q. Right. So as long as there is an outside bidder, a bidder who is not part of the Penguin Random House imprint family, the imprints are free to compete against each other?

A. They're free to—correct.

Q. And often do?

A. Correct. Well, I don't know about often. What do you mean by "often"?

Q. Well, let's just leave it. That they're free to compete with each other?

A. Correct.

Q. And they drive bids up on each other; correct?

A. I wouldn't say that, because I think if you removed the independent bidder, then they couldn't go higher. So it's that presence of the independent bidder that is allowing the bid to go up.

Q. In all situations where there is an independent bidder, the imprints fight with each other and they drive their bids up; correct?

A. Again, the way I interpret it is if we imagine we have a rounds auction and from Round 2 onwards there's only one independent publisher present—and let's say we go to Round 7—that value in Round 7 only happened because of the presence of the independent publisher.

Q. But you would agree with me that until the outside bidder drops out, the top two bids could be two Penguin Random House imprints fighting with each other; correct?

A. I haven't seen examples of that. Dr. Snyder had some in his report, but it turned out that other bidders were the second- or first-highest bidder, but there may be examples of it.

Q. And in the best-bid situation, just to clarify to an even simpler concept, when the bids are submitted, the individual imprints have no idea who they're bidding against most of the time; correct?

A. Your last bit there was most of the time?

Q. Well, perhaps all the time. But I'm just trying to—

A. Well, sometimes—

Q. In a best-bid situation, you submit a bid, most of the time you do not know who you're bidding against; correct?

A. There are situations where that's true. I can't put a number on it for you, because there are situations where the Penguin Random House imprints discuss and coordinate prior to the bidding what they wish to bid. I—I don't have a number for you about how frequent that is compared to bidding without knowledge.

Q. But you know that there are best-bid situations where the top two bidders have been two imprints from Penguin Random House; correct?

A. Correct.

Q. And the winner has been chosen between the two?

A. I don't know—I can't characterize it that way, but I will say that the author has picked one of the Penguin Random House imprints.

Q. Okay. And you know that this is a long-standing business practice of Penguin Random House?

A. I believe so.

Q. And, in fact, you believe that it is economically—it can well be profit maximizing to have this structure?

A. I think the structure can have advantages, if you allow the competition—if you take rounds auctions—I think is the easiest way to think about it—allow the imprints to bid against—to bid independently until they run up to a point where there's no competition left, and that additional bidding is negative.

Q. But in its simplest forms, you would agree with me that the current structure at Penguin Random House of allowing its imprints to compete with each other may be profit maximizing; correct?

A. Yes, could be.

Q. And you also understand that Hachette has the same system?

A. I don't recall Mr. Pietsch's testimony on that point. I apologize. I know Simon & Schuster has a slightly different—I just don't recall Hachette or Macmillan or HarperCollins.

Q. But they're not—Penguin Random House is not the only publisher operating today that allows imprint competition?

A. I—I—I'll take your word for it. I just don't recall.

Q. Okay. Let's take a quick look back at a slide that was used, I believe, from your presentation. Pam, this is Tab 7. This is not confidential. And I believe this was Slide 39 of the government's deck on the presentation.

A. I'm there.

Q. Okay. You recognize this slide? This is your slide?

A. I do.

Q. And—and I just draw your attention to the highlighted language to the line there that says, " . . . if this book"—"if this book made its way to 1745 Broadway [Penguin Random House's address], we are talking 300–400 baseline." What did you understand that to mean?

A. This is someone at Simon & Schuster saying that if this book were to go to the open market or to get to Penguin Random House, then the—Penguin Random House would be willing to offer a significant amount relative to the values we see on the right.

Q. Right. And then it says, " . . . and if Knopf/not-so-little Random/Doubleday start all going after it, 500–750 easy." Do you see that?

A. I do.

Q. So here this—the point is being made by the vice president at Simon & Schuster that the imprint competition that could ensue once this gets over to Penguin Random House could drive the bidding up even higher than it was; correct?

A. With a minor—you said vice president of Simon & Schuster. I think this is just the vice president of the imprint.

Q. Pardon me. Correct. But you would agree with that comment?

A. The—the—this vice president is saying Penguin Random House would be very interested in this book; correct.

Q. And its imprints would compete with each other and drive the price up; correct?

A. I don't know if I would say that necessarily.
Q. It's your slide. So I'm not sure, but it—you don't read it that way?
A. I—no. I—
Q. Okay. Let's switch and talk about your theory of harm and unilateral effects.
A. Okay. Unilateral effects?
Q. Yes.
A. Sure.
Q. Now, the theory, in general, relies on the bidders being one and two; correct?
A. No. That's true in rounds—rounds auctions, but not necessarily in other formats.
Q. Well, let's be clear. The theory of unilateral effects you're talking about does not predict harm if Penguin Random House and Simon & Schuster never bid against each other; correct?
A. That's—well, that would be fair in auctions, yes.
Q. Well, auctions is the model you used to model the entire set of acquisitions in the SSA; correct?
A. That's true.
Q. All right. So—and the theory does not predict harm if the number of bidders is reduced where PRH and Simon & Schuster weren't one and two; correct?
A. I'm sorry. Are we talking about the SSA, or are we talking about—
Q. No. I'm talking about your theory of harm in general at this point.
A. No, I don't agree with that.
Q. Let's take a situation where Penguin Random House, Simon & Schuster, HarperCollins, and Norton bid before the merger. Okay? It's just—
A. Sure.
Q. No merger. Simon & Schuster is a separate company. So it's Penguin House [sic], Simon & Schuster, HarperCollins, and Norton. Okay?
A. Okay.
Q. Now, if Norton won that hypothetical auction, your unilateral effects theory doesn't tell you anything about whether there will be harm even if post-merger Simon & Schuster couldn't bid on the book?
A. It may. I mean, it—are you talking about best bids or rounds?
Q. Either.
A. Well, no. So in a best-bids there can be the second-order effect of—the parties can—so in—in the—
Q. Let me stop you.
A. Sure.
Q. Can you answer the question without respect to second order? Then I'll ask you about second order.
A. Yeah. The answer is no. Or wait. I can't remember the question. But there can still be a loss of competition in that setting, because Norton may perceive this—if it's a best-bid competition, they perceive the softening of the competition, and so they bid less aggressively.
Q. So I'm clear, when you say "second order," you're referring to a situation where parties other than Penguin Random House and Simon & Schuster somehow soften their bidding because they're observing behavior by the merged entity?
A. There—that is an effect, yes.
Q. And you haven't modeled that effect anyplace; correct?
A. It's not—well, it's discu-—I mean, the best-bids auctions are capturing this general idea. The best-bids GUPPI is looking at the idea of if we have a best-bid setting, what is likely to be the effect.
Q. But it is not examining this softening effect on parties other than the merging parties; correct?
A. Correct.
Q. Okay. And neither is the second-score auction; correct?
A. Correct.
Q. Okay. And—and neither of your models predicts harm just because there's one fewer bidder; correct?
A. Could you—could you say more?
Q. In other words, your analysis examines harm only in situations where Penguin Random House and

Simon & Schuster are number one and number two; correct?
A. I don't agree with that.
Q. Okay. Your models are not telling you that there's a—that there's a reduction in harm simply by eliminating one of the publishers in the publisher population; correct?
A. I disagree.
Q. Now, you're aware that other publishers in this case have testified that they don't intend to reduce their advances after the merger; correct?
A. Correct.
Q. And you don't have any reason to doubt that, do you?
A. Well, I think the—the testimony, at least as I have heard it from HarperCollins and—well, I—I have to be careful here. I would say both HarperCollins and Macmillan have concerns about whether they'll be able to compete as they might wish to after the transaction is completed.
Q. Right. But you don't have any—
A. Other—
Q. You don't have any question about the fact that the publisher executives who testified in this trial, that they don't intend to reduce their bids or are telling you what they believe; correct?
A. It's a pretty broad statement. Could you be more specific? I'll put it this way. Maybe this will help. I'm not aware of any executive testifying after the transaction I intend to reduce my bids.
Q. All right. Now, your—your prediction is that advances are going to go down by roughly 6 percent for PRH and S&S authors if the merger is approved; correct?
A. Yeah, about 4 percent for Penguin Random House and—but, again, I would caution against putting too much weight on the specific number.
Q. Right. And—and you said that could go down to as low as 3 percent? I think you said that. And I said that there's a true effect that we're trying to estimate using a variety of things, and the—the 4 percent for Penguin Random House and 11 and a half for Simon & Schuster are estimates of that. But, again, I don't put a great deal of weight on them being the precise number.
Q. All right. But you agree it could go down to 3 percent?
A. The true number could be 3; it could be 10. My best estimate is what you see in the report—or my conservative estimate is what you see in the report. I don't—you know, it's an estimate of the—whatever the true value is.
Q. Okay. And do you recall—we talked a little bit yesterday about your testimony in the United States v. Sugar [sic] case?
A. Correct.
Q. Okay. And in that case, did you testify that the government was asserting that the merged firm would have a 3 to 4 percent price increase?
A. My models were under 0.5 percent. The government had a range of models, some of which went under 1 percent and some of which were higher. I think their second-score auction model might have been in that range.
Q. And do you recall testifying that a 3 to 4 percent price effect for the merged firm in that case was not significant?
A. I don't recall using that language.
Q. Okay. Let's talk about implementing the model. We talked yesterday about the fact that the market shares you calc-—under the market shares you calculated, almost nine times out of ten, Penguin Random House and Simon & Schuster would not be first and second; correct?
A. Could you repeat that, please?
Q. Sure. That according to the market shares you calculated, almost nine times out of ten, Penguin Random House and Simon & Schuster would not be first and second?
A. You mean if you're assuming diversion according to share?
Q. Correct.
A. Yeah, I believe it's around about 12 percent.
Q. Okay. And so if Penguin Random House lowered advance offers for every book acquisition with the

idea that S&S is no longer operating as their main competitive constraint, they'd be wrong about 88 percent of the time; correct?

A. You're using the aggregate calculation. You would get a different percentage for both Simon & Schuster and Penguin Random House.

Q. But, overall, for the merged entity, they would be wrong about 88 percent of the time; correct?

A. I haven't thought it through. I—I mean, I don't—so I wouldn't think of it as being wrong, I guess, is what I would say. If you imagine a situation where you have a best-bids competition and I know I'm competing against—frequently against, let's say, HarperCollins and HarperCollins is removed, then it is optimal for me to reduce my bids even if I'm not always losing to HarperCollins, or even if I don't lose to them as much as 40 percent or 50 percent of the time.

Q. Well, if—if you're—if you put yourself in the position now of the merged firm and you're looking at an auction, the place where you're going to have limited competition is where Simon & Schuster and Penguin Random House would have been one and two previously; correct?

A. I disagree, again. In the—and if I may, I just—in the best-bid setting or negotiations, you're thinking about how often is this other party competing with—with me a significant percentage of the time. It's not like the second-score setting where it is—first and second is the key question.

Q. So if you're contemplating any type of auction—let's take—let's take the blind-bid auction or the best-bid auction—and you knew that Simon & Schuster was a runner-up in prior bidding, you wouldn't know whether they were going to turn up again in the next bid; correct?

A. Correct. You're using your knowledge of the past to make a prediction about how likely it is they will compete with you. If that's very rare, then you may not change your bid a lot. If it's very frequent, you may change your bid more frequently.

Q. And what is the mechanism by which the merged entity could implement this ability to lower overall advances by 6 percent? How do they do that?

A. So if you're competing frequently with an opponent in auctions or negotiations and they are removed from the competition, it is profit maximizing to take account of the fact that competition has been lessened and to lower your bids, in general, in best bids, and negotiations to be less aggressive. In rounds auctions you don't really need to take any action. You continue to bid the way you did before, and some auctions will just end before they otherwise would have, and you will pay less.

Q. But take the best-bid auction, you don't know whether—you don't know who is going to show up at the auction; correct?

A. Right. But you also don't know that today, and you make an inference about how much competition is out there when you're forming your bid. If that competition has been lessened, you bid less post-merger. It's the same intuition as what you do today.

Q. And so for you, this turns on whether the person placing the bid has a perception that a particular competitor is going to appear on the scene, either to make a bid in a best-bid or to make an actual bid in an auction or to be the outside option in a bilateral negotiation; that it's that publisher's perception of who their primary competition is?

A. In my—it doesn't have to be their primary competition. So, again, in my experience with firms, when they're looking across their industry or they're looking at particular markets they compete in, they have a sense of the intensity of the competition in that market. And they adjust their bidding and their behavior based on that. If it's very competitive, they're more aggressive. If it's uncompetitive, they're less aggressive. And when there's a change in competition, either because of a merger or a firm goes out of business, they will modify their behavior accordingly.

Q. Isn't it true that–

THE COURT: Mr. Oppenheimer, I feel like we're plowing the same ground a lot. Can we move forward?

MR. OPPENHEIMER: If I may, Your Honor, just—just one last—

THE COURT: Okay.

BY MR. OPPENHEIMER:

Q. Do the publishers typically know who was second in a bid? Do they have that information?

A. No. They typically—I would say generally they don't. They usually know the winner, but they don't generally know who's second.

Q. Okay. If—if—let me take us to a situation where we're in a bilateral negotiation for a repeat author, somebody with whom we have an existing relationship.

A. Sure.

Q. Okay. And let me further assume that that author is at the high end of the advance scale, somebody who's making—historically has made large advances. Okay?

A. Okay.

Q. All right. We can agree that that's probably an important negotiation to the publisher?

A. If it's profitable, yes.

Q. All right. And at—at the very highest levels for the parties that are making not $250,000 in advances, but many millions of dollars in advances, do you believe that those negotiations will also—the bidders or the negotiators in those negotiations will shave their offers after the merger because of this 6 percent pricing effect?

A. Well, the 6 percent is the prediction of the model. The question, rather, is today Simon & Schuster knows that Penguin Random House wins four out of ten books, and when they're thinking I've got an author coming up for negotiation, how aggressive do I want to be in terms of the offer I make, they're thinking about their competition. What other options might the author have if I can't reach a satisfactory agreement with the author?

Q. They're also thinking about the fact that if they lose an author at those very high echelons, they also potentially lose their incumbency and the benefit of the future work of those authors; correct?

A. That's correct.

Q. Would you think, as an economist, that they would have to have a very substantial price advantage to make a reduction in their normal offering strategy in that situation?

A. Could you repeat the wording, please.

Q. Yeah. Do you—do you think in a situation in which you're negotiating for the continuation of an incumbent relationship with a very high-profile author, that it would be very important to you to not lose that contract?

A. So we've seen examples of the parties losing these types of authors to each other, and I believe there were examples of HarperCollins losing these types of authors to the parties. Established authors do switch. And the—this is a business, and you—based on how much competition you think there would be, you come to a determination about your bid but also about the factors you're talking about. We have a relationship. We may wish to keep this author.

Q. And do you—

A. Or—so if I may, just looking for the runner-up study, you see both sides of this coin. There are cases where a party will say, this is a strong author for us; we're very motivated to keep them. And there are other cases where they say, this author has seen some declining sales. We love them, but this is time for them to take a haircut. In both of those settings, the author who's very popular, there's also a stronger incentive for a rival to steal them. And in the case with the author who has to take a haircut, if they are unhappy, then that may be an opportunity for a rival. So I can't characterize that certain of those established relationships will have more or less aggressive bidding by the incumbent.

Q. Let's talk about coordinated effects, briefly.

A. Sure.

Q. Okay. You have not estimated any sort of price impact from any sort of coordinated effects in this case; correct?

A. That's correct.

Q. And you haven't calculated a percentage likelihood that publishers will coordinate post-merger; correct?

A. That's correct.

Q. And you're not able to tell us how much more likely coordination is post-merger than it was premerger; correct?

A. Correct. I can't quantify it.
Q. You—you can't tell us whether it's more than 50/50 or any other thing; correct?
A. That's correct.
Q. Okay. Are you aware of any current coordination that's occurring in the industry?
A. I am not.
Q. To be clear, you're not offering any opinion that publishers will coordinate on the timing of payments; correct?
A. I am not offering any such opinion. And I am, in general, not saying—we can go on to your questions. Sure.
Q. Not offering an opinion that publishers will enter into no-poach agreements; correct?
A. Correct.
Q. Let's talk about printing briefly.
A. Sure.
Q. You have not rendered an opinion on printing in this case; correct?
A. That is correct.
Q. Of any kind; correct?
A. Correct.
Q. Okay.
MR. OPPENHEIMER: Your Honor, that's all I have.
THE COURT: Okay. Thank you, Mr. Oppenheimer. Any redirect?
MR. STEVENSON: Yes, just a few questions.

REDIRECT EXAMINATION

BY MR. STEVENSON:

Q. Dr. Hill, on—excuse me. On Monday you testified that you tried to build a best-bids auction model using something like the agency data and ended up with significantly higher price effects, and they were enough that you didn't think they were credible based on what you knew about the market, and so you used the second-score auction model. Do you remember that?
A. I do.
Q. And then yesterday you testified that you experimented with the first-price auction. You weren't able to get results that you thought were credible, and you also thought—and you also didn't make a great deal of progress with the negotiations model, and there were a couple other types you considered. And the Court asked, "So your choice of model depended in part on what the results were and if they looked right to you?" Do you recall that?
A. Yes.
Q. Was the first-price auction you referred to yesterday with results that you didn't think were credible the same one that you described on Monday that predicted higher price effects than what you thought was credible?
A. Yes.
Q. Do you reject any models in your analysis of this merger because the harm predicted by the model was too low?
A. I did not.
Q. Dr. Hill, at the outset of Mr. Oppenheimer's questions this morning, he asked about a hypothetical where Penguin Random House and Simon & Schuster, despite their market shares, don't compete. Do you recall that?
A. I do. The one on the overhead?
Q. On the ELMO, yeah. Is that hypothetical at all consistent with the evidence and analysis you've conducted in this case.
A. No. I don't think it's likely that Penguin Random House and Simon & Schuster never compete with one another in an auction.
MR. STEVENSON: I have no further questions.

THE COURT: Okay. Thank you. Anything else?
MR. OPPENHEIMER: Just briefly, Your Honor.

RECROSS-EXAMINATION

BY MR. OPPENHEIMER:

Q. Doesn't the inability that you confronted to build a first-price model, negotiating model, show that the industry may be unmodelable?

A. I think it shows there are challenges in modeling first-price auctions in general, but I—again, I think we've been over this ground. I feel like the second-price auction and then, subsequently, the GUPPI models are a reasonable way to estimate whether there's likely to be a unilateral effect.

And you mentioned the GUPPIs again. You—you do not have a GUPPI for the bilateral; correct? You only have the hybrid GUPPI; correct? There's the hybrid and then the two model ones—auction ones, yes.

Q. Right. But you do not have a GUPPI for the bilateral negotiation context; correct?

A. Correct.

Q. Okay.

A. I mean, except to the extent that the hybrid includes it, yes.

Q. Okay. And then, Pam, if we could quickly put up Slide 68. This was a slide that you used in your—your opening comments. I'm going to spend a very short time based on what you just said. With respect to the various entries that you–

MR. STEVENSON: Objection. This is beyond the scope of my redirect.

THE COURT: Sustained.

MR. OPPENHEIMER: Okay. Thank you, Dr. Hill.

THE WITNESS: Thank you.

THE COURT: Okay. Anything else from you, Mr. Stevenson?

MR. STEVENSON: May I just suggest that—we intend to call Dr. Hill in rebuttal, and I suggest—to save our paralegals a little bit of time and maybe a couple trees—that we save the binders of his reports that, I suspect, will be passed out again.

THE COURT: Okay. That's fine. All right. You can step down for now.

THE WITNESS: Thank you, Your Honor.

THE COURT: We'll see you later. Thank you, Dr. Hill.

REBUTTAL OF NICHOLAS HILL

MR. READ: The United States calls what it anticipates will be its only rebuttal witness, Dr. Hill.

MR. STEVENSON: Good morning, your Honor. Ethan Stevenson for the United States. May we pass out some notebooks?

THE COURT: Yes.

MR. STEVENSON: (Tenders documents to counsel and the witness.) May I proceed?

THE COURT: You may. Thank you.

BY MR. STEVENSON:

Q. Good morning, Dr. Hill.

A. Good morning, Mr. Stevenson.

Q. We did this before; but just for the record, will you please state your name.

A. Sure. Nicholas Hill.

Q. Have you been keeping up with the trial, Dr. Hill?

A. I have been.

Q. Did you observe Dr. Snyder's testimony this week?

A. I did.

Q. Did you prepare a slide presentation to assist with your testimony today?

A. I did.

MR. STEVENSON: Your Honor, may we publish the slide presentation?

THE COURT: You may. For the record, does that have a number?

MR. STEVENSON: Demonstrative No. 8. U.S. Demonstrative 8.

BY MR. STEVENSON:

Q. Dr. Hill, I'd like to start our conversation this morning by focusing on market definition. Do you recall testifying last week that about 70 percent of publishers' spending on advances is on anticipated top sellers?

A. Yes, I do.

Q. And have you heard the Defendants' statistic that only 2 percent of all new trade book titles are anticipated top sellers?

A. Yes, I have.

Q. What, if anything, do you make of the difference between the proportion of advance spending on anticipated top sellers versus the proportion of new titles that are anticipated top sellers?

A. So I think those two numbers show, your Honor, that anticipated top sellers are treated differently in the industry. They're 2 percent of all titles and they are 70 percent of all advances.

Q. And last week I think you testified that one way anticipated top sellers are treated differently is that they tend to receive more marketing. Do you recall that, Dr. Hill?

A. I do. And if you could please advance one more slide. So this is the slide from my report. And, your Honor, here in the far left, the first bar, this is the average title marketing spend for non-anticipated top sellers. And then we see the average spending for anticipated top sellers with advances from $250,000 to $500,000 and then so on. And you can see that the advance—the anticipated top sellers have significantly more marketing spend. And also, the marketing spend increases with the advance amount.

Q. Are you aware of testimony from some of Defendants' witnesses that marketing personnel at the publishers generally don't know advance amounts when they're making decisions about how to market books?

A. Yes.

Q. How did you react to that testimony?

A. So my reading of the testimony was somewhat mixed. I understood they generally don't know. I wasn't entirely clear from the testimony how much oversight there was. But if we take it as a given fact that the marketing folks do not know the advance amount when they're deciding on marketing for a book, they're nevertheless identifying the anticipated top sellers and treating them differently.

Q. In your initial testimony, you discussed that authors of anticipated top sellers primarily publish with the Big 5. Other than what we covered last week, have you observed any additional evidence of why that is?

A. Yes. If you can please advance one more slide. These are just some quotes, your Honor, talking about the advantages of the Big 5 for anticipated top sellers. And I would direct you in particular to the left-hand column here, to the comments from this author talking about the things that the Big 5 are able to do that he believes the non-Big 5 are not able to do.

Q. Now, this week, Dr. Snyder testified a few times, I think, that in his view anticipated top sellers can't be targeted. Did you hear that?

A. I did.

Q. What do you make of that testimony?

A. I don't agree with Dr. Snyder on that point. When a publisher sees a manuscript, they form an expectation of the sales and they have a sense of whether they believe this is anticipated to be a top seller.

Q. Have you seen any additional evidence on that point other than what we covered last week?

A. Yes. If you could please advance one more slide. So these are some quotes on this point, your Honor. I think the one on the left is particularly helpful. This is from a literary agent saying: I think there are recognizable qualities in—in books that people who have been in the business for a long time would easily recognize. And so would you say for some books there's a consensus that this is going to be a successful book?

A: Yes. And I think that's consistent with the idea that people in the industry have a sense of books that are likely to be anticipated top sellers.

Q. Did you hear Dr. Snyder's testimony arguing that your $250,000 threshold is arbitrary?

A. Yes.

Q. What did you think of Dr. Snyder's evidence on this point?

A. So if you could advance one more slide, please. I think it's helpful to look back at Dr. Snyder's evidence on this point.

This is Dr. Snyder's chart. And he—my initial chart, your Honor, looked at zero to 250 and then 250 plus. So it's anticipated top sellers and non-anticipated top sellers.

Dr. Snyder broke that into zero to $50,000, $50,000 to $1 million and then $1 million-plus. So the second bar here is a mixture of those I defined as non-anticipated top sellers and anticipated top sellers. If we could please advance one more slide.

If you recut these data and separate them into four bins, so here, your Honor, on the right-hand side, we have two bins that concern anticipated top sellers, one from $250,000 to $1 million and one from $1 million upwards. And those two bars look very similar to one another.

On the far left, your Honor, we have the zero to $50,000 that Dr. Snyder identified. And that bar looks very different.

And then in between those two, your Honor, is this bar from $50,000 to $250,000. And here, it looks like a transition period where it looks more—it's going in between the zero to $50,000 and the anticipated top sellers. And so I think this is consistent with my initial report, where for the $250,000-plus, the competitive conditions look very different when you cut it either of these two ways.

Q. Dr. Hill, I'd like to bring up a slide—oh, excuse me. For the record, this is Slide 6 of U.S. Government—U.S. Demonstrative 8.

Now I'd like to show you a slide from Dr. Snyder's presentation, which is Defendants' Demonstrative 18. That's Slide 32, please. Did you observe Dr. Snyder's testimony regarding this slide?

A. I did.

Q. What was your reaction?

A. So I think the point that I'm making here in response to the question is correct, that the hypothetical monopsonist test tells you whether the market you have defined is a properly defined antitrust market. And the market with the $250,000 threshold passes that test.

But as it also says here, it doesn't necessarily tell you that there may not be a market at other cutoffs. And, your Honor, that's why I also performed market definition, concentration and market shares and some modeling for other cutoffs, to see if my results were sensitive to this particular demarcation.

Q. Have you previously defined markets for targeted customers?

A. Yes. I would target—defining markets around targeted customers is very common. I did it in the Tronox litigation. I've done it frequently in the course of my career.

Q. I'd like to talk now about Dr. Snyder's arguments regarding market shares. Did you agree with Dr. Snyder that market shares in this market are not very informative of the competitive significance of publishers?

A. No. I don't agree with Dr. Snyder there.

Q. Why not?

A. So for two major reasons: First, I think that the market share data we have here are comprehensive. We have all the anticipated top sellers, and they are reflecting contemporaneous competition. So it's a rich source of information about market shares.

Second, we see that those market shares are stable over time, which gives us more confidence that they are accurately reflecting competitive conditions.

Q. What evidence have you seen that these market shares are stable over time?

A. So if we could please return to the deck and advance one slide. Thank you. So this slide is from my reply report. And here, your Honor, we're looking in blue at the market share of Penguin Random House and Simon & Schuster; in black, we're looking at other Big 5; and in purple, we're looking at the non-Big 5. And we're seeing market share values for 2019, 2020 and 2021.

And we can see as we look across the graph, the market shares here are stable. And similarly, in my report, I looked at concentration measures for 2019, 2020, 2021 and the combination of years. And those used year-specific market shares. And again, all of those results were consistent with one another.

MR. STEVENSON: Your Honor, this slide is a re-creation of PX 0994. I move to admit PX 0994.

THE COURT: Any objection?

MR. OPPENHEIMER: No objection.

THE COURT: That will be admitted. (Whereupon, Plaintiff's Exhibit No. 0994 was entered into evidence.)

BY MR. STEVENSON:

Q. Dr. Hill, did the horizontal merger guidelines discuss the stability of market shares at all?

A. Yes. If you could please advance one more slide. This is some language, your Honor, from the merger guidelines. And it says: The agencies give more weight to market concentration when market shares have been stable over time, especially in the face of historical changes in relative prices or costs. And this is telling us when you have stable market shares, it allows you to put more weight on your market concentration measure.

Q. Dr. Snyder gave a statistic in his testimony that in his agency data, 23 percent of the time non-Big 5 publishers are winner or runner-up. Did you hear that?

A. I did.

Q. What do you make of that statistic?

A. So I think I can clear up some of the discussion of that statistic. I think what Dr. Snyder did, because this was in one of his reports, he took market shares that ranged from zero to 100. So everyone got a market share, including the non-Big 5. So that sums to 100. Then he took shares of the time that a particular firm was the runner-up. And that share—that summed to 100.

So he's got a base of 200, because the market shares sum up to 100 and the percentage of the time each firm was a runner-up sums up to 100.

So Dr. Snyder took the proportion of the time that the non-Big 5 were the winner or the runner-up, and that added up to 23 percent. If you divide that by 200, which is the base, you get 11.5 percent, which is similar to their market shares in my market share data.

Q. So just to—

THE COURT: Can you just say that one more time?

THE WITNESS: Sure. So Dr. Snyder is putting together two different things that sum to 100: the market shares and also the percentage of the time that the firm is a runner-up. And so he finds combined, if you add up the percentage of the time the non-Big 5 win and the percentage of the time they're the runner-up, it sums up to 23.

THE COURT: Oh.

THE WITNESS: But if I sum that up for all the firms, for Penguin Random House—and I don't have the exact numbers for them, but their market share is around 40 percent. If they're runner-up around 40 percent, you'd get 80 percent for them using this metric. And for another firm, the second-largest, it might be about 50 percent. You add all those up and they add up to 200. So if you want to understand the relative sizes of the players based on that statistic, you should divide the 23 percent by 200.

THE COURT: I see. Thank you.

BY MR. STEVENSON:

Q. And just for a clear record, what is the 23 divided by 200?

A. It's about 11 and a half.

Q. Is that number similar to the market shares you calculated?

A. The market share for the non-Big 5 is about 9 percent. So yes. Those numbers are similar.

Q. Do you view that 23 percent number as meaningful to your analysis?

A. No, I don't.

Q. Why don't you?

A. So I think, your Honor, we have two different—it's combining two different numbers that are useful. One is the—or one number is useful and one can be useful. So the market share number, your Honor, is a useful measure of competitive significance. How often do you actually win when all is said and done?

Then there's a separate number for unilateral effects, which is a diversion ratio. When one firm wins, how often does it lose to the other firm?

Dr. Snyder's number is taking a market share and the total number of times that the other firm is runner-up. So if some other publisher like HarperCollins were to win, he's counting: How often is the other firm the runner-up?

But for unilateral effects, we focus on diversion ratio. When one firm wins, how often does the other firm lose?

And he's combining the information that's important in there, which is the diversion ratio, with information about when, for example, HarperCollins wins and somebody else is runner-up. So it's mixing two useful numbers into a new number that doesn't—I'll say this: I've never seen that figure used before in the course of my career, because it's not entirely clear what it's reflecting.

THE COURT: The figure of—the percentage of time that you're either the winner or the runner-up, that number, what he said was 23 percent, which you say is 11.5 percent, you think it's not useful because it combines two concepts that aren't really combinable?

THE WITNESS: Yeah. And—yeah. Exactly, your Honor. Because with the runner-up, you don't know who you are runner-up to. If Simon & Schuster was runner-up all the time to some member of the non-Big 5, that would be different than if you knew it was runner-up to Penguin Random House. But the figure is just combining those things. And the diversion ratio is getting at that more directly.

THE COURT: Thank you.

BY MR. STEVENSON:

Q. Now I'd like to switch to a related but slightly different topic, still on Dr. Snyder's agency data.

Dr. Snyder testified that the merging parties are winner and runner-up only 7 percent of the time and further testified that this is less than the 12 percent implied by the parties' market shares. Do you recall that testimony?

A. I do.

Q. What did you make of that testimony?

A. So I think that the number again has the conceptual problem I've just been talking about. It's combining market shares and diversions. And I also think that the calculation is not properly done. So—sorry.

Q. Why don't you think the calculation is properly done?

A. So if we could please advance one more slide. So, your Honor, this is a demonstrative that's taken—it's based on Dr. Snyder's demonstrative. And down here in the green box, we have the total number of books in which one party was the winner and one party was the runner-up. And so to perform his calculation, Dr. Snyder divides that amount by the 150 books in which there's a known runner-up and the 149 books sold in a single-bidder process in which the runner-up is not known.

And I think the more appropriate calculation here is reflected on the left, is to divide the 21 books by the 150 books.

And yeah. And just trying not to belabor it too much, you can see in the 360, that's not equal to 149 or 150, because there's 61 books Dr. Snyder excluded. Those were multi-bidder processes in which there was an unknown runner-up. And so he didn't include them. But he did include the blue box. And I don't think including the blue box is appropriate.

Q. Now, you mentioned a conceptual problem that I think you were discussing earlier. But do you think that 13 or 12 percent statistic is meaningful to your analysis?

A. No. I think again the important—there's two separate numbers here that are useful: There's a market share, which is how often a firm wins, and it's a commonly used measure of competitive significance.

And then separately there's a diversion ration, which looks at when one firm wins, how often does the other lose? And here, this number is combining that information with other information about when a third party wins and some other third party is the runner-up, for example.

Q. Do the horizontal merger guidelines touch on this issue at all?

A. Yes. If you could please advance one more slide.

This is a couple of quotes from the merger guidelines, your Honor. I'll—I think they're both informative, but I'll just focus on the second here. It says: Diversion ratios between products sold by one merging firm and products sold by the other merging firm can be very informative for assessing unilateral price effects with higher diversion ratios indicating a greater likelihood of such effects.

Diversion ratios between products sold by merging firms and those sold by non-merging firms have at most secondary predictive value.

So this is my point, that the 12 percent is including these diversion ratios that have secondary value; and it's also including diversion between non-merging firms and non-merging firms.

THE COURT: But you had in your analysis the 12.5 percent rate. Isn't that the same calculation as the 13 percent that we've now determined is the better calculation for Dr. Snyder?

THE WITNESS: The 12 percent was calculated by the Defendants, your Honor; it was not my calculation.

THE COURT: Oh, I thought you had a 12.5 percent calculation.

THE WITNESS: No. The Defendants performed that calculation using my market shares. But it is not a calculation I relied on.

THE COURT: Oh, I see. So that's a defense calculation using your market shares, whereas his calculation was using his agency data?

THE WITNESS: That is correct, your Honor.

THE COURT: Okay.

BY MR. STEVENSON:

Q. Dr. Hill, I'd like to focus our attention now on the Penguin Random House merger from 2013. Did you examine any evidence on how the Penguin Random House merger may have affected authors of anticipated top sellers?

A. I did.

Q. At a high level, would you please describe the evidence you considered.

A. Sure. I looked at average advances over time for anticipated top sellers for Penguin Random House. We didn't have any data for other publishers, your Honor, going back to 2013. So everything here I talk about is going to be Penguin Random House.

Q. Why did you look at average advances?

A. So if we could advance one more slide, please. This was the metric that Dr. Snyder chose in his report. So he said: A natural first step is to examine whether PRH advance amounts changed, if at all, after the 2013 merger. For example, if average advances were increasing prior to 2013, but then flatten out or decrease thereafter, that could be an indication that the 2013 Penguin Random House merger had the effect of reducing author advances.

So this is in Dr. Snyder's rebuttal report. He adopted this framework. Just to minimize disagreement, I used the same framework. It seemed reasonable to me and it didn't seem—and I also used his data, similarly to avoid disagreements.

Q. Dr. Snyder testified on Monday that when looking at the 2013 merger, the number one thing as an economist I would be interested in is what effect it had on output. Did you hear that?

A. I did.

Q. Did Dr. Snyder analyze Penguin Random House's effect on output in any of his expert reports?

A. He did not.

Q. Did average advances for anticipated top sellers change after the Penguin Random House merger?

A. After the Penguin Random House merger, average advances for anticipated top sellers fell.

Q. Why do you believe that to be the case?

A. So both Dr. Snyder and I found this to be true. Your Honor, Dr. Snyder found that advances were falling before the merger and continued to fall after. And he tested: Was there any significant change after the merger? And his answer is no. I used a different methodology as he described, and we'll get into that in a minute. And I also found that average advances fell after the merger.

Q. Could you share with us Dr. Snyder's analysis on this point?

A. Sure. I believe the Court has seen this before. But this next slide here is from Dr. Snyder's rebuttal report.

And this is looking at average advance amounts for using different thresholds. And the black line, your

Honor, is books with an advance above $500,000 and the red line is books with an advance above $250,000. And along the horizontal axis, which is marked Year, we have years; and then in the vertical axis we have average dollars per title. So this is taken from Dr. Snyder's analysis.

He tests the $250-and-above line and finds that it was decreasing pre-merger and it continued to decrease post-merger.

But I should say, he would say: I didn't find any change in the rate of decrease. And so it was decreasing after the merger the same as it was decreasing before the merger.

THE COURT: How is that decreasing? Because if you look from 2013 to 2014, it's all going up.

THE WITNESS: Yes. So what he's testing is the overall trend, your Honor. If you start with the 2010 data and you go down to 2021, he was testing: Is there a downward slope in this line? On average, if you plot the best fit through that line, it's going to be a downward-sloping line. And then he tested: If I look at the line for the first three dots here and then I look at the line for the other dots, do those lines have different slopes?

And he found they don't. They're both downward-sloping. But I think it might be helpful, actually, if we advance to the next slide, your Honor.

This is a summary of—this is what I looked at, your Honor. I looked at a shorter time period. I looked at 2010 to 2012, which is before the merger, and 2014 to 2016, which is after the merger. So commonly when looking for the effect of an event, like a merger, you try to limit the time period. I also did this for the two years before and the two years after.

And you can see here in the first line, your Honor, for anticipated top sellers, the average advance went from—I probably shouldn't read these numbers, actually. But you can see the Penguin Random House average advance for anticipated top sellers went down by about $100,000.

BY MR. STEVENSON:

Q. This slide referred to average advances for other books. Why did you calculate average advances for non-anticipated top sellers?

A. Yeah. So, your Honor, to examine the potential effect of the merger—and I think Dr. Snyder testified about this—I used a common econometric technique known as difference in differences. And to understand the technique, I think it helps to think about it's an attempt to do something similar in the social sciences to a randomized control trial.

So if you imagine that a firm is testing whether a drug, new drug, is effective, there's a treated population who gets the drug and there's a control population who get placebo. And you test whether there has been an effect of the drug by seeing whether the treated population is different—has a different experience than the control population.

So here, what I was trying to do—and we can talk in a second about the results—was anticipated top sellers could potentially have been affected by the merger. There was a merger from the Big 6 to the Big 5. We've seen that those publishers compete more intensively for anticipated top sellers. So I wanted to see if there was an effect on them. And as my control group I picked "other books," books that are not anticipated top sellers, where we've seen the non-Big 5 compete more aggressively.

And so that was my experimental design, to ask the question: If I compare those two groups, do they have the same outcome? And just like in a control trial, your Honor, you want your treatment group and your control group to otherwise be as similar as they can be. So we don't—in social sciences, one doesn't do control trials for very good reasons. And you try to pick the best control group you can. They're never perfect.

And I wouldn't claim that "other books" is perfect. But I think it's a reasonable way to look at the issue. And you can see that the "other books" in this time period, the advances stay flat or maybe a tiny bit upward.

Q. Did you prepare a graphical depiction of this analysis?

A. Yes, I did. So if you could please advance one more slide. So this is the full-time series here, your Honor. In my analysis I'm going to look at 2010 to 2012 and 2014 to 2016.

But you can see on the horizontal axis here, we have years. And on the vertical axis, we have average advance per title indexed to 2012.

So a value here of 100 percent, that's the value for average advances for Penguin Random House in 2012. And then if you see a value above 100, that means average advances have gone up compared to 2012. If you see a number below 100, that tells you average advances have gone down compared to 2012.

The red vertical line is depicting the date of the merger. The green line here is anticipated top sellers over time. So it moves from 100 roughly down to about 60 to 70 by 2021. The non-anticipated top sellers are largely flat and then rise up to about 130 by 2021.

THE COURT: Why do you choose 2012 instead of 2013?

THE WITNESS: For the date of the merger, your Honor, or you mean the comparison?

THE COURT: As the starting—

THE WITNESS: For indexing?

THE COURT: Because the merger happened in 2013.

THE WITNESS: Right. So it's common in these kinds of studies to exclude the time period in which the transaction itself is happening, because that year has some time in which the parties were independent and some time in which they were together. And so I took the last most recent year in which the parties were still independent entities.

THE COURT: I see.

THE WITNESS: If we advance one more slide, please, just to finish this discussion off. This is a summary of what it looked like when I calculated first for anticipated top sellers. So advances for Penguin Random House went down by about 5 and a half percent. Advances for other books went up by 9.5 percent. And the—so the difference-in-differences estimate here is saying: Comparing the treated group to the control group, advances went down for authors of anticipated top sellers by about 15 percent.

BY MR. STEVENSON:

Q. What conclusions did you draw from the difference-in-differences analysis?

A. So I think this is an indication that the merger may have had a negative effect on the advances for anticipated top sellers.

Q. Did you perform any statistical tests to determine whether this result was statistically significant?

A. Yes. These results are highly statistically significant.

Q. How much weight do you put on this evidence that the merger may have had a negative effect for authors of anticipated top sellers?

A. So it is a piece of evidence that for Penguin Random House its advances to anticipated top sellers went down. But there's a lot of information that we are missing when we're trying to evaluate this overall.

So, your Honor, I don't know market shares. I don't know concentration levels. I don't know diversion ratios. I don't have a fulsome qualitative record.

So is this indicative that there may have been a negative effect? Yes. Is it dispositive? No. Because I'm just—and further, as I said, your Honor, "other books" is the best control group I had available. I think it has a reasonable basis for being used. But no control group is perfect.

THE COURT: My question about this is it seemed like there was a big difference between 2012 and 2013. If you start from 2013, it looks like it went up. If you start from 2012, it looks like it went down.

THE WITNESS: Yeah. I looked at this also using 2011 and 2012 compared to 2014 and 2015. But 2013 has—I didn't look at that, your Honor, because it mixes time periods when they were—part of that time period they were merged and part of it they were not.

THE COURT: I see.

BY MR. STEVENSON:

Q. Dr. Hill, let's discuss imprint competition now. Did you hear testimony from Dr. Snyder about imprint competition?

A. I did.

Q. What did you understand Dr. Snyder's arguments about imprints to be?

A. I think his argument is that imprint competition is an important factor that will help mitigate any anticompetitive effect.

Q. What's your view of that argument?

A. I don't agree with Dr. Snyder.

Q. Why don't you agree with Dr. Snyder?

A. I think that the competition provided by—well, first, I think that there's clear evidence that publishers limit competition between imprints. So if we look at Penguin Random House, there are the Penguin Random House bidding rules. Penguin Random House imprints can and do coordinate with one another.

Penguin Random House imprints are unlikely to steal top selling authors from one another. And some of the adult divisions of Penguin Random House in rounds auctions have house bids. So there are these limitations on the ways in which Penguin Random House imprints can compete with one another compared to how they can compete with independent publishers.

Q. We discussed this a little bit last week. But have you seen any additional evidence about how Penguin Random House constrains competition among its imprints?

A. Yeah. If you can please advance one more slide. This is, your Honor, another auction from 2018 for a nonfiction book. And this is—it represents Penguin Random House imprints coordinating with one another in the process of the auction.

And there's a lot of information here, but I'll cut down to the last bullet, where it says: So it seems best for everyone to go with $1,050 to have the best shot. No bonus. North American rights. Quarterly payouts. So they're laying out here the bid and other terms, ancillary terms, to the bid.

And then you can see in red that the Penguin Random House imprints indeed submitted identical offers in the last round. If these were independent publishers, this sort of behavior would not be permitted.

Q. Have you seen any examples of imprints across different PRH divisions coordinating in best bid auctions?

A. Yes. I believe there's some examples in my report.

Q. Dr. Hill, I'm going to have Mr. Masri pull up Page 51 of your reply report. Without revealing the author or title of the book, could you describe what you observed in this instance?

A. Yes. This is a best bids auction, single-round, involving a book. And this is discussions among Penguin Random House personnel to figure out the collective Penguin Random House approach to bidding in this auction.

I'll—without reading it, your Honor, I'll direct you down to the last complete sentence here, and then there's a fragment here, just talking about the successful coordination in this case.

Q. You mentioned that imprints don't compete with each other in the same way that they do with independent publishers. Is there a theoretical reason behind that?

A. Yes. Your Honor, if you imagine two imprints at Penguin Random House competing with one another, if Imprint A loses to Imprint B, the expected profit from the book stays within Penguin Random House. It moves from Imprint A to Imprint B. If Imprint A loses a book to Simon & Schuster, the expected profit leaves Penguin Random House. So it's just a fundamentally different level of threat posed by independent publishers vis-à-vis other imprints.

Q. Did Dr. Snyder present any examples of what he considers to be valuable imprint competition?

A. Yes.

Q. Have you reviewed those examples?

A. Yes. He provided four in his rebuttal report and one in his testimony.

Q. What is your opinion of those examples?

A. I think that on the whole those examples show the value of competition between independent publishers rather than between imprints.

Q. Would you please give us an example of what you mean?

A. Sure. If we could please advance one more slide.

This is an example from Dr. Snyder's rebuttal report, your Honor. It's a rounds auction. And in the first column, we have publisher; in the second column, we have the imprint. And then we have bids in each round and then finally a column for the winner.

And I've coded the highest bid or joint highest bid in each round green and the second-highest bid yellow. So in this competition, we can see that the highest bid or second-highest bid in every round is either the first Penguin Random House imprint or an imprint from another Big 5 publisher.

The second Penguin Random House imprint is never the highest bidder or the second-highest bidder. And indeed, the imprint exits the auction after the third round when the highest bid is—I won't characterize it, but you can see, your Honor, between that exit point and Round 6, there's a substantial inflation in the total amount. That's driven by competition between the Penguin Random House imprint and an imprint from an independent publisher.

So from my perspective, this exhibit, this example, shows the value of publisher competition. It doesn't show the value of imprint competition.

Q. Do you have a sense as to what the advance for this book might have been had the independent publishers not competed for it?

A. Yes. If we could please advance another slide.

Here, your Honor, I've taken out the two independent publishers and asked: What would have happened? And Penguin Random House imprints cannot bid against one another when they're the last two in an auction.

So what we're seeing here is that the winner would have been at a much lower level. And that difference is summarized for your Honor in the gray box towards the bottom of the slide.

Q. Now, this is just one of Dr. Snyder's examples. Did you examine the others?

A. Yes. There were two other examples in his rebuttal report that are similar to this. They were rounds auctions that I believe show the value of publisher competition rather than imprint competition. And then once in his rebuttal report and once in his testimony, he cited examples of best bid auctions where Penguin Random House finished first or second.

Q. Did those auctions show the value of imprint competition?

A. I don't believe so. The example that Dr. Snyder testified about, we saw that there was a very large difference between the first and second-highest bid. And Dr. Snyder also testified that at the time of bidding, publishers don't know who they're competing with. So when they're forming their bid, they are thinking about: How much might my rivals bid here?

And seeing that after the merger, after the bidding is finished, that a Penguin Random House imprint is first and second, I think it's hard to conclude that that second Penguin Random House imprint is what that first Penguin Random House imprint had in mind as the competitive threat when it was forming its bid, particularly in Dr. Snyder's example that he testified about, when there was a very large difference between the valuation of the highest bidder and the second-highest bidder.

Q. Did you hear Dr. Snyder's testimony about—I believe he called it a work-around to stimulate imprint competition?

A. I did.

Q. What did you make of that?

A. So in the course of doing the runner-up survey, your Honor, I reviewed a lot of documents, emails between publishers, within publishers, between agents and publishers, a lot of data.

I didn't see—the evidence that I saw was that in general, agents are respectful of the Penguin Random House bidding rules and they will, when asked, give truthful information about whether Penguin Random House is the last two bidders. I didn't see any evidence of a work-around.

And I also see some tension between the idea—Dr. Snyder's idea that there is this work-around that agents know such that the Penguin Random House bidding rules are invalidated and Mr. Dohle's promise: If this merger goes through, we won't extend the Penguin Random House bidding rules to Simon & Schuster.

If it was true that agents already knew how to circumvent the bidding rules, there would be no need for a letter saying: Don't worry. We're not going to extend the bidding rules. So I think there's a tension there.

THE COURT: But he was relying on an actual email that said: We're going to do this. I was interested that it was sort of publicly stated. It was an email to all the auction participants that they were going to—I think it actually says: If PRH are the top two, we're going to move forward on an independent bidder.

THE WITNESS: It was—you mean Mr. Dohle's promise?

THE COURT: No. I'm talking about the evidence that Dr. Snyder relied upon to talk about the work-around was an actual auction rules process, where the agent informed all the bidders that they were going to do this.

THE WITNESS: I was in the gallery, your Honor. I'm sorry. I didn't see that document. In general, in my review of the record, I have not seen other examples of that. But apparently there is one that I wasn't aware of.

BY MR. STEVENSON:

Q. I'd like to move on and now focus on entry and expansion, particularly the role of non-Big 5 publishers. This week, Dr. Snyder testified about non-Big 5publishers winning large contracts for anticipated top sellers. Do you recall that?

A. I do.

Q. Have you seen any evidence on how frequently the non-Big 5 compete for large contracts as compared to the Big 5 publishers?

A. Yes. If we could please advance one more slide. This is a figure taken from my reply report. And, your Honor, there are—the first column here is publishers. The second column is calculating the share of $1 million-plus contracts. So let's see how often for these large contracts each of the publishers is winning.

And you can see, your Honor, that the shares look very similar to the shares we see for anticipated top sellers in general. The only notable difference is the non-Big 5 win about 6 percent of these as compared to 9 percent of all anticipated top sellers.

The second column takes a different look at this issue and says: These data go from 2019 to 2021. So there are 36 months that we observe. It asks the question: How often does each one of these publishers—in how many of these months did each publisher win at least one contract of a million dollars or more?

And you can see. The answer for Penguin Random House is all 36. For Simon & Schuster, it's 33 of the 36. And then the other Big 5 look similar, or smaller in the case of the Publishers 2 and 3. And then the non-Big 5 have much lower numbers.

So winning a $1 million-plus contract is a common occurrence for the Big 5. It's significantly rarer for the members of the non-Big 5, which is consistent with their market shares.

Q. Now, on the opposite side of the spectrum, Dr. Snyder—or on the advance spectrum, if you will, Dr. Snyder testified that there are several publishers who compete below $250,000 and are poised to expand. Do you recall that?

A. I do.

Q. What do you understand Dr. Snyder's argument to be?

A. So I understand his argument to be—and in his report, I believe he identifies 21 publishers who have won a book for an advance between $100,000 and $250,000. And his view is that these publishers are poised to enter the market for anticipated top sellers.

Q. And do you agree that these publishers are poised to enter?

A. I don't agree with him on this point. If we could please advance one more slide.

There's a figure from my reply report analyzing this. And here, your Honor, I've broken that range from $100,000 to $250,000 into six bins of equal size. And you can see that 75 percent of these publishers have never won a book for more than $175,000 and only one of them has ever won a book above $225,000.

So when we look at this group of 21 publishers, we see they're heavily skewed towards the lower end of this $100,000-to-$250,000 range.

Q. Changing gears a little bit, have you seen evidence on how much of the books published by non-Big 5 publishers are anticipated top sellers?

A. Yes. So if we could please advance one more slide. This slide is also from my reply report. Here, I'm asking a slightly different question than I have before, your Honor, which is: If we just look at the titles won by publishers, what proportion of them are anticipated top sellers?

And you can see the answer for Penguin Random House is about 27 percent. For Simon & Schuster, it's 19 percent. And then the other Big 5 publishers I won't read, but you can see their values. And for the non-Big 5 publishers, it's 4 percent.

So those anticipated top sellers are a very important part of the business for the Big 5 publishers.

They're a significantly smaller part of the business for these non-Big 5 publishers.

MR. STEVENSON: Your Honor, this is a re-creation of PX 0995. I move to admit PX 0995.

THE COURT: Any objection?

MR. OPPENHEIMER: No objection, your Honor.

THE COURT: That will be admitted. (Whereupon, Plaintiff's Exhibit No. 0995 was entered into evidence.)

BY MR. STEVENSON:

Q. Now, Dr. Hill, we've heard some testimony from Defendants' witnesses, including Dr. Snyder, that four smaller publishers—who I won't name for confidentiality purposes, but I'll refer to in an exhibit in a minute—and those four have recently entered the market for anticipated top sellers.

Are you familiar with the testimony at a general level?

A. Yes.

Q. Have you seen any evidence regarding the competitive significance of these publishers?

A. Yes. So if we could please advance one more slide. And I'll refer to them as the Group of 4 to stay out of trouble with their particular names. This slide, your Honor, is for 2019, 2020 and 2021, looking at the share of contracts for Penguin Random House in blue, Simon & Schuster in green and then each of the four members of the Group of 4 in red, yellow, light blue and pink. And you can see that these firms are not a significant part of the market for anticipated top sellers.

Q. And for the record, this is part of PX 0968, which I believe has been previously admitted. Do you know how the share of these four entrants stacks up with the rest of the market?

A. Yes. If we could please advance one more slide. This is from my reply report, your Honor. Here, 2019—we have 2019, 2020 and 2021. The dark blue is showing the Big 5 share of contracts; the purple is showing the share of contracts for the other Big 5—or the other non-Big 5; I apologize—and the red is showing the share for the Group of 4.

And you can see here, too, this group are very small compared to the Big 5 and they're also small relative to the other members of the non-Big 5.

THE COURT: So maybe you're going to address this later. But I think what Dr. Snyder was saying is that it doesn't matter if they're less-frequent winners. But if they as a group are operating at 9 percent—he's aggregating them all—they have the same way of constraining market power as a group as some of the other Big 5, because that 9 percent that represents everybody else is similar to what some of the Big 5 people have on their own.

And so his view was: In an auction, you don't know which one it's going to be. But if you know that there's an X percent chance that some non-Big 5 person is in, that's constraining competition anyway as a group aggregated.

THE WITNESS: Yeah. And so two thoughts on that, your Honor: The 9 percent is included in my modeling. So I do give—the non-Big 5 publishers collectively have 9 percent. It's included in market shares; it's included in diversions. So I'm including that in all of their—the calculations for them.

What I think we're seeing here in all of these demonstratives is that the non-Big 5 do see significant barriers to expansion. And over time, they haven't materially changed their share.

If you count them as an aggregate group and you do the concentration numbers, then, as Dr. Snyder testified, the concentration numbers would be even higher than they actually are. So I think it's—they're included in the analysis. I think the point here, rather, for this Group of 4 is just they are not a significant part of the total market.

THE COURT: Not by themselves?

THE WITNESS: Right.

THE COURT: But as part of the aggregate, Dr. Snyder would say they are.

THE WITNESS: Right. And collectively, I'm treating them according to their shares when doing my analysis.

THE COURT: Okay.

BY MR. STEVENSON:

Q. You mentioned that the smaller publishers are included in your modeling. And I think Dr. Snyder said this, that every publisher bids in the—in every auction of your second-score auction model. Is that a fair summary?

A. Correct.

Q. So does that mean that in your modeling, Princeton University Press is bidding in every auction?

A. No. In the model, I believe I combine the non-Big 5 into one group and give them a 9 percent market share.

Q. So they're bidding as a sixth bidder. Am I understanding that right?

A. Correct.

Q. Why did you analyze these four publishers? Why did you pick them?

A. They were mentioned in Dr. Snyder's rebuttal report as an example of entrants who are likely to expand or successful entrants. And that's why I looked at them in particular.

Q. Setting aside these four publishers in particular, Dr. Snyder testified that several publishers have expanded in recent years. Did you hear that testimony?

A. I did.

Q. What do you make of that testimony?

A. So in his report—and we talked about this a little bit in my initial presentation—Dr. Snyder identified a Group of 13 publishers that he said grew their market share from 2019 to 2021.

When I looked at that group, there were a couple of problems. So the first one was, Dr. Snyder calculated market shares excluding Penguin Random House and Simon & Schuster. So he found—some of his 13 that he said grew, when you calculate market shares using all market participants, actually lost market share. So the 13 was a little bit high to begin with.

Second, we've seen that the share of the non-Big 5 has not changed over time. And indeed, some members of the non-Big 5 grew and other members of the non-Big 5 decreased by about the same amount.

And then finally, your Honor, when we looked at the group of 13, I looked to see how many of those publishers had sustained growth. So they increased their market share from 2019 to 2020 and from 2021 to—sorry—from 2020 to 2021. And the answer was only two of the 13 showed the sustained growth.

Q. I think you got to this just a minute ago. But Dr. Snyder also testified that the number of publishers who were acquiring anticipated top sellers is increasing. What did you make of that?

A. Yeah. I mean, I think he presented a figure on that in his rebuttal report. And I don't have any reason to dispute it. But despite that increase in the number of publishers, the collective market share of the non-Big 5 did not change, which must mean that the average share of a member of the non-Big 5 decreased.

But regardless, I think the correct measure is: What's the total market share here? And that did not change materially.

Q. I'd like to briefly discuss diversion ratios, which you mentioned earlier. After hearing from Dr. Snyder this week, have any of your conclusions regarding diversion ratios changed?

A. No.

Q. Would you please remind us what your baseline measure of diversion ratios between the merging parties are?

A. Sure. So my baseline measure is diversion according to market share.

Q. Why is your baseline measure diversion according to market share?

A. So if we could please advance one more slide. This is a table that I believe we have seen before. This is looking at the total number of observations that underlines the five measures of market share that I discussed earlier. And you can see that diversion proportional to share has the highest number of observations.

And the agency data, if you look at the number of observations that it uses to estimate diversion from S&S to Penguin Random House, it gives 22 observations. As Dr. Snyder testified, that sample is not representative. So I think that number in particular should be taken with a grain of salt.

So I like the proportional-to-share numbers, because they're based on a large sample. And I also like them because for PRH diversion from Penguin Random House to Simon & Schuster, all of the five measures give similar diversion numbers, your Honor. For Simon & Schuster to Penguin Random House, the diversion proportional to share is a midpoint between the higher estimates and the lower estimates. So I think it's a reasonable choice.

Q. Now, I think you misspoke. You said that these are five measures of market share. Did you mean diversion ratios?

A. I apologize. Yes.

MR. STEVENSON: Your Honor, on this slide is a re-creation of PX 0996. I move to admit PX 0996.

THE COURT: Any objection?

MR. OPPENHEIMER: No objection, your Honor.

THE COURT: That will be admitted. (Whereupon, Plaintiff's Exhibit No. 0996 was entered into evidence.)

BY MR. STEVENSON:

Q. You mentioned that diversion according to shares is still your baseline calculation. Have you observed any qualitative evidence during the course of this trial suggesting that that's a reasonable assumption?

A. Yes. If we could please advance one more slide. These, your Honor, are some quotes from publishers talking about their diversion. I'll just focus on the first. It says: The publishers we're competing with most frequently align with market share. We compete most frequently with Penguin Random House. And then they list—then the respondent lists a number of other publishers.

These are consistent with diversion according to share. And the same is true for the other two quotes here.

Q. I'd like to focus now on unilateral effects. Did you hear testimony from Dr. Snyder that your theory of harm is only concerned with auctions in which the merging parties are winner and runner-up?

A. Yes.

Q. What was your reaction to that testimony?

A. I don't agree with Dr. Snyder on that point.

Q. Why don't you agree with Dr. Snyder?

A. So if we think about it at a very high level, your Honor, in negotiations, the competition that can be lost here is, when Penguin Random House is negotiating with an author, one of the threats the author has at her disposal is to switch to Simon & Schuster.

And Penguin Random House may not know who is number one and number two; but they know in general how often they are losing to other rivals.

Similarly, in best bids—we were talking about this earlier—when a publisher is forming its bid or an imprint, it's thinking about the possibility of losing to other publishers. And that—it may not know exactly who in this best bids is the closest challenger, but it knows in general with whom it is competing closely.

So in those settings, it is not the case that they have to be number one and number two. In rounds auctions, the theory here is based on number one and number two. Those are the situations in which there's likely to be harm for that particular setting.

Q. Do the horizontal merger guidelines address this issue at all?

A. Yes, they do. If we could please advance one more slide. And if we could go down to the last paragraph, please.

So it's a little bit long, your Honor, but I think it's worth going through: The mechanisms of these anticompetitive unilateral effects and the indicia of their likelihood differ somewhat according to the bargaining practices used, the auction format and the sellers' information about one another's costs and about buyers' preferences.

For example, when the merging sellers are likely to know which buyers they are best and second-best placed to serve, any anticompetitive unilateral effects are apt to be targeted at those buyers. When sellers are less well-informed, such effects are more apt to be spread over a broader class of buyers.

So this last clause here about when sellers are less well-informed, but the harm is spread over a broader class of buyers, this is the idea I was talking about with negotiations. When Penguin Random House performs a negotiation today, it's aware of the constraint imposed by Simon & Schuster.

Post-merger, that constraint is lost; and similarly for Simon & Schuster with respect to Penguin Random House.

Q. Do any of your models predict harm to authors in situations other than when the merging parties are winner and runner-up?

A. Yes. So the GUPPI models look at best bids, your Honor, and at hybrid situations. And these are situations where it may not be the case that the parties are number one and number two; it's rather the potential threat of losing to the parties.

And with respect to the second-score auction model, we don't need to retread this ground, I think. But there I'm taking the second-score auction model as a more general statement about competition and what will be lost.

Q. Dr. Snyder discussed this at length, I think, yesterday, about the merging parties being able to predict when they're number one and number two.

In your view, will the merging parties need to be able to predict when they would have been the top two bidders for a book for the merged firm to successfully lower advances?

A. No, not necessarily. So again, in a best bids setting, your Honor, one firm—let's take Simon & Schuster—today, they lose on the order of 42 percent of the time to Penguin Random House in a best bids context. And I'm taking that as an estimate using—across all their losses.

They know post-merger that threat has been diminished. And so that is going to affect their behavior even though in a particular auction they may not know that Penguin Random House is the next most enthusiastic about the book.

And it's equivalent—it's similar to the situation you sometimes observe in consumer products, your Honor, where if when Anheuser-Busch InBev is thinking about pricing Bud Light, it doesn't literally know who the next-favorite beer of all of its customers is.

But if it was to buy SABMiller, it would say: Many of our customers like SABMiller. Now we know that if we lose a sale to SABMiller, it stays within the corporate family, so we can be a little less aggressive in our pricing when we're pricing Bud Light. That is the intuition for best bids in negotiations.

And you don't need to know Nicholas Hill's favorite beer is Bud Light followed by Miller Lite to raise prices to consumers.

Q. Did you hear testimony from Dr. Snyder about the research connecting market concentration to price?

A. I did.

Q. And what was your understanding of Dr. Snyder's testimony on that point?

A. I thought his argument was that studies linking higher concentration to higher prices had been debunked, I think he said.

Q. What was your reaction to that?

A. I don't agree with Dr. Snyder.

Q. Why not?

A. There was a literature in the 1950s that looked at this and there is a modern literature that is looking at the effect of concentration on prices. And I have a paper in *The Journal of Health Economics* looking at this very issue.

So we looked at Part D prescription drug plans. And, your Honor, these are available in 34 regions around the country. We looked at—I believe it was a 2013 merger between two providers of these plans. They competed in some regions and they didn't compete in others. So we asked: What happened to their premiums as a function of whether or not they were both present in a region?

And what we found was that their premiums went up in the regions where they were both competing compared to the regions where they were not.

And what's more, we then took the regions where they were competing and we split them into two buckets, your Honor: ones that were moderately concentrated or higher and ones that were unconcentrated. And in the moderately concentrated or higher regions, we saw a larger effect than we had previously seen. And we saw no effect in the regions where they competed but the market was unconcentrated.

And I don't mean—this is a—I have a coauthor on this paper, Mathis Wagner, whom I should mention. And this is not the only paper in the literature. There are many other papers looking at how concentration can affect price.

Q. I'd like to briefly discuss a couple of Dr. Snyder's more technical arguments regarding your second-score auction model. And let's start with profit margins. Do you agree with Dr. Snyder's characterization of your profit margins?

A. I do not.

Q. Why not?

A. So I think the disagreement between—or as I perceive it, the important disagreement here is about variable costs versus fixed costs. And my belief is that variable costs are what one should include in the model. And that is what I did for Simon & Schuster in my initial report and in my reply report.

As Dr. Snyder said, in my initial report for Penguin Random House, I included direct operating expenses, which are a mixture of variable and fixed. So there were some fixed costs included.

In my rebuttal report, I reran—sorry. In my reply report, I reran the model excluding those costs so that they were not present. And I think that is the appropriate treatment for Simon & Schuster and it's the appropriate treatment for Penguin Random House.

THE COURT: I think I remember now that the reason you included it the first time is you were just trying to be conservative, because you didn't know which ones were fixed and which ones were variable, so you assumed they were all variable. Is that right?

THE WITNESS: That's correct, your Honor. With hindsight, I wish I had just gone through and tried to characterize them as exactly what percentage is fixed, is variable. But I think that the estimates in my initial report and the estimates in my reply report tell us the range. It's somewhere between this conservative number in the initial report and the number in the reply report, which is more aggressive.

THE COURT: What about Dr. Snyder's testimony that it's not theoretically correct not to include at least some of the fixed costs, because you have to over time account for them?

THE WITNESS: Yes. So in economics, we—the second-score auction model, for example, is explicit that you should include variable costs. And the GUPPI methodology is explicit that you should include variable costs. And that is because when you're thinking on the margin about that additional book, which is what the model is interested in, you should not be worrying about your fixed costs.

And this is consistent with the testimony from Ms. McIntosh, who I understand is the CEO of Penguin Random House in the U.S., the United States. She testified that she is—encourages her editors to look at the variable costs. That is the right measure to think about when you're competing for a book.

THE COURT: But the P&Ls include fixed costs.

THE WITNESS: So the acquisition P&Ls have a target margin and they have fixed costs, including in that calculation. What I used to calculate margins were the actual P&Ls, what actually happened to the book rather than the acquisition P&Ls. But you're correct, your Honor: They include a target margin and they include some fixed costs in them.

THE COURT: And I guess that means that they're taking fixed costs into account when they're bidding for advances, et cetera. So how does that fit in with what you're doing?

THE WITNESS: So I would—it is present in their acquisition P&L. But when you look through their bidding histories, the place where they draw the line on "We can't bid any further here" is when the contribution margin or the variable cost gets to zero. So they have a target margin.

And then there's an example in my report, in Section 5.1 of my reply report, involving Mr. Karp and the memoir of a musician, where he's saying: We're not going to cover our fixed costs, but this still covers—this is above our variable costs, so we should acquire this book. This is still worthwhile for us. And in general, looking through these competitions, there are many examples like that.

THE COURT: Thank you.

BY MR. STEVENSON:

Q. Did you hear Dr. Snyder's testimony regarding the fit of your second-score auction model based on the actual and predicted margins?

A. Yes, I did.

Q. What was your reaction to that testimony?

A. So I disagree with Dr. Snyder. If we could go back to the deck, please, and advance one more slide. So this, your Honor, is comparing actual and predicted margins in my model for Penguin Random House and Simon & Schuster. And this is using the baseline conservative model. You can see that the match is good.

If we could advance one more slide, please. This is the comparison when I exclude—when I treat direct operating expenses as fixed. Here, the match is less good but still acceptable. Somewhere in between these two figures is where the truth is, because the direct operating expenses are a mix of fixed and variable.

So in my view, this is a perfectly acceptable match. Dr. Snyder in his presentation implemented the model in a different way and then calculated predicted and actual margins. And his slide as I recall showed that for the baseline model the match is still close. It's less close for this model. And then it's very different when you use his margins.

But for the model I ran and implemented, the match between the margins is good.

Q. So—

THE COURT: I'm sorry. So what did Dr. Snyder do differently? Because he says that in the second round, when it was corrected, it was found unreliable. I'm just trying to understand what he did compared to what you did.

THE WITNESS: Yeah. So when I implemented the model, your Honor, I took a blended margin of Penguin Random House and Simon & Schuster and used that to calibrate the model. So you put one margin in.

He then in his demonstrative took either Penguin Random House's margin or Simon & Schuster's margin. He did not use the blended margin, which is what I actually used when I was estimating my model.

THE COURT: Well, his model would have included the fixed costs, because he thinks you're supposed to include that. Right?

THE WITNESS: Yes. If you remember, his demonstrative had the three columns, your Honor. In the middle column, that was using Dr. Snyder's margins. And the first and third columns used my margins.

And then there's a separate question when you're—what's called parameterizing the model or setting it up. You give it information about market shares so it can estimate diversions and then you give it information about margins so it knows how competitive the industry is.

THE COURT: Is that one input, the margins?

THE WITNESS: Yes. You input the margin for just one firm. And so when I did it—and I used a blended margin for Penguin Random House and Simon & Schuster.

THE COURT: The third time?

THE WITNESS: So in both of—yeah. This is the results here, your Honor, on the screen.

THE COURT: Both times you blended it, but you just blended different numbers?

THE WITNESS: Yes. Exactly. Because the direct operating costs had been treated as variable once and is fixed in the other. That's exactly right. Dr. Snyder in his Column 2 here used his margins for S&S and his margins for Penguin Random House. And—

THE COURT: But did he blend them?

THE WITNESS: No. So in the—when he's parameterizing the model, that's the rows here, your Honor. The first row is, this is when he parameterizes it using PRH's actual margin.

THE COURT: I see.

THE WITNESS: The one below is when he does it using S&S's actual margin. And he didn't present the results here when he parameterized it using the blended margin, which is what I actually did in estimating the model.

THE COURT: So these are just his numbers, because he didn't blend ever. So he just did one for Simon & Schuster and one for Penguin Random House?

THE WITNESS: That's correct in this chart. And I'm not aware of it in his reports.

THE COURT: Okay. Thank you.

BY MR. STEVENSON:

Q. Now, I want to be very quick about this. But Dr. Snyder referred a couple times during his testimony about common components of a book's value. Can the second-score auction model handle common components of a book's value?

A. Yes, it can. They can be incorporated without changing the results.

Q. Aside from the technical issues raised by Dr. Snyder, he raised some general arguments that I think we discussed at length last week. So I'll be very brief.

Have you observed any additional evidence since we spoke last week regarding any similarities in how publishers compete in negotiations versus auctions?

A. Yes. If we could please return to the deck and advance one slide. So—sorry. One extra. Apologies. So while we're waiting for the slide, when we get to the slide, it has two quotes on it, your Honor. On the top, this is a quote from a literary agent who testified about how she's thinking about negotiations when she's negotiating with a publisher. And she has this idea of: The value I try to get from the publisher I'm negotiating with is the value I think I could get from the next-best alternative out there.

So she refers to it as a BATNA, B-A-T-N-A. And it says: And the best way to get the best deal from the publisher you're negotiating with is to improve your BATNA, your best alternative to what's in front of you. And so I spend a lot of time in my head and in the information-gathering and the like figuring out what the BATNA is and try to get it this way.

So she's walking through this idea of negotiations: I'm negotiating with one publisher and I'm trying to get as much value as I think I could get if I went to my next-best alternative. That's the quote from the literary agent about how she performs negotiations.

If we go below, there's a quote from Dr. Miller's paper about the second-score auction model where he says: The second-score approach is strategically equivalent to a specific form of bargaining in which buyers play suppliers off against each other up to the point at which the utility offered by the highest-surplus supplier cannot be matched profitably by the next-best supplier.

So what he's saying there is, the second-score auction model is identical to a particular form of multilateral negotiation, where the person selling the object gets the valuation of the second-highest alternative, which is exactly the outcome that happens in the second-score auction model.

And it reflects what this literary agent is saying about how she thinks about negotiations.

Q. I'd like to share a slide from Dr. Snyder's presentation with you, which is Slide 59 of Defendants' Demonstrative 18. Did you hear Dr. Snyder's testimony regarding this slide?

A. I did.

Q. What was your reaction?

A. I don't agree with the characterization on this slide.

Q. Why not?

A. So if we focus first on the—we'll work from bottom to top, your Honor: The rival publishers' relevance—and he says they're not relevant in the SSA and they're not relevant in the GUPPI.

In both of these frameworks, rival publishers' market shares affect the market shares of the publishers—of the parties and hence diversions. And the extent to which rival publishers compete also affects the margins that are realized in the model.

So they absolutely affect the predictions of the model.

Similarly, the idea that imprints compete and that agents play an important role, these are reflected in the current margins. If there is a tremendous amount of competition because of the large number of imprints, we'd expect to see very low margins. And the margins are reflecting both of these forces that occur in the market.

And then to the very variety of acquisition processes, I think when testifying he actually said "all possible acquisition processes." So two thoughts there: One, building a model that has every acquisition process would be very challenging. But the GUPPI model does address best bids, hybrid negotiations and second-score auctions.

And the SSA addresses second-score auctions and, as we just saw, a very particular kind of multilateral bargaining.

So it's true: It does not cover all of them. But I think it's unfair to say that they're not covering more than one.

Q. I'd like to flip—

THE COURT: Wait. What about the agent?

THE WITNESS: Yes. So I put the agents in the same category. I think we saw some of this in my initial testimony. If agents are omnipotent, then we would expect to see publishers not earning any real margins because agents are able to extract all the value they can from publishers.

But in fact, agents are good at helping extract the value that's created by competition. And that's reflected in the margins that the publishers are earning.

BY MR. STEVENSON:

Q. I'd like to flip to the next slide in Dr. Snyder's presentation, Slide 60.

Now, there was some discussion about this yesterday, I believe, on pass-through. What is pass-through?

A. So the way I think about pass-through, your Honor, is you could start abstracting from GUPPI in general and just think: If I'm a firm and my costs go up, how much of that cost increase is reflected in my price?

If pass-through is 100 percent, when my costs go up by a dollar, my price goes up by a dollar. If pass-through is zero, a dollar increase in my costs shows no increase in price. So at a high level, that is what pass-through is measuring.

Q. How does that relate to the GUPPI?

A. So in the GUPPI framework, the way I think about this is you have two firms who are independent, Publisher A and Publisher B. Pre-merger, if Publish A loses a sale to Publisher B, that profit is gone.

Post-merger, when they're one firm, it recognizes: Oh, I didn't actually lose that book at all. It just got recaptured by one of—my sister agency here. And so that is an opportunity cost from the perspective of the firm.

It used to be if I raised price and I lost 40 books to Publisher B, I just lost all that money. But now it's just transferred over. And some authors don't leave and I get to pay them lower advances. So there's an opportunity cost created by internalizing the removal of our competition with each other.

THE COURT: Why is that an opportunity cost?

THE WITNESS: So people sometimes think about it that way, your Honor, because pre-merger, I picked the optimal price that balances the chance that an author leaves and the—which is bad news; and if I raise the price, I get more margin, which is good news. So I was perfectly balanced.

Now, Publisher B, if I raise price, I still get the benefits of the higher price. But the cost is lower, because I don't actually lose some of them.

And so there's an opportunity for me to say: Wait a minute. I need to raise price to get these things back into balance with each other. And so I have an opportunity that the individual firms don't think about, but when they're merged they do.

So here, pass-through is how much of this opportunity cost will be passed through by the merged firm to its customers, or authors in this case.

THE COURT: Opportunity costs as measured by the raised price?

THE WITNESS: That's right. The incentive. How much of the incentive will get passed through.

THE COURT: I understand.

BY MR. STEVENSON:

Q. How did you arrive at the pass-through rates you used in the GUPPI models?

A. So here I used the pass-through rates that CRA used when they derived the model.

Q. Who is CRA, just to be clear?

A. I apologize. The economists working on behalf of the merging parties during the advocacy phase.

Q. Now, at the top of this slide it says that GUPPI is calculated based on a single formula that would be applied to any industry. Do you see that?

A. I do.

Q. Are you aware of GUPPI being used to diagnose unilateral effects in industries that feature negotiations?

A. Yes. It's a widely used tool, and it was used in a litigated context in the Sanford/Mid Dakota Clinic case that involved the FTC and was accepted by that court.

Q. Now, I'd like to step away from Dr. Snyder's criticisms of your second-score auction model. Would you remind us at a conceptual level what the merger guidelines say about merger simulations such as a second-score auction model?

A. Sure. If you could please advance one more slide. Your Honor, this is some language from the merger guidelines on merger simulations. And we've talked about this before, the idea being that the specific predictions of the merger simulation are less important than whether it consistently predicts substantial price increases; in this case, substantial advance decreases.

Q. We can be quite quick. Would you please remind us what your baseline second-score auction model predicts?

A. Sure. So if we could advance one more slide, please. This is a summary of the effects in the baseline model: About 4 percent for Penguin Random House authors, a 4 percent reduction in advances; about 11 and a half percent for Simon & Schuster authors.

Q. Remind us what the second-score auction model predicted treating direct operating expenses as fixed.

A. Right. So if we can please advance one more slide. Here, we see for Penguin Random House authors, it's about 6 percent. For Simon & Schuster authors, it's about 15 percent. And if we could advance one more slide, please. We'll see here a similar result using Dr. Snyder's margins: 3 percent and 8 percent.

And if we advance one more slide, we'll see the results using Dr. Snyder's agency data in the model for the market shares. And there, the effects are about 5 percent and 15 percent.

Q. Stepping back, what is your conclusion based on the collective results of your model?

A. So these results combined with the other versions of the model that I ran in my initial report and my reply report consistently predict a significant reduction in unilateral competition. And that's consistent, your Honor, with the other buckets of evidence that I had looked at: concentration evidence, qualitative evidence and diversion evidence. And then the simulation evidence as well all point consistently towards a substantial lessening of competition.

MR. STEVENSON: Your Honor, I think I made one oversight. And that's—I failed to admit PX 0966. I move to admit that at this time. 0966.

THE COURT: Any objection?

MR. OPPENHEIMER: No objection, your Honor.

THE COURT: That will be admitted. (Whereupon, Plaintiff's Exhibit No. 0966 was entered into evidence.)

MR. STEVENSON: And I have no further questions. I pass the witness.

THE COURT: Thank you. I guess the only thing I would note is on the GUPPI numbers, when you ran it with Dr. Snyder's numbers, he would say that those are unreliable based on the reliability—oh, wait. That's the second-score auction.

THE WITNESS: Yes.

THE COURT: So there's no check on the GUPPI analysis for reliability?

THE WITNESS: Yes. I believe Dr. Snyder presented—he ran it using his margins. And he found—so I think he found price increases of about a 4 and a half percent and 2.3 percent effect.

THE COURT: Okay.

THE WITNESS: Do you have this slide from Dr. Snyder? While we're waiting for—

THE COURT: So are your GUPPI numbers—are your GUPPI analyses based on his numbers using blended rates while his are separate? Or what is different between what you did and what he did?

THE WITNESS: So I ran it using the margins I use in my baseline second-score auction model, so the more conservative margins. Then he ran it using margins from—his calculated margins for Simon & Schuster and Penguin Random House.

THE COURT: Which includes the fixed costs?

THE WITNESS: That's correct, your Honor.

THE COURT: And you used—you input one number in GUPPI?

THE WITNESS: In GUPPI, you actually use always the single firm's—you use one firm's margin or the other firm's margin.

THE COURT: Okay.

THE WITNESS: Because in GUPPI, the formula—oh, these are the results, your Honor, if you're interested. Column 1 here are my results and Column 2 are Dr. Snyder's results. And—

THE COURT: But his are less than 5 percent. He said 5 percent is the cutoff.

THE WITNESS: Yeah. So actually, I think he misspoke there. It's a 5 percent GUPPI, not a 5 percent price increase. So when Dr. Shapiro proposed his safe harbor, it was a 5 percent GUPPI value instead of a 5 percent price increase.

THE COURT: Is this a GUPPI value or a price increase?

THE WITNESS: My understanding, these are price increases, your Honor.

THE COURT: Okay.

THE WITNESS: And if you assume 50 percent pass-through, then the price increase is half the size of the GUPPI. So the 4.7 here would correspond to 9.4 percent GUPPI.

THE COURT: Oh, so that would be significant. It would be above 5?

THE WITNESS: Correct, your Honor.

THE COURT: Thank you.

MR. STEVENSON: Your Honor, if I may ask one more question.

THE COURT: Yes.

BY MR. STEVENSON:

Q. Dr. Hill, do you know what the logic of the safe harbor was by Dr. Shapiro?

A. Yeah. Dr. Shapiro's idea was that in many mergers there may be some efficiencies and entry and expansion. And so he proposed the 5 percent to allow for the possibility that there will be efficiencies or entry. Absent those, the 5 percent is not a safe harbor. If you knew for sure there were no entry and no efficiencies, then there's no 5 percent safe harbor. But that's my understanding of what Dr. Shapiro said.

MR. STEVENSON: No further questions.

BRIAN MURRAY, CEO, HARPERCOLLINS

HarperCollins CEO Brian Murray said on the stand that News Corp.'s bid for Simon & Schuster "was not close" to Bertelsmann's offer and that he was "shocked" that they were willing to pay $2.175 billion. "We've probably done five or so acquisitions and tend be very disciplined in our financial modeling, so we could not find a way to have a return at that price." (We'll say it one more time: Publishers Lunch has previously reported that people familiar with the same said the underbidder was Vivendi, not HarperCollins.)

In his direct examination, Murray asserted that PRH was three times the size of HarperCollins' "general trade books" in the US, according to "market share" and what he has "been told by our booksellers as well." That estimate excludes both Harper Christian and at least parts of Harlequin, which Murray categorized as publishing mass market series romance, even though the division has been developing its trade business. By the same measure of general trade, Murray said compared to S&S, "sometimes they're a little bigger and sometimes we're a little bigger. We're a similar size," but it "depends on the year."

Echoing testimony from Hachette and Macmillan CEOs, Murray said that Harper competes most frequently with PRH, then S&S. "S&S we've found to be very aggressive and often we're going head-to-head with them as well," he said.

Later S&S's counsel Stephen Fishbein showed that in HarperCollins's "budget book"—the plan for their fiscal year 2021—that internal analysis of market share in 2019 showed that PRH was twice the size of Harper, when Christian and Harlequin are included. Fishbein also noted that the government's expert believes that PRH is double the size of Harper in trade frontlist. Murray explained that the numbers become confusing because some of Harper Christian's titles are trade, but the division also includes an $80 million Bible business. Later, Fishbein quipped, "So like a Bible that was obviously written a long time ago and has been in print for a long time, that's not part of the frontlist, right?"—drawing laughs from the crowd—but Murray explained that some, with updated covers, forewords, and gift packaging, are.

Under cross-examination Murray was evasive or non-committal on a number of topics. Will the publisher continue to "be very aggressive in acquiring books" after the merger, as he declared a year ago, when consumer spending on books was rising quickly? "It's hard to say." Is that spending contingent on merger? "I don't know. I can't speculate what's going to happen in the future." In Murray's deposition, however, he had said that Harper's aggressive acquisitions strategy will continue after the merger.

Fishbein produced an early 2022 document of HarperCollins business projections, anticipating increasing advances for new books from 2020 through 2024. Numbers weren't discussed in open court and Murray said he'd "have to do the math" to determine the percent increase. Then Fishbein asked, "Have you ever discussed with anyone at [HarperCollins or] News Corp. that author advances could decrease as a result of the Penguin Random House-Simon & Schuster merger?" and "Has HarperCollins reduced any budget or projection of author advances based on the merger?" The answer to both was no.

Judge Pan wondered what happens when acquisitions are going better than budgeted, asking, if "it turns out you are acquiring the books you wanted and paying less than you thought you would have had to because all the advances have come down, what would you do with that excess money?"

Murray said it would be hard to know that as it's happening, since they aren't calculating an over or under in real time. "Auctions are going fast and furious. It's not really until you get to the end of the year when you total up and say how did we do, did we do better, did we do worse. Often it can be the difference of two or three books totally changes the financial performance of the company."

Fishbein also tried to get Murray tangled up on the significance of having your own distribution. During direct examination, Murray explained that sales teams get books into stores around the country, and those stores are "gatekeepers" for their local communities. He asserted that client publishers that are distributed by another company are at a disadvantage. "If you outsource your sales team, you now could be one of thousands of books in a bag that you are trying to sell." Since Harper doesn't have any client publishers, the sales force is focused on their own titles, so "our bag is small." Harper does use Lakeside to handle a portion of their fulfillment, and Lakeside offers that service to other publishers. That segment, Murray said, is pick, pack, and ship—just labor, not sales and strategy. He doesn't think that Harper is at a disadvantage in that situation.

In a particularly tense exchange, Fishbein asked Murray, "You're a businessman right?" "Yeah." "Doesn't it stand to reason that you should make all of your books successful?" "No." Murray tried to explain that publishers "get a pool of money, and they have to decide how to allocate that money across the books." "Your testimony is that you pay advances for books that you don't want to be successful?" "No."

As Murray continued flipping through the binder with his deposition, Fishbein said, "We're going to leave that. If you want to keep reading it, let me know, but I am ready to move on." "I am just missing the context," Murray replied and closed the binder.

Like all the other executives, Murray was questioned about whether "Amazon is a major problem, a major competitor for HarperCollins?" Here, his eventual answer was different than most others, acknowledging: "Certainly on the romance front," and he noted they mostly only competed in genre fiction. "They have not been a competitor for big books. . . . We've not come up against them in any auctions. I'm not aware of any books we've lost against Amazon when bidding for big books."

Murray also discussed the costs of putting out a book. He estimated that it takes 2000 hours of employee time (seemingly office workers, rather than warehouse staff) to publish a book "taking our creative people who publish books, seeing how many books they do, looking at the number of people, and just doing the math." While noting "it could vary widely," he suggested that writing a book also takes 2000 hours on average, and "we spend about the same amount of time as authors may spend creating their work."

Murray also gave some insight into the company's business details. Two realms where Harper doesn't compete with other Big 5 publishers are series romance and Harper Christian titles. Even trade titles under the Christian division—"Christian lite" or titles about "heartland values"–are "not usually published by New York City-based publishers." Later, he described the company's overall business plan. "We always try to have a plan where we grow faster than the market" and determine how they're going to do it. Then they "put more money into those areas."

"Would it be fair to say that even if the merger does through you'll still be very aggressive?" Answer: "It's hard to say."

Towards the end, Judge Pan asked why Murray publicized the plan to pay higher advances. "Why wouldn't you just go into the auctions, spend more, and win more books?" she asked. He said that, while some companies were "pulled back" during the pandemic, they were "moving in the other direction" and "saw increase in consumer spending." "There's no better way to make a statement like that to get the message out to all the agents in the industry," he said.

TESTIMONY OF BRIAN MURRAY, CEO, HARPERCOLLINS

DIRECT EXAMINATION

BY MR. BEN MATELSON:

Q. Good morning.

A. Good morning.

Q. Would you state your name for the record, please.

A. Brian Murray.

Q. And, Mr. Murray, where are you employed?

A. At HarperCollins in New York.

Q. And what is your title?

A. I'm the chief executive officer.

Q. How long have you been with HarperCollins?

A. About 25 years.

Q. And what positions did you hold with HarperCollins before you became the CEO?

A. I was group president. Before that, I was the chief executive officer of our Australia, New Zealand business. And before that, I had a business strategy role within the general books group in New York.

Q. You mentioned group president. What was the group that you were president of?

A. I was responsible for about half the company's worldwide operations when I was group president, so, yeah, about half the revenues.

Q. All right. And in what year did you become the CEO?

A. 2008.

Q. And can you outline your responsibilities as the CEO of HarperCollins?

A. Sure. I am responsible for working with all our leaders around the world to develop and execute growth plans. We publish in over 20 countries and we publish in over 16 languages. And together with my leadership team we are focused on finding ways to grow our publishing business. And I am involved in all the day-to-day activities and managing that big publishing organization.

Q. And then just focusing on the U.S. publishing business, can you just describe for us how that business is organized?

A. Sure. We have a general books group which has—it's sort of a division. It has three different publishers and presidents that are responsible for building our general books group. We have a children's division that's separate from that. And then we have a Christian publishing company as well.

Q. All right. And is Harlequin also part of the HarperCollins?

A. Harlequin is headquartered and run out of Canada, but it publishes significant business into the U.S. as well.

Q. All right. And if you could just give us maybe a thumbnail sketch of the types of books that each of those groups publishes starting with the general books group.

A. Sure. The general books group publishes books for consumers, for readers of all types, very much broad-based general interest titles, fiction, nonfiction, cooking, lifestyle a very, very broad base of books that you would find in a Barnes & Noble or a local independent store. It's a very, very broad-based general interest publishing business.

Q. All right. And then in the children's publishing group?

A. Yeah. The children's business for us is a lot of fiction, some picture books. We focus on teen, young adult, middle grade, and some board books. And, yeah, it's a great business. We don't do education. It's really, again, books that you would find for sale in a Barnes & Noble or independent bookstores.

Q. All right. And then moving on to the Christian books business, can you give us an overview of that?

A. Sure. Our Christian business is an evangelical Christian publishing company. It really focuses on publishing for that audience. It's a very large audience in the United States.

But over the recent years, they have broadened a little bit doing what we call more kind of what we call American heartlands, American values type publishing. Those businesses are all run out of Nashville and Grand Rapids, Michigan, so very much a middle of the country sensibility, and they publish for that audience.

Q. All right. And then Harlequin, if you could give us an overview of Harlequin?

A. Sure. Harlequin is one of the best well-known book brands in the world. It's known for publishing series romance. Those are the books that you might have seen in Walmarts or Targets or grocery stores. Very commercial, targeted to women. And then, like I said, that's very much a global brand. We publish out of Toronto and London for a global audience, and that brand is known very much all around the world.

Q. And then I think with respect to the general books group, I think you mentioned that there are three sort of subdivisions within that.

A. Correct.

Q. What are those?

A. There's kind of the Harper group of imprints. There is a Morrow group of imprints. These are kind of management structures. And then there's a Harper One group of imprints.

Q. Do the heads of those three groups report to you?

A. They do.

Q. We heard earlier in this trial from a HarperCollins' executive Liate Stehlik. Where does she fit into the organization?

A. She runs our Morrow group, which is one of the larger groups within HarperCollins.

Q. And do the heads of the Harper Christian and Harper children's and Harlequin groups also report to you?

A. They do.

Q. And moving on to acquisitions of books, what is your role, if any, in the acquisition of books for HarperCollins?

A. So every year I work together with my direct reports to determine what the right publishing program would be, where we are going to grow.

And then during the course of the year, I approve the size of the bids that they are going to be making on a kind of day-to-day basis.

Q. All right. And I don't want to mention any numbers in the public session, but is there—are there certain steps in the approval process that require your personal approval?

A. Yes.

Q. And can you just give us, again without mentioning numbers, what are the steps that require your approval?

A. What are the steps?

Q. The steps.

A. You mean the process they go through?

Q. Yes.

A. So our editors and our publishers would, if they are interested in a book, they will review the book, talk to our sales team. They will come up with a projection of what we think that book could sell. And eventually that book, if it's an expensive book, will find its way to me.

And I may have a discussion with the publisher and president of that division if it's above a certain level, and I would approve it or we would have a discussion about whether to go forward or not.

Q. And just to clarify, is your approval required to make an offer at a particular dollar level?

A. Correct, yes. Basically to make an offer, that's right.

Q. So we will get into the numbers in closed session.

A. Sure.

THE COURT: Can I ask a question quickly? Have you been involved at the lower levels of this process as an editor or sort of a publisher at the lower levels?

THE WITNESS: I have not been an editor, no. I have come up the business side.

THE COURT: Okay.

THE WITNESS: And when I ran our business in Australia and New Zealand, I was involved in all of the decisions there. And when I was in the general books group, I was involved in all of the decisions in that division. But in my CEO role, I am not in the actual going talking to agents about, you know—

THE COURT: Right.

THE WITNESS:—where are we on this. My presidents and publishers are involved in that.

THE COURT: Okay. So have you never done that part of the job, just the actual negotiating and bidding?

THE WITNESS: Yes. I am involved in approving. There's the occasional one where I may be involved, but that's not the standard practice.

THE COURT: I see. Thank you.

BY MR. MATELSON:

Q. Just to follow up, do you try to keep yourself informed about the books that are being acquired by your various divisions?

A. Yes.

Q. Okay. How do you keep yourself informed?

A. Well, I mean, I am meeting with and talking with my team all the time. There's—any given day, there could be a number of books that we are bidding on that are above that level. And then we are constantly forecasting, looking at our business, and trying to figure out how to adjust course and how to grow our business. So there's a lot of—I mean, there's a lot of conversation about how are we tracking against our plans.

Q. Now, going back to the personal approval of offers at a certain level, how long has that requirement for your personal approval been in place?

A. A very long time.

Q. And did you introduce that requirement?

A. I think it was there before I became CEO, yeah.

Q. Okay. Why is there a requirement to have your personal approval to make certain offers?

A. There's limited capital. And in our plan we are held accountable for delivering revenues. There's only so much capital that can be spent on acquiring books. And we also want to make sure that we are delivering on our profit goals. So if you misallocate the capital or you overspend too frequently, it becomes we are unable to hit our targets. So those approvals come back to me, and I will either give the approval or refuse the approval.

Q. Just in general, can you talk about how the sort of financial risks that you are talking about differ or how they compare for books that are at your approval level or above versus ones that are below your level?

A. Sure. The more that you commit in an advance on a particular project, the greater the risk of failure. And so you can only take so many big bets in the course of a year. And so that's a big part of our discussion is how many bets are we taking. Are we taking enough or are we taking too many. And then we want to make sure that we don't have all our bets in one area. We don't want to have all our bets in fiction or all our bets in nonfiction. We want to make sure that there's an appropriate kind of almost allocation of where our risk is so that if things change we are not going to be hurt by that.

Q. I'm trying to understand sort of what types of costs there are, what types of costs HarperCollins incurs to acquire a new book and then bring it all the way to market. Can you give us an overview of that?

A. Yes. Obviously there is the amount of money you commit as a guarantee. That's what we call that, an advance. There's a fair amount of time that our team spends developing that book. They don't come to us often—sometimes we don't even have a manuscript. We might have a table of contents. We might have a sample chapter. There's a significant amount of time my creative teams will spend to bring that idea or manuscript to fruition. And then there's marketing required to get the word out. We have people who are dedicated to market the book, to publicize the book. And then we have two large sales teams in the United States, one for the Christian division, one for our general books and children's division. And the sales team spends a significant amount of time trying to generate orders. So there's a tremendous amount of time and expense. And, of course, we have to print, produce the books. So the bigger the book is, the bigger the risk is on the inventory and the printing and the logistics of getting those books out to the various customers. So there's quite a bit of expense involved in bringing an idea to readers.

Q. Has HarperCollins ever tried to calculate how much employee work—how many hours of employee work goes into a book?

A. Yeah, we did it some time ago. I did it when I was in Australia. I did it when I was in the U.S. You know, rough time, it averages out to about 2,000 hours for every book. That's taking our creative people who publish books and seeing how many books they do, looking at the number of people, and just doing the math. So roughly we kind of think about the amount of time and overhead of our own employees in terms of how much they spend bringing a book to market. It's about 2,000 hours. And, yeah, sometimes if an author writes a book a year and they are a professional writer, they may be spending 2,000 hours. It could vary widely if it's a short book or a long book, but we spend about the same amount of time as authors may spend creating their work.

Q. And in general, is there any relationship between the sales you project for an acquisition and the advance level that you offer to authors?

A. Yes. So when we run our projections we have an editor's perspective on what we think a book can sell based on their vision, and then we also have input from our sales team and we have public information from BookScan that gives us comparable titles. And all of these inputs go into a title projection, and that generates a way to figure out what we might be able to pay for a particular project.

Q. And then once you have a sales projection for a book, what kinds of tools are available to sell the

book to meet those projections that you have set?
A. When we are actually—when the book is made and we are going to market?
Q. Yes.
A. Well, we have relationships with almost every book seller in the United States as well as with distributors. We ship books all across the country to get them out. And then we have publicists who have relationships with television and radio producers. We have digital marketers who are active on all the social media platforms. And we have traditional marketers who help us try to get the word out. And then we have, as I mentioned, the two large sales teams, which is a part of our—I think it's a very important part of what we do is to generate interest and buzz with the booksellers to give that book the greatest potential to achieve the sales we have in our title P&L.
Q. And do the sales goals you set for a book influence at all the level of marketing and publicity that you do for that book?
A. Yes. My publishers and presidents are all—their incentives are all aligned around hitting their goals. And if they have asked me for a large advance there's a lot of risk riding on those big books. There's less risk riding on the small books. And so for them to achieve their results and to participate in the incentive plans, we have created alignment around trying to make sure that the likelihood of those books hitting their full potential are met.
Q. I think you referred to this a moment ago with respect to printing, but I just wanted to clarify. When you are expecting to sell—or when you are—yeah, when you are expecting to sell more copies of a given book, do you also print more advanced copies of the book to sell?
A. Yes, we may. Yeah, advanced copies are a tool that are used for certain books to get early buzz, to give them to reviewers or book sellers or social media influencers. So that's one of the tools that we have.
Q. Okay. And just more generally, in terms of the number of copies you print, is there a relationship between the sales you project—
A. Yes.
Q.—and the number of books you print to be able to distribute?
A. Yes. If expectations are big, we are going to print more books. We would—yes.
Q. Let me ask you a little bit about competition for author content. And just based on your experience, is there a publisher that you—that HarperCollins competes with most frequently for general trade book author content?
A. That would be Penguin Random House.
Q. And then after Penguin Random House, who would you say would be the next most significant competitors?
A. Simon & Schuster.
Q. And then do you consider Hachette and Macmillan also to be competitors?
A. Yes.
Q. And why would you—when you mention PRH first and Simon & Schuster second, why do you rank them that way?
A. Penguin Random House is very large. They are maybe three times larger or a little more than HarperCollins. So they are very active in all the bidding. I mean, they are almost always—there could be multiple editors or imprints or divisions bidding on books. So they are always there. And Simon & Schuster we've found them to be aggressive, and often we are going head to head with them as well.
THE COURT: I'm sorry, you said that Penguin Random House is three times larger—
THE WITNESS: Yes.
THE COURT:—than HarperCollins? By what measure?
THE WITNESS: I think if you look at market share of general trade books, and I have been told by our book sellers as well that they are three to three and a half times larger.
BY MR. MATELSON:
Q. So just to clarify that, are there certain divisions at HarperCollins you consider to be not in the category of general trade books?
A. A lot of the series romance, the Harlequin, that business, series romance, we are not competing with

Penguin Random House. Our Christian business does compete with them a little bit, but we publish, like I said, for evangelical Christians, we publish a lot of Bibles, we publish a lot of Christian theologians. We have a dedicated Christian sales force. So we are really in kind of a little bit of a different business. We do go head to head sometimes with them but more on what I call the heartland values, kind of Christian-lite books. But the vast majority of our Christian business is not usually published by New York City-based publishers.

Q. Thinking about books that sell for higher advance levels, so let's say the level of your approval or above, what does a publisher need to have to successfully compete for for acquiring those kinds of books?

A. First of all, you have to have significant capital because these are big bets, and if they go wrong, you can lose a fair amount of money, quite a bit of money. You have to have an expertise and a reputation. It helps if you have published authors that are publishing to the similar readers so you can point to similar books that maybe you published one, two, or three years ago that were successful. And so when you are pitching for a new project, you can demonstrate that your team is very capable, and you can talk about what made those previous books successful. It's very important to have broad sales distribution and to have great partnerships with your printers so that if something starts to really sell quickly, that you are able to get books printed as fast as possible so that you don't go out of stock.

There's a lot to it. There's a lot of expertise and a track record, I think, that are very important for an author to sign with an author (sic). If you can demonstrate all of those capabilities and you have the capital and the team you have a good shot.

THE COURT: I'm sorry, can I just go back for a moment to what you said about the general trade book market.

THE WITNESS: Sure.

THE COURT: And you said that Penguin Random House is three to three and a half times your size in that particular part of the market.

THE WITNESS: Correct.

THE COURT: What about Simon & Schuster, do you think they are bigger than you or smaller than you in general trade books?

THE WITNESS: I think it depends on the year. Sometimes we are a little bigger, and sometimes they are a little bigger. It's very similar size.

THE COURT: I see. Thank you.

BY MR. MATELSON:

Q. All right. I think the first thing you said had to do with capital. I just wanted to ask, is the revenue you get from your backlist a factor in being able to compete for these higher advance books?

A. Yes. The size of a publisher's backlist is critical to their financial stability and your ability to take these big risks with new projects, with new authors. If you don't—because it's almost like an annuity. Once books are successful, sometimes children's books will be three generations, people have been buying them over and over again, and so that backlist catalog is really, really important to pay for the overhead of your publishing teams and then also to take the risks on the new books. So without a backlist I think it's very hard to compete with these big books.

Q. And then I think you also mentioned the sales force. Why is having your own sales force relevant to competing for these higher advance books?

A. You want to be able to penetrate the entire American market in order to get your authors' books on the best seller list. And there could be three to four hundred critical independent book sellers that report to *The New York Times*. And all of our authors want to be *New York Times* best sellers. So having the reach across the country is important to get those books appropriately stocked and promoted at independent bookstores. They are also, the bookstores, the independent bookstores and some of the chains, are also really important gatekeepers for their local communities and their local readership. So you really want to get them excited about a new author or a new book so that they will hand-sell it to their customers. If you don't have your own sales force, what happens is a book becomes one of thousands in the bag. There's a saying about how many—a sales rep for a publisher would talk about how big their bag is. That's how many books are they selling to an independent book seller in a season. And at HarperCollins, we just have our books that we are selling, and that's it. We don't have clients or other third parties. So our bag is small, and our sales reps can be very focused. If you outsource your sales team, you now could be one of thousands of books in a bag that you are trying to sell, so the likelihood of that book getting the same attention and hand-selling, I think, goes down.

Q. I believe you also mentioned reputation or track record. What's the relevance of that?

A. Authors want to be part of a publishing company where their literary heroes have been published. The reputation of a publishing company—I mean, we are over 200 years old. When authors, prospective authors, or authors come to HarperCollins for the first time, they come and they see—and we really promote in our office space these literary giants that we have published in our 200-year history. And you can't underestimate the impact of a prospective author thinking they could be published by the same house that published Mark Twain, for example. It does matter.

Q. And then I think one of the factors you mentioned was a printer or having access to a printer. Can you just explain a little bit more about why that's relevant?

A. Sure. When books hit and they become successful in the marketplace after week one or after something happens later on, if there's some major publicity or something happens in the news, often we scramble to print more copies to get them out to the book sellers as fast as possible. And having really good relationships with your printers so that they can give us press time immediately and then ship them out to our book sellers becomes a core capability.

If you don't have that relationship, your books could be out of stock for a long time while there's demand. And so being able to respond quickly and replace inventory when there's tremendous interest in a book is very, very important.

Q. We have heard during this trial about some recent publishing startups. I think one that's been mentioned in court is Zando. There have been a few others. Are you familiar with these companies?

A. I have heard of them, yes.

Q. Okay. How would you assess the ability of startups to compete for books at the higher advance levels compared to a major publisher like HarperCollins?

A. I think it would be very difficult as a general rule. They might be able to buy one or two, but I think as a general rule, it would be very, very difficult.

Q. Why do you say it would be difficult?

A. Because of the risk profile of placing big bets. Most of the bets don't pay off, and I think you would need a lot of capital. In our experience, even when we start imprints within HarperCollins, new imprints, it can take more than five years before you are profitable. And even at the five-year point, you haven't recouped all the investments of the previous four years.

So it's just a long time to become profitable because there's no backlist. And so they can certainly buy a book or two, but in the main, I don't think they are a competitor.

Q. I want to change gears and ask a few questions about the 2020 bidding for Simon & Schuster. When Simon & Schuster was put up for sale in 2020, did News Corp. participate in the bidding?

A. Yes.

Q. And what role, if any, did you have?

A. My job with my team was to determine a go-forward plan, if we bought Simon & Schuster, how would we bring the two companies together, and to come up with a plan and how we would go to market, and also to work on developing what we thought the business was worth in order to make a recommendation on what the News Corporation board should do or could do.

Q. All right. And then, again, I will save the specific numbers for the closed session, but did—and News Corp. is your parent company?

A. Correct.

Q. And did they submit a bid for Simon & Schuster?

A. They did.

Q. And did you later learn of the winning bid for Simon & Schuster?

A. Yes.

Q. To your understanding, was the News Corp. bid close to beating out the Bertelsmann bid for Simon

& Schuster?

A. It was not close.

Q. And when you learned the purchase price that Bertelsmann paid, what was your reaction to it?

A. I was shocked.

Q. And why was that your reaction?

A. We had data on comparable multiples of publishing M&A activity over the last ten years or so, and it was far outside that range.

Q. Would that same price have made sense for HarperCollins from your perspective?

A. It's really a News Corp. board question, but I did not recommend—I would not have recommended that. But really the board is the one who decides how to allocate their capital.

Q. Understood. What was your thinking about why you would not have recommended that same price?

A. We've probably done five or so acquisitions, and we tend to be very disciplined in our financial modeling. And so we could not find a way to have a return at that price.

Q. All right.

MR. MATELSON: Your Honor, I have now reached the end of the questions I wanted to ask in public session.

THE COURT: Okay.

MR. MATELSON: And I will pause to allow defense counsel to proceed with cross-examination of public topics.

THE COURT: That's fine. Thank you. I just had a couple of questions. In terms of your budget for acquiring books, is that determined by how profitable you were last year or do you get some capital from your parent company or what limits your ability to spend money on books?

THE WITNESS: So each year we put forward a plan. And in that plan, the amount of spending for new books is in that plan. And we need to have a plan that we try to grow faster than the market. That's one of our aspirations. And we look at the number of books that we may be doing. We may be growing the number of books. And we have to make sure we have enough kind of fire power to buy books. And yet I still need to hit other metrics. This is where the balancing comes in. I still need to have profits. I can't ask just overspend for books to buy revenue and not have profit or cash happen as well. So there's a little bit of a financial model where we fine-tune how fast do we think we can grow and still achieve profits and then deliver cash to our parent company. We self-finance. We don't need capital from our parent company for day-to-day operations. But if we are doing an acquisition, we might—how we source capital then is a parent company decision.

THE COURT: So your projections of how much you are going to spend are very much correlated to how much you have made?

THE WITNESS: How much we have made and how confident we are about the future.

THE COURT: And the backlist, what's going to happen?

THE WITNESS: The backlist is a key element because that generates guaranteed revenues, profits, and cash, and then we reinvest that in new works.

THE COURT: Thank you. My other question was, you said that your sales force only sells for your own books.

THE WITNESS: Correct.

THE COURT: And there seem to be other people in the industry who sell for smaller publishers. Have you made—and I guess they get paid to do that?

THE WITNESS: Correct.

THE COURT: Have you made the decision not to do that because it's better for your books or—

THE WITNESS: Yes, that has been our decision.

THE COURT: I understand. Thank you. Any questions based on my questions?

MR. MATELSON: Nothing from me, Your Honor. Thank you.

THE COURT: All right. Thank you.

CROSS-EXAMINATION

BY MR. FISHBEIN:

Q. Good morning, Mr. Murray.
A. Good morning.
Q. Mr. Murray, if this merger goes through, the Penguin Random House, Simon & Schuster merger, you intend to compete as hard as you can, don't you?
A. We intend to compete, yes.
Q. Do you plan to hold back in competing with Penguin Random House, Simon & Schuster if the merger goes through?
A. No, I don't intend to hold back. No.
Q. And you said that you supervise your publishers and editors, right?
A. Correct.
Q. And they are the ones that are doing bidding, correct?
A. Yes.
Q. And so will you instruct them, if the merger goes through, to hold back in the amount that they bid in auctions?
A. I guess it depends on what happens. It's hard for me to say. It's hard for me to say.
Q. But as you sit here now, do you have any plans to instruct your staff to bid less than they otherwise would if there is a merger?
A. No.
Q. And does that apply also to exclusive negotiations where you are negotiating with, for example, a repeat author?
A. No.
Q. In other words, do you have any plans now post-merger to tell your editors and publishers, hey, bid less, offer less in an exclusive?
A. No. We have not changed anything because we don't know if the merger is going through so . . .
Q. Now, you acquired another publisher in 2021. That was HMH correct?
A. Correct.
Q. And at the time, they were one of the largest independent publishers, is that right?
A. Yes.
Q. And so leading up to that acquisition, did you discuss internally at HarperCollins that that deal would allow you to bid less in auctions for works?
A. No.
Q. Did you discuss that that deal would allow you to offer less to authors in exclusive negotiations?
A. No.
Q. And as a result of your acquisition of HMH, has HarperCollins, in fact, lowered advances to authors because of that merger?
A. No.
Q. Now, you said you wanted HarperCollins to acquire Simon & Schuster, right?
A. Yes. That was my—yes.
Q. And you were disappointed when you were unable to acquire Simon & Schuster, right?
A. Yes.
Q. And if this deal gets blocked, HarperCollins would still be interested in acquiring Simon & Schuster, is that right?
A. Yes.
Q. And you understand that if HarperCollins acquired Simon & Schuster, what's known as the Big 5 would then be four, right?
A. Yes.
Q. And do you believe that consolidation from five to four is by itself anticompetitive?
A. No.
Q. Do you believe that a merger between HarperCollins and Simon & Schuster would result in lower

advances to authors?

A. No.

Q. Now, let me ask you about the market shares, because isn't it true that certainly in all book sales, HarperCollins is second to Penguin Random House, correct?

A. I think last year, yes, yeah.

Q. Okay. Well, you measure market share yourself internally, right?

A. We do.

Q. And so what is like, for example, U.S. general books? Is that trade books?

A. U.S. general books would be, yeah, that would our general books group as well as our children's division.

Q. Are those trade books?

A. Yes.

Q. Okay. I want to show you some exhibits. Mr. Murray, just while those are being passed out, there's a binder, and I am going to refer to exhibits by exhibit number and also by the tab number that is in your binder there. So if you go to tab 10, Defense Exhibit 105, do you recognize that?

A. Yes.

Q. What is it?

A. Pardon?

Q. What is it?

A. This was our budget book for our fiscal year 2021.

Q. What is a budget book?

A. It is the annual plan that we put together.

Q. And what is it used for?

A. It's used to develop our publishing plan and our business plan for the following year.

Q. Do you have anything to do with putting together budget books?

A. Yes.

Q. What is your role?

A. I would oversee the building of the plan, the book, and then it would be presented to our parent company.

MR. FISHBEIN: Your Honor, I offer Defense Exhibit 105.

THE COURT: Any objection?

MR. MATELSON: No objection.

THE COURT: 105 will be admitted. (Defendant's 105 received in evidence.)

BY MR. FISHBEIN:

Q. If you turn, Mr. Murray, to slide 63, please, U.S. general books, and you see there's a chart, market share 2019?

A. Yes.

Q. And there, at least, Penguin Random House is–

A. Page 63?

Q. Yeah.

A. Yeah. Okay.

Q. By that measure, Penguin Random House is about double HarperCollins, is that right?

A. Yes. But that includes our Christian business. All right. So if you subtract the Christian business and if you subtract Harlequin, that's where I am getting the three times.

Q. Okay. But for your internal purposes, you include those in your general book category, right?

A. No, not really. I mean, this chart does, but—the chart does.

Q. The title of the page is U.S. general books, right?

A. Yes.

Q. And then there's a market share, and that includes Christian and Harlequin?

A. Yes.

Q. Okay. There was testimony by the expert called by the government in this case that reflected a

market share for Penguin Random House. This is trade frontlist and backlist for 2020 of Penguin Random House at around 27 percent and HarperCollins around 13.8. Again, about two to one. Do you dispute that as a market share for trade frontlist and backlist sales 2020?
A. I don't know. I don't know the expert's data. I have no idea.
Q. Okay. And I think you said—well, let me ask you. You have about 125 imprints, is that right?
A. Yes.
Q. How many titles per year does HarperCollins do?
A. It would be about 10,000 or so globally.
THE COURT: I'm sorry, can I just ask a question? When people talk about trade books, does that include Christian?
THE WITNESS: No.
THE COURT: So like BookScan or anyone, they wouldn't include that?
THE WITNESS: No. So we have an $80 million Bible business. Yeah, so there's books our Christian division does that would never be sold in a bookstore.
THE COURT: I see.
THE WITNESS: And then there's a Christian bookstores channel that's a large channel where they only sell Christian content, and that's a completely different channel. So BookScan will pick up Christian sales if they are sold through Barnes & Noble or Amazon, but it misses a very large part of the Christian business.
THE COURT: I see.
THE WITNESS: So, yeah, the data is not perfect.
THE COURT: I see. Thank you.
BY MR. FISHBEIN:
Q. But part of your Christian publishing is trade, isn't it?
A. Some is, yes.
Q. In other words, you include in Christian what you would refer to as inspirational content?
A. Yes.
Q. That could be nonfiction or even fiction books with a Christian theme?
A. Correct.
Q. And those are trade books, right?
A. They are.
Q. Now, you mentioned some attributes of some of the major publishing companies in terms of editorial, marketing, distribution, et cetera. Do you remember that?
A. Yes.
Q. And I think you mentioned track record as well, right?
A. Yes.
Q. Now, you believe that you can compete with Penguin Random House on all those levels, right?
A. Yeah, yes.
Q. In other words, you are just as good at editorial as any major publisher, right?
A. I think so.
Q. And your marketing is as good as any major publisher, right?
A. Yes.
Q. And your track record is as good as any major publisher?
A. Yes.
Q. So when you say, going forward you are going to compete with Penguin Random House and others, you have the tools to do that, right?
A. We do.
Q. Now, on distribution, does HarperCollins do its own distribution?
A. We do some but not all.
Q. Okay. What percentage do you not do?
A. We have outsourced pick, pack, and ship operation to our printer. I don't know the exact percentage.

Q. I mean, is it a trivial percentage, or is it a significant percentage?
A. No, it would be a significant percentage.
Q. So a significant percentage of your distribution is done by a third party?
A. Correct.
Q. And that third party is whom?
A. It's Lakeside.
Q. Lakeside or LSC?
A. Yes.
Q. Does Lakeside or LSC offer that service to other publishers?
A. Yes.
Q. In addition to Lakeside and LSC, there are companies like Ingram that also do third party distribution, right?
A. Correct.
Q. Do you feel like you are at a disadvantage against other publishers because you outsource your distribution?
A. We only outsource the pick, pack, and storage. All of the IT, all of the credit collections, all of the strategic elements we retain. It's just the labor and the actual racking in the warehouse. So, no, I don't feel that I am at a disadvantage.
Q. But to be clear, you haven't had to invest in warehouses, right?
A. Not recently, no.
Q. In other words, to the extent that you outsource, they are taking care of the warehouse operations, not you, right?
A. Again, we have a warehouse—we own and operate a warehouse in Buffalo which today does our Harlequin business, it does a little bit of Christian business, and we do all our own returns processing. We are in a major investment right now in London for a brand-new facility after four years, so it's mixed.
Q. Listen carefully. For your outsource distribution business, do you have warehouses for that?
A. Yes.
Q. So what does the third party do?
A. We have multiple warehouses.
Q. What does the third party distributor do for you, Mr. Murray?
A. They do the picking and the packing. The labor in the warehouse, they do that.
Q. Okay. So to the extent that employees are required to pack, to ship, and to do other things associated with a warehouse, HarperCollins does not employ those people, right?
A. Not the Lakeside employees, correct.
Q. Right. So Lakeside does that for you, right?
A. Yes.
Q. And other publishers could also take advantage of that service from Lakeside, right?
A. Yes.
Q. And do you feel like you are at a disadvantage because you use Lakeside for those services instead of doing it yourself?
A. No.
Q. Would you agree with me, Mr. Murray, that HarperCollins is a strong competitor in the U.S. publishing industry?
A. Yes.
Q. Now, do you personally get involved in setting budgets like marketing budgets for specific books?
A. No.
Q. Do you know how the editors do it?
A. I know what the general guidelines are. I am not involved in the title-by-title marketing, no.
Q. So do the general guidelines include any line of demarcation above which you are supposed to market and below which you don't have to put an effort into marketing?
A. No.

Q. And certainly a $250,000 advance, for example, does not separate the amount of marketing that you are going to do on a book, is that fair?
A. You know what, you would have to—I am not the right person to answer that.
Q. To your knowledge, as the person who gives guidance, have you ever given guidance that you should treat a book for $300,000 advance different from a book for $200,000 advance?
A. No. Again, I'm not involved in the title-level marketing decisions.
Q. Isn't it fair to say, Mr. Murray, that in your guidance, you tell your editors and publishers that they should promote all of your books?
A. It's up to them. I mean, they get a pool of money, and they have to decide how to allocate that money across the books so . . .
Q. You mentioned that you put capital at risk, right; you want to get a return, right?
A. Correct.
Q. And you are a businessman, right?
A. Yeah.
Q. Doesn't it stand to reason that you should try to make all your books successful?
A. No.
Q. No?
A. No.
Q. Okay.
A. My team has a—they have to decide how to allocate their resources.
Q. So your testimony is that you pay advances for some books that you don't want to be successful?
A. No.
Q. Okay. You mentioned some terms, and I just wasn't sure what you meant. You said big books and big risks. Is there a policy at HarperCollins that defines what a big book is or a big risk?
A. No.
Q. And certainly there's no guidance, formal or informal, that separates big books and big risks at an advance level of $250,000, right?
A. Sorry, say that again.
Q. In other words, there's no guidance either in writing or informal that says a book above a $250,000 advance is a big risk or a big book?
A. No.
Q. It's subjective, right?
A. Yes.
Q. And while we are talking about risk, I mean, there are some books with larger advances that are not so risky, for example, a repeat author who you have a track record with and you have some confidence as to what the sales of their next book is going to be, right?
A. Some are less risky than others, but it's hard—I just have to say it depends.
Q. It depends on a lot of factors, right?
A. Yeah.
Q. And one of those factors, for example, is whether it's a repeat author with a track record?
A. In fiction, yes. Nonfiction, less so.
Q. Okay. But in fiction, if you have a series and you know how the first four in the series did, the fifth is probably less risky, right?
A. Correct.
Q. And those advances could be in the millions, right?
A. They could be, yes.
Q. And then there could be a lower advance book that's a first-time author, nonfiction that is risky, right?
A. Yes.
Q. Mr. Murray, HarperCollins has been very aggressive in acquiring book rights from authors in recent years, is that true?

A. Yes.
Q. And, in fact, you have stated publicly that HarperCollins will be very aggressive in buying books, right?
A. Yes.
Q. And did you want the market to know that HarperCollins was out there and bidding aggressively?
A. Yes.
Q. And when you say very aggressive, that means that you have been increasing title output, right?
A. Yes.
Q. And also increasing the amount of money that you spend acquiring new authors, right?
A. Yes.
Q. And that includes authors with advances above $250,000, right?
A. Yes.
Q. Would it be fair to say that you are trying to sign up the best books that you see in the marketplace?
A. Yes.
Q. And that strategy that you have announced publicly about being aggressive, is that contingent at all on whether the Penguin Random House, Simon & Schuster merger goes through?
A. I don't know.
Q. I'm sorry?
A. I don't know. I can't speculate what's going to happen in the future.
Q. Okay. But as you sit here now, do you plan to vary that strategy depending on whether the merger goes through?
A. I don't know.
Q. Well, would it be fair to say that even if the merger goes through, your strategy of being very aggressive will continue?
A. It's very hard to say.
Q. You gave a deposition in this case, right?
A. Yes.
Q. Could you look in the back of your binder. There's a tab with your deposition, if you could look at page 32. And when you are there, let me know and I will direct you to the lines.
A. 32?
Q. Yes.
A. Yep.
Q. So looking at lines 14 to 18, were you asked the following question and gave the following answer?
Question, in other words, even if that merger goes through, your strategy that we have been talking about, about being aggressive acquiring rights from authors, that will continue, is that right? Answer, yes. Did you give that answer to that question?
A. Yes.
Q. Was it truthful?
A. I have to see what else I said here.
Q. Please do.
MR. FISHBEIN: Your Honor, I would offer lines 14 through 18 page 32 in evidence as a prior inconsistent statement under oath.
THE COURT: Any objection?
THE WITNESS: Okay. Yes.
THE COURT: Just a moment.
MR. MATELSON: I'm sorry. We don't object.
THE COURT: That will be admitted.
BY MR. FISHBEIN:
Q. It was truthful, right, Mr. Murray?
A. Yes.
Q. Now, you said that you constantly, as part of your job, prepare projections and think about the future

growth of the company, is that right?
A. Yes.
Q. And do you review those projections? We are going to leave that. If you want to keep reading it, let me know, but I am ready to move on.
A. No. I am just missing the context. Go ahead.
Q. Do you review those projections with anybody more senior than you?
A. Which projections?
Q. About the future financial performance of HarperCollins.
A. Let's see. We do review them with our CFO.
Q. Okay. Sir, your CFO meaning the CFO of HarperCollins?
A. No, the CFO of News Corporation.
Q. The parent company?
A. Yeah, the parent company.
Q. If you could take a look at Defense Exhibit 279. It's tab 2 in your binder. Do you recognize this document?
A. Yes.
Q. What is it?
A. This was a strategy update. We tend to do them every January.
Q. What year?
A. '22.
Q. 2022?
A. Yes.
Q. And were you involved in the preparation of this document?
A. Yes.
Q. Were you involved in presenting this document to someone?
A. Yes.
Q. Who did you present it to?
A. My boss Robert Thompson as well as the parent company CFO.
Q. So you presented it to the CEO and CFO of News Corp, is that right?
A. Correct.
MR. FISHBEIN: Your Honor, defense offers Defense Exhibit 279.
THE COURT: Any objection?
MR. OPPENHEIMER: No objection.
THE COURT: It will be admitted. (Defendant's 279 received in evidence.)
BY MR. FISHBEIN:
Q. If you could turn with me, Mr. Murray, to slide 25. And I am not going to ask Mr. Murray to state any specific numbers. And we have got a code, our Rosetta Stone code thing, which is in the front flap of everybody's notebook. I will explain, Mr. Murray, how we are going to use that when we get to it.
Do you see that this slide is titled, investing in author advances to drive organic growth?
A. Yes.
Q. By the way, this presentation was put together after the announcement of the Simon & Schuster and Penguin Random House merger, correct?
A. Correct.
THE COURT: What's the Bates number on that?
MR. FISHBEIN: It's slide 25, and it's Bates number ending in 3214.
THE COURT: Thank you.
MR. FISHBEIN: Let me know, Your Honor, if you have any trouble finding it.
THE COURT: I've got it. Thank you.
BY MR. FISHBEIN:
Q. It's called, investing in author advances to drive organic growth, right?
A. Yes.

Q. Right below that, it says, organically growing trade publishing output. Do you see that?
A. Yes.
Q. By organic, what does that mean?
A. Not through acquisitions of companies.
Q. And, in fact, if you look at the note at the bottom left, it says excludes HMH acquisition, right?
A. Yes.
Q. So this takes out any growth that's just by virtue of an M&A transaction, right?
A. Correct.
Q. All right. And then on the left side, there's some bars under the title trade, title count. Do you know what that represents?
A. Yes.
Q. What is that?
A. That would be original works of trade titles.
Q. Okay. And on the bottom of each bar, you see the first one says FY 20? Do you see that?
A. Yes.
Q. And that's your fiscal year 2020, right?
A. Correct.
Q. And then the next one is fiscal year 2021, et cetera, through fiscal year 2024, right?
A. Yes.
Q. And so if I'm reading it right, the number at the top of the first bar, which is a number that ends with 39, do you see that?
A. Yes.
Q. I don't want to read out the number, but it's a number that ends in 39.
A. Yes.
Q. And that's the number of new titles in fiscal year 2020, right?
A. Yes.
Q. And then you have a projection, because this was done in 2022, all the way through fiscal year 2024, right?
A. Yes.
Q. And for fiscal year 2024, it's the number at the top that ends in 18, right?
A. Yes.
Q. And have you calculated what percent growth you were projecting?
A. Growth in what?
Q. In title count.
A. Bullet point says about—yes.
Q. Okay. I thought we had discussed—anyway, it doesn't matter. If you look at DX409—excuse me. If you look in the cover flap of your binder, we have a sheet that will allow you to identify a percentage without saying it out loud. Do you see that?
A. Yes.
MR. FISHBEIN: That's been marked as Defense Exhibit 409 which, Your Honor, I would offer solely for the purpose of knowing what he's referring to in terms of the numbers in his testimony.
THE COURT: Okay. That's fine.

BY MR. FISHBEIN:

Q. So, Mr. Murray, on Exhibit 409, can you identify the letter associated with the percentage growth of title count?
A. We said approximately.
Q. Okay. Now, title advance spend, what does that reflect?
A. That would reflect the amount of money in our plans going forward for new projects.
Q. And it's advances, right?
A. Correct.
Q. So that's advances for new books going forward, right?

A. Yes.
Q. And it's just the advance; it's not the royalties, right?
A. Right.
Q. So same thing, it goes from fiscal year 2020 through fiscal year 2024, correct?
A. Yes.
Q. And just so we are clear, for fiscal year 2020, the amount of committed advance is a number that ends in 7?
A. Yes.
Q. And for fiscal year 2024, the projection is—it's a number that ends in 8, right?
A. Yes.
Q. If you look at Defense Exhibit 409, approximately what percentage increase is that for the advance spend?
A. I don't know. I would have to do the math.
Q. So you haven't done that?
A. No.
Q. So if we wanted to do it, obviously we would take the difference between 2024 and '20, right, and we would calculate that as a percentage of fiscal year 2020, right?
A. Yes.
Q. Okay. When you made this presentation to your bosses at News Corp., did you caveat it in any way to the effect that author advances could go down if the Penguin Random House, Simon & Schuster merger went through?
A. No.
Q. And, in fact, Mr. Murray, have you ever discussed with any of your colleagues at HarperCollins that author advances could decrease as a result of the Penguin Random House, Simon & Schuster merger?
A. No.
Q. Have you ever discussed with anyone at News Corp.—have you ever discussed with anyone at News Corp. that author advances could decrease as a result of the Penguin Random House, Simon & Schuster merger?
A. No.
Q. Has HarperCollins reduced any budget or projection of its future author advances based on the Penguin Random House, Simon & Schuster merger?
A. No.
Q. Now, you have been in the industry for a while, right? And so do you have a sense over the last ten years directionally as to whether advances for authors have gone up or down or stayed the same?
A. In the aggregate, it's hard for me to know. I think right now, it's the—consumer spending is what's really—to me that's been the biggest change is, during the pandemic, the consumer spending on books has dramatically ramped up.
Q. So I am asking you about advances, not consumer spending. And I am asking about the last ten years as opposed to just the last two years. Do you have a view as to whether advances have gone up or down?
A. I don't, no.
Q. If you could look at your deposition, page 50, it's in the back there. Tell me when you're there.
A. Page 50. Okay.
Q. So page 50, line 17, were you asked the following question and gave the following answer:
Based on your experience in the publishing industry, Mr. Murray, have you noticed any trend in author advances over the last ten years in terms of whether it increased or decreased? Answer, no, they have been increasing. Do you see that?
A. Yes.
Q. Did you give that testimony at your deposition?
A. Yes.
MR. FISHBEIN: Your Honor, I would offer that as a prior inconsistent statement under oath.
THE COURT: Any objection?

MR. MATELSON: Objection—

MR. FISHBEIN: He said he didn't know.

THE COURT: I am going to overrule the objection. That's admitted.

BY MR. FISHBEIN:

Q. You are also aware, Mr. Murray, that during that same, ten-year period, there has been consolidation in the publishing industry, correct?

A. Yes.

Q. So you believe that advances to authors have been increasing notwithstanding consolidation in the industry, right?

A. Yes. I guess I'm just getting confused when you are talking about advances in aggregate and when you are talking about advances on a title level. I think that's kind of part of the discrepancies, but anyway sorry.

Q. Okay. But—

A. I'm just telling you it's hard for me to know what's going on over ten years.

Q. Do you believe that advances in the aggregate have been increasing during this ten-year period that there's been consolidation?

A. Again, it's hard for me to know.

Q. So if you could look at your deposition transcript, page 51.

A. Yes.

Q. Tell me when you're there.

A. 51, yep.

Q. And looking at lines 10 through 17—19, you were asked: Are you aware that there's been consolidation in the publishing industry in the last ten years? Answer, yes.

And you believe that author advances have increased notwithstanding that consolidation, is that right? Answer, yes. Did you give that testimony?

A. Yes.

Q. Let me show you another exhibit, Mr. Murray. If you can look at Defense Exhibit 299, which is tab 3 in your binder. Do you recognize that document?

A. Yes.

Q. What is it?

A. It's the News Corp. 10-K.

Q. So that's a securities filing by your parent corporation, correct?

A. Correct.

Q. And in it there's a description of HarperCollins' business, right?

A. Yes.

MR. FISHBEIN: Your Honor, I offer Defense Exhibit 299.

THE COURT: Any objection?

MR. MATELSON: No objection.

THE COURT: That will be admitted. (Defendant's 299 received in evidence.)

BY MR. FISHBEIN:

Q. Mr. Murray, do you know how the description of HarperCollins' business in this 10-K is written?

A. I believe my CFO at HarperCollins works with the parent company to draft that.

Q. Okay. So the CFO of HarperCollins is involved in the description of HarperCollins' business in the 10-K, right?

A. Yes.

Q. And do you meet with the CFO regularly–

A. Yes.

Q.—about HarperCollins' business?

A. Yes.

Q. And do you also meet with News Corp. regularly about HarperCollins' business?

A. Yes.

Q. And you understand that filings with the SEC are supposed to be accurate, right?
A. Yes.
Q. So if you can go with me to page 9 of the 10-K, tell me when you are there.
A. Yep.
Q. And do you see there's a paragraph at the top that starts, the book publishing business?
A. Yes.
Q. And let me ask you first, the book publishing business, does that refer to HarperCollins?
A. Yes.
Q. Does News Corp. have any other book publishing business apart from HarperCollins?
A. No.
Q. This is a description of HarperCollins, right?
A. Yes.
Q. It says, the book publishing business operates in a highly competitive market that is quickly changing and continues to see technological innovations. Do you see that?
A. Yes.
Q. And do you agree that HarperCollins operates in a highly competitive market?
A. Yes.
Q. Do you agree that the highly competitive market in which HarperCollins operates is quickly changing?
A. Yes.
Q. Do you agree that the book publishing market continues to see technological innovations?
A. Yes.
Q. What are they, by the way, the technological innovations?
A. Social media is having a big impact on the business. Digital audio continues to grow. There's two examples.
Q. Social media, you are referring, for example, to TikTok influencers?
A. Correct.
Q. And so those—that would be the ability to sell a lot of books through TikTok followings, right?
A. Correct.
Q. And so if a HarperCollins author has a big TikTok following, does HarperCollins incur any expense when the author puts out on TikTok that a new book is coming out?
A. No.
Q. So that's kind of a built-in marketing, right?
A. Yes.
Q. And do you pay advances to some of your TikTok authors more than $250,000?
A. I don't know.
Q. Have you ever heard the term BookTok influencer?
A. Yes.
Q. What is that?
A. Someone who's on TikTok and reviews and promotes books that they love.
Q. Fair to say that they are quite influential these days, right?
A. Some of them have been, yes.
Q. And that wasn't true ten years ago, right?
A. Correct.
Q. Now, if we continue with the 10-K, the next sentence says, HarperCollins competes with other large publishers such as Penguin Random House, Simon & Schuster, and Hachette Livre. Do you see that?
A. Yes.
Q. And that's some of the other large publishers. Would you agree that you also compete with Macmillan?
A. Yes.
Q. And I think you said—Simon & Schuster is listed there. And would you also agree that you compete

with Scholastic?
A. Yes.
Q. And would you characterize them as a major publisher?
A. Children's publisher, yes.
Q. Major children's publisher, fair?
A. Yes.
Q. And then the sentence continues, as well as with numerous smaller publishers for the right to works by well-known authors and public personalities. Do you see that?
A. Yes.
Q. Do you agree that HarperCollins competes with numerous smaller publishers for the rights to works by well-known authors and public personalities?
A. Yes.
Q. So an example of that would be Norton, right?
A. It could be.
Q. Are you familiar with Norton?
A. Yes.
Q. They are a smaller to medium-sized publisher, right?
A. Correct.
Q. And you compete with them, right?
A. Yeah, yes.
Q. Okay. And then continuing the sentence, it says, competition could also come from new entrants as barriers to entry in book publishing are low. Do you see that?
A. Yes.
Q. And do you agree that that is a correct statement?
A. Yes.
Q. Now, Amazon is a book publisher as well as a distributor, right?
A. Yes.
Q. In fact, Amazon is the biggest book distributor in the United States, right?
A. Yes.
Q. Does Amazon, in your view, use its strength in book distribution as part of its marketing pitch to authors to use their publishing services?
A. Yes.
Q. How?
A. They will talk about their ability to make the Amazon-published books very visible on the Amazon website.
Q. Can you explain to the court what the significance of that is? Why is that part of their pitch?
A. Well, I mean, obviously if you have visibility on Amazon, the possibility of sales on Amazon goes up.
Q. And Amazon is a big retail outlet for books, right?
A. Correct.
Q. A huge amount of books are sold on Amazon, correct?
A. Yes.
Q. And so do you believe that Amazon uses as a competitive advantage the fact that it can prioritize its own published books when people search on Amazon?
A. Yes.
Q. And that's a competitive advantage that they have, right?
A. Yes.
Q. If you could look with me at another exhibit, this one is 327, it's your tab 5, and tell me what that is.
A. Okay.
Q. What is that document?
A. This was a budget plan for fiscal 2020.

Q. And is this another budget that you participated in?
A. Yes.
MR. FISHBEIN: Your Honor, I offer Defense Exhibit 327.
THE COURT: Any objection?
MR. MATELSON: No objection.
THE COURT: That will be admitted. (Defendant's 327 received in evidence.)
MR. FISHBEIN: This is confidential. So I would ask that the monitors not show the page I am going to refer the witness to.

BY MR. FISHBEIN:

Q. But, Mr. Murray, if you could look at slide 12 and tell me when you're there.
A. Yes.
Q. The title of the slide is, changing competitive landscape, right?
A. Yes.
Q. And here you detail—and, again, this was presented to your bosses, right?
A. Correct.
Q. So you told your bosses about retail environment, right?
A. Yes.
Q. And then competitors, correct?
A. Yes.
Q. And those are competitors in book publishing, right?
A. Yes.
Q. And so you list three competitors here, right?
A. Yes.
Q. One is Penguin Random House, correct?
A. Yes.
Q. One is a publisher that is active outside the United States, right?
A. Correct.
Q. And the other, who is the other publisher that you list as a competitor?
A. Sorry, say that again.
Q. Who is the other publisher that you list as a competitor?
A. Amazon.
Q. And it says, Amazon continues to expand publishing operations. So what do you understand that to mean, that when you present it to your bosses about competitors, you said that Amazon continues to expand publishing operations?
A. Well, this was 2019, I think, when we—it would have been early 2019. I'm not sure when this was prepared. It was some time ago.
Q. Okay. What did you mean when you were telling your bosses about the competitors that Amazon continues to expand publishing operations?
A. They had launched some imprints where they were acquiring English language rights to some of the foreign language—they were expanding their direct publishing, I think, at the time.
Q. Right. And that included getting rights from major authors, correct?
A. Yes.
Q. And you said this was some time ago, but doesn't Amazon continue to compete with HarperCollins, for example, in the romance genres?
A. Yes.
Q. I'm sorry, the answer was?
A. They compete in romance, yes.
Q. It's broader than romance. Are you familiar with the category called genre fiction?
A. Yes.
Q. And that would include romance, science fiction, fantasy, westerns, mystery, correct?
A. Yes.

Q. And would you agree that to this day, Amazon is a major problem for HarperCollins, a major competitor?
A. Certainly on the romance front.
Q. You agree with that?
A. Yeah.
Q. So in connection with your bid for Simon & Schuster, did HarperCollins do any analysis around the issue of synergies?
A. Yes.
Q. And you were asked some questions by the government about the purchase price and your reaction to it. Do you remember that?
A. Yes.
Q. By the way, are you experienced in M&A. transactions?
A. Yes.
Q. Have you been involved in a number of them over your time?
A. Yes.
Q. Was part of your background that you were a business consultant?
A. Yes.
Q. And would you agree that the price that makes sense to pay for an asset can vary depending on who's purchasing it?
A. Yes.
Q. And the reason for that is because different purchasers can achieve different levels of efficiencies with the asset they purchase, is that one reason?
A. Could be, yes.
Q. So in other words, your own internal calculation of synergies can affect what makes sense for you in terms of how much you are going to offer for the asset, right?
A. Yes.
Q. And so when you were looking at Simon & Schuster, you did your own synergies analysis, right?
A. Correct.
Q. Did you have any—you, Mr. Murray, were you involved in that in any way?
A. Yes.
Q. What was your role?
A. I oversaw all of the analytical work that was done to try to develop a price.
Q. What was the process that was used to determine—and I am not going to ask you to say out loud the synergies number. I just wanted to ask about the process. What was the process that was used?
A. It's both top down and bottom up. So in some cases we can easily understand what kind of costs, additional costs, HarperCollins might have to incur to absorb parts of a target company.

So, for example, in the UK and Australia, it's very easy for us to figure out what our costs would be. We already distribute Simon & Schuster in the UK and Australia, so that's a very easy calculation for us. And then in the United States we can look at our own staffing models. And we know how many titles Simon & Schuster is publishing. We can make estimates about what kind of publishing staff we think we would need. And then in the back office in the support areas, we are able to, again, determine what incremental costs would be required for us to support that volume of business.
Q. Did you have an internal team at HarperCollins that worked on the synergies analysis?
A. Yes.
Q. Did you also have external advisers?
A. No.
Q. So it was just internal?
A. Yes.
Q. Okay. And just very roughly, how many people were involved in this exercise?
A. Maybe 15.
Q. And over what period of time did they conduct the synergies analysis?

A. I think we have done it every other year for ten years so . . .
Q. On Simon & Schuster?
A. Yes.
Q. Okay. So a lot of work went into it, fair?
A. Yeah.
Q. And focusing on the U.S., what are—you mentioned some of them. You mentioned back office was one area, right?
A. Correct.
Q. You mentioned employees was an area, right?
A. Yes.
Q. Did you look at real estate savings in the United States?
A. We did.
Q. Okay. Are there any other areas, real estate, employees, back office, anything else that you looked at that contributed to your synergies analysis?
A. No. It was all of—no, that sounds about right.
Q. Okay. If you could look at Defense Exhibit 143, please. It's tab 8.
MR. FISHBEIN: And, again, this is a confidential document, Your Honor, so we won't publish it.
THE WITNESS: Tab 8?
BY MR. FISHBEIN:
Q. Yes.
A. Okay.
Q. Do you recognize this?
A. Yes.
Q. What is it?
A. At the top, it looks like—I mean, it's a long email chain. So at the top, it's from Charlie Redmayne to me.
Q. Is this an email chain in which you give a recommendation to the CEO of HarperCollins relating to the Simon & Schuster purchase, potential purchase?
A. It's from me to the CEO of News Corporation.
Q. And it relates to the Simon & Schuster—potential Simon & Schuster acquisition, right?
A. Yes.
MR. FISHBEIN: Your Honor, I would offer Defense Exhibit 143.
THE COURT: Any objection?
MR. MATELSON: No objection.
THE COURT: That will be admitted. (Defendant's 143 received in evidence.)
BY MR. FISHBEIN:
Q. Mr. Murray, if you can look at your email on November 7, at 8:41 a.m, it's on the second page. Do you see it?
A. Yes.
Q. Okay. And in the second paragraph, I don't want you to read out the figure, but there's a sentence that says HC—it's the second sentence, I believe. It says, HC at, and then there's a figure in millions. Do you see that?
A. Yes.
Q. S&S at, and then there's a figure. Do you see that?
A. Yes.
Q. And then it says, full synergies of, and there's a figure. And then it says, over time. Do you see that?
A. Yes.
Q. So there's a number between the phrase full synergies of and over time. Do you see it?
A. Yes.
Q. What does that number reflect, Mr. Murray?
A. That would have been the cost synergies anticipated of a Simon & Schuster and HarperCollins

merger.
Q. Okay. That was the result of the work that you just described?
A. Correct, yeah.
Q. And then later down, I think it's the one, two, three, four, fifth paragraph, do you see one that says, synergy risks are minimal? Do you see that?
A. Yes.
Q. Did you believe that, at the time, that the synergies you calculated, the risks were minimal?
A. Yes.
Q. By that, what do you mean that the risks were minimal, the risk of what?
A. Achieving those synergies.
Q. So in other words, the risk that you would not actually achieve those synergies, correct?
A. Right.
Q. Have you calculated synergies in other deals?
A. Yes.
Q. Do you have kind of like sort of a baseline to go off of to figure out what synergies are possible?
A. Yes.
Q. Based on that experience, when you wrote to the CEO of News Corp., you believed your figure—you had confidence in it, right?
A. Correct.
Q. You had mentioned Bibles before. And can I just make sure I understand. Like, we talk about frontlist and backlist sometimes, right?
A. Yes.
Q. So like a Bible that was obviously written a long time ago and has been in print for a long time, that's not part of the frontlist, right?
A. How much time do you have? They republish Bibles all the time. So the Bibles are constantly being refreshed with—it could be new translations, new forwards. They're gifts. There's new covers. Bibles do—we do have a frontlist for Bibles.
Q. Would you say, though, most of your Bible sales are frontlist, backlist, do you know?
A. Backlist.
Q. Backlist. Okay.
MR. FISHBEIN: I have nothing further for now, Your Honor until the closed session.
THE COURT: Yes. I understand. Any direct for the open session?
MR. MATELSON: Yes. May I proceed?
THE COURT: Yes.

REDIRECT EXAMINATION

BY MR. MATELSON:

Q. Just a few additional questions, Mr. Murray, to follow up on the cross. Can I ask you to turn again to tab 2 in your binder. It was DX279.
Q. If you look at page 25, there was a bar chart or two bar charts there. Do you recall that?
A. Yes.
Q. All right. Do you have that in front of you? I just wanted to ask you a few questions about the data. Is the data for title count showing a U.S. title count?
A. I believe that's global.
Q. And how many countries does HarperCollins operate in?
A. Over 20.
Q. And then the same thing, same question with respect to the advance spend. Is that also global?
A. Also global.
Q. And then if you take a look at the advance spend chart on the right and look at the year-over-year growth that was projected for fiscal '22 to fiscal '23, how does that growth rate compare to the growth rate from previous years?

A. It's moderated.

Q. And then if you also look at 23—I'm sorry, when you say moderated, what do you mean by that?

A. The growth rate has slowed significantly.

Q. All right. And how would the rate of growth for '23, fiscal '23 to fiscal '24, compare to the previous years?

A. It's also a slower growth rate.

Q. And the growth that you are projecting for HarperCollins in the future, is that—are you projecting that would replace the volume of output that Simon & Schuster has today?

A. No.

Q. And then has HarperCollins changed its thinking at all on future growth rates or projections since DX279 was created?

A. Yes. Again, the biggest driver is consumer spending. That's—we have had tremendous growth, and that growth has been moderating. And so we are evaluating the rate of growth.

Q. I think I want to get into more specifics in the closed session, so I won't ask about that further right now. You were asked about whether or not advances had been increasing over the last ten years.

First, do you know whether the merger between Penguin and Random House in 2013 had any impact on advances in the industry one way or the other?

A. I don't know.

Q. I believe you were trying to clarify a point with Mr. Fishbein about the advance levels and what you were thinking. Can you explain what you were trying to clarify?

A. Yes. Sometimes advances, and maybe I misheard, but sometimes they can refer to individual projects, whether the advances go up or down or whether it's an aggregate for HarperCollins or whether it's an aggregate for the industry. So sometimes, I wasn't quite sure what the question was.

Q. You were also asked about a recent acquisition of the HMH trade book business. I was wondering if you could compare sort of the relative size of that business to the size of Simon & Schuster's trade business?

A. Yeah. It's about probably a little less than a quarter of the size.

Q. You were also shown an annual report written by News Corporation. And there was a statement, I think you were shown, about, well, competition and barriers to entry. Do you recall that?

A. (Nodding head.)

Q. Was the annual report addressing at all the market that we are discussing in this trial sort of the higher advance trade books?

A. No. I believe it was written by my CFO with regard to the entire HarperCollins global business.

Q. You were also asked a few questions about synergies that you projected in 2020 for a potential merger acquisition between Simon & Schuster.

As part of that exercise, did you project any revenue synergies that would accrue to HarperCollins?

A. We did not.

Q. And do you typically include revenue synergies in merger projections?

A. We do not.

Q. What is the rationale? Why don't you do that?

A. It's very difficult to size them, and we try to focus on the cost side of the equation because we are very certain when we size synergies we know what we can do on the cost side. And then if we have revenue opportunities, that's just—that's great. But we don't count on them in our financial modeling.

Q. Do you model a change or an improvement in the return rates of books in your synergies analysis?

A. I don't believe we did with Simon & Schuster, no.

Q. Have you looked at or updated the Synergies analysis for Simon & Schuster since the fall of 2020?

A. No.

Q. All right. So would you have any knowledge of whether Simon & Schuster's cost structure may have changed since then?

A. No.

Q. I believe you were also asked a little bit about Amazon Publishing. And I think you were shown a

2020 budget document on that. Do you recall that?

A. Yes.

Q. And can you just clarify, when does the fiscal year begin and end for HarperCollins?

A. It begins July 1 and ends June 30, and we just began fiscal year '23 this past month.

Q. So the budget for fiscal year 2020 would be set when approximately?

A. In 2019.

Q. All right. And since that document was written, do you have an assessment of—what is your current assessment of Amazon Publishing as a competitor for general trade books, particularly, I guess, at the higher advance levels that we are talking about in this case?

A. They have not been a competitor for big books.

Q. And what's your basis for saying that?

A. We've not come up against them in any auctions. I am not aware of any times we have lost any books to Amazon or that they have even been bidding for big books.

THE COURT: When you say big books, how are you defining that?

THE WITNESS: Basically when it comes up to my threshold, those are the ones I would be aware of.

MR. MATELSON: Your Honor, I think I have concluded with my public redirect. Unless there are other questions, I am happy to move into closed session at this point.

THE COURT: I have a couple of questions. There were some questions posed to you about your decision to offer bigger advances and that you publicized that you were going to do that. And I was just wondering, why would you publicize that? Why wouldn't you just go into the auction, spend more, and win more books?

THE WITNESS: At the time, we saw this amazing increase in consumer spending in books as the pandemic hit, and we wanted to put everyone on notice in the industry, the agents, prospective authors, that we were being aggressive during this time.

Some other publishers during the pandemic, I believe, pulled back a little bit, and we were going in the opposite direction. We felt that with the pie of spending, the amount of money consumers were spending in the U.S. growing that much, it was a terrific time to be expanding organically. So there's no better way than to make a statement like that to get the message out to all the agents in the industry.

THE COURT: And you sort of have a budget that you have projected that you are going to spend on advances each year. If the overall level of advances went down because of this merger or otherwise, what would you do? Would you just spend below your budget, or would you just use your budget and acquire more books than you otherwise would have? How would that affect your budgeting?

THE WITNESS: It's so hard to say. So when we do a budget, the budget is detailed for the next fiscal year. And it's almost title by title. And so we know exactly what our fiscal '23 plans are. And when we get out to '24 and '25, there's a lot of estimating that's going on. So we take a view on what do we think—how fast is the market going to grow. Our job is to grow faster than the market and to develop a plan to do that. And so some of the outcomes of that are, again, cash, the amount of money we are going to spend on infrastructure, the amount of money we are going to spend on author advances. It has to be—our model, when you get to the outer years, has to be internally consistent. It has to make sense.

THE COURT: Even for next year, say, you are in a year and it turns out you are acquiring the books you wanted and paying less than you thought you would have had to because all the advances have come down, what would you do with that excess money?

THE WITNESS: Oh, again, I mean, it's hard for me to say, because it's not like we are going to know that we are—we are not going to know, oh, we got these 50 books for less money than we otherwise would have. I don't know if I would know that in a quarter or two after an advance, after a possible merger. It would take time for us to see, how is our business performing, what kind of flow-through from our revenues are we getting in profits, and then also cash because your profits don't always translate into cash. It just depends on the mix of your books. So it's not a—there's not a, I'm going to know at a certain point in time how am I going to change how I run the business or how would I reallocate the cash flow that comes out of the business.

THE COURT: So you are not getting sort of realtime reports back, we are winning these and we are prepared to offer X, but we only had to pay Y and make decisions midyear?

THE WITNESS: No.

THE COURT: You wait until the end of the year and decide for next year?

THE WITNESS: Yeah. Auctions are going fast and furious. It's not really until you get to the end of the year when you total up and say how did we do, did we do better, did we do worse. Often it can be the difference of two or three books totally changes the financial performance of the company. It's often hard to generalize about what we are going to do in the future. But our plan, we always try to have a plan where we are going to grow faster than the market, and we figure out, how are we going to do it, in which areas, where do we feel like we have opportunity. And we usually put more money into those areas to try to grow the business.

THE COURT: I see. Thank you. Any questions based on my questioning?

MR. MATELSON: Nothing from me, Your Honor.

MR. FISHBEIN: No, Your Honor.

PART THREE: TESTIMONY OF DEFENSE WITNESSES

JENNIFER RUDOLPH WALSH

The defense opened their case with former literary agent Jennifer Rudolph Walsh, whom they compensated handsomely for her declaration and testimony. Walsh told the court how important love, dreams, and art are to the publishing industry, rather than just the financials, and the informal nature of most business deals—all of which seemed to surprise Judge Pan.

Walsh explained that an agent is a "curator" for a publisher who finds the content, and has a fiduciary relationship with authors. They are "honor bound to act in the best interest of our clients." In explaining exclusive submissions and pre-empts, she said that making a "perfect match" is "like a badge of honor."

Contrary to every working member of the business who has testified so far, Walsh did not consider "best bids" to be an auction. "An auction to me is where people are bidding against one another. Whereas, a best-bids is each editor is just coming forward with their best offer and they're not bidding against one another. . . . So to me that's not an auction."

Under that definition, she didn't hold many auctions as an agent. And her best bids situations required "just one enthusiastic editor"—a single bidder, not three or more. She also wouldn't necessarily send to a large number of potential bidders, since that would get an unfinished work out more widely. "Remember, it's a draft."

Judge Pan asked if there are confidentiality agreements or ethics about submissions. "There's ethics," Walsh said, but there are also scouts, and "it's their job to sort of try to grab material. And so you just have to be careful." But "we don't sign an NDA with our editors. It's a good faith business."

Later, Walsh also explained to the court how options work, and that authors who want to switch publishers respect the option clause to be "honorably released" from their publisher. "Is there an actual formal release from the option?" Pan asked. Not usually, it's informal [like everything.] "If you have an author who wants to move and you just send her to another editor, is that poaching?" Pan asked. Walsh said poaching is "one of those funny words that sounds bigger than it actually is." "Does that mean you can move an author from one Penguin Random House imprint to another Penguin Random House imprint?" "Yes."

Walsh also said that the best deal for a book is not necessarily for the most money—which is why "every agent that I'm aware of closes the [auction] letter with, we reserve the right to decide what constitutes the best offer." She was "not always looking to get every dollar out of an editor." "We want to get to a place where the editor is maybe paying, ideally, a little more than they wanted to and the author is getting more than she expected to, but that the relationship feels healthy and everybody is excited and sort of rowing in the same direction."

Pan asked, "how's that consistent with your fiduciary duty to your author that you're not trying to get the most money for that author?" Walsh said that the duty was to find the best deal for a client. "The best offer is not necessarily the highest offer," she said.

Walsh believes that, if PRH were to renege on their bidding pledge, it would be detrimental enough to their relationships with agents that there would be an effect on competition. "That broken trust would be costly," she said. "I think that agents would not feel comfortable in the same way with that broken trust, and they would communicate that with their authors. And I feel that the editors would also feel like they had been misled and could potentially leave, and authors and agents would follow them."

Walsh supported the defense's assertions that small publishers, Amazon, and self-publishing are all competitors to the Big 5. "It's an exciting time for new entrants in the publishing industry," her examples even including, "There's a publishing house called Open Road which was traditionally an ebook publisher, but their new CEO, David Steinberger, is extremely dedicated to books, so I would say watch the space on that as well." More on point, she said that Zando's forthcoming novel *The Butcher and the Wren*, by Alaina Urquhart sold 43,000 pre-orders "with a single post on Instagram."

Amazon's publishing business wasn't popular in the industry, Walsh said. "It almost became like selling to them was like crossing a petition line," she said, but they could course correct. "They have the money and the marketing power." She also said that she "gasped" when she heard the $40 million total of Brandon Sanderson's Kickstarter. "I think it will be a wave of the future." At the same time, under cross,

Walsh confirmed Dr. Hill's finding that only about 10 percent of ATSB go to publishers outside of the Big 5: "I think it's because they pick their shots, and they don't bid at that level often, but when they do, I think they are very effective. Ten percent of the time, that sounds right to me."

When asked if a large publisher's backlist gives them a greater ability to absorb losses, Walsh said, "A backlist is just money. So it's not like a backlist helps you any other way except that it's funding. So a well-funded organization, whether it's small or new, can absorb the same thing."

Often, Walsh disagreed with literary agent Ayesha Pande's testimony from earlier in the trial. Pande said that when lots of publishers are bidding, usually smaller publishers aren't involved. "It's just not consistent with my experience. It's really specific to the project," Walsh said. While Pande said that she always submits to both PRH and S&S when she sends her books wide, Walsh said, "Agents submit to editors and imprints. So when you're making a submission list, you're not only thinking of the umbrella level. It would not be necessary for us to think in terms of what the umbrella company was. The answer for me would be no." (Though if Walsh always submits to editors at any of PRH or S&S's combined 138 imprints, the answer would be yes.)

Defense attorney Abby Rudzin asked Walsh about Dr. Hill's assertion that "agents don't have a magic wand." She replied, "I actually do have a magic wand that was given to me by my author Sue Monk Kidd who said I was magic." On the main point, however, Walsh actually agreed with Hill: When Pan asked, "In a situation, hypothetically, where the publisher was willing to pay $750,000 and the agent just asked for 250 and that's what they got, would you think that that agent had done a good job in that deal?" Walsh said no.

One line of cross-examination established for the record that once upon a time, advances were paid in advance of publication, in two installments, and now PRH and others commonly pay a guarantee, in four installments.

In a tense back-and-forth, Judge Pan insisted on Walsh admitting the difference between "hope" and "expectation" of an anticipated top seller.

Judge Pan: Okay. I just want to push you on that. You are saying that you never anticipate that a book that you are marketing is going to be a best seller or top seller?

Walsh: I would say I always anticipate that what I am working on is going to be a best seller. . . .

Judge Pan: So you think every book you work on is going to be a best seller or a top seller? I just want to make sure I'm understanding this.

Walsh: No. I think every book that I work on has the potential to break out.

Judge Pan: That's not the question. It's called anticipated best sellers that you expect to be a best seller. And you are telling me every book you work on you anticipate to be a top seller? I just want to make sure I'm understanding you.

Walsh: Again, this is a category that doesn't exist. For me, I don't have an anticipated top seller category, so I am putting myself in the mind space of that. I will say that I don't sell books that I think this will be okay. I sell books that I believe in and think that they have an ability to find a big audience or find a prize-worthy mention or I—you know, that's the way I approach my representation. . . . What I meant to say is all of them could be, is how I meant it.

Pan: Right, but that's not the question.

Walsh: I understand the distinction.

Counsel later asked why Walsh wanted to testify in this trial (presumably aside from her declared fee of at least $250,000, against a rate of $2,000 per hour and $10,000 per day at trial, which she reconfirmed in cross-examination). "Because this is about an industry that I love and that is sacred to me," she said. "And I felt that there was a fundamental misunderstanding as if we were describing the forest without the root systems, without the understory and the overstory, which is one of, you know, love and a calling. And so I just wanted to represent that here."

TESTIMONY OF JENNIFER RUDOLPH WALSH

DIRECT EXAMINATION

BY MS. ABBY RUDZIN:

Q. Ms. Walsh, can you please state your full name for the record.

A. Jennifer Rudolph Walsh.

Q. Please tell us how you started in publishing.

A. I started as a summer intern for Virginia Barber at the Virginia Barber Literary Agency my junior year in college. And I fell so in love with book publishing—and, fortunately, Virginia fell in love with me too. So she hired me to work full-time, and from my senior-year dorm room, I was her assistant. And then I graduated on a Saturday and began work full-time for her that Monday, and that was 1989.

Q. How long did you stay at the Virginia Barber Literary Agency?

A. I stayed there until I bought the business in 1997 and renamed it the Writers Shop.

Q. And how long were you at the Writers Shop?

A. I was at the Writers Shop from '97 to 2001 when I sold the Writers Shop to William Morris Agency.

Q. And what is William Morris Agency?

A. The William Morris Agency is the oldest entertainment agency in the world, over 120 years old.

Q. After you sold the Writers Shop to William Morris, did you continue to work there?

A. I did. I went over there as the head of their book division.

Q. And did you have a title or other roles at William Morris?

A. Yes. I was the global head of the book division; and I also had the honor of being the first woman ever on the board of directors, as well as the youngest person ever.

Q. While you had these executive responsibilities, did you continue to act as a literary agent?

A. Always.

Q. About how many deals would you say you did?

A. It would vary year to year, but between, I'd say, 50 and a hundred.

Q. Per year?

A. Per year.

Q. What was the size of the literary department at WMA?

A. When I got there, it was quite small. But during the course of my tenure, we grew and grew and, ultimately—sort of, 20 to 25 agents altogether and then support staff.

Q. Did you have a role in supervising those 20 to 25 agents?

A. Yes, I did.

Q. What was that role?

A. I oversaw all of their deals, and I strategized for growth possibilities. I did their evaluations and I weighed in on their bonuses.

Q. Did you personally get involved in any of their actual deals?

A. I did. I had a thing that I would say to them, which is, "Come to me for the four Cs." So the first C was the creation of the relationship, or otherwise known as signing. The second one was contracts. Anything that had to do with contractual issues. The third was crisis, which is pretty self-explanatory. And the fourth was celebration. So that was where I would be.

Q. Okay. And just to be clear, when you talk about the creation of the relationship and the signing, what are you talking about?

A. Agents signing clients.

Q. So before the agent has sold any books?

A. Exactly or—yes.

Q. And how long did you work at William Morris?

A. I worked at William Morris from 2001 to 2009 when I was on a small executive board committee that merged William Morris with Endeavor, forming WME.

Q. And did you continue to work at WME after the merger?

A. I did.

Q. What was your role?
A. I remained a literary agent, and I remained the global head of the book division. And I added lectures and theater to my oversight.
Q. Did you remain on the board?
A. I did.
Q. What can you tell us about WME's book division?
A. It's amazing. It's the largest content provider. It publishes about 200 books a year, a third of which are *New York Times* best sellers, and it does about a thousand deals globally per year.
Q. A thousand book deals?
A. Yes.
Q. Thank you. Are you still at WME today?
A. I'm not.
Q. And why have you left?
A. I left at the end of 2019 to focus on a women's tour that I had founded four years earlier called Together Live; and this was a tour that went around the country with a diverse and inclusive group of women sharing their stories of courage and resilience. And so I left to focus on that.
Q. And are you still working on Together Live?
A. Sadly, I closed it during the pandemic.
Q. So what have you been doing with your time since then?
A. Well, I've been selling—smelling the roses for the first time in my entire life. I published a book of essays from the speakers from Together Live called *Hungry Hearts* that I wrote the introduction for, and I've been doing a tiny amount of consulting.
Q. And what are you here to testify about today?
A. I'm here to testify about the publishing industry as a whole and, specifically, the literary agent's role within that industry.
MS. RUDZIN: Your Honor, based on this foundation of Ms. Walsh's experience and qualifications, defendants move that Ms. Walsh be accepted as an expert on the publishing industry and the role of the agent in it.
THE COURT: Any objection?
MR. READ: No objection to being qualified as an expert as a literary agent—Experience as a literary agent in the industry; experience in that sense.
THE COURT: Okay. Were you planning to go beyond that at all, Ms. Rudzin?
MS. RUDZIN: No.
THE COURT: Okay. Then I will qualify her as an expert as a literary agent. Thank you.
BY MS. RUDZIN:
Q. Ms. Walsh, can you please describe for the Court the role of the literary agent in the publishing industry.
A. The literary agent finds the author, then helps the author decide what is the form that they want to submit to a publisher, and then helps make the match between the author and the publisher. And once that match is made, the literary agent stays involved through the publication; as well as exploits other ancillary rights of the book, like movie rights, foreign translation rights, TV rights, podcast rights, et cetera.
Q. Do literary agents owe any duties to their clients?
A. Yes. Literary agents are a fiduciary, which means that we are honor bound to act in the best interest of our clients.
Q. So I think you said that one of the things literary agents do is sell book rights. Can you tell us about that process.
A. Absolutely. So—well, a majority—if you're an experienced agent, a majority of the book deals that you're doing are likely to be for authors who already have a publisher. So if that's the case, you would be negotiating with the existing publisher, perhaps; or if it's a new author or an author who does have a track record but wishes to move. That's—those are the most common three things that a literary agent is doing.
Q. So let's talk about the process for a debut author. How does that start?

A. Well, it starts when you find the author, which is an important role that literary agents play for the publisher, is that we're the curator. We receive many, many submissions, and we only choose the things that we are very enthusiastic about. So when you decide to sell a book, the first thing you do is start talking about it, and you—we call this pre-seeding or creating buzz. You go out for lunch with editors, you talk about the book, and you start getting feedback. And you might start getting some information about comparison titles or the perfect editor.

Q. What happens after the agent pre-seeds the marketplace?

A. Then the agent works with the author to determine what is the best form of the submissions. So it could be a sample chapter. It could be a table of contents. It could be a partial manuscript. So essentially, the submission is a sales tool. So you want to put your best foot forward. So you try to determine what that is.

Q. For fiction authors, is it generally a complete manuscript?

A. You know, I would say commonly, for a first-time author, it would be a complete manuscript, but even with first-time authors, you can submit a partial if it's really strong.

Q. What does the agent do next after it determines the actual form of the submission?

A. Then the agent decides how they want to submit it. So do they want to submit it exclusively to one person or to two people, or do they want to go out—we call it wide.

Q. If the agent goes wide, does the agent include more than one editor at the same publishing house on the list of people to send it to?

A. Oh, absolutely. An agent isn't submitting to a publishing house. An agent is submitting to editors and imprints.

Q. How many imprints are there for agents to consider making submissions to?

A. Hundreds.

Q. And how many editors are available for the agent to submit to?

A. Hundreds.

Q. How many editors does the agent typically submit a book to?

A. There is no typical. And I know that's strange, but every book is different; and, therefore, every submission process is different. So we're not—we're not looking for the largest amount of submissions. We're looking for the perfect match.

Q. How does the agent decide whom to include on the submission list?

A. Well, a big—a big responsibility of an agent is having relationships in the publishing business. And so agents know editors very well, and they know their background, and they know what books they love and what books they've published or missed out on. So that deep knowledge helps us create what I call a bespoke submission list. So if I'm doing a book about a cult and I happen to know an editor who grew up in a cult, then, you know—then I have information that would help me make that perfect match.

Q. Ms. Walsh, have you been watching the trial?

A. I was here Monday and Tuesday.

Q. Have you read transcripts of the last week?

A. I've reviewed partial transcripts.

Q. Did you review Ms. Pande's testimony?

A. Yes, I did.

Q. Ms. Pande testified that when she submits her books widely, she always submits to Penguin Random House and Simon & Schuster. Do you recall that testimony?

A. Yes.

Q. In your view, do agents always submit their books to both Penguin Random House and Simon & Schuster?

A. Agents submit to editors and imprints. So when you're making a submission list, you're not only thinking of the umbrella level. So it would not be necessary for us to think in terms of what the umbrella company was. The answer for me would be no.

Q. You mentioned that an agent might submit projects to only a single editor. Why would an agent ever do that?

A. I know this is going to sound very counterintuitive, but it's very exciting for us to make a perfect match. And if you feel that you know exactly who's right for the book and you send it to them, it's like a badge of honor. So we love to do that.

Q. And why are agents focused on finding what you call the perfect match rather than just selling the book to someone who will pay a lot of money for it?

A. Well writers are artists, and whatever they've created represents their heart. It's a sacred work of art, and so it really matters. And not only that, but the collaboration between the editor and the author has a very outcome in terms of the books. So a good match is good business.

Q. What happens if the agent sends the project to only one editor and they can't do a deal?

A. Well, likely in that situation, the editor will have given generous editorial feedback, because editors are incredibly generous about books. So it might be that you take that feedback and tweak the project a little. I've done that and gone back to the same editor—or you move on. There are plenty of fish in the sea.

Q. What would you do if you were moving on?

A. Well, it depends if I thought I want to go another single submission or if I want to go out wider. So for the sake of this, let's say I'm going out wider. Then I would create my submission list.

Q. And what happens after the agent has created her submission list?

A. Then you call everybody on the list and you pitch the book verbally. And that's giving you more information. I mean, an editor will say to you on the phone, I think this sounds better for a colleague of mine, or an editor you can see just isn't responding. So the whole time you're making your calls, you're polishing your final submission list.

Once you're done with that, then you write the personalized cover note. And that's just "Great to have lunch with you the other day. You know, as discussed . . ." And then you have an elevator pitch, for lack of a better word, describing the book. You'll use some favorable comparison titles. We call those comps. And then you press send and you—with all your best hopes, and you wait.

Q. Does the author ever meet any of the editors?

A. Yes. So once the editors start coming to you with their reactions, you determine whether you think an author meeting would be a good idea, and sometimes you suggest meetings. Sometimes the editor suggests meetings. But you don't always let the author meet with everybody, because, for one thing, it's a fragile part of the process. And if an editor has a strong constructive criticism that you feel like is not going to be in alignment with the author, you sort of try to—you want the author to have the truth, but you also protect the process so that the fragility of that early creative period is not crushed.

Q. But, presumably, editors want to meet the author before they make a bid. So if you're limiting the meetings, you're limiting the numbers of bidders; right?

A. Yeah, you could be, because—again, with the counterintuitive; but more isn't necessarily more in this process. And so you just want to make sure that you're really making the best matches. And then it's from the matches that you look for the best offer. But the match is certainly multiple truths. It's just as important as the—as the advance level, and in some cases even more important.

Q. Okay. So the author has meetings with editors. Now it's a more narrowed list. Then what happens?

A. So sometimes after one of these meetings, an editor is so excited and the author is so excited that you just say, okay, this is the one this is—this is my true love, and this is what I want. And the agent might decide to just negotiate exclusively with that editor. Some people call that inviting a preempt, just to give you the language.

Q. Why would the agent invite a preempt or choose to negotiate with just a single editor when there are potentially other editors interested?

A. Well, if it's an absolute dream match for the author, if both the editor and the imprint are exactly right for the author's priorities and even dreams, then it's really just about coming to a good number where everybody feels happy. And the agent goes into it with a pretty good working understanding of what the book is worth. And the agent has been collecting information the whole way, you know; hearing from every editor, getting their feedback. So they've honed that expectation. And, honestly, preempts, sometimes you actually even do better than if you had gone to auction. Because it's very exciting for the editor to preempt a process, and you get to a very good place, and you declare a victory. Everybody is very happy in those situations.

Q. Well, assuming the author wants a particular editor and everybody is happy and all that kind of stuff, how does the agent know that she's getting the most advance she can get from that editor?

A. Well, experience and skill helps. But the truth is that we're not always looking to take every single dollar out of the editor's pocket. We want to get to a place where the editor is maybe paying, ideally, a little more than they wanted to and the author is getting more than she expected to, but that the relationship feels healthy and everybody is excited and sort of rowing in the same direction.

THE COURT: Can I ask how's that consistent with your fiduciary duty to your author that you're not trying to get the most money for that author?

THE WITNESS: Thank you so much for that question. Because our closing note; every agent that I'm aware of closes the letter with 'we reserve the right to decide what constitutes the best offer.' So it tells you a lot about our culture that we all use this sentence. Because the best offer may not necessarily be the highest dollar amount, but it's the best offer from the best editor at the best imprint for that author.

THE COURT: So you interpret fiduciary duty to be the best offer, but not necessarily the most money?

THE WITNESS: Exactly. The best offer isn't necessarily the highest offer. It can be, but it's not necessary for it to be. And all imprints are not created equal for the author. So if you're a literary author, being with Knopf or Farrar, Straus, might bring you prizes and things that are ultimately worth more to you in the fullness of time.

THE COURT: Thank you.

BY MS. RUDZIN:

Q. I think you said maybe an editor would pay a premium in a preempt. Do you have an understanding as to why?

A. Well, they don't want to risk losing the book. And if the book goes to an auction or to a best-bid situation there's risk; and if they really love it, they're really going to fight hard for it.

Q. You seem to be—have just distinguished between a best-bids and an auction. Isn't a best-bids a type of auction?

A. You know, not in my opinion. In my opinion, it's a process. So an auction to me is where people are bidding against one another. Whereas, a best-bids is each editor is just coming forward with their best offer and they're not bidding against one another. It's just they're bidding directly for the book. So to me that's not an auction.

THE COURT: So I was thinking about what you said about your fiduciary duty. But wouldn't it be your fiduciary duty to get that editor—the one that's the best fit for the most money?

THE WITNESS: Well, we are trying to get the most money from that editor but, do we know if we've gotten every last dollar? No. It's an art and a science. So you push it as far as you can until you get to a place where—again, these are people you know and you've done business with in the past—until you get to the place where you feel like this is—this is the right stop. And as I said, it's an art and a science. It's something that you feel.

THE COURT: Why wouldn't you go to auction and test the market and then try to get more money out of the one you want to go with anyway?

THE WITNESS: Well, once I've gone to auction, then I've lost my ability to have this hope and potential with this—with this one person who's very excited and very aggressively willing to take it off the table. I can't put the genie back in the bottle. So once I've gone to auction, I've lost my ability to have white space for where the advance is.

THE COURT: Could you explain that, because I thought they can also participate in the auction, too?

THE WITNESS: Well, they can, but if they come to the auction—let's put best bids aside for a second. If they come to the auction and I have a lot of people that are bidding low and slow, they might feel they don't have to go anywhere near what that original preemptive number was. So I've lost that ability to go back and negotiate exclusively.

THE COURT: Okay. So I guess it could go either way, because the auction could go above the preempt.

THE WITNESS: It can. It can. You just don't know. It's a chance that you're taking. And so with your experience and with your skill, and with your relationships and your understanding of the marketplace, you make your best educated guess.

THE COURT: And is your guess mostly based on comps?

THE WITNESS: It's comps. But since no two books are alike, comps are not really a perfect best guess. So for many agents, they use other things as well. It matters who the author is. It matters what their platform is. It matters who they know. It matters how charismatic they are. So you're kind of factoring all that stuff in, and you come to a—come to a place that you feel like it's a generous, fair number. And if you get that number from the right editor at the right imprint, then it's obviously the author's final decision, but you support that decision.

THE COURT: Okay. Thank you.

THE WITNESS: Thank you.

BY MS. RUDZIN:

Q. So turning to the auction or best bids, does the agent ask for anything in terms of a bid besides the advance amount?

A. Yes. Agents generally ask for a marketing plan, a love letter. They want to know what the scope of rights are that the—that the person is buying. In other words, world rights or U.S./Canada or whatever the scope is. They want to know how many books they're looking to buy. And all of that is presented at once in a best-bids situation.

Q. So let's talk about a couple of those. Why would the agent ask for a marketing plan?

A. Well, it's aspirational. And I know you've learned about the P&L's also aspirational. But it gives the author and the agent some sense of how the editor and the publisher is seeing the book.

Q. How, if at all, does that marketing plan that comes with the bids resemble how the bid—the book is actually marketed?

A. Well, actually, probably not so much because it could be one to three years later when the book is being published. So a marketing plan that was three years ago wouldn't have TikTok on it, for example. So things change a lot, and the book is often acquired. It's just—it's just a partial or it's a proposal. Now it's a full manuscript and a full book, and the publisher is getting reads from their booksellers and from people in their publicity department. They have a much better sense at that time what the actual marketing plan will be.

Q. Does the agent ever go back to the marketing plan that was submitted with the bids and say to the editor: You promised to do this. Why aren't you doing this?

A. If it served our author, we would, but, no, I can't think of an instance where we've done that. I mean, in the old days where you used to get a guaranteed—if you got a guaranteed ad in *The New York Times*, which was the big gold ring years ago, then, of course, that's something that you would go back and say: Hey, where's my ad? But nobody runs ads in *The New York Times* in the same way anymore.

Q. And in your experience when you're negotiating contracts, do you get a commitment from the publisher about how much money will be spent on marketing in the future?

A. It's rare, but you can.

Q. You also referred to a love letter. What does that mean in this context?

A. Well, you've heard a lot of people talk about love and passion in this courtroom. And a love letter could be the deciding factor for an author. It's written by the editor about how they feel about the work and why they want to publish it. And sometimes it has some feedback too and compares it to other books. And, I mean, those letters mean the world to authors.

Q. Turning back to best bids, what information does a bidding editor have about other potential bidders in a best-bids process?

A. None. They bid completely blind.

Q. How many editors need to be interested in a book for there be to a best-bids process?

A. Just one enthusiastic editor.

Q. Would the agent tell the editor she's the only bidder?

A. I can't imagine why she would.

Q. Ms. Pande testified that she would need more than two interested editors to run a best-bids process.

Do you recall that testimony?

A. Yes.

Q. And what is your response?

A. I don't understand it. Because in the best-bid process, the way I understand it, they're just putting the bid on the table; so I don't know why you would need more than one.

Q. Is it true that the more bidders the agent has participating in a best-bids process, the higher the advance offers will be?

A. It's actually not true. And, again, I know this is counterintuitive, but more is not necessarily more. And one of the reasons I love best bids and so many agents love best bids is because you're not getting competition with an editor competing with another editor. You're just seeing their clean take of the book. And you'll get one offer for a hundred thousand dollars, say three for $200,000, and then one for a million, and you're like, wow. This person sees this book very differently. And beauty is in the eye of the beholder.

Q. Is every best-bids process a single round?

A. No. There's another variation on best bids, which I would call an auction, which we call better best. And that tends to be a two-round auction, although even that can go a third round, if that's what the agent wants.

Q. In that multi-round best-bid auction, does every editor that wants to get to move on to the next round?

A. Well, it depends on what the agent decides. So sometimes, yes, all are welcome; and sometimes agents tell the bidders in advance that only two people are going to go to the next round. And she'll do that to create some competitive pressure so that people don't come in with a low first bid.

Q. Wouldn't it be to the agent's advantage to have more bidders even in the second round?

A. I'm going to sound like a broken record here. More isn't necessarily more. What the agent is trying to do is to get the most enthusiastic editor from the best imprint for that book and then create the best opportunity for a good offer or a great offer from that person. So the enthusiasm is a very big piece of that, and so it only takes two to keep going.

Q. In a multi-round best bid, does the agent tell the editors how many bidders there were in the previous round or how many are being invited to the next round?

A. You know, the agent decides this, but unless it's in the author's best interest to pass on the information, they don't.

Q. Does the agent tell editors going into the next round what the bids were in the previous round?

A. Again, it's agent-specific; but, generally no. They would probably just be more directional. Like, you're going to have to come up; but, generally, no.

Q. So let's turn to round-robin auctions. How many rounds are they usually?

A. There's no usual. Every situation is different.

Q. How does a round-robin auction end?

A. Well it can end a few different ways. Perhaps the agent feels that people are running out of gas; and you can feel that. They're taking longer to call you back. They're coming up in smaller increments. So you get a sense that they're losing some momentum.

Sometimes, also, you might see that you're heading into a situation where the only bidders that are left are imprints of PRH. And PRH has a policy where the imprints could bid against each other in a round-robin auction until it's just PRH imprints. So there has to be an external bidder. So if the agent feels like they might be losing their external bidder, they might just go to best bids as a way of ending the auction. And it's also possible that at any time during the auction, the agent just decides to negotiate with one person exclusively.

Q. If the agent calls for best bids when she believes that only Penguin Random House imprints will put in a better bid, is that a violation of the Penguin Random House rule?

A. Not to my understanding.

Q. Will the agent ever share how many bidders there are in a round-robin auction?

A. You know, it's the agent's decision to share, but unless it really serves their author, they don't. And finding out the number can cut both ways.

Q. How so?

A. Well again, intuitively, you think the more people the better. But, actually, it sometimes has the unintended consequence of making people feel like they don't want to compete. And it also gets your material out there in a way that you can't control. And, remember, this is still just a draft.

Q. Will the agent ever share who the other bidders are in a round-robin auction?

A. Very rarely. I mean, it would have to serve the author. Maybe so if there were some rivalry that they were trying to spur on, perhaps, but very rarely.

THE COURT: Aren't there confidentiality agreements about the draft? You said once you put the draft out, you can't control it. Aren't there ethics about that?

THE WITNESS: Well, there's ethics, of course, but—I don't want to get too confusing. But there's a thing called literary scouts, and they work for TV companies, film companies, foreign publishers, and it's their job to sort of try to grab material. And so you just have to be careful. We don't sign—we don't sign NDAs with our editors. It's a trust—it's a good-faith business.

THE COURT: Okay. Thanks.

BY MS. RUDZIN:

Q. Have you read Mr. Pietsch's testimony?

A. Yes.

Q. Mr. Pietsch testified that round-robin auctions are the most common form of auction. Do you recall that testimony?

A. Yeah. I was surprised by that.

Q. Why?

A. Because it's—it's been so many years since, really, that was the common way of doing things. And most of my colleagues and most of my associates seem to do best bids or better best.

Q. And why do you think there's been that shift of best bids?

A. I think people like the idea of just sort of seeing the whole story and—rather than seeing how people could potentially get auction fever about something and end up with remorse because they ended up paying for something that doesn't come in the way they wanted it to; and it could—it could negatively affect the book.

Q. Once the deal is final, does the agent share the outcome with other bidders in the auction?

A. The agent decides. You know, many don't, and at most, they would share just the winner.

Q. So we've been talking about the process for a debut author. Is it different for a repeat author that wants to leave her publisher?

A. Yes and no. So if it's a repeat author that wants to leave their publisher, they have something in their contract called an option clause. And the option clause, while it's not binding, most agents respect and honor that clause. So even if the author wishes to leave, you still might submit a synopsis of a book or try to get into some conversation with the existing publisher. And you don't have to take any offer. You just want to respect that period of time and, sort of, be honorably released from your option clause. And then it depends. You might do an exclusive submission to somebody who's been a fan of that author for a long period of time, or you might decide to go out slightly wider.

THE COURT: I'm sorry. Is there an actual formal release from the option clause?

THE WITNESS: No. It's informal. I mean, sometimes people ask for it in writing, but it really isn't necessary.

THE COURT: So can you explain that. You send it to your former editor, and then there has to be an actual conversation you are released?

THE WITNESS: Yes. Yes.

THE COURT: Okay.

THE WITNESS: I mean sometimes you leave and tell the editor from the beginning: This person doesn't want to continue. And often if it's gone wrong, it could be mutual, in which case they won't even review the material and they'll just say go with God.

THE COURT: Okay.

BY MS. RUDZIN:

Q. Does the option clause require the author to sell the book to the publisher with the option?

A. No.

Q. It's just for that first look; right?

A. It's a first look and an exclusive period. You can even accept an offer less than from—if they make an offer and you don't accept it and then you go out and accept an offer less than, that's fine too.

Q. If you have an author who wants to move and you just send her to another editor, is that poaching?

A. First of all, it's not. Poaching is one of those funny words that sounds bigger than what it actually is. I mean really what poaching is is telling somebody you're a fan of their work, which editors do all the time. You know, I know so-and-so is under contract, but I'm a big fan. And all that means is that when it's time to move, you know who the fans are, and you factor that fandom into your submission strategy.

Q. Does that mean you can move an author from one Penguin Random House imprint to another Penguin Random House imprint?

A. Yes.

Q. So let's just finish up with repeat authors. You said most book deals are for repeat authors. Do you have a more precise estimate?

A. Well if you're 30 years into your career, 75 to 80 percent of your authors are repeat. And a big role of the literary agent is keeping publishers and agents—pardon me—and authors in happy relationships. So an ideal is that you find a home for life.

Q. And if the author does want to stay with her editor, how does the agent sell the right to the author's next book?

A. In an exclusive negotiation with that editor.

Q. Does the agent threaten to take the author elsewhere to get the editor to put more money on the table?

A. Let's think of it this way: Competition is a dial, and the agent has their hand on the dial the whole entire time. So if we want to, call a rounds auction a ten on the dial, because it's the most overt competition. An exclusive negotiation, it might be at a one to two, but the editor is still completely aware of the fact that the agent can take the author elsewhere. So, no, you would very rarely threaten to leave. Because, remember, these are close, intimate relationships. An editor might stay at an author's house for a few days while they're editing their book together.

These are generally—in the best-case scenario, these are happy, intimate relationships, and so it's not a contentious thing.

Q. Have you reviewed Dr. Hill's testimony from yesterday?

A. Yes.

Q. Or, actually, now it might be the day before.

A. I just lost track of days, but, yes.

Q. Dr. Hill testified that agents don't have a magic wand to prevent harm to authors and cited as evidence of that examples where from the documents he could tell that an editor had money left in her pocket after she acquired a book. Do you recall that testimony?

A. I do.

MR. READ: Objection, Your Honor.

THE COURT: And what's the objection?

MR. READ: The motion *in limine* that—your motion *in limine* that she's not qualified to give opinions about economic testimony. She's a 701 witness for opinions.

THE COURT: Yes. Yes. It's not clear to me that this is economic testimony yet. So I'd like to hear the foundation a bit more.

THE WITNESS: I'm sorry. Could you repeat the question.

BY MS. RUDZIN:

Q. Sure. Dr. Hill testified that agents don't have a magic wand. Do you recall that?

A. Yes.

Q. What's your reaction to that?

THE COURT: I'm sorry. I need more context for what that meant.

MS. RUDZIN: I'll read a little bit more of his testimony. He said that agents " . . . don't have a magic wand." They can't prevent harm to authors because there are—this is an exact quote. " . . . there are examples of competitions where the publishers were willing to pay more than they eventually did." " . . . if agents were so good at preventing any harm to authors, you wouldn't expect to see that."

THE COURT: I'm going to overrule the objection. You can comment on that.

THE WITNESS: Okay. Well, I actually do have a magic wand that was given to me by my author Sue Monk Kidd, who thought I was magic. So what I would say is that agents have tools to get to the best offer from the best editor and the best imprint. There are times when, indeed, the—the editor would have paid more. Also, there are times when the editor has to pay more than they want to. But as long as the author has gotten to a place where they feel happy with the offer and the editor and the imprint, I don't consider that a loss because, in the aggregate, there's a better book. Remember, the pie—there is a pie that is the book. The advance is one—the North American advance is one—is one wedge of that pie. If we picked an editor that the collaboration is very successful, the book will be better as a result. It will sell more; so royalties. But also internationally, it will sell more in more territories, which is money that goes directly to the author, as well as potentially more likely to get a book or a a film or TV deal. So that's the full pie.

THE COURT: Can I ask you: So in a situation, hypothetically, where the publisher was willing to pay $750,000 and the agent just asked for 250 and that's what they got, would you think that that agent had done a good job in that deal?

THE WITNESS: No, I would not. No, I would not. I mean, not all agents are equal in their skill—in their skills, just like not all writers are equal. So—but, generally, I think you might find they had a little bit left in their pockets sometimes, and sometimes you take a little bit more out of their pocket than they wanted to give.

THE COURT: Okay. Thank you.

BY MS. RUDZIN:

Q. I realized, Ms. Walsh, that when I talked to you this morning about your credentials, I didn't ask you, what are some of the notable books that you have sold as an agent?

A. Thank you for asking that. Many to think about, but some that come to my mind are *The Secret Life Of Bees* by Sue Monk Kidd who bought me my magic wand, *The Glass Castle* by Jeanette Walls, *Lean In* by Sheryl Sandberg. My mind has gone blank. I'm sorry.

Q. That's all right. Those are three pretty good ones.

A. Okay. Oh, Brene Brown, all of Brene Brown's books.

Q. Who were the largest publishers you have sold books to?

A. Who are the largest publishers I have sold book to? PRH, HarperCollins, Simon & Schuster, Hachette, and Macmillan.

Q. Are you familiar with Scholastic?

A. Yes.

Q. I take it you haven't sold a lot of books to them. You don't do children's, right?

A. I do do some of children's, but no. We do a lot of business with them, and I knew the CEO quite well and was very impressed, but, no, I didn't have a chance to do a lot of business there.

Q. How many imprints are there at the larger publishers like Penguin Random House and HarperCollins?

A. I think over a hundred.

Q. And what about the other large publishers like Hachette and Macmillan?

A. They each have dozens. I'm not exactly sure. The number probably fluctuates slightly.

Q. Do all those imprints compete against each other?

A. Fiercely.

Q. We talked about the largest publishers. What are some of the midsized publishers you have worked with?

A. Norton, Grove Atlantic, Kensington, Chronicle, Abrams, Hay House.

Q. And what about smaller publishers, have you dealt with any of those?

A. Sure. There's Graywolf. There's the university presses, Andrews McMeel.

Q. Do those midsized and small publishers compete for the same books as the large publishers?

A. Absolutely. They don't compete necessarily as frequently, but when they compete, they compete certainly as fiercely.

Q. And how do agents think about those midsized and small publishers when preparing their submission list?

A. It really depends on the book, because if they are the perfect place for a book, they could be at the top of the list. Agents are thinking about editors and imprints. So they are really looking to make that perfect match wherever it is.

Q. Do those smaller and midsized publishers ever win the rights to expensive books?

A. Oh, absolutely.

Q. Why would an author ever choose a smaller publisher over a best in class like Penguin Random House?

A. Well, I mean, first of all, they are best in class too. So just because they are smaller doesn't mean that they are not as impeccable in every way. Why would someone pick Amherst over Harvard? Not everyone wants to be at a big school. Some people prefer a smaller, more familial type situation, thinking about Grove Atlantic who has literary giants as authors, but also a very small familial feeling that people like. If you are a self-help author or wellness author, you may prefer Hay House because they have this cruise and these conferences that make a really, really successful lecture business for a lot of these authors. So if you want to go to a place like Norton because you have written maybe a soft science book or narrative nonfiction book, they are excellent at getting attention. So there's different reasons someone might choose a different route.

Q. Do those smaller publishers ever actually outbid one of the larger imprints?

A. They do. As I said, they pick their bets, but when they go, they go the distance.

Q. We have heard the smaller publishers called farm teams during this trial. What is your response to that?

A. The smaller publishers are called farm teams? First of all, it's rude, but it's also untrue because I think farm teams, it means that everybody is looking to go to the majors everybody is looking to go up. And that's not the case with people that are published by these midsized and smaller publishing houses. You know, many very successful authors that could go anywhere choose to remain at these houses for their whole careers. The editors are extraordinary. And there are times where people go from a large one of the Big 5s to one of the midsized or smaller publishing houses.

Q. Can you give us an example of someone who has chosen to stay at one of the smaller firms through several books?

A. Sure. Richard Powers, I think, was at Morrow and moved to Norton where he's remained. Mary Roach has been at Norton her whole career.

Q. What about authors that have moved from big to small?

A. From big to small, Colette Baron-Reid, a best-selling author that moved from Crown to Hay House. Gabrielle Bernstein, another best-selling author that moved from, I think, maybe also Crown, definitely inside the PRH building, to Hay House. You know, it happens. It's not unheard of by any stretch.

Q. Ms. Pande testified that when multiple editors are interested in a book, smaller publishers are, in her words, very rarely involved. Do you recall that testimony?

A. I do.

Q. Do you have a response to it?

A. Well, if it's just a matter of interest, I'm not sure how the other publishers would have that information. But certainly as an agent, she's getting that information. And it's just not consistent with my experience. It's really specific to the project.

Q. We have heard in this case that larger publishers have an advantage in acquiring books because they have a better reputation than smaller publishers. What's your view on that?

A. I mean, it just feels like a fundamental misunderstanding. I mean, bigger is not necessarily better. You know, the head of Grove Atlantic, Morgan Entrekin, is literally a legend. You can't have a better reputation than he has. I can understand how it would look like that from the outside, but it's just not the case.

Q. Mr. Pietsch testified that one advantage Hachette has over smaller publishers is its stronger relationship with media. Do you recall that testimony?

A. Yes, I do.

Q. And what's your response?

A. Well, I mean, old media for sure. But that's a disintegrating relationship because nobody cares about a newspaper ad or article or a network package. So it's really shifted to new media. And all of those relationships are new and everybody is figuring it out. I think that historically maybe that was true, but I think it's much less true now.

Q. We have also heard that larger publishers have an advantage in marketing that authors need. Do you have a view on that?

A. I am going to be repetitive here, but I think they had a historical advantage that is also eroding because if an author can sell thousands of books with a single Instagram post, an author with the right platform, then what marketing department do you need? You need a single entrepreneurial person, ideally somebody who really understands social media.

Q. Mr. Pietsch testified that Hachette's strong relationships with retailers are an advantage Hachette has over smaller publishers. Do you recall that testimony?

A. I do.

Q. And what's your response to that?

A. I don't want to sound like a broken record here, but Amazon is the biggest retailer and everybody has access. There's no preferential treatment there. Anybody can distribute—could sell through Amazon. So I love independent bookstores, but I think it's not exactly where the growth in the books sales are going.

MR. READ: Objection, foundation.

THE COURT: I am going to sustain that objection.

BY QUESTIONER: We have heard people say in this trial that the larger publishers have an advantage in distribution. Do you agree?

A. The larger publishers actually distribute some of the smaller publishers, so the distribution is actually exactly the same. And I think if I'm correct, HarperCollins actually doesn't even distribute their own titles. So in that sense, I'm not sure if that really is an advantage.

Q. Does a publisher's printing capabilities matter to the decision about which editor to go with for a book?

A. Their ability to print the book?

Q. Yes.

A. No.

Q. Has it ever come up in a meeting between an author and an editor or an agent and editor?

A. I can't say it has.

Q. Mr. Pietsch testified that Hachette has a greater ability to absorb losses than smaller publishers because of its bigger revenues and backlist. Do you recall that testimony?

A. I do.

Q. And do you have a response?

A. Well, I have two responses. First of all, a backlist is just money. So it's not like a backlist helps you any other way except that it's funding. So a well-funded organization, whether it's small or new, can absorb the same thing. The other thing is I'm not so sure, as an author, as an author's representative, how good it feels to know that absorbing losses is not a big deal because I think authors prefer to feel like it's all or nothing and maybe this midsized and smaller houses sort of really treat it that way as well. I'm not sure.

MR. READ: Objection, foundation.

THE COURT: Sustained. That will be stricken.

MS. RUDZIN: Your Honor, I have a decoder if I could hand it out, please.

THE COURT: Yes.

BY MS. RUDZIN:

Q. Ms. Walsh, have you ever sold a book in Dr. Hill's proposed market of book rights that go for $250,000 or more to smaller publishers?

A. I have.

Q. Can you give us some examples, please?

A Yes. Author A I sold to Hay House for a seven-figure advance in quite a competitive situation.

Q. Do you know why the author chose Hay House?

A. Yeah. He wanted to be part of their lecture series. And also at Hay House, a lot of the authors have big online communities, and when a new book comes out, they all post for that person. So I think he really desired to be part of that community as well.

Q. Can you give us another example, please?

A. Yes. Author B moved from a Big 5 publisher where he had been a *New York Times* bestseller to Harvard Business Press for over $500,000 in also a competitive situation.

Q. You've got a couple more on the list. Why don't you run through those.

A. Sure. No problem. I just wanted to say that, in that particular case, Harvard Business Press has an excellent reputation for getting directly to the business community and so that served a larger mission for him with his—you know. So, yes, C is an example of a quirky literary novel that also had a lot of interest but ultimately ended up at Abrams for over that figure and was tremendously successful. And then on D and E, Your Honor, I wanted these examples to show you that these two authors both went to a coffee table book publisher called Phaidon. And they hired a commercial editor, a veteran of the Big 5, and she was known for popular culture. So then they shifted into doing popular culture books of big celebrities. And in both cases, those advances were well north of $500,000.

Q. Do you think any of these authors made the wrong choice in choosing these smaller publishers?

A. No, I don't. I think they were very happy with their decision.

Q. Do you think any of them received inferior services?

A. Absolutely not.

Q. Have you sold as many books to these smaller publishers as you have to the larger what's been called the Big 5?

A. No, I have not.

Q. Have you seen any new entrants come into the market?

A. Yes. It's an exciting time for new entrants in the publishing industry. We have seen Spiegel & Grau, Zando, Catapult, Astra, and I'm also going to put on the new entrants, although it's not strictly true, there's a publishing house called Open Road which was traditionally an ebook publisher, but their new CEO, David Steinberger, is extremely dedicated to books, so I would say watch the space on that as well.

Q. Let's just talk about a couple of those. What do you know about Spiegel & Grau?

A. Spiegel & Grau was founded by two veterans of the publishing industry, Julie Grau and Cindy Spiegel. I know I read in an article that they were oversubscribed for their funding, and I think it's early days, but they are off to a great start. I think the first book they published was called *Fox and I*, and I believe it was an instant *New York Times* best seller.

Q. Is that the only *New York Times* best seller they have had?

A. I think they have published three or four books. So in the early days, they are off to a very good start.

Q. What can you tell us about Zando?

A. Zando is also founded by a veteran of the Big 5, Molly Stern. I believe she is also quite well-funded, and she's also kind of off to a great start.

Q. Can Zando—

MR. READ: Objection, foundation, well-funded.

THE COURT: Sustained.

BY MS. RUDZIN:

Q. Ms. Walsh, how do you know that Zando is well-funded?

A. Well, I know that it's well-funded because they are buying books at a big clip. I know she's part of the SISTER corporation, which is owned by Elisabeth Murdoch. And from what I have read, she's very dedicated to the book business.

Q. When you say she's very dedicated to the book business–

A. Elizabeth Murdoch, from what I have read, Elizabeth Murdoch and the SISTER company. So an example of—

THE COURT: There's no question pending. Go ahead.

BY MS. RUDZIN

Q. Can you tell us, has Zando had any successful books?

A. Yeah. So an example from Zando which I particularly love is a book that they are getting ready to publish in September called *The Butcher and the Wren.* And this is very much, I think, what Zando's whole profile is, is partnering with people and brands that already have a platform.

But this particular author has a big following, and with a single post on Instagram, she presold over 40,000 books. So, I mean, that's just staggering from a per copy perspective, and it pretty much guarantees a number one spot on the *New York [Times]* best seller list when it's published in September.

Q. Is that the only success Zando has had?

A. That hasn't been published yet, but I think they have published a couple other books and I think they are doing well.

Q. What can you tell us about Astra?

A. Astra is also from a veteran of the Big 5. His name is Ben Schrank, and I actually worked with him on the *Sisterhood of the Traveling Pants* series. He's wonderful, and we will see.

Q. None of these publishers is particularly well-established, so why would agents submit books to them?

A. You know, as I mentioned to you earlier, agents submit to editors. And these are all peopled, all of these places are peopled by editors who have a long history of success and who have great relationships in the industry. Their authors love them, and the agents will be happy to support them.

Q. Let's turn to large companies that are not exclusively focused on book publishing like Disney and Amazon. Do agents sell books to them?

A. Yes. I mean, Disney certainly in the children's space. You know, they did have an adult space for a while which they sold, but right now they are very successful in the children's space.

Q. We have heard mixed messages about Amazon as a competitor. What is your view?

A. I don't think Amazon handled the rollout of their publishing house well. I think they told people in the industry that they were not going to be publishers, and then they became publishers and that trust was crushed. And hard to grow, easy to break. I think they hired the wrong people. And they really didn't act diplomatically with the independent book sellers and small bookstores. It almost became like selling a book to them was like crossing a petition line, so people aren't going to do that.

Q. Could Amazon course correct?

A. Absolutely. They have all the money and all the resources and all the marketing power. If they wanted to course correct, they absolutely could. And I think we are already seeing a little bit of that with a book that I recently read about that was actually a book of theirs that actually was sold in the independent bookstores. And that's a big softening.

Q. Let's turn to self-publishing. Do you see it as a viable option for authors?

A. I do. I do.

Q. Why?

A. Well, I think there's a lot of white space there. So I think that people are making traction with self-publishing. I made the mistake of gasping about the $40 million Kickstarter campaign that I heard about because I think that's remarkable and I think it will be a wave of the future. I had a situation prior to my leaving WME with author G where Amazon made an unsolicited audio offer for a very high price. And we had an accepted offer from one of the Big 5 publishers, but they didn't want to do it without the audio rights. So in consultation with us, we decided to actually set up our own publishing for him to self-publish. So we hired a freelance editor. We hired a ghost writer. We hired a book packager who physically makes the book. And we hired Ingram to distribute. And so in that situation, for not a very big investment, for the right author who could—you know, his platform is very big and he could sell presumably hundreds of thousands of books, he was very excited about going this route. So it's not the self-publishing route where you are uploading a book. It was actually going to be a fully published book.

Q. And what happened?

A. He unfortunately changed his mind about the project.

Q. Do you have any clients who have actually self-published?

A. Yes. Author F, who was a number one *New York Times* best seller from one of the Big 5, decided he wanted to publish a book, self-publish a book. And he's entrepreneurial and he believed his name would make a difference. So in the same way, we helped him get that together. And he published a book that he was very proud of and he was very happy with the financial side of it as well.

Q. Shifting gears, Dr. Hill has used the term anticipated top seller. What is your reaction to that?

A. Well, his use of it was the first time I ever heard of it.

Q. Do you understand it?

A. Yes. I get what he's saying. I mean, we say best sellers, but yes. You know, the other thing too, and I can let you in on a little secret here, everybody in the book industry believes that every single book that they sell has the potential to be a best seller. So for us, I guess every book you work on we would put in that category regardless of the advance.

Q. When the agent is putting together the submission or deciding on whether to have best bids or an auction, can the agent tell whether the book is an anticipated top seller?

A. You mean at that arbitrary level that Hill drew up? No, absolutely not. I mean, you have a sense. You have high hopes. But you really don't know what's going to happen until the auction or the best bid or the exclusive negotiation takes place.

THE COURT: Okay. I just want to push you on that. You are saying that you never anticipate that a book that you are marketing is going to be a best seller or top seller?

THE WITNESS: I would say I always anticipate that what I am working on is going to be a best seller.

THE COURT: How many books do you sell for less than a hundred thousand advance?

THE WITNESS: I do. And certainly earlier in my career, all the time. And now I try to find new authors, and it's—you know, we spend years working on a title. We wouldn't work on something if we didn't believe it had the ability to break out or to be a prize winner.

THE COURT: No, not ability; anticipated top seller. You think they are all the same? You never think some will do better than others?

THE WITNESS: I do think some are going to do better than others, but I think they all are going to do well. Hope springs eternal. I believe everything I am working on is going to break out. I do believe that. And I think many of my colleagues feel the same way.

THE COURT: So you think every book you work on is going to be a best seller or a top seller? I just want to make sure I'm understanding this.

THE WITNESS: No. I think every book that I work on has the potential to break out.

THE COURT: That's not the question. It's called anticipated best sellers that you expect to be a best seller. And you are telling me every book you work on you anticipate to be a top seller? I just want to make sure I'm understanding you.

THE WITNESS: Again, this is a category that doesn't exist. For me, I don't have an anticipated top seller category, so I am putting myself in the mind space of that. I will say that I don't sell books that I think this will be okay. I sell books that I believe in and think that they have an ability to find a big audience or find a prize-worthy mention or I—that's the way I approach my representation.

THE COURT: No, I understand that. It's just there's a difference between hoping it will be a top seller and expecting it to be a best seller. I'm just trying to understand your testimony in terms of expecting it to be a top seller. You don't expect every single book you work on to be a best seller or top seller?

THE WITNESS: Right. I hope.

THE COURT: So the questions are not about hope. The questions are about expect.

THE WITNESS: Okay. Then please ask me the question again.

MS. RUDZIN: Your question or my question?

THE COURT: So her answer, what I heard, was that she thinks all of them are, and that's why I wanted to stop and make sure she understood the question.

THE WITNESS: What I meant to say is all of them could be, is how I meant it.

THE COURT: Right, but that's not the question.

THE WITNESS: I understand the distinction.

BY MS. RUDZIN:

Q. Can the agent know whether a book will be a top seller?

A. Well there are franchise authors, for example. James Patterson, John Grisham yes, you know it's going to be a top seller. And you have a strong track record that also gives you that fact pattern. And then there are giant celebrities Michelle Obama where you know it's going to be a top seller. Even celebrities though sometimes you think it's going to be a big best seller, and it flops. It happens.

Q. Do you have a sense of what kind of advance per book that James Patterson or John Grisham gets?

A. Oh, in the millions, many millions.

Q. Can a book that everyone expects to be a top seller, expects to sell well, flop?

A. Absolutely. It happens commonly. I mean, Andrew Cuomo's book was sold at the height of his being America's governor during the COVID crisis. I mean, that book was sold for $5 million, I believe. I don't know for a fact. But by the time it came out, the nursing home scandal had happened, the Me Too issues, and the book didn't do any business. I have had that with other celebrities as well. And sometimes it's just a timing issue, like Marie Kondo. Marie Kondo did a book about—*Joy at Work*, about making your office sparked with joy because it's not cluttered. It published in March of 2020. So these things happen, and there's nothing you can do about it. You know, also a lot of times when a first book is a big breakout, it sells lots and lots of copies, and so the publisher pays a ton of money for the next book. And there's something called the sophomore slump, and sometimes that sophomore slump lasts. So these are all different ways where our expectations are dashed, and I guess that's sort of where I go into the hope place. I understand the distinction you are making, but you can't really be a hundred percent sure, and so yeah.

Q. Do you find that there's some kind of consensus among editors you submit a book to about whether that book will sell well?

A. What I feel is that sometimes there is more of a consensus, but just as often—again, we are not talking about these mega mega celebrities, or are we still talking about mega mega celebrities?

Okay. Oftentimes there's a cluster of people who feel it's one level, and then there's usually one person who sees it at a higher level and one person who sees it at a way lower level. That's the spectrum, because it's a co-creational experience, and a big piece of it is how the editor sees it.

Q. What publishers can compete effectively for books that everyone thinks will sell well?

A. All of them.

Q. Well, how would a small publisher pay Stephen King, for example?

A. Well, for one thing, there are things beyond just an advance. Sometimes as—you know, Stephen King is an example. They use joint ventures or profit sharing. You know, there are different ways. If for whatever reason an author wants to be with a certain editor and a certain imprint or a certain small publisher, there are ways that you can make it work. And also, again, it's just about securing financing.

Q. What about Ms. Obama who presumably commands tens of millions of dollars in advance, are you saying a smaller publisher could acquire that?

A. It's possible. I mean, Zando's CEO is Michelle Obama's former editor. If that was the route that Zando wanted to go, I'm sure they could secure capital. It's a good bet.

Q. Ms. Pande testified that she would treat books that she thinks will sell well differently than other books by sending them out to more editors. Do you recall that testimony?

A. Yes, I do.

Q. Do you have a response to it?

A. I mean, every agent does things differently, but that's the opposite of what I do when I feel like I have a book that I know is going to do very well on the marketplace. If I know in my heart that this is going to really be a big book, then I really target my list to editors that I feel like are going to be a perfect match for my author.

Q. Is there anything different about books that receive an advance of $250,000 as compared to books that receive an advance below that amount?

A. You know, I recognize that that is an arbitrary number, and it's certainly arbitrary to me. It's not as if we serve, you know, paper plates to the people with advances of under $250,000 and fine china to those advances over $250,000. They are the same people. And we provide, the publishing house and the agencies, provide the identical service. And actually, yesterday, Brian Murray testified that every single book that they work on takes approximately 2,000 hours to work on. And I loved that he said every single book. He didn't say the big books take 2,000 hours and the little books take 1,000 hours. It's just an indication of how people in the publishing industry treat books like sacred objects. They take it very seriously, and the treatment is the same regardless of the advance level.

Q. Is there a separate set of authors who sell books above $250,000?

A. No. I mean, a lot of my authors that are above that number started way below and then grew book over book, which is a very traditional thing you see in book publishing.

Q. Is there any difference in how agents sell books with expected advances above and below $250,000?

A. No. We are using the same tools.

Q. Are there different editors who buy the books that go for more than $250,000?

A. No. I mean, every editor is capable of buying a book at the level that they are supported by their publisher. So it's just a matter of finding that match. And once the passion and enthusiasm is there, they just need to get the support from their house.

Q. Are there different agents who sell books who receive advances of up to $250,000?

A. No. I mean, obviously the newer agents are developing their lists, so it may be less common. But they could also get one right out of the gate. It's all the same people.

Q. Would the agent expect a bigger marketing spend for a higher advance book?

A. Yes, traditionally. But when I think about that Instagram example, I mean, there's one post and it sold 43,000 copies. So it's possible that in some of the cases, the reason they are paying big money is because the person has a big platform. And if that platform is there for the advertising, then the spend might be lower.

Q. Are terms like royalties and bonuses negotiable only when the advance is above $250,000?

A. No. Royalties are generally negotiated in something called a boiler plate, so every agency has a separate boiler plate with every publishing house. And those royalties are negotiated by the agency. So any author that would be at, in my case, formerly WME, but any agency gets the same royalties. So if you are a poetry author for a $25,000 advance or you are a mega celebrity with a multimillion dollar advance, you are using the same boilerplate. Bonuses was the second half of your question. And publishers, I think publishers, I don't know, I can't say like, because I have never worked at a publishing house, but I do think they like to give them to both small and medium-sized and large advances, because by the time an author is earning bonuses, it means everybody is making money and it's kind of a win-win for everybody.

Q. You talked about the agency boiler plate. Are you saying there's no customization for particular authors?

A. No. Of course there's customization. When you are negotiating on any author's behalf, you are reflecting the author's needs to the editor and working around—you know, the payout might be different. It might be central to this author that the publisher make a contribution to their philanthropic endeavor. It could be first-class air fair. We have heard a lot about glam here. It could be that. I mean, there are different needs. But while it's generally correlated not necessarily. I was just thinking about a celebrity I did a book with. It was a small book. And it wasn't under the 250—it was under the $250,000 range, but I negotiated glam because—and first class because that was specific to that author's needs.

THE COURT: So your answer is it's generally correlated with the size of the advance but not always?

THE WITNESS: Yes, exactly.

BY MS. RUDZIN:

Q. In your experience, do Penguin Random House and Simon & Schuster compete significantly with one another for what Dr. Hill calls anticipated top sellers?

A. Do they compete? Well, first of all, again, those are two umbrella companies. I am always looking at the imprint level. Competition is fierce throughout all the imprints, but I don't think of Simon & Schuster and PRH as being any more fiercely competitive—you know, competed against one another than Hachette and HarperCollins.

Q. When you were an agent, how often would you see a Penguin Random House imprint and a Simon & Schuster imprint as the last two bidders for books?

A. Well, me personally, that would be never because I did best bids, so I would never have two last bids like that. But I have no doubt that, if you search for it, you could find examples of it. But I just think it's as random as any other variation of imprints.

Q. Do you recall Ms. Pande's testimony that none of her sales, over $50,000 in the past four years, would have been affected by the merger of Penguin Random House and Simon & Schuster?

A. Yes, I do remember that.

Q. Did that surprise you?

A. No, not really.

Q. Why not?

A. Because, as I said, there's so many variations, and also authors—agents have tools, so like, for example, switching to best bids. So, no, it doesn't surprise me.

Q. How often does an agent submit books to two different imprints under the same corporate umbrella?

A. Regularly.

Q. And is that because imprints at the same publishing house compete against each other?

A. Yes, they compete fiercely.

Q. Do you believe that there would still be competition between Penguin Random House imprints and Simon & Schuster imprints after the merger?

A. Absolutely, because PRH already has three divisions that fiercely compete. Simon & Schuster is a fourth division. It will also fiercely compete. They have gone this extra mile to say that it will be treated as an external bidder, which essentially says nothing will change.

Q. Have you seen instances where Penguin Random House has tried to reduce the competition between its imprints?

A. Has Simon & Schuster tried to—sorry.

Q. Have you seen instances where Penguin Random House has tried to reduce the competition among its own imprints?

A. Not at all. I mean I think that the way that they think about it, and I really appreciate this, is that if you have three imprints or five imprints all competing for something, two things. Number one, you are five times more likely because you have that many dogs in the hunt. And I think for my purposes, more importantly is the most passionate editor is getting the book, the person who has the biggest and most vibrant vision for that book.

Q. So you mentioned the Penguin Random House promise that Simon & Schuster would be considered an external bidder. Would there be a competitive effect if that promise were broken?

A. I think there would be. I mean, to go back to the Amazon thing trust takes many years to build and one moment to break. I think that broken trust would be costly.

I think that agents would not feel comfortable in the same way with that broken trust, and they would communicate that with their authors. And I feel that the editors would also feel like they had been misled and could potentially leave, and authors and agents would follow them.

Q. Okay. But what about effects on competition, would there be effects on the competitive dynamics that the agent is dealing with—

A. Oh.

Q. Let me finish the question–

A. Sorry.

Q.—if Penguin Random House goes back on its promise to keep Simon & Schuster an external bidder?

A. Even if that happened the imprints still bid against one another, and in that final round, the agent has the ability to go to best bids, so I don't think there would be.

Q. Going back to a little bit earlier on distribution, in your experience, does an author favor an imprint

because of its corporate umbrella's distribution capabilities?
A. I can't imagine that being a factor.
Q. Does an author favor an imprint because the umbrella publisher has better relationships with retailers?
A. I don't see that.
Q. What about the publishers' relationship with media, does that make a difference to an author choosing an editor?
A. You know, it could. It could. But as I said, I think those old media relationships are less and less powerful. And I think the new media—you know, everybody's making new relationships right now, so I don't know. You know, people care about media obviously a lot.
Q. If the merger closes, do you expect agents to be unable to create good submission lists and find an author's perfect match?
A. I don't understand why they would be unable to. Nobody's going away. I mean, Simon & Schuster has its imprints. Their editors are there. You know, I don't see the competition being affected.
Q. Ms. Pande testified that the merger would limit the number of editors and imprints that would be a good home for her clients. Do you recall that testimony?
A. Yes, I do.
Q. And what is your reaction to it?
A. I don't understand it. I mean again, if Simon & Schuster were to disappear, which would be very sad there would still be many options for people. But that's not what's happening here, so I'm not exactly sure what she means by that.
Q. Do you expect author advances to go down as a result of the merger?
A. I don't. You know, in 2013, when Random House merged with Penguin, there was a lot of anxiety around it at that time. And in the fullness of time, we see that advances continue to rise and authors are very happy. And so I always think about the best predicter of future is past, so I feel very confident.
Q. Why did you want to testify in this case?
A. Well, because this is about an industry that I love and that is sacred to me. And I felt that there was a fundamental misunderstanding as if we were describing the forest without the root systems, without the understory and the overstory, which is one of love and a calling. And so I just wanted to represent that here.
Q. Thank you.
MS. RUDZIN: Your Honor, I would like to enter the decoder sheet into evidence as Defendant's Exhibit 411, please.
THE COURT: All right. Thank you. That will be admitted.
MS. RUDZIN: Thank you. (Defendant's 411 received in evidence.)

CROSS-EXAMINATION

BY MR. READ:

Q. We have a few binders, Ms. Walsh.
A. Sure.
Q. Good afternoon. My name is John Read.
A. Hello.
Q. When you get the binders, don't be dismayed. They are thick because of your prior testimony.
A. Okay.
Q. But I am going to work to shorten the number of questions I ask you and try to keep this a little more abbreviated for your time and for the court's time. Ms. Walsh, you testified earlier about a dial of competition that an agent can have, right?
A. Yes.
Q. They can turn it from one to two or up to ten, right?
A. Correct.
Q. I wanted to ask you just a couple of follow-up questions about that. As the agent turns the dial up to

ten to try to get the maximum benefit of competition, can the agent control which publisher bid on the books that you have submitted?

A. The agent can't control somebody falling in love with a book, but an agent can find the right matches and then use that dial accordingly.

Q. Right. And the agent can't control how much the editor or the publishing house chooses to submit for the bid, right?

A. Sorry. Can you reframe that question? I don't understand what you are asking.

Q. Yeah. As the agent is turning up the dial on competition, they can't control how much the publisher chooses to bid?

A. Correct. It's not a money dial. It's an overt or covert competition dial.

Q. Just a couple questions about marketing which you touched on.

A. Sure.

Q. Your experience is that the marketing budget is the most important lever to get the book out in the world and get people's attention, right?

A. Not necessarily. You know, if you have, like, the platform like we were talking about, then the budget is irrelevant.

Q. Let me ask that again. The marketing budget is the most important lever that an agent has to get the book out in the world and get people's attention?

A. Okay. I mean, marketing is. Marketing is the most important lever.

Q. Okay. And as a result, when you are negotiating the sale of a book, in addition to asking for an advance amount and the right match, you ask for a marketing plan, right?

A. Correct.

Q. And you negotiate with the publisher about the amount of money they will commit to marketing the book, right?

A. Well, marketing commitments are pretty rare, but we do get them.

Q. Do you often negotiate with a publisher about the amount of money committed to marketing a specific title?

A. Often, no.

Q. Would you turn—we are going to actually use this binder now.

A. Okay. Great.

Q. Would you turn to the tab that has your deposition.

A. Yes. Walsh deposition. Okay. Got it.

Q. Would you turn to page 155, please.

A. Yes.

Q. Line 8, the question is, did you ever negotiate with a publisher about the amount of money they committed to marketing a specific title? Answer, often. Did I read that correctly?

A. You did.

Q. And you did that deposition under oath, did you not?

A. I did, sir.

Q. And you expect higher marketing commitments for higher advance books, correct?

A. Yes.

Q. Let's talk about some of the terms in the contract that an author has. I want a little context over time. When you started in the business, Ms. Walsh, the advances paid out to authors in two periods, in halves, correct?

A. Correct.

Q. And then on delivery—on the signing of the contract and then on delivery and acceptance of book, right?

A. Correct.

Q. And then it became common for the payout to the author of the advance to be paid out in thirds?

A. Correct.

Q. And then when you left WME in 2019, the boiler plate agreement with Penguin Random House was

payments in fourths, right?
A. You showed me something. I mean, I can't be sure of it, but I saw something that certainly indicated that that you showed me.
Q. So payouts today are in four installments, are they not?
A. Commonly.
Q. And the last installment comes a year after the book is published, right?
A. Yes.
Q. So that's a change that's happened over time with regard to authors and the contract terms they have with publishers?
A. That's correct.
Q. Now, you concluded your testimony with a question about wanting to testify here, correct?
A. Correct.
Q. You are being paid for your testimony, right?
A. Yes, I am.
Q. A quarter of a million dollars?
A. Yes.
Q. You testified about advances, I think, after the 2013 merger?
A Yes.
Q. When you were at WME, you never calculated the average advance that was obtained for your clients?
A. No, I didn't calculate it.
Q. Yeah. And in 2019, you left WME?
A. Yes.
Q. And you haven't reviewed any data about advance levels at a high level?
A. No, I have not.
Q. You testified a little bit about some of these small publishers and their ability—actually, I am going to pass on those. I don't think that's necessary. You talked about some of your clients that you have represented.
A. Yes.
Q. I think Jeanette Walls was one you mentioned?
A. Yes.
Q. Brene Brown was one you mentioned. Sheryl Sandberg was one you mentioned. These all bring a smile to your face?
A. Yes.
Q. These are all clients whose books, adult books, you sell to the Big 5? They all sell adult books to the Big 5?
A. All of those books are imprints owned by the Big 5, correct.
Q. Right. And you placed all those authors with Big 5 publishers because you thought the Big 5 would be the best home for those authors?
A. I thought the editors and the imprints that I chose were the best homes.
Q. And those are editors and imprints within the Big 5?
A. Correct.
Q. You mentioned, I think, author G on the–
A. Yes.
Q. He's not an author, right?
A. He's actually just got a children's book, I think.
Q. Okay. He's got a children's book. He's known for–
A. He's a celebrity.
Q. He's a celebrity?
A. Yes.
Q. And you gave a story about the effort to self-publish, right?

A. Correct.
Q. And I just wanted to make clear, that book never got published?
A. No, it never got published.
Q. Okay. Let me put on the screen Dr. Hill's—I think this is PX963 we are going to put on the screen.
A. Where do I find PX963?
Q. It will be in one of the tabs.
A. Okay.
Q. It's tab 3.
A. I don't see my tabs numbered 1, 2, 3.
THE COURT: It's on your screen.
THE WITNESS: Okay. Thank you. Sorry.
BY MR. READ:
Q. I don't know we are going to go long, but you followed the trial.
A. Yes.
Q. And you read Dr. Hill's reports–
A. Yes.
Q.—before your deposition. And so I really wanted your help with this graph–
A. Okay.
Q.—right? The right side of the graph shows the small publishers, the non-Big 5 having 45 percent—having won 45 percent of the contracts—There's a redacted version if we can publish it to the audience. The small publishers have won 45 percent of the books below $250,000, right?
A. When you say won, are you talking about exclusive negotiations or for repeat authors or just auctions?
Q. They have contracted for 45 percent.
A. Okay.
Q. And then for anticipated top sellers, books above 250, they have won 9 percent. Do you see that?
A. I do.
Q. Here is my question to you with your experience. Why is it that small publishers have been able to secure 45 percent of the titles below 45 percent but only been able to secure contracts titles above—only 9 percent above $250,000?
A. I think it's because they pick their shots, and they don't bid at that level often, but when they do, I think they are very effective. 10 percent of the time, that sounds right to me.
Q. So they pick their spots in places where they will be the best home?
A. Yes.
Q. Let me ask just a few more questions. You called into question the CEO of Hachette's testimony about how often auctions occur. Do you recall that?
A. I don't think I called it into question. I just said it wasn't consistent with my experience.
Q. Okay. Let's be fair about that. So your experience is auctions are rare, right, from your colleagues and—
A. Round robin.
Q. Round robins?
A. Yes.
Q. But you don't dispute that, as a CEO of Hachette, he's got a broad view—he can have a different perspective?
A. I apologize. I don't dispute that.
MR. READ: No further questions, Your Honor.
THE COURT: Thanks. I had just one question. One thing that I didn't hear in your testimony was the way agents are compensated. Can you talk about that?
THE WITNESS: Yes. I am happy to. So it varies from agency to agency. Some of the smaller agencies have their agents on something—not a guaranteed salary. You just make money off of the commissions that you bring in. It's called a draw. That's what we call it. I'm sure there are other names for it. The

larger agencies have people on salaries, and then they give them discretionary bonuses.

THE COURT: So agencies receive a commission, and then individual agents might be compensated with a salary with discretionary bonuses?

THE WITNESS: Yes.

THE COURT: But all the agencies get paid by commission?

THE WITNESS: Correct.

THE COURT: And what is the level of commission generally?

THE WITNESS: In the literary business, it's generally 15 percent domestically and 20 percent internationally.

THE COURT: So if you negotiate for international and domestic rights, is it a different commission?

THE WITNESS: Yes. The author pays a different commission. And the reason for that is because a lot of agencies might have a French subagent that they are paying 10 percent of the commission to, and then they only keep 10 percent of the commission. So it's because often there's a subagent in between.

THE COURT: Okay. So given the way the compensation is structured, isn't the incentive of the agent to sell the book for the highest advance possible?

THE WITNESS: You know, there's multiple truths here. You want the best advance, but you want it from the best editor and the best imprint. And the reason for that is because a good collaboration makes a better book, and a better book sells more copies and makes it worth more in all the other places of the pie. So that good match is good business. So you might be taking a little bit less, let's just say, on the U.S., Canada advance rights, but it's a decision that you believe will be worth more in the fullness of time.

THE COURT: And is that your opinion about all agents, or is that just the way you do it?

THE WITNESS: Oh, everybody, everybody.

THE COURT: So your testimony is that all agents are not trying to necessarily maximize the advances paid to the authors?

THE WITNESS: I'm saying it's not the sole priority when you are trying to find that match, that perfect match. The match itself can be as important as the advance. Every situation is different and every author is different. But a majority of the authors want to have long-term careers and they want to be in successful relationships with the publisher where their books are lucrative. And so they—they are choosing accordingly, and they are looking at the past books that the editor has published and how the authors' trajectories have gone. And there are editors that add real value, monetary value, to their projects.

THE COURT: No, I understand that. But you are telling me that agents are not trying to get the top advance?

THE WITNESS: I'm saying it is not always the exclusive priority. There are some authors who are just like, all I care about is the money, so in those cases—

THE COURT: Let me ask you a different way. Are agents always trying to get the top advance?

THE WITNESS: No. They are always trying to get the best deal.

THE COURT: Okay. Any questions based on my questioning?

MS. RUDZIN: Just one quick one, Your Honor.

REDIRECT EXAMINATION

BY MS. RUDZIN:

Q. Why are you so confident that other agents are also not just considering the advance?

A. Well, 30 years in the business, I have many friends that are agents that work in different places, and I also supervise 20 to 25 agents, many of whom came from different agencies. So I think I have a pretty strong sense of the market. And I don't think that every agent would end their closing letters with, we reserve the right to decide what constitutes the best offer if the best offer was always the highest offer.

MS. RUDZIN: Thank you.

THE COURT: Anything else?

MR. READ: No.

THE COURT: Thank you so much. You can step down.

THE WITNESS: Thank you.

JENNIFER BERGSTROM, SVP, GALLERY BOOKS GROUP

Gallery Book Group SVP, publisher Jennifer Bergstrom said that 65 percent of Gallery's acquisitions are under $50,000 advances, 30 percent are between $50,000 and $1 million ("The $150,000–$250,000 range is a bit of a sweet spot for me"), and 5 percent are over $1 million. "What my team and I really spend the most time on are that 65 and 30 percent," she said. "That's where we are putting in the most elbow grease."

Bergstrom detailed a number of successful books—some that Gallery didn't pay much for, and some that they did, such as Amy Schumer's memoir, which they paid millions for. "We try to find the widest possible audience for our books regardless of how much we paid."

Bergstrom also discussed the entrepreneurial spirit of the imprint, and said that about 75 percent acquisitions come from approaching celebrities, politicians, athletes, the "celebrity adjacent," etc. That way, "we can control the content. It's our idea. It's also we have a culture of—like I said, we are entrepreneurial. Our CEO—we like to reward enterprise. We love when editors think for themselves and generate ideas." She said they participate in auctions the other 25 percent of the time, but she doesn't like them because "they can be time-consuming" and "we can't really control the content."

On the topic of competing with smaller publishers, Bergstrom said that they would love to publish Sarah J. Maas, "but she's with Bloomsbury." They also compete with Hay House for motivational books. Self-publishing may be a threat as well, as Gallery author Anna Todd moved to self-publishing (though Todd began her career writing on Wattpad, and recently returned to set up an imprint at Wattpad Books).

This was the first time conservative publishers came up in the conversations about small and mid-size publishers. "We publish on both sides of the political aisle," Bergstrom said, so they compete with Post Hill Press, Regnery, Skyhorse, and All Seasons Press, "started by my ex-boss," former Gallery president and publisher Louise Burke. No one mentioned that Post Hill, Regnery, and Skyhorse are all distributed by Simon & Schuster.

Bergstrom said that Gallery always requires audio rights—which is why they lost Author W, a comedian, to Abrams. "Very significant format," she said. "I need audio."

In addition to editorial meetings, Bergstrom also said that her group has a weekly meeting called "What's Hot" to discuss trends. "I used to be the hippest person in the room," Bergstrom said, but now "half the time I'm taking notes."

The lightest moment of the day occurred when Bergstrom misspoke about an author who is a reality TV star, who she said was on Broadway, not Bravo. "Broadway? She wishes." "Don't we all," replied defense counsel Ryan Shores.

Blind Items

Much of Bergstrom's testimony was about advances, acquisitions, and marketing plans for recent or forthcoming books, and she gave quite a bit of information on books that had been anonymized. The full transcript will let you try to match some of the titles and authors. (Author V, for example, was "a former press secretary" who went to Post Hill for over $1 million, which sounds like Kayleigh McEnany. Ultimately, Threshold did not bid because CEO Jonathan Karp did not support buying the book, as "He didn't think highly of her. . . . Mr. Karp is happy that we are not publishing author V.")

TESTIMONY OF JENNIFER BERGSTROM, SVP, GALLERY BOOKS GROUP

DIRECT EXAMINATION

BY MR. RYAN SHORES:

Q. Good afternoon, Ms. Bergstrom.

A. Good afternoon.

Q. Could you please state your full name for the record.

A. Yes. I am Jennifer Bergstrom.

Q. And, Ms. Bergstrom, what is your current job?

A. I am the senior vice president and publisher of the Gallery Books Group.

Q. Can you give us a brief background on your education and your work history.

A. Sure. I graduated from Barnard with a bachelor's in English. And luckily I have figured out that I could make a career out of my love of reading.

After graduation, my first job in publishing was at Putnam where I was the assistant to the publisher in the children's division.

Q. And when was Gallery launched?

A. We launched Gallery 13 years ago.

Q. And what was your role when Gallery was launched?

A. When we launched and today, I oversee the editorial, marketing, publicly, and sales of our entire list.

Q. And have you continued to maintain those responsibilities until today?

A. Yes, I have.

Q. Now, as part of your job history, can you give us a sense of how many years you have overseen acquisitions of book titles?

A. 13 years.

Q. And approximately how many books have you overseen the acquisition of?

A. Thousands.

Q. What distinguishes Gallery from other divisions at Simon & Schuster?

A. Gallery is one of five imprints in the adult division. We are perhaps the imprint with the greatest range. We publish everything from fiction, nonfiction. We do crime, thrillers, women's book club fiction, celebrities, athletes, journalists. We do sci fi, horror. So really we are known for our pop culture, but our lists are very, very varied.

Q. Can you give us an example or two of your pop culture stars that you have published?

A. Sure. Well, our biggest or mega celebrity to date has been Amy Schumer. And yet we also publish a lot of lesser-known celebrities, YouTubers, Instagrammers, that don't have the kind of platform that an Amy Schumer has.

Q. About how many books does Gallery publish per year?

A. A hundred, give or take.

Q. Ms. Bergstrom, we have been careful to preserve confidentiality in this case. I am going to hand you up a document that's a decoder, and it will be used during your testimony to talk about advances and specific authors.

Now, Ms. Bergstrom, you mentioned Amy Schumer. Did she receive a significant advance?

A. Yes. She received millions of dollars.

Q. And is that a typical advance paid by Gallery?

A. No, it is not. Only about 5 percent of our list is in that million plus range.

Q. And in that million dollar plus range, when you pay an advance at that level, do you anticipate the book will sell well?

A. I certainly hope so.

Q. Does it always happen?

A. No. We have had our duds for sure. But I expect, when I am acquiring someone like Amy Schumer, that her fans are going to come to the book. And we actually published her when she was really at the height of her career.

Q. And let's talk about, when you pay an author an advance below a million dollars, can you give us a sense of what types of books you are publishing in that range?

A. We are publishing all kinds of books in that range, everything, like I said, from unknown YouTubers to Instagram stars, books on politics, very, very wide range.

Q. And using the decoder that's in front of you, Ms. Bergstrom, can you give the judge a sense of a few of the authors that are kind of in the below million-dollar range that you publish?

A. Sure. Author A is a reality TV star. She's a housewife on Broadway—excuse me, Broadway? She wishes. Bravo.

Q. Don't we all?

A. Yes. Author B was the star, he is now in prison, of a major Netflix show. We paid 175 for that.

Author C is someone who we have not yet published. He is actually a Swedish journalist who has been studying climate change, and this is a novel that he has written that we will be publishing simultaneously with a number of publishers around the world. But he's a debut novelist. And, yeah, that would be it.

Q. And, Ms. Bergstrom, is it fair to say that these are the types of authors that you publish in the less than million-dollar range, a mix of celebrities, fiction, nonfiction?

A. Yes.

Q. And let's go back to the million dollar plus category. When you are paying an author a million dollar plus advance, how do you think about the risk involved in that circumstance?

A. I mean, there's always risk. I get it wrong. My team and I get it wrong. But, again, I am hoping that I have calculated that there's an audience there, that they have a fan base.

Q. Okay. And do you think about the risk differently at lower advance levels than the million-dollar advance level?

A. I actually do. I find the lower advance levels, even the three that we just spoke of, to be I am uncertain, I don't have a track record, or my group is very good at identifying talents before the rest of the world knows how big they are. So there's a lot of uncertainty there, more so than actually the million plus.

Q. Are there examples of authors below—that you paid below a hundred thousand dollar advance that have gone on to sell a lot of books?

A. Yeah. One of my biggest authors, author D on this list, we bought her first book for $95,000. It has sold over 1.3 million copies. She's on her sixth book with us, and she's sold five and a half million across. So this was someone that we really blew up.

Q. Thank you, Ms. Bergstrom. What factors do you consider in deciding what to offer an author in terms of an advance?

A. The passion of the editor, which I'm sure you have heard a lot about, is very important to me. Obviously the platform of the author, whether they are a radio, TV show host or, like I said, a reality TV star or journalist. And the most important is the actual content of the book. Is it good.

Q. And we have heard a lot about P&L statements in this trial. Do you use a P&L in trying to formulate an advance offer?

A. Yes, we do. We run a P&L for every acquisition. Our P&Ls, we plug in our projected sales, our projected unit costs, and based on our profit margins, we figure out what we think the advance should be.

Q. And you mentioned projected sales. How do you determine the projected sales?

A. We look at competitive titles, comp titles as we call them. Let's say for an Amy Schumer, we would be looking at other female comediennes who published recently. But it's an art. It's not a science by any means.

Q. Is there ever disagreement among your staff about the potential sales for an individual book?

A. All the time, and with my boss.

Q. And why is that?

A. Because it's so subjective. And some of us have been doing it longer than others, but it's a guesstimate.

Q. Ms. Bergstrom, do you ever acquire a book for less than the advance reflected in your profit and loss statement? Does that happen?

A. Yes.

Q. What about the opposite situation, are there ever situations where you have an advance level set out in the P&L, and you end up paying more than is reflected in that?

A. Yes.

Q. Can you give us an example?

A. Amy Schumer.

Q. And can you just give us a sense of how much you went over your P&L level in that case?

A. Millions.

Q. Have you ever heard the term anticipated top seller, Ms. Bergstrom?

A. Not until this trial.

Q. Is there any way to anticipate, other than the million dollar plus that you mentioned, is there any way to accurately anticipate what a top selling book would be?

A. No. I mean, you try, but you are taking some bets. I mean, with an Amy Schumer, yes, I feel pretty confident that I can make her a best seller. But like I said, there's a lot of other books at the lower end that aren't as easy.

Q. And do you think about $250,000 advance is any type of demarcation point for your expectations relative to book sales?

A. No.

Q. Ms. Bergstrom, in general terms, how does Gallery acquire books?

A. Two ways. One is one-on-one negotiations and then auctions where we compete with others.

Q. And can you just roughly explain what percentages you do of one-on-one negotiations versus auctions?

A. Yeah. Auctions really only comprise about 25 percent of our business. The majority of our business, the other 75 percent, are really—our editors and I are entrepreneurial. We are approaching authors and celebrities and politician and athletes for ideas. So it's really we are on the look. We are scouts in a lot of ways.

Q. And how long does that process of seeking out a celebrity or somebody you want to write a book, how long does that process take?

A. The longest it's taken me—we had an author Mike Rowe. He is actually the star of Discovery Channel's Dirty Jobs. And it took me ten years to convince him to write a book.

Q. Now, you mentioned that this is one of your primary ways of acquiring books. Why is that? Why is this outreach method a primary way that you acquire books?

A. First of all, we can control the content. It's our idea. It's also we have a culture of—like I said, we are entrepreneurial. Our CEO—we like to reward enterprise. We love when editors think for themselves and generate ideas.

Q. And how does the negotiation occur in this context that you are referring to? How are the terms negotiated?

A. It's one on one. We have presented an opportunity, so the agent is usually very—we come to a fair agreement. It can take days. It can take two hours.

Q. And what role does competition from other publishers play when you are negotiating these terms?

A. I assume I am negotiating exclusively, but I always have my competition in my rearview mirror. But it's one on one. And sometimes we don't come to terms, and sometimes they will go to someone else.

Q. Other than this outreach method, are there other ways you engage in one-on-one negotiations to acquire content?

A. Sure. We have options, so we will negotiate with an author who we have published their first book for a second book. And, again, that's one on one with the agent. And both sides are usually very motivated to come to a deal because we are both looking at the same numbers.

Q. Do you always come to a deal?

A. No.

Q. And what factors play into those negotiations with repeat authors?

A. The factors, again, are the sales and whether or not we think we can grow and whether we want to continue working together.

Q. Are there any other ways that you acquire content in a one-on-one context?

A. Exclusives are when authors or agents will just come to us because they like the way we have published someone else on our list or they want to work with a particular editor.

Q. Now, you mentioned auctions, you use those about 25 percent of the time. Why that low?

A. We don't like auctions. They can be time-consuming. And, again, we can't really control the content. And they can sometimes be time-consuming. Did I say that?

Q. You did. What type of auctions do you participate in, Ms. Bergstrom?

A. Best bids, round robin, and then, of course, there can be hybrids of both depending on how the agent wants to play it.

Q. And in the best bids situation, do you typically know who you are competing against during the best bids process with other publishers?

A. No.

Q. So how do you factor in competition in that best bid situation?

A. I can't. I mean, I have to assume that I am competing with everyone. And given the range of our list, I usually—we usually are.

Q. Does Gallery sometimes offer earn-out bonuses to authors?

A. Yes, we do. Author E on the list is someone who wrote a horror novel. We paid $125,000 with a $25,000 earn-out bonus.

Q. Does your willingness to offer an earn-out bonus depend on the level of the advance?

A. No, it does not.

Q. Do you negotiate royalty rates at times?

A. Yes, we can.

Q. How does that occur?

A. Again, if an agent wants to negotiate it, we can be flexible. On a hard cover royalty rate, for instance, we can give them a flat 15 percent rather than escalating from 10 to 15. It's rare, but we do it.

Q. Is your willingness to negotiate on the royalty rate, does that depend on the advance level you are offering the author?

A. No, it doesn't.

Q. Let's talk a little bit about marketing and publicity. What type of marketing does Gallery do for authors?

A. All kinds. We do influencer mailings to Instagram stars. We do online advertising. All of our books get galleys. We pay for newsletters. There's a big range.

Q. And do you include—I'm sorry, let me ask you about this. What about publicity? I skipped over that. What kind of publicity do you do?

A. Publicity, again, our publicists are trying to book our authors on radio, TV. We are looking for reviews. And we are also back to the good old-fashioned author tour now where we put our authors on the road, and they will do bookstore signings or ticketed events.

Q. And do you include an estimate of marketing and publicity spend in the profit and loss statement that you discussed?

A. When we are acquiring books, yes, we do. We put a, it's a guesstimate, into each P&L. And it's a guesstimate because oftentimes we aren't publishing that book for many years. So it's not until—we are usually about ten months from publication, from actual pub date, that we start our planning for how we are going to market and publicize that book.

Q. Are you the person who puts, I think you called it, a guesstimate of the cost into the profit and loss statement; do you do that personally?

A. Yes, it's me, or it's the editor and I approve it. But I'm ultimately responsible for it.

Q. And you mentioned that there is a time lag that's ten months before publication. Can you give us a sense of, from the time of an acquisition P&L to the time the next time you reconsider marketing and publicity spend, how long can that be in between?

A. It can be a year, but it's usually more than that because we can't determine our marketing and publicity plans until we have all had a chance to read that finished book. And so much changes. I am usually hoping that an author's platform may have grown since we acquired the book so that might affect how we market the book. It makes it easier to market the book.

Q. And let's fast-forward to the point where you are making a marketing and publicity spend decision closer to the time of publication. Who's involved in that decision?

A. I usually have my publicity director, our marketing director, our associate publisher, and I are all in a room. And we are very familiar with the list at that point. And we figure out what each individual book needs.

Q. And can you give us some of the factors or give us a flavor of the discussion, what plays into your ultimate decision?

A. Well for author D who we bought for $95,000 for her first book by the time we were making that decision, she had written the manuscript. It had a lot of in-house reads and enthusiasm. And there was another book in a similar vein at that point that was really taking off. It had an unreliable narrator. And it was just like what readers were craving. So we leaned into that, and we spent a lot of marketing and publicity dollars on that book.

Q. And do you typically discuss the advance level in these meetings when you are making a decision about how much to spend?

A. No. Our marketing and publicity people don't know the advances for the books.

Q. Has the advent of social media changed the way you market and publicize books?

A. Yes. It's been a game changer. Obviously there's TikTok, YouTube, but it's free, and it absolutely has changed the way we market.

Q. Is it all free, all social media is free?

A. No. We need to spend money on, for instance, I call it the Instagram box where you watch celebrities open it. The costs for that are for the product. But, no, we are not paying Instagram influencers to cover our books.

Q. Ms. Bergstrom, I am going to walk you through or have you walk us through some of the authors that are listed here in their marketing and publicity spend. I just want you to describe to the judge your approach to marketing and publicity.

Let's start with author F. Without disclosing the author's name and the title of the book, can you give us a flavor of the genre or what type of book this is?

A. Sure. This is a writer that—she's paranormal, so it's sexy vampires. This book was probably her 21st book. So she's what I would call a franchise author. She's very established. Though we spent $1.2 million on the book, we spent about $62,000 on the marketing and publicity because she had such an established fan base, we knew how to reach her readers. And I had published her before, so I could see what worked. The author G—

Q. Before we go there, Ms. Bergstrom, did this book sell well?

A. Yes, it sold very well.

Q. Okay. And I know you are an English major. I am a history major. But just doing the math, the advance level for this particular book is $1.2 million, and the marketing and publicity spend is $62,000. So that's about a 5 percent, right, 5 percent of the advance?

A. (Nodding head.)

Q. Okay. Now, I didn't mean to interrupt you. Please go to G.

A. Sure. So G is a celebrity-adjacent author, but also her platform was on social media. So we paid $450,000 for her book, and we spent $36,000 on the marketing and publicity. We didn't need to spend more than that because she was getting on all—she had a lot of national media for—that we were considering—excuse me, that she had already booked at that point on Good Morning America, The Today Show. So publicity drove that, and that didn't cost us.

Q. And how did this book sell?

A. Very well. It was one of our biggest selling books of '21.

Q. And just so I am doing the math again for the record, you spent $36,000 about on marketing and publicity. That's about 10 percent of the overall advance level, $450,000, is that right?

A. Yes.

Q. Let's take a look at H. Can you tell us—

THE COURT: Can I ask a question, Mr. Shores?

MR. SHORES: Yes.

THE COURT: I'm just thinking this through, but is what's relevant here what they ultimately spend or what their marketing plan is during the auction phase and what the authors are expecting during the auction phase? Are we looking at the right timeframe in this line of questioning?

MR. SHORES: Is that a question for me or—

THE COURT: I guess the question is, is all of this relevant to what we are talking about in this trial?

MR. SHORES: I believe it is because one of the arguments that's been made is the one thing that distinguishes so-called anticipated top selling authors is they demand a higher level of marketing and publicity spend.

THE COURT: Right, but at the auction phase, not ultimately, right?

MR. SHORES: I think you could think about it both ways. I think both could be relevant. I think one thing Ms. Bergstrom was explaining was it is a guesstimate at the P&L stage.

THE COURT: Oh, we have learned that.

THE WITNESS: But I could also add that I really tend not to give any marketing promises in the acquisition. I never promise any financial. I really don't. If we are in what I call a beauty contest where we are competing with someone else, yes, I will tip—I will talk about what I have done for other authors. But it's too early in the process when we are acquiring a book to know what we are going to market and spend on it.

THE COURT: So there's been testimony that, in a beauty contest, people have to submit a marketing plan.

THE WITNESS: Yes.

THE COURT: That's not a promise of how much you are going to spend or what you are going to do in the marketing realm?

THE WITNESS: In that case, it would be a promise. It doesn't happen—it happens very rarely for us at Gallery.

THE COURT: And do you find that authors have different expectations about marketing?

THE WITNESS: Oh, yes.

THE COURT: Can you talk about that, which different authors feel that way?

THE WITNESS: Yes. Some authors, they are very, very in tune with—and it's usually the franchise authors who have been doing it for a long time, what works and what they want. And, of course, it's a challenge to continue book on book to improve their sales. But a lot of my list because it's pop culture is very publicity driven too. So the authors' expectations are a little bit in line with ours.

THE COURT: All right. Thank you. You can go ahead, Mr. Shores.

MR. SHORES: Your Honor, just in response, one more point I wanted to make is the Department of Justice's own expert looks at actual spend actual marketing and publicity spend, so I think they believe it's relevant in this case. That's one reason we are talking about it.

THE COURT: Okay. That's fine.

BY MR. SHORES:

Q. When you provide a marketing plan to an author, what are some of the things that might entail?

A. Again, it would be a marketing and publicity plan. So we would list our ideas. Like I said, it could be anything from online advertising to newsletters to actual media tours or book signings.

Q. And do you typically provide a financial commitment that you as the publisher will contribute to the author's book?

A. That is very rare.

Q. Okay.

A. Very rare.

Q. And we were going through the set of authors. And I believe we were down to H on your list, Ms. Bergstrom.

A. Yes.

Q. I just want to go through those quickly. Can you give the judge a sense of the author at H, again without disclosing the name or the title of the book?

A. Yes. This is an author who, with this book actually, we really had an incredible opportunity. This author had written about 25 books with us. This was—at one point she was a debut author that we really grew into a homegrown, as I like to say. So this particular book, it came in. It was just the book, I think, of this career, of this author's career. So we went big. We went all in.

Q. And what was the advance for this author?

A. $200,000, and the marketing PR was $93,000.

Q. And that's about 45 percent, right, of the advance?

A. Yes, that sounds about right.

Q. And then, Ms. Bergstrom, when you say go big, what are the types of things you might do for an author like this?

A. This author, we put them on the road. We spent some extra money on Goodreads, extra money on Facebook, really got them on some podcasts, and got more profiles on them. We expanded the review coverage. But we really—it was a concerted effort, and it paid off.

Q. And let's look at author I. Can you give us a sense of who author I is?

A. Yes. This author writes historical fiction. And this, I think, is about her third or fourth book with us. But historical fiction is red hot, so we decided again that we would spend a decent size amount of money on her marketing and publicity.

Q. What was the advance for this particular author?

A. $175,000, and the marketing and PR was $54,000.

Q. Okay. So the marketing and PR represented about 30 percent of the overall advance of $175,000, is that right?

A. Yes.

Q. And all of these authors F through I, are all of these successful authors for Gallery?

A. Yes. They are all best sellers in terms of their sales.

Q. Ms. Bergstrom, do some authors that you work with get glam budgets?

A. Author J does. It's very rare. J and A. One is a reality TV star, and the other one is a major pop star. So it's rare. But essentially if fans are used to seeing these two authors on TV, we need to make sure they look the same in real life.

Q. And does your willingness to offer a glam budget depend on the advance level?

A. No, it does not.

Q. I want to turn to the sales aspect of your business. Does Gallery sell through different sales channels depending on the advance level of the book?

A. No. We try to find the widest possible audience for all of our books regardless of how much we paid.

Q. Does Gallery identify a group of books for particular sales efforts or sales emphasis?

A. Yes. Three times a year, as we head into sales conference, I will pick what I call focus titles and will share them with the sales force. There's some examples too.

Q. Before we get to the examples, can you give us a little bit of flavor of how you choose particular titles to be focus titles?

A. It's—yeah, it's very subjective, but as publisher, I see an opportunity in these books whether it's because something else similar is working or whether the author's platform, like I said, is bigger than when we even acquired it. So it's my, essentially, call on what I think we should drill down and focus on. It doesn't mean the other titles don't get focus, but it's just these are our great opportunities.

Q. And what happens after you identify a title as a focus title?

A. Well, the sales force will then go and sell that title, but we—yeah.

Q. You said, I think you mentioned, that there were some focus titles on this document here. Can you identify those for us?

A. Sure. K through Q. K through Q. were—or excuse me, are focus titles from my spring '21 list.

Q. Spring '21?

A. '22.

Q. Okay. And by my count, there are three of your focus titles that have an advance above $250,000, is that right?

A. Yes.

Q. And four have an advance at $100,000 or less, is that right?

A. Yes.

Q. Let's take a look at the author M. Can you explain to us a little bit about that author and why you identified that particular author for a focus title?

A. It's an incredible book. It checks all the boxes for me. It's psychological suspense, which is very big. We know how to publish this kind of book very well based on some of the other authors we have on our list. Sales force read it, picked it as one of their favorites, so we ended up investing a significant amount of money in marketing for it.

Q. And what is the advance for the author at M?

A. $65,000.

Q. And when you are engaging in these discussions about focus titles, do you discuss the advance level too?

A. No.

Q. Okay. And these are all focus titles from 2022, right?

A. Yes.

Q. Okay. Ms. Bergstrom, I want to move to a new topic. Who do you consider to be Gallery's competitors for acquiring books?

A. Everyone.

Q. Have you ever heard the term Big 5?

A. Yes.

Q. Is that a term you use in Gallery?

A. Not particularly, no.

Q. And do you—can you tell us who the Big 5 are?

A. Yes, Simon & Schuster, Hachette, Macmillan, PRH, and Harper.

Q. Do you also compete against smaller publishers?

A. Yes.

Q. And can you list some of those for us?

A. Sure. Abrams, Skyhorse, Post Hill Press, Bloomsbury, just to name a few.

Q. And do you ever learn who your competitors are after an auction when you participate?

A. Sometimes. Sometimes the agent will tell us. Sometimes they won't. Sometimes the first time I find out about it is when I see the book in a store.

Q. And that was going to be my next question. Sometimes do you find out who published a book that you may have lost by seeing it in a store in a publication?

A. Yes.

Q. And based on that sense you develop, would you say that you compete against Penguin Random House in the final stages of an acquisition frequently?

A. No, it's rare.

Q. Do you compete against HarperCollins?

A. Yes. I lost three very significant books to them just over the past two years, year and a half.

Q. And looking at your sheet, can you identify some losses to HarperCollins?

A. Yes. Author R. It's still painful. This was a big book, big loss for us. We bid $3.125 million. And Harper won it. They won it for more. Author S, also a big loss for us. We bid $2.75 million, and Harper won that.

And the last one, author T, is actually someone that I published before, had the option, couldn't come to terms, agent took her to auction, and Harper—excuse me, our highest bid was $3.3 million, and Harper beat us.

Q. And are these some of your larger bids over the last couple years?

A. Yes. Those are three of the largest losses. Personally too.

Q. Personally. Do you compete against imprints at Hachette?

A. Yes, we do.

Q. Can you give us some examples, again, looking at your list?

A. Sure. Author U is someone that we bid half a million dollars on for her memoir, again celebrity-adjacent, and Hachette beat us.

Q. Is author N also an example of that, Ms. Bergstrom?

A. Author?

Q. Is author N also an example—

A. Yes. N is a Netflix star, big show. We actually won this, though we were the underbidders. Hachette was the high bid.

Q. Why don't we talk a little bit about the mid-sized and smaller publishers. What types of books do you compete for against those publishers?

A. All kinds, political, celebrity, novels, sci fi, all genres and types.

Q. Let's start with the political. What smaller publishers do you compete with in the political space?

A. Well, we publish on both sides of the political aisle. So author V would be an example of a former press secretary who we wanted to acquire, but it sold for over a million dollars to—I'm sorry, Post Hill Press.

Q. Are there other competitors in the political space other than Post Hill Press?

A. Yes. There's Regnery. There's actually an imprint that my ex-boss and an ex-editorial director from Hachette formed. Those are the three that come to mind.

Q. Is that last one also—

A. And Skyhorse and Post Hill.

Q. The one you mentioned that your former boss formed, is that All Seasons?

A. That's All Seasons.

Q. What about in the sci fi space, do you compete against any smaller and mid-sized publishers in that space?

A. Bloomsbury has an author named Sarah Maas who we would love to publish, but she's with Bloomsbury.

Q. What about for celebrity books. You have mentioned a lot of celebrity books. Do you compete against smaller and mid-sized publishers in that space?

A. Yes.

Q. Can you give us an example of a publisher you compete against?

A. I don't see—oh, there she is. Author W is a comedienne, Netflix comedienne. We bid $250,000, and Abrams actually won this book. The author said she wanted to be a big fish in a small pond.

MR. SHORES: At this point, Your Honor, I would like to introduce an exhibit. May we pass it up?

THE COURT: Yes.

BY MR. SHORES:

Q. Ms. Bergstrom, if you could take a look at this exhibit that's been marked DX286. And when you have an opportunity, just tell us what this document is.

A. This is an email exchange from the editor who was attempting to acquire author W. And she is filling me in on the auction.

Q. Okay. And the top email is from Natasha Simons to you, and it's dated February 18, 2021, is that correct?

A. Yes.

Q. And is Natasha Simons the editor that you were mentioning works for you?

A. Yes.

MR. SHORES: I would like to offer DX286 into evidence.

THE COURT: Any objection?

MS. RIKER: No objection.

THE COURT: That would be admitted.

MR. SHORES: We would like to have this admitted under seal, Your Honor.

THE COURT: All right. (Defendant's 286 received in evidence.)

MR. SHORES: May I publish a redacted copy of this document, Your Honor?

THE COURT: You may.

BY MR. SHORES:

Q. Ms. Bergstrom, I want to point you to the top of this email and the sentence that starts, the agent. Do you see that?

A. Yes.

Q. And do you understand this to be the agent letting you know that this particular author went with another publisher?

A. Yes.
Q. Okay. And the email says, why. It's in quotes, right? The language is in quotes? And it says, quote, ultimately it was a combination of two factors, a slightly more favorable offer with PR and a substantial audio bonus and the feeling that it might benefit her to be the bigger fish in the smaller pond. Do you see that?
A. Yes.
Q. And then it also says in parentheses, also the separate audio offer which was admittedly appealing, end parentheses. Do you see that?
A. Yes.
Q. And you referenced earlier the idea of being a bigger fish in a smaller pond. Is this what you were referring to?
A. Yes.
Q. Did this author also choose Abrams in part because of their PR offering?
A. Yes. Abrams—this author was asking for us to hire a private publicist, which I don't like to do, and also asking to retain—or to ask for an audio bonus and slightly more favorable offer.
THE COURT: Can I ask you, demands like this, like glam fee, audio bonus, private publicist, do you get demands like that from particular types of authors like authors who think their book is really hot and has the sense that it's going to sell well basically?
THE WITNESS: Yes. We get these asks across the board, not asking for private PR that much, but again, I don't need them to—I'm not going to pay for that. Although, some of them do have their personal publicists that we work with. But, yeah, these are just a few factors that come into negotiations.
THE COURT: So putting aside advance levels, are there just some books that you think are going to sell well, there's like buzz about them, other editors seem to think they are going to sell well, and do those books get treated differently from other books?
THE WITNESS: That's a great question. When we acquire books at Gallery, we assign a marketer, a publicist, and obviously an editor to it. Each one of our books has—I call them the SWAT team. So each book truly gets published with care and enthusiasm. Again, some will take off. Some won't. But our attitude really is that that's what each book deserves, and we are able to do it.
THE COURT: And so this has kind of come up with other witnesses as well. I understand all books have hope and potential, and you publish them or you sell them because you believe in them. But it just seems to me a matter of economics. And I'm just wondering if it's true that the books where there's the most competition, where there's the most expectation surrounding them are sort of in a different category from other books that don't have those expectations or beliefs of sales. I mean, I know everybody believes in the book and hopes that it will sell well. But the ones that you expect to sell well, are those in a different category?
THE WITNESS: The books that we expect to sell well sometimes don't sell well.
THE COURT: No, I understand that.
THE WITNESS: So in a different category, as far as in my business, the advance really doesn't determine—
THE COURT: I'm saying put the advance aside.
THE WITNESS: Put the advance aside.
THE COURT: Just books that people think are going to sell well. It strikes me this business is a risk-taking business. Every book is a gamble.
THE WITNESS: It's fickle.
THE COURT: So the ones that you think are going to pay off, aren't you going to try to make sure they pay off?
THE WITNESS: Yes, of course I want them to pay off. The big, big, big advances, they can keep me up at night. I want them to work. But I'm—usually there's less risk for me because I know what I am buying. At that level there is—either it's an author who is on TV every night or there is something that can help me mitigate that risk. It's the ones below it that I really do take more chances with or have to.
THE COURT: Yes, you mentioned that. You said when they have a track record, you have something to

base your decision on. That's one thing. But when they have no track record, it's more like you are trying to figure out what the market would be without knowing in advance what it's going to be—

THE WITNESS: The other thing—

THE COURT:—that is the difference?

THE WITNESS: That is the difference. The other thing is just 65 percent of my acquisitions are under $50,000 advances. 30 percent are between $50,000 and a $1 million, and then 5 percent over. So what my team and I really spend the most time on are those—that 65 and 30 percent. That's where we are putting in the most elbow grease. I mean, that's where we have just an opportunity to take an author—and I have done it with author P on this list. He's a sci fi author. His first book with us, we paid $25,000. When it came in, I read it, and we said he could be the next Stephen King. So we really, really went big on that. So that's—in the course of our day, that's where we are really focusing. Amy Schumer might keep me up at night because I think, oh, my God, that's big, but I can also take a deep breath because I know her popularity.

THE COURT: And the authors that do have the track record where you can identify the market more readily, they are the ones that get the higher advances?

THE WITNESS: I would say most of—in my fiction or even in nonfiction, that 150 to 250 range is a bit of a sweet spot for me. But, again, the risk is that I have picked an author whose platform isn't growing at the rate that I thought it would, and I have duds there too.

THE COURT: Okay. Thank you.

MR. SHORES: May I follow up, Your Honor?

THE COURT: Yes.

BY MR. SHORES:

Q. Other than track record, what are some of the other factors you are considering when you are giving this elbow grease, as you called it, to those types of books?

A. Well, it's the book itself. Did it deliver. I often say the title is the strongest marketing tool we have. Is it a great title? Did we package it correctly? Are we getting good reviews?

Q. And do you often discuss those issues with your staff?

A. Yes.

Q. And is there always agreement with your staff on all those issues?

A. No, there's not always agreement.

Q. And do you exchange ideas about those things?

A. Yeah, we listen to everyone in the room at Gallery. We really do. We have a special—in fact, we have an editorial meeting every week, and we have many a meeting called 'what's hot' where we go around the room and say what's hot. I used to be the hippest one in the room, but I no longer am. So half the time I'm taking notes because I'm hearing about these people for the first time but—

Q. Ms. Bergstrom, does everyone agree what's hot?

A. No. In fact, sometimes I don't agree and the editor does and the editor will prove me wrong.

Q. Ms. Bergstrom, we were talking about celebrity books and competition in that area. What about motivational books, do you compete against small and mid-sized publishers for motivational books?

A. Yes. Hay House is a formidable competitor for us. We lost author X to them. We published her first book, again didn't come to agreement on the option, and the agent took it to market, we bid a million dollars, and Hay House outbid us.

Q. Does self-publishing play a role with authors at Gallery?

A. Yes, particularly in romance. One of our top selling authors Anna Todd is now self-publishing. I had author H, just recently on our last contract, the agent told me the author wanted to use a pseudonym and write a new series and wanted to self-publish it. So I essentially had to compete and buy the book. I didn't want her to self-publish, so we offered on that. It's actually coming out next week.

Q. I want to ask you one final question, Ms. Bergstrom. Do you understand that there's an allegation in this case that if this merger of Penguin Random House and Simon & Schuster goes through, publishers like yourself will be able to identify a group of authors called anticipated top sellers and target them to reduce their advances? Do you understand that?

A. Yes, I do.
Q. What is your view of that?
A. My view is I struggle to identify what those top sellers are. And even if I could, no agent or author would want to work with me if they knew that I couldn't compete, so it would hurt my business.
MR. SHORES: I pass the witness.
THE COURT: Okay. Thank you. Any cross?
MR. SHORES: Your Honor, before I do that, I should have moved into evidence, the key, the Rosetta Stone, as DX412.
THE COURT: Okay. Thank you. That's in.
MR. SHORES: Under seal, please.
THE COURT: Yes. (Defendant's 412 received in evidence.)
MS. RIKER: Lauren Riker for the United States. May I proceed, Your Honor?
THE COURT: Yes.

CROSS-EXAMINATION

BY MS. RIKER:
Q. Good morning, Ms. Bergstrom.
A. Good afternoon.
Q. Nice to meet you. And I would like to follow up on a few points made by your counsel. Counsel asked you about losses to small publishers. But you don't keep track of who you lose to, right?
A. Correct, we don't.
Q. So you don't know who you lost to most frequently, right?
A. No.
Q. And so you don't know whether you lose more frequently to non-Big 5 publishers when the advance is below $250,000 than when it's above, right?
A. Yes. We don't keep copious notes, so no.
Q. So you don't know, correct?
A. I have a—no, I don't know.
Q. Your counsel asked you about author H in the Rosetta Stone, and you said that Gallery paid $200,000 for the advance in the book listed.
A. Yes.
Q. The total contract for that author is more than $200,000, correct?
A. Yes. I actually looked at this contract last night, and it's 200 for this title.
Q. Were there other books included on that title?
A. Yes. We have multiple contracts with this writer. This is the writer who has written over 25 books with us. And can I go back to your question?
Q. Sure. Well, your counsel can ask follow-up questions during his time.
A. Okay.
Q. Ms. Bergstrom, when you are trying to acquire a book, you don't tell the agent the max you are willing to pay, correct?
A. Sometimes I do. Sometimes I have.
Q. And agents don't always get you to pay the max price you are willing for a book, correct?
A. Correct.
Q. And agents can't force you to exclude audio from the scope of rights, can they?
A. Well, agents can do anything, but I can't remember ever acquiring a book that I didn't have audio for.
Q. Because you always get audio rights, correct?
A. Yes. They are a significant format. I need audio.
Q. And the author—I will try to use the same—author W, in DX286 wanted to retain audio rights, but Gallery wouldn't agree to it, correct?
A. Correct, especially not for a comedian.

Q. You don't negotiate to exclude audio rights, correct?
A. I don't exclude audio rights, correct.
Q. Your counsel asked you about author V, and you said that Gallery wanted to acquire author V's book, correct?
A. Correct.
Q. The Gallery editor who wanted to buy that book sought Jonathan Karp's blessing before offering it, right?
A. I think so. I can't remember. I'm sorry.
Q. Do you recall whether the editor sought—
A. Oh, I thought you said she did. We would have needed Jon Karp's blessing.
Q. Mr. Karp did not support bidding on author B's book, correct?
A. I don't remember that to be the case, but here comes the email.
Q. Ms. Bergstrom, if I showed you a copy of the email with Mr. Karp, would that refresh your recollection?
A. Well, what will—I am probably—Mr. Karp would not have liked us to buy this book, so I would not be surprised that he had an opinion on it.
Q. So it would not surprise you that Mr. Karp did not support purchasing author V's book, correct?
A. Correct. He didn't think highly of her.
Q. And did Gallery even bid on author V's book?
A. It wasn't Gallery. It was Threshold. And I don't remember what we bid on it. I know it sold for over a million to Post Hill, and the editor may have told me that.
Q. But you don't even know if Gallery's imprint Thresholds attempted to acquire this book, correct?
A. Well, by attempted—
MR. SHORES: Your Honor, I don't mean to interrupt, but I think there's confusion here about what Ms. Bergstrom's referring to. I think they were talking about B, and there's some confusion about what's happening. I don't want to interrupt.
THE COURT: You think they are talking about different books?
MR. SHORES: I think they are talking about different authors.
THE COURT: We are talking about author V as in Victor.
MR. SHORES: I'm sorry. I thought I heard B, so we just wanted to—
THE COURT: So your testimony was about V or B?
THE WITNESS: My testimony is about V.
THE COURT: Okay. That's what I understood as well.
MS. RIKER: I was asking about V.
THE COURT: Okay. I think we've got it. We are talking about V. So you didn't bid for V?
THE WITNESS: Just today when I testified, V is an example of a political book that was bought by a smaller house that we were interested in. I don't think we bid a million dollars, but it went for over a million dollars.
BY MS. RIKER:
Q. And you don't even know if—
A. Well, most of Threshold's business is done as exclusives. So agents—the political conservative space is a space that a lot of people do not want to play in. So what happens is agents will call our Threshold editor and say what do you think about this. We then run it up the flagpole internally. So that is an author that—let's put it this way. Mr. Karp is happy that we are not publishing author V.
THE COURT: But your previous testimony that you bid for it was not correct?
THE WITNESS: We didn't bid for it. It went for over a million dollars to a smaller publisher.
THE COURT: I understand. Go ahead, Ms. Riker.
MS. RIKER: Your Honor, no further questions.
THE COURT: Thank you. Any redirect?
MR. SHORES: No further questions, Your Honor.
THE COURT: Okay. Thank you. Thank you for your testimony. You may step down.

CHARLES DUHIGG, AUTHOR

Author of *The Power of Habit* Charles Duhigg served as a curious and somewhat baffling witness for the defense. The upshot is, he is a very happy Random House author, and he has made so much money he really doesn't care about his advances. Also, despite having an MBA and having written about economics, he does not appear to understand the nuts and bolts of business very well.

Duhigg has had a rewarding and valued partnership with his editor, Andy Ward. On the process of writing *The Power of Habit*, Duhigg said, "It would not be unfair to have Andy Ward's name on the title alongside mine. It only succeeded because of Andy." So for his third, forthcoming book, with *Power of Habit* having sold millions of copies, Duhigg happily took a $2 million advance from Random House, even though Andrew Wylie expected they would get $4 million to $5 million if they shopped it. "And I specifically said I did not want to do that. It's a very, very bad idea to take a very large advance."

Duhigg tried to represent that most authors he knows feel the way he does, big advances are bad, and "the royalties are the big thing." Apparently no one has explained to Duhigg the windfall profits a publisher makes by paying him standard royalties on books that achieve his level of success. Challenged by Judge Pan, he actually said this: "For someone who is an expected bestseller, you anticipate that you will earn royalties in excess of your advance. Like that's the whole point of being a bestseller."

Asked on cross, "If the advance wasn't as important as the royalty, why did you seek a $1.5 million advance for your third book instead of higher royalty rates?" or seek a profit-sharing deal? Guess what the MBA and Wylie client said? "Because it didn't occur to me. I don't know. I mean, that was not an option that was given to me."

Judge Pan, who was charmed by Stephen King, was appropriately suspect of Duhigg. "You've given me very interesting testimony. But is it typical of authors? There's a lot of data that I've been presented with in this case that suggests that you are not typical."

She said later, "I feel you may be atypical for what we're focusing on here, which is advances and things of that nature, because if you—you sort of have the luxury of saying: I'm going to get royalties later, so I don't care as much about what the advance is now. I just need enough to write this book."

When he evaded her questions, she tried again: "But if you were an author who can't expect necessarily to earn out their advances, wouldn't they need more of an advance to make sure they can keep supporting their writing? Because they have more risk."

TESTIMONY OF CHARLES DUHIGG, AUTHOR

DIRECT EXAMINATION

BY MS. SMITH:

Q. Good morning, Mr. Duhigg.

A. Good morning.

Q. Can you please state your name for the record.

A. My name is Charles Duhigg.

Q. Mr. Duhigg, do you have a job?

A. I do. I'm a journalist and I write books. I do that via writing books for Andy Ward at Random House and by writing magazine articles for primarily *The New Yorker* magazine.

Q. And how long have you been writing professionally, Mr. Duhigg?

A. I became a journalist after graduating from business school in 2003 and I've done it since then. So almost 20 years.

Q. Can you tell us a little bit about your writing career?

A. Sure. I got an MBA, and halfway through my MBA decided that I'd much rather be a journalist than be a businessperson. And so after graduating, I got a job at the *Los Angeles Times*, where I wrote for the outdoors section and then for the business section. And then I moved to *The New York Times*, where I was an investigative business writer, and was there until 2017.

I wrote my first book and then my second book while a reporter at *The New York Times*.

And then in 2017, I left the *Times* in order to concentrate more on writing books and to write for *The New Yorker*.

Q. And, Mr. Duhigg, have you won any awards for your writing?

A. I have. In 2013, I was part of a team that at the time had won a Pulitzer Prize for our coverage of Apple and international economics. And then there's a number of other prizes, but I don't think most people are familiar with those. So I can describe them if you want me to, but they'll probably be meaningless names to you.

Q. Mr. Duhigg, you mentioned that you're an author of books. How many books have you published?

A. I've written two books with Andy Ward. So I wrote a book called *The Power of Habit* and another book called *Smarter Faster Better*. And I'm working on a third book right now.

Q. Let's start with your first book. Can you tell us a little bit about it?

A. Sure. Absolutely. Let me just take a—sorry. I'm a little nervous. Let me take a sip of water, if that's okay.

THE COURT: That's fine.

BY MS. SMITH:

Q. I'll take this opportunity, Mr. Duhigg, to ask you to slow down just a little bit—

A. Oh, I'm sorry. Sure.

Q.—because our court reporter is—

A. Sure.

Q.—having—

A. Sure. I'll speak a little bit more slowly. So the first book that I wrote is named *The Power of Habit*. And it's about the science of habit formation, how habits emerge within our brains from a neurological perspective, how they exist within our lives and our societies and our organizations and how we can understand those habits to try and change ourselves, but also change society.

Q. You mentioned Andy Ward. Is Andy Ward your editor?

A. He is. Yes.

Q. Where does Mr. Ward work?

A. He works for Little Random, which is what they call the Random House imprint inside Random House the company.

Q. When you first sold your first book *The Power of Habit* to Andy Ward, had you written the full book?

A. No. And this is pretty typical for nonfiction writers, because you need to spend a lot of time reporting and writing the book. What I did is I wrote a proposal, which again is pretty typical. It took me about a year to write that proposal outside of, you know, my day job at *The New York Times*.

It was about—it was about 50 or 60 pages long.

It sort of explains what I hope to achieve with the book, like where I think my reporting will take me in a plan and gives hopefully a taste of what the writing will be like. And so I had written that proposal before bringing it to my agent, who brought it to publishing houses.

Q. So you mentioned your agent. Did you have an agent at the time you prepared your proposal for *The Power of Habit*?

A. Not for most of it. There was actually an agent that I was trying to convince to represent me and she was not interested in representing me. So I didn't have an agent as I was writing the proposal.

And then I wrote an article for *The New York Times* magazine about the psychology of credit cards. And someone at the Wylie Agency saw that article and they contacted me and they said: Would you like to write a book about the psychology of credit cards?

I said: That sounds like the worst book ever. I do not want to write that book, but I'm really glad you called because I actually have this proposal I've been working on. And so I went to the Wylie Agency and I met with Scott Moyers, who was at that time an agent. He's now the publisher of Penguin.

And Scott said he would be willing to represent me, and things kind of went from there.

Q. Can you tell us a little bit about how you sold *The Power of Habit* to Random House?

A. Sure. So we put together the proposal. Scott helped to polish it and get it to the right place. And then he sent it to a number of editors, I think, just to kind of get—like to whet their appetite. And he called me and he said: You know, there's this one guy, Andy Ward, who actually hasn't even started working at Random House yet. He's a magazine editor who's going to be working at Random House. They just announced that. He is interested in buying this book on a preemptive basis, like he'll make an offer and sort of like prevent us from having an auction or a bidding war.

And I didn't know anything about Andy Ward. And so I asked him about Andy Ward and I asked some friends. And the word that came back is that Andy Ward is like the greatest editor and just a wonderful person, but more importantly a very, very good editor who can elevate your prose. And my feeling was that if I could work with a great editor, that would be wonderful. And so on Scott's advice, I agreed to give the book in a preemptive way to Andy Ward.

Q. You mentioned that Mr. Moyers, your agent, submitted the book to a handful of other people.

A. Yeah.

Q. Who were those editors?

A. I actually don't know. I might have known at the time, but I might also not have known.

Q. Does that mean that you don't typically as an author ask your agent for kind of a blow-by-blow of the acquisition and submission process?

A. Yeah. Unlike—I think of it like when you buy a house, like the realtor tells you everything all the time. Right? This is very different. The agent is a real professional. And so usually you sort of let them handle all of the knife work of getting an advance and getting a book on track done. You get to sort of stay out of it, which is nice and important.

So yeah. Certainly anything that I want to be informed of, they will inform me of. Anything I need to be informed of, my agents will inform me of. But it's not a blow-by-blow because that's their job.

Q. And you accepted Mr. Ward's preemptive offer for *The Power of Habit*?

A. I did.

Q. Did you know Mr. Ward before you accepted that offer?

A. No. I had never met or spoken to him.

Q. Did you consider any other editors?

A. I mean, not really, because my belief was that if I had a—I've worked with editors as a newspaper reporter quite a bit. And I know that if you work with a great editor—a writer can write something that's good, but the best a writer can do is good. To be great, you really need an editor who makes it great. And so I wanted to find an editor who would make it great.

And I spoke to people who had worked with Andy Ward at his magazine—at *GQ* and *Esquire*. And they said: This is a guy who makes you great.

Q. Mr. Duhigg, how much money did Mr. Ward offer for *The Power of Habit*?

A. They offered an advance of $750,000.

Q. And how did you feel when you received that preemptive offer for a $750,000 advance against royalties?

A. The main way I felt was happy; obviously, very happy. But also relieved, because you don't get the whole check at once. Right? They don't give you $750,000. They give it to you over four years, and they deduct 15 percent for your agent and 30 percent for taxes. So it meant that the first check I got would be $115,000. And that $115,000, that's the first of four. That meant I could take a year off from *The New York Times* to write the book. Right? That's about what I was earning as my salary at *The New York Times*. And we had just had a baby, and so it meant that I could take a year to write this book. And I felt like it needed a year to read a great book—or to write a great book.

Q. Did you write the book expecting to only earn as much per year as you would as a journalist?

A. No. I mean, so I came up with the idea for this book right before my first son was born. And I had—after working for ten years, I had $40,000 in savings and I was living in New York. And so I wrote this book to make money because otherwise we could not afford—we couldn't afford to buy a house; we couldn't afford to do anything.

So no. When I wrote this book, it was not to get the advance. It was to write a great book that would hopefully sell millions of copies, because that's where the real money comes from: It comes from selling a lot of books.

And then there's all these other things that appear. Right? You can give speeches. You sell foreign rights. You sell your—the IP to companies that take it and do things with it.

So no. I had hoped to earn much more than the advance.

Q. And did you have an expectation before you received Mr. Ward's preemptive of what a publisher would pay for *The Power of Habit*?

A. I mean, no. Not really. I was—I wanted to earn enough—I wanted to get an advance that was large enough to allow me to take a year to write this book.

Q. And was the amount of the advance the primary reason you decided to sell your book *The Power of Habit* to Random House?

A. No, not at all. I think this is true for me. It's true for every author I know, and I have a lot of friends who are authors. The advance is like—I mean, it's money. Right? Like everyone likes money. But it's like Issue No. 7 on the criteria of how you make this decision.

The biggest issue is: Do I like this editor? Do I think this editor is going to elevate my work and help me write a great book? Because if I write a great book, it doesn't matter how big the advance is. I'm going to sell a lot of books. And that's where the money is going to come from.

But equally, am I working with a publishing house that represents my values? Am I working with a publishing house that seems aligned with promoting my book in the way that I think it's going to be successful? Am I working with people who allow me the freedom to write the book that I want to write, that matters to me? There's so many other things that matter beyond the advance.

And I know that there's been a huge focus on the advance in this trial. But as—for authors, the advance is—it is one part of the puzzle and it's a very unimportant part of the puzzle because if the book works, you make so much more money from things beyond the advance. That's what you're focused on, is writing a book that people want to read.

Q. And how did *The Power of Habit* perform after it was published?

A. It's performed well. We've been—we had some lucky breaks. And it's—I can't remember the exact—I think it sold over 4 million copies now in North America and then many more overseas.

Q. And did your editor contribute to making *The Power of Habit* a success as you hoped he would?

A. Yeah. Oh, absolutely. I mean, this book would not—it would not be unfair to have Andy Ward's name on the title alongside mine. It only succeeded because of Andy.

Q. What did Mr. Ward do to make your book a success?

A. I mean, everything from like—before I write a chapter, I write him a huge memo saying: I think this is what the chapter should do. And he gives me pages and pages of feedback on that. Right? And we strategize together and we think together. How do I report this? Who do I go after?

And then I'll write a first draft, and he'll go through and he'll line-edit every single sentence and he'll write things in the margins like—he never writes, "This is good." It's only negatives things like, "This is terrible. No. Don't do this."

So after I emotionally recover from reading that, then I go back and edit it. And then he does it again and again and again. I mean, a good editor is sitting by you for every single page and is helping you see the possibilities that you can't see on your own to elevate that prose into something that's genuinely meaningful.

Q. Mr. Duhigg, did Random House, the publisher, do anything to make your book a success?

A. Yeah. Absolutely. I mean, there's like a thousand things, most of which I wasn't even aware of or am not aware of. But, like, take the book jacket. Right? They came up with something like 13 or 15 different mockup book jackets to try and figure out like which one is going to attract the reader's eyes when it's sitting there on a shelf and get them to pick it up.

Once the book was published and it started going out, they assigned two publicists to me and a marketer or maybe—I'm sorry—two marketers and a publicist. I always get them mixed up. And those people worked tirelessly, like, to get me on Terry Gross and to tell me which podcasts I should do and to help me understand, like: It's well worth going and speaking to this bookstore, but you don't need to speak at this bookstore.

There was this huge sales staff who, like, knew all of this stuff about, you know: This is how you talk to the Costco in Des Moines to get them to put the book on the shelves. But Books Are Magic, which is my favorite bookstore in Brooklyn, like you have to talk to them differently. I mean, there were literally like hundreds of people who knew something precise and helped—were able to step in and help me.

Q. When in the publication process did Random House provide you with this support?

A. All the market—that stuff I was talking about?

Q. Yes.

A. Mostly after. So basically, like, it was me and Andy writing—when I'm writing the book. And then the book jacket folks come in and like there's people to sort of bounce titles off of and things like that.

But then once the book was published, and particularly once it starts selling, like once it's clear that it is working, that there's something in it that resonates with the audience, that's when most of the sort of marketing and promotion, they really like lean in. So it wasn't—so the book has to earn that support.

Q. Mr. Duhigg, you mentioned that you talked to lots of other authors and you have friends who are authors. Right?

A. Yes.

Q. And do you talk to your peers about your publisher?

A. Yeah. Oh, I mean, the only thing writers like more than writing is gossiping about writers. So I spend a lot of time talking about editors, talking about other writers, talking about—yes.

Q. And do you believe that since you received an advance of $750,000 for *The Power of Habit* that you received any special attention from Random House in connection with that book?

A. No. No. I mean, they were very explicit. I mean, I was—because I was new to this, I sort of asked, like: Can they make promises, like We're going to spend so much on marketing and X, Y and Z? And the answer was: No. Like we judge the book based on, like, what—the book you've written and we will support it if it seems like it's—the market—the readers are responding.

Q. And, Mr. Duhigg, do you measure the success of *The Power of Habit* by the amount of an advance you received?

A. No. No. No. The goal of being a writer is not to get the biggest advance possible. The goal of being a writer is to write something that is beautiful and true that people want to read and to figure out how to inform people that this book exists.

And if you do that, if you write something that is true and that touches people, they will buy it. And then you will get the royalties. And the royalties will be so much larger than that advance and the speaking fees and the IP sales, all of it.

The goal is to write a beautiful book. And that is what makes the whole system work. It's not to see if you can con some publisher into giving you a large advance in the hopes that, like—no. That's not what anybody in my job wants.

Q. Mr. Duhigg, did you earn out your advance for *The Power of Habit*?

A. I did.

Q. And without getting into specifics, about how much money have you made from that book?

A. I made in excess of $5 million from *The Power of Habit.*

Q. And does that include the speaking fees and the foreign rights that you're mentioning?

A. No. I'm sorry. Let me be more clear. No. That's just North American royalties. So from Random House, I've earned in excess of $5 million. And then there's speaking fees in addition to that. We've sold *The Power of Habit* into 40 different countries, not Random House, like other publishers in other countries. And each of them pay me royalties and paid an advance. So it's been—I've been very fortunate. It's been very remunerative.

Q. Let's move on to your second book, Mr. Duhigg. Can you tell us a little bit about your second book?

A. Sure. It's named *Smarter Faster Better*. And it's about the science of productivity. So it kind of builds on *The Power of Habit*, but it's about why some people and some companies are more productive than others.

Q. How did you sell your second book, Mr. Duhigg?

A. So that was actually completely different. And I'm sorry if I'm speaking too fast.

THE COURT REPORTER: If you could slow down a bit, please.

THE WITNESS: Thank you. So what happened was, after I had finished writing *The Power of Habit*, but before it was published, I had a phone call with Andy Ward and I said: You know, like productivity keeps coming up. We should write a book about productivity.

And then he contacted Andrew Wylie, who was then my agent. Scott Moyers had left. And he told Andrew Wiylie: We'll buy that second book for the exact same contract as the first book.

So I didn't have a proposal for that one, which to any writers I do not recommend doing that, because it makes writing the book really hard. But they basically said: Look, we liked what you turned in. And so if you want to do another one, we'll do it with you.

Q. So you got the same advance for *Smarter Faster Better* as you had for *The Power of Habit*?

A. That's right.

Q. And was there any other financial terms built into your contract for *Smarter Faster Better*?

A. I think that there was this, like, provision that they would speed up the release of the advance on *The Power of Habit*, like as a little, like, bonus. So they didn't give me any extra money. They just gave me the money from *The Power of Habit* a little bit faster, if I'm remembering that correctly. But it wasn't a big deal. It wasn't like something that—it was just kind of a nice, like: You're doing a good job. So attaboy.

Q. Did you expect to receive that advance amount for *Smarter Faster Better*?

A. Did I expect to receive. .?

Q. That advance, the $750,000 advance for *Smarter Faster Better*.

A. I mean, I didn't expect anything. Again, I was relieved because it meant that I would get a check that was about equal to one year of salary at *The New York Times*, and that meant that I could take another year off to write the second book. It meant that we could actually buy a house. So it was nice.

Q. And did you try to negotiate a higher advance for *Smarter Faster Better*?

A. No. No. I think I asked Andrew Wylie to ask if they would sign up for a two-book deal, because then I'd be, like, guaranteed that I could write two more books. But they were not interested in that. So no. I didn't—I didn't want anything more.

Q. Was the size of the advance the reason that you decided to sell *Smarter Faster Better* to Random House?

A. No. No. Not at all. In fact, I remember at that point because we had written *The Power of Habit*, because *The Power of Habit* was good—it hadn't come out yet, but I think there was a recognition that, like, it was a good book—Andrew Wylie said: You know, if we go to other publishing houses, we can get more—we can run up—we can get a bigger advance.

But I wanted to work with,—again, the advance is not the primary motivator. I wanted to work with Andy.

Q. Were you contractually required to sell your second book to Penguin Random House?

A. No, I was not. And maybe they would like a right of first refusal. But I'm not even certain that's right.

Q. And you testified that Mr. Wylie was your agent at this point because Mr. Moyer had left. What did you mean by that?

A. So Scott Moyer left the Wylie Agency as an agent and became the publisher of Penguin. So he became—which he had previously been a bookseller instead of an agent or a book maker.

Q. And what role did Mr. Wylie play in selling your second book to Random House?

A. I mean, he, like, answered the phone. Andy Ward called him. I don't know. I mean, there might have been, like, a lot of conversations. But basically the author doesn't want to negotiate. Right? These are people that I need to have the most intimate relationship, one of the most intimate relationships of my life with. I don't want to be arguing about money with them. So that's what Andrew Wylie does.

Q. And was *Smarter Faster Better* published by Random House?

A. It was.

Q. And was it successful?

A. Yes. It was not as successful as *The Power of Habit*, but it sold in excess of a million copies.

Q. And did *Smarter Faster Better* earn out its advance?
A. It did. The royalties from that have been in excess of the advance. They've been over a million dollars. Just from—again, this is North American royalties. So for *Smarter Faster Better*, we also sold—Andrew Wylie on my behalf also sold that into, I think, 37 other countries, not with Random House. And there are speeches associated with *Smarter Faster Better*. So I've earned more than a million dollars. But I've earned over a million dollars in royalties.
Q. And—
A. Sorry if I'm giving too much.
Q. Without getting into specifics, about how much money do you earn from the speaking fees and the foreign rights compared to what you earn from your advance in royalty payments—
A. So—
Q.—in New York America?
A. I'm sorry. So are you talking about royalties or advances?
Q. Both.
A. So they're about equivalent. So I would say for my first two books, what happened outside of North American is about equal—combined is about equal to what happened in North America.

So it worked out that, like, the advance from Random House—it was just Random House at that point—was $750,000. I earned another $750,000 in advances from outside of North American.

But again, the royalties are really—that's—the royalties are the big thing. And those came in, and that's about equal to North America.

And then speaking fees, I mean, speaking fees can get great. Like it's tens of thousands of dollars per speech. And it's not untypical to give, like, 30 speeches a year. So it's very remunerative. Not just for me; for many people.

THE COURT REPORTER: Sorry. You said it's not atypical to give 30 speeches?
THE WITNESS: So it's not atypical. Yes. I'm sorry.
BY MS. SMITH:
Q. And you're a nonfiction writer. Right, Mr. Duhigg?
A. Yes.
Q. So from your conversations with your peer group and your understanding of how they work, is it true that fiction writers can also earn the same kind of additional income from publishing books?
A. Yeah. Usually through different venues. So they oftentimes—instead of giving speeches to companies, they give speeches to MFA programs and they teach MFA programs. They oftentimes go to conferences.

And if you write science fiction, there's this endless list of sci-fi conventions you can go to. And you get paid to do that.

And then oftentimes, for fiction writers, actually, which nonfiction doesn't have quite as much, is Hollywood. Right? Hollywood buys the rights to all these books, even if they're not going to make them into a movie. And they pay really well for that.

Q. And, Mr. Duhigg, you said you're also working on a third book. Have you—
A. I have.
Q.—sold that book?
A. Yes.
Q. I'm just going to ask you to let finish my question—
A. Oh, sure.
Q.—before you start your answer—
A. I'm sorry. Yeah.
Q.—just for the benefit of Ms. Reporter.
A. Sorry.
Q. At a high level, what is that book about?
A. That book is about the science of communication and conversation.
Q. And to whom did you sell that book?

A. I sold that book to Andy Ward.
Q. How much did Random House pay to acquire the rights to publish your third book?
A. So they gave me an advance of $2 million for that book.
Q. And were you contractually obligated to sell that book to Random House?
A. No.
Q. Then why did you sell your book to Random House?
A. Because I want to work with Andy. I mean, honestly, not only do I enjoy working with Andy, but I'm going to sell the most books working with Andy. And selling the most books is both spiritually rewarding and financially rewarding.
Q. I notice that you keep referring to Mr. Ward when I ask you questions about Random House. Is there a reason for that?
A. I mean, yeah. Because I work—I like—I don't really work for Random House; I work for Andy Ward. Like that is the relationship.
Q. If Mr. Ward left Random House and went to another publisher, what would you do?
A. I would—if he would have me, I would follow him to another publisher.
Q. Regardless of which publisher he went to?
A. I mean, yeah. I mean, essentially, yeah. I don't know. If he went to, like, some, like, far-right publisher, maybe not. But Andy wouldn't do that. I don't know. Yes. Anywhere that Andy would go, I would want to go with Andy.
Q. Mr. Duhigg, is your close relationship with your editor, with Mr. Ward, is that unusual compared to your peers that you know?
A. No. Many—most writers will say that, outside of their marriage, their closest and most intimate relationship is with their editor. And I think there's a huge devotion when you find a good one.
Q. Mr. Duhigg, do you think that the $2 million advance paid by Random House for your third book was the highest advance you could have received?
A. No. I could have received far, far more. And I specifically asked my agent—I told my agent, actually, that I would be happy if he could just get me $1.5 million. If we had gone—yeah. We could have earned a lot more. But I didn't want that.
Q. Did anyone else offer you money to publish your third book before you sold it to Random House?
A. Not formally. But Audible had indicated that they would, sight unseen, pay a million dollars or more for the audio rights. And other publishers have made clear that if I'm ever unhappy that they would welcome me both emotionally and financially.
Q. So you mentioned a conversation with Audible. Did you use that conversation in your negotiations with Random House about your third book?
A. So I don't really do the negotiations with Random House. Andrew Wylie does them on my behalf by design. I did mention to Andy Ward that Audible had been very encouraging, and I did that because I hoped that it would help him internally in rallying the troops to buy my next book.
Q. Did it work?
A. I don't know. I don't know. You would have to ask them. But I think so, because I've been told since then—and this is a little—sorry. This is a little bit in the weeds, so tell me to stop. When Random House bought my first two books, it came from Little Random, that makes print books. And we sold a lot of audio books. And so within Random House, audio got a lot of money for my books, but they didn't pay for my advance.

And so I had told Andy Ward about this Audible thing in the hopes that they could—instead of Little Random paying my full advance, the audio division of Random House could also pay part of the advance, which would be more equitable.

Q. And, Mr. Duhigg, you mentioned that you believed you could get a much higher advance from your third book.
A. Yes.
Q. Did you want a higher advance?
A. No. So Andrew Wylie put together an analysis of what we could expect if we went to markets.

Right? That indicated we could probably get between $4 and $5 million in an advance for my third book. And I specifically said I did not want to do that. It's a very, very bad idea to take a very large advance.

Q. Why did you think it was a bad idea to take a very large advance?

A. Because if you're like me, this is a career. Right? I'm not writing one book; I'm writing hopefully ten, 12 books over my career. And I want a partnership. I want a partnership where my partner succeeds along with me, which means that I don't want them to take on a huge risk and I don't want them to ask me to take on a huge risk. I want us to make choices that are sensible together.

And what I needed in an advance is I needed an advance that was big enough to give me in this case two years to write a book, because I thought that that's what this book would take. And if I wrote a great book, it would sell millions and millions of copies. So it doesn't matter how big the advance is. The prize is the end of the rainbow. Right? When this book sells for years and years and years.

And I felt like $1.5 million was plenty of money to give me the time and the space to write that book. And Andrew Wylie being Andrew Wylie, like, he is a man who can, like, squeeze blood from a rock. Like he got $2 million. Right? Because he,—because probably because he can't stop himself. But I was pleased with that. But I was very clear I did not want more than $2 million. It's an advance. It's not the economic point of writing the book.

Q. Mr. Duhigg, do you think it's unusual to have that feeling about an advance among your peer group?

A. Not among people who write more than one book in their lifetime. Like this is a constant conversation among—you know, Michael Lewis is famous for taking very modest—

MR. KELLEY: Objection, your Honor. This question calls for hearsay.

THE COURT: Sustained.

THE WITNESS: Okay.

BY MS. SMITH

Q. Mr. Duhigg, can you tell us about anyone—withdrawn. Mr. Duhigg, do you believe that your agent has a duty to get the highest advance for you?

A. No. No. They have the exact opposite duty. They have a duty to find a place for your book where it is going to do best. And oftentimes, that means not taking the largest advance. This happens with overseas. I've sold this book—all my books have been sold in the overseas markets. Each country has its own little, like, deal.

And very often, the agent who—this guy named James Poland, who works within Andrew Wylie's offices, will come to me and he'll say: I got three offers on this book. I think you should turn down the two top offers because this third publisher, he's only—he's not offering as much money in an advance, but they will sell more of your book.

They are better positioned; they understand your book; they understand you; they understand how to market this kind of book. They will make it more of a success.

From my perspective, what I'm saying is, that actually means I will make more money, right? Because it's about sales. It's not about advances; it's about sales.

Q. Mr. Duhigg, do you expect your third book to earn out its advance?

A. I mean, I hope so. Look, it is inevitable that I will have a book that is a flop. I mean, I will hopefully write enough books that I'll have a book that is a flop.

Everybody has a flop. And so I am very hopeful that it does earn out this advance. I'm hopeful that it's profitable for Random House and for me. There is absolutely no guarantee that it will be.

But I also believe that even if it isn't, that I have—because I haven't tried to extort Random House, that I have a relationship with them, where they will say, This didn't work, but we are still with you; we want to do your fourth book and we're going to figure out how to make that one better.

Q. Mr. Duhigg, do you believe that the Penguin Random House and Simon & Schuster merger will disadvantage you in some manner?

A. No. Exactly the opposite.

Q. Why?

A. I was thinking about this. There was a bunch of coverage about the fact that Stephen King had come in and talked to this Court. And, like, everybody knows who Stephen King is. All Stephen King has to do is just tweet that he's written a new book and everyone's going to line—I will line up to buy it. I love Stephen—I read Stephen King when I was 8 years old.

But nobody knows who I am. Like nobody knows who Charles Duhigg is. And the market—like, the world is different now that you can't be Stephen King. You can't even be Malcolm Gladwell. Like it's just—that age is over.

And so the only thing, the best insurance I have that my book will be read, is to try and find a company that hires data geeks who figure out that someone in Des Moines who works in tech likes books like mine and that if we serve them an ad on Facebook at 7:00 p.m., they might see that ad. But that if it's someone in San Francisco and they don't work in tech, then what we need to do is serve them an ad on Twitter, and to do that in 10,000 different ways. Discoverability. Telling readers that this book exists that they want to read. That is the hardest thing.

And my experience is, I was with Random House before Random House merged with Penguin. And their capabilities at data analysis and data analytics and access to data and their investment in creating tools that help authors sell their books, it became so much more sophisticated after that merger. And, like, I was told it was more sophisticated because they now can be more sophisticated.

And I believe that if this merger goes through that it will make it—it will—Random House wants to sell books. It wants to help its authors. It wants to make the world better for writers. I think expanding that to a new group of writers, the Simon & Schuster writers, will make the world a better place. And if it doesn't happen, it will be disastrous for Simon & Schuster, because they will get acquired by private equity. And I covered private equity for a decade at *The New York Times*, and I saw what happened with newspapers. And they will gut that company.

Q. Mr. Duhigg, if the combined Penguin Random House and Simon & Schuster offered you a lower advance after they merge, what would you do?

A. If they offered me a lower advance?

Q. Yes.

A. Like if I felt that was unjust?

Q. Yes.

A. Oh, I would go on Twitter and I would say: They have now violated their promise that they are going to—that this isn't going to change things. Like—I mean, not only just me. Like, I would go on Twitter. I'd go to *The New York Times*, to *Publishers Weekly*. Andrew Wylie would go to all those publications. Like, the hue and cry would be enormous.

But I believe my editor would do that. Like Andy Ward would stand up and threaten to resign in protest. Like the company has promised that they will maintain competition, that they will protect competition, that they'll encourage competition. And this is a profession rooted in truthfulness and trust. If they violated that, it would be—have very significant consequences.

Q. Even if the company hadn't made that promise, would that change your support for the merger?

A. Yeah. I mean, the fact that they made that promise is great. But yeah. Even if they hadn't made that promise, because, look, the thing that I know about Andy Ward and I know about everyone who works in Random House is they love authors. These are people who have spent their entire life trying to sell more books, to convince the public to read and to buy books. They have spent their whole life trying to protect authors so that we have the freedom to write what we want to write. And I have never seen them do anything that is not with the author's best interest in mind. And if they started behaving without the author's best interest in mind, they would get abandoned by the entire industry immediately.

Q. So I just want to clean up, because I think I asked you a question that you may have misheard.

A. Oh.

Q. Even if Penguin Random House hadn't made that promise, would you still support the merger?

A. Yes. I would support the merger. I'm sorry.

Q. Thank you, Mr. Duhigg.

A. I might be a little longwinded.

MS. SMITH: No further questions. I pass the witness.

THE COURT: Thank you. Any cross?

MR. KELLEY: Good morning, your Honor. Collier Kelley from the United States.
THE COURT: Good morning.
MR. KELLEY: May I proceed?
THE COURT: Yes.

CROSS-EXAMINATION

BY MR. KELLEY:

Q. Good morning, Mr. Duhigg.
A. Good morning.
Q. So you spoke a lot about advances. And my general—tell me if this is correct. Your general perspective is that advance doesn't matter that much. Correct?
A. Well, I wouldn't say it doesn't matter. I mean, look, it's the money that allows me to write a book. So it's not that it's, like, totally immaterial. But if you're asking me, like, what I think about a book as an economic unit, the royalties matter—the royalties are what matter. The advance is just the publishing house giving me an advance on those royalties.
Q. So if the advance wasn't as important as the royalty, why did you seek a $1.5 million advance for your third book instead of higher royalty rates?
A. Because it didn't occur to me. I don't know. I mean, that was not an option that was given to me.
Q. And you mentioned the advance for your three books has helped you several times. I believe you said it's helped you write your previous two books you published and it's helping you write your third book. Is that fair?
A. Yes, sir.
Q. And it's helped you and it's allowed you to take time off from your other jobs?
A. Yes.
Q. It's also—I think you mentioned with *The Power of Habit* the advance helped you—you had had a new child. Right?
A. Yes.
Q. And the advance helped you pay the—you know, all the baby stuff, basically?
A. Yeah.
Q. Okay. And your second advance, it helped you buy a house. Correct?
A. I mean, we had saved up some money at that point. And we were very—I never knew if I was going to get fired from *The New York Times*. And so selling that second book meant that it was like: Okay. We can go ahead and buy that house. We're not going to get foreclosed on. Like, even if I get fired from *The Times*, like, there is this income stream that gives us a little bit of a cushion. Does that make sense?
Q. Yes. So the advance has helped you with your living expenses and it's allowed you to write these books. Correct?
A. Yeah. It provided income while I was doing the reporting and the writing for the books.
Q. Okay. And—
A. And—I'm sorry.
Q. Continue.
A. And promotion. Like, once you publish the book, your job isn't done. It's actually—you have a whole other job.
Q. Okay. And it sounds like the marketing at Penguin Random House has been very important to you. Correct?
A. Yes. Yeah.
Q. And it's been a big draw for you to continue to publish books at Penguin Random House. Correct?
A. I would say actually the draw is Andy Ward. It's the editing. There's—I mean, there are many publishers that could provide very similar marketing and promotion as Random House. So it's really been—Andy Ward is really the reason I'm there.
Q. I think you also mentioned you almost prefer a small advance to a larger advance. Is that correct?
A. I mean, not just almost. Yeah. In other words, there's a certain—there's a certain size of advance that

makes sense. In excess of that is dangerous.

Q. And that is because you earn out your advance—or you have earned out your advance for your previous two books. Correct?

A. I'm sorry. Say it again. I'm not sure I understand the question.

Q. So you don't seek a higher advance because you always expect your book to earn out the advance. Correct?

A. I don't seek a higher advance because I don't—the advance should be sized to provide the money I need in order to write the book.

Like what I do is I sit down and calculate, like, this book is going to take two years. Like how—what size of an advance do I need where I can take two years off of earning money from magazine writing to write this book? And then my—if I write a great book, then I think it's going to sell enough copies that it'll—what I earn will be larger than the advance.

But in addition, it's not just the book. So the best way to sell an old book is to write a new book. Right? So when I go and I write a new book, I know that sales of *The Power of Habit* are going to rise, because it just reminds people that I exist.

And on each book, you can like speak for about three—you can be on the speaking circuit for about three years. But unless you write a new book, they stop asking you to speak. And speaking is really remunerative. Some of my colleagues earn, like, $100,000 a speech. And so if you write this book, you can say, Oh, I think that I'm probably going to have, you know, hopefully a year, maybe three years of giving speeches and earning from that.

So—I'm sorry. Did I answer your question?

Q. I'll move on.

A. Okay.

Q. So you only receive royalty checks if your advance earns out. Correct?

A. I'm not sure about the checks part. But yes. What happens as far as I understand it is I'll get like a statement that'll say: You've earned $300,000 in royalties and your advance was $750,000. And so once you get to $750,000 and one dollar, we're going to give you that dollar. But until then, we keep it to repay the advance.

Q. So if you do not earn out your advance, you will not receive royalty checks. Is that fair?

A. I believe so. Yeah.

Q. Okay. You don't actually know how often authors earn out their advance, do you?

A. No, I don't.

Q. You have not looked into studies as to how many authors earn out their advance, have you?

A. No, I have not. I don't know if those studies exist. But no. I have not seen them.

Q. So if I were to tell you that a majority of authors do not earn out their advance, you wouldn't be able to dispute that, would you?

A. No. I would not be able to dispute that.

Q. And so the authors who do not earn out their advance, they're not going to receive the royalties that you rely on that has shaped your opinion. Correct?

A. I'm sorry. Say the question again.

Q. So the authors who do not earn out their advance, they do not get royalties. Correct?

A. I believe—right. I don't think they get the next dollar. Yes. I think you're right.

Q. And you've primarily said that you don't seek a high advance because you rely on royalties. Correct?

A. Yeah. I mean, I think most authors—like you don't write a book saying, Gosh, I only hope it sells 10,000 copies, but I can convince some publisher to give me a big advance. You write a book because you want people to read it.

And you're hopeful. You go into this saying: I want an advance that's large enough to let me write a great book. But if I write a great book, like, I think people are going to read it and they're going to buy it.

And I think that's what all authors—and you're right: There's a number of authors for whom that doesn't—and this will happen to me. Some book I write will not earn out its advance. But this is about a career; it's not about one book.

Q. And then so in the hypothetical situation you just said, where you don't sell enough copies to earn out your advance, you'd be thankful you got that advance, though, wouldn't you be?

A. No. I would actually—I would be very scared that it means that Random House would not want to work with me anymore, because they lost money.

Q. But financially, you personally would have less money?

A. I personally would have less money?

Q. If your book did not earn out, if you did not receive the royalties. So you would prefer to have a higher advance just in case you don't earn out. Correct?

A. No. I mean, everyone in this room could go to something that paid them more money. Right? Like you guys are government lawyers. You could earn more money. We're not trying to maximize money. We're not trying to—like, I assume. The goal here is not—you do this because you believe in justice. And I write books because I want people to read those books, not to try and maximize my bank account. And, and, if I believe that more people will read my books because I take a smaller advance, then I'll take that smaller advance. And I think it's going to pay off in my benefit over time, even if it doesn't on this book.

Q. So moving on, you stated that—

A. Sorry. I didn't mean—I hope that wasn't—

Q. Earlier, you stated that a private equity firm might buy Simon & Schuster. But you have no personal knowledge of that, do you?

A. I have—no. I have not spoken to the bidders myself. But I did cover private equity for a number of years.

Q. And you also mentioned—I think you said the word "data geeks"?

A. Yeah. Like data analytics experts.

Q. So we can call it data analytics.

A. Sure.

Q. Do you know if Simon & Schuster has data analytics?

A. I think every publisher has people who are looking at data.

Q. And so do you know if small publishers have data analytics?

A. Yeah. Absolutely. I know small publishers have data analytics. I mean, nowadays you can sort of buy some aspects of it off the shelf.

Q. You also mentioned Audible.

A. Yes.

Q. But you never actually considered Audible as an option for audio rights, did you?

A. What do you mean, "consider"? I mean, certainly if Random House had not been interested in my audio rights, then Audible would have been the place I would have wanted to take them.

Q. You always intended for Random House to acquire the audio rights to your third book. Correct?

A. I was hopeful they would acquire audio rights.

MR. KELLEY: No further questions at this time.

THE COURT: Thank you. I think it's a good time for us to take a break. So let's take 15 minutes at this time. Please don't talk to anybody about your testimony during the break.

MS. SMITH: Your Honor, I have no redirect, unless you have questions.

THE COURT: I do have some questions, actually. Let me ask you a few questions and then I'll let you go.

THE WITNESS: Sure. Or we can take—whatever. I have the whole day set aside.

THE COURT: Thank you. So you've spoken a lot about all authors want this, all authors want that. But it seems to me that your experience, of course, is colored by your own success.

THE WITNESS: Absolutely.

THE COURT: And congratulations on your success.

THE WITNESS: Thank you.

THE COURT: So what about authors who don't earn out their advances? And we've heard in this trial that 85 percent of books don't earn out their advances. What if you're an author who didn't earn out their advance but you want to write a second book?

THE WITNESS: So I think if you're an author who didn't—and this happens a lot. I have a number of friends who, whether it's their second book or their third or fourth, like, it's going to happen to me. There's some book I write that won't earn out its advance. So I guess—I'm sorry. What's the question?

THE COURT: But also 98 percent of the books apparently are not—

THE WITNESS: Right.

THE COURT:—top sellers.

THE WITNESS: Yeah.

THE COURT: We've heard lots of statistics. You know, 4 percent of the books account for 60 percent of the profits. And so I feel like you maybe are not a typical author.

THE WITNESS: So here's—I think that's—let me answer that a couple ways.

THE COURT: Okay.

THE WITNESS: And I hope—tell me if this answers the question. So I think for folks like myself, I'm very typical. Right? So I'm a professional writer. I have 20 years of writing experience. And I'm a nonfiction writer. You're not going to find a lot of *New York Times* reporters, for instance, who write books that don't succeed in some way. Right?

THE COURT: You guys are a very small portion of the–

THE WITNESS: Yeah.

THE COURT:—[indiscernible] market.

THE WITNESS: I think—

THE COURT: You—

THE COURT REPORTER: I'm sorry, Judge. I didn't hear your question.

THE COURT: I said: And you guys are a small portion of the author market. My line of questioning basically is, you've given me very interesting testimony. But is it typical of authors? And there's a lot of data that I've been presented with in this case that suggests that you are not typical. So go ahead.

THE WITNESS: What I would say is, I'm not certain that there's anyone who's typical. Right? There's people who publish poetry books. And those people know that their sales are going to be very small no matter how talented they are. There's people who publish science fiction. And in science fiction, the way the market works is, like, basically if someone loves you, then they tell someone else and you can become this huge hit overnight.

And people will write ten books that never sell and then their eleventh book is a huge hit. There's people like me who are professional writers who want to make a career of this. And I think they're very similar to me. They're very typical to me. There's a whole bunch of other people who write books essentially as a sideline. And for them, they never anticipate. They never really want to be huge writers.

There's writers who write bad books—not bad books, but they don't write great books because they know that they'll get invited on the lecture circuit. I know, like, five or six of these guys. And they're great. Right? They give great lectures. But you need a new book to, like, remind people that you give good lectures.

And so the thing I would say is, you're right: I am atypical. But every author is atypical. Like the most you can do is you can create like a thousand little groups—

THE COURT: Of course.

THE WITNESS:—of people that you're like.

THE COURT: But the focus on this trial is on something in particular. I feel you may be atypical for what we're focusing on here, which is advances and things of that nature, because if you—you sort of have the luxury of saying: I'm going to get royalties later, so I don't care as much about what the advance is now. I just need enough to write this book.

But if you were an author who can't expect necessarily to earn out their advances, wouldn't they need more of an advance to make sure they can keep supporting their writing? Because they have more risk.

THE WITNESS: So again, my—I'm not a lawyer, so I don't understand a lot. But my understanding was that the group that we're talking about are likely expected bestsellers. For someone who is an expected bestseller, you anticipate that you will earn royalties in excess of your advance. Like that's the whole point of being a bestseller. And to your point, it would be—if a publishing house came to me and they said, We will give you exactly the amount of money that you need to just write this book, then I would say actually, That's really dangerous for me, because what I need something in excess of that, because it's not just writing this book; it's that once the book gets published, I'm going to spend a year promoting the hardcover and then I'm going to spend a year promoting the paperback. And during that time, I'm going to start writing my next book.

So $750,000 is actually a good amount of money because not only it gives me four checks of $115,000 or whatever it is, you know, that lets me write that first book, but to the point you just raised, it actually is the seed fund to allow me to write the next book. And I don't think it's untypical for people—it's not untypical for people who think they're going to write a bestseller to think that way.

In fact, I mean, I talk with a lot of my colleagues about this, people who don't sell a lot of books. And this is how they do it. They sort of—it's this chain, chain link. Right? Like: I get the book on track. I write this book. I use the advance to finance writing the next book. Hopefully, the book I just wrote, the revenues—royalties start coming in eventually, and so that's how I pay for my kids' college.

But I have enough—it's—you get that money over four years. And that's long enough to write a book and to start working on the next book.

Does that answer your question?

THE COURT: No. It's helpful. And so I guess my closing question would be: If you were an author—and I don't know if you can put yourself in this position. But if you were an author that wasn't from *The New York Times*, didn't have a sense that this is—that people are going to read this necessarily, a bigger risk for you, would you want a higher advance than you would if you think you were going to earn out?

THE WITNESS: If I believed in my book? I mean, if I anticipate that I'm going to be a bestseller, if I anticipate that—

THE COURT: No. I'm just saying—

THE WITNESS: So if—

THE COURT: I'd like you to kind of put that aside, because it's not really about anticipated bestsellers.

THE WITNESS: Oh, okay. Okay.

THE COURT: That's not what this is about. But if you were somebody who considered this a bigger risk in terms of how successful your book is going to be, would you need a higher advance to finance your writing?

THE WITNESS: If I was going to write one book, and that is all I want to do with my life, is write one book—

THE COURT: That's not what I'm saying.

THE WITNESS: So for the other—for anyone else who wants to write multiple books, you don't want to put your publishing house, your partner, in a position where they believe that you are a bad bet, because I'm going to be coming back to them again and again and again and saying: Bet on me again. Like, this time it's going to work. Please bet on me. Like, believe with me that we can make this work. And so I'm not going to ask for a huge amount of money because it means the next time I come, they're going to say: Look, it's just too big a risk. We can't do this again. We've lost too much money on you.

And I've seen this with my fiction writer friends, who it's not untypical for them to write four books that don't sell at all until the fifth book suddenly makes their career. And they say the same thing. They say, like: Look, I don't want the biggest advance possible. I don't want to get as much money as I can. I want an amount of money that lets me write this book and that makes sense for you, my partner, so that if it doesn't work, if this flops, when I come back to you and say, Let's try it again, you don't say, It's just too expensive. I've already lost too much on you. My boss won't let me do it because your P&L will never come out positive.

Everyone has the same attitude if this is a career for you. Like you don't want to buy a million-dollar house and get a $10 million loan on it. You know that that's bound to fail.

And by the same token, of course, there's no author who wants to get more money than they can possibly repay or earn out because it means you're never going to write another book. And for us, this is a career.

Does that answer your question?

THE COURT: Yes. Thank you.
Any questions based on my questions?
MR. KELLEY: No more questions.
MS. SMITH: No.
THE COURT: Thank you very much.
THE WITNESS: Thank you. Thank you for having me. This is a real honor. I really appreciate it.
THE COURT: Thank you. You may step down. (Witness excused.)

SALLY KIM, SVP AND PUBLISHER, PUTNAM

Like many other imprint publishers, Putnam publisher Sally Kim confirmed on the stand that her boss Ivan Held approves any advances up to $250,000; thereafter he needs approval from Penguin Publishing Group president Allison Dobson (and above $1 million, Dobson needs approval from PRH US CEO Madeline McIntosh).

More unusually, Kim reported that, "At Putnam, I would say about 80 percent we buy through one-on-one negotiations with agents. And then the rest we buy at auction. . . . We consistently buy books at auction at about less than 20 percent. So I was actually surprised to find that out myself."

To government's contention about price levels, annual Putnam Title Profitability charts do list books by advance levels, we were shown—including the advance level for "significant deals" of $250,000 to $499,999. And, "There are three advance levels below the $250,000 to $499,999 range. Right?" (We know this one: Yes, right. Good, Very Nice, and Nice.)

As the government pointed out, "there's a correlation between the advance level and the marketing spend?" Indeed, Kim conceded, "I have looked at it. And, you know, it's interesting to see that when you look at averages, there is a general correlation." And Judge Pan noticed a row of data showing, "It's sort of even more extreme that the higher-advance-level ones accounted for a greater percentage of sales."

She recalled the happy success of buying *Where the Crawdads Sing* for "mid-six figures," when other interest might not have been that high. "Through our conversations with the agent, we started to get the sense, as I mentioned before, that there weren't a lot of editors banging down his door to make an offer. So we decided to try to preempt and we made a preempt offer and he accepted it."

Like some others on the stand, she said the other PRH imprints are "probably my fiercest competitors, actually." (Was this helping their case, that PRH is already/only the strongest competitor to PRH? By the close of the trial, the government's John Read pointed out the problem.) She added, "My sense, I think, is we actually lose more to an internal peerage imprint than we do external."

TESTIMONY OF SALLY KIM, SVP AND PUBLISHER, PUTNAM

DIRECT EXAMINATION

BY MS. RUDZIN:

Q. Good morning, Ms. Kim. Can you please state your name for the record?

A. Sally Kim.

Q. And please tell us about your job at Penguin Random House.

A. I am senior vice president and publisher of Putnam, which is an imprint of the Penguin Publishing Group division.

Q. And what do you do as the publisher of Putnam?

A. I oversee a team of editors who acquire and edit books and I also oversee the marketing and publicity departments. I also acquire and edit several books a year myself.

Q. I just want to make sure the court reporter can hear you. If you'd speak into the microphone, please.

A. Oh, sure.

Q. Can you please give us a brief overview of your career in publishing?

A. So I've been in publishing for about 30 years. I started in 1995 as an assistant at the Sandra Dijkstra Literary Agency. About a year after that, I moved up to Harper San Francisco, where I was an editorial assistant. And then in 1998, I moved to the New York office of HarperCollins. And then since then, I've held various editorial positions at several different publishers, including St. Martin's Press, which is an imprint of Macmillan; Crown, which is an imprint of Random House; back to HarperCollins; and then Touchstone, which was an imprint of Simon & Schuster at the time. And then in 2015, I moved over to head up Putnam.

Q. How long have you been in a role in which you acquire book rights?

A. About 25 years. 1998 was when I became an acquiring editor at HarperCollins.

Q. And what types of books do you personally like to acquire?

A. I like to describe them as upmarket commercial fiction, which is really an industry term, but it's the cross between for me literary fiction and commercial fiction. So that means I'm always looking for a certain quality of writing that can win awards and critical acclaim, but can ultimately really appeal to a wide audience.

Q. Are there any books you're particularly proud of having acquired and edited?

A. So many. But the ones that come to mind really are the ones where I really felt like I was reading something new for the first time. One example is *Sharp Objects*, by Gillian Flynn, which we published at a time when dark psychological suspense wasn't really as popular as it is now, written by women.

And the other is a book called *The Prophets* by Robert Jones, Jr., which is just a groundbreaking book about the love between two enslaved men during Antebellum South.

This is a book when I read it for the first time, I felt like I was reading a classic in the making and that in many ways I felt like I worked my whole career for the opportunity and the responsibility to publish this book. So it was a finalist for the National Book Award last year.

Q. Congratulations. Have you personally received any awards?

A. I have. Earlier this year, the Poets & Writers organization honored me with the editor's award.

Q. What does that award recognize?

A. It recognizes sustained contribution to literary prose. So it recognizes an editor who has contributed to that.

Q. Congratulations on that, too. Let's turn to Putnam. What can you tell us about Putnam?

A. So Putnam is the oldest imprint in the industry. It was founded in 1838. For many, many, years, it was—it maintained a very strong reputation for publishing very big commercial blockbusters. And it's maintained its status. We've maintained our status in that we have more hardcover *New York Times* bestsellers than any other imprint consistently, year after year.

Q. And what brought you to Putnam?

A. So I was recruited to help—to come to Putnam and to help sort of revitalize from sort of its more mass-market commercial list to include more diversion fiction and different categories of fiction, including literary fiction, women's fiction. We also have turned some of our focus to nonfiction.

Q. How did you go about broadening Putnam's list?

A. Well, it was a process. I mean, really ultimately when you're creating a list or expanding a list, you really need editors at the helm to really attract books to that imprint. So I really looked to find some editors who had strong reputations for, you know, books in these categories that we were looking to expand into, but also strong relationships with agents, where they could attract those books.

Q. Have you been successful in broadening Putnam's list?

A. I'd like to think we have been. It's ever-evolving, so we're constantly working towards it.

But yes. We still have a very strong franchise list, a very strong commercial list, but we have been really successful in publishing into new fiction categories; as I mentioned, literary fiction, women's fiction. And on the nonfiction side, we have a strong prescriptive and narrative nonfiction list.

Q. So if I understood what you were saying, Putnam still publishes franchise authors. Right?

A. Yes. We are very proud to still publish John Sandford, Clive Cussler, Tom Clancy, Lisa Scottoline, among others.

Q. Putnam also now publishes some literary novels?

A. Yes. Some of the books that we always like to tout: *The Immortalists*, by Chloe Benjamin, which was one of the first books I bought at Putnam; *Such a Fun Age*, by Kiley Reid, which was long-listed for the Booker Prize; *The Prophets*, which I mentioned earlier, which I should note that it was our first—Putnam's first National Book finalist since 1989; and *Booth*, by Karen Joy Fowler, which we just learned a couple weeks ago was long-listed for this year's Booker Prize.

Q. And are you responsible for all of Putnam's acquisitions?

A. Yes. I don't edit and acquire each one myself, but I do approve and oversee all the acquisitions that we make.

Q. So let's talk about the process for acquiring book rights. How many books have you personally acquired or tried to acquire over the course of your career?

A. Hundreds.

Q. How does Putnam usually acquire books?

A. At Putnam, I would say about 80 percent we buy through one-on-one negotiations with agents. And then the rest we buy at auction.

Q. So the 80 percent figure, based on what we have heard in the trial, seems really high for just negotiations. Is Putnam somewhat unique in that?

A. Yes. I think it has a lot to do with the fact that we are very—still a franchise-heavy list. Also, not only with our franchises, but we have a lot of authors that are repeat authors that we publish regularly. So those negotiations tend to be one-on-one.

We also, like a lot of imprints—but we do get a lot of exclusive submissions from agents. So that means we're looking at these exclusively and the negotiations ultimately become one-on-one negotiations.

So—and then, you know, I think auctions tend to be emotional and dramatic, so I think sometimes auctions do sort of stick out in people's minds more than they do. But—so I actually am always curious how many we end up buying at auction, and I had looked. And we consistently buy books at auction at about less than 20 percent. So I was actually surprised to find that out myself.

Q. Do you find that on occasion a book is sent out widely to editors, so not exclusively to Putnam, but Putnam still just negotiates with the agent?

A. Yes. That actually happens probably most of the time. We're part of a multiple submission. A lot of editors in the industry get the book, but we end up being the only publisher that's interested. That happens quite often. And then that ends up being a one-on-one negotiation with an agent.

Q. Does Putnam end up offering on every book that is submitted to it?

A. No. We want to buy books that we love, but also books that we feel fit the vision for the list. So not every book falls into those categories. So no. We don't offer on every book.

Q. So let's discuss auctions briefly, because they're a minority of your acquisitions. In an auction, do you know whom you're bidding against?

A. No. Not usually.

Q. Do you know the number of other bidders in an auction?

A. No, not usually. I mean, we'll always ask. We always like to ask agents as many questions as we can. We don't usually get the answers to those questions, but . . .

Q. When the agent tells you how many bidders are participating in an auction, does that affect how you bid?

A. It can. But really, we approach each auction, each situation, individually and differently. So if we really, really want a book—and that happens a lot—we'll bid what we want or what we need or what we think we need to buy that book. It only really takes one passionate editor at another imprint to win that book away from us. And we're very aware of that.

Q. If it's one of those situations you mentioned, where you learn that Putnam is the only interested imprint, let's start with: How would you know that?

A. We don't always exactly know. We do—we're in constant contact with the agent once we receive a submission. We're talking to them constantly. So sometimes it's really a nuance. It could be, you know, we're on the phone with them and we get—sometimes it's like the tone of her voice or how enthusiastically she's pushing us to make an offer. We take little nuances like that and it informs our thinking.

Q. If you think Putnam is the only imprint interested in a book, even though the agent has submitted it widely, does Putnam then bid at a lower level?

A. Well, no, not necessarily, because as I mentioned, we want to win the book. The goal is always to win the book. And even if it's a one-on-one negotiation, we know the agent can decide to send it to five more editors; and among those five editors there could be one editor who decides they want this book, too. So we're constantly aware that there's competition. We need to bid what we feel we want to—you know, what we think we can—how we can win the book and go for it forthright.

I also think, you know, this is such a relationship business; and there are agents that I have known for 20-plus years that I still do business with. And if I consistently low-balled them or didn't get them fair offers, I would not be able to do business with them anymore. They really, you know, rely on us to be able to have fair and open negotiations. So that is always front of mind for me.

The other is the author. We want to pay a fair price and value for their book, and we want them to come and be happy about the deal. We want to start off on the right foot. I always say: At Putnam, we want authors to come to us with full hearts. And so, you know, we keep that in mind when we're making offers.

Q. We've heard that Viking passed on the *Where the Crawdads Sing* and that Putnam has made it a huge success. Can you tell us the story of how Putnam acquired it?

A. So that was a book that was submitted widely. The editor at Putnam who received it read it, loved it, shared it with all of us, ran up and down the halls. And through our conversations with the agent, we started to get the sense, as I mentioned before, that there weren't a lot of editors banging down his door to make an offer. So we decided to try to preempt and we made a preempt offer and he accepted it.

Q. And just generally, what was the preempt offer?

A. Mid-six figures.

Q. When Putnam submitted its offer for the book, did the offer include a marketing plan?

A. No. We generally don't do that. I would say it's hard to predict, you know. We do think about marketing as we get closer to the publication of a book. So often we're buying books either, you know, as a proposal, on an outline, you know, or in the case of even fiction, even if we have a full manuscript, that book is going to get revised and edited.

Any good editor will want to get their hands on it. And sometimes it's years before we are actually turning our heads to actually publishing that book.

So, you know, it's really—it doesn't make a lot of sense to commit to any sort of marketing at the time of acquisition. I mean, who knew that BookTok was going to be a big thing just a year ago? There's no way you could account for that and guarantee something like that in a contract.

Q. What if the agent actually asks for a marketing plan as part of a bidding process?

A. They'll sometimes ask. And we'll politely demur, because specifically at Putnam we do pride ourselves on our, you know, bespoke marketing campaigns for each book. Every book is very different. We don't do cookie-cutter campaigns. That's one of the things we, you know, always tout. So we explain to them, you know, at this point, when this book is only a proposal, it's only an outline, we can send you a marketing plan, but it's going to be very generic. The book hasn't been written. No one's read it yet. No one loves it yet.

So, you know—and oftentimes, agents understand that because they really want—they understand that the books are living, breathing things.

Q. So back to *Where the Crawdads Sing*, how did Putnam turn that into a book that sold a lot of copies?

A. Well, we didn't know. I mean, we always hope it's going to be a success, but we didn't know when we first published that book. Our first initial print for that book was 25,000 copies. People loved it. You know, people are starting to read it.

Q. Let me just ask, is 25,000 copies a lot of copies?

A. You know, it's not—it wouldn't have been enough to earn back the advance. I'll say that. You know, every book is different. But I will say for a debut novel, we were very happy with that number. And we were very proud to have this book on our list. And then Reese Witherspoon picked it for her book club and the skies opened up.

Q. Did that happen before or after publication?

A. After publication. The buzz just started, skyrocketed, and then we put a lot of marketing support behind the book. And marketing is interesting, because you can't create demand out of thin air with just marketing. When you have a book that has some traction, has some buzz going, marketing can really amplify that. And it increases it and exposes that book to, you know, a whole host of new readers. So that's what we did. And then the book just continued and continued to just create more and more buzz, more and more word of mouth, and it became a huge success.

Q. As of today, about how many copies have you sold?

A. In the U.S., about 10 million.

Q. So now looking at the other side of the coin, can you tell us about a book that you passed on that ended up selling well?

A. That list is very long. But I would—one that comes to mind is *The Girl on the Train* by Paula Hawkins.

Q. Do you know how many copies of that have sold?

A. I don't. But I would venture to say millions.

Q. You didn't think it was going to sell well?

A. I just didn't personally connect with it as a reader.

Q. How do you value a book Putnam is considering acquiring?

A. Well, really, there are a couple questions I really first ask myself: Is this a book I love, that we love? Is this a book that fits the vision of our list? And if the answer is yes to both, then we will start thinking about the value and we start running a P&L.

Q. We've heard about P&Ls. They start with a number of copies of the book that the imprint thinks it can sell. How do you estimate that?

A. Well, we start by looking at what we call comp books, comparable books, whether they're books that have similar editorial content or a book that we feel appeals to a similar audience and to the book that we're trying to buy.

For example, if we're trying to buy a World War II historical novel, we'll look at other World War II historical novels and see how generally they have sold. And then we'll use those numbers to base our P&L around.

Q. Is there kind of a direct correlation between the P&L—sorry—the comps you pick and the number of copies you actually sell?

A. Well, no. It's just an educated guess. It's really a guide. I mean, the way I always describe P&Ls is we go in with a number that we really feel on advance that we think we are going to try to be able to offer. And then we use P&L and the comps to sort of see: Where do we end up? Really, you know, how many copies should we reasonably expect to have to sell in order to make money off that level of advance?

So sometimes the P&L will tell us: No, you're not going to make a lot of money off that advance. And that obviously, you know, creates a conversation on our end. Should we—sometimes we'll pull a different comp to justify that level. Or sometimes we'll say: Okay. We know we're not going to make, you know, X amount of profit off this book. We still are going to offer this advance.

So really I always feel like the P&L, it's not dictating; it's a guide. It's a guide that tells us where we should expect to be.

Q. Why would you offer an advance that your P&L tells you would not allow Putnam to make money?

A. If we love the book, we're going to want it. But there are other considerations. I mean, sometimes I mentioned that Putnam was going through a little bit of an evolution. There might be a book that we—in a category that we publish well into. So that book we know or we hope will sell well, and so we're going to put a certain high value on it.

Conversely, if it's a book in an area that we don't publish into much, but we really want to get into that business, you know, the horror category, for example, that book is going to be worth a little more to me in that moment than maybe to another publisher. So I take that into consideration.

I think about prestige. There are books that we have a sense, you know, might win an award or garner really great critical acclaim. And I'm always thinking about Putnam's reputation, you know, in the industry, particularly as we're evolving. And so to me, that book might be worth more to me and worth stretching for.

We're also always looking at authors as sort of a long-term investment. So if it's an author who we really feel has ten books in them, you know, this is an author we can really grow and develop, we might stretch to get that first book, to have that author on our list.

Q. Turning back to the P&Ls, besides the number of copies, what are the other fields in the P&L?

A. So we put in, you know, price, what we think the dimensions of the book might be, how many pages we think it's going to be ultimately when it's written. So we fill in fields like that that kind of give us a little bit of a sense. And then there are other fields that we don't touch that are sort of cost-related, you know: the price of paper and printing and binding—we call that PPB—freight costs, shipping costs, marketing costs.

Q. And you said you don't put those in. Where do all those costs come from?

A. They're fixed by finance. The finance department controls those.

Q. Do you know how the finance department estimates the marketing cost of P&L?

A. I don't know exactly. But I do know it's sort of a function that's sort of a percentage of expected sales revenue.

Q. In your experience, how common is it for different imprints to value the same book differently?

A. Very common. I mean, I think I mentioned comps earlier. It's such—even pulling comps is such a subjective thing. You talk to three different editors; they'll pull three different comps for a book. So I think that is one variable.

But the list of things I mentioned earlier about, you know, all the considerations I'm taking in, you know: Is this a book I want to publish? A category I want to get into? You know, a book that's going to bring prestige? I mean, these are questions that editors have different answers to. So inevitably you're going to get a different valuation in the end.

Q. Do you ever learn that your valuation was wildly different from others?

A. Often. You know, sometimes I'll see—there'll be a book that I was in an auction for and we won't win and then we'll see it reported in a place like Publishers Marketplace and I'll see that it indicates maybe it went for seven figures, and maybe I had only run my P&L and thought I would bid to low six figures. Conversely, I'm sure I know sometimes at the end of an auction I'll get a sense from the agent that maybe when I win an auction that I paid a lot more than the last bidder.

Q. Does it frustrate you when you learn that you might have overpaid for the book?

A. No. I don't really think of it as overpaying. I think of it as the price I needed to pay to win the book, because again the goal for us is always we want to win, especially if it's a book that we really see for the list.

Ultimately, I'm never going to make an offer that I can't live with. So if I find out that another editor or editors valued it much lower, I just—I don't really care that much, to be honest.

Q. Are there other financial terms Putnam offers in competing for a book besides the advance?

A. Yeah. We offer sometimes, you know, different royalties, bonuses.

Q. Can you just explain what a bonus is? Is it just extra money?

A. The way I always describe bonuses is it is very much an additional advance. So—and they kick in at certain sales performance thresholds.

Q. Is your willingness to negotiate those terms, a bonus or different royalty rates, based on the advance level?

A. No. We have bonuses in different rates for a range of all advances. It really actually has less to do with the actual individual advance and more to do with the agent that we're negotiating with.

Q. How so?

A. Well, agents can be persuasive. But also, you know, we have again longstanding relationships with a lot of them, and so some of them have the ability to convince us to agree to certain terms. And some of them, you know, their contracts—the agent contracts with us, you know, and the boilerplate includes some of these terms already. So it doesn't matter if it's a quote-unquote small book or a big book. They'll get those terms.

Q. Is there anything else Putnam does to try to win the book besides offer attractive financial terms?

A. Passion. We often try to meet—we almost always meet an author, you know, before we make an offer. And that meeting I feel like is the most crucial part of all of this.

I always describe it as sort of almost like a two-way job interview because we're assessing the author and her ability, you know, to promote the book and talk about the book and her vision. But we're also pitching ourselves and how great we would be to work with.

So these are things that we always are constantly on the agent about throughout the whole process. We're calling; we're pouring on the love; we're talking about how innovative we'll be. And all the things that come up a lot in the meeting we'll reiterate throughout the whole negotiation process.

In fact, you know, when we send in an offer, we always—almost always include what we call a love letter, where we highlight all these things and talk about all the ways in which we are going to be such a great partner for this author. So we rely on passion to really kind of take us over the edge sometimes.

Q. When Putnam is touting itself to win the book, does it ever talk about Penguin Random House's access to printing facilities?

A. No.

Q. Does Penguin Random House's access to printing facilities ever come up in conversations with authors or agents?

A. No, they don't.

Q. Does Putnam ever win an auction even though the advance it offers is lower than an advance offered by another publisher?

A. It does, and it happens a lot. And I think that has a lot to do with, I guess, the meeting, you know, that I mentioned earlier, that vision-setting. And I think a lot of times that's when that first—the chemistry between an author and an editor really—I've seen it happen. I've felt it myself. That's when it's really born.

And so when that vision is clear and that connection is really tight, you know, that will drive an author to come to an imprint even if it means taking a lower advance. One example is—I think it's Author G here.

When I won that book, at the end of that auction, the agent revealed to me that the author turned down a higher advance of several hundred thousand dollars to come with us because he really felt that Putnam and—he felt he had a mind-meld with me and that it was—he was giving the responsibility of his book to us.

Q. Switching gears, who do you consider to be Putnam's competitors?

A. I consider all publishers to be our competitors.

Q. Do you worry about losing a book to an imprint at HarperCollins?

A. Yes.

Q. Do you worry about losing a book to an imprint at Macmillan?

A. Yes.

Q. Do you worry about losing a book to an imprint at Simon & Schuster?

A. Yes.

Q. Do you worry about losing a book to an imprint at Hachette?

A. Yes.

Q. Do you worry about losing a book to other Penguin Random House imprints?

A. Yes. I would say they're probably my fiercest competitors, actually.

Q. Do you have any sense of how many of your losses have been to other Penguin Random House imprints?

A. My sense, I think, is we actually lose more to an internal peerage imprint than we do external.

Q. Do you worry about losing a book to one of the smaller publishing houses?

A. I do. And I think in some of the—again, it's that connection with the author and the agent, author and editor. You can't really understate [sic] that.

I think some of the newer imprints that have started, you know, Zando and Spiegel & Grau, those are editors with very fine reputations in the industry, longstanding reputations with agents. So you'll see that authors will want to go there because they know that these editors have those reputations.

In fact, I published a writer named Lara Williams, her first book, *Supper Club*, a few years ago. We didn't come to terms for her second book, and I discovered that Zando actually bought that second book and published it earlier this year. I think it was one of their lead titles.

Q. And so that was an author that Putnam had published her first book and then she went to Zando for her second book?

A. I published her second book and she went to Zando for her third. She published her first book elsewhere.

Q. When you lose at auction, do you ask whom you lose to?
A. Yes. We always ask. We don't always get the answer, but we ask.
Q. Why do you ask?
A. It's a data point that we always like to know. We're always looking at ways in which we can differentiate ourselves from other publishers. So it's just always helpful to know. And to be honest, it's just fun to know who you're up against in auction.
Q. Switching gears again, how does Putnam decide the level of marketing support a book will receive?
A. Well, it really depends on each book. Every book gets some sort of marketing support. We do put a lot of support behind the books that we really feel have the potential to succeed.
Q. When does Putnam make that decision?
A. Pretty close to publication. By that time, the book has been written; it's been edited; it's been revised; we've shared it around internally; our sales department starts to buzz about it. And we have a sense of kind of what the traction or reaction the book will get out there in the world.
And also, the market, you know, what's happening in the world? I mentioned BookTok earlier. You know, the book could suddenly be publishing into a category that's very trendy. You know, which books are really hot this year. Who would have guessed two years ago when you signed up a witch book that this would be a witch book moment?
So those are—that's—those are reasons why we really do pay attention to not only the individual book, but what's happening at that time. So as we get closer to the publication, we really start to hone in and think about the important things that will help move that book.
Q. When you are acquiring a book, does Putnam ever commit in contract to provide a certain level of marketing?
A. No. Generally, no.
Q. What, if any, relationship is there between the size of the advance for a book and the amount of marketing support it receives?
A. I mean, there is some correlation. I like to believe that we are right some of the time and when we expect a book to work well that it will.
But really, more than anything, it depends on the book. And it doesn't really matter what the advance is. It's: We're going to do this type of marketing that we feel will position that book well to find its readers and succeed.
Q. Okay. I'd like you to look at the demonstrative, which is confidential, please. So I'll ask you first, do you recognize all of these books?
A. Yes. These are all books published by Putnam.
Q. Let's talk about the first book, Book A. Can you tell us about that book?
A. So Book A is a book we bought for $50,000. It's a book that we loved. And it's a book when it—after it was revised and it came in, people really—it was a book we all loved at the imprint. But really the sales team, the sub-rights team, everybody started to really just go crazy for this book. So we put more marketing behind it. We thought: Okay. We have something here. It's really—we're getting a little focus test here internally.
And the book really started to work. This was also one that Reese Witherspoon picked for her book club eventually when it went into paperback. So we ended up spending all told $185,000 on marketing, which is—my math is not great, but I will say it's almost I think four times as much as we spent on the advance.
Q. Do you know the marketing cost that was estimated by the P&L for that book?
A. No.
Q. Is there a document that would refresh your recollection?
A. The P&L has a field for that.
Q. Would that be a P&L that you would have reviewed when you were deciding whether to acquire Book A?
A. Yes; at the time of acquisition.
MS. RUDZIN: Your Honor, may I hand it up?
THE COURT: You may.

MR. VANCE: Your Honor, Defendants produced certain documents for the first time yesterday. So to the extent that one of these documents that they're using to refresh the witness was produced yesterday, we would object.

MS. RUDZIN: To be clear, your Honor, I'm not planning on moving it into evidence.

THE COURT: I'm sorry. Your objection is you didn't receive this until yesterday. Are you saying they shouldn't be able to use it?

MR. VANCE: It wasn't produced in the case until yesterday. So we don't think they should be able to use it.

THE COURT: Why wasn't this produced earlier?

MS. RUDZIN: Because it's outside the discovery period. This book was purchased before 2018.

THE COURT: I'm going to sustain the objection.

BY MS. RUDZIN:

Q. Let's talk about Book F, please.

A. Okay.

Q. How much did Putnam pay for that book?

A. $4 million.

Q. And how much did Putnam spend marketing that book?

A. $90,000.

Q. How does the $90,000 in marketing spend compare to the size of the advance?

A. Again, you're questioning my math here.

Q. It's actually on the page.

A. Oh, I'm looking here. I see it. 2.3 percent.

Q. What did the P&L for Book F estimate as the marketing cost?

A. You mean in the P&L?

Q. Yes.

A. I'm not sure. I don't have that P&L in front of me.

Q. Is there a document that would refresh your recollection?

A. The acquisition P&L.

Q. Is that a P&L you reviewed when Putnam acquired Book F?

A. Yes.

MS. RUDZIN: Your Honor, may I hand it up?

THE COURT: Yes.

MS. RUDZIN: (Tenders document to the Court and the witness.)

BY MS. RUDZIN:

Q. Ms. Kim, what did the P&L estimate as the marketing cost for Book F?

A. $176,000.

Q. So Putnam ultimately spent only half as much as the P&L estimated. Is that correct?

A. Yes.

Q. Let's talk about Book B, please.

A. Okay.

Q. What can you tell us about Book B?

A. So Book B is another book we really loved. We bought that for $75,000.

Q. How much did Putnam put into marketing it?

A. We spent $75,000. My math is good enough to say that's 100 percent of what we spent on the advance.

Q. By the way, on Books A and B, do you have a sense of what the P&L estimate would have estimated for marketing costs, given those advance sizes?

A. Yeah. I mean, I've reviewed so many P&Ls. It would have been a lot lower than what we ended up spending.

Q. Do you have any sense what—the magnitude of how much lower?

A. Oh, probably in the low five figures.

Q. Thank you. Let's turn to Author E, Book E.
A. Okay.
Q. What can you tell us about that book?
A. So this is a book that we paid a million dollars to acquire. It was the second book by this author and following a nice—very nice success.
Q. How much did Putnam spend on marketing this book that it paid a million dollars for?
A. $35,000.
Q. It looks like that is the book that Putnam spent the least on in terms of marketing. Do you agree on this slide?
A. Yes.
Q. Why did Putnam spend so little to market that?
A. We really didn't need to spend that much more money to market this book because the author has a high profile. It was following the success of a book similar to it that did very well. So we didn't really need to spend excess money to get it to the readers and the attention of the readers who would buy it.
Q. Do you know what the P&L for Book E estimated as the marketing spend?
A. No. I don't have it off the top of my head.
Q. Is there a document that would refresh your recollection?
A. The P&L.
Q. Is that a P&L you reviewed when Putnam acquired Book E?
A. Yes.
MS. RUDZIN: Your Honor, may I hand it up?
THE COURT: You may.
MS. RUDZIN: (Tenders document to the Court and the witness.)
BY MS. RUDZIN:
Q. Ms. Kim, what did the P&L for Book E estimate as the marketing expense?
A. $215,000.
Q. So that would be significantly more than the actual spend Putnam put into the book?
A. Yes.
Q. Ms. Kim, do you know why the P&L estimated a marketing spend of $215,000 for Book E that got a million-dollar advance and a lower amount—I think you said 175—for Book F, which got a $4 million advance?
A. It's related to—well, it's a percentage of the expected sales revenue. So that's how it's calculated.
Q. So even though Book F got a four-times-larger advance than Book E, the expected sales revenue was not four times larger?
A. It's sort of based on the fixed costs of the P&L. So it's not a variable field that we touched.
Q. Does the marketing support Putnam puts behind a book have any connection to the marketing costs estimated in the acquisition P&L for the book?
A. No. You know, as I mentioned, you know, obviously we hope that there's some correlation with books that we feel are going to sell well. But no. We look at each book individually. We look and see, based on what the book—what we feel it needs to be able to be marketed successfully, we do those things. And so it has no bearing on how much we paid for the book.
Q. We've heard others in this trial use the term "lead title." Are you familiar with that term?
A. I am.
Q. What does it mean?
A. Well, we have three seasons in a year. So every season, we have two or three titles that we really designate as lead titles, titles that we feel we really want the sales team to really love and read, books that we feel we want to put a lot of attention on and marketing support for. So that's sort of what a lead title refers to.
Q. Does Putnam's choice of a lead title have anything to do with the advance it paid for the book?
A. No. Generally, you know—I'll give you an example: On our fall '22 list, we have a debut novel that we paid $100,000 for which was our lead title for that season. Then just the past spring list of this year,

we had another debut novel that we paid $175,000 for. That was our lead title.
Q. I'd like to turn to some questions about the $250,000 advance threshold issue in this case.
A. Okay.
Q. Are the negotiations over a book that will cost more than $250,000 different than negotiations over a book that will cost less than $250,000?
A. No.
Q. Do books acquired for over $250,000 receive a different level of sales support than books acquired for less than $250,000?
A. No.
Q. Do books acquired for over $250,000 receive a different level of printing and distribution support than books acquired for less than $250,000?
A. No. No.
Q. Would your answer change to any of those questions if the figure was lower, like 100 or 150?
A. No.
Q. Would it change if it was higher, like $350,000 or $500,000?
A. No.
Q. In your experience, have you observed whether the average advance received by authors over the past ten years has changed?
A. It's got—they've gotten higher. I've been acquiring books during that period, and they've definitely gotten higher.
Q. Based on your experience, do you believe you will be able to buy books by paying lower advances if Penguin Random House acquires Simon & Schuster?
A. No.
Q. Does Putnam plan to bid any differently if the merger goes through?
A. No. As I said, you know, we're always worried about just one editor anywhere being our competition. So no. We're not going to be changing the way we bid for books.
MS. RUDZIN: Thank you. I'll pass the witness.
THE COURT: Thank you. Any cross?
MR. VANCE: Good morning, your Honor. Robert Vance for the United States.
THE COURT: Good morning.
MR. VANCE: I'm going to hand out some binders first.
(Tenders documents to the Court)
MR. VANCE: May I proceed, your Honor?
THE COURT: Yes.

CROSS-EXAMINATION

BY MR. VANCE:

Q. Good afternoon, Ms. Kim. I'm Bobby Vance. I represent the United States. You've worked at Penguin Random House since 2015. Correct?
A. Yes.
Q. You've worked at the Putnam imprint that entire time?
A. Yes.
Q. There are approximately seven people at Putnam who acquire or edit books?
A. Yes.
Q. And you've been the publisher of Putnam for a little over two years. Right?
A. Yes.
Q. You report to Ivan Held?
A. Yes.
Q. Mr. Held is the president of three imprints?
A. Yes.
Q. Those would be Putnam, Dutton and Berkley imprints. Correct?

A. Yes.
Q. Do you have any responsibilities at the Dutton and Berkley imprints?
A. No.
Q. Mr. Held reports to Allison Dobson. Correct?
A. Yes.
Q. Ms. Dobson is the president of the Penguin Publishing Group?
A. Yes.
Q. Penguin Random House has approximately 90 imprints in the U.S. Correct?
A. Approximately. Yes.
Q. And you don't have any responsibilities at those other imprints. Right?
A. No.
Q. So your responsibilities are limited to Putnam?
A. Yes.
Q. You require Mr. Held's approval for the amount that you can bid on a book. Right?
A. Yes.
Q. That's true regardless of the amount?
A. Yes.
Q. And Mr. Held requires approval from Ms. Dobson for any offer at $250,000 or above. Right?
A. Yes.
Q. And any advance above $1 million requires approval from Madeline McIntosh. Correct?
A. I believe so. I'm not certain.
Q. Ms. McIntosh is the CEO of Penguin Random House U.S.?
A. Yes.
Q. I want to talk about the performance of books that Putnam has published. Let me direct your attention to your binder. In your binder, there's a folder labeled PX 989. In the folder, you're going to see what has been marked for identification purposes as Plaintiff's Exhibit 989. So let me explain how this is organized first.
A. Okay.
Q. There is an email with two attachments. The email should be on top. The attachments are both Excel files, and both Excel files have multiple sheets or tabs. We had to print this on very large paper for readability.
A. I, do, too, when I review these.
Q. Each attachment is stapled together. As I mentioned, there are multiple tabs. So what we did was in the bottom left-hand corner we put the tab name and then we put the corresponding year, just to keep us organized.
A. Okay.
Q. Does that make sense?
A. Yes.
Q. Let's look at the email first.
MR. VANCE: Your Honor, the email is not confidential, but the two attachments are.
Permission to publish the cover email of PX 989 to the screen?
THE COURT: Yes. Go ahead.
BY MR. VANCE:
Q. This is an email from Tina McCormick dated September 24th, 2021. Right?
A. Yes.
Q. Ms. McCormick is the vice president of business management at Penguin Random House. Correct?
A. Yes.
Q. And can you tell the Court the nature of your interactions with Ms. McCormick or people under her supervision, please?
A. So we're in frequent contact with people in our finance group.
Q. What do you discuss with the people in your finance group?

A. Mostly, you know, they review our P&Ls when we're looking at our assumptions for certain books and kind of guiding us that way. They also, you know—we route our contract requests through them as well, so they're involved in that routing process. And generally, they're our numbers people, so we go to them with questions all the time.
Q. The recipients of the email are Mr. Held. Correct?
A. He's one of the recipients.
Q. That's your boss. Right?
A. Yes.
Q. You also received this document?
A. Yes.
Q. Ms. McCormick also sent this to Benjamin Lee?
A. Yes.
Q. Mr. Lee is the senior vice president associate publisher of paperbacks and backlists at Putnam?
A. Yes.
Q. And she sent it to Ashley McClay. Right?
A. Yes.
Q. Ms. McClay is Putnam's director of marketing. Right?
A. Yes.
Q. Then everyone in the CC is Penguin—in Penguin's finance department. Correct?
A. Correct.
Q. And there are two attachments, one titled Putnam 2019 Title Profitability and the other titled Putnam 2020 Title Profitability. Correct?
A. Yes. Yes.
Q. Let's look at the first paragraph of the email. Ms. McCormick is explaining to you that she's attaching the post-pub P&Ls for Putnam's 2019 and 2020 publication lists. Right?
A. Right.
Q. She states that you usually meet to review these over the summer. Correct?
A. Yes.
Q. In the second paragraph, she writes: Since you will either be reviewing these on screen or printing them out yourselves, I sent you the Excel files rather than .pdfs. Right?
A. Right.
Q. Then if you drop to the third paragraph, she explains that these files follow the same format that Penguin Random House has been using over the past several years. Correct?
A. Right.
Q. Then Bullet 1 says: The first tab summarizes key performance indicators (net sales, advance, percentage unearned and contribution profit) by subject category, advance level and key author. Did I read that correctly?
A. Uh-huh.
THE COURT REPORTER: Is that yes?
THE WITNESS: Yes.
MR. VANCE: Your Honor, I'd move to admit PX 989 into evidence.
THE COURT: Any objection?
MS. RUDZIN: No objection.
THE COURT: That will be admitted. (Whereupon, Plaintiff's Exhibit No. 989 was entered into evidence.)
BY MR. VANCE:
Q. Now we're going to break out the Excels. I want you to look at the attachment titled Putnam 2020 Profitability.
A. Okay.
Q. This should be the one with the really large paper.
A. Yes.

MR. VANCE: Your Honor, this attachment is fully confidential. Permission to publish it on the screen without showing it to the public gallery?

THE COURT: Yes.

BY MR. VANCE:

Q. Ms. Kim, I'm going to ask a few questions about this document, but I want to make sure we're on the same page.

A. Uh-huh. Literally.

Q. This is completely confidential.

A. Okay.

Q. You see there are categories and row titles?

A. Yes.

Q. We can say those out loud, but we can't say the numbers.

A. Okay.

Q. So I'm going to point you to specific cells and try to ask questions that way. If you look at the top left-hand corner, it says: Summary Putnam Adult 2020 pubs. Correct?

A. Yes.

Q. This is an analysis of Putnam's 2020 publication list. Right?

A. Yes.

Q. Did you review this attachment after Ms. McCormick—

THE COURT: The one on the screen is 2019. Did you want to do 2020?

MR. VANCE: Yes.

BY MR. VANCE:

Q. This is the analysis for Putnam's 2020 publication list. Right?

A. The one I'm looking at. Not the one that was on screen, but the one in front of me, yes.

MR. VANCE: Oh, sorry. Perfect. Let's go to Page 1.

THE COURT: I think we're still on 2019 on the screen, according to the bottom left-hand corner. You want to look at 2020. Right?

MR. VANCE: Perfect. We've got it now. Sorry about that.

BY MR. VANCE:

Q. Did you review this attachment after Ms. McCormick sent it to you?

A. Yes.

Q. On the first page, there is a section titled By Advance Level. Right?

A. Oh, yes. At the bottom. Yes.

Q. There are seven advance levels listed. Correct?

A. Yes.

Q. The middle advance level is $250,000 to $499,999. Correct?

A. Yes.

Q. Then let's look at Column B. This is the title count. Correct?

A. Uh-huh. Yes.

Q. So these are the number of weeks that Putnam sold in each of these advance levels. Correct?

A. The number of titles we published. Yes.

Q. Published. Thank you. Then if you look at Row 3 up at the top, you can see the Excel is divided by categories that correspond to total numbers and categories that correspond to average numbers. Do you see that?

A. Yes.

Q. I want to focus you on Column I.

A. Okay.

Q. Column I are average net sales. Correct?

A. Yes.

Q. So let's look back at the By Advance Level part of the page and look at the advance level of $250,000 to $499,999. Are you there?

A. Yes.

Q. Now, look at Column I for this advance level. I'm just going to say the cents so I know we're in the same cell.

A. Okay.

Q. It ends in 83 cents. Right?

A. Yes.

Q. It is correct that as you move up each advance level from here, the average net sales continue to increase. Right?

A. From that cell going down, yes.

Q. There are three advance levels below the $250,000 to $499,999 range. Right?

A. Yes.

Q. And it is correct that the average net sales for each of those advance levels are lower than the average net sales for all advance levels at $250,000 or above. Right?

A. They are lower. Yes.

Q. Using the same attachment, I want you to turn to the tab titled Title Detail. It starts on Page 3.

A. Uh-huh.

Q. This page or two pages lists all the books that Putnam published in 2020. Right?

A. Yes.

Q. Then look at Column AK. That shows the marketing spend for each title. Right?

A. Yes.

Q. Have you ever studied Putnam's data to determine if there's a correlation between the advance level and the marketing spend?

A. I have looked at it. And, you know, it's interesting to see that when you look at averages, there is a general correlation. But when you drill down to title by title, it really is a range.

So, you know, we looked at that chart before that we—where with certain five-figure advance books, we spend a disproportionate amount on marketing. And sometimes with the very, very high advance books, for example, we spend not that much, you know, relatively. So there is a correlation, I think, in the way there should be. You know, I like to believe that we're—we can predict with some sense that, you know, certain books will work. But for the most part, you know, the way we approach marketing is every book is different. Every situation is different. Every moment is different.

Q. I want to turn to the demonstrative and ask you a few questions about that. You can—we're done with the Excel.

A. Okay.

Q. So if you could pull out the demonstrative that you reviewed.

THE COURT: Can I ask one question about that spreadsheet—

MR. VANCE: Oh, sure.

THE COURT:—if you don't mind?

MR. VANCE: Sure.

THE COURT: It looks to me from Column B, which is the number of titles on the summary page, that in Row 27, that's only eight titles. But it's accounting for so much more than on the previous line, 18 titles. Am I reading that correctly? The number of titles in Column B, Row 26, is more than twice as high as Row 27.

THE WITNESS: Yes.

THE COURT: But Row 27 accounted for so much more in sales. This isn't adjusted for—per title. So this is just—it's sort of even more extreme that the higher-advance-level ones accounted for a greater percentage of sales.

THE WITNESS: Well, I think in this case, too, you have—there is a correlation with expected sales with some of these titles, obviously. But, you know, it's also a grouping of, in the case of 27, eight titles. So how those individual eight titles individually performed is—there's a wide spectrum. And ditto for Row 26.

THE COURT: Correct. Thank you. Go ahead.

BY MR. VANCE:

Q. So I want to ask you a few questions about the demonstrative that you covered with counsel.
A. Okay.
Q. There are six books here. Right?
A. Right.
Q. Let's start with Author A. The book listed here was published in 2017. Correct?
A. I believe so. Yes.
Q. And then Books B through D were published in 2018. Right?
A. Yes.
Q. Authors E's book was published in 2020?
A. Yes. I believe so.
Q. Author F's book was published in 2021?
A. Yes.
Q. So you selected books from a five-year period. Right?
A. Yes.
Q. Putnam typically publishes about 60 books a year. Correct?
A. 60, 65, sort of on average.
Q. So over a five-year period, Putnam approximately—maybe a little over 300 books. Correct?
A. Everyone's testing my math today. Yes. I will say of those 65, though, a good portion of those are repeat authors, you know, authors—franchise authors that we regularly publish every year, sometimes twice a year.
Q. Let's start with Book A, which was published in 2017. Did Putnam publish about 60 books in 2017?
A. Probably. Yeah.
Q. Did you compare the advances of each of those approximately 60 books to the actual marketing spend to see if there was a relationship?
A. Not every single book. But I think as sort of this chart will show, every book really does kind of represent—you know, every book is kind of a different book. It's hard to really categorize and make assumptions about a certain level of advance, having each book kind of perform, and for us to actually spend the same amount for each one of those books.
Q. For the year 2017, did you compare the actual marketing spend to the approximately 60 books that you published and those advances?
A. I'm sorry. I'm not following the question. Did I compare those marketing spends to—
Q. The advances for the books in 2017 that you published.
A. Not every single book. No.
Q. About how many?
A. I would say a handful.
Q. Let's talk about Author E. Author E is famous, correct?
A. Yes.
Q. You'd agree that Author E has a huge platform to promote Book E on Author E's own. Correct?
A. She has a national platform. Yes.
Q. Switching gears a little, on direct, I believe you said, "I'm always thinking of Putnam's reputation in the industry." Does that sound right?
A. Yes.
Q. Why is that?
A. Because we want to be known for publishing quality books. We want to be known for publishing successful books and books—we also want to be known for books, you know, that span a wide range of categories. We want to be a well-rounded publisher. So that includes publishing commercial books that sell well, but also books of prestige and books of quality. Our goal is always to have books that people are still going to be reading ten years from now, 20 years from now.
Q. Do you think Putnam has a good reputation?
A. I believe so.

Q. Do you think Putnam's reputation is important to its authors?
A. Yes.
Q. Why is that?
A. For the same reason. I think authors want to be published by publishers with good reputations, good standing, you know, with booksellers and media. They want to be a part of a list that they can be proud to say they're a part of. So—and I think also generally speaking, there is a correlation between good editors with good reputations and good histories with publishing good books. Being at an imprint, they add, you know, value to that imprint by being there and attracting those books and authors.
Q. I want to talk about the book acquisition process now. You've acquired books for less than what Mr. Held has approved you to bid. Right?
A. I'm sorry. Say that again.
Q. You typically ask Mr. Held to clear you to bid on a book. Right?
A. Yes.
Q. And you've acquired books for less than Mr. Held has cleared you to offer. Right?
A. Oh, yes.
Q. Let's look at an example. Ms. Kim, I'm directing you back to your binder. In the pocket we also have a key. We're going to talk about Book 42 on the key.
A. Okay.
Q. So for confidentiality reasons, I'll refer to it as Book 42 and the author as Author 42. You're familiar with Book 42, correct?
A. Yes.
Q. Please turn to Tab PX 42 of your binder. Let me know when you have that document in front of you.
A. Okay. I do.
Q. In Tab PX 42, you will see what has been marked for identification purposes as Plaintiff's Exhibit 42. PX 42 is an email chain with the top email dated October 21st, 2020, from Ivan Held to you and others at Penguin Random House about the auction for Book 42. Right?
A. Yes.
MR. VANCE: Your Honor, permission to publish a redacted version of PX 42 on the screen?
THE COURT: Yes.
BY MR. VANCE:
Q. Let's look at Page 3—
A. Okay.
Q.—at your email to Mr. Held on October 14th at 2:56 p.m. Do you see that?
A. Yes.
Q. You sent this email to Mr. Held because you needed his signoff on your bid for Book 42. Right?
A. Yes.
Q. In the first line of the email—again, we can't say this out loud, so that's why I'm doing it this way—there's a first and last name. Do you see that?
A. Yes.
Q. That's the agent for Book 42. Right?
A. Yes.
Q. Have you purchased books from this agent before?
A. Personally, no. But I have worked with editors who have acquired books from him and his agency.
Q. At Putnam?
A. Putnam? Nothing is specifically coming to mind. But I am familiar with this agent.
Q. You explain that the agent for Book 42 was conducting a best bids auction. Right?
A. Yes.
Q. A best bids auction is when an agent asks you to submit your best offer on the first round. Correct?
A. And it's intended to be the first and only round.
Q. Let's look at Paragraph 2 of the email. You asked Mr. Held to authorize you to bid up to $350,000 for Book 42. Correct?

A. Yes. That's what I'm asking to be cleared to.
Q. You also informed him in that email that you planned on bidding $250,000 or $275,000. Correct?
A. That's what I was thinking at the time.
Q. You explained that you wanted the extra room in case the bids were matched and you had to nudge up. Right?
A. Yes. We often ask for clearance for a certain amount, and we don't always end up offering that amount.
Q. Also in Paragraph 2, you relayed to Mr. Held that the agent for Book 42 told you he was expecting two bidders. Correct?
A. Yes. That's what we're reporting that the agent told us.
Q. Those two bidders were Putnam and a non-PRH house. Right?
A. That's—again, we're reporting what he told us.
Q. Putnam ultimately acquired Book 42 for $275,000. Correct?
A. Yes.
Q. The final advance amount for Book 42 was $75,000 less than the $350,000 advance amount that Mr. Held had approved you to bid in this best bids auction. Right?
A. Yes.
Q. There is a lot of math today. I apologize.
A. Yes, there is.
Q. Let's turn back to PX 42, the first page. Please look at your email to Ms. Dobson at 12:38 p.m. Do you see that?
A. Yes.
Q. You explain that Atria was the—you send an email that Putnam won the book. Right?
A. Yes.
Q. You explain that Atria was the underbidder in the auction for Book 42. Correct?
A. That's what the agent had told us.
Q. Did you have any information suggesting that wasn't accurate?
A. No.
Q. Atria is a Simon & Schuster imprint. Correct?
A. Yes.
MR. VANCE: Your Honor, I move to admit Plaintiff's Exhibit 42 into evidence.
THE COURT: Any objection?
MS. RUDZIN: No.
THE COURT: That will be admitted. (Whereupon, Plaintiff's Exhibit No. 42 was entered into evidence.)
BY MR. VANCE:
Q. The standard royalty rate for Penguin Random House for hardcopy books, the top end is 15 percent. Correct?
A. The standard, yes.
Q. Have you ever negotiated above 15 percent?
A. Personally, I have not.
Q. The standard for paperback is 7 and a half percent?
A. Yes.
Q. Have you ever negotiated above that?
A. Not in a long, long time. But there has been an instance of that in the past.
Q. But not in a long, long time?
A. Not for a long, long, long time.
Q. You'd agree that you don't lose to non-Big 5 publishers more than Big 5 publishers. Correct?
A. I do lose to non-Big 5 publishers.
Q. No. As a whole, you would agree that you don't lose to non-Big 5 publishers more than Big 5 publishers. Correct?

A. As a whole, I would say, you know, I'm up against as far as I know all sorts of publishers. But no. I don't really necessarily track that in that way. But no.

Q. So I understand, is the answer no, you do not lose to non-Big 5 publishers more than Big 5 publishers?

A. I think if I were to tally it, probably the number would be higher in that. But I actually don't really keep a track of that. But I'm not saying that I don't lose to—

THE COURT: Can you just ask the question again? I'm confused.

BY MR. VANCE:

Q. Is it correct that Putnam loses to Big 5 publishers more than non-Big 5 publishers?

A. I would say that we lose to Big 5 publishers frequently.

Q. You were deposed in this matter, correct?

A. Yes.

Q. You provided testimony under oath, right?

A. Yes.

Q. Please, in the back of your binder, there's your deposition transcript. If you could turn to Page 390, please. Let me know when you're there. I'm going to read Lines 390, 12 through 18. Question: Is there another publisher that Putnam loses to with more frequency than any member of the Big 5? There's an objection. Witness: There is not one that comes to mind, no. Did I read that correctly.

THE WITNESS: Uh-huh.

THE COURT REPORTER: Is that yes?

THE WITNESS: Yes. Sorry.

BY MR. VANCE:

Q. Were you asked that question and did you give that answer?

A. Yes.

MR. VANCE: Your Honor, I'd move to admit for impeachment and substance.

MS. RUDZIN: I object. It's not impeaching. His question was about the non-Big 5 collectively and this is about a specific—

THE COURT: Your objection is overruled.

MR. VANCE: I reserve time for recross, your Honor.

THE COURT: Thank you.

MS. RUDZIN: Nothing further, your Honor.

THE COURT: Thank you. Ms. Kim, you can step down. Thank you for your testimony today.

THE WITNESS: Thank you.

ELYSE CHENEY, LITERARY AGENT

Elyse Cheney was the first of three agents to take the stand in succession, followed by Andrew Wylie and Gail Ross. They discussed auctions and negotiations, how they retain their power, and the effect of the possible merger on their clients.

Cheney echoed what many other witnesses have said when asked why Big 5 publishers acquire books for $250,000+ more often than non-Big 5 do. "I think the non-Big 5, you know, are just not going to play in that sandbox too many times. They don't have the same scale." But when they do acquire ATSB, smaller publishers have sometimes been "phenomenal." "I would say they're either really outstanding, but otherwise pretty equal. . . . It's a process of bringing a book to market—everybody's travel to the bookstores is pretty similar."

Cheney said that, to her recollection, all 12 of her books that went to round-robin auctions ended in a best bids situation—which she, like Jennifer Rudolph Walsh, doesn't really consider an auction. Of those, five went to PRH or S&S, but none of them had both S&S and PRH as first and runner-up.

Like Walsh, Cheney doesn't think about submissions in terms of the Big 5, but rather the individual imprints, and unlike Ayesha Pande, she doesn't always submit to S&S and PRH imprints when going wide with a title. "I don't think of it as PRH and Simon & Schuster. I think per imprint, and for particular books, I'm going to try to find the imprint that's going to be best suited for—and the editors best suited for the material. So I might decide to send it to, you know, Macmillan, Norton, and someone else. I don't always have to include everybody in every auction that I do or every submission. I just try to keep it limited to the people I know would do a great job with the book."

Cheney also explained how the best deal for a book is not necessarily the highest, and why editors want to maintain a relationship with her. "If I go to somebody with this one particular project that I think is very valuable, I'm going to the person who has the highest success rate with that kind of book. I'm going to the person who understands how to position that book in the world. I'm going to the person who knows how to work with my author to get the best book possible out of them. If that person, that editor, and I see eye to eye, we're both going to see the maximum value of that particular project," she said. " . . . If they're going to make it really painful for me or they're going to start lowballing me, I'm probably just not going to ever take them exclusive again."

Cheney explained how she can get more money for a client, even in a direct negotiation, by "reframing" the project for the editor. When one of her sub-agents got a pre-empt for $700,000 from a PRH imprint, Cheney urged them to go back to the editor and eventually landed at $1 million.

Defense attorney Daniel Petrocelli asked, again, if the advance was the most important part of a deal. "It's really not," Cheney said. "I mean, of course, everybody wants to make a lot of money. Obviously, I do as well, but I regularly suggest that people don't take the largest advance, and that could be a half-a-million-dollar cut. It could be a $200,000 cut." She went on, "There's another story, actually, where at an auction and everybody else was about $500,000 less than this one other publisher, that publisher went way beyond in a best [bids] . . . And I thought, oh, all right. Well, maybe I should do this more often. And then, literally, I had to work every single day for the next three years in order to help make that project right. And it just never was right, and it was incredibly frustrating because they just didn't understand how to do this particular kind of book."

When Judge Pan asked whether she cares about competition if she's hand-selecting editors, Cheney spoke to the power of agents, the proverbial "magic wand" as Hill put it. "If there were only one publisher, I think I would still have leverage because I have what they need," she said "In order for them to survive, I have those keys to the kingdom. So I still have leverage."

Cheney also surmised that the potential merger would have a "neutral to positive effect on her clients." "I do think that Simon & Schuster could benefit from some of the tools that Penguin Random House has developed over time." She said that, if advances went down from PRHSS, she would take her 200 clients elsewhere. (Though the question and answer did not speak to Hill's assertion that advances industry-wide will go down.) She'd do the same if PRHSS reneged on their bidding pledge.

In the cross-examination, Cheney was asked, "Markus Dohle . . . is a friend of yours; right?" And the follow-up was, "You've had multiple discussions with Mr. Dohle about this merger; right?"

"A few," Cheney said.

The prosecution pointed out that 25 of 28 ATSB deals Cheney made from 2018 through 2021 were with Big 5 publishers—and 17 of those went to Penguin Random House.

TESTIMONY OF ELYSE CHENEY, LITERARY AGENT

DIRECT EXAMINATION

BY MR. PETROCELLI:

Q. Ms. Cheney, please state your name for the record.

A. Elyse Cheney.

Q. What is your occupation?

A. I'm a literary agent, and I own a literary agency.

Q. How long have you been a literary agent?

A. About 26 years.

Q. What's the name of your agency?

A. The Cheney Agency.

Q. When did you start it?

A. January 2005.

Q. How many agents work with you?

A. There are four of us total.

Q. So going back, can you trace what you did before you started your own agency?

A. Sure. I was an agent at Sanford Greenburger Associates for eight years. I was an agent for eight years. Sorry.

Q. Before you started your firm, you were a literary agent for eight years?

A. Yes.

Q. And before that?

A. I was two years working part-time as, kind of, a reader for a small literary agency on the Upper East Side.

Q. Okay. You—what kind of authors do you represent?

A. Primarily serious nonfiction and occasionally fiction.

Q. Okay. And can you look at the first demonstrative that I'm going to put on the—on the monitor; and that will be Demonstrative 3.

MR. PETROCELLI: Defendants' Demonstrative 3, Your Honor.

THE COURT: All right.

BY MR. PETROCELLI:

Q. Are these some of the books and authors whom you represent?

A. Yes.

Q. Is there any particular type of book or author whom you represent?

A. I mean, again, tends to be in the serious nonfiction category. Some memoirs, some individuals who may have unique experiences.

Q. Now, could you turn to the other exhibit you have in front of you, which is Plaintiff 749. I also have as a demonstrative a color-coded version of that just to make it a little bit easier for you and for us to go through it. But you have 749 in front of you?

A. I do.

Q. And what is that?

A. It's a chart of my deals from—my personal deals from 2018 to 2021.

Q. Okay.

MR. PETROCELLI: Your Honor, I'd ask to admit Plaintiff's 749.

THE COURT: Is there any objection?

MR. GOLDSMITH: No objection.

THE COURT: And this is under seal?
THE COURT REPORTER: Can I get your name?
MR. GOLDSMITH: Jonathan Goldsmith.
THE COURT REPORTER: Thank you.
THE COURT: Is this under seal?
MR. PETROCELLI: Oh. Thank you. It is, Your Honor. Thank you.
THE COURT: All right. Thank you. It will be admitted under seal. (PX Exhibit 749 admitted into evidence.)
MR. PETROCELLI: And, also, I'm going to mark the color-coded version as Defendants' Demonstrative 4.
THE COURT: All right. It says 6 on it.
MR. PETROCELLI: Excuse me?
THE COURT: It says Defendants' Demonstrative 6 on the copy I got.
MR. PETROCELLI: Well, I think it's because we were anticipating some others to come before it.
THE COURT: Okay.
MR. PETROCELLI: Let's call it Defendants' Demonstrative 6, then, since it's already on the document.
THE COURT: Okay.
MR. PETROCELLI: Thank you.
BY MR. PETROCELLI:
Q. So these are the deals that you did between 2018 and 2021; right?
A. Yes. I think that there are two books that I personally did not sell, but someone else in my agency did.
Q. So there's some corrections to this?
A. Yes.
Q. Okay. Let's—why don't you tell us what those corrections are.
A. Number 15.
Q. And what's the correction on 15?
A. That was sold by somebody else at my agency, but I don't have all the—
Q. And did you have any other corrections?
A. Number 34.
Q. 15 was done by someone else, and—
A. Yeah.
Q. And No. 34 was done by someone else; is that correct?
A. Correct.
Q. So—and then did you have any additions that you noted should be added?
A. Yeah. There's one more that's missing that was done with Bloomsbury.
Q. And if you look at Demonstrative 6, the color-coded version of Plaintiff's 749, you'll see that that's been added at the end; right?
A. Yes.
Q. That's a deal that you did with Bloomsbury you said. Okay?
A. Correct.
Q. So just to speed this along, we've made a—a list of the deals that you have done based on Exhibit 749, as you have just corrected, above $250,000 and below $250,000. So I'd like to mark that as the next demonstrative.
MR. PETROCELLI: And I'll use Demonstrative 4 for that one, Your Honor.
THE COURT: All right.
MR. PETROCELLI: And I think this can be displayed publicly.
BY MR. PETROCELLI:
Q. You have that in front of you?
A. I do.
Q. Okay. And with the corrections that you made, this sets forth the various deals that you have done

with publishers from 2018 to 2021 for $250,000 advances and above. And then the second column is all your deals; correct?

A. Yes.

Q. Okay. And you'll see here that you did 28 out of 44 deals for $250,000 and above?

A. Yes.

Q. And this indicates, for the record, that you did zero with Hachette?

A. Correct.

Q. Two with HarperCollins?

A. Right.

Q. Three with Macmillan?

A. Right.

Q. Two with Norton?

A. Yes.

Q. One with other? Do you know who that is?

A. I do.

Q. Who is that?

A. Workman.

Q. Was that prior to the time it was acquired?

A. Yeah.

Q. And 17 with Penguin Random House?

A. Yes.

Q. And three with Simon & Schuster; right?

A. Right.

Q. And then all deals adds the additional ones that you did below 250; right?

A. Uh-huh.

Q. And do you happen to remember who the publishers were for the four all deals? We know one is—one is Workman. Two—well, why don't you tell us, if you can remember.

A. Workman, and Bloomsbury, Yale University Press, and—

Q. And there's an additional Workman; right?

A. Oh, right. That's right. Yes.

Q. So—

A. Additional Workman.

Q.—two Workmans, one Yale, and one Bloomsbury make up that column; right?

A. Yes.

Q. Okay. Thank you. Now, with respect to the 250 and-above deals that you did with the non-Big 5, what's your view of the level of service that your author clients received from those publishers as compared to services rendered by the Big 5?

A. In some cases, they've been phenomenal. I mean, Workman is an incredible publisher, and they put tremendous resources behind their publications. I would say they're either—you know, in that case, really outstanding, but otherwise pretty equal.

Q. In your experience, have you observed any qualitative differences in the publishing services rendered by the Big 5 versus the non-Big 5?

A. Broadly, no. It's pretty similar. I mean, it's a process of bringing a book to market, to—everybody's travel to the bookstores is pretty similar.

Q. Why is it, then, that as we've seen in this trial, there are so many deals 250 and above that are done with the Big 5 as opposed to the non-Big 5? Do you have a view about that?

A. I think the non-Big 5, you know, are just not going to play in that sandbox too many times. They don't have the same scale. The Big 5 have—you know, I don't—to be honest, I don't think about it as the Big 5. So if I think about Penguin Random House, I'm thinking about—I don't know—have 15 imprints I might be working with. Same with Simon & Schuster. Whereas, if it's Norton, you're pretty much going to Norton. If it's Workman, you're going to Workman. So the scale is very different.

Q. So other than scale, have you, in your experience, observed any qualitative differences in the work performed by these publishers?

A. No, not at all.

Q. Okay. So we've done another cut of your—of your 44 deals, and that is going to be set forth on Defendants' Demonstrative 5 [sic], and this can be publicly displayed as well.

A. Uh-huh.

Q. And what does this reflect, Ms. Cheney?

A. The format of how I sold the book, of each book.

Q. So the formats being auction, preempt, option, and exclusive?

A. Right.

Q. Okay.

THE COURT: I think—should this be Demonstrative 7? I already had something done as Demonstrative 5.

MR. PETROCELLI: It'll be 7. Thank you, Your Honor.

THE COURT: Thank you.

BY MR. PETROCELLI:

Q. So with respect to these different formats, by "auction," what kind of auctions are we talking about? The eight auctions for 250 and above.

A. What format auction, because there's different—

Q. Yeah.

A. I mean, just to clarify, auction, I think in a lot of people's minds means, you know, a bunch of people in a room raising paddles. In this case, an auction usually can take primarily two forms.

One is a traditional auction of going round by round where there's initially—everybody puts in a blind bid and then you go back to the lowest bidder with the high bid and you go in rounds. Even there you can stop and say—reserve the right to go to best bids at any time.

Or you can do what's still called an auction, but I think probably isn't really an auction, which is called best bids. And that's where you send out instructions to interested publishers and you say: By noon tomorrow, please give us your best offer. In which case, each publisher is flying blind, and they're coming up with an offer that they think is based on what they can sell, whether they want to sign the author up for the long term. They may have lots of different reasons for coming up with their bid, but they're basically going in with what they think it's worth.

Q. So how many of your eight auctions for 250 and above were round-robin auctions that went the whole distance as a round-robin instead of ending with a best-bid or a better best bid?

A. I believe none.

Q. And same question for the—the additional four below 250, if you remember.

A. I don't remember not ever just ending, sort of expiring with—it always goes to best bids pretty much.

Q. Okay. And in these 12 auctions that you have listed on Demonstrative 5 [sic], do you know if in any of them PRH or S&S was the winner?

A. I'm not sure.

Q. Okay.

A. I'm sure—

Q. If we looked at your—

A. Right, right, right.

Q.—color-coded chart—

A. Uh-huh.

Q.—if you look at the red, that tells you it's an auction. If you look at the purple or the white, that tells you if it's S&S and PRH. And to speed this up, if I told you that of the 12 auctions Penguin Random House or Simon & Schuster was the winner in five of them; does that sound right?

A. Yes.

Q. And if I told you those were Books 23, 24, 30, 31, and 32, would you agree with that?

A. Yes. That's correct.

Q. Okay. And of those five auctions in which either Penguin Random House or Simon & Schuster acquired the book, did any result in Penguin Random House and Simon & Schuster finishing one and two?

A. No. There's one that I'm not entirely sure, but I'm pretty sure the number two was Harper.

Q. Which one is that?

A. *The Uprising*. Sorry.

Q. What number?

A. Oh, number. Sorry.

Q. Is that 31?

A. 31, yeah. But I'm pretty sure the answer remains no for all five.

Q. You think no, but, maybe, possibly No. 31?

A. Small possibility. Yeah.

Q. Okay.

A. Based on my records.

Q. We'll leave it there.

A. Okay.

Q. In your experience, do you include PRH and Simon & Schuster in every acquisition format?

A. No.

Q. Why not?

A. Really, first, again, just—I don't think of it as PRH and Simon & Schuster. I think per imprint, and for particular books, you know, I'm going to try to find the imprint that's going to be best suited for—and the editors best suited for the material. So I might decide to send it to, you know, Macmillan, Norton, and someone else. I don't always have to include everybody in every auction that I do or every submission. I just try to keep it limited to the people I know would do a great job with the book.

Q. As we see on Defendants' Demonstrative 7, you have 20 of the $250,000-and-above deals conducted other than by auction. Do you see that?

A. Yeah.

Q. Okay. Preempt option and exclusive?

A. Right.

Q. In—in each of those three circumstances, is the acquisition process, essentially, a direct negotiation with a single publisher?

A. Yes, definitely. For option and it's an exclusive negotiation, you're not allowed to, you know, shop the offer to someone outside of the—whoever you have the contract with. And then for—my—my screen just went off.

For a preempt, like, that's a publisher coming forward and saying: I want to take this off the table before there's any auction. We are so excited about this. We have to have it. Here's X amount of money.

So they're—usually what they're doing is saying we see this as a really big project and so we're going to throw down our best shot and hope you're going to take it. And so then you either decide you're interested in negotiating with them or you're not.

Q. So let me follow up on these direct negotiations. Since you're not doing a competitive auction, either a full round-robin or one that ends in a—some type of best bid, how do you know when you're just negotiating with one publisher that you're getting the best deal for your client?

A. Well, I mean, I think we should define what the best deal for my client means. In my mind, the promise that we make to authors is we're going to try to help you find the widest audience possible for your books. So in order to do that, that may mean going with the publisher who has the highest bid, but it might also mean going with the publisher who has the most experience in that kind of project, and that—the imprint, and—and the editor who has the most experience and success rate for that kind of project.

Q. When you said it may mean going to the publisher with the highest bid, if you don't have an auction, how do you know if there's a better bid out there, a higher bid out there, when you're pursuing a direct negotiation?

A. Well, I think—just to back up for a minute. I think that there's a misapprehension that the primary determinant of the value of the project is competitive auctions or competitive bidding. Really, when I start working on a project, it's far in advance of any kind of submission. I'm working on the project in order to create something that has inherent value for the culture. So I'm working on something that I hope is going to become a nondeniable proposition in the mind of the editor. So something that's so exciting or so important to the political culture or so moving that they call me and they say: I have to have this. What do I have to pay for it? Can you repeat the question again just so I can—

Q. Yeah. I'm exploring the notion that in this book acquisition process—

A. Uh-huh.

Q.—that we've learned so much about during this trial—and since this is a trial about competition—you represent a client; right?

A. Uh-huh.

Q. You have to answer audibly, by the way.

A. Oh, yes. Yeah. I just need a reminder of the question so I can go back.

Q. I'm going to get to it—

A. Okay.

Q.—but I want you to understand where I'm going.

A. Okay.

Q. You—and you work on a commission; right?

A. Yes.

Q. So the more money you can get for the author, the more money you make; right?

A. Yes.

Q. So you, like your client, the author, have an incentive to get the most amount of money; right?

A. Yes.

Q. Okay. So when you're pursuing a direct negotiation as opposed to a competitive auction process—which apparently happens here most of the time according to your chart—how can you be assured that you're getting the most amount of money for your client?

A. Well, I think there's several, kind of, hidden factors in this kind of relationship. If I go to somebody with this one particular project that I think is very valuable, I'm going to the person who has the highest success rate with that kind of book. I'm going to the person who understands how to position that book in the world. I'm going to the person who knows how to work with my author to get the best book possible out of them. If that person, that editor, and I see eye to eye, we're both going to see the maximum value of that particular project. So I'm going to them and saying, you know, I've got this. Now, they're not just bidding on that project. I have 200 other clients waiting behind me. So if they want to do business with me and they want to do—get the kind of projects that I represent, then—and they're interested, obviously, in the particular project, they're going to bid, you know, strongly in order to continue that relationship, to continue to get successful books that, hopefully, I'm representing.

If they're going to make it really painful for me or they're going to make it—start lowballing me, I'm probably just not going to ever take them exclusive again.

Yeah. So that's—those are the different components that are going into—the other thing is that I think that sometimes auctions—I think publishers prefer auctions because it's a much safer route for them.

Q. Why?

A. But not for the author.

Q. Why is an auction safer for a publisher?

A. Well, the publishers always say, you know, we prefer to do an auction because then we can kind of go up incrementally, and then, you know, there will be an auction fever and, you know, you'll probably end up getting more money. And I'm like, that has not been my experience at all. Again, it's not—we're not all sitting in a room and I'm saying you, you, you, and everybody is going up in some kind of emotional contagion. It's actually a very protracted process where I call so-and-so. I tell them the bid that they have to beat. They go to their boss. They call me two hours later. This is not impulsive. So I actually don't—I think that's kind of a myth, the whole auction thing, and sort of overplayed. Plus, if I have an auction—let's say I go two rounds of that auction and I'm at $300,000 and I'm thinking, well, maybe at this point I should go to best bids because I know so-and-so, you know—a few of those—few of these bidders might be dropping out in the next round. So—but I know Bidder 4 probably has $600,000. So if I go to best bids, I still might not get that $600,000 because I'm ending Round 2 at 300.

However, if I decide to go exclusively to the person that I know is the best person for this—maybe that person is not going to give me every single cent that I want, but I know it's the best person because they're going to give me the right price, which is almost as important.

I can explain that. Why? If I do an auction either as a best-bids or I do it exclusively, then I'm getting the guy who has 600 no matter what because he's going to—he thinks it's worth 600. So I'm not ending up at 450, where I might not end up at 450 with an auction. I think the auction idea is a little overplayed.

Q. When you have conducted direct negotiations for any number of these reasons as you've indicated, have you ever found out afterwards that you left a fair amount of money on the table? Has a publisher ever called you and said—or an editor said, by the way, you know, I stole this from you? That ever happen?

A. The only thing that's happened, actually, is that I knew—in one case, I left money on the table at an auction situation, and if I had gone for the person who I knew I sort of had, but the author really wanted to meet everyone, I could have gotten probably $150,000 more.

So I was bummed about that, but, generally, no. I mean, I think if you could look at the number of deals I've had that are for a lot of money, I think it sort of speaks for itself.

Q. When you're doing direct negotiations, are you—in the back of your mind or even the front of your mind, are you thinking about the competition, if you're not able to make a deal? And, in particular, are you thinking about the competition in proportion to their market shares?

A. Market share, I mean, absolutely not. What I'm always thinking about is: Is this book going to sell in the stores? Can this book connect with readers? Is it going to change their minds? Is it going to change their hearts about something? Is it going to change—you know, wake them up to some reality that they didn't realize? So I'm thinking, who is going to help my author get to the most readers as possible. That's what I'm thinking of it. I'm sorry. Yeah.

Q. Do you track market share—not downstream retail sales, I mean—but market share of the various publishers with respect to the acquisition of books?

A. It's totally irrelevant to me, to be honest.

Q. Do you track that?

A. No.

Q. Okay. When you're doing these negotiations and you—

THE COURT: I'm sorry. Can we get an answer to the question? When you're doing direct negotiations, are you thinking about the competition? Are you thinking that you can get more in a direct negotiation if there are other people who want this book? I think that was the question.

THE WITNESS: No. I mean, for example, I do—as you can see, I do a lot of exclusive negotiations, and often, you sort of get to know who is willing to pay, who is not, who understands the kind of books that you do, who doesn't, who does them well. So you kind of know where they're going to come in at some point. You have an idea if you're going to them where you can get them, and you have an idea that usually that person is probably going to pay top dollar for that kind of book.

So I'm not thinking about—in fact, I know that if I went to another publisher who is purely thinking about sell, sell, sell—and maybe I'll get a couple hundred thousand more—that in the end I could have a big bomb, and that really, actually, hurts the author's career.

So, in other words, if you go to a place—if you go to—and this is one of the reasons that I am very cautious about auctions. If you go to—round by round, best bids, whatever, and you end up getting, like, an insane amount of money from a publisher that you don't actually think is the right publisher and then it becomes hard for the author to turn it down, you can really kind of screw the author up and screw the potential of success, because there's a huge range of talents and a huge range of skill sets in the industry and amongst the imprints.

BY MR. PETROCELLI:

Q. When you're doing these exclusive negotiations, though, are you—are you telling the publishers that the—if they're not meeting your price that you're going to go elsewhere?

A. No. I mean, what you're trying to do is reframe things for them. So, recently, a younger person in my office got a preemptive offer for like 700. I'm like, go back. She went back. She got 800. And she's like, okay. I'm done. You know, this is it. They said it's final. And I was like, no, you're not done, actually. Let's talk about what this book is.

So we talk about the book. And then I start to think, how can we reframe this so that the editor understands just—they have the artillery to get it because they want it. How can I give them what they need to sell it to their boss, because I'm going to reframe exactly how they're thinking about it. So it's partly a generative process. That's how I get more money. Everybody thinks—you know, it's not standard, sort of, negotiation.

Q. Well, look, we're talking—we're in this trial because there's going to—if—there may be a merger of two—

A. Right.

Q.—big publishers—right?—Simon & Schuster and Penguin Random House, depending on the outcome of this case. You understand that; right?

A. Yes.

Q. So right now when you're having these direct negotiations—and let's say you're talking to Penguin Random House, you know that out there somewhere is Simon & Schuster and you may be able to go there if you're not able to make a deal with Penguin Random House. I mean, that enters your thinking?

A. I'm pretty determined. So if I decide that I want this particular editor to do this book, I'm usually—it would be a surprise to me if they didn't and that we couldn't come to a deal. Because you kind of get to know people. You get a feel for it. You know how to ride it.

Q. Do you feel these direct negotiations—if this merger goes through and Simon & Schuster and Penguin Random House are now owned by the same corporate parent—

A. Uh-huh.

Q.—that in those direct negotiations that you were having premerger, now the day after the merger, do you believe in some way you're going to be disadvantaged?

A. No. I mean, the—the one I was just telling you about where we went from 700 to a million was with a Penguin Random House, you know, imprint. It's just—I'm not thinking about Simon & Schuster. I'm just not thinking about them, because I want a very particular person to do the project, because I know who the best people are going to be, and that's the most important thing to me and usually my author.

Q. Okay. And is the advance the most important part of the—of the deal?

A. It's really not. I mean, of course, everybody wants to make a lot of money. Obviously, I do as well, but I regularly suggest that people don't take the largest advance, and that could be a half-a-million-dollar cut. It could be a $200,000 cut.

Q. Let me stop you there.

A. Sure.

Q. I'm not in your business. That sounds—that sounds implausible in a way that you could leave a half a million dollars. You get a piece of that. Your client gets—

A. Yeah.

Q.—a much bigger piece of that.

A. Yeah.

Q. I assume you would do that with your client's consent?

A. Of course.

Q. Okay.

A. Yeah.

Q. So why would you do that?

A. I mean, I have sophisticated clients; so they want to work with the best people. They're—the reason they're doing the book is because they have a story to tell, and they're trying to make meaning of something. They're trying to communicate something. And the editor who can help them bring—make the richest, most robust project, that means the world to them.

It's huge.

It's like—and then how that editor then communicates—and that editor is sort of like the orchestra leader. How that editor communicates what this book is about and how important it is to their sales force, to the marketing department, to the publicity department, that is so essential to the success of the book.

I mean, I could give you example after example after example of places where, you know, there was—there's another story, actually, where at an auction and everybody else was about $500,000 less than this one other publisher, that publisher went way beyond in a best—it was off rounds and then we went to best bids, $500 spread—$700,000 spread. And I thought, oh, all right. Well, maybe I should do this more often. And then, literally, I had to work every single day for the next three years in order to help make that project right.

And we took—and it just never was right, and it was incredibly frustrating because they just didn't understand how to do this particular kind of book. And it's so sensitive and subtle, and, you know, that has made a—has—that's bad because, basically, the book ended up selling a pittance compared to the advance—and that's not good for the authors.

Q. Okay. I just have a couple of—

THE COURT: Can I ask a question: Are you saying that competition doesn't matter in book acquisition because you hand select editors and you don't consider competition?

THE WITNESS: The main thing that I'm considering and the main thing that I think adds value is really the—the thing that drives the most value is the quality of the project, the timeliness of the project, the ability for it to last, you know, the ability for it to become something that's adopted in colleges and—

THE COURT: No, I understand that, but my question is: Are you telling me that you think that competition doesn't matter in book acquisition because you are hand selecting editors based on these factors that you know about?

THE WITNESS: I mean, would I say it a hundred percent doesn't matter, like if there were only one publisher, I think I would still have leverage because I have what they need?

THE COURT: Right.

THE WITNESS: In order for them to survive, I have those keys to the kingdom. So I still have leverage. You know, I think right now there's absolutely enough competition, if I need to go out to multiple people in order to sort of, create value, but that's not the primary thing I'm thinking about, yeah.

THE COURT: So you think competition doesn't matter?

THE WITNESS: Does or doesn't?

THE COURT: Does not matter.

THE WITNESS: I don't think it's the most important factor.

THE COURT: From what you said, it sounded like you don't think it matters.

THE WITNESS: I wouldn't say I don't think it matters at all. I just don't think that's the primary determinative of the price.

THE COURT: Okay.

BY MR. PETROCELLI:

Q. So just a couple of other topics. One is there's been reference at this trial to something called anticipated top selling books. Is that a term with which you're familiar, at least prior to this case?

A. No.

Q. How do you—let me ask you this, then: How do you decide what kind of money to ask for when you're representing an author and you're—you're seeing a proposal or a manuscript or whatever it is that you have in front of you? How do you decide how to start pricing that?

A. Well, usually it's—you know, what you're going to get is variable, and it could have a—there could be a huge range in terms of, you know, where something might end up. You could have somebody literally spending a million dollars more than somebody else.

So what I'm thinking of is what's the best in class here? What's the book in this category that has really rocketed to success? And as long as it's not a ridiculous comparison, that's what I'm—you know, because it was such a runaway—a best seller. I'm thinking, okay, so that book sold that many copies. Then let me do the numbers and let me think of, you know, where I can go then based on the numbers of other—of the comps.

Or—but there are other factors too, because perhaps I know that HarperCollins really needs to fill their fall list and they're looking for a big book. That's the signal of, oh, we're going to pay—overpay for something if you give us something if it's slotted in there. So then I'm thinking, okay, I have this price, but I could add maybe $200,000 or $300,000 dollars on to it because they want—they want something for right now.

Q. In your experience, is $250,000 or any number thereabouts some kind of dividing line above which books are treated differently than below that line?

A. $250,000 is not—certainly doesn't fit into the top seller category. It's just not a relevant number.

Q. Is there some other number that separates books in a qualitative way such that they're treated differently if they're above that number and treated differently if they're below that number? Is there any bright line number?

A. You would think that would be the case. You would think that a book that had—that sold for $1.1 million would get different treatment than a book that sold for $200,000. That seems like a logical conclusion; right?

Q. And what different—

A. And yet it's not.

Q. What different treatments would you expect?

A. You would think that the publisher would spend, sort of, more marketing money on it. You think the—you would think that the publisher might, for example, do a special advance reading copy for—for the million-dollar book. But, in fact, that's not the case.

I just recently have two books, one over a million, one over 700; one of them extremely timely. And—and this is where I don't think marketing is, frankly, that big of a category—of a driver of sales. In both, I asked the editor: Can you do a, sort of, fancier ARC rather than this galley, which is kind of like—they can do it pretty cheaply and it looks cheap. No. I was told no twice.

Now, you would think—they've just made a huge investment in both of these books. They're not even going to do a really beautiful galley to send out to reviewers? No. No. I had to call three times. Finally, I called the head of the company, and I was like: This is what we need. And they said: Okay. Fine.

But—and you would think that they would be ahead in terms of—you know, another thing you could do—and these are all things that the margins—another thing you could do is, like, the editor is ahead and they're, like, let's go out and get endorsements now so that we can put them on the galley so that people in sales and people at the bookseller level will see that famous author has just blurbed this book. Half the time they're not even—it just happened to me. Same book. No, we don't even have the list together.

So I'm the one who's doing that. I'm the one who's driving it half the time. I mean, I did a deal with, actually, the same publisher, $1.1 million, and I said to her afterwards—because it's always—it's actually a point of frustration, I think, for a lot of agents. Why didn't you spend more money on marketing? And she said: Well, we just spent it all on the advance.

And why do people get that advance? People get that advance, in part, because the author has their own marketing—they already have an audience that is, sort of, built in. They're coming, in a way, with their own marketing machine. They're—they're probably going to get attention because of who they are or because they have unique information to transmit.

So the publishers kind of know it's not—they're not the ones through marketing to drive this book. Publicity is what sells books.

Q. Final questions I have: What impact, if any, do you think the merger between Penguin Random House and Simon & Schuster will have on your clients?

A. I would say it's neutral to positive. Do you want me to elaborate?

Q. How so?

A. Well, I think, in general, Penguin Random House has really—has made a commitment to books over a very, very long period of time, and because they're a private company, they can invest long-term in things like infrastructure, printing, whatever. Whereas, a company like Simon & Schuster, which is shareholder driven and quarterly-report driven, it cannot make those kinds of investments. So I do think that Simon & Schuster could benefit from some of the tools that Penguin Random House has developed over time. So that's one thing. That's what's coming to mind right now, but—

Q. And what if post-merger the merged firm sought to reduce advances that you typically would have expected from—I realize every book is different; right?

A. Yeah.

Q. But let's say it's the type of book you would have expected $300,000 for premerger and now post-merger they're offering you 250 or 260. You have—in your judgment, you think it's worth more and you would have gotten more before. That's my—that's my hypo. Are you with me?

A. I am.

Q. Is there anything—

A. It's a little hard because the difference is not that much, you know.

Q. Well, okay. You can make up any numbers you want.

A. It would have to be something that would be more dramatic.

THE COURT REPORTER: Hold on. One at a time.

THE WITNESS: Sorry.

BY MR. PETROCELLI:

Q. My question to you is whether you think post-merger if you were faced with what you perceived to be a lowering of advances, you could resist it, especially given, you know, the size of the merged firm?

A. So what I'm hearing is—you're saying if I started to notice a pattern of reduced advances?

Q. Yes.

A. Which would probably mean there was some coordination at the top of a company, because how else—because it's a decentralized company, I'm not sure how that reduction would happen.

Q. Let's assume it happened.

A. Okay. So it happened. That would be unfortunate, but it would mean I would need to take my 200 authors and, you know, call up Hachette, call up HarperCollins, call up, you know, Norton. Call up these places and say: We're not getting this. Plus, we're not getting what we used to have, and, you know, this—there was an implicit promise that, in fact, our authors were supposed to get more money if this merger happened. So what happened to that promise?

Q. Speaking of promises, the last thing I'm going to ask you about is Defendants' 236—which I think you have in front of you—which is a letter to the literary agent community from Markus Dohle. Do you have that?

A. I do.

Q. And this is a letter you received at or about the date that it bears, February 4, 2022?

A. Right.

Q. Okay.

MR. PETROCELLI: Your Honor, I would ask that this be admitted into evidence.

THE COURT: All right. Any objection?

MR. GOLDSMITH: No objection.

THE COURT: That'll be admitted. (DX Exhibit 236 admitted into evidence.)

BY MR. PETROCELLI:

Q. How—I assume you read this letter?

A. Yes.

Q. And what role, if any, has it played in your thinking about this merger?

A. I mean, I was already—felt comfortable with the merger before this letter came about. This letter is great, but I—you know, I had already supported it.

Q. Okay.

A. I mean, this is wonderful information, but, you know, I was already on board.

Q. And so one more hypo. Assume that after this merger—maybe not the day after, but sometime after—the company reneged on this letter and said, no, we're not going to treat Simon & Schuster as an external bidder, which they would have the legal right to do.

A. Uh-huh.

Q. So what would you do about that, if anything? Or what could you do about that, if anything?
A. Well, I mean, I think we have to remember, this is a very relationship-based business. So if—it's very trust-based. Like I said, we don't—when we're doing an auction, we're just doing it by phone and everybody is trusting that everybody else is being aboveboard. Because if somebody starts to break a trust, then you don't really want to do that much business with them.
So if that happened, I think there would be a number of different tools that I would have in my tool kit to deal with it. First of all, you know, right now I have with Penguin a book that was number one on the best seller list. And I would probably call Michael Pietsch and say, this guy has had two number one best sellers. Maybe you're interested in the next book. Let's make a deal.
Q. Call whom?
A. I would call the head of Hachette.
Q. Oh. Michael Pietsch you said?
A. Yeah, Michael Pietsch. Yeah. So slowly there would be a dribble away from Penguin Random House, and I—you know, I have 200 clients, but I'm a small—you know, medium-sized agency compared to a lot of other agencies, which might have a thousand or 800 clients. If those people start to leave as well, that would have a real impact on Penguin Random House's business. I mean, that betrayal would be a big issue.
And, I mean, I represent the media. I represent people all over *The New York Times*, *The Atlantic*, every single major newspaper and magazine. And I would be on the phone with them very quickly. I would have no problem doing that.
Q. Okay. Thank you, Ms. Cheney.
MR. PETROCELLI: Pass the witness, Your Honor.
THE COURT: All right. Thank you. Any cross?
MR. GOLDSMITH: Yes, Your Honor. Good afternoon, Your Honor.
THE COURT: Good afternoon.
MR. GOLDSMITH: Jonathan Goldsmith for the United States. May I proceed?
THE COURT: Yes.

CROSS-EXAMINATION
BY MR. GOLDSMITH:
Q. Good afternoon, Ms. Cheney. I'd like to start by continuing to discuss the same slides, defendants' demonstrative, that we were just looking at.
A. Sure.
Q. So the first page, I have at least stickered Defendants' Demonstrative 3. Are you looking at that?
A. These are my books?
Q. Yes. The title is Works Represented by Elyse Cheney.
A. Yes.
Q. And earlier you described these as some of the authors you represent; right?
A. These are books that I've represented. At this point I don't represent—there's one author that I don't represent anymore—actually, two—but they're from, like, 20 years ago.
Q. Every one of these books on this list was sold to either Penguin Random House or Simon & Schuster; is that right?
A. Yes.
Q. Can we move on to the next page.
A. Sure.
Q. Earlier you said that the one deal above $250,000 sold to other was to Workman, who you mentioned was acquired after this deal; is that right?
A. Yeah. Correct. Right.
Q. Workman was acquired by one of the Big 5 publishers; is that right?
A. Yes.
Q. And 25 of your 28 deals from 2018 through 2021 with advances of $250,000 or more went to Big 5

publishers; right?
A. I—I'm assuming you're correct.
Q. And for this same group, your deals from 2018 through 2021 with advances of $250,000 or more, 17 out of the 28 went to Penguin Random House; right?
A. Yes.
Q. So that's 60 percent?
A. Uh-huh. Yes.
Q. And earlier you called the industry a relationship business; right?
A. I did.
Q. You have important relationships with editors; right?
A. Yep.
Q. And important relationships with multiple editors at the same publisher; right?
A. Yes.
Q. And these relationships factor into the acquisition process; right?
A. Yeah.
Q. Based on the number of deals you do with Penguin Random House, would it be fair to say that you have many important relationships with editors at Penguin Random House?
A. I do.
Q. In addition, Markus Dohle, the CEO of Penguin Random House, is a friend of yours; right?
A. Yep.
Q. You've had multiple discussions with Mr. Dohle about this merger; right?
A. A few.
Q. You can put that document aside. I'd like to look at the color-coded version of your deal chart that was marked, I think, as Defendants' Demonstrative 6.
A. Uh-huh. 7-—749?
Q. Yes. So it's 749 with the—with the color coding.
A. Yeah.
Q. Looking at page 1—as you previously said, this is sorted by advance; right?
A. Yes.
Q. So looking at page 1, the first three deals with the lowest advances are all children's books; right?
A. Yes. Actually, no, because the—No. 46 was not a children's book, and that's—I believe it's $70,000.
Q. Okay. So three—so Nos. 1, 2, and 3 were all children's books; right?
A. Yeah. The numbers here, yes.
Q. And the book in Row 5 is a cookbook; right?
A. Yes. Oh, you know what? Actually, that number is wrong. Oh, no, it's not wrong. No, no, no. Sorry. I just did another deal for her. It's—it's right.
Q. Like I said, the book in Row 5 is a cookbook; right?
A. Yeah.
Q. The book in Row 7 is another children's book or young reader book?
A. Yes.
Q. That's a young reader version of another book on your list, the book in Row 42; is that right?
THE COURT REPORTER: Can you repeat that question, please.
MR. GOLDSMITH: Sure.
BY MR. GOLDSMITH:
Q. That's a young reader version of another book on your list, the book in Row 42; right?
A. Yes.
Q. And the advance for the adult version is more than ten times greater the advance for the young reader version; right?
A. Correct.
Q. Back on the first page, the book in Row 9 is another children's book; right?
A. Yes.

Q. And all of these books that we just discussed are below $250,000; right?
A. Yes.
Q. And they're all below $150,000; right?
A. They are. I mean, there are a couple others on the list that aren't children's books that are less than $150,000, but yeah.
Q. There are no cookbooks on this deal sheet with advances at or above $250,000; right?
A. Right.
Q. And none of your children's or young adult books you sold in this time period had advances at or above $250,000?
A. That's correct. I mean, I'm not—just to clarify, I'm not in the children's book business. It's usually an ancillary, you know, thing that you build off of the—a successful book.
Q. But the handful of children's books that you did sell during this time period all had advances below $150,000; right?
A. Yeah. They're spin-offs.
Q. None of your deals in this time period were with Scholastic; right?
A. Yeah. This is—usually if you have a book that's kind of a spin, like in the one you were talking about just now, No. 7, usually you're going to the same publisher who did the adult book.
Q. None of the deals that you had in this time period were with Amazon; is that right?
A. Right.
Q. In fact, you've never sold a deal to Amazon as a publisher for a print format book; right?
A. Right.
MR. GOLDSMITH: Thank you. No further questions at this time, Your Honor.
THE COURT: Thank you. I had a question. In response to Mr. Petrocelli's questions about what you would do if advance levels got lowered—
THE WITNESS: Uh-huh.
THE COURT:—you said you would take your books to another publisher.
THE WITNESS: Right.
THE COURT: Why would you do that when you also testified that the editor is the most important thing and the advances don't determine which publisher you choose?
THE WITNESS: Well, it's like a give-and-take relationship. I mean, I'm not planning on doing it for the rest of my career, hopefully, but you're sending a message. So I've actually done this very thing before. I had a situation with one of my authors—
THE COURT: If I may, I—I think I'm asking: Why would you care to do anything about this when it doesn't affect the way you do your business?
THE WITNESS: Can you explain—can you repeat the question, then.
THE COURT: I understood your testimony to be that you're just looking for the best editor.
THE WITNESS: Uh-huh.
THE COURT: And the advances are not as important, and it's not about competition for you; that it's—it's these other factors that based on your expertise you're finding the best home for the book—
THE WITNESS: Uh-huh.
THE COURT:—et cetera. So why would you respond to lowered advances when that's not the way you run your business? You're looking for editors. So you would leave the editors that you were saying are the best because of lowered advances that you don't rely on?
THE WITNESS: I think we're talking about a gradation. So you—if the advances were suddenly cut in half, I would absolutely—you know, that would be a really big problem for me. If the—so I'm not saying the money is not important, but there are other editors at each—you know, at Macmillan that—that are—for example, with serious nonfiction, there's some phenomenal people at Penguin Random House. There's also great people at Macmillan. So I'd probably go there.
THE COURT: Okay. Thank you.
MR. PETROCELLI: Nothing, Your Honor.
THE COURT: All right. Thank you.

Thank you for your testimony. You can step down.
THE WITNESS: Thank you.

ANDREW WYLIE, LITERARY AGENT

In his testimony, Andrew Wylie revealed that he has not sold a book since 2018 where both PRH and S&S bid, and he claimed the Wylie Agency doesn't conduct "auctions"—by which he means they don't have rules for soliciting bids, though they do submit to multiple publishers in multiple rounds.

"How do you satisfy yourself that you're getting the very best deal when you're only negotiating with one party?" Petrocelli asked.

"Well, I've been doing it for 42 years, and I can calculate with a high degree of accuracy the amount we would be able to achieve through a multiple submission; and if we can achieve that through a single submission, then we do a single submission," Wylie said.

Wylie thinks the merger would have a positive impact on his authors "Because what is important, in my view, for Simon & Schuster is to have its enterprise supported by an understanding parent company. So if it were, for instance, to go to private equity, as happened originally with Houghton Mifflin, the private equity company wouldn't understand the business it was in; would, say, load it with debt as Blackstone did to Houghton Mifflin, basically destroying the publishing house so that it was sold at a discount later to one of the Big 5." (This account is not correct; the ruination of Houghton Mifflin began when a consortium of private equity firms that bought the company from Vivendi sold it to the smaller Irish software company Riverdeep, which vastly overpaid to keep the publisher going public. Riverdeep's heavy borrowings headed the company inevitably to bankruptcy—but they reorganized and came back to public markets with a once-hot stock. Management mistakes and additional business issues led to the slimming of the company and the sale of the quite successful trade division.)

Wylie said that the agency does "not represent top selling authors," trying to draw a distinction between John Grisham and Danielle Steele and Wylie's clients, because "what we are aspiring to do, to be selfish, is enjoy the work that we're representing, enjoy reading it, and not to have our primary goal be purely financial but, rather, to be literary. And I would argue that the performance of works of interest is stronger over time than the purely commercial work, which flares and dies quite rapidly." Of course, Wylie clients such as Paul Beatty, Judd Apatow, T Kira Madden—whose most recent book sold in a significant deal—and Charles Duhigg, also a witness for the defense, are in fact top sellers.

A significant amount of cross-examination referred to Wylie's quickly diminished 2010 project Odyssey Editions, which directly published ebook editions of 20 backlist books (through an Amazon exclusive to start). Since most of the books included were published in print by Random House, the publisher announced very publicly it would put new business on hold with Wylie worldwide. After various counter-threats, a month later Wylie gave the digital rights to Random House—where they still earn a standard 25 percent royalty. The questioning, which highlighted Wylie's concern over not being able to do business with Random House or "any other substantial publisher" seemed designed to show that Wylie, at least, doesn't ultimately have bargaining power over major publishers and their firm business policies.

TESTIMONY OF ANDREW WYLIE, LITERARY AGENT

DIRECT EXAMINATION

BY MR. PETROCELLI:

Q. Please state your full name for the record.
A. Andrew Wylie.
Q. What do you do for a living?
A. I'm a literary agent.
Q. Where do you work?
A. At the Wylie Agency.
Q. How many other agents work with you?
A. Total number of employees is about 50. And agents, about 20.
Q. Approximately how many authors does your agency represent?
A. Fifteen hundred.

Q. Approximately how many do you personally represent?

A. Probably 80 to a hundred, although I would say that the number is significantly higher because I—I closely consult on most of the arrangements made through the agency.

Q. Can you tell the Court a little bit about your background.

A. I grew up in New England. I went to Harvard. I had a traveling fellowship after college and went to Europe and came back and had a bookstore in New York for a couple years and interviewed people for magazines. And then I began the agency in 1980.

Q. And what did your father do?

A. He was a publisher at Houghton Mifflin. He was editor and then Editor in Chief.

Q. How long have you been a literary agent?

A. Forty-two years.

Q. Okay. What type of books do you generally sell?

MR. PETROCELLI: And, Your Honor, I've been messing up these numbers, but I think we're at Defendants' Demonstrative 8.

THE COURT: Okay.

MR. PETROCELLI: If we can display that.

BY MR. PETROCELLI:

Q. You want to tell us a little bit about your clients. You can brag a little bit, if you want.

A. From the beginning, we seek out books of high quality, both in fiction and nonfiction. It interested me that the books that received the highest advances and the most prominent distribution were not books that I deemed to be of great quality, and I felt that the—the highest quality books were not either well represented or well published. So that was the area that we looked at, and we've continued on that path for 42 years.

Q. And by estates, we are referring to authors who are deceased?

A. Yes.

Q. And—and you represent their personal representatives in connection with their literary works?

A. Yes.

Q. Okay. So you have in front of you, Mr. Wiley, two trial exhibits. One is Plaintiff's Exhibit 857. The other is Plaintiff's 856. Starting with 857, you recognize this document?

A. Yes.

Q. What is it?

A. It's a record of contracts entered into by clients of ours; contracts that we have represented, that we've negotiated.

MR. PETROCELLI: Your Honor, I'd ask that this be admitted into evidence.

THE COURT: Any objection?

MS. CROSS: No.

THE COURT: That will be admitted.

MR. PETROCELLI: And this is under seal, Your Honor.

THE COURT: Okay.

MR. PETROCELLI: And so is the next one as well, when I get to it. (PX Exhibit 857 was admitted into evidence.)

BY MR. PETROCELLI:

Q. So if you look at the 14 pages, there are different initials on the left-hand side under staff. What does that signify?

A. The agent in charge of a particular client.

Q. Okay. And if you look at pages 15, 16, and 17, at the bottom left it says, "AW deals." I take it those are your deals?

A. Yes.

Q. Okay. And I'm not going to ask you to count. I'll represent to you that there are 158 deals on pages 15, 16, and 17. Okay?

A. Yep.

Q. Now—
THE COURT: I'm sorry. What period of time are we talking about?
BY MR. PETROCELLI:
Q. 2018 through 2021; is that right, Mr. Wylie?
A. Yes.
Q. Okay. Now, Exhibit 856, do you recognize this document?
A. Yes.
Q. What is it?
A. I'm sorry?
Q. And what is it?
A. It's a record of sales made by the agency.
Q. Now, it might assist your recollection if I represent to you that these are—these are 52 of your deals in which Penguin Random House or Simon & Schuster acquired the book.
A. Okay.
Q. Would you agree with that?
A. Yes.
Q. Okay.
MR. PETROCELLI: And, Your Honor, I would ask that Exhibit 856 be admitted also under seal.
THE COURT: Any objection?
MS. CROSS: No.
THE COURT: That will be admitted. (PX Exhibit 856 admitted into evidence.)
BY MR. PETROCELLI:
Q. Okay. I'm going to focus on 856 for the moment, your deals where Penguin Random House and Simon & Schuster, one or the other, acquired the book. Okay?
A. Yes.
Q. Again, not making you count them up, but there are 36 of the 52 in which under the column "Single or multiple submission?" it states "single."
A. Okay.
Q. What does that mean?
A. That means the proposal or book was submitted only to one editor at one publishing house.
Q. And then there are 16 in that same column where it states "multiple." What does that mean?
A. That means that the project was submitted to more than one editor at one publishing house.
Q. And then the last column says "Other bidders." To what does that refer?
A. Other publishers who bid for the project but failed to acquire the rights.
Q. And sometimes next to multiple, under "Other bidders," it says "None." What does that mean?
A. No other house bid for the project.
Q. I note that Penguin Random House is not listed as the other bidder for any of the books won by S&S.
A. Right.
Q. Nor is Simon & Schuster listed as another bidder for any book won by Penguin Random House.
A. Correct.
Q. Okay. Does that mean that you have not sold a book since 2018 in which both Penguin Random House and Simon & Schuster submitted a bid for the book?
A. That's correct.
Q. And I notice that there are no auctions listed here.
A. We don't conduct auctions.
Q. Now, who is the "we"?
A. Our agency.
Q. The Wylie Agency, some 20 agents or so, including yourself, your testimony is that the firm does not conduct auctions in transacting book sales to publishers?
A. Correct.
Q. Okay. I'm going to follow up on that, but before I do, does it follow that given that Simon &

Schuster and PRH—Penguin Random House—have not both submitted a bid for one of your books, that they've never finished one and two in any acquisition process?

A. I don't think it's ever happened.

Q. Okay. Now—

THE COURT: So can I understand: When it says "multiple" here, that just means you sent it out to more than one editor?

THE WITNESS: Yes.

THE COURT: And then you did a one-on-one negotiation?

THE WITNESS: Well, in a multiple submission, we submit to more than one house. The houses we submit to either decline to offer or place offers. We take a look at them, and if—if one offer is markedly stronger than another and the house has an editor we feel would be ideally suited to edit the book, then we—we would accept that bid on behalf of the author.

THE COURT: So is—that's not a best-bids auction?

THE WITNESS: I'm sorry. What?

THE COURT: That is not a best-bids auction?

THE WITNESS: No, no. No. An auction has rules and compels the agent and author to accept the strongest bid. The strongest financial terms offered do not compose, necessarily, the best offer, in my view, because you also have to consider the editor who would be working with the author and the context from which the book would come; what else the publisher is publishing, and the strengths or weaknesses of the publishing house.

THE COURT: Thank you. My question is: How is what you do different from a best-bids auction?

THE WITNESS: My understanding is that other agents say this is an auction. They have rules. You place first bids by Tuesday. You will then be asked to place second bids by Friday, and third bids next week; and the strongest financial offer will be accepted.

THE COURT: And you send out to a bunch of editors, and they make bids to you, and then you pick the one you like the best, but there are no rules?

THE WITNESS: No rules.

THE COURT: Okay.

BY MR. PETROCELLI:

Q. So can you just elaborate a little bit more on that, because we're trying to understand the difference between a formal auction where there's a best-bid process in place, which involves multiple bidders all making bids, and presumably the one who makes the best bid is the winner. And you're not calling it an auction—right?—but you are submitting it to multiple bidders, and you're getting multiple responses back. And are you always picking the best one?

A. No.

Q. So how do you choose?

A. We—we are picking one that we feel presents the strongest combination of financial terms plus editorial engagement and context for the author.

Q. Well, why don't you conduct an auction, a more formal auction, in which you try to, you know, drum up more direct competition, let's say, in the form of a round-robin auction?

A. Well, to achieve our goals, we would have to say: Submit your bid and your editor's name. And then if we were to select one house over another house—and let's say that that house had a lower financial offer but a better editor, then we would be offending people unnecessarily.

Q. I notice in your answers, you've been using the term "financial terms."

A. Hmm.

Q. Are there financial terms that you negotiate for your author clients besides the advance?

A. Yes, indeed. Territorial rights, royalty rates, division of revenue for second serial rights. Multiple aspects of a contract are negotiated.

Q. There's been testimony in this case that the advances that we've been essentially dealing with are the North America rights. You understand that?

A. Well, I understand that we're talking about North American rights. For our agency, we operate globally, operate directly into all markets around the globe. So about 50 percent of our business is—is in the U.S., and the other 50 percent in the rest of the world combined.

Q. So to be clear, in the representation of your clients, do you, on behalf of your clients, convey the worldwide rights or just the North America rights?

A. In talking to publishers in the U.S., we convey only North American rights, except in the case of photographic work, where production considerations dictate that it should be a global deal.

Q. And then do you negotiate similar deals with countries outside the U.S.?

A. Yes.

Q. And those deals have nothing to do with the U.S. publisher?

A. Correct.

Q. Okay. And that's and your—your author clients get additional compensation from those deals?

A. Yes, they do.

Q. Okay.

A. And the balance is roughly half the author's revenue comes from the U.S. and the other half comes from the rest of the world combined.

Q. Are you doing this, essentially, all around the same time, or are you—first do the U.S. and then wait for the book to come out and then do the rest of the world?

A. Depends entirely on—on the—on the project involved. We represent authors—Italian authors, German authors, French authors, Japanese authors, and in those cases, we would usually negotiate first in the author's home territory and then spread around the world. So the U.S. could be the third or fourth publisher we turn to.

And even with U.S. resident authors, we sometimes make arrangements outside of the U.S. first to indicate to U.S. publishers the strength with which the project is viewed outside of the U.S.

Q. We talked a bit about your multiple-bidder process. What about the single-bidder process? What—what—what circumstances are they?

A. Well, either if an author has been published by an editor and publisher and has had a happy experience and wants to remain with that editor and publisher, or if we feel that the ideal match between author and editor and publisher is identifiable and we calculate the price we would like the author to be paid as an advance for the book, then we go to a single submission. And in most cases, the deal is done with one editor without broadening the submission or having discussions outside of that editor and publisher.

Q. So focusing on the single submissions, given your work in trying to get your client the very best deal, how do you satisfy yourself that you're getting the very best deal when you're only negotiating with one party?

A. Well, I've been doing it for 42 years, and I can calculate with a high degree of accuracy the amount we would be able to achieve through a multiple submission; and if we can achieve that through a single submission, then we do a single submission.

Q. Well, how—how do you take into account what you might achieve outside of that single submission in order to judge whether you're getting a reasonable proposal from the publisher with whom you're negotiating?

A. Experience.

Q. Is there any rule of thumb?

A. Not really, no. It's—it's just detailed knowledge of the business, of the publishers, and of the editors in the industry.

Q. So you understand this is a trial about whether Penguin Random House and Simon & Schuster can merge and thereby be owned by one corporate parent?

A. Yes.

Q. Okay. Do you have—what impact, if any, do you believe this merger would have on—on your business, on your representation of your clients, and your ability to get them the best possible deal?

A. Generally speaking, I think it would be a positive result.

Q. And why is that?

A. Because what is important, in my view, for Simon & Schuster is to have its enterprise supported by an understanding parent company. So if it were, for instance, to go to private equity, as happened originally with Houghton Mifflin, the private equity company wouldn't understand the business it was in; would, say, load it with debt as Blackstone did to Houghton Mifflin, basically destroying the publishing house so that it was sold at a discount later to one of the Big 5.

Q. Now, you mentioned the Big 5. I'm reminded—and I was going to ask you: Looking through your sheet, your deal sheet, almost all of your, you know, higher amounts of—of advances are with Big 5 firms. Why is that?

A. Well, I think they have the broadest talent editorially. They are generally well financed, and their production and distribution is expert.

Q. Do you make deals from time to time with non-Big 5 firms?

A. Absolutely. To take an example, years ago Al Gore, whom we represent, came to see me carrying a computer and gave me a slide presentation of a lecture, which he thought could possibly become a book. He had in mind to call it *An Inconvenient Truth*, and he asked me about how it—I told him I thought it would be an important book. And he asked me who the best publisher would be and what the best arrangement would be, and I said Rodale. And we submitted only to Rodale and made an arrangement with Rodale to publish that book.

Q. In your—

A. The ramification—

THE COURT: Is that—I'm sorry. Is—is Rodale an imprint from a Big 5 publisher or—

THE WITNESS: I'm sorry. I can't hear you.

THE COURT: I'm just trying to understand who Rodale is. Is that an imprint for a Big 5 publisher, or is it a smaller independent one?

THE WITNESS: No. It was at the time an independent publisher which had a magazine publication and—and related environmental interests.

THE COURT: Thank you.

BY MR. PETROCELLI:

Q. In your experience in dealing with non-Big 5 publishers, irrespective of the amount of the advance, what's—what's your view been about the quality of the services that they provide?

A. Generally, the services provided by non-Big 5 publishers are—are professional and—and really quite—quite strong.

Q. There's been talk in this trial about something called anticipated top selling books. Is that an expression in the course of your career with which you are familiar?

A. I am familiar with it, but it is not part of the business that we are active in.

Q. What do you mean by that?

A. We don't represent top selling authors. We don't represent authors like John Grisham or Danielle Steel or—

Q. Why not?

A. Because what we are aspiring to do, to be selfish, is enjoy the work that we're representing, enjoy reading it, and I—and not to have our primary goal be purely financial but, rather, to be literary. And I would argue that the performance of works of interest is stronger over time than the purely commercial work, which flares and dies quite rapidly.

Q. Thank you, Mr. Wylie.

MR. PETROCELLI: I pass the witness, Your Honor.

THE COURT: All right. Thank you.

(Recess taken.)

THE COURT: Good afternoon. I see you have another binder. Excellent.

MS. CROSS: We do, but it's a thin one, Your Honor.

THE COURT: Okay.

MS. CROSS: May it please the court. Anna Cross for the United States.

THE COURT: Good afternoon.

CROSS-EXAMINATION

BY MS. CROSS:

Q. Good afternoon, Mr. Wylie.

A. Good afternoon.

Q. Mr. Wylie, one clarification on a question that Mr. Petrocelli asked you. You testified that you published Al Gore's *An Inconvenient Truth* through Rodale.

A. I didn't publish it. I represented it.

Q. Okay. So Rodale published that book; is that correct?

A. Yes.

Q. And Rodale is now owned by Penguin Random House?

A. Correct.

Q. And I'm not sure it came up in your testimony, but you represent authors Charles Duhigg and Andrew Solomon; is that right?

A. Yes.

Q. And Charles Duhigg publishes with Penguin Random House; is that right?

A. Yes.

Q. And Andrew Solomon publishes with Simon & Schuster?

A. Yes.

Q. You view it as your role as an agent to try to get an advance that the author doesn't earn out; isn't that right?

A. I think I've said that with levity as much as profundity.

Q. Do you believe it's your role as an agent to try to get an advance that an author doesn't earn out?

A. Well, if the book is going to earn a hundred dollars and the author is paid $200, then the author is happier than if the book earned a hundred dollars and the author was paid $50. So yes.

Q. And very few of the books you represent earn out their advance; is that right?

THE COURT: I'm sorry. Did we get—

WITNESS: It was a few years ago, but it's not anymore.

THE COURT: I'm sorry. Did we get an answer to the question?

THE WITNESS: I'm sorry.

THE COURT: Did you answer the question is—whether your role is to get an advance that the author does not earn out?

THE WITNESS: I'm sorry. I can't hear you.

THE COURT: Sorry. I believe counsel asked you if you view your role as getting an advance for your client that the author does not earn out, and I wasn't sure I heard an answer to the question and what you said.

THE WITNESS: Well, I—I mean, it's a complicated question, in my view, because, ideally, the author would earn out, and both publisher and author would be very happy. If the author does not earn out, then the author's appraisal of the job the agent has done is that the agent has secured more money for the author than the author would otherwise have obtained. And so that's advantageous to a certain degree. But that's a short-term view.

BY MS. CROSS:

Q. And just so I understand your position, do you believe it's your role as an agent to try to get an advance that an author doesn't earn out?

A. Not necessarily.

Q. Okay. You gave a deposition in this matter on April 21st, 2022; is that right?

A. Yes.

Q. Could you please turn to the tab in your binder marked deposition, and then turn to page 31. I'm going to read from lines 19 through 22.

"Question: Do you believe it's your role as an agent to try to get an advance that an author doesn't earn out? "Answer: Correct." Did I read that correctly?

A. You did.

MS. CROSS: Your Honor, I move to admit page 31, lines 19 through 22 from Mr. Wylie's transcript into evidence.
THE COURT: Any objection?
MR. PETROCELLI: No, Your Honor.
THE COURT: That's admitted. (Wylie Deposition Transcript page 31, lines 19 through 22 admitted into evidence.)
BY MS. CROSS:
Q. And you have estimated that 5 percent of your books—of the books you represent earn out their advance; is that right?
A. That's probably right.
Q. For most authors you represent, the advance level matters to their daily existence; is that right?
A. Yes.
Q. You testified about financial terms other than the advance before the break. Do you recall that?
A. Yes.
Q. Okay. I want to talk specifically about digital royalties, ebook royalties.
A. Mm-hmm.
Q. There are standard digital royalty rates in the publishing industry; is that right?
A. Yes.
Q. And I want to take you back to 2010 to a project you started called Odyssey Editions. Do you recall that project?
A. Yes.
Q. In 2010 publishers were paying ebook royalties of 25 percent; is that right?
A. Some. Some were paying less, and some were paying more.
Q. You decided to create Odyssey Editions because you thought the royalty rate for ebooks should be higher than 25 percent; right?
A. Yes. And I also felt that were it not increased by publishers, that they ran the risk of losing control of those rights because the authors would publish digitally outside of their print publishing agreements, and that would be damaging to the fundamentals of the publishing industry.
Q. You had conversations with publishers about increasing the ebook royalty rate prior to launching Odyssey Editions; right?
A. Yes.
Q. And you couldn't get a publisher to agree to a higher ebook royalty; right?
A. Correct. Yeah.
Q. And so you were trying to improve ebook royalties through Odyssey Editions; right?
A. Well, I was trying to show what could happen if the authors' concerns, which I felt were legitimate, were not addressed.
Q. And let's talk about what Odyssey Editions was. You selected 20 books to be distributed electronically, exclusively through Amazon, and you called that Odyssey Editions; right?
A. Yes. Well, there was a distribution agreement for two years with Amazon.
Q. Random House was the original print publisher of many of the books you tried to distribute on Amazon through Odyssey Editions; right?
A. Yes.
Q. Authors received 100 percent of the digital royalties for Odyssey Edition ebooks and paid you a commission; is that right?
A. Yes.
Q. After you launched Odyssey Editions, Random House announced through *The New York Times* that they would no longer do business with you as a result of Odyssey Editions; right?
A. Yes.
Q. You were concerned about not being able to do business with Random House; right?
A. As I would have been with any other substantial publisher, yes.
Q. And after *The New York Times* announcement by Random House that they would no longer do

business with you, you had meetings with Markus Dohle, who was the CEO of Random House at the time; is that right?

A. Yes.

THE COURT: Can I just ask: You're saying Random House, do you mean Penguin Random House, or do you mean the imprint Random House?

MS. CROSS: Your Honor, this was in 2010, prior to the merger of Penguin Random House—

THE COURT: Okay. I see. Thank you.

MS. CROSS:—and so it was his position at the time.

THE COURT: Thank you.

MS. CROSS: Yeah.

BY MS. CROSS:

Q. After the meetings with Mr. Dohle, you withdrew the Random House books that you had been trying to distribute through Odyssey Editions from Amazon; is that right?

A. Yes.

Q. And the digital rights for the books Random House had published in print form that you put on Odyssey Editions went to Random House after your conversations with Mr. Dohle; right?

A. Yes.

Q. It's fair to say Odyssey Editions doesn't go into conflict with publishers anymore; right?

A. Yes.

Q. And most publishers still offer a 25 percent digital royalty; right?

A. Yes.

Q. Penguin Random House offers a digital royalty of 25 percent?

A. Yes.

Q. And you—you still think that a 25 percent digital royalty is unfair to authors; right?

A. I feel it could be higher because the publisher is not bearing an equivalent cost of production to that involved in print publishing, book publishing.

Q. And just to make sure I get an answer to my question: Do you think 25 percent for a digital royalty rate is fair to authors?

A. No.

Q. Turning to another topic, you don't think self-publishing is an effective way to publish; is that right?

A. Yes.

Q. And you haven't sold any print titles to Amazon?

A. No.

Q. If one of your authors wanted to publish with Amazon, you'd try to talk them out of it; is that right?

A. Yes.

Q. You testified in response to Mr. Petrocelli's questioning that you don't do auctions, and I just want to clarify a point about that. As you testified, you do multiple submissions; is that right?

A. Yes.

Q. And sometimes you do submit proposals or manuscripts to as many as 15 different editors; is that right?

A. Yes.

Q. Okay. And sometimes you submit them in waves if you don't in the first round of submissions get an offer that you want; is that right?

A. Yes.

Q. You generally sell books to the highest bidder; right?

A. Generally, but there are a number of exceptions to that.

Q. You only rarely sell books to an underbidder; right?

A. It's not that rare.

Q. Do you recall giving a ballpark for how often do you sell to an underbidder of 7 and a half percent?

A. That sounds about right, yeah.

Q. Let's turn to the backlist. You believe that the backlist is important for a publisher; right?

A. Yes.
Q. In fact, you've analogized the backlist to the basement of a house. It plays the same role for a house you live in for the publishing house; right?
A. Yes.
Q. And you've also noted that if you don't have a solid basement, your house is unstable; is that right?
A. Tends to blow away in a storm, yes.
MS. CROSS: No further questions.
THE COURT: Thank you. Any redirect?

REDIRECT EXAMINATION

BY MR. PETROCELLI:

Q. Following up on the questions regarding Odyssey, did I understand that you wanted to withhold audio rights—or digital rights—excuse me—from the publisher and transact separately with Amazon?
A. No. The calculation was that for the books that we digitally distributed through Odyssey, the contracts had been entered into prior to ebook production. So we were conveying rights that were not covered in the print publishing agreement between the author and the publisher at the time of publication of the books.
Q. You took the position that since the contracts were drafted before the advent of ebooks, that ebooks were not within the scope of rights conveyed?
A. Exactly.
Q. Okay. And there was a dispute about that?
A. Yes.
Q. And did you resolve it?
A. Yes.
Q. How did you resolve it?
A. To my satisfaction.
Q. Of course. With respect to the 20 books, was there some kind of compromise reached?
A. The discussion and the agreement are confidential by—
Q. But there was an agreement reached?
A. Yes.
Q. Okay.
MR. PETROCELLI: Thank you, Your Honor. Nothing further.
THE COURT: Thank you. I just have sort of a general question for you about your business and negotiating these deals.
THE WITNESS: Yeah.
THE COURT: And my understanding is that all these deals are different.
THE WITNESS: Uh-huh.
THE COURT: And like in any bargaining situation, do you sometimes feel like you have more leverage and sometimes you feel like you have less leverage in any individual deal?
THE WITNESS: Yes.
THE COURT: So what kind of factors go into giving you more leverage?
THE WITNESS: Really the quality of the—of the project.
THE COURT: And that's subjective, though, is it not?
THE WITNESS: Yes. But I think there are recognizable qualities in books that people who have been in the business for a long time would easily recognize.
THE COURT: And so would you say for some books there's a consensus that this is going to be a successful book?
THE WITNESS: Yes.
THE COURT: And those types of negotiations, can you just describe how those negotiations differ from others, if they do?
THE WITNESS: Well, yes. To give an example, if there's a young writer who has not previously

published who may be at the Iowa Writers' school [sic] and who has a collection of stories, which we deem to be worthy, the reception in the publishing community can vary by—by quite a margin. Some publishers would say we're not going to publish stories. Other would say I will only offer on this book of stories if I get the next book, which must be a novel. And still others would say the writer is a genius and I must acquire this book, probably with an option clause on the next book.

THE COURT: And how do you—so you've identified this is a book that—

THE WITNESS: Yeah. So we would go—

THE COURT:—could be successful. So how do you deal with this?

THE WITNESS:—probably to a broader number of publishers with that collection of stories coming out of the Iowa Writers' Workshop than we would with the next novel of a young Irish writer called Sally Rooney, let's say.

THE COURT: Okay. So you would go broader with something that looks like it could generate interest among—

THE WITNESS: I'm sorry. What?

THE COURT: You would go broader with something that looks like it could generate interest among—

THE WITNESS: I didn't hear the beginning of that. I'm sorry.

THE COURT: You would go broader with a project that you determine—

THE WITNESS: Yeah. In a way, the less sure we are of the value of a project, the broader the submission. If we know pretty much exactly what the book will receive or would receive through an auction or multiple-submission process, we will usually go to the ideal editor and publisher on a single-submission basis.

THE COURT: I see.

THE WITNESS: And if they meet our goal, then that's that. The deal is done.

THE COURT: And last question: So if it's a situation where you want to go broad, it's because sometimes there's going to be an editor who says I must have this—

THE WITNESS: Uh-huh.

THE COURT:—versus other people who are going to say don't want it?

THE WITNESS: Yeah.

THE COURT: Does it help to have more, I guess, choice in who you send it to because you're looking for that editor that loves this particular book?

THE WITNESS: Yes, because everyone has—has different tastes and judgment. So—and sometimes people who you believe would respond positively to a project don't do so. And—and—and others whom you think would be hesitant to be enthusiastic are wildly enthusiastic.

THE COURT: Okay. Thank you. Any questions based on my questioning?

MR. PETROCELLI: No, Your Honor.

THE COURT: All right. Thank you. Anything from you? No. All right. Thank you so much. Thank you for your testimony. You can step down.

THE WITNESS: Okay.

GAIL ROSS, LITERARY AGENT

In her testimony, Gail Ross introduced to the trial the term BATNA, or Best Alternative to a Negotiated Deal. Ross said "the best way to get the best deal" from a publisher is to "improve your BATNA." The BATNA includes nonfinancial terms, "all these ephemeral things like an editorial relationship and a love of a particular house or the fact the book wasn't there," she said.

If the merger were to happen, PRH attorney Daniel Petrocelli asked, "do you think you would be thinking about this BATNA or your other competitive alternatives in a different way?" No, Ross said. "It only takes one competitor in a sense or the idea of one competitor to make my negotiations strong. And if we're going out more widely, then there are plenty of competitors."

She said PRH's relationships with independent bookstores and systems would be a boon for S&S authors, and she doesn't expect the combined company to lower author advances. On Paramount Global—which has owned S&S in one form or the other for decades, and where the house has grown to record sales and profits in recent years—in her view, "I'd clearly say that they are punching above their weight, but they are understaffed and need an infusion." (She may have missed the past where Markus Dohle expressed admiration for how Simon & Schuster is "super lean" in how it acquires and has "done certainly better than Penguin Random House has" so PRH could "potentially learn from them and adopt that.")

On S&S publicity staff, she said "They work really hard. They work so hard, but they don't have a lot—they don't have the staff that the other publishers tend to have." (Here she may have missed PRH's post-merger "efficiencies model" with its "de-duplication" plans.)

Upon cross-examination, Ross confirmed that she always submits to both PRH and S&S imprints, unless a book is an option or exclusive submission.

TESTIMONY OF GAIL ROSS, LITERARY AGENT

DIRECT EXAMINATION

BY MR. PETROCELLI:

Q. Good afternoon.

A. Good afternoon.

Q. Please state your full name for the record.

A. Gail Ross.

Q. What do you do for a living?

A. I am a literary agent and media lawyer.

Q. Media lawyer?

A. Yes.

Q. Okay. Where do you practice?

A. I'm the president of the Ross Yoon literary agency, and I am a partner in the law firm of Trister, Ross, Schadler & Gold here in the District.

Q. You live and work here in Washington?

A. I do.

Q. Okay. Now, when did you become a lawyer?

A. I graduated from Georgetown in 1980.

Q. 1980?

A. Uh-huh.

Q. And how long have you been a literary agent?

A. I started—I sold my first book in 1986.

Q. Okay. And as between your work as a lawyer and your work as a literary agent, what's the breakdown?

A. Oh, I try to practice law as little as possible. It varies week to week. It might be a couple hours a week. It's usually work—I review publishing law contracts for academics who might come in, a university press contract or something like that, or I do some work for clients at the agency who negotiate their consulting agreements with CNN or something like that, but it's a minimum. It's minimal.

Q. Okay. So your primary work is as a literary agent?

A. Yes.

Q. And you're not an antitrust lawyer, are you?

A. No.

Q. Okay. So let me ask you to refer to what I have marked as Defendants' Demonstrative 9. And can you identify for the Court what this is?

A. Yes. This is a selection of books that I represented.

Q. Is there any particular type of book or genre that you specialize in?

A. I represent primarily nonfiction. Just an occasional novel. I love to read them, but I can't sell them. And my nonfiction breaks down into categories. I'm lucky enough that it breaks down into categories I care a lot about, and so it tends to be politics, history, science, social justice issues, women's issues, environment, psychology, a little religion.

Q. The Ross Yoon literary agency, that's the name of your firm?

A. Yes, it is.

Q. And how many agents work with you?

A. One—we are pretty lean and mean. There are one, two—there are only five of us, currently.

Q. Including yourself?

A. Yes.

Q. Okay. Now, you have also in front of you Plaintiff's Exhibit 838.

A. The famous lists.

Q. Yeah. And could you identify to the Court what that is?

A. The first page or all of it or?

Q. Well, just the entire document, and then I'll go through the different pages with you.

A. Oh. The document represents a compendium of different breakdowns of sales of mine—just mine—during the relevant years that—2018, 2019, 2020, and 20—no. 2020 and 2021.

Q. 2018 to 2021?

A. '21. Correct.

Q. Your deals?

A. Just my deals, yes.

Q. Okay. And those deals—and I will represent to you—total 89 and are listed on pages 1, 2, and 3.

A. That's correct.

Q. Okay. Then we get to page 4, which is not easy to read.

MR. PETROCELLI: And this a confidential document, Your Honor. And by the way, I'd ask that this be admitted under seal.

THE COURT: Any objection?

MR. VANCE: No objection.

THE COURT: All right. This will be admitted. (PX Exhibit 838 admitted into evidence.)

BY MR. PETROCELLI:

Q. Okay. So 1, 2, and 3 are the totality of the deals. I think they number 89; right?

A. Correct.

Q. Now, on page 4, which is the tiny print, what is that?

A. I don't know. No. Kidding. This list represents my sales during that relevant period to an imprint at either PRH or Simon & Schuster.

Q. Okay. I'll represent to you that there are 43 deals there. And these, again, are deals in which the books were sold either to Penguin Random House or Simon & Schuster; is that right?

A. That's correct.

Q. Okay.

A. Although I have to say, I can't see it very well, but I see it at the bottom it says that.

Q. Well, you have the monitor in front of you.

A. Oh, there we are. Okay.
Q. So I just want to make sure we understand some of the columns here.
A. Yes.
Q. So under "Manner Sold," you can see that there are references to option, exclusive submission, auction?
A. Yes.
Q. And preempt; right?
A. Yes.
Q. Okay. And so based on what we heard throughout this trial, you need not explain, you know, what those types of submissions are, but suffice it to say, that three of them, options, exclusive submissions, preempts, involve direct negotiations as opposed to an auction; right?
A. Correct.
Q. Okay. And with respect to the auctions, how do you conduct your auctions?
A. They typically fall into two categories, at least how I do it. I'm a little old-fashioned. So I do two types: rounds, which I can explain, and best-bids. The rounds begin—do you want me to explain how rounds work?
Q. Please.
A. The rounds begin—and all this is spelled out in a memo that's gone to the participants that says what the rule—my rules for conducting the auction. So if it's a rounds auction, it begins with publishers submitting blind first bids, either by phone or electronically. And then I take the first-round bids and put them in ascending order, such that—to go to Round 2, the high—the lowest bidder in Round 1 has to beat the highest bidder in Round 1 by a prescribed percentage or dollar amount usually, and that's also in the rules. I tend to do $10,000 increments, but other people do 10 percent increments.
Q. Let me just pause right there.
A. Sure.
Q. Do the participants—and by participants, you mean the publishers; right?
A. Yes.
Q. And you don't invite all publishers, do you?
A. No.
Q. Okay. So the first step is you identify who you want to invite?
A. Well, I have—at that—by the point I'm going to an auction, it's been a fairly, you know, long process by which I made decisions about where I'm going to submit, the imprints to which I'm going to submit to, the proposal. I've worked on this incredible book proposal with my wonderful client, and then we submit it to the appropriate imprints. And then we typically have meetings—or used to go to New York with my clients and spend days running around Manhattan. That has not happened since March of 2020 because of COVID.
Q. Because of the pandemic; right?
A. Yes. So—
Q. And this is all prior to the auction; right?
A. Yes. This is way—very much prior to the auction. And I don't set auction dates or anything and the like when I submit the proposals. I'm really—I'm working with what comes to me as it comes to me. All the—try to collect all the information as the process proceeds.
Q. Do you submit to more publishers than you invite to the auction?
A. I mean, really, the invitations to the auction depend on them and not on me. I submit to people I think are appropriate. And then we see after these meetings, and whether it's going to go to auction. Sometimes I only have one interested party. Sometimes my author has fallen in love with someone based on these editorial discussions and meetings that we've had and says to me: Go see if you want to solicit a preempt because I'd love to be there.

And then vice versa. After the meetings and maybe more discussions, a particular publisher—imprint, I should say, will want to make a preemptive bid prior to my even sending out the rules. I mean, a preempt can happen at any time between a submission of the proposal to the beginning of the auction.

Q. Now, once the—once you start the auction, send out the rules, do you tell the publishers how many are participating and who they are?

A. No.

Q. Do you tell them how many are participating?

A. If it serves my client's interests. I don't have to. I get to control that kind of information, unless, of course, you know, you get into the rules of imprints bidding against imprints within houses and those things, but aside from that, I tell them nothing.

Q. Okay. And you—your reference to unless you get into internal imprinting, were you referring to the rule at some publishers that allow imprints to internally compete provided there's an external bidder?

A. That, and also some of the houses go to house bids. And so they will ask if someone—if another imprint—there's a—HarperCollins, for example, and Simon & Schuster currently do house—if they have more than one imprint involved and—at similar levels of interests, they'll do a house bid. So in order to coordinate that house bid, we have to tell them of the interest.

Q. Those are the two firms that you have to tell because they only do house bids?

A. Yes.

Q. Okay. So—okay. So we were talking about the auction, and you were explaining how the rounds work.

A. Yes.

Q. Okay. And do you let the—the round—that's a round-robin auction. Do you let it go the distance, all the way to the end?

A. Rarely. I haven't let it go the distance in memory. And based on—this sheet was very helpful. I want to thank the government for making me see some of my history. And I haven't gone to the end because it—we always say in our memos that we reserve the right at any time to ask for best bids. And best bids isn't necessarily the highest bid, but best bids is when you would end the rounds, perhaps after Round 3 or Round 4.

It's really a feel that I have for the strategy. And then tell everyone—tell the people who are left that they get to make a best bid, which would include the whole gamut of everything they want to say, editorial letters that are consistent with what the—my client and the editor have discussed, promotion plans, and any other things that are of interest.

Payouts can be different in terms of—in terms of proportionality. Some of the payouts are in quarters, but they're—four payments, but they're not in quarters.

Q. So when you call for best bids, do I understand you're not just getting, like, a number back, but you're getting more of a fulsome proposal?

A. I ask for as much as they want to give me at that point. I want to listen to everything because the more that comes in for my client, the more we're better to—we're better able to determine the real—I mean, best bids means the best place for them to be.

Q. Why do you go to best bids rather than just let the round-robin go to conclusion?

A. There usually comes a point in an auction when you're, sort of—everybody is kind of saying uncle. And you want to respect that and also get everything you can in front of the client. I mean, it's—you know, it's really the author's decision.

Q. Okay. So if you turn to page 5—

A. Yes.

Q.—of Exhibit 838.

A. This one I can see.

Q. Okay. And do I understand that these are just the auctions taken from the prior page of 43 transactions in which—in which either Penguin Random House or Simon & Schuster acquired the book?

A. That's right. But I would like to, if I could—it was one of the great things about the deposition was I was able to go back and—and find some changes I wanted to make, clarifications, if I could.

Q. Please.

A. The—we talked in the deposition about *Sandy Hook*—oh, I wasn't supposed to say that.

Q. Well—

A. The one on 5/1/2019. Sorry.
Q. 5/1/2019.
A. Correct.
Q. You mean the date?
A. The date of the auction. Right.
Q. The auction date of May 1, 2019, on page 5 of Exhibit 838. What about it?
A. All I want to say about that is it was a preempt.
Q. Okay.
A. Okay. I discussed in the deposition that the two players that are listed as the final bidders were very interested, but in going back, I saw that I hadn't sent an auction memo out yet, and so that would be a preempt.
Q. Okay. So that takes us down to—from 16 then to 15. But you have another correction?
A. Right. Yes. I have one more correction. It just should have been an asterisk on the—there was a deal on—I'm sorry.
Q. Page 4?
A. Yes. On page 4. Thank you.
Q. Is it the fourth —
A. Fourth one down. I did that—
Q. The fourth one down—hold on.
A. I co-—
Q. I just want to identify—
THE COURT REPORTER: Hold on. You're speaking over each other.
BY MR. PETROCELLI:
Q. I just want to identify for the record—
A. I'm so sorry.
Q. Just for the record, I just want to identify what you're referring to. So it's page 4 of Exhibit 838, and it's the fourth item from the top?
A. That's correct.
MR. PETROCELLI: This is confidential, by the way.
THE COURT: Uh-huh.
MR. PETROCELLI: Okay.
BY MR. PETROCELLI:
Q. You can see it on your monitor, though; right?
A. Yes.
Q. And that one—what about that one?
A. I meant to include an asterisk because I conducted—I was a co-agent on that. It's two authors, and the other author had a different agency, and the other agency did most of the auction because I had—I was sick or—I can't remember, but I didn't have enough paperwork. So I just put an asterisk to say that I—that I didn't conduct it. And so I didn't really have enough to show you.
Q. Okay. But that was an auction won by Simon & Schuster?
A. Correct. Yes.
Q. So that would, then, bring our total back on page 5 from 15 to 16?
A. Correct.
Q. Okay. And by my count, there are 9 of the 16 in which Penguin Random House acquired the book and 7 with—when Simon & Schuster did. Does that sound right to you?
A. Yes.
Q. Okay. Now, of these 16 auctions in which either Penguin Random House or Simon & Schuster acquired the book, was there ever an occasion when they were runners-up, one and two, in the auction?
A. Yes.
Q. How many times?
A. The auction on 5/7/2021.

Q. Hold on. This is page 5 again—right?—of—

A. Yes.

Q. What was that date?

A. 5/7/2021.

Q. Okay. Second from the bottom; right?

A. That's correct.

Q. Okay. Now, with respect to the—you said of the 43 on your deal sheet in which Penguin Random House or Simon & Schuster acquired the book, 16 were auctions. So that would leave 27 that were not auctions. Okay?

A. Uh-huh.

Q. And those 27 fall in the category of direct negotiations?

A. Correct.

Q. Okay. So I want to ask you some questions about that. So in direct negotiations, can you please explain why you believe that you are getting your client the best possible deal without conducting an auction.

A. For a variety of reasons. Part of it depends on the needs of my client. I—by the time I'm deciding how to sell it, I've worked very hard with the client on a—on the proposal. I know their needs, their wants, their expectations. Sometimes there's just the perfect editor at a given imprint.

But in terms of how do I get to that number? I mean, it all goes back to—I teach this to my clients too. I—when I got out of law school, I took the Harvard negotiation project training, and I—and I took a mediation training. And I always—I always think about the idea of the best alternative—the BATNA, which is from the negotiation project where you have an agreement in front of you or a person—or a publisher in this case—that you're negotiating with. And the best way to get the best deal from them is to improve your BATNA, your best alternative to what's in front of you.

And so I spent a lot of time in my head and in information gathering and the like figuring out what that BATNA is and trying to get it this way. And sometimes it's—it's a give and take. But for a variety of reasons, my client either has been—if it's an option, they've been with that publisher and they want to have the books together. I mean, there's a huge, huge advantage to have your book—Book 1 and Book 2 together. Because when Book 2 comes out, then you get a whole other round of promotion on Book 1. So ofttimes that's a factor if they've been at the same publisher.

If they—if they need a certain kind of editing or they want a certain kind of list, a particular list, they—you know, it's—it's just—it comes from experience and knowledge of the business and what a particular editor might be able to do.

Q. Does your BATNA take into account nonfinancial terms?

A. I mean, it always does because you want to—because in order to get to this negotiated agreement, that's totally taking into nonfinancial terms—right?—all these ephemeral things like an editorial relationship and a love of a particular house or the fact the book wasn't there.

I mean, obviously, my BATNA can't—can't give me the—the passbook if we're negotiating just with someone who bought Book A. Book A is here with the publisher in front of me, and the BATNA can't provide that support between their books; right?

Q. You understand that—

THE COURT: I'm sorry, what does BATNA stand for?

THE WITNESS: I'm sorry. It's a term that the Harvard negotiation project uses in a book called *Getting Yes* [sic]. And it means the best alternative to the negotiation you're having. Okay. So—if the better your BATNA is, if you can walk away from something, then it's easier to push to the terms that you think are fair and right, and so I try to use that.

Sometimes you can—I mean, it's always easier to walk if you know what you're walking to. And in this business, there's always the other competitor. Whether it's—whether they're bidding or not, they're always there.

BY MR. PETROCELLI:

Q. Well, that's where I wanted to go. Right?

A. Okay. Sorry.
Q. Okay. So you know this is a trial about competition?
A. Yes. Of course.
Q. And it's a trial about whether Simon & Schuster and Penguin Random House can merge; right?
A. Yes.
Q. And I'm sure you understand that right now they're two separate corporate entities, but post-merger, they would be owned by the same corporate parent; right?
A. Correct. Yes.
Q. So when you're doing your direct negotiations and you're thinking through the—the best alternative to a negotiated agreement, are you taking into account not only who the other publishers out there who could possibly be interested but also what their market shares are in the acquisition market?
A. I'm embarrassed to admit this, but I don't know what their market shares are.
Q. Okay. So let me follow up on that. And to be clear, I'm not talking about downstream retail sales.
A. Oh, okay.
Q. I'm talking about, like, how—what their—the percentage of books that one publisher acquires from authors relative to other publishers. That's not something you track; right?
A. No.
Q. Okay. So when you're thinking about these other publishers, these other competitors, you're—are you thinking that you can't make a deal, you know you have other alternatives?
A. Yes.
Q. Okay. Are you ranking them in some way or—I mean, how are you thinking about these other competitors?
A. Well, we're—are we just now talking with when I'm—
Q. I'm talking about the premerger world right now.
A. Right. But we were also just talking about when I'm in a direct negotiation. Still—
Q. Yes.
A. No. I mean, there's certain information you gather. I have authors who other editors at different imprints and different publishers have expressed interest in in the past, and—or I know that somebody else might be really interested in that author. So, I mean, you're just always—I'm always gathering information. You know, I'm sort of a—it all comes in, and I have to use my best judgment. Because at the end of the day, it's all about what's the best place for my client to go at that moment.
Q. So if this merger were to occur—and we're now in a world where a Simon & Schuster and Penguin Random House are owned by the same corporate parent—do you think you would be thinking about—and I know this is a hypothetical, but do you think you would be thinking about this BATNA or your other competitive alternatives in a different way?
A. No. There's plenty of competitors out there.
Q. What do you mean by that?
A. Well, I mean that, I mean, I only—it only takes one competitor in a sense or the idea of one competitor to make my negotiations strong. And if we're going out more widely, then there are plenty of competitors.
Q. Who are the competitors—who are the publishers who compete for works that you sell?
A. I do a fair amount of work with Hachette—do you want the imprints or—because I think of everything in terms of editors and imprints and not—not Big 4 or Big 5.
Q. I'm embarrassed to say that if you name the imprint, I might not know the—
A. Okay.
Q.—corporate publisher. So maybe you can give me the parent name.
A. Sure. Well, I work with all—I sell to all of the—the Big 5, Big 4, and then I—I submit an—a lot to Norton. I did a lot with Houghton Mifflin before HarperCollins bought them. I submit often to Grove Atlantic. This book *Solitary* that's on here was wonderfully published by Grove Atlantic. It was a National Book Award finalist. He just passed away last week so it makes me sad. And I submit to Blooms-—I do books with Bloomsbury, and I just sold a book to Nat Geo books. So—

Q. In your experience, the Big 5 buy more books than the other publishers; fair?
A. Sure.
Q. Okay.
A. They're bigger and they need—they have larger lists, and they need to fill those lists. So of course.
Q. So when you do deal with a publisher outside that group, is it—what's your experience with the quality of the publishing services that they render?
A. I try not to submit my books to anybody who doesn't have the capacity to publish with quality and vigor. So I think it—you know, but they have to pick different slots. I mean, the bigger publishers have more slots, if you will. The other—the smaller publishers have—pick their slots a little bit more carefully in the sense that they have less—less slots to fill.
Q. That's scale?
A. Yes. Of course.
Q. The—let me go back to the auctions again. You are familiar with the rule at Penguin Random House as—I think Hachette may have it also—
A. Of course.
Q.—where the imprints can bid so long as there's an external bidder; right? So what—and then if there are no external bidder, you have to then tell the publisher—in this case Penguin Random House—there's no external bidder?
A. Yes.
Q. Are you with me?
A. Yes.
Q. How often, if at all, does it happen in your auctions that you have to make that notification to Penguin Random House?
A. I've had it happen once in 36 years.
Q. Once?
A. Yes.
Q. And—
A. It was over a decade ago.
Q. And why is it that it happened only once?
A. Because people like myself who represent authors that go to auction like this know how to—that's one of the reasons you go to best bids at a certain time. If you're in an auction, you go to best bids because you know—you can see where it's going, and you—and you want to keep a non-PRH player in the auction.
Q. And—and best bid is one way to accomplish that?
A. Yes.
Q. There's been a lot of discussion in this trial about something called anticipated top sellers. Prior to, you know, being involved in this case as a witness, had you ever heard of that before?
A. No. The first time is when I read the complaint.
Q. And do you generally know what's being referred there, books that you can tell in advance are going to be top sellers? I'll just characterize it that way for purposes of my questions.
A. Right.
Q. Is there—is there something like that in your industry?
A. You know, I always say the phrase publishing business is an oxymoron. And in this case, it's very difficult. It's very difficult. There's factors that aren't—you're not in control of. And, I mean, look, as agents you take—you have a certain—I try in my mind to—to take on books that I can afford to take on unless I'm—I have to do it because something—you know, a social cause or something that I feel that I can find a very small publisher for them and I want to help somebody.
But I'm typically taking on books that I think are going to go from high-five figures to millions of dollars. So there—I have that. But that's more gut than anything else. And—and it's looking at similar kinds of books. It's looking at the marketplace that exists now and trying to project the marketplace that exists two years from now, but—when the book may be published, but we don't have a crystal ball.

Q. Is—in your—in your world, in your business, is there some kind of demarcation by the reference to an advance level—let's say $250,000—where the industry treats books above that amount in a certain way in contrast with how they would treat books below that amount?

A. No.

Q. And if I asked you the same question but just putting in another number, either a hundred or 400 or 600 or any number, is there any such line in—that—that exists in your business?

A. There's no bright line like that that I know of. There are many books that have had great success with a hundred-thousand-dollar advance, and there are many books with a million-dollar advance that have been a flop.

The worst day of a life of an agent and an author is when they've gotten a large advance and you go on BookScan and you see their first few months' sales and it says 4,000 copies or something like that. It happens. It happens more than any of us would like.

Q. What impact, if any, do you believe this merger would have on your clients?

A. Well, I'm focusing primarily on my Simon & Schuster clients. I have a lot of Simon & Schuster clients whose books will be published in the next several years. And I think—I think it will be terrific for them because, you know, Simon & Schuster has sort of been on the—for sale for quite some time, even though the actual sale didn't—you know, didn't happen until March of—March of 2020 when it was—they were official.

But we've known that Viacom didn't want them for a long time, and they are doing very well. I mean, I would—I'd clearly say that they are punching above their weight, but they are understaffed and need—need an infusion. And if this doesn't work, it seems to me, then we're talking about private equity, and that won't happen. I mean, that would be terrible, in my opinion. And so I think that Random House and Simon & Schuster, particularly the imprints that I do the most with are—

Q. When you said "Random House," again, do you mean Penguin Random House?

A. Excuse me. PRH.

Q. Okay. I apologize. Continue.

A. Yeah. The imprints at PRH and at Simon & Schuster that I work the most with are—have—I mean, it's—they're both places that care a lot about books and authors, and the ecosystem is so author friendly and focused. And PRH just has better systems than Simon & Schuster does. And they—and the other thing that's really important to me about my clients is a lot of my clients do very well in independent bookstores. And I go around the country and I ask bookstore people about their various publishers. And, you know, everyone thinks that PRH has the best relations with the independent bookstores in the business. And I'm just looking forward to that for my Simon & Schuster authors.

MR. VANCE: Your Honor, we object to the testimony about private equity as speculation.

THE COURT: That's sustained.

BY MR. PETROCELLI:

Q. The—do you have a concern that this merged company being much bigger than either one today would be in a position to lower author compensation?

A. No, I don't, because my understanding is—is that PRH really wants to invest in Simon & Schuster and the people at Simon & Schuster, who—I mean, the people I know at Simon & Schuster are very much looking forward to this. And the idea would be that they'd be—have more money than they have now to offer in advances, to work with bookstores, to do the—the—you know, the—their publicity and social media stuff is just not as good as most of the other—

Q. Whose?

A. Simon & Schuster. I'm sorry.

Q. I'm sorry. Whose publicity?

A. Simon & Schuster.

Q. Okay.

A. They work really hard. They work so hard, but they don't have a lot—they don't have the staff that the other publishers tend to have.

Q. But if—to make it a hypothetical—

A. Sure.
Q.—if they did over time try to lower advances on your authors, is there anything you could do about that?
A. Well, I'd be spending more time across town with the other publishers than Simon & Schuster and PRH. I don't think it's going to happen. I—I don't remember—it just—the idea of this lowering advances across the board is something—you know, the economy could tank and then everybody will lower advances, but because of the merger, no, I don't see it.
Q. Well, let me follow up on that back to the time when Penguin and Random House merged back, I think, in 2013. You were working actively in your business at that time; right?
A. Yes.
Q. And did you over the ensuing years observe any impact on author advances following that merger?
A. Certainly not negative. I mean, my business has grown and grown and grown. So to the extent that I do some percentage of the business with PRH, I have not seen anything negative.
Q. Okay.
MR. PETROCELLI: Your Honor, did I seek to admit Plaintiff's Exhibit 838 under seal? If I haven't, I now do.
THE COURT: All right. That'll be admitted. (PX Exhibit 838 admitted into evidence.)
MR. PETROCELLI: Okay. Thank you. And I'll pass the witness.
THE COURT: Okay. Thank you.
MR. VANCE: May I proceed, Your Honor?
THE COURT: Yes.

CROSS-EXAMINATION

BY MR. VANCE:

Q. Ms. Ross, nice to see you again.
A. Nice to see you too, sir.
Q. I want to start with PX 838, which was the document that Mr. Petrocelli was reviewing with you.
A. Yep.
Q. If you could turn to page 2 of that document.
A. Yes.
Q. You see the first 2000—I mean 2021 sale is listed to Macmillan?
A. Yes. I've changed that.
Q. That should be PRH; correct?
A. That's correct. That was changed before the deposition.
Q. Then if you could turn to page 5, please.
A. Yes.
Q. And—
A. Oh, I'd like to change—could I—is it okay if I change—tell you one other thing that I found after I went over our deposition? We need to take Celadon out of the—you pointed out—and I found out afterwards—Celadon dropped out right before the best-bid round. Okay. This is for 5/7/2021.
Q. Do you mean 3/1/2019?
A. I'm sorry?
Q. Sorry. You said 5/7/21. That's a different auction.
A. Oh. I'm on a different page. I'm on page 5.
Q. Let me—let me start—so you previously with Mr. Petrocelli corrected the one on 5/7/21; right?
A. Oh, I did? Oh, I'm sorry. I thought I corrected—no, I corrected 5/1/2019.
Q. All right. You'd agree—let's look at the second from the bottom.
A. Yes.
Q. The one at 5/7/21.
A. Yes.
Q. You would agree that Celadon—

A. Dropped out before the—
Q.—dropped out?
A. Yeah, we went through that. And you were right.
Q. All right.
A. Thank you.
Q. And then look at one more. The one on 3/1/2019.
A. Right.
Q. Do you see that one?
A. Yes.
Q. Do you agree Celadon had dropped out of that one?
A. No. I double-checked that after our deposition, and that is—it did not.
Q. You were deposed in this matter; right?
A. Yes.
Q. The last tab of your—
MR. VANCE: Oh, excuse me. Could we hand out our binders? I apologize.
THE WITNESS: Oh, it's not this one?
MR. VANCE: Your Honor, may we approach with binders, please?
THE COURT: Yes.
THE WITNESS: Don't I get a binder?
THE COURT: Yes.
THE WITNESS: Thank you.
BY MR. VANCE:
Q. Let me direct you to the last tab of the binder, which is your deposition transcript—
A. Yes.
Q.—to page 83. And let me know when you're there.
A. Okay.
Q. All right. So I'd like you to read lines [sic] 83, 22 through 25 to yourself. I'm not going to read them out loud because they're marked as confidential, but let me know when you're done.
A. Okay.
Q. Were you asked that question, and did you give that answer?
A. What I said then—what I should have said then—I mean, I don't have the paperwork in front of me. I'll—if this is impeachable, go ahead. But, I mean, this is one thing—
Q. Were you asked that question, and did you give that answer?
A. When Ms. Raab responds that she's bowing out; correct. Yes.
MR. VANCE: Your Honor, I move to admit the testimony at page 83, line 22 through 25, into evidence as impeachment in substance.
THE COURT: I'm really not sure what this is impeaching, Mr. Vance.
MR. PETROCELLI: Your Honor, I'm not sure what the answer was to which this is being—
THE COURT: Exactly.
MR. VANCE: So—sure. So on page 5 of PX 838—
THE COURT: Okay.
MR. VANCE:—there's three final bidders listed in the row with the date 3/1/2019.
THE COURT: Oh, I see.
MR. VANCE: And one is listed as Celadon.
THE COURT: Yes.
MR. VANCE: Which we reviewed at Ms. Ross's deposition. And then this testimony is establishing that Celadon had, in fact, dropped out.
THE COURT: Okay. For what it's worth, I'll admit that. (Ross Deposition Transcript page 83, lines 23 through 25 admitted into evidence.)
THE WITNESS: I'm sorry to say, but I—
THE COURT: It's okay. Ma'am, you're not here as a lawyer. You're a witness. Okay. Go ahead, Mr.

Vance.

BY MR. VANCE:

Q. So I want to move on to our version of this chart. We have a different exhibit in your binder. If I could ask you to turn to PX 837, and let me know when you're there.

A. Okay.

Q. So you'll see what has been marked for identification purposes as PX 837 in your binder. This is also the document that you produced in the—in response to the DOJ subpoena; correct?

A. Yes.

Q. All right. You see at the bottom left it says "All sales"; right?

A. Yes.

Q. So this tab reflects all your deals for the year 2018 through 2021; correct?

A. Well, except for the changes that we—yes.

Q. Okay.

MR. VANCE: Your Honor, I move to admit PX 837 into evidence.

THE COURT: Any objection?

MR. PETROCELLI: No.

THE COURT: 837 is admitted. (PX Exhibit 837 admitted into evidence.)

BY MR. VANCE:

Q. So to make these next questions a little easier, we've prepared a highlighted version behind the green slip sheet, and we've numbered the rows. I'm trying to avoid making you count here. So we're going to use this version for a few questions.

A. This is—this is in the—this—after this green sheet?

Q. Yes.

A. Okay. Go ahead.

Q. All right. So you understand the term Big 5 publisher to include Simon & Schuster, Penguin Random House, Macmillan, Hachette, and HarperCollins; right?

A. Yes.

Q. Can you confirm that in blue are your deals with the Big 5 publishers?

A. Yes.

Q. Can you confirm in white are your deals with the non-Big 5 publishers?

A. Yes.

Q. So let's count the deals with the non-Big 5 publishers. There are two in 2018; right?

A. Correct.

Q. There are two in 2019; correct?

A. Yes.

Q. There are two in 2020; right?

A. Yes.

Q. There are two in 2021; correct?

A. Yes.

Q. Of the 89 deals listed here for the years 2018 through 2021, only eight are with a non-Big 5 publisher; correct?

A. Yes.

Q. Two of those deals are with HMH; right?

A. Correct.

Q. HMH is now owned by HarperCollins; correct?

A. That's correct.

Q. Of the eight deals you had with a non-Big 5 publisher, only two received advances of more than $250,000; correct?

A. In those years, yes.

Q. And one of those two deals was with HMH; right?

A. Correct.

Q. For the years 2018 through 2021, you didn't sell the publishing rights to any books to Disney; right?
A. No.
Q. For the years 2018 through 2021, you didn't sell the publishing rights to any books to Amazon; correct?
A. No.
Q. If eight of your 89 deals for the years 2018 through 2021 are with non-Big 5 publishers, then 81 of your 89 deals for those years are with a Big 5 publisher; correct?
A. Uh-huh.
Q. There's no—
A. Yes.
Q. There's no question that the Big 5 publishers are where most of your clients do business; right?
A. That's correct.
Q. The reasons that most of your clients do business with the Big 5 are because of their editorial, sales, and promotional capabilities, along with the ability to pay higher advances; right?
A. Sure. But I will say there have been other years the—this—the breakdown is different. This is for those four years, but—
Q. I want to talk about your book submission process. You sell a lot of books to Penguin Random House and Simon & Schuster; right?
A. Yeah. I—I used to know the percentage, but I don't right now.
Q. Except for options and exclusive submissions, you've always offered a book that you were selling to Penguin Random House; correct?
A. Not necessarily.
Q. All right. I'd like you to turn to your deposition transcript.
A. No, no, but I thought you said—
THE COURT: Ma'am, you are a witness.
THE WITNESS: I'm sorry.
THE COURT: Please turn to your deposition transcript.
BY MR. VANCE:
Q. Page 196, line 2 through 6. "Question: Have you sold proposed books without offering them to Penguin Random House? "Answer: There are a lot of imprints of Penguin Random House. I have, yes, but those were exclusive submissions or option." Did I read that correctly?
A. Uh-huh.
Q. That was the question. You gave that answer?
A. (Nods head.)
MR. VANCE: Your Honor, I'd move to admit the lines as impeachment in substance.
THE COURT: Any objection? Those are admitted. (Ross Deposition Transcript page 196, lines 2 through 6 admitted into evidence.)
BY MR. VANCE:
Q. Except for options and exclusive submissions, you've always offered a book that you were selling to Simon & Schuster; correct?
A. During this period? I—I'd have to study that.
Q. All right. Let's look back at 196, lines 2 through 9. "Have you sold . . . books without offering them to Penguin Random House? "There are a lot of imprints of Penguin Random House. I have, yes, but those were exclusive submissions or option. "Have you sold proposed books without offering them to Simon & Schuster? "Well, the same answer." Did I read those questions and answers correctly?
A. Yes. I'm just trying to figure out whether you're talking about in general or—
THE COURT: Ma'am, could you just answer the question that the attorney asked you.
THE WITNESS: Yes.
MR. VANCE: Your Honor, I move to admit the testimony into evidence.
THE COURT: Any objection?
MR. PETROCELLI: No.

THE COURT: It's admitted. (Ross Deposition Transcript page 196, lines 2 through 9 admitted into evidence.)

BY MR. VANCE:

Q. I want to talk to you about your earlier testimony now about the effect of the Penguin and Random House merger on author competition. That opinion was based on your anecdotal experience; correct?

A. Yes.

Q. You haven't conducted an industrywide study of how the Penguin and Random House merger impacted author compensation; right?

A. No.

MR. VANCE: I reserve time for recross.

THE COURT: All right. Thank you.

MR. PETROCELLI: Nothing.

THE COURT: All right. Thank you. Let's see. I have a couple questions for you. Mr. Petrocelli asked you some questions about anticipating sales.

THE WITNESS: I'm sorry?

THE COURT: Mr. Petrocelli asked you some questions about anticipating what the sales level of a book would be.

THE WITNESS: Yes.

THE COURT: And you said that that's very hard to do. But isn't it true that all of the advances that are being offered are based on estimates of expected sales? Can you explain your answer in that context.

THE WITNESS: Sure. We—just like publishers have profit and loss statements, we all make estimates of what they think they can sell, what the other books like that have sold, what kind of track record my client has with other books or—you look at things like the—as—as the—the platform of the author, what they have the ability—you know, we talk about concentric circles of audiences and the—you know, besides your—the smaller group that you work in, a lot of my authors have, you know, an ability to get to other audiences. And that, you know, out here is a huge seller.

But in here you want to make sure you get to the other—if it's a psychologist, you want to get to the other psychologists, you want to get to psychiatrists, you want to get to the social workers; you want to make sure you get to those audiences. And some clients bring a really good apparatus, if you will, or some sort of platform where they can help get to audiences. So that's weighed in by the authors as well—by the imprints and editors as well.

THE COURT: And so some of those clients are expected to have strong sales based on those audiences?

THE WITNESS: There's a—we have expectations of strong sales. Unfortunately, the market doesn't often always get us to those expectations.

THE COURT: Okay. And when you're negotiating for a book, it seems that sometimes you have more leverage and sometimes you have less. Can you talk about what factors go into whether you have more leverage?

THE WITNESS: Sure. You have to look at—well, one thing is how the author has done in the past. If the author has written books in the past that have not sold—you know, there's an old saw, that you're only as good as your last track—right?—sales track.

Then—then there's a burden on the—that the next book idea has to be that much better, and the publisher has to—the imprints have to fall in love with that idea and see it as—as making up for the last track. So, you know—and part of it depends on externals, like what's going on in the world.

My client just—client of mine a couple weeks ago won the Pulitzer Prize. So that—that's—it's all—what's going on—you know, I had—I made four book deals right after Donald Trump was elected President that weren't even in the ideas—in the heads of my clients. But the externals happened. And thank goodness I didn't have a Hillary Clinton book at that time. So there's so many factors that go into that.

THE COURT: And in terms of the factors that go into it, do you sometimes see there's a consensus among editors that—about these factors that this is going to be a good book?

THE WITNESS: Yes.

THE COURT: Okay. Any questioning based on my questioning?
MR. PETROCELLI: Not from me, Your Honor.
MR. VANCE: No, Your Honor.
THE COURT: All right. Thank you for your testimony.
THE WITNESS: I'm sorry about that.
THE COURT: That's okay.
THE WITNESS: I sometimes can't keep my mouth shut.
THE COURT: Not at all.

ALEXANDER BERKETT, EXECUTIVE VP, CHIEF CORPORATE DEVELOPMENT AND STRATEGY OFFICER, VIACOMCBS

Most of ViacomCBS executive Alex Berkett's testimony was in closed session. But he confirmed for the record that the final three bidders for Simon & Schuster were PRH, Vivendi and HarperCollins. The other invited bidders in the first round were "another strategic buyer" (e.g. a company in publishing), and a financial buyer, identified as based on "relationships that we had with certain human beings at one of the private equity firms and their background in the publishing business." (This means, presumably, Richard Sarnoff at KKR). And "there was a very small strategic buyer that had a financial backer"; the backer was a "sovereign wealth fund."

TESTIMONY OF ALEXANDER BERKETT, EXECUTIVE VP, CHIEF CORPORATE DEVELOPMENT AND STRATEGY OFFICER, VIACOMCBS

DIRECT EXAMINATION

BY MR. FISHBEIN:

Q. Good morning.

A. Good morning.

Q. Can you state your full name and spell it for the record, please.

A. My full name is Alexander Julian Berkett. It's spelled A-1 -e-x-a-n-d-e-r J-u-1 -i-a-n B-e-r-k-e-t-t.

Q. Mr. Berkett, how are you currently employed?

A. I'm employed by Paramount Global.

Q. What kind of company is Paramount Global?

A. It's a media and entertainment company.

Q. And has Paramount Global been known by any other name in recent years?

A. It was known as ViacomCBS from the period December 2019 until February of this year.

Q. And just so that we get a little corporate history, what happened in 2019 with respect to that company?

A. Viacom, which was its own company, and CBS, which was its own company, merged in December of 2019.

Q. Did Simon & Schuster, the publishing company, have a relationship with either Viacom or CBS prior to 2019?

A. Simon & Schuster was owned by CBS for many years prior to the merger with Viacom.

Q. And what was the name of the new company once Viacom and CBS merged in 2019?

A. ViacomCBS, one word.

Q. So am I correct that ViacomCBS became the owner of Simon & Schuster by virtue of that merger in 2019?

A. That is correct.

Q. And you said ViacomCBS changed its name to Paramount Global in February of 2022; is that right?

A. That's correct.

Q. I'm going to refer to your current employer as ViacomCBS or Viacom, if it's before 2019, because that's the way we've been referring to it in this case. Okay?

A. Okay.

Q. Mr. Berkett, when did you first start working for ViacomCBS or its predecessors?

A. I began to work for Viacom, predecessor ViacomCBS, in the summer of 2015.

Q. And if you could just briefly describe what kinds of positions you've held within Viacom since 2015.

A. I joined as the SVP of corporate development, which, essentially, means overseeing the merger and acquisition or M&A activity of the company. Shortly after, later in 2015, I also added a strategy role. And I've held similar roles with different titles since then at Viacom and subsequently at ViacomCBS.

Q. What is your current title at ViacomCBS?

A. Executive vice president, chief corporate development and strategy officer.

Q. And so, broadly speaking, what have you been responsible for over your—about seven years with ViacomCBS?

A. The strategy of the company and various strategic initiatives, as well as all of its M&A or merger and acquisition activity.

Q. Again, just briefly, can you tell the Court what your career history or background was before you joined Viacom in 2015.

A. After graduating from undergraduate, I worked as an investment banker for 12 years; a little shy of 12 years. After that, I partnered with some folks and we started a company called Townsquare Media, which we grew. And then I was recruited from that company, Townsquare Media, to go to Viacom in 2015.

Q. Which firms did you work for when you worked in investment banking?

A. Bear Stearns and J.P. Morgan.

Q. Mr. Berkett, did you have a role in ViacomCBS's sale of Simon & Schuster to Bertelsmann?

A. Yes, I did.

Q. What was your role in the process?

A. I was one of the people leading or coordinating the effort.

Q. And when you said "coordinating," with whom were you coordinating? Who was on the team?

A. People from my corporate development or M&A team; people in our legal department; people in our HR department; people in our tax department; people in our accounting department; or a variety of people at the corporate portion of our company; as well as many executives at Simon & Schuster: our executive team, our board of directors, and our financial advisors and, to a lesser extent, our legal counsel.

Q. If you could, just maybe move the microphone a little bit closer, just to make sure everybody can hear you. You mentioned that there were financial advisors. Who did ViacomCBS use as its financial advisors?

A. LionTree.

Q. And what is your position with respect to, I think you said, the corporate—was it corporate development team at ViacomCBS?

A. I was the leader of that team and still am.

Q. Okay. And did you report to anybody with respect to your activities with respect to the sale of Simon & Schuster?

A. When the merger of Viacom and CBS closed, I reported to Bob Bakish, the CEO of ViacomCBS.

Q. Okay. And then did that change at all?

A. When Naveen Chopra joined us as chief financial officer in the summer of 2020, I began reporting to Naveen.

Q. Okay. Now, you said that you were one of the leaders of ViacomCBS's effort to sell Simon & Schuster; is that correct?

A. That is correct.

Q. Why does ViacomCBS want to sell Simon & Schuster?

A. As we approached the completion of the merger in 2019—

Q. And which merger are you talking about?

A. I'm talking about the merger of Viacom and CBS.

Q. Okay.

A.—we, the continuing management team, together with the board of directors, undertook a review of the assets of the company to make determinations about what of those assets were core to what our strategic priorities were going to be. And our strategic priorities then and now center on building a streaming video business and producing the world's best video content.

And in that review, we determined a number of our assets were not core to that mission, not supportive to that mission, not additive to that mission. And some of those assets, in addition to not being supportive to that mission, didn't have a lot of connectivity to other parts of our business. Simon & Schuster was determined to be one of those assets, ultimately, and we took a recommendation to the board of directors saying that and suggesting that we should divest ourselves of the business and reallocate the capital to our strategic priorities.

Q. And what is it about Simon & Schuster that renders it not core to ViacomCBS's business?

A. As a trade book publisher, it's a fantastic business, but it does not provide us content, video content, for our streaming activities or our television and film activities.

Q. But don't books have some content that, I guess, could be used for streaming or otherwise?

A. There's a tremendous wealth of intellectual property in books, and, in fact, many books are made into movies. But it's important to note that the rights for books are bought by book publishers, but they do not come with, generally, the rights to make derivative video work, whether that's film, television, or episodic content, out of that intellectual property.

In fact, the authors or owners of the underlying intellectual property of books, in their representation, sell those rights separately. And so there is no inherent advantage to us owning Simon & Schuster to access the intellectual property of the books in respect to film or television or streaming projects.

Q. Now, has Viacom made any public statements to investors, shareholders, whatever, regarding the strategy as it relates to Simon & Schuster?

A. Yes.

Q. And when was that first done?

A. In March of 2020.

Q. What happened in March of 2020?

A. Bob Bakish, the company CEO, was speaking at a Morgan Stanley investor conference, and he announced that the company had made the determination that Simon & Schuster was not core to our mission. It's a great asset, but not additive to our strategic priorities in video specifically, and that we had made that determination and that when market conditions improved, we would proceed with a sale of the asset.

Q. And after Mr. Bakish's public comments in March of 2020, did the company make any additional comments publicly about its intentions with respect to Simon & Schuster?

A. Yes.

Q. And what were those?

A. I would say, generally, at each quarterly earnings presentation and conference call, at a number of investor events interceding the period of time, the companies consistently reiterated the conclusion we determined about the strategic value of Simon & Schuster to us and the fact that it was noncore and that we intended to divest it, consistently and on multiple occasions from many members of the management team.

Q. Mr. Berkett, if ViacomCBS is not permitted to sell Simon & Schuster to Bertelsmann, what will ViacomCBS do with Simon & Schuster?

A. ViacomCBS will sell Simon & Schuster to another buyer.

Q. And why is that?

A. Because the determination that was made in 2020 remains fully true for all the same reasons it was then today, and we foresee that being the state of affairs going forward. And we've told the market that we intend to sell it for those reasons. We would like to reallocate capital out of that business towards our strategic priorities and balance sheet management, and we intend to do that as soon as possible.

Q. You mentioned that you've already told the market of your plans. What significance does that have in terms of what you do in the future?

A. It would be very difficult for us to turn around and tell the market something different. In fact, I think it would challenge the credibility of the management team, particularly because I think it's self-evident to the marketplace that nothing about the conclusions that led us to determine that we needed to divest the asset have changed.

Q. Mr. Berkett, you said that it was first announced in March 2020 by the CEO that Simon & Schuster would be sold. Did something happen after that that affected the timing of the sale?

A. Yes. Sort of just beginning to germinate at that moment in time, the global pandemic was certainly a timing consideration, and it was calibrated into Bob's initial messaging, which was to say when market conditions improve—and I don't remember the exact language, but something along those lines—we would undertake a sale process.

Q. Did there come a time when—when you did undertake a formal sale process?

A. Yes.

Q. And when was that?

A. In the fall of 2020.

Q. And, again, just high level, what kind of process was it?

A. Some people might describe it as an auction, but it was a process where we solicited interest from buyers, a group of buyers, proceeded with management presentations to help to explain the business to those buyers, solicited bids, and went from there.

Q. And how many rounds of bids did you accept from potential purchasers?

A. Ultimately, we did two rounds of bidding.

Q. Which companies participated in this process through the end, meaning that they submitted bids in both rounds?

A. Bertelsmann and its subsidiary Penguin Random House; News Corporation and its subsidiary HarperCollins; and a company called Vivendi.

Q. And did Vivendi have any interest in book publishers at the time, to your knowledge?

A. I believe it owned a book publisher called Editis.

Q. Okay. And was there a relationship—we've heard testimony about a company called Hachette. Is there any relationship between Vivendi and Hachette?

A. Yes. There's a relationship between Vivendi and Hachette's parent company Lagardère where Vivendi is today a significant shareholder of that business.

Q. Now, you mentioned the three companies, Bertelsmann, Vivendi, and News Corp. Were there other potential buyers who looked at Simon & Schuster but did not make it all the way to the end of the process?

A. Yes.

Q. And without naming specific entities, what type of companies were those?

A. There was another strategic buyer, there was a financial buyer, and there was a very small strategic buyer that had a financial backer; so a little bit of a hybrid.

Q. And I'm going to ask you about some of those terms in a second, but is—were there only three others, or are you just giving examples?

A. Those are the three that I remember today.

Q. Okay. And you used the terms financial and strategic buyer. Can you just explain what that means in the context of this deal.

A. I can. In the context of this deal and, frankly, most M&A deals, a strategic buyer is a buyer who owns similar assets to the assets that are being sold. A financial buyer is a, generally, private equity fund, hedge fund, growth equity fund, a venture capital fund, someone that's an investor that doesn't necessarily own assets similar to the assets being sold.

Q. And why do you distinguish between strategics and financial in an M&A transaction like this?

A. Because their motivations and their ability to pay may be different and generally are different.

Q. Okay. And maybe you could just explain that. What's the difference and why in a transaction like this?

A. A strategic buyer, which has assets similar to the assets that are being sold, very often, if not always, has an opportunity to realize synergies or cost-savings efficiencies, sometimes revenue, uplift, that a financial buyer does not have access to by virtue of the fact that they don't own similar assets to harvest those synergies together with.

Q. And does that affect the value that the various types of buyers can pay?

A. Yes.

Q. How so?

A. Synergies and synergy opportunities oftentimes increase quite—sometimes quite substantially the value of a set of assets to a buyer.

Q. And, Mr. Berkett, when—when was this process, the sale process that you mentioned, completed? In other words, when was it announced that Viacom and CBS and Bertelsmann had signed a deal?

A. In late November of 2020.

Q. What—what criteria did ViacomCBS use in evaluating the three final bids for Simon & Schuster?

A. We had four goals in our evaluation of the bids and, frankly, before that going into the process. The first was to maximize the value that we would receive and the consideration and cash that we would receive as a result. The second was deal certainty. Making sure that the counterparty would have the ability and the capability to pay and the ability to live up to its obligations and fulfill its obligations under the contract. We wanted the asset to find a good home with an owner that would invest and continue the legacy of the business that was almost a hundred years old at the time. And we wanted the buyer to be a good home for the employees and executives at Simon & Schuster.

Q. Now, if you're selling Simon & Schuster, if I may ask, why do you care whether it finds a good home as long as you get the value that you want?

A. Well, I think most businesses do care about the home for the asset and their employees. I would admit that perhaps price and deal certainty are more important considerations, but they certainly are considerations for a number of reasons, but not least of which is reputational and to the extent that you're discarding businesses in a careless way to buyers who might not be the right home for the business that will have reputational impacts across a number of different constituencies, including employees and potential employees.

Q. Mr. Berkett, who—which of the three offers offered the highest price for Simon & Schuster?

A. The Bertelsmann/Penguin Random House bid was the highest price.

Q. And what was your assessment of Bertelsmann in terms of financing and willingness to close?

A. I was certain that they could finance the business and would live up to their obligations.

Q. And then what about—what was your assessment of Bertelsmann on the third and fourth criteria, about good home for the business and employees?

A. I thought they'd be an excellent home for the business, for the legacy of the business, and for the employees and executives.

Q. And what is that based on? How did you come to that conclusion?

A. Based on conversations we had with the company, based on Bertelsmann/Penguin Random House's reputation in the marketplace.

Q. And had you had similar conversations with other bidders? In other words, as part of the management presentations, did you meet with representatives of the other bidders?

A. Yes.

MR. FISHBEIN: Your Honor, that's all I have for the open portion.

THE COURT: Okay. Thank you. Any cross?

MR. MATELSON: Good morning, Your Honor. Ben Matelson for the United States.

THE COURT: Good morning.

MR. MATELSON: I just have very, very few questions in open session, and then the bulk of what I need to cover will be confidential.

THE COURT: Okay.

CROSS-EXAMINATION

BY MR. MATELSON:

Q. Good morning, Mr. Berkett.

A. Good morning. Good to see you again.

Q. You too. You mentioned the four goals you had for the transaction, and I just wanted to elaborate a little on the second one, deal certainty. And one of the things that you considered to be under the heading of deal certainty was the ability to achieve regulatory approvals for the deal; correct?

A. Correct.

Q. All right. And just to be clear, we're talking about regulatory approval includes approval by the U.S. antitrust agencies; correct?

A. Correct.

Q. Now, you talked about the sales process. You mentioned the firm called LionTree. Could you just explain what tasks you assigned LionTree to do in connection with the sale.

A. LionTree were our financial advisor. They're a well-known investment bank in the media entertainment space. They helped us prepare the materials to present to potential buyers, explain the Simon & Schuster business. They helped us populate a data room with information to satisfy the due diligence process. They helped us think about who the potential buyers were and which potential buyers might be the ones who could fulfill our objectives to the highest degree.

They helped us organize the actual sale process in the fall of 2020 and helped advise us with the considerations related to that and the negotiations related to that.

Q. All right. And then when it came time to solicit offers, am I correct that you decided to invite a select group of companies to submit expressions of interest?

A. I believe that we invited a select group of people to participate in management presentations and thereafter invited that group of people to solicit—or, rather, to proffer offers in the first round.

Q. Okay. So even to get the meeting for the management presentation, I believe you—at that stage, you—you invited just a select—a small select group of interested bidders; correct?

A. Correct.

Q. And I think you mentioned that financial buyers were part of that group?

A. There was one financial buyer and one small strategic that had a reasonably large financial backer.

Q. All right. So it's fair to say that you believe that a financial buyer was potentially a good home for Simon & Schuster; right?

A. I think amongst the group of people we invited to the first round, we had much more skepticism that a financial buyer would ultimately prove to be the winning bidder, really even a finalist. There were discrete reasons for the two invitations that involved financial buyers that related to—on the one hand, relationships that we had with certain human beings at one of the private equity firms and their background in the publishing business. And on the second hand, there was a sovereign wealth fund backing a smaller strategic that we thought might be someone who might do something attractive economically to us. There was a small chance.

Q. All right. But just in terms of the third and fourth criteria you mentioned, about a good home—

A. Uh-huh.

Q.—you believe that a financial buyer could potentially be a good home for Simon & Schuster at the outset of the process; right?

A. Could potentially. I think there's a little bit more skepticism on private equity firms, particularly on the fourth of those scores, related to head count reduction and whether that means they're a great home for the asset, but I do agree with your assertion, potentially.

Q. All right. And you also mentioned Vivendi and their current relationship with Hachette. I just wanted to clarify, back in November 2020, Vivendi did not have an ownership interest in Hachette or its parent company; correct?

A. That—that may be correct. I don't remember. It's been a bit of a long and back-and-forth history between the companies, and there was a period of time where Lagardère was facing a sort of a hostile approach by a hedge fund based in the United Kingdom. And if recollection serves, Vivendi was playing the role of a white knight and took a stake in Lagardère. But I can't, Ben, tell you whether it was before November or after November from my memory today.

Q. All right. And at the time you were accepting offers from Vivendi, they did not have a publishing business in the United States; correct?

A. I know that their publishing business, Editis, is headquartered in France. I don't—I can't say I know what percentage of their business was in the United States, if any.

Q. Thank you. I will pause my questions there and resume in closed session. Thank you.

A. Thank you.

MR. FISHBEIN: So I guess now we'll need to close the courtroom.

THE COURT: Okay. We can do that. How long do you expect the closed session to last?

MR. FISHBEIN: I think mine will be about 20 minutes.

THE COURT: And Mr. Matelson?

MR. MATELSON: Probably about the same. Hopefully, less.

THE COURT: Okay. So, we're going to close the courtroom at this time for approximately 40 minutes, and so—until about 10:40. And so I am going to ask the members of the public to please exit the courtroom at this time.

(Proceedings held in closed court.)

MADELINE MCINTOSH, CEO, PENGUIN RANDOM HOUSE U.S.

PRH US CEO Madeline McIntosh spent much of her testimony on a level-headed explanation of many of the financial, strategic and procedural nuts and bolts of publishing.

There were a lot of numbers, but one number stood as representing just how big PRH already is as a company. McIntosh approves all advances at the company of $1 million or more, and annually, "on average, I directly approve about 200" such deals. So of the approximately $1 billion market the government says ATSB represent—and the roughly $370 million they say PRH accounts for—a substantial portion of those are books for $1 million or more. (It was not declared in court how many of those approved offers for over $1 million PRH actually won.) That group includes many multi-million-dollar deals, as a document we could only see partially was provided, showing the biggest deals year by year: In 2010, one for $40.3 million; another for $27 million; in 2011, one for $8.5 million, another for $18.8 million; in 2021, one for $35.5 million; one for $14.5 million; one for $17.3 million; and one for $12.5 million.

Confusingly, however, when Judge Pan asked McIntosh later in the day how much "you pay in total for author advances generally each year," McIntosh was not sure. "I want to say it's a $100 million, but I could also have that number wrong. . . . It might be $200 million." They will "get back to [her] with the accurate number." Maybe the confusion is over pay versus approve?

Markus Dohle already provided the court much larger numbers in the trial, with confidence: PRH paid out "a little more than $1 billion globally" in advances and royalties in 2021, he testified, roughly two-thirds of that paid by PRH US. Dohle also said that in 2021, PRH US committed an "all-time high" of around $650 million in author advances.

Another sign of where Judge Pan is in interpreting the information that had been presented, and how McIntosh's clear testimony help her cut through some of the prior equivocations: "From your testimony, it seems to me that your industry is very much driven by expected sales of books. Do you think that's correct?"

McIntosh answered, "I would say we spend a lot of time trying to guess the expected sales of books. And if you are asking about—is that something we can focus on, absolutely we focus on it, and we try to drive towards maximizing that number."

Earnings and Earn Out

Though you had to be listening carefully since the discussions were spread throughout the session, McIntosh did get close to explaining to the court that big books do not have to earn out to make money for the company—and that when paying big advances, it is not even her expectation that they will earn out.

Asked "the advance level that you would typically expect" for a book projected to sell 300,000 units in the first year, she said: "So I would actually expect a book that is selling 300,000 units in a year is probably going to sell at least 400 or 500 thousand over its life, once you [add] backlist in there too. So—I don't know—4 million, 5 million dollars advance." (That's an advance allocating roughly $10 a unit, across all units.)

Generally, McIntosh said at another point, "We can feel that we're in comfortable, profitable territory at around 70 percent of earnout for most books." (But the estimate above would not seem to yield that earnout—even if all the units were $30 hardcovers, and of course the units will be spread across lower-priced formats, that would drive only $1.8 million of earned royalties on a 400,000-unit sale).

Also, as she noted, there are "authors who absolutely can deliver hundreds of thousands of readers over—over one book after another after another. Their agents, understandably, are going to use that track record to ensure that we are paying a high advance. And I've certainly heard agents say to me that they hope in those cases that . . . those authors don't earn out because they will know that they've done the right job in terms of negotiating the advance."

When reviewing P&Ls McIntosh is, "looking at the contribution number and the EBITDA number; those are two different financial thresholds. And then I'm looking at the total advance number and the sales expectations." And in reviewing deals with editors, "I often find myself directing their attention to the contribution number because I want them to think about what is the incremental impact of making this bet on our company. . . . So the contribution lets you look to see what is the incremental, and as long as that's in solidly positive territory, then I would encourage them to feel good about that path."

All that math helps you understand what was one of the best turns of phrase so far in the trial, when she suggested to the court that the books that drive much of their profit are "the unanticipated best sellers." They drive "the lion's share of our profit because they had advances that were relatively low compared to the very high sales achievement."

But as Judge Pan elicited, these are not necessarily books that were bought for little or no money or for which there were not some expectations and enthusiasm, but rather titles like Where The Crawdads Sing or Girl On the Train (or even Charles Duhigg's books, since he doesn't want oversized advances)—bought for well into ATSB territory—that become gigantic hits.

Crown and Penguin Reorganizations

On her decision to merge the Crown Publishing Group in the Random House group in 2018, McIntosh said: "It was my evaluation that Crown was really struggling to succeed. They had a very dispersed set of categories in which they were publishing, and they were really struggling to make the kind of marketing investments that were needed to support those very diverse books and imprints. And I felt that Random House had the strongest marketing team, really, in the—certainly I feel in the—in the company, but also in the industry, and that by pairing them, that the Crown editors and books would benefit from the stronger marketing support that Random House could provide."

As a result, "Crown books have—I think have been published better, sold better. Agents have been more—felt more supported for their clients. The feedback that I receive from agents has been quite positive."

On the separate reorganization she enacted at Penguin—particularly in mass market—McIntosh explained: "Based on my measurement, I found that we were acquiring hundreds of books for very little advance. We were investing no marketing money to support them. We were putting covers on them that were very, very old-fashioned . . . and that while we were printing these and in some cases shipping a couple of hundred, we were getting most of them back.

"So I made the decision with the team to significantly curtail that approach to publishing, and we regrouped. We reassessed how we could publish particularly in the romance category. And over a couple of years . . . we repositioned in particular Berkeley as being a home to much more contemporary-feeling romance stories . . . with much more fashion-forward covers often in the trade paperback format. And we have been steadily increasing the title counts since then." At Berkley, she said, "the sales and profit results have been fantastic." (No one connected the dots that one of the big authors PRH lost to another house—Nora Roberts—was directly related to the 2016 "realignment" as Roberts' longtime editor, president of the Berkley Publishing Group Leslie Gelbman left as a result.)

Lead Titles, Priority Books and Opportunity Books

McIntosh explained two types of books that get a lot of attention as they move their way to launch: There is "the priority book—meaning that this is one where we have very aggressive sales goals, and so we—we really—it is a priority for us to meet those goals." And then there's "an opportunity book . . . where at first glance, it might not seem as obvious as sales success, but where the—again, the people who've read it are starting to develop some excitement for it, and we think if we rally around it, we might be able to make something good happen."

Under cross later, the government showed a 2020 document from Maya Mavjee—referencing an admittedly "out of date" Crown policy from 2012—that defined four categories of titles. Category one "lead titles" had a sales goal of 75,000 units or higher and/or advance over $500,000. Category two "opportunity titles" are defined as having a sales goal of 25,000 to 75,000 units and/or advance of $150,000 to $500,000. The document shows at the time how lead titles got the most marketing—multi-city author tour where appropriate up to 15 markets, social network and target search advertising, etc.—

and category three and four titles did not.

Earlier in her direct testimony, though, McIntosh explained their current marketing plans and expenditures are based on "an agile mindset. So we measure the performance of the activities that we're conducting. And if—say we've done an online ad campaign and it's successfully translating to sales, then we're going to expand that campaign. If we're doing something and it is seemingly having no results, then we're going to stop throwing good money after bad. So we're adapting in real time based on the results."

Fiction Shares; Avoid Upbidding

As with their interview of Markus Dohle, much of the government's questioning of McIntosh was really focused on entering documents into the record and having her confirm them.

A multi-year evaluation from 2015 through 2019 of the US physical marketplace for fiction prepared by sales analyst Reid Welsh, who reports to Jackie Updike, identified "top authors" as those who sell more than 500,000 units in a year. For retail dollar market share, PRH had at 42 percent to 44 percent share of the top end of the fiction market those five years, while non-Big 5 publishers had only 5 to 6 percent.

For "non-top authors," PRH had a share of about 31 percent, and here the non-Big 5 had a share of about 27 percent.

Another series of documents explored the extent to which PRH might or might not coordinate in-house bids from across divisions. In a late 2018 document McIntosh had written about "increased background coordination in auctions to leverage internal demand information better and avoid internal upbidding." But she had said pre-emptively, since the defense knew this was coming, "This is again at the beginning of my time as CEO where . . . we were all feeling a little bruised from some acquisition experiences in what was then the more recent past where we felt a little overly manipulated by an agent in an acquisition or two and that it turned out all of the demand that the agent had was within Penguin Random House and that we had significantly paid more than we really should have paid for a couple of acquisitions."

Still, later, in one 2020 deal for an author wanting to move within the company, there was interest from multiple imprints, and McIntosh wrote, "I feel we should coordinate. Shouldn't be forced into bidding against each other for existing authors." Here, she said, PRH still paid the author more than they had received previously. These two documents would figure heavily into the government's arguments about PRH's true behavior and policies regarding internal bidding.

During her direct testimony, McIntosh explained: "My general belief and what I tried to instill when I came in as the CEO is that the publishing divisions had a long history in some cases of really using quite sharp elbows against each other and that I thought it was important for our company culture going forward that my board, the publishers who report to me, the publishing division heads, that they compete to achieve the best results for their division but also to acknowledge that we are one company and that we are all working together to achieve the best results for the company." Now, she believes, her top reports "have developed much more of a habit of helping each other on any number of strategic issues. And this does relate to consultations from time to time on acquisitions."

She underscored, "Even with the top level of the company working more collaboratively and even with those occasional consultations, I think it has not translated to any lowering impact on the advances that we have paid. In fact, the opposite."

Approvals

Among more numbers, the approval levels across PRH are similar to the rest of the Big 5: At Random House, all acquisitions are approved by president and publisher Gina Centrello, apparently regardless of advance level. As we had learned previously, all Penguin Publishing Group publishers can approve advances up to $250,000, after which they need sign-off from president Allison Dobson.

At Knopf Doubleday, Maya Mavjee recently "decided to adopt the Penguin level" of $250,000 for her publishers. (Previously, we understand, Mavjee approved all deals herself, as Centrello does. The change was to give her publishers some independent authority.)

At Random House Children's, the threshold is $150,000, after which it goes to a management meeting.

And at Penguin Children's, the approval level for imprint publishers is $100,000.

Also as previously disclosed, group heads can approve advances up to $1 million, above which they go to McIntosh for approval.

More Stats

Children's books comprised 27 percent of PRH's sales in 2021. That's about $725 million—so roughly double the size of Scholastic's trade division, and more or less equal on its own to all of Macmillan or HBG (pre-Workman).

Christian books accounted for 2 percent.

TESTIMONY OF MADELINE MCINTOSH, CEO, PENGUIN RANDOM HOUSE U.S.

DIRECT EXAMINATION

BY MR. PETROCELLI:

Q. Good morning, Ms. McIntosh.

A. Good morning.

Q. Can you please state your full name for the record.

A. Madeline McIntosh.

Q. Can you please tell the Court a bit about your background.

A. I've worked in book publishing my whole adult life. I got into it after graduating from college as an art history major. As soon as I found out that you could actually work in books, I was hooked, and I've done that pretty much ever since.

Q. You need to get the microphone a little closer to you.

A. Sorry.

Q. Thank you. And do I understand your husband is also an author?

A. My husband is an author, yes. We met at work, when he worked in publishing. Now he's a writer.

Q. And who publishes—what's his name?

A. Chris Pavone.

Q. And who publishes your husband?

A. Macmillan.

Q. What is your current role at Penguin Random House?

A. I'm the CEO of Penguin Random House U.S.

Q. How long have you worked for the company?

A. I started at the predecessor company, which was called Bantam Doubleday Dell in 1994. And except for 18 months when I worked at Amazon, I've been there ever since.

Q. Can you slow down just a little bit and give us your complete history in the publishing business, starting with your first job.

A. Sure. I started as a temp at HarperCollins, and then my first permanent job was at Norton as an editorial assistant. From there I got interested, in the early '90s, in the meeting point of old media and new media. So I moved to Bantam Doubleday Dell to the new media department. I, from there, got into what became online sales and eventually moved to the sales department to lead up online sales.

Q. Did you—what did you do after that?

A. Excuse me. After I led online sales, I got promoted to be the head of the adult sales group for Random House, which we were called at that point, and eventually I moved to be the Random House audio publisher.

Q. And then what happened?

A. I left the company in 2008 to move to Luxembourg to work for Amazon to lead the—I was the director of content acquisition for the international launch of the Kindle.

Q. How long were you at Amazon?

A. For 18 months.

Q. Then what did you do?

A. After that Markus Dohle recruited me back to Random House to a newly created position as president of sales, operations, and digital.

Q. And then after that job, what happened?

A. That job, the content of the job stayed the same, but I was promoted and titled to COO. So I was COO at the time that we merged with Penguin in 2013.

Q. And then after the 2013 merger, what was your next position?

A. I was the COO of the new Penguin Random House for about a year, and then in 2014, I moved to be the president of Penguin Publishing.

Q. And that's one of the adult divisions?

A. Yes.

Q. And how long did you have that position?

A. I was there from the fall of 2014 until the spring of 2018 when I moved into my current job.

Q. And you've been CEO of Penguin Random House U.S. since 2018?

A. Yes.

Q. What are your responsibilities as CEO?

A. I'm responsible for all aspects of our business in the United States. So, of course, that includes a primary focus on all aspects of publishing, from acquisition through editorial development, marketing, sales, operations, fulfillment, third-party distribution; everything that relates to our author and employee experience in the United States.

Q. To whom do you report?

A. To Markus Dohle.

Q. What are your responsibilities regarding the company's acquisition of books?

A. I oversee the teams who are responsible for publishing them. And so that means I could be involved in an ad hoc basis on any number of different topics, but I directly approve acquisitions at the million-dollar threshold and above.

Q. Do you ever get involved from time to time in acquisitions below $1 million?

A. Yes, certainly. On an informal basis, not a routine basis, publishers consult with me regularly.

Q. As the CEO, about how many title acquisitions are you involved in on an annual basis?

A. I directly approve—obviously, the number varies over time, but on average, I directly approve about 200.

Q. When you were president of the Penguin Publishing Group from 2014 to 2018, what was your participation then in the company's acquisition of books from authors?

A. I probably approved several hundred, if not a few thousand acquisitions.

Q. Okay.

MR. PETROCELLI: Your Honor, may I hand up a small binder?

THE COURT: Yes.

MR. PETROCELLI: Thank you. May I approach the witness?

THE COURT: Yes.

MR. PETROCELLI: Thank you.

THE COURT: Thank you.

MR. PETROCELLI: Pam, can you put up the first demonstrative, which is Defendants' Demonstrative 10.

BY MR. PETROCELLI:

Q. So I'd like to talk a bit about the lifespan of a book, starting from acquisition. And what are these four icons that we put on this demonstrative?

A. These are just—this is a generalized way to show the different phases of a book moving from acquisition to publication.

Q. Okay. Now, we've spent a lot of time on acquisition. So let me zero in on something more specific. Let's assume we're at the point where the editor wants to acquire the book. How does—how do your editors determine how much to offer for the advance?

A. They build a P&L.

Q. Okay. And how do they determine the amount of the advance based on the P&L?
A. They would make an estimate of how many copies they believe they can sell. And so the combination of the copies that they can sell by format and the price would translate to an output that would let them know the level of advance they can pay.
Q. So from time to time, do you receive P&Ls from multiple editors at multiple imprints for the same title?
A. Yes.
Q. And when you receive multiple P&Ls for the same title, do the numbers vary, or are they the same?
A. They vary.
Q. And why do they vary?
A. Because these are not—these aren't widgets that we're producing. The valuation is a highly subjective process, and so it's a reflection of that particular editor's vision and belief in the book project.
Q. So if you get a P&L for a title for $1,100,000 and another one for 1.2 and another one for 1.3, just by way of a hypothetical, all for the same book, how do you handle that?
A. I approve all three.
Q. So you're approving a title at 1.1 even though you are authorizing your company to pay 1.3 for the same title?
A. Yes.
Q. Do you tell the 1.1 person that you've approved the 1.3?
A. No.
Q. And so why do you do it that way?
A. Because I want them to—for the most part, to remain true to their vision. So if one of them is seeing it much more aggressively, I—for one thing, I think that—that vision, that more aggressive number is likely to be reflected onto the market too. So, I'm not going to do anything to pull that number down because I want us to win the book.
Q. Okay. Well, let's turn to a P&L.
MR. PETROCELLI: And this is going to be displayed not public facing, Pam. This is a confidential document. It's Defendants' Exhibit 414.
BY MR. PETROCELLI:
Q. Do you recognize this?
A. I do.
Q. And what is it?
A. This is a P&L that was created for an acquisition that I believe we completed in 2018, but this is the standard P&L template.
Q. Has this book been published yet?
A. No.
Q. Okay.
MR. PETROCELLI: Your Honor, I think you should have the decoder, which is marked at Defendants' 433.
THE COURT: Yes.
BY MR. PETROCELLI:
Q. And, Ms. McIntosh, do you have this decoder as well in your binder?
A. Is it in here? Yes, I do.
Q. Am I correct that this is Book H?
A. Yes.
Q. Okay. So, what I'd like to do is really have you walk us through this P&L, with particular emphasis on what the editor does versus what the computer program does.
A. Yeah.
Q. Okay. First of all, what publishing division are we in here?
A. We're in the Penguin Publishing Group.
Q. Okay. And what's the name of this particular P&L program? Do you know?

A. Abacus.
Q. Abacus. And do each of the publishing divisions have its own P&L program?
A. Abacus is a program that Penguin used prior to our merger, and some of the other divisions have adopted it. Some have their own slightly different variations on it, but the majority use this one.
Q. Now, this particular P&L has at the top, under draft, the advance of $4 million. Do you see that?
A. Yes.
Q. Okay. But when an editor starts out on the P&L, is there an advance already listed?
A. No. The advance—the advance would be one of the inputs that they make.
Q. So when the editor is first filling this out, do they fill it out without first putting in the advance, just so they can see how this is going to pencil out?
A. They may—different editors may start in different spots, but my understanding is that they're going to start by identifying the format and probably they pick a price that they think is reasonable. They put that in, and then they're going to start to play with the sales expectations—
Q. And then ultimately—
A.—the sales estimates.
Q.—there will be a suggested advance?
A. Yes. So the—
Q. Okay.
A. So the sales estimates that they are going to put in are going to then be measured against an advance, which they—
Q. Okay. Well, I'd like to go through this a little bit more slowly.
A. Okay.
Q. So, initially, there's a—first item is list price; right? The editor chooses the list price?
A. Yes.
Q. How does the editor choose the list price?
A. They would think about whether this is a long book or a short book. They would think about the prices that seem like fairly common price points for that level, and certainly, in terms of the price, that would be since checked by their business manager.
Q. And then I notice here, if we go down to net sales units, it's a round number.
A. Yes.
Q. Do you see that? It's 150,000 units; right?
A. Yes.
Q. Is that a number that the editor selects?
A. Yes. This editor has made a bet that the book will sell 150,000 copies.
Q. Now, where does the editor get that number from? Or how does the editor come up with that estimate?
A. So it would depend a lot on the kind of book it is, but if it's a book by a repeat author, someone who we've published in the past, then the editor is going to have that author track record to go on. But they're really most frequently going to be relying on what we call comp titles or comparable titles to kind of triangulate; we think the audience for this is about the same size as the audience for this other book. This seems like a good bet.
Q. So that's the—that's really the judgment of the editor at that point?
A. Yes.
Q. Now, I've been focusing on the hardcover format, but this P&L covers all formats; is that right?
A. This particular P&L is showing all the print and ebook formats.
Q. But not audio?
A. In this case, audio is reflected as an asset offset, which just means its actual sales are not reflected on this P&L.
Q. So the sales—the estimated units that are reflected for each of the formats going across the page to lifetime totals, that's the editor's assessment of what—how many units it could sell in each format?
A. Yes.

Q. Over the life of the book?

A. The—I believe—and sorry. The blow-up boxes are masking the top, but I believe that the first few columns are showing the first year's projected sales, and then the—if you move that one down further, I'll be able to see. Yes. So the first four columns are showing the first-year projections, and then lifetime would include additional backlist sales.

Q. Okay. And, now, unit shipped is an odd number, and I'll just for now focus on the hardcover column. Okay?

A. Okay.

Q. Unit shipped is an odd number. There's a return percentage indicated. And is the program then computing what the returns would be—the return units would be based on the return rate that's embedded in the program?

A. Exactly. So the editor can't adjust the return percentage; that is set by the finance director based on the average returns for that format and that imprint. And so, the editor in this case has put in the 150,000 as a net sales number, and the program is calculating based on their average return rate of 28 percent what that unit's shipped number would be.

Q. Now, that return rate that's embedded in the program is one of a number of percentages or formulas embedded in the program that the editor cannot alter; is that right?

A. Correct.

Q. How often—well, how are those various percentages derived, and how often are they updated?

A. They're derived based on the imprint or the division's overall actual spending over time. And so the—they are kind of a trailing indicator of our costs and the finance director's—I'd say they—they maybe make adjustments to those costs on an annual basis.

Q. You said finance director. Each division has a finance director?

A. Yes.

Q. Okay. Now, the next item here is gross sales. And to be clear, is that sales of dollars to Penguin Random House, not at the cash register; right?

A. Correct.

Q. And that's derived by multiplying the list price times the unit shipped; right?

A. And then take it less the—the margin—the discount to retail, yes.

Q. Okay. And that's roughly 50 percent?

A. Roughly, yes.

Q. And then we have the same calculation for returns, and then we get down to incentives, and that's another odd number. Does that mean that's a computer-derived number?

A. That's a computer-derived number that is based on the—the retail arrangements that we—the terms of sale we agree to with retailers sometimes include incentives, which do not vary by book, and they're baked in as a formula here.

Q. Okay. So incentives are what? Sales discounts?

A. It could be promotional discounts, merchandising. Different retailers have different kinds of incentives.

Q. Okay. Then we have net sales after the deduction of incentives and returns. And then we have a series of cost items. Plant. What's plant?

A. So plant—I think of plant as being our cost for creating the first book, the first copy of the book. So it's all of the—for example, the art or the permission for the art on the jacket. It's the development costs for the content itself.

Q. Work for hire, doesn't apply here?

A. In this case, it's—it doesn't apply.

Q. And what's PPB?

A. That's paper, printing, and binding. So that is the variable cost to make each incremental unit.

Q. Are plant and PPB, again, based on the data in the program?

A. It's based on the data in the program. The only—the variation would be if—for example, if this were a really high-end illustrative book, then the plant and PPB would be set to be a higher percentage.

Q. Okay. Now, we get to royalties earned and unearned advances. And to be clear about this, if no advance had been put into the system at this point; right? Is royalties earned—what is royalties earned?
A. Royalties earned is just the calculation based on the royalty rate per unit that's applicable in the contract. That is showing for this number of copies sold times that royalty rate. This is what the royalties earned would be.
Q. So it would be—if you go all the way over to the lifetime total column, you see royalties earned of $1,348,339; right?
A. Yes.
Q. And that would be—as though there were no advance at all, that would be the royalties earned on the estimated units sold?
A. Correct.
Q. Okay. Now, there is—I'll come back to the unearned. I just want to go through the other cost items. Now, we—
THE COURT: I'm sorry. Let me just make sure I understand. The royalty rate is times the net sales?
THE WITNESS: Yes.
THE COURT: Okay. Thank you.
BY MR. PETROCELLI:
Q. And royalty rates are different for each of these formats?
A. Yes.
Q. And the computer is aggregating them?
A. Yes.
Q. Okay. And doing it by format; right?
A. Correct.
Q. Okay. So gross profit then, if we—if we work our way down, is what?
A. Gross profit is going to be, essentially, going to be the revenue minus the costs of this—
Q. Including the advances?
A. Including the advances, yes.
Q. Now, here the gross profit is negative, and that's because not only do we have the royalties earned, but we have this unearned advance; right?
A. Yes.
Q. Now—
A. Well, I'm sorry. The gross profit here is negative just for the hardcover. Over the lifetime, it's showing a positive gross profit.
Q. Thank you for that clarification. I was just focusing on the hardcover.
A. Okay.
Q. So maybe at this time what I'll do—because it can get a little confusing—is at some point after completing this, the editor has chosen a royalty of what—excuse me, an advance of what?
A. In this case, the editor has input an advance of $4 million.
Q. Okay. Now, if you go to the last column under lifetime totals and you add up royalties earned in—in the unearned advance, they add up to $3 million. Do you see that?
A. Sorry. The zoom here is making it harder for me to see. Could you restate the question, please?
Q. Yeah. Lifetime totals, royalties earned, and unearned advance come to $3 million—approximately $3 million, not 4?
A. That's correct, yes.
Q. So why is there a $3 million advance embedded in this P&L rather than the $4 million?
A. In this case—and this is what you could sort of see going on at the top of the page there, what they are counting on is being able to offset part of that advance to the audio publisher. They're assuming the audio publisher is going to take part of this asset onto their own balance sheet. And that because they're buying world rights here, they're going to be able to sublicense to other publishers in other territories.
Q. So just to—just to be clear about that, the total advance is 4, but it's for worldwide rights, not just North America?

A. Correct.
Q. And so there's going to be income coming in from the worldwide exploitation, and then audio is going to carry some of the advance?
A. Correct.
Q. But for this P&L, a $3 million number was used; right?
A. Correct.
Q. And the unearned advance, is that the difference between $3 million and what the royalties would be on a straight percentage basis?
A. Right. It's the royalties earned plus the royalties unearned equals the advance.
Q. Okay. And—okay. So then, that's part of the subtraction that goes into the total costs of goods sold; right?
A. Correct. Yes.
Q. Now we can go back to gross profit. And it's negative in the hardcover format, but by the time we get all the way over to the right, it's positive to the lifetime totals; right?
A. Yes.
Q. Okay. And then we have outbound freight. What that is?
A. That's our cost to ship books to retailers.
THE COURT: I'm sorry. Can I just ask: Shouldn't royalties earned plus unearned advances equal $4 million?
THE WITNESS: Well—
THE COURT:—or $3 million? It equals neither.
THE WITNESS: The royalties earned of the 1.—if you look at the right-hand side where it says 1.348—
THE COURT: Yeah.
THE WITNESS: 1.348 plus 1.651—those two should total to 3.
THE COURT: Okay. So, the royalties earned is a sum of the royalties across all the different types of formats, including ebooks, trade paperbacks, et cetera?
THE WITNESS: Exactly.
THE COURT: But the unearned is only across hardcover?
THE WITNESS: Well, yes, you're right. It's—I think the—my guess is that on this—on the form, it's just that—it's just really using that as a—the unearned is not calculating by format. It's just that is the unearned. We usually try to—if we have excess unearned advance, we tend to take that onto our balance sheet in the first year after publication. I think that's why they've done it this way.
THE COURT: Okay. Thank you.
BY MR. PETROCELLI:
Q. Outbound freight is the shipping of the books to the stores; right?
A. Yes.
Q. And for ebooks, you don't have that, obviously?
A. Correct.
Q. And then—now, is that a computer-derived number, or is that something the editor inserts?
A. The outbound freight is going to be set in the template. The editor cannot adjust it.
Q. Okay. Now we have marketing, which is, in this case, under the hardcover format, $150,000; and then there's some odd numbers. And in the lifetime totals, it's $308,916. What's going on there?
A. This is a placeholder number. It's really generated again, by the percentage you see on the right-hand side, the 5.8 percent. That is set at the publishing division level across all of their P&Ls. They could certainly adjust that over time, but it's just their way of making sure that the editor is accounting for some marketing cost in the P&L.
Q. Okay. What is the next item, contribution to total overhead?
A. That's showing just what is the variable impact of this—what is the incremental impact of this publication on our results.
Q. Is a simple way of thinking about that, that's what your variable costs are?
A. That's the variable costs for this publication, yes.

Q. Okay. And then we're going to get down to some overhead figures, and is a way to think about that, those are fixed costs?
A. Yes. In the P&L, this direct overhead is reflecting the cost of the imprint that's publishing the book, and then the allocated overhead is reflecting what the rest of the company costs.
Q. And those—those percentages are, again, computer derived based on what the finance director has—has inputted?
A. Yes. Those are hard coded in.
Q. And then we have the subtraction down to net profit; right?
A. Yes.
Q. And this is showing with a $3 million advance a net profit of 2.1 percent; is that right?
A. Yes.
Q. And now we have—let me go over a box at the bottom called Suggested Advance. And I'm seeing three choices that you're—the editor is being given by this program: 10 percent, 12 and a half percent, and 15 percent. And what is that about?
A. That's just a calculation that runs automatically as the editor is putting in price and units. And so it is basically doing the math for the editor to understand that if she was hoping to achieve a 10 percent profit percentage, then the advance would be the $2.5 million.
Q. So if the—if an editor had not put in any advance number yet in this program and wanted to see what the suggested advance would be for 15 percent net profit, then it would give you that number; right?
A. Correct.
Q. And it would also give you the number for 12 and a half percent and 10 percent; right?
A. Correct.
Q. And at 10 percent, the suggested advance would be $2.575 million. Do you see that?
A. Yes.
Q. Which, of course, is less than the $3 million advance that was actually input; right?
A. Yes.
Q. And so that's why we have a lower profit margin, net profit margin than the 10 percent?
A. Correct.
Q. Okay. So just to recap on this P&L, Defendants' 414, the editor is putting in the list price and the unit shipped, in this case the net units; right?
A. Yes.
Q. And the computer is pretty much doing everything else; is that right?
A. Yes.
Q. Are there some of these categories, like marketing, for example, that the editor can override by putting in a different number than the computer would generate by the percentage?
A. I think they could override marketing. I don't think it's something they do.
Q. Okay. Did—did you approve this P&L?
A. I did.
Q. Well, so here we have a situation where a 10 percent net profit margin would have yielded a suggested advance of $2.5 million, but you approved $4 million?
A. Yes.
Q. $3 million embedded into this P&L, and then you have that other million that's being allocated, I guess, in part to audio; right?
A. Yes.
Q. So why would you approve a P&L where you're only making 2 percent?
A. I recall in this case certainly discussing with the editor, would there be a way to buy this for a little bit less and have a little more cushion in the P&L. But she was absolutely very convincing that this was a book she absolutely wanted to publish and that the agent was very firm on the price required.
Q. Okay. Who was the agent?
A. Andrew Wylie.
Q. So the author got $4 million in this situation?

A. Yes.
Q. Okay. And only counting the $3 million into the P&L, you're at 2.1 percent?
A. Yes.
Q. Okay. Now, if by the way, this merger were cleared by the Court, and assume that, for example, overhead is lower, what effect would that have?
A. If overhead is lower, than the editor would feel more confident at a higher advance. The formula would allow a higher advance to be generated.
Q. If overhead is lower post-merger, does the net profit go up or down?
A. If everything else stays the same, then net profit goes up.
Q. And what does that do to the suggested advance?
A. It allows a higher advance.
Q. Okay. We can put that away. When you review an acquisition P&L, such as this one, what are you looking for?
A. I'm looking at the contribution number and the EBITDA number; those are two different financial thresholds. And then I'm looking at the total advance number and the sales expectations.
Q. Does an author need to earn out her advance for the book to be profitable to Penguin Random House?
A. No. We can feel that we're in comfortable, profitable territory at around 70 percent of earnout for most books.
Q. Here was a situation where if the author had earned out, you would have only received 2.7 percent profit, and that's at the $3-million-advance level?
A. At the—yes.
Q. So what's the direction that you give your editors about profit expectations and their impact on suggested advances?
A. I generally focus their attention on the contribution number for—particularly situations where we're really having to consider, can we pay this advance? Is it worthwhile to make this investment in this book? I often find myself directing their attention to the contribution number because I want them to think about what is the incremental impact of making this bet on our company. So we are, obviously, going to have zero incremental benefit if we don't publish it at all. So the contribution lets you look to see what is the incremental, and as long as that's in solidly positive territory, then I would encourage them to feel good about that path.
Q. By contribution, you mean overhead? I'm sorry. You mean variable costs—
A. The variable costs of that publication.
Q. And does that—with that advice, are you—or that direction, are you intending to encourage them to be more liberal or more conservative in the advances that they pay?
A. More liberal. More conservative approach would have us always aiming to be in positive net profit or EBITDA on every single book because we do need to cover our overhead costs. But particularly for the bigger bets, like the one that we were just reviewing, I would be comfortable as long as we were in positive contribution territory.
MR. PETROCELLI: Okay. So, Pam, could you put up the next demonstrative, which is Defendants' Demonstrative 11.
BY MR. PETROCELLI:
Q. What does this demonstrative depict?
A. This illustrates the various approval thresholds within the company for acquisitions.
Q. Do any of these approval thresholds have to do with a view that an anticipated top seller is a book at a certain level of advance?
A. No, it does not.
Q. Okay. And that would be true if the advance—suggested advance level were $250,000 or any other number, for that matter; is that right?
A. Correct. It's not reflecting that at all.
Q. Okay. So just making sure we understand the chart, under Random House, what's the approval level

there?
A. All acquisitions are approved by the division head.
Q. The division head?
A. The division head.
Q. And that person is whom?
A. That's Gina Centrello.
Q. And Ms. Centrello reports to whom?
A. To me.
Q. And so there's no lower threshold there?
A. No.
Q. In her group?
A. Not for her group, no.
Q. And what about—the next two look like they have the same approval levels in the Penguin Publishing Group and The Knopf Doubleday Publishing Group?
A. Yes, the Penguin Publishing Group has had this approach for a long time prior to the Penguin Random House merger; that the imprint publisher has leeway up to $425,000, and then it goes up to the division head. Knopf, which is that next column, used to look like Random House, in that the head of Knopf approved every acquisition, but when Maya Mavjee took over the group a couple of years ago, she decided to adopt the Penguin level.
Q. An imprint publisher refers to whom?
A. That's the publisher of a given imprint, like Brian Tart is the publisher of Viking.
Q. And editors report to that publisher?
A. Yes.
Q. And so that level is—the publisher imprint level for Penguin and Knopf is what?
A. That is $250,000.
Q. And then above that, the next person is the head of that division?
A. Yes.
Q. For those divisions, and what number is that?
A. They can approve up to $1 million.
Q. And who are "they"?
A. Who are the people who head those divisions?
Q. Yes.
A. So Allison Dobson heads the Penguin Publishing Group. Maya Mavjee heads the Knopf Doubleday Publishing Group.
Q. You want to spell Maya's last name, please.
Q. And what about the two children's groups, Random House Children's Books and Penguin Young Readers Group?
A. So Random House Children's, the imprint publisher, can make a decision on a contract up to $150,000. And above that level, as you see, it says meeting. That means that the whole management team gets together, along with the division head, to make the decision up to a million dollars.
Q. And who heads up the Random House Children's book division?
A. That's Barbara Marcus.
Q. Okay. And the final one?
A. Then Penguin Young Readers—which is led by Jen Loja—in her group, the imprint publishers decide up to a hundred thousand dollars, and beyond that level it goes to her for approval.
Q. And you get it at a million, you indicated; right?
A. Correct.
Q. And then if it's more than 2, who reviews it?
A. Then Markus reviews it.
Q. Up to $75 million?
A. Yes.

Q. Now, when it exceeds your level, like the example we just saw, do you also review those P&Ls before it goes to Mr. Dohle?

A. Yes.

Q. Okay. So we can go back, then, to Defendants' 10. And we talked about acquisition. Let's talk a bit about the editorial process. And the editorial process, just briefly, how long does that take?

A. That could take any amount of time, from after acquiring the rights, in some rare cases, we could publish the book a couple months later, but in most cases it could take years, maybe even a decade, to get to the final work.

Q. When is the—at least the initial date of publication of the book first set?

A. So that's set when the editor is able to project with high degree of confidence that the book will be available at a certain time. And at that point, the imprint publisher is going to assign a publication date to the book.

Q. And is the publication date based solely on when the book will be available, when it will be written?

A. No. That's one input, but they're also going to be looking at a number of different factors. If this is a book—like seasonality plays into it. So, if this is a book that we want to sell at Mother's Day, then we need to have the book available at retail before that. We could also look to see what are the other books that are going on sale in a given period. So if we feel that this book is—has a very similar readership to another book, then we would probably try to avoid stacking them right next to each other.

Q. Does the publication date have anything to do with the advance?

A. No.

Q. Can the publication date change once it's set?

A. Yes.

Q. Why?

A. It often does. It could change either because it turns out the book is not ready. It could change because there's a particular media endorsement or event that we're trying to tie into. It could change because we have feedback from retailers recommending a change.

Q. Are any other decisions about the book made during the editorial process?

A. Related to the planning of the book?

Q. Yes.

A. They're going to think about what the jacket looks like. They're really focused just on making the book, though. So that's what I think of as the editorial process.

Q. Is there something called a publication goal or a pub goal?

A. Yes, the pub goal is a number that is—it depends a little bit on different parts of the company, but generally that is the number that the sales director and the publisher are agreeing is their—what they're aspiring to in terms of shipping to bookstores.

Q. You mean number of prints?

A. Number of copies, yeah.

Q. So since we saw a number of copies on the P&L, is the pub goal print number based on what's in the P&L?

A. No.

Q. Why not?

A. There—for one thing, the pub goal is established in a completely different context. It's—as I said, it could be years later, but also the sales numbers that are used in the P&L as we looked at it, those are really driving to the whole life of the book; whereas, a pub goal is really just talking about what is the number that we're going to ship on day one of the publication.

Q. Okay. Going to the next phases here, what we're calling the prepublication and publication phases, there are different steps that are indicated on the demonstrative. What's the launch meeting?

A. So the launch meeting is the first time that the editor is presenting the book to his or her colleagues. Usually, that's the editor presenting to publicity, marketing, design, and often to salespeople. And that's the organizing principle for that launch is it's going to be all the books that fit into a particular season. So when you assign a pub goal—a pub date, rather, you're assigning the book to a season or span. And all of those books are going to be presented together in a series of these meetings that you see illustrated here.

Q. You called it a season a span?

A. A span.

Q. How many spans are there in a year?

A. We have three. We pretend winter is not a season, but we have fall, spring, and summer.

Q. Are all the books scheduled to be published in that particular span discussed in this launch meeting?

A. Yes, every book is launched.

Q. What's the strategy meeting, and how does it differ from the launch meeting?

A. So from the launch meeting, then, through to the sales conference meeting—I'm skipping over one. So sales conference is going to, again, be where you present all of the books to all of the salespeople, but the strategy meeting sits in between that. And that's really—I mean, I think of that's the one where the sausage is made. That's the meeting that is going to be a discussion of the titles for which the publisher either has the highest sales expectation or where there's—we think there's a particular opportunity to—to achieve an expectation if we—if we—if we play our cards right. So there's going to be maximum feedback in that meeting. That's where often you find out that there's a disconnect, where actually the sales channel heads do not see the potential for the book that the publisher is describing or often that's the book where you start to get a sense of very positive developments, where more people have now read the finished book and you start to see buzz happening.

Q. At the strategy meeting, are only a select number of books discussed?

A. They tend to be the books where there's something that really has to be hashed out. So, again, different imprint publishers are going to play this in different ways in terms of how they use that meeting, but it is a subset of the list in the strategy meeting.

Q. Do you call these books priority books?

A. There are priority books. There could be opportunity books. Again, it's a little bit that different personalities of the different groups are going to use their own judgment in deciding what to bring into the strategy meeting.

Q. What's the difference between a priority book and an opportunity book?

A. Well, there's no set definition of these. In just a very general way, I think of the priority book meaning that this is one where we have very aggressive sales goals, and so it is a priority for us to meet those goals. Whereas, an opportunity book would be one where at first glance, it might not seem as obvious as sales success, but where the—again, the people who've read it are starting to develop some excitement for it, and we think if we rally around it, we might be able to make something good happen.

Q. Do advance levels play a role in selecting priority or opportunity books?

A. No. The most important number that is being used in this whole series of meetings is the sales goal number, the sales expectation. So those sales expectations, there certainly could be consistency. If we had a really high sales expectation at time of acquisition and then by the time we're ready to publish the book, we still have a high sales expectation, then it would seem logical to me that there could be a high advance attached to that. But these meetings never are referring to the advance. They're referring to what is our sales goal.

Q. Do the salespeople know the advance levels as a general rule?

A. No. It's considered confidential information.

Q. What then goes on at these next couple of meetings: sales conference, rep account, publicists?

A. So what are these?

Q. Yeah. What are these?

A. So sales conference, this is the—by the time you get to sales conference, hopefully you have a pretty robust first draft of how you're going to go to market with these books. You have jacket designs. You have fairly firm pub dates. And so in the sales conference, this is where you are formally presenting to the sales reps across all channels all the information they need to then go to market. So that next step is where you have sales reps who are going out into their different channels to present the list, the individual titles, the whole span, to their accounts; at the same time as publicists are going to be playing that same role but with the media, trying to secure positive review attention or future attention for the authors.

Q. What are advance copies, and to whom do they get sent?

A. Advance copies are an important tool that we use to generate interest in the book. They're absolutely not relevant for all books, but they're relevant to most narrative books. Sometimes they're digital copies. Sometimes they're early print copies. We regularly send these to—not just to reviewers, but also to booksellers, as a way to generate positive buzz.

Q. And then it takes us to printing and shipping.

A. Yes. So by the time we get to the print meeting, hopefully we have a pretty accurate sense of what the feedback is from booksellers and what the media plan is for the author. So at that point, we're either reviewing the sales estimates or the actual orders from—on an account-by-account basis and using that number to send an order to the printer.

Q. Now, as of this point in time when you're printing and taking orders and starting to ship out to booksellers, is the marketing plan or the publicity plan or both put in place?

A. I'd say that the first—it's very much an iterative process. So certainly, in the earlier meetings that you see on the left-hand part of the slide—the strategy meeting, for example, that's really where, kind of, the first draft of those plans is being hashed out. But, again, depending on whether we have increased excitement for a book, whether booksellers are demonstrating their willingness to support the book in store, ideas that come from the market into us, those are used to shape the plans. And that that shaping and iteration goes on, really, all the way up until the pub date. And, actually, I should say, it really goes beyond that, but certainly we have plans by the time we publish the book.

Q. And what role does the advance play in the development of the marketing plan as of the time the books are being shipped?

A. It does not play a role. It's really the entire conversation and all of the planning is around the number of books we want to sell.

Q. I'll come back to that in a moment. After the book is put on sale, is there any further iteration of the marketing plan based on results?

A. Yes. We, particularly over time, have really evolved to be in much more of an agile mindset. So, we measure the performance of the activities that we're conducting. And if, say we've done an online ad campaign and it's successfully translating to sales, then we're going to expand that campaign. If we're doing something and it is seemingly having no results, then we're going to stop throwing good money after bad. So we're adapting in real time based on the results.

Q. Why isn't the marketing plan as it evolves tied to the advance?

A. Well, as I described, the marketing plan is very much tied to the sales goal; the sales, the number that we want to sell. And if everything is very consistent in the world, then it would make sense that a book with very high sales goals may very well have had a large advance. But it's also true that different kinds of books require different kinds of support. So, we could have two books that have very similar advance levels across different categories. And one, if it's a debut novel that we really want to believe in the book and, again, we're starting to receive that positive buzz, then we would invest quite a lot in launching that book versus a book that is by an author with an established platform. We don't have to spend as much money to achieve those sales.

Q. And you've actually seen that occur in your work?

A. All the time.

Q. When given, especially, very high advances, where the company is making a big investment, taking a bet, as you put it, isn't the company going to want to do more, work harder, do everything in its power to make sure that that higher-advance book sells so the company doesn't lose money?

A. The way I think about it is that, again, hopefully, we're making good decisions at the time of acquisition, and that if we're investing a lot in an advance, that's just not a momentary thought. That that's a conviction that we have that is going to remain true. However, a lot of times things do change, and even if we have committed to a high advance, the reason that that shouldn't drive the marketing spend is that that is essentially a sunk cost at that point. I've already committed that—I'm paying that $4 million, for example. That money is already gone. I can't do anything about that money. What I can do something about going forward is the number of copies that I'm going to aim to sell, and I am going to think about the marketing spend related to that number.

Q. And what do you find in your experience to be the most effective lever at marketing and enhancing the sale of a book?

A. We organize ourselves around—I think of them as three legs of the stool, of how we support books, how we launch books. There's paid marketing, which the easiest way to think of that is advertising. There's publicity, which is—we call earned media. So that is stuff we can't pay for. We have to earn, the book has to earn it. And then the third is bookseller support.

So across all three of those departments—marketing, publicity, and sales—I believe all three of them are going to very strongly agree that the most important is publicity and that the second most important is bookseller support. And that the problem with marketing is that we cannot spend money in a way that is going to translate to sales. We would if we could, but paid marketing is the least effective way to generate sales.

Q. I'd like to show you a government exhibit. It is Government Exhibit 986.

MR. PETROCELLI: Is this confidential?

THE WITNESS: Is that—I'm sorry. Is that in my binder?

MR. PETROCELLI: Yes. This should not be public facing. What is—oh, by the way, Your Honor, I neglected to move into evidence the P&L, which is Exhibit 414, and I would ask that it be received into evidence.

THE COURT: All right. Any objection to that?

MS. CROSS: No, Your Honor.

THE COURT: That will be admitted under seal.

MR. PETROCELLI: Thank you. (PX Exhibit 414 admitted into evidence.)

MR. PETROCELLI: This is not confidential, Your Honor. This is Exhibit 986. Do you have it?

THE COURT: I do have it.

MR. PETROCELLI: Yeah, and I think it's going to be on the screen.

BY MR. PETROCELLI:

Q. It starts out with an email from Maya Mavjee to you in April of 2020 about an attachment back in April of 2012. Do you see that?

A. I do see that.

Q. And what is this email and its attachment?

A. This email is—she's sharing with me, in 2020, a document that had been created in 2012—so about eight years before that—when she was then head of the Crown Publishing Group.

Q. Okay. Now, just briefly through this document, what I'm seeing here are different categories. Category 1 is lead titles with sales goals of 75,000 units or higher and there are advances over half a million. Do you see that?

A. I do see that.

Q. And then you have another, Category 2. If you could—with lower numbers than three, four, and all the way down to five. What do you understand this to be, and why was it being sent to you?

A. My understanding of what this was—that in 2012, Crown was trying to better organize themselves around marketing.

Q. And why are you mentioning Crown?

A. Because it was created in the Crown Publishing Group, which doesn't exist anymore.

Q. It was created in the Crown Publishing Group—

A. Yes.

Q.—before the merger with Random House?

A. No. It was part of the Crown Publishing Group in 2012, was before the merger of Penguin.

Q. When you say it doesn't exist anymore—we'll get to that later on—but—

A. Yes.

Q.—why doesn't Crown exist anymore as a separate division?

A. Because I combined it in 2018 with the Random House Publishing Group.

Q. So what used to be the Crown publishing division is now in the—

A. Part of the Random House publishing division.
Q. Okay. So, I want to get back to this document, then.
A. Yes. So, my understanding is that as part of the Crown team's attempts to better organize their marketing efforts, they had kind of used this as a brainstorming document, I guess is the best way to describe it. But I think it's something that they created, and it was never really used.
Q. To your knowledge, was it used when you took over Penguin, for example?
A. I never saw anything like this at Penguin.
Q. Or when you were COO?
A. I never saw anything like this until this document.
Q. And has this been used at all, to your knowledge, in the last ten years?
A. No. I don't even think it was really much used at Crown. I don't know that, but certainly, when they were combined with Random House, Random House doesn't use anything like this.
Q. Do you know why whoever created this document had different marketing categories tied to sales goals or advance levels?
A. I can understand having the activities attached to sales goals, but I don't understand why they would have put the advance in here.
Q. So is there any kind of system in place now or that has been in place in the last ten years or so where marketing is directly tied to advance levels?
A. No.
Q. By the way, do you know what percentage of spend was marketing in the past year?
A. I believe it was 2 percent for Penguin Random House as a whole in the U.S. last year, as a percentage of our sales.
Q. Across all formats?
A. Across the whole company, I believe it was 2 percent.
Q. So to be clear, actual marketing spent—
A. Actual was 2 percent of sales.
Q. Was 2 percent.
MR. PETROCELLI: Okay. Thank you. You can take that document down.
BY MR. PETROCELLI:
Q. And just to be clear, do you have any kind of separate marketing, publicity, or sales teams associated for books that were acquired for more than $250,000?
A. No, I do not.
Q. And you understand that in this trial there's been a lot of talk about anticipated top selling books?
A. Yes, I've heard that.
Q. Right. And what's your understanding of that term as used either in your company or industry-wide?
A. It's not a term that I was familiar with.
Q. Okay. I'm going to follow up on that. You understand that the position that the government takes in this is that it can be defined to mean books acquired for advances of $250,000 or greater?
A. I understand that's their definition.
Q. So putting aside the words anticipated top sellers, is there any part of the company's business that's tied to certain levels of advance?
A. No.
Q. Like editorial? Sales? Distribution? Marketing? Anything?
A. No.
Q. Is there any special documentation that's required for advances above $250,000?
A. No.
Q. Or, frankly, any other level besides the P&L?
A. We do the P&L for every acquisition.
Q. At any level?
A. At any level.
Q. Now, without getting tied to the words anticipated top selling books, which you've said it's not

something that you've heard of before this case, are there books that just in the ordinary course of your work and the company's business, that when you are negotiating and acquiring those books you expect to be top selling books, you have a very high degree of confidence that those books will sell lots and lots of copies?
A. Yes. I would say books by big, best-selling names that are on the bestseller list every year. Big franchise author names. The ones who sell millions of copies, I would expect them to continue to sell millions of copies.
Q. Besides top franchise-type authors, are there any other circumstances when at the acquisition stage, you have a very high degree of confidence that that book is going to sell lots and lots of copies, going to be one of your top sellers?
A. The connections start to get a little bit more tenuous, but certainly celebrity books or books that are by people who are already famous, whether that's for entertainment or politics or what have you. So people who are genuine celebrities, we would expect that the number of people who know who they are and are interested in them will then be reflected in selling a lot of copies.
Q. So looking past the acquisition stage to what actually happens with the sale of the books, as it turns out, are there categories of books that you have seen that consistently are the top sellers, and are there categories that are consistently not the top sellers?
A. No.
Q. What about these franchise authors and celebrities, for example?
A. Well, so, if we're calling those a category of books, franchise authors are top sellers. Celebrities—we certainly have made many very painfully expensive bets on celebrities who turned out not to be able to sell the books. But I understood your question to mean are there categories of books, like, subject categories of books that are going to translate to top sellers or not, and I would say there's not.
Q. What advance levels are typically associated with the franchise author books and the celebrity books that you indicated you do expect to sell at very high volumes?
A. I mean, millions of dollars of advance. I think a way to look at it is for Penguin Random House books last year, if I look at the top 10 percent of the books, I think—if I get down to that 10 percent level of our top—of going from most successful to least successful for sales, that 10 percent level gets you to about 300,000 copies sold in that year. And if you told me I'm definitely going to sell 300,000 copies in a year, I would spend many millions of dollars to get that book.
Q. So you're saying when you see a P&L that's at the 300,000-unit level, you think that you have a pretty good handle on that?
A. Yeah. If we have a fair degree of confidence in that 300,000-unit copy level, then, sure, I would feel confident in a multimillion-dollar advance.
Q. So 300,000 units, if you get a P&L—and I'm just generalizing here, of course; right?
A. Yeah.
Q. But if you get a P&L at 300,000 units, what is the advance level that you would typically expect to see associated with that volume?
A. So in, in the example I was just citing, it was 300,000 in just a given year. So, I would actually expect a book that is selling 300,000 units in a year is probably going to sell at least 400 or 500 thousand over its life, once you get backlist in there too. So, I don't know, 4 million, 5 million dollars advance.
Q. And you review sales data, both company-wide and industry-wide, as part of your job?
A. Yes, I do.
Q. And by the way, do you track acquisition market shares at all as part of your business?
A. I don't think there's a way for me to track that.
Q. Okay. But you track downstream?
A. Yes.
Q. And what are some of—the work that you do with that?
A. The most granular way we can look at industry data is using BookScan data. So I get a lot of reports of BookScan data. And one of the reports I've looked at is on the industry basis; the top thousand books that performed in the market over the course of the year. I would look to see which of our books hit that

top thousand.

Q. And what do you typically see with respect to how Penguin Random House's books do with respect to thousand titles industry-wide or the top—I understand you said the top thousand.

A. Right. So for the top thousand, if we're talking in terms of the connection between those top thousand and advance levels, I think it's interesting that advance levels are all over the map in terms of our books that are on that top thousand list. There are some that we've paid many millions of dollars for, but there are plenty of books that we spend a million dollars on the advance and published them last year and they did not even make the top thousand on BookScan.

Q. But do you have an estimate of let's say the advances that you pay in excess of a million dollars, what percentage of those books make the top 1,000?

A. The books that we spent a million dollars on?

Q. Or higher.

A. Or higher. I think it's less than 45 percent of those books end up on that thousand best seller list.

Q. And what about under a million, what percentage—

A. The percentage goes down.

Q. What percentage—let me just finish my question. What percentage of your books with advances under a million dollars make that top 1,000 list?

A. I believe it's 10 percent or below.

Q. Under a million?

A. Under a million, yeah.

Q. Okay.

THE COURT: I'm sorry. Can you give me a sense of how many books you're talking about? Like, what's the denominator? How many books are you publishing?

THE WITNESS: I'm sorry. I don't actually have that number offhand.

THE COURT: Okay.

MR. PETROCELLI: Your Honor, was your question how many books above or below a million?

THE COURT: For either. Because she's saying 45 percent of her books of a million or more are on the list and 10 percent of her books below a million, but I don't know how many that is.

BY MR. PETROCELLI:

Q. Do you have any estimate of that?

A. I'm trying to understand what the—I was talking about the thousand titles in the industry. And of the books that we published that had advances of a million and above, they were—I think—I would really want to verify my numbers. I'm sorry. But the higher percentage of books was for the million and above, and the lower percentage was for lower-level advances.

Q. And you don't know how many of the books are a million and above? Is it a hundred? Is it 200?

A. I don't know the number offhand, so I don't want to misstate it.

Q. Okay. Fair enough. Is there any particular type of book that receives a very high advance but doesn't earn out?

A. Is there any type of book that receives a very high advance and doesn't earn out?

Q. Yes.

A. Yes. Yes, certainly.

Q. What are they?

A. Certainly the books by—I've referred now to the franchise authors. So, authors who absolutely can deliver hundreds of thousands of readers over one book after another after another. Their agents, understandably, are going to use that track record to ensure that we are paying a high advance. And I've certainly heard agents say to me that they hope in those cases that those authors don't earn out because they will know that they've done the right job in terms of negotiating the advance.

Q. I want to ask you a couple questions about profitability of books as opposed to units sold. Okay?

A. Uh-huh.

Q. In your experience, are Penguin Random House's profit margins higher or lower for books sold with larger advances?

A. Profit margins are lower at the higher advance levels.
Q. Consistent with what we saw in that P&L?
A. Yes.
Q. I'd like to show you a document that's already in evidence as Exhibit 151. It was a Penguin Random House deck for a very well-known political figure, and we don't want to mention any names. And if you could turn to Slide 9—and this would not be public facing. Slide 9, Bates number ending in 8286. Do you have that in front of you?
A. I do.
Q. Okay. And this—you see the example given, that out of every hundred books published, a certain number are profitable; right?
A. Yes.
Q. And then you see in the second box there, it says, you know, a certain percentage of those profitable books—not of the total books, but of the profitable books—drive a fairly high percentage of profitability. Do you see that?
A. I do.
Q. Okay. And why is that?
A. The way I think of it is that in terms of our—the books that sell the most—there are the ones where we have predicted those high sales at time of acquisition, and so that number has been baked into probably a high advance. And those are less profitable for us.
Then there's the other basket of titles that sell a lot, which are the books that we did not anticipate. So, they're the unanticipated bestsellers, and those account for the lion's share of our profit because they had advances that were relatively low compared to the very high sales achievement.
Q. You're saying the unanticipated top selling books account for the lion's share of the profit?
A. That's correct.
Q. And is that consistent with what you see in that third box there?
A. Yes. These are unpredictable breakout books with significant overperformance to expectations and investment.
Q. Okay.
THE COURT: I'm sorry. So, what percentage of your books are the unpredictable breakouts, and what percentage are the ones that you, kind of, knew?
THE WITNESS: Well, this illustration is showing 35 percent are profitable, and of that, 4 percent are these, the ones driving the breakout profit. So it would be just a couple of books in every hundred are driving that degree of profit. Because it's—
THE COURT: I'm sorry. A couple of books are the breakout books?
THE WITNESS: A couple of books are the breakout books, yes.
THE COURT: The unexpected breakout books?
THE WITNESS: Yes.
BY MR. PETROCELLI:
Q. Can you give some examples, by the way?
A. *Where the Crawdads Sing* is a great current example. *Fifty Shades of Grey*, *Gone Girl*, *Girl on the Train*. These are—you know, *Midnight Library* is another current one. *Atomic Habits*. Even if we had high hopes for them at the time of acquisition, we may even have made a significant investment on them at time of acquisition, but still the sales performance so outstrips our expectation, that they deliver most of the profit to the company.
THE COURT: I'm sorry. So, you're saying if there's one or two that are breakout, that means there are 33 that were the ones that you sort of expected.
THE WITNESS: So, I don't want to get lost on the slide too much, but the 4 percent here is showing 4 percent of the 35. So, 35 are profitable. Period. And of those, just 4 percent of that 35—so I think it's, like, twoish books account for the lion's share of profitability, and all the rest—so 45 percent of the profitability would be accounted for by the 33 or so books in that hundred.
THE COURT: So you're saying the 4 percent that drives 60 percent are all breakout books?

THE WITNESS: Yes, that's what I'm saying.
THE COURT: Okay.
MR. PETROCELLI: Should I continue, Your Honor?
THE COURT: Yes.
MR. PETROCELLI: I was going to change subjects, unless you had any further questions.
THE COURT: I'm sorry. Let me ask one more question because that surprises me. So, you're saying the 4 percent that drive 60 percent of profitability are all breakout books, meaning you didn't expect them to do as well as they did, and they are all the ones—some of them are not anticipated top sellers that did even better than you expected. All of them are complete surprises, is that what you're saying?
THE WITNESS: No. I'm saying that whatever the degree of advance was, whatever the level of advance was, that the performance so outstrips the expectations of it that are reflected in that advance that they are driving outside profits.
THE COURT: Correct. So it's not that those 4 percent are all the complete shocks. Some of them are ones that you thought would do well, but some of them did even better than you expected?
THE WITNESS: I think that's fair to say.
THE COURT: Okay. That makes a lot more sense to me. Thank you. Go ahead.
MR. PETROCELLI: Okay. I'm glad we clarified that, Your Honor.
THE COURT: Okay.
BY MR. PETROCELLI:
Q. So I'm going to turn to the subject of direct negotiations and auctions for a bit. Now, there's been a lot of testimony already about how books are acquired through auctions, round-robin, best bid, direct negotiations, with respect to option negotiations or exclusive submissions or preempts. So we don't need to go over that. You're well familiar with all of that; right?
A. Yes.
Q. In your experience, are auctions more common for debut authors or established authors?
A. They're more common for debut authors.
Q. In your experience, do you believe auctions result in publishers paying more than in other formats?
A. In this case—I'm sorry. Do you mean round-robin auctions?
Q. Round-robin.
A. Do round-robin auctions? No, I would say that round-robin auctions are actually preferred by editors because it lets them feel a little bit more confidence in the advances that they're paying.
Q. Why is that?
A. Because they can validate what they're bidding relative to what the other market players are bidding. Whereas, in a best-bid auction, you have to figure out not only what is your top number that you're willing to pay, you also have to guess what is the top number that any other individual player out there is willing to bet. And you have to put all of your bets out there right away. Whereas, in a round-robin auction, you can start low and feel your way up.
Q. In your experience, do agents have a preference for round-robin auctions?
A. I know that round-robin auctions have been declining in popularity, and that's driven by the agents.
Q. Do you believe that in round-robin auctions that go the distance on a round-robin basis, that your editors will end up paying less than in another type of transaction?
A. I don't know for sure. I think that in best-bid situations, those are the situations where we often end up overpaying, so round-robin auctions seem like safer bets to me, but I couldn't tell you the percentage outcome that way.
Q. And in direct negotiations, how do your editors and you, approving what they do, assess whether that's a reasonable offer to make given that there's no direct competition?
A. Do you mean if we're renewing with an existing author, for example? Well, there's going to be the author's track record, either established through our last books with them or maybe they're coming to us from another house. So, there's established track record that, certainly, the agent is going to use, either in their argument why this next book is going to sell better than that last one did. Even if the last one is a disappointment, they will come up with reasons why the next book is going to defy gravity, so to speak.

Q. Besides the estimated number of copies that you expect to sell, in having a negotiation for a book, is there any other factors that enter into the thinking of an editor and you, in your supervisory role, besides the estimated copies?
A. When we're deciding to buy any book or—
Q. Let's say a repeat author first.
A. Once we've already invested in an author's career, we definitely have a preference to keep the author. We pride ourselves in working over long careers. So, part of it is about the personal connection. It's a very close working relationship between an author or publisher and the editor. So there's a personal connection but even more than that, there is a desire to continue to work and reap the benefits of the investments we've already made in that career.
Q. Given how some authors and editors have very close relationships, isn't that something that the editor can actually take advantage of, knowing the author doesn't really want to depart from the editor and thereby allow you to offer a lower advance?
A. I don't think the agents really let that happen. We want to be in an arrangement that is fair. So if we lowball our offer to the author, the agent is going to threaten to take their client elsewhere.
Q. What about from the perspective of the editor, however? How do you understand the editor's view about lowballing an existing author?
A. Editors do not like to lowball the authors. It just feels like—
Q. Why not?
A. Again, it's a very close relationship. They develop a lot of trust in each other. The editor's investing a lot of her work in the book, and the author is investing a lot of trust in us. And the editor would be embarrassed to make a lowball offer.
Q. Is there any reputational impact if the editor or the company loses an author—an existing author?
A. Yes. It can be embarrassing if we lose an author, particularly if that author then goes on to achieve great sales for our competitor. So, it's both an emotional one and a business one, since we're trying to maximize our sales. We're trying to maximize our market share. Working to establish an author and then having them go and have another competitor reap those benefits, that's bad.
Q. Has PRH ever lost authors to other publishers?
A. Unfortunately, yes.
Q. Can you give some examples?
A. Nora Roberts, Harlan Coben.
Q. Where did they go?
A. Harlan Coben went to Hachette. His editor had left us to go there. Nora Roberts, the editor also went to Macmillan in that case, and we lost her to Macmillan.
Q. Were those significant authors?
A. Yes.
Q. And are they still with those publishers?
A. Yes.
Q. Have you ever lost any authors to non-Big 5 publishers?
A. We've lost authors to Amazon.
Q. Who?
A. Who are the authors? Dean Koontz, Mindy Kaling. Those are the two really prominent ones. We recently lost an armada-sales author named Rhys Bowen, I believe has gone to Amazon.
Q. Where did he go?
A. She—
Q. She.
A.—went to Amazon.
Q. All three?
A. Yes.
Q. When did that happen?
A. Dean Koontz and Mindy Kaling were a number of years ago. Rhys Bowen was recently.

Q. And who do you consider Penguin Random House's competitors?
A. Who do I consider our competitors to be?
Q. Yeah.
A. Big 5 and non-Big 5 publishers.
Q. And why non-Big 5?
A. Because, while I would say that in most competitive situations where we're bidding on books, that we do encounter all the other Big 5 in those situations, we also come across non-Big 5 publishers, whether that is Norton or Disney or Scholastic. There are start-up publishers that also have been spending big to acquire books.
Q. Have you lost any books to any start-up publishers in recent years?
A. There are books that we were planning to try to acquire, and as the editor was working on their P&L, the—you know, Riverhead recently was planning to bid on one and Zando preempted the book for, according to the agent, a million dollars.
Q. Okay. Let's talk about children's books. You indicated there were two children's divisions; right?
A. There are, yes.
Q. And about what percentage of Penguin Random House's trade books is represented by children's books?
A. I know in 2021 it was 27 percent. Twenty-seven percent.
Q. And do you ever acquire children's books for advances in excess of $250,000?
A. Yes.
Q. And in excess of a million dollars?
A. Yes.
Q. And who do you compete with on the children's book side?
A. In addition to the Big 5, as I said, there's certainly Scholastic, Disney, Abrams, Candlewick. There are a number of pure-play children's publishers.
Q. And did you say Scholastic and Disney?
A. I did.
Q. Okay. And then you said a number of others?
A. Yes.
Q. Are Scholastic and Disney, you know, quantitatively—
A. Yeah, in the children's space, it's really—people refer to the Big 7 because it's the, quote, unquote, Big 5 publishers plus Disney and Scholastic.
Q. And do you compete against Simon & Schuster in the children's space? By that I mean, are they a close competitor?
A. My understanding from the children's colleagues is that the two that they see more often in competition are HarperCollins and Scholastic.
THE COURT: Can I ask: Of the children's books, what percentage, approximately, of those have advances in excess of $250,000?
THE WITNESS: The percentage? I'm sorry. I don't know that offhand.
THE COURT: Is it a lot or just a few?
THE WITNESS: Children's books tend to be less expensive acquisitions. So, while I don't know the percentage, I would say it would be more common for a children's book to have a lower advance than an adult book would.
THE COURT: Okay.
BY MR. PETROCELLI:
Q. Have you lost any children's books at high-advance levels to any start-ups?
A. Similar to the Riverhead situation, I know that Zando has been very aggressive in acquisitions.
Q. What about Christian publishing? What percentage—your company publishes Christian books, religious books; right?
A. Yes, we have four imprints that publish in that space.
Q. Approximately what percentage of your trade book sales are Christian books?

A. For us, it's 2 percent. They're a higher percentage of the market of the industry as a whole. I think they're more like 6 percent of the industry as a whole, but for Penguin Random House, it's 2 percent.

Q. So you under-index?

A. Yes.

Q. And both for children's and Christian books, is the acquisition process the same as other books?

A. Exactly.

Q. And do you see Christian books being acquired for advance commitments greater than $250,000?

A. Absolutely.

Q. And to the judge's question, do you know the numbers?

A. My sense of the Christian category books is they can be just as expensive as the rest of the adult trade advances. I don't think the spread is any different. We've paid $2 million for a Christian book. We've paid a hundred thousand dollars for a Christian book.

THE COURT: Can I just ask: When you talk about Christian books, are you talking about the books that are sold exclusively in Christian stores and not in regular, I guess, retail outlets? Are you talking about the sort of—what, I guess, HarperCollins would call, sort of, Christian adjacent books, just sort of, the whole values-type books.

THE WITNESS: Yeah, we call them crossover books. So, the answer is both. The reason we have the four imprints is that they're positioned slightly differently in terms of their degree of conservatism in the Christian space, but some of them are going to sell maybe only in Christian stores and Amazon. The others could sell in Walmart. And the trend in those categories has been away from the Christian-only bookstores to general retail and Amazon.

THE COURT: Okay. Thank you.

BY MR. PETROCELLI:

Q. Do you compete against Simon & Schuster in the Christian book market?

A. No.

Q. Why is that?

A. I don't think they have any Christian publishing.

Q. Who do you compete against?

A. HarperCollins is the major competitor. Hachette is a major competitor. But it's a fairly dispersed set of publishers. So, there are some that are only Christian publishers. Tyndale, Baker, B&H, and there are others. We can encounter any of them in auctions.

Q. After you became CEO in 2018—

A. Uh-huh.

Q.—I think you testified earlier that that's when you reorganized the Crown division into the Random House division; right?

A. Yes.

Q. And why did you do that?

A. It was my evaluation that Crown was really struggling to succeed. They had a very dispersed set of categories in which they were publishing, and they were really struggling to make the kind of marketing investments that were needed to support those very diverse books and imprints. And I felt that Random House had the strongest marketing team, really, in the company, but also in the industry, and that by pairing them, that the Crown editors and books would benefit from the stronger marketing support that Random House could provide.

Q. And in your estimation, has that been a success?

A. Yes.

Q. In what way?

A. Crown books have, I think have, been published better, sold better. Agents have felt more supported for their clients. The feedback that I receive from agents has been quite positive.

Q. Ms. McIntosh, I want to talk about internal competition within the different divisions. Going back to the 2013 Penguin Random House merger, Penguin had its own children's division?

A. Yes.

Q. And Random House had its own?
A. Yes. Children's division, yes.
Q. And when the companies merged, did you combine them or keep them separate?
A. We kept them separate.
Q. And have they continued to remain separate?
A. Yes, they have.
Q. And do they bid against one another in auctions for books?
A. They do.
Q. Now, we have heard a fair amount of testimony so far that the policy at Penguin Random House is to allow imprints to compete with one another across divisions provided there's an external bidder in the process. Is that right?
A. Yes.
Q. Okay. Now, just to be clear, on imprints within a single division, if multiple editors within one of the divisions had been approached and want to bid, how does that work?
A. They can each submit a bid. Within a division, they each have their own approach to how they manage the communication with the agent, but it is a common occurrence that multiple imprints within the same division would be bidding for the same work.
Q. Isn't that a situation that requires, under your policy, a single house bid?
A. For that division, it requires that division to submit the bids together to the agent. As I said, they handle it in variable ways, but in the Penguin division, for example, the imprints communicate to a central person in that division what number they want to bid. And that person, as long as there are multiple imprints, that person manages the communications of those bids which are sometimes the same and sometimes different to the agent.
Q. So just so I'm clear, I am only focusing now on a situation where there are multiple imprints in one division and one division only, right?
A. Yes.
Q. And let's say three editors from different imprints are approached. They fill out three P&Ls?
A. Yes.
Q. And let's say they had three different numbers. Would all three numbers be communicated to the agent?
A. It depends on the auction structure. If it is a rounds auction, then normally what would happen is there would be a Penguin group, Penguin Publishing group, number submitted on behalf of imprint A, B, and C. And then as those rounds progress, it could be that imprint C decides just to hold, that they are not going to progress to a higher bid, they want to keep their number active and aware, you know, to the agent, but that the other two are going to continue to progress. If it turns out that there's only one Penguin imprint that is still in the auction, then that imprint communicates directly with the agent on their own.
Q. We are talking about an auction now, right?
A. In this case we are talking about a rounds auction, yes.
Q. Let's stick with that. It's a round auction, and we have three different bids coming from the same division. This person who communicates to the agent, does the person communicate all three numbers or just one number?
A. They could do either. If it's a rounds auction, usually they would communicate just one number. But I was trying to point out that if imprint C, for example, doesn't want to pay as much but still wants to be considered, then they might be communicating those different numbers to the agent at the same time.
Q. What happens if the author, for whatever—
THE COURT: I'm sorry. Then Penguin would have two numbers in the auction?
THE WITNESS: In that case, yes, that's correct.
BY MR. PETROCELLI:
Q. What would happen then if the author said, hey, I want to stick with imprint A, but C in the same division offered the highest number?
A. Uh-huh.

Q. Can the author then get the highest number but with the preferred imprint?

A. It's up to each of the imprints to decide if they are willing to go up to that higher number. And imprints have different feelings about their appetite for different acquisitions. There could be an imprint that might think that higher number is just too much to pay, so they might say I would love to publish you, but I am only going to go to this number.

Q. So you can't force the issue, right?

A. No.

THE COURT: I'm sorry, so do they each have a budget? Why would they not just pay the higher one since ultimately it's coming from the same place?

THE WITNESS: Because they don't have individual acquisition budgets. We don't have acquisition budgets in that way. But they might just feel that advance is too high for—they might have different sales expectations, for example. They might think that, if we pay that much, that's putting too much risk on this—maybe it's a debut novel—we are putting too much risk on this author's debut. I think there's a risk that we could end up in an unhappy situation if we don't sell enough copies. So, they might think there's too much heat in that advance number.

BY MR. PETROCELLI:

Q. Does the editor get compensated in part based on how he or she did with the sale of a book relative to the advance?

A. No. No. Our compensation structure is there's a base salary and then there's a bonus. And the bonus is, for bonus-eligible employees, is calculated on the same basis for everyone in the company. Certainly if an editor has a repeated track record of big, successful books that are very profitable for the company, then I would expect that editor would bring that up at the time of their salary negotiation. But there's no direct tie between a book's performance and that editor's compensation.

Q. Is there a post mortem done on each and every book acquisition whereby at some point in time after the book has been on sale for a while and you can see how it performed, you go back, or someone goes back, and compares it to the P&L and gives it a grade of some sort, says, well, you really paid too much for this or you paid too little? Is there any kind of post-mortem like that that's done on a regular systematic basis?

A. Post-mortems can be run anytime. And it is a fairly routine thing to run a post-mortem. It would be a post-mortem P&L. I don't think the business manager who is running it would necessarily be comparing it to the time of acquisition. They would be doing an actual P&L based on the actual cost and revenue of that book. And different groups within the company do this in different schedules. There's no set time of year when everybody has to run their post-mortem P&Ls.

Q. Is there a system in place whereby an actual P&L is rendered at some point after the sale and then compared to the original estimate or guess in the acquisition P&L?

A. There's no systematic approach to that. I think if you run a post-mortem P&L and it's showing very negative results, then my prediction would be that person would go back and say, well, where were we wrong, at the time of acquisition, what did we get wrong, because we are always trying to learn as we go forward. But there's no—these are tools that are readily available, and different parts of the company are going to use them in different ways.

Q. Do you require and receive regular post-mortem reports of comparisons back to the original P&Ls?

A. No, I don't.

Q. So sticking with the internal bidding, it is the case that imprints can bid against other imprints in other divisions without going through this house bid procedure?

A. Agreed, yes.

Q. Okay. Now, is there a system in place at the company whereby whenever any editor receives a submission, that editor lets everyone else know that he or she has received the submission?

A. No.

Q. Is there a system in place whereby whenever an editor actually wants to make a bid for a book, that editor contacts the editors or someone in the other imprints throughout the company to give notification?

A. No. The editor would, if they want to bid on a book, they would communicate with their publisher and possibly their division head depending on the level. And it would be a common thing then for there to be some degree of communication within the division so that they know that this many of us within this division are interested in the book. But there's—to answer your question, there's no system or systematic approach or process that triggers them to communicate with the other divisions about that.

Q. How long has this internal bidding been going on?

A. At Random House, which is the part of the company I came from, it's gone on for as long as I have been aware of bidding. It's a longstanding practice within Random House.

Q. And then when the Penguin company merged with Random House, was Penguin then allowed as a publishing group to compete against the other divisions?

A. Yeah, they adopted what had been the Random House approach.

Q. Okay. Now, why do you do this given that you might have different editors in different divisions bidding up a book and causing the company to pay more?

A. While that could happen, the value in having these very diversified opinions expressed about the value of a book is—I think it increases our chance of getting it right. As I have been pointing out, because books are not a commodity, there's a variable way to come to a perspective on the value of the product. So it is important to me as the person running the company to know that we are bringing to bear the whole kind of intellectual framework of the company in making their own decisions about whether they think a book is worth working on and to what degree they are willing to stake their claim to it.

Q. Do you think it helps the company win more books?

A. I think so.

Q. Why do you have the external bidder rule?

A. Why do we have the external bidder rule?

Q. Yeah. In other words, why don't you just let them bid against each other without regard to whether there's an external bidder left? And I guess we are talking about an auction now, right?

A. Yeah. I mean, we have had that rule for such a long time, my understanding of it in principle is that once there are only Penguin Random House imprints left in the auction, then the idea of the fact is that Penguin Random House has won that auction and it is left then for the author and the agent to—they can ask the different Penguin Random House parties to come up to the highest bid if they want to. Those parties are going to decide, as I said, whether they want to, but if there are only Penguin Random House parties left in the auction, then we have already won the auction, and then it's, as I said, up to the author to pick which imprint they want to work with.

Q. Now, does it turn out that in spite of these policies that you have, that sometimes imprints communicate or coordinate with one another with respect to an auction?

A. It doesn't happen a lot, but it does sometimes happen.

Q. Okay. And was there some particular event or point in time when you actually encouraged that there be some level of communication or coordination?

A. It doesn't usually happen that I would be encouraging it; although, that sometimes has happened. A division could be looking for information from the other divisions as a way to gather more market data. Maybe the other divisions know something that could be helpful in their own valuation of the book. And there could be other circumstances in which it happens, but I can't underline enough the degree to which these imprints and divisions are very competitive with each other. So I think the best way to describe the dynamic is that an imprint who is interested in winning the book is looking for information and is interested in getting information, but they are not necessarily interested in divulging information to others, whether those—certainly not out-of-house competitors, but also the people they see as intense internal competitors.

Q. Isn't there a person in your company who, as part of her responsibilities, helps to coordinate or communicate among imprints?

A. There's one of my colleagues, Nina Von Moltke, you may be thinking of. She's our president of strategic development. And she acts as a right hand for me in all sorts of—or backup for me in all sorts of different situations. And when I started in this role in 2018, because I was particularly concerned that I imagined I would be very busy and pressed in different directions and I didn't want publishers ever to have to wait for me if they had questions about their approach to a bid, and so I encouraged them to work with Nina the same way they would work with me.

Q. There are emails and other evidence indicating that, from time to time, Ms. Von Moltke coordinates, with your knowledge, various imprints in connection with an auction. Are you aware of that?

A. I am.

Q. Why does that happen?

A. In some cases it's really about strategizing around their first bid in an auction. If you have an appetite to buy a book, the agent has said there are going to be multiple round best bids, there's going to be elimination bids, then Nina might help the division head or heads to figure out, how do we optimize the chances that we stay in this auction and not just, you know, spend all of our money in the first round. So that's one kind of competitive strategy situation.

Q. Before you go on to the next one, are you saying that in that situation, it might be suggested that a lower opening number be offered?

A. It might be suggested that you not spend your total. If you have asked for a million and a half as approval and I have given the approval, it might be suggested that you not make your opening bid too high a number, in which case you are going to probably not make it beyond that, that your ultimate number is going to have to be higher than what you've already been approved to.

Q. In what other circumstances might this communication or coordination occur?

A. It would certainly come up and, frankly, should come up if an agent approaches one of our publishers about a house author, somebody we are already publishing. We have no policy against authors moving from one imprint to another, and it absolutely does happen. I've facilitated it happening in the past to help make the author happy, but it shouldn't happen kind of behind the back of the first publisher. So if an agent comes to you and says I am offering this author that used to be published by this other part of your company, in those cases, I think the division heads should be checking with each other to make sure that the option really has been exercised and to see if there are any other extenuating circumstances we should be aware of.

Q. Is it the case though that in certain circumstances, as a result of a level of communication or coordination, the company might win a book at a lower level than had there been no coordination or communication?

A. I don't think so. I think in the patterns that I have seen, certainly in the time I have been in this role, the patterns that I have seen is that the more you know about internal bids—you don't go to the lowest common denominator. You go to the highest common denominator.

So, if you know that one of your internal competitors is willing to spend more than what you had originally had in mind, then you are likely to increase the number that you are asking for approval on. And that happens regularly.

Q. Did you not take the position with the company after you were on the job for about a year, the CEO job, that you now have more open communications during competitive auctions than you've had in the past and a more PRH-wide approach to problem solving?

A. Certainly my general belief and what I tried to instill when I came in as the CEO is that the publishing divisions had a long history in some cases of really using quite sharp elbows against each other and that I thought it was important for our company culture going forward that my board, the publishers who report to me, the publishing division heads, that they compete to achieve the best results for their division but also to acknowledge that we are one company and that we are all working together to achieve the best results for the company. And so, whereas in the past, I think they had never really looked to each other to share expertise. In the years since, I think they have developed more of a practice of—and I am really talking about the very top level of the company, these are the people who report directly to me—that they have developed much more of a habit of helping each other on any number of strategic issues. And this does relate to consultations from time to time on acquisitions.

Q. Did you also at some point take the position with the company that increased background coordination in auctions to leverage internal demand information has been better in avoiding internal upbidding?

A. I think what you are referring to is the feeling that we had in 2018. This is again at the beginning of my time as CEO where we had had—we were all feeling a little bruised from some acquisition experiences in what was then the more recent past where we felt a little overly manipulated by an agent in an acquisition or two and that it turned out all of the demand that the agent had was within Penguin Random House and that we had significantly paid more than we really should have paid for a couple of acquisitions. And the feeling at the time was that if we talk to each other a little bit more, maybe we could avoid those embarrassing, costly, unprofitable missteps. I should say that, in practice, my experience has been that even with the top level of the company working together more collaboratively and even with those occasional consultations, I think it has not translated to any kind of lowering impact on the advances that we have paid. In fact, the opposite.

Q. Okay. The final topic I wanted to address with you is the period of time after the 2013 Penguin Random House merger. Did you observe any impact on, first of all, title reductions?

A. The Penguin genre fiction titles were—title count was certainly impacted a couple of years after the merger. It was not because of the merger.

Q. And how were they impacted?

A. I decreased them.

Q. Why did you do that?

A. Because Penguin had been particularly strong in commercial fiction. About more than 60 percent of our sales at that point had been in commercial fiction and in particular in the genre fiction space, so this is romances, mysteries, and science fiction, but particularly romances.

And many of these books were published in mass market, which is the small format paperback. That format was significantly being disrupted by a combination of the growth of ebooks which had big impact in those categories, the consolidation amongst the mass merch retailers and wholesalers, and also authors deciding that, in those categories, that they would prefer to be self-published. So, all of these things combined were translating to Penguin had kind of been trying to muscle their way through the fact that there were market changes and not take them into account. But the fact was that, when I—based on my measurement—I found that we were acquiring hundreds of books for very little advance. We were investing no marketing money to support them. We were putting covers on them that were very, very old-fashioned, kind of make good cowboys, et cetera, and that while we were printing these and in some cases shipping a couple of hundred, we were getting most of them back. So it was my determination that, while I would be happy to keep publishing those books, I couldn't keep publishing them if there was no one who wanted to buy them.

Q. So you made a decision to curtail them?

A. So I made the decision with the team to significantly curtail that approach to publishing, and we regrouped. We reassessed how we could publish particularly in the romance category. And over a couple of years, and it did take a couple of years, but over the course of a couple of years, we repositioned in particular Berkeley as being a home to much more contemporary-feeling, you know, romance stories, happily ever afters but where the characters are people like me and my neighbors or you and your neighbors, that they are contemporary in feel with much more fashion-forward covers often in the trade paperback format. And we have been steadily increasing the title counts since then.

Q. On that subject, could you take a look at defendants' demonstrative 12. And can you explain to the court what this is?

A. This is illustrating what I was just describing where the bottom row is showing selections from our current Berkeley list of trade paperbacks, and the upper row is showing what typical books looked like in this category prior to our change.

Q. And as a result of this change, have you seen any shift in results for these sorts of books?

A Yes. Happily, Berkeley has really become very successful at this combination of—they invest more per book. They pay higher advances. They actually work to support the authors in the market. And these covers, I think any layman would notice, are more aligned with kind of what might appeal to current consumers. And the sales and profit results have been fantastic.

Q. And after the Penguin Random House merger, did you observe any impact on advances paid by your company?

A. Yes. They went up.

Q. Okay. If you were to take the average of advances in the ensuing years, would there be any variability year to year?

A. Yes. Of course there is variability particularly—variability can be caused by the highest level advances that we pay. There are some of our highest paid authors. We don't negotiate a new contract every year. We could have a contract that has many years -worth of books on a single contract. And so depending on the year in which that contract is established, that could impact our average. Our averages can also, of course, be impacted if we lose a franchise author. I have already described a couple who we lost to our competitors or in a happier circumstance when we woo away from a competitor a new franchise author and make an investment in them.

Q. I would like you to take a look at defendants' demonstrative 13. There's a public version of this that's anonymized.

MR. PETROCELLI: And then Your Honor has a–

THE COURT: Okay. Thank you.

MR. PETROCELLI:—a version that is not anonymized.

BY MR. PETROCELLI:

Q. With respect to these numbers, first of all, what are these numbers?

A. These are a selection of our highest paid authors. It's not all of our highest paid authors, but it's showing certainly authors in whom we have some of our very biggest investments.

And this is showing the contract from these authors that were put in place in each of these years.

Q. Were you involved in these deals?

A. Not every single deal, but certainly I have been involved to some extent in all of them.

Q. And so do these deals, like author A from 2010, $40.3 million; author B, $27 million, is that for one book or multiple books?

A. In both of those cases, those are for multiple books, I believe.

Q. 2011, $8.5 million, $18.8 for the same two authors, multiple or single books?

A. I think that in the 2011, author A, that might be a single book. And author B, I believe that is multiple books.

Q. Just to get these into the record, in 2012, we have author A, $35.5 million; author B, $14.5 million; author C, $17.3 million; and author F, $12.5 million?

A. Yes.

Q. These are multiple book deals?

A. Some of them may be single book deals, but I believe they are generally multibook deals.

Q. Okay.

MR. PETROCELLI: Your Honor, rather than to say all this, I would just ask that the numbers be reflected from the demonstrative.

THE COURT: That's fine.

MR. PETROCELLI: Okay.

BY MR. PETROCELLI:

Q. You will see that in some years, there are fewer big contracts than in other years, right?

A. Yes.

Q. Okay.

THE COURT: And just to give me a sense, how much are you paying in total for author advances generally each year?

THE WITNESS: I want to say it's a hundred million dollars, but I could also have that number wrong. That's a number that just jumped to mind for me. It might be $200 million. I'm sorry.

THE COURT: Is it 200?

THE WITNESS: I, again, don't want to say the wrong number, but—can we get back to you with the accurate number?

MR. PETROCELLI: Your Honor, I actually didn't hear the question. What was it?

THE COURT: How much is she paying in total author advances in each year so I can get a sense of what percentage of the total are these.

THE WITNESS: And I just don't want to say the wrong number.

BY MR. PETROCELLI:

Q. 2016, is that the year that you lost one of the well-known authors Nora Roberts?

A. Yes, 2016.

Q. 2016. Okay. One last document, and that's Defendants Exhibit 22. It's an email thread with an analysis. Can you briefly describe to the court what this is.

A. Yes. I had been invited by The Authors Guild to participate in a panel. The topic of the panel was—and this is in 2018. The topic of the panel was author compensation. And so, I was getting prepared for that panel.

Q. Now, this was back in 2018, right?

A. Yes.

Q. Now, The Authors Guild was putting this together?

A. Yes.

Q. And did The Authors Guild express a concern to the industry about author compensation?

A. Yes.

Q. What was the expressed concern?

A. They expressed a concern that author compensation was going down.

Q. And by author compensation going down, was The Guild referring to just advances or total compensation?

A. They were referring to total compensation.

Q. Okay. And then you were asked to speak at a panel to address that issue?

A. Yes.

Q. And then you had this report prepared?

A. Yes.

MR. PETROCELLI: Your Honor, I would ask that Defendants' 22 be admitted into evidence.

THE COURT: Any objection?

MS. CROSS: No, Your Honor.

THE COURT: That will be admitted. (Defendant's 22 received in evidence.)

BY MR. PETROCELLI:

Q. Turning to the graph or the chart, can you explain to the court what the first line is referring to?

A. The first section, the first graph?

Q. Yes. There are four bullets there, right?

A. Yes, there are four bullets. So as the comment says to the right of the graph, this is showing that over these four years, the overall annual new advance commitments was up since 2015.

Q. And by the way, is this just Penguin Random House?

A. Yes.

Q. Okay.

THE COURT: So, this shows the total amounts you are paying in advances?

THE WITNESS: This does, yes.

BY MR. PETROCELLI:

Q. And the years were 2015 to 2018?

A. Yes. Sorry, it's a little fuzzy on the screen, but yes.

Q. Okay. And then if you could go to the next bullet, what is that about?

A. The next is showing that—so in all of the rest of these, the data—the person preparing the data is trying to understand are there variations by type of book or size of book. And I should point out also here that the headline of the graph points out that there's one author contract that's been excluded from the data. But this is showing that the higher annual advance commitments is driven by higher advance levels primarily on the adult publishing side.

Q. By the way, is this all trade books or is this fiction or just—

A. This is all Penguin Random House books.
Q. Okay. And the third bullet?
A. The third is showing that the higher advance level was not just being driven by the biggest deals, that the median advance was also up on the adult side, whereas, as you can see there on the children's side, it had remained steady.
Q. And the final bullet?
A. It showed that, compared to 2015, that after 2015, there was a slight dip in the number of new contracts and works that had been negotiated for, but that the numbers were up from 2016 through 2018.
Q. Since the time that The Authors Guild expressed that concern, has The Guild continued to express concerns about author compensation?
A. Yes.
Q. And have you had any further occasions to respond?
A. Yes. I have responded, as I did then, by sharing what the Penguin Random House advance in royalty development has been. And they have acknowledged to me or I have understood that because they are looking at total compensation, they are also concerned about some sources of author compensation that have nothing to do with publishing, so, for example, magazine contracts or other kinds of teaching gigs that authors could use to earn money.
MR. PETROCELLI: Your Honor, I pass the witness.
THE COURT: Okay. Thank you.
MS. CROSS: Good afternoon, Your Honor. Anna Cross for the United States.
THE COURT: Yes. Good afternoon.
MS. CROSS: Is it all right if we pass up some binders?
THE COURT: Yes.
MS. CROSS: Your Honor, before we get started, the exhibits I will be introducing do have redacted versions, so if we could turn on the public screen which I don't think has been on so far.
THE COURT: Okay.

CROSS-EXAMINATION

BY MS. CROSS:

Q. Good afternoon, Ms. McIntosh.
A. Good afternoon.
Q. I would like to begin by talking about some of Penguin Random House's strengths. One of Penguin Random House's strengths is that it has the largest sales force in the industry, is that right?
A. In my opinion, that's one of our strengths, yes.
Q. And you believe that agents care about a publisher having a strong network of sales representatives, right?
A. I believe so, yes.
Q. You view having a large sales force as a competitive advantage for Penguin Random House in discussions with agents, right?
A. I do.
Q. And you sometimes get involved in trying to acquire books at your approval level or above, is that right?
A. I do sometimes, yes.
Q. Okay. Could you please turn to PX218 in your binder. This is an email you wrote in November 2021 to an agent, is that right?
A. Yes.
MS. CROSS: Your Honor, I move to admit PX218. THE COURT: Any objection?
MR. PETROCELLI: No.
THE COURT: That will be admitted. (Plaintiff's 218 received in evidence.)
MS. CROSS: Let's publish a redacted version, please.

BY MS. CROSS:

Q. You were writing here to the agent with an improved offer for a book PRH was trying to acquire, right?

A. Yes.

Q. I would like to focus on the fourth paragraph. You wrote, I know you're already aware of these advantages from your work with us on other projects, but simply for emphasis, with Penguin Random House, the author's name is redacted, would have the support of the largest and smartest and best resource sales force in the industry, the most robust supply chain, and a state-of-the-art consumer marketing operation. You went on to write, we have direct relationships with more book sellers than anyone. We have direct relationships with more consumers than any other publisher. And in my humble opinion, we have the most brilliant editors and creative marketing teams. You were summarizing PRH's advantages to an agent there, is that right?

A. That's right.

MS. CROSS: And could we go to the third and last page of the same exhibit, please.

BY MS. CROSS:

Q. You attached to your email to the agent a Penguin Random House advantage document, right?

A. Yes.

Q. And in the top left corner, you identified Penguin Random House as the number one global publisher?

A. Yes.

Q. On the right-hand side, you identified it as having 500-plus *New York Times* best sellers per year, is that right?

A. Yes.

MS. CROSS: We can take that exhibit down.

BY MS. CROSS:

Q. I would like to turn to the role of the backlist for Penguin Random House. PRH had the largest backlist in the industry, is that right?

A. I believe so, yes.

Q. And it's fair to say that backlist is valuable to PRH, right?

A. It is valuable to PRH, yes.

Q. PRH's backlist accounts for the majority of its revenue?

A. Yes.

Q. You would agree with me that buying new books is a very risky enterprise, right?

A. There's definitely risk with new book purchases, yes.

Q. Having a backlist allows PRH to take risks on new acquisitions, right?

A. Having all of our revenue, which is inclusive of backlist and frontlist, is what allows us to invest in new books, yes.

Q. Okay. The fact that PRH has the largest and richest backlist in the industry is what gives it latitude to take risks with new acquisitions every day, right?

A. That is how we work. That is how we make our investments, yes.

Q. You testified in response to Mr. Petrocelli's questions about your involvement in the Penguin Random House merger, is that right?

A. Yes.

Q. After the 2013 Penguin Random House merger, PRH market share declined, right?

A. Yes. I believe our market share has declined almost every year.

Q. Part of the reason for PRH market share loss was that editors were not aggressive enough in their bidding for new acquisitions, right?

A. I don't know if that's the reason, but it's one of the possible reasons.

Q. All right. In your opinion, the conservatism of editors being too focused on the bottom line was part of the reason for the loss of market share, right?

A. I think a way for us to grow market share is to make sure we are being aggressive in acquisitions.

Q. And so just so I'm clear, the conservatism of editors in focusing on the bottom line contributed to the loss of market share, is that right?
A. Is there a particular time frame you are referring to?
Q. After the 2013 merger.
A. So any time from 2013 to 2022 has it.
Q. Let's take it to about 2018. I think you've testified that there has been a change in what you have told editors, but was there a time when editors were not being aggressive enough in seeking new acquisitions?
A. I don't think I would say they weren't aggressive enough. I think our editors are very good at taking acquisitions, and I don't want to make it sound like I'm criticizing them. I think that they were becoming concerned or were concerned about the bottom line more than I wanted them to be. And I encouraged them to, as I have already described, to focus more just on the variable cost of this publication and leave the overhead concerns to the managers.
Q. I would like to turn to your role in acquisitions. As you testified before lunch, you have to approve offers to acquire books with an advance of a million dollars or more, is that right?
A. Yes.
Q. And you are rarely involved in acquisitions below that level, is that right?
A. It's certainly on an ad hoc basis below that level.
Q. Is it fair to say that you are only rarely involved in acquisitions below one million dollars?
A. I would say much less frequently than on acquisitions above a million dollars.
Q. Okay. Is it fair to say you are rarely involved in those?
A. I think that's fair to say.
Q. Okay. When you are involved in book acquisitions, Penguin Random House most frequently competes with HarperCollins, Simon & Schuster, Hachette, and Macmillan, is that right?
A. Yes, I believe that's the case.
Q. You don't have any statistics about how frequently Penguin Random House competes against others for an advance of a million dollars or less, do you?
A. I don't have any statistics like that at any level.
Q. And you testified about what you characterized as the declining frequency of round robin auctions. You haven't done anything to track the frequency of auction formats in the industry, have you?
A. No, I have not.
Q. Could you please turn to PX190 in your binder. This is an email chain from April 6, 2021 involving you and others at Penguin Random House, is that right?
A. Yes.
MS. CROSS: Your Honor, I move to admit PX190. THE COURT: Any objection?
MR. PETROCELLI: No.
THE COURT: That will be admitted. (Plaintiff's 190 received in evidence.)
MS. CROSS: Could we publish the redacted version, please.
BY MS. CROSS:
Q. I would like to focus your attention on the second email from the top from Aaron Wehner. Is that the right pronunciation of his name?
A. Yes.
Q. Mr. Wehner is the publisher of Clarkson Potter and Ten Speed Press, is that right?
A. Yes.
Q. Those are within the Random House division, right?
A. Yes. They are our cookbook publishers within PRH.
Q. Let's look at the first paragraph. In the third line, Mr. Wehner wrote, many of our competitors pay in thirds or sometimes even halves, and some cover photo budgets out of plant costs as well. That said, a Chronicle or an HMH or Artisan doesn't bring nearly as much to the table as we do beyond better payout, which all the major agents recognize. Did I read that correctly?
A. Yes.
Q. And then I would like to take you to the fifth paragraph where Mr. Wehner wrote, for higher level

advances, the payout difference tends to be much less of an issue. The smaller publishers tend not to compete. The first two payments are much larger, et cetera. Did I read that correctly?
A. Yes.
Q. You responded to Mr. Wehner, is that right?
A. I did.
Q. Let's go to the top email. You wrote to him, okay. Thanks. This is really helpful. I will hear her out and report back. Is that right?
A. Yes.
Q. Could you please turn to PX438 in your binder. And there is a decoder sheet at the front of your binder should we need it. We won't be saying the name of the author or the book here.
A. Okay.
Q. And the redacted version on the screen can guide us once it's up. PX438 is an email chain from February 2019 that includes you in parts of it, is that right?
A Yes.
MS. CROSS: Your Honor, I move to admit PX438.
THE COURT: Any objection?
MR. PETROCELLI: No.
THE COURT: 438 will be admitted. (Plaintiff's 438 received in evidence.)
MS. CROSS: Let's publish the redacted version, please.
BY MS. CROSS:
Q. This email chain is about a request from Tony Chirico to you for guidance on bidding on a book, is that right?
A. Yes.
Q. Mr. Chirico at this time was the publisher at Knopf Doubleday Publishing Group?
A. Yes.
Q. I would like to focus your attention on Mr. Chirico's. February 23 email at 8:11, please. He wrote there, and it's at the bottom of our screen, if we are going to coordinate payout and royalties, we will need that early Monday. I don't know how many bidders there will be. Did I read that correctly?
A. Yes.
Q. And you responded to Mr. Chirico in the top email, right?
A. Yes.
Q. You wrote, I'm guessing besides us, it's Ecco and maybe Little, Brown. If at a lower level, I'd think of Norton, but it's hard to picture them playing at this level. Did I read that correctly?
A. You did.
Q. And Ecco is an imprint of HarperCollins, is that right?
A. Yes.
Q. Little, Brown is an imprint of Hachette?
A. Yes.
Q. You found it hard to picture Norton bidding at the advance level discussed in this email, is that right?
A. Certainly for a cookbook, it seemed unlikely to me.
Q. Please turn to tab PX176 in your binder. This is an email chain involving you and several other Penguin Random House employees, the date on the top email being September 11, 2020, is that right?
A. Yes.
MS. CROSS: Your Honor, I move to admit PX174.
THE COURT: Any objection?
MR. PETROCELLI: No.
THE COURT: That will be admitted. (Plaintiff's 174 received in evidence.)
MS. CROSS: If we can publish the redacted version, please.
THE COURT: Yes.
BY MR. PETROCELLI:
Q. Turn to the bottom email on the page, August 6, 2020 at 8:47 a.m. That's an email from you. And

based on the context of the email above, you were writing to Reid Welsh, Nina Von Moltke, and Jackie Updike, is that right?

A. Yes.

Q. You testified earlier about Ms. Von Moltke. She's the president and director of strategic development for Penguin Random House U.S., right?

A. Yes.

Q. And Reid Welsh is a sales analyst at PRH who reports to Jackie Updike?

A. Yes.

Q. At the top of the email, you can see the titles of two attachments to this email. Do you see those?

A. Yes.

Q. I would like to turn to the second one, the title of which is draft 2020 U.S. marketplace update, fiction analysis, part 2. And it's the number, the Bates number, in the bottom—the top right in our binders that ends in 2021. Actually, let's start at 2020 just to get the titles right.

A. Okay.

Q. The title of this slide prepared by Mr. Welsh is marketplace update U.S. physical marketplace, fiction, part 2, and it's dated August 2020, is that right?

A. Yes.

Q. Let's go to the next page, please. The introductory slide identifies two goals; one, revisit historical market landscape for fiction; two, discuss current year-to-date performance. Do you see that?

A. I do.

Q. This slide also discusses definitions that are used in the analysis in the bottom portion including a definition of top author. Do you see that?

A. Yes.

Q. The definition of top author is an author that sells more than 500K units in a single year, 2015 to 2019. Do you see that?

A. I do.

Q. And so that's referring to titles that sold 500,000 copies in a single year in that time frame between 2015 to 2019, is that correct?

A. Yes.

Q. And that's a category of books that Mr. Welsh analyzed in this presentation, right?

A. Yes.

MS. CROSS: Let's look at slide 2056, please. That's page 99.

BY MS. CROSS:

Q. And the title of this slide is, top versus non-top authors YTD performance. That's year-to-date performance, right?

A. Yes.

Q. Let's go to the next slide ending in 057. The title of this slide is marketplace print overall fiction top authors. Do you see that?

A. I do.

Q. I want to focus on the graphs on the right-hand side of the page under the heading, retail dollars market share. The top half of that has the PRH divisions broken out. Do you see that?

A. I do.

Q. And so it has Knopf Doubleday, Penguin Publishing Group, Random House Publishing Group, and the other divisions as other. Do you see that?

A. I do.

Q. Mr. Welsh here totaled up the PRH market share for these top authors with the numbers right under PRH. Do you see those?

A. Yes.

Q. Those range 42.2 percent to 44.1 percent for those three years?

A. Yes. I'm sorry, yes, that's correct.

Q. And the non-PRH market share for top authors is underneath. Do you see that?

A. I do.
Q. Okay. And the market shares form Hachette, HarperCollins, Macmillan, and S&S are broken out. Do you see that?
A. I do.
Q. And underneath those are all others. Is it your understanding that that is all the non-Big 5 publishers' market share for top authors?
A. Yes.
Q. And for 2018 to 2020, the non-Big 5 market share for top authors ranges from 5.2 to 6.3 percent, is that right?
A. Yes.
Q. And if you look at one column, so 2020, for example, the numbers for PRH and non-PRH add up to 100 percent, right?
A. Yes.
MS. CROSS: Let's turn to the slide ending in 060, please.
BY MS. CROSS:
Q. The title of this slide is, marketplace print overall fiction non-top authors. Do you see that?
A. Yes.
Q. And I want to turn to the graphs that mirror the ones we just looked at. On the right-hand side, you see retail dollars. The PRH market share is identified as being between 31 and 31.7 percent for those three years, is that right?
A. Yes.
Q. And for non-PRH, and specifically the non-Big 5 publishers, it's between 26.6 and 27.6 percent for non-top authors, is that right?
A. Yes.
MS. CROSS: And could we put the two graphs side by side now for pages 058 and 060, please.
BY MS. CROSS:
Q. I would specifically like to compare the figures for the non-Big 5 in terms of market share for top authors which range between 5.2 percent and 6.3 percent and then for non-top authors which range from 26 percent to 27.6 percent. Do you see that?
A. I do.
Q. Based on this presentation, the non-Big 5 have significantly less market share for top authors than for non-top authors, is that fair?
A. Yes.
MS. CROSS: You can take that down.
BY MS. CROSS:
Q. You review best seller lists, is that right?
A. I do.
Q. And PRH performs well on best seller lists, right?
A. It varies quite a bit week to week.
Q. PRH performs better at the top of the best seller lists than it does for books overall, right?
A. I believe that we do better at the top of the list than we do over the long tail, yes.
Q. Let's turn to coordination. Mr. Petrocelli asked you questions about house bids within a division, right?
A. Yes.
Q. And he also asked you about competition among divisions. Do you recall that?
A. Yes.
Q. I want to ask some questions about how the PRH adult divisions in particular interact with each other when several divisions are interested in acquiring a book during an auction. Do you understand that?
A. Yes, I do.
Q. The Penguin Random House divisions are allowed to communicate with each other during auctions, right?

A. They are allowed to, yes.
Q. In fact, you have encouraged communication among divisions at PRH during auctions to avoid internal upbidding, right?
A. I have encouraged the division heads to communicate with each other when they deem it appropriate.
Q. Could you turn to PX411, please. PX411 is a November 2, 2018 email from you to Mr. Dohle attaching a presentation for Penguin Random House shareholder board, is that right?
A. Yes.
MS. CROSS: Your Honor, I move to admit PX411.
THE COURT: Any objection?
MR. PETROCELLI: No.
THE COURT: That's admitted. (Plaintiff's 411 received in evidence.)
MS. CROSS: Publish a redacted version, and please turn to the second page, which is the presentation.
BY MS. CROSS:
Q. The title of the presentation is, Penguin Random House U.S. insights and outlook. Do you see that?
A. I do.
Q. You helped prepare the presentation?
A. Yes.
MS. CROSS: Let's turn to the slide that ends in 204, please.
BY MS. CROSS:
Q. And to set the stage, this is a presentation from November 2018, is that right?
A. Yes.
Q. And you had taken over as CEO in April 2018, is that right?
A. Yes.
Q. Okay. So the title of this slide is, what's happened since April. Is it fair to say this is a summary of things that had happened since you took over as CEO?
A. Yes.
Q. Okay. And let's look at the second item and go to the bottom bullet of it which reads, increased background coordination in auctions to leverage internal demand information better and avoid internal upbidding. You presented this information about leveraging internal demand information to the PRH shareholder board, is that right?
A. Yes.
Q. Internal upbidding refers to driving up the price through competition among PRH divisions?
A. Yes.
Q. That bullet was the result of your feeling that different PRH divisions had, through their competition against each other, driven up the advance of the book, right?
A. This is what I was describing before, that there were a couple of occasions where I felt that that had happened.
Q. Where the divisions had driven up the advance?
A. Yes.
Q. I think you testified on direct there are times where you are personally involved in coordinating bids from different PRH divisions at auctions, right?
A. Occasionally it has happened, yes.
Q. Where you are not available, Nina von Moltke is tasked with performing that role, is that fair?
A. Yes.
Q. And you want information shared across divisions that will help PRH win books, right?
A. I want us to do what we need to do to win books, yes.
Q. And the publishing heads do share information with Ms. Von Moltke about their bidding strategies, right?
A. Sometimes they do and—some of them do. Some of them do sometimes is a better way to answer.
Q. And, again, if we need the decoder at the front of your binder, you can pull that handy. Let's turn to PX107 in your binder, please. This is an email chain from June 10, 2020 involving you, Ms. Mavjee, and

Mr. Thomas and Ms. Von Moltke regarding bidding for a book that for confidentiality reasons I'll refer to as book 77. Is that all right?

A. Yes.

MS. CROSS: Your Honor, I move to admit PX107.

THE COURT: Any objection?

MR. PETROCELLI: No, Your Honor.

THE COURT: That will be admitted. (Plaintiff's 107 received in evidence.)

MS. CROSS: Publish the redacted version.

BY MS. CROSS:

Q. Mr. Mavjee and Mr. Thomas are both within the Knopf Doubleday Group, is that right?

A. Yes.

Q. In the fourth email from the top, at 2:12, Mr. Thomas sent you an acquisition P&L for book 77, is that right?

A. Yes.

Q. And in the third email from the top, at 2:18, you wrote, "hi. I feel we should coordinate. Shouldn't be forced into bidding against each other for existing authors. Nina is reaching out to RH." That's Random House, right?

A. Yes.

Q. You asked Ms. Von Moltke to reach out to Random House to coordinate the Doubleday and Random House bids here, is that right?

A. Yes.

Q. Let's look at the next email up the chain at 3:20, it's two emails up, from you at 3:20, you wrote, reached Gina. Gina is Gina Centrello, right?

A. Yes.

Q. She's the publisher of the Random House Publishing Group?

A. Yes.

Q. And you wrote, she's trying to reach Kara who, with Whitney, are the ones bidding. Agreed it should be the same number, whatever you guys decide the number should be. She will come back to you. Did I read that correctly?

A. Yes.

Q. So you and Ms. Centrello here agreed the same advance should be offered by the Knopf Doubleday group and Random House group, right?

A. For this house author, yes, for which we had an option, yes.

Q. In the top email, Ms. Mavjee wrote, we are coordinated. Bill and Kara will agree to a number, and both offer same. Thanks for pulling us together. Did I read that correctly?

A. Yes.

Q. And Knopf Doubleday and Random House here offered the same number for the book, right?

A. Yes, they agreed to a higher number.

Q. And PRH successfully acquired book 77, right?

A. Yes, for more than they had paid for the author's last book, I should note.

Q. Let's turn to Page 116, please. This is an email chain from October 2020 that includes emails to you about what to offer for several books in an auction, is that right?

A. Yes.

MS. CROSS: Your Honor, I move to admit PX116.

THE COURT: Any objection?

MR. PETROCELLI: No.

THE COURT: That will be admitted. (Plaintiff's 116 received in evidence.)

MS. CROSS: Could we publish it, please.

BY MS. CROSS:

Q. Let's look at the bottom email on the first page from Mr. Aykroyd, October 27, 7:28. At this time, Mr. Aykroyd was the director of business operations at Penguin Random House, is that right?

A. At the Knopf Doubleday Group.
Q. And Mr. Aykroyd was seeking approval from you to bid on two books, two cookbooks?
A. Yes.
Q. Mr. Aykroyd here copied Ms. Mavjee and Ms. LeCates, is that right?
A. Yes.
Q. And both of them are from the Knopf Doubleday Group, right?
A. Yes.
Q. In the second paragraph, Mr. Aykroyd wrote, we would like to lock up the author's next two cookbooks. The author's name is redacted. In a two-step best bid auction, we would likely go in at $600K per book, $1.2M total. We would like approval to offer as much as $750K dollars per book, 1.5M dollars total in the final round. Did I read that correctly?
A. Yes.
Q. And Mr. Aykroyd was asking you for approval to bid $1.5 million total for two books for Knopf Doubleday, is that right?
A. Yes.
Q. And he indicated he was planning to go in at $600,000 per book as an opening bid, right?
A. Yes.
MS. CROSS: Could we go up to the 9:07 email, please.
BY MS. CROSS:
Q. You approved Mr. Aykroyd's request there, right?
A. Yes.
MS. CROSS: Let's keep scrolling up to the 9:27 p.m. email from Ms. Von Moltke.
BY MS. CROSS:
Q. Ms. Von Moltke emailed you and asked whether to advise Knopf Doubleday to start their bidding lower in order to keep the final bid lower, right?
A. She—what her actual email says is that—to go in a bit lower in round one. I worry that if they go in at 600 each, it will go for more than 750 per book, which is what they were asking for.
Q. Okay. And in the next line, she wrote, TSP Potter were planning $350K per book in round one with the same upper threshold for approval. That's her telling you that other Random House imprints within the Random House group were bidding and were bidding lower, is that right?
A. They are asking for the same upper level, but in that first round, they were planning to bid lower.
Q. Okay. And so this email chain is about two separate divisions, Knopf Doubleday and Random House, competing for the same book and coordinating, is that right?
A. Yes.
Q. Let's look at your 9:58 email. 9:57, sorry. You wrote, it's a good point. Do you want to suggest it to Ms. Von Moltke. Right?
A. Yes.
Q. And she responded, sure, happy to. Right?
A. Yes.
Q. Okay. Let's look at another exhibit related to the same auction, PX121, please. This is an email chain from October 28 and 29, 2020 relating to the same books that we just looked at, right?
A. Yes.
MS. CROSS: Your Honor, I move to admit PX121.
THE COURT: Any objection?
MR. PETROCELLI: No. (Plaintiff's 121 received in evidence.)
THE WITNESS: I'm sorry, I want to make sure I'm looking at the correct—
MS. CROSS: You know what, I—
THE COURT: This appears to be a different book?
MS. CROSS: I can clarify, I think.
BY MS. CROSS:
Q. I will focus your attention to the second email from the top. I think two different acquisitions are

discussed in this email.

A. Okay.

Q. In Ms.Von Moltke's Thursday, October 29 email, in the second paragraph, that's the language we will look for—

MS. CROSS: Could we go ahead and publish the redacted version, please.

BY MS. CROSS:

Q. She wrote, on the other big auction today, title redacted, both RH and KDD want to go up to $1.6M plus bonuses in round two coordinated in this case $800K per book. This was a request to increase the approval from the first approval you had granted for these two cookbooks, right?

A. Yes.

Q. For both Random House and Knopf Doubleday?

A. Yes.

Q. And in the top email, you granted approval for them to increase their coordinated bids, right?

A. My understanding, yes. What happened is that Knopf was initially going to hold at 1.5, but when they learned that Random House was willing to go to 1.6, they increased their bid to 1.6 and I approved both of them going to 1.6.

Q. And they submitted a bid for the same amount?

A. Yes.

MS. CROSS: Let's turn to PX421, please.

BY MS. CROSS:

Q. This is an email chain from December 12, 2018 involving you and Ms. Von Moltke, and it concerns book 79, is that right?

A. Yes.

MS. CROSS: Your Honor, I move to admit PX421.

THE COURT: Any objection?

MR. PETROCELLI: No.

THE COURT: That's admitted. (Plaintiff's 421 received in evidence.)

MS. CROSS: Let's publish a redacted version, please.

BY MS. CROSS:

Q. I would like to look at the email from the agent at 3:57 on December 12. In his second paragraph, he wrote, we have three top offers at $600,000. They are all from Penguin Random House, so the bidding is done. Now, author's name redacted, has the very challenging job of deciding between six top editors. So there were three offers from Penguin Random House at the same amount, $600,000, is that right?

A. Yes. Apparently they were all the top offers.

Q. And that was one from each of the adult divisions at Penguin Random House, right?

A. I don't know that to be the case.

Q. At any rate, there were three bids at the same amount from different Penguin Random House bidders, and there were several house bids in there, right?

A. According to this email, yes.

Q. Okay. At 4:00 p.m., Casey Blue James forwarded the email from the agent to Nina von Moltke. Do you see that?

A. I do.

Q. At 5:49 the same day, she forwarded it to you and wrote, glad we didn't go higher. This one definitely benefited from the coordination. Did I read that right?

A. Yes.

Q. And you responded, I'll say. Thank you. Did I read that correctly?

A. Yes.

MS. CROSS: Let's turn to PX986, please.

BY MS. CROSS:

Q. PX986 is an email from Ms. Mavjee to you, is that right?

A. Yes.

Q. Mr. Petrocelli asked you about this document earlier today, is that right?

A. Yes.

MS. CROSS: I wanted to follow up on it, but first, Your Honor, I move to admit PX986.

THE COURT: Any objection?

MR. PETROCELLI: No.

THE COURT: That will be admitted. (Plaintiff's 986 received in evidence.)

MS. CROSS: Could we publish a redacted version, please.

BY MS. CROSS:

Q. I think you testified earlier, Ms. Mavjee had headed up Crown for a number of years, is that right?

A. Yes.

Q. And in 2020, she was forwarding you guidelines from Crown relating to marketing support to be given to certain titles, right?

A. As I described, it was a document from 2012 at Crown, yes.

Q. And she described it as follows: I know this is out of date, but it was useful as a guideline. Once everyone including editors understood the parameters for each category, it made the author care conversation more manageable. This was more to get us all on the same page. M. Did I read that correctly?

A. Yes.

Q. Okay. And I want to take a quick look at the categories that are in here. There are five categories. Category one on page 362 is lead titles identified as having a sales goal of 75,000 units or higher and/or advance over $500,000. Do you see that?

A. I do.

Q. Then on page 364, there are category two opportunity titles which are defined as having a sales goal of 25,000 to 75,000 units and/or advance of $150,000 to $500,000. Do you see that?

A. I do.

Q. On page 366, there's a category three with a sales goal of 10,000 to 25,000 units and/or advance of $50,000 to $150,000. Do you see that?

A. I do.

Q. And finally, category four is sales goal of 5,000 to 10,000 units and/or advance of $50,000 or less. Is that right?

A. Yes.

Q. And this time for real finally is category five, paperback conversions by a medium print run. Do you see that?

A. I do.

Q. I would like to compare the marketplace rollout offered for category one lead titles with the marketplace rollout offered for category four titles.

MS. CROSS: Could we pull up those be sections, please. Thank you.

BY MS. CROSS:

Q. For lead titles, the first bullet under marketplace rollout is, multi-city author tour where appropriate up to 15 markets. For category four, there's no multi-city author tour provided. Is that right?

A. That's correct in this document, yes.

Q. And the fourth bullet on the left-hand side for category one, social network and target search advertising, that service was not provided for category four books according to this document, is that right?

A. That's part of what seemed so out of sync to me, but, yes, I agree that that's what the document says.

Q. And there's a bullet—the fifth bullet is, publisher sponsored promotion at appropriate retail venues. That's not something provided according to this document for category four books, is that right?

A. Again, according to this document.

Q. Okay. And if you go down six lines or so on the category one side, it says, submit work for various national book awards as appropriate. That, again, is not something included for the category four titles, is that right?

A. According to this document, yes.
MS. CROSS: We can take that down.
BY MS. CROSS:
Q. In 2018—changing topics. And I think this is something you talked about on direct. In 2018, you decided to merge Crown and Random House, right?
A. Yes.
Q. And you oversaw the Crown integration into Random House in 2019?
A. Yes.
Q. Do you recall that Gina Centrello, the publisher of Random House, drafted an integration memo?
A. Yes.
MS. CROSS: Let's turn to PX241, please.
BY MS. CROSS:
Q. This is an email from January 18, 2019 from you to Mr. Dohle attaching the Crown integration memo, is that right?
A. Yes.
MS. CROSS: Your Honor, I move to admit PX241.
THE COURT: Any objection?
MR. PETROCELLI: No.
THE COURT: 241 is admitted. (Plaintiff's 241 received in evidence.)
MS. CROSS: Let's publish that and turn to the second page, please.
BY MS. CROSS:
Q. The second page is titled, Random House Crown integration memo. Do you see that?
A. Yes.
Q. And five lines from the top, Ms. Centrello wrote, we are focusing the editorial profiles of each group as follows. And she then described the new editorial profiles for Ballantine Bantom Del, Crown, and Random House. Do you see that?
A. I do.
Q. The memo describes the new focus areas for those groups. For Ballantine Bantam Dell, it's primarily commercial fiction, right?
A. Yes.
Q. For Crown, it's nonfiction, lifestyle, and Christian publishing?
A. Yes.
Q. And for Random House, it's literary fiction and narrative nonfiction, is that right?
A. Yes.
Q. You were reducing the overlap and focus among the three components of Random House, is that right?
A. I would describe it more accurately as about focusing the teams around what we consider them to be good at.
Q. On the second page in the sixth entry, it says, Random House and BBD will continue to do a house bid, and Crown would bid separately so the agents will not lose a bid. Of course, there will be less internal competition with the focused editorial profiles in our three divisions. Did I read that right?
A. You did.
Q. As part of the integration of Crown into Random House, you discontinued some imprints, right?
A. Yes.
Q. One of those was Spiegel & Grau?
A. Yes.
Q. And you described that discontinuation on the second page of the integration memo, the Spiegel & Grau imprint will be discontinued. We will publish out their books through 2019 as Spiegel & Grau titles contingent on their permission. All future titles will be reassigned to other divisions.
A. Yes.
Q. When you discontinued Spiegel & Grau, PRH kept its backlist, right?

A. Yes.
Q. And in connection with this Crown integration, Editor Molly Stern left PRH, is that right?
A. Yes.
Q. She ended up founding her own publishing company Zando, is that right?
A. Yes.
Q. And the backlist she had developed at Crown stayed with Penguin Random House?
A. Yes.
Q. Could you please go to PX68 in your binder. This is an email string from December 2019 with the subject, Writers House presentation. Do you see that?
A. I do.
MS. CROSS: Your Honor, I move to admit PX68.
THE COURT: Any objection?
MR. PETROCELLI: No objection.
THE COURT: That will be admitted. (Plaintiff's 68 received in evidence.)
BY MS. CROSS:
Q. Writers House is a large literary agency, is that right?
A. Yes.
Q. And you were preparing a presentation for Writers House describing PRH's capabilities here?
A. Yes.
MS. CROSS: There's a slide deck attached to present to Writers House if we could turn to the next page.
BY MS. CROSS:
Q. That's the title page for the presentation you made for Writers House, is that right?
A. Yes.
Q. I would like to turn to the agenda for the meeting, which is at 934. Do you see that? According to the agenda here, you discussed with Writers House how PRH creates demands, how it—demand, how it fulfills demand, its audio capabilities, and ancillary author services. Is that right?
A. Yes.
MS. CROSS: You can take that one down.
BY MS. CROSS:
Q. Mr. Petrocelli asked you about an Authors Guild advance data presentation. Do you recall that?
A. I'm sorry, an author what?
Q. An Authors Guild presentation you were preparing for. Do you recall that?
A. Authors Guild, yes. I'm sorry, I misheard.
Q. And that was DX22, is that right?
A. Sure.
Q. Go ahead and turn to it. Yes. Thank you.
A. Yes.
Q. And you testified about the new deals' advance commitments that are included as an attachment to that email, right?
A. Yes.
Q. Are you aware that this presentation got revised after this email was sent?
A. No, not—that's—I don't know if it was or not. Sorry.
Q. Would it refresh your recollection to see an email from this time period?
A. Yes.
MS. CROSS: Your Honor, may I approach?
THE COURT: Yes.
THE WITNESS: I'm sorry, do you have the revised version?
BY MS. CROSS:
Q. I don't.
A. Okay.

Q. You can put that away, and I will just repeat the question. Do you understand that the advance data was revised after December 9, 2018?

A. Certainly according to this email that I am reading right now.

MS. CROSS: No further questions at this point, Your Honor.

REDIRECT EXAMINATION

BY MR. PETROCELLI:

Q. Just briefly, you were shown Plaintiff's Exhibit 174. Do you have that handy? Turn to the page bearing Bates No. 2021. If you look at the binder the government gave you–

A. Yes.

Q.—Ms. McIntosh, it would be Exhibit 174. And actually, can you turn to—yeah, this is the page. It's on the screen.

Q. Okay. So with respect to this top author reference–

A. Yes.

Q.—500,000 units in a single year, first of all, this is all about the fiction category, right?

A. Yes.

Q. And these are—do you know approximately how many authors there are across the industry with 500,000 units or more during this four-year period?

A My understanding is that it was about 50.

Q. About 50 authors—

A. Yes

Q.—across the publishing industry who during this four-year period sold more than 500,000 units in a single year?

A. Yes.

Q. And in terms of Penguin Random House's group of authors, among the 50, would they include, for example, the authors identified on demonstrative 13, which is—

A. Demonstrative 13 is which one?

Q.—with the various authors and the large advances?

A. Absolutely.

MR. PETROCELLI: Your Honor, I neglected to identify and seek to admit DX433, which is the Rosetta for demonstrative 13.

THE COURT: Okay.

MR. PETROCELLI: I would also ask that demonstrative 13 be admitted in lieu of my having to read all the numbers into the record.

THE COURT: Yes. Those will be admitted under seal. (Defendant's 433 received in evidence.)

MR. PETROCELLI: Thank you, Your Honor.

BY MR. PETROCELLI:

Q. These top authors that are referenced in Plaintiff's Exhibit 174 for 500,000 units in a single year, what type of advance levels would that typically correspond to?

A. $5 million, $4 million, $5 million, $6 million, and more.

Q. Okay. Thank you.

MR. PETROCELLI: Nothing more, Your Honor.

THE COURT: All right. Thank you. I had a few questions for you, Ms. McIntosh. From your testimony, it seems to me that your industry is very much driven by expected sales of books. Do you think that's correct?

THE WITNESS: I would say we spend a lot of time trying to guess the expected sales of books. And the if you are asking is that something we can focus on, absolutely we focus on it, and we try to drive towards maximizing that number. Our actual outcomes, the profits, are driven by what we—not only what are those books that are selling and how many copies, but what have we paid for the books that are selling.

THE COURT: Yes. So, it seems to me, and correct me if I'm wrong, that starting from when you acquire the books, you are trying to project the expected sales of books, and then even after that, you are saying it's sort of an iterative process where you are reassessing based on new information what the expected sales of books will be?

THE WITNESS: Correct.

THE COURT: And then you determine what resources you will spend based on what the expected sales of books will be, but that could be different from your initial expectation. Your expectations could change, but it is always driven by the expected sales of books is what it sounds like to me.

THE WITNESS: It's the combination of the expected sales of books and the type of book. I would just add that nuance to it. If it's the type of book where in order to get those sales, we really need to establish the author for the first time, there could be essentially a disproportionately large amount of resources invested in that.

THE COURT: Okay. Thank you. And in your experience with auctions, how often do underbidders win the title?

THE WITNESS: I think usually the top bid wins, but certainly I hear of cases where the underbidder has won. I hear about that when it's one of our publishers. But I don't have any data to tell you how many times that happens.

THE COURT: Would you say that's rare?

THE WITNESS: I would say it's rare.

THE COURT: Okay. So, in terms of your market share, there's been evidence in this trial that HarperCollins is the second largest publisher, but there's also been testimony that if you take into account their Christian sales and that the Christian sales add to their market share, but they don't really compete with you on Christian sales. So, there's been testimony that if you take out their Christian sales, you are like three times their size on trade books. Do you have a sense of that?

THE WITNESS: I think they do compete with us on Christian sales. I think Harper is one of the main competitors that we have for Christian acquisitions and sales.

THE COURT: Except, I guess, the testimony is that you have so little of that compared to them.

THE WITNESS: Well, we have been working hard to increase that over time, so that's been a key area that we have been investing in.

THE COURT: So, if you take out Christian sales, do you think you're three times the size of HarperCollins on trade books?

THE WITNESS: I'm sorry, I don't know. I don't have that number on the top of my head.

THE COURT: Okay. In terms of advanced copies, how do you decide which books you have advanced copies for?

THE WITNESS: Yeah. For one thing, you don't need advanced copies for books that are not narrative books. So advanced copies are going to be primarily for books where we really want, whether it is sales reps or book sellers or media, to read the book ahead of time and to get excited. So those advanced copies could be digital, they could be print galleys which is kind of a cheaper produced version of a print book, or it could be actually advanced versions of the final book. So I would just describe them as narrative oriented books.

THE COURT: But you don't give advanced copies for all your narrative books, so how do you decide which ones?

THE WITNESS: Generally, I would say it probably concentrates more on books where support from bricks and mortar book sellers is important. So independent bookstores in particular want to read the books that they are going to be supporting. It is less likely to be books by established franchise authors because they're thought of as being a little bit more of a known proposition. But we are going to really focus the advanced copies. And it's not just about producing them, but it's about encouraging people to read them, so focusing their attention on the books where we really believe, even if you don't know this author, you just have to read this, you are going to fall in love. It's that kind of a feeling.

THE COURT: So, are those books that you expect will sell well?

THE WITNESS: They often are books that bubble up during those meetings that I was describing. The sales reps read everything in digital form, and they will make suggestions to us of, let's make sure we do physical galleys on this one. I really want us to do a big mailing on this one. I would say if there is a

category, it is fiction books that we are hoping are going to do well in independent bookstores.
THE COURT: Okay. But it is mostly based on the recommendations of your sales reps?
THE WITNESS: Yes.
THE COURT: Thank you. Any questions based on my questioning?
MR. PETROCELLI: No, Your Honor. Thank you.
THE COURT: Thank you so much for your testimony. You may step down.
THE WITNESS: Thank you.

MANUEL SANSIGRE, SENIOR VICE PRESIDENT OF M&A, PENGUIN RANDOM HOUSE

PRH SVP of M&A Manuel Sansigre gave interesting—but ultimately inadmissible—testimony on developing PRH's bid for S&S and their post-merger "efficiencies model" of anticipated savings and sales performance after the two companies are integrated.

When Viacom announced the sale of S&S in March 2020, Sansigre's team began creating an efficiency model—analyzing duplications between the two companies—(and continued even when the sale was on pause through the spring and summer due to COVID) with publicly available info about S&S. Around Labor Day 2020, Viacom restarted the sale process and gave Sansigre access to raw S&S data—"P&Ls by country, by different divisions, and also additional cost breakdowns from Simon & Schuster"—which he mapped so it was comparable to PRH's data.

When PRH moved into "the second round of the process" in October 2020, Viacom provided additional information about S&S—specifically, "intel information" on all S&S employees, about 1400 in the US. Sansigre the created an "op ex matrix" that "mapped each position to the equivalent position at the same department level of Penguin Random House to really make sure that the departments were comparable." He used this data to create the official efficiency model and investment proposal in November, which Bertelsmann used to approve the transaction.

Sansigre explained that two departments at Bertelsmann—M&A and ZI, the "department of money"—looked at his models line by line to challenge his assumptions: "It was very intense." We also learn that, throughout this process, "Silk is the code name that we gave to the acquisition of Simon & Schuster." (Remember that S&S's bankers called it Project Typeface.)

Sansigre's model included financial information from S&S for 2017–2019, and projections for 2020 (since the year wasn't complete at the time). S&S provided a projection for 2021, but he didn't use it. "I asked a lot of questions why they were modeling 2021 in that way. But I created my own set of projections for 2021. And I think it's important to understand that when a seller is putting out their certain projections, precisely because they are selling the company, you want to develop your own opinion about how the condition would evolve."

Some of Sansigre's testimony involves describing columns in a spreadsheet and the calculations he used to determine financial projections. ("You just gave me a mathematical formula," Judge Pan said at one point.) Ultimately Sansigre found four areas of "synergies" between the two companies: "Teal estate savings, operating expenses savings, variable cost savings, and increase in sales," which would lead to savings of $159 to $208 million on average per year until 2025 worldwide, or $137 million–$175 million in the US alone.

With respect to real, "The best majority of the savings are linked to our headquarters in New York City," he said. "Both Penguin Random House and Simon & Schuster, we have both headquarters based in New York City. And after the transaction, we will not need both offices." So about 90 percent of those savings will come from moving S&S employees to the PRH offices. Sansigre confirmed that the PRH offices could accommodate all of S&S's NYC employees, and the merged company could sublease the S&S offices until their lease expired. He calculated a $26 million spend to refit the Rockefeller Center space to be usable for subleasing.

Based on a number of mergers, particularly the 2013 integration of Penguin with Random House, Sansigre's model showed overlaps—and thus potential cuts—in "headcount and non-headcount," i.e. personnel and consultants, after the merger. "It's very important to highlight that they're always with the philosophy of leaving creative untouched," he said. "Basically, any personnel or services that are linked to the books themselves, those are untouched." He estimated 12.3 percent savings "based on our experience."

Sasigre's Op Ex Matrix calculated the "average compensation of both organizations" in assessing redundant positions because "Our philosophy in these kind of mergers is that at the end of it, you want to take the best people from both sides. So at the end of the day, the combined entity, right, it needs to be the average of both organizations."

Judge Pan extensively questioned Sansigre's model and how he determined the savings he reported, determining that he put 12.3 percent into the model because that's what was achieved with Penguin, then "looked at the actual numbers to see that that was realistic."

"I had conversations with Mr. Dohle and Mr. [Nihar] Malaviya, going over it with them, they've done it in the past," Sansigre said. But, "I still wanted to go one step ahead and calculate in detail what was these overlapping functions to really go back and give the comfort to our board, like we're responsible and this is achievable."

He continued, "It's a normal practice to keep those percentages fixed as you move, right, because then you have new information. And again, if inflation goes up, the synergies will go up."

"Absolutely, I understand," Judge pan said. "It's a normal practice for what you're doing, which is figuring out if it makes sense to acquire another company."

Sansigre looked at "marketing, sales and merchandising, fulfillment, production, IT, administration, editorial, and art departments" and said that actual decisions on staff cuts won't be made until after the companies are integrated. Here is his testimony by department:

IT: Paramount provides some IT services for S&S, which post-merger will save $10 million, and some in-house IT staff seem likely to be kept. "We wanted to be conservative, we estimated some incremental cost linked to bringing Simon & Schuster on board," Sansigre said.

Fulfillment: PRH doesn't need to add all three of S&S's warehouses and would likely close all but the largest, Riverside—which over time they estimate might be slimmed to only about 40 percent of its current capacity. They would also eliminate the third-party contractor that S&S uses to process returns.

Sales: "So in my analysis, Penguin Random House has a sales force that is five times larger than Simon & Schuster. It's very important to note that we basically have—90 percent of our clients overlap. So therefore, as part of the transaction, we will not need basically a lot of positions to cover the same clients." A PRH spokesperson clarified afterwards this pertained only to duplicative sales management, rather than people on the ground.

Editorial and Art: Sansigre testified that he found there are 70 executives who overlap between S&S and PRH in the editorial and art departments, and that some of them would be cut. A spokesperson for PRH clarified that the plans actually identified just five managerial positions that would be eliminated, and none of those people touch the books.

On the topic of variable cost savings, Sansigre expects that S&S's freight costs and returns rate will go down once they're integrated into PRH's supply chain, based on the experience of past acquisitions. He also said that ad spend will go down since many of the programs are run through the same platforms. All of this savings, Sansigre said, will go to authors in the form of royalties. "Given that we are projecting additional revenues and improving returns, every additional dollar that we create in increased sales we automatically share with authors. So this is basically the contribution, right, how much additional payment we will be paying to authors based on the efficiencies."

Sansigre also attested that, looking at a P&L, advance numbers will go up 10 percent for PRH and S&S authors with the decrease in allocated overhead costs.

Sansigre also anticipates an overall sales increase of about 0.7 percent, particularly in special markets, indie bookstores, and international exports. "Our sales organization is five times larger. The capillarity of our sales force is getting to basically all independent bookstores, right. And it's anchored on our experience because of our supply chain. As we mentioned, also if we reduce return rates, we'll have the ability to also increase sales."

In concluding his direct testimony, Sansigre said that PRH's "philosophy" is "So we leave creative untouched. That basically means not to cut any editors, and of course not to cut any services to authors. And we actually want to do the opposite, we want to give them the maximum quality services."

Following Sansigre's testimony, an S&S spokesperson reached out to clarify and correct a couple of points.

When Sansigre told the court, "We learned from the management presentation of Simon & Schuster that they have presence in 100 countries" and added that "in our case, we have presence in more than 200 countries," he was speaking about sales of physical books only. S&S reports that for print books and ebooks combined, their titles are available in over 200 countries. PRH has its own "dedicated sales reps across the globe," whereas S&S uses wholesalers and distributors in some international markets.

Additionally, for audiobooks—which Sansigre targeted as the largest area of forecast revenue enhancements after the merger—he said their "understanding" was that "Simon & Schuster largely outsourced the production of audiobooks. . . . They don't have their own audio studios, they don't have the same capabilities that we have."

The S&S spokesperson clarified they do have "an in-house studio" as well as "a superb staff of producers, editors, marketing/publicity folks," noting, "We actually have a thriving audio business."

TESTIMONY OF MANUEL SANSIGRE, SENIOR VICE PRESIDENT OF M&A, PENGUIN RANDOM HOUSE

DIRECT EXAMINATION

BY MR. FRACKMAN:

Q. Mr. Sansigre, can you tell us your name and your position.

A. Sure. My name is Manuel Sansigre. I am the senior vice president of M&A for Penguin Random House.

Q. How long have you held that position?

A. Since basically the summer of 2015.

Q. And who do you report to at Penguin Random House?

A. Markus Dohle.

Q. What are your responsibilities?

A. I am in charge of all acquisitions for Penguin Random House.

Q. Do you have a team that works with you?

A. Yes.

Q. How many people are on your team?

A. Two people.

Q. When did you join Penguin Random House?

A. I joined in 2015.

Q. And before 2015, what did you do?

A. I was a banker in three different investment banks, both in the U.S. and also in Europe.

Q. Could you tell the court your educational degrees.

A. Sure. I hold an undergrad of law and an undergrad in business administration from Carlos III University of Madrid. I also hold a master's in advance finance from IE Business School, Instituto Empresa Madrid.

Q. Any other degrees?

A. I also hold a master's in business analytics from NYC Stern School of Business.

Q. How many merger and acquisition transactions have you worked on in your career as an investment banker together with your time at Penguin Random House?

A. I have worked on over 200 transactions in my career.

Q. Were any of those transactions that you worked on when you were an investment banker in the publishing industry?

A. Yes. I actually advise Penguin Random House in acquisition of a publisher in Spain. Actually, that's the way I started at Penguin Random House.

Q. What transaction was that in connection with?

A. There was an acquisition of Santillana.

Q. And that's a publisher, right?

A. Yes.

Q. Okay. Now, at Penguin Random House, how many transactions have you worked on?

A. I have worked on over 100 transactions reviewing publishing companies.

Q. And how many of those 100 transactions have closed?

A. 26.
Q. So now let's turn to the Simon & Schuster transaction. What was your involvement in the decision to acquire Simon & Schuster?
A. Sure. So my team and I, we were primarily involved in modeling the PRH and Simon & Schuster efficiencies.
Q. Now, you used the words efficiencies. We are also going to hear the word synergies. In your practice, do you make any distinction between those two terms?
A. No. Efficiencies or synergies are terminology that we use interchangeably.
Q. What do efficiencies or synergies refer to in your usage in connection with acquisitions?
A. It means benefits created a second sequence of transaction.
Q. Let's turn to the timeline of your involvement. I will have Ms. Radford bring up the timeline that you have helped us prepare. Let's briefly walk through your modeling work and how you developed your model. Let's start at the beginning. When did ViacomCBS announce the sale of Simon & Schuster?
THE COURT: Does this have an exhibit number for the record?
MR. FRACKMAN: This is defendants' demonstrative 14, Your Honor.
THE COURT: Okay.
THE WITNESS: So ViacomCBS announced the sale of Simon & Schuster in early March.

BY MR. FRACKMAN:
Q. And what did you do at that point?
A. Well, as soon as they announced, I started thinking about how I would model efficiencies basically.
Q. When you model efficiencies, are there stages that you usually undertake?
A. Yes. Normally there's different stages to get to, let's say, the final model, right, that you are going to use for the transaction. In this situation, we actually went through three stages.
Q. So before we get to that, I think you told the court that you have closed 26 transactions at Penguin Random House. But how many transactions have you done synergies modeling or financial modeling in connection with?
A. So in all the transactions, at the end of the day, I've done a lot of times synergy analysis, projections. It is a very common M&A tool, right, or M&A—It's a normal tool when you are assessing opportunities.
Q. All right. You said that there were three stages in the development of your work on this transaction. What was the first stage?
A. So the first stage was creating the architecture of the model. Okay. So, I knew that this was a transaction with a lot of information, so it was important to create a template, right, that eventually would become a model. So, I started thinking what would be the information that I would need from the Penguin Random House and from Simon & Schuster in order to create efficiencies model.
Q. When did you start that work?
A. I started right away.
Q. Did you have any Simon & Schuster confidential information at that point in time?
A. No. At that time we didn't have the access to any private information. It was only publicly available information.
Q. And you are talking about March 2020 at this point, right?
A. Yes.
Q. So what happened after you started preparing the skeleton or framework for your model?
A. So the bankers of Simon & Schuster told us that because of COVID they were putting the sell process on hold.
Q. Did you stop your work at that point, or did you continue?
A. No. I used this opportunity to keep developing the architecture of the model. And, for example, I started pulling all the Penguin Random House data and really making sure that the mechanics of the model were—that it was working well.
Q. At this point in time, did you look at any prior transactions?
A. Yes. As I and my team would do in every single transaction, we look back to this experience of 26

transactions and the other ones that we have worked to really understand how we model synergies, how we model projections, et cetera.

Q. Okay. So that was your first stage. When did you move into the second stage of work on the efficiencies model?

A. So by the end of summer of 2020, the bankers came back to us and told us that they were about to restart the process and that most likely they will start populating the data after Labor Day.

Q. And was that around Labor Day?

A. It was around Labor Day, yes.

Q. Okay. So, did you get access to the Simon & Schuster data room at that point?

A. Yes, we did.

Q. And what did you do with that data?

A. So once that I had access to, quite honestly, a lot of information about Simon & Schuster information, the first very important process is about trying to normalize the Simon & Schuster data to be comparable with Penguin Random House data.

Q. Was that a big job, small job?

A. It was a huge job. Basically, my team and I were totally devoted full time to this project day and night. And the idea was really to make sure that we could look at Penguin Random House and Simon & Schuster through the same lenses.

Q. So we are going to put up now Plaintiff's Exhibit 405 for identification. It is confidential data.

MR. FRACKMAN: And I will ask Ms. Radford to go to the Silk US worksheet on PX450.

BY MR. FRACKMAN:

Q. Mr. Sansigre, could you tell the court what we are looking at on this worksheet of PX405?

A. This is the mapping spreadsheet that we created, as I just mentioned.

Q. How many worksheets or tabs are there in PX405?

A. It has over 100 tabs.

Q. What's contained in these tabs? That's a lot of tabs, 100.

A. So basically Simon & Schuster raw data, so P&Ls by country, by different divisions, and also additional cost breakdowns from Simon & Schuster. The idea on this file was to again try to map Simon & Schuster P&L to be comparable to us.

MR. FRACKMAN: Your Honor, I offer PX405 into evidence.

THE COURT: Any objection?

MS. LEAL: No objection, Your Honor.

THE COURT: That will be admitted. (Plaintiff's 405 received in evidence.)

BY MR. FRACKMAN:

Q. Mr. Sansigre, how long did the mapping project take that resulted in PX405?

A. Two very intensive weeks after the data room was open.

Q. Once you had the data mapped in PX405, what did you do next?

A. So I took the mapped P&Ls, and I inserted all these data into the efficiencies model.

Q. Was there anything else that you did in this, what you called second stage, other than the weeks of mapping of data?

A. Well, now that we have efficiencies model with both Penguin Random House and the mapped Simon & Schuster data, then we could start make the projections on the efficiencies model itself.

Q. When did you begin the third stage of your development of your model?

A. The third stage started when basically ViacomCBS communicated to us that we were moved into the second round of the process and they not only open—or they provide us with additional financial information on Simon & Schuster, but also more deeper breakdowns for the company. But additionally we got access to confidential information in the clean data room.

Q. Let me stop you right there.

MR. FRACKMAN: I would ask Ms. Radford to bring back up the timeline if we can. This is again defendants' demonstrative 14, slide 2.

BY MR. FRACKMAN:
Q. When did this third stage begin?
A. Around October 15th of 2020.
Q. What type of information did you get in the third stage—Simon & Schuster information did you get in the third stage that you didn't have prior to October?
A. Especially the information in the clean data room.
Q. And what information was in the clean data room?
A. It was the intel information of all Simon & Schuster employees.
Q. How many employees did you receive data for from Simon & Schuster?
A. It was all of them, around 1,400 in the United States.
Q. What did you do with this data once you got it?
A. Well, I went line by line, and I basically mapped each position to the equivalent position at the same department level of Penguin Random House to really make sure that the departments were comparable.
Q. Do you have a name for this worksheet or workbook or spreadsheet, whatever you want to call it?
A. Yes. The name of this document is called the op ex matrix.
MR. FRACKMAN: Let's pull up PX406 for identification. And I will ask of Ms. Radford to go to the summary worksheet or summary tab.
BY MR. FRACKMAN:
Q. Mr. Sansigre, what is the court—what are we looking at here in PX406?
A. This is the op ex matrix that I created.
Q. How many worksheets are in PX406?
A. Around 50, 50 tabs.
Q. And we are going to come back and look at this in greater detail.
MR. FRACKMAN: At this point I will just offer it in evidence, and we will proceed.
THE COURT: Is this data all from Simon & Schuster?
THE WITNESS: A good part of this information is from Simon & Schuster, yes.
THE COURT: Is there also PRH information on this?
THE WITNESS: Yes.
THE COURT: It's both?
THE WITNESS: Both.
THE COURT: Okay.
MR. FRACKMAN: I don't believe there is any objection. This is on the plaintiff's exhibit list, PX406.
THE COURT: Any objection to PX406?
MS. LEAL: No objection, Your Honor.
THE COURT: That will be admitted. (Plaintiff's 406 received in evidence.)
BY MR. FRACKMAN:
Q. How long did it take you to create the op ex matrix?
A. It took me also 24/7, couple of weeks to create this document.
MR. FRACKMAN: Let's go back to the timeline, Ms. Radford.
BY MR. FRACKMAN:
Q. All right. So you got access to Simon & Schuster data, Simon & Schuster clean room data, you developed your op ex matrix. What did you do next?
A. So once we built the op ex matrix, I was able to finalize basically the efficiencies model that was used for the approval of the transaction by Bertelsmann.
Q. When was the work on the efficiencies model completed?
A. It was completed by basically the beginning of November, around like November 6.
Q. And is that the document that has been referred to as the official model?
A. Yes.
MR. FRACKMAN: Pam, could you put up PX168, please, and go to the Silk IS US output tab or worksheet.

BY MR. FRACKMAN:

Q. Mr. Sansigre, what are we looking at in PX168?

A. This is the November of 2020 official model that was used to approve the transaction by Bertelsmann.

MR. FRACKMAN: Your Honor, I offer PX168 in evidence.

THE COURT: Any objection?

MS. LEAL: No objection, Your Honor.

THE COURT: That will be admitted. (Plaintiff's 168 received in evidence.)

BY MR. FRACKMAN:

Q. We will come back to PX168 a little bit later. Let's go back to the timeline. How was the official model's conclusions, that is PX168's conclusions, used?

A. So with those conclusions, we were able to identify the potential benefits out of this transaction that we could create and basically arrive to the valuation that serve us basically to sign the transaction.

Q. Did you communicate PX168, your model, to Bertelsmann?

A. Absolutely. This is the document—the final version of this model, what we call the official model, was sent to them basically for the final approval, but actually, they were reviewing and vetting my assumptions very early on in the process.

Q. You have on the timeline something called the investment proposal, PX148. What is that?

A. So the investment proposal is basically the document where, in this case, Penguin Random House is proposing the acquisition of Simon & Schuster to be approved by Bertelsmann.

MR. FRACKMAN: And, Ms. Radford, would you pull up PX148, please, for us to look at.

BY MR. FRACKMAN:

Q. Mr. Sansigre, what is PX148 that we are looking at?

A. This is the resolution of Bertelsmann supervisory board approving the Simon & Schuster transaction.

Q. And does this, PX148, include the investment proposal that was submitted to Bertelsmann by Penguin Random House incorporating the synergy or conclusions of your modeling?

A. Yes.

MR. FRACKMAN: We offer PX148 in evidence.

THE COURT: Any objection?

MS. LEAL: No objection, Your Honor.

THE COURT: That will be admitted. (Plaintiff's 148 received in evidence.)

MR. FRACKMAN: So if you would turn to page 8 of PX148, Ms. Radford.

BY MR. FRACKMAN:

Q. Is this the investment proposal that you just mentioned?

A. Yes.

Q. All right. And what do these pages show in a general sense?

A. So the philosophy of the integration and the calculation of the synergies.

Q. What are the big buckets of synergies that you identified and were incorporated into PX148, the investment proposal?

A. Basically the four categories were real estate savings, operating expenses savings, variable cost savings, and increase in sales.

Q. And we are going to come back to each of those, but in total, how much did you identify in efficiencies in the investment proposal, PX148?

A. Between 159 to $208 million per annum by 2025.

Q. Per annum, that's annual savings. Are those worldwide or just in the U.S.?

A. They were worldwide.

Q. What is the number, the annual savings or synergies, that you projected for the U.S. alone?

A. For the U.S., the range was between 137 million and 175 million dollars per annum by 2025.

Q. By 2025? You modeled it over a four-year horizon?

A. Yes.

Q. Let's go back to the timeline if we could, defendants' demonstrative 14, page 2. And I want to turn to the box or the section at the bottom in orange. What are you showing there?

A. This is basically trying to show how Bertelsmann was reviewing and vetting what assumptions and efficiencies is modeled across the process.

Q. Right. So, this is entitled, Bertelsmann review of PRH efficiencies, and you have it starting in May and continuing to November. Why don't we start in May? What was Bertelsmann's involvement in your work at that point?

A. So after the process was put on hold, we went actually to Bertelsmann to basically tell them that we wanted to explore the project. And we did that in a meeting with them, and they confirmed that they wanted us to go ahead and explore the transaction. And for that also they started supporting us or supporting the process by creating two different groups to review and vet all the work that we were doing for this transaction.

Q. Are you saying that the Bertelsmann—well, what are the groups that you are referring to?

A. They are basically—in this situation, they set up two different groups. One is the Bertelsmann M&A group, so basically the department of money for Bertelsmann. And the other one is called ZI. That's the way they called it.

Q. ZI?

A. ZI, which is basically the controlling risk management group of Bertelsmann.

Q. And what was the involvement of the M&A, Bertelsmann M&A group, and the Bertelsmann controlling group in your modeling work over the summer and into the fall?

A. It was very intense. They were both analyzing line by line so that particularly there was no mistakes in the model, and all the formulas and review also, of course, projections and assumptions and challenging them.

Q. How many individuals were involved in working with you or reviewing your work from Bertelsmann?

A. So in the case of the ZI group, I believe they had one full-time person, Mr. Sullwold, and also they have Java Hepton (phonetic) also dedicated to this project, but also the head of ZI was all the time also reviewing all this information.

MR. FRACKMAN: Now, let's turn to the next—let's turn to defendants' demonstrative 14, page 6.

BY MR. FRACKMAN:

Q. What are you showing here on slide 6 of defendants' demonstrative 14?

A. This is showing conceptually how Bertelsmann review efficiencies.

Q. What is this four eyes principle that we have noted here?

A. So especially in important transactions, Bertelsmann wants to make sure that there are different departments independent from each other to look into the transaction to make sure that everything is reviewed.

Q. And those are two eyes from M&A and two eyes from ZI, is that what you are saying?

A. Basically.

Q. Okay. And I want to just focus on the involvement of the ZI person. You mentioned his name was Mr. Sullwold. What did he do with you on a day-to-day basis while you were working on the model?

A. It was a really intense review of the 100 tabs that we discussed from the documents. So, he was literally going line by line making sure the calculations were accurate and also challenged the assumptions and the calculations of the efficiencies.

Q. And when you got data in the fall, both the original data following Labor Day and then some of the clean room data, did Bertelsmann have access to any of that data?

A. They had access to all the data except the clean team data.

MR. FRACKMAN: Okay. Let's pull up defendants' demonstrative 14 at 7, which is an image of DX416.

BY MR. FRACKMAN:

Q. What is this, Mr. Sansigre? I mean, it's an email, but who is Timo [Sullwold], and what does it concern?

A. This is the person from ZI that we just discussed sending me an email asking me basically to provide him with the mapping file that we discussed before and also basically the documents that were linked to the efficiencies model.

Q. Is this the only communication between you and Mr. Sullwold in which he asked for data to support your model, or are there others and this is just an example?

A. There is a lot of emails back and forth, and we also had like conversations every other day.

MR. FRACKMAN: Your Honor, I offer DX416 into evidence.

THE COURT: Any objection?

MS. LEAL: No objection.

THE COURT: That will be admitted. (Plaintiff's 416 received in evidence.)

MR. FRACKMAN: Let's turn, Pam, to page 8 of demonstrative 14. This is an image of DX415 for identification.

BY MR. FRACKMAN:

Q. What is this, Mr. Sansigre?

A. This is an email from Florian Protschky. He's like a member of the M&A department of Bertelsmann.

Q. What is Mr. Protschky asking for here?

A. He wanted to have additional questions around the operations of Simon & Schuster and also around synergies in order to help us with the—For the operational—for the operations of the company.

Q. This is dated September 22, 2020. What was going on at that point?

A. We were starting to ask questions to Simon & Schuster management and basically put together all these questions to gather additional information to better understand how Simon & Schuster operate compared to Penguin Random House.

Q. And how often would Mr. Protschky or someone else from the Bertelsmann M&A group contact you with questions about the work you were doing in connection with the transaction?

A. Very similar to the ZI group, it would be emails very frequent, and we will have conversations every other day.

MR. FRACKMAN: Your Honor, I offer DX415 into evidence.

THE COURT: Any objection?

MS. LEAL: No objection.

THE COURT: That will be admitted. (Defendant's 415 received in evidence.)

MR. FRACKMAN: So let's go back, Pam, to slide 6 in the demonstrative.

BY MR. FRACKMAN:

Q. Other than the M&A group and the ZI controlling group at Bertelsmann, who else reviewed your work on the efficiencies model?

A. So once we basically sent the investment proposal to Bertelsmann, they needed to move that investment proposal through their different committees. In this case, first investment committee, then the executive committee, and finally the supervisory board.

Q. By the way, did the ZI group generate any independent appraisal or valuation of the transaction, or did they just rely on your work?

A. They created their own independent assessment.

MR. FRACKMAN: And let's look at slide 9 of demonstrative 14. This is PX864.

BY MR. FRACKMAN:

Q. What are we looking at, Mr. Sansigre?

A. This is the ZI appraisal that they created.

MR. FRACKMAN: Your Honor, we offer PX864 into evidence.

THE COURT: Any objection?

MS. LEAL: No objection.

THE COURT: That will be admitted. (Plaintiff's 864 received in evidence.)

BY MR. FRACKMAN:

Q. Where did the ZI group get the information to form the view that the magnitude of cost synergies appears reasonable when comparing to former larger Penguin Random House mergers as stated in PX864

to your knowledge?
A. So they reviewed, of course, all the work that we had done. They also reviewed similar transactions that we have done in the past. And also they had direct access to all the information that Simon & Schuster was providing except the clean team information that was provided.
Q. Was this an independent appraisal, or was it just rubber stamping what you had done?
A. It was, my opinion, it was really a real appraisal.
Q. Now, why did Bertelsmann spend all this time double-checking your work with four different—two different sets of eyes, four different eyes?
A. It's a large transaction, and their money was on the line.
Q. So this ZI appraisal, PX864 that we are looking at, did you provide any input into it?
A. I couldn't. I gave some comments, but it was—that document, it was not under my control.
Q. Would they have permitted you to have input into it if you had wanted to?
A. I don't think so.
Q. And that's because their job was to do an independent evaluation?
A. Yes.
Q. Okay. With that background, let's go back to the November 2020 official model, PX168. How much time did you and your team spend building the November 2020 official model, PX168, in total?
A. It was basically since the beginning in March when I started creating the architecture of the model until we signed the deal in November.
Q. How many drafts or versions of PX168 did you create before you got to the final one?
A. About a hundred versions.
Q. You have worked at investment banks. Did the approach—how did the approach that you took in preparing PX168 compare with what you did when you were a banker?
A. It's the same. I have applied the same practices as when I was a banker working in all these transactions.
Q. Why did you need a hundred iterations of this model before it was final?
A. So throughout the process, we are learning more and more information about Simon & Schuster, the way they operate. Simon & Schuster would provide us with additional breakdowns and information to really better understand honestly everything in the way they work, right. So, a lot of this information was not provided at the beginning, but basically mostly at the end of the process.
Q. Now, you testified earlier that there are a hundred worksheets in PX168, I think, if I have that right.
A. Yes.
Q. What are the two that are most important for our discussion today and for the court?
A. Yeah, I think those would be the Silk US IS output, and the other one would be Silk US.
Q. So let's talk about the Silk US IS output first. I know the court probably knows this, but US refers to what?
A. The United States.
Q. And what does IS refer to?
A. Income statement.
Q. What is contained—so that's the Silk US IS worksheet. What about the Silk US worksheet?
A. That's basically the top where the large majority of the calculations of efficiencies is done.
Q. Those are two out of a hundred tabs. What are the other 98 doing?
A. Other supporting documentation. Also this was a global transaction, so basically it contains information from other countries.

BY MR. FRACKMAN:

Q. So while we are interested here in the Silk US IS output, you have tabs for other geographies as well, right?
A. Yes.
Q. And then do you have other tabs in which you are doing calculations that are rolled up into the summary spreadsheet that we are looking at, Silk US IS output?
A. Yes.

Q. With the court's indulgence, let's keep our focus on this Silk US IS output summary tab. I want to take you through some of the information here to orient the court in case the court would like to go back and look at it later. Let's start at the left-hand column, the one that starts with gross fiscal sales and then continues down. What do those rows refer to?
A. So these rows are the different items of the profit and loss.
Q. Based on the P&L of the two companies as you map them for your model?
A. Yes.
Q. Okay. So—
THE COURT: I'm sorry, so this is combined?
THE WITNESS: No. This is just Simon & Schuster.
THE COURT: Okay.
BY MR. FRACKMAN:
Q. Now let's go across the top here. You have three columns under heading, historical, 2017A, 2018A, and 2019A. What are those?
A. Those are the actuals, 2017 actual, 2018 actual, and 2019 actual of Simon & Schuster.
Q. And where did you get the information to populate those three historical columns?
A. From Simon & Schuster business records.
Q. Okay. Now let's go to the one right next to that to the right that says, forecast 2020F. What does that refer to?
A. This also refers to—it's 2020 forecast basically.
Q. Why is it called a forecast in contrast to the three historical years you had next to it?
A. Well, we were modeling throughout 2020, so 2020 was not closed yet. So, this forecast actually incorporated nine months of actuals until September of 2020 and the last quarter of 2020 as a forecast.
Q. Who provided the forecast? Was that from Simon & Schuster, or was that from yourself?
A. It was basically from Simon & Schuster.
Q. Now, to the right of that, you have a column, this is I, column I, that says, estimate 2021E. What does that refer to?
A. This is the estimate, the projection, for 2021, and it was the first, let's say, year that we projected.
Q. And how did you come up with the projection for 2021? Where did you get the information?
A. Well, we based on a lot of information and discussions how the market was evolving, the books that were coming. At the same time we were doing a lot of due diligence on Simon & Schuster, so we were learning a lot about how the company was performing.
Q. Did Simon & Schuster provide you with an estimate for 2021?
A. Yes.
Q. Did you use it, or did you refine it?
A. I didn't use it. I asked a lot of questions why they were modeling 2021 in that way. But I created my own set of projections for 2021. And I think it's important to understand that when a seller is putting out their certain projections, precisely because they are selling the company, you want to develop your own opinion about how the condition would evolve.
Q. And is that because, in your experience, sellers might puff their projections?
A. Sometimes. But in general, you really want to have your own opinion of how the company is going to evolve.
Q. Is that consistent with how you approached estimates of future financial results when you were an investment banker?
A. Yes.
Q. Okay. Now, let's keep going.
THE COURT: Sorry. Can I ask, so is your estimate what Simon & Schuster would do as a standalone company, or does it incorporate revenue synergies from PRH?
THE WITNESS: So 2021 is still independent, let's say, standalone. Is now, when we get to 2025, the columns we are going to discuss now, where I model projected the three states of the world.
THE COURT: I see.

BY MR. FRACKMAN:

Q. I also am quite confident the court knows what CAGR refers to in the next two columns, but why don't you just tell us for the record.

A. It means compounded annual growth rate.

Q. And you have it both for the year 2017 to 2019 based on the actual data from Simon & Schuster, the historical data, and you also have it in column K for 2019 to 2021 based on both the historical for 2019 and the forecast for 2020 and your estimate for 2021, is that right?

A. Yes.

Q. Now let's go to the three worlds that you have modeled here, and let's start with M, column M, base case standalone 2025. What does that refer to?

A. This is the first state of the world that I model. That is basically how the company will evolve over the years until 2025.

Q. Is this as a standalone company or as part of Penguin Random House?

A. It's as a standalone.

Q. And then to the right of that, you have the percentage growth, which is, I assume, the average growth rate for those years based on that projection?

A. Yes.

Q. Let's go all the way to the right. We are going to come back to the target column. Let's first go to the upside case Silk with synergies in columns Y and Z. Before we start, what does Silk refer to?

A. Silk is the code name that we gave to the acquisition of Simon & Schuster.

Q. Okay. And let's look in column Y. You have Silk upside case, Silk with synergies 2025E. What does that—what do the numbers in that column refer to?

A. This is the second state of the world that I projected which was Simon & Schuster under PRH management including the synergies and efficiencies that we have identify we could achieve as part of this transaction.

Q. And to the left of that, you have a base case with also similar estimates for 2025 and percentage growth for the period '21 to '25. How does the base case compare to the upside case, and why do you have both here?

A. Sure. So at the end of the day, it's impossible to predict the future. That's why we tend to work with ranges. So the base case basically was a plan a discount to all these efficiencies in order to get to that range.

Q. How much discount is in the base case from the upside case that you modeled?

A. So it's generally the discount is around 80 percent except for certain items in sales and also for real estate.

Q. So you said the discount is 80 percent, the base case is 80 percent of the upside?

A. Yes.

Q. A reduction of 20 percent–

A. Yes.

Q.—approximately Which is the projection that you modeled as the likely outcome of the merger, the upside case or the base case?

A. The base case is the one that was used for Bertelsmann approval, and that's also the set of numbers that we will be held accountable by them.

Q. But which one–

A. The base case.

Q. That's the base case. So why do you even have the upside case?

A. Well, we are very confident that we will achieve the upside case, but we just want to be conservative.

Q. You modeled the upside case because that's what you think you are going to accomplish, achieve, but you discount it for purposes of approval taking a more conservative estimate; is that what you are saying?

MS. LEAL: Objection.

THE COURT: I am going to sustain the objection.

BY MR. FRACKMAN:

Q. Why do you discount the upside case to the base case for purposes of getting approval for the transaction?

A. As I said, it's impossible to predict the future, so it's very common in M&A to create ranges. So we wanted to have more conservative basically low bound, and that is what the base case represents.

Q. Okay. Now let's turn to columns S and T, and let's focus on S. That's target synergies base. And just for ease of discussion, let's take one row, gross fiscal sales, and can you explain to the court how the value in that cell, S8, is calculated.

A. Yes. This cell is calculated by subtracting the two states of the world of base case minus standalone, so basically V8 minus M8.

Q. So if you subtract M8 from V8, you get S8?

A. It is V8 minus M8, but yes.

Q. The difference between base case, which is how you project Simon & Schuster will perform as part of Penguin Random House, less compared to how it would perform as a standalone basically?

A. Yes.

THE COURT: I'm sorry, but what does that number represent in terms of synergies? You just gave me a mathematical formula. How did you figure out that that was the amount of synergies?

THE WITNESS: So we have another tab, which I think—I mean, that has the calculation for every single line and how we targeted the synergies. This is just a summary.

MR. FRACKMAN: Your Honor, we are about to go through some specific examples for the Court to answer that question.

THE COURT: Okay.

BY MR. FRACKMAN:

Q. Does the math follow, that we just reviewed, follow for all of the rows in this worksheet?

A. Yes.

MR. FRACKMAN: And if you go down to the very bottom, Pam, of the worksheet, of the tab in the box there, you see 137 and 175.

BY MR. FRACKMAN:

Q. What do those numbers reflect?

A. That is the range of U.S. efficiencies that we projected for Simon & Schuster.

Q. There are a lot of lines here. Can you describe the four big buckets that the synergies fall into for the court?

A. Sure. So the first one is real estate savings. The second one is operating expenses savings. The third one is variable cost savings. And the last one is increased sales.

MR. FRACKMAN: And I will ask Ms. Radford to bring up slide 10 of demonstrative 14.

BY MR. FRACKMAN:

Q. What are you showing here on slide 10?

A. This is the base case targeted synergies by those four categories that I just described.

Q. The left-hand column are the categories you just described, and the right-hand column are the projected synergies derived from PX168 that we were just looking at, is that right?

A. Yes.

Q. So now with that introduction, let's look at a few examples. And I would like to start with real estate synergies. Where on PX168, and again we are on the Silk US IS output tab, where on this tab are the real estate synergies reflected? What is the line? What is the row?

A. You can find it in line 60.

Q. Row 60 or line 60, D&A. Why is it D&A and not real estate?

A. D&A means depreciation and amortization. I apologize. There has been a change a couple of years ago where the expenses of real estate are no longer part of operating expenses, per se. They are considered amortization of the right of use of an asset. Therefore, those expenses are embedded in the D&A line.

Q. So if we go across on the D&A line, that's row 60, to columns S and T, we see two values. What are those values? I mean, not the number, but what do those represent?

A. Those represent the real estate savings that we project.

Q. In contrast to most of the rows, you have the same value in both the base case and the upside case for the real estate synergies. Why is that?

A. We were really confident that we will get the numbers, so that's why we kept the same in both scenarios.

Q. We are going to go in a moment and look at the data that you reviewed in order to come up with the value for real estate. But just tell the court, as a general matter, what are we talking about here in real estate savings?

A. The best majority of the savings are linked to our headquarters in New York City. Both Penguin Random House and Simon & Schuster, we have both headquarters based in New York City. And after the transaction, we will not need both offices.

Q. Does this refer mostly to the savings you expect to get from the Simon & Schuster headquarters in New York City?

A. Yes.

MR. FRACKMAN: Let's look at slide 11 of demonstrative 14.

BY MR. FRACKMAN:

Q. Can you take the court through the steps that you undertook in order to come up with that projection for real estate savings for the Simon & Schuster headquarters space?

A. Yes. So first I reviewed the Simon & Schuster New York City office lease to understand information from that list, but also what were the options, what we could do with that list.

Then I discussed with Penguin Random House real estate team and also with the rest of the management to confirm that there was a space for Simon & Schuster personnel. Then we discussed with a real estate broker in New York City to reanalyze the market conditions. This was in the middle of the pandemic at the time. And finally, we also asked JP Morgan to assess the subleasing opportunities.

Q. Now let's look at the backup for each of these. Where did you get the information for the Simon & Schuster lease or about the Simon & Schuster lease?

A. From the data rooms or from their business records.

Q. Is that information reflected in any of the exhibits that we have reviewed so far?

A. Well, it's part of PX168 or part of the mapping that is not in—

Q. What about PX405? That's the mapping document.

A. It's part of the mapping document, yes.

MR. FRACKMAN: Okay. Let's go to the next slide, Pam. This is slide 12 of defendants' demonstrative 14. This is a page from PX405, Your Honor.

BY MR. FRACKMAN:

Q. What tab are we looking at at PX405, Mr. Sansigre?

A. This is the tab facilities cost. And basically what I did here is, once I downloaded the documents from the data room, I basically copy paste into the spreadsheet as a reference. You can see my name and the date when—

Q. Let me just slow you down there. This is a document that was made available to you by Simon & Schuster in the data room, right?

A. Yes.

Q. And what you are saying is you took it and cut and pasted and incorporated it into your mapping document PX405?

MS. LEAL: Objection.

THE COURT: Sustained. Let the witness testify, Mr. Frackman, not you.

MR. FRACKMAN: Just trying to move it along.

THE COURT: I understand, but he needs to testify.

BY MR. FRACKMAN:

Q. Let's look at the information you have here that's highlighted. What information is that, Mr. Sansigre?

A. This is the information from the headquarters in New York City, and you can see the facilities expanse between 2017 and 2020.

Q. Is this the lease amount?

A. This is the P&L—yeah, it's the lease amount going through the P&L.

MR. FRACKMAN: Your Honor, this is found, as Mr. Sansigre said, at the facilities cost worksheet of PX405, row 26.

THE COURT: I'm sorry. So, the bottom is PRH's expenses, or is that Simon & Schuster?

THE WITNESS: All of these are Simon & Schuster expenses.

THE COURT: Okay.

BY MR. FRACKMAN:

Q. Now, what do you have—that's the information on the left that you got from Simon & Schuster that's highlighted, the amount of the lease. What do you have on the right under the heading key legal terms?

A. These basically represent specifically for the headquarters, the expiration date, the square footage of the office, and some clauses from the lease linked to what were the options and what to do with this space. And then the last one, you can see some of the terms, the lease terms, that they were entering into a contract.

Q. So after you got the square footage, the lease terms, and the lease amount, what did you do next?

A. Well, the first thing is that we realized that we couldn't just terminate the contract potentially. After discussing with the advisers, we realized that we could only sublease it. So what we did then was to understand how many people were in these offices and—understand how many people were in these offices—

Q. Let me stop you right there. How did you get the information of how many employees were at the Simon & Schuster headquarters at Rockefeller Center?

A. All that information, operational information, about the space was in the data room.

Q. Did you then confirm whether Penguin Random House had enough space at its offices in New York to accommodate the employees that you anticipated bringing over from Simon & Schuster?

A. Yes, we did.

Q. How did you do that?

A. So we have conversations with our real estate team analyzing the head count that was in those offices, and even our head of real estate visit their offices to really understand their layout and the way they were working.

Q. And what did you determine as to whether you needed any of the Simon & Schuster headquarters space after the merger closed?

A. That we could accommodate all of Simon & Schuster employees in New York.

Q. Okay. You mentioned you then consulted with a real estate broker, Cushman & Wakefield. And what did they tell you?

A. Well, they basically told us that the market conditions were what they were given COVID, but that the space was in a good place to be subleased.

Q. Did you incorporate into your model the savings from the entirety of the Simon & Schuster lease once you determined you didn't need their space, or did you incorporate a lower amount?

A. I incorporated 50 percent of the lease amount.

Q. What was the basis for the 50 percent number?

A. We additionally got JP Morgan to assess the subleasing opportunities in Manhattan.

Q. What was JP Morgan's involvement in the transaction?

A. They were our financial advisers.

Q. And let me show you the next slide. This is slide 13 of demonstrative 14, which is a page from DX417. What is this, Mr. Sansigre?

A. This is a presentation that JP Morgan created to basically assess the different options and opportunities, and they concluded that we would be able to at least recover 50 percent of the lease.

MR. FRACKMAN: Your Honor, we offer DX417 in evidence.

THE COURT: Any objection?
MS. LEAL: No objection.
THE COURT: That will be admitted. (Defendant's 417 received in evidence.)
THE COURT: But 10 is not 50 percent of 18.
THE WITNESS: This is the large majority, right. The 10 is composed of other smaller things.
THE COURT: I'm sorry?
THE WITNESS: The ten, besides the New York offices, it has other leases and other savings. But the large majority of that saving is the New York headquarters.
THE COURT: Okay.
BY MR. FRACKMAN:
Q. Did you incorporate the JP Morgan appraisal information and other lease information that you got from Simon & Schuster into your model, PX168?
A. Yes.
Q. And where in the model is it reflected?
A. I created a tab called real estate benchmark, which was detailing the leases one by one, and I inputted all these numbers.
MR. FRACKMAN: So, Ms. Radford, let's go to PX168, the real estate benchmark worksheet. And I will direct Mr. Sansigre to row 21.
BY MR. FRACKMAN:
Q. What is reflected on row 21 of this worksheet, Mr. Sansigre?
A. You can see the different information from the headquarters like expiration date, the number of employees, the square footage, and then you can also see the lease payment.
Q. And over to the right, in column N, what is reflected there?
A. Is 50 percent.
Q. There are other facilities that also appear on this worksheet. What do they refer to?
A. This is other small spaces that we were not anticipating to use when the lease expired.
Q. Is it fair to say that most of the total here comes from the savings of the headquarters space?
A. Yes.
Q. Are there any costs associated with subleasing Simon & Schuster's headquarters?
A. Yes. We will need to obviously do the move. And also they are refitting the space and also investing into the space in order to be able—in good condition to be subleased.
Q. Did you take that cost into account in your model?
A. Yes. We calculated $26 million of refitting.
Q. By the way, what percentage of the total real estate savings that you modeled comes from the subleasing of the Simon & Schuster headquarters space?
A. Like 90 percent basically.
Q. Okay. Before we leave real estate, I want to ask you a question about hard coding that the court has heard references to. The court, I know, knows what a hard coded cell in Excel is, but for the record, could you explain what hard coding means in Excel?
A. Hard coded means that it's a cell that is not linked either to another document or to another spreadsheet or that has a formula.
Q. Does hard coding in your experience mean that the data is unreliable?
A. No, not at all.
Q. Are the real estate savings on PX168, on the summary spreadsheet that we just looked at, hard coded?
A. Only the 50 percent.
Q. All right. So, the information is not hard coded except for your 50 percent number, and that's derived from JP Morgan's recommendation that we just looked at, right?
A. Yes.
THE COURT: And for all the other real estate holdings, did you also pull the leases, figure out if you could get out of them, do a market survey for each of these?

THE WITNESS: We reviewed the leases for all of them, but we didn't do a market assessment for all of them, that those were allowing the leases to expire. It was not about recouping the lease.

THE COURT: Okay.

BY MR. FRACKMAN:

Q. Do you have a view as to whether the 50 percent number that is hard coded, that cell on N21, is it fact-based and is it reliable?

A. It is reliable, and it is based on worth of data and facts in this situation based on an assessment that—

Q. What is your response to the criticism from the government that you used hard coded assumptions in your model PX168?

A. Well, I honestly say that after all these months preparing these models, they are not at all just created out of thin air. It's really a lot of research, a lot of discussions with management, look at historical information, and in discussions also with Bertelsmann, right, vetting all these numbers.

Q. Could the real estate synergies that you modeled, the savings, have been achieved without the merger?

A. No.

Q. Why do you say that?

A. Because I guess Simon & Schuster will continue to need the headquarter in New York City.

Q. Okay, Your Honor. Why don't we turn back to Defendants' Demonstrative 14, page 14. This is where we ended up yesterday with real estate, the first category of efficiencies that we covered. And we're going to turn now to OpEx. Mr. Sansigre, you mentioned that you did a calculation of OpEx savings. What does OpEx include?

A. OpEx and operating expenses both include headcount and non-headcount expenses.

Q. In your experience—which you have a lot of, are OpEx savings common in mergers and acquisitions?

A. Yes, they are very common. They are easy to identify and easy to implement.

THE COURT: I'm sorry, you said it's headcount and non-headcount?

THE WITNESS: Headcount and non-headcount expenses, so third party charges, other kind of costs that are not linked to the personnel per se.

THE COURT: I'm sorry, what are the non-headcount expenses?

THE WITNESS: For example, when you receive a charge—you hire a third party to give you services on IT, for example, or you hire a consultant to help you with something or your auditors, those are what we consider generally non-headcount expenses.

THE COURT: So the consultant expenses?

THE WITNESS: Basically, yes, they are consulting expenses.

MR. FRACKMAN: And we'll get a look at some of those in greater detail, Your Honor.

THE COURT: Okay.

BY MR. FRACKMAN:

Q. So Mr. Sansigre, have you prepared a slide to—well, why don't we bring up slide 15 of Demonstrative 14. What are you showing here, Mr. Sansigre?

A. We're showing in operating expenses the fact that we analyze the reduction of duplicative functions, both in headcount and non-headcount.

Q. And then you have in the third—the second large bullet a list of departments. What are those departments, and how do they relate to your OpEx work?

A. So we make this analysis for headcount and non-headcount for the vast majority of the departments of the target company. In this case, marketing, sales and merchandising, fulfillment, production, IT, administration, editorial, and art departments. And it's very important to highlight that they're always with the philosophy of leaving creative untouched. Basically, any personnel or services that are linked to the books themselves, those are untouched.

Q. So let's dig into this in a little bit more detail. When you look at OpEx savings, what is the first source of information that you look at?

A. So first we ground it in experience. I mentioned yesterday that we have closed 26 transactions, and we've reviewed more than 100 publishing companies. So we understand the cost structure and the way publishing companies work. At the end of the day, they have very, very similar operations. So what we do is to look back and analyze all the transactions to see what kind of efficiencies we achieved in the past.

Q. Is there one transaction that you focused on when you did the OpEx work for the Simon & Schuster efficiencies model?

A. We reviewed several transactions, but in terms of size, we anchor in the Penguin Random House merger.

Q. So let's look at that 2013 merger. What OpEx synergies did Penguin Random House achieve in that transaction?

A. So the best way to look at it from a related perspective is by looking at the combined cost structure of both companies, and what were the savings that we achieved for the combined entity.

Q. Is there a range of OpEx savings that you've realized in your historical acquisitions, apart from the 2013 Penguin acquisition?

A. Yes, we have reviewed a lot of these transactions, and the range goes between 12 and 14 percent being the Penguin Random House merger in the low end of that range.

Q. So yeah, I was going to ask you that question. Specifically with respect to the 2013 Penguin merger, what was the OpEx savings that Penguin Random House achieved?

A. We were able to achieve 12.3 percent of the combined entity, basically by these duplicative functions on the back end of both companies.

Q. How do you know that number, like where did you get it?

A. So we have business records of all the transactions that we have done. And specifically, for the Penguin Random House merger, given the size, there was like synergies tracking that Bertelsmann, independently from us, would create to monitor how we achieved the synergies.

Q. Were you familiar with the synergies tracker that Bertelsmann—the synergies tracker before you started on the modeling for the Simon & Schuster transaction?

A. Yes.

Q. When did you review, and is there a document that you reviewed to get the specific OpEx savings from—the synergies and OpEx savings from the 2013 merger?

A. I reviewed a specific document, yes.

Q. And what is that document?

A. It's called the 2016 Synergies Tracking.

Q. Let's pull up—let me ask a couple of other prefatory questions on this. How long did Bertelsmann track the efficiencies flowing from the 2013 merger?

A. For three years.

Q. And why did Bertelsmann stop that work after three years?

A. Well, after three years, it starts being bothersome to keep tracking, because three years have passed. Also, the synergies achieved by 2016—that was the last year that it was created, the synergies were already over achieved.

Q. Let's pull up DX-301, Pam, and we'll focus on tab Overview FC2. Mr. Sansigre, what are we looking at here in DX-301? Well, what is DX-301?

A. This is the Penguin Random House merger integration synergies tracking file.

Q. And this worksheet that we're looking at, Overview FC2, what does it contain?

A. It contains the different savings by geography, and also comparing what originally was budgeted. This shows the actual synergies achieved.

Q. There is a column H entitled Passed on Savings to BAU. What does that reflect?

A. Those are the actual synergies achieved.

Q. That is line—

A. H8.

MR. FRACKMAN: H8. Your Honor, I offer DX-301 into evidence.

THE COURT: Any objection?

MS. LEAL: No objection.

THE COURT: That will be admitted. (Defendants' Exhibit 301 admitted into evidence)
THE COURT: I'm sorry, what is BAU?
THE WITNESS: BAU, that means business as usual.
BY MR. FRACKMAN:
Q. So that is the efficiencies that Bertelsmann confirmed were achieved as a result of the 2013 merger. What was the projected—what were the projected efficiencies at the time of the merger?
A. Originally the number was substantially lower.
Q. Do you remember the categories in which you achieved these synergies?
A. The same categories, de-duplications of overlap, overlapping functions.
Q. Pam, would you pull up DX-273, please. And let's just look at the front page. Mr. Sansigre, what is DX-273?
A. This is a presentation that we prepared in the summer of 2020 to pitch potential investors to participate in the Simon & Schuster potential acquisition with us.
Q. And did you in fact use DX-273 and present it to potential investors?
A. Yeah, my team and I created this document together with other departments of Penguin Random House. And yes, we used this document to show to external investors.
MR. FRACKMAN: Your Honor, we offer DX-273 into evidence.
THE COURT: Any objection?
MS. LEAL: No objection.
THE COURT: That will be admitted. (Defendants' Exhibit 273 admitted into evidence)
BY MR. FRACKMAN:
Q. Let's turn to slide—page 35 of DX-273. What is reflected on this page?
A. This reflects the overall synergies achieved by nature, by category.
Q. And you have OpEx synergies at the top and variable costs below?
A. Yes.
Q. And these are the categories, the subcategories of OpEx savings that were realized as a result of the 2013 merger, right?
A. Yes.
Q. While we're on the topic of the 2013 merger—and we'll come back to how you used the OpEx experience for 2022, I want to ask you one other question. Did Penguin Random House experience revenue synergies as a result of the 2013 merger?
A. No.
Q. And were any revenue synergies anticipated or modeled at the time of the merger?
A. No.
Q. The Court has heard about a revenue decline in the years following 2013. Are you familiar with what was going on in the business at that time that affected the revenue decline?
A. Yes, I performed an analysis for that.
Q. And what did your analysis show?
A. Well, what I realized is that there was like a revenue decline linked to an erosion linked to market conditions, especially in commercial fiction.
Q. Did that relate to the merger or did it relate to other things going on in the industry at the time?
A. This had nothing to do with the merger.
Q. Have you heard anyone at the company—that is, Penguin Random House, refer to this revenue decline as revenue dis-synergies?
A. Yes, I have heard that.
Q. Do you agree with the use of that term?
A. No, I don't agree.
Q. Did you use that term?
A. No, I haven't used that term for that specific situation.
Q. So you testified about the Bertelsmann synergies tracker, and the OpEx savings recognized in that tracker that we see here on DX-273.35. How did you use that information in modeling the efficiencies

projected from the current transaction?
A. So I anchor of course on these numbers. So what these numbers are what help me calculate the 12.3 percent that were referred to before; but also helped me, together with discussions with Mr. Dohle and Mr. Malaviya, to identify the different categories of synergies.
Q. So you came up with this 12 percent OpEx savings from your prior transactions, in particular the Penguin merger?
A. In particular this one, yes.
Q. And then what did you do with that 12 percent?
A. Well, that 12 percent ground me. Again, it was a range between 12 and 14. But given the size, that 12 percent ground me in order to start calculating what could be the potential efficiencies achieved with Simon & Schuster.
Q. Let's pull up slide 16 from Demonstrative 14. What is shown on slide 16, Mr. Sansigre?
A. This is embedded into PX-168, so the efficiencies model in the Silk US worksheet. As I said yesterday, this is where the vast majority of the efficiencies calculation happened. And in this particular area, what you can see is the different departments with the Penguin Random House cost structure; then the Simon & Schuster cost structure; then what would be the combined cost structure of both companies. And then at the end, you can see the targeted dollar savings for those departments. And then in the total, you can see the total efficiencies that we projected. And you can see there the 12.3.
Q. And this is in the Silk US worksheet, rows 59 to 69 of PX-168?
A. Yes.
Q. Did you just plug this 12.3 percent number into your model?
A. No, I had several conversations, again, with Mr. Dohle and Mr. Malaviya that actually achieved the Penguin Random House merger. So they have extensive experience in achieving these efficiencies. But additionally, I did a totally separate analysis to confirm the reliability of my projections.
Q. And what is that analysis called?
A. That analysis is called the OpEx matrix.
Q. And we've introduced that, Your Honor, as PX-406. Let's turn to that now. Pam, will you pull up PX-406, summaries worksheet. Mr. Sansigre, tell the Court what we're looking at here.
A. This is the OpEx matrix.
Q. And this is the summary page, right?
A. Yes.
Q. How many worksheets do you have in PX-406?
A. Around 50 I would say.
Q. Around 50 you say?
A. Yes.
Q. And just on a very high level, I'd direct your attention to E52. What is reflected on this summary page?
A. E52 is the total synergies that I calculated in this analysis.
Q. And you testified earlier that there was both a headcount component and a non-headcount component. Let's first look at row 48. What's reflected there?
A. Those are the synergies—the headcount synergies projected for this transaction.
Q. And the total is in E48; is that right?
A. Yes.
Q. And then you said that there was a non-headcount component?
A. Yes.
Q. Where is that reflected?
A. We can see the total in E51.
Q. Okay. So, let's start with the headcount component. Can you explain at a high level the work you performed to calculate the savings reflected in cell E48?
A. Sure. So, each company records their departments in a different way, so it was very important to really understand their department structure in order to compare Penguin Random House and Simon &

Schuster departments one by one. So, what I did is almost at the end of the process, I received information from the clean team where I have basically the full roster of employee data for all the employees of Simon & Schuster.

Q. So, let me stop you right there. Could we pull up Demonstrative 14, page 17, please. So Mr. Sansigre, what is shown on this slide?

A. This is the confidential document with anonymized data for Simon & Schuster employees with their location, department, title, but also their salary, benefits and other relevant information.

Q. This page of the data has information for about a dozen employees. How many employees did you receive such data for?

A. I received this for all Simon & Schuster employees in the U.S., there are about 1,400.

Q. Okay. So, once you got the detailed compensation data for all of the Simon & Schuster employees, what did you do with that information?

A. I went line by line, employee by employee matching their position at what would be the equivalent Penguin Random House department and sub department.

Q. And once you had completed that mapping exercise, what did you do?

A. I was very careful with this information, because only my team had access to this document. So, I aggregated the data by the Penguin Random House departments with the information, and I used that information to plug it into the OpEx matrix.

Q. So you incorporated it into PX-406?

A. Yes.

Q. Let's turn to that next slide, Pam. This is a page from PX-406 entitled U.S. S&S Payroll Worksheet. What are you showing here, Mr. Sansigre?

A. This is the people that I created from the previous document that you just showed. This is the people that I was mentioning that then I plugged into the PX-406. You can see the different departments and sub departments in the way PRH look at them, with the number of headcount, the compensation, the benefits, tenure.

Q. Okay. So, you have this information in one of the worksheets of PX-406. What did you do with it?

A. So this was the basis for aligning Penguin Random House departments and sub departments with the Simon & Schuster ones. And with that, I was able to identify the overlapping functions.

Q. With the Court's indulgence, we'll look at a couple of the detailed worksheets for the different departments that Mr. Sansigre examined, and we'll start with administration. Let's turn to PX-406, the administration worksheet. And Pam, let's go to the top first and just orient ourselves. Mr. Sansigre, you have some information at the top under a heading with an orange heading that says PRH U.S. Gross Spending Administration.

What is in the orange block on this slide, and on all the other sub slides?

A. So this is the area where I inputted the Penguin Random House information. And what you can see is the expenses and the headcount by—the expenses by nature, and also then by sub departments. That's why it's called a matrix.

Q. Yes, I wanted to get to that. So first of all, this information in the orange blocks on the different worksheets are from PRH, right?

A. Yes.

Q. That's PRH data, okay. And although this is in the administration department, you have a whole bunch of sub departments to the right. What do those reflect?

A. These departments reflect the sub departments within administration.

Q. You have executives?

A. You have executives, corporate services, finance, HR, IT security, legal, contracts, RMS—which means royalties management system, corporate shared and other.

Q. And are these all within administration?

A. Yes.

Q. Now let's go down—

THE COURT: Is this still all headcount?

THE WITNESS: This is all still headcount, yes.

BY MR. FRACKMAN:

Q. Let's go down to the green block. What is reflected in the green block that starts at row 28 and goes to row 34?

A. So thanks to my mapping, I was able to basically do the same exercise for Simon & Schuster. So I broke the different Simon & Schuster employees by sub department exactly aligned—as you can see by each column, exactly aligned with each PRH sub department. And also I had enough information to break the spending linked to headcounts between employee and non-employee.

Q. So let's turn to row 45 that's entitled HC-Synergies. Just take the Court through the information that appears on row 45. Let's start with the number in E45. What does that reflect?

A. This is the total headcount synergies projected for the admin department.

Q. For the administration department. And then if you go to the right, you have a group—a series of negative numbers in each of the sub departments. What does that reflect?

A. Those are the overlapping positions identified.

Q. And is that just an addition formula that adds those up to the number in E45?

A. Yes.

Q. Now let's go down to E48. What is reflected there?

A. Here is reflected the potential savings from those overlap positions. Basically, it's a formula that calculates the overlapping positions identified, multiplied by the average compensation of both organizations, both Penguin Random House and Simon & Schuster.

Q. And why did you use the average compensation of both organizations for calculating the headcount efficiencies?

A. Our philosophy in these kind of mergers is that at the end of it, you want to take the best people from both sides. So, at the end of the day, the combined entity, right, it needs to be the average of both organizations.

Q. All right. Let's go to the non-headcount synergies, row 51. First let's start with cell E51. What's contained there?

A. This is the total non-headcount synergies that we projected.

Q. And again, you have it allocated across different sub departments; is that right?

A. Yes.

Q. How did you—well, first, what are the non-headcount synergies that are included in the administration department efficiencies calculation?

A. Just to clarify, I did not locate the expenses. The expenses are from Simon & Schuster business records. So then what I did is go sub department by sub department identifying the different third party charges that clearly were overlapping. For example, we don't need two insurance, we don't need bank charges, right, we don't need so many bank accounts, for example. There's those kind of charges that we're saving here.

Q. Is the detail for the non-headcount savings reflected on the summary sheet included in PX-406?

A. Yes, if you go to the top, U.S. non-employee G&A cost categories.

Q. Just slow down, slow down. U.S. non-employee G&A cost categories. Okay, Ms. Radford opened up that tab. What do you have here?

A. It's the non-employee expenses broken by each item basically.

Q. By each department?

A. By each department, but also by each item.

Q. Okay. So that's an overview of what you did in administration. Let's look at another one, if we could, Your Honor. Let's look at IT. And first let's go to the IT tab in 406. I think we can go right down to row 52. What's reflected in cell E52, Mr. Sansigre?

A. The total synergies projected for the total IT department, but also by sub department within IT.

Q. And going up to E48, what's reflected there?

A. This is the headcount savings projected.

Q. Now, in the case of IT, the non-headcount savings are far greater than the headcount savings. Can you explain to the Court why that is?

A. In the case of IT, at Random House, we have our own IT organization that is specialized for book publishing. In the case of Simon & Schuster, they were largely dependent on ViacomCBS. So ViacomCBS was providing the IT and the services to Simon & Schuster.

Q. And the rationale is that after the merger—

A. Well, we have scalable systems. ViacomCBS is not going to continue to charge us for those services, but also they are not going to provide the further services. And things that we have disintegrated, a scalable IT system, we're going to be able to bring all Simon & Schuster into our system basically.

Q. Where did you get the detail to calculate the non-headcount synergy numbers for IT, where did it come from?

A. So again, it comes from Simon & Schuster business records.

Q. Let's turn to slide 19 of Defendants' Demonstrative 14.

THE COURT: I'm sorry, so the question from Mr. Frackman was to calculate the synergy numbers. My understanding was that all of this data goes into what were the costs of Simon & Schuster and what were the costs of Penguin Random House. But then on the summary slide, it seems like you just applied a percentage. So, to me, the synergy calculation is the percentage.

So where did we get the percentages, I think, is the more relevant question?

THE WITNESS: So, the summary—well, we have seen two business information, right, the early one which is in the efficiencies model, and then this one is in the OpEx matrix. In the OpEx matrix, that summary that we saw is just linked to this detailed analysis that we just came from for admin, for IT.

THE COURT: So, I understand, but you would just have a percentage like 12 percent—which I think you said was hardwired?

THE WITNESS: It doesn't work that way. So, when I finalized the OpEx matrix, first of all, what I realized is that the 12.3 percent was very sound. And then what I did is, given that I was very—it confirmed the 12.3 percent, what I did is I took the dollar amount from the OpEx matrix, and that is what basically I put it into the efficiencies model. In order to get that dollar amount, I just put the percentages, the 12 percent and all these percentages that you show.

The reason why that is important is because—and it's a very common practice in M&A, is as you update the model with new information—because there's new actuals, new forecasts, et cetera, you want to anchor on those percentages so that the synergies move as you have new information. That is the best way of making the efficiencies model really reliable.

THE COURT: Yes, but the synergy percentage itself, that was hardwired, right?

THE WITNESS: It was informed on the OpEx matrix.

THE COURT: It was informed by the matrix, but it's a hardwired number, 12 percent, that you came up with, for example; am I correct?

THE WITNESS: It was implied. I knew by each department what is the dollar amount that we were targeting.

THE COURT: Yes, but the percentage is hardwired?

THE WITNESS: Yes.

THE COURT: Can you pull up No. 6 demonstrative, I just want to make sure—

MR. FRACKMAN: Demonstrative 6?

THE COURT: I think it was number—was that 6 that you—the one you started with today that had the—slide 16, I'm sorry.

MR. FRACKMAN: Slide 16, Pam.

THE COURT: The percentages, those are hardwired?

THE WITNESS: Those are hardwired, yes.

THE COURT: Okay, that was my question.

BY MR. FRACKMAN:

Q. Maybe this would help—which jumps ahead in the discussion, but why don't we bring up slide 21 from Defendants' Demonstrative 14. Mr. Sansigre, what are you showing here on slide 21? The department column is pretty clear. What does the second column, the one entitled 11/4/2020 draft model, refer to?

A. So on the left side, you can see the different departments, categories. Then you're going to see three columns with projected efficiencies. The first column was the efficiencies that were projected before I finalized the OpEx matrix; then what were the conclusions of the OpEx matrix in PX-406; and then the dollar amount of the November 2020 final model in PX-168.

Q. And explain to the Court again how you used the OpEx matrix to reach the final numbers in the November 2020 model.

A. So, again, from a practical perspective, I wanted to put exactly the same dollar amounts—that's what you need to anchor, the same dollar amounts in the efficiencies model. But again, because you—and that's what I did. In order to get there, you need to hard code the percentages. But that is very common and very normal, and it's grounded on this analysis.

And again, I repeat, it's very important because as you update the model, you want to keep updating the model with new information. The percentages stay the same. If there's more inflation, for example, then the synergies are going to go up. If for whatever reason there's lower costs, then the synergies will run down. That's the best way to show that the model is reliable for all time.

Q. Let's go back to the IT—

THE COURT: So, can I just ask one thing?

MR. FRACKMAN: Sure.

THE COURT: So, it sounds like when you updated the model, you were taking into account all the new information about costs, like say they opened the clean room and you get more information and you would update the model. So, the parts that were updated were the cost numbers, like how much is Simon & Schuster paying for IT, how much is Simon & Schuster paying for whatever.

THE WITNESS: Exactly, yes.

THE COURT: But the expectation of synergies as a percentage is a hardwired number that you came up with using your judgment and based on experience?

THE WITNESS: It's based on—it's very important to recall what I said before. What is important is the total amount, the 12.3. We have all this experience with all these transactions, especially the Penguin Random House merger. That is the one that I was very comfortable with, because it's what we have done in the past and it's our experience. But I went a step farther to say, you know what, given that I have all this additional information, let's try to actually go department by department and create a document bottoms-up where you can actually really calculate this information so that you can issue a report.

THE COURT: So, you're saying that it would have been an appropriate assumption that you could achieve 12.3 because you've achieved it before, but you just tried to back it up by looking at all the numbers to see if it would come out to about 12.3?

THE WITNESS: I didn't back it up, because if the—again, the 12 percent is based on our experience. If the OpEx matrix would have resulted in a lower amount, then I would have raised a hand and say, well, now that I've been able to get more in deep, actually maybe we need to put down the—reduce the synergies. But the conclusion of the OpEx matrix was the other way around, was like not only confirmed that the 12.3 percent was valid, but also I was able to go department by department and get that comfort. Your Honor, they—

THE COURT: So how would it be different, though, if you put in the percentages based on experience?

THE WITNESS: It would have been the same basically. But the difference is that each company has marketing or IT or sales and merchandising in—they calculate or they do it in a different way. That's why the focus always is the total combined, right, the 12.3.

THE COURT: Right. So, your focus was very much on figuring out what the actual expenses were. But I'm saying that the percentages of synergies that you predicted, you put in those percentages based on your experience, but didn't you put in percentages that would result in a 12.3 percent overall?

THE WITNESS: Well, yes, I mean, I had conversations with Mr. Dohle and Mr. Malaviya, going over it with them, they've done it in the past. So, before the OpEx matrix, we will go to administration, IT, and then they will see the dollar amount and say, well, that makes sense with what we achieved. We will look at what is the dollar amount that we achieved in the Penguin Random House merger. And I say, oh, sales, if we achieve like similar—I don't want to say the number, a similar amount or even a higher amount, that seems reasonable, right. And all that basically added up to the 12.3 that they were talking about. But additionally, again, because of all the accountability—and I'm very professional and I really—we're very responsible. This is important decisions, right. So, I still wanted to go one step ahead and calculate in detail what was these overlapping functions to really go back and give the comfort to our board, like we're responsible and this is achievable.

THE COURT: Yes. And just to make sure I understand, though, when you put in the percentages of synergies, you put them in so that you would end up with a 12.3 which is what you expected; then you went and looked at the actual numbers to see that that was realistic?

THE WITNESS: That is basically what happened. But again, I want to come back to this concept that we signed November 2020. Then in 2021, we started receiving new information from Simon & Schuster and Penguin Random House, right, and we are almost two years after. And it's a normal practice to keep those percentages fixed as you move, right, because then you have new information. And again, if inflation goes up, the synergies will go up.

THE COURT: Absolutely, I understand. It's a normal practice for what you're doing, which is figuring out if it makes sense to acquire another company.

THE WITNESS: Yes.

THE COURT: Okay, thank you.

BY MR. FRACKMAN:

Q. So let's go back to IT. Let me ask a question to follow up with the Court's questioning. When you did the detailed headcount savings identifying the number of employees who would no longer be needed—let's say in the administration department, and you went sub department by sub department, did you look at the individual employee overlap or did you use a percentage?

A. I did both. I mean, I went sub department by sub department seeing what are the kind of positions. And I know the Penguin Random House organization pretty well, so I basically was able to identify the overlapping positions.

Q. Okay. Let's go back to IT. We were looking at the basis for your IT savings. I believe you said, Mr. Sansigre, that you got that information from Simon & Schuster. Let's look at slide 19 of Demonstrative 14. This is from PX-406, the corporate allocations worksheet. What is reflected here, Mr. Sansigre?

A. Here is reflected a document from the data room from Simon & Schuster business records. You can see there the date and my name, because it's coming from the data room. And this is basically the breakdown of the ViacomCBS allocation to Simon & Schuster.

Q. Did you just incorporate that full amount into your OpEx matrix or did you refine it in any way?

A. Well, again, I analyzed the expense line by line. I had conversations with Mr. Malaviya who also oversees IT. And we have conversations with the head of IT of Penguin Random House to really understand these expenses, and basically to see what would be the process of us integrating Simon & Schuster into our IT systems.

Q. The Court will see, if Your Honor wants to go back, that the non-headcount IT synergies number is lower than what is reflected on the corporate allocations worksheet that we're looking at now. Mr. Sansigre, why didn't you just incorporate the total amount?

A. Yeah, I had this conversation with Mr. Malaviya. ViacomCBS will stop charging us for these services, even though we have scalable IT systems and we are very confident that we will bring Simon & Schuster at nominal costs. At the end of the day, we wanted to be conservative, so we estimated some incremental cost linked to bringing Simon & Schuster on board.

Q. Let's look at one other. Pam, let's go to the fulfillment tab in PX-406, please. So, Mr. Sansigre, we—Pam will take us to the left. A little bit farther down, please. So, you have here total synergies in E52 again. Can you explain how you calculated that? I mean, the mechanics I think the Court already understands, but the input for it.

A. So in the case of fulfillment, it was a little bit different. Because we needed to analyze their different distribution centers, and to really understand their expenses and how they were managing their volumes basically.

Q. And where did you identify that there would be both headcount and non-headcount savings in the fulfillment area?

A. So, I have conversations with Mr. Malaviya that is in charge of fulfillment. And what we realized is that Penguin Random House, we have already four warehouses—and very important, we have four warehouses across the United States. We didn't need to add another three warehouses. That's actually anchored also on experience of the Penguin Random House merger where we closed warehouses.

Q. How, if at all, are third party vendors for returns incorporated into your fulfillment synergies number?

A. So interesting, in the case of Simon & Schuster, we learned that they don't basically record or process their own returns. They get a third-party company to do their returns.

Q. And what cell calculates the savings from eliminating the third party returns that Simon & Schuster is currently paying for?

A. Q51.

Q. Let me ask briefly about a couple of the other departments. Did you look at sales and marketing—sales and merchandising?

A. Yes, I did.

Q. And why don't we pull up the summary sheet for that, Pam. No, not that—well, I didn't mean—I meant in PX-406. Sales, right? Yeah, thanks. Now, this is a smaller number of savings. Can you explain to the Court the basis for the projections here?

A. So in my analysis, Penguin Random House has a sales force that is five times larger than Simon & Schuster. It's very important to note that we basically have—90 percent of our clients overlap. So therefore, as part of the transaction, we will not need basically a lot of positions to cover the same client.

Q. And I think the question that the Court asked is did you just take 13 percent or did you actually look at the numbers first?

A. First, the important thing is the dollar amount, right. That is the number that is calculated on—that affects basically the efficiencies model. In order to calculate the price, the percentage is important, as I mentioned, for the mechanics of the model, how the model keeps updating us as we move along.

Q. Yes, I guess my question was bad. Did the number of headcount reductions that you projected derive from the fact that you were putting in 13 and a half percent or did you build it up from the number of individuals that you identified as overlapping?

A. I build it up by the number of overlapping positions, yes.

Q. Okay.

THE COURT: I'm sorry, let me ask about that, too, because this was something that was discussed before. I understand there's evidence in the record that this is not a bottoms-up analysis, it's a top-down analysis. Is that your understanding?

THE WITNESS: So, the efficiencies model, the other document, is largely top-down, okay. This exercise is what most people would call bottoms-up.

THE COURT: So, did you actually identify which employees you're going to cut?

THE WITNESS: That is a part of integration planning that always happens after closing.

THE COURT: And did you identify how many you were going to cut?

THE WITNESS: Yes, it's in the document.

THE COURT: So can I see that?

BY MR. FRACKMAN:

Q. Sure. Well, we can look at it while we're on the fulfillment tab. If you can go to E45. What is reflected in E45, Mr. Sansigre?

A. This is the headcount efficiencies that we estimated for the reduction of warehouses and volumes through Simon & Schuster warehouses.

Q. And what are the subcategories that you modeled to the right that total the number in E45?

A. So when we modeled this, there were three distribution centers for Simon & Schuster. We realized that, if anything, we will just need the larger one called Riverside. And within Riverside, we really didn't need as much capacity as they had, because at Penguin Random House, our supply chain is really scalable. We have invested a lot of money in making it scalable that you can put a lot of units. We are also adding clients every year, right. So, we're very comfortable with moving all these volumes through the Penguin Random House distribution centers.

Q. And what if the total number in E45 had amounted to 7 percent instead of what you have in E47, what would you have done? How would that affected your model?

A. I would have needed to reduce the synergies in the efficiencies model. As I said, at the end of the day, I'm going to be held accountable. And we are very responsible people, we're not going to be making this analysis not grounded on the actual experience. And again, this document was to give me the comfort in regards to a third party potentially to show that my analysis was grounded on detailed analysis.

THE COURT: Can I ask, though, these numbers that are broken down on the right, those are based on percentage reductions, correct?

THE WITNESS: In the case of distribution specifically, yes, because it's very linked to volumes, right. It depends on the volume. So yes, you can see on the right, the 40 percent that you can see is basically the capacity that we were expecting that we will need from Riverside. And the rest of the volume we would be able to accommodate into the Penguin Random House warehouses.

THE COURT: Again, it's that you looked and saw what the costs were, you saw that there was overlapping, and then you estimated a percentage reduction that you could make?

THE WITNESS: Yes.

THE COURT: And so the percentage you made, that was informed by the percentage you originally thought for distribution?

THE WITNESS: No. What we did is we have information about the volumes that Simon & Schuster had, their returns. And I was able to discuss that with Mr. Malaviya that is in charge of all the distribution. And I had also conversations with PRH management that are in charge of understanding the warehouses. And given the technology that we have in the Penguin Random House warehouses, we knew that we could move all that volume into our warehouses.

THE COURT: But then you came up with a percentage that you thought you could save?

THE WITNESS: Yes. It's grounded on our experience and in the Penguin Random House merger, yes.

THE COURT: And is that the percentage that's on slide 16?

THE WITNESS: This was to calculate the dollar amount of savings. And then in the efficiencies model, we just anchor on that dollar amount, and we apply the percentage in order to get to the dollar amount to be the same.

THE COURT: Did you change the percentages on slide 16 depending on what was happening here?

THE WITNESS: Yes. The overall number was the same, it was 12.3, so I was comfortable overall when that took place. But then I said, you know what, I have done all this analysis, I'm going to also go department by department and align it. And in order to align it, I basically needed to put the percentages that will get to the dollar amount. And as I said, the methodology of the percentages is because as you move along with new actuals, you can anchor those percentage savings.

THE COURT: I'm trying to understand how this all fits in. The management judgment was 12.3 percent. That's what you were expecting, and it was kind of your guideline where you thought you should be?

THE WITNESS: Yes.

THE COURT: And then you went back and looked at the numbers, and you expected all of the synergies in each category ultimately to add up to 12.3 total?

THE WITNESS: No, that's what I was saying, like if the numbers would have been lower, I would have raised a hand and said listen, we anchor on the 12.3. But my experience, if the numbers would have gone down, I would have said, you know, we cannot achieve the 12.3. But it was the other way around, right. My analysis showed that the 12.3 was grounded, and that's what happened, right. But if it would have gone down, I would have needed to go back to the management and to Bertelsmann and say we need to bring down the synergies, because I'm worried that we're not going to be able to achieve it.

THE COURT: Yes, and it seems to me—and I'm just trying it figure out exactly how this worked, you were as precise as possible in the actual numbers in terms of costs and people. But then the percentage you applied was a management judgment: We can reduce that by 40 percent, we can reduce that by 20 percent?

THE WITNESS: It's basically anchored on our experience, yes, we can reduce that. But I have all the overlapping positions and all the charges, right, so I could go one by one and really understand. So you're absolutely right, it's based on judgment, but with a wealth of data, a wealth of conversations and discussions. This particular spreadsheet, the aggregated information, I actually shared it with Mr. Dohle and Mr. Malaviya. And they have the experience, right, they've done it, so it gave me a lot of comfort.

THE COURT: So overall, a lot of the work that was put into this was based on putting in the correct numbers and updating them, and then it was discussing among the management what percentages you could glean in savings?

THE WITNESS: Yes, based on our experience, yes.

THE COURT: And then putting it all in was a way of checking yourself to see if it came out to around 12.3 percent, which is what you would have expected based on your prior experience?

THE WITNESS: Yes.

THE COURT: But the actual synergies in each category were percentages based on management judgment among you and all the other managers, with the idea that it should come out to 12.3 percent?

THE WITNESS: Yes. But again, if this analysis would have concluded that we should target a lower amount, I would have needed to reduce the amount.

THE COURT: Yes. If you had seen numbers which indicated there's no overlap between the people, for example, in IT, then that particular sub synergy, you would have taken it out?

THE WITNESS: Yes, and I would be—

THE COURT: You'd be making adjustments in all the different categories?

THE WITNESS: Exactly.

THE COURT: But it was all management judgment as to the percentage?

THE WITNESS: And because, again, we are also conservative, because we're going to be held accountable. I think that if the numbers would have been a little bit higher, most likely we would not have kept increasing because we wanted to be conservative, right. If you look at our 26 transactions, we have this concept of look-backs. So, we project in a way very conservative, and Bertelsmann comes back after three years and they review the numbers.

THE COURT: You want to be right.

THE WITNESS: I want to be right, I want to be right, trust me. And we do look-backs and we say, well, they really do an incredible job of understanding how we projected where is the company. And in those look-backs, our projections have been always above what we projected, because we're conservative and, again, we're responsible. We are trying to do this for the right reasons. It's not just guesses or anything, it's actual projections based on our experience.

THE COURT: Okay, I think I understand that.

BY MR. FRACKMAN:

Q. Let me just cover one related point. Let's pull up—I'm not going to take the Court through every one of these slides–

THE COURT: I think I understand the general procedure now, so I don't think we need to get into all the details.

BY MR. FRACKMAN:

Q. Let's just pull up slide 20 of Demonstrative 14, Pam. What do you show here, Mr. Sansigre?

A. This is the projected efficiencies in the OpEx matrix by department.

Q. And I just want to ask one question about IT. How much of the number reflected in the IT synergies relates to the elimination of the payments to ViacomCBS, those corporate assessments for IT that the parent provided Simon & Schuster?

A. The full amount.

Q. Was there any management judgment in connection with that determination?

A. No, they're going to stop charging us the $10,000,000.

Q. Let's go to the next slide, if we could. I just have one more question on slide 21. We looked at this before. When you updated the November 4 draft OpEx synergies after doing your OpEx matrix work, Mr. Sansigre, did you adjust both the numbers and the percentages or just one or the other?

A. Yes, as I mentioned, now that I have the dollar amounts, I basically aligned the dollar amounts in the efficiencies model with the OpEx matrix.

Q. Now, why didn't you use the exact numbers from your OpEx matrix, PX-406, in the November 2020 final model? There are some differences here, small.

A. So the OpEx matrix included a lot of confidential information from individuals. I wanted to be—I'm very delicate with the situation of not sharing information. Not only because of the agreement with ViacomCBS related to the clean team, but also because sometimes these models get shared, right, and I'm very protective of that information. So I didn't want to incorporate the OpEx matrix analysis into the efficiencies model.

Q. Why didn't you just link it?

A. The same reason. Again, like at the end of the day, this was a separate analysis that was giving me the confirmation, and it was grounding my analysis.

Q. I want to turn to a question arising from your deposition. It's obvious you did quite a bit of work on headcount and OpEx.

Do you recall at your deposition being asked whether you used Simon & Schuster headcount and salary information in your November 2020 model, PX-168?

A. Yes, I remember that.

Q. And what did you answer?

A. I said no.

Q. Can you explain to the Court why you said no when we just reviewed the work you did and how it did affect the numbers in PX-168?

A. We had two depositions, right, and a lot of hours with the Government. We spent a lot of time in the efficiencies model, and I interpreted the question as is the headcount information embedded into the spreadsheet. I mean, the efficiencies model has over 100 stats, and none of these stats have headcount information for the reasons that I just said. If the Government would have asked me what is this analysis, right, I would have totally explained the reasons of that document.

Q. Did the Government in those two depositions show you Plaintiff's Exhibit 406, your OpEx matrix, at any point?

A. No.

Q. Okay, so next slide. We've covered real estate and operating expenses. Let's turn to variable costs and return rates. What are the variable costs that you included in your model?

A. I included return rates, freight, PPB—which means paper, printing and binding, and marketing spend.

Q. And when you talk about return rates, are you referring to return rates on physical books or on physical and digital?

A. It's only on physical.

Q. Only on physical, okay. Tell us the importance of lower return rates to Penguin Random House, or any publisher for that matter.

A. Well, return rates is a very idiosyncratic thing that we have in book publishing. At the end of the day, retailers can return—so we sell our books on a returnable basis. So basically, retailers can return the book any time they want if they have not sold it or just if they want. That coupled together with the fact that predicting demand is really complicated in book publishing, to really understand the demand of each book. That leads to retailers to over order. The most important thing for a retailer is that they don't lose a sale. So therefore, they have this incentive of over ordering. At the end of the day, if they over order, the publishers, we are the ones that need to print the book, we need to ship the book. And then if they return it back to us, basically we need to also take care of holding the inventory and destroying potentially—

Q. Yeah, I wanted to ask you that question. What are the costs that Penguin Random House bears for returned books?

A. Of course, the paper, printing and binding; shipping it to the retailers; holding the inventory, right. It has like a cost, right, holding the inventory for all time. And then as I mentioned, potentially scrap the book.

Q. Is return rates an important metric for Penguin Random House?

A. It is important for us and for any publisher.

Q. Does Penguin Random House track return rates?

A. Yes.

Q. So how did you use or model return rates in PX-168, your efficiencies model?

A. So maybe to explain a little bit more on returns, the way the return rate is calculated is because retailers tend to over order, right—for example, you will ship 140 books only to sell 100, right. Therefore, you get 40 back. That would be a 40 percent return rate. But if in order to sell the same 100 books we could only ship 120, therefore we will only get returned 20 percent—or 20 books which is 20 percent, right. So that return rate is important for publishers, and that's why we track it, right. So what I did is to look into the return rate of—the actual return rates of Simon & Schuster and Penguin Random House, and see the differential between both return rates.

Q. Let's pull up your—we're going to PX-168, your model, the Silk US IS output summary worksheet. I'll direct you to row nine. What is reflected on row nine?

A. This is the summary—I mean, this is the line for returns.

Q. And row 10?

A. And row 10 is the return rate.

Q. And the savings that you modeled—and we'll get to how you modeled it. The savings for how you modeled are reflected in cell S—

A. S9.

Q. S9. So to move this along, you said you compared the Simon & Schuster return rate with the Penguin Random House return rate?

A. Yes, I took a variety of steps to calculate this potential efficiency.

Q. Let's just focus on this, the difference. Where did you get the information for the Simon & Schuster return rate?

A. Well, it was in their P&Ls and in their business records.

Q. Did you speak to Simon & Schuster management to confirm the rate?

A. Yes, in the management presentation, I confirmed the rate with the CFO.

Q. And on PX-168 that we have in front of us, where is the Simon & Schuster return rate reflected?

A. Well, so historical, it would be in line—from E10 to H10, E10 to H10. That is historical return rate.

Q. And the base case standalone projection for the Simon & Schuster return rate, where do you have that?

A. In M10.

Q. And where is the Penguin Random House return rate reflected on PX-168?

A. Well, it's not reflected exactly here, but basically, it's illustrated in V10.

Q. V10, that's the base case—that's what you project Simon & Schuster's rate would be post-merger?

A. Yes.

Q. And how did you use the difference between V10 and M10 in your calculations?

A. So I looked at the historical return rates, and I compared the same historical return rates for Penguin Random House and Simon & Schuster. And I got an average of 4 percent, and that is basically what I used. Also, again, I did more things, but that is basically what I used to target the potential improvement as soon as Simon & Schuster would join our supply chain.

Q. And the number—the percentage in V10 base case, how does that number compare with Penguin Random House's own return rate as you projected it at this time?

A. It is the same. The assumption was that Simon & Schuster return will converge with—

Q. What was the basis for the assumption that you would bring Simon & Schuster's return rate down to Penguin Random House's return rate?

A. So we have a lot of examples. Starting with the Penguin Random House merger itself, we were able to bring the Penguin return rate by more than 8 percent down. We have a variety of other transactions like

Little Tiger, like Santillana in Spain. We have several transactions where we have been able to reduce return rate, but also—which is I think very important, our experience with third party distribution clients.

Q. So let me stop you right there. If I could, you just referred to several transactions?

A. Yes.

Q. And then you said third party distribution clients. What are you referring to by the phrase third party distribution clients?

A. This is other publishers that they basically rely on our supply chain in order to sell their books.

Q. So this is other publishers that Penguin Random House provides the distribution services for, right?

A. Yes.

Q. And what has been the experience at Penguin Random House with respect to return rates for third party publishers who come into the Penguin Random House supply chain?

A. It's interesting, because it's like a controlled experiment. Because we bring all these third-party solution clients that come from different supply chains, and as soon as they are part of our philosophy—of our integrated machine as we call it, the return rates go down. And also, we experience a sales lift with a lot of them. But basically, we weren't able to reduce their return rates on all of them.

Q. So you mentioned you also grounded it in the 2013 Penguin merger experience. Let's pull up DX-273, which is in evidence. This is the management presentation from July 2020. I'll ask Pam to go to page 36. Mr. Sansigre, let's look at the information on the left hand side of page 36. What is shown there?

A. This is showing the Penguin return rate and the Random House return rate over time.

Q. And the top line, the orange line, whose is that?

A. Penguin is the orange, and Random House is the gray one.

Q. And what does this show?

A. This is showing how we were able to bring down the return rate of Penguin and converge with Random House.

Q. Are you aware that the DOJ has criticized—Ms. Hammer, their expert—has criticized your return rate calculation, because since 2020, Simon & Schuster's return rate has already come down some?

A. Yes, I'm aware of that.

Q. What's your response to that?

A. Well, first of all, the most important thing is to identify what is the gap. It's not about the return rate only itself, it's about the gap between the return rate of PRH and the return rate of Simon & Schuster.

Q. Have you looked at the gap between Penguin Random House's return rate and Simon & Schuster's from 2017 to 2021?

A. Yes.

Q. Let's pull up Demonstrative 14, page 24. What are you showing here on—well, first of all, where is this information contained in your model?

A. This information is contained in DX-168 up to 2019, because 2020 and 2021 are actuals. So up to 2019 is in PX-168. But in later versions of the model, we would have actuals for 2020 and 2021.

Q. Tell us what this shows for 2020—for the different years with respect to the difference between Penguin Random House's return rate and Simon & Schuster's?

A. So the historical average was 4 percent. You can see a decline in 2019 to 2.5, and that's exactly what we were more or less targeting of improvement. And then, yes, in 2020 and 2021, the Simon & Schuster return rates went down, but ours went substantially more down. As you can see, 8 percent and 11.8 percent. However, because all this information is based on the pandemic which is not—in my opinion from a modeling perspective and thinking about the future of the company, is not as reliable as to thinking about the company before the pandemic. So that's why we didn't increase also the targeted return rate in the company, because our expectation is that this will normalize in the future.

Q. Let me just make sure the record is clear on this. The difference between Penguin's return rate and Simon & Schuster's return rate in 2021 is over 10 percent, right?

A. Yes.

Q. How much did you model for the improvement of Simon & Schuster's return rate in your efficiencies model?

A. 2.6.

Q. Now, I believe the Government also has complained that the return rate number that we were just looking at in PX-168 is hard coded. What is your response to that?

A. It is hard coded in the spreadsheet, but it's based on this analysis and numerous conversations, and also the experience, of course.

Q. Now, there are some other variable cost savings that you have in PX-168. Why don't we jump back to that summary sheet. Again, we're looking at the Silk US IS output tab of PX-168.

And we're not going to go through all of these, Mr. Sansigre, but can you describe for the Court how you calculated the savings for freight, for instance?

A. A similar approach.

Q. And what about the marketing programs savings, what does that even refer to?

A. This is the outspend basically, and it was also a similar approach.

Q. Well, how do you know that the outspend is going to come down at all?

A. Well, at the end of the day, a lot of our ad programs are run through the same platforms, so we expect consolidation in those suppliers so we're going to be able to save money.

Q. Now, you also have here in the variable costs category royalties, row 26. What do you model for the changes in royalties as a result of the merger?

A. So given that we are projecting additional revenues and improving returns, every additional dollar that we create in increased sales we automatically share with authors, with royalties. So this is basically the contribution, right, how much additional payment we will be paying to authors based on the efficiencies.

Q. Let's go to Demonstrative No. 14, page 25. We've covered three of the four categories of efficiencies. Let's turn to revenue enhancements. As a way to summarize or expedite the discussion, I want to show you a page from Ms. Hammer's report. This is going to be reflected on our Demonstrative 14, page 26. This is from her table one in her report. Are you familiar with this summary?

A. Yes.

Q. Does this accurately reflect the revenue enhancements that you projected coming from the merger?

A. Yes. This is the revenue enhancements net of the cost of delivering that same increase in revenues.

Q. The top group are the revenue increases, and then the bottom group you have here are the costs associated with those revenue increases?

A. Yes.

Q. So let's focus on gross physical sales. Let's go back to PX-168. Again, the same Silk US IS output tab, row eight. What do you show on row eight?

A. This is the gross physical sales line.

Q. Tell the Court the basis—well, before we get to the basis, how large is this increase that you project?

A. Well, again, it's not—this is the summary top. Actually, the calculations are in Silk US. But what this projected is an additional, let's call it, sales lift of 0.7 percent a year.

Q. Less than 1 percent a year?

A. Yes. And in the aggregate, it's like a lift around 3 percent.

Q. And if someone wanted to see the mechanics of that, they would go to, you said, the Silk US tab?

A. Exactly.

Q. We don't have to go there at the moment. Okay. So although that's a small increase, it's an increase. What is the basis for that projection?

A. So I think as I mentioned before, our sales organization is five times larger. The capillarity of our sales force is getting to basically all independent bookstores, right. And it's anchored on our experience because of our supply chain. As we mentioned, also if we reduce return rates, we'll have the ability to also increase sales.

Q. So let me just stop you there on the historical experience. What historical experience are you referring to?

A. So transactions, Little Tiger also is a very—what I call experiment. We're experimenting how getting a company with the same titles in a different supply chain as soon as they got into our supply chain distribution and sales organization, that we basically realize a lift.

Q. The Court may not know what Little Tiger refers to. Can you explain that?

A. So Little Tiger is a children's book company. Although it's based in the UK, a large portion of their business is in the U.S.

Q. And was this a company that Penguin Random House acquired?

A. Yes.

Q. And what was the experience from that acquisition with respect to sales lift?

A. So we were able to double their—the sales in two years.

Q. And what about the experience with third party distribution customers, did that experience also inform your sales lift projection?

A. Yes, absolutely.

Q. And just explain that again for the Court, please.

A. As I mentioned, as you are able to get all that content into a sales force as big as we have—and especially with the capillarity, getting to all this in the bookstores, but also trying to get the book wherever there is going to be a consumer. That is basically why we're able to achieve this sales lift.

Q. What are the specific areas in which Penguin Random House believes it can improve or increase Simon & Schuster's physical sales?

A. So based on conversations with management, we were able to identify four areas of improvement. International exports. We were able to think about increasing special markets.

Special markets is what we call to retailers that normally they don't carry books, okay. The third one is independent bookstores, right, that capillarity that I was mentioning. And the last one is what we call backlist optimization.

Q. Could you repeat that?

A. Backlist optimization.

Q. So let's quickly run through the foundation for each of those. Let's start with international exports. Why do you think you can improve Simon & Schuster's sales in the international arena?

A. So we learned from the management presentation of Simon & Schuster that they have presence in 100 countries. They might have the ability to reach to other countries, right, more than 100 countries. But in our case, we have presence in more than 200 countries.

Q. What's the difference between using direct sales, as Penguin Random House does, or using wholesalers or middlemen?

A. So we have dedicated sales reps across the globe, right. So they are in these different countries, and they're taking care of the retailers in those countries. So the books are not distributed through distributors, we have actual presence dedicated to get Penguin Random House books into all these countries.

Q. And is there a dollar value, in addition to what you just mentioned, associated with eliminating the wholesalers in these countries?

A. That would be beneficial. In a way, it's basically getting rid of the wholesaler in the middle, right. So that will help not only to increase sales, but also that would mean more royalties to authors.

Q. How do you know that Simon & Schuster has an on-the-ground presence in only 100 countries compared to Penguin Random House's 200?

A. So we—I mean, I saw that in their management presentation document, but also, we had conversations with Simon & Schuster management.

Q. And when you say management presentation document, you're referring to what you got from Simon & Schuster?

A. Yes.

Q. Okay. Let's turn to the next category which are specialty stores. Give an example of a store that falls into this category.

A. Yeah, stores like Williams-Sonoma or West Elm, for example.

Q. Why do you think you're going to be able to improve Simon & Schuster's sales in those types of stores?

A. Well, we have invested in developing those relationships, and to know exactly what these retailers want and need. And that's why we certainly think that we will be able to get these books. And also, because in a few of these, we don't see that Simon & Schuster has any presence.

Q. Does Penguin Random House have a dedicated sales team for these, I guess you call them, non-traditional bookstores, book outlets?

A. Yes, we have sizable special markets organization.

Q. What is your understanding as to whether Simon & Schuster has a dedicated team for these types of stores?

A. They have, but not to the extent that we have.

Q. Let's turn to independent bookstores. Why do you believe that you can increase sales of Simon & Schuster titles to independent bookstores?

A. So we—as I mentioned before, the capillarity, we almost don't use wholesalers, we go directly to all these independent bookstores. And we have programs to serve them books as fast as possible, et cetera. However, Simon & Schuster uses more wholesalers, right. They don't have the same level of attention, right, in order to distribute those books.

Q. And then you said—I think you said backlist optimization. What does that refer to?

A. So in the last 10 years, we have invested a lot in technology. As I just mentioned before, we have an independent dedicated IT organization. We have been investing a lot into artificial intelligence, and technology and tools to help that. In this case, backlist optimization is about using an algorithm to really understand what are the key words that are critical online, right. So that basically helps us to identify what are the best keywords in order to make the books more discoverable and available in these online platforms.

Q. In addition to those areas of improvement that you just described, did you do any quantitative analysis of Penguin Random House's sales reach as compared to Simon & Schuster's?

A. Yeah, I wanted to do also a confirmatory analysis of the sales lift, so I created an analysis. This is also in PX-168.

Q. Okay. Let's go to Demonstrative 14, page 27. This is in the U.S. physical sales lift worksheet of PX-168. Can you explain what this worksheet shows?

A. In order to analyze what would be the potential sales lift, I asked my team—specifically Cara Deedy, that had access to the clean team room—which that part of the information I didn't have access. She was able to look at—

Q. Let me just stop you right there, if I could. You have here: "S&S top nine physical customers as percentage total U.S. physical sales." What does that refer to?

A. Yes, this is the percentage of the total U.S. physical sales for the top nine customers as a percentage of the total for both Simon & Schuster and Penguin Random House.

Q. And it shows a difference between the percentage of the companies' sales in those top nine outlets, right?

A. Yes.

Q. How much is that difference?

A. About 7 percent.

Q. And what does that mean to you in terms of modeling sales lift?

A. This is to me the potential sales lift. As I was mentioning before, we cover 90 percent of the same accounts. But there's some accounts that Simon & Schuster doesn't cover, right. So this is a way to really understand what is the lift that could be achieved as soon as Simon & Schuster titles go through our supply chain.

Q. You have underneath there a U.S. gross sales opportunity calculation. What does that reflect?

A. So I calculated that the midpoint—I didn't take the end of the range, right, so I took like a midpoint of a potential lift to understand the dollar amount of that lift of 4.5 percent.

Q. Did you just plug that 4.5 percent into your model?

A. No, again, this is just to confirm the 0.7 percent that we were discussing at the beginning per annum.

Q. This was just one of your confirmation tests?

A. Yes. And we also have, as you can see, analysis depending on the written rate.

Q. Explain to the Court why you drew the conclusion that Simon & Schuster could not achieve this sales lift on its own, and that therefore it is, what we would, call merger-specific?

A. At the end of the day, over the last 10–15 years, we have invested over $250,000,000 in our supply chain integrated IT sales force, right, that is, as we just mentioned, five times larger. So in discussions with management, they didn't confirm to us or they didn't have any plans of investing the same amount of money to try to get to similar a supply chain that we have.

Q. Let's move on from the sales lift, go to slide 28 of the demonstrative. I want to just cover one last item on the OpEx matrix, PX-406, just to make sure the record is clear on this. Pam, can you bring up the summary worksheet again, please. Take a look, Mr. Sansigre, at cell E45. What does that cell reflect?

A. Those represent the total headcount efficiencies projected in the OpEx matrix.

Q. That's headcount reduction?

A. Headcount.

Q. We don't have to use a euphemism, headcount reductions. How did you calculate them?

A. I calculate department by department, grounded on experience and really understanding the overlapping positions in each department.

Q. Did you just apply a percentage or did you go department by department and sub department by sub department to identify the overlap?

A. So for sales, fulfillment, IT and admin, I went sub department by sub department. For production and marketing, it's a little bit different because they're more homogeneous, there's not so much different there. But still I went basically headcount by headcount to understand the overlapping positions.

Q. Could Simon & Schuster, in your view, have achieved these headcount reductions absent the merger?

A. No.

Q. Let's now go to page 28 of Defendants' Demonstrative 14. What are we showing here, Mr. Sansigre?

A. This is the total annual benefits created as a consequence of the transaction by 2025.

Q. And these are the different categories that we've reviewed with the Court, right?

A. Yes.

Q. Is this the base case or is this the upside case?

A. This is the base case.

Q. So let's put this aside for a moment. I want to turn to a new topic with you, which are subsequent iterations of your model. And we'll turn to page 29 of Defendants' Demonstrative 14. This is from Ms. Hammer's report, and it compares the three different iterations of your model, right?

A. Yes.

Q. You're familiar with this?

A. Yes.

Q. So I want to focus first on June 2021, which is the middle column. What was going on in spring 2021 that relates to the—what is called here the June 2021 model?

A. So at that time, Bertelsmann requested for me to model a special scenario, and that special scenario was potential additional cash injection of Bertelsmann in all of its divisions. So basically I want a special iteration, and I use the same spreadsheet, given that the same spreadsheet already had all the information together.

Q. What was the impact of the contemplated Bertelsmann cash infusion on the June 2021 model?

A. So it implies an additional growth and an additional investment. Basically, we projected that we'll have even more sales for both Penguin Random House and Simon & Schuster.

Q. And does that explain the large increase in projected gross physical sales from your official November 2020 model to this June 2021 iteration?

A. Yes.

THE COURT: I'm sorry, what were the new assumptions you were making for that model?

THE WITNESS: So Bertelsmann was starting to plan an additional cash injection for all the different divisions. And they basically went to all the divisions, including us, and said, well, if we were to invest all this amount of money, how much potentially Penguin Random House and Simon & Schuster including—would the company grow.

THE COURT: I'm sorry, how much was that?
THE WITNESS: The lift—the additional sales?
THE COURT: No, I'm just trying to understand what this model is supposed to represent.
THE WITNESS: So this model represents that basically they were saying we have like $6 billion to invest in all our businesses globally. And of course, Penguin Random House is a content business, one of the content business. Basically, they say, well, we don't know yet how we're going to inject all that money. But basically, they ask to all the divisions can you calculate in a scenario, if you were to receive money, how would you invest it, right.
So here, the idea was to invest more money in authors and making other investments additionally in supply chain. The consequence of that modeling was increased sales. But it was a separate analysis that they ask us to look at. This was after the deal was already signed.
THE COURT: I understand.
BY MR. FRACKMAN:
Q. While we're on gross physical sales, let's turn to the January '22 model—or iteration of your model. Let me ask you first, why did you do one at this point in time, around January 2022?
A. So Bertelsmann, every year, once they do transaction, they want the numbers to be refreshed with new information. So by January 2022, we already have actual data for both Penguin Random House and Simon & Schuster. So they wanted basically for me to refresh the model.
Q. Why did the gross physical sales projection come down so dramatically from the June 2021 iteration to the January 2022 version?
A. So the pandemic had created a lot of volatility, both for Penguin Random House, Simon & Schuster and the industry in a way. So what happened was that in both 2020 and 2021, they were record years for both companies. As I explained before, when you model to the long term, you need to normalize, be more conservative about the future. So instead of taking as year of projection the new higher number or the new record year number, I basically decided to be more conservative on the synergies achieved.
Q. My question was a bad one, Mr. Sansigre. Does the January 2022 iteration still reflect this contemplated Bertelsmann cash infusion?
A. I'm sorry, no.
Q. So I just want to cover one other thing about the June '21 iteration. Are you aware that that June 2021 version was the basis for a response to the DOJ's request for additional information in June 2021?
A. Yes, I'm aware.
Q. So do you know why that version was used if it contained this one-time Bertelsmann cash infusion that was contemplated at the time?
A. So I think it's a legal matter primarily, because at that point I had already produced or already gave the efficiencies model, and they asked me for the most recent one. I shared that exactly at the time, the one that was—the most recent one, coincidentally, was the additional cash investment that I just explained.
Q. Let's put the June '21 aside for a moment and compare the November 2020 official one with the more recent January 2022 one. And we'll go to the next tab. We've simplified this by taking out that one-time June one. You explained why you updated it in January 2022. When was the work actually done that's reflected in this January '22 version?
A. So I incorporated both Penguin Random House and Simon & Schuster actuals for 2020 and for 2021.
Q. Now, there are some changes, and we're going to cover a few of them, but let me ask you the summary question. What is your view as to whether these changes between the official model and the January 2022 model change your view on the reliability of the 2020 official version?
A. In my opinion, the November 2020 model continues to be the most reliable for a couple of reasons. The first—
Q. So let me just ask you, even though it's a year and a half out of date?
A. Yes, absolutely.
Q. Or old—out of date, I used Ms. Hammer's terminology. Okay. So why do you still think the November 2020 official model is the right one to look at?

A. So as I was saying, there is too many reasons. The first reason is that the November 2020 model is based on pre-pandemic data. The pandemic has basically changed a lot of return rates as we saw before. And also there was like excess demand for some months when people were in lockdown. So 2020 and 2021—I mean, in a way, a little bit 2022, they're not a representation of what would be the long term of the company, right. So in my opinion, the historical view of Simon & Schuster is still a stronger representation of what the future would look like.

The second one is that the November 2020 model was heavily vetted and reviewed by Bertelsmann, as we discussed yesterday. And that's it. But in any case, I refreshed with this new information. And if I would have identified a big gap in these projections, I think as I mentioned before, I would have needed to go back to Bertelsmann.

Q. Is the total change in your model from the official one to this January '22 one material for your purposes?

A. No.

Q. Let's look at a couple of the changes. We're not going to go through all of it, Your Honor, but I do want to have the record clear on what some of the changes were. Let's start with the change in gross physical sales that came down a small amount from the 2020 official model to the one in January 2022. Why?

A. So as I mentioned, 2020 and 2021, they were record years for both Penguin Random House and Simon & Schuster. And as I just mentioned, I don't think it's the right representation of the future for both companies.

Q. Is this a COVID pandemic issue?

A. It's COVID related in a way. So because 2021 was the new starting point of the revised—or this iteration, if I would have just plugged the 2021 record year and just assumed the same synergies, then the synergies would have gone substantially up, right. But again, because they were a record year, I wanted to be conservative, so I just brought down the growth.

Q. Let's go down to the total variable cost and returns row. There's an increase there from your November 2020 model to the January '22 version. What accounts for that?

A. So at the end of the day, these models are—almost all lines are linked down to contribution. So cost of shipment, freight, marketing programs, returns, they are based on the revenue. So if you change the revenue, automatically it's going to change. This also included the fact that inflation was starting to hit in a lot of these lines, so that's why the number changed.

Q. And do you have a view as to which of the two total variable cost numbers is the more reliable one to use for projecting the synergies from the transaction?

A. In my opinion, I think like the—I don't know, somewhere in the next year the industry will normalize. And that's why I still believe that the pre-pandemic averages and historical information is more representative of the future of the company.

Q. Let's look at the—

THE COURT: Can I ask a question about that, Mr. Sansigre. This looks strange to me, because you would think the variable costs would be correlated with the gross physical sales, but the gross physical sales are down and the variable costs are up. Why? Because I don't think the costs would be associated with ebooks and audio, it's mostly gross physical sales, right, for variable costs?

THE WITNESS: Yes.

THE COURT: So why are gross physical sales down so much and variable costs up so much?

THE WITNESS: That's exactly because of inflation. So what happens is because the inflation has been affecting printing and the cost of printing, because you're targeting a certain percentage of savings, then because of inflation, theoretically you will be able to save more money.

THE COURT: I see. But because of inflation, though, wouldn't 2022 be the more accurate model? It's not going back to—

THE WITNESS: No, actually our experience at the beginning of 2022 is that inflation, specifically for our business, is actually starting to come down. Freight, for example, is based on—

THE COURT: The rate of inflation is coming down, but the costs are not going to go down to the levels they were at before, are they?

THE WITNESS: Not in total, but as a percentage of sales, that is our expectation. Freight, for example, is very linked to oil, right, because it's transport. So oil is down again, right. With printing, there was a lot of supply chain issues across America and China, especially for children's. These are very important, kind of like printers. There was a little bit of bottleneck in all the supply chain. As we go out of—a little bit of the pandemic, those supply chains will normalize. Therefore, because there's not that much traffic, the rates as a percentage of sales will normalize again.

THE COURT: Okay, thank you.

BY MR. FRACKMAN:

Q. Let's turn to OpEx quickly. What's going on here in the differences in the OpEx categories?

A. So there's a few things going on here. The first is that, as I just mentioned, all these numbers are impacted by inflation. So the total cost base of Simon & Schuster of 2021, in a way compared to the previous year, was 8.5 percent higher. Okay, so that's one. So that is the effect of inflation. The second effect is after the deal was signed, going back to review again the numbers in detail, I realized that some of the savings that I have targeted and that we have analyzed in editorial, art and production departments for Simon & Schuster were incorporated in administration. So it was just a reclassification of the—

Q. Yeah, let me just make sure we're on the same page here. The editorial and art OpEx numbers came way down in your model from November 2020 to January '22. Did that reflect an actual reduction in the savings or just a reclassification within the model?

A. It was just a reclassification.

Q. And where did those expenses get moved to?

A. To admin.

Q. Now, there is one big item here that changed—well, how about production, same thing?

A. The same thing with production.

Q. There's one big item that changed, which is fulfillment. Why don't you describe—explain to the Court what the changes were that affected the OpEx savings for fulfillment.

A. So what happened here is I had conversations with Mr. Malaviya around the situation of distribution in general in the United States. What we realized is that given the additional volumes of books that we needed to handle, we would need more space on Riverside. Therefore, we need it at full capacity.

Q. Let me stop you right there. What is Riverside?

A. Riverside is the largest warehouse of Simon & Schuster.

Q. And you had modeled a 40 percent reduction there; is that right?

A. We modeled originally 40 percent capacity; not reduction, capacity.

Q. And what you're saying is that you determined that you might need more of the Riverside warehouse?

A. Yes, we actually said let's assume 100 percent capacity. And the reason was that precisely, again, because the pandemic is not representative of the long term of book publishing. What happened is when the readers went on lockdown and the bookstores were closed, the vast majority of the books were sold online. When you sell online, basically you as a publisher need to hold a larger inventory, right. The physical bookstores, they have the inventory, right. But when they were closed and everything was going online, we as publishers need to hold a longer period of inventory for all these titles. So that's why we realized that we needed more space.

But as we again go back out of the pandemic and bookstores start opening and start building their inventories, then we expect that our capacity needs will go back to basically the similar thing that we projected.

Q. So do you have a view for the Court as to which of those fulfillment numbers is the correct, most reliable one for calculating synergies from the transaction?

A. I still believe that is the November 2020.

THE COURT: Why?

THE WITNESS: Because again, the pandemic made all bookstores close, so everybody was ordering online.

THE COURT: Right. But I thought you said the more reliable ones are the non-pandemic numbers, but the bigger number is the pandemic number, right, 20.77?

THE WITNESS: The November model is based on the past before the pandemic in a way, because we started the model in March and we finished by November. So the full impact of the pandemic was not incorporated in the model.

THE COURT: Oh, I see. But you say because of the pandemic you need more warehouse space, so that's why I thought the bigger number was the pandemic number.

THE WITNESS: So, this is the saving, right. So, when you need less capacity—

THE COURT: Oh, this is the savings, that's why.

THE WITNESS: This is the savings, right. So, if you need less capacity, then you can reduce basically that capacity and have that savings.

THE COURT: I see, okay. I've got it, thank you.

BY MR. FRACKMAN:

Q. What is the total percentage change in your EBIT number from the November 2020 official model to the January '22 model, Mr. Sansigre?

A. I think it's—I mean, it's less than 10 percent.

Q. Let's turn to a new topic, we can take that down. What does your November 2020 model project with respect to author compensation?

A. It only projects the automatic royalty payments that we will need to pay to authors.

Q. And let's pull up PX-168, the Silk US IS output tab again. Let's look at row 26. Is that what you just were referring to?

A. Yes.

Q. What does your model say, if anything, about how Penguin Random House or Bertelsmann will use any of the other synergies or savings that you modeled resulting from the Simon & Schuster acquisition?

A. Nothing, this model is not modeling any of that.

Q. That would be something outside of your model?

A. Yes.

Q. Let me show you something that was introduced in court the other day. This is DX-414. And I'll ask you while that's coming up: Are you familiar with the Penguin Random House P&L format?

A. Yes, I am.

Q. This is a P&L that was shown to the Court the other day, DX-414, for an author. And I just want to focus on two lines with you. The first is about seven from the bottom, and it says: "Allocated O/H percentage." What does that refer to?

A. This is the percentage of allocated overhead that is charged to basically every acquisition P&L that basically the auditors use to evaluate the events.

Q. And that percentage, 14 percent, what does that reflect?

A. This is based actually on actuals from Penguin Random House business records. It's basically the percentage of allocated costs over net sales.

Q. Now I want to go down to another line, which is at the bottom, third from the bottom, suggested advance. What does that refer to?

A. This basically is a scenario analysis based on the cost structure and the targeted margin, what would be the different suggested advances for this author.

Q. What is the relationship in this P&L between the allocated overhead cost, the 14 percent, and the various suggested advances reflected here?

A. Well, it's totally related. If you were to charge more or less of that 14 percent, that will affect the amount of suggested advance.

Q. So if the allocated overhead came down, what would be the impact on the suggested advance numbers?

A. *Ceteris paribus*, or all things being equal, it would increase the advance—the suggested advance basically.

Q. And just so the record is clear, who sets the allocated overhead figure? By that I mean, does the editor have any control over that or is that fixed in the P&L model?

A. No, no one has control of it because it's based on the actual costs.

Q. What would be the impact on the suggested advances modeled—set forth in this P&L form of synergies resulting from the merger as you have calculated them?

A. So I didn't do a super extensive analysis, but just calculating the basically $137,000,000 that we just saw. And if specifically we focus on the allocated overheads, that 14 percent will go down to 11 percent.

Q. And then the impact on the suggested advances would be what?

A. It will be almost 10 percent increase for both books from Penguin Random House or Simon & Schuster.

Q. Just to close—and we can take this down. We've spent a lot of time on the modeling and the efficiencies. What changes to the creative aspects of the business do you project in your model?

A. Totally untouched, actually quite the opposite. We want to keep all the services that all Simon & Schuster authors have. And whenever we can improve them, we will improve them.

Q. And let's pull up—So you were talking about whether your model reflects any changes in the creative aspects of the business?

A. No.

Q. Let's pull up—you mentioned the Penguin Random House philosophy. What are you showing here?

A. This is the philosophy that we have applied in basically all the transactions that we have closed.

Q. And what does it say about what happens to the creative part of the business when you have a transaction?

A. So we leave creative untouched. That basically means not to cut any editors, and of course not to cut any services to authors. And we actually want to do the opposite, we want to give them the maximum quality services.

Q. Is this consistent with what you told Bertelsmann in the investment proposal back in November 2020?

A. Absolutely.

Q. Let's pull up PX-148 in evidence and turn to page nine. Could you highlight the top line, the very top line. Is this what you were referring to as being consistent with the investment proposal itself?

A. Yes, I wrote this.

Q. And this says, Penguin Random House informed Bertelsmann, its parent, in connection with the proposal that it plans to leave the creative aspects of the company untouched, right?

A. Yes.

Q. And is that what your model reflects?

A. Yes.

MR. FRACKMAN: I pass the witness, Your Honor.

THE COURT: Okay, thank you. Any cross?

MS. LEAL: Good afternoon, Your Honor. Jessica Leal for the United States.

THE COURT: Good afternoon—well, good morning still.

CROSS-EXAMINATION

BY MS. LEAL:

Q. Good afternoon, Mr. Sansigre.

A. Good afternoon.

Q. We've spent some time on Zoom together, it's nice to see you in person.

A. Same.

Q. Mr. Sansigre, I believe yesterday you discussed with Mr. Frackman your hard coded 50 percent number generating your real estate synergy estimates; is that right?

A. Yes.

Q. And do you remember going over the JP Morgan materials with Mr. Frackman?

A. Yes.

Q. Reading from the transcript of yesterday's hearing at page 243—I'm sorry, 2439 (sic), lines 18

through 22, Mr. Frackman asked you: "Did you incorporate the JP Morgan appraisal information and other lease information that you got from Simon & Schuster into your model, PX 186?" And you answered: "Yes." Do you remember that?
A. Yes.
Q. Mr. Sansigre, you gave a deposition in this matter on March 11th, 2022; is that right?
A. Yes.
Q. And you were under oath, just as you are today?
A. Yes.
THE COURT: Am I supposed to have the binder?
MS. LEAL: Actually, I'm going to play a clip for us right now, Your Honor. (Video played)
BY MS. LEAL:
Q. Mr. Sansigre, was that your testimony on March 11th, 2022?
A. Yes.
MS. LEAL: Your Honor, the United States would move to admit these pages—this page, 224, lines 17 through 25, from Mr. Sansigre's deposition into evidence as impeachment and a party admission.
THE COURT: Any objection.
MR. FRACKMAN: Objection, Your Honor, to the introduction of the deposition pages for this purpose. The record is whatever—claimed impeachment is the record. The pages for the deposition are not evidence apart from the impeachment of Mr. Sansigre.
THE COURT: Overruled. Go ahead.
MS. LEAL: Your Honor, may we approach with the binders?
THE COURT: Yes.
MS. LEAL: May I proceed, Your Honor?
THE COURT: Yes.
BY MS. LEAL:
Q. Mr. Sansigre, your November 2020 model was prepared for use in the investment proposal when Penguin Random House was seeking approval to acquire 100 percent of Simon & Schuster?
A. Yes.
Q. And you hoped your model was going to support Bertelsmann's willingness to pay over $2 billion to acquire Simon & Schuster, correct?
A. I hoped.
Q. In your model, when you were creating it, you weren't attempting to perform an analysis of cognizable efficiencies under the Department of Justice and Federal Trade Commission's 2010 Horizontal Merger Guidelines?
A. No.
Q. I want to talk briefly about the modeling approach to forecasting you used. Do you remember discussing bottoms-up and top-down models during the deposition?
A. Yes.
Q. You called the November 2020 model a top-down model?
A. Largely, yes. It's largely a top-down model.
Q. Did you refer to as anything other than a top-down model?
A. Yes, because the vast majority is top-down models, so that's why it's called top-down model.
Q. You expect to do a bottom-up model after the deal closes, if it does?
A. That's common practice to do bottoms-up for the old efficiencies after closing as integration plan.
Q. After the deal closes, if it closes, that's the point when you expect to perform a bottoms-up model?
A. We will have enough information to provide a bottoms-up of all categories.
Q. And that's because today you don't have access to all the information you would need to perform a bottom-up model?
A. No.
Q. Can you turn to the deposition binder you have, it should be marked as the 30(b)(6) deposition of February 2nd, 2022.

A. Which deposition?
Q. The February 2nd, 2022 one.
A. Yes, okay.
Q. I just want to make sure that I understood this correctly. You agree that you do not have access to all the information you would need to perform a bottoms-up model today?
A. I don't have access to 100 percent of the efficiencies, no.
Q. You're waiting for the deal to close, if it closes, before you're going to create an integration plan, right?
A. Yes.
Q. You can only really identify in detail what synergies you will be able to achieve once the transaction closes?
A. That is not accurate.
Q. I'm sorry?
A. That is not accurate.
Q. In the deposition binder there, do you see—flip to page 61.
THE COURT: I'm sorry, what page was that?
MS. LEAL: Page 61, Your Honor, beginning at line seven.
THE WITNESS: Page 61?
BY MS. LEAL:
Q. That's right. The question was asked: "Is there an expectation the synergies will increase from November 2020 to your expectation today?" Answer "There has been no discussion about that. At the end of the day—about that. At the end of the day, our model is a top-down model. And in order to really identify in detail a lot of these synergies, we can only really, let's say, update and really know, right, if we can even ever achieve those synergies once we close a transaction and we're able to get private and confidential information, and also have discussions with Simon & Schuster management. But we have been unable to do that." Did I read that right?
A. Yes. What I meant here—
Q. Did I read that right?
A. You read it right, yes.
Q. I want to go back a little further in time. I believe you told Mr. Frackman you started work on your model in March 2020; is that right?
A. Yes.
Q. And that was within days of Viacom's announcement that Simon & Schuster was going to be available for sale?
A. Yes.
Q. Would you please turn to PX-162 in your binder.
A. PX-162?
Q. That's right. Thank you.
A. Okay.
Q. Is this an email you sent on Sunday, March 8th to Mr. Malaviya and some of your other colleagues?
A. Yes.
MS. LEAL: Your Honor, I'd move to admit PX-162.
THE COURT: Any objection?
MR. FRACKMAN: No objection.
THE COURT: That will be admitted. (Plaintiff's Exhibit 162 admitted into evidence)
BY MS. LEAL:
Q. You see where you wrote: "Hi guys, so I have been working on the pitch"?
A. Yes.
Q. Was the pitch you were working on a proposal to Bertelsmann about being invited to the process to invest or potentially acquire Simon & Schuster?
A. Yes.

Q. Do you see where you wrote: "Please find attached the pro forma P&L. And I have been working with an initial take at synergies. We need to review with Nihar and divvy up if possible"?
A. Yes.
Q. At this time, were you anticipating modeling three synergies cases of base, upside and downside?
A. Yes.
Q. Earlier you mentioned the clean team could access certain information in the Simon & Schuster clean room?
A. Yes.
Q. Other than yourself, the only person on your team who could access clean room data was Cara Deedy; is that right?
A. Yes.
Q. And you, yourself, actually had limited access to information in the clean room that Ms. Deedy had access to, but you did not?
A. Yes.
Q. You did not have access to the details of Simon & Schuster's customer information?
A. No, I did not have access.
Q. I wanted to ask a clarifying question earlier. Did you say that your synergy analysis included information from the clean room that was in your OpEx matrix file?
A. It was aggregated, and after consulting with counsel, they tell me what is fine to aggregate that data and insert it into the OpEx matrix.
Q. So it was only aggregated, it wasn't the detailed clean room information?
A. Yes.
Q. Just briefly, because I don't want to belabor the point, the June 2021 model that you discussed with Mr. Frackman, this is one of the many dozens of iterations that occurred after November 2020; is that right?
A. Yes.
Q. And it was actually created in April 2021; does that sound familiar?
A. I don't recall.
Q. If you could take a look at tab 140 in your binder. Do you recognize PX-140?
A. There are so many versions that I'm going to assume that this is that version, yes.
Q. Just taking one quick step back, PX-140 was the model that underlied the Bertelsmann response to the Department of Justice back in June 2021; is that your understanding?
A. Today, I don't know. I always communicated through my lawyers that the November 2020 was the official model. And at the time, they asked me for the latest version, and honestly I don't recall what is the exact version that I provided.
Q. Okay. Can you turn to tab PX-886 in your binder. This should be the response of Bertelsmann to request for additional information and documentary material issued on March 12th, 2021. Do you see that?
A. I can see that on the screen now.
Q. So Mr. Sansigre, you are aware that there was an investigation by the Department of Justice on the proposed merger before this lawsuit was filed?
A. Yes.
Q. And you're aware the Department of Justice inquired during the investigation about Penguin Random House's efficiencies claims with the merger with Simon & Schuster?
A. Yes.
Q. If you flip to page 101 there, you'll see Specification 31?
A. Yes.
Q. Was Bertelsmann's response to Specification 31 there on pages 101 to 105?
A. Yes.
Q. Specification 31 was where the Department of Justice asked Bertelsmann for a description of any benefits that Bertelsmann anticipates will result from the acquisition of Simon & Schuster, including cost

savings, economies, new products, product improvements or other efficiencies or synergies; is that right?
A. Yes.
Q. And you, yourself, helped prepare Bertelsmann's response to Specification 31, correct?
A. Actually, I barely—I mean, I participated in the process, yes, by sending the documents that they told me.
Q. You understand the response was going to be provided to the Department of Justice in or around June 25th, 2021?
A. Absolutely.
MS. LEAL: Your Honor, I move to admit the answer to Specification 31 on pages 101 to 105 of PX-886.
THE COURT: Any objection?
MR. FRACKMAN: No. I'd note it's confidential, it's—
THE COURT: That will be admitted under seal. (Plaintiff's Unnumbered Exhibit admitted into evidence under seal)
BY MS. LEAL:
Q. Now if you could go back to the PX-140 we were discussing prior to the narrative response. Just for clarity, do you recognize this as the model that supported the figures in the June 25th, 2021 response to Specification 31?
A. You're in PX-140, right?
Q. Yes.
A. Yes, I can see it.
Q. And that's the one that was supporting the narrative response?
A. I didn't put together the documents that were provided for Specification 31. I produced or I sent very early on the official models and the documentation, including the OpEx matrix and the documents that we have reviewed so far. But at the time they asked me also: Give me all the versions of the models. And I gave, I think, probably around eight versions.
Q. So is it your testimony you didn't read the response that was being written in Specification 31 in your preparation?
A. I reviewed, but I think that the Specification 31 was around the most updated model.
Q. And those numbers were actually lower than what was in your November 2020 model, right?
A. They were down by less than 6 percent, which—
Q. They were less; is that right?
A.—confirmed the reliability of the model.
Q. Were they less, Mr. Sansigre?
A. Excuse me?
Q. Were they less than your November 2020 model?
A. They were less, yes.
THE COURT: I'm sorry, my realtime is down again. (Brief interruption)
MS. LEAL: May I proceed, Your Honor?
THE COURT: Yes.
BY MS. LEAL:
Q. On the PX-140 tab in front of you, do you see the name of your model there printed on the first page? It's actually the PX-140 tab in front of that. Yeah, sorry about that. Is it—
A. Yeah.
Q.—the 210401 Silk model, version 62?
A. Yes.
Q. Is that the file name?
A. Yes.
Q. And what was the 210401 and version 62 supposed to be referencing in the file name?
A. So sometimes, not always, we just put the latest date of the information. So maybe when this document was finalized was not exactly coinciding with the date in the document.

Q. So is it your understanding that this version 62 was finalized as version 62 on April 1st, 2021?
A. No.
Q. Do you know what date it was finalized?
A. Again, I provided all the models, so I guess it will be whenever it was closed.
Q. Do you know the date?
A. I did like hundreds of iterations, so I don't know the date, I'm sorry. The only one that I know is the final one, the official one.
Q. The official one of November 9th, 2020, is that the date?
A. Yes.
Q. I want to talk about the 12.3 percent, just a couple questions here. You had been targeting the 12.3 percent well before you had access to Simon & Schuster's confidential information, right?
A. I think as we explained today, we have closed 26 transactions, and the range is between 12 and 14 percent. And we anchor it in the Penguin Random House merger, and that percentage was 12.3.
Q. I don't believe that answered the question. You had been targeting the exact 12.3 percent before you had access to Simon & Schuster's confidential information; is that right?
A. That is not right.
Q. Can you turn to PX-163 in your binder. And before I ask a question about the document, Mr. Sansigre, the first time you got Simon & Schuster's confidential information was when the data room was opened in September 2021?
A. Yes.
Q. Do you see here on PX-163 an email of May 22nd, 2020?
A. Yes.
Q. I think I misspoke earlier, Your Honor, I said September 2021. But Mr. Sansigre, it was September 2020, right?
A. I understood.
Q. Thank you. So this is a few months before the data room with the confidential information was provided?
A. Absolutely.
Q. Do you recall this PRH strategy and business committee meeting of May 26th, 2020 referenced in the email?
A. Yes, I remember it.
Q. You're a recipient of this materials for this—it's called the SBC?
A. Yes.
MS. LEAL: Your Honor, we move to admit PX-163.
THE COURT: Any objection?
MR. FRACKMAN: No objection.
THE COURT: That will be admitted. (Plaintiff's Exhibit 163 admitted into evidence)
BY MS. LEAL:
Q. And you participated in that meeting; is that right?
A. Yes.
Q. Can you turn to page 54 of this presentation at the meeting you were at. Do you see the 12.3 percent there as the percentage of savings over combined OpEx that was identified?
A. Yes, I can see it.
Q. So at this time, May 2020, you'd already identified the 12.3 percent number?
A. But I was not targeting 12.3 percent.
Q. Is this the same 12.3 percent number that you've been discussing with Mr. Frackman?
A. I think at the time, again, we had been reviewing several transactions. And it's not only Penguin Random House, as I said, it's a range between 12 and 14 percent. Yes, I was targeting savings, but in my mind, it was not 12.3 percent.
Q. But it was written down as 12.3 percent, right?
A. It was written down, yes.

Q. A quick question about your editorial and art comments earlier to Mr. Frackman. I can't go into the specifics, but correct to say there are millions of dollars in cuts in editorial and art that are assumed in your November 2020 model?

A. Very small amount, and it was not linked to creative.

Q. There are millions of dollars that have been identified for the editorial and art function in your November 2020 model, correct?

A. There is small amounts, and they were linked to executives that they make money enough to grant those savings.

Q. And how many of those executives made that amount of money?

A. There's a few that can get to those kind of amounts, yes.

Q. Do you know how many?

A. I mean, probably like 70.

Q. Seventy people were going to be—executives were going to be cut from editorial and art—

A. No—

Q.—to make that savings?

A.—what I mean is that there are 70 people with those kind of level of compensations.

Q. And was there a plan to cut those 70 people in order to achieve those cuts?

A. No.

Q. You actually testified earlier, though, that that editorial and art scenario was a black box to you. Does that sound familiar?

A. I didn't use those words.

Q. Can we go ahead and turn to your deposition binder.

THE COURT: I'm sorry, did we figure out what the millions of cuts in editorial and art were for, then?

THE WITNESS: So similar to other transactions, there's—within editorial positions, people that are not touching the books, there is also overlapping of positions. So we're talking about those specific kind of overlapping positions at the really high executive level.

THE COURT: Right. And then when Ms. Leal asked you if you were going to cut them, you said no, so I was left confused.

THE WITNESS: She said that if I was going to cut the 70, I said no. But yes, we had identified certain overlap in those departments.

THE COURT: So you would cut executives in editorial and art?

THE WITNESS: Yes.

THE COURT: Okay, thank you. Go ahead.

BY MS. LEAL:

Q. And no one's actually given you any feedback on who would be cut should the merger proceed?

A. No. As I mentioned before, it's going to be a matter of putting both companies together and identify who's best on both sides.

Q. And that hasn't happened yet, and can't happen until the integration plan occurs; is that right?

A. No, but I understand that—I understand the importance of going one by one and really understanding. But at the end of the day, that kind of bottoms-up approach is going to be outdated very quickly. Because if someone retires—

THE COURT: Okay, I'm going to instruct the witness to answer the question.

THE WITNESS: I'm sorry, okay.

THE COURT: Ask again, Ms. Leal.

BY MS. LEAL:

Q. Sorry, Your Honor, I lost track of the exact question I asked, but I can ask it in a different way. No one's given you any guidance on who will actually be terminated if the merger is allowed to proceed?

A. No, it's based on numbers and historical information.

Q. So if you can turn to your binder there, the deposition binder, to when you were sitting as a designee of Penguin Random House on February 2nd, 2022, and go to page 211. Beginning at line 21, I asked you: "Was there any exercise to look at, like, Simon & Schuster employees' titles to determine sort of redundancy"—

A. Sorry, I think I'm in the different—sorry, I'm in the other deposition, sorry. What page of the first deposition?

Q. The first deposition at page 211, starting at line 21.

A. Which line?

Q. 21.

A. 21, okay. Thank you.

Q. I asked you: "Was there any exercise to look at, like, Simon & Schuster's employees' titles to determine sort of redundancy that would work towards these percentages reduction in editorial? For example, any of these categories, is there any sort of review at that level?"

You answered: "So I think—actually, you bring specifically for editorial and art, editorial and art, the philosophy of this transaction—and basically all our transaction, is always to leave what we call creative untouched. At this—and this was a scenario where it was really a black box to me, because we didn't really know if the overhead—or basically the managerial right and the managerial—which are not creative, on the publishing divisions for Simon & Schuster, they were in the editorial line or the admin line, right." Did you refer to it as a black box, Mr. Sansigre? Yes or no, please.

A. I referred to that as a black box, yes.

MS. LEAL: Your Honor, we move to admit that testimony—as Mr. Sansigre was sitting as a designee of Penguin Random House at the time, into evidence.

THE COURT: Any objection?

MR. FRACKMAN: Which part?

THE COURT: The part that was just read.

MR. FRACKMAN: Well, I think the whole excerpt should come in then.

THE COURT: Do you have any objection to that?

MS. LEAL: No objection to that, Your Honor. (Brief interruption by the court reporter)

MR. FRACKMAN: I'm fine with it coming in, Your Honor, but it should be the complete answer which continues to line 14 on page 213.

MS. LEAL: No objection, Your Honor.

THE COURT: That will all come in. Just give me a moment to read it. (Plaintiff's Unnumbered Exhibit admitted into evidence)

BY MS. LEAL:

Q. I also asked you in your deposition if there was something in particular that led you to quantify the specific hard coded number for art in your November 2020 model. Do you remember me asking you that?

A. I don't remember.

Q. Do you remember telling me that you did not take information, aggregating it and then apply it to the model?

A. I don't recall having said that.

Q. It's right there on page 214 in the same deposition transcript you're looking at. Starting on line 13, I asked: "Was there something in particular you saw that led to this percentage itself? Because it sort of seems like just an odd number to me, that it would be selected. I'm sort of wondering how you got to this percentage. If it was based on experience or if there was some specific description of Simon & Schuster's art department that led you to quantify it as this percentage?" Your answer: "So again, without using expressly, right—I think you asked this morning your question about in the information, where did you have access to their org charts, right. So, I do have access to their org charts, right, but I am not taking that information, aggregating it and then applying to a model. But from an assumption perspective in my mind, is, oh, when I saw the org chart of art, I saw that there's a head of art, that is right. So, my assumption is the org chart coincides with this line, and that's where I see duplicity."

Is that what you said, Mr. Sansigre?

A. Yes.

MS. LEAL: Your Honor, we move to admit this as well as party admission.

THE COURT: Any objection?

MR. FRACKMAN: No objection, Your Honor.

THE COURT: That will be admitted. (Plaintiff's Unnumbered Exhibit admitted into evidence)

BY MS. LEAL:

Q. Mr. Frackman asked you about the IT savings that were predicted as synergies in your model. Do you recall that?

A. Yes.

Q. And isn't it true that there are no specific plans on how Penguin Random House will implement the IT transition after acquiring Simon & Schuster to reach the projected millions of dollars of IT synergies?

A. So after closing of the transaction, ViacomCBS will no longer charge the $10,000,000, and we will integrate it then. We are doing every year integration of companies, and we know how to do it.

Q. I don't think you answered the question. There are no specific plans on how Penguin Random House will implement the IT transition after acquiring Simon & Schuster to reach the predicted millions of dollars of IT synergies?

A. We have specific plans, but not at the level of an integration plan.

Q. Can you please turn to page 234 in the deposition that's in front of you.

A. Which page, sorry?

Q. 234. Beginning on line 15, I asked you: "Has Penguin Random House had any plans on how it will implement the IT transition after acquiring Simon & Schuster to reach the millions—or other number, at this time?"

Your answer: "So no specific plans. But, there was some discussions before the lawsuit. There were some discussions, I'm thinking—it was not linked to the survivability of the synergies, it was more linked to the TSA. So to really understand, we wanted to understand if we were to close the transaction, how fast we could—we needed to jump into our TSA. But no specific plans were created or developed." Did I read that right?

A. Yes.

MS. LEAL: Your Honor, I'd move to admit this testimony as well as impeachment and as a party admission.

MR. FRACKMAN: No objection.

THE COURT: That will be admitted. I'm sorry, what is a TSA?

THE WITNESS: Excuse me?

THE COURT: What is a TSA?

THE WITNESS: TSA is a transition service agreement. (Plaintiff's Unnumbered Exhibit admitted into evidence)

BY MS. LEAL:

Q. Just one question on the return rates, Mr. Sansigre. Each of Penguin Random House's distribution clients have their own individual return rates despite relying on the same Penguin Random House distribution system; is that right?

A. Yes.

Q. On freight and marketing departments, those are both synergies you have estimated in your variable costs synergies, right?

A. Yes.

Q. You have no clue what Simon & Schuster's contracts say about freight?

A. We don't have clue. But it's a standard practice, we know all those contracts, what they look like basically. It's our experience.

Q. But you have never looked at the Simon & Schuster freight contracts, correct?

A. Our advisors review the contracts, and yes, I have not looked at specifically the contracts.

Q. In fact, you didn't even look at Penguin Random House's freight contracts when you were modeling in November 2020?

A. It was not just me, it was a group, and I participated with Mr. Malaviya that actually has a good understanding of all those contracts.

Q. You don't know if Mr. Malaviya looked at the freight contracts when you were modeling your

November 2020 synergies?
A. I'm pretty confident that he looked at it.
Q. You don't know that, do you?
A. I don't know.
Q. You, yourself, never looked at any freight contracts when you were doing your November 2020 model, correct?
A. No.
Q. For your revenue enhancements, I'd like to talk about audiobooks. This is actually the largest category of your revenue enhancements is synergies; is that right?
A. Yes.
Q. Can you turn to PX-168, with an asterisk. It has a printout of the sheets from the November 2020 model. So you actually have to go a couple of pages in where you'll see the one that has the stamp Silk US at the bottom, and at the top it has KPI's sales. Do you see that?
A. Yes.
Q. The millions of dollars of audio revenue synergies predicted in your November 2020 model are reliant on this hard coded number you see here at cell Z30; is that right?
A. No, it was relying on all of information.
Q. Does the calculation of your audio synergies depend upon this Z30 number that we see on the screen that's highlighted?
A. Yes.
Q. And that's hard coded, correct?
A. Yes.
Q. And the millions of dollars of audio growth that are claimed as a synergy are attributed to Penguin Random House following a merger, right?
A. Can you rephrase the question?
Q. Sure. The millions of dollars that are generated from using this percentage number are calculated as synergies attributable to Penguin Random House if the merger does proceed?
Q. But they're called a synergy, right?
A. They're called efficiencies and synergies, yes.
Q. And you testified in your deposition that you selected this hard coded percentage number here for audio growth, because you thought Simon & Schuster would grow with the industry; is that right?
A. I don't recall having said that.
Q. Would looking at your prior testimony help refresh your recollection? If so, I can point you to it.
A. Excuse me?
Q. Would looking at your prior testimony help refresh your recollection?
A. The first deposition?
Q. I'm just asking if you read it, would it refresh your recollection?
A. Actually, I didn't.
Q. It's okay, we'll try this. If you'd like to read—to yourself, not out loud, on the 30(b)(6) deposition, page 173, and beginning on line 19. Just read that to yourself to see if it—and I'll see if it refreshes your recollection.
(Witness reads the document)
A. Yes, I can see it.
Q. So is it correct that you testified in your deposition you selected this hard coded number, the Z30 cell that we're looking at, for audio growth, because you thought Simon & Schuster would grow with the industry?
A. So the important—okay, yes.
Q. That's growth rate that would happen naturally without a merger making a difference; is that right?
A. No, I need to give more context to the 10 percent.
Q. So looking back here at the screenshot of the KPI's that you have in your binder, you see audio there is a category called management under AA30?

A. Yes.
Q. Was that Simon & Schuster's internal prediction of what their audio growth would be?
A. Yes.
Q. It's actually higher than what you predicted it would be; is that right?
A. Yes.
Q. So in this case, your November 2020 model assumes Simon & Schuster will grow in audiobooks more slowly combined with Penguin Random House than Simon & Schuster expected to grow on its own?
A. Yes, basically.
Q. And nevertheless, your November 2020 model, if we take it at face value, it calls Simon & Schuster's growth here a synergy; is that right?
A. We develop our own estimates of the company, so yes, these would be the synergies on top of our own estimate of how Simon & Schuster would perform.
Q. And your own estimate is reflected there in the base case, Y30, that low number there, that was your prediction of what Simon & Schuster would do on its own?
A. Yes.
Q. And your synergy is what you're calling the growth between that number and the Z30?
A. So it would be 80 percent of the 10 percent minus the 3 percent, so it's 5 percent left.
Q. And you call that a synergy?
A. Yes.
THE COURT: I'm sorry, I just don't understand this document. Can you just explain base, upside and management, what those columns mean?
THE WITNESS: Management, it was just basically to input what the bankers have created in the model for Simon & Schuster. So that was management projections that the bankers put in the model, right. And again, normally you don't take for granted whatever the bankers are putting. Then based on upside, that represents basically the base is equivalent to the standalone growth. And the upside is the synergies that we are targeting. So the differential between upside and base is basically the synergy or the lift.
THE COURT: I see, okay. Thank you. But this is all numbers for Simon & Schuster?
THE WITNESS: All Simon & Schuster, yes.
THE COURT: Okay, thank you.
BY MS. LEAL:
Q. Looking at the same chart, the expectation of Penguin Random House's growth was in the T column; is that right?
A. Yes.
Q. So Penguin Random House's growth for audio was far less than what you predicted for Simon & Schuster?
A. Yes.
Q. I want to ask just a couple of questions about the U.S. physical sales lift sensitivity test you discussed with Mr. Frackman. You said that the assumption was there was going to be increased sales in indies, special market and international that's modeled there?
A. And backlist optimization.
Q. I'm sorry?
A. And backlist optimization.
Q. Can you turn to your deposition of February 2nd, 2022, as the designee for Penguin Random House, and go to page 159. Do you see where I asked: "An assumption here is that the increase in sales will be indies, special market and international?" You answered: "Yes." I asked: "Is there more?" You said: "No, the assumption are those three for the specific U.S. physical lift." Did I read that correctly?
A. Yes.
MS. LEAL: Your Honor, we move to admit this testimony as impeachment and as a party admission.
MR. FRACKMAN: No objection.
THE COURT: That will be admitted. (Plaintiff's Unnumbered Exhibit admitted into evidence)

BY MS. LEAL:

Q. Your sensitivity test did not have any specific information from Simon & Schuster about all of the independent bookstores or special markets that Simon & Schuster sold to, correct?

A. No.

Q. You modeled millions of dollars of increased sales, but no amount from that was divided between what would be from independent bookstores, what would be for special markets or what would be for international sales, correct?

A. Similar to what we have done in the past, yes.

Q. In fact, Simon & Schuster could be selling a larger percentage of total physical books to its customers—top customers, because it's doing a better job at focusing on its biggest accounts than Penguin Random House?

A. I don't think so.

Q. You haven't tested that possibility, have you?

A. I have not tested that possibility.

Q. You don't have the data to disprove that, do you?

A. I don't have an anchor on basically other transactions I have or what.

Q. And you've not quantified how much more discoverable Simon & Schuster's books will be if it has access to Penguin Random House's supply chain?

A. No.

Q. You do not have the information to perform an analysis to quantify how many more Simon & Schuster's books Penguin Random House can sell internationally as a combined entity than Simon & Schuster can sell on its own?

A. No.

Q. Now, Mr. Frackman asked you a lot of questions about the 2013 merger. I just have a few. Am I correct saying your November 2020 model targets year-over-year increases in net sales?

A. Yes.

Q. To the contrary, the 2013 merger synergy plan actually assumed an overall loss in net sales for two years, correct?

A. Yes.

Q. Was that because there was a concern that the regular course of business might be slightly disrupted due to factors such as uncertainty in job security, managers investing time in integration efforts and a loss of some authors?

A. Yes, it was a merger of equals, so we have that concern at the time.

Q. And looking at revenues from pre-2013 and post-2013 merger, there has been millions of dollars of revenue decline, right?

A. Yes.

Q. Can you turn to PX-92 in your binder. Apologies, it was the one we flagged.

A. I have it in front of me.

Q. Thank you. Is PX-92 a copy of July 2nd, 2020 email exchanges between you and Mr. Malaviya?

A. Yes.

Q. Are you discussing market share and sales development topics in preparation of a Silk management presentation?

A. Yes.

MS. LEAL: Your Honor, I move to admit PX-92.

THE COURT: Any objection?

MR. FRACKMAN: No objection.

THE COURT: That will be admitted. (Plaintiff's Exhibit 92 admitted into evidence)

BY MS. LEAL:

Q. I won't go into the specifics out loud, because I understand there may be some confidentiality concerns. But at this time, were aggregated net sales and advances, pre-2013 merger and post-2013 merger, reflected in charts in the email chain?

A. Yes.
Q. And you can put that aside. You did not use Penguin Random House's experience with the 2013 merger to estimate your November 2020 model's year-over-year increases in net sales, correct?
A. We reviewed it.
Q. You did not use Penguin Random House's experience with the 2013 merger to estimate your November 2020 model's year-over-year increases in net sales?
A. We reviewed it, and we used it.
Q. You did use it?
A. We learned from that situation, yes.
Q. You agree it's important to note that the Penguin Random House merger was in 2013, since a lot has changed since then?
A. Yes, the market is more stable now.
Q. And the market's evolved?
A. Yes, but it was not as disruptive at the time.
Q. You agree there were certain market realities at the time of 2013 that are different in 2020?
A. Yes, self-publishing was coming up, and it ate a lot of our revenues.
Q. And from a market perspective, it was a different situation in 2013 versus what it is in 2020 or today?
A. Yes, right now we have a wealthy coexistence between formats and business models.
Q. There have been a lot of changes in the market since the pandemic began in March 2020 as well, right?
A. Yes, but not related to formats in a way or related to business models.
Q. Would you agree there's been a lot of changes, Mr. Sansigre?
A. Yes, but not—
Q. I'd like a yes or no.
A. There have been changes, yes
Q. Due to the timing of your work, your November 2020 model did not have the benefit of Simon & Schuster's 2020 or 2021 year-end financials?
A. I agree
Q. You have received the final year-end—or have you received the final year-end financials since November 2020?
A. Yes.
Q. And you've seen that Simon & Schuster's been performing even better than the performance you estimated they would have with Penguin Random House in your November 2020 model?
A. Yes.
Q. And that's better as a standalone company without any use of Penguin Random House's supply chain?
A. Yes. We will be able to improve it.
Q. And input in your November 2020 model that impacts how many synergies will be generated was a prediction of what Simon & Schuster's sales would be as a standalone company, right?
A. Yes.
Q. And Simon & Schuster has had millions of dollars more in sales in 2021 than you anticipated in your November 2020 model?
A. Yes.
Q. So your assumptions about Simon & Schuster's sales in 2021 are no longer accurate?
A. That is not true.
Q. Are the sales you predicted for Simon & Schuster in 2021 what ended up matching the actuals for 2021?
A. No.
Q. So they're not accurate; is that right?
A. For that specific year, no.
Q. And everything models year-after-year in your model, correct?

A. But important thing is the long term.
Q. Did they model each year after year; so if there's a mistake in one year, then the next year would have a mistake as well; is that right?
A. Yes.
Q. Even though you know these assumptions are now no longer true, for 2021 at least, you have not gone back to the board with any revised synergies for review about how Penguin Random House will supposedly improve Simon & Schuster's standalone excellent performance?
A. No, I have not.
Q. You have not modeled what a 2022 standalone Simon & Schuster looks like before determining what synergies can be added on top?
A. We have refreshed the model with actuals. And yes, we've been discussing this morning those numbers actually.
Q. And what was the date that you did that?
A. By the end of—beginning of 2022, yes.
Q. The beginning of January—
A. January of 2022.
Q. That's the date that you completed the January 2022 model, are you sure?
A. There's a lot of iterations, I don't know exactly the date.
Q. You don't know the date of that January 2022 model, correct?
A. I don't recall exactly.
Q. You don't know if it has Simon & Schuster's 2021 final year-end numbers in it, do you?
A. I think it incorporated somehow that, because through counsel, they told me basically the number.
Q. The Simon & Schuster 2021 year-end financials were not completed by January 2022 when you did your model, were they?
A. But my—
Q. Please answer yes or no.
A. Not the complete financials, no.
MS. LEAL: Those are all my questions right now, Your Honor.
THE COURT: Okay, thank you. Any redirect?

REDIRECT EXAMINATION

BY MR. FRACKMAN:

Q. Thank you, Your Honor. Just a couple of questions. Pam, could you bring up PX-163, please, the page that the Government showed Mr. Sansigre. It's page 54. So, Mr. Sansigre—next page, please. These are the estimates that were in your initial May 2020 presentation to Bertelsmann, right?
A. Yes.
Q. Are these the numbers that ended up in your final model for your upside case savings?
A. No, they were guesses.
Q. Did they change?
A. Substantially.
Q. And let's look at—let's go to PX-168, Pam—let's just make a note here. You have here a number for fulfillment, right. Let's make a note of that, without saying it out loud, and now let's go to PX-168 in the summary tab again. Maybe Pam can bring them up right next to one another.
A. What are you looking for?
Q. I'm looking for the comparison of your upside synergies or efficiencies calculation in the official model, PX-168, compared to what you had in this early one. But you might know it off the top of your head?
A. Here—first of all, this is global, so it's a little bit complicated to compare apples to oranges. The presentation is global, and the spreadsheet that we've been discussing is U.S. But again, certainly the numbers are not the same.
Q. And why are they not the same?

A. Because they were not representing the actual business records of Simon & Schuster.

Q. In the course of your work, did you get additional information that helped you develop a more accurate projection of the savings that you were anticipating from the transaction?

A. Yes, we got all the financial statements of Simon & Schuster, additional breakdowns, as we discussed today. And all this vetted, again, by Bertelsmann independently.

Q. I'd like to turn quickly to the audio sales projections that Ms. Leal asked you about. She didn't give you a chance to explain how you came up with your audio projections for the sales.

A. So we have our own internal studios, and we have been investing a lot of technology in audio. Our understanding, Simon & Schuster largely outsourced the production of audiobooks. Therefore, there's quote, unquote a middleman, right, that is managing those titles. And that also makes them not be as nimble and agile in producing those audios.

Q. Ms. Leal showed you a projection that had come from Simon & Schuster's bankers, but you didn't have a chance to explain why you discounted that projection. Can you explain to the Court why?

A. Well, again, I think they were bankers, they don't have the same experience as my team does. And it doesn't make any sense that they were projecting down physical sales and audio growing at 14 percent. Because at the end of the day, there's an important correlation between printed titles and the audio version, right. So it doesn't make any sense that print revenues goes down substantially, and then they're able to grow out 14 percent.

Q. Have you had experience in the past with respect to the reliability of sellers,' investment bankers' projections?

A. Yes.

Q. And what is that experience?

A. Well, the experience is they are trying to sell the company. And I think in this particular case, yeah, they were trying to show that audio, right, it was basically the new engine. But they don't have their own audio studios, they don't have the same capabilities that we have, so I was a skeptic about their projections.

Q. Ms. Leal asked you about a JP Morgan document, and whether you had incorporated that in any way into the model. The questioning in the deposition at that point, as the record will show, referred to Exhibit 27. Why don't we pull up Defendants' Exhibit 27. Let's go to the second page. Mr. Sansigre, are you familiar with this exhibit?

A. Yes.

Q. Was this the same JP Morgan document that you testified you used in connection with your real estate synergies calculation?

A. No.

MR. FRACKMAN: No further questions.

MS. LEAL: No questions, Your Honor.

THE COURT: All right, thank you. You can step down. Thank you very much, Mr. Sansigre. You can step down, your testimony's completed.

EDWARD A. SNYDER, WILLIAM S. BEINECKE PROFESSOR OF ECONOMICS AND MANAGEMENT, YALE UNIVERSITY

The antitrust trial took a pretty striking turn for anyone trying to gauge where the case actually stood as it entered its third and final week. The defense was questioning their economic expert, Yale professor Dr. Edward Snyder, who was duly explaining why he believes the government's expert Dr. Nicholas Hill got almost everything wrong: "The government has not proven that there will be a substantial lessening of competition as a result of the merger."

That will likely be the question on which the case hinges. Yes, the merger will give the combined firm half of the market for ATSB, but can or has the government shown that will result in lower advances for authors—and will that reduction, if expected, be sufficient in scale to block the deal?

Judge Florence Pan took over a good portion of the middle of Dr. Snyder's testimony, pushing back on his inferences and articulating in a series of exchanges what would seem to be her view—of both Dr. Hill's analysis, and the assessment of the potential effect of the merger on competition for anticipated books and advances offered for those top books.

Notably, the defense kept trying to limit the DOJ to an allegation of "unilateral effects analysis" and insisting that the only competitive situations of relevance are the modest number in which PRH and S&S are the winner and runner-up. Otherwise, "then you don't have head-to-head competition," Dr. Snyder said.

Here is where Judge Pan first jumped in: "Why is that not head-to-head competition? They're both in the competition. They just didn't win." Snyder answered, "The two parties are winner and runner-up 21 times, according to the data. So that's infrequent. And that, I think, is informative about the question."

Judge Pan came back to that point this way: "So my understanding . . . is that general competition affects each of the different types of acquisition models. Because if you're in a one-on-one negotiation, knowing that this author could walk at any moment and go to somebody else, that can affect the amount that you offer in your one-on-one negotiation.

"If you are in an auction, knowing there are more competitors or knowing there's a lot of interest in the book could affect how much you offer. And that doesn't depend on if you're number one or number two. And in the situations where there's imprint bidding, there has to be some kind of a third party in the mix for those two imprints to keep competitively bidding. And that doesn't depend on if you're number one or number two; that just depends on if there's more people involved. So I'm wondering how all that fits into what you're talking about."

Snyder allowed that, " . . . yes, I can understand this idea of general weakening of competition. But when I look at the actual numbers of rivals and the frequency with which other Big 5 are bidding and so on and so forth, it would be hard for me to understand how that would actually get traction, how it would be implemented."

Judge Pan stayed with her view: "It just seems to me there's just a lot more than you need to be number one or number two to affect competition. That's why I'm a little, I guess, confused by the testimony."

While Dr. Snyder pressed on the flaws and limited expectations of Dr. Hill's Second Score auction model—and really, all of his models, Judge Pan answered for Hill, showing her takeaway: "So his focus is not on the precise manner in which things are happening in the real world. He's just trying to get a sense of competition between these two and is using a rough-cut way of modeling the competition between these two. And removing the competition between these two would result in some harm.

"And he's saying—he said: I don't put a lot of weight on the exact number. That's not what I'm going for here. It's more about, you know, to show there would be harm and cross-referencing it with all these other things he's done to build sort of more of a mosaic, not just relying on the second score auction. I think that's what I interpreted him to be explaining."

Snyder said simply, "My opinion is that the [second score] model should be left behind. It has no value. It is fundamentally flawed with respect to fit."

The judge returned, "I don't think anybody thinks it fits exactly."

She was stirred sufficiently by the exchanges that she did more research during the short recess, and resumed her questioning of—or was it really lecturing to?—Dr. Snyder:

"So I looked at my notes over the break, including my notes on Dr. Hill's testimony. And he did not rely only on the merging parties being number one and number two, according to my notes. Under the win-loss ratio, he asked: When Simon & Schuster lost, how often did Penguin Random House win? And that was 59 percent of the time. And when Penguin Random House lost, how often did they lose to Simon & Schuster? That was 19 percent of the time.

"And they didn't have to be number one and number two under that way of looking at it. And he also made the points that I was making about general competition in his testimony, according to my notes."

While the judge has clearly inferred some reduction in competition, Snyder balked at where that leads and how you quantify it: "What does softening of competition mean? It means that there's some process, some set of cascading actions, where individual editors and publishers will cut their bids, will reduce their advance offers. That requires—well, there's been no analysis of that."

Later Snyder added pointedly, "When will firms actually cut their advances in this market? Maybe I should be more succinct. They don't know. And the problem is, they have so many rivals there, it would not make sense as an across-the-board pricing strategy. It would result in mistakes where you do loss of business. And I don't see that the competitive conditions generate that process of softening of competition in this context because of the strength of competition."

Judge Pan expanded her theory in turn: "This is something I've been thinking about. I don't think that the theory requires a conscious decision to lower advances. Wouldn't it be that you're just winning at lower levels because there's less competition? There's less competition, so people aren't bidding up the prices.

"So you're not going in thinking: I'm going to start lowering my advances. But everybody wants to acquire the book at the lowest price they can pay in order to win. And now they're just going to win at an earlier point in time because there's less competition. Isn't that the way advances get lowered, not as a result of a conscious decision to lower advances?"

Then she noted, "I'm saying that there will be no decisions to cut advances, but you'll get to pay lower advances and still win because there's less competition."

Dr. Snyder answered, "I think this isolates the issue. I don't see that there's going to be a lessening of competition here."

Judge Pan returned, "That's the ultimate question."

Indeed—but the exchange kept going!

Snyder wanted to get his points in: "You still have the Big 3, the other top firms. They're saying they're not going to cut advances. The CEO of–"

Judge Pan cut him off: "Because that's how it works. You don't say, I'm going to cut advances. You just keep bidding and it turns out you can win at lower levels because there are fewer people bidding now. I think that's the theory."

Later, she expanded again: "So it seems to me from the testimony that I've heard that the publishers and editors kind of go in thinking: I can go up to a certain amount. But I'm going to start at this lower amount and I'm just going to keep, you know, bidding up, depending on the form of the negotiation or the auction and try to get it at the lowest price that I can. But I'm willing to go pretty high. I'm willing to go to some high number.

"And if there's less competition, they end up paying less because, even though they were willing to go high—so they've not made a conscious decision to come in with lower advances; they're just able to win at an earlier point in the process because, for example, if Penguin Random House had been in the process or if Simon & Schuster had been in the process, maybe they would have bid something that would have forced you to bid higher. But they're not there anymore. So now, look, I can win at a lower rate.

"And systemically, over time, this results in a general lower level of advances because there are fewer people competing. You don't have to compete as high or as long to get to the end result. The end result is generally lower."

Snyder suggested that she just meant round robin auctions—and the defense is still trying to argue that those are rare, but Judge Pan made clear: "But it's true in a one-on-one negotiation, too, because you might come in lower and realize you don't have to go as high because there's less competition out there. I mean, I think it goes across formats potentially."

Shortly thereafter Dr. Snyder was allowed to get back to his intended testimony, which included walking through all of the ways in which he found the market for ATSB to include many serious players and options beyond the Big 5, at least in isolated circumstances.

While the PRHSS combined market share for ATSB of 50 percent is daunting—and the government argues, presumptively illegal—Snyder did hit the essence of the case: "Market share tells me how frequently they're winning. It doesn't tell me, can they lower advances? And that's when I talked about the fundamental forces in all markets. You've got to take into account the behavior of agents and the responses of rivals."

In his data collected from 18 agencies, covering just under 1,000 deals from 2018 through 2021, publishers making significant deals or better numbered 29 in 2019 and 33 in 2020.

"Market power on the buying side of the market is not a significant concern if suppliers have numerous attractive outlets for their goods or services." Across the full time period, he found 20 different publishers that paid advances of $1 million or more at least once.

He also "calculated that mid-sized and smaller publishers as winners or runners-up in the $250,000-plus segment between 2019 and 2021 are winner or runner-up 23 percent of the time."

This would prove to be a controversial—and pesky—point of contention that was revisited multiple times, up through the defense's closing arguments, at which Judge Pan made it clear she disagreed with the statistic.

The 23 percent came from Snyder's smaller set of agency data, in which he found 150 auctions with multiple bidders, where you could identify the runner-up, and 149 single bidder acquisitions. Of the 150 auctions, 9 were won by non-big-fives (6 percent), but he could not identify how many times they were runners-up. His math on the stand suggested that number should be 60 to get to his 23 percent, but the Judge and others did not find that credible. "That seems very high." Indeed, revisited on Thursday, Dr. Snyder admitted, "That was a mistake I made yesterday." Doing the math again, he concluded the other publishers were underbidders about 30 times (25, really, by the arithmetic. In the same subset of books, S&S or PRH won 96 of those auctions. (Dr. Snyder said the houses were over-indexed in that sample.)

But rebuttal testimony later from Dr. Hill demonstrated that the 23 percent should really be divided in half—to 11.5 percent—since the pool of winners and underbidders is 200, not 100.

Once again, when it got to another technical measure, Judge Pan spoke for us all when she said, "Nobody has explained how the GUPPI analysis actually works; it's hard for me to understand." ("You have made Professor Snyder's day," defense attorney Randy Oppenheimer said.)

Dr. Snyder tried to show that it's a general measure of the lost sales (or opportunities) after a merger, some of which are "diverted to the party you acquire" as an "exercise of market power" that tries to "take into account how profitable it is for the other party that gets those sales."

But he said a GUPPI analysis will always show some kind of harm, and suggested it's a "screening device" to see if you should move on to other calculations and analyses.

Overall, Dr. Snyder rejects the idea that you can create any useful models—Second Score auction; GUPPI; etc.—to model the publishing business and this merger. "I think the whole modeling and calculation exercise is difficult." But that would leave the court with the various datasets on sales of big books, which probably does not favor the defense. Except Dr. Snyder isn't really troubled by high market shares either, as was teased out later in the day. Under cross-examination, it was established that he also did not produce any models to calculate potential harm that might counter the government's estimates. "I concluded it wasn't possible to get insights into important elements in a model: Market share, willingness of authors and agents to make substitutions; and the potential response of rivals. . . . ."

He added, "One of the real problems in modeling this industry is the role of agents in selecting among the mix of acquisitions; I couldn't figure out how to do that." And, "I stopped thinking about it in active way because my empirical analysis didn't indicate that there would be harm." See no harm, model no harm, look for no harm.

As to the data collected by DOJ expert Dr. Hill, he found total advances paid of $4.4 billion to $4.5

billion over a three-year period. About $3.2 billion of that went to ATSB—hence the argument already heard that those books comprise over 70 percent of all advances.

The DOJ's lawyer Mel Schwarz explained later—to the dismay of any who might see it—that of the universe of 58,000 total titles published a year that they have been discussing, fully half of those titles "sell fewer than one dozen books."

"My book isn't in that category," Dr. Snyder replied to the court's amusement. More broadly, Schwarz said, of the top half (or 29,000 titles), 90 percent of those books sell fewer than 2,000 units. "I didn't study it," Dr. Snyder said, even though he dismissed the idea of ATSB as representing a tiny percentage of the market (e.g. just two percent of books published).

In perhaps his most effective juggling of the data, earlier in his testimony, Snyder had shown that 694 contracts—or 231 a year—were for $1 million or more. And 45% of the advances were associated with those seven-figure contracts. He suggested that would be a market unto itself, and one where the authors are so successful already (or so sought after) that they have the leverage, and will be bound to attract competition. He starts to see the market concentrate at advances of over $50,000 (very nice deals), so although he doesn't "like the idea of a price cutoff" at any level, he posited this as a better market to study (since, with the lower threshold, it has more active competitors).

Judge Pan, as indicated previously, is pretty convinced on the government's level of $250,000 plus, and the discernible dominance of the Big 5 at that level and above: "I think the evidence reflects that at $250,000 you are less likely to get non-Big 5 competitors." The other publishers are "the ones being priced out at higher advance levels." She asked, "Can it be a different market just because at certain levels people are not likely to compete? Can that help define a market?"

Snyder allowed that, "Conceptually that may be the case; it's possible. That's not what I see here. What economics tells us to do is . . . check the numbers; the number of competitors by itself is important." He added, "The numbers show more than 30 publishers securing contracts above $250,000." He would return to this theme repeatedly during the day. While the numbers show the non-Big 5 market comprising less than 10 percent of these big deals, Snyder sees dozens of publishers, lots of new entrants, agents and authors with leverage, internal competition, and three remaining big publishers, all at play.

He countered that the non-Big 5 publishers are the winner or runner-up 23 percent of the time, suggesting they play a bigger role in driving bids. But in further examination, he could not support his number and where it came from. (NB, reporting on all of the statistical data is challenging, since much of it is confidential and shown only to the participants, and even the sharable data passes quickly on a screen and is not posted anywhere for close examination. So those of us who know the business well have no ability to scrutinize the data being presented.)

That 23 percent pertained to his smaller set of agency data, in which he found 150 auctions with multiple bidders, where you could identify the runner-up, and 149 single bidder acquisitions. Of the 150 auctions, 9 were won by non-Big 5s (6 percent), but he could not identify how many times they were runners-up. His math on the stand suggested that number should be 60 to get to his 23 percent, but the Judge and others did not find that credible. "That seems very high."

Indeed, revisited on Thursday, Dr. Snyder admitted, "That was a mistake I made yesterday." Doing the math again, he concluded the other publishers were underbidders about 30 times (25, really, by the arithmetic. In the same subset of books, S&S or PRH won 96 of those auctions. (Dr. Snyder said the houses were over-indexed in that sample.)

Rebuttal testimony later from Dr. Hill demonstrated convincingly (to the Judge, at least) that the 23 percent should really be divided in half—to 11.5 percent—since every deal has a winner and an underbidder, so the pool of winners and underbidders is 200, not 100. A calculation of 11.5 percent would conform better to Hill's expectations—and a different set of raw numbers that were shared in court.

Further, Hill saw it was an incorrectly compounded equation anyway: "Dr. Snyder is taking a market share and the total number of times the other firm is the runner up," whereas in determining "unilateral effects" of a merger "we focus on diversion: When one wins, how often does the other lose?" Of Snyder's assertion, Hill claimed, "I've never seen that number used in the course of my career because it's not clear what it represents."

The 23 percent figure would remain pesky and controversial up until the defense's closing arguments—where they continued to rely on that percentage as saying something significant, until Judge Pan made it clear that she was persuaded by Dr. Hill that the correct calculation was 11.5 percent.

There were other unanswered discrepancies in Snyder's testimony as well. About 1200 ATSB are acquired each year. But in Dr. Snyder's report—presumably based on his smaller dataset of agency data?—he lists "yearly averages of about 884 [ATSB] for the two merging parties; 991 for the rest." Asked "any idea why" that adds up to much more than 1200, he said, "I'm not seeing it right now.

In another challenge to Dr. Snyder's math during Cross-Examination, the government said non-Big 5s won only 154 out of 3600 ATSB, "maybe about 5 percent." And they said it was found that those publishers made 262 offers. There wasn't always data about underbidders, but those numbers were also offered to refute the idea that smaller publishers can win or rank as underbidder in 23 percent of deals. (Here that comes out to more like 11.5 percent.)

Under cross, Snyder also conceded some of the government's points about the Big 5's advantages: "There's a comfort level for potential bestselling authors among the Big 5. That doesn't mean that those individual Big 5 competitors don't face a lot of competition; I believe they do. . . . They're bigger; they have more resources, and as I testified earlier today they have reputation."

In one of the many fruitless exchanges during cross-examination, the DOJ and then eventually Judge Pan both tried to get Dr. Snyder to concede that a reduction in a small group of dominant players in a business will reduce competition. "Is three bidders better than two?; is four better than 3?" asked Schwarz. Even when the judge asked, Snyder would only say, "I can't answer that question, without the specific competitive conditions."

She probed in a number of ways: "At some point, does it become important how big the largest competitor is? Like, if you have one player who dwarfs all the other players, but there's still lots of players, does that matter?"

He answered, "My view on that is, yes, there is a general relationship out there between concentration of market shares and lessening of competition. . . . Given the competition within the Big 5 now, Big 4 going forward, given the potential role for entry and imprint competition, we're not at a point where that relationship changes." He also tried to point to vastly different emerging/fast-changing markets like electric vehicles (Tesla) and streaming (Netflix) to rebut the idea that even with a "top player [with] 90 percent of the market share" others could still have the "capacity to compete and constrain."

Ultimately, when asked, "Do you think that two publishers bidding for a book is sufficient in all circumstances to lead to a competitive outcome?," he said, "You have at least one competitive constraint." That epitomized his inclination to find competitive constraints somewhere, and anywhere.

On Thursday morning, there was another exchange that highlighted Judge Pan's view of the testimony versus Dr. Snyder's appraisal of the market forces. Mr. Schwarz was asking if the document in which Madeline McIntosh had written about "increased background coordination in auctions to leverage internal demand information better and avoid internal upbidding" affected Dr. Snyder's view of the internal competition among PRH editors—and it did not.

Judge Pan pressed, "That doesn't affect your analysis?. . . . They've appointed someone to internally coordinate bidding at PRH. There's testimony to that effect." Or at least that was her impression. (PRH counters, out of court, that the transcript shows Madeline McIntosh saying she was "occasionally" involved in coordinating, and when she is not available Nina von Moltke fills in for her.) "And there are emails of editors saying: 'Let's all go up this amount or Let's all bid the same amount.'"

"That doesn't affect your analysis? Because I thought you were assuming that they were all competing with one another internally, like independently. But they may not be?"

Snyder still felt, "Without having this implemented, I can't really speculate. And maybe I should just say: We'll see." He insisted editors are entrepreneurial and competitive, and had a series of qualifications—even if one person is overseeing and approving the bids. But eventually, he allowed, "It could have an effect on some situations, based on what I'm hearing this morning."

There was still one more exchange Thursday in which Snyder resisted playing ball. The DOJ keeps reminding us about the Apple ebook case, in which the court found that publishing CEOs had regularly met privately "in order to discuss the common challenges they face" (whether or not this is true, that was Judge Denise Cote's finding). The DOJ has demonstrated that stretched payment of advances into four portions and policies against splitting off audio rights are blanket policies agents and authors are unable to counteract, and keeps suggesting that a reduced number of big publishers will make such policies—which they view as "coordination"—easier to perpetuate and build on. They even suggest there could be an agreement not to poach each other's authors.

Judge Pan pressed Dr. Snyder a few times here as well, since she—and Mr. Schwarz—were asking, "We're interested in whether the coordination can happen. Your answer seems to be focused on why this is a bad idea, and we're focused on whether the coordination can happen." He kept suggesting editors would resist, even if the CEOs came to an agreement. Judge Pan asked if his view was "premised on your belief that the editors would not comply with the directive of the CEO to not poach?" Ultimately, Snyder said, "I don't think the Big 5 would be able to come up with a mechanism that would distinguish among the types you're talking about." More importantly, but not to the point of the question, "What would the Big 5 be doing? They would just be hurting themselves."

Back to the end of Wednesday's testimony, the DOJ and Snyder reviewed the actual size of some smaller competitors. The much-admired and discussed Norton trade list has totaled 120 to 150 titles a year. Astra has about 40 employees, and aspires to get to 50 in a year or so. Confidential Amazon documents from head of publishing Mikyla Bruder suggested that "they face challenges" in expanding their trade line and have "been considering reducing . . . title count"—the DOJ said their "share of ATSB has been dropping in recent years." The DOJ showed that Dr. Snyder seemed to have mixed up Chronicle with Blackstone (the latter of which "tripled the amount of advances made between 2014 and 2021"). And while Snyder was impressed that Spiegel & Grau "in a short period of time . . . committed a large amount of money to three contracts," a NYT account said they planned to publish only 15 to 20 books a year. To Snyder, "That would indicate that they are in the market and they are competing." To the government, which has heard many reports on individual ATSB bought by independents and new publishers, it still all adds up to less than 10 percent of the market.

Dr. Hill's Rebuttal Testimony

Following Dr. Snyder's examination, the government was able to bring back their expert Dr. Hill for rebuttal and the final word. After addressing the controversial 23—or 11.5—percent issue covered earlier, there was still more discussion about imprint competition (or not) within PRH. Hill found "clear evidence" that "imprints can and do coordinate with each other" at least at times. "If these were independent publishers, this kind of behavior"—e.g. emails in which an executive says it "seems best for everyone to go with" a certain bid— "would not be permitted." And there was still more about GUPPIs and Second Score Auctions.

In one final bit of industry terminology and strategy, we were taught still more about the auction strategy known as The Workaround. Dr. Snyder had cited one agent's email on bidding conditions as "very clear testimony that the agents can set the auction rules to extend external competition and thereby sustain within-firm imprint competition."

That was accomplished by declaring, "If in any round all the top bidders are in the same corporation, then I will include the next-highest bidder." The point being to ensure that there remains the appearance of an outside bidder so that the PRH imprints can continue to bid against each other.

Dr. Hill was asked about this in his rebuttal: "Would you agree with me that this is describing a mechanism by which the PRH requirement of an outside bidder being present in order to continue imprint competition could effectively be thwarted?"

Earlier, he had said, "The evidence that I saw was that in general, agents are respectful of the Penguin Random House bidding rules and they will, when asked, give truthful information about whether Penguin Random House is the last two bidders. I didn't see any evidence of a work-around. And I also see some tension between the idea—Dr. Snyder's idea that there is this work-around that agents know such that the Penguin Random House bidding rules are invalidated and Mr. Dohle's promise: If this merger goes through, we won't extend the Penguin Random House bidding rules to Simon & Schuster. If it was true that agents already knew how to circumvent the bidding rules, there would be no need for a letter saying: Don't worry. We're not going to extend the bidding rules."

But the Judge noted that Snyder "was relying on an actual email that said: We're going to do this. I was interested that it was sort of publicly stated" to the auction participants. Hill admitted that he hadn't seen that email.

On the supposed power of agents, at one point Dr. Hill observed, "If agents are omnipotent, we'd expect to see publishers not earning any margins." Rather, "Agents are good at extracting the value that's created by competition," and the lessening competition constrains that ability.

The defense continued to push on Dr. Hill's evaluation of harm and his definition of the ATSB, but at this stage of the proceedings it felt like an exercise in futility. Dr. Snyder's attempt to shift the markets to under $50,000; $50,000 to $1 million; and over $1 million only helped lead the judge to posit that there could be multiple tiers of books by price, including those with modest anticipated sales, or a "mid-tier market." But that only helped reinforce the posited market for ATSB.

The defense also probed Dr. Hill about the exact mechanisms and practices under which bids and advances might actually go down after a merger.

Judge Pan said to Dr. Hill: "You just said you would expect them to start offering less, on average 11 percent less. But wouldn't it really play out that there's less competition so you might—you might come in at a lower initial bid, but you wouldn't have to go up to your max because there's fewer people bidding, so the auctions will end earlier? There's just—I just feel like there would be downward pressure, not from people consciously thinking 'I'm lowering,' but more just from the lack of bidding."

Her second, and final, question, was on the specificity of the $250,000 threshold for ATSB, following the defense's renewed efforts to show it's a made-up notion that simply demarcates the place where the government could find concentration and try to construct a theory of harm.

The judge asked of Dr. Hill, "My understanding was that you were just trying to figure out the top selling books, and these are the ones that need more distribution, that need more sales support, need more marketing, have authors that might have different expectations from people who are not expecting their books to do as well. And I thought you were saying you just used 250[,000] because it's a proxy for the amount of sales because all the advances are based on expected sales and that's why you did it at 150 and 500 and 1 million. I didn't think, correct me if I'm wrong, that 250 was actually that important."

Dr. Hill confirmed: "That's a correct summary. There's a group of these books that exist in the industry. As the person analyzing it, I picked 250 to try to identify that group. And I tested whether above or below made a big difference, and it did not. So I was comfortable with that 250 as my method for finding this general group of anticipated top sellers."

TESTIMONY OF EDWARD A. SNYDER, WILLIAM S. BEINECKE PROFESSOR OF ECONOMICS AND MANAGEMENT, YALE UNIVERSITY

DIRECT EXAMINATION

BY MR. OPPENHEIMER:

Q. Would you state your name for the record, please.

A. My name is Edward A. Snyder.

Q. And would you describe briefly your academic background.

A. I went to school in Maine, Colby College, and then I earned my master's degree in public policy and my Ph.D. in economics from the University of Chicago.

Q. As an economist, what is your area of specialization?

A. Industrial organization. IO is the field of economics that deals most directly with competitor interactions and pricing and antitrust issues.

Q. What is your current profession?

A. I am the William S. Beinecke professor of economics and management at Yale University.

Q. Do you hold any secondary appointments?

A. I do; in the economics department at Yale.

Q. And could you briefly walk us through your academic career.

A. Yes. I earned tenure at University of Michigan's business school, and then I became dean of three top business schools, where I worked over roughly a two-decade time period. The first was University of Virginia's Darden School; second was the University of Chicago's *Booth* School; and then most recently, the Yale School of Management.

Q. Have you also been teaching?

A. Yes. I've taught, actually, from the beginning of my career, pretty much throughout my career. And since I stopped deaning three years ago, I've developed a new course on economic analysis of high-tech industries, an exciting topic and quite successful course. Prior to that, I taught courses on microeconomics. When I was at Michigan, I developed a course that basically leveraged IO content called competitive tactics. And then I had the great joy of teaching with Nobel laureate Gary Becker for nine years, a course on major policy issues.

Q. And do you continue to do research?

A. I do. I find it rewarding. I have a published article very recently on the vertical merger guidelines. I have a chapter that's coming out in an annual book on antitrust cases. And I recently submitted a paper to a journal for their traditional lined review.

Q. And have you ever served in government?

A. Yes. I started my professional career at the U.S. Department of Justice in the antitrust division.

Q. Have you served as an expert in antitrust cases?

A. Yes; in a wide variety of industries, ranging from high-tech, pharmaceuticals, medical technologies, financial matters.

Q. And have you previously been designated as an expert and qualified as an expert in these cases?

A. Yes.

Q. Have any of your roles involved monopsony issues?

A. Yes. Three come to mind. One is the litigation involving dairy farmers. The second one is litigation involving cranberry farmers. And the third one is high-tech employees.

Q. Was the dairy farmers case 2019, Vermont?

A. I believe so. Yes.

Q. Have you recently testified on coordination issues?

A. I did. I testified two times earlier this year on coordination issues in federal court in Denver involving allegations of price-fixing in the broiler chicken industry.

Q. And have you worked on behalf of plaintiffs and defendants?

A. Yes. I've not testified recently on behalf of plaintiffs. However, in the last four years, I've been retained by three different plaintiffs, two in the high-tech context, one being video streaming and the other within gaming, and the third one involving a specific medical technology.

Q. Have you served as an economics expert in a merger?

A. The work that I've done on mergers corresponds to what Dr. Hill referred to as the advocacy phase. And I've gone before the agencies on three separate occasions. One involved a particular medical technology. Another one involved fleet cards. Those are basically credit cards that firms use for their fleets of vehicles. And I can't remember the third right now. Oh, it was hotel services.

Q. And do you have experience in financial accounting?

A. I have a lot of experience with financial accounting and decisions involving investments and programs and so forth.

MR. OPPENHEIMER: Your Honor, at this time we'd move to qualify Professor Snyder as an expert on economics.

THE COURT: Any objection?

MR. SCHWARZ: No objection, your Honor.

THE COURT: He will be so qualified.

BY MR. OPPENHEIMER:

Q. Professor Snyder, have you prepared a slide presentation to assist with your testimony today?

A. I have.

MR. OPPENHEIMER: Your Honor, we will not use any portion, of course, that was the subject of earlier colloquy. But subject to that, and subject to confidentiality, may we publish as we proceed those slides?

THE COURT: Yes.

MR. OPPENHEIMER: Thank you. Let's put up Slide 2, Pam. Thank you.

THE COURT: For the record, what is this exhibit?

MR. OPPENHEIMER: Pardon me?

THE COURT: For the record, what is this exhibit?

MR. OPPENHEIMER: Your Honor, this is a demonstrative. This is the first part of the slide show.

THE COURT: It doesn't have a number?

MR. OPPENHEIMER: It does not, your Honor. We can designate this as Slide 2.

THE COURT: I think you already have a Defendants' demonstrative—

MR. OPPENHEIMER: Demonstrative 16, your Honor.

THE COURT: We already have a Demonstrative 16, I think. 18.

MR. OPPENHEIMER: 18, your Honor. Demonstrative.

THE COURT: All right.

BY MR. OPPENHEIMER:

Q. Dr. Snyder, Professor Snyder, what were you asked to do in this case?

A. I was asked to assess the likely competitive effects of the proposed merger and, of course, to respond to the opinions and the analyses offered by the Government's expert, Dr. Nicholas Hill.

Q. And did you reach conclusions?

A. I did. My overall conclusion was very simple: The Government has not proven that there will be a substantial lessening of competition as a result of the merger. And then I have identified some additional more specific opinions. That's what's here on this slide.

Q. Let's start with No. 1. Can you explain your first opinion and briefly the basis for it?

A. Well, this is actually more of an observation than an opinion. It's simply that there's no allegation of harm to consumers in the sale of books that would result from this merger.

Q. And for your analysis, what's the implication of that?

A. Simply that the issues concerning this matter focus on the upstream, the acquisition of books.

Q. Can you explain your second conclusion and the basis for it?

A. My second opinion is that there's no harm to authors in the broad market of all trade books. The main basis for that is that there is a lot of competition in that industry to acquire books and the merger is not going to reduce that competition.

Q. When you refer to the broad market, can you just explain for us what you mean by that?

A. Yes. "All trade books" refers to all kind of books that most people are interested in reading: fiction, nonfiction, historical books, biographies, science fiction. It does not include academic textbooks, for example, but it's the broad category of books that consumers read.

Q. Is it subject to any advance level cutoffs?

A. No.

Q. Let's go to your third conclusion, where you say: Books with advances of $250,000 or more are not a valid market. Would you elaborate on that?

A. Yes. I've reached the conclusion that the proposed market segments starting at $250,000 for anticipated top sellers is not a valid market. I have several reasons for that. As Dr. Hill correctly identified, I believe that it is indeed an arbitrary cutoff. I do not see that firms operate differently below and above that threshold. The competitive conditions for an author who ends up getting a $100,000 advance, I don't see that those are different from an author who gets a $400,000 advance. The other aspect of the market definition that is, I think, maybe not appreciated fully in this matter is that it has the word "anticipated" in it. And the question of the anticipation—I'll go through this in more detail—gets at whether it's possible for publishers, editors, to identify and then target authors. And this is a fundamental problem with the proposed market.

Q. Do you believe in this industry as you've studied it that publishers can identify and target authors?

A. As I wrote in my report, the question of targeting or identification—excuse me—identification, which is closely connected to the idea of anticipation, that's a question of by whom and when. And certainly it is the case that for some authors we all know they're going to be bestsellers when their book comes out. But it's—that then raises the question of: Are those also the authors that there's any chance of targeting, meaning cutting their advances?

And that's the important part of this combination of identification and targeting, because those are the authors we all agree are anticipated, but they're also the ones who have all the leverage. So it's unlikely that you would get both identification and targeting. Now, for others, yes. It's going to be the case that maybe you can identify, anticipate; but it's not going to be done consistently, especially with an ex post approach to defining the market.

Q. We'll get into that a little bit more a little bit later. What is your fourth opinion?

A. The fourth conclusion is that there's no harm to authors who receive advances of $250,000 and above. This price segment as well as the broad market is highly competitive. It's going to remain so. Not only do you have PRH and S&S; you've got the other so-called Big 3. You have a large number of middle and smaller publishers. You've got imprint competition. You have agents who represent authors who are soliciting bids, and a large number of publishers are responding to those bids. The other fact that I would want to point out here is that PRH and S&S are rarely the winner and runner-up. And that is the essential element of the Government's claim, that there will be a loss of head-to-head competition and there will be so-called unilateral effects that result. Those are straight out of the Government's complaint; and I think Dr. Hill and I agree those are the necessary conditions for harm. But if you take Dr. Hill's market share data or my market share data, the prediction is that the two parties will be winner and runner-up in only 12 percent of the time. That means that in 88 percent of the time, that condition for harm doesn't exist.

Q. Professor Snyder, why is that an important observation with respect to the Government's theory?

A. It raises the question that is not answered by the models that Dr. Hill has offered, which is: How will this theory of cutting advances work in practice? How will editors actually know when to cut advances when that necessary condition of winner and runner-up is only met 12 percent of the time?

Q. You mentioned models. What is your view of Dr. Hill's second score auction model?

A. The second score auction model is in this setting a wrong fit for the industry. It's unreliable in terms of how it's been estimated, and the results from it are really quite striking. What goes into that model are of course market shares and margins. Once those are in the model, it's important to understand—I think, your Honor, you understand this—but no publisher changes their bid in the model. There's no competitive response inside the model. Agents play no role inside the model. So, the results of the model are really disconnected from the industry, especially when we take into account that the model presumes an acquisition format, rounds to completion, that so-called round-robin format, that agents rarely choose. So, I'm putting aside the issues with inputs for now, but this is really a bad fit with the industry.

Again, competitor responses: Not there. The parties get a free lunch, exercise of monopsony power and no loss of market share. Authors are harmed, but there are no responses by competitors. And agents don't do anything.

Q. You did allude to inputs, so I want to pause on that for a minute. Do you have a view on the inputs that were used with respect to the second score auction model?

A. Well, the inputs, as I mentioned, are market shares and margins. Market shares have to go into this model. That's just a requirement. So, Dr. Hill uses market shares, and I really don't have an objection to that. My focus is more on the issue of margins. And his approach to margins was inconsistent at the outset. And then when he responded to my criticism and he developed consistent margins, the results of the SSA model are that it fails the reliability test that the developer of the model, Nathan Miller, specified. So, in my view, both efforts in Dr. Hill's first report and in his third report fail, one on inconsistency and the other one on reliability.

Q. Taking these factors into account and mindful of the output of the second score auction model, what is your overall assessment of the model?

A. Well, based on its lack of fit, again, agents are stuck with a format that they rarely choose. There's no competitor response. And then when you actually estimate the model, it's either based on inconsistent inputs or unreliable results. I don't find that the SSA model in this context offers any value in terms of the fundamental economic analysis.

Q. Is your opinion of the model influenced by the degree of harm it purports to identify?

A. Well, the harm that it identifies is a little bit less than $30 million annually. So my observation would be simply that's not a very large number in the context of a billion-dollar annual advance level. And by the way, I should just make it clear: Of course, Dr. Hill's estimation of the model is for his proposed pricing. It's above $250,000, not the broad market. So that's not a very large number. If one were to really think about using that estimate, I believe sound adjustments to the model would bring that down from that $30 million annual amount as you would, for example, include imprint competition, as you would include the different margins. So, I have a view about what margins should be included. Dr. Hill may disagree. But mine are consistent, and they are grounded in the book-level P&Ls that the parties actually use when they're bidding. So, I think I have a very strong argument for using the margins the way I identified them. And when you incorporate those sound adjustments—I'm not talking about efficiencies—that brings down that $30 million annual estimate to a much lower number.

Q. Now, in his subsequent report after your report, Dr. Hill applied the GUPPI calculations to his analysis. What is your opinion of Dr. Hill's use of the GUPPI index?

A. His calculations of the GUPPI index do not confirm the SSA model. Before I get into that, I'd just observe that if one were to think about doing a GUPPI calculation, that's a screening device. That's typically used at the outset. And then it's followed by, as the developers of the GUPPI index have said, then you get into modeling further analysis, including merger simulations. So, one of the things that struck me was, this is an odd thing to come in the third report to attempt to confirm the original SSA model. In terms of whether it can do that, the answer is no. It's got the same problems with lack of fit to the industry. It's got the same problems with respect to inputs. It also cannot account for agent behavior. There's no competitor response. So, I don't find the GUPPI model at all persuasive in this context. Again, it's a screening device.

THE COURT: Can you explain what you mean by competitor response?

THE WITNESS: Well, in the SSA model, your Honor, no publisher changes any bids. The effect of harm comes from elimination of bids due to the merger; and you slide down to the next-second-best, which determines the price.

THE COURT: So you're saying it's a one-round auction?

THE WITNESS: It's a one-round auction. Automatic harm. No publisher changes their bids in the SSA model.

THE COURT: Because it's a one-round auction?

THE WITNESS: Correct. They bid their maximum from the outset. And agents can't go to them and say anything, because they've already bid their max. The GUPPI calculation also has no competitor responses. There's no agent role. And it's not what economists would call an equilibrium, because any equilibrium in any real market has to take into account how parties on each side of the market are adjusting their behavior. And in the GUPPI model, we have no agent, no author adjustments. They're stuck. They're either in the single bidder or hybrid or whatever. And then on the rival side, there's no competitor response. So, this is not what economists would refer to as an equilibrium model, which goes back to the point I mentioned earlier: It's a screening device that then is intended, according to its developers, former chief economists Farrell and Shapiro—it's intended to then lead to further analysis to get at, well, how will this actually work in taking into account actions on both sides of the market?

BY MR. OPPENHEIMER:

Q. Let's switch to a different area, coordinated effects. Would you describe your fifth conclusion, no coordinated effects, and the basis for it?

A. Well, coordinated effects is part of what the DOJ alleges. And Dr. Hill makes the case for coordinated effects. I have to disagree, however. According to the guidelines, what's important for coordinated effects are a mechanism of harm, the ability to detect and monitor. And in this context, these are one-off acquisition processes with many dimensions that are not observable by other rivals.

Eventually, on this point—I agree with Dr. Hill—eventually, the identity of the winner is known. However, that does not tell you what you need to know to coordinate during the acquisition processes. And as I said, there are just so many dimensions of competition during the acquisition process. So, this claim has no conceptual force grounded in the guidelines and in fundamental economics.

Q. What role in your analysis did the 2013 merger of Penguin and Random House play?

A. Well, Mr. Oppenheimer, you referred to that as the natural experiment earlier this afternoon. That is something that economists would look at, a merger in 2013, to see what happened. The number one thing as an economist that I would be interested in seeing is what effect it had on output. And then a second thing would be: What effect did it have on advances, both in total and based on averages? And what I see with respect to output is output increases in terms of titles and contracts. Total advances increase. And this is the analysis that I think was discussed before I started testifying. But when you look at buckets, categories of advances—

Q. Professor Snyder, I'm going to ask you not to go into that. That was the subject of colloquy with the Court. So, we'll continue on to the next topic.

A. Okay.

Q. How did you approach your assignment?

A. Well, the first thing I did was I studied the industry. That's what I do in every case I take on.

Q. What did you do after that?

A. After that, I conducted empirical analyses. And they tied into what I was just talking about earlier: What adjustments are being made on the author's side and the agent's side with respect to selecting, acquisition formats, making adjustments? And what publishers do they consider when they engage publishers, seek responses from them and ultimately contract with? And then the second set of empirical analyses focuses on, well, what's the source of competition here from the publisher side? That's imprints; it's competition among the top publishers; it's also competition with middle and smaller publishers who are already bidding and winning contracts; and then it's also publishers that are operating right below the $250,000 threshold. They've already got operations set up to be a competitor. What's different for them is they have not yet secured a contract above 250. So, I focused on all those things on the publishing side.

Q. And what information and data did you use for that analysis?

A. I reviewed a lot of information from a lot of different sources. Of course, the examples that have been presented in the complaint are a source of information. There's documentary evidence. But there are also six different data sets here. And Dr. Hill, to his credit, he and his team developed some important data sets. I've developed a data set around the so-called agency data. And so I've reviewed all those data and, where appropriate, I used them.

MR. OPPENHEIMER: May we bring up Slide 4, Pam?

BY MR. OPPENHEIMER:

Q. Based on your study, what are the features of the publishing industry that are important to your economic analysis?

A. I know your Honor has heard a lot of this. On the agency side, I would just point out that the agents are critically important. They choose among a mix of acquisition processes. And there's a mix of authors and agents, some of which are repeat players when it comes to successful authors. Other authors have different profiles, of course. For example, there are celebrities. And then there are also authors who are more of the classic debut authors.

MR. OPPENHEIMER: May we put up Slide 5?

BY MR. OPPENHEIMER:

Q. Does this identify, this slide, some of the characteristics you've identified in connection with agents?

A. Yes. Given what I just said, I don't need to read this slide. I think I would just call out that whatever acquisition process they pick, agents can change it. And as Dr. Hill has explained, agents sometimes start out with a rounds auction but then switch to a best bids auction. And that's called a hybrid. And he and I agree on that.

Q. And so, let's go back to your industry future summary slide.

MR. OPPENHEIMER: Slide 6, Pam.

BY MR. OPPENHEIMER:

Q. What did you learn about publishers that is relevant to your economic analysis?

A. Well, again, this is well-known. I mean, editors end up to varying degrees co-developing books with authors. The other thing that is striking about this industry, though, is that many publishers combine firm-wide capabilities with entrepreneurial and creative efforts at the imprint level. That's the second bullet point there.

Q. Well, what are you addressing with your last bullet point under publishers?

A. Well, there's just a great diversity of publishers. Yes, there are the so-called Big 5, but there are many publishers with different profiles, with different approaches to engaging prospective authors and contracting with them.

Q. What did you learn about consumers that is relevant to your analysis?

A. I think the most interesting thing about this industry is that what consumers read is what publishers acquire. So, you've got a very one-to-one relationship between the downstream and the upstream.

Q. From an economic perspective, do the industry features you've identified pose challenges for industry participants?

MR. OPPENHEIMER: That'll be Slide 7, please.

THE WITNESS: Yes. And I have a demonstrative on this. There are many different challenges. But oftentimes, I do like to think about: What are salient challenges for the economic analysis? And the first one I have here is matching authors to editors.

BY MR. OPPENHEIMER:

Q. What is the significance of that for you?

A. Well, again, this has been well-established. But this is a market where that creative match between editors and authors ends up being a driving force; and indeed, editors, when they do find a potential match with an author, that's when they're likely to bid and bid more. This is a central component of the industry. And it ties in, of course, to the way firms are organized. Again, not all firms, but many firms use imprints to increase their chances of a successful match.

Q. And what role do agents play in matching authors to editors?

A. Well, they are the agents who can contact and basically provide potential vision and profile of the author and engage editors to spark their interest and generate the potential match.

Q. Would you describe for us what economic matching theory is and its relevance to your analysis in this case? Pam, may we have Slide 8?

A. Well, it's good to every once in a while pay attention to Nobel prize winners. I just wanted to make it clear that economists for a long time didn't think about the role of matching, but over the last two decades economists have. And two American economists, Roth and Shapley, won the Nobel Prize for their work on matching. And it's in contexts where price doesn't by itself clear the market. So, I just wanted to make sure that it's—this is not an unheard-of or certainly completely unusual feature of an industry. Matching is important.

Q. And do publishers organize themselves to address this matching issue?

A. Yes. That's what the idea of the hybrid organization, combining firm-wide capabilities with entrepreneurial efforts at the imprint level, is all about. It's a way to empower editors to be creative, to be entrepreneurial; and that is in the interest of the publisher because it increases the likelihood that there will be a match and they'll eventually win the contract.

Q. Slide 9.What is the second challenge that must be addressed as part of your economic analysis?

A. It's what to bid. These products are uncertain in terms of what their value is. The profiles of the authors vary greatly. So, this is a fundamental problem. And even if an editor is particularly excited about the book, she won't necessarily know how much to bid.

Q. What does economic theory tell us about the approach to valuing truly unique products like books?

A. Economics organizes this answer based on the following distinction: Editors have two types of factors that influence the maximum that they're willing to bid. One is so-called common factors. So it's a well-known author, a long track record, observable prior work; comps are known. You can put that into your book-level P&L. Those are common factors because everybody can see them. They're common across potential bidders. The other kind of factor is individual factors that vary across editors. And those concern things like: What's the vision for the book? What's the likely receptivity in the market to the book? And these—this is an important insight for me because the mix of common factors and individualized factors varies. And when you take the very high end, profile authors with long track records, common factors are going to denominate. You're going to have very similar valuations.

You still can have differences, but you'll tend to have more similar valuations. And I think this is consistent with the testimony by Mr. Wylie. And then as you go to the more classic debut author, individualized factors before more important. So the mix of the two varies across advance levels.

Q. Slide 10, please. And you indicated you observed this in some of the testimony. Is this another example of that that you've seen in the testimony to date?

A. Yes. The testimony from Jennifer Bergstrom—I'll just identify the bottom statement. She's talking about authors for whom she doesn't have a track record. But she says: There's a lot of uncertainty there. Much more so—excuse me—more so than actually the million-plus.

Q. Professor Snyder, this distinction between the identification of common factors and private individualized factors, do you see anything significant in your work about authors who are paid advances in excess of $250,000 with respect to that distinction?

A. Well, it goes back to the issue of identification, which is tied to who's anticipated to be a top seller. And it goes to the issue of targeting. And I don't want to repeat myself; but with the benefit of common factor versus individualized factors, that distinction in mind, there are going to be some authors who can be anticipated to be bestsellers, but those are the ones for whom common factors are going to denominate or be more important, at least, in the valuations. And as a result, there's going to be more—tighter distribution of willingness to pay and, of course, those are the ones with respect to targeting who have the leverage.

Q. You've indicated that the industry has some distinctive features. But are there underlying economic fundamentals that are important to your analysis?

A. Industry features help explain how competition will unfold. But the underlying competitive factors are the same in every industry and every market I've ever looked at.

Q. Slide 12, Pam. Do you believe that observation is reflected in the horizontal guidelines, horizontal merger guidelines?

A. I do. And if we were to take the more typical antitrust issue of sellers providing goods and services downstream to consumers, the two core economic forces relate to what I said earlier, which is on the buy side, what alternatives do buyers have? And what is their willingness to make substitutions? And then on the supply side, it's the responses of rival suppliers. Those are the two things. Both sides of the market: demand and supply.

Q. Now, given that we're focused on the upstream acquisition of books in this case, can you put these two fundamental forces into this context for us?

A. Yes. In the monopsony context, the issue is: Can authors and agents make adjustments and find alternatives to avoid the exercise of monopsony power? And then the second factor is: Are there competitors, rival publishers, who can discipline the potential exercise of monopsony power?

Q. Did this framework guide your empirical analysis?

A. Absolutely.

Q. Can you explain that?

A. On the author/agent side, I wanted to understand how agents choose the acquisition processes that they select and the frequency with which they select them. And I also wanted to identify: To what extent were authors and agents willing to choose among different publishers? We of course hear about the two merging parties. We've got the other three, the Big 5. We also have the middle and smaller publishers. So, I looked at: Are there from the point of view of at least a substantial number of authors alternatives to any of the above?

Q. Could you use a model rather than conduct these empirical analyses?

A. So that's a good question. And I certainly have sympathy with Dr. Hill's observations about the challenges of modeling the different acquisition formats. I think I heard his testimony to the effect that he considered but wasn't able to model, for example—I think it was single-bidder or one-on-one negotiations. What makes this a difficult challenge to model is that you've got the different acquisition formats; you have the agents doing the selection; and you have a very multidimensional, one-book-at-a-time set of acquisitions.

Q. Do either of the SSA model or the GUPPI calculation embody the fundamental economic forces that you identified in your earlier answer?

A. No. There's no agent role in selecting and making adjustments and there are no competitive responses. And that's, I think, one of the most important points for me when I evaluate the SSA model and when I evaluate the GUPPI calculations. Those two fundamental forces are absent.

Q. So I know we've talked a lot about data in this case. And you've talked about data. I'd like to go over some of the data sets that you and Dr. Hill have been using, sometimes jointly.

Pam, if we could bring up Slide 13.

Professor Snyder, could you describe what this slide is showing us?

A. Yes. And I should just preface this by saying there are other data snippets and sources, for example, on particular acquisition processes and so forth. But these are the primary data sets that I think have been discussed in the course of the trial. And I'll start on the left. The number one data set is the advance data, organized by Dr. Hill. And sometimes, your Honor, I may refer to these as the acquisition data because they're the ones that we also used to generate market shares. But I'll just refer to them here as the advance data. And Dr. Hill's data go from 2019 through midway 2021. That's analogous to the advance data in Column 5 that I developed. The only difference is that I extended those data to complete 2021. So those two data sets have a lot of observations, 24,000 in the case of Dr. Hill and nearly 30,000 in the case of my advance data. And then the number of observations in the proposed segment are identified in the bottom row.

Q. What is the win-loss data?

A. 2, 3 and 4—let's start with 2. These are the more curated data sets that Dr. Hill developed. The win-loss data use information from the two merging parties, PRH and Simon & Schuster. It covers this time period identified here. 924 observations are identified in the broad market, 206 in the proposed market with advances above $250,000. To get this information, there's a lot of work to evaluate information from the two parties. And it was done from each of their points of view.

Q. And what are the editorial minutes?

A. The editorial minutes also involved a lot of work, also relied on information from the parties. So, Dr. Hill and his team reviewed editorial minutes over the time period indicated here.

The number of observations, 784, these are not by definition going to give you all the observations because at the meetings, members of the meetings don't talk about every acquisition. But the result here is 284 observations in the $250,000 segment.

Q. And the runner-up data?

A. The runner-up data, again, a lot of work. Dr. Hill developed these data for one year, 2020. As he testified, he started from the top, the maximum advances, and worked his way down. When he got to $500,000, my understanding from his testimony is that he did look at some observations below $500,000 down to $250,000, but he didn't develop those data systematically. So these data go from as a result $500,000 on up and do not include $250,000 to $500,000.

Q. We may get into this in more detail later. But just generally, does that affect the results of analyses done on the runner-up data?

A. I'm sorry. What was the end of the question?

Q. Yes. The fact that they analyzed data from advances of $500,000 and up, does that affect the conclusions that can be derived from the runner-up data?

A. I think the data are useful. The data sets have various limitations. I think when each of us has been using the data sets, I think we've been aware of these limitations. But you try to get to various insights. But you're right: I mean, you have to keep in mind that each data set has some limitations. And this one is not complete with respect to that range.

Q. Let's go to the Slide 14, please. So here we have the same data sets arrayed with certain features. Can you explain, what are we seeing in Slide 14?

A. Well, I wanted to identify in Slide 14: What data do you see from each data set? And so this slide has the five that I've already discussed, plus it adds in the agency data that I developed and my team developed. And along the rows I've got: Well, what do we see? Do we see the runner-up? Well, it turns out that two data sources, Dr. Hill's runner-up data and the agency data, generate insights about runner-up. What about other bidders and their bids? The first five data sets—and that includes my data set on advances—does not provide that information.

Do we know whether the process was at least—was a multi-bidder or single process? You could go into more fine-grained categorizations. But do you get insights on that? You do in Dr. Hill's runner-up data, but not in the other data sets, 1 through 5. And do you get any insights about imprint competition? No. And it's because of these features of the databases that I've identified, 1 through 5. That's what led me to say: Maybe we could get better data, more complete, more 360-style data, by looking at this from the point of view of agents.

Q. Would it be a fair summary that the agency data is the only data that addresses winner, runner-up, other bidders and bids, multi- or single-bidder process and imprint competition?

A. Yes.

Q. What is the feature of the agency data that allows it to address all of those issues where the other data sets cannot?

A. Well, as I mentioned, for example, when you look at the win-loss data or the editorial minutes data, you're looking at those questions from the point of view of only two parties, PRH and S&S. But the agency data allow you to look at it from the point of view of the agents. They're in effect like the hub and they've got spokes to not just those two parties, but to others.

Q. Have you heard the observation that the agency data are not representative?

A. Well, it's a small data set. And I'll get into more details about that. They are not representative in one important respect. I think Dr. Hill and I agree on this. And that's that the agency data end up overrepresenting PRH and S&S. And depending on the metric that I use, it's a substantial overrepresentation of the merging parties. Maybe it's 15—I can't recall, but maybe 15 to 20 percent.

Q. Can you identify some of the—just very briefly—some of the consequences of that overrepresentation?

A. Well–

THE COURT: I'm sorry. What is the 15 or 20 percent?

THE WITNESS: So if, your Honor, I look at either Dr. Hill's advance data or my advance data, you can get pretty reliable measures of market share. And I think those market shares are in the range of 47 to 49 percent, combined. But if you look at the agency data, then their combined market share goes to 57 percent. I might not have done the math right, but the numbers that I just gave are right.

THE COURT: I see. I see.

BY MR. OPPENHEIMER:

Q. Would it be a fair summary that there are occasions when relying on the agency data will overstate the shares of Penguin Random House and Simon & Schuster?

A. Yes.

Q. Stepping back, which data sets did you primarily use for your empirical work?

A. I used different data sets for different purposes.

Q. And can you give us an overview of how you approached the different data sets in your work?

A. Well, I was, consistent with my earlier testimony, very interested in the mix of acquisitions. And that's something that I could see observed in the agency data. I could see imprint competition, because the agents are engaging imprints from within the same publisher. You can see that there. So, several of my analyses focused my attention on: Well, what will the agency data show?

Q. Let's talk about that–

THE COURT: When you say "mix of acquisitions," what do you mean?

THE WITNESS: I mean whether they are single bidder or multi-bidder. And when I present the agency data, your Honor, I'll just use that—those two categories. But one can see in the agency discovery a richer set of acquisition formats and you can see the adjustments and get a really good feel for the role of agents in orchestrating the acquisition processes, not just going through a door and say, I'm going to have to stay there, but I'm going to test that and maybe make adjustments.

BY MR. OPPENHEIMER:

Q. Just to clarify, do the agents have information that is unavailable to the publishers?

A. Yes, because they are the hub. If they've engaged 14 different editors, that information will not be available in the data sets No. 5 as well as the ones to the left.

Q. So let's take a look at the agency data a little more closely. What is the—Let's bring up Slide 15. What is the scope of the agency data you analyzed?

A. Well, the agency data come from agents, 18 different agents, who responded to a broad discovery request. And—

Q. May I interrupt you, Professor Snyder, just one second? You said 18 agents. Did you mean agencies?

A. Yes. Sorry. It covers a four-year time period, starting in 2018 to 2021. Total observations there are 973. You'll note 2018 was light in terms of observations, because the discovery request didn't lead to as many observations in the earlier year, 2018. And the other thing on this slide is just—it identifies the split between on the left-hand side the number of observations below—it ended up with advances below $250,000, and on the right-hand side the number that ended up with advances above $250,000. So, focusing on the right-hand side, with the proposed segment, the agency data yield 360 of the 973 total.

Q. So we brought up a slide now that I believe focuses on that group of titles that you selected over 250. Can you walk us through what this slide is telling us about the way you managed and dealt with this data?

A. Well, I was interested in learning a few things. And I won't go into all of them right now, but if I may I'll point out three. Number one, I did want to understand: Do I see a mix of acquisitions in the data? And in the upper left-hand side, you see the single bidder. 149 of those out of—I should explain this. I'm sorry. Let me start again. If you look at the yellow-orange at the top, there are 360 observations above $250,000. 61 of them I and my team could not develop reliable information for. That leaves 299. Going back to the point about the mix of acquisitions, 149 of them are single and 150 involve multi-bid auctions with known runner-up.

Q. And before you go beyond that, just a quick question: How many of the acquisition processes in this data set that you examined were pure round robins?

A. Very few. And I don't think there's a reliable number across all of the data sets and all of the information. But in the course of reviewing the 360 on the right-hand side, we saw very few. And I've seen very few from other sources of material, leading me to believe that rounds auctions, where they begin at rounds and go to completion, are very rare, probably less than 10 percent.

Q. When you say "go to completion," you mean go to completion as a round?

A. Correct; as opposed to, as Dr. Hill explained, some of these start out at rounds and then they switch to best bids. Those are hybrids, not pure round-robin auctions to completion.

Q. And you said "very few." Can you give us some sense of the magnitude of how many were observed?

A. A handful. A few. Less than—certainly less than ten that I can recall seeing in any context here.

Q. Now—

THE COURT: Can I ask you a question?

MR. OPPENHEIMER: Sure.

THE COURT: Can you capture how many observations there were where both Penguin Random House and S&S bid but neither won? That seems to be missing from this chart.

THE WITNESS: Good catch, your Honor. Because the observation in orange-pink won by PRH or S&S, that's 96. The other party didn't bid in 45 of those. But you're asking the question—could you repeat the question?

THE COURT: I guess the question is: Did you capture—are there instances where both PRH and S&S bid but they did not win? That would give a better picture of how often they are actually competing, because this only captures when one of them won. There could be more times where they're competing but neither of them won.

THE WITNESS: One of the problems I had in constructing this chart is that there are a lot of ways to divide the chart. I can check to see if I can provide that information.

THE COURT: Okay. Thank you.

BY MR. OPPENHEIMER:

Q. Professor Snyder, given the Government's theory of harm in this case under their unilateral effects analysis, is it important to you to know when Penguin Random House and Simon & Schuster are involved in bidding when they are neither winner nor runner-up?

A. Yes, because then you don't have head-to-head competition, if I understand your question.

THE COURT: Why is that not head-to-head competition? They're both in the auction. They're competing. They just didn't win.

THE WITNESS: I might have misunderstood Mr. Oppenheimer's question.

BY MR. OPPENHEIMER:

Q. Well, but her Honor's question is really to the point. So, if PRH and S&S are both in a competition for books at an auction and neither wins and neither is the runner-up, does that have relevance for your analysis of the Government's unilateral effects case?

A. I think it's useful to point out the bottom-left number. So, we have a total of 299 observations; let's call it 300. The two parties are winner and runner-up 21 times, according to the data. So that's infrequent. And that, I think, is informative about the question. But I just don't see it on the chart here.

Q. Under the Government's theory of harm, is it relevant data when the parties are both in an auction but neither ends up being first or second?

A. Yes. That means that neither is a relevant competitive constraint. To be a competitive constraint, according to the DOJ's theory and the basic idea of unilateral effects in this context, they have to be winner or runner-up to exert competitive influence.

Q. Under the Government's theory, if they're neither winner nor runner-up, is there any competitive constraint recognized by the analysis?

A. Well, there's no change in the relevant competitive constraint. What's happening is, HarperCollins and Norton are one and two. And nothing will change as a result of the merger.

Q. Is it—

THE COURT: So what you're talking about right now is just about the second score auction model, which is not the entirety of the Government's theory. Right?

THE WITNESS: Well, may I put aside coordinated effects here? You're talking about—

THE COURT: I just think that what you two are talking about is about the second score auction model. Am I correct?

THE WITNESS: It's about the second score auction, but not only about that, because when I read the Government's complaint, it's about the loss of head-to-head competition.

And that's going to matter when the parties are winner or runner-up. If they're not winner or runner-up, then the loss of head-to-head competition does not generate harm. And it's not just inside the SSA model; it's the basic idea of the case.

THE COURT: So, my understanding—maybe it's not captured in what you're talking about—is that general competition affects each of the different types of acquisition models. Because if you're in a one-on-one negotiation, knowing that this author could walk at any moment and go to somebody else, that can affect the amount that you offer in your one-on-one negotiation. If you are in an auction, knowing there are more competitors or knowing there's a lot of interest in the book could affect how much you offer. And that doesn't depend on if you're number one or number two. And in the situations where there's imprint bidding, there has to be some kind of a third party in the mix for those two imprints to keep competitively bidding. And that doesn't depend on if you're number one or number two; that just depends on if there's more people involved. So I'm wondering how all that fits into what you're talking about.

THE WITNESS: That's a big question. I'll just say the following: I think what you're getting at is this general idea of the outside auction, and is there a lessening of the outside auction that would actually impact competition? And if you're talking about a single bidder, a one-on-one negotiation situation, the challenge I would have is really just understanding: Well, how will that actually affect that negotiation when there's so many different potential bidders? And the agent will not confront that question unless the negotiation fails. So it seems to me to be in theory something that, yes, I can understand this idea of general weakening of competition. But when I look at the actual numbers of rivals and the frequency with which other Big 5 are bidding and so on and so forth, it would be hard for me to understand how that would actually get traction, how it would be implemented.

THE COURT: It just seems to me there's just a lot more than you need to be number one or number two to affect competition. That's why I'm a little, I guess, confused by the testimony.

THE WITNESS: I think, your Honor, when we go away from that, we're moving away from unilateral effects. And I'll just say my understanding of the Government's complaint: We're moving into something that's broader; and as you rightly say, it's not in the model for sure. But I see it as a more general argument about whether there's going to be this softening of the outside constraint and that could have some effects. Am I at least hearing your question correctly?

THE COURT: I think that's part of it. Yes.

THE WITNESS: I think my bottom-line view is, post-merger, we still have PRH imprints competing. I mean, I know legally they could stop that. But I believe there's every reason to believe that's going to continue. I believe that, based on the testimony, other so-called Big 5 are going to be in there competing. The data show that 90 percent of the time when PRH and S&S bid, they've got competition from one other of the so-called Big 5. And then you have all of these other numerous mid-sized and lower-tier publishers. And agents already go to them, and they already respond. They're very much in the mix.

BY MR. OPPENHEIMER:

Q. Professor Snyder, do the—let me break this into a couple of parts as well. Do the Government's models identify harm in any context where Penguin Random House and Simon & Schuster are not one and two?

A. The answer is no.

Q. And are you aware of any empirical analysis done by Dr. Hill outside the models that establishes unilateral harm?

A. No.

Q. We'll come back to this. You had mentioned that 47 percent of the time when one of Penguin Random House or Simon & Schuster bids, that the other did not bid. Do I have that correct?

A. Yes. In terms of the slide, the 96 is in the pink-orange. And then you see underneath that other party did not bid, the second gray at the bottom. That's 45. That's how you get the 47 percent of the time that the contract was won by one of the two parties. The other one did not bid. And this is all within the context of multi-bidder auctions.

Q. Do you believe that the analyses produced by the second score auction can be analogized to bilateral negotiations?

A. No. And I think on this point, I mean, Dr. Hill and I agree that there's no model that's been developed and offered for bilateral negotiations. As to whether it can be generalized, that's a different question. And I think what's important to understand is that the model—and I paid attention, your Honor, to your, I think, framework—the model has inputs. The market share captures how the parties are doing in all kind of situations. So that part, I think, would say: Yeah. Well, maybe the model can work. The problem is with what's inside the model. And when you go inside the model, the machinations of the model that generate harm automatically are all based on an acquisition process that we very rarely see. So it's not possible in my opinion to generalize from a model that is so disconnected from what agents and authors actually do.

And you have to go back to the fundamental question: If agents aren't choosing rounds auctions with any substantial frequency, where they start from the beginning and end, why model harm based on that format? It's got to generate an overestimate of harm.

THE COURT: So, I asked Dr. Hill this very question.

THE WITNESS: I was here, your Honor.

THE COURT: And his response was that he's not trying to model exactly what's going on in the real world. He's using a more simplified version and inputting, based on market shares, this is how often you would expect to see these two entities compete with one another. And based on the margins, this is how aggressively they would bid. And he's just trying to get a very general sense. He's not trying to be specific. He doesn't think the actual number is important. It's just more of a sense. And that's why he's trying to compare it to all these other things, like the GUPPI, but also his nonquantitative assessments. Like he's just trying to paint an overall picture and say: All of these things are consistent. So, his focus is not on the precise manner in which things are happening in the real world. He's just trying to get a sense of competition between these two and is using a rough-cut way of modeling the competition between these two. And removing the competition between these two would result in some harm. And he's saying—he said: I don't put a lot of weight on the exact number. That's not what I'm going for here. It's more about, you know, to show there would be harm and cross-referencing it with all these other things he's done to build sort of more of a mosaic, not just relying on the second score auction. I think that's what I interpreted him to be explaining.

THE WITNESS: That's what I heard as well. Very often he said a mix of things that he looked at; this was directional and so forth. Your Honor, I would just say, if you're going to rely on—you know, you can look at it from the point of view of the other types of evidence one could look at. You could just start with market shares and say 12 percent of the time, based on market shares, you're going to have the parties winner and runner-up. You don't need a model for that.

What I'm—my opinion is that the model should be left behind. It has no value. It is fundamentally flawed with respect to fit. And I can go into more detail, but I think you already get the sense of why I believe it's not a fit.

THE COURT: I don't think anybody thinks it fits exactly

THE WITNESS: Okay. And then in terms of giving some guidance, it's $30 million annually with inputs that in this first try are inconsistent and in the second try result in unreliable results based on the person, Dr. Nathan Miller who developed the model. And on his second try, those results are unreliable. So I understand your Honor's question and your characterization of how he's approaching it. But what I'm saying is, the SSA model, whatever—it adds no value to the other stuff. It needs to be in my opinion completely left behind.

THE COURT: I get that. So, let's not talk about the SSA anymore.

THE WITNESS: Thank you, your Honor. Understood.

BY MR. OPPENHEIMER:

Q. So let's do something else. Let's move back and talk a little bit about the broader market. Okay? Very good.

THE COURT: Is now a good time for a break? I feel like we should give the court reporter some break this afternoon. Maybe now is a good time.

MR. OPPENHEIMER: Sure.

THE COURT: So, let's take a break right now. We'll return in 15 minutes, at 4:00.

(Thereupon a recess was taken, after which the following proceedings were had:)

THE COURT: Good afternoon. So, I looked at my notes over the break, including my notes on Dr. Hill's testimony. And he did not rely only on the merging parties being number one and number two, according to my notes. Under the win-loss ratio, he asked: When Simon & Schuster lost, how often did Penguin Random House win? And that was 59 percent of the time. And when Penguin Random House lost, how often did they lose to Simon & Schuster? That was 19 percent of the time. And they didn't have to be number one and number two under that way of looking at it. And he also made the points that I was making about general competition in his testimony, according to my notes.

MR. OPPENHEIMER: Perhaps I could explore that a little bit, your Honor.

THE COURT: Sure.

MR. OPPENHEIMER: Great.

BY MR. OPPENHEIMER:

Q. So, Professor Snyder, let's follow this line of inquiry that we started. Under the Government's theory of unilateral harm, is it required for there to be harm that Penguin Random House and Simon & Schuster be in head-to-head competition?

A. That's my understanding. Yes.

Q. And what do you understand head-to-head competition to be in that context?

A. I consider that to be sort of the first step in getting at the relevant conditions for harm. So you have to be head-to-head, which means—let's be clear—you're both competing for the same acquisition. That—unless that happens, it's not possible to have both parties be one and two. So that's a step towards under what circumstances you would get unilateral effect harm.

But it's not the condition that I see in the Government's complaint.

Q. Before we get into how that would play out, just following this, does the Government compute any harm in any circumstances where Penguin Random House and Simon & Schuster are not in one and two competition with each other?

A. When you say "compute," Mr. Oppenheimer, do you mean in terms of the model?

Q. Any form of computation.

A. With respect to the SSA and to the GUPPI calculations, both rely on diversion, which is premised by—which is premised on the condition where you're one and two or two and one.

Q. And is there any basis for inferring a softening of competition under the Government's theory without an analysis of the times when Penguin Random House and Simon & Schuster are number one and number two?

A. Well, I think that goes to your Honor's question. And my view is, when you go to the more general arguments about softening of competition, I won't repeat myself, but you leave the model behind. I think that's clear. Then the question is: What does softening of competition mean? It means that there's some process, some set of cascading actions, where individual editors and publishers will cut their bids, will reduce their advance offers. That requires—well, there's been no analysis of that. But the most important thing for me is, how—it's completely unclear how Dr. Hill imagines this cascading starts when, from the point of view of PRH and S&S, they're only hitting each other 12 percent of the time. And the same analysis applies to anybody else. If you cut your advances and the competitive conditions for harm aren't met, meaning you're not—you don't actually have a lessening of competition, then you can be making a mistake. So, the core of this is: When will firms actually cut their advances in this market? Maybe I should be more succinct. They don't know. And the problem is, they have so many rivals there, it would not make sense as an across-the-board pricing strategy. It would result in mistakes where you do loss of business. And I don't see that the competitive conditions generate that process of softening of competition in this context because of the strength of competition.

Q. So—about.

THE COURT: May I inquire?

MR. OPPENHEIMER: Of course.

THE COURT: This is something I've been thinking I don't think that the theory requires a conscious decision to lower advances. Wouldn't it be that you're just winning at lower levels because there's less competition? There's less competition, so people aren't bidding up the prices. So, you're not going in thinking: I'm going to start lowering my advances. But everybody wants to acquire the book at the lowest price they can pay in order to win. And now they're just going to win at an earlier point in time because there's less competition. Isn't that the way advances get lowered, not as a result of a conscious decision to lower advances?

THE WITNESS: I understand your Honor's theory. It—

THE COURT: It's a question. Isn't that the way markets work? Isn't that the way it should work?

THE WITNESS: Well, no. It doesn't work in terms of actual decisions to cut your advances because it doesn't make sense to cut your advances if you're going to lose business.

THE COURT: I'm saying that there will be no decisions to cut advances, but you'll get to pay lower advances and still win because there's less competition.

THE WITNESS: I think this isolates the issue. I don't see that there's going to be a lessening of competition here. You still have—

THE COURT: That's the ultimate question.

THE WITNESS: Right. You still have the Big 3, the other top firms. They're saying they're not going to cut advances. The CEO of—

THE COURT: Because that's how it works. You don't say, I'm going to cut advances. You just keep bidding and it turns out you can win at lower levels because there are fewer people bidding now. I think that's the theory.

THE WITNESS: That's the theory. But again, it goes to how this industry actually works and where there will be an actual reduction of competition. If your idea—and I think this is Dr. Hill's general idea, that you're going to have this opportunity. But you have to ask the question: Will it actually present itself? Will there be any reduction of competition when agents control the acquisition processes and we have imprint competition, we have competition from the other Big 3 and we have competition, as I'll get to at some point, from a large number of other publishers? So, I understand, well, maybe in some circumstances the result that you're identifying could happen. But then you have a very interesting question: Why did I win? Is that something I want to replicate? It's really hard to implement the intuition that Dr. Hill—the general intuition about the tradeoff. Well, there's less competition out there, and therefore I will reduce my bid when the competitive conditions vary so much across situations. And you really don't know when you should. You're going to be wrong most of the time, and you can't learn from what the outcomes are.

THE COURT: So, it seems to me from the testimony that I've heard that the publishers and editors kind of go in thinking: I can go up to a certain amount. But I'm going to start at this lower amount and I'm just going to keep, you know, bidding up, depending on the form of the negotiation or the auction and try to get it at the lowest price that I can. But I'm willing to go pretty high. I'm willing to go to some high number. And if there's less competition, they end up paying less because, even though they were willing to go high—so they've not made a conscious decision to come in with lower advances; they're just able to win at an earlier point in the process because, for example, if Penguin Random House had been in the process or if Simon & Schuster had been in the process, maybe they would have bid something that would have forced you to bid higher. But they're not there anymore. So now, look, I can win at a lower rate. And systemically, over time, this results in a general lower level of advances because there are fewer people competing. You don't have to compete as high or as long to get to the end result. The end result is generally lower.

THE WITNESS: I think I now understand your Honor's question.

THE COURT: That's what I'm saying.

THE WITNESS: So, what that process has in mind, I think, is that you have these rounds situations and they progress and you don't have to keep raising your offer. You get it earlier.

I think that's—

THE COURT: But it's true in a one-on-one negotiation, too, because you might come in lower and realize you don't have to go as high because there's less competition out there. I mean, I think it goes across formats potentially.

THE WITNESS: I can only do one at a time.

THE COURT: Okay.

THE WITNESS: But in the rounds situation, that's why it's important to realize we don't see that going to completion. It's very rare. And if it was a good auction format for agents, they would be choosing it. They don't choose it, based on my understanding. I know there's one bit of testimony that said it's still used a lot. I didn't see it in any of the data and in the information I looked at. So what that's telling me is that the agents have tools to avoid the situation that you described, because then if you go to—from rounds to best bid, how do you know if you're an individual editor that you should reduce your bid? That's—you're going to be wrong far more than you're going to be right. And where you're wrong or right, you're not going to learn and figure out how to do it. This is a very different market from the electronic vehicle market, where you're setting prices and you're getting a variable response in terms of quantity demanded. This is yes or no. Should I or not? Do I win? Do I lose?

THE COURT: Okay. Depending on the format, I guess.

THE WITNESS: So yeah. If it's a negotiation, then I think we established before the break there's the issue of, well, maybe there is a reduction in the outside option, the strength of the outside option. But even there, if I'm in a negotiation with an author, an agent, do I really know that there has been a lessening of competition, given the other imprint competition, the other Big 3 competition and all of the other publishers out there? I get the idea. But I don't believe that editors—especially because they're going to want to get the book. That's what they're motivated to do. I don't see it. One last point, your Honor. There are situations, yes, where an imprint gets a book for less than the maximum willingness to pay. But that's not an indicator of lack of competition in my opinion, because you also get outcomes where the agent and author are getting way more than what their reservation price was. That's just the nature of one-on-one negotiations.

THE COURT: Thank you.

BY MR. OPPENHEIMER:

Q. So, Professor Snyder, in this context, I want to come back to the Government's theory of unilateral effects. Do you have that in mind?

A. Yes.

Q. Okay. And could you describe for us briefly how the Government's theory is treated under the horizontal merger guidelines? What is the theory focused on?

A. It's the—unilateral effects refers to how the merging parties will alter their behavior post-merger to the detriment of competition.

Q. And is it focused on the competitive interactions of the two merging parties?

A. The basic idea is that post-merger, before—in this context, the publisher is thinking about lowering advances, say, across the board. They know that if they do that, they're going to lose business to rivals. But now, in the context of post-merger, some of that lost business doesn't go to rivals; it goes to the party with whom you've merged.

Q. So, for purposes of unilateral effects—let's take an example: In analyzing this merger with Penguin Random House and Simon & Schuster, does it matter if PRH is the runner-up to, say, HarperCollins in a certain percentage of the acquisitions?

A. No. The unilateral effects conditions are one and two. The two parties have to be one and two.

Q. So the theory itself is based on the proposition that it is the elimination of the competition between the two merging parties. Is that fair to say?

A. Yes, and how they change their behavior as a result. The model—well, I'll just stop there.

Q. And in that context—strike that. Is there any analysis by Dr. Hill of unilateral effects that does not rely upon measuring the competition specifically between Penguin Random House and Simon & Schuster?

A. No.

Q. Is there any specific analysis in Dr. Hill's work that measures or defines soft competition outside of that relationship?

A. And the first part of your question was, is there any modeling?

Q. Or analysis of the softening of competition outside of the relationship between Penguin Random House and Simon & Schuster.

A. There's no analysis, no modeling. That's what he says, his description of softening of competition. But from my listening to his analysis, there's no explanation of how this would actually work. And the implementation of when an editor—when she's going to cut advances is necessary. And he has not addressed that.

Q. Again, I'll come back to that. Put aside modeling. Is there any identification of harm in Dr. Hill's theories regarding unilateral effects other than with respect to the elimination of competition between Penguin Random House and Simon & Schuster?

A. I'm not sure that you're asking me a different question from a couple questions ago. The answer is no.

Q. I want to skip over market for a second, Professor Snyder. You've alluded a couple of times to your view that there is ample competition, including in the portion of the market that involves authors who receive advances in excess of $250,000. Do you have that in mind?

A. Yes.

Q. Okay. We'll come back to it. But just to set the table, do you believe that there is a cognizable market for anticipated top sellers measured by advances in excess of $250,000?

A. I don't.

Q. So we're just using that now for purposes of focusing on that segment which is in the Government's argument.

Is it your view that there will be no substantial reduction in competition in that market segment with the merger?

A. That's correct. Competition is strong, and it's going to remain strong. Imprints are not going to go away. The other Big 3 are present in the vast majority of situations where Penguin Random House and S&S bid. You've also got a large number of other publishers that are bidding, winning and constraining.

Q. So let's talk about each of the things that you've just mentioned. Do you have some demonstratives that show some of the evidence you've identified regarding the current competitive significance of the other major publishers?

A. Yes.

Q. Let's go to 35. What's the observation you make with respect to HarperCollins?

A. CEO Murray said: I don't intend to hold back post-merger. We have the tools to go forward.

Q. Let's go to 36. And with respect to Mr. Weisberg from Macmillan, what is your analysis? How does this fit into your analysis?

A. Well, beyond the statements, it goes to the point that from an editor's point of view within PRH or S&S, post-merger, they're running into Macmillan and Hachette and HarperCollins with very high frequency. And at least you have to credit to some extent the statements that they're not going to cut back. And individual publishers, including within these three and others, have plans to expand and gain market share.

Q. 37, please. What is the significance to you—first of all, is the data on this slide correct based on your understanding?

A. These data are derived from the agency data. And I alluded to this earlier. When PRH or S&S bid, at least one of the other so-called Big 5, HarperCollins, Hachette, Macmillan, bid 90 percent of the time.

Q. What's the significance to you of that for purposes of competition in the market segment over $250,000?

A. Well, it's one of the reasons why if you're taking the point of view of the S&S or PRH editor and saying, Has my competition been relaxed, before you answer yes, you'd better recognize that you're going to face competition from these others. And this doesn't get into imprint competition. It doesn't get into competition outside the Big 5.

Q. Well, doesn't the fact that the combined entity will have nearly half of the market share of this $250,000-and-up price segment demonstrate that the merger will reduce competition?

A. Market share tells me how frequently they're winning. It doesn't tell me, can they lower advances? And that's when I talked about the fundamental forces in all markets. You've got to take into account the behavior of agents and the responses of rivals.

Q. You mentioned a couple of times mid-sized and smaller publishers that compete at the higher advance levels.

Q. Let's take a look at Slide 38, please. Can you describe for us what we're seeing on Slide 38?

A. First of all, the source of these data are my advance data, which again are similar to Dr. Hill's advance data, except for it now covers all of 2021. And from those data I identified the number of publishers acquiring contracts with advances of at least $250,000 over this three-year time period. And that number is 29 for 2019 and then it grows to 33 in 2021. Again, this is not just bidding; this is winning.

Q. Is that a relevant consideration under the horizontal merger guidelines?

A. Yes. The guidelines the way I read them stress the importance of numbers of options.

Q. We've just put up a portion of the horizontal merger guidelines. Can you explain the significance of this to your analysis?

A. Yes. I mean, granted, high market shares, but the potential market power is talked about in this context. Market power on the buying side of the market is not a significant concern if suppliers have numerous attractive outlets for their goods or services.

Q. And are the publishers that you're talking about in the competitive landscape able to commit large amounts to acquire books?

A. Yes. I've studied that; and the answer is yes.

MR. OPPENHEIMER: Your Honor, the next slide is confidential, so we'll block it from public view.

THE COURT: All right.

MR. OPPENHEIMER: May we have Slide 40?

BY MR. OPPENHEIMER:

Q. And is this a slide showing some of the evidence you've gathered about publishers' willingness to enter into large contracts?

A. Yes. Using the same data set, the advance data over three years, 2019, 2020 and 2021, from those data, I identified the number of publishers who entered into contracts with advances of $1 million or more. And I found that there were 20 during this time period. So they are committing at least a million dollars for a single contract. And just to be clear, the so-called Big 5 are among the 20, and there are 15 others committing at least that level of financial resources.

Q. And that's 15 who are non-Big 5?

A. Correct.

Q. Well, along with the number of publishers willing to participate and able to participate at this level of advance, what else is relevant?

A. Well, I see in this list—and I realize I'm not allowed to identify the names—I was not surprised to find certain publishers who are part of large enterprises, public companies, able to do this and actually doing it. But I was surprised to see a lot of other smaller publishers able to commit at least a million dollars.

Q. So we have numbers running down the left side of Slide 40. Can you identify just a few that you have in mind by number?

A. Yes. So, for example, No. 6: Over $9.6 million committed to a single contract. No. 10: A very well-known publisher. $2 million. And then down to, for example, No. 15 and 16: At or above $1.2 million.

Q. So how often do you see smaller publishers as a group entering into contracts for $250,000?

A. So as group, if you combine their share, I have a slide on that. That's the next slide.

MR. OPPENHEIMER: It's confidential, your Honor.

THE WITNESS: So, what this slide identifies—and this is using Dr. Hill's advance data—is the number of titles acquired by the individual members of the so-called Big 5 along with non-Big 5 publishers as a group. And what it shows is the non-Big 5 publishers as a group in red, that group is roughly comparable to Simon & Schuster, to Macmillan and to Hachette.

BY MR. OPPENHEIMER:

Q. We've heard the observation made that there's something inappropriate when analyzing competition about looking at the non-Big 5 publishers as a group. Do you agree with that?

A. Well, it's hard not to, given the prevalence of the term and the idea of, well, maybe these others are—should be lumped together. But these 15 publishers based on the earlier slide—and it's many more based on the numbers slide that I presented; it's over 30—excuse me—it's over 25 in 2021—they have different strategies. They're being engaged by different agents at different points in time. And they are important competitive influences on acquisitions in this proposed segment.

Q. If the non-Big 5 publishers are competing in the $250,000-and-up range at the same rate as Macmillan and Hachette and Simon & Schuster and a little less than HarperCollins, should they only be thought of in terms of their individual levels of participation as individual publishers or is it also relevant to think of them as a group effect on competition?

A. Well, when you don't know who are going to be your rivals, it might be hard to figure out who among the non-Big 5 is going to be there. But these data show that collectively they're important. But it's also relevant to look at them individually and understand their competitive influence.

Q. Now, have you taken a look at how often smaller and mid-sized publishers are runner-up in bidding in this price segment?

A. Yes. That was to me an important question with respect to unilateral effects and where does the competitive constraint come from. So, using the agency data, I wanted to go beyond just how often do these mid-sized and smaller publishers win, but I also wanted to identify the frequency with which they were winner or runner-up because, again, that's central to the theory of unilateral effect harm.

Q. So if I understand Slide 42, you've calculated that mid-sized and smaller publishers as winners or runners-up in the $250,000-plus segment between 2019 and 2021 are winner or runner-up 23 percent of the time?

A. That's right. And this is going back to the earlier exhibit with the forks in the road, the agency data overview. This is—your Honor, the number here is 150. So it's 23 percent of that number based on the agency data.

Q. And have you also taken a look at how frequently the non-Big 5 as a group participate in acquisition processes even when they're not winners?

A. Yes. I have a slide on that.

Q. Let's go to 43. Would you tell us what we're seeing here?

A. This is from the agency data. $250,000-and-above advances on a per-title basis for the same three-year period. What's shown here is simply the percentage of time that mid-sized and smaller publishers are bidding on these potential acquisitions. And it's 54 percent of the time.

So again, you go back to—from the point of view of an individual editor, you expect them to compete against you more than half the time.

Q. So if we put these two charts together in more than half of the multi-bidder situations, the non-Big 5 as a group are participating and they're winner or runner-up in roughly 23 percent of those—of the total situations?

A. Based on the agency data, that's right. And again, just to be clear, that's the only source of data that can illuminate this question. Dr. Hill's runner-up data shows runner-up, but not for these small and mid-sized publishers.

THE COURT: Is your 23 percent comparable to his runner-up data?

THE WITNESS: Where the data have overlapped observations, we get the same results, which is good. The—

THE COURT: His runner-up only looked at the two merging parties. Right?

THE WITNESS: Yes.

THE COURT: So, you can't compare that to your 23 percent?

THE WITNESS: Correct.

THE COURT: I see.

THE WITNESS: So we have observations in the agency data that are not included in his data and vice versa.

BY MR. OPPENHEIMER:

Q. Doesn't this just show that they bid a lot but lose a lot?

A. I don't know that we have systematic data on bidding by the full set of publishers. But my read of the overall record is that publishers bid a lot and they lose a lot. And this isn't just the small and mid-sized.

Q. So let's turn a second to authors and agents. What did you conclude about their willingness to consider a broad range of publishers for works that end up in Dr. Hill's proposed market?

A. Again, this is one of the two fundamental questions. Are authors and agents willing to choose alternatives outside a particular group, whether it's the two merging parties or the so-called Big 5? So I studied that using the advance data from the three-year period. And I've just identified a selected group of authors who have chosen to publish with non-Big 5 publishers.

Q. Professor Snyder, we've got one of your slides up, Slide 44.

MR. OPPENHEIMER: And that's confidential.

BY MR. OPPENHEIMER:

Q. But can you tell us what we're seeing here that's of significance for your work?

A. Well, if you could advance the slide to show the second part of it. So, these two slides identify this set of authors—I'm trying to remember. I'm not claiming this is a representative set, but I think it's 37 in number. And then what I've identified is: Who have they decided to contract with to have their works published? And it may be that some of these individual authors had no Big 5 option. There's the famous story about J. K. Rowling; and I'm not saying she's on this slide. But, you know, she had trouble getting traction with her work. But when I look at this list, I see a lot of savvy, well-known authors choosing to go outside the Big 5. And that's the point.

Q. What does that tell you?

A. The—

THE COURT: So, I'm sorry. You said "choosing." But this is just a list of people who publish with non-Big 5. You didn't actually look to see whether they had a Big 5 option in each case?

THE WITNESS: That's correct.

THE COURT: Okay.

THE WITNESS: And I probably shouldn't have mentioned anybody by name. But it's possible that individual authors, especially debut authors, would not have a Big 5 option. But again, if you look at this list, there are a large number of very well-known people on the list. I would be surprised if they didn't have Big 5. But you're right, your Honor: I don't know for sure.

BY MR. OPPENHEIMER:

Q. What does it tell you about the services that can be provided by non-Big 5 publishers?

A. Well, in the bottom analysis, these high-profile, savvy authors are willing to go with them. They are viable alternatives. That's the key point.

Q. What does it tell you about publishers such as Chronicle and Norton in terms of whether they're a competitive constraint in this market?

A. This goes back to: Are they a relevant option? Now and post-merger, the answer is yes.

Q. But isn't it true that they also have smaller market share?

A. Yes.

Q. And what does that tell you about whether they're a competitive constraint in the market?

A. Market shares are different from ability to constrain. And you go back to the earlier evidence. They're able to make large financial commitments. You take the non-Big 5 as a group. They're in there constraining 23 percent of the time. That's the kind of analysis that goes beyond market share. There are a lot of firms that have big market shares at one point or another. You've got Tesla as an example from my class. You've got NetFlix as an example from my class. They had big market shares. But they're in very rivalrous situations that constrain their market power.

Q. Let's move on to your second observation about competition in the $250,000-and-up segment. 47, Pam. You say publishers are entering and expanding. How does this support your conclusion with respect to competition in this segment?

A. Well, part of the competitive constraint comes from the potential for new entry. And here, this is confidential. Is that correct?

Q. This slide is not.

A. Oh, I have a slide if I could advance.

Q. Sure. We'll advance to—we will advance to Slide 47, which is not confidential. And is this the slide that you had in mind, Professor?

A. Thank you. Yes. So in the left-hand side, I've just identified three recent new entrants. And in the middle column, I've identified publishers that have recently expanded. They were already operating in the $250,000-plus advance category. And then what I've identified on the right are publishers that are operating just below the $250,000 threshold and they're very successful. So they have the potential to move into the 250 plus category.

Q. To be clear, those are entities that are already in the market to acquire books. Correct?

A. They're in and they're succeeding. Yes.

Q. Let's go to Slide 48. This is confidential. So, Professor Snyder, can you walk us through this without mentioning names and tell us what it is these data convey in terms of your analysis?

A. So the set of publishers—I hope I can at least say it's a mix, Big 5, non-Big 5. Each one of these pieces of testimony indicate that the publisher intends to expand and compete aggressively. So, for example, the fourth one, quote—and I'm just quoting from a slide: This particular publisher, quote, "has tripled the amount of advances it paid between 2014 and 2021 and anticipates continued growth through increasing audio books, advance amounts and the number of books acquired." That's from deposition testimony. And the other statements are variants on that theme.

Q. And why is the competitor's ability to expand relevant to the question of whether the combined company can reduce advances?

A. The basic idea here is that even if you have a big market share—I'm going to put aside the imprint and competition for a moment right now—whether you can exercise market power depends on the elasticity of supply among rivals. That's the technical term. Are there a lot of them? Do they have the capacity? Are they already succeeding? Do they have the plans?

And that's what this speaks to. And when you have robust supply of rivals, that constrains any potential exercise of monopsony power.

Q. Let's go to your third observation. And I know you've been putting aside imprint competition, but let's go to it now. 49. What are your observations regarding imprint competition?

A. Just very quickly I'll go back to the importance of matching. It's in the interest of publishers, many publishers, to use imprints, to delegate to them, encourage them to compete to find authors and match with authors and win contracts. So, they're encouraged to be entrepreneurial and they are not constrained in most acquisition processes. That—specifically, they're not constrained at all in one-on-one negotiations, in preempts, in best bids or hybrids.

My understanding of what's in the record is that there are constraints in situations where you have round acquisitions and there are no external bidders. I'll just note there's also testimony that suggests that that is rare; and when it happens, agents have a work-around.

Q. As long as you've mentioned that, can we bring up Slide 54?

THE COURT: What's the work-around?

MR. OPPENHEIMER: I can take us there, too, your Honor.

THE COURT: I'm just wondering. What's the work-around?

THE WITNESS: Oh, I'm sorry. Sorry, your Honor. I thought—the work-around is that if an agent gets to a situation where, say, they're—where the two top bidders are from within the same house, say two PRH bidders, they don't have to notify PRH according to practice if they carry forward another external bidder, even if the bidder's number three.

So, the agent has a way to not reveal the information about the two PRH imprints being number one and number two. And then the agent can in that situation—and this is what I learned from the record—then the agent has the ability to shift to best bid, for example. And the imprints from PRH are in the situation where they have to decide how much to bid.

BY MR. OPPENHEIMER:

Q. So if I understand, in a situation where you have two PRH imprints and a third party, the third party can be the third—the bottom rung of the bidding. As long as they're there, the two PRH imprints have to keep competing against each other?

A. Well, they don't know that they shouldn't. That's for sure. The rule doesn't kick in. And there's very clear testimony that the agents can set the auction rules to extend external imprint—excuse me—external competition and thereby sustain within-firm imprint competition.

Q. So we've brought up Slide 53 from your deck in response to her Honor's question about work-around. This is a note of bidding rules that was sent out by one of the agents. Can you describe for us what we're seeing here, Professor Snyder?

A. Well, this is indeed the work-around. Quote: If in any round all the top bidders are in the same corporation, then I will include the next-highest bidder. That—by doing so, this agent doesn't have to let PRH, for example, know your imprints are the last two. And this agent further says what is standard, what I see in all the contracts: The agent has the right to accept or reject any bid at any time.

Q. I mean, I may be missing something. But does that not effectively completely end-run the limitation on imprint bidding by the requirement of there being an outside bidder?

A. Correct. And that's why the testimony is so clear that it happens so rarely that the rule is actually put into force.

THE COURT: I guess it depends on how many bidders there are.

THE WITNESS: Correct.

MR. OPPENHEIMER: If we could bring up Slide 54.

BY MR. OPPENHEIMER:

Q. You had mentioned testimony that it is very seldom that notification is given by agents to Penguin Random House that would stop the imprint bidding. Is this an example of the evidence you had in mind, the testimony that's displayed on 54?

A. Yes. I'm not saying that the rule is never put into force. But when I read testimony like this, this particular agent has been in the business a long time. How often does it happen that you have to notify Penguin Random House? I've had it happen—I've had it happen once in 36 years. Again, that might be a skewed result. But it's a striking result. And the actual number of examples that I read about in the complaint and in Dr. Hill's reports, it's striking that it does confirm that the rules only kick in late in the process and then only sometimes. And then even late in the process they don't always have an effect and the imprints still continue to bid aggressively.

Q. Let's take an example of one of those that I know is near and dear to the heart of a colleague of mine.

MR. OPPENHEIMER: Can we bring up Slide 52? And this is confidential, your Honor.

BY MR. OPPENHEIMER:

Q. So, Professor Snyder, what are we looking at here in imprint competition on this identified title? And please don't mention the name of the book or the names of the imprints. But you can identify whose company they're from and the amounts.

A. Okay. I think I've got the rules. This example came out of the agency data work. Each one of the 900-plus acquisitions involved studying the process, who bid and the amounts. And what we see in this particular situation is that the top two bidders are from the same publishing house. And there's a huge gap between the number one imprint from that publishing house and the number two imprint from that publishing house. And this is at best bid, so what was bid is what was paid, which is what the author received.

Q. So, the imprint competition here resulted in one of the Penguin Random House imprints paying a million more than the next highest bid?

MR. SCHWARZ: Objection. Leading.

THE COURT: Sustained.

BY MR. OPPENHEIMER:

Q. And so going back to the theory of harm in this case, Professor Snyder, who in this example is pushing up the bidding?

A. I could answer that narrowly and say the number two imprint. But I think what's going on here is that the agent has really struck a good relationship with the top bidder and the top bidder is very excited about it when it goes to best bids. They bid a lot.

MR. SCHWARZ: Your Honor, pure speculation. He has no idea what—

THE COURT: I'll sustain the objection.

BY MR. OPPENHEIMER:

Q. Professor Snyder, it's the end of the day and it was actually a trick question. And I shouldn't do that because I end up only tricking myself. But I want to take you back to the fact that this is a best bids auction.

A. Yes.

Q. So what is the competitive constraint in the best bids auction that we're seeing here?

A. Well, there's no obvious competitive constraint. The best bid wins. And if the party that had bid the top amount bid lower, then the competitive constraint would have been the second one.

Q. And what—in this best bids situation, what do the three Penguin Random House imprint publishers and the two outside publishers who submitted their bids—what do they—what do they know about their competition?

MR. SCHWARZ: Your Honor, again, I don't know that he can possibly tell us what they know.

THE COURT: I'm going to sustain the objection.

MR. OPPENHEIMER: Let me rephrase, your Honor, please, if I may. I'm just trying to get at the structural question.

BY MR. OPPENHEIMER:

Q. Assuming only, Professor Snyder, that they have been invited to a best bids auction and they know nothing else, they've had no other communications other than their assessment of this particular book, and that's all each of them knows, are they able to evaluate the effect on their bid of the presence of other bidders in this best bids situation?

A. Apparently not. That's all I can say.

THE COURT: Is this a good time to break for the day?

MR. OPPENHEIMER: Certainly, your Honor.

THE WITNESS: Of course.

THE COURT: So, let's break for the day and we'll resume tomorrow at 9:30.

BY MR. OPPENHEIMER:

Q. Professor Snyder, good morning.

A. Good morning.

Q. In our last session, we were talking about the unilateral effects case. And I want to go—to continue on that same vein. In Dr. Hill's report, he quoted the merger guidelines, horizontal merger guidelines, paragraph 6.2, that pertains to this. And he observed, quoting those guidelines 6.2, in the auction context, anticompetitive unilateral effects are likely in proportion to the frequency or probability with which, prior to the merger, one of the merging sellers had been the runner-up when the other won the business. Is that your understanding of what Dr. Hill's unilateral effects analysis is based on? And I'm not referring to SSA models. I'm referring to the general theory of harm under unilateral effects.

A. Yes. The approach, as I understand Dr. Hill's testimony to reflect, is that you look at market shares and you use them to predict the frequency with which the parties are one and two.

Q. And is it the case under the unilateral effects theory that we have just identified that it would only makes sense for the merged parties to reduce bids in the future in those situations where they would have been runner-up and winner to each other?

MR. SCHWARZ: Objection, leading.

THE COURT: Sustained. Could you rephrase.

BY MR. OPPENHEIMER:

Q. Professor Snyder, based upon the unilateral effects guidance in 6.2, can you tell us, what is the relevance of determining who is the winner and the runner-up with respect to determining how people would bid in the future?

A. So with unilateral effects, the issue is will there be a reduction in competition, will there be targeting by which we mean reductions in offers made to authors.

And what the unilateral effects theory is about is tied to the earlier question, the frequency with which the parties are winner and runner-up. And just to be clear, this is different from coordinated effects. It's different from general ideas about softening of competition.

Q. So to what degree does the theory of unilateral effects in the horizontal merger guidelines rely on the notion that the merging parties are winner and runner-up to each other?

A. My understanding is that that's what they say.

Q. Would it be fair to say that the theory of unilateral effects is predicated on determining when there is head-to-head competition, meaning winner and runner-up?

MR. SCHWARZ: Objection, leading, Your Honor.

THE COURT: Sustained. Let the witness testify.

MR. OPPENHEIMER: Yes, Your Honor.

BY MR. OPPENHEIMER:

Q. Yesterday we were discussing Dr. Hill's win, loss, and editorial minutes data. Do you have that in mind?

A. I do.

Q. Okay. Now, do either of Dr. Hill's win, loss, or editorial minutes database tell you who is winner or runner-up?

A. No.

Q. Let me ask you this. Under the data in those data sets, is it possible that Simon & Schuster lost to Penguin Random House in some of those situations but that another bidder was the runner-up?

A. Yes. I mean, that's—and it's not a criticism of the data. It's just that the data cannot reveal the situation where, for example, a Simon & Schuster imprint lost to a Penguin Random House imprint, but there was an intervening bid that was higher.

Q. And would vice versa be true, that PRH could have lost S&S but that actually other bidders were ahead of PRH?

A. Yes.

Q. What is the significance of that to the theory of unilateral effects in this case?

A. Well, the runner-up data and the editorial minutes data, and I think I made that clear when I presented the advantages of the agency data and also Dr. Hill's runner-up data, it's just simply the case that those other data sets do not provide information about the conditions related to unilateral effects.

Q. Professor Snyder, you should have a notebook with your reports on your desk, if you could look for that.

MR. OPPENHEIMER: Your Honor, this is a notebook that contains Professor Snyder's reports, and I am going to be looking with the professor at his rebuttal expert report of June 3, 2022.

BY MR. OPPENHEIMER:

Q. Professor, before you do that, one correction. You just referred to the runner-up database which I was not asking about. Were you referring to the win-loss database?

A. I was trying to contrast the win-loss database and the editorial minutes database versus Dr. Hill's runner-up data.

Q. Thank you for that clarification. If I could ask you to look at your rebuttal expert report of June 3, 2022, I would like to draw your attention to page 184 of that report and specifically to a table that's depicted on that page identified as Exhibit X.8.

A. Yes.

Q. Professor Snyder, what are you showing in Exhibit X.8 on 184?

A. I am identifying just a selection of titles from Dr. Hill's win-loss records where they are not informative about the issue of who is the runner-up.

Q. Can you identify for the court whether there are any, based on that exhibit, X.8, whether there are any accurate depictions of winner and runner-up on that table?

A. It might be helpful to go through the first one. Am I allowed to refer to the specific title, or should I just identify the first row?

Q. Let me see if I can—no, I prefer not. Let me see if I can direct your attention.

If you look at the fifth title down, would you explain to us what that row is describing. It starts with the title of the work and the author. We won't mention those. But then if you would, describe for the court, what does the rest of that row identify?

A. Yes. So what I am doing with this table just by way of background is using the agency data to identify the runner-up. And then I am identifying what information is provided in the win-loss data that Dr. Hill includes for these various titles. So, the fifth one down, the source of the data is Simon & Schuster. The winning publisher is an imprint at PRH. And then the runner-up, according to the agency data, is Simon & Schuster.

Q. And with respect to all of the other entries, is it the case that Simon & Schuster is not the runner-up?

A. Well, in five of the other seven listed in this exhibit, a party other than—a party other than the two merging parties is the runner-up. And then a seventh, I can't tell from the agency data.

Q. How does this help inform us whether the win-loss records enable us to identify whether Penguin Random House and Simon & Schuster are winner and runner-up?

A. I think Dr. Hill and I agree on this. These data are useful for some things, but you simply don't have the information to identify who is the runner-up.

Q. May I direct your attention to page 190 of the same report a few pages down. Is this a comparable analysis of the editorial meeting minutes?

A. It is.

Q. And what is it telling us?

A. Again, the information from the editorial minutes is reflected in the third column in the sense of what is the source. And then the winning publisher is identified in the next column. And the first four of those, it's PRH. And the fifth one is Simon & Schuster. And then the insight that is provided by the agency data concerns the last column. And you can see that in four out of the five presented here, some other party is the runner-up.

Q. So do these analyses inform your conclusion that Dr. Hill's win-loss records and editorial meeting minutes do not provide information with respect to when Penguin Random House or Simon & Schuster are winner or runner-up to each other?

MR. SCHWARZ: Objection, leading.

THE COURT: Sustained. I would rather hear the testimony from the witness than in the form of a leading question.

MR. OPPENHEIMER: Understood, Your Honor.

BY MR. OPPENHEIMER:

Q. Can you tell us how these two charts inform your judgment about their usefulness in determining when Penguin Random House and Simon & Schuster are one and two in the empirical data?

A. Well, these two data sets, of course, are drawn only from the parties' discovery. So, you can only identify their bidding and their winning. And to get information about runner-up, you have to go through another process to access information about who actually was runner-up. You may guess, but you are going to guess right and wrong.

Q. Based on your answer, Professor Snyder, would you describe for us whether it would be appropriate to calculate diversions based on the data in these two data sets?

A. I will not calculate diversions based on data that does not include information about who the runner-up actually was. And you can't tell that from the win-loss data nor can you from the editorial minutes.

Q. Can the data about—in your opinion, can the data regarding diversions derived from Dr. Hill's win-loss and editorial minutes databases be directly compared to your agency data set?

A. No.

Q. Can it be used to directly compare with Dr. Hill's diversion proportional to market share approach in this case?

A. Well, proportion to market shares is based on multiplying the market shares to each other. That gives you a prediction. Whether or not it's accurate depends on circumstances. You could have a predicted diversion that's correct, could be correct, using market shares, but it could be way off. It could be that two firms are bidding all the time and they are, just in the duopoly context, they are winner and runner-up all the time.

Actually, that would give you a case where you would get wildly divergent predictions, but it also could be the case that two firms have substantial market shares, but they are not actually in head-to-head competition and actually winner and runner-up. So that's the basic insight with respect to market share. Absent other information, using market shares to predict diversion is what economists often do. In this case, 12 percent is the predicted diversion. I think you asked something else in the question.

Q. No, no, that's fine. I will come back to it now because I want to stay focused for a minute on these two data sets. Do they tell you whether Penguin Random House and Simon & Schuster were competing for the same books?

A. No. Again, I'll just reference the predictions by market share. Whether those are right or wrong, you don't get insights about that looking at win-loss or editorial minutes.

Q. In those circumstances, in those records, when Penguin Random House and Simon & Schuster both show up in bidding, would you conclude that they were bidding for the same book?

A. When they do show up in Dr. Hill's databases?

Q. Yes.

A. Yes.
Q. Just that they were bidding for the book?
A. Yes.
Q. Okay. Do they tell you whether they are operating these two data sets? Do they tell you whether either company is operating as the competitive constraint against the other?
A. No.
Q. Would you explain why.
A. Again, I think maybe I'm not explaining it well enough, but you just can't identify who is the runner-up when one of the parties wins unless you have a data source that identifies the bids from other publishers. And as Dr. Hill acknowledges, I don't think there's any dispute about this, the editorial minutes and the win-loss data are just looking at the two parties. So, you obviously cannot identify whether that information corroborates an assumption about who is runner-up or not because that information is simply not in those data.
Q. You mentioned a moment ago and we heard about it yesterday that the implied rate at which Penguin Random House and Simon & Schuster are number one and number two in acquisitions, multi bidder acquisitions in Dr. Hill's data, is 12 percent. Do you have that in mind?
A. Yes.
Q. On your own analysis based upon the agency data, do you have a different conclusion about how often Penguin Random House and Simon & Schuster are one and two in multi bidder situations?
A. It's lower, but, of course, the data set is not a perfect data set. It starts with almost a thousand observations. But when I can identify winner and runner-up for books that have advances in excess of $250,000, the frequency of winner and runner-up is lower than 12 percent.
Q. All right. Now, I would like to come back to your earlier answer where you indicated that, under the unilateral effects theory in these analyses, it only makes sense for the merged parties to reduce bids in the future in those situations when they would have been winner and runner-up to each other. Do you have that in mind?
A. I do.
Q. Okay. Let's go through a couple of configurations in terms of the acquisition of books. In terms of the unilateral harm theory of the case, in the situation where Simon & Schuster lost to Penguin Random House but was not the runner-up, if you could identify that those situations existed when you were bidding in the future, would it make sense for Simon & Schuster to reduce its bid?
A. No.
Q. Would you explain why.
A. They are not winner and runner-up. The relevant competitive constraint comes from somebody else.
Q. So just so I understand, if we have five bidders for a book in a multi bidder situation and Simon & Schuster is third or fourth but not one or two in the bidding process, are you saying that that is not a competitive constraint? And if so, would you explain that.
A. So from the point of view of the Penguin Random House imprint editor and publisher point of view, you are asking the question would it make sense to reduce their bid in that circumstance? If they knew that Simon & Schuster was not the relevant competitive constraint, then of course it would be optimal not to make any change.
Q. In that situation, would Penguin—would it be economically rational for Penguin Random House to stop bidding any sooner just because hypothetically Simon & Schuster wasn't in that bidding?
A. No.
Q. Would you explain why.
A. Again, this is looking at the problem prospectively and asking the question when would it make sense to cut advances. And what your question reveals is that whether it's optimal depends on who is the relevant competitor and whether that's been weakened. And if the bidder knows that it's someone else, it's Hachette Workman or Hachette Little, Brown, competitive conditions don't change and it doesn't make any sense to alter the bid.
Q. Yesterday we had some questions regarding whether or not an auction might just end earlier if

Penguin Random House and S&S merged. Is there a reason to be concerned about harm in that situation under the unilateral effects theory?

A. No, because the auction will continue until you get to that point where you have winner and runner-up. This is putting aside agent adjustments.

Q. Again, staying focused on the unilateral effects theories, would it be rational to lower bids in a best bids acquisition?

A. No.

Q. And, again, why is that?

A. In a best bids situation, unless you know that there's been an elimination of competition by the merger where the next bidder has been eliminated, it's not rational to cut the bid. And then that gets into the question of what do you know in that particular circumstance. The problem is you are only going to be right, well, in 12 percent of the aggregate cases to see that lessening of the competition.

Q. When you say that, I infer that you will be, quote/unquote, wrong in 88 percent of the circumstances. Is that correct?

A. In 88 percent of the circumstances, just focusing on this decision, focusing on the unilateral effects, it would not make sense to alter the bid.

THE COURT: Can I ask a question? I am just very interested in what you are saying. It seems like you are saying, because when you enter an auction, you don't know who else is in it, you are not going to alter your behavior because maybe the other merger party wouldn't have been the second runner-up, so it shouldn't affect your behavior because you don't know who else is in the auction. Is that right?

THE WITNESS: Correct. And conversely, if you did know, then you would be able to execute the targeting in lowering the advance.

THE COURT: Okay. So, what if we were talking about consolidation that leads us to only two big players in the market or three, like some very small number, you still think it wouldn't make a difference because you still wouldn't know in each auction who else is in it? At some point does it matter that there's just a much smaller number of possible bidders?

THE WITNESS: I understand your question, Your Honor. With it being 12 percent, that makes it very difficult to implement the strategy of lowering bids. If you were to go to a completely different or a more concentrated picture, then the probability of getting it right goes up and the probability of getting it wrong goes down.

THE COURT: So, there is a correlation between concentration and possibility, but you are just saying we are not at that level yet?

THE WITNESS: If you take the point of view of, say, Hachette imprint—and I think it's useful to think about someone else as well, not just the merging parties—and you look at it from the point of view of one of their imprint editors, I just mentioned Workman acquired last year, Little, Brown, Grand Central, they are going into that bidding process, and I think Your Honor's question goes to, well, will they want to pull their punches and not bid aggressively because, say, Simon & Schuster is not there anymore. And the problem that they have is one of probabilities. It really goes right to your intuition in terms of where would it be rational to actually employ the strategy. And from their point of view, who is the relevant next bidder. Is it a PRH imprint? Is it HarperCollins? Is it Macmillan? Is it Norton, Astra, Chronicle, et cetera? And it's just not a safe bet to go in and change your bidding given the highly competitive conditions, the number of parties, the frequency with which non-Big 5 compete against each other, and the frequency with which agents engage non-Big 5 and that they respond.

THE COURT: No, I understand. But you do think that at some point, at a very high concentration level, the probabilities would improve to lower your bids, like your chances would improve of having a successful result by lowering your—

THE WITNESS: Certainly, if you got to two. And depending on the—whether they actually are in head-to-head competition, but I think your question presumes that they are—

THE COURT: So—

THE WITNESS:—then the probabilities of getting it right go way up.

THE COURT: Yes. So have you heard the testimony in this trial that the market shares are actually underestimating the power of Penguin Random House because the market shares include Christian books for Hachette? It's like a large percentage of Hachette's revenues, Christian books. But those Christian books are not sold in regular retail outlets. They are only sold in Christian stores. And so if you were to take away Christian books, Penguin Random House would be three times the size of Hachette in revenue. And if that were true, would that affect your analysis?

THE WITNESS: First of all, I didn't—I heard that testimony. I wasn't able to verify it. I understood that there was this, wow, where's the three times coming from. But I can only respond in terms of actual competitive conditions. And my response doesn't depend so much on the particular market shares. And I don't want to belabor the point, but you have very robust competition within the so-called Big 5. That's not going to change post-merger. There will be one fewer but very robust competition. And then you have the midsized publishers who are bidding very frequently, winning, constraining.

THE COURT: You are fighting my hypothetical.

THE WITNESS: Pardon?

THE COURT: You are fighting my hypothetical, as we say in law school.

THE WITNESS: Sorry, Your Honor.

THE COURT: My hypothetical is it's not things are as you have analyzed it. I am saying what if we changed one of the variables which is that there's much more market concentration than you had assumed here. You are saying there's a 12.5 percent chance of head-to-head. But if the number one leader in the industry is three times the size of the number two, which is not an assumption that you made in your analysis, I am just wondering how that would affect your analysis.

THE WITNESS: That goes to the whole issue of is the market valid, and the $250,000 market definition is something with which I have a lot of problems but—and I assume we will get to that later but—

THE COURT: It's a separate issue.

THE WITNESS: Well, all of these questions come up in the context of this proposed cutoff being $250,000. And that's on that basis you are calculating shares. I understand now your question. You are saying, instead of it being market shares that produce the 12 percent, maybe they are higher in that segment. But once you get to that point, I don't want to fight the hypothetical, you want to look at competitive conditions that will continue post merger. And, again, everything I hear is that the other big three are going to be competing aggressively, imprint competition within PRH is going to continue, and you have the non-Big 5.

THE COURT: Okay. Thank you.

BY MR. OPPENHEIMER:

Q. Professor Snyder, just to clarify a few things, the 12 percent of the time that Penguin Random House and Simon & Schuster are one and two to each other, that's not your number, correct?

A. No. That's based on Dr. Hill's advance data from which he derives market shares, and it's very consistent with the market share data that you would derive from my advance data with the—I haven't checked it exactly, but those are based on a lot of data from both sets of advance data.

Q. Right. And as I understand it, so your data or your percentage for the times that Penguin Random House and Simon & Schuster are one and two is lower, but for present purposes, you are saying they are in the ball park. But I also want to ask you to explain, when we see market shares, whatever those market shares are, is that telling us how often Penguin Random House and Simon & Schuster are number one and number two, or do the 12 percent and your 7 and 6 percent, are they looking—are they derived differently, or are they just the market share?

A. The market shares give you a prediction, and it can be a good prediction. It can be off on the high side. It can be off on the low side. I mean, two firms could get a certain level of market share without ever being in head-to-head competition, which means there would zero probability that they would be winner and runner-up. It's not a criticism of starting with that, but I just want to recognize that there are limitations to relying on it.

Q. And just for purposes of clarification, market share is not the percentage of time that these parties encounter each other one and two?

A. That's right. I mean, you could—correct. I will just stop there.

Q. Okay. Now, I want to talk about one-on-one negotiations as well. You have been explaining to us why certain decisions don't make economic sense for the merged party going forward because of the risks they would be taking and that they would be wrong 88 percent of the time if they generally applied a reduction in advances. What is the analysis as it applies to bilateral negotiations?

A. Well, I think Your Honor asked about this. And I only answered one part of the question yesterday. But it concerns this idea of might there be a perception that the competitive constraint, the outside option, so to speak, has weakened in the context of a one-on-one negotiation. And, Mr. Oppenheimer, are you wanting me to focus just on unilateral or more broadly?

Q. If it would help you to focus more broadly, please do so.

A. I think it was an important question and would, say, take the point of view of a Hachette imprint like Workman, Little, Brown, and they are in a one-on-one negotiation with an author, and would that affect how they negotiate. That, I think, is an important question. I would just observe before going any further the SSA model, of course, doesn't provide any insights. I would just point out this is not confined to unilateral effects. It's not about coordinated effects. It's about this more general idea of would there be a softening of competition based on perception.

Under current competitive conditions, the Little, Brown editor at Hachette has to think about, well, has there been a production competition from the merger or is the outside option unidentified going to end up being Macmillan or Norton. And they don't know. And that's the problem of implementation of this idea that, oh, we are going to get a cascading set of effects.

I'm asking where is it going to happen. I think it's unrealistic in that situation where you have already a provisional match. You are in a one-on-one negotiation for a reason, and then you are going to say, no, I'm not sure, but there could be a lessening of competition out there, I am going to pull punches.

I don't see that, because if you do that, you are going to risk losing that book and getting it wrong far more than you are going to get it right.

Q. Is that what you meant by your reference to 88 percent of the time you could be wrong?

A. Well, 88 percent of the time is more narrowly focused on unilateral effects involving PRH and S&S. I was trying to broaden the answer to respond to Your Honor's question yesterday.

Q. By the way, when you are in a bidding situation, do you know at the outset, is there any way to know whether you are in the 12 percent situation or the 88 percent situation?

A. No. And you may not get any feedback that helps you. The agents are the ones who control the information flow.

Q. May we put up slide 57, Pam. You have prepared a demonstrative for us, Professor Snyder. Can you tell us what we are looking at and how this relates to the 88 percent risk.

A. These are four scenarios, each of which would contribute to the 88 percent.

So, scenario one, neither Simon & Schuster or Penguin Random House wins. So with respect to the likelihood or potential harm from unilateral effects, that's a no situation. There's no incentive to adjust bids when there's somebody else who is ahead of you. And then scenario two, one of the merging parties wins and the other does not even participate, from the agency data on multi bid situations, that's 47 percent of the time, as I recall. I'm not saying that those data are representative, but that's an indication that you don't always even have the head-to-head competition. Scenario three, PRH wins and S&S is not the competitive constraint. And four is the reverse. Those are the situations where, if you knew you were in those, you would not want to make any adjustment to how you compete for acquisitions.

Q. Do any of these four scenarios correspond in a general level to bilateral negotiations?

A. I think they do, and this goes to the question of who is the relevant constraint. So PRH, S&S are in the bilateral negotiation. They are the prospective winner. It's theirs to lose. Who is the competitive constraint? It's a version of three and four.

Again, going back to the Hachette, Little, Brown competitor situation—they are in a one-on-one negotiation with somebody conditioned on a match—are they going to reduce their offer based on the perception that competition has weakened? That's the question.

THE COURT: Is now a good time for a break, Mr. Oppenheimer?

MR. OPPENHEIMER: Certainly, Your Honor.

THE COURT: Let's take a 15-minute break at this time. Thank you.

(A recess was taken at 11:29 a.m.)

BY MR. OPPENHEIMER:

Q. Professor Snyder, it's good see you again. Before the break there was a little bit of colloquy with respect to Christian books.

MR. OPPENHEIMER: Your Honor, for the record, you mentioned Macmillan. I think it's HarperCollins in the testimony.

THE COURT: Yes.

MR. OPPENHEIMER: Okay.

BY MR. OPPENHEIMER:

Q. Just a quick question for you, Professor Snyder, about your data. Would you turn again or stay within, this time, your rebuttal expert report, June 3.

A. Okay.

Q. And I would like to have you, when you have it, turn to appendix C, page C1. Is that one of the appendices in your report for the acquisition data you have described?

A. Yes. And, again, at the outset I identified the fact that sometimes you see these two data sets referred to as advance data and sometimes as acquisition data.

Q. And if I could draw your attention to C7 of your appendix C.

A. C7, yes.

Q. Yes. And if I could draw your attention down to No. 30, the entry No. 30 for HarperCollins, do you see that?

A. Yes.

Q. So do you see the reference there to general and Christian divisions, all advance levels?

A. I do.

Q. Does that indicate that you included all of Christian when you did your market share calculation?

A. Yes.

Q. Is it your understanding that Dr. Hill did the same thing?

A. Yes.

Q. So it's included in your current share calculation?

A. Yes.

Q. With respect, not to shares now, but to the incidents, the frequency with which Penguin Random House and Simon & Schuster are number one and number two, just so we have it in the record, can you tell us what your percentage—the percentage you arrived at looking at the agency data?

A. It will take me a moment to find it.

Q. Professor Snyder, if I could direct you to page 76 of your report.

A. It's also reflected in slide 16, the earlier demonstrative.

Q. Could you read the number into the record for us.

A. Again, could you repeat the question.

Q. Yes. What is your percentage—we know it's not 12 percent. You have said it's lower. What is your percentage for the frequency of time that Penguin Random House and Simon & Schuster are one and two?

A. I recall, without redoing the calculation, about 6 or 7 percent.

Q. Okay. Do you recall a difference between the 6 and 7 percent, what accounted for the one point difference?

A. I think it was imprint competition.

Q. So the lower 6 percent is taking imprint competition into account; the 7 percent is not?

A. That's my recollection.

Q. Okay. Thank you.

THE COURT: If I could ask, I thought you said the agency data over-included PRH and S&S. How does this number become lower?

THE WITNESS: Oh, you're right. They do overrepresent PRH and S&S. I think the figures were going from roughly 49 percent in the advance data to 57 percent. But within the agency data, I understood the question to be when are they winner and runner-up. And that's not 12 percent. It's 6 to 7 percent.

THE COURT: So 12 percent is what would be expected?

THE WITNESS: Correct.

THE COURT: Based on the larger data set?

THE WITNESS: That's correct.

THE COURT: Based on the specific agency data set, their market shares are overrepresented, but it turns out they are head-to-head only 6 or 7 percent of the time.

THE WITNESS: Head-to-head and produce—

THE COURT: One and two.

THE WITNESS: Correct.

THE COURT: 6 or 7 percent.

BY MR. OPPENHEIMER:

Q. Professor Snyder, just so we are clear–

THE COURT: I'm clear.

MR. OPPENHEIMER: Okay.

BY MR. OPPENHEIMER:

Q. Let's talk a little bit about softening competition. I would like to go back to Dr. Hill's theory about that for a second. What is your understanding of that theory?

A. It's pretty much what I said before the break. It's not about unilateral effects. It's not about coordinated effects. It's not modeled. It's the idea that, as Your Honor said, there could be some kind of cascading of effects based on perception, based on knowledge that the merger has taken place, and it happens—it has to start with reductions in advances by rivals.

Q. Is there any empirical analysis that you are aware of in Dr. Hill's work about softening?

A. No.

Q. Is there any modeling that pertains in Dr. Hill's work to that softening?

A. No. I thought I mentioned that, but definitely not.

MR. OPPENHEIMER: Your Honor, I know, I think, by popular claim, we all decided to spend no more time on the second score auction model if we could. Procedurally, we've got a lot of potential slides and whatnot for the rebuttal case to go back into it. There were certain areas that I did not go into, specifically the inputs to that model and the description of the critical threshold calibration test that Professor Snyder alluded to briefly but did not go into. What I would like to do now, and I just want to be mindful of the Court's admonition, to go through those quickly but to dispose of those two issues.

THE COURT: That's fine.

BY MR. OPPENHEIMER:

Q. Let's start with inputs to the second score auction model. Do you have any disagreements with the inputs that Dr. Hill used?

A. Yes.

Q. What are those briefly?

A. The two inputs into the second score auction model are market shares of the two parties. You can't put in an alternative diversion ratio, so that's just a requirement. You use market shares. And sometimes the description of that input gets a little bit confused with actual diversion ratios, but he's using market shares, and that's one input. And my overall view about the SSA model isn't that it rises and falls on the inputs, but I do have a definite concern about the other input which is margins.

Q. Would you briefly explain that.

A. Yes. Dr. Hill in his first report estimated the SSA model with inputs for the two parties that were inconsistent. In the case of PRH, he included operating expenses in the calculation of the margin. And by including those, of course, that reduced the margin based on that compared to the alternative. By contrast, with Simon & Schuster, he excluded operating expenses. So, he got results in his first report based on those two margins being the inputs. And the model can be estimated different ways. Without going into too much detail, you can estimate the model with one party's margin the other party's margin or an average of both. I pointed out in my second report that these two inputs were inconsistent. And what I did was pick margins that included operating expenses for both PRH and S&S. And I recalibrated his results. And I also pointed out the inconsistency in Dr. Hill's first report. In his final report, his third report, Dr. Hill went in a different direction. He got consistency, but he got it a different way, by excluding operating expenses from both firms' margins. So now we have consistent margins conceptually, but they are not grounded in the actual book level P&Ls that the parties use to make bids. So, consistency not grounded in P&Ls. And I mentioned this maybe quickly in passing yesterday, but the test of reliability developed by Dr. Nathan Miller, who developed the SSA model, it passed for the first iteration of Dr. Hill's estimation in his first report, and then when he responded to my criticism and he redid it, he solved the consistency problem; however, the model becomes unreliable based on Dr. Miller's reliability test.

Q. Let me break those in two and we will go through it quickly.

THE COURT: And that reliability test is you compare the actual margins to what the model would predict to be the margins?

THE WITNESS: Correct, Your Honor.

THE COURT: Okay.

BY MR. OPPENHEIMER:

Q. What is the effect of having higher margins on the SSA's assessment of harm?

A. So in general, the greater the margins, the greater the harm.

MR. OPPENHEIMER: Pam, could we get slide 58. Your Honor, we will not be adverting to obviously any of the efficiencies bars.

BY MR. OPPENHEIMER:

Q. Professor Snyder, I just want to draw your attention to this slide, which is the estimated percent decreased and combined entities' average author compensation 2015 to 2020. Can you tell us, what is it that we are seeing in this? And just direct your comments, please, to the first two bars, those being adjustments with Dr. Hill's margins, and then with corrected margins.

A. Yes. Focusing on the first two, what I was referring to as Dr. Hill's results from his first report, that's depicted in the first column. And the average is—average predicted reduction in author compensation is 6.1 percent. And that's an average of roughly an 11 percent prediction downward for Simon & Schuster and about a 4 percent predicted reduction for Penguin Random House. And that corresponds to an aggregate harm. Even though Dr. Hill did not report it in his first report, I think he doesn't disagree that that corresponds to 29.3 million in annual harm.

THE COURT: Can you just tell me, that's 6.1 percent of what? I thought this was like a billion-dollar market, so I am getting confused now about where we are getting these numbers.

THE WITNESS: The percentage reduction refers to the average percentage reduction in author compensation post merger for Penguin Random House and Simon & Schuster. So, if you predict an average of 6 percent for them—

THE COURT: So. you are adding up what their author compensation was?

THE WITNESS: Correct.

THE COURT: Okay. And it's 6.1 percent of that, of just the two merged parties?

THE WITNESS: Correct.

THE COURT: Okay.

THE WITNESS: And I admit I can't remember the specific details, but I think the way Your Honor described it was right. And recall that in the SSA model, there is no loss in market share for the parties, so I don't think you need to make an adjustment for a change in base.

THE COURT: Okay.

THE WITNESS: Should I continue?

BY MR. OPPENHEIMER:

Q. Yes. Tell us what the second bar depicts.

A. The second bar is what I presented in my second report replying to Dr. Hill. And when I say with corrected margins, that's my version of corrected. Now they are consistent with respect to operating expenses. They are included in both. And by including operating expenses, consistent with the answer I gave earlier, when you input to the model lower margins, it reduces harm. And here it reduces the average percent author compensation from 6.1 percent down to 4.3 percent, and then the aggregate annual harm falls by a corresponding amount.

Q. Okay. And you mentioned the reliability test for the second score auction model. First of all, I understand the judge understands the basic mechanism of that test, but would you clarify for us, what is the purpose of that test? What is the consequence of failing that test?

A. Well, there's no specific cutoff that says the test is not reliable based on a divergence between the predicted margin and what the individual firm's margin is. Dr. Hill and I agree on that. It turns out that, in his first iteration, the predicted margins for each were very close.

Q. Before you go on, maybe we can help put this in context for you. We will bring up for you to talk off of slide 60. Try slide 64. Thank you.

Would you tell us what this is. It says Hill's SSA model fails reliability test, but would you describe this grid for us.

A. Sorry I'm pausing. There was a slight divergence with my hard copy. But as I was referring to his first iteration, that's obviously the left-hand column, the row here is S&S margin prediction error. So S&S margin predicted by the model was 5 percent below its actual margin and vice versa for the prediction margin with respect to PRH. When you go to his third report where he now has consistency but higher margins because he's excluding operating expenses from both PRH and S&S, the predictions versus actuals diverge greatly. So, the top row, the model is predicting an S&S margin that is 50 percent higher than its actual margin, and the lower, the second row, is predicting a 33 percent lower margin for PRH compared to actual. This is telling you whether the model is making sense of the inputs and the outcomes. And what this failure of the reliability test means is that the results are not reliable.

Q. Thank you. Let's move on now quickly, and we can close up on the GUPPI.

MR. OPPENHEIMER: And, Your Honor, for the same reason, some of this may, I guess, come up in rebuttal.

BY MR. OPPENHEIMER:

Q. Do you have an opinion as to whether Dr. Hill's GUPPI analysis addresses the issues you have identified in the second score auction?

A. It does not.

Q. Just very briefly, why is that? And may we bring up slide 15.

So, we are going to skip over the equation mercifully. It's an equation that applies to any industry. It's a calculation. I said it's not an equilibrium. It doesn't account for competitor responses or for author agent adjustments. But in terms of the core issue of does it fit, it has the same problems with SSA. It doesn't account for the full extent of the mix of acquisition processes. The GUPPI calculations don't cover, for example, one-one-one negotiations. It doesn't account for agents' ability to select among acquisitions and make adjustments. It doesn't account for imprint competition. And there are no rival responses.

Q. Did you also perform some analysis whereby you corrected the inputs to the GUPPI model?

A. I did.

Q. Did you prepare a demonstrative to show us the results of that analysis?

A. I did.

Q. We should perhaps pause one second, the famous formula. We will go to 64. There we go. Okay.

Can you tell us what we are looking at here? And, Professor Snyder, you can ignore the third column because that has a calculation for efficiencies.

A. Yes.

THE COURT: I'm sorry, can you just explain—nobody has explained how the GUPPI analysis actually works.

MR. OPPENHEIMER: Oh.

THE WITNESS: Then may I go to the equation?

THE COURT: Yes, because it's hard for me to understand how it works without understanding the equation.

MR. OPPENHEIMER: You have made Professor Snyder's day. Could we go to 62. Thank you. There you go, Your Honor.

THE WITNESS: So, this is the single formula that would be applied to any industry; electric vehicles, pharmaceuticals, video streaming.

MR. SCHWARZ: You said 62?

THE WITNESS: I think it's 60.

THE COURT: Can you explain like on a broad level what it's trying to do?

THE WITNESS: Yes. So, what it's trying to do is answer the question, okay, I'm a firm, I am thinking about exercising market power before the merger, and I've got this series of competitors out there. And before the merger, you take into account the loss of sales if you were to reduce in this context advances or loss of acquisitions. And then it's asking the question, okay, now what if you merge with one party. Some of those lost sales are diverted to the party you acquire. So good, good, I'm more likely to exercise market power. And then how valuable is that diversion. Well, I want to take into account how profitable it is for the other party that gets those sales that's now part of my own firm. That's basically the numerator here.

THE COURT: Okay.

THE WITNESS: And the diversion is measured here so it could be here, from Simon & Schuster would be A, to Penguin Random House, B, and then the margin for Penguin Random House. That's the basic intuition.

THE COURT: Okay. So that's a percentage of the premerger author comp?

THE WITNESS: Right.

THE COURT: What's pass-through?

THE WITNESS: Pass-through could be a variety of numbers based on market conditions. Dr. Hill, when he calculated the GUPPI, he used two different pass-through rates.

THE COURT: But what is pass-through?

THE WITNESS: Oh, it's the pass-through to, in this context, authors, how much does this affect them.

THE COURT: Meaning—can you explain that more.

THE WITNESS: If in the context of multi round auctions you got a reduction of 4.7 percent in advances, after the merger, Dr. Hill assumes that all of that would be harm to authors, a hundred percent of it would mean harm.

THE COURT: What would be the alternative?

THE WITNESS: The alternative would be, I think, to take into account the baked-in competitor pricing. So not all of the diversion would be to just the party you acquire. Some of it would be to other parties, and you would have less loss to authors. And he makes a 50 percent assumption—

THE COURT: So, you are saying- if the diversion would go, not just to the party you are acquiring, but to other competitors?

THE WITNESS: It does go to—in the GUPPI index, it goes to other parties. So, if the diversion in the numerator from A to B is 15 percent—

THE COURT: Then 85 percent is going to other parties?

THE WITNESS: Correct, Your Honor.

THE COURT: I'm trying to understand the pass-through though. The alternative to all the harm going to authors is the harm going where?

THE WITNESS: Some of it gets, in effect, mitigated by the fact that there are other rivals, that those other rivals are not changing their prices. But the way I understand Dr. Hill's view is that basically mitigates some of the harm. This question might be better posed to Dr. Hill, but I'm giving you my understanding of what he did.

THE COURT: Okay. I'm not sure I totally understand that, the pass-through part of it, but I kind of understand this. Go ahead, Mr. Oppenheimer.

BY MR. OPPENHEIMER:

Q. Is there a GUPPI—does the GUPPI formula apply to bilateral negotiations, for example?

A. No. And Dr. Hill didn't calculate it for bilateral or so-called one-on-one negotiations.

Q. And does the GUPPI calculation typically across all of its versions produce a lower harm figure than the second score auction model?

A. I think that depends on the particular formats and assumptions. Both models—excuse me. Both the SSA model and the GUPPI calculations always predict some harm. That direction is something that always happens.

THE COURT: I thought he said that he did a GUPPI calculation that was hybrid which would take into account bilateral negotiations.

THE WITNESS: My understanding was that his—this slide would show single round and hybrid on the bottom, and that's where I think he dealt with the shift to best bids. I'm not sure if I am answering your question, Your Honor.

THE COURT: I understand. I thought he said that. I might be wrong.

THE WITNESS: If we can go back to the other slide.

BY MR. OPPENHEIMER:

Q. Formula?

A. No, for the results.

Q. Yes. If we can switch back to the results, let me just—this is the slide correcting some of the flaws in Dr. Hill's GUPPI, yield small harm, that slide?

A. I just wanted to add there's no row here for one-on-one negotiations or preempts.

Q. Can you explain what you are showing on this chart. And if you would, for the record, read in the numbers as you go.

MR. OPPENHEIMER: This is slide 60.

THE WITNESS: Yes. So, the first column is labeled number one, but I just wanted to point out that, again, this is produced in Dr. Hill's third report, but he's using the same margins as input as he did in the SSA model in his first report.

BY MR. OPPENHEIMER:

Q. Dr. Snyder, just so we are clear, on the far left-hand column, you divided this into multi round, single round hybrid?

A. Based on what Dr. Hill did.

Q. Thank you.

A. He calculated it for these two groups.

Q. Thank you.

A. And his predicted result is 10.3 percent for the multi round. And for the single round slash hybrid, it's 5.2 percent. And these are converted from negative numbers to, going back to the formula, to positive numbers.

Q. And what is column two?

A. Column two is the adjustment I get when I use, instead of the diversion according to share, I use the agency prediction. And we talked about that being about 7 percent versus 12. And when I use the margins that I used in my second report, and those margins are the ones that include operating expense for both parties, the results there are multi round price pressure is 4.7 percent, and 2.3 percent for single round slash hybrid.

Q. So taking the 2.3 percent for the single round hybrid, you are saying, with adjusted margins, that is the harm predicted by that run of the GUPPI?

A. That's right. And you will see the same relationship in Dr. Hill's column number one. And that difference reflects the different pass-through rates. What you see in column two with my alternative inputs are numbers that are lower, but they have the same relationship, two to one relationship, because of the—I'm following Dr. Hill's assumptions there about a hundred percent pass-through versus 50 percent pass-through. And if I may, what's important here is, again, this model always produces some harm. All GUPPI calculations do. Here what we are seeing is lower price pressures as a result of the merger when you use these alternative inputs. And there is not, Your Honor, a clear consensus on what's the trigger line where you say, aha, this is a problem. As the originators of the GUPPI calculations commented, this is much more of a screening device. But with respect to when do you actually proceed to further modeling and, for example, merger simulations and so on and so forth, I believe that the consensus is 5 percent. So with these corrections, the GUPPI calculations are saying, it's my understanding, people may disagree, would say let's stop there.

Q. When you say let's stop there, I just want to be clear, when you refer to this as a screening device, not even do further empirical or modeling work?

A. If this is all you did, you would stop.

Q. And can you combine in some way the different harm predictions for multi round from the different harm predictions for single round hybrid?

A. Are you talking about combine the first row and the second row?

Q. Sure, yes.

A. I don't know. I haven't tried to do it.

Q. Has Dr. Hill provided a mechanism to do that?

A. I don't recall.

Q. If you were to apply this type of even screening analysis to all of the acquisition transactions in the publishing world at any market segment, it doesn't matter, would you have to know, in order to apply it, what percentage of acquisitions were multi round and what were single round hybrid?

A. I think you would want to take that into account, but that goes to a deeper issue that I think—forgive me. I think the whole modeling and calculation exercise in this context is difficult because agents choose, and none of these approaches account for what agents select, and then agents adjust and sometimes go in one path and then go into another path. So I wouldn't press that too far.

Q. Let's talk a little bit about the market. What is your understanding of the market that Dr. Hill has identified?

A. Dr. Hill, he identifies the broad market, but he proposes a market segment based on advances of $250,000 or higher and he identifies these as anticipated top sellers.

Q. And did you reach an opinion about whether Dr. Hill's proposed market for so-called anticipated top sellers is a relevant antitrust market?

A. I concluded that it is not, and there are four main reasons that I have in my head about what the fundamental problems are.

Q. Let me ask you this. Do you have a view on the use of price, just price, to define a market?

A. My view on price is that price can help you corroborate a proposed market, but it should not be and I don't believe it has been used as the sole means of identifying a market segment.

Q. Do you see a logic for the proposed market using a cutoff of $250,000 advances?

A. No. And if I could just go through some of the basic reasons, one is when you observe the market above and below that level, the basic industry functions are the same. If you publish a book for an advance of a hundred thousand or a million, it's the same basic steps. So, the functions aren't different.

In addition, publishers as well as agents don't operate differently above and below the threshold. So, before I return to just the function part, my view is, if you just think about those two factors, it calls into question the validity of this market. The functions are the same, industry participate—excuse me, industry participants don't operate differently. That's in contrast to other situations where you see the differences above and below a certain threshold or you see differences with respect to different customers, but you don't have those differences here. With respect to the functions, the slide is up, I don't think I need to go through them, but they are the same below and above.

Q. What is the economic significance of the fact that the functions don't differ below and above the $250,000 threshold?

A. Well, it gives you a more robust view of what competition is. One of the factors I mentioned yesterday is that there is a large number of publishers who operate just below the $250,000 threshold. Those are publishers by definition that are already doing all these functions, and it's just a question of, instead of spending, for example, a million dollars on five contracts, might they go to $400,000 on two and then the remainder on another. That would put them in the market. That's one difference.

Q. There's been some discussion about marketing, and you mention it in your demonstrative here. What about the point that has been discussed that sometimes publishers market books with higher advances with different levels of marketing, how do you assess that in your analysis?

A. Well, here I think it's important to keep in mind the basic distinction between the marketing functions and the marketing spend. The functions are going to be basically the same. In today's world, you do the search optimization.

Ideally you get some social media traction. You try to get the book reviewed. With respect to brick-and-mortar retailers, you try to get the book on the shelf and ideally on the display table. I forgot if I mentioned you try to get the book reviewed. But you want to generate publicity about the book. So, the basic functions are not different. The marketing spend does vary with advance level. And I agree with that general proposition. Dr. Hill presented some data showing that the marketing spend after the fact increases by certain buckets of advance levels. So, there's a positive relationship based on actual spending. I'm not surprised to see that, but, I mean, if you think about it, if a publisher commits to a million-dollar advance versus a $200,000 advance, the publisher is going to need to recoup that so they are going to spend more money at the outset. And if the book gets traction in the sense that a book for which they spent a lot of money ends up being a real best seller, they are going to keep spending. So that's going to generate that positive relationship. But there's all kinds of variants around that relationship. A very well-known author might be able to basically sell the book herself or himself. So that relationship is going to have a lot of variables or noise. But in the end, I don't see anything surprising in what Dr. Hill presented. I don't disagree with the numbers. It just doesn't tell me that you should use a cutoff of $250,000.

Q. Let's put up demonstrative slide 28. This is a demonstrative that we exchanged with the government recently. Would you tell us what we are looking at here, Professor Snyder.

A. Yes. So, the top of this exhibit is a reproduction of what Dr. Hill presented in his third report, his reply report. It draws on my advance data which, as I have indicated, goes through the end of 2021. So, the time period here is 2019 to 2021. And it reflects his proposed cutoff. So, on the left-hand side are market shares, and that's what's shown vertically. But on the left-hand side, that's for the 0 to $250,000 range. And then the right-hand side, it shows those market shares for his proposed market segment. Before going back to the market shares, if I could just point out that I supplemented this market share analysis that he presented with information that I think helps clarify what are we talking about in terms of number of contracts and total advance dollars. This came up very early in the trial. In the 0 to $250,000 segment, the number of contracts over this three-year period is almost $26,000. In the right-hand side for contracts that pass the $250,000 threshold, about $3,500, if you divide by 3, we get the numbers that we have heard talked about in the range of 11 or 12 hundred books that—or contracts that fall into that category. On the bottom I have used the advance data that Dr. Hill relied on to identify the total advances. And what you see on the left-hand side is 1.2 billion for the category from 0 to $250,000. I will mention that, because the data don't include all publishers, that might be a little bit low, but it's fine. And then on the right-hand side, that's where much more of the dollar advance action is. It's $3.2 billion. If you add those up together, it's $4.4 billion to $4.5 billion in that three-year time period for both segments.

Q. And what point was Dr. Hill making with this to justify the division of the market segment at $250,000?

A. I think this is a, you know, maybe the core of his argument or at least one of them. What he's saying is look at this break. And he says look at the change in market shares, they must be telling me something. Now, when you go from the left-hand column to the right-hand column, what you see very dramatically is that the non-Big 5 publishers, their share drops from 45 percent down to 9 percent. And conversely, the group of Big 5 grows substantially to the right.

Now, there's some interesting details here that I think are worth noting. Hachette's share goes down. They are light blue. The others are for Macmillan, not a big change. For Simon & Schuster, an increase from 9 to 12. What's really interesting is look at HarperCollins. It goes from 11 percent to 25 percent.

Q. Excuse me. These data are confidential.

A. Sorry.

MR. OPPENHEIMER: Your Honor, perhaps it would simplify things—I don't believe that we have objection to this, but if we put this demo into evidence as Plaintiff's 963A. 963 has already been admitted. I don't think there's any dispute about any of the numbers. And then we could refer to the blocks. We wouldn't have to read in any of the numbers and Your Honor would have it.

MR. SCHWARZ: It's already in evidence. No objection.

MR. OPPENHEIMER: Okay, Your Honor.

THE COURT: Okay.

MR. OPPENHEIMER: If we can call this with the number of contracts in total advance dollars at the bottom 963A, we would move its admission at this time.

THE COURT: That's admitted.

MR. SCHWARZ: No objection. (Plaintiff's 963A received in evidence.)

BY MR. OPPENHEIMER:

Q. Professor Snyder, if we just discuss the conclusions without reference to the specific percentages. Thank you.

A. Is it okay to proceed by just identifying them by number 1 through 5 with the different colors?

Q. Yes. Are you numbering from the top or bottom?

A. From the top.

Q. Sure.

A. So light blue is No. 1. The publisher I was just mentioning is No. 4 in maroon increases its share from 11 percent below $250,000 to 25 percent above.

So, when I see this, it goes back to the fundamental question is this threshold arbitrary. And I think Dr. Hill's argument is that it's not arbitrary. We see this divergence, these changes in market shares, at $250,000. That change must be telling us something fundamental about the market. But when I look at this, why is it 250? Why–

THE COURT: He did a number of different advance levels, not just 250.

THE WITNESS: He did for things like the HMT and other—he did.

THE COURT: I thought his report said 250 is not a magic—

THE WITNESS: It's not a magic number.

THE COURT: It works—his analysis, he says, works at 100, 250, 500, 1 million.

THE WITNESS: Let's take a look at the next slide, see if it works for 50. I think, Your Honor, I'm not disagreeing that the market shares change, and maybe that doesn't pose a problem. But for me it does. Why use one threshold? Why not use two? Why use 250? Why not use 50? And what's depicted on the next slide is a different cut, and that's zero to $50,000 and then $50,000 to a million, and then a million and above. And if Dr. Hill's analysis works all the time, let me just look at this and see if that actually plays out, I don't think so, or at least raises questions.

BY MR. OPPENHEIMER:

Q. Are you comparing the drop of the non-Big 5 at $50,000 on this slide No. 29 to the prior drop on Exhibit 963?

A. That's one of the things I would look at, yes.

Q. Just focusing on that, what is your observation about that?

A. Well, on the previous slide, and this is, I think, sort of a basic agreed-upon fact, above $250,000, the non-Big 5 have 9 or 10 percent share. When we go to this presentation, you ask the question where does that drop really happen. Most of it happens at $50,000. The non-Big 5 go from 58 percent share below $50,000 down most of the way to 9 or 10 at the $50,000 threshold. So, they go from 58 down to 17.

Q. And can you describe for us the observations you make about the number of contracts in total advance dollars at these different cutoffs than Dr. Hill made?

A. Yes. I find this useful to understand where the contracts are, where are the dollars. And I won't read the numbers. Maybe I should.

MR. OPPENHEIMER: Your Honor, may we go ahead without objection and admit slide 29 in evidence? That way he won't have to articulate the numbers.

THE COURT: Any objection.

MR. SCHWARZ: No objection, Your Honor.

THE COURT: That will be admitted.

BY MR. OPPENHEIMER:

Q. You can proceed.

A. Thank you. So, in the 0 to $50,000, we have over 17,000 contracts. In the $50,000 to $1 million, we have roughly 11 and a half million contracts. And then the one million and above, we have 694. So over three years, that's an average of 231 contracts annually. On the advances, recall that the total advances in the previous slide was 4.4.

Q. We don't have to articulate the numbers because Her Honor will have these. If you go column, that will be fine.

A. 45 percent of the advances are in the right-hand column, the total advance dollars, associated with those 694 contracts.

THE COURT: Can I just ask, are markets ever defined by who the main players are in the market?

THE WITNESS: I think who is your competitor, who are you more likely to compete with, is one of the ways that you can corroborate a market. I don't want to offer too much in the way of obviously any kind of legal opinion on that, but I think my reading is that's one of the things you look at, who do you compete against and how often.

THE COURT: Including who your primary competitors are? I'm just—in economics, is that something? Is that a thing in economics?

THE WITNESS: It wouldn't be the first thing I would go to to define a market. But I think it is useful to ask, does it make sense in terms of who is competing.

So, for example, if you had a merger in the accounting world and you said, well, we are going to look at the top accounting firms in the world, and there is going to be a merger for a group of customers who are—who have different characteristics, the top accounting firms would be the ones most likely to compete. So I would get the logic in that context.

THE COURT: Okay. Go ahead.

BY MR. OPPENHEIMER:

Q. Do you get the logic in this context, Professor Snyder?

A. I don't. If I may, I found this striking because if you go back to the fourth of the Big 5 on this chart, and recall from the previous slide that particular entity was gaining a lot of share if you looked at it at the 250 cutoff.

Q. These are the red bars?

A. These are the red bars. Go back to Your Honor's question. Now go to the next slide and say, well, at what threshold does that particular publisher become a much more frequent winner. It's not at 250. It's at 50. So, this doesn't negate the idea that you want to look at, you know, what are the shares and so forth, but to me, it establishes that this is just arbitrary, because if you are looking for changes in the number of competitors or the shares of competitors, there's nothing special about $250,000.

THE COURT: So, I think the evidence reflects that at higher advance levels, you are less likely to get the non-Big 5 publishers competing because they just don't have as much money. And so, I'm just wondering, like within economics, can be you define a market by, I guess, the number of people who are able to compete at a certain level?

THE WITNESS: And, Your Honor, you talk about something—a different threshold above 250—

THE COURT: I'm not really thinking so much about thresholds. I'm just thinking about—I think the most relevant, and correct me if you disagree, bar is the purple one. That's the one that—because they are the ones who may be priced out at the higher advance levels. And the question is, can it be a different market just because, at certain levels, people are not competing or not likely to compete, can that help define a market?

THE WITNESS: So if—

THE COURT: Without thinking about the numbers, I'm just saying, are there some markets where, although they compete on a broad market, they just don't compete on a higher end scale because they can't?

THE WITNESS: Conceptually that may be the case. It's not what I see here because—

THE COURT: Conceptually it's possible?

THE WITNESS: It's possible. But what economics tells us to do and what the guidelines tell us to do is check the numbers. The numbers of competitors by itself is important. And then I think Your Honor's question goes to do they have the capacity to compete, can they actually do it. So, the numbers show more than 30, increasing number of publishers securing contracts above $250,000, and then you recall the analysis that I did on the maximum contracts that individual publishers are making over a certain time period, and 15 of them are making contract deals in excess of a million dollars.

THE COURT: So it has to take into account everyone who can compete and not the ones who do?

THE WITNESS: Correct, because when you get to the issue of the exercise of market power, you have to ask will there be constraining influences even from parties that don't have a big market share. So, I also did the analysis that showed that even though the non-Big 5 only won a certain percent, they were winner or runner-up 23 percent of the time. So, all of my analysis fits together to establish that there's a lot of competition above that particular threshold. The other thing I just want to say is post merger, we are not going to eliminate imprint competition, in my opinion, within PRH, and we are not going to eliminate competition with the other three firms, Hachette, HarperCollins, and Macmillan.

THE COURT: Thank you.

BY MR. OPPENHEIMER:

Q. If we were to use the method from Dr. Hill's chart of looking to see where market share of the non-Big 5 falls off, where do you see it falling off most significantly, at $250,000 advance level or at the $50,000 advance level?

A. Non-Big 5 share drops off much more substantially at the $50,000 level just in terms of numbers.

Q. And if we were to measure market concentrations of the acquisition of books with advances of $50,000 and up, would we have a concentrated market?

A. I can't do the HHI calculations in my head, but you would have a substantially less concentrated market. Am I correct your question was about 50 to a million?

Q. Yes.

A. Substantially less concentrated. I should just mention, though, I am not proposing this as an alternative market definition. And I know you asked me to think about the effect on concentration. Given what I said earlier about functions and operations, I don't like the idea of any price cutoff.

Q. And would you agree with me that there is no structural presumption for the acquisition book market that includes all advance levels?

A. That's correct. If I can remember the basic numbers, post-acquisition, the HHI is roughly 1,100 or 1,200 and the change is under 400. So, if you apply the grid that Dr. Hill used, and it reflects the merger guidelines, that's outside the range where there would be any presumption of harm.

Q. You have also raised the issue of whether books generating a $250,000 advance are anticipated to be top sellers. What is your concern there?

A. Well, this is the adjacent part of the market definition. It's not just about the dollar cutoff. It's the idea that there are books that you can anticipate that will be in this category and the—excuse me, the guidelines provide guidance around so-called price discrimination markets. And what is required is identification, meaning, okay, we all anticipate such and such an author is going to be a best seller. That's the identification part. And then the second part is targeting.

The issue raised by this claim that this is a price discrimination market calls into question can you reliably anticipate? I would say for some, yes. Can you target? Very difficult given competition.

Q. And why is that? Why is it difficult even if you could identify the target?

A. Well, Your Honor, I would just focus on the right-hand side there. It's more likely that the authors who get a million dollars or more are going to fall into the category of anticipated. I mean, there's probably more of a consensus.

I'm not saying everybody agrees, but it's more likely that the answer to the question do publishers anticipate the author to be a top seller, there's going to be more likelihood that there's a consensus, that they are going to say yes.

But then on the right-hand side, that raises the question of targeting, right? Okay. These are anticipated. We can identify them. Are publishers actually going to be able to lower advances to authors would generate about 230 books a year? Who are they?

A lot of them are going to be very well-known authors or celebrities, authors with track records, and it's exactly those authors who have the most leverage. It's also those authors for whom, as I testified yesterday, common factors in terms of valuation are going to be relatively more important. So, if you are talking about an author with a very strong track record, he or she's going to have—may have a relationship with one publisher, but other publishers would look very fondly on the prospect of getting that author because they can see the track record. Common factors are more important.

Q. By the way, does Dr. Hill ever actually identify a retail sales level for books that he identifies as top sellers?

A. I don't recall that being in the record.

Q. Let's bring up slide 31. Does Dr. Hill see a one-on-one relationship between anticipated top seller and the books that make the cutoff into his $250,000 market?

A. No. This is his trial testimony, and I will just read the very last part after the dash. Some books are in our market, but they are probably not anticipated top sellers and vice versa.

Q. Just briefly on the hypothetical monopsonist test, did you analyze it?

A. I did.

Q. What conclusions can you draw, if any, from Dr. Hill's hypothetical monopsonist test?

A. I think he testified that it doesn't necessarily validate his demarcation point, and I would agree with him. The hypothetical monopsonist test in this contest is past at any dollar threshold $1,000, $1 million. So it's not much of a test if the test is always passed. It tells us that the way he set it up, self-publishing is not a relevant alternative. It doesn't constrain potential exercise of monopsony power here. But given that it passes at all dollar thresholds, it's not informative about what threshold to select.

Q. Have you seen anything in the modeling or empirical or theoretical work that Dr. Hill provided that would enable you as an economist to segment the market for the acquisition of books into subsets of some kind based on advance levels?

A. Based on advance levels, the answer is no.

Q. Is there an allegation in this case of harm to consumers in the sale of books?

A. No.

Q. Does that have any relevance to your economic analysis?

A. Not much. As I pointed out, consumers read what publishers acquire. There's a one-to-one relationship between books and the acquisition rights. But there's no allegation of harm. It just focuses attention on the so-called upstream market.

THE COURT: I think there is an allegation that lower advance levels could lead to a less variety and a smaller number of books. That's in the record.

THE WITNESS: I stand corrected. I don't recall that allegation in Dr. Hill's analysis, but it may have been made by somebody else.

BY MR. OPPENHEIMER:

Q. Putting aside the allegation, Professor Snyder, have you seen anything in Dr. Hill's work that models that issue or deals with it as an empirical matter?

A. Of that, I'm pretty sure the answer is no.

THE COURT: Can I go back to relevant market for a minute. It seems to me reasonable to think that not all books are equal in the market. There's such a wide variety of them. There's so many of them and so many different contracts. And it does seem that this is an industry that's very focused on anticipated sales. It's kind of the driving force in this industry which books are going to sell because it's a business. And there's been a lot of testimony about kind of a portfolio of business, you are looking for the ones that are going to hit big, that a large percentage of the profits are generated by a small number of books. So, this whole industry appears to be driven by anticipated sales. And so that's the factor that determines what you bid for the advance level. And then later on they are always assessing that's the factor that determines how much we are going to market the book. If they see that it looks like the sales are going to go well, later in the process after the auction, they increase their marketing budgets, they try to create the buzz. Everything is about sales. It just seems to me reasonable that the books are not all the same, and some books are going to be treated differently because they are expected to sell well. And then the question is just, how do you identify those books? Because I guess the ones that are going to sell well do require more sales, more distribution, more marketing, right? Because if your book is not going to sell, you don't need all that. It just seems to me intuitive that there should be some kind of a segmentation based on the number of sales and that the higher selling books might need different services and that the authors who wrote those books might have different expectations. So putting aside advance levels, doesn't that—is that consistent with your view of this market?

THE WITNESS: Short answer is yes, Your Honor. There is something about books that are anticipated to be best sellers, and authors and the agents who represent them are going to be looking for a set of services. One of the advantages that individual firms in the Big 5 have is that they have reputations because they have been in business a long time and fundamentally economists talk about reputations being a function of repetition. So, I get that and I accept that.

But that doesn't—then the issue for me would be how do we draw a cutoff. Is it concentrated. And then also whatever cutoff we make, or two cutoffs, do authors have—are they vulnerable to targeting, I think I have made that clear, especially at the high end. I think that's a very dubious proposition.

The other thing I would point out is that while reputation and that comfort level with known Big 5s, I get, I accept, there are other publishers that are really credible with anticipated top sellers. I mean, I am not an industry expert, but I get the impression Norton is viewed as super high quality.

THE COURT: Yes.

THE WITNESS: And then you have interestingly entrants who don't have any track record, but they are proceeding to launch their businesses with reputable editors. So, again, I am going to what's—are there relevant competitive constraints on individuals in the Big 5. And of course, you are going to get competition within them, but there's also going to be competition from outside.

But I think you're right, there is this comfort level that draws authors and agents to for sure consider the Big 5, but it's not only them, and then there's competition within them.

THE COURT: Thank you.

BY MR. OPPENHEIMER:

Q. Have you determined any differences in the any of the services you have identified, any of the functionalities that would enable you to draw a line in the market at a particular advance level?

A. No. And I mentioned I distinguish between marketing spend and marketing function. I agree the marketing spend is going to be higher as you go to higher advance buckets, as Dr. Hill depicted.

Q. We have also heard testimony that for books that are acquired at lower advance levels, that they can get—they can themselves generate buzz, they might come out at a particular time when the topic that they address is hot, and that marketing spend will adjust to go up for them too. How, if at all, does that factor into your analysis?

A. So in general my view is that if you think about this from the point of view of the acquiring publisher, they make a decision about what they are willing to spend. That puts them in a situation where right out of the gate they are going to want to spend more and put in more effort for books in the higher advance category. There are exceptions to that. Maybe, as I mentioned, there are authors who make that really easy, and the effort to get publicists and reviewed and shelf space really just go smoothly. But the distinction here is you've got the upfront efforts, but then you have the ongoing efforts. And there the paths diverge a little on how well the book is doing. So, I see the positive relationship, but again, it's about spending. It's not about different functions. I will just go back to the point that now all books you are going to try to optimize on search mechanisms.

Q. Let's talk a little bit about the broad market for the acquisition books, just close that off. What is your view on the acquisition—on the market for the acquisition of all books of this merger?

A. It's competitive, highly competitive, and it will remain so post acquisition.

Q. Let's bring up slide 22. Professor Snyder, what are we looking at here in slide 22?

A. This is market shares for the—

Q. And let's not call them out. Just describe them. Don't call the numbers out.

A. Okay. This is market shares for the two parties. And then it shows in the blue box they are combined. And this is for the broad market over the time period 2019 to 2021, and it uses as a data source my advance data.

MR. OPPENHEIMER: Your Honor, this is Defendants' 382 in demonstrative form. We would move its admission.

THE COURT: Any objection?

MR. SCHWARZ: No objection.

THE COURT: This will be admitted. (Defendants' 382 received in evidence.)

MR. OPPENHEIMER: And it will be a confidential exhibit, Your Honor.

THE COURT: Yes.

BY MR. OPPENHEIMER:

Q. Did you examine the concentration in the market for the acquisition of all the books, Professor Snyder?

A. I did. And I have a slide depicting the HHI calculation and the change in HHI calculation. I tried to do this from memory a little while ago, and I think I was basically right. Post-acquisition the market will remain unconcentrated with the HHI being less than 1,200 and the change, which is on the vertical axis, is 353. That puts this far away from the area where there is a structural presumption of anticompetitive harm.

MR. OPPENHEIMER: Your Honor, this is Defendants' 426 in demonstrative form. I move its admission.

MR. SCHWARZ: No objection.

THE COURT: This will be admitted. (Defendants' 426 received in evidence.)

BY MR. OPPENHEIMER:

Q. Professor Snyder, I would like to turn to a different topic now, and that the 2013 merger of Penguin and Random House. Do you have that in mind?

A. Yes.

Q. Is that merger informative for you in analyzing the likely effects of the current merger?

A. It's informative, but that was in 2013. So, if you look at the history before and after, I mean, things have changed. But it is informative at some level.

Q. Are there—first of all, what is your basic conclusion with respect to the 2013 merger that would be most directly applicable to our analysis today of this merger?

A. So the number one thing and number mum two thing that I looked at was output and advances. Output measured by titles increased by 13 percent using Dr. Hill's three years before, leave out 2013, three years after. So, if you just compare the three years before to three years after, titles increased by 13 percent. So as an economist, that's really fundamental to just look at output. It increased.

Q. Professor Snyder, is that in the $250,000 and up segment?

A. Yes.

Q. Any other observations, general observations, from the 2013 merger?

A. When I look at average advances, I think I am allowed to describe this, Your Honor, without the table, what I found was that if you—instead of treating the whole range $250,000 and up, if you think about it in terms of buckets, I looked at the bucket from 250 to 500 thousand, average advances increased. I looked at the bucket from $500,000 to a million, average advances increased. And when I look at it from a million to two million, average advances increased. I am doing this from memory. When you go beyond that level, the data are really noisy because small numbers and the averages don't increase.

MR. OPPENHEIMER: Pam, if you could put up Defendants' 385. Your Honor, we would like to move for the admission of Defendants' 385. There's no objection as I understand it.

MR. SCHWARZ: Let me see it. No objection.

THE COURT: All right. (Defendants' 385 received in evidence.)

BY MR. OPPENHEIMER:

Q. What are we looking at in Defendants' 385, Professor Snyder?

MR. SCHWARZ: Excuse me. I don't actually have a copy, but I think it's in—

MR. OPPENHEIMER: The only notes it has are mine.

BY MR. OPPENHEIMER:

Q. What are we seeing in Defendants' Exhibit 385, Professor Snyder?

A. We are looking at average advances per title over the time period 2010 to 2021, and these aren't by bucket. These are by different thresholds. So the bottom in light blue is for all categories. And then you move to the green, that's for average advances above a hundred thousand dollars. And then the next one up, red is for average advances for $250,000 and above. And then the top one is for average advances for $500,000 and above.

Q. And what does this tell you?

A. It's a different way to look at what I just described. I actually prefer, as I have reflected on it, looking at these as buckets rather than different thresholds.

I gave a summary of what I learned looking at the different buckets, but what you see is that average advances overall, and the key reference point is 2013, I don't see any systematic reduction in average advances using this methodology. In fact, I see increases or flat.

Q. And you had alluded—Take that down, Pam. Thanks. You alluded earlier to the fact that there's some high variation in both the $4 million level of the advance testimony data because of small numbers. What did you mean by that?

A. Sorry, Mr. Oppenheimer, would you—

THE COURT: I don't think we need to understand that. Is this a good time for a lunch break?

MR. OPPENHEIMER: Yes.

DIRECT EXAMINATION (Continued)

BY MR. OPPENHEIMER:

Q. We were on the 2013 merger, I think we're getting pretty close to the end here. Does Dr. Hill have a criticism of your use of the 2013 merger?

A. Well, he forwards a so-called difference-in-difference analysis that is intended to reach a different conclusion about the effects of the merger.

Q. Could you briefly describe that criticism for us, and then I'm going to ask you some questions about it.

A. So his analysis looks at the—what's going on in the zero to $250,000 segment as a so-called benchmark for the $250,000 and above segment. And he basically wants to establish the conclusion that the difference between how things went in the above $250,000 segment indicates that there was some problem with that segment post-merger.

Q. And when you say some problem, is he comparing the above $250,000 segment with the below $250,000 segment with respect to average advances?

A. Yes.

Q. And what does he say about that?

A. He says that if you look at the difference, average advances went up as I recall slightly for the below $250,000 segment. And then that is not apparent in the above $250,000 segment, and therefore he attributes that to the merger. You know, I may not be doing justice to his argument, but I think that's the core of it. So, again, it uses the experience below $250,000 as a benchmark.

Q. And what is your view of that—by the way, is that the difference-in-difference approach?

A. Yes.

Q. Okay. And what is your view of that?

A. The difference-in-difference approach is a standard tool. It's within the broad category of benchmarking. One of the key things is selection of the benchmark. It's odd that here, having made the distinction—or claimed to make the distinction between the below 250 and above 250, one would use below 250 as a benchmark. But in implementing a benchmark analysis or a difference-in-difference analysis, a couple things that you look for. Prior to the event, is there stability in the benchmark. There can be a trend up or down, but if you see that benchmark bouncing around in terms of average titles, to me, that's time out, don't use that, because it's not going to be a reliable benchmark post-event. The other issue in executing a difference-in-difference analysis, or any benchmark analysis, is to just check is there anything happening in the benchmark reference that may lead you to a conclusion that's not valid. And the key thing there is taking into account things that are happening in the benchmark below $250,000 category compared to what's happening in the above $250,000 category.

Q. And was there something happening in the under $250,000 category that reflected on whether it was a good benchmark or not?

A. Yes, the mass merchandise titles that part of the market—my understanding is that several firms were moving away from that market. That's a lower price segment in terms of advances within the $250,000 category, which means that if you eliminate the lower end of that range, it's going to project the remainder to go up. Not because—well, just simply because of that composition.

Q. As opposed to the merger?

A. Well, that's the benchmark. I think his focus on the benchmark is really just to set up the comparison with the above $250,000. But the benchmark average advances are going up because of that composition effect.

Q. And again, by composition effect, you're talking about the reduction in mass market sales?

A. Yes, which tends to increase the average title below $250,000.

Q. And in conclusion ultimately, then, what is the impact of Dr. Hill's difference-in-difference analysis on your conclusions that—with respect to average advances after the 2013 merger?

A. Well, I didn't do a complete analysis of the benchmarking in the difference-in-difference. As I said, I wouldn't have done it because of the variability in the benchmark pre-event. But if you just correct for that one factor, his results become insignificant.

Q. Statistically insignificant?

A. Correct.

Q. Let's turn to coordinated effects now. Just tell us, in general, what is your opinion about coordinated—the coordinated effects claim in this case?

A. Coordinated effects in this context are unlikely. In addition, I don't see that there will be any increase in the likelihood of coordinated effects as a result of the merger. And that goes to core ideas reflected in the guidelines about coordinated effects.

Q. Pam, may we bring up slide 66. Let me direct your attention to slide 66 of your presentation. Is this what you had in mind about the merger guidelines, and if so, could you elaborate?

A. Yes. One of the requirements for coordination is that you have to have a coordination mechanism. So, the first part of this quote refers to that. Coordinated interaction can involve the explicit negotiation of a common understanding of how firms will compete or refrain from competing. So that's the first step. You have to have something that you want to agree on and implement. Conditional on that, what the guidelines call out is the importance of detection, monitoring and enforcement. Meaning, are firms agreeing to whatever mechanism they have selected to reduce competition, and can deviations from that agreement be detected through monitoring. And then ultimately, is there a way for parties in the industry to respond and, quote, punish.

Q. What is your opinion regarding the likelihood of coordination among publishers post-merger in this case?

A. I'm going to put aside the idea concerning poaching authors, if I may. All of the other ideas around coordination fall victim to the basic economic principles here. How would rival publishers agree not to compete given the complexity of each acquisition process. So, one example there is the claim that, well, we'll pay advances out according to a different schedule. Well, that just tells you the intervals over which time advances will be paid out. It doesn't tell you how much. So, that's not a good coordination mechanism. Plus, you have other dimensions of the—each acquisition, including bonuses and which rights and so forth. So, the complexity of the deal, the multiplicity of dimensions makes both picking a coordination mechanism, but also finding ways—finding out whether a party is deviating from the mechanism. This is one of the most opaque industries in terms of acquisition processes to understand why did somebody win, why did somebody lose. And it's completely insufficient to say that, well, eventually the identity of the winner is known. But again, I agree, at some point that's revealed, but that is not sufficient to identify a coordination mechanism of monitoring and detection and punishment.

THE COURT: Can I ask a question. Could there be coordination on other parameters? Like, there's certain industry standards in terms of like royalty rates, for example, or the payout structure of a contract, it's less desirable for the authors to be paid in quarters versus thirds, things of that nature? Could there be coordination in things like that as opposed to in individual auctions?

THE WITNESS: The potential for coordination on those dimensions seems to me to be zero, because there are too many dimensions on which to compete. So, the payout schedule doesn't tell you how much. So, somebody could adhere to a changed payout schedule but still compete for authors. And it's all about is there an effective mechanism that actually results in a bottom-line reduction in competition.

THE COURT: So, it's not clear how something like that could play out in terms of them detecting it in each other and enforcing it?

THE WITNESS: Correct.

THE COURT: Because it does seem like there are some certain things that the industry tacitly all kind of agrees on, which is like they don't want the audio rights split off from the general rights, and everybody uses that same contract term. Do you see what I'm saying? And nobody wants to deviate from that, there seems to be like an industry standard.

THE WITNESS: But that—sorry, Your Honor.

THE COURT: Go ahead. So, if you wanted to compete with somebody, you might say, okay, I'll unhook the audio rights, but nobody does it.

THE WITNESS: Fair point, Your Honor. But there's so many other ways to compete, that what good does it do the rivals to agree on audio rights—we want those bundled—when it doesn't limit competition on many other dimensions, most important of which is advances.

THE COURT: So, it doesn't matter in terms of merger analysis from your perspective if they coordinate on one aspect of contract negotiations as long as they can still compete freely on other aspects?

THE WITNESS: I think Your Honor's question helps, because you can in theory think of a coordination mechanism, but you have to ask the second question: Does it actually result in a net reduction in competition. And you're right, that's the point I'm making.

THE COURT: I see.

BY MR. OPPENHEIMER:

Q. And why would it be difficult for publishers in this business to coordinate on advances specifically?

A. Advances vary all over the place. And if the idea was, well, we all want to cut our advances 10 percent, that wouldn't tell you what that number should be. So even if you find out what the advance is, that doesn't tell you whether the parties are adhering to some mechanism.

Q. Do you understand Dr. Hill to have made a prediction on how likely it would be for there to be coordination post-merger?

A. I don't believe so. I don't think he has an opinion about the likelihood, the baseline likelihood.

Q. And Your Honor referred to industry standards. Are industry standards, or common practices, evidence of coordination?

A. No. Oftentimes you see contracts spelling out particular terms in a somewhat standard way, but there's still many dimensions of competition.

MR. OPPENHEIMER: Your Honor, I have no further questions at this time. I'd reserve for redirect. I would make a quick proffer on his testimony on efficiencies: That he would testify as indicated in his reports on the merger specificity issues and the pass-through issues that are the subject of those reports.

THE COURT: I understand, thank you.

MR. OPPENHEIMER: Thank you, Your Honor.

THE COURT: I have a question that I've been thinking about, and that is: Is it a concern to you, the relative size of the different competitors? Because it seems to me that your analysis very much focuses on the number of competitors. At some point, does it become important how big the largest competitor is? Like, if you have one player who dwarfs all the other players, but there's still lots of players, does that matter?

THE WITNESS: So, this ties into condition on the threshold and whether you use one or two. Putting that aside, I understand the question. Higher shares goes back to, I think, your earlier question about if the shares get high, won't the probability that I was referring to of being 12 percent, won't that become 15 percent or won't that become 20 percent. I'll pause there and see if I'm on track.

THE COURT: Yes, yes. I guess that is related, yes.

THE WITNESS: Right. So, my view on that is, yes, there is a general relationship out there between concentration of market shares and lessening of competition. But it's not a relationship that simply always goes up every step of the way. And given the number of competitors, I do think that's important. Given the competition within the Big 5 now, Big 4 going forward, given the potential role for entry and imprint competition, we're not at a point where that relationship changes.

THE COURT: So, let's take a hypothetical. What if the top industry player had 90 percent of the market share, but there are lots and lots of competitors comprising the other 10 percent. What would that do to your analysis?

THE WITNESS: So that's a really good example. Because you look back and you say, well, look at Tesla, they had a very big share for a while. Now they've got competition from Ford. Go back and say Netflix, they had a really big share. Now they've got competition, and they're being forced to change their fundamental business model to be ads. So you have to go beyond share—that's what economics teaches us—and look at the number and their capacity to compete over time. So, 90 percent share sounds very dramatic. But even in that case I would ask: Well, who are they; do they have the capacity to compete and constrain.

THE COURT: The other 10 percent, you mean?

THE WITNESS: Yes, Your Honor.

THE COURT: And so, in your view, the size in itself is not a problem, it depends really on what's going on with the 10 percent, not with the 90 percent? Because if the 10 percent contains people who can constrain and compete, then it doesn't matter to you if somebody has 90 percent or even 95 percent?

THE WITNESS: Well, a merger that went to 90 percent, of course you'd want to take a very close look at. Because that puts much more of a burden on the remaining 10 percent, whoever represents that market share. But I don't see that as an issue here for the reasons I mentioned. We're not at that level.

We've got imprint competition; competition within the Big 5, very reputable; non-Big 5, with capacity and a demonstrated ability to win. They are numerous. Plus, you have authors who are represented by agents who can adjust acquisition processes.

THE COURT: I understand that. I'm just trying to isolate size, and does it matter or not. And I think you're saying given the size of where we're at now, it doesn't matter here. But I'm just trying to figure out, at some level it does matter is what you're saying, because it does put pressure on the remaining competitors to constrain a bigger, I guess, leader in the industry.

THE WITNESS: This goes back, Your Honor, to studies that I looked at when I was young about concentration and price. And there was a big debate about it, but some economists, at least, came to the conclusion about, well, there's this broad relationship over time, across industries whereby if you increase concentration, you get price increases. That's—that whole body of literature has been pretty much—I don't want to say debunked, but it's given way to a recognition that you have to look at this more carefully and see if there is a lessening of competition in a particular setting. And that broad-based relationship may or may not hold. So I wouldn't want to have a merger go to 90 or 95 percent and rely necessarily on numbers in capacity, in imprint competition and so forth. But right now, we've got a lot of competition. I don't see that changing post-merger.

THE COURT: Okay, thank you. Any cross?

MR. SCHWARZ: Yes, Your Honor.

THE COURT: It's time for binders?

MR. SCHWARZ: Yeah, well, I can keep moving in the meantime, if that doesn't bother Your Honor.

THE COURT: Sure.

MR. SCHWARZ: I can do something with respect to a demonstrative while we're passing those things out to economize time.

CROSS-EXAMINATION
BY MR. SCHWARZ:

Q. Would you go back to your demonstrative charts, and particularly to pages 28 and 29.

A. Yes, Mr. Schwarz.

Q. And I should have said good afternoon, Dr. Snyder. We've met before.

A. That's okay.

Q. I apologize for that. If you would actually take a look at 29. There you picked as your middle section, or chart if you will, the 50 to 999,000 column. Do you see that?

A. Yes.

Q. Are you aware that Dr. Hill testified that he saw a difference in the level of competition and competitor shares here at the $150,000 level, not the $50,000 level?

A. And when you—just to clarify, you're asking about $150,000 all the way up?

Q. Yes, sir.

A. So one threshold, one cutoff, yes.

Q. That was a measure where he started to see a change; are you aware of that?

A. Yes, I do recall that.

Q. So is there a particular reason, then, why you picked 50 as your starting point instead of 150?

A. No, I wanted to investigate, you know, just the question of whether there is a unique point where you see a change in market shares, which I understood to be one of his core arguments. And 50 is where one sees it. So this seems like an important observation.

Q. You made a point about the fact that the red competitor there—I won't name it, started to have a big increase at $50,000. And I—let me finish my question. And I wonder how you can possibly conclude that, when it could just as easily be that in fact nothing changed for that particular competitor until you got to 100 or 125. How do I know where the break starts within that $900,000 category?

A. Yes, I understand. The point is not to say this is the magic number, but simply to say $250,000 buttressed by observed changes in market share is arbitrary, because we see it at 50.

Q. Is it arbitrary to try to find the place, roughly speaking, where competition seems to change for authors? Is that arbitrary, or is that what we're supposed to be doing here?

A. Well, that goes to a lot of issues about whether there is something different about the anticipated top selling authors, and where to look for the break. I don't want to give you my full testimony all over again, but Dr. Hill did look at different thresholds. My understanding, my recollection is that he always looked at them with just one threshold at a time. He didn't consider the question of whether it might be two. And I think it is relevant to explore that issue, especially because when you do, you can isolate the roughly 230 authors annually in the top category and pose the question that I posed, which is: Yes, they can be identified, but can they be targeted.

Q. Well, I was asking about the 150 category and up, and why you picked 50, so let's look at another document which we'll pass out, with Your Honor's permission?

THE COURT: Yes.

BY MR. SCHWARZ:

Q. PX-960, which is already admitted into evidence I'm told. You may have recognized this because it was in Dr. Hill's original report, Dr. Snyder?

A. Yes.

Q. You see there that he did do a chart at 150 and up?

A. Yes. I just would just make it clear, these are all a single threshold and up.

Q. That's correct, I understand. That's what we're trying to find here. And you see that at that point, you start to see—from that point up, going up to—and he did $1,000,000 and up as well, all the way up to $1,000,000 and up, that the percentages become relatively stable at that point; would you agree?

A. If you use a single threshold at these various cutoffs, and you're asking just look left to right, there's a fair amount of stability, yes.

Q. Indeed, perhaps most importantly, there's stability with respect to the non-Big 5, and it is at the—I believe it's a public number, at roughly the 10 percent level. In fact, it goes down as you go up to $1,000,000.

A. When you start at 150 and use a single cutoff, the answer's yes.

Q. Now let's go back to your demonstrative, page 29, which Mr. Oppenheimer asked you about to some extent. I just want to—sorry, it's 28. I meant 28, not 29.

A. Yes.

THE COURT: I'm sorry, where is this?

MR. SCHWARZ: In the demonstrative set that Mr. Oppenheimer was using, Your Honor, the 85 pages. It's on the screen, too.

THE COURT: Oh, okay.

MR. SCHWARZ: And we may have called it 963-A, I'm not sure. Didn't you add an A to it?

MR. OPPENHEIMER: I may have.

BY MR. SCHWARZ:

Q. In any event, 963. There—and you may recall I asked you this in the deposition. At the below 250 threshold, the non-Big 5 have a 45 percent share, and the—at the above 250 threshold, they have a 9 percent share, correct, do you see that?

A. Correct.

Q. And the question I asked you was: Do you not take any significance from that difference? Doesn't that require an explanation?

A. I think this goes to Your Honor's question about do the market shares at the high end tell us something. And I think I said, yes, there's a comfort level among potential bestselling authors with the Big 5. It doesn't mean, however, that those individual Big 5 competitors don't face a lot of competition. I believe they do.

Q. Well, I think I was getting at a little bit different point, which is when I asked you that question in your deposition, I was trying to get at why you thought there was this distinction. And you answered size and reputation. Do you remember that? Or if you don't, I can get it out.

A. No, I believe that's—I do recall that. They're bigger, they have more resources. Plus, as I testified earlier today, they have reputation, because they've been in business a long time and there's repetition. So those two things generate reputation.

Q. We'll come back to reputation in a second. But if their size is important here, why don't you see that reflected in the zero to 250 category?

A. There was competition throughout. The fact that there are these other—you're talking about the non-Big 5 having a bigger share?

Q. Yes, sir. I'm trying to get at why do you think the non-Big 5 have 45 percent of the below 250 category. And I don't understand how size doesn't impact that category as well—

A. I'm sorry.

Q. There must be something else, isn't there?

A. I agree, there's more non-Big 5 competition at the lower end.

Q. And I'm trying to get you to help me—if you have a view, if you don't, tell us, why that is.

A. It reflects the fact that there are larger numbers competing at the lower end. It's not necessarily at the 250 and below, but this is where the cut is. And when you go above, you have—even though you have larger—you still have a large number, over 30—and that number includes the Big 5, and it's increasing, but they win less. They have fewer resources.

Q. Isn't risk and capital—risk of losing capital a major factor in that explanation?

A. I understand that argument, and I think Dr. Hill identified that as one of his barriers to entry. But I don't believe that it is here. When I look at the empirical analysis that shows the willingness of even small publishers to enter into million-dollar contracts, I don't think that's what's going on here. I think the Big 5 have more resources.

Q. Yes, I agree with that. The Big 5 do have more resources, don't they. So, let's go back to reputation. Do you have any view on how long it takes to build up a reputation for success in the—let's call it the best seller category, since you don't like the word anticipated?

A. That's a good question.

Q. I try.

A. Of course it takes time to build up reputation, if the means by which you build up reputation is having observations in the marketplace where you're buying a lot over a long period of time. As I said, one simple way to think about how one can—not the only way—build reputation is to do more and win more, and then you build up a reputation. However, there are, as I said earlier, highly reputable publishers like Norton—I don't think anybody would say they don't have a strong reputation. But there are also—and this is I think instructive, there are alternative ways to assure the market that you're going to follow through. And the reputation may not come from that long history, but it may be individual editors who go off and start a new publisher, which has happened.

Q. You mentioned Norton—you've mentioned them more than once. Do you happen to know how many trade books they publish a year?

A. I don't, but—I'm not sure if I'm allowed to say this, but they were very well represented on the list of authors that—

Q. We'll get there, we'll get there. I just asked you a question if you knew how many trade books they published a year, and I—

A. Fair enough. I don't. I mean, their share is low. As I recall, in the proposed segment it's maybe 1 percent, which would correspond to—

Q. And has that changed significantly in the last five or 10 years, as far as you know?

A. I haven't studied the time series there.

Q. Would you—I'm not sure, Your Honor, if I'm allowed to say the number, though it's in the deposition. But would you accept the notion that it's less than 200 a year in trade books?

A. In all trade books?

Q. Norton.

A. I wouldn't be surprised. I don't have that number.

THE COURT: Was that 1 percent of the 250 and above market or of the entire market?

MR. SCHWARZ: Well, I'm making up a number that's higher than it actually is. It's like 200 out of 10,000.

THE COURT: Okay.

MR. SCHWARZ: For all trade books.

MR. OPPENHEIMER: I'm sorry, Your Honor. I don't want to quarrel with a hypothetical. There's no foundation.

MR. SCHWARZ: Well, I'm happy to do that later. I'm trying to avoid not putting the number into the record.

THE COURT: That's fine.

THE WITNESS: I'm sorry to interrupt, Your Honor, I don't know if I'm allowed to clarify what I meant by 1 percent?

THE COURT: Sure. What did you mean?

THE WITNESS: I meant it in the 250k and above.

THE COURT: Okay.

BY MR. SCHWARZ:

Q. We're going to look at your chart on that, so rest assured we'll come to that. Now, I want to start in a little bit more orderly fashion with the market and market definition, okay. We'll try to go through the normal steps of the way at least the government economists normally think of things, market, and then market share, and then harm, et cetera. Do I—I'm not sure I know the answer to this question actually, even after all this time. Do you believe that there is a properly defined market for all publishers of books in the United States, of trade books?

A. I do, yes.

Q. Did you do a hypothetical monopsonist test to determine that that was the case?

A. No, but I found Dr. Hill's HMTs to indicate that self-publishing was not a relevant alternative at many different advance levels. The test works virtually down to zero.

Q. I think what you're saying is you accepted his HMT, at least for that broad market?

A. His HMT yields the insight that when you're looking at all trade books, self-publishing is not a relevant competitive constraint.

Q. So I think you've said that you accept the existence of the—what we'll call the broad market,

because that's what you call it, correct?
A. Yes.
Q. And did you attempt to do an HMT with respect to the Government's market of $250,000 and up advances for trade books?
A. So I just have to make sure I understand. You're asking me—
Q. Did you do an HMT for the Government's alleged ATS market?
A. So all trade books, but above $250,000?
Q. Yes.
THE COURT: So what do you mean by HMT?
BY MR. SCHWARZ:
Q. I'm sorry, I'm lapsing into lingo. It's hypothetical monopsonist test, Your Honor.
A. I did not do it, I saw Dr. Hill did it. I don't have any disagreement with his calculation.
Q. Okay. And but you do have a quarrel with his claiming that what we would call—the Government would call a sub market exists for ATS trade books with respect to the purchase of trade manuscripts at $250,000 and up?
A. Yes.
Q. If—let me give you a hypothetical so we can see if we can figure this out together. If there were only one publisher who, for whatever reasons—legal, economic, the only one who was willing to pay $250,000 or more for a manuscript, would you consider that likely to cause competitive harm to the authors trying to sell their books to that publisher?
A. Unless there is extremely ready entry, if a firm has a hundred percent, I would expect them to be able to exercise monopsony power given the fact that self-publishing is not a relevant constraint.
Q. And while we're at it, you mentioned ready entry. Do you know what the merger guidelines discuss as being sufficiently ready to count for purposes of entry?
A. I've read that part, but I can't quote it to you.
Q. Does two to three years sound right?
A. That sounds right.
Q. By the way, on page 22 of your demonstrative, you have a 28 percent average market share—I don't know if I'm supposed to say it out loud, but I just did. A market share there which is for an average over that three-year period. Do you see that?
A. Yes, and that's in the broad market.
Q. Right. And do you happen to remember—because you did have a chart on this in your rebuttal report, what the number was for 2021?
A. By itself, no, I don't remember.
Q. Over 30 percent, does that ring a bell?
A. I don't remember. I don't dispute that number.
Q. I believe if you—I think you have up there—you may have a hard time finding it amidst all that, but page 87 of your rebuttal report has the Exhibit 7.2 where you break it out by year.
A. Do you have a page number on that, Mr. Schwarz?
Q. Yes, 87.
A. Yes, for the combined parties, it's 30.6.
Q. In 2021?
A. Correct.
Q. And it has been going up, then, over those three years?
A. Yes.
Q. Do you understand there to be—this relates to a number of different analyses that both you and Dr. Hill did. Is there a difference between a count of contracts above $250,000 and titles above $250,000?
A. It's messy. The fact is—
Q. Why is it messy? I'm just asking you is there a difference.
A. Well, there is a difference sometimes. Sometimes the contract only covers one title, other times the contract covers multiple titles. And it's not always apparent what's going on. And where a contract covers

more than one title, do you take an average advance. Are there data around specific books getting something other than the average. That's why I said it's messy.

Q. Okay. So just—I'd just like to clarify the issue, and then ask another question. If—when we count by contracts—or when you did, let's just speak about yourself. When you say you do a contract count, do you count a contract where there may be two or more books where the total payment is $250,000 and up?

A. So two specific analyses come to mind. One is the maximum dollar contract where I had the identity of a large number of publishers entering into contracts above a million dollars. I did not identify whether those were multiple titles or not. So that's one. Both—I'm trying to remember, I was about to remember the other one. Oh, the time series on output by PRH before the 2013 merger, and then continuing, that increase in output was 13 percent based on contracts.

Q. Okay, thank you. I'm trying to get at a different point, so let me ask a better question. If—when you use the word by contracts—you know, in other words, you're categorizing this by contracts above 250, does that mean you include any contract, whether it's one or more than one book, where the total advance is 250 or more; and when you say by title, you mean one book getting an advance of 250 or more?

A. Yes. And I think you'll see that in Dr. Hill's reports as well.

Q. Okay. I just want to be sure that that's—so when we all, including the Court, look at these, we need to be careful to look whether it's you're saying by contract or by title, because you can get a different answer.

A. I don't think you need to be all that careful. Maybe you can convince me otherwise. The data are messy, and the messiness goes in both directions. I haven't found this issue to be something that leads to results that differ.

Q. Well, let me point out one that remains confusing to me. On page—excuse me, paragraph 131 of your rebuttal report—that's page 92. There you say—

A. I'm sorry, you just have to slow down a little bit.

Q. You probably can answer this question without looking, but go ahead.

A. So rebuttal report, page—

Q. 92, paragraph 131.

A. I'm sorry, repeat that.

Q. Paragraph 131, page 92. The question will be—

A. Okay, it starts on page 91. Thank you

Q. Well, the question—all I'm asking you—so just I think if I tell you the question, it will short circuit this. I think there you say that there are about 1,200 anticipated top selling books acquired each year?

A. Yes.

Q. Now, on page 120 of that same report, Exhibit 9.2, you have a line there that shows the averages of 884 for the two merging parties, and 993 for the rest. And my math—which this is about as far as I can go, is 1,875 total on an annual basis. I'm just wondering there—I noticed that you talk about acquired from contracts, so I'm just wondering, that's a pretty big spread, and I'm trying to understand the difference.

A. So which two numbers are you adding up?

Q. 884.

A. Yes.

Q. Yearly average of the two merging parties, and 991. That's a lot different than 1,200?

A. It is.

Q. Any idea why?

A. Not sitting here right now.

Q. Okay. But there you're talking about contracts, right, that's your title?

A. Yes.

Q. So might part of the answer, at least, be that there may be multiple titles in each contract?

A. I don't know

Q. Okay. While you're in that area there, paragraph 131 of your rebuttal report, you talk about something we've mentioned several times which is ATS books, the market the Government's talking about, constitutes 2 percent of the 58,000 titles published in your broad market annually. It's towards the end of that paragraph.

A. Yes, I see it.

Q. Do you have any idea—perhaps that may have been in one of your charts that went into evidence on your direct, what percentage of the total amount of advances annually that 2 percent constitutes?

A. Yes.

Q. How much?

A. I'm doing this from recall, but that was I believe number 28 in my deck.

Q. Okay, that's pretty good. Let's take a look.

A. And this of course, again, is Dr. Hill's report on the top.

Q. No, I'm sorry, I don't think you're—if I might be so bold to suggest, that's not my question. I was asking you how much of the total number of—the dollar amount of advances are the 2 percent. Is that—oh, I'm sorry, you're right. I apologize, you're correct, it's at the bottom there. You were going to say, I interrupted you?

A. So, in rough numbers, the total advance dollars across the two categories, which cover everything—

THE COURT: I'm sorry, I don't know what document you're looking at.

MR. SCHWARZ: It's the bottom of page 28, Your Honor, of his demonstrative now on the screen.

THE COURT: Oh, okay.

MR. SCHWARZ: I believe he's referring to the bottom numbers, not the chart itself.

THE COURT: Okay.

BY MR. SCHWARZ:

Q. Go ahead.

A. Yes. So, at the bottom, the total advances across the two categories that cover all trade books is 4.4 billion—as I recall, it's 4.4 billion plus, but let's just call it 4.4 billion. And the right-hand side accounts for 3.2 billion. And this is over a three-year time period. And that's—as I recall, that's pretty consistent with some of the numbers that came in early in the trial to the effect that the above $250,000 advance segment accounts for 70 plus percent of the total.

Q. I'm sorry, I got distracted. Did you give a percentage in your answer?

A. I can do it if you'd let me, but I think it's above 70 percent.

Q. Yeah, yeah, it looks about like three-quarters there, but okay. At any rate, that's fine, thank you.

A. I'm sorry, Mr. Schwarz, I just meant—I don't want to slow you down, but it may be that the lower end isn't completely inclusive. But it's over 70 percent.

Q. Okay, thank you. Do you have any idea about the—if you cut those 58,000 volumes a year, how many books—let's say half of those—the bottom half of those books, how many they sell in a given year? So the bottom half.

A. You're talking about the books—

Q. The 58,000 that are published, have you looked at all as to the cut of how many any given slice of that 58,000 sells in a given year?

A. I don't think so, because I also don't recall any evidence on how the books above $250,000 sell downstream. So you're asking—

Q. I was asking you about all 58,000; that's ATS and non-ATS.

A. I'm sorry, what's the question?

Q. Well, let me just ask it straight out. Would it surprise you to know that half of those 58,000 books sell fewer than one dozen books?

A. My book was in that category. Sorry.

Q. And if I had more time, I'd ask you to name the other 24,000 and a half there—excuse me, 29,000, there's my math. Would it surprise you to know that 90 percent sell fewer than 2,000 books?

A. I didn't study it.

Q. You just don't know?

A. I didn't study it. I don't think there's any evidence on the record. I would not be surprised.

Q. You have a chart that I have elsewhere, but I think you had it in your demonstrative, so I'd prefer to use that. I've found it on page 41 of your demonstrative.

A. Yes.

Q. And there you put the non-Big 5 into—you add it all together?

A. Correct, using Dr. Hill's advance data.

Q. But Dr. Hill didn't add it all together, did he?

A. Well, I think in his market share calculations he did.

Q. Well, in any event, you do that, and you do it in a few other exhibits in your reports, don't you?

A. I do, with the qualification that it's useful for some purposes, but you also have to recognize it's a lot of different publishers.

Q. Do you ever try to calculate the Herfindahl-Hirschman Index for the market that you depict here, 41?

A. Assuming that the non-Big 5 are one firm?

Q. Yes, sir.

A. I did not.

Q. Would it surprise you if I told you that on that basis, they're in the red zone for presumptively illegal?

A. No.

Q. So it's fair to say, you really shouldn't be able to have it both ways, should you, Dr. Snyder? You can't put them together for some purposes you like and not for others, can you?

A. I think it's useful to ask the question as a group how important are they. But it's also important to realize that they don't operate as a group, they have different strategies and they compete against each other.

Q. Well, if you want us to look at it as a group, we can. But then even by your broad market standards, you would have an illegal merger, wouldn't you? Have you looked at that category?

A. Mr. Schwarz, I'm getting confused.

Q. Well, let me—I can take you back to that category. But if you do the—have you done the HHIs for any situation where you put all the non-Big 5 into one category?

A. No. And I might have misspoke, because earlier, a couple of questions ago, you asked me if I had done something. And I thought you were just asking me about the above $250,000.

Q. Well, have you—and I tried to clarify that just now by asking you have you done an HHI calculation for either the broad or the ATS market with all the non-Big 5 put into one bucket?

A. No, I don't believe so.

Q. I don't think you have either. I'm asking you if you did. But my second point is, then, but you do calculate the HHI for the broad market, and you found it to be in the safe zone. And in that situation, you thought it appropriate to separate the non-Big 5, correct?

A. And I think that's right

Q. Correct?

A. Yes.

Q. Yes, that's what you did, okay. Now let's talk about the anticipated top seller market. You don't like the anticipated part of that, because you don't think it's easy to anticipate these top sellers. Is that at least part of what you said?

A. What I said is the issue of the anticipation is a question of by whom and when. Some books can be anticipated, others less reliably.

Q. But at its most basic level, sir, isn't it the fact that every editor, when they put $250,000 on the table, they're anticipating that this book is going to sell, correct?

A. That's my point, that particular—

Q. That's my point. What is your point?

A. Sorry, Mr. Schwarz, a little bit of talking over here.

Q. Sorry.

A. When that particular editor puts $250,000 on the table, it becomes a book in the proposed segment, and it reflects the anticipation by one. That's what we can infer. Maybe there are others who also anticipate it, but we only know one does in your example.

Q. If we have an auction where they're bidding round-robin, we know there will be more than one because they're bidding each other up, correct?

A. Yes. And that's an interesting situation where you go in and you're not sure if others share your view. But the agent may give you feedback that then leads you to think, oh, it's not just me, there's—based on the agent feedback, there are others who also highly value this book.

Q. And to some extent, I may—this may overlap with something I asked you early on in the cross-examination. But if we had a monopsonist publisher in the United States, one buyer, could they target authors who might receive $250,000 or more?

A. I believe they could, subject to what we talked about earlier, entry. The issue that I've raised is for some authors, especially celebrity and authors with track records, recall I said they're the ones who have the leverage. But what you're saying is wait, if it's a monopsonist, single firm, they can't say, well, if you don't pay me what I deserve—and this goes back to Mr. Wylie's testimony, I'm going to go to somebody else. So in your hypothetical, there's nobody else to go to, so that leverage is negated.

Q. Yeah, but aren't you also accepting the notion that the monopsonist can target the anticipated—or I can take out that word, the best seller authors if they want to, because they know what they're going to pay—they, the monopsonist?

A. Yes. I don't have any disagreement with that hypothetical.

Q. The Court asked you a number of questions, and I confess, I came away a bit confused. Do you think that two bidders, two publishers bidding for a book, is sufficient in all circumstances to lead to a competitive outcome?

A. All I can tell you is if you have two bidders, then you have at least one competitive constraint. That's what you know.

Q. But is one competitive constraint as good as two or three or four?

A. Well, agents often go to one.

Q. I asked you a different—I didn't say the word agent. Is three better than two, is four better than three bidders or negotiators or multi-round bidders?

A. Well, I think it is relevant to note that what agents do matters in this industry. So agents—

Q. I'm sure you can be asked that on redirect, but I've asked you a different question.

A. Go ahead, I don't have anything to add.

Q. The question was: Is three bidders better than two when you're trying to sell your manuscript; is four better than three; is five better than four?

A. This is a question out of the 1960s. It's just simply a numbers game—

Q. I was alive then, so go ahead.

A. So was I, I started studying then. We're both dating ourselves. So this—I'm sorry, I have to bring in agents. How many do they actually choose; what is the relevant competitive constraint. So you have to not ask this general question, you have to put it in the industry context.

Q. Okay, fine.

A. And three might be perfectly sufficient. Competition among Hachette, Macmillan, HarperCollins might be absolutely sufficient.

THE COURT: Can you answer the question just generally, in a competitive bidding situation, is three better than two or four better than three?

THE WITNESS: If the agent has many to choose from or—

THE COURT: I'm just saying generally. Not in the book industry, just in any competitive bidding situation, is it better to have more bidders?

THE WITNESS: I can't answer that question without looking at the specific competitive conditions.

BY MR. SCHWARZ:

Q. Well, suppose I'm an agent who would love to have five competitors, and I end up only having four. Would you grant in that circumstance that I might be unhappy with this merger?

A. But there's over 30 who compete for these contracts.

Q. But I want somebody who has a great reputation for success.

A. And post-merger there will be four, right, plus others like Norton and S&G. And I think that's enough, yes.

Q. Yeah, but you told me the agent is the one who has good control over this, and I'm the agent and I want five.

A. There are five—

Q. Are you telling me I don't know what I'm doing?

A. There's going to be imprint competition post-merger. We have competition among the other Big 5, plus others. So, you're changing, I think, your hypothetical to a world where there's only five options. Is that right?

Q. Five with a great reputation for success, yeah.

A. There's—and there's fierce competition among Penguin Random House; there's competition within Penguin Random House; you've got Hachette, Macmillan, HarperCollins. My answer is that's sufficient.

Q. So—

A. It's not limited, the competition is not limited to that.

Q. Implicitly what you just said is that you know better than the agent, even though you've been saying the agent knows better than you?

A. Well, some agents choose one, some agents enlist many. I think the situations and the approach by agents vary. I think you were asking me—I thought, in a more general sense, and I don't think your general description applies.

Q. Okay, we'll move on. I think you said, both in your report and on your direct, that you really hadn't seen a market or a sub market, if you will, defined by price—or at least not exclusively by price?

A. Yes, without other indicators.

Q. I'm not sure what that means, but let me explore it in that regard. I believe you're familiar with the case of Federal Trade Commission vs. Qualcomm?

A. Yes.

Q. You were a testifying expert in that case?

A. Yes.

Q. And do you remember there was a broad market there—to use the terminology of this case, CDMA modem chips?

A. I do recall there was a broad market.

Q. CDMA is a code for some type of chip, right, some standard? We don't have to get into that, but just so the record's clear.

A. Yes.

Q. And do you remember there was a sub market that the Court found there?

A. Yes, for—yes, I do. I can describe it if you'd like, but yes.

Q. Well, I'll say it, and you tell me if I'm wrong. It's premium LTE modem chips, a subset of the CDMA chips?

A. That subset of modem chips had superior performance characteristics used in high end smartphones.

Q. I'm just trying to get the name of it out there. Premium LTE modem chips. By the way, this is at 411 F.Supp.3d 658. It is the Northern District of California, 2019, bench trial. And do you know how premium was defined so that—in other words, how did the Court define premium LTE modem chips?

A. It wasn't only by price, because it was designated as a subset based—my recollection, based on LTE. And there were performance differences for that segment compared to the broader market. And then, the Court also recognized that these typically sell for above a certain amount. I can't remember if it was 400 per chip or 250, I simply don't remember. But there was then, conditional on that, a price cutoff.

Q. Well, I believe it was defined as chips that go into $400 or higher handsets.

A. Thank you.

Q. Is that right?

A. You're refreshing my recollection, I agree with that.

Q. So there was a dollar definition of a sub market of CDMA chips that the Court found, and it was a case in which you testified—not for the plaintiff I'll grant you, but you're aware of that case?

A. I don't accept your characterization, however. My recollection is that the LTE chips had different performance features which made them attractive for smartphone—high end smartphones. And then based on that, it used a price cutoff, not for the chip, but for the phone. So the use of a price cutoff was conditioned on other factors that distinguished the product.

Q. But $399 LTE modem chips were not in the market, and $401 ones were?

A. Given that you've refreshed my recollection, it was based on the smartphone, not the chip.

Q. You get my point, there was an arbitrary cut: 399 out, 401 in?

A. Conditional on these being higher performance chips, and designated as LTE within the category—the broader category.

Q. And do you know the Ninth Circuit affirmed with respect to that market definition? I know they reversed on other grounds.

(Brief interruption by the court reporter)

MR. OPPENHEIMER: Your Honor, I think this is argument, and also verging on just calling for a legal opinion. He's testified as to the factual basis.

THE COURT: I'm going to overrule the objection, just probing the expert's knowledge.

BY MR. SCHWARZ:

Q. I'm simply asking you whether or not that market definition, based on price, was affirmed by the Ninth Circuit, if you know?

A. I'm just repeating the same point. I apologize, I don't agree with your characterization based on price. You're leaving out, again, the higher performance features of the LTE chips. And conditional on that, the Court did—my recollection, which goes to the do I recall this being approved by the Court or used by the Court, yes.

Q. By the way, Dr. Snyder, did the Court find your testimony to be unreliable in that case?

A. I don't recall.

Q. You don't recall, okay. Well, I'll refresh your recollection: "Snyder did not even evaluate Qualcomm's conduct, so the Court finds that Dr. Snyder's opinions are not reliable." That's at page 820. That doesn't ring a bell?

A. It rings a bell insofar as my assignment was different. It wasn't to evaluate Qualcomm's conduct. I don't recall—I don't think I've read that particular sentence. I have no reason to dispute it.

Q. And I think you did also—while we're talking about this subject, you did early on in your direct testimony reference the Sitts vs. Dairy Farmers case in Vermont?

A. Yes.

Q. And that was—happened to be a monopsony case—

A. Yes.

Q.—involving, I think, milk?

A. Dairy farmers.

Q. Well, and their milk, yeah.

A. And their other products.

Q. Okay. And that—in an opinion—the relevant opinion I'm talking about, although there are several others, is a 2020–1 trade cases, paragraph 81276; also, 220 WL 3467993. There, that judge, in what would have been a jury trial, also found that your testimony, quote, does not fit the facts of this case, and your testimony was not permitted before the jury?

A. I don't know what that means. I can tell you what I understand the judge's objection to be to the work that I did. And it was on the identification of potential options as opposed to doing more work to find out whether a particular option was really available.

Q. Can we look at your—I guess what you call your waterfall. And I guess we can just look at your demonstrative. Page 16, Your Honor.

THE COURT: I just don't know where these demonstratives are.

MR. SCHWARZ: I don't know where yours are, but that was what Mr. Oppenheimer was using frequently. So we can probably also put it on the screen.

BY MR. SCHWARZ:

Q. So if I understand this chart correctly, you were able to discern 150 auctions with multiple bidders

where you could determine the runner up; is that correct?
A. That's correct.
Q. And there were 149 single bidders contracts—excuse me, acquisitions where because they were single bidder auctions you couldn't, of course, determine the runner up, correct?
A. Correct, there was no known identified runner up.
Q. I'm not arguing, I'm just trying to lay the foundation. And of the 150 multi-bidder with known runner up, you found 96 that were won by PRH or Simon & Schuster, correct?
A. Yes.
Q. That's almost two-thirds. That's quite a high percentage, isn't it?
A. Yes.
Q. And of those 96, S&S or PRH, depending on which one of those two won, the other one was runner up, correct?
A. I just want to make sure I understand which—
Q. Twenty-one out of 96, I'm just reading off of your chart.
A. Yes.
Q. And by my math, that means 22 percent of the time the merging parties were runner up to each other?
A. No.
Q. Okay. What's wrong with my math?
A. Well, you're just focusing on the multi-bid.
Q. I know, but you can't—I don't—I have no idea about the other ones. I'm only looking at the ones that you can identify the runner up, correct? If I look at the other ones, why would I count them?
A. There's no known runner up.
Q. So is that a penalty for this argument? Does that mean we can't look at the places where we do know something?
A. I guess it's a matter of interpretation. I see this as—I understand your point, that in a multi-bidders context where we have a known runner up, your numbers are right. All I'm saying is there are these other contracts where you also don't have a known runner up.
Q. So you spent a lot of time with Mr. Oppenheimer talking about the fact that PRH and S&S are seldom runners up when the other wins—seldom in terms of a low number. I think you even said 6 or 7 percent ultimately as a number, right?
A. Yes.
Q. Okay. And you spent a lot of time telling us that only runners up count for meaningful competition, right?
A. That's right. And you can estimate that by market shares, and it's 12 percent.
Q. So I'm looking at what I can know—I can't know what I can't know. But with respect to what I know, you tell me there are 96 occasions when I can know something, right? And 21 of those times the other party's a runner up. So isn't that 22 percent a meaningful number?
A. Well, there's so many different things to say. Your calculation is right. I think the fact that there's not a known runner up in 149 others I think is relevant. We can disagree. I also think that we have to keep in mind that PRH and S&S are over represented here. We have to keep in mind that in 47 percent of the time, when one wins, the other doesn't even bid.
Q. Well, if we were an all-knowing agent who handled all the single bidders, and we—it's just as possible that in every one of those 149 occasions, S&S was runner up to PRH or vice versa; you don't know and I don't know, right?
A. In those situations—
Q. Right, am I right? You don't know and I don't know, yes or no?
A. I'll give you a yes or no. In those situations, one cannot know, so that's the simple fact. You can't identify them.
Q. And so are you in the business of trying to count things that you can't figure out the—that you don't know the answer to?

A. Well, if you can't know it, they're not runner up

Q. I don't—how can you possibly say that under oath? They could be the runner up, you don't have any idea, do you?

A. You don't know.

Q. Correct.

A. If you want to use—excuse me, if you want to use market share, then you could apply 12 percent to that.

Q. No, I'm trying to use your numbers, which you tell me are what I should look at. And when you came up with that 6 or 7 percent number, you were including the 149 in your denominator, weren't you?

A. That's correct.

Q. Thank you. Dr. Snyder, would you please look at page 43 of your demonstrative—I'm sorry, 42, 42.

A. Okay.

Q. There you say that 23 percent is the share of contracts with non-Big 5—I assume that means publishers, as winners or runners up in the ATS market?

A. Based on the agency data, yes.

Q. I'm trying to understand how you calculated that. If I—is this related to the data on—in your waterfall, page I think it's 15 of the demonstrative?

A. It's not reflected in that particular waterfall, but water can flow in a lot of different categories. But it's basically a reflection of how often these other publishers win, plus, as indicated in the data, how often are they runner up.

Q. Let me understand what it's a percentage of. Am I correct in—let's assume I'm making up a number, a hundred occasions that you're looking at where you can determine the runner up—I guess we know what the answer was, 150. Is that the same data we're looking at that's in your waterfall, 150 examples?

A. I believe so. I can check. I believe that's right.

Q. It's on page—just so the Court understands and the record is clear, we're looking at the waterfall on page, what, 15? No, 16. So it's the green rectangle there with 150. Is that the number of known multi-bidders with known runners up, I should say?

A. Yes.

Q. So that would be the denominator, if you will?

A. Yes.

Q. And, again, my arithmetic is not great, but if I understand this, in theory then there could be as many—if the non-Big 5 publishers were, purely hypothetically, to have been the winner and runner up on every one of those 150, you could score 300, right?

A. Two hundred I think. Maybe I'm not getting your question.

Q. Two hundred—

THE COURT: Can you explain that, Mr. Schwarz?

MR. SCHWARZ: Can I explain it?

THE COURT: Your question, I'm not sure I understand it.

BY MR. SCHWARZ:

Q. My question was if there are 150 known occasions where we can identify who the runner up and the winner were in your sample, then there are in theory, at least in terms of data points, as many as 300 winners, so to speak, if you will?

A. So you're confusing—

THE COURT: Oh, you're saying winner and runner up?

MR. SCHWARZ: Yes, Your Honor.

THE COURT: So two spots–

MR. SCHWARZ: Yes, I'm sorry.

THE COURT:—in 150. I got it, okay.

MR. SCHWARZ: It took me a long time to have this explained to me myself.

THE WITNESS: And if you can convert it to percentages, it would be 200 percent would be the max.

BY MR. SCHWARZ:

Q. Exactly. So is it the—if, if I look at the waterfall there, you have nine of those 150 were won by the non-Big 5—Demonstrative 16?

A. Yes.

Q. So that—then what I'm struggling to understand is how many times did the non-Big 5 have to be runner up in order to get to 23 percent?

A. More often than they won, and you see that in other data.

Q. Okay. But can you give us a precise number if we know the denominator and we know the methodology and we know one of the two variables? We know the nine. We know the denominator is 150. Is it—are we talking about 14 or are we talking about—

A. I can do it, but just an interim step here. The denominator would be 300.

Q. Okay.

A. Not 150.

Q. Great.

A. And then they win nine times, and then your—the percent calculation is 23 percent. So, we need roughly 69 total in the numerator, 69. And if I've got my calculation right, that means they won nine times and they were runner up 60. I'm sorry, I did that incorrectly. It has to be 35. Will that get us there?

Q. I have no idea.

A. Hold on a sec. The numerator has to be 46. Nine times the one, and that means 37 times they need to be runner up. So nine plus 37 equals 46—I'm sorry, I'm still doing it incorrectly, because the—I was closer the first time. The denominator's 300.

Q. So my rough math tells me you've got to get up to 60 something to get 23 percent.

A. Well, 60 additional times roughly. So their runner-upness, if I could coin a new phrase, exceeds the frequency with which they win.

THE COURT: I'm sorry, that's 60 times out of 150?

THE WITNESS: Well, the denominator now is 300. So it's total count.

THE COURT: I see.

BY MR. SCHWARZ:

Q. There's some multiplication and some division going on here, and I still don't understand it. But it strikes me as extremely unlikely that 60 times out of 150 they were—the non-Big 5 were runners up.

THE COURT: So, I want to make sure I understand this. So, you're saying the non-Big 5 won nine times, and they were runner up 60 times out of the 150 multi-bidder situations where we know the runner up. That seems very high.

THE WITNESS: It is high, Your Honor. But when you look at individual publishers like Norton, which was mentioned earlier, and Astra, their share is 1.1 percent combined. And elsewhere in my analysis, the data indicate that they are winner and runner up roughly 7 percent. So, it does happen when you look at individual publishers.

BY MR. SCHWARZ:

Q. So if you used 150 as your denominator, it would be something like 25 times they were runner up?

A. Well, this is combining them to be 23 percent.

Q. I understand that.

A. So it's nine over 150 plus, I believe, 60 over 150, converted into 300.

Q. All right, let's look at something we perhaps all can understand a little better, which is Exhibit 6.5 of your rebuttal report, which is at page 80.

A. Yes.

Q. So if I read this right, Dr. Snyder—and I'm sure you'll tell me if I don't, this shows that for multi-bidder contracts won by PRH—and now I'm looking at 6.4, putting together all 74 contracts, Simon & Schuster was the runner up 20 percent of the time?

A. The right-hand column?

Q. Yes, sir.

A. That's the number I read, 20 percent on a base of 74 contracts.

Q. And this is your chart, right, I mean, this is what you came up with?
A. Yes.
Q. And in 6.5 is the occasions among the multi-bidder contracts over $250,000 in advances where Simon & Schuster won, and depicting who the runner up was. And recognizing it's only 22 contracts, you calculate 27—yeah, 27 percent of the time Penguin Random House is the runner up?
A. Yes.
Q. And if I've got my math right, that means Penguin Random House is the most frequent runner up to Simon & Schuster in all these bids, correct?
A. In those 22, yes.
Q. I mean, I assumed you picked all the ones you could identify?
A. I'm just—yes, in those 22 bids—or contracts.
Q. We'd love to know more, but we don't. As far as you know, we don't know any more than that, correct?
A. Correct.
Q. Because you've told us your concerns about the various other data points we have, the win-loss reports, the editorial reports, et cetera?
A. I'm not sure if there's a question there.
Q. This is the best data you could find, correct?
A. No—
Q. To show runners up?
A. That's not my testimony. I'm okay with diversions according to share; I said that that's okay. But let's look at the other data to see if there could be divergences. And the agency data are one of the two sources where you can get at the runner up, and therefore diversion.
Q. But in terms of actual data showing runners up, this is what we've got that you think is reliable, correct?
A. Well, I think you get insights from Dr. Hill's runner up. But you have to take into account that it's only based on discovery from the two parties.
Q. Okay. This is from discovery from agents, correct?
A. Correct.
Q. This being the charts we just looked at, so the record's clear?
A. Yes.
Q. Did you attempt to put together any model of potential harm in the anticipated top seller market?
A. No
Q. And did you try?
A. No, and I can explain why if you'd like.
Q. I think, as I recall, in your deposition you said you thought about it to some extent, correct?
A. Yes, and I have thought about it.
Q. And did you conclude that it was impossible?
A. I concluded that it was possible to get insights around important elements in a model: Market share, ability and willingness of authors and agents to make substitutions, and the potential supply responses of rivals. Those three components are often input into models that illuminate—hopefully illuminate, the potential exercise of market power. And you see that in the application of models to situations where you're looking at two firms that are merging, a group of firms that are potentially a cartel, and then you take into account those competitive forces. But I did not do a model.
Q. Well, let me see if I can get at this another way. To the extent that you could—you've thought about it, did you come up with any potential way to do a model that might be able to be done given the data we have?
A. Two things. One is, as I've testified, one of the real problems in modeling this industry is the role of agents, for example, in selecting among the mix of acquisitions. I couldn't figure out how to do that. But the other thing I would just say is I stopped thinking about it in any active way, because my empirical analyses didn't indicate that there would be harm. And having considered Dr. Hill's model, I didn't—I

was not persuaded that his SSA model yielded any relevant insights because of reasons that I've testified to.

Q. When you say your empirical analyses formed part of that conclusion, I'm not sure I understand what empirical analyses you're referring to.

A. All of the empirical work I did on the mix of acquisitions used by agents; the willingness of authors and agents to choose non-Big 5 publishers; the non-quantitative inquiries into the record about qualitative evidence of how agents behave. So that's on the agent/author side. And then on the publisher side, it's numbers of bidders; imprint competition; the number—the ability of non-Big 5 to commit substantial resources; empirical inquiry into recent entry; identification of potential entrants who are operating successfully below the $250,000 threshold. So these together are what economists look at on both sides of the market. I may have left something out, but that's the core of it.

Q. But economists looking to see if there's harm frequently do try to put together a model of some kind, don't they?

A. As I said, I—

Q. That's a yes or no question. I don't think we need to go through all this again if you've said it. Can you answer that yes or no?

A. Well, I would just refer you back to my previous testimony.

Q. Well, so you can't answer it yes or no

A. Sometimes they do, sometimes they don't.

Q. Would you take a look at page 52 of your demonstrative.

A. Yes.

Q. There we're talking about particular bids for this particular book, *Neruda on the Park*. And you gave some testimony about this subject.

THE COURT: It's confidential.

BY MR. SCHWARZ:

Q. Yeah, I wasn't going to get into it. We don't—we're not supposed to talk about the numbers, okay, and it shouldn't be on the public screen.

A. I think I might have testified earlier about the numbers, but who's going to piece it all together.

Q. Okay, I'm sorry. Well, then you and I won't repeat the numbers. But there you see that there is—you took this to indicate to us the importance of imprint competition, correct?

A. Yes.

Q. Showing that everything is in the eye of the beholder, I looked at this and I saw, wow, somebody bid a huge amount above everybody else; is that correct? That is what happened, correct, somebody bid a very large amount above three—four other bidders?

A. Yes.

Q. Now, in the world in which I live in, I call that a maverick, somebody who looks at the value of what they're buying and sees a very much higher price than everybody else. What do you call that person?

A. I wouldn't identify this as maverick behavior.

Q. You would call them a fool? I mean, what would you call them?

A. I think the term maverick reflects behavior—

Q. Well, what would you call them? Forget maverick.

A. I wouldn't call them maverick, and—

Q. I said forget maverick, what would you call them?

A. I would characterize it as a situation where the editor for that particular imprint was really excited about acquiring this book, and they had a large maximum value in mind. And they bid a high level, and it turns out apparently to be much higher than others.

Q. And in that situation—putting aside the question of different imprints, and I take your point about that, you have an author who was tremendously benefitted by having five bidders instead of four, correct?

A. I think this author was primarily benefitted by having one who was really excited about the match.

Q. One out of five, would you concede that much?

A. There are five here.

Q. Okay, great, we agree. And if that very enthusiastic editor were not available to bid for whatever reason, that author might end up with a much, much, much lower advance, correct?

A. Yes, if you hold the other four constant, no agent behavior, yes.

Q. Well, I mean, the way you've described competition, what matters is who's one and two. There's a big gap between one and two, correct?

A. Yes.

Q. Now let's go back to a hypothetical, just for a change of pace here. I'm talking about agents now. If there were a monopsonist publisher who was the only buyer of manuscripts in the United States, do you think agents have enough ability to overcome whatever harm that monopsonist might try to accomplish in the market?

A. Probably not.

Q. So there are some limits to the agent's ability?

A. Definitely.

Q. Okay. And I take it another limitation is that the agents, absent a gun, cannot force a publisher to bid?

A. Correct, all they can do is invite.

Q. Right. And I take it they can't force them to bid higher once they bid?

A. I don't know what the word force means. Agents have—

Q. With a gun, any—

MR. OPPENHEIMER: Your Honor, he should be allowed to finish his answer.

BY MR. SCHWARZ:

Q. Okay, fine. Finish your answer.

A. They have tactics, not guns.

Q. And if a publisher has been told that they can go up to X dollar amount, do you think that the agents have the ability to get them to go beyond that amount?

A. Beyond their maximum?

Q. Yes.

A. No.

Q. Do you think that an author who has an agent who can't get them more than $25,000 in an advance has a lousy agent?

A. No, I wouldn't reach that conclusion based on just that information.

Q. Do you think that the level of competition among publishers has an effect on the amount of the advance that an agent is able to get for his client or her client?

A. Not if the potential publishers have low valuations. The agent can't manufacture higher maximum valuations.

Q. Okay, I agree with that. Now, you—one of your quarrels with the second-score auction models that Dr. Hill performed is that he uses the wrong margin—profit margin calculations, correct? And you went through that at length with Mr. Oppenheimer, right?

A. Yes.

Q. And a major part of that quarrel between you is that Dr. Hill chose to use, as best he could determine it, variable costs rather than fixed costs—at least you understand that to be what he was trying to do?

A. I think he should testify on that. That's not my—

Q. Did you—

A.—concern.

Q. Okay, sorry, finish. Did you include operating costs, in whole or in part, in your margin calculations to correct Dr. Hill's calculations?

A. Am I allowed to give a real answer here or just you want yes?

Q. I hope so.

A. Yes. In my rebuttal report, having identified that Dr. Hill used inconsistent approaches to margins in his first report, I chose to recalibrate the model with consistent margins across the two parties that included operating expenses.

Q. Do you think including operating expenses is appropriate to determine profit margins for normal corporate operations?

A. In this situation, absolutely, because the imprints are distributed—there are a hundred of them for Penguin Random House. If you have a hundred different entrepreneurial creative activity—excuse me, operations, you better make sure that they are bidding in a way that allows PRH as a whole to recover operating expenses.

Q. Did you hear or read any of Madeline McIntosh's testimony?

A. I don't recall that I did.

Q. Would you be surprised to know that, I believe, she testified that she was encouraging her editors to bid above variable costs to at least recover some operating costs, even if they don't factor in all operating costs?

A. That can be a strategy in some situations. But if you're in a situation where you've got lots of this entrepreneurial activity distributed throughout the firm, if everybody does that, that's a recipe for a big problem with the overall activity.

Q. Are you—I assume you're familiar with a fellow named Paul Krugman who won a Nobel Prize?

A. I don't know him personally, but I'm familiar with him for his Nobel Prize-winning research and his column.

Q. In your book, your book of exhibits—I think you should have one of these, we're going to start looking at this book.

A. Oh, Government's exhibits?

Q. Yes.

A. Sorry.

Q. In there, it's under a tab called Microeconomics Excerpt, and it follows the tabs for Spiegel & Grau. It's about midway through, a little bit short of midway. The cover page looks like that.

A. I'm not there yet. Now I've got the right notebook, so please direct me.

Q. Yeah, it's got a tab saying Microeconomics. There is an index, but it's easier just to find it. It's about a third of the way through right after Spiegel & Grau.

A. The binder I have in front of me is United States exhibits for the—for my examination.

Q. Yeah. Has it got a bunch of tabs in it?

A. Sorry, this is the wrong one, rebuttal report and deposition transcripts.

Q. It's a little bit thinner—a lot thinner. Not that thin I don't think—maybe. You want to help him. Your Honor, might—

THE COURT: Yes, please.

THE WITNESS: Thank you. I did not have this, but now I do.

BY MR. SCHWARZ:

Q. That's our fault, I'm sorry. So if you'd turn to page 369. We put the cover page in just so you can see this is a microeconomics 101 textbook. At the top of the page: "When price is greater than minimum average variable costs, however, the firm should produce in the short run." Is that a proposition you agree with?

A. Yes.

Q. Lower down right in the middle, there's a paragraph—the fifth paragraph begins with it's worth: "It's worth noting that the decision to produce when the firm is covering its variable costs, but not all of its fixed costs, is similar to the decision to ignore some costs." And then the next paragraph: "In the short run, a production decision fixed cost is, in effect, like a sunk cost, it has been spent and it can't be recovered in the short run." Do you agree with those statements?

A. Yes, in econ 101.

Q. I'm reminded to read another sentence, which says: "You may recall from chapter nine that a sunk cost is a cost that has already been incurred and cannot be recouped. And because it cannot be changed, it should have no effect on any current decision." Do you agree with that?

A. This is—you're talking about a sunk fixed cost, not operating expenses, right?

Q. So would you consider the salary of the CEO, Mr. Dohle, to be a sunk cost or an operating cost?

A. It's an ongoing cost, it's not a one-time fixed sunk cost.

Q. Do you think that that cost varies with the amount of books that are published?

A. No.

Q. But you nevertheless think it's a variable cost?

A. It's an ongoing operating expense that the distributed units need to take into account. And if they don't take into account ongoing operating expenses, the result will be problematic. It won't be problematic if you do it for the 101st book, provided that you've been recovering and contributing to operating expenses for the previous hundred.

Q. So I take it what you're saying is you need to pay back your share of operating costs before you can price a variable cost?

A. In the context of a distributed organization like PRH and Simon & Schuster, I am not at all surprised to see guidance reflected in the book level P&Ls where they are supposed to account for shares of operating expenses that are ongoing.

Q. But we're talking about Nathan Miller's second-score auction model. And in that regard, do economists consider the CEO's salary or other administrator's salaries to be part of the variable costs that they're supposed to exclude from margin? We're not talking about how PRH operates, we're talking about how you do a second-score auction model.

A. I didn't realize we were talking about that.

Q. I'm sorry, I thought I started that way. Can we start—we're talking about your concerns about Dr. Hill's profit margin calculations in the second-score auction model, okay, are you with me?

A. Yes.

Q. So in that regard, you seem to have a quarrel with how he calculates margin. And as I understand it, you think he should exclude the CEO's salary as margin?

A. I realize that that's—that that particular cost is something that you want to keep going back to, but operating costs in a distributed situation need to be covered. And it's reflected in the P&Ls, book level P&Ls, that guide bidding by individual agents—excuse me, individual editors. This is exactly what I would expect. It's absolutely consistent with economics. If you want to bring in a Nobel Prize-winning economist, bring in Oliver Williamson who won the Nobel Prize based on how you organize activity in organizations that have this feature of distributed operational units combined with firm-wide infrastructure.

Q. Let me try again, something that I think we got distracted from. My question being, so does there come a point in time where a particular imprint has paid its fair share of operating costs and can then price at variable cost?

A. I can definitely imagine that there can be a situation where an imprint is developing over a course of time acquisitions at prices that cover operating costs, and then are encouraged to price more aggressively. But the body—what I'm saying is that the body of their activity, and activities across imprints, better cover operational expenses that are ongoing.

Q. Okay. Do you think barriers to entry into the ATS market—that is, bidding 250 and up, are low in this market?

A. I do.

Q. And that's because you think it's easy to get size and reputation and capital to bid 250?

A. We see entry increasing—excuse me, reflected in the increasing number of active participants in the market based on winning. We see their ability to make big financial commitments. So yes, I think that you see entry, and you see their ability to commit resources. We also see a large number of, what I call, savvy authors saying yes to those publishers. And you also see agents inviting them to bid, and they respond and they bid. And sometimes they win, sometimes they lose, and other times they constrain.

Q. Why don't you take a look at your—the binder of exhibits, the same book that had Paul Krugman's thing. You'll find closer to the middle, past Paul Krugman's excerpt, PX-80-E?

A. Yes.

Q. I believe we want to look at page 13 in the deck. Does this look familiar to you at all, Dr. Snyder? This document, I believe, has been admitted. Are you on page 13?

A. I'm on page 13. I don't recall seeing this document.

Q. Okay. If you look at—this is a capital allocation report of Bertelsmann, 2020 to 2022. If you look at under market characteristics, talking about the purchase of Simon & Schuster. Do you see that at the top of the page?

A. Yes.

Q. Are you with me?

A. And you're talking about business characteristics?

Q. Market's characteristics.

A. Oh, markets, yes.

Q. Second section. It says: "Structure: Oligopoly. In addition to PRH, only four other major trade publishers." And then it says, "Barriers to entry high, especially reputation and sales." It sounds a whole lot like what you said, reputation and sales. Does that—the fact that your merging party thinks this is the case have any effect on your view?

A. Oligopoly, yes. Barriers to entry high, no, I don't change my view. The data shows successful entry, increasing number of entrants, capacity to make substantial financial commitments, and authors willing to consider them, and in many cases contract with them.

Q. So you would agree that this is an oligopoly?

A. Any industry with anything less than a large, large, large number falls into the category of oligopoly.

Q. Really, okay. So, I gather from your answers to those questions that you consider yourself to be more knowledgeable about these issues than the merging parties—or at least PRH?

A. I don't know who wrote this, and so on and so forth. All I can tell you is based on the empirical work that I've done, and looked at how firms are entering, I do not agree with the proposition that barriers to entry are high.

THE COURT: Can I ask a question. Can there be a difference in terms of entering a market between being somebody who can enter the market and be a consistent player versus someone who can enter and win one or two books? Because I think that's where there's a disconnect between what you're saying and what Mr. Schwarz is saying.

THE WITNESS: You can have one-hit wonders, if I may. However, then you also have firms like Chronicle that are getting a lot of traction. So I'm not claiming all of them are going to enter and become successful, long term players, but they're entering and they are acquiring and they're winning.

THE COURT: But they're acquiring just a few books whereas the major players are acquiring lots of books.

THE WITNESS: That's right.

THE COURT: So how are you defining the market that they're trying to enter, just occasionally winning or being a consistent player in the market?

THE WITNESS: Well, the guidelines say you have to look at the number, and then the second thing that I look at is ability to compete. And one of the measures is willingness to commit large dollars amount. And I studied that and confirmed that they are willing to do so. And then I also looked at whether, as I said, these various authors are willing to go with them, and are agents willing to engage them. And all those indicators say yes. I agree that they don't win as much as the Big 5.

THE COURT: So even if they're just doing a couple books a year, you would consider them in the market, and that proves that there's no barrier to entry?

THE WITNESS: It indicates that barriers to entry are certainly not high the way that economists—at least, I think about barriers to entry being high. It's not about the capital. I do agree that there are differences in reputation, but I think I've already covered that.

THE COURT: Okay.

BY MR. SCHWARZ:

Q. Is there a difference between barriers to entry and barriers to successful entry so that they can meaningfully compete with the Big 5?

A. There can be. And then you have to look at how individual entrants are doing, and whether they're getting traction; and whether smaller publishers that have been around a little bit longer like Chronicle are moving forward. And they are, I think the evidence was that they were tripling advances.

Q. We're going to come to those points right now, but let me—let's start down that road with your Exhibit 9.1, which is page 119 of your rebuttal report. That's the fatter binder that has your deposition in it as well.
A. So this is labeled rebuttal report and deposition transcripts?
Q. Yes, sir, that's it, that's it. Page 119 of the first document. It's on your screen now, if that's easier.
A. Okay.
Q. So there, just so we understand what we're looking at, that's the frequency of $250,000 and above offers made and contracts signed by non-Big 5 publishers in the three-year period 2019 to 2021. Did I get that right?
A. Yes.
Q. Now, I note that this says contracts signed. Does that mean what it says, not titles but contracts?
A. I believe so.
Q. So, in other words, that could be a contract in which—just take one example, Norton paid $250,000 for two books?
A. Yes.
Q. Meaning, therefore, an average of 125 per book?
A. Yes.
Q. So if I understand it, you found—and I don't know that I'm allowed to read these out loud. I suspect not, so I won't. But you see there that the top publisher—and going on down towards zero as the actual contracts signed?
A. Yes.
Q. And I think I'm allowed to anonymize and use the bottom—the aggregate. So you have 154 in total, correct?
A. Yes.
Q. Now let's stop there. What's—I think we've said—and again, I'm not sure if we should use 1,865 or 1,200 as the denominator per year. We had that issue, and you couldn't help me with that. But let's take 1,200 to be conservative, okay. 1,200 books a year is 3,600. Are you with me?
A. Yes.
Q. It sounds like a low number to me since you're using contracts here, but I'll give you that. 154 into 3,600 is what percent?
A. Maybe about 5 percent, I think you're right.
Q. Yeah. And then you have a column for offers made, right?
A. Yes.
Q. To the left of that. Does that 262 include—I assume it includes the 154?
A. Yes.
Q. So my first comment is that kind of calls into question that waterfall calculation we were doing where you had the non-Big 5 having a very large runner up since the number of offers they made is not a whole lot—the fraction isn't all that much greater than the contracts signed. Any explanation for that?
A. I think you'd have to go through the footnotes here to understand that there are data other than the agency data.
Q. Well, what data are you using to come up with 154 and 262?
A. That is spelled out in footnote 294 which goes on a long ways.
Q. Okay, thank you. And you would say, I think—I hope you're consistent enough to say that the competition matters only for these non-Big 5 publishers that you list here if those offers made were runners up?
A. Yes.
Q. Okay. So I'm going to give them a hundred percent credit, every one of those 262 was a win or a runner up.
A. Okay.
Q. What's 262 into 3,600?
A. I think it—it's under 10 percent.

Q. It certainly is. So, it's below the market share that we've otherwise attributed to these folks?
A. Based on these data.
Q. Okay. Well, it's your data, I didn't make it up. Okay, so let's talk about—let me—I'm sorry, before we talk about individual names here, did you exclude other non-Big 5 publishers that had any sizable contracts signed in that time period, in the relevant ATS market?
A. Yes, because I didn't have sources of information for some of them.
Q. Okay. So we're unsure if they had additional contracts or not; is that fair?
A. No, we're sure that there are others who won, but these are data that also take into account offers. And I don't have that for publishers—
Q. So there are other contracts—
A. Excuse me.
Q. Sorry, my fault.
A. It's hard for me to follow your questions if I can't complete my thought.
Q. You finish.
A. So just to be clear, my recollection is that we didn't have information for important publishers such as Scholastic and Chronicle and others.
Q. So this is the data you had for this chart?
A. To get into this chart, it wasn't just that they won, I had to have information on offers made.
Q. Okay. Now let's talk about some of these individual publishers, divorced from any of those numbers. We're not going to talk about the numbers connected with the names, because that would be inappropriate, okay. I'm just talking about confidentiality purposes. I'm just looking at the left column names and asking you questions.
A. Okay.
Q. Do you have any idea how many books a year—I guess I asked you how many books a year—how many trade books a year Norton publishes?
A. I think I said I don't know, because you're now going to the broad market.
Q. So let's take the—
A. Excuse me, sir.
Q. I'm sorry.
A. I need to be able to finish very short sentences at a minimum.
Q. I thought you said you didn't know, but go ahead, finish.
A. I think I tried. Go ahead.
Q. So we have a whole series of names here, and there's an index at the beginning. I take it you did not read the testimony of the person from Norton?
A. I've read testimony about Norton. Can you be more specific?
Q. Well, there's only to my knowledge—I could be wrong, there's only one deposition, Mr. Glusman?
A. I did read parts of that.
Q. And if you take a look in there under the Norton tab—
A. Where are you, Mr. Schwarz?
Q. In your binder of exhibits.
A. The United States exhibits?
Q. Yes, sir. Well, you tell me when you've found the tab.
A. I found the Norton tab.
Q. So the first page is page 64?
A. Yes.
Q. Are you aware that Norton is an employee-owned company?
A. I didn't hear the question.
Q. Are you aware that Norton is owned by its employees?
A. I think I heard that, but it's not a fact that I kept in mind. But I see it here on this page.
Q. All right. And on the next page, do you see that they publish about 150 trade titles per year? It's been between 120 and 150 for many years.

A. I see the number 150 titles in response to that question.
Q. Well, isn't—don't you think that's relevant to consider how much of a competitor they're going to be in the marketplace if this merger takes place?
A. Well, competitor is, again, according to the basic theory of unilateral facts, a function of winning and being runner up.
Q. They can't win more than 150 if that's all they win, right?
A. I don't disagree with that.
Q. Okay. And let's just—I think it might be easier, rather than going through your list, I'll just go through—I'll cover all of them in one way by just going from start to finish in my book, how's that? That makes life easier to find. So Astra, that's the first one. Do you know anything about Astra? Do you know how many employees they have?
A. Here's what I know about Astra: They're a relatively recent entrant. Their share is very small. And they've been gaining traction. And they are more of a competitive influence based on the information I have about how often they bid and are runner up.
Q. And do you see here on page 27 of the Astra deposition, they're hoping to get up to 50 employees?
A. Yes.
Q. Do you consider that to be a substantial competitive threat to the Big 5?
A. I think you might have misstated here. It says: "How many employees does Astra currently have?" They say: "Somewhere between 40 and 50." I don't see a projected number.
Q. "And how many people do you expect to hire in 2022?" "Ten."
A. I see that.
Q. And at the bottom it says: "Do you want to continue to hire more individuals in the coming years?" Answer: "Astra Publishing House has no opinion on that."
A. Yes.
Q. And you consider Astra to be a serious competitive threat to the Big 5?
A. What I would say is simply that their share is small, and it understates, based on the information I have, how often they are winner or runner up. I wouldn't identify them as a major competitive constraint.
Q. Let me eliminate a couple that I think you can answer without depositions. And that is Baker Publishing, have you heard of them? I don't think I have a tab on them, but I was hoping you might know. Baker and Tyndale are occasionally referred to in some of your testimony or your report. Are they Christian publishers exclusively?
A. I'm not sure. That sounds right, but I'm not positive.
Q. Let's flip ahead for a minute to Chronicle. We'll skip over Blackstone for a minute. That's another one of the—your identified small publishers.
A. Okay.
Q. What do you know about Chronicle, if anything?
A. I think there's testimony to the effect that they've tripled the amount of advances paid between 2014 and 2021, and that they anticipate growing.
Q. I think you may be confused, because you're referring to page 48 of your demonstrative which says what you just said, and cites Joshua Stanton's deposition. Do you see that?
A. Yes.
Q. Would it surprise you to know that Joshua Stanton works for Blackstone, not Chronicle?
A. If you're pointing it out, I assume you're right.
Q. Well—
A. Because I'm looking at the—
Q. If you don't—if you doubt me, take a look at your Blackstone tab, and you'll see the deposition of Blackstone is Joshua Stanton.
A. Yes, you're right.
Q. And Chronicle is a specialist in illustrated books, isn't it? And not just books, but photographs, children's books, puzzles, games, toys.
A. I think that is answered on the next tab: "Chronicle Books was founded in 1967. It has been, for

probably 40 years of that, a general trade publisher, primarily illustrated books. We publish a vast range of categories: Cookbooks, lifestyle, art, design, photography, children's, et cetera, 300 titles a year."

Q. And I won't read out loud, but if you'd turn the page to page 100, you and the Court can see the reference to a smaller number of trade books that they publish a year?

A. Yes, 170.

Q. And of course that is—we don't know how many of those are ATS books, but presumably a fraction?

A. Since they're publishing—this answer does not correspond to the price segment, it would be a fraction.

Q. Right. Now, you also described Amazon in your—page 48 of your demonstrative where you say that Mikyla Bruder agreed that Amazon Publishing is going to continue to look for opportunities to lure top selling authors to its publishing house. Do you know who—I assume it's Ms. Bruder, is?

A. I don't recall.

Q. Well, somewhere in here—perhaps towards the end, is Amazon. It looks like it's a third of the way through, and even I'm having a hard time finding it. It's after Abrams, but Abrams is not alphabetical.

A. Yes, I have it.

Q. And again, I have to deal with confidentiality issues. And you were aware—putting this aside for a second, are you aware that Amazon's share of ATS books has been dropping in the last—in recent years? Do you recall Dr. Hill's chart that we discussed in your deposition?

A. I did see that the share dropped.

Q. And if you would look on page 63 of the deposition—and this is—you have the correct person, this is Ms. Bruder's testimony, the question was asked: "Why has Amazon been considering reducing its title count?" And I will not read the answer out loud, but you can read it to yourself. Did you consider that answer in your Exhibit 48—page 48, I should say?

A. Yes.

Q. Don't you think, then, that your statement here is misleading?

A. What statement?

Q. The one that I just read, Ms. Bruder, page 48. I read it out loud.

A. I take that statement to mean they're not going to go away. They're acknowledging that they face challenges, one of which, of course, is not funding.

Q. Would it be other things, then? Do you have any view about what their other problems are?

A. I haven't studied it. All I can do is read this and see that it says—it refers to a particular challenge.

Q. You have Amazon and Chronicle, by way of example, listed under advance—publishers already paying 250 and up advances—excuse me, $250,000 and up advances, plan to expand?

A. Yes.

Q. Do you see any testimony here that says they're planning to expand any of these people? I'll go through all of them if you'd like.

A. Not in the—you're asking me about Amazon. Not in the three pages that you selected.

Q. Let's look at Candlewick, if we can find that one. It's relatively alphabetical at the beginning there. Page 22 of the deposition of Candlewick Press through Karen Lotz, L-O-T-Z, on page 22.

A. Yes.

Q. Lines—you can read the question on line 17 and the answer through line 23. Do you think that testimony is consistent with an intention to expand?

A. Yes.

Q. "Candlewick Imprint, in particular, is not planning to increase our title count." Is that expansion, sir?

MR. OPPENHEIMER: Your Honor, the rest of that answer should be read into the record.

BY MR. SCHWARZ:

Q. "But some of our imprints will be increasing the title count." Do you know how much?

A. No. I see the various testimony, and I can't quantify it.

Q. Do you know if Candlewick Imprint is their largest imprint?

A. I believe so.

Q. And what do you know about Spiegel & Grau?

A. A recent entrant, they have the benefit of having well-known editors. And they're competing in the proposed segment.

Q. Do you know how many books they intend to publish a year or otherwise?

A. Not off the top of my head.

Q. Well, did you look at their deposition, sir?

A. I looked at a lot of depositions, I don't—I can't tell you if I looked at this particular one.

Q. Well, let's see, here it is. Well, since this is highly confidential, Your Honor, at the Spiegel & Grau tab, there's a response to the DOJ's subpoenas and they list precisely what they have, and I won't read it out loud. Did you consider looking at any press statements by Spiegel & Grau?

A. So just to be clear, you're moving away from the—

Q. Yeah, I can't read it out loud, so I—

A. Well, I think some things are pretty clear. In a short period of time, they committed a large amount of money for three contracts, two of which fit the proposed segment. Maybe I'm misreading this. And when I say short period of time, it's less than two months. That's the way I'm reading this. I could be wrong.

Q. I mean, I will point you—there's a—after that testimony, there's a *New York Times* article of an interview with Spiegel & Grau. And in there, it says: "In its revamped form, Spiegel & Grau will produce 15 to 20 books a year." Is that relevant at all to your consideration of whether they're meaningful competitors to the Big 5?

A. I don't know *The New York Times* article.

Q. Well, if I—if we take as a hypothetical that they're trying to do 20 books a year, would that affect your view of them as a meaningful competitor to the Big 5—or the Big 4?

A. I can't extrapolate from what's here. Two out of three in a two-month time period are in the segment. What was *The New York Times* number?

Q. Fifteen to 20 books of any kind a year.

A. That would mean that they're in the market and they're competing.

Q. And you think that PRH and S&S editors are going to be concerned about their competition if they know they're doing 20 books a year?

A. Well, what we know is that more than half the time, as I recall, a non-Big 5 is invited and responds to bids in the ATS segment. And then, of course, you have within Big 5 competition more than the half the time.

Q. Let's shift gears, okay. We're going to look at one of your—we're not going to be talking anymore, for the moment at least, about these small publishers.

THE COURT: Then maybe it's a good time for us to break for the day, it's 5:00 o'clock?

MR. SCHWARZ: Oh, it's that time?

BY MR. SCHWARZ:

Q. Dr. Snyder, good morning.

A. Good morning, Mr. Schwarz.

Q. Mel Schwarz for the United States. I'll take this mask off.

Dr. Snyder, I'd like to go back to something that was a challenge yesterday, which was Page 42 of your demonstratives, which—I think you have your demonstrative exhibits in front of you. That was the 23 percent figure that we were struggling to figure out. Do you remember that?

A. Yes.

Q. Now, maybe it would be easier if you—I don't want to—we can't put two things on the screen. But we need to look back while we have this in mind to Page 16, your waterfall in the demonstrative binder.

MR. SCHWARZ: Do you have the demonstrative binder?

MR. OPPENHEIMER: Yes. Your Honor, may I approach and provide Dr. Snyder with the demonstrative binder?

THE COURT: Yes. That's fine.

MR. OPPENHEIMER: Thank you.

(Tenders document to counsel and witness.)

MR. SCHWARZ: Thank you.

BY MR. SCHWARZ:

Q. Are you with me, sir?

A. Yes. I see both.

Q. Thank you. Am I right that the 23 percent calculation came from the data which is in Page 16?

A. Yes. From the agency data.

Q. Right. And now just looking at 16, we have 150 multi-bidder acquisitions with known runners-up of which, if I'm reading this right, 96 were won by PRH or Simon & Schuster and 45 were won by the remaining Big 5. Correct?

A. Yes.

Q. And my math tells me that is 141 out of 150.

A. Yes.

Q. And that's 94 percent, roughly?

A. Yes.

Q. And do you think that the fact that the Big 5 won all but nine of those 150 contracts is at least part of the explanation why the non-Big 5 were runners-up quite frequently?

A. I didn't catch the last part of your question.

Q. The non-Big 5 seem to be runners-up perhaps 14 times. I can't be sure what—about the percentage calculations. But that strikes me with respect to the rest of the data we have as a fairly high number. And I'm trying to see if that is affected, if that number went up percentage-wise, because the Big 5 won 94 percent of the time.

A. 96 were won by the two parties and 45 by the other Big 5.

Q. Correct.

A. I mentioned, I think, very early on that these data overrepresent the parties. So that's one explanation. And then you're right: What you're seeing here is a relatively small number for the non-Big 5. It's less than what their share is based on the big data sets that Dr. Hill and I developed, the so-called advance data.

THE COURT: Where did you get 14?

MR. SCHWARZ: I'm—

THE COURT: You said they seem to be runners-up perhaps 14 times.

MR. SCHWARZ: Your Honor, to be fair, that was just—that was my subtraction of nine from 23 percent. But that—you remember we had a long colloquy about this yesterday.

THE COURT: Oh. So 14 percent.

MR. SCHWARZ: I have no idea if that's right. And Dr. Snyder was—

THE COURT: Okay.

BY MR. SCHWARZ:

Q. I don't mean—I don't mean to denigrate you, but you were not completely able to explain how we got to that.

A. No. I think I did.

Q. Okay.

A. And I explained—

Q. How many—

A. Excuse me. The—

MR. OPPENHEIMER: Your Honor—

THE WITNESS: May I?

THE COURT: Wait a minute. We can't all talk at the same time. Is there an objection?

MR. OPPENHEIMER: Yes, your Honor.

THE COURT: If there is, then come to the microphone.

MR. SCHWARZ: I hadn't posed a question.

MR. OPPENHEIMER: Your Honor, I would request that counsel not interrupt the witness so that a complete answer can be given.

MR. SCHWARZ: I'll withdraw the question, your Honor.

BY MR. SCHWARZ:

Q. Are you able now to tell us on how many occasions the non-Big 5 were runner-up within the 150 known runners-up?

THE COURT: Didn't we do this calculation yesterday and come up with 67?

MR. SCHWARZ: Yes. I've only—if your Honor wants to know, I'm happy to do that. But if—

THE COURT: Go ahead, Mr. Snyder, if you want to confirm.

THE WITNESS: There are—the base we agree on. The denominator is 150. They win in nine. So what we need is to infer the number of times that they were runner-up such that nine plus that number equals 23 percent of 150. I think that's about 30 times that they were runner-up, in that ballpark.

MR. SCHWARZ: Okay.

THE COURT: Yesterday you said 67.

THE WITNESS: And I gave an incorrect answer.

BY MR. SCHWARZ:

Q. Let's move on, then. There were a few non-Big 5 publishers that I didn't ask you about, and I'll try to move that along quickly. Do you know the publisher Regnery, spelled R-E-G-N-E-R-Y?

A. I've heard of it.

Q. Do you know them to publish conservative books, books on the right side of the political spectrum?

A. I don't recall. And I can check, if you want, the binder. But I don't recall.

Q. And do you have any idea of how many ATS advances they do in a given year?

A. Their share is small.

Q. Would one to five be about what you are aware of?

A. Not without checking the numbers.

Q. Well, then, let's look at the deposition of Regnery in your binder of exhibits. That's the one with all the tabs in it, sir.

A. Yes. I see it.

Q. I'll confess that I did not mark the precise lines in which there is an answer of one to five, but it should be in here. This one might have gotten past us. So I will not belabor the point. We'll figure this out. Oh, I see my problem. My problem is very simple: I have the wrong page. Let's move on. It seems to be the wrong page. Let's talk about Abrams. Do you know what Abrams does?

A. It's one of the non-Big 5 publishers that operates in the proposed segment.

Q. Do you know what they specialize in, if anything?

A. I do recall that they publish children's books. But I don't recall exactly to what extent that is their emphasis.

Q. And do you know whether they also specialize in illustrated books?

A. I don't recall.

Q. And do you know how many—about how many books of any kind, trade books, that they publish in a given year?

A. Well, just looking at the tab, I see a number 350 to 375.

Q. And you have no reason to dispute that, do you?

A. No.

Q. And you wouldn't know how many of those are anticipated top sellers?

A. No, I don't, without checking the data.

Q. And with respect to Chronicle, did you look at the deposition of the Chronicle witness?

A. At some point, I did. Yes.

Q. Did you note that they testified they had no plans to increase their production?

A. I don't recall that. What I do recall is that they had been increasing their production.

Q. Well, take a look at the tab for Chronicle at—the answer on Page 100, Lines 7 to 21. In particular, the question at Line 19: And does Chronicle intend to increase the number of trade books that it publishes each year? Answer: No.

A. Yes. I see that. As I mentioned, my other understanding about Chronicle is that they had increased the number of acquisitions and advance spend considerably up to the time that this deposition was taken.

Q. And with respect to Candlewick, did you take note of the fact that they had no plans to increase their acquisition rate for books?

A. Mr. Schwarz, I thought that you asked me about this yesterday. And I can read the full answer again if you'd like.

Q. Well, I'd like you to take a look at page—if you have it in your book—Page 120. If not—

A. So yesterday you asked me about Page 22. And that's where there was information about their plans with respect to growth. I see on Page 120 another question regarding plans to acquire books for $250,000 or more.

Q. I'm glad you found that. And the answer was: No. I do not have plans to increase that. At Line 10. Correct?

A. It's—the question was: Do you have any plans to increase the number of offers—It makes—

Q.—to acquire books at $250,000 or more? Answer: No?

A. The answer is no. And, of course, that relates to current competitive conditions.

Q. Right. Do you have your rebuttal report in one of the larger binders?

A. Yes.

Q. Would you turn, then, to Exhibit 9.2, Page 120.

A. Yes.

Q. And what are you depicting there, if you can summarize it briefly?

A. The title of Exhibit 9.2 is Annual Number of Books Acquired From Contracts With Advances of At Least $250,000 For the Years 2019 Through 2021.

Q. And you're attempting to put together the maximum production in those years?

A. In the first three columns, it's just the simple numbers. And then there is a calculation of the yearly average.

Q. And the right-hand column is the maximum year's increase above average year. Right?

A. Yes.

Q. So looking at the second column from the right, the sum of publishers' yearly maximum, is that an indication at least for those three years of the maximum production of Penguin Random House, Simon & Schuster and all the other publishers for ATS books?

A. It's the highest observed number for that—for a given year—

Q. Okay.

A.—over that three-year time period.

Q. And have you made an effort to calculate what the share of that highest production is as between the merging parties and everybody else? In other words, 1,005 is what percentage of the total of roughly 2,227?

A. It seems to me about 40 percent. But I could actually—

Q. Maybe a little bit higher. But not much different than their market share as we calculate it in the anticipated top seller market. Correct?

A. Correct.

Q. Let's talk about—

THE COURT: Mr. Schwarz, I'd like to go back to that formula for the 23 percent. If now is not a good time, I can wait. But I'm looking at it, and I think—

MR. SCHWARZ: If it's a good time for you, it's a good time for us.

THE COURT: Okay. You said nine plus X equals 23 percent of 150. But we're looking for runners-up. So shouldn't it be 300?

THE WITNESS: That was a mistake I made yesterday, your Honor. Here it's just: Of the total number of actual contract competitions, how often are they winner or runner-up?

THE COURT: I see. So it should be 23 percent of 150.

THE WITNESS: Correct. I apologize for the error.

THE COURT: Okay. Okay. Got it. Thank you.

BY MR. SCHWARZ:

Q. But I think you said that that number could be skewed a bit because the data overrepresents PRH and

Simon & Schuster as well as having the Big 5 win 94 percent of the 150 occasions?

A. I think you said a particular number being overskewed. I might have misheard. So which number are you asking about?

Q. I think—I just wanted to go back to the point that you were saying that this 150, the data, skewed higher for PRH, Penguin Random House and Simon & Schuster, than the norm.

A. Yes.

Q. And in terms of our market share information, the fact that the Big 5 won 94 percent of the time is slightly higher than we might otherwise expect, which was 91 percent on other occasions when we were calculating that number?

A. I see it somewhat differently. But I understand your question. If PRH and S&S are overrepresented—

Q. Yes.

A.—then the other Big 5 and non-Big 5 are underrepresented.

Q. But the fact that the Big 5 wins 94 percent of the time might skew the runner-up—runner-up occasions of the non-Big 5 higher than it normally might be?

A. I don't see how that would necessarily follow.

Q. Okay.

THE COURT: But the 23 percent is based on the agency data, which seems to be skewed?

THE WITNESS: It overrepresents PRH and S&S. It underrepresents everybody else.

You see that in the—compared to Dr. Hill's advance data shares, my advance data shares. And you just look at the titles and shares in the agency data. You see them overrepresented.

And, your Honor, I believe it's because of—the production came in response to requests from the parties and then I think it might have been supplemented by the Government. But the agencies provided the data. It's possible, at least, that they focused more on acquisitions that the parties were involved with and won.

THE COURT: But the request was for all of their data. And you're saying that they might have not—

THE WITNESS: I probably shouldn't speculate. I can only see that they're overrepresented.

THE COURT: Okay. But in other words, the agency data is not a representative set of data?

THE WITNESS: Correct, in terms of overrepresenting the parties. It's also not representative with respect to average advances. My recollection is that the average advances in the agency data are lower.

But for my purposes, seeing the mix of acquisitions, seeing the percentage of time that one of the parties wins, does the other party bid, those dimensions of not being representative do not affect my analysis.

THE COURT: Thank you.

BY MR. SCHWARZ:

Q. At the risk of going through this too much, one other point comes to mind. I think we established that the non-Big 5 won nine out of 150 contracts. Correct?

A. These are 150 multi-bidder contracts for which we have an identified runner-up.

Q. I understand that. I'm just trying to get to the math. Nine over 150 is about 6 percent?

A. Correct.

Q. And that is less frequent than the 9 percent we have seen in other data as the share of ATS books acquired by non-Big 5?

A. Yes. The other data show 9 to 10 percent.

Q. Now, one more question, then. If that number, 6 percent, is underrepresenting the non-Big 5, you wouldn't be surprised to see that they end up being runner-up more often than normal?

A. I'm sorry, Mr. Schwarz. I don't see how you can go from that to your provisional result.

THE COURT: Because the market share isn't about runner-up. Market share—

MR. SCHWARZ: Yes, your Honor. You're absolutely right. The market shares are with respect to wins. But if you win less frequently than normal, perhaps—well, I don't want to testify.

THE COURT: Okay.

MR. SCHWARZ: And I'm not the economist.

THE COURT: Okay.

BY MR. SCHWARZ:

Q. So with respect to imprints—we're changing gears now; we'll get off math for a while—are you aware of any legal impediments to Penguin Random House or Simon & Schuster after the merger changing their imprint policy with respect to various imprints bidding for the same book?

A. No.

Q. And are you aware of certain occasions when the editors do coordinate their bids so as not to—so as to come up with a single bid for a particular book?

A. In certain situations. I didn't see any in the context of one-on-one negotiations, imprints or best bids. And I only saw those examples in rounds auctions after a certain point.

Q. And you're aware, of course, that, for example, at Penguin Random House most of these editors work in the same building together? At least they did before COVID?

A. They're colleagues across the organization, independent of COVID.

Q. And we would never know if they spoke to each other in the hallway, would we, about a particular book?

A. We would not.

Q. I think I asked you this yesterday in a different context, whether you had heard or read Ms. McIntosh's testimony.

A. I do recall your question.

Q. Yeah. And the answer was, I think, yes, at least to some extent?

A. To some extent.

Q. Did you happen to notice the document, which is PX 411, which was a deck, and on Page 4 of which she said that—Ms. McIntosh said she wanted to increase background coordination to leverage internal demand information better and avoid internal upbidding?

A. I'd like to just find the document, Mr. Schwarz, if you could direct—

Q. I'm not sure that that's in your binder. But I only ask you: Are you aware of that at all as you sit here?

A. I don't recall that testimony.

Q. So would it affect your view of the importance of imprint competition if you knew that the head of PRH U.S. would like to reduce the amount of upbidding by the various imprints?

A. You're asking about testimony that I'd like to see before I make—

Q. Just assume that—and if I'm wrong, I'm wrong. But assume that was the testimony.

A. And could you restate what the assumption is?

Q. The assumption is that Ms. McIntosh at PRH, head in the U.S., wanted to leverage internal demand information better and avoid internal upbidding.

A. Compared to the current situation, I'm not sure what that means. But I understand that she—I'm assuming that you're right.

Q. Yes, you are. That's my question. If I'm wrong, then I'm wrong.

A. And then what's the question?

Q. Does that affect your view about the importance of imprint competition within Penguin Random House or Penguin Random House and Simon & Schuster?

A. Not really. I mean, Penguin Random House has 100 imprints. The editors are very entrepreneurial. The firm is set up for them to be—to go out and engage potential authors.

To have somebody at the top of that saying they would like to potentially coordinate more, I don't—based on what I understand about the organization, that would not change the intensity of imprint competition.

Q. So you don't think that the CEO wanting to change policies in any way will have any effect on editors?

A. What I know about editors is that they are creative and entrepreneurial. Could it have some effect in some situations? Sure. But with 100 imprints and one person saying they'd like to coordinate, no. I don't see how that can materially affect the extent of imprint competition.

Q. Let's change gears again here—

THE COURT: Wait. Can I follow up on that?

MR. SCHWARZ: Of course.

THE COURT: So they appointed someone to start coordinating bids internally, according to some of the testimony. And there are emails of them coordinating bids, like different editors and publishers in different situations saying: In this one, let's just go up by this amount or Let's all bid the same amount. That doesn't affect your analysis? Because I thought you were assuming that they were all competing with one another internally, like independently. But they may not be?

THE WITNESS: I'm not assuming that there's no coordination. And I'm also aware that for one of the Penguin Random House divisions, there is a structure in place to coordinate and provide house bids in a similar way to Simon & Schuster.

THE COURT: No. This is not the house bids; this is actually—they've appointed someone to internally coordinate bidding at PRH. There's testimony to that effect. And there are emails of editors saying: Let's all go up this amount or Let's all bid the same amount.

THE WITNESS: And is that for all of PRH?

THE COURT: It's for various divisions within PRH coordinating. And the person who's appointed, my understanding, is for PRH for all of North America.

THE WITNESS: Okay.

THE COURT: Does that affect your analysis?

THE WITNESS: Without having this implemented, I really can't speculate.

And maybe I should just say: We'll see. But my understanding of what editors do is that, again, they are entrepreneurial. And if there's too much coordination in a situation like that, the firm is going to reduce the motivation for editors.

So with that predicate, I'd have to think about—and I think the best thing to do would be to see if that actually had any effect.

THE COURT: But if you assume that they do that, that still doesn't affect your analysis?

THE WITNESS: Well, the question is: How much coordination? What actual restrictions on advances would occur? And in what circumstances? Is the coordination going to involve best bids? That would be a very sharp departure. Is the coordination going to involve one-on-one negotiations?

THE WITNESS: I doubt it. So we're talking about one particular auction format, if I understand the assumption.

THE COURT: I think not bilateral, but I think it affects everything else. Okay.

THE WITNESS: Again, agents always have the option to pick the format and make adjustments.

THE COURT: Okay.

THE WITNESS: So it could have an effect in some situations, based on what I'm hearing this morning.

THE COURT: Thank you.

MR. SCHWARZ: May I change gears, your Honor?

THE COURT: Yes.

MR. SCHWARZ: Thank you.

BY MR. SCHWARZ:

Q. You testified to some extent about the Penguin Random House merger as to some extent indicative of the fact that a merger did not have a negative effect on advances. Is that perhaps a too shorthand summary of where you were with Mr. Oppenheimer?

A. For the three buckets of advances from 250 to 500, 500 to a million and a million to two, the three-year period before and the three-year period after 2013, it shows an increase in average advances for those three buckets. And the ones above that, average advances does not show an increase.

Q. I think you're referring to DX 385, so I'm going to—I'm not sure if that's in front of you. But in any event, I would like to look at DX 385, so I'm going to hand that up to you.

MR. SCHWARZ: With your Honor's permission.

THE COURT: Yes.

MR. SCHWARZ: If I may approach. (Tenders document to the witness.)

THE WITNESS: Thank you.

BY MR. SCHWARZ:

Q. This is a chart that you prepared, is it not?

A. Yes.

Q. And it's hard to see exactly the numbers, because they're just pinpoints. But the way I look at this, if I'm reading it right, in the $500,000-and-above category, the average advances drop between 2010 and 2021. Likewise, for the average advances of 250—$250,000 and above. Am I reading that correctly?

A. And your start year is not 2013; it's 2010?

Q. I'm looking at your chart, sir. Yes.

A. Sir, I'm just asking the—

Q. And you started at 2010. Yes.

A. Thank you. Yes. I see that.

Q. So I'm reading it correctly? They went down. Yes?

A. For—

Q. For those two categories, 250 and above and 500 and above.

A. From 2010 to 2021, yes.

Q. Right. And I think even the one from $100,000 and above went down slightly. Correct?

A. I can't tell.

Q. It's a little bit lower. And how about the zero and above? I assume—so is that zero to $100,000, that chart, that bar at the bottom?

A. No. If I may just explain: That's why I redid the calculations by buckets. This is just a dollar amount and above.

In the earlier question, where I gave the summary, I think it provides much more insights about the buckets because, as we know, when you get to the high numbers, high advance levels, that—you're influenced greatly by choppiness in the data. So if you look at buckets, the three buckets that I identified earlier, the advance levels go up.

However, I'm not doing it for the whole time period, which is why I wanted to clarify why—that you're starting at 2010.

Q. Right. It would be great if you would just answer my questions. And if your counsel wants you to expound, he'll have redirect. My question was: Is the category zero dollars and above, is that everything from zero up?

A. Yes.

Q. Up to whatever? Millions?

A. So it's influenced by everything.

Q. And—but the $500,000 and above is also influenced by everything, too. Correct? Everything above it?

A. Correct.

Q. Okay. So you can help me with the math if I'm wrong. But if you have the—the only one going up is the zero and above. And the only thing that you're adding to it is zero to 250. Everything else is already indicated above that. The only thing that could affect those numbers are zero to 250. Correct? And so it must be that the zero-to-250 category is the part that's increasing that chart?

A. I'm sorry. This is influenced by the high end.

Q. I know that, sir. All of them are influenced by the high end, according to your testimony.

So therefore, it must be—I think—that the zero to 250 is the part that's being added on the bottom and it must be the one going up?

A. No. And the answer is very simple. If you look at the buckets from 250 to 500, they are going up. If you look at the bucket from $500,000 to a million, they are going up. So it's not—with these data, you can't—in fact, you would make a mistake drawing that inference.

Q. Okay. If you think so. Would you look in your binder of exhibits, our exhibits, which is the one that's got all the tabs in it, at PX 92?

MR. SCHWARZ: And this was admitted into evidence, I believe, with Mr. Sansigre.

BY MR. SCHWARZ:

Q. Now, I'm just—the first question, I guess, would be: Do you recall ever seeing this before today?

A. I just need a moment, Mr. Schwarz.

Q. Certainly.

A. I don't recall seeing this right now. I've seen data along these lines, but I don't recall this page.

Q. Well, take a look at the bottom of the first page there. You see there's a chart that indicates net sales and advances. Do you see that? The bottom of the page. It's nice and big on your screen.

A. Yes.

Q. And you see the column, second from the right, 2011 to 2019?

A. Yes.

Q. And 2011 is before the Penguin Random House merger?

A. Yes.

Q. And 2019 is after?

A. Yes.

Q. And 2019 is before the pandemic. Right?

A. Yes.

Q. Okay. And you see there that for those years, total net sales went up. I assume that's millions, $46 million?

A. I can't make that assumption. I'm not sure what "net sales" here means. Are you just—can you represent that this is downstream?

Q. I'm asking you if it says that net sales for fiction, nonfiction and juvenile books went up $46 million. That's what it says, anyway, isn't it?

A. I'm just asking what net—it says those words. I'm just asking you if you know if this refers to downstream sales. I assume it does.

Q. I believe it's referring to net sales income of Penguin Random House—excuse me—before the merger, Random House; after, Penguin Random House.

A. Okay.

Q. And it's talking about advances in the same column at the bottom. It shows a minus 73. Do you see that? I assume again it's millions.

A. Yes.

Q. So is it fair to draw the conclusion from that that for those years, net sales went up and advances went down?

MR. OPPENHEIMER: Your Honor, object to the question. No foundation for this witness. It's not his document.

THE COURT: Overruled.

THE WITNESS: As depicted for these three rows, fiction, nonfiction, juvenile, that's what it shows. I don't know if there's a particular cutoff here or not. And I don't know how it would take into account the change in strategy with respect to mass merchandise.

BY MR. SCHWARZ:

Q. Okay. You can put that to the side. Lastly, I'd like to talk about coordinated effects. Okay? Do you have an understanding of whether or not the horizontal merger guidelines are also concerned with legal tacit coordination as well as unlawful coordination?

A. I don't think it says those words. But I understand what you're saying. The concern is not just what is illegal, but also what might be potentially tacit coordination.

Q. To refresh your recollection, I'll read a couple sentences from the merger guidelines:

Coordinated interaction alternatively can involve parallel accommodating conduct not pursuant to a prior understanding. Parallel accommodating conduct includes situations in which each rival's response to competitive moves made by others is individually rational and not motivated by retaliation or deterrence, nor intended to sustain an agreed-upon market outcome, but nevertheless emboldens price increases and weakens competitive incentives to reduce prices or offer customers better terms.

Coordinated interaction includes conduct not otherwise condemned by the antitrust laws.

Does that refresh your recollection about the concern of the merger guidelines?

A. It doesn't refresh it. I think I answered it correctly before.

Q. Do you have an understanding of whether or not royalty rates for hardcover books are relatively standard across the industry?

A. As a percentage of retail price.

Q. Yes. 15 percent is the norm?

A. Yes.

Q. And do you also have an understanding that it has come to be the case that at least the Big 5 publishers insist on receiving audio rights when they negotiate contracts?

A. It's not just the Big 5. This is, I think, the trend in a more global world and a more digital world, to go for a broader set of rights.

Q. And I wasn't sure what you were saying when we were talking about installment payments. You're aware that advances are typically paid in installments?

A. Yes.

Q. And were you saying that you think it was inconsequential that payments went from three tranches to four?

A. Well, just to clarify, they didn't go from three to four in terms of contracts already in place. Right? So—

Q. Right.

A.—the change was for new contracts. And what I was saying in terms of interaction with Your Honor was that if you have a change in the time intervals and the number of payments, that is relevant, but it doesn't—because when you get paid, of course, matters. But it leaves out how much. And the advance level is negotiated going forward with the change.

So that single change does not lead to a reduction in competition unless there is also a constraint on advances. And then if there's a constraint on advances, what about bonuses, et cetera?

Q. So you think that when payments got changed from three to four quarterly payments, that presumably advances went up in order to compensate for the lost interest or time value of money?

A. I'm just pointing out that that as a coordination mechanism according to the guidelines has to be put in context of the dimensions of competition. And it would not be sufficient to lessen competition because there are so many other dimensions on which publishers compete.

Q. Are you aware of whether or not when the change was made from three payments to four for advances as a matter of norm that advances went up to compensate for the lost value of the money or the time value of money?

A. Well, that's sort of the point: You can't know. And no one could know. No rival could know if a publisher was altering advances or bonuses or anything else. That's why the other part of the coordination is about detection, monitoring and punishment. There's no way anybody would know. And especially not me.

Q. All right. Let's turn to actual coordination for a minute. Have you read the Court of Appeals decision in United States versus Apple?

A. I know the case.

Q. All right. And just for the record, that's 791 F.3d 290, 2015.

And referencing—I'm going to read you a passage from it, sir. I haven't made it an exhibit, but I'm going to just ask you about a discrete fact.

The Court wrote at Page 300: Conveniently, the Big 6 operated in a close-knit industry and had no qualms communicating about the need to act together.

Of course, at this time, Penguin was part of the Big 6.

As the District Court found, based on the publisher Defendant's own testimony, quote—and now quoting the district court: "On a fairly regular basis, roughly once a quarter, the CEOs of the Big 6 held dinners in the private dining rooms of New York restaurants without counsel or assistants present in order to discuss the common challenges they faced." Are you aware of that happening?

A. Yes.

Q. And the CEOs of the Big 6 were the Big 5 plus Penguin. Correct?
A. I don't think that's correct with respect to Penguin Random House.
Q. Do you think there's another—a different sixth than Random House?
A. All I'm saying is I don't know if it included all six. I mean, if—
Q. So you're quarreling with the Court's finding?
A. I'm just saying I can't square that with some other information that I'm aware of.
Q. All right. And—
A. I'm not trying to quarrel with anybody.
Q. Well, let us assume with your noted exception that all six did meet for private dinners. I'm not—I understand Random House was not a defendant in this case. But I read you the facts as described by the Court. Let's assume they did that. Is it possible, given that they talked about the concerns of the day that they faced, that they might have talked about things such as advances?
A. I don't know.
Q. We'll never know, will we?
A. I don't know.
Q. It was the case, however, that these six along with Apple were able to conduct a conspiracy in which they made a great effort to get the prices of ebooks up. Correct?
A. That's my understanding. Yes.
Q. And they were able to do that by coordinating among those six, weren't they?
A. Apple did the coordination and the prices were observable.
Q. And the other six—putting aside Random House—went along, correct, happily?
A. I can't get inside the conspiracy. I know the basic allegations.
Q. Right. And so let's—in your testimony with Mr. Oppenheimer, you kept putting aside poaching, if I recall. Correct? Poaching authors.
Is it not possible that those CEOs could get together and make a deal to not poach each other's anticipated top selling authors or actually top selling authors?
A. So just repeat the last part. The actual or potential . . . ?
Q. Or potential. I was just trying to distinguish between anticipated and actual. So let's make it the ones that they know are top sellers.
A. The reason why I separated that, just to be clear, your Honor, is in that situation, detection would happen right away. If there was a deviation from the agreement, if an incumbent author was poached, the editor and the publisher would learn about it. So this is different from the other things.
But then the question is—and I think this is answering your question, Mr. Schwarz—is it possible for them to do that and implement it? Not in the real world, no.
Q. You, I think, said you were an expert in the high-tech litigation. Am I correct? Out in California?
A. Yes.
Q. And that related to antipoaching agreements among Silicon Valley employers, did it not?
A. I think it was a broad set of employers, not just in the Valley.
Q. And they were able to implement nonpoaching arrangements amongst themselves, were they not? At least allegedly?
A. Not in a consistent way. There were allegations and there were—obviously, there was attempts to establish that there had been restraints.
Q. So is it your testimony that if the Big 5 CEOs got together at dinner on a quarterly basis and agreed that they weren't going to poach each other's top selling authors, that that might not be effectuated?
A. I don't see how it would. So an agent contacts an editor and says: You know, my top selling author has a broken relationship with his or her editor. And this author is in play. Do you want to talk to me? And then the editor is going to say: No. I don't want to?
I can't see that happening. And I don't think a no-poaching agreement would in fact be effective, given those circumstances.
Q. Are you saying it would not be or it would be if they did have that agreement?
A. It would not be effective, because the circumstances that lead somebody to move will come up

independently. And then the question is: How in the world are editors going to respond? Are they just going to say: No, no thank you? And then wait for some other of the 30 publishers to say: No. I'm not going to follow this agreement. I want to pick up that author?

Q. So you think—

A. I don't—

Q. You think the CEOs of these corporations have limited or no control over their employees? Is that basically what you're saying?

A. You have to understand—

Q. Is that what you're saying? Yes or no.

A. I think I get to give more than a "yes" or "no" answer. You may disagree. But if the Court wants to instruct me, then of course. So what was the question?

Q. Do you think that the CEOs of these Big 5 publishers have less control over their employees than the typical CEOs of major corporations?

A. Not in a way that would affect this idea of poaching when you have 25 other publishers who would be very happy to get authors who are currently published by the Big 5.

And I can go on, but I realize you don't want to have me continue.

THE COURT: Well, I think maybe the hypothetical is somewhat different from what you've answered. Could they make an agreement that they won't go after each other's authors as opposed to authors approaching them and turning them down? Could they make an agreement that we won't affirmatively, you know, approach any of your authors?

THE WITNESS: And that, your Honor, is exactly the kind of thing that came up in high-tech. Were there situations where somebody initiated a move or was it poaching? What was the communication that was required to distinguish the two of somebody saying "I want to move" versus somebody saying, "Hey, would you possibly move?"

That's what I mean. I think in practice this is a nonstarter.

THE COURT: Because in practice, you can't distinguish between the two readily?

THE WITNESS: Mr. Schwarz's question was focused on the Big 5. Even within the Big 5, I don't see how individual editors would say, you know: This great author, we have an agreement among the Big 5. We're not going to poach.

But if in fact—and it's hard for the agent to know. If in fact this is a situation where the author's relationship with the imprint and the editor is broken, they're going to leave.

So I think it's just too much of a risk to say: No. I'm going to follow the agreement. And I don't think the CEOs would want to have their editors follow that agreement.

THE COURT: So your answer is premised on your belief that the editors would not comply with the directive from the CEO to not poach?

THE WITNESS: I don't think it would be in the interest of the CEOs to try to reach this agreement if there were five because—

THE COURT: Putting that aside, if they reached that agreement, you think it wouldn't work because the employees would not follow the directive?

THE WITNESS: They might follow the directive. But the impact on competition is not just poaching from them; it's all the other 25. This would be a great opportunity for any number of other publishers to get an established author.

THE COURT: So your answers seem to be focused on why this is a bad idea. We're just trying to understand the coordination, like can the coordination happen?

THE WITNESS: It would be a bad idea because the CEOs I don't think would—

THE COURT: We're not interested in bad ideas; we're interested in whether the coordination can happen.

THE WITNESS: And I don't think it can happen because in terms of affecting competition, I don't think the five would be able to come up with a mechanism that would distinguish among the types that your Honor talked about.

And even if they did, there would be many other competitors that are very happy. So the impact on competition would not be there. And what would the Big 5 be doing? They would just be hurting themselves.

THE COURT: Okay. Thank you.

MR. SCHWARZ: I was going to pass the witness, your Honor.

THE COURT: Thank you.

MR. SCHWARZ: Thank you.

MR. OPPENHEIMER: Good morning, your Honor.

THE COURT: Good morning.

REDIRECT EXAMINATION

BY MR. OPPENHEIMER:

Q. Good morning, Dr. Snyder. How are you?

A. Good morning, Mr. Oppenheimer.

Q. I don't think this will be long. Let's start where you and Mr. Schwarz just left off and just finish that up quickly.

In your analysis, did you—with respect to coordination, did you consider Dr. Hill's opinion regarding the ebooks case?

A. I did.

Q. And may we bring up Slide 68, Pam? Does the ebooks case in your opinion show that the market for acquisition of books, the market for acquisition of books from authors upstream, is vulnerable to coordinated conduct?

A. No. In fact, the differences are instructive.

Q. Okay. Would you elaborate by reference to your demonstrative that we have on the screen?

A. As I mentioned earlier, one difference is Apple. You had a coordinating firm, the so-called hub and spoke.

The second major difference is that this conspiracy as alleged concerned downstream prices which were observable. Neither of those two things are present in the context of the acquisitions of book rights.

Q. And are there any other factors that you observed?

A. Well, those are the two main factors. And I don't want to get into the—back into the question of Random House's role. My understanding is that they were not a defendant.

Q. Understood. Going to the colloquy with Mr. Schwarz with respect to following the orders of a CEO, just talking about practice now, would it be your understanding that as a matter of the economics of coordination that literally every acquiring publisher would have to be told about this coordination?

A. Well, maybe not every one, but you'd have to get more than a small number.

Q. And would it be the case that in every instance in which there was—let me rephrase.

Describe for us, if you would, what the process would need to be for each editor to determine whether they were dealing with a situation where the author that was approaching them had made an independent decision to leave their prior publisher.

A. That gets back to your Honor's question. It's possible that the CEOs—let's go with this theory—are going to say: We're not going to poach. And there's five of them.

But then they want to carve out an exception: Well, it's okay if we're approached.

Well, can that be—can that approach be manufactured? How do you distinguish between when somebody is adhering to the agreement? Per the guidelines, when are the deviations from the agreement detectable? And what is the punishment going to be?

In this situation, unless you say "No poaching, never, we're never going to," then the issue of detection becomes really important. And then if it's that conspiracy, then I go back to: Why would a small number of publishers do that unless they had everybody on board or nearly everybody on board?

Q. In your work—by the way, Professor Snyder, you've testified as an expert in other cases with respect to coordination. Is that correct?

A. High-tech employees.

Q. And in your work in this area and in this case, have you ever seen reports of coordination in the upstream acquisition market for books?

A. No. And I don't think Dr. Hill has said that he sees anything either in terms of the baseline type of coordination.

Q. Let's change gears. I want to ask you some questions. Now we're getting into a bit of housekeeping, Professor Snyder. We're close to the end here. I appreciate your patience.

But I want to talk a little bit about margins.

And you were questioned yesterday by Mr. Schwarz regarding the inclusion of operating costs when calculating margins. Do you have that question-and-answer sequence in mind?

A. I certainly have the topic in mind.

Q. All right. And have you had an opportunity to review Simon & Schuster's Mr. Karp's trial testimony on this point?

A. Yes. Parts of it, at least.

Q. And do you recall that Mr. Karp testified regarding S&S having targets in the acquisition P&Ls for both gross margin and operating income margins?

A. My recollection is that both parties reflect operating expenses in that way.

Q. Can you tell us the significance of that or the way in which you treated margins in your analysis?

A. Well, I wanted to follow their practice as reflected in the book-level P&Ls, recognizing that what I called the Economics 101 approach does not work in the context where you have a large number of operating units making bids. And if all of them were to be willing to bid to a margin that did not allow for some recovery of operating expenses, that would be unsustainable.

Q. And would you explain why, briefly?

A. By exception, it's fine. But if you do it—I think this came up very early on. Suppose you've got 100 books published and now you look at the 101st. Well, the marginal costs of that are low. The margins are high.

But if you did that for all 101, the problem would be the firm would not be through the activities of these distributed imprints capturing enough of their operating expenses, including Mr. Schwarz's, you know, example of the CEO salary.

But in general, what firms have to do is not just price for the 101st book; they have to price in a way that sustains the organization.

Q. And do you recall the general standard that Simon & Schuster wants to achieve for operating income in their acquisition P&Ls?

A. Could you repeat that?

Q. Sure. Do you recall the general standard that S&S wants to achieve for operating income margin in their acquisition P&Ls? And I don't believe an exact number was used.

A. I don't recall.

Q. Do you recall whether it was positive?

A. Yes.

Q. What is the significance of that for you?

A. Well, it's instructive about—you know, this is Management 201, not Econ. 101. You have—I'm just repeating myself.

Q. Pardon me.

MR. OPPENHEIMER: Pam, if we can bring up Plaintiff's Exhibit 577. Your Honor, this has already been admitted.

THE COURT: Okay.

BY MR. OPPENHEIMER:

Q. I want to draw your attention—let's see. We want to move a couple of pages back. This is the P&L. Here we go. Do you recognize this as a portion of the book-level P&L that you examined in your work in this case?

THE COURT: This is confidential, correct?

MR. OPPENHEIMER: Yes, your Honor. Thank you.

THE WITNESS: Yes. This is a book-level P&L.

BY MR. OPPENHEIMER:

Q. And I'd like to draw your attention—we've highlighted it—it's about two-thirds of the way down the page. There's a gross margin line. Do you see that?

A. I do.

Q. And then below the gross margin line, there are six categories of fixed expenses. Do you see those?

A. Fixed expenses. They include editorial, warehousing, non-titled advertising, production, selling, and the last one is G&A.

Q. And would you classify those as ongoing operating expenses?

A. Yes

Q. Would you explain why?

A. Well, for example, warehousing. To be in the book business, you have to figure out a way to distribute the books. So that's an ongoing expense. Selling is an ongoing expense. G&A is a general category.

So these are operating expenses that occur on an ongoing basis. And what's reflected here and what I see consistently is that S&S and PRH are given guidance, not that it can't be put aside by exception, but the guidance here is price in a way that allows us to cover these ongoing operating expenses. And this is what I mean by Management 201.

Q. And below those entries, do you see the line for operating income?

A. Yes. It's 13.6 percent.

Q. And is the operating income being calculated after accounting for those ongoing operating expenses?

A. Yes.

Q. What does this tell you about how Simon & Schuster treats ongoing operating expenses when calculating profit margins in title-level P&Ls?

A. Unsurprisingly, in this kind of organization that Nobel laureate Oliver Williamson described, where there's delegated authority down to operating units as opposed to top-down control of everything, you end up with a mechanism like this where you provide guidance in the form of book-level P&Ls, guidance that then informs how the individual editors should bid and what targets they have to hit.

THE COURT: Can I ask, are you saying that Dr. Hill in his analysis used the gross margin line, that very high number, instead of the operating income line, which is a much, much lower number?

THE WITNESS: Your Honor, in his first report, for PRH, he included operating expenses; and for Simon & Schuster, he did not. I pointed—

THE COURT: For Simon & Schuster, he was using the gross margin line?

THE WITNESS: Yes. That's my—now—"yes" is the short answer. Yes.

THE COURT: Thank you.

BY MR. OPPENHEIMER:

Q. And then in closing on this issue, Mr. Snyder, how does this relate to your testimony yesterday that in creating the profit margins to correct Dr. Hill's model inputs, you need to include ongoing operating expenses?

A. I believe the practice here for both companies leads you to when you're selecting margins to include margins that reflect the importance of capturing these ongoing operating expenses. So in terms of the exhibit, you would go to the lower number, operating income margin of, in this particular example, 13.6 and not use the larger one.

I would just add, though, even if you disagree, you should do it consistently. He did not do it consistently in his first report. He did it consistently in his second report—I'm sorry—in his third report. But as I testified earlier, those results are completely unreliable based on the reliability test that Dr. Nathan Hill—Miller, rather—provided to people using his model.

That's based on the predicted margin versus actual.

Q. Thank you. Now, just one of the last, I think, housekeeping matters: There's been some discussion over the last day or so about whether in the market that's being proposed for books over $250,000 we're talking about 1,200 books a year or 1,800 books a year. So let me ask you a couple questions about that. First, do you and Dr. Hill agree that there are approximately 1,000 to 1,200 books acquired at or over a

$250,000-per-book advance annually?

A. Could you slow down a little bit on the number there?

Q. I apologize. Are you and Dr. Hill in agreement that there are approximately 1,000 to 1,200 books acquired at the 250-and-up category level?

A. That's the number that I keep hearing about, somewhere around that number. And again, both Dr. Hill and I have to struggle with contracts versus titles.

Q. Just to close on that point, with respect to your work overall, is the distinction between contracts and titles one that changes any of your outcomes in any material way?

A. No. I identified the issue as a source of messiness, but it doesn't impact my fundamental analyses in any way.

Q. Okay. And then just to close off on this, if you could go to your notebook that has the reports, I'd like to have you take a quick look at Dr. Hill's initial report. That's the May 10 report. And I know you have a lot of notebooks there, but you should have one with his reports in it. Excellent.

A. His initial report?

Q. Yes. And what I'd like to do is draw your attention to a figure that's in Appendix E, Page E-1. This is confidential. This is Dr. Hill's Figure 25, just to close off the numbering. Do you have that? I think we have it on the screen as well.

A. Yes.

Q. So this figure, 25, from Dr. Hill's report covers three years. I'll represent to you that 2021's a partial year in his data.

And if I draw your attention down to the bottom, where it says Total Advances Count, do you see there that for the years 2019 and 2020 we're looking respectively for 2019, a count of 1,132 and for 2020, 1,294? Do you see those?

A. I do.

Q. Is this consistent with your understanding that this segment sees about 1,000 to 1,200 titles a year?

A. That's correct. And you were right about the 2021 figure: His data go through the first six months of that calendar year.

Q. Now, a few general questions and then we're done. I want to go back to best bids briefly, single-round best bid auctions. Do you have those in mind?

A. Yes.

Q. Just some general questions: In a single-round best bid auction, what causes the highest bidder to pay the most?

A. It can be influenced by a large number of factors, one of which is the maximum value that the editor and publisher are willing to pay conditioned on the match, provided that that maximum meets the—in general—the financial guidance reflected in the book-level P&Ls with respect to operating expenses.

Q. Is it influenced by other bidders in the best bids auction format?

A. It can be. Not in a specific way, because you don't know who's bidding. However, you may have a sense that there will be a lot of interest in a particular book. You may have a sense that maybe not.

Q. And what is the competitive constraint in a single-round best bids auction?

A. Well, in the best bids situation, the top bid pays what they bid. And if—but to be the top bid, they have to beat out the second bid, second-highest.

Q. And referring now to the best bid situation, Professor Snyder, the single-round best bid?

A. Single-round best bid, for you to win it, you have to beat the second.

Q. I see. I'm sorry. My question is not well designed. Let me ask you this: Is there an economic basis for believing that the amount other bidders offer in a best bid affects the winning bid in a single-round best bid auction?

A. It depends.

Q. Is there an economic basis for believing that the number of other bidders affects the winning bid in a single-round best bid auction?

A. Well, in general, when you go into the best bid situation, you don't know the number of bidders. Again, you may have some sense of how much interest there will be in a book.

And this goes back to what I described earlier as the role of—the combination of common factors and private factors. If it's a well-known author, it's probably not going to go to a single-round best bid. But in general, for certain authors, the common factors play a bigger role.

Q. I think you said that in a single-round best bid situation, the participants do not know who the other bidders are. Is that correct?

A. Maybe by exception. But no. And you see that in the testimony offered by the agent Pande, where she's inviting multiple imprints from PRH and others to engage. And in general, when they respond, they don't know who else is involved. They may have a general sense that: Well, HarperCollins is likely to be in this or maybe Chronicle will be in this. But they don't know.

Q. And in a single-round best bid situation, do the bidders know the bids of the other participants?

A. No.

Q. And do they—again, assuming a single-round best bids situation, do they ever know that before the winning bid is determined?

A. Put it this way: The agent wants to call best bids, and the agent's not going to provide that information. The agent wants to get the best bid.

Q. Do you understand one of the Government's theories is predicated on a belief that there will always be, always be, one less competitor participating in every acquisition process?

A. The—

Q. Let—pardon me.

A. Here we go from the world inside the model where there is always one less bidder to the real world. And in the real world, I think the Government's overall complaint wouldn't say "always." But it focuses on when there is a reduction.

Q. And within the model itself, the second-score auction model, it does always assume that there is—that every publisher's bidding in every acquisition?

MR. SCHWARZ: Objection. Leading. It sounds like you're telling him what the answer is.

MR. OPPENHEIMER: Your Honor, it was—

THE COURT: I'm going to overrule that objection.

MR. OPPENHEIMER: Okay. And I'll withdraw my statement

THE COURT: It was leading, but it's so clear that I don't think it's—

THE WITNESS: I think I've testified about this. But maybe not. Yes. The model assumes that all the bidders bid, but there is no imprint competition. So all that's reflected is a particular bid for one publishing house.

They all bid. And then the merger reduces the number of bidders by one in every case.

In contrast to the real world—call that big number N. In the real world, agents pick and engage a smaller number. Call it P. And whether there's a reduction depends on the circumstances following the merger. And even if there is, the agent can go to others to replace that bidder.

MR. OPPENHEIMER: No further questions, your Honor.

THE COURT: Thank you. Anything else from you, Mr. Schwarz?

MR. SCHWARZ: No. I'm finished, your Honor.

THE COURT: Thank you. Thank you for your testimony, Dr. Snyder.

THE WITNESS: Thank you, your Honor.

THE COURT: You may step down. (Witness excused.)

MR. PETROCELLI: Your Honor, with that, Defendants rest.

RULING ON THE INADMISSIBILITY OF PRH'S EFFICIENCIES MODEL EVIDENCE

THE COURT: Good morning, Mr. Fishbein. We had agreed yesterday that we would begin today by addressing the matter of the government's motion to exclude the defendants' efficiencies. So, I am prepared to hear oral argument on that issue and to issue a ruling at this time.

MR. SCHWARZ: Good morning. Mel Schwarz for the United States. May it please the Court. I don't want to belabor this issue too much with a lot of case discussion, but I am prepared to go into as much detail as you like with respect to the cases. I think there are two essential reasons why the efficiencies claims, and I will call them that because the law is a little unclear about whether it's an actual affirmative defense or burdens of proof, but we will just call them claims, the two reasons why it fails. First of all, putting aside the independent expert, if we just went on what we have heard, it fails. It's neither verified nor verifiable. We are looking at a financial model prepared, as Your Honor heard, for the purposes of purchasing Simon & Schuster. It was prepared by someone who doesn't know anything about the horizontal guidelines. That's no fault of his, but that's the truth of the matter, and it is based on November 2020 data. Even though it was updated innumerable times, I don't even think Mr. Sansigre knows how many times, for some reason which I can't explain, perhaps Mr. Frackman can, the November 9 model becomes the holy grail for them. I don't understand it. So, we don't have any updates of actual data which obviously would be relevant to many things because, as Your Honor heard, the 12.3 percent on operating expenses is hard coded, hard wired. Whatever term you want to use, you get the point. So beyond that, he uses hard coding from a seven-year-old, seven years old in 2020, merger of Penguin and Random House in which—and Your Honor hasn't heard. There's a lot more evidence about dis-synergies in terms of revenue. We haven't heard that evidence. In any event, even if we looked at that, the world has changed dramatically since 2013. We had the rise of ebooks and audio books, and we have 26, I think the witness said, mergers in the meantime, including major independents like Workman and HMH. So those numbers are simply not sufficient. And the coup de grace on all this is that Mr. Sansigre testified in his deposition that you don't know the exact numbers until you do an integration plan, which is perfectly logical, because he did not and could not go through one by one and say we want to keep this employee, we want to get rid of this employee, this person stays, this one goes and, of course, their salaries are different. So, you can't make these judgments until afterwards.

Why they didn't hire an independent expert, which is point two, again, I can't speak to that. But the law has been clear since the 2010 guidelines that you need to have independent verification. Judge Howell said that shortly after this. There are three other cases that I can cite for Your Honor, which say that point blank. The D.C. Circuit in the Anthem case is extremely skeptical of all these things, which is another issue. If we had to, Your Honor, at the end of this trial, we will tell Your Honor there is no efficiencies defense in this circumstance where you have the number one company trying to buy the number three. They don't need efficiencies. Frankly, if anything, the evidence would be, if we keep going, that S&S is leaner than PRH, but that's another story.

THE COURT: Can I ask with you, Mr. Schwarz, based on your argument, we could never have efficiencies evidence in a merger trial because you are saying we would never know until after the merger is complete. We would never have good enough data for you until that point. There must be something short of that. The degree of precision you are demanding can't be required.

MR. SCHWARZ: That is not the case, Your Honor. It would have been very easy for them to hire McKinsey. Dr. Israel is the name of an expert who comes up frequently on the defense side of many of these cases. It would have—I'm sure, particularly after the contract was signed, they could have sent them in, as they did by the way in the Anthem case, and go through and come up with things that could well be cognizable efficiencies. There's also lots of cognizable efficiencies that one could imagine that are fairly clear. If you have, you know, somebody who doesn't have a factory that is state of the art and can move there, you could envision something that is fairly clear. But you would still need—and I couldn't imagine, you know, if I were sitting up there, Your Honor, which I never will be, but—

THE COURT: You never know, Mr. Schwarz.

MR. SCHWARZ:—how I would figure out without the aid of experts on both sides poking holes in this to figure this out. We need to have an expert. It is perfectly possible to do this after the contract is signed. The reason Mr. Sansigre can't do it is because if the deal falls apart, they are competitors and he can't see all this confidential data. He can't see the employees' salaries because there would be poaching going on. If Dr. Israel or McKinsey came in, it would be perfectly plausible for them to do that. And that's what happens in cases where these merger efficiencies are considered. I would be the first to admit that it's extremely rare for efficiencies defenses to carry the day even in the best of circumstances, and you will hear a lot of argument about that if we go further down this road. But there is one and only one case—I am going to lay it straight out for Your Honor. There's one case that they cite in which—and this is Judge Hogan and before the merger guidelines, 25 years ago in the first Staples case where he heard—he heard evidence from a management witness, and then he proceeded to listen to the defense witness and completely discredit the management expert and found, and I'm quoting, defendant failed to produce the necessary documentation for verification. And that was at 970 F.Supp 1058 at page 1089. That is it. That is the one case where this evidence went to a consideration by the judge.

THE COURT: Okay.

MR. SCHWARZ: And two holdings, Judge Howell's case and Judge Chutkan case, the Wilhelmsen case, are holdings in which they said, because there's no independent expert, we will not credit, even though there was an effort to present that evidence. Unless Your Honor has questions, that's all I have to say.

THE COURT: Thank you, Mr. Schwarz.

MR. SCHWARZ: Thank you.

THE COURT: Mr. Frackman.

MR. FRACKMAN: Good morning, Your Honor.

THE COURT: Good morning.

MR. FRACKMAN: I have some slides that I might use, but let me start by addressing a few questions. Every witness that the Court has heard discussing this transaction, I am not just talking about the Penguin Random House witnesses, the Simon & Schuster witness, the HarperCollins witness, the Hachette witness, they have all testified that there are likely tens of millions of dollars of synergies flowing from an acquisition of Simon & Schuster by another publishing house, not a few million, tens of millions. I won't say on the record. The Court has heard that testimony. The Penguin Random House estimate, although different in some respects, is not out of line with the estimates of these other potential acquirers and of Simon & Schuster itself, point one.

Point two, the test is not mathematical precision. We are predicting the future. Even the best models have a component of uncertainty to them. There is no case that says you have to have mathematical precision with respect to any forward-looking projection including efficiencies. Third, there is no case that mandates an expert to prove efficiencies. They are used sometimes. They weren't used in Staples. They weren't used in Peabody, the recent 2020 case from the Eastern District of Missouri. And we all know that as good as experts are in certain respects, paid experts, experts are experts. They are not independent, court-appointed neutrals. To suggest that an expert is more reliable than a fact witness when it comes to estimating efficiencies of this type is, I think, highly speculative.

THE COURT: What did you mean by court-appointed neutrals?

MR. FRACKMAN: Well, I mean, there are cases where the court appoints its own expert to assist the court in making findings. Judge Kaplan did that a few years ago in the Southern District of New York to assist on economic matters in an antitrust case. But as independent as experts are, I think it is illusory to think that they are required for this type of proof. They may be helpful, but they are not the only way to prove facts about efficiencies. No court has said they are. No court has mandated them. The test is that we have to prove that the projected efficiencies are likely to be accomplished. That's a factual matter. It requires findings by the Court. We can present those facts in different ways as long as they are reliable. Okay. So how does one predict the future when there is some degree of uncertainty? And both the DOJ and the cases have observed that the best place to ground those projections are in reliable past experience. This is the district court in FTC versus Peabody Energy. Horizontal merger guideline section 10, by contrast, efficiency claims substantiated by analogous past experience are likely to be credited. 2006 commentary on the horizontal guidelines, the best way to substantiate an efficiency claim is to demonstrate that similar efficiencies were achieved in the recent past from similar actions. The reliance on Penguin Random House's history of acquisitions, and in particular, the 2013 one, merger with Penguin, is a very reliable basis. It is maybe the best basis for predicting what will happen in the future.

THE COURT: Can I ask you about that, Mr. Frackman?

MR. FRACKMAN: Sure.

THE COURT: Then why did Mr. Sansigre project so many revenue synergies when there were none in the 2013 merger?

MR. FRACKMAN: A fair question, Your Honor. The evidence from the fact witnesses and Mr. Sansigre, but you also heard it from Mr. Dohle, is that the revenue reductions that Penguin Random House experienced actually starting in 2012 and continuing in the years after the merger with Penguin Random House—with Penguin related to reductions in mass market titles. It was an industry-wide change in response to, among other things, ebooks.

THE COURT: Yes.

MR. FRACKMAN: And that's why, with respect to projecting revenues going forward, that experience was not reliable enough for Mr. Sansigre to base his projections on.

THE COURT: Yes, I heard that testimony, but I think the revenue projections are ones that are not based on past experience and are a good example of one that's just based on management judgment which is not verifiable.

MR. FRACKMAN: I would say, Your Honor, that the testimony was that it is based on past experience such as with the other acquisitions, Little Tiger, such as with third party distribution clients that come into the Penguin Random House machine or a distribution system, and that, therefore, the very small forward-looking projections on revenue growth that Mr. Sansigre used in his model were based on past experience. It is undoubtedly correct that when you are talking about forward-looking revenue projections as opposed to cost savings, there's an additional element of uncertainty. We can't dispute that. That is just a fact. It's axiomatic with respect to that type of projection. However—

THE COURT: Mr. Frackman, it seems to me that it is possible to verify some of the work that Mr. Sansigre did. And it was very detailed work. So, an expert could or an independent person trying to verify what he did could look at all the inputs that he put into the spreadsheets, which were very detailed, they could interview him and the other people he talked about about what assumptions he made and determine if those were reasonable assumptions. And I think much of the work could be verified. I don't think that happened here, and I am kind of wondering why. But then there are some things that I don't think are really verifiable, things like the revenue projections where he's picking and choosing among the prior precedents. This is not like the Penguin Random House merger, but it is like the Tiger acquisition. He's exercising judgment that's not verifiable. So what am I supposed to do with that?

MR. FRACKMAN: Well, the Court, of course, was perceptive enough to notice that when we started with Mr. Sansigre, we started with those that were easily verifiable such as real estate savings.

THE COURT: Got it. Some of it can be but—

MR. FRACKMAN: Return rate differentials.

THE COURT: Got it.

MR. FRACKMAN: I think, Your Honor, this is why this type of issue, I don't think there's any case where the court has tried to grapple with it mid case because it does require a fine tooth comb. We are going to have to look at the individual categories. It is certainly possible that the Court could conclude that some, if not the preponderance, of the efficiencies we claim, real estate, IT, return rate differentials, and other items, are verifiable and are reliable, reasonably reliable, without having to find that with respect to all of it.

THE COURT: I want to make sure I am understanding you. Are you saying that I can pick and choose among these efficiencies and credit some and not others?

MR. FRACKMAN: Absolutely.

THE COURT: But none of them are verified. How am I supposed to do that?

For example, Mr. Sansigre said he, for the real estate, he looked at leases and determined what the amounts were, and then he looked at reports that said we can assume 50 percent savings because we can sublease. I am not looking at the leases. I don't want to look at that. I don't want to look at the report that told him 50 percent. I'm not in a position to verify that Mr. Sansigre did what he said he did. I don't see how a court can do the type of verification that's necessary here because I don't think a court should just take a merging party's word for it.

MR. FRACKMAN: This is why we provided, and it's embedded in Mr. Sansigre's exhibits, the factual foundation to substantiate those items. Real estate is a good example.

THE COURT: But you are expecting me to go into the spreadsheets and look at those things and then look at the leases and make sure he's correct?

MR. FRACKMAN: Well, it's one lease in particular. The amount of the lease is set forth clearly in the papers. The Court has our—his testimony that points exactly where the amount of the lease is, the expiration date, and the Court has—

THE COURT: Why would you expect me to do that? Why didn't you get an expert to do this for me? I don't see why it's the Court's role to do this.

MR. FRACKMAN: Your Honor, that would be the conclusion, that you must—a party must have an expert in order to prove efficiencies.

THE COURT: You don't have to but—I don't think you necessarily have to as a rule according to the horizontal merger guidelines, but as a practical matter, it's your burden and you can't expect a court to go through, as you said, with a fine tooth comb what your clients have done. I don't understand why you wouldn't get an expert to verify this because otherwise you can't meet your burden.

MR. FRACKMAN: There's nothing more for an expert to, quote, verify. The amount of the lease is set forth in the documents. The termination date is set forth in the documents. The support for the 50 percent re-leasing, re-letting assumption is set forth in the documents.

THE COURT: Okay. Let's take a step back, Mr. Frackman. I think the reason courts have wanted verification and have been quite stringent in their requirements is because merging parties have an incentive to be optimistic about what the efficiencies are going to be. And a lot of the paperwork and spreadsheets you are relying on were prepared for different purposes, you know, to justify buying the company. It wasn't for the purpose that we are now using these spreadsheets for. And given that—and it's not to say that the parties weren't acting in good faith, but of course they are optimistic about what's going to happen. That's why they want to do this deal. And the case law is clear that they could just project fantastical efficiencies, as Judge Howell said. And if we are going to look at efficiencies, we are going to be careful and rigorous and make sure that they are independently verified, verified by somebody, not the parties who have an incentive to be very rosy in their expectations. Okay. And on this record, there is no independent party that has verified these efficiencies. And you are saying let's take Mr. Sansigre's word for it. And I think Mr. Sansigre seemed very competent and did a very careful job, but he can't verify himself. And I don't think a court is in a position to do the type of very careful, rigorous verification that is required to rely on this evidence.

MR. FRACKMAN: Well, Your Honor, the test is verifiable—

THE COURT: And verified. Cognizable efficiencies are verified according to the horizontal merger guidelines.

MR. FRACKMAN: In every one of the cases that address efficiencies, the Court has reviewed and made findings with respect to the specific efficiencies. The Court always has to make those findings, and that's why it's verifiable and whether they are likely to be achieved. With respect to real estate, it's a great one to start with, what more could we do, Your Honor? We have—

THE COURT: You could have an independent expert look at the leases and look at whatever JP Morgan study he was relying on and verify that that was correct because I can't do it.

MR. FRACKMAN: Look, Your Honor, it is totally reasonable in my view, in our view, for the projection to be based on the recommendation of JP Morgan.

THE COURT: I agree, but I don't know what that recommendation was. I am not verifying and looking at what it was.

MR. FRACKMAN: Well, it's in the record, Your Honor. The actual document from JP Morgan that said greater than 50 percent is in the record. Mr. Sansigre took only 50 percent.

THE COURT: Okay. I think I understand your argument, Mr. Frackman.

MR. FRACKMAN: IT is another example, Your Honor.

THE COURT: Okay.

MR. FRACKMAN: The amount assessed by Simon & Schuster—by Paramount to Simon & Schuster is stated in the documentation in the model with the backup the actual line items charged, assessed by the parent.

THE COURT: So, I take it that this is just a strategic choice that the defendants have made, that they decided not to have an independent expert verify this because they chose to ask the Court to go through all of the underlying documents to verify the efficiencies of the November 2020 model. Is that what you are saying?

MR. FRACKMAN: I don't think that's correct, Your Honor, at all. Obviously it was a choice like all choices in a case. We believe that Mr. Sansigre's analysis is detailed, fact-based, reliable, more than sufficient for the Court to find that they are likely or more likely to occur than not. And, actually, I don't think an expert would relieve the Court ultimately of having to make some decisions about that.

THE COURT: All right. Can you address the fact that the model is not up to date, that it doesn't include the most recent actual numbers?

MR. FRACKMAN: Yes. So, first of all, as Mr. Sansigre testified yesterday, the difference between the November 2020 and January '22 amounts are minimal. I think he said 6 percent. But more importantly, the core testimony here and the rationale for using the November 2020 is that the last two years have been so idiosyncratic because of the pandemic and the impact in particular, well, on many businesses, but particularly on the publishing industry, that it would be less reliable to project going forward based on the last two years than on the actual historical trends predating the pandemic.

THE COURT: How do we know that? How do we know that that's a reasonable prediction, because none of us have a crystal ball, and I think it's really not reasonable to assume that the world is going to go back to pre-pandemic levels.

MR. FRACKMAN: Well, this, of course, would relate primarily to the revenue enhancements. The cost savings are the same and the—

THE COURT: The 2022 to the 2020 model, they are not the same.

MR. FRACKMAN: Most of them are the same with the exception of fulfillment.

THE COURT: No, I don't think so.

MR. FRACKMAN: They are very, very close, Your Honor. Fulfillment is the one that changed. If the Court were to find that, with respect to fulfillment, the more recent projection is the more reliable, then the Court would use the more recent projection.

THE COURT: Which are also not verified, but that's another story. So, I kind of wrote this down. The January 2022 model predicts gross physical sales of 16.01 million compared to $19.66 million in the November 2022 model.The January 22 model predicts 9.57 million in fulfillment savings compared to 20.77 million in November 2020. Savings on administration is 30.57 million as compared to 18.1 million in November. I understand that includes editorial and art, but the additions from those lines don't account for that whole change. These numbers are very different. And when you tell me that they are close, you are just saying the bottom line is close, but the actual line items are very different.

MR. FRACKMAN: Well, there are two things. One is the bottom line is close. Second of all, the—

THE COURT: I'm not sure why the bottom line being close is the operative factor because the merger guidelines say you have to justify each efficiency.

MR. FRACKMAN: Correct. This is why I said—it is true that there are some small changes within the groups. Particularly I want to focus on the spending for a moment. Yes, it is not a dollar-to-dollar correction if you move the op ex for editorial art and production into administration, but it's the large part of it. And one line item that has what I would call a significant change is fulfillment. And Mr. Sansigre testified as to why that number has changed. Yes, if the Court were to find or conclude that it is more likely than not that we will not revert to pre-pandemic times and, therefore, the merged company is going to need the warehouse space that is anticipated in January '22 as opposed to crediting Mr. Sansigre's testimony that that is an outlier because the historical experience with the warehouse needs are more reliable, then we would use and the Court could use the 2022 fulfillment number.

THE COURT: Mr. Frackman, I just—I'm just really at a loss as to why I should be doing the work that you should have gotten an expert to do. Like, why should I be doing that?

MR. FRACKMAN: That assumes that the test, Your Honor, and the requirement is that we have an independent expert—an expert—no expert is completely independent—an expert.

THE COURT: I mean, you don't have to, but then you are risking a judge telling you, I don't want to do the verification for you.

MR. FRACKMAN: The Court is perfectly capable of making findings on the reliability of financial numbers. Courts do it all the time—

THE COURT: This is not a question of reliability. It's a question of verifiability. So let me step back for a moment. I think we are in a different world in the merger area versus regular Rule 702 where we talk about more general reliability because we have the horizontal merger guidelines and we have several cases that are persuasive in this actual jurisdiction that talk about verifiable and verified efficiencies. Can you name a single precedent where a court has done what you are asking me to do, that is, I should do the work of verifying a very detailed November 2020 model with hundreds of tabs to make sure that it's correct and reasonable? And is that, in your view, a good use of the Court's time?

MR. FRACKMAN: Every court that has analyzed efficiencies have looked at specific items and—

THE COURT: I am going to do that. I have listened to the testimony. But I still can't satisfy myself that all of this is verified. I have heard what Mr. Sansigre said he did, but I am not in a position to verify it.

MR. FRACKMAN: Your Honor, if the holding of the Court is that an expert is required as a matter of law, I can't argue with that. If the—you know, but if the question is is the factual support sufficient to establish that the efficiencies are likely to occur or substantial amounts of the efficiencies are likely to occur, then that finding can be made absent an expert's gloss on it. And, in fact, the horizontal merger guidelines themselves say that efficiency claims substantiated by past experience in the business, the actual business calculations, are more reliable than when they are generated outside of the usual business context.

THE COURT: I understand that. Thank you.

MR. FRACKMAN: Thank you.

THE COURT: Anything else from you, Mr. Schwarz?

MR. SCHWARZ: No, Your Honor. Just for the record I would like to say that the Peabody Energy case, which he cited, there was an expert in that case, and the court still rejected most of the efficiencies in any event. And I think the law is clear from the D.C. Circuit in Anthem on the fact that these cannot be vague, speculative, or otherwise cannot be verified by reasonable means. That's at 359. And I don't think this is reasonable at all.

THE COURT: Okay. Thank you. The Court has heard the evidence on this issue and the arguments of the parties and is prepared to rule. Dr. Snyder is an expert witness for the defendants who is offered to testify on merger-related efficiencies. His expert opinion relies on a projection of synergies produced in November of 2020 by Manuel Sansigre, a senior vice president at Penguin Random House who's in charge of mergers and acquisitions. Mr. Sansigre produced his synergy projections to help Random House evaluate whether it should acquire Simon & Schuster. Dr. Snyder's expert report offers three primary conclusions about Mr. Sansigre's projections. First, that the projected synergies are the type that economists would recognize given the features of the publishing industry. Second, that the projected synergies are merger-specific efficiencies. Third, that the projected synergies would benefit authors through higher income and consumers through greater availability of books. Significantly, however, Dr. Snyder concedes that he did not, quote, independently verify specific dollar amounts, unquote, and did not, quote, independently derive estimates, unquote, of Mr. Sansigre's projected synergies. Thus, the parties agree and stipulate that Dr. Snyder did not verify the projections from the November 2020 model that form the basis of his expert opinion on efficiencies.

The government filed a motion *in limine* to exclude Dr. Snyder's testimony on efficiencies under

Federal Rule of Evidence 702. The government argued, among other things, that Dr. Snyder's reliance on unverified projections rendered his efficiencies testimony inadmissible under Rule 702, the horizontal merger guidelines, and cases applying the horizontal merger guidelines.

The Court essentially deferred ruling on the motion to preclude the expert testimony on efficiencies determining that it should hear the evidence about Mr. Sansigre's projections before deciding whether the alleged efficiencies are verifiable and verified as required by the horizontal merger guidelines and persuasive case law. The Court decided to hear the evidence during the trial given that this is a bench trial but instructed the parties to arrange the presentation of evidence so that the verifiability of Mr. Sansigre's projected synergies could be considered and argued and the Court could then rule on the government's motion before hearing the totality of Dr. Snyder's expert testimony on efficiencies. The Court determined that it would be more efficient to proceed in this fashion because if defendants were unable to meet their burden to show that the efficiencies were substantiated, verifiable, and verified under the horizontal merger guidelines, then it would be unnecessary to consider any of the other aspects of the efficiencies evidence. The Court has now heard the evidence on the projected efficiencies and arguments from the parties, and it will grant the motion to preclude the efficiencies evidence because the efficiencies projected by Penguin Random House are not substantiated and verified. Although many of the projections may be verifiable, some are not verifiable. Moreover, the efficiencies have not, in fact, been independently verified by anyone, and they, therefore, are not cognizable under the horizontal merger guidelines and are not reliable under Rule 702.

Finally, the Court concludes that the efficiencies projections in the November 2020 model are unreliable because they are out of date and include 2021 projections that have been proved to be inaccurate.

The applicable legal standards are as follows: Federal Rule of Evidence 702 concerning testimony by expert witnesses provides, quote, a witness who is qualified as an expert by knowledge, skill, experience, training, or education may testify in the form of an opinion or otherwise if, A, the expert's scientific, technical, or other specialized knowledge will help the trier of fact to understand the evidence or to determine a fact in issue; B, the testimony is based on sufficient facts or data; C, the testimony is the product of reliable principles and methods; and D, the expert has reliably applied the principles and methods to the facts of the case, unquote. Rule 702 incorporates the Supreme Court's guidance in Daubert versus Merrell Dow Pharmaceuticals, Inc. which called upon trial judges to serve a gatekeeping role in ensuring that an expert's testimony both rests on a reliable foundation and is relevant to the task at hand.

Also in Kumho Tire Company, Limited versus Carmichael, the Supreme Court clarified that the gatekeeper role extends to all expert testimony. And this is confirmed by Rule 702's advisory committee note to the 2000 amendment. The party seeking to introduce expert testimony must demonstrate its admissibility by a preponderance of the evidence. Courts take a flexible approach to deciding Rule 702 motions and have broad discretion in determining whether to admit or exclude expert testimony. Horizontal merger guideline section 10. The horizontal merger guidelines outline the analysis and enforcement practices of the Department of Justice and the Federal Trade Commission with respect to horizontal mergers under the federal antitrust laws including section 7 of the Clayton Act. See horizontal merger guideline section 1. Federal courts frequently use the guidelines to develop legal standards in antitrust litigation. See, for example, FTC versus H.J. Heinz Company, 246 F.3d 708. That's a D.C. Circuit case from 2001. Section 10 of the horizontal merger guidelines discusses efficiencies. The guidelines observe that efficiencies are difficult to verify and quantify in part because much of the information relating to efficiencies is uniquely in the possession of the merging firms. Moreover, efficiencies projected reasonably and in good faith by the merging firms may not be realized. Therefore, the merger guidelines say, it is incumbent upon the merging firms to substantiate efficiency claims so that the agencies can verify by reasonable means the likelihood and magnitude of each asserted efficiency. Courts interpret this requirement of substantiation and verification to encompass, quote, how and when each efficiency would be achieved and any costs of doing so, how each efficiency would enhance the merged firm's ability and incentive to compete, and why each would be merger specific, end quote. That's from United States versus H&R Block, 833 F.Supp.2d 36 at 89. That's a D.D.C. case from 2011, and it is quoting the horizontal merger guidelines section 10. Under the guidelines, projected efficiencies are generally less credible when generated outside the usual business planning process, and they are more credible when substantiated by analogous past experience.

Ultimately, efficiencies must be cognizable to be considered under the guidelines. Quote, cognizable efficiencies are merger-specific efficiencies that have been verified and do not arise from anticompetitive reductions in output or service. A cognizable efficiency claim must represent a type of cost saving that could not be achieved without the merger, and the estimate of the predicted saving must be reasonably verifiable by an independent party. And that's quoting the horizontal merger guidelines and also, I believe, H&R Block. Case law provides that the Court must undertake a rigorous analysis of the kinds of efficiencies being urged by the parties in order to ensure that those efficiencies represent more than mere speculation and promises about post-merger waiver. That's H&R Block at 89. So, thus, in sum, the foregoing legal standards and precedents place the burden on defendants to establish that the projected efficiency relied upon by Dr. Snyder are substantiated, that they are reasonably verifiable by an independent party, and that they are, in fact, verified.

Where efficiencies are not independently verifiable and verified, no court in this jurisdiction has ever given any weight to such efficiencies evidence. See H&R Block, 833 F.Supp.2d 36, D.D.C. 2011; United States versus Aetna, 240 F.Supp.3d, D.D.C. 2017; FTC versus Sysco Corporation, 113 F.Supp.3d, 1, D.D.C. 2015; FTC versus Wilhelmsen Holding, ASA, 341 F.Supp.3d 27, D.D.C. 2018; FTC versus Staples, 970 F.Supp 1066, D.D.C. 1997. This is because it is the parties' interest to be aggressive and optimistic in the projection of efficiencies to justify their own merger. Because courts are not well-positioned to verify such projections, independent verification is critical in order to allow a court to determine whether such projections are reliable. Without verification, the efficiencies analysis could swallow the analytical framework required by the Clayton Act. See H&R Block at 91. The Court's findings and conclusions are as follows: Number one, many of the projected efficiencies in the November 2020 model may be verifiable, but at least some are not verifiable. According to the testimony of Mr. Sansigre, he and his team worked very hard to derive the efficiencies model. They began in March 2020 by including detailed data about Penguin Random House. When data became available from Simon & Schuster in September 2020, he added that data to the model. When additional data became available in October 2020, he included that data as well. The data and assumptions in the model were closely checked by executives in the Bertelsmann M&A group and the ZI risk management group including Markus Dohle and Nihar Malaviya.

Mr. Sansigre estimates that the model was revised a hundred times before it became final. All of Mr. Sansigre's judgments and assumptions were based on his broad experience in M&A and in particular in M&A in the publishing industry.

And the Court has no doubt that Mr. Sansigre is very competent, an expert in these matters. Mr. Sansigre uses the term synergies and efficiencies interchangeably. His model identified four categories of synergies; real estate, operating expenses, variable costs, and revenue. The real estate efficiencies were largely based on expected consolidation of Simon & Schuster's New York headquarters with Penguin Random House's New York headquarters. Mr. Sansigre consulted with managers within Penguin Random House and determined that the personnel of Simon & Schuster could be accommodated in Penguin Random House's New York office space. He then examined Simon & Schuster's lease and consulted with real estate experts who advised him that he could sublet Simon & Schuster's office space for 50 percent of the rental payments owed under the lease. He also examined other real estate holdings and estimated some additional savings from allowing other leases to expire. Based on those calculations, he projected approximately $10 million in savings per year, almost all of which are from consolidating the New York office space.

The operating expense synergies reflect efficiencies in headcount and non-headcount expenses, essentially personnel costs. Mr. Sansigre's November 2020 model projected $ in annual operating expense synergies in 2025. You know, I didn't think of this before, parties, but I do have numbers in this. Is it okay for me to be reading this publicly?

MR. FRACKMAN: As the Court knows, we actually made quite an effort to keep the numbers confidential. And I think both Simon & Schuster and Penguin Random House believe they are confidential. They affect personnel issues and subsequent events.

THE COURT: I am going to black out the numbers then, and we will issue a blacked out—I will just black out the numbers and then read on the record. Thank you. I'm sorry about that. Okay. So Mr. Sansigre's November 2020 model projected a certain amount in annual operating expense synergies in 2025. Mr. Sansigre began by predicting a percentage decrease in operating expenses. And this figure was based on prior operating expense synergies in 26 prior acquisitions including the 2013 Penguin Random House merger which had operating expense synergies of a certain percentage as well as consultation with Penguin Random House executives like Mr. Malaviya and Mr. Dohle. Then Mr. Sansigre looked at the data examining costs department by department to identify where operating expense synergies actually might be achieved.

In some departments such as sales, IT, and administration, Mr. Sansigre looked at specific employee roles and third party contracts to determine which kinds of positions or contacts might be redundant to estimate headcount and non-headcount savings. In some other departments such as fulfillment, Mr. Sansigre used his judgment to project a percentage of savings based on considerations like Penguin Random House's ability to scale its distribution to meet a portion of Simon & Schuster's distribution demand. After reviewing the department-by-department data, Mr. Sansigre compared the cumulative projected synergies of that analysis with the expected percentage of synergies that he had used based on prior transactions and management judgment, and the two projected synergies number matched. Mr. Sansigre's November 2020 model projected a certain amount of annual variable cost synergies in 2025. As part of the variable costs, Mr. Sansigre considered return rates. He found that Penguin Random House had lower return rates than Simon & Schuster by certain percentage points between 2017 and 2021. He reviewed records of improved rates from the 2013 merger from Penguin and Random House, the acquisition of smaller publishers like Little Tiger, and experiences of Penguin Random House's third party distribution clients. He also consulted Simon & Schuster and Penguin Random House management. Based on those considerations, Mr. Sansigre used his judgment to predict a certain percentage of improvement in Simon & Schuster's post-merger return rate by 2025. Penguin Random House's investments in a supply chain were a significant factor in those projections. Mr. Sansigre's November 2020 model projected a certain amount of annual revenue synergies in 2025. The most significant projected revenue synergies came from gross physical sales and audio. After accounting for certain rising costs, most significantly royalties and advance write-offs, he came up with a particular number that was a projected increase in sales. And the sales projections are based on Mr. Sansigre's judgment and experience. Penguin Random House's large sales force was a significant factor in Mr. Sansigre's gross physical sales projections. He believed this large sales force would get Simon & Schuster books into more stores and, thus, increase sales, namely in independent books stores, specialty stores, and international retailers.

Simon & Schuster relies on its top customers for a greater proportion of its sales than Penguin Random House does. Mr. Sansigre interpreted this to mean that Penguin Random House could improve Simon & Schuster's sales among it's non-top customers. Considering past acquisitions, Mr. Sansigre noted that Penguin Random House doubled the sales of Little Tiger's imprints within two years after acquiring the smaller publisher. Notably, however, Mr. Sansigre's sales projections do not align with the historical data from the 2013 merger of Penguin and Random House which is more similar in scale to the proposed merger of Penguin Random House and Simon & Schuster. After the 2013 merger, sales declined. Mr. Sansigre discounts the sales results of the 2013 merger because of changed market conditions including the decline of commercial fiction around 2013 in which Penguin was heavily invested at the time. In audio, Mr. Sansigre predicted that Penguin Random House's significant investments in in-house audio production would let it improve Simon & Schuster's audio revenue because Simon & Schuster relied on third parties for much of its audio revenue.

Mr. Sansigre used his judgment to predict that Simon & Schuster would have a certain percentage increase in audio revenue post merger through essentially growing with the market and benefiting from Penguin Random House's in-house capabilities. Mr. Sansigre discounted Simon & Schuster's management's relatively high predictions for a Simon & Schuster standalone future audio revenue because he wanted to independently analyze the value of the merger.

So in sum, Mr. Sansigre's projected synergies are based on educated management judgments mostly based on past experience and applied to whatever detailed data about the businesses of Penguin Random House and Simon & Schuster that was available to him. Many of the projections about cost savings are arguably verifiable because theoretically an independent party could look at all the underlying data about the costs of each entity that Mr. Sansigre compiled and inputted into his spreadsheets. They could get detailed explanations about the assumptions that Mr. Sansigre made in coming up with his percentage estimates of savings, and they could determine whether those assumptions were reasonable and based on past experience. Relying on past experience is favored by the horizontal merger guidelines. Some of the projections, however, most notably the revenue projections, are not verifiable and are not based on past experience. The November 2020 model projects sales synergies after the merger even though past experience does not support any sales synergies because after Penguin and Random House merged in 2013, they experienced a decrease in sales. There were other merger experiences of Penguin Random House that supported the idea of sales synergies, but Mr. Sansigre picked and chose among the different precedents and he justified his sales projections not relying on Penguin and Random House merger based on his evaluation of changed marketing conditions. Therefore, the actual percentages that Mr. Sansigre chose to apply to revenues as synergies are not verifiable. Indeed, the defendants have conceded that revenue synergies are the least easy to predict, and one of Mr. Sansigre's own emails in the record acknowledges that the sales efficiencies are difficult to predict. Ultimately, however, the projected sales synergies are derived from Mr. Sansigre's personal judgment, and they are not consistent with the most prominent past experience and, thus, the projected sales synergies in particular are not verifiable. Number two, none of the efficiencies are independently verified. The parties agree and stipulate that, regardless of whether the model was verifiable, it was not, in fact, verified by anyone outside of Penguin Random House. Thus, there was no independent verification as the horizontal merger guidelines and prior case law contemplate. Defendants argue that the Court may verify the projections by hearing how they were derived and satisfying itself that Mr. Sansigre put in a lot of work and made reasonable assumptions, but the Court strongly disagrees that this is what is contemplated by horizontal merger guidelines and the case law.

The Court is not in a position to fact-check what Mr. Sansigre says that he did or to determine whether his assumptions were reasonable. Notably, none of the cases that have considered this issue support the notion that the Court should provide the independent verification necessary to support efficiencies evidence proffered by defendants. Defendants have said that there's no case that says an expert is necessary. And I think that's true. Nobody has said that explicitly. But the defendants have the burden to establish that these efficiencies were independently verified, and they assume a risk in litigation in arguing to a court that a court should do that work that in many precedents was performed by experts with much more knowledge about the industry and expertise in dealing with financial models and assumptions than a court could reasonably be expected to have. This Court notes that in the Sysco case, that court found that the expert had not verified whether efficiencies predicted by a consulting company were merger specific and for that reason among others declined to consider the efficiencies evidence. That court did not attempt to verify the merger specificity on its own. And this Court is not aware of any other precedent where a court has undertaken the kind of rigorous verification that is necessary in order to rely on efficiencies in an antitrust case. Number three, subsequent updates of the November 2020 model undermine its reliability.

After the November 2020 model was created, Mr. Sansigre continued to update and refine the model. Most notably, new iterations of the model were created in June 2021 and January 2022. The new iterations have some drastically different projections with respect to efficiencies. The Court focuses on the January 2022 model because defendants contend that the June 2021 model was about a special circumstance, a possible large infusion of cash to the business.

Looking at the January 2022 model, that model predicts an increase in gross physical sales of as compared to in the November 2022 model. The January 2022 model predicts—I'm sorry, I should not have said those numbers. The January '22 model predicts a certain number in fulfilling savings as compared to a much larger number predicted in November 2020, and savings on administration in the 2022 model is far larger as compared to the number in the November 2020 model. And I understand that that includes editorial and art, but the additions of those lines does not account for the magnitude of the change. Furthermore, certain projections of the November 2020 model were proved inaccurate by the actual performance of Simon & Schuster in 2021. While the November 2020 model made certain predictions of synergies for a merged company based on inputs regarding Simon & Schuster's expected performance as a standalone company, the actual standalone performance of Simon & Schuster exceeded the predictions. This indicates that the November 2020 model is both out of date because it does not include actual updated performance numbers and also that the November 2020 model relied on provably wrong projections and predictions.

Mr. Sansigre testified that the November 2020 model is still the most reliable because it reflects pre-pandemic market conditions. It appears to be his judgment that the future will look more like the pre-pandemic world than the present world. The Court rejects that testimony because Mr. Sansigre cannot possibly know what the post-pandemic world will be like and whether the book industry will revert to pre-pandemic levels of sales and costs. Even with the benefit of industry expertise, it is clear to this Court that we are in uncharted waters. Thus, the Court concludes that the November 2020 model is unreliable because its inputs are not updated and its projections are provably inconsistent with actual numbers for Simon & Schuster in 2021. The Court finds that Mr. Sansigre's justifications for continuing to use the November 2020 model are unpersuasive. The Court, thus, finds that the November 2020 efficiencies model contains some projected efficiencies that are not verifiable and that, in any event, none of the efficiencies have been verified as required by the horizontal merger guidelines and persuasive case law. Moreover, the model is unreliable because it is not updated and makes provably inaccurate projections. As a result, Dr. Snyder's expert report based on the November 2020 model is not based on sufficient facts and data under Rule 702 and must be excluded.

Five precedents in this jurisdiction unanimously support this conclusion. Those precedents are H&R Block, Wilhelmsen, Staples, Aetna, and Sysco. In United States versus H&R Block, the court rejected efficiencies evidence where the projected efficiencies, quote, were largely premised on defendant's managers' experiential judgment about likely costs rather than a detailed analysis of historical data. The court noted that, while reliance on the estimation and judgment of experienced executives about costs may be perfectly sensible as a business matter, the lack of a verifiable method of factual analysis resulting in the cost estimates renders them not cognizable by the court. If this were not so, then the efficiencies defense might well swallow the whole of section 7 of the Clayton Act because management would be able to present large efficiencies based on its own judgment and the court would be hard pressed to find otherwise. In this case, many of the efficiencies projections are also premised on management expectations and judgment. In FTC versus Wilhelmsen Holding ASA, the court rejected efficiencies evidence where the projected efficiencies were based on, quote, a series of significant assumptions, percentage reductions in cost, percentage increases in productivity, or assumed cost product equivalencies that were doing all the work in calculation of the estimates.

There the critical issue was that because the bases for the assumptions the expert identified and their role in the efficiencies analysis were unclear, the reasonableness of the assumptions along with the ultimate determinations could not be verified with any degree of rigor. Significantly, the court in that case noted that, quote, references to the merging parties' past practices, managerial expertise, and incentives or internal verification processes, unquote, could not, quote, serve to substantiate any efficiencies, unquote, because a court cannot substitute defendants' assessments and projections for independent verification.

So here, while Penguin Random House's internal process was rigorous, that internal process cannot substitute for independent verification.

In FTC versus Staples, the court rejected efficiencies evidence where, quote, the defendants' projected base case savings of $5 billion were in large part unverified or at least the defendants failed to produce the necessary documentation for verification, unquote. Here the efficiencies also are unverified. And although the defendants will say that they produced the documentation for verification, as the Court has already stated, the Court does not have the capability, the time, or resources to perform the verification.

In United States versus Aetna, the court rejected efficiencies evidence where the defendants' experts failed to review the underlying provider contracts after the merging parties approached—after the merging parties projected efficiencies based on the contracts, and that was criticized. Instead, the expert noted simply that a third party consultant had taken a large haircut to the total savings estimated and without much analysis concluded that the savings were verifiable.

The court deemed that insufficient. The court said, without a more robust analysis which the companies have not provided, the court cannot conclude that these network efficiencies are verifiable and likely to be passed on to consumers.

Here, like in that case, Dr. Snyder also failed to look closely at the underlying data and did not do any robust analysis to verify the efficiencies. Finally, in FTC versus Sysco, the court rejected efficiencies evidence where defendants' expert relied on synergy projections made by McKinsey, the consulting firm which was hired by Sysco to determine the prospective value of acquiring U.S. Foods.

The court there did not question the rigor and scale of the analysis conducted by McKinsey but noted that the expert had not verified that the synergies were merger specific. The court stated that it was not clear what independent analysis the expert did to reduce McKinsey's projected savings to merger-specific savings.

The court also noted that in one example, the expert relied exclusively on documents created by either McKinsey or defendants. He performed no independent analysis to verify those numbers. Again, similarly in this case, Dr. Snyder did not perform any independent analysis to verify the numbers. And in that case, the court did not undertake to do the verification itself. As a result, the Court will exclude Dr. Snyder's testimony on efficiencies. No independent party could reasonably verify the magnitude of at least some of the asserted efficiencies in Mr. Sansigre's projected model, especially the sales synergies, and Dr. Snyder made no attempt to provide a quantitative verification of the synergies. Because Dr. Snyder's testimony was not based on sufficient facts and data, that testimony cannot help the trier of fact to determine a fact at issue and, therefore, is not admissible under Rule 702. Although the Court's reasoning is firmly grounded in precedents applying the horizontal merger guidelines, it bears mentioning that the Court's analysis under Rule 702 is also consistent with the application of that rule in other contexts. It is well established that expert testimony may be excluded under Rule 702 where the expert relies uncritically on information provided to them by the party or parties for whom they are working. In the Title VII case, Campbell versus National Railroad Passenger Corporation, the court excluded the testimony of plaintiffs' expert who relied on a summary of testimony prepared by plaintiffs' counsel to form his opinions without independently reviewing or verifying that testimony. That case is at 311 F.Supp.3d 281 from 299 to 300. That's D.D.C. 2018. The court reasoned, quote, such blind reliance on facts provided by plaintiff's counsel combined with his failure to review other sources of information renders his expert report unreliable, unquote. That's at 300. See also McReynolds versus Sodexho Marriott Services, Inc., 349 F.Supp.2d 30 at 38, D.D.C. 2004, allowing in a Title VII case testimony of plaintiffs' expert who relied on data prepared by the opposing party instead of by the same party who retained the expert. And see also United States ex rel Morsell versus NortonLifeLock, Inc. That's 568 F.Supp.3d 248 at 276, D.D.C. 2021, where expert and false claims case explicitly disclaimed verification of assumptions, the expert was allowed to opine only conditionally assuming the government succeeds in proving the assumptions upon which the opinions rely.

All of these cases support the proposition that an expert's opinion may be excluded as unreliable when the opinion blindly rests on evidence provided by the party that retains the expert. A party may not cloak unexamined assumptions in the authority of expert analysis. See Ask Chemicals, LP versus Computer Packages, Inc, 593 F.Appx. 506, 510, Sixth Circuit, 2014.

For all the foregoing reasons, the Court grants the government's motion to exclude the defendants' efficiencies evidence. Does any party want any additional findings or conclusions for the record?

MR. SCHWARZ: No, Your Honor.

MR. FRACKMAN: I think that covers it, Your Honor.

THE COURT: Okay. Thank you.

SUMMARY OF VIDEO TESTIMONY

Five government witnesses and one for the defense appeared in videotaped testimony only, which was not live, but recorded earlier during depositions and edited for the court. The parties presented written transcripts to the judge, but those transcripts were not entered into the court transcripts—and good portions of the testimony were shown in closed sessions.

Here we capture just a few reported notes from the public portions of some of those videotapes.

Prosecution Witnesses

Liate Stehlik, Morrow Group president and publisher

Like other big houses, at Morrow Stehlik can approve deals up to $350,000 and above that she gets approval from HarperCollins CEO Brian Murray. She said PRH is her biggest competitor and S&S her next biggest competitor. They usually don't see a lot of competition from independent houses such as Norton, Chronicle or Bloomsbury at the highest advance levels—more at $100,000 and below. Like her peers, except perhaps at S&S, she believes HarperCollins' scale and deep resources do give it an advantage over smaller publishers. And so on.

Michael Jacobs, Abrams CEO

Jacobs amusingly noted that Abrams was not invited to bid on Barack and Michelle Obama's books, cheerfully admitting, "We're not used to paying those kinds of advances." They have had enormous success with Jeff Kinney's *Wimpy Kid* series—which has sold over 270 million copies around the world in almost 70 languages.

Like many others, he was not familiar with the government's precise term anticipated top selling books, but he certainly understood the idea, as comparable to "a lead title." He has no position on the merger, but conceded that, "We get outbid all the time . . . It's just the reality of things. We have to make choices and there's a limited number of things we can really lean into and do well by." They "like to make more prudent business decisions" for themselves. "It's about resources."

Andrew Solomon, Author

Solomon seemed to be another curious witness for the prosecution, since he is happily published by Scribner and is not concerned that the merger will affect him. "I feel fairly secure in my position in the literary world," he said, drawing chuckles from the gallery.

Solomon had written to the DOJ in support of the merger, at the request of PRH CEO Markus Dohle. "I agreed to be supportive because I think it's a good idea," Solomon said, and noted that Dohle was a friend. (The DOJ neglected to inquire if Solomon and Dohle might know each other through PEN America, where Solomon is a board member and former president, and Dohle is currently executive vice president of the board and a generous supporter.)

Christy Fletcher, literary agent

Much of Fletcher's testimony was tied to her expressed opinion of Random House's 2013 acquisition of Penguin, which was absorbed into a combined Penguin Random House.

"The way that Penguin was integrated into Random House should not be the model, in my view, of how a potential acquisition of Simon & Schuster should be handled if you want to maintain a robust marketplace for authors," she said. Instead, it would take "careful consideration." She also said that she believes the Penguin integration did have a negative effect.

Fletcher said that she didn't know if she experienced downward pressure on advances after the PRH merger, but does believe that if S&S were incorporated as a division, rather than being "left as a separate entity" it would lead to downward pressure. "With fewer bidders it's hard to drive the advances up," she said. She also said that if S&S were folded into PRH, as Penguin was, "that would make it harder potentially to hold back rights, the rights you'd negotiate over in those deals." When asked if her authors have benefitted from S&S being a third party bidding against PRH, she said "I believe that to be true."

Fletcher clarified the bidding policies for a number of major publishers. For PRH, S&S, and HarperCollins, agents must disclose if there is interest from another editor at the same parent company. The rules are "more ambiguous" at Hachette, she said. Her primary concern is that the bidding process would remain in a possible PRHSS. Her other concern is how internal competition—i.e. poaching—would be handled.

She also said, "If there's no third party to drive them up, they stop at their initial bids. It can be very punishing for authors writing on the initial quarter that's paid" referring to PRH's policy of splitting advances into four payments.

Ultimately, Fletcher said in her deposition that "if the merger is handled in the way that it's described, I don't have the concerns I had when it appeared" that the merger was going to be handled the way the Penguin acquisition was.

Though Fletcher said that the proposed merger would not lead to increase competition, she could see some benefits in the merged company. "I think the ability for S&S to benefit from the way Penguin Random House has structured their marketing and promotional departments would be beneficial to authors who are published by Simon & Schuster. I think the ability for the combined entity to support the retail environment, independent bookstores in particular, and also to negotiate with powerful players in the business like Amazon, I think there's potentially some benefit to that." Also, "I think Simon & Schuster being part of a privately owned company that is committed to the book business is generally a benefit to authors who are published by them." She hypothesized that then they would not be "submitted to the pressures of quarterly earnings reports."

Questioning turned to the consolidation of Random House and Crown imprints. Fletcher said that the restructuring of marketing and promotional departments "gave them much greater capabilities." "In the end they're actually much better publishers now," she said.

Lawyers continued to ask about why an author would go with a small publisher over a big one. "Just because a big publisher has the capabilities to perform at a certain level doesn't mean they will," she said. "Sometimes a smaller publisher will care about a book more" and that it's about the "care and feeding" of an author. Still, she later confirmed that the majority of books she sold in the last five years went to Big 5 publishers. It's a "book by book" situation, she said.

Defense Witness

John Glusman, Norton VP, Editor in Chief

Glusman was the only defense witness to be appear by videotaped deposition. He proudly declared, Norton is "one of the best publishers in the business."

When asked what benefit authors get from publishing with Norton over a bigger house, Glusman pointed to the company's ownership structure, which they tell authors when acquiring. "We're an independent employee-owned publisher and the largest such trade publisher in America," he said. Why is that a selling point? "The fact that we're independent means we're not beholden to corporate interests and not beholden to stock valuations on a quarterly basis, and the company has a history which is probably the most stable in the business due to our unique ownership structure. That stability is enormously attractive to agents and authors alike."

Glusman said that the majority of their books are acquired through auctions; only 20–25 percent are not. They work with the same agents as major publishers and compete for the same books—though "not always." "When Norton wants to compete it is able to compete with the Big 5 publishers," he said.

When asked whether, post-merger, the greater resources of PRH and S&S combined would "make it harder to acquire the book because of the cost," Glusman replied, "That's one of the likely scenarios."

PART FOUR: CLOSING STATEMENTS

CLOSING ARGUMENT OF THE UNITED STATES

MR. READ: May it please the Court. As I begin, I'm sure defendants will join me in thanking Your Honor for taking the time to hold this hearing in August during vacation. I don't think it's lost on any of us that you had the opportunity to—with the nomination, to find someone else to do this trial who may not have had time. And I think both sides are grateful that you made the time for this, even though it requires writing a fast opinion, so that both sides could have their day in court. I think we're all grateful for that.

As I begin, I want to state how, on one level, straight forward and simple this case is. Simon & Schuster compete today to acquire rights from authors. That merger will end that competition which benefits the authors. And authors will earn less money for what they write, whether the great American novel or a nonfiction that inspires. Contrary to what you heard during trial, this case is not about the publishers' love of books and authors. It's not about small authors winning a few books here and there. It's not about a surprise breakout star or a small advance on their first novel. None of that is surprising, but those outliers don't make a trend.

This merger is about the largest publisher, Penguin Random House, cementing its dominant position, eliminating a major competitor in a highly concentrated market, giving it 50 percent market share, which is all presumptively illegal.

And the defendants will have failed to rebut that presumption.

Your Honor, I'm going to organize my remarks around the Baker Hughes case and how it outlines burdens. So I will start with market definition and market shares, and talk about the merger being presumptively illegal. And then I'll talk about the defenses the defendants have raised to try and rebut that presumption. And I'll close with the anticompetitive effects in case Your Honor believes they have rebutted the presumption.

Before doing all that, I just want to talk about this industry and the seeming argument that normal rules of economics and antitrust don't apply. We've heard statements that editors and authors have a passion for books, and they do. It's almost like they're claiming that the value of books is not determined by expected sales or competition from other publishers, but by alchemy I think was one of the words. One defense witness said publishing business is an oxymoron. The suggestion that normal laws of economics and competition don't apply just isn't right. And taken to its extreme, could lead to an industry that devolves to two firms, a duopoly with lots of imprints and a great loss of competition. Put differently, the good intentions of defendants don't save this merger or don't save the industry from a duopoly or a monopoly.

Competition matters, and book publishing is a business. Penguin Random House and Simon & Schuster are very successful, very profitable at acquiring books and authors—books from authors and selling them. We brought this case, the United States did, because the best protection for authors is robust competition, independent firms vying for the right to publish the best works that the authors put their hearts and souls into creating, and being rewarded for that effort for acquiring the right books. The love of books is not on trial nor the passion of the authors. In fact, Your Honor, antitrust is full of examples of nonprofits and other entities where social welfare aims and the nonprofit didn't excuse the anticompetitive loss from applying.

I thought we would start with a slide after this one to remind you of the head-to-head competition. I thought about going through some stories of that, but I think Your Honor's heard plenty. But I think there's value in seeing—this is from Anna Porro's summaries where she went through and found 25 head-to-head stories. I wanted you to see what's at stake for these authors, and the amounts of money to each individual that matters if head-to-head competition is decreased.

Let's turn now to the Baker Hughes criteria, and the order in which they set out the burdens. So that begins with product market. There's been hours of testimony on product market, and it's actually kind of a straight forward proposition. Let me illuminate how we consider pre-complaint the evidence and decide to describe the authors who would see less of competition. It became clear that in this world, those authors at the very high end have different needs and have different competitive opportunities than those at the very low end. And I think there's little debate about that. I think Dr. Snyder essentially conceded that.

You've heard words to describe the high end. I think sometimes they're called franchise authors, key authors, giant celebrities. The works they do are sometimes called lead titles. At the other end—maybe not at the low end, but you hear midlist authors and midlist titles. And given that they have differences at both ends, the question was how you analyze that, how you look at that, and how you describe those at the high end that have a different set of competitive conditions.

When we looked in the data—and Your Honor saw this with PX-963, the next slide, we saw just a difference in how the firms competed. And that left us with the question of how we distinguish and how do we draw the line between those two. We drew guidance, as Your Honor knows, from precedent. We located a case in a creative industry like this one where courts focused on the most valuable works created in that industry, and that's Syufy, which Your Honor knows about and has probably read. It's not a merger case, but the Court needed to find a relevant market. It found that industry anticipated top grossing films met that definition.

There, the Court was worried about 30 movies a year that had particularly strong demand, and how to differentiate those from the movies that have little demand. The defendants there argued, like plaintiffs do here, that the definition there was ad hoc. The Syufy defendants said the top grossing films were, quote, "Simply those films that proved to be highly successful in the marketplace, but they possessed no special characteristics that differentiate them from less successful films, from an ex-ante perspective." The Ninth Circuit ended up disagreeing. Anticipated top grossing films were distinct, just like anticipated top selling books are distinct from those at the time the rights are acquired.

So let's look at some of the criteria Syufy used for anticipated top grossing films, and how they map to the anticipated top selling books. You can see the size of the investment initially in production budget or in advance maps; the frequency of big name stars or well-known authors; large marketing budgets; longer playtimes or print runs; and improved contract terms.

With the Syufy criteria in mind, I thought I would spend some time with Your Honor on the elicited testimony about the distinctions between anticipated top selling books and others. We note that higher advance books are correlated with higher expected sales. There was ample testimony from industry participants, including CEOs. We cite Jon Karp here who testified that the sales are the main factor on which advances are based.

Next, even though defendants tried to walk away from this, there's a correlation between high advances and higher marketing support. Author Andrew Solomon testified to that. He said that publishers devote more publicity and marketing resources to books that they expect to sell well. Third, there's a correlation between books expected to sell well and the initial print run. The CEO of HarperCollins testified to that. And fourth, there's a correlation between advance levels and the publisher's willingness to negotiate with the author over customized contract terms. Ms. Walsh testified to that.

She talked about terms like glam, airfare, contributions to charitable organizations that are generally correlated with advance levels.

Beyond looking at the criteria set out in Syufy, I wanted to note for Your Honor what's not in the Ninth Circuit opinion. There's no discussion there of whether industry anticipated top grossing films was a phrase articulated by Hollywood executives in exactly those terms. That appears to have been irrelevant to the real question the Court was facing of whether those 30 popular films each year would be an antitrust problem. In this case, the real question is whether authors at that high end of anticipated top selling books will be harmed.

The other concept not in the Syufy opinion, but on which we have spent a lot of time at trial, is any lingering discussion of whether the product market fails because there's some movies that were expected to do well but flopped, and some movies that had surprising success, which happens in that industry. It would be unreasonable to expect that predictions translate to reality a hundred percent of the time. That's why there's risk in this business. The anticipation of success was good enough for product market purposes for the Ninth Circuit, and we believe should be here.

In this matter, while buying books has great risk, the experience of the industry insiders and the P&Ls

they create to justify their purchases help them determine the monetary value of the books, and whether they can expect commercial success of the books they're trying to acquire. From defendants' own witnesses, Your Honor heard how the industry predicts the worth of a book. Ms. Madeline McIntosh, the CEO of Penguin Random House U.S., agreed with Your Honor that the publishing industry in general is, quote, "Very much driven by the expected sales of books." And agent Andrew Wylie, called by the defendants, testified that he's been negotiating for, quote, "42 years, and I can calculate with a high degree of accuracy the amount we would be able to achieve through a multiple submission. And if we can achieve that through a single submission, then we do a single submission." Like the movies, we have a difference at the high and low ends of the authors and their books, and it turns on anticipated success.

Now let me discuss the harder issue: How you turn that idea of anticipated top selling books at the high end into a concept which economists can bring data to and do their analysis. The Government's proposed relevant market in this case is based on economic analysis confirming that the market meets the hypothetical monopolist test, the Brown Shoe factors and common-sense. It's not arbitrary. Dr. Hill determined that using an advance level threshold of $250,000 would be a reasonable demarcation. We define the market around the practical indicia relevant to those top selling authors. We use both the hypothetical monopolist test to establish a market, and we look to Brown Shoe to solidify and help. Either on its own is legally sufficient, but we do both.

As Your Honor asked some questions about this, the hypothetical monopolist test gets directly to the ultimate question of whether there are substitutes sufficiently close to the products that even a monopolist could not profitably worsen price. And the Brown Shoe factors are kind of qualitative things that get to that same question of whether there's reasonably interchangeable substitutes outside the market.

Let's talk about the hypothetical monopolist test a little first. This really isn't in dispute. There are no reasonably interchanged substitutes for authors of anticipated top selling books. Self-publishing was the only alternative put forward in this case, and it's not reasonably interchangeable for the vast majority of anticipated top selling authors or, frankly, authors throughout most of the spectrum. Defendants' expert Dr. Snyder conceded that the hypothetical monopolist test is satisfied at any threshold, so I'm not going to dwell on that issue. By establishing the hypothetical monopolist test, we've defined a market, meaning we've defined an area that merits further inquiry.

I'll now turn to the—how this market satisfies the Brown Shoe factors. First, as we consider the Brown Shoe, the case law is clear that market definition is supposed to be pragmatic and factual, it's not supposed to be formal and legalistic, and the markets are not to be measured by metes and bounds. So here's some of the factors in Brown Shoe. The first one is industry recognition. There's evidence in the industry that the industry uses $250,000 to draw lines for various purposes. So it's recognized in the industry.

Publishers Marketplace uses $250,000 to define significant deals. Jon Karp chose $250,000 as his level of approval.

Ms. McIntosh said that Penguin Random House Publishing Group and Knopf Doubleday require approvals at $250,000. Ms. Kim—and this is the slide that's confidential, gathered data in the regular course of her work that broke out the performance of Putnam's books by advance level. I don't know if you have the notebook there, but you'll see the chart. This is, I think, slide 17.

THE COURT: Got it, thank you.

MR. READ: This is a demonstrative that puts forward the exhibit that was put in with her in which there was questioning about—we put that in not solely to show a correlation between advances and marketing spend, but to also show the buckets of advances that they looked at in their ordinary course of documents. As you see, $250,000 is a level. And you also see that advances start to—the slope starts to change around $250,000. So that seems to be an area where there's some importance.

Finally, with regard to $250,000, Your Honor saw PX-87 where Mr. Dohle was questioned. And he was trying to get Ms. McIntosh to get involved in acquisitions at the $250,000 level and the $500,000 level. The point there is he thought advances at that level could materially grow Penguin Random House's market share. His thinking shows that the acquisition of books at those levels is meaningful to Penguin Random House and its business.

Agents and editors recognized anticipated top selling books as well. Andrew Wylie testified that publishing veterans like him are able to determine in advance which books are likely to be successful, because there are, quote, "Recognizable qualities in books that people who have been in this business for a long time would readily recognize."

The second indicia from the Brown Shoe Supreme Court case is unique needs. We see top selling authors requiring stronger marketing and publicity to achieve the full potential of their work. Several witnesses, including Jon Karp, testified that the Big 5 publishers have stronger publicity and marketing capabilities, and that these stronger capabilities provide a significant edge in turning books into best sellers. Authors of anticipated top selling books also depend on the Big 5 publishers' larger sales force to maximize the sales of their books.

The third indicia is distinct prices. Under the Government's market definition that the advance is higher for anticipated top selling books than for other books, and some authors seek and obtain special terms such as guaranteed marketing and "glam" budget.

The fourth criteria is price sensitivity. This is similar to the hypothetical monopolist test. Anticipated top selling authors can be targeted because they're not as sensitive to price. They don't have alternatives that they can switch to if they suffer an adverse price change. As discussed—well, as I've chose to just glide over, self-publishing is a weak substitute.

Finally, the fifth—one of the fifth indicia here of Brown Shoe is special characteristics. Anticipated top selling authors are often authors of successful books in the past.

They've appeared on best seller lists often. They have a successful track record. They may be recognized with past awards or have notoriety from their social media endeavors. And as we discussed earlier, agents and editors can identify those authors based on the literary quality in their submissions. So they are identified by special characteristics. The bottom line, Your Honor, is that anticipated top sellers is a market under either the hypothetical monopsonist test or the Brown Shoe indicia.

Now, Dr. Snyder criticizes Dr. Hill and us for using a price number to define the product market—or a number.

Turning to the next slide, courts have consistently used numerical thresholds to define markets. The first three I discussed in the opening: Wilhelmsen that focused on 10 fleets; Anthem which focused on 5,000 employees; and Staples, on customers with $500,000 annual spend in office supplies.

Brown Shoe, which we just talked about, identified distinct prices as an indicia. So we look at Whole Foods where the market consisted of core customers who paid distinct prices at premium supermarkets. We listed here as well—because there are markets that are harder to find with numbers, but get at the same thing, is international boxing where the Supreme Court held that boxing championships—the championship could be separated from other boxing matches, because it had higher revenues and rights fees and greater popularity among viewers. And finally in the world of amateur athletics, in the recent O'Bannon case, they focused on elite athletes, which at some level is hard to define, but you know when you see it—at least the people in the industry do. Similar to these cases and the numerical information in them, we used advances to identify particularly valuable creative works at issue.

If I could, I'd like to turn to the argument about the 2 percent issue and the volume of commerce. Even with this argument that we only cover 2 percent of the titles, we're talking about a large and meaningful market. First of all, with regard to the other 98 percent, Dr. Snyder admitted it wouldn't surprise him that those 56,000 titles have sold fewer than 12 copies, and 90 percent sold less than 2,000 copies. The existence of so many books with negligible sales doesn't hide the harm to the authors we've been focused on. The market, we alleged, is where the money is. Advances contracted to be paid to the authors are a billion dollars, and it's 70 percent of the advances at stake, as has been talked about.

This is an industry, probably like movies, where a small fraction of the books drive profitability.

I'd like to talk about one case. The claim the Government cannot prevail because it's only talking about 2 percent of the titles is a losing argument. It lost in Staples. There, Judge Sullivan had a market that was national business-to-business customers, and those customers only accounted for 1 percent of the sales—of the business customers of Staples. The customers at issue were 1 percent. They accounted for a large volume of commerce, 35 percent. The Court ended up enjoining the merger, because the harmed 1 percent of customers accounted for a disproportionate number of sales because it was material. And that argument of immateriality should fail here.

If we could move to shares, Your Honor. There's no dispute that after this merger, Penguin Random House will be more dominant than it already is—borrowing from Mr. Dohle's words, cementing its number one position in the market.

Dr. Hill testified Penguin Random House and Simon & Schuster will have a 49 percent share of our market, the Big 5 will combine for 90 percent. None of the non-Big 5 will have more than 1 percent. And cumulatively, all those small publishers are 10 or 9 percent. There's no material variation to these market shares if we choose different advance thresholds, whether it's 150, 350, 500 or a million.

Defendants have presented through the three weeks of trial no evidence that any purchasers of anticipated top sellers were omitted from the dataset, nor have defendants shown that these market shares changed substantially over time other than through the march of acquisitions of smaller publishers by the Big 5 over the past decade. To the contrary, as Dr. Hill explained yesterday, the combined share has increased—of the merging parties has increased in recent years, while the other Big 5 have slightly lost share, and the non-Big 5, all those small publishers, has been flat. The evidence has shown that the shares reflective here—reflected here are reflective of current competitiveness and the likelihood of success of these companies. As the Bertelsmann board recognized in 2019, the U.S. publishing market is an oligopoly. There will be five—there are currently five firms controlling 90 percent of this market, and the merger would take it down to four.

So the next issue is, is the merger presumptively illegal. Under Baker Hughes and its burden shifting framework, if a transaction results in a high concentration and significant increase, there's a presumption that it will substantially lessen competition. There's no dispute by Dr. Snyder that if anticipated top sellers is a market, the HHIs are sufficient under the guidelines for a presumption of illegality. To reiterate Dr. Hill's testimony, regardless of the specific advance used or the year used, the mergers above the guidelines level of market concentration require to establish a presumption. And under Baker Hughes, once the Government establishes that presumption, the burden, quote, "Then shifts to the defendants to rebut the presumption by offering proof that the market share statistics give an inaccurate account of the merger's probable effect on competition in the relevant market."

Before I go further and cover the defenses to see if they've done that, I'd like to spend a few moments regarding the defendants' characteristic that the presumption is weak. In fact, it's usually outcome determinative. The following cases from this circuit are all cases where, even after the Court took evidence of efficiencies and entry and testimony about unique features of the market, the Court held defendants had not properly rebutted the presumption.

So let's turn to the defenses and see if defendants have properly rebutted. There's four principal defenses that we've gleaned from this case. Your Honor has already ruled on efficiencies, so I won't discuss that, and will discuss the other four. They are entry, promise and buyer power, and then the 2013 merger seems to be a defense, too. Let's start with entry. The question this defense poses is whether suddenly new publishers would enter or existing publishers would expand to replace the competitive significance of Simon & Schuster. The legal test is whether the entry or expansion would be timely, likely and sufficient in magnitude, character and scope to replace the lost competition. The evidence will show that the entry of new firms and expansion won't satisfy that test.

There are high barriers to achieving scale in this industry and acquiring the rights of anticipated top sellers. Among those are reputation, as you see, funding for the book, hiring skilled professionals and publicity and marketing professionals. And in the supply chain, especially printing.

There's no dispute that in the past 30 years, no publisher has entered the market and become as strong as the Big 5. For good reason: The competitive advantages of the Big 5 are difficult to duplicate. Building a large backlist takes a long time, because only a small number of titles each year turn into that reliable backlist titles. New entrants seeking to compete against the Big 5 have a variety of other disadvantages. Particularly, they have to solve the reputation of having a long track of success. Defendants' own documents recognize this. Mr. Dohle was—to a famous public figure, him and his team were teaching them about getting into the publishing business and providing background instruction in this document.

And they told this public figure no history of company starting from scratch have achieved profitability in the three- to five-year time period. And he also told them that the idea of creating a separate publishing company, even with Penguin Random House's help, was not a viable option. The better option would be an imprint within Penguin Random House.

Bertelsmann board documents later recognized that reputation creates a high entry barrier for a publishing company. And Ms. Kim confirmed that when she testified, quote, "I think authors want to be published by publishers with good reputations, good standing, you know, with booksellers and media. They want to be part of a list that they can be proud of—that they can be proud to say they're a part of."

Looking at recent history on entry is informative. It's shown that new publishers struggle to gain scale. It's difficult to become profitable and routinely produce best sellers. The parties stretched to find some brand new entry that they could claim change everything, and is timely and sufficient. And one of the companies they focused on was Spiegel & Grau, a publisher that re-founded itself a couple of years ago and has published a handful of books.

It's informative that in its original incarnation, Spiegel & Grau published important books at Penguin Random House. But when it closed their imprint and retained their backlist, they had to go and start a new company. It's improbable that fine publishers who they didn't think they did not want to keep are now a great competitive threat to them.

The expansion of small publishers by a handful of titles each year won't solve the competitive problems. We have—there's example after example of how small publishers don't have the resources or the inclination to expand. Most of that was in closed testimony, so I'll refer you to the testimony of some of the small publishers and their statements about their willingness to expand and the challenges they face.

Even Amazon has not succeeded. Here's one of the largest corporations on earth. It tried to expand its presence in publishing a decade ago in the type of books at issue here, and did not succeed. They have reduced their title count in recent years and are not considered a threat. Consequently, while some publishers may have grown, others have shrunk. And the data show that the non-Big 5 publishers as a group have been flat over the last three years.

One last point on entry before I move on, and that's printing. Printing capacity is an issue for everyone, even Penguin Random House, and makes it hard to expand, especially if you're going to be beholden to Penguin Random House. In this exhibit, Ms. Reidy stated that Simon & Schuster did not want to be 100 percent beholden to a competitor. She was concerned that Penguin Random House might deprioritize Simon & Schuster's book. When Mr. Eulau testified, he said, quote, "If authors hear that you can't print books, they wouldn't want to be published by you." These sentiments of a defendant are not unique. You've heard and seen those concerns in closed sessions by a number of publishers who have genuine concerns about getting the printing they need to compete.

Let me turn to the second defense to try and rebut the presumption that defendants make. It's the promise of Mr. Dohle and the existence of lots of imprints. First, you heard the testimony of the CEO of Kensington that the promise makes no economic sense for a businessman. And there are reasons it shouldn't be trusted here. The promise is unenforceable, it's revocable. Yet, even if Penguin Random House were to adhere to the letter of the promise, it wouldn't stop Penguin Random House and Simon & Schuster from being able to lower advances or sidestep it. For example, they can close imprints; they can merge imprints; they can refocus imprints so they're less likely to compete directly with sister imprints for the same authors. Penguin Random House can reduce title counts, fire editors, control imprint budgets. It can admonish editors to take less risk in acquiring books, and then refuse to approve editor requests for large advances when it's in competition with itself. All these measures can be done internally without violating the letter of the promise, or Penguin Random House can quietly violate its promise without detection.

The Court has heard evidence of how today, Penguin Random House divisions sometimes coordinate their bid despite Penguin Random House's policy not to. Mr. Tart testified to an example where the divisions coordinated, slowed their bidding, despite there being an external bidder. And Ms. McIntosh presented to her board one of her plans to increase the background coordination and auctions, to leverage internal demand information better, and avoid internal up-bidding.

Even—which is all legal, but just not consistent with the promise. Even if the merger were to proceed and the promise held to, when Penguin Random House bids on books, it would do so knowing that there's one less independent bidder out there that could drive the price up. And there's some economic testimony that that will affect its offer. This promise by defendants is unlike any other commitment a court has accepted as a defense to rebut a presumption of illegality and should not be accepted here.

The third defense, the power of agents. The Court has heard a great deal of testimony about agents in this case.

Defendants would have this Court believe that sophisticated agents hold all the power and the leverage in the relationship. Your Honor should note that this defense was provided and failed in Anthem in this circuit. There, the national corporations that needed—companies that needed insurance for their employees, they had access to skilled, sophisticated brokers or consultants that would help them bid for—get bids for their insurance purposes or negotiate one-on-one with insurance companies.

Judge Jackson found that those skilled agents, even with alternative means of bidding or negotiating, could not mitigate the harm from the loss of a major insurer. She wrote—and affirmed by the circuit: "As noted above, the evidence also shows that loss of one competitor from the four major carriers alters the RFP, the request for a proposal, the bid, and negotiating dynamic. Even with strong advocates on the other side"—which were the agents that they were talking about, "this loss of leverage undermines the defense contention that customers will be able to wield their seasoned human resource managers and consultants to counteract the anticompetitive effects of the merger." Defendants want the Court to assume that the literary agent has the power to prevent harm, just like defendants claimed in Anthem. But after weeks at trial, we have evidence as to who holds the power between the agents and Penguin Random House, and it's Penguin Random House.

I refer you to the testimony of their witness, Mr. Wylie. He experienced Penguin Random House back when it was smaller and only Random House in 2010. He tried to convince Penguin Random House that EBIT growth rate should be above 25 percent. He couldn't get them to do that, so he went to Amazon with his Odyssey project to try and create some pressure. When Random House found out, they announced in *The New York Times* that they would no longer do business with him and his agency. He pulled his books from Amazon, the Odyssey project, and the digital rights then went to Random House.

Random House won and offers the digital royalty rate of 25 percent they wanted. He testified that that rate is unfair, but he doesn't have the power to change it with all his skill and whatever leverage he has. His agency needed to do business with Penguin Random House or he would have risked losing clients.

If agents had all the power, all the leverage over the Big 5, as claimed by the defendants, then why have payout terms shifted over time from halves to thirds to quarters, and now with the core payment not happening until a year after the book is published, final payment. Over the years, authors have had to wait longer and longer for their advance to be paid. And audio rights, why did they used to be negotiable, and now no longer are for Penguin Random House and Simon & Schuster. The evidence is the power lies more with Penguin Random House and Simon & Schuster than with agents. And what leverage agents have today will be reduced with one less independent bidder.

The final defense is the Penguin Random House merger. Given this merger happened over a decade ago, and the industry has become more concentrated, and the market has changed in many ways, we would understand if Your Honor preferred not to resolve the actual effects of that merger. But we think there's significant evidence contrary to what defendants say that it harmed authors. You heard testimony from Christie Fletcher and Ayesha Pande. Christie Fletcher testified the Penguin Random House merger harmed authors because they stopped bidding against each other. Ayesha Pande talked about how the Penguin Random House, and then the Crown Random House, mergers made it more challenging, quote, "to sell her clients' books because there was less choice." And then on the screen is Dr. Hill's regression which suggests that anticipated top selling books suffered after the merger. At a minimum, this evidence creates a red flag that defendants' attempt to point to the 2013 merger as pro-competitive and as rebutting the presumption of illegality fails.

Your Honor, we turn to the next issue. If, under Baker Hughes, Your Honor thinks they have rebutted the presumption, what evidence is there that there is harm, or at least there is a reasonable probability of harm, the authors may be harmed. Let me talk first about some direct evidence that the economists—that don't require economics. You heard Mr. Dohle's testimony of how he currently encourages Penguin Random House to be more aggressive. He wants them to take more risk in bidding, to pay larger advances. And the reason is he wants them to grow their share, which is terrific. We want Penguin Random House to try to grow its share and compete harder in doing that that way. He conceded, however, that once the merger is consummated, Penguin Random House's incentives to grow its share will lessen, implying that Penguin Random House would no longer feel as great a need to take as much risk and to bid quite as aggressively and to pay quite as much in advances. That change in incentives is evidence the merger may lead to harm. And you can couple that with one of the exhibits from Jon Karp where he wrote that merging with a competitor will arguably be bad, quote, "for the larger book publishing ecosystem."

Now we can turn a little bit more to the—well, before we turn to the economic evidence, there is a common economic logic that fewer bidders means lower advances. You heard testimony from that early on from Michael Pietsch, the CEO of Hachette. He testified that the number of bidders—the larger it is, leads to, quote, "more upward pressure in auctions in general. The price paid at auction can increase because of the number of participants," end quote. And the manner the book is acquired, whether through rounds auctions, best bids, preempts or negotiations doesn't change that fundamental logic. You heard testimony that when a publisher is acquiring a book, even through a negotiation, the publishers know the agent has the ability to shop the book if they're not happy with the offer. And so you heard the testimony of Gail Ross, one of defendants' agent witnesses, talk about BATNA, the best available alternative, and how that's important to getting a fair deal. If, in negotiating with Simon & Schuster, Penguin Random House is currently the best alternative for fair financial terms today, common-sense says it won't be as much of a threat or an option that the agent can use as effectively after the merger.

Now to all the challenging economic modeling testimony. We'd remind the Court that none of it is required, as the Government need only prove a reasonable probability of harm. And there's no need for precise economic modeling. And since Your Honor heard this testimony just yesterday, I'm going to touch on it lightly—unless Your Honor has questions.

THE COURT: That's okay.

MR. READ: Dr. Hill used a second-score auction model, as you know, to simulate the effect of the merger. He used conservative inputs. He found that PRH authors on average will have their advances reduced by about $45,000 per book, and Simon & Schuster authors on average, in the anticipated top selling market, will have their advances reduced by about $105,000 per book. And you can see the statistics before you. Dr. Snyder criticized the fit of his second-score auction model in the publishing industry, so Dr. Hill used a GUPPI model developed by the merging parties' own economists that was modified for this industry. And those models predicted similar results.

Dr. Hill acknowledges that his model isn't a perfect fit with all the way the books are sold, but it's a reasonable choice given the data that's available to everybody. As he explained, the purpose of estimating harm is less about the precision and more to see if there's something substantial.

And remember, he did not use those models that estimated and present to Your Honor the highest harm. He presented what he had the most confidence in and thought were the best predictors.

The second-score auction model he used is consistent with the work of other economic experts relied on by courts in this district. Similar models, even if not exactly identical, were used by government's economic experts in Anthem, Wilhelmsen and Sysco. And in Anthem, as the prior quote showed, there was both bidding and negotiation going on in that industry. In both Anthem and Wilhelmsen, government economists also used—government experts used the GUPPI model, and they were approved in those courts as well. Though the defendants have made arguments about the poor fit of the model, they failed to provide the Court or prove with another model that has a better fit anything materially different. In fact, as you heard from Dr. Snyder, he didn't even try to create a model in this case, an alternative model.

The harm is substantial. Defendants argue that the measurable harm from these numbers is too small to enjoin the merger. That's wrong. Let me first, before we get to this slide, tell you about Stephen King—or remind you about him. He flew here voluntarily because he understood the impact on younger up-and-coming authors, including his son. He explained that continued consolidation from the Big 5 to the Big 4 means it, quote, "becomes tougher and tougher for writers to find enough money to live on." Dr. Hill's estimates were 4 percent and 11 percent of harm, and that's in line with the estimates you see before you from other cases in this circuit—in this district, and from the Hackensack case in the Third Circuit.

They all have roughly similar harm estimates, and all those mergers were enjoined.

In addition to the quantifiable harm, there's harm that's harder to measure. That includes the increased leverage to negotiate important terms like marketing or quicker payout for an advance. It also includes, if we step back a bit, the effect that ensues with diversity: Books that are never written; or nonfiction books that aren't researched as accurately; new voices that will never get heard. As Mr. Dohle conceded, diminished author compensation will be fewer authors staying in the business, and fewer diverse stories being written.

Your Honor, my final topic will be coordination. As defendants concede, once the United States has demonstrated that this merger will create market concentration levels that mandate a presumption of illegality, there's a presumption of anticompetitive coordinated effects. Defendants bear the burden that the presumption by—that the presumption fails because there's proof of structural barriers that make tacit coordination or direct coordination possible in this industry. They failed to present such evidence.

Rather, the presumption of significant coordinated effects has been reinforced by unusually powerful evidence of explicit coordination among the Big 5 publishers. As found in the Second Circuit, the CEOs of then the Big 6 secretly met quarterly without lawyers or staff to discuss whatever was on their minds. They unlawfully coordinated with Apple to raise ebook prices. Those actions alone demonstrate a willingness and ability to achieve their anticompetitive goals, even when there were six competitors. Reducing to four will make that even easier to orchestrate.

And contrary to Dr. Snyder's views that editors will ignore their CEO instructions, there's every reason to believe that successful coordination among the remaining big CEOs to restrict acquisitions is feasible. An agreement simply to stop poaching each other's authors, each other's most successful authors among the Big 4, could be readily agreed to, implemented and enforced; particularly after this merger when Penguin Random House has half the market and the ability to counter-poach anybody who breaks the agreement and punish them; and has access to printing that it can use to delay the printing of its rival's books if they don't abide by the agreement.

We've been also presented with strong evidence of tacit coordination over the years, which is a major concern in the guidelines, in the case law. And contrary to Dr. Snyder's unique viewpoint, the development of industry uniformity about advance levels from three to four tranches, the standardization of royalty rates of 15 percent for hard cover books, and the non-negotiability of audio rights, those are all points that an industry rife with the ability to tacitly coordinate could do and could harm authors. The merger would reduce the number of players needed to agree, needed to monitor, and clearly exacerbates the risk of coordination in this market.

Let's end where we started. We showed you the list of head-to-head competition early, and the amount of money the competition generated for those authors. Some were $75,000, $140,000 and even $800,000. That's compensation and real work, creative work that fuels social discourse and progress. These numbers mean something to those that work hard to generate books, and they're at stake if this merger is permitted to proceed. The Clayton Act protects this work and ensures the market generates these numbers for people who perform this work, which is why the United States respectfully requests that the Court enjoin the merger.

REBUTTAL CLOSING ARGUMENT OF THE UNITED STATES

MR. READ: May it please the Court. Starting with the end of Mr. Fishbein, he argued about coordination. What you didn't hear, though, was that—you know, none of his arguments apply to the poaching or the contract terms that we specifically called out. There's no argument that the future Big 4 won't know what kind of contract terms there are about to payouts and negotiation of audio and other rights. And there's no discussion or recognition that you will also know if people are poaching your authors. And it's going to be far easier to have a follow the leader strategy post-merger with Penguin

Random House so dominant and the other smaller publishers.

Then I want to turn to the last thing that Mr. Petrocelli said. He took on, surprisingly to me, the claim that Simon & Schuster and Penguin Random House aren't rivals, and contrasted that with other cases where he said it was obvious they were rivals. I would just like, Your Honor, as you reflect on that, to go back to Mr. Karp's testimony—I think it was the second day of trial, where he went document after document about Simon & Schuster losing to Penguin Random House; and telling document after document about the frustration they felt, the bids they lost, the stalking horse worry that agents were using Penguin Random House to get their bids up. And when you're Simon & Schuster and facing Penguin Random House, that's your rival, and that's what they're worried about. The idea that they're not direct rivals is surprising on this record. I think Mr. Karp's testimony is the best place to go for that.

Mr. Petrocelli also encouraged you to think about the imprints, and the fact that they compete and try to get authors for themselves. I would suggest, Your Honor—I am an antitrust lawyer, I don't know all the cases, but I cannot think of a case where a merger was allowed because the corporate parent allowed subsidiaries to compete with each other. I'm struggling to think of a concept where that would be and you could rely on. And it's telling me to they have not presented one, a case for Your Honor on that issue.

And secondly, there is testimony from Jonathan Karp, again. He admitted in his testimony that having multiple imprints from the same publisher bidding on the same book rarely drives up the advance. So it's not the imprint competition that's driving up the advance, according to the CEO of Simon & Schuster. And there was an interesting quote that Ms. Kim made where she said her fiercest competitor is Penguin Random House and other imprints. I've been reflecting on that, and wondered if that just doesn't speak to the size of Penguin Random House already: That she's losing opportunities to other editors who are bidding about the same but get some business, and don't think the solution to that is letting Penguin Random House get bigger. Your Honor has heard more than enough testimony—well, Your Honor's heard a lot of testimony about the 12 percent and the 23 percent. I think I don't need to spend any time there, other than to say that the testimony was from Dr. Hill about 11 and a half being the right number for the second place bid, which comports with the market shares again, right. It's another indication that the non-Big 5, at their 10 percent share, are having about the impact you would expect that a 10 percent share would bring.

Mr. Fishbein talked about advances going up. First of all, there's testimony from agents—Ms. Fletcher and Ms. Pande, that advances have been going down. So there's conflicting testimony. Second of all, you would expect, all else equal, as more people are buying books, and therefore expected sales of books are going up, that that would be reflected somewhat in the advance. So to really do an analysis of that Penguin Random House merger and whether it was so good it inoculates this merger, you'd need more a complicated analysis, and that just hasn't been done. I think the red flags are there, again, to have that not rebut the presumption.

I think maybe the biggest argument—and I want to try to spend the remaining time on, is product market, and this idea that there's a gradual continuum, and then therefore there's almost the argument that there's no line that can be drawn. I think the best thing to do would be go back to first principles of why define a market. We're looking to find out are there authors here, are there a group of authors that are vulnerable. And under the statute, with any line of commerce, if there's a group of authors that are vulnerable and don't have competitive options that are sufficient, we ought to take a look at them. And that the hypothetical monopolist can be satisfied at different places just tells you there's a group of authors that can be fairly wide ranging about where you can focus the analysis. We thought the most relevant analysis, therefore the relevant product market, is those at $250,000 and up. Because they—you know, part of the problem is they don't see the non-Big 5 as a substantial help for them. The non-Big 5 pick their shots and aren't able to provide the resources on a consistent basis there. And again, the statute there goes back to any line of commerce. And so you can have multiple sub markets, and as long as there's one that's a problem and it's material and substantial, a merger should not be allowed.

I think I'll be brief, there was one other case that Mr. Petrocelli put up about—early in his presentation about super premium ice cream. And the story there was does fancy super premium ice cream compete with the cheaper ice cream.

That is a different question than ours of authors at high end and low end, because they're not competing against each other, right. So these examples of premium products that compete with non-premium products are different than where we're looking at is there a targeted group.

And so that may lead me to my final point. In this district, as far as I know, in the last decade—and we'll provide the evidence in our post-trial conclusions of law, I cannot think of a case where the plaintiff has failed on product market without there being an adequate substitute. So the losses where the plaintiff has failed on their proof have been because there is something that arguably the victims could turn to as an alternative. And that's just not here. It's conceded that there's no—if you're an author wanting to sell your manuscript, there's no other viable option if the merger monopolizes—if the industry monopolizes. And so that leads to the further inquiry that then we go into.

Thank you for your time, Your Honor. It's been a pleasure to present evidence and be an advocate for competition in this industry.

THE COURT: Thank you. I want to thank the litigation teams in this case. I want to say that I think both sides did an excellent job presenting their evidence and their arguments. I think the parties were very well represented. I very much appreciate all the work that has gone into presenting this case to the Court. I will take the matter under advisement, and I look forward to seeing your post-trial briefing. Thank you.

CLOSING ARGUMENT OF BERTELSMANN AND PENGUIN RANDOM HOUSE

MR. PETROCELLI: Your Honor, Daniel Petrocelli for Defendants Bertelsmann and Penguin Random House. On behalf of my clients, I wish to thank you for your hard work and the hard work of your staff in diligently conducting these trial proceedings, keeping us on time, and diverting I'm sure very valuable time that you could have spent elsewhere. So we very much appreciate it.

We're obviously now at the end of a long road in which the defendants here have sought to put these two great publishing houses together creating enormous benefits for readers and authors alike. And as we've seen, the Government has tried its best to show that this merger will decrease advances for a tiny set of transactions under long-settled analysis the DOJ and the courts use to determine whether a merger will cause a price decrease or in this case—a price increase, or in this case, a price decrease. And we submit that after three weeks of trial, the Government has not come close to making that showing. And I'll summarize the reasons why, Your Honor. And along the way, we took note that Your Honor asked a lot of important questions. And we would like—I would like, together with Mr. Fishbein, to try to answer some of those questions. But of course, in our post-trial submission, we'll have more opportunity to address the issues fully.

So let me begin with the legal standard. I want to go back to the opening statement of the Government here—Pam, if you could put up slide one—because I was somewhat surprised to hear in the Government's opening statement that it stated that it need only show that a substantial reduction in competition may occur or that there's an appreciable danger.

And that is simply not the law in the D.C. Circuit, and has not been for decades. The Government has to prove, and Your Honor has to find, that a substantial lessening of competition is likely to result. And I submit, perhaps the Government has asserted that lower standard because it hasn't shown, and cannot show, that this merger is likely to cause the harms the Government alleges.

And as this trial unfolded, it seemed obvious, at least to me, that there was a significant retreat by the Government and by Dr. Hill from core principles of unilateral effects in his models. Instead, what we heard a fair amount of was the Government contending that competition may be softened in some generalized, unknown and unquantifiable way. Without a viable unilateral effects analysis, the Government is left only with this general directional effect. But Your Honor, that is not proof of likely harm, and it's certainly not proof of substantial harm, which is perhaps why the Government has resisted this settled standard.

Now let me tell you what I'm going to discuss, Your Honor, and it largely tracks Mr. Read's structure. I'm going to talk about the market definition. And then I'm going to talk about the evidence that rebuts the structural presumption, and then discuss unilateral effects. And Mr. Fishbein has a number of other points that he will address to the Court.

Clearly, the market definition issue is critical, and perhaps case dispositive here.

The Government, as the Court knows, has the burden to prove the existence of a distinct legally cognizable product market. By its terms, the Government's anticipated top seller market here is drawn by price: Books that yield advances for $250,000 or more. The Government claims this is a sub market of the market for all books, and it's solely on the basis of this alleged sub market that the Government can trigger the presumption of harm. As has been acknowledged in the case, the presumption does not arise based on the broader market for all trade books.

And the cases, Your Honor, are clear, they are consistent, that a product market cannot be defined solely by one price along a continuum of prices. Instead—and you can see some of the authorities on this point, to qualify as a market, the Government has to prove that its price segment captures a distinct category of products or customers. Here, that would be authors. And the Government has to prove the Brown Shoe industry reality factors, which the Court applies to evaluate any alleged antitrust market. And that's what the courts have done in all the cases that you've heard.

And if you take a look at this slide—which is just a high level summary of some of the key cases on this critical market definition issue, you will see here that the Government's alleged market, based on the evidence in the trial, really satisfies none of these requirements. In fact, I submit that the evidence is largely, if not entirely, undisputed that none of these distinctive characteristics exist in this case. No one that you heard testify uses the concept of anticipated top seller to segregate books into a distinct category. No one has even heard of that before this case, by that or any other name. No one in the industry provides specialized services, only to books that garner advances of $250,000 or more.

What we heard throughout, Your Honor, was regardless of the advance level, we see the same bargaining processes; the same editorial processes; the same editors; the same marketing and publicity methods; the same printing; the same distribution; the same sales processes; and the same book selling retailers. Mr. Read mentioned and called out specifically the Syufy case, Your Honor, where there was a market for anticipated—industry anticipated top grossing films. I suggest that case demonstrates why the Government's market fails here.

In that case, ex-ante, before, there was no question that you could identify what those films were. They had famous movie stars in them. They had top directors in them. They had large, large budgets. They are advertised on print and ad budgets in excess of sometimes the production budget of those films. This was obvious to anybody. There wasn't any lack of clarity as to what those top grossing or anticipated top grossing films were. And they could only be exhibited in certain theaters that were suitable to pictures like that. So we have none of those characteristics here, Your Honor.

The Government—and yesterday Mr. Hill—Dr. Hill, excuse me, made clear that he was relying on evidence outside his model such as approval levels of the various publishers.

If you could put up slide 35, Pam. These approval levels do nothing to identify the Government's claimed market. There are a number of different approval levels, depending on what governance requirements any particular publisher has. And they vary up and down the range. There's nothing suggesting that $250,000 is an internal approval level because it identifies any market.

Likewise, Dr. Hill mentioned the various categories of *Publishers Weekly* [Ed: Nope], one of which—I think one of six or seven of which is $250,000. That's of no moment, Your Honor.

They're not contending that each of those categories constitutes a separate market. Those are just different deal buckets to describe different types of deals. At the end of the day, I think what the Government is really relying on is the correlation between advances and predicted sales.

And to be clear, we have never disputed that there is a general correlation between advance levels and predicted sales. After all, the profit and loss statements, Your Honor, are based on estimated sales. But there's nothing qualitatively different about those estimations, whether you're at the $250,000 advance or $50,000 advance or $1,000,000 advance. These are just advances along a price continuum based on different sales expectations. And a general correlation does nothing in and of itself to justify the definition of a distinct market along any particular point in that continuum.

Second, to the extent that there's any reason, Your Honor, to think that the industry does treat certain books or authors as if they're in a different category from other books or authors, the Government's proposed market doesn't capture that distinction. And we can see this at both ends of the price segment that the Government defines in its market boundary.

So according to Dr. Hill, the bottom of the Government's market is roughly $250,000, and perhaps down to $150,000. And we're not suggesting mathematical precision is required here. But the reason Dr. Hill draws the line in that range is because he claims that's where there is a dramatic change in market shares that he says occurs right around that spot. He claims that's where competitive conditions are different, below and above his line. And he relies prominently on this chart.

But as we showed the last couple of days, Your Honor, when you actually break that data down below the $250,000 mark, what you see is that the Big 5 continued to lead the market as it grew until you get all the way down to $50,000. So if you could—you can see it right here, and we can break that down even further. And the only dramatic change here, if there is any, Your Honor, is at the $50,000 mark. Thereafter, it's relatively stable. And our point is not that we should draw the line at $50,000. What we're saying is that by the Government's own logic, if the market for anticipated top selling books is defined mainly by the point at which the vast majority of buyers drop out of most acquisitions, then the market boundary has to be $50,000. And if you define it there,

Your Honor, there's been no evidence that the presumption would be triggered. Dr. Hill performed no calculations, as I believe, below the $100,000 level.

Let's take a look at the other end of the telescope, at the upper range. And as you know from the Sysco case, one way to think about whether a price segment captures distinct products is whether there's an industry consensus that the products are different in some way. And I recall Your Honor asked questions of some of our witnesses about whether such a consensus exists. And even recently, Your Honor noted that it seems to be intuitive that there should be some kind of segmentation based on the number of sales; and that higher selling books might need different services; and that authors who wrote those books might have different expectations.

I'd make a couple of points in response to that. I don't think it's intuitive that there must be a segmentation at some level of the kind that matters for antitrust purposes, I think we're mainly talking about a continuum, as I've explained. But perhaps more relevant to the way you may be thinking about it is that if there is any distinct segmentation of books where there is an industry consensus, books that are truly likely to succeed, the evidence showed that it's books in basically two categories. One, repeat franchise authors with a track record of success where you can predict with a high degree of probability that those books are going to sell well.

And similarly, celebrity authors who have an existing following that you can predict translates into book sales. And we received testimony from witnesses about this.

And the point here, Your Honor, is that these books garner advances vastly in excess of $250,000. We're talking about advances in the multiple million dollar range. I have here an excerpt from Ms. McIntosh's testimony where she said, you know, if someone's estimating with one of these types of authors that we're going to sell 300,000 copies, yeah, I'm going to spend millions of dollars. 300,000 copies, Your Honor, is far, far, far in excess of anything that would pencil out to a $250,000, $350,000, $500,000 advance.

In this kind of range where I think the Government is trying to land their definition, sort of in this 200 to maybe even up to million dollar range, that's where there's the most uncertainty. That's where, if anything, those would be unanticipated top sellers. That's where the risks and gambles are being taken that you heard so much about. And here's Ms. Bergstrom from Simon & Schuster who made that point, Your Honor.

Now, the Government of course could have tried to come in here and block this merger based on a market defined by those advance levels where there was a high degree of predictability. But that would have failed also, Your Honor, because the authors in that price advance level have the most leverage since they have the books that, by definition, everyone wants to buy. Related to this idea, Your Honor, is—and we didn't hear about it in the closing, but we did in Mr. Read's opening when he talked about a price discrimination; or when we heard some testimony, I think, by Dr. Hill about targeting authors.

Again, this requires the Government to prove that publishers can and do identify in advance a distinct category of authors who need the services that can be provided only by certain publishers: Those publishers who pay advances of $250,000 or more. The idea being that these authors are captive to those select publishers, and can be targeted for price decreases.

This price discrimination theory, as we'll amplify in our post-trial submission, is simply an application of the Brown Shoe industry factors, Your Honor, it's not a departure from it. But just going down that line for a moment. If you could identify the market at which authors mostly receive services from the Big 5, then that market boundary, as I indicated, needs to be defined at around $50,000. Because that's where the dramatic cliff occurs, not 250 or even 150 or even 350. If you can define the market by authors that truly can be identified in advance based on objective criteria, such as in Syufy, we're talking about the franchise and celebrity authors, not a market defined by advances as low as $250,000 or $150,000. But, Your Honor, those authors, as I indicated, they might be identifiable, but they can't be targeted. They have the most leverage, and they're not susceptible to pricing decreases. I mean, I enjoyed listening to Stephen King, but no one is cutting his compensation. I mean, there are authors in the Government's price market who are billionaires. I mean, I think Stephen King could buy Simon & Schuster if he wanted.

So beyond that point, Your Honor, there are—despite the Government's attempt to be dismissive of them, there are other publishers—it's not just the Big 5—who provide services equivalent to those by the Big 5 publishers. Some are better than others. Obviously, the Big 5 have more money and do more things, buy more books. But that's not a categorical difference in services. I mean, look at the testimony of the various people that you saw, Your Honor. None of them downgraded or degraded the services of companies like Abrams, Norton—who's been around for a hundred years, or Kensington, Disney, et cetera. No one indicated that these—the services rendered by these publishers were inferior.

If you look at the next slide, you can just get a sense of some of the books and authors. This slide is confidential. It's confidential because some of this came out in closed session, Your Honor. But this is a who's who list of books and authors here by firms other than the Big 5. So there's really no credible evidence at all that only the Big 5 can serve authors who want larger advances, the Big 5 just do more of them.

Now, Ms. McIntosh addressed an issue that the Government raised throughout the trial, which was about marketing spend. Because the Government was contending through some of their testimony that, well, you can tell by marketing spend which ones are the anticipated top sellers. But as we learned, there's a straight flat percentage put in these P&Ls for marketing spend that might have, once again, a general correlation to actual spend. But, certainly, the actual spend is not at all based on what's in the P&L. Ms. McIntosh walked through the process, as did Ms. Kim—and perhaps other witnesses as well, and explained that a publisher decides to spend on a book what the publisher learns as the book approaches publication—which can be years after the acquisition, based on feedback from salespeople, from retailers and others. And most of the time, the marketing folks don't even know what the advance level is.

So you can't define—you can't rely on the marketing as a basis for defining something in the acquisition market, it happens much later, and there's no causal connection to the advance. At most, there's a loose correlation. And the Government has never identified any level of marketing expenditures that reflect some distinct category of books or consensus understanding that these books differ from others.

Now, we heard a little bit about "glam," but that's because you're dealing with a celebrity author. That has nothing to do with the advance, Your Honor. Indeed, I think Ms. Walsh testified that she got "glam" for one of her clients who got an advance under $250,000.

So look, we think it's quite clear what's happening here, Your Honor. As I indicated in the opening—my opening statement, the Government found no harm whatsoever in the place where they always look, and that is in the downstream market.

There's no undue concentration, there's no harm. Then they went upstream, and they looked at the market for all trade books, which is the right place to look. And they found, once again, there is no harm in that market. And so they've come up with this price boundary, and it's the only way that they can trigger the presumption. And this boundary is simply arbitrary.

I don't know why Dr. Hill talked about the hypothetical monopsonist test, because, as he pointed out, it passes the test at any advance level. It doesn't indicate anything, it's utterly meaningless other than addressing whether there's an outside option in the form of self-publishing, which nobody was arguing in this case. And I think the fact that the hypothetical monopsonist test passes at any level means there is no sensible line to draw. So I think that's supportive of our position.

So, again, when all is said and done, the only real market here, Your Honor, is the obvious one, and that's the one for all trade books. And as the Government concedes, that's not concentrated. And as I said in my opening statement, and I'll repeat again, the only reason we're here is because the Government has created an artificial market to create artificial concentration to create artificial harm.

So let me talk about the harm.

THE COURT: Before you do that, can I ask you to address one aspect of Dr. Hill's testimony. You've said that it might make more sense to draw a relevant market for the celebrity authors, the above a million authors, or at $50,000. He said that the existence of other markets does not necessarily mean that the one that was chosen is not also a relevant market. Can you address that?

MR. PETROCELLI: Yeah, Your Honor, I heard that, I think it was yesterday. The Government has never pled that market. They've never tried to prove that market. And that market is, I think—if there is such a sub market at that level, it demonstrates that the $250,000 line is arbitrary.

There's nothing distinguishing these books in these different price segments. The only difference is where the Big 5 kick in as the more dominant buyers of the books. And so, yeah, they could have come in and said there's a couple of sub markets in here: There's one from 50 to 250, there's one from 250 and above. But I think that that would have been very difficult for them to maintain any sort of credibility about the 250 line. And so that's just not a case that we were presented, and I think that there would be no basis for carving up the market in so many different ways.

Because, again, the books are negotiated and edited and published the same way along any of these price points. It's just a matter of these Big 5 buy more than the other publishers. That's it; that's it. And I'm not aware of any case, Your Honor—I like to say I'm not an antitrust expert, but I'm not aware of any case, Your Honor, that defines a market just by the number of competitors. And I don't think any has been cited.

So going to the presumption. Again, if we accept the Government's market definition, then the presumption is triggered. And then our burden is to—as I indicated in the opening, it's a burden of production, not of persuasion, of course. And I believe the evidence in this case readily, readily shows that the presumption has been rebutted. And here's just a summary of some of the reasons why, if you'd turn to the next slide, Pam.

So I'll briefly go over these points, Your Honor. Let me start with the merger guidelines. They tell us that in a market for differentiating products and individual bargaining—which is what we're dealing with here, the likelihood of harm is determined not by market concentration, but by the degree to which the merger eliminates competition between the merging parties; defined to mean when they were the top two bidders, or the first and second choice. So right off the bat, you need to know more than shares. And the Government's case here relies almost entirely on shares. But shares are not a true indicator of competitive effects in this case for these various reasons. And again, I point out the statement of Judge Mehta in the Sysco case that we saw in my opening.

And when we do this analysis of taking into account the shares, how often do these two firms actually meet head-to-head one and two. Professor Snyder's analysis shows us that the merging parties were the first and second choices in only about 6 percent. And even in Dr. Hill's analysis, it was only 12 percent. So right off the bat, under either of those experts, we're dealing with the idea that pretty much 90 percent of the time, 90 percent of the time, these two companies are rarely one and two.

The second reason market information is not indicative is because the agents control the acquisition formats and the number of bidders. And I know that Mr. Read made some comments about this. But it is undisputed, Your Honor, that it is the agents, and only the agents, who decide who to submit proposals to, who to ask for bids, who to invite to an auction, how the rules for those auctions were set up. They have the complete discretion to change those rules. They decide when they're going to conduct direct negotiations. So it is the agents who are driving this bargaining process. I'm not saying the publishers don't have leverage either, I'm pointing out that it is the agents who are the drivers of the process.

And unlike some of the assumptions made in these models, the agents do not obviously invite all publishers.

They invite selected publishers. And not even publishers, Your Honor, that's another point I'll get to. They're not inviting these monolithic companies, they're inviting particular editors at particular imprints. And there probably are hundreds, hundreds of these imprints spread around the various publishing houses. And they're looking, obviously, for the right match.

So the important point here is that if the merger did functionally eliminate one potential participant, it will not necessarily change the dynamic of any given auction. Because that publisher may not have participated in the first place, or because the agent can readily replace that publisher with another bidder. And I think as Dr. Hill himself acknowledged, more than half—I think he said as high as 60 percent of all acquisitions, occur by bilateral negotiations rather than by auctions. Another 20, 30 percent are best bid auctions, and the remainder might be a round-robin. Almost every witness agreed that parties do not make advance offers and demands in accordance with market share estimates. None of them ever track market share estimates in the acquisition market. It's not something that's ever been done, to my knowledge, before this case. They only know that there are many other parties that could win the book if they don't bid high enough. And we saw quite a bit of testimony about this.

Next is imprint competition, Your Honor. Market shares are also not good indicators, because several of the so-called Big 5 rely—as part of their chosen business models, to permit internal imprint competition. And this, as I indicated before, creates many more potential acquirers than market shares reflect. And in terms of this internal imprint competition, you know, there was that sort of catchy line, I guess, by Mr. King about: It's like a husband and wife bidding against each other for a house. I had to chuckle at that, because frankly, I've had some tough negotiations with my wife over our house.

But that aside, Your Honor, imprint competition exists because it's good for business. Publishers use imprint competition all the time. The Government's first witness, Mr. Pietsch, on whom they heavily rely, explained that Hachette allows imprint competition. In fact, if you recall that document with his scorecard of losses to other firms for advances in excess of $500,000, there were, I think, four or—I can't remember exactly the number, that were lost to another imprint in Hachette. And Penguin Random House has been doing this for decades. And I think Macmillan does it, Simon & Schuster and HarperCollins I believe do single house bids.

But these publishers believe that allowing imprints to separately and competitively bid increases their chances of winning the book; not only winning the book, but importantly, matching up with the author. And that could turn into, you know, the next Stephen King—or at least a long-standing author-publisher relationship, which in the long run is much more profitable. So that's why they do it, it's economically rational to do it. And they do have the rule that says we're not going to allow the internal bidding if we're the only ones left. But as you heard, the agents can readily avoid that circumstance by including an outside bidder, an external bidder. And rarely, if ever, have gotten into a circumstance where they had to give that notification—in fact, I think we heard from Gail Ross that she's only had to give the notification once in some 30 years over her entire career.

THE COURT: So Mr. Petrocelli, I agree that imprint competition is an important factor to be considered. But does it undermine the Government's reliance on market shares? Because the market shares include the imprint competition.

MR. PETROCELLI: Well, it does, because—in the sense that the Government is suggesting there are only five bidders, now there's going to be four. But we're talking about multiple, multiple bidders. So the market shares reflect all the wins of each of the publishing houses, right.

THE COURT: Including the imprints?

MR. PETROCELLI: Yes, which include all the imprints. But it doesn't really reflect how the acquisition process occurs, and it doesn't give any credit for internal competition. You know, the agents are not provoking a competition among five large publishers—and a sixth one if you want to aggregate everybody else into that other category. They're provoking competition among dozens and dozens of imprints, and the market shares don't really reflect that reality.

The last point I want to make about internal imprint competition is the answer to the Government's effort to show that it's illusory. They pointed to in Ms. McIntosh's testimony, I don't know, three or four or five instances where there was internal communication. Let's be clear, there are thousands of author submissions over the last few years. I don't know how many millions and millions of documents in this case have been produced, Your Honor, and they had five or six—or whatever, instances where there was coordination. I won't go through them all. But I think in most of those instances, they didn't result in any lower bid. Some of them had to do with the strategy of how to open the bidding process.

And I think as you heard when I examined Ms. McIntosh, there is no system in Penguin Random House where whenever a proposal comes in to an imprint or an editor, they're to notify everybody in order to mobilize some overarching coordination process. That doesn't occur. And these imprints zealously compete against each other. You heard testimony that on occasion, one of the Penguin Random House individuals, Ms. von Moltke, was involved in these communications on the emails. To be clear, she has a high-level job. She was not hired or tasked to be some kind of overarching coordinator or tzar of coordination. She has gotten involved in bids from time to time when the circumstances called for communication for one reason or the other. Ms. McIntosh made clear that it's not common, it happens rarely. And when you think about it, why would they impose an internal structural coordination system that would literally override decades of their internal imprint competition, which they have decided is in the best interest of their business.

Another point I want to make about the rebuttal of the structural presumption is, again, it assumes that things are static and they don't change. But, you know, we have, first of all, three other major publishers who, as you heard, are going to compete fiercely to win these books post-merger, just like they do premerger. Intense competition from three major publishers. This is not a Sysco case; this is not a CC Holdings case; this is not a Wilhelmsen case where you have these two gigantic companies merging, and everybody else is a far distant third. And it's easy to see, intuitively there, why that would be a problem, because they're almost always going head-to-head. But we don't see that here, because Simon & Schuster is not at the size of Penguin Random House. And in fact, as you heard from the testimony, Simon & Schuster's addition to the company would just effectively replace the lost market share the company suffered after the 2013 merger with Penguin.

So we heard testimony about new entrants. And yes, they're small, but these are prominent people who are getting books, and paying even seven figures for them. But perhaps more to the point, Your Honor, we have a number of these existing firms—not just the remaining members of the Big 5, but all the other firms, who have a reputation, who have the skill, who have the infrastructure, who can fill the void if there's an effort to win more books. It's not like they have to wait three, four, five years to develop a backlist. I think what Mr. Read was suggesting were characteristics applicable to new entrants, not existing entrants who can readily expand.

And the last point I'm going to make on the presumption, and why market shares distort the constraining effects, has to do with the non-Big 5 publishers again. And I'm not going to focus on the 10 percent of all acquisitions that they win. And by the way, 10 percent is not an immaterial number, because it's bigger than—in the aggregate, some of the other Big 5 members. So it poses serious competition in the aggregate.

And remember, every one of these books is a new product. Every one of these books is something that never existed before. There's no inherent known value to these books. So anybody at any time can show up and win a book. That's why you see 10 percent, which is a significant number. But what we also heard yesterday—and I know there was some debate about the math, I think Dr.—I think Professor Snyder's calculation was more accurate than Dr. Hill's. But you have the Big 5 either winning or placing second 23 percent of the time. And that's not—that's meaningful, Your Honor, because the second bid is obviously constraining the winner.

There was a debate, like I said, about what the right denominator was: Was it 21 over 150 or 21 or 299. But I think as Dr. Hill acknowledged, if you're looking at what are all the actual auctions in which the non-Big 5 either win or come in second, he agreed with that number as 23 percent. He used his fraction to describe another dynamic—which off the top of my head I can't remember. But I do remember that he agreed that if you're just looking at the acquisitions, the 23 percent holds up. And if you wanted to cut it in half, it would still be—

THE COURT: I don't think so. I don't think that's where we landed, Mr. Petrocelli. We landed at 11.5 percent.

MR. PETROCELLI: Well, I think Professor Snyder's 23 percent, Your Honor—maybe I'm wrong—

THE COURT: That's what Dr. Snyder says, but I was persuaded by Dr. Hill that the number is 11.5.

MR. PETROCELLI: Well, whether it's 23 or half of that, Your Honor, it's a significant constraint. Because it's not just—the point I was trying to make is that it's not just the wins, it's the times they're also coming in second because they're constraining the winner, okay.

Now, those are the reasons why I think market shares don't reflect the true competitive effects. And I think the presumption is rebutted, and I think the Government then has to resort to proving up their case without the benefit of the presumption.

And on that point, Your Honor, let me go back to basics here. When the Government filed this case, it was very clear that it was based strictly on the loss of competition between the merging parties: The direct head-to-head one and two, of competition that would be eliminated by virtue of the merger. And that was clearly—that was clearly what they alleged, and that was how Dr. Hill proposed to analyze the competitive effects. However, it did seem that as the trial evolved, we did hear testimony by Dr. Hill—and even somewhat in Mr. Read's closing remarks, about a general softening of competition, and whether competition is harmed here just by the elimination of one bidder.

Now, you know, we go from five—putting aside the imprints, we go from five to four, right. Is that alone enough to show a reduction in competition. And the answer is that it is not, not at all. I mean, the guidelines recognize that the only transactions that could be affected, even in theory, are those where both the merging parties were one and two. And it's only in that situation that the merger can affect the outcome. And if you'd put up the slide, Pam.

What we see here is that in all these scenarios—and these are scenarios where the merging parties were not one and two, where somebody else wins; where one of the merging parties wins, but the other doesn't participant; where Penguin wins, but Simon & Schuster is not the second runner up; Simon wins, Penguin Random House is not. I mean, these are really all of the scenarios that can occur outside of the two firms being one and two. And this is the only way in which competition can be harmed. And that's what all the cases that deal with the unilateral effects address, whether we're talking Sysco, CC Holdings and the rest of them.

The guidelines obviously don't assume that just by eliminating one competitor there's some automatic softening or weakening of competition. The concern is whether the combined firm will be able to decrease its own prices without losing authors to non-merging firms. And that requires, Your Honor, an economic and quantitative analysis to determine whether reducing the number of competitors will actually reduce prices given the market conditions.

Now, Dr. Hill tried to do exactly that. But we submit his model and analysis fell short, because they don't fit. And if the models don't fit here, absent concrete projections of harm afforded by some other model or in some other way, the Government simply cannot show that the merger is likely to cause a substantial reduction in competition. So I'm not going to get into the details of Dr. Hill's model. And in terms of the profit margin issue, Mr. Fishbein is going to address that.

But Dr. Hill did attempt to model something other than by way of the second-score auction model. He tried to model bilateral negotiations; he couldn't do that. He tried to model best bids; that didn't work. And so the best he could do, I think he said, was to do the rounds model under the SSA format. And to be clear, I don't think there's much debate that that doesn't really fit, because very few, if any, of the auctions actually go to a full round. They usually end with a best bid, even when an auction is convened.

And so Dr. Hill's—I think his point, at the end of the day, was that there's a general downward pressure that you could kind of assume is going to apply post-merger. I think that that, in many ways, has it backwards for this reason. The one thing that I think we know from the way these auctions are conducted, and the way the agents run these processes, is that the agents and authors consider bilateral negotiations and best bids to be different and better for authors than multi-round auctions.

And I think it's obvious, because if they thought that multi-round auctions and round-robin auctions would best suit their interests, they would use them. But they rarely do. So any model focused on round-robin auctions cannot logically say anything meaningful about the way that agents and authors choose specifically to avoid round-robin auctions. As I've said, Mr. Fishbein will talk about the input issue.

We know that Dr. Hill did not select, in the first instance, his GUPPI model, but he went back to it in rebuttal after Dr.—after Professor Snyder's criticisms. And again, without getting into the details—and we can cover more of this in our briefing, Your Honor, the GUPPI suffers from the same limitations and flaws as the SSA; including not taking into account imprint competition, responses of other publishers, the role of agents. And obviously it does not cover at all direct negotiations. And then we heard testimony that, based on Professor Snyder's calculations, there may be a safe harbor that shows no harm.

And to be clear, we heard—I'm not sure there's evidence in the record on that, so I'm going to stop right there. That takes me now, Your Honor, to coordinated effects, but Mr. Fishbein is going to address that.

So with that, let me just conclude by saying a couple of other factors that I think show why this merger will not reduce author advances, and then I will be done. You may recall that in the Sysco case, there were extensive ordinary course business documents consistently identifying the merging parties as the only other's main competitor or main rival. And again, it was very easy it infer from that that the mergers of the two were going to enable that firm to exercise monopoly power.

Here, Your Honor, despite a lot of documents that we've seen—and I think there's probably around 200 documents in the exhibit list, there are no documents at all showing or indicating or suggesting that Penguin Random House and Simon & Schuster are direct rivals, none. And they're not, because Simon & Schuster is smaller, and HarperCollins, among others, is bigger. I know that Your Honor rejected the efficiencies presentation, but the one thing I will point out about that in the hundreds of tabs and cells there, that there was no proposal to cut advances. You saw nothing in there that post-merger there would be a savings by reducing advances. That's not something that the company ever contemplated, and wouldn't make any sense.

And to the contrary, from the witnesses, Your Honor, I think we heard that the other major competitors, they don't intend to change their behavior post-merger. We even heard that from Ms. Pande. In fact, several predicted that advances will increase—which I suggest is the most likely outcome here, because these companies are going to be motivated to compete against a firm with greater resources. And in order to win those books, they're going to have to pay more; because if you don't win the book, you don't have anything to sell. And we heard testimony to that effect from Brian Murray and John Glusman. I think there's a confidential slide there showing excerpts of their testimony.

And then also the next slide, Your Honor, where a number of the publishers testified that they will not change—they will not change bidding strategies at all. As Mr. Glusman put it: If anything, the merger might increase advances. Now, that takes us back to one final point, and that's the 2013 merger. And all I'm going to say about that is that there were witnesses like Mr. Glusman and others, like Mr. Zacharius, like Mr. Murray who all agreed that advances across the industry did not decrease following that merger. And we have an output increase of some 13 percent for books in the Government's market. More books were published, hundreds of millions of dollars were spent.

We saw that chart that Mr. Read showed that Dr. Hill prepared. But that does not account for the mass market turn below $250,000, and doesn't account for the variability at the top end for advances in the $4,000,000 and above range. So we don't think that chart is an accurate depiction of what happened.

We will address these issues in more detail in our post-trial submissions. Again, let me thank Your Honor and your staff. This is an incredibly important case. We know the Court is going to review the evidence and the law very carefully in reaching its decision. We submit that when you do, that the only decision here that is correct and just is to deny the Government's motion. Thank you.

CLOSING ARGUMENT OF VIACOMCBS AND SIMON & SCHUSTER

MR. FISHBEIN: Thank you, Your Honor. I think we're going to pass up some slides, and there will be some confidential slides which I'll identify. You'll see them; the gallery, I believe, will not.

Your Honor, as I mentioned yesterday, my clients ViacomCBS and Simon & Schuster, we have an independent interest in seeing this merger through. You heard from the leadership, from the CEO of Simon & Schuster, from the top M&A executive at ViacomCBS, they want this deal not only because Bertelsmann offered the best price, also Penguin Random House they concluded was the best—a great home for Simon & Schuster.

But also because they felt that the deal will benefit Simon & Schuster authors. And that's what I want to focus on today.

So let me start with a legal principle that I think we've referred to, but I think is important: And that is that the analysis under Section Seven, substantially to lessen competition, is forward-looking; it focuses on the future. Why do I say that? I mean, we've heard a lot about market shares and diversion ratios. And those are, of course, the current market shares. That's what happened in the past. And those are useful to the extent they predict the future. But if there's reason to believe that things are changing, if there's reason to believe that incentives may be different—and Mr. Read mentioned that the merged entity, as a larger entity, may have different incentives. Well, the other competitors may have different incentives, too, and that's what I want to look at.

And I think that's especially important in this industry, because I think everybody agrees that it's rapidly changing. I mean, we've seen it in a variety of sources.

There's the HarperCollins 10-K; the Department of Justice argued, just a couple of days ago, the world has dramatically changed since 2013. We've heard about technological innovations, all sorts of things. So in a changing environment, I think it's especially important not to simply assume that market shares, diversions, competitive dynamics are going to stay the same tomorrow as they are today.

Now, to make this concrete, so what are we sort of up against. With Simon & Schuster—and you've heard this, the calculation that comes out of the Government's models, what they're alleging here, is that on average, we will pay the authors of anticipated top selling books $100,000 less per book. That's a lot of money. And that includes not only these very, very top authors listed here, but everybody. Now, they've said it's an average, they're not saying it's a hundred for each book. But presumably, if you pay less—if you don't lowball Bruce Springsteen, you're going to have to raise it somewhere else lower down. And my point is that it's significant, and so it puts—you know, what they're really saying is it puts Simon & Schuster editors in this kind of situation.

And we used best bids here, because the testimony was that that's a frequent method, the agents can choose it. If they're not getting what they want through rounds auctions, they can go to best bids. And you have your Simon & Schuster editor in the bottom right there, and they have to think about a lot. They have to think about the other Big 5. They have to think about other publishers, there are others that may be inspired by this book. And they have to think, can they get away with, can they get away with a reduction.

And Your Honor, I want to sort of draw a comparison with commodity markets. Dr. Hill made a couple of references—I think he must have worked on a case involving beer, so he mentioned beer. So when you're in a commodity and you're making lots of sales of the same product over and over and over again, it gives you a little leeway to sort of try out price reductions. You could reduce your price on beer for a week or something, see how the market reacts. If worse comes to worst, you lose some sales for a week.

But books are not like that. The best bids here is one round. And if you don't get the Springsteen book, you never get it. And you can't say in the future that you're the leader of the singer-songwriters, et cetera. So it's a different dynamic. And what those editors are really thinking about is can I take the risk, can I take the risk of softening. That would be a difficult proposition under current situation.

But what I submit to the Court is, when you look at it from the perspective of now there's going to be this combined entity, there's going to be this merged entity, how is that going to change the thinking of the other competitors; especially if the merged entity is trying to hold down values by a hundred thousand dollars per book, which is significant.

And I submit, Your Honor, and what I want to spend some time on is, what does that do to the incentives of the others to come in, fill that gap and take away market share from the combined entity if they're going to lower advances. Because again, all the models assume that the market shares stay the same. What I'm saying is that incentives can change, and that you have some other competitors here that are ready, willing and able to step into the gap.

The next slide is confidential, but I want to spend a little time with this, Your Honor. And by—and we're not talking here about entry. Mr. Read spent a fair amount of time debunking the idea that new entrants can easily come in. I don't want to belabor the point. But obviously HarperCollins is number two, so they already have a reputation, they already have an infrastructure, they're already there. And I know Your Honor's familiar from other cases where we instruct juries, that trying to discern what somebody's intent is in the future, what they're going to do in the future, can be difficult. It's also often subject to circumstantial evidence. I think it's quite remarkable that in this case, there is such strong and compelling direct evidence of what this second competitor is going to do, because they've said it.

So on the bottom left, you remember that Mr. Murray publicly said that they were going to be very aggressive. That was a statement that was made well after the merger was announced. It got the attention of the other publishers, which goes back to my cartoon of people sitting around the table: They're going to have to think about HarperCollins being aggressive. On the right here—and I won't say the numbers, that comes out of HarperCollins' January 2022 strategy update that's well over a year after the deal was announced. They had plenty of time to think about it. This was presented to leadership of News Corp—so Mr. Murray, the CEO, is presenting to his leadership, he's accountable for it. And they project increasing titles, increasing advance spends, and increasing advance per title. So on all metrics, it's going up.

And I specifically asked him: Did you caveat it; did you say if the merger goes through, then we can't accomplish any of this? And he said no. So the contemporary business judgment, with the merger in mind, is that they're going to increase, they're going to be aggressive. And if there's any doubt about it, any doubt about what their intentions are—if there's changed incentives, there's changed motives, if there's changed conduct as a result of the merger, I actually asked him directly about that in his testimony.

And I can't repeat it, again, because it's confidential. But if you look at the top, the blue underlined and then the question and answer below that, he was directly asked: "What do you intend to do with respect to this merger?"

And now taking a step back and going beyond HarperCollins, I think we have clear evidence here that it is not going to be a static situation, as the Government's models predict. You are going to have other empowered competitors motivated to take advantage of any softening or reduction that they see. And they have said that. And the DOJ models just don't account for that, and for that reason are quite counter-factual.

Now, Your Honor asked, and it came out of a statement that Mr. Murray made—and I do want to just spend a minute on it, on this issue of, well, how strong really is HarperCollins. And there was this issue of Christian and romance, and should it be counted. The way it actually arose in the testimony is that Mr. Murray said that one of his vendors told him that. So we're talking about downstream sales through a single vendor—albeit an important vendor, who told him that Penguin Random House was three times his size. So that's a downstream market from the one vendor's point of view. The important thing is we're obviously concerned about the upstream, the acquisition of rights from authors.

THE COURT: Well, the market shares are downstream.

MR. FISHBEIN: The market share is actually—that I believe all the experts are using are upstream, they're based on the advance database.

THE COURT: Oh, I see, yes.

MR. FISHBEIN: And they're different than the downstream. So what we care about here, being a monopsony case, is the upstream market shares.

THE COURT: But they're correlated.

MR. FISHBEIN: They are correlated. They're correlated, and not exactly the same. But I think the point is, is that Mr. Murray repeating what a vendor told him in a negotiation—where obviously the vendor has an incentive to say you don't have a lot of leverage, is not a substitute for what the two experts did in this case. And they agree—they disagreed on a lot, but they both used Christian and romance as part of their data in computing market shares.

THE COURT: Yes.

MR. FISHBEIN: So Your Honor has a question?

THE COURT: I'm absorbing what you're saying, which is interesting, Mr. Fishbein. It just seems to me that the reason I kind of focused on this testimony was because—and you make a good point, that the market shares we've looked at in this case is about advances, and this is a point about downstream.

But it struck me as an important consideration that the market shares, at least in the downstream market, would overstate—I'm sorry, would understate the power of Penguin Random House, and even Simon & Schuster, because this publisher's market share includes all these books that Penguin Random House and Simon & Schuster don't compete in.

And I think that there is going to be some correlation—perhaps not as strong as I originally thought, because we're talking about upstream versus downstream, between that. And I think that this could translate into also an understatement of the power of the combined entity in the advance market, given the correlation between the two.

MR. FISHBEIN: So let me address that—and I fully understand the point. So first point, which I think we've covered, is that the most relevant market is the upstream. You see the graph here. This is from both experts' data, and PRH is roughly 50 percent bigger than HarperCollins on that measure. The second one, if you look at the bottom chart, that is downstream. So now I'm shifting to what Your Honor's talking about is downstream. This is HarperCollins' internal market share division, and they include Christian and romance. I mean, it's specifically footnoted there. That's HarperCollins Christian Publishing and romance. And so PRH is not double the size, it's whatever—I mean, triple the size, it's roughly double the size. And there's a reason for that, Your Honor.

THE COURT: But I guess my question is what would it be if you took out the Christian—

MR. FISHBEIN: Well, why take it out? In other words, what I'm getting at is—

THE COURT: Because they don't compete in those.

MR. FISHBEIN: No, but most Christian, most Christian is not Bibles. Most Christian is what they call inspiration or spiritual, and Penguin Random House does compete in that, they do.

THE COURT: Only—no, there's three categories. There's the Bibles; there's the Christian that are sold only in the specialty Christian stores—which Penguin Random House does not compete very much in at all, if at all; and then there's sort of the values—more general market ones, what they call crossover. And I thought the evidence was clear that they're not really competing on Christian.

MR. FISHBEIN: I think Ms. McIntosh—and obviously anybody can go back and look, I believe she testified that they do compete in the—

THE COURT: 2 percent.

MR. FISHBEIN:—in the spiritual part.

THE COURT: In the spiritual part, but very small.

MR. FISHBEIN: Okay. But the only way you get to three-to-one is if you exclude all of the Christian and all of the romance. And I don't think there's any evidence that—I mean, obviously everybody competes in romance. And the other thing, Your Honor, is that those—

THE COURT: But not those—not the Harlequin romance, which is sold in the—not in the regular retail bookstores, but in other markets.

MR. FISHBEIN: So I'll come back to that in a second. But I think we all sell romances, okay, and it's not broken down here what portion of that is Harlequin versus anything else. Now, the other thing, Your Honor, is that if you're going to—

THE COURT: I don't want to quibble about it.

MR. FISHBEIN: No, go ahead.

THE COURT: I don't want to get into too much detail on the testimony on this, but I get your general point.

MR. FISHBEIN: And look, let me—I'm just going to make two other points, which is if you take out Christian and romance from HarperCollins to make the comparison, you also have to take it out of Penguin Random House in—

THE COURT: Exactly, and it's zero—it's close to zero. That's why it's interesting to me.

MR. FISHBEIN: Okay. Well, yeah, the record will reflect. And I would just say, when you go back and look at the record, please distinguish between the different types of romance and the different types of Christian.

THE COURT: Absolutely.

MR. FISHBEIN: And then the final thing, Your Honor, we're talking about here is the market for anticipated top selling books, which the Government defines with an advance level of 250. Now, the subgroup you're talking about, these pocket romance series that sell in drugstores, we've not seen any of them on the list of advances of above 250. I just don't think it's a factor at all.

THE COURT: But the Christian books are.

MR. FISHBEIN: I'm sorry?

THE COURT: But the Christian books are in there, the ones that they don't compete on.

MR. FISHBEIN: Well, okay. The Bibles aren't in there.

THE COURT: No, but the—

MR. FISHBEIN: The inspirational ones are. But we do compete on there. So anyway, I think you understand my point.

THE COURT: I do, I got it.

MR. FISHBEIN: There's a number of facets to this, and I don't think it's as simple as Mr. Murray saying one of his vendors told him he was three times the size.

Okay, let's go to—so I talked about HarperCollins. And now Macmillan and Hachette, the other two of the Big 5, very, very similar story. They're ready, willing and able. You can see the quotes here. And, you know, I sort of tried to imagine, well, what would Dr. Hill say about this. You know, he would say, well, the competition with the Big 5 is already baked into the market share. But again, that's the existing market share, and so he'd be wrong on sort of two counts. One is that Macmillan is already, already trying to take market share from the Big 5, as indicated here. And they had a spectacular year in 2021. You might remember Mr. Weisberg talking about how proud they were that they were taking market share.

And again, like HarperCollins, there's a desire, there's a stated intent to continue to claw market share away from the others, which will only be enhanced if there's that big, new formidable competitor trying to do better for their authors. They're going to want to do the same. And that's where the current market shares just do not predict the future. They do not account for three well-funded, deeply experienced, highly motivated rivals ready to pounce on any sign of softness or weakening.

Your Honor, the same is true for the smaller ones. And I'm not going to dwell on this, because Mr. Petrocelli touched on it. I do want to cover one aspect. This is just some more evidence, some more specifics about how the non-Big 5 publishers certainly are able to compete. That first one from Norton I think is particularly interesting where, if you remember, Mr. Karp said they lost a big book above 250 to Norton specifically because the author was impressed with the marketing plan. And then with Abrams, it was also marketing and publicity.

And this is interesting, too, the feeling that it might benefit the author to be the big fish in a smaller pond. And so they have advantages. You know, if you're not a big fish in a small pond, then I guess you're a small fish in a big pond and you're kind of a guppy. And I don't think authors are interested at this point in being guppies.

THE COURT: Different kind of guppy.

MR. FISHBEIN: Yeah, exactly, exactly. Okay. Now, we've tended to think about the non-Big 5 as this large group of smaller entities. And when Mr. Read talks about expansion, of course he focuses on Zando and some of these smaller ones. But there are several—and I think this is important to point out—and are you guys getting the confidential ones? Okay, yeah.

So you've got Amazon, you've got Scholastic, you've got Disney are not part of the—aren't part of the Big 5. All three of them have experience—let's take Amazon. And there's no dispute about this, we all know that they, at a certain point in time, made a big play—I listed the books down here: Dean Koontz, Patricia Cornwell, Mindy Kaling, made a big push, multimillion advances. They have the imprints, they have the editors. They drew back for whatever reason.

There's some indication that, more recently, Mr. Karp said he saw them in an auction. There's one of the Colleen Hoover books that's now being distributed at Barnes & Noble. So they ebb and flow to some extent.

But there's no doubt that they have the resources, they have the expertise, they have a track record having done it before. And so they're poised to compete. And I would submit that if you have a new, big merged entity that is trying to soften advances, that is a motivation for them to come in and fill the gap. Mr. Read talked about entry, I guess, happening over a period of two or three years. As you can see here, Mr. Weisberg said Amazon can, again, become a formidable competitor at any given moment. That seems timely; that seems timely enough. And we saw the same thing with Scholastic, they poached $2,000,000 authors from Simon & Schuster. Disney, I can't say the number of titles or the specifics, but you can see it there specifically said that they had plans. And so again, added on to the existing Big 5, how do the motivations change; are they going to fill the gap if the merged entity tries to do what the Government says.

And then finally, I do—on this topic—and this is just—again, I won't dwell on this, because Mr. Petrocelli discussed it. But obviously some of the other smaller publishers also have plans to expand. I have to come back to the farm teams, because I told you I would in my opening, and because I have some associates who would be very angry if I didn't spin the metaphor out further. So what the DOJ said in their opening, you know, there was that farm teams comment.

Okay, and it's kind of funny, it's the baseball thing. But they really did swing for the fences in the opening. And Mr. Read went out of his way to say that the metaphor is especially apt, and really stressed that they're really there for nothing else than to feed the Big 5, is what he said. And, you know, I think there's a reason. I think he chose his words carefully, and he wanted to prove that.

And it was important, because he didn't want this to be collectively another Big 5. You've got Scholastic as another Big 5 in children's. And then you've got all these smaller and medium as another Big 5. All of a sudden, it starts to be six and seven, and it's just not the same argument that they wanted to make. So it's an important issue, and I submit, Your Honor, just it fell flat. So strike one: They obviously compete head-to-head. That's not a farm team situation. They're going for the same talent. The minor league teams don't recruit the same talent as the major league teams. There's many bestselling authors who stay at these small and medium publishers, and we've given some examples here of some of the best known authors around at Abrams, Norton and otherwise. And, you know, farm teams, the whole concept is as soon as you get called up to the majors you go. But that's not the situation.

And then even more so, there's some who switch from the Big 5 to the smaller ones. And that's certainly never happened, to my knowledge, in the major leagues, that somebody got elected to the all star team and said I'm going to spend the next season in the minors. So these are real competitors, they're a real force, and I think Your Honor really has to think about this market and what I'm saying about others filling in the gap as three significant other Big 5.

Scholastic, very, very strong in children's. And then another Big 5 equivalent, again, poised and ready to fill the gap if there's an attempt to lower advances.

Okay, so let me—and then just kind of as a reality check, you know, is this theory that when there's combinations, when there's M&A, others step in; does that have any validity. And there was the natural experiment with the 2013 Penguin Random House merger. As Mr. Read, I think, said, the evidence was a little bit inconclusive—or at least the experts were arguing with each other. But I don't think there's any disagreement at all, I don't think any of the participants in the industry who came here and testified said that advances have gone down over the last 10 years. Everybody said advances have gone up.

There's of course been a number of combinations, significant ones, and I think that's relevant. And you have Mr. Murray in the middle being very, very clear advances have gone up notwithstanding consolidation in the industry. And it's to similar effect, from agents, publishers, et cetera.

And so I think that's just kind of corroboration for what I'm saying, that when there's combinations, if there's any temptation to hold down advances, there's changed incentives and motivations for everybody else.

Let me address printing, because the Government did raise this, and I think that printing really is not an issue here. So, first, if the Government wanted to make the case that there's some kind of foreclosure, that Penguin Random House really can disadvantage competitors through its ownership of—its purchase of those Quad printing facilities, you'd have to do some kind of foreclosure analysis. You'd have to look at what the options are in the market, substitutability, is it just the U.S. or can you go to printers in Europe. And Dr. Hill did not do that. There was no expert analysis in this case, so we don't know really market shares. We have anecdotal information that I'll get to, but we don't have any formal analysis of the issue—which, if they wanted to prove it, that's really what they would have to do.

The second is, yes, there are capacity constraints. I mean, everybody said that, that especially during the pandemic, demand was up and the printers just couldn't keep up. They couldn't keep personnel, they had various issues. But that was not caused by the merger. I mean, there's nothing about the merger that added to this capacity issue. If anything, Bertelsmann's purchase of those failing Quad plants helped retain capacity. You remember Quad wanted to merge with LSC, the government blocked it. They closed their plants for a little while, and then Bertelsmann came in and rescued them.

So the merger is not responsible for that.

I think some of the witnesses said that some of the people complaining, the other publishers, said, well, if—if the merger goes through, then maybe Bertelsmann will self-preference its own printing. There's no evidence of that. That was really just speculation. And I asked the Macmillan guy, I asked the HarperCollins guy, no one had any examples.

They said, look, for now it's going fine; we're worried about this in the future. I just think that's speculation. There's no evidence to support that.

And then finally, on the fundamental question of, well, what would happen if Bertelsmann did do that—even though there's no evidence of it, there are plenty of other options. I think it's a little ironic, I guess, that Mr. Read illustrated this point with the email from Simon & Schuster from Mr. Eulau, where Mr. Eulau, the CFO, was saying: We don't want to be beholden to Bertelsmann, and so they went off and signed a contract with LSC. And what Mr. Eulau testified—I don't know if you remember it, because I asked him a series of questions, how have you addressed this issue of not wanting to be beholden to Bertelsmann. And he said: Well, we put a bunch of capacity with LSC; we sent some overseas; we went to small and medium publishers in North America, and we have successfully dealt with the situation. So Simon & Schuster successfully dealt with it. And I can't read the bottom left one out loud, but other publishers have also said that in the hard cover and soft cover print, there are other options.

On the right here, you have, again, an excerpt from a publisher's very, very recent strategy update indicating how they have successfully—they call it: "We're performing better than competitors on bestselling titles," because they were successfully able to replace their U.S. printing with other printing. So the big picture here, Your Honor, is there's options; there's no foreclosure analysis; there's really only speculation. I just don't think the printing is a relevant issue in this case.

I do want to talk about the margin, as Mr. Petrocelli mentioned. So there's two inputs to Dr. Hill's models—and this is true for both the GUPPI and the second-score auction, as I understand it. One is market share, and we don't—I don't think there's—there's not a disagreement on current market shares, so those are what they are. But the other one is the margins, and it makes a big difference. So as Dr. Hill testified, the higher the margin, the higher the harm. Because if you have low margin, you assume that all these buyers are clustered right around where they think the value is. And the difference between the first and second isn't very big. When you have a big margin, they're spread out and the harm is much higher. So it makes a big difference.

Now, Dr. Hill wants to use the higher level of margin, gross margin, which is the margin after variable costs, but before you take out any fixed costs. So originally he used—I guess it was the variable margin for Simon & Schuster—I think I'm getting this right. He used gross margin for one.

He couldn't categorize some costs, so he used the lower level margin for the other. Snyder pointed out that that's not right, it's not consistent. And so in the second effort, he used the higher level margin for both, just the variable costs. And he explained on the stand—

THE COURT: No, I think he still used variable costs for Simon & Schuster, but he assumed—I think he told me he used the same for Simon & Schuster.

MR. FISHBEIN: That's correct, he stuck with the variable costs for Simon & Schuster. But then for Penguin Random House, he went closer to variable costs so that they were consistent for the second time around.

THE COURT: Right, it was about his assumptions about what is a variable cost.

MR. FISHBEIN: That's exactly right. It wasn't—in other words, he's all in on the idea that it should be the variable cost margin, and not what we would call net income or operating income margin.

THE COURT: Yes, and he says that's what the models require.

MR. FISHBEIN: He did say that. He did say that. So the question is what to do if the industry shows you that the relevant measure is net income margin, but the model says you have to use gross margin. And I respectfully submit that you find another model. You don't change the industry facts to fit the model, you've got to form the model around the industry.

THE COURT: I think the industry models—the industry facts are disputed, because—

MR. FISHBEIN: Okay, so let's—

THE COURT:—Ms. McIntosh talked about variable costs.

MR. FISHBEIN: Well, I think we should—let's address that, and that's what's on this slide. So the first point is that you have the these P&Ls—and you've seen enough of these P&Ls, Your Honor, they're ubiquitous, right. So the left one is Simon & Schuster, and the right one is Penguin Random House. They both have the two measures. And so, look, it's an inference, but I think it's a pretty good one, that why would you set up a P&L to tell editors when they're determining advances, right, why would you set it up to also have the calculation of the net income or operating income if nobody cares and it doesn't matter. I think it's there for a reason, and—

THE COURT: Okay, I was just going to say these P&Ls are flexible, at best, and they don't seem to really rely very much on—

MR. FISHBEIN: Well, they are flexible, I'm not going to disagree with that. There are exceptions. I mean, we did hear in Simon & Schuster's case about an exception of, I think it was, an $8,000,000 memoir where they were willing to take a negative, I think it was, 3 percent operating income margin.

But the discussion around that I think was sort of like the exception that proves the rule, like should we do it, should we do it. And, look, Mr. Karp testified—and he was not challenged on this at all, and I have the quote here, that the guidance is to be positive, and that it should be double digit. So I think the combination of they set up the P&L to show it, the guidance is to be positive in double digits, I mean, that's not disputed on the Simon & Schuster side.

You are right, Ms. McIntosh had a different view—which I'm going to get to in a second. The P&L, though, is the same. The P&L on the Penguin Random House also has the EBIT margin. She did say—I think what she said was: Editors were so focused on the EBIT margin, I had to sort of course correct; and she said it was especially with the higher value books. And I think that's true. I mean, nobody disputes that for one or two books, or even three or four, some number of books, you can depart as long as you make it up on the other.

But you cannot run a business like this and always be short on the EBIT margin, you will go out of business.

So I think fairly taken as a whole, Ms. McIntosh's testimony is that the default is that you want positive net—well, whatever they call it, positive net profit, that there came a time when people were so focused on that, she wanted to have a correction and focus them on the gross margin, especially for the higher titles. But I don't think that's suggests that the net income is not what's relevant. And given the structure of the business, given what's clearly true on the Simon & Schuster side, undisputed, choosing gross margin, that higher number, is a mistake.

THE COURT: So I would say all businesses have fixed costs, and that model asks for variable costs only. Why?

MR. FISHBEIN: I'm sorry?

THE COURT: All businesses have fixed and variable costs, but the model requires variable costs. So you're saying it's not consistent with this market. I don't think it's consistent with any business.

MR. FISHBEIN: Well—

THE COURT: So why does the model require variable costs only?

MR. FISHBEIN: I didn't create the model, I just don't know. I'm not going to pretend I know why they chose that for that model. Some of it does have to do with the structure of the business. In other words, if it's—what I believe Dr. Snyder said is that if there's a business with very, very strong central control where the same people are responsible for the fixed costs—the executives and the people that sort of manage fixed costs at headquarters are also the ones doing the sale, I guess the theory is they'll have in mind the fixed costs and they don't have to worry about the variable costs.

What Dr. Snyder was saying when you distribute it among all these imprints, you can't tell them just ignore fixed costs because they'll drive you to bankruptcy.

THE COURT: I understand the argument, Mr. Fishbein. I just think that it's a model that is applied across all industries. All industries have fixed costs as well as variable, but the model requires variable costs. So I don't think it undermines the model to say: But in our industry, we have fixed costs.

MR. FISHBEIN: Okay, no, I think what I'm saying is a little different. Every industry—I agree with you. Every industry has variable costs and fixed costs. I cannot speak to any other industry as to whether they make their pricing decisions based on variable or fixed. There may be commodity industries where they view their fixed costs as sunk costs, and they just don't care about them; and when they tell their salespeople to set price, they say do it on the variable costs. I can't speak to that, because I don't know other industries. All I know is that in this industry we actually have the P&Ls, hundreds of them, and they focus on the fixed costs as well. And we have testimony from the executives. So it's not a fit here. I can't explain to you why it is or is not a fit anywhere else.

THE COURT: Okay. I think this is something we don't have evidence about. We should have asked the expert about it. But since we didn't, I'm not sure what to do with it.

MR. FISHBEIN: Well, I'm sure. I mean, they—

THE COURT: I'm sure you should have asked him.

MR. FISHBEIN: Yeah, okay. They bear the burden of proof, and I think they have to establish that the model they picked works for this industry.

THE COURT: Absolutely. But if you're going to tell me it doesn't work for this reason, I'm not sure what to do with it if we don't have any testimony from an expert about the model.

MR. FISHBEIN: Okay. I'll just end with this: I think where Your Honor's coming from—and, look, it's common-sense, I totally understand it. You're saying it kind of proves too much; if it doesn't work here, what about then doesn't it not work everywhere else, and then what's the point of the model. And I'm just saying in a court of law where they bear the burden and we're trying to accomplish a merger that we believe in, and they're coming to us and saying you cannot—they're coming to my client and saying: You got the highest price, you can't do it, right; you can't do it, you can't sell to the one that's going to be the value for your shareholders. They have to prove that it's the right fit. I don't have to prove that it's not a right fit somewhere else or that it is somewhere else.

THE COURT: Absolutely. But if you want to challenge an economic model for the reasons that you're saying, you need evidence to challenge it. You can't, I guess, tell me that you're the expert in economics, telling me why this doesn't work here. That's all I'm saying. I don't think I have evidence on this.

MR. FISHBEIN: And I'm going to move on. The evidence is on this slide, that's all I'm saying. The evidence is on this slide that it should be fixed costs.

THE COURT: But the significance of it, I don't have expert testimony about it.

MR. FISHBEIN: Okay, I understand. I think we've had our say on this.

THE COURT: We understand each other.

MR. FISHBEIN: We understand, we do, we do. I want to try to answer one other question that Your Honor posed, and then I'm going to wrap up, which is about the—well, no, then I'm going to get to coordinated effects and the sub markets, but I'm almost done. You asked about the sub markets, right, is it okay to have multiple sub markets. And I think there are cases that can talk about different—like, for example, different types of products in sub markets. But what you can't do, though, is if you just have a continuum, and even with every additional $10,000 in anticipated sales you could say that you would expect more marketing, you would expect more attention, you would expect a higher advance. So if it's an even continuum like that, the danger is the Government can then just choose their sub market at any level they want. And that's the problem. That's what you can't allow. You can't allow them to cherry pick at any point they want, because obviously they could just go to the area on the curve where there's the least competitors and it fits the HHI. So you can't have kind of a know it when I see it, it has to be attached to some product difference that's clearly differentiated at some point. There could be three of them, but you'd really have to be able to say below this level is fundamentally different than above this level. And that's not true if you go up by $10,000, $10,000, $10,000. So I would offer that.

THE COURT: So I think that there is some recognition, even on the defense side, that all books are not created equal. And Mr. Petrocelli has acknowledged the really top sellers, the celebrities and the authors with a track record. And I think—and you can correct me if you disagree, that what Dr. Hill said was he was just trying to find those books, the anticipated top sellers, regardless of the advance level; just the ones that need more marketing, more sales because they're expected to reach a very wide audience, et cetera. And he just chose 250 to identify those books.

So it's not so much that the market is relying on the 250—although it does, because he had to draw a line someplace. He's looking for those top selling books, and that's why he did his analysis, not just at 250, but also at I think 100, 150, 250, 500 and a million. And he said it was all consistent. So if you define the market as just the top selling books, we're not exactly sure exactly where it is, but this approximates it. And then it passes all the relevant market tests in terms of I guess horizontal monopsonist—although, in this case, we all agree that all of the segments would pass that. And then he says you can draw this many different places, but that doesn't take away from the validity of where I drew it, because it's consistent at this level.

Then he would say this is appropriate.

MR. FISHBEIN: Yeah, and all I'm saying is that if that gets carried so far, as it is in this case, where you could say the same thing about 50, 100, 150, all the way up—and you could, because at each of those breaks, you anticipate more sales, you'd like to have more marketing. You saw on the charts of the competitors, as you go down in advance level, there's more of those non-Big 5 competitors. So it's a gradual continuum, and so that means the Government, under that logic, could really choose anything. They could choose to make it at 50, at 75, at 100. And if you get to that point, they can just pick and choose. They can just pick and choose wherever the competition is such that it passes the presumption. And I think that's a problem. I think it has to be rooted in something more objective, some clear break off, if you're going to use those considerations.

On coordinated effects, Your Honor, I think the merger guidelines are pretty clear on this. And what I want to emphasize is there's been discussion of whether coordination has already occurred. There was a fair amount about audio, I think the payout structure. So those things already happened, and maybe they could still happen afterwards. That's not the issue. If you look here at 7.1, the agencies examine whether a merger is likely to change the map. So, again, it's merger-specific. Is the merger going to make the vulnerability or the possibility of coordination worse. And then there's a bunch of factors that are set here that both experts, I think, agree to. And on all of these—transparency, ability to monitor, ability to punish, homogeneous products, none of that changes because there's one less competitor. It's still non transparent. You can't really monitor it. You don't know exactly what the competitors paid for or bid. It's obviously not a homogeneous product, and so the only thing that's really different is what I think Mr. Read said, which is if you want to get together, there's one less person to invite. That would be true in any merger. That would be true in any reduction.

And I think that's making light of a pretty serious issue. Obviously people know if they meet and fix prices, it's a real problem. So to sort of say that the fact that there's one less person to invite is going to make it more likely that they're going to do it I think is farfetched. And on this ebooks case, that was 10 years ago. That's obviously a downstream case. This is an upstream case, which is fundamentally different, because there is price transparency there. That was the price of ebooks, which everybody could see. There was—Apple was right in the middle as a hub. The personnel were different. The representative from Simon & Schuster that was alleged to be involved is deceased. Penguin Random House wasn't involved. So it's a very different situation, very long time ago, downstream versus upstream. I just don't think it's applicable or really should be controlling here.

And so, Your Honor, for me to wrap up on the fundamental point that I started with, which is my clients want this merger because they truly believe that it's a good deal for all concerned, including authors. Obviously you heard that it's a cultural fit, that Penguin Random House is wholeheartedly committed to books. And that's what Mr. Karp and Mr. Berkett said. But it wasn't only us—and you have on here what some of the other publishers—and, again, I can't quote directly. But some of the other publishers who actually were complaining about the deal—I mean, they are opposed to the deal, but what was their rationale. Their rationale was that this was going to be a formidable competitor that would get good distribution deals and increase the discoverability and the visibility and the sale of its authors. And they felt disadvantaged. They felt disadvantaged because the new entity would do a better job promoting its authors than they could they felt. And I asked him specifically, like, you know, and so does that help Simon & Schuster and Penguin Random House authors, and they agreed. So even their criticism, I think, shows why this is better. Now, as far as their criticism—and they're right about that, the merged entity will have scale and is going to do a great job for authors. And so these other publishers—and I have to use some of their spectacular profits that we heard about in the last couple of years, to step up and compete the way they have said that they're going to do. And that's competition, that's competition. That's what we're here for. And maybe author Charles Duhigg said it best: He said, "The world will be a better place."

And I will leave it with that, Your Honor.

PART FIVE: POST-TRIAL BRIEFS AND REBUTTALS

UNITED STATES FINDINGS OF FACT AND CONCLUSIONS OF LAW

INTRODUCTION

As its CEO admitted, Penguin Random House's ("PRH") proposed acquisition of Simon & Schuster ("S&S") would "cement Penguin Random House as number one in the United States." The acquisition would establish a single firm with nearly 50% of the market in a concentrated industry that has a history of coordination. PRH, along with the remaining "Big Five" publishers, would control approximately 90% of the relevant market. The proposed acquisition is precisely the march toward concentration and monopsony power that Congress enacted the Clayton Act to prevent.

One entity's control of almost half of the nation's anticipated top-selling books threatens competition in multiple ways. Authors' advances would fall—advances that they use to pay their bills and that reflect compensation for their work. The contractual terms publishers offer authors would worsen. Authors would have one fewer independent outlet for their work, and, as PRH's CEO acknowledged, as advances fall the diversity of stories being told would narrow.

These are not abstract concerns. They are shared by many agents, authors, and even Defendants' executives. PRH and S&S themselves recognized the serious antitrust concerns inherent in their proposed merger. Contemporaneous documents predicted regulatory hurdles, and it is therefore no surprise that PRH agreed to pay a significant premium to acquire S&S.

The United States has satisfied its burden under prevailing Supreme Court precedent. Due to the high level of concentration, the proposed merger triggers a presumption of illegality. There is no real dispute that if the relevant market is the market for the acquisition of publishing rights to anticipated top-selling books, then the proposed merger is presumptively illegal. That is the case here, and Defendants have not and cannot rebut that presumption. The proposed merger may substantially lessen competition. Therefore, the acquisition violates Section 7 of the Clayton Act and should be enjoined permanently.

Merger analysis begins with the framework-setting exercise of market definition. This exercise is not a rigid formulaic one requiring measurement by "metes and bounds," but is instead an analytical tool to evaluate competition. Market definition is a relatively narrow issue here, as Defendants concede that: (1) there is a market for the acquisition of all trade books in the United States as self-publishing is not an adequate substitute to defeat a significant reduction in advances by publishers in that market; and (2) self-publishing is not an adequate alternative to defeat a reduction in advances among anticipated top sellers—defined as books obtaining advances of $250,000 and above. Defendants' argument against the United States' product market is simply that the $250,000 threshold for that submarket is "arbitrary" and unrecognized by publishers.

The United States proved that the relevant market here is anticipated top sellers, *i.e.* books that receive an advance of $250,000 or more. This market was established by Defendants' own documents, witness testimony describing whom the Defendants compete against, Defendants' internal approval processes, and how authors of anticipated top-selling books choose their publishers, the "practical indicia" described in *Brown Shoe Co. v. United States,* 370

U.S. 294 (1962), and the economic analysis presented by the United States' economic expert, Dr. >Nicholas Hill. The incontrovertible reality is that authors of anticipated top sellers—because they have more substantial financial, marketing, reputational and distribution needs—face a far more limited market of purchasers of their manuscripts than other authors. Market definition is one of many tools to assess whether the merger in question will cause competitive harm to an identifiable segment of market participants. Precedent in this Circuit is clear that whether the segment exists is more important than precisely where the line is drawn.

Once the relevant market is defined, this is a straightforward case: the merger would eliminate a key competitor to the top player in the market and lead to a nearly 50% market share for the combined entity. This easily clears the thresholds used in this Circuit to identify mergers presumed to be illegal. These metrics account for the relative competitive significance of smaller publishers, acknowledging that they can occasionally compete for a handful of titles.

But those smaller publishers do not win often enough—nor have any realistic prospect of doing so in the near future—to create any doubt about the enduring market power of a combined PRH and S&S. This is borne out by the evidence; in the last thirty years, no new publisher has cracked the ranks of the Big Five.

The record evidence shows that competition among the Big Five publishers is what drives advance levels for anticipated top-selling books. The idea that "everything is random" in the publishing industry and therefore there can be no value attributed to how and where publishers set advance levels is contradicted by the everyday dealings of the publishing industry. PRH, S&S, and other publishers are large companies run by sophisticated executives who are accountable to corporate owners, shareholders, and investors. These publishers invest substantial time, capital, and energy to identify books that are likely to sell well, win awards, and contribute to the marketplace of ideas. Identifying these anticipated top sellers is what their editors do—quite successfully—for a living, and they compete vigorously to acquire these books. Indeed, it is an economic and business rationale that motivated this merger. PRH's CEO was clear that PRH had lost market share and one way to regain market share was through merger, here with one of its most significant competitors.

The evidence is clear that head-to-head competition between the parties significantly increases advances for anticipated top-selling books. Defendants' own expert admitted that PRH is the principal competitor of S&S and that S&S is the runner up to PRH at least 20% of the time. Non-Big Five publishers play a minimal role, winning less than 10% of anticipated top sellers, whereas they win a much larger percentage of books outside of the anticipated top-seller market.

Defendants had an opportunity to rebut the presumption by showing how it might not reflect commercial realities. But they did not come close to meeting their burden. First, they failed to show how new firms could timely enter or other firms could expand to replace the competition from S&S and defeat any effort by the merged parties to exercise their market power. Defendants themselves recognize that barriers to entry into the relevant market are high, undercutting their own argument. New and smaller publishers face many hurdles to entry or expansion, including a lack of a reputation for success, the absence of a backlist, difficulty publicizing books, and weaker relationships with retailers. The fact that on some occasions, small publishers win big books does not change this fact. Indeed, those occasions are all the more notable because they are not common. That even Amazon is no longer considered a competitive threat by Big Five publishers when it comes to acquiring anticipated top sellers underscores the high barriers to successful entry into the market.

Second, Defendants attempted to argue that literary agents can control and manufacture competition as well as extract higher offers from unwilling publishers. The record shows that, even now, agents' leverage is limited. Agents cannot force editors to bid on a book, let alone to bid above the editors' authorized limit. And the record contains numerous examples of publishers' ability to insist on terms that are beneficial to them and detrimental to authors: standardized royalty terms, mandatory transfer of audio rights, lengthened payout timetables, and reduced digital royalty rates.

Third, Defendants argued that internal competition among Defendants' imprints could eliminate the harm from the merger. This runs contrary to common business sense and legal precedent and is similarly unsupported factually. Publishers monitor how their imprints bid for books and limit competition between them, even in situations where the imprints nominally have some autonomy. Indeed, the CEO of PRH's U.S. operations specifically sought to reduce "internal up-bidding" by PRH imprints in recent years.

Defendants' attempt to save the merger with a unilateral, unenforceable, and revocable promise to compete against itself post-merger does not stand up to scrutiny. Real-world business realities and PRH's current internal bidding policies show that it is in PRH's interest to limit internal competition, and the record shows that internal competition among imprints is no substitute for robust competition among independent publishers. And, of course, there are numerous challenges in the details of implementation for such a promise when the Defendants control the existence of imprints, those imprints' budgets and editorial focus, and so forth.

Defendants' failure to rebut the presumption ends the analysis and requires a judgment in the United States' favor. But even if Defendants were able to rebut the presumption—which they are not—the United States still carries its burden on the strength of the evidence showing that the merger may cause anticompetitive effects. The record shows numerous examples where authors have benefited from the competition between PRH and S&S that the merger will extinguish. In addition to that evidence, Dr. Hill performed a number of analyses utilizing multiple data sets and various sensitivities. The trend was consistent: the proposed merger will harm authors by reducing advances for anticipated top sellers. Specifically, Dr. Hill's quantitative analysis predicts that if the merger is allowed to proceed, advances for anticipated top sellers will decline by about 4% for PRH authors, and about 11.5% for S&S authors. In real terms, this means that authors stand to lose on average tens of thousands of dollars, if not more, per book.

Even when using quantitative economic models proposed by Defendants' own economists during the investigative phase (the GUPPI models), Dr. Hill predicted similar reductions in author compensation. Defendants' expert, Dr. Snyder, offered no model of his own to counter these harm estimates.

The loss of S&S as an independent bidder will not just be felt in head-to-head bidding scenarios. S&S will no longer be a stalking horse that agents can point to as an alternative when negotiating one-on-one with an editor or soliciting bids in a single-round auction.

This merger will also enhance the ability of major publishers to tacitly coordinate their actions towards authors. For example, they may refrain from poaching each other's authors, thereby reducing author income. Or they may further change standard contract terms to the detriment of authors. Such coordination need not be particularly elaborate or involved; simply by cementing PRH as the "leader" that other publishers follow, the merger will affect other firms' behavior and endangers competition and authors' livelihoods.

For the reasons detailed below, the Court should find that PRH's proposed acquisition of S&S may substantially lessen competition and thus violates Section 7 of the Clayton Act. The evidence and law support a permanent injunction. The Court should block the merger.

I. FACTUAL BACKGROUND

A. The Merging Parties, Jurisdiction, and Venue

1. PRH is the largest trade book publisher worldwide and in the United States. Trial Tr. 741:14–16 (Dohle); Trial Tr. 595:20–22 (Karp). Headquartered in New York, New York, PRH is owned by Bertelsmann SE & Co. KGaA ("Bertelsmann"), an international media and services company headquartered in Gütersloh, Germany. Dkt. 119–7 at 2 (Joint Pre-Trial Statement, Exhibit G, Statement of Uncontested Facts ¶¶ 1–3). PRH has close to 100 U.S. publishing imprints (a trade or brand name for a specific editorial group such as Viking, Riverhead, and Crown) across six publishing divisions. Trial Tr. 812:5–11 (Dohle). PRH publishes over 2,000 new titles annually in the United States, more than any other publisher. Dkt. 56 at 9 (Am. Answer ¶ 18); Dkt. 56 at 11 (Am. Answer ¶ 28). Its 2020 U.S. publishing revenues surpassed $2.4 billion. Dkt. 56 at 9 (Am. Answer ¶ 18).
2. S&S, also headquartered in New York, New York, is the third-largest trade book publisher in the United States. Dkt. 119–7 at 3 (Joint Pre-Trial Statement, Exhibit G, Statement of Uncontested Facts ¶ 5); PX-530 at 2 (describing S&S as the third largest publisher of general interest books for adults and children); Trial Tr. 106:14–19 (Pietsch) (same); DX-105 at 64 (same); PX-663 at 92 (showing 2019 US trade publishing market share); PX-829 at 2 (showing revenue shares of the Big Five for December 2021 year-to-date). Paramount Global, the global media and entertainment company (formerly known as ViacomCBS), owns S&S. Dkt. 119–7 at 3 (Joint Pre-Trial Statement, Exhibit G, Statement of Uncontested Facts ¶¶ 7–8). S&S operates around 50 U.S. imprints across three publishing groups and publishes over 1,000 new titles annually in the United States. PX-663 at 89; Trial Tr. 473:20–474:1 (Karp); Dkt. 56 at 9 (Am. Answer ¶ 20). Its 2020 U.S. publishing revenues exceeded $760 million. Dkt. 56 at 9 (Am. Answer ¶ 20).
3. This Court has personal jurisdiction over each Defendant under Section 12 of the Clayton Act, 15 U.S.C. § 22. Dkt. 56 at 9 (Am. Answer ¶ 15). PRH and S&S both transact business within this District. Dkt. 56 at 9 (Am. Answer ¶ 15).
4. Venue is proper in this District under Section 12 of the Clayton Act, 15 U.S.C. § 22, and 28 U.S.C. § 1391. Dkt. 56 at 9 (Am. Answer ¶ 16).
5. PRH and S&S are engaged in interstate commerce, Dkt. 56 at 9 (Am. Answer ¶ 14), and as shown throughout this trial, their activities substantially affect interstate commerce.

B. Overview of the Proposed Transaction

6. PRH and S&S are two of what the industry refers to as the "Big Five" publishers, a group of the largest trade book publishers in the United States that also includes HarperCollins Publishers, Hachette Book Group, and Macmillan Publishing Group, LLC. Trial Tr. 106:14–19 (Pietsch); Trial Tr. 344:12–24 (Eulau).
7. The Big Five have been consolidating the publishing industry for decades. Trial Tr. 334:5–9 (King). Bertelsmann entered the U.S. publishing market in 1977 by acquiring Bantam Books, and continued to grow by merging with other large U.S. publishers including Doubleday Dell in 1986, Random House in 1998, and most recently Penguin in 2013, creating the current entity Penguin Random House. Dkt. 119–7 at 2 (Joint Pre-Trial Statement, Exhibit G, Statement of Uncontested Facts ¶ 4); Trial Tr. 818:8–16 (Dohle). Since the 2013 merger, PRH has continued to acquire new imprints, including Rodale and Little Tiger. Trial Tr. 2522:19–2523:1 (Sansigre); *see also* PX-163 at 46–47 (U.S. publishers partially or fully acquired by PRH since 2013 include Sasquatch Books, Rodale, Little Tiger, F&W Media, and Sourcebooks).
8. Other members of the Big Five have followed PRH's example, acquiring mid- sized publishers in the United States in recent years. Trial Tr. 169:10–17 (Pietsch) ("Each time the smaller publishers of scale, you know, in recent years, you know, are continually being acquired by other Big Five publishers. . . ."). Hachette acquired a number of independent publishers over the last decade, including most recently Workman Publishing in September 2021, along with Worthy, Perseus, and Black Dog & Leventhal. Trial Tr. 102:13–103:4 (Pietsch); Trial Tr. 204:3–19 (Pietsch). Similarly, HarperCollins acquired Houghton Mifflin Harcourt (HMH), one of the largest remaining independent publishers, in 2021. Trial Tr. 1386:12–17 (Murray). Rodale, Workman and HMH previously competed on occasion with the Big Five for anticipated top-selling books in the United States. *See, e.g.,* Trial Tr. 2075:14–20 (Cheney) (Workman); Trial Tr. 2095:10–2096:6 (Wylie); Trial Tr. 2098:11–12 (Wylie) (Rodale); Trial Tr. 2129:24–2130:17 (Ross); Trial Tr. 2144:7–18 (Ross) (HMH); Trial Tr. 309:7–20 (Pande) (HMH); Trial Tr. 192:6–193:15 (Pietsch) (explaining that approximately half of Hachette's losses to non-Big Five publishers for books with advances above $500,000 were to HMH). Macmillan, the smallest of the Big Five, has seen its market position decline relative to the rest of the Big Five as it has pursued organic growth rather than mergers and acquisitions. Trial Tr. 1079:23–1080:18 (Weisberg).
9. The proposed acquisition of S&S by PRH continues this trend of consolidation. In March 2020, ViacomCBS (now Paramount Global) CEO Bob Bakish announced that S&S would be put up for sale. Trial Tr. 2182:14–2183:2 (Berkett). While a "fantastic business" as a trade book publisher, ViacomCBS determined S&S was not core to its strategic interests. Trial Tr. 2181:20–24 (Berkett).
10. After ViacomCBS announced its plans to sell S&S, PRH management described S&S as "one of the last high-quality, scaled assets remaining in the [U.S. publishing] market." PX-163 at 52. PRH CEO Markus Dohle advocated that Bertelsmann be willing to pay a substantial premium over the next largest bidder for S&S. Trial Tr. 740:23–741:5 (Dohle).
11. In the fall of 2020, ViacomCBS solicited bids during a two-round bidding process in which the final second-round bidders were Bertelsmann/PRH, News Corp/HarperCollins, and Vivendi. Trial Tr. 2185:2–15 (Berkett). ViacomCBS had four criteria when evaluating the final bids: value maximization, deal certainty (*i.e.,* ability to satisfy the transaction terms), finding a good home for the business, and finding a good home for the employees and executives, with price and deal certainty being the more important considerations. Trial Tr. 2187:22–2188:25 (Berkett). Bertelsmann/PRH submitted the highest bid. Trial Tr. 2189:1–14 (Berkett). [REDACTED] the deal team recommended Bertelsmann/PRH. Trial Tr. 2224:15–2225:1 (Berkett).
12. On November 24, 2020, ViacomCBS entered into a Share Purchase Agreement with Bertelsmann and Penguin Random House. *See* PX-885. Under this agreement, Bertelsmann and PRH would acquire S&S for $2.175 billion in cash. PX-885 at 23. Bertelsmann agreed to certain contractual terms related to deal certainty, particularly the apportionment of the antitrust risk,[REDACTED] Trial Tr. 2219:16–22 (Berkett). [REDACTED] The deal was announced to the public in late November 2020. Trial Tr. 2187:17–21 (Berkett).
13. The acquisition would cement Penguin Random House as the number one trade publisher in the United States—one of PRH's strategic goals for the merger. Trial Tr. 742:2–4 (Dohle); PX-162 at 1 ("Strategic rationale . . . Cement PRH as #1 in the US"). The combined firm would benefit from outsized influence over the U.S. publishing industry with a market share at least twice that of its next closest competitor in the Big Five, [REDACTED] *See* [REDACTED] *seealso* PX-959 at 1 (combined firm's upstream market

share (49%) nearly twice that of [REDACTED]

C. How a Book Is Acquired and Published

14. Publishers compete to acquire the rights from authors to publish books in the United States. In exchange for the right to publish the work, publishers pay authors an advance, which is frequently the author's entire compensation for the book. Trial Tr. 254:18–21 (Pande). An advance is a guarantee of payment typically paid out in installments and represents prepaid royalties that accrue from the sale of a book to a publisher. Trial Tr. 106:20–107:25 (Pietsch). Over time, if a book "earns out" by earning royalties equal to the amount of the initial advance, the author receives additional payments from further sales as periodic royalty payments. Trial Tr. 106:20–107:25 (Pietsch); Trial Tr. 1945:7–17 (Duhigg); *see* Trial Tr. 321:15–17 (King). As discussed *infra,* more than 85% of author contracts for anticipated top-selling books never earn out their advance. Trial Tr. 1239:25–1240:8 (Hill).
15. An anticipated top-selling book is simply that: a book expected to generate significant sales. Trial Tr. 1226:5–7 (Hill). The authors of those books want, need, and can often obtain, significant marketing and distribution support, as well as an editor with a reputation for quality and success. Trial Tr. 1231:13–19 (Hill); *see also* DX-21 at 5. An author of an anticipated top-selling book can also demand and obtain a sizeable advance given that their book is expected to have sizable sales. The market of anticipated top-selling books is roughly a $1 billion market and accounts for 70% of all advance spending on general trade books. *See* Trial Tr. 1239:10–24 (Hill); Trial Tr. 2819:19–2820:2 (Snyder); Trial Tr. 2904:17–2905:3 (Snyder).
16. Authors are typically represented by literary agents to sell the publishing rights to their book (or books) in the form of a proposal or a completed manuscript. PX-151 at 5. Literary agents are typically compensated with a 15% commission of the author's earnings. Trial Tr. 245:18–25 (Pande); *see* PX-151 at 5.

1. *Methods of Selling a Book*

17. It can take an author several years of refining a manuscript to get it ready for submission to publishers. Trial Tr. 245:1–17 (Pande); Trial Tr. 246:23–257:6 (Pande).
18. Once the manuscript is ready to be sent to prospective publishers, the author and agent choose editors to whom they will send the manuscript. Trial Tr. 246:1–8 (Pande). Agents consider "which might be the most qualified editors and publishing houses to submit" the manuscript. Trial Tr. 246:1–8 (Pande). Factors include the reputation and track record of the editor and publisher for publishing similar books and the "ability of a publishing company to pay an appropriate compensation for the work." Trial Tr. 246:9–16 (Pande); Trial Tr. 1379:10–21 (Murray). It is common for agents to submit manuscripts to a variety of editors at different publishing imprints. PX-151 at 5. For some repeat authors, the project is subject to an option clause from their previous publishing contract. Trial Tr. 113:5–18 (Pietsch). An option clause gives a publisher a 30- or 60-day window to bid on the author's next book before the agent submits the proposal to other publishers. Trial Tr. 113:5–18 (Pietsch); PX-2002 at 57–58 (Stehlik Dep. 145:24–146:8).
19. Depending on the level of interest from editors, the literary agent will determine how to solicit offers. Trial Tr. 251:8–11 (Pande). The method of sale can range from exclusive negotiations to submissions to multiple publishers culminating in single or multi-round auctions. PX-151 at 5; *see also* Trial Tr. 2087:2–23 (Wylie); Trial Tr. 2088:9–16 (Wylie); Trial Tr. 2088: 24–2089:22 (Wylie); Trial Tr. 2048:9–13 (Cheney) (identifying the formats of selling a book as auction, preempt, option, and exclusive).
20. In exclusive negotiations, the agent negotiates with one publisher for acquisition rights. That can happen because the publisher has an option in a prior contract, because the agent chooses to submit the project to a single publisher, or because a single publisher is interested after a manuscript has been widely submitted. Trial Tr. 954:18–955:4 (Tart).
21. If there are enough interested bidders, an agent can choose to set up an auction. Trial Tr. 252:13–15 (Pande); Trial Tr. 253:12–19 (Pande). Auctions take various forms. Some common methodologies in the publishing industry include 1) rounds or round-robin auctions, where publishers bid against one another in rounds; 2) best-bid auctions, where there may be a single round; and 3) hybrid auctions, which may be some combination of the two. Trial Tr. 1265:2–13 (Hill); Trial Tr. 112:4–113:4 (Pietsch); Trial Tr. 2116:10–2117:9 (Ross); Trial Tr. 2048:21–2049:19 (Cheney). The auction structure an agent uses for any given project differs based on the competitive variables at play, agency practices, agent preference, and the author's priorities. *See* PX-2007 at 11 (Fletcher Dep. 36:2–3, 36:5–13); Trial Tr. 253:12–24 (Pande) (the auction structure selected "really depends on how many editors at different publishing houses have expressed interest").

22. Sometimes, after submitting a manuscript widely, the author may accept a preempt. Trial Tr. 252:18–253:1 (Pande). A preempt is an offer to preemptively acquire the book before it goes to auction. Trial Tr. 252:18–253:1 (Pande); Trial Tr. 303:5–15 (Pande). An author may accept a preempt where there is a good editorial fit and "the money [is] so high that they fe[el] like they [are] getting a premium above what the bidding would be. . . ." PX-2007 at 69 (Fletcher Dep. 156:18–157:8); *see also* Trial Tr. 303:5–15 (Pande) ("[P]reemptive offers tend to be quite high because it has to incentivize us to be willing to take the book off the table and not offer it in a competitive situation."). Other times, after an agent has submitted a book widely and only received one offer, the author will decide to take the bid in hand instead of face the uncertainty associated with an auction. PX-2007 at 69 (Fletcher Dep. 156:18–157:8).

2. Expected Sales and Competition Drive How Much Publishers Offer for a Book

23. Publishers determine how much to offer for an author's work—namely, the size of the advance—by putting together projected profit-and-loss statements known as "P&Ls" for the proposed book(s). Trial Tr. 1973:12–22 (Kim); Trial Tr. 200:1–18 (Pietsch); Trial Tr. 569:1–13 (Karp); *see also* DX-414 at 1. These P&Ls include the expected list price for the book in various formats, production and marketing costs, and—the key factor—anticipated sales based on previous sales of comparable titles (referred to as "comp titles" or "comps"). *See* Trial Tr. 1971:4–14 (Kim); Trial Tr. 200:1–18 (Pietsch); Trial Tr. 916:3–8 (Tart) (anticipated sales based on comp titles are input and calculated to get a "suggested advance"); Trial Tr. 2393:21–2394:14 (McIntosh) (PRH "spend[s] a lot of time trying to guess the expected sales of books"). Comp titles are those with similar characteristics to the proposed book, such as subject matter, literary merit, and author background. Trial Tr. 1971:4–14 (Kim); Trial Tr. 2066:1–2067:1 (Cheney) (explaining the use of comps when deciding how much she thinks she can sell a project for). Publishers consider these indicative of a new book's projected sales and use the commercial success of comp titles to help determine how large an advance to offer for an author's work. Trial Tr. 1971:15–1972:10 (Kim). P&Ls represent the publisher's best estimate at the time of acquisition. Trial Tr. 1041:11–19 (Tart).

24. The relationship between the level of advance and projected sales is "extremely close" because publishers are "willing to pay a higher advance when [they] think [they] can sell more copies." Trial Tr. 110:19–111:1 (Pietsch); *see also* Trial Tr. 749:15–17 (Dohle); Trial Tr. 458:9–14 (Karp); Trial Tr. 1039:25–1040:8 (Tart).

25. In addition to the anticipated sales, competition among publishers is the key driver of the price paid by the publisher in the form of an advance. *See, e.g.,* Trial Tr. 114:25–115:6 (Pietsch) (in negotiations "we end up bidding against what we imagine the market would be if the book were taken out [to other publishers]. So it can lead to us increasing our offers quite significantly."); Trial Tr. 596:5–597:4 (Karp) (the threat that the agent could shop a book to other publishers affects the advance that S&S pays in exclusive negotiations and preempts); Trial Tr. 253:2–6 (Pande) (if an agent or author views the preempt as insufficient, they can decline and seek offers from other publishers).

26. Even when a book is sold via an option or exclusive negotiation, publishers know that their offers need to be attractive enough to keep the manuscript "off the marketplace." Trial Tr. 1122:24–1123:6 (Weisberg); *see* Trial Tr. 113:5–115:6 (Pietsch) (most option clauses do not include binding terms or set the price for future advances so if the agent and the publisher cannot reach a mutual agreement under the option, the agent can take the project elsewhere).

3. Advances Are the Most Important Contract Term

27. Authors' agreements with publishers include many contract terms, some of which are the subject of negotiations with publishers. The most important contract term is the advance; however, the contract also includes the royalty rates for different formats, the scope of rights the publisher is seeking to acquire (including territories, translation rights, and formats such as audio), and the payout structure for advances (*e.g.,* quarters or thirds). Trial Tr. 254:9–17 (Pande); Trial Tr. 254:25–255:14 (Pande). As publishers have consolidated, many contract terms have become less advantageous to authors and more difficult for agents to negotiate. *See infra* V.E.

28. The advance is the "single most important contract term" because, "in a large number of cases, it may be the only compensation that the author will receive for their work." Trial Tr. 254:11–21 (Pande). Very few authors earn out their advances. Trial Tr. 254:18–24 (Pande) (estimating on the "generous side" 20% of her agency's authors have earned out their advance); Trial Tr. 2101:3–5 (Wylie) (estimating 5% of his clients' books earn out); *see also* PX- 989 at 2–3, 8–9 (columns E and F of the summary tabs identify authors that have un-earned royalties). Dr. Hill calculated that more than 85% of author contracts for anticipated top-selling books never earn out their advance, even several years after

publication, making the advance all the more important for these authors. Trial Tr. 1239:25–1240:8 (Hill).

29. The amount of the advance is often critical for authors. Trial Tr. 2101:6–8 (Wylie) (agreeing that for most authors he represents the advance level matters for their daily existence). Authors use advances to take time off from their jobs to research and write their book(s), as well as support their children, buy houses, and for general living expenses. *See, e.g.,* PX-656 at 1; Trial Tr. 1916:7–21 (Duhigg); Trial Tr. 1942:22–1943:1 (Duhigg); Trial Tr. 1925:12–22 (Duhigg) ("I was relieved because it meant that I would get a check that was about equal to one year of salary at *The New York Times,* and that meant that I could take another year off to write the second book. It meant that we could actually buy a house . . ."); *see also* Trial Tr. 334:10–14 (King) (noting that in 2018, the average full-time writer earned below the poverty line); PX-2002 at 69–70 (Stehlik Dep. 163:14–164:10). As a HarperCollins publishing executive testified, "typically the most important thing for an agent representing authors is to get the most amount of money up front." PX-2002 at 66–67 (Stehlik Dep. 157:20–158:12).
30. Because authors of anticipated top sellers seldom earn out their advance, literary agents and authors focus on the amount of the advance in negotiations with publishers and rarely negotiate royalty rates that would apply beyond the advance. Trial Tr. 109:12–110:10 (Pietsch); PX 2002 at 66–67 (Stehlik Dep. 157:20–158:23); *see also* Trial Tr. 1941:16–20 (Duhigg) (testifying that seeking a higher royalty rate was "not an option given to [him]")
31. Authors usually receive their advances in a four-payment structure, under which the publisher makes the fourth payment a year after the book is published. Trial Tr. 1829:2–18 (Walsh); *see also* Trial Tr. 254:25–255:3 (Pande); Trial Tr. 256:22–25 (Pande); PX-862 at 7 (describing PRH's adult books payout guidelines).
32. Standard royalty rates are determined by media type, format, territory, and language. Trial Tr. 2249:1–13 (McIntosh) (PRH's royalty rates differ by book format). Generally, hardcover books receive a 10% royalty rate for the first 5,000 copies sold, 12.5% for copies 5,000 to 10,000, and 15% thereafter, while paperback books earn a straight 7.5% royalty. Trial Tr. 255:24–256:20 (Pande). Standardization of royalty rates has extended even to e-books, which at one point received royalty rates around 50% of net sales but were lowered to 25% across the industry. Trial Tr. 775:14–776:10 (Dohle); Trial Tr. 2101:15–17 (Wylie); Trial Tr. 255:24–256:20 (Pande). Audio and digital downloads also earn 25% of net sales. Trial Tr. 256:3–20 (Pande).
33. Some higher profile authors are able to negotiate profit share deals, either in addition to or instead of an advance; however, profit share deals are not common. Trial Tr. 324:19–325:8 (King).
34. Under the advance on royalty compensation structure, an author does not earn additional compensation until the book earns out the advance paid. *See, e.g.,* Trial Tr. 107:14–21 (Pietsch). Publishers, on the other hand, enter "profitable territory at around 70 percent of earnout for most books." [REDACTED] Trial Tr. 2258:21–25 (McIntosh); *see also* Trial Tr. 1240:9–12 (Hill).

II. SECTION 7 LEGAL FRAMEWORK

A. Section 7 of the Clayton Act Proscribes Mergers That *May* Substantially Lessen Competition; Doubts Are to Be Resolved Against the Transaction

35. Section 7 of the Clayton Act "creates a relatively expansive definition of antitrust liability," and "subjects mergers to searching scrutiny." *California v. Am. Stores Co.*, 495 U.S. 271, 284–85 (1990).
36. Section 7 bars mergers or acquisitions "the effect of [which] may be substantially to lessen competition, or to tend to create a monopoly" in "any line of commerce or . . . activity affecting commerce in any section of the country." 15 U.S.C. § 18. As Section 7 makes plain, Section 7 bars mergers or acquisition that may substantially *lessen* competition. 15 U.S.C. § 18. The court does not need to find that the proposed transaction may *eliminate* competition to enjoin it.
37. Further, as the Supreme Court has explained, Congress used the word "may" in Section 7 "to indicate that its concern was with probabilities, not certainties," *Brown Shoe,* 370
38. U.S. at 323 (1962), because Congress "intended to arrest anticompetitive tendencies in their 'incipiency.'" *United States v. Phila. Nat'l Bank,* 374 U.S. 321, 362 (1962) (quoting *Brown Shoe,* 370 U.S. at 317).
39. Accordingly, it is not necessary to prove that the proposed acquisition *will* cause competitive harm. Rather, a showing "that the merger create[s] an appreciable danger of [anticompetitive consequences] in the future" is legally sufficient to block a merger. *FTC v. H.J. Heinz Co.,* 246 F.3d 708 (D.C. Cir. 2001) (quoting *Hosp. Corp. of Am. v. FTC,* 807 F.2d 1381, 1389 (7th Cir. 1986)). "A certainty, even a high

probability, need not be shown," and "doubts are to be resolved against the transaction." *FTC v. Elders Grain, Inc.*, 868 F.2d 901, 906 (7th Cir. 1989); *see also FTC v. Advocate Health Care Network,* 841 F.3d 460, 467 (7th Cir. 2016).

40. This standard makes sense because the "fundamental purpose" of Section 7 is "to arrest the trend toward concentration, the tendency to monopoly, before the consumer's alternatives disappear[] through merger." *Phila. Nat'l Bank,* 374 U.S. at 363. The Supreme Court has held that "a trend toward concentration in an industry, whatever its causes, is a highly relevant factor in deciding how substantial the anti-competitive effect of a merger may be." *United States v. Pabst Brewing Co.,* 384 U.S. 546, 552–53 (1966); *see also United States v. Cont'l Can Co.,* 378 U.S. 441, 461–62 (1964).
41. Defendants argued in their closing that *United States v. AT&T, Inc.,* 916 F.3d 1029, 1032 (D.C. Cir. 2019) overruled the plain text of the statute and controlling Supreme Court precedent and requires a Plaintiff to prove that the proposed merger will substantially reduce competition with some degree of certainty. *See* Trial Tr. 3261:9–21 (Defendants' Closing); Bertelsmann & PRH Closing Slides at 2. They are wrong. Defendants quoted the language in *AT&T* stating that the government must show that the proposed merger is "likely to substantially lessen competition" (Defendants' Closing Slides at 2), but selectively omitted the language immediately following that quote, which confirms that this standard "encompasses a concept of 'reasonable probability.'" 916 F.3d at 1032. Defendants also ignore that, in that same paragraph, the *AT&T* court explicitly stated that Section 7 prohibits mergers where "the effect of such acquisition may be substantially to lessen competition," 916 F.3d at 1032 (quoting 15 U.S.C. § 18), and that "Congress acted out of concern with 'probabilities, not certainties.'" 916 F.3d at 1032 (quoting *Brown Shoe,* 370 U.S. at 323). Section 7 prohibits anticompetitive mergers between buyers, and courts have enjoined such mergers when they may harm competition. *United States v. Rice Growers Ass'n of Cal.,* No. S–84–1066 EJG, 1986 WL 12562 (E.D. Cal. Jan. 31, 1986) (blocking merger of purchasers of paddy rice); *United States v. Pennzoil Co.,* 252 F. Supp. 962 (W.D. Pa. 1965) (enjoining merger of purchasers of crude oil); *Boardman v. Pac. Seafood Grp.,* 822 F.3d 1011, 1021–22 n.8 (9th Cir. 2016) (affirming injunction against merger harming competition in "seafood processors' purchase of fish from fishermen"). The evaluation of mergers of buyers, or "buy-side" mergers, involves "essentially the [same] framework" as mergers involving the selling side of a market. U.S. Dep't of Justice & Fed. Trade Comm'n, *Horizontal Merger Guidelines* § 12 (2010), ("Merger Guidelines"); *see also Weyerhaeuser Co. v. Ross-Simmons Hardwood Lumber Co.,* 549 U.S. 312, 321–22 (2007) (due to the "close theoretical connection" between monopoly power and monopsony power, "similar legal standards should apply").
42. In a buy-side case, the United States needs to show only that the merger may lessen competition at the buyer level. That is, there is no requirement that the United States prove downstream effects on consumers to block a proposed merger. *See Mandeville Island Farms, Inc. v. Am. Crystal Sugar Co.,* 334 U.S. 219, 235 (1948) (finding a buy-side price-fixing scheme illegal "even though the price-fixing was by purchasers, and the persons specifically injured under the treble damage claim are sellers, not customers or consumers.").

B. Courts Analyze Section 7 Claims Through a Burden-Shifting Framework

43. To effectuate the "searching scrutiny" of mergers prescribed by Congress, courts have developed a burden-shifting approach. "First[,] the government must show that the merger would produce 'a firm controlling an undue percentage share of [a] relevant market, and [would] result[] in a significant increase in the concentration of firms in that market.'" *Heinz,* 246 F.3d at 715 (quoting *Phila. Nat'l Bank,* 374 U.S. at 363). "Such a showing establishes a presumption that the merger will substantially lessen competition." *Id.* (quotation marks omitted).
44. Next, "[t]he burden then shifts to the defendant to rebut the presumption by offering proof that 'the market-share statistics [give] an inaccurate account of the [merger's] probable effects on competition in the relevant market.'" *FTC v. Sysco Corp.,* 113 F. Supp. 3d 1, 23 (D.D.C. 2015) (quoting *Heinz,* 246 F.3d at 715). Defendants' burden is dependent on the strength of the prima facie evidence: "the more compelling the prima facie case, the more evidence the defendant must present to rebut it successfully." *Heinz,* 246 F.3d at 725 (internal quotation marks omitted). Further, "if a Government's prima facie case anticipates and addresses the respondent's rebuttal evidence," then the government's case is "significantly strengthened" and "the respondent's burden of production on rebuttal is also heightened." *Chicago Bridge & Iron Co. N.V. v. FTC,* 534 F.3d 410, 425–26 (5th Cir. 2008).
45. If Defendants rebut the plaintiff's prima facie case, "the burden of producing additional evidence of anticompetitive effect shifts to the [plaintiff], and merges with the ultimate burden of persuasion, which

remains with the [plaintiff] at all times." *United States v. Anthem, Inc.*, 855 F.3d 345, 350 (D.C. Cir. 2017) (internal quotations omitted).

III. THERE IS A RELEVANT MARKET FOR THE ACQUISITION OF U.S. PUBLISHING RIGHTS TO ANTICIPATED TOP-SELLING BOOKS

A. Applicable Legal Standards

1. General Principles of Market Definition

46. As a general matter, "[m]erger analysis starts with defining the relevant market." *Sysco,* 113 F. Supp. 3d at 24. Defining a relevant market is not an end unto itself, but an analytic tool or framework used to ascertain the "locus of competition," *Brown Shoe,* 370 U.S. at 320–21, and "'recognize competition where, in fact, competition exists,'" *Cont'l Can Co.,* 378 U.S. at 453 (quoting *Brown Shoe,* 370 U.S. at 326) (internal quotations omitted); *see also* Merger Guidelines § 4.1.1 ("[T]he purpose of defining the market and measuring market shares is to illuminate the evaluation of competitive effects."). This is why the Supreme Court held that the Clayton Act market definition exercise was intended by Congress to be "a pragmatic, factual" analysis and "not a formal, legalistic one." *Brown Shoe,* 370 U.S. at 336.
47. A relevant antitrust market has two components: (1) the relevant product market; and (2) the relevant geographic market. *United States v. Anthem, Inc.*, 236 F. Supp. 3d 171, 193 (D.D.C. 2017). The Supreme Court instructs that "[t]he outer boundaries of a product market are determined by the reasonable interchangeability of use or the cross-elasticity of demand between the product itself and substitutes for it." *Brown Shoe,* 370 U.S. at 325. The focus of this analysis is "on customers' ability and willingness to substitute away from one product to another in response to a price increase or a corresponding non-price change such as a reduction in product quality or service." Merger Guidelines § 4; *see also Sysco,* 113 F. Supp. 3d at 25–26.
48. In a buy-side case, the market definition analysis is a "mirror image" of that in a sell-side case, so "the market is not the market of competing sellers but of competing buyers." *Todd v. Exxon Corp.*, 275 F.3d 191, 202 (2d Cir. 2001) (Sotomayor, J.) (quotation marks omitted). Thus, the proper inquiry is "the commonality and interchangeability of the buyers, not the commonality or interchangeability of the sellers." *Id.* (quotation marks omitted). Here, the focus is the "commonality and interchangeability" of publishers and the ability and willingness of authors to switch from a publisher to a substitute in the face of a decrease in advances.
49. Courts find labor markets to be relevant markets for antitrust purposes. For example, in *O'Bannon,* the court found a relevant market of "FBS football and Division I basketball schools" that compete for "elite football and basketball recruits." *O'Bannon v. NCAA,* 7 F. Supp. 3d 955, 965–67 (N.D. Cal. 2014).
50. Contrary to Defendants' protestations about the precise boundaries of the relevant market, binding Supreme Court precedent acknowledges that "[t]he market, as most concepts in law or economics, cannot be measured by metes and bounds." *Anthem,* 236 F. Supp. 3d at 193 (quoting *Times-Picayune Publ'g Co. v. United States,* 345 U.S. 594, 611 (1953)). It is expected that there may be some imprecision about the precise location of the outer boundaries of a market. *FTC v. Tronox Ltd.,* 332 F. Supp. 3d 187, 202 (D.D.C. 2018) ("The Supreme Court has wisely recognized there is 'some artificiality' in any boundaries, but that 'such fuzziness' is inherent in bounding any market.") (quotation marks omitted). Such expected and normal imprecision does not doom a market definition as suggested by Defendants.

2. Courts May Define Relevant Sub-Markets Around Groups of Targeted Sellers

51. "A broad market may also include relevant submarkets which themselves may 'constitute product markets for antitrust purposes.'" *FTC v. Whole Foods Mkt., Inc.,* 548 F.3d 1028, 1037–38 (D.C. Cir. 2008) (quoting *Brown Shoe,* 370 U.S. at 325).
52. Such sub-markets can be based on a set of "targeted customers." *FTC v. Wilh. Wilhelmsen Holding ASA,* 341 F. Supp. 3d 27, 46 (D.D.C. 2018); *accord Anthem,* 236 F. Supp. 3d at 195 ("Case law provides for the distinction of product markets by customer."); *FTC v. Staples, Inc.,* 190 F. Supp. 3d 100, 117–118 (D.D.C. 2016) ("*Staples II*"); *Sysco,* 113 F. Supp. 3d at 48. In a sell-side case, a "submarket exists when sellers can profitably raise prices 'to certain targeted customers but not to others,' in which case regulators 'may evaluate competitive effects separately by type of customer.'" *Anthem,* 236 F. Supp. 3d at 195 (quoting Merger Guidelines § 3); *see also* Merger Guidelines § 4.1.4. Conversely, in a buy-side market, a submarket exists where the merging parties can profitably lower prices to a certain group of targeted suppliers.

53. In a buy-side case, there are two economic conditions necessary to define a targeted seller market: (1) buyers must be able to pay different prices to the members of the targeted group of sellers than to other sellers; and (2) sellers must not be able to engage in arbitrage, or opportunistic re-selling. *See* Merger Guidelines § 3; *Staples II,* 190 F. Supp. 3d at 117–18.
54. Multiple sub-markets may exist within a broader market. *See Cont'l Can Co.,* 378 U.S. at 457–58; *United States v. Aluminum Co. of Am.,* 377 U.S. 271, 275 (1964). The fact that one sub-market can be established by the evidence does not exclude the possibility that the record may also support the existence of other markets. *Cont'l Can Co.,* 378 U.S. at 457–58. Likewise, the existence of a sub-market is not disproven by evidence that a broader market could also be properly defined. *Aluminum Co. of Am.,* 377 U.S. at 275; *see also Brown Shoe,* 370 U.S. at 325; *Anthem,* 236 F. Supp. 3d at 254.

3. A Price Level Is an Appropriate Way to Identify Targeted Sellers

55. Courts have consistently used numerical cutoffs to define submarkets. *See Wilhelmsen,* 341 F. Supp. 3d at 51 (market consisting of customers owning fleets of 10 or more vessels of a particular type); *Anthem,* 236 F. Supp. 3d at 195 (market of companies with 5,000 or more employees); *Staples II,* 190 F. Supp. 3d at 118 (market of customers who spend $500,000 or more annually on office supplies). Numerical cutoffs are not designed to be rigid bright lines, but rather are used "[f]or analytical purposes." *Staples II,* 190 F. Supp. 3d at 118 & n.10. In *Wilhelmsen,* the court found a submarket of "Global Fleets"—defined as a fleet with "10 or more globally trading vessels"—even though the numerical value of 10 "was not intended as an exact statement of the threshold" and was chosen "for its roundness and simplicity." *Wilhelmsen,* 341 F. Supp. 3d at 54–55. The FTC's economist used this number "as a starting point for developing a series of statistical estimates." *Id.* at 55. The consistent results of these analyses confirmed that owners of Global Fleets are a "distinct customer group." *Id.*; *see also Staples II,* 190 F. Supp. 3d at 118 & n.10 (noting that government's expert chose $500,000 in annual office supply purchases as a cutoff "[f]or analytical purposes" and citing testimony "that there is no 'magic place that's the right place' to draw the line"); *Anthem,* 236 F. Supp. 3d at 197–98 (acknowledging that some industry participants used different employee cutoffs to define "national accounts" than the 5,000 employee cutoff proposed by plaintiff).
56. Likewise, courts have held that it is appropriate to use price levels to help identify a relevant submarket. In *Brown Shoe,* the Supreme Court identified "distinct prices" as one of the "practical indicia" courts may use to identify the existence of a submarket. 370 U.S. at 325. Judge Brown in *Whole Foods* applied this principle to a targeted customer market, stating that "distinct prices" for the targeted group (referred to as "core" customers) "indicates the existence of a submarket of core customers." 548 F.3d at 1038–39.
57. Courts have also found relevant product markets consisting of premium product segments based on "distinctions in degree" across a broader range of products. *Int'l Boxing Club of New York, Inc. v. United States,* 358 U.S. 242, 249–52 (1959) (affirming market of championship boxing contests as distinct from non-championship contests, based on factors such as their higher revenues/rights fees and greater popularity among viewers); *see also Syufy Enterprises v. American Multicinema, Inc.,* 793 F.2d 990, 994–95 (9th Cir. 1986) (affirming market of "industry-anticipated top-grossing films"); *Whole Foods,* 548 F.3d at 1041 (market of "premium" natural and organic supermarkets); *O'Bannon,* 7 F. Supp. 3d at 986 (finding relevant market in which colleges compete for "elite football and basketball recruits"), *aff'd in relevant part,* 802 F.3d 1049 (9th Cir. 2015).
58. Defendants argue that markets cannot be identified by price, citing *In re Super Premium Ice Cream Distribution Antitrust Litig.,* 691 F. Supp. 1262 (N.D. Cal. 1988), which rejected a proposed market for "super premium" ice creams. But *Super Premium Ice Cream* is simply an example of a situation where a proposed market defined by price and quality characteristics failed the hypothetical monopolist test; the record there indicated that consumers of super premium ice creams could substitute to ice cream brands "lower in the spectrum of price or quality" in the event of a price increase, and thus those lower-cost options would discipline any price increase. *See id.* at 1268. Here, by contrast, the market for anticipated top-selling books satisfies the hypothetical monopsonist test, because authors of anticipated top sellers have no reasonable substitutes to turn to in response to a decrease in advances by a monopsonist publisher. From the perspective of an author, selling her book for a low advance is not a reasonable substitute for selling her book for a high advance, unlike customers who did view low-price ice cream as a reasonable substitute for high-price ice cream.

4. *Courts May Rely on Economic Analysis and Practical Indicia to Determine the Relevant Product Market*

59. Courts look to two main types of evidence in defining the product market: "the hypothetical monopolist test, the application of which is frequently the subject of testimony from experts in the field of economics, and the practical indicia described by the Supreme Court in *Brown Shoe*." *Wilhelmsen,* 341 F. Supp. 3d at 47 (internal quotations and citation omitted). Both economic analysis and the *Brown Shoe* indicia are tools to answer the same question: whether a product outside the proposed relevant market is "reasonably interchangeable" with the products within the proposed market. Reasonable interchangeability turns on whether a price increase in the proposed market likely would "drive consumers to an alternative product" such that "that product must be reasonably substitutable for those in the proposed market and must therefore be part of the market, properly defined." *Whole Foods,* 548 F.3d at 1038; *see also United States v. H & R Block, Inc.,* 833 F. Supp. 2d 36, 55 (D.D.C. 2011) ("key question" for court is whether products outside the proposed market "are sufficiently close substitutes to constrain any anticompetitive . . . pricing" on products within the proposed market).
60. Both types of evidence show that authors of anticipated top sellers can be targeted and constitute a sub-market.

5. *Defendants Rely on Inapposite Product Market Caselaw*

61. In every case cited in Defendants' Pre-Trial Brief or closing arguments where a court rejected a proposed product market, the court found that reasonably interchangeable substitutes existed *outside* the proposed market. *See United States v. E.I. du Pont de Nemours & Co.,* 351 U.S. 377, 404 (1956) (holding that cellophane faces "competition and interchangeability with other wrappings"); *HDC Med., Inc. v. Minntech Corp.,* 474 F.3d 543, 547 (8th Cir. 2007) (undisputed that multiple-use dialyzers and single-use dialyzers have "identical uses," such that there is "reasonable interchangeability" between the products); *Crestron Elecs.* Inc. *v. Cyber Sound & Sec. Inc.,* 2012 WL 426282, at *5 (D.N.J. Feb. 9, 2012) (plaintiff failed to define the market "with [any] reference to the rule of reasonable interchangeability"); *United States v. Oracle Corp.*, 331 F. Supp. 2d 1098, 1131 (N.D. Cal. 2004) ("evidence at trial established that . . . customers have choices outside" the proposed market); *FTC v. Arch Coal, Inc.,* 329 F. Supp. 2d 109, 121–23 (D.D.C. 2004) ("evidence of significant interchangeability between 8800 Btu and 8400 Btu coal"); *United States v. Sungard Data Systems, Inc.,* 172 F. Supp. 2d 172, 183 (D.D.C. 2001) (users may switch to alternative forms of disaster recovery); *United States v. Gillette Co.,* 828 F. Supp. 78, 83–84 (D.D.C. 1993) (pen consumers would substitute to other modes of writing for fountain pens); *Super Premium Ice Cream,* 691 F. Supp. at 1268, *aff'd sub nom. Haagen-Dazs Co., Inc. v. Double Rainbow Gourmet Ice Creams, Inc.,* 895 F.2d 1417 (9th Cir. 1990) (concluding that "all grades of ice creams compete with one another"); *United States v. Joseph Schlitz Brewing Co.,* 253 F. Supp. 129, 146 (N.D. Cal. 1966) (finding a "'competitive overlap' between premium and non-premium beers").
62. That is not the case here. Because the United States alleged a market that includes all publishers as buyers of anticipated top-selling books, there exist no reasonable substitutes outside the defined market, and Defendants have not attempted to propose any alternative product or service that authors of anticipated top sellers would turn to as a reasonable substitute when faced with a significant price increase. Self-publishing, as discussed below, is not a credible alternative and Defendants concede as much. Trial Tr. 3272:17–25 (Defendants' Closing). Therefore, the cases cited by Defendants are not applicable here.

B. The Anticipated Top Seller Market

63. The acquisition of U.S. rights to anticipated top sellers is a relevant product market. Both the economic analysis and practical indicia support this conclusion.
64. The government's economic expert, Dr. Nicholas Hill, concluded that the market for anticipated top sellers is a relevant market. *See* Trial Tr. 1225:1–2 (Hill); Trial Tr. 1250:20–1251:1 (Hill). Dr. Hill defined an anticipated top seller as a book that receives an advance of $250,000 or more. Trial Tr. 1232:13–21 (Hill). Dr. Hill used an advance threshold to identify anticipated top sellers because the advance a publisher pays is correlated with that publisher's expected sales for the book. Trial Tr. 1232:22–1233:2 (Hill). This threshold was intended to serve as a practical way to identify a group of books whose authors have different preferences and face different competitive conditions as indicated by the available data. Trial Tr. 1237:21–1239:7 (Hill); Trial Tr. 3202:4–23 (Hill). None of Dr. Hill's opinions are sensitive to the exact threshold used to define an anticipated top seller. Trial Tr. 1233:14–

20 (Hill); Trial Tr. 1238:7–14 (Hill); Trial Tr. 3202:4–23 (Hill). And, as discussed in more detail below, Dr. Hill performed numerous sensitivity tests to confirm that his analysis holds at different thresholds.

65. The choice of the $250,000 threshold is supported by the industry's recognition of $250,000 as a meaningful number. For example, Publishers Marketplace, an industry publication, classifies deals over $250,000 as significant or major deals. And $250,000 is an internal threshold used by some publishers to trigger additional managerial review. Trial Tr. 1233:3–13 (Hill). Further, PRH imprints analyze key performance indicators by advance level, including a $250,000 to $499,999 advance level. *See, e.g.,* PX-989.
66. Dr. Hill chose to define a market around this subset of sellers because authors of anticipated top sellers (1) have different preferences for publishers and self-publishing than other authors, and (2) face different competitive conditions than other authors. Trial Tr. 1231:5–10 (Hill). Authors of anticipated top sellers have stronger preferences than other authors for publishers with strong distribution, marketing, and reputation that allow their books to reach a broad consumer market. Trial Tr. 1231:11–1232:11 (Hill); Trial Tr. 1236:6–10 (Hill); Trial Tr. 1549:11–21 (Hill). Authors of anticipated top sellers also face different competitive conditions as demonstrated by the significantly different market shares that the non-Big Five have for anticipated top sellers (10%) compared to non-anticipated top sellers (45%). Trial Tr. 1233:21–1234:6 (Hill); PX-963 at 1.
67. Though Dr. Snyder disagreed about whether defining a market around a subset of sellers applies to this case, he acknowledged the relevance of such considerations for market definition. Trial Tr. 2824:14–2825:10 (Snyder). He testified that he would "get the logic" of defining a market based on the primary competitors to serve a group of customers in a different context: "if you had a merger in the accounting world and you said . . . there is going to be a merger for a group of customers who . . . have different characteristics, the top accounting firms would be the ones most likely to compete." Trial Tr. 2824:14–2825:10 (Snyder).
68. The market for anticipated top sellers is significant, with advances committed by publishers for these books representing approximately 70% of all commitments for advances, or roughly $1 billion in commerce annually. Trial Tr. 1239:13–24 (Hill); Trial Tr. 2904:17–2905:8 (Snyder).

C. Authors of Anticipated Top-Selling Books Can Be Targeted for a Reduction in Advances

69. A properly defined market around a group of targeted sellers, *i.e.* a "price discrimination" market, must satisfy two conditions: differential pricing and limited
70. arbitrage. Merger Guidelines § 3; Trial Tr. 1229:11–15 (Hill); *see also Wilhelmsen,* 341 F. Supp. 3d at 46–47. Differential pricing is the ability "to price differently to targeted [sellers] than to other [sellers]." Merger Guidelines § 3. In this context, it requires that publishers have the ability to (1) identify different sellers, and (2) charge them different prices. Trial Tr. 1229:16–19 (Hill). Arbitrage would be an attempt by authors to avoid targeting by selling to a third person who is then in turn able to sell to the publishers. Trial Tr. 1230:7–12 (Hill).
71. The market for anticipated top sellers satisfies the criteria for differential pricing and limited arbitrage. Trial Tr. 1230:24–1231:4 (Hill). Publishers are able to price to authors of anticipated top sellers differently than other authors because book deals are individually negotiated. When deciding what to offer for a book, publishers form an expectation of a book's anticipated sales, thus identifying the book as an anticipated top seller (or not). Trial Tr. 1541:21–24 (Hill); Trial Tr. 3046:7–16 (Hill). Also, arbitrage is not feasible. *See* Trial Tr. 1230:13–23 (Hill).
72. Defendants effectively agree. First, though Dr. Snyder disputes whether individual publishers could identify anticipated top sellers, he agrees that the hypothetical monopsonist would be able to do so. Trial Tr. 2909:17–2910:11 (Snyder). That admission suffices for market definition purposes, where the question is "whether the hypothetical [monopsonist] can engage in price discrimination." *See* Carl Shapiro, *The 2010 Horizontal Merger Guidelines: From Hedgehog to Fox in Forty Years,* 77 Antitrust L.J. 49, 93 (2010); *see also Sysco,* 113 F. Supp. 3d at 46 ("As the Merger Guidelines state, markets for targeted customers may exist 'when prices are individually negotiated and suppliers have information about customers that would allow a hypothetical monopolist to identify customers that are likely to pay a higher price for the relevant product.'") (quoting Merger Guidelines § 4.1.4). Second, Defendants do not dispute that arbitrage is not occurring in this market. *See* Trial Tr. 1545:23–1546:6 (Hill).
73. Dr. Snyder is nevertheless incorrect that individual publishers could not identify anticipated top sellers. *See* Trial Tr. 2630:19–2631:13 (Snyder). For purposes of analyzing whether the market for anticipated top-selling books is a valid product market, it does not matter whether a publisher's prediction of success proves to be true or whether all publishers share the same view of every book. As Dr. Hill

explained, when an editor reviews a book, he or she forms "an expectation of the sales" for that book. Trial Tr. 3046:12–16 (Hill). In doing so, the publisher determines whether the book is likely an anticipated top seller. Trial Tr. 3046:12–16 (Hill); *cf.* Trial Tr. 2393:21–2394:14 (McIntosh); *infra* III.E.1. That identification suffices under the government's definition of an anticipated top seller.

74. To illustrate: when a publisher submits a bid of $250,000 or more for a book, the publisher has determined the book is an anticipated top seller and therefore knows that few other publishers are likely to be able to effectively compete with that bid. *Cf.* Trial Tr. 2908:22–2909:8 (Snyder).
75. Similarly, Defendants' greater marketing spend on anticipated top sellers, *see infra* III.E.1a., indicates that anticipated top sellers are identifiable by publishers. Defendants' executives testified that advance amounts are irrelevant when making marketing decisions. *See,* e.g., Trial Tr. 2271:24–2272:3 (McIntosh). Yet higher advance books receive more marketing than lower advance books. *See, e.g.,* PX-972 at 1. Taken together, as Dr. Hill explained, "if we take it as a given fact that the marketing folks do not know the advance amount when they're deciding on marketing for a book, they're nevertheless identifying the anticipated top sellers and treating them differently." Trial Tr. 3045:7–20 (Hill).
76. It is not necessary for all industry participants to agree on what an anticipated top seller is for price discrimination to be feasible. A publisher just needs to know whether *it* believes the book is an anticipated top seller. Nevertheless, the record demonstrates that there is often agreement, *ex-ante,* about the likelihood that a book will sell well. For example, Mr. Wylie testified that publishing industry veterans are able to determine in advance which books are likely to be successful, and that there are books for which there is a consensus that the book is likely to be successful. Trial Tr. 2108:10–24 (Wylie) ("there are recognizable qualities in . . . books that people who have been in the business for a long time would easily recognize."); *see also infra* III.E.1.
77. Finally, Defendants argue that book sales are "random," *see* Trial Tr. 803:3–6 (Dohle), and that publishers cannot anticipate sales, but this argument addresses whether publishers can identify *actual* top sellers, a market not alleged, not *anticipated* top sellers. Defendants also overstate the point. While there certainly is some unpredictability in book publishing, there is also a correlation between advances and sales. *See* PX-151 at 11 ("In general, **higher advance levels are correlated with more book sales**—however, there are always exceptions") (bolded in original); PX-2002 at 50 (Stehlik Dep. 134:8–15) (testifying it is uncommon for top-selling books to come from authors who are paid low advances). Moreover, Defendants' consistently high market shares, *see* PX-994 at 1, healthy profit margins, *see* Trial Tr. 781:3–5 (Dohle); Trial Tr. 1492:2–3 (Hill), and decades of success indicate that they must have at least some aptitude for anticipating what is likely to sell well.

D. The Hypothetical Monopsonist Test Establishes That the Acquisition of U.S. Publishing Rights to Anticipated Top-Selling Books Is a Relevant Product Market

78. The hypothetical monopsonist test is the buy-side counterpart to the "hypothetical monopolist test," which evaluates whether a market is too narrowly defined by examining whether a candidate market excludes important substitutes. Trial Tr. 1241:4–7 (Hill); Merger Guidelines §§ 4.1.1, 12; *see also, e.g., H & R Block,* 833 F. Supp. 2d at 51 ("An analytical method often used by courts to define a relevant market is to ask hypothetically whether it would be profitable to have a monopoly over a given set of substitutable products. If so, those products may constitute a relevant market."); *Wilhelmsen,* 341 F. Supp. 3d at 47. In targeted-seller markets, the hypothetical monopsonist test also addresses whether the targeting of certain sellers is feasible. Trial Tr. 1546:10–23 (Hill); *see supra* III.C. The test asks whether a hypothetical monopsonist—the only buyer of the products in the alleged market—would find it profit-maximizing to impose a small but significant and non-transitory reduction in price ("SSNRP") for at least one product in the market. *See* Merger Guidelines § 4.1.1. If the hypothetical monopsonist test passes, the candidate market constitutes a relevant product market. *See id.* As the Merger Guidelines explain, "The hypothetical [monopsonist] test ensures that markets are not defined too narrowly, but it does not lead to a single relevant market." *Id.*; *see also* Trial Tr. 3048:20–3049:9 (Hill). *Any* relevant market that satisfies the test may be evaluated for competitive effects, "guided by the overarching principle that the purpose of defining the market and measuring market shares is to illuminate the evaluation of competitive effects." *See* Merger Guidelines § 4.1.1.
79. In this context, the hypothetical monopsonist test answers the following question: if all competition among market participants were eliminated—*i.e.,* all publishers were combined into a single monopsonist publisher—would advances decrease by a significant amount? Trial Tr. 1241:14–1242:9 (Hill). The key inquiry is whether enough authors of anticipated top sellers would switch to self-publishing if faced with a SSNRP such that it would not be profitable for the hypothetical monopsonist

to impose a SSNRP. *See* Trial Tr. 1242:10–1243:9 (Hill).

80. Both the government and Defendants' experts agree that the market for anticipated top sellers passes the hypothetical monopsonist test, including that the hypothetical monopsonist could target authors of anticipated top sellers. *See* Trial Tr. 1230:24–1231:4 (Hill); Trial Tr. 1248:21–22 (Hill); Trial Tr. 2897:14–2898:2 (Snyder); Trial Tr. 2898:8–18 (Snyder); Trial Tr. 2909:17–2910:11 (Snyder). Therefore, the market is properly defined.

1. Qualitative Evidence Shows That Self-Publishing Is a Poor Substitute to Traditional Publishing

81. For authors of anticipated top-selling books, self-publishing is the only theoretical alternative that is outside of the proposed market. But, as Defendants conceded, competition from self-publishing will not suffice to prevent a small but significant price decrease. *See* Trial Tr. 3272:17–25 (Defendants' Closing) ("nobody was arguing in this case" that self-publishing is an "outside option" for authors).

82. The qualitative evidence at trial demonstrated that self-publishing is not a meaningful alternative to the services provided by traditional publishers, particularly for authors who would otherwise receive an advance above $100,000 or $250,000. For example, Mr. Pietsch testified that self-publishing was not a threat "at all" for books with an advance above $100,000 and that it is "not competitive with what we do." Trial Tr. 173:7–174:2 (Pietsch); *see also* Trial Tr. 355:13–15 (Eulau) (self-publishing not a threat to a publisher's core business); Trial Tr. 356:7–9 (Eulau); PX-2004 at 51–52 (Solomon Dep. 83:20–22, 84:8–85:18); PX-445 at 3.

2. The Market for Anticipated Top Sellers Formally Passes the Hypothetical Monopsonist Test

83. Dr. Hill concluded that the market for anticipated top-selling books passes the hypothetical monopsonist test. *See* Trial Tr. 1248:21–22 (Hill). To reach his conclusions, Dr. Hill implemented the hypothetical monopsonist test using the aggregate diversion ratio methodology. Trial Tr. 1244:23–25 (Hill); Trial Tr. 1245:14–1246:9 (Hill).

84. If diversion to self-publishing is sufficiently high—and reaches what economists call the "critical diversion" ratio—it would not be profitable for the hypothetical monopsonist to impose a substantial reduction in advances. Trial Tr. 1245:14–1246:9 (Hill).

85. Dr. Hill therefore estimated what "actual diversion" would be for this market—*i.e.,* the percentage of authors who actually would switch to self-publishing. If actual diversion is lower than the critical diversion ratio, then a price decrease would be profitable and the relevant market passes the hypothetical monopsonist test. Trial Tr. 1245:14–1246:9 (Hill). The actual diversion ratios calculated by Dr. Hill were both far below the critical diversion ratio. Trial Tr. 1247:24–1249:6 (Hill); PX-969 at 1. Therefore, the hypothetical monopsonist test passes.

86. As noted above, Defendants and their economic expert do not dispute these results. *See* Trial Tr. 2898:8–18 (Snyder); Trial Tr. 3272:17–25 (Defendants' Closing). The economic and factual evidence supports a finding that the government's market passes the hypothetical monopsonist test. As a result, the market for anticipated top sellers constitutes a relevant antitrust market.

E. Practical Indicia Establish That Authors of Anticipated Top-Selling Books Are Unique Customers with Unique Needs

87. Along with economic analysis, "practical indicia" articulated by the Supreme Court in *Brown Shoe* may be used to determine the boundaries of a submarket. Those indicia include "industry or public recognition of the submarket as a separate economic entity, the product's peculiar characteristics and uses, unique production facilities, distinct customers, distinct prices, sensitivity to price changes, and specialized vendors." *Brown Shoe,* 370 U.S. at 325. In targeted customer cases, courts also consider whether the targeted group is "a distinct group with distinct needs," as compared to the broader universe of customers. *Wilhelmsen,* 341 Supp. 3d at 52; *accord Anthem,* 236 F. Supp. 3d at 195 (finding that national accounts are "a unique set of customers with unique needs").

88. The *Brown Shoe* factors "are not necessarily criteria to be rigidly applied[,]" and courts can find that submarkets exist when "only some"—but not all—of the "practical indicia" are present. *FTC v. Swedish Match,* 131 F. Supp. 2d 151, 159 (D.D.C. 2000); *see also FTC v. Staples, Inc.*, 970 F. Supp. 1066, 1075 (D.D.C. 1997) ("*Staples I*") (same). As this Court has recognized, "*Brown Shoe*'s practical indicia were meant as 'practical aids rather than with the view that their presence or absence would dispose, in talismanic fashion, of the submarket issue.'" *Staples I,* 970 F. Supp. at 1075 (quoting *Int'l Tel. & Tel. Corp. v. Gen. Tel. & Elecs. Corp.*, 518 F.2d 913, 932 (9th Cir. 1975)). The record includes practical indicia that support the conclusion that anticipated top-selling books are a distinct market:

1. The Publishing Industry Recognizes Anticipated Top Sellers

89. The industry recognizes that advances are based on the sales that a publisher anticipates for a particular book. For example, Mr. Pietsch testified that the relationship between projected sales and advances is an "extremely close one." Trial Tr. 110:19–111:1 (Pietsch). Similarly, Mr. Karp testified that predicted sales are the "main factor" on which advances are based. Trial Tr. 458:9–14 (Karp). Several other witnesses testified similarly. See Trial Tr. 916:19–21 (Tart) (higher projected sales correspond to higher advances); PX-2002 at 64 (Stehlik Dep. 154:13–16) (larger potential audience results in willingness to pay higher advances); Trial Tr. 1371:22–1372:7 (Murray); [REDACTED] Trial Tr. 2239:16–22 (McIntosh); PX-151 at 11 ("In general, higher advance levels are correlated with more book sales—however, there are always exceptions.").
90. It is clear that the concept of expected sales is very important to the publishing industry. As Ms. McIntosh testified, PRH "spend[s] a lot of time trying to guess the expected sales of books"; expected sales is something PRH "absolutely" focuses on; and PRH works diligently to project expected sales throughout the publishing process. Trial Tr. 2393:21–2394:14 (McIntosh); *see also* Trial Tr. 2148:16–2149:15 (Ross) (explaining agent's process for forecasting expected sales); Trial Tr. 749:7–22 (Dohle); Trial Tr. 1039:25–1040:8 (Tart).
91. Agents, authors, and publishers have testified that anticipated top sellers are identifiable and recognized as competitively different. Mr. Wylie testified that publishing industry veterans are able to determine in advance which books are likely to be successful, because there are "recognizable qualities in . . . books that people who have been in the business for a long time would easily recognize." Trial Tr. 2108:10–24 (Wylie). For that reason, as Mr. Wylie admitted, for some books, there is a consensus in advance that a particular book is likely to be successful. Trial Tr. 2108:22–24 (Wylie); *see also* Trial Tr. 310:12–24 (Pande) (testifying that she treats books that she thinks will get a lot of attention differently than other books).
92. Conversely, the industry also recognizes categories of books that are not anticipated top sellers. For example, Mr. Karp testified about "midlist" books, which are anticipated to have a lower level of sales and thereby receive lower advances. Trial Tr. 593:3–594:8 (Karp). Similarly, bestselling author, Stephen King, testified that occasionally some of his books are not "crafted best seller[s]" and do not "fit the mold," so he publishes those books with smaller publishers for smaller advances. Trial Tr. 327:17–331:15 (King). Generally, the industry acknowledges that the competitive conditions are different for anticipated top sellers. For example, the CEO of Macmillan, Mr. Weisberg, testified that "big mega price books" are a "different business" than the other 98% of books. Trial Tr. 1129:24–1130:11 (Weisberg).
93. Anticipated top-selling books differ from other books in other ways:

2. Greater Marketing Support

94. Anticipated top-selling books generally receive more marketing support. *See, e.g.,* Trial Tr. 490:15–492:15 (Karp); Trial Tr. 1069:18–1070:10 (Weisberg); Trial Tr. 1373:1–11 (Murray); Trial Tr. 2001:12–2002:4 (Kim) (there is a general correlation between average advance level and marketing spend); PX-989 at 10–11; Trial Tr. 258:11–21 (Pande) ("[T]here's a pretty clear relationship between the level of the advance and the amount of resources that the publisher invests in the marketing and publicity of the book."). Publishers designate high advance books as "lead titles," which are books that receive the most marketing support. *See* PX-986 at 2 ("Category 1: Lead Titles[:] Sales goal of 75,000 units or higher and/or Advance over $500,000"); Trial Tr. 1071:13–1072:15 (Weisberg) (testifying that lead titles can be picked because they were acquired for a large sum and/or because the book has received good reviews). Similarly, the CEO of Abrams defined "expected top seller[s]" as "lead titles, as titles that were the biggest potential books in terms of selling." PX-2005 at 24–25 (Jacobs Dep. 89:14–90:7). In addition, in some cases, agents negotiate for marketing commitments for particular books; and for those books, agents negotiate for larger commitments for higher-advance books. *See* Trial Tr. 1827:10–1828:18 (Walsh) (expects higher marketing commitments for higher advance books).
95. Finally, the merging parties' data shows a strong correlation between advances and marketing spending. Dr. Hill analyzed the merging parties' actual marketing spend for individual books in title-level P&L data (as opposed to predicted spending reflected in acquisition P&Ls). Trial Tr. 1236:18–1237:8 (Hill). His analysis showed that for books that received advances less than $250,000, the merging parties spent an average of $10,000 per title on marketing. *See* PX-972 at 1 (Figure 1). By contrast, average marketing spend was nearly five times higher for books that received an advance between $250,000 and $500,000. *See* PX-972. And marketing spend was nearly ten times higher for titles with advances

between $750,000 and $1 million (compared to spending for books with advances of less than $250,000). *See* PX- 972 at 1; *see also* Trial Tr. 1236:11–1237:8 (Hill); Trial Tr. 2818:4–7 (Snyder); Trial Tr. 2835:18–25 (Snyder); Trial Tr. 2836:9–12 (Snyder).

Figure 1. Average Marketing Expenditures by Advance Amount, PRH and S&S (PX-972)

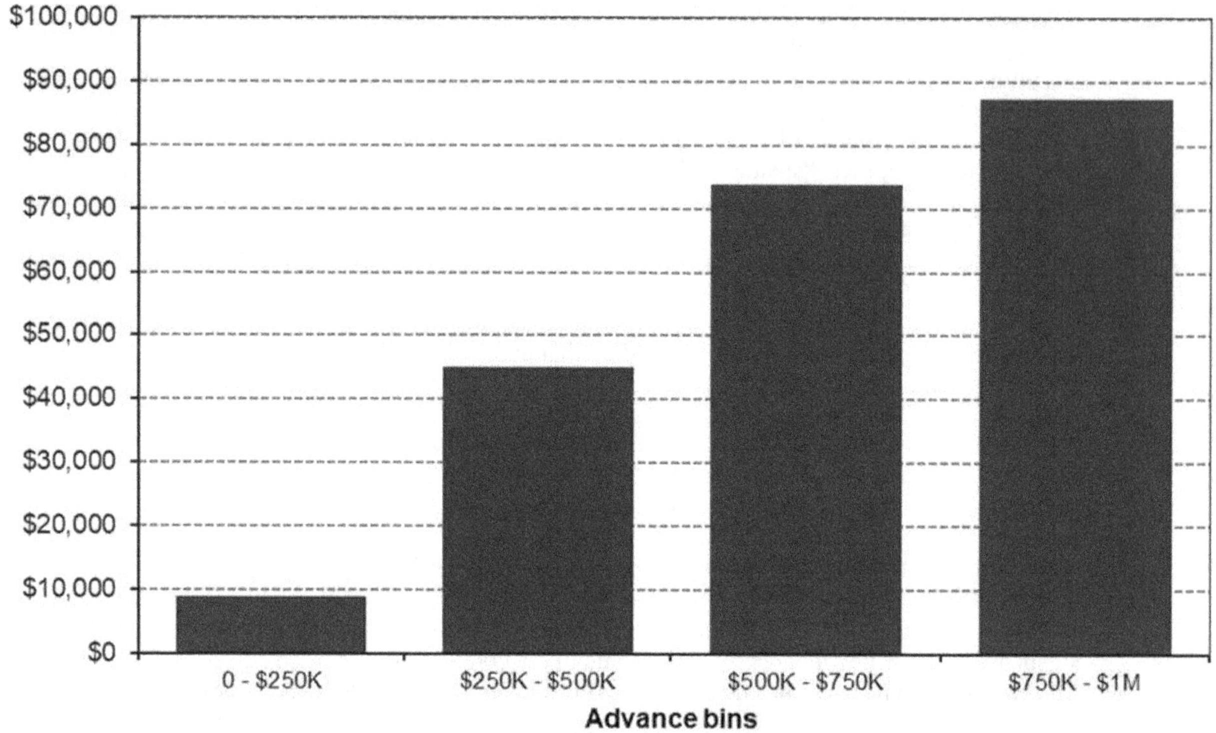

a. *Executive Approval*

96. Both Defendants require higher-level executive approval for high-advance books. In particular, both S&S and two of the three PRH adult divisions require high-level approval for offers that include an advance of $250,000 or more. *See* Trial Tr. 459:5–8 (Karp); Trial Tr. 2261:12–2262:5 (McIntosh); Trial Tr. 914:22–915:2 (Tart); Trial Tr. 1993:1–3 (Kim); *cf.* PX-87 at 3 (request for more senior management involvement in acquisitions "greater than 250/500k$"). Other publishers have similar executive approval levels. *See* [REDACTED] Trial Tr. 232:21–233:2 (Pietsch) (Hachette publishers have varying executive approval level, but they are all around $250,000).

b. *Higher Risk*

97. Higher-advance books are riskier than other books. *See* Trial Tr. 1369:14–1370:4 (Murray) ("The more that you commit in an advance on a particular project, the greater the risk of failure."); *see also* Trial Tr. 1371:1–3 (Murray) ("[T]he bigger the book is, the bigger the risk is on the inventory and the printing and the logistics of getting those books out to the various customers."); Trial Tr. 1373:5–7 (Murray) ("[I]f [editors] ask me for a large advance, you know, there's a lot of risk riding on those big books. There's less risk riding on the small books."); *cf.* Trial Tr. 155:4–17 (Pietsch) (Workman sought to acquire books with low advances because it did not want to "take on unearned advance risk").

c. *Print Orders*

98. Publishers make larger print orders for books that they expect to sell at higher volumes. Trial Tr. 1373:21–1374:3 (Murray); PX-2005 at 26 (Jacobs Dep. 91:6–13). Publishers also print more advance copies, *i.e.,* books given to reviewers, booksellers, or social media influencers, of books they expect to sell well. Trial Tr. 1373:12–20 (Murray).

d. *Tracking*

99. Publishers also track high-advance books separately from other books—or, similarly, track their performance in various advance buckets or tiers. *See* PX-790 at 1–36 (Hachette tracker of losses above

$500K); PX-989 at 2 (tracking sales, profitability, and margin for books in various advance buckets); *cf.* PX-174 at 100, 103 (tracking market shares separately for top-selling authors and non-top-selling authors). Publishers also measure their success based on bestseller lists. *See* PX-218 at 3 ("500+ NYT bestsellers per year[;] 60+ Nobel Prize laureates"); PX-68 at 32; Trial Tr. 887:23–888:5 (Dohle); Trial Tr. 1090:2–7 (Weisberg); Trial Tr. 1378:7–14 (Murray); DX-217 at 8; Trial Tr. 1961:14–22 (Kim) (boasting that Putnam has more hardcover *New York Times* bestsellers than any other imprint); Trial Tr. 2370:7–16 (McIntosh) (testifying that she reviews bestseller lists and that PRH performs better at the top of list than they do at the bottom of the list).

3. *Anticipated Top-Selling Writers Have Unique Needs*

100. Authors of anticipated top-selling books have unique needs. *See* Trial Tr. 1548:10–1549:6 (Hill). Market share data show that authors of anticipated top-selling books make different choices from authors of other books. Trial Tr. 1233:21–1235:21 (Hill). For anticipated top-selling books, authors choose non-Big Five publishers approximately 10% of the time of the time. PX-963 at 1 (Figure 2). For other books, authors choose non-Big Five publishers roughly five times as often (*i.e.,* nearly 50% of the time). PX-963 at 1. These market shares suggest that authors of anticipated top-selling books most often choose a Big Five publisher because they possess the strong reputation, distribution, and marketing needed to maximize the sales of an anticipated top seller. Trial Tr. 1231:11–1232:11 (Hill); Trial Tr. 1235:10–24 (Hill); Trial Tr. 1236:6–10 (Hill); Trial Tr. 1549:11–21 (Hill).

Figure 2. Market Shares by Contract for Anticipated Top Sellers and Non-Anticipated Top Sellers (2019–2021) (PX-963)

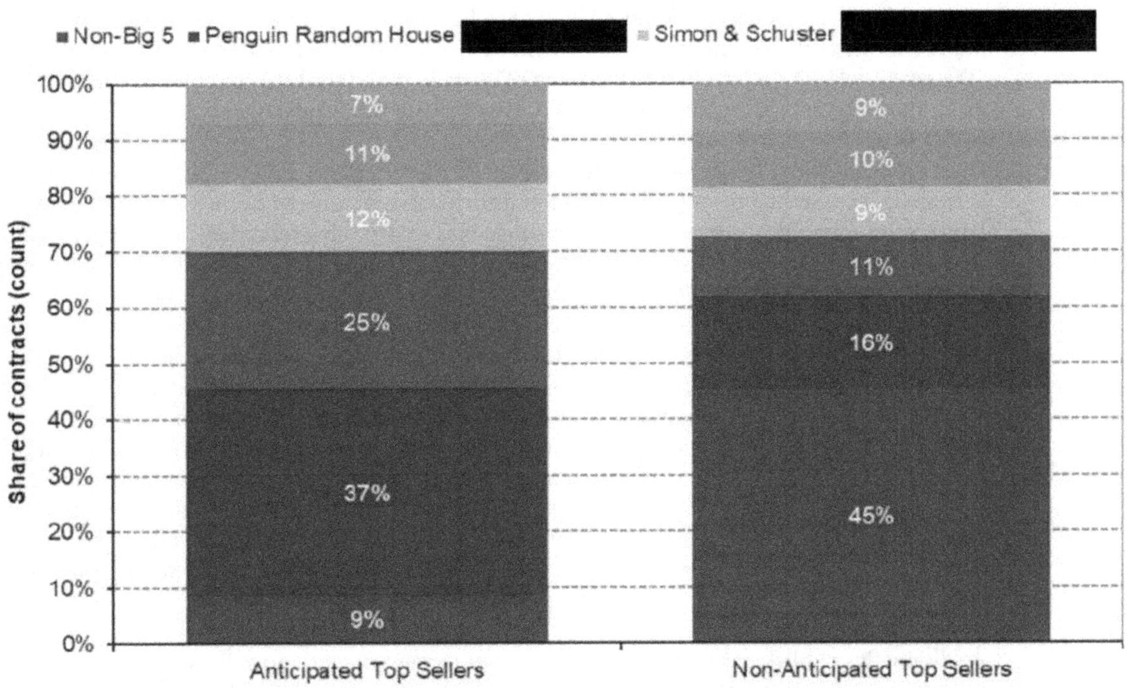

101. As put by Dr. Snyder, "There is something about books that are anticipated to be best sellers, and authors and the agents who represent them are going to be looking for a set of services. One of the advantages that individual fnms in the Big Five have is that they have reputations because they have been in business a long time and fundamentally economists talk about reputations being a function of repetition. So I get that and I accept that." Trial Tr. 2834:9–16 (Snyder).

102. Late S&S CEO Carolyn Reidy wrote that the Big Five are S&S's "biggest competitors, *especially for books by already bestselling authors and celebrities,* since they am the most likely to come up with high advance payments required and are known for their strong editorial and publishing skills." PX-530 at 2 (emphasis added); *see also* Trial Tr. 353:1- (Eulau) (understanding that "publishing skills refers to everything you do to publish a book and get it out there such as marketing and sales").

103. Defendants do not dispute that market shares look very different within the government's market than outside of it. When asked about this difference at trial, Defendant's agent expert, Jennifer Walsh, agreed with the basic premise, stating that non-Big Five publishers "don't bid [above $250,000] often" and adding that the government's market share calculations "sound[] right to me." Trial Tr. 1833:7–14 (Walsh). Dr. Snyder also agreed that the market shares for "the group of Big 5 grows substantially" above the $250,000 advance level while the shares of the non-Big Five publishers drops "very dramatically" at this level, from 45% to 9%. Trial Tr. 2820:9–13 (Snyder).

104. Market shares reflect that authors of anticipated top sellers demand "publisher[s] [that are] ready to commit incredible energy and resources." DX-21 at 5. Witnesses testified that the Big Five publishers have stronger publicity and marketing capabilities—stronger capabilities that give them an edge in turning books into bestsellers. *See, e.g.,* Trial Tr. 153:20–154:14; (Pietsch); Trial Tr. 158:11–159:6 (Pietsch) ("[T]he publicists for our publishing imprints get noticed. Their calls get returned [REDACTED] [T]hey have a presence; they have reputation; they have valuable connections. The smaller publishers simply don't have the same scale. They can't count on getting the attention of these influencers in the same way."); Trial Tr. 335:13–336:8 (King). For example, Mr. Karp admitted that, for new print books, the Big Five publishers' publicity and marketing assets give them an advantage in creating bestsellers. Trial Tr. 451:22–454:9 (Karp). Similarly, best-selling author Andrew Solomon testified that Big Five publishers are more successful with best-selling books because, when "your book comes out [REDACTED] you want to be on NPR, you want to be on Good Morning America or the Today Show, [REDACTED] And any publisher can sort of try. The publishers at the Big Five houses have more ready access to all of that. . . . There's just a whole industry that responds better to Big Five publishers." PX-2004 at 63–64 (Solomon Dep. 102:5–103:18); *see also* PX-2004 at 18–19 (Solomon Dep. 41:1–42:2).

105. Similarly, Ms. Pande testified that when one of her authors has been successful publishing with a small publisher, the author often prefers to publish his or her next book with a Big Five publisher, because "the next book would have a better chance of success with more substantial resources being brought to promoting and publishing the book from one of the Big 5." Trial Tr. 291:10–292:1 (Pande). [REDACTED]

106. Big Five publishers' larger sales forces also make them better suited towards maximizing sales of anticipated top-selling books. Mr. Solomon testified that he picked S&S's Scribner in part because of its larger sales force; this mattered to him because "[a] larger sales force reaches a larger number of sales outlets and is more persuasive with their interaction with them." PX-2004 at 19 (Solomon Dep. 42:3–21); *see also* PX-2004 at 54 (Solomon Dep. 93:5–20); Trial Tr. 326:20–327:6 (King) (King picked Scribner because "[t]hey had salespeople everywhere . . . I realized that I was going to reach book stores from coast to coast and that was great [REDACTED] They are a muscular firm. They were not going to just be in specialty book stores.They were going to be everywhere.").[REDACTED]

107. PRH knows that its strong marketing, publicity, and sales capabilities are important to authors and agents, as evidenced by its presentation to the literary agency, Writers House, in December of 2019. *See generally* PX-68 at 1–42. In that presentation, PRH highlighted its consumer insights and marketing for celebrity authors, its partner platforms (*e.g., The New York Times,* Goodreads, and Amazon), and its retail relationships. *See* PX-68 at 6–12. Publishers also highlight their marketing, publicity, and sales capabilities to prospective anticipated top-selling authors by submitting marketing plans during the acquisition process. Mr. Karp agreed that anticipated top-selling authors expect a certain level of marketing, publicity, and sales attention. Trial Tr. 491:11–13 (Karp).

108. Additionally, publishers' larger marketing spend for anticipated top sellers, *see supra* III.E1.a., indicates that strong marketing can better maximize sales for anticipated top sellers than other books. Publishers spend marketing resources on the books they believe will benefit most from those resources. As put by Mr. Tart, "I don't find that marketing money can create a success. I think it can amplify it." Trial Tr. 981:21–23 (Tart). Therefore, the large marketing spend on anticipated top sellers reflects publishers' judgment that anticipated top sellers will benefit more from marketing support than other books.

109. Books with higher advances also involve a significant amount of risk because many high-advance books do not sell well, resulting in publisher losses. *See, e.g.,* Trial Tr. 1369:14–1370:4 (Murray). Larger publishers are better positioned to take on this risk because they can spread it out over a larger set of books and imprints and because they have amassed large backlists that serve as a financial cushion. *See, e.g.,* Trial Tr. 156:5–20 (Pietsch); Trial Tr. 157:25–158:10 (Pietsch); PX-2002 at 83–84 (Stehlik Dep. 177:16–20, 177:23–178:6, 178:8–15,178:17–25); Trial Tr. 912:13–913:2 (Tart). Thus, according to Mr.

Pietsch, large publishers like Hachette have "more range for taking these risks onbooks that could become significant bestsellers." Trial Tr. 156:5–20 (Pietsch).

4. *Anticipated Top Sellers Have Specialized Vendors*

110. A distinct group of publishers serves anticipated top sellers. Of the "hundreds" of publishers who operate in the broader market for all trade books, *see* Dkt. 56 at 4 (Am. Answer ¶ 7), only 33 acquired an anticipated top seller in 2021, Trial Tr. 2684:10–19 (Snyder). And compared to their presence in the broader market, the Big Five dominate the market for anticipated top sellers. As discussed above, the Big Five acquire more than 90% of anticipated top sellers while acquiring only 55% of other books. *See* PX-963.

111. Executives of both merging parties recognize that there are fewer strong competitors for anticipated top sellers than for other books. *See* PX-530 (Reidy: "[The Big Five] are our biggest competitors, *especially for books by already bestselling authors and celebrities.*") (emphasis added); Trial Tr. 602:18–23 (Karp); PX-438 at 1 (McIntosh: "If at a lower level I'd think of Norton, but it's hard to picture them playing at this level."); *see also supra* III.E.2.

112. Third-party publishers also recognize this dynamic. [REDACTED] *see also* PX-2002 at 91–92 (Stehlik Dep. 185:20–186:19) (small publishers such as Norton, Chronicle, and Bloomsbury don't usually bid above $250,000, but Norton and Chronicle more commonly bid below $100,000).

113. Similarly, Scholastic is, according to Mr. Dohle, "as large as Macmillan and Hachette." Trial Tr. 737:19–738:1 (Dohle). But in the market for anticipated top sellers, Scholastic is several times smaller than both Macmillan and Hachette, and [REDACTED] *See* PX-959. And Workman Publishing, before it was acquired by Hachette, was one of the largest non-Big Five publishers. Trial Tr. 169:18–23 (Pietsch). But it rarely competed to acquire books with an advance of $200,000 or higher, because it sought to avoid the risks associated with publishing high-advance books. Trial Tr. 155:4–17 (Pietsch). The fact that all three of these firms—Kensington, Scholastic, and Workman—are successful in the broader book publishing industry but much less so for anticipated top-selling books shows that competitive conditions are different inside the market, compared to the rest of the business.

114. Additionally, a much greater proportion of all books published by Big Five publishers are anticipated top sellers compared to non-Big Five publishers. For example, 27% of PRH's books and 19% of S&S's books are anticipated top sellers, whereas only 4% of non-Big Five publishers' books are anticipated top sellers. PX-995 (Figure 3); Trial Tr. 3077:9–3078:1 (Hill).

Figure 3. Anticipated Top Sellers as a Percentage of Dr. Snyder Advance Data Titles by Publisher (2019–2021) (PX-995)

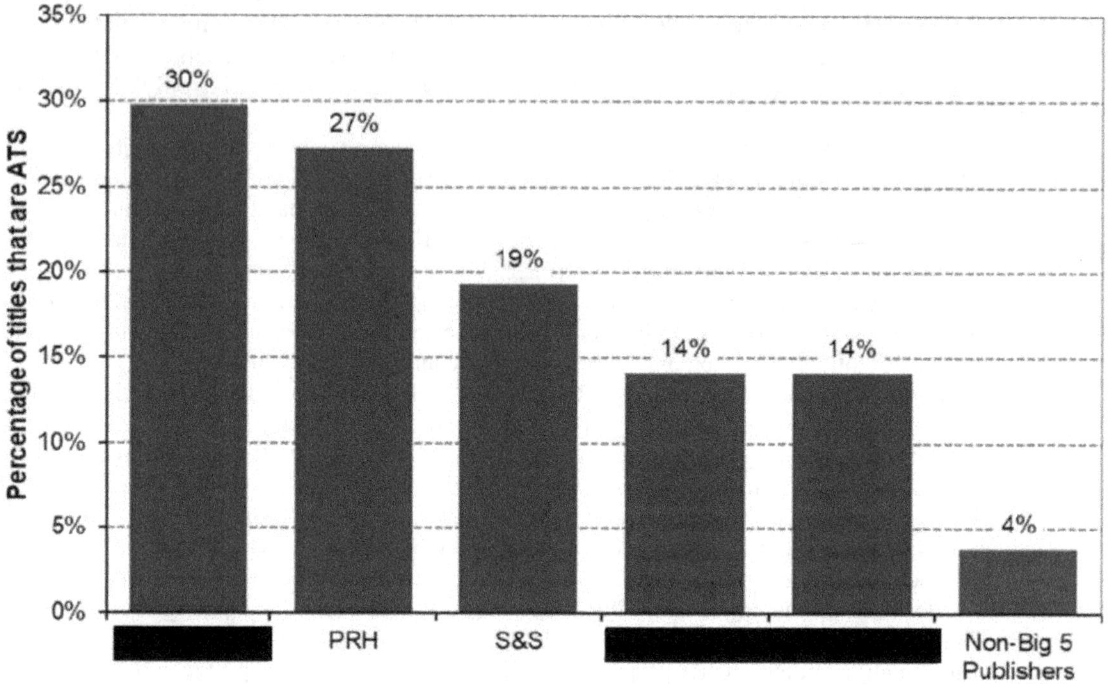

5. *Anticipated Top Sellers Have Distinct Prices*

115. Anticipated top-selling books have distinct prices. As discussed above, in this market the "price" for the book is essentially the advance. Anticipated top sellers receive higher advances because they are expected to sell more.

116. Anticipated top-selling authors demand specialized te1ms that are not often available to other authors. For example, an anticipated top-selling author secured a "SOK budget for glam, travel expenses, and outside PR." DX-21 at 2. For that same author, S&S offered to provide business class airfare, four-star hotel accommodations, and a $5,000 reading fee for the audiobook. DX-21 at 5. Ms. Walsh testified that these specialized contract te1ms-such as guaranteed ma1·keting, airfare and donations to charitable causes-am conelated with advances. Trial Tr. 1819:9–1820:2 (Walsh); Trial Tr. 1827:19–22 (Walsh). Mr. Karp testified that "glam budgets" and "as-is" clauses are not standard terms and that only authors of anticipated top sellers can demand them. Trial Tr. 575:7–576:5 (Karp). Mr. Weisberg, confirmed that special terms, such as bonuses and front-loading of payments, are usually only secured by "top end" authors. Trial Tr. 1132:17–23 (Weisberg). Mr. Tart testified he will only negotiate hardcover royalty rates for the more desirable books and he will only negotiate royalty rates for other formats "at the very, very top tier advance level." Trial Tr. 988:2–989:8 (Tart). Furthermore, anticipated top-selling authors sometimes receive bonuses when their books make bestseller lists. *See* [REDACTED] at 2 (showing bestseller bonus for books by [REDACTED] at 13.

6. *Anticipated Top-Selling Authors Are Not Sensitive to Price Changes*

117. *Brown Shoe*'s price sensitivity factor is akin to the inquiry undertaken in the hypothetical monopsonist test. *See Swedish Match,* 131 F. Supp. 2d at 159–60. As has been addressed above, a small but significant change in advances will not cause authors of anticipated top-selling books to shift in a significant way to self-publishing. *See supra* III.D.

7. *Anticipated Top-Selling Books Have Special Characteristics*

118. Anticipated top-selling authors are more likely to have track records of success, reach bestseller lists, and receive awards. Ms. McIntosh confirmed that agents of franchise authors "use [] track record[s] to ensure that [Penguin Random House is] paying [] a high advance." Trial Tr. 2285:23–2286:14 (McIntosh). Publishers identify anticipated top sellers as books that "could sell and hit the bestseller

lists." PX-2002 at 66 (Stehlik Dep. 157:2–16) (uses the phrase "big book" instead of anticipated top seller).

119. Publishers anticipate which books might win an award or receive critical acclaim, which causes them to offer higher advances because awards generate sales. Trial Tr. 1972:11–1973:11 (Kim); *see also* Trial Tr. 921:3–5 (Tart); Trial Tr. 969:13–21 (Tart) (publishers consider whether a book might win an award when constructing a P&L). Also, an author is more likely to receive a higher advance if her previous book won an award. *See* Trial Tr. 313:19–314:11 (Pande).

120. In *Syufy,* 793 F.2d 990, the Ninth Circuit delineated a product market around those approximately 30 films per year "anticipated" to be "top grossing." The Ninth Circuit focused on criteria similar to *Brown Shoe*'s practical indicia, but specifically geared for the creative industry of movies. *Id.* at 994.

121. The "anticipated top sellers" market proposed for books aligns closely with the approved "industry anticipated top grossing" market for films:

- There the movie studies invested more in the production of "anticipated top- grossing" films; here the publishers invest more in "anticipated top-selling" books including by paying larger advances;
- There "anticipated top-grossing" films tended to have big name stars, or directors, or producers; here "anticipated top selling" books tend to be associated with "franchise" authors, celebrities, or authors with potential to win major literary awards;
- There "anticipated top grossing" films were associated with larger advertising budgets; here "anticipated top selling" books with larger marketing spend (*see supra* III.E.1.a);
- There longer play times; here larger print runs (*see supra* III.E.1.d); and
- There more lucrative contract terms; here better contractual terms (*see supra* III.E.4).

Similarities between this case and *Syufy* confirm that the market for anticipated top sellers is a properly defined market.

F. Defendants' Argument About the Phrase "Anticipated Top Sellers" Is Misguided

122. Defendants argue that "anticipated top sellers" cannot form the basis for a product market because it is not a term used by publishers. They are wrong. There is no requirement that a relevant market be drawn around existing terminology in a particular industry. Such a requirement would immunize mergers that harms groups of customers or sellers as long as industry participants did not have a specific name for that group. In *Wilhelmsen,* for example, the court upheld a product market around "Global Fleets" despite the defendants' protests that "neither [defendant] use[s] the FTC's definition of that term." 341 F. Supp. 3d at 51–52. As the court explained, it was sufficient that "Global Fleets" constituted a "construct" providing a "useful way to discuss and predict economic conditions;" as long as it "capture[d] key aspects of the economic reality facing fleets" and allowed the court to "measure how the result of a merger would affect customers within [a relevant] subset" of the market. *Id.* at 52. Likewise, in upholding the plaintiff's proposed market of "industry anticipated top-grossing films," the court in *Syufy* never considered whether the term was commonly used by the movie industry. 783 F.2d at 882–883; *see also Le v. Zuffa, LLC,* 216 F. Supp. 3d 1154, 1165–66 (D. Nev. 2016) (allowing plaintiffs to proceed with a market based on "elite professional MMA [mixed martial arts] fighters" over defendants' objection that it is "a term not used in the industry and apparently created solely for the purpose of this [antitrust] litigation").

123. As in *Wilhelmsen,* the government has shown that anticipated top sellers provides a useful construct here. Multiple publishers have testified that there are books that publishers and agents expect to generate high sales and that, for those books, publishers will put in extra effort to boost sales. *See* Trial Tr. 1813:20–1814:3 (Walsh) ("there are franchise authors . . . yes, you know it's going to be a top seller . . . [a]nd then there are giant celebrities . . . where you know it's going to be a top seller"); Trial Tr. 575:10–576:5 (Karp) (agreeing with the Court that "you can't demand [a budget for glam and wardrobe] unless you are a top selling books author" and it is "a fair assumption to make" that an "as-is" term is "something you would only offer to an anticipated top selling books, not just to anybody").

G. The Acquisition of Publishing Rights to All Books Is Also a Relevant Product Market

124. Alternatively, the market can be defined more broadly to include all trade books, but not self-published books. Defendants appear to agree that this constitutes a relevant market. *See* Trial Tr. 2629:1—22 (Snyder); Trial Tr. 2897:5–13 (Snyder).

H. The Relevant Geographic Market Is Worldwide

125. The relevant geographic market is worldwide—meaning that the government has included all acquisitions of U.S. publishing rights in the market, regardless of the location of the author or publisher. *See* Dkt. 2 at 16 (Compl. ¶ 40); Dkt. 56 at 13 (Am. Answer ¶ 40). Defendants have not contested this definition.

IV. THE PROPOSED ACQUISITION OF SIMON & SCHUSTER IS PRESUMPTIVELY UNLAWFUL

A. Applicable Legal Standards

126. "A merger which produces a firm controlling an undue percentage share of the relevant market, and results in a significant increase" in market concentration is presumptively illegal. *Phila. Nat'l Bank,* 374 U.S. at 363–65 & n.42; *Sysco,* 113 F. Supp. 3d at 52. Courts use two different measures of market concentration to trigger the presumption. One is based on the percentage of the relevant market that would be controlled by the merged firm, and the other is a statistical measure of market concentration known as the Herfindahl-Hirschman Index ("HHI"). Starting with the combined firm's market share, in *Philadelphia National Bank,* the Supreme Court held that a significant change in concentration that results in a combined market share of at least 30% is sufficient to establish the legal presumption that a merger violates Section 7. 374 U.S. at 331, 364 (merger to a 36% market share with the top four banks controlling a combined 78%); *see also Heinz,* 246 F.3d at 711, 715–717 (holding FTC established presumption where defendants would have a combined share of 32.8% in a concentrated market); *Hosp. Corp.,* 807 F.2d at 1383 (finding transaction unlawful that raised defendant's market share from 14% to 26% and the market share of the four largest firms from 79% to 91%).

127. Courts also routinely assess a proposed merger's presumptive illegality using the Merger Guidelines and employing HHIs. *See, e.g., Sysco,* 113 F. Supp. 3d at 52–53; *Swedish Match,* 131 F. Supp. 2d at 166–67. HHIs are calculated by summing the squares of each market participant's individual market share both pre- and post-acquisition. *Sysco,* 113 F. Supp. 3d at 52; *United States v. H & R Block,* 833 F. Supp. 2d at 71–72; Merger Guidelines § 5.3. Under the Merger Guidelines, if an acquisition (1) increases the HHI of a relevant market by more than 200 points and (2) results in a post-acquisition HHI exceeding 2500, it is presumptively anticompetitive. *H & R Block,* 833 F. Supp. 2d at 71–72 (enjoining transaction that would have given the combined firm only a 28.4% market share because the transaction would have resulted in a highly concentrated market as demonstrated by an increase in the HHI of more than 200 and a post-acquisition HHI that would have exceeded 2500); Merger Guidelines § 5.3.

B. The Merger Presumptively Violates Section 7 in the Relevant Market

128. The merger easily clears the applicable thresholds here. The government's expert, Dr. Hill, calculated market shares based on a comprehensive set of data from more than sixty publishers. Trial Tr. 1251:12–1252:3 (Hill). According to these calculations, the merging firms account for nearly half (49%) of the market for anticipated top-selling books, and the Big Four combined will control approximately 90%. Trial Tr. 1254:3–6 (Hill); PX-959 at 1 (Figure 4). Dr. Hill also calculated market shares at different advance thresholds and found similar results. *See* PX-960 at 1 (Figure 5). The post-merger HHIs would be 3,111, with an increase of 891, well in excess of the thresholds required to establish the presumption under the Guidelines. Trial Tr. 1256:24–1258:11 (Hill); Trail Tr. 1259:4–12 (Hill). Moreover, post-merger HHIs (and the post-merger increase) are above the presumption thresholds at a variety of other advance cut- offs (*e.g.,* $150,000, $350,000, $500,000, or $1 million). Trial Tr. 1254:7–25 (Hill); *see also* PX-960 at 1.Figure 4. Share of Purchases of Anticipated Top Sellers (January 2019-June 2021) (PX- 959)

Figure 4. Share of Purchases of Anticipated Top Sellers (January 2019–June 2021) (PX-959)

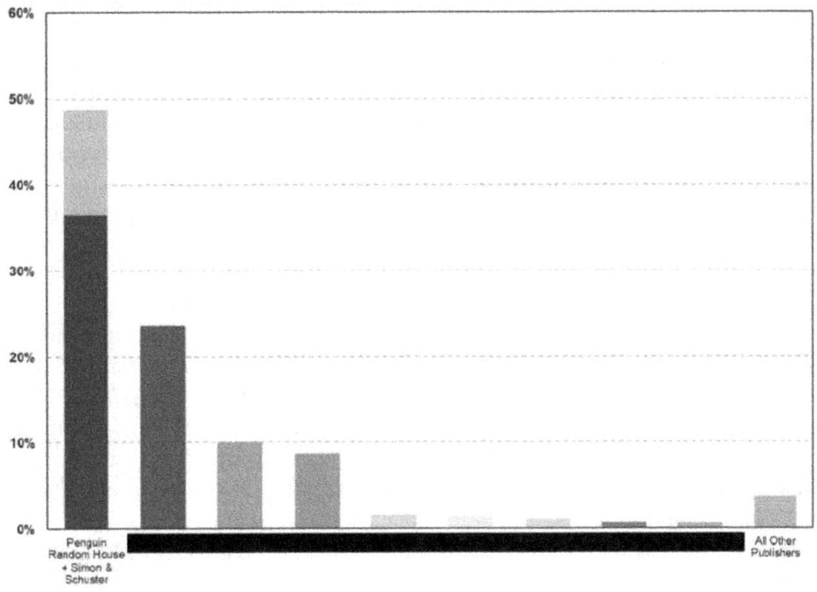

Figure 5. Share of Purchases of Anticipated Top Sellers Using Different Advance Cutoffs (January 2019–June 2021) (PX-960)

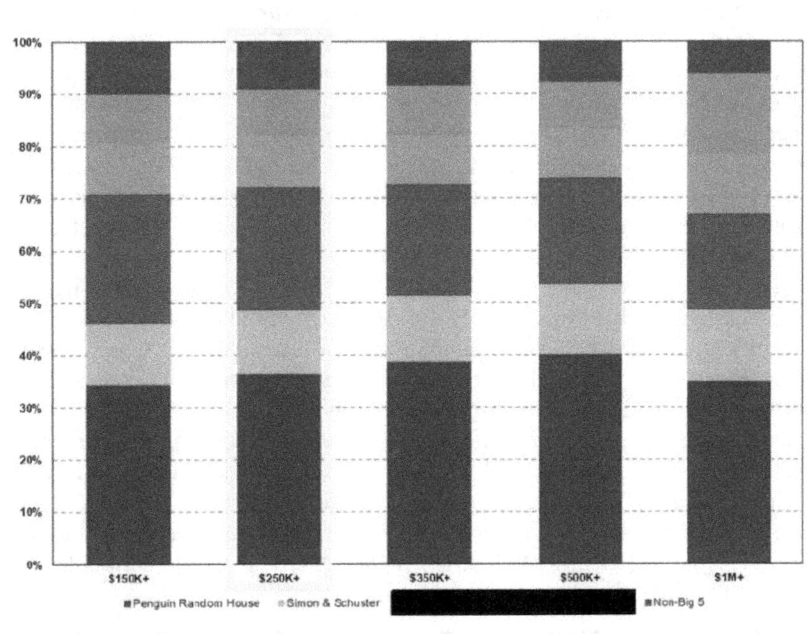

129. While Defendants dispute the market definition of anticipated top-selling books, Defendants do not dispute those market shares or HHI calculations.

C. The Presumption Is Almost Always Sufficient to Block a Merger

130. Defendants' characterize the legal presumption as "weak." Dkt. 131 at 35–36 (Defendants' Pre-Trial Brief). But the caselaw demonstrates that triggering the presumption is usually outcome-deten:ninative because defendants, as here, are unable to rebut it. *See, e.g., FTC v. H.J Heinz Co.,* 246 F.3d 708 (D.C.

Cir. 2001); *FTCv. Tronox Ltd.,* 332 F. Supp. 3d 187 (D.D.C. 2018); *FTC v. Wilh. Wilhelmsen Holding ASA,* 341 F. Supp. 3d 27 (D.D.C. 2018); *United States v. Aetna Inc.,* 240 F. Supp. 3d 1 (D.D.C. 2017); *FTC v. Sysco Corp.,* 113 F. Supp. 3d 1 (D.D.C. 2015); *FTC v. Staples Inc.,* 190 F. Supp. 3d 100 (D.D.C. 2016); *United States v. H & R Block, Inc.,* 833 F. Supp. 2d 36 (D.D.C. 2011); *FTC v. Libbey, Inc.,* 211 F. Supp. 2d 34 (D.D.C. 2002); *FTC v. Swedish Match,* 131 F. Supp. 2d 151 (D.D.C. 2000).

131. The presumption applies to mergers that raise concerns about unilateral effects—the loss of direct competition between the merging parties. Merger Guidelines § 6 (unilateral effects). And the presumption applies to mergers that raise concerns about increased coordination among remaining firms in the market, *i.e.* coordinated effects. Merger Guidelines § 7 (defining coordinated effects). Because Defendants appear to concede that HHIs can support a presumption of harm in coordinated effects merger cases, *see* Dkt. 131 at 37 (Defendants' Pre- Trial Brief) (arguing only that the HHI cannot support the presumption for unilateral effects), this brief will focus only on its application to unilateral effects.

132. The caselaw is clear that the presumption of illegality applies when mergers raise concerns about unilateral effects. *See Whole Foods,* 548 F.3d at 1035 ("The district court should bear in mind the FTC will be entitled to a presumption against the merger on the merits" in a unilateral-effects case); *Heinz,* 246 F.3d at 716 (applying presumption in unilateral-effects case); *Wilhelmsen,* 341 F. Supp. 3d at 62 (same); *Aetna,* 240 F. Supp. 3d at 43 (evidence of unilateral effects supports application of the presumption); *Anthem,* 236 F. Supp. 3d at 192, 231 n.28 (applying presumption in unilateral-effects case); *Staples II,* 190 F. Supp. 3d at 131 (same); *Sysco,* 113 F. Supp. 3d at 55 (same); *H & R Block,* 833 F. Supp. 2d at 81 (same).

D. Aggregating the Fringe Competitors Strengthens, Rather than Weakens, the Presumption

133. Defendants claim that practically the proposed merger reduces the number of competitors from "*six* (the five largest plus all others in aggregate) to *five,*" rather than five to four, due to the presence of smaller non-Big-Five competitors. Dkt. 131 at 40 (Defendants' Pre- Trial Brief); *see also* Trial Tr. 3304:6–7 (Defendants' Closing) ("And then you've got all these smaller and medium [publishers] as another Big 5"). Defendants cannot cite any authority for this unconventional proposition. Rather than "aggregate" fringe competitors, courts instead observe the reality of their unique competitive force and assign them appropriate weight. *See, e.g., FTC v. Hackensack Meridian Health, Inc.,* 30 F.4th 160, 172 (3d Cir. 2022) (assessing HHI based on a post-merger combined share of 47%, with the next two closest competitors having 21% and 9% shares; court did not treat remaining competitors—comprising 23% of the market—as a single firm); *Staples II,* 190 F. Supp. 3d at 128 (concluding merger was presumptively illegal because it would result in "one dominant firm with a competitive fringe"; court did not treat "competitive fringe" as an aggregate competitor in the market); *H & R Block,* 833 F. Supp. 2d at 71–72 (assessing HHI to be 4,291, with top three firms comprising 90% of the market; court did not treat the "numerous smaller firms" that comprised the remaining 10% of the market as a single firm). In any event, characterizing the merger as one from six-to-five does not magically remove its presumption of illegality. *See, e.g., Elders Grain, Inc.,* 868 F.2d at 905 (enjoining merger from six to five firms after noting the relevant market "was already highly concentrated before the acquisition, with only six firms of any significance") (Posner, J.); *United States v. Rockford Mem'l Corp.,* 898 F.2d 1278, 1284–85 (7th Cir. 1990) (Posner, J.) (same, where record showed six hospitals in a service area—and an additional one nearby—accounted for 83% of hospitalizations).

134. In fact, aggregating the fringe into one imagined unified competitive force leads to higher concentration measures that paint an even *worse* picture for defendants. The reason is the HHI squares *each firm's* market share. Squaring the share of one larger, combined firm (of about 9%) yields a larger post-merger HHI than squaring the shares of a number of smaller firms and then later adding them together. *See* Trial Tr. 1572:10–25 (Hill); PX-959 at 1; PX-963 at 1. This would entitle the government to an even stronger presumption of anticompetitive harm.

V. THE DEFENDANTS CANNOT REBUT THE PRESUMPTION

A. Market Shares Accurately Reflect Competitive Conditions

135. Defendants bear the burden of showing that the market shares and the associated presumption of illegality inaccurately reflect competitive reality. *United States v. Baker Hughes Inc.,* 908 F.2d 981, 991 (D.C. Cir. 1990). Here, Defendants do not question the accuracy of Dr. Hill's market shares, either in the data he used or the methodology used to calculate them. Instead, they try to argue that there are reasons to think that the market shares of firms, whether members of the Big Five, smaller publishers, or

even firms that have yet to publish their first book, have greater competitive significance vis-à-vis PRH and S&S than their market shares would indicate. However, when the record evidence is examined, it is clear that Defendants' arguments fall flat, and that the market shares are, in fact, an accurate representation of the publishing industry's market structure when it comes to anticipated top sellers and the likely effect of the merger on competition.

136. Both Dr. Hill and Dr. Snyder gathered data from a variety of data sources for their analysis, and market shares calculated using both experts' data are consistent with competitive conditions in the market for anticipated top sellers that justify finding the merger presumptively illegal. For example, as discussed more fully below, Dr. Hill compiled several different sets of data showing how frequently the merging parties compete with each other and with other publishers, including "win/loss" data from PRH and S&S tracking when they win or lose opportunities, Trial Tr. 1247:13:19 (Hill), and "runner-up" data that identifies, when PRH or S&S won a book, the runner-up publisher. *See infra* VI.C.1. These data sets describe a competitive dynamic consistent with publishers' market shares. For example, as market shares would predict, when S&S loses a book to a competitor, it most often loses to PRH. *See* Trial Tr. 1280:17–1281:17 (Hill).

137. Similarly, data collected by Dr. Snyder from literary agents subpoenaed during the course of this lawsuit ("agency data") show that non-Big Five publishers are winners or runners up at a frequency consistent with their relative market share. *See infra* VI.C.1. And a win/loss tracker maintained by Hachette also depicts results consistent with what market shares would predict—that roughly 90 to 95% of Hachette's losses above $500,000 are to the other Big Five publishers. PX-790 (Hachette loss tracking document showing that Big Five publishers account for approximately [REDACTED] of Hachette's losses above $500,000); Trial Tr. 191:16–194:24 (Pietsch) (describing loss tracking document).

138. As described at trial, the government's shares are based on hundreds of contracts—approximately 1,200 per year. Trial Tr. 1588:20–25 (Hill); Trial Tr. 2818:18–2819:18 (Snyder). As reflected in that broad set of contracts, market shares have not changed year-over-year. Trial Tr. 1482:15–1483:17 (Hill); Trial Tr. 3049:16–3050:21 (Hill); PX-967 at 1; PX-994 at 1 (Figure 6). This stability suggests that more weight should be placed on market shares. Trial Tr. 3051:5–15 (Hill); Merger Guidelines § 5.3 (agencies give more weight to market concentration when shares have been stable over time).

Figure 6. Share of Contracts (PX-994)

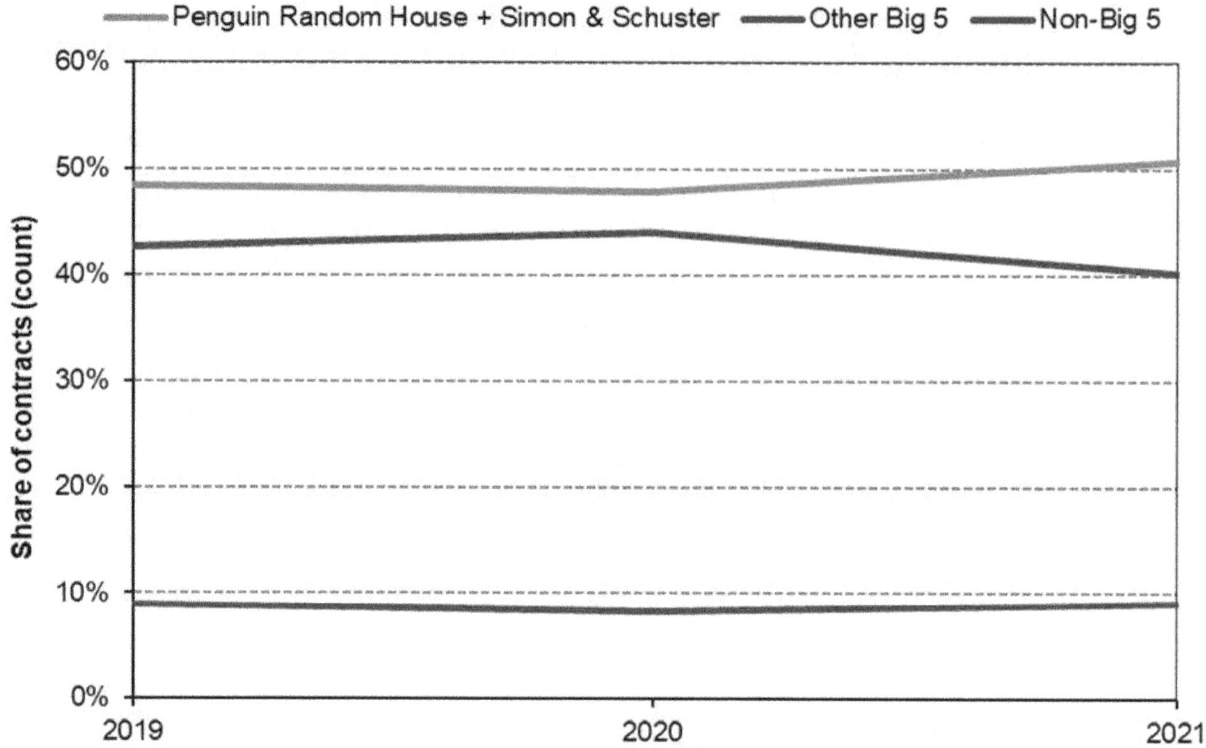

139. Defendants argue that market shares are not good indicators because they understate the competitive significance of smaller publishers and the market is dynamic and changing over time. While the evidence does show that the market has changed in some aspects—for example, audiobooks have become more popular recent years, change has been far slower for the essential features of competition. As discussed more fully regarding entry, below, over at least the last three decades, no firm has entered the market and become a strong competitor for the Big Five. And there is no evidence that the non-Big Five publishers are likely to change that reality in the near future. For these reasons, while change occurs in this market like any other, the evidence does not show that the government's market shares are an unreliable guide as to what might happen after the merger.

B. The Big Five Publishers Are the Main Competitors in the Anticipated Top- Seller Market

140. The Big Five publishers are the main competitors in the market for the acquisition of anticipated top-selling books. *See* Trial Tr. 153:5–13 (Pietsch); PX-157 at 1 ("Large publishers are our (main) competitors [REDACTED] "); PX-2002 at 71–72 (Stehlik Dep. 165:15–166:13) (HarperCollins imprint Morrow Group's main competitors are first PRH, then S&S, and sometimes Hachette and Macmillan). This is consistent with their relative market shares.

141. The industry itself recognizes that the Big Five dominate this market. At trial, top executives from several Big Five publishers testified that the other Big Five publishers are the publishers that they compete with—and lose to—most frequently. *See, e.g.,* Trial Tr. 152:11–153:4 (Pietsch); Trial Tr. 449:19–25 (Karp); Trial Tr. 451:13–16 (Karp); Trial Tr. 794:16–795:7 (Dohle); Trial Tr. 2360:20–23 (McIntosh); Trial Tr. 1374:4–23 (Murray); PX-2002 at 98 (Stehlik Dep. 197:1–11) (Harper Collins' Morrow Group loses most frequently first to PRH and second to S&S); Trial Tr. 351:21–352:14 (Eulau).

142. The evidence shows that smaller publishers rarely compete for anticipated top sellers. *See, e.g.,* Trial Tr. 153:14–22 (Pietsch) (Hachette loses to non-Big Five publishers "quite rarely" above $250,000); PX-790 at 1–36 (Hachette loss tracking document showing that Big Five publishers account for approximately [REDACTED] of Hachette's losses above $500,000); PX-530 at 2 (smaller publishers "rarely compete with [S&S] in auctions for new properties," but instead are "farm teams for authors who then want to move to a larger, more financially stable major publisher"). For example, Kensington is one of the largest mid-sized publishers and is quite successful in the genres it focuses on (*e.g.,* romance books), but

it has a very small market share in the market for anticipated top-selling books. PX-2000 at 8 (Zacharius Dep. 52:5–24); [REDACTED] Similarly, Scholastic is a very large publisher for children's books, and mentioned often by Defendants at trial, but it too has a very small market share in the market for anticipated top-selling books. *See* PX-959 at 1 (market shares; [REDACTED]); *see also* Trial Tr. 196:15–22 (Pietsch) (explaining that Perseus and Workman rarely offer advances above $250,000). Indeed, literary agent, Elyse Cheney acknowledged that the Big-Five are best-positioned to win anticipated top- selling books: "I think the non-Big 5, you know, are just not going to play in that sandbox too many times. They don't have the same scale." Trial Tr. 2047:16–18 (Cheney).

143. Publishers acknowledged at trial that while smaller publisher compete in the broader market for the acquisition of publishing rights, their presence in the market for anticipated top selling books differs markedly. S&S CEO Jonathan Karp admitted that (at least for auctions), there are fewer competitors at higher advance levels. Trial Tr. 602:18–23 (Karp); *see also* PX-2002 at 91–93 (Stehlik Dep 185:9–187:7) (non-Big Five publishers compete "very rarely" at advance levels of $250,000 or higher, but do compete more frequently at lower levels); Trial Tr. 169:24–170:20 (Pietsch) ("[S]ignificant independent publishers" generally do not "try[] to compete in this high-risk area"); *cf.* PX-2005 at 42 (Jacobs Dep. at 157:11–17) (explaining Abrams is "outbid all the time by publishers who are [] willing to pay . . . more for books than we are. You know, it's just the reality of things.").

144. Defendants' internal documents are consistent with this fact. In her description of S&S's business, then-CEO Carolyn Reidy wrote that Big Five publishers are S&S's "biggest competitors, especially for books by already bestselling authors and celebrities"—or, in other words, anticipated top-selling books—"since they are the most likely to come up with high advance payments required and are known for their strong editorial and publishing skills." PX- 530 at 2. Similarly, PRH executives recognize that "[f]or higher level advance [REDACTED] [t]he smaller publishers tend not to compete. . . ." PX-190 at 1; *see also* PX-438 at 1 ("If at a lower level I'd think of Norton, but it's hard to picture them playing at this level.").

145. For anticipated top-selling books, Big Five publishers have several important competitive advantages over other publishers. These advantages include:

1. Big Five Publishers Have the Size and Resources Necessary to Absorb Losses and Manage Risk

146. Paying a significant advance carries the risk that a publisher will lose money if the book does not sell well. *See, e.g.,* Trial Tr. 156:5–20 (Pietsch); Trial Tr. 456:1–456:5 (Karp); Trial Tr. 917:13–25 (Tart); PX-2002 at 90–91 (Stehlik Dep.184:21–185:8); Trial Tr. 1375:24–1376:5 (Murray). The Big Five publishers, due to their larger size, are better positioned to absorb the losses from underperforming high-advance books. *See, e.g.,* Trial Tr. 156:21–157:14 (Pietsch); PX-2002 at 91 (Stehlik Dep. 185:9–23); Trial Tr. 456:6–9 (Karp) (broader range of books/imprints helps S&S manage risk of advances). If a book with a large advance financially underperforms, that loss can have a bigger negative financial impact on smaller publishers. *See, e.g.,* Trial Tr. 156:21–157:14 (Pietsch). This makes it harder for small publishers to compete for anticipated top-selling books. *See, e.g.,* Trial Tr. 153:20–154:14 (Pietsch); PX-2002 at 81–82 (Stehlik Dep. 175:3–176:3) (Big Five publishers can "place more bets" than non-Big Five publishers); PX-2005 at 42–43 (Jacobs Dep. 157:11–158:8) (testifying the Abrams can only compete at higher advance levels for a very small number of books because of a resource issue).

2. Big Five Publishers Have Robust Backlists

147. The Big Five publishers have, over decades, amassed a steady stream of revenue from "backlist" sales—meaning sales of books published in previous years. Trial Tr. 117:19–118:14 (Pietsch). These sales are particularly profitable, as backlist sales involve fewer costs (*e.g.,* their marketing costs are lower) and they have lower return rates than frontlist books. Trial Tr. 157:15–158:10 (Pietsch); Trial Tr. 361:16–362:2 (Eulau). Big Five publishers use the revenue they receive from backlist sales as a financial cushion that helps them afford to pay higher advances and manage the risk associated with high-advance books. Trial Tr. 156:5–20 (Pietsch), Trial Tr. 157:25–158:10 (Pietsch); PX-2002 at 83–85 (Stehlik Dep. 177:16–178:25); Trial Tr. 2357:23–2358:19 (McIntosh); Trial Tr. 360:8–14 (Eulau); Trial Tr. 1377:14–1378:3 (Murray) ("The size of a publisher's backlist is critical to their financial stability and your ability to take these big risks with new projects, with new authors [REDACTED] So without a backlist, you know, I think it's very hard compete [for] these big books."); Trial Tr. 1384:11–13 (Murray). For this reason, the Big Five publishers' large backlist gives them an important competitive advantage over other publishers.

3. *Big Five Publishers Have Sophisticated Publicity and Marketing Resources*

148. Big Five publishers have larger and more sophisticated publicity and marketing teams, as well as better relationships with media executives and other professionals who help publicize books. *See, e.g.,* Trial Tr. 153:20–154:14 (Pietsch); Trial Tr. 158:11–159:6 (Pietsch); These teams and relationships give Big Five publishers an important competitive advantage over other publishers, because they are better able to promote a book through their connections with media executives and others. *See, e.g.,* Trial Tr. 158:11–159:6 (Pietsch); Trial Tr. 451:21–454:9 (Karp) (marketing and publicity teams give Big Five publishers a competitive advantage for new print bestselling books); PX-2004 at 19–20 (Solomon Dep. 42:8–43:16); PX-2002 at 82–83 (Stehlik Dep. 176:21–177:15) (Big Five publishers have more data to create more effective marketing campaigns); Trial Tr. 335:13–336:1 (King); Trial Tr. 259:13–260:4 (Pande). As Mr. Solomon testified, "your book comes out and . . . you want to be on NPR; you want to be on Good Morning America or the Today Show. . . . And any publisher can sort of try. The publishers at the Big Five have more ready access to all of that [REDACTED] There's just a whole industry that responds better to Big Five publishers." PX-2004 at 62–64 (Solomon Dep. 101:22–103:18).

4. *Big Five Publishers Have Extensive Sales Forces*

149. The Big Five publishers have larger retail facing sales teams, and they supply retailers with many bestselling books. *See* Trial Tr. 159:7–160:1 (Pietsch). These assets allow Big Five publishers to do a better job of getting their books displayed (*e.g.,* "on an end cap or a visible display"), promoted, and sold through retailers. Trial Tr. 153:23–154:14 (Pietsch); Trial Tr. 159:7–160:1 (Pietsch) ("smaller publishers without that volume of successful publishing simply don't have that leverage; don't have that kind of relationship with retailers and don't have those kinds of [display and display space] commitments"); PX-2004 at 17–19 (Solomon Dep. 40:15–42:21) ("A larger sales force reaches a larger number of sales outlets and is more persuasive with their interaction with them. And you know, in that arena, I think bigger is better."); PX-2002 at 82 (Stehlik Dep. 176:5–13) (Big Five publishers have an advantage in "get[ting] placement into different stores"); PX-2002 at 94 (Stehlik Dep. 188:17–22) (Big Five "more reach"); *see also* PX-2002 at 121 (Stehlik Dep. 246:6–16); Trial Tr. 334:20–335:7 (King) ("There are a number of independent publishers, but . . . the indies who look at works like my son's work who are new writers who don't have a reputation . . . , there are fewer and fewer of them because they are being squeezed. And the reason they are being squeezed is because they don't get the shelf space that they used to in the bookstores because the majors take a lot of that shelf space up. And that's like the minor leagues for writers."); Trial Tr. 2355:15–22 (McIntosh) (having the largest sales force is a competitive advantage for PRH); PX-218 at 1; PX-218 at 3 (similar); Trial Tr. 1378:4–1379:9 (Murray) (strong sales force is necessary to compete successfully for higher-advance books).

5. *Big Five Publishers Have Variable Cost Advantages*

150. The Big Five have better terms with retailers and printers that put them in a better position to compete for anticipated top sellers. *See* Trial Tr. 154:7–14 (Pietsch); Trial Tr. 159:7–160:1 (Pietsch); Trial Tr. 163:7–18 (Pietsch) ("We negotiate the financial terms with each of the retailers and wholesalers that we work with. And, given our scale, we have terms of a certain favorableness. When we acquire smaller companies, we see that their terms are not nearly as favorable."); *see also* PX-2002 at 80–81, 82 (Stehlik Dep. 175:3–9, 176:14–20). Smaller publishers may struggle to distribute their books to some retailers. *See* [REDACTED]

6. *Big Five Publishers Benefit from Their History of Success*

151. Big Five publishers have a long track record of success, as they have published many, many successful authors for a long period of time. *See, e.g.,* Trial Tr. 454:15–18 (Karp). This track record can give them an important competitive advantage in acquiring new books, particularly at higher advance levels. *See, e.g.,* Trial Tr. 454:11–22 (Karp); Trial Tr. 920:7–21 (Tart); Trial Tr. 2005:15–2006:18 (Kim); Trial Tr. 353:20–25 (Eulau); Trial Tr. 1375:24–1376:23 (Murray); Trial Tr. 1379:10–21 (Murray); PX-2002 at 86–90 (Stehlik Dep. 180:25–184:19); *see also* Trial Tr. 2834:12–16 (Snyder) ("One of the advantages that individual firms in the Big 5 have is that they have reputations because they have been in business a long time and fundamentally economists talk about reputations being a function of repetition."); Trial Tr. 535:7–20 (Karp) (noting that Macmillan's division Farrar, Straus & Giroux has "a long reputation" which can help in acquiring authors); PX-411 at 11 (explaining that imprints with historical credibility in literary fiction can more easily influence independent booksellers, reviewers, and prize committees, which allows them to acquire books at "more reasonable advance levels.").

7. *Non-Big Five Publishers Are at a Competitive Disadvantage Against the Big Five*

152. All of these advantages collectively make it materially harder for non-Big Five publishers to compete with Big Five publishers to acquire anticipated top-selling books. For example, [REDACTED] Similarly, Mr. Solomon testified that "the Big Five publishers . . . have a capacity that smaller companies don't have. I mean, in the same way that Apple is better at selling computers than someone who makes them in his garage in Vermont." PX-2004 at 54 (Solomon Dep. 93:5–20); *see also* PX-2004 at 43–45 (Solomon Dep. 74:10–20, 76:14–77:1) ("I believe the scale of [S&S] means that they have the resources to really throw themselves behind the books that they put out. [REDACTED] [S]cale had been enormously helpful."); PX-2004 at 60–61 (Solomon Dep. 99:11–100:9) ("It is possible for a non-Big Five publisher to do extremely well, but it's a lot harder and it happens less frequently. And even when it does happen, I think the scope and spread is not comparable."); PX-2005 at 42 (Abrams Dep. at 157:11–17) (Abrams "get[s] outbid all the time"). Mr. King also testified that the Big Five publishers are more appealing to authors because of "[t]he distribution for one [REDACTED] They can pay, if they choose, huge advances. They have a publicity network. They have publicity departments. And they are able to tap into the social media now. They are able to tap into—they are able to get advanced copies out to reviewers and they are able to put up a platform." Trial Tr. 335:13–22 (King).

153. In contrast to the large number of losses the Big Five publishers have to each other each year, the losses of anticipated top-selling books to non-Big Five publishers are infrequent. *See, e.g.,* Trial Tr. 153:14–22 (Pietsch) (Hachette loses to other publishers "quite rarely" above $250,000); PX-790 at 1–36 (H [REDACTED] hachette loss tracking document showing that Big Five publishers account for approximately [REDACTED] of Hachette's losses above $500,000); Trial Tr. 191:16–194:24 (Pietsch) (describing loss tracking document); PX-530 at 2 (former S&S CEO Reidy saying that smaller publishers "rarely compete with [S&S] in auctions for new properties," but instead are "farm teams for authors who then want to move to a larger, more financially stable major publisher"); *see also* Trial Tr. 795:11–796:9 (Dohle) (cannot name specific instances in which PRH lost to non-Big Five publishers); PX-2002 at 26–30 (Stehlik Dep.73:10–74:6, 75:18–77:4); PX-2002 at 74–75 (Stehlik Dep. 168:6–169:11); PX-2002 at 92–93 (Stehlik Dep. 186:2–187:7); PX-2002 at 122, (Stehlik Dep. 247:18–24); Trial Tr. 1029:19–1030:12 (Tart); Trial Tr. 253:25–254:8 (Pande); Trial Tr. 2047:16–18 (Cheney) ("I think the non-Big 5, you know, are just not going to play in that sandbox too many times. They don't have the same scale.").

154. Defendants point to examples where non-Big Five publishers beat one of the merging parties to acquire books, including anticipated top sellers. These examples prove less than Defendants assert. The government does not dispute that the merging parties sometimes lose to non-Big Five publishers; that follows from the fact that the non-Big Five publishers do have some market share. Trial Tr. 1551:4–8 (Hill) ("So, again, there's 10 percent of the market is accounted for the non-Big 5. So I'm not saying they can never do it. I'm just saying there are barriers to them doing it as regularly and competing as effectively as the Big 5 do."). But none of Defendants' examples show that non-Big Five publishers frequently win anticipated top- selling books or are more competitive than their share would indicate. To the contrary, for some of Defendants' examples, S&S's publishing executives expressed surprise that those non-Big Five publishers competed at high advance levels, further reinforcing that this type of competition is relatively rare and unlikely to affect the strategy of Big Five publishers like S&S when acquiring books. *See* DX-38 at 1 (Pelz: "We lost this one to Hay House (!)"; McGuire: "Wow I didn't know they pay big advances"); DX-131 (Cheiffetz commenting on loss to Princeton: "The [REDACTED] buy one big book a year"; McGuire: "Wow I had no idea they pay that much"). These anecdotes do not constitute a trend—the evidence is clear-that non-Big Five publishers do not frequently acquire anticipated top-selling books.

155. In addition, some of the non-Big Five publishers' market share can be attributed to the fact that some authors started with particular non-Big Five publishers, developed close personal relationships with those publishers, and do not intend to switch to another publisher.[REDACTED] The fact that non-Big Five publishers are able to retain some authors with whom they have long-standing close personal relationships does not mean that their share understates their competitive impact

8. *Dr. Snyder Presented Misleading Data Regarding the Competitive Significance of Small Publishers*

156. Despite a low market share, Dr. Snyder argues that non-Big Five publishers still serve as significant competitive constraints because they are the winner or runner-up 23% of the time for the acquisition of anticipated top-selling books. Trial Tr. 2688:24–2689:6 (Snyder); Trial Tr.); Trial Tr. 2693:20–2694:2

(Snyder). Dr. Snyder's figure is misleading, however, because it is not an actual percentage that measures the relative significance of the non-Big Five. To do so using this statistic, it must be halved. Trial Tr. 3051:16–3053:17 (Hill). This is because the 23% figure is actually the combined numerator from two percentages: the shares of all publishers' (a) wins and (b) runner up bids. Adding the numerators, each with a denominator of 100%, means that the "23%" is relative to a denominator of 200%. Trial Tr. 3051:16–3053:8 (Hill). After halving the 23% to 11.5%, Dr. Snyder's statistic is similar to the non-Big Five's 9% market share. Trial Tr. 3051:16–3053:17 (Hill). Therefore, Dr. Snyder's statistic, when corrected, is consistent with the market shares calculated by Dr. Hill that support the presumption that the merger is illegal.

C. Entry and Expansion by Non-Big Five Publishers Would Not Be Timely, Likely, or Sufficient

1. Legal Standard for Entry and Expansion

157. To successfully rebut a presumption of harm, Defendants must demonstrate that entry into the relevant product market would be "timely, likely, and sufficient in its magnitude, character, and scope to deter or counteract the competitive effects of concern." *H & R Block,* 833 F. Supp. 2d at 73 (quoting Merger Guidelines § 9); *see also Anthem,* 236 F. Supp. 3d at 222 (entry must "fill the competitive void" resulting from the merger) (quoting *Sysco,* 113 F. Supp. 3d at 80); *Staples II,* 190 F. Supp. 3d at 133. Merely pointing to the existence of potential entrants or publishers that might expand is insufficient to rebut the presumption of illegality. *See Chi. Bridge,* 534 F.3d at 436; *H & R Block,* 833 F. Supp. 2d at 73–77.

158. To be timely, Defendants must show that entry and expansion would be "rapid enough to make unprofitable overall the actions causing those effects." *Merger Guidelines* § 9.1. When expansion would take a period of years, it will not deter anticompetitive activity by the merged entity. *See Elders Grain,* 868 F.2d at 905; *United States v. Visa U.S.A., Inc.,* 163 F. Supp. 2d 322, 342 (S.D.N.Y. 2001), *aff'd,* 344 F.3d 229 (2d. Cir. 2003); *see also Staples II,* 190 F. Supp. 3d at 133 ("The relevant time frame for consideration in this forward looking exercise is two to three years.").

159. "The history of entry into the relevant market is a central factor in assessing the likelihood of entry in the future." *Anthem,* 236 F. Supp. 3d at 222 (quoting *FTC v. Cardinal Health,* 12 F. Supp. 2d 34, 56 (D.D.C. 1998)). The absence of significant entry in the market can indicate that there are high barriers to entry. *See Heinz,* 246 F.3d at 717 (rejecting ease of entry defense where district court found that "there had been no significant entries in the baby food market in decades"); *Cardinal Health,* 12 F. Supp. 2d at 56 (noting that history of entry and expansion in wholesale drug distribution market "does not suggest that any form of entry in the future is very likely").

160. Entry must be at sufficient scale to prevent anticompetitive effects from the merger. *See H & R Block,* 833 F. Supp. 2d at 73. Similarly, where Defendants allege there will be an expansion of existing competitors, they must be able to demonstrate that such expansion can act as a constraint on the merged company. *See id.* at 73–77 (finding the eighteen companies offered by defendants as expansion candidates post-merger insufficient because they were unlikely to replace the competition that would be eliminated by the acquisition); *Sysco,* 113 F. Supp. 3d at 81 (rejecting defendants' argument that existing regional firms could expand to serve national customers because "like new entry, successful expansion is extraordinarily capital intensive and demands a long time horizon").

161. "Entrants must be significant enough to compete effectively, *i.e.,* affect pricing." *Anthem,* 236 F. Supp. 3d at 222 (quotation omitted). That is, they must be "of a sufficient scale to compete on the same playing field" as the merged firm. *Id.* (quoting *Chi. Bridge,* 534 F.3d at 430); *see also Sysco,* 113 F. Supp. 3d at 81 (rejecting defendant's argument about expansion by regional players); *Cardinal Health,* 12 F. Supp. 2d at 58 (finding that the lack of another national wholesaler after the merger was "too great a competitive loss—which the regional wholesalers cannot sufficiently replace").

162. Courts have recognized numerous barriers to entry that are present here, including reputation and the need for significant upfront investments. "Reputation can be a considerable barrier to entry where customers and suppliers emphasize the importance of reputation and expertise." *Anthem,* 236 F. Supp. 3d at 222 (quoting *FTC v. CCC Holdings Inc.,* 605 F. Supp. 2d 26, 54–55 (D.D.C.)); *see also id.* at 223 ("To sell to national accounts, the insurer must develop a strong enough reputation to be recommended by the consultants guiding the employers through the contracting process.[REDACTED]"); *Sysco,* 113 F. Supp. 3d at 80 (finding incumbency "a powerful force in the foodservice distribution industry"); *H & R Block,* 833 F. Supp. 2d at 75 ("Building a reputation that a significant number of consumers will trust requires time and money."); *Cardinal Health,* 12 F. Supp. 2d at 57 ("The sheer economies of scale and strength of reputation that the Defendants already have over these wholesalers serve as barriers to

competitors as they attempt to grow significantly in size.").

2. *Entry Barriers Are High*

163. In this market, barriers to entry are high. In the past thirty years, no publisher has entered the market and become a strong competitor for the Big Five. *See* Trial Tr. 163:2–6 (Pietsch). And for good reason. New entrants face a variety of disadvantages—they lack a backlist, have a harder time publicizing books, have weaker relationships with retailers, and cannot point authors and agents to a sustained history of success. *See* Trial Tr. 163:7–165:6 (Pietsch).

164. Moreover, the competitive advantages of the Big Five are difficult to duplicate, particularly in the immediate term. Building a large backlist is a years-long endeavor because only a small number of new titles each year turn into reliable backlist titles. Trial Tr. 165:20–167:5 (Pietsch); PX-2002 at 85 (Stehlik Dep. 179:18–20, 179:23–25). Building relationships with the media executives and other professionals that help publicize a book also takes a long time; the Big Five have spent many years developing these relationships and building their credibility. Trial Tr. 163:21–164:17 (Pietsch); Trial Tr. 167:6–168:8 (Pietsch). And building a strong track record of success can also take many years. *See* PX-2002 at 90 (Stehlik Dep. 184:10–13, 184:16–19). Finally, no entrant has come close to building the scale necessary to manage the risk of high-advance books as effectively as the Big Five publishers do today. *See* Trial Tr. 168:17–169:17 (Pietsch).

165. For these reasons, industry participants recognize that entry is not easy. For example, Hachette CEO Michael Pietsch testified that entry in this market is "very difficult." Trial Tr. 168:0–169:1 (Pietsch). Similarly, HarperCollins CEO Brian Murray stated that it would be "very, very difficult" for a startup to compete for high-advance books, for a variety of reasons, including the "risk profile of placing big bets" and lack of access to a backlist. Trial Tr. 1380:12–1381:8 (Murray); *see also* Trial Tr. 249:20–250:9 (Pande) ("[I]t takes a long time for a publisher to establish itself in the industry . . . all of these [new entrant] publishers are still too new to have really proven themselves."); Trial Tr. 339:6–10 (King) ("If you are saying could a new publisher suddenly show up in the marketplace, they show up all the time and they don't have a great deal of success because they don't have the traction that the Big 5 do. The Big 5 are pretty entrenched.").

166. Bertelsmann itself recognizes the difficulty of entry. A Bertelsmann board presentation states that "[b]arriers to entry" in the U.S. publishing market are "[h]igh" due to reputation and distribution requirements. PX-80-E at 13. And in 2019, PRH advised that starting their own publishing company was "[n]ot a viable option," noting that there is "[n]o history of companies starting from scratch achieving profitability in 3–5 year time period." PX-79 at 8; *see* Trial Tr. 755:4–15 (Dohle). PRH further explained that creating a profitable publisher would take many years because there is a years-long lag between when books are acquired and when they are published—and because it would take many additional years after that before the publisher would accrue a backlist large enough to insulate the publisher against the risk associated with high-advance frontlist books. PX-151 at 33 (showing an initial three-year phase with "losses driven by investment in books that are not yet published," and an additional four-year period where "[l]osses [are] driven by book(s) with high advances not performing," with the publisher not reaching the "steadier-state phase" until years seven through ten); Trial Tr. 750:6–751:12 (Dohle) (similar); *see also* Trial Tr. 1380:12–1381:8 (Murray) ("It can take more than five years for an imprint to become profitable.").

167. As writer Andrew Solomon explained, the publishing business is a "long game" because "you have to invest a lot of money at an early stage in order to get a book to do well" and even successful books can take 10 years to earn a publisher more than a negligible profit. PX-2004 at 57–58 (Solomon Dep. 96:12–17, 96:20–97:12, 97:14–18, 97:22). The Big Five publishers are best positioned to play that long game. PX-2004 at 57–58 (Solomon Dep. 96:12–17, 96:20–97:12, 97:14–18, 97:22).

3. *Expansion by Existing Publishers Will Not Be Sufficient, Timely, or Likely*

a. *Expansion or Repositioning by Non-Big Five Publishers is Unlikely*

168. Non-Big Five publishers have small market shares that have not changed over time. They face barriers to expansion—including reputation, lack of a strong backlist, ability to manage risk, breadth of marketing and distribution, strong relationships with retailers—and are unlikely to expand. Trial Tr. 1481:15–1482:12 (Hill); *see generally* Trial Tr. 1475:21–1483:17 (Hill) (discussing barriers to expansion non-Big Five publishers face).

169. Mr. Pietsch testified that it would be "very, very hard" for non-Big Five publishers to grow to the point where they could compete on an even playing field with the Big Five in this market, noting that this

type of expansion has not happened in his 45 years in the publishing business. Trial Tr. 169:2–170:20 (Pietsch). [REDACTED] And, in fact, some small or mid-sized publishers that tried to compete with the Big Five eventually decided to abandon those efforts and sell themselves to Big Five publishers instead—or simply exited the business. Trial Tr. 169:2–170:8 (Pietsch); Trial Tr. 334:20–335:3 (King) (there are "fewer and fewer" independent publishers "because they are being squeezed");[REDACTED]

170. Relatedly, at trial, multiple non-Big Five publishers testified either that they do not plan to expand or that they plan to expand only in a very limited way.*see also* [REDACTED]

b. Expansion by The Remaining Big Five Is Also Unlikely

171. The remaining Big Five publishers lack the incentive to expand in response to a post-merger price decrease. Trial Tr. 1486:25–1487:6 (Hill). In multi-round auctions, these publishers will have an incentive to maintain their current bidding behavior, and in other acquisition types, they will have an incentive to bid similarly or *less* aggressively, not more. Trial Tr. 1486:25–1489:9 (Hill).

172. To start with, the Big Five publishers do not all bid in every auction. *See* PX- 933B at 1 (PRH and S&S only bidders); PX-937B at 1 (PRH and S&S only bidders). There are many instances in which the other three Big Five publishers dropped out of multi-round auctions and competition between PRH and S&S, as the only remaining bidders, forced advances to go up. *See, e.g.,* PX-935B at 1 [REDACTED] PX-943B at 1 PX-557 at 6 [REDACTED] *see also* Trial Tr. 427:5–430:17 (Karp) (describing auction discussed in PX- 557; competition between PRH and S&S pushed the advance up from $650K to $825K after the last non-party bidder dropped out); Trial Tr. 176:2–17 (Pietsch). Nothing about the merger will cause the remaining large publishers to bid more aggressively, or offer higher advances. At most, they will continue to drop out of auctions at the same level that they have in the past. Trial Tr. 177:1–15 (Pietsch); Trial Tr. 1088:8–14 (Weisberg) (Macmillan does not have plans to change how it bids or the number of books it acquires because of the merger); Trial Tr.1486:25–1487:18 (Hill); *cf.* [REDACTED] PX-2005 at 30 (Jacobs Dep. 118:2–6 (similar). For that reason, expansion by the Big Five publishers is unlikely to prevent the harm from the merger in many multi-round auctions.

173. An example illustrates this point. As described more fully above, today, there are some auctions where a third bidder, like Hachette, drops out at a particular level, like $500,000, and competition between the merging parties continues until the advance increases to, say, $700,000. *See, e.g.,* PX-588 at 1 (describing auction where last third-party bidder dropped out around $650K and competition between PRH and S&S pushed advance up to $825K); PX-941-B at 1; *see also* PX-938-B at 1 (summary of auction for [REDACTED] in which two [REDACTED] imprints dropped out after bidding $500,000 and competition between PRH and S&S pushed the advance up to $750,000); PX-943-B at 1 (summary of auction for [REDACTED] in which [REDACTED] bid $150,000 in Round 1 and competition between PRH and S&S pushed the advance to $390,000). In those sorts of auctions, if $500,000 is the limit Hachette set for itself at the start of the auction, it is likely that Hachette would still drop out once the auction hit that level after the merger. Trial Tr. 177:1–15 (Pietsch). Once Hachette drops out, there would be no other competition to force S&S or PRH to increase to $700,000.

174. In other acquisition types, such as best-bid auctions, negotiations, and some hybrid auctions, the remaining Big Four will have an incentive to compete *less* aggressively after the merger. Trial Tr. 1487:19–1489:9 (Hill). Publishers will recognize over time that the combined PRH-S&S is bidding less aggressively, and, as put by Dr. Hill, "[i]f you recognize that competition has been softened but you are less likely to lose an auction for a book on average, then your incentive is to take some of that as a high probability of winning and take of it as a higher margin if you win. So you take a little bit of both, and that means you bid a little bit less aggressively than you did prior to the merger." Trial Tr. 1488:8–18 (Hill); *see also* Trial Tr. 1268:22–1269:24 (Hill); Carl Shapiro, *The 2010 Horizontal Merger Guidelines: From Hedgehog to Fox in Forty Years,* 77 Antitrust L.J. 49, 71 n.81 (2010) (stating, with regard to rival responses in sell-side mergers: "[r]ivals usually have an incentive to raise the prices of their products in response to the higher demand they face when the merged firm raises the prices for its products"). *Cf. H & R Block,* 833 F. Supp. 2d at 77–78, 88 (holding that expansion or repositioning by the largest competitor, Intuit, was unlikely because it did not have incentive to defeat an anticompetitive elimination of free products after the merger).

c. The Merger Will Not Affect the Future Plans of HarperCollins, Hachette or Macmillan, and Their Shares Have Been Declining

175. In addition to their economic incentives, other evidence confirms that the remaining Big Five publishers are unlikely to expand sufficiently. First, the combined market share of HarperCollins, Hachette, and Macmillan declined from 2019 to 2021, indicating that they have not grown more competitively

significant in recent years. PX-994 at 1.

176. Second, these publishers testified that the merger will *not* affect their future plans, or that they do not plan to expand faster than they have been (which would be captured by existing market shares). *See* Trial Tr. 177:1–15 (Pietsch); Trial Tr. 1088:8–14 (Weisberg). Hachette's CEO, Michael Pietsch explained that Hachette will not change how it evaluates and bids on books after the merger. Trial Tr. 177:1–15 (Pietsch); Trial Tr. 217:7–11 (Pietsch). Macmillan's CEO, Weisberg testified similarly. Macmillan has no plans to change how it bids for books or the number of titles it seeks to acquire if PRH were to acquire S&S. Trial Tr. 1088:8–14 (Weisberg). Because Hachette and Macmillan will continue to operate as they do today, they are unlikely to expand or in any way replace the loss of competition the market will suffer.

177. Nor will HarperCollins expand sufficiently. HarperCollins CEO Brian Murray testified that it plans to grow more slowly than it has in recent years. Trial Tr. 1429:15–1430:10 (Murray); DX-279 at 25. And the existing plans project annual growth rates in advance spending from fiscal years 2022–2024 of [REDACTED] , which do not necessarily mean that it would grow faster than the market, given the trade book business's significant growth in recent years. *See, e.g.,* DX-279 at 3 (showing [REDACTED] annual growth). [REDACTED]

d. Defendants' Unsupported Arguments About Expansion at Closing Arguments Cannot Justify Rebutting the Presumption

178. At closing, counsel for ViacomCBS claimed that a number of firms are "poised" to expand to fill in the gap created by the merger. *See* Trial Tr. 3300:15–3304:19 (Defendants' Closing). In addition, he argued that the merger will change the incentives of the remaining publishers, causing them to compete more aggressively than they did prior to the merger. *See* Trial Tr. 3292:20–3293:8 (Defendants' Closing). To rebut the presumption of harm, Defendants must offer proof that the merger will induce expansion by these publishers. *See* Merger Guidelines § 9. Such proof does not exist in the record.

179. First, the unstated premise of these arguments is that it would be easy for another Big Five publisher to expand to such a degree that it would replace the competitive significance of S&S. This is simply not the case. Publishers are not commodities and S&S's competitive significance is the result of decades of effort to establish a reputation, brand, and relationships with authors and editors. *See, e.g.,* 454:11–18 (Karp) (S&S has "decades of credibility and success for nonfiction books"). If it were so easy to replace (or replicate) that competitive significance, then there would be no reason for PRH to pay $2 billion to buy it. Nor would it make sense for PRH to conclude that the merger would "cement" its position as the number one publisher. Trial Tr. 742:2–4 (Dohle); PX-162 at 1 ("Cement PRH as #1 in the US").

180. Second, the United States called six witnesses from five different non-party competitors—including the three CEOs of the remaining Big Five publishers and the CEOs of two relatively large non-Big Five publishers. None of them said that the merger will cause them to change their bidding strategies or induce them to expand. *See supra* V.C.3.a–b. And it is clear that those publishers will have no greater incentives—and perhaps diminished ones—to compete vigorously for advances.

181. Finally, because they cannot rely on testimony from the non-party publisher witnesses who did appear at trial about what they would do, Defendants instead point to speculation about potential expansion by non-testifying publishers, like Disney, Amazon and Scholastic. Trial Tr. 3302:11–3303:13 (Defendants' Closing). The Court should not credit unsupported, speculative claims about future plans by other publishers. If such evidence existed, Defendants could have presented it.

182. Indeed, much of the evidence cited by counsel does not relate to expansion at all—instead, it relates to the existing competition between publishers, which is also captured by current market shares. For example, as evidence of a "Competitive Response to [the] Merger," counsel cited testimony from Mr. Pietsch that the merger would *not* change Hachette's bidding strategy. *See* Trial Tr. 3300:15–3301:2 (Defendants' Closing); ViacomCBS & S&S Closing Slides at 8. But the existence of other competitors does not rebut the *Philadelphia National Bank* presumption. *See, e.g., Tronox,* 332 F. Supp. 3d at 194–195, 207–210 (enjoining five-to- four merger).

4. Printing Is an Additional Barrier to Entry and Expansion

183. Lack of access to printing capacity also serves as a barrier to entry and expansion. In recent years, the industry has faced a printing capacity crunch, as the number of books printed and sold has continued to increase while book printing capacity has remained flat. Trial Tr. 758:3–5 (Dohle); Trial Tr. 121:8–19 (Pietsch); Trial Tr. 364:1–9 (Eulau); [REDACTED] Lack of access to printing capacity creates several problems for publishers. Without timely access to printing capacity, publishers' books may go out of stock at retailers, which can lead to lost sales. Trial Tr. 759:6–9 (Dohle); Trial Tr. 362:16–23 (Eulau);

Trial Tr. 1379:22–1380:11 (Murray). This is especially true if a book becomes an unexpected success and the publisher cannot meet the demand for a book because it is unable to get copies printed on short notice. In addition, publishers may be forced to push back the release date of a book, which can also lead to wasted marketing and publicity efforts, lost sales, and frustrated authors and agents. Trial Tr. 758:18–759:9 (Dohle); Trial Tr. 362:9–15 (Eulau); Trial Tr. 363:13–25 (Eulau). Access to printing capacity is important when competing for authors, and losing access would adversely impact the publisher's ability to attract authors. Trial Tr. 363:8–12 (Eulau); Trial Tr. 363:19–22 (Eulau).

184. PRH's parent company, Bertelsmann, owns a book printing company. No other major or mid-sized publisher does. *See* PX-983 at 1 ("[w]e are the only publisher with a printer in the family. . . ."); Trial Tr. 760:18–21 (Dohle); Trial Tr. 762:11–17 (Dohle). And alternatives to Bertelsmann are limited. For one-color trade book printing—*i.e.,* the printing of standard-size black and white books—the only other large printer in the United States is LSC, which may not have capacity available and which may give preferential treatment to Big Five publishers. *See* [REDACTED] And smaller printers do not have the scale required to efficiently serve the needs of large and mid-sized publishers. [REDACTED] Trial Tr. 364:19–365:14 (Eulau).1 For mass market books, publishers' options are even more limited-Be1ielsm.ann owns the only major U.S. mass market book printing company. [REDACTED]

185. Without access to sufficient printing capacity, new and existing publishers alike may find expansion more challenging-in fact, they may even be forced to retrench. *See also* PX-682 at 2 (S&S ''would not want to be 100% beholden to a competitor for printing."); PX-983 (PRH's relationship with a printing group gives it a "huge competitive advantage in attracting authors . . ."); Trial Tr. 764:22–765:6 (Dohle) (acknowledging that other publishers have "a genuine concern" that they will be at a competitive disadvantage in acquiring authors); Trial Tr. 363:5–22 (Eulau); Trial Tr. 368:7–369:12 (Eulau).

186. In fact, several publishers have testified that the problems caused by their dependence on Bertelsmann for printing may worsen after the merger with S&S. [REDACTED]

5. Amazon's Limited Success Shows How Difficult Entry Is

187. Notably, even Amazon has tried to marshal its considerable resources to enter the market and made very little headway in acquiring authors. *See* Trial Tr. 356:10–18 (Eulau). Amazon launched a publishing business called "Amazon Publishing" over a decade ago. Trial Tr. 171:24–173:6 (Pietsch). It made a few headline-grabbing acquisitions but met with limited success and then retrenched. Trial Tr. 171:24–173:6 (Pietsch); PX-2002 at 101–102 (Stehlik Dep. 201:17–202:1) (Amazon has become less aggressive in recent years). As Mr. Pietsch described it, Amazon "started an Amazon publishing program that was intended to be competitive. . . . And they closed it down . . . very quickly after some very visible failures." Trial Tr. 172:17–25 (Pietsch).

188. As a potential competitor, Amazon faces all of the disadvantages (*e.g.,* lack of backlist, limited publicity resources, etc.) of other new or small competitors. Trial Tr. 171:4–23 (Pietsch). In addition, it faces a unique competitive disadvantage that does not affect other potential entrants: its ability to sell Amazon-published books at book retailers Amazon does not own is very limited. Trial Tr. 171:17–23 (Pietsch) (Amazon's ability to sell books via other retail channels, such as chain stores, independent books stores, Target, and Walmart is "extremely limited"); PX-2000 at 36–37 (Zacharius Dep. 142:22–143:24); PX-2002 at 99–101 (Stehlik Dep. 199:10–201:19).

189. Today, Amazon's competitive significance remains limited. As several industry participants testified, it is not a significant competitor, particularly for anticipated top-selling books. Trial Tr. 170:23–173:6 (Pietsch); PX-2005 at 43–44 (Jacobs Dep. 158:14–159:4); PX- 2002 at 33–34 (Stehlik Dep. 80:25–81:3) (Amazon is not a competitor for HarperCollins for the acquisition of books); Trial Tr. 1433:4–17 (Murray) (HarperCollins has not competed against Amazon for "big books"); Trial Tr. 1107:4–8 (Weisberg); DX-422 at 28 (Glusman Dep. 102:14–20); DX-422 at 70 (Glusman Dep. 219:6–11, 219:16–18) (Norton does not view Amazon or Audible as a competitor; cannot recall Amazon being part of any of Norton's auctions; that would be "highly unusual"). Agents also testified that they rarely sell books to Amazon. PX- 2007 at 23–24 (Fletcher Dep. 55:20–56:10) (Ms. Fletcher has only sold one book to Amazon publishing and does not regularly submit to Amazon); Trial Tr. 2144:22–24 (Ross) (Ms. Ross did not sell the publishing rights to any book to Amazon between 2018 and 2021); Trial Tr. 2079:17–22 (Cheney) (Ms. Cheney has never sold a print deal to Amazon). In fact, Amazon's share in the relevant market was [REDACTED] in 2021. [REDACTED] Trial Tr. 1486:3–11 (Hill). And Amazon's sharE [REDACTED]

6. Other Recent Entrants Have Made Little Headway

190. Defendants mostly point to three companies as examples of new entrants who have had success in

publishing anticipated top-selling books: Spiegel & Grau, Zando, and Astra. Spiegel & Grau and Zando are small publishers started recently by former PRH editors and do not have a backlist. Trial Tr. 756:7–757:1 (Dohle); Trial Tr. 2388:9–17 (McIntosh). Astra is a small publisher owned by Thinkingdom Media Group. Trial Tr. 556:15–20 (Karp). Despite these individual editors' impressive professional successes in prior roles, these potential entrants have made little headway. Their share in the market is, collectively, [REDACTED] and there is no evidence that they compete with the merging parties with any degree of frequency. *See* PX-2002 at 29–30 (Stehlik Dep. 76:12–77:4) (unaware of any instances in which Morrow competed with Zando or S&G); Trial Tr. 249:20–250:9 (Pande) (Pande typically does not include S&G, Zando, or Astra in her submissions because "these publishers are still too new to have really proven themselves"); Trial Tr. 552:21–557:3 (Karp) (unable to identify any blockbuster books published by Zando or Astra; when asked about Astra: "I don't know about their track record"; identified only one instance in which S&S competed with S&G and none for Zando or Astra); PX-790 [REDACTED] DX-422 at 60 (Glusman Dep. 182:16–18) (Astra is not a significant competitor); DX-422 at 66 (Glusman Dep. 188:1–4, 188:20–22) (S&G and Zando are not significant competitors); Trial Tr. 1380:17–1381:8 (Murray) (startup publishers can "buy a book or two, but in the main, I don't think they are a competitor"). In fact, even Dr. Snyder acknowledged that Astra is not a "major competitive constraint." Trial Tr. 2953:4–9 (Snyder).

7. *Dr. Snyder's Analysis of Entry and Expansion Is Unpersuasive*

191. Defendants' expert attempted to create several analyses suggesting that entry and expansion are likely here. None are persuasive.

192. Dr. Snyder testified that a group of publishers are "operating just below the 250,000 threshold" and "have the potential to move into the 250-plus category." Trial Tr. 2694:24–2695:2 (Snyder). But placing this evidence in context shows that this group is unlikely to meaningfully constrain the merged firm. Of the 21 publishers identified in Dr. Snyder's report who had won a book for an advance between $100,000 and $250,000, 75% have never won a book for more than $175,000, and only one has ever won a book for more than $225,000. Trial Tr. 3076:9–3077:8 (Hill).

193. Second, Dr. Snyder collected data showing that a select group of non-Big Five publishers grew, to some extent, in the proposed market between 2019 and 2021. *See* Trial Tr. 1482:15–22 (Hill). But, as Dr. Hill explained, this growth was almost entirely offset by a decline by other non-Big Five publishers, leaving the collective market share of non-Big Five publishers essentially unchanged. Trial Tr. 1482:15–1483:17 (Hill); Trial Tr. 3082:5–3083:6 (Hill); PX- 977 at 1; PX-967 at 1; PX-994 at 1. And, of course, none grew to the point where their share even approaches that of any of the Big Five. *See* PX-959 at 1. The fact that a few non-Big Five publishers grew a small amount, while others shrunk by a similar amount, evidences churn amongst the non-Big Five publishers but fails to show that significant expansion by the non-Big Five is possible. *See Anthem,* 236 F. Supp. 3d at 224 (rejecting Defendants' argument that growth by 32 small entrants showed entry was timely, likely, and sufficient, noting that only one had attained a double-digit market share, while others lost share).

194. Similarly, Dr. Snyder testified that the number of publishers who have acquired anticipated top sellers has increased from 2019 to 2021. Trial Tr. 2684:10–19 (Snyder). But merely counting the number of firms in the market is rarely relevant to antitrust analysis without considering other measures of their competitive significance. *Cf. H & R Block,* 833 F. Supp. 2d at 50 (stating that 10% of the market was "divided amongst a plethora of smaller companies"). Instead, as Dr. Hill explained, the market shares of non-Big Five publishers is more informative than their number. Trial Tr. 3083:7–20 (Hill). And those market shares, when aggregated, remained flat from 2019 to 2021. PX-994 at 1. Indeed, the competitive significance (here, average market share) of any given publisher within that group may actually have decreased if, in fact, the number of firms acquiring anticipated top sellers increased as Dr. Snyder alleged. Trial Tr. 3083:7–20 (Hill).

195. Finally, some of Dr. Snyder's testimony about expansion appears to reflect a misunderstanding of the record. Dr. Snyder at first highlighted Chronicle as his most notable example of a small publisher that has expanded significantly; he testified that he thought that Chronicle has tripled its spending on advances in recent years. Trial Tr. 2695:9–23 (Snyder) (referring to Chronicle); Trial Tr. 2945:10–18 (Snyder) (Chronicle is "moving forward . . . I think the evidence was that they were tripling advances."); Trial Tr. 2953:22–25 (Snyder) (similar); *see also* Trial Tr. at 2943:24–2955:9 (Snyder). But Dr. Snyder later acknowledged that his testimony was based on a misunderstanding of the record. In fact, his opinion was based on deposition testimony from an executive from a different (and much smaller) publisher, Blackstone. Trial Tr. 2953:18–2954:13 (Snyder).

196. In addition, the argument that post-merger competition from the remaining Big Four will suffice to prevent the harm is inconsistent with the law. Courts have enjoined mergers even where the merging parties are not the two only—or even the main two—competitors. For example, in *Anthem,* the court enjoined a merger of a firm with a 40% share and a competitor with an 8% share based on the reasoning that the merger would eliminate a significant amount of head-to-head competition between the two firms. *See Anthem,* 236 F. Supp. 3d at 208 (market shares); *see also id.* at 216–221 (unilateral effects analysis). The fact that other strong competitors existed—including another competitor that was the "closest" competitor for at least one of the firms—was beside the point, because competition between the merging parties was significant. *See id.* at 216–221. In addition, as the court found, "reducing the number of national [competitors] from four to three is significant." *Id.* at 220.

197. Similarly, in *Swedish Match,* the court found that the existence of two remaining large competitors was not enough to prevent the harm from the merger because "a unilateral price increase . . . is likely after the acquisition because it will eliminate one of Swedish Match's primary direct competitors." 131 F. Supp. 2d at 169. And several other cases have similarly enjoined mergers, despite the existence of continued competition from two or three large competitors, based on the conclusion that unilateral and/or coordinated effects are likely when a merger unites a firm with one of its most important rivals. *See, e.g., Hackensack Meridian Health,* 30 F.4th at 172–174 (enjoining merger based on unilateral effects theory where merging parties had post-merger market share of 47% and at least two other non-party hospitals remained in the market); *Elders Grain,* 868 F.2d at 902–903, 905 (reducing number of competitors from six to five "will make it easier for leading members of the industry to collude on price and output"); *Hosp. Corp.,* 807 F.2d at 1384 (enjoining merger where, after the merger, the four largest firms would have held a combined market share of ~90%); *Tronox,* 332 F. Supp. 3d at 194–195, 207–210 (enjoining five-to-four merger).

D. Defendants' Purported Efficiencies Are Not Verifiable and Cannot Rebut the Presumption of Harm

198. On July 8, 2022, the United States filed a Motion *in Limine* pursuant to Federal Rule of Evidence 702 to exclude testimony by Dr. Snyder regarding efficiencies. Dkt. 97. During the July 25, 2022 argument on the motion, Defendants argued that the Court needed to hear evidence about the projection of synergies in a financial model on which Dr. Snyder based his testimony before making an evaluation of Defendants' efficiencies claim. Final Pretrial Conference Tr. 47:23–48:14. The Court instructed the parties to arrange the presentation of evidence during trial so that the projected synergies' verifiability could be considered and argued before hearing the totality of Dr. Snyder's expert testimony on efficiencies. Final Pretrial Conference Tr. 60:22–61:4; Trial Tr. 2751:4–10. The Court determined that it would be more efficient to proceed in this fashion because if Defendants were unable to meet their burden to show that the efficiencies were substantiated, verifiable, and verified under the Merger Guidelines, then it would be unnecessary to consider any of the other aspects of the efficiencies evidence. Trial Tr. 2751:11–16. After hearing the testimony of the financial model's author, PRH's Senior Vice President of M&A Manuel Sansigre, the Court found that Defendants failed to establish that the projected efficiencies relied upon by Dr. Snyder are substantiated, and failed to show that those projected efficiencies are reasonably verifiable by an independent party or that the projected efficiencies are, in fact, verified. Trial Tr. 2749:13–2772:19. The Court granted the United States' Motion *in Limine* and excluded Defendants' efficiencies evidence. Trial Tr. 2770:20–2771:4; Trial Tr. 2772:17–19.

E. Literary Agents Cannot Counteract the Likely Anticompetitive Effects of the Proposed Merger

199. The record does not support Defendants' assertion that the skill and power of agents will rebut the potential for harm from the merger. Instead, the record is replete with evidence showing that agents will not have sufficient bargaining leverage to eliminate the harm that this merger likely will cause. *See generally* Trial Tr. 1491:3–19 (Hill); *cf.* Trial Tr. 338:13–25 (King) (agents cannot maintain competition after the merger because "there are only so many shops").

1. *"Sophisticated Seller" Is No Defense*

200. It is no defense that some authors may be represented by sophisticated agents in negotiations. As a legal matter, courts "have not considered the 'sophisticated [seller]' defense as itself independently adequate to rebut a prima facie case" and view "the economic argument for even partially rebutting a presumptive case, because a market is dominated by large [sellers]," as "weak." *Chicago Bridge,* 534 F.3d at 440; *see also Anthem,* 236 F. Supp. 3d at 221; *cf. Phila. Nat'l Bank,* 374 U.S. at 370 (rejecting "the concept of 'countervailing power'" where defendants claimed that a merger would enable competition with

other banks).

201. The mere "presence of some large sophisticated [sellers]" is not sufficient to defend against anticompetitive harm. *Cardinal Health,* 12 F. Supp. 2d at 58 ("courts have not yet found that power buyers alone enable a defendant to overcome the government's presumption of anti-competitiveness" in Section 7 cases). Defendants must show not only the existence of powerful authors or agents, but also that these authors or agents can "counteract" anticompetitive harms to the market. *See Anthem,* 236 F. Supp. 3d at 221.

202. In *Anthem,* the court rejected the defendants' argument that some customers could push back against anticompetitive harm, even though those customers were "typically sophisticated companies with substantial resources," which "benefit[ed] from the assistance and advice of brokers and consultants" (similar to the roles agents play for authors) during the negotiation process. *Anthem,* 236 F. Supp. 3d at 221. The evidence in this case likewise indicates that the "loss of one competitor" would "alter[]" the "negotiating dynamic, even with strong advocates on the other side." *Id.*

203. As in *Anthem,* the "loss of leverage" authors and agents will suffer as a result of the merger "undermines the defense contention that [these authors and agents] will be able to . . . counteract the anticompetitive effects of the merger." *Id.* There is limited evidence that individual authors and agents possess sufficient market power to counter harm resulting from the combined entity at all—much less that these authors and agents can offset harms to competition as a whole. An example demonstrates the real power dynamic at play: as discussed more fully below *infra* V.E.6, even a high-profile agent such as Mr. Wylie was unable to withstand Random House's market power. After attempting to publish e-books with Amazon through an endeavor called "Odyssey Editions," Random House announced in *The New York Times* it would not do business with Mr. Wylie. Trial Tr. 2103:6–9 (Wylie). As a result, Mr. Wylie met with Mr. Dohle. Trial Tr. 2103:14–18 (Wylie). After this meeting, Mr. Wylie pulled his Odyssey Editions books from Amazon, and Random House received the digital rights for the books for which it already had the print rights. Trial Tr. 2104:5–2104:12 (Wylie).

2. The Agency Landscape Is Fragmented

204. The fragmentation of the agency landscape also undercuts Defendants' optimistic prediction of agent power. The cases involving a "power buyer" defense usually involve an industry where a small number of buyers have a large market share. *See Cardinal Health,* 12 F. Supp. 2d at 59 (discussing cases). That is not the case here. To the contrary, the literary agency segment is unconcentrated. *See* PX-151 at 5 ("Agent landscape fragmented with a few big agencies, but large number of small players. . . ."). This fact undercuts Defendants' claim that agents' bargaining leverage will suffice to prevent the harm from the merger. The experience of the agents Defendants called to the stand represent examples of the fragmented agent landscape. They accounted for a very small proportion of the approximately 4,800 book contracts that would occur over a 4-year period given that there are approximately 1,200 anticipated top selling books acquired per year. *See* PX-838 at 2–4 (Ross listed approximately [REDACTED] deals during 2018–2021); PX-749 at 1–4 (Cheney listed [REDACTED] deals during 2018–2021); PX-857 at 16–18 (Wylie listed [REDACTED] deals during 2018–2021).

3. Margin and Bargaining Evidence Shows That Agents' Leverage Is Limited

205. The record also shows that, even in the pre-merger world, agents' leverage is limited. As Dr. Hill explained, publishers' margins are fairly significant. Trial Tr. 1491:20–1492:8 (Hill). If agents held all of the bargaining leverage, one would expect that agents would capture almost all of the publishers' margins. Trial Tr. 1491:20–1492:8 (Hill). The fact that this does not happen undermines Defendants' prediction that, post-merger, agents will suddenly be empowered to exercise more influence and power than they have historically. Indeed, even Dr. Snyder agreed that literary agents are not omnipotent, explaining that agents would not be able to overcome harm to authors from a hypothetical monopsonist publisher. Trial Tr. 2933:24–2934:7 (Snyder).

206. Relatedly, publishers often acquire books for less than they were willing to pay. *See* Trial Tr. 2006:19–2007:3 (Kim); Trial Tr. 1491:20–1492:8 (Hill); Trial Tr. 1844:19–2 (Bergstrom); Trial Tr. 2678:13–15 (Snyder) ("There are situations, yes, where an imprint gets a book for less than the maximum willingness to pay."); *see also* Trial Tr. 1758:1–13 (Walsh) (agents do not know if obtained what publisher was willing to pay). For example, in one auction, PRH (Putnam) employees asked for clearance to bid up to $350,000 but ultimately won the book for $275,000. Trial Tr. 2009:3–2010:3 (Kim); PX-42 at 1, 3; *see also* Trial Tr. 1492:9–1493:3 (Hill) (summarizing example where publisher was approved to offer $500,000 but acquired the title for $350,000). This, too, suggests that there are limits to agents' power. If agents held all of the cards, they would always or almost always push

publishers to spend the maximum amount of money that they are willing to spend. *See* Trial Tr. 1492:5–8 (Hill).

207. Agent witnesses and Dr. Snyder also concede that agents cannot force editors to bid or increase their maximum bid. *See* Trial Tr. 2934:6–2935:10 (Snyder); Trial Tr. 1875:17–19 (Bergstrom). And Ayesha Pande testified that there is nothing she can do to control the number of editors who express interest in a book, how many editors make an offer to acquire a book, or how much an editor offers to acquire a book. Trial Tr. 251:12–20 (Pande); *see also* Trial Tr. 1826:21–24 (Walsh) (agreeing that agents can't control what a publisher chooses to bid on a book).

208. For PRH in particular, its outsized presence requires literary agents to deal with its editors. Ayesha Pande testified that she "always" submits books to more than one editor at PRH because they have so many imprints. Trial Tr. 251:12–20 (Pande). Ms. Pande testified that she would not be able to discipline PRH by refusing to submit projects to any of their editors because "I don't believe I would be doing my clients any favors by not submitting to Penguin Random House when on average they make up approximately 30 or so percent of my submissions. So leaving them out would really shrink the possibilities." Trial Tr. 250:10–251:3 (Pande).

4. Agents Do Not Have the Leverage to Hold Back Audio Rights

209. Publisher treatment of audio rights over time provides an instructive example of relative bargaining power between large publishers and literary agents. Agents would often prefer to sell print rights (*i.e.,* the rights to publish a print book) to one publisher and audio rights to another publisher. Ayesha Pande explained that she would always prefer to sell audio rights separately from print rights because if she sells both to the same publisher, "any revenues from those [audio] rights will only come to my client after the entire advance earns out." Trial Tr. 257:21–258:2 (Pande). But if an agent can separately sell audio rights to an audio publisher, the agent can "provide a separate income stream directly to" the client. Trial Tr. 258:3–6 (Pande); *see also* Trial Tr. 622:20–22 (Karp) (agents sometimes ask S&S to buy a book without also acquiring audio rights). PRH and S&S both have a policy of always, or almost always, refusing to acquire a book without also acquiring audio rights. Trial Tr. 622:17–19 (Karp); PX-328 at 1 ("For at least the last five years, but more likely the last ten years, we have bought everything with Audio."); Trial Tr. 1876:5–6 (Bergstrom). Agents do not have the leverage to force the merging parties to abandon this position in favor of authors. To the contrary, as Mr. Tart explained in an internal email, PRH "turned down big book after big book until agents realized we would not play in an auction without Audio. And now they always sell us audio." PX-328 at 1–2. PRH's unwillingness to bid for titles unless audio rights are included in the sale shows that PRH, not agents, have leverage over these valuable rights.

210. In a recent auction over a highly-sought after book, [REDACTED], an agent's attempt to hold back audio rights from the bundle of rights offered to publishers quickly failed. An S&S editor described the project as "a book we would all love to publish, but I hope we will walk away if audio rights are not part of the deal." PX-652 at 2. Without audio rights, S&S declined to bid, with one S&S executive commenting: "It will be very interesting to see whether PRH, Hachette, Harper or Macmillan participate. MY understanding is that they too have the 'no audio, no deal' rule." PX-652 at 2. The strategy to hold to the industry line succeeded. After initially excluding the audio rights from the auction, the agent for this title restarted the auction with audio rights included. *See* PX-568 at 1–2; Trial Tr. 625:21–626:6 (Karp); *see also* PX-320 at 1 (PRH editor suggesting that the agent probably restructured the auction because everyone bid on audio). Both S&S and PRH bid on the project, with PRH making the winning bid of [REDACTED] PX-944-B at 1.

5. Agents Could Not Prevent Disadvantageous Shifts in Author Payout Structures

211. Just as with audio rights, agents have not had the leverage to prevent publishers from paying authors in smaller increments over longer periods of time. Authors used to receive advances in two installments—half on signing of the contract and half on the delivery and acceptance of the book (*i.e.,* before it is published). Trial Tr. 1828:19–1829:1 (Walsh). Over time, publishers worsened the deal they offered their authors. First, they changed to a three- payment structure, and now to a four-payment (quarters) structure, under which the publisher makes the fourth payment a year after the book is published. Trial Tr. 1829:2–18 (Walsh); *see also* Trial Tr. 254:25–255:3 (Pande); Trial Tr. 256:22–25 (Pande); PX-862 at 7 (describing PRH's adult books payout guidelines). Ayesha Pande explained that now it can take three to four years for an author to receive her entire advance. Trial Tr. 255:15–18 (Pande). [REDACTED] Despite that, she could not recall a specific example where she was able to negotiate a payout with PRH that was not in quarters. PX-2007 at 32 (Fletcher Dep. 74:9–12, 14).

6. *Agents Could Not Improve Digital Rights—Odyssey Editions*

212. Finally, the history of Mr. Wylie's failed "Odyssey Editions" project further confirms the limitations on agents' leverage. In 2010, Mr. Wylie tried to convince Random House to raise the e-book royalty rate from 25%. Trial Tr. 2101:21–2102:9 (Wylie). He failed. Trial Tr. 2102:10–12 (Wylie). Mr. Wylie then turned to Amazon with his Odyssey Editions project, in which Amazon would be the exclusive e-book distributor of twenty books; Random House held the print rights for many of these titles. Trial Tr. 2101:18–2103:5 (Wylie). Under this proposed plan, authors would have received 100% of the digital royalties for Odyssey Edition e-books (less a commission paid to the Wylie Agency). Trial Tr. 2103:2–5 (Wylie). In response to the launch of Odyssey Editions, Random House announced in *The New York Times* that it would not do business with Mr. Wylie, blackballing him. Trial Tr. 2103:6–9 (Wylie). As a result, Mr. Wylie met with Mr. Dohle. Trial Tr. 2103:14–18 (Wylie). After this meeting, Mr. Wylie pulled his Odyssey Editions books from Amazon, and Random House obtained the digital rights for the books for which it already had the print rights. Trial Tr. 2104:5–12 (Wylie). Today, Penguin Random House continues to offer a digital royalty rate of only 25%—a rate that Mr. Wylie described as unfair. Trial Tr. 2104:16–2105:5 (Wylie).

F. Intra-Publisher Competition Does Not Rebut the Presumption of the Harm from the Merger

1. *Intra-Firm Competition Is Legally Irrelevant*

213. The law assumes that a corporation's wholly-owned subsidiaries and divisions pursue "the common interests of the whole" and categorically rejects arguments that individual units of a corporation are "separate economic actors, pursuing separate economic interests." *Copperweld Corp. v. Indep. Tube Corp.,* 467 U.S. 752, 769–70 (1984). Rather, a corporation and its division or wholly-owned subsidiary "have a complete unity of interest. Their objectives are common, not disparate; their general corporate actions are guided or determined not by two separate corporate consciousnesses, but one." *Id.* at 771; *see also* Phillip E. Areeda & Herbert Hovenkamp, *Antitrust Law: An Analysis of Antitrust Principles and Their Application* ¶ 964b (5th ed. 2022) ("Antitrust generally presumes that a firm maximizes its profits in the environment in which it finds itself. . . ."). "They share a common purpose whether or not the parent keeps a tight rein over the subsidiary; the parent may assert full control at any moment if the subsidiary fails to act in the parent's best interests." *Copperweld,* 467 U.S. at 771–772.

214. Defendants cite no case where a Court has approved a merger based on a claim that defendants permit its subsidiaries to compete with each other. Indeed, courts have rejected such commitments as potential remedies in merger cases. *See, e.g., St. Alphonsus Med. Ctr. v. St. Luke's Health Sys.,* 778 F.3d 775, 793 (9th Cir. 2015) (holding that district court did not abuse discretion when choosing a divestiture remedy instead of defendants' proposal to establish "separate bargaining units to negotiate with insurers"); *Promedica Health Sys., Inc. v. FTC,* 749 F.3d 559, 572–73 (6th Cir. 2014) (discussing the FTC's disfavor towards behavioral or conduct remedies; affirming FTC's divestitures; rejecting the merging parties' proposal to form separate negotiating teams for each merging hospital to negotiate with insurers). Even if intra-publisher competitive bidding were relevant, it is insufficient to counteract the presumption because it is: (1) revocable or alterable at any time for any reason; and (2) predicated upon a number of operational and logistical choices, discussed below, that only PRH controls. There would be no legal or factual impediment to changing, sidestepping, ignoring, or revoking the promise and so the Court cannot assume that any such bidding, even if relevant, would continue or be genuine.

2. *Even if Intra-Firm Competition Was Legally Relevant, Defendants Cannot Show That It Will Eliminate the Harm Caused by the Merger*

215. In addition, as a factual matter, Defendants cannot show that intra-publisher competition will eliminate the harm caused by the merger. While some imprints are allowed to bid separately in some situations, this competition will not suffice to prevent the harm the merger may likely cause, for a variety of reasons.

216. A publisher has an economic incentive to limit competition among its imprints that would drive up the publisher's costs. Trial Tr. 1494:24–1495:14 (Hill) (discussing the deposition testimony of PRH's President of Crown Publishing Group; "because ultimately we are the same company so, frankly, we would just be driving up the price of an auction amongst ourselves. So this is summarizing the incentive to try to limit competition when the competition is just down to Penguin Random House imprints."); *see generally* Trial Tr. 1494:24–1495:14 (Hill) (discussing publisher incentives to avoid competitive intra-publisher competition).

217. If a PRH imprint loses a book to another PRH imprint, PRH still retains any profit the book earns. Trial

Tr. 3069:21–3070:7 (Hill). But if a PRH imprint loses a book to an external publisher, PRH loses the entire profit for that book. Trial Tr. 3069:21–3070:7 (Hill). That gives PRH imprints an incentive to compete less aggressively with each other than with external publishers. *See* Trial Tr. 3068:21–3070:7 (Hill).

218. Consistent with these incentives, publishers limit competition among imprints in several ways:

a. Publishers Place Formal Limits on Intra-Publisher Bidding

219. First, publishers place formal limits on the extent to which imprints can bid independently. S&S and HarperCollins do not allow imprints to bid separately for the same book; they all bid together. *See* Trial Tr. 463:11–13 (Karp); PX-2002 at 75–76 (Stehlik Dep. 169:24–170:2, 170:4–6, 170:8–20). By contrast, Hachette allows its imprints to bid independently, but only when a non-Hachette publisher is also bidding; when the only remaining imprints in an auction are from Hachette, they do not bid independently. Trial Tr. 239:11–23 (Pietsch).

220. PRH follows a similar policy to Hachette: it allows imprints from different divisions—the Penguin, Random House, and Knopf Doubleday divisions—to bid independently when other publishers are also competing, but not when they are the only remaining bidders. *See* PX-332 at 1–2; Trial Tr. 943:3–18 (Tart); Trial Tr. 2331:21–25 (McIntosh). Once they are the only remaining bidders, the bidding stops and does not replicate the bidding that takes place between independently competing publishers.

b. PRH's Imprints Coordinate Their Bids to Avoid Real Competition

221. Second, internal coordination among imprints—which is expressly contemplated and permitted pursuant to *Copperweld*—can limit competition between them even in situations where PRH's claimed internal competition policy permits them to continue bidding. A board presentation prepared by Ms. McIntosh makes this point explicitly, noting that PRH had "increased background coordination in auctions to . . . avoid internal up-bidding." PX-411 at 4; Trial Tr. 2372:17–2373:8 (McIntosh). Consistent with Ms. McIntosh's presentation, the record includes several examples of intra-PRH coordination. For example, when PRH author [REDACTED] sought bids

222. from multiple PRH divisions—including Knopf Doubleday and Random House (which under PRH's claimed internal policies are supposed to bid separately)—Ms. McIntosh asked them to "coordinate," adding that PRH "shouldn't be forced into bidding against each other for existing authors." PX-107 at 1. One of her direct reports reached out to both divisions and ensured that they followed Ms. McIntosh's instructions, noting: "We are coordinated. Bill [Random House] and Kara [Knopf Doubleday] will agree to a number and both offer same." PX-107 at 1; *see also* Trial Tr. 2373:25–2376:6 (McIntosh). Similarly, in another situation, when PRH thought it was the "main driver of value" in an auction, Knopf Doubleday and Crown (which at that time was an independent PRH division) "agree[d] to move up slowly." PX-336 at 2; *see also* Trial Tr. 1051:12–1054:21 (Tart) (describing bidding for the book discussed in PX-336 and agreeing that PRH divisions can coordinate on bids). This would constitute price-fixing if done by separate firms. Because PRH divisions are all owned by one company, however, such conduct is legal. But it undercuts the argument that imprints amount to independent competitors.

c. Publishers Take Additional Steps to Avoid Intra-Publisher Competition

223. Third, publishers can also take other steps to reduce internal publisher competition, even when they allow their imprints to bid separately. They can, for example, instruct imprints to focus on acquiring different types of books, reduce the title count or restrict acquisition budgets of particular imprints, fire editors, or just informally instruct the leaders of imprints not to bid too aggressively against each other. *See* DX-71 at 2 (Karp tells S&S publishers "Collegiality matters more than internal competition. We will thank and honor editors who defer to more enthusiastic colleagues [REDACTED] Try to bail out on submissions in which there are more than two imprints in the building pursuing the project [REDACTED] ");

224. The most notable example of this relates to PRH's internal merger of the Random House and Crown divisions. Prior to that internal reorganization, Crown and Ballantine Bantam Dell (which is part of the Random House division) had both published fiction and non-fiction books. After the merger, however, PRH instructed Ballantine Bantam Dell to focus on fiction and told Crown to focus on non-fiction. PX-241 at 2–3. According to an internal PRH analysis, this would result in "less internal competition" even though (at the time) Ballantine Bantam Dell and Crown were allowed to continue to bid separately. PX-241 at 3.anticompetitive effects. At first, Dr. Snyder suggested that Ms. McIntosh's efforts to limit imprint competition wouldn't "materially affect the extent of imprint competition." Trial Tr. 3001:25–3002:6 (Snyder). He then stated that coordination across imprints in best-bid auctions "would be a very

sharp departure" from current practice, Trial Tr. 3003:25–3004:1 (Snyder), despite evidence that such coordination occurs in best-bid auctions today, Trial Tr. 3069:6–20 (Hill). Ultimately, Dr. Snyder conceded that PRH's current efforts to coordinate bids "could have an effect in some situations, based on what I'm hearing this morning." Trial Tr. 3004:11–12 (Snyder).

d. Imprint "Competition" Does Not Likely Lead to Increased Author Compensation

225. Whatever imprint competition that exists after publishers' limitations likely does not generate higher author compensation. Dr. Hill testified that "[i]f there is a tremendous amount of competition because of the large number of imprints, we'd expect to see very low margins." Trial Tr. 3100:25–3101:2 (Hill). Yet PRH earns a healthy margin, Trial Tr. 781:3–5 (Dohle); Trial Tr. 1492:2–3 (Hill), which suggests that competition among the dozens of PRH imprints is not equivalent to competition among independent bidders and does not materially increase author compensation.

226. Similarly, Mr. Karp, who has worked at S&S, Hachette, and Random House, *see* Trial Tr. 415:2–11 (Karp), testified that intra-firm competition rarely drives up the advance for a book. Trial Tr. 463:22–464:6 (Karp). He further testified, "I don't believe that internal competition has any effect on what we ultimately offer." Trial Tr. 600:5–7 (Karp). For all these reasons, Defendants cannot show that intra-firm competition will meaningfully mitigate the harm caused by the merger.

G. Mr. Dohle's Unenforceable Letter Does Not Rebut the Presumption

1. Promises to Not Use Acquired Market Power Are Legally Insufficient

227. A revocable behavioral promise cannot rebut a prima facie case. The Clayton Act prohibits attaining market power by acquisition without requiring a specific showing that the dominant merged firm intends to exercise that market power. *See Phila. Nat'l Bank,* 374 U.S. at 362–63; *Hosp. Corp.,* 807 F.2d at 1389 (proof of higher prices is not required); *see also Heinz,* 246 F.3d at 719.

228. Courts have consistently rejected promises by merging parties not to exercise their acquired market power in merger cases such as this. *See St. Luke's Health Sys.,* 788 F.3d at 793; *ProMedica Health Sys.,* 749 F.3d at 573; *H & R Block,* 833 F. Supp. 2d at 82 ("While the Court has no reason to doubt that defendants would honor their promise [to maintain the acquired firm's current prices for three years post-merger], this type of guarantee cannot rebut a likelihood of anticompetitive effects in this case."); *Cardinal Health,* 12 F. Supp. 2d at 64. When a corporation states an intention to maintain an acquired entity as separate and permit them to continue to function in the future as they had been doing, "[t]here can be little, if any, reliance upon the statement in the face of well-known tendencies of human conduct." *Pennzoil Co.,* 252 F. Supp. at 984. Further, an action that a defendant takes during the pendency of an investigation into their acquisition should be viewed with skepticism, especially when it may have been made to improve their litigating position. *Cf. Hosp. Corp.,* 807 F.2d at 1384 ("Post-acquisition evidence that is subject to manipulation by the party seeking to use it is entitled to little or no weight."). The fact that Defendants are willing to make such a promise "strongly supports the fears" of anticompetitive effects. *Cardinal Health,* 12 F. Supp. 2d at 67.

229. Even if viewed as a self-help remedy for the anticompetitive effects of the merger, the announced bidding policy is not the type of unilateral remedy that courts might consider, as it does not change or affect the acquisition at issue. *See, e.g., FTC v. Libbey, Inc.,* 211 F. Supp. 2d 34, 45–46 (D.D.C. 2002) (finding that an amended acquisition agreement that "supercede[d] and nullifie[d]" the original merger agreement "becomes the new agreement that the Court must evaluate in deciding whether an injunction should be issued.").

2. Mr. Dohle's Unenforceable Letter Fails to Rebut or Offset the Harm from Defendants' Merger

230. The factual record in this case supports the conclusion that Mr. Dohle's unilateral, revocable promise should be given no weight. Mr. Dohle's letter is neither binding nor legally enforceable. *See, e.g.,* Trial Tr. 770:5–8 (Dohle). If PRH violates the terms of the letter, agents and authors would have no formal recourse or enforcement mechanism. In addition, Mr. Dohle, his successor, or his superiors could rescind or modify the promise at any time for any reason, including self-serving ones or rationales based on demands of corporate leadership and PRH's owners. Trial Tr. 770:13–21 (Dohle).

231. The letter also has limited application. By its terms, it applies only to auctions, DX-236 at 1; Trial Tr. 771:11–25 (Dohle)—a puzzling omission given that Defendants frequently argue in other aspects of this litigation that many or most books are acquired outside of auctions.

232. In addition, the letter's promise can be sidestepped. PRH can take a variety of measures to reduce intra-firm competition without violating the promise even when permitting S&S legacy imprints to bid

independently. *See supra* V.F.2.b. For example, Mr. Dohle's letter does not stop PRH from simply instructing PRH and/or S&S imprints to refocus on categories of books that would reduce potential competition with their sister imprints (as it did after the Crown/Random House merger). *See* Trial Tr. 767:24–768:19 (Dohle); *supra* V.F.2.c. Nor does it stop PRH from reducing competition through a variety of other means, like closing imprints, reducing title count, or just informally discouraging intense intra-firm competition. *See* Trial Tr. 765:24–766:2 (Dohle); Trial Tr. 767:24–768:19 (Dohle). And PRH's history of allowing coordination among PRH imprints—even when those imprints are supposed to bid independently—also casts doubt on the effectiveness of Mr. Dohle's promise. *See supra* V.F.2.b.

233. Defendants' promise is further suspect because it initially arose at the end of the government's pre-Complaint investigation and is related to the current litigation. While Defendants initially tried to suggest otherwise, *see* Dkt. 104 at 2 (Defendants' Opposition to United States' Motion *In Limine* To Preclude Evidence of Penguin Random House's Announced Bidding Policy) ("PRH announced the policy . . . without even knowing whether the merger would be challenged."), Defendants' explanation is not credible. An earlier version of the promise was announced less than a month before the United States filed this lawsuit, during a period of time when PRH and S&S were working to convince the government not to file its lawsuit. *See* Dkt. 104 at 3–4 (Defendants' Opposition to United States' Motion *In Limine* To Preclude Evidence of Penguin Random House's Announced Bidding Policy). Mr. Dohle's letter itself was released during the pending litigation. DX-236 at 1. Moreover, Mr. Dohle conceded that he made the promise because agents were concerned about the proposed merger. Trial Tr. 770:1–4 (Dohle). Accordingly, skepticism of the promise is appropriate. *Cf. Hosp. Corp.,* 807 F.2d at 1384 ("Post-acquisition evidence that is subject to manipulation by the party seeking to use it is entitled to little or no weight.").

H. Defendants' Intent Is Irrelevant

234. Defendants' assertion that they do not intend to lower author compensation if this merger is consummated is legally irrelevant. The United States is not required to prove bad intent, so a counterargument suggesting salutary intent does not advance analysis of this proposed merger.

235. "It is not requisite to the proof of a violation of § 7 to show that restraint or monopoly was intended." *E. I. du Pont de Nemours,* 353 U.S. at 607 *accord United States v. Bazaarvoice, Inc.,* 2014 WL 203966, at *11 (N.D. Cal. Jan. 8, 2014) ("[I]ntent is not an element of a Section 7 violation"). Rather, Section 7 prohibits any acquisition whose "*effect* . . . may be substantially to lessen competition." 15 U.S.C. § 18 (emphasis added). Thus, a proposed acquisition that, as here, "is reasonably likely to cause anticompetitive effects" is unlawful, *H & R Block,* 833 F. Supp. 2d at 49 (quotation marks omitted), irrespective of the parties' intent.

I. Defendants' Attempt to Gain Market Share Through the Merger Does Not Rebut—and Actually Reinforces—the Presumption Against the Merger

236. Defendants seek to justify their merger by proffering that they are merely seeking to gain market share. Trial Tr. 741:17–23 (Dohle); Trial Tr. 876:25–877:2 (Dohle) ("We are basically paying $2.2 billion to actually replace our lost market share in this case."). But the structural presumption exists because acquiring market share of the size of PRH's proposed acquisition of S&S is likely to reduce competition. *See Phila. Nat'l Bank,* 374 U.S. at 363 (describing mergers "which produce[] a firm controlling an undue percentage share of the relevant market" as "inherently suspect" under Section 7).

237. The law contemplates that companies grow by competing in the market and winning additional business through the provision of superior goods and services. As the Supreme Court explained, "one premise of an antimerger statute such as § 7 is that corporate growth by internal expansion is socially preferable to growth by acquisition." *Phila. Nat'l Bank,* 374 U.S. at 370. This preference protects consumers from anticompetitive harm because "expansion through merger," as compared to expansion via internal growth, "is more likely to reduce available consumer choice while providing no increase in industry capacity, jobs or output." *Brown Shoe,* 370 U.S. at 345 n.72; *see also Hiland Dairy, Inc. v. Kroger Co.,* 402 F.2d 968, 975–76 (8th Cir. 1968) ("As a general proposition internal expansion is preferable to growth by merger or purchase"). Bertelsmann's strategy to "refill [its] market share" after losing market share to its competitors therefore underscores the dangers of the proposed merger. Rather than competing with its rivals to gain market share, PRH has chosen to buy its close competitor and eliminate competition that benefits authors. *See* Trial Tr. 741:17–742:4 (Dohle); Trial Tr. 802:12–18 (Dohle). That rationale is not a valid defense.

J. The Effects of the 2013 Merger Do Not Rebut the Presumption

1. *Lack of Provable Effects from an Earlier Merger Does Not Rebut a Presumption of Harm for This Merger*

238. Defendants have suggested that the 2013 Penguin/Random House merger did not have an effect on competition for books and therefore rebuts the allegations of anticompetitive effects for this merger. But that argument is unavailing. First, that merger did not result in the concentration increase the present merger will cause. At the time, the Penguin/Random House merger reduced the Big Six down to the Big Five. Additionally, to adopt a policy that a failure to find harm from a prior merger would rebut the presumption of harm would simply mean that a merger in a consolidating industry could not be stopped until *after* at least one merger in the industry unambiguously showed harm—which is too late. Such a policy would fly directly in the face of the intent of Congress "to arrest anticompetitive tendencies in their 'incipiency.'" *Phila. Nat'l Bank,* 374 U.S. at 362 (quoting *Brown Shoe,* 370 U.S. at 317).

2. *The Penguin/Random House Merger May Have Harmed Authors*

239. Contrary to Defendants' arguments about the 2013 merger, there is ample evidence suggesting that it may have harmed authors. First, there is testimony from those in the industry that experienced harm from the Penguin/Random House merger. Agent Christy Fletcher testified that the merger harmed her authors because Penguin and Random House no longer bid against each other. [REDACTED] PX-2007 at 33–34 (Fletcher Dep. 76:18–77:10); PX-2007 at 40–42 (Fletcher Dep. 87:12–89:19); PX-2007 at 43–44 (Fletcher Dep. 90:13–91:20); PX-2007 at 57–58 (Fletcher Dep. 119:24–120:5). Similarly, agent Ayesha Pande testified that the merger led to editorial layoffs and made it "more challenging to sell [her] clients' books because there was less choice." Trial Tr. 293:1–294:3 (Pande).

240. Second, it should be undisputed that PRH paid lower average advances for anticipated top sellers after the 2013 merger. Dr. Hill, Dr. Snyder, and PRH management all came to that same conclusion. *See* Trial Tr. 3060:4–16 (Hill); Trial Tr. 3009:25–3010:14 (Snyder) (acknowledging PRH document showing PRH's advance payments decreased even though its net retail sales increased); [REDACTED].

241. Third, Dr. Hill studied the data and found that the 2013 merger led to a statistically significant reduction in advances for anticipated top-selling books. Trial Tr. 3066:2–10 (Hill). Dr. Hill's difference-in-difference analysis compares the change in advances for anticipated top sellers to the change in advances for other books before and after the 2013 merger of Penguin and Random House. *See* PX-966 at 1. By statistically comparing these two groups, Dr. Hill estimates that advances for authors of anticipated top sellers fell by approximately 15% relative to advances for others books after the merger. Trial Tr. 3065:16–25 (Hill). Dr. Hill testified this analysis is indicative of a negative effect from the 2013 merger, but not dispositive, due to the quality of data available for this historical time period. Trial Tr. 3066:11–3067:1 (Hill).

242. Finally, even though Dr. Snyder stated that "[t]he number one thing as an economist that I would be interested in seeing is what effect [the 2013 merger] had on output," Trial Tr. 2638:25–2639:14 (Snyder), he never analyzed the Penguin/Random House merger's effect on output in his expert reports. Trial Tr. 3059:21–3060:3 (Hill). And Dr. Snyder ignored evidence that PRH's output had actually decreased after the merger. *See* Trial Tr. 218:13–17 (Pietsch) (observing a 1,000-title reduction in a PRH division's title count following the 2013 merger). To the extent that Dr. Snyder's late argument that PRH's output increased was correct, he failed to compare PRH's putative change in output to the rest of the market. Because Defendants claim that PRH's retail market share declined after the 2013 merger, one can infer that the putative increase in output suggested by Dr. Snyder happened as the rest of the retail book market (including the sale of coloring and other books) was growing even faster, underscoring that PRH behaved differently than the rest of the market after the 2013 merger. Consequently, the disputed results of the 2013 merger cannot rebut the presumption.

VI. THE EVIDENCE OF ANTICOMPETITIVE EFFECTS IS SUFFICIENT TO BLOCK THE PROPOSED TRANSACTION

243. Even if Defendants are able to rebut the presumption that the proposed merger is unlawful, Plaintiff has introduced sufficient additional evidence of both unilateral and coordinated anticompetitive effects to meet the ultimate burden of persuasion.

244. If Defendants rebut the presumption, the Court next examines the evidence to determine whether harm is reasonably probable. *Heinz,* 246 F.3d at 715. Defendants' own statements and documents and the economic evidence show that the parties compete fiercely for the rights to anticipated top selling books, and that eliminating direct competition between them is likely to harm authors. *See id.* at 717 ("[T]he

FTC's market concentration statistics are bolstered by the indisputable fact that the merger will eliminate competition between the two merging parties."); *Sysco,* 113 F. Supp. 3d at 65 ("Evidence of probable unilateral effects strengthens the FTC's *prima facie* case that the merger will lessen competition in the national customer market.").

245. Moreover, PRH's own CEO has admitted that its incentives to grow (*i.e.,* compete more vigorously for market share) will change if is allowed to acquire S&S. Today, Mr. Dohle is focused on the importance of growing PRH's market share. Trial Tr. 797:19–25 (Dohle). To do so, he encourages PRH editors to be more aggressive in acquiring books by increasing their appetite for risk. Trial Tr. 799:22–800:5 (Dohle); Trial Tr. 801:8–20 (Dohle) (desiring PRH now pay "much more" to win books). But Mr. Dohle also recognized that an alternative way to grow is to acquire a company with sizable share—a company like S&S, Trial Tr. 801:21–23 (Dohle)—and conceded that once PRH buys S&S *it will not have as strong a need to grow its share.* Trial Tr. 802:11–18 (Dohle). That is, based on the PRH CEO's own description of what it would take to acquire more books and how acquiring market share would generate the same effect, it is clear that after the merger PRH will no longer need to be as aggressive or increase its appetite for risk as it competes with remaining publishers for books. This predictably harms authors.

A. Applicable Legal Standards for Unilateral Effects

246. Mergers necessarily eliminate the competition between the merging companies. *See Heinz,* 246 F.3d at 717. The inevitable loss of that competition supports the finding that the merger may result in a substantial lessening of competition. *See Sysco,* 113 F. Supp. 3d at 61–62 ("Courts have recognized that a merger that eliminates head-to-head competition between close competitors can result in a substantial lessening of competition.") (citing cases and Merger Guidelines § 6); *Aetna,* 240 F. Supp. 3d at 9 ("direct evidence of head-to-head competition" supported presumptive unlawfulness of the merger).

247. This is particularly true in a "highly concentrated market," where the loss of "significant head-to-head competition" is "an important consideration when analyzing possible anti-competitive effects." *Staples I,* 970 F. Supp. at 1083.

248. In particular, a merger between direct competitors that eliminates head-to-head competition may lead to "unilateral anticompetitive effects," meaning "the acquiring firm will have the incentive to raise prices or reduce quality after the acquisition, independent of competitive responses from other firms." *Aetna,* 240 F. Supp. 3d at 43 (quoting *H & R Block,* 833 F. Supp. 2d at 81).

249. Unilateral effects commonly arise in markets where "buyers and sellers negotiate to determine prices and other terms of trade" via auctions or other negotiation processes. Merger Guidelines § 6.2. "In such a market, '[sellers] commonly negotiate with more than one [buyer], and may play [buyers] off against one another.'" *Sysco,* 113 F. Supp. 3d at 62 (quoting Merger Guidelines § 6.2). "If two competitors merge, [sellers] will be prevented from playing the [buyers] off one another in negotiations." *Id.* "This alone can significantly enhance the ability and incentive of the merged entity to obtain a result more favorable to it, and less favorable to the [seller], than the merging firms would have offered separately absent the merger." Merger Guidelines § 6.2.

250. A merger may cause harmful unilateral effects even if the merging firms are not the two largest in the market or each other's closest competitors. *Sysco,* 113 F. Supp. 3d at 62 ("[T]he merging parties need not be the top two firms to cause unilateral effects."); *see also Aetna,* 240 F. Supp. 3d at 43; *Anthem,* 236 F. Supp. 3d at 216. In *H & R Block,* for example, a nonparty to the proposed merger had a market share of over 60% and was the closest competitor to both merging companies, but the court nonetheless enjoined the merger. 833 F. Supp. 2d at 44, 83–84. Similarly, in *Heinz,* the D.C. Circuit enjoined the merger of two baby food manufacturers even though a third company was the largest and closest competitor of both defendants. 246 F.3d at 718–19, 727.

B. The Merger Would Eliminate Head-to-Head Competition Between PRH and S&S

3. *Authors Benefit from Direct Competition between PRH and S&S*

251. There can be no dispute that the merging parties compete intensely with each other to acquire books. PRH is S&S's closest competitor and the publisher against whom S&S's editors compete most frequently. *See* Trial Tr. 595:23–25 (Karp) ("Q. So you would expect Penguin Random House to be the publisher you bid against the most, correct? A. I think so, yes."); Trial Tr. 1280:17–1281:17 (Hill) (S&S win/loss data shows that S&S loses to PRH ~60% of the time). Similarly, S&S is one of PRH's most important competitors, *see* Trial Tr. 2360:20–23 (McIntosh); Trial Tr. 1275:25–1276:6 (Hill), and is a particularly strong competitor for certain categories of books, including, most notably, biographies, memoirs, political non-fiction and books about current events. *See* Trial Tr. 454:23–455:3 (Karp); Trial

Tr. 455:8–11 (Karp); PX-326 at 2 ("S&S has political bestseller chops like no other right now.").

252. Authors benefit from Defendants' fierce and frequent head-to-head competition for the rights to anticipated top-selling books. The record includes numerous examples showing the extent to which competition between the two firms can benefit authors, including:

a. [REDACTED] . In January 2019, S&S offered $5 million for a memoir by [REDACTED] a few days later, it increased its offer to $6 million. Trial Tr. 418:13 18 (Karp); PX-643 at 2. PRH's Crown imprint then offered $7.5 million. Trial Tr. 419:24–420:8 (Karp); PX-958-B at 1; PX-643 at 2; PX-863 at 2. [REDACTED] told S&S that [REDACTED] would not go back to Crown if S&S increased its offer to $8 million. Trial Tr. 420:9–13 (Karp); PX-643 at 2. To prevent the agent from going back to PRH, S&S bid $8 milliion to secure the book. PX-613 at1; Trial Tr. 425:2–8 (Karp); PX-958-B at 1. Competition from PRH was directly relevant to S&S's decision to increase its offer from $6 million to $8 million. *See* Trial Tr. 423:22–424:4 (Karp); *see also* Trial Tr. 425:2–5 (Karp) (PRH was the "stalking horse" that the agent used to increase the offer to $8 million).

b. [REDACTED] The auction for- [REDACTED] initially included up to six bidders, but narrowed to two bidders-PRH and S&S—-once the bidding reached approximately $650,000. Trial Tr. 427:5–428:2 (Karp); PX-557 at 6; PX-941-B at 1. Even after the other bidders dropped out, S&S and PRH continued to bid against each other for several rounds. Trial Tr. 428:3–428:20 (Karp); PX-557 at 1–6; PX-588 at 1. In the final rounds of the auction, PRH bid $805,000, S&S matched that offer, and PRH increased its bid by $20,000 to win. Trial Tr. 430:8–18 (Karp); PX-588 at 1. For direct competition between PRH and S&S drnve up the final advance by $175,000, from $650,000 to $825,000. Trial Tr. 430:19–23 (Karp); *see also* PX-941-B at 1.

c. . [REDACTED] The auction for book started with multiple bidders but narrowed to just two-PRH and S&S-after S&S bid $475,000. PX-324 at 1; PX-944-B at I (summary of auction for). Even after the other bidders dropped out, Defendants continued to increase their bids through several auction rounds until S&S bid $650,000. At that time, the agent called for the parties to submit their final best bid. *See* PX-326 at 2; PX-569 at 1. Viking (PRH) Associate Publisher Wendy Wolf assumed that Viking was bidding against S&S, adding that "S&S has political bestseller chops like no other right now." PX-326 at 2. When Mr. Tart suggested PRH increase its bid to $775,000 to have a "shot," Ms. Wolf agreed, writing "there just is literally no telling what the opponents hold in their hands, esp[ecially] if it's S&S and they're looking at their winning streak in politics." PX-326 at 1.Viking then bid $775,000 and won the book. Trial Tr. 929:11–13 (Tart); PX-39 at 1. After winning, Ms. Wolf described PRH as having "prevailed over a house bid from . . . S&S." PX-39 at 1. Mr. Tart replied: "we got this one, and over stiff competition." PX-39 at 1.

d. [REDACTED] . S&S offered $750,000 for[REDACTED] Trial Tr. 446:2–4 (Karp). After receiving S&S's bid, the agent decided to conduct an auction and gave S&S "topping rights," meaning S&S could acquire the book if it made an offer that was 10% higher than the highest bid in the auction. Trial Tr. 446:6–11 (Karp); PX-729 at 1. PRH's Portfolio imprint submitted the highest bid in the auction, at $1 million. Trial Tr. 446:14–22 (Karp); PX-729 at 1; PX-863 at 2–3. S&S then exercised its "topping rights" with a bid for $1.1 million and won the book. Trial Tr. 447:1–5 (Karp). The author had previously published books with S&S. When justifying his recommendation to increase to $1.1 million, Mr. Karp wrote that he didn't "want to let PRH steal an author we've invested in and developed." PX-729 at 1.

253. These examples are illustrative; the record includes many other instances of head- to-head competition between the merging parties. *See, e.g.,* PX-559 at 1 (S&S lost three "beauty contest[s]" in one week to PRH); PX-624 at 1 ("I did everything I could and we lost to Random House. [REDACTED] Frustrating."); PX-716 at 1–3 (PRH and S&S only bidders in last two rounds for book by [REDACTED]); PX-590 at 1 ("The author is deciding between Hillary Redmon at Random House and Karyn Marcus at Gallery [S&S]"); PX-700 at 1 ("It was down to PRH and Atria [S&S] in the final best bid part of the auction [REDACTED] "); PX-697 at 1 (S&S and two PRH imprints were the three highest bidders); PX-574 at 1 (similar); PX-2007 at 38–39 (Fletcher Dep. 84:24–85:15; 85:18) (testifying her authors benefited from having S&S bid against PRH).

254. The government's summary witness, Adriana Porro, prepared exhibits summarizing 27 competitive episodes, including some of those discussed above, in which PRH and S&S were the final two bidders (or, sometimes, the only two bidders) for a particular book. *See* Trial Tr. 660:16–17 (Porro); Trial Tr. 663:9–15 (Porro); Trial Tr. 664:8–10 (Porro) (describing Ms. Porro's review); PX-932-B at 1 (summary of bidding for [REDACTED]); PX-934-B at 1 (same, for [REDACTED]); PX-935-B at 1 (same, for

[REDACTED]); PX-936-B at 1–2(same, for [REDACTED]); PX-937-B at 1 (same, for [REDACTED]); PX-938-B at 1–2 (same, for [REDACTED]); PX-939-B at 1–3 (same, for [REDACTED]); PX-940-B at 1–2 (same, for [REDACTED]); PX-943-B at 1 (same, for [REDACTED]); PX-945-B at 1 (same, for [REDACTED]); PX-946-B at 1–2 (same, for [REDACTED]); PX-947-B at 1 (same, for [REDACTED]); PX-948-B at 1–2 (same, for [REDACTED]); PX-950-B at 1–2 (same, for [REDACTED]); PX-951-B at 1 (same, for [REDACTED]); PX-952-B at 1 (same, for [REDACTED]); PX-954-B at 1–2 (same, for [REDACTED]); PX-955-B at 1 (same, for [REDACTED]); PX-956-B at 1 (same, for [REDACTED]); PX-957-B at 1 (same, for [REDACTED]).

255. As these examples illustrate, there is a substantial history of direct head-to-head competition between PRH and S&S that has resulted in increased payments to authors. The post-merger loss of this competition significantly increases the likelihood of anticompetitive effects. *See, e.g.*, *Staples II,* 190 F. Supp. 3d at 131–132 (examining instances of past head-to head competition over customers between defendants); *H & R Block,* 833 F. Supp. 2d at 81–82 (historical instances where one defendant considered offerings and prices of the other in setting its own offerings and prices); *Heinz,* 246 F.3d at 718 (concluding defendants compete with each other because of "evidence that the two do in fact price against each other").

4. Authors Benefit from Competition Between S&S and PRH When Defendants Are Not the Highest Two Bidders in an Auction

256. The benefits of competition between PRH and S&S for author advances are not limited to auctions where Defendants are the two highest bidders. This is because having a larger number of bidders participating in auctions can lead to higher advances more generally. For example, Hachette CEO Michael Pietsch testified that a larger number of bidders leads to "more upward pressure in auctions . . . in general, . . . the price paid at auction can increase because of the number of participants." Trial Tr. 180:20–181:11 (Pietsch); *see also* Trial Tr. 499:6–500:12 (Karp); PX-2002 at 78–79 (Stehlik Dep. 172:1–17, 172:20–25, 173:1–2, 173:4–7);Trial Tr. 338:23–25 (King) ("You know, the baseball players have a saying, you can't hit them if you can't see them. And you can't sell books competitively if there are only so many people in competition"); PX-2007 at 12–14 (Fletcher Dep. 40:21–23, 41:1–10, 41:13–19, 41:23–25, 42:2–3) (for auctions, "we prefer to have an array of editors from different houses participating"; want a minimum of three for a rounds auction); Trial Tr. 1268:2–5 (Hill); *Anthem,* 236 F. Supp. 3d at 220–221 (enjoining merger in part because "reducing the number of national carriers from four to three is significant"; relying on testimony that having more bidders leads to better prices during negotiations even before negotiations narrow to the two best options).

257. The potential positive effect of having an increased number of bidders is particularly important in an auction for book rights because the bids that a publisher makes for a particular book are subjective—meaning that one publisher or editor can sometimes value a book higher or even significantly higher than other publishers or editors. Trial Tr. 479:9–480:5 (Karp); Trial Tr. 601:9–16 (Karp). Having more bidders thus increases the chance that one of the bidders has a higher valuation for a work. Trial Tr. 601:17–25 (Karp); *see also* Trial Tr. 1305:24–1306:3 (Hill) (greater variation in bids leads to more harm in second-score auction model); Trial Tr. 2109:22–2111:5 (Wylie) (in situations where there are likely to be significant differences in how publishers value a work, it helps to have more choice in terms of publishers to whom the book can be submitted); PX-2007 at 12–13 (Fletcher Dep. 40:21–23, 41:1–10, 41:13–19); PX-2007 at 36 (Fletcher Dep. 82:7–10, 82:12–13); Trial Tr. 2931:16–2933:23 (Snyder) (discussing the best-bid auction for [REDACTED] in Defendants'Demonstrative 18 at 25 in which the highest bidder bid [REDACTED] in a field of five bidders).

5. Authors Benefit from Competition Between PRH and S&S in Single- Round Best-Bid Auctions

258. Competition between the merging parties is also important in single-round best- bid auctions, where agents require each publisher to submit their best and final bid in the first round and publishers are not given a chance to later improve their bids. Trial Tr. 2008:25–2009:2 (Kim) (describing best-bid auction format). As with other auction types, in best-bid auctions having more bidders often leads to higher advances. As Mr. Karp agreed, "anytime there is a competitive situation," including best-bid auctions, "competition raises advance levels, less competition lowers them." Trial Tr. 499:6–500:12 (Karp); *see also* Trial Tr. 1267:13–1268:21 (Hill) (discussing two examples in U.S. Demonstrative 4 at 37 that illustrate the correlation between bid levels and the number of bidders in best-bid auctions). This is because publishers bidding in a single-round best-bid auction are more likely to submit a higher bid

when there are more competitors, as the presence of more competitors reduces the publisher's odds of winning any given bid. Trial Tr. 1268:22–1270:12 (Hill); Trial Tr. 1487:21–1488:1 (Hill); PX-2002 at 77–79 (Stehlik Dep. 171:11–24, 172:1–17, 172:20–173:2, 173:4–8) (larger number of bidders in two-round best-bid auction leads to higher bids because bidders have a lower chance of winning). For that reason, if the merger eliminates an important bidder, one would expect advances to go down for books acquired in a one-round best-bid auction. *See* Trial Tr. 3088:20–3089:25 (Hill).

259. Defendants' claim that one-round best-bid auctions give agents more leverage than other types of auctions is unsupported by the record. In at least one instance, PRH pushed an agent to end a multiple-round auction by moving to best bids. Trial Tr. 928:5–23 (Tart) (discussing PX-326 at 3). If best-bid auctions were inherently better for agents and worse for publishers, PRH presumably would not press agents to move to that format.

6. Authors Benefit from Competition Between PRH and S&S for Books Acquired Outside of Auctions

260. Competition among publishers, including PRH and S&S, affects the advances offered for books acquired outside of auctions. This includes situations where only one publisher has submitted a bid for a particular work, such as exclusive negotiations, options contracts, and preempts. In these bidding situations, publishers know that the agent can always shop the book to other publishers if the publisher's offer is not high enough. *See, e.g.,* Trial Tr. 113:19–115:6 (Pietsch); Trial Tr. 596:10–597:4 (Karp); Trial Tr. 1847:1–6 (Bergstrom) (even in exclusive negotiations she always has her "competition in [the] review mirror [REDACTED] [S]ometimes [they] don't come to terms, and sometimes they will go to someone else."). Accordingly, the threat that the agent could take a book to auction or other publishers—*i.e.* the threat of competition from other publishers—directly influences the advances publishers offer even in exclusive or other one-on-one negotiations. *See, e.g.,* Trial Tr. 113:19–115:6 (Pietsch); Trial Tr. 596:10–597:4 (Karp); Trial Tr. 1966:13–24 (Kim) ("[E]ven if it's a one-on-one negotiation, we know the agent can decide to send it to five more editors. . . . . . So we're constantly aware that there's competition."); Trial Tr. 2127:7–13 (Ross) ("[I]f you can walk away from something, then it's easier to push to the terms that you think are fair and right, and so I try to use that . . . [I]t's always easier to walk away if you know what you're walking to. And in this business, there's always the other competitor. Whether it's—whether they're bidding or not, they're always there."); Trial Tr. 1271:19–1272:12 (Hill) (discussing U.S. Demonstrative 4 at 38).

261. Similarly, when a publisher seeks to acquires a book through a "preempt," the publisher must submit a bid that is high enough to entice the agent and author to forego further bidding. *See, e.g.,* Trial Tr. 115:7–116:15 (Pietsch); Trial Tr. 596:5–9 (Karp); PX-2002 at 59–61 (Stehlik Dep. 147:19–21, 147:23–149:4); Trial Tr. 303:5–11 (Pande); *see also* Trial Tr. 921:6–11 (Tart) (preempts are a "competitive situation"). Also, agents can invite several publishers to make competing preempt offers. PX-2002 at 60 (Stehlik Dep. 148:4–10); DX-188 at 2 ("[Agent] has an aggressive editor trying to preempt the book now and is subtly inviting us to counter preempt."); Trial Tr. 1271:19–12 (Hill) (discussing U.S. Demonstrative 4 at 39).

262. Publisher competition to recruit or poach authors away from their current publishers also affects author advances and represents another type of competitive acquisition format. PRH tracks "key authors," which include authors the company wants to recruit. When asked about PRH's recruitment of other publishers' authors, Mr. Dohle explained that "[i]f we have an opening and a chance to get attractive authors on board, we immediately go in and try to get them to Penguin Random House, sure." Trial Tr. 884:1–18 (Dohle). Poaching of authors between the merging parties "[r]esults in better terms for authors. It gives established authors a chance to realize benefits of competition." Trial Tr. 1272:13–1273:3 (Hill). After highlighting examples of poaching between the merging parties, Dr. Hill explained that poaching demonstrates "there's substantial head-to-head competition between the parties" and that such head-to-head competition can "be important for different acquisition formats." Trial Tr. 1272:21–1273:11 (Hill).

7. Eliminating the Competition Between PRH and S&S Will Harm Authors

263. Because authors benefit from competition between PRH and S&S, the elimination of that competition will likely harm authors. Though the effect of eliminating this competition will be most acute for PRH and S&S authors, it is not necessarily limited to authors of those publishers. As Dr. Hill explained, for certain acquisition types, "[t]hird parties may also have a second-order effect, where they observe that the merged firm is less aggressive and so they can also bid as they were before or even bid a little less aggressively because their probability of winning has also gone up." Trial Tr. 1269:20–24 (Hill); *see*

also Trial Tr. 1487:19–1489:9 (Hill).

264. At trial, several industry participants testified that they expected that the proposed merger would lead to a reduction in competition. For example, the CEO of Kensington stated that he "personally expect[s] that advances will go down since there will be less competition . . ." PX-2000 at 3 (Zacharius Dep. 20:6–13); *see also* Trial Tr. 1085:3–1086:2 (Weisberg) (advances will go down because of "[l]ess competition. It's as simple as that."). Similarly, Ms. Pande testified that the proposed merger would limit the choices her authors have to publish their books and that "overall advances" for her clients "would be suppressed." Trial Tr. 294:4–295:16 (Pande). And Ms. Fletcher testified about the concern that if PRH and S&S merged in the same way that Penguin and Random House integrated, it would make it harder for agents to withhold certain rights, such as territories or formats, as they customarily do now. PX-2007 at 37–38 (Fletcher Dep. 83:7–25, 84:3–10). These conclusions should come as no surprise even to Defendants' senior executives. For example, the CEO of S&S predicted that the Department of Justice would not allow PRH to acquire S&S—and also stated that a merger with a competitor would arguably be harmful for the book publishing ecosystem. PX-655 at 1; PX-634 at 1.

C. Economic Analysis Shows That Eliminating Competition Between S&S and PRH Will Lower Advances and Harm Authors

265. Economic analysis presented by the government's expert, Dr. Hill, confirms that the merger is likely to lead to significant unilateral effects. Dr. Hill conducted several different types of economic analyses. Each analysis, when taken alone, is subject to various limitations and caveats, which Dr. Hill acknowledged. Viewed collectively, however, these analyses reinforce the conclusions set forth by the qualitative evidence discussed above—*i.e.,* that the merger is likely to lead to a significant reduction in competition in the market for anticipated top sellers.

1. Diversion Ratios Indicate That There Is Significant Competition to Be Lost Between the Merging Parties

266. Economists often use "diversion ratios" to estimate how closely merging parties compete with each other. Trial Tr. 1263:1–3 (Hill); *see also* Merger Guidelines § 6.1. A "diversion ratio" is an attempt to quantify the following question: if one of the merging parties tries to raise prices (or, here, lower advances), how often would an author switch to the other merging party relative to other firms? Trial Tr. 1274:13–1275:4 (Hill). The higher the diversion ratio, the more often customers in that scenario are predicted to switch to the other merging party. A higher diversion ratio indicates that the merging parties are close competitors and, therefore, that a merger is more likely to lead to harm. Trial Tr. 1274:2–12 (Hill); *see also* Merger Guidelines § 6.1. More broadly, diversion ratios can be thought of as one way to estimate the significance of the competition between the merging parties. *See* Merger Guidelines § 6.1.

267. Dr. Hill estimated diversion ratios by undertaking four studies, each based on a different set of data: (i) market shares; (ii) win/loss data; (iii) "runner-up" data; and (iv) minutes from the parties' editorial meetings. Trial Tr. 1275:5–24 (Hill). All four studies lead to the same conclusions: first, that diversion between the merging parties is significant, and second, that diversion from S&S to PRH indicates that PRH is S&S's closest competitor. *See* Trial Tr. 1275:25–1276:6 (Hill); PX-970 at 1.

268. First, Dr. Hill analyzed diversion according to market shares—meaning that he estimated what diversion would be if one assumes that diversion is proportional to market shares. Trial Tr. 1276:18–1277:4 (Hill). Based on that approach, Dr. Hill estimated that if PRH were to lower advances, about 20% of its lost authors would divert to S&S and about 40% of S&S's lost authors would divert to PRH. Trial Tr. 1276:7–17 (Hill); PX-970 at 1.

269. Dr. Hill also explained that diversion according to share is a widely used approach in antitrust economics. Trial Tr. 1276:18–1277:16 (Hill); *see also H & R Block,* 833 F. Supp. 2d at 86. Using market shares to calculate diversion is particularly appropriate here because the documentary and testimonial evidence shows that the merging parties compete just as intensely as their market shares would suggest and that publishers generally compete in accordance with their market shares. Trial Tr. 1277:20–1279:22 (Hill); *compare* Trial Tr. 3085:15–3086:3 (Hill); Trial Tr. 150:20–151:2 (Pietsch); PX-2002 at 71 (Stehlik Dep. 165:15–20); Trial Tr. 595:23–25 (Karp) *with* PX-959 at 1. Diversion according to share is also based on the largest data set. Trial Tr. 1293:20–1294:11 (Hill). Accordingly, Dr. Hill viewed diversion ratios proportional to market shares as his baseline diversion estimate. Trial Tr. 3084:1–3085:2 (Hill).

270. Second, Dr. Hill analyzed sets of win/loss data maintained by the merging parties. These data show

which publishers the merging parties lose to most often. *See* Trial Tr. 1281:5–18 (Hill). According to these data, when PRH bids on a book and loses, it loses to S&S approximately 20% of the time. Trial Tr. 1280:17–1281:17 (Hill); PX-970 at 1. And when S&S bids on a book and loses, it loses to PRH approximately 60% of the time. Trial Tr. 1280:17–1281:17 (Hill); PX-970 at 1.

271. Win/loss data are commonly used to estimate diversion ratios. Trial Tr. 1281:19–1282:1 (Hill); *see also* Merger Guidelines § 6.1; *Wilhelmsen,* 341 F. Supp. 3d at 65; Carl Shapiro, *The 2010 Horizontal Merger Guidelines: From Hedgehog to Fox in Forty Years,* 77 Antitrust L.J. 49, 83 (2010).

272. Third, Dr. Hill conducted a "runner-up" study. For this study, Dr. Hill compiled as much evidence as he could regarding the bidding for all of the books that PRH and S&S acquired for $500,000 or more in 2020. Trial Tr. 1284:11–1285:12 (Hill). The "runner-up" study showed that for books acquired by PRH, S&S was the runner-up approximately 25% of the time. Trial Tr. 1282:15–24 (Hill); PX-970 at 1. And for books acquired by S&S, PRH was the runner-up approximately 60% of the time. Trial Tr. 1282:15–24 (Hill); PX-970 at 1.

273. Finally, Dr. Hill conducted a study based on the merging parties' editorial minutes. Editorial minutes are business records kept of each party's editorial staff meetings where the parties discuss books they are interested in, books they bid on, and books they won or lost. *See* Trial Tr. 1286:13–22 (Hill). Dr. Hill used these minutes to identify a set of books that each of the merging parties bid on and then used acquisition data from all publishers (including non-parties) to determine how frequently one merging party bid on a book and lost to the other merging party. Trial Tr. 1286:13–1287:11 (Hill). According to this study, when PRH bid on a book and lost, it lost to S&S about 20% of the time. *See* Trial Tr. 1286:6–12 (Hill); PX-970 at 1. And when S&S bid on a book and lost, it lost to PRH about 55% of the time. *See* Trial Tr. 1286:6–12 (Hill); PX-970 at 1.

274. The following chart, based on PX-970, summarizes the results of these four studies.

Figure 7. Summary of Dr. Hill's Diversion Estimates (PX-970)

Type of Analysis	Diversion from PRH to S&S	Diversion from S&S to PRH
Diversion according to share	19%	42%
Win/loss data	19%	59%
Runner-up study	27%	59%
Editorial minutes	21%	54%

275. As suggested by the above chrut, though these four studies differ methodologically, they all point in the same direction. *See* Trial Tr. 1287:14–16 (Hill). They all show that there is a significant amount of competition between the merging parties-and, in particular, that PRH is S&S's most frequent competitor. *See* Trial Tr. 1275:25–1276:6 (Hill); PX-970 at 1. In addition, this evidence is also consistent with the qualitative evidence, described more fully above, *see supra* VI.B., which also shows that the palties compete frequently with each other. Trial Tr. 1263:15–1265:1 (Hill).

276. Diversion estimates calculated by Defendants' economic expelt, Dr. Snyder, are broadly consistent with those calculated by Dr. Hill in the four studies described above. Trial Tr. 1289:16–20 (Hill); Trial Tr. 1292:25–1293:19 (Hill) (discussing U.S. Demonstrative 4 at 48–49). Dr. Snyder found that the diversion ratio from PRH to S&S is 20% and the diversion ratio from S&S to PRH is 27%. Trial Tr. 2927:4–25 (Snyder). Based on those calculations, Dr. Snyder also found that PRH is S&S's closest competitor. *See* Trial Tr. 2928:1–10 (Snyder). However, the diversion ratio from S&S to PRH that Dr. Snyder estimated is smaller than the diversion ratios from S&S to PRH that Dr. Hill estimated from his four data sources. *See* Trial Tr. 1293:9–19 (Hill).

277. Dr. Snyder used data collected from agents, the agency data, as his sole method for estimating diversion. But Dr. Snyder's agency data is flawed because it is not representative, *i.e.,* books in his data set differ in important ways from the population of all anticipated top- selling books, Trial Tr. 1289:22–

1291:14 (Hill) (discussing U.S. Demonstrative 4 at 47); Trial Tr. 2997:17–22 (Snyder), and is based on a small sample size. In particular, Dr. Snyder's estimate of diversion from S&S to PRH is based on a sample of 22 books over four years, the smallest sample of all the data sets used to estimate diversion. Trial Tr. 1291:15–1292:12 (Hill); Trial Tr. 1707:20–1708:1 (Hill); PX-996 at 1.

278. In contrast, Dr. Hill's analysis was based on several sources of data that painted a consistent picture. *See* PX-970 at 1. Though each data set had its limitations, Dr. Hill explained that taken in the aggregate the studies tried "to get a holistic understanding of what diversion might look like." Trial Tr. 1294:20–1295:4. Similarly, while Dr. Snyder's agency data diversion ratios are not worthless, they should be considered as just one of five estimates, not the only estimate as Dr. Snyder suggests. *See* Trial Tr. 1289:7–15 (Hill). Treating Dr. Snyder's ratios as such supports Dr. Hill's baseline diversion estimate, diversion according to share. Trial Tr. 1293:20–1294:11 (Hill) (discussing U.S. Demonstrative 4 at 50).

2. Dr. Hill's Economic Modeling Provides Results That Are Consistent with the Prediction That the Merger Is Likely to Lead to a Significant Reduction in Competition

279. Dr. Hill used various economic models to quantify the expected harm from the merger. Although no one model perfectly fits the publishing industry, these models are still useful to assess the likelihood of substantial anticompetitive harm in this setting. Taken together, Dr. Hill's models confirm that the merger is likely to lead to a significant reduction in competition. *See* Trial Tr. 3106:5–15 (Hill); Merger Guidelines § 6.1 (discussing how the DOJ and FTC use merger simulations). Following the merger, Dr. Hill's model predicts that advances for anticipated top sellers would be reduced by about 4% (or $44,000) for PRH authors and about 11.5% (or $105,000) for S&S authors. Trial Tr. 1311:7–1312:20 (Hill); PX-964 at 1–2.

280. First, Dr. Hill used a "second-score" auction model to simulate the effect of the proposed merger. Trial Tr. 1295:21–22 (Hill). This model is designed to analyze the competitive effects of mergers in industries where auctions are common and where the full history of bidding is often not available. Trial Tr. 1295:23–1296:4 (Hill). The model predicts harm in situations where the merging parties are the first- and second-place bidders, since the effect of the merger is to eliminate the second-highest bid, making the third-place bid the one that sets the amount of advance. *See* Trial Tr. 1299:17–1302:19 (Hill); Trial Tr. 1303:7–22 (Hill).

281. Similar or identical models have been used by the government's economic experts in successful merger challenges in this district, including in industries that feature negotiations. *See Wilhelmsen,* 341 F. Supp. 3d at 64–65; *Anthem,* 236 F. Supp. 3d at 217–20; *Sysco,* 113 F. Supp. 3d at 24, 66–67 (noting that customers were awarded contracts through requests for proposal or "bilateral negotiations").

282. Dr. Hill calibrated the model using two inputs: market shares and variable profit margins. 1305:5–1306:3 (Hill). The model uses market shares to infer the frequency with which the merging parties are runner up when the other wins an auction. Trial Tr. 1305:5–17 (Hill). The model uses variable profit margins to infer the distance between the second- and third-place bidders. *See* Trial Tr. 1305:5–1306:3 (Hill); Trial Tr. 1471:1–11 (Hill). Generally speaking, higher margins suggest that there is greater variation among bids and hence greater harm. *See* Trial Tr. 1305:18–1306:3 (Hill); *see also* Merger Guidelines § 6.2 ("[Anticompetitive unilateral effects] tend to be greater, the more profitable were the pre-merger winning bids."); Carl Shapiro, *The 2010 Horizontal Merger Guidelines: From Hedgehog to Fox in Forty Years,* 77 Antitrust L.J. 49, 83 (2010). Dr. Hill corroborated the model's inference about the variation among bids using Dr. Snyder's agency data. Trial Tr. 1303:23–1304:12 (Hill).

283. Dr. Hill used the merging parties' title-level P&L data (based on realized sales of anticipated top sellers) to calculate variable profit margins. Trial Tr. 1311:7–13 (Hill). To be conservative, he treated a cost category in PRH's P&Ls—"direct operating expenses"—as costs that were completely variable even though some of those costs were likely fixed. Trial Tr. 1311:18–1312:6 (Hill). By treating these costs as variable, it reduced PRH's margin and hence the model's prediction of harm. Trial Tr. 1311:25–1312:6 (Hill).

284. Dr. Hill also ran the model treating direct operating expenses as fixed costs for PRH. Under that iteration, the model predicts greater harm—a 6% reduction in advances per book, or about a $60,000 reduction per book for PRH, and a 15% reduction per book, or about a $140,000 per book reduction for S&S. Trial Tr. 1314:10–20 (Hill).

285. The second-score model leads to broadly similar results even if the market is defined with different advance thresholds of $150,000 or $350,000 to identify anticipated top sellers. Trial Tr. 1315:7–15 (Hill).

286. After criticism from Dr. Snyder about the second-score auction model's fit with the industry, Dr. Hill

corroborated the results of the model using a series of models based on the "gross upward pricing pressure index" ("GUPPI"). Trial Tr. 1315:16–1316:10 (Hill). The GUPPI models used by Dr. Hill were originally created by the Defendants' economists in the pre-complaint investigation of this merger by modifying the traditional GUPPI formula to fit three book acquisition types: a best-bid auction, a multi-round auction, and a hybrid approach, which was a multi-round auction followed by negotiations. *See* Trial Tr. 1316:2–1317:13 (Hill); Trial Tr. 1633:15–1634:11 (Hill).

287. GUPPI, or a variant thereof, "Upward Pricing Pressure" (UPP), has been used by the government's economic experts in several successful merger challenges. *See Wilhelmsen,* 341 F. Supp. 3d at 64; *Anthem,* 236 F. Supp. 3d at 212; *FTC v. Sanford Health,* No. 1:17-cv-133, 2017 WL 10810016, at *12–13 (D.N.D. Dec. 15, 2017), *aff'd.,* 926 F.3d 959 (8th Cir. 2019).

288. Like the second-score model, the GUPPI models use diversion ratios and margins as inputs. Trial Tr. 1318:2–13 (Hill). In the models, higher diversion ratios and higher margins will lead to a higher prediction of harm. Trial Tr. 1318:14–19 (Hill). For diversion ratios, Dr. Hill ran the GUPPI models using both diversion proportional to share and Dr. Snyder's diversion ratios based on his agency data. Trial Tr. 1318:20–24 (Hill). For margins, Dr. Hill used his original, conservative, margin calculation. Trial Tr. 1318:25–1319:6 (Hill). As described in the chart below, Dr. Hill found that the GUPPI models predicted similar effects to the second-score auction model and that the merger likely will lead to a significant reduction in author compensation. *See* PX-964 at 1–2; Trial Tr. 1637:21–1638:4 (Hill); Trial Tr. 1639:7–24 (Hill).

Figure 8. Dr. Hill's Estimates From Second-Score Auction and GUPPI Models (PX-964)

Model	Diversion Assumption	% Reduction in Author Compensation	
		PRH	S&S
Second-score auction model	Diversion according to share	4.3%	11.6%
Multi-round auction GUPPI	Diversion according to share	7.3%	19.2%
Multi-round auction GUPPI	Snyder diversion ratios	7.4%	12.8%
Single-round and hybrid GUPPI	Diversion according to share	3.7%	9.6%
Single-round and hybrid GUPPI	Snyder diversion ratios	3.7%	6.4%

3. Dr. Snyder's Criticisms of the Second-Score Auction Model Do Not Undermine the Model's Prediction that The Merger Is Likely to Substantially Harm Authors.

289. Defendants' expert, Dr. Snyder, did not create or implement any alternative models to estimate harm. Nor did he try to do so. Trial Tr. 2929:8–12 (Snyder). Dr. Snyder did, however, offer several criticisms of Dr. Hill's models. As discussed below, these criticisms are immaterial or incorrect.

290. *First,* as mentioned previously, Dr. Snyder criticized Dr. Hill's use of the second- score auction model on the grounds that the model most directly applies to a specific type of auction (with a format similar to that of round robin auctions) and is not applicable to other types of acquisitions. Trial Tr. 2632:21–2633:19 (Snyder). But Dr. Hill's application of the second- score auction model was not meant to suggest that all anticipated top sellers are sold via second- price auctions. Trial Tr. 1296:13–21 (Hill); Trial Tr. 1597:16–1598:23 (Hill). Instead, the model generates a prediction for the market for anticipated top sellers based on aggregate information about how often the parties compete. Modeling every type of acquisition would, for a variety of reasons, be infeasible. Trial Tr. 1597:16–1600:6 (Hill).

291. In addition, the intuition behind the second-score auction model—*i.e.,* that harm is more likely where the merging parties are close competitors and margins are higher—applies to other types of acquisitions, too. Trial Tr. 1599:16–1600:6 (Hill); Trial Tr. 1610:21–1611:1 (Hill). The second-score auction model does apply to a specific form of negotiation, the dynamics of which are similar to those in the publishing industry, where the price obtained through the negotiation is set by the next best alternative. Trial Tr. 3098:10–3100:3 (Hill). Dr. Hill also explained in his testimony the similarities to how best-bid auctions would likely be affected by the merger. Trial Tr. 1726:19–1730:4 (Hill). For these reasons, Dr. Hill found the second-score auction model to be useful as one method for estimating harm from the

transaction. Trial Tr. 1726:19–1730:4 (Hill).

292. Moreover, as described above, in response to Dr. Snyder's criticism regarding the applicability of Dr. Hill's second-score auction model, Dr. Hill ran multiple iterations of a GUPPI analysis to corroborate his initial analysis. *See* Trial Tr. 1316:2–1317:13 (Hill). As set forth above, Dr. Hill found that the GUPPI models were similar to his earlier findings by predicting similar effects to the second-score auction model. *See* PX-964 at 1–2; Trial Tr. 1637:21–1638:4 (Hill); Trial Tr. 1639:7–24 (Hill). Both the second-score auction model and the GUPPI models confirm that the merger likely will lead to a significant reduction in author compensation.

293. *Second,* in addition to his high-level criticisms about fit, Dr. Snyder also criticized Dr. Hill's implementation of the second-score auction and GUPPI models. Dr. Snyder mistakenly argues that Dr. Hill should have accounted for fixed costs when calculating the merging parties' variable profit margins. As Dr. Hill explained, both the second-score auction model and the GUPPI models are "explicit" that one should use firms' variable, not fixed, costs to implement the models. Trial Tr. 3092:23–3093:15 (Hill); *see also* Nathan Miller, *Modeling the effects of mergers in procurement,* 37 Int'l J. Indus. Org. 201, 203, 206 n.9 (2014) (specifying the model inputs are marginal costs, which depend on variable costs, not fixed costs); Joseph Farrell & Carl Shapiro, *Antitrust Evaluation of Horizontal Mergers: An Economic Alternative to Market Definition,* 10 B.E. J. Theoretical Econ. 1, 7 (2010) (same). This is because these models (like most in economics) assume that publishers make decisions on whether to acquire one more book on the margin. In other words, economists assume publishers ask whether the marginal profits of acquiring one more book exceed the marginal costs. Trial Tr. 3092:23–3093:9 (Hill).

294. Dr. Snyder notes, however, that the merging parties must cover fixed costs in the long run and that their acquisition P&Ls include fixed costs. Trial Tr. 2935:17–2940:7 (Snyder). Yet because all firms have fixed costs, it is hardly surprising that publishers are interested in covering them. When making decisions about what a publisher's maximum willingness is to pay for a particular book, publishers should consider variable costs and not fixed costs. Trial Tr. 3092:23–3094:16 (Hill).

295. This intuition is corroborated by testimony from Defendants' executives. For example, under questioning by Defendants' counsel, Ms. McIntosh testified that she tells her editors to "focus their attention on the contribution number . . . because I want them to think about what is the incremental impact of making this bet on our company." Trial Tr. 2259:5–20 (McIntosh). In fact, she explicitly rejected Dr. Snyder's suggested approach of looking at how a book contributes to a publisher's fixed costs. Trial Tr. at 2259:24–2260:7 (McIntosh).

296. Nevertheless, even adopting Dr. Snyder's incorrect margins, the second-score auction model predicts meaningful harm to authors: a 3% reduction in compensation for PRH authors and an 8% reduction for S&S authors. *See* Trial Tr. 3105:17–25 (Hill).

297. Dr. Snyder's other criticisms of Dr. Hill's margin calculations are similarly incorrect. As discussed above, in his initial report, Dr. Hill identified that a group of PRH's costs had a mix of fixed and variable costs. Trial Tr. 1311:18–24 (Hill). To be conservative, he treated all those costs as variable. Trial Tr. 1311:25–1312:6 (Hill). In response to Dr. Snyder's criticism that those costs should appropriately be treated as fixed, Dr. Hill reran his models in his reply report doing just that—and found an even greater prediction of harm. Trial Tr. 1314:10–20 (Hill). For this second iteration, Dr. Snyder claimed that the actual margins of the publishers did not match the margins predicted by Dr. Hill's second-score auction model and therefore the results of Dr. Hill's model were unreliable. Trial Tr. 2804:24–2806:9 (Snyder). But the actual and predicted margins presented by Dr. Snyder were based on a methodology Dr. Hill did not actually use. Trial Tr. 3095:21–309724 (Hill). When comparing the actual and predicted margins using the methodology Dr. Hill *did* perform, the model presented an acceptable match. Trial Tr. 3094:19–3097:25 (Hill).

4. *Dr. Hill's Harm Estimates Are Consistent with Other Times Courts Have Blocked Anticompetitive Mergers*

298. Dr. Hill's harm estimates are consistent with those other courts have found sufficient to enjoin a merger. Courts have found estimates of quantifiable harm in the single digit percentage range, including estimates lower than Dr. Hill's here, to be substantial enough to enjoin a merger. *See, e.g., FTC v. Hackensack Meridian Health, Inc.,* 2021 WL 4145062, at *22n.26 (D.N.J. Aug. 4, 2021), *aff'd,* 30 F.4th 160 (3d Cir. 2022) (5.7% price effect for the merging parties' patients); *Sysco,* 131 F. Supp. 3d at 53–54, 66 (reflecting 4.6% to 5% market-wide price effect without efficiencies or the planned divestitures, or 3% to 3.2% market-wide price effect after accounting for those mitigating factors);26 *H & R Block,*

833 F. Supp. 2d at 87 (2.2–2.5% price effect for the acquiring firm's customers and a 10.5–12.2% price effect for the acquired firm's customers).

299. Further, Defendants' claim that the number of authors and books potentially harmed by this merger represents a "tiny corner" of the market not worthy of concern, Trial Tr. 60:21–61:3 (Defendants' Opening Statement), is contradicted by *Staples II,* which noted that "[a]ntitrust laws exist to protect competition, even for a targeted group that represents a relatively small part of an overall market." 190 F. Supp. 3d at 126. There, the targeted group consisted of just 1,200 large customers, or 1% of all business-to-business customers, within a business segment that represented "approximately thirty-five percent of Defendants' sales." *Id.* at 112, 126, 132, 138. The court rejected the defendants' argument that blocking the merger to protect this segment of large customers was misplaced because 99% of all business-to-business customers would allegedly benefit from the merger. *Id.* at 126, 137.

5. The Merger Will Likely Lower Output and Harm Readers

300. The Sherman Act does "not confine its protection to consumers, or to purchasers, or to competitors, or to sellers" and is meant to be "comprehensive" in "protecting all who are made victims of the forbidden practices." *Mandeville Island Farms,* 334 U.S. at 235–36. Accordingly, the proposed merger between PRH and S&S must be enjoined because it will substantially lessen competition among purchasers in the relevant market (*i.e.,* publishing companies) in their effort to acquire anticipated top selling manuscripts.

301. There is no requirement that the government also prove effects from the merger on consumers. *See Mandeville Island Farms,* 334 U.S. at 235 (finding a buy-side price fixing scheme illegal "even though the price-fixing was by purchasers, and the persons specifically injured under the treble damage claim are sellers, not customers or consumers."); *Telecor Commc'ns, Inc. v. Sw. Bell Tel. Co.,* 305 F.3d 1124, 1133–34 (10th Cir. 2002) (rejecting the defendants' argument that the government needed to show harm to end consumers because "[t]he Supreme Court's treatment of monopsony cases strongly suggests that suppliers . . . are protected by antitrust laws even when the anti-competitive activity does not harm end-users."); *Todd,* 275 F.3d at 213–14 ("In an oligopsony, the risk is that buyers will collude to depress prices [or salaries to laborers], causing harm to sellers [laborers]."); *Rice Growers Ass'n,* 1986 WL 12562 at *11–12 (holding merger unlawful due to harms on buy-side without analyzing downstream harm); *Heinz,* 246 F.3d at 719 ("[N]o court has ever held that a reduction in competition for wholesale purchasers is not relevant unless the plaintiff can prove impact at the consumer level.").

302. Plaintiff has nonetheless demonstrated harm to readers from the proposed transaction. As Mr. Dohle admitted, if advances go down it will lead to lower output, have a negative impact on the diversity of stories that are being published, and ensure that fewer authors will be able to make a living from writing. Trial Tr. 772:1–25 (Dohle); *see also* Trial Tr. 295:23–296:5 (Pande) (the proposed merger may make it more difficult for certain authors to publish their books because they "may get advances that will not allow them to move forward with the publication of their book"); Glusman Dep. 247:21–249:14 (the merger will lead to less diversity of books).

303. Reduced advances will lead to lower output or reduced quality of books because being paid less for their work will cause some authors to decide not to write a book at all, or possibly to write a lower quality book by, for example, deciding not to hire a researcher or photographer. Trial Tr. 460:11–462:12 (Karp); *cf.* Trial Tr. 1941:6–15 (Duhigg) (the advance is "the money that allows [authors] to write a book"); PX-2002 at 69–70 (Stehlik Dep. 163:14–15, Stehlik Dep. 163:17–20, Stehlik Dep. 163:33, Stehlik Dep. 163:25–164:10) (authors sometimes use advances to pay for living expenses or hire a researcher, photographer, or co-writer). For example, a journalist with a proposal to write a non-fiction book who receives an offer for a lower advance might decide it does not make financial sense to take time off from work to write the book. PX-656 at 1; Trial Tr. 462:9–22 (Karp); *cf.* Trial Tr. 1912:13–1913:1 (Duhigg); Trial Tr. 1916:4–21 (Duhigg) (explaining that the advance of $750,000 he was offered for his first book, split into four payments, allowed him to take a year off from *The New York Times* to write the book because the $115,00 he received as an initial payment, after taxes and paying the agent commission, could replace the salary he was earning as a journalist).

D. The Proposed Transaction Will Increase the Likelihood of Coordinated Effects

1. Applicable Legal Standard

304. "Merger law 'rests upon the theory that where rivals are few, firms will be able to coordinate their behavior, either by overt collusion or implicit understanding. . . . '" *Heinz,* 246 F.3d at 715 (quoting *FTC v. PPG Indus.,* 798 F.2d 1500, 1503 (D.C. Cir. 1986)). Mergers that result in a sufficiently high level of concentration therefore establish a presumption of anticompetitive coordination. *Id.* at 715–717;

see also H & R Block, 833 F. Supp.2d at 77. Accordingly, once the "government has established its prima facie case, the burden is on the defendants to produce evidence of 'structural market barriers to collusion'" specific to the book publishing industry that would "defeat the 'ordinary presumption of collusion' that attaches to a merger in a highly concentrated market." *H & R Block,* 833 F. Supp.2d at 77 (quoting *Heinz,* 246 F.3d at 725). Defendants cannot meet that burden here.

305. Coordinated effects are not limited to explicit collusion; rather, there are "numerous forms of coordination." Merger Guidelines § 7.1. Indeed, the presumption is motivated, in part, by the concern that a merger may result in tacit agreements and other parallel accommodating conduct that softens competition but does not amount to an explicit agreement not to compete. Such tacit coordination is difficult to detect and is often not actionable under the Sherman Act. *See* Merger Guidelines § 7; *see also Heinz,* 246 F.3d at 725; *Elders Grain,* 868 F.2d at 905; *Hosp. Corp.,* 807 F.2d at 1387 ("The fewer competitors there are in a market, the easier it is for them to coordinate their pricing without committing detectable violations of [S]ection 1 of the Sherman Act, which forbids price fixing.").

306. Accordingly, tacit collusion, more so even than express collusion, is "feared by antitrust policy" because "even when observed, [tacit collusion] cannot easily be controlled directly by the antitrust laws." *Heinz,* 246 F.3d at 725 (citation omitted); *see also Elders Grain,* 868 F.2d at 905 (six to five merger increased likelihood "leading members of the industry [would] collude on price and output without committing a detectable violation of section 1 of the Sherman Act" . . . since competitors "may not have to communicate or otherwise collude overtly in order to coordinate their price and output decisions"); *Hosp. Corp.,* 807 F.2d at 1387 (similar).

307. Competitors often find it easier to coordinate when it can "be enforced by detection and punishment of deviations that would undermine the coordinated interaction." Merger Guidelines § 7. For some types of coordination to occur, there needs to be "some form of common understanding" that firms will "pull [their] punches," the "ability to monitor and detect" whether other firms are adhering to the coordination, and some kind of punishment mechanism. Trial Tr. 1327:6–1328:5 (Hill); *see also* Trial Tr. 2638:2–21 (Snyder) ("what's important for coordinated effects are a mechanism of harm, the ability to detect and monitor.").

308. Coordinated effects are more likely where there is enough transparency for firms to successfully monitor an anticompetitive agreement or implicit understanding. *See, e.g., H & R Block,* 833 F. Supp. 2d at 78. Similarly, markets with high barriers to entry are more likely to result in coordinated effects. *Heinz,* 246 F.3d at 724 (courts view the "combination of a concentrated market and barriers to entry [as] a recipe for price coordination.").Not all forms of coordination, however, require both detection and punishment.

309. Parallel accommodating conduct requires neither. Instead, parallel accommodating conduct covers situations where "each rival's response to competitive moves made by others is individually rational, . . ., but nevertheless . . . weakens competitive incentives to reduce prices or offer customers better terms." Merger Guidelines § 7. And, in fact, several cases have enjoined mergers based on a coordinated effects theory without explicitly analyzing whether a specific punishment mechanism exists. *See, e.g., H & R Block,* 833 F. Supp. 2d 36, 77–81; *Elders Grain,* 868 F.2d at 905–906.

310. Courts have found a history of collusion or attempted collusion highly probative of likely harm from a merger; a history of collusion "establishes a precondition to effective collusion—mutual trust and forbearance. . . ." *Hosp. Corp.,* 807 F.2d at 1388; *see also Elders Grain,* 868 F.2d at 906 ("The theory of competition and monopoly that has been used to give concrete meaning to section 7 teaches that an acquisition which reduces the number of significant sellers in a market already highly concentrated and prone to collusion by reason of its history and circumstances is unlawful in the absence of special circumstances."); *H & R Block,* 833 F. Supp. 2d at 78; *Tronox,* 332 F. Supp. 3d at 208–212; Merger Guidelines § 7.2. Past coordination indicates that firms within the market have been able to overcome the obstacles that might otherwise make coordination difficult. *See, e.g., Heinz,* 246 F.3d at 724 (defendants' argument that structural barriers would prevent coordination "undermined by the record evidence of past price leadership in the baby food industry"). And a market already "prone to collusion" is "even more prone to collusion" after the proposed merger of two large competitors—leading to significant competitive harm. *Elders Grain,* 868 F.2d at 906; *see also Hosp. Corp.,* 807 F.2d at 1389 ("Considering . . . , the history of collusion in the industry [among other factors]," the FTC properly determined the hospital merger would "create an appreciable danger" of anticompetitive effects).

2. This Merger Is Likely to Increase the Risk of Coordination Among Publishers

311. Evidence demonstrates that the increasing levels of market concentration, especially with only four

remaining meaningful significant competitors, as well as the publishing industry's history of coordination pose a severe risk of tacit or even direct post-merger coordination of competition among the remaining Big Four. The industry's structure and the elimination of S&S as an independent competitor will, as Dr. Hill concluded, "likely [] increase the risk of coordination." Trial Tr. at 1328:10–11 (Hill); *see generally* Trial Tr. 1260:7–11 (Hill); Trial Tr. 1326:3–1331:4 (Hill).

312. First, as Bertelsmann itself recognized, the U.S. publishing industry is already an "oligopoly" with "only 4 further large publishers" beyond PRH. PX-80E at 13; *see also* Trial Tr. 2943:2–16 (Snyder). The proposed transaction would reinforce that oligopolistic market structure and render it even more susceptible to coordination by reducing the number of major competitors from five to four. Trial Tr. 1328:24–1329:1 (Hill). The elimination of an independent S&S will make it easier to reach a common understanding, monitor adherence to the understanding and detect deviations, and punish those who do not play along.

313. And as discussed more fully above, barriers to entry and expansion are significant, making it less likely that a new, disruptive entrant would be able to limit coordination by the remaining Big Four. *See supra* V.C.2.

314. Second, the trade book publishing industry has an established history of collusion. Between 2009 and 2010, five of the then Big Six publishers, including Penguin (but not Random House), coordinated with each other to raise e-book prices. This coordination involved "numerous exchanges *between* executives at different Big Six publishers," including "frequent telephone calls among the Publisher Defendants." *United States v. Apple, Inc.*, 791 F.3d 290, 302 (2d Cir. 2015) (emphasis in original); *see also id.* at 319 ("That the Publisher Defendants were in constant communication regarding their negotiations with both Apple and Amazon can hardly be disputed."). The Second Circuit held this conduct to be *per se* unlawful, describing it as "express collusion." *Id.* at 316, 321–29.

315. Third, industry-wide changes to the number of installments for author compensation payouts, the forced bundling of audio rights with publishing rights, and the uniform movement to 25% royalties on e-book sales all suggest that the Big Five publishers already engage, at least, in parallel behavior that allows them to obtain concessions that result in less favorable contractual terms and lower compensation for authors. *See supra* V.E.4. (describing how publishers insist on obtaining audio rights at the same time they obtain publishing rights even though that deprives authors of direct payments from audio publishers); *supra* V.E.5. (describing how publishing industry has shifted to structure advances so that they are paid in smaller average amounts over longer periods of time); Trial Tr. 775:5–15 (Dohle) (e-book royalty rates shifted from 50% to 25%); *see also* Trial Tr. 776:22–25 (Dohle) (agreeing that he took credit for leading an industry shift in e-book royalty rates).

316. The industry's history of coordination shows that competitors have the ability to reach some form of common understanding and the market is already susceptible to coordination. Trial Tr. 1329:8–17 (Hill).

317. Beyond its enduring oligopoly and history of collusion, several other structural features of the book publishing business make it susceptible to coordination. First, it is a "close- knit" industry where key executives often have professional relationships with executives from other publishers. *See Apple,* 791 F.3d at 300 ("[T]he Big Six operated in a close-knit industry and had no qualms communicating about the need to act together.").

318. Second, the evidence shows that competitive outcomes are transparent. *See infra* ¶ 329 (collecting evidence on transparency). The Big Five can easily monitor and detect adherence to common understandings. Publishers acknowledge that they can observe which publisher poached an author or won a book in an auction or other competitive event. That is, they have "an ability to know to whom [they a]re losing." Trial Tr. 1330:11–22 (Hill).

319. After detection, the industry has punishment mechanisms. Many publishers depend on the Big Five for distribution, and some depend on Bertelsmann for printing. *See* [REDACTED] Trial Tr. 119:12–25 (Pietsch) (describing services that Hachette performs on behalf of its distribution clients); PX-682 at 2 ("We would not want to be 100% beholden to a competitor for printing."). These contractual arrangements create deeper relationships among competitors, which can facilitate coordination and enable punishment. *Cf. Hosp. Corp.,* 707 F.2d at 1389 ("The management contracts between" hospitals "illustrate the unusual degree of cooperation in this industry [REDACTED] ").

320. Moreover, if the one of the publishers recruits or poaches an author, it can be punished by having its own authors targeted for poaching. Targeting a particular publisher for poaching or more aggressive competitive actions could be a punishment for deviating from a common understanding to make the

standard contract terms more beneficial to publishers or to refrain from poaching.

321. The market is also vulnerable to coordination because it involves frequent purchases for relatively small amounts. Dr. Hill noted that there are over 1,000 contracts per year within the anticipated top-seller market. Small, frequent purchases "make coordination easier," whereas larger purchases make coordination harder to sustain because of the temptation to deviate from the common understanding to secure particularly lucrative sales. Trial Tr. 1330:1–3 (Hill); *see also* Merger Guidelines § 7.2 (explaining that a firm can be deterred from defecting from the agreement "if sales are small and frequent").

322. Finally, the post-merger dominance of PRH is not something than can readily be ignored. As discussed above, PRH is a powerful industry player today. After the merger, with nearly 50% of the market and important stakes in the distribution and printing businesses, PRH would be in a pole position to act as a leading firm whose decisions the other players would likely follow. In addition, after the merger, PRH and HarperCollins alone would control almost 75% of the relevant market. As courts have recognized, such a market structure makes coordinated effects particularly likely. *See Tronox,* 332 F. Supp. 3d at 209 (merger makes coordinated effects more likely through "sheer market power" in part because the "post-merger market would feature two firms that control roughly three quarters" of the market); *see also Heinz,* 246 F.3d at 724 n.23 (recognizing that "price leadership" is "a danger" in a "duopoly" market).

3. Defendants' Arguments Regarding Structural Barriers are Unsubstantiated and Ignore Likely Forms of Coordination

323. Defendants cannot meet their burden to rebut the presumption of coordinated effects here. Defendants' arguments and Dr. Snyder's assumptions regarding the two most likely forms of post-merger coordination—on contractual terms or not to poach authors—are unsubstantiated and belied by case law, the evidence, and common sense.

324. First, Dr. Snyder opined that coordination on contractual terms such as audio rights and payout structure is immaterial because possible coordination on such terms "doesn't limit competition on many other dimensions, most important of which is advances." Trial Tr. 2882:5–19 (Snyder).

325. The Supreme Court disagrees with Dr. Snyder. In *Catalano v. Target Stores,* 446 U.S. 643, 647 (1980), competing beer distributors agreed to change the terms under which they sold beer to retailers by no longer extending credit to retailers and instead requiring upfront payments. The beer distributors defended their agreement on credit terms by claiming there was no agreement on the price of the beer itself, even though those contractual changes made the overall bundle of terms and price less favorable to retailers. The Court held the agreement *per se* illegal because "[i]t is more realistic to view an agreement to eliminate credit sales as extinguishing one form of competition among the sellers." *Id.* at 649. That the price of the beer remained outside the agreement to fix credit terms did not save the agreement from legal condemnation. *Cf. United States v. Socony-Vacuum Oil Co.,* 310 U.S. 150, 222 (1940) (agreements regarding price formulas are illegal because "they are related to the market prices" even when the ultimate price is not fixed).

326. Here, the reasonable danger that the remaining competitors could more easily coordinate—or act in parallel by accommodating each other's updated standard contract terms—presents a harm to authors even if the advance amount itself is not subject to coordination.

327. Defendants also argue that "there[is] no way for publishers to coordinate or follow prices [or] other deal terms," in part because certain information about the acquisition process is not fully transparent. Trial Tr. 85:7–10 (Defendants' Opening Statement). This assertion is not supported by the record.

328. The evidence presented at trial shows that, in recent years, several deal terms have become standardized across the industry (or, at least, the Big Five), including audio and royalty rates, often to the detriment of authors. *See, e.g.* PX-652 at 1–3 (audio); Trial Tr. 255:24–256:10 (Pande); Trial Tr. 257:14–18 (Pande) (audio and royalty rates); Trial Tr. 1941:16–20 (Duhigg) (testifying that he did not know he could negotiate over royalty rates); Trial Tr. 1828:21–1829:18 (Walsh) (payouts shifted from halves to fourths); Trial Tr. 256:22–25 (Pande) (similar), Trial Tr. 775:5–15 (Dohle); *see also* Trial Tr. 776:22–25 (Dohle). These changes have been transparent to industry participants. *See e.g.,* PX-652 at 1 ("It will be very interesting to see whether PRH, Hachette, Harper or Macmillan participate. MY understanding is that they too have the 'no audio, no deal' rule."). Taken together, further consolidation increases the likelihood of future consensus regarding contract terms such as royalty rates, payouts, and the types of rights authors can reserve—all of which already reflect a high degree of standardization within the relevant market.

329. Second, there are no structural barriers that would prevent the future Big Four from tacitly agreeing not to poach each other's major authors. Poaching is a competitive action that increases author compensation. In the publishing industry, poaching is transparent and easily detected: when one publisher steals an author away from another publisher, the losing publisher learns the identity of the winner either through early reporting by industry trade press, Trial Tr. 1233:3–13 (Hill), or when the new publisher publishes the author's book. *See* Trial Tr. 1330:11–22 (Hill); *see also* Trial Tr. 2295:10–19 (McIntosh) (describing major authors who moved from PRH to Hachette and Macmillan); DX-423 at 15–16 (Glusman Dep. 210:22–211:25) (describing authors Norton lost to PRH). When asked to explain why coordination would be unlikely after the merger, Dr. Snyder differentiated coordination regarding author poaching from other types of coordination, stating "I'm going to put aside the idea concerning poaching authors, if I may. All of the other ideas around coordination fall victim to the basic economic principles here." Trial Tr. 2880:14–2881:18 (Snyder).

330. Dr. Snyder's later testimony that any no-poach agreement would cause the Big Five to lose authors to smaller publishers, Trial Tr. 3018:22–3021:13 (Snyder), ignores the evidence, detailed above, establishing that non-Big Five publishers face a number of important competitive disadvantages in the relevant market. *Supra* V.C.3.a. Dr. Snyder's argument that editors would ignore a directive from their CEOs to refrain from poaching is similarly unsubstantiated. *See* Trial Tr. 3017:14–3018:1 (Snyder). The record provides no basis to conclude that employees in this business are particularly unlikely to ignore the instructions of their corporate leaders. In fact, to the contrary, the evidence suggests that the merging parties' editors do, for example, follow corporate-wide rules against acquiring books without audio rights. PX-652 at 1–3. And they also follow corporate guidance limiting intra-firm competition. *See, e.g.,* PX-54 at 2 ("We would like to invoke the PRH policy/rule where other imprints can bid on this but not more than our $150k."); PX-107 at 1 (PRH CEO asks divisions to coordinate; they later report that they will "agree to a number and both offer same").

331. Similar to Defendants' arguments regarding transparency, any suggestion that future coordination is unlikely because there is no plausible punishment mechanism misses the mark. Trial Tr. 2880:9–13 (Snyder). Given its large size, a combined PRH/S&S could be especially well situated to punish violations of any tacit or explicit agreement by, for example, punishing deviations from a no-poach agreement by retaliating in a tit-for-tat manner whenever a rival tries to poach authors from it. In addition, because its parent company Bertelsmann controls access to scarce printing capacity in the United States, PRH (through Bertelsmann) could discipline publishers who violate an agreement by withholding or restricting access to printing capacity. *See* PX-983 at 1; Trial Tr. 760:18–21 (Dohle); Trial Tr. 762:11–17 (Dohle); [REDACTED] Regardless, coordinated effects do not require a showing that punishment is likely. To the contrary, coordinated effects can occur where the major competitors mutually recognize that it is not in each other's interest to aggressively compete in a particular way, even in the absence of an obvious punishment mechanism. *See* Merger Guidelines § 7.

332. For the foregoing reasons, Defendants cannot overcome the presumption of coordinated effects here.

CONCLUSION

The evidence shows that the proposed merger between PRH and S&S likely would substantially lessen competition in the market for the acquisition of U.S. publishing rights to anticipated top-selling books in violation of Section 7 of the Clayton Act. The Court should therefore permanently enjoin PRH from merging with S&S.

Respectfully submitted,

Dated: September 1, 2022

John R. Read (DC Bar #419373) United States Department of Justice Antitrust Division
450 Fifth Street, NW, Suite 4000
Washington, DC 20530
Counsel for Plaintiff United States of America

UNITED STATES POST-TRIAL BRIEF

INTRODUCTION

Penguin Random House's ("PRH") proposed merger with Simon & Schuster ("S&S") should be enjoined. This is a straightforward case: the merger would eliminate the significant head-to-head competition between the two companies that benefits authors today and result in a highly concentrated market for the acquisition of anticipated top-selling books. Pursuant to this Circuit's precedents, the merger is presumed to be unlawful.

Rather than persuasively counter the substantial factual record and Dr. Nicholas Hill's quantitative analysis, Defendants obfuscate. They misstate the law and fail to provide relevant and credible evidence to rebut the presumption. They seek to focus the Court's attention on outlier examples that are simply exceptions that prove the government correctly defined the market, demonstrated the merger is presumptively illegal, and proved the merger will likely harm authors.

The legal standards put forth by Defendants are inaccurate, and would hold the government to an impossibly high burden while requiring Defendants to provide the thinnest veneer of a defense to rebut the presumption of illegality. Such a framework inaccurately represents the law in this Circuit, as exemplified by *Anthem* and *Baker Hughes,* and would defeat the purpose of a burden-shifting exercise altogether. The government has met its burden to identify a relevant product market—the market for rights to publish anticipated top-selling books—and shown high levels of concentration sufficient to establish a presumption that the merger will substantially lessen competition.

Defendants have failed to satisfy their burden to rebut this presumption. Instead, in arguing the government's product market and evidence that the merger will lessen competition are incorrect, Defendants use statistical sleight-of-hand to suggest that Dr. Hill's analysis is incorrect and rely on exceptions and outliers that do not represent the way that competition typically works in the market for anticipated top sellers. As demonstrated at trial and described in the United States' Proposed Findings of Fact and Conclusions of Law ("United States' Proposed Findings"), testimony, documents, and the economic analysis of Dr. Hill all provide ample evidence that the merger's effects "may be substantially to lessen competition," in the words of the Clayton Act, 15 U.S.C. § 18. Accordingly, the merger should be enjoined.

I. DEFENDANTS MAKE SIGNIFICANT CONCESSIONS IN THEIR PROPOSED FINDINGS

333. Defendants make several significant concessions that support finding that the merger is presumptively illegal and that the United States alleged a proper relevant market.

A. Defendants Concede That Dr. Hill's Market Share and HHI Calculations Are Correct

334. Defendants do not dispute that the government's shares for the market for anticipated top-selling books are correctly calculated. In their Proposed Findings ("Defs. PFOF"), Defendants acknowledge that both Dr. Hill and their expert Dr. Snyder agree on the market shares for the market for anticipated top-selling books. *See* Dkt. 178 at 52 (Defs. PFOF ¶ 113); Trial Tr. 2655:6–10 (Snyder); *see also* Dkt. 178 at 51 (Defs. PFOF ¶ 110). Defendants do not contest that the combined PRH and S&S will control approximately 49% of the market for anticipated top-selling books. *See* PX-959; Trial Tr. 1254:3–6 (Hill). Thus, Defendants concede the merger would result in a combined market share that far surpasses the 30% share the Supreme Court found sufficient to establish a presumptive violation of Section 7. *United States v. Phila. Nat'l Bank,* 374 U.S. 321, 364 (1963); *see FTC v. H.J. Heinz Co.,* 246 F.3d 708, 711, 715–717 (D.C. Cir. 2001) (holding FTC established presumption where defendants would have a combined share of 32.8% in a concentrated market); *Hospital Corp. of Am. v. FTC,* 807 F.2d 1381, 1384 (7th Cir. 1986) (finding transaction unlawful that raised defendant's market share from 14% to 26% and the market share of the four largest firms from 79% to 91%).

335. Additionally, Defendants do not contest that Dr. Hill correctly calculated the HHIs in the market for anticipated top-selling books. Dr. Hill found the HHIs in the relevant market were above the level necessary to create a presumption against the merger, as established by courts and the U.S. Department of Justice & Federal Trade Commission, Horizontal Merger Guidelines (2010) ("Merger Guidelines"). Trial Tr. 1256:24–1258:11 (Hill); Trial Tr. 1259:4–12 (Hill) (establishing that the pre-merger HHI is 2,220 and the post-merger HHI is 3,111); Merger Guidelines § 5.3; United States v. H & R Block, Inc., 833 F. Supp. 2d 36, 71–72 (D.D.C. 2011). While Defendants contest the government's definition of anticipated top sellers—see infra III for an explanation of why Defendants' criticisms are baseless—Defendants do not contest that if the government's market definition for anticipated top sellers is correct, the HHIs are correctly calculated and sufficient to establish that the merger is presumptively anticompetitive.

B. Defendants Do Not Contest That They Are Close Competitors and That Significant Evidence Supports the Relevant Market

336. While Defendants argue that market shares are not reliable indicators of competitive effects by stating that S&S is not PRH's closest competitor (which is itself a misleading statement, as S&S is one of PRH's closest competitors, *see infra* V.B), even they do not contest that PRH is S&S's closest competitor. Mr. Karp conceded that PRH is the publisher that S&S's editors most frequently compete against. *See* Trial Tr. 595:23–25 (Karp) ("Q. So you would expect Penguin Random House to be the publisher you bid against the most, correct? A. I think so, yes."). And both Dr. Hill's and Dr. Snyder's data sets confirm that PRH is S&S's closest competitor—Dr. Hill's data sets show that S&S loses to PRH approximately 60% of the time, and Dr. Snyder's data set indicates that PRH is the most frequent runner-up to S&S. *See* Trial Tr. 1280:17–1281:17 (Hill); Trial Tr. 2927:17–2928:4 (Snyder).

337. Defendants acknowledge commercially relevant factors distinguish books at different advance levels, Dkt. 178 at 26 (Defs. PFOF ¶ 46) ("*Every factor relevant* to commercial reality shows only a price continuum, not a distinct submarket of books defined anywhere around the $250,000 advance level.") (emphasis added), and concede that there are meaningful differences among books based on advance level. For example, Defendants admit that there is a "general positive correlation" between higher advances and higher expected sales, more marketing support, higher initial print runs, and customized contract terms. Dkt. 178 at 125 (Defs. PCOL ¶¶ 23–24); Trial Tr. 3265:12–15 (Defs.' Closing Statement) ("And to be clear, we have never disputed that there is a general correlation between advance levels and predicted sales. After all, the profit and loss statements, Your Honor, are based on estimated sales."); Dkt. 178 at 26 (Defs. PFOF ¶ 45).

C. Defendants Admit That Mr. Dohle's Letter "Is Not Legally Binding"

338. Defendants concede that Mr. Dohle's promise made concerning PRH and S&S's competition post-merger "may not be legally binding." *See* Dkt. 178 at 76–77 (Defs. PFOF ¶ 210). This is in contrast to their Pre-Trial Brief, in which Defendants suggested that Mr. Dohle's promise could rebut the presumption if it was "credible, concrete, and supported by evidence." *See* Dkt. 159 at 50 (Defs. Pre-Trial Brief). Defendants all but abandoned this argument in their proposed findings—spending a single paragraph on the promise, which cites no law—and effectively concede, as made clear in the United States' Proposed Findings, a mere promise not to abuse acquired market power is legally insufficient to rebut the government's prima facie case. *See* Dkt. 177 at 84–85 (U.S. PFOF ¶¶ 227–229).

D. Defendants Do Not Contest That S&S Understood the Transaction Carried Antitrust Risk

339. The fact that the parties are before the Court today is not surprising. It is undisputed that Defendants understood their merger—a merger that would transform the Big Five to the Big Four—risked violating the antitrust laws. As a result, [REDACTED].

II. DEFENDANTS CONTINUE TO MISSTATE THE APPROPRIATE LEGAL STANDARDS

340. Defendants' Proposed Conclusions of Law misstate several applicable legal standards and attempt to add additional elements of proof to a Section 7 case. The Court should reject Defendants' invitation to alter the standards established by the Supreme Court and the D.C. Circuit, and their attempts to avoid the presumption of illegality that applies to this merger.

341. First, the Court should reject Defendants' suggestion that the language in Section 7 prohibiting mergers where the effect "may be substantially to lessen competition" requires the United States to prove harm with a heightened degree of certainty. Defendants assert that a plaintiff must prove "a concrete, fact-based projection of substantial harm," and that here the United States is advocating for a standard of

"speculation about the possibility of some harm." Dkt. 178 at 116 (Defs.' PCOL ¶ 3). Defendants are wrong on both counts: the United States' Proposed Findings sets forth the correct standard—the reasonable probability standard courts have applied for decades (*see Brown Shoe Co. v. United States,* 370 U.S. 294, 323 & n.39 (1962) (the Clayton Act is "concern[ed] with probability, not certainties" and proscribes "mergers with probable anticompetitive effects"))—and explains why Defendants' effort to change the required level of proof is at odds with the settled caselaw. Dkt. 177 at 27–29 (U.S. PFOF ¶¶ 35–40). The United States is not arguing for a change of the Section 7 standard, and the evidence presented in this case clearly satisfies the existing standard.

342. Second, the Court should reject Defendants' attempt to add a new element of proof in a Section 7 case by claiming that "the merger cannot be enjoined under § 7 unless the government proves that likely substantial harm is imminent." Dkt. 178 at 152–3 (Defs. PCOL ¶ 96). Defendants' new "requirement" purportedly "demands more than a speculative possibility that advances may be reduced by an unspecified amount over some unspecified period of time"—without citing a source. Dkt. 178 at 152–3 (Defs. PCOL ¶ 96). When courts in this district have used the phrase "sufficiently probable and imminent," it has been in the context of discussing the general burden of proof in a Section 7 case, in order to clarify that it is something more than "ephemeral possibilities" and something less than a "certainty." *See, e.g., FTC v. Wilh. Wilhelmsen Holding ASA,* 341 F. Supp. 3d 27, 43 (D.D.C. 2018); *FTC v. Arch Coal, Inc.,* 329 F. Supp. 2d 109, 115 (D.D.C. 2004). The cases Defendants cite do not support the claim that courts require separate proof of "imminent harm" before enjoining a merger, and Defendants point to no cases holding that a plaintiff failed to make out a Section 7 claim solely because of a lack of "imminent harm." In any event, there is no doubt on this record that authors face imminent harm from this merger—publishers are competing for new books every day, and the loss of S&S as an independent competitor would affect such competition immediately upon consummation of the merger.

343. Third, the Court should reject Defendants' claim that the presumption of harm established by the government's prima facie case "[h]as [m]inimal [f]orce" and that it is a "low bar" that can be rebutted with a "minimal evidentiary showing." Dkt. 178 at 118 (Defs. PCOL ¶ 7); Dkt. 178 at 138 (Defs. PCOL ¶ 55). Defendants provide no legal support for this "minimal" standard.2 They also ignore that the quantum of proof required in rebuttal is not fixed. As the D.C. Circuit explained in *Baker Hughes,* "[t]he more compelling the prima facie case, the more evidence the defendant must present to rebut it successfully." *United States v. Baker Hughes Inc.,* 908 F.2d 981, 991 (D.C. Cir. 1990). Courts in this district subject rebuttal evidence to rigorous analysis and frequently reject it as insufficient. For example, in *Heinz,* the D.C. Circuit rejected all of the defendants' proffered rebuttal arguments. With respect to the defendants' efficiencies rebuttal, the *Heinz* court required "proof of extraordinary efficiencies" given the high concentration levels resulting from the merger—a standard the defendants failed to meet. *Heinz,* 246 F.3d at 720. Likewise, the court rejected the defendants' "innovation" rebuttal argument because of "the absence of *reliable and significant evidence*" to justify it. *Id.* at 723 (emphasis added); *see also Wilhelmsen,* 341 F. Supp. 3d at 68 (finding defendants failed to carry burden on ease of entry where claim was "at odds with" record evidence and "defies basic economic principles"); *United States v. Aetna Inc.,* 240 F. Supp. 3d 1, 52–59 (D.D.C. 2017) (rejecting ease of entry rebuttal claim after conducting in-depth "assessment of the expert and non-expert evidence for each specific element of the entry analysis"). This is far from the "low bar" that Defendants claim.

344. Defendants also misstate the standard for making this rebuttal showing, suggesting they need only provide evidence "indicating" that the market shares the United States presents are not representative. Dkt. 178 at 138 (Defs. PCOL ¶ 55). This is incorrect. As the D.C. Circuit has stated, rebutting a presumption of illegality requires more: a defendant "must provide sufficient evidence that the prima facie case 'inaccurately predicts the relevant transaction's probable effect on future competition,' or it must sufficiently discredit the evidence underlying the original presumption." *United States v. Anthem, Inc.,* 855 F.3d 345, 349 (D.C. Cir. 2017) (quoting *Baker Hughes,* 908 F.2d at 991).

345. Fourth, this Court should reject Defendants' attempt to argue that the presumption of illegality should be ignored here because "[t]he government cites no case rejecting a merger on the basis of market shares alone where five market participants remained in active competition." Dkt. 178 at 146 (Defs. PCOL ¶ 76). While it is unclear what Defendants mean by "on the basis of market shares alone," there can be no doubt that there are numerous cases blocking a merger despite the fact that there would have been five remaining "market participants" (or many more) post-merger. Indeed, the case that established the Section 7 presumption, *Philadelphia National Bank,* held a merger to be presumptively illegal based on market shares of 30% despite the fact that there existed "40 other banks in the Philadelphia market."

374 U.S. at 363–64, 367; *see also H & R Block,* 833 F. Supp. 2d at 73 ("defendants note there are eighteen companies" in the relevant market); *Wilhelmsen,* 341 F. Supp. 3d at 60 (pie chart showing numerous other suppliers with total share of 9%); *Hosp. Corp.,* 807 F.2d at 1387 (seven competing hospitals remained after the acquisition); *FTC v. Elders Grain, Inc.,* 868 F.2d 901, 905 (7th Cir. 1989) (five firms remaining post-merger). However, as explained in the United States' Proposed Findings, "merely counting the number of firms in the market is rarely relevant to antitrust analysis without considering other measures of their competitive significance." Dkt. 177 at 101 (U.S. PFOF ¶ 194). It is not the number of firms that drives the relevant inquiry. As precedent shows, the critical question is the extent to which each market participant is capable of constraining the merged firm.

346. Defendants continue to attempt to distinguish this case from "any other where a merger has been blocked" by citing a handful of cases where the merging parties were "the top two competitors in the industry" or it was a "merger to duopoly." Dkt. 178 at 142 (Defs. PCOL ¶¶ 64–65). But Defendants argument is unavailing. First, it is not necessary in a unilateral effects case that the merging parties be either the top two competitors in a market or each other's closest competitor. Dkt. 177 at 102–103 (U.S. PFOF ¶¶ 196–97); Dkt. 177 at 125 (U.S. PFOF ¶ 250) (discussing cases). Nor is it necessary that the merger result in a duopoly or monopoly market structure. In fact, courts have found that a merger violates Section 7 even where, as here, there would be four or more significant competitors after the merger. *Elders Grain,* 868 F.2d at 902–903, 905 (merger reducing number of competitors "of any significance" from six to five); *Hosp. Corp.,* 807 F.2d at 1387 (the "four largest firms came to control virtually the whole market" as a result of acquisitions at issue); *FTC v. Tronox Ltd.,* 332 F. Supp. 3d 187, 207 (D.D.C. 2018) (enjoining merger resulting in four competitors); *Aetna,* 240 F. Supp. 3d at 9–10 (blocking merger). Courts have also found Section 7 violations where the merged firm would have market shares similar to those here. *FTC v. Hackensack Meridian Health, Inc.,* 30 F. 4th 160, 172 (3d Cir. 2022) (merged firm would have 47% share, with "next two closest competitors" at 21% and 9%, respectively); *Anthem,* 236 F. Supp. 3d at 207–09 (merged firm market share of approximately 50% in four-competitor market). There is nothing to suggest that the facts of the cases cited by Defendants are necessary, rather than sufficient, conditions to block a merger.

III. DEFENDANTS' PRODUCT MARKET CLAIMS ARE WRONG

A. The Cases Defendants Cite Are Inapposite

347. *Defendants heavily rely on Oracle,* a case from a different circuit that they claim is "similar" to the proposed market definition here. Dkt. 178 at 121 (Defs. PCOL ¶ 14). But *Oracle* is not similar to this case at all. First, *Oracle* did not involve a submarket of targeted customers. Rather, the issue was whether particular types of software products were reasonably interchangeable for buyers. *Oracle* therefore provides no guidance on how to properly identify the members of a targeted customer submarket, the issue on which the Defendants seek to apply the case here. *See United States v. Oracle Corp.*, 331 F. Supp. 2d 1098, 1154 (N.D. Cal. 2004) (noting the government argued the case based on unique "product characteristics;" not characteristics of the customers). Second, *Oracle* does not stand for the proposition that "a submarket cannot be defined solely on the basis of price differences among otherwise comparable products," as Defendants claim. Dkt. 178 at 119–20 (Defs. PCOL ¶ 12). There, the court found that "there were no generally available data" that would allow an expert to reliably calculate market shares in the proposed market—not that markets can never be defined by reference to prices. 331 F. Supp. 2d at 1148, 1158–59. The *Oracle* court's concerns about the availability of data to identify market participants and calculate shares do not apply here, where both experts agree that the data are accurate and complete. Moreover, courts in this circuit do not follow *Oracle* when defining targeted customer markets. For example, courts do not require the targeted group to have "objectively observable characteristics" (*FTC v. Sysco Corp.,* 113 F. Supp. 3d 1, 45–46 (D.D.C. 2015)), and the fact that a proposed customer group may be somewhat "over-inclusive" does not render the submarket invalid. *Id.* at 45 (finding defendants' "national customer" lists to be a "useful proxy" despite claim they were "over-inclusive").

348. bottom, *Oracle* is simply another in the line of cases Defendants cite where a proposed product market failed because there were reasonably interchangeable substitutes outside the candidate market. *See id.* 331 F. Supp. 2d at 1158 (finding multiple substitutes for "high function" software); Dkt. 177 at 37–38 (U.S. PFOF ¶¶ 61–62). In that way, *Oracle* is similar to *In re Super Premium Ice Cream Distribution Antitrust Litig.,* 691 F. Supp. 1262 (N.D. Cal. 1988), where the court held that ice cream options that were lower on the price/quality spectrum constrained the price of high-quality ice cream. That is not the

case here, where authors would not switch to writing books with only a niche readership as a substitute for writing and selling anticipated top sellers in order to defeat lowered advances. *See* Dkt. 177 at 35–36 (U.S. PFOF ¶ 58). Ultimately, both *Oracle* and *Super Premium Ice Cream* dealt with a different issue than the one the Court is deciding here. Those cases addressed whether certain products were reasonably interchangeable with each other and therefore must be grouped in the same relevant product market. They were not about how to identify a group of customers (or sellers) *within* a broader product market who could be targeted after the merger, which is the question the Court is addressing here.

349. Defendants have not identified a single case that contradicts the United States' statement at closing that "in this district, as far as I know, in the last decade . . . I cannot think of a case where the plaintiff has failed on product market without there being an adequate substitute." Trial Tr. 3324:25–3325:4 (U.S. Closing).

B. The Relevant Product Market Encompasses All Authors of Anticipated Top Sellers, Not Only Franchise Authors and Celebrities

350. Defendants have attempted to twist the market at issue in this case by suggesting that the United States is only interested in protecting the interests of the "elite of the elite" authors. Dkt. 178 at 9–10 (Defs. PFOF ¶¶ 5–6) (falsely claiming the United States narrowed its case to "'franchise' authors who write multiple successful books, popular or notorious celebrities, and authors with prior books that won the acclaim of literary awards"). Contrary to Defendants' claim, the United States' product market includes all books whose expected sales would justify an advance of at least $250,000, Dkt. 177 at 38 (U.S. PFOF ¶ 64); not solely books from franchise and celebrity authors. A $250,000 advance paid out over three to four years after the deduction of the typical 15% agent commission will earn an author between $53,000 and $71,000 per year. *See also* PX-656 at 1 ("I believe [the agent] is telling you the truth when she says they can't [write the book] for less than $350,000. Assume they're each making $150,000 a year and they want to take a full year off. They're just trying to break even after paying the [agent's] commission.").

351. It does not matter whether "everyone recognizes" the books in the United States' market as likely best sellers. *See* Dkt. 178 at 10–11 (Defs. PFOF ¶ 8). It only matters that publishing professionals—editors and agents—can recognize books that are expected to sell a lot of copies and appeal to a large audience—a fact for which there is ample proof. Trial Tr. 1541:21–25 (Hill); Dkt. 177 at 40 (U.S. PFOF ¶ 70); Dkt. 177 at 47–48 (U.S. PFOF ¶¶ 89–91); Trial Tr. 1134:14–1135:3 (Weisberg); Trial Tr. 1229:20–1230:6 (Hill). As Dr. Hill articulated, "the threshold is identifying a group of books and authors that are different than other authors." Trial Tr. 1239:4–6 (Hill).

352. The summaries Ms. Porro created illustrate some examples in which PRH and S&S agreed—based on their final bids—that a book was an anticipated top seller. *See, e.g.,* PX- 932-B at 1 (both bidding $300,000); PX-955-B (both bidding $1.5 million); PX-954-B at 1 (three PRH divisions and S&S all bidding $1.05 million); PX-938-B at 1 (both bidding $750,000); PX- 950-B at 1 (bidding $675,000 (PRH) and $700,000 (S&S)); PX-943-B at 1 (bidding $390,000 (PRH) and $350,000 (S&S)); PX-935-B at 1 (bidding $350,000 (PRH) and $368,000 (S&S)). Only one of the competitive episodes summarized by Ms. Porro involved an author who is inarguably famous selling a work for millions of dollars—[REDACTED]—and none involved franchise writers. Moreover, the United States presented evidence showing how many authors in this market would be harmed by a merger of PRH and S&S, including non-franchise authors, debut authors, non-fiction authors, and even a few celebrities of various levels of fame and advance level. Dkt. 177 at 126–129 (U.S. PFOF ¶¶ 252–254); Dkt. 177 at 140–141 (U.S. PFOF¶¶ 279, 284).

353. Defendants describe <u>Where the Crawdads Sing</u> as an example of an "unanticipated best seller." Dkt. 178 at 32 (Defs. PFOF ¶ 82). <u>Where the Crawdads Sing</u>, however, sold to PRH for [REDACTED], DX-413 at 1, placing it squarely within the market for "anticipated top sellers." The other three books cited—<u>Gone Girl</u>, <u>Fifty Shades of Gray</u>, and <u>The Life-Changing Magic of Tidying Up</u>—were sold to PRH nearly a decade or more ago with no record evidence of their advance level.

C. Authors of Anticipated Top Sellers Can Be Targeted for a Decrease in Advances

354. Defendants suggest that authors of anticipated top sellers cannot be targeted because they do not share "objective," or "easily identifiable" characteristics. *See, e.g.,* Dkt. 178 at 38–39 (Defs. PFOF ¶¶ 78–79); Dkt. 178 at 131 (Defs. PCOL ¶ 38). But as the court explained when rejecting a similar argument in *Sysco,* "price discrimination can occur even when customers do not have common observable characteristics." *Sysco,* 113 F. Supp. 3d at 45–46; *see also id.* at 46 ("Price discrimination can occur in such a marketplace, even if the customers do not share specific identifiable traits"). Instead, price

discrimination was feasible because the *Sysco* defendants "engage[d] in individual negotiations with their national customers and possess[ed] substantial information about them." *Id.* at 46.

355. The same is true here. Book deals are individually negotiated. *See* Dkt. 56 at 12 (Defs. Am. Answer ¶ 33). And publishers have "substantial information about" books before they bid on them. *See Sysco* 133 F. Supp. 3d at 46. When deciding what to bid, publishers typically have a finished manuscript, partial manuscript, or book proposal. *See* Trial Tr. 245:5–17 (Pande); Trial Tr. 246:23–247:6 (Pande); Trial Tr. 1750:4–7 (Walsh); 1912:13–1913:1 (Duhigg); Trial Tr. 2105:19–21 (Ross). Publishers often know the sales history of the author's previous books, *see, e.g.,* [REDACTED] and the author's social media following or platfonn, *see* Trial Tr. 1111:18–25 (Weisberg); DX-21 at 5.4 Publishers also often meet with the author or agent before bidding. *See* Trial Tr. 1754:3–24 (Walsh). Publishers have the sales history of comparable titles to project a book's sales, including some provided by the author's agent. *See, e.g.,* Trial Tr. 1753:12–1754:2 (Walsh); PX- 2002 at 62–63 (Stehlik Dep. **151:**18–152:11); PX-42 at 5.

356. Publishers already use this information to project the book's sales and hence determine what they will pay for the book. Thus, publishers are already identifying whether a book is an anticipated top seller, and publishers can target authors of anticipated top sellers. *See* Dkt. 177 at 40–43 (U.S. PFOF ff 69–76). This is the case regardless of the degree of precision with which publishers can anticipate the sales of a book at the time of acquisition. The moment that a publisher submits a bid of $250,000 or more for a book, the publisher knows that this book is an anticipated top seller, **and** that few other independent publishers are likely to be bidding competitive—and one fewer after the merger of PRH and S&S.

D. Targeted Customers Can Be Harmed When They Lie On a "Continuum"

357. Defendants concede that for "every factor relevant to commercial reality," books differ based on the advances they receive. See Dkt. 178 at 26 (Defs. PFOF 46); Dkt. 178 at 125–26 (Defs. PCOL ¶¶ 24–25). Nevertheless, Defendants argue that because such differences occur along a "continuum" and do not sharply differ above and below the $250,000 threshold, the government's market is not properly defined. See Dkt. 178 at 26 (Defs. PFOF ¶ 46); Dkt. 178 at 125–26 (PCOL ¶¶ 24–25). Such a difference is not required by this Court's targeted customer cases or the Merger Guidelines.

358. Similar to the "continuum" at issue in this case, the Court described a continuum of insurance customers in *Anthem:* "the larger a customer becomes, it requires greater, customization, sophistication and network coverage, as its range of choices narrows." *See United States v. Anthem, Inc.,* 236 F. Supp. 3d 171, 199 (D.D.C. 2017). The *Anthem* Court found that the existence of such a continuum *supported* the government's market definition of "national customers," *i.e.,* employers with 5,000 or more employees, not the opposite, as Defendants argue here. *See Anthem,* 236 F. Supp. 3d at 199–200; Dkt. 178 at 26 (Defs.' PFOF ¶ 46).

359. In *Wilhelmsen* and *Staples II,* this Court defined markets around targeted customers using a numerical threshold without finding that the government's threshold represented a sharp break point. *See Wilhelmsen,* 341 F. Supp. 3d at 52–56; *FTC v. Staples, Inc.,* 190 F. Supp. 3d 100, 118 & n.10 (D.D.C. 2016) ("*Staples II*"). And the government's expert in *Wilhelmsen* performed an analysis to show that his 10-ship threshold was *not* drawn at a sharp boundary between "global fleets" and other fleets. *See Wilhelmsen,* 341 F. Supp. 3d at 54–56.

360. The Merger Guidelines explicitly contemplate that mergers can harm a group of targeted customers situated along a continuum. In a discussion of "Targeted Customers and Price Discrimination," the Guidelines describe a hypothetical merger harming small buyers but not large buyers, while noting that price discrimination targeted at small buyers "can occur *even if* there is no discrete gap in size between the classes of large and small buyers." Merger Guidelines § 3 (emphasis added). Requiring—as Defendants suggest—proof of sharp differences above and below the government's threshold in a targeted customer case is inconsistent with this Circuit's precedents and the Merger Guidelines, and would immunize mergers that unquestionably harm some sellers but not others so long as the group of affected sellers don't have sharp distinctions from the unaffected group.

E. $250,000 Is an Appropriate Threshold to Identify Anticipated Top Sellers

361. Anticipated top sellers are defined as books that receive an advance of $250,000 or more. Dkt. 177 at 38 (U.S. PFOF ¶ 64). Authors of anticipated top sellers face different competitive conditions as demonstrated by the significantly different market shares that the non- Big Five have for anticipated top sellers (10%) compared to non-anticipated top sellers (45%). Dkt. 177 at 39 (U.S. PFOF ¶ 64).

362. Defendants argue that the government should have used a $50,000 threshold, claiming market shares for non-Big Five publishers materially change at that level. Supporting this argument, Dr. Snyder presented

market shares in three advance ranges: below $50,000, from $50,000 to $999,999, and $1,000,000+. Dkt. 178 at 22–23 (Defs. PFOF ¶¶ 36–37).

363. Defendants are wrong for several reasons. As an initial matter, defining a market for anticipated top sellers using an advance threshold of $250,000 does not preclude the existence of other markets, such as a $50,000 to $249,999 market. *See* Trial Tr. 3172:17–3173:6 (Hill); Merger Guidelines § 4.1.1; Dkt. 177 at 33–34 (U.S. PFOF ¶ 54).

364. Next, a closer look at Dr. Snyder's exhibit shows that the $250,000 threshold captures the distinct preferences and competitive conditions of anticipated top sellers. Dr. Hill demonstrated this by splitting Dr. Snyder's $50,000 to $999,999 range—which mixed anticipated top sellers with other books—into two ranges: $50,000 to $249,999 and $250,000 to $999,999. This created a total of four ranges: $0 to $49,999, $50,000 to $249,999, $250,000 to $999,999, and $1,000,000+. The market shares in the two ranges that concern anticipated top sellers ($250,000 to $999,999 and $1,000,000+) look very similar to one another, yet different from both the $0 to $49,999 and $50,000 to $250,000 ranges. Trial Tr. 3047:6–3048:12 (Hill) (discussing slide 6 of U.S. Demonstrative 8). This is not to say that market shares in the $0 to $50,000 range are identical to market shares in the $50,000 to $250,000 range. As Dr. Hill acknowledged, for books that receive advances between $50,000 and $250,000, there is a "transition period" in which the non-Big Five's share is less than their share for books below $50,000. *See* Trial Tr. 3048:6–12 (Hill).

365. More fundamentally, Defendants misconstrue the purpose of the advance threshold in Dr. Hill's analysis. It was not meant to identify the precise point at which competitive conditions and author preferences change from a zero dollars per book to something else; as Defendants admit, these changes likely happen along a "continuum." *See* Dkt. 178 at 26 (Defs. PFOF ¶ 46). Instead, the threshold was meant as a practical way to identify a group of authors who are more likely to be harmed by the merger than others because of that group's preferences and the competitive conditions they face. *See* Trial Tr. 1228:18–1229:10 (Hill); Trial Tr. 1231:5–19 (Hill); Trial Tr. 3202:4–22 (Hill); *see also* Merger Guidelines § 3. The $250,000 threshold successfully does that. Dkt. 177 at 31–63 (U.S. PFOF ¶¶ 46–125). To check that his results were not sensitive to the exact threshold used, Dr. Hill calculated market shares at various other thresholds ($150,000, $350,000, $500,000, and $1 million) and found that these alternatives generate similar results. Dkt. 177 at 38 (U.S. PFOF ¶ 64); Dkt. 177 at 64–65 (U.S. PFOF ¶ 128). This stability around Dr. Hill's $250,000 threshold supports his choice, rather than undermines it as Defendants suggest. *See Wilhelmsen,* 341 F. Supp. 3d at 55–56; *see also supra* III.E.

366. Finally, the Court's rejection of an analogous argument in *Anthem* further supports the government's threshold. In *Anthem,* the defendants argued that instead of the 5,000- employee threshold used by the government to define a "national customer," a better definition would be 1,000 or 3,000. *Anthem,* 236 F. Supp. 3d at 199. The Court acknowledged that some employers with fewer than 5,000 employees may have "needs and characteristics similar to" those with 5,000 or more. *Id.* But the suite of reasonable options available to Anthem's largest customers (some with more than 200,000 employees) were more limited than customers at defendants' proposed threshold, who had more insurance products to choose from. *Id.* at 200. The Court found the government's threshold superior because it "focuses the competitive analysis on the products that industry participants appear to agree are preferred by customers with more than 5000 employees." *Id.*

367. The same is true here. The options for an author who receives a $50,000 advance are quite different than an author receiving a multi-million-dollar advance. For example, many publishers have paid advances of at least $50,000 but never $250,000 or more. The vast majority of publishers have never even paid more than $175,000 for a book, *see* Trial Tr. 3076:21–3077:8 (Hill) (discussing U.S. Demonstrative 8 at slide 20), suggesting that they are not viable options for authors who receive the largest advances. Lowering the market threshold to $50,000 would assign market shares to publishers who cannot serve many authors in the market for anticipated top sellers. Therefore, assigning these publishers market share would paint a misleading picture about the likely competitive effects of the merger for many authors of anticipated top sellers. By drawing the line at $250,000, a threshold where market shares are stable, *see* PX-960, the government's threshold "focuses the competitive analysis on the [publishers] that industry participants appear to agree are preferred by" authors who receive advances of $250,000 and more. *Anthem,* 236 F. Supp. 3d at 200; *see also* Merger Guidelines § 4.1.1 (the "overarching principle" of "measuring market shares is to illuminate the evaluation of competitive effects").

F. The Government Correctly Applied the "Narrowest Market" Principle

368. In addition to arguing that the government's proposed market is too narrow, Defendants now argue that

it is too broad. Defendants now claim that because a market for books with advances of at least $1,000,000 passes the hypothetical monopsonist test, the government's market violates the "narrowest market rule." Dkt. 178 at 130–31 (Defs. PCOL ¶¶ 36–37). This argument misconstrues the "narrowest market" principle.

369. The "narrowest market" principle is used by the Department of Justice and the Federal Trade Commission to determine the substitutes that should be included in the product market (specifically those substitutes that can defeat the hypothetical monopolist test and therefore need to be included in the market versus those substitutes that are too weak and therefore are generally excluded). *See* Merger Guidelines § 4.1.1 (explaining the logic that otherwise "the relative competitive significance of more distant substitutes is apt to be overstated by" their market shares). That is what the government did here when it excluded self-publishing.

370. The issue is different, however, when identifying the targeted customers that should be included in the market and determining whether the government should focus on the fewest customers who could be targeted, as Defendants implicitly suggest. Here, the Merger Guidelines embrace analyzing targeted-seller markets using a broader group of sellers than the narrowest possible one, and state, "[i]f prices are negotiated individually with" sellers—as they are here—the hypothetical [monopsonist] test may suggest relevant markets that are as narrow as *individual* [sellers]. . . . . Nonetheless, the Agencies often define markets for *groups* of targeted [sellers], *i.e.,* by type of [seller], rather than by individual [seller]. By so doing, the Agencies are able to rely on aggregated market shares that can be more helpful in predicting the competitive effects of the merger." Merger Guidelines § 4.1.4 (emphasis added). The government followed this approach here: instead of analyzing individually each author (or small slice of authors) who could be harmed (as would be the narrowest market along the dimension Defendants contest), the government properly grouped a manageable set of similarly-situated authors together from whom market shares could meaningfully be drawn and analyzed—authors of anticipated top sellers.

G. The Relevant Market Properly Excludes Self-Publishing

371. Despite conceding in their closing arguments that "nobody was arguing in this case" that self-publishing is an "outside option" for authors, Trial Tr. 3272:17–25 (Defs. Closing Argument), Defendants now try to do just that. Dkt. 178 at 75–76 (Defs. PFOF ¶ 181–185). The record is clear that they were right the first time: self-publishing is not a reasonable alternative for the vast majority of authors, and instances such as Brandon Sanderson's Kickstarter campaign are outliers rather than a competitive trend. *See* Dkt. 177 at 35–36 (U.S. PFOF ¶¶ 81–82; *see also* Trial Tr. 2898:15–18 (Snyder); Trial Tr. 1076:4–10 (Weisberg).

IV. DEFENDANTS OFFER NO REAL REBUTTAL

372. Defendants' attempts to rebut the presumption of illegality fail. They do not contest, let alone discredit, the market shares or HHIs used to measure market concentration that were calculated by Dr. Hill, nor do they show that the presumption inaccurately predicts the merger's probable effect on future competition. *Anthem,* 855 F.3d at 349; *Baker Hughes,* 908 F.2d at 991. Though Defendants quibble at the margins, their focus on outliers does not change the facts that underly the core of the government's case and the presumption of illegality.

373. As discussed above (*supra* ¶ 11), Defendants misstate the legal standard by asserting that they need only make a "minimal evidentiary showing" to rebut the government's prima facie case. Dkt. 178 at 138 (Defs. PCOL ¶ 55). Defendants make this claim in spite of *Anthem*'s and *Baker Hughes*'s plain language that "[t]he more compelling the prima facie case, the more evidence the defendant must present to rebut it successfully." *Anthem,* 855 F.3d at 349–350 (quoting *Baker Hughes,* 908 F.2d at 991). When assessed under the proper standard, Defendants' arguments lack substantial, if any, actual evidentiary support and are insufficient to rebut the presumption that their merger is illegal.

A. The Government's Market Share Calculations Meaningfully Explain How Competition Works in the Relevant Market

374. Instead of offering evidence that market shares overstate the extent of competition between PRH and S&S—such as evidence that the two publishers specialize in different genres—Defendants focus on misleading statistics to support their assertions.

375. First, they assert that PRH and S&S are winner and runner-up in "only" 6–7% (or, alternatively, 12%) of acquisitions. *See* Dkt. 178 at 141 (Defs. PCOL ¶ 61). This statistic is both incorrectly calculated and lacks context. As Dr. Hill testified, and as Defendants appear to acknowledge, Dr. Snyder inflated his denominator by including in it instances in which there was no known runner-up, which halved the

correct calculation from 13% to 7%. *See* Trial Tr. 2918:12–2919:24 (Snyder); Trial Tr. 3055:11–3056:18 (Hill).

376. Even the corrected statistic, *i.e.,* 12 or 13%, fails to offer insight for unilateral effects analysis unless it is placed in context. To the government's knowledge, no court has ever performed this calculation to evaluate the likely unilateral effects of a merger. If they had, however, many would have found calculations similar to Defendants' 12%, showing that, if anything, Defendants' calculation *supports* the government's contentions regarding unilateral effects. One can perform this calculation using diversion ratios and market shares as shown in the footnote. In *H & R Block,* fewer than 5% of customers viewed the merging parties as their top two choices. In *Hackensack,* it was 12%.8 And in *Anthem,* it was about 15%.9 In each case, the court found that the proposed mergers were likely to cause unilateral effects despite "only" 5–15% of customers viewing the merging parties as their top two options.

377. Specifically, Defendants point to their 12% calculation as proof that the merging parties' market shares are "highly misleading." *See* Dkt. 178 at 140–41 (Defs. PCOL ¶¶ 60–61). This claim is wrong. By Defendants' own admission, the 12% calculation is derived using only the merging parties' market shares. *See* Dkt. 178 at 77 (Defs. PFOF ¶¶ 187–188). Defendants' calculation comes from an equation that, as a matter of arithmetic, will transform Defendants' 49% share into a small-seeming number. *See supra* note 6. They therefore cannot prove that market shares are "highly misleading." *See* Dkt. 178 at 140–141 (Defs. PCOL ¶¶ 60–61).

378. Second, Defendants state that that the non-Big Five are winners or runners-up in 23% of auctions, which they claim shows that the non-Big Five are a competitive constraint more than twice as often as market shares indicate. *See* Trial Tr. 2689:22–2690:5 (Snyder); Dkt. 178 at 70 (Def's PFOF ¶ 166). Once again, this is misleading.

379. Contrary to Defendants' assertions, their 23% statistic is not directly comparable to market shares. *See* Trial Tr. 3052:24–3053:8 (Hill). Since the total of market shares and the runner up shares each sum to 100%, to directly compare the 23% to non-Big Five publishers' market shares it should be divided by 2. Trial Tr. 3051:16–3052:13 (Hill); *see* Dkt. 177 at 83 (U.S. PFOF ¶ 156). With the proper adjustment, the 23% corresponds to 11.5%, which is similar to the market share of the non-Big Five publishers. *See* Trial Tr. 3053:11–17 (Hill). Rather than prove that the non-Big Five compete more than their shares suggest, as Defendants allege, Defendants' statistic does the opposite. *See* Dkt. 177 at 83 (U.S. PFOF ¶ 156).

380. Third, Defendants assert that the non-Big Five submit bids in 54% of multi-bidder auctions, which implies they are more significant competitors than their market shares suggest. *See* Dkt. 178 at 70 (Defs. PFOF ¶ 166). They are wrong. Defendants' 54% number includes instances in which non-Big Five publishers bid in an auction's early rounds but dropped out far before its conclusion. *See, e.g.,* PX-935-B (book sold for $350,000; Norton bid $105,000); PX- 941-B (book sold for $825,000; Norton and Bloomsbury bid $100,000 and $75,000 respectively). For example, even if a non-Big Five publisher bid a dollar, this would be counted in Defendants' 54% statistic. *See* Trial Tr. 3148:12–3149:14 (Hill). Such bids don't measure competitive significance.

381. Fourth, instead of reporting the diversion ratios calculated by their expert, Defendants repeatedly cite DX-436, a figure taken out of context from Dr. Hill's reply report that Dr. Hill used to rebut a specific point from Dr. Snyder's rebuttal report. *See, e.g.,* Dkt. 178 at 76–77 (Defs. PFOF ¶ 186); Dkt. 178 at 77 (Defs. PFOF ¶ 188); Dkt. 178 at 91 (Defs. PFOF ¶ 221); Dkt. 178 at 109 (Defs. PFOF ¶ 267). DX-436 presents runners-up from Dr. Snyder's agency data for only a subset of the time period Dr. Snyder analyzed. *See* DX-436 (2019–2021); Trial Tr. 2657:7–25 (Snyder) (2018–2021). The diversion ratio from S&S to PRH is smaller than Dr. Snyder's complete results, and the diversion ratio from PRH to S&S is about the same. *Compare* DX-436 *with* Trial Tr. 2927:4–25 (Snyder) (discussing Snyder Rebuttal Report Exhibits VI.4 and VI.5). Thus, Defendants' claims based on DX-436 are derived from diversion ratios from a subset of an undisputedly unrepresentative sample of 22 contracts. *See* Dkt. 177 at 139 (U.S. PFOF ¶ 277); Trial Tr. 2997:17–22 (Snyder). Had Defendants presented the diversion ratios their expert actually calculated, they would have shown a diversion ratio for S&S to PRH that is consistent with Dr. Hill's estimates—which show substantial head-to-head competition between the merging parties—and that suggests that PRH is S&S's closest competitor. *See* Dkt. 177 at 138–39 (U.S. PFOF ¶ 276); Trial Tr. 2927:4–2928:10 (Snyder).

B. Defendants Failed to Show That Entry of New Publishers and Expansion of Current Publishers Will Constrain PRH Post-Merger

382. The Merger Guidelines and this district's precedents require that a defendant show that entry by new

competitors or expansion by incumbent competitors be "timely, likely, and sufficient in its magnitude, character, and scope to deter or counteract the competitive effects of concern" posed by a merger. *H & R Block,* 833 F. Supp. 2d at 73 (quoting Merger Guidelines § 9). Defendants must provide evidence that satisfies their burden with each of these hurdles. Defendants have provided insufficient evidence to clear any of them.

4. There Is No Evidence That Expansion by the Remaining Big Five Publishers Is Likely to Constrain PRH Post-Merger

383. Defendants try to point to HarperCollins,' Hachette's, and Macmillan's plans to continue to compete just as they did pre-merger as evidence those companies are likely to increase their presence post-merger. The CEOs of HarperCollins, Hachette, and Macmillan, however, all testified that the merger itself will *not* cause them to be more aggressive in acquiring books. *See* Dkt. 177 at 92–93 (U.S. PFOF ¶¶ 175–177). Citing to plans written before the merger was announced or referring to statements about what a company would *like* to do ignores concerns expressed by those same publishers that the merger will affect their ability to compete against the combined company. *See, e.g.,* Trial Tr. 1086:6–1087:5 (Weisberg) (ability to acquire books generally); [REDACTED]

384. If it were easy for HarperCollins, Hachette, or Macmillan to win books over PRH and S&S, they would have done so already. Instead, they have lost share since 2019, *see* Dkt. 177 at 62–63 (U.S. PFOF ¶ 138 & Fig. 6 (PX-994)). Defendants did not, and cannot, point to any evidence showing that HarperCollins, Hachette, or Macmillan are likely to expand their market shares against a combined PRH and S&S sufficiently to replace S&S's competitive significance. Growing with, or slower than, the market's organic growth is not sufficient to replace the lost competition. *See* Dkt. 177 at 92–93 (U.S. PFOF ¶¶ 176–177).

5. There Is No Evidence That Expansion by Non-Big Five Publishers Is Likely to Constrain PRH Post-Merger

385. Defendants also posit that certain smaller publishers *might* be able to expand and become a new, major publisher. However, the evidence Defendants cite does not show that expansion by these publishers will be timely, likely, or sufficient. For example, defense counsel questioned Dr. Hill by using a news report about Disney that was not admitted into evidence, suggesting that Disney would re-enter the adult trade book category and "within five years, aims to release 50 to 60 titles through" its Hyperion imprint. *See* Dkt. 178 at 57–58 (Defs. PFOF ¶ 126); Trial Tr. 1569:2–6 (Hill). Dr. Hill's acknowledgement of the news article is not evidence that proves Disney will replace S&S's competitive significance. Even if Disney's intentions as represented by Defendants are taken at face value, there is no evidence regarding its plans to acquire books with advances above $250,000 per year, and the five-year time horizon is well outside the two-to-three years used to evaluate entry. *See Staples II,* 190 F. Supp. 3d at 133.

386. Defendants also assert Amazon is "a significant non-Big Five competitor [that] is only becoming more competitive." Dkt. 178 at 73 (Defs. PFOF ¶ 177). This description is contrary to the trial testimony, including from publishers cited by Defendants in their Proposed Findings, *compare* Dkt. 177 at 97–98 (U.S. PFOF ¶¶ 187–189) *with* Dkt. 178 at 58 (Defs. PFOF ¶ 127), and Defendants' own executives. Trial Tr. 356:10–18 (Eulau). These assessments of Amazon's competitive significance in the market for anticipated top sellers are based on observations of Amazon's retrenchment after several of their high-profile author signings failed. *See, e.g.,* Trial Tr. 171:24–173:6 (Pietsch); PX-2002 at 101–102 (Stehlik Dep. 201:17–202:1). Defendants do not meet their burden by claiming Amazon could theoretically compete more. Rather, they must show that Amazon is likely to expand its presence in acquiring anticipated top sellers in a timely and sufficient way to counter the merger's likely anticompetitive effects. Defendants have not done so.

6. There Is No Evidence That New Publishers Are Likely to Enter at Sufficient Scale to Constrain PRH Post-Merger

387. With no evidence in the record sufficient to show that current publishers will replace S&S's competitive significance, it is not surprising that Defendants similarly cannot point to any evidence that a new publisher could do so either. Though they provide a handful of examples of new publishers acquiring anticipated top sellers, these examples are notable because they are exceptions that prove the rule—that entry is difficult. By focusing on these outliers, Defendants once again fail to provide any grounds for the Court to find that a new publisher will replace S&S's competitive significance.

388. Defendants' use of Spiegel & Grau, Zando, and Astra as examples, *see* Dkt. 178 at 59–60 (Defs. PFOF ¶¶ 130–132), illustrates the problems new publishers face. These publishers have yet to take any

significant share, and there is no evidence in the record that they, or any other new publisher, could grow at such a rate that they could replace S&S's competitive significance, and thereby rebut a presumption of illegality. *See Anthem,* 236 F. Supp. 3d at 222; *H & R Block,* 833 F. Supp. 2d at 73. That Spiegel & Grau, Zando, Astra, or any other publisher can publish one or two successful books does not show that their market shares understate their competitive significance, or that any one of these firms will turn into an S&S- sized publishing house in the time frame required. To assume that any of these new firms will be able to replace S&S is idle, optimistic speculation, especially since no publisher has joined the ranks of the Big Five in the past thirty years. *See* Dkt. 177 at 86 (U.S. PFOF ¶ 163); Trial Tr. 163:7–165:6 (Pietsch).

389. Defendants rely on the unfounded assertions of former literary agent Jennifer Walsh for their claims related to the expansion plans of various smaller publishers. *See* Dkt. 178 at 54–55 (Defs. PFOF ¶ 144). Ms. Walsh, however, has no basis to testify as to any publisher's financial position or ability to invest in new acquisitions. *See* Dkt. 178 at 54 (Defs. PFOF ¶ 144). The United States' agent witness, Ayesha Pande was more credible on this topic when she explained why she typically excluded publishers like Spiegel & Grau, Zando, and Astra from her first wave of submissions: "[A]ll of these publishers are still too new to have really proven themselves." Trial Tr. 250:2–9 (Pande); *see* Dkt. 177 at 90 (U.S. PFOF ¶ 190). There is no direct evidence about any expansion plans, if they exist, for any small publishers.

7. Intra-Firm Competition Among a Publisher's Subsidiary Imprints Does Not Replace Competition Among Independent Publishers

390. PRH claims that post-merger "S&S editors and imprints would not disappear and would still be available for submissions and bids." Dkt. 178 at 68 (Defs. PFOF ¶ 162). However, this is directly contradicted by PRH's history of reorganizing imprints following the Penguin-Random House merger and its plans for headcount reductions following this merger. *See* Trial Tr. 767:24–768:11 (Dohle); Trial Tr. 2562:1–2563:20 (Sansigre) (testifying about PRH's plans for headcount reductions of executives in the combined firm's editorial and art functions).

391. An imprint is nothing more than a publisher's subsidiary. Imprints may ostensibly be allowed to bid against each other, drawing off the same corporate parent resources, but that is not a substitute for "separate economic actors, pursuing separate economic interests" vying against one another for a book, *i.e., actual* competition. *See Copperweld Corp. v. Indep. Tube Corp.,* 467 U.S. 753, 769–770 (1984). As a result, Defendants cited to no example of a PRH imprint bidding more aggressively than they otherwise would have to beat another PRH imprint. And Defendants can cite no case that supports their view that the Court should treat competition among subsidiaries as equivalent to competition among independent companies. *Cf.* Dkt. 177 at 111–112 (U.S. PFOF ¶¶ 213–214).

C. Agents Cannot Protect Authors from the Merger's Anticompetitive Effects

392. As discussed in the United States' Proposed Findings, the presence of certain sophisticated sellers is insufficient as a matter of law to rebut the presumption. Dkt. 177 at 104–105 (U.S. PFOF ¶¶ 200–203). Even before this proposed merger, agents have had limited leverage and have been unable to hold back publisher demands to acquire audio rights, shift the payout structure for advances, or lower e-book royalties. Dkt. 177 at 106–110 (U.S. PFOF ¶¶ 205–212). Agents' role in the book acquisition process and the tools they have to encourage publishers to acquire a book will not change if the merger is allowed to proceed. To the extent that agents have any power over the current bidding process to protect their authors, Defendants provide no evidence describing how agents' power will increase or somehow prevent publishers from altering how they bid for books post-merger.

D. Defendants Failed to Demonstrate the Merger Would Increase Advances PRH Will Pay Authors

393. Defendants cite testimony from Madeline McIntosh to claim that efficiencies will allow the company to increase the advances it pays authors. Dkt. 178 at 17–18 (Defs. PFOF ¶ 25). However, the Court has already found that Defendants' efficiency claims are "unreliable," Trial Tr. at 2767:3 (Court) and "unverified." Trial Tr. at 2769:4 (Court). Defendants, therefore, cannot claim that that these purported efficiencies would benefit authors, and Ms. McIntosh's testimony regarding those efficiencies cannot be used to rebut the presumption.

E. There Is No Evidence that Changes in Retail Bookselling Affect the Market for Anticipated Top Sellers

394. The advent of social media as a tool used to publicize, market, and sell books to readers has not

removed barriers to entry in publishing anticipated top sellers. To the extent Defendants argue otherwise, they provide no support for this proposition. Dkt. 178 at 35–36 (Defs. PFOF ¶ 69). New ways to market books on social media networks like Instagram or Tik- Tok do not change the need for publishers to have sufficient resources, reputations, and printing capabilities to effectively publish books that can take advantage of such author-driven marketing. Marketing via endorsements by celebrities or "influencers" is not new. As Mr. Weisberg testified, "this is a business of one to one word of mouth. It's never been anything else and it's still not, just the devices have changed." Trial Tr. 1068:24–1069:4 (Weisberg). The effects of social media on the market for anticipated top sellers and the ability of smaller publishers to compete for such attention has already been reflected in the (uncontested) market shares in this case, the documents and testimony describing the competitive dynamic for anticipated top sellers, and Dr. Hill's quantitative analysis. Dkt. 177 at 76–78 (U.S. PFOF ¶¶ 148–149).

395. Moreover, Defendants' assertions about the effect of online retail on the small publishers, Dkt. 178 at 57 (Defs. PFOF ¶ 151), is almost entirely unsupported by the factual record and, even if true, irrelevant to the claims in this case. Any trend toward online sales has not occurred recently, but over the past two decades. And yet, in the past thirty years no publisher has become a strong competitor for the Big Five. *See* Trial Tr. 163:2–6 (Pietsch).

F. Bertelsmann Controls Printing Assets Needed by Competitors

396. Defendants assert that Bertelsmann has not yet exercised its control over printing assets to disadvantage rival publishers. PRH's rivals, however, fear that control as they compete against PRH. [REDACTED] Bertelsmann's ability to cut off other publishers from printing their books, making it harder for them to expand or compete in the future, is not strongly contested.

V. DEFENDANTS' UNILATERAL EFFECTS ARGUMENTS ARE WRONG

A. Defendants Misconstrue Fundamental Principles of Unilateral Effects

397. Defendants claim that a merger can adversely affect competition only when the merging parties were consumers' top two choices. Dkt. 178 at 135–136 (Defs. PCOL ¶ 49); Dkt. 178 at 139–140 (Defs. PCOL ¶ 59). This is incorrect. In best-bid auctions, for example, S&S is likely to reduce its bid in any auction where S&S perceives that PRH would have been a competitor for that book, regardless of whether PRH would have been the actual runner-up bidder (and vice-versa). See Trial Tr. 3086:4–3087:2 (Hill). This is because the competitive constraint in a best-bids auction is the winner's expectation of competition, not the actual runner-up bid. See Trial Tr. 3155:7–3156:18 (Hill).

398. In these types of auctions, losing an important competitor generates lower bids overall, not just when the merging parties are winner and runner-up. The more important the competitor being acquired, the greater the effect on bids made by the other party. The same is true for many books acquired outside of auctions. See Dkt. 177 at 132 (U.S. PFOF ¶ 260).

399. Defendants misleadingly quote the following passage of the Merger Guidelines to support their claim that a merger can adversely affect only those authors for whom the merging parties were the winner and runner up: "Anticompetitive unilateral effects in [bargaining and auction] settings are likely in proportion to the frequency or probability with which, prior to the merger, one of the merging sellers had been the runner-up when the other won the business." Merger Guidelines § 6.2 (emphasis added); see Dkt. 178 at 139 (Defs. PCOL ¶ 59). Rather than limiting unilateral effects to the particular instances where the merging parties are winner and runner-up, the Guidelines state that unilateral effects as a result of the merger are in proportion to the frequency with which one of the merging parties is the runner up when the other wins. This frequency or probability is just the "bidding analog of the diversion ratio," not a special requirement for bargaining and auction settings. See Carl Shapiro, The 2010 Horizontal Merger Guidelines: From Hedgehog to Fox in Forty Years, 77 Antitrust L.J. 49, 83 (2010).

400. It is true that the merger is likely to harm authors whose books are sold in a multi- round auction where PRH and S&S are the top two bidders. But this does not suggest that for authors whose books are acquired in best-bids auctions, the only harm will be to those authors for whom the merging parties were winner and runner-up. As explained by Dr. Hill and the Merger Guidelines, in settings in which the merging parties are explicitly bidding each other up, such as round robin auctions, harm for each individual author will be particularly great, whereas for authors whose books are acquired via a best-bid auction, harm to each individual author will be less, but the harm will be spread over a greater number of authors. See Trial Tr. 3086:4–3088:7 (Hill) (discussing Merger Guidelines § 6.2).

401. Similarly, Defendants' attempt to paint their executives or employees as too naïve to exercise market power defies common sense and the fundamental tenets of the antitrust laws. See, e.g., Dkt. 178 at 89–

92 (Defs. PFOF ¶¶ 219–24); Trial Tr. 3291:6–3292:19 (Defs. Closing Argument).12 First, in some auctions and negotiations, the auction or negotiation will end earlier as a result of eliminating competition between PRH and S&S, and no conscious decision to lower advances would be required. See Trial Tr. 1728:18–1729:5 (Hill); Trial Tr. 3201:9–3202:3 (Hill); see also Trial Tr. 180:2–182:1 (Pietsch).

402. Second, lowering bids in a best-bid auction or negotiation is far from alchemy. Today, Defendants bid more aggressively when they perceive more competition and less aggressively when they perceive less competition. See Trial Tr. 1267:13–1268:21 (Hill) (discussing two examples in which the merging parties planned to bid less aggressively because they perceived less competition). S&S's own CEO agreed that "anytime there is a competitive situation," including best-bid auctions, "competition raises advance levels, less competition lowers them." Trial Tr. 499:6–500:12 (Karp). Reducing offers in best-bid auctions or negotiations is merely a corollary of what Defendants already do.

403. When asked by Defendants' counsel how the merged firm would lower advances post-merger, Dr. Hill explained, "if you're competing frequently with an opponent in auctions or negotiations and they are removed from the competition, it is profit maximizing to take account of the fact that competition has lessened and to lower your bids, in general, in best bids, and negotiations to be less aggressive." Trial Tr. 1728:18–1729:1 (Hill). Defendants' CEOs do not contest that they compete frequently with each other. Mr. Karp testified that S&S bids against PRH more than any other publisher. Trial Tr. 595:23–25 (Karp). Ms. McIntosh testified that for book acquisitions where she plays a role, S&S is one of PRH's most frequent competitors. See Trial Tr. 2350:20–23 (McIntosh). And despite Defendants' claims that they don't know who they compete against, see Dkt. 178 at 89 (Defs. PFOF ¶ 219), Mr. Karp testified that after auctions conclude, "agents usually tell us who we were competing against. They very rarely don't." Trial Tr. 495:25–496:4 (Karp); see also PX-790. Similarly, two of Dr. Hill's diversion ratio calculations—using win/loss data and editorial minutes data—were based on documents kept by the merging parties. See Dkt. 177 at 137–38 (U.S. PFOF ¶¶ 270, 273). Both of those calculations showed that the merging parties compete with each other frequently. See PX-970. In the case of S&S, they show that when S&S loses, it loses to PRH 55–60% of the time. See PX-970. One does not need a crystal ball to intuit that if your most frequent competitor, who wins the majority of your losses, is eliminated it would be profit maximizing to lower your bids.

404. Because Defendants know that they compete against each other frequently—or have the information necessary to know—it will be profit maximizing for them to lower advances post-merger in best-bid auctions and negotiations. As a result, whatever "conscious decision" Defendants assert must take place to lower advances, see Dkt. 178 at 159 (Defs. PCOL ¶ 112), it is already assumed by the antitrust laws, and is not an element of the government's proof. As put by the leading antitrust treatise: "As a general proposition business firms are (or must be assumed to be) profit maximizers, which means that they constructively 'intend' to take the course of action that maximizes their returns. . . ." Phillip E. Areeda & Herbert Hovenkamp, Antitrust Law: An Analysis of Antitrust Principles and Their Application ¶ 113 (5th ed. 2022).

B. PRH and S&S Are Close Competitors to Each Other

405. Defendants argue that "overall market shares are a highly misleading indicator of competitive effects because PRH and S&S are not particularly close competitors." Dkt. 178 at 140 (Defs. PCOL ¶ 60). This claim is wrong. The record shows that PRH is the closest competitor for S&S—and that S&S is one of PRH's main competitors.

406. These conclusions are supported by testimony of senior executives at both firms and by Dr. Hill's analysis. As discussed in the United States' Proposed Findings, Mr. Karp testified that PRH likely is the firm that S&S competes with most frequently, while Ms. McIntosh stated that S&S is one of the competitors that PRH competes with the most. Dkt. 177 at 126 (U.S. PFOF ¶ 251) (citing Trial Tr. 595:23–25 (Karp) and Trial Tr. 2360:20–23 (McIntosh)). In addition, Dr. Hill analyzed the closeness of competition between the firms using three different sets of data: win/loss reports, the "runner up" data, and a database based on Defendants' editorial meeting minutes. All three studies showed either that PRH and S&S competed as closely as market shares would predict—or, actually, more closely. *See* Dkt. 177 at 136–138 (U.S. PFOF ¶¶ 270–274). And, according to this data, approximately 55–60% of S&S's losses are to PRH. *See* Dkt. 177 at 137–138 (U.S. PFOF ¶¶ 272–273).

407. Neither of the two arguments Defendants rely on to support their claim undercuts the evidence discussed above. First, Defendants argue that PRH and S&S are not close competitors for Christian books. Dkt. 178 at 80 (Defs. PFOF ¶ 196). But Christian books only make up 2% of PRH's total

business. Trial Tr. 2299:14–19 (McIntosh). For that reason, evidence regarding Christian books has no bearing on how often S&S and PRH compete for the vast majority of PRH's anticipated top sellers. Significantly, under any measure—win/loss, runner up, and editorial minutes—the result is the same: PRH and S&S are close competitors.

408. Second, Defendants rely on testimony from a few agents stating that PRH and S&S rarely were the top two bidders for particular books. Dkt. 178 at 79 (Defs. PFOF ¶¶ 192–194). But these agents account for a small portion of the market. *See* PX-749 (Cheney deal sheet shows that she only sold [REDACTED] anticipated top sellers per year); Trial Tr. 2043:16–2044:12 (Cheney) (making a few corrections to PX-749) PX-856 at 2 (Wylie, [REDACTED]). By contrast, the data that Dr. Hill relies on is far more systematic; his win-loss, runner-up, and editorial minutes analyses are based on approximately 350 multi-bidder acquisitions. PX-996.

409. Finally, Defendants argue that unilateral effects are only possible where the merging parties are the only (or maybe the main) competitors. Dkt. 178 at 141–142 (Defs. PCOL ¶¶ 63–64). As discussed above, the caselaw does not support this argument. *See supra* II. Neither do the relevant economic principles. Under the Merger Guidelines and economic theory, a merger can result in unilateral effects even when the merging parties are not the only two competitors. *See* Guidelines § 6.1 ("A merger may produce significant unilateral effects for a given product even though many more sales are diverted to products sold by non-merging firms than to products previously sold by the merger partner."); Merger Guidelines § 6 ("[U]nilateral effects are by no means limited" to "merger[s] to monopoly"); Trial Tr. 1581:7–20 (Hill). Instead, the key question is whether there is a significant amount of competition between the two firms. *See* Merger Guidelines § 6.1 ("The extent of direct competition between the products sold by the merging parties is central to the evaluation of unilateral price effects."); Trial Tr. 1274:2–12 (Hill). And here, because PRH is S&S's closest competitor and S&S is one of PRH's main competitors, it clearly is the case that there is a significant amount of competition to be lost between PRH and S&S.

C. Defendants' Criticisms of Dr. Hill's Models Are Unavailing

410. Defendants make several criticisms of Dr. Hill's models, many of which were already addressed in the United States' Proposed Findings. *See* Dkt. 177 at 143–46 (U.S. PFOF ¶¶ 289–97). None undermine the fundamental conclusion shared by his models: the proposed merger is likely to substantially harm authors of anticipated top sellers.

411. Defendants state that Dr. Hill's models only measure harm where PRH and S&S are the first and second-place bidders in multi-round auctions. Dkt. 178 at 87 (Defs. PFOF ¶ 215). That is incorrect. Trial Tr. 3088:8–22 (Hill). Both the best-bids and hybrid GUPPI models predict harm outside those scenarios, and Dr. Hill interpreted his second-score auction model more broadly. Trial Tr. 3088:8–22 (Hill).

412. Defendants attempt to discount Dr. Hill's second-score auction model by asserting that in best-bid auctions and bilateral negotiations, a publisher must pay "an amount at or near" its maximum willingness to pay. Dkt. 178 at 100 (Defs. PFOF ¶ 249). The implication is that a merger could not reduce advances in best-bid auctions or negotiations because in these settings publishers always, regardless of perceived competitive conditions, offer the author the absolute maximum that they would be willing to pay for the book. Dr. Hill, however, reviewed examples of Defendants' employees bidding lower when they expect to have few competitors—the opposite behavior of what Defendants allege. *See* Trial Tr. 1267:13–1268:21 (Hill). If Defendants' assertions were correct that publishers always pay their maximum amount when making a best bid or negotiating, agents should never sell books via multi-round auction because they would consistently yield inferior results, yet they do. *See, e.g.,* Trial Tr. 112:4–9 (Pietsch).

413. Defendants further allege that when using Dr. Snyder's preferred inputs, the GUPPI models fall below a "safe harbor" articulated by the former Deputy Assistant Attorney General for Economics and co-creator of the GUPPI, Carl Shapiro. This argument is misleading and incorrect. First, the output of Dr. Snyder's GUPPI calculation cannot be verified because he did not produce any backup. Trial Tr. 3142:3–6 (Hill). As a result, it is unclear whether the "safe harbor" is triggered at all. Dr. Snyder only presented a GUPPI of the weighted average for S&S and PRH, which was 4.7%, instead of individual GUPPIs for PRH and S&S as Dr. Hill did. *See* PX-964. But the putative "safe harbor" applies only when the GUPPI value of *all* the merging firms' products (*i.e.* all the individual GUPPIs)—*not* the weighted average GUPPI—is below 5%. Carl Shapiro, *Update from the Antitrust Division,* 24 (2010), *at* https://www.justice.gov/atr/file/518246/download. Given that S&S's GUPPI was materially larger than PRH's under Dr. Hill's calculations and Dr. Snyder's average GUPPI was 4.7%, it is likely that Dr.

Snyder's GUPPI for S&S was above 5% and outside the putative safe harbor. *See* PX-964; Trial Tr. 3141:8–20 (Hill).

414. Second, to arrive at this result, Dr. Snyder used incorrect margins and unreliable diversion ratios. He subtracted fixed costs from profit margins, an approach at odds with the GUPPI formula. Trial Tr. 3093:2–6 (Hill); Dkt. 177 at 144–45 (U.S. PFOF ¶ 293). As discussed *supra* at ¶ 49, Dr. Snyder's diversion ratio from S&S to PRH is based on an unrepresentative sample of 22 S&S wins over a four-year period. Relying on this limited sample to fall under the putative "safe harbor" by 0.3% would be incorrect. Moreover, the logic of the "safe harbor" is that there might be some entry or efficiencies. Trial Tr. 3109:14–23 (Hill). But here, Defendants failed to present cognizable efficiencies or show that substantial entry will occur post-merger.

D. Defendants Overstate the Competitiveness of Non-Big Five Publishers.

415. Defendants make several claims about competition from the non-Big Five publishers. These arguments are inconsistent with both the record and economic theory.

1. Big Five Publishers Do Have Competitive Advantages Over Other Publishers

416. First, Defendants argue that non-Big Five publishers provide the "same quality editorial, publicity, marketing, and sales services necessary to successfully publish" anticipated top-selling books. Dkt. 178 at 33–34 (Defs. PFOF ¶ 65). This ignores the testimony of S&S's CEO, who admitted that Big Five publishers have a competitive advantage in marketing and publicity, Trial Tr. 451:21–454:9 (Karp), and the author Mr. Solomon, who testified at length about the advantages of the Big Five in marketing, publicity, and sales. PX-2004 at 54 (Solomon Dep. 93:5–20); *see also* PX-2004 at 62–64 (Solomon Dep. 101:22–103:18) (describing advantages of Big Five in publicity/marketing); PX-2004 at 17–19 (Solomon Dep. 40:15–42:21) (sales); PX-2004 at 95:4–96:10 (publicity/marketing). And, of course, Defendants also ignore a mountain of other evidence presented at trial regarding the advantages of the Big Five in these (and other) areas, including documents and/or testimony from S&S's former CEO, PRH's U.S. CEO, Hachette's CEO, and a variety of other industry participants. *See* Dkt. 177 at 75–81 (U.S. PFOF ¶¶ 145–152) (collecting evidence on the competitive advantages of the Big Five); PX-530 at 2.

417. In addition, while Defendants rely heavily on testimony from three agents about the services of non-Big Five publishers, Dkt. 178 at 33–34 (Defs. PFOF ¶ 65), Defendants ignore these agents' actual behavior as these agents direct their clients to the Big Five Publishers, thereby undercutting Defendants' claims that the non-Big Five offer the "same" quality. Two of the agents that Defendants rely on—Ms. Fletcher and Mr. Wylie—sold [REDACTED] of their anticipated top sellers to Big Five publishers, respectively. PX-874 (Fletcher deal sheet shows that she sold of her anticipated top sellers to the Big Five); PX-857 at 16–18 (Wylie,[REDACTED] And Defendants' other agent witnesses, Ms. Ross and Ms. Cheney, also sold approximately [REDACTED] of their anticipated top-selling books to the Big Five. PX-838 (Ross, [REDACTED] PX-749 (Cheney [REDACTED]. Trial Tr. 2043:16–2044:12 (Cheney) (making a few corrections to PX-749.

2. *Defendants' Aggregation of Non-Big Five Publishers Is Incorrect*

418. Defendants argue that this is an "effective 6–5 merger" and that the Court should "aggregate" all the small publishers and treat them as one large competitor. Dkt. 178 at 142 (Defs. PCOL ¶ 640; Dkt. 178 at 146 (Defs. PCOL ¶ 76). The United States explained in its Proposed Findings why aggregating the fringe into a single competitor is wrong and why the Court should properly view this as a five-to-four merger of significant competitors, with a fractured fringe of numerous small publishers who are unable to constrain the majors. Dkt. 177 at 60–61 (U.S. PFOF ¶¶ 133–134). Accordingly, it is not legally or economically correct to treat scores of small independently-operated publishers as the equivalent of a single competitor. *Id.*

419. Defendants also falsely claim that Hachette's win/loss tracker (the "Ones that Got Away") proves that the small publishers are collectively as competitively significant as S&S, HarperCollins, and Macmillan individually. *See* Dkt. 178 at 72 (Defs. PFOF at ¶ 171) (claiming the tracker "demonstrates that, collectively, the non-Big Five publishers represent as much of a competitive threat to Hachette as any one of the other Big Five publishers"). The tracker does not show that. The win/loss document tracks more than 300 losses and allots ~30 of them to Houghton Mifflin Harcourt (HMH) and other small publishers. In their filing, Defendants omit the fact that almost half of those 30 losses were to HMH, which HarperCollins has since acquired. PX-790; Trial Tr. 192:15–193:5 (Pietsch). That means only 5–6% of the losses are to *current* non-Big 5—which is far less than the losses to any of HarperCollins, S&S, and Macmillan. In addition, the tracker supports the government's product market. It is another

example of *Brown Shoe* support because Hachette treats high-advance books differently—tracking them separately. Trial Tr. 1907:7–18 (Pietsch); *see also* Dkt. 177 at 42–43 (U.S. PFOF ¶ 99) (noting additional evidence).

VI. DEFENDANTS MISSTATE THE FACTS AND THE LAW ON COORDINATED EFFECTS

420. Defendants misstate the facts and law on coordinated effects. First, Defendants incorrectly imply that the presumption of harm from greater coordination does not apply because the government's expert did not discuss "current coordination in the industry" and failed to "quantify any price impact from purported coordination." Dkt. 178 at 112 (Defs. PFOF ¶ 274). The law requires no such showing, and Defendants cite no case that demands one. *See, e.g., Heinz* 246 F. 3d at 724 (finding a "recipe for price coordination" based on market concentration, barriers to entry, and "past price leadership"). Moreover, Defendants ignore the evidence, discussed in the United States' Proposed Findings, regarding parallel behavior with respect to audio rights and contractual terms. Dkt. 177 at 154 (U.S. PFOF ¶ 315–316).

421. Second, Defendants do not, and cannot, square Dr. Snyder's assertion that there would be no harm to authors if publishers—in a coordinated fashion—worsened contract terms because the advance would still be negotiable, Dkt. 178 at 114 (Defs. PFOF ¶ 281) (quoting Dr. Snyder as testifying it would not "actually result in a bottom line reduction in competition"), with the Supreme Court's decision in *Catalano v. Target Stores,* 446 U.S. 643 (1980). *See* Dkt. 177 at 157 (U.S. PFOF ¶ 325). Nor do Defendants explain why publishers, like PRH and S&S, currently modify contract terms in ways that are worse for authors (*e.g.,* lengthening the time for the payout of the advance or lowering the digital e-book royalty) if the modifications have no material financial impact because the advance is still negotiable.

422. Third, Defendants' suggestion that courts are concerned only about whether the merger would increase the risk of "illegal" coordination is wrong. *See, e.g.,* Dkt. 178 at 159 (Defs. PCOL ¶¶ 134–135) (Section III.C: "The Merger Will Not Increase The Likelihood That Hachette, Macmillan, and Other Publishers Will Enter Illegal Anti-Poaching Agreements"). Courts are concerned when mergers increase the likelihood that industry participants can reach tacit understandings that do not rise to violations of the antitrust laws. Dkt. 177 at 150–151 (U.S. PFOF ¶¶ 305–06). Such an understanding could be as simple as the dominant PRH/S&S realizing it no longer needs to be as aggressive to grow share, Trial Tr. 802:11–18 (Dohle), and choosing not to engage in a "zero sum" game where it tries to poach the best authors from Hachette, Macmillan, and HarperCollins as long as they do not poach PRH/S&S's authors. If, however, one of those publishers does not follow the dominant firm's lead and begins to recruit its authors (as [REDACTED] did when it offered [REDACTED] to move from PRH, *see* Dkt. 178 at 94–95 (Defs. PFOF ¶ 233), PRH can retaliate by aggressively using its deep pockets to poach authors and/or Bertelsmann can threaten to make printing more difficult as feared by multiple CEOs. *See* Dkt. 177 at 155 (U.S. PFOF ¶ 319) (collecting testimony).

423. Fourth, Defendants misstate their own burden and assert that they can prevail as long as they can point to "cartel problems." Dkt. 178 at 158 (Defs. PCOL ¶¶ 127, 132). To rebut the presumption, however, Defendants must prove that the alleged "cartel problems" are "*much greater* in the [publishing industry] than in other industries." *Heinz,* 246 F. 3d at 724 (emphasis added) ("But the district court made no finding that any of these 'cartel problems' are so much greater in the baby food industry than in other industries that they rebut the normal presumption."). For the reasons outlined in the United States' Proposed Findings, Defendants did not make such a showing here. *See* Dkt. 177 at 143–151 (U.S. PFOF ¶¶ 311–332).

424. To the contrary, the evidence shows that industry players have already figured out how to solve "cartel problems" and will be able to do so more easily after the merger. For example, product differentiation and a lack of transparency on retailer contract terms did not prevent collusion in the e-books case. *United States v. Apple, Inc.,* 791 F.3d 290 (2d Cir. 2015); *see also Heinz,* 246 F.3d at 724–25 (finding likelihood of coordinated effects in product market differentiated by brand; holding evidence of past price leadership "undermined" expert testimony about "cartel problems"); *see also H & R Block,* 833 F. Supp. 2d at 78 ("[W]hile collusion may, in some instances, be more likely in markets for homogenous products than differentiated products, product differentiation in this market would not necessarily make collusion more difficult."); *Hosp. Corp.,* 807 F.2d at 1389–90 (upholding injunction against merger based on coordinated effects theory even though the relevant services were "complex and heterogenous"). Moreover, *Apple* shows that coordination can be successful and harmful without every

publisher participating (as neither Random House nor any small publishers participated). This history contradicts Defendants' claim that "a no-poach agreement . . . would be ineffective" without the smaller publishers' participation. Dkt. 178 at 115 (Defs. PFOF ¶ 284).

VII. CONCLUSION

425. The evidence shows that the proposed merger between PRH and S&S likely would substantially lessen competition in the market for the acquisition of U.S. publishing rights to anticipated top-selling books in violation of Section 7 of the Clayton Act. The Court should therefore permanently enjoin the merger.

Respectfully submitted,

Dated: September 7, 2022

John R. Read (DC Bar #419373)
Meagan K. Bellshaw
Anna Cross
Brittney A. Dimond
Jonathan S. Goldsmith
Collier E. Kelly
Owen M. Kendler
Ihan Kim
January Kim
Kevin Krautscheid
Jessica N. Leal
Sarah H. Licht
Bennett J. Matelson
Lauren G.S. Riker
Lisa A. Scanlon
Melvin A. Schwarz
Ethan D. Stevenson
Amanda M. Strick
Robert Vance
Jeffery G. Vernon
United States Department of Justice Antitrust Division
450 Fifth Street, NW, Suite 4000
Washington, DC 20530
Counsel for Plaintiff United States of America

DEFENDANTS' FINDINGS OF FACT AND CONCLUSIONS OF LAW

INTRODUCTION

1. Under Clayton Act § 7, a merger can be blocked only if the government proves that it will likely cause substantial and imminent harm to competition in a relevant, well-defined market. The government has not made that showing.
2. Antitrust law operates on the basic premise that competition is the best means for ensuring low prices, which generally benefits consumers, and maximizing output, which generally benefits workers.
3. The government did not bring this case to address concerns that the proposed merger of storied publishing houses Penguin Random House ("PRH") and Simon & Schuster ("S&S") might increase consumer book prices or reduce the number of books published every year. The case has never been about competitive harm to readers or booksellers.
4. Instead, the government has always focused on alleged harm to authors. Specifically, the government claims that the merger will reduce the component of compensation paid to them in the form of advances on royalties from eventual book sales. But the government ultimately abandoned any claim that the merger would reduce advances paid to *all* authors. By the time of trial, the government was focused only books that yielded advances of $250,000 or more—the top two percent of all books, representing only about 1000 authors. The government paid no heed to whether the merger would improve the sales, distribution, and visibility of books written by the many thousands of other authors who receive less than $250,000 for their hard work and creative efforts.
5. Trial brought even more clarity to the government's claim. It turns out that the government is not even concerned with all authors who receive advances of $250,000 or more. According to the government, its suit focuses on only a subset of that high-end category: authors easily identifiable by their proven track records and existing fan bases, i.e., "franchise" authors who write multiple successful books, popular or notorious celebrities, and authors with prior books that won the acclaim of literary awards.
6. These are not the authors being paid advances of $250,000, or $500,000, or even $1,000,00These authors sign multi-million dollar deals. They are the elite of the elite. As such, they are the least in need of protection by the antitrust laws, because their well-deserved compensation reflects a simple market reality: they write the books publishers will always compete hardest to acquire.
7. Yet protecting these authors is what this case has come to. The government at trial could not identify any other way to plausibly define or describe the market its case addresses. The trial confirmed that industry participants draw no categorical distinctions between books acquired for advances lower than $250,000 and books acquired for higher amounts. The government then tried to assert that its targeted market could be identified by the advance threshold where the Big Five publishers acquire the overwhelming majority of books. But the evidence showed that threshold to be just $50,000—a threshold that would likely preclude the government from trying to make its case based on statistical concentration alone.
8. All of which leaves the government with only one real argument: the market it wants to protect is characterized by the franchise, celebrity, and prize-wining authors who write books everyone recognizes as likely best-sellers. But the government has provided the court no workable quantitative metric that captures the advances paid to those select authors while excluding advances paid to other authors without similar track records or platforms. The law requires the government to draw the narrowest market that can be drawn to distinguish the products that require antitrust protection from those that do not. The $250,000 advance threshold cannot be reconciled with that rule. It is an arbitrary price line with no practical, competitive, or legal significance.
9. The government's effort to prove competitive harm to the most successful authors suffers from similarly arbitrary and unsupported claims. Among other things, the government's economic expert, Dr. Nicholas Hill, sought to prove that the merger would lower advances through a statistical model that admittedly examined the merger's effects only on one type of book acquisition: a "round-robin" or "rounds" style auction, where multiple editors each submit offers through multiple bidding rounds. Yet the agents who control the bidding rules rarely choose such formats, because such formats are usually not in authors' best interests, financial and otherwise. Dr. Hill nevertheless extrapolated the results of his rounds-only model across all bargaining formats to reach a broad conclusion about the merger's effects industrywide. To justify the extrapolation, Dr. Hill speculated that bidding in all formats is subject to roughly similar competitive considerations, even though he is not an expert on bargaining in the

publishing industry—as this Court emphasized—and even though agents overwhelmingly choose other formats precisely because they do *not* generate the same bargaining results as the round-robin auctions examined in his model.

10. The extrapolation of a model focused on round-robins to other formats is insupportable. And it cannot be rehabilitated by Dr. Hill's further speculation about how the merger might affect competition in acquisitions he never studied—the vast majority of acquisitions in the industry.
11. For these and the many other reasons set forth below, the government did not prove that the merger is likely to cause a substantial and imminent adverse effect on competition in any well-defined market.

PROPOSED FINDINGS OF FACT

I. BACKGROUND OF THE PARTIES AND THE DEAL

1. 1. On November 25, 2020, Penguin Random House ("PRH") and Bertelsmann SE & Co. KGaA ("Bertelsmann") announced plans to acquire Simon & Schuster, Inc. ("S&S").
2. The Department of Justice conducted a lengthy investigation of the merger, and on November 2, 2021, filed a complaint seeking to enjoin the merger under Section 7 of the Clayton Act. *See* Compl. (Dkt. 1). The case was tried and included 12 days of testimony, concluding on August 19, 2022.
3. *Story of Penguin Random House.* PRH's mission is "to create the future of books
4. and reading . . . for generations to come." Tr. 806:11–14 (Dohle (PRH)). PRH believes that "books matter," that "reading matters." Tr. 806:21–22 (Dohle (PRH)).
5. PRH is made up of about 100 imprints, both "small- and medium-sized publishing houses" that it operates in the United States. Tr. 812:5–11 (Dohle (PRH)).
6. 5. PRH is owned by Bertelsmann, which itself is majority-owned by the nonprofit Bertelsmann Foundation, and minority-owned by the sixth generation of the Mohn family, who founded the company. Tr. 808:20–23 (Dohle (PRH)). The Bertelsmann Foundation—the largest operating nonprofit in Europe, with an office in Washington, D.C.—was founded 45 years ago and aims to help governments and institutes make data-driven decisions tackling major issues like the environment, healthcare, and education. Tr. 808:24–809:22 (Dohle (PRH)). Bertelsmann's commitment to its publishing business means that the company reinvests its profits into its business divisions, including by making significant investments into PRH. Those investments include—first and foremost—PRH's investment in content. In 2021 alone, PRH paid over one billion dollars in author advances and royalties. Tr. 810:18–25 (Dohle (PRH)). As Mr. Dohle testified, Bertelsmann gives PRH "unlimited access to cash flow to invest into our business. I've never seen them limit us in any way . . . in terms of investments." Tr. 809:23–811:3, Tr. 815:18–21 (Bertelsmann imposes no budget on what PRH can spend to acquire books; "As much as we want.").
7. *Story of Simon & Schuster.* S&S was founded in 1924 by Richard Simon and
8. Max Schuster. Tr. 473:11–12 (Karp (S&S)). The company publishes adult, children, and audio books. Tr. 473:16–19 (Karp (S&S)). About 75 percent of S&S's business takes place in the United States. Tr. 474:2–6 (Karp (S&S)). S&S is made up of nearly 50 imprints and publishes around a thousand new books each year. Tr. 473:20–474:1 (Karp (S&S)).
9. S&S built its "origins in going out and getting the books." Tr. 475:25–476:1 (Karp (S&S)). The company tries to maintain the same spirit it held in 1939 of seeking out its "own books" as "exclusive opportunities," Tr. 475:25–476:6 (Karp (S&S)), often through approaching authors directly or receiving exclusive submissions from agents. Tr. 475:22–24, Tr. 476:7–10 (Karp (S&S)).
10. CBS owned S&S for many years. CBS merged with Viacom in 2019 and changed its name to ViacomCBS. Tr. 2177:16–22 (Berkett (Paramount f/k/a ViacomCBS)). ViacomCBS continued to own S&S. Tr. 2177:23–25 (Berkett (Paramount)). ViacomCBS then changed its name to Paramount Global, the current name of the owner of S&S. Tr. 2177:23- 2178:3 (Berkett (Paramount)).
11. Following the merger between Viacom and CBS, the management team decided that S&S was no longer a strategic priority, and the company would "now center on building a streaming video business and producing the world's best video content." Tr. 2180:23–2181:19 (Berkett (Paramount)). The management team discussed with the company's board of directors pursuing the sale of S&S. Tr. 2181:10–19 (Berkett (Paramount)).
12. Three strategic buyers made it to the end of the two-round bidding process to purchase S&S. Tr. 2185:8–2187:9 (Berkett (Paramount)). Bertelsmann/PRH bid the highest price. Tr. 2189:1–4 (Berkett (Paramount)). Certain that Bertelsmann could "finance the business and live up to their obligations"—

including being a great home for S&S's business, legacy, and employees—Paramount decided to sell S&S to Bertelsmann. Tr. 2189:5–19 (Berkett (Paramount)).

13. *The Publishing Industry.* The publishing industry has changed in recent years. Tr. 1067:17–1068:3 (Weisberg (Macmillan)); DX-299 at 9 (News Corp. 10-K stating that the book publishing business "is quickly changing and continues to see technological innovations"). The shift to online retail has "made publishers more profitable and leveled the playing field," changing the risk assessment for smaller publishers in particular. Tr. 837:2–838:6 (Dohle (PRH)). With the advent of "social media and TikTok, all of the different ways you can market a book virally," publishers are trying to find an audience for a book using "every device possible to find that audience." Tr. 1067:19–25, 1108:22–1109:24, 1113:1–17 (Weisberg (Macmillan)).
14. The market for the acquisition of books is highly competitive. Tr. 1298:21- 1299:10 (Murray (HarperCollins)) (HarperCollins will compete aggressively for books); PX- 2002 (Stehlik (HarperCollins) Dep.) 71:17–72:16; DX-299 at 9 (News Corp. 10-K describing the "book publishing business" as "operat[ing] in a highly competitive market"); Tr. 552:10–20 (Karp (S&S)) (publishing is "a dynamic landscape"); Tr. 1805:15–22 (Walsh) ("It's an exciting time for new entrants in the publishing industry"); PX-2005 (Jacobs (Abrams) Dep.) at 51:23- 52:3 (Abrams' "strategic plan" is to "grow our business and to be very strong in categories in which we publish and to try new things, keep growing our children's publishing aggressively and, you know, be a—a profitable independent midsized publisher.")
15. Amidst all of this, advances publishers pay to authors are rising. PX-2002 (Stehlik (HarperCollins) Dep.) at 51:11–16, 51:18–52:1; DX-422 (Glusman (Norton) Dep.) at 130:14–131:3, 131:9–19.; Tr. 991:5–19 (Tart (PRH)); Tr. 1990:4–9 (Kim (PRH)).
16. Publishers plan to spend more on author advances in the future, not less, including in plans developed after the PRH/S&S merger was announced. PX-2002 (Stehlik (HarperCollins) Dep.) at 49:11–51:5; DX-188 at 1 (June 16, 2021 email noting HarperCollins CEO publicly stated that HarperCollins "was going to be more aggressive in its offers" for books "because the market is growing");[REDACTED] Tr. 1092:6–10, 1098:5–18 (Weisberg (Macmillan)) (Macmillan plans to spend more on author advances in coming years in efforts to grow its retail market share).
17. Between 2020 and 2021, PRH and S&S lost retail market share, while other "Big Five" publishers gained. PX-829 at 2; Tr. 1094:1–6 (Weisberg (Macmillan)); DX-217.0006 (noting that "year to date," Macmillan has "taken approximately 2 points of market share from the other Big Five publishers").
18. Macmillan is a strong publishing company, with multiple well-known imprints, led by CEO Don Weisberg. Tr. 1057:14–19, 1089:4–17 (Weisberg (Macmillan)). Macmillan opened its Flatiron imprint within the last eight years. Tr. 1089:23–1090:7 (Weisberg (Macmillan)). That imprint is affiliated with Oprah Winfrey, who has a book club that both attracts authors and helps sales. Tr. 1090:8–25 (Weisberg (Macmillan). In the past two years, Macmillan has had record-breaking, unprecedented growth and profit. Tr. 1091:4–12 (Weisberg (Macmillan)); PX-829 at 2 DX-217.0004 (Macmillan internal presentation showing that Macmillan grew its market share within the "Big Five," based on Bookscan data, from about 10.4 percent to 12.2 percent year over year).
19. Hachette Book Group is another large and successful publisher. Hachette has multiple imprints that compete against each other in book auctions. Tr. 227:2–8 (Pietsch (Hachette)); Tr. 1796:21–23, Tr. 1797:10–15 (Walsh). Hachette is led by CEO Michael Pietsch. Tr. 95:22–96:4 (Pietsch (Hachette)).
20. HarperCollins, led by CEO Brian Murray, is owned by News Corporation and is the second largest publisher in the industry. Tr. 1362:10–1365:9, 1401:21–24 (Murray (HarperCollins)). HarperCollins competes with other Big Five publishers as well as non-Big Five publishers for content. DX-299 at 9.
21. *Plans to Sell S&S.* The decision to sell S&S is a firm one. Paramount's leadership has made repeated public statements to investors that S&S will be sold and divested from the company because it is no longer a strategic priority. Tr. 2182:14–2183:15 (Berkett (Paramount)) (describing public comments made by CEO Bob Bakish and others). If S&S cannot be sold to PRH, Paramount will sell it to another buyer "as soon as possible." Tr. 2183:16–2184:2 (Berkett (Paramount)).
22. Paramount believes that a sale to PRH would be the best outcome for the company. ViacomCBS used four criteria for evaluating the offers it received for S&S: price, deal certainty, stewardship, and whether the buyer is a "good home for the employees and executives at Simon & Schuster." Tr. 2188:1–12 (Berkett (Paramount)). Alexander Berkett—EVP, Chief Corporate Development and Strategy Officer at Paramount—testified that, "[b]ased on conversations we had with the company, based on Bertelsmann/Penguin Random House's reputation in the marketplace," he "thought they'd be an

excellent home for the business, for the legacy of the business, and for the employees and executives." Tr. 2189:9–19; Tr. 584:15–585:-4 (Karp); DX-154 (Karp "delighted" with transaction outcome).

23. Literary agents believe PRH's acquisition of S&S is a superior outcome to the alternative of an acquisition by a private equity company. Tr. 2094:20–2095:2 (Wylie (Wylie Agency)) ("Because what is important, in my view, for Simon & Schuster is to have its enterprise supported by an understanding parent company. So if it were, for instance, to go to private equity, as happened originally with Houghton Mifflin, the private equity company wouldn't understand the business it was in; would, say, load it with debt as Blackstone did to Houghton Mifflin, basically destroying the publishing house so that it was sold at a discount later to one of the Big 5."). Agent Elyse Cheney explained that the merger will be "neutral to positive" for her clients because "Penguin Random House has really—has made a commitment to books over a very, very long period of time, and because they're a private company, they can invest long-term in things like infrastructure, printing, whatever, you know. Whereas, a company like Simon & Schuster, which is shareholder driven and quarterly-report driven, it cannot make those kinds of investments." Tr. 2069:12–24.
24. Best-selling author Charles Duhigg also testified that an acquisition of Simon & Schuster by a private equity firm would be "disastrous for Simon & Schuster writers." Tr. 1938:18–23 ("And I covered private equity for a decade at *The New York Times,* and I saw what happened with newspapers. And they will gut that company.").
25. _Story of the Deal._ Bertelsmann and PRH decided to pursue the acquisition of S&S because they were convinced PRH was the best home for S&S. They believed that—as with the merger of Random House and Penguin—Bertelsmann could bring PRH's industry- leading supply chain to bear on S&S's books, enabling S&S to obtain more retail shelf space, enjoy higher sales, and reach more readers. Tr. 878:1–22 (Dohle (PRH)). And they believed that savings from the merger would allow the combined company to spend more money to acquire books and thereby compete better for retail sales. *Id.;* Tr. 2258:3–13 (McIntosh (PRH)) (if merger reduces overhead costs for combined company, formula for calculating advances will generate higher advance offers to authors).
26. Other publishers who considered or attempted to acquire S&S also believed an acquisition would create significant benefits. Tr. 208:12–14 (Pietsch (Hachette)). HarperCollins, the second biggest publisher in the industry, sought to acquire S&S for that reason, DX- 288.0017; Tr. 1421:23–25 (Murray (HarperCollins)); DX-143.0002, and it is now concerned that [REDACTED]
27. Other industry participants anticipate other author benefits apart from increased advances. In particular, they expect that S&S authors will benefit from PRH's superior distribution system, retail relationships, and marketing and promotional departments. PX-2007 (Fletcher (Fletcher & Company) Dep.) at 140:22–142:3; Tr. 2134:11–20 (Ross (Ross Yoon Agency)) (Q. "What impact, if any, do you believe this merger would have on your clients?" A. "Well, I'm focusing primarily on my Simon & Schuster clients. I have a lot of Simon & Schuster clients whose books will be published in the next several years. And I think—I think it will be terrific for them [REDACTED]"); Tr. 2135:9–20 (Ross (Ross Yoon Agency)) ("[A] lot of my clients do very well in independent bookstores. And I go around the country and I ask bookstore people about their various publishers. And, you know, everyone thinks that PRH has the best relations with the independent bookstores in the business. And I'm just looking forward to that for my Simon & Schuster authors.").
28. As literary agent Elyse Cheney testified, "Penguin Random House has really—has made a commitment to books over a very, very long period of time, and because they're a private company, they can invest long-term in things like infrastructure, printing, whatever, you know. Whereas, a company like Simon & Schuster, which is shareholder driven and quarterly- report driven, it cannot make those kinds of investments. So I do think that Simon & Schuster could benefit from some of the tools that Penguin Random House has developed over time." Tr. 2069:18–2070:1.

II. THE GOVERNMENT'S PROPOSED RELEVANT SUBMARKET

29. The government has sought to block the merger under Clayton Act § 7, but it has not attempted to prove that the merger will increase consumer prices or reduce output in the sale of books to readers downstream. Tr. 1539:11–25 (Hill).
30. The government also did not show—or even attempt to show—that the merger would likely harm competition in the upstream market for all trade books. The government originally alleged such a claim, *see* Compl. ¶¶ 32–35, but it abandoned the claim at trial. Tr. 1536:16–1537:2 (Hill). Defendants' expert Professor Edward Snyder agreed that the market for all U.S. trade books is a relevant market but,

testified that there is "no harm to authors in the broad market of all trade books. The main basis for that is that there is a lot of competition in that industry to acquire books and the merger is not going to reduce that competition." Tr. 2629:7–22, Tr. 2837:1–4 (Snyder) (Q. "What is your view on the acquisition—on the market for the acquisition of all books of this merger?" A. "It's competitive, highly competitive, and it will remain that way."); DX-382 (market shares for the broader market for all trade books, 2019- 2021). The government's expert, Dr. Nicholas Hill, agreed. Tr. 1535:16–1536:22 (Hill).

31. Unable to show harm from the transaction in the market for the acquisition of all trade books, the government instead sought to prove harm only in an arbitrarily-defined submarket, which it described as the market to acquire rights to "anticipated top selling books," defined as U.S. trade books acquired for advances of $250,000 or more. Compl. ¶¶ 36–39.
32. The alleged price-segmented submarket is not well defined, as explained in the following findings. While a price can help "corroborate" a proposed product market, "it should not be . . . used as the sole means of identifying a product market." Tr. 2815:20–25 (Snyder).

A. The Alleged Submarket Is Both Underinclusive And Overinclusive

33. Dr. Hill testified that, in defining his market for anticipated top selling books, "an anticipated top seller is a book that is expected to sell a significant number of copies." Tr. 1226:5–7 (Hill). But Dr. Hill never analyzed what it means to be an "anticipated top seller" in terms of sales—he defined the term simply "using the advance amount." Tr. 3176:20–3177:10 (Hill) (Q. "You have never—in your work, you have never actually, other than with respect to the price cutoff, you haven't defined with specificity what it means for a book to be a top seller in your reports, correct?" A. "Correct. I defined it using the advance amount or identify it using the advance amount, I would say." Q. "When you were asked in your deposition, well, what is an anticipated top seller expected to do in retail sales, you said it would generate what you called significant sales, correct?." . . . A. "Yeah. And I identified that this is about 20 percent of all books in the sample qualify for this." Q. "But that you did not have a definition of what significant copies was, correct?" A. "That's correct."). And, in defining his alleged submarket, Dr. Hill did not study whether the amount of sales that would support an advance of $250,000 or more in a P&L varies across publishers. Tr. 3177:10–22 (Hill) (Q. "And you did not know what quantity of downstream sales, for example, at Penguin Random House supports an advance of $250,000 or more?" A. "That's correct." Q. "And you haven't studied whether the number of estimated book sales needed to justify a $250,000 advance varies across publishers?" A. "Correct." Q. "And there's no specific level of estimated sales that you can identify that's associated with your price segment threshold of $250,000?" A. "Correct.").
34. Instead of using a threshold for the alleged submarket that is based on sales, Dr. Hill used an advance of $250,000 as the boundary of the market. Tr. 3176:24–25 (Hill) ("I defined it using the advance amount or identify it using the advance amount."). This price- defined submarket is both over- and underinclusive for the category of books it claims to cover. Tr. 1238:15–1239:8 (Hill) (admitting that "[s]ome anticipated top sellers are in our market, but they're not—or some books are in our market, but they're probably not anticipated top sellers, and vice versa").
35. Dr. Hill asserted that the $250,000 advance threshold demarcates a line above which the Big Five publishing houses have a dominant aggregate market share of book acquisitions. Tr. 3169:24–3170:17 (Hill). According to Dr. Hill, that larger market share proves that authors "are making different choices" above and below that threshold. Tr. 1233:3–13, 1235:12–21 (Hill). The government relied on PX-963 to argue that the $250,000 threshold reflects a change in competitive conditions because authors of books acquired for more than $250,000 have fewer publisher options:

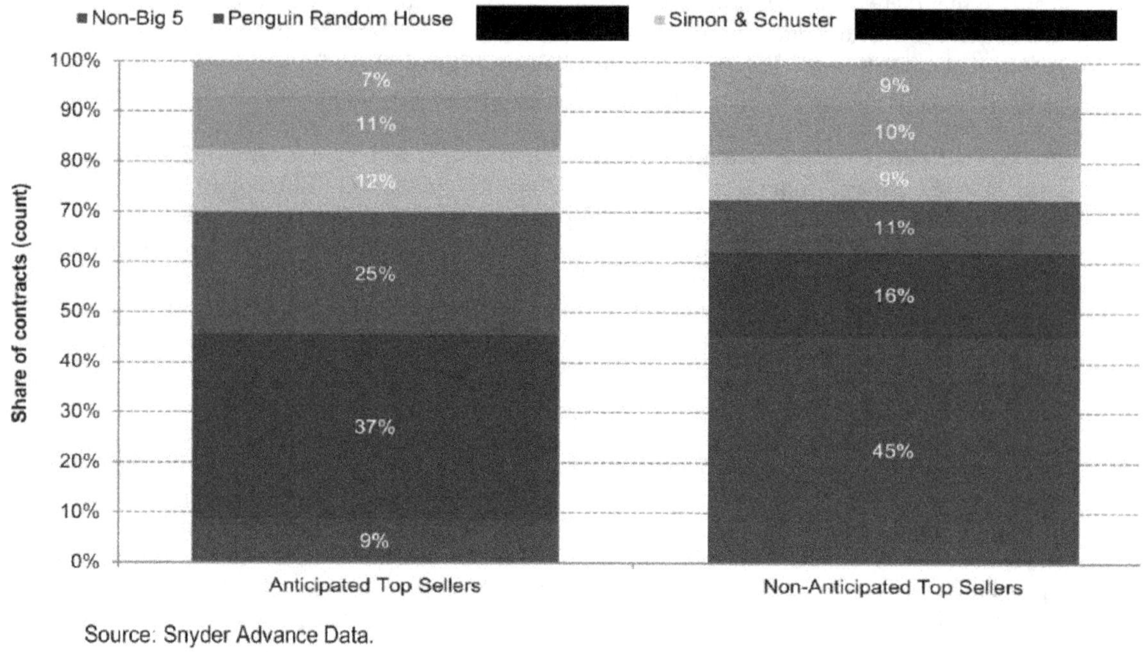

Source: Snyder Advance Data.

US v. Bertelsmann
1:21-cv-0866-FYP
PX 0963

t.Shares 1 of 1 DOJ-LIT-000000927

36. The data actually show that if there is a relevant price cutoff above which the Big Five make up a large majority of book acquisitions, it is much lower than $250,000, closer to $50,000:

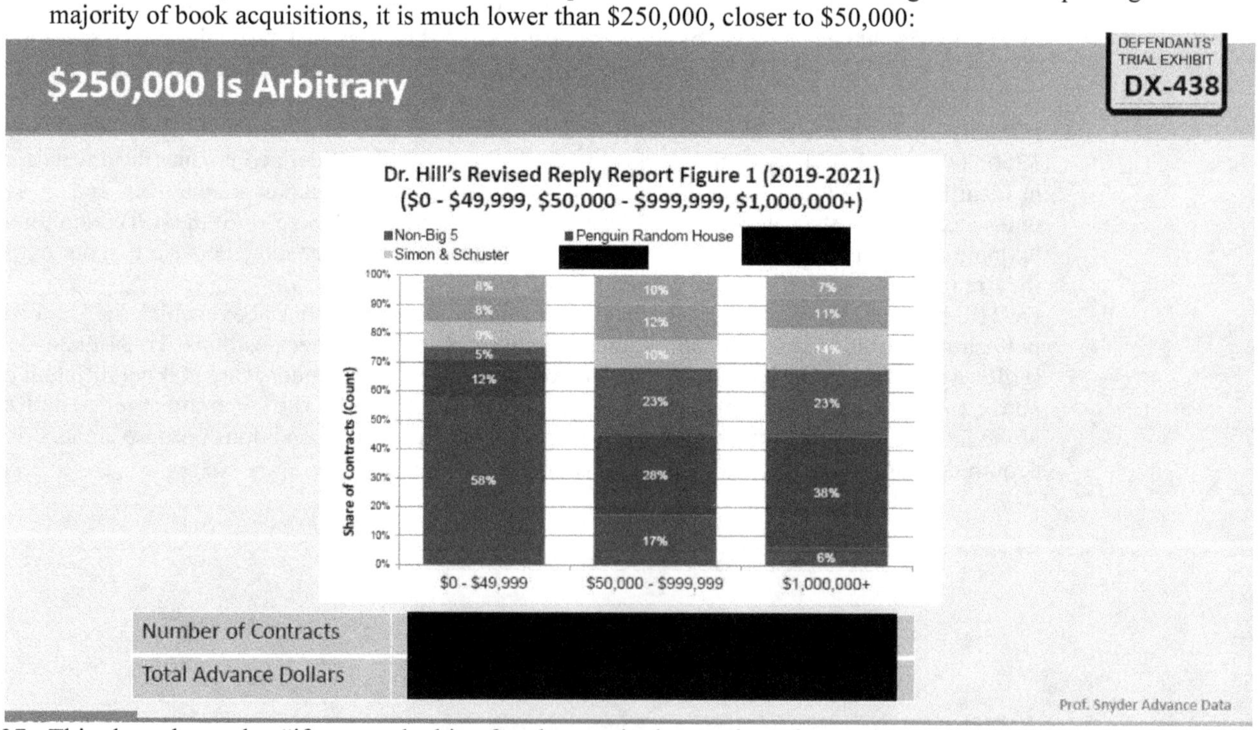

37. This chart shows that "if you are looking for changes in the number of competitors or the shares of competitors, there is nothing special about [$]250,000." Tr. :23–2826:2 (Snyder); 1816:21–1817:17 (Walsh). To the contrary, the data establish that *if* competitive conditions differ based on market shares and author preferences, the difference begins with books acquired for advances of $50,000 or more. Tr.

2822:14–2823:18 (Snyder); DX-438. In other words, under Dr. Hill's theory that the market share difference defines the proper boundary of a submarket for "anticipated top selling books," the boundary must be drawn at the $50,000 advance level.

38. If a market were properly defined—according the government's own criteria—at the $50,000 advance level, the government could not establish likely substantial harm in that market. The HHI for this broader market would show a "substantially less concentrated market." Tr. 2828:11–2829:6 (Snyder). Dr. Hill did not attempt to measure concentration in the market for books acquired for $50,000 or more. Tr. 1536:10–15 (Hill).
39. The government's $250,000 advance-level market boundary fails to properly capture "anticipated top selling books" in another respect. The government contended in closing arguments that "anticipated top sellers" share certain easily identifiable "special characteristics": they are books written by repeat authors with a successful "track record" (often "franchise" authors), celebrity authors with "notoriety," and authors "recognized with past awards." Tr. 3241:10–14 (closing). Jennifer Bergstrom, Publisher of Gallery Books at S&S, explained that when she acquires a book by a celebrity author like Amy Schumer, she expects the author's platform to result in high sales. Tr. 1841:8–19 (Bergstrom (S&S)). Jennifer Walsh also acknowledged that with "giant celebrities," like Michelle Obama, and franchise authors like James Patterson, "you know it's going to be a top seller." Tr. 1813:20–1814:3 (Walsh). Agent Andrew Wylie testified that he would understand "anticipated top selling books" as referring to well-known, repeat, "top selling authors," like "John Grisham or Danielle Steel." Tr. 2096:16- 23; *see* Tr. 2281:8–17 (McIntosh (PRH)) (franchise authors are "top sellers").
40. These books by established, franchise, celebrity, and prize-winning authors tend to be acquired for millions of dollars, not for anything close to $250,000. Tr. 2281:18–2282:7 (McIntosh (PRH)); *see also* Tr. 984:14–23 (Tart (PRH)) (Q. "[T]his case is about books that go for $250,000 advance or more. Is that a high level advance to you?" A. "[N]o. I don't consider 250—a high level advance. You know, I consider seven figures mid—multiple seven figures being a high level advance."); Tr. 1842:10–16 (Bergstrom (S&S)) (Q. "Is there any way to anticipate, other than the million dollar plus that you mentioned, is there any way to accurately anticipate what a top selling book would be?" A. "No."). If there is any difference in negotiating conditions, it exists only in the high million-dollar advance arena. Tr. 985:3–8 (Tart (PRH)). The government's market-defining advance threshold of $250,000 thus encompasses a vast collection of books that would not be broadly recognized in the industry as any type of "anticipated top seller."
41. The government asserted that 90 percent of books acquired for under $250,000 sell fewer than 2000 copies—they are essentially bottom-tier books. Tr. 2905:9–2906:9 (Snyder); Tr. 3242:22–24 (closing). The majority of *mid-list* books, then, must be found above the government's $250,000 threshold. As the witnesses testified, the only industry-consensus top-sellers, with the distinct, easily-identifiable characteristics the government emphasizes, generally receive advances well exceeding $1 million.
42. If the government had attempted to allege a well-defined submarket of books written by established, franchise, celebrity, and prize-winning authors, that submarket would have been subject to analysis of competitive harms very different from the submarket the government did allege. These authors have the most leverage in negotiations with publishers and are therefore the least likely to be targeted. Tr. 2685:16–2686:5, 2830:18–23 (Snyder) ("[A]n author with a very strong track record, he or she's going to have—may have a relationship with one publisher, but other publishers would look very fondly on the prospect of getting that author because they can see the track record."). As successful author Andrew Solomon observed: "I have a proven sales history and a proven history of winning prizes. And I think the publishers are always going to be interested in that and drawn to it." PX-2004 (Solomon Dep.) at 108:5–15; *see* Tr. 2830:13–15, 2646:21–2647:12 (Snyder) ("[T]here are going to be some authors who can be anticipated to be bestsellers, but [REDACTED] those are the ones with respect to targeting who have the leverage."). The leverage these authors have is evident in the fact that the books sold for the highest advances are generally less profitable than "mid-list" books acquired for lower advances. Tr. 2287:10–2288:2 (McIntosh (PRH)); Tr. 589:24–591:9 (Karp (S&S)) ("I think there's a fairly common truth that publishers hold which is that you make money on the midlist books.").
43. Dr. Hill admitted that he did not consider whether authors who sell books for tens of millions of dollars would have more bargaining leverage than authors who sell books for $250,000. Tr. 1544:3–10 (Hill).

B. The "Hypothetical Monopsonist" Test Does Not Establish Any Well-Defined Submarket Based Solely On Price

44. The hypothetical monopsonist test ("HMT") does not justify using the $250,000 advance-level

threshold to define a submarket because the test would pass at any submarket at any price level. Tr. 2821:14–25 (Snyder). Dr. Hill agreed that the HMT "tests whether the market you've chosen passes the [m]onopsonist test, but it doesn't necessarily validate your demarcation point at 250,000 or more." Tr. 1243:12–1244:15, 1548:3–7 (Hill) (Q. "[Y]ou're not claiming that your hypothetical monopsonist test required you to choose 250- or any other specific advance level as a cut-off, correct; that we agree on?" A. "Correct.").

C. The Alleged Submarket Does Not Reflect Industry Realities

45. The $250,000 price boundary does not reflect the commercial realities of the publishing industry. While advance payments may loosely correlate with expected sales, advances simply increase along a continuum—there is no categorical divide at the $250,000 level, or anywhere close, where industry participants negotiate or otherwise treat books differently based on sales expectations. Above and below the $250,000 threshold, all basic industry functions are the same—publishers, agents, editors, and authors do not operate differently above and below that threshold. Tr. 1816:25–1817:4 (Walsh) (books above and below $250,000 are provided "the identical service" from agencies and publishers); Tr. 2816:1- 18, 2889:5–2890:2 (Snyder) ($250,000 threshold is "arbitrary"). Indeed, publishers and agents do not track publishers' market shares for the acquisition of books for advances over $250,000, or at any advance level. Tr. 823:18–824:4 (Dohle (PRH)) (PRH does not track market shares for the acquisition of books and he is not aware of any industry publications that provide such information); Tr. 2128:1–7 (Ross (Ross Yoon Agency)) (does not know what publishers' market shares are in acquisition market).
46. Every factor relevant to commercial reality shows only a price continuum, not a distinct submarket of books defined anywhere around the $250,000 advance level.

1. Books Acquired For Advances Of At Least $250,000 Receive No Unique Services Or Treatment

47. Industry participants do not treat books differently depending on whether they were acquired for an advance above $250,000 or below that amount. Tr. 1989:11–1990:3 (Kim (PRH)) (no difference in negotiations over book that will cost more or less than $250,000; no difference in sales support based on that acquisition amount; no difference in printing or distribution based on that acquisition amount). There is no distinct set of agents who only sell books for over $250,000, and no distinct set of editors who only acquire books for over $250,000. Tr. 1817:18–1818:7 (Walsh); Tr. 2133:17–22 (Ross (Ross Yoon Agency)) (Q. "[I]n your business, is there some kind of demarcation by the reference to an advance level—let's say $250,000—where the industry treats books above that amount in a certain way in contrast with how they would treat books below that amount?" A. "No."); PX-2002 (Stehlik (HarperCollins) Dep.) at 134:24–135:10 (no special evaluation processes for books in different potential advance categories).
48. Nor do publishers have distinct editorial, publishing, sales, or marketing departments that service books receiving advances of $250,000 or more. Hachette CEO Michael Pietsch opposes the merger and testified for the government. He nonetheless admitted, with respect to marketing books with $250,000+ advances: "We do not divide our company that way." Tr. 232:16–20 (Pietsch (Hachette)); DX-422 (Glusman (Norton) Dep.) 137:22–138:5; Tr. 985:19–21, 989:18–25 (Tart (PRH)); Tr. 2278:23–2279:1 (McIntosh (PRH)) (Q. "[A]nd just to be clear, do you have any—any kind of separate marketing, publicity, or sales teams associated for books that were acquired for more than $250,000?" A. "No, I do not."); Tr. 1868:5–17 (Bergstrom (S&S)) (THE COURT: "So putting aside advance levels, are there just some books that you think are going to sell well . . . and do those books get treated differently from other books?" A. "When we acquire books at Gallery, we assign a marketer, a publicist, and obviously an editor to it. Each one of our books has—I call them the SWAT team. [REDACTED] Again, some will take off. Some won't. But our attitude really is that that's what each book deserves, and we are able to do it.").
49. *Marketing Spend and Marketing Plans.* Marketing spend is not a feature that distinguishes "anticipated top sellers" from other books publishers acquire. Marketing spend is not determined by the advance, and marketing spend does not separate books into any distinct identifiable categories.
50. The estimated marketing spend figure identified in the acquisition "profit and loss" ("P&L") statements is a "placeholder number." Tr. 2253:14–24 (McIntosh (PRH)); Tr. 918:18–21 (Tart (PRH)); Tr. 1850:1–1850:9 (Bergstrom (S&S)) (Q. "And do you include an estimate of marketing and publicity spend in the profit and loss statement that you discussed?" A. When I am—when we are acquiring books, yes, we do. We put a, it's a guesstimate, into each P&L. And it's a guesstimate because oftentimes we aren't publishing that book for many years. So it's not until—we are usually about ten months from

publication, from actual pub date, that we start our planning for how we are going to market and publicize that book.").

51. Publishers do not often create marketing plans to submit with their acquisition offers. Tr. 1855:6–13 (Bergstrom (S&S)) (Gallery at S&S "rarely" submits marketing plans with offers). Whether they do or not has nothing to do with the advance level. After all, when a marketing plan is created to present with an offer, the publisher does not yet know how much the book will ultimately be acquired for, or who will acquire it. Tr. 576:17–578:3 (Karp (S&S)); Tr. 1854:23–1855:5 (Bergstrom (S&S)) ("I really tend not to give any marketing promises in the acquisition. I never promise any financial. I really don't. If we are in what I call a beauty contest where we are competing with someone else, yes, I will tip—I will talk about what I have done for other authors. But it's too early in the process when we are acquiring a book to know what we are going to market and spend on it.").
52. The actual marketing plan for a book is not derived from or developed with reference to the advance paid for the book. Tr. 2271:24–2272:3 (McIntosh (PRH)) ("advance level does not play a role in the development of the marketing plan"); Tr. 2278:7–10 (McIntosh (PRH)) (Q. "So is there any kind of system in place now or that has been in place in the last ten years or so where marketing is directly tied to advance levels?" A. "No."). In fact, the individuals at S&S in charge of marketing and publicity "often don't know" and "our sales force rarely knows" how much was paid to acquire a book. Tr. 493:13–19 (Karp (S&S)). Likewise, the salespeople at PRH rarely know the advance levels of the books they are tasked with selling because the advance levels are considered confidential. Tr. 2268:22–2269:24 (McIntosh (PRH)); *see* Tr. 1921:13–19, 1922:3–14 (Duhigg) (explaining absence of special marketing attention for book that received $750,000 advance).
53. Publishers instead determine their marketing plan near the *publication* date, "as late as possible, often six weeks before [they're] about to publish a book." Tr. 976:21–22 (Tart (PRH)). That is because the marketing spend depends on the finished book and its reception in the marketplace, not the advance. Tr. 976:23–977:24 (Tart (PRH)) (explaining three key factors that determine book marketing spend). Publishers do not typically even decide how much they are going to spend to market a book until *after* reader reactions have come in. Tr. 574:4–11 (Karp (S&S)); Tr. 1850:15–25 (Bergstrom (S&S)) (publisher "can't determine our marketing and publicity plans until we have all had a chance to read that finished book"). PRH's Putnam imprint follows substantially the same approach. Tr. 1981:1–7 (Kim (PRH)) (discussing the decision about the level of marketing support to provide for a book) (Q. "When does Putnam make that decision?" A. "Pretty close to publication. By that time, the book has been written; it's been edited; it's been revised; we've shared it around internally; our sales department starts to buzz about it. And we have a sense of kind of what the traction or reaction the book will get out there in the world."). As Viking Editor Brian Tart explained, any marketing plans a publisher might submit with a bid become "pretty obsolete by the time we publish." Tr. 984:1–13.
54. Government witness Ayesha Pande agreed that the key time marketing decisions are made is "the month immediately leading up to publication, when the publisher starts pitching the book to news outlets and other media, and then in the six to eight weeks right after publication." Tr. 258:11–259:2.
55. Marketing spend is also not a distinguishing feature of a distinct anticipated top- seller category because books sold for drastically different advance levels can and do receive identical marketing and promotion downstream. Tr. 990:1–991:4 (Tart (PRH)) (providing example of $1,000,000 and $100,000 book with same marketing and sales). Although publishers hope marketing spend will be correlated "with books that we feel are going to sell well," publishers nonetheless "look at each book individually," and so marketing spend ultimately "has no bearing on how much we paid for the book." Tr. 1988:6–15 (Kim (PRH)); *see* Tr. 491:13–22 (Karp (S&S)); Tr. 1114:1–24 (Weisberg (Macmillan)).
56. Books acquired for particularly high advances actually can require *less* marketing spend because such authors are often public figures who generate publicity and therefore do not need marketing. Tr. 1986:7–18 (Kim (PRH)) (describing $35,000 spend on million-dollar advance book, Book E); DX-413 (book title decoder for Kim testimony). Agent Elyse Cheney explained: "People get that advance, in part, because the author has their own marketing—they already have an audience that is, sort of, built in. They're coming, in a way, with their own marketing machine." Tr. 2069:2–5. For example, S&S's current best-selling author, Colleen Hoover, does not have a high marketing budget at S&S because she is "the queen of TikTok, and so she has a huge following on TikTok." Tr. 572:19–20 (Karp (S&S)). The highest advances certainly do not always reflect the highest marketing spend. Tr. 1858:25–1859:2 (Bergstrom (S&S)) (marketing and publicity spends for best-selling authors ranged from five percent to thirty percent of advance level).

57. As literary agent Elyse Cheney testified, while one might think that a publisher would spend "more marketing money" for books acquired for higher advances, "in fact, that's not the case." Tr. 2067:17–22. Cheney explained the story of two books she sold recently, "one over a million, one over 700; one of them extremely timely." Tr. 2067:23–25. In both situations, she asked the editor for special treatment in the form of "fancier" advanced copies for reviewers, and was "told no twice" before complaining to the head of the publishing company who said "Okay. Fine." Tr. 2068:1–10, 2068:18–21 (Cheney (Cheney Agency)) ("Half the time they're not even—it just happened to me. Same book. No, we don't even have the list together. So I'm the one who's doing that. I'm the one who's driving it half the time."); Tr. 2068:22–2069:1 (Cheney (Cheney Agency)) ("I mean, I did a deal with, actually, the same publisher, $1.1 million, and I said to her afterwards—because it's always—it's actually a point of frustration, I think, for a lot of agents. Why didn't you spend more money on marketing? And she said: Well, we just spent it all on the advance.").
58. Marketing spend will vary for all of these reasons, regardless of the advance paid upfront. Sally Kim, SVP and Publisher of PRH's Putnam imprint, testified to several examples of books with marketing spend that did not directly correlate with the advance spend. Tr. 1985:9–22 (describing advances versus marketing spend for Book F and Book B), *see also* DX- 413 (book title decoder for Kim testimony).
59. As Professor Snyder testified, to the extent high advances correlate with higher marketing spends at all, that correlation reflects the publishers' efforts to recoup the money spent at the outset. But there are many "variants around that relationship. A very well-known author might be able to basically sell the book herself or himself." Tr. 2818:11–13 (Snyder); *see also* Tr. 1818:8–15 (Walsh). Ultimately, regardless of the actual marketing spend, the marketing *functions* are the same for all books regardless of advance. Tr. 2817:8–2818:17 (Snyder).
60. <u>*Negotiation Processes and Contract Terms.*</u> Publishers do not employ a different negotiation process for books that sell for advances above $250,000. Tr. 984:24–985:2 (Tart (PRH)).
61. The top 2 percent of the advance market is not more "competitive" than the other 98 percent. Government witness Don Weisberg (Macmillan) characterized the 98 percent as "just as competitive." Tr. 1131:18–25 ("I don't think there's anybody, any editor that you'd meet that doesn't want to find that future story that they worked on.").
62. The same boilerplate contracts are used for authors of books that sell for above and below $250,000, and there are no contract terms that are negotiable only for authors of books that sell for above $250,000. Tr. 1818:16–1819:8 (Walsh).
63. The so-called "glam budget" occasionally included in a contract is not a feature that defines anticipated top-selling books as a market, either. Viking Publisher Brian Tart explained that a "glam budget" is discussed only for certain "kinds of books, like celebrity books . . . you don't ever talk about glam with fiction really or certain other kinds of books that you're doing, it's really a specific kind of book that you would be negotiating that. So I don't really consider it so much advance based as I do kind of type of book." Tr. 987:6–12; Tr. 1859:3- 1859:12 (Bergstrom (S&S)) (testifying that it is "very rare" for authors to get "glam budgets and "willingness to offer a glam budget" does not depend on advance level); Tr. 575:20–23 (Karp (S&S)) (THE COURT: "It's not a standard term in a book contract?" THE WITNESS: "Thankfully, no. John Irving isn't asking for a glam budget."); Tr. 1819:9–1820:2 (Walsh) (negotiated "glam" for a celebrity book sold for under $250,000 because "that was specific to the author's needs").
64. Negotiations over royalty rates and bonuses do not vary according to advance level either. These benefits depend on the competitive dynamics in each particular acquisition process; they can be wrested by agents with particular leverage in negotiations. As Brian Tart testified, things like bonuses and royalties can come up "[w]hen there's leverage" and the agent says "if you give me this or that, then it's yours . . . that's usually when I'll negotiate to get the book. And so, you know, bonuses come up, even at the five-figure level." Tr. 1045:7–14. Agents often try to reach a six-figure payout by simply negotiating a bonus on top of a five- figure advance—as a result, publishers "do talk bonuses" at lower advance levels. Tr. 1045:15- 18 (Tart (PRH)).

2. *Non-Big Five Publishers Provide Equivalent Publishing Services*

65. Big Five publishers do not provide unique publishing services that cannot be provided by numerous other elite publishers among the top 30 publishers. These other publishers can and do provide the same quality editorial, publicity, marketing, and sales services necessary to successfully publish authors of books at all advance levels, including above $250,000. PX-2007 (Fletcher (Fletcher & Company) Dep.) at 171:25–172:19 (services offered by smaller companies can be "superior" to services offered by larger

publishers; "just because a big publisher has the capabilities to perform at a certain level doesn't mean they will [REDACTED] And a smaller publisher may value a particular book more and be willing to throw a disproportionate amount of resources behind that book."); Tr. 2096:9–15 (Wylie (Wylie Agency)) ("[T]he services provided by non-Big 5 publishers . . . are professional and . . . really quite—quite strong."); DX- 422 (Glusman (Norton) Dep.) at 66:2–8, 66:10; Tr. 2047:7–12 (Cheney (Cheney Agency)) (Q. "In your experience, have you observed any qualitative difference in the publishing services rendered by the Big 5 versus the non-Big 5?" A. "Broadly, no. It's pretty similar. I mean, it's a process of bringing a book to market, to—everybody's travel to the bookstores is pretty similar."); Tr. 1551:9–13 (Hill) (Q. "So you don't dispute . . . that publishers outside of the so- called Big 5 are perfectly capable of rendering those services, they just don't do it as often?" A. "Yeah, in some circumstances, they can do it, yes."); Tr. 1563:16–23 (Hill) (Q. "But you're not saying that the services that those publishers actually render are inferior to the services provided by the Big 5?" A. "For a particular book that is acquired by the non-Big 5, the author has decided that—assuming that the Big 5 competed, that that—for that book, that non-Big 5 publisher is the best choice. And given the respective advance amounts offered."); Tr. 2834:23- 2835:3 (Snyder) ("there are other publishers that are really credible with anticipated top sellers"); Tr. 1798:12–16 (Walsh) (non-Big Five publishers "are best in class too. So just because they are smaller doesn't mean that they are not as impeccable in every way.").

66. It is not disputed that non-Big-Five companies, collectively, compete as a sixth bidder for books above the government's $250,000 advance threshold. Tr. 3081:12–23 (Hill) (A: "In the model, I believe I combine the non-Big 5 into one group and give them a 9 percent market share." Q. "So they're bidding as a sixth bidder. Am I understanding that right?" A. "Correct."); Tr. 1574:8–18 (Hill) (THE COURT: "[F]rom the perspective of a Big 5 publishing house in an auction, are they thinking, we're just as likely to have one non-Big 5 firm, whichever one it is, as likely as Hachette, which has, like, a similar share?" THE WITNESS: "That's right. If you take them all collectively, that's roughly correct.").
67. Although Dr. Hill asserted that non-Big-Five publishers have less ability to bear risk than Big Five publishers, he did not study the issue and had no basis for opining on publisher financing. Tr. 1565:15–25 (Hill) (he has not studied the capital constraints of publishers in the industry, and is "not aware of the funding of all the non-Big 5 publishers").
68. The fact that Big Five publishers enter *more* deals than individual non-Big-Five publishers above $250,000 advances simply reflects their greater appetite and resources, not qualitative difference in the services they provide to authors. Tr. 2047:7–18 (Cheney (The Cheney Agency)) (Q. "Why is it, then, that as we've seen in this trial, there are so many deals 250 and above that are done with the Big 5 as opposed to the non-Big 5? Do you have a view about that?" A. "I think the non-Big 5, you know, are just not going to play in that sandbox too many times. They don't have the scale."); Tr. 2047:25–2048:3 (Cheney (The Cheney Agency)) (Q. "So other than scale, have you, in your experience, observed any qualitative differences in the work performed by these publishers?" A. "No, not at all."). The weight of the evidence does not support the theory that the non-Big Five publishers' lower frequency of participation in the alleged submarket demonstrates that they provide a lower quality of service to authors in that market.
69. Depending on an author's goals, non-Big Five publishers may be preferable. Tr. 1798:12–1799:4 (Walsh). Larger publishers do not necessarily have competitive advantages when it comes to reputation, marketing, distribution, or printing. First, many editors at smaller publishers—just like editors at larger publishers—have stellar reputations. Second, any advantages larger publishers might have once had in marketing and publicity have eroded as dynamics have shifted to favor new technologies like Instagram and TikTok over traditional print media. Third, smaller publishers use the same distribution channels as larger publishers. Fourth, to the extent Big Five publishers have any greater access to printing services (which they do not, *see infra* FF ¶¶ 134–43), printing is simply not a factor for authors in choosing a publisher. Tr. 1799:19–1800:22, 1801:12–20, 1802:19–1803:1 (Walsh); Tr. 1977:18–21 (Kim (PRH)) (Q. "Does Penguin Random House's access to printing facilities ever come up in conversations with authors or agents? A. "No, they don't.")
70. The evidence showed that non-Big Five publishers publish many top-selling authors. *See* DX-376 (list of noteworthy authors who signed contracts for at least $250,000 with non-Big Five publishers). For example, [REDACTED]
71. [REDACTED] And Abrams now publishes "the most successful middle grade series in the world," Jeff Kinney's *Diary of a Wimpy Kid.* That publication "helped [the] company grow significantly" over the last 15 years, and the series remains under contract at Abrams for additional books. PX-2005 (Jacobs

(Abrams) Dep.) at 61:21–63:2.

72. Norton also publishes many well-known authors, including several books by Michael Lewis, all of which became bestsellers. DX-422 (Glusman (Norton) Dep.) at 58:2–10, 59:1–2, 59:4–6. Indeed, Norton is "one of the best publishers in the business," with "one of the most serious nonfiction lists in the business on a consistent basis, award winners ranging from the Pulitzer Prize to the Nobel Prize to the National Book Award to the National Book Critics Circle Award." Norton's long, stable history is "enormously attractive to agents and authors alike." DX-422 (Glusman (Norton) Dep.) at 63:14–64:1, 65:2–4, 65:6–18; *see also* Tr. 1415:12- 1416:3 (Murray (HarperCollins)) (discussing Norton).
73. Major authors like Michael Lewis, Mary Roach, and Richard Powers have chosen to continue to publish with Norton despite opportunities to move to a Big Five publisher. These authors choose to stay with Norton out of loyalty, and because of their excellent marketing capabilities, among other reasons. Tr. 541:8–544:24, 550:19–551:13 (Karp (S&S)); DX-054 (July 2019 email demonstrating author chose Norton over S&S "because of their marketing team, who . . . conveyed a compelling plan"); Tr. 1799:9–1800:8 (Walsh) (identifying authors who have chosen to remain with smaller publishers or to switch to smaller publishers from Big Five publishers);[REDACTED]
74. Authors, too, acknowledge that non-Big Five publishers, such as Graywolf, can "do extremely well" by their authors, and that their books can win "extraordinary number[s] of Pulitzer prizes and national book awards." PX-2004 (Solomon Dep.) at 99:11–20.

3. The $250,000+ Advance Threshold Does Not Correspond To Any Distinct Set Of Authors Or Particular Book Characteristics

75. "Every book is unique, every book is individual." Tr. 1068:12–13 (Weisberg (Macmillan)). And "every author is atypical." Tr. 1952:20–25 (Duhigg (best-selling author)).
76. There is no specific category of authors who write books that sell for $250,000 or more. Some authors sell books for under $250,000 early in their career, and for above $250,000 once they have established themselves. Tr. 1817:13–19 (Walsh).
77. Books acquired for over $250,000 come from all genres. As of 2021, 27 percent of PRH's trade book publishing program consisted of children's books, representing over a quarter of PRH's trade book publishing program. Tr. 2297:12–15 (McIntosh (PRH)). PRH acquires some of those children's books for over $250,000, and even over $1 million. Tr. 2297:16–20 (McIntosh (PRH)). Christian books, which are a much smaller segment of the trade books market than children's books are, constitute about two percent of PRH's trade book publishing program, and are likewise sometimes acquired for advances exceeding $250,000. Tr. 2299:14–19, 2299:25–2300:2 (McIntosh (PRH)). The acquisition processes for children's and Christian books are exactly the same as for other trade books. Tr. 2299:22–24 (McIntosh (PRH)).
78. Apart from certain easily identifiable established, franchise, celebrity, and prize- winning authors, agents and publishers generally have no objective criteria for reaching in advance an consensus on whether a book is likely to be a top selling book. One editor or agent may have a sense the book will do well, or hope that it will, but normally there is no consensus. Tr. 2133:15–16 (Ross (Ross Yoon Agency) ("[W]e don't have a crystal ball."). And they use the same tools to negotiate the sale of any book, regardless of one individual's subjective expectations. Tr. 1811:3–10, 1817:18–20 (Walsh).
79. Nor, apart from the few exceptions already discussed, can publishers cannot easily predict top sellers, and there is no "magic advance number" that corresponds to books that sell well. PX-2002 (Stehlik (HarperCollins) Dep.) at 134:18–21. Books acquired for below $250,000 sometimes unexpectedly evolve into "breakout" books after winning major awards. DX-422 (Glusman (Norton) Dep.) at 136:21–23, 136:25, 137:1–2, 137:5–20; Tr. 573:2–574:3 (Karp (S&S)) (testifying about unexpected bestseller acquired for low advance); Tr. 1843:9–16 (Bergstrom (S&S)) (Q. "Are there examples of authors below—that you paid below a hundred thousand dollar advance that have gone on to sell a lot of books?" A. "Yeah. One of my biggest authors, author D[REDACTED] on this list, we bought her first book for $95,000. It has sold over 1.3 million copies."). The government's own witness, Macmillan CEO Don Weisberg, rejected the premise—essential to the government's submarket theory—that there are identifiable "criteria" that determine when a book will become a "big book": "Sometimes it's determined by the advance you pay, sometimes it's determined by the passion you have for the books. So we may buy a book for less money but because everybody in house reads it and loves it, it becomes a big book. So it's not always defined by the same criteria." Tr. 1070:18–24; *see also* Tr. 316:15–18, 317:4–6, 318:22–319:4 (King) (testifying that his book *Carrie* received $2,500 advance and became a bestseller).

80. In fact, editors do not always agree on which books are likely to be bestsellers. *Where the Crawdads Sing* exemplifies this phenomenon. The book was submitted widely but Viking editor Brian Tart's team "didn't think it was going to be a big book" and "didn't even make a bid on it." Tr. 970:15–22. An editor at PRH's Putnam imprint, though, "read it, loved it, shared it with all of us, ran up and down the halls. And through our conversations with the agent, we started to get the sense, as I mentioned before, that there weren't a lot of editors banging down his door to make an offer." Tr. 1967:17–22 (Kim (PRH)). Putnam made a preempt offer in the mid six-figures. Tr. 1967:25–1968:1 (Kim (PRH)). Although Putnam "always hoped" *Crawdads* would be successful, it still initially printed only 25,000 copies—not even enough for the author to earn back her advance. Tr. 1969:12–19 (Kim (PRH)). But "then Reese Witherspoon picked it for her book club and the skies opened up." Tr. 1969:23–24 (Kim (PRH)). As of today, the book has sold "about 10 million" copies in the U.S. Tr. 1970:12–13 (Kim (PRH)).
81. Mr. Tart told a similar story about the highly successful book *The Life-Changing Magic of Tidying Up* by Marie Kondo: "I didn't know what to make of it. And I didn't even make a bid on that book. And ultimately that's kind of changed the world in some way and sold millions of copies in the process." Tr. 971:2–7; Tr. 971:7–8 (Tart (PRH)) (Q. "Were those books anticipated top sellers?" A. "Not to me.").
82. Madeline McIntosh, CEO of PRH U.S., testified that those breakout titles—those "unanticipated best sellers"—are in fact the titles that "account for the lion's share of [PRH's] profit because they had advances that were relatively low compared to the very high sales achievement." Tr. 2287:10–2288:5. For books like *Where the Crawdads Sing, Fifty Shades of Gray,* and *Gone Girl,* the "sales performance so outstrips [PRH's] expectation, that they deliver most of the profit to the company." Tr. 2289:2–10 (McIntosh (PRH)); Tr. 748:11–23 (Dohle (PRH)).
83. For all the foregoing reasons, individual editors may value a book at vastly different levels. *See* Tr. 1815:5–16 (Walsh). When editors create P&Ls to determine what advance they should offer, they include projected sales based on comparable books, known as "comp titles." Tr. 1844:7–12 (Bergstrom (S&S)). But determining the comp titles is an "art," "not a science." Tr. 1844:12 (Walsh). There is frequently disagreement among editors at the same publishing company about the potential sales for an individual book because "it's so subjective," it's a "guesstimate." Tr. 1844:13–18 (Bergstrom (S&S)); Tr. 2240:1–8 (McIntosh (PRH)) (Q. "And why do they vary?" A. "Because . . . these aren't widgets that we're producing. . . . . [T]he valuation is a highly subjective process, and so it's a reflection of the—that particular editor's vision and belief in the book project."); *see also* Tr. 1555:6–21 (Hill) (discussing book [REDACTED] where one non-Big Five publisher bid above $250,000 but remaining publishers, including PRH and S&S, bid below $250,000).
84. Because editors strive to develop lasting relationships with authors they want to publish, advances are not always correlated with editors' expectations of how a particular book will sell. Don Weisberg testified that sometimes Macmillan is "paying more for a book that we might not think might benefit us at the time of publication but we think the author is somebody we want to publish forever and we think down the road will be special so we'll spend extra. I mean, it's hard for me to make statements about this that are accurate in every case because every auction is different." Tr. 1135:6–20.
85. And even if a book obtains a high advance, that advance does not necessarily correspond to a book's ultimate sales. Books that everyone expects to sell well, and that obtain high advances, frequently flop. Tr. 1814:7–1815:4 (Walsh); Tr. 2134:2–10 (Ross (Ross Yoon Agency) ("It happens more than any of us would like"); Tr. 2281:8–17 (McIntosh (PRH)) ("[W]e certainly have made many very painfully expensive bets on celebrities who turned out not to be able to sell the books.").
86. When pressed, competing publishers could not identify any meaningful characteristics that correspond to the $250,000 advance threshold. The government's own witness, Don Weisberg (CEO of Macmillan), testified that the difference between the top 2 percent of advances and the other 98 percent is dollars: "The difference is primarily in the financial level." Tr. 1129:2–12. Auctions take place "every day," even for lower-advance books. *See* Tr. 1129:13 (Weisberg (Macmillan)). The only thing that distinguishes the other 98 percent are that they are "not the big mega price books." *See* Tr. 1129:24–25, 1130:12–23 (Weisberg (Macmillan)) (THE COURT: "I see. And so you're saying these are sort of a different set of authors, more ones that you're developing and investing in?" THE WITNESS: "Well—or we can develop and invest in an author from a higher level too, but, yes." THE COURT: "But are you discovering them, is that the difference?" THE WITNESS: "Discovering is a strong word. I mean, we're investing in them. At the end of the day, as a publisher, all we're about is our authors.").

4. Industry Participants Do Not Recognize A Separate Submarket For The Acquisition Of "Anticipated Top Sellers" Defined By A $250,000 Advance Threshold

87. The publishing industry does not recognize a market for "anticipated top selling books" defined by an advance threshold anywhere in the $250,000 range. As John Glusman, editor-in-chief at Norton testified, if there were a common industry understanding of anticipated top-selling books, "we'd all be rich by now." DX-422 (Glusman (Norton) Dep.) at 134:24- 135:1.
88. Among publishers, there is no industry-wide agreement on what the term even means. PX-2002 (Stehlik (HarperCollins) Dep.) at 134:2–7 (testifying that she has never heard and does not use the term "anticipated top-selling book"); PX-2005 (Jacobs (Abrams) Dep.) at Tr. 89:11–90:1 (Q. "Does Abrams use the term 'expected top seller'"? A. "No." Q. "Do you know what the term 'expected top seller' means?" A. "I would imagine or guess that it means what we might call a lead title." Q. "[Y]ou're speculating on what that may mean, because it's not a term that you use or are familiar with, correct?" A. "No. I don't think I've ever used the term 'expected top seller.'"); Tr. 975:19–24 (Tart (PRH)) (advance level of $250,000 for book has no significance, and does not indicate how well book will sell); Tr. 1845:10–19 (Bergstrom (S&S)) (Q. "And do you think about $250,000 advance is any type of demarcation point for your expectations relative to book sales?" A. "No."); Tr. 1133:7–14 (Weisberg (Macmillan)) (testifying that anticipated top-seller is not a category used at Macmillan).
89. Agents do not recognize any distinct market for "anticipated top-selling books" defined by a $250,000 advance threshold either. They are not familiar with any common industry understanding of the term or what it might mean, and do not know of any "formula" for determining whether a book is an "anticipated top-seller." PX-2007 (Fletcher (Fletcher & Company) Dep.) at 179:14–16, 179:18, 179:20–180:6; Tr. 1810:17–19 (Walsh) (this case is first time she has heard term "anticipated top seller"); Tr.2132:14–22 (Ross (Ross Yoon Agency)) (first time encountered term anticipated top sellers "is when I read the complaint."); Tr. 2065:21- 25 (Cheney (Cheney Agency)) (not familiar with term prior to this case).
90. The market-defining $250,000 advance boundary also is not a line used in the industry to separate books into separate categories for different treatment. For example, Hachette keeps track of books that it lost for *$500,000* or more—not $250,000. PX-790 (showing that between 2017 and mid-2021, Hachette lost at least 30 books for $500,000 or more to *non*-Big Five publishers, while only losing 23 to Macmillan). HarperCollins has no guidance—formal or informal—suggesting that a book acquired for an advance of $250,000 or more is bigger or riskier than any other book. Tr. 1397:15–20 (Murray (HarperCollins)).
91. To the extent that authors anticipate *themselves* to be best-sellers, the advance against royalties is far less relevant than the long-term royalties those authors expect to earn. "For someone who is an expected bestseller, you anticipate that you will earn royalties in excess of your advance. Like that's the whole point of being a bestseller." Tr. 1953:14–18 (Duhigg); *see also* Tr. 1927:13–21 (explaining that his second top-selling book was less successful in sales, but still earned him royalties in excess of the advance) (Q. "And was *Smarter Faster Better* published by Random House?" A. "It was." Q. "And was it successful?" A. "Yes. It was not as successful as *The Power of Habit,* but it sold in excess of a million copies." Q. "And did *Smarter Faster Better* earn out its advance? A. "It did. The royalties from that have been in excess of the advance. They've been over a million dollars. Just from—again, this is North American royalties.").
92. A key example of this was government witness Stephen King, who testified that he has earned royalties in excess of advances for his bestselling books such as *Carrie, The Shining,* and *Night Shift.* Tr. 319:2–14 (A. "*Carrie* was a best seller in paperback. *The Shining* was the first hard cover best seller. And *Night Shift* was also a best seller." Q. "And I take it you earned out your advance on those books?" A. "Yes." Q. "And received royalties hopefully?" A. "Yes." Q. "Okay. Good. Are any of those books still in backlist with Doubleday?" A. "Yes, they are still in the backlist." Q. "And they continue to earn money for Doubleday and for you, I hope?" A. "Yes."); *see also* Tr. 321:13–17 (King) (Q. "Okay. And you recall whether those ten were best sellers?" A. "They were all best sellers, yes." Q. "And did all of them earn out, that is, you received royalties beyond the advance in those cases?" A. "Yes, sir.").
93. *Internal Approval Thresholds.* Some publishers do have internal thresholds at which editors must obtain clearance before they can make advance offers. Those thresholds do not correlate with the view that any particular advance level indicates a book is an anticipated top seller. Tr. 2260:14–17 (McIntosh (PRH)).
94. These approval levels are not tied to the advance for any book; they are based on the full *contract* size for a book deal. In other words, if the publisher offers $300,000 for a two- book deal, and each book

receives an advance of $150,000, S&S's CEO must still approve that deal because the total deal is over $250,000. Tr. 488:13–489:4 (Karp (S&S)); The same is true for the PRH divisions that require approval of certain advance levels. DX-169.0002 (PRH document showing "Title acquisition process descriptions" and noting for Penguin: "Imprint publisher can approve *deals* up to $250k," while "*Deals* over $250k advance value get submitted to division head for review/discussion (no set format for that, can be formal or informal, depending on *deal size and complexity*" (emphases added)).

95. The amounts at which approval is required vary among and even within different publishers. At PRH, the approval levels vary among imprints and divisions from $100,000 to $75 million. Tr. 2260:14–2263:18 (McIntosh (PRH)); DX-169.0002. [REDACTED]

96. Even when Mr. Dohle encouraged Ms. McIntosh to get more involved in PRH's acquisitions at the $250,000 or $500,000 level, it was not because those particular advance levels had any correlation to "anticipated top selling books." Mr. Dohle chose those thresholds randomly to signal to Ms. McIntosh that it was important that she encourage more content acquisition to stem PRH's market share loss. Tr. 799:8–800:12, 803:12–15 (Dohle (PRH)).

97. *Lead Titles.* Some industry participants recognize "lead titles." PX-2005 (Jacobs (Abrams) Dep.) at 90:4–7, 90:21–91:5. These are books that a publisher expects to sell well. PX- 2005 (Jacobs (Abrams) Dep.) at 91:1–5; Tr. 1071:23–24 (Weisberg (Macmillan)) ("THE COURT: How would you define lead title?" THE WITNESS: "Top of the list."). Indeed, when asked whether there was a "shorthand for identifying the books that you really want to put a priority on," Don Weisberg (Macmillan) testified, "[T]here are lead titles versus—we don't have any—there's not really a term that comes to my mind because each one of the publishers are different. And so, believe it or not, the semantics change even within house. So nothing comes to mind." Tr. 1071:4–12.

98. Although the phrase "lead title" is recognized, nobody testified that the phrase has any connection to books that receive advances of $250,000 or more. *See, e.g.,* Tr. 1113:18- 1114:24 (Weisberg (Macmillan)) (testifying that he is "not aware of" any dollar cutoff or advance level where Macmillan begins to offer marketing, advertising, and publicity tours).

99. Lead titles are *not* associated with a particular dollar amount of advance. No publisher was familiar with the idea of assigning lead titles according to advances paid. Rather, the term "lead title" is associated with marketing, printing, and other retail-market aspects of how a book is treated within a publishing company. PX-2005 (Jacobs (Abrams) Dep.) 91:22–92:7; Tr. 1989:1–7 (Kim (PRH)). "Lead titles" are books that publishers market "more aggressively." Tr. 1072:7–8 (Weisberg (Macmillan)). To be sure, some lead titles are books that received advances of $250,000 or more. But not every book that receives an advance in that price segment becomes a lead title. As government witness Don Weisberg (Macmillan) testified, a lead title is "not defined by the fact that we might spend a lot of money on it. It might be a title that we bought for not a lot of money but because person after person that has read it has raved about it and it becomes a lead title." Tr. 1072:2–6.

100. And like the marketing spend, the "lead title" moniker is not determined at acquisition. The "lead title" status attaches only after the book is ready to be sold and marketed downstream. Books "take on a life of their own as they go through the process" toward downstream sales. Tr. 1071:19–20 (Weisberg (Macmillan)). And as Michael Jacobs, CEO of Abrams Books, explained, a lead title is a "title in which the company was—was taking an aggressive stand in terms of its marketing, its projected first printing distribution of the book into the marketplace and—and the resources in terms of marketing and publicity that—that the company would put against the—against the property." PX-2005 (Jacobs (Abrams) Dep.) at 91:7–13.

101. 101. Ms. Bergstrom testified that Gallery Books chooses "focus titles" each season that represent great opportunities to find major success. The Spring 2022 focus titles were acquired for advances ranging from $50,000 to $1 million, with more acquired for below $100,000 than above $250,000. Tr. 1859:23–1860:8, 1860:20–25 (Bergstrom (S&S)). Sally Kim testified that Putnam recently had lead titles that were acquired for only $100,000 and $175,000. Tr. 1989:1- 7.

102. And Ms. McIntosh testified that different PRH publishing groups might select "priority" and "opportunity" books to focus sales efforts on. Those selections have nothing to do with advance level, and everything to do with sales goals for the books. In fact, the salespeople at PRH do not even know the advance levels of the books they are tasked with selling because the advance levels are considered confidential. Tr. 2268:22–2269:24 (McIntosh (PRH)). Priority and opportunity books are selected at strategy meetings held well after the book is acquired. Tr. 2266:14–2268:21 (McIntosh (PRH)).

5. *Publishers Cannot Adjust General Bidding Conduct In Response To Competitors' Pricing*

103. Books acquired for advances of $250,000 or more also are not subject to collective targeting based on other publishers' pricing decisions. It is effectively impossible to respond to the other publishers' pricing conduct from one acquisition to another because book valuation is so individualized and because publishers rarely know who they are bidding against, if anyone, or what amounts they are bidding.

104. Each book is unique and subject to highly individualized, subjective valuations that may range by hundreds of thousands of dollars for each book. *See supra* FF ¶¶ 75–86. As PRH Viking Publisher Brian Tart testified, valuing books is "as much an art as a science." Tr. 967:5. Multiple witnesses explained that different publishers, imprints, and editors place significantly different values on books when they are bidding. Tr. 217:12–20 (Pietsch (Hachette)) (Q. "It's also the case when you are bidding for books against other publishers, it's quite common that with respect to the same book, different publishers and different editors could value it very differently. True?" A. "Absolutely. Absolutely." Q. "And that happens often. Right?" A. "That is—that is—"Q. "And that's because every book is unique. Correct?" A. "Absolutely correct."); Tr. 479:9–480:5, 601:13–16 (Karp (S&S)) ("Well, in a word, subjectivity. I think that people read differently, and they have different enthusiasms, they have different interests and they have different metabolic reactions to the book. But I also think that certain editors and publishers have a kind of inner confidence about certain kinds of books. And so sometimes they'll bid more because they've had success with a certain kind of book. Conversely, they may bid more because they really want to carve a niche that they haven't yet succeeded at. So sometimes people pay more because they have a lot of books like that, and other times they pay more because there are a lot of books that they don't have any books like that."); Tr. 1844:13–18 (Bergstrom (S&S)) (Q. "Is there ever disagreement among your staff about the potential sales for an individual book?" A. "All the time, and with my boss." Q. "And why is that?" A. "Because it's so subjective. And some of us have been doing it longer than others, but it's a guesstimate."); Tr. 1974:7–13 (Kim (PRH)) (Q. "In your experience, how common is it for different imprints to value the same book differently?" A. "Very common. I mean, I think I mentioned comps earlier. It's such—even pulling comps is such a subjective thing. You talk to three different editors; they'll pull three different comps for a book.").

105. Because book valuations are so subjective and individualized, publishers can learn little if anything from the bidding decisions of other publishers from one acquisition to the next. Winning or losing a negotiation for one unique book tells an editor nothing about how much to bid to win the next completely different book. Tr. 489:20–21 (Karp (S&S)) ("I wouldn't be able to assess what the other people thought the books were worth, because they'd have the same subjective frame."). Because each book and each negotiation differs, "you can't learn from what the outcomes are." Tr. 2675:5–15 (Snyder).

106. The problem is compounded by the fact that editors rarely know who they are bidding against when making a bid. Tr. 216:12–17 (Pietsch (Hachette)); Tr. 1965:11–17 (Kim (PRH)) (Putnam does "not usually" know who they are bidding against in an auction, or how many bidders there are); PX-2007 (Fletcher (Fletcher & Company) Dep.) at 162:20–23 (Q. "[D]o you ever release the identities of auction participants to each during an auction?" A. "No."); Tr. 495:18–24 (Karp (S&S)) (Q. "While a book auction is in progress and before it's concluded, what kind of information do you typically have about who the competitors are?" A. "We rarely know anything. Sometimes we know the number of people we're bidding against, but sometimes the agents don't even disclose that."); Tr. 2119:1–4 (Ross (Ross Yoon Agency)) (Q. "[D]o you tell the publishers how many are participating and who they are?" A. "No."). As a result, a publisher cannot learn from one acquisition how much value any other bidder placed on the book (except the winner's value, if the amount is even known).

107. Given the individualized valuation of books and the absence of information in almost all acquisitions about who else was bidding and what amounts they bid, acquisitions do not normally provide publishers meaningful information about other publishers' pricing decisions or competitive conditions more generally. Brian Murray, CEO of HarperCollins, testified that because acquisitions are "fast and furious," HarperCollins does not even assess whether its advance spending has increased or decreased until the end of each year. Tr. 1435:10- 1436:21. Publishers thus have no way, in subsequent blind acquisitions for different unique books, to respond accurately to pricing conduct from prior acquisitions, whether at the $250,000 level or any other. Tr. 2786:2–12 (Snyder) (THE COURT: "It seems like you are saying, because when you enter an auction, you don't know who else is in it, you are not going to alter your behavior because maybe the other merger party wouldn't have been the second runner-up, so it shouldn't affect your behavior because you don't know who else is in the auction. Is that right?" THE

WITNESS: "Correct."); Tr. 1764:11–15 (Walsh) (regarding passing information on to publishers, "the agent decides this, but unless it's in the author's best interest to pass on the information, they don't").

III. ABSENCE OF LIKELY SUBSTANTIAL AND IMMINENT HARM

108. The evidence does not show a likelihood of substantial and imminent harm in the alleged submarket for the acquisition of "anticipated top-selling books."

109. The government's theory of harm relies heavily on the respective market shares of the many publishers that acquire books for advances of $250,000 or more. But as discussed in greater detail below, market shares alone do not capture the competitive conditions that will continue to prevail in every acquisition for every one of the books in the government's alleged submarket—which, after all, constitutes the books that the government claims everyone is most certain will be bestselling titles (and would, therefore, be the most sought after books). Following the merger, the combined entity will face stiff competition—either explicit or implicit—for every one of those books it is invited and chooses to consider. Its rivals will include HarperCollins, the large and aggressive number two publisher with immediate plans to expand, Hachette and Macmillan, and elite houses like Norton, Disney, Abrams, Scholastic, and many others. *See infra* FF ¶¶ 164–80. And agents would be choosing not just from among those many elite publishers, but from a much larger field of *imprints*—Hachette and PRH between them have more than a hundred separate imprints that could make independent offers in any best bid auction or bilateral negotiation. *See infra* ¶¶ 198–202. In these and many other ways, the combined entity's market share by itself says nothing about how much competition there will be to win the books most likely to succeed. As Professor Snyder testified, you "have to go beyond share . . . and look at the number and . . . capacity to compete over time." Tr. 2885:7–21 (Snyder).

110. The parties disagree about the significance of market share statistics, but the parties and their experts have never disagreed about how to calculate market shares in the alleged submarket for "anticipated top selling" books.

111. In contrast to the considered market-share analysis of both experts, at trial, HarperCollins CEO Brian Murray proffered for the first time an unsupported hearsay claim that PRH's market share is actually three and a half times larger than HarperCollins' market share because HarperCollins' market should exclude its romance series and Christian books. Tr. 1374:15–1375:23. That claim is not more credible than the experts' shared understanding for multiple reasons.

112. First, Murray's vague market share claim is based entirely on unreliable hearsay statements from [REDACTED] Tr. 1324:24–1325:23, Tr. 1440:16–21 (Murray (HarperCollins)). Second, Murray's testimony referred to *downstream* market shares for the sale of books, not the relevant upstream shares (which no one in the industry had collected or measured before Dr. Hill or Professor Snyder). Tr. 1700:24–1701:13 (Hill); Tr. 826.15–19 (Dohle (PRH)) (HarperCollins' estimate of PRH's downstream share differs from those PRH tracks as part of its business operations). Regardless, Murray testified that BookScan does not account for a very large part of HarperCollins' Christian sales, *see* Tr. 1390:24–1391:14, which means that HarperCollins' downstream market share is actually *understated.* [REDACTED] *Id.* Fourth, any market share assessment based on eliminating Christian books and romance series books would need to remove those books from all competitors' sales before recalculating their market shares, a process that no expert or anyone else did in this case. Fifth, there is no evidence that the types of books that Murray claimed should be excluded from general trade books—e.g. Bibles and mass market romance series, which Murray said were not sold in traditional bookstores—garner advances above $250,000 and are therefore relevant to the market at issue in this case.

113. Most importantly, both parties' economists include Christian and romance books in the upstream market share measurements. Tr. 2796:20–2797:7 (Snyder). Although Dr. Hill studied market share data for months and had every incentive to reduce HarperCollins' market shares if it could be credibly done and helped the government's case, Dr. Hill's market-share assessment was the same as Professor Snyder's. Tr. 2655:6–10 (Snyder). Dr. Hill at no time opined that Christian books and romance books should be excluded from market share calculations, and admitted that he included those books in his market share calculations. Tr. 1473:3–1474:6 (Hill). The analyses of the expert economists—who found rare common ground on this issue—carries greater weight than the hearsay-based assertion of a rival publishing company's CEO.

114. Although the parties agree on how to calculate market shares, they do not agree on whether market shares by themselves prove that the merger is likely to substantially reduce competition. They do not.

Market shares do not fully reflect many conditions in the industry that will affect competition after the merger.

A. Industry Participants Recognize That The Merger Will Not Reduce Competition For The Most Sought-After Books

115. The direct evidence from industry witnesses shows that the merger will not lead to lower author advances or reduced title counts. Tr. 583:13–19 (Karp (S&S)) (testifying that S&S has no plans to decrease author advances or reduce title count post-merger because they "have a growth mindset"); Tr. 1407:24–1408:12 (Murray (HarperCollins)) (HarperCollins has had no discussions about author advances decreasing as a result of the merger). PRH itself has no plans to save money on author advances post-merger. *See infra* FF ¶ 120.

116. Rival publishers consistently testified that the merger will have no effect on their bidding strategies or the amounts of their bids. Tr. 1385:9–15 (Murray (HarperCollins)) (HarperCollins does not "intend to hold back" in competing post-merger or to bid less for books); Tr. 211:9–13 (Pietsch (Hachette)) (Q. "To be clear, what you're saying is that, merger or not, your bidding would be the same as before. Right? You're going to bid as much as you think it's worth and not more. Right?" A. "That is correct."). Agents likewise testified that the merger would not change their bidding strategies or the outcomes of their deals. Tr. 308:13–16 (Pande (Ayesha Pande Literary)) (THE COURT: "Ms. Pande, is it correct that if Simon & Schuster and PRH were merged, it wouldn't have affected any of the deals on this list?" THE WITNESS: "Correct."); Tr. 2135:25–2136:3 (Ross (Ross Yoon Agency)) (Q. "[D]o you have a concern that this merged company being—being much bigger than either one today would be in a position to lower author compensation?" A. "No, I don't [REDACTED]"); 1823:21–1824:2 (Walsh) (Q. "If the merger closes, do you expect agents to be unable to create good submission lists and find an author's perfect match?" A. "I don't understand why they would be unable to .[REDACTED]").

117. In fact, ordinary-course business documents and trial testimony show that industry participants expect advances to increase.

118. In a 2022 document presented to its parent company News Corp. after the merger of PRH and S&S was announced, HarperCollins forecasted that its title count and advance spending would [REDACTED] over a five-year period. DX-279.0025.

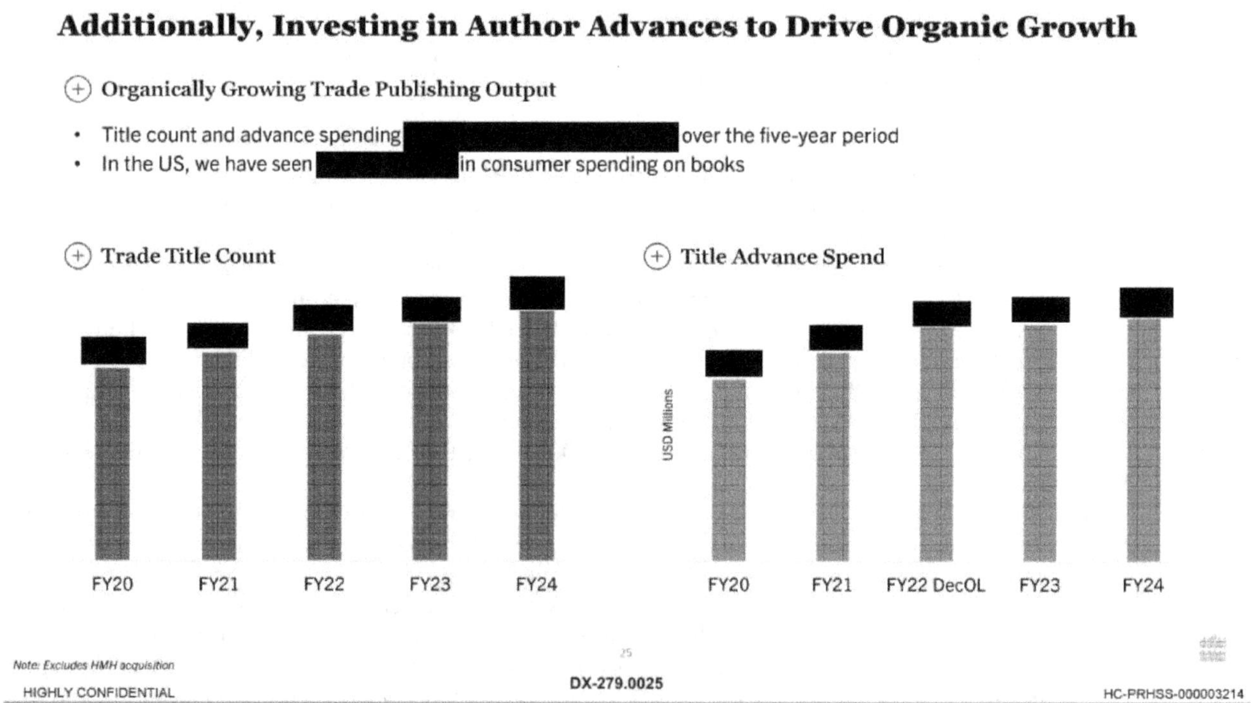

119. Don Weisberg, CEO of Macmillan, effectively admitted his concern that advances and other benefits to authors would *improve* because of the merger. According to Weisberg, the merged PRH and S&S would "try to benefit from its scale with customers, with vendors" (Tr. 1116:22–24), thereby gaining an advantage in distribution and discoverability (Tr. 1117:15–18, Tr. 1117:23–1118–13). That advantage

in distribution and discoverability would benefit authors. Tr. 1117:15–22 (Weisberg (Macmillan)) (if PRH were favored in distribution and discoverability by Amazon, it would be a benefit to PRH and S&S authors); Tr. 1937:2–1938:23 (Duhigg) (merger will increase "[d]iscoverability," which is crucial for authors' success and "the hardest thing" for authors to achieve in an online world). As a result, rival publishers are concerned that the merged entity could "get any book" it wanted "in almost every situation if they want to pay enough." Tr. 1088:6–7 (Weisberg (Macmillan)). In response to the question whether he was "concerned . . . that the combined entity would have resources such that they could outbid you in auctions," Weisberg answered, "Yes." Tr. 1118:14–17.

120. PRH's own ordinary-course documents show that it does not expect the merger to cause a reduction in author advances. It is telling that, when modeling likely cost-savings from the merger, PRH did not account for any such reduction. Manuel Sansigre, Senior Vice President & Head of Global Mergers & Acquisitions, led PRH's efforts to model the efficiencies from the acquisition of S&S. Tr. 2400:4–6; 2402:5–9 (Sansigre (PRH)). Over the course of eight months, Mr. Sansigre created over 100 drafts of the model used to project the benefits from the transaction, which Bertelsmann relied on to approve the $2.2 billion investment. Tr. 2411:19- 2412:14, 2421:9–16 (Sansigre (PRH)). Notably, author compensation is a major cost center for publishers, consistently accounting for over half of S&S's and PRH's variable costs. *See* PX- 168 at Tabs Silk US IS Output cells C26:H27, PRH US cells B40:J41. But in the model he prepared in the ordinary course of business, Tr. 2411:13–2412:14 (Sansigre (PRH)), Mr. Sansigre identified no potential cost-savings from reduced author compensation.

121. To the extent Weisberg and other rivals claimed otherwise, they admitted it was only speculation. Tr. 1119:1–6 (Weisberg (Macmillan)) (admitting speculation); Tr. 1085:25- 1086:5 (Q. "And what's your—what's the reasoning behind your thought that advances will go down?" A. "Less competition. It's simple as that." Q. "Is that based on any of your experiences in the industry?" A. "No, it's just gut."); PX-2000 (Zacharius (Kensington) Dep.) at 71:15–18, 71:20–22 (view that advances may go down after the merger is "just a feeling" he has).

122. The government also attempted to elicit evidence of "harm" from self-interested Big Five publisher witnesses who admitted that their own companies will attempt to purchase Simon & Schuster if PRH's acquisition falls through. Tr. 1387:4–12 (Murray (HarperCollins)) (testifying that "if this deal gets blocked, HarperCollins would still be interested in acquiring" S&S); Tr. 205:13–16 (Pietsch (Hachette)) ("I would be very happy for my parent company to acquire it. Yes."). Despite their admitted interest in acquiring S&S, neither HarperCollins' CEO nor Hachette's CEO believe that—if they were to acquire it—their companies would reduce advances paid to authors. Tr. 206:17–21 (Pietsch (Hachette)); Tr. 1387:19–21 (Murray (HarperCollins)). Hachette's CEO did not even perform any analysis informing his parent company that Hachette *could* reduce title count or author advances should it acquire S&S. Tr. 207:25–208:11 (Pietsch). Rather, these companies calculated synergies—just as PRH did—to justify their bids for S&S. Tr. 1421:1–1422:6 (Murray (HarperCollins); *see* DX-288.0017 (Hachette presentation regarding synergies of potential acquisition of S&S).

123. Author Andrew Solomon testified that he is "not concerned that the merger . . . will negatively affect" him. PX-2004 (Solomon Dep.) at 107:2–11. The authors whose books sell for high advances are precisely the authors whose books are the most desirable, whose "proven sales history and proven history of winning prizes" means that they will always have publisher options. PX-2004 (Solomon Dep.) at 108:9–109:4 (testifying that the merger will not affect him as an author).

B. Large Existing Rivals Plan To Expand And Can Easily Do So

124. The publishing industry is dynamic and thriving. Tr. 758:3–5 (Dohle (PRH)) ("the book market has been growing 20 percent"); Tr. 552:10–20 (Karp) (publishing is "a dynamic landscape"); Tr. 1805:15–22 (Walsh) ("It's an exciting time for new entrants in the publishing industry"); Tr. 2684:10–19 (Snyder) ("[F]rom those data I identified the number of publishers acquiring contracts with advances of at least $250,000 over this three-year time period. And that number is 29 for 2019 and then it grows to 33 in 2021. Again, this is not just bidding; this is winning.").

125. Existing publishing companies are taking advantage of the dynamic environment with plans to expand. Macmillan's CEO testified that his company plans to spend more on author advances in coming years in efforts to grow its retail market share. Tr. 1092:6–10, 1098:5–18 (Weisberg (Macmillan)). HarperCollins' CEO has publicly stated that his company is "going to be more aggressive in its offers" for books "because the market is growing." DX-188; PX-2002 (Stehlik (HarperCollins) Dep.) at 49:11–14, 49:16–22, 50:4–51:5. Mr. Jacobs testified that Abrams intends to grow. PX-2005 (Jacobs (Abrams) Dep 51:23–52:3 (Q. "What is Abrams' strategic plan?" A. "To, you know, grow our business and to be

very strong in categories in which we publish and to try new things, keep growing our children's publishing aggressively and, you know, be a—a profitable independent midsized publisher.").

126. As Dr. Hill was forced to concede, [REDACTED].
127. The industry also perceives Amazon to be growing as a publisher and becoming a more effective competitor. It has 50 editors working in multiple imprints to acquire and publish award-winning books in a variety of genres. Tr. 558:16–559:6 (Karp (S&S)); Tr. 1419:15–21 (Murray (HarperCollins)) (testifying that Amazon was expanding its publishing operations," including by launching new imprints). Amazon "getting more aggressive" in the acquisition of books, and competes for books at high advance levels. Tr. 457:3–10, 559:21–560:2, (Karp (S&S)) (testifying that in July 2022, S&S competed with Amazon in a seven-figure auction for a book).
128. Any competitive advantages the traditional publishers may have once had over Amazon are eroding. Amazon has superior access to consumer data to inform its publishing program, and independent booksellers—once reluctant to carry Amazon-published books—now have Amazon titles on their best seller lists. Amazon's penetration into the independent retail space demonstrates that "a rubicon has been crossed"—Amazon is "more of a threat" than traditional publishers may have previously thought. Tr. 559:7–20, 560:18–561:11 (Karp (S&S)); Tr. 1808:24–1809:6 (Walsh); Tr. 1107:13–19 (Weisberg (Macmillan)) (Q. "And, in fact, you fear that Amazon can again become a formidable competitor at any given moment; isn't that fair?" "Yes." Q. "And that's because they could expand, right, they could change what they're doing now?" A. "Right. Yes.").
129. New publishing houses are also entering the market to take advantage of opportunities to acquire and publish books. Tr. 552:10–20 (Karp (S&S)) (testifying that publishing is "a dynamic landscape" with "new publishing companies" that have entered in the last few years); Tr. 1805:15–22 ("It's an exciting time for new entrants in the publishing industry."); DX-299.0011 (News Corp. 10-K indicating that HarperCollins' competition "could also come from new entrants as barriers to entry in book publishing are low"); Tr. 2296:24- 2297:1 (McIntosh (PRH)) (testifying that "start-up publishers . . . also have been spending big to acquire books").
130. Recent entrants have already been winning high-advance books over Big Five publishers. For example, Michael Pietsch, CEO of Hachette, testified that Spiegel & Grau is a new publisher that recently bid more than $500,000 to win Alison Smith's *Echoes Within.* Tr. 231:5–22; *see also* Tr. 757:2–22 (Dohle (PRH)) (testifying that Spiegel & Grau is founded by two ex-PRH editors and is "buying big books"); Tr. 552:21–24 (Karp (S&S)) (Spiegel & Grau is an "upstart company"). Spiegel & Grau only just launched in 2019, but the very first book they published, *Fox and I,* was a *New York Times* bestseller. Tr. 554:22–555:2 (Karp (S&S)); Tr. 1805:23–1806:9 (Walsh).
131. Zando is another new publishing company, founded by former PRH publisher, Molly Stern. Zando pursues an innovative business strategy by creating imprints centered around public figures with large followings. Tr. 555:7–556:14 (Karp (S&S)). Zando is brand new, but it is already competing in auctions for books above the $250,000 advance-level and publishing successful books that achieve high sales. *Id.;* Tr. 1807:5–18 (Walsh).[REDACTED] Tr. 2297:2–8 (McIntosh (PRH)). Zando has also been "very aggressive" in acquiring books in the children's space. Tr. 2299:5–8 (McIntosh (PRH)).
132. Astra House, financially backed by a large parent company, is another new publishing company that has rapidly expanded to have multiple imprints. Tr. 556:15–20 (Karp (S&S)). Like Zando and Spiegel & Grau, Astra is also helmed by a publishing industry veteran. Tr. 1807:19–23 (Walsh).
133. The government tried to show barriers to *entry* are high, but none of the cited barriers would impede *expansion* by existing publishers, which are already equipped with the skilled editors, good reputations, and logistical resources needed to fulfill their growth plans.

1. Printing

134. The government asserts that access to printing is a barrier to entry, but Dr. Hill did not analyze or render any opinion on the effects of access to printing capacity on competitive forces. Tr. 1734:1–7 (Hill). The government did not show that access to printing would impede expansion plans by existing publishers or pose an obstacle to growth even for smaller publishers.
135. All publishers—including PRH [REDACTED]—have faced shortages of printing capacity in the United States. Tr. 817:25:818:4 (Dohle (PRH)); Publishers acknowledge that their concerns about printing capacity pre-exist any potential merger of PRH and S&S and will persist even if the merger does not go through. *See, e.g.* [REDACTED],
136. [REDACTED]
137. [REDACTED]

138.[REDACTED]

139.[REDACTED]

140.Although the government has tried to elicit evidence that Bertelsmann will use its ownership of printing facilities to raise rival publishers' costs or to favor PRH, no such allegations were made in the complaint, much less proved at trial. The evidence showed Bertelsmann Printing Group does not give PRH preferential treatment compared to other publisher clients. Tr. 817:25–818:4 (Dohle (PRH)); [REDACTED]

141.[REDACTED]

142.[REDACTED]

143.None of these concerns demonstrates favoritism toward PRH by Bertelsmann. In fact, the evidence showed that Tr. 817:12–818:4 (Dohle (PRH)).

2. *Backlist*

144.The government attempted to show that backlists are crucial to publishers' business models and therefore represent a barrier to new entrants. But, again, the barrier has no bearing on expansion by existing publishers, which have large backlists. And, the evidence shows that a backlist is merely one source of revenue among others—including the front list—that allow publishers to invest in new books. Tr. 2358:11–14 (McIntosh (PRH)) (Q. "Having a backlist allows PRH to take risks on new acquisitions, right?" A. "Having all of our revenue, which is inclusive of backlist and frontlist, is what allows us to invest in new books, yes."); Tr. 1803:2–10 (Walsh) ("a backlist is just money"). And, of course, existing publishers with big names such as Disney and Amazon, do not face funding constraints. *See, e.g.,* Tr. 2956:10–14 (Snyder) (noting that Amazon does not consider funding to be a concern); Tr. 1808:24–1809:6 (Walsh) (Amazon has "all the money and all the resources and all the marketing power. If they wanted to course correct, they absolutely could."). New entrants can obtain the financial security that comes from backlists in other ways. Spiegel & Grau, for example, is a brand new entrant and already oversubscribed for funding. Tr. 1805:23–1806:6 (Walsh). Zando is also well- funded. 1806:10–22 (Walsh).

145.In any case, publishers can acquire entire backlists through mergers and acquisitions if they deem it important, and even *one* particularly successful backlist title can be as effective as one hundred other backlists titles. *See* PX-2002 (Stehlik (HarperCollins) Dep.) at 230:19–22, 230:24–231:2, 232:4–14.

3. *Reputation*

146.The government also attempted to show that publishing houses need to build reputations before they can compete to acquire books. That concern again has no application to existing publishers that compete in the $250,000+ price segment—all have strong reputations. Further, authors care more about the reputations of the individual editors and publishers they work with than the publishing houses in general. Tr. 739:21–740:8 (Dohle (PRH)).

147.And those individual editors can—and do—start their new publishing companies. "Upstart" company Spiegel & Grau was founded by two former PRH publishers with track records of major successes. Tr. 552:21–553:20 (Karp (S&S)); Tr. 2835:5–7 (Snyder) ("[Y]ou have interestingly entrants who don't have any track record, but they are proceeding to launch their businesses with reputable editors."); Tr. 2958:1–4 (Snyder) (Q. "And what do you know about Spiegel & Grau?" A. "A recent entrant, they have the benefit of having well-known editors. And they're competing in the proposed segment."); Tr. 1805:23–1806:6 (Walsh) ("Spiegel & Grau was founded by two veterans of the publishing industry."); Tr. 1806:10–13 (Walsh) ("Zando is also founded by a veteran of the Big 5, Molly Stern.").

4. *Distribution*

148.Access to distribution channels is irrelevant to expansion for existing publishers—they already have access to distribution infrastructure. Many publishing companies—including HarperCollins, the second-largest publisher—engage third-party distribution companies to distribute their books to retail stores. Tr. 1392:25–1393:18 (Murray (HarperCollins)). New entrants can also contract for distribution services. S&S and PRH both handle distribution for many smaller publishers. Tr. 553:25–554:6 (Karp (S&S); Tr. 828:12–828:22 (Dohle (PRH)). In fact, S&S offered to distribute books for Spiegel & Grau, but Spiegel & Grau instead chose to affiliate with Ingram for distribution. Tr. 553:21–554:19 (Karp (S&S)); Tr. 1802:14–15 (Walsh) ("The larger publishers actually distribute some of the smaller publishers.").

C. Downstream Competition Drives Competition For The Acquisition Of Books

149.It is uncontested that the downstream—or retail—market for the sale of books to readers is unconcentrated and fiercely competitive, and that it will remain so post-merger. Tr. 1539:1–25 (Hill).

The government accordingly could not—and did not—bring a claim focused on downstream harm to consumers.

150. This competitive dynamic is illustrated by the trends in publishers' retail market share. [REDACTED] Meanwhile, smaller and mid-size publishers' retail market shares have been increasing over the same period of time. Tr. 832:6–833:9 (Dohle (PRH)); DX-76.0004 (December 2019 PRH presentation showing PRH's loss of market share from 2013 to 2019). In fact, in 2021, 50 percent of books sold in the United States were sold by non-Big Five publishers. Tr. 833:12–24 (Dohle (PRH)).

151. The reason the retail market has been trending towards fragmentation, towards smaller publishers, and away from the Big Five publishers, is that consumers began shifting to online book purchases instead of in-store book purchases. At least 50 percent of book sales are now made online. This trend has leveled the playing field between smaller publishers and larger publishers for several reasons. First, online retailers like Amazon can carry 1000 times more titles than a standard independent bookstore. Second, online retailers use algorithms rather than human salespeople to determine what books are presented to consumers, which has removed some of the Big Five's advantages in terms of visibility to consumers. Third, online retailers are much more efficient, helping smaller publishers save money on printing, binding, and other costs of producing excess stock. Tr. 834:2–19, 835:18–836:22, Tr. 837:2–838:6 (Dohle (PRH)).

152. This downstream competition drives publishing houses to compete "aggressively" to acquire the books that will make them more competitive downstream. Tr. 799:14–800:5 (Dohle (PRH)) (Dohle "encouraged" McIntosh to get more involved in editors' acquisitions of books "given the importance of getting the books that are in demand with end consumers, to [s]top the market share loss").

153. To that end, in 2021, PRH committed an all-time high of $650 million in author advances, representing a major push to acquire books that consumers want to buy. Tr. 811:11–16 (Dohle (PRH)).

D. Agents Control The Competitive Conditions Of Specific Acquisition Processes

154. There are no set rules for book acquisitions. Agents devise the rules for each acquisition process, depending on what the agent thinks will achieve the best result for her client's particular book. PX-2007 (Fletcher (Fletcher & Company) Dep.) at 36:2–3, 36:5–13 ("It really depends on the variables in play in that particular project. How many people you anticipate offering, who those people are, how much financials play into the author's decision making."); Tr. 112:25–113:4 (Pietsch (Hachette)) ("Agents are all independent operators who . . . set up . . . the sale of the books they represent and the way that they think is going to be most effective for them and their client."); Tr. 1613:6–1614:15 (Hill) (acknowledging agent's role in deciding the type of acquisition process).

155. Agents choose how many editors to submit a book or book proposal to, based on various factors, such as the editor's track record with comparable books, editorial sensibilities, and their expectations of how much the editor might bid. PX-2007 (Fletcher (Fletcher & Company) Dep.) at 160:10–161:14. Agents do *not* choose which publishing companies to submit a book to based on those companies' respective shares in the market for the acquisition of books. Tr. 2128:1–7 (Ross (Ross Yoon Agency)).

156. They choose what information—if any—to share with publishers, including the number and identities of other bidders, and even the rules for the acquisition process. PX-2007 (Fletcher (Fletcher & Company) Dep.) at 161:17–20, 161:25–162:5, 162:18–23; Tr. 495:4–24 (Karp(S&S)); Tr. 1764:21–1765:14, 1765:19–1766:10 (Walsh). As agent Gail Ross testified, she only tells editors how many other editors are participating in an acquisition process "if it serves my client's interests. . . . I get to control that kind of information." Tr. 2119:5–10.

157. When agents hold auctions—which they do in less than half of acquisitions, *see infra* FF ¶ 163—they control the entire auction process. PX-2000 (Zacharius (Kensington) Dep.) at 119:2–3, 119:5; Tr. 183:23–184:14 (Pietsch (Hachette)).

158. The entire acquisition process is fluid. Agents change the rules and determine how to close the process in real time, depending on the feedback they receive on the book. PX- 2007 (Fletcher (Fletcher & Company) Dep.) at 155:2–20. For example, agents might start an acquisition process as a round-robin auction, but reserve the right to end the auction and ask for best bids at any time. Tr. 2120:3–19 (Ross (Ross Yoon Agency)); Tr. 1615:7–12 (Hill) (Q. "But you would agree with me, though, that the acquisition process, whether it's an auction or some other form, can be changed mid-stream by the author and agent?" A. "Yeah, I've seen settings where they'll say, we're doing a two rounds auction, and then they will call for best bids at the end, having not previously announced that.").

159. Having more bidders in an auction does not guarantee higher advances—an auction can be competitive with even just two bidders. PX-2007 (Fletcher (Fletcher & Company) Dep.) at 256:6–10, 12–18.

160. Even in auctions, agents reserve the right to accept an underbidder, because the best offer for an author might not be the highest offer. Tr. 1756:13–1757:8, Tr. 1836:5–1837:2 (Walsh); [REDACTED] DX-422 (Glusman (Norton) Dep.) at 256:6–18. Agent Andrew Wylie testified that he is looking for an offer "that we feel presents the strongest combination of financial terms plus editorial engagement and context for the author." Tr. 2090:11–23. Likewise, "best bids" does not necessarily mean the "highest bid," but the best all-around bid for the book. Tr. 2120:9–2121:25 (Ross (Ross Yoon Agency)). Even the government's own witness, Ayesha Pande, testified that she has sold books to underbidders. Tr. 304:16–24.

161. In fact, an agent's goal is not always to extract every possible dollar from an editor in the advance. The publication of a book requires a healthy relationship between editor and author, so an agent wants to strike a deal that allows everyone to feel they are on the same team. Tr. 1756:2–12 (Walsh). As Ms. Walsh explained, "a majority of the authors want to have long-term careers and they want to be in successful relationships with the publisher where their books are lucrative." Tr. 1835:14–1837:2.

162. Multiple agents testified that the merger will have no effect on their ability to create submission strategies that achieve the best results for their clients. The S&S editors and imprints would not disappear and would still be available for submissions and bids, and if agents did lose one potential bidder, they could easily submit to any of the numerous other editors at dozens of other publishing houses that compete in the government's alleged market. Tr. 1823:21- 1824:2 (Walsh); Tr. 2094:14–18 (Wylie (Wylie Agency)) (Q. "Do you have—what impact, if any, do you believe this merger would have on—on your business, on your representation of your clients, and your ability to get them the best possible deal?" A. "Generally speaking, I think it would be a positive result."); Tr. 2129:12–23 (Ross (Ross Yoon Agency)) (testifying that "if this merger were to occur, "[t]here's plenty of competitors out there" and "it only takes . . . the idea of one competitor to make my negotiations strong. And if we're going out more widely, then there are plenty of competitors"); Tr. 2136:21–25 (Ross (Ross Yoon Agency)) (if PRH and S&S tried to lower advances, "I'd be spending more time across town with the other publishers"); Tr. 2070:22–2071:16 (Cheney (Cheney Agency)) ("[I]t would mean I would need to take my 200 authors and, you know, call up Hachette, call up HarperCollins, call up, you know, Norton."). As Ms. Ross testified, "[I]n this business, there's always the other competitor. Whether it's—whether they're bidding or not, they're always there." Tr. 2127:11–13.

163. Despite agents' choice not to include every publisher in an auction and their ability to replace lost bidders, Dr. Hill's economic model does not account for that commercial reality. Tr. 1630:20–1631:18 (Hill). As Professor Snyder explained, the model assumes that "all [publishers] bid" in all acquisitions, then assumes "the merger reduces the number of bidders by one in every case," and then uses market shares to determine the effect eliminating that one bidder. Tr. 3036:11–12. But in "the real world," agents do not invite all publishers; they instead "pick and engage a smaller number." Tr. 3036:13–18 (Snyder); *see also* Tr. 1750:24–1751:4 (Walsh) ("we're not looking for the largest amount of submissions. We're looking for the perfect match."). The elimination of one publisher via merger thus does not necessarily affect all or even most acquisitions—whether the number of bidders is reduced "depends on the circumstances," and even if S&S would have been a bidder, "the agent can go to others to replace that bidder." Tr. 3036:11–12 (Snyder). Dr. Hill's market-share based model does not account for that dynamic. This is particularly important given that the majority of acquisitions involve only one publisher in a bilateral negotiation with an agent and author. Tr. 1608:20- 1609:3 (Hill) (agreeing that about 60 percent of acquisitions for advances over $250,000 are bilateral negotiations).

E. Non-Big Five Publishers Collectively Impose A Significant Competitive Threat

164. Publishers outside the Big Five also pose a serious threat in any given acquisition, especially when viewed collectively.

165. The data demonstrate that—as a group—the non-Big Five publishers are comparable in size as a competitive constraint to Macmillan or Hachette. Tr. 2686:23–2687:9 (Snyder). During the time period analyzed by Dr. Hill, non-Big-Five publishers collectively acquired as many titles for advances of $250,000 or more as Hachette did. Tr. 1583:18–23 (Hill). In 2021, non-Big-Five publishers collectively acquired roughly as many titles as S&S in the $250,000 and above price range—and they acquired more than Hachette or Macmillan. Tr. 1584:5–17 (Hill). When aggregated, the non-Big-Five publishers are as likely to win as Hachette or Macmillan and have the same market share as S&S. Tr. 1572:10–16 (Hill) (Q. "And if we look over to 2021, the non-Big 5 collectively have a larger market share than Hachette and Macmillan; is that correct?" A. "If you aggregate them into one firm, yes." Q. "And they have—collectively, they have the same market share as Simon & Schuster, correct?" A. "Correct.").

166. In fact, the data show that 54 percent of multi-bidder auctions for deals over $250,000 included at least one bid from a non-Big Five publisher, and non-Big Five publishers were either the winners or the runners-up in 23 percent of those multi-bidder auctions. Tr. 2689:22–2690:5, 2827:13–23 (Snyder). In other words, the non-Big Five compete well above their weight—while they collectively have a not-insubstantial 10 percent market share, they are an even more significant *competitor,* making the winning or second-place offer in almost one- quarter of all multi-bidder auctions. Dr. Hill observes that the 23 percent figure does not reflect the *relative* size of non-Big Five publishers compared to the Big Five, Tr. 3204:9–17, which is true but irrelevant: the 23 percent figure simply shows *how often* non-Big Five publishers are one of the top two bidders, and it shows that they impose a competitive constraint *more than twice as often* as the market shares might indicate, as Dr. Hill finally conceded. Tr. 3147:17-3148:3 ("If you are using it to say in literally what proportion of auctions were they first or second, then the 23 is a percent.").

167. The data confirm the real-world evidence that "high-profile, savvy authors are willing to go with" non-Big Five publishers. They are "viable alternatives," which means they represent "a competitive constraint in this market," regardless of their market share. Tr. 2693:2- 19 (Snyder); Tr. 1798:12–1799:4 (Walsh) (authors sometimes pick smaller publishers over PRH).

168. Literary agents regularly submit books to non-Big Five publishers. Tr. 247:22- 248:7 (Pande (Ayesha Pande Literary)) (she "frequently" submits books to publishers like Bloomsbury, Grove, and Norton to achieve a higher advance for her clients); Tr. 1797:16–23 (Walsh) (she has worked with Norton, Grove Atlantic, Kensington, Chronicle, Abrams, Hay House, Graywolf, and others); Tr. 2095:10–20 (Wylie (Wylie Agency)) (he "absolutely" makes deals with non-Big 5 publishers); Tr. 2130:9–17 (Ross (Ross Yoon Agency)) (she often submits books to Grove Atlantic, Norton, and Bloomsbury). Accordingly, non-Big Five publishers regularly compete with Big Five publishers to acquire books at all advance levels. PX-2000 (Zacharius (Kensington) Dep.) at 53:3–6, 56:18–24, 57:2 (acknowledging that Kensington regularly competes with Big Five publishers); Tr. 546:3–5 (Karp (S&S)) (S&S "regularly" competes with Scholastic for books with advances of $250,000 or more); DX-299.0010–11 (News Corp. 10-K stating that HarperCollins competes with "numerous smaller publishers for the right to works by well-known authors and public personalities"); Tr. 1797:24–1798:2 (Walsh) (midsized and small publishers compete "fiercely" for the same books as larger publishers); DX- 422 (Glusman (Norton) Dep.) at 103:17–20 (Q. "So Norton's biggest competitors are the Big 5 publishers and imprints of those Big 5 publishers, is that fair?" A. "Yes."); Tr. 2296:20–2297:1 (McIntosh (PRH)) (testifying that "in most competitive situations where we're bidding on books, that we do encounter all the other Big 5 in those—in those situations, we also come across non- Big 5 publishers, whether that is Norton or Disney or Scholastic").

169. Ms. Bergstrom testified that Gallery competes against mid-sized and smaller publishers for "all kinds" of books—"political, celebrity, novels, sci fi, all genres and types." Tr. 1864:2–1864:6.

170. Non-Big Five publishers do not just compete for books for advances of $250,000 and above—they frequently win them. *See, e.g.,* [REDACTED] Tr. 547:3–548:3 (Karp (S&S)) (S&S has lost books for over $250,000 to Hay House); DX-038 (demonstrating S&S loss to Hay House for $700,000 book); Tr. 548:4–549:20 (Karp (S&S)) (S&S has lost books for over $250,000 to academic presses); DX-131 (demonstrating S&S loss to Princeton University Press for high advance book); Tr. 1799:5–8 (Walsh) (smaller publishers outbid larger publishers); Tr. 973:3–974:10 (Tart (PRH)) (describing PRH Viking losses to Norton and Hay House); Tr. 1555:6–21 (Hill) (demonstrating win by Astra House over Big Five publishers). As of 2021, 33 publishers entered deals for $250,000 or more—up from 29 publishers in 2019. Tr. 2684:10–19 (Snyder).

171. Between 2017 and mid-2021, Hachette lost at least 30 books for $500,000 or more to *non*-Big Five publishers, while losing only 23 to Macmillan and 38 to S&S. PX-790; Tr. 229:4–231:14 (Pietsch) (explaining Hachette's losses to Chronicle, Abrams, Grove Atlantic, Disney, and Spiegel & Grau). This demonstrates that, collectively, the non-Big Five publishers represent as much of a competitive threat to Hachette as any one of the other Big Five publishers.

172. Smaller publishers can also win books as the underbidder in auctions, because the size of the advance is not always the determinative factor in what leads an author to publish a book. As Mr. Jacobs, explained, Abrams can "lend[] a certain amount of panache . . . to the publication," and authors sometimes "have a relationship with the—the editor that they feel is—is one in which they—their creative vision to be executed [sic] in a way." PX-2005 (Jacobs (Abrams) Dep.) at 75:4–76:3.

173. John Glusman testified that Norton sometimes wins auctions as the underbidder due to a "combination

of factors," including "the editorial, the sales, the publicity, the promotional and marketing talent and our ability to sell books as effectively—and in some cases, more effectively depending on the book of any publisher in the industry." DX-422 (Glusman (Norton) Dep.) at 255:2–14, 16–25. This further shows that there isn't a qualitative difference in terms of the services that non-Big-Five publishers can offer. *See supra* FF ¶¶ 65–74.

174. Non-Big Five publishers that compete against the Big Five include smaller and mid-sized publishers like Abrams, Kensington, and Grove, but they also include large players like Amazon and Scholastic. PX-2005 (Jacobs (Abrams) Dep.) at 33:25–34:1, 34:3–9, 34:11–17; Tr. 1105:18–1106:1 (Weisberg (Macmillan)).

175. Scholastic is a "giant" of children's publishing and a competitor of the Big Five, with annual revenue in the billions. Tr. 545:10–14 (Karp (S&S)). Scholastic is "in some cases larger than the Big 5," with respect to children's books. Tr. 1105:5–23 (Weisberg (Macmillan)). S&S "regularly" competes with Scholastic for books that ultimately sell for over $250,000. S&S has lost books by best-selling authors Cassandra Clare and Scott Westerfeld to Scholastic when Scholastic offered higher advances. Tr. 546:3–13 (Karp (S&S)).

176. Disney, too, is a major competitor for children's books. Tr. 2297:21–2298:1 (McIntosh (PRH)). In fact, in the children's space, the industry recognizes the "Big Seven" publishers, because Scholastic and Disney are such significant competitors. Tr. 2298:4–8 (McIntosh (PRH)).

177. Amazon is also a significant non-Big Five competitor and is only becoming more competitive. *See supra* FF ¶¶ 127, 128; PX-2000 (Zacharius (Kensington) Dep.) at 106:17–20 (Amazon "absolutely" is "a direct competitor to book publishers"); Tr. 1107:13–19 (Weisberg (Macmillan)) (Q. "And, in fact, you fear that Amazon can again become a formidable competitor at any given moment; isn't that fair?" A. "Yes." Q. "And that's because they could expand, right, they could change what they're doing now?" A. "Right. Yes."); PX-2002 (Stehlik (HarperCollins) Dep.) at 82:24–83:2, 83:12–84:15, 199:18–199:22 (HarperCollins competed with Amazon to publish Patricia Cornwell and Dean Koontz); Tr. 561:12–562:3 (Karp (S&S)) (S&S competed against Amazon for seven-figure books by Colleen Hoover, Dean Koontz, and others); Tr. 1419:25–1420:16 (Murray (HarperCollins)) (Amazon is a "major competitor" for HarperCollins, particularly in the romance genre).

178. PRH has lost major authors to Amazon's publishing program in recent years. Tr. 2295:24–2296:5 (McIntosh (PRH)) (PRH lost Dean Koontz, Mindy Kaling, and Rhys Bowen to Amazon).

179. For these reasons, the government's reliance on a draft presentation written by the late Carolyn Reidy of S&S—referring to non-Big Five publishers as "farm teams" for authors—is misplaced. As an initial matter, the trial evidence showed that the presentation was drafted in an effort to make S&S's outlook seem "positive enough" for senior management. Tr. 375:17- 376:2 (Eulau); DX-405. The only testimony the government could elicit about this document came from Dennis Eulau, S&S CFO and COO, who—*first*—had no memory of receiving, discussing, or even reading the document (Tr. 371:15–372:4), and—*second*—admitted to having no personal knowledge of what it is like to compete on the book acquisition side of the business, having never held an editorial position during his career at S&S. Tr. 369:25–370:10, 370:19- 371:5 (recounting no conversations with agents about acquisitions and no participation in any book acquisitions throughout his career), 372:5–15 (Q. "Mr. Eulau, do you know which publishers compete in auctions with Simon & Schuster?" A. "Which compete, I do not." Q. "Because you don't follow auctions or who's bidding and that sort of thing, correct?" A. "I do not." Q. "And you don't know how often various publishers compete in auctions with Simon & Schuster?" A. "Or in the mix, I do not. I do not know.").

180. In any case, S&S's *current* CEO, Jonathan Karp, disagreed with Ms. Reidy's characterization of non-Big Five publishers "because usually when you are on a farm team, you want to get off the farm team and you want to get to the majors," but non-Big Five publishers "publish a lot of authors [S&S] would love to publish and a lot of authors who actually have come to [S&S] and then gone back to" their previous non-Big Five publishers. Tr. 550:6–18.

F. Self-Publishing Is Also A Competitive Threat, Especially For Celebrity And Romance Authors

181. Self-publishing is a viable option for authors. Tr. 1809:7–9 (Walsh); Tr. 1108:2–9 (Weisberg (Macmillan)) (Q. "Don't a lot of people self-publish through Amazon? A. "Yes." Q. "And Amazon has a platform where you basically load up what you wrote and then they distribute it for you electronically right?" A. "Yes." Q. "As an e-book, right?" A. "Yes.").

182. Self-publishing is a particularly viable option for celebrity or well-known authors who already have a built-in following on social media or elsewhere. Tr. 1109:2–24 (Weisberg (Macmillan)) (Q. "Would

you agree that self-publishing is especially attractive for authors who have a built-in following?" A. "I think so. Yes." Q. "When I say a built-in following or built- in audience, you mentioned social media, right?" A. "Yeah." Q. "And that's changed a lot in the industry recently, hasn't it?" A. "Yeah." Q. "In other words, there are personalities who are Internet influencers or have a big TikTok following, right?" A. "Sure." Q. "That can be very helpful in selling books?" A. "Absolutely." Q. "That's one of the things you look at, right, when you're looking at acquiring an author, right?" A. "Yes.").

183. Authors have access to online platforms to sell books in ways that would not have been predicted years ago. Tr. 1113:1–11 (Weisberg (Macmillan)). Recently, Brandon Sanderson—who also publishes books with Macmillan—raised around $40 million in a self- publishing campaign on Kickstarter. Tr. 1112:4–25 (Weisberg (Macmillan). This phenomenon could well be the "wave of the future" in publishing. Tr. 1807:10–15 (Walsh).

184. Self-publishing is also a particularly attractive option to romance authors, as Jennifer Bergstrom testified. Tr. 1872:21–1873:4 (Q. "Does self-publishing play a role with authors at Gallery?" A. "Yes, particularly in romance. We have a—one of our top selling authors Anna Todd is now self-publishing. I had author H, just recently on our last contract, the agent told me the author wanted to use a pseudonym and write a new series and wanted to self- publish it. So I essentially had to compete and buy the book. I didn't want her to self-publish, so we offered on that. It's actually coming out next week.").

185. Even best-selling authors published by the Big Five are turning to self-publishing. Tr. 1810:9–16 (Walsh).

G. PRH And S&S Do Not Frequently Compete Head To Head As The Top Two Bidders In Acquisitions

186. PRH is certainly viewed as the "major competition" for most publishers, Tr. 3184:20–3185:3 (Hill), but PRH and S&S do not frequently compete head to head as the top two bidders in acquisitions. HarperCollins is a powerful and aggressive second-place competitor. PX-163 at BPRH-004177288 (showing HarperCollins market share) [REDACTED]; *see also* DX-299 (News Corp. 10-K). S&S, on the other hand, is "part of another group" (Tr. 3185:1 (Hill)), in which each member represents about 10 percent of the market (Hachette, Macmillan, S&S, and other publishers collectively). Tr. 2687:3–9 (Snyder) ("So what this slide identifies—and this is using Dr. Hill's advance data—is the number of titles acquired by the individual members of the so- called Big 5 along with non-Big 5 publishers as a group. And what it shows is the non-Big 5 publishers as a group in red, that group is roughly comparable to Simon & Schuster, to Macmillan and to Hachette.").

187. The data show that PRH and S&S are rarely the winner and runner-up. As Dr. Hill concedes, his own market shares for books above $250,000 imply that PRH and S&S are the top two choices for authors in only about 12 percent of all acquisitions. Tr. 1588:7–19 (Hill). According to Professor Snyder's real-world agency data, the two are the top two bidders in only 6–7% of acquisitions where a winner and runner-up actually exist and can be identified. Tr. 2797:20–2798:6 (Snyder). At a minimum, then, some publisher *other* than PRH or S&S either wins or makes the constraining second-place bid in 88 percent of all acquisitions. Tr. 1588:7–19 (Hill).

188. As Professor Snyder summarized, "PRH and S&S are rarely the winner and runner-up. . . . [REDACTED] [I]f you take Dr. Hill's market share data or my market share data, the prediction is that the two parties will be winner and runner up in only 12 percent of the time. That means that in 88 percent of the time, that condition for harm doesn't exist." Tr. 2632:1–12 (Snyder). As further proof that the merging parties are not particularly close competitors, 47 percent of the time, when one of PRH or S&S wins a book in a multi-bidder auction for over $250,000, the other company does not bid at all. Tr. 2665:20–2666:4 (Snyder); Tr. 1579:11–17; 1692:5–10 (Hill). In fact, Dr. Hill's own analysis of Professor' Snyder's agency data, DX-436, entitled "Share of runner-up status for competitors to Penguin Random House and Simon & Schuster in anticipated top seller wins (2019–2021)" demonstrated that, when PRH won an anticipated top seller during this period, [REDACTED] were the runner-up in multi-bidder auctions more frequently than S&S. Conversely, when S&S won, [REDACTED] were more frequently the runner up than PRH.

189. The Horizontal Merger Guidelines define diversion ratios as "the fraction of unit sales lost by the first product due to an increase in its price that would be diverted to the second product." Guidelines § 6.1. Market shares are not always a useful assumption when calculating diversion ratios—particularly where the evidence suggest that diversion rates are "not proportional to share." Tr. 1277:17–1278:19 (Hill). Market shares only indicate the amount of wins a publisher has—they do not reflect how often a publisher serves as the competitive, runner-up constraint in actual acquisitions, and the idea that

diversion is proportional to share is just an assumption. Tr. 1687:18–1688:3, 1691:7–10, 1692:11–1693:20, 1694:8–18 (Hill). Indeed, as Dr. Hill admitted, PRH and S&S could have the same market shares they do now, and yet *never* compete against each other. Tr. 1689:23–1690:12 (Hill). While, of course, real-world data shows that the merging parties do compete against each other in a limited set of auctions each year, this shows the limitations of the inferences that can be made based on market shares alone.

190. The testimonial evidence from industry participants confirms that PRH and S&S are rarely the top two bidders for a book. As S&S CEO Jon Karp testified, PRH and S&S are the final competitors for a book only a "small fraction" of the time. Tr. 497:21–25.

191. Even more compelling is the experience of literary agents, the only industry players with a view into all the bidders for a particular book. Tr. 1707:8–16 (Hill). And not one agent witness testified that PRH and S&S appeared as first-and-second bidder regularly in their business. Even the government's own witness, Ayesha Pande, admitted that PRH and S&S were the final two bidders for *none* of the eight books she has sold for over $250,000 since 2018. Tr. 301:6–8, 301:20–23 (Pande (Ayesha Pande Literary)); DX-263 (Pande deals sheet). As a result, if PRH and S&S had been merged, nothing about those eight deals would have been different—including the advance levels. Tr. 308:13–16 (Pande (Ayesha Pande Literary)).

192. Agent Elyse Cheney of The Cheney Agency testified that between 2018 and 2019, 28 out of her 44 books sold for $250,000 or more. Tr. 2045:6–13; PX-749 (Elyse Cheney deals sheet). Of those 28 deals, only eight were sold through auction. Tr. 2045:11–13, 2052:5- 10; PX-749 (Cheney deals sheet). Out of those eight, five were won by either PRH or S&S. Tr. 2050:14–22. But out of those five, none—with the possible exception of one that Ms. Cheney could not fully remember—involved PRH and S&S as the final two bidders in the auction. Tr. 2050:23–2051:12 (Cheney).

193. Similarly, literary agent Andrew Wylie of The Wylie Agency testified that he does not think PRH and S&S have ever finished first and second in an acquisition process for a book his agency was selling. Tr. 2088:17–22. In fact, since 2018, Wylie has not sold any book in which both PRH and S&S submitted a bid for the book. Tr. 2088:5–8; PX-856 (Wylie deals sheet).

194. Literary agent Gail Ross of Ross Yoon Agency has sold just one book since 2018 for which PRH and S&S were the top two bidders. Tr. 2124:11–17; PX-838 at 5 (Ross deals sheet).

195. Other evidence showed that PRH and S&S frequently lose books for over $250,000 to other Big Five publishers. Tr. 533:09–534:23, 536:8–18 (Karp (S&S)) (S&S lost books that sold for over $250,000 to Macmillan and Hachette, including books by Jamie Foxx and Ben Carson); Tr. 506:11–25 (Karp (S&S) (S&S has lost "plenty of books" to HarperCollins, including seven-figure deals). Other large publishers have many imprints to which agents can submit books. Tr. 1797:7–15 (Walsh). Competition is fierce among all the imprints, and S&S and PRH imprints are not more fiercely competitive against each other than they are against imprints at other publishing companies, like Hachette or HarperCollins. Tr. 1820:4–15 (Walsh). Further, when PRH or S&S bid, 90 percent of the time, one of the other three Big Five members also bids. Tr. 2665:2–5 (Snyder).

196. For example, Ms. McIntosh, CEO of PRH U.S., testified that PRH's children's book divisions see much more competition from HarperCollins and Scholastic than they do from S&S. Tr. 2298:9–13. Ms. McIntosh also testified that S&S is not a competitor against PRH in the Christian book market. Instead, PRH's main competitors for Christian books are HarperCollins, Hachette, and non-Big Five publishers like Tyndale, Baker, and B&H. Tr. 2301:2–12.

197. The government introduced summaries and anecdotal evidence showing approximately 33 instances in which PRH and S&S finished first and runner up. Tr. 416:24- 448:11 (Karp (S&S)), PX-932-B through PX-958-B (Rule 1006 summaries created by Porro). But of course there will be times when S&S is runner up to PRH, which, after all, acquires the most books—that is what it means to be the largest publisher. But those few anecdotal instances do not trump the overwhelming data showing that PRH and S&S in fact rarely are the first and second place bidders in book acquisitions. Additionally, several of the summary exhibits include best bid auctions, *see* PX-0933-B, PX-0942-B, PX-0949-B, where the specific publisher finishing as the runner up does not actually serve as the competitive constraint, Tr. 2702:6- 2703:5 (Snyder).

F. Internal Imprint Competition Significantly Broadens The Competitive Landscape

198. Competition among imprints within the same publishing company is common in the industry. Hachette allows its imprints to compete so long as there is one outside bidder remaining in an auction. Tr. 225:6–9 (Pietsch (Hachette)). There is evidence that Macmillan also allows its imprints to compete against

each other in auctions. PX-938-B (showing bids from multiple Macmillan imprints).

199. For decades, Random House and then PRH, too, have allowed their imprints across divisions to bid separately for books, so long as one bidder from another publishing company remains in the auction. Tr. 839:1–10 (Dohle (PRH)); Tr. 297:18–23 (Pande (Ayesha Pande Literary)); Tr. 2331:21–25, 2338:4–13 (McIntos(PRH)) (Q. "[H]ow long has this internal bidding being going on?" A. "At Random House, which is the part of the company that I came from, it's gone on for as long as I have been aware of bidding. It's a long, longstanding practice within Random House." Q. "And then when the Penguin company merged with Random House, was Penguin then allowed as a publishing group to compete against the other divisions?" A. "Yeah, they adopted what had been the Random House approach.").

200. For example, when Penguin and Random House merged in 2013, both companies had their own children's division. After the merger, the two children's divisions continued to operate separately and to bid against each other in auctions. Tr. 2331:7–20 (McIntosh (PRH)).

201. Agents repeatedly testified that when they decide to whom they will submit a book for sale, they think in terms of individual editors and their imprints, not in terms of publishing houses. Accordingly, when agents opt to submit a book widely to multiple potential acquirers, they often submit to multiple editors and imprints within the same publishing house. Tr. 1750:13–17 (Walsh); Tr. 2130:1–3 (Ross (Ross Yoon Agency)) ("I think of everything in terms of editors and imprints and not—not Big 4 or Big 5"); Tr. 2051:17–2052:4 (Cheney (The Cheney Agency)) (Q. "In your experience, do you include PRH and Simon & Schuster in every acquisition format?" A. "No." Q. "Why not?" A. "Really, first, again, just—I don't think of it as PRH and Simon & Schuster. I think per imprint, and for particular books, you know, I'm going to try to find the imprint that's going to be best suited for—and the editors best suited for the material."); Tr. 3–4:5–8 (Pande (Ayesha Pande Literary)) (testifying about book proposal submitted to five different PRH imprints).

202. There are hundreds of editors and imprints for an agent to choose from. Tr. 1750:18–23 (Walsh).

203. Although each PRH division has its own approach to how its imprints manage communication with agents, it is still common for different imprints within a single division to bid for the same book. Tr. 2332:1–19 (McIntosh (PRH)). There is no system in place within PRH by which an editor alerts other editors at the company that she has received a particular submission or intends to make a bid. Tr. 2337:11–2338:3 (McIntosh (PRH)). As a result, PRH editors view some of their colleagues at other PRH imprints as their fiercest competitors for the acquisition of books. Tr. 771:3–10 (Dohle (PRH)).

204. PRH and other publishers encourage internal competition because they believe that it is good for business. Mr. Dohle explained that the policy facilitates the "perfect match" between author and editor, which hopefully translates to more sales of the book. Tr. 839:11- 840:4 (the "essence of publishing . . . is that every book idea finds the most passionate editor with the largest vision for the book. And the largest vision for the book, the biggest passion for the book, has a high correlation to the advance . . . the editor wants to pay for the book. And with that, hopefully, also in more sales.").

205. When asked why PRH maintains this policy even though it might result in different editors within the company bidding each other up, causing the company to pay more, Ms. McIntosh explained that while "that could happen, the value in having these very diversified opinions expressed about the value of a book is—I think it increases our chance of getting it right." Tr. 2338:14–19.

206. The policy also helps publishing companies win more books. Tr. 2339:3–4 (McIntosh (PRH)) (Q. "Do you think it helps the company win more books?" A. "I think so."). As Mr. Pietsch, Hachette's CEO, explained: "We want our publishers to be competitive, and in some cases that includes being competitive with each other. That causes them to move faster and work harder and have better chances of winning the book." Tr. 227:6–15.

207. These policies align with Nobel-prize winning economists' matching theory, which posits that price alone is not outcome-determinative. As Professor Snyder testified, matching theory is consistent with how publishing companies are organized: "That's what the idea of the hybrid organization, combining firm-wide capabilities with entrepreneurial efforts at the imprint level, is all about. It's a way to empower editors to be creative, to be entrepreneurial; and that is in the interest of the publisher because it increases the likelihood that they will—that there will be a match and they'll eventually win the contract" Tr. 2643:22–2645:1, 2696:18- 2697:4 (Snyder) ("It's in the interest of publishers, many publishers, to use imprints, to delegate to them, encourage them to compete to find authors and match with authors and win contracts. . . . they're not constrained in most acquisition processes. That—specifically, they're not constrained at all in one-on-one negotiations, in preempts, in best bids or hybrids."). Dr. Hill admits that imprint competition can be profit-maximizing. Tr. 1719:4–16 (Hill) (Q.

"But in its simplest forms, you would agree with me that the current structure at Penguin Random House of allowing its imprints to compete with each other may be profit maximizing; correct?" A. "Yes, could be.").

208. Consistent with those goals, Ms. McIntosh, CEO of PRH U.S., testified that if multiple editors come to her for approval to bid on a book, all seeking approval for a different bid amount, she will approve all three levels without telling each editor that she approved a different—and maybe higher—amount for another editor. She does this because "if one of them is seeing it much more aggressively . . . that more aggressive number is likely to be reflected onto the market too. So I'm not going to do anything to pull that number down because I want us to win the book." Tr. 2240:9–24.

209. Although both Hachette and PRH allow imprint competition only when there is an outside bidder, that restriction is rarely relevant, for various reasons. For one, it does not apply at all to best bids, a very common acquisition format. Tr. 1765:5–18 (Walsh). In addition, agents have plenty of outside options, and even in rounds auctions they can always avoid the rule by calling for best bids before the last outside bidder drops out. Agent Gail Ross testified that she has only *once,* in 36 years, had to notify a PRH imprint that no external bidder remained in the contest, in part because she can always call for best bids. Tr. 2131:12–2132:13; *see* Tr. 1765:10- 12 (Walsh) ("if the agent feels like they might be losing their external bidder, they might just go to best bids as a way of ending the auction"). An agent can avoid the rule even when the last outside bidder is lower than competing internal imprints, simply by keeping the outside bidder in a final best bids round. One agent's written rules for a particular auction made this approach explicit: "If in any round all of the top bidders are in the same corporation, then I will include the next highest bidder." DX-440.

210. PRH's post-merger policy will go even further, allowing PRH and S&S to compete regardless of whether an outside bidder remains in an auction. Tr. 768:23–769:6 (Dohle (PRH)). The aim is to keep PRH and S&S "as external and independent as possible." Tr. 771:24–25 (Dohle (PRH)). The commitment to preserve S&S as an independent bidder may not be legally binding, but PRH also cannot simply renege on the promise. Dohle testified that, based on his decades of experience, once a publisher commits something to authors and agents, it is "practically" impossible to take it away without "damag[ing]" the publisher's important relationship with authors and agents, and therefore, damaging its business. Tr. 873:18–874:10. Ms. Walsh, with decades of experience as an agent, agreed. Tr. 1822:9–19.

211. But even if PRH were to go back on its promise to treat S&S as an external bidder—which the evidence shows is highly unlikely—there is no evidence that PRH would abandon its decades-long business practice of allowing the combined company's imprints to compete against each other as they do now, in best bids and in rounds auctions, until there is no external bidder, and the agents would still have the same tools at their disposal to achieve the best results for their clients. Tr. 1822:20–1823:6 (Walsh).

212. Because of the internal competition policies at PRH, it is very rare that PRH imprints communicate with one another about an auction, which, as noted (*supra* FF ¶ 163), make up less than half of the total acquisitions. Tr. 1608:23–1609:3; 1609:19–1610:3 (Hill). When it does happen, it is usually because a highly motivated imprint is looking for information to help it win the book. Tr. 2339:23–2340:20 (McIntosh (PRH)). It might also come up if an agent approaches one of PRH's publishers about a PRH author moving to another imprint within PRH. While PRH has no policy against such a move, the current publisher should be aware of the situation to ensure that any option clauses in the author's contract have been exercised, and to share any extenuating circumstances. Tr. 2342:9–24 (McIntosh (PRH)). Ms. McIntosh testified that these instances of internal communications generally result in the bids going to the *highest* common denominator, not the lowest. Tr. 2342:25–2343:12.

213. Ms. McIntosh further testified that while she encourages competition among the imprints at the different divisions, since she became CEO, she has sought to reduce the use of especially "sharp elbows" within the company. In particular, she has sought to encourage the different division heads to work towards what is best for their division, but also to share expertise and acknowledge that PRH is one company working together to achieve the best results. She also testified that, in response to some acquisitions in which agents improperly manipulated PRH imprints into bidding against each other with no external bidder participating, she has occasionally encouraged division heads to communicate to avoid such embarrassing scenarios. Tr. 2343:13–2345:1. In her role as President of Strategic Development, Nina Von Moltke serves as Ms. McIntosh's "right hand" in all sorts of situations—including occasionally facilitating communication among imprints in the rare circumstances where such communication is warranted. Tr. 2340:21–2341:23. Contrary to the government's suggestion, Ms. Von Moltke was not

hired to coordinate all internal bidding, which would defeat any benefits the company gains from internal competition. *See supra* FF ¶¶ 204–07. And again, Ms. McIntosh testified that "in practice, my experience has been that even with the top level of the company working together more collaboratively and even with those occasional consultations, I think it has not translated to any kind of lowering impact on the advances that we have paid. In fact, the opposite." Tr. 2345:2–7.

I. The Evidence Does Not Show That Advances Will Be Substantially Reduced Through A "Softening" Of Competition

214. The government at trial argued, for the first time, that eliminating S&S from the market would cause a general "softening" of competition market-wide. The government alleged that this softening would cause all publishers—not just the merging parties—to reduce their bids over time in all acquisitions. As between the merging parties, Dr. Hill speculated that PRH and S&S editors will be able to "bid less aggressively" without losing books, even in bilateral negotiations and best bids, because the number of potential, unknown competitors will be reduced by one. Tr. 1270:6–12 (Hill). He further speculated that there could be a "second order" softening in which other publishers in the alleged market also may lower their bids for the same reason. Tr. 1723:15–19, 3182:23–3183:12 (Hill)

215. But Dr. Hill admits that his models only measure harm where PRH and S&S are the first and second-place bidders in multi-round auctions. Tr. 1584:24–1585:2, 1585:10–20 (Hill). His second-score auction ("SSA") model does not actually measure any first-order "softening" where PRH and S&S are not the first and second-place bidders, and neither his SSA model nor his GUPPI calculation examines one-on-one bilateral negotiations. Tr. 1620:16- 1621:4, 1626:22–1627:20 (Hill) (admitting he did not analyze whether the SSA could be applied to processes other than second-score auctions); Tr. 1736:16–23 (Q. "But you do not have a GUPPI for the bilateral negotiation context; correct? A. Correct."). He also admits he did not model or quantify any second-order softening effect to predict what other publishers might do post-merger. Tr. 1723:20–1724:4, 3183:13–21 (Hill). Nor is Dr. Hill an expert on publishing industry bargaining processes. Tr. 1554:12–21 (Court). He accordingly was not qualified to opine on whether and how the elimination of one potential competitor would affect editor responses in blind bidding formats, including bilateral negotiations and best bids. The government thus adduced no competent evidence establishing even the existence of a competitive response to the elimination of one relatively small competitor, much less establishing that the speculative softening effect would likely create a substantial lessening of competition.

216. Dr. Hill recognized that the elimination of one competitor could reduce advances in blind acquisition formats only to the extent editors consciously recognize and account for absence of the former competitor in calculating their offers. Editors would need to "take account of the fact that competition has been lessened" and then decide to "to be less aggressive" in bidding Tr. 1728:18–1729:1 (Hill). Each editor's response in a given acquisition thus depends on her subjective "perception of current competition" with the merged company pre-merger. Tr. 3192:12–24 (Hill) ("Post merger they are going to perceive that there's less competition facing them, so they will bid less aggressively."); Tr. 3183:25–3184:5 (Hill) ("It's in the best bids [and] the negotiations, you have that weakening in anticipation. I frequently compete with this person, I don't think they are competing with me anymore, so I'm going to bid less aggressively.").

217. Although Dr. Hill thus recognized that any "softening" effect from a merger of depends on how rivals both perceive and respond to the effect of eliminating of one competitor with a ten percent market share, he did not proffer a model to analyze that reaction, though he acknowledged that models are available to do so. Tr. 3182:22–3183:3–6 (Hill). Dr. Hill also proffered no real-world mechanism by which editors could learn from prior acquisitions how much they could safely reduce bids without losing books to the remaining competitors with 90 percent market shares. Tr. 2680:9–22 (Snyder) (Dr. Hill offers "no explanation of how this would actually work"). The closest he came was speculating that firms would hire a "management consultant" to help them decide if, when, and how much to lower their bids—an idea that no one in the industry ever discussed existing or being contemplated. Tr. 1594:20- 1595:4 (Hill).

218. Dr. Hill's "management consultant" suggestion illustrates the importance of industry expertise in establishing the existence and effect of any market response to the elimination of a single competitor. Dr. Hill lacks such expertise. He nevertheless drew a halting comparison to the beer industry to explain how softening would occur. Tr. 3195:21–3196:16, 3197:2–23 (Hill). But bargaining to acquire books in the publishing industry differs in material ways that make comparisons to such commodity industries inapt. As Professor Snyder observed, this "is a very different market from the electronic vehicle market,

where you're setting prices and you're getting a variable response in terms of quantity demanded." Tr. 2677:15–21.

219. Unlike beer and electronic vehicles, every book that publishers acquire is wholly unique and subject to widely varying, individualized valuations. *See supra* FF ¶ 104. And unlike commodity transactions, bargaining for books is largely conducted without knowing who else is bidding or the amounts of their bids. *See supra* FF ¶ 106. These twin factors mean that acquisition processes give editors little information about their competition that they can use to inform their offers in the next blind bidding process for a completely different book—whether in a bilateral negotiation or a best bid format, which collectively constitute the overwhelming majority of book acquisition processes. *See supra* FF ¶ 107; Tr. 1608:23–1609:3, 1609:19- 1610:3 (Hill).

220. To the extent Dr. Hill focused only on the possibility that PRH or S&S *themselves* would reduce offers in blind bidding formats because their editors perceive a reduced competitive threat, he acknowledged that this more limited form of softening requires each editor to revise her offers based on an understanding of how often she has encountered and lost to the other party. Tr. 1268:9–21 (Hill) ("If Penguin Random House never lost to Simon & Schuster, then in these best bid settings it may say post-merger: We never lost to these guys anyway, so we're not going to change our behavior. If Penguin and Random House always lost to Simon & Schuster, they could say post-merger: This is great. The competition has softened significantly. And then somewhere in between is the middle ground where they competed sometimes, but not always. And so you may soften—feel competition softened. How much it softened depends on how often you compete with the other party."). The data show that PRH lost to S&S and vice versa in only about 12 percent of all acquisitions, according to Dr. Hill (if it is assumed that all acquisitions are auctions with an identifiable runner up), and about 6–7% of acquisitions, according to Professor Snyder when taking into account the actual variety of acquisition formats, including bilateral negotiations. *See supra* FF ¶ 187. In all other acquisitions, another publisher won the book or was runner up ahead of the other merging party. *See supra* FF ¶ 187. There is no evidence that any editor at either publisher is aware of that figure, but the testimony of industry participants uniformly recognized that PRH and S&S are rarely first and second place bidders. *See supra* FF ¶¶ 190–94. And the diversion ratios that Dr. Hill referenced, which are unknown to editors in the ordinary course of business, also don't tell editors the extent of competition between the parties in the overall market because they do not show the frequency with which books are acquired in situations where PRH and S&S are actually the first and second place bidders.

221. Dr. Hill did not and could not show how, given that data, editors would know how to safely reduce their offers without losing books to other rivals. As Professor Snyder testified, "the problem is, they have so many rivals there, it would not make sense as an across-the-board pricing strategy. It would result in mistakes where you do [have] loss of business." Tr. 2671:22- 2672:25. Dr. Hill speculated, for example, S&S editors, knowing they would no longer be outbid by PRH, would on average reduce their offers by about 11.5 percent in all acquisition processes, including bilateral negotiations and best bids. Tr. 1312:7–15 (Hill). But he has no analysis demonstrating that if S&S editors imposed such a reduction, the lower bid would still exceed offers made by (best bids) or potentially available from (negotiations) HarperCollins, Hachette, Macmillan, Norton, or any of the other publishers that acquire books in the government's alleged submarket. And "from an editor's point of view within PRH or S&S, post-merger, they're running into Macmillan and Hachette and HarperCollins with very high frequency." Tr. 2682:21–24 (Snyder); DX-436. Dr. Hill has only a "general intuition about the tradeoff" between reducing offers and losing books, as Professor Snyder testified, and it is "really hard to implement [REDACTED] Well, there's less competition out there, and therefore I will reduce my bid when the competitive conditions vary so much across situations. And you really don't know when you should. You're going to be wrong most of the time, and you can't learn from what the outcomes are." Tr. 2674:15–2675:15 (Snyder); Tr. 2672:11–18 (Snyder) ("But the most important thing for me is, how—it's completely unclear how Dr. Hill imagines this cascading starts when, from the point of view of PRH and S&S, they're only hitting each other 12 percent of the time. And the same analysis applies to anybody else. If you cut your advances and the competitive conditions for harm aren't met, meaning you're not—you don't actually have a lessening of competition, then you can be making a mistake.").

222. Further, the costs of miscalculating how much advances can be shaved without losing the books are not like the consequences a brewery faces when it raises beer prices briefly to test consumer reactions. Every time an editor miscalculates and loses a book by even the smallest margin, the book is gone forever, and the author may be as well. "It would result in mistakes where you do [have] loss of

business." Tr. 2671:22–2672:25 (Snyder); Tr. 2673:23- 2674:3 (Snyder) ("It doesn't make sense to cut your advances if you're going to lose business."). The stakes for editors in losing such business by miscalculating their offers would be especially high because, by the government's own account, these books and authors are the most attractive in the entire industry. And, softening advances would create opportunity for new entrants and smaller publishers—who already compete for high-advance books, *see supra* FF ¶¶ 164–80—to step in and win books.

223. Publishers recognize these risks and uniformly testified that they did not expect to be lowering their offers after the merger. Tr. 1873:5–16 (Bergstrom (S&S)) (Q. " Do you understand that there's an allegation in this case that if this merger of Penguin Random House and Simon & Schuster goes through, publishers like yourself will be able to identify a group of authors called anticipated top sellers and target them to reduce their advances? Do you understand that?" A. "Yes, I do." Q. "What is your view of that?" A. "My view is I struggle to identify what those top sellers are. And even if I could, I can't—no agent or author would want to work with me if they knew that I couldn't compete, so it would hurt my business."); Tr. 1088:3–7 (Weisberg (Macmillan)); [REDACTED] DX-422 (Glusman (Norton) Dep.) 134:18–23. 226.

224. Dr. Hill's speculation that S&S, PRH, and other editors in the industry would perceive and respond to reduced competition in blind bidding by substantially reducing their offers for the most sought-after books, secure in the knowledge they would not be lost to aggressive rivals, is unsupported by data, trial testimony, or common sense.

J. The 2013 Merger Of Random House With Penguin Did Not Cause A Reduction In Author Advances

225. In 2013, Random House merged with Penguin. The rationale for that merger was the same as the rationale for the merger of PRH and S&S: Random House believed that it could deliver synergies by bringing its superior supply chain and distribution capabilities to the sale of Penguin books. Tr. 818:23–819:6 (Dohle (PRH)).

226. To economists, the 2013 merger of Random House and Penguin is highly relevant to the evaluation of the merger of PRH and S&S because it represents a "natural experiment." The effects the 2013 merger had on output and advances is highly predictive of what effects the instant merger will have on output and advances. Tr. 2638:25–2639:14 (Snyder).

227. The 2013 merger of Penguin and Random House did not result in reduced advances. Tr. 218:6–8; 237:6–8; 237:9–12 (Pietsch (Hachette)); 2841:4–8 (Snyder).

228. In fact, in the period coinciding with the merger of Random House and Penguin, publishers competed even more fiercely, setting off a "frenzy" to acquire books. DX-188.0001; Tr. 503:8–504:5 (Karp (S&S)) (testifying that "around 2013," HarperCollins "made a strategic decision to increase their market share by bidding aggressively"); DX-422 (Glusman (Norton) Dep.) at 131:9–19.

229. Advances industry-wide actually *increased,* despite an anxiety in the industry that advances would decrease, because other publishers had to bid *more* to compete with the combined Penguin and Random House, which was itself paying more in advances. Tr. 2347:24- 2348:1 (McIntosh (PRH)) (Q. "And after the Penguin Random House merger, did you observe any impact on advances paid by your company?" A. "Yes. They went up."); DX-435.0007 (showing annual advance commitments increasing since 2015, driven by higher advance levels); Tr. 1824:13–20 (Walsh); DX-422 (Glusman (Norton) Dep.) 133:7–9, 133:11–23; Tr. 2137:10–15*sae*Ross (Ross Yoon Agency)). Professor Snyder's analysis of the 2013 merger also demonstrated that the average advances above $250,000 increased or stayed consistent after the merger. Tr. 2839:13–25; DX-385 (PRH average advances committed per title 2010–2021).

230. Professor Snyder's analysis confirmed that, when examining buckets of advance size, from $250,000 to $500,000, $500,000 to $1,000,000, and $1,000,000 to $2,000,000, average advances *increased* or stayed flat from the pre-2013 period (2010–2012) to the post-2013 period (2014–2016). Tr. 2838:16–2841:8 (Snyder).

231. Nor did the 2013 merger result in a reduction in titles published by the newly combined company. Tr. 820:15–19 (Dohle (PRH)); Tr. 2345:8–14 (McIntosh (PRH)) (title reduction "was not because of the merger").

232. Rather, after the merger, PRH reduced the number of lower-advance titles it published due to market forces unrelated to the merger. Readers of genre fiction—especially romance and science fiction—switched to purchasing e-books and self-published titles, which were available at lower price points than traditionally published mass-market paperbacks. As a result, in 2014 and 2015, retailers began stocking

fewer mass-market books. Some of PRH's imprints were over-indexed in the declining mass-market format, and they had to adjust to the shift in market demand. Tr. 820:20–822:2 (Dohle (PRH)). As Ms. McIntosh testified, she decreased Penguin's publication of mass-market paperback format books in the genre fiction space after assessing that Penguin had been trying to "muscle their way through the fact that there were market changes," by continuing to acquire and publish these types of books without any marketing investments and with old-fashioned covers, and even though retailers were returning most of the books. She determined that, "while I would be happy to keep publishing those books, I couldn't keep publishing them if there was no one who wanted to buy them." So- called "mass market" fiction books typically receive very low advances. Tr. 2345:17–2346:18.

233. In the years following the 2013 merger, PRH also lost some very significant authors who commanded very large advances—like Nora Roberts and Harlan Coben—to rival publishers. Tr. 2295:10–19, 2348:2–16, 2351:3–5 (McIntosh (PRH)). These authors continued to be highly successful with other publishers. Tr. 1099:9–1100:18 (Weisberg (Macmillan)) (Nora Roberts moved from PRH to Macmillan; [REDACTED].

234. The decline in demand for mass-market paperback books, and the resulting reduction in publication of those books, was an industry-wide phenomenon not limited to PRH or connected to the 2013 merger. Tr. 218:18–219:8 (Pietsch (Hachette)) (testifying that he observed a reduction in PRH's title count after the 2013 merger, and agreeing that at the same time a trend in the industry caused some publishers to "cut[] back on their mass-market publishing").

235. Ms. McIntosh testified that her strategy with respect to genre fiction after the previous merger worked: Within a couple of years, the repositioning of Penguin's imprints has resulted in "much more contemporary-feeling" romance books and a steady increase in title counts. Tr. 2346:19–2347:6; 2347:14–23 (testifying that Berkeley (PRH imprint) "has become very successful . . . they invest more per book. They pay higher advances. They actually work to support authors in the market. And these covers . . . are more aligned with kind of what might appeal to current consumers. And the sales and profit results have been fantastic."). Professor Snyder's analysis of the 2013 merger likewise demonstrates that output of titles acquired for $250,000 or more increased by 13 percent in the three years following that merger. Tr. 2838:25- 2839:12 (Snyder).

236. When Dr. Hill analyzed the 2013 merger's effect on advances, he compared average advances for books above and below the $250,000 threshold before and after the 2013 merger and estimated a drop in average advances above $250,000, both in absolute terms and compared to advances below $250,000, but he did not analyze whether the mass market decline, and reduction in output of books at the lowest advance levels, affected the validity of his calculations, nor did he examine the impact of the unevenness in high advance contracts during these time periods on the average advances. Tr. 3187:16–3189:19 (Hill); Tr. 2839:15–25 (Snyder); *see also* DX-385 (showing higher variability of average advances in higher advance contracts).

237. In fact, Professor Snyder demonstrated that Dr. Hill's approaches to analyzing the 2013 merger omitted two key facts. First, that if one were to exclude the so-called "mass market" fiction books with advances below $50,000, Dr. Hill's "difference in difference" analysis comparing books with advances below $250,000 with books with advances above $250,000 and below $4,000,000 in the three years before and after the merger the results were statistically insignificant. Tr. 2876:9–2879:13 (Snyder).

238. Second, Professor Snyder found that Dr. Hill's average advance calculations pre- and post-2013 were heavily affected by the presence or absence of a few extremely high advance contracts in both time periods. Professor Snyder's analysis confirmed that average advances rose post-merger for advances in the $250,000 to $500,000, $500,000 to $1,000,000, and $1,000,000 to $2,000,000 ranges. Tr. 2838:16–2841:8 (Snyder). It was only when looking at advances above $2 million, and in particular above $4 million, that the average advance data become noisy due to small numbers and the timing of large contracts with repeat authors. *Id.; see* Tr. 2348:2- 16 (McIntosh (PRH)) ("[V]ariability can be caused by the highest level advances that we pay. There are some of our highest paid authors. We don't negotiate a new contract every year. We could have a contract that has many years['] worth of books on a single contract. And so depending on the year in which that contract is established, that could impact our average. Our averages can also, of course, be impacted . . . if we lose a franchise author. I have already described a couple who we lost to our competitors or in a happier circumstance when we woo away from a competitor a new franchise author and make an investment in them."); DX-439 (table showing significant variability in annual author contracts from 2019 to 2021).

239. Dr. Hill did not analyze whether the mass market decline affected the validity of his calculations. Tr.

3188:6–14 (Hill). He did not even calculate whether the number of book contracts increased or decreased after the merger. Tr. 3185:16–18 (Hill). He admitted, though, that such trends might have affected his conclusions. Tr. 3188:24–3189:19 (Hill). He further admitted that his analysis did not show that the effects he calculated were caused by the merger—just that they occurred after the merger. Tr. 3188:1–2 (Hill).

K. The Government's Economic Models Did Not Prove A Likelihood Of Substantial Harm To Competition

240. Consistent with the unilateral effects claim asserted by the government, Dr. Hill analyzed the potential for harm through an economic model focused only on auctions in which the merging parties are the first and runner-up bidders. Tr. 1299:20–23, 1301:15–23, 1302:21- 1303:6, 1584:24–1585:2, 1585:10–23, 3163:17–23 (Hill).

241. To model such harm, Dr. Hill principally used the SSA model. The SSA model, by design, will *always* show some harm when any two competitors merge. Tr. 1629:1–5 (Hill); Tr. 2810:25–2811:19 (Snyder). Consistent with its function, Dr. Hill admits that the harm estimated by his SSA model is "more directional than . . . entirely precise." Tr. 1654:5–9 (Hill). He estimated authors would see their advances reduced by 4 percent for authors contracting with PRH and 11.5 percent for S&S authors, for an overall average of about 6.1 percent, but admitted that the overall harm could be as low as 3 percent. Tr. 1654:14–1655:13 (Hill); Tr. 2802:24- 2803:15 (Snyder). Although the model was designed specifically to examine round-robin style auctions, Hill applied his projections to all acquisitions won by either PRH or S&S. Tr. 1298:16- 19, 1586:10–14, 1597:11–13. The overall reduction projected by applying the model's results across all formats is approximately $29.3 million in annual reduced advances for PRH and S&S authors. Tr. 2802:24–2803:15 (Snyder).

242. The evidence revealed a variety of problems with the SSA model.

1. The SSA Does Not Reflect Most Real-World Acquisitions

243. Dr. Hill selected the SSA model not because it was a sound fit for the publishing industry or is typically used to model the bilateral negotiations and best bid formats that dominate bargaining in the industry. To the contrary, Dr. Hill testified that a bilateral negotiation model would have been his first choice, but he could not build one that generated meaningful results. Tr. 1618:5–21. He also tried a best bid model, but lacked the information necessary for that model. Tr. 1322:19–1324:1 (Hill); Tr. 1633:5–14 (Hill) (Q. "You did look at the first score auction model and rejected it, correct?" A. "I tried a number of first price auctions and rejected them." Q "So were you just looking at auction models?" A. "No, I also looked at negotiations. As I said, I tried to build a model that included all of the mechanisms in one grand model and it—sadly, for my chances of winning the Nobel prize, I failed in that endeavor.").

244. Dr. Hill instead used the SSA model because, unlike models more appropriate to real-world bargaining conditions, the SSA model was "easy to solve." Tr. 1322:19–1324:1 (Hill) (explaining he used SSA because "it's very easy to solve" and though it is "not guaranteed" to give the "same predictions as best bid auctions or other formats," Hill lacked information needed to run other models for this industry); Tr. 1611:20–1612:15 (Hill) (THE COURT: "So your choice of model depended in part on what the results were and if they just looked right to you?" THE WITNESS: "It depended on whether I could get a model I could solve.").

245. Dr. Hill admitted that the SSA model was designed to examine round-robin style auctions, not bilateral negotiations or best bids. Tr. 1616:17–19, 1605:21–24, 1627:13–20 (Hill). He also admitted that as far as he is aware, no other economist has ever applied an SSA model to make predictions about the effect of a merger on bargaining outcomes in best bids and bilateral negotiations. Tr. 1620:16–1621:4 (Hill).

246. As Professor Snyder explained, the SSA "is in this setting a wrong fit for the industry," because it fails to account for agents' roles in acquisitions, publishers' responses to competition, and the diversity of acquisition formats. Tr. 2632:21–2633:19 (Snyder); Tr. 2634:12–22 (Snyder) ("I don't find that the SSA model in this context offers any value in terms of the fundamental economic analysis."). In particular, Professor Snyder emphasized, "the model presumes an acquisition format, rounds to completion, that so-called round-robin format, that agents rarely choose." Tr. 2632:21–2633:19 (Snyder).

247. Indeed, the vast majority of books are not sold to publishers through the round- robin auctions that Dr. Hill modeled. Dr. Hill himself estimates that only about 20 percent of all acquisitions use rounds auction formats, much less round-robins—the rest are bilateral negotiations or best bids. Tr. 1608:23–1609:3, 1609:19–1610:3 (Hill). Professor Snyder estimated that multi-bidder acquisitions that finish as a round robin comprise "probably less than 10 percent" of all acquisitions. Tr. 2658:19–2659:9 (Snyder). Other witnesses testified similarly from practical experience. Tr. 475:10–476:10 (Karp (S&S))

(testifying that the majority of S&S acquisitions are not acquired via auction); Tr. 2088:13–16 (Wylie (The Wylie Agency)) (Q. "The Wylie Agency, some 20 agents or so, including yourself, your testimony is that the firm does not conduct auctions in transacting book sales to publishers?" A. "Correct."); Tr. 2292:10–13 (McIntosh (PRH)) (Q. "In your experience, do agents have a preference for round-robin auctions?" A. "I know that round-robin auctions have been declining in—in popularity, and that's driven by the agents."); Tr. 1767:2–9 (Walsh) (testifying that most of her colleagues use best bids or better-best, not round robins).

248. The rarity of rounds or round-robin auctions shows authors generally do not perceive that such formats generate results that are in their best interest. If such processes typically maximized author interests, they would be a widespread form of acquisition, not the least common. Although a process where multiple publishers "bid up" the advance might at first seem favorable to authors, the evidence made clear why authors and agents generally do not favor this format. Tr. 2056:8–25 (Cheney (The Cheney Agency)) (idea that auctions will compel higher end prices is "kind of a myth" when it comes to publishing); Tr. 1758:14–1759:6 (Walsh).

249. In a multi-round auction, the auction may end before the bidding reaches the amount the winning publisher would have paid. Tr. 2291:12–2292:9 (McIntosh (PRH)) (round robin auctions do not necessarily result in publishers paying more because "in a round robin auction, you can start low and feel your way up"); Tr. 1759:1–6 (Walsh) ("If they come to the auction and I have a lot of people that are bidding low and slow, they might feel they don't have to go anywhere near what the original preemptive number was."). By contrast, in the increasingly common best bid format, the publisher does not know any other bid amounts and likely will have only one chance to win the book. Tr. 477:25–479:08 (Karp (S&S)); Tr. 1757:18- 25, 1762:10–1763:1 (Walsh); Tr. 2702:3–2703:5 (Snyder). The publisher accordingly must bid an amount at or near its maximum bid (hence the term "best bid"). Tr. 1763:2–6 (Walsh) (Q. "Is it true that the more bidders the agent has participating in a best-bids process, the higher the advance will be?" A. "It's actually not true."); Tr. 2292:3–21 (McIntosh (PRH)) ("I think that in best-bid situations, those are the situations where we often end up overpaying. . . ."). Similarly, in a bilateral negotiation, the publisher does not know what other publishers are willing to pay, so it must again ultimately offer at or near its maximum amount to "keep it off the marketplace," as Weisberg put it. Tr. 1122:23–1123:11 (Weisberg (Macmillan)); Tr. 1758:14–1759:6 (Walsh).

250. For these reasons, as agent Elyse Cheney explained, "there's a misapprehension that the primary determinant of the value of the project is competitive auctions or competitive bidding." Tr. 2053:20–23 (Cheney (Cheney Agency)). In Cheney's experience, publishers tend to "prefer auctions because it's a much safer route for them," but other negotiation formats are better for authors. Tr. 2056:8–11 (Cheney (Cheney Agency)). Among the 28 books that agent Elyse Cheney sold for $250,000 between 2018–2021, 20 of those books were sold through a manner other than a multi-bidder auction. Tr. 2052:5–10 (Cheney (Cheney Agency)).

251. The majority of books are sold through one-on-one bilateral negotiations with just one editor. Tr. 2124:24–2125:5 (Ross (Ross Yoon Agency)) (more than 60 percent direct negotiations, not auctions); Tr. 2088:13–16 (Wylie (The Wylie Agency)); Tr. 1963:20–23 (Kim (PRH)) (80 percent of PRH's Putnam imprint acquisitions via bilateral negotiation); Tr. 1609:8- 13 (Hill) (Q. "I think we're in agreement in essence, which is that the majority of the acquisitions are not auctions, they're bilateral negotiations?" THE COURT: "The majority are. They're 60 percent." THE WITNESS: "Yeah, I would say somewhere around 50 to 60 percent will be negotiation.").

252. There are various reasons agents usually choose to submit to and negotiate exclusively with one editor rather than solicit bids from multiple editors. PX-2007 (Fletcher (Fletcher & Company) Dep.) at 155:21–156:17. Among other reasons, agents pursue bilateral negotiations because authors have long-term objectives—including financial objectives—beyond the immediate maximization of a one-off advance. For example, literary agent Gail Ross explained that there is a "huge, huge advantage" to authors publishing their first and second books with the same publisher, because when the second book is published, the first book gets a new round of promotion. Tr. 2126:3–9. Established authors likewise tend to stay with same editors or imprints that enabled their career success, Tr. 1748:24–1749:9 (Walsh), as illustrated by the Putnam imprint's experience, Tr. 1963:20–23 (Kim (PRH)).

253. Similarly, agents often pursue bilateral negotiations with a single editor because the editor and author have made a particular connection that will produce the best possible book, facilitate a long-term lucrative partnership, or both. As author Charles Duhigg explained: "The biggest issue is: Do I like this editor? Do I think this editor is going to elevate my work and help me write a great book? Because if I

write a great book, it doesn't matter how big the advance is. I'm going to sell a lot of books. And that's where the money is going to come from." Tr. 1917:22–1918:10; Tr. 1956:7–10 (Duhigg) ("And so I'm not going to ask for a huge amount of money because it means the next time I come, they're going to say: Look, it's just too big a risk. We can't do this again. We've lost too much money on you."); *see* Tr. 2293:17- 2294:1 (McIntosh (PRH)) ("[I]t's a very close working relationship between an author or—publisher and the editor. So there's a personal connection but even more than that, there is a desire to continue to work and reap the benefits of the investments we've already made in that career.")

254. Agent Elyse Cheney similarly testified "I could give you example after example" of where the wrong editor ruined a book project. Tr. 2063:18–25. In one case, she chose the highest-bidding publisher and "then, literally, I had to work every single day for the next three years in order to help make that project right. And we took—and it just never was right, and it was incredibly frustrating because they just didn't understand how to do this particular kind of book." Tr. 2063:25–2064:4. As a result, "the book ended up selling a pittance compared to the advance, like—and that's not good for the authors." Tr. 2064:6–8; *see* Tr. 2063:5–14 (Cheney (The Cheney Agency)) (her authors "want to work with the best people" because "they have a story to tell, and they're trying to make meaning of something. And the editor who can help them bring—make the richest, most robust project, that means the world to them. It's huge. It's like—and then how that editor then communicates—and that editor is sort of like the orchestra leader.").

255. "Top-selling" authors might not even bother to shop their books around to multiple publishers, preferring instead to accept preempts or continue publishing with their current publisher. Tr. 322:12–20, 324:11–18, 326:8–11 (King) (testifying that he accepted an offer from Scribner without talking to other publishers, and has not tested the market for his books with other publishers). Duhigg sold his first book through a preempt to Andy Ward at Random House based on the recommendation of his agent, Tr. 1913:21–1914:17 (Duhigg), and sold his second book to the same editor at Random House without soliciting any offers from other publishers. Tr. 1924:4–23 (Duhigg).

256. Agents ultimately are looking not just for the maximum one-off advance amount, but to get the "best deal" for their clients, which includes maximizing their *long*-term financial benefit. In Elyse Cheney's words: "I think we should define what the best deal for my client means. In my mind, the promise that we make to authors is we're going to try to help you find the widest audience possible for your books. So in order to do that, that may mean going with the publisher who has the highest bid, but it might also mean going with the publisher who has the most experience in that kind of project, and that—the imprint, and—and the editor who has the most experience and success rate for that kind of project." Tr. 2053:7–15. Andrew Wylie agreed: "The strongest financial terms offered do not compose, necessarily, the best offer, in my view, because you also have to consider the editor who would be working with the author and the context from which the book would—would come; what else the publisher is publishing, and the strengths or weaknesses of the—of the publishing house." Tr. 2089:15–22. So did Charles Duhigg: "When I wrote this book, it was not to get the advance. It was to write a great book that would hopefully sell millions of copies, because that's where the real money comes from: It comes from selling a lot of books. And then there's all these other things that appear. Right? You can give speeches. You sell foreign rights. You sell your—the IP to companies that take it and do things with it. So no. I had hoped to earn much more than the advance." Tr. 1916:22- 1917:15; Tr. 1772:24–1773:7 (Walsh) ("[T]here is a pie that is the book. The advance is one—the North American advance is one—is one wedge of that pie. If we picked an editor that the collaboration is very successful, the book will be better as a result. It will sell more; so royalties. But also internationally, it will sell more in more territories . . . as well as potentially more likely to get a . . . film or TV deal. So that's the full pie.").

2. Dr. Hill Used Flawed Inputs In The SSA

257. Not only do Dr. Hill's analyses fail to reflect the real competitive conditions in the publishing industry, they incorporate significant input flaws that further underscore their lack of connection to the real world, and the inapplicability of the SSA model, and which results in an overstatement of the alleged harm.

258. *Margin Inputs.* In Dr. Hill's first report, he used inconsistent inputs to calculate the parties' profit margins: he included ongoing operating expenses for PRH, which reduced PRH's profit margin, but excluded them for S&S. Professor Snyder pointed out the inconsistent treatment and he recalibrated the SSA model by using profit margins that included ongoing operating expenses for both PRH and S&S, Tr. 2801:1–18 (Snyder), resulting in a 30 percent reduction in alleged harm. Tr. 2802:16–2804:23 (Snyder).

259. In response, Dr. Hill chose to use profit margins that *excluded* operating expenses for both merging parties in his reply report, Tr. 2801:19–22 (Snyder), although he admitted that this approach to calculating margins was likewise inaccurate, Tr. 1645:8–18 (Hill) ("The truth here is somewhere in between . . . the figure in my initial report, which is conservative, and the figure in my reply report is aggressive . . . so somewhere in between there is what I think is the truth.").

260. Exclusion of operating expenses is not consistent with how publishers operate. Operating expenses are a key component of the book-level P&Ls that publishers build to inform their bids for books. Tr. 2801:23–2802:7 (Snyder). Professor Snyder explained that in this context, including operating expenses to determine profit margins is appropriate because PRH operates through about 100 different imprints, and when "you have a hundred different entrepreneurial creative . . . operations, you better make sure that they are bidding in a way that allows PRH as a whole to recover operating expenses." Tr. 2936:10–2937:5 (Snyder). If no advances were calibrated to recover some operating expenses, the company could not cover its costs. That is why the book-level P&Ls incorporate operating expenses into the advance recommendation. Tr. 3025:7–3026:23 (Snyder); Tr. 2253:25–2254:17 (McIntosh (PRH)) (describing line item for fixed costs in book-level P&L); Tr. 570:12–571:14 (Karp (S&S)) (describing line item for operating income margin after fixed expenses, and testifying that S&S always wants the operating income margin to be positive and in the double digits); Tr. 3029:20- 3030:14 (Snyder) ("I believe the practice here for both companies leads you to when you're selecting margins to include margins that reflect the importance of capturing these ongoing operating expenses."). Professor Snyder recalculated Dr. Hill's results for the SSA by including operating expenses for both PRH and S&S. Tr. 2801:15–17 (Snyder).

261. Dr. Hill admitted that by excluding operating costs to calculate higher profit margins, his calculations suggested more harm from the merger. Tr. 1305:24–1306:3 (Hill) ("So a higher variable profit margin leads to greater variation in bids or is associated with greater variation in bids and leads to more harm. And smaller margins means more tightly clustered bids and it means less harm"); Tr. 1309:10–16 (Hill) ("But the general point I was just trying to make here is just that when there's higher profit margins, there's generally going to be more harm."). Merely by correcting that input to include ongoing operating costs in the determination of the profit margins for both firms, the estimated harm under Dr. Hill's SSA would decrease from 6.1 percent to 4.3 percent for the combined firm, with a commensurate reduction in the $29.3 million dollars in estimated annual harm. Tr. 2802:16–2804:23 (Snyder).

262. Equally important, Dr. Hill's initial approach to calculating profit margins (including ongoing operating costs for PRH, but excluding them for S&S) is the only way in which he could get the actual and predicted margins to acceptably match in the SSA model—which he and Professor Snyder agree is a key test of the reliability of the model according to its creator. Tr. 1646:12–14, 1647:3–8 (Hill); Tr. 2633:20–2634:8; 2802:1–7 (Snyder). It was only by taking this inconsistent approach to ongoing operating expenses that Dr. Hill could get the actual and predicted margins to come within five percent of each other for both companies. Tr. 2805:15–2806:9 (Snyder). As Professor Snyder explained, when Dr. Hill treated margins consistently by excluding operating expenses from PRH and S&S's margins, "the predictions versus actuals diverge greatly." Tr. 2805:24–2806:5 (Snyder). "[T]he model is predicting an S&S margin that is 50 percent higher than its actual margin, and the lower, the second row, is predicting a 33 percent lower margin for PRH compared to actual." Tr. 2806:2–5 (Snyder). And "what this failure of the reliability test means is that the results [of the model] are not reliable." Tr. 2806:7–9 (Snyder).

263. Dr. Hill's variable approach to ongoing operating expenses in his initial and reply reports highlights an aspect of the SSA model obscured by his testimony. The SSA model (and the GUPPI calculations) do not demand a particular type of margin to function. The article proposing the SSA model discusses marginal costs, but only because "it is a dominant strategy for the suppliers to submit offers at marginal cost." Nathan H. Miller, *Modeling the Effects of Mergers in Procurement,* 37 INT'L J. OF INDUS. ORG. 201, 203 (2014). It does not require the use of marginal costs when they are not actually the relevant costs. On the basis of what margins are identified, the SSA model then infers differences in bids from the profit margins, because that margin is the difference between the maximum a firm is willing to bid, and the value it actually pays. Thus, as Professor Snyder stated, for the profit margin to be a meaningful input into the analysis, it *must* represent the actual way firms determine their maximum bid, which is why it is proper to look at whether and how ongoing operating costs are treated in the acquisition P&Ls that help guide the bidding process. Tr. 2936:10–18 (Snyder).

264. Notably, the SSA model *did not* "reject" Dr. Hill's PRH margins when he chose to include ongoing

operating expenses in the PRH margin in his initial report. The model simply accepts the margins given as a measure of the maximum willingness to pay. The crucial issue for the reliability of the model is that the actual margins input into the model must match the margins the model predicts for each entity. And whether operating expenses are included (as Dr. Snyder testified should be included, given how advances are estimated in acquisition P&Ls by including fixed cost contributions) or excluded (as Dr. Hill chose to do after his inconsistent approach was criticized), the actual and predicted margins are not sufficiently close to be reliable here.

265. Ultimately, both of Dr. Hill's SSA model attempts fail. His first attempt fails because of the inconsistent treatment of the margin inputs, and the second attempt fails because even after adjusting the margin inputs, the model failed the reliability test established by the model's developer. Tr. 2633:20–2634:11 (Snyder).

266. *Market Shares and Runner-Up, Win-Loss, and Editorial Minutes Data as a Check.* The next input error involves the data used to identify how often PRH and S&S were the top two bidders in the modeled auctions—an essential factor in the SSA analysis. Dr. Hill relied on the parties' market shares for all acquisition formats combined (rather than seeking to derive market shares related to auctions, much less round robin auctions) for this input, notwithstanding the fact that the record evidence demonstrates that these overall market shares overstate the degree of winner and runner-up competition between PRH and S&S. *See supra* FF ¶ 187. Dr. Hill did so based in part on his belief that market shares are a conservative measure based on "diversions" from two other data sources that failed to even show who the winner and runners up were in various acquisition processes, and thus shed no light on the actual amount of head to head competition between the parties. Tr. 1283:6–21 (Hill) (admitting that win loss data does not show who was runner up or "second closest bidder"); Tr. 1712:20–23 (Hill) (same); Tr. 1696:13- 1697:3 (Hill) (admitting that editorial minutes do not show who was runner up); Tr. 1698:18-1699:7 (Hill) (same). Two of Dr. Hill's key data sources were notes from publishing company editorial meetings, and win-loss data from publishing companies. Yet he admitted that both sources identify only which publisher won a given auction and provide no information about the runner-up; he merely assumed that either PRH or S&S was the runner up if the other firm won. As for editorial minutes: "Q. And could you actually tell from looking at the editorial minutes who was number one and number two?" A. "No." Tr. 1696:19–1697:3 (Hill); *see* Tr. 1699:1–7 (Hill) ("Q. "But in each of these specific cases, you couldn't tell for the book that was the subject of the minutes you reviewed who was actually one and two?" A. "That's correct."). And for win-loss data: "In the win-loss data, we know that Penguin Random House records that it lost and Simon & Schuster won. But we don't necessarily know that Penguin Random House was the second closest bidder; we just know they competed." Tr. 1283:6–21 (Hill). While Dr. Hill also relied on runner-up data, those data were limited to just the acquisitions that the merging parties won for more than $500,000, thereby providing an inaccurate picture of real- world competition in the government's alleged $250,000+ market. Tr. 1284:11–14 (Hill). The runner-up data also do not compare how frequently the two encounter each other in the marketplace overall. Tr. 1283:23–1284:3 (Hill) (explaining that runner up data focused on books won by the parties).

267. The data on which Professor Snyder relies—collected from literary agencies—are superior because they provide insight into not only the winning bids for transactions across the marketplace, but also the runner-up bids and the full set of acquisition formats used to sell books to publishing companies. Tr. 2654:6–15, 2656:15–20 (Snyder). When diversion ratios are measured using Professor Snyder's superior agency data, it becomes clear just how much Dr. Hill's diversion ratios—which rely on his flawed data inputs—overestimate diversion. *See* DX- 436 (using agency data to show most frequent runners-up when PRH or S&S win contracts for over $250,000).

3. The SSA Model Does Not Account For Imprint Competition

268. Because Dr. Hill's SSA analysis relies on market shares, it incorrectly assumes that every pre-merger acquisition involves every publisher—the Big Five plus the other non-Big Five publishers. And it likewise incorrectly assumes that every post-merger acquisition will involve one fewer competitors. That's not the competitive reality. As Professor Snyder explained, in the SSA model, "the merger reduces the number of bidders by one in every case." Tr. 3036:11–12 (Snyder). That's [i]n contrast to the real world—call that big number N. In the real world, agents pick and engage a smaller number. Call it P. And whether there's a reduction depends on the circumstances following the merger. And even if there is, the agent can go to others to replace that bidder. Tr. 3036:13–18 (Snyder).

269. Furthermore, as everyone agrees, the majority of book acquisitions involve bilateral negotiations—which Dr. Hill failed to model at all. Tr: 1611:2–12 (Hill); 1736:16–23 (Hill); *see also supra* FF ¶ 163.

And, even among the subset of books acquired in some auction format, as already shown, Dr. Hill is extremely over-inclusive in assuming that every auction involves every publisher with a represented market share. But he is also grossly under-inclusive in assuming that *only* five (then four) publishers are available as competitive options for any given acquisition. In fact, because agents can separately invite publishers' internal imprints to compete independently for acquisitions, there are more than one hundred competitive options available to agents for any given acquisition. *See supra* FF ¶¶ 198–202. And the merger will not eliminate any of the that imprint-level competition at all. Dr. Hill's model thus errs fundamentally in analyzing competition only at the market share level.

4. *Dr. Hill's GUPPI Calculations Are Marred By The Same Errors As The SSA*

270. In response to Professor Snyder's criticisms of the fit of Dr. Hill's second score auction model, Dr. Hill employed a GUPPI calculation in an attempt to confirm the results of the SSA model. As an initial matter, the GUPPI is not a confirmation device; it is a "screening device" that is "used at the outset" to determine whether a merger should be further scrutinized. Tr. 2636:6 (Snyder). More significantly, though, "[i]t's got the same problems with lack of fit to the industry. It's got the same problems with respect to inputs. It also cannot account for agent behavior. There's no competitor response." Tr. 2635:23–2636:18 (Snyder). As Dr. Hill admitted, GUPPIs are not equilibrium models, which take into account the actions of rivals post- merger. Tr. 3164:23–25 (Hill) (Q. "And the GUPPI models don't assume any competitive response, correct?" A. "That's correct."). Nor did Dr. Hill create a GUPPI calculation for books acquired through bilateral negotiations. Tr. 1736:16–23 (Hill) (Q. "But you do not have a GUPPI for the bilateral negotiation context; correct?" A. "Correct."). And because Dr. Hill did not determine the prevalence of particular acquisition formats in the industry, he was unable to use his format-specific GUPPI results to actually calculate industry-wide price effects akin to what he attempted to do with the SSA model. Tr. 3165:16–3166:20 (Hill) (Q. "And you have not performed any calculation that amalgamates the results of the individual GUPPIs, right?" A. "Correct. . . ." Q. "And you didn't provide any framework for combining those three results?" A."That's fair.").

271. Both the SSA model and the GUPPI calculation, by design, will *always* show some harm when any two rival publishers merge. Tr. 1629:1–5 (Hill); Tr. 2810:25–2811:19 (Snyder). Consistent with that design, Dr. Hill admits that the harm estimated by his SSA model is "more directional than . . . entirely precise." Tr. 1654:5–9 (Hill). He estimated the downward pricing pressure to be approximately 4 percent for PRH and 11.5 percent for S&S, but admitted that the overall harm could be as low as 3 percent. Tr. 1654:14–1655:13 (Hill); Tr. 2802:24- 2803:15 (Snyder) (Hill's average reduction in author compensation is 6.1 percent, which corresponds to $29.3 million in annual harm).

272. As Dr. Hill testified, he relied on the same flawed inputs for his GUPPI calculation as his SSA model. Tr. 1318:2–13 (Q. "How do these inputs compare to the second score auction models?" A. "So they're the same. In the second score auction model, we used market shares to estimate diversion. In GUPPI, we can—we also have a diversion estimate. And then both models take the variable profit margin."). For example, the margins he inserted in his GUPPI calculations used the same inconsistent approach to operating expenses that he used in his initial report—including ongoing operating expenses for PRH and excluding them for S&S. Tr. 1643:5–23 (Hill). Likewise, he used diversions according to overall market share for all acquisition formats for each of his specific GUPPI calculations. Tr. 1318:8–24 (Hill). However, when the GUPPI calculations are corrected using Professor Snyder's inputs, *see supra* FF ¶¶ 260, 267, they suggest harm of less than five percent for both multi-round and single round/hybrid formats, as Dr. Hill admitted. Tr. 3107:7–12 (Hill). The figures fall within the GUPPI "safe harbor," which is designed to acknowledge that even though the GUPPI always predicts harm, mitigating market conditions—like ease of entry and expansion—may make that harm prediction inaccurate. Tr. 1629:6–25, 3109:14–23 (Hill); Tr. 2813:24–2814:10 (Snyder).

IV. COORDINATED EFFECTS

273. Although the government alleges the merger will facilitate coordination among the remaining Big Five publishers, Compl. ¶¶ 52–53, the evidence demonstrated that the market is not conducive to coordination.

274. Dr. Hill admitted that he did not study the likelihood of increased coordination post-merger, is not aware of any current coordination in the industry, and did not quantify any price impact from purported coordination. Tr. 1733:4–15 (Hill). Instead, Dr. Hill speculates that coordination may be more likely because some publishing companies were previously found liable for participating in a conspiracy orchestrated by Apple to raise downstream retail prices of e-books. But Dr. Hill acknowledges that case

found collusion in "a different market." Tr. 1329:4–1330:20 (Hill). Moreover, Random House was not alleged to have been involved in the conspiracy orchestrated by Apple. Tr. 774:14–775:3 (Dohle (PRH)).

275. In particular, this market is characterized by "one-off acquisition processes with many dimensions that are not observable by other rivals," which means there is no ability to "detect and monitor" rivals' adherence to the agreed-upon behavior. Tr. 2638:2–21 (Snyder). It is not enough that the identity of the winner is eventually known, based on public announcements or publication of the book, because the deals are so complex. As Professor Snyder testified, even an agreement to pay advances on a different schedule is not a workable "coordination mechanism," because "that just tells you the intervals over which time advances will be paid out. It doesn't tell you how much." Tr. 2880:14–2881:11 (Snyder).

276. Michael Pietsch (CEO of Hachette), who opposes the merger, admitted that the merger will not change Hachette's bidding strategy for books going forward—Hachette editors will bid as much as they think a book is worth and do not intend to coordinate pricing. Tr. 211:9–13; 217:7–11; 217:21–24; 237:23–238:5 (Pietsch); *see also* PX-2002 (Stehlik (HarperCollins) Dep.) at 135:24–136:2, 136:4–7, 136:9 (Q. "And if the Simon & Schuster/Penguin Random House merger goes through, do you believe it will be any more likely that Morrow Group will coordinate or discuss author advances with other publishers?" A. "No."); [REDACTED]

A. Books Are Non-Homogeneous And Subjectively-Valued

277. Because books are non-homogenous, publishers cannot send or receive price signals based purely on the advance level paid for a book. Dr. Hill agreed that "greater transparency typically makes coordination[] easier because it aids in the monitoring and punishment." Tr. 1329:22–25 (Hill). But the publishing industry is "one of the most opaque industries in terms of acquisition processes to understand why did somebody win, why did somebody lose." Tr. 2881:5–7 (Snyder). Given the complexity of book deal terms and the "multiplicity of dimensions" in deals, signaling to and coordinating on terms with rival publishers would be ineffective and unlikely. Tr. 2881:2–25 (Snyder). Given the subjective and individualized valuation of books and the lack of information available about bidders' identities and offer amounts, it is impossible to send and receive pricing signals from one acquisition to the next. *See supra* FF ¶¶ 104–07.

278. Estimates of potential sales in the P&L are just that: estimates. Editors are "very rarely spot on with those estimations," and tend to skew in a "really wide range." Tr. 918:1–6, 967:22–24 (Tart (PRH)) ("Q. And as you discussed with the Judge, you don't usually get it right, right? A. Correct, it's really a guess."). Although the expected sales are informed by "comp" titles used in the P&L, that number is an "educated guess." Tr. 1971:15–25 (Kim (PRH)).

B. Publishers Compete Over Non-Price Terms

279. Agents negotiate with publishers over terms beyond the advance amount, including payout structure, territorial rights, royalty rates, division of revenue for second serial rights, and other non-price terms. Tr. 2091:10–13 (Wylie (Wylie Agency)); [REDACTED] 66:1–2; PX-2007 (Fletcher (Fletcher & Company) Dep.) at 66:4–5, 66:8.

280. Authors also often choose publishers based on non-price factors like their connection with the editor. *See supra* FF ¶ 253.

281. Professor Snyder testified that the "potential for coordination on these [non-price] dimensions seems to me to be zero, because there are too many dimensions on which to compete. . . . And it's all about is there an effective mechanism that actually results in a bottom line reduction in competition." Tr. 2881:12–25.

C. New Publishers Can Easily Enter The Market

282. As set forth in Part III.B., *supra,* barriers to entry are low, meaning new entry and expansion into the market is easy.

D. The Merger Will Not Facilitate No-Poaching Agreements

283. Nor will the merger facilitate agreements among publishers not to poach authors from each other. Dr. Hill did not even offer an opinion that the merger will facilitate no-poach agreements. Tr. 1733:23–25 (Hill).

284. And as Professor Snyder testified, it is simply unrealistic to expect publishing companies to act against their own interests by refusing to explore opportunities to publish authors published by other companies. Tr. 3016:5–3018:1 (Snyder). In any case, a no-poach agreement among the remaining Big Five publishers would be ineffective in the face of non-Big Five publishers' track record of winning

authors from Big Five publishers. *See supra* FF ¶¶ 170, 171, 178.

E. Downstream Competition Reduces Any Incentive To Coordinate Upstream

285. As set forth above in Part III.C., *supra,* it is uncontested that publishers compete fiercely downstream to sell books to consumers. This downstream competition drives publishers' revenue, and reduces incentives to coordinate upstream, which would constrain their abilities to compete in that downstream market.

PROPOSED CONCLUSIONS OF LAW

286.1. Section 7 of the Clayton Act prohibits a merger only "where in any line of commerce or in any activity affecting commerce in any section of the country, the effect of such acquisition may be substantially to lessen competition, or to tend to create a monopoly." 15 U.S.C. § 18. This standard requires the government to "show that the proposed merger is *likely* to *substantially* lessen competition." *United States v. AT&T, Inc.,* 916 F.3d 1029, 1032 (D.C. Cir. 2019) (first emphasis added). The government also must prove that substantial harm is "imminent." *United States v. Marine Bancorp,* 418 U.S. 602, 623 n.22 (1974); *see FTC v. RAG- Stiftung,* 436 F. Supp. 3d 278, 290 (D.D.C. 2020).

287. The government asserts that § 7 does not require it to prove that a merger is "likely" to cause substantial harm to competition, only that harm "may" occur. Tr. 31:23–32:4 ("The standard here is what may occur, not what is likely to happen."). The law in the D.C. Circuit and elsewhere has been to the contrary for more than 30 years. *See AT&T,* 916 F.3d at 1032; *FTC v. H.J. Heinz,* 246 F.3d 708, 719 n.17 (D.C. Cir. 2001); *United States v. Baker Hughes,* 908 F.2d 981, 985, 991 (D.C. Cir. 1990); *FTC v. Sysco Corp.,* 113 F. Supp. 3d 1, 65 (D.D.C. 2015); *FTC v. Arch Coal,* 329 F. Supp. 2d 109, 115 (D.D.C. 2004); *United States v. Oracle Corp.,* 331 F. Supp. 2d 1098, 1109 (N.D. Cal. 2004). Congress used the term "may" in the statute not to establish a standard lower than "likely" harm, but simply "to indicate that its concern was with probabilities, not certainties," *Heinz,* 246 F.3d at 713 (quoting *Brown Shoe Co. v. U.S.,* 370 U.S. 294, 323 (1962)). The government's effort to apply a lower standard to this merger is baseless.

288. The difference between the D.C. Circuit standard and the government's standard is not just semantics—it is the difference between a concrete, fact-based projection of substantial harm and speculation about the possibility of some harm. By eliminating one market competitor, almost any merger in theory *could* diminish competition in some way. And it is easy enough for the government to speculate that a change in the number of competitors might lead to some "softening" of overall competition that might reduce prices by some unknown amount. But "§ 7 deals in 'probabilities,' not 'ephemeral possibilities.'" *Marine Bancorp,* 418 U.S. at 622–23 (quoting *Brown Shoe,* 370 U.S. at 323). For this reason, "antitrust theory and speculation cannot trump facts" and merger challenges "must be resolved on the basis of the record evidence relating to the market and its probable future," *Arch Coal,* 329 F. Supp. 2d at 116–17, not on the basis of what *might* or *could* occur.

289. In a merger challenge, "the ultimate burden of persuasion . . . remains with the government at all times." *Heinz,* 246 F.3d at 715 (quoting *Baker Hughes,* 908 F.2d at 983). The government must prove "every element" of a § 7 claim, and "a failure of proof in any respect will mean the transaction should not be enjoined." *Arch Coal,* 329 F. Supp. 2d at 116.

290. A three-step proof structure applies. First, the government must prove that the "transaction will lead to undue concentration in the market for a particular product in a particular geographic area." *Baker Hughes,* 908 F.2d at 982. This stage itself includes multiple subsidiary steps. To show undue concentration in a relevant market, the government "bears the initial burden of (1) defining the appropriate product market, (2) defining the appropriate geographic market, and (3) showing that the merger will lead to undue concentration in the relevant product and geographic market." *FTC v. Tronox Ltd.,* 332 F. Supp. 3d 187, 197 (D.D.C. 2018).

291. If the government satisfies those elements, it gives rise to "a presumption that the transaction will substantially lessen competition." *Arch Coal,* 329 F. Supp. 2d at 129; *see also Baker Hughes,* 908 F.2d at 982. The statistical presumption imposes on defendants only a burden to produce evidence showing that market shares alone do not adequately capture themarket's competitive conditions. *Baker Hughes,* 908 F.2d at 991. "[B]ecause the burden of persuasion ultimately lies with the plaintiff, the burden to rebut must not be 'unduly onerous.'" *United States v. Anthem, Inc.,* 855 F.3d 345, 349–50 (D.C. Cir. 2017) (quoting *Baker Hughes,* 908 F.2d at 991); *see Baker Hughes,* 908 F.2d at 981, 989–92 (describing evolution of law away from presumptions and structural analysis toward focus on real-world facts and economic analysis).

292. If defendants surmount the low bar of showing that market-share statistics alone do not prove likely harm to competition, the presumption drops out, and the government must produce "additional evidence of anticompetitive effect" sufficient to carry its burden of persuasion, which again "'remains with the government at all times.'" *Heinz,* 246 F.3d at 715 (quoting *Baker Hughes,* 908 F.2d at 983).

I. THE GOVERNMENT DID NOT CARRY ITS BURDEN OF ESTABLISHING A WELL-DEFINED SUBMARKET

293. The government "bears the burden of proof and persuasion in defining the relevant market." *RAG-Stiftung,* 436 F. Supp. 3d at 291 (quoting *Arch Coal,* 329 F. Supp. 2d at 119). The relevant market is the "area of effective competition" where the defendants operate. *United States v. E. I. du Pont de Nemours & Co.,* 353 U.S. 586, 593 (1957) (quoting *Standard Oil Co. of Cal. v. U.S.,* 337 U.S. 293, 299 n.5 (1949)). "Defining the relevant market is a necessary predicate to finding a Clayton Act violation because the proposed merger must be one which will substantially lessen competition within the area of effective competition.'" *RAG- Stiftung,* 436 F. Supp. 3d at 291 (quotation omitted). "Without a well-defined relevant market, a merger's effect on competition cannot be evaluated," *FTC v. Tenet Health Care Corp.,* 186 F.3d 1045, 1054 (8th Cir. 1999), because the market definition "dictates the analysis of market power and the merger's anticompetitive effects," *RAG-Stiftung,* 436 F. Supp. 3d at 291; *see FTC v.* Freeman Hosp., 69 F.3d 260, 268 (3d Cir. 1995). The government's failure to properly define a market by itself compels rejection of a merger challenge. See, e.g., RAG-Stiftung, 436 F. Supp. 3d at 292; FTC v. Thomas Jefferson Univ., 505 F. Supp. 3d 522, 557 (E.D. Pa. 2020); Oracle, 331 F. Supp. 2d at 1109; United States v. SunGard Data Sys., Inc., 172 F. Supp. 2d 172, 182–83 (D.D.C. 2001); United States v. Long Island Jewish Med. Ctr., 983 F. Supp. 121, 137–140 (E.D.N.Y. 1997).

294. The principal "area of effective competition" between PRH and S&S (at least upstream) is the market for the acquisition of all U.S. trade books, which indisputably is a "well- defined market" for antitrust purposes. FF ¶ 30. But while the government initially claimed that a merger between PRH and S&S would substantially harm competition in that market, it abandoned that claim by the time of trial. FF ¶ 30.

295. The government instead focused on a "submarket" within the broader market. The law recognizes that within a broader market, "well-defined submarkets may exist which, in themselves, constitute product markets for antitrust purposes." Brown Shoe, 370 U.S. at 325.

296. The government intended its submarket to capture only "anticipated top selling books," and it picked an advance threshold of $250,000 to define that submarket for purposes of identifying market shares and proving competitive harm. FF ¶ 31. The government does not claim mathematical precision in that amount, but neither does it disclaim the need for line- drawing altogether: Dr. Hill opined only that "a small change away from [$]250,000" does not make a "significant" difference in his market definition analysis. Tr. (Hill) 1233:17–20 (emphasis added).

297. To the extent the government means to define its submarket by price alone, the proposed market fails—a submarket cannot be defined solely on the basis of price differences among otherwise comparable products. See Brown Shoe, 370 U.S. at 326 ("It would be unrealistic to accept Brown's contention that, for example, men's shoes selling below $8.99 are in a different product market from those selling above $9.00."); Oracle, 331 F. Supp. 2d at 1158 (rejecting government effort to define market as "any sale in excess of $500,000"); In re Super Premium Ice Cream Distrib. Antitrust Litig., 691 F. Supp. 1262, 1268 (N.D. Cal. 1988) (price and quality distinctions "are economically meaningless where the differences are actually a spectrum of price and quality differences"), aff'd, 895 F.2d 1417 (9th Cir. 1990); HDC Med., Inc. v. Minntech Corp., 474 F.3d 543, 547 (8th Cir. 2007); Crestron Elecs. Inc. v. Cyber Sound & Sec. Inc., 2012 WL 426282, at *5-*6 (D.N.J. Feb. 9, 2012); United States v. Joseph Schlitz Brewing Co., 253 F. Supp. 129, 145 (N.D. Cal. 1966). As these precedents indicate, price matters only to the extent it reflects substantive differences among products that cause consumers to treat otherwise similar products differently within their different price categories. In other words, to establish a submarket defined by a price divide, the government must prove that "products across that divide do not compete with each other," Crestron, 2012 WL 426282, at *6, in accordance with all the usual factors applied to identify product interchangeability.

298. The government now seems to agree that a submarket cannot be defined by price alone. Its theory now is that books that yield advances of at least $250,000 generally comprise a qualitatively different category of books than books acquired for lower advances. As the government argued during closing, industry participants describe the "high end" books encompassed by its market as those by "franchise

authors, key authors, giant celebrities." Tr. 3233:17–19 (closing). According to the government, these "[a]nticipated top selling authors are often authors of successful books in the past. They've appeared on best seller lists often. They have a successful track record. They may be recognized with past awards or have notoriety from their social media endeavors." Tr. 3241:10–14 (closing). The government contrasts the high end of "anticipated top selling books" with "midlist authors and midlist titles," which differ from "those at the high end that have a different set of competitive conditions." Tr. 3233:20–24; see Tr. 3173:2–3 (Hill) (describing "market for 50 to 250" as "mid-tier market"; Tr. 3172:17–22 (Court) (referring to "another relevant market of mid-selling books between 50 and 250").

299. The government's market definition theory is similar to the theory rejected by Judge Vaughn Walker in Oracle. In that case, the government tried to define a market "limited to so-called high function [software]" sold by certain vendors, which was supposed to exclude "mid-market software" and other potentially competitive software solutions. 331 F. Supp. 2d at 1158. According to the government's expert economist, "high function" software included "any sale in excess of $500,000." Id. That price threshold, however, swept in many products the market was supposed to exclude. Id. The court thus held that the expert's sales data was "unreliable in establishing a distinct and articulable product market." Id. at 1159. In addition, the court emphasized, the government's expert admitted that the proposed market had "no 'quantitative metric' that could be used to determine the distinction between a high function product and a mid-market product"; instead, the expert simply "kept telling the court that there is 'something different' about the products sold" by certain vendors. Id. That vague assurance was insufficient: "[T]he court cannot delineate product boundaries in multi-billion dollar merger suits based upon the mere notion that there is 'something different' about the merging products and all others, especially when that 'something different' cannot be expressed in terms to make a judgment of the court have meaning. More is required." Id.

300. Much the same analysis applies here, as shown below. First, the government's economist essentially asserts that there is "something different" about books acquired for advances of $250,000 or more, but industry participants in fact recognize no distinctions among books acquired for advances above and below that level. See infra CL ¶ 21. There are certainly differences among books, but the differences do not separate books into distinct price-defined market categories—they at most merely reflect the unexceptionable spectrum of price and quality that exists in any market of differentiated products. Second, the $250,000 quantitative metric fails to distinguish between high-end books and mid-market books even by its own terms. If, as the government contends, such books are distinguished from each other by how often the Big Five acquire, then the proper market boundary would be a $50,000 advance threshold, which is the threshold where the Big Five begin acquiring the clear majority of books. See infra CL ¶ 31. Third, as in Oracle, the government's quantitative metric sweeps in a vast number of "mid- tier" books that its market is supposed to exclude, thereby violating the "narrowest market" rule that governs the market definition analysis, see infra CL ¶ 34.

301. In sum, just as the "sale in excess of $500,000" quantitative metric failed to establish a well-defined market in Oracle, the $250,000 advance threshold fails here as well, as the following sections demonstrate.

A. The Government's Alleged Submarket Does Not Reflect Industry Reality

302. The central issue in defining a product market is drawing a boundary where products outside the market cannot be reasonably substituted for products inside the market. *See* Sysco, 113 F. Supp. 3d at 25. Courts generally use two tests to determine whether the government has established a well-defined market boundary.

303. One test is the multifactor analysis of "practical indicia" identified in Brown Shoe, which seek to account for the "economic and commercial realities" of the industry. FTC v. Cardinal Health, Inc., 12 F. Supp. 2d 34, 46 (D.D.C. 1998). These factors reflect the core premise that "determination of the relevant market in the end is a matter of business reality . . . of how the market is perceived by those who strive for profit in it." Id. (quotation omitted); see Rothery Storage & Van Co. v. Atlas Van Lines, Inc., 792 F.2d 210, 219 n.4 (D.C. Cir. 1986) ("we assume that economic actors usually have accurate perceptions of economic realities"). The factors include "industry or public recognition of the relevant market as a separate economic entity," the "peculiar characteristics and uses" of a product, "unique production facilities," "distinct customers," "distinct prices," "sensitivity to price changes," and "specialized vendors." United States v. H & R Block, 833 F. Supp. 2d 36, 51 (D.D.C. 2011).

304. In addition to the qualitative Brown Shoe factors, courts also often consider a quantitative measure of product substitution known as the "hypothetical monopolist test" or "HMT." See Sysco, 113 F. Supp.

3d at 33. That test hypothesizes that there is only a single seller of all products in the alleged market, and asks whether that seller "could profitably raise prices on those products" without losing customers to substitute goods. Id. at 33–34 (citing Guidelines § 4.1.2).

305. Dr. Hill conceded that the HMT does not operate to draw any meaningful market-defining boundary in this case. According to Dr. Hill, the HMT did not address whether books at different advance levels could be substitutes for each other. FF ¶ 44. He also admitted that the HMT could be used to define any price segment as its own submarket. FF ¶ 44. If the HMT sufficed to define a submarket based solely on price, the government could wield the HMT to cherry-pick a submarket among otherwise identical products merely by identifying some price segment where there was enough concentration to claim a presumption of harm. The HMT is supposed to distinguish different products, not facilitate an infinite set of price-segmented submarkets among the same products. The HMT thus does not provide a sound legal basis for distinguishing books in the $250,000+ segment—or in any other segment—from books acquired in any other range of advances.

306. The factors relevant here are the industry-reality Brown Shoe factors. The evidence underlying those factors is largely undisputed. Nobody in the industry uses the term "anticipated top sellers." FF ¶¶ 87–92. Not only is the phrase meaningless, there is no such substantive category either, certainly not as defined by a boundary anywhere around the $250,000 advance level. Id. No publishing company organizes itself, its imprints, or its personnel around the advance level paid to acquire books. FF ¶ 47. Nobody categorically distinguishes between books that receive advances of $250,000 or more and those that receive lower advances, whether in terms of editorial personnel, editing processes, negotiating tactics, printing services, distribution mechanisms, marketing support, or retailer placement. FF ¶¶ 47–48. No special imprints or divisions cater specially to books that yield advances of $250,000 or more. FF ¶ 48. The $250,000 advance level itself does not separate books or authors according to any special characteristics. FF ¶¶ 75–86. Internal management approval requirement and deal thresholds vary widely, and they are triggered by total deal amounts, not individual title amounts. FF ¶¶ 93–102. In all these respects, the record evidence "failed to demonstrate a consensus among the industry's players regarding the boundaries of the product market." Sysco, 113 F. Supp. 3d at 33.

307. The government asserts two main arguments in response. Neither has merit.

B. The Unsurprising Correlation Between Advances And Expected Sales Does Not Establish A Distinct Submarket

308. The government's first argument is that a distinct submarket for anticipated top-sellers exists because author advances are generally correlated with sales expectations and, therefore, with expenditures on certain publishing services:

Characteristics of Books with Higher Advances

- **Correlated with higher expected sales**
  - > Karp Trial Tr. 458:9 – 14
  - > Pietsch Trial Tr. 110:19 – 111:1
  - > PX 0151 at slide 9
- **Correlated with more marketing support**
  - > Karp Trial Tr. 490:15 – 492:15
  - > Dohle Trial Tr. 843:2 – 10
  - > Solomon Litigation Deposition, April 28, 2022 at 31:3 – 8, 31:10 – 20, and 31:22 – 33:1
  - > Walsh Trial Tr. 1827:10 – 1828:18
- **Correlation between initial print runs and expected sales**
  - > Murray Trial Tr. 1373:21 – 1374:3
- **Correlated with customized contract terms**
  - > Walsh Trial Tr. 1819:25 – 1820:2

12

309. Defendants do not deny the existence of a general, positive correlation for each of these metrics. To be sure, it is not a perfect correlation along any of them, and correlation alone does not establish causation. For example, with respect to marketing, the evidence showed that marketing commitments are not fixed in the contract in conjunction with the advance—marketing expenditures are always determined long after the acquisition (when the advance is determined), and the marketing and sales teams typically do not even know the amount of the advance. FF ¶¶ 49–59. And "glam" promises in the contract have no connection at all to advance levels or expected sales. FF ¶ 63.

310. But, much more important, the general correlation between advances and expected sales and certain publishing expenditures does not prove the existence of a *separate, distinct submarket* for books at any point along the advance-level spectrum. The correlation merely shows that books—like all differentiated products—are valued along a *continuum.* As shown, however, market-defining criteria must do more than reflect a spectrum of price or value among otherwise comparable products in a market—they must establish a lack of substitutability between the products or otherwise identify a substantive distinction among the products recognized by real-world market participants. *See supra* CL ¶ 12.

C. The Government's Alleged "Targeted Sellers" Market Is Not Well Defined

311. The government also asserts a "targeted sellers" or "price discrimination" submarket. Some courts have recognized such markets where, for example, there is a distinctly identifiable group of "core consumers" whose "particular circumstances dictate that a product is the only realistic choice," or who "find a particular product uniquely attractive." *FTC v. Whole Foods Market, Inc.,* 548 F.3d 1028, 1039 (D.C. Cir. 2008) (opinion of Brown, J.). As the *Sysco* court emphasized, this principle is "not without controversy," because taken to its logical extreme, "price discrimination against a single customer might be used to justify blocking a merger." 113 F. Supp. 3d at 39 & n.20. For that reason, it is essential to identify "limiting principles or factors" that allow the court "to distinguish a 'targeted' group of customers from customers in general." *Id.* at 39 n.20.

312. The government invokes a version of the core customer principle here, asserting that the category of franchise, celebrity, and prize winning authors is both easily identifiable and vulnerable to targeted advance decreases because they have unique needs and preferences that only certain publishers can satisfy. According to Dr. Hill, their books "are aimed at a broad market" and they "have more of a taste for strong distribution, strong marketing and a strong reputation." Tr. 1231:13–15. "And similarly, on the supply side . . . the number of publishers that regularly compete to purchase these books is different for authors of anticipated top sellers than for other authors." Tr. 1231:16–19; Tr. 1232:5–8 (Hill) ("[I]f

you're a major political figure and you're having your 15 minutes of fame, you want your book everywhere and get it sold. And you may have different preferences than authors who are doing different things.").

313. In the government's view, the $250,000 advance level captures the distinction between books that require unique services, on the one hand, and books acquired under different competitive conditions where authors have more publishing options, on the other. Tr. 3233:6- 3235:25. The government is wrong in two respects.

1. The $250,000 Advance Level Does Not Reflect Changed Competitive Conditions

314. To prove that the $250,000 advance level reflects the point at which author preferences differ and

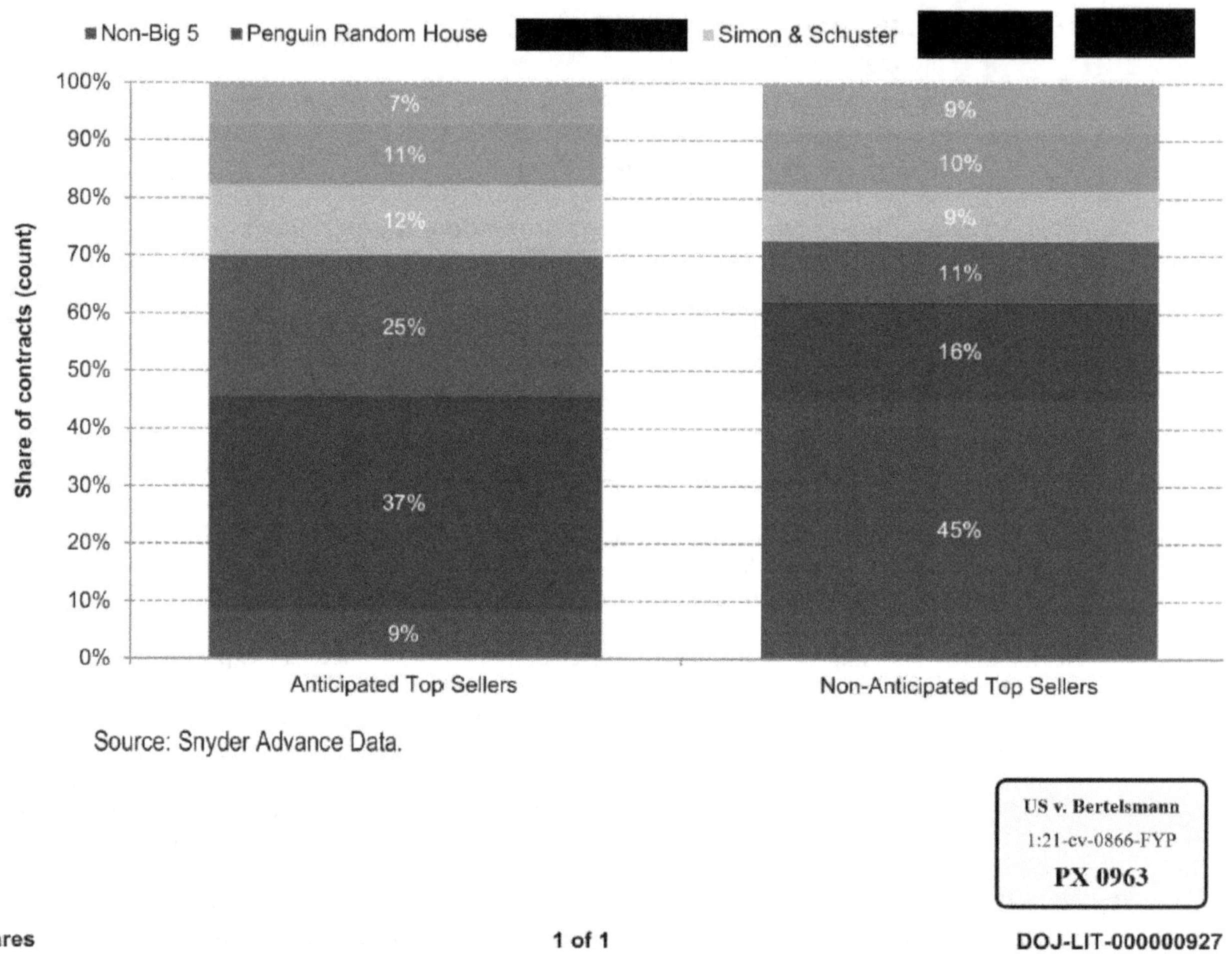

competitive conditions change, the government relies heavily on the following chart:

315. The two bars show market shares above and below the $250,000 threshold, and they appear to suggest that the Big Five have significantly larger aggregate market shares above that threshold. According to Dr. Hill, the market-share difference is important to his market definition because it shows that "the authors of anticipated top sellers are making different choices than other authors," Tr. 1235:20–21, which in his view proves that they have a distinct need for "marketing, distribution and reputation" that he thinks only the Big Five can provide, Tr. 1236:9–10. In addition, the government contends that authors selling books that yield advances below $250,000 have more publishing options and thus cannot be as easily targeted by publishers for advance decreases. According to the government, the chart reflects "data" that shows "a difference in how the firms competed" for books at the "high end" compared to other books. Tr. 3233:17–3234:2 (closing).

316. The data collected in the chart actually prove the opposite. Defendants' expert Professor Snyder analyzed the same data and demonstrated that the Big Five publishers' aggregate market share actually changes materially at about the *$50,000* level, which is therefore where the market-defining boundary

exists under the government's own market-share-based theory. The following chart illustrates that

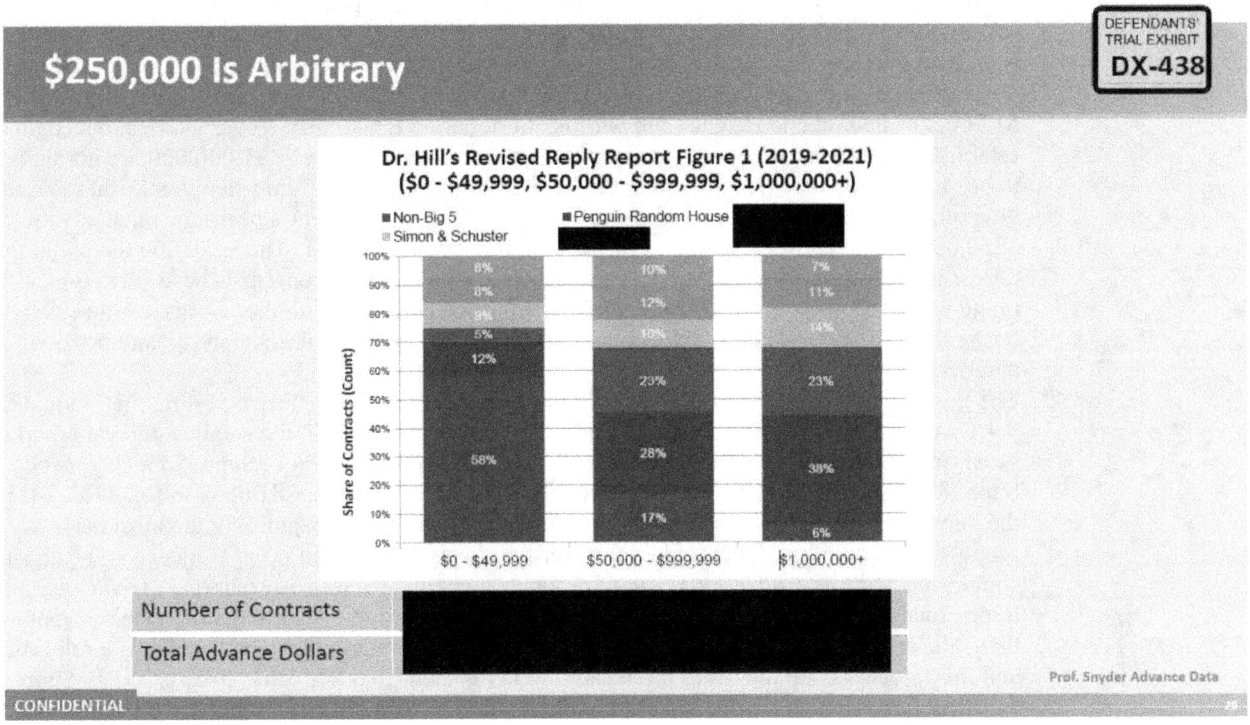

dynamic:

317. By Dr. Hill's and the government's own account, their submarket is properly defined by the advance level at which competing publishers' market shares reveal that "the authors of anticipated top sellers are making different choices than other authors." Tr. 1235:20- 21 (Hill). Those different choices are what allegedly facilitate "targeting" and price discrimination. But on that theory, the chart above shows that the market-defining line exists at $50,000—all authors above that price level are subject to essentially the same alleged threat of targeting, because they all supposedly depend equally on the Big Five to serve their "taste" for certain publishing services. Put differently, any line at an advance level above $50,000 fails to identify the substantive difference in competitive conditions and author "choices" and "preferences" that supposedly justify a distinct submarket.

318. Drawing the line at $50,000, however, results in a submarket that would be substantially less concentrated. FF ¶ 38. Indeed, it is telling that the government declined to measure HHIs using any threshold below $100,000. Tr. 1536:10–15 (Hill). The absence of a clear record shows why courts insist the government prove a well-defined market at the outset: the market definition is essential to correctly analyzing "the merger's anticompetitive effects." *RAG-Stiftung,* 436 F. Supp. 3d at 291.

319. Dr. Hill suggested that even if the $50,000 line accurately captures anticipated top-selling book authors' supposed "preferences" for Big Five publishing services, the $250,000 line still works because there may simply be *another* "submarket" for "mid-tier" books between $50,000 and $250,000. Tr. 3173:1–3174:8; *see* Tr. 3324:12–15 (closing) ("you can have multiple sub markets, and as long as there's one that's a problem and it's material and substantial, a merger should not be allowed"). The separate submarket suggestion is a non sequitur. The problem is not that the government ignored a distinct submarket—it is that the $250,000+submarket the government *did* allege fails to distinguish books subject to one set of competitive conditions from books subject to different competitive conditions. Rather, on the government's own market-share-based theory, books are subject to the *same* competitive conditions all the way down to the $50,000 threshold. Under the government's own market-definition criteria, then, that threshold should determine its submarket.

2. The $250,000 Advance Level Is Not Narrowly Defined Around Franchise, Celebrity, And Prize-Winning Authors

320. The government's alleged market fails in another, independent respect. As noted above, the alleged market principally seeks to encompass books being sold by "franchise authors, key authors, giant celebrities." Tr. 3233:17–19. If the evidence showed anything approaching "a consensus among the

industry's players" (*Sysco,* 113 F. Supp. 3d at 33) as to books likely to perform well, that consensus would center only on books by such franchise, celebrity, and prize-winning authors—authors easily identifiable by their track records or platforms. FF ¶¶ 39–40, 78. According to the government, because such books are easy to identify, they are uniquely subject to "targeting" for a price decrease.

321. The evidence uniformly showed, however, that advances paid for such books generally well exceed $1,000,000, and tend to range in the *millions* of dollars. FF ¶ 40. The government adduced no evidence establishing any kind of industry consensus that books sold for *under* $1,000,000 are normally expected to be "top selling" books, rather than the kind of "mid- selling" or "mid-tier" books that fall outside the government's alleged market. *See supra* CL In fact, the government's position is that advances below $250,000 almost entirely represent very *low* selling books. FF ¶ 41. The $250,000 threshold thus necessarily captures most *mid*-tier books, with any true industry-consensus bestsellers typically in a range well exceeding $1,000,000. The $250,000 price boundary, in other words, captures vastly *more* books than just easily-identifiable, consensus top-sellers by franchise, celebrity, and prize-winning authors.

322. The government's submarket accordingly violates the Guidelines' "narrowest market" rule. Guidelines § 4.1.1 ("market shares and concentration" should be examined "in the smallest relevant market satisfying the hypothetical monopolist test"); *see RAG-Stiftung,* 436 F. Supp. 3d at 292; *Sysco,* 113 F. Supp. 3d at 26–27; *United States v. H&R Block, Inc.,* 833 F. Supp. 2d 36, 58–60 (D.D.C. 2011). Under the narrowest market rule, market definition analysis "begins by examining the most narrowly-defined product or group of products sold by the merging firms to ascertain if the evidence and data support the conclusion that this product or group of products constitutes a relevant market." *Arch Coal,* 329 F. Supp. 2d at 120. If the "most narrowly defined" product group does not qualify as a relevant market, then "the analysis shifts to the next broadest product grouping to test whether that is a relevant market," and the "process continues until a relevant market is identified." *Id.; see Oracle,* 331 F. Supp. 2d at 1158–59 (government's price threshold failed to define "distinct and articulable market" where threshold encompassed products market was supposed to exclude).

323. The government here made no effort to satisfy the narrowest market rule. Its price boundary is not tailored at all to the books and authors it seeks to encompass, i.e., books by franchise and celebrity authors and others with a similar consensus of expected success. The boundary instead indisputably extends the market far more broadly, embracing mid-tier and other books that do not share the easily-identifiable characteristics of books likely to become bestsellers.

324. As explained above, the government cannot justify its failure to prove a proper submarket at the $250,000 boundary by arguing that it could have tried to prove a *different* submarket for the acquisition of books for advances exceeding $1,000,000 or $2,000,000 or $5,000,000. Even if a valid submarket could be tailored to encompass only multimillion-dollar acquisitions of books by franchise, celebrity, and prize-winning authors, the charts above indicate it likely would capture an insignificant number of acquisitions each year—"an insubstantial amount of commerce." *Oracle,* 331 F. Supp. 2d at 1120.

325. The anticompetitive effects analysis in such a hypothetical submarket would also be qualitatively different. The government would have to prove, for example, that S&S competes frequently enough with PRH in such rarefied space for the merger to have materially adverse unilateral effects among the relatively few transactions that exist in that space. Further, authors winning multi-million dollar contracts have much more leverage in bargaining, as shown by the fact that such books are less profitable for publishers. FF ¶ 42. Given that leverage, while such authors can be more easily identified, they likely cannot be easily targeted for price decreases. The government, in any event, did not conduct this analysis, and the government bears the burden of proof. The defendants cannot be required to disprove the likelihood of harm in a market the government did not proffer in the first place.

326. In short, if the government had actually sought to define a submarket by an advance level that reflected its asserted substantive distinctions among books and authors—i.e., either at $50,000 and above to reflect allegedly changed competitive conditions, or at $1,000,000 and above to reflect the easily-identifiable top-selling books—it would have had serious difficulty proving the likely competitive harm needed to block the merger. The Court need not reach such issues, of course, and it lacks the evidentiary record to do so, given the government's litigation choices. The simple, dispositive point is that the government sought to prove harm only in a price-segment submarket that is not properly defined. Its case accordingly fails at the threshold.

D. The Government's Caselaw Does Not Support Its Inadequate Market Definition

327. The cases cited by the government do not justify defining a submarket by a boundary untethered to any

of the substantive distinctions that allegedly warrant a submarket.

328. The best example is the government's lead case, *United States. v. Syufy Enterprises, Inc.*, 793 F.2d 990 (9th Cir. 1986). That case involved alleged monopolization of a local market for the exhibition of "industry anticipated top-grossing films" in theaters in San Jose, California. *Id.* at 994. The Ninth Circuit in that case upheld a jury's market definition finding, because the evidence showed that the already-completed films in the alleged market shared such characteristics, all easily identifiable "ex ante," as "longer playtimes, guaranteed rentals, famous stars, directors and producers, booking in first class theatres, and lucrative terms offered for the pictures by exhibitors." *Id.* at 995. None of those ex ante factors exists here—notably, the *Syufy* court did not define a market based on the price of the movie *script,* which would be analogous to the book manuscripts (sometime uncompleted) at issue here. At the time a manuscript is acquired, no distribution or marketing plan is known, no shelf space is reserved, no copies are pre-ordered, and the author may or may not be famous. The last factor is the only potential basis for an analogy to *Syufy,* because one might compare an expected movie blockbuster with marquee actors to a manuscript by a franchise or celebrity author—even an incomplete manuscript by such an author could generate industry consensus about its expected success. But the government's market is not narrowly tailored to such books.

329. The analysis in cases like *Staples, Wilhelmsen,* and *Anthem* is similar. The courts in those cases used "numerical thresholds to define markets," Tr. 3241:23–24 (closing), but the threshold was never a negotiated price paid for a product or service; it was instead a threshold reflecting a substantive distinction among products and customers the courts were trying to capture. *See FTC v. Wilh. Wilhelmsen Holding ASA,* 341 F. Supp. 3d 27, 55 (D.D.C. 2018) (using number of vessels to distinguish global shipping fleet from smaller regional fleets, based on statistics showing that numeric definition closely aligned with substantive customer needs); *Anthem,* 855 F.3d at 351 (defining "national account" as health insurance for 5,000 employees in more than one state, to distinguish from small intrastate markets); *FTC v. Staples,* 190 F. Supp. 3d 100, 110–21 (D.D.C. 2016) (using $500,000 annual office-supply spend to distinguish large "business to business" customers from individual customers with small retail needs).

330. Another case cited by the government, *O'Bannon v. NCAA,* 7 F. Supp. 3d 955 (N.D. Cal. 2014), *rev'd in part,* 802 F.3d 1049 (9th Cir. 2015), illustrates the same point in a different way. As the government observes, the court there approved a market "in which NCAA Division I schools compete to sell unique bundles of goods and services to elite football and basketball recruits." 7 F. Supp. 3d at 986. The government contends that "elite" athletic recruits are comparable to the elite authors in its submarket—the status may be hard to define, but in both cases "you know when you see it—at least the people in the industry do." Tr. 3242:12–15. But the elite athletic recruits in *O'Bannon* were easily identified by their prior track records of success. Importantly, the *O'Bannon* court did not try to draw a similarly arbitrary numerical boundary to distinguish "elite" recruits from other recruits; rather, the court simply labeled as "elite" *all* the Division I football and men's basketball recruits who received the unique bundle of goods and services. Here, there is no comparable distinction in the publishing services provided to different authors—no category of authors at any price level receives "unique" services. FF ¶¶ 47–59, 63. At best, the government could have tried to define its market by an advance-level boundary that genuinely segregates easily-identifiable "elite" authors, i.e., franchise, celebrity, and prize-winning authors with proven track records and/or existing fan bases. But instead the government drew a $250,000 price boundary that sweeps in many authors who do not share the same characteristics as authors whose books are expected to be best sellers.

331. Neither *O'Bannon* nor any other case cited by the government holds that a submarket can be defined by a quantitative boundary that comes nowhere close to capturing the qualitative distinctions between product or consumer characteristics that allegedly justify a separate submarket.

II. THE GOVERNMENT HAS NOT PROVED THAT THE MERGER WILL SUBSTANTIALLY LESSEN THE VIGOROUS COMPETITION TO ACQUIRE BOOKS BY FRANCHISE, CELEBRITY, AND PRIZE-WINNING AUTHORS

332. Nobody disputes that publishers today compete vigorously to acquire books written by franchise, celebrity, and prize-winning authors. If anything, competition is especially intense for such books, as shown by the lower profits publishers realize on the books with the highest advances. FF ¶ 42. When defined (inaccurately and overbroadly) by the $250,000 price boundary, five large publishers routinely compete to acquire books in this price segment, and another thirty or so compete as an aggregate as

often as three of the Big Five. FF ¶¶ 164–178. These authors have no difficulty triggering interest among one or more of the hundreds of editors working at the publishing imprints that compete for such books. FF ¶ 42.

333. The government did not prove that the merger is likely to substantially lessen that competition by diminishing the incentives or ability of publishers to continue vying aggressively for these most sought-after books.

334. Apart from its distinct "coordinated effects" theory, *see infra* Part III, the government asserts only one theory of likely harm from the merger—the "unilateral effects" analysis prescribed by the Guidelines for analyzing mergers in markets involving differentiated products and individualized bargaining. Guidelines §§ 6.1, 6.2. A unilateral effects analysis does not ask whether or how eliminating one competitor from a market affects the general competitive incentives and conduct of all other competitors. There is no general competitive "softening" or "weakening" analysis. Rather, a unilateral effects claim focuses much more specifically on the elimination of competition *between the merging parties:*

The extent of direct competition between the products sold by the merging parties is central to the evaluation of unilateral price effects. Unilateral price effects are greater, the more the buyers of products sold by one merging firm consider products sold by the other merging firm to be their next choice.

Guidelines § 6.1. And where prices are determined by individual bargaining processes, "[a]nticompetitive unilateral effects in these settings are likely in proportion to the frequency or probability with which, prior to the merger, one of the merging sellers had been the runner-up when the other won the business." Guidelines § 6.2.

335. Applying those long-settled Guidelines principles, the government's complaint focused on the effect of the merger in eliminating "head-to-head" competition. Compl. ¶¶ 9, 42- And every example the complaint listed of such head-to-competition alleged that PRH and S&S were the top two bidders in an auction. Compl. ¶¶ 44–49. The evidence ultimately showed, however, that PRH and S&S are the top two choices for authors in only, at most, about 12 percent of all acquisitions. FF ¶¶ 187–188. As a result, the merger would have no effect on 88 percent of all acquisitions in the government's alleged market. FF ¶ 187.

336. For that reason and others set forth below, the government failed to prove that merging PRH and S&S would cause substantial harm to competition.

A. The Statistical Presumption Has Minimal Force

337. Assuming that a $250,000 price boundary establishes a well-defined submarket of books widely recognized in the industry as likely top sellers, it is not disputed that the merger triggers the purely statistical presumption of harm based on the Herfindahl-Hirschman Index ("HHI") of increased market concentration. But rebutting that presumption is never unduly onerous and it is not dispositive here.

338. The Guidelines expressly warn against overreliance on HHI and other purely statistical thresholds as proof of harm, because the "purpose of these thresholds is not to provide a rigid screen to separate competitively benign mergers from anticompetitive ones." Guidelines § 5.3; *see* Areeda & Hovenkamp ¶ 930 (HHI indices "may have some utility, but only if their significant limitations are kept in mind" and they are used "very tentatively"). The HHI simply identifies concentration levels that "raise concerns," providing "one way" to distinguish between those "mergers unlikely to raise competitive concerns," and those "for which it is particularly important to examine whether other competitive factors confirm, reinforce, or counteract the potentially harmful effects of increased concentration." Guidelines § 5.3. It would contradict the Guidelines' plain terms to give conclusive force to an HHI presumption without closely examining the "other competitive forces" affecting the market. *See* Carl Shapiro, *The 2020 Horizontal Merger Guidelines: From Hedgehog to Fox in Forty Years,* 77 Antitrust L.J. 49, 55- 56 & n.25 (2010) (co-author of 2010 Guidelines explaining that Guidelines adopt "integrated approach" to antitrust analysis that "does not necessarily . . . base predictions of competitive effects primarily on market concentration," reflecting "the gradual decline of the structural presumption").

339. The government suggests that defendants bear the burden of persuasion both to rebut the statistical presumption and to disprove other aspects of the government's prima facie case. That suggestion misconstrues the *Baker Hughes* proof structure. *Baker Hughes* and its progeny make clear that courts ordinarily should not block mergers solely on the basis of market concentration statistics. "The government does not maximize its scarce resources when it allows statistics alone to trigger its

ponderous enforcement machinery." *Baker Hughes,* 908 F.2d at 992 n.13. Put simply, the HHI "cannot guarantee litigation victories." *Id.* at 992; *see New York v. Deutsche Telekom AG,* 439 F. Supp. 3d 179, 206 (S.D.N.Y. 2020) ("[M]arket shares and HHIs establish only a presumption, rather than conclusive proof of a transaction's likely competitive impact."). For that reason, the HHI presumption imposes on defendants only a "burden of producing evidence," not a burden of persuasion. *Baker Hughes,* 908 F.2d at 991.

340. The defendants' evidentiary burden is not "unduly onerous," *Anthem,* 855 F.3d at 349–50 (quoting *Baker Hughes,* 908 F.2d at 991), and it does not require defendants to affirmatively disprove the government's prima facie case. Rather, "the ultimate burden of persuasion . . . remains with the government at all times." *Heinz,* 246 F.3d at 715 (quoting *Baker Hughes,* 908 F.2d at 983). The defendants' burden instead is limited to rebutting the *statistical* presumption: defendants need only produce evidence indicating that market shares, *without more,* "produce an inaccurate account of the merger's probable effects on competition in the relevant market." *Arch Coal,* 329 F. Supp. 2d at 116 (citing *Heinz,* 246 F.3d at 715). After defendants make that minimal evidentiary showing, the statistical presumption itself drops from the case, and the government must rely on "additional evidence of anticompetitive effect" to carry its burden of persuasion, which again "'remains with the government at all times.'" *Heinz,* 246 F.3d at 715 (quoting *Baker Hughes,* 908 F.2d at 983).

341. Defendants may rely on a wide range of evidence to show that market shares alone do not provide all the information required to fully assess the likely competitive effects of a merger. Such evidence may include "the absence of significant entry barriers in the relevant market," *Baker Hughes,* 908 F.2d at 984, and factors like changing market conditions, special features of the product or negotiating process, and the conduct of other firms in the market, *see id.* at 985–86; *Deutsche Telekom,* 439 F. Supp. 3d at 207.

B. The Presumption Is Rebutted Because Evidence Shows That Concentration Statistics Alone Do Not Accurately Predict The Competitive Effects Of The Merger

342. As shown in this section, overwhelming evidence of real-world dynamics shows that market shares alone do not capture the full competitive conditions in the publishing industry and do not accurately predict the merger's likely effects on author advance levels. The statistical presumption thus is rebutted, and the government must carry the burden of proof and persuasion to establish likely substantial harm through "a broader inquiry into future competitiveness" that requires "weighing a variety of factors to determine the effects" of the merger on competition. *Baker Hughes,* 908 F.2d at 984; *see Brown Shoe,* 370 U.S. at 322 n.8 ("only a further examination of the particular market—its structure, history and probable future—can provide the appropriate setting for judging the probable anticompetitive effect of the merger").

1. *Market Shares Alone Are Misleading Because PRH And S&S Are Not Close Competitors—They Are Rarely First And Second Place In Bidding*

343. HHI concentration levels are an especially unhelpful indicator of competitive effects where, as here, the government asserts a unilateral effects claim focused on competition between the merging parties. Market shares are neither a necessary nor sufficient component of such a claim (at least absent a merger creating one entity with monopoly power). For example, a unilateral effects claim requires analysis of the merging parties' margins, *see infra* CL ¶¶ 119–21, so market shares alone cannot accurately predict competitive outcomes.

344. Even more importantly, as explained above, a unilateral effects challenge to a merger under Guidelines §§ 6.1 and 6.2 addresses the effects of eliminating consumers' options *between the merging parties' products or services. See supra* CL ¶ 49. The premise of Guidelines §§ 6.1 and 6.2 is that regardless of market shares, when prices are individually negotiated, a merger can adversely affect only those transactions in which the merging parties were consumers' top two choices: "Anticompetitive unilateral effects . . . are likely in proportion to the frequency or probability with which, prior to the merger, one of the merging sellers had been the runner-up when the other won the business." Guidelines § 6.2. In all other transactions, only two outcomes are possible: either one of the merging parties wins and another publisher was runner-up, in which case the merger has no effect; or another publisher wins, in which case the merger has no effect. Tr. 2662:9–20 (Snyder) (if PRH and S&S are not "winner or runner-up" in acquisitions, "then the loss of head-to-head competition does not generate harm"). It follows that "even if the merging parties had large market shares, if they were not particularly close competitors, then the market shares might overstate the extent to which the merger would harm competition." *Sysco,*

113 F. Supp. 3d at 62; *see Oracle,* 331 F. Supp. 2d at 1122 ("a strong presumption of anticompetitive effects based on market concentration is especially problematic in a differentiated products unilateral effects context"); Herbert Hovenkamp & Carl Shapiro, *Horizontal Mergers, Market Structure, and Burdens of Proof,* 127 Yale L.J. 1996, 2014 (2018) (unilateral effects claims "pose[] a challenge for the structural presumption").

345. In this case, overall market shares are a highly misleading indicator of competitive effects because PRH and S&S are not particularly close competitors. While many publishers view PRH as their "major competition," Tr. 3184:24–25 (Hill), [REDACTED] is and will remain a powerful and aggressive second-place competitor. FF ¶ 186. S&S, on the other hand, is "part of another group," Tr. 3184:24–3185:1 (Hill), each of which represents about 10 percent of the market [REDACTED]FF ¶¶ 165, 186. It is not an especially strong competitor to PRH.

346. The data confirm that PRH and S&S are rarely the final two competitors for books. According to Dr. Hill's own estimates, PRH and S&S are the top two choices in only about 12 percent of all acquisitions in the $250,000+ price segment. FF ¶¶ 177–178. According to Professor Snyder's more robust set of granular, real-world agency data, the two are the top two bidders in only 6–7 percent of such acquisitions, specifically those where an actual winner and runner-up exist and can be identified. FF ¶ 187. Even taking a rough average of the two, some *other* publisher wins or makes the constraining second-place bid in about 90 percent of all acquisitions.

347. The data are confirmed by industry participants who testified that in their many years of experience, very few acquisitions involved a final choice between PRH and S&S. FF ¶¶ 190–196.

348. The government has identified approximately 33 individual transactions where PRH and S&S were the top two bidders, out of thousands over the same time period. FF ¶ 197. Those anecdotes do not show that both parties are *each other's* main competitor, as in *Sysco* and *Heinz,* which is the key to a unilateral effects claim. In fact, the agency data show that when either PRH or S&S wins, the most common runner-up is [REDACTED] DX-436. And when S&S wins, PRH is the third most common runner-up. *Id.* It is of course inevitable that S&S will sometimes lose books to PRH, and vice versa. But those few instances do not trump the full data showing that, proportional to all acquisitions in the government's alleged market, PRH and S&S are rarely the top two bidders.

349. As Dr. Hill acknowledged, this case is unlike *Sysco* and *Peabody,* where the merging parties were not just each other's biggest rivals, but were the top two competitors in the industry. Tr. 3184:20–3185:12. Nor is it like *FTC v. CCC Holdings, Inc.,* 605 F. Supp. 2d 26, (D.D.C. 2009), which involved a 3–2 "merger to duopoly," where the only two remaining firms would control 99 percent of the market, *id.* at 33, rather than the effective 6–5 merger (based on market shares) at issue here. It is also unlike *Heinz,* where the parties were not the top two competitors in the whole market, but they were the *only* competitors in the wholesale market for "second position on the supermarket shelves." 246 F.3d at 717. The merger thus was likely to cause price increases by removing the constant, direct competition between them for that important second-place position. *Id.*

350. The competitive dynamic between PRH and S&S is nothing like the competition at issue in those cases or in any other where a merger has been blocked. And that dynamic certainly is not captured accurately by overall market share statistics.

2. Market Share Statistics Do Not Account For Ordinary Course Business Documents Demonstrating That Industry Participants Do Not Expect The Merger To Reduce Author Compensation

351. Courts routinely rely on ordinary-course business documents from the merging parties and other industry participants to draw inferences about the likely competitive effects of a merger. In *Heinz,* the D.C. Circuit emphasized that "Heinz's own documents recognize the wholesale competition and anticipate that the merger will end it." 246 F.3d at 717. In *Sysco,* Judge Mehta relied heavily on numerous documents from both merging parties and industry analysts expressly recognizing that the two merging parties were each other's strongest competitors, making adverse unilateral effects almost inevitable. 113 F. Supp. 3d at 64–65. And in *Tronox,* the court discussed a plethora of ordinary-course documents showing the parties' recognition that reducing output would be an effective strategy. 332 F. Supp. 3d at 208–10.

352. In this case, there are no comparable documents demonstrating an industry expectation that the merger will reduce author advances. The documents show the opposite. For example, a board-level business-planning document prepared by [REDACTED] demonstrates its expectation that advances will *increase.* FF ¶ This document is especially credible—it reflects an understanding of market conditions

formulated by a highly sophisticated industry actor to guide its fundamental business decisions.

353. PRH's own documents are equally significant. The record includes extensive evidence of PRH's own merger planning documents and analysis, which includes detailed assessments and quantification of every conceivably relevant savings from the merger. Author compensation is a major cost center for any book publisher, and it is thus an enormous opportunity for savings. FF ¶ 120. Yet nowhere does any merger-planning spreadsheet include any entry identifying how much PRH is likely to save in reduced author advances. FF ¶ 120. If increased market concentration were likely by itself to cause a substantial reduction in advances, it is impossible that the company would have overlooked such a significant source of likely savings in its detailed accounting of the merger's expected benefits.

3. Competitive Incentives Arising From Downstream Sales Competition Will Constrain Publishers From Reducing Advances For The Most Sought-After Books

354. The government does not deny that publishers compete fiercely to sell their books to readers downstream. Nor does the government contend that the merger will diminish that strong downstream competition. That continued competition matters upstream because publishing companies only make money by selling books to consumers—if they do not compete aggressively to acquire books from authors, they will lose out in the aggressive competition to sell them to readers. FF ¶¶ 149–153.

355. In short, competitive incentives upstream are driven almost entirely by competitive pressures downstream. And because downstream competition will concededly be unaffected by the merger, increased concentration in the upstream market is much less likely to reduce competition than in other markets lacking such exogenous competitive pressures.

4. Market Share Statistics Do Not Account For Agents' Ability To Influence Competition By Controlling The Bargaining Processes

356. Market concentration statistics also ignore the competitive effect of agents' control over the bargaining process. In markets where all or most participants actively bid in all or most product transactions, the elimination of one competitor might have some quantifiable effect on prices corresponding in some way to market shares. *See infra* CL ¶ 104 (discussing auction model). But in this price segment of the publishing market, very few acquisitions involve multibidder, multiround auctions, and none involves active participation by all market participants. FF ¶¶ 163, 247. Rather, the agent decides which editors to invite, and how many, based on a host of individualized factors. FF ¶ 155. They certainly do not decide whom to invite based on market shares. FF ¶ 155. In fact, it is undisputed that in this price segment, the agent usually chooses to negotiate with only *one* publisher, because bilateral negotiations maximize authors' competitive outcomes. FF ¶¶ 252–253.

357. As a result, even if a merger eliminated one competitor from the overall market, the effect would not be consistent across all acquisitions in accordance with market shares. Eliminating one publisher would have *no* competitive effect on acquisitions to which that publisher would not have been invited or would not have made the winning or runner-up bid. *See supra* CL ¶ 59 (discussing "softening" theory). And even where the publisher might have competed, the agent often can replace the lost bidder. FF ¶ 163. Given agents' control over the competitive conditions applicable in each acquisition, it is essential to analyze the merger's effects at the acquisition level, rather than at the more abstract level of overall market concentration.

358. In emphasizing the significance of agent control over bargaining, defendants do not contend that agents "create competition where none exists," as the government asserts. Indeed, according to the government's own theory, agents do not *need* to create competition—if there are books that the everyone in the industry knows will be top-selling books downstream, they are necessarily books publishers will compete aggressively for, especially given the highly competitive arena downstream. The point is that in deciding which publishers may vie for these most sought-after books, and the rules under which they will compete, agents profoundly affect acquisition-level competitive forces in ways not captured by high-level market concentration statistics alone.

5. Most Acquisitions Are Subject To The Collective Competitive Pressure Of The Entire Market, Not Individual Competitive Threats Measured By The Participant's Market Share

359. The vast majority of acquisitions are either one-on-one negotiations or "best bid" and "better/best bid" formats. FF ¶ 251. In neither situation is the publisher bidding directly against known bidders or bids. The publisher accordingly must bid as if it is competing against the *entire collection* of unknown rivals that *could* submit bids. Market shares have little to do with that competitive threat—because the publisher does not know which or how many rivals it is bidding against, it cannot measure their

competitive threat by their identity or market share. And nobody tracks market shares in the acquisition market, let alone share segments by advance amounts. FF ¶ 45. The publisher instead knows only that it faces the collective threat of the entire market, including any rival that might acquire the book if the publisher does not bid high enough to win it. *See infra* CL ¶ 109 (discussing competitive differences between auction-style bidding against known bids and non-auction bargaining against entire market).

360. Even after the merger, for any given book—especially one that enjoys an industry consensus of likely success—that threat comprises potential bids from many quarters. *See Arch Coal,* 329 F. Supp. 2d at 150 (continued presence of "significant number of competitors" weighs against finding merger anticompetitive). HarperCollins, Hachette, and Macmillan by themselves will pose a major competitive threat in any given acquisition for these most-valued books. In multi-bidder acquisitions where the advance was at least $250,000 and PRH and/or S&S bid, at least one of the other Big Five also bid 90 percent of the time. FF ¶ 195.

361. The next fifteen largest publishers will also continue to be a major threat. They include name brands—like Amazon, Disney, Scholastic, and Norton—that regularly bid in multi- round auctions, pay large advances, and win prominent authors. FF ¶¶ 164–178. In this price segment, these publishers as a group acquired as many or more titles in 2021 than each of Hachette, Macmillan, and S&S. FF ¶ 165. Even without considering continued imprint competition, the merger changes the effective number of potential acquirors for any given book from at least six (the five largest plus all others in aggregate) to at least five. The government cites no case rejecting a merger on the basis of market shares alone where five market participants remained in active competition.

6. Market Concentration Statistics Ignore The Much Broader Competitive Field Created by Imprint Competition

362. Market shares also do not accurately capture market conditions because they do not reflect the full competitive landscape created by internal imprint competition in the industry. FF ¶¶ 198–213. Hachette's imprints compete actively against each other. FF ¶ 198. PRH's imprints have done so for decades. FF ¶ 199. There is also evidence that Macmillan permits imprint competition. FF ¶ 198. Market share analysis must comport with "business realities," *Sysco,* 113 F. Supp. 3d at 37, and imprint competition is unquestionably a reality in the publishing industry.

363. Like Hachette's rule, PRH's imprint competition rule requires the presence of an outside bidder for a multi-round auction, but that rule does not apply to the very common single- round best bid format. FF ¶ 209. And even in multi-round auctions, agents easily avoid the rule by calling for best bids as participants narrow down to just PRH imprints. FF ¶ 209.

364. Even though each publisher's total market share is partly the product of its internal imprint competition, market shares do not capture the effect of imprint competition on overall market dynamics. Relying on market-share statistics would compel the assumption that for each acquisition in this price segment, there are at most six potential bidders for any given book. *See supra* CL ¶ 76. The business reality is completely different. Because of imprint competition, each author with an industry-consensus top-seller in fact has *more than a hundred* potential options for publishing her book. FF ¶ 202. And the merger of PRH and S&S would not reduce the number of bidding imprints at all. FF ¶ 162. The correct question in this case, then, must be whether and how a merger between PRH and S&S would materially affect author advances in *that* competitive landscape—a much broader and more diverse landscape than market shares alone suggest.

7. Planned Expansion By Rivals Makes Static Market Shares An Unreliable Basis For Evaluating The Likely Future Effects Of The Merger

365. Static, backward-looking market shares are an unreliable measure of the future effects of this merger because existing large, successful, aggressive, well-resourced rivals are already planning to spend more money purchasing more books, and there are no objective barriers that will hinder their plans. "Barriers to entry are important in evaluating whether market concentration statistics accurately reflect the pre- and likely post-merger competitive picture." *Heinz,* 246 F.3d at 717 n.13; *see* Guidelines § 5.2.

366. The publishing industry is dynamic and thriving. FF ¶¶ 14–16, 124. Existing large and aggressive rivals are actively planning to exploit the moment by expanding their own retail market shares [REDACTED] FF ¶¶ 125–126. Industry participants also recognize expansion by Amazon as a growing threat. FF ¶¶ 127–128. As Macmillan's CEO testified, Amazon is poised to be a "formidable" competitor "at any given moment." FF ¶ 128.

367. None of the barriers to entry cited by the government would deter these existing well- resourced,

successful, and aggressive publishers from executing on their plans to acquire more of the most sought-after books. They can all handle printing and distribution as they always do, they all have strong reputations and skilled editors, and they all have backlists or other sources of financial support. FF ¶¶ 133–148. The government did not show how any of those factors could hinder the existing growth plans of HarperCollins, Macmillan, and Disney, or how they could impede a juggernaut like Amazon if it decided to expand its acquisitions.

368. The planned growth by these significant rivals makes purely backward-looking market shares an unsound basis for predicting how future book acquisitions will be affected by the merger. By their own design, publishers like HarperCollins, Macmillan, Disney, and Abrams will be making themselves available as options to agents in more acquisitions and they will be willing to pay higher amounts to acquire books. Static market share figures ignore that dynamic.

8. Market Concentration Statistics Do Not Reflect The Natural Experiment Of The 2013 Penguin And Random House Merger, Which Did Not Cause A Reduction In Advances

369. The Guidelines state that a "recent merger[] . . . in the relevant market" can represent a "'natural experiment[]'" that is "informative regarding the competitive effects of the merger" under review. Guidelines § 2.1.2; *see NRDC v. Jackson,* 650 F.3d 662, 665 (7th Cir. 2011) (surest "way to test a model is to compare its projection against real outcomes").

370. In 2013, Random House merged with Penguin. At the time, they were the first and second largest publishers respectively, with a combined market share in downstream trade-book sales similar to that of PRH and S&S today. To the extent those shares correlate with upstream shares, that merger should have caused a reduction in author advances similar to—if not greater than—the reduction the government predicts from the merger of PRH and S&S.

371. The 2013 merger had no such advance-reducing effect. FF ¶¶ 225–239. PRH did not reduce advances paid to authors after the 2013 merger of Penguin and Random House. FF ¶¶ 229–230. Industry participants observed no decrease in advances after the merger, and some recognized an increase. FF ¶¶ 227–229.

372. Professor Snyder confirmed that average advances increased after the merger for all advances below $2 million. FF ¶ 230. Professor Snyder also showed that output of titles acquired for $250,000 or more increased significantly in the years following the merger. FF 235.

373. Dr. Hill contended that advances in the $250,000+ price segment decreased after the merger compared to books with lower advances. FF ¶ 236. But his data showed only a difference in advances between the segments—he did not attempt to show that the difference was *caused by the merger.* FF ¶ 239.

374. The merger did not cause the difference. Market forces did. Starting around the time of the merger, the entire industry began experiencing a precipitous decline in consumer demand for mass-market paperback books. FF ¶¶ 232, 234. PRH was compelled by these market forces to pull back significantly from the acquisition of such books. FF ¶¶ 232, 234–235. But because such books overwhelmingly are acquired for very low advance amounts—well under $250,000—the reduced acquisitions of these books had the effect of *increasing* the average advances for all books under $250,000. FF ¶¶ 232, 237. By contrast, because books produced exclusively as mass-market paperbacks rarely if ever appear among books acquired for $250,000 or more, the decline in acquisition of such books had no effect on advance levels in that price segment, which continued to steadily increase after the merger. Dr. Hill admitted that he was unaware of the industrywide decline in demand for mass-market paperback books and thus did not consider its effect on advances for books above and below $250,000. FF ¶ 239.

375. Further, the average advance reduction Dr. Hill cites for all books with advances of $250,000 did not occur for books in the $250,000 to $2,000,000 range. FF ¶¶ 238. The average reduction for all books includes major changes for a very few books over $2,000,000, which resulted from the timing of these large contracts and the loss of one very high-advance author to competition. FF ¶¶ 233, 238.

376. The natural experiment of the 2013 merger, in short, reveals no evidence that it caused a reduction in author advances at any level, and substantial evidence that it caused or contributed to an increase in advances. At a minimum, the 2013 merger shows why concentration statistics alone do not conclusively prove that a comparable merger is likely to substantially reduce author advances.

C. The Government's Theory Of General "Softening" Of Competition Is Inconsistent With Its Unilateral Effects Claim, Unsupported By The Evidence, And Inadequate To Prove A Likely Substantial Lessening Of Competition

377. Consistent with the Guidelines §§ 6.1 & 6.2, the government's complaint challenges the merger on the

ground that merging two allegedly close competitors will have the "unilateral effect" of allowing the combined entity to reduce prices in transactions with authors for whom the merging parties were the two top choices. To establish that claim, Dr. Hill invoked an auction model that, in his view, proves that the merger would likely reduce advances for those authors. Dr. Hill admits that his auction model analyzes the merger's effects on prices only in auctions where the merging parties are the first and runner-up bidders. Tr. 1299:20–23, 1301:15- 23, 1302:21–1303:6, 1584:24–1585:2, 1585:10–23 (Hill). His auction model predicts an average 6 percent advance reduction for authors contracting with PRH and S&S, which he admitted could be as low as 3 percent. FF ¶ 241. His model did not predict reductions for any other author advances. FF ¶¶ 215, 240.

378. At trial, however, the government developed a different theory of harm, one that predicts the merger will likely reduce *all* author advances through a general "softening" of competition resulting merely from the elimination of S&S as a potential bidder in all acquisitions. Tr. 1489:6–9, 3182:9–3184:19 (Hill). As the Court described the government's softening theory, if the merger eliminates S&S as a potential bidder, advances will be lowered in all auctions—by an unspecified amount over an unspecified period of time—because "there's less competition, so people aren't bidding up the prices." Tr. 2673:9–20 (Court). In other words, "they're just going to win at an earlier point in time because there's less competition." *Id.; see* Tr. 2674:15–18 (Court) ("it turns out you can win at lower levels because there are fewer people bidding now"). The government's theory further posits that "systemically, over time, this results in a general lower level of advances because there are fewer people competing. You don't have to compete as high or as long to get to the end result. The end result is generally lower." Tr. 2676:8–12 (Court).

379. The general softening theory on its face does not apply to best bids or one-on-one negotiations—by far the most common acquisition formats—because neither format involves publishers actively "bidding up prices" and there is no opportunity for bidding to end "at an earlier point in time." But as the Court described it, the government's theory applies "in a one- on-one negotiation, too, because you might come in lower and realize you don't have to go as high because there's less competition out there." Tr. 2676:21–25 (Court); *see* Tr. 3183:3- 3184:19 (Hill) (best bids)). There are multiple problems with this theory.

380. First, while mathematical precision is not required, a merger cannot be blocked unless the government proves that it is likely to cause a *substantial* reduction in competition. *See supra* at Introduction ¶ 1. And the government admittedly never tried to quantify, by any measure, the amount that advances would be reduced by "softening," even though Dr. Hill acknowledged that economic models were available to do so. Tr. 3183:13–21 (Hill). Because Dr. Hill did not use any model to quantify an alleged softening effect, even roughly, it is impossible to predict a "substantial" reduction. In fact, Dr. Hill suggested that any softening effect would *not* be substantial—he testified that other publishers' bidding behavior "may be unchanged or they may have a small diminution in their aggressiveness." Tr. 1489:5–9; *see* Tr. 3183:13–17 ("I have not calculated it, but generally [the second order effect is] significantly lower in most models" (Hill).

381. Second, the merger cannot be enjoined under §7 unless the government proves that likely substantial harm is *imminent. See supra* at Introduction ¶ 1. Yet the government made no effort to prove how long it will take—even in broad-brush terms—for overall prices to be substantially reduced as a result of general "softening." The imminent-harm requirement demands more than a speculative possibility that advances may be reduced by an unspecified amount over some unspecified period of time. The requirement recognizes that dynamic market forces can easily change over time for various reasons, especially when the premise of harm is that market prices will become "substantially" supra- or infracompetitive, inviting expansion, entry, and repositioning.

382. Third, the government's "softening" theory is internally inconsistent. As the Court described the theory, such harm is not caused by publishers consciously choosing to pay lower advances: "You don't say, I'm going to cut advances. You just keep bidding and it turns out you can win at lower levels because there are fewer people bidding now. I think that's the theory." Tr. 2674:15–18. But elsewhere Dr. Hill asserted that "softening" harm would occur *only* because publishers in best bids and one-on-one negotiations would make a *conscious* decision to respond to an *observed* "weakening" of competition by submitting lower bids. Tr. 1269:20–24 ("Third parties may also have a second-order effect, where they observe that the merged firm is less aggressive and so they can also bid as they were before or even bid a little less aggressively because their probability of winning has also gone up."): Tr. 3183:4–6 ("other players seeing that competition has been weakened will, themselves, weaken their competitive

response"); Tr. 3183:25–3184:4 ("It's in the best bids [and] the negotiations, you have that weakening in anticipation. I frequently compete with this person, I don't think they are competing with me anymore, so I'm going to bid less aggressively.").

383. Fourth, assuming the government asserts only the latter position based on Dr. Hill's admissions that conscious competitive responses are required, the softening claim is unsupported by the record. Dr. Hill is not an expert on bargaining in the publishing industry, FF ¶ 215, and thus he is not qualified to opine on how editors determine the amount of their bids in blind formats and bilateral negotiations. He did not and could not explain how often publishers would decide they could safely reduce their offers, or by how much, or under what circumstances. FF ¶ 214–222. His expertise *does* include economic modeling, but he did not invoke that expertise to use readily available models to analyze how the market, as a whole, would respond the elimination of S&S as a separate potential bidder.

384. Nor did industry participants testify that they planned to make lower bids after the merger. To the contrary, publisher witnesses consistently testified that they did *not* plan to bid lower than they otherwise would have, and some made clear that they expected advances to increase. FF ¶¶ 16, 118, 223, 276.

385. Finally, as Professor Snyder explained, eliminating S&S would not give publishers in best bids and bilateral negotiations the incentive or ability to reduce their offers without losing books. FF ¶¶ 220–222. S&S has only about a 10 percent market share. The remaining five bidding sources (and many more counting imprints) that win 90 percent of all acquisitions will remain a collective threat to every publisher in every acquisition—especially for the most sought-after books in the industry. No publisher can be confident that because one 10 percent player is no longer competing, it can safely reduce bids substantially for the highest- demand books without risking loss to one of the many players among the other 90 percent: given S&S's relatively small market share, "you're going to be wrong far more than you're going to be right." Tr. 2677:15–17 (Snyder). And because every book is unique and subjectively valued, and publishers have little to no information about the identity of other bidders (if any) in bargaining, they cannot "learn" from one blind bargaining experience how much value other editors will place on the next entirely unique book. FF ¶¶ 103–107, 221. Whether "you're wrong or right, you're not going to learn and figure out how to do it. This is a very different market from the electronic vehicle market, where you're setting prices and you're getting a variable response in terms of quantity demanded." Tr. 2677:15–17 (Snyder). Indeed, HarperCollins CEO Brian Murray testified he cannot even evaluate bargaining outcomes until year end, when they can be viewed in the aggregate—an aggregate outcome that is "[o]ften" driven by just "two or three books." Tr. 1436:9–21. Such untimely, broad-brush, erratic information plainly does not give allow editors to make sound judgments in real time about how much they can safely reduce specific bids in particular bargaining over unique books against unknown rivals.

386. Further, as Dr. Hill acknowledged, the consequences of any miscalculation are significant: if an editor reduces her offer for one high-demand book and loses it to a rival, the book is lost forever, and the publisher may lose that author—by definition a top-selling author—forever as well. Tr. 1731:17–21 (Hill) (Q. "[Publishers are] also thinking about the fact that if they lose an author at those very high echelons, they also potentially lose their incumbency and the benefit of the future work of those authors; correct?" A. "That's correct."); *see* FF ¶ 222. Dr. Hill did not explain why or how often editors would take such risks, especially given their lack of concrete information about their bidding rivals.

D. The Government's Unilateral Effects Models Do Not Establish That The Merger Is Likely To Cause A Substantial Reduction In Advances

387. Rather than attempting to analyze whether and how eliminating one competitor would influence all acquisitions in the market, Dr. Hill invoked a statistical model that analyzes price effects only in acquisitions where he assumed that PRH and S&S were the two top bidders. FF ¶ 240.

388. To predict those price effects, Dr. Hill's initial expert judgment was that the publishing industry is best modeled using a "second score auction" ("SSA") model. He used the SSA because it was "easy to solve," whereas he could not make other available models work. Tr. 1322:19–1324:1; Tr. 1611:20–1612:15 (Hill) (THE COURT: "So your choice of model depended in part on what the results were and if they just looked right to you?" THE WITNESS: "It depended on whether I could get a model I could solve.").

389. The SSA model attempts to predict how a merger will affect the prices of products sold in one very specific auction scenario, i.e., completed multi-round, round-robin auctions when the merging parties were the two final bidders. FF ¶ 240. The model seeks to determine whether and how eliminating one of

the bidders would affect the outcome of those auctions, and only those auctions. FF ¶ 240–241, 245. Because eliminating one of those two bidders will necessarily affect prices in some of those auctions, the SSA model, by design, will *always* show some harm when any two competitors merge. FF ¶ 241.

390. Although the model itself analyzes only multi-round, multi-bidder formats, Dr. Hill assumed that its projections apply equally to any and all bargaining formats in which PRH or S&S acquires a book. FF ¶ 241. Applying the SSA's results to all such acquisitions, he calculated that advances for all authors who contract with PRH in the $250,000+ price segment would decline approximately 4 percent on average, and advances for S&S authors would decline about 11.5 percent. FF ¶ 241. Those percentages work out to a total predicted reduction of just $29.3 million in total annual author compensation, out of PRH and S&S combined total average annual author compensation of [REDACTED] million in this price segment, and billions of dollars in total author compensation market wide. FF ¶ 241. Dr. Hill conducted no formal analysis of potential effects on acquisitions won by other publishers. FF ¶ 215. He asserted only that the effect would be nonexistent or small. *See supra* CL ¶ 95.

391. For the reasons that follow, the SSA's projections cannot be applied to acquisition formats other than round-robins and the results are unreliable on their own terms.

1. *The SSA Model At Best Applies Only To Round-Robin Auctions And Its Predictions Cannot By Extended To Other Acquisition Formats*

392. Dr. Hill admits that the SSA is designed to model only multi-round, multi-bidder auctions like round-robins. FF ¶¶ 215, 241. He further acknowledges that the SSA was not designed to apply to bilateral negotiations or best bids. FF ¶¶ 243, 245. According to Dr. Hill, other models exist to examine the effects of a merger on such bargaining formats, and he would have preferred to use one of those models. FF ¶ 243. In fact, Dr. Hill tried using several of the models developed to examine bilateral negotiations and best bids, but he was to make them work. FF ¶ 243.

393. Dr. Hill thus returned to the SSA model and simply applied its results to all acquisition formats. FF ¶ 215, 241. The Guidelines specifically warn that different bargaining formats can lead to different competitive effects. Guidelines § 6.2 ("The mechanisms of these anticompetitive unilateral effects, and the indicia of their likelihood, differ somewhat according to the bargaining practices used, the auction format, and the sellers' information about one another's costs and about buyers' preferences."). Dr. Hill nevertheless applied the SSA model's predictions equally across all formats because he assumed that bargaining dynamics and outcomes are functionally similar enough to justify treating them all the same. Tr. 1598:8–11, 1599:18–1600:6 (Hill).

394. Dr. Hill's assumption that bargaining dynamics are ultimately the same regardless of format is contrary to commercial reality. Industry participants do not consider bargaining dynamics in all formats to be equivalent—if agents and authors believed that round-robins maximized their outcome, round-robins would be the norm in the industry, rather than the rarest of all acquisition formats. In fact, agents and authors overwhelmingly use bilateral negotiations and best bid formats because they believe that such formats better serve author interests, including their long-term financial interests. FF ¶¶ 247–256. It makes no sense to assume that the outcome of a round-robin bargaining model can fairly predict the outcome of other bargaining formats that are employed specifically because their outcomes are *not* equivalent to round-robin bargaining.

395. No economic model is a perfect fit for the market it examines. But it must be a close enough fit to generate reliable predictions about real-world outcomes. In this case, the SSA model might reasonably fit the round-robin auctions it is designed to examine, but Dr. Hill seeks to extend the SSA's predictions to acquisition formats utilized precisely because they are *not* round-robins. And the key difference centers on the one point *most important* to the SSA model: the existence of a constraining runner-up bid. The whole point of the SSA model is to examine the effect of eliminating one competitor among multiple buyers that are "bidding up" prices by bidding against known offers. FF ¶ 241. But a central reason agents and authors overwhelmingly eschew round-robin formats is that the dynamic of bidding against known bids often works against author interests, in part because bidding can end too early, before the winner makes its best bid. FF ¶ 249. Agents and authors accordingly use formats that leverage the omnipresent competitive threat of the *entire market*—rather than just a single known bid amount—which generally forces a buyer to make close to its maximum bid up front. FF ¶ 249.

396. The effect of eliminating one competitor from a collective market threat depends on dynamics different from those in play when specific bidders are competing through multiple rounds of known bid amounts. In the latter scenario, eliminating one competitor will cause certain price outcomes to be lower automatically (when the eliminated competitor was one of the two top bidders)—the point of the SSA

and other models is to assess the extent of that effect. By contrast, eliminating one competitor from the market has a completely different effect on best bids and bilateral negotiations.

397. As Dr. Hill himself admits, the questions of whether, and how much, eliminating one competitor affects a given negotiation depend entirely on whether a bidder decides to respond by making a *conscious decision* to "bid less aggressively." Tr. 1270:6–12; Tr. 1302:2–7 ("[I]n a best bids auction, the question is: Has the competition with the field decreased? Do I think there's less competition? And if I know that someone I compete with a lot has been eliminated, I may say: Okay. Now there's less competition. And I can bid less aggressively than I used to."); Tr. 1728:23:1729:1 (Hill) ("it is profit maximizing to take account of the fact that competition has been lessened and to lower your bids, in general, in best bids, and negotiations to be less aggressive"). And Dr. Hill further admits that whether and to what extent a given bidder consciously decides she can safely lower a bid without losing the book can depend on specific context. Tr. 3191:17–22 (Q. "So does that mean that they would bid less aggressively in every blind bid that they entered?" A. "It would depend on the particular subject matter of the book potentially and the editor's perception of how often they compete with Penguin Random House, but, yes, it could affect all blind bid competition."); Tr. 3194:3–8 (Q. "I want to make sure I understand. Are you saying that in every form of acquisition, any type of auction, any type of bilateral negotiation, that it would be economically rational for the S&S editors to lower their bid?" A. "Again, I said, I think, from the beginning, it's going to depend on the specific S&S editor and their perception."). Indeed, Dr. Hill testified that a firm deciding whether and how much to lower bids may even need to "hire a management consultant," who can assess the market conditions and "say, now that this competition is being removed, you can do these different things." Tr. 1595:21–1596:4. Economists likewise understand that bargaining dynamics in non-auction scenarios differ materially, which is why they use models *different* from the SSA to examine outcomes in non-auction bargaining. FF ¶ 243, 245.

398. Dr. Hill nevertheless applied the model's results to justify his opinion that even in bilateral negotiations he "would expect [S&S editors] on average to reduce [bids] by the 11.5 percent" predicted by the SSA model. Tr. 3199:7–11. But he proffered no mechanism by which editors in bilateral negotiations and best bids could safely reduce bids so dramatically without losing acquisitions—acquisitions for the most sought-after books in the industry. Models do exist for predicting how mergers are likely to affect such transactions, but Dr. Hill did not apply any of them here. He instead could only speculate that editors would accurately assess competitive conditions in these transactions and successfully make lower bids without losing any books. But he is admittedly not an expert on bargaining in the industry, FF ¶ 215, and thus is not qualified to opine on how editors make decisions about how much to bid, what kind of competitive knowledge they normally act on, how much they can learn from prior acquisitions, and so on.

399. Dr. Hill's theory might apply intuitively to a high-information, high-liquidity "efficient market," where it is appropriate to presume that market participants can fully and accurately incorporate all publicly available information into pricing decisions. *See, e.g., Coburn v. Evercore Trust Co., N.A.,* 844 F.3d 965, 969 (D.C. Cir. 2016). The publishing industry is, if anything, the polar opposite of an "efficient market": the real-world facts show that because every book is unique and bidding is almost always blind, it is essentially impossible for editors to learn from the acquisition of each unique book how much value other unknown editors place on different books in other acquisition processes. FF ¶ 104–107. Lacking either expertise in the industry or an economic model of bargaining conduct in such conditions, Dr. Hill could only speculate that the results of his SSA model apply equally to all transactions, despite their fundamentally different bargaining dynamics. But "antitrust theory and speculation cannot trump facts." *Arch Coal,* 329 F. Supp. 2d at 116–17.

400. The fact that Dr. Hill could not obtain results from properly applicable models does not justify the use of an inapplicable model. Nor does it justify retreat to unanalyzed and unsupported speculation about how individual negotiators and bidders make decisions about how much to offer when they are competing against the collective threat of the entire industry.

2. *Dr. Hill Used Inappropriate Inputs In Applying The SSA Model*

401. Dr. Hill also used inappropriate inputs in applying the SSA model.

402. First, Dr. Hill used inadequate market-share data to estimate how often PRH and S&S were the top two bidders in the auctions modeled by the SSA. Market shares necessarily reflect only which publisher won a given acquisition, not who was runner up. And they are a product of all acquisition processes, not just auction formats. Professor Snyder's agency data make clear that market shares significantly overstate how often PRH and S&S are actually winner and runner-up. FF ¶ 187.

403. Dr. Hill invoked other data sources to try to confirm the market shares, but those sources did not shed additional light. He compiled and relied on editorial minutes and win-loss data, but neither source identified runners-up, as he admitted. FF ¶ 266. So Dr. Hill simply assumed that when one entity won and the other also bid, the other was runner-up—an unsupported assumption contradicted by the real-world agency data. FF ¶ 266, 267. Dr. Hill also collected runner-up data, but it too was incomplete: it omitted a large portion of the alleged market, and it did not compare how frequently the two encounter each other in the marketplace overall. FF ¶ 266.

404. Second, Dr. Hill used incorrect data to estimate the parties' book-acquisition margins, another essential factor in a unilateral effects claim. Dr. Hill's first report initially included operating expenses in PRH's margins, but excluded them for S&S. After Professor Snyder identified the inconsistent treatment, Dr. Hill chose to estimate profit margins by excluding operating expenses altogether for both merging parties. FF ¶¶ 258–259 .

405. The exclusion of operating expenses results in margins that are significantly inflated and wholly inconsistent with commercial realities. Dr. Hill incorrectly asserted that the model requires the use of only variable costs, but the assertion contradicts his own analysis, which initially *included* operating costs for PRH. FF ¶ 258. If Dr. Hill actually understood that the model prohibits the inclusion of operating expenses in estimated margins, he would not have included them in his model at the outset. In fact, as Professor Snyder explained, what the model "requires" is the use of predicted margins that reflect *the actual margins used by the parties* in their pricing decisions. Tr. 2805:15–2806:9 (Snyder); FF ¶ 263. One might speculate that companies in other industries focus only on variable costs when they calculate expected margins to make offers, but the undisputed evidence here shows that in the publishing industry, operating expenses are considered an essential component of the book-level P&Ls that publishers build to inform their advance offers. FF ¶ 263.

406. By excluding operating costs from margin estimates, Dr. Hill estimates margins that are much higher than the actual margins publishers use to calculate their advance offer. Using the correct margin figures results in much lower predicted advance-reduction harm. FF ¶ 261.

3. Dr. Hill's GUPPI Calculations Do Not Bolster His Inapplicable And Flawed SSA Analysis

407. In response to Professor Snyder's showing that the SSA does not generate reliable predictions of the merger's effects for the vast majority of acquisitions, Dr. Hill employed GUPPI calculations to try to model the effects in bargaining formats other than round-robins. FF ¶ 270. But the GUPPI calculations do not show reliable predictions either.

408. As an initial matter, the GUPPI is not a confirmation device; it is a "screening device" that is "used at the outset" for evaluating whether a merger should undergo more in- depth analysis. FF ¶ 270; *see* Jan M. Rybnicek & Laura C. Onken, *A Hedgehog in Fox's Clothing? The Misapplication of GUPPI Analysis,* 23 Geo. Mason L. Rev. 1187, 1193 (2016) (GUPPI does not provide "a direct indication of the likely effects of a merger"). In addition, "[i]t's got the same problems lack of fit to the industry. It's got the same problems with respect to inputs. It also cannot account for agent behavior. There's no competitor response." Tr. 2635:23–2636:18 (Snyder).

409. Dr. Hill also failed to create a GUPPI calculation—or any model at all—for bilateral negotiations, FF ¶ 270, which his own runner-up data show account for more than 60 percent of all acquisitions for PRH and S&S. FF ¶ 163.

410. Dr. Hill also used the same flawed inputs in his GUPPI calculations that he used in the SSA model. FF ¶ 272. Using Professor Snyder's inputs, the GUPPI calculations in fact suggest harm of less than 5 percent for both multi-round and single-round and hybrid acquisition processes, as Dr. Hill admitted. FF ¶ 272. Predicted pricing pressure below 5 percent falls within the recognized "safe harbor" for the inherently imprecise GUPPI calculation. The Department of Justice typically employs a safe harbor because a GUPPI calculation always shows harm. FF ¶ 272. Where, as here, a GUPPI calculation predicts an effect below 5 percent, it signals that harm is unlikely to result from the transaction and further investigation is not warranted. FF ¶ 272.

III. THE GOVERNMENT DID NOT PROVE THAT THE MERGER WILL LIKELY CAUSE A SUBSTANTIAL DECREASE IN ADVANCES THROUGH COORDINATED EFFECTS

411. The government's final theory of harm is that the merger will lead to "coordinated conduct" among the remaining publishers in the market for anticipated top-selling books.

A. Coordinated Effects Claim Requires Proof That A Merger Increases The Ability Of Industry Participants Both To Reach An Express Or Implied Agreement And To Punish Deviations From The Agreement

412. Coordination—sometimes referred to as "tacit collusion" or "conscious parallelism"—is the process "by which firms in a concentrated market might in effect share monopoly power . . . by recognizing their shared economic interests and their interdependence with respect to price and output decisions." *Brooke Grp. Ltd. v. Brown & Williamson Tobacco Corp.,* 509 U.S. 209, 227 (1993). Coordination between rivals can occur only if the firms can solve what economists call "cartel problems," i.e., the difficulties of maintaining a consensus to take actions that would *not* be in each company's individual interest absent coordination. *See* George J. Stigler, *A Theory of Oligopoly,* 72 J. Pol. Econ. 44, 44–46 (1964). These problems make the "anticompetitive minuet" of tacit coordination "most difficult to compose and to perform." *Brooke Grp.,* 509 U.S. at 227–28.

413. The first step—establishing a tacit consensus—"requires harmonizing the incentives of participating firms and mitigating firm uncertainty concerning rival firms, so that they can effectively coordinate their behavior." *In re B.F. Goodrich Co.,* 110 F.T.C. 207, 295 (1988), *as modified by* 112 F.T.C. 83 (July 18, 1989). The second step—enforcing the consensus—is equally critical, because without "mutual trust and forbearance . . . an informal collusive arrangement is unlikely to overcome the temptation to steal a march on a fellow colluder by undercutting him slightly." *Hosp. Corp. of Am. v. FTC,* 807 F.2d 1381, 1388–89 (7th Cir. 1986). Consequently, firms will not coordinate unless they can "retaliate effectively if and when cheating occurs." *Goodrich,* 110 F.T.C. at 295. To block a merger based on a likelihood of coordinated effects, then, the government must prove that "market conditions, on the whole, are conducive to [1] reaching terms of coordination and [2] detecting and punishing deviations from those terms." *H&R Block,* 833 F. Supp. 2d at 77.

414. The government also must show that the merger is "*likely to change* the manner in which market participants interact, inducing *substantially more* coordinated interaction." Guidelines § 7.1 (emphasis added); *see* Areeda & Hovenkamp ¶ 919 (merger must "change firms' incentives to coordinate their behavior").

B. The Merger Will Not Increase The Likelihood Of Coordinated Compensation Terms

415. During opening argument, the government's sole coordinated effects theory was that the merger would enable other industry participants to "play follow the leader in their choices about how to compensate authors or the terms in which they set for authors." Tr. 49:12–14. To establish that theory, the government acknowledged, it would have to prove that the combined entity would be able to "punish any other publisher it believes is acting as a maverick and not following the industry lead." Tr. 50:13–14.

416. The government at trial did not adduce any evidence showing that the merger will make it easier at all—much less substantially easier—for aggressive market rivals to reach and enforce any implied "follow the leader" agreement on any author compensation terms. Nor did the government fulfill its promise to prove that the combined entity could "punish" any individual "maverick" who deviated from such an agreement. In fact, Dr. Hill admitted that he did not study the likelihood of increased coordination post-merger. FF ¶ 274. Dr. Hill testified only that the existing market is "vulnerable" to coordination, but his key bases for that conclusion were the Ebooks precedent, Tr. 1329:11–13 (Hill), which is irrelevant, *see infra* CL ¶ 136, and transparency of pricing, Tr. 1330:14–122 (Hill), which is demonstrably incorrect, *see infra* CL ¶. He also did not explain how the merger would likely facilitate substantially *more* coordination, which is the relevant inquiry.

417. The merger does not increase the likelihood of coordination over advances and other compensation terms because books are non-homogenous, pricing is non-transparent, and deals are too complex. Tr. 2880:14–2883:12 (Snyder). As the Guidelines state, coordination is likely to succeed only when "each competitively important firm's significant competitive initiatives can be promptly and confidently observed by that firm's rivals," which is "more likely" when price terms "are relatively transparent" and products are "relatively homogeneous." Guidelines § 7.2; *see Arch Coal,* 329 F. Supp. 2d at 141–42, 144–45 (non-transparent pricing leads to "limited, imperfect, and largely unreliable and untimely" information about rivals' conduct, making coordination "unlikely to succeed," and heterogeneity likewise "limit or impede the ability of firms to reach terms of coordination"); *Deutsche Telekom,* 439 F. Supp. 3d at 239; *Oracle,* 331 F. Supp. 2d at 1113. Because advance information is at best sparse and untimely, publishers cannot reliably send or respond to "follow the leader" signals. FF ¶ 277. Likewise,

because books are so differentiated and their value is so subjective, even when a publisher does discover compensation terms, it cannot use that information to make a judgment about what terms to offer a different author for an entirely different book. FF ¶ 277. Relatedly, non-price competition undermines the ability to send and follow signals (since non-price subjects are even more subjective and non-transparent), *see Deutsche Telekom,* 439 F. Supp. 3d at 235, 240, and authors often pursue subjective non-price preferences in acquisitions, FF ¶¶ 279–281. Further, the ease of expansion by smaller firms, FF ¶ 282, precludes larger rivals from enforcing a tacit agreement. *See* Guidelines § 7.2 (coordination less likely when market includes "participants with small market shares and little stake in the outcome resulting from the coordinated conduct, if these firms can rapidly expand their sales in the relevant market").

418. The government speculates that access to printing could be used to punish deviations, but Dr. Hill did not provide any support for that speculation: he did not opine that the merged firm could identify deviations, nor did he opine that it would be profitable for the merged firm to withhold printing as punishment, given the availability of printing services elsewhere.

C. The Merger Will Not Increase The Likelihood That Hachette, Macmillan, And Other Publishers Will Enter Illegal Anti-Poaching Agreements

419. In examining Professor Snyder, the government challenged him to explain why the merger would not make it more likely that rival publishers would enter into illegal and possibly criminal anti-poaching agreements, i.e., CEOs getting "together at dinner on a quarterly basis and agree[ing] that they weren't going to poach each other's top selling authors." Tr. 3017:14–17.

420. As an initial matter, the government adduced no evidence demonstrating that its own witnesses like Hachette's Michael Pietsch or Macmillan's Don Weisberg would be more likely after the merger to risk their personal freedom by entering into such illegal horizontal agreements. Nor did the government show how changing the number of lunch partners from five to four (with, perhaps, a fifth rotating seat for Norton or Disney or Abrams and so on) would make it substantially more likely publisher CEOs would expressly collude over poaching. Even leaving aside the specter of criminal liability, the government adduced no expert or real-world evidence establishing either that publishers would have an economic incentive to avoid poaching the most-sought after authors, or that they would have a mechanism for punishing deviations from such an agreement. As Professor Snyder explained, publishing CEOs would have no economic incentive to avoid poaching because there are too many competitive options for authors and CEOs would "just be hurting themselves" if they did not take the opportunity to contract with a top-selling author. Tr. 3021:6–13.

D. The Ebooks Case Does Not Show That The Merger Will Increase The Likelihood Of Coordination

421. The government's coordination claim relies heavily on *United States. v. Apple, Inc.,* 791 F.3d 290 (2d Cir. 2015), which affirmed a judgment that Apple had orchestrated a conspiracy with certain major publishers to increase *downstream* retail prices of digital books ("ebooks"). The case involved a "hub-and-spoke" conspiracy, organized by Apple at the "hub" and imposed through the "spokes" of its separate contracts with publishers, each of which agreed that Apple's ebook outlet would charge specified retail prices. Although each price agreement individually was contrary to the publisher's financial interest, the court held that Apple induced them all to agree by organizing communications and engineering a collusive understanding that each would accept the same term, thereby promoting their collective long-term interest in avoiding low-price ebooks competition from Amazon. *Id.* at 318 ("Apple consciously played a key role in organizing their express collusion.").

422. The finding that Apple orchestrated a conspiracy concerning downstream price competition for ebooks is not relevant. For one thing, neither Random House nor Bertelsmann was even accused of participating in the conspiracy. The government at trial even congratulated PRH's CEO for having kept Random House out of the conspiracy. Tr. 774:24–775:3. For another, the Guidelines state that prior coordination in a different product market matters only if "the salient characteristics of that other market at the time of the collusion are *closely comparable* to those in the relevant market." Guidelines § 7.2 (emphasis added). The dynamics of retail bookselling are not at all comparable—much less *closely* comparable—to the acquisition of book rights. Unlike retail book prices, book-acquisition pricing is completely non-transparent, subjective, and individualized, precluding monitoring and enforcement of any tacit agreement. FF ¶¶ 77–85; *see supra* CL ¶ 132. Finally, there is no third-party entity here with the incentive and ability to organize collusive behavior to serve its own independent business

objectives.

423. In sum, the government has failed to carry its burden of proving that the merger of PRH and S&S is likely to "substantially lessen competition" in any market.

Dated: August 31, 2022
Respectfully submitted,
By: Daniel M. Petrocelli (appearing *pro hac vice*)
M. Randall Oppenheimer (appearing *pro hac vice*)
O'MELVENY & MYERS LLP
1999 Avenue of the Stars
Los Angeles, CA 90067
Andrew J. Frackman (appearing *pro hac vice*)
Abby F. Rudzin (appearing *pro hac vice*)
O'MELVENY & MYERS LLP
Seven Times Square
New York, NY 10026
Jonathan D. Hacker (D.C. Bar No. 456553)
Julia Schiller (D.C. Bar No. 986369)
O'MELVENY & MYERS LLP
1625 Eye Street, NW
Washington, D.C. 20006
Deborah L. Feinstein (D.C. Bar No. 412109)
Jason Ewart (D.C. Bar No. 484126)
ARNOLD & PORTER
601 Massachusetts Ave., NW
Washington, D.C. 20001
Attorneys for Defendants Bertelsmann SE & Co. KGaA and Penguin Random House LLC
By: Stephen R. Fishbein (appearing *pro hac vice*)
Jessica K. Delbaum (appearing *pro hac vice*)
SHEARMAN & STERLING LLP
599 Lexington Avenue
New York, NY 10022
Ryan Shores (D.C. Bar No. 500031)
Michael Mitchell (D.C. Bar No. 1531689)
SHEARMAN & STERLING LLP
401 9th Street, NW, Suite 800
Washington, D.C. 20004
Rachel E. Mossman (D.C. Bar No. 1016255)
SHEARMAN & STERLING LLP
2828 North Harwood Street, Suite 1800
Dallas, TX 75201
Attorneys for Defendants Paramount Global (f/k/a ViacomCBS Inc.) and Simon & Schuster, Inc.

DEFENDANTS' POST-TRIAL BRIEF

The government's Proposed Findings of Fact and Conclusions of Law (Dkt. 177) confirms the government's failure to prove that the merger between Penguin Random House ("PRH") and Simon & Schuster ("S&S") would likely cause a substantial lessening in competition in any well-defined market.

The government's brief is an anachronism. Before its first thorough modernization in 1992, the Horizontal Merger Guidelines focused principally on concerns about concentration in markets for homogenous products. A central premise of the 1992 Guidelines is that markets for differentiated products require a different analysis, focused less on market concentration and more on the effects of eliminating head-to-head competition between the merging parties. That premise was fortified and elaborated in the current 2010 version. *See generally* Carl Shapiro, *The 2010 Horizontal Merger Guidelines: From Hedgehog to Fox in Forty Years,* 77 Antitrust L.J. 701 (2010) (co-author of 2010 Guidelines).

The government's brief seeks to escape the current Guidelines and resurrect a bygone era. It focuses overwhelmingly on market concentration, insisting that market shares alone conclusively prove the anticompetitive effects of the merger and obviate any need even to *consider* whether head-to-head competition between PRH and S&S tells a different story about competitive effects. The government even embellishes the facts, repeatedly describing the merger as if it were fusing five separate rival publishers into a single dominant collective with a 90 percent share. Contrary to the government's depiction, this merger is a not a "merger to monopoly," or anything like it. The industry will remain rife with competition—there will be four large, aggressive rivals, and numerous other elite publishers that are collectively equivalent to a fifth threat competitor in bargaining for the most sought-after books.

This merger will not substantially lessen competition, but will enhance it. Among other things, the merger will incentivize PRH and S&S's many rivals to compete even harder to win the books readers most want to read. The contemporaneous, ordinary-course business documents of industry participants uniformly recognize that advances will continue to increase, either despite the merger or because of it. When pressed on the stand, witnesses from rival publishers were forced to admit that they either planned no advance reductions, or affirmatively recognized that the merged entity would be able to increase advances, forcing a competitive response that rivals plainly would rather avoid.

The government eventually acquiesces to the Guidelines' focus on head-to-head competition between the merging parties, but its case founders there as well. First, despite what market shares might facially indicate, PRH and S&S hardly ever compete with each other head- to-head as the top two choices for authors. Second, when they do so, it is hardly ever in the form of round-robin-style auctions. Even though such auctions are the rarest form of bargaining in the industry, the government's expert, Dr. Hill, used a model designed specifically to examine only round-robin auctions—its entire point is to examine how a merger affects bargaining outcomes when all bidders know and respond to the amounts they are bidding against, and the merger eliminates one of the bidders. Despite that essential condition of his own model, Dr. Hill extrapolated its projections to the "blind" bargaining formats—bilateral negotiations and best bids—that comprise some 80 to 90 percent of acquisitions, *none* of which involves bidding against known amounts. According to Dr. Hill, the model's projections apply equally to these blind-bidding formats, based entirely on his own speculation that editors and agents would perceive and consciously respond to post-merger changes in competitive conditions as if they *did* know exactly what amount they were bidding against. Dr. Hill cited no authority justifying this extrapolation, conducted no study to support it, and lacked any publishing-industry expertise on which to ground it. And the evidence directly refuted his assumption that a model about known- bid bargaining could apply to blind-bid bargaining: in fact, editors in the latter formats have none of the information they would need to adjust their offers, as he assumes they would. And if they started bidding less aggressively absent accurate information about whom they are bidding against for a book and how much their rivals are valuing it, they would immediately start losing bestselling books and authors. And not just for that acquisition, but likely forever. For these reasons, editors in blind-bargain book acquisitions cannot make the kind of experimental, market-guessing price adjustments that, according Dr. Hill, are the norm in everyday consumer product markets, where goods are commonly priced and sellers *do* have accurate, detailed, timely information on what consumers purchased, how much, and the prices they paid.

Competition matters in both markets, to be sure, but the competitive conditions in the markets are fundamentally different. That difference is precisely why the Guidelines long ago recognized that mergers in markets with individually bargained prices require a different analysis. Dr. Hill's assumption that the dynamics of pricing consumer goods are similar to the dynamics of individualized bargaining for unique, unpublished manuscripts cannot be reconciled with that principle.

The government's brief resists long-settled antitrust principles in another important way. Courts have held for decades that to block a merger, the government cannot just claim harm to competition in general—it must prove that the merger is likely to cause substantial harm to competition *in a well-defined market.* Unless a market is properly identified, the parties cannot know what the relevant market shares are or what specific competitive forces will be affected by the merger.

After incorrectly asserting that market definition is merely one among many "tools" used to assess competitive harm—in fact, it is an essential predicate to any merger challenge—the government searches *within* the market for the acquisition of all U.S. trade books for a "submarket" where it can find an adverse effect on advances. The government claims to have found such a submarket—its own separate economic unit—in the acquisition of books for advances of $250,000 or more. But the proposed $250,000 market-defining threshold does not survive even the government's own justifications for it.

On the one hand, the government contends that the submarket must be defined by the advance level where the Big Five collectively possess the strong majority of market shares, because that difference in market shares ostensibly shows a difference in competitive conditions and a difference in author preferences. The evidence showed, however, that the advance level at which the Big Five possess a strong majority of market share occurs at the *$50,000* threshold. The market-share difference justification thus fails to provide a sound basis for defining a submarket at the $250,000 level.

On the other hand, the government describes its submarket in substance as capturing books by franchise, celebrity, and prize-winning authors, because such books are easily identifiable *ex ante* and there is an industry consensus that they will likely be top sellers. The evidence showed, however, that such books typically receive advances well exceeding $1,000,000. The industry-consensus justification thus also fails to provide a sound basis for defining a submarket at the $250,000 level.

In short, the government's submarket is far too small if it is meant to capture a market- share difference, and far too big if it is meant to capture an industry consensus about certain books easily identifiable as likely bestsellers. Indeed, among the potential market-defining thresholds discussed at trial, the boundary that makes the *least* sense is the $250,000 threshold the government elected to build its case upon. No industry participant recognizes $250,000 as an amount that divides competition for books into separate economic units. No industry participant structures its personnel, imprints, divisions, or services around unpublished manuscripts or proposals acquired at or around that level. No special contract template is triggered. Some manuscripts of course garner advances higher than others—the inevitable result of competition and individualized bargaining over entirely unique products. And higher advances generally reflect higher sales expectations, which sometimes translate into a higher marketing spend, *if* the book still looks like a winner as it nears publication. But a broader market characterized by a predictable *continuum* of different prices for different books is, if anything, the opposite of a market that segregates books into distinct *categories* that operate as separate submarkets.

Because the government did not prove that the $250,000 threshold it used to analyze competitive effects constitutes a well-defined submarket, its challenge fails as a matter of law.

I. THE GOVERNMENT MUST PROVE THAT SUBSTANTIAL HARM IS LIKELY TO OCCUR

The government persists in contending that it must prove only that harm "may" occur, not that the merger is "likely" to cause substantial competitive harm. Dkt. 177 at 28–29 (¶ 40); Tr. 31:23–32:4. That contention ignores three decades of precedent, Dkt. 178 at 116 (Defendants' Proposed Conclusions of Law ("CL") ¶ 2), as well the Guidelines, which require "an assessment of what will likely happen if a merger proceeds," U.S. Dep't of Justice & Fed. Trade Comm'n, *Horizontal Merger Guidelines* § 1 (2010).

Contrary to the government's assertion, the D.C. Circuit in *FTC v. H.J. Heinz Co.,* 246 F.3d 708 (D.C. Cir. 2001), did not adopt an "appreciable danger" standard that is lower than "likely" harm. The *Heinz* court in fact expressly applied the settled "likely" standard. *Id.* at 717 n.13, 719 n.17. The court made only a passing reference to "appreciable danger" embedded within a parenthetical quotation from *Hospital Corp. of Am. v. FTC,* 807 F.2d 1381 (7th Cir. 1986) ("*HCA*"), which the government also misreads. The *HCA* court referred to an "appreciable danger" standard only to emphasize that the government need not show *already- existing* harm from a *consummated* merger. *Id.* at 1389. The government need only show future harm, but to make that showing, the court emphasized, it must prove that "the challenged acquisition is *likely* to hurt consumers." *Id.* at 1386 (emphasis added). The "appreciable danger" of harm standard is thus functionally equivalent to the "likely" harm standard.

Finally, the government cites the D.C. Circuit's statement in *United States v. AT&T, Inc.,* 916 F.3d 1029 (D.C. Cir. 2019), that blocking a merger requires proof that it "is likely to substantially lessen competition, which encompasses a concept of 'reasonable probability.'" *Id.* at 1032 (quoting *Brown Shoe Co. v. United States,* 370 U.S. 294, 323 n.39 (1962)). Contrary to the government's suggestion, that passage does not announce a *lower* standard—it *equates* "reasonable probability" with the "likely" standard, as the court makes clear in the very next paragraph, which repeatedly invokes the "likely" harm standard. *Id.* The Court's meaning is also clear from its citation to *Brown Shoe* footnote 39, which distinguishes "reasonable probability" from an incorrect "mere possibility" standard—a standard akin to the low "may occur" standard the government urges this Court to apply. 370 U.S. at 323 n.39.

II. THE GOVERNMENT'S $250,000 ADVANCE THRESHOLD DOES NOT ESTABLISH A WELL-DEFINED MARKET FOR ANTICIPATED TOP- SELLING BOOKS

In a § 7 case, the government must begin at the threshold by proving the existence of a "well-defined" market where the merger will allegedly harm competition. Dkt. 178 at 118–19 (CL ¶ 8). The government again seeks to evade a long-settled burden, asserting that market definition is merely "one of many tools" used to assess competitive harm. Dkt. 177 at 11. It is more than a "tool"—it is a "necessary predicate" that the government must prove in every case, *FTC v. RAG-Stiftung,* 436 F. Supp. 3d 278, 291 (D.D.C. 2020), because "[w]ithout a well- defined relevant market, a merger's effect on competition cannot be evaluated," *FTC v. Tenet Health Care Corp.,* 186 F.3d 1045, 1051 (8th Cir. 1999). The failure to prove a well-defined market dooms a § 7 challenge. Dkt 178 at 118–19 (CL ¶ 8).

The government here sought to prove harm only in one submarket within the broader market for all U.S. trade books: an alleged submarket for "anticipated top-selling books." Because that phrase concededly has no industry meaning (Dkt. 177 at 62–63 (¶¶ 122–23)), it provides no basis, in itself, for identifying market shares or assessing the merger's competitive effects. The government accordingly invoked a quantitative metric—an advance level of $250,000—to distinguish books within the submarket from other books.

The government concedes that to establish a well-defined market, a price-defined boundary like its $250,000 threshold must have substantive content., i.e., it must either identify a "submarket of core customers" whose needs make certain products subject to differential pricing, Dkt. 177 at 34–35 (¶ 56) (quotation omitted), or it must identify categorical distinctions among products within "a broader range of products," *id.* at 35 (¶ 57). In this case, the government contends that the $250,000 advance level is "an appropriate way to identify targeted sellers." *Id.* at 34 (emphasis and capitalization altered). According to the government, the $250,000 advance level segregates "a group of books whose authors have different preferences and face different competitive conditions." Dkt. 177 at 38 (¶ 64); *see id.* at 39 (¶ 66). The "different competitive conditions" the government refers to are the "significantly different market shares" that supposedly exist below and above the $250,000 advance level. *Id.* at 39 (¶ 66). The same is true for authors' "different preferences": the supposed difference in market share data above and below the $250,000 advance threshold "show that authors of anticipated top-selling books make different choices from authors of other books." *Id.* at 52 (¶ 100); *see* Tr. 1235:17–21 (Hill) (market share difference at $250,000 level shows that "authors of anticipated top sellers are making different choices than other authors"); Tr. 1549:15–18 (Hill) (market shares reflect authors' "revealed choices that they have a stronger preference for the Big 5 vis-à-vis the non- Big 5 than do . . . authors of other books").

The $250,000 advance level does not establish a well-defined market based on different "competitive conditions" and different "preferences" for multiple reasons.

A. The **$250,000 Advance Level Does Not Reflect A Change In Market Shares**

As just shown, the fundamental premise of the government's $250,000 market-defining advance level is that above that level, the Big Five have a strong majority of market shares, and below that level, they do not. That premise is unambiguously false. As defendants have already shown, the market-share dynamic changes at *$50,000.* Dkt. 178 at 128 (CL ¶¶ 31–32). It is accordingly at that level—and only that level—where it is possible even in theory to claim that authors have different "revealed preferences" and that their books are subject to different competitive conditions. In other words, the government's own defense of its quantitative metric proves why that metric does *not* establish a well-defined submarket. And because the government never defined a submarket according to the $50,000 threshold dictated by its own "targeted seller" criteria, the government did not and could not identify any HHI presumption at that level, nor did it conduct any analysis of the merger's competitive effects in a market defined by a $50,000 advance threshold. The government's own flawed litigation choices about what submarket to analyze, and how to define it, compel judgment for defendants.

B. The $250,000 Advance Level Is Not Narrowly Defined To Capture Only Anticipated Top Selling Books

As defendants have shown, the government was obligated to identify an advance level that defined a submarket narrowly enough to exclude books that are not "anticipated top selling books." Dkt. 178 at 131 (CL ¶¶ 37–38); *see United States v. Oracle Corp.*, 331 F. Supp. 2d 1098, 1158 (N.D. Cal. 2004) (rejecting market defined by $500,000 price that included many products that the market is supposed to exclude). The government's brief only confirms its failure to do so.

The government's brief reiterates that the $250,000 advance level is supposed to exclude "'midlist' books," Dkt. 177 at 48 (¶ 92); *see* Dkt. 178 at 120–21 (CL ¶ 13), which are assertedly in a "different business" than the "big mega price books" in the government's submarket. Dkt. 177 at 48 (¶ 92) (quotations omitted). Yet the government itself insists that almost all books below $250,000 sell fewer than 2,000 copies, and the vast majority sell only a few dozen. Dkt. 178 at 24 (Defendants' Proposed Findings of Fact ("FF") ¶ 41). In other words, the segment below $250,000 almost entirely comprises *low* selling books. It necessarily follows that most of the anticipated *midlist* books supposedly excluded from the government's submarket are in fact found above the $250,000 threshold. *Id.* That inference is supported by testimony that only "seven figure[]" advances are considered "high level advance[s]," Dkt. 178 at 24 (FF ¶ 40), confirming that six-figure advances tend to reflect midlist expectations.

Further confirming the overbreadth problem, the government's brief doubles down on its trial theory that books in the alleged submarket can be distinguished from others by the status of their authors as franchise authors, celebrities, or prize winners. Dkt. 177 at 61 (¶ 121). In describing the "special characteristics" that make these books and authors easily identifiable and hence subject to targeting, the government emphasizes that the market comprises authors who "are more likely to have track records of success, reach bestseller lists, and receive awards." *Id.* at 60 (¶ 118); *see id.* at 61 (¶ 121) (books in submarket "tend to be associated with 'franchise' authors, celebrities, or authors with potential to win major literary awards"); *id.* at 62–63 (¶ 123) (citing testimony referring to "franchise authors" and "giant celebrities"). The government also adds emphasis to Carolyn Reidy's assertion that "*books by already bestselling authors and celebrities*" require especially skilled publishing services. *Id.* at 53 (¶ 102) (quoting PX-530 at 2 (emphasis by government)). And the government cites agent Andrew Wylie's statement that "for some books, there is a consensus in advance that a particular book is likely to be successful," *id.* at 47–48 (¶ 91), which Wylie illustrated with the example of a book by widely-acclaimed, award-winning author Sally Rooney.

Books by such franchise, celebrity, and prize-winning authors may fit within the government's substantive market-definition criteria. But the evidence shows that such books are acquired for advances well exceeding $1,000,000, often in the multimillion dollar range. Dkt. 178 at 130 (CL ¶ 36). The government established no connection between such easily- identifiable, industry-consensus top-sellers and advances in the $250,000-$1,000,000 range. To the contrary, its own witness testified that the $100,000-$500,000 advance range includes "first time" authors, authors who are not "celebrities," and authors who do not write "blockbusters." Tr. 1133:15–1134:7 (Weisberg). The $250,000 advance level again fails to establish a well- defined market under the government's own criteria.

The government suggests, however, that determining which books constitute "anticipated top-selling books" depends not on any industry-consensus criteria, but on each individual publisher's decision to pay an advance of $250,000 or more. Dkt. 177 at 21, 41–42 (¶¶ 15, 72, 75). The argument is perfectly circular: its market is well defined, the government says, because any book acquired for an advance of $250,000 is automatically a book within its submarket, and any book acquired for less is automatically outside its market. If the government's approach were right, its 32-page discussion of market definition would be largely meaningless: the fact that publishers choose to pay advances of $250,000 or more for certain books would be enough, by itself, to put those books in the submarket the government seeks to define.

More to the point, the government's approach is contrary to law, including the precedent the government presses most heavily, *Syufy Enterprises v. American Multicinema, Inc.,* 793 F.2d 990 (9th Cir. 1986). In *Syufy,* the court upheld a submarket of "*industry* anticipated top-grossing films," which were all completed films defined by characteristics that made them identifiable and distinct "ex ante." *Id.* at 994–95 (emphasis added). The court thus required exactly the kind of industry-consensus criteria the government says are not required here. Similarly, the court in *FTC v. Sysco Corp.,* 113 F. Supp. 3d 1 (D.D.C. 2015), upheld a market definition defined by a quantitative metric because the evidence "demonstrate[d] a consensus among the industry's players regarding the boundaries of the product market." *Id.* at 33. As Judge Mehta warned, unless a court applies substantive "limitations" on an alleged price-discrimination market, the government could define a market around a single customer (here, seller). *Id.* at 39 n.20. The government's circular theory that the submarket is properly defined by whatever any one publisher decides to pay for a book implicates precisely that concern.

As Judge Mehta recognized, the correct way to determine whether the government has established a well-defined "targeted sellers" market is to apply the same objective criteria courts always apply in market definition analysis. *Id.* at 40. Those criteria do not support the government's effort to draw a price-defined submarket at the advance threshold of $250,000.

C. Practical Indicia Do Not Provide Any Basis For Distinguishing Books Acquired For $250,000 Or More From Other Books

As already shown, if there is any industry consensus around objective criteria for identifying, *ex ante,* books likely to be top sellers, those criteria point only to books acquired for advances well exceeding $1,000,000. The government made no effort to identify a price level reasonably tailored to capture those books and exclude midlist and other books. Nor did the government attempt to establish that advance levels in that untested market would be adversely affected by the merger.

The only market the government did try to identify and analyze was defined by the $250,000 advance threshold, but as the trial made clear, nobody in the industry recognizes that threshold—or anything close to it—as distinguishing one category of books from another for separate competition. Dkt. 178 at 124 (CL ¶ 21). Just as "[e]vidence of industry or public recognition of the submarket as a separate economic unit matters because we assume that economic actors usually have accurate perceptions of economic realities," *United States v. H & R Block, Inc.,* 833 F. Supp. 2d 36, 53 (D.D.C. 2011), the converse must be true as well: the complete absence of *any* industry recognition that books acquired for advances of $250,000 or more constitute "a separate economic unit" constitutes strong evidence that no such separate unit exists.

The government's contrary argument relies chiefly on the premise that the industry does recognize a correlation between advances and anticipated retail sales. Dkt. 177 at 47 (¶ 89). The government then spends many pages trying to show that advances correlate with increases in marketing and other services publishers provide to top-selling books. But as defendants have already shown, a certain degree of correlation between expected sale, advances, and publishing services is not evidence that the industry separate books into *different categories* at any particular advance level. Dkt. 178 at 125–26 (CL ¶¶ 24–25).

If anything, the correlations cited by the government *refute* its premise that the publishing industry treats manuscripts acquired for advances of $250,000 or more as a "separate economic unit" from other manuscripts. According to the government, this case differs from *In re Super Premium Ice Cream Distribution Antitrust Litig.*, 691 F. Supp. 1262 (N.D. Cal. 1988), because in that case, the lower priced ice cream competed with the premium ice cream and thus could be substituted for it if premium prices were increased. *Id.* at 1268. The government says that here, if a "hypothetical monopsonist" reduced high advances, no author would turn to an even lower advance as a substitute. Dkt. 177 at 35–36 (¶ 58). The government is right about that much, which establishes only the circularity and uselessness of the "hypothetical monopsonist test" ("HMT") in this context. *See infra* at 14–15. During closing, however, the government distinguished *Super Premium* in a different way, asserting that the ice cream types there competed with each other, whereas here "authors at high end and low end" are "not competing against each other." Tr. 3324:20–21.

The argument is instructive. Authors do, of course, compete with each other to sell their books to publishers. And as the government's closing argument suggests, a central aspect of the market definition analysis is whether the $250,000 line separates authors and books into *distinct spheres of competition,* where books above the line largely do not compete with books below the line. Not one industry witness testified that the $250,000 threshold distinguishes books in that way. Neither that advance threshold nor any other is used to divide books into different bargaining processes or distinct categories of editorial, marketing, printing, or other services. Some books of course are acquired for advances higher than others, and some books that show a promise of success as they near publication obtain more sales, marketing, and publicity support. Dkt. 178 at 29–31 (FF ¶¶ 52–58). But the evidence is undisputed that publishers generally do not commit to marketing spends when they acquire a manuscript—marketing is determined months or years later, when the book is completed and nearing publication, and sales agents are receiving early reactions. *Id.* at 29–30 (FF ¶ 53). In all events, no evidence shows that industry participants divide books by advance amounts and place those that garner advances for, say, $150,000 into a different economic unit than books that garner advances for $400,000 or $600,000 or $800,000. The evidence is uniformly to the contrary. *Id.* at 26–27 (FF ¶¶ 47–48).

The only real-world evidence cited by the government that even *mentions* the figure $250,000 is the various deal-approval thresholds used by some publishers for corporate governance purposes and the multiple categories of concluded deals reported in Publishers Marketplace. Dkt. 177 at 30 (¶ 65). But the government admits that these thresholds are only for "deals," not for individual books. *Id.* They thus do not reflect *any* assessment that $250,000 per book is a meaningful *advance* threshold. And the thresholds at which different publishers require approvals vary widely. Dkt. 178 at 44–45 (FF ¶¶ 94–95). The $250,000 threshold sometimes used for approving and reporting deals has no more significance than any of the many other thresholds used for the same purpose.

D. The HMT Does Not Identify A Substantively Distinct Submarket

The government asserts that because a price-segmented submarket defined at the $250,000 advance level "formally passes" the HMT—which nobody disputes—the market is properly defined. Dkt. 177 at 46 (¶ 86). As noted above, the government asserts that the HMT properly defines a market because if a hypothetical monopsonist reduced advances within any given price segment, no author would reject the reduced advances for *even lower* advances. *Id.* at 35–36 (¶ 58). To state the argument is to refute it. As Dr. Hill admitted at trial, the HMT's operation would justify a submarket within *any* price segment along the advance continuum. Tr. 3173:7–13 (Hill) (THE COURT: "Well, the hypothetical monopsonist test would work on any of these levels except maybe the very lowest ones because self-publishing isn't really an alternative for most books, right?" THE WITNESS: "I would say it does."); Tr. 1548:3–7 (Hill) (Q. "[Y]ou're not claiming that your hypothetical monopsonist test required you to choose 250- or any other specific advance level as a cut-off, correct; that we agree on?" A. "Correct."). $500,000 to $505,000. Each segment would "formally" satisfy the HMT for the same reasons the $250,000 does: if a hypothetical monopsonist reduced advances within the segment, no rational author would respond by substituting lower advances or self-publishing. As Professor Snyder observed far too generously, a test that validates any price-defined market at any advance threshold is "not much of a test." Tr. 2831:19–20. Indeed, it is not a "test" at all.

III. THE PURELY STATISTICAL HHI PRESUMPTION IS REBUTTED HERE

A. The Presumption Does Not Shift The Burden To Defendants To Prove The Absence Of Competitive Harms

The government contends that under the *Baker Hughes* three-step proof structure, the purely statistical presumption is by itself "usually outcome-determinative." Dkt. 177 at 67–68 (¶ 130). That contention is refuted by *Baker Hughes* itself, which strongly condemned reliance on market concentration statistics, without more, as the basis for blocking a merger. *United States v. Baker Hughes, Inc.,* 908 F.2d 981, 992 & n.13 (D.C. Cir. 1990); *see United States v.* Gen. Dynamics Corp., 415 U.S. 486, 498 (1974) (although "market share and concentration" can be "of great significance," they are "not conclusive indicators of anticompetitive effects").

It is likewise inconsistent with Baker Hughes to say that the government may buttress its purely statistical case by sprinkling in additional evidence of alleged harm and then force defendants to rebut the presumption by affirmatively disproving the government's additional evidence. That approach would effectively shift the burden of persuasion to defendants, contrary to Baker Hughes. Heinz, 246 F.3d at 715. Defendants' sole burden instead is to produce evidence showing that market-share statistics alone "give an inaccurate account of the merger's probable effects on competition." Id. at 715 (cleaned up). And defendants need only identify facts adequate to "cast doubt[] on the persuasive quality of the statistics to predict future anticompetitive consequences." Id. at 715 n.7 (emphasis added).

The government cites several district court cases holding that the presumption was not rebutted. But in those cases, the concentration statistics alone gave rise to a much stronger inference than exists here—in many, the post-merger HHI would have been more than double the post-merger HHI of 3111 here. Several cases are addressed at Dkt. 178 at 142 (CL ¶ 64), others include:

- FTC v. Wilh. Wilhelmsen Holding ASA, 341 F. Supp. 3d 27 (D.D.C. 2018): merging parties occupied the "number one and number two market positions," represented each other's "primary competition," and together would control almost 90 percent of the market, with the next closest competitor at 4 percent, resulting in post-merger HHI of 7214. Id. at 60, 62, 63.
- United States v. Aetna, 240 F. Supp. 3d 1 (D.D.C. 2017): merging parties were "close competitors," and in vast majority of counties, merger would create HHI exceeding 5000, with outright monopoly in some counties. Id. at 42–43.
- FTC v. Staples, Inc., 190 F. Supp. 3d 100 (D.D.C. 2016): merging parties were the first- and second-largest suppliers, with the third company having less than one percent of the market, resulting in a post-merger market with HHI of 6265, reflecting just "one dominant firm with a competitive fringe." Id. at 128, 136.
- United States v. H & R Block, Inc., 833 F. Supp. 2d 36 (D.D.C. 2011): merging parties were two of three largest providers, which collectively accounted for 90 percent of market, resulting in a post-merger HHI of 4691. Id. at 44, 72.
- FTC v. Libbey, Inc., 211 F. Supp. 2d 34 (D.D.C. 2002): merging parties were first- and third-largest providers in a market of four, resulting in a post-merger HHI of 6241. Id. at 39, 50–51.
- FTC v. Swedish Match N. Am., Inc., 131 F. Supp. 2d 151 (D.D.C. 2000): merging parties were first- and third-largest sellers, resulting in post-merger HHI of 4733. Id. at 153–54, 166–67.

The market-share statistics here are nothing like the statistics in those cases. But of course every case ultimately must be examined on its own facts and merits. And whatever was true in those cases, the record here—as shown below—includes vastly more than enough evidence to "cast doubt[] on the persuasive quality of the statistics to predict future anticompetitive consequences." Heinz, 246 F.3d at 715 n.7.

B. The Evidence Casts Serious Doubt On The Reliability Of Market Shares As Conclusive Proof Of Competitive Harm

4. *The Government Wrongly Focuses On The Big Five's Collective Market Share*

In attempting to show that concentration statistics alone conclusively prove the merger's anticompetitive effects, the government principally focuses on the market shares of the Big Five publishers as a collective. According to the government, the Big Five publishers are "the main competitors" in the government's alleged submarket, because they collectively have approximately 90 percent of the market, and elite publishers like Norton, Abrams, Scholastic, Disney, and others collectively share about 10 percent of the market. Dkt. 177 at 73 (¶ 140); see Dkt. 178 at 70 (FF ¶ 166). The government then spends many pages reciting evidence that the Big Five publishers have certain advantages over most small publishers.

The entire discussion misses the point. This merger is not a "merger to monopoly," leaving only a single entity—"BIG FIVE PUBLISHING, INC."—with a 90 percent share and a smattering of scattered, feeble fringe competitors. The merger instead will leave four large and aggressive rivals with 90 percent of the market competing for the most sought-after books—inaddition to the merged entity, there will be HarperCollins with [REDACTED], Macmillan with[REDACTED], and Hachette with [REDACTED] . PX-963. And they would all face additional powerful competition from rivals in the remaining 10 percent, many with storied legacies, strong reputations, and skilled editors, with author and title lists to match. Dkt. 178 at 33, 36–37 (FF ¶¶

Each of the advantages the government cites to distinguish the Big Five are rooted in the simple fact that the Big Five are, to state the obvious, the five biggest publishers. Their backlists are "just money," id. at 62–63 (FF ¶ 144) (quoting Walsh), as DOJ essentially admits, Dkt. 177 at 76 (¶ 147). Money and scale might allow the Big Five to hire extensive sales forces and marketing teams and to negotiate advantageous agreements with retailers, but they say nothing about the quality of the non-Big Five's publishing services. The government's expert admitted that he has not studied publishers' capital constraints or non-Big Five publishers' funding. Dkt. 178 at 35 (FF ¶ 67) (quoting Dr. Hill). And the government itself acknowledges that scale is a main reason the Big Five win more high-end books. Dkt. 177 at 73–74 (¶ 142) (quoting Cheney: "I think the non-Big 5, you know, are just not going to play in that sandbox too many times. They don't have the same scale."); id. at 79–80 (¶ 152) (citing Big Five's "resources" and "scale"). DOJ also cites reputation as a Big Five advantage, id. at 79 (¶ 151), but there can be no doubt that many elite smaller publishers and new entrants have stellar reputations, as evidenced by their impressive title and author lists. Dkt. 178 at 27, 55 (FF ¶¶ 69, 146–47). 65, 70–74). Those facts alone may not fully determine the competitive effects of the merger, but neither does the government's misplaced focus on the Big Five's collective market share.

The Guidelines make clear that the merger's competitive effects depend not on market concentration alone, but on whether elimination of head-to-head competition between the merging parties will result in harm to authors. Guidelines § 6.2 ("Anticompetitive unilateral effects" are "in proportion to the frequency or probability with which, prior to the merger, one of the merging sellers had been the runner-up when the other won the business."); id. § 6.1 ("Unilateral price effects are greater, the more the buyers of products sold by one merging firm consider products sold by the other merging firm to be their next choice."); see also Sysco, 113 F. Supp. 3d at 61 ("Courts have recognized that a merger that eliminates head-to-head competition between close competitors can result in a substantial lessening of competition."). The government itself ultimately recognizes that analysis of head-to-competition—not a simple recitation of market share statistics—is central to evaluating the merger's competitive effects. Dkt. 177 at 124, 125 (¶¶ 246, 248).

Market shares are not an adequate measure of that head-to-head competition. See Sysco, 113 F. Supp. 3d at 62 ("[E]ven if the merging parties had large market shares, if they were not particularly close competitors, then the market shares might overstate the extent to which the merger would harm competition."); Dkt. 178 at 78 (FF ¶ 189). That is why the HHI presumption has little force in unilateral effects cases: the presumption arises solely from concentration statistics and does not reflect in any way the extent of pre-merger or post-merger head-to-head competition. See Christopher Conlon & Julie Holland Mortimer, Empirical Properties of Diversion Ratios, 52 RAND J. Econ. 693, 694 n.1 (2021) ("Researchers have pointed out concerns with using concentration measures or functions of market share to capture the strength of competition. For example, such measures . . . do not capture the closeness of competition when products are differentiated."). For this reason, Professors Hovenkamp and Shapiro—the latter of whom co-authored the Guidelines and frequently appears as an expert for the government—warn that a unilateral effects claim "pose[s] a challenge for the structural presumption." Herbert Hovenkamp & Carl Shapiro, Horizontal Mergers, Market Structure, and Burdens of Proof, 127 Yale L.J. 1996, 2014 (2018). The government accuses defendants of misciting Professors Hovenkamp and Shapiro for the proposition that the statistical presumption does not apply at all in unilateral effects cases, Dkt. 177 at 68–69 (¶ 132 n.6), but neither defendants nor the professors said any such thing. The point, rather, is that because unilateral effects focuses on a factor—head-to-head competition—that market shares do not always capture accurately, the presumption should be especially easy to rebut in unilateral effects cases. As the professors observe, the presumption persists only insofar as its "basic contours . . . have been adapted to unilateral effects analysis, where the primary inquiry is not based on overall market concentration but rather on the relative degree of substitution." Hovenkamp & Shapiro, supra, at 2014; see generally Shapiro, supra at 707–08 & n.25 (2010 Guidelines approach "does not necessarily . . . base predictions of competitive effects primarily on market concentration," reflecting "the gradual decline of the structural presumption"). The government makes no effort to "adapt" the presumption here—it simply cites the Big Five's collective market shares and tries to declare victory.

The government's emphasis on the Big Five's collective shares not only ignores head-to- competition, but also misstates the competitive effect of the smaller publishers. As defendants have shown, the non-Big Five publishers actually pose a competitive constraint on the final advance amount in 23 percent of auctions, which is how often non-Big Five publishers win or come in second in auctions with multiple bidders in the alleged submarket. Dkt. 178 at 80 (FF ¶ 166). The government continues to assert that the 23 percent figure does not accurately represent the relative size of non-Big Five publishers, Dkt. 177 at 83 (¶ 156), but the argument misses the point: the 23 percent figure does not address the relative size of non-Big Five publishers, but how often they serve as a competitive constraint on other publishers by either winning or providing the runner-up "price to beat." The government's misunderstanding of the figure shows just how misleading market shares can be. It also starkly illustrates the challenges editors face in interpreting competitive threats in blind-bidding formats, as discussed below, infra at 31–34. If the government and its expert, after studying the market as extensively as they have in this case, can err so obviously in relying on market shares to infer that non-Big Five publishers pose a meaningful threat in only one out of ten cases, it is impossible to see how editors—who do not even possess that market share information, misleading as it is—can be expected to make accurate assessments of the competitive threats they face .

5. *<u>PRH And S&S Are Not Close Head-To-Head Competitors</u>*

The government ultimately recognizes that the question of competitive harm principally focuses on the frequency with which PRH and S&S compete head to head as the top two bidders for books in the alleged submarket. To prove the extent of that competition, however, the government begins not with the readily available data addressing that question, but with the very few anecdotes it could find illustrating specific instances of head-to-head competition between PRH and S&S. Dkt. 177 at 126–30 (¶¶ 252–55). These examples—which amount to just over 30, Dkt. 178 at 141 (CL ¶ 63)—are a tiny fraction of the 1200 or so acquisitions that Dr. Hill admitted occur each year in the alleged submarket. Tr. 1588:20–25. Defendants have never denied that some amount of such head-to-head competition occurs. Of course it does—in any merger, the merging parties will have engaged in some amount of direct competition. The relevant issue is how much, and what is its effect on market-wide competition. Here, as Dr. Hill admitted at trial, market shares indicate that PRH and S&S should be the top two bidders in, at most, only 12 percent of acquisitions. Dkt. 178 at 77 (FF ¶ 187).

Because such head-to-head competition between PRH and S&S is so rare, the government now seeks to retreat from Dr. Hill's admission, asserting instead that the various diversion ratios that Dr. Hill calculated are the proper measure. Dkt. 177 at 136 (¶ 267). But diversion ratios do not, alone, identify the frequency with which the merging parties actually meet head-to-head as the top two bidders—the fact most essential to evaluating the unilateral effects of a merger. For example, market shares—the principal basis on which Dr. Hill calculated diversions—necessarily identify only who won an acquisition, not who was runner-up. And Dr. Hill admitted that two of his other methods likewise did not identify who the runner-up bidder was, while the third provided no information for acquisitions between $250,000 and $500,000. Tr. 1283:6–21, 1284:11–14, 1712:20–23, 1696:13–1697:3, 1698:18–1699:7. None of his diversion analyses, in short, provides adequate information about runner-up bidders, a fact essential to determining how often PRH and S&S were winner and runner-up to each other. It is irrelevant that his diversion analyses "all point in the same direction," Dkt. 177 at 138 (¶ 275), because they all fail to establish the most important fact: the identity of runner-up bidders. The government cannot escape Dr. Hill's own acknowledgment, based on more than diversions alone, that PRH and S&S are the top two bidders in, at most, just 12 percent of acquisitions.

Finally, the government's assertion that "diversion from S&S to PRH indicates that PRH is S&S's closest competitor," Dkt. 177 at 136 (¶ 267), is belied by Dr. Hill's own analysis of the agency data. Defendants' trial exhibit DX-436, which is an exhibit from Dr. Hill's own expert report, shows that when S&S won a book in the government's alleged submarket, [REDACTED] Dkt. 178 at 141 (CL ¶ 63); DX-436. Dr. Hill's own analysis shows a stark divergence between what happens in the real world and what a market-share approach suggests.

6. *Static Market Shares Fail To Account For Rivals' Planned Expansion*

Because the government's analysis relies on static market shares, it cannot adequately account for future expansion or entry in the market—very little of which is needed to actually replace any potential lost competition. The government agrees that future expansion or entry of other firms into the relevant market can mitigate anticompetitive effects. Dkt. 177 at 83–84 (¶ 157). But the government wrongly asserts that expansion or entry matters only if defendants prove that it will be induced by the merger. Id. at 93 (¶ 178). The D.C. Circuit recognizes that even "a firm that never enters a given market can nevertheless exert competitive pressure on that market," such that even "the threat of entry" (or expansion) can rebut the statistical presumption. Baker Hughes, 908 F.2d at 988; see Heinz, 246 F.3d at 717 n.13 ("threat of outside entry can significantly alter the anticompetitive effects of the merger"). There is ample evidence in the record that existing, well-resourced rivals are already planning to exploit this moment of growth in the industry to expand their own market shares. Dkt. 178 at 57–58 (FF ¶¶ 124–28). There is also indisputable evidence of recent, significant entry by aggressive new firms that are spending heavily to acquire books in the government's proposed market. Id. at 59–60 (FF ¶¶ 129–32).

This entry and expansion are more than sufficient to fill any "competitive void" resulting from the merger. Dkt. 177 at 83 (¶ 157) (quoting United States v. Anthem, 236 F. Supp. 3d 171, 222 (D.D.C. 2017)). PRH and S&S are the top two bidders in only 12 percent of acquisitions, supra at 22, which means that only 120 to 145 acquisitions per year might be affected by the merger. See Tr. 1588:20–1589:11 (Hill). Even assuming that those few transactions will be affected adversely by the merger (which defendants dispute), very little expansion by existing rivals or entry by new rivals would be needed to offset that small effect. The data show that other publishers have the capacity to counteract any advance decreases because they do not always acquire the maximum number of book deals they could for $250,000 or more. See DX- 369 (showing other publishers do not always acquire up to their capacity); see also Tr. 2826:20- 2827:12 (Snyder). In other words, they are able to expand, and the record shows they are ready to as well. [REDACTED] Dkt. 178 at 57 (FF ¶ 126). Macmillan's CEO testified that his company plans to spend more on author advances in coming years, and HarperCollins' CEO has publicly stated that his company intends to bid more aggressively. Abrams also intends to grow its business. Id. at 57 (FF ¶ 125).

7. *Market Shares Fail To Account For Agents' Role In Driving Competition*

Because static market shares reflect only prior wins, they could have meaning in themselves only to the extent all publishers participated in all past acquisitions and will all participate again in all future acquisitions post-merger. In that scenario, market shares alone might be instructive as to how eliminating one participant will affect future acquisitions. The assumption does not hold, however, because literary agents indisputably control the basic structure of bargaining—they decide who will receive a manuscript, who may bid, and what bargaining format applies. Dkt. 177 at 21–22 (¶¶ 18–19); Dkt. 178 at 65–67 (FF ¶¶ 154–58). The evidence shows that agents rarely select multi-bidder, multi-round auction formats. Dkt. 178 at 101 (FF ¶ 251). The evidence also shows that agents never invite all potential market participants to engage in an acquisition, and that agents do not select invited participants based on their market shares. Id. at 66, 68 (FF ¶¶ 155, 163). Agents' control over bargaining participation shows why market shares alone do not conclusively determine the merger's competitive effects. Id. at 144–45 (CL ¶¶ 71–73).

Contrary to the government's caricature, defendants do not argue that agents hold "all of the bargaining leverage," Dkt. 177 at 106 (¶ 205), or that agents could use their leverage to unilaterally eliminate any harm the merger might cause. Id. at 104 (¶ 199). Defendants' point is simply that agents' control over the bargaining process gives them great influence over the competitive conditions that govern any given acquisition—including who is actually competing—and that market shares alone do not account for that influence.

8. *Market Shares Do Not Capture The Competitive Significance of Imprint Competition*

Market share statistics also fail to capture intra-publisher competition, which dramatically broadens the competitive landscape. Hachette permits active competition among its imprints. Dkt. 178 at 80–81 (FF ¶ 198). PRH has done so for decades. Id. at 81 (FF ¶ 199). The evidence suggests that Macmillan does, too. Id. at 80–81 (FF ¶ 198). Any analysis that fails to take this competition into account fails to comport with "business realities." Sysco, 113 F. Supp. 3d at 37.

The government does not deny that intrafirm imprint competition is a reality in the publishing industry, but contends that the Court must disregard it because the government could not find another merger decision relying on a similar industry reality. Dkt. 177 at 111 (¶¶ 213- 14). But the absence of such decisions suggests only that intrafirm competition is not a commercial reality in most other industries—not that it must be ignored where it is a standard practice. The reality in the publishing industry is there are more than one hundred imprints to which agents can submit books to drive competition. Market shares alone falsely suggest a much more limited field of potential bidders for a book. Dkt. 178 at 147 (CL ¶ 79).

9. *The 2013 Merger Did Not Cause A Decrease In Author Advances*

The government very much wants this Court to ignore the 2013 merger of Penguin and Random House. Dkt. 177 at 121 (¶ 238). But the Guidelines and the caselaw make clear that such "natural experiments" are directly relevant in merger analysis. Dkt. 178 at 149 (CL ¶ 84); see FTC v. Foster, 2007 WL 1793441, at *38 (D.N.M. May 29, 2007) ("'Natural experiments,' i.e., evidence that the posited harm has occurred under circumstances similar to the proposed transaction, are relevant to merger analysis."). The government downplays the 2013 merger because under its own theory, that merger—which involved similar downstream market shares—should have caused the kind of advance reduction the government projects here. Dkt. 178 at 149 (CL ¶ 85).

It did not. Following the 2013 merger, output of books acquired for $250,000 or more increased, and PRH did not reduce advances. Rather, average advances increased for all advance segments under $2 million. Id. at 92–97 (FF ¶¶ 225–39). Dr. Hill's contrary results are explained entirely by broader market dynamics he did not consider and by normal variations in a few of the very highest-end, multimillion dollar advances. Id. at 97 (FF ¶ 239).

The outcome of the 2013 merger "natural experiment" is strong evidence that this merger, too, will have no adverse competitive effect. And it is conclusive evidence that market share statistics should not be the sole basis on which to assess the competitive effect of this merger.

10. *Ordinary Course Documents Show No Expectation Of Decreased Advances*

The government contends that defendants' "intent" with respect to author compensation is irrelevant. Dkt. 177 at 119 (¶ 234). As an initial matter, the cases the government cites hold only that the government need not prove an intent to lessen competition—not that the merging parties' intent is categorically irrelevant. See United States v. E.I. du Pont de Nemours & Co., 353 U.S. 586, 607 (1957) ("It is not requisite to the proof of a violation of [§] 7 to show that restraint or monopoly was intended."); United States v. Bazaarvoice, Inc., 2014 WL 203966, at *11 (N.D. Cal. Jan. 8, 2014) ("Intent is not an element of a Section 7 violation.").

In fact, § 7 cases consistently rely on contemporaneous, ordinary course documents showing the merging parties' and other industry participants' understanding of the market conditions and their expectations of the effects of the merger. See, e.g., Heinz, 246 F.3d at 717 (noting that "Heinz's own documents recognize the wholesale competition and anticipate that the merger will end it"); Wilhelmsen Holding ASA, 341 F. Supp. 3d at 63 (considering strategic planning email, among other ordinary course documents, stating that if defendant were to "[a]cquire WSS chemical business, take away [its] main competitor and win back this space fully for [Drew Marine], this could increase our ability to charge far better prices and win across all segments"); Sysco, 113 F. Supp. 3d at 64–65 ("The FTC presented ordinary course documents, from both Defendants and third parties," demonstrating that the merging parties were "particularly close competitors"); FTC v. Tronox Ltd., 332 F. Supp. 3d 187, 208–10 (D.D.C. 2018) (considering ordinary course documents showing parties' recognition that reducing output would be an effective strategy).

The same types of ordinary course documents in this case demonstrate that neither the merging parties nor their rivals are expecting reduced advances as they make their most important business decisions. Dkt. 178 at 54, 55 (FF ¶¶ 118, 120). These documents hold far more weight than the government witnesses' made-for-litigation statements, which are plainly motivated by rival publishers' fear that the merger will result in increased competition, which in turn will compel them to increase their bids to compete against the combined company. Id. at 55 (FF ¶ 119); see United States v. AT & T Inc., 310 F. Supp. 3d 161, 211 (D.D.C. 2018) ("Caution is . . . necessary in evaluating the probative value of the proffered third-party competitor testimony."), aff'd, 916 F.3d 1029 (D.C. Cir. 2019). In fact, the government cites no contemporaneous statements from rival publishers indicating any expectation of decreased advances. Rival publishers who wanted to acquire S&S themselves actually admitted that they did not consider the potential for decreased advances in constructing their proposals for the acquisition of S&S. See Dkt. 178 at 56 (FF ¶ 122) (describing Murray and Pietsch testimony).

IV. THE GOVERNMENT'S UNILATERAL EFFECTS ANALYSIS DID NOT PROVE THE MERGER IS LIKELY TO CAUSE SUBSTANTIAL HARM

To prove that the merger is likely to cause "substantial" harms, the government touts Dr. Hill's opinion that, post-merger, "advances for anticipated top sellers will decline by about 4% for PRH authors, and about 11.5% for S&S authors." Dkt. 177 at 15. According to the government, this percentage reduction translates to a per capita $44,000 average reduction for PRH authors in the alleged market, and $105,000 for S&S authors, Dkt. 177 at 140 (¶ 279), for an aggregate average reduction of $29.3 million annually, Dkt. 178 at 97 (FF ¶ 241).

The government reached its overall quantitative harm projection through a two-step analysis. First, its expert Dr. Hill ran his "second-score auction" model to predict the percentage price reduction for PRH and S&S authors in acquisitions subject to the model—i.e., "rounds" or round-robin auctions—where he predicted PRH and S&S would be the top two bidders. That model generated predicted 11.5 and 4 percent reductions for S&S and PRH authors, respectively.

Second, Dr. Hill then applied those specific percentage reductions across *all* acquisitions won by either PRH or S&S. According to Dr. Hill, after the merger, S&S and PRH editors would all perceive a reduced threat of competition. *Id.* at 88 (FF ¶ 216). Assuming—with no evidence—that editors would perceive reduced competition roughly consistent with the market-share-based assumptions he used in the SSA model, Dr. Hill then opined that S&S editors would respond to the elimination of competition from PRH by reducing their average offers in all formats by about 11.5 percent, without losing books, and that PRH editors would similarly respond to the merger by reducing their average offers by about 4 percent, again without losing books. Tr. 1312:18–25, 3198:9–13, 3199:7–11 (Hill); Dkt. 178 at 90–91 (FF ¶ 221).

Both steps in the government's method for estimating harm to PRH and S&S authors are fundamentally flawed. First, even accepting the SSA model's predicted average advance reductions for round-robin auctions, such auctions are a rare acquisition format, and there is no basis for extrapolating the projection harm in those formats to the other, non-round-robin formats that comprise 80 to 90 percent of all acquisitions. In fact, Dr. Hill admitted that he is unaware of any other economist who has used a second-score auction model to examine other bargaining formats. Dkt. 178 at 90 (FF ¶ 245). Second, the model itself is flawed; correcting its errors further diminishes the projected harm into statistical insignificance—certainly not enough to show a "substantial" competitive harm.

A. The Government's Attempt To Extrapolate The Results Of The SSA Model To Formats Not Modeled By The SSA Is Insupportable

The government admits that the SSA model, by its terms, applies only to "a specific form of negotiation," i.e., one "where the price obtained through the negotiation is set by the next best alternative." Dkt. 177 at 140 (¶ 279) (citing Tr. 3098:10–3100:3 (Hill)). As Dr. Hill put it in the cited testimony, the SSA analysis "is strategically equivalent to a specific form of bargaining in which buyers play suppliers off against each other," until the second-best bidder cannot match the highest bid. Tr. 3099:14–20; *see* Tr. 1297:8–18 (Hill) (equating SSA to "open outcry auction," where "there's an object and I say, I'll pay $10 and you say, I'll pay $15, and we keep bidding" and "eventually, at some point, everybody drops out but the winner"). All agree that the "specific form of bargaining" modeled by the SSA is rounds or round-robin bargaining, and that such formats comprise only about 10 to 20 percent of all acquisitions. Dkt. 178 at 98–99 (FF ¶¶ 243–47). The remaining 80 to 90 percent are either bilateral negotiations (the majority) or "best bid" formats, neither of which involves agents "playing off" editors against each other through known bidding levels until the second-to-last bidder drops out. *Id.* at 99 (FF ¶ 247). Dr. Hill nevertheless extrapolates the SSA's "known bid" results to all "blind bid" formats and projects that advances for all acquisitions will be reduced, on average, by 11.5 percent (S&S authors) and 4 percent (PRH authors), for an overall average of 6 percent.

Dr. Hill's overall harm projection thus depends entirely on his ability to justify extrapolating the SSA's percentage harm projection to the 80 to 90 percent of formats that, unlike round-robin formats, do not involve bidding against a known bid amount. It is not enough to say that the SSA reveals a "directional" effect of decreased advances—the SSA will *always* show a negative price effect. *Id.* at 97 (FF ¶ 241). What matters is how much effect it shows and how far it applies. If Dr. Hill's extrapolation cannot be justified, his harm projection is reduced by at least the 80 to 90 percent attributable to projected effects in blind-bidding formats.

Dr. Hill's extrapolation is indefensible. In round-robin auctions, the SSA predicts a price reduction automatically, as a mathematical matter: whenever the merging parties are the final two bidders, eliminating one of them will necessarily cause a price reduction in certain cases (depending on the amount of the third-place bid). The SSA calculates the mathematical effect of eliminating one of those final two bidders. In that situation, the effect occurs without conscious response by either party, as Dr. Hill observes: "In rounds auctions you don't really need to take any action. You continue to bid the way you did before, and some auctions will just end before they otherwise would have, and you will pay less." Tr. 1729:2–5.

In blind formats, by contrast, Dr. Hill concedes that the effect, if any, of eliminating one competitor occurs through an entirely different mechanism: editors must *perceive* diminished competition and react to that perception by *consciously* reducing the amount of their offers. In "the best-bid setting or negotiations," Dr. Hill speculates, "you're thinking about how often is this other party competing with . . . me," and you "us[e] your knowledge of the past to make a prediction about how likely it is they will compete with you" for a given book. Tr. 1728:3–20. In Dr. Hill's view, if an editor thinks she was "competing frequently with an opponent in . . . negotiations and they are removed from the competition," it would be "profit-maximizing" for her "to take account of the fact that competition has been lessened and to lower [her] bids, in general, in best bids, and negotiations to be less aggressive." Tr. 1728:21–1729:1. As a result,

Dr. Hill imagines, "when there's a change in competition . . . because of a merger," editors "will modify their behavior accordingly." Tr. 1730:2–4; *see* Tr. 3183:1–3184:4 (Hill) ("It's in best bids and negotiations, you have that weakening in anticipation. I frequently compete with this person, I don't think they are competing with me anymore, so I'm going to bid less aggressively."); Tr. 3201:25–3202:1 (Hill) ("information is learned, people react, and they adjust their behavior").

There is no basis for Dr. Hill's speculation that S&S and PRH editors will have either the incentive or the ability post-merger to reduce their offers in blind bargaining formats at all, let alone by an average of 6 percent. First, Dr. Hill is not an expert on bargaining in the publishing industry, Dkt. 178 at 87 (FF ¶ 215), and thus is not qualified to proffer opinions on how agents and editors determine their offers in blind bargaining, i.e., what information they have, what factors they consider, what weight they give various factors, how much they "learn," and so on.

Second, the evidence Dr. Hill cites to prove that editors would reduce their offers in best bids and bilateral negotiations because they perceive diminished competition shows nothing of the kind. Dr. Hill relies on a single agent, Gail Ross, who testified about how *she* approaches bargaining in non-rounds formats. Tr. 3099:2–11 (Hill). According to Ms. Ross, she tries to consider her best available alternative, a technique she was taught when she took a "Harvard negotiating project training" course after law school. Tr. 2125:17–24 (Ross). Dr. Hill says that technique is similar to round-robin auctions, where the parties are bidding against a specific known amount—i.e., the best available alternative—which to him justifies extrapolating the SSA's harm projections to all other formats.

Ms. Ross's testimony does not remotely justify that extrapolation. Dr. Hill cited no evidence that editors are, like agent Ross, lawyers specifically trained in the Harvard negotiation project approach. What is more, Ms. Ross did not testify *how* she analyzes her next best option in bilateral negotiations, where she does not know whom the other option might be or how they would value the unique book at issue. Even more important, she did not explain how *editors* evaluate the next best option in both negotiations and best bids, given that they have no information about whom they are bidding against or how their unknown rivals value the book.

In that key respect, the formats fundamentally differ on the one point most critical to the SSA and round-robins: in blind best bids and negotiations, the editor does *not* know the agent's best available alternative, and thus cannot bargain against that specific amount. Ms. Ross's testimony is entirely consistent with the testimony of other witnesses that in blind formats, editors can only bid against the *general threat* of competition from the *entire* market, which can "lead to [publishers] increasing [their] offers quite significantly." Tr. 115:6 (Pietsch). Because an editor in blind bargaining does not know whom she is bidding against, or what subjective valuation any other editor would place on the book, the publisher is incentivized to go "all in" to win the book. Dkt. 178 at 100 (FF ¶ 249). By contrast, in a round-robin auction, everyone knows exactly what they must beat, and the bidding may end before the amount reaches the winner's maximum willingness to bid. *Id.*

In short, even if all editors use the Harvard bargaining strategy of basing bids on the next best option—and there is no evidence they do—the next best option in a blind format is indisputably *not* the same as the next best option in a round-robin format: rather than being a specific known amount, it is the maximum amount that *could* be offered by *anyone* that *could* be interested in the particular book. And given that books are subject to widely varying valuations, it is impossible to treat the highly individualized, unknown next best option in non-rounds formats as equivalent to the very specific, known next best bid in a round robin. *Id.* at 48–50 (FF ¶¶ 104–07). It is easy to see why Dr. Hill was unaware of any other economist who considered the SSA model applicable to bargaining formats that lack a known next best bid.

Third, the record refutes Dr. Hill's speculation that even if PRH and S&S editors do not know the specific amounts they are bidding against, they nevertheless will know enough to reduce their offers in blind bidding by an average of 6 percent, without losing bestselling books and authors to unknown and aggressive rivals. Indeed, Dr. Hill's own speculation proves the opposite. According to Dr. Hill, an S&S editor "today . . . knows that Penguin Random House wins four out of ten books," and after the merger the editors would take account of that fact and reduce offers, on average, by 6 percent. Tr. 1731:9–16. But any editor of the merged entity who followed Dr. Hill's approach would be guaranteed to lose books—bestselling books, by authors the company likely will never see again. The information an editor needs is not how often PRH or S&S previously won in general, but how often and when PRH and S&S were the top two bidders—in every other case, another publisher *necessarily* won or came in second. *See* Dkt. 178 at 55–56 (FF ¶¶ 220–21). In the latter situation, reducing bids by an average of 6 percent would mean either still losing (if another publisher would have won), or creating a huge risk of losing a book it previously would have won (if the runner-up bid would have exceeded the reduced bid). And of course an editor has no way of knowing exactly who would have been the winner or runner up, or how much their bids would have been. If there is any reasonable prospect HarperCollins or Macmillan or any other rival would have been the second-place bidder, reducing bids by 6 percent will in many cases simply gift these rivals new victories for the most sought-after books in the industry.

The government cites no basis on which editors could confidently reduce bidding given their lack of information about winners and runners-up. Dr. Hill's own estimations are based on market share data unknown to anyone in the industry. *Id.* at 25, 89 (FF ¶¶ 44, 220). Certainly nobody knows the 12 percent head-to-head competition figure his analysis generates. Given that figure, any former S&S editor who reduces her bids based on her observation that PRH previously won about 40 percent of the time overall (based simply on its market share) will make it *more likely another publisher will win* 88 percent of the acquisitions.

Nor is there any way to accurately identify the true scope of PRH and S&S head-to-head competition anecdotally from repeat bargaining—i.e., there is no way to "learn" the necessary information, as Dr. Hill speculates. *See supra* at 30–32. Bilateral negotiations are the most common form of acquisition, and editors ordinarily glean no information about any potential rival bidding in that process. In best bids, agents rarely if ever tell editors who they were bidding against and how much they bid, so editors learn little information there, as well. Dkt. 178 at 66 (FF ¶ 156). Even in round robins, editors usually do not learn who the non-prevailing bidders were or how much they bid. *Id.* And even when an editor does learn in a given acquisition how much another publisher bid, Dr. Hill cannot explain how the editor can use that information in the next acquisition to determine how much rivals are subjectively valuing a different, unique book. *Id.* at 88 (FF ¶ 217); *id.* at 154 (CL ¶ 100). Without all this information—all of which is known in a round-robin format—there is no way editors post-merger could confidently make the kind of decisions about bidding "less aggressively" that would reduce advances to the level Dr. Hill projects.

Finally, Dr. Hill does not account for the stakes involved. Unlike the "consumer products" markets Dr. Hill analogized to, Tr. 3089:13 (Hill), publishers cannot "test" the market with price reductions and quickly recover lost market share if too many authors flee. When a publisher loses an anticipated bestselling book, the book is gone forever, and the author probably is too, taking with her all her future downstream sales. *Id.* at 91 (FF ¶ 222); *id.* at 154 (CL ¶ 101). Editors of the combined entity post-merger thus will have strong incentives *not* to reduce advances, because doing so risks losing books and authors to publishers that previously would have come in second, especially given that editors have almost no information about whom the potential second-place publisher might have been or how much it would have bid.

For these reasons and others defendants have already identified, *id.* at 157–61 (CL ¶¶ 107–15), there is no sound basis for extrapolating the projected harm from the SSA model to acquisitions that lack the known-competing-bid feature essential to the SSA. Dr. Hill's speculation that the combined entity's editors will know enough from their perceptions of diminished competition to reduce their bids by an equivalent amount is unsupported and insupportable.

Industry participants recognize that round-robin auctions differ fundamentally from blind-bidding formats like bilateral negotiations and best bids. Agents and authors overwhelmingly choose the latter formats precisely because they are *not* like round-robins—they serve other interests and objectives and ultimately generate better results for authors. *Id.* at 100- 01 (FF ¶¶ 248–50). If round robins were similarly effective, they would not be the rarest of all bargaining formats.

Economists likewise recognize the differences, which is why when they study the effects of mergers on blind-bidding formats, they use models different from the SSA, as Dr. Hill admitted. *Id.* at 98–99 (FF ¶¶ 243, 245). Economists also may use a device—known as the "revenue equivalence theorem" ("RET")—to determine whether an SSA's projections can be legitimately extrapolated to at least best bid auctions, if not to bilateral negotiations. Tr. 1626:22–1627:21 (Hill). As Dr. Hill explained, if the RET's conditions were satisfied here, "it would mean you could apply the second score auction to best bid auctions." Tr. 1627:15–16. Although this recognized method was readily available to test the validity of his extrapolation (at least in part), Dr. Hill admittedly did not even attempt to determine whether the RET justified the extrapolation. Tr. 1627:13–14.

In short, nothing in Dr. Hill's analysis or in the trial evidence justifies extrapolating his SSA's results to blind-bargaining formats that lack the one feature most essential to the auctions modeled by the SSA—actual knowledge of rival bid amounts. And without that extrapolation, almost all of the harm Dr. Hill projects—some 80 to 90 percent or more—reduces to zero.

B. Dr. Hill's SSA Model Fails On Its Own Terms

Not only did Dr. Hill err in applying the SSA model's results to blind-bargaining formats, but the SSA fails on its own terms even as to the round-robins it is supposed to examine.

Two inputs go into the SSA model: market shares and margins. Tr. 1305:5–18 (Hill). Both inputs are flawed, resulting in a faulty calculation of harm.

First, the backbone of the SSA model is the assumption that the winner pays the price of the second-place bid. Tr. 1299:25–1300:2 (Hill). Dr. Hill admits that, according to the model, "an author can be harmed" only "when the parties are the first and second closest bidders." Tr. 1300:6–7 (Hill). It is thus essential to determine, as accurately as possible, not only who won the bidding, but also who was runner up. Dr. Hill employed market shares in the model, but market shares reflect only who won, not who was the runner up, and they do not accurately predict runners-up here. Dkt. 178 at 77, 108–09 (FF ¶¶ 187, 266–67). The model's results accordingly are unreliable.

Second, Dr. Hill also used faulty margin information. Dr. Hill's first report initially included ongoing operating expenses in PRH's margins, but excluded them for S&S's margins. *Id.* at 104 (FF ¶ 258). After Professor Snyder objected to the inconsistent treatment, Dr. Hill elected to estimate profit margins by excluding operating expenses altogether for both merging parties. *Id.* at 104–05 (FF ¶¶ 258–59). But by excluding ongoing operating costs from margin estimates, Dr. Hill estimates margins that are much higher than the *actual* margins publishers use to calculate their advance offers. Using the correct margin figures that account for operating costs—just as publishers do when determining their offer amounts—results in much lower predicted advance-reduction harm, as Dr. Hill acknowledges. *Id.* at 105–06 (FF ¶¶ 260- 61).

The government now asserts that the SSA model is "explicit" that "one should use firms' variable, not fixed, costs to implement the model[]." Dkt. 177 at 144–45 (¶ 293). That assertion is refuted by Dr. Hill himself, who included fixed operating expenses in PRH's margins when he first ran the model and reported its results in his initial report. Dkt. 178 at 104 (FF ¶ 258). It is also refuted by the academic article on the SSA cited by the government, Nathan Miller, *Modeling the effects of mergers in procurement,* 37 Int'l J. Indus. Org. 201, 203, 206 n.9 (2014). That article does not say the model allows only for the use of marginal costs—in fact, the very footnote cited by the government is applying the model using a margin that includes *more than marginal costs. See id.* As even the government concedes, the SSA model employs marginal costs only because economists "assume" that businesses make purchase decisions on the basis of marginal cost. Dkt. 177 at 144–45 (¶ 293). The government thus contends that Dr. Hill properly excluded fixed costs because when publishers decide how much they are willing to pay, they "*should* consider variable costs and not fixed costs." *Id.* at 145 (¶ 294) (emphasis added). But when seeking an accurate estimate of a merger's effect on real-world pricing decisions, what matters is not what an economist thinks publishers *should* do in the abstract, but what publishers *actually* do. Dkt. 178 at 162 (CL ¶ 120). And ongoing operating expenses—which include some but not all "fixed" costs—are a key component of the P&L statements publishers use to generate their advance decisions. *Id.* at 105 (FF ¶ 260).

The government asserts that PRH executive Madeline McIntosh "explicitly rejected" the premise that ongoing operating costs are part of the P&L analysis. Dkt. 177 at 144–45 (¶ 295). Not so. The government omits the rest of her testimony explaining that when she urged her editors to focus on the "contribution number," she was encouraging PRH publishers to be "more liberal" in their approach "for the bigger bets," where she thinks it suffices for PRH to be in "positive contribution territory," because if PRH does not bid aggressively and win the book, then there is no incremental benefit at all. Tr. 2260:5–6,

2259:16 (McIntosh). Under a "[m]ore conservative approach," she observed, PRH is "aiming to be in positive net profit or EBITDA on every single book because we do need to cover our overhead costs." Tr. 2260:2–5. That approach is consistent with S&S's practice—its P&L objective is for operating income margins, after fixed expenses, to be positive. Tr. 571:4–14 (Karp). The fact that Ms. McIntosh adopts a more nuanced approach to costs in certain situations does not justify a categorical rejection of the *general* practice that publishers follow in calculating their advance offers.

By using costs that differ from actual costs publishers use, the model's predicted margins fail the reliability "check" prescribed by the model's author. *See* Miller, *supra,* at 203. The government contends otherwise, but only by confusingly criticizing Professor Snyder's critique of Dr. Hill's method. Dkt. 177 at 146 (¶ 297). The problem is simple. The SSA article urges the modeler to conduct a "first check" on the reliability of a firm's margin estimates by comparing it to data on real-world margins "for other firms." Miller, *supra,* at 203. Dr. Hill did not do so. He instead used the average margin of *both firms.* Tr. 3095:21–3097:14 (Hill). His margins thus improperly validated themselves. Analyzed correctly, the margins fail the SSA reliability check, as Professor Snyder showed. Dkt. 178 at 106 (FF ¶ 262).

C. The GUPPI Calculations Do Not Cure The SSA's Defects

The government contends that Dr. Hill's GUPPI calculations "corroborated" the SSA's results. Dkt. 177 at 142 (¶ 286). To be sure, the GUPPIs generated similar results, but the results suffer from the same inadequacies and defects as the SSA. For one thing, Dr. Hill did not create a GUPPI calculation for books acquired through bilateral negotiations, which compromise the majority of book acquisitions. Dkt. 178 at 110 (FF ¶¶ 269); Tr. 1736:16–23, 3164:14–16 (Hill). And the GUPPIs—like the SSA—are not "equilibrium models" that actually account for the kind of post-merger competitive responses Dr. Hill could only speculate about. Dkt. 178 at 110–11 (¶ 270); Tr. 3164:23–25 (Hill). The GUPPI calculations thus do no more work than the woefully inadequate SSA.

Dr. Hill's GUPPI calculations also use the same flawed margin inputs he used in the SSA. Dkt. 178 at 111–12 (FF ¶ 272). Using Professor Snyder's diversion calculations and margins, which properly account for ongoing operating expenses as the merging firms do, the results "suggest harm of less than five percent for both multi-round and single round/hybrid forms, as Dr. Hill admitted," which "fall within the GUPPI 'safe harbor.'" *Id.;* Tr. 1629:6–25, 3107:7–12, 3109:14–23 (Hill); Tr. 2813:24–2814:10 (Snyder).

More generally, the government substantially overstates the capabilities of a GUPPI calculation. Dkt. 177 at 142 (¶ 286). It is merely a "screening device that is used at the outset to determine whether a merger should be further scrutinized." Dkt. 178 at 110–11 (FF ¶ 270). In other words, GUPPI is not a model but is merely a calculation used at the early stages of a merger investigation to determine if further investigation is warranted. If GUPPI calculations had probative force, Dr. Hill surely would have employed them in his initial report.

D. No Evidence Supports The Government's Speculative Theory Of Harm Through A "Second Order Effect" Of Softening Competition

In addition to addressing harm to authors who contract with either PRH or S&S, the government passingly asserts that potential harm is "not necessarily limited to authors of those publishers," because there could be a "second-order effect" based on the competitive responses of *other* firms. Dkt. 177 at 134 (¶ 263); *see id.* at 91–92 (¶ 174). According to Dr. Hill, just as PRH and S&S editors might respond to a perceived reduction in competition by bidding less aggressively, other publishers might also observe reduced competition and choose to bid less aggressively. *Id.* But to block the merger on that basis, the government must prove that this second-order effect is both likely and substantial—it is not enough to speculate that harm might be "not necessarily limited" to authors who contract with PRH and S&S. And even the testimony from Dr. Hill the government cites observes only that, *if* rivals observe reduced competition, they could "bid *as they were before* or even bid a little aggressively." *Id.* at 134 (¶ 263) (quoting Tr. 1269:20–24 (Hill)); *see* Tr. 1489:6–9 (Hill) (rivals' bidding behavior "may be unchanged or they may have a small diminution in their aggressiveness"); *see* Dkt. 178 at 152 (CL ¶ 95). In other words, rivals might lower bids a little, or they might not lower them at all—hardly a basis for blocking a $2 billion merger.

Another witness cited by the government, agent Ayesha Pande, similarly conceded the failure of the "second-order softening" theory. After speculating that her clients would be harmed by reduced competition, Dkt. 177 at 134–35 (¶ 264), she was forced to admit that the merger would not have affected a single one of the acquisitions she cited, Dkt. 178 at 53–54 (FF¶ 116).

On top of the admissions by its key witnesses, the government makes no effort to show how editors in specific acquisitions can accurately predict and respond to their rivals' valuations, especially given its *own admission* that "the bids a publisher makes for a particular book are subjective—meaning that one publisher or editor can sometimes value a book higher or even significantly higher than other publishers or editors." Dkt. 177 at 130–31 (¶ 257); *see id.* at 155 (¶ 154) (citing evidence showing that executives "expressed surprise" at how high rival bids were). The problem of individualized and unpredictable valuations is compounded by the fact that editors rarely even know who is vying for a given book and or who else might be interested. Dkt. 178 at 48–49 (FF ¶ 104). Especially given the exceedingly high stakes of losing an expected bestselling book and author, *id.* at 90–92 (FF ¶¶ 221–22); *id.* at 155 (CL ¶ 101), the idea that other editors will have the incentive and ability to lower bids substantially in response to blind, subjective bidding over individualized books is not just speculative, but contrary to the commercial realities of the industry. *Id.* at 153–55 (CL ¶¶ 98–101).

V. THE MERGER WILL NOT INCREASE THE LIKELIHOOD OF COORDINATION

The relevant question in coordinated effects analysis is whether the merger is "likely to *change* the manner in which market participants interact, inducing *substantially more* coordinated interaction." Guidelines § 7.1 (emphasis added); *see* Areeda & Hovenkamp, *Antitrust Law* ¶ 919 (merger must "change firms' incentives to coordinate their behavior"). According to the government, the "two most likely" avenues for post-merger coordination are coordination on "contractual terms or not to poach authors." Dkt. 177 at 156–67 (¶ 323). The government has not shown that coordination on contractual terms or poaching is likely in this market—let alone that the merger will lead to "substantially more" of such conduct.

A. Contractual Terms Are Not A Plausible Avenue For Coordination

At trial, Professor Snyder opined that an agreement not to compete on audio rights would make little sense in the publishing industry, because competition exists on "many other dimensions" in book negotiations. Tr. 2882:18–19. The government argues that Professor Snyder was wrong because of *Catalano, Inc. v. Target Sales, Inc.*, 446 U.S. 643 (1980). There, the Supreme Court held that an agreement by beer distributors to stop extending credit to retailers was a form of *per se* unlawful price-fixing. *Id.* at 649. The Court explained that because credit terms were "inseparable" from price terms, defendants' agreement to stop extending "interest-free credit" amounted to price-fixing. *Id.* at 648.

Catalano is irrelevant here. Professor Snyder's point was that *coordination*—which concededly requires firms to monitor and detect cheating, Dkt. 177 at 151 (¶ 307)—is unlikely to occur along one element of a multifaceted set of contract terms. Coordination on audio rights would be nonsensical, because it would be rational and easy for any industry member to cheat on the agreement by competing on other negotiable contract terms. In other words, there is a structural barrier to coordinating on contract terms in the publishing industry: contract terms are developed through "opaque" negotiation processes, making it difficult to determine who cheated, on what, and how. Tr. 2881:5–7 (Snyder) ("This is one of the most opaque industries in terms of acquisition processes to understand why did somebody win, why did somebody lose."); *see also id.* at 2881:2–5 (Snyder) ("So the complexity of the deal, the multiplicity of dimensions makes both picking a coordination mechanism, but also finding ways—finding out whether a party is deviating from the mechanism."). No one is arguing, as defendants did in *Catalano,* that an explicit agreement to coordinate on a contractual term would be lawful. The point is that it would be implausible, given the structure of this industry.

The government also misses the mark by arguing that the standardization of various contract terms (i.e., audio rights, royalty rates, and payout installments) means that the Big Five "already engage, at least, in parallel behavior." Dkt. 177 at 154 (¶ 315). There are obvious alternative explanations for why contract terms would become standardized in book publishing. Audio rights are the clearest example: the negotiation of these rights presents a classic free-rider problem that each publisher has an individual incentive to solve. Witness Brian Tart explained this point at trial without contradiction. Tr. 932:6–7. He testified that because "[t]he audio book benefits entirely from the book's publicity, marketing, packaging, positioning, editing, et cetera," giving up audio rights as a publisher means that the "outside audio players do almost zero marketing, certainly nothing approaching our marketing and publicity, [and] they get a free ride." Tr. 952:10–12, 952:15–17 (Tart) (quoting PX-328). It is no surprise that publishers would independently reach the same decision to request audio rights when acquiring a book. Nor is it any surprise that other subsidiary terms have become largely standardized, given that the "single most important contract term" is the *advance,* as the government itself insists. Dkt. 177 at 25 (¶ 28). Indeed, "in a large number of cases," the advance "may be the only compensation that the author will receive for their work." *Id.* (quoting Tr. 254:11–21 (Pande)). The standardization of other terms merely reflects their relative insignificance to authors during bargaining.

B. The Merger Will Not Make Anti-Poaching Coordination More Likely

The government separately asserts that there are "no structural barriers" that could prevent the Big Four from "tacitly agreeing not to poach each other's major authors." *Id.* at 158- 59 (¶ 329). Yes, there are: the same structural barriers that hinder coordination on contract terms would hinder no-poach coordination as well. In particular, publishers would have little to no information about why authors *stay* with their respective publishers over time. The decision of an author to stay with her publisher could mean that other publishers have refrained from poaching, but it could also mean that other publishers have regularly attempted to poach and failed, leading the author to negotiate better terms with her own publisher through the same "opaque" and complex negotiations that characterize this industry. *See supra* at 43. Given the lack of information about deal terms, publishers have no effective means of monitoring compliance with a no-poach agreement, and nothing about the merger will change that fact.

C. The Ebooks Case Is Irrelevant

As defendants have explained in previous filings—*see* Dkt. 178 at 168 (CL ¶ 136); Dkt. 131 at 56–57 (Defs. Pre-Trial Brief 49–50)—*United States. v. Apple, Inc.,* 791 F.3d 290 (2d Cir. 2015), has no bearing on the coordination question in this case.

Under the Guidelines, previous coordination in a different market matters only if the "salient characteristics of that other market at the time of the collusion are closely comparable to those in the relevant market." Guidelines § 7.2. *Apple* involved a conspiracy to increase retail prices in a different market: the downstream market for the retail sale of ebooks. 791 F.3d at 318. Downstream retail prices are transparent and readily capable of being monitored for deviation from any tacit or explicit agreement. Upstream acquisition prices are the opposite. Tr. 2881:5–7 (Snyder) (acquisition processes are "opaque"). And Random House and Bertelsmann were not even defendants in the *Apple* case—a point that the government congratulated Mr. Dohle on during trial. Dkt. 178 at 168–69 (CL ¶ 137) (citing Tr. 774:24–775:3). If the *Apple* case suggests anything, then, it is that Mr. Dohle, Bertelsmann, and PRH would likely steer the company *away* from collusive conduct, just as they did in *Apple.* And if the government is right that PRH will be a "leading firm whose decisions the other players would likely follow" in the industry, Dkt. 177 at 156 (¶ 322), then collusion by others is less likely too.

In any event, PRH's size in itself cannot make coordination more likely when the requirements for coordination—transparency, the ability to monitor and punish, and a relevant history of coordination—are absent from the market the government has alleged. Size alone would not give PRH or others the ability to send or respond to the necessary signals, nor would PRH's size enable PRH or others to ensure they would not lose huge amounts of money passing up bestselling books and authors while they wait to see whether their rivals somehow understand the signal and do the same in their own contracting decisions—decisions others will know little about.

CONCLUSION

For the foregoing reasons, and the reasons previously stated, the government's § 7 challenge should be rejected and the merger should be allowed to proceed.

Dated: September 7, 2022

Respectfully submitted,

By: Daniel M. Petrocelli (appearing *pro hac vice*)
M. Randall Oppenheimer (appearing *pro hac vice*)
O'MELVENY & MYERS LLP
1999 Avenue of the Stars
Los Angeles, CA 90067
Andrew J. Frackman (appearing *pro hac vice*)
Abby F. Rudzin (appearing *pro hac vice*)
O'MELVENY & MYERS LLP
Seven Times Square
New York, NY 10026
Jonathan D. Hacker (D.C. Bar No. 456553)
Julia Schiller (D.C. Bar No. 986369)
O'MELVENY & MYERS LLP
1625 Eye Street, NW
Washington, D.C. 20006
Deborah L. Feinstein (D.C. Bar No. 412109)
Jason Ewart (D.C. Bar No. 484126)
ARNOLD & PORTER
601 Massachusetts Ave., NW
Washington, D.C. 20001
Attorneys for Defendants Bertelsmann SE & Co. KGaA and Penguin Random House LLC
By: Stephen R. Fishbein (appearing *pro hac vice*)
Jessica K. Delbaum (appearing *pro hac vice*)
SHEARMAN & STERLING LLP
599 Lexington Avenue
New York, NY 10022
Ryan Shores (D.C. Bar No. 500031)
Michael Mitchell (D.C. Bar No. 1531689)
SHEARMAN & STERLING LLP
401 9th Street, N.W., Suite 800
Washington, D.C. 20004
Rachel E. Mossman (D.C. Bar No. 1016255)
SHEARMAN & STERLING LLP
2828 North Harwood Street, Suite 1800
Dallas, TX 75201
Attorneys for Defendants Paramount Global (f/k/a ViacomCBS Inc.) and Simon & Schuster, Inc.

PART SIX: MEMORANDUM OF OPINION

MEMORANDUM OF OPINION

As Judge Florence Pan makes painfully clear in her now-issued full "memorandum opinion" blocking Penguin Random House's acquisition of Simon & Schuster, in her view it was never a close case: She finds in favor of all of the government's key arguments and building blocks, and positively scoffs at many of the defendants' "medley of other arguments."

Along the way, she provides multiple burns — of PRH in particular and the Big Five in general, including the contention the merger would have no effect on advances ("incredible"); PRH's bidding pledges ("the Court gives no weight to this unenforceable promise"); PRH's "coordinat[ion of] their bids within the same auction, artificially suppressing advances"; plus their expert's "counterintuitive and apparently erroneous testimony" and "reliance on the limited and unrepresentative" data set he collected from 18 agencies; while also noting "the industry-wide standardization of certain contract terms…in ways that favor authors over publishers."

The Conclusion

Judge Pan's summary in her 80-page opinion concludes, "The government has presented a compelling case that predicts substantial harm to competition as a result of the proposed merger of PRH and S&S. It has properly defined a relevant market–focused on the publishing rights for anticipated top-selling books–that encompasses 70 percent of the advances that publishers pay to authors. The post-merger concentration of the relevant market would be concerningly high: The merged entity would have a 49-percent market share, more than twice that of its closest competitor. [HarperCollins has a 24 percent share.]"

"…The defendants have failed to show that the relevant market is not well defined; have failed to establish that the market-share data inaccurately reflects market conditions; and have failed to rebut the government's affirmative evidence of anticompetitive harm." As for their other arguments, "The Court is unpersuaded by the defendants' arguments that the market-share does not accurately reflect conditions in the relevant market because it does not account for constraints that would be imposed by existing and new competitors, literary agents, and internal imprint competition."

Particular Points

Befitting her conduct as reported during the trial, Judge Pan's full opinion and assessment of how publishing works is clear and lucid, and she was not distracted by any of the ambivalence or imprecision offered on the stand by various witnesses and defense attorneys.

As she writes early in the opinion, "The Court is unconvinced by the testimony of certain defense witnesses who stated that advance levels are not the most important factor in book acquisitions, and that the author's 'fit' and comfort level with the editor are more significant [referring to the testimony of Jennifer Rudolph Walsh and Elyse Cheney]. While that may be true in a small number of cases, books generally are sold to the highest bidder. While the choice of an editor is undoubtedly significant, the agent typically has submitted the book only to a pre-screened list of suitable editors and thus may choose the highest bid among those editors. The overwhelming weight of the evidence supports the conclusion that advances levels are the primary focus of book acquisitions."

While the judge writes at length about her reasoning in accepting the government's "relevant market" of authors for anticipated top-selling books and grounds it well in logic and case law ("consistent with cases in which courts have recognized the 'high end' of other broad markets as distinct submarkets for antitrust purposes"), she also states the case as pretty obvious. "The Court has no trouble recognizing that anticipated top-selling books are distinct from the vast majority of books that do not carry the same expectations for success…. Evidence strongly supports the conclusion that, from the perspective of editors and publishers, not all books are created equal."

Despite all the discussions at trial of the modest instances in which the largest publishers lose a big author or a big book to someone else, "It is the Big Five who have the backlists and the marketing, publicity, and sales advantages necessary to consistently provide the high advances and unique services that top-selling authors need. It is precisely those specialized needs that make the authors of anticipated top-selling books vulnerable to targeting for price reductions."

Stated again in a similar way, underscoring the potential harm to authors from a merger, "Because they [authors] have no reasonable substitute, authors can be targeted for and impacted by a decrease in prices…."

More on Harm

With her acceptance of the relevant market of anticipated top-selling books, and the unchallenged data showing PRH and S&S combined would have a 49 percent share of such a market, Judge Pan easily accepts that the government has a "prima facie case," the merger is per se illegal and should be blocked, absent the defense being able to "demonstrate that the market share and the associated presumption of illegality inaccurately reflects competitive reality."

Regarding the potential harm of the merger, again Judge Pan relies on both the factual record and the obvious inference that eliminating one of the top three competitors will lessen competition. "Consistent with their market shares, when S&S loses a book, it most often loses to PRH; and when S&S wins a book, its most likely runner-up is PRH." But more broadly, "Even when the merging parties were not the top two bidders, S&S's participation strengthened competition across all auction formats…. A book's perceived value may vary significantly among different editors and publishers, and an unusually high bid for a book is likelier when there are more bidders…. The loss of S&S as an independent bidder would weaken bidding incentives and reduce the frequency of events like these."

In a footnote, she reaches even further: "The Court finds testimony that the merger will have either no effect or positive effects on advances incredible. The Court instead credits the much stronger evidence that advances will decrease after the merger, based on the market-share data, economic analyses, and the more credible testimony regarding market dynamics…."

The Judge also points out in her reasoning that authors can be negatively affected even if advances do not decline concretely, from the general lessening of competition: "It is not necessary for advances to decline in absolute terms for authors to be harmed. The relevant market has been growing rapidly in recent years in response to strong consumer demand, and advances have been rising, consistent with that growth. If the merger goes through, the rate of growth might be offset by competitive harm, allowing publishers to acquire books for more than they do now but for less than they would have absent the merger."

And More Skepticism

As noted in our opening, this opinion is full of doubts and concluding the worst about the parties involved, both these publishers and all big publishers.

On PRH CEO Markus Dohle's bidding pledge and other revised thoughts on bidding policy changes from the stand, "The Court gives no weight to this unenforceable promise. Indeed, the promise calls to mind the criminal-law concept of 'consciousness of guilt.': Mr. Dohle's extraordinary pledge appears to reflect his awareness of how threatened the combined entity would be to authors and agents…. It appears that the promise was made just to get the deal done, and once the merger is executed, there will be no economic incentive to maintain the policy."

On PRH's argument about agents holding all the power, "Agents cannot create competition where it does not exist, and competition is what ultimately increases authors' advances…. In any event, as a general matter, agents do not have the power to effectively discipline larger publishers. Time after time, when agents have attempts to curb the Big Five's exercise of market power, the agents have failed."

That refers back to another finding, on "coordinated effects" within publishing that make any concentration at the top suspect. Here Judge Pan saw that: "Recent years have seen the industry-wide standardization of certain contract terms — involving payment structure, audio rights and e-book royalties — in ways that favor publishers over authors, suggesting that the top publishers have engaged in coordinated conduct… Thus, in an industry where the competition to acquire anticipated top sellers is intense, the competing publishers nevertheless choose, almost always, not to gain advantage by offering more favorable contract terms. This phenomenon bespeaks a tacit agreement among the publishers to compete only on the basis of advance levels because it collectively benefits them not to yield on other contract terms. The Court finds that the Big Five publishers have engaged in tacit coordination that is profitable for those involved."

She adds, "It is significant that in a market already prone to collusion, where coordinated conduct already appears to be rampant, PRH's acquisition of S&S would reinforce the market's oligopsonistic structure and create a behemoth industry leader that other market participants would easily follow."

As always, the full opinion is posted below. The forcefulness of Judge Pan's ruling and her lack of doubt on nearly every aspect of the defendants' case may weigh heavily on any negotiations between Paramount and Bertelsmann on whether to extend the term of the original purchase agreement pending an appeal. It also may weigh significantly on how other bidders might view the regulatory landscape. (A potential acquisition by HarperCollins would give them a 36 or 37 percent share of ATSB, above the 30 percent threshold for potentially too much concentration, but about equal with PRH's current share of 37 percent.)

She even pokes at the argument that a sale to a private equity firm would be harmful to S&S, noting that "the expressed concerns about a private-equity acquisition are highly speculative" and "it is just as likely that another publishing company will prevail in a future sale" — also suggesting that she does not believe her ruling blocks an acquisition by another publisher.

At the same time, her opinion deploys the same restrained "velvet hammer" that she used during the trial. While the DOJ aimed to set new precedent as a building block for future cases and declared the ruling "a victory for workers more broadly," the term "worker" does not appear anywhere in the opinion. Rather, Judge Pan takes pains to portray this as a non-controversial finding about "market concentration in the publishing industry" that happens to "sound[s] in 'monopsony' "but in most respects fits naturally within all of the major precedents in the DC Circuit. Rather than break new ground, she works hard to root her ruling in established practice (and therefore diminish any grounds for appeal).

UNITED STATES DISTRICT COURT FOR THE DISTRICT OF COLUMBIA Civil Action No. 21-2886-FYP MEMORANDUM OPINION

John Steinbeck famously said, "I guess there are never enough books." He apparently meant that in the figurative sense, as a comment on the power of books to educate, to enrich, and to explore. But today, his statement also rings true in the economic sense: The retail market for books in the United States was over $11.5 billion in 2019 and has only continued to expand. People want to read. And book publishers have the enormous power and responsibility to decide which books–and therefore which ideas and stories–will be made broadly available to the public. A publishers' marketplace of ideas is also a marketplace of book sales, production costs, and market share. It is this commercial market, so inextricably intertwined with the intellectual life of our nation, that the Court examines in this case.

Penguin Random House ("PRH") is by far the largest book publisher in the United States. Owned by Bertelsmann SE & Co. KGaA ("Bertelsmann"), an international media and services company, PRH annually publishes over 2,000 new books in the U.S. and generates nearly $2.5 billion in revenue. Simon & Schuster, Inc. ("S&S"), owned by the media giant Paramount Global (formerly Viacom CBS), is the third-largest publisher in the U.S. S&S publishes about 1,000 new titles yearly and reported over $760 million in net sales in 2020.

In March 2020, ViacomCBS announced that it planned to sell S&S. Following a multi-round bidding process, Bertelsmann and PRH signed an agreement with ViacomCBS and S&S in November 2020 to purchase S&S for $2.175 billion. The acquisition of S&S would cement PRH's position as the "number one" publisher in the United States, increasing its retail market share to almost three times that of its closest competitor.[1] Trial Tr. at 741:17-742:4 (Dohle).

---

[1] In 2019, PRH had a. [REDACTED] percent share of the market for U.S. book sales and S&S had a [REDACTED] percent share. *See* ECF No. 177 (United States' Sealed Corrected Proposed Findings of Fact and Conclusions of Law ("Govt. PFOF-PCOL") i 13 (citing Defendants' Exhibit No. DX") 105 at 64); *see also* ECF No. 184 (government's redacted post-trial brief). Thus, the combined entity would have a market share of approximately [REDACTED] percent. The merged company's next closest competitor would be [REDACTED] which had an [REDACTED] share of the market for book sales in 2019. *See* Govt. PFOF-PCOL i 13 (citing DX 105 at 64).

In November 2021, the Antitrust Division of the United States Department of Justice ("the government") brought this action against PRH, S&S, and their parent companies ("the defendants"), seeking to block the merger of PRH and S&S under Section 7 of the Clayton Act. The government's case sounds in "monopsony," a market condition where a buyer with too much market power can lower prices or otherwise harm sellers. Essentially, the government alleges that the merger will increase market concentration in the publishing industry, which will allow publishing companies to pay certain authors less money for the rights to publish their books.

The case proceeded to trial on August 1, 2022. For twelve days, the Court heard evidence and argument about how PRH's acquisition of S&S would affect competition in the "upstream" market for publishing rights. The Court heard testimony from authors, publishers, literary agents, and industry executives, and admitted over 230 exhibits.[2] After a thorough review of the record and careful consideration of the parties' arguments, the Court concludes that PRH's acquisition of S&S is likely to substantially lessen competition to acquire "the publishing rights to anticipated top-selling books," which comprise the relevant market in this case. The Court therefore will enjoin the proposed merger of PRH and S&S.

I. BACKGROUND

A. The Industry

The book industry is dominated by five major publishing houses–PRH, HarperCollins Publishers, S&S, Hachette Book Group, and Macmillan Publishing Group, LLC–which are known as the "Big Five." Together, the Big Five held nearly 60 percent of the market for the sale of trade books in 2021 *(i.e.,* books intended for general readership, as opposed to specialized books like textbooks or manuals). *See* DX 382; PX 663 at 92.

The Big Five have achieved their market dominance in part by acquiring other publishers, contributing to a trend toward consolidation in the industry. Bertelsmann entered the U.S. publishing market by acquiring Bantam Books in 1977, which merged with Doubleday Dell in 1986 and with Random House in 1998. PRH itself was formed in 2013 when Random House acquired Penguin Books. Since 2013, PRH has continued to acquire other publishers, including Sasquatch Books, Rodale, Little Tiger, F&W Media, and Sourcebooks. Meanwhile, Hachette has acquired several independent publishers in the last decade, such as Workman Publishing, Worthy, Perseus, and Black Dog & Leventhal. *See* Trial Tr. at 102:13-103:4 (Pietsch), 204:3-19 (Pietsch). In 2021, HarperCollins acquired Houghton Mifflin Harcourt, which previously was one of the largest among the mid-size, independent publishers. *See* Trial Tr. at 1386:12-17 (Murray), 192:6-193:15 (Pietsch). The remaining Big Five publisher, Macmillan, has pursued organic growth. *See* Trial Tr. at 1079:23-1080:18 (Weisberg).

Some smaller publishers are well respected in the industry and compete against the Big Five–in both the upstream market for acquiring books for publication and in the downstream market for selling books to

---

[2] The Court appreciated hearing the testimony of many dedicated professionals who work in the publishing industry. The Court heard from authors Charles Duhigg, Stephen King, and Andrew Solomon. Publisher witnesses included: Jennifer Bergstrom, Senior Vice President and Publisher of the S&S imprint Gallery Books Group ("Gallery"); Sally Kim, Senior Vice President and Publisher of the PRH imprint G.P. Putnam's Sons ("Putnam"); Liate Stehlik, President and Publisher of Morrow Group, HarperCollins Publishers; and Brian Tart, President and Publisher of the PRH imprint Viking Penguin ("Viking"). The following literary agents testified: Elyse Cheney, Christy Fletcher, Ayesha Pande, Gail Ross, Jennifer Rudolph Walsh (expert witness), and Andrew Wylie. The Court also heard from top industry executives, including Markus Dohle, CEO of PRH; Dennis Eulau, Executive Vice President and COO of S&S; John Glusman, Vice President and Editor in Chief of W.W. Norton & Company ("Norton"); Michael Jacobs, President and CEO of Abrams Books; Jonathan Karp, President and CEO of S&S; Madeline McIntosh, CEO of PRH in the U.S.; Brian Murray, CEO of Harper Collins Publishers; Michael Pietsch, CEO of Hachette Book Group; Don Weisberg, CEO of Macmillan Publishers; and Steven Zacharius, CEO of Kensington Books. The government's economic expert was Dr. Nicholas Hill, and the defendants' economic expert was Professor Edward Snyder. Finally, Adriana Porro, a statistician for U.S. Department of Justice, Antitrust Division, also testified.

The following witnesses testified by video: Christy Fletcher, John Glusman, Michael Jacobs, Andrew Solomon, Liate Stehlik, and Steven Zacharius. *See* Government's Exhibit No. ("PX") 2008 (Fletcher Dep.); Trial Tr. at 1740:16-17 (noting that video of Fletcher's deposition was played at trial); DX 422 (Glusman Dep.); DX 423 (Glusman sealed); Trial Tr. at 1880:4 (noting that video of Glusman's deposition was played at trial); PX 2005 (Jacobs Dep.); Trial Tr. at 701:13-23 (noting that video of Jacobs's deposition was played at trial); PX 2004 (Solomon Dep.); Trial Tr. at 689:7-8 (noting that video of Solomon's deposition was played at trial). PX 2002 (Stehlik Dep.) at 64-65; Trial Tr. at 628:23 (noting that video of Stehlik's deposition was played at trial); PX 2000 (Zacharius Dep.); Trial Tr. at 385:11 (noting that video of Zacharius's deposition was played at trial).

consumers. For instance, Scholastic is one of the largest children's book publishers and works with some of the same authors as the Big Five, *see* Trial Tr. at 118:20-22 (Pietsch), 545:10-547:2 (Karp); while Kensington, one of the largest remaining independent publishers, is a prominent purveyor of romance novels. *See* PX 2000 (Zacharius) at 8; PX 2002 (Stehlik) at 64-65. In addition, Norton is a prestigious publishing house specializing in narrative nonfiction and is favored by some best-selling authors like Michael Lewis. *See* Trial Tr. at 540:24-541:24 (Karp), 544:17-25 (Karp), 550:22-551 :4 (Karp); DX 422 at 7. Other players in the industry include well capitalized, mid-sized publishers like Amazon and Disney, which each bring in over $100 million in annual revenues from publishing. *See* Trial Tr. at 737:22-738:11 (Dohle).

Each publishing company is organized as an umbrella organization that houses various "imprints." An imprint is a trade name or brand name for an editorial group. Imprints specialize in publishing certain types of books and thus develop reputations for success in particular genres. *See* PX 530 at 2. The editors within each imprint select and acquire manuscripts for publication; and then collaborate with authors to develop and finalize their books. *See* Trial Tr. at 97:1-6 (Pietsch), 1915:10-25 (Duhigg), 1919:8-1920:3 (Duhigg). PRH has close to 100 U.S. publishing imprints within six publishing divisions. *See* Trial Tr. at 812:5-11 (Dohle); Govt. Demo. 1 (PRH organizational chart). Its best-known imprints include Viking, Penguin Press, Doubleday, Riverhead, Random House, and Putnam. S&S operates three publishing groups with around 50 imprints, including Simon and Schuster, Atria Books, Scribner, and Gallery Books. *See* PX 663 (materials for prospective S&S buyers) at 91, 101.

All publishers and editors are highly motivated to secure the rights to publish new books; indeed, identifying and acquiring books that people want to read is the essence of the business. Yet only 35 out of 100 books tum a profit, and breakout titles drive revenues–the top 4 percent of profitable titles generate 60 percent of profitability. *See* PX 151 (presentation by PRH executives on publishing industry) at 11; Trial Tr. at 747:16-18 (Dohle), 2289:2-10 (McIntosh) ("*Where the Crawdads Sing* is a great current example. *Fifty Shades of Grey, Gone Girl, Girl on the Train* [their] sales performance so outstrips our expectation, that they deliver most of the profit to the company."). Publishing has therefore been described by insiders as a "portfolio business": The business model is to acquire a large number of high-quality books, knowing that a substantial percentage of the titles will not be profitable. *See* Trial Tr. at 747:5-9 (Dohle). As PRH CEO Markus Dohle put it, publishers are "angel investors" that "invest every year in thousands of ideas and dreams, and only a few make it to the top." *Id.* at 747:5-9. The books that do "make it to the *top*" and sell well, especially over a number of years, allow the companies to take risks in acquiring new books and enable publishers to manage the uncertainty inherent in "betting" on new titles. *See id.* at 747:5-7 (Dohle); PX 151 at 11. Books that continue to sell after the first year of publication comprise a publisher's "back list," which can provide an important source of stable revenue. Back lists allow publishers to play the "long game" because some books take a while to become profitable. *See* PX 2004 at 55. By contrast, the "front list," which consists of books not yet released or on the market for under a year, is risky and has poorer margins, due to the expenses of marketing and roll-out associated with the new titles. *See* Trial Tr. at 118:15-119:11 (Pietsch).

B. Acquiring Books for Publication

Books begin, of course, with authors. Authors often spend years developing their ideas, conducting research, and refining their manuscripts or proposals before submitting them for publication. A project that is acquired may still take months or years of work before it becomes a completed book that is ready for distribution. *See, e.g., id.* at 1916:14-21 (Duhigg). To support themselves, authors often rely on "advances" from their publishers. *See id.* at 1925:15- 22 (Duhigg), 1941:9-1943:1 (Duhigg) (advance allowed him to take time off from his job to write, support his newborn child, buy a house, and pay living expenses). An advance is an upfront payment against the royalties that an author may earn in the future.[3]

[3] Royalties are payments made to the author based on a book's sales. *See* Trial Tr. at 106:20-107:25 (Pietsch). For example, authors earn 7.5 percent of sales for paperback books. *See id* at 255:24-256:20 (Pantle), 2011:9-10 (Kim). An advance is an upfront payment of those anticipated royalties; the author is not required to pay back the advance even if the book's actual royalties never exceed the amount of the advance. *See id* at 106:20- 107:25 (Pietsch). Advances are paid in installments, typically in quarters. Generally, the first installment is paid upon the signing of the

The advance is the "single most important" term in a contract for publishing rights because in a "large number of cases, it may be the only compensation that the author will receive for their work." *Id* at 254:18-24 (Pantle); *see also* PX 2002 (Stehlik) at 67. Indeed, most authors do not "earn out" their advances, *i.e.,* ultimately earn royalties that exceed the amount of their advances.[4] In addition to the advance, authors care about working with editors who share their vision for the book and who can help them to "bring the book into the world." Trial Tr. at 97:2-6 (Pietsch); *see also id* at 1918:5-24 (Duhigg), 1943:13-17 (Duhigg) (editor is "the reason I'm there" at PRH), 2055:10-2056:9 (Cheney), 2063:5-17 (Cheney).

Authors generally are represented by literary agents, who use their judgment and experience to find the best home for publishing a book. They typically begin the process by submitting the book (which might be a full or partial manuscript, or just a proposal) to multiple imprints or editors on a preliminary basis, to gauge the level of interest in the project. *See id.* at 246:11-22 (Pande), 2105:22-25(Wylie); PX 151 at 5. Agents use their expertise to determine which imprints and editors to target, based on factors such as the kinds of books the imprint previously has published, how effectively they have published those kinds of books, and the ability of the company to pay appropriate compensation. *See* Trial Tr. at 246:9-22 (Pande), 2117:8-2118:25 (Ross). Agents prioritize submitting manuscripts and proposals to Big Five imprints because of their ability to pay; an agent might send out a second round of submissions that includes more smaller publishers if interest among the Big Five is not strong. *See id.* at 246:17-22 (Pande), 248:15-249:10 (Pande). Given the size of PRH and S&S, and the number of imprints they represent, some agents "always" submit to multiple PRH imprints and to S&S. *See id.* at 250:10-251 :3 (Pantle), 260:16-21 (Pantle).

Agents try to maximize the advances paid to authors: They not only have a fiduciary duty to achieve the best deal, *see id.* at 494:7-17 (Karp), 1748:21-23 (Walsh), but they also are paid on commission (typically 15 percent of the advance). *See id.* at 245:18-25 (Pantle); PX 151 at 5. Indeed, one prominent agent has stated that it is his job to "get an advance that an author doesn't earn out," Trial Tr. at 2100:5-25 (Wylie); while a publisher explained that "typically the most important thing for an agent representing authors [is] to get the most amount of money up front," *see* PX 2002 (Stehlik) at 67.

Other common terms in a book contract include royalty rates, audio rights, and payment structure *(i.e.,* the number and timing of the installments in which an advance is paid). *See* Trial Tr. at 255:11-17 (Pantle), 255:24-256:20 (Pantle). Yet many of those other terms have become standardized across the industry, making advance levels even more important. For instance, each book format has a standard royalty rate that is rarely altered. *See id.* at 106:20-107:13 (Pietsch).[5] Audio rights are now always included in book contracts and may not be sold separately. *See id.* at 257:14-258:6 (Pantle), 622:17-25 (Karp); PX 328 (internal PRH email) at 1-2 ("We have to get those [audio] rights."). Finally, even though authors prefer to receive "frontloaded" advances–payments that are made sooner, and in fewer installments–the industry norm has shifted in the opposite direction, from payouts in thirds to payouts in quarters. *See* Trial Tr. at 254:25-255:3 (Pantle), 256:22-25 (Pantle), 1829:11-18 (Walsh);[REDACTED] at 19-20.

The Court is unconvinced by the testimony of certain defense witnesses who stated that advance levels are not the most important factor in book acquisitions, and that the author's "fit" and comfort level with the editor are more significant. *See* Trial Tr. at 1756:2-1757:8 (Walsh), 1836:5-1837:2 (Walsh), 1935:14-20 (Duhigg), 2055:5-2056:9 (Cheney), 2063:4-17 (Cheney). While that may be true in a small number of cases, books generally are sold to the highest bidder. *See id.* at 2395:2-10 (McIntosh) (underbidder

---

book contract; the second payment is made upon delivery and acceptance of the manuscript; the third installment is paid upon publication; and the fourth payment is made twelve months later. *See id* at 777:1- 19 (Dohle), 1829:11-15 (Walsh), 255:1-25 (Pande). It can take three to four years for an entire advance to be paid to an author. *See id.* at255:15-18 (Pantle), 777:1-19 (Dohle).

[4] *See* Trial **Tr.** at 108:2-12 (Pietsch) ("Roughly half the time. About half the books we [Hachette] publish earn out their advances."), 254:20-24 (Pande) (20% of authors represented by Pande's agency earned out advance), 1239:25-1240:8 (Hill) (more than 85% of author contracts for anticipated top-selling books never earn out their advance), 2101:3-5 (Wylie) (5% of books he represents earn out their advances).

[5] Generally, paperback books receive a 7.5-percent royalty rate; e-books and audio or digital downloads receive 25 percent of net sales; and hardcover books get a IO-percent rate for the first 5,000 copies sold, 12.5 percent for copies 5,000 to 10,000, and 15 percent of sales exceeding 10,000 copies. *See* Trial Tr. at 255:24-256:20 (Pantle), 2011:4-15 (Kim).

winning an auction is "rare"), 2090:20-23 (Wylie) ("[W]e are picking one that we feel presents the strongest combination of financial terms plus editorial engagement and context for the author."), 2106:1-7 (Wylie) (sold books to the highest bidder about 93% of the time). While the choice of an editor is undoubtedly significant, the agent typically has submitted the book only to a pre-screened list of suitable editors and thus may choose the highest bid from among those editors. *See id.* at 246:1-22 (Pande). The overwhelming weight of the evidence supports the conclusion that advance levels are the primary focus of book acquisitions.

Most books are sold in exclusive negotiations between the agent and a single editor or imprint.[6] Such negotiations come about because (1) a publisher has an "option" from a prior contract with the author, which allows the publisher to take the first look at the author's next project and submit an exclusive bid within a limited period; (2) a publisher is willing to pay a premium to "preempt" the book from being offered to others; (3) an agent approaches a single editor that is a particularly good fit for a book and enters negotiations with that editor and their imprint; or (4) only one imprint is interested after the agent has completed a round of submissions. *See id.* at 475:13-476:10 (Karp), 954:18-955:7 (Tart). Alternatively, an agent might decide to utilize an auction format, which requires imprints to bid against each other to acquire the book. Auctions may be organized in (1) a "round robin" format, where the agent accepts competing bids in several "rounds," eliminates the lowest bidders before proceeding to the next round, and continues until only one bidder remains; (2) a "best bids" format, where all bidders submit their highest bid in a single round; or (3) a hybrid format, such as "better best," where the bidding starts as a "round robin" and then shifts to a final round of "best bids." *See id.* at 111:8-113:4 (Pietsch), 2049:1-19 (Cheney), 2116:10-2117:9 (Ross).

A publisher that hopes to acquire a desirable book must offer a competitive advance to be in the running. Editors and publishers determine how much their imprint is willing to pay for a given book. *See id.* at 97:1-6 (Pietsch). To make that determination, they estimate the profitability of the book by generating a profit and loss statement ("P&L"). Such a statement suggests an appropriate advance after considering (1) the anticipated sales of the book and its expected list price (in various formats); and (2) predicted production and marketing costs. *See* DX 414 (P&L Sheet); Trial Tr. at 915:5-918:21 (Tart). The most important input in a P&L- and the driving force behind the advance offered- is the publisher's estimate of book sales. *See* Trial Tr. at 917:13-16 (Tart) ("the higher sales equate to a higher advance in the P&L"), 110:19-111:1 (Pietsch) (relationship between the level of advance and projected sales is "extremely close"). The sales prediction is based on the demand for comparable titles (referred to as "comp titles" or "comps"), which have similar characteristics to the proposed book in terms of subject matter, literary merit, or author background. Publishers also often confer with their sales, publicity, and marketing teams about expected demand for a book. *See id.* at 842:15- 843:10 (Dohle), 914:11-18 (Tart), 1036:13-16 (Tart). But publishers do not rely only on the P&L to determine an appropriate advance. They also consider factors like the editor's enthusiasm, their relationship with the author, whether the book might win an award, and whether the book is in a growing category- if they really want a book, they will "stretch" beyond what a P&L suggests would be profitable. *Id.* at 969:4-970:14 (Tart), 967:3-10 (Tart).

Publishers' sales estimates, broadly speaking, are reasonably reliable. Ultimately, there is a correlation between high advances and high book sales. Books that sell well tend to have garnered high advances, and books that receive high advances tend to sell well. *See id.* at 749:4- 22 (Dohle); PX 151 at 11.

C. The Competition for Books

Regardless of the method used to acquire a book's publishing rights, the amount that is paid is inexorably determined by competition. In an auction, a skillful agent can capitalize on enthusiasm for a book and play bidders off against one another, knowing that a publisher will "bid what [it] need[s] to buy

---

[6] More than half of books are sold through negotiations. *See* Trial Tr. at 1608:20-1609:1 (Hill) (explaining that 60% of books with advances over $250,000 involve negotiations, with the remaining 40% being auctions); *see also id.* at 478:15-479:1 (Karp) (explaining that less than half of acquisitions are auctions because S&S has "so many repeat authors), 771:11-14 (Dahle) (auctions are "small sliver of the overall deals we do, especially the expensive deals we do"), 1963:20-1964:18 (Kim) (explaining that Putnam imprint buys 80% of books through one- on-one negotiations and attributing the higher percentage to its number of "franchise" authors).

that book" because "it [only] takes one passionate editor at another imprint to win that book away." Trial Tr. at 1965:21-25 (Kim). Although the perceived value of a book is subjective and may vary among editors, there is often a consensus among industry players about which books will be successful. *See id.* at 2108:14-24 (Wylie) ("I think there are recognizable qualities in–in books that people who have been in the business for a long time would easily recognize."), 310:12-24 (Pande) (agent explaining that she treats an anticipated strong seller differently, such as by "sending it out as widely as I possibly can").

It is not uncommon for editors and publishers to experience a "kind of auction fever," in which they change their sales expectations for a book and increase what they are willing to pay for it during a competitive round-robin auction. *Id.* at 180:20-181:11 (Pietsch). "[T]he interest of other parties validates [a publisher's] own sense of what a book is worth." *Id.* The record contains numerous examples of books that sold for unexpectedly high advances and achieved other favorable terms for their authors due to the bidding frenzy incited by competitive auctions. For instance, in a hybrid auction of rounds followed by best bids, [REDACTED], initially received bids of between $150,000 and $400,000 from four publishers. *See* PX 944-B (Porro bidding summary); Trial Tr. at 923:16-930:18 (Tart) (discussing book's acquisition); PX 320 (emails). After six rounds of bidding, PRH's Viking imprint more than doubled its initial bid and won the book for $775,000 "over stiff competition." PX 39 (email from Tart); *see also* PX 944-B (Porro bidding summary); Trial Tr. at 923:16-930:18 (Tart). At the best-bids stage, Viking decided to "stretch" from its initial bid clearance of $700,000 because "there just is literally no telling what the opponents hold in their hands." PX 326 at 1 (emails between Tart and Viking editor Wendy Wolf). Another example is [REDACTED]–which also benefitted from a rounds auction. *See* PX 948-B (Porro bidding summary). In the first round, there were three bids, ranging from $200,000 to $300,000. *See id.* Yet after five rounds, [REDACTED] received $535,000 plus a $100,000 bonus. *See id.;* Trial Tr. at 433:24-435:17 (Karp) (discussing bidding process); PX 632 (emails discussing auction). The record contains at least 11 other examples that illustrate the sharp increase in prices engendered by competitive auctions, with advances increasing at least $100,000 by the end of the auction.[7]

Competition is also a key factor in one-on-one negotiations, where publishers must offer high advances because they know that the agent always has the option of breaking off negotiations and selling the book on the market. *See* Trial Tr. at 955:11-20 (Tart) (explaining that in one-on-one negotiations "you know there's competition out there"), 1847:1-6 (Bergstorm) ("I assume I am negotiating exclusively, but I always have my competition in my rearview mirror. But it's one on one. And sometimes we don't come to terms, and sometimes they will go to someone else."), 1966:17-24 (Kim) ("[E]ven if it's a one-on-one negotiation we're constantly aware that there's competition ")1,14:21-115:6 (Pietsch). Some publishers consider individual negotiations to be the most challenging way to acquire a book, because "you are basically bidding against the author's expectations and the agent's expectations," and there are "no other market inputs [but] you know there's competition out there." *Id.* at 955:11-20 (Tart). In such situations, agents have bargaining leverage because the threat of taking the book to other publishers always lurks in the background. This is particularly true where a publisher is attempting to preempt the auction process. *See, e.g., id.* at 115:21- 116:5 (Pietsch) ("When we're calculating a preempt, we want to bring an advance that we believe the agent will consider a good advance; that they will think, yes, there's a chance that if I take this to auction, I might not get this much or this is the range that it might end up at. And so we try to offer a high advance that we think will be compelling to–to the agent ") 3;03:13-15 (Pande) ("So preemptive offers tend to be quite high because it has to incentivize us to be willing to take the book off

[7] *See* PX 937-B (one-round and best-bid auction with beginning high bid of$375,000 and winning bid of $550,000); PX 938-B (four-round and best-bid auction with beginning high bid of$250,000 and winning bid of $750,000); PX 716 (addressing auction summarized in PX 938-B); Trial Tr. at 435:21-437:19 (Karp) (same); PX 939-B (seven-round auction with beginning high bid of$300,000 and winning bid of$1.5 million); PX 940-B (five- round and best-bid auction with beginning high bid of $400,000 and winning bid of $1.1 million for two books); PX 941-B (eight-round auction with beginning high bid of$550,000 and winning bid of$825,000); PX 947-B (two- round and opportunity-to-improve auction with beginning high bid of$500,000 and winning bid of$600,000 and bonuses for two books); PX 950-B (three-round and best-bid auction with a chance to improve, with beginning high bid of$250,000 and winning bid of$700,000); PX 951-B (best-bid and opportunity-to-improve auction with initial preempt offer of $750,000 and winning bid of$1.1 million); PX 954-B (three-round and best-bid auction with beginning high bid of$750,000 and winning bid of$1.05 million); PX 955-B (one-round auction with opportunity to improve, with beginning high bid of$800,000 and winning bid of$1.5 million); PX 729 (book initially received $750,000 preemptive offer from S&S, went to auction, and then S&S made an offer 10% higher than final auction bid, for offer of $1.1 million); Trial Tr. at 445:5-448:11 (Karp) (addressing book in PX 729).

the table and not offer it in a competitive situation."). As agent Gail Ross stated: "[I]n this business, there's always the other competitor. Whether they're bidding or not, they're always there." *Id.* at 2127:11-13.

Agents often submit a book to more than one imprint within a publishing company, *see id.* at 250:10-251:3 (Pande), and publishers sometimes allow their imprints to bid against one another in auctions. For example, PRH allows competitive bidding between its divisions, so long as there also is an external bidder; but for imprints within the same division, PRH requires the division to submit a "house bid." *See id.* at 769:2-20 (Dohle), 935:20-936:1 (Tart), 943:3- 24 (Tart); PX 332 (email from PRH staff to agent explaining imprint bidding rules). A house bid is a single bid made on behalf of more than one imprint from a particular publisher; the house bid allows the agent to choose which imprint to work with, and each imprint might also submit a "pitch," *i.e.,* a letter or memo describing its editorial and other services. *See* PX 2002 (Stehlik) at 75-76. Hachette also allows its imprints to bid against one another if there is an external bidder, *see* Trial Tr. at 239:11-23 (Pietsch), and Macmillan appears to allow some imprint competition, *compare* PX 938-B (showing separate bids from two Macmillan imprints), *with* PX 941-B (showing house bid from Macmillan imprints), *and* PX 954-B (showing one bid from Macmillan imprints). S&S and HarperCollins, however, do not allow competitive bidding among their own imprints but instead require their imprints to submit house bids. *See* Trial Tr. at 463:11-13 (Karp), 600:8-10 (Karp), 2119:11-24 (Ross); PX 2002 (Stehlik) at 75-76. Allowing sibling imprints to compete against each other increases the publisher's chances of winning a title; gives the editors from each imprint the freedom to pursue their desired projects, and allows authors more choice in finding the most "comfortable home" and best editorial match for their books. Trial Tr. at 839:11-840:4 (Dohle).

Although internal competition may yield benefits to publishers and authors, it is not in a publisher's economic interest to allow its own imprints to drive up the price of an acquisition, and publishers therefore take steps to limit internal competition. *See* PX 411 (presentation by Madeline McIntosh to PRH Board) at 4 (explaining that McIntosh had "[i]ncreased background coordination in auctions to leverage internal demand information better and avoid internal upbidding"); Trial Tr. at 239:11-23 (Pietsch) ("Once we have only Hachette imprints bidding, then continuing to bid each other up would hurt the company's collective P&L."). Ample evidence in the record demonstrates that PRH imprints often coordinate their bids within the same auction, artificially suppressing advances. *See id.* at 2341:9-2345:7 (McIntosh), 2373:9- 2382:8 (McIntosh); PX 107 (email from McIntosh) ("I feel we should coordinate– shouldn't be forced into bidding against each other for existing authors"); PX 121 (emails between McIntosh and PRH executive Nina von Moltke) (coordinating imprint bids). For example, PRH imprints sometimes agree to submit the same bid. *See* PX 107 ("We are coordinated. Bill [Knopf Doubleday] and Kara [Random House] will agree to a number and both offer same."). They also sometimes arrange to start their bidding from a lower number. *See* PX 116 (emails between von Moltke and McIntosh) (deciding that PRH imprints "go in a bit lower in round 1"). Finally, PRH imprints sometimes decide to collectively "move up slowly" in their bidding, particularly if PRH is the "main driver of value." PX 336 (email from PRH executive to Tart). PRH appears to take pride in its successful program of bid coordination. *See* PX 421 (email from von Moltke to McIntosh) (discussing auction where three top bids at $600,000 were from PRH imprints and noting she was "[g]lad we didn't go higher (this one definitely benefitted from the coordination!)"). This type of behavior from independent companies would be illegal. *Cf United States v. Apple, Inc.,* 791 F.3d 290,339 (2d Cir. 2015).

In competing for the most attractive new books, the Big Five have significant advantages over smaller publishers. Most critically, the Big Five have the capital to take chances and place bigger bets on a book's success; that is, they can offer higher advances for more books. Indeed, agents and authors choose the Big Five because "they are most likely to pay an appropriate advance," *see* Trial Tr. at 246:19-22 (Pande); and at least one mid-size competitor observes that the Big Five often "overpay" for books. *See* DX 422 (Glusman) at 76. The Big Five can afford to take on more risk by paying higher advances because they have the most substantial back lists, which are highly profitable. A book that does not sufficiently earn out its advance is a "loss" for the publisher,[8] but a publisher that has a steady income stream from its back list has a higher tolerance for absorbing such losses. *See* Trial Tr. at 156:5-158:10 (Pietsch), 160:7-161:7 (Pietsch), 1066:22-25 (Weisberg) ("It[] obviously has an impact on the bottom line if [your] unearned advances are too large."). PRH has the largest back list in the industry, and its back list is the most significant source of its revenue. *See id.* at 2358:2-7 (McIntosh).

The Big Five also offer significant advantages in ensuring a book's presence in the media and visibility to its target audience. The Big Five publishers and their individual imprints have teams dedicated solely to selling, marketing, and publicizing books, which have built critical relationships with booksellers and the media. *See* PX 2004 (Solomon) at 64 ("There's just a whole industry that responds better to Big Five publishers."); Trial Tr. at 259:13-260:4 (Pande), 840:5-841:12 (Dohle), 983:12-25 (Tart). Big Five publicity teams "engage with the media to promote the book." Trial Tr. at 1047:16-20 (Tart). Those teams can secure author interviews on prominent programs like the Today Show, Good Morning America, or NPR, and can persuade senior book reviewers to closely read and review the book. *See* PX 2004 (Solomon) at 63-64.[9]

The Big Five's sales teams can help ensure that stores not only buy books but place them in prominent displays. *See* Trial Tr. at 174:19-175:5 (Pietsch), 1372:11-25 (Murray), 1378:4- 1379:9 (Murray); PX 2002 (Stehlik) at 112 ("I would say generally the Big Five seem to have more visibility in stores than other smaller publishers."). The Big Five edge extends to the virtual marketplace; for instance, PRH hires data scientists to study Amazon's search algorithms and spends money to get books better positioned in Amazon's search results. *See* Trial Tr. at 893:6-16 (Dohle); PX 2002 (Stehlik) at 112.

Meanwhile, marketing teams are responsible for paid advertising and use "every device possible to find that [book's] audience." *See* Trial Tr. at 1067:17-1068:14 (Weisberg). In service of that goal, they produce market research and data analytics, as well as send marketing materials to traditional outlets or social media influencers. *See id.* at 983:12-25 (Tart), 1849:13- 25 (Bergstrom), 1938:5-12 (Duhigg). The Big Five can even ensure that books look better when they reach an audience, providing multiple versions of cover art for an author to choose from. *See* PX 2001 (Zacharius) at 37 ([REDACTED] Trial Tr. at 1920:4-13 (Duhigg) ("[Random House] came up with something like 13 or 15 different mock-up book jackets to try and figure out like which one is going to attract the reader's eyes when it's sitting there on a shelf and get them to pick it up.").

By contrast, smaller publishers might have a handful of staff doing all the editing, marketing, publicity, and sales work on a book. *See id.* at 259:13-260:4 (Pantle). Although some of their books do well, that success is harder won and less frequent. *See* PX 2004 (Solomon) at 64 ("[T]here's some fabulous books that are published by other houses and some of them end up being successful. But it's harder when you have fewer resources. It's easier when you have more resources."). Authors want the easy advantages offered by the Big Five's strong publicity, marketing, and sales teams.[10] Authors know that "when a publisher really gets behind a book, particularly a big publisher, the chances are that that book is going to probably succeed on some level." *See* Trial Tr. at 335:23-336:1 (King).

Successful authors who first publish with smaller publishers often prefer to publish their next book with a Big Five publisher. *See id.* at 291:10-292:25 (Pantle). Along with their substantial resources, Big Five publishers have developed a valuable reputation for having strong editorial staff with experience working with the best books and authors. *See* PX 530 at 2 (opining that Big Five "are known for their strong

---

[8] A book need not earn out its entire advance for a publisher to profit; publishers begin to profit "at around 70 percent of earnout for most books." *See* Trial Tr. at 1240:9-12 (Hill), 2258:21-25 (McIntosh).

[9] *See* PX 2004 (Solomon) at 63-64. ("You know, your book comes out and what do you want; you want to be on NPR, you want to be on Good Morning America or the Today Show, you want to ... do a radio interview with Terry Gross.... The publishers at the Big Five houses have more ready access to all of that. And ... if there is a new book that [S&S imprint] Scribner said is a really major title, it will at least be closely read by the editors of book reviews in a way that a book coming from a more obscure press is likely to go to a junior reader"); Trial Tr. at 1047:16-20 (Tart), 167:17-168:9 (Pietsch) ("And so to get [the media] to pay attention to your emails or return your phone calls or come out to lunch or come to your pitch event, it takes a long time in developing a lot of credibility."), 1372:11-25 (Murray) ("And then we have publicists who have relationships with television and radio producers.").

[10] *See* PX 2002 (Stehlik) at 101 ("Most authors want to have their books in as many locations as possible."), 112 (suggesting that visibility is one reason "why many agents and authors prefer to go with bigger publishers").

editorial skills").[11] Thus, a second book with a Big Five publisher gives the author a better chance of an even bigger success. *See* Trial Tr. at 291:10-292:25 (Pantle). The Big Five view the smaller publishers as a "farm team" for spotting writing talent, and routinely lure authors away from the non-Big Five publishers with higher advances and the promise of superior marketing, distribution, and even cover design. *See* PX 530 at 2 (explaining that small publishers "become farm teams for authors who then want to move to a larger, more financially stable major publisher"); Trial Tr. at 291:10-292:25 (Pande), 335:412 (King) (describing smaller publishers as the "minor leagues for writers"). The trial record contains many examples of authors who moved from non-Big Five publishers to the Big Five after establishing a track record of success. *See* Trial Tr. at 292:6-12 (Pande) ("I have had several authors who have moved from small publishers to larger publishers. One of the authors' names is Lad[ee] Hubbard. Her first book was published by Melville House. And for her second book, she moved to [HarperCollins]. My author Lisa Ko moved from Algonquin to Penguin Random House."); DX 423 (Glusman) at 15-19 [REDACTED] Of course, there are exceptions, as the defendants point out. *See, e.g.,* ECF No. 178 (Defendants' Sealed Proposed Findings of Fact) ¶ 70 (citing PX 2001 (Zacharius) Law) ¶¶ 9-10).[12] [REDACTED] *see also* ECF No. 182 (Defendants' Redacted Proposed Conclusions of Self-publishing is not a significant factor in the publishing industry. Self-published books are rarely published in print and are typically limited to online distribution. *See* Trial Tr. at 173:13-23 (Pietsch), 1108:2-9 (Weisberg). The authors of self-published books cannot pay themselves an advance. *See id.* at 173:8-15 (Pietsch) (remarking that for advances above $100,000, "I do not consider [self-publishing] a threat at all because [s]elf-published authors can't pay themselves an advance against royalties"). Moreover, individual authors generally do not have relationships with media or distributors necessary to ensure that their books are visible to a potential audience. *See id.* at 173:13-23 (Pietsch) ("Self-published authors don't have the ability to attract the attention of media. Imagine how hard it is for one person who has a book they published entirely on their own to say: Give me your attention. Review my book. Promote my book. And so they simply don't have access to the general-interest market that we and the other Big 5 publishers address routinely. That's our business."). In short, self-publishing cannot compete with the experience and resources of publishing companies. *See id.* at 173:13-174:2 (Pietsch); PX 2004 (Solomon) at 52-53 ("I think a commercial publisher sells more books, gamers more reviews, gains more attention, does all kinds of things I [as an author] don't have all of those business competencies that are involved."); *see also* Trial Tr. at 2898:8-18 (Snyder) (positing that "self-publishing is not a relevant constraint").

II. LEGAL STANDARDS

Section 7 of the Clayton Act prohibits mergers and acquisitions "where in any line of commerce or in any activity affecting commerce in any section of the country, the effect of such acquisition may be substantially to lessen competition." 15 U.S.C. § 18. The "fundamental purpose" of Section 7 is "to arrest the trend toward concentration, the tendency to [monopoly or monopsony], before the [buyer's or seller's] alternatives disappear through merger "*United States v. Phila. Nat'l Bank,* 374 U.S. 321,367 (1963). Thus, Congress "sought to assure the courts the power to brake this force at its outset and before it gathered momentum." *Brown Shoe Co. v. United States,* 370 U.S. 294, 317-18 (1962).[13]

---

[11] *See also* Trial Tr. at 353:8-25 (Eulau) (acknowledging that "reputation is important" for attracting authors), 454:11-22 (Karp) (agreeing that S&S's decades of credibility and success attracts authors), 535:7-20 (Karp) (noting that a Macmillan imprint has "a long reputation, so they can claim that when they publish a writer, that writer will be following in the tradition of other great award-winning Nobel laureates"), 1375:24-1376:23 (Murray) ("[To acquire top authors,] [y]ou have to have ... expertise and a reputation. It helps if you have published authors that are publishing to the similar readers, you know, so you can point to similar books that maybe you published one, two, or three years ago that were successful."), 2005:15-2006:18 (Kim) ("[A]uthors want to be published by publishers with good reputations, good standing, you know, with booksellers and media. They want to be a part of a list that they can be proud to say they're a part of.").

[12] Defendants proposed conclusions of fact and law are contained in the same document (ECF No. 178) but are separately enumerated. The Court will refer to the proposed conclusions of fact as "Defs. PFOF" and proposed conclusions of law as "Defs. PCOL."

[13] The government's theory is that the combined defendants would exercise market power on the buy-side of the publishing market, *i.e.,* monopsony. Although most antitrust law has developed under sell-side theories of harm, *i.e.,* monopoly, monopsony analysis relies on similar principles. Under the Horizontal Merger Guidelines, discussed *infra* at n.15, "to evaluate whether a merger is likely to enhance market power on the buying side of the market, the Agencies employ essentially the framework described ... for evaluating whether a merger is likely to enhance market power on the selling side of the market." U.S. Dept. of Justice & Fed. Trade Comm'n, Horizontal Merger Guidelines *§* 12 (2010), https://www.justice.gov/sites/default/files/atr/legacy/2010/08/19/hmg-2010.pdf ("Merger Guidelines"). "The kinship between monopoly and monopsony suggests that similar legal standards should apply to claims of monopolization and to claims of monopsonization." *Weyerhaeuser Co.*

To this end, "Congress used the words *may* be substantially to lessen competition to indicate that its concern was with probabilities, not certainties." *FTC v. HJ Heinz Co.,* 246 F.3d 708, 713 (D.C. Cir. 2001) (emphasis in original) (quoting *Brown Shoe,* 370 U.S. at 323). The government "must prove the alleged Clayton Act violation by a preponderance of the evidence," *i.e.,* that the merger would more likely than not violate the statute; but "'[S]ection 7 does not require proof that a merger or other acquisition will cause higher prices [or anticompetitive effects] in the affected market. All that is necessary is that the merger create an appreciable danger of such consequences in the future.'" *United States v. Anthem, Inc.,* 236 F. Supp. 3d 171, 192 (D.D.C. 2017) (first quoting *United States v. SunGard Data Sys., Inc.,* 172 F. Supp. 2d 172, 180 (D.D.C. 2001); and then quoting *Hosp. Corp. of Am. v. FTC,* 807 F.2d 1381, 1389 (7th Cir. 1986).[14]Section 7's probabilistic standard "creates a relatively expansive definition of antitrust liability" and "subjects mergers to searching scrutiny." *California v. Am.Stores Co.,* 495 U.S. 271,284 (1990).[15]

Although "Congress neither adopted nor rejected specifically any particular tests for measuring the relevant markets [where commerce is affected] [n]or [defined] the word 'substantially,' *Brown Shoe,* 370 U.S. at 320-21, the D.C. Circuit has taken a burden-shifting approach to Section 7 cases. *See AT&T, Inc.,* 916 F.3d at 1032; *Heinz,* 246 F.3d at 715; *United States v. Baker Hughes Inc.,* 908 F.2d 981, 982-83 (D.C. 1990). The *Baker Hughes* test, as it has come to be known, has a preliminary requirement and three steps. At the threshold, the government must demonstrate the existence of a relevant market. *See Marine Bancorp.,* 418 U.S. 602, 618 (1974); *FTC v. RAG-Stiftung,* 436 F. Supp. 3d 278, 291-92 (D.D.C. 2020). Once it has done so, the first step of the test allows the government to establish a prima facie case and a presumption of anticompetitive effects by demonstrating undue concentration within that relevant market. *See Anthem,* 855 F.3d at 349; *Heinz,* 246 F.3d at 715. The second step shifts the burden to the defendants, who must demonstrate in rebuttal that real-world conditions make market concentration alone an unreliable predictor of the merger's anticompetitive effects. *See Anthem,* 855 F.3d at 349-50; *Heinz,* 246 F.3d at 715. If the defendants successfully rebut the prima facie case, the burden shifts back to the government in the third step "and merges with the ultimate burden of persuasion, which remains with the government at all times." *Baker Hughes,* 908 F.2d at 983; *accord Anthem,* 855 F.3d at 350.

III. ANALYSIS

The government contends that the merger of PRH and S&S would harm competition to acquire the publishing rights to "anticipated top-selling books," resulting in lower advances for the authors of such books and less favorable contract terms. The defendants do not dispute that if advances are significantly decreased, some authors will not be able to write, resulting in fewer books being published, less variety in the marketplace of ideas, and an inevitable loss of intellectual and creative output. *See* Trial Tr. at 772:8-25 (Dohle). The defendants vigorously contest, however, whether advances would decrease after the merger: They contend that competition would not be harmed and that advances would actually rise.

---

v. Ross-Simmons Hardwood Lumber Co., 549 U.S. 312, 321-22 (2007). "Monopsony and monopsony power are the equivalent on the buying side of monopoly and monopoly power on the selling side." *United States v. Syufy Enters.* 903 F.2d 659, 663 n.4 (9th Cir. 1990) (quotations omitted).

[14] Although defendants quote *United States v. Marine Bancorporation,* 418 U.S. 602, 623 n.22 (1974), for the proposition that a merger's anticompetitive effects must also be "imminent" to violate the Clayton Act, *see* Defs. PCOL, 1, the full quotation from that case is that "the loss of competition 'which is *sufficiently* probable and imminent' is the concern of§ 7," *Marine Bancorp.,* 418 U.S. at 623 n.22 (emphasis added) (citation omitted). The Court understands that description of the standard to be functionally indistinguishable from the D.C. Circuit's formulation of the Section 7 standard, as described above.

[15] In *United States v. AT&T, Inc.,* the D.C. Circuit described the Section 7 standard of proof as follows: "[T]he government must show that the proposed merger is likely to substantially lessen competition, which encompasses a concept of 'reasonable probability."' 916 F.3d 1029, 1032 (D.C. Cir. 2019) (emphasis deleted) (quoting *Brown Shoe,* 370 U.S. at 323 n.39). The parties dispute the meaning of this language. The defendants argue that AT&T require[s the government] to prove that a merger is 'likely' to cause substantial harm to competition, [not] only that harm 'may' occur." Defs. PCOL 2. The government points to *AT&T's* explanation "that this standard encompasses a concept of 'reasonable probability," 'arguing that *AT&T* requires something less than what the defendants propose. *See* Govt. PFOF-PCOL 38, 40; *see also id* 38 (arguing for an "appreciable danger" standard). The root of these competing formulations may be uncertainty over how the government's preponderance-of-the-evidence burden interacts with Section 7's already probabilistic standard; combined, the two standards require the government to prove "by a preponderance of the evidence" that the effect of a challenged merger or acquisition "may be substantially to lessen competition." *Anthem,* 236 F. Supp. 3d at 192. Like the district court in *AT&T,* this Court "need not further toil over discerning or a1iiculating the daylight, if any, between 'appreciable danger,' 'probable,' 'reasonably probable,' and 'likely' as used in the Section 7 context." *United States v. AT&T,* 310 F. Supp. 3d 161, 189 n.16 (D.D.C. 2018). The selection of any of the competing pe1mutations is not outcome-determinative in this case.

A. Market Definition

The first step in merger analysis is the identification of a relevant market. *See Marine Bancorp.,* 418 U.S. at 618. Market definition "helps specify the line of commerce and section of the country in which the competitive concern arises"; and allows the Court to evaluate any anticompetitive effects by "identify[ing] market participants and measur[ing] market shares and market concentration." Merger Guidelines§ 4.[16] "Determination of the relevant market is a necessary predicate to a finding of a violation of the Clayton Act because the threatened monop[sony] must be one which will substantially lessen competition 'within the area of effective competition.'" *United States v. E.1 du Pont de Nemours & Co.,* 353 U.S. 586, 593 (1957) (quoting *Standard Oil Co. of Cal. v. United States,* 337 U.S. 293, 299 n.5 (1949). But defining a relevant market is not an end unto itself; rather, it is an analytical tool used to ascertain the "locus of competition." *Brown Shoe,* 370 U.S. at 320-21; *see also* Merger Guidelines *§* 4.1.1 ("[T]he purpose of defining the market and measuring market shares is to illuminate the evaluation of competitive effects."). Accordingly, the Supreme Court has emphasized that market definition under the Clayton Act was intended by Congress to be "a pragmatic, factual" analysis and "not a formal, legalistic one." *Brown Shoe,* 370 U.S. at 336.

Market definition has two components: the relevant geographic market and the relevant product market. *See Brown Shoe,* 370 U.S. at 324; *Anthem,* 236 F. Supp. 3d at 193. Here, the parties agree that the relevant geographic market is the global market for the acquisition of U.S. publishing rights. *See* Govt. PFOF-PCOL 125; ECF No. 1 (Complaint) 40; ECF No. 56 (Amended Answer) 40 (agreeing "that Penguin Random House and Simon & Schuster compete with each other and with many other publishers to acquire rights to publish books in the United States and that authors who sell U.S. publishing rights can reside anywhere in the world."). The parties strenuously dispute, however, the boundaries of the appropriate product market.

The government defines the relevant product market as the one for publishing rights to anticipated top-selling books. *See* Govt. PFOF-PCOL 15, 63. Anticipated top-selling books are those that are expected to yield significant sales, and for which authors therefore receive higher advances. *See id.* 15. The government contends that such books have distinctive characteristics, including the need for extra marketing, publicity, and sales support to allow them to reach broader audiences. *See id.* 15, 64-68, 87, 93-119.

The proposed market for anticipated top-selling books is a submarket of the broader publishing market for all trade books. *See id.* 124; *see also* Defs. PCOL 9-10 (explaining that the "market for the acquisition of *all* U.S. trade books" is an appropriate, broader market). Under the government's monopsony theory, the authors of anticipated top-selling books are "targeted sellers" against whom the merged defendants might lower the prices paid for the authors' wares. *See* Govt. PFOF-PCOL ¶¶ 55-58, 69-76; *see also* Merger Guidelines§ 4.1.4 (If a monopsonist could "profitably target a subset of [sellers] for price [de]creases, the [government] may identify relevant markets defined around those targeted [sellers]."); *cj FTC v. Wilh. Wilhelmsen Holding ASA,* 341 F. Supp. 3d 27, 46-47 (D.D.C. 2018) ("[A]ntitrust markets can be based on targeted customers"); *Sysco,* 113 F. Supp. 3d at 38-40 (discussing definition of markets based on targeted customers). In the monopsony context, "[a] submarket exists when [buyers] can profitably [cut] prices to certain targeted [sellers] but not to others, in which case regulators may evaluate competitive effects separately by type of [seller]." *Anthem,* 236 F. Supp. 3d at 195.

Courts evaluate relevant product markets in the monopsony context in two ways: by considering qualitative, "practical indicia" as described by the Supreme Court in the *Brown Shoe* case, 370 U.S. at 325; and by examining "supply substitution" and applying the "hypothetical monopsonist test," which are discussed in detail, *infra.* The parties in this case focus their arguments on whether "practical indicia" support the finding of a market to publish "anticipated top-selling books." Because the parties choose to

[16] The Merger Guidelines "outline the principal analytical techniques, practices, and the enforcement policy of the Department of Justice and the Federal Trade Commission" for merging competitors under federal antitrust laws. Merger Guidelines *§* I. They "describe the principal analytical techniques and the main types of evidence on which the Agencies usually rely to predict whether a horizontal merger may substantially lessen competition." *Id* Although the Merger Guidelines are not binding, courts have consistently looked to them for guidance in merger cases. *See, e.g., FTC v. Sysco Corp.,* 113 F. Supp. 3d 1, 38 (D.D.C. 2015).

fight on the battlefield of "practical indicia," that is where the Court begins its analysis.

1. Practical Indicia

"[W]ithin [a] broad market, well-defined submarkets may exist which, in themselves, constitute product markets for antitrust purposes. The boundaries of such a submarket may be determined by examining such practical indicia as industry or public recognition of the submarket as a separate economic entity, the product's peculiar characteristics and uses, unique production facilities, distinct [sellers], distinct prices, sensitivity to price changes, and specialized vendors." *Brown Shoe,* 370 U.S. at 325. These indicia are "practical aids" as opposed to "talismanic" criteria "to be rigidly applied," *FTC v. Swedish Match,* 131 F. Supp. 2d 151, 159 (D.D.C. 2000); thus, "submarkets can exist even if only some of these factors are present." *FTC v. Staples, Inc.,* 970 F. Supp. 1066, 1075 (D.D.C. 1997) *("Staples* I").

Brown Shoe's practical indicia also may help identify a market of targeted sellers. *See FTC v. Whole Foods Market, Inc.,* 548 F.3d 1028, 1038-39 (D.C. Cir. 2008) (citing *Brown Shoe,* 370 U.S. at 325). For example, a market of "distinct [sellers]," as posited by the government, may find "a particular [set of buyers] 'uniquely attractive' and "the only realistic choice" for their products. *Id.* (first citing *Brown Shoe,* 370 U.S. at 325; then quoting *Nat'l Collegiate Athletic Ass'n v. Bd. of Regents of the Univ. of Okla.,* 468 U.S. 85, **111** (1984); and then quoting *SuperTurj,· Inc. v. Monsanto Co.,* 660 F.2d 1275, 1278 (8th Cir. 1981).

1. i. The $250,000 Threshold

To identify the books that are anticipated to sell well, the government focuses on the criterion of "distinct pricing": For analytical purposes, it defines anticipated top-selling books as those for which publishers pay an advance of at least $250,000. *See* Govt. PFOF-PCOL, ¶ 64; *Brown Shoe,* 370 U.S. at 325 (explaining that "distinct prices" are probative in market definition); *see also Whole Foods,* 548 F.3d at 1038-39 (explaining distinct prices paid by targeted group of customers "indicate[] the existence of a submarket of core customers"); *Syujy Enters. v. Am. Multicinema, Inc.,* 793 F.2d 990, 995 (9th Cir. 1986) (considering "lucrative terms offered for the pictures by exhibitors" to define relevant market). Books that meet the $250,000- advance threshold comprise only 2 percent of all book acquisitions, but they account for 70 percent of all advance spending, amounting to $1 billion annually. *See* Govt. PFOF-PCOL ¶¶ 15, 68 (citing Trial Tr. at 1239:10-24 (Hill), 2904:17-2905:3 (Snyder). Government's Exhibit 963 shows that the market shares of industry participants in the proposed publishing market for anticipated top-selling books are far more concentrated than in the market for publishing books at lower advance levels:

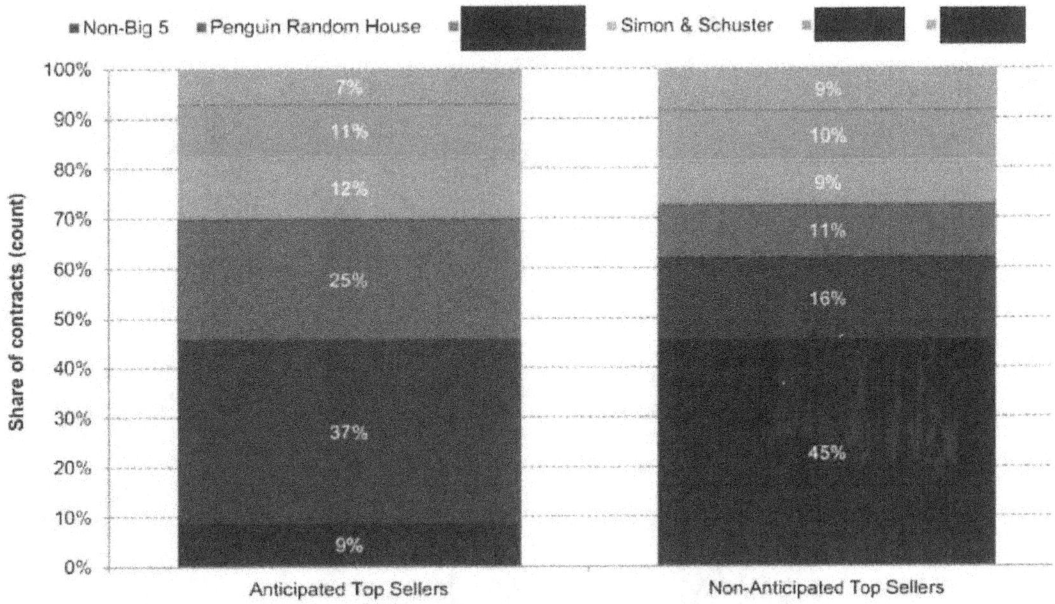

Source: Snyder Advance Data.

In the publishing market for anticipated top-selling books, the Big Five publishers hold 91 percent of the market share, while smaller publishers collectively hold only 9 percent PX 963. By contrast, in the publishing market for books that earn advances below $250,000, the non-Big Five publishers have a much more substantial market share of 45 percent. *Id.*

As an initial matter, the government's use of high advances as a proxy for anticipated book sales is logical and supp01ted by market realities. In publishing, advances are correlated with expected sales because books that are expected to sell well receive higher advances. *See supra* Section J.B. In fact, advance levels are set by using P&L's, and the defining feature of a P&L is the sales estimate. *See id.;* Trial Tr. at 917:13-16 (Tru1) ("[T]he higher sales equate to a higher advance in the P&L."). Moreover, industry practices indicate that $250,000 is a reasonable place to draw the line: S&S and two of the three PRH adult divisions require approval from senior publishers or executives for advance offers of $250,000 or more; and *Publishers .Marketplace,* a major industry publication, categorizes deals for $250,000 or more as "significant."[17] *See* Trial Tr. at 1233:5-135 (Hill), 459:5-8 (Karp), 1993:1-3 (Kim), 914:22-915:2 (Tali), 2261:12-2262:5 (McIntosh); PX 989). [REDACTED] This evidence is probative of "industry or public recognition" of a distinct category of books that receive advances at or above the $250,000 level. *Brown Shoe,* 370 U.S. at 325.

The defendants take aim at the $250,000 threshold that the government has chosen to b01md the market. *See* Defs. PCOL ¶ 23-25, 28-41. Most significantly, they argue that the $250,000 threshold is either too high or too low to define a submarket for anticipated top selling books. *Id.* 28-41; Defs. PFOF ¶¶ 33-43. Specifically, the defendants rely on their Exhibit 438 to argue that the advance threshold should be set at

[17] As for other Big Five publishers. Hachette does not have a company-wide approval policy, but its different imprints require approval for offers from above $100,000 to above $250,000. *See* Trial Tr. at 232:21-233:5 (Pietsch) ("All om publishers have advance approval levels and they are clustered right around [$250,000]"). Hachette also tracks the books it lost for advances of $500,000 or more. *See* PX 790. [REDACTED]. *See* Trial Tr. at 1438:8-11 [REDACTED] 1102:13 (Weisberg); DX 408.

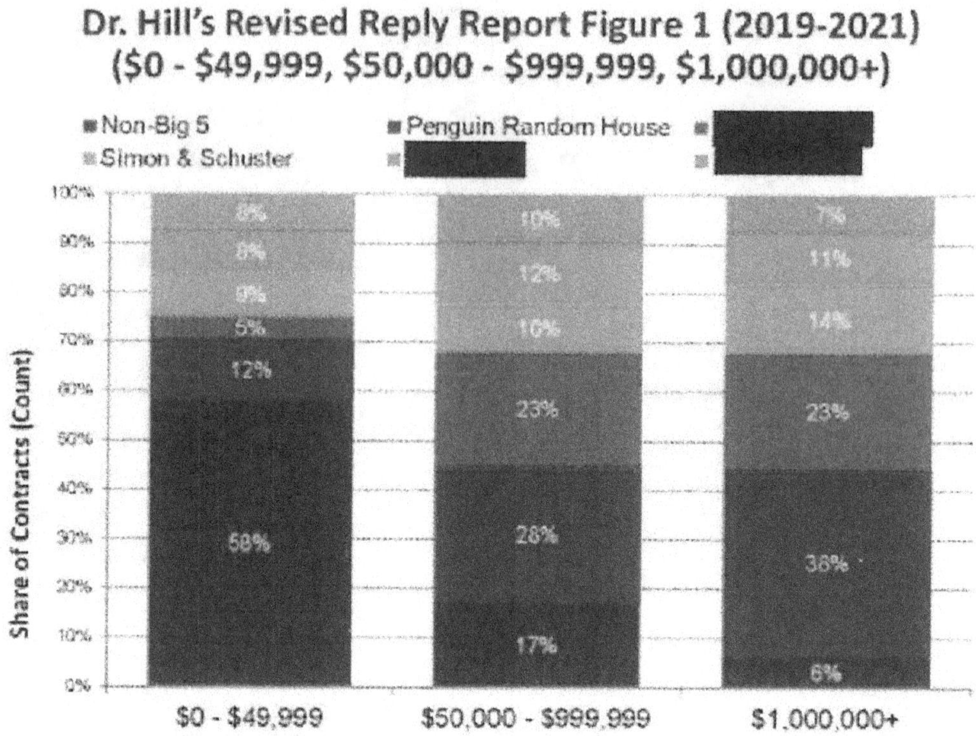

$50,000 to capture the point at which the Big Five begin to dominate the market for acquiring books. *See* Defs. PFOF, ¶ 37 ("[T]he data establish that *if* competitive conditions differ based on market shares and author preferences, the difference begins with books acquired for advances of $50,000 or more," where the market share of non-Big Five publishers is reduced from 58% to 17%.); Defs. PCOL ¶¶ 31-34. Alternatively, the defendants contend that the threshold should be set at $1 million to identify the books by celebrity, franchise, or award-winning authors that are most clearly destined for success. *See* Defs. PFOF ¶¶ 37-40; Defs. PCOL ¶¶ 35-41. If the relevant market were properly defined at the lower ($50,000) or higher ($1 million) advance level, the defendants urge, the government could not show a sufficient decrease to competition or harm to authors. *See* Defs. PFOF ¶¶ 38, 42-43.

The defendants' excessive concern over the specific dollar threshold betrays a misunderstanding of why the threshold was chosen. The market that the government seeks to define is the one for anticipated top-selling books, and the $250,000 demarcation was adopted only as an analytical tool to help it group together the books in question. The government's economic expert, Dr. Nicholas Hill, also conducted his analyses at other numerical thresholds (including $150,000, $250,000, $500,000, and $1 million) and observed consistent outcomes at those various high-dollar amounts. *See* PX 960; Trial Tr. at 1254:7-25 Hill), 1259:2-12 (Hill), 1233:14-20 (Hill). Thus, the $250,000 cutoff is merely useful; it is not intended to be a rigid bright line, but rather is helpful "[f]or analytical purposes" to facilitate the assessment of anti-competitive effects. *FTC v. Staples, Inc.*, 190 F. Supp. 3d 100, 118 & n.10 (D.D.C. 2016) *("Staples II")* ("[T]here is no 'magic place that's the right place' to draw the line." (quoting government expert's testimony). Accordingly, the Court rejects this argument against the government's defined market.

The Court is unswayed by the defendants' tactic of enumerating other markets or submarkets in which competition would not be harmed by the merger. In addition to proposing submarkets at the $50,000- and $1 million- advance levels, the defendants also declare that the government could not prove anticompetitive effects from the merger in the broad market of publishing rights for all U.S. trade books, or in the downstream market for retail book sales. *See* Defs. PFOF ¶¶ 29-31. Those protestations are beside the point because the Clayton Act prohibits mergers that may substantially lessen competition "in *any* line of commerce or in *any* activity affecting commerce." 15 U.S.C. § 18 (emphasis added). Thus, even if alternative submarkets exist at other advance levels, or if there are broader markets that might be analyzed, the viability of such additional markets docs not render the one identified by the government unusable. *See United States v. Cont'l Can Co.,* 378 U.S. 441, 456-58 (1964) (validating a relevant product market of glass and metal containers, even though "there may be a broader product market made up of metal, glass and other competing containers"); *United States v. Aluminum Co. of Am.,* 377 U.S. 271, 275 (1964) (explaining that even though insulated aluminum conductor and insulated copper conductor could both be in "a single product market," that "does not preclude their division for purposes of [Section] 7 into separate submarkets"); *see also Brown Shoe,* 370 U.S. at 325; *Anthem,* 236 F. Supp. 3d at 201-02.

Ample precedent supports the government's use of a numerical cutoff to identify a submarket. It is common for courts to use seemingly arbitrary criteria to home in on a segment of a broader industry. *See Wilhelmsen,* 341 F. Supp. 3d at 51 (market of customers with fleets of 10 or more global maritime vessels); *Anthem,* 236 F. Supp. 3d at 195 (market of companies with 5,000 or more employees); *Staples II,* 190 F. Supp. 3d at 118 (market of customers who spend $500,000 or more annually on office supplies). In *Wilhelmsen,* Judge Chutkan approved a relevant market "defined around the FTC's preferred set of targeted customers"– "Global Fleets." 341 F. Supp. 3d at 48, 58. The government characterized "Global Fleets" as "fleets of 10 or more globally trading vessels." *Id.* at 51. Although the defendants argued "that the Global Fleets construct is premised on arbitrary thresholds," the court found that such fleets "are a distinct group with distinct needs," even though the "choice of ten globally trading vessels was arbitrary in the sense that the number ten is not compelled by a specific market reality." *Id.* at 51-54. Judge Chutkan explained that the government's expert "chose ten as a starting point for developing a series of statistical estimates, the non-statistical implications of which support the appropriateness of regarding Global Fleets as a distinct customer group." *Id.* at 55. In other words, the cutoff of ten ships to define "Global Fleets" was an appropriate analytical tool, just as the choice of a $250,000-minimum advance level to define "anticipated top-selling books" is appropriate for analytical purposes. At bottom, such "construct[s]" provide a "useful way to discuss and predict economic conditions" because their "key aspects correspond to elements of the existing marketplace that would make it possible to profitably target a subset of customers [or sellers] for price increases [or decreases] post-merger." *Id.* at 52 (quoting *Sysco,* 113 F. Supp. 3d at 38).

The government's focus on anticipated top-selling books also is consistent with cases in which courts have recognized the "high end" of other broad markets as distinct submarkets for antitrust purposes. *See, e.g., Int'l Boxing Club of NY, Inc. v. United States,* 358 U.S. 242,251 (1959) (affirming district court's conclusion "that non-championship fights are not 'reasonably interchangeable for the same purpose' as championship contests" and explaining that defining the relevant market "involves distinction in degree as well as distinctions in kind"); *Whole Foods,* 548 F.3d at 1032 (recognizing relevant submarket of "premium, natural, and organic supermarkets" that "generally target affluent and well educated customers"); *O'Bannon v. Nat'l Collegiate Athletic Assn,* 7 F. Supp. 3d 955, 986-88 (N.D. Cal. 2014) (recognizing relevant submarket of "elite football and basketball recruits"), *relevant part on other grounds,* 802 F.3d 1049 (9th Cir. 2015). Thus, the relevant market defined here falls comfortably within the parameters set by numerous applicable precedents.

The defendants nevertheless fault the government for defining its submarket by "price alone," contending that any correlation between advance level and expected sales shows only that books "are valued along a *continuum.*" *See* Defs. PCOL ¶¶ 12, 24-25 (emphasis in original). They argue that the existence of "a spectrum of price or value" is insufficient to establish a submarket and, accordingly, that the government's market is not appropriately defined. *Id.*[18] Once again, such arguments overlook the

[18] In support, the defendants primarily rely on *In re Super Premium Ice Cream Distribution Antitrust Litig.,* 691 F. Supp. 1262 (N.D. Cal. 1988), *aff'd sub nom. Haagen-Dazs Co. v. Double Rainbow Gourmet lee Creams, Inc.,* 895 F.2d 1417 (9th Cir. 1990), and *United States v. Oracle Corp.,* 331 F. Supp. 2d 1098 (N.D. Cal. 2004). The Court finds both *In re Super Premium Ice Cream* and *Oracle* inapposite. Neither case concerns a market of targeted sellers or buyers, as relevant to this case. Further, in *In re Super Premium lee Cream,* the evidence showed that consumers who bought higher-priced "super premium" ice cream could and would buy lower-quality ice cream as a substitute. *See* 691 F. Supp. at 1268. Here, authors of anticipated top-selling books have no alternative to selling their books to a publisher because, as addressed in Section I.C, self-publishing is not a realistic alternative. Because they have no reasonable substitute, authors can be targeted for and impacted by a

purpose of the $250,000 threshold as an analytical tool that facilitates the examination of market shares and anticompetitive effects. The threshold number need not represent an exact point at which the market begins to distinguish a product. *See Wilhelmsen,* 341 F. Supp. 3d at 54-55; *Anthem, Inc.,* 236 F. Supp. 3d at 200 (accepting a 5,000-employee threshold to define "national accounts" even though the "threshold may exclude some products that would meet the needs of smaller employers"); *Staples II,* 190 F. Supp. 3d at 118 & n.10 ("[T]here is no 'magic place that's the right place' to draw the line." (quoting government expert's testimony). Rather, a threshold will necessarily represent a "starting point" for "statistical estimates, the non-statistical implications of which support the appropriateness of regarding" anticipated top-selling authors as a "distinct [seller] group" that buyers can target. *Wilhelmsen,* 341 F. Supp. 3d at 55.

2. ii. The Remaining Brown Shoe *Factors*

Aside from distinct pricing, the government argues that the remaining *Brown Shoe* factors demonstrate that there is a relevant submarket for the publishing rights to anticipated top-selling books. *See* Govt. PFOF-PCOL ¶¶ 87-114, 117-121. The government contends that such books have "peculiar characteristics and uses," in that they require stronger marketing, publicity, and sales support, which allow them to reach a broader audience of readers. *Id.* ¶¶ 87 (quoting *Brown Shoe,* 370 U.S. at 325), 93-95. In addition, authors of anticipated top-selling books are "distinct sellers," in that they (1) care more about their publishers' reputation and services, which ensure wider distribution of their books; (2) may receive more favorable contract terms than other authors; and (3) face different competitive conditions, as demonstrated by the dominant market share of the Big Five (91%) in publishing anticipated top sellers. *See id.* 66, 93-114, 117-119. For all those reasons, the government argues, anticipated top-selling books are in a different category from books that are expected to sell relatively few copies, and publishers can target their authors for price decreases.

The defendants, however, insist that all books are in the same market. They argue that books at all advance levels go through an identical editing, marketing, and distribution process; that there is no difference in the personnel who handle such books; that the contracts for all books are negotiated in the same way; and that any special terms in the contracts for some books simply result from an agent's leverage. *See* Defs. PFOF ¶¶ 47-67; Defs. PCOL ¶ 21. Further, they contend that publishers cannot predict which books will be top sellers. *See* Defs. PFOF ¶¶ 78 ("[P]ublishers generally have no objective criteria for reaching in advance a consensus on whether a book is likely to be a top selling book."), 79 (arguing that publishers "cannot easily predict top sellers," other than books by celebrity, franchise, or prize-winning authors), 75 (asserting that every book is individual and author atypical) (citing Trial Tr. at 1068:12-13 (Weisberg), 1952:20-25 (Duhigg); Defs. PCOL ¶ 21.

The Court has no trouble recognizing that anticipated top-selling books are distinct from the vast majority of books that do not carry the same expectations for success. Obviously, the entire publishing industry is dedicated to selling books; and all editors and publishers naturally are very focused on discovering and acquiring the books that they believe will drive sales. Evidence strongly supports the conclusion that, from the perspective of editors and publishers, not all books are created equal. Beyond advances, contracts for books that are expected to sell well are more likely to include favorable terms like higher royalty rates, higher levels of marketing support, "glam" packages *(e.g.,* for hair, makeup, and wardrobe services), and airfare for authors.[19] *See* Trial Tr. at 988:2-8 (Dohle) ("Very rarely, if ever, will I negotiate the other royalty rates, but if it were to happen, it would be at that very, very top tier advance

---

decrease in prices, in a manner that ice-cream customers could not have been targeted by a price increase. As for *Oracle,* there, the government attempted to define a market of "high function" software and tried to use a minimum sale price of$500,000 to identify such software. *See* 331 F. Supp. 2d at 1158. Yet there were several flaws in the data analyzed and presented by the government's expert. *See id* at 1158-59. Nor did the government offer any other qualitative or quantitative evidence to define the market. *See id.* Here, Dr. Hill's data suffers from no similar flaws and the government has marshalled evidence beyond the advance price to show practical indicia of a submarket for the publishing *rights* to anticipated top-selling books

[19] For example, Crown, a former publishing division of PRH that later merged with the Random House division, produced guidelines for marketing support based on expected sales and advance levels. *See* PX 986; Trial Tr. at 2275:19-2278:1 (McIntosh). Under those guidelines, books with expected sales of more than 25,000 units or advances of more than $150,000 were to receive a dedicated publicist, book tours with stops in 5 to 15 markets, extensive national media engagement, prominent placement on PRH and partner websites, and targeted social media pushes. *See* PX 986 at 2-4. By contrast, books with advances and sales under those thresholds were to have only a contact in the publicity department, smaller book tours (if any), and limited media engagement. *See id* at 5-9.

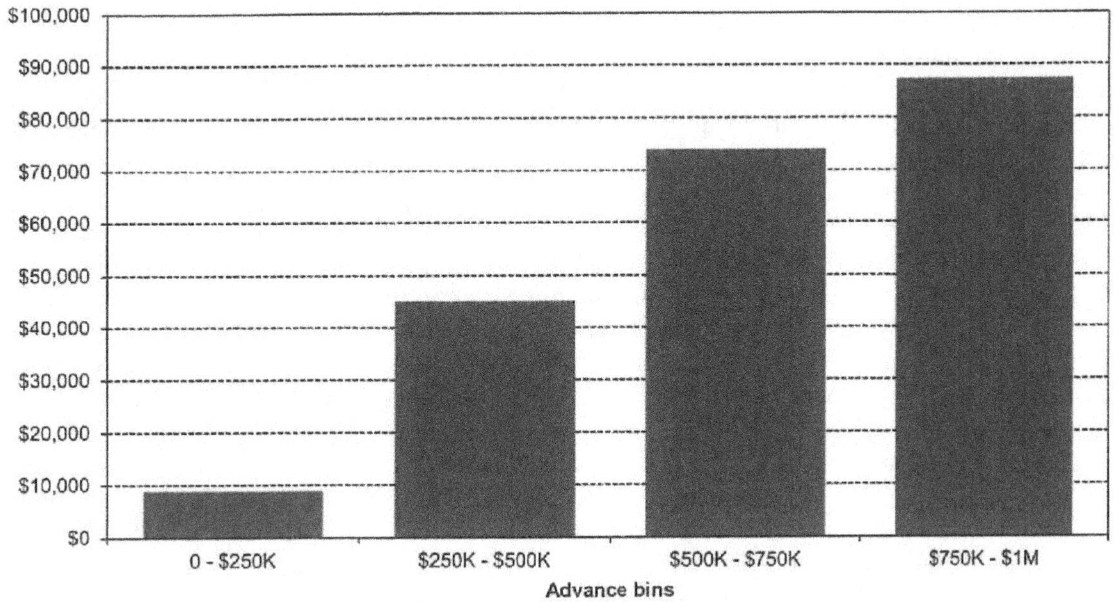

level."), 1132:17-23 (Weisberg) ("top end" authors can negotiate terms such as payment schedules, bonuses, and glam budgets), 1819:9-1820:2 (Walsh) (customization of contract terms is generally correlated with higher advances), 1828:8-18 (Walsh) (higher marketing commitments are expected for higher advance books); DX 21 at 5 (agent demanding "a publisher ready to commit incredible energy and resources"). Publishers print more of the books they think will do well; circulate more advance copies of such books to reviewers or influencers to create excitement; push for interviews with more media outlets; and schedule book-tour appearances in more locations.[20] *See* Trial Tr. at 1373:12-1374:3 (Murray); PX 986. Anticipated top-selling books also get more attention from marketing and sales teams.[21] For example, Dr. Hill determined that S&S and PRH spend, on average, under $10,000 on marketing for books with advances under $250,000, and between $40,000 and $90,000 on marketing for books with advances over $250,000. The fact that the Big Five publish 91 percent of anticipated top sellers also supports a finding that the authors of such books have unique needs and preferences. *See* PX 963.

Although smaller publishers can sometimes put out an anticipated top-selling book, it is the Big Five who have the back lists and the marketing, publicity, and sales advantages necessary to consistently provide the high advances and unique services that top-selling authors need. *See supra* Section I.C (discussing Big Five's publishing advantages). It is precisely those specialized needs that make the authors of anticipated top-selling books vulnerable to targeting for price reductions. Publishers of anticipated top-selling books know that such authors are not able to find adequate substitutes for publishing their books because of their unique needs and preferences. *See id.* Those publishers therefore can target authors of anticipated top-selling books for a decrease in advances (prices) because it is not as likely that such a price decrease will cause the publishers to lose a book. *See Wilhelmsen,* 341 F. Supp. 3d

[20] Some of the defendants' witnesses testified that all books are anticipated to sell well. *See* Trial Tr. At 576:17-24 ("[A] good editor worries about every book that he or she acquires, making every book profitable."), 1810:17-1812:4 (Walsh) ("I would say I always anticipate that what I am working on is going to be a best seller."). That assertion is not credible. Although an agent, author, or publisher may "hope" every book will be a hit, that is not the same as anticipating or expecting that a book will do well. *See id* at 1813:4-6 {The Court: "You don't expect every single book you work on to be a best seller or top seller?" Walsh: "Right. I hope."); *see also id* at 328:2-10 (King) (explaining that he chose a smaller publisher for a book that "wasn't a crafted best seller"), 593:21-594:8 (Karp) (recognizing that some books are "midlist" books that publishers are "hoping," but not anticipating, will be hits).

[21] *See* Trial Tr. at 258:14-21 (Pantle) ("I would say that there's a pretty clear relationship between the level of the advance and the amount of resources that the publisher invests in the marketing and publicity of the book."), 490:13-492:4 (Karp) ("[T]he big obvious books that we spent a lot of money for, they definitely have to be marketed and publicized aggressively."), 1373:1-11 (Murray), 2001:12-2002:4 (Kim); PX 989 (Putnam post- publication P&L sheet) (showing general correlation between advance level and marketing spending).

at 56-57 (finding targeted buyer market where market was characterized by individual negotiations and customers had unique needs and preferences); *Staples II,* 190 F. Supp. 3d at 127 (finding targeted buyer market where industry recognized customers as a distinct group that needed specific prices and services); *see also* Merger Guidelines § 4.1.4.

Although the defendants proclaim that no one in the industry uses the term "anticipated top seller," Defs. PFOF ¶¶ 87-88, that does not mean that such books do not exist. *See Wilhelmsen,* 341 F. Supp. 3d at 51-52 (rejecting defendant's argument "that the definition of Global Fleets does .not accord with commercial reality, given that [defendants do not] use the FTC's definition of that term ") *see also Lev. Zujfa, LLC,* 216 F. Supp. 3d 1154, 1159, 1165-66 (D. Nev. 2016) (denying motion to dismiss that was based in part on defendant's argument that "Elite Professional MMA fighters" is not a term used in the industry). In fact, market participants have other names for expected top sellers, such as "lead titles" or "priority titles."[22] Regardless of nomenclature, clear evidence demonstrates that the practice of identifying and giving special support to the books that will drive sales is common. The government's defined market thus reflects "commercial realities" in the publishing industry. *United States v. Grinnell Corp.,* 384 U.S. 563,572 (1966).

The defendants' position that individual publishers are unable to anticipate which books will be top sellers is unsupportable. That contention is contradicted by the universal industry practice of making a sales estimate for every single book before offering an advance, and credible testimony that there is often consensus among editors and publishers about which books will be popular with readers. *See supra* Section LC; Trial Tr. at 2108:14-24 (Wylie) ("But I think there are recognizable qualities in books that people who have been in the business for a long time would easily recognize."). The defendants' high share of the book-acquisition market and their substantial profit margins strongly indicate that they are successfully choosing books that people want to read. *See* PX 994; Trial Tr. at 781:3-5 (Dohle), 1492:2-3 (Hill). To be sure, editors often offer a range of advances for any given book, and the defendants correctly note that there are many examples of books that were unexpected best sellers, such as Stephen King's *Carrie,* or Marie Kondo's *The Life-Changing Magic of Tidying Up. See* Defs. PFOF ¶¶ 79, 81. But it is commonplace for multiple editors to gravitate to the same book, as evidenced by the routine occurrence of competitive auctions; and the defendants do not dispute that there is a general correlation between author advances and book sales, *see* Trial Tr. at 749:4-22 (Dohle); PX 151 at 11. That is strong evidence that the book-acquisition process is not random. Indeed, whenever a publisher submits a bid of $250,000 or more for a book, that publisher has determined that the book is likely to be a top seller and knows that the competitors for the book are likely to be limited to the Big Five. *See* Trial Tr. at 153:10-13 (Pietsch) (other Big Five publishers are Hachette's main competitors for books with advances over $250,000); PX 530 at 2 (Big Five publishers are S&S's "biggest competitors since they are the most likely to come up with high advance payments required "). These practical indicia in the publishing industry strongly support the existence of the identified relevant market.

One high-end submarket case that the Court finds highly relevant is *Syufy Enterprises v. American Multicinema, Inc.* In *Syufy,* the Ninth Circuit upheld a relevant submarket "for [the] exhibition of industry anticipated top-grossing motion pictures in the San Jose area." 793 F.2d at 994. Anticipated blockbusters, the court explained, "are identifiable on the basis of such criteria as national advertising support, longer playtimes, guaranteed rentals, famous stars, directors and producers, booking in first class theatres, and lucrative terms offered for the pictures by exhibitors." *Id.* at 994-95. Those indicia are analogous to some of the features of anticipated top-selling books, such as: more substantial marketing, publicity, and sales

---

[22] "Lead titles" or "priority titles" are expected to sell well and receive more significant marketing, publicity, and sales support. *See* PX 986 (Crown internal guidance identifying "lead titles" as books with a sales goal of 75,000 units or advances of$500,000, and advising increased marketing, sales, and publicity support for those titles); PX 2005 at 24-27; Trial Tr. at 1071:4-1072:15 (Weisberg) (defining lead title as "top of the list"), 1988:19- 25 (Kim) ("So every season, we have two or three titles that we really designate as lead titles, titles that we feel we really want the sales team to really love and read, books that we feel we want to put a lot of attention on and marketing support for."). They also generally receive high advances. *See* Trial Tr. I 071:4-1072: 15 (Weisberg) ("[I]f we spend a lot of money on a book and it's a book that everybody loves, it becomes a lead title."), 2268:9- 2269:22 (McIntosh) ("[I]f we had a really high sales expectation at time of acquisition and then by the time we're ready to publish the book, we still have a sales–a high sales expectation, then it would seem logical to me that–that there could be a high advance attached to that.").

support; authors who are prominent or have a track record of success; and higher advances. Moreover, the appellant in *Syufy* challenged the existence of the market for "anticipated top-grossing motion pictures" by making arguments similar to those pressed by the defendants here, insisting that the market was "ex post facto and ad hoc," that "all first run films are in substantial competition with each other," and that such films "possess no special characteristics that differentiate them from less successful films from an *ex ante* perspective." *Id.* at 994. This Court joins the Ninth Circuit in rejecting such arguments. As discussed, distinctive characteristics set anticipated top-selling books apart from the rest of the pack.

In sum, this case demonstrates that "[w]hatever the market urged by the [government], the other party can usually contend plausibly that something relevant was left out, that too much was included, or that dividing lines between inclusion and exclusion were arbitrary." *FTC v. Tronox Ltd.,* 332 F. Supp. 3d 187,202 (D.D.C. 2018) (quoting 2B Phillip E. Areeda & Herbert Hovenkamp, *Antitrust Law* 1 530d (4th ed. 2014) [hereinafter Areeda, *Antitrust Law]).* Yet "[t]he Supreme Court has wisely recognized there is 'some artificiality' in any boundaries, but that 'such fuzziness' is inherent in bounding any market." *Id.* (quoting Areeda, *Antitrust Law* 1530d); *Anthem,* 236 F. Supp. 3d at 193 ("The 'market,' as most concepts in law or economics, cannot be measured by metes and bounds." (quoting *Times-Picayune Publ'g Co. v. United States,* 345 U.S. 594, 611 (1953). Market definition is more art than science, *see RAG-Stiftung,* 436 F. Supp. 3d at 312-13, and it is critical to remember that the goal of the exercise is to enable and facilitate the examination of competitive effects. *See Brown Shoe,* 370 U.S. at 320-22; *Cont'l Can,* 378 U.S. at 452-55. In this Court's view, the government has easily cleared the bar.[23]

2. *Supply Substitution*

The traditional way to define a relevant market in the monopsony context would be to examine "the commonality and interchangeability of the buyers" of a certain good. *Todd v. Exxon Corp.,* 275 F.3d 191, 202 (2d Cir. 2001). Indeed, '"the outer boundaries of a product market are determined by the reasonable interchangeability of use or the cross-elasticity of [supply] between the product['s buyers, in the case of monopsony,] and the substitutes for [such buyers].' Accordingly, the touchstone is [supply] substitution." *See Wilhelmsen,* 341 F. Supp. 3d at 45 (quoting *Brown Shoe,* 370 U.S. at 325).

To test the proposed market boundaries, courts commonly turn to the "hypothetical [monopsonist] test." *Sysco,* 113 F. Supp. 3d at 38. The hypothetical monopsonist test "ensures that markets are not defined too narrowly," on the theory that if the test identifies substitute buyers for the product in question, such buyers should be included in the market. *See* Merger Guidelines *§* 4.1.1 (describing hypothetical monopolist test). The hypothetical monopsonist test assumes that there is only one buyer in the proposed mark.et and asks whether that hypothetical buyer, freed from price regulation, "could profitably target a subset of [sellers] for price [decreases]." *Sysco,]* 13 F. Supp. 3d at 38 (quoting Merger Guidelines§ 4.1.4). If such a hypothetical monopsonist could profitably impose what economists call a "small but significant and non-transitory [decrease] in price" of at least five percent in the proposed market, that indicates the existence of a relevant market. *Id.* at 33-34 (quoting Merger Guidelines§ 4.1.4).

Here, the government includes all publishing firms in the market to acquire the publishing rights for anticipated top-selling books. *See* Govt. PFOF-PCOL ¶ 79. Applying Judge Mehta's explanation of the test to the instant facts, we arrive at the following analysis:

> *If enough [authors] are able to substitute away from [selling their books to] the hypothetical [publisher monopsonist] to another [way of distributing their books] and thereby make a [decrease in advances] unprofitable, then the relevant market cannot include only the [publisher monopsonist] and must also include the substitute [method of distribution]. On the other hand, if the hypothetical [publisher monopsonist] could*

[23] To define a market around a targeted seller, sellers must not only be identifiable by buyers for differential pricing but also must be unable to engage in arbitrage or opportunistic re-selling. *See Staples 11,* 190 F. Supp. 3d at 117-118; Merger Guidelines § 3. The foregoing discussion establishes that anticipated top-selling books are subject to differential pricing. Authors of those books also cannot realistically engage in arbitrage by selling their books to a third party who would then sell the books to publishers for a better price. *See* Trial Tr. at 1230:7-23 (Hill). As Dr. Hill testified, publishers would still need to read the book or proposal and value it in the same manner as if the book were submitted directly by the author. *See id.*

profitably [lower advances to authors] by a small amount, even with the loss of some [authors], then economists consider the [publishers] to constitute the relevant market.

See Sysco, 113 F. Supp. 3d at 33; *see also* Merger Guidelines§ 12 ("In defining relevant markets [in buy-side cases], the Agencies focus on the alternatives available to sellers in the face of a decrease in the price paid for by a hypothetical monopsonist. Market power on the buying side of the market is not a significant concern if suppliers have numerous attractive outlets for their goods or services.").

The government's expert, Dr. Hill, estimated what "actual diversions" would be for the defined market, *i.e.,* the percentage of authors who would switch to self-publishing in the face of a "small but significant and non-transitory [de]crease" in advances paid for anticipated top-selling books. He found that even if some small number of authors switched to self-publishing, it would be profitable for publishers to decrease advances–that is, the defection of authors in response to the lowered advances would be far less than what would be necessary to make the decrease unprofitable. *See* Trial Tr. at 1245:14-1246:9 (Hill).

The defendants do not dispute that the relevant market of "publishing rights to anticipated top-selling books" passes the hypothetical monopsonist test. *See* Trial Tr. at 2897:18-2898:18 (Snyder). They instead argue that the test is inapposite here because it does not address the alleged arbitrariness of the $250,000 threshold for bounding the market, *see id.;* Defs. PFOF ¶ 44; indeed, submarkets at all but the lowest advance thresholds should pass the hypothetical monopsonist test because self-publishing generally is a poor substitute for the services of an established publisher. *See* Trial Tr. at 2898:8-18 (Snyder) ("[S]elf-publishing is not a relevant constraint."); *supra* Section LC (further detailing inadequacy of self-publishing). The incongruence of the hypothetical monopsonist test here is not surprising because it examines substitutes for the *buyers* in the market, while the government's proposed market is one of "targeted *sellers": *In this case, the test and the market-definition dispute are focusing on different sides of the market.[24] Although the Court agrees that the hypothetical monopsonist test sheds no light on the contested issues in this case, it is sufficient to note for present purposes that the test is a standard analytical tool in merger cases; and that it concededly supports the government's definition of the relevant market. Defendant's other objections to the relevant market have been addressed *supra.*

B. Prima Facie Case

I. Market Concentration

Once the relevant market has been established, the next step is straightforward: "[T]he government must show that the merger would produce 'a firm controlling an undue percentage share of the relevant market, and would result in a significant increase in the concentration of firms in that market." *See Heinz,* 246 F.3d at 715 (quoting *Phila. Nat'l Bank,* 374 U.S. at 363 (alterations omitted). Market concentration is fundamental to merger analysis. "That competition is likely to be greatest when there are many sellers, none of which has any significant market share, is common ground among most economists, and was undoubtedly a premise of congressional reasoning about the antimerger statute." *Phila. Nat'l Bank,* 374 U.S. at 363; *see also Heinz,* 246 F.3d at 715 ("[W]here rivals are few, firms will be able to coordinate their behavior, either by overt collusion or implicit understanding, in order to restrict output and achieve profits above competitive levels." Thus, demonstrating post-merger 'undue' market concentration "establishes a 'presumption' that the merger will substantially lessen competition." *Heinz,* 246 F.3d at 715 (first quoting *Phila. Nat'l Bank,* 374 U.S. at 363; and then quoting *Baker Hughes,* 908 F.2d at 982). In *Philadelphia National Bank,* the Supreme Court held that a significant change in concentration that results in a combined market share of at least 30 percent is sufficient to establish the legal presumption

---

[24] For this reason, the defendants' argument that the government has not defined the "narrowest market," as required by some case law, lacks merit. *See* Defs. PCOL ,r¶ 3 5-41 (citing Merger Guidelines *§* 4.1.1; *RAG-Stiftung,* 436 F. Supp. 3d at 292; *Sysco,* 113 F. Supp. 3d at 26-27; *United States v. H & R Block, Inc.,* 833 F. Supp. 2d 36, 58-60 (D.D.C. 2011); *FTC v. Arch Coal, Inc.,* 329 F. Supp. 2d 109, 120 (D.D.C. 2004). The cases relied upon by the defendants focus on defining the market by reference to demand substitution and applying the hypothetical monopolist test, while the instant case concerns a market defined by targeted sellers as articulated by the Merger Guidelines. *See* Merger Guidelines *§* 4.1.4 ("If prices are negotiated individually with customers, the hypothetical monopolist test may suggest relevant markets that are as narrow as individual customers Nonetheless, the Agencies often define markets for groups of targeted customers, i.e., by type of customer, rather than by individual customer. By so doing, the Agencies are able to rely on aggregated market shares that can be more helpful in predicting the competitive effects of the merger.").

that a merger violates Section 7. 374 U.S. at 331,364 (merger to a 36% market share with the top four banks controlling a combined 78%); *see also Hosp. Corp.,* 807 F.2d at 1384 (determining that FTC's finding that transaction was unlawful was supported by substantial evidence where defendant's market share was raised from 14% to 26% and the market share of the four largest firms from 79% to 91%); *cf Heinz,* 246 F.3d at 711, 715-17 (holding FTC established presumption through statistics about the change in market concentration where defendants would have a combined market share of 32.8%).

The government's expert, Dr. Hill, calculated market shares based on a comprehensive set of data from more than sixty publishers. *See* Trial Tr. at 1251:12-1252:3 (Hill). According to his calculations, the merging firms account for nearly half (49 percent) of the publishing market for anticipated top-selling books, and the newly constituted "Big Four" that would emerge after the deal would control approximately 91 percent. Trial Tr. at 1254:3-6 (Hill). Government's Exhibit 959 graphically depicts the post-merger market shares:

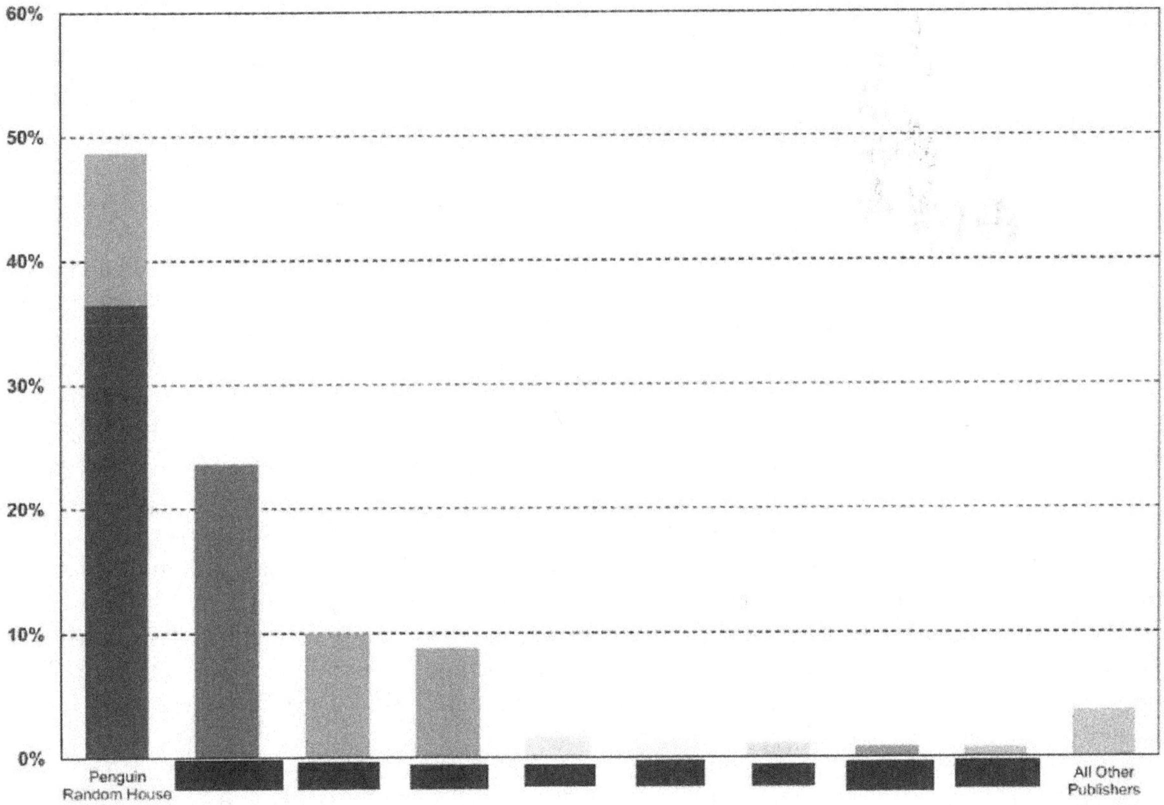

The second-largest market participant post-merger would be [REDACTED]with 24 percent of the market, while- and- would have 10 percent and 9 percent, respectively. *See* PX 959. The non-Big Five would have the remaining 9 percent. *See id* Dr. Hill also calculated market shares using different advance thresholds to bound the relevant market and found similar results. *See* PX 960. The post-merger market shares undoubtedly portray a highly concentrated market dominated by four main players, with the leading, merged company holding an "undue percentage share." The 49-percent share that the post-merger PRH would hold is far above the levels deemed too high in other cases. *See, e.g., Phila. Nat'l Bank,* 374 U.S. at 364 (36%); *cf Heinz,* 246 F.3d at 711, 715-17 (32.8%). The substantial market share of the proposed combined entity justifies a strong presumption of anticompetitive effects. *See Baker Hughes,* 908 F.2d at 991 ("The more compelling the prima facie case, the more evidence the defendant must present to rebut it successfully."). Moreover, the high concentration must be considered in the context of an undeniable trend in consolidation in the publishing industry. *See United States v. Pabst Brewing Co.,*

384 U.S. 546, 552-53 (1966) ("[A] trend toward concentration in an industry, whatever its causes, is a highly relevant factor in deciding how substantial the anti-competitive effect of a merger may be.").

The post-merger market also would be unduly concentrated under the Herfindahl- Hirschman Index ("HHI"), a measure commonly used to evaluate market concentration. *See RAG-Stiftung,* 436 F. Supp. 3d at 310 n.26 (explaining calculation of HHI). The HHI is a formula "used to estimate the competitiveness of the market on the basis of the number and size of the films." Areeda, *Antitrust Law* ¶ 930a. It provides a "short cut to establish a presumption of anticompetitive effect through statistics about the change in market concentration." *AT&T, Inc.,* 916 F.3d at 1032. "The HHI estimates market concentration by summing the squares of the market share of every firm in the market. When one assesses the competitive impact of a merger, the important numbers are (1) the *post-merger* HHI; and (2) the amount the merger increases the HHI." Areeda, *Antitrust Law* ¶ 930a (emphasis in original). An increase in the index above certain levels "establish[es] the [government's] prima facie case that a merger is anti-competitive." *Heinz,* 246 F.3d at 716. Under the Merger Guidelines, if an acquisition (I) increases the HHI of a relevant market by more than 200 points and (2) results in a post-acquisition HHT exceeding 2500, it is presumptively anticompetitive. *See* Merger Guidelines § 5.3; *see also Staples II,* 190 F. Supp. 3d at 128; *H & R Block,* 833 F. Supp. 2d at 71-72 (enjoining transaction that would have given the combined firm only a 28.4 percent market share because the transaction would have resulted in an increase in the HHI of more than 200 and a post-acquisition I-IHI that would have exceeded 2500). Here, the post-merger HHT would be 3,111, with an increase of 891, well above the thresholds required to trigger the presumption under the Guidelines. Trial Tr. at 1256:24-1258:11 (Hill), 1259:4-12 (Hill).[25]

Based on the market-share analysis and the HHI analysis, the government has met its burden to establish that the proposed merger between PRH and S&S would produce "a firm controlling an undue percentage share of the relevant market, and [would] result in a significant increase in the concentration of firms in that market." *Phila. Nat'l Bank,* 374 U.S. at 363. That showing alone is sufficient to establish a prima facie case. *Heinz,* 246 F.3d at 716 ("Sufficiently large HHI figures establish the FTC's prima facie case that a merger is anti-competitive." (citing *Baker Hughes,* 908 F.2d at 982-83 & n.3). Notably, the defendants do not question the accuracy of Dr. Hill's market-share calculations, nor his application of the I-IHI.

The government further notes that the market shares reflect the actual competitive dynamics in the market. *See* Govt. PFOF-PCOL ¶¶ 135-97. Dr. Hill compiled several different data sets to evaluate how frequently the merging parties compete against each other and against other publishers. As discussed in more detail below, *see infra,* Section II.B.2.i, the data tracks the instances where the merging parties lost books to one another, and where they were "runners-up" to each other in book acquisitions. Dr. Hill's analysis of the data reveals that, as market shares would predict, the Big Five in fact dominate book acquisitions in the relevant market.

Consistent with their market shares, when S&S loses a book, it most often loses to PRH; and when S&S wins a book, its most likely runner-up is *PRH. See* Trial Tr. at 1282:15-24 (Hill) (indicating that for books acquired by S&S, PRH was the runner-up approximately 60% of the time); PX 970 (showing diversion ratios); *see also* Trial Tr. at 2927:17-2928:4 (Snyder) (PRH is also the most frequent runner up to S&S according to Professor Snyder's data set). Moreover, an independent deal tracker maintained by Hachette for acquisitions above $500,000 also depicts results consistent with market shares: Roughly 90 to 95 percent of Hachette's losses in that advance range were to other Big Five publishers. *See* PX 790 (tracking Hachette's losses to these publishers); Trial Tr. at 191:16-194:24 (Pietsch).

Also significant is the stability of the market shares held by the primary market participants over time. Based on Dr. Hill's comprehensive data set, which included information from approximately 1,200 book contracts per year, the market shares of the Big Five in acquiring anticipated top-selling books has remained stable for the past three years. *See* PX 967.

Furthermore, the Big Five's market shares versus the non-Big Five have also been consistent: The data

---

[25] Moreover, post-merger HHIs (and the post-merger increase) also are above the presumption thresholds if the relevant market is defined using a variety of other advance cutoffs *(e.g.,* $150,000, $350,000, $500,000, or $1 million). Trial Tr. at 1254:7-25 (Hill); *see also* PX 960.

demonstrate that the aggregate market share of non-Big Five publishers has been "essentially flat." Trial Tr. at 1482:15-25. This stability suggests that more weight should be assigned to market shares, *see* Merger Guidelines§ 5.3 ("The Agencies give more weight to market concentration when market shares have been stable over time") and thus reinforces the presumption of anticompetitive effects based on market concentration.

2. Other Evidence

The government does not rely solely on the high degree of market concentration that would result from the merger, and the attendant presumption of anti-competitive harm; instead, the government also "bolster[s] its prima facie case by offering additional evidence." *Wilhelmsen,* 341 F. Supp. 3d at 59. The government presents evidence that (1) the merger will cause anticompetitive effects from the elimination of competition between PRH and S&S, and (2) the higher concentration in the post-merger market will increase the risk of coordinated anticompetitive conduct by the largest publishers. *See* Govt. PFOF-PCOL ¶¶ 135-97.

3. i. Unilateral Effects

Mergers necessarily eliminate the competition between the merging companies. *See Heinz,* 246 F.3d at 717. The government contends that PRH and S&S currently compete "fiercely" to publish anticipated top-selling books, and that eliminating direct competition between them is likely to harm authors. Govt. PFOF-PCOL ¶ 244. Indeed, "[c]ourts have recognized that a merger that eliminates head-to-head competition between close competitors can result in a substantial lessening of competition." *Sysco,* 113 F. Supp. 3d at 61; *see also Wilhelmsen,* 341 F. Supp. 3d at 59. "Unilateral effects" are those that result directly from the elimination of competition between the merging parties. *Anthem,* 236 F. Supp. 3d at 216. As explained by the Merger Guidelines, "[a] merger can enhance market power simply by eliminating competition between the merging parties. This effect can arise even if the merger causes no changes in the way other firms behave." Merger Guidelines § 1. Unilateral effects may be especially acute in a "highly concentrated market." *Staples I,* 970 F. Supp. at 1083.

4. a. Head-to-Head Competition

The analysis of unilateral effects focuses on how closely the merging firms currently compete, in order to extrapolate the effects of eliminating that competition. *See* Merger Guidelines *§* 6.2. Evidence in the record demonstrates that PRH and S&S are close competitors for anticipated top-selling books. Specifically, PRH is the publisher against which S&S competes the most frequently and to which S&S loses the most. *See* Trial Tr. at 595:23-25 (Karp) (agreeing that PRH is the "publisher [S&S] bid[s] against the most"), 1280:17-1281:17 (Hill) (reviewing win/loss data showing that S&S loses to PRH about 60% of the time). Meanwhile, S&S is a significant competitor to PRH, *see id.* at 2360:20-23 (McIntosh), 1275:25- 1276:6 (Hill), and makes a particularly strong showing in biographies, memoirs, political nonfiction, and books about current events, *see id.* at 454:23-455:3 (Karp), 455:8-11 (Karp); PX 326 at 2 ("S&S has political bestseller chops like no other right now.").

The government's expert, Dr. Hill, conducted a variety of economic analyses that assess how closely PRH and S&S compete. Dr. Hill used four different methods to calculate "diversion ratios," which measure head-to head competition between the merging parties by asking the following question: If one merging party lowered advance levels, what percentage of its authors would "divert" their business to the other merging party, as opposed to diverting to other firms in the industry? A higher diversion ratio indicates that the merging parties are close competitors and that the merger is more likely to lead to harm. *See* Trial Tr. at 1274:2-12 (Hill); *see also* Merger Guidelines § 6.1.

Dr. Hill calculated diversion ratios based on: (1) diversion proportional to market shares, which is the largest data set; (2) win/loss data, which examines which publishers the merging parties lose to the most often; (3) runner-up data, which shows how often the other party was the "runner-up" when one of the merging parties won an acquisition; and (4) minutes from the parties' editorial meetings, which provide a window into how frequently one merging party bid on a book and lost to the other party. Recognizing that each methodology has limitations, Dr. Hill performed multiple tests "to get a holistic understanding of what diversion might look like." Trial Tr. at 1294:20-1295:4. All the methodologies employed by Dr. Hill pointed to the same conclusion: that PRH is S&S's closest competitor, and that S&S is a significant

Figure 7. Summary of Dr. Hill's Diversion Estimates (PX-970)

Type of Analysis	Diversion from PRH to S&S	Diversion from S&S to PRH
Diversion according to share	19%	42%
Win/loss data	19%	59%
Runner-up study	27%	59%
Editorial minutes	21%	54%

competitor to PRH. Specifically, Dr. Hill's diversion ratios indicate that if PRH lowered advances, between 19 and 27 percent of its authors would divert to S&S; and that if S&S lowered advances, between 42 and 59 percent of its authors would divert to PRH. The government summarized the results of the four studies as follows: The defendants' expert, Professor Snyder, calculated his own diversion ratios, using a less reliable data set assembled from the records of eighteen agents who responded to subpoenas ("agency data").[26] Although Professor Snyder's ratios were lower, he also found that PRH is S&S's closest competitor. Professor Snyder determined that the diversion ratio from PRH to S&S is 20 percent, and the diversion ratio from S&S to PRH is 27 percent. Trial Tr. at 2927:4- 25 (Snyder).

The competition between PRH and S&S benefits authors by increasing advances paid for their books, and industry participants predict that the loss of that competition would be harmful to authors. Kensington's CEO, Steven Zacharius, testified, "I personally would expect that [advances] would go down since there will be less competition for those authors." PX 2000 at 3. Macmillan's CEO Don Weisberg testified, "My guess is less competition will long-term probably bring the advance levels down." *See* Trial Tr. at 1085:3-24. Agent Ayesha Pande testified, "I think overall [the merger] will limit the choice, the number of editors and imprints and publishing houses that would be a good home for my clients And I believe overall advances for my clients would be suppressed." *See id.* at 295:3-16.[27]

The merger would cause an inarguable loss of competition from the elimination of situations where PRH and S&S would have been the top two or the only two bidders for an anticipated top seller. Dr. **Hill** calculates that this should happen in approximately 12 percent of book transactions based on market share, while Professor Snyder calculates that it happened only 6 to 7 percent of the time in his data set.

[26] Professor Snyder's agency data is less comprehensive than Dr. Hill's data set. The eighteen literary agencies that provided information in response to subpoenas are only a subset of the agents in the industry. *See* Trial Tr. at 2657:7-25 (Snyder). Of the 973 contracts examined by Professor Snyder, from 2018 to 2021, only 360 earned advances per title of $250,000 or more. *See id.* Of those 360 contracts, Professor Snyder could not identify a clear runner-up in 61 instances. *See* Trial Tr. at 2658:12-15 (Snyder). The remaining pool of data, relatively small and unrepresentative as it was, *see* Trial Tr. at 1289:22-1292:12 (Hill), indicated that PR and S&S were the winner and runner-up in only 7 percent of the cases, while market shares would have predicted that they would be winner and runner-up in 12 percent of the cases. *See* Trial Tr. at 1588:7-19 (Hill), 2797:20-2798:6 (Snyder). Notably, Professor Snyder's estimate of diversion from S&S to PRH is based on a sample of only 22 books over four years, the smallest sample of all the data sets used to estimate diversion. Trial Tr. at 1291:15-1292:12 (Hill), 1707:20- 1708: l (Hill); PX 996 at 1.

[27] Defendants presented testimony to the contrary, suggesting that the lost competition between PRH and S&S would not harm authors or their advances; and that it instead might lead to an increase in advance levels. *See* Defs. PFOF ,r¶25-26 (suggesting that savings from the merger would allow the combined company to spend more money to acquire books, which in tum would force competitors to offer higher advances), 115-116 (stressing that PRH and competitors have no plans to lower advances). For example, S&S CEO Jonathan Karp testified that the company has no plans to decrease author advances or reduce title count post-merger, *see* Trial Tr. at 583:13-19; and PRH Head of Global Mergers & Acquisitions Manuel Sansigre did not consider the potential for reduced author compensation when projecting the merger's efficiencies for PRH, *see id* at 2532:25-2533:12. In addition, HarperCollins CEO Brian Murray stated that his com an had not discussed author advances decreasing due to the merger, *see id.* at 1407:24-1408:12; and that [REDACTED], *see i* . at 1447:3-19, 1452:9-14. The Court finds testimony that the merger wil l have either no effect or positive effects on advances incredible. The Court instead credits the much stronger evidence that advances will decrease after the merger, based on the market-share data, economic analyses, and the more credible testimony regarding market dynamics discussed *supra.*

See id. at 1588:7-19 (Hill), 2797:20-2798:6 (Snyder). The government's evidence included 27 summaries of competitive episodes, over three and a half years, in which PRH and S&S drove up advances through direct, head-to-head competition. *See id.* at 660:16-25 (Porro), 664:8-10 (Porro), 686:9-22 (Porro). For example, as the only two bidders for one book, PRH and S&S drove the advance offered from $6 million to $8 million. *See* PX 958-B. As the last two bidders for another book, PRH and S&S drove the advance offered from $685,000 to $825,000. *See* PX 941-B. The loss of such head-to-head match-ups undoubtedly would harm the authors whose advances would have been bid up by the direct competition. *See generally* Merger Guidelines§ 6.2. The defendants argue, however, that the incidence of harm would be too infrequent to be considered substantial. *See* Defs. PCOL ¶¶ 58- 65.

Even when the merging parties were not the top two bidders, S&S's participation strengthened competition across all auction formats–round-robin, best-bid, and hybrid. Hachette CEO Michael Pietsch testified that a larger number of bidders leads to "more upward pressure" so that "in general the price paid at auction can increase because of the number of participants." *See* Trial Tr. at 181:7-11 (Pietsch). Dr. Hill con-filmed that when a large number of imprints participate in an auction, all of them understand that they need to be more aggressive in their bidding to prevail. *See id.* at 1268:2-8 (Hill) ("So this is a correlation between when you have a large number of bidders, you may need to be more aggressive in your bidding.");[28] *see also Anthem,* 236 F. Supp. 3d at 220-21 ("reducing the number of national carriers from four to three is significant" because of its likely effect on bidding behavior). A higher number of bidders also increases the chances that an author will receive an "outlier" high bid. A book's perceived value may vary significantly among different editors and publishers, and an unusually high bid for a book is likelier when there are more bidders. *See* Trial Tr. at 601:20-25 (Karp), 1305:18-1306:3 (Hill), 2109:3-21 (Wylie). In one notable example, one bidder offered an advance four times higher than the next closest bidder, reflecting the winner's unique view of the book's potential. *See id* at 2931:16-2933:19 (Snyder). The loss of S&S as an independent bidder would weaken bidding incentives and reduce the frequency of events like these.

As previously noted, competition among publishers influences advances even in individual negotiations between an agent and one publisher. *See supra* Section I.C. That is because publishers know that agents can shop the book to other publishers if the publisher's offer is not high enough. *See id.* Therefore, the loss of PRH as an outside competitor would weaken authors' leverage in one-on-one negotiations with S&S, and the loss of S&S as an outside competitor would weaken authors' leverage in one-on-one negotiations with PRH. This conclusion is consistent with Dr. Hill's expert testimony, *see* Trial Tr. at 1270:13-1271:18 (Hill), as well as the Merger Guidelines. *See* Merger Guidelines § 6.2 ("A merger between two competing [buyers] prevents [sellers] from playing those [buyers] off against each other in negotiations.").

Finally, the evidence suggests that the acquisition of S&S would reduce PRH's motivation to compete for publishing rights. PRH CEO Markus Dohle testified that there are two ways to increase market share in the industry: publish more successful books or acquire other companies that publish successful books. *See* Trial Tr. at 801:18-23. PRH has most recently pursued a strategy of bidding more aggressively and acquiring more "big books" to organically increase its market share. *See id.* at 800:15-801:3 (Dohle), 2259:5-20 (McIntosh). The acquisition of S&S would give PRH an alternative means of increasing its market share that would remove the pressure on PRH to acquire more books. *See id.* at 802:11-18 (Dohle). Thus, accomplishing its goal of increasing market share through the merger would cause PRH to bid less aggressively for books than it otherwise would. *See id.* (Q: "After this merger, Penguin Random House will not have as strong a need to grow its share?" Dohle: "Yes.").

5. b. Economic Models

Dr. Hill used economic models to attempt to quantify the expected harm to authors from the merger. He

[28] Dr. Hill gave two examples that demonstrate how the number of bidders influences a publisher's bidding strategy in best-bids auctions. In a 2019 best-bids auction for a young adult novel, an S&S editor wrote that, because there were only three bidders, "I think we can be more guarded in our bidding." *See* Trial Tr. at 1267:15- 22 (Hill). In a 2020 best-bids auction for a book by a musician, a PRH editor wrote, "Another editor and I discussed bringing our offer significantly down yesterday based on the sense I got from the agent that she doesn't have many interested bidders." *See id.* at 1267:23-1268:1 (Hill).

conceded that the models are imprecise and do not perfectly reflect the way books are acquired in the publishing industry; but he performed the analyses to glean additional information about the likelihood of anticompetitive harm. *See id.* at 1653:25-1654:9 (Hill). Dr. Hill's primary model predicts that the merger would cause advances for PRH authors to decrease by about 4 percent (or $44,000); and would cause advances for S&S authors to decrease by 11.5 percent (or $105,000). *See id.* at 1312:10-20 (Hill); PX 964 at 1-2. Although the defendants challenge the applicability of the models and some of the inputs used by Dr. Hill, they fail to convince the Court that the models are worthless. The economic models generally corroborate the other evidence in the record that author advances would decrease in the wake of the merger.

Dr. Hill primarily relied on a "second-score auction" model to quantify the merger's potential harm to authors. *See id.* at 1295:21-22 (Hill). The model assumed that all book rights are allocated using auctions, *see id.* at 1298:13-1302: 19 (Hill); and it used a market-share input to estimate how often the merging parties would be the top two bidders in an auction, *see id.* at 1305:9-17 (Hill). The model used an input of variable-profit margins to estimate the variation among the bids: Using higher variable-profit margins generally would cause the model to predict greater harm, *i.e.,* a bigger decrease in advance level.[29] *See id.* at 1305:18-1306:3 (Hill). To measure the effect of the merger, the model looked at the instances when the merging parties would be the top two bidders and then eliminated the second-highest bid, thereby making the third-place bid the one that would set the amount of the advance (on the theory that the winning bid would now only need to beat the third-place bid). *See id.* at 1303:7-22 (Hill).

The defendants argue that Dr. Hill's second-score auction model is flawed because (1) it inaccurately assumes that all book transactions involve auctions, and (2) Dr. Hill used the wrong input for variable-profit margins. *See* Defs. PFOF 1215; Defs. PCOL 11106-121; ECF No. 183 (Defs. Objections to Govt. PFOF-PCOL) at 29-36. Although the defendants are correct that the model does not precisely reflect how book contracts are allocated among publishers, its exclusive reliance on auctions is a reasonable simplification. *See* Trial Tr. at 1296:16-21 (Hill) (explaining why he interprets the model more broadly). The market-share data captures the rate at which the parties are winning book contracts–through negotiations, auctions or otherwise; and market shares also reasonably predict how often the merging parties would be the winner and runner-up. *Compare* PX 970, *with* Trial Tr. at 2927:8-25 (Snyder) (diversion according to share produces diversion ratios broadly consistent with Dr. Hill's runner-up study and Professor Snyder's agency data). Moreover, as previously discussed, competition affects advance levels even in one-on-one negotiations, so the model's use of auctions to simulate the result of negotiations has some basis in market reality. Finally, similar or identical models have been used in other antitrust cases involving industries that feature negotiations. *See Wilhelmsen,* 341 F. Supp. 3d at 64-65; *Anthem,* 236 F. Supp. 3d at 217-20; *Sysco,* I 13 F. Supp. 3d at 24, 66-67 (noting that customers were awarded contracts through "a request for proposal or bilateral negotiations"). The Court understands that the second-score auction model provides only a rough approximation of expected harm but nevertheless finds it useful. As for Dr. Hill's allegedly mistaken inclusion of fixed costs in some of his variable-profit margins, that was the more conservative approach: Including the extra costs lowered the margins and reduced the model's prediction of harm. *See* Trial Tr. at 1311:18-1312:6 (Hill). Although Professor Snyder also suggested that Dr. **Hill** should have included fixed costs **in** all the variable-profit margins, *see id.* at 3027:5-3030:4 (Snyder), Dr. Hill explained that the model explicitly calls for the use of variable, not fixed, costs.[30]

In response to Professor Snyder's criticism that the second-score auction model was a poor fit for the publishing industry, Dr. Hill also ran a series of models based on the "gross upward pricing pressure index" (GUPPI). *See id.* at 1315:16-1316:10 (Hill). The GUPPI models use diversion ratios and margins as inputs, with higher diversion ratios and higher margins leading to a higher prediction of harm. *See id.*

[29] Variable-profit margin is equal to revenue minus variable costs. The metric does not account for, *i.e.*, subtract, fixed costs. See Trial Tr. at 1310:2-25 (Hill).

30 Both the second-score auction model and the GUPPI models, discussed *infra*, are "explicit" that one should use firms' variable, not fixed, costs to implement the models. Trial Tr. at 3092:23-3093:15 (Hill). This is because the models assume that publishers ask whether the marginal profits of acquiring one more book exceed the marginal costs. See id.

Figure 8. Dr. Hill's Estimates From Second-Score Auction and GUPPI Models (PX-964)

Model	Diversion Assumption	% Reduction in Author Compensation	
		PRH	S&S
Second-score auction model	Diversion according to share	4.3%	11.6%
Multi-round auction GUPPI	Diversion according to share	7.3%	19.2%
Multi-round auction GUPPI	Snyder diversion ratios	7.4%	12.8%
Single-round and hybrid GUPPI	Diversion according to share	3.7%	9.6%
Single-round and hybrid GUPPI	Snyder diversion ratios	3.7%	6.4%

at 1318:2-7 (Hill); *see also supra* Section III.B.2.i.a (explaining diversion ratios). But the GUPPI models used by Dr. Hill are more difficult for the defendants to challenge because those models were originally adopted by the defendants' own economists during the pre-complaint investigation of the instant merger. *See* Trial Tr. at 1633:15-23 (Hill). The GUPPI models also predict a reduction in author advances due to the merger, across different auction formats and using various diversion ratios, including those calculated by Professor Snyder. The government summarized Dr. Hill's findings as follows: *See* Govt. PFOF-PCOL ¶ 288 (citing PX 964). There is ample precedent for using GUPPI and similar models to predict harm in antitrust cases. *See Wilhelmsen,* 341 F. Stipp. 3d at 64; *Anthem,* 236 F. Supp. 3d at 212; *see also FTC v. Sanford Health,* No. 1:17-, v-133, 2017 **WL** 10810016, at *12-13 (D.N.D. Dec. 15, 2017), *aff'd.,* 926 F.3d 959 (8th Gir. 2019).

6. iii. Coordinated Effects

Another avenue for the government to prove competitive harm is by showing a likelihood of "coordinated effects," which occur when market participants mutually decrease competition in the relevant market. *AT&T,* 310 F. Supp. 3d at 246 ("A proposed merger may violate Section 7 by enabling or encouraging post-merger coordinated interaction among firms in the relevant market that harms customers."; *see also* Merger Guidelines§ 7 ("Coordinated interaction involves conduct by multiple firms that is profitable for each of them only as a result of the accommodating reactions of the others."). Coordinated effects can arise from an express or implied agreement among competitors, *see* CCC *Holdings,* 605 F. Supp. 2d at 60; or from "parallel accommodating conduct" among competitors without a prior agreement, Merger Guidelines § 7. Parallel accommodating conduct involves "situations in which each rival's response to competitive moves made by others is individually rational, and not motivated by retaliation or deterrence nor intended to sustain an agreed-upon market outcome, but nevertheless emboldens price [decreases] and weakens competitive incentives to [raise advances] or offer [authors] better terms." *Id.*

Coordinated effects are likelier in concentrated markets; indeed, the idea that concentration tends to produce anticompetitive coordination is central to merger law. *See Heinz,* 246 F.3d at 716 ("Merger law 'rests upon the theory that, where rivals are few, firms will be able to coordinate their behavior, either by overt collusion or implicit understanding, in order to restrict output and achieve profits above competitive levels.'" (quoting *FTC v. PPG Indus.,* 798 F.2d 1500, 1503 (D.C. Cir. 1986). Therefore, when the government has shown that a merger will substantially increase concentration in an already concentrated market–as it has done here, *see supra* Section III.B.1–"the burden is on the defendants to produce evidence of 'structural market barriers to collusion' specific to this industry that would defeat the 'ordinary presumption of collusion' that attaches to a merger in a highly concentrated market." *H & R Block,* 833 F. Supp. 2d at 77 (quoting *Heinz,* 246 F.3d at 725).

As an initial matter, a history of collusion or attempted collusion is highly probative of likely harm from a merger. *See Hosp. C01p.,* 807 F.2d at 1388; *see also FTC v. Elders Grain, Inc.,* 868 F.2d 901,906 (7th Cir. 1989) ("[A]n acquisition which reduces the number of significant sellers in a market already highly concentrated and prone to collusion by reason of its history and circumstances is unlawful in the absence of special circumstances."); *H & R Block,* 833 F. Supp. 2d at 78; *Tronox,* 332 F. Supp. 3d at 208-210; Merger Guidelines § 7.2. Thus, it is significant that in *United States v. Apple, Inc.,* the Second Circuit upheld a finding that between 2009 and 2019, all the "Big Six"[31] publishers, except for Random House, participated in a "horizontal conspiracy to raise e-book prices." *See* 791 F.3d at 339. This coordination involved "numerous exchanges between executives at different Big Six publishers," "constant communication" among the publishers "regarding their negotiations with both Apple and Amazon," and "frequent telephone calls among the Publisher Defendants." *Id.* at 302,318. "[T]he Big Six operated in a close-knit industry and had no qualms communicating about the need to act together." *Id.* at 300. The Second Circuit concluded that the publishers engaged in "express collusion" that was a *per se* violation of antitrust law. *Id.* at 316, 321-29. Although Random House did not participate in the conspiracy, Penguin Books and S&S both did, *see id.* at 308, and this "history of successful cooperation establishes a precondition to effective collusion- mutual trust and forbearance." *See Hosp. Corp.,* 807 F.2d at 1388. The case portrays an industry already "prone to collusion," which may become "even more prone to collusion" after the proposed merger of its largest and third-largest competitors. *See Elders Grain,* 868 F.2d at 905-06.

The *Apple* case provides the backdrop for trends in the industry that appear to demonstrate that the Big Five are already engaging in tacit collusion or parallel accommodating conduct when acquiring books. Recent years have seen the industry-wide standardization of certain contract terms–involving payment structure, audio rights, and e-book royalties–in ways that favor publishers over authors, suggesting that the top publishers have engaged in coordinated conduct. Advances used to be paid to authors in two installments, but publishers uniformly moved to paying them in three installments and then four installments, thereby delaying authors' compensation. *See supra* Section J.B. After audiobooks became a significant source of revenue in the industry, publishers uniformly refused to acquire books without audio rights included, thereby limiting authors' ability to maximize their compensation and preventing authors from diversifying their sources of income. *See id.* In addition, during the early years of e-books, publishers uniformly shifted e-book royalty rates from 50 percent to 25 percent, thereby reducing authors' compensation. *See* Trial Tr. at 774:6-776:21 (Dohle). Thus, in an industry where the competition to acquire anticipated top sellers is intense, the competing publishers nevertheless choose, almost always, not to gain advantage by offering more favorable contract terms. This phenomenon bespeaks a tacit agreement among the publishers to compete only on the basis of advance level because it collectively benefits them not to yield on other contract terms. *Accord H & R Block,* 833 F. Supp. 2d at 77-78 ("[A] highly persuasive historical act of cooperation between [competitors]" supports the theory that "coordination would likely take the form of mutual recognition that neither firm has an interest in an overall 'race to free' ").

One example involving audio rights is illustrative. When selling the publishing rights to–highly sought-after book, her agent attempted to hold an auction that excluded audio rights. S&S wanted the book but refused to bid because "[t]he only way to prevent agents from breaking off audio rights like this is to hold firm to our policy of no deals without audio rights." PX 652 at 2. An S&S editor ruminated, "It will be very interesting to see whether PRH, Hachette, Harper or Macmillan participate. M[y] understanding is that they too have the 'no audio, no deal' rule." *Id.* The agent was forced to restart the auction with audio rights included, *see* PX 568 at 3, presumably because the book received insufficient offers or only received offers that included audio. *See* PX 320 at 1 (in the first round, PRH bid for bundled audio rights in violation of the auction's initial rules). In the renewed auction that included audio rights, the bidding was fervid and reflected vigorous competition.[32] This episode starkly demonstrates that the publishers, despite their great enthusiasm for the book, initially engaged in parallel conduct to deny the author the ability to exclude audio rights from the auction. The parallel conduct was effective and mutually beneficial, as the publishers all retained the opp01iunity to acquire the book, with their preferred contract

---

31 This was before Penguin Books and Random House merged, so there was a "Big Six" instead of a "Big Five."

[32] As previously discussed, there were six rounds of bidding between four bidders, with a high bid of $400,000 in the first round and a winning bid of$775,000 from PRH's Viking imprint, which was $75,000 more than Viking's initial bid clearance. *See supra* Section LC.

te1m concerning audio rights. Based on this evidence, the Court finds that the Big Five publishers have engaged in tacit coordination that is profitable for those involved.

Finally, it is significant that in a market already prone to collusion, where coordinated conduct already appears to be rampant, PRH's acquisition of S&S would reinforce the market's oligopsonistic structure and create a behemoth industry leader that other market participants could easily follow. *See* PX 80E (translation of PX 80, materials for Bertelsmann board presentation) at 13 (describing publishing industry as an oligopoly). The Big Five publishers already control 91 percent of the relevant market. *See* PX 963. The merger would distill the Big Five to a Big Four, with an overwhelmingly dominant top firm, PRH-S&S, controlling 49 percent of the market and dwarfing its nearest competitors. In the newly reconfigured market, the top two firms, the merged entity and [REDACTED] would have a 74-percent market share. *See id.* Under such circumstances, coordinated effects are likely through "sheer market power" because the "post-merger market would feature two firms that control roughly three quarters" of the market. *Tronox,* 332 F. Supp. 3d at 209; *see also Heinz,* 246 F.3d at 724 n.23 (recognizing that "price leadership" is "a danger" in a "duopoly" market). The merger would thus increase the market's already high susceptibility to coordination. *See* Trial Tr. at 1329:18-21 (Hill).[33]

C. Rebuttal

The government is entitled to a presumption of anticompetitive effects and has also met its burden to establish a prima facie case. The defendants, therefore, now have the burden to rebut the government's case by "show[ing] that the prima facie case inaccurately predicts the relevant transaction's probable effect on future competition." *See Baker Hughes,* 908 F.2d at 981. It is the defendants' task to demonstrate that the market shares and the associated presumption of illegality inaccurately reflect competitive reality. *See id.; see also Heinz,* 246 F.3d at 715 ("To rebut the presumption, the defendants must produce evidence that shows that the market-share statistics give an inaccurate account of the merger's probable effects on competition in the relevant market."

"There is no science to weighing the factors at play in an antitrust analysis," and the defendants may rebut the government's prima facie case with any relevant "real-world evidence." *RAG-Stiftung,* 436 F. Supp. 3d at 312. For example, the defendants may meet their burden of rebuttal by demonstrating low barriers to entry in the relevant market, *see, e.g., Wilhelmsen,* 341 F. Supp. 3d at 68; *Staples II,* 190 F. Supp. 3d at 133; or sophisticated counterparts (here, authors and agents) who can blunt the impact of consolidation, *see, e.g., RAG-Stiftung,* 436 F. Supp. 3d at 315.

"[B]ecause the burden of persuasion ultimately lies with the plaintiff, the burden to rebut must not be 'unduly onerous.'" *United States v. Anthem, Inc. ("Anthem If'),* 855 F.3d 345, 350 (D.C. Cir. 2017) (quoting *Baker Hughes,* 908 F.2d at 981, 991). However, "[t]he more compelling the prima facie case, the more evidence the defendant must present to rebut it successfully." *See Baker Hughes,* 908 F.2d at 991. Here, the government has "made out a strong prima facie case" based on the highly concentrated market and affirmative evidence of likely anticompetitive effects. *See Wilhelmsen,* 341 F. Supp. 3d at 66. The defendants, therefore, "must make out a correspondingly strong rebuttal showing." *See id.*

1. Existing Competition

The defendants assert that existing competition can and will constrain the merged company more than market shares or the government's evidence would suggest. *See, e.g., Sysco,* 113 F. Supp. 3d at 78. The defendants point to competition from other publishers, competition from self-publishing, and internal competition within publishing houses. *See* Defs. PFOF ¶¶ 115-23, 164-85, 198-213; Defs. PCOL ¶¶ 74-79.

---

[33] Other factors that courts have found relevant to an evaluation of the likelihood of coordinated effects include: differentiated products, transparent competitive outcomes, punishment mechanisms, and frequent purchases for small amounts. *See H & R Block,* 833 F. Supp. 2d at 77-79; CCC *Holdings,* 605 F. Supp. 2d at 62; *Arch Coal,* 329 F. Supp. 2d at 144-45 . The Court sees no need to march through a discussion of those factors. Merger analysis is industry-specific and fact-intensive. *See Brown Shoe,* 370 U.S. at 321-22 ("Congress indicated plainly that a merger had to be functionally viewed, in the context of its particular industry." (footnote omitted). Where, as here, there is a strong risk of collusion based on history, current practices, and extreme market concentration, the Court finds it unnecessary to explore peripheral issues.

7. *i. Other Publishers*

The defendants argue that a combined PRH and S&S would be constrained by other publishers, who do not plan to lower their advance offers or change their bidding strategies. *See* Defs. PFOF ¶¶115-23; Defs. PCOL ¶¶ 74-76. For example, HarperCollins's CEO Brian Murray testified that his company would not "hold back" in competing with the merged entity. *See* Trial Tr. at 1385:9-15 (Murray). Consistent with that testimony, HarperCollins did not project a decrease in its title count or its advance spending after the PRH-S&S merger was announced. *See* DX 279 (HarperCollins strategy presentation for 2022) at 25. The CEOs of other competitors, including Hachette and [REDACTED] also stated that they would not change their bidding strategies in response to the merger. *See* Trial Tr. at 211:9-13 (Hachette CEO Michael Pietsch); [REDACTED]) at 31. Therefore, the defendants argue, other existing publishers stand ready to prevent any unilateral anticompetitive effects from the merger.

The defendants' reliance on such assurances from their competitors is insufficient. It is not necessary for other publishers to change their maximum advances or bidding strategies for anticompetitive unilateral effects to occur. First, and most obviously, with respect to book acquisitions where PRH and S&S would have been the winner and runner-up, the merged entity will acquire such books for lower advances regardless of the other publishers' bids. *See supra* Section III.B.l, Section III.B.2.i.

Second, in situations where PRH or S&S would have won a book, regardless of the runner-up, the merged entity might submit a lower bid due to its decreased motivation to achieve organic growth. *See supra* Section III.B.2. In such a case, another publisher could win the book instead, for a lower advance than what PRH or S&S would have offered as standalone entities.

Third, publishers do not immediately offer their maximum advance when attempting to acquire books; moreover, they initially offer higher advances when they think there is more competition, and lower advances if they think there is less competition. *See supra* Section III.B.2.i.a; *see also* Trial Tr. at 499:6-500:12 (Karp), 1267:13-1268:8 (Hill). The general softening of competition with the elimination of S&S as a standalone bidder, leading to the perception of less competition in book acquisitions, would likely lead publishers to make lower initial advance offers. *See supra* Section III.B.2. If subsequent bids that would have come from PRH or S&S as separate entities are not forthcoming, or are lower than they otherwise would have been, the other publishers could acquire books for lower advances simply by following their existing bidding strategy.

Fourth and finally, it is not necessary for advances to decline in absolute terms for authors to be harmed. The relevant market has been growing rapidly in recent years in response to strong consumer demand, and advances have been rising, consistent with that growth. *See* PX 2002 (Stehlik) at 16-17; DX 422 (Glusman) at 37-38; Trial Tr. at 991:5-19 (Tart), 1990:4-9 (Kim). If the merger goes through, the rate of growth might be offset by competitive harm, allowing publishers to acquire books for more than they do now but for less than they would have absent the merger. That would result in harm to authors even if there were no decline in advances, or even if there was some (slowed) growth in the total advances paid.

The defendants also argue that non-Big Five publishers would be a significant competitive constraint on a combined PRH and S&S. *See* Defs. PFOF ¶¶164-80; Defs. PCOL ¶¶ 74-76. The evidence shows, however, that the smaller publishers lack the resources to compete regularly in the market for anticipated top-selling books. *See supra* Section LC; Trial Tr. at 2047:13-18 (Cheney). Individual publishers outside the Big Five rarely acquire books for advances at or above $250,000. *See* PX 963.

The defendants take the novel approach of aggregating all the non-Big Five publishers and characterizing them as a single force with a 9-percent market share–which allegedly makes their collective power to constrain the merged company comparable to that of a Big Five publisher. *See* Defs. PFOF ¶ 164 ("When aggregated, the non-Big-Five publishers are as likely to win as [REDACTED]") Defs. PCOL ¶ 64 (arguing that an "effective 6-5 merger (based on market shares) [is] at issue here"); *see also* Trial Tr. at 2906:10-2907:14 (Snyder).[34] The defendants offer no precedent to support this economic sleight of hand, and the methodology appears dubious. If market shares can be so readily manipulated by

[34] Although Dr. Hill combined the non-Big Five's market shares in his economic models as a reasonable simplification, *see* Trial Tr. at 3081:12-23 (Hill), he did not treat them as one competitor in his overall analysis.

aggregating unaffiliated companies, why not aggregate all the publishers that are not PRH and S&S into a single, massive counterweight with a 51 percent market share? The defendants' approach appears incompatible with the way antitrust law approaches market concentration and its presumed effects on competition. *See supra* Section III.B.l. Generally, a firm with lower market share is assumed to wield less market power, and market concentration would be considered low in an industry with many individual firms with small market shares. *See* Merger Guidelines *§* 5.3 ("The Agencies may measure market concentration using the number of significant competitors in the market. This measure is most useful when there is a gap in market share between significant competitors and smaller rivals ").For example, applying a *HHI* analysis shows that 100 firms that each have a I-percent market share (which would produce an HHI of 100) do not represent the same competitive landscape as two firms that each have a SO-percent market share (which would produce an I-IIII of 5000).[35] Indeed, the government points out that aggregating the non-Big Five publishers does not help the defendants' case because it yields a higher HHI and depicts a more concentrated market. *See* Govt. PFOF-PCOL ¶ 134.

Professor Snyder gave counterintuitive and apparently erroneous testimony about the significance of non-Big Five bidders in competitive auctions. He claimed that the non-Big Five publishers, with a combined market share of 9 percent, are nevertheless the winner or runner-up in 23 percent of auctions for anticipated top-selling books; while PRH and S&S, with a combined market share of 49 percent, are the winner and runner-up only seven percent of the time. *See* Trial Tr. at 2689:22-2690:5 (Snyder), 2827:13-23 (Snyder). The Court finds the 23- percent figure unreliable because it was the subject of much contradictory testimony at trial, including the credible assertion by Dr. Hill that the number should be halved. *See id.* At 3051:16-3053:17 (Hill). And overall, Professor Snyder's reliance on the limited and unrepresentative "agency data" weakened the credibility of his analyses. *See supra* Section lll.B.2 (note 26). Thus, the defendants' expert fails to cast doubt on the reliability of the market-share statistics presented by the government. *See Heinz,* 246 F.3d at 715.

8. ii. Internal Competition

The defendants argue that internal imprint competition increases competition in the market beyond that represented in market shares. *See* Defs. PFOF ¶¶ 198-213; Defs. PCOL¶¶ 77-79. That argument is undermined by the presumption that "[c]ompanies with multiple divisions must be viewed as a single actor, and each division will act to pursue the common interests of the whole corporation." *AT&T,* 916 F.3d at 1043. This presumption "was adopted as a principle of antitrust law," *id.,* in *Copperweld Corp.* v. *Independence Tube Corp.,* 467 U.S. 752, 771 (1984) ("[T]he coordinated activity of a parent and its wholly owned subsidiary must be viewed as that of a single enterprise A parent and its wholly owned subsidiary have a complete unity of interest."). Consistent with economic principles and common sense, internal imprint competition should be considered only to the extent that it maximizes the profits of the publishing house. *See* Areeda, *Antitrust Law* ¶ 964b ("Antitrust law generally presumes that a firm maximizes its profits in the environment in which it finds itself ").

Although internal competition among imprints is currently permitted by some publishers in round-robin auctions, such competition is far from unrestrained. To the extent imprints compete internally within the confines of a house bid, they can provide more editorial choices to authors, but there is no price competition that allows authors to achieve the highest possible advance level. *See supra* Section LC. Even this non-price competition is discouraged. *See* DX 71 at 2 (email from S&S CEO Karp regarding editor guidelines) ("Duplicating work is not a productive expenditure of one of our most valuable resources–time. You can acquire more books if you aren't all chasing the same ones. Try to bail out on submission in which there are more than two imprints in the building pursuing the project."). In cases where internal imprints do compete financially, such competition is confined to situations where there is an external bidder. Moreover, as previously discussed, there are numerous examples in the record of PRH using "background coordination in auctions to avoid internal up-bidding." PX 411 at 4; *see also* Trial Tr. 2372:17-2373:8 (Mclntosh); *supra* Section I.C. Thus, internal competition would have a very limited

[35] Summing the squares of each firm's market share, the first HHT is calculated as 100 x 12 = 100, and the second HHI is calculated as 2 x 502 = 5000. *See supra* Section ill.A.2.

impact in mitigating anticompetitive effects in the industry. To achieve the highest advances for authors, internal imprint competition is no substitute for competition among independent publishers.

The defendants assert that the merged company would go even farther in permitting internal competition than current policies allow. *See* Defs. PFOF 1210; DX 236. They note that PRH CEO Dohle has promised, in a letter to agents, that S&S legacy imprints will bid against PRH imprints even when there are no external bidders. *See* Defs. PFOF 1210; DX 236. The Court gives no weight to this unenforceable promise. Indeed, the promise calls to mind the criminal-law concept of "consciousness of guilt": Mr. Dohle's extraordinary pledge appears to reflect his awareness of how threatening the combined entity would be to authors and agents. The promise lacks credibility for three reasons:

First, the proposed policy would not be profit-maximizing and is thus unreliable evidence of future conduct. *See* Areeda, *Antitrust Law* 1 964b. It is unclear how the new feature of the policy–allowing internal competition even without an external bidder–would financially benefit the combined entity. Instead, it appears that the promise was made just to get the deal done, and once the merger is executed, there will be no economic incentive to maintain the policy.

Second, the promise can be broken at will. Mr. Dohle, his successor, or his superiors could legally change or rescind the new policy at any time. The defendants argue that such behavior would harm the merged entity because of backlash from agents, *see* Defs. PFOF 1210, but evidence shows that agents have limited power over the large publishing houses, *see infra* Section III.C.3.i. A unilateral promise by PRH that it will not use its market power if it acquires S&S cannot rebut the government's prima facie case. *See H & R Block,* 833 F. Supp. 2d at 82 (Even if "the Court has no reason to doubt that defendants would honor their promise [to maintain the acquired firm's current prices for three years post-merger], this type of guarantee cannot rebut a likelihood of anticompetitive effects in this case.").

Third, the promise would not prevent the merged entity from reducing internal imprint competition. Despite the promise, PRH could coordinate bids with legacy S&S imprints in the same way that PRH currently does among its own imprints. *See supra* Section LC. The promise also would not stop the merged company from consolidating PRH and legacy S&S imprints, as PRH did when it reorganized the divisions within Random House in 2019, so that "there [would] be less internal competition with[in] the focused editorial profiles in [its] divisions." *See* PX 241. Finally, the merged entity could direct its imprints to focus on non-competing genres, thereby preventing the imprints from pursuing the same books. *See id.* For all the foregoing reasons, Mr. Dohle's promise does little to rebut the government's prima facie case or the presumption of anticompetitive effects.

9. iii. Self-Publishing

The defendants argue that self-publishing is a competitive constraint on the market, particularly for celebrity and romance authors.[36] *See* Defs. PFOF ¶¶181-85; *see also* Trial Tr. at 566:1-11 (Karp). But, as previously discussed, self-publishing is not a reasonable substitute for traditional publishers in the market for anticipated top-selling books. *See supra* Section LC, Section II.A.2. Anecdotes about author Brandon Sanderson raising $40 million on Kickstarter, or author Colleen Hoover having success with self-publishing, do not change the overall picture of the industry. Sanderson's success with self-publishing was "rare," "a feat," and "so incredible." Trial Tr. at 1076:4-10 (Weisberg), 1077:4-7 (Weisberg). Similarly, Hoover is "a cultural phenomenon" and "the hottest author in the country." *Id.* at 524:18-25 (Karp), 560:5- 10 (Karp). Sanderson and Hoover are exceptions that prove the rule: For the overwhelming majority of authors in the relevant market, self-publishing is no real substitute for using a publishing house, and self-publishing therefore does little to constrain anticompetitive effects.

2. Barriers to Entry and Expansion

The defendants argue that there are few barriers to entry that would prevent new or existing publishers from competing effectively with the merged company. *See* Defs. PFOF ¶¶ 69, 124-48; Defs. PCOL ¶¶ 80-83. New entrants to the market would presumably give authors alternative outlets to publish their books, thereby preventing the merged entity from lowering advances. "The existence and significance of

[36] Defendants admitted in their closing argument that self-publishing was not a true option for authors. *See* Trial Tr. at 3272:17-25 (arguing that hypothetical monopsonist test is "utterly meaningless other than addressing whether there's an outside option in the form of self-publishing, which nobody was arguing in this case"). In their post-trial briefing, however, they surprisingly assert that self-publishing is a competitive threat.

barriers to entry are frequently crucial considerations in a rebuttal analysis. In the absence of significant barriers, a company probably cannot maintain [sub]competitive pricing for any length of time." *Baker Hughes,* 908 F.2d at 987. To constrain the new entity, "entry [by new competitors] must be timely, likely, and sufficient in its magnitude, character, and scope to deter or counteract the competitive effects of concern." *Wilhelmsen,* 341 F. Supp. 3d at 66-67 (quotations omitted). "The expansion of current competitors is regarded as essentially equivalent to new entry, and is therefore evaluated according to the same criteria." *Id.* at 66 (quotations omitted).

Contrary to the defendants' contentions, the evidence demonstrates that there are substantial barriers to entry and expansion in the publishing market for anticipated top-selling books. Established publishers have many advantages that are not easily replicated, including: (1) back lists that generate substantial and consistent revenue, which in turn suppo1ts risky acquisitions of high-advance books, *see* Trial Tr. at 156:5-157:14 (Pietsch); (2) large and effective marketing, sales, and distribution teams that have relationships with media and retailers, *see* [REDACTED] at 6-7; (3) excellent reputations and track records of success that attract authors, *see* Trial Tr. at 454:11-22 (Karp); and (4) lower variable costs due to economies of scale, *see id.* at 2047:16-18 (Cheney); *see also* Section LC. In addition, numerous publisher witnesses expressed concern about a lack of access to sufficient printing capacity, which limits the number of books that publishers can physically produce and thus limits opportunity for expansion. *See id.* at 758:3-5 (Dohle), 121:8-19 (Pietsch), 364:1-9 (Eulau); [REDACTED] at 3. Industry insiders, including PRH executives, candidly acknowledged in trial testimony and ordinary-course documents that barriers to entry are high in the publishing business. *See* Trial Tr. at 168:9-169:1 (Pietsch), 755:4-15 (Dohle), 1380:12-1381:8 (Murray); PX 80-E at 13; PX 79 (presentation by PRH executives on publishing industry) at 8.

The best proof that would-be new competitors face formidable barriers to entry is the stability of market shares in the industry: No publisher has entered the market and become a strong competitor against the Big Five in the past thirty years. *See* Trial Tr. at 163:2-6 (Pietsch). Moreover, the Big Five's market share in acquiring anticipated top-selling books has remained stable for the past three years. *See* PX 967. Thus, there is little evidence that new or existing publishers will grow at a pace and magnitude that would allow them to discipline a merged PRH and S&S. *See Wilhelmsen,* 341 F. Supp. 3d at 68 ("The fact that the merging parties have been able to maintain high margins and market shares without witnessing notable entry and expansion suggests that the market is characterized by significant barriers to entry."; Merger Guidelines § 5.3 ("The Agencies give more weight to market concentration when market shares have been stable over time ").The Big Five's market shares are built on "decades of credibility and success," Trial Tr. at 454:11-22 (Karp), and they cannot be easily challenged by less-established publishers.

Although the defendants argue that social media like "BookTok"[37] and Amazon's online bookstore level the playing field for smaller publishers, those platforms are not new and are far from "game-changing." *See id.* at 1069:1-4 (Weisberg) ("[T]his is the business of one-to-one word of mouth. It's never been anything else and it's still not, just the devices have changed."). Despite the current availability of "BookTok" and virtual storefronts, the Big Five still consistently acquire the publishing rights for 91 percent of anticipated top-selling books, demonstrating that the playing field has not been leveled in any meaningful way. *See* PX 994. For example, PRH utilizes its superior resources to maximize sales even on Amazon. *See supra* Section I.C (PRH hires data scientists to study Amazon's search algorithms and spends money to get books better positioned in Amazon's search results.).

The defendants nevertheless point to new entrants like Zando, Spiegel & Grau, and Astra House, which have had some success in acquiring publishing rights to anticipated top-selling books. *See* Defs. PFOF ¶¶ 129-32, 144, 147. Although those publishing houses are associated with successful and well-respected editors, they lack many of the other advantages enjoyed by the Big Five: big back lists; extensive marketing, sales, and distribution teams; and scale. As a result, those new entrants have barely made a dent in the relevant market- their collective share is less than one percent, *see* PX 968, and no one in the

[37] BookTok refers to activity on the social media platform TikTok where users review and promote books to one another. *See* Trial Tr. at 1414:12-16 (Weisberg).

industry views them as substantial competitors to the Big Five. *See* Trial Tr. at 249:20-250:90 (Pande), 552:21-557:3 (Karp).

Moreover, the growth of those new competitors was accompanied by a countervailing shrinkage in the market shares of other non-Big Five publishers: The stability of the overall market share of non-Big Five publishers indicates that the new entrants have done little to change the competitive landscape, and that barriers to entry and expansion remain high. *See id.* at 1482:15- 1483:17 (Hill); PX 977.

The defendants contend that Big Five rivals like HarperCollins and well-funded companies like Disney are poised to expand in the relevant market. *See* Defs. PFOF ¶¶ 124-48; Defs. PCOL ¶¶ 81-83. To be sure, Big Five rivals face low barriers to expansion because they have many of the same advantages that PRH and S&S have. But there is no evidence that HarperCollins, Hachette, or Macmillan could or would compete more aggressively with the merged company. *See* Trial Tr. at 177:1-15 (Pietsch), 1088:8-14 (Weisberg), 1385:9-1386:11 (Murray). The distribution of market shares among PRH, S&S, and the other Big Five publishers, has remained relatively constant in recent years. *See* PX 994. The Court has every reason to believe that all the industry players are already doing their best to compete; it is therefore unlikely that the non-merging Big Five publishers could suddenly expand sufficiently to prevent the anticipated competitive harm.

Two well-funded companies outside the Big Five highlighted by the defendants are Amazon and Disney. Amazon acquired several high-priced books when it first started its publishing business about a decade ago, but it has failed to make significant headway in the industry. *See* Trial Tr. at 172:17-25 (Pietsch). From 2019 to 2021, Amazon's share in acquiring the publishing rights to anticipated top-selling books declined from under-[REDACTED] to under [REDACTED]. *See* PX 968 at 2. Amazon also struggles with selling its books outside of its own platform. *See* Trial Tr. at 171:17-23 (Pietsch). The Court therefore is not convinced that Amazon is a significant competitive constraint in the relevant market. The defendants argue that [REDACTED]. *See* Defs. PFOF ¶ 126. While Disney may have the motivation and financial resources to execute the alleged plan, it will still face many of the previously discussed barriers to entry.

There is no evidence to suggest that Disney is better equipped than Amazon to succeed in the relevant market. Tn addition, it is a strain to characterize Disney's five-year aspirational plan as evidence of "timely" market entry. *See Staples II,* 190 F. Supp. 3d at 133 ("The relevant time frame for consideration in this forward-looking exercise is two to three years.").

3. Additional Arguments

The defendants raise a medley of other arguments based on (1) the power of literary agents to constrain anticompetitive behavior by publishers; (2) efficiencies from the merger that will offset anticompetitive effects; (3) the lack of negative effects from the last major merger in the publishing industry; and (4) the parties' interest in finding the "best home" for S&S. The Court will consider each of these in turn.

10. i. Power of Agents

The defendants argue in post-trial briefing that the market-share data used by the government does not account for the control that agents wield over acquisition formats, which renders the data unreliable. *See* Defs. PCOL ¶¶71-73 ("Market concentration statistics also ignore the competitive effect of agents' control over the bargaining process."). To the contrary, the market-share data necessarily reflects agents' existing practices with respect to acquisition formats. The market-share numbers aggregate individual book deals, each of which was presumably subject to an acquisition format that was determined by an agent.

The defendants also have argued that agents can constrain the competitive harm of the merger through their control over acquisition formats. The defendants have suggested that even if some imprints are eliminated or consolidated after the merger, agents can readily find substitutes for the missing imprints in any given auction. *See* Trial Tr. at 3276:8-3277:21 (Defs. Closing) ("[T]here probably are hundreds, hundreds of these imprints spread around the various publishing houses [I]f the merger did functionally eliminate one potential participant, it will not necessarily change the dynamic of any given auction because the agent can readily replace that publisher with another bidder."). Indeed, the defendants seem to treat agents as the buy-side analogue to "power buyers." "Courts have noted that the existence of power buyers-sophisticated customers who retain strategies post-merger that may constrain the ability of the merging parties to raise prices–is a factor that can serve to rebut a prima facie case of anti-competitiveness." *Wilhelmsen,* 341 F. Supp. 3d at 70 (quotations omitted).

But agents cannot create competition where it does not exist, and competition is what ultimately increases authors' advances. *See* Trial Tr. at 114:25-115:6 (Pietsch), 596:5-597:4 (Karp), 251 :4-251:20 (Pande). The proposed merger would reduce the number of imprints available to bid independently for any given book, so agents' ability to play prospective publishers against one another would weaken. *See* Merger Guidelines *§* 6.2 ("A merger between two competing [buyers] prevents [sellers] from playing those [buyers] off against each other in negotiations. This alone can significantly enhance the ability and incentive of the merged entity to obtain a result more favorable to it, and less favorable to the [seller], than the merging firms would have offered separately absent the merger.").

In any event, as a general matter, agents do not have the power to effectively discipline large publishers. Time after time, when agents have attempted to curb the Big Five's exercise of market power, the agents have failed. For example, agents were unsuccessful in attempts (1) to increase e-book royalties, *see* Trial Tr. at 2101:12-2105:5 (Wylie) (boycott of Wylie by Random House ended his attempt to secure higher e-book royalties for authors); (2) to unlink audio rights from publishing rights, PX 328 at 2-3 ("Remember when Amazon was offering seven figures on Audio before books were sold to publishers? We turned down big book after big book until agents realized we would not play in an auction without Audio. And now they always sell us Audio."); and (3) to prevent publishers from changing payment structures, *see* Trial Tr. at 1828:19-1829:18 (Walsh) (describing publishers' shift from paying out advances in halves to paying them out in quarters); PX 2008 (Fletcher) at 19-20 [REDACTED] All those contract terms were important to authors and agents, but they were forced to back down in response to pressure from the Big Five.

11. *ii. Efficiencies*

The defendants argued at trial that efficiencies would limit the merger's anticipated competitive harm. Efficiencies alone might not suffice to rebut a prima facie case, but they "may nevertheless be relevant to the competitive effects analysis on the market required to determine whether the proposed transaction will substantially lessen competition." *Sysco,* 113 F. Supp. 3d at 82 (quotations omitted). The Court, however, precluded the defendants' evidence of efficiencies, after determining that the defendants had failed to verify the evidence, as required by law. *See* Trial Tr. at 2749:12-2772:24. Efficiencies therefore play no role in the instant analysis.

12. *iii. The 2013 Penguin-Random House Merger*

The defendants argue that the 2013 Penguin-Random House merger was a "natural experiment" that did not cause a decrease in advances paid for anticipated top-selling books. *See* Defs. PCOL 184 (quoting Merger Guidelines§ 2.1.2); *see also* Defs. PFOF ¶ 226. They are correct that analogous historical events are useful for considering the likely effects of a merger. *See* Merger Guidelines § 2.1.2.

But the parties hotly dispute how the 2013 merger affected author advances. The defendants assert that advances for anticipated top-selling books did not decrease due to the merger, because they were already declining before the merger and continued to do so afterward. *See* Defs. PFOF ¶ 227; Trial Tr. at 2841:4-8 (Snyder), 2638:25-2639:14 (Snyder). The government counters that advances paid for anticipated top-selling books decreased more relative to other books' advances after the 2013 merger. *See* Govt. PFOF-PCOL 11238-42; Trial Tr. at 3066:2-10 (Hill); PX 966. Ultimately, the Court finds the evidence about the 2013 merger inconclusive. The contraction in mass-market paperbacks around 2013 muddies the analysis, and the intervening nine years have brought important shifts in the industry, such as continued consolidation. *See* Trial Tr. at 169:2-170:20 (Pietsch). Thus, the aftermath of the 2013 merger does not affect the Court's analysis.

13. *iv. A "Good Home" for S&S*

Defendants have argued that *PRR* is the best home for the authors, editors, and staff of S&S. *See* Defs. PFOF ¶¶ 22-24. Witnesses have noted that S&S authors would gain many advantages from working with the combined entity, including access to PRH's distribution network. *See, e.g.,* Defs. PFOF ¶ 25 (PRH could bring its "industry-leading supply chain to bear on S&S's books, enabling S&S to obtain more retail shelf space, enjoy higher sales, and reach more readers." (citing Trial Tr. at 878:1-22 (Dohle). Moreover, the defendants have suggested that if the sale to *PRR* is enjoined, Paramount Global might sell S&S to a private equity firm that would take on debt and "gut" the company. *See* Defs. PFOF ¶¶ 23-24; *see also* Trial Tr. At 2094:20-2095:2 (Wylie) ("So if it were, for instance, to go to private equity , the private equity company wouldn't understand the business it was in; would, say, load it with debt as Blackstone did to Houghton Mifflin, basically destroying the publishing house so that it was sold at a discount later to one of the Big 5."), 1938:18-23 (Duhigg) ("And if [the merger] doesn't happen, it will be disastrous for Simon & Schuster, because they will get acquired by private equity [a]nd they will gut that company.").

Those arguments are not relevant to the Court's analysis of the government's claim under the Clayton Act. The Court is required to assess the anticompetitive effects of the merger under the applicable statute and case law, which do not contemplate consideration of the preferences of the merging parties' employees and stakeholders, or their distaste for other potential buyers of the assets in question. The focus of the Court's inquiry is harm to competition in the relevant market. *See, e.g., E. I du Pont de Nemours,* 353 U.S. at 589,592. Nevertheless, the Court notes that the expressed concerns about a private-equity acquisition are highly speculative. Other potential buyers from the publishing industry have shown interest in acquiring S&S, and it is just as likely that another publishing company will prevail in a future sale. *See* Trial Tr. at 2185:2- 15 (Berkett). Nor is the Court moved by the desire of S&S and its employees to be acquired by PRH. It comes as no surprise that S&S would like to benefit from the extraordinary market power and other advantages that the combined entity would enjoy. The Court, however, must focus on harm to competition in the relevant market.

CONCLUSION

The government has presented a compelling case that predicts substantial harm to competition as a result of the proposed merger of PRH and S&S. It has properly defined a relevant market—focused on publishing rights for anticipated top-selling books—that encompasses 70 percent of the advances that publishers pay to authors. The post-merger concentration of the relevant market would be concerningly high: The merged entity would have a 49-percent market share, more than twice that of its closest competitor. Moreover, the top two competitors would hold 74 percent of the market; and the top four market participants would control 91 percent. The government has buttressed its market-share analysis with strong evidence of likely unilateral effects and coordinated effects that would hurt competition.

The defendants have failed to show that the relevant market is not well-defined; have failed to establish that the market-share data inaccurately reflects market conditions; and have failed to rebut the government's affinitive evidence of anticompetitive harm. Contrary to the defendants' contentions, the relevant market appropriately identifies a submarket of targeted sellers–the authors of anticipated top-selling books. Those authors have unique needs and preferences, have fewer outlets that can satisfy their requirements, and therefore are vulnerable to anticompetitive behavior. The Court is unpersuaded by the defendants' arguments that the market-share data does not accurately reflect conditions in the relevant market because it does not account for constraints that would be imposed by existing and new competitors, literary agents, and internal imprint competition. Nor have the defendants presented admissible evidence of efficiencies or any other evidence that changes the Court's view of the competitive landscape.

Accordingly, the Court finds that the proposed merger of *PRH* and S&S violates Section 7 of the Clayton Act because it is likely to substantially lessen competition in the market for the publishing rights to anticipated top-selling books. The Court therefore will enjoin the merger. A separate order will issue this day.

FLORENCE Y. PAN
United States Circuit Judge
(Sitting by designation in the United States District Court for the District of Columbia)

MEMORANDUM OF OPINION

Dated: October 31, 2022

APPENDICES

APPENDIX A: ORIGINAL COMPLAINT

UNITED STATES DISTRICT COURT FOR THE DISTRICT OF COLUMBIA
UNITED STATES OF AMERICA
U.S. Department of Justice Antitrust Division
450 Fifth Street, NW, Suite 4000
Washington, DC 20530,
Plaintiff,
v.
BERTELSMANN SE & CO. KGaA
Carl-Bertelsmann-Strasse 270
33311 Gütersloh, Germany,
PENGUIN RANDOM HOUSE, LLC
1745 Broadway
New York, NY 10019,
VIACOMCBS, INC.
1515 Broadway
New York, NY 10036,
And
SIMON & SCHUSTER, INC.
1230 Avenue of the Americas
New York, NY 10020
Defendants.

COMPLAINT

The United States of America brings this civil action to stop Penguin Random House, LLC—the world's largest book publisher—from buying its publishing rival, Simon & Schuster, Inc. If Defendants' proposed merger is allowed to proceed, Penguin Random House would be, by far, the largest book publisher in the United States, towering over its rivals. The merger would give Penguin Random House outsized influence over who and what is published, and how much authors are paid for their work. The deal, which was arranged by the two publishers' parent companies, Bertelsmann SE & Co. KGaA, ("Bertelsmann") and ViacomCBS, Inc. ("ViacomCBS"), would likely harm competition in the publishing industry and should be blocked. The United States alleges as follows:

INTRODUCTION

Authors are the lifeblood of book publishing. Without authors, there would be no stories; no poetry; no biographies; no written discourse on history, arts, culture, society, or politics. In the words of Penguin Random House's U.S. CEO, "[B]ooks have the power to sustain us, particularly in challenging times . . ." Penguin Random House's Global CEO put it more simply, "Books matter . . ."

Penguin Random House's proposed acquisition of Simon & Schuster would result in substantial harm to authors, particularly authors of anticipated top-selling books. Today, Penguin Random House and Simon & Schuster compete vigorously to acquire publishing rights from authors and provide publishing services to those authors. This competition has resulted in authors earning more for their publishing rights in the form of advances (*i.e.*, upfront payments made to authors for the rights to publish their works), and receiving better editorial, marketing, and other services that are critical to the success of their books. In 2020 alone, publishers paid authors over $1 billion in advances. Authors rely on these advances to fund their writing and pay their bills.

Penguin Random House is the world's largest book publisher, and Simon & Schuster is the fourth-largest U.S. book publisher. Together their U.S. revenues would be twice that of their next closest competitor. Indeed, one of Penguin Random House's strategic goals for the merger is to "cement Penguin Random House as #1 in the U.S."

Penguin Random House and Simon & Schuster are two of what the industry calls the "Big 5" U.S.

publishers. The Big 5 and their predecessors have long dominated the U.S. publishing market. In evaluating a potential acquisition of Simon & Schuster, a Bertelsmann board presentation characterized the U.S. publishing industry as an "oligopoly" of Penguin Random House and "only 4 further large publishers."

Publishing is a risky business. Only a fraction of books published become commercially successful. Publishers pay significant advances to authors whose books they expect will have commercial success. In most cases, the advance represents an author's total compensation. One reason the Big 5 are able to offer authors higher advances than smaller publishers is because they can spread the costs—and risks—of their investment over a larger number of books and authors. They also are able to offer authors the extensive editorial, production, marketing, and publicity support generally needed to produce a top- selling book, and the sales and distribution networks necessary to place books into readers' hands. Publishers other than the Big 5 cannot regularly pay the high advances and provide the unique bundle of services needed to secure the publishing rights to anticipated top-selling books and maximize their chances of becoming commercially successful. Simon & Schuster's late CEO likened non-Big 5 publishers to "farm teams for authors" from which the Big 5 could cherry pick talent. In contrast, she described the other Big 5 publishers as "our biggest competitors, especially for books by already bestselling authors and celebrities, since they are the most likely to come up with the high advance payments required and are known for their strong editorial and publishing skills."

If consummated, this merger would likely result in substantial harm to authors of anticipated top-selling books and ultimately, consumers. Penguin Random House would control close to half of the market for the acquisition of publishing rights to anticipated top-selling books. Penguin Random House's next largest competitor would be less than half its size. Post-merger, the two largest publishers would collectively control more than two-thirds of this market, leaving hundreds of authors with fewer alternatives and less leverage. As illustrated by the chart below, when measured by total advances paid to authors for rights to anticipated top-selling books, the combined Penguin Random House-Simon & Schuster (shown in dark blue and orange) would far outstrip the remaining Big 5 publishers and the largest independent publishers (shown in lighter blue), and enjoy substantial market power in its negotiations with authors:

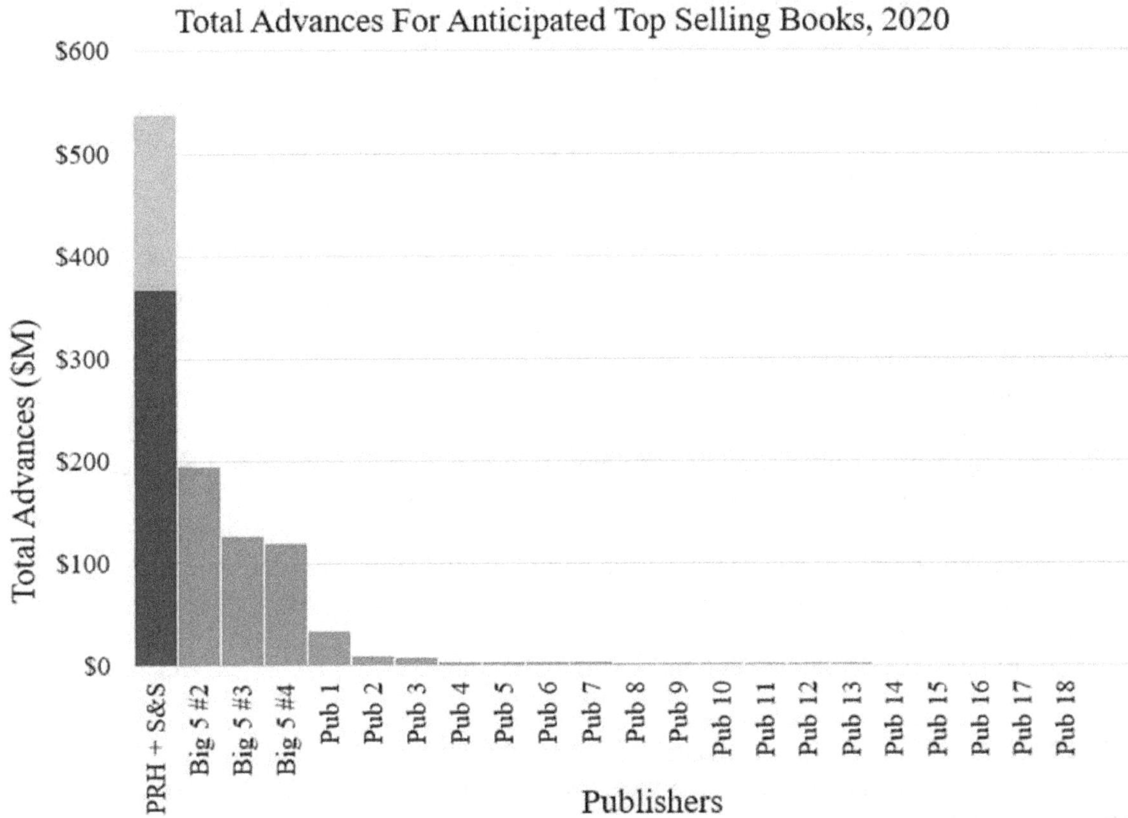

Penguin Random House and Simon & Schuster compete head-to-head to acquire publishing rights to hundreds of books every year, and this competition has resulted in substantial benefits for authors of anticipated top-selling books. Penguin Random House and Simon & Schuster are frequently invited by agents to bid in auctions for the rights to these books, and they are often the final two bidders. Competition between Penguin Random House and Simon & Schuster has resulted in higher advances, better services, and more favorable contract terms for authors.

The proposed merger would eliminate this head-to-head competition, enabling the merged firm to pay less and extract more from authors who often work for years at their craft before producing a book. As a senior Penguin Random House executive remarked to a colleague: "I would not want to be a big author at Simon & Schuster now . . ." The colleague responded, "I agree. Especially when the price tag [for acquiring Simon & Schuster] is going to be so high." By harming authors, the merger is also likely to harm consumers. Penguin Random House's Global CEO has recognized the principle that reducing author pay means "[f]ewer authors will be able to make a living from writing" which, in turn, "will have an impact on the output." By reducing author pay, this merger would make it harder for authors to earn a living by writing books, which would, in turn, lead to a reduction in the quantity and variety of books published.

There is no reason to accept the harm to competition threatened by this merger. Although Defendants have publicly suggested that the merger is necessary to create a stronger counterweight to Amazon, Penguin Random House's Global CEO privately admitted that he "never, never bought into that argument" and that one "[g]oal" after the merger is to become an "[e]xceptional partner" to Amazon.

Penguin Random House and Simon & Schuster both recognized that a merger of their companies would give rise to substantial antitrust risk. When Simon & Schuster announced that it was up for sale in March 2020, its current CEO wrote to one of its best- selling authors: "I'm pretty sure that the Department of Justice wouldn't allow Penguin Random House to buy us, but that's assuming we still have a Department of Justice." That same month, the Chairman of Bertelsmann, Penguin Random House's parent, acknowledged that Penguin Random House posed greater "antitrust risks" than any other potential buyer of Simon & Schuster. As a consequence of that risk, Bertelsmann understood that it would have to pay a significant premium over other bidders to acquire Simon & Schuster.

Authors and consumers should not be asked to bear the risk and suffer the harm from this anticompetitive merger. For the reasons set forth in this Complaint, Penguin Random House's proposed acquisition of Simon & Schuster is likely to substantially lessen competition in violation of Section 7 of the Clayton Act and should be enjoined.

JURISDICTION AND VENUE

The United States brings this action under Section 15 of the Clayton Act, as amended, 15 U.S.C § 25, to prevent and restrain Defendants from violating Section 7 of the Clayton Act, 15 U.S.C. § 18. This Court has subject matter jurisdiction over this action under Section 15 of the Clayton Act, 15 U.S.C § 25, and 28 U.S.C. §§ 1331, 1337(a), and 1345.

Defendants Penguin Random House and Simon & Schuster are engaged in interstate commerce and in activities substantially affecting interstate commerce. Penguin Random House and Simon & Schuster acquire publishing rights from authors and provide publishing services, including editing, marketing, sales, and distribution of general trade books, to authors throughout the United States.

This Court has personal jurisdiction over each Defendant. Bertelsmann and ViacomCBS have consented to personal jurisdiction in this District. Penguin Random House and Simon & Schuster also are corporations that transact business within this District through, among other things, their acquisition of content from and provision of publishing services to authors.

Venue is proper in this District under Section 12 of the Clayton Act, 15 U.S.C. § 22, and 28 U.S.C. § 1391.

DEFENDANTS AND THE PROPOSED TRANSACTION

Bertelsmann is an international media and services company, headquartered in Gütersloh, Germany. Bertelsmann has numerous subsidiaries, including Penguin Random House and the Bertelsmann Printing Group, a major supplier of book printing services in the United States.

Penguin Random House is headquartered in New York, New York. Penguin Random House was formed from the 2013 merger of Penguin and Random House, which were founded in 1935 and 1927, respectively. Penguin Random House has more than 90 U.S. imprints (a trade or brand name for a specific group of editors, such as Doubleday), across seven publishing groups. Penguin Random House is the largest U.S. trade book publisher. It publishes over 2,000 new titles every year in the U.S. In addition to publishing, Penguin Random House sells distribution services to third-party publishers. In 2020, Penguin Random House earned over $2.4 billion in U.S. publishing revenues.

ViacomCBS is an international media and entertainment company, headquartered in New York, New York. ViacomCBS's assets include the Paramount film and television studios, the CBS television network, cable networks, streaming services, and Simon & Schuster.

Simon & Schuster, headquartered in New York, New York, is a wholly-owned subsidiary of ViacomCBS. Founded in 1924, Simon & Schuster is the fourth-largest U.S. trade book publisher. It has over 30 U.S. imprints across three publishing groups and publishes over 1,000 new titles annually in the U.S. In 2020, Simon & Schuster earned over $760 million in U.S. publishing revenues.

On November 25, 2020, Bertelsmann and ViacomCBS announced that Penguin Random House would acquire Simon & Schuster from ViacomCBS in an all-cash deal valued at approximately $2.175 billion.

BACKGROUND

U.S. General Trade Book Publishing

The term "general trade books" (hereinafter "books") is widely used in the publishing industry and refers to books that are published for wide public consumption, including both fiction and a variety of non-fiction such as biographies, cookbooks, travel guides, and self-help books. It does not include, for example, academic texts or professional manuals. Bringing a book to market in the United States requires the participation of many different entities, including authors and their agents, publishers, printers, distributors, wholesalers, retailers, and ultimately, readers.

Book publishing is a collaborative effort between authors and publishers. An author writes a manuscript or proposal for a book and generally hires an agent to solicit competing bids from publishers and negotiate a license for the book's publishing rights with the winning bidder. The licenses obtained by publishers generally include the right to publish a book in various formats (print, ebook, audiobook) within a particular geographic area. Publishers compete for these rights on a number of different dimensions. In addition to paying authors advances and royalties, publishers provide editorial, design, marketing, publicity and other services to authors. Publishers also arrange for printing and distribution of books to wholesalers and retailers.

Authors are compensated in the form of an advance and royalties. An advance is essentially an up-front payment of royalties expected to accrue from future sales of the book. The royalty rate is a fixed percentage of sales that is set by the publisher and is rarely negotiated. If a book "earns out" by earning royalties that exceed the amount of the advance, the author receives additional payments from further sales at the agreed upon royalty rate. Most authors do not earn out their advance and thus their advance generally constitutes their entire earnings from their book. Consequently, the key financial determinant in most negotiations is the size of the advance and its payout structure (*e.g.,* the number of installments the advance is divided into, and the timing of each such payment).

Authors' agents seek to maximize the amount paid to authors for licensing the rights to publish their clients' books. In order to secure the most favorable terms for their clients, agents typically submit a book proposal, which can be a complete manuscript, an outline for a book, or just an idea for a book, to several publishers seeking offers. If there are enough interested publishers, agents can set up a competitive bidding situation such as an auction where multiple publishers bid to acquire the rights to the book.

In the United States, books are sold through several retail sales channels, including online retailers such as Amazon, national bookstore chains such as Barnes & Noble and Books-A-Million, independent bookstores such as The Strand and Politics & Prose, big-box stores such as Target, Walmart and Costco, and specialty retailers such as Anthropologie and Bass Pro Shops. In the United States, books also are sold to retailers and institutional buyers (including schools and libraries) through wholesalers such as Ingram and Readerlink. Publishers set the cover or "list price" of a book and sell the books to retailers at a standard discount from the list price (a little less than half-off for most types of print books). Publishers also may offer retailers marketing and other promotional discounts in addition to the standard discount off of list.

Penguin Random House and Simon & Schuster are Two of the Big 5 Book Publishers in the United States

The book publishing market in the United States is dominated by the Big 5 publishers. In the words of Simon & Schuster's former CEO, the Big 5 are one another's "biggest competitors." In addition to strong editorial and publishing capabilities, the Big 5 generally offer larger marketing and promotional budgets, and employ dedicated teams of sales representatives who service retailers and promote an author's books.

In order to solicit the most attractive bids for their clients, authors' agents typically submit manuscripts to some or all of the Big 5 publishers—especially Penguin Random House, which has, by far, the largest number of imprints and publishes the most new books in the United States. Authors generally choose to work with a publisher they believe will bring them the best chance of success, usually based on a combination of advance and other financial terms and, as Simon & Schuster's former CEO put it, "editorial match, a feel the editor and [publishing] house understands what they are writing, and publishing vision as to how to bring the book to market and create an audience for it."

Smaller Publishers are Limited in their Ability to Compete Effectively with the Big 5

Smaller publishers lack the resources and capabilities of the Big 5 publishers, and thus they are limited in their ability to compete for the publishing rights to anticipated top-selling books. Smaller publishers typically have smaller "backlists" (*i.e.*, inventories of older titles that continue to generate sales) than the Big 5, which are a critical source of revenue that allow the Big 5 to pay more and higher advances to authors. Smaller publishers also lack scale in book sales. With fewer titles to rely on for sales, smaller publishers lack the financial resources to (1) regularly pay the advances required to secure publishing rights to anticipated top-selling books, and (2) absorb the financial losses from books that do not meet their sales expectations. While smaller publishers occasionally win auctions for anticipated top-selling books, it is the exception rather than the norm. Smaller publishers typically have lower marketing and promotional budgets, fewer experienced sales representatives, and less robust in-house distribution capabilities compared to the Big 5. Authors of anticipated top-selling books generally seek publishers who have the prestige, reputation, experience, and ability to maximize the book's chances of becoming commercially successful. Therefore, authors of anticipated top-selling books generally do not view smaller publishers as competitively significant options compared to the Big 5.

The Defendants recognize that smaller publishers are limited in their ability to compete with the Big 5 for the rights to publish anticipated top-selling books. In the words of the late CEO of Simon & Schuster, the "myriad smaller publishers" in the United States "rarely compete with us in auctions for new properties. Often these publishers become farm teams for authors who then want to move to a larger, more financially stable major publisher."

RELEVANT MARKETS

A typical starting point for merger analysis is defining a relevant market, which has both a product and a geographic dimension. Courts define relevant product markets to help determine the areas of competition most likely to be affected by the merger.

The proposed acquisition would result in the lessening of competition in each of the two product markets described below. Each of these products constitutes a line of commerce as that term is used in Section 7 of the Clayton Act, 15 U.S.C. §18, and each is a relevant product market in which competitive effects can be assessed. As recognized by the Supreme Court and the U.S. Department of Justice and Federal Trade Commission *Horizontal Merger Guidelines*, the focus in defining product markets is the extent of substitution in response to changes in price. One tool used to assess substitution in markets composed of buyers of goods is known as the "hypothetical monopsonist" test. This test, as described in the *Horizontal Merger Guidelines*, asks whether a firm that was the only buyer of a product (a hypothetical monopsonist) would profitably impose a price reduction— specifically, a small but significant and non-transitory reduction in price (a "SSNRP")—on at least one product purchased by the merging firms in the relevant market. As described below, each relevant product market satisfies this hypothetical monopsonist test.

Product Markets

The Acquisition of U.S. Publishing Rights to Books from Authors is a Relevant Product Market

The acquisition of U.S. publishing rights to books from authors (hereinafter referred to as "content acquisition") is a relevant market and line of commerce within the meaning of Section 7 of the Clayton Act. In this market, authors sell the rights to publish their works in the United States, and publishers agree to provide editorial, design, printing, sales and distribution, marketing, publicity, or other services to authors. The market is differentiated, meaning that publishers have differing capabilities and resources they can offer to authors. In addition, advances are individually negotiated, which allows each publisher to bid higher or lower depending on its perception of the competition it faces in seeking to acquire the rights for any given book. A hypothetical monopsonist of the U.S. publishing rights to books would profitably decrease the advances paid to authors by a small but significant, non-transitory amount.

Self-publishing is not a reasonable alternative for most authors seeking to sell the publishing rights to their books in exchange for an advance. By definition, self-publishing does not pay authors advances, which authors often use to fund their writing. Self-publishing also does not include the breadth of editorial, distribution, and marketing services that are important factors in whether a book will become commercially successful. Indeed, an internal Simon & Schuster document acknowledged that "[s]elf-publishing is not viewed as a threat to [our] core business." Authors of books would not substitute to self-publishing in sufficient numbers to deter a hypothetical monopsonist from imposing a small, but significant, and non-transitory decrease in advances.

Some publishers hire authors on a "work-for-hire" basis to draft books conceived of by the publisher, not the author. The publisher, and not the author, owns the publishing rights in a work-for-hire arrangement. Moreover, such authors generally are compensated differently than authors who sell the rights to publish their books in exchange for an advance and royalties. Authors of books would not substitute to work-for-hire arrangements in sufficient numbers to deter a hypothetical monopsonist from imposing a small, but significant, and non-transitory decrease in advances.

The Acquisition of U.S. Publishing Rights to Anticipated Top-Selling Books is also a Relevant Product Market

The acquisition of the U.S. publishing rights to anticipated top-selling books is a relevant product market and line of commerce under Section 7 of the Clayton Act. The market for the acquisition of U.S. publishing rights to anticipated top-selling books is narrower than, and included within, the market for the acquisition of U.S. publishing rights to books.

The authors of anticipated top-selling books generally command higher advances than other authors. Penguin Random House and Simon & Schuster typically require senior executives to review and approve such purchases based on projected profit-and-loss statements ("P&Ls") prepared by editors. These P&Ls include the sales expected to be derived from the book based upon the sales history of comparable books or other works by the same author, production and marketing costs, and the book's expected list price. The higher the anticipated sales, the higher a publisher is generally willing to bid on the advance.

It is appropriate to define relevant product markets around purchases made from certain types of sellers, such as authors of anticipated top-selling books. The publishing industry displays the characteristics identified in § 3 of the *Horizontal Merger Guidelines* for when markets may be defined in this way: prices (*i.e.,* advances) are individually negotiated and publishers have information that allows them to identify authors that have fewer competitive options. Publishers know based on experience that if the bidding for a particular book exceeds a certain advance level, they are likely bidding against a limited set of competitors that have the financial wherewithal to pay for the advance, the publishing expertise to attract and serve authors of anticipated top-selling books, and the capability to generate sufficient sales to justify the advance. Publishers take this into account when deciding how much to bid on advances for a particular book. Given the individualized nature of the negotiations, publishers can target authors of anticipated top-selling books by offering lower advances and authors cannot arbitrage to avoid lower advances. As a result, a hypothetical monopsonist of anticipated top-selling books would profitably reduce advances paid to authors of anticipated top-selling by a small but significant, non-transitory amount.

Self-publishing and work-for hire arrangements are not reasonable alternatives for authors seeking to sell the rights to publish their books in exchange for an advance. As noted above, self-published and work-for-hire authors typically do not receive advances for their work. Moreover, authors who publish their own books retain the publishing rights, while work-for-hire authors do not possess publishing rights to begin with. In other words, neither self-publishing nor work-for-hire arrangements involve the *acquisition* of publishing rights from authors. Not enough authors of anticipated top-selling books would switch to self- publishing or work-for-hire arrangements to deter a hypothetical monopolist from imposing a small but significant, non-transitory decrease in advances.

Geographic Markets

Penguin Random House and Simon & Schuster compete to acquire the rights to publish books in the United States. Authors who sell U.S. publishing rights are predominantly located in the United States but can reside anywhere in the world. The market includes publishers who acquire U.S. publishing rights even when those publishers are located outside the U.S. Accordingly, the relevant geographic markets for content acquisition are global.

ANTICOMPETITIVE EFFECTS

The proposed merger would eliminate a major competitor to Penguin Random House, already the market leader, and create a firm that controls a substantial share of the relevant markets. The merger would also result in significantly increased concentration in the relevant markets, which have experienced significant consolidation in recent years. Post-merger, the market for the acquisition of U.S. publishing rights to anticipated top-selling books would be highly concentrated. The merger is presumptively unlawful.

A. The Proposed Merger Would Eliminate Head-to-Head Competition Between Penguin Random House and Simon & Schuster, Depressing Author Pay and Reducing the Quantity and Variety of Titles Published

If Defendants' proposed merger is allowed to proceed, Penguin Random House would account for close to half of the market for the acquisition of U.S. publishing rights to anticipated top-selling books. Penguin Random House's next largest competitor would be less than half its size. Post-merger, the merged firm and its next largest competitor would account for more than two-thirds of that market.

Penguin Random House and Simon & Schuster compete closely to acquire the rights to anticipated top-selling books. They almost always are invited to bid in auctions for anticipated top-selling books, are often the top two bidders, and frequently lose to each other. For example, in September 2019, after learning that Simon & Schuster lost an auction to Penguin Random House, Simon & Schuster's then-President and current CEO wrote to his boss: "This was the third [book] we lost this week to PRH [and] . . . [t]here may have been a fourth."

The head-to-head competition between Defendants has allowed authors of anticipated top-selling books to secure higher advances and other favorable terms. For example, in January 2019, Simon & Schuster tried to acquire the memoir of a Grammy Award-winning singer and avoid competing in an auction by making a pre-emptive offer for $5 million. After this initial offer was rejected, Simon & Schuster increased its bid to $6 million, and Penguin Random House countered with $7 million plus $2.5 million in potential bonuses. Upon hearing of Penguin Random House's bid, Simon & Schuster's then-President emailed his boss: "I'm concerned that if we offer less than $8 million, [the author's agent] will go back to PRH. She said they were willing to offer more." Simon & Schuster eventually won with a bid of $8 million.

In mid-2019, Penguin Random House, Simon & Schuster, and Hachette were invited to bid on a book proposal based on a Broadway play. Penguin Random House and Simon & Schuster submitted equivalent bids; Hachette's was lower. The author's agent then asked for "best bids" from Penguin Random House and Simon & Schuster, both of which knew they were competing against the other. Simon & Schuster submitted a bid of $1.4 million, whereas Penguin Random House's bid was closer to $1.25 million. Upon learning this, Penguin Random House's U.S. CEO agreed to match Simon & Schuster at $1.4 million. At that point the auction was a dead-heat, with each publisher trying to win the "beauty contest" between them by pointing to the superior services each could provide to the author, including marketing, publicity, and editorial support. As Simon & Schuster's current CEO summed it up: "The choice is between Simon & Schuster and RH and we'll find out today." The author eventually chose Penguin Random House.

That same month, an agent sent a proposal to four of the Big 5 publishers for a book on the Mueller investigation. Only Simon & Schuster and Penguin Random House submitted offers. After hearing that its bid of $625,000 was lower, Simon & Schuster increased its bid to $1.5 million. A senior Simon & Schuster executive told the agent that Simon & Schuster had not offered her agency "an advance of this magnitude to a new author in the nine years I've been here." Penguin Random House increased its offer to $1.5 million plus up to $500,000 in sales bonuses. After hearing that the author chose Penguin Random House, the Simon & Schuster executive wrote the CEO: "I did everything I could and we lost to Random House … Frustrating."

In 2020 Penguin Random House and Simon & Schuster competed in an auction for a book on gender inequality. After the first round, three bidders remained, including Penguin Random House and Simon & Schuster, with Simon & Schuster submitting the highest bid at $475,000. After the third bidder dropped out, Simon & Schuster and Penguin Random House drove the bidding up to $625,000 and $650,000 respectively. Subsequently, the agent asked for best and final bids, and Simon & Schuster bid $750,000. Suspecting that it was bidding against Simon & Schuster, Penguin Random House stretched its bid to $775,000. After winning the contract, the acquiring editor emailed her colleague: "we prevailed over . . . S&S." Her colleague replied: "[W]e got this one, and over stiff competition."

Penguin Random House and Simon & Schuster again went down to the wire in another fierce contest for an author's debut novel. After multiple rounds of bidding, the author's agent announced that only the two top bidders would be allowed to continue. Penguin Random House and Simon & Schuster were the two highest at $510,000 and $525,000, respectively. They continued bidding against one another for several additional rounds. Upon hearing that the other bidder had put in a final offer just shy of $700,000, Simon & Schuster increased its offer from $525,000 to $700,000 and won the auction.

Penguin Random House and Simon & Schuster also competed for a book on the opioid epidemic in an auction in early 2020. When the bidding reached $645,000 after several rounds, the other bidders dropped out leaving Penguin Random House and Simon & Schuster as the only remaining bidders. Penguin Random House and Simon & Schuster then went back and forth with competing bids for multiple rounds, with Penguin Random House eventually prevailing with a winning bid of $825,000.

In the broader product market for content acquisition, the merger would harm a wide spectrum of authors who benefit from competition between Penguin Random House and Simon & Schuster today. While smaller publishers can be competitive alternatives for some authors whose works are not anticipated to be top sellers, the merger is likely to harm any author who views Penguin Random House and Simon & Schuster as close substitutes and would benefit from head-to-head bidding by these competitors. For example, Penguin Random House and Simon & Schuster were the final two bidders for a book by a freelance science journalist, and their direct competition drove the final advance up substantially above Penguin Random House's initial offer. Penguin Random House's successful final bid was $15,000 higher than Simon & Schuster's best bid, a difference the author indicated would help pay for her son's college tuition. The fact that smaller publishers may be an acceptable alternative for certain authors will not protect other authors who have benefitted from competition between Penguin Random House and Simon & Schuster, and would continue to benefit in the future if the merger is enjoined.

By eliminating the head-to-head competition between Penguin Random House and Simon & Schuster, the proposed merger would likely result in authors earning less for their books. Because many authors do not earn out their advances, the advance often represents the sum total of an author's compensation. A reduction in author compensation is likely to lead to fewer authors being able to make a living from writing and fewer and less diverse books being published.

B. Penguin Random House's Proposed Acquisition of Simon & Schuster Would Facilitate Coordination Among the Remaining Big 5 Publishers

In addition to eliminating head-to-head competition, the proposed merger is also likely to reduce competition by facilitating coordination between the remaining major publishers. The market structure of the publishing industry already is conducive to coordinated behavior. A few large players dominate the industry and the terms of author contracts, other than advances, have become fairly standardized over time. For example, royalty rates are typically identical among the Big 5 publishers and are rarely negotiable. Similarly, audio rights used to be negotiated separately but the Big 5 publishers now generally demand that authors bundle audio rights with print and electronic rights. If this merger is allowed to proceed, the Big 5 would be reduced to the Big Four, with the merged firm nearly twice as large as its next largest competitor. Penguin Random House would thereby cement its position as the key leader for other publishers to follow. With fewer players and an obvious leader, the Big Four would likely find it easier to reach and sustain a consensus that harms authors through coordination. For example, the new Big Four could tacitly agree to extract a broader scope of rights by requiring authors to sell worldwide publishing rights (instead of U.S. or North American-only publishing rights), or they could pay out advances in smaller increments or over longer periods of time. Information about rival publishers' actions is widely available in this industry, and communications between employees of rival publishers is common, making deviations from any industry understanding or agreement more easily detectable.

The risks of post-merger coordination are substantial. The Big 5 have a history of collusion. In 2012 the United States filed a complaint in the District Court for the Southern District of New York alleging that five publishers—including Penguin and Simon & Schuster—conspired with Apple to increase the prices of ebooks. After a trial, the District Judge found that Apple and the publishers had indeed engaged in a price-fixing conspiracy in violation of Section 1 of the Sherman Act, a judgment that was affirmed by the Second Circuit.

LACK OF COUNTERVAILING FACTORS

A. Entry Barriers are High and Will Increase With this Merger

There are high barriers to economically meaningful entry or repositioning in the markets for content acquisition, and thus new entry or repositioning by existing competitors is unlikely to prevent or counteract the proposed acquisition's likely anticompetitive effects. It can take many years and significant financial investment for a publisher to accumulate a stable of backlist titles, which are a crucial source of revenue used to fund author advances for new books. In addition to sufficient financial resources, infrastructure and scale, a publisher needs name recognition and a demonstrated track record to convince authors of anticipated top-selling books to consider switching publishers. Because authors must entrust their work to a publisher for the entire lifecycle of a book (often spanning years), it is important to authors of anticipated top-selling books that a publisher has a proven track record of producing commercially successful books. One internal Bertelsmann analysis of the potential merger succinctly described the barriers to entry as "high (mainly reputation, distribution)."

In addition, many smaller publishers lack distribution capabilities and depend upon Penguin Random House and Simon & Schuster for distribution services. These services include: selling books to retailers and other customers; warehousing; order fulfillment and shipping (often referred to as "pick, pack, and ship"); invoicing and collections; and returns processing. The merged firm would have even greater control over distribution services, giving it more power over competitors and allowing Defendants to raise competitors' costs or enhance barriers to entry or re-positioning.

B. There Are No Merger-Specific Efficiencies that Outweigh the Likely Harm to Competition from this Merger

Defendants have claimed that the proposed acquisition would generate synergies by combining the operations of Penguin Random House and Simon & Schuster. But Penguin Random House's own executives have raised doubts about these synergy claims. For example, Penguin Random House's COO, who is charged with integrating Simon & Schuster into Penguin Random House, has characterized the "synergies task" as "extremely aggressive." Similarly, Penguin Random House's Global CEO testified that he is "not convinced" that Penguin Random House's U.S. management will take the steps necessary to achieve the planned synergies. To the extent the proposed transaction would result in any verifiable, transaction-specific efficiencies in the alleged relevant markets, such efficiencies are unlikely to outweigh the transaction's likely anticompetitive effects.

C. This Merger Will Not Provide a Counterweight to Amazon's Alleged Buying Power

Although Penguin Random House has publicly stated that the merger with Simon & Schuster will provide a counterweight to Amazon's alleged buying power, its internal documents tell a different story: Penguin Random House plans to embrace Amazon even more closely after the merger. For example, in seeking approval from Bertelsmann's Supervisory Board to pursue Simon & Schuster, Penguin Random House executives stated that the acquisition would advance their "[g]oal" to be an "[e]xceptional partner for Amazon." Penguin Random House's Global CEO has also refuted this claim. When asked whether he viewed the proposed merger as a counterweight to Amazon, he replied: "No, I've never, never bought into that argument… I am convinced it is not the case in the coming together of Penguin Random House and Simon & Schuster."

D. Penguin Random House's Proposed "Fix" Would Not Preserve Competition Between Defendants

Aware of the competitive concerns raised by agents and authors, as well as the ongoing antitrust scrutiny of this merger by the United States, Defendants have tried to salvage their deal by making an unenforceable promise to continue competing after the merger is consummated. On September 20, 2021 Penguin Random House announced that, after the merger, it would allow Penguin Random House imprints and legacy Simon & Schuster imprints to continue bidding against one another up to an unspecified amount. In short, after securing nearly half the market for publishing rights to anticipated top-selling books, Penguin Random House asks this Court to trust that Penguin Random House will not use its market power to maximize profits for the benefit of its shareholders but rather, it will essentially compete with itself to reduce those profits. This proposal defies economic sense, can be evaded or violated without detection, and is unenforceable.

VIOLATIONS ALLEGED

If allowed to proceed, Penguin Random House's proposed acquisition of Simon & Schuster would eliminate competition between Penguin Random House and Simon & Schuster and would likely lessen competition substantially in the markets for content acquisition in the United States in violation of Section 7 of the Clayton Act, 15 U.S.C. § 18.

1. Among other things, the transaction would:
    a. eliminate competition between Penguin Random House and Simon & Schuster;
    b. facilitate coordination between the combined firm and the remaining Big 5 publishers;
    c. likely cause author income to be less than it would be otherwise;
    d. likely cause a reduction in the quantity and variety of books published by the merged firm; and
    e. likely reduce quality, service, choice, and innovation.

REQUEST FOR RELIEF

2. The United States requests:
    a. that Penguin Random House's proposed acquisition of Simon & Schuster be adjudged to violate Section 7 of the Clayton Act, 15 U.S.C. § 18;
    b. that the Defendants be permanently enjoined and restrained from carrying out the proposed acquisition of Penguin Random House by Simon & Schuster or any other transaction that would combine the two companies;
    c. that the United States be awarded costs of this action; and
    d. that the United States be awarded such other relief as the Court may deem just and proper.

Dated: November 2, 2021 Respectfully Submitted,
RICHARD A. POWERS
Acting Assistant Attorney General Antitrust Division
KATHLEEN S. O'NEILL
Senior Director of Investigations and Litigation
CRAIG W. CONRATH
Director of Civil Litigation
OWEN M. KENDLER

Chief Financial Services, Fintech, and Banking Section
YVETTE F. TARLOV (DC Bar #442452)
Assistant Chief, Financial Services, Fintech, and Banking Section
JOHN R. READ (DC Bar #419373)
Brittney Dimond
Jonathan S. Goldsmith (DC Bar #1044315)
Collier Kelley
Ihan Kim
January Kim (DC Bar #1035032)
Kevin Krautscheid
Jessica N. Leal
Sarah H. Licht (DC Bar #1021541)
Bennett J. Matelson (DC Bar #454551)
Lisa A. Scanlon
Ethan Stevenson
Jeffrey G. Vernon (DC Bar #1009690)
Attorneys for the United States
United States Department of Justice Antitrust Division
450 Fifth Street, NW, Suite 4000

APPENDIX B: DOJ PRE-TRIAL BRIEF

UNITED STATES DISTRICT COURT FOR THE DISTRICT OF COLUMBIA
UNITED STATES OF AMERICA,
Plaintiff,
v.
BERTELSMANN SE & CO. KGaA, PENGUIN RANDOM HOUSE, LLC, VIACOMCBS, INC., and SIMON & SCHUSTER, INC,
Defendants.

Introduction

Penguin Random House's proposed acquisition of Simon & Schuster would further entrench the largest publishing giant in the United States (and the world) and give the merged company control of nearly half of the market to acquire anticipated top-selling books from authors. Penguin Random House admits that the merger would "[c]ement PRH as #1 in the US" and strengthen the "oligopoly" of large publishing houses. Indeed, the post-merger combined Penguin Random House/Simon & Schuster would share control of 90% of the relevant market with just three other companies. The evidence will show that the proposed merger would likely result in authors of anticipated top-selling books receiving smaller advances, meaning authors who labor for years over their manuscripts will be paid less for their efforts and fewer authors will be able to earn a living from writing. The proposed merger creates such an obvious risk of harm to competition that Simon & Schuster's CEO, Jonathan Karp, admitted in an email: "I'm pretty sure the Department of Justice wouldn't allow Penguin Random House to buy us, but that's assuming we still have a Department of Justice." This concern was prescient.

If allowed to proceed, the proposed transaction would eliminate competition between two of the last remaining major publishers. Penguin Random House and Simon & Schuster are legendary businesses responsible for publishing some of the most esteemed works of fiction and non-fiction in this country's history. Today, they compete fiercely to win the rights to publish anticipated top-selling books. The evidence will show that many authors have benefitted from this competition, which would disappear if the proposed merger were allowed to proceed, likely leading to lower advances and worse contract terms for authors.

The proposed merger also is the latest and most aggressive march towards concentration in an industry with a history of consolidation and coordination and would solidify the dominant position and power of the leading player, Penguin Random House. Today, the publishing industry is an "oligopoly" dominated by the "Big 5" publishers. The late Simon & Schuster CEO Carolyn Reidy described the Big 5 as one another's "biggest competitors," in contrast to smaller publishers, which she characterized as "farm teams for authors who then want to move to a larger, more financially stable major publisher."The Big 5 make up 90% of the relevant market because they are the only firms with the capital, reputations, editorial capacity, marketing, publicity, sales, and distribution resources to regularly acquire anticipated top-selling books. The proposed merger would further increase consolidation in this concentrated industry, make the biggest player even bigger, and likely increase coordination in an industry with a history of coordination among the major publishers.

The Clayton Act prohibits mergers if the effect of the transaction "may be" substantially to lessen competition. 15 U.S.C. § 18. The Supreme Court has explained that the words "may be" are intentional to show that the statute is concerned with "probabilities, not certainties,"

Brown Shoe Co. v. United States, 370 U.S. 294, 323 (1962), because Congress "intended to arrest anticompetitive tendencies in their 'incipiency.'" *United States v. Phila. Nat'l Bank,* 374 U.S. 321, 362 (1963) (quoting *Brown Shoe,* 370 U.S. at 317). The Supreme Court has made clear that courts need not wait until the harms of consolidation have already been cemented; rather, the Clayton Act can be used as a proactive tool to thwart consolidation before it worsens. Where, as here, the relevant market is already highly concentrated and the merging parties' market shares are substantial, both the Supreme Court and DC Circuit have recognized that the proposed acquisition is presumptively anticompetitive. *Phila. Nat'l*

Bank, 374 U.S. at 364 (holding that significant change in concentration that resulted in a combined market share of 30% was sufficient to establish that transaction was presumptively illegal); *FTC v. H.J. Heinz Co.*, 246 F.3d 708, 711, 716-17 (D.C. Cir. 2001) (finding FTC established prima facie showing of anticompetitive effects where defendants would have a combined share of 32.8% in a concentrated industry).

The presumption of illegality empowers the Court to reject a proposed merger unless and until the Court finds that the Defendants present significant countervailing evidence to disturb that presumption. Here, Defendants have not and cannot meet that weighty burden. First, Defendants themselves recognize that barriers to entry into the relevant market are high, undercutting their arguments that new or smaller publishers could enter or expand in a manner timely, likely, and sufficient to restore competition lost by the merger. Second, Defendants grossly overstate the ability of literary agents to maximize value for their author clients in the absence of a competitive environment. Literary agents cannot create competitive conditions where there are none. Third, Defendants' purported efficiencies defense fails for several reasons (if it is even legally permissible) because their purported efficiencies are neither cognizable nor sufficient to overcome the likely anticompetitive harm that will arise should the Court permit the proposed merger to be completed. Finally, Penguin Random House's last-ditch, made-for-litigation effort to save its proposed merger with an unenforceable, unilateral promise to compete against itself post-merger is irrelevant, illogical, and should be ignored.

Accordingly, the United States respectfully requests that the Court permanently enjoin Penguin Random House's proposed acquisition of Simon & Schuster.

Factual Background

A. The Parties

Penguin Random House ("PRH") is the largest trade book publisher worldwide and in the United States. Headquartered in New York, New York, PRH is owned by Bertelsmann SE & Co. KgaA ("Bertelsmann"), an international media and services company headquartered in Germany. PRH has more than ninety U.S. publishing imprints (a trade or brand name for a specific editorial group such as Viking, Riverhead, and Crown) across six publishing divisions. PRH publishes over 2,000 new titles every year in the U.S. Its 2020 U.S. net sales surpassed $2.6 billion.

Simon & Schuster ("S&S"), also headquartered in New York, New York, is the fourth- largest book publisher in the United States as measured by total sales. S&S is owned by international media and entertainment company Paramount Global (formerly known as ViacomCBS). S&S has over thirty U.S. imprints across three publishing groups and publishes over 1,000 new titles annually in the U.S. Its 2020 U.S. net sales were [REDACTED]. Bertelsmann executives described S&S as "one of the last high-quality scaled assets in the US [publishing] market" in advocating for its acquisition by Bertelsmann, which "would solidify PRH's position in the US, our key market."

PRH and S&S are two of what the industry refers to as the "Big 5" U.S. publishers, a group which includes HarperCollins Publishers, Hachette Book Group, and Macmillan Publishing Group, LLC. Together, the Big 5 publishers are one another's "biggest competitors... since they are the most likely to come up with high advance payments required and are known for their strong editorial and publishing skills." The Big 5 dominate U.S. book publishing and account for over 90% of the market for the acquisition of publishing rights to anticipated top-selling books. The Big 5 have existed for decades, some dating back to the early 1900s, and have grown mostly through acquisitions of smaller competitors. Defendants' internal documents acknowledge there have been "no successful startups in the last decade," in part due to "[h]igh barriers to entry." The publishing industry has undergone significant consolidation in incremental measures over recent years. The impact of that consolidation has further cemented the dominant position of the Big 5. PRH itself is a result of the 2013 merger between Penguin and Random House. Other recent examples of consolidation include the 2021 acquisition of Houghton Mifflin

Harcourt's trade book division by HarperCollins, Inc. for $349 million, and Hachette Book Group's 2021 acquisition of Workman Publishing for $240 million.

B. How a Manuscript is Acquired and Published

Authors typically partner with a literary agent to sell the publishing rights to their book (or books) when they are in the form of a proposal or manuscript. This process usually relies on competition to secure the best outcome for the author, and ranges from exclusive negotiations, to submissions to multiple publishers, to fast-moving auctions. Auctions may take various forms, including best bid auctions, a one-round process in which each interested publisher submits its best bid; rounds auctions, in which the literary agent holds several rounds of bidding as publishers with the lowest bids are eliminated from contention; or other hybrid auction formats. Authors whose books are anticipated to attract especially high bids and generate significant sales typically will submit their proposal through an agent to a variety of editors at multiple publishing houses and conduct a competitive auction to maximize the value of their work. In an effort to secure the best outcome for their clients, literary agents frequently submit proposals to imprints at some or all of the Big 5 publishers, especially for books that are expected to sell well.

Authors are primarily compensated through an advance against royalties. An advance is a guaranteed payment typically paid out in installments over several years and represents prepaid royalties that accrue from the sale of a book to a publisher. Over time, if a book "earns out" by earning royalties equal to the amount of the initial advance, the author receives additional payments from further sales as periodic royalty accountings. Royalties are determined by media type, format, territory, and language. In addition to the amount of the advance, authors and their agents also look for a strong editorial relationship, robust marketing and publicity plans, and an extensive distribution network.

Publishers determine how much to offer for an author's work—namely, the size of the advance—by putting together projected profit-and-loss statements known as "P&Ls" for the work. These P&Ls include the expected list price for the book in various formats, production and marketing costs, and—the key factor—anticipated sales based on previous sales of comparative titles (referred to as "comp titles" or "comps"). Comp titles are those with similar characteristics to the proposed book, such as subject matter, literary merit, and author background. Publishers consider these the best estimates of a new book's projected sales and use the commercial success of comp titles to help determine how much to offer for an author's work.

C. Anticipated Top-Selling Books

An anticipated top-selling book is expected to generate significant sales, which typically requires strong editing, marketing, and distribution support. An author of an anticipated top-selling book typically receives a generous advance. More than 85% of author contracts for anticipated top-selling books never earn out their advance, even several years after publication. Thus, the amount of the advance is all the more important because the vast majority of authors never receive royalties beyond the amount of the initial advance. Indeed, because authors of anticipated top-selling books seldom earn out their advance, literary agents and authors focus on the amount of the advance in negotiations with publishers and rarely negotiate royalties beyond the advance. [REDACTED]

Authors of anticipated top-selling books are overwhelmingly published by Big 5 publishers, including PRH and S&S. The Big 5 have the financial wherewithal, editorial, marketing, sales, and distribution support that these authors strongly prefer to put them in the best financial position possible. This phenomenon is borne out by the numbers: the Big 5 control over 90% of the market for anticipated top-selling books. In 2020, that meant the Big 5 controlled 90% of a $1 billion market for advances contracted to be paid to authors. Authors of anticipated top-selling books typically look to the Big 5 publishers when selling the rights to publish their books, rather than smaller publishers. Authors of anticipated top- selling books also do not typically consider self-publishing a feasible alternative because it requires authors to leave a sizable guaranteed advance on the table while also taking on all the publishing responsibilities themselves, including potentially significant costs. Indeed, many self-published books sell very few or no copies at all.

D. The Big 5 Dominate the Publishing Industry and are the Main Competitors for Anticipated Top-Selling Books

The Big 5 publishers are best able to acquire and publish anticipated top-selling books because their size and resources allow them to better manage risk and facilitate a book's commercial success. First, publishing anticipated top-selling books usually requires the ability to pay large advances and assume the risk that the book will not sell well. The dynamics of publishing anticipated top-selling books leverage the Big 5's dominance because they have the capital, market position, and other assets that enable them to spread the costs—and risks—of their investment over a larger number of books and authors. The Court will hear testimony from Penguin Random House Global CEO Markus Dohle describing the publishing business as a "portfolio business" and confirming that PRH can better manage its risk relative to a smaller publisher because it publishes many books and is not dependent on a few.

Second, the Big 5 are best able to offer authors the extensive and sophisticated infrastructure of editorial, production, marketing, and publicity support needed to produce a top- selling book, and the sales and distribution networks necessary to place a book into the hands of readers. For example, a marketing presentation titled "The Penguin Random House Advantage" touts the company's "industry-leading supply chain and specialized sales team for eve1y kind of retail channel" as a competitive advantage and proclaims, "we get om books into consumers' hands faster and more reliably than our competition."

Third, because the Big 5 publishers have superior marketing, distribution, and sales strengths compared to smaller publishing competitors, they are more likely to help a book succeed commercially. Because Big 5 publishers are more likely to sell a large number ofbooks than their rivals, they can afford to pay authors of anticipated top-selling books larger advances than smaller publishers can. For that reason, internal S&S documents drafted in connection with the merger of Viacom and CBS confirm that Big 5 publishers—and not smaller firms—are one another's "biggest competitors, especially for books by already bestselling authors and celebrities, since they are the most likely to come up with high advance payments reqrnred and are known for their strong editorial and publishing skills." The same document confirms that publishers outside the Big 5 are "farm teams for authors who then want to move to a larger, more financially stable major publisher" because the smaller publishers cannot regularly offer high advances or the unique bundle of services that the authors of anticipated top-selling books expect. PRH executives agree that "for higher advance levels the smaller publishers tend not to compete."

E. Penguin Random House and Simon & Schuster Compete Fiercely to Acquire the Rights to Publish Anticipated Top-Selling Books

Given the dynamics among the Big 5 generally, it is no surprise that PRH and S&S fiercely compete head-to-head. This competition has inured to the benefit of authors, resulting in higher advances, better services, and more favorable contract terms for authors of anticipated top-selling books. The Court will hear from the parties and see Defendants' documents about this fierce competition, including several instances of head-to-head competition, discussed further *infra* at 33. For example, PRH imprint Viking celebrated winning over a house bid from S&S by declaring it had won over "stiff competition." Further, the Court will hear testimony from the government's expert witness, Dr. Nicholas Hill, explaining how the extensive record of head-to-head competition between PRH and S&S confirms that the merger is likely to substantially lessen competition. Even Defendants' economic expert Dr. Edward Snyder concedes the existence of this head-to-head competition at comparable levels to Dr. Hill's analysis.

F. The Proposed Transaction

On November 25, 2020, ViacomCBS announced that it had agreed to sell S&S to Bertelsmann for $2.175 billion in cash. The combined firm would dominate the U.S. publishing industry with revenues twice that of its next closest competitor in the Big 5, HarperCollins. The acquisition would "[c]ement Penguin Random House as #1 in the US"—one of PRH's strategic goals for the merger.

Top executives on both sides of the proposed transaction recognized that a deal between two otherwise fierce competitors in the Big 5 may have anticompetitive consequences. For example, before the deal was announced, Simon & Schuster CEO Jonathan Karp assured one of his authors, "I'm pretty sure the Department of Justice wouldn't allow Penguin Random House to buy us…." Bertelsmann's Chief Executive Officer likewise expressed that Bertelsmann faced "a disadvantage in the auction due to antitrust risks, which are likely to be greater in our case than with all other bidders." In an effort to surmount those "antitrust risks," Bertelsmann paid hundreds of millions of dollars over the next-highest bidder.

G. The Proposed Transaction Will Cede Nearly Fifty Percent of the Market for Anticipated Top-Selling Books to the Combined Firm, Which Will Harm Competition by Lowering Author Advances and Diminishing Output, Creativity, and Diversity

The proposed merger would eliminate significant head-to-head competition between two firms who are already members of the Big 5. Should the Court allow the proposed merger to proceed, the combined firm would be a giant in the market for the acquisition of publishing rights to anticipated top-selling books, with a market share of 49%. Post-merger, PRH's even more dominant position in the market would provide it additional leverage in negotiations with authors, resulting in the combined firm's extracting lower advances and greater concessions from authors. And although the United States need not show harm to consumers, *see Telecor Commc'ns, Inc. v. Sw. Bell Tel. Co.*, 305 F.3d 1124, 1133–34 (10th Cir. 2002), readers inevitably would be harmed: by reducing author compensation, the quantity and variety of books published will fall as well. This harm is neither conjectural nor hypothetical. As the Court will hear from witnesses, including the Penguin Random House Global CEO himself, reducing author compensation will likely reduce the output of books published and limit consumer choice by limiting what stories readers hear.

Argument

I. Legal Standard

A. Legal Standard: Section 7

Section 7 of the Clayton Act "creates a relatively expansive definition of antitrust liability," and "subjects mergers to searching scrutiny." *California v. Am. Stores Co.*, 495 U.S. 271, 284–85 (1990). Section 7 specifically bars mergers or acquisitions "the effect of [which] may be substantially to lessen competition, or to tend to create a monopoly" in "any line of commerce or … activity affecting commerce in any section of the country." 15 U.S.C. § 18. As the Supreme Court has explained, Congress used the word "may" in Section 7 "to indicate that its concern was with probabilities, not certainties," *Brown Shoe*, 370 U.S. at 323, because Congress "intended to arrest anticompetitive tendencies in their 'incipiency.'" *United States v. Phila. Nat'l Bank*, 374 U.S. 321, 362 (1962) (quoting *Brown Shoe*, 370 U.S. at 317).

Accordingly, it is not necessary to prove that the proposed acquisition *will* cause competitive harm. Rather, a showing "that the merger create[s] an appreciable danger of [anticompetitive] consequences in the future" is legally sufficient to block a merger. *Heinz*, 246 F.3d at 719 (quoting *Hosp. Corp. of Am. v. FTC*, 807 F.2d 1381, 1389 (7th Cir. 1986)). "A certainty, even a high probability, need not be shown," and "doubts are to be resolved against the transaction." *FTC v. Elders Grain, Inc.*, 868 F.2d 901, 906 (7th Cir. 1989). This standard makes sense because the "fundamental purpose" of Section 7 is "to arrest the trend toward concentration, the tendency to monopoly, before the consumer's alternatives disappear through merger." *Phila. Nat'l Bank*, 374 U.S. at 363. Indeed, the Supreme Court has held that "[a] trend toward concentration in an industry, whatever its causes, is a highly relevant factor in deciding how substantial the anti-competitive effect of a merger may be." *United States v. Pabst Brewing Co.*, 384 U.S. 546, 552–53 (1966); *see also United States v. Cont'l Can Co.,* 378 U.S. 441, 461 (1964).

The application of Section 7 is not limited to mergers between sellers; the statute also prohibits anticompetitive mergers between buyers, and courts have enjoined such mergers when likely to harm competition. *United States v. Rice Growers Ass'n of Cal.*, No. S–84–1066 EJG, 1986 WL 12562 (E.D. Cal. Jan. 31, 1986) (blocking merger of purchasers of paddy rice); *United States v. Pennzoil Co.*, 252 F.

Supp. 962 (W.D. Pa. 1965) (enjoining merger of purchasers of Penn Grade crude oil); *Boardman v. Pac. Seafood Grp.*, 822 F.3d 1011, 1021–22 (9th Cir. 2016) (affirming injunction against merger harming competition in "seafood processors' purchase of fish from fishermen"). The evaluation of mergers of buyers, or "buy-side" mergers, involves "essentially the [same] framework" as mergers involving the selling side of a market. *Merger Guidelines* § 12; *see also Weyerhaeuser Co. v. Ross-Simmons Hardwood Lumber Co.*, 549 U.S. 312, 321–22 (2007) (due to the "close theoretical connection" between monopoly power and monopsony power, "similar legal standards should apply").

In a buy-side case, the United States needs to show only that the merger may lessen competition at the buyer level. That is, there is no requirement that the United States prove downstream effects on consumers to block a proposed merger. *See Mandeville Island Farms, Inc. v. Am. Crystal Sugar Co.*, 334 U.S. 219, 235 (1948) (finding a buy-side price fixing scheme illegal "even though the price-fixing was by purchasers, and the persons specifically injured under the treble damage claim are sellers, not customers or consumers.").

To effectuate the "searching scrutiny" of mergers prescribed by Congress, courts have developed a burden-shifting approach. If a transaction (1) "produces a firm controlling an undue percentage share of the relevant market," and (2) "results in a significant increase in the concentration of firms in that market," that creates a presumption that the merger will substantially lessen competition. *Phila. Nat'l Bank*, 374 U.S. at 363; *Heinz*, 246 F. 3d at 715.

Once the government shows that the merger is presumptively unlawful, "[t]he burden then shifts to the defendant to rebut the presumption by offering proof that 'the market-share statistics [give] an inaccurate account of the [merger's] probable effects on competition in the relevant market.'" *FTC v. Sysco Corp.*, 113 F. Supp. 3d 1, 23 (D.D.C. 2015) (quoting *Heinz*, 246 F.3d at 715). The defendants' burden is dependent on the strength of the prima facie evidence: "The more compelling the prima facie case, the more evidence the defendant must present to rebut it successfully." *United States v. Baker Hughes Inc.*, 908 F.2d 981, 991 (D.C. Cir. 1990).

B. Legal Standard: Defining Relevant Product Markets

As a general matter, "[m]erger analysis starts with defining the relevant market." *Sysco*, 113 F. Supp. 3d at 24. A relevant antitrust market has two components: (1) the relevant product market and (2) the relevant geographic market. *United States v. Anthem, Inc.*, 236 F. Supp. 3d 171, 193 (D.D.C. 2017). The Supreme Court has recognized that the definition of the relevant market in a Clayton Act case was intended by Congress to be "a pragmatic, factual" analysis and "not a formal, legalistic one." *Brown Shoe*, 370 U.S. at 336. This reflects the fact that "the market, as most concepts in law or economics, cannot be measured by metes and bounds." *Anthem*, 236 F. Supp. 3d at 193 (quoting *Times-Picayune Publ'g Co. v. United States*, 345 U.S. 594, 611 (1953)); *see also FTC v. Tronox Ltd.*, 332 F. Supp. 3d 187, 202 (D.D.C. 2018) (recognizing that some "fuzziness is inherent in bounding any market"). Market definition is not an end in itself: "Defining the market is not the aim of antitrust law; it merely aids the search for competitive injury." *Oltz v. St. Peter's Cmty. Hosp.*, 861 F.2d 1440, 1448 (9th Cir. 1988). It can help a court ascertain the "locus of competition" in which anticompetitive effects are to be assessed. *Brown Shoe*, 370 U.S. at 320–21. Thus, the tools of market definition analysis "are not to be used to obscure competition but to 'recognize competition where, in fact, competition exists.'" *Cont'l Can Co.*, 378 U.S. at 453 (quoting *Brown Shoe*, 370 U.S. at 326).

The Supreme Court instructs that "[t]he outer boundaries of a product market are determined by the reasonable interchangeability of use or the cross-elasticity of demand between the product itself and the substitutes for it." *See Brown Shoe*, 370 U.S. at 325. The focus of this analysis is "on customers' ability and willingness to substitute away from one product to another in response to a price increase or a corresponding non-price change such as a reduction in product quality or service." *Merger Guidelines* § 4; *see also Sysco*, 113 F. Supp. 3d at 25–26.

In a buy-side merger such as this one, the market is not composed of competing sellers but of competing *buyers* (here, book publishers). *Todd v. Exxon Corp*, 275 F.3d 191, 202 (2d Cir. 2001) (Sotomayor, J.) (holding that the proper focus in a buy-side market is "the commonality and interchangeability of the buyers, not the commonality or interchangeability of the sellers.").

Creative industries can pose different challenges given that the industry is not about fungible items like widgets, but about art or ideas. As a result, in creative industries, courts have defined relevant markets around *anticipated* success. In *Syufy Enterprises v. American Multicinema, Inc.*, the court concluded that the exhibition of "industry anticipated top-grossing films" was an appropriately defined relevant market based on criteria such as national advertising support, longer play times, bookings in first class theaters, and lucrative terms offered for the films by exhibitors. 793 F.2d 990 (9th Cir. 1986). Using technical and formal parameters in lieu of common-sense industry realities to define a relevant market in a creative industry is not only unmoored from the law, but also detrimental to analyzing harm to participants in those industries.

C. Legal Standard: Defining Submarkets Around Targeted Groups

Under longstanding precedent, "[a] broad market may also include relevant submarkets which themselves may 'constitute product markets for antitrust purposes.'" *FTC v. Whole Foods Mkt., Inc.*, 548 F.3d 1028, 1037–38 (D.C. Cir. 2008) (quoting *Brown Shoe*, 370 U.S. at 325).

Thus, "the mere fact that a firm may be termed a competitor in the overall marketplace does not necessarily require that it be included in the relevant product market for antitrust purposes." *FTC v. Staples, Inc.*, 970 F. Supp. 1066, 1075 (D.D.C. 1997) (holding that, while all sellers of office supplies "must, at some level, compete with one another," there is a relevant product market limited to office supply superstores); *see also Anthem*, 236 F. Supp. 3d at 193 ("plaintiffs' relevant market need not include all potential customers or participants.").

Such narrower markets can be based on a set of "targeted customers." *FTC v. Wilh. Wilhelmsen Holding ASA*, 341 F. Supp. 3d 27, 46 (D.D.C. 2018); *accord Anthem*, 236 F. Supp. 3d at 195 ("Case law provides for the distinction of product markets by customer."); *FTC v. Staples, Inc.*, 190 F. Supp. 3d 100, 117–118 (D.D.C. 2016) ("*Staples II*"); *Sysco*, 113 F. Supp. 3d at 48. As explained by the *Anthem* court, "[a] submarket exists when sellers can profitably raise prices to certain targeted customers but not to others, in which case regulators 'may evaluate competitive effects separately by type of customer.'" *Anthem*, 236 F. Supp. 3d at 195 (quoting *Merger Guidelines* § 3); *see also Merger Guidelines* § 4.1.4. In a buy-side market, this test is reversed: the question is whether buyers can profitably decrease payments to certain targeted sellers. The submarket can be based on numerical distinctions, such as company size or annual spending. *Wilhelmsen*, 341 F. Supp. 3d at 51 (market consisting of customers owning fleets of 10 or more vessels of a particular type); *Anthem*, 236 F. Supp. 3d at 195 (market of companies with 5,000 or more employees); *Staples II*, 190 F. Supp. 3d at 118 (market of customers who spend $500,000 or more annually on office supplies).

II. There is a Relevant Product Market for the Acquisition of U.S. Publishing Rights to Anticipated Top-Selling Books

The evidence at trial will show that the proposed merger is likely to lessen competition substantially in at least one relevant product market: the market for the acquisition of publishing rights to anticipated top-selling books. This relevant market is a "targeted customer" market (here, a "targeted seller" market) in which authors, as sellers, are the targeted group. Anticipated top-selling books can be identified by the advances publishers pay to authors because those advances are based on the publishers' assessment of the volume of future book sales. The United States will show that a $250,000 advance payment is an appropriate cutoff to identify anticipated top-selling books, although, as discussed below, other reasonable advance level cutoffs above and below this level also show that authors will likely be harmed. This product market is a significant one: advances contracted to be paid to authors of anticipated top-sellers totaled over $1 billion in 2020. This is roughly 70% of all advance spending by the publishers who produced data in this case.

At trial, the United States will present two categories of evidence supporting this product market. First, "practical indicia," rooted in the facts of the industry, and second, expert economic analysis from Dr. Hill. *See Sysco*, 113 F. Supp. 3d at 27 (noting that "practical indicia" and expert economic testimony are the "two main types of evidence in defining the relevant product market"). Both types of evidence establish that the relevant product market here is the sale of publishing rights to anticipated top-selling books.

A. Practical Indicia Establish that Authors of Anticipated Top-Selling Books are Unique Customers with Unique Needs

Practical indicia show that authors of anticipated top-selling books are a unique set of sellers with unique needs. *See Anthem*, 236 F. Supp. 3d at 195–197 (finding that national employers are a "unique set of customers with unique needs" that constitute "a distinct subset of the health insurance market"). To attract authors of anticipated top-selling books and successfully publish them, a publisher must have a high level of editorial, marketing and publicity expertise, and the sophisticated sales and distribution capabilities required to make the book a success. Publishers also need the financial wherewithal—including the ability to spread financial risk across a portfolio of books and a steady revenue base fed by substantial sales of previously published books—to take on the very significant risks of paying such high advances to authors. Successfully promoting and marketing top-selling books to consumers is also expensive and risky. In addition, publishers that can demonstrate to authors a sustained track record of success with top-selling books have a competitive advantage over publishers who cannot.

Publishers who lack these attributes are not "seen by sellers [*i.e.,* authors] as being reasonably good substitutes," and thus are limited in their ability to compete. *Todd*, 275 F.3d at 202. As Defendants and other industry participants recognize, there are few publishers who possess these attributes *and* who are regularly competing for (and winning) these top books— overwhelmingly, the Big 5. The former CEO of S&S wrote, "[t]he publishing market is made up of what is known as the 'Big 5' ... These are our biggest competitors." This is because "they are the most likely to come up with high advance payments required and are known for their strong editorial and publishing skills," whereas non-Big 5 publishers "rarely compete with us in auctions for new properties" and often serve as "farm teams for authors who then want to move to a larger, more financially stable major publisher." PRH executives likewise recognize that "[l]arge publishers are our (main) competitors" and "[f]or higher level advances... smaller publishers tend not to compete." These statements reflect the reality that no small publisher has successfully entered or expanded to threaten the dominance of the Big 5.

The Court will hear testimony from other industry witnesses, including literary agents and executives from other publishing houses, that the Big 5 have the editorial, marketing, publicity and sales skills, the long track record, the financial capacity, and the other key attributes that give them a powerful advantage in winning anticipated top-sellers from authors. The strong preference of authors of anticipated top-selling books for publishers who possess this particular set of attributes is highlighted by the fact that the Big 5 publishers have consistently maintained a 90% share of this market. While Defendants may try to confuse the record by pointing to isolated instances of a non-Big 5 publisher winning a particular book, the market share data tell the story: smaller publishers are not sufficient competitive constraints on the Big 5, and they cannot replace the competition that would be lost by allowing the Defendants to merge to a 50% share of the market. Indeed, the dominance of the Big 5 over the rest of the publishing market is so stark that Bertelsmann, in materials presented to its Board, called the U.S. market an "oligopoly" made up of PRH and "only 4 further large publishers."

B. Authors of Anticipated Top-Selling Books can be Targeted by Publishers

There are two conditions necessary to define a targeted seller market: (1) buyers must be able to identify members of the targeted group of sellers; and (2) sellers must not be able to engage in arbitrage, or opportunistic re-selling. *See Merger Guidelines* § 3; *Staples II*, 190 F. Supp. 3d at 117–118. Both conditions are satisfied here. First, publishers identify the members of the targeted group of sellers when they project future sales and create P&L analyses for each book to determine what advance to offer. Because book deals are individually negotiated, prices are not uniform and publishers can individually target sellers. *See Merger Guidelines* §§ 3, 4.1.4. Publishers can profitably lower advances to this group of authors because their competitive options are far more limited than for authors of books that are not anticipated top-sellers.

Second, authors of anticipated top-sellers have little ability to avoid targeting by publishers through arbitrage. Nor would authors be able to avoid targeting by switching to self-publishing. As the Court will hear at trial, there is ample evidence that self-publishing is not a meaningful competitor to traditional publishing, especially for authors who have earned higher advances. This is also reflected in Defendants' ordinary course documents—for example, the former S&S CEO stated that "self-publishing is not viewed as a threat to [Simon & Schuster's] core business."

C. An Advance Level of $250,000 is an Appropriate Way to Identify Targeted Authors of Anticipated Top-Selling Books

As discussed above, there is ample precedent in the caselaw for using a numerical cutoff to identify a group of targeted customers (or here, sellers). In this case, it is appropriate to use the amount of an advance because of the close connection between advances and anticipated sales. As Dr. Hill explains, "there is consistent evidence that publishers offer large advances for books that are expected to sell more copies. This means that a book that is awarded a large advance is very likely to have large anticipated sales." The forward-looking sales expectations of the market participants are the key determinant of price competition at the time of acquisition.

Data shows that the competitive landscape is very different for advances over $250,000 than it is for advances below that threshold. Dr. Hill finds that the Big 5 have a 90% share of advances over $250,000 and non-Big 5 publishers only begin to have meaningful shares at levels below $250,000. In fact, Defendants' expert's own agency data reveal that the Big 5 dominate the market for anticipated top-sellers with a collective 94% market share. This conclusion is reinforced by testimony the Court will hear from other publishing industry professionals. For example, [REDACTED]

Other practical indicia also support the use of a $250,000 advance level to identify authors of anticipated top-selling books. As the Court will hear at trial, both PRH and S&S recognize $250,000 as a significant threshold in their ordinary business operations: they require higher-level approvals and additional documentation to make an offer of $250,000 or more for a book. This type of internal business practice is recognized in the caselaw as a basis for defining a market. *See Anthem*, 236 F. Supp. 3d at 197–98 (using 5,000-employee cutoff to define "national accounts," where defendants used the 5,000 threshold in the "ordinary course of business operations."). Other publishers use the same threshold for additional approval. For example, industry journal *Publisher's Weekly* [Ed.: Publishers Marketplace] uses thresholds to categorize book deals, and uses $250,000 to define a "significant deal" when agents and publishers submit announcements of their deals.

Importantly, although the evidence supports that $250,000 is an appropriate threshold, changing the threshold for observing the likely effects of this merger does not change the results: Dr. Hill's analysis shows that his conclusions hold across a wide range of average advances. His report analyzes cutoffs of $150,000, $350,000, $500,000, and $1 million and finds that "market shares do not change meaningfully even when the precise definition of an anticipated top-seller is significantly changed."Thus, using $250,000 is appropriate here given that the outcome is not sensitive to reasonable variations in the boundary. *See Wilhelmsen,* 341 F. Supp. 3d at 54– 56; *see also Tronox,* 332 F. Supp. 3d at 202 ("The Supreme Court has wisely recognized there is 'some artificiality' in any boundaries, but that 'such fuzziness' is inherent in bounding any Courts have recognized that, because there is not always a clear break point between submarkets, it is appropriate to select a reasonable cutoff as a starting point for further analysis to confirm the robustness of the results. For example, in *Wilhelmsen*, the FTC's economist used 10 vessels "as a starting point for developing a series of statistical estimates, the non-statistical implications of which support the appropriateness of regarding Global Fleets as a distinct customer group." *Wilhelmsen*, 341 F. Supp. 3d at 55; *see also Staples II*, 190 F. Supp. 3d at 118 & n.10 (noting that government's expert chose $500,000 in annual office supply purchases as a cutoff "[f]or analytical purposes" and citing testimony "that there is no 'magic place that's the right place' to draw the line").

Defendants' argument that it is inappropriate to use price to help identify a relevant submarket has been rejected by the caselaw. In *Brown Shoe*, the Supreme Court identified "distinct prices" as one of the "practical indicia" courts may use to identify the existence of a submarket. 370 U.S. at 325. The D.C. Circuit in *Whole Foods* applied this principle to a targeted customer market, holding that "distinct prices" for the targeted group (which the *Whole Foods* court referred to as "core" customers) "indicates the existence of a submarket of core customers…." *Whole Foods*, 548 F.3d at 1038–39. In *United States v. Gillette Co.*, 828 F. Supp. 78, 81 (D.D.C. 1993), the court found a separate market for premium writing implements priced between $50 and $400, expressly rejecting the defendants' argument that "a relevant product market cannot be defined by reference to a narrow price range along a broader continuum of prices."

Defendants' claim that it is arbitrary to impose a cutoff where there is a "continuum of advance payment amounts" is also contrary to precedent. The caselaw supports using numerical cutoffs to identify a group of customers in a relevant submarket, and courts routinely determine where to draw a line based on the commercial realities of competition in the industry. *See, e.g., Anthem*, 236 F. Supp. 3d at 197–202; *Wilhelmsen*, 341 F. Supp. 3d at 54–56; *Staples II*, 190 F. Supp. 3d at 118–127. Courts have also found relevant product markets consisting of premium product segments based on "distinctions in degree" across a broader range of products. *Int'l Boxing Club*, 358 U.S. at 249–252 (holding that championship boxing contests are a distinct market from non-championship contests, based on factors such as their higher revenues/rights fees and greater popularity among viewers); *see also Syufy*, 783 F.2d at 882–883 (affirming market of "industry-anticipated top-grossing films"); *Whole Foods,* 548 F.3d at 1041 (market of "premium" natural and organic supermarkets); *O'Bannon v. NCAA*, 7 F. Supp. 3d 955, 986 (N.D. Cal. 2014) (finding relevant market in which colleges compete for "elite football and basketball recruits"), *aff'd in relevant part*, 802 F.3d 1049 (9th Cir. 2015).

The key question in assessing whether the proposed group of targeted customers is a properly defined submarket is whether the "construct is a useful way to discuss and predict economic conditions" because "its key aspects correspond to elements of the existing marketplace that would make it possible to profitably target a subset of customers for price increases." *Wilhelmsen,* 341 F. Supp. 3d at 52 (citation omitted). For the reasons discussed above, the definition of anticipated top-selling books corresponds to the marketplace realities here.

D. Economic Analysis Establishes that the Acquisition of U.S. Publishing Rights to Anticipated Top-Selling Books is a Relevant Product Market

The hypothetical monopsonist test is the buyer-side counterpart to the "hypothetical monopolist test," which courts routinely apply in sell-side cases to define a product market. *See Merger Guidelines* § 12; *Wilhelmsen*, 341 F. Supp. 3d at 47, 57–58 (applying hypothetical monopolist test); *Staples II*, 190 F. Supp. 3d at 121–122 (same); *Sysco*, 113. F. Supp. 3d at 33–34 (same); *H&R Block*, 833 F. Supp. 2d at 51–52 (same); *see also Todd*, 275 F.3d at 201–02 (analyzing "whether a 'hypothetical cartel' would be 'substantially constrain[ed]' from increasing prices by the ability of customers to switch to other producers.").

The test asks whether a hypothetical monopsonist—the only present and future buyer of the products in the alleged market—would find it profit-maximizing to impose a small but significant and non-transitory reduction in price ("SSNRP") for at least one product in the market. *See Merger Guidelines* § 4.1.1. A hypothetical monopsonist would likely impose a SSNRP if sellers could not reasonably substitute to buyers outside the proposed market in response to the price reduction. That means that buyers outside the proposed market do not serve as a competitive constraint on the hypothetical monopsonist. In such circumstances, the proposed market is properly defined for antitrust purposes. *Id.* If, on the other hand, the hypothetical monopsonist likely would *not* impose a SSNRP, because sellers are able to substitute to other buyers that have been excluded from the proposed market, the proposed market is too narrow to constitute a properly defined antitrust market.

At trial, Dr. Hill will testify that the relevant market for the acquisition of U.S. publishing rights to anticipated top-sellers satisfies the hypothetical monopsonist test. Dr. Hill defined the hypothetical monopsonist as all publishers, with self-publishing as the buying option outside the market. Dr. Hill's analysis demonstrates that a hypothetical monopsonist publisher would likely reduce advances to authors of anticipated top-sellers because an insufficient number of those authors would switch to self-publishing in response to such a reduction, so as to make it unprofitable for the hypothetical monopsonist to impose a SSNRP.

III. The Relevant Geographic Market is Global

The relevant market is composed of both the relevant product market, described *supra* at Section II, and the relevant geographic market. "The 'relevant geographic market' identifies the geographic area in which the defendants compete in marketing their products or services." *H&R Block*, 833 F. Supp. 2d at 50 n.7; *Merger Guidelines* § 4.2. The relevant geographic market must "correspond to the commercial realities of the industry" as determined by a "pragmatic, factual approach" to assessing the industry. *Brown Shoe*, 370 U.S. at 336 (internal citation omitted). Here, the parties do not dispute that the relevant geographic market for the acquisition of U.S. publishing rights to anticipated top-sellers is global.

IV. Bertelsmann's Acquisition of Simon & Schuster Is Presumptively Unlawful

A. The Proposed Transaction is Presumptively Illegal Because It Would Create Extraordinarily High Market Shares and Concentration in the Relevant Market

A merger that significantly increases concentration in an already concentrated market is presumptively illegal. *Phila. Nat'l Bank*, 374 U.S. at 363–65 & n.42; *Sysco*, 113 F. Supp. 3d at 52. In *Philadelphia National Bank*, the Supreme Court found that a significant change in concentration that resulted in a combined market share of 30% was sufficient to establish that presumption. 374 U.S. at 364; *see also Heinz*, 246 F.3d at 715–717 (finding FTC established prima facie showing of anticompetitive effects where defendants would have a combined share of 32.8% in a concentrated market); *Hosp. Corp.*, 807 F.2d at 1383 (finding transaction unlawful that raised defendant's market share from 14% to 26% and the market share of the four largest firms from 79% to 91%).

Courts also assess a proposed merger's presumptive illegality using the *Merger Guidelines* and employ a statistical measure of market concentration called the Herfindahl- Hirschman Index ("HHI"). *See, e.g., Sysco*, 113 F. Supp. 3d at 52–53; *FTC v. Swedish Match*, 131 F. Supp. 2d 151, 166–67 (D.D.C. 2000). HHIs are calculated by summing the squares of each market participant's individual market share both pre- and post-acquisition. *Sysco*, 113 F. Supp. 3d at 52–53; *Merger Guidelines* § 5.3. Under the *Merger Guidelines*, if an acquisition (1) increases the HHI of a relevant market by more than 200 points and (2) results in a post- acquisition HHI exceeding 2500, it is presumptively anticompetitive. *H&R Block*, 833 F. Supp. 2d at 71–72 (enjoining transaction that would have given the combined firm only a 28.4% market share because the transaction would have resulted in a highly concentrated market as demonstrated by the fact that it would have increased the HHI by more than 200 and the post- acquisition HHI would have exceeded 2500); *Merger Guidelines* § 5.3.

Starting with market share, Dr. Hill will testify that PRH currently controls 37% of the market for anticipated top-sellers and S&S controls approximately 12%. If this merger is permitted to proceed, the combination of PRH and S&S would result in a dominant publisher that controls roughly half the market with a combined **49%** share—significantly higher than the 30% the Supreme Court found concerning in *Philadelphia National Bank*. That newly- minted combined firm would also enjoy twice the market share of its next largest competitor, HarperCollins, which has a 24% market share. The merged firm would also have more than *five times* the market share of *all* publishers outside the Big 5 combined, whose collective market share is only 9% with no single publisher outside the Big 5 having more than 2% market share. With respect to HHI, Dr. Hill will testify that the proposed merger would result in an 891 increase in the HHI and a post-merger HHI of 3113. These results are well above the threshold (increase of more than 200 points in HHI and a post-merger HHI of 2500) to trigger a presumption of illegality under the *Merger Guidelines*. *See United States v. Anthem, Inc.*, 855 F.3d 345, 349 (D.C. Cir. 2017) (citing *Merger Guidelines* § 5.3). These troubling outcomes are the same if the $250,000 advance threshold is raised or lowered. In fact, Dr. Hill calculated the HHI at multiple advance levels and across different time periods. The result did not change: each of those scenarios resulted in HHI figures that trigger the *Merger Guideline*'s presumption that the proposed transaction will substantially reduce competition. Dr. Snyder does not (and cannot) dispute Dr. Hill's market share or HHI calculations. Instead, although market shares are routinely used in antitrust analysis (including in the *Merger Guidelines* § 5.2) to evaluate a firm's competitive significance, Dr. Snyder argues it is more informative to measure how frequently firms compete or firms' capacity to compete than their share of wins. Aside from speculating on potential better measures of analysis, Dr. Snyder does not offer competing calculations. Further, his own agency data show that a non-Big 5 publisher is the runner-up in roughly 10.5% of the competitions for anticipated top seller contracts, which is similar to the frequency that market shares predict, thus disproving Dr. Snyder's claims about market shares.

B. The Record Evidence Corroborates the Presumption of Illegality

The parties' own ordinary-course documents and testimony from their executives, as well as documents and testimony from other industry participants, corroborate the presumption that the merger will substantially lessen competition.

14. *Industry Participants Recognize That the Big 5 Are Especially Close Competitors and Smaller Publishers Struggle to Compete*

The Court will hear from numerous industry participants who will testify that should this merger be allowed to proceed, it is likely to reduce competition, largely because publishers outside the Big 5 are not viable alternatives for most authors of anticipated top-selling books. These smaller competitors—who together make up only 9% of the market, representing their minimal competitive significance going forward—simply will not be able to constrain a post- merger combined firm that controls 49% of the relevant market. Defendants' own documents and testimony from executives recognize that publishers outside the Big 5 are "farm teams for authors." Simon & Schuster's current CEO Jonathan Karp is expected to testify that S&S bids most frequently against and loses most to other Big 5 publishers (and to PRH most of all). Simon & Schuster's Chief Financial Officer Dennis Eulau is expected to testify that other Big 5 publishers are the "most able to afford to" compete at high advance levels. PRH executives confirmed that for "higher level advances ... smaller publishers tend not to compete."

Literary agents and authors will likewise testify that publishers outside the Big 5 cannot consistently compete on an equal playing field for anticipated top-selling books. For example, when asked by an author if she had ever "been in an auction that has gone above $500K where any of the non-Big 5 were still in on it? $250k?! [REDACTED] literary agent Christy Fletcher responded, "[n]ever that I can remember." Author Andrew Solomon will testify that Big 5 publishers are more likely to be successful publishers of a top-selling book than smaller publishers due to the superior resources and contacts of the Big 5. Executives at publishers outside the Big 5 themselves recognize that they struggle to compete for anticipated top-selling books. For example, Abrams CEO Michael Jacobs will testify that Abrams gets "outbid all the time by publishers who are willing to pay... more for books than we are" because Abrams has limited resources and there is a "limited number" of things Abrams can "really lean into" and "make investments that make sense for us." The evidence demonstrating that the Big 5 are close competitors who leave small publishers far behind in competing for anticipated top-selling books matters because it illustrates that those smaller publishers will not be a meaningful competitive constraint on the combined firm such that they could overcome the presumption of illegality.

15. Examples of Head-to-Head Competition

"[M]ergers that eliminate head-to-head competition between close competitors often result in a lessening of competition.... And this is true even where the merging parties are not the only two, or even the two largest, competitors in the market." *See Anthem,* 236 F. Supp. 3d at 216 (internal quotation and quotation marks omitted); *see also Sysco*, 113 F. Supp. 3d at 61 ("Courts have recognized that a merger that eliminates head-to-head competition between close competitors can result in a substantial lessening of competition."); *Merger Guidelines* § 6. The evidence at trial will depict numerous instances of head-to-head competition between PRH and S&S. For example:

In 2020, PRH and S&S competed in a multi-round auction for a book focused on gender inequality. After the first round, three bidders remained with S&S submitting the highest bid at $475,000. After the third bidder dropped out, PRH and S&S competed against each other to drive the bidding up to $650,000 and $625,000, respectively. At that point, the literary agent asked for each publisher's best and final bid, and S&S bid $750,000. Suspecting that it was bidding against S&S, PRH stretched its final bid to $775,000 and won the book. After learning they had indeed beaten S&S, PRH editors celebrated their win "over stiff competition." Also in 2020, PRH and S&S competed in an auction for a book regarding the opioid epidemic. All other bidders dropped out when the bidding reached $645,000 after several rounds, leaving the two merging parties as the only remaining competitors. PRH and S&S went back and forth with competing bids over multiple rounds, with PRH ultimately prevailing with a winning bid of $825,000.

These instances of head-to-head competition inform the likelihood of anticompetitive effects if the proposed transaction is permitted to move forward.

16. Industry Participants Recognize That the Proposed Transaction Is Likely to Lead to Lower Advances for Authors of Anticipated Top-Selling Books

Industry participants anticipate that the merger is likely to lead to lower advances for authors. For example, Hachette CEO Michael Pietsch is expected to testify that [REDACTED] and Kensington CEO Steven Zacharius has testified that he "would expect that [advances] go down since there will be less competition for those authors."The Court will hear testimony from several literary agents that they expect the merger will lead to lower advances for authors. For example, literary agent Christy Fletcher testified that "[w]ith fewer bidders, it's harder to drive the advances up." Executives from the remaining Big 5 publishers will testify that the combined firm will be so dominant that it will be able to employ exclusionary tactics such as restricting printing capacity or access to distribution networks to make it more difficult for the remaining Big 5 publishers to compete against the combined firm.

17. Industry Participants Recognize That the Proposed Merger Is Likely to Reduce the Overall Output and Diversity of Books

To be clear, the United States need not prove any harm to consumers to prevail in this matter (*see* Legal Standard, *supra* at 14). Nevertheless, it bears noting that industry participants also recognize that by lowering author advances, the proposed merger is likely to diminish overall output, creativity, and diversity among books published. Penguin Random House Global CEO Markus Dohle is expected to testify that compensating authors less would mean that fewer authors will be able to make a living from writing, which would negatively impact the output of overall books written.Moreover, Mr. Dohle is expected to testify about the correlation between author income and the diversity of stories that are published, such that if author income is significantly diminished, the diversity of stories published would also be diminished.

Author Stephen King is also expected to testify that the proposed merger would reduce competition and likely reduce the diversity of books being published.Author Andrew Solomon will testify that even authors who are paid large advances receive those payments in "dribs and drabs" over several years, which can make it challenging if not impossible for an author to make a living solely by writing.Further, literary agent Ayesha Pande will testify that the proposed merger likely will make it more difficult to get sizeable advances for authors from diverse backgrounds because there will be fewer editors to whom she can submit diverse stories.

18. There is Evidence That the 2013 Merger Between Penguin and Random House May Have Harmed Competition and Authors

Some evidence suggests that the 2013 merger of Penguin and Random House, *see supra* at 5, harmed authors of anticipated top-selling books by reducing advances and the overall output of books published. Literary agents have testified that the 2013 merger reduced competition for authors' works and resulted in lower author advances; they expressed concern that the proposed acquisition of S&S could lead to similar "downward pressure" on advances. Internal PRH documents confirm the anticompetitive harm from the 2013 merger.

Dr. Hill will testify that the merger between Penguin and Random House led to lower compensation for authors of anticipated top-selling books. The relevant data shows that authors of anticipated top-selling books earned on average just under $100,000 *less* per advance in the two years following the 2013 merger than they did in the two years leading up to the merger. Furthermore, average advances for authors of anticipated top-selling books decreased by about 15% compared to advances for authors of all books. Such anticompetitive consequences will only be more significant with the proposed acquisition of S&S by PRH, which will result in a 49% combined share in the relevant market.

C. Economic Analysis Corroborates the Presumption of Illegality

Dr. Hill will testify at trial that he quantified the extent of head-to-head competition between PRH and S&S for anticipated top-selling books by estimating diversion ratios between the parties that show S&S is a significant competitor to PRH. Here, diversion ratios measure the proportion of anticipated top-sellers that a merging party would acquire of those that the other merging party would lose if it offered lower advances. Because the merged firm will now earn profits on books that are diverted from one merging partner to the other, the higher the diversion ratio between the merging parties, the more likely the merged firm is to lower advances. *See H&R Block*, 833 F. Supp. 2d at 86 ("[T]he diversion rate from TaxACT to HRB measures the proportion of customers that would leave TaxACT in response to a price increase and switch to HRB."); *FTC v. CCC Holdings*, 605 F. Supp. 2d 26, 70 (D.D.C. 2009) ("[T]he diversion ratios are the best indicators of whether a significant share of the market views CCC and Mitchell as their first and second choices, and Audatex a more distant third."); *Swedish Match*, 131 F. Supp. 2d at 169 ("[T]he diversion ratio is important because it calculates the percentage of lost sales that go to National. High margins and high diversion ratios support large price increases, a tenet endorsed by most economists."); *Merger Guidelines* § 6.1.

Dr. Hill estimated diversion between the merging parties in four different ways. The methods are based on different datasets, including market share data and extensive party data that provide different angles from which Dr. Hill examined how frequently the merging parties lose to each other for anticipated top-sellers. All four methods reveal that the proposed transaction will likely lead to substantial anticompetitive unilateral effects. For example, in analyzing anticipated top-sellers that S&S would lose if it lowered advances, Dr. Hill estimates that approximately 42% to 59% would be lost to PRH. Today, the threat that S&S could lose these authors to PRH keeps S&S from reducing advances. Post-merger, however, these authors would be recaptured by the merged firm. As Dr. Hill will explain, "[t]his greatly reduces the competitive pressure on Simon & Schuster to keep advances at their current level and will create a strong incentive for it to lower advances."

Dr. Hill also calibrated a second-score auction model to evaluate how the proposed merger may affect competition for anticipated top-sellers. The model formalizes a competitive dynamic that is generally present when a book is sold, regardless of the method of acquisition: the publisher that acquires the book seeks to pay only as much as is necessary to beat out its strongest rival. The model uses high-level information about competition in the entire market for anticipated top-selling books to quantify the extent to which the elimination of competition between the merging parties will lead to lower advances. The model is calibrated using two inputs to estimate the effect of the merger on advances for anticipated top-selling books: market shares and profit margins. Using a PRH margin that is likely a significant underestimate, the model conservatively predicts a decrease in advances paid by PRH of 4.3% and by S&S of 11.6%. The model predicts a decrease in advances paid of 5.8% for PRH and 15.3% for S&S if one uses a PRH margin that is likely closer to PRH's true margin. In addition, Dr. Hill estimated the effect of the proposed merger using alternative models, and found that (1) they produce results consistent with the results of his second-score auction literary agencies. This dataset is smaller than any of the datasets Dr. Hill employed to calculate diversions. At trial, Dr. Hill will testify that the dataset is not representative. But even if it were representative, Dr. Snyder's estimates are largely consistent with Dr. Hill's. Hill Reply Rep., §§ 4.4 & 4.6. model and (2) all predicted that the proposed merger would lead to substantial anticompetitive effects. Dr. Hill used Gross Upward Pricing Pressure Index ("GUPPI") models developed by Defendants' economists in the pre-complaint investigation to modify the traditional GUPPI formula to fit different book acquisition formats. The models predicted advance decreases of 3.7–7.3% for PRH and 9.6–19.2% for S&S. Even incorporating Dr. Snyder's own diversion ratios, these models still predicted substantial harm to authors of anticipated top-sellers. Moreover, those results were consistent with the results of the second-score auction model.

D. Coordinated Effects: The Proposed Transaction Will Increase the Likelihood of Tacit Coordination Among Publishers Regarding Content Acquisition

"Merger law rests upon the theory that, where rivals are few, firms will be able to coordinate their behavior, either by overt collusion or implicit understanding, in order to restrict output and achieve profits above competitive levels." *Heinz*, 246 F.3d at 715 (internal quotation marks omitted). Mergers can "diminish competition by enabling or encouraging post-merger coordinated interaction among firms in the relevant market that harms customers." *Merger Guidelines* § 7. A century of antitrust law recognizes that "oligopolistic market structures" dominated by only a few firms are likely to result in "tacit coordination," *Heinz*, 246 F. 3d at 725 (quoting Areeda & Hovenkamp, Antitrust Law: *An Analysis of Antitrust Principles and Their Application* (2021), ¶ 901b2), where a few major firms can engage in "interdependent pricing ... by recognizing their shared economic interests with respect to price and output decisions." *Id.* at 724 n.23.

Tacit collusion, more so even than express collusion, is "feared by antitrust policy" because "even when observed, [tacit collusion] cannot easily be controlled directly by the antitrust laws." *Id.* at 725 (quoting Areeda ¶ 901b2); *see also Hosp. Corp.* 807 F.2d at 1389 ("The fewer competitors there are in a market, the easier it is for them to coordinate their pricing without committing detectable violations of [S]ection 1 of the Sherman Act, which forbids price fixing."). For this reason, "[i]t is a central object of merger policy to obstruct the creation or reinforcement by merger of such oligopolistic market structures in which tacit coordination can occur." *Id.* (quoting Areeda ¶ 901b2). In evaluating the possible acquisition of S&S, Bertelsmann itself recognized the U.S. publishing industry as an "oligopoly" with "only four other major trade publishers" beyond PRH. The proposed transaction would reinforce that oligopolistic market structure, rendering it even more susceptible to tacit coordination.

Once the government has established its prima facie case, the burden is on Defendants to produce evidence of "structural barriers" specific to the publishing industry that would defeat the "ordinary presumption of collusion" that "attaches to a merger in a highly concentrated market." *CCC Holdings*, 605 F. Supp. 2d at 60 (quoting *Heinz*, 246 F.3d at 725). Defendants have not and cannot identify any such structural barriers here, especially in light of the recent history of express collusion over ebook prices among Defendants and their competitors. *See United States v. Apple, Inc.*, 791 F.3d 290, 320 (2d Cir. 2015) (upholding finding that the current members of the Big 5, with the exception of then-independent Random House, conspired with Apple, Inc. to "eliminate retail price competition and to raise ebook prices.").

Courts have found that a history of collusion—like that affirmed by the Second Circuit in *United States v. Apple*—is relevant to an evaluation of a merger's likely coordinated effects; a market that is "prone to collusion" is "even more prone to collusion" after the proposed merger of two large competitors. *See, e.g., Elders Grain,* 868 F.2d at 905–906. A history of collusion also "establishes a precondition to effective collusion—mutual trust and forbearance." *Hosp. Corp.*, 807 F. 2d at 1388; *Elders Grain*, 868 F.2d at 906 (mergers "which reduce the number of significant sellers" in markets "already highly concentrated and prone to collusion by reason of its history and circumstances is unlawful in the absence of special circumstances.").

The history of collusion in the publishing industry would therefore further render the market susceptible to tacit coordination following the proposed transaction. *See Heinz*, 246 F.3d at 725. Moreover, the presence of entry barriers in this concentrated market as discussed *infra* at page 42 add to the likelihood of coordinated effects that would occur if the proposed merger is permitted to proceed. As noted in *Heinz*, "[t]he combination of a concentrated market and barriers to entry is a recipe for price coordination." *Id.* at 724.

V. Defendants Cannot Rebut the Strong Presumption of Illegality

"If plaintiffs establish the prima facie case, defendants must present evidence to rebut the presumption by affirmatively showing why a given transaction is unlikely to substantially lessen competition, or by discrediting the data underlying the initial presumption in the government's favor." *Anthem*, 236 F. Supp. 3d 192 (internal quotation marks omitted); *see also H&R Block*, 833 F. Supp. 2d at 72; *CCC Holdings*, 605 F. Supp. 2d at 46.

A. Entry and Expansion Would Not be Timely, Likely, Or Sufficient

Ease of entry into the relevant product market "can be sufficient to offset the government's prima facie case of anti-competitiveness," *Sysco*, 113 F. Supp. 3d at 80, but only if it is "timely, likely, and sufficient in its magnitude, character, and scope to deter or counteract the competitive effects of concern," *H&R Block*, 833 F. Supp. 2d at 73 (quoting *Merger Guidelines* § 9). "Defendants bear the burden of demonstrating the ability of other distributors to 'fill the competitive void' that will result from the proposed merger." *Sysco*, 113 F. Supp. 3d at 80 (quoting *Swedish Match*, 131 F. Supp. 2d at 169).

Here, there are high barriers to economically meaningful entry or repositioning in the anticipated top-seller market. As described *supra* at page 5, entry at the scale of the Big 5 has been limited, which is evidence that entry or expansion by a non-Big 5 publisher is unlikely. *See FTC v. Cardinal Health, Inc.*, 12 F. Supp. 2d 34, 56 (D.D.C. 1998) ("The history of entry into the relevant market is a central factor in assessing the likelihood of entry in the future."). This is exemplified by the failure of even Amazon—which has a wealth of resources—to expand materially in the market. Today, more than a decade after launching its publishing business, Amazon rarely succeeds in acquiring anticipated top-sellers. Although it has the second largest market share of any non-Big 5 publisher, its share is still only 1%.

Publishers outside the Big 5 are limited competitors for anticipated top-sellers. Non-Big 5 publishers collectively account for only about 9% of anticipated top-seller acquisitions, with no single small publisher having more than 2% market share. Further, from 2019 to 2021, the non-Big 5's market share of anticipated top-sellers has increased by only 0.1%, and Amazon's market share has declined over this period. *See Anthem*, 236 F. Supp. 3d at 244 (finding entry unlikely where only one of 32 entrants had grown to attain a double-digit market share, and the company with the second highest share stood at 6%). In addition, Dr. Hill will testify that based on the parties' win-loss-data, neither Defendant loses more than 11% of anticipated top-sellers to non-Big 5 publishers. Moreover, at trial, the other Big 5 publishers and smaller publishers will testify about the non-Big 5's relative inability to compete for anticipated top-sellers. Defendants can point to no record evidence that any publisher outside the Big 5 intends to expand to the extent necessary to counteract the anticompetitive effects of the proposed merger.

One reason that non-Big 5 publishers struggle to gain market share is that they are financially constrained from competing with the Big 5, especially for anticipated top-selling books. As detailed *supra* at pages 8–10 and 19–21, anticipated top-selling books are risky because they are based on sales numbers that can be difficult to achieve. The risks involved in acquiring anticipated top-sellers makes timely or sufficient expansion by smaller publishers unlikely, as diversifying risk by publishing many anticipated top-sellers is not a realistic option for many non-Big 5 publishers. *See supra* at pages 8–10, 19–21. Further, Big 5 publishers, unlike smaller publishing companies, can also mitigate risk through backlist sales.

Backlist books are those no longer considered new releases, generally published at least one year earlier. Backlist sales are a significant portion of Big 5 publishers' revenues and are typically higher margin than front list sales. In 2020, PRH earned 58% of its revenue from backlist books and S&S earned of its revenue from backlist books. An entrant, however, would have no backlist, and small publishers have substantially smaller backlists than Big 5 publishers. Anticipated top-selling books are also expensive to market and distribute. The Big 5 have large and experienced marketing departments, which give them a competitive edge over smaller publishers in competing for anticipated top-sellers. In addition, all of the Big 5 handle their own sales and marketing, and all but one of the Big 5 handle their own distribution. All of the Big 5 publishers also have robust sales teams and well-established sales relationships. In contrast, smaller publishers typically do not have the scale to handle all aspects of distribution in-house and must outsource distribution functions. These publishers must rely on third parties—in many cases, the Big 5 publishers with which they compete—to distribute their books. For a smaller publisher, third-party distribution services can be the highest cost of publishing a book outside the cost of acquiring the book. Moreover, the Big 5 publishers have been in business for decades and have strong reputations across a broad range of genres and subgenres. It takes many years, numerous literary prizes, critical acclaim, and commercial success to build up the kind of prestige that PRH and S&S have built. Smaller publishers do not have the same track of record of success with anticipated top-sellers. Indeed, when asked why the Big 5 had such a high percentage of anticipated top-selling books, Dr. Snyder admitted that reputation was a major reason. *See CCC Holdings*, 605 F. Supp. 2d at 54–55 ("Reputation can be a considerable barrier to entry where customers and suppliers emphasize the importance of reputation and expertise").

Significant expansion or repositioning by other members of the Big 5 is also unlikely. Dr. Hill will testify that the merged firm will bid less aggressively than the companies would bid pre-merger because its probability of winning has increased due to the elimination of S&S as an independent rival. This, in turn, incentivizes rival publishers to bid less aggressively for books to increase their likelihood of winning the same books at lower cost, enabling higher margins. Further, as described *supra* at page 35, the Court will hear evidence that the combined firm will be so dominant that it will be able to employ exclusionary tactics, such as restricting printing capacity or access to distribution networks, that will make it more difficult for other publishers to compete against the combined firm.

B. Literary Agents Cannot Counteract the Anticompetitive Effects of the Proposed Merger

Defendants assert that because agents can choose the process by which they sell the rights to a book and which publishers to invite to compete for a book, the proposed merger will not harm authors. But courts "have not considered the 'sophisticated [seller]' defense as itself independently adequate to rebut a *prima facie* case" and view "the economic argument for even partially rebutting a presumptive case, because a market is dominated by large [sellers]" as "weak". *Chicago Bridge & Iron Co. N.V. v. FTC*, 534 F.3d 410, 440 (5th Cir. 2008); *see also Anthem,* 236 F. Supp. 3d at 221.

Moreover, testimony at trial will show that Defendants' argument is not grounded in reality. Agents are not powerful sellers that can counteract the anticompetitive harms from the merger. As Defendants' purported expert Jennifer Walsh admitted at deposition, literary agents are part of a fragmented industry. They are numerous and diffuse, with agents belonging to many different agencies, including many small or even solo agencies. Most literary agents have more limited resources compared to PRH and S&S, which are part of multibillion-dollar companies that have access to business development and strategy teams and vast amounts of data.

Further, agents are not omnipotent. Agents cannot control whether publishers are interested in a book. Agents cannot control a publishing house's internal bidding rules, including whether it prohibits its imprints from bidding against each other for a book. Nor can an agent control how a publisher values a book. Agents cannot control how much a publisher bids for a book. Agents cannot even always control the scope of rights that they can sell; a recent example is that the Big 5 publishers have all but refused to acquire books unless audio rights are included. Moreover, contrary to Defendants' assertion, agents do not always have control over the process of selling the book rights. For example, a lack of interest in a book may leave an agent without the ability to conduct an auction, and require the agent to accept an offer without the benefit of a competitive process (or no offer at all). Agents cannot manufacture competition. In addition, an agent cannot conduct an auction if the only imprints that are interested in a book are all in the same publishing house. Similarly, an agent may be required to conduct a best bids auction, instead of a rounds auction, if there are an insufficient number of independent bidders for a book.

Defendants also frequently acquire books for less than their P&Ls project the books are worth. If agents currently exercised outsized real competitive leverage that substituted for publishers' market power, as Defendants suggest, this would not happen; rather, a publisher would consistently pay the maximum value that its individual book P&L supported.

Accordingly, agents cannot extract the maximum value for books even pre-merger. Defendants do not suggest agents' power will increase post-merger, and there is no reason to believe that it would. Thus, the evidence belies Defendants' assertion that agents will be able to extract the maximum value for books from Defendants simply by adjusting auction rules.

C. Defendants' Efficiencies Defense Fails

Defendants claim that the proposed merger would create a more efficient publisher and the resulting higher profits would be passed on not only to PRH's owner, Bertelsmann, and its shareholders, but also to authors. From the earliest cases decided after the amendment of the Clayton Act to apply it to mergers, the Supreme Court has focused on preserving competition rather than optimizing economic efficiency. *See Brown Shoe Co. v. United States*, 370 U.S. 294, 344 (1962); *see also Phila. Nat'l Bank*, 374 U.S. at

371. This is because "a merger which produces a firm controlling an undue percentage share of the relevant market, and results in a significant increase in concentration of firms in that market is so inherently likely to lessen competition substantially that it must be enjoined in the absence of evidence clearly showing that the merger is not likely to have such anticompetitive effects." *Phila. Nat'l Bank*, 374 U.S. at 363, *see also FTC v. Procter & Gamble Co.*, 386 U.S. 568, 580 (1967) ("Possible economies cannot be used as a defense to illegality. Congress was aware that some mergers which lessen competition may also result in economies but it struck the balance in favor of protecting competition."). This Circuit has followed the Supreme Court's guidance and taken a highly skeptical view of efficiencies as a potential merger defense. *See Anthem,* 855 F.3d at 353 ("[I]t is not at all clear that [efficiencies] offer a viable legal defense to illegality under Section 7."); *Heinz*, 246 F.3d at 721 (expressing concerns about efficiencies claims that are "mere speculation and promises about post-merger behavior"). This skepticism is heightened where a market leader acquires another competitor. Efficiencies analysis has never on its own justified an otherwise anticompetitive acquisition by a dominant company. *Sysco*, 113 F. Supp. 3d at 81 ("The court is not aware of any case ... where the merging parties have successfully rebutted the government's *prima facie* case on the strength of the efficiencies."). The skepticism is particularly warranted here where PRH, the market leader, seeks to acquire one of its largest competitors, thereby cementing PRH's dominance.

The caselaw and *Merger Guidelines* recognize that only certain types of efficiencies have the potential to enhance a merged firm's ability and incentive to compete, and thus potentially offset the anticompetitive effects of a merger. These efficiencies, referred to as "cognizable efficiencies," must be substantiated by the merging parties, reasonably verifiable by an independent party, achievable solely via the merger, and not arise from anticompetitive reductions in output or service. *See H&R Block,* 833 F. Supp. 2d at 89; *Merger Guidelines* § 10. As detailed in the United States' Motion *in Limine* to Exclude Testimony of Dr. Edward Snyder Regarding Efficiencies (Dkt. No. 97) and Plaintiff's Expert Summary § 8, which the United States incorporates here by reference, the analysis by Defendants' efficiency expert Dr. Snyder fails each of these criteria.

D. Defendants' Unenforceable Promise to Allow Simon & Schuster to Bid Independently for Books Does Not Resolve the Proposed Transaction's Anticompetitive Harm

PRH attempts to shift the focus from the plain anticompetitive effects of the proposed merger by offering the Court what amounts to little more than a hope and a promise. Contrary to economically rational decision-making, PRH now promises to change its current bidding practice to allow S&S to compete against PRH for a book, even if there is no third-party publisher competing for the book. In other words, PRH promises to bid against itself to drive up the price of acquiring books. PRH's nonsensical proposal is a self-serving, transparent litigation strategy, and the United States addresses its failure to resolve the anticompetitive effects of the proposed merger in the Unites States' Motion *in limine* to Preclude Evidence of Penguin Random House's Announced Bidding Policy (Dkt. No. 95), which it incorporates by reference here.

Conclusion

Defendants' presumptively illegal proposed transaction would unite two powerhouses among the Big 5 publishers and eliminate longstanding competition that has benefited authors of anticipated top-selling books. Accordingly, the United States respectfully requests that this Court find that the proposed acquisition of Simon & Schuster by Penguin Random House violates Section 7 of the Clayton Act, 15 U.S.C. § 18, issue a permanent injunction restraining Penguin Random House and Bertelsmann from carrying out the proposed acquisition of Simon & Schuster or any other transaction that would combine the companies, award the United States costs of this action, and award any such other relief as the Court may deem just and proper.

Respectfully submitted,

Dated: July 15, 2022
John R. Read (DC Bar #419373)

Sarah Licht (DC Bar #1021541)
Bennett J. Matelson (DC Bar #454551)
Robert P. Vance, Jr.
United States Department of Justice Antitrust Division
450 Fifth Street, NW, Suite 4000
Washington, DC 20530
Counsel for Plaintiff United States of America

CERTIFICATE OF SERVICE

I certify that on July 15, 2022, I served the foregoing and all accompanying documents on the below individuals by electronic mail:

For Defendants Bertelsmann SE & Co. KGaA and Penguin Random House LLC:
Daniel M. Petrocelli
M. Randall Oppenheimer
O'Melveny & Myers LLP
1999 Avenue of the Stars, 8th Floor
Los Angeles, CA 90067
Andrew J. Frackman
Abby F. Rudzin
Eamonn W. Campbell
O'Melveny & Myers LLP
Times Square Tower
7 Times Square
New York, NY 10036
Julia Schiller
O'Melveny & Myers LLP
1625 Eye Street, NW
Washington, DC 20006
Debbie Feinstein
Arnold & Porter
601 Massachusetts Ave., NW
Washington, DC 20001
599 Lexington Avenue New York, NY 10022
Ryan Shores
Michael Mitchell
Shearman & Sterling LLP
401 9th Street NW, Suite 800
Washington, DC 20004
Rachel Mossman
Shearman & Sterling LLP
2828 North Harwood Street, Suite 1800
Dallas, TX 75201
Sarah Licht
U.S. Department of Justice Antitrust Division
450 Fifth Street, NW, Suite 4000
Washington, DC 20530
Counsel for Plaintiff United States of America

APPENDIX C: DEFENDANTS PRE-TRIAL BRIEF

UNITED STATES DISTRICT COURT FOR THE DISTRICT OF COLUMBIA
UNITED STATES OF AMERICA
Plaintiff,
v.
BERTELSMANN SE & CO. KGaA, PENGUIN RANDOM HOUSE, LLC, VIACOMCBS, INC., and SIMON & SCHUSTER, INC.
Defendants.

INTRODUCTION

The U.S. publishing industry is robust and highly competitive. More readers are reading books than ever before, and the number grows every year. Publishers compete vigorously to reach those readers, and the only way they can compete effectively is to find, acquire, and publish the books readers most want to read—books that might be written by established best-selling authors, public figures with a "story to tell," or previously unknown authors whose debut novel captures the public's imagination. Publishers compete to acquire these books across a variety of objective and subjective dimensions, including royalty advances, editorial relationships, niche-genre experience, marketing visions, and other factors. Publishers of all sizes compete to acquire and sell books of all kinds at all advance levels. To be sure, the largest publishers predictably acquire more books at all advance levels, including the highest, but smaller publishers acquire books at all levels as well. Collectively, in fact, smaller publishers— which include elite publishers like Norton and Scholastic, and global giants like Amazon and Disney—outpace one or more of the largest publishers in acquisitions every year. Slice and dice the market any way you want, and you will find vigorous competition to acquire books, especially books that one or more publishers believe are most likely to succeed with consumers.

The merger at issue in this case will encourage even more competition and growth in the U.S. publishing industry. The transaction originated when the owner of Simon & Schuster ("S&S"), ViacomCBS (n/k/a Paramount Global), stated publicly that it would be divesting S&S as part of a broader strategy to shed non-core assets and focus on film, television, and streaming. ViacomCBS's sale of S&S created an opportunity for Penguin Random House ("PRH") to compete better in hotly competitive consumer markets, where large rivals are expanding and—to an even greater extent—smaller competitors and entirely new publishers are rapidly gaining share. S&S is a storied publishing house with an attractive list of authors, skilled and experienced editors, and a strong backlist of popular titles, but it lacks access to PRH's larger, industry-leading distribution structure and administrative systems. PRH recognized that if it combined S&S's high-quality assets with PRH's premier logistics, PRH could expand distribution of S&S titles to the benefit of authors and consumers alike, while also improving PRH's ability to compete against its many bookselling rivals.

Unsurprisingly, after investigating the merger, the government found no evidence that combining PRH and S&S would diminish competition in any consumer market. If anything, by making the combined entity a stronger bookselling competitor, the merger will incentivize other publishers to compete even harder for consumer attention. The government will not even attempt to prove otherwise at trial.

But it still wants to block the merger. Unable to prove any downstream harm to consumers, the government instead seeks to focus solely on the merger's alleged effects in the *upstream* market to *acquire* the books that publishers compete to sell downstream. Yet the government does not actually allege harm to that upstream market either. While its complaint initially alleged that the merger would harm competition in the market to acquire U.S. book rights, its expert has abandoned that claim—he admits that the market will remain unconcentrated, and he conducted no analysis purporting to establish harm to that market.

The government instead has narrowed its focus down to one very small *segment* of the market to acquire U.S. book rights: the set of about 1200 books acquired annually for advances of at least $250,000, or about 2% of all books published by commercial publishers. The government treats this tiny price segment as a "sub-market" and gives it a label—the market for the rights to "anticipated top-selling books"—that is entirely unknown to industry participants.

But even then, the government does not allege the merger will adversely affect *all* advances within that small price segment. Its focus tightens even further, narrowing down to advances paid when either PRH or S&S acquires the book. And yet according to the mathematical model the government invokes to prove harm, not even advances for all of *those* books will decline. By its terms, the model applies only to a specific kind of transaction—one very uncommon in the publishing industry. Based on the best available data, the type of transaction modeled by the government accounts for only approximately *85* books acquired annually, out of more than 55,000 total books published annually, and out of approximately 1200 books acquired annually for advances of $250,000 or more.

To block a merger under Clayton Act § 7, the government must prove that it is likely to cause a "substantial lessening of competition" in a "line of commerce." Alleged harm to 85 books does not constitute a substantial lessening of competition by any definition. To find a § 7 violation in such a tiny corner of the market, the government makes three claims. None will survive scrutiny at trial.

First, the government tries to erase 98% of the market, shriveling it down to the small segment of books that are acquired for advances of at least $250,000. But that price segment is just that—a price segment, not a cognizable "market." Courts have consistently rejected price-defined product markets in antitrust cases when the alleged price boundary does not reflect any real-world *substantive* difference in how industry actors treat the products. And the evidence will show that publishing industry actors do not treat the acquisition of books differently based on the amount of the advance that might ultimately be negotiated. Publishers across the entire industry compete to acquire books of all kinds, and neither editors nor agents nor authors treat books that yield advances in one price segment differently from books that yield lower (or higher) advances. The advance for each unique book is driven primarily by how particular editors perceive that book's potential success, and different editors have different expectations for any given book. The wide variation in advances that inevitably results is, if anything, the *opposite* of a clear, market-defining product categorization. The government's failure to define a cognizable market is fatal to its claim.

Second, after shifting focus to a corner of the book-acquisition market, the government then tries to show that the merger will reduce some of the advances within that artificially shrunken market. But the government will not prove even that constricted theory of harm. The government starts with a purely statistical *presumption* of harm, based on post-merger shares of its small market segment. The D.C. Circuit has repeatedly held, however, that the statistical presumption is weak at best, and easily overcome by evidence showing that market shares do not adequately reflect real-world competitive forces. Such evidence here will be overwhelming.

Among other competitive factors that market shares cannot account for, acquisitions in this industry are controlled by agents, who use their skill and experience to decide which publisher(s) to invite to consider a given book and which acquisition format will best serve their clients' interests. Book-acquisition market shares—a statistic unknown to anyone in the industry—do not figure into either decision, nor do they affect how publishers compete if and when they are selected to participate in a given acquisition.

Where market shares alone do not prove a § 7 case, the government must conduct an actual analysis of real-world competitive conditions to identify likely harm. When it turns to that task here, however, the government either ignores or mischaracterizes the real world it is supposed to examine. The government's theory is that the merger will reduce advances in acquisitions where PRH and S&S would have been the final two bidders for a book, on the basic premise that removing one of them via merger will make the final advance lower. To make that case, the government will rely on two categories of evidence.

The government first will invoke a handful of anecdotes about acquisitions where PRH and S&S were the highest bidders, suggesting that eliminating one of them would have reduced the final advance amount. Nobody disputes, of course, that PRH and S&S *occasionally* have the two highest bids. But the evidence will show that they are *rarely* the top two bidders—only in about 7% of acquisitions involving advances of $250,000 or more. Anecdotes about *some* of those acquisitions out of thousands of books published each year cannot establish substantial harm to competition.

Recognizing as much, the government will also try to make a more comprehensive, quantitative prediction of marketwide harm based on a mathematical model that purports to show how eliminating either S&S or PRH through the merger will systematically affect real-world bargaining. But the model rests on assumptions that do not remotely reflect the reality of book acquisitions. For example, the model assumes that in all acquisitions, the winning bid amount was constrained by the runner-up bid, which in turns leads to the critical inference that if the runner-up bid were removed, the winning bidder would make a lower bid and still prevail. In the real world, however, agents structure the vast majority of book acquisitions as either a one-on- one negotiation or a single-round "best bid" auction, neither of which involves a constraining runner-up bid. A model need not "fit" the real world perfectly, but it must at least *represent* the real world in a meaningful way. The government's auction model here comes nowhere close. It accordingly does not reliably represent the effects of the merger on real-world acquisitions. And that foundational defect, while dispositive in itself, is only the first of many other flawed assumptions, omissions, and data errors that underlie the model.

Third, at the outset of this case, the government contended that even if the merger will not enable the combined entity to make significant unilateral reductions in advance levels, the merger at least will enable publishers as a group to coordinate various aspects of the book- acquisition process. The government's expert, however, has effectively abandoned this claim— he will not testify that the merger will more likely than not facilitate coordination. Rightly so: none of the conditions required for coordinated effects is present here.

The merger between PRH and S&S will not substantially lessen competition, either in the market to acquire U.S. book rights, or in the small segment of that market involving books that ultimately yield advances of $250,000 or more. The merger instead will enhance competition by creating efficiencies that will enable the combined entity to make better offers to more authors, especially for those books most likely to succeed with consumers. And by making the combined entity a stronger competitor downstream, it will incentivize other publishers to compete harder to acquire the books they, too, need to win sales among consumers. Blocking this merger would harm authors and consumers alike. The government's effort to enjoin the merger should be denied.

FACTUAL BACKGROUND

Some 57,000 to 64,000 books are published in the United States each year by one of more than 500 different publishing houses (another 10,000 to 20,000 are self-published).

Publishers compete vigorously to sell these books to consumers. The government does not contend otherwise, nor does it contend that the merger will reduce competition in the consumer bookselling market. That competition among publishers to sell books to consumers gives every publisher a strong incentive to compete aggressively in acquiring the rights to publish books, especially the rights to books they believe readers most want to read.

The trial evidence will show that, given the significant competition to *sell* books, the market to *acquire* books is also extremely competitive, at all advance levels. As in any competitive industry, of course, some firms publish more books than others. In the publishing industry, the five largest individual publishing houses based on consumer book sales are PRH, HarperCollins, Macmillan, S&S, and Hachette—which some colloquially refer to as the "Big 5." The next five largest include global behemoths Amazon and Disney, as well as renowned publisher Scholastic, and the next ten include such prominent firms as Norton, Abrams, and Chronicle. While the five largest publishers by definition acquire and sell the most titles, other publishers compete and win books of all kinds at all advance levels, including bestselling books from prominent authors like JK Rowling, Michael Lewis, Dolly Parton, and Paul Krugman. In the aggregate, smaller publishers acquire more books than one or more of the Big 5 every year, and they have been gaining share among consumers for years.

As that growth shows, there are no meaningful barriers to expansion by existing rivals or entry by new competitors. The evidence will show that other Big 5 publishers are actively planning to grow their shares across advance levels. They already have the tools—skill, experience, and reputation—and they do not need to add facilities (publishers generally obtain printing services from third parties). Entirely new publishers can easily enter as well: established editors have left incumbent publishers to begin their own imprints, and investors have proven more than willing to finance new ventures from well-known editors. In just the past three years, at least three new publishers—Astra, Spiegel & Grau, and Zando—have entered the market and have acquired books at all advance levels. Zando and Spiegel & Grau have already published major best-sellers and have plans to expand.

Competition in the publishing industry differs from most other industries. One critical difference is that books, unlike most other consumer products, are highly differentiated, with entirely subjective and individualized assessments of "value." Except for a few books published each year by well-established or celebrity authors, it is impossible to predict with any certainty whether a given book will perform well. There is thus no intrinsic value for the rights to any book, nor is there an identifiable "market" price—there is only the actual compensation paid in each specific acquisition. That compensation usually includes (but often is not limited to) a percentage royalty on sales of the book, with a royalty "advance" individually negotiated and paid up front. An author will "earn out" her advance if the book sells well enough to pay royalties exceeding the advance, in which case the author continues earning royalties.

But acquisitions are about more than just the advance. Authors (through agents) negotiate other terms, such as the scope of the rights (allowing the author to profit elsewhere from excluded rights), higher royalty rates, accelerated payments, and other financial perks. Authors also may bet on themselves and forgo an advance in favor of a profit-sharing arrangement that might provide higher upside payments. And monetary terms are only one part of the story. Authors also care about the relationship with the editor: they seek an editor who shares the author's vision for the book and often an editor who will be a good partner for a long- term writing career. Because authors highly value the editor herself and their connection, it is not uncommon for an author to choose a publisher that has not offered the highest advance.

Another critical feature of the industry is that acquisitions are controlled by literary agents acting on authors' behalf. The agent determines the "rules" for each acquisition, decides which publishers may compete for each acquisition, and controls what information about bidding to share. When an author brings her agent a book, the agent uses her skill and experience to determine how and to whom to pitch the book. Given each book's subjective nature, a good agent uses different tools for different books to serve her clients' interests.

One critical agent tool is the acquisition format. The agent can choose to make an "exclusive submission" to a single publisher, either because the author prefers to stay with his current editor, or because the agent uses her experience and relationships to identify a particular editor she thinks is likely to value the book most highly. In either case, the agent simply negotiates with that editor (and her publisher) to see if they can agree on terms. If they cannot, the agent can always look elsewhere. And even when an agent chooses to submit a book more widely—i.e., to multiple editors at different publishers (or different imprints within the same publisher)—the book still may be acquired without any competitive bidding. An interested publisher can respond with a generous offer to "preempt" an auction. Or, if the author is enthusiastic about working with a particular editor—usually based on a meeting between them to assess the potential relationship—the agent can solicit a preempt offer. Either way, the agent and publisher negotiate deal terms one-on-one.

In the minority of acquisitions involving multiple bidders, agents usually do not choose the kind of format common in other industries that use auction-type bidding. Agents typically use "best bid" auctions—either one-round only, or with a chance to improve the bid—where each interested publisher simply makes its maximum bid (or almost maximum, if there will be a chance to improve), not knowing how many other bidders there are, who they might be, or how much their "best" is. And auctions that start as more traditional round-robin auctions—perhaps because the agent wants to generate "buzz" for a book—usually conclude with a call for each finalist's best bid. Few auctions involve round-robin bidding through to the end.

Still another important industry feature is the prevalence of intra-firm competition.

Economists recognize the benefits of allowing business sub-units to compete with each other, though it is not common in other industries. It is in the publishing industry: several publishers with multiple imprints allow them to bid independently for books. One of them is PRH, which for decades has allowed imprints in separate divisions to bid independently, unless and until the agent advises that only PRH imprints are left bidding (the limitation has little significance in a best bid auction or in a round-robin auction that progresses to a call for best bids—i.e., most auctions—and thus is rarely triggered). PRH has publicly assured agents that after the merger, it will not only apply its independent bidding policy to S&S imprints, but will go further and allow S&S imprints to bid against PRH imprints even absent an outside bidder.

Agents and others have recognized the value PRH will bring to S&S authors, editors, and readers. The evidence will show that S&S is not going to remain a subsidiary of ViacomCBS— it will be divested one way or the other. Agents and editors will testify that among potential acquirors, PRH will be the best steward of S&S's legacy and assets. Other options would be another Big 5 parent company (such as News Corp. or Vivendi), a similarly well-resourced company already in the publishing industry (such as Disney or Amazon), or a finance firm with no publishing tradition at all. None of these other entities can claim Bertelsmann's centuries- long history in the publishing industry and the profound commitment it shares with PRH to improving public readership. Other potential acquirors may be more likely to squeeze short-term profits from S&S, rather than make long-term investments that will help develop new, diverse authors and strengthen valued author relationships. PRH and Bertelsmann intend to make exactly those investments, just as they always have.

ARGUMENT

Section 7 of the Clayton Act prohibits a merger only "where in any line of commerce or in any activity affecting commerce in any section of the country, the effect of such acquisition … may be substantially to lessen competition, or tend to create a monopoly." 15 U.S.C. § 18. Section 7 requires a predictive exercise, but it "deals in probabilities not ephemeral possibilities." *FTC v. Arch Coal*, 329 F. Supp. 2d 109, 115 (D.D.C. 2004) (quoting *FTC v. Tenet Health Care Corp.*, 186 F.3d 1045, 1051 (8th Cir.1999)); *see U.S. v. Baker Hughes, Inc.*, 908 F.2d 981, 984 (D.C. Cir. 1990) (Section 7 "involves probabilities, not . . . possibilities"). The government must therefore prove that "the challenged acquisition [is] *likely* substantially to lessen competition." *Arch Coal*, 329 F. Supp. 2d at 115 (emphasis added); *see U.S. v. Marine Bancorp.*, 418 U.S. 602, 623 n.22 (1974) (alleged harm to competition must be "sufficiently probable and imminent" to warrant relief); *U.S. v. Oracle Corp.*, 331 F. Supp. 2d 1098, 1109 (N.D. Cal. 2004) (rejecting merger challenge because government failed to prove "merger will *likely* lead to a substantial lessening of competition"). In any merger challenge, "the ultimate burden of persuasion … remains with the government at all times." *FTC v. H.J. Heinz*, 246 F.3d 708, 715 (D.C. Cir. 2001) (quoting *Baker Hughes*, 908 F.2d at 983).

Courts generally apply a multi-stage proof structure to determine whether the government can establish that a merger will likely cause an imminent and substantial lessening of competition. The first stage involves identifying concentration in a "relevant market": the government must prove that the "transaction will lead to undue concentration in the market for a particular product in a particular geographic area." *Baker Hughes*, 908 F.2d at 982. This stage itself includes multiple subsidiary steps. To show undue concentration in a relevant market, the government "bears the initial burden of (1) defining the appropriate product market, (2) defining the appropriate geographic market, and (3) showing that the merger will lead to undue concentration in the relevant product and geographic market." *FTC v. Tronox, Ltd.*, 332 F. Supp. 3d 187, 197 (D.D.C. 2018).

If the government satisfies those elements, it gives rise to "a presumption that the transactions will substantially lessen competition." *Arch Coal*, 329 F. Supp. 2d at 129; *see also Baker Hughes*, 908 F.2d at 982. But where the government relies on the "short cut" of market concentration statistics, *U.S. v. AT&T, Inc.*, 916 F.3d 1029, 1032 (D.C. Cir. 2019), the resulting presumption of harm is weak at best, *see infra* at 28-29. "[B]ecause the burden of persuasion ultimately lies with the plaintiff, the burden to rebut must not be 'unduly onerous.'" *U.S. v. Anthem, Inc.*, 855 F.3d 345, 349-50 (D.C. Cir. 2017) (quoting *Baker Hughes*, 908 F.2d at 991). The presumption imposes on defendants only a burden to produce evidence showing that market shares alone do not adequately capture the market's competitive conditions. *Baker Hughes*, 908 F.2d at 991. And when the government presents "a less-than-compelling prima facie case," even "less of a showing is required from defendants." *Arch Coal*, 329 F. Supp. 2d at 129; *see Baker Hughes*, 908 F.2d at 981, 989-92 (describing evolution of law away from presumptions and structural analysis toward focus on real-world facts and economic analysis).

If defendants surmount the low bar of showing that market-share statistics alone do not prove likely harm to competition, the presumption drops out, and the government must produce "additional evidence of anticompetitive effect" sufficient to carry its burden of persuasion, which again "'remains with the government at all times.'" *Heinz*, 246 F.3d at 715 (quoting *Baker Hughes*, 908 F.2d at 983). The government always bears "the ultimate burden of persuasion" on "every element of [a] Section 7 challenge, and a failure of proof in any respect will mean the transaction should not be enjoined." *Arch Coal*, 329 F. Supp. 2d at 116.

The government will not carry its burden of persuasion on any element of its § 7 challenge. Part I below demonstrates that the small price segment of books that yield advances of $250,000 or more is not a cognizable "market" for antitrust purposes. Even if it were, Part II shows that the government will not establish a substantial lessening of competition within that small price segment. Finally, Part III explains why the government cannot show likely substantial harm through its separate "coordinated effects" claim.

I. THE GOVERNMENT CANNOT SHOW THAT THE $250,000+ PRICE SEGMENT IS A COGNIZABLE PRODUCT MARKET

Defining a product market is "a necessary predicate to finding a Clayton Act violation," because the government must show that "it is likely the proposed merger will substantially lessen competition *in a relevant market*." *FTC v. RAG-Stiftung*, 436 F. Supp. 3d 278, 287, 291 (D.D.C. 2020) (internal quotation marks omitted; emphasis added). Market definition is the "first step" in any merger case, and it is "key to the ultimate resolution of this type of case, since the scope of the market will necessarily impact any analysis of the anticompetitive effects of the transaction." *U.S. v. SunGard Data Sys., Inc.*, 172 F. Supp. 2d 172, 181 (D.D.C. 2001); *see U.S. v. Gillette Co.*, 828 F. Supp. 78, 81 (D.D.C. 1993). An improperly-defined product market prevents an accurate assessment of a merger's competitive effects. The government has the burden of proving the existence of a distinct, legally-cognizable market. *See SunGard*, 172 F. Supp. 2d at 181.

"Because the ability of consumers to turn to other suppliers restrains a firm from raising prices above the competitive level, the relevant market must include all products reasonably interchangeable by consumers for the same purposes." *U.S. v. Microsoft Corp.*, 253 F.3d 34, 51– 52 (D.C. Cir. 2001) (internal quotation marks and citation omitted). A "market" for antitrust purposes is thus defined by "all goods that are reasonable substitutes, even though the products themselves are not entirely the same." *FTC v. Sysco Corp.*, 113 F. Supp. 3d 1, 25 (D.D.C. 2015). The "general rule" in defining a product market is that the "outer boundaries" of the market "are determined by the reasonable interchangeability of use" between defendants' products and competing products, also known as "the cross-elasticity of demand." *Brown Shoe Co. v. U.S.*, 370 U.S. 294, 325 (1962); *see also FTC v. Staples, Inc.*, 970 F. Supp. 1066, 1077 (D.D.C. 1997).

In other words, courts consider "whether two products can be used for the same purpose, and if so, whether and to what extent purchasers are willing to substitute one for the other." *Arch Coal*, 329 F. Supp. 2d at 119. If customers are willing to switch "from one product to another" in the event of a price or quality change, then the market must encompass both products. *RAG- Stiftung*, 436 F. Supp. 3d at 292.

Courts have applied "two main analytical approaches" when defining a product market: the "practical indicia described by the Supreme Court in *Brown Shoe*," and a "hypothetical monopolist" test. *FTC v. Wilh. Wilhelmsen Holding ASA*, 341 F. Supp. 3d 27, 47 (D.D.C. 2018) (internal quotation marks omitted); *see Sysco*, 113 F. Supp. 3d at 27. *Brown Shoe*'s "practical indicia" are a set of factors that function as "proxies for proof of substitutability" between products. *Wilhelmsen*, 341 F. Supp. 3d at 47; *see Sysco*, 113 F. Supp. 3d at 27. The "hypothetical monopolist" test examines, through statistical modeling, whether a single company controlling an entire product market "could profitably raise prices" in that market. *Sysco*, 113 F. Supp. 3d at 33; *see* Phillip E. Areeda & Herbert Hovenkamp, *Antitrust Law: An Analysis of Antitrust Principles and Their Application* ¶ 536 (4th and 5th eds. 2021). These same market-definition standards apply in cases where, as here, the government asserts that a merger will reduce competition to *buy* inputs from upstream sellers. *See* U.S. Dep't of Justice and Fed.

Trade Comm'n, *Horizontal Merger Guidelines* § 12 (2010) ("Guidelines"). The question is "whether and to what extent" the sellers of an input (here, authors) will switch to other buyers (here, publishers) if input prices decline. *Arch Coal*, 329 F. Supp. 2d at 119.

Unable to identify any harm to competition in the market for the acquisition of all book rights, the government shifts its focus to one tiny corner of that market—the segment of books acquired for advances of $250,000 or more, which the government treats as a "sub-market" for the "acquisition of U.S. publishing rights to anticipated top-selling books." Dkt. 1 at 14 (Compl. 36).

Courts have generally rejected efforts to define markets solely by price differences among otherwise comparable products. *See Brown Shoe*, 370 U.S. at 326 ("It would be unrealistic to accept Brown's contention that, for example, men's shoes selling below $8.99 are in a different product market from those selling above $9.00."); *HDC Med., Inc. v. Minntech Corp.*, 474 F.3d 543, 547 (8th Cir. 2007) ("Price is only one factor in a user's choice between one product or the other. That there are price differentials between the two products … are relevant matters but not determinative of the product market issue.") (cleaned up); *In re Super Premium Ice Cream Distrib. Antitrust Litig.*, 691 F. Supp. 1262, 1268 (N.D. Cal. 1988) (price and quality distinctions "are economically meaningless where the differences are actually a *spectrum* of price and quality differences"), *aff'd sub nom, Haagen-Dazs Co. v. Double Rainbow Gourmet Ice Creams, Inc.*, 895 F.2d 1417 (9th Cir. 1990); *accord Crestron Elecs. Inc. v. Cyber Sound & Sec. Inc.*, 2012 WL 426282, at *5-*6 (D.N.J. Feb. 9, 2012); *U.S. v. Joseph Schlitz Brewing Co.*, 253 F. Supp. 129, 145 (N.D. Cal. 1966). As these precedents recognize, price alone cannot define a market's boundaries—price matters only to the extent it reflects *substantive differences among products* that cause consumers to treat otherwise similar products differently within their different price categories. In other words, to establish a market defined by a price divide, the government must prove that "products across that divide do not compete with each other," *Crestron*, 2012 WL 426282, at *6, in accordance with all the usual factors applied to identify product interchangeability.

The court's analysis in *Staples* exemplifies the correct approach. In that case, the government challenged a merger as likely to harm competition in a sub-category of large "business-to-business" ("B-to-B") transactions directed at large enterprise customers. The government, however, did not define the market merely by citing a particular price boundary, but instead made a persuasive factual showing, based on standard market-definition criteria, that real-world market participants substantively treated large B-to-B services as categorically separate from smaller-scale services provided at lower price-points. 190 F. Supp. 3d at 111-21. In particular, the court found that "the sale and distribution of consumable office supplies to large B-to-B customers is a proper antitrust market because the evidence supports the conclusion that: (1) there is industry or public recognition of the market as a separate economic entity; (2) B-to-B customers demand distinct prices and demonstrate a high sensitivity to price changes; and (3) B-to-B customers require specialized vendors that offer value-added services." *Id.* at 127.

None of those factors is true here. To the contrary, as discussed in Parts I.A. and I.B. below, the evidence will show that nobody in the industry—not authors, not publishers, not agents—approaches competition differently for books that yield advances of $250,000 or more. The analysis applied in *Staples* thus compels the opposite conclusion here: there is no distinct market for the acquisition of books that yield advances in this small price segment.

A. The *Brown Shoe* Factors Do Not Support Treating The Price Segment Of Books Acquired For $250,000+ Advances As A Distinct Market

Courts treat the "practical indicia" under *Brown Shoe* as important guidelines for market definition. *SunGard*, 172 F. Supp. 2d at 182. The factors include "industry or public recognition of the relevant market as a separate economic entity," the "peculiar characteristics and uses" of a product, "unique production facilities," "distinct customers," "distinct prices," "sensitivity to price changes," and "specialized vendors." *U.S. v. H & R Block*, 833 F. Supp. 2d 36, 51 (D.D.C. 2011). None of these factors supports the government's contention that a distinct market exists for the acquisition of books that yield advances of $250,000 or more.

1. The Publishing Industry Does Not Recognize A Separate Market For The Acquisition Of Books For $250,000+ Advances

Evidence that the industry or general public recognizes a given market "matters because we assume that economic actors usually have accurate perceptions of economic realities." *Rothery Storage & Van Co. v. Atlas Van Lines, Inc.*, 792 F.2d 210, 219 n.4 (D.C. Cir. 1986).

Defining the relevant market is "in the end ... a matter of business reality—how the market is perceived by those who strive for profit in it." *SunGard*, 172 F. Supp. 2d at 182 (cleaned up).

The evidence will show that there is no industry-wide understanding that the market for U.S. book rights is divided either into "anticipated top-sellers" and "other books," or into price- defined segments of books acquired for advances of at least $250,000 and those acquired for less. Industry actors do not employ objective criteria to identify the books that will receive advances of $250,000 or more and then treat them differently from others. Testimony from numerous witnesses—including agents, editors, and representatives of multiple publishing houses—will demonstrate that members of the industry have very different expectations about which books will perform well. Even when one editor is willing to pay an advance of $250,000 or more, other editors likely assign the book much lower value, if any at all.

The government will also cite some publishers' internal requirements for additional approval of advances exceeding certain amounts (sometimes $250,000), the evidence will show that these approval thresholds are also arbitrary—i.e., they have never been fixed to collect a set of books with unique shared characteristics—and have varied over time.

The government focuses on a price segment defined entirely by the *outcome* of individualized and subjective acquisition processes for differentiated books. But the government can cite no precedent defining a market in which participants share no common understanding as to which products are inside the market, even as those participants supposedly act differently when they compete over those products.

2. Books In This Price Segment Lack "Peculiar Characteristics And Uses"

The government will not prove that books in the $250,000-plus price segment share any "strong physical and functional relationship" that justifies treating them separately from other books. *Rothery*, 792 F.2d at 219 n.4. Books in this segment do not share common narrative, thematic, or other literary features that distinguish them from books that ultimately yield lower advances. They come from everywhere and every genre—cookbooks, religious books, literary fiction, children's books, and more. They are written by celebrities, professors, franchise authors, and debut writers. The only shared feature of books in this price segment is that at least one editor somewhere ultimately decided it was worth paying an advance of $250,000 or more for the book—a decision that includes not only that editor's subjective assessment of the book's likely success, but many other individualized factors affecting her valuation of the book.

3. Acquiring Books In This Price Segment Requires No Unique Facilities

A market can be defined around a product that "requires unique production facilities," because if the producer raised prices, "the ability of other producers to shift resources to make the product would be limited." *Rothery*, 792 F.2d at 219 n.4; *see General Foods Corp. v. FTC*, 386 F.2d 943 (3d Cir. 1967). The evidence will show that publishers do not devote special production facilities to books acquired for advances of $250,000 or more. They are edited, printed, and distributed using the same people and instruments as all other books.

4. There Is No Distinct Set Of Authors Selling Only $250,000+ Books

Under certain circumstances, a "core group of particularly dedicated, 'distinct customers,' paying 'distinct prices,' may constitute a recognizable submarket." *FTC v. Whole Foods Mkt., Inc.*, 548 F.3d 1028, 1039 (D.C. Cir. 2008) (quoting *Brown Shoe*, 370 U.S. at 325). A market thus can be defined by a set of "distinct customers with distinct needs." *Wilhelmsen*, 341 F. Supp. 3d at 57. Consistent with the focus on actual market realities, this factor considers whether companies cater to distinct customers by, for example, providing "higher levels of customer service," a "unique environment," or appealing to the "core values" of those customers through services provided. *Whole Foods*, 548 F.3d at 1039. In *Whole*

Foods, for example, the FTC argued for a distinct market of "premium, natural, and organic supermarkets" ("PNOS") by "describ[ing] the core PNOS customers, explain[ing] how PNOS cater to these customers, and show[ing] these customers provided the bulk of PNOS's business." *Id.* at 1032, 1041.

The government cannot make a comparable showing here. As noted above, industry participants do not apply common objective criteria to identify which authors to target as likely to receive advances of $250,000 or more. There are no separate publishers who target such authors, and no separate imprints or departments within publishers that cater separately to such authors. To be sure, some well-established or celebrity authors may predictably command large advances, but those advances vastly exceed $250,000. And apart from the most successful authors, repeat authors in general do not command predictable advances. Offers vary widely to debut and repeat authors alike: even within the same publishing house, editors may submit drastically different bids on a book that eventually sells for $250,000 or more.

The most one can say about this price segment is that larger publishers *more often* acquire books than do smaller publishers. But that fact—which is true at all price levels—does not demonstrate either that the largest publishers distinctly target books in this segment, or that authors treat such publishers as a distinct market. It means only that the companies with the most capital tend to spend more money more often, which is a truism applicable in almost any market. In any given acquisition in this price segment, however, many publishers—the top twenty at least—pose a credible competitive threat to win the title. *See infra* at 32-33.

For similar reasons, the government cannot define a distinct "targeted customers" sub- market. Such markets can exist where sellers can profitably "target for price increases" a distinct subgroup of customers who cannot substitute away to other products. *Staples*, 190 F. Supp. 3d at 127. Because sellers can discriminate in their pricing between distinct consumer segments—i.e., they can profitably raise prices in a distinct price category—these markets are also known as "price discrimination" markets. *Sysco*, 113 F. Supp. 3d at 38 (quoting Guidelines § 4.1.4).

The analogous market here would be a targeted *sellers* market. To establish such a market, the government must prove that publishers can (a) identify and segregate authors selling books for advances of at least $250,000, and (b) decrease advances for those books without losing the authors to other publishers. Guidelines § 3; *see also Staples*, 190 F. Supp. 3d at 118. The government will not make either showing.

As already explained, the trial evidence will show that no objective criteria exist for identifying in advance and separately "targeting" those authors whose books will be acquired for advances of at least $250,000. The inherent subjectivity of all books is partly why agents must intermediate—the agent best knows how to match a book with the potential acquirors who will value it most highly and structure an acquisition format for that will achieve maximum value for the author. But neither the agent nor the author typically knows how the negotiation will turn out, or whether any publisher will ultimately agree to pay an advance of $250,000 or more. As to the few authors whose books easily *can* be identified as likely to garner high advances—e.g., a brand-name author like John Grisham or a starpower public figure like Michelle Obama—they are among the most sought-after sellers in the industry, and their advances vastly exceed $250,000. If a publisher tried to segregate these authors and impose an across-the-board price reduction on their advances, there would be many publishers to whom they could turn for better offers. Indeed, these authors have the *most* leverage against publishers, making them *least* likely to be targeted for a price decrease. Forcing price reductions on the most popular authors would be a losing strategy for any rational publisher.

5. *Brown Shoe's "Distinct Prices" Factor Is Meaningless Here*

Distinct product pricing is one feature suggesting that products belong in their own separate market. *See H & R Block*, 833 F. Supp. 2d at 52-53; *see also* Julian O. von Kalinowski, 2 *Antitrust Laws and Trade Regulation* § 24.02 (2d ed. 2022) ("distinct prices may place products in separate submarkets"). But in this case, *price itself* is the defining boundary of the market. Because any book sold for $250,000 or more is, by definition, a book sold in a "distinct price" category, this factor does no work to define this market. Put differently, this factor would allow the government to define a market at *any* price segment: a boundary of $1,000 would encompass "distinct prices," as would a boundary of $1,000,000 or $10,000,000.

6. Publishers Cannot Set General Price Levels Against Competitors

Under *Brown Shoe*, a market definition can be supported by evidence that market participants set their prices in response to prices of other products within the alleged market, and contrariwise "do *not* respond to changes in the prices of other alleged substitutes" *outside* the market. Kalinowski, *Antitrust Laws and Trade Regulation* at § 24.02; *see also Staples*, 970 F. Supp. at 1075–76 (discussing "compelling evidence" that Staples priced certain products in comparison to comparable products at other office superstores). This factor, too, confirms the absence of any cognizable market defined by books that yield advances of $250,000 or more.

The evidence will show that publishers cannot impose across-the-board price adjustments in response to rival pricing behavior. Given the highly subjective, uncertain nature of predicting a book's success, what Publisher A pays for Book Y cannot affect what Publisher B pays for Book Z. And even if a publisher somehow did try reducing all advances within one price segment by, say, 5%, rivals could not know whether that target was achieved in any given acquisition and thereby could not adjust their own acquisitions in response.

7. There Are No "Specialized Vendors" In The $250,000+ Advance Segment

The government cannot demonstrate that publishers who acquire books for advances of $250,000 or more have "special characteristics." *Staples*, 970 F. Supp. at 1078. This factor requires more than the circular observation that larger entities are larger—it requires evidence of "uniqueness" among market participants; differences in the "type of customers targeted and served"; or visible differences in "appearance, physical size, [or] format" of vendors in the market. *Id.* As Judge Mehta observed in describing the asserted market in *Sysco*, "[n]o one entering a systems, specialty, or cash-and-carry outlet would mistake it for a broadline distribution facility." 113 F. Supp. 3d at 28.

The opposite is true here. Among the several dozen largest publishing houses, no one entering a given office would know whether it has paid advances of at least $250,000, or how often. Many large and established companies outside the Big 5 acquire books within this price range—including Disney, Amazon, Norton, and Scholastic. New entrants do as well.

Even among the Big 5 alone, there are no specialized editors or unique imprints that serve *only* books acquired for advances of $250,000 or more—every editor acquires and shepherds books at a wide range of advance levels.

B. The "Hypothetical Monopsonist Test" Does Not Justify Recognition Of A Discrete Market For Books Acquired For $250,000+ Advances

In addition to the qualitative *Brown Shoe* factors, courts also often consider a quantitative measure of product substitution known as the "hypothetical monopolist test" or "HMT." *See Sysco*, 113 F. Supp. 3d at 33. That test hypothesizes that there is only a single seller of all products in the alleged market, and asks whether that seller "could profitably raise prices on those products" by imposing a "small but significant and non-transitory" increase in price (or "SSNIP") on products in the market, "typically assumed to be five percent." *Id.* at 34 (citing Guidelines § 4.1.2). If the hypothetical seller could impose a SSNIP without losing many consumers to substitute goods, then the products may define a relevant market. *See id.* By contrast, if the price increase would cause the hypothetical monopolist to *lose* so many buyers to substitute goods that the price increase became unprofitable, "then the relevant market cannot include only the monopolist's product and must also include the substitute goods." *Id.* at 33. In this case, the test involves a hypothetical *monopsonist*—i.e., a single *buyer* of all book rights in the alleged market—and the price conduct at issue is a "small but significant non-transitory *reduction* in price," or "SSNRP."

The HMT does not support the government's price-defined market here for two reasons.

First, the test is tautological in a market defined only by price. Because the government here defines its proposed market to encompass only publishers who will pay advances of $250,000 or more, any publisher *outside* the market *by definition* will not pay an advance of that amount.

Applied to that alleged market, the HMT asks whether, if a hypothetical single publisher paying advances of at least $250,000 imposed a SSNRP, authors would turn to substitute publishers who will *not* pay that amount. But no author would rationally turn to a source that pays *less than* $250,000 as an alternative to a source that pays *more than* $250,000, even if the latter imposes a SSNRP (so long as the price remains above $250,000). The same dynamic would hold for *any* price-defined market: if the market boundary is defined at $500,000 or $1,000,000, no rational author in that market would respond to a SSNRP by turning to a publisher who only pays less than the market-defining boundary. The HMT thus would confirm a market at *any* price definition, making it a meaningless test in this context.

Second, the hypothetical monopsonist test does not account for the real-world ease of expansion and entry by competing publishers. The evidence will show that other publishers can easily expand their acquisitions in the $250,000-plus price segment—they already have the needed skill, experience, and reputation, and they are already planning to grow. *See infra* at 31. New publishers have also recently entered and are growing. *See infra* at 31. Existing and new rivals would have an especially strong incentive to expand or enter if a hypothetical monopsonist tried to impose a SSNRP on the books considered most likely to succeed, thereby creating an opportunity for rivals to capture those books. The HMT thus provides no basis for inferring the real-world existence of a discrete market for books in the $250,000-plus price segment.

* * * *

The foregoing analysis shows why the government will not be able to prove the existence of a cognizable market for the acquisition of books that yield advances of $250,000 or more. But even if this price boundary satisfied the technical requirements for defining a market, it ends up with a market "defined so narrowly that it encompasses an insubstantial amount of commerce." *Oracle*, 331 F. Supp. 3d at 1120. It is important not to define a market "so narrowly it fails to capture the potential effects of the merger"—for example, by "focus[ing] on a single city in analyzing the effects of a merger between sellers who compete on a much larger scale." *Id.* The government does exactly that here. It focuses narrowly on a price segment that is only about *2%* of the overall book-acquisition market, while ignoring the merger's effects on the remaining 98% of the market, and completely ignoring its effects on 100% of consumers. This merger instead should be evaluated on the much larger scale in which PRH and S&S actually compete, i.e., the market for the acquisition of all U.S. book rights. And the government will not even attempt to show harm to competition in that market.

II. THE GOVERNMENT WILL NOT ESTABLISH A LIKELIHOOD OF SUBSTANTIAL HARM TO COMPETITION IN THE ERSATZ MARKET FOR THE ACQUISITION OF BOOKS FOR ADVANCES OF $250,000 OR MORE

The government's theory of competitive harm here is not quite entirely unprecedented, but it is unusual. Because the "principal objective of antitrust policy is to maximize *consumer* welfare by encouraging firms to behave competitively," *Kirtsaeng v. John Wiley & Sons, Inc.*, 568 U.S. 519, 539 (2013) (emphasis added), merger challenges—like antitrust law more generally—almost always address likely harms to competition in *downstream* markets, in the form of higher prices or reduced output, *see* Areeda & Hovenkamp ¶ 910h (interest "antitrust policy cares about most" is "consumer welfare as measured by price and output"). In this case, however, after extensive investigation, the government could identify no likely harm to the consumers, because the sale of books will remain highly diffuse and competitive.

But rather than close the investigation, the government turned its attention *upstream*, to the "supply" or "input" market in which publishers acquire book rights. Merger challenges based on alleged upstream harms are rare—and hence there is very little caselaw addressing them—because as the FTC has explained, "[o]nly in special circumstances does an increase in power in negotiating input prices adversely impact consumers." Statement of FTC Concerning the *Proposed Acquisition of Medco Health Solutions by Express Scripts, Inc.*, FTC File No. 111- 0210, at 7 (Apr. 2, 2012) ["*Express Scripts* Closing Statement"]. Normally the ability to obtain lower input prices is good for consumers, because "aggressive but competitive buying" tends to "yield higher output." Areeda & Hovenkamp ¶ 983; *see also* Herbert Hovenkamp, *Federal Antitrust Policy*, 1.2b (6th ed. 2020); Areeda & Hovenkamp ¶ 983 ("If a large buyer is able to obtain lower prices by reducing transaction costs, the buyer will generally buy *more* rather than less."); Areeda & Hovenkamp ¶ 575 ("hard bargaining that reduces costs or drives prices down toward the competitive level results in *increased* output on the buying side"). But the kind of "special circumstances" referenced by the FTC may arise when a merger gives the combined entity enough power in the input market that it can reduce the *overall supply* of inputs, because reducing supply will tend to reduce output in the downstream consumer market, thereby raising consumer prices. Areeda & Hovenkamp ¶ 575 ("The monopsonist, like the monopolist, 'exercises' its power by reducing output, in this case in the market in which it purchases."); *see also id.* ("Unlike the competitive buyer, the monopsony buyer can reduce the purchase price by scaling back its purchases. The important and often overlooked consequence of monopsony power is *reduced output* ...." (emphasis altered)). But absent reduced supply in the input market, consumers suffer no harm: neither "competition [nor] consumers suffer when the increased bargaining power of large buyers allows them to obtain lower input prices without decreasing overall input purchases." Statement of FTC, *In re Caremark Rx, Inc./Advance PCS*, FTC File No. 031 0239, at 2 (Feb. 11, 2004); *see also Express Scripts* Closing Statement, at 8 (closing merger investigation after concluding that "even if the transaction enables the merged firm to reduce" payments to upstream suppliers, there was "no evidence that this would result in reduced output or curtailment" of downstream consumer services).

The government challenges the merger here without seeking to prove that it will reduce the overall supply of books. That failure in itself justifies rejection of the merger challenge.

But even looking past that foundational legal defect, the trial evidence will show that the government's narrow theory that the merger will reduce some advances in a tiny price segment of the market fails on its own terms, purely as a matter of fact. The government will seek to establish harm to advances on three bases. First, the government will rely heavily on market share statistics to argue, based on market concentration alone, that the merger will give the combined entity enough market power to reduce advances in this price segment. But as Part II.A. shows, market shares provide at best only a weak initial "presumption" of likely harm, and it is easily rebutted here. Next, the government will recite anecdotes showing that PRH and S&S sometimes are the two highest bidders, which of course is true, but obscures the relevant point that PRH and S&S are *rarely* the two highest bidders, as Part II.B. shows. Finally, the government will invoke an abstract mathematical model that purports to show how eliminating either PRH or S&S through the merger will affect real-world acquisitions. But as shown in Part II.C, the model's projections bear no connection to real-world book acquisitions, which are nothing like the auctions examined in the government's model. Part II.C. further shows that the model is rife with other errors and omissions in its assumptions and inputs. Given the government's failure to model real-world acquisitions or otherwise reliably show how those acquisitions would be harmed, the government's § 7 challenge must be rejected.

A. The Government Cannot Rely On A Statistical Presumption Of Likely Substantial Harm

The Complaint and discovery make clear that the government intends to rely heavily on estimates of post-merger market concentration to show harm to the price segment of books acquired for advances of at least $250,000. According to the government, one measure of such concentration—the Herfindahl-Hirschman Index "(HHI")—will by itself justify a presumption that the merger will substantially lessen competition in that price segment. That contention is incorrect. The HHI statistical presumption is a weak presumption, which courts recognize as easily rebuttable by the merging parties. It certainly is easily rebutted here.

1. The HHI Has Limited Probative Value In General

The HHI and other concentration indices "may have some utility, but only if their significant limitations are kept in mind," and they are used "very tentatively." Areeda & Hovenkamp ¶ 930; *id.* ¶ 930d (if "used too rigidly," concentration indices "may in fact hinder rather than promote competitive analysis of mergers"). Such statistics are, after all, "artificial creations with no intrinsic claim to correctness." *Id.* ¶ 931a3. Because the HHI can be "overly responsive" to mergers, Areeda & Hovenkamp ¶ 931a3, overreliance on it risks doing "considerably more harm than good by preventing firms from developing to their most efficient size" through acquisitions, *id.* ¶ 930c. The Guidelines themselves specify that HHI thresholds are not "rigid screens," but are merely tools for identifying circumstances that warrant full analysis of all factors relevant to assessing potential anticompetitive effects. Guidelines ¶ 5.3.

Given the HHI's limited utility, the D.C. Circuit has emphasized that rejecting a merger based solely on market concentration figures would grossly inflate the role of statistics in § 7 actions, and would upend settled principles governing the burden of persuasion in civil litigation. *Baker Hughes*, 908 F.2d at 992. Put simply, the HHI "cannot guarantee litigation victories." *Id.*; *see also New York v. Deutsche Telekom AG*, 439 F. Supp. 3d 179, 206 (S.D.N.Y. 2020) ("[M]arket shares and HHIs establish only a presumption, rather than conclusive proof of a transaction's likely competitive impact."); *In re AMR Corp.*, 625 B.R. 215, 256 (Bankr. S.D.N.Y. 2021) ("HHI calculations alone are only a starting point in an antitrust inquiry.").

When the weak statistical presumption of harm arises in a merger case, defendants must produce evidence showing why market shares alone do not capture competitive conditions, but the burden is not "unduly onerous." *Anthem*, 855 F.3d at 349-50 (quoting *Baker Hughes*, 908 F.2d at 991). Courts impose no artificial constraints on the kind of evidence defendants may identify. Because "only examination of the particular market—its structure, history, and probable future—can provide the appropriate setting for judging the probable anticompetitive effects of the merger," *U.S. v. General Dynamics*, 415 U.S. 486, 498 (1974), § 7 "requires evaluation of a merger's competitive effects under the totality of the circumstances," *Deutsche Telekom*, 439 F. Supp. 3d at 208. Defendants can therefore identify many different ways in which concentration statistics "produce an inaccurate account of the merger's probable effects on competition in the relevant market." *Arch Coal*, 329 F. Supp. 2d at 116 (citing *FTC v. H.J. Heinz*, 246 F.3d 708, 715 (D.C. Cir. 2001)). Such evidence may include "the absence of significant entry barriers in the relevant market," *Baker Hughes*, 908 F.2d at 984, and factors like changing market conditions, special features of the product or negotiating process, and the conduct of other firms in the market, *id.* at 986; *see Deutsche Telekom*, 439 F. Supp. 3d at 207.

As the following sections show, there are many reasons market shares do not themselves prove an anticompetitive effect here.

2. *The HHI Is Not Relevant To A "Unilateral Effects" Analysis*

The HHI is an unhelpful predictor of the competitive impact of this merger because the government's theory of competitive harm relies on "unilateral effects" analysis. Dkt. 1 at 4-5 (Compl. ¶¶ 7-9). In a merger between buyers, a unilateral effects analysis focuses on the merger's effects on transactions where sellers strongly prefer to sell only to one of the two merging parties (enabling the buyer to lower prices without losing sellers). Market concentration has nothing to do with that analysis. *See* Guidelines ¶ 6.1; *Oracle*, 331 F. Supp. 2d at 1122 ("a strong presumption of anticompetitive effects based on market concentration is especially problematic in a differentiated products unilateral effects context"); Herbert Hovenkamp & Carl Shapiro, *Horizontal Mergers, Market Structure, and Burdens of Proof*, 127 Yale L.J. 1996, 2014 (2018) (cases alleging unilateral effects "pose a challenge for the structural presumption"). The HHI-based presumption of harm accordingly should play no role in determining whether the government carried its burden of proving likely harm through "unilateral effects."

3. *The Government's Reliance On Static, Backward-Looking Market Shares Does Not Account For The Ease Of Expansion And Entry*

The government's case assumes that the current market shares define the competitive landscape that will exist after the merger—the same participants and shares, except that PRH and S&S shares will be combined. But when there are low barriers to expansion by existing rivals or entry by new rivals, it is error to rely on past market shares to draw inferences about post-merger competition. As the Guidelines recognize, market-share analysis must account for firms outside the market that can provide "rapid" response to a price reduction, Guidelines § 5.1, because even "the *threat* of entry can stimulate competition in a concentrated market, regardless of whether entry ever occurs," *Baker Hughes*, 908 F.2d at 987; *see Deutsche Telekom*, 439 F. Supp. 3d at 226 (realistic threat of entry "constitute[s] a substantial incentive to competition" post-merger).

The evidence will show that existing Big 5 rivals can easily expand and actively plan to do so. Other rivals among the top twenty also can easily increase their acquisitions—they already possess the needed talent, experience, and reputation. Numerous top twenty rivals plan to meaningfully expand, including

Disney, Chronicle, Candlewick, and others. And entirely new publishers started by well-known editors have recently gained share and become increasingly effective competitors. Given this ease of expansion and entry, market shares are a highly unreliable predictor of post-merger competitive conditions.

4. Market Shares Alone Do Not Account For Multiple Other Factors That Drive Competition In Real-World Acquisitions

The government's reliance on current market shares also ignores numerous other factors that will continue to profoundly affect competition after the merger.

First, the evidence will show that publishers compete ferociously downstream to sell their books to readers. They compete for shelf space in independent bookstores and in superstores like Barnes & Noble, Walmart, and Target. They compete for visibility in online marketplaces like Amazon. Ultimately, the publishing companies make money from the sale of books to consumers—if they do not compete aggressively to acquire the books from authors, they will lose out in the competition to sell them to readers. The government itself does not contest the highly competitive nature of the downstream sale of books. Upstream market share statistics alone do not reflect the effect the concededly competitive downstream marketplace has on incentives to compete upstream.

Second, market concentration also ignores the competitive effect of agents' control over the acquisition process. Publishers do not participate in acquisitions proportionally to their market shares—the agent decides which publishers to invite, and how many. Those invitations are not based on market shares, which are not even known to the agent. They are instead based on a host of individualized factors, including the agent's judgment about which editors are most likely to connect with the book and author. And even where an agent perceives that a bidder has been "lost," the agent often can invite a new bidder to replace the lost bidder. Increased market concentration thus has little to no bearing on participation in specific acquisitions.

Third, the vast majority of acquisitions are structured either as exclusive submissions, where there is no bidding competition at all, or "best bid" and "better/best bid" formats, where a publisher does not know the amount of other bids. In both formats, each publisher must bid as if it is competing against the *entire collection* of unknown rivals that *could* submit bids. Increased concentration would not affect that bargaining dynamic.

What matters instead is the collective threat posed by the many potential rivals that might acquire the book if the publisher does not. For any given book—especially one a publisher thinks is likely to succeed—that threat comprises potential bids from many quarters. *See Arch Coal*, 329 F. Supp. 2d at 150 (continued presence of "significant number of competitors" weighs against finding merger anticompetitive). The other three members of the Big 5—HarperCollins, Hachette, and Macmillan—by themselves pose a major competitive threat in any given acquisition. In multi-bidder acquisitions where the advance was at least $250,000 and PRH and/or S&S bid, at least one of the other Big 5 also bid 90% of the time. And those three publishers collectively won only slightly fewer titles than PRH and S&S combined. The next fifteen largest publishers are a major threat as well. They include numerous name brands— like Amazon, Disney, Scholastic, and Norton—that regularly bid in multi-round auctions, pay large advances, and win prominent authors. For contracts in this segment, these publishers as a group acquired more titles in 2019-2021 than each of the other three Big 5 publishers.

In short, the merger at most reduces the number of publishers that pose a meaningful competitive threat in any given acquisition from "very many" to "still very many, but one fewer." Even viewed strictly through the government's structural lens, the merger changes the effective number of potential acquirors for any given book from *six* (the five largest plus all others in aggregate) to *five*. And the government has not cited any case rejecting a merger on the basis of market concentration alone, where five market participants remained in active competition. But again, market shares here are especially unreliable indicators of competitive forces: given how agents structure acquisitions and control publisher participation, competition is generally driven by the collective threat of competition from all possible acquirors, rather than by any specific threat posed by individual rivals in accordance with their market shares.

B. Anecdotes Of Individual Head-To-Head Competition Do Not Show Substantial Harm To The Market

Based on its complaint and discovery strategy, it is clear the government at trial will rely heavily on anecdotes about individual multi-bidder acquisitions where PRH and S&S were the two highest bidders. Such anecdotes do exist, of course, just as they would in any competitive market. But individual anecdotes are not the equivalent of marketwide data. Defendants will provide the Court with much more complete acquisition data, reflecting *thousands* of acquisitions beyond the few anecdotes the government will recite. The data show that, beyond the government's anecdotes, S&S and PRH are rarely the top two bidders—only about 7% of all acquisitions with advances of $250,000 or more. In all other acquisitions in that segment, either there was no bidding competition at all (i.e., the book was acquired through one-on-one negotiations) or other publishers provided the direct competition. The government's anecdotal stories about some acquisitions where PRH and S&S were the top two bidders reflect only a minuscule percentage of actual acquisitions. *See infra* at 37.

The government's anecdotes are also flawed even on their own terms. Some are simply incorrect and do not represent acquisitions where PRH and S&S were runners up to each other. Many appear to involve best-bid or better-best formats, where the runner up bid is unknown and thus poses no competitive constraint. And even in the few instances where they were knowingly the two final bidders, there is no basis for assuming that in that acquisition, the winner's bid necessarily would have been different if the runner up had not been present—especially considering that the agent could well have replaced the lost bidder with publisher. Finally, and in any event, the merger will *not* eliminate S&S as an independent bidder, *see infra* at 43, so the anecdotal examples of pre-merger competition actually reflect the post-merger world as well.

C. The Government's Model Does Not Prove The Merger Will Cause Harm

The government's unilateral effects theory of harm relies on a mathematical device known as a "second score auction" model ("SSA"). The SSA model attempts to predict how a merger will affect the prices of products sold in one very specific auction scenario, i.e., multi- round, multi-bidder auctions when the merging parties were the two highest bidders. The model seeks to determine whether and how eliminating one of the bidders through merger would affect the outcome of those auctions. Although the SSA by its terms applies only to a specific acquisition format, the government's expert, Dr. Nicholas Hill, assumes that its results can be applied to *all* acquisitions won by either S&S or PRH. Dr. Hill projects that in such acquisitions, the merger would reduce advances by about 6% on average. Dr. Hill admits this projected percentage translates to a reduction of just $29.3 million in total annual author compensation, out of PRH and S&S combined total average annual author compensation of $473 million in this price segment, and total author compensation marketwide of many hundreds of millions more.

The trial evidence—including the opinions of Defendants' expert, Edward Snyder, the William S. Beinecke Professor of Economics and Management at the Yale School of Management—will show that for multiple reasons, even the relatively small effect Dr. Hill projects from the SSA model is entirely unreliable.

1. Dr. Hill's Model Does Not Reflect Real-World Acquisitions

As noted, the SSA model expressly applies only to acquisitions involving multi-bid, multi-round formats—the only formats that have two "final" bidders and thus can be subject to the model, which depends on the existence (and elimination) of a runner-up bidder that constrains the winner's price. In the real world, however, the vast majority of acquisitions are structured as either a one-on-one negotiation or a best-bid auction, neither of which involves a final round where the top bidder is constrained by the runner-up. Dr. Hill nevertheless assumes that the SSA model's output applies to all acquisitions where PRH or S&S prevailed, as if every one of those acquisitions involves a competitive dynamic identical to a multiple-bidder, multiple- round auction. That assumption is facially nonsensical, and indeed is specifically rejected by the academic literature Dr. Hill cites, which demonstrates that different acquisition formats lead to different competitive effects. The Guidelines agree: "The mechanisms of these anticompetitive unilateral effects, and the indicia of their likelihood, differ somewhat according to the bargaining practices used, the auction format, and the sellers' information about one another's costs and about buyers' preferences." Guidelines § 6.2. Dr. Hill does not and cannot justify applying his model to acquisitions that lack the one feature most important to the auctions his model examines: the presence of a constraining runner-up bidder.

2. *Dr. Hill Makes Significant Errors In All Three Inputs Used In His Model*

As Dr. Hill presents it, the SSA model requires three key data inputs. Dr. Hill makes profound errors as to all three. *Diversion Ratio/Market Shares*. One key input of the SSA model is market share, which the SSA uses to determine "diversion ratios" between S&S and PRH. This ratio is essentially the estimated proportion of sales that would have been won by one of the merging buyers, but would be diverted to non-merging buyers if one of the merging buyers were eliminated. The larger the diversion ratio, the more likely it is sellers would turn to non-merging buyers, giving the combined entity less power to impose a profitable price reduction.

To determine the diversion ratio, the SSA uses market shares to estimate how often PRH and S&S were the top two bidders in acquisitions, which ostensibly identifies the frequency of post-merger diversion. But market shares significantly overpredict how often PRH and S&S are the top two bidders in book acquisitions, causing the model to overstate projected harm here.

Using market shares, Dr. Hill estimates that S&S and PRH would be the top two bidders in about 12% of acquisitions involving advances of at least $250,000 in the last several years. That percentage itself is low, but actual data from agents show that from 2018 to 2021, PRH and S&S were the top two bidders in only 21 acquisitions out of 299 in this price segment, or just *7%* of acquisitions. That low percentage reflects both the strength of other competitors and the fact that, for the multi-bidder contracts in this segment where either PRH or S&S won, the other company did not even bid for almost half of them (47%). In other words, PRH and S&S very often do not pursue the same book, even when it draws multiple bidders.

Market shares do not accurately estimate how often PRH and S&S were the top two bidders because shares do not capture the competitive makeup of individual acquisitions, which causes another error in Dr. Hill's analysis. In relying on market shares, he assumes that all publishers participate in all acquisitions in proportion to their market shares, and would continue to do so after the merger, except that one bidder in every auction would be eliminated. That assumption is categorically false—it ignores the real-world role of agents, who *choose* how many and which publishers to invite to auction (when the agent holds one). Market shares thus do not reflect how often the "lost" bidder actually participated in auctions. Market shares also cannot account for the agent's ability to replace a lost bidder by simply inviting another publisher to participate. Because Dr. Hill overlooks the likelihood of bidder replacement in real-world acquisitions, his conclusions say little about the real-world effects of the merger.

Profit Margins. A second necessary input to the SSA model is at least one of the merging parties' profit margin on book acquisitions. The margin combines with the diversion ratio to determine the extent to which the merged entity could profitably reduce advances. To simplify slightly, the higher the margin, the easier it would be for the combined entity to profitably reduce advances, even though doing so would cause some authors to divert elsewhere. If the margin is inflated, the model will necessarily exaggerate the harm by overstating the profit incentive to reduce advances.

To predict PRH and S&S margins, Dr. Hill uses data that do not reflect the actual margins they use to determine their bids in acquisition processes. He initially excluded certain marketing costs from PRH's margin, and he excluded operating expenses altogether from S&S's margin (while conversely including those same costs in the PRH margin). He later tried to cure the problem by removing operating expenses from both margins, but the resulting predicted margins still do not align with actual margins. As a result, Dr. Hill's projected harm is overstated and unreliable.

Third-Best Bid Data. Dr. Hill also uses the SSA model to quantify the projected price effect. The model assumes that the price for an asset sold at auction is determined by the *second* highest offer, because the winning bid need be only nominally higher to prevail. The second-best bid thus effectively determines how high the winning bid must be. To test the effect of a merger on the second-highest bid, the model assumes if the second-highest bidder drops out, the price would have been effectively determined by the *third*-best bid. If that bid is close to the second-highest bid, the quantifiable harm is negligible or nonexistent, as Dr. Hill himself admits. To quantify the price effect, the model assumes that shares and profitability data can be used to infer the level of the third-highest bid.

Dr. Hill's initial analysis relied on that assumption and thus offered no evidence identifying real-world differences between the second-best bid and the third-best bid, when PRH and S&S were the two highest. He again subsequently tried to cure that omission using the agent-generated data on actual acquisitions Defendants relied on, but his analysis of that data was selective and unreliable. Dr. Hill accordingly has failed to corroborate his model's assumption-based harm quantification.

3. Dr. Hill Does Not Account For Author Benefits From Merger Efficiencies

As Dr. Hill applies it, the SSA model will *always* project some price reduction, because the diversion ratio is necessarily positive—there are *some* sellers who would divert to the other merging buyer when their preferred buyer is eliminated, and the model predicts that *at least* for those sellers, eliminating the constraining runner-up bid will reduce the prices they pay. Of course, it is entirely implausible that all mergers cause adverse price effects purely by mathematical fiat. To the contrary, as the Guidelines recognize, "a primary benefit of mergers to the economy is their potential to generate significant efficiencies and thus enhance the merged firm's ability and incentive to compete," leading to better "prices, improved quality, enhanced service, or new products." Guidelines § 10. For this reason, a static market-share based model like Dr. Hill's cannot reliably assess a merger's full competitive effects. It is instead essential to evaluate the extent to which the combined entity will attain the efficiency benefits any merger seeks. Such benefits are "relevant to the competitive effects analysis of the market," and form part of the "comprehensive and holistic assessment of whether the proposed merger is likely to create or enhance market power or facilitate its exercise." *Arch Coal*, 329 F. Supp. 2d at 124, 151; *see Tenet Health Care*, 186 F.3d at 1054 (efficiencies must be considered "in the context of the competitive effects of the merger").

Courts take into account efficiency benefits that are merger-specific, verifiable, and do not arise from anticompetitive effects of an acquisition. *Anthem*, 855 F.3d at 354-56. To be merger-specific, a claimed efficiency benefit must not be "achiev[able] by either company alone" through "practical alternatives" to the merger. *Id.* at 356. But even if merger-specific, efficiency benefits "will not be considered if they are vague, speculative, or otherwise cannot be verified by reasonable means." Guidelines § 10; *see also Sysco*, 113 F. Supp. 3d at 86. Merging parties thus must "present substantiation" showing that claimed efficiency benefits are concrete and non-speculative, but the merging parties need not secure independent verification of them. Dep't of Justice & Fed. Trade Comm'n, *Commentary on the Horizontal Merger Guidelines*, at 52 (Mar. 2006). Efficiencies "substantiated by analogous past experience" are the "most likely to be credited." *Deutsche Telekom*, 439 F. Supp. 3d at 213, 216–17 (quoting Guidelines § 10). Efficiencies resulting from consolidating operations among separate facilities are also especially "susceptible to verification." *Id.* at 213 (quoting Guidelines § 10).

To evaluate the merits of acquiring S&S, senior PRH executives with experience in analyzing business combinations thoroughly analyzed the merger's costs and benefits. The resulting "PRH Efficiencies Model" identifies four distinct ways in which the merger will improve the combined entity's net income over what each entity could achieve separately. First, the merger will increase the number of books sold at retail by providing S&S authors access to PRH's premier supply chain. Absent a merger, the investments required by S&S to create such a system would be costly, time-consuming, and impractical. Second, the merger will reduce variable costs, including especially the significant costs incurred when unsold books are returned to the publisher. PRH has consistently reduced the "return rates" of previously acquired companies by incorporating their books into PRH's distribution system, and it expects to do the same for S&S's return rate. Third, the combined company will decrease operating expenses by reducing duplicative sales, marketing, and administrative positions. PRH does not eliminate editorial roles after acquisitions—it considers editorial expertise additive, not redundant—but "de-duplicating" other positions will reduce costs significantly. Finally, the combined company will save real estate costs by reducing redundant properties and consolidating employees into existing PRH offices.

As the trial evidence will show, none of these efficiencies could reasonably be achieved by either entity absent the merger, and none of them stems from anticompetitive reductions in output or quality. They are not speculative, but instead are verified by past experience: in prior mergers, PRH achieved efficiency benefits even *greater* than expected, creating access to more money it has deployed to win the most attractive books and thereby better compete downstream.

Professor Snyder will show how the foregoing gains from cost savings and revenue enhancement will directly benefit authors. Given the intensity of downstream competition, publishers always have strong incentives to use their gains to win more titles, especially those considered most likely to succeed. With greater net income, the combined company will not only offer higher advances, it will also bid on more books from more authors—an author benefit the government ignores entirely. The historical pattern at both PRH and S&S shows the effect of this incentive: as Professor Snyder will demonstrate, based on the observed correlation between each entity's net income and total author compensation, authors have consistently received 60% or more of each firm's resources gained. That relationship between publisher income and author compensation reflects basic industry economics. A publisher's willingness to pay for any given book is largely a function of its expected revenues from sales of the book, minus the variable and operating costs associated with the book. For each potential acquisition, these revenue and cost factors are reflected in a "profit and loss" ("P&L") projection prepared before the editor she makes an offer for a book. When publisher income rises because revenues are enhanced and costs are reduced, the projected profit margin on each book increases automatically, giving the editor room to offer a higher advance for a given book without diminishing the profit the publisher would have received pre-merger. And publishers will seize that opportunity, because acquiring successful books is the best way to compete effectively in selling books to consumers.

Based on the cognizable efficiencies quantified in the PRH Efficiencies Model (with reductions conservatively made by Professor Snyder for efficiencies he did not consider adequately merger-specific), Professor Snyder will opine that the merger will produce gains for the merged entity that will translate to an increase in total annual author compensation for all U.S. book rights of $75 million to $107 million in 2025. Dr. Hill's model simply ignores those gains. On its own terms—leaving aside the flaws described above—the model implies that the merger will reduce total author compensation in the segment of books acquired for advances of at least $250,000 by only $29.3 million. Accordingly, depending on exactly how the merger's gains to authors are distributed across all price segments, the merger could well *increase* author compensation in this price segment. And the merger need achieve only a fraction of the gains PRH anticipates to wipe out Dr. Hill's projected harms. At a minimum, any fair accounting for the merger's gains to authors would drive his projected harms down toward zero, eliminating any confidence that his model projects enough marketwide harm to justify blocking the merger.

4. No Bidder Will Be Eliminated By The Merger

A § 7 merger challenge involves a predictive judgment, and here the government's predictions rest on the crucial assumption that after the merger, S&S will no longer exist as an independent bidding force. The government will not be able to substantiate that assumption. In fact, S&S will remain an independent bidding entity, consistent with longstanding PRH practice, the practice of other publishers, and recognized business organization theory.

A key value for PRH is internal competition, which PRH views as good for business: it increases the likelihood that PRH—via one of its imprints—will acquire the book, and it ensures that the book and its author are matched with the best editor for the project. Consistent with its longstanding internal competition policy, PRH has publicly announced to its agent-partners that it will allow PRH imprints to bid against S&S imprints (and vice versa), even when they are the only bidders in an auction. *See supra* at 10.

When evaluating the competitive effects of a merger, courts take such commitments into consideration. *See, e.g., FTC v. Butterworth Health Corp.*, 946 F. Supp. 1285, 1298 (W.D. Mich. 1996) (concluding that hospital merger was unlikely to harm competition in part because of "formal assurances" hospitals made regarding prices, which bespoke "a serious commitment by defendants … to refrain from exercising market power in ways injurious to the consuming public"), *aff'd*, 121 F.3d 708 (6th Cir. 1997) (per curiam). To be sure, a commitment to certain post-merger conduct does not factor *automatically* into predictions about post-merger effects.

The commitment must be credible, concrete, and supported by evidence—just like any other prediction or assumption about the post-merger world. *See U.S. v. Aetna Inc.*, 240 F. Supp. 3d 1, 60 (D.D.C. 2017) ("[E]vidence about the likelihood of the [post-merger] divestiture goes to the weight of the evidence regarding the divestiture's effects.").

Here, the evidence shows that S&S will in fact remain an independent bidding force after the merger. As noted, internal bidding competition is a longstanding PRH policy—a strategy that helped lead to its industry-leading position. Other publishers pursue similar internal competition strategies. Well-recognized business organization theory validates reliance on internal competition to maximize enterprise performance. And PRH made a public commitment to agents that S&S would be treated as an independent bidder after the merger (even absent an outside bidder). Reneging on that assurance would violate the trust between PRH and its author- agent partners that is essential to PRH's ability to compete successfully for book rights.

These facts demonstrate conclusively that PRH's commitment to treating S&S as an independent bidder is not illusory or a policy manufactured merely to obtain merger approval. It is a serious business commitment that will govern its post-merger conduct.

5. Dr. Hill's Model Does Not Reflect Experience From PRH's Prior Merger

The 2013 merger of Random House and Penguin confirms that this merger will not reduce author advances. The Guidelines recognize that a "recent merger ... in the relevant market" can represent a "'natural experiment'" that is "informative regarding the competitive effects of the merger" under review. Guidelines § 2.1.2. Put more sharply, the surest "way to test a model is to compare its projection against real outcomes." *NRDC v. Jackson*, 650 F.3d 662, 665 (7th Cir. 2011).The government's model of harm fails that test. When Random House and Penguin merged, they were the first and second largest publishers respectively, with a combined market share in tradebook sales similar to that of PRH and S&S today. Based on those market shares and assuming comparable margins, the government's model would have projected a reduction in advances comparable to, or even greater than, the model predicts here. The evidence will show, however, that the 2013 merger had no negative effect on author advances. In fact, advances trended *upwards* in subsequent years. The 2013 merger did not cause the harm the government's model would project because that model does not accurately capture the real-world conditions of this industry. *See supra* at 35-36.

III. THE GOVERNMENT WILL NOT PROVE AN INCREASED LIKELIHOOD OF COORDINATION AFTER THE MERGER

The government's final theory of harm is that the merger will lead to "coordinated conduct" among the remaining publishers in the market for anticipated top-selling books. Coordination—sometimes referred to as "tacit collusion" or "conscious parallelism"—is the process "by which firms in a concentrated market might in effect share monopoly power ... by recognizing their shared economic interests and their interdependence with respect to price and output decisions." *Brooke Grp.*, 509 U.S. at 227. Coordination between rivals can occur only if the firms can solve what economists call "cartel problems," *i.e.*, the difficulties of maintaining a consensus to take actions that would *not* be in each company's individual interest absent coordination. *See* George J. Stigler, *A Theory of Oligopoly*, 72 J. Pol. Econ. 44, 44-46 (1964).

These problems make the "anticompetitive minuet" of tacit coordination "most difficult to compose and to perform." *Brooke Grp.*, 509 U.S. at 227-28.

The first step—establishing a tacit consensus—"requires harmonizing the incentives of participating firms and mitigating firm uncertainty concerning rival firms, so that they can effectively coordinate their behavior." *In re B.F. Goodrich Co.*, 110 F.T.C. 207, 295 (1988), *as modified by* 112 F.T.C. 83 (July 18, 1989). The second step—enforcing the consensus—is equally critical, because without "mutual trust and forbearance ... an informal collusive arrangement is unlikely to overcome the temptation to steal a march on a fellow colluder by undercutting him slightly." *Hosp. Corp. of Am. v. FTC*, 807 F.2d 1381, 1388-89 (7th Cir. 1986). Consequently, firms will not coordinate unless they can "retaliate effectively if and when cheating occurs." *Goodrich*, 110 F.T.C. at 295. To block a merger based on a likelihood of coordinated effects, then, the government must prove that "market conditions, on the whole, are conducive to [1] reaching terms of coordination and [2] detecting and punishing deviations from those terms." *H & R Block*, 833 F. Supp. 2d at 77 (cleaned up).

The government will not make that showing. The government's own expert concedes as much: Dr. Hill will testify at trial that he cannot say the merger is more likely than not to cause increased coordination. And indeed it will not, as the evidence will show.

A. Multiple Features Of The Publishing Industry Preclude Coordination

1. *Differentiated Products And Non-Transparent Pricing*

It is well recognized that a merger is unlikely to increase coordinated conduct where the product is non-homogenous and pricing is non-transparent. As the Guidelines put it, coordination is likely to succeed only when "each competitively important firm's significant competitive initiatives can be promptly and confidently observed by that firm's rivals," which is "more likely" when price terms "are relatively transparent" and products are "relatively homogeneous." Guidelines § 7.2; *see Arch Coal*, 329 F. Supp. 2d at 144-45 (non-transparent pricing leads to "limited, imperfect, and largely unreliable and untimely" information about rivals' conduct, making coordination "unlikely to succeed," and heterogeneity likewise "limit or impede the ability of firms to reach terms of coordination"); *Deutsche Telekom*, 439 F. Supp. 3d at 239 (coordination more likely in markets where pricing is "more transparent"); *Oracle*, 331 F. Supp. 2d at 1113 ("Factors that increase the likelihood of coordination include product homogeneity, pricing standardization and pricing transparency.").

As discussed, books are the most non-homogenous, subjectively-valued products one can imagine. Because the monetary terms for every unique book depend on individualized judgments about its "value," knowing how much a rival paid for a given book reveals nothing about whether that publisher departed from an implicit agreement or conveyed a signal about future acquisitions of other unique books. To be sure, agents and editors often try to identify loosely comparable books as baselines for their valuation, but such "comps" are hardly precision devices, and even identifying useful "comps" is itself a highly subjective endeavor—different editors within the same publisher often choose different "comps" for the same book.

Non-transparent pricing also precludes coordination. Given agents' control over bidding information, there is little opportunity to coordinate or signal in real time. *See Arch Coal*, 329 F. Supp. 2d at 144 ("The emphasis on sealed bids and confidentiality [during bidding] is an important aspect of the market structure and dynamics that would frustrate coordination among producers."). Final advance amounts are sometimes reported after the fact, but usually only in general ranges, and even that information is sporadic and unreliable, precluding timely responses. *See id.* at 145 (coordination unlikely where "cheating" and "punishment" would not occur "until well after the fact"). Terms like advance payout timing and royalty rates are also independently negotiated and non-public, precluding tacit agreement on such terms.

2. *Non-Price Competition*

Another factor precluding coordination is competition over non-price terms, which makes coordination less likely when such terms are subjective, variable, and undisclosed. *See Deutsche Telekom*, 439 F. Supp. 3d at 235, 240. Because authors often pursue subjective non-price preferences in acquisitions, *see supra* at 8, it is impossible to determine from the advance alone exactly what pricing strategy the publisher applied, how that strategy would apply to other books, and whether the advance deviated from a tacit understanding about acquisition terms.

3. *Ease Of Entry And Expansion*

Coordination by incumbents is difficult when new firms can easily enter and take up slack created by non-competitive coordination. *See Deutsche Telekom*, 439 F. Supp. 3d at 237; *cf. Arch Coal*, 329 F. Supp. 2d at 138 ("Barriers to entry ... increase the likelihood of coordinated interaction."). The same dynamic applies when smaller firms can easily expand.

Guidelines § 7.2 (coordination less likely when market includes "participants with small market shares and little stake in the outcome resulting from the coordinated conduct, if these firms can rapidly expand their sales in the relevant market"). The easy of expansion and entry here, *see supra* at 31, further precludes any likelihood of coordination.

B. Given Strong Downstream Competition To Sell Books, Publishers Would Have Little Incentive To Coordinate Upstream

To establish that a merger is likely to result in coordinated conduct, the government must prove that the merger would increase incumbent rivals' incentives to coordinate their pricing.

See supra at 46. The government cannot make that showing here, especially given the strong incentive to succeed in the vigorous competition to sell books to consumers. That downstream competition—which the merger will not diminish in any way—gives every publisher an incentive to compete aggressively against rivals to acquire books upstream, especially those books predicted to perform well among readers. Even if it were possible to reach some tacit understanding on advances, every publisher would have a strong incentive to undercut that agreement wherever possible, in order to outcompete rivals and grow market share downstream.

C. The Merger Will Not Increase The Incentive Or Opportunity To Coordinate In Author Recruitment

The government also asserts that the merger will increase the likelihood publishers will tacitly agree not to "poach" successful authors from existing relationships. But the same strong interest in competing downstream that disincentivizes coordination on pricing would also strongly incentivize publishers to deviate from any agreement not to poach the most successful authors. And the same ease of entry and expansion that makes any pricing agreement effectively unenforceable would mean the same for an anti-poaching agreement.

D. The Ebooks Case Does Not Show That The Merger Will Increase The Likelihood Of Coordination

The government's tacit coordination theory relies heavily on *U.S. v. Apple, Inc.*, 791 F.3d 290 (2d Cir. 2015), which affirmed a judgment that Apple had orchestrated a conspiracy with certain major publishers to increase *downstream* retail prices of digital books ("ebooks"). The case involved a "hub-and-spoke" conspiracy, organized by Apple at the "hub" and imposed through the "spokes" of its separate contracts with publishers, each of which agreed that Apple's ebook outlet would charge specified retail prices. Although each price agreement individually was contrary to the publisher's financial interest, the court held that Apple induced them all to agree by organizing communications and engineering a collusive understanding that each would accept the same term, thereby promoting their collective long-term interest in avoiding low-price ebooks competition from Amazon. *Id.* at 318 ("Apple consciously played a key role in organizing their express collusion.").

The finding that Apple orchestrated a conspiracy concerning downstream price competition for ebooks is not relevant here. For one thing, neither Random House nor Bertelsmann was even accused of participating in the conspiracy. For another, as the Guidelines state, prior coordination in a different product market matters only if "the salient characteristics of that other market at the time of the collusion are *closely comparable* to those in the relevant market." Guidelines § 7.2 (emphasis added). The dynamics of retail bookselling are not at all comparable—much less *closely* comparable—to the acquisition of book rights. Retail book prices are wholly transparent and easily monitored for any deviation from express or implied agreement. By contrast, book-acquisition pricing is completely non-transparent, subjective, and individualized, precluding monitoring and enforcement of any tacit agreement. *See supra* at 46-48. Finally, there is no third-party entity here with the incentive and ability to organize collusive behavior to serve its own independent business objectives.

CONCLUSION

For all the foregoing reasons, and based on the evidence to be adduced at trial, this Court should grant judgment for Defendants and permit this merger to proceed.

Dated: July 15, 2022

Respectfully submitted,

Attorneys for Defendants Bertelsmann SE & Co. KGaA and Penguin Random House LLC

Daniel M. Petrocelli (appearing *pro hac vice*)

M. Randall Oppenheimer (appearing *pro hac vice*)
O'Melveny & Myers LLP
1999 Avenue of the Stars
Los Angeles, CA 90067
Andrew J. Frackman (appearing *pro hac vice*)
Abby F. Rudzin (appearing *pro hac vice*)
O'Melveny & Myers LLP
Seven Times Square
New York, NY 10026
Courtney Dyer (D.C. Bar No. 490805)
Julia Schiller (D.C. Bar No. 986369)
O'Melveny & Myers LLP
1625 Eye Street NW
Washington, D.C. 20006
Deborah L. Feinstein (D.C. Bar No. 412109)
Jason Ewart (D.C. Bar No. 484126)
Arnold & Porter
601 Massachusetts Ave. NW
Washington, D.C. 20001
Attorneys for Defendants Paramount Global (f/k/a ViacomCBS Inc.) and Simon & Schuster, Inc.
Stephen R. Fishbein (appearing *pro hac vice*)
Jessica K. Delbaum (appearing *pro hac vice*)
Shearman & Sterling LLP
599 Lexington Avenue
New York, NY 10022
Ryan Shores (D.C. Bar No. 500031)
Michael Mitchell (D.C. Bar No. 1531689)
Shearman & Sterling LLP
401 9th Street, N.W., Suite 800
Washington, D.C. 20004
Rachel E. Mossman (D.C. Bar No. 1016255)
Shearman & Sterling LLP
2828 North Harwood Street, Suite 1800
Dallas, TX 75201

APPENDIX D: SELECTED TRIAL EXHIBITS

Overview of Exhibits from The Trial

At the conclusion of the trial, the parties published to the docket about 150 exhibits officially entered into evidence, comprising about 800 pages in all. We examined all of those documents and present an edited selection of about 30 exhibits.

Some documents were important reference points during the trial and are shown here in full – to the extent that we can, given the redactions – to provide a little more context. From PRH, those include pitches to authors, and internal memos about such topics as: Leveraging Bertelsmann printing assets, regaining lost market share, avoiding "internal upbidding," various examples of coordination of auction bids, and marketing efforts for big "lead" and "opportunity" titles. From S&S, those include Carolyn Reidy's memos explaining her business to CBS leadership and discussing changes in the printing landscape, along with Jonathan Karp's correspondence with John Irving and his request that ViacomCBS consider selling to a financial buyer.

A number of documents included figures and statistics of broad interest, including an analysis of the decline in PRH's fiction sales, a calculation of synergies following the Penguin Random House merger, information on advances paid to PRH authors over the years, and a number of charts prepared by the two economics experts who testified.

Those data are all well worth closer examination. The fiction data shows variations in sales among formats and divisions and underscores big changes in genre fiction markets. The advance trends show that PRH talks about advance commitments two ways: Actual advances $508 million in 2018 – as well as refreshers and bonuses (for another $61 million that year).

We also learn that in 2018, average advances for new works at PRH were $305,000 for adult books and a little under $50,000 for children's books (with the Obama deal set aside). The median advances for the two groups were $100,000 for adult books and $20,000 for children's books. PRH executed a little over 2,500 contracts that year. You will glean many other facts like these from the data exhibits.

And a few documents are included here for historical interest (a memo explaining the integration of Crown into Random House) or general insights into the publishing process (including discussions of the payout of advances). There is also an agent's auction letter that exemplifies "The Workaround," used to keep auctions going even when PRH imprints are the top bidders. It also exposes the defense's notions about the significance of "best bids" auctions, since it's "a three-round best bids auction" with a possible fourth round at the end – which is therefore not best bids at all, but a different way of bidding in rounds.

There are still other interesting details that we learned from some of the exhibits not included here, such as:

In one document responding to requests from the government, PRH represents it has spent "nearly $257 million on supply chain improvement, including estimated up-front and annual spend" since 2009. About $159 million cumulatively was spent following the 2013 merger with Penguin.

PRH reports that it was April 2020 when it "issued global audio policy guidelines to PRH affiliates throughout the world" describing their longstanding US policy of generally requiring audio rights when they acquire a book (while saying they have made "exceptions of a case-by-case basis, usually for authors who have pre-existing audio relationships"). The same document details their payout guidelines for different divisions.

In a separate response to the same set of government queries, S&S noted that it pays advances of between $100,000 and $1 million in four parts. Larger deals are paid out in fifths, and they "may exercise greater flexibility" on the payout of smaller advances.

We learned from two documents that the "financial partner" Bertelsmann considered partnering with to help finance the purchase of S&S was New York-based investment firm Atairos—though they decided in early November 2020 that doing the deal on their own "had significantly more potential to enhance value for Bertelsmann."

Date: Tuesday, October 22, 2019 10:25 AM
Subject: Agenda and documents for the preparation of Board of Directors meeting 10/19 on 29 October 2019 in Gütersloh 11
From: Guerra, Esther
To: Dahle, Markus
CC: Sawhney, Divya Oberdorf, Anya
Attachments: TO_VS_10-2019.pdf; TOP02_Rabe_Nachgenehmigung pdf; TOP02_Rabe_Nachgenehmigung pdf; TOP03_Kapitalallokation_2020-2022_1019.pdf

Subject: Agenda and documents for the preparation of the Executive board meeting 10/19 on October 29, 2019 in Gütersloh

Gentlemen,

In preparation for the short-notice Board of Directors meeting scheduled for October 29, 2019, we have attached the agenda and prepared documents.
The documents for TOP 2 will be discussed in detail at the Investment Committee meeting, to which you have already been invited.
The necessary resolution will be made in the subsequent meeting of the Board of Directors.

The documents obtained for TOP 3 "Capital Allocation" are also attached.

Best wishes, Silke Tilk

Dear Sirs,

In preparation for the Executive Board meeting scheduled for 29 October 2019, we are sending you the agenda and preparatory documents attached.
The documents for Item 2 will be discussed in detail at the meeting of the Investment Committee to which you have already been invited.
The required resolution will be made in the subsequent meeting of the Executive Board.

The documents for TOP 3 "Capital Allocation" are also attached.

Best regards
Silke Tilk

Esther Guerra
Penguin Random House

US v. Bertelsmann
1:21-cv-0866-FYP
PX 0080-A

CONFIDENTIAL **BPRH-002749205**

BPRH-002749205-T001

Capital Allocation 2020-22

October 2019

Bertelsmann
4(c)-30
Jan. 8, 2021

BERTELSMANN

CONFIDENTIAL COMMERCIAL INFORMATION PURSUANT TO 28 C.F.R. § 16.7

US v. Bertelsmann
1:21-cv-0866-FYP
PX 0080-E

CONFIDENTIAL

BPRH-002749216

BPRH-002749216-T001

PRH B1/B2: Purchase of competitor (here: Simon & Schuster) – **Valuation of > €1bn expected; relief in subsequent years through synergy effects and cash flow contribution**

Classification of projects

Strategic thrust	1 Boosting core businesses - Consolidation -
Market characteristics	size (2018): US$ 17.1m[1] Growth: +3% annual (2018 vs. 2016) Structure: Oligopoly, in addition to PRH only four other major trade publishers[2] Cyclicality: Small, stable business Barriers to entry: High (especially reputation, sales)
Business characteristics (Simon & Schuster)	Market position: #5 Publishing house worldwide Market share: ~4-5%[3] (2018) in the USA[1] EBITDA-Marge: [redacted] Scalability: High Risks: Amazon's market position and falling stationary trade lead to or require margin concessions on the part of the publishers
Value-added concept	Synergies through consolidation, for example, central functions and logistics; stronger counterweight vs. Amazon; Increase attractiveness for authors

Possible financial impact[4], in €m

	1 Total S&S acquisition			2 Partial S&S acquisition[5]		
	T0	T1	T2	T0	T1	T2
Sales	717	717	717	359	359	359
Op. EBITDA (adj.) standalone	[redacted]	[redacted]	[redacted]	[redacted]	[redacted]	[redacted]
Synergies[6]	[redacted]	[redacted]	[redacted]	[redacted]	[redacted]	[redacted]
Op. EBITDA (adj.) combined	[redacted]	[redacted]	[redacted]	[redacted]	[redacted]	[redacted]
D&A (adj.) before any Start-ups	[redacted]	[redacted]	[redacted]	[redacted]	[redacted]	[redacted]
Adjustments	[redacted]	[redacted]	[redacted]	[redacted]	[redacted]	[redacted]
Op. EBIT	[redacted]	[redacted]	[redacted]	[redacted]	[redacted]	[redacted]
FCF	[redacted]	[redacted]	[redacted]	[redacted]	[redacted]	[redacted]
Purchase Price	[redacted]	[redacted]	[redacted]	[redacted]	[redacted]	[redacted]
EV/EBITDA '18 (100%)	[redacted]	[redacted]	[redacted]	[redacted]	[redacted]	[redacted]
Present value synergies	[redacted]	[redacted]	[redacted]	[redacted]	[redacted]	[redacted]
Effects Financial Margin, in €m	[redacted]	[redacted]	[redacted]	[redacted]	[redacted]	[redacted]

1) US publishing sales of print books, e-books and audio downloads as well as Amazon/self-publishing sale s2) Hachette, Harper Collins, Macmillan and S&S 3) No regional sales breakdown available; if US share between 70-100% 4) Assumptions: Constant update P&L S&S 2018 (including central overhead CBS allocation) + integration effects, CCR 100%, Integration from 01/01/2021 5) 50% assumption 6) K 10% cost savings with 3 year start-up

DEFENDANTS' TRIAL EXHIBIT
DX-076

Date:	Saturday, December 14 2019 03:51 PM
Subject:	Re: US Developments Deck
From:	Sawhney, Divya
To:	Dohle, Markus ; Von Schilling, Claire
CC:	Malaviya, Nihar
Attachments:	US Deck - 12.13.19_Final.pptx; US Deck - 12.13.19_Final.pdf

Hi Markus and Claire,

Here is the US Market and PRH Development deck Markus was referring to.

- The **US Market data** covers 2013 through 2019, with 2019 a combination of YTD and an estimate for the remaining months. Markus – in your printout, we had noted our fiction share is down 5% - this should unfortunately be 7% down and has been adjusted here.
- The **PRH US data** on slides 7 and 8 cover 2014 through 2018.

Our suggestion is to hold off on taking these slides into the TR meeting. Nihar is already working on some fiction cuts as he mentioned.

Please let us know if you have additional questions.

Divya

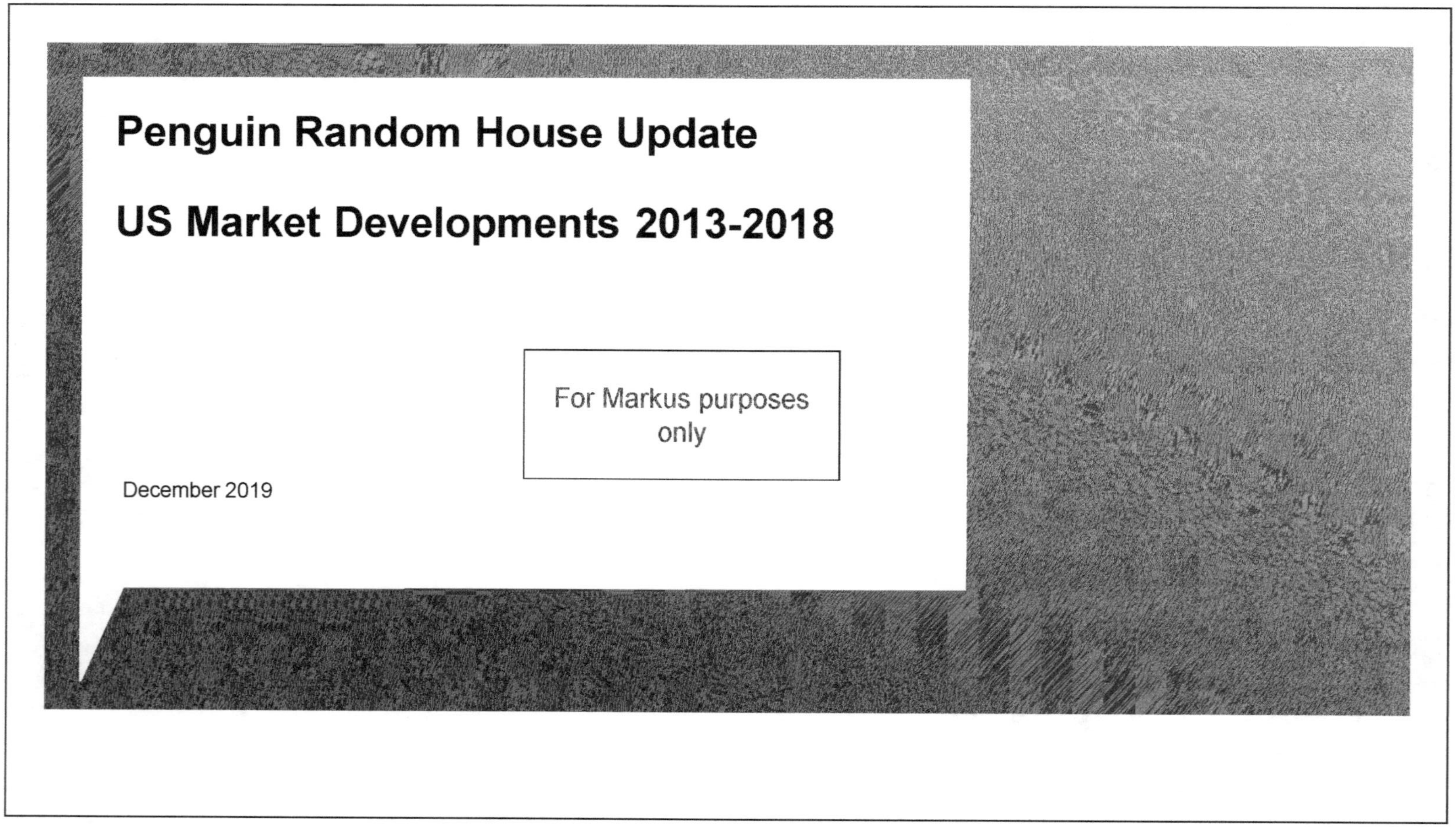
Penguin Random House Update
US Market Developments 2013-2018
For Markus purposes only
December 2019

Case 1:21-cv-02886-FYP Document 181-8 Filed 09/08/22 Page 3 of 3

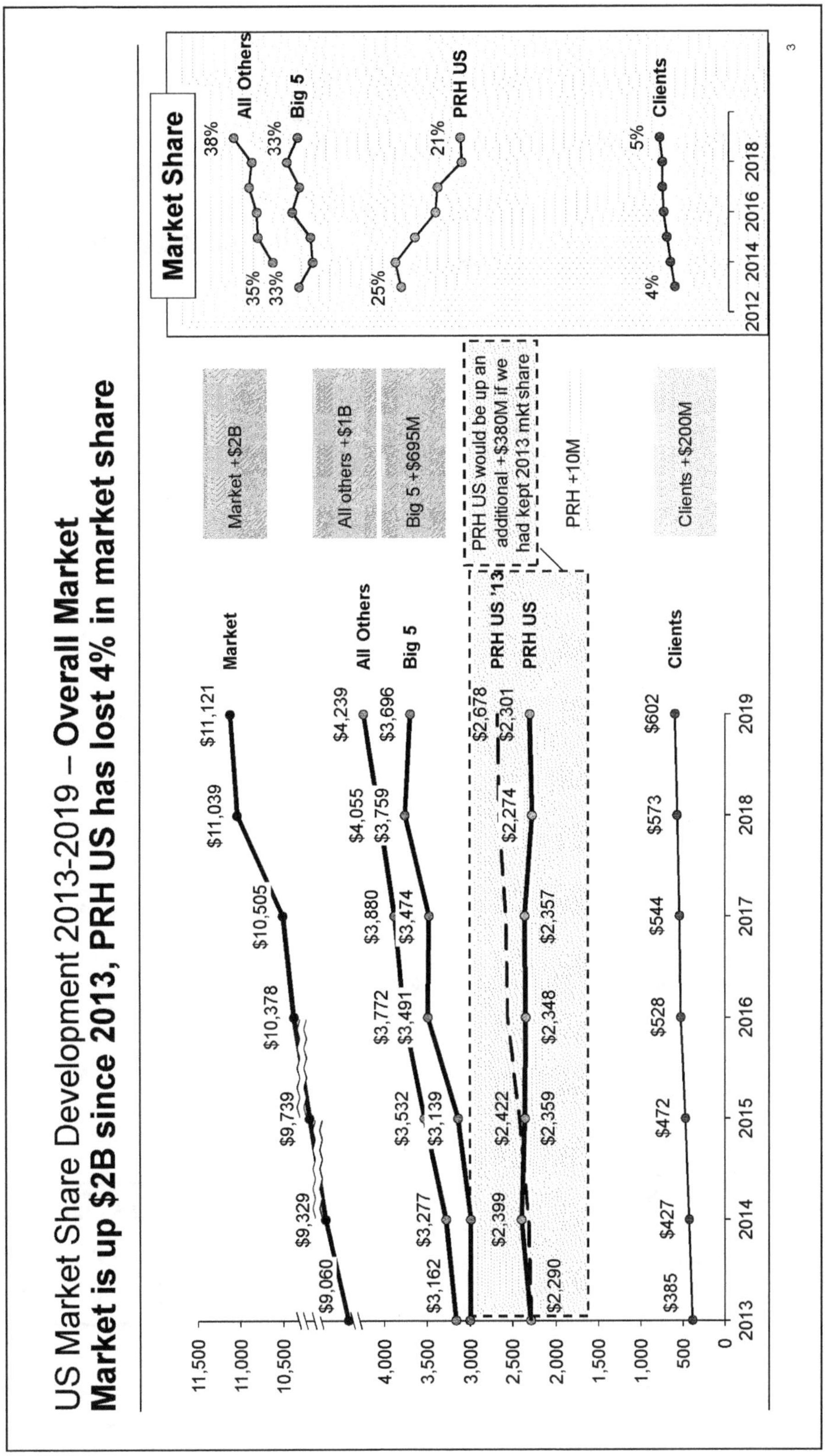

CONFIDENTIAL

DX-076.0004

BPRH-002756362

Date:	Thursday, July 2 2020 10:12 AM
Subject:	RE: Silk Management Presentation (Wed 7/1)
From:	Malaviya, Nihar <[redacted]>
To:	Sansigre, Manuel <[redacted]>; Dohle, Markus <[redacted]>; Deedy, Cara <[redacted]>; Johnston, James <[redacted]>; Sawhney, Divya <[redacted]>; Oberdorf, Anya <[redacted]>; Stoeger, Lea <[redacted]>; Polinsky, Lev <[redacted]>;
CC:	Steinecke, Anke <[redacted]>;
Attachments:	image001.png

Hi Manuel,

Thanks for doing this great analysis.
I think that we can add in two more factors in here to make the story richer.

1. Sales – audio – we should include in audio in the picture below – as probably the majority of the audio sales are substituting from other formats. Unfortunately, we won't be able to separate out Penguin and Random House from an Audio perspective as they are combined in a single division, however at the total level – audio in fiction has grown by 60 million over this time frame – it that does reduce the sales decline in Fiction to be near ~200 million level – which is still very high.
2. Advances - our advance investment in Fiction has also gone down between these years – we spent around $285 million in advances on fiction titles whose first format was published in 2011 vs $190 million on fiction titles whose first format was published in 2020. This is not a perfect proxy for sales – as we're only measuring part of the frontlist and does not represent all commitments that we entered into that year – but it does show that the $200 million reduction in sales was accompanied by almost a $100 million reduction in advances for this category. Incidentally, advance for the titles published in non fiction and juvenile went up collectively by $30 million over the same time period – so overall advances did go down by $70 million.

I created the following table showing the sales development across all formats by category along with the advance developments. There's not a 1 to 1 match between overall sales in a given year and advances paid on the titles published in that year – but there's a definite relationship (and especially if we ignore the growth in backlist).
A couple of caveats to consider here:

1. The numbers won't match exactly what you pulled – as it depends on which parameters that were used. But they are consistent with each other (e.g. the same parameters were used for 2011 vs 2019)
2. 2011 was a low point for net sales for the combined company – with $2.02 billion in net sales. Both 2010 and 2013 (excl. 2012 craziness) were $2.16 billion. So the sales comparison is somewhat favorable to us with 2011 as a baseline. I added in 2010 also as a comparison point

Net Sales	**2010**	**2011**	**2019**	**2011 vs 2019**	**2010 vs 2019**
Fiction	1000	975	777	-198	-223
Non Fiction	727	610	777	167	50
Juvenile	432	435	512	77	80
Total	**2159**	**2020**	**2066**	**46**	**-93**

Advances	**2010**	**2011**	**2019**	**2011 vs 2019**	**2010 vs 2019**
Fiction	293	286	190	-96	-103
Non Fiction	197	172	183	11	-14
Juvenile	27	35	47	12	20
Total	**517**	**493**	**420**	**-73**	**-97**

US v. Bertelsmann
1:21-cv-0866-FYP
PX 0092

CONFIDENTIAL BPRH-002878013

So if we just focus on the totals – we can say that we have become more efficient as a company – even using 2010 as a baseline – our sales decline basically matches our advance decline (and as there are other variable costs to consider – so, our profitability has improved). If we use 2011 as baseline – the same story gets even stronger.
One further caveat is that I'm ignoring the growth in backlist between 2010/2011 vs 2019 for the time being – if we factor that in – the story is not as strong (frontlist is down about $200 million between 2011 and 2019 – all in fiction, while advances are only down $100 million – so we can still make a similar story but it's just not as strong).

Any further thoughts?

Nihar

From: Sansigre, Manuel
Sent: Thursday, July 2, 2020 12:08 AM
To: Dohle, Markus <[redacted]>; Deedy, Cara <[redacted]>; Johnston, James <[redacted]>; Sawhney, Divya <[redacted]>; Oberdorf, Anya <[redacted]>; Stoeger, Lea <[redacted]>; Polinsky, Lev <[redacted]>; Malaviya, Nihar <[redacted]>
Cc: Steinecke, Anke <[redacted]>
Subject: RE: Silk Management Presentation (Wed 7/1)

Hi all,
Just wanted to close the loop on our discussion about losing market share and mass market in the US. I ran an analysis on the fiction sales, excluded audio and just for core US (no intercompany nor international).
As you can see below, Fiction Net Sales were $933m in 2011 vs $658m in 2019, so a loss of $275m. The erosion is both cross format (audio is excluded but added $75m net sales for fiction) and for both Penguin and RH.

Fiction Net Sales (USD mn)	2011	2019	change
Core Penguin	**453.5**	**318.9**	**(134.7)**
Electronic	149.3	127.0	(22.3)
Hard Cover	100.0	88.3	(11.7)
Mass Market	97.3	36.0	(61.3)
Trade Pbk	106.9	67.6	(39.3)
Core RH	**480.4**	**339.2**	**(141.2)**
Electronic	166.9	108.4	(58.5)
Hard Cover	128.3	109.4	(18.9)
Mass Market	77.9	30.9	(47.1)
Trade Pbk	107.3	90.5	(16.8)
Grand Total	**933.9**	**658.1**	**(275.8)**

This erosion was basically created by 4 categories: Fantasy, Mystery, Romance and Sci-Fi; specifically Mystery. And also not just in mass market.

Net Sales	2011					2019			
(USD mn)	Fantasy	Mystery	Romance	SCI-FI	Total	Fantasy	Mystery	Romance	SCI-FI
Core Penguin	**44.2**	**55.4**	**53.2**	**7.0**	**159.6**	**11.6**	**9.9**	**13.8**	**3.6**
Electronic	19.4	13.2	26.8	2.5	61.9	7.4	7.5	10.3	1.9
Hard Cover	14.8	25.0	4.4	1.2	45.4	0.7	(0.2)	0.3	0.2
Mass Market	7.5	13.9	15.2	2.7	39.2	2.1	1.1	1.6	0.9
Trade Pbk	2.5	3.3	6.8	0.5	13.1	1.4	1.5	1.7	0.6
Core RH	**54.9**	**90.8**	**25.9**	**18.0**	**189.5**	**21.1**	**8.0**	**7.1**	**11.8**
Electronic	17.0	31.0	11.9	6.2	66.1	6.1	5.1	4.5	4.4
Hard Cover	12.5	31.5	4.3	4.6	52.9	3.6	0.2	0.1	0.7
Mass Market	18.6	13.1	8.6	4.4	44.7	8.1	0.4	0.7	1.8
Trade Pbk	6.7	15.2	1.2	2.8	25.8	3.2	2.2	1.8	5.0
Grand Total	**99.0**	**146.1**	**79.1**	**24.9**	**349.2**	**32.6**	**17.9**	**20.8**	**15.5**
Electronic	36.4	44.2	38.6	8.8	128.1	13.5	12.6	14.7	6.3
Hard Cover	27.3	56.5	8.7	5.8	98.3	4.3	0.0	0.4	0.9
Mass Market	26.1	27.0	23.7	7.1	83.9	10.2	1.5	2.3	2.7
Trade Pbk	9.1	18.4	8.1	3.3	38.9	4.6	3.7	3.5	5.6

So, bottom line it seems that we loss $262m in commercial fiction, that if we use an average contribution margin of (maybe lower) is basically an erosion of in contribution.

As this is a bridge between 2019 and 2011, I am not sure if the story is that RH did that rationalization first and then we did Penguin.

I would love to hear your thoughts and see if this story makes sense

Thanks
Manuel

-----Original Appointment-----
From: Dohle, Markus < >
Sent: Monday, June 29, 2020 2:35 PM
To: Dohle, Markus; Deedy, Cara; Johnston, James; Sawhney, Divya; Oberdorf, Anya; Stoeger, Lea; Sansigre, Manuel; Polinsky, Lev; Malaviya, Nihar
Cc: Steinecke, Anke
Subject: Silk Management Presentation (Wed 7/1)
When: Wednesday, July 1, 2020 12:00 PM-2:00 PM (UTC-05:00) Eastern Time (US & Canada).
Where: Webex Below

-- Do not delete or change any of the following text. --

When it's time, join your Webex meeting here.

Meeting number (access code):
Meeting password:

Date: Friday, September 11 2020 11:16 AM
Subject: FW: fiction & MS generally
From: McIntosh, Madeline
To: [redacted]
Attachments: FINAL - 2019 US Marketplace Analysis - Adult Fiction.pdf; DRAFT - 2020 US Marketplace Update - Fiction Analysis Pt II - August 2020.pdf

---

From: Welsh, Reid
Sent: Thursday, August 6, 2020 3:32 PM
To: Updike, Jaci < [redacted]; Von Moltke, Nina [redacted] McIntosh, Madeline [redacted]
Subject: RE: fiction & MS generally

Hi all,

As mentioned, I am attaching our current working draft of the Fiction Analysis Pt. 2 as well as the original fiction deck discussed back in February. Our current draft covers most of the main topics of discussion, with the exception of pricing which we are currently looking into and will include in a final version.

Looking forward to talking tomorrow! Thanks

Reid

From: Updike, Jaci [redacted]
Sent: Thursday, August 6, 2020 11:14 AM
To: Von Moltke, Nina [redacted]; McIntosh, Madeline < [redacted]
Cc: Welsh, Reid [redacted]
Subject: RE: fiction & MS generally

Reid and I discussed yesterday and will have something to share with us today. I think the work done will line up really well with what you might be doing Nina. Madeline – Reid is going to send us both the updated work, as well as the previous presentation for us to have as a comparison.

From: Von Moltke, Nina [redacted]
Sent: Thursday, August 6, 2020 8:54 AM
To: McIntosh, Madeline [redacted]
Cc: Welsh, Reid [redacted] Updike, Jaci [redacted]
Subject: Re: fiction & MS generally

That would be great!
Tomorrow preferred on my end if possible due to wifi issues.
Thanks!
Nina

US v. Bertelsmann
1:21-cv-0866-FYP
PX 0174

> On Aug 6, 2020, at 8:47 AM, McIntosh, Madeline [redacted] wrote:
>
> Hi. I believe you're both working on an update related to marketshare assessment by category (Reid focused on performance in fiction, Nina focused on the additional angle of content pipeline).
>
> Understanding you may only have very partial work so far, I wondered if there would be value in getting together today

CONFIDENTIAL BPRH-004441958

or tomorrow? I know Jaci would love to join but can't due to lack of power.

Do you have availability today or tomorrow? Preference?

Madeline McIntosh
Penguin Random House

Top vs. Non-top Authors

YTD Performance

Bookscan POS

Marketplace – **Print – Overall Fiction (Top Authors)**

NPD Bookscan

Retail $$ | 2019-20 Variance, PRH vs. Non-PRH

PRH top authors fell behind the rest of the industry

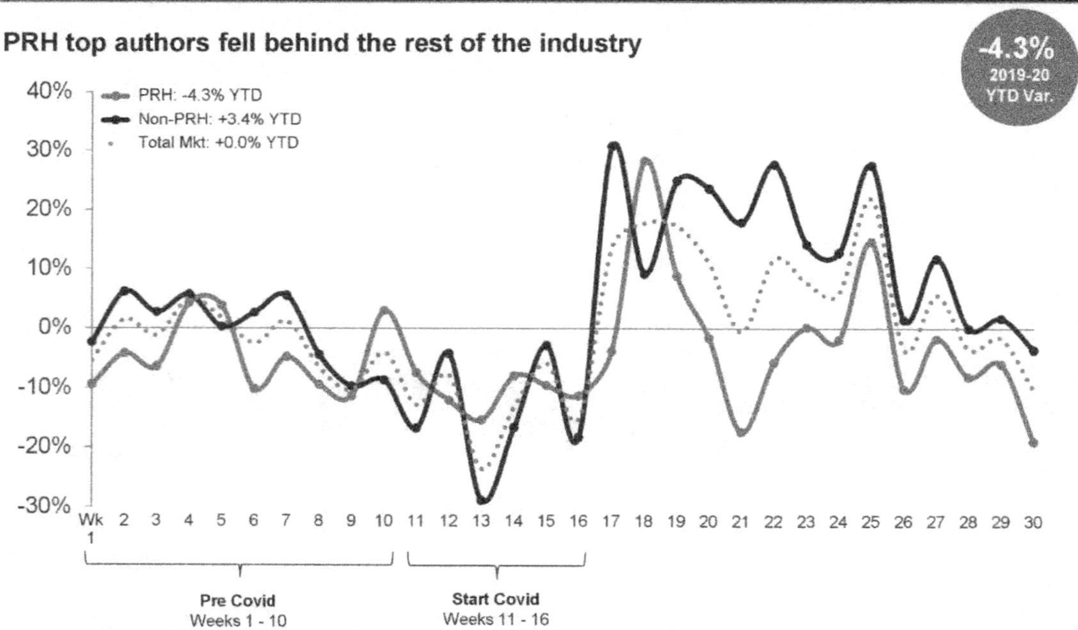

Retail $$ | Market Share

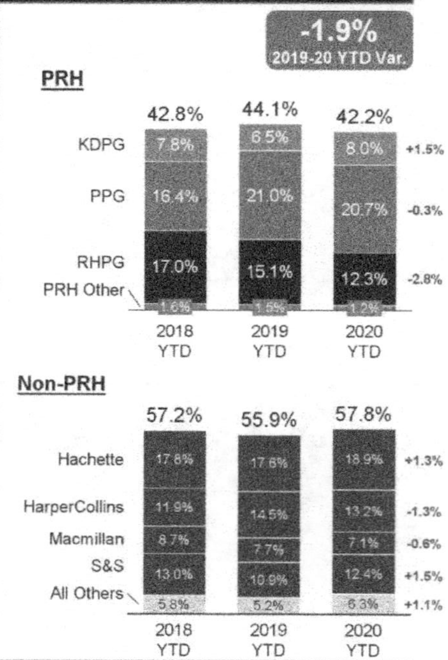

38 Privileged and Confidential

Parameters: Excludes Comics & Graphic Novels; NPD Bookscan Retail $$s Weeks 1-30

CONFIDENTIAL

BPRH-004442057

Bookscan POS

Marketplace – **Print – Overall Fiction (Non-top Authors)**

NPD Bookscan

Retail $$ | 2019-20 Variance, PRH vs. Non-PRH

PRH non-top authors outpaced the industry

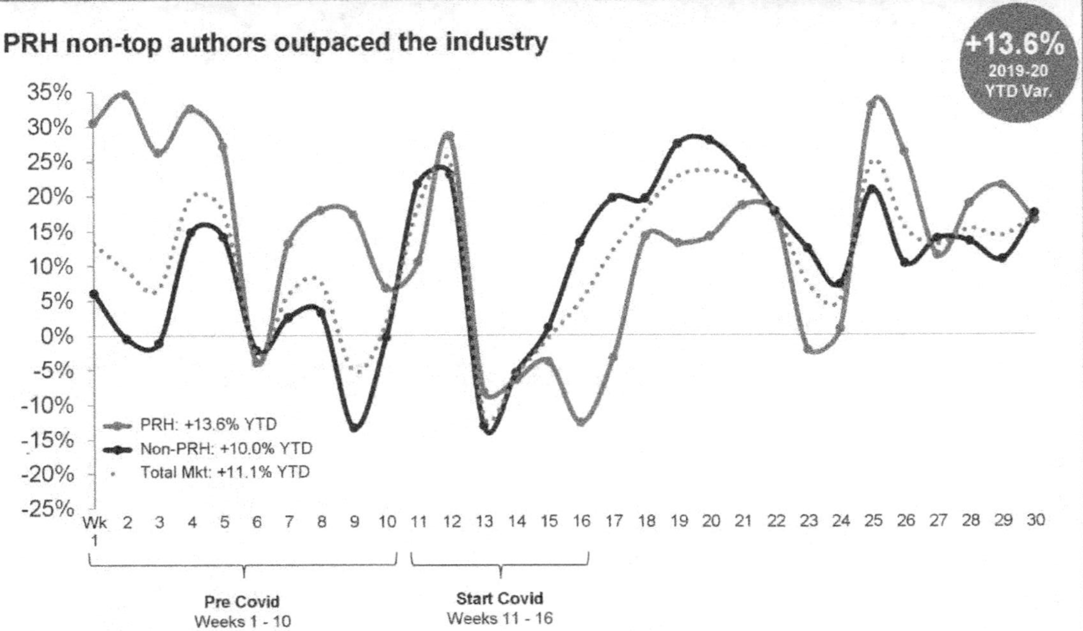

Retail $$ | Market Share

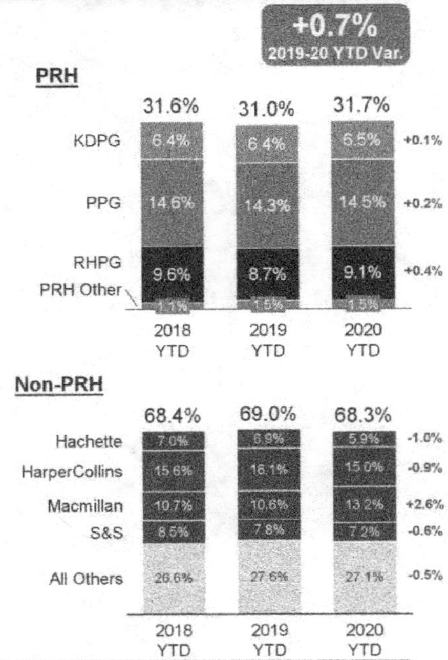

41 Privileged and Confidential

Parameters: Excludes Comics & Graphic Novels; NPD Bookscan Retail $$s Weeks 1-30

CONFIDENTIAL

BPRH-004442060

DEFENDANTS' TRIAL EXHIBIT
DX-273
Case 1:21-cv-02886-FYP Document 181-16 Filed 09/08/22 Page 1 of 3
Penguin Random House
Management Presentation
July 2020
Penguin Random House
DX-273.0001

Integration: Penguin Random House | **Overall Synergies**

Realized $144mn in synergies from multiple cost areas around the world

Operating expenses

Area	Rationale	Synergies Realized
Admin / other	Several overlapping functions	$59mn
IT / systems	Migrate to Random House's best-in-class systems	$22mn
Distribution	Consolidate warehouses to reduce labor	$15mn
Sales	Consolidate sales forces (customer base ~90% | the same)	$14mn

Variable costs

Area	Rationale	Synergies Realized
Production	Strike better agreements with printers and paper suppliers	$34mn

Total Synergies ($mn)
$110
+
$34
$144

DX-273.0035

Integration: Penguin Random House | **Results: US Variable Cost Synergies**

Meaningful reduction in returns and cost of shipment

Significant reduction in Penguin's return rate

US physical dollars return rate (%)[1]

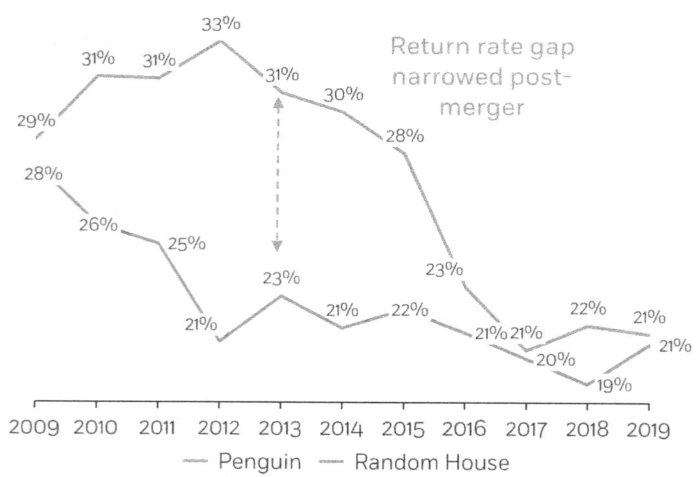

Penguin's return rate reduced from a high of 31% to nearly 20% post-merger

Cost of shipment reduction over time

US net physical sales / cost of shipment development

Net physical sales ($mn)	$1,697	$1,653	$1,637	$1,638

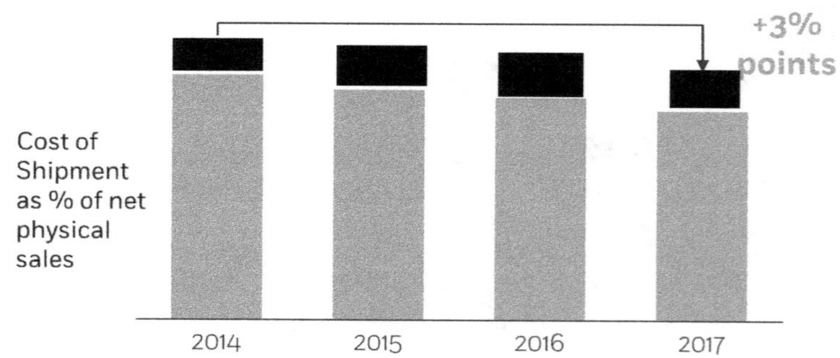

Lower cost of shipment resulted in 3% improvement in profitability

36 Source: PRH US internal data
[1]PRH US billings, hardcover and paperback only

DX-273.0036

July 2020 – Highly confidential | Penguin Random House

US v. Bertelsmann
1:21-cv-0866-FYP
PX 0157

Date: Wednesday, April 1 2020 05:59 PM
Subject: Markus's GEC blog
From: Dohle, Markus
Dohle, Markus [redacted] McIntosh, Madeline [redacted] Weldon, Tom [redacted] Cabutí, Núria [redacted] Burland, Julie [redacted] Cheng, Azia [redacted] Steve Connolly [redacted]>; Shrinagesh, Gaurav
To: [redacted] Cochrane, Kristin [redacted] Johnston, James [redacted] Steinecke, Anke [redacted] Von Schilling, Claire [redacted] Sawhney, Divya [redacted] Sansigre, Manuel [redacted] Mallia, Jo [redacted] Malaviya, Nihar [redacted] Coesfeld, Carsten [redacted];

"Uber-resource your most important priorities!"

This is a mindset and mantra I learned very early in my career on the job in turnaround and crisis situations - and then later again from Eli Goldratt, the management guru and father of the "Theory of Constraints".
For the last twenty plus years I've used this mindset when I talked about Amazon. Around 2000 it became clear that Amazon would become the world's largest and first truly global bookseller. Thus Amazon was becoming "the most important priority" in terms of our book sales (besides preserving the diversity of booksellers and ensuring a competitive market place for books in the future).
So I started to ask the question how we can best serve the fastest growing and soon largest bookseller in the world - in order to grow with them as fast as we can.

I then introduced that mindset when I came to New York in May 2008 to run Random House. From the get go - some of you might remember it - I never bought into the negative view of (almost) all industry constituencies on Amazon's growth. I've always viewed us as supplier of and service provider for Amazon. And I always wanted to provide them with the highest service levels in all areas of our business in order to grow with them - locally and globally - as much as we can, and using the profit/contribution to support the entire book selling ecosystem. Large publishers are our (main) competitors - Amazon is (mainly) our customer, in all book formats. So why always "competing with and complaining about them" (like the entire industry has done)?

Nihar said it very well early on: "If you think that Amazon will destroy the industry and with that your company one day you can influence it - in other words: you still have a (the ultimate) choice. You just stop doing business with them!"
Well, that means that most publishers would have and should have stopped doing business with them in the last twenty years...the alternative would have (and should have) been to just stop complaining - because "complaining is not a strategy!"

I think our positive, realistic and professional view on Amazon that we have adopted early on has served us very well - and believe me, I know first hand how difficult they can be on a macro and micro level (so kudos to our teams serving them around the globe on a daily basis). I've always told our companies and teams around the world to "uber-resource their departments and projects serving Amazon" following my own experience and Eli's fantastic theory (laid out in his book "The Goal").

You guys know that the question I've been asking Jeff Weber (frequently for many years:) when I see him in our New York offices is: "How many people have you already hired today?" Sure, it's a running gag - but then again it's not....

I've outlined a few times in the last weeks that in the last month we've reached a market place that we have been discussing for the last twenty years - a market place with few(er) bookstores and Amazon as "the quasi only shop in town" (I know that still differs from territory to territory). We tried to prepare our companies and

CONFIDENTIAL BPRH-003705600

organizations for this moment - the moment of an "online" dominated world. And here you go - in real time we find ourselves in this (new) reality. Now is the time to make a difference - a tangible difference. Now is the time to make use of and leverage the preparation and all the hard work we've put into becoming Amazon's (and other online platforms') best partner in town - around the world - in all formats (and especially in sales, marketing and publicity!).

This is our moment friends. Let's grasp the opportunity and gain market share in these difficult times as we steer our companies through this unprecedented crisis (the WHAT).

I'm looking forward to discussing ideas and ways to achieve this goal with you and your Amazon leads tomorrow on our call (the HOW).

Amazon/online is our most important priority right now - so please uber-resource our services to these channels!

Cheers and speak tomorrow.
Yours Markus

PS: You can share this note with your teams (and especially the online teams in advance of tomorrow's call) as you see fit...

US v. Bertelsmann
1:21-cv-0866-FYP
PX 0983

Date: Friday, April 26 2019 12:32 PM
Subject: MEETING RECAP - 4/25 BVG/PRH Fall planning update
From: Malone-Barber, Sue
To: Weiss, Mitch, Coral Graphics; Sawyer, Chris, BVG; Dohle, Markus; Malaviya, Nihar; Bleemer, Kirk; DeFazio, Michael; Driskill, Susan

Thanks again for the productive discussion yesterday. Here is a recap of things we talked about and next steps. Please let me know if anything is missing or understood differently...

Dave's update:

- New Kolbus is on the floor and training starts next week (4/29)
- Planning to buy 2 new jkt machines from UK and Spain. May take 4-6 weeks (Dave is uncertain of timing as of now)
- 2 trimmers arriving within 2-3 weeks
- Crewing: Have had some successes (Increased supervision) but still not where Dave wants to be and they continue recruitment efforts. As of now, OT will still be required
- High confidence in improved binding function and capacity which (at times) is now outpacing what the press room can deliver
- Press room needs work. Presses are old and Dave is looking to order new ones (for next year) as well as looking at supervision.
- Identifying and replacing/improving all the weakest links throughout the print/bind process
- They are seeing a [redacted] unit increase in output YTD – HC and SC
- Dave is generally confident in the Fall outlook. He cautioned he doesn't expect perfection and there will be issues (usual mfg issues coupled with old equipment)
- They are striving to give [redacted] weekly HC units to PRH, with a goal of [redacted] total HC units in Fall
- Dave indicated they are backing off 3rd party work this fall

PRH concerns:

- PRH is currently seeing an average output of [redacted] HC units a day ([redacted]/week), with a great deal of volatility. We continue to need to move del dates and split runs
- Adding the additional Kolbus HC units of [redacted] a week to the current average output of [redacted]/week, only gets us to [redacted] units/week
- Kirk highlighted that in order to hit [redacted] HC units, BVG would need to increase their output by ~[redacted] which seems aggressive
- In light of the ongoing volatility we are experiencing, the pressure of getting all the improvements and crew in place in the next 2 months, and the Kolbus only getting us to [redacted] units, PRH is nervous about BVG's ability to consistently hit [redacted] units/week in the fall
- PRH asked if [redacted] HC units is guaranteed and/or can BVG give us a HC unit guarantee?
- PRH is willing to give a performance-based financial incentive, calibrated to a mutually agreed upon unit guarantee

Markus reiterated the importance of, and strategic advantage of, acting like vertically integrated company:

- We have a combined [redacted] profit to defend ([redacted]) and we must consider the [redacted] lever: Every $1.00 for BVG is [redacted] for PRH (BVG loses $1.00, we lose [redacted])
- We are the only publisher with a printer in the family and that is a huge competitive advantage in attracting authors (our ability to get books and supply the market better than anyone else)
- Critically important for BVG and PRH to focus on improvement now, and ensure we've taken every pragmatic step we can take before entering the fall season - even if it means incurring costs (For example, PRH is buying more paper, holding more inventory, etc.).
- He encouraged Dave not to run too tightly and invest in incentives for weekends
- PRH is willing to help with financial incentives to increase our capacity and make it financially attractive to print PRH's allocated units, even if overall capacity goes down

NEXT STEPS:

- **Dave and Mitch to think about what the guaranteed HC unit number is. Our next regularly scheduled meeting is Monday, 5/6. We can discuss at that meeting if that works. Kirk will follow up.**
- **We will have a final Fall check-in with Markus around 6/20 (prior to 6/23). Sue will work on getting that scheduled**

CONFIDENTIAL BPRH-002729574

US v. Bertelsmann
1:21-cv-0866-FYP
PX 0087

Date: Saturday, August 15 2020 10:28 AM
Subject: PRH US - key priorities - confidential
From: Dohle, Markus
To: McIntosh, Madeline
Attachments: PRH US Agenda 2020.pdf; ATT00001.htm

Dear Madeline,
Just wanted to follow up on our great discussion on Monday - I really appreciated the openness of it and look forward to following up with you soon. There is a lot summarize - I hope it's okay to capture my thoughts on this so we are aligned:

1. As we have discussed, profitable market share growth continues to be THE key metric for our owners (and for us). If we look at the amount of market share we have lost since you and I began having conversations about market share in the US, it's minus 1.5% (from 2017 to 2019). In other words: if we had just grown with the market, we would have more revenue and EBIT ( ). Further, year to date July, we are again 0.2% down in market share in a growing market (plus 3.9% YTD). I know that not achieving our key success factor is frustrating for both of us, and it is urgent and important to turn this around for the US business performance and because it's the key metric for our shareholder.

I'd like to follow up on some of the topics above and attached in the next weeks and will schedule a few meetings to discuss the status with you. Please feel free to reach out to me at any time as well.

I would like to thank you again for our open discourse about the key priorities - as always you have my full support to deliver on the expectations above and attached.

With my best wishes — Markus

PRH US priorities for the next 2-3 years

2. Content acquisition focus and involvement

— More deep involvement with content acquisitions; team meetings for acquisitions greater than 250/500k$ to get more content

Case 1:21-cv-02886-FYP Document 181-41 Filed 09/08/22 Page 1 of 1

Date:	Tuesday, April 14 2020 07:30 PM
Subject:	Re: Two acquisitions to note
From:	Dobson, Allison < >
To:	Tart, Brian < >;
CC:	Ziga, Katharine < >; James, Casey Blue < >;

Hi —

Thanks for the note.

RE: - happy to talk about this one. I should preface that I am super skeptical of right now — I think the are realizing that books are so they are pulling things out of the woodwork. Plus - I am sitting on two huge deals in that same zone with which are years late and the agents have absolutely no juice to make them actually materialize, and we've just gotten nowhere with them on the renegotiations for their . If there's something that really is irresistible then let's talk, but I want to be sure this is real before we bid and I want to be really cautious and realistic about what we bid.

And thanks for the update on — what a disappointment. We certainly put best foot forward on that one, so I am very sorry to hear this result. The PRH rule is that if an agent next goes exclusively to a PRH division, they would have to live within our bid. However, if he takes it to an action, within the auction situation with competitive bidders, by the rule, Knopf or RH could bid to the level of the market. I imagine, given the track, that $150K is the market. But technically, if Simon and Schuster were willing to pay $500K, another PRH division could go to $501K if they saw it at that level. That said, there are some books where there are bad feelings and we just ask the other divisions to back off. We try to do that infrequently — lest we get it done to us — but it does happen. We did it when decided to leave, for example. It's sort of an academic question until we understand what is going to do with it, but let me know how you are feeling about it.

Happy to jump on the phone tomorrow to discuss any and all.

A

Allison Dobson

> On Apr 14, 2020, at 5:12 PM, Tart, Brian < > wrote:
>
> We have in the proposal. turned down $1.5M already and thinks it will go up to $2M. It's a Very slight, but emotional. said she might want to do book and even add a full to this, which would bring the advance level up to $5M or so...Just a head's up. We are talking tomorrow morning about where we stand on it.
>
> author of sent in her option book. We paid $225k for and it is was worth around $100k. We offered $150k for the new novel and they turned us down and are going out widely with it. We would like to invoke the PRH policy/rule/process where other imprints can bid on this but not more than our $150k. is the agent. We poured a lot into the publication of to even get to the sales level we got to, so it is disappointing that they turned down our offer of $150k. But that is really the outside of what this book is worth.
>
> Brian
>
> Sent from my iPad

US v. Bertelsmann
1:21-cv-0866-FYP
PX 0054

CONFIDENTIAL BPRH-000453622

Date: Wednesday, June 10 2020 03:37 PM
Subject: Re: Acq P&L - [redacted] by [redacted]
From: Mavjee, Maya [redacted]
To: Von Moltke, Nina [redacted]
CC: McIntosh, Madeline [redacted] Thomas, William [redacted]

We are coordinated. Bill and Kara will agree to a number and both offer same. Thanks for pulling us together. M

Sent from my iPad

> On Jun 10, 2020, at 3:23 PM, Von Moltke, Nina [redacted] wrote:
>
> Ok, great – I was just about to reach out to her too. That's good to know.
>
> **From:** McIntosh, Madeline [redacted]
> **Sent:** Wednesday, June 10, 2020 3:20 PM
> **To:** Thomas, William [redacted] Mavjee, Maya [redacted]
> \>
> **Cc:** Von Moltke, Nina [redacted]
> **Subject:** Re: Acq P&L [redacted]
>
> Reached Gina. She's trying to reach Kara who (with Whitney) are the ones bidding. Agreed it should be the same number. Whatever you guys decide the number should be. She'll come back to you.
>
>> On Jun 10, 2020, at 3:02 PM, Mavjee, Maya [redacted] wrote:
>>
>> Thank you. M
>> On Jun 10, 2020, at 2:18 PM, McIntosh, Madeline [redacted] wrote:
>>
>> Hi. I feel we should coordinate – shouldn't be forced into bidding against each other for existing authors. Nina is reaching out to RH.
>>
>> **From:** Thomas, William
>> **Sent:** Wednesday, June 10, 2020 2:12 PM
>> **To:** McIntosh, Madeline [redacted] Von Moltke, Nina < [redacted]; Mavjee, Maya [redacted]
>> **Subject:** Fwd: Acq P&L - [redacted]
>>
>> Here is the p&l.
>>
>> Sent from my iPhone
>> Begin forwarded message:
>>
>>> **From:** "Whitaker, Corbin" [redacted]
>>> **Date:** June 10, 2020 at 10:32:31 AM EDT
>>> **To:** "Thomas, William" [redacted] "Ackroyd, Cameron" < [redacted]
>>> **Cc:** "Kraska, Katie" [redacted] "Easton, Sarah" < [redacted]

US v. Bertelsmann
1:21-cv-0866-FYP
PX 0107

CONFIDENTIAL BPRH-003046557

DEFENDANTS' TRIAL EXHIBIT
DX-435

Date:	Monday, December 10 2018 08:48 AM
Subject:	RE: Invitation to join panel at NYPL on December 10th
From:	Von Moltke, Nina
To:	Von Schilling, Claire ; McIntosh, Madeline
CC:	Malaviya, Nihar James, Pauline
Attachments:	Author Comp Dev_overview 2015-2018.pptx

Resending with one correction and a break out of bonus/refresher advance commitments that Pauline helpfully suggested this morning.

From: Von Moltke, Nina
Sent: Sunday, December 09, 2018 11:28 PM
To: Von Schilling, Claire
Cc: McIntosh, Madeline Malaviya, Nihar
>; James, Pauline
Subject: RE: Invitation to join panel at NYPL on December 10th

Hi. Wanted to pass on some info on our overall author payments in the last few years. There are different angles to look at, but we've tried to summarize the most relevant ones on the attached slide. Happy to give more context when we meet tomorrow afternoon.

On Speakers Bureau:

Hope that's helpful.
Nina

From: Von Schilling, Claire
Sent: Thursday, December 06, 2018 5:39 PM
To: Von Moltke, Nina
Cc: McIntosh, Madeline Malaviya, Nihar
>
Subject: Re: Invitation to join panel at NYPL on December 10th

Nina - Would it be possible to also look at any growth in the speakers bureau and increased revenues for authors thru this service that we provide? It's just come up on the prep call Madeline and I are on with the AG.
Thank you.
Sent from my iPhone
On Dec 5, 2018, at 9:54 AM, Von Moltke, Nina wrote:

> I can compile an overview of evolution of author comp (advances/royalties paid) from our end.
> Claire, can you send the link to their study?
> To your question about "general compensation for artists overall in the digital world" - that has a lot of facets of course. Assume we should focus on book authors and not other types of writers that participate in the digital world at large?

From: Von Schilling, Claire
Sent: Wednesday, December 05, 2018 9:44 AM
To: McIntosh, Madeline [REDACTED]
Cc: Von Moltke, Nina [REDACTED] Malaviya, Nihar <
Subject: Re: Invitation to join panel at NYPL on December 10th

I've got the answers to questions covered so just need a general analysis of their study and its flaws and overview / context of general compensation for artists overall in digital world.

On Dec 5, 2018, at 8:55 AM, McIntosh, Madeline [REDACTED] wrote:

> Hi. As Claire knows, I'm on a panel on Monday sponsored by the Authors Guild. Overall theme is about content monetization, with the underlying assumption that authors are earning less.
>
> That earnings stat comes from the AG's survey of its author members, and so I'm sure it's true, but of course it also reflects the nature of their membership (mainly adult fiction and narrative nonfiction authors). In other words, they skew in the same way PRH skews, and I think that's something I can point out.
>
> I should be prepared with a couple of simple points & facts (simple enough that I can remember them without notes) that address the bigger picture:
>
> - Book sales are up overall, but variable by category & format. Areas that are down disproportionately impact a publisher like PRH and an author population like AG's.
> - Some statement about the shift of retail online & what that means for pubs and authors. But let's think carefully (given our net effective discount position and other Amazon & Audible dynamics) about what I should say.
> - Nina: anything worth pointing out about what trends we see in author compensation?
> - Some words of warning about allowing content to be used as loss leader/ subscription driver/ platform marketer. Without naming Audible or Kindle Unlimited, I should address what the danger is for authors in those kinds of deals.
> - Something about the impact of self publishing and how we look at it.
> - What else?
>
> ---
>
> **From:** Paul W. Morris [REDACTED]
> **Sent:** Tuesday, December 4, 2018 2:55 PM
> **To:** McIntosh, Madeline [REDACTED] Von Schilling, Claire <
> **Cc:** Flanagan, Bernadette [REDACTED]
> **Subject:** Re: Invitation to join panel at NYPL on December 10th
>
> Hi Madeline, apologies to you and Claire for leaving her off the last email.
>
> Thanks for this reply. We are finishing up some talking points for Rick and will be able to send you general and specific questions tomorrow or Thursday morning at the latest. For now, the general flow of the program will likely go as follows:
>
> 1) Introduction and some statistics from our recent authors income survey
> 2) Some of the causes for why authors' incomes are down
> 3) Is this a problem, and why we should care (i.e., what books might be getting written as a result?)
> 4) What are other ways for authors to earn a living while writing? How to find the right balance; the role awards/prizes and residencies play for writers, and for publishers in the marketplace...
> 5) With more books being sold than ever before, what is the role technology plays in helping or hindering authors' ability to reach new audiences, and in creating a sustainable career as a professional writer
>
> Rick will be adding his own thoughts to this flow and we will send you an update soon. A call would be ideal, if

we can arrange, perhaps at least with you, me, Mary, and Rick, if not the other panelists. Thanks for letting me know what you think.

My best,
Paul

p

Paul W. Morris
Vice President, Membership & Outreach
The Authors Guild

From: "McIntosh, Madeline" [redacted]
Date: Tuesday, December 4, 2018 at 1:59 PM
To: "Paul W. Morris" [redacted] "Von Schilling, Claire" <
Cc: "Flanagan, Bernadette" [redacted]
Subject: RE: Invitation to join panel at NYPL on December 10th

Hi Paul. Adding Claire von Schilling, my colleague who's going to try to make sure I have my act together before the panel ☺

I don't think I have any points in mind that I'd want to make, but I'd be happy to get on the phone ahead of time to prepare. Do you know if Rick already has a sense of where he will take the conversation or which questions he might throw my way?

From: Paul W. Morris [redacted]
Sent: Tuesday, December 4, 2018 12:28 PM
To: Flanagan, Bernadette [redacted]
Cc: McIntosh, Madeline [redacted]
Subject: Re: Invitation to join panel at NYPL on December 10th

Dear Bernadette and Madeline,

I hope you're both well and enjoyed a nice Thanksgiving holiday. I believe the library has been in touch with you about logistics for Monday's event? There's a chance we might try to get you, or as many of you as we can, on a call together before the event, if you think you have the time this week.

Also, as we prepare some talking points for Richard Russo and the evening generally, I am writing to see if there's anything specific you'd like to share regarding this topic, questions or concerns of particular interest to you personally or professionally. If so, please feel free to include anything you'd like me to pass along to Rick so he's made aware.

Finally, the NYPL has asked us for a recommended reading list on this topic so they can direct attendees to their collections. Is there a title or two you might suggest? Our first event on the series, focusing on journalism, had no shortage of books for further reading (see below). No problem if none come to mind, but wanted to give you the opportunity to weigh in.

Thank you, sending best for now,
Paul

Democracy's Detectives: The Economics of Investigative Journalism by James T. Hamilton
The End of Competitive Advantage: How to Keep Your Strategy Moving as Fast as Your Business by Rita Gunther McGrath
The Curse of the Mogul: What's Wrong with the World's Leading Media Companies by Jonathan A. Knee, Bruce C. Greenwald, and Ava Seave
The Content Trap: A Strategist's Guide to Digital Change by Bharat Narendra Anand
Who Owns the News? A History of Copyright by Will Slauter (2019)
Move Fast and Break Things: How Facebook, Google, and Amazon Cornered Culture and Undermined Democracy by Jonathan Taplin
World Without Mind: The Existential Threat of Big Tech by Franklin Foer
Saving the Media: Capitalism, Crowdfunding, and Democracy by Julia Cagé
The Media and Public Life: A History by John Nerone
The Creation of the Media: Political Origins of Modern Communications by Paul Starr
Deciding What's True: The Rise of Political Fact-Checking in American Journalism by Lucas Graves
Making News: The Political Economy of Journalism in Britain and America from the Glorious Revolution to the Internet edited by Richard R. John and Jonathan Silberstein-Loeb

---
Paul W. Morris
Vice President, Membership & Outreach
The Authors Guild

From: "Flanagan, Bernadette" [redacted]
Date: Tuesday, November 20, 2018 at 1:15 PM
To: "Paul W. Morris" [redacted], "McIntosh, Madeline" < [redacted]
Cc: "Von Schilling, Claire" [redacted]
Subject: RE: Invitation to join panel at NYPL on December 10th

Dear Paul,

Thanks for your note!

Here is Madeline's bio:
Madeline McIntosh was appointed CEO of Penguin Random House U.S. in April 2018. Her previous work in the company includes leadership roles in Penguin Publishing, Random House Audio, Random House Sales, and serving as the first COO of Penguin Random House. She started in the company as an assistant in the New Media department in 1994.

Madeline serves on the Board of Directors for Poets & Writers, the nation's largest nonprofit organization serving creative writers. She graduated from Harvard University with a BA in Fine Arts in 1991. She lives in New York with her husband, author Chris Pavone, and their twin sons.

Madeline's email is [redacted] You can also contact me in case you need anything – my email is [redacted] and phone number is [redacted]

Please let me know if you need anything else!

Best,

Bernadette

From: Paul W. Morris [redacted]
Sent: Monday, November 19, 2018 4:50 PM
To: McIntosh, Madeline [redacted]
Cc: Flanagan, Bernadette [redacted]; Von Schilling, Claire <[redacted]>
Subject: Re: Invitation to join panel at NYPL on December 10th

Dear Madeline,

Thank you for agreeing to participate in this event. We are in the process of preparing a more detailed update for you, but for now, I wanted to share with you the event page that the NYPL just made live on their site: https://www.showclix.com/event/whoownstheword2/tag/pub

We will be promoting this heavily in the coming weeks and will write again soon with further info. In the meantime, could you share a short bio with me? The NYPL has requested it, along with your email address, as they will be handling logistics with you, like arrival, security, etc.

Many thanks, sending best for the holiday weekend ahead,
Paul

Paul W. Morris
Vice President, Membership & Outreach
The Authors Guild

From: Mary Rasenberger <[redacted]>
Date: Monday, November 12, 2018 at 11:11 PM
To: "McIntosh, Madeline" [redacted]>
Cc: "Paul W. Morris" [redacted] "Flanagan, Bernadette" <[redacted], "Von Schilling, Claire" <[redacted]
Subject: RE: Invitation to join panel at NYPL on December 10th

That is fabulous! We will get you more information soon.

From: McIntosh, Madeline [redacted]
Sent: Monday, November 12, 2018 8:48 PM
To: Mary Rasenberger [redacted]
Cc: Paul W. Morris [redacted]; Flanagan, Bernadette [redacted]
>; Von Schilling, Claire [redacted]>
Subject: Re: Invitation to join panel at NYPL on December 10th

Hi Mary. Thanks for the invitation. I'll be delighted to join.

All the best,
Madeline
On Nov 12, 2018, at 6:57 PM, Mary Rasenberger [redacted] wrote:

> Hi Madeline,

I hope this finds you well! I am emailing to invite you to participate in a forum **on December 10, 6:30pm** at the **New York Public Library's main branch at 42nd St** on the ecosystem of book publishing today. It is part of a special series of events that the Authors Guild is co-hosting with the New York Public Library, called *Who Owns the Word*, focusing on the economics of authorship and how it is changing. The series will be moderated by novelist Richard Russo, Vice President of the Authors Guild, and each event will take a close look at the current economic landscape for writers in three different fields: journalism, book publishing and writing for the screen. The idea is to look at the economies of writing and publishing from all angles, allowing multiple perspectives to emerge. It promises to be an exciting, honest discussion about the future of the written word and we would love for you to be involved.

The December 10th forum will focus on book publishing, and I thought you'd be perfect for it. We would like to have speakers from large and a small publishers. Speakers potentially lined up include authors Alex Chee, Kurt Anderson and TJ Stiles. We can send full details if you would like to know more. An honorarium is available and we can help with transportation costs.

I hope that you are interested and available! If you have any questions, please feel free to reach out to me.

All the best,
Mary

Who Owns the Word: Three Forums on Authorship and the Future of The Written Word

The digital revolution has drastically altered the way books and other creative works are distributed and experienced. This change has resulted in an enormous rise in the net worth of technology companies, and a corresponding drop in income for the creative sector as a whole, authors and the publishing community included.

In partnership with the New York Public Library, the Authors Guild will conduct a series of three public forums exploring the current state of authorship and the role technology plays in both helping and hindering the advancement of literary culture.

With this series, we hope to engage today's leading thought-leaders and influencers in fostering a dialogue and turning the tide. The panelists will bring together in conversation journalists, authors, and screenwriters; newspaper, book publishers and TV/film producers, as well as representatives from the technology companies. The panels will focus on the confluence of the creative and tech sectors in each of the three distinct area of the literary arts: 1) book, 2) journalism, and 3) motion picture. Topics will explore ownership and authorship of creative works and how they are monetized and protected, as well as the impact that tech companies are having on the creative sector and on the writers who produce the content that drives traffic to the major Internet platforms. Each forum will address how creators, corporations, and cultural institutions can all play an active role in sustaining a society that relies on the freedoms that creative expression makes possible.

Mary E. Rasenberger
Executive Director
The Authors Guild
31 East 32nd Street, 7th Floor
New York, NY 10016

NEW DEALS (ADVANCE COMMITMENTS)

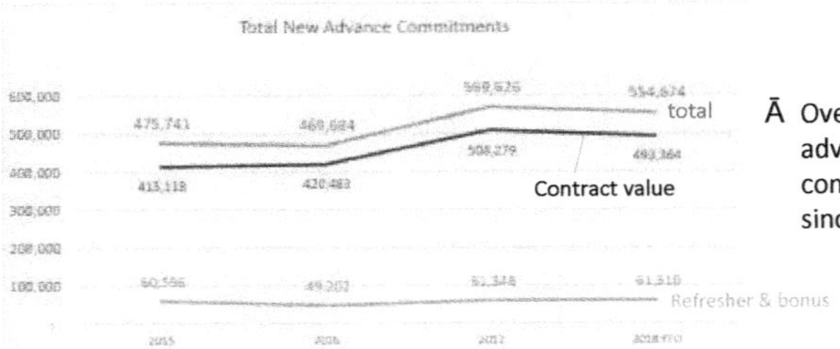

Ā Overall annual new advance commitments up since 2015

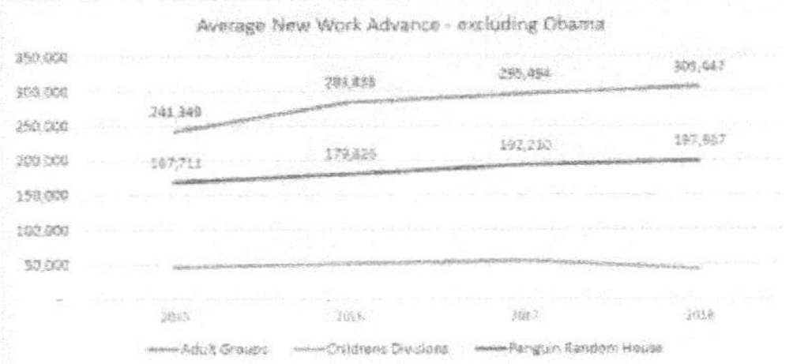

Ā Driven by higher advance levels on the adult side

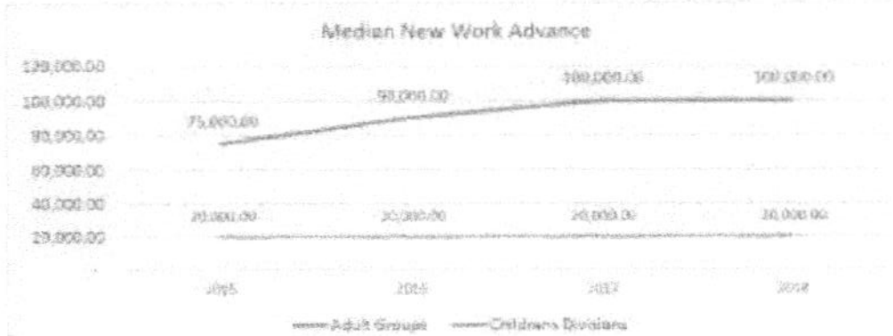

Ā Higher advance level not only driven by biggest deals – median advance also up (for adult titles)

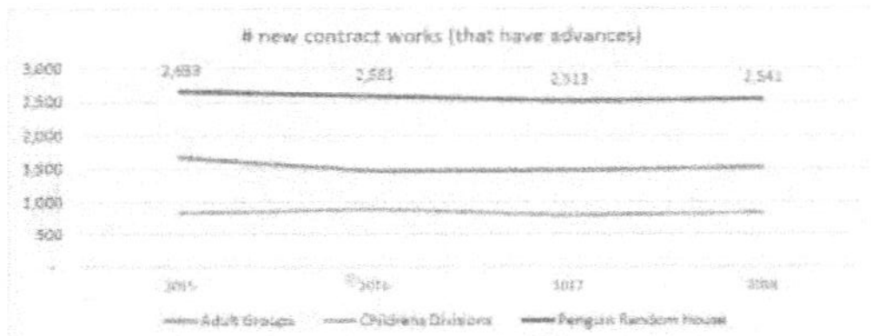

Ā # of new contracts / new works is down slightly from 2015, but steady since 2016

ALL AUTHORS / PUBLISHED TITLES – ACTUAL ROYALTY PAYMENTS

Ā Overall earned royalties decreased after 2015 (outlier year), stable since then
Ā Payable share down slightly due to higher advances (higher advance titles take longer to earn)

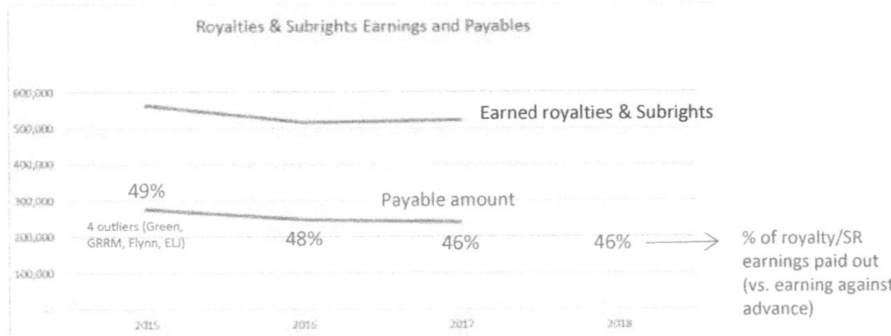

Ā However, if we exclude the extreme ends of the range (over $1M and under $500 p.a.), we seen an increase in the average royalty payment by author

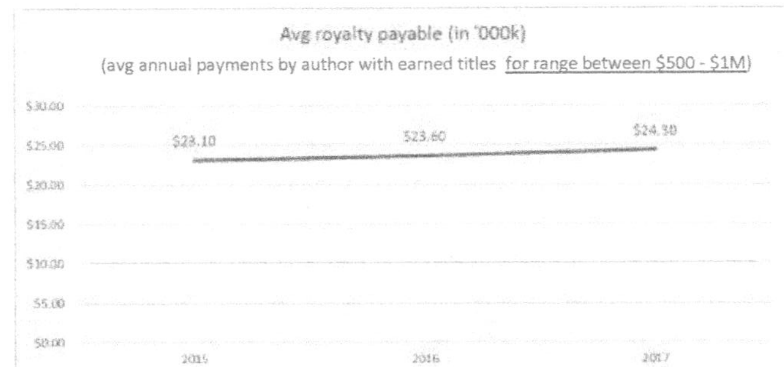

!"#$%&'(()

Significant Variability in Annual Author Contracts

	2010	2011	2012	2013	2014	2015	2016	2017	2018	2019	2020	2021
Author A	$40.3M	$8.5M	$35.5M			$49M		$48M		$60M	$6M	$45M
Author B	$27M	$18.8M	$14.5M	$15M	$19.2M							
Author C			$17.3M						$18.8M			$5.8M
Author D												$52M
Author E								$65M		$35M		$8M
Author F			$12.5M					$11.5M				
Author G							$9.5M					

Extracted from BPRH-LIT-006488175

6

Date: Thursday, August 8 2019 02:43 PM
Subject: [redacted] Books update
From: Dohle, Markus [redacted]
To: McIntosh, Madeline [redacted]>;
Attachments: Penguin Random House Offer_Imprint Presentation_August 14th, 2019.pptx; Penguin Random House Offer_Imprint Presentation_August 14th, 2019.pdf

---

Hi Madeline,

Attached, please find the presentation for the [redacted] imprint meeting next week. David has reviewed with Gina, and we will send to [redacted] later today.

If you have any questions, please reach out to me or to David.

Looking forward to getting together on Monday.

Markus

US v. Bertelsmann
1:21-cv-0866-FYP
PX 0151

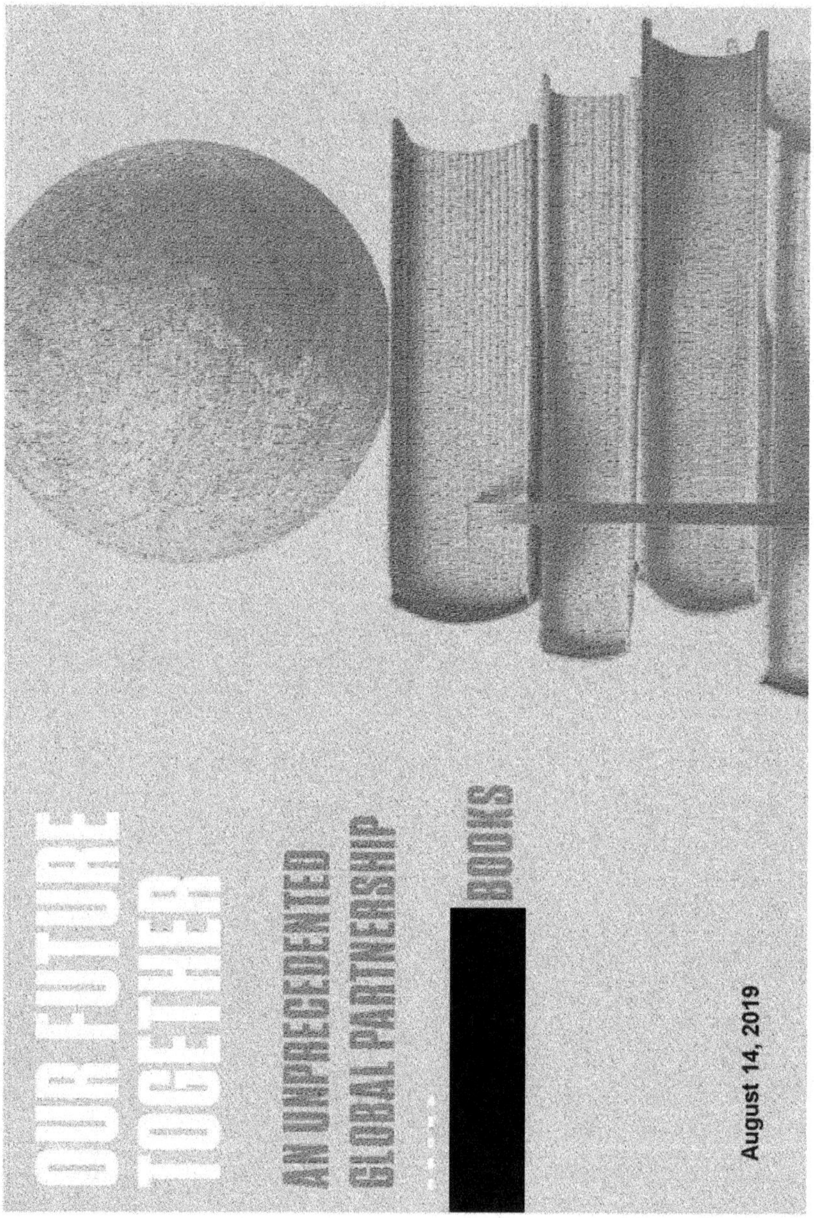

Confidential – not to be distributed or shared

Content Rights Landscape

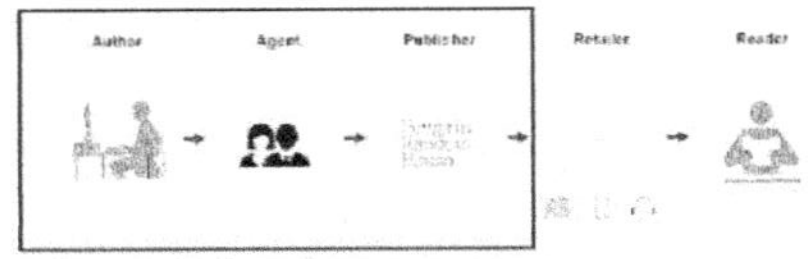

Author

Agent

- Most authors have agents or other representation
- Agents typically submit manuscripts to multiple publishers but sometimes make exclusive submissions
- Agent sells publication rights to a property in exchange for advance and royalties
  - Rights for a property are split by media type (books, performance, interactive, merchandise), territory (World, US, UK), and language
- Agents typically take 15% of advance; representatives have different models
- Agent landscape fragmented with a few big agencies but large number of smaller players along with non-agent representatives

Publisher

Penguin Random House

- Publishers have deep connections with wide variety of agencies
- In most cases, publishers acquire rights in fast-moving competitive auctions
- Publishers pay an advance to agents and authors in exchange for a bundle of rights
  - In vast majority of cases, publisher secures only book rights (physical, audio, and eBook), worldwide or in a collection of territories, and in a single or all languages
  - If a studio has interest in performance / video or interactive rights (i.e. AR / VR, gaming), it usually acquires those rights separately from the author / agent

 BPRH-003688280

Publisher Activities to Reach Consumers

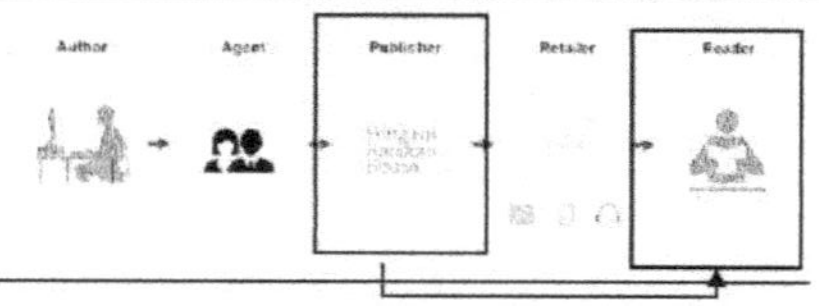

Content Marketing

Imprint-level marketers

- Each book and / or author is a brand on its own that requires creating reach and awareness
- Every individual book or author requires its own marketing campaign
- Marketing and publicity investment is a significant driver of consumer awareness and sales
- Each imprint has dedicated marketing and publicity support, sometimes centrally managed

Programmatic Marketing

Corporate-level marketers

Consumer Insights & Analytics

Creative Strategy, Campaigns & Partnerships

Consumer Platforms & Engagement

Design & Video

PRH's Corporate Marketing team supports imprint book marketers in a variety of ways:

- Building or licensing tools, technology, and data to support book marketing
- Running analysis to understand and plan for our largest brands
- Managing corporate channels and key consumer segment programs on Facebook, across the web, and through email
- Running training programs to improve our ability to execute campaigns on a title level

8

Confidential – not to be distributed or shared

CONFIDENTIAL BPRH-003688285

Publishing is a portfolio business, with profitability driven by a small percentage of books

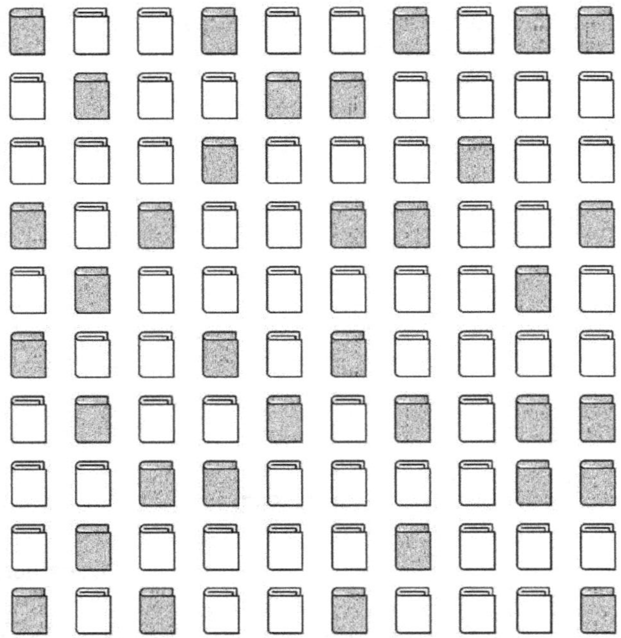

Out of every

100

books published,

35

are profitable

Book profitability is primarily driven by **revenues generated** and **advance paid**

▼

Top 4% of profitable titles drive 60% of profitability

▼

These are **unpredictable breakout books** with **significant over-performance** to expectations and investment

▼

In general, **higher advance levels are correlated with more book sales** – however, there are always exceptions

9 *Confidential – not to be distributed or shared*

Overall New Imprint Profitability

ILLUSTRATIVE

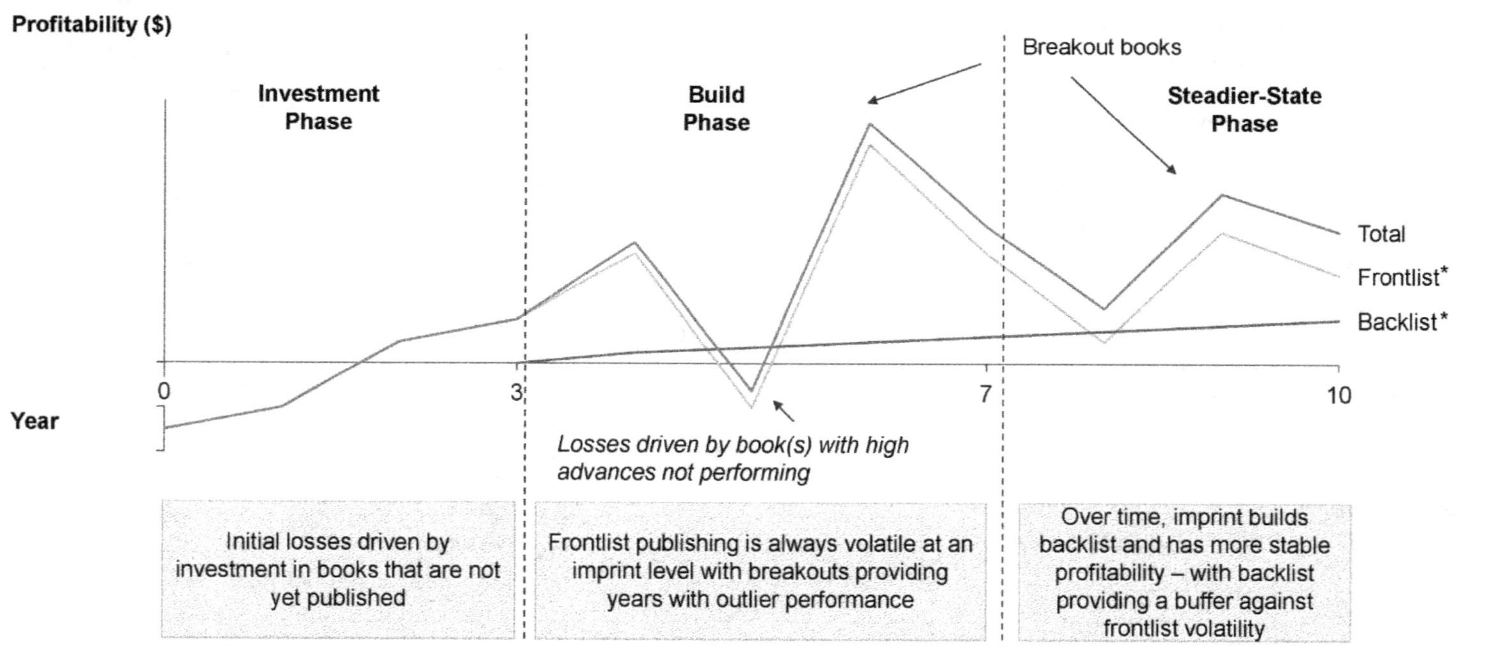

** Frontlist is books in first year of publication, backlist is books post first year of publication*

10

Confidential – not to be distributed or shared

CONFIDENTIAL

BPRH-003688308

Date: Saturday, September 14 2019 11:28 PM
Subject: RE: [REDACTED] meeting (Sunday)
From: Sawhney, Divya [REDACTED]
To: Deedy, Cara [REDACTED] Dohle, Markus [REDACTED] >; Malaviya, Nihar [REDACTED] Steinecke, Anke [REDACTED] Drake, David [REDACTED] Sansigre, Manuel [REDACTED]
Attachments: Penguin Random House Offer_Imprint Presentation_September 20th 2019_v42.pdf; Penguin Random House Offer_Imprint Presentation_September 20th 2019_v42.pptx

Hi everyone,

Here is an updated deck for us to walk through tomorrow.

(No change to the agenda.)

Divya

From: Deedy, Cara [REDACTED]
Sent: Friday, September 13, 2019 6:21 PM
To: Dohle, Markus [REDACTED] Malaviya, Nihar [REDACTED] Sawhney, Divya [REDACTED] Steinecke, Anke [REDACTED] Drake, David [REDACTED] Sansigre, Manuel [REDACTED]
Subject: RE: [REDACTED] meeting (Sunday)

All,

Please see attached for the discussion materials for Sunday's call. Agenda below:

Agenda for Sunday Call

1. **Update on Meeting Details (David)**
   - Any Request for advance materials?
   - Who are their attendees?
     i. [REDACTED]
     ii. [REDACTED]
2. **Review Deck**
3. **Next Steps**
   - Confirm schedule for next week: Wednesday 11-12:30, Thursday 2-3:30
   - Copyediting plan
   - PRH attendees?

Regards,
Cara
-----Original Appointment-----
From: Dohle, Markus [REDACTED]
Sent: Wednesday, September 11, 2019 1:12 PM
To: Dohle, Markus; Malaviya, Nihar; Sawhney, Divya; Steinecke, Anke; Drake, David; Sansigre, Manuel; Deedy, Cara
Subject: [REDACTED] meeting (Sunday)
When: Sunday, September 15, 2019 1:00 PM-2:00 PM (UTC-05:00) Eastern Time (US & Canada).
Where: Dial-in [REDACTED] | Participant [REDACTED]

USA [REDACTED]
GERMANY [REDACTED]

LEADER PASSCODE: [REDACTED]

US v. Bertelsmann
1:21-cv-0866-FYP
PX 0079

CONFIDENTIAL BPRH-002744486

OUR FUTURE
TOGETHER
AN UNPRECEDENTED
GLOBAL PARTNERSHIP
BOOKS
September 20, 2019
Confidential – not to be distributed or shared

Considerations on Key Takeaways

Potential routes to build enterprise value

Potential routes		Industry context	Assessment
A Create	Imprint	• Imprints usually created for long term (i.e. 10+ years)	Only proven-long term business model in publishing but difficult to exit
A Create	Company	• Company will always have a higher cost structure than an imprint and will take a longer time to achieve profitability • No history of companies starting from scratch achieving profitability in 3-5 year time period	**Not a viable option**
B Acquire	Imprint	• Limited secondary market for imprint acquisition (distressed situations only) • Typically, imprints are shut down or stay with a publishing company	**Not a viable option**
B Acquire	Company	• Significant number of deals happen annually in publishing industry • Typical multiple 0.8x-1.0x revenue	• Quickest way to build EV • Comes with backlist and team • Requires capital outflow • Opportunistic, depends on availability of target + right fit

7

Confidential – not to be distributed or shared

Penguin Random House

CONFIDENTIAL BPRH-002744493

Date:	Tuesday, November 2 2021 10:24 AM
Subject:	improved offer
From:	McIntosh, Madeline
To:	
CC:	Dobson, Allison ; Centrello, Gina ;
Attachments:	PRH Advantage.pdf; image003.png

Dear

Thanks for your call yesterday and for letting me know we need to improve our offer in order to remain competitive. We remain determined to become publisher, and so I'm happy to revise our offer with the addition of significant bonuses, triggered prior to earn-out. **Together with the existing advance of this is now a total package of** Details below.

We've left our profit share option intact. Similar to the discussions we have about the value of standard royalty rates in preserving equitable treatment for all our authors, we feel that it's important to maintain our standard approach to the profit share model. This model is one that has been accepted by others with substantial audiences, as well as by some with smaller audiences. At both ends of the spectrum, the feeling has been that our approach is fair for all, and we'd like to keep to that.

As we discussed, the decision for the author clearly comes down to optimizing his share of upside at the front or back end. No matter which model is used, we will be motivated, committed, and elated to drive this book to the top of the market and keep it going over the long term. We believe this can be a very special book, and I very much want us to be the publisher fortunate enough to partner with to bring it to life.

I know you're already aware of these advantages from your work with us on other projects, but simply for emphasis, with Penguin Random House, would have the support of the largest (& smartest & best resourced) sales force in the industry, the most robust supply chain, and a state of the art consumer marketing operation. We have direct relationships with more booksellers than anyone. We have direct relationships with more consumers than any other publisher. And, in my humble opinion, we have the most brilliant editors and creative marketing teams.

If you'd like more information about any part of what the PRH experience would be like for please don't hesitate to ask. For ease of reference, I've attached a summary.

As far as the finances, we're offering two options:

- **advance plus bonuses: total package of**

If within 12 months of initial publication, total cumulative earnings from all sources reach PRH will pay a bonus advance of We will pay an additional recoupable bonus at the cumulative earnings thresholds below, if the earnings threshold is reached within 12 months of reaching the previous threshold:

initial advance			
	earnings threshold	bonus advance	cumulative advance

Total potential bonus:

- **Profit Share:** of net profits

US v. Bertelsmann
1:21-cv-0866-FYP
PX 0218

Net profits calculation:

= Net Profits

Author will not be liable for losses.

The author will be granted meaningful consultation on the marketing.

I hope this will help provide with all the information he needs into making his decision. We're looking forward to hearing back.

Best,
Madeline

Penguin Random House

The Penguin Random House Advantage

- #1 Global Publisher
- 270+ imprints worldwide
- 600 million books sold every year
- 500+ NYT bestsellers per year
- 60+ Nobel Prize laureates

What Sets Us Apart

Broadest Sales and Distribution Reach

With an industry-leading supply chain and specialized sales teams for every kind of retail channel—including non-traditional, B2B and educational accounts—**we get our books into consumers' hands faster and more reliably than our competition.**

- Largest publishing sales force **(400+ reps)** with deepest, most extensive account relationships
- Distribution to **28,000 US retail locations**, more than any other publisher
- Biggest international sales force in the industry, with global reach to readers in **175+ countries**
- Only publisher shipping to Amazon multiple times per day, seven days a week

Reaching Your Readers

With **more consumer relationships than any book publisher** or dedicated book retailer, we are the best at finding the right audience for each of our books, no matter the genre or topic.

- **22 million** consumers reached monthly across web, social and email outreach
- **16.6 million** email subscribers in our consumer database
- **310+ million** fans across our corporate, divisional and authors' social media
- **70,000-member online reader panel** to inform successful positioning of our titles

Beyond the Book

We offer a variety of other services to help our authors expand their audience reach and revenue beyond the book.

- **Grammy-winning** Audio Team with 15 recording studios, 13 producers, ...
- **Author Portal** featuring weekly sales figures, royalty statements, graphing tools and bestseller data, exclusive author discount, and a wealth of publishing resources and tutorials from in-house experts to help you engage fans, grow audience, and drive book sales
- **PRH Speakers Bureau:** Booked **850+ events** with **220+ authors** and sold **180k+ books in 2019**
- **Video Team:** 1,000+ videos produced via in-house digital studio with over **27 million views in 2019**
- **E-courses and Podcasts:** Work with array of strategic partners to develop and distribute online course and podcast content for authors and drive incremental book sales
- **Licensing and Merchandising:** Out of Print Clothing® sells literature-inspired apparel, accessories and novelties directly to consumers online and in over 1,000 wholesale accounts, in 90+ countries

Social Responsibility

With **$10 million** in U.S. charitable donations, author ambassador opportunities with partner organizations like Save the Children, First Book, and PEN, and a variety of ongoing diversity and sustainability initiatives, we are a publishing partner our authors can be proud to work with.

HIGHLY CONFIDENTIAL BPRH-LIT-000029920

Date: Friday, November 2 2018 06:31 PM
Subject: PRH Board - Nov 2018 - US Update_11-2_no appendix.pdf
From: McIntosh, Madeline <[redacted]>
To: Dohle, Markus <[redacted]>
Attachments: PRH Board - Nov 2018 - US Update_11-2_no appendix.pdf

Hi Markus. Attached is the current draft of the US update for the board meeting. Still some more tweaking to do Monday, but this is certainly the general idea. Please let me know if you think it looks ok or have suggestions.

Good meeting with Thomas today. We mainly talked about the RH/Crown change and about the more complicated puzzle that is Knopf Doubleday. Nothing unexpected.

I'll be in the office Monday morning before flying out to Berlin. So we can talk by phone Monday or I'll see you Tuesday.

Thanks.

US v. Bertelsmann
1:21-cv-0866-FYP
PX 0411

Penguin Random House

U.S. – Insights and Outlook

Penguin Random House Board of Directors
November 13, 2018

Confidential Business Information-To Be Distributed to Penguin Random House Board of Directors Only

Penguin Random House

What's happened since April?

What I knew I had to tackle in 2018:	1. Understand why we were losing market share and what to do about it	2. Try to minimize impact of terms pressure and find ways to mitigate	3. Manage downtown move
What happened so far:	• Listening Tour: employees & agents (ongoing) • Town Halls (covering all US employees) • Elevated two strategically critical areas to US Board level: - Consumer Marketing (appointed Sanyu Dillon) - Audio (Amanda D'Acierno) • Promoted Nina von Moltke to Pres., Strategic Development • Created market development structure in Sales (led by Amanda Close) • Unified adult and kids educational sales teams • Opportunity assessments: Juvenile (Publishing, Education, China) and Adult Non-fiction	[redacted] • VSO (facilitated reductions in sales, fulfillment, ops/IT, royalties, contracts) • Prioritized physical pricing initiative (new publishing-focused tools close to roll-out) • Increased background coordination in auctions to leverage internal demand information better and avoid internal up-bidding	• Interim moves to allow for construction • Final move in December

← • Random House & Crown announcement →

 Confidential Business Information -To Be Distributed to Penguin Random House Board Members Only

Penguin Random House

HIGHLY CONFIDENTIAL

BPRH-LIT-002537204

Date: Tuesday, April 6 2021 02:57 PM
Subject: RE: cookbook payouts
From: McIntosh, Madeline [REDACTED]
To: Wehner, Aaron [REDACTED] Centrello, Gina [REDACTED] Sanford, David [REDACTED] Von Moltke, Nina [REDACTED] Flaxman, Jill [REDACTED]

OK, thanks. This is really helpful. I'll hear her out and report back.

From: Wehner, Aaron
Sent: Tuesday, April 6, 2021 2:55 PM
To: McIntosh, Madeline [REDACTED] Centrello, Gina [REDACTED] >; Sanford, David [REDACTED] Von Moltke, Nina [REDACTED]
Cc: Flaxman, Jill [REDACTED]
Subject: Re: cookbook payouts

Hi Madeline,

Sorry to hear [REDACTED] landed in your box on this fun topic. Payouts are an issue in every negotiation with [REDACTED] we lost something just last week w/her over payout; Norton offered thirds, with everything paid by publication). Many of our competitors pay in thirds (or sometimes even halves), and some cover photo budgets out of plant cost as well. That said, a Chronicle or a HMH or Artisan doesn't bring nearly as much to the table as we do beyond better payout, which all the major agents recognize. It's pretty rare we lose something over payout.

For context, on the typical mid-range/modestly frontloaded cookbook deal of [REDACTED] the advance breakdown from us would look as follows:

[REDACTED] paid on sig
[REDACTED] paid on d&a *[approximately [REDACTED] of total [REDACTED] paid at this point would have been paid by Author to photographer]*
[REDACTED] paid on pub
[REDACTED] paid 12 months post-pub

Whereas for a Norton at this level, the author would have [REDACTED] total by d&a and not have to cover photo costs. If the author relies solely on their book advances/revenue, the Norton deal is clearly much more appealing. Whereas for authors who have a broader revenue stream, they can afford to weight other factors in the decision (and we usually prevail in those cases).

For higher level advances, the payout difference tends to be much less of an issue. The smaller publishers tend not to compete, the first two payments are much larger etc.

For whatever reason [REDACTED] has decided that our policy of four payments are a deep offense. We have worked out a frontloaded payout structure with her (and we almost always adjust the four payments on most low to mid-level acquisitions to reflect the significant up-front costs that cookbook authors bear). And [REDACTED] still routinely sells books to us; as she's acknowledged to me and others, we are by far her main source of business.

I'd be happy to gather to discuss later in the week, and can enlist Jill to join as well (cc'd here). Thanks much...

A

From: "McIntosh, Madeline" [REDACTED]
Date: Tuesday, April 6, 2021 at 10:56 AM
To: "Wehner, Aaron" [REDACTED] "Centrello, Gina" <

US v. Bertelsmann
1:21-cv-0866-FYP
PX 0190

CONFIDENTIAL BPRH-005152040

"Sanford, David" , "Von Moltke, Nina"
Subject: cookbook payouts

Hi. I have a message from that she wants to talk to me about payouts on cookbooks "which is becoming more of an issue for PRH." Any idea what's triggering her?

I'll set up time for later in the week.

Madeline McIntosh
Penguin Random House

cell

Date: Friday, January 18 2019 12:16 PM
Subject: confidential: RH/C integration
From: McIntosh, Madeline [redacted]
To: Dohle, Markus [redacted]
Attachments: Crown Integration Memo 1-18-19.pdf

Hi Markus. Attached is the summary of the changes that we discussed. I'll also share this afternoon what the communication plan looks like.

The news re: fiction moving to RH and BBD has already taken place to VERY positive responses from agents. Andrew Wylie, Molly Friedrich, Stefanie Rostan, all others: happy to have Susan and Kara overseeing their authors and keeping their editors.

US v. Bertelsmann
1:21-cv-0866-FYP
PX 0241

RANDOM HOUSE – CROWN INTEGRATION MEMO

January 17, 2019

Random House

Random House is the name of our group, and there are three main divisions:

1) Ballantine Bantam Dell
2) Crown
3) Random House

We are focusing the editorial profiles of each group as follows:

1) **Ballantine Bantam Dell** (BBD) – Primarily commercial fiction
   - Imprints:
     - * Publisher: Kara Welsh
       - Ballantine Books
       - Bantam Books
       - Dell
       - Delacorte Press
     - * Publisher: Scott Shannon
       - Del Rey
   - Editors Julian Pavia and Hilary Teeman will join BBD
   - BBD will no longer be acquiring prescriptive nonfiction
   - Marnie Cochran transferred to the Harmony/Rodale team working under Diana Baroni and acquiring prescriptive nonfiction to increase our market share in that category.

2) **Crown** – Nonfiction, lifestyle, and Christian publishing
   - Imprints:
     - * Co-Publishers: David Drake and Aaron Wehner
       - Crown Trade
       - Clarkson Potter
       - Harmony
       - Rodale Books
       - Ten Speed Press
     - * Publisher: Tina Constable
       - Convergent
       - Currency
       - Image
       - Multnomah
       - WaterBrook

- Crown Archetype will publish out titles already announced under this imprint; going forward, celebrity titles will be acquired under Crown Trade.
- Forum will publish out titles already announced under this imprint and then will be quietly discontinued. We will continue publishing select conservative voices under Crown Trade and otherwise cede the category to Sentinel.
- Regardless of editorial transfers, fiction titles will stay on the Crown list through 2019 with their existing editors, publicists, and marketing persons, but will be supported by the BBD marketing team.
- If we own future books of fiction by a Crown author, with the approval of author and agent, we will move it to the BBD list. If we own a future nonfiction book by a BBD author, we would move to Crown if the author approves.
- In the future, agents would submit to the editor of their choosing on the appropriate list.
- Random House and BBD will continue to do a house bid, and Crown would bid separately, so the agents will not lose a bid. Of course, there will be less internal competition with the focused editorial profiles in our three divisions.
- Clarkson Potter is mostly unaffected.
- Christian publishing is currently unaffected. We will be analyzing this publishing program.

3) **Random House** (RH) – Literary fiction and narrative nonfiction

- Imprints:

  * Publisher: Susan Kamil
    - The Dial Press
    - Hogarth
    - Random House

  * Publisher: Tom Perry
    - Modern Library

  * Publisher: Chris Jackson
    - One World

- The Spiegel & Grau imprint will be discontinued. We will publish out their books through 2019 as Spiegel & Grau titles (contingent on their permission). All future titles will be reassigned to other divisions.
- We are phasing out our e-only publishing program.

The structure of our support departments follows:

4) The **Finance**, **Production**, and **Subrights** departments will be combined, reporting to Bill Takes.

- **Finance** will be led by Patsy Tucker (VP, Director of Business Operations & Analytics).
  - * Jill Flaxman will now be SVP, Deputy Publisher of Clarkson Potter, Harmony, Rodale, and Ten Speed Press, reporting to Aaron Wehner.
- **Production** will have two teams:
  - * Derek Gullino: 4-color publishing
  - * Lisa Feuer: 1-color publishing
- **Subrights** will have co-directors: Denise Cronin and Lance Fitzgerald.

5) The **Art** department will be combined into a single team led by Paolo Pepe (SVP, Creative Director).

6) The combined **Marketing and Publicity** departments will be led by Theresa Zoro.

- Donna Passannante will be moving to PRH Audio.
- Carisa Hays will be heading the Speakers Bureau

Reductions

- Editorial: [redacted]
- Digital: [redacted]
- Finance: [redacted]
- Subrights: [redacted]
- Production: [redacted]
- Art: [redacted]
- Marketing & Publicity: [redacted]

[redacted] terminations
[redacted] enior positions eliminated [redacted]
[redacted] open positions eliminated
Savings & Benefits: [redacted]

HIGHLY CONFIDENTIAL BPRH-LIT-000094381

Date: Tuesday, April 7 2020 09:20 AM
Subject: CPG- 12345 Categories 04-03-12.doc
From: Mavjee, Maya [redacted]
To: McIntosh, Madeline [redacted]
Attachments: CPG- 12345 Categories 04-03-12.doc

Hi there. I know this is out of date. But it was useful as a guideline. Once everyone, including editors, understood the parameters for each category it made the author care conversation more manageable. This was more to get us all on the same page M

US v. Bertelsmann
1:21-cv-02866-FYP
PX 0986

CATEGORY 1: Lead Titles
Sales goal of 75,000 units or higher and/or Advance over $500,000

Beginning at acquisition:

- Creation of consumer identity profile to guide marketing efforts for pre-pub, publication, and post-publication efforts
- Conceptualize visual narrative for the book
- Provide author with access to RH Author Portal and Crown Author Questionnaire to help establish and refine author's online and offline platform designed to maximize book sales, followed up with ongoing conversations with Crown team
- Identify and pitch as appropriate key conferences/trade shows where author may have a presence (FYE, BEA, SXSW, TED, etc)

Engaging accounts (6-9 months prior to publication):

- Title included in Crown Publishing Group online and print (where appropriate) catalogs
- Dedicated publicist assigned to work with the author
- SEO-optimized book-specific terms selected for use throughout the life of the book in online and print marketing campaign, flap copy, etc
- Extensive solicitation material as appropriate to the individual title
- Galleys or color advance reading copy creation where appropriate
- Focused collaboration with and support of author's platform partners
- Creation of point of purchase display materials
- Cover image, author photo, author links, blurbs, press quotes, reading group guides, teacher's guides, excerpts, TOC, flap copy, ebook copy, author biography, awards (if applicable) posted on www.RandomHouse.com, www.CrownPublishing.com, and edelweiss.abovethetreeline.com.
- All content above is sent weekly to our online retailers
- Pitch appropriate key conferences/trade shows/book festivals where author may have a presence

Engaging consumers (3-6 months prior to publication):

- Search-optimized press release developed in consultation with author for use with media
- Targeted, category specific galley mailing to appropriate long lead media, including publishing trades
- Leverage author's media contacts via galley mailing
- Long-lead media luncheons and desk-side meetings in New York, as appropriate
- Outreach and galley or finished copy mailings to category- or topic- appropriate special interest groups, including retailers, professional organizations, bloggers and bookgroups
- Identify and pitch publications for first and second serial excerpts
- Bookseller dinners in target regional markets to be set up where appropriate
- Creation or updating of author's website to maximize book's presence
- Ongoing support of author's online platform and social media development, including search engine optimization for author's site
- Creation of title-specific digital assets to bolster author web presence and online account detail pages
- Social network and targeted search advertising and promotion as appropriate
- Excerpts posted on scribd.com
- Press release and associated assets posted on Crown website and social media platforms as appropriate
- Continued book festival pitching as appropriate

Marketplace roll-out:

- Multi-city author tour where appropriate; up to 15 markets
- Television and/or Radio Satellite Tour (s)where appropriate
- Consumer book advertising in appropriate venues including print, online, electronic, outdoor and/or transit

- Social network and targeted search advertising and promotion as appropriate
- Publisher-sponsored promotion at appropriate retail venues
- Targeted, category-specific finished book mailing to appropriate media nationwide, including print and online reviewers and bloggers as well as appropriate TV and radio outlets
- Extensive national and regional media follow-up
- Leverage author's media contacts via finished book mailing
- Interviews actively solicited in author's home and tour markets, with publicist to arrange all tour market travel via Random House Travel
- Blogger tour or Twitter "party" arranged either internally or with outside vendor as appropriate
- Tie-in with author lecture schedule and facilitate book sales for those events as necessary
- Submit work for various national book awards as appropriate
- Submit book for appropriate national TV, print and online Holiday gift book round-ups
- Academic marketing outreach to category- or topic-appropriate teachers and professors
- Book focus on CPG-owned media verticals and RH Inc corporate platforms, as appropriate
- Featured in RH Inc and Crown Publishing Group e-newsletters (such as WhatsNew@RandomHouse, Read It Forward, The Recipe Club, Crafternews, Books for Better Living, as appropriate)
- eBook version promoted in all PR, advertising, promotion and social media outreach
- Book specific "widget" created, for embedding on partner websites
- Any author events listed on websites
- Author event materials as needed
- Reading group guide created and posted online where appropriate

Driving sales (ongoing post-publication efforts):

- Ongoing analysis – what's working?
- Ongoing promotion at appropriate retail venues
- Ongoing consumer book advertising in appropriate venues on an ROI basis
- Tie-in with author lecture schedule and facilitate book sales for those events as necessary
- Submit work for various national book awards as appropriate
- Submit book for appropriate national TV, print and online Holiday gift book round-ups
- Publicist to target ongoing media interviews opportunistically and to coordinate ongoing media requests

CATEGORY 2: Opportunity titles
Sales Goal of 25,000 — 75,000 units and/or Advance of $150,000 - $500,000

Beginning at acquisition:

- Creation of consumer identity profile to guide marketing efforts for pre-pub, publication, and post-publication efforts
- Conceptualize visual narrative for the book
- Provide author with access to RH Author Portal and Crown Author Questionnaire to help establish and refine author's online and offline platform designed to maximize book sales, followed up with ongoing conversations with Crown team
- Identify and pitch as appropriate key conferences/trade shows where author may have a presence (FYE, BEA, SXSW, TED, etc)

Engaging accounts (6-9 months prior to publication):

- Title included in Crown Publishing Group online and print (where appropriate) catalogs
- Dedicated publicist assigned to work with the author
- SEO-optimized book-specific terms selected for use throughout the life of the book in online and print marketing campaign, flap copy, etc
- Solicitation material as appropriate to the individual title
- Galleys where appropriate
- Focused collaboration with and support of author's platform partners
- Creation of point of purchase display materials as appropriate
- Cover image, author photo, author links, blurbs, press quotes, reading group guides, teacher's guides, excerpts, TOC, flap copy, ebook copy, author biography, awards (if applicable) on www.RandomHouse.com, www.CrownPublishing.com, and edelweiss.abovethetreeline.com.
- All content above is sent weekly to our online retailers

Engaging consumers (3-6 months prior to publication):

- Search-optimized press release developed in consultation with author for use with media
- Targeted, category specific galley mailing to appropriate long lead media, including publishing trades
- Leverage author's media contacts via galley mailing
- Long-lead media luncheons and desk-side meetings in New York, as appropriate
- Outreach and galley or finished copy mailings to category- or topic- appropriate special interest groups, including retailers, professional organizations, bloggers and book groups
- Identify and pitch publications for first and second serial excerpts
- Updating of author's website to maximize book's presence
- Ongoing support of author's online platform and social media development, including search engine optimization for author's site
- Creation of title-specific digital assets to bolster author web presence and online account detail pages
- Social network and targeted search advertising and promotion as appropriate
- Excerpts posted on scribd.com
- Press release and associated assets posted on Crown website and social media platforms as appropriate

Marketplace roll-out:

- Multi-city national author tour where appropriate; up to 5 markets
- Radio Satellite Tour where appropriate
- Consumer book advertising in appropriate venues, potentially including print and online
- Social network and targeted search advertising and promotion as appropriate
- Publisher-sponsored promotion at appropriate retail venues
- Targeted, category specific finished book mailing to appropriate media, including print and online reviewers, bloggers as well as appropriate TV and radio outlets
- Extensive national and regional media follow-up
- Leverage author's media contacts via finished book mailing
- Bookseller dinners in target regional markets to be set up where appropriate
- Interviews actively solicited in author's home and tour markets, with publicist to arrange all tour market travel via Random House Travel
- Any interview requests generated by mailing that are local to the author or can be set up by phone or via satellite will be scheduled
- Blogger tour or Twitter "party" arranged either internally or with outside vendor as appropriate
- Tie-in with author lecture schedule and facilitate book sales for those events as necessary
- Book festival pitching as appropriate
- Submit work for various national book awards as appropriate
- Submit book for appropriate National TV, print and online Holiday gift book round-ups
- Academic marketing outreach to category- or topic-appropriate teachers and professors
- Book focus on CPG-owned media verticals and RH Inc corporate platforms, as appropriate
- Featured in RH Inc and Crown Publishing Group e-newsletters (such as WhatsNew@RandomHouse, Read It Forward, The Recipe Club, Crafternews, Books for Better Living, as appropriate)
- eBook version promoted in all PR, advertising, promotion and social media outreach
- Book specific "widget" created, for embedding on partner websites
- Any author events listed on websites
- Author event materials as needed
- Reading group guide created and posted online where appropriate

Driving sales (ongoing post-publication efforts):

- Ongoing analysis – what's working?
- Ongoing promotion at appropriate retail venues
- Ongoing consumer book advertising in appropriate venues on an ROI basis

CATEGORY 3
Sales Goal of 10,000 — 25,000 units and/or Advance of $50,000 — $150,000

Beginning at acquisition:

- Creation of consumer identity profile to guide marketing efforts for pre-pub, publication, and post-publication efforts
- Conceptualize visual narrative for the book
- Provide author with access to RH Author Portal and Crown Author Questionnaire to help establish and refine author's online and offline platform designed to maximize book sales, followed up with ongoing conversations with Crown team
- Identify and pitch as appropriate key conferences/trade shows where author may have a presence (FYE, BEA, SXSW, TED, etc)

Engaging accounts (6-9 months prior to publication):

- Title included in Crown Publishing Group online and print (where appropriate) catalogs
- Dedicated publicity contact assigned to handle any publicity queries.
- SEO-optimized book-specific terms selected for use throughout the life of the book in online and print marketing campaign, flap copy, etc
- Solicitation material as appropriate to the individual title
- Galley creation where appropriate
- Cover image, author photo, author links, blurbs, press quotes, reading group guides, teacher's guides, excerpts, TOC, flap copy, ebook copy, author biography, awards (if applicable) on www.RandomHouse.com, www.CrownPublishing.com, and edelweiss.abovethetreeline.com.
- All content above is sent weekly to our online retailers

Engaging consumers (3-6 months prior to publication):

- Search-optimized press release developed in consultation with author for use with media
- Targeted, category specific galley mailing to appropriate long lead media, including publishing trades
- Outreach and galley or finished copy mailings to category- or topic- appropriate special interest groups, including retailers, professional organizations, bloggers and book groups
- Identify and pitch publications for first and second serial excerpts
- Ongoing support of author's online platform and social media development, including help with search engine optimization for author's site
- Creation of title-specific digital assets to bolster author web presence and online account detail pages
- Social network promotion as appropriate
- Press release and associated assets posted on Crown website and social media platforms as appropriate

Marketplace roll-out:

- Targeted, category specific finished book mailing to appropriate media nationwide, including print and online reviewers, bloggers as well as appropriate TV and radio outlets
- Extensive national and regional media follow-up
- Regional author tour, as appropriate (up to 4 markets)
- Publicist to schedule media interviews with author in their home market, by phone, and via satellite as appropriate
- Local market author events and media to be set up where appropriate
- Social network promotion as appropriate
- Maximize media coverage through Crown's social media platforms
- Submit book for appropriate national TV, print and online Holiday gift book round-ups
- Academic marketing outreach to category- or topic-appropriate teachers and professors
- Book focus on CPG-owned media verticals and RH Inc corporate platforms, as appropriate

- Featured in RH Inc and Crown Publishing Group e-newsletters (such as WhatsNew@RandomHouse, Read It Forward, The Recipe Club, Crafternews, Books for Better Living, as appropriate)
- eBook version promoted in all promotion and social media outreach
- Book specific "widget" created, for embedding on partner websites
- Any author events listed on websites
- Author event materials as needed
- Reading group guide created and posted online where appropriate
- Press release and associated assets posted on Crown website and social media platforms as appropriate

Driving sales (ongoing post-publication efforts):

- Ongoing analysis – what's working?

Message

From:	Eulau, Dennis [/O=EXCHANGELABS/OU=EXCHANGE ADMINISTRATIVE GROUP (FYDIBOHF23SPDLT)/CN=RECIPIENTS/CN=702A649498F94D16BBD47E90D2D1E89B-EULAU, DENN]
Sent:	5/6/2019 8:05:01 PM
To:	Reidy, Carolyn [/o=ExchangeLabs/ou=Exchange Administrative Group (FYDIBOHF23SPDLT)/cn=Recipients/cn=c433dce50ac94802aae488127181ab5c-Reidy, Caro]
Subject:	FW: cONSTELLATION
Attachments:	Publishing Call.docx
Importance:	High

I would Change this to say we were planning the out years of eaudio where planned at [REDACTED] growth – so we feel our LRP stands...

ALTHOUGH OUR LONG RANGE PLAN SUPPOSED THAT DIGITAL AUDIO WOULD CONTINUE TO GROW AT [REDACTED] WE ARE SEEING A DECELERATING SO FAR THIS YEAR. IT'S TOO EARLY TO DETERMINE HOW MUCH OF THIS DECLINE IS DUE TO TITLES – A VERY SUCCESSFUL DIGITAL AUDIO TITLE CAN SELL SIGNIFICANTLY MORE THAN THE AVERAGE TITLES – BUT ITS LOOKING LIKE GROWTH THIS YEAR COULD BE DOWN TO [REDACTED]

From: Reidy, Carolyn [REDACTED]
Sent: Monday, May 06, 2019 7:40 PM
To: Eulau, Dennis [REDACTED]
Cc: Reidy, Carolyn [REDACTED]
Subject: cONSTELLATION
Importance: High

DENNIS: Can you read this and see if you think I have any errors/things I shouldn't say, or suggestions of what I SHOULD say?

Many thanks.

CKR

US v. Bertelsmann
1:21-cv-0866-FYP
PX 0530

VCBS-00454200

Project Constellation
Diligence Discussion Agenda
STRICTLY CONFIDENTIAL

PUBLISHING

1. Business Overview and Differentiation
    a. Competition: Describe the competitive landscape and the threat from other large publishers (Penguin Random House, Hachette, HarperColllins, Macmillan) vs. smaller, independent publishers vs. self-publish alternatives

AS YOU NOTE, THE US PUBLISHING MARKET IS MADE UP OF WHAT IS KNOWN AS THE 'BIG FIVE' – PRH DOMINATES WITH THE LARGEST MARKET SHARE, FOLLOWED BY HARPER COLLINS AND THEN S&S. HACHETTE IS A CLOSE FOURTH, FOLLOWED BY MACMILLAN. THESE COMPANIES ARE OUR BIGGEST COMPETITORS, ESPECIALLY FOR BOOKS BY ALREADY BESTSELLING AUTHORS AND CELEBRITIES, SINCE THEY ARE THE MOST LIKELY TO COME UP WITH HIGH ADVANCE PAYMENTS REQUIRED AND ARE KNOWN FOR THEIR STRONG EDITORIAL AND PUBLISHING SKILLS. LIKE S&S, EACH OF THESE COMPANIES IS MADE UP OF SMALLER PUBLISHING IMPRINTS, EACH WITH ITS OWN EDITORIAL FOCUS WHICH GIVES IT A REPUTATION BOTH FOR EDITORIAL AND PUBLISHING SUCCESS. AND OUR MARGINS ARE THE BEST OF THE BIG FIVE PUBLISHERS.

AUTHORS GENERALLY CHOSE TO GO WITH A PUBLISHING HOUSE THAT THEY BELIEVE WILL BRING THEM SUCCESS, AND THEIR CHOICE IS USUALLY BASED ON A COMBINATION OF EDITORIAL MATCH, A FEEL THE EDITOR AND HOUSE UNDERSTANDS WHAT THEY ARE WRITING, AND PUBLISHING VISION AS TO HOW TO BRING THE BOOK TO MARKET AND CREATE AN AUDIENCE FOR IT.

PUBLISHING HOUSES AND IMPRINTS GAIN REPUTATIONS BASED ON THE SUCCESSES THEY HAVE PUBLISHED. S&S FOR EXAMPLE HAS BEEN SEEN AS THE PREMIER SERIOUS NONFICTION PUBLISHER FOR DECADES – AS THE PUBLISHER OF ALL THE PRESIDENTS MEN (AND ALL OF BOB WOODWARD'S SUBSEQUENT TITLES), DAVID MC CULLOUGH, DORIS KEARNS GOODWIN – AS EXAMPLES. AS TO CELEBRITIES, OUR SUPERB PUBLISHING OF BRUCE SPRINGSTEEN AND HILARY CLINTON – FROM TWO VERY DIFFERENT CATEGORIES – STAND US WELL IN COMPETITION FOR THE NEXT MAJOR BOOK. SCRIBNER'S REPUTATION FOR LITERARY FICTION GOES BACK TO THE 1920S AND F SCOTT FITZGERALD AND HEMINGWAY AND THEY STILL ARE RECOGNIZED AS ONE OF THE PREMIER LITERARY FICTION PUBLISHERS AT WORK IN THE MARKET.

BY AND LARGE, WHEN WE WANT TO WIN AN AUCTION OR 'BEAUTY CONTEST' AS IT'S CALLED WHEN THE MONIES INVOLVED ARE CLOSE, WE DO. OUR EDITORS AND OUR PUBLISHING SKILLS ARE THE MATCH OF ANY OF OUR MAJOR COMPETITORS AND IN INDIVIDUAL CASES EXCEED THEM.

OF COURSE THE FIVE MAJOR PUBLISHERS MAKE UP ABOUT HALF OF THE TRADE MARKET AND THERE ARE MYRIAD SMALLER PUBLISHERS, SOME WITH ONLY A SINGLE TITLE UNDER THEIR NAME. THEY TOO CAN COMPETE WITH US FOR THE BESTSELLER LIST AT ANY ONE TIME, AS THEY IDENTIFY BOOKS THAT TAP INTO THE CULTURAL ZEITGEIST, BUT THEY RARELY COMPETE WITH US IN AUCTIONS FOR NEW PROPERTIES. OFTEN THESE PUBLISHERS BECOME FARM TEAMS FOR AUTHORS WHO THEN WANT TO MOVE TO A LARGER, MORE FINANCIALLY STABLE MAJOR PUBLISHER.

Project Constellation
Diligence Discussion Agenda
STRICTLY CONFIDENTIAL

AND LAST BUT NOT LEAST IS THE NEW MARKET OF SELF PUBLISHING. THE ONLY GENRE THAT HAS MIGRATED ALMOST EXCLUSIVELY TO SELF PUBLISHING IS THE ROMANCE MARKET, WHICH USED TO BE THAT BEDROCK FOR MASS MARKET PUBLISHING, WHICH HAS DECLINED DRAMATICALLY IN THE LAST FEW YEARS. MOST SELF PUBLISHED BOOKS ARE SOLD AT EXTREMELY LOW PRICES – LESS THAT $5. WE HAVE ADJUSTED OUR PUBLISHING PROGRAM AS A RESULT OF THE RISE OF SELF PUBLISHING AND WE ONLY PUBLISH ROMANCE WRITERS WHOM WE FEEL CAN SUSTAIN A SIGNIFICANT SALES VOLUME IN TODAY'S WORLD IN BOTH PRINT AND DIGITAL FORMATS.

HOWEVER, THE SELF PUBLISHING MARKET IS ALSO AN OPPORTUNITY FOR US – WE HAVE A SMALL SELF PUBLISHING IMPRINT WITH AUTHOR SOLUTIONS, CALLED ARCHWAY, AND BOTH THROUGH THAT IMPRINT AND ALSO BY LOOKING AT THE BESTSELLER LISTS FOR SELF PUBLISHED TITLS, WE CAN FIND AUTHORS WHO WANT TO MOVE TO A MAINSTREAM PUBLISHER WHO CAN PUBLISH THEM IN ALL FORMATS.

I'D LIKE TO ALSO NOTE THAT SINCE TRADE PUBLISHING IS A RELATIVELY FLAT MARKET – AND HAS BEEN FOR THE LAST TEN YEARS OR SO – MAINTAINING MARKET SHARE IS ITSELF AN ACCOMPLISHMENT, BECAUSE GROWTH, IF IT COMES, COMES FROM TAKING MARKET SHARE AWAY FROM OTHER PUBLISHERS. SO WE ARE PROUD OF THE FACT THAT SIMON & SCHUSTER HAS MAINTAINED IT'S 7% MARKET SHARE THROUGHOUT THE DECADE – A REAL ACCOMPLISHMENT WHEN YOU REALIZE THAT ████ OF OUR SALES VOLUME IS CREATED EACH YEAR FROM NEW TITLES – ABOUT ████ OF OUR SALES VOLUME IS BACKLIST, THE REST IS ORIGINATED EACH YEAR.

i. How does S&S differentiate itself to win rights for well-known authors and public personalities? EDITORIAL STRENGTH AND PUBLISHING VISION

b. Changing Distribution: Comment on the impact of new digital distribution models and how S&S is positioned to better monetize IP of its authors given these trends

THE NEW DIGITAL DISTRIBUTION MODELS HAVE DEFINITELY BENEFITED OUR BUSINESS

FIRST OF ALL, DIGITAL DISTRIBUTION MEANS THAT ALL OF OUR TITLES ARE AVAILABLE EVERYWHERE IN THE WORLD AT ANY TIME. THANKS TO DIGITAL SHORT RUN PRINTING, THIS MEANS OUR BOOKS ARE AVAILABLE BOTH IN DIGITAL FORM, AS EBOOKS, AND ALSO IN PHYSICAL FORM. ALL 20,000 OF OUR BACKLIST TITLES CAN BE PURCHASED BY INTERESTED CONSUMERS – WHEREAS BEFORE YOU HAD TO HAVE SALES OF SEVERAL THOUSAND COPIES A YEAR IN ORDER TO ECONOMICALLY KEEP THEM IN PRINT IN A WAREHOUSE, THERE IS NOW NO NUMERICAL REQUIREMENT TO KEEPING A BOOK IN PRINT.

SECONDLY, THE ABILITY TO HIGHLIGHT A TITLE THROUGH DIGITAL MEANS HAS LED TO A MUCH BROADER RANGE OF TITLES SOLD. ANY EVENT CAN LEAD US TO CHANGE THE METADATA ON A TITLE, MAKING IT POSSIBLE THROUGH THE DIGITAL DISTRIBUTION CHANNELS OR THROUGH SOCIAL MEDIA TO INTEREST CONSUMERS BECAUSE AN OLDER TITLE – WHICH MAY NOT ACTUALLY BE PHYSICALLY IN ANY BOOKSTORE, NOR TOP OF MIND TO THE MEDIA – IS RELATED TO SOMETHING HAPPENING IN THE WORLD.

Project Constellation
Diligence Discussion Agenda
STRICTLY CONFIDENTIAL

THIRD, THERE ARE NEW DIGITAL MODELS OF SALE. ONE EXAMPLE IS SUBSCRIPTION SELLING: WE HAVE OUR BACKLIST OFFERED THROUGH SCRIB'D AND ARE PAID UPON CONSUMER READS AS IF WE SOLD THE BOOK, AND WE FIND THAT UP TO [REDACTED] OF OUR TITLES ARE ORDERED BY AT LEAST ONE CONSUMER EACH YEAR. THIS IS AN ENTIRELY NEW SALES MODEL AND WE FIND [REDACTED] REGULAR TRADE SALES OF THE BOOKS. IN ADDITION THERE ARE SITE SUBSCRIPTIONS FOR SCHOOLS, VARIOUS TYPES OF LIBRARIES – AND AGAIN, WE DON'T [REDACTED] OF READERS WHO ARE DISCOVERING AND ENJOYING A WIDE RANGE OF OUR TITLES.

THERE ARE OTHER MODELS – CHUNK SELLING, CHAPTER SELLING, OTHER EXPERIMENTS – BUT NONE HAVE YET GOTTEN REAL TRACTION. NEVERTHELESS WE ARE OF COURSE EXPERIMENTING WITH ANY IDEA THAT COMES ALONG THAT SEEMS TO HAVE PROMISE.

i. Market research suggests that printed book sales are projected to decline 10% annually. Is this consistent with S&S experience / projections and if not why is the trend different for S&S

WE DO NOT SEE THIS TREND IN THE TRADE PUBLISHING BUSINESS, ALTHOUGH THE EDUCATIONAL MARKET HAS SEEN DECLINES OF AROUND 10% OR HIGHER ANNUALLY OVER THE LAST FEW YEARS. THE U.S. TRADE MARKET, ACCORDING TO THE AAP, SHOWED PHYSICAL BOOK GROWTH OF 4.1% IN 2018 AFTER A LOSS OF 0.2% IN 2017 AFTER A GROWTH OF 4.7% IN 2016. SIMON & SCHUSTER DID NOT SEE GROWTH IN PHYSICAL BOOK SALES IN 2018, BUT THAT WAS AFTER A GROWTH OF [REDACTED] IN 2017.

c. Content Rights and Cross Distribution (S&S to Constellation): Describe your agreements with content creators. Do you have the ability to own or manage rights to S&S's consumer books for monetization opportunities across the Constellation mediums and owned distribution platforms (e.g., successful book turned into a Constellation TV series on Constellation All Access)?

IN GENERAL, WE SIGN CONTRACT WITH AUTHORS FOR BOOK AND AUDIO RIGHTS. WE RARELY ACQUIRE FILM RIGHTS FOR OUR TITLES, ALTHOUGH IT IS POSSIBLE THAT ONE COULD IF OUR CORPORATE PARTNER WAS INTERESTED IN DOING SO. BY AND LARGE, AUTHORS HAVE SEPARATE AGENTS FOR BOOK AND FILM RIGHTS AND THOSE AGENTS RARELY WANT TO CONFUSE A BOOK AUCTION BY DEALING WITH SOME PURCHASERS FOR BOOK RIGHTS ONLY AND OTHERS FOR COMBINED BOOK/FILM RIGHTS. IN TERMS OF FAMOUS AUTHORS – SUCH AS STEPHEN KING – [REDACTED] IN ADDITION, THERE ARE DIFFICULTIES ON THE FILM SIDE WITH TRYING TO BUNDLE THE RIGHTS IN AN AUCTION: FIRST IS THE SPEED AT WHICH WE HAVE TO MOVE TO MAKE A DECISION TO ACQUIRE A BOOK. SECONDLY, MANY OF THE BOOKS WE BUY ARE NOT YET FULLY WRITTEN AND FILM PURCHASERS WOULD PREFER TO WAIT AND SEE HOW SUCCESSFUL THE FINAL BOOK IS.

IF HOWEVER CBS IS INTERESTED IN ONE OF OUR TITLES, WE WORK TO PERSUADE THE AUTHOR TO GIVE CBS PARTICULAR FAVOR IN DECIDING TO WHOM TO SELL THE FILM RIGHTS AND CAN FACILITATE MEETINGS AND DISCUSSIONS WITH THE AUTHOR AND HIS OR HER REPRESENTATIVE.

Project Constellation
Diligence Discussion Agenda
STRICTLY CONFIDENTIAL

HAVING SAID ALL THAT, WE HAVE CREATED A SYSTEM TO ALERT ALL THE CBS MEDIUMS AND PLATFORMS OF BOTH THE BOOKS WE ACQUIRE AND THE BOOKS THAT GO TO OTHER PUBLISHERS THAT MIGHT INTEREST THEM. WE WORK CLOSELY WITH BOTH THE NETWORK, INCLUDING DAYTIME AND UNSCRIPTED, STUDIOS, ALL ACCESS, SHOWTIME, AND THE VARIOUS PODS WITH TERM DEALS. SO FAR THIS YEAR, FOR INSTANCE, WE HAVE PITCHED MORE THAN 100 TITLES TO THEM, RESULTING IN 25 PROJECTS CURRENTLY UNDER DEVELOPMENT, RANGING FROM NANCY DREW TO THE PEACH TRUCK COOKBOOK (AN INCREASE OF OVER 30% OVER LAST YEAR).

IN ADDITION, WHEN CBS SIGNS UP A PROJECT THAT IS BASED ON AN S&S BOOK, WE WORK VERY CLOSELY WITH THEM TO MARKET THE TITLE: TWO PRIME EXAMPLES BEING UNDER THE DOME BY STEPHEN KING AND THE DOVEKEEPERS BY ALICE HOFFMAN PLUS THE MOTION PICTURE, AMERICAN ASSASSIN.

d. Cross Distribution (Constellation to S&S): Provide examples in which S&S was able to monetize IP of certain Constellation businesses through consumer books.

TWO OF OUR VERY SUCCESSFUL CONSUMER BOOK PROGRAMS BASED ON CBS CONTENT HAVE VERY DIFFERENT PROFILES. FIRST IS STAR TREK. WE HAVE PUBLISHED TIE IN STAR TREK NOVELS, CREATED BY S&S BASED ON THE CHARACTERS AND VARIOUS 'WORLDS' OF STAR TREK, FOR OVER __ YEARS AND HAVE WORKED WITH PARAMOUNT AND THEN CBS TO HELP KEEP THAT BRAND ALIVE. WE ARE CURRENTLY CREATING NEW TRADE PAPERBACKS TO TIE INTO THE ALL ACCESS PROGRAM. SECONDLY WE HAVE THE RECENT FIVE FEET APART: SIMON & SCHUSTER MADE A NOVEL OUT OF THE SCRIPT FOR THIS MOVIE, PUBLISHED IT AS A STAND ALONE NOVEL IN ADVANCE OF THE FILM'S RELEASE, AND THEN PUBLISHED A MOVIE TIE IN EDITION. THE RESULT IS A NOVEL THAT HAS SPENT TO DATE 21 WEEKS ON THE NYTIMES YOUNG ADULT BESTSELLER LIST, 8 OF THEM AS #1.

IN ADDITION, WE HAVE PUBLISHED COMMEMORATIVE/ANNIVERSARY BOOKS FOR SHOWS SUCH AS 60 MINUTES AND INSIDE EDITIONS. LAST YEAR WE PUBLISHED NOTE TO SELF BY GAYLE KING, BASED ON A CBS THIS MORNING SEGMENT. WE ALSO PUBLISHED WITH STEPHEN COLBERT, WHOSE BOAT IS THIS BOAT, WHICH HAS RAISED OVER $2 MILLION FOR HURRICANE RELIEF. THERE HAVE ALSO BEEN SOME TITLES FROM TELEVISION STARS, SUCH AS COOKBOOKS BY PAULEY PERRET, OF NCIS (FOR WHICH WE HAVE IN THE PAST PUBLISHED BOTH ADULT AND CHILDREN'S NOVELIZATIONS), AND A FORTHCOMING ONE FROM

I'D ALSO LIKE TO MENTION THAT IN BOTH OUR CHILDREN'S AND ADULT DIVISIONS WE ARE CREATING MORE WHOLLY OWNED IP THAT CAN BE AVAILABLE TO CBS, IN HOPES WE CAN DEVELOP SOME PRODUCTS THAT ARE NOT SUBJECT TO THE VAGARIES OF AGENT PREFERENCES. AN ADULT PRODUCT, [REDACTED] FOR INSTAND, HAS BEEN OPTIONED AT CBS. AND WE HAVE MORE THAN TEN CHILDREN'S SERIES THAT ARE VERY POPULAR IN PRINT AND ARE AVAILABLE FOR DEVELOPMENT.

i. What type of content have you found to be the most successful in this regard?

BY FAR THE MOST SUCCESSFUL PROJECTS THAT WE'VE WORKED ON WITH CBS ARE BASED ON TRADE FICTION, AS IT IS THE NARRATIVE DRIVE THAT MOST INTERESTS THE FILM DIVISIONS. HOWEVER, WE HAVE ALSO BEEN WORKING ON TALENT DEVELOPMENT WITH DAYTIME, AND HAVE HAD SEVERAL AUTHORS COME CLOSE TO

Project Constellation
Diligence Discussion Agenda
STRICTLY CONFIDENTIAL

DEVELOPMENT DEALS WITH THE STUDIO. WE WERE DR. PHIL'S PUBLISHER BEFORE HE BECAME A CBS PROPERTY, AND SO WE'D LIKE TO FIND THE NEXT DR. PHIL BEFORE HE OR SHE IS FAMOUS.

BUT AS YOU CAN SEE FROM THE BREADTH OF TITLES WE'VE ALREADY PUBLISHED WITH CBS, THERE ARE MANY AREAS WHERE BOOKS CAN BE SUCCESSFUL – SOME OF MUCH LARGER IMPACT THAN OTHERS – AND SINCE OUR LISTS HAVE A WIDE RANGE OF TITLES AND SALES NUMBERS, WE CAN FIND VERY SUCCESSFUL PRODUCTS IN MANY DIFFERENT AREAS.

ii. Is it reasonable to assume there is a similar opportunity for certain Venus content?

THERE IS ABSOLUTELY NO DOUBT ABOUT IT. AFTER ALL, WE PUBLISHED MTV BOOKS WITH MTV YEARS AGO AND STILL HAVE SOME EXTREMELY SUCCESSFUL BACKLIST TITLES IN PRINT FROM THAT IMPRINT (MOST FAMOUS BEING PERKS OF BEING A WALLFLOWER). THE IMPRINT WAS CLOSED DOWN WHEN CBS AND VIACOM SEPARATED, [REDACTED] AND DIDN'T FEEL IT WAS WHERE THEY WANTED TO FOCUS. EVEN AT THE TIME WE FELT THERE WERE MANY POSSIBILITIES OF BOOKS FROM THE THEN-EXISTING PROGRAMMING AND EVEN SOME THAT BUILT ON THE BRAND OF MTV ITSELF.

IN ADDITION, THE VIACOM CHILDREN'S BRANDS LEND THEMSELVES TO BOOKS – WE DID PUBLISH THE NICKELODEON TITLES FOR MANY YEARS, ALTHOUGH THEY ARE NOW LICENSED ELSEWHERE – AND I AM SURE WE COULD DISCOVER NEW AREAS OF PUBLICATIONS THROUGHOUT THE VIACOM UNIVERSE.

e. Revenue Concentration and Key Relationships: The Constellation 10-K mentions that S&S's top two accounts drive a significant portion of its revenue – please provide more details on S&S's revenue concentration, recent historical and expected trends in these top accounts, and overall relationship status with top accounts

AMAZON AND BARNES & NOBLE ARE OUR TWO MAJOR ACCOUNTS, WHICH COMBINED MAKE UP APPROXIMATELY [REDACTED] OF OUR DOMESTIC BOOK SALES. AMAZON HAS BEEN INCREASING MARKET SHARE (IN 2018 THEY WERE [REDACTED] OF OUR NET SALES, UP FROM [REDACTED] IN 2017) AND WE EXPECT IT TO PROBABLY CONTINUE TO GROW MARKETSHARE OVER TIME. BARNES & NOBLE HAS SUFFERED ALONG WITH MOST RETAIL OUTLETS AND HAS SEEN ITS SHARE OF OUR SALES DECLINE FROM [REDACTED] IN 2017 TO [REDACTED] IN 2018. B&N IS CURRENTLY EXPLORING A SALE – WE HOPE THEY CONTINUE TO OPERATE, AS THEIR 670 STORES ARE KEY SHOWROOMS FOR OUR PRODUCT – BUT IF IT DOES EXIT THE MARKET, [REDACTED]

HAVING AMAZON AND B&N MAKE UP [REDACTED] OUR SALES IS NOT UNUSUAL IN OUR MARKET---BEFORE IT WENT BANKRUPT IN 2011, BORDERS AND B&N WERE ABOUT [REDACTED]

WE HAVE EXCELLENT RELATIONSHIPS WITH BOTH ACCOUNTS. ALTHOUGH AMAZON IS A TOUGH NEGOTIATOR, [REDACTED] WE HAVE A GREAT PARTNERSHIP WITH THEM AND MANY OF THE WAYS IN WHICH THEY CAN SEEM DIFFICULT ARE DEMANDS THAT MAKE US BETTER AS PUBLISHERS AND [REDACTED] WE HAVE FOR MANY YEARS HAD A STRONG RELATIONSHIP WITH B&N, AT ALL LEVELS AND AREAS OF THE COMPANY. THEY ARE

Project Constellation
Diligence Discussion Agenda
STRICTLY CONFIDENTIAL

GREAT BOOKSELLERS,

I'D ALSO LIKE TO POINT OUT THAT OF OUR SALES ARE WITH OTHER CUSTOMERS – WALLMART, TARGET, AND INDEPENDENTS, ALL OF WHICH HELP US GET CONSUMER ATTENTION FOR OUR BOOKS AND EACH OF WHICH ON CERTAIN TITLES CAN HAVE AN INFLUENCE GREATER THAN THEIR OVERALL MARKET SHARE.

2. Financials
   a. Is it possible to provide revenue and operating income broken down by: 1) domestic vs. international (further breakdown as available), 2) direct vs. indirect distribution, and 3) print vs. digital (visual vs. audio) content?

OVER THE LAST FIVE YEARS, DOMESTIC REVENUES HAVE BEEN OF OUR REVENUES AND OF OUR OI. CAN YOU TELL US WHAT FURTHER BREAKDOWN YOU'D LIKE TO SEE?

WE ARE UNCLEAR WHAT YOU MEAN BY 'DIRECT VS INDIRECT DISTRIBUTION.' [DO THEY MEAN THROUGH WHOLESALERS AS OPPOSED TO DIRECT SHIPPING?]

      i. Digital content represented of 2018 publishing revenues – what is your expectation for how that will trend over time and what is the impact to the projected financials in terms of operating income?

OVER THE LAST FOUR YEARS, EBOOK SALES HAVE DECLINED RATHER DRAMATICALLY – IT APPEARS THAT THE INITIAL ENTHUSIASM FOR EBOOKS HAS WANED, OUR THEORY BEING DIGITAL FATIGUE – CONSUMERS SEEM TO WANT TO USE THEIR PHONES AND IPADS FOR FILM MORE THAN FOR READING, AND THE POSITIVE ASPECTS OF THE PHYSICAL BOOK HAVE BECOME MORE PRONOUNCED. MEANWHILE, DIGITAL AUDIO HAS INCREASED DRAMATICALLY AND MEANT THAT OVERALL DIGITAL CONTENT AS A PERCENTAGE OF OUR REVENUES HAS REMAINED FAIRLY CONSTANT. NOW THAT EBOOKS ARE WELL BELOW OF OUR SALES VOLUME, WE EXPECT THAT THEIR PORTION OF OUR SALES WILL BEGIN TO DIGITAL AUDIO WILL AND WE ARE PROJECTING PHYSICAL BOOK SALES REVENUE TO GROW SOMEWHERE AROUND A YEAR.

AS TO THE EFFECT OF THESE CHANGES ON OUR ECONOMICS, THAT IS COMPLICATED BECAUSE ONE HAS THE QUESTION OF HOW YOU APPORTION

ONE THING TO NOTE IS THAT EBOOKS

AS YOU MIGHT IMAGINE.

Project Constellation
Diligence Discussion Agenda
STRICTLY CONFIDENTIAL

WHEN WE CONSIDER OUR BUSINESS, [REDACTED] THE ORIGINATING COSTS – THE LARGEST OF WHICH ARE [REDACTED] —WHICH COVERS BOTH PHYSICAL AND DIGITAL FORMATS – DO NOT AS A PERCENTAGE FLUCTUATE MUCH AS A RESULT OF FORMAT SHIFTS.

b. Constellation management presentation called out 1) Digital Audio and 2) Data-driven Publishing as key growth drivers – please provide additional detail on these initiatives
   i. In 2018, digital audio sales grew at [REDACTED] and in 2017 they grew [REDACTED] - how has this been trending over time? Is growth decelerating?

ALTHOUGH OUR LONG RANGE PLAN SUPPOSED THAT DIGITAL AUDIO WOULD CONTINUE TO GROW AT [REDACTED] WE ARE SEEING A DECELERATING SO FAR THIS YEAR. IT'S TOO EARLY TO DETERMINE HOW MUCH OF THIS DECLINE IS DUE TO TITLES – A VERY SUCCESSFUL DIGITAL AUDIO TITLE CAN SELL SIGNIFICANTLY MORE THAN THE AVERAGE TITLES – BUT ITS LOOKING LIKE GROWTH THIS YEAR COULD BE DOWN TO [REDACTED]

WE HAVE OVER THE LAST THREE YEARS DRAMATICALLY INCREASED OUR TITLE OUTPUT (BY [REDACTED] – WE NOW CREATE AN AUDIOBOOK OF EVERY TITLE WE PUBLISH THAT IS IN THE LEAST AUDIO-FRIENDLY; WE HAVE ADDED SOME ORIGINALS; AND WE'VE EVEN EXPERIMENTED WITH CBS WITH A PODCAST (MOBITUATIRES, WITH MO ROCCA OF CBS SUNDAY MORNING) THAT WILL ALSO BECOME A BOOK. WE ARE FOCUSED ON MAKING SURE THAT WE MAXIMIZE POSSIBILITIES IN THIS MARKET. NEW PLAYERS, SUCH AS APPLE AND GOOGLE, SHOULD ALSO HELP THE MARKET CONTINUE GROWING AS THEY COMPETE WITH THE MARKET LEADER, AUDIBLE.

DATA DRIVEN PUBLISHING IS AN ORGANIC GROWTH INITIAIVE BY S&S. THE CONCEPT OF THIS NEW IMPRINT, CALLED TILLER, IS TO USE DATA AVAILABLE THROUGH THE WEB – SOCIAL MEDIA, BOOK SALES THROUGH DIGITAL PLATFORMS, ONLINE INTERESTS – TO DETERMINE AUDIENCES FOR BOOKS THAT DO NOT YET EXIST, AND THEN TO CREATE BOOKS FOR THOSE AUDIENCES, OFTEN USING INFLUENCERS WITH PRE-EXISTING PLATFORMS AS AUTHORS. NORMALLY WE BEGIN WITH AN AUTHOR AND FINISHED MANUSCRIPT AND CREATE AN AUDIENCE AND MARKET FOR THE BOOK. TILLER PRESS BEGINS WITH THE AUDIENCE AND MARKET AND THEN MAKES A BOOK TO FULFILL THE NEED. THIS IS AN ATTEMPT TO USE THE POWER OF DIGITAL INFORMATION AOBUT CONSUMER TASTES AND DESIRES TO CREATE PRODUCT. ALL THAT WE CREATE FOR TILLER WILL ALSO HELP US MARKET OUR EXISTING AUTHOR DRIVEN PRODUCT MORE EFFECTIVELY. TILLER IS PROJECTED TO BE MAKING A SIGNIFICANT CONTRIBUTION IN 2021. WE BEGAN BUILDING THE INFRASTRUCTURE AND HIRING STAFF FOR TILLER AT THE END OF LAST YEAR, FIRST BOOKS WILL BE PUBLISHED IN JUNE, AND A FULL PUBLISHING PROGRAM SHOULD BE IN PLACE BY MID 2020.

c. Provide additional detail on the $[REDACTED] outlined in the Constellation Transformation document (VDR 2.4.17)

THIS ONE I LEAVE TO DENNIS AND GAUTUM!!

Project Constellation
Diligence Discussion Agenda
STRICTLY CONFIDENTIAL

i. Confirm how much of these [redacted] are included in the publishing projections provided in the Constellation LRP
ii. Describe expected changes in the publishing cost structure going forward beyond these expected [redacted] – we note that most expense items appear consistent [redacted] change and is it sustainable?

FIRST OF ALL, [redacted] WE IMPLEMENTED REVENUE RECOGNITION ACCOUNTING CHANGES AND APPROXIMATELY [redacted] OF COSTS PREVIOUSLY RECORDED AS [redacted] IS NOT INCLUDED IN THE REVENUE LINE OFFSETTING SALES. WHAT WE CONSIDER [redacted]

AS TO EXPECTED CHANGES IN THE PUBLISHING COST STRUCTURE: THERE ARE TWO WAYS IN WHICH WE HAVE BEEN WORKING TO INCREASE OUR MARGINS OVER THE YEARS.

FIRST OF ALL, WE FOCUS ON OUR WORK FLOWS, DIGITIZING MANY OF THEM, MAKING OURSELVES MORE EFFICIENT AND EFFECTIVE, CONSTANTLY REVIEWING OUR ORGANIZATIONAL STRUCTURE TO MAKE SURE THAT OUR HEADCOUNT IS DEPLOYED AS NEEDED. EACH YEAR WE GIVE OURSELVES A SAVINGS TASK THAT WE ACHIEVE BY THIS FOCUS ON HOW WE OPERATE AND WHERE WE CAN TAKE COSTS OUT OF OUR PROCESSES.

SECONDLY, WE HAVE HAD A FOCUS ON INCREASING OUR DISTRIBUTION CLIENT BUSINESS, LEVERAGING OUR STRONG SALES ORGANIZATION, OUR SYSTEMS, AND OUR WAREHOUSING CAPABILITIES AT LITTLE ADDITIONAL COST TO S&S TO SERVICE SMALLER PUBLISHERS, MANY OF WHOM CAN NO LONGER SUPPORT THEIR OWN SELLING OPERATIONS. WE HAVE SIGNIFICANTLY INCREASED OUR DISTRIBUTION CLIENT INCOME OVER THE LAST FIVE YEARS, (BY [redacted] THE SIZE OF OUR MAIN WAREHOUSE AND, IN JANUARY, OPENING A NEW WAREHOUSE TO HOLD CLIENTS.

WE ARE NOW THE SECOND LARGEST DISTRIBUTION SERVICES PUBLISHER IN THE US, SECOND ONLY TO PRH, AND WE ARE CONTINUING TO GROW. WE EXPECT TO DOMINATE THIS PART OF THE BUSINESS AS THE INDUSTRY CONTINUES TO CONSOLIDATE. WE ARE ALSO EXPANDING SIGNIFICANTLY OVERSEAS WITH DISTRIBUTION CLIENTS, MANY FROM THE US, WHICH WILL ALSO HELP STRENGTHEN THE RETURNS OF OUR OVERSEAS UNITS.

Reference Exhibits:

Project Constellation
Diligence Discussion Agenda
STRICTLY CONFIDENTIAL

Project Constellation
Diligence Discussion Agenda
STRICTLY CONFIDENTIAL

Publishing Market Overview and Competitive Landscape

Digitalisation Has Not Reached a Peak Yet, and is Predicted to Continue to Change and Disrupt Industries

- The global print publishing industry, including educational literature, was expected to generate $130Bn in revenue in 2018
- Its primary characteristic is a strong concentration among few markets, where the six largest book markets account for 66% of the worldwide publishing business, with the largest players being the United States, China and Germany
- Publishing, with a focus on books, can be divided into three sub-verticals: the **Audiobook Market**, the **E-Book Market** and the **Physical Book Market**

Audiobook Market Overview

- Audiobooks are the fastest growing segment within the digital publishing industry, with the US being the biggest market for the audio format in 2017
- In 2018, the global audiobook market was expected to generate ~$3.5Bn in revenue, with growth in audiobooks predicted to continue
- Audiobook sales have doubled in the UK in the past five years, rising by 12% in volume and 15% in value in 2017
- The growing popularity of the audiobook is also proven by the fact that the New York Times now publishes an audio bestseller list

Key Competitors

E-Book Market Overview

- E-books were widely popularised when Amazon launched its e-book reader, Kindle, in 2007
- Today, most publishing houses such as Penguin Random House, Hachette Livre, HarperCollins, and Simon and Schuster produce books in the e-book format
- In North America and the UK, e-books had a share between 15-25% of the largest publishers' sales in 2013, which has been declining due to the rise of Amazon and self-publishers
- Distributors of e-books have caught on with the trend, developing their own e-reading tables

Key Competitors

- Publishing Houses
- E-Reading Tablet Providers

Physical Book Market Overview

- The market is primarily composed of a small number of large international publishers like Penguin Random House, Hachette Livre, HarperCollins, and Simon & Schuster
- Unlike inherently global entertainment forms like music and video, the physical book market is characterised by strong local publishers and distributers
- This mainly reflects the disruption caused by the advancement of e-commerce, particularly Amazon

Key Competitors

Sources: Company information, BookMap – How Big is the Global Publishing Industry?, Good e-Reader – Global Audiobook Trends and Statistics for 2018, Ruediger Wischenbart Content and Consulting – Global eBook Report 2017

VIACOMCBS INC. Case 1:21-cv-02886-FYP Document 181-96 Filed 09/08/22 Page 1 of 2 CONFIDENTIAL TREATMENT REQUESTED

Message

From: Eulau, Dennis [/O=EXCHANGELABS/OU=EXCHANGE ADMINISTRATIVE GROUP (FYDIBOHF23SPDLT)/CN=RECIPIENTS/CN=702A649498F94D16BBD47E90D2D1E89B-EULAU, DENN]
Sent: 2/4/2020 4:22:45 PM
To: Bulger, Joe [/o=ExchangeLabs/ou=Exchange Administrative Group (FYDIBOHF23SPDLT)/cn=Recipients/cn=2906fac85b3c4bf88aaded75a64d6091-Bulger, Joe]; Stambaugh, Doug [/o=ExchangeLabs/ou=Exchange Administrative Group (FYDIBOHF23SPDLT)/cn=Recipients/cn=dc31db8d077f4579bc1e79d95142c6bc-Stambaugh,]
Subject: Fwd: Printing Contract for Approval

Sent from my iPhone

Begin forwarded message:

From: "Bakish, Robert" [redacted]
Date: February 4, 2020 at 4:20:45 PM EST
To: "Spade, Christina" [redacted], "Reidy, Carolyn" [redacted]
Cc: "D'Alimonte, Christa" [redacted] "Jordan, Veronica" [redacted], "Byrnes, David" [redacted] "Eulau, Dennis" [redacted]
Subject: RE: Printing Contract for Approval

Pending the answers to chris' questions I am comfortable with this

B

From: Spade, Christina [redacted]
Sent: Tuesday, February 4, 2020 3:12 PM
To: Reidy, Carolyn [redacted]>; Bakish, Robert [redacted]
Cc: D'Alimonte, Christa [redacted]; Jordan, Veronica [redacted]; Byrnes, David [redacted]>; Eulau, Dennis
Subject: RE: Printing Contract for Approval

Carolyn -

A couple questions: 1) what are the terms of the rate increases for the [redacted] with LSC? 2) Is this consistent with your assumption for printing costs in 2020 Budget?

Thank you - Chris

US v. Bertelsmann
1:21-cv-0866-FYP
PX 0682

From: Reidy, Carolyn [redacted]
Sent: Tuesday, February 4, 2020 3:06 PM
To: Bakish, Robert [redacted]
Cc: Spade, Christina [redacted] D'Alimonte, Christa [redacted]; Jordan, Veronica [redacted]>; Byrnes, David [redacted]>; Eulau, Dennis [redacted]
Subject: Printing Contract for Approval

VCBS-04811264

Dear Bob:

We have negotiated a deal with LSC Communications, one of the printers with whom we deal. This contract commits us to spending [redacted] a year for the next [redacted]. This [redacted] represents approximately 50% of our standard US Domestic Hardcover and Trade paperback work. Obviously, I need your approval for us to sign.

We have been negotiating this deal for some time but suddenly we are getting pressure to sign from LSC. We believe part of their urgency is related to our current manufacturer, Ouad, with whom we have a contract that runs through 2020 and who recently asked us to change terms on the remaining year of the contract, with a [redacted] increase in rates. After we refused, it put itself up for sale. We expect an announcement of a sale any day now and think LSC is worried the new owner will approach us. Strong indications are that Quad will be selling its Book Trade business to Bertelsmann who owns Penguin Random House. We would not want to be 100% beholden to a competitor for printing. Because there is very limited printing capacity in the marketplace right now, we are working to make sure we reserve printing time/space. This deal not only gives us favorable pricing (and, we believe, can be almost cost neutral with our current rates) but also allows us reserved printing time.

The summary of the deal is below. Our team has reviewed all with Dave Byrnes. If you want any additional details, don't hesitate to ask.

Carolyn

LSC Deal Summary:

- [redacted] year deal: [redacted]
- New deal includes annual commitment to LSC of [redacted]
- S&S Option to increase work to [redacted]
  - Option allows Quad sale to play out (Berryville/Bertelsmann looking promising), and we can go either way with other 50%
  - Also provides safety net for 2020 volume if Quad falters (recent developments make that less likely)
  - [redacted]

VCBS-04811265

VIACOMCBS INC.
CONFIDENTIAL TREATMENT REQUESTED
Corporate Development
DEFENDANTS' TRIAL EXHIBIT
DX-339
Case 1:21-cv-02886-FYP Document 181-22 Filed 09/08/22 Page 1 of 7
VIACOMCBS
PROJECT TYPEFACE:
COST SYNERGIES
OVERVIEW
May 2020
DX-339.0001
VCBS-02774576

COST SYNERGIES OVERVIEW

- In collaboration with the S&S senior management team, and with the benefit of detailed S&S financial reports, we have refined the view of potential cost synergies achievable in a combination of S&S with one of the other top 4 US trade publishers
  - Employee compensation savings based on a review of headcount data by department and team
  - Other operating expense savings based on review of granular 2019 expense detail
- Preliminary estimate of annual "run-rate" EBITDA synergies is [redacted]
  - Excludes costs to achieve synergies
- We have identified and scoped the following areas of synergies:
  1. **Employee**: compensation expense savings associated with reduction in headcount across business units and S&S overhead
  2. **Occupancy**: reduction in rent expense resulting from site consolidation, enabled by headcount reduction referenced above
  3. **Shared Services**: reduction in shared services expenses provided by CBS Corporate, primarily in tech
  4. **Other Operating Expenses**: reduction of various expenses across Warehouse, Advertising, Editorial, Production, Selling, and G&A
  5. **COGS:** improvement in terms with key suppliers across edition costs, freight, advertising and royalties
- Based on S&S management input, analysis does not contemplate any of the following synergies:
  - [redacted]
  - [redacted]

VIACOMCBS

DX-339.0002

VCBS-02774577

COST SYNERGIES: CURRENT VS. 2019 ANALYSIS

($ in '000s)	Current Analysis	2019 Analysis
Employee		
Occupancy		
Shared Services		
Other OPEX		
Operating Expense		
COGS		
Total Expense		
Returns Reserve		
Total Synergies		

DX-339.0003

VIACOMCBS

VCBS-02774578

COST SYNERGIES: EMPLOYEE

3

Indicates that synergy was calculated using highlighted %s

1

($ in '000s)	Employ.	Employee Cost[1]	% Synergies Low	% Synergies High	$ Synergies Low	$ Synergies High	Methodology Notes
Editorial							
Art & Design							
Production							
Publisher (Adult)							
Publishing & Production							
Sales							
Advertising & Mark.							
Publicity							
Sales & Marketing							
Ops. Dist. Center							
Cust. Ops.							
Inv. Mgmt. (Children's)							
Ops. Supply Chain							
Warehouse & Supply Ops							
Administration							
G&A							
Mgmt. & Execs							
Business Develop.							
Business Administration							
Accounting							
CFS							
Finance							
Royalties							
Accounting & Finance							
Human Resources							
Legal							
Other							
Total							

Note: based on underlying analysis with greater level of granularity than summarized here.

VIACOMCBS

VCBS-02774579

COST SYNERGIES: OCCUPANCY, SHARED SERVICES, OTHER

4

Indicates that synergy was calculated using highlighted %s

($ in '000s)	2019 Total Cost	Reduction Low	Reduction High	$ Synergies Low	$ Synergies High	Methodology Notes
2 Occupancy						
New York, NY						Based on estimated employee cost savings analysis on a headcount basis by location. Assumes rent cost on leased properties decreased proportionally to decrease in seats. Does not assume any decrease in the avg sq. ft. / HC for the employees who remain.
U.K.						
Parsippany, NJ						
Canada						
Australia						
Avon, MA						
India						
TN, Delanco NJ, Concord MA, CA						
Occupancy Expense						
3 Shared Services						
Enterprise Services						
IS&T Application Support						
Internet Security Group						
Application Licensing / Hosting						
HR/Payroll, Legal, Oracle						
Other						
IS&T Service Fees						
Other (HR, Legal, Facilities)						
Shared Services (Corp Alloc.)						
4 Other OPEX (Ex. Employ., Occup., S						
Warehouse						
Non Titled Advertising						
Editorial						
Production						
Amazon ASAP						
Other Selling						
Selling						
G&A						
Other Operating Expenses						

Note: based on underlying analysis with greater level of granularity than summarized here.

DX-339.0005

VIACOMCBS

VCBS-02774580

COST SYNERGIES: COGS

5

($ in '000s)	2019 Total Cost	% Savings Low	% Savings High	$ Synergies Low	$ Synergies High	Methodology Notes
Paper						
Binding						
Whole Book Purchases						
Printing						
Whole Book Purchases - POD						
Covers and Jackets						
Other Edition Costs						
Edition Expense						
Editorial Freelance Costs						
Freelance Copyediting & Pro						
Cover & Jacket Art						
Other Plan Costs						
Plant Expense						
Amazon						
Barnes & Noble						
Other Coop Expense						
Titled Adv Accrual						
Customer Payments						
Advertising Space						
Other Titled Advertising						
Titled Advertising Expense						
Ground Motor Transportation						
Outbound UPS						
Other (incl. Client Allocation)						
Freight Expense						
Royalty Expense						
Royalty Write-Off						
JV Co-Pub Expense						
Total COGS						

DX-339.0006

VCBS-02774581

VIACOMCBS INC. CONFIDENTIAL TREATMENT REQUESTED

DX-339.0007

VCBS-02774582

VIACOMCBS INC. Case 1:21-cv-02886-FYP Document 181-88 Filed 09/08/22 Page 1 of 2 CONFIDENTIAL TREATMENT REQUESTED

Message

From: Karp, Jonathan [/O=EXCHANGELABS/OU=EXCHANGE ADMINISTRATIVE GROUP (FYDIBOHF23SPDLT)/CN=RECIPIENTS/CN=02DE0354F13444D7BCB58CD0F8031C04-KARP, JONAT]
Sent: 9/11/2020 11:46:14 AM
To: Berkett, Alex [ ]
Subject: RE: S&S sale

```
Perfect.  Thanks.  I'm at .

-----Original Message-----
From: Berkett, Alex < >
Sent: Friday, September 11, 2020 11:06 AM
To: Karp, Jonathan >
Subject: RE: S&S sale

3:45?

-----Original Message-----
From: Karp, Jonathan >
Sent: Friday, September 11, 2020 10:58 AM
To: Berkett, Alex >
Subject: Re: S&S sale

Thanks. Maybe 1:30 or 3:30?  I'm at .

> On Sep 11, 2020, at 9:10 AM, Berkett, Alex > wrote:
>
> Let's find 15 minutes to discuss today.  Any windows that work?
>
> On Sep 11, 2020, at 5:34 AM, Karp, Jonathan > wrote:
>
> Alex:  Thanks for clarifying with Julia, and for including me in the conversation.  I'll maintain all
of your confidence.
>
> Two thoughts for you:
>
> 1.  The original Wall Street Journal story on March 4 reported, "The company will seek at least $1.2
billion for Simon & Schuster...."
>
> 2. Although I really do understand why strategics are the most likely option, if there is a financial
buyer who is willing to match the top bid, that outcome would be better for the employees of S&S and
arguably the larger book publishing ecosystem.  You mentioned  yesterday and I've read more about
> Jon
>
>
> -----Original Message-----
> From: Berkett, Alex < >
> Sent: Thursday, September 10, 2020 11:06 PM
> To: Phelps, Julia < >
> Cc: Karp, Jonathan < >
> Subject: Re: S&S sale
>
>
 "what's going on with the S&S sale?"
>
> I believe our answer heretofore was, "as we previously stated, we have determined the asset is not
strategic and, when market conditions stabilize, we will pursue a sale process".
>
> The nuance now is, we launched the sale process today, so that answer is no longer quite right.  Yet,
we probably don't want to acknowledge that we have launched a sale process.
>
> Perhaps something like:
> "As we previously stated, we have determined the asset is not strategic and we have received
significant in bound interest.  The inbound interest is not surprising, given that Simon & Schuster is
such an iconic asset and its performance this year has been fantastic.  When we have further developments
to report, we will do so."
>
>
>
> On Sep 10, 2020, at 7:19 PM, Phelps, Julia > wrote:
```

US v. Bertelsmann
1:21-cv-0866-FYP
PX 0634

VCBS-01985466

>
> Hi Jonathan - [redacted]

>
> Sent from my iPhone
>
>> On Sep 10, 2020, at 7:55 PM, Berkett, Alex <[redacted]> wrote:
>>
>> I suggested Jonathan echo Bob's messaging in his communications, as he will increasingly be asked about the process.
>>
>> On Sep 10, 2020, at 5:48 PM, Karp, Jonathan <[redacted]> wrote:
>>
>> Hi Julia,
>>
>> Alex Berkett said that Bob Bakish will be making comments early next week about the sale of S&S and that you're working on that messaging. Can you share it with me at the appropriate time so we're aligned and I characterize his comments accurately?
>>
>> Jon

VIACOMCBS INC. Case 1:21-cv-02886-FYP Document 181-91 Filed 09/08/22 Page 1 of 1 CONFIDENTIAL TREATMENT REQUESTED

Message

From: Karp, Jonathan [/O=EXCHANGELABS/OU=EXCHANGE ADMINISTRATIVE GROUP (FYDIBOHF23SPDLT)/CN=RECIPIENTS/CN=02DE0354F13444D7BCB58CD0F8031C04-KARP, JONAT]
Sent: 3/5/2020 10:40:07 AM
To: John Irving
CC:
Subject: RE: About being sold...

Thanks, John! I'm pretty sure that the Department of Justice wouldn't allow Penguin Random House to buy us, but that's assuming we still have a Department of Justice.

Enjoy the homestretch!

J.

From: John Irving
Sent: Thursday, March 5, 2020 9:33 AM
To: Karp, Jonathan
Cc:
Subject: About being sold...

External Email

Dear Jon,

and I appreciate the heads-up you gave us. I'm actually surprised, and somewhat relieved, to hear that any publishing house is "quite desirable" nowadays; my sense of the desirability of literary fiction is somewhere between a dinosaur and Harvey Weinstein. As for your estimation of knowing the outcome of the sale—"which could be in 2-6 months"—I'm guessing this may roughly coincide with when I finish But, on both counts, we'll see.

Naturally, I'm inclined to imagine an ironic sale; generally, irony is more satisfying in fiction than in real life. Such as: S.&S. is bought by Penguin Random House, and I find myself back in the hands of publishers I thought I left—I mean, in the U.S. and the U.K. But that's how I imagine things in fiction: ironically.

All the best,
John

On Mar 5, 2020, at 8:24 AM, Karp, Jonathan wrote:

Dear John,

I assume told you that we're for sale. I called her yesterday because I didn't want to disrupt your writing day. There's really nothing to do about it or glean from it until we know the outcome, which could be in 2-6 months. Apparently, we're quite desirable, but time will tell.

All my best,
Jon

US v. Bertelsmann
1:21-cv-0866-FYP
PX 0655

VCBS-03055376

DEFENDANTS' TRIAL EXHIBIT
DX-154

From: Karp, Jonathan
Sent: Wednesday, November 25, 2020 1:03 PM
To: John Irving
Subject: RE: Full circle

Dear John,

Your German is a lot better than mine. I'll muddle through!

J.

From: John Irving [redacted]
Sent: Wednesday, November 25, 2020 12:44 PM
To: Karp, Jonathan [redacted]
Cc: [redacted]
Subject: Re: Full circle

External Email

Dear Jon,

Yes, the backlist matters. I'm not sure exactly when it was—maybe in September 2019, at the time of the Toronto International Festival of Authors—but I was having a beer with Markus Dohle at the annual Penguin Random House cocktail party. With halfway decent prescience, I should have said, *"Ich kenne ein wirklich gut Verlag Sie kaufen sollen"*—or something along those lines. But I can tell Markus thinks my German is pretty bad, so I didn't say it. Not even in English, which would be: "I know a really good publishing house you should buy."

"*Willkommen nach Bertlesmann,*" as they say—"Welcome to Bertlesmann."

John

> On Nov 25, 2020, at 12:16 PM, Karp, Jonathan [redacted] wrote:
>
> Dear [redacted]
>
> The backlist matters! We will coordinate! And yes, I'm delighted by the outcome.
>
> J.
>
> **From:** [redacted]
> **Sent:** Wednesday, November 25, 2020 12:13 PM
> **To:** Karp, Jonathan [redacted]
> **Cc:** John cell Irving [redacted]
> **Subject:** Re: Full circle

<External Email>

Dear Jon: The first thought I had was a very selfish one: maybe now PRH will market John's backlist in the US! My second thought was to check in with you and make sure you're feeling good about this. Sounds like you are. Have a Happy Thanksgiving! Best, [redacted]

On Nov 25, 2020, at 12:03 PM, Karp, Jonathan [redacted] wrote:

Dear John and [redacted]

And so we return to the world of Joe Fox! Rest assured that this entire $2.175 billion dollar deal was merely an excuse to unify your backlist! See the Bertelsmann press release attached!

All my best,
Jon

Jonathan Karp
President &
Chief Executive Officer

November 25, 2020

Dear Colleague,

In March, when ViacomCBS announced its plan to sell Simon & Schuster, we did not know that shortly thereafter we would also be weathering a deadly pandemic, displacement from our offices, disruption in the bookselling marketplace, and the sudden death of our longtime and revered CEO, not to mention high-profile lawsuits seeking to quash publication of two of our books. Through it all, we have persevered, adapted and innovated, maintained a keen focus on our authors and our books, and produced some of our best results in recent years. Now, eight months later, I am delighted to announce that Simon & Schuster will be joining together with Penguin Random House for the next chapter in our storied publishing history.

From our company's inception, there has been much cross-pollination between Simon & Schuster and Penguin Random House. In fact, the founder of Random House, Bennett Cerf, met Max Schuster when they were both students at Columbia Journalism School. (Richard Simon was an undergraduate at Columbia University at the time.) They all shared an entrepreneurial approach to book publishing and founded their companies within years of each other. I learned these details from my personal copy of Bennett Cerf's memoir, At Random, which was given to me on my first day as a Random House employee. I spent 16 rewarding years at Random House can personally attest to what a great work culture it is, and what a deep commitment the organization has to its employees and authors. From our first meeting with Markus Dohle and his team, it was clear that he wants to bring Simon & Schuster into the Bertelsmann family with the same thoughtful respect for our creative independence that accompanied the merger of Penguin and Random House – an integration that took years and was handled with exceptional professionalism.

We expect the transaction will likely close in the second half of 2021 at the earliest, subject to customary closing conditions, including regulatory approval. I understand that many of you will have questions about how this transition to new ownership will affect your work, and your benefits. I assure you that as this process unfolds we will share information with you , but understand that this will be a long process. Expect no sudden changes beyond the normal decisions we make in our regular course of business. As we head into 2021, our upcoming list of books holds the promise of being every bit as exhilarating a year of publishing as 2020 has been, and I know that we will continue to do our best for our authors and our distribution clients.

I want to thank Bob Bakish, Alex Berkett, and everyone else at ViacomCBS and LionTree for managing our sale with such intelligence and consideration of our business. I also want to thank those of you at Simon & Schuster who worked so diligently to provide a comprehensive view of our company to prospective buyers.

Successful companies are dynamic and change can be galvanizing. In our 96-year history, Simon & Schuster has had seven owners. From these transformations we have adjusted to new management, welcomed other companies into our fold, and always emerged stronger, with an enduring commitment to excellence in book publishing. When we join Penguin Random House after closing, we can look forward to benefitting from exciting new relationships and opportunities that will enhance our ability to provide authors with the best possible publication they can receive.

You can read more about our news in the attached press release from Bertelsmann and Markus Dohle's note to all Penguin Random House staff. Once again, my thanks for all you have done to make Simon & Schuster such an outstanding and valuable company.

Sincerely,

Jonathan Karp

Jonathan Karp
President and Chief Executive Officer
Simon & Schuster
1230 Avenue of the Americas
New York, N.Y. 10020

<M Dohle Letter-FINAL.docx><Bertelsmann PR - Final.pdf>

DEFENDANTS' TRIAL EXHIBIT **DX-071**

Message

From:	Karp, Jonathan [/O=EXCHANGELABS/OU=EXCHANGE ADMINISTRATIVE GROUP (FYDIBOHF23SPDLT)/CN=RECIPIENTS/CN=02DE0354F13444D7BCB58CD0F8031C04-KARP, JONAT]
Sent:	11/17/2019 8:02:18 PM
To:	Bergstrom, Jennifer [/o=ExchangeLabs/ou=Exchange Administrative Group (FYDIBOHF23SPDLT)/cn=Recipients/cn=5c09a7770c5e48489fac8b389128bbbe-Bergstrom,]; Ferrari-Adler, Jofie [/o=ExchangeLabs/ou=Exchange Administrative Group (FYDIBOHF23SPDLT)/cn=Recipients/cn=efd8c38543ca4f2994c882b965a946f8-Ferrari-Adl]; Nan Graham [redacted] [/o=ExchangeLabs/ou=Exchange Administrative Group (FYDIBOHF23SPDLT)/cn=Recipients/cn=b6c55e49bfee4ec8b7264c5be7258e1e-Graham, Nan]; McGuire, Libby [/o=ExchangeLabs/ou=Exchange Administrative Group (FYDIBOHF23SPDLT)/cn=Recipients/cn=e524fc851dba49feb728c5bfb609936e-McGuire, Li]
Subject:	Guidelines for editors on acquisitions, time management, title count, and multiple submissions

Thanks for the good conversation on Friday. I've adapted some of the points we discussed and added new ones, based on your feedback.

I recommend that you review these points verbally with editors at an editorial meeting. (If you want to hand out printed copies, that's fine, but I'd rather not have you circulate it via email.)

Nothing below should be considered an edict. My hope is that we can change the culture of acquisition here for the better.

I'm making these suggestions with an open mind and an awareness that there is no uniform way of doing business. As long as we're excited to publish the book, we should go for it, however we can.

Objective: To create a culture in which we empower you to acquire 10 to 12 new titles a year in the most efficient way – books you are excited to work on and confident we can publish profitably.

1. You will be rewarded for enterprise and imagination and for creating your own opportunities. The highest praise will go to those who make things happen and acquire projects before they are submitted widely. Most of our biggest titles are not acquired in fevered auctions. Our most successful authors tend to be writers we build over time or acquire in routine ways (outreach, options, limited submissions).

2. Whether or not there is wisdom in crowds, being part of a pack is not the best way to distinguish yourself. The editors who stand out and excel define themselves in the eyes of authors and their representatives by articulating what they want to publish and by identifying those authors through individual outreach. Let agents know you'll be supported to make a good offer (or pre-empt) if you have a strong vision for publishing the book.

DX-071.0001

VCBS-00650323

3. Collegiality matters more than internal competition. We will thank and honor editors who defer to more enthusiastic colleagues (or to those who have established a prior relationship with the author on submission). Duplicating work is not a productive expenditure of one of our most valuable resources – time. You can acquire more books if you aren't all chasing the same ones.

4. Simon & Schuster will be a better publishing company if we're driven by editors who think for themselves and acquire the books they want to buy, without focusing on the competition or needing to have their judgment validated by other bidders. We prize editors who follow their curiosity and instincts and have conviction about their acquisitions.

5. Never request submissions from agents if you see in company editorial minutes that those projects have been submitted to other S&S imprints.

6. If you hear about a project from a scout and you want to receive the submission, first find out from the agent whether other imprints have it before asking that it be submitted to you. Agents do not want to burn any bridges by refusing to submit to you, but in all likelihood, if you weren't on the original submission list, you're not going to win the book and you'll be wasting your own time and the time of colleagues at the imprint. It would be much better to let agents know that you'd like to receive comparable submissions in the future. It's always better to establish the relationship with the agent before the submission rather than during or after.

7. Try to bail out on submissions in which there are more than two imprints in the building pursuing the project (especially if you think your chances aren't as good as the other two imprints in the building.)

DEFENDANTS' TRIAL EXHIBIT
DX-440

From: Karp, Jonathan
Sent: Friday, July 26, 2019 8:30 AM
To: Davis, Dawn
Subject: RE: -- Closing Instructions

DD: If you decide you want to bid, yes, you should send me a P&L with sales figures on two or three comp titles. That should be the process for every acquisition.

J.

From: Davis, Dawn < >
Sent: Thursday, July 25, 2019 5:10 PM
To: Karp, Jonathan < >
Subject: -- Closing Instructions

Jon,
I think you know about this from Sean but the auction for the story collection is on Monday. I believe Sean ran p&ls at 300 and 500. Kathy (Scribner) at $350 and $450. They had 9 meetings.

Do you need me to send you a P&l as well. I am thinking about what level I want to spend for one book (we were hoping it would be a two book deal). Do you want to /need to read any of the stories. What do you need from me?

Thanks,

Dawn L. Davis
VP & Publisher, 37 INK, an imprint of Simon & Schuster

1230 Avenue of the Americas
New York, NY 10020

From:
Sent: Thursday, July 25, 2019 10:40 AM
To: Davis, Dawn <
Subject: -- Closing Instructions

External Email

Dear Dawn,

I'm excited to invite you to an auction for [redacted]
You made my job easy -- When I told [redacted] we'd be meeting with you, he already knew your work, and admired both the writers you publish and how you've published them. Here are my instructions for tomorrow's auction:

RIGHTS

I'm offering North American Print, Electronic, and Audio.

FORMAT

We will conduct a three-round, best bids auction.

First Round bids should be delivered by phone or email by 10:00 AM on Monday, July 29th.

The top five (5) bidders in the First Round will proceed to the second round. Second Round bids should be delivered by Noon.

The top three (3) bidders in the Second Round will proceed to the Third and final round. Third Round bids should be delivered by 3:00 PM.

If the final round's bids are even, then I might request one more round to create separation. I also reserve the right to slightly alter the number of progressing publishers, should circumstances require.

BIDS

All bids must include payouts. Payments due on Hardcover Publication must be guaranteed no later than 12 months after D&A. Paperback payments -- if you include them -- must be guaranteed no later than 24 months after D&A. If in any round all of the top bidders are in the same corporation, then I will include the next highest bidder. [redacted] reserves the right to accept or reject any bid at any time.

[redacted] final decision will be made on Advance and Payout Schedule, Royalties, Editorial Notes, Marketing Plans, Bonuses, Publication Plans and Schedule, and any other information that bidders find useful. [redacted] and I see this as is the beginning of a long, collaborative relationship, and we welcome your participation. We are available to discuss any questions as we approach the closing time, and I thank you for your continued interest.

All best,

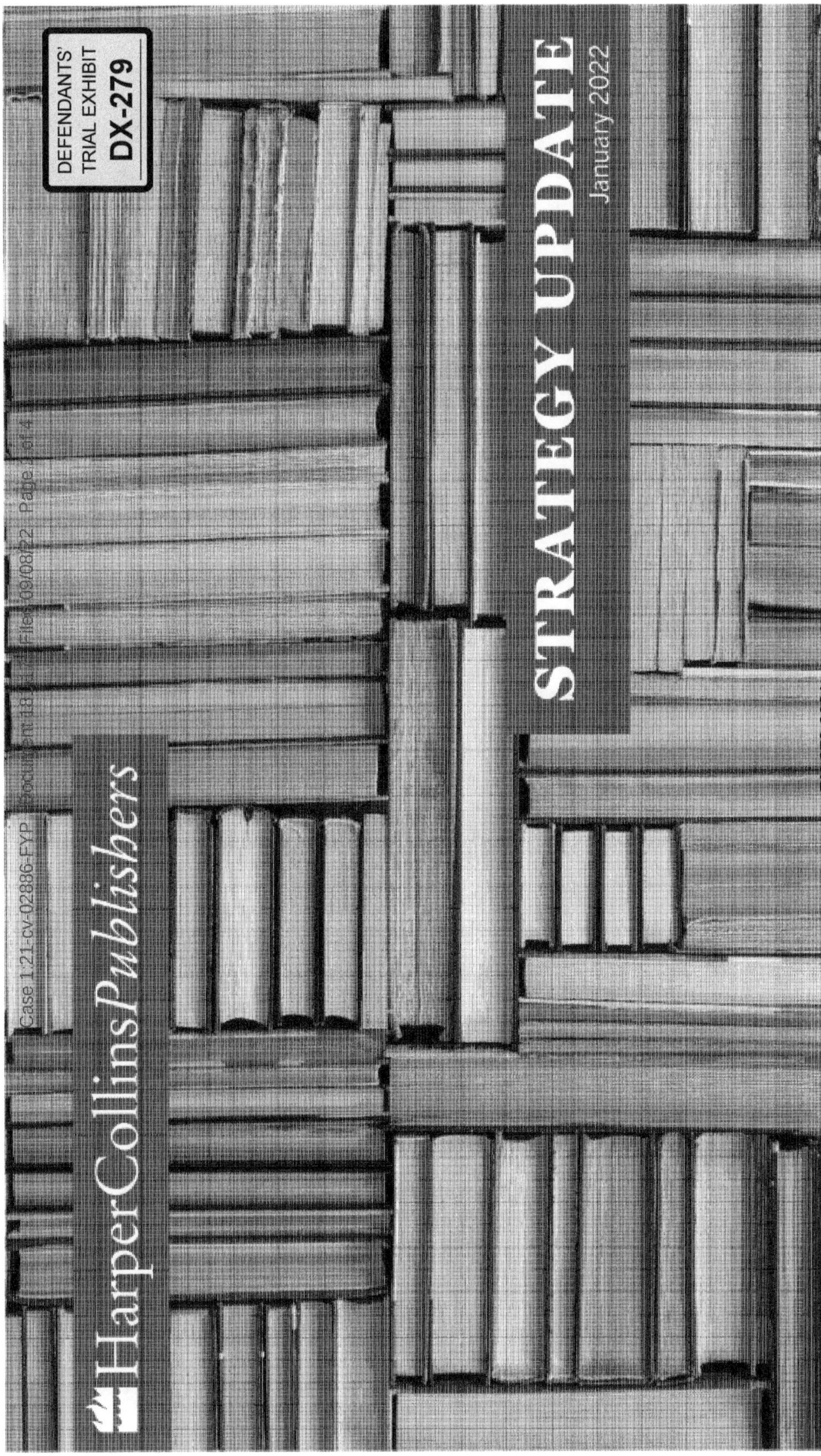

HC-PRHSS-000003190

DX-279.0001

HIGHLY CONFIDENTIAL

Additionally, Investing in Author Advances to Drive Organic Growth

⊕ Organically Growing Trade Publishing Output

- Title count and advance spending increasing approximately ███ over the five-year period
- In the US, we have seen ████ growth in consumer spending on books

⊕ Trade Title Count

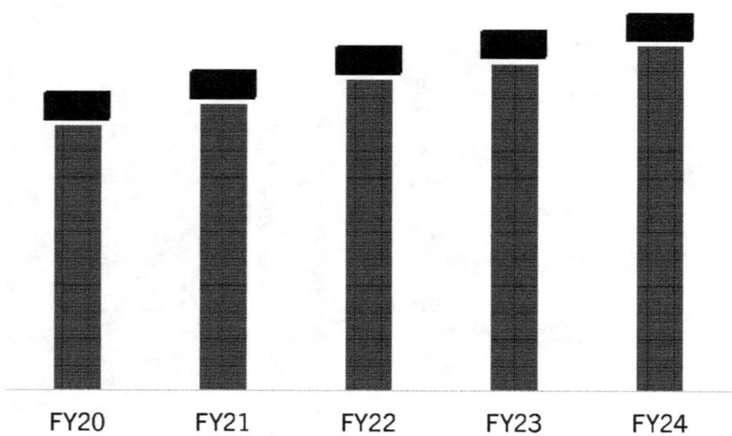

⊕ Title Advance Spend

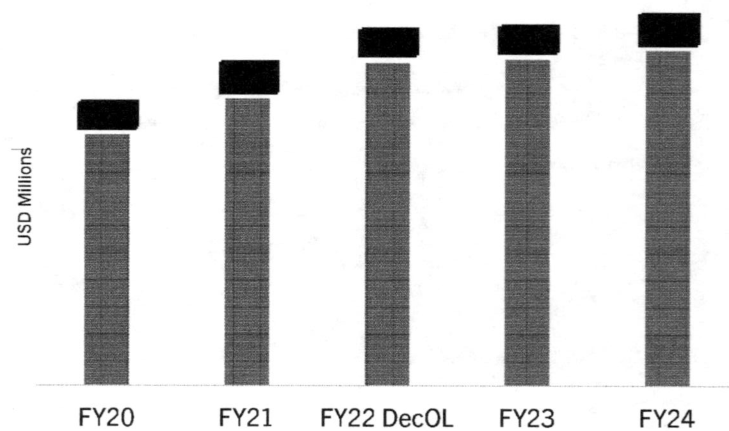

Note: Excludes HMH acquisition

HIGHLY CONFIDENTIAL

25

DX-279.0025

HC-PRHSS-000003214

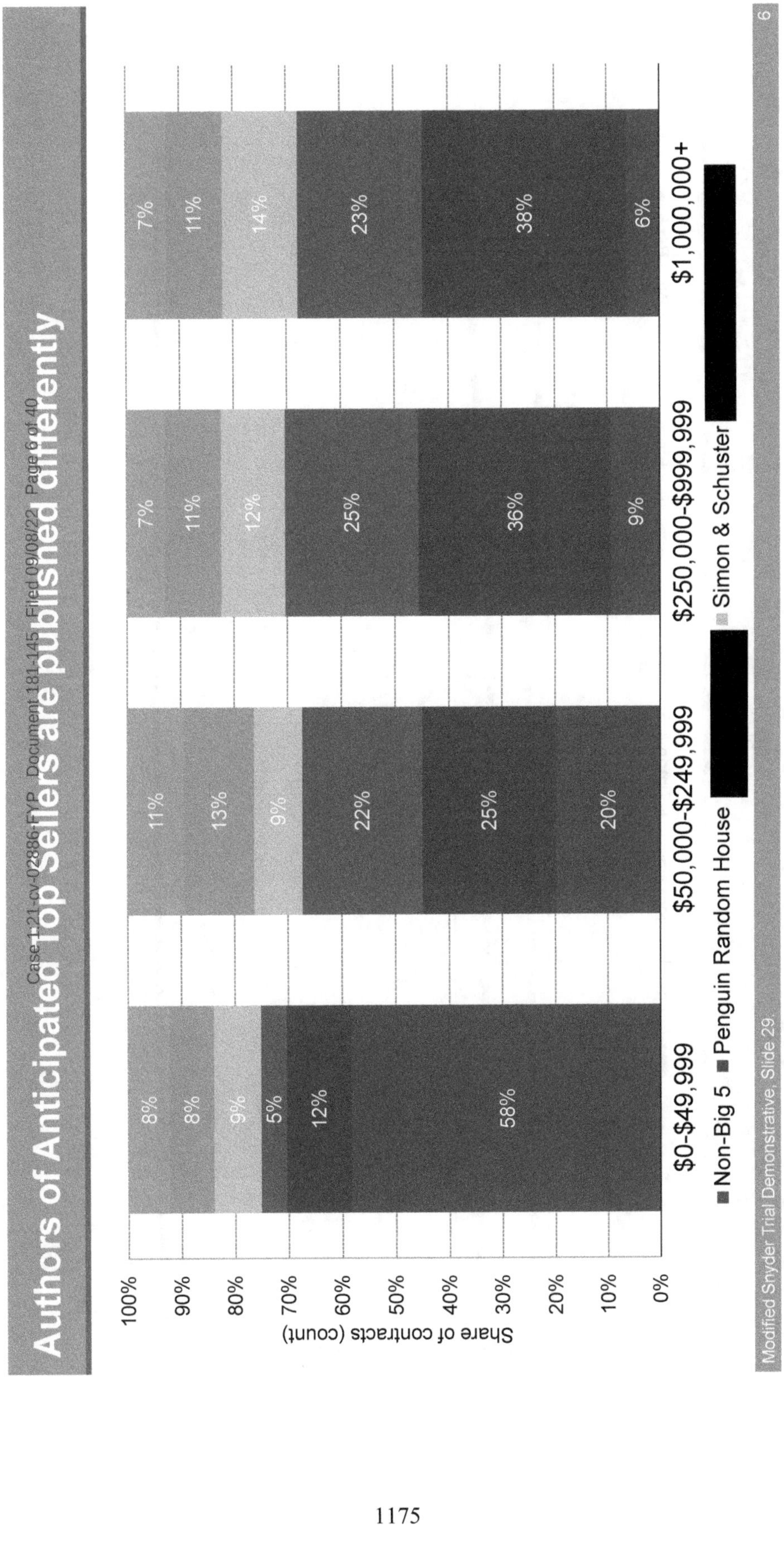
Case 1:21-cv-02886-FYP Document 181-145 Filed 09/08/22 Page 6 of 40
Authors of Anticipated Top Sellers are published differently
Share of contracts (count)
100%
90%
80%
70%
60%
50%
40%
30%
20%
10%
0%
$0-$49,999
$50,000-$249,999
$250,000-$999,999
$1,000,000+
8%
8%
9%
5%
12%
58%
11%
13%
9%
22%
25%
20%
7%
11%
12%
25%
36%
9%
7%
11%
14%
23%
38%
6%
Non-Big 5
Penguin Random House
Simon & Schuster
Modified Snyder Trial Demonstrative, Slide 29
6

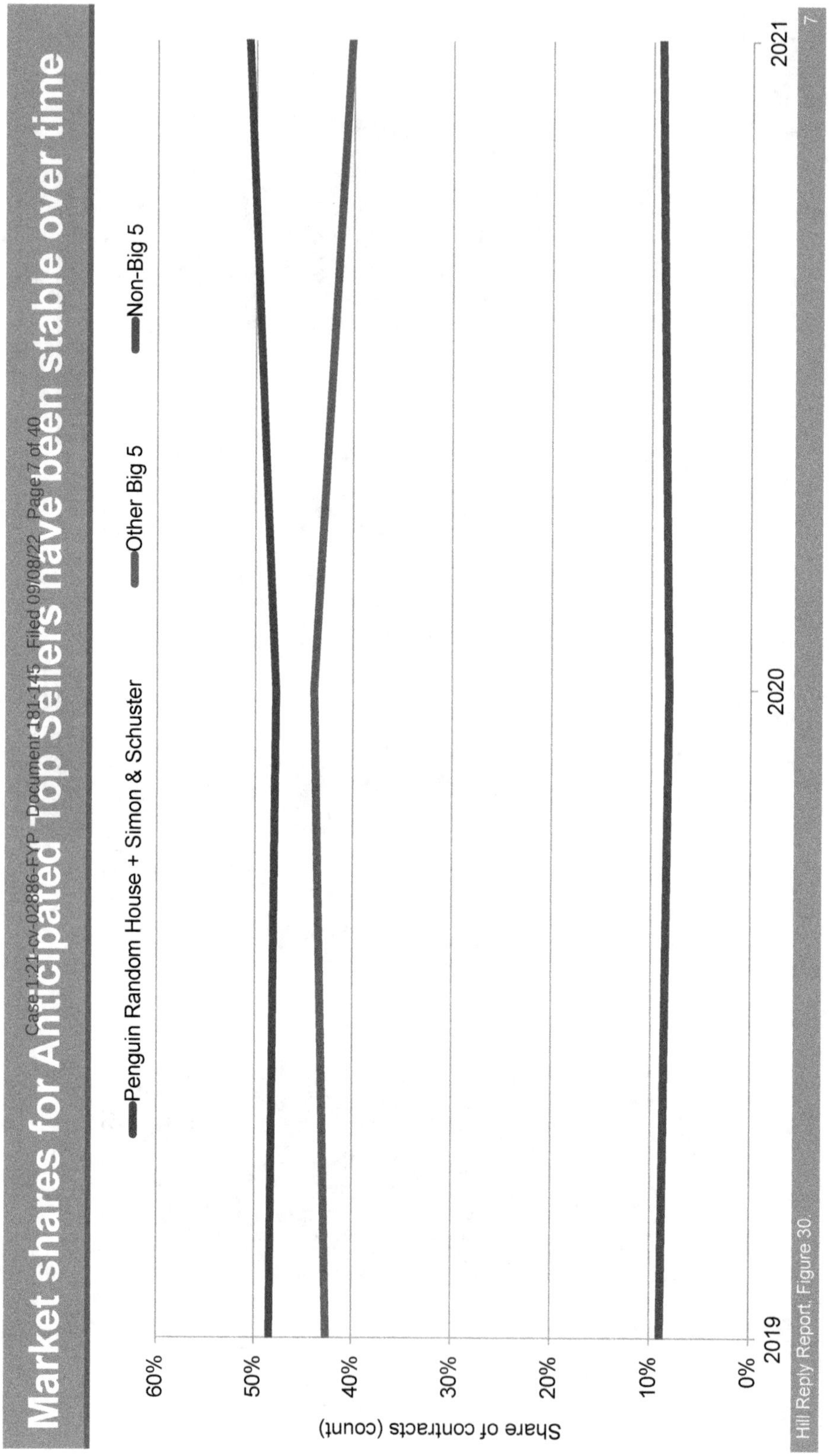
Market shares for Anticipated Top Sellers have been stable over time
Case 1:21-cv-02886-FYP Document 181-145 Filed 09/08/22 Page 7 of 40
Penguin Random House + Simon & Schuster
Other Big 5
Non-Big 5
Share of contracts (count)
60%
50%
40%
30%
20%
10%
0%
2019
2020
2021
Hill Reply Report, Figure 30.
7

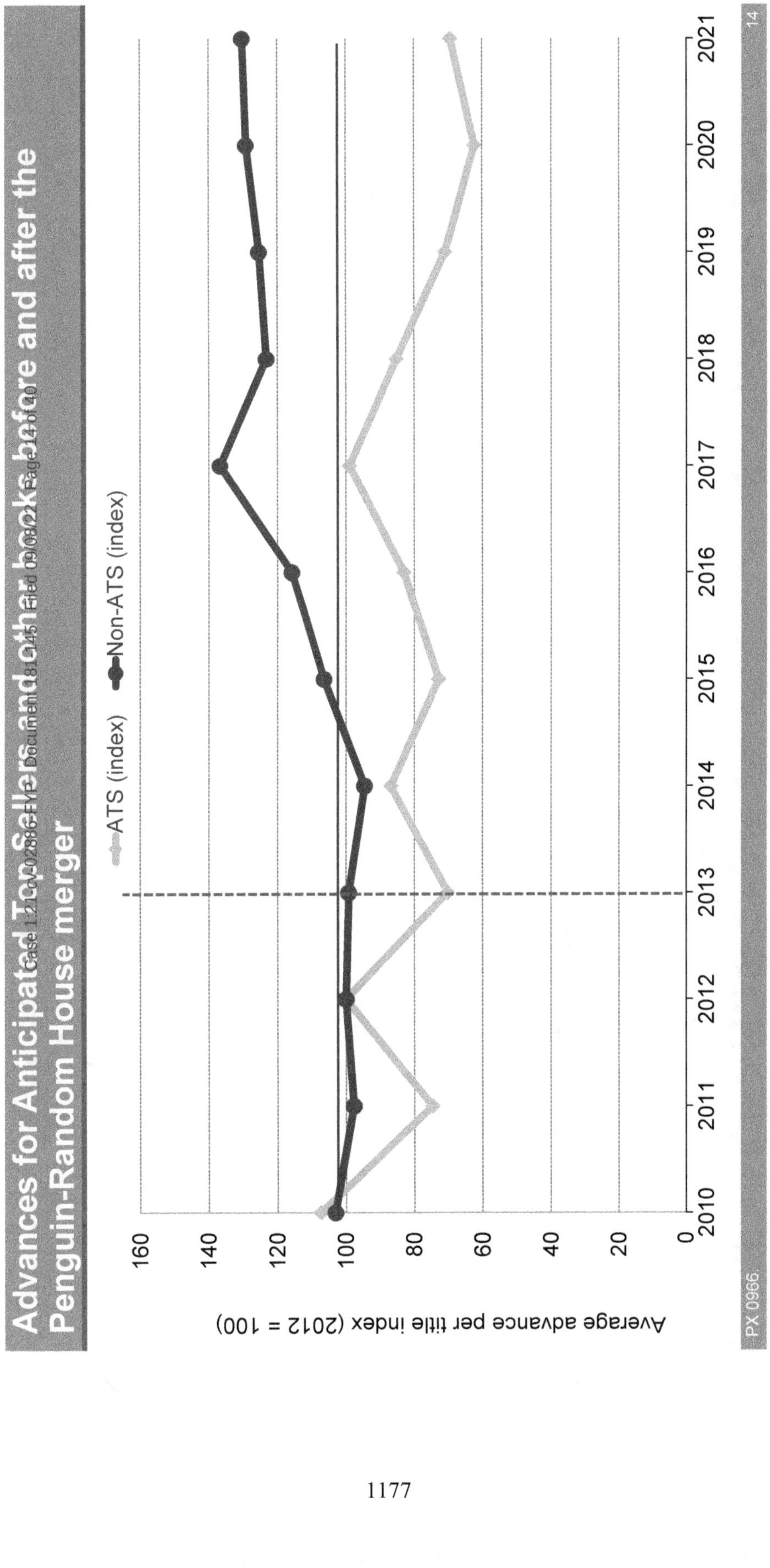
Advances for Anticipated Top Sellers and other books before and after the Penguin-Random House merger
Case 1:21-cv-02886-FYP Document 181-145 Filed 09/08/22 Page 14 of 40
ATS (index)
Non-ATS (index)
Average advance per title index (2012 = 100)
160
140
120
100
80
60
40
20
0
2010
2011
2012
2013
2014
2015
2016
2017
2018
2019
2020
2021
PX 0966
14

Advances for Anticipated Top Sellers decreased after the Penguin-Random House merger

Competitive situation	Estimated change in advance over time	Difference-in-differences estimate
Anticipated top sellers	-5.6%	-15.3%
Other books	9.6%	

Hill Reply Report, Figure 25.

15

Penguin Random House imprints coordinate bids

2018 auction for non-fiction book

"I'm sorry to say I didn't catch [another editor] in time to stop a first bid . . . but maybe there's still time for coordination once the money gets higher?"

"I'm starting to wonder how real the 4th bidder is. This is the perfect situation where we risk driving up price. Wondering if we shouldn't tell Crown to match the 885 and Penguin the same if they go to them next. . . . Would avoid us bidding each other up."

"[Penguin Random House] is now the main driver of value here. So we're agreeing [to] move up slowly. Crown intends to bid $890k (up only $5k). When it comes back to [Penguin Publishing Group]... we also go up a mere $5k...."

"So it seems best for everyone to go with $1050 to have the best shot. No bonus. North America [rights]... Quarterly payouts."

Three Penguin Random House imprints and Simon & Schuster competing in last rounds

Penguin Random House imprints coordinate identical offers of $1,050,000 in last round

BPRH-LIT-000492563 at -563; PX 0398; PX 0336 at -784; PX 0221 at -542

16

The Big 5 most frequently sign large contracts

Publisher	Share of $1 million+ contracts	Months with $1 million+ contracts
Penguin Random House	38.3%	36
HarperCollins		
Simon & Schuster	14.1%	33
Macmillan		
Hachette		
Non-Big 5		
Scholastic		
Amazon		
Blackstone		
Disney		
Hay House		
Baker		
Kensington		
WW Norton		
Wiley		
Abrams		
Bloomsbury		
Chronicle		
National Geographic		
Regnery		
Sterling		

Hill Reply Report, Figure 41.

19

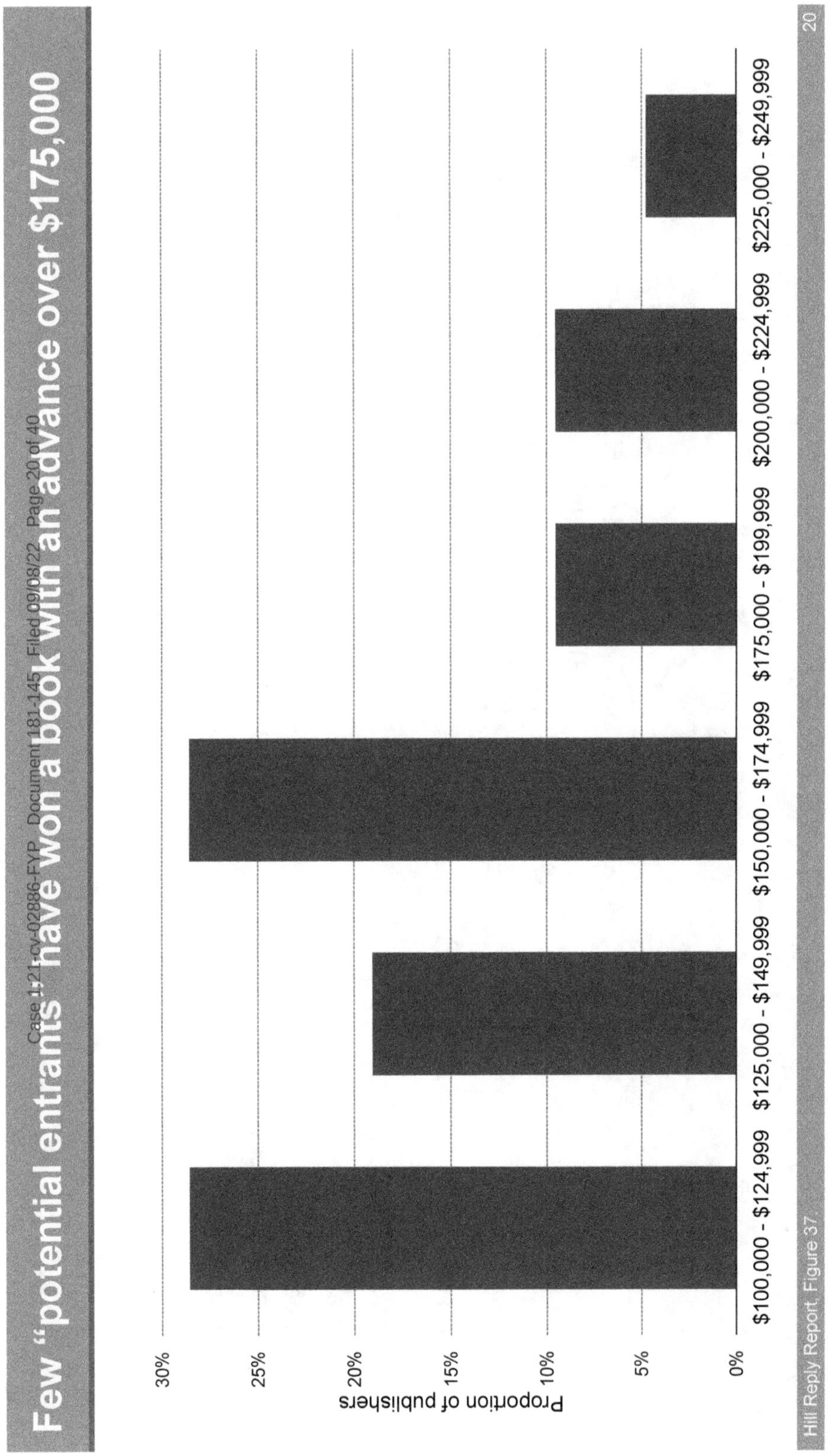
Few “potential entrants” have won a book with an advance over $175,000
Case 1:21-cv-02886-FYP Document 181-145 Filed 09/08/22 Page 20 of 40
Proportion of publishers
30%
25%
20%
15%
10%
5%
0%
$100,000 - $124,999
$125,000 - $149,999
$150,000 - $174,999
$175,000 - $199,999
$200,000 - $224,999
$225,000 - $249,999
Hill Reply Report, Figure 37
20

Six Data Sets

	Dr. Hill				Prof. Snyder	
	(1) Advance Data	(2) Win-Loss Data	(3) Editorial Minutes	(4) Runner Up Data	(5) Advance Data	(6) Agency Data
Time Period	2019-6/2021	2018-2021	2020-2021	2020	2019-2021	2018-2021
Number of Obs. – Broad Market	23,940	924	784	287	29,344	973
Number of Obs. – $250,000+ Advances	3,163	206	284	287	3,540	360

Dr. Hill Advance Data; Dr. Hill Win-Loss Data; Dr. Hill Editorial Minutes; Dr. Hill Runner Up Data (Dr. Hill Corrected Initial Report, ¶ 185); Prof. Snyder Advance Data; Prof. Snyder Agency Data (DX-377)

13

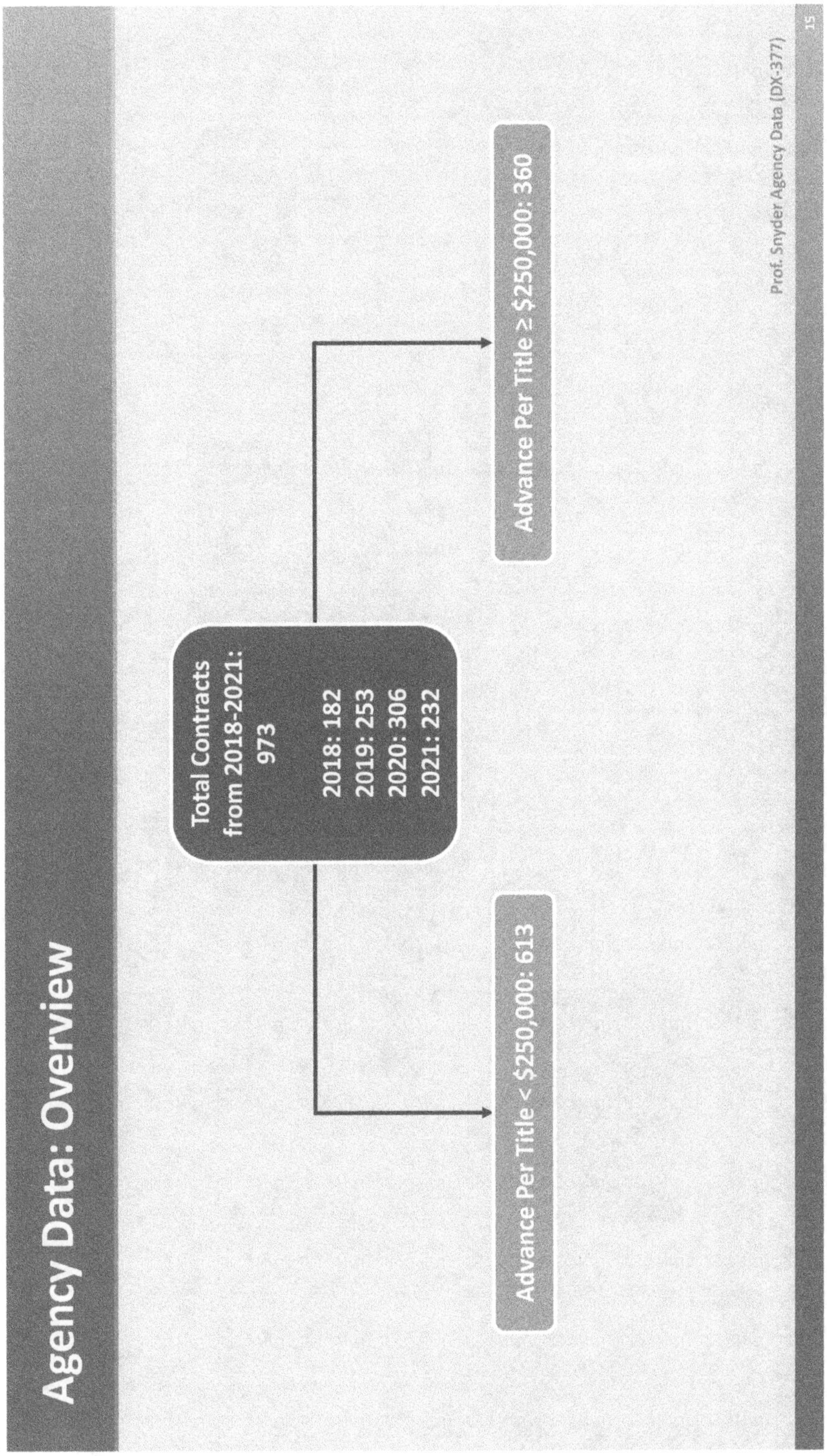
Agency Data: Overview
Total Contracts from 2018-2021: 973
2018: 182
2019: 253
2020: 306
2021: 232
Advance Per Title < $250,000: 613
Advance Per Title ≥ $250,000: 360
Prof. Snyder Agency Data (DX-377)
15

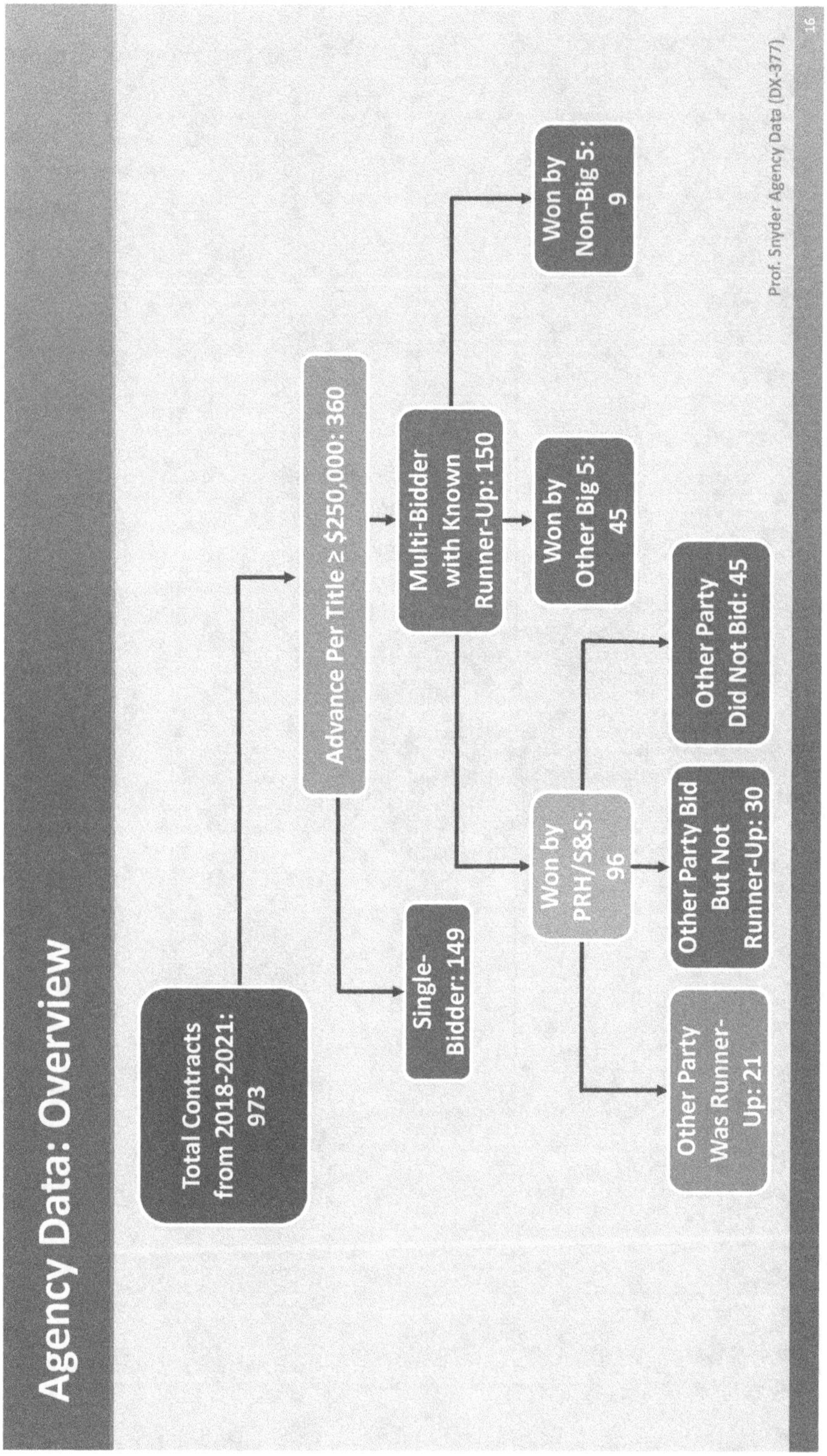
Agency Data: Overview
Total Contracts from 2018-2021: 973
Advance Per Title ≥ $250,000: 360
Single-Bidder: 149
Multi-Bidder with Known Runner-Up: 150
Won by PRH/S&S: 96
Won by Other Big 5: 45
Won by Non-Big 5: 9
Other Party Was Runner-Up: 21
Other Party Bid But Not Runner-Up: 30
Other Party Did Not Bid: 45
Prof. Snyder Agency Data (DX-377)
16

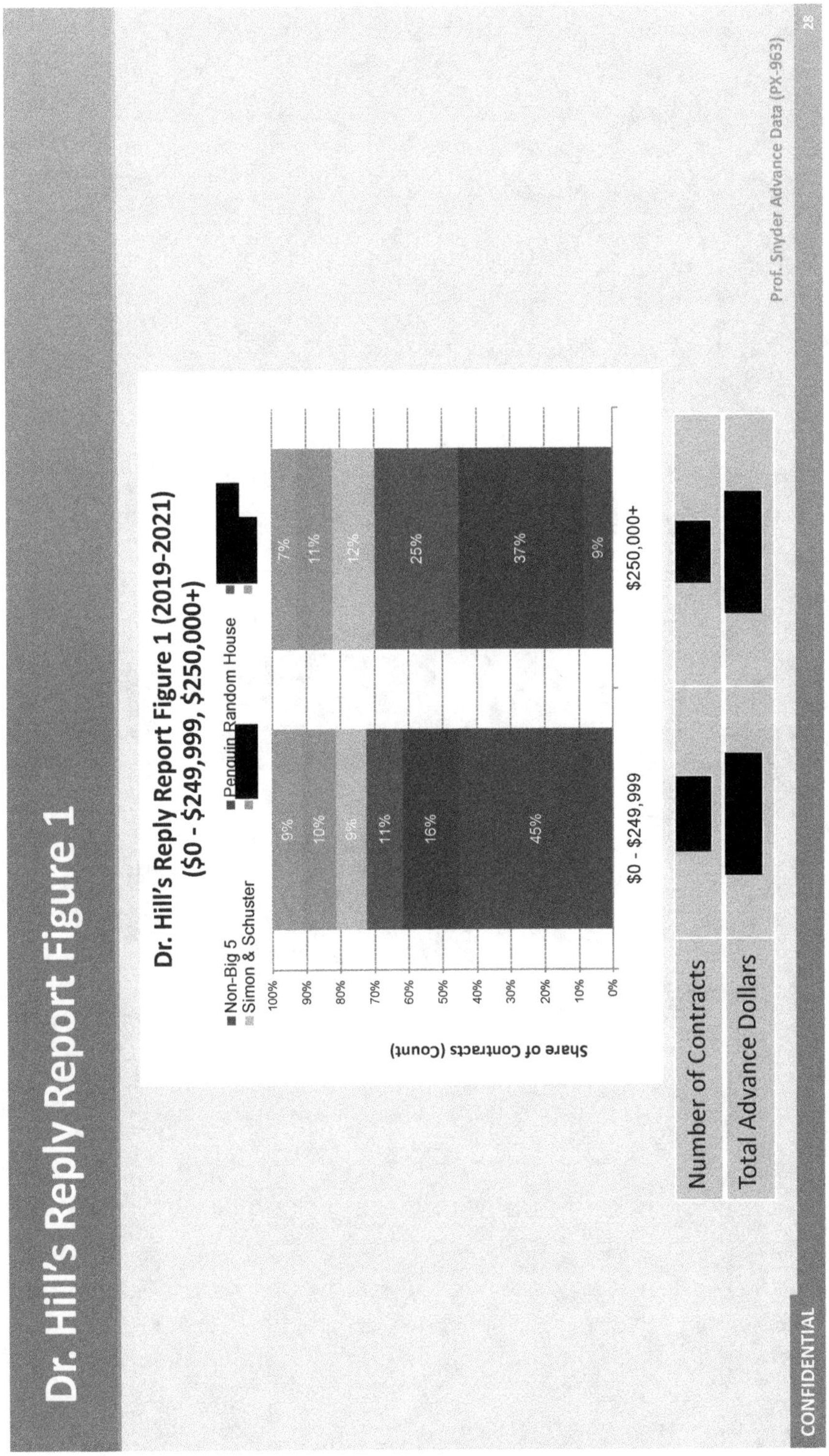
Dr. Hill's Reply Report Figure 1
Dr. Hill's Reply Report Figure 1 (2019-2021)
($0 - $249,999, $250,000+)
Non-Big 5
Simon & Schuster
Penguin Random House
Share of Contracts (Count)
100%
90%
80%
70%
60%
50%
40%
30%
20%
10%
0%
9%
10%
9%
11%
16%
45%
7%
11%
12%
25%
37%
9%
$0 - $249,999
$250,000+
Number of Contracts
Total Advance Dollars
Prof. Snyder Advance Data (PX-963)
CONFIDENTIAL
28

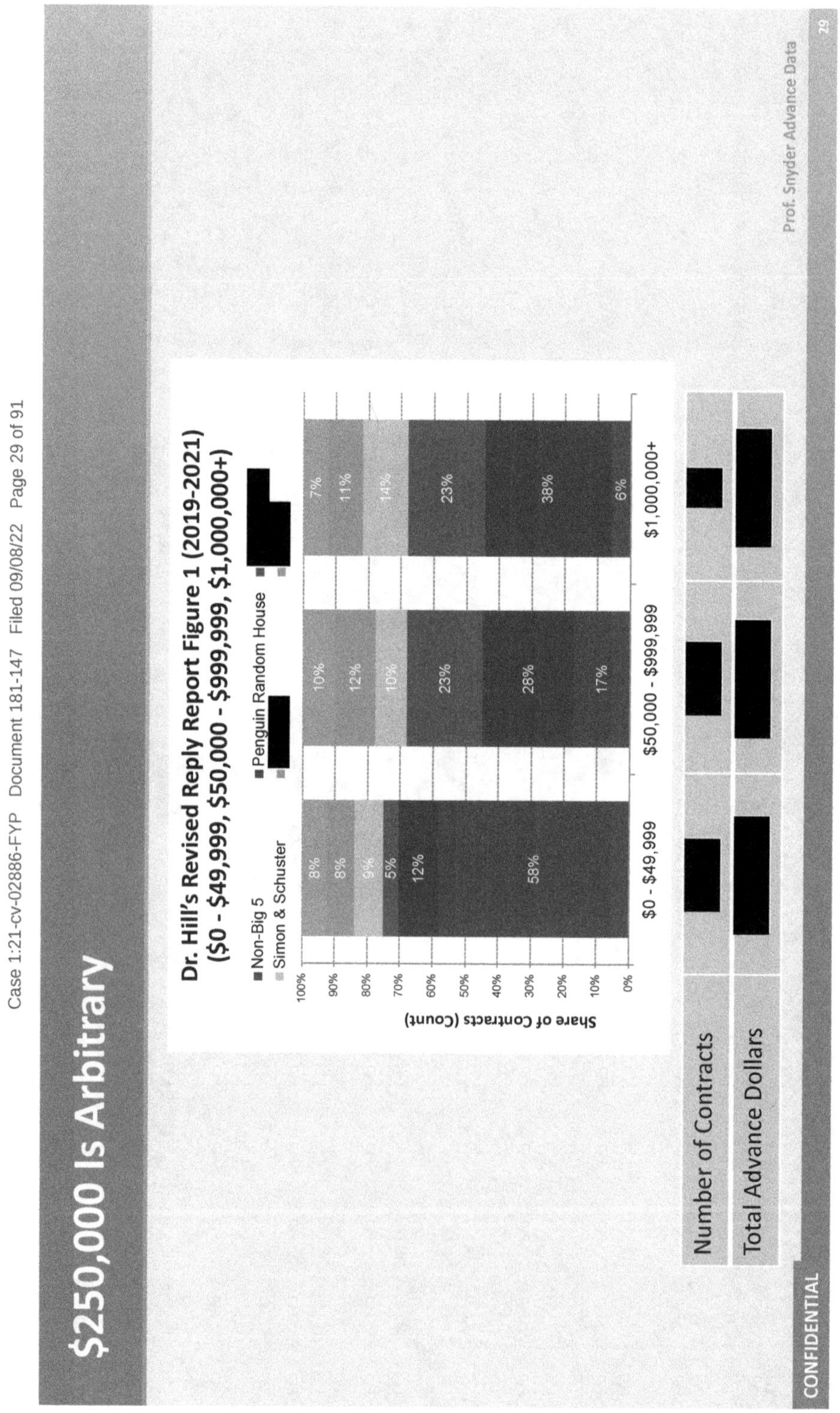
Case 1:21-cv-02886-FYP Document 181-147 Filed 09/08/22 Page 29 of 91
$250,000 Is Arbitrary
Dr. Hill's Revised Reply Report Figure 1 (2019-2021)
($0 - $49,999, $50,000 - $999,999, $1,000,000+)
Non-Big 5
Simon & Schuster
Penguin Random House
Share of Contracts (Count)
100%
90%
80%
70%
60%
50%
40%
30%
20%
10%
0%
8%
8%
9%
5%
12%
58%
10%
12%
10%
23%
28%
17%
7%
11%
14%
23%
38%
6%
$0 - $49,999
$50,000 - $999,999
$1,000,000+
Number of Contracts
Total Advance Dollars
CONFIDENTIAL
Prof. Snyder Advance Data
29

Case 1:21-cv-02886-FYP Document 181-147 Filed 09/08/22 Page 41 of 91

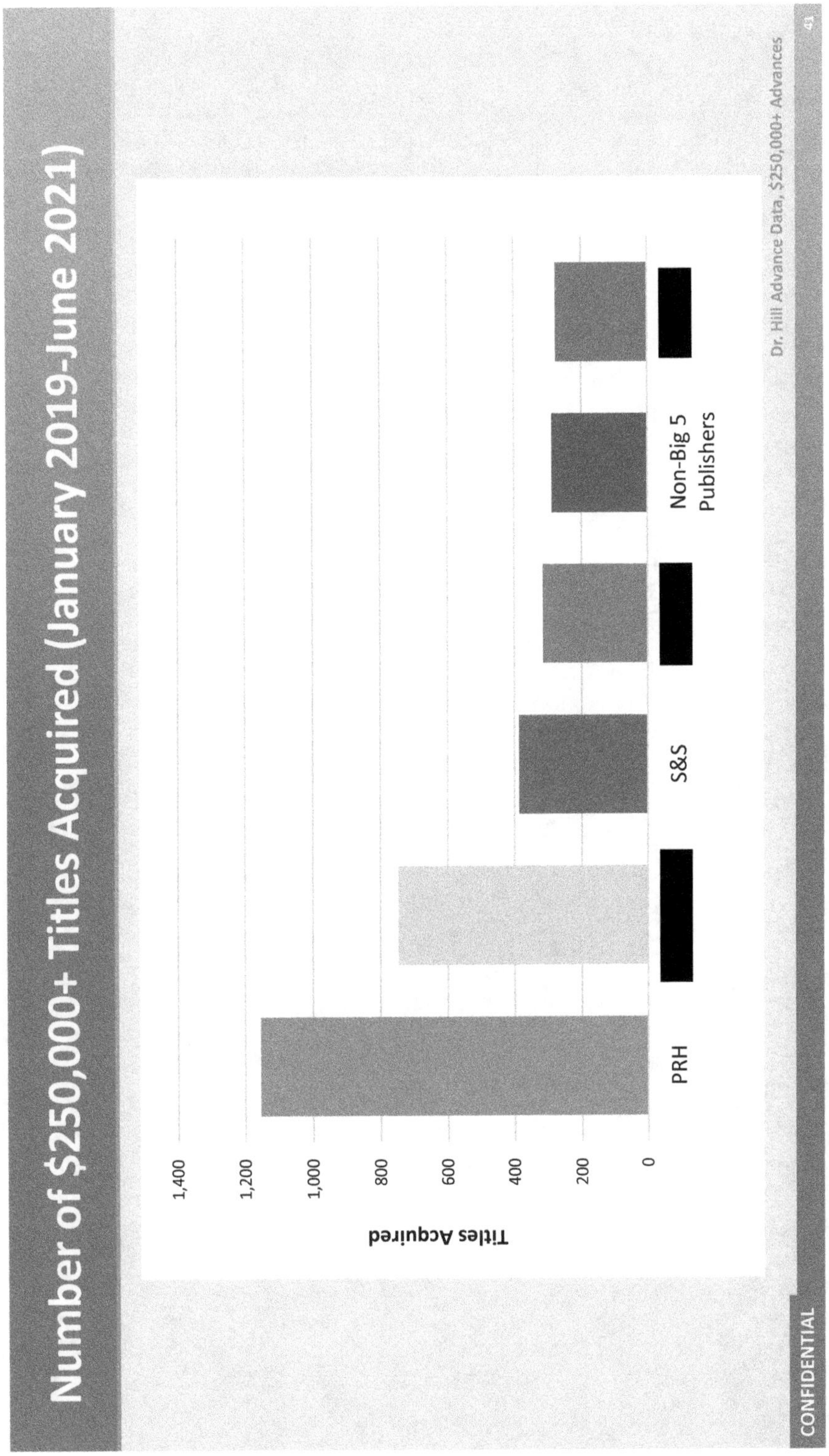

PRH's Output Increased Post-Merger

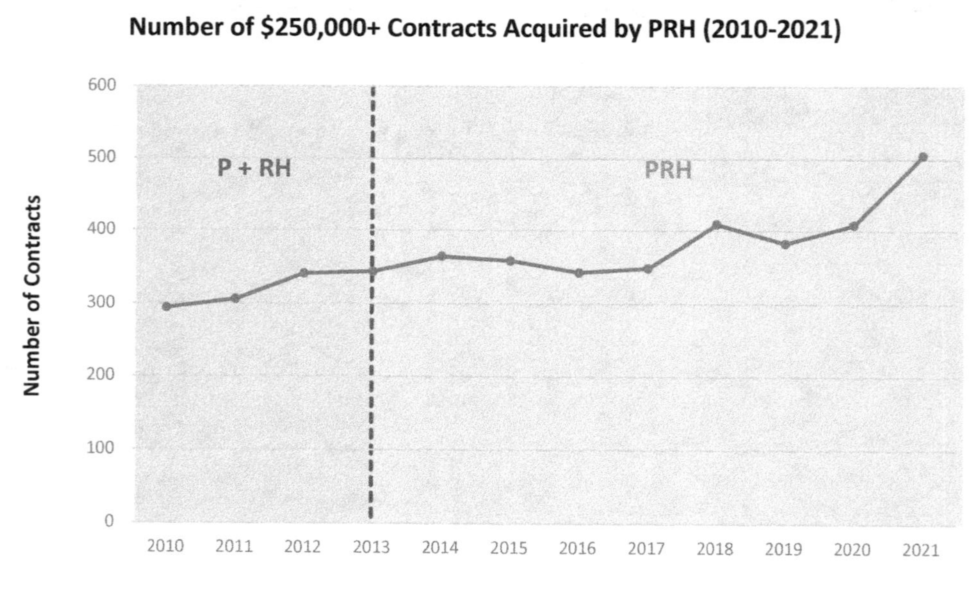

Prof. Snyder Advance Data, $250,000+ Advances

CONFIDENTIAL

86

www.ingramcontent.com/pod-product-compliance
Lightning Source LLC
LaVergne TN
LVHW081413160926
848178LV00067B/93
9781948586559